lonely planet

Canada

THIS EDITION WRITTEN AND RESEARCHED BY

Korina Miller

Kate Armstrong, James Bainbridge, Anna Kaminski, Adam Karlin, John Lee, Carolyn McCarthy, Phillip Tang, Ryan Ver Berkmoes, Benedict Walker

PLAN YOUR TRIP

TOTEM POLE, HAIDA GWAII
P761

DANITA DELIMONT / GETTY IMAGES ©

FORILLON NATIONAL PARK
P313

RON WATTS / GETTY IMAGES ©

ON THE ROAD

Contents

ON THE ROAD

PHUNG CHUNG CHYANG / SHUTTERSTOCK ©

AURORA VILLAGE P800, YELLOWKNIFE

Contents

UNDERSTAND

SURVIVAL GUIDE

SPECIAL FEATURES

Welcome to Canada

Canada is more than its hulking-mountain, craggy-coast good looks: it also cooks extraordinary meals, rocks cool culture and unfurls wild, moose-spotting road trips.

The Great Outdoors

The globe's second-biggest country has an endless variety of landscapes. Sky-high mountains, glinting glaciers, spectral rainforests and remote beaches are all here, spread across six times zones. It's the backdrop for plenty of *ah*-inspiring moments – and for a big cast of local characters. That's big as in polar bears, grizzly bears, whales and, everyone's favorite, moose.

The terrain also makes for a fantastic playground. Whether it's snowboarding Whistler's mountains, surfing Nova Scotia's swells or kayaking the white-frothed South Nahanni River in the Northwest Territories, adventures abound. There are gentler options, too, like strolling Vancouver's Stanley Park or swimming off Prince Edward Island's pink-sand beaches.

Captivating Cultures

Sip a *café au lait* and tear into a flaky croissant at a sidewalk bistro in Montréal; head to an Asian night market and slurp noodles in Vancouver; join a wild-fiddling Celtic party on Cape Breton Island; kayak between rainforest-cloaked Aboriginal villages on Haida Gwaii: Canada is incredibly diverse across its breadth and within its cities. You'll hear it in the music, see it in the arts and taste it in the cuisine.

Foodie Fare

Canada is a local food smorgasbord. If you grazed from west to east across the country, you'd fill your plate like this: wild salmon and velvety scallops in British Columbia, poutine (golden fries topped with gravy and cheese curds) in Québec, and lobster with a dab of melted butter in the Maritime provinces. Tastemakers may not tout Canadian food the way they do, say, Italian or French fare, so let's just call the distinctive seafood, piquant cheeses, and fresh, seasonal fruits and veggies our little secret. Ditto for the award-winning bold reds and crisp whites produced from the country's vine-striped valleys.

Artistic Flair

The arts are an integral part of Canada's cultural landscape. You'll find it from the International Fringe Theater Festival (the world's second-largest) in Edmonton to mega museums like Ottawa's National Gallery. Montreal's Jazz Festival and Toronto's star-studded Film Festival draw global crowds. And did you know Ontario's Stratford Festival is the continent's largest classical repertory theater? Even places you might not automatically think of – say, St John's or Woody Point – put on renowned shindigs (an avant-garde 'sound symposium' and a big-name writers festival, respectively).

Why I Love Canada

By Korina Miller, Writer

I've traveled to three dozen countries and never found anywhere more beautiful than Canada. And when I'm gone, what do I miss? Flights that take you low over the sky-clawing Rockies. Catching sight of an orca from a ferry deck. Driving across the prairies where wheat blows like an endless sea. Listening to the Tragically Hip on the radio and drinking a good, strong cup of tea. Candy smoked salmon, sharp cheddar cheese and Okanagan wine. A vastness that compels you to explore. I'm Canadian and I love Canada. And I'm not even going to apologize for it.

For more about our writers, see p896

Above: Bull moose, Banff National Park (p586)

Canada

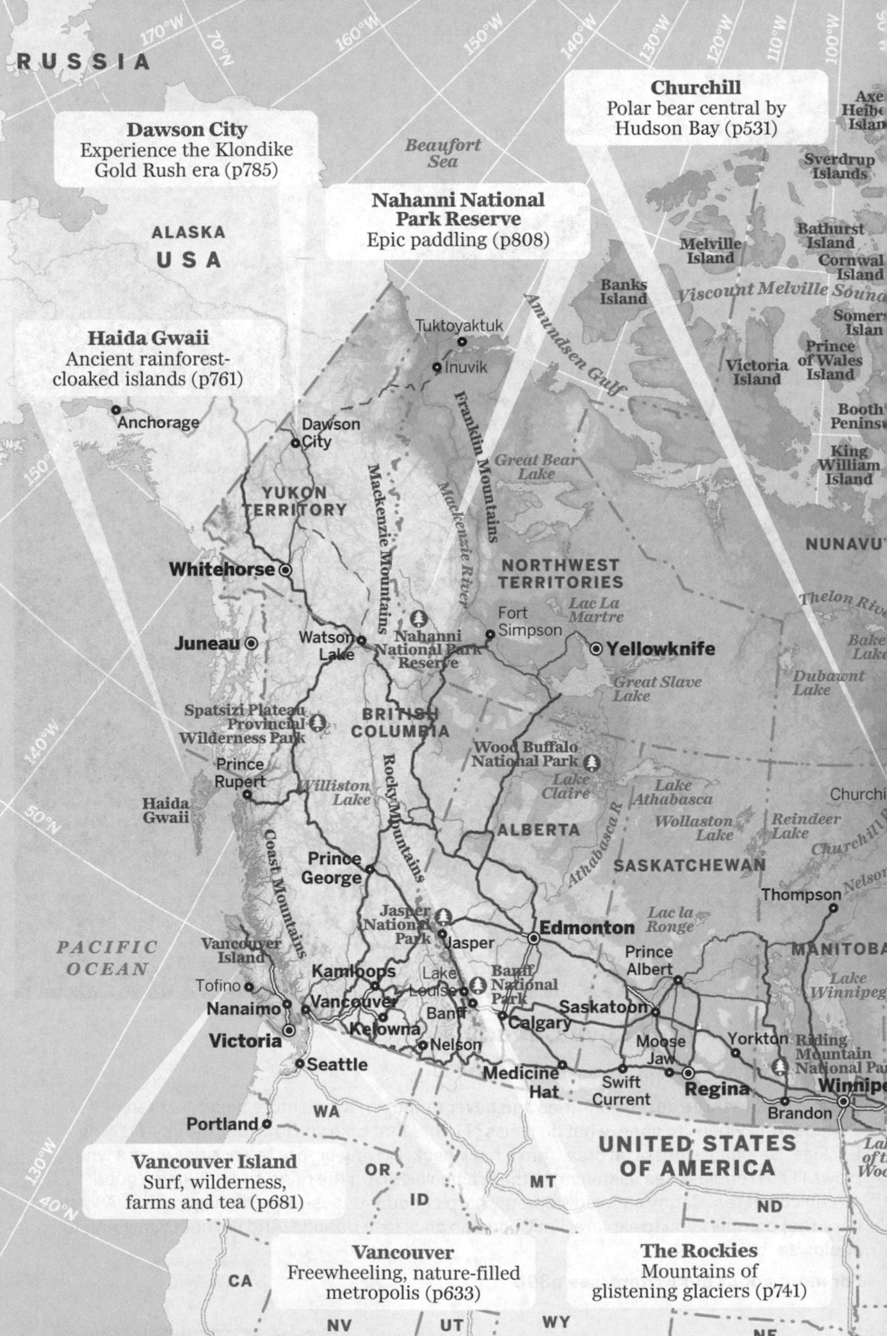

Churchill
Polar bear central by Hudson Bay (p531)
Dawson City
Experience the Klondike Gold Rush era (p785)
Nahanni National Park Reserve
Epic paddling (p808)
Haida Gwaii
Ancient rainforest-cloaked islands (p761)
Vancouver Island
Surf, wilderness, farms and tea (p681)
Vancouver
Freewheeling, nature-filled metropolis (p633)
The Rockies
Mountains of glistening glaciers (p741)
RUSSIA
ALASKA
USA
Beaufort Sea
Tuktoyaktuk
Inuvik
Anchorage
Dawson City
YUKON TERRITORY
Whitehorse
Juneau
Watson Lake
Mackenzie Mountains
Mackenzie River
Franklin Mountains
Nahanni National Park Reserve
Fort Simpson
Yellowknife
NORTHWEST TERRITORIES
Great Bear Lake
Great Slave Lake
Lac La Martre
Amundsen Gulf
Banks Island
Melville Island
Victoria Island
Viscount Melville Sound
Sverdrup Islands
Bathurst Island
Prince of Wales Island
King William Island
NUNAVUT
Spatsizi Plateau Provincial Wilderness Park
BRITISH COLUMBIA
Prince Rupert
Haida Gwaii
Williston Lake
Rocky Mountains
Coast Mountains
Wood Buffalo National Park
Lake Claire
Lake Athabasca
Athabasca R
Wollaston Lake
Reindeer Lake
Dubawnt Lake
ALBERTA
SASKATCHEWAN
Prince George
Jasper National Park
Jasper
Edmonton
Lac la Ronge
Thompson
MANITOBA
Lake Winnipeg
PACIFIC OCEAN
Vancouver Island
Tofino
Nanaimo
Victoria
Kamloops
Vancouver
Kelowna
Lake Louise
Banff National Park
Banff
Nelson
Calgary
Prince Albert
Saskatoon
Moose Jaw
Regina
Yorkton
Riding Mountain National Park
Brandon
Medicine Hat
Swift Current
Seattle
Portland
WA
OR
ID
MT
ND
CA
NV
UT
WY
NE
UNITED STATES OF AMERICA

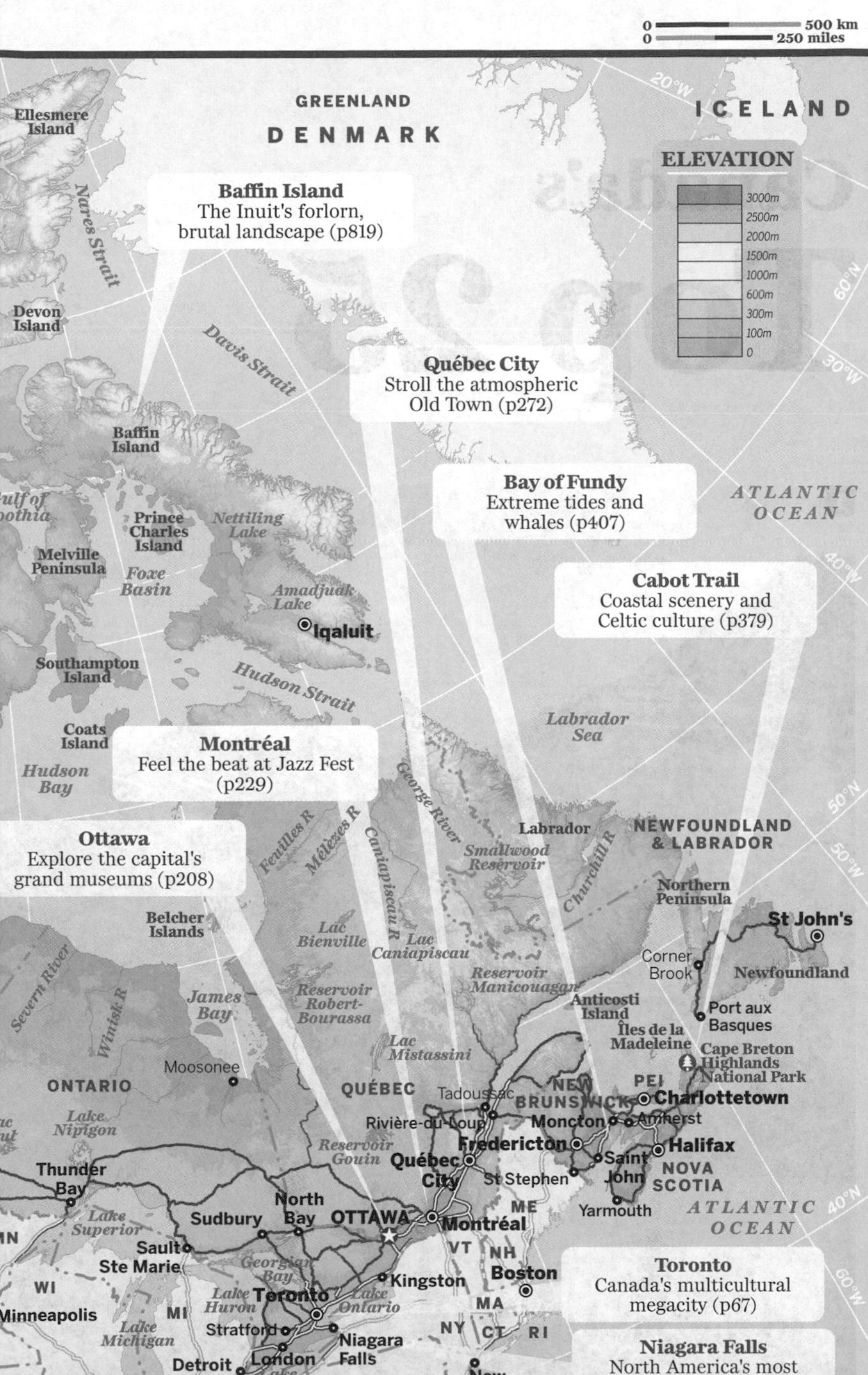
0 500 km
0 250 miles
GREENLAND
DENMARK
ICELAND
ELEVATION
3000m
2500m
2000m
1500m
1000m
600m
300m
100m
0
Baffin Island
The Inuit's forlorn, brutal landscape (p819)
Québec City
Stroll the atmospheric Old Town (p272)
Bay of Fundy
Extreme tides and whales (p407)
Cabot Trail
Coastal scenery and Celtic culture (p379)
Montréal
Feel the beat at Jazz Fest (p229)
Ottawa
Explore the capital's grand museums (p208)
Toronto
Canada's multicultural megacity (p67)
Niagara Falls
North America's most voluminous cascade (p118)
Ellesmere Island
Nares Strait
Devon Island
Davis Strait
Baffin Island
Gulf of Boothia
Prince Charles Island
Nettiling Lake
Melville Peninsula
Foxe Basin
Amadjuak Lake
Iqaluit
Southampton Island
Hudson Strait
Coats Island
Hudson Bay
Labrador Sea
ATLANTIC OCEAN
George River
Feuilles R
Mélèzes R
Caniapiscau R
Labrador
Churchill R
Smallwood Reservoir
NEWFOUNDLAND & LABRADOR
Northern Peninsula
St John's
Corner Brook
Newfoundland
Port aux Basques
Belcher Islands
Lac Bienville
Lac Caniapiscau
Reservoir Manicouagan
Anticosti Island
Îles de la Madeleine
Cape Breton Highlands National Park
Severn River
Winisk R
James Bay
Reservoir Robert-Bourassa
Lac Mistassini
Moosonee
ONTARIO
QUÉBEC
Tadoussac
NEW BRUNSWICK
PEI
Charlottetown
Lac Seul
Lake Nipigon
Rivière-du-Loup
Moncton
Amherst
Fredericton
Halifax
Reservoir Gouin
Québec City
Saint John
NOVA SCOTIA
St Stephen
Thunder Bay
North Bay
Sudbury
OTTAWA
Montréal
ME
Yarmouth
ATLANTIC OCEAN
Lake Superior
MN
Sault Ste Marie
VT
NH
Georgian Bay
Kingston
Boston
WI
Lake Huron
Toronto
Lake Ontario
MA
Minneapolis
MI
Lake Michigan
Stratford
NY
CT
RI
Niagara Falls
Detroit
London
Lake Erie
PA
New York
IA
Chicago
20°W
30°W
40°W
50°W
60°W
60°N
50°N
40°N

Canada's Top 25

1

The Rockies (BC/Alberta)

1 The sawtooth, white-topped mountains straddling the British Columbia (BC)–Alberta border inspire both awe and action. Four national parks – Banff, Yoho, Kootenay and Jasper – offer countless opportunities to delve into the lush wilderness with ribbons of hiking trails, rushing white water and powdery ski slopes. The Rockies Rail Route (p46) provides another popular way to experience the grandeur: luminous lakes, jumbles of wildflowers and glistening glaciers glide by as the steel cars chug up mountain passes and down river valleys en route to points east or west.

Below: Peyto Lake (p592)

Haida Gwaii (BC)

2 Once known as the Queen Charlotte Islands, this dagger-shaped archipelago (p761) 80km off BC's coast is a magical trip for those who make it. Colossal spruce and cedars cloak the wild, rain-sodden landscape. Bald eagles and bears roam the ancient forest, while sea lions and orcas cruise the waters. But the islands' real soul is the resurgent Haida people, best known for their war-canoe and totem-pole carvings (pictured below). See the lot at Gwaii Haanas National Park Reserve, which combines lost villages, burial caves and hot springs with some of the continent's best kayaking.

ALISON RIDGWAY ©

2

DON JOHNSTON / GETTY IMAGES ©

Vancouver (BC)

3 Vancouver (p633) always lands atop the 'best places to live' lists, and who's to argue? Sea-to-sky beauty surrounds the laid-back, cocktail-lovin' metropolis. With skiable mountains on the outskirts, 11 beaches fringing the core and Stanley Park's thick rainforest just blocks from the glass skyscrapers downtown, it's a harmonic convergence of city and nature. It also mixes Hollywood chic (many movies are filmed here) with a freewheeling counterculture (a popular nude beach and the Marijuana Party political headquarters) and buzzing multicultural communities.

Niagara Falls (Ontario)

4 Crowded? Cheesy? Well, yes. Niagara (p118) is short, too – it doesn't even crack the top 500 worldwide for height. But c'mon, when those great muscular bands of water arc over the precipice like liquid glass, roaring into the void below, and when you sail toward it in a mist-shrouded little boat, Niagara Falls impresses big time. In terms of sheer volume, nowhere in North America beats its thundering cascade, with more than one million bathtubs of water plummeting over the edge every second.

3.

VADIM PETROV / SHUTTERSTOCK ©

NOEL HENDRICKSON / GETTY IMAGES ©

Cabot Trail (Nova Scotia)

5 The 300km Cabot Trail (p379) winds and climbs over coastal mountains, with heart-stopping sea views at every turn, breaching whales just offshore, moose nibbling roadside and plenty of trails to stop and hike. Be sure to tote your dancing shoes – Celtic and Acadian communities dot the area, and their foot-stompin', crazy-fiddlin' music vibrates through local pubs.

Nahanni National Park Reserve (Northwest Territories)

6 Gorgeous hot springs, haunted gorges and gorging grizzlies fill this remote park (p808) near the Yukon border, and you'll have to fly in to reach them. Only about 1000 visitors per year make the trek, half of them paddlers trying to conquer the South Nahanni River. Untamed and spectacular, it churns 500km through the Mackenzie Mountains. Thirty-story waterfalls, towering canyons and legends of giants and lost gold round out the journey north.

Bottom right: Kraus Hot Springs (p809)

ASCENT/PKS MEDIA INC. / GETTY IMAGES ©

Driving the Trans-Canada Highway

7 Canada's main vein (p37) stretches 7800km from St John's, Newfoundland, to Victoria, BC, and takes in the country's greatest hits along the way. Gros Morne National Park, Cape Breton Island, Québec City, Banff National Park and Yoho National Park are part of the path, as are major cities including Montréal, Ottawa, Calgary and Vancouver. It takes most road-trippers a good month to drive coast to coast, so what are you waiting for? Fuel up, cue the tunes, and put the pedal to the metal. Top left: Banff National Park (p586)

Charlevoix (Québec)

8 A pastoral strip of rolling hills northeast of Québec City, the Charlevoix (p291) region harvests much of the province's food. Gastronomes road-trip out, knowing that the produce from the farms and orchards that flash by will end up as part of their next meal in true farm-to-table fashion. Village inns and alehouses serve the distinct, locally made wares: think tomato aperitif with foie gras or pear ice wine served with fresh sheep cheese. Artsy towns such as Baie St-Paul and La Malbaie make good bases for exploration. Top right: Farmers market, Charlevoix (p291)

Manitoulin Island (Ontario)

9 The largest freshwater island in the world and floating right smack in Lake Huron's midst, Manitoulin (p165) is a slowpoke place of beaches and summery cottages. Jagged expanses of white quartzite and granite outcroppings edge the shoreline and lead to shimmering vistas. First Nations culture pervades, and the island's eight communities collaborate to offer local foods (wild rice, corn soup) and eco-adventures (canoeing, horseback riding, hiking). Powwows add drumming, dancing and storytelling to the mix. Bottom right: Bridal Veil Falls (p165), Manitoulin Island

Montréal Jazz Festival (Québec)

10 Where else can you join more than two million calm, respectful music lovers (no slam dancing or drunken slobs) and watch the best jazz-influenced musicians in the world, choosing from 500 shows, of which countless are free? Only in Montréal, Canada's second-largest city and its cultural heart. BB King, Prince and Astor Piazzolla are among those who've plugged in at the 11-day, late-June Montréal Jazz Festival (p243). You might want to join them after your free drumming lesson and street-side jam session. The good times roll 24/7.

Hockey

11 Hockey (p844) is Canada's national passion, and if you're visiting between October and April taking in a game is mandatory (as is giving a shout-out to the nation's 2014 Olympic gold medal–winning team). Vancouver, Edmonton, Calgary, Toronto, Ottawa, Winnipeg and Montréal all have NHL teams. Minor pro teams and junior hockey clubs fill many more arenas with rabid fans. And if you're still looking for a fight, pond hockey brings out the sticks in communities across the land. Bottom: The gold medal–winning Canadian Women's ice hockey team at the 2014 Winter Olympics

Northern Lights

12 Canada has a lot of middle-of-nowhere, high-latitude places, from the Labrador (p506) coast to Arctic villages. They may not seem like much during the day, but at night, drapes of green, yellow, aqua, violet and other polychromatic hues flicker and dance across the sky. Traditionally, some Inuit peoples believed the northern lights (aka the aurora borealis) were the spirits of hunted animals while others feared they were the lanterns of demons chasing lost souls. Seen from September to March, darker skies make the coldest winter months the best for viewing.

Rideau Canal (Ontario)

13 This 185-year-old, 200km-long waterway – consisting of canals, rivers and lakes – connects Ottawa and Kingston via 47 locks. It's at its finest in wintry Ottawa (p208), when it becomes the world's largest skating rink (pictured bottom). People swoosh by on the 7.8km of groomed ice, pausing for hot chocolate and scrumptious slabs of fried dough called beavertails. February's Winterlude festival kicks it up a notch when townsfolk build massive ice sculptures. Once it thaws, the canal becomes a boater's paradise.

Churchill (Manitoba)

14 The first polar bear (pictured top) you see up close takes your breath away. Immediately forgotten are the two bum-numbing days on the train that took you beyond the tree zone onto the tundra, to the very edge of Hudson Bay. Churchill (p531) is the lone outpost here, and it happens to be smack in the bears' migration path. From late September to early November, tundra buggies head out in search of the razor-clawed beasts, sometimes getting you close enough to lock eyes. Summer lets you swim with beluga whales.

Toronto (Ontario)

15 A hyperactive stew of cultures and neighborhoods, Toronto (p67) strikes you with sheer urban awe. Will you have dinner in Chinatown or Greektown? Five-star fusion or a peameal bacon sandwich? Designer shoes from Bloor-Yorkville are accessorized with tattoos in Queen West. Mod-art galleries, theater par excellence, rockin' band rooms and hockey mania add to the megalopolis. It is far and away Canada's largest city, as well as its most diverse – about half of its residents were born in another country.

RONNIE CHUA / SHUTTERSTOCK ©

Drumheller (Alberta)

16 Dinosaur lovers get weak-kneed in dust-blown Drumheller (p614), where paleontological civic pride runs high thanks to the Royal Tyrrell Museum, one of the planet's preeminent fossil collections. The World's Largest Dinosaur (pictured above; p623) is here, too – a big, scary, fiberglass T-rex that visitors can climb up and peer out (through its mouth). Beyond the dino-hoopla, the area offers classic Badlands scenery and eerie, mushroom-like rock columns called hoodoos. Scenic driving loops take you past the good stuff.

Green Gables (PEI)

17 It may be the tiny, rural town of Cavendish (p454) and its big star, Anne of Green Gables, that draw you to Prince Edward Island (PEI). Written by Lucy Maud Montgomery in 1908 about a red-haired orphan named Anne, it's still one of the island's biggest money-makers. But once here, it's the seaside villages, creek-crossed woods, gabled farmhouses, rolling hills and rose-colored beaches that captivate. The fresh oysters and lobsters are simply the icing on the plum puffs. Nicknamed the Gentle Island, PEI will soothe you into holiday mode. Top right: Green Gables Heritage Place (p454)

The Prairies

18 Solitude reigns in Canada's middle ground. Driving through the flatlands of Manitoba and Saskatchewan (pictured bottom right; p536) turns up uninterrupted fields of golden wheat that stretch to the horizon, melting into the sunshine. When the wind blows, the wheat sways like waves on the ocean, punctuated by the occasional grain elevator rising up like a tall ship. Big skies mean big storms that drop like an anvil, visible on the skyline for kilometers. Far-flung towns include arty Winnipeg, boozy Moose Jaw and Mountie-filled Regina, sprinkled between with Ukrainian and Scandinavian villages.

Fall Foliage

19 Canada blazes come autumn, which should come as no surprise in a country that's half-covered by forest. Québec's Laurentian Mountains (p258) flame especially bright from all the sugar maple trees (which also sauce the nation's pancakes). Cape Breton, Nova Scotia, flares up so pretty they hold a festival to honor the foliage – it's called Celtic Colours and it's in mid-October. New Brunswick's Fundy Coast and Ontario's Muskoka Lakes area pull in leaf peepers, too. Top: La Mauricie National Park (p271), Québec

Old Québec City (Québec)

20 Québec's capital (p272) is more than 400 years old, and its stone walls, glinting-spired cathedrals and jazz-soaked corner cafes suffuse it with atmosphere, romance, melancholy, eccentricity and intrigue on par with any European city. The best way to soak it up is to walk the Old Town's labyrinth of lanes and get lost amid the street performers and cozy inns, stopping every so often for a *café au lait*, flaky pastry or heaping plate of poutine (fries smothered in cheese curds and gravy) to refuel.

19

20

Baffin Island (Nunavut)

21 The forlorn, brutal landscape of the Inuit, Baffin (p819) is home to cloud-scraping mountains and a third of Nunavut's population. The island's crown jewel is Auyuittuq National Park – whose name means 'the land that never melts' – and indeed glaciers, fjords and vertiginous cliffs fill the eastern expanse. The park is a siren call for hardcore hikers and climbers, and more than a few polar bears. Baffin is also a center for Inuit art; studios for high-quality carving, printmaking and weaving pop up in many wee towns. Bottom: Ice fishing, Baffin Island

Vancouver Island (BC)

22 C'mon, can a place really 'have it all'? Yes, if it's Vancouver Island (p681). Picture-postcard Victoria is the island's heart, beating with bohemian shops, wood-floored coffee bars and a tea-soaked English past. Brooding Pacific Rim National Park Reserve sports the West Coast Trail, where a wind-bashed ocean meets a mist-shrouded wilderness, and surfers line up for Tofino's (pictured above opposite) waves. Then there's the Cowichan Valley, studded with welcoming little farms and boutique wineries, prime for wandering foodies.

22

Viking Trail (Newfoundland)

23 The Viking Trail (p492), aka Rte 430, connects Newfoundland's two World Heritage sites on the Northern Peninsula. Gros Morne National Park, with its fjordlike lakes and geological oddities, rests at its base, while the sublime, 1000-year-old Viking settlement at L'Anse aux Meadows (pictured bottom left; p496) – Leif Eriksson's pad – stares out from the peninsula's tip. The road is an attraction in its own right, holding close to the sea as it heads resolutely north past Port au Choix's ancient burial grounds and the ferry jump-off to big, bad Labrador.

Bay of Fundy

24 This ain't your average bay, though lighthouses, fishing villages and other maritime scenery surround it. The unique geography of Fundy (p407) results in the most extreme tides in the world, reaching 16m (56ft), about the height of a five-story building. They stir up serious whale food, with gin, humpback, endangered North Atlantic right whales and blue whales swimming in to feast, making a whale-watch here extraordinary. Tidal bore rafting, where outfitters harness the blasting force of Fundy's waters, is another unique activity.

Dawson City (Yukon Territory)

25 End-of-the-road Dawson (p785), with its brightly painted Klondike-era buildings, once drew thousands in the search for gold. Today, instead of miners after the shiny stuff, the city attracts artists and rugged individualists and has a doors-always-open feel about it that makes you feel like a returning local. Give gold panning a go in the icy rivers or try your hand at poker at the historic saloon where cancan dancers still kick up their heels. Then soak up some of the spectacular sub-Artic scenery that surrounds Dawson. Magic. Opposite: Downtown Hotel (p790)

24

25
DOWNTOWN
HOTEL
JACK
LONDON
GRILL
GRACE'S
GIFT SHOP
1026

Need to Know

For more information, see Survival Guide (p855)

Currency

Canadian dollar ($)

Languages

English, French

Visas

Currently, visas are not required for citizens of 46 countries – including most EU members, Australia and New Zealand – for visits of up to six months.

Money

ATMs widely available. Credit cards accepted in most hotels and restaurants.

Cell Phones

Local SIM cards can be used in unlocked GSM 850/1900 compatible phones. Other phones must be set to roaming.

Time

Atlantic Standard Time (GMT/UTC minus four hours)

Eastern Standard Time (GMT/UTC minus five hours)

Central Standard Time (GMT/UTC minus six hours)

Pacific Standard Time (GMT/UTC minus eight hours)

When to Go

High Season

(Jun–Aug)

- Sunshine and warm weather prevail; far northern regions briefly thaw.
- Accommodation prices peak (up 30% on average).
- December through March is equally busy and expensive in ski resort towns.

Shoulder

(May, Sep & Oct)

- Crowds and prices drop off.
- Temperatures are cool but comfortable.
- Attractions keep shorter hours.
- Fall foliage areas (eg Cape Breton, Québec) remain busy.

Low Season

(Nov–Apr)

- Places outside the big cities and ski resorts close.
- Darkness and cold take over.
- April and November are particularly good for bargains.

Useful Websites

Destination Canada (en.destinationcanada.com) Official tourism site.

Environment Canada Weather (www.weather.gc.ca) Forecasts for any town.

Lonely Planet (www.lonelyplanet.com/canada) Destination information, hotel bookings, traveler forum and more.

Government of Canada (www.gc.ca) National and regional information.

Parks Canada (www.pc.gc.ca) Lowdown on national parks.

Canadian Broadcasting Corporation (www.cbc.ca) National and provincial news.

Important Numbers

Country code	☎1
International access code	☎011
Emergency	☎911
Directory assistance	☎411

Exchange Rates

Australia	A$1	C$1
Europe	€1	C$1.45
Japan	¥100	C$1.29
NZ	NZ$1	C$0.95
UK	UK£1	C$1.71
USA	US$1	C$1.29

For current exchange rates see www.xe.com.

Daily Costs

Budget: Less than $100

- Dorm bed: $25–40
- Campsite: $25–35
- Self-catered meals from markets and supermarkets: $8–12

Midrange: $100–250

- B&B or room in a midrange hotel: $80–180 ($100–250 in major cities)
- Meal in a good local restaurant: from $20 plus drinks
- Rental car: per day $35–65
- Attraction admissions: $5–20

Top End: More than $250

- Four-star hotel room: from $180 (from $250 in major cities)
- Three-course meal in a top restaurant: from $50 plus drinks
- Skiing day pass: $50–80

Opening Hours

Opening hours vary throughout the year. We've provided high-season opening hours; hours will generally decrease in the shoulder and low seasons.

Banks 10am–5pm Monday to Friday; some open 9am–noon Saturday

Restaurants breakfast 8–11am, lunch 11:30am–2:30pm Monday to Friday, dinner 5–9:30pm daily; some open for brunch 8am to 1pm Saturday and Sunday

Bars 5pm–2am daily

Clubs 9pm–2am Wednesday to Saturday

Shops 10am–6pm Monday to Saturday, noon–5pm Sunday; some open to 8pm or 9pm Thursday and/or Friday

Supermarkets 9am–8pm; some open 24 hours

Arriving in Canada

Toronto Pearson International Airport (p116) Trains ($12) run downtown every 15 minutes from 5.30am to 1am; taxis cost around $60 (45 minutes).

Montréal-Pierre Elliot Trudeau International Airport (p257) A 24-hour public bus ($10) runs downtown. Taxis cost a flat $40 (30 to 60 minutes).

Vancouver International Airport (p662) Trains ($7.50 to $9) run downtown every six to 20 minutes; taxis cost around $40 (30 minutes).

Land Border Crossings The Canadian Border Services Agency (www.cbsa-asfc.gc.ca/bwt-taf/menu-eng.html) posts wait times (usually 30 minutes).

Getting Around

Car An extensive highway system links most towns. The Trans-Canada Hwy stretches from Newfoundland to Vancouver Island. Away from the population centers, distances can be deceivingly long and travel times slow due to single-lane highways. All major rental car companies are readily available.

Train Outside the Toronto–Montréal corridor, train travel is mostly for scenic journeys.

Ferry Public ferry systems operate extensively in British Columbia, Québec and the Maritime provinces.

Air Regional and national carriers crisscross the country, taking days off travel time and reaching northern towns inaccessible by road.

For much more on **getting around**, see p867

What's New

National Music Centre, Alberta

Calgary's fabulous new museum takes you on a ride through Canada's musical history with fun artifacts and interactive displays. Test your skill at the drums, electric guitar or in a recording room. (p575)

Eau Claire Distillery, Alberta

Tiny Turner is turning heads with its award-winning craft distillery. Using Alberta grain and custom-crafted German stills, this cool place pours tastings of gin and vodka infused with natural flavors like prickly pear and lemon. (p585)

Ancient Forest/Chun T'oh Whudujut, British Columbia

Follow boardwalks through this ancient forest, passing 2000-year-old red cedars, waterfalls and rare orchids. Found 120km east of Prince George, it was designated a provincial park in 2016. (p767)

Lighthouse Lodgings

Newfoundland has opened the doors of its lighthouses to overnighters. While you'll be sleeping in the historic lightkeeper's home rather than the lighthouse itself, it's still some of the most atmospheric lodgings in the country. (p497)

Sea to Sky Gondola, British Columbia

Hop a gondola to 885m above sea level for panoramic views over the Coastal Mountains and Pacific Ocean. Once at the top, set off into the lush forest on one of the countless trails. (p668)

Skywood Eco Adventure, Ontario

Fancy trekking at the tops of the trees? Set in Thousand Islands, this new park has the country's largest aerial adventure and zipline route. There's everything from a treehouse playground for three-year-olds to adventures that will make the bravest adult's knees knock. (p203)

Mosaic Stadium, Saskatchewan

Regina's CFL team – the much loved Roughriders – are getting a new home where 40,000 of their closest fans can cheer them on. (p543)

Rogers Place, Alberta

Regularly referred to as the Oilers Centre, this will be the home for the city's hockey team and the focus of regeneration in Edmonton's downtown. The arena is super high-tech and designed to max out your hockey-watching experience. (p571)

Jasper Dark Sky Preserve, Alberta

Designated a Dark Sky Preserve by the Royal Astronomical Society of Canada, Jasper has some of the starriest night skies you'll ever see. Come for the observatory, the Dark Sky Festival or just to see the twinkly lights. (p609)

For more recommendations and reviews, see **lonelyplanet.com/canada**

If You Like...

Adrenaline Activities

Whistler If you want to ski or snowboard Canada's best, Whistler reigns supreme. (p670)

Tofino Little Tofino packs big adventure with its Pacific coast surfing, kayaking, hiking and storm watching. (p704)

Banff Queen of the Rockies, Banff has it all: skiing, hiking, rafting, horseback riding, mountain biking...phew! (p586)

Laurentians The mountain villages speckling the landscape outside Montréal let you ski, luge and rock climb. (p258)

Marble Mountain Skiing and snow-kiting in winter, caving and kayaking in summer, and ziplining year-round in Newfoundland. (p499)

Wine & Spirits

Winter Festival of Wine Slip, slide and slurp candy-sweet ice wines at the Okanagan's Sun Peaks resort in January. (p31)

Niagara Wine Tours International Cycle back roads from winery to winery on guided trips tailored to all fitness levels. (p129)

Taste Trail Take a self-guided driving tour through rural Prince Edward County's farms and vineyards. (p194)

Myriad View Distillery Visit a moonshine producer and put hair on your chest with its 75% alcohol elixir. (p449)

Merridale Estate Cidery Sip apple cider or brandy in Vancouver Island's verdant Cowichan Valley. (p697)

Historic Sites

L'Anse aux Meadows Poke around the Viking vestiges that Leif Eriksson left behind in Newfoundland around AD 1000. (p496)

Québec City History is palpable throughout the walled city where the French put down stakes in 1608. (p272)

Louisbourg Munch soldiers' rations and bribe guards at Nova Scotia's re-created 1744 fortress. (p388)

Batoche See the prairie site where Métis leader Louis Riel clashed with the Canadian army in 1885. (p556)

Klondike Sites Preserved structures in Dawson City tell the tale of the Klondike gold rush. (p785)

Live Music

Montréal The city hosts Canada's most prolific indie rock scene, known for its boho, underground clubs. (p229)

North by Northeast Nearly 1000 bands spill off stages throughout Toronto for a rockin' week in June. (p91)

Horseshoe Tavern Toronto's legendary venue is the place for emerging acts to cut their teeth. (p110)

George Street This St John's street has a music festival named after it, with day and nighttime performances. (p471)

Red Shoe Pub World-renowned Celtic fiddlers scorch the strings on Cape Breton Island. (p378)

IF YOU LIKE...SURFING

Tofino on British Columbia's west coast attracts surf fans. Learn to ride some waves at a surf school (p705).

Lighthouses

Point Prim Lighthouse This gorgeous historic lighthouse is the oldest one on Prince Edward Island. (p441)

Peggy's Cove Near Halifax, this lighthouse is absolutely picture perfect. (p348)

Point Amour Atlantic Canada's tallest lighthouse features killer views over Labrador's black-rock landscape and iceberg-strewn sea. (p508)

Cape Enrage The 150-year-old clifftop tower presides over the highest, meanest tides in the world. (p420)

Swallowtail On New Brunswick's Grand Manan Island, looming atop a moss-covered cliff with seals swimming below. (p410)

Roads Less Traveled

Route 132, Québec Rocky shores, glinting silver churches and wooded hills from Ste-Flavie to Forillon National Park. (p302)

Highway 17 along Lake Superior, Ontario Fjordlike passages, hidden beaches and primeval forests coated in mist on the lake's northern shore. (p173)

Route 199, Québec Wee coastal road past sand dunes and fishing villages on the Îles de la Madeleine. (p324)

Highway 37A to Stewart, BC Vintage toasters and converted school-bus restaurants along with the requisite glaciers. (p768)

Route 470, southwest Newfoundland Rippled coastal ride past windswept terrain and fishing hamlets. (p505)

Highway 742 through Kananaskis Rough, gravel road through deep forests where wolves, moose and bears regularly wander. (p586)

Wildlife-Watching

Churchill Polar bears rule the tundra at Hudson Bay's edge; beluga whales chatter in the river. (p531)

Long Island Endangered North Atlantic right whales, blue whales, humpbacks and seals swim offshore from Nova Scotia. (p360)

Gros Morne They say there are six moose per square kilometer in Newfoundland's premier park. (p492)

Khutzeymateen Grizzly Bear Sanctuary The refuge, near Prince Rupert, BC, is home to more than 50 big guys. (p759)

Wood Buffalo National Park Shaggy bison and packs of huge wolves play out nature's deadly dance. (p806)

Icefields Parkway The scenic road in the Rockies pretty much guarantees bear and elk sightings. (p591)

Algonquin Provincial Park Moose and loons provide quintessential Canadian viewing; howling wolves provide the soundtrack. (p187)

Victoria Resident pods of killer whales ride the local waves. (p681)

Art

National Gallery of Canada The Ottawa museum holds the world's largest collection of Canadian and Inuit art. (p209)

Art Gallery of Ontario Rare Québecois religious statuary, First Nations carvings and works by the famed Group of Seven. (p77)

UBC Museum of Anthropology Vancouver's top collection centers on soaring, beautifully carved totem poles. (p644)

Sunshine Coast Gallery Crawl Studios stud the British Columbia coast. A purple flag fluttering over a property means the artist is in. (p677)

Cape Dorset This small, wintry town in Nunavut is the epicenter of Inuit art. (p821)

Seafood

Digby Foodies from around the globe salivate over the giant, butter-soft scallops from this Nova Scotia town. (p361)

Lobster Supper Don a bib and crack into a crustacean in a Prince Edward Island church basement. (p453)

Malpeque Tiny PEI town where the namesake oysters come from, famed for their moist, briny taste. (p454)

Red Fish Blue Fish This takeout shack on Victoria's waterfront serves sustainably caught seafood. (p688)

Markets

Kensington Market It's a blast rummaging through the vintage shops of this offbeat Toronto neighborhood. (p81)

Panda Market Taste-trip through steaming Malaysian, Korean, Japanese and Chinese food stalls near Vancouver. (p666)

Marché Jean-Talon Farmers from the countryside bring their fruits, veggies, cheeses

Top: Kensington Market (p81), Toronto

Bottom: Cape Enrage lightstation (p420)

Polar bear on the tundra

and sausages to Montréal's lively marketplace. (p256)

St Lawrence Market Butchers, bakers and pasta-makers fill Toronto's awesome 1845 market hall. Art and antiques, too. (p75)

Salt Spring Island Saturday Market Gobble island-grown fruit and piquant cheeses while perusing local arts and crafts. (p716)

Halifax Seaport Farmer's Market With 250 vendors, this market is a prime spot to buy organic produce and seafood. (p345)

Beaches

Basin Head Beach Many Prince Edward Island locals rate this sweeping stretch of sand as their favorite. (p446)

Sauble Beach This shore near Southampton, Ontario, was voted Canada's best freshwater beach. (p144)

Eastern Shore Beaches Several white-sand beaches with life-guards, boardwalks, swimming and even surfing brush the coast near Halifax. (p334)

Greenwich Follow the board-walk over marshlands and dramatic dunes onto Prince Edward Island's most unspoiled, pink-sand beach. (p447)

Long Beach Located near Tofino, the pounding Pacific waves draw surfers and beach bums alike. (p704)

English Bay Beach This sandy curve in downtown Vancouver bustles with buskers, sunbathers and volleyballers. (p636)

Starry Nights

Moose Factory No roads to this speck on the Ontario map, just a small Cree settlement and eco-lodge. (p182)

Torngat Mountains National Park Labrador's raw, chilly tip has no towns in sight for hundreds of kilometers. (p509)

Yellowknife The Northwest Territories' far-flung, kitted-out capital lets you see the lights while dogsledding. (p796)

Churchill Visit around October and you'll have northern lights with a side of polar bears. (p531)

Whitehorse The Yukon's arty main town has outfitters who'll take you out under the night sky. (p773)

Month by Month

TOP EVENTS

Montréal Jazz Festival, June

Québec City's Winter Carnival, February

Stratford Festival, April–November

Dark Sky Festival, October

Festival Acadien, August

January

Ski season is in full swing, and many mountains receive their peak snowfall. Toward the end of the month, cities begin their winter carnivals to break the shackles of cold, dark days.

Ice Wine Festivals

British Columbia's Okanagan Valley (www.thewinefestivals.com) and Ontario's Niagara Peninsula (www.niagarawinefestival.com) celebrate their ice wines with good-time festivals. The distinctive, sweet libations go down the hatch alongside chestnut roasts, cocktail competitions and cozy alpine-lodge ambience.

February

Yes it's cold, as in 'coldest temperature ever recorded' cold (that'd be Snag, Yukon, on February 3, 1947: −62.8°C). But that doesn't stop folks from being outdoors. February is a party month, filled with all kinds of wintry events.

Chinese New Year

Dragons dance, firecrackers burst and food sizzles in the country's Chinatowns. Vancouver (www.vancouver-chinatown.com) hosts the biggest celebration, but Toronto, Calgary, Ottawa and Montréal also have festivities. The lunar calendar determines the date.

Québec City's Winter Carnival

Revelers watch ice-sculpture competitions, hurtle down snow slides, go ice fishing and cheer on their favorite paddlers in an insane canoe race on the half-frozen, ice-floe-ridden St Lawrence River. It's the world's biggest winter fest (www.carnaval.qc.ca).

Winterlude in Ottawa

A snowy bash along the Rideau Canal, where skaters glide by on the 7.8km of groomed ice. When they're not sipping hot chocolate and eating beavertails (fried-dough pastry), the townsfolk build massive sculptures entirely of ice (www.pch.gc.ca/winterlude).

Yukon Quest

This legendary 1600km dog-sled race (www.yukonquest.com) goes from Whitehorse to Fairbanks, Alaska, through February darkness and -50°C temperatures. It's the ultimate test of musher and husky. Record time: 10 days, 2 hours, 37 minutes.

World Pond Hockey Tournament

Small Plaster Rock, New Brunswick, plows 20 rinks on Roulston Lake, rings them with straw-bale seating for 8000-odd spectators and invites 120 four-person teams to hit the puck. Teams travel from as far as the UK, Egypt and the Cayman Islands (www.worldpondhockey.ca).

Northern Manitoba Trappers' Festival

The Pas puts on a weekend of frosty anarchy featuring dogsled races, snowmobiling, ice sculptures, torchlight parades and trapping games (www.trappersfestival.ca). Bundle up: the daily mean temperature is -16.1°C.

Vancouver International Wine Festival

Vancouver uncorks 1700 wines from 200 vintners at the Vancouver International Wine Festival (www.vanwinefest.ca), a rite of spring for oenophiles. You're drinking for art's sake, since the event raises funds for the city's contemporary theater company.

March

Snow lessens and temperatures moderate from the brunt of winter. Ski resorts still do brisk business, especially mid-month when kids typically have a week-long school break.

Sugar Shacks

Québec produces three-quarters of the world's maple syrup, and March is when trees get tapped. Head out to local sugar shacks, scoop up some snow, put it on a plate and have steaming syrup from a piping cauldron poured on.

Regina Powwow

Students at First Nations University of Canada initiated this Saskatchewan powwow (www.fnuniv.ca/pow-wow) 30-plus years ago to celebrate spring and give thanks for the land's rebirth. Dancers arrive from around North America, and traditional crafts and foods abound.

April

Apart from the far north, winter's chill fades and spring sprouts. It's a good time for bargains since ski season is winding down but the summer influx hasn't yet begun.

Stratford Festival

Canada's Stratford, a few hours outside Toronto, nearly outdoes England's Stratford-upon-Avon. The Stratford Festival (www.stratfordfestival.ca) plays a monster season from April to November. Four theaters stage contemporary drama, music, operas and, of course, works by Shakespeare. Productions are first-rate and feature well-known actors.

World Ski & Snowboard Festival

Ski bums converge on Whistler for 10 days of adrenaline events, outdoor rock and hip-hop concerts, film screenings, dog parades and a whole lotta carousing (www.wssf.com). Heed the motto: Party in April. Sleep in May.

Hot Docs

Want to learn more about Ontario's Hwy 7? Millionaires who live in Mumbai's slums? Belly dancers working in Cairo? Toronto hosts North America's largest documentary film festival (www.hotdocs.ca), which screens 170-plus docos from around the globe.

May

May is a fine time for shoulder-season bargains and wildflower vistas. The weather is warm by day, though nippy at night. Victoria Day at month's end marks the official start of summer.

Tiptoe Through the Tulips

After a long winter, Ottawa bursts with color – more than three million tulips of 200 types blanket the city for the Canadian Tulip Festival (www.tulipfestival.ca). Festivities include parades, regattas, car rallies, dances, concerts and fireworks.

Chocolate Festival

Plays about chocolate, painting with chocolate, jewelry making with chocolate – are you sensing a theme? Québec's Fête du Chocolat de Bromont (www.feteduchocolat.ca) is all about the sweet stuff. The best part: eating the chocolate. Bromont lies 75km east of Montréal.

June

Take advantage of long, warm days to hike, paddle and soak up the great outdoors (but bring repellent for black flies). Attractions don't get mega-busy until later in the month, when school lets out for the summer.

Luminato

For 10 days in early June, big-name musicians, dancers, artists, writers, actors and filmmakers descend on Toronto for a celebration of creativity that reflects the city's diversity (www.luminatofestival.com). Many performances are free.

North by Northeast

Around 1000 emerging indie bands spill off the stages in Toronto's coolest clubs. You might catch the

Top: Pouring out maple syrup on snow at a sugar shack

Bottom: Pride Toronto

rock stars of tomorrow. Film screenings and comedy shows add to the mix. Over its 20-year history, NXNE (www.nxne.com) has become a must on the music-industry calendar.

Montréal Jazz Festival

Two million music lovers descend on Montréal in late June, when the heart of downtown explodes with jazz and blues for 11 straight days (www.montrealjazzfest.com). Most concerts are outdoors and free, and the party goes on round the clock.

Pride Toronto

Toronto's most flamboyant event (www.pridetoronto.com) celebrates all kinds of sexuality, climaxing with an out-of-the-closet Dyke March and the outrageous Pride Parade. Pride's G-spot is in the Church-Wellesley Village; most events are free.

Elvis Festival

If you're in Penticton, BC, in late June and you keep seeing Elvis, rest assured it's not because you've swilled too much of the local Okanagan Valley wine. The town hosts Elvis Fest (www.pentictonelvisfestival.ca) with dozens of impersonators and open-mike sing-alongs.

Sakatchewan Jazz Festival

Come show your soul patch at this jazzy 10-day festival (www.saskjazz.com) at venues throughout Saskatoon. Blues, funk, pop and world music are also on the agenda. Herbie Hancock and Ziggy Marley are among the acts that have trekked to the prairie.

July

This is prime time for visiting most provinces, with the weather at its warmest, a bounty of fresh produce and seafood filling plates, and festivals rockin' the nights away. Crowds are thick.

Country Music in Cavendish

Some of the biggest names in country music come to Prince Edward Island for the Cavendish Beach Festival (www.cavendishbeachmusic.com). This is one of the largest outdoor music festivals in North America, and the island swells with people.

Montréal Comedy Festival

Everyone gets giddy for two weeks at the Just for Laughs Festival (www.hahaha.com), which features hundreds of comedy shows, including free ones in the Quartier Latin. The biggest names in the biz yuck it up for this one.

Calgary Stampede

Raging bulls, chuckwagon racing and bad-ass, boot-wearing cowboys unite for the 'Greatest Outdoor Show on Earth.' A midway of rides and games makes it a family affair well beyond the usual rodeo event, attracting 1.1 million yee-hawin' fans (www.calgarystampede.com).

Winnipeg Fringe Festival

North America's second-largest fringe fest (www.winnipegfringe.com) stages creative, raw and oddball works from a global line-up of performers. Comedy, drama, music, cabaret and even musical memoirs are on tap over 12 days.

Arctic Art

The Great Northern Arts Festival (www.gnaf.org) in Inuvik, Northwest Territories, draws scores of carvers, painters and other creators from across the circumpolar world. It's an ideal place to buy arctic art, watch it being made or participate in workshops.

Stan Rogers Folk Festival

Honoring a legendary Canadian folk singer, the three-day Stanfest (www.stanfest.com) in Corso, Nova Scotia, has drawn dozens of artists for over two decades. Over 10,000 fans flock to the tiny town to strum, dance and croon.

August

The sunny days and shindigs continue. Visitors throng most provinces, and prices reflect it. It can get downright hot and humid away from the coasts.

Acadian Celebration

Acadians tune their fiddles and unleash their Franco-Canadian spirit for the Festival Acadien (www.festivalacadien.ca) in Caraquet, New Brunswick. It's the biggest event on the Acadian calendar, with singers, musicians and dancers letting loose for two weeks in early August.

Newfoundland Rowing Regatta

The streets are empty, the stores are closed and everyone migrates to the shores of Quidi Vidi Lake for the Royal St John's Regatta (www.stjohnsregatta.org). The rowing race began in 1825 and is now the continent's oldest continuously held sporting event.

Edmonton Fringe Festival

Edmonton's Fringe Festival is North America's largest fringe bash, staging some 1600 performances of wild, uncensored shows over 11 days in mid-August. Acts are democratically chosen by lottery (www.fringetheatreadventures.ca).

Canadian National Exhibition

Akin to a state fair in the USA, 'The Ex' (www.theex.com) features more than 700 exhibitors, agricultural shows, lumberjack competitions, outdoor concerts and carnivalia at Toronto's Exhibition Place. The 18-day event runs through Labour Day and ends with a bang-up fireworks display.

September

Labour Day in early September heralds the end of summer, after which crowds (and prices) diminish. But the weather is still decent in most places, making it an excellent time to visit. Plus, moose mating season begins!

Prince Edward Island Fall Flavours

This island-wide kitchen party merges toe-tapping traditional music with incredible seafood over the course of three weeks (www.fallflavours.ca). In Charlottetown, don't miss the oyster-shucking championships or the chowder challenge.

Toronto International Film Festival

Toronto's prestigious 10-day celebration (www.tiff.net) is a major cinematic event. Films of all lengths and styles are screened in September, as celebs shimmy between gala events and the Bell Lightbox building. Buy tickets well in advance.

Newfoundland Coastal Cookout

The wee town of Elliston in eastern Newfoundland gathers many of Canada's best chefs and has them cook at stations set up along a gorgeous 5km coastal trail. Foodies flock in to eat and hike and eat some more (www.rootsrantsand roars.ca).

Canadian Deep Roots Festival

Tune in to Mi'kmaw, Acadian, African–Nova Scotian and other unique music – all with local roots – in the fun university town of Wolfville, Nova Scotia (www.deeprootsmusic.ca). Workshops are available with some of the performers, so you can learn to drum, strum or fiddle.

October

With fall foliage flaming bright and the weather cool but comfortable, October welcomes lots of visitors. Grab a stick, because hockey season gets underway.

Celtic Colours

With foot-stompin' music amid riotous foliage, this roving festival in Cape Breton attracts top musicians from Scotland, Spain and other countries with Celtic connections (www.celtic-colours.com). Community suppers, step-dancing classes and tin-whistle lessons round out the cultural celebration.

Oktoberfest in Ontario

Willkommen to this nine-day beery Bavarian bash in Kitchener, supposedly the largest Oktoberfest outside of Germany (www.oktober fest.ca). The sauerkraut, oompah bands, lederhosen and *biergartens* bring 500,000 people to clink steins under the tents.

Dark Sky Festival

In late October, Jasper's Dark Sky Festival (jasper darksky.travel) fills two weeks with events celebrating space. Hear talks by astronauts and celebrities like Bill Nye, listen to the symphony under the stars, see the aurora borealis reflected in a glacial lake and gaze through a telescope into the great beyond.

December

Get out the parka. Winter begins in earnest as snow falls, temperatures drop and ski resorts ramp up for the masses. 'Tis the holiday season too.

Mountain Time

Powder hounds hit the slopes from east to west. Whistler in British Columbia, Mont-Tremblant in Québec and the Canadian Rockies around Banff, Alberta, pull the biggest crowds, but there's downhill action – and cross-country – going on in every province.

Niagara Festival of Lights

The family-friendly Winter Festival of Lights (www.wfol.com) gets everyone in the holiday spirit with three million twinkling bulbs and 125 animated displays brightening the town and the waterfall itself. Ice-skate on the 'rink at the brink' of the cascade.

Itineraries

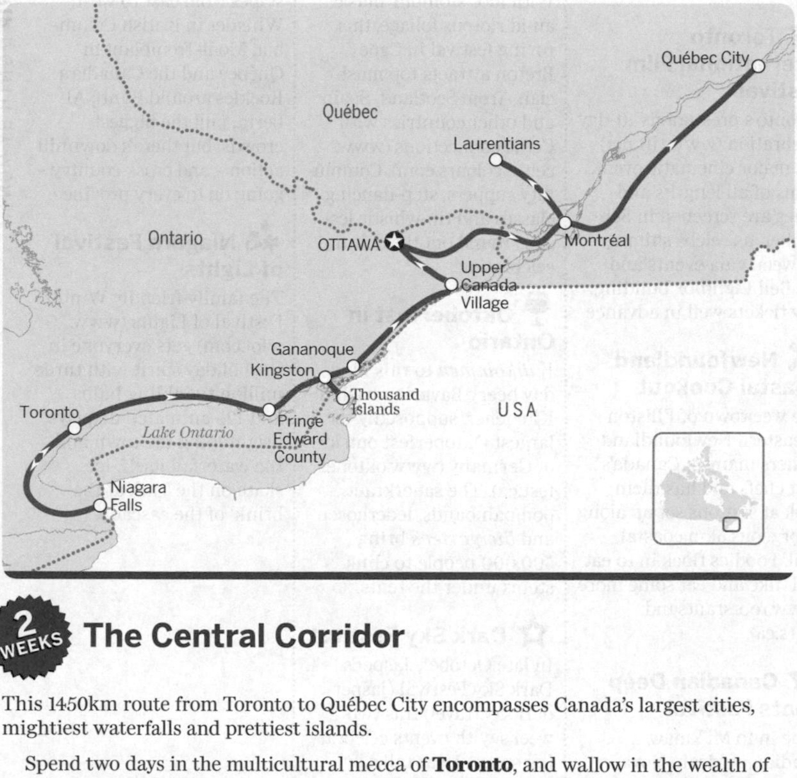

The Central Corridor

This 1450km route from Toronto to Québec City encompasses Canada's largest cities, mightiest waterfalls and prettiest islands.

Spend two days in the multicultural mecca of **Toronto**, and wallow in the wealth of architecture, art museums, restaurants and nightclubs. Spend day three at **Niagara Falls**, then begin your eastward haul. The Loyalist Parkway (Hwy 33) rambles shoreside in winery-laden **Prince Edward County** and pulls into colonial **Kingston**. From there, the misty, mansion-covered **Thousand Islands** dot the St Lawrence River; **Gananoque** makes a good break for a day in their midst. Make a half-day stop at **Upper Canada Village**, a re-created 1860s town, before heading to **Ottawa** for a couple of days to get your culture fix at the national museums. Save room for your next stop, **Montréal**, where the French exuberance seduces via Euro-cool clubs and foodie-beloved cafes. Had your fill? Swing over to the **Laurentians** to spend a day or two and hike, cycle or ski yourself back into shape. Finish in **Québec City** – the charismatic Old Town, walled and dramatically poised on a bluff, will leave an impression long after you return home.

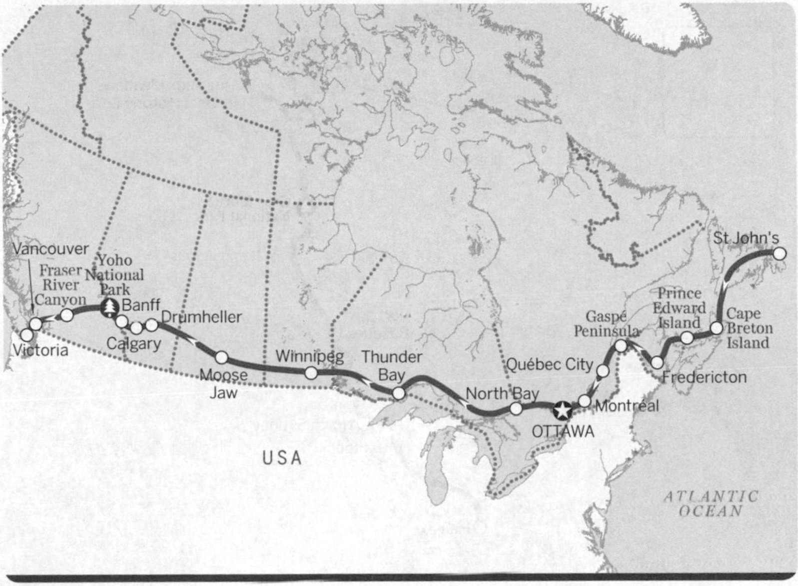

Trans-Canada Highway

The world's longest highway – a 7800km belt of asphalt cinched around Canada's girth – is technically a patchwork of provincial roads. Scenic stretches alternate with mundane ones; many of the best sights require a detour off the highway.

The road begins in **St John's**, Newfoundland, Canada's oldest city and a heck-of-a-pub-filled good time. It rolls all the way through the province until it hits the sea, at which point you must ferry over to North Sydney, Nova Scotia, where the road resumes on beautiful **Cape Breton Island**. Continue to New Brunswick – or take the longer route to **Prince Edward Island** – then follow the St John River via **Fredericton** to Québec. The **Gaspé Peninsula** entices as a pastoral side-trip east. Otherwise, the highway follows the mighty St Lawrence River and reaches romantic **Québec City**.

Carry on the urban theme in **Montréal**, where the *pâtisseries* and *café* will keep you lingering, before plunging into Ontario at museum-fortified **Ottawa**. From there, follow in the fur traders' footsteps to **North Bay**, the gateway to the Algoma wilderness that inspired the Group of Seven painters. Savor the superb stretch of road skirting Lake Superior to **Thunder Bay**. And voilà, there goes week two.

Next the highway enters the prairie flatlands of Manitoba, where **Winnipeg** rockets up and provides an enlivening patch of cafes and culture. The road dawdles under Saskatchewan's big skies until reaching bad-ass **Moose Jaw**, where Al Capone used to hide his bootlegged booze. In Alberta, dinosaur junkies can detour to **Drumheller**. And put on your cowboy boots before arriving in **Calgary**, a former cow town that's become one of Canada's fastest-growing cities. So passes week three...

You're in the Rockies now. They offer a dramatic change of scenery as the highway meanders through **Banff** before entering British Columbia at **Yoho National Park** and reaching its highest point (1643m) at Kicking Horse Pass. The mountains eventually give way to river country. The most memorable section leads through the **Fraser River Canyon** from where it's only a quick jaunt to mod, multicultural **Vancouver** and the ferry to **Victoria**. Snap a picture at the Mile 0 sign. You made it!

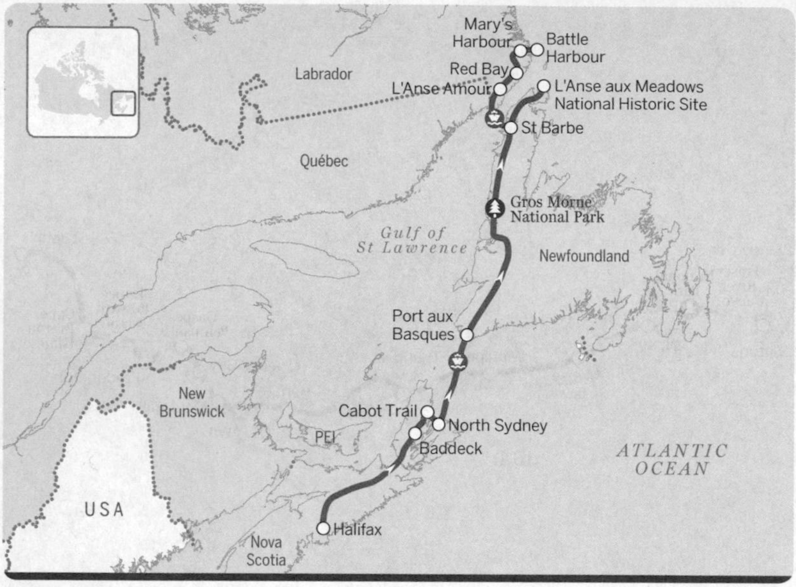

Cabot & Viking Trails

Wild, windswept and whale-riddled, this 1700km route through Nova Scotia, Newfoundland, Labrador and Québec unfurls sea-and-cliff vistas, Viking vestiges and much more.

Start in **Halifax** and spend a few days enjoying the beer, farmers markets and cosmopolitan life. Then hit the road to Celtic-tinged Cape Breton Island for two days. It's about a five-hour drive, and there's no ferry involved, as a causeway connects the mainland to the island. You won't have time to traverse Cape Breton in depth, but you can certainly get a feel for its beauty in pastoral **Baddeck** and along the art-studio-dotted **Cabot Trail**. Industrial **North Sydney** is nearby for the ferry to Newfoundland.

It's a six-hour sail over the Cabot Strait to **Port aux Basques**. The ferry goes daily, but be sure to book in advance. Spend a day in the sleepy town, then steer for **Gros Morne National Park**, about four hours north on the Trans-Canada Hwy. This World Heritage site is rich with mountain hikes, sea-kayak tours, fjord-like lakes and weird rock formations. After soaking it up for three days, continue on the Viking Trail to its awe-inspiring endpoint: **L'Anse aux Meadows**. This was North America's first settlement, where Leif Eriksson and his Viking pals homesteaded 1000 years ago. Poke around for a day before backtracking about two hours to **St Barbe**, where the ferry for Labrador departs. Reservations are wise for the daily, two-hour crossing.

And then you're in the Big Land. (Actually, the ferry lands in Québec, but more on that province later.) Turn your wheels northeast and head for **L'Anse Amour**, intriguing for its tall lighthouse and shipwreck-strewn hiking trail. Further along is **Red Bay**, Canada's newest World Heritage site, which preserves a massive, 16th-century whaling port. To really get away from it all, drive 90km onward to Mary's Harbour and spend the night on the offshore island that holds **Battle Harbour**, a restored village. After a few days in Labrador, it's time to head back. Before getting on the ferry, detour for a few hours down Rte 138 in Québec. It makes a beautiful drive past waterfalls and overlooks the crashing surf. Afterward, you'll need a couple of (long) days to retrace your path to Halifax.

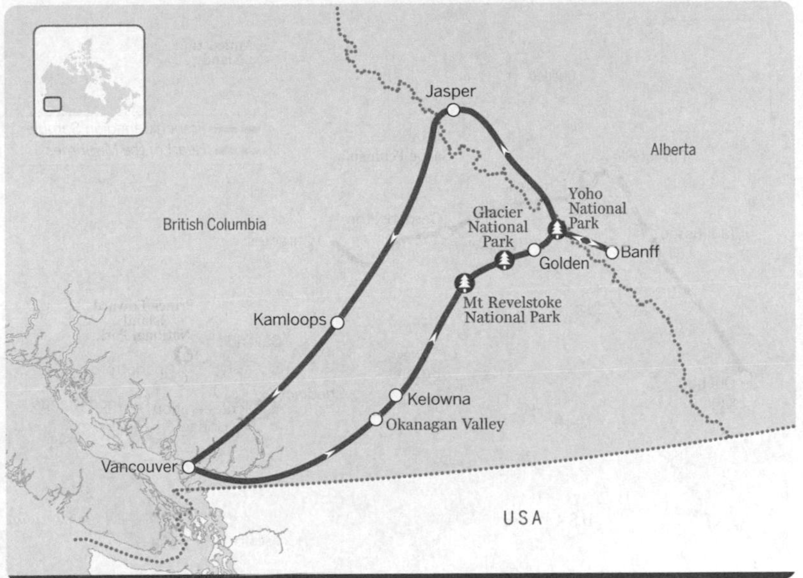

The Rockies

Prepare to feast on a smorgasbord of scenic delights on this 2000km trek, which loops through British Columbia and Alberta.

Start with a couple of days in mountain-meets-the-sea **Vancouver**, where you'll be spoiled by urban hiking, biking and other activities, plus western Canada's best culinary scene. Make the wine pilgrimage east through rolling hills to the lake-studded **Okanagan Valley**, famous for its fruit orchards, crisp whites and bold reds. **Kelowna** makes a good sipping base in the area.

Next it's time to get high in BC's Rocky Mountains. A trio of national parks pops up in quick succession, each providing plenty of 'ah'-inspiring vistas. **Mt Revelstoke** has a cool scenic drive and hikes. **Glacier** has 430 of its namesake ice fields. And **Yoho** is home to looming peaks and crashing waterfalls. **Golden** is a convenient base.

Cross the border into Alberta, and park it in **Banff**. You won't be able to stop the cliches from flying forth: grand! majestic! awe-inspiring! Allot plenty of time – at least three days – for hiking, paddling, gawking at glaciers and spotting grizzly bears (best done from a distance). Sapphire-blue Lake Louise is a must, surrounded by alpine-style teahouses that let you fuel your hikes with scones, beer and hot chocolate.

From Banff, the Icefields Pkwy (Hwy 93) parallels the Continental Divide for 230km to **Jasper**. Try to keep your eyes at least partially on the road as you drive by the humongous Columbia Icefield and its numerous fanning glaciers. Foaming waterfalls, dramatic mountains and the sudden dart of a bear (or was that a moose?) are also part of the journey. Jasper itself is bigger and less crowded than Banff, and offers superb hiking, horseback riding, rock climbing, mountain biking and rafting.

It's a shame to have to leave, but we must return to Vancouver. The Yellowhead Hwy (Hwy 5) plows south to **Kamloops**, a handy spot to spend the night before motoring back to the City of Glass.

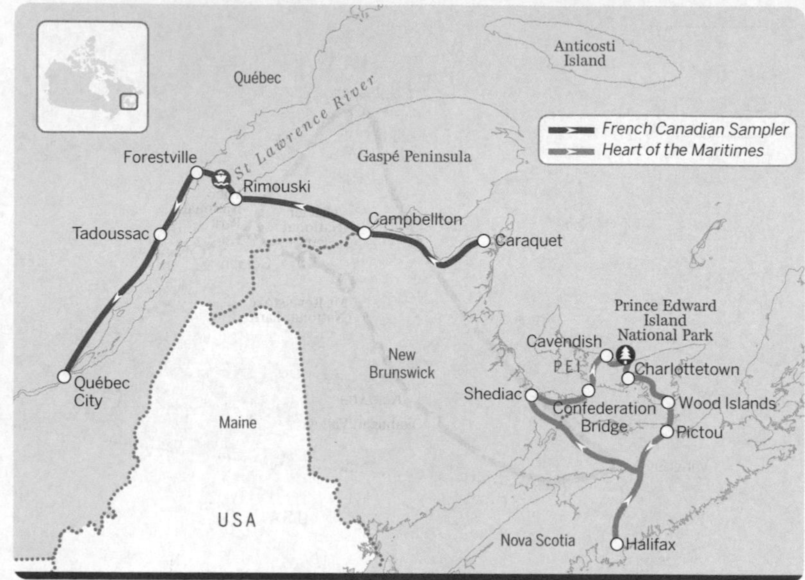

1 WEEK French Canadian Sampler

Get a taste of Gallic Canada on this 700km jaunt through New Brunswick and Québec.

Start in **Caraquet** and immerse yourself in Acadian culture at the historic sites and via local foods like *pets de sœur* ('nun's farts' in English – try one to see if you can figure out why). If you visit in August, the fiddle-fueled Festival Acadien takes over the town.

Ramble east through **Campbellton** and cross into Québec. **Rimouski**, on the St Lawrence River, is your target. Explore its intriguing museums and delicious cafes, and day-trip east up the **Gaspé Peninsula** on Rte 132, where fluttering Acadian flags, tidy farming hamlets and rocky shores flash by.

From Rimouski, a ferry crosses the river to **Forestville**, from where you can head south to welcoming **Tadoussac**. It's all about whale-watching in this boho little town; zodiacs motor out to see the blue whales that patrol the area.

Finish your trip in atmospheric **Québec City**. Check in at a cozy inn, wander the Old Town's labyrinth of lanes and stop often to sip in the corner cafes.

Heart of the Maritimes

This 650km loop lassos the core of the Maritime provinces (Nova Scotia, New Brunswick and Prince Edward Island).

Eat and drink your way through **Halifax**, then make a break northwest for New Brunswick. Festive **Shediac** is home to the world's biggest lobster sculpture and – no surprise – the cooked version of the creature gets served in eateries all over town.

Barrel over the 12.9km **Confederation Bridge** that links New Brunswick to PEI and begin the pilgrimage to Anne's Land. Anne, of course, is the fictional red-headed orphan of Green Gables fame, and **Cavendish** is the wildly developed town that pays homage to her.

Continue the red theme by exploring the red sandstone bluffs at **Prince Edward Island National Park**; there's birdwatching, beach walking and swimming too. Stop in PEI's compact, colonial capital **Charlottetown** before taking the ferry from **Wood Islands** back to **Pictou** in Nova Scotia. You can stroll Pictou's boardwalk and, if you're lucky, the town might be hosting its First Nations Powwow. It's about two hours from here back to Halifax.

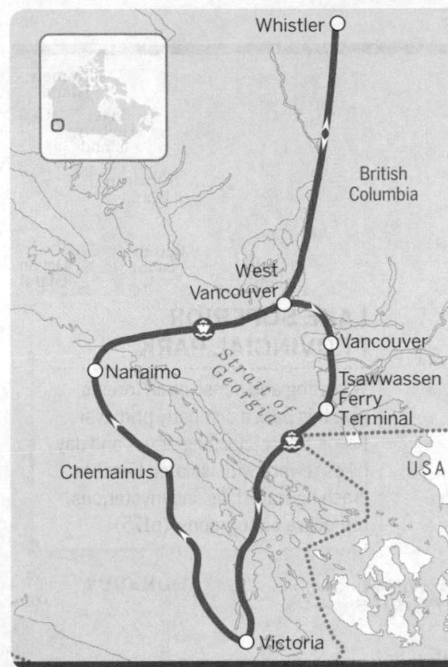

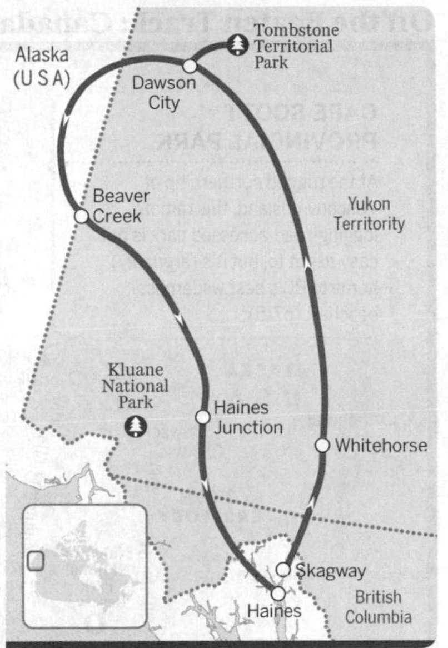

Bite of British Columbia

You don't have to drive far to experience a range of heart-leaping landscapes in southern BC. Ocean, mountains, forests, islands – all present and accounted for in roughly 550km.

Begin in **Vancouver** and take a couple of days to check out the indie shops, the foodie fare and the forested seawall vistas of Stanley Park. On day three, drive to the Tsawwassen ferry terminal for the dreamy boat trip to Swartz Bay on Vancouver Island. Zip over to **Victoria**, spending an overnight exploring the picture-perfect capital and its historic buildings. On day four, drive north up the island on Hwy 1, stopping off at **Chemainus**, a former logging settlement that's reinvented itself as an art town. Continue north for a late lunch and an overnight in **Nanaimo**, then, next morning, catch the ferry back to the mainland's Horseshoe Bay terminal in **West Vancouver**.

From here, the Sea to Sky Hwy (Hwy 99) runs cliffside through formidable mountains to **Whistler**. The resort town has heaps of adrenaline activities and fun, ski-bum bars to occupy your final few days. It's 130km back to Vancouver.

Klondike Highway & Around

Heed the call of the wild, and set your wheels for this epic roadway. Know it'll be a lot of driving for one week (approximately 30 hours), but the road *is* the main attraction of the trip.

Start in **Skagway, Alaska**, as the Klondike Hwy does. Soon you'll leave the cruise ships behind and enter the rugged land Jack London wrote so much about. Follow the road to lively **Whitehorse**, which has groovy arts and organic bakeries. From there continue north to offbeat **Dawson City**. Linger a few days and check out the gold rush historic sites, take a mine tour and blow a kiss to the dancing girls. Day-trip to **Tombstone Territorial Park** for its wide, steep grandeur.

Next, follow the Top of the World Hwy (Hwy 9) across mountain tops to the Alaskan border, and connect down through the US and onto the Alaska Hwy in the Yukon at **Beaver Creek**. The road between here and well-stocked **Haines Junction** is sublime, paralleling Kluane National Forest and the St Elias Mountains. The gawk-worthy Haines Hwy rolls in to **Haines**, Alaska, where your journey ends.

Off the Beaten Track: Canada

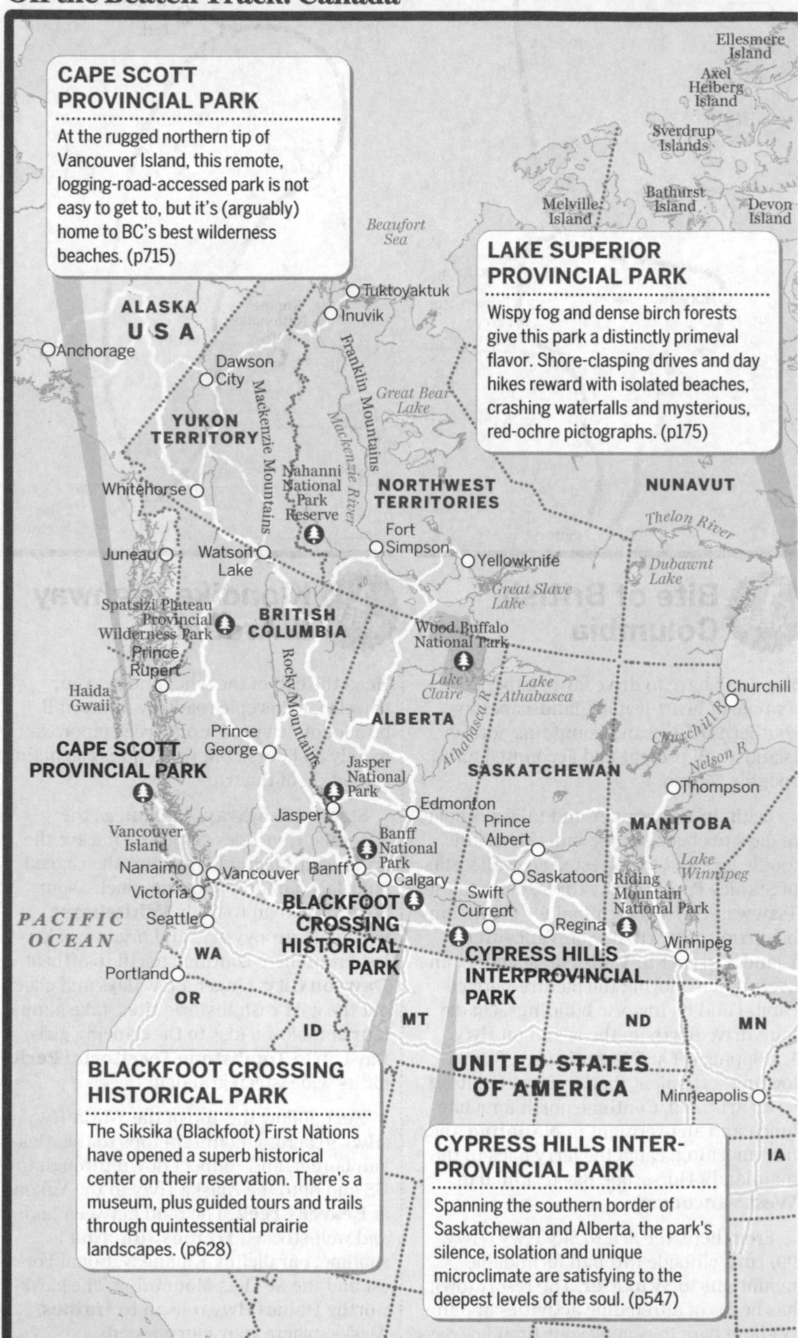

PANGNIRTUNG

This artistic Baffin Island Inuit community is the gorgeous launching pad to the soaring cliffs and utterly spellbinding magnificence of Auyuittuq National Park. (p819)

TORNGAT MOUNTAINS NATIONAL PARK

You'll have to fly or boat in to Labrador's chilly tip, home to polar bears and some of the highest peaks east of the Rockies. Local Inuit guides lead the way for otherworldly hiking and flightseeing. (p509)

GASPÉ PENINSULA

This is the windswept, rocky spot where Jacques Cartier landed in 1534, surrounded by steep limestone cliffs, pebble beaches, whales, seals and the ever-crashing sea. (p308)

TAYLOR HEAD PROVINCIAL PARK

This beachy park on Nova Scotia's undeveloped eastern shore juts out into the Atlantic, offering trails of wildflowers and beach grass and plenty of perfect sheltered coves for kayaking. (p390)

Jasper National Park (p606), Rockies Rail Rout

Plan Your Trip

Scenic Drives & Train Trips

Canada – blessed with a huge expanse of wild landscapes that have highways unfurling right through the good parts – is made for road-tripping. Spiky mountains, ocean vistas, moose and Tim Hortons doughnut shops flash by. Even if you have just one day, you can take a gobsmacking journey. With more time you can really roll.

Best Experiences

➡ Dance at a traditional ceilidh on the Cabot Trail

➡ Visit a misty, gothic castle on the Thousand Islands Parkway

➡ Hike and bike on the Sea to Sky Hwy

➡ See whales from shore on the Cabot Trail

➡ Gape at dazzling mountain views on the Rockies Rail Route

Major Sights

➡ Jasper National Park (Rockies Rail Route)

➡ The Chief (Sea to Sky Hwy)

➡ Thousand Islands National Park (Thousand Islands Pkwy)

➡ Cape Breton Highlands National Park (Cabot Trail)

Key Starting Points

➡ Vancouver or Whistler, British Columbia (Sea to Sky Hwy)

➡ Gananoque or Brockville, Ontario (Thousand Islands Pkwy)

➡ Chéticamp or Baddeck, Nova Scotia (Cabot Trail)

➡ Jasper, Alberta or Prince Rupert, British Columbia (Rockies Rail Route)

Sea to Sky Highway

Otherwise known as Hwy 99, this cliffside roadway offers a heart-leaping, humbling drive from Vancouver's ocean to Whistler's peaks. It begins at sea level, clasping the shore of Howe Sound, before twisting into the Coast Mountains and climbing through old-growth rainforests. You'll rise 670m (2200ft) during the 130km route, with plenty of opportunities for scenic vistas, waterfall gaping and outdoor activities along the way.

Highlights

In West Vancouver, not long after you cross the Lion's Gate Bridge, drop by Lighthouse Park to see the namesake structure along with shimmering sea views. Next you'll pass Horseshoe Bay, where ferries glide in and out for the 20-minute ride to Bowen Island – a rustically charming retreat populated by writers and artists.

Back on Hwy 99, about 30km north is the kid-friendly Britannia Mine Museum. Descend into the former copper pit for an underground train tour, followed by gold panning. About 6km onward you'll hear the rushing waters of Shannon Falls Provincial Park. Pull into the parking lot and stroll the 10-minute trail to British Columbia's third-highest waterfall, which gushes 335m down the rock face.

Continuing your drive, you'll soon see a sheer, 652m-high granite rock face looming ahead. It's called the 'Chief' and it's the highlight of Stawamus Chief Provincial Park. Climbers go ga-ga over it. The town just beyond is Squamish, a haven for mountain bikers, hikers, kiteboarders and microbrew aficionados. It's a great spot to hang out for a day.

Nearby Brackendale attracts thousands of salmon-hungry eagles in winter. Hikers will want to pit stop at Garibaldi Provincial Park. Pull over at any of the designated trailheads to meander past scenic alpine meadows and breathtaking mountain views.

Back on the road, you'll be in Whistler before you know it. Canada's favorite ski resort combines a gabled, Christmas-card village with some jaw-dropping dual-mountain terrain. Skiers and snowboarders will be in their glory in winter, while summer is almost as busy with mountain bikers and hikers.

When to Go

This is a beautiful, well-maintained drive any time of year.

Time & Mileage

It's 130km from Vancouver to Whistler on the Sea to Sky Hwy. You can drive it in under two hours. But why hurry? It works best when stretched into a two- or three-day jaunt.

Western Road & Rail

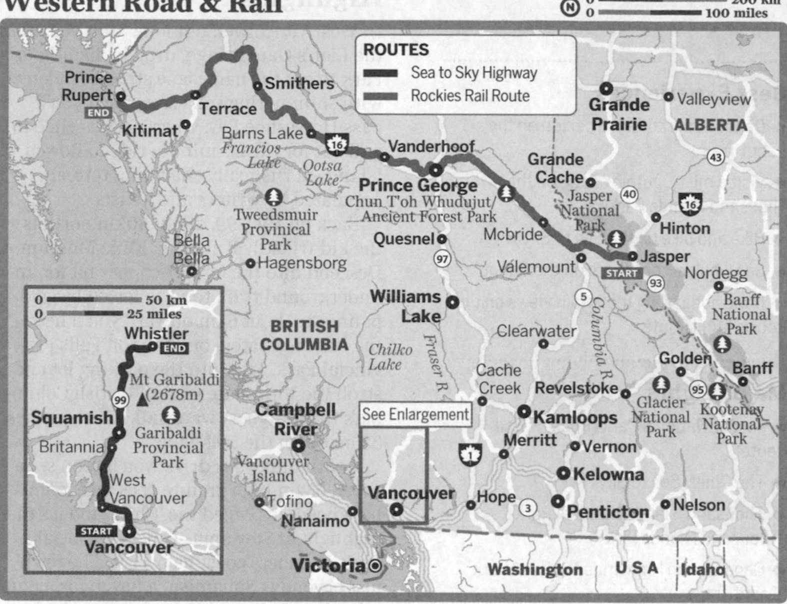

ADVANCE PLANNING

- ➡ Join an automobile club that provides 24-hour emergency roadside assistance and discounts on lodging and attractions.
- ➡ Some international clubs have reciprocal agreements with Canadian automobile associations, so check first and bring your member card from home.
- ➡ International travelers might want to review Canada's road rules and common road hazards.
- ➡ Make sure your vehicle has a spare tire, a tool kit (eg jack, jumper cables, ice scraper, tire pressure gauge) and emergency equipment (eg flashers).
- ➡ Bring good maps, especially if you're touring off-road or away from highways. Don't rely on a GPS unit – in remote areas it may not even work.
- ➡ Always carry your driver's license and proof of insurance.

Resources

Tourism BC (www.hellobc.com/driving-routes/31/sea-to-sky-highway-route.aspx) Driving directions for the route and stop-off points along the way.

Mountain FM Radio (107.1) Provides handy traffic and road-condition updates en route.

Drive BC (www.drivebc.ca) Driving conditions and alerts.

Rockies Rail Route

Rail buffs consider the Jasper to Prince Rupert train a must-do journey. It traverses epic Canadian scenery, from the cloud-wrapped peaks and glacial streams in Alberta's Rockies to the hauntingly beautiful Pacific coast of British Columbia. In between a whole lot of pine, spruce and hemlock trees whiz by, as do rustic settlements, rivers and sawmills. But then – did you see it? A black bear loping trackside. And totem poles that mark an ancient Aboriginal village veiled by trees. And unbelievably turquoise lakes glistening in the valleys...

Highlights

The train – a retro silver bullet from the 1950s – chugs during daylight hours only, so you see the landscape in all its glory. (You spend the night in Prince George, a long-standing lumber town at roughly the halfway point.)

The route traces an old Aboriginal trading path. It climbs over the Yellowhead Pass at 1130m, and follows the Skeena River to the ocean. The train gently sways and fabled images flash by: the ancient red cedars of Chun T'oh Whudujut, daring bridges, deep canyons, dark tunnels and snowy mountains.

The trip starts and ends with a scenic bang. Jasper National Park has the white-dipped peaks and glistening glaciers you see on postcards, while Prince Rupert is a misty, unspoiled town with an intriguing aboriginal heritage. Both are hot spots for adventure seekers.

When to Go

Mid-June to late September is peak period, when 'touring class' tickets (which include tour guides, meals and access to the train carriage with a panoramic dome) are available. The rest of the year only 'economy class' seats are available.

Time & Mileage

The train runs year-round, departing three times a week on Wednesday, Friday and Sunday. The 1160km trip between Jasper and Prince Rupert, including an overnight stay in Prince George, takes 33 hours.

Resources

Via Rail (www.viarail.ca) Prices and specifics on train routes.

Prince George Tourism (www.tourismpg.com) Lodging listings for your overnight stay.

Prince Rupert Tourism (www.visitprincerupert.com) For help planning onward adventures.

Thousand Islands Parkway

The Thousand Islands Pkwy rolls along a pastoral strip by the St Lawrence River, where a fog-cloaked constellation of 1800 islands floats between Kingston and Brockville, Ontario. The road offers dreamy vistas and dainty Victorian towns, where you can pull over to spend the night at an inn or take a boat ride through the isles, many of which hold rambling old mansions and castles. It's a mist-kissed trip into a slower, gentler era.

DAVID P LEWIS / SHUTTERSTOCK ©

Sea to Sky Hwy (Hwy 99)

Highlights

Even though the islands start around Kingston – a pretty, historical town with loads of museums on everything from shipbuilding to penitentiaries – the scenic drive doesn't really pick up until the town of Gananoque, some 33km east along Hwy 401. That's where the parkway dips south of the highway and rolls into gorgeous territory.

Gananoque is the area's star for ambience, filled with quaint inns and manicured gardens. It's also the jump-off point for boat cruises through the islands, especially to Boldt Castle, a turreted, Gothic palace by the gent who was the original proprietor of New York City's famous Waldorf Astoria Hotel. It's technically in the USA, so bring your passport.

Eastern Excursions

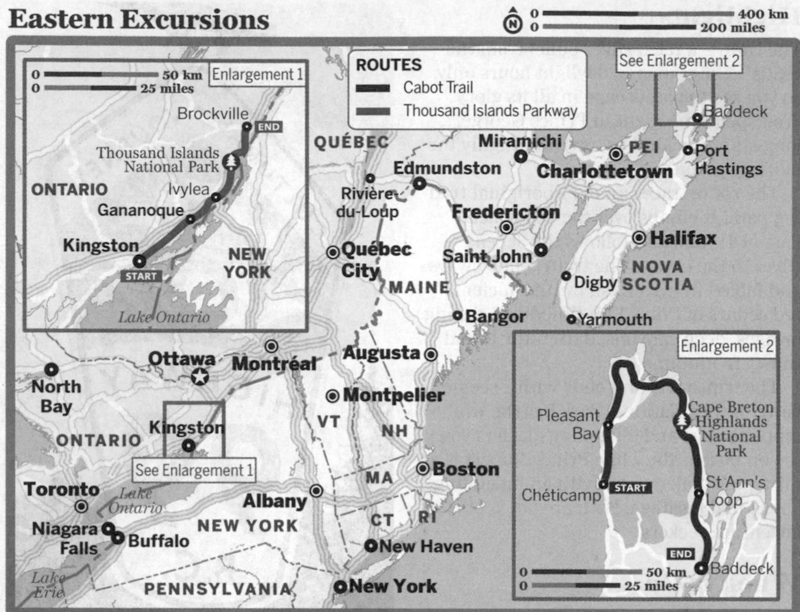

Ivylea is 22km onward, where soaring bridges link Ontario to New York State over several islands. Halfway across there's an observation deck with killer views (mists permitting). If boat tours aren't your thing, you can keep driving over the bridges and reach Boldt Castle by car.

Back on the parkway, the road continues to snake along the river, with furry green islands dotting the water beside it. In 18km you'll come to Mallorytown, the home base for Thousand Islands National Park. Twenty rugged, pine-laden islands are protected, home to lumbering turtles and peregrine falcons. It's a sublime area for backcountry camping and kayaking.

The parkway moseys on, hugging the river for a few more kilometers before rejoining Hwy 401 for the final approach into Brockville. This is another atmospheric town, with opulent 19th-century manors and vintage-looking streets where you can imagine the clip-clop sounds of carriage horses that used to ring through the area.

When to Go

June through September is peak season when the weather is most pleasant. May and October are good shoulder-season times. Many boat companies and activity outfitters close between November and April.

Time & Mileage

The parkway runs for 35km between Gananoque to just north of Mallorytown. The islands themselves stretch from Kingston to Brockville (about 90km). With boat trips or detours into the USA, you'll need a full day, and it's well worthwhile to spend the night along the way.

Resources

1000 Islands Gananoque Visitor Services Centre (www.1000islandsgananoque.com) Activity, restaurant and lodging info.

Top: Thousand Islands National Park (p203)

Bottom: Peregrine falcon

CHRIS HILL / SHUTTERSTOCK ©

Cabot Trail

The Cabot Trail rings Cape Breton Island, Nova Scotia's lush tip. Driving it is a singular, brake-smoking journey. The road twists and climbs over coastal mountains, and around every bend something awesome reveals itself: ocean views, dramatic cliffs, breaching whales just offshore or moose snacking by the roadside. Celtic and Acadian communities dot the area, and their crazy-fiddlin' music vibrates through local pubs. Their unique foods get heaped on local plates too, so loosen the belt for a full cultural immersion.

Cabot Trail (p379)

Highlights

Most road trippers start at Chéticamp, a deeply Acadian fishing community known for its crafty hooked rugs and lively music. It's also the gateway into Cape Breton Highlands National Park, where moose and bald eagle sightings are common. To stretch your legs, the park's hiking trails zigzag to spectacular, edge-of-cliff sea vistas. And how about some Acadian stewed chicken and potato pancakes with molasses? Chéticamp's eateries are prime for sampling.

Next along the roadway you'll reach Pleasant Bay, known for its whale-watching tours and Tibetan Buddhist monastery, where the monks give tours. Little fishing towns, world-famous golf courses, lighthouses and divine seafood houses pop up as you keep heading around the Cabot

TOP ROAD TRIP ALBUMS

These Canadian artists – some old, some new, spanning genres and provinces – will provide the proper soundtrack for your trip. Load up your favorites, hit shuffle and 'keep the car running,' as the first group on our list sings.

- Arcade Fire *Neon Bible*
- Tragically Hip *Fully Completely*
- Neil Young *Massey Hall 1971*
- The New Pornographers *Mass Romantic*
- Drake *Hotline Bling*
- Rush *Moving Pictures*
- Great Big Sea *Road Rage*
- Feist *The Reminder*
- Bachman-Turner Overdrive *Bachman-Turner Overdrive II*
- Stompin' Tom Connors *Ballad of Stompin' Tom*
- Jill Barber *Chansons*
- Great Lake Swimmers *Where in the World Are You*
- Drake *Take Care*
- The Weeknd *Beauty Behind the Madness*

Lighthouse in Chéticamp (p379), Cabot Trail

GO BIG OR GO HOME

Canada is a big place – and not every little town has a lot going for it. In a bid to attract tourists, communities across the country have created sights that may not be grand, but that are certainly BIG, proving that, to Canadians, size does matter. Here's just a few of the World's Biggest that you might encounter:

Hockey Stick 62.5m (Duncan, BC)

Cuckoo Clock 6.7m (Kimberley, BC)

Pierogi 7.6m (Glendon, Alberta)

T-Rex 26.2m (Drumheller, Alberta)

Moose 9.7m (Moose Jaw, Saskatchewan)

Nickel 9.1m (Sudbury, Ontario)

Axe 14.9 (Nackawic, NB)

Trail. And keep your eyes peeled for pods of frolicking pilot whales. The area around St Ann's is a center for Celtic arts. Baddeck is the unofficial end of the road, a beautiful spot to wind down and take in a traditional ceilidh (gathering for fiddling and dancing) in the town parish hall.

When to Go

July and August are peak season, with the nicest weather. September and October are good months to go, especially the latter for the Celtic Colours festival. Many places close from November through May.

Time & Mileage

The Cabot Trail winds for 300km around Cape Breton Island's northeastern tip. The highlights lie on the coastal portion between Chéticamp and Baddeck. You can do the drive in a day, but that's pushing it, as the road is narrow, hilly and slow-going most of the way.

Resources

Cabot Trail Working Association (www.cabottrail.travel) Lists accommodations, restaurants and events for towns along the way and has a useful interactive map.

Tourism Nova Scotia (www.novascotia.com) Look under 'Regions' for listings info.

Plan Your Trip

Travel with Children

Deciding where to go with your kids in Canada can be a daunting decision. Mountains, prairies, beaches and easy-going cities are strewn across six time zones. Between wildlife sightings, cowboy encounters, hands-on pirate history, hunting for dinosaur fossils and ice-skating on mountain lakes, it's impossible to make a bad choice.

Best Regions for Kids

Vancouver (British Columbia)

Sandwiched between sea and mountains, build a sandcastle one day and go snowboarding the next while enjoying the comforts of the city.

Canadian Rockies

Hike, ski, camp or snowshoe while looking out for moose, bear, elk and whistling marmot.

Montréal (Québec)

Get a taste of Québecois *bonheur* in the historic streets, year-round ice-skating, inner-city beach and the Biôdome full of critters.

Maritime Provinces

Climb a lighthouse, sail on a pirate ship, whale-watch and beach hop in summer; see the trees turn red, orange and gold in fall.

Toronto (Ontario)

Chase through parks in summer, ice-skate in winter and don't forget to visit Niagara Falls!

Canada for Kids

As if seeing moose, eagles and whales or running around in the snow, on the beach or in the woods all day isn't fun enough, everywhere you turn, those crafty Canadians have cooked up some hands-on learning experience, living history lesson or child-oriented theater.

Museums & Monuments

Most large Canadian cities have science museums that specialize in hands-on activities, while at historic sites strewn across the country costumed thespians get you right into the period and often have demonstrations of everything from blacksmithing to cooking. At some of these places there are also puppet or theatrical performances for children and other events such as hayrides. Teens usually enjoy these sites as well since they are often large and diverse enough for self-exploration and touch on subjects they've studied at school.

Outdoor Activities

Canada is all about open spaces, fresh air, rivers, lakes and mountains, snow, sand and wildlife.

➡ Most Canadian cities are endowed with parks and promenades set up for even the tiniest **cyclists**, but finding a child-sized bike rental can be hit or miss. For a cycling-oriented holiday try the mostly flat Confederation Trail that traverses bucolic Prince Edward Island or the traffic-free Kettle Valley Trail (KVR; British Columbia) that's one of the least strenuous stretches of the Trans Canada Trail.

➡ The Canadian National Park system contains easy strolls as well as longer **hiking trails** that teens might enjoy. **Horseback riding** is widely on offer and can be especially fun in cowboy country around Calgary.

➡ Most lake areas offer **canoe** rentals perfect for leisurely family outings, while seafront regions are packed with **kayak** outfits. For a bigger adrenaline rush for older kids, try **white-water rafting** or **'playboating'** spots, particularly on the Ottawa River in Beechburg.

➡ There are plenty of **fishing** lodges, but you'd be surprised at how lucky you can get just casting into any lake or river. Likewise, try **clamming** (Prince Edward Island and British Columbia are tops) – ask locals where to go and bring a shovel and a bucket.

➡ On the coasts and the Bay of Fundy, **whale-watching** can be thrilling, but be prepared with seasickness pills, extra snacks, sunscreen and warm clothes.

➡ The tiny summer waves on the east and west coast are an excellent way to start learning to **surf**; rent a board or wetsuit or take a class.

➡ Heading out **skiing** or **snowboarding** is an obvious family choice. Children under six often ski for free, ages six to 12 usually pay around 12% to 50% of the adult price and ages 12 to 18 pay a little more than 33% to 75% of the adult price. Then, of course, there's also **ice-skating**, **sledding** and **snowshoeing**.

Eating Out

Everywhere you turn in Canada you'll find fast food and fried fare. If you're health conscious, a hurdle can be finding more wholesome options in small towns; however, you can usually find at least one cafe with sandwiches and wraps or you can self-cater. Fortunately, there are plenty of cabin and family suite–style options that allow you to cook for yourself, and some B&Bs will also let you cook. In cities, every restaurant option is available from vegan to steakhouses.

Easy-to-find Canadian foods your kids will love if you let them include poutine (French fries topped with brown gravy and cheese), fish and chips, Montréal-style bagels (wood-fired, dense and slightly sweet), pancakes or French toast with maple syrup, bear-claw doughnuts, butter tarts, and Nanaimo bars (crumb crust topped with custard and then melted chocolate). You may all gain a few kilos on this trip!

Most Canadian restaurants offer booster seats and child-friendly servers as soon as you steer your progeny through the door. However, families with even the most well-behaved children may not feel comfortable at fine-dining establishments.

Children's Highlights

History Lessons

➡ **Dinosaurs** Royal Tyrrell Museum of Palaeontology, Drumheller (Alberta)

➡ **Aboriginal Peoples** Haida Gwaii (British Columbia), Head-Smashed-In Buffalo Jump World Heritage site (Alberta), Aboriginal Experiences (Ottawa), Wanuskewin Heritage Park (Saskatchewan)

➡ **European Colonization** L'Anse aux Meadows (Newfoundland), Louisbourg National Historic Site (Nova Scotia), Fort William Historical Park (Ontario), Fort Edmonton (Alberta)

Winter Wonderlands

➡ **Winter Carnivals** Québec City Winter Carnival, Cavalcade of Lights (Toronto), Vancouver Festival of Lights

➡ **Ice-Skating** Rideau Canal (Ottawa), Lake Louise (Alberta), Harbourfront Centre (Toronto), Lac des Castors (Montréal)

➡ **Skiing, Snowboarding & Sledding** Whistler-Blackcomb (British Columbia), Norquay (Banff), Mont-Ste-Anne (Québec)

➡ **Dogsledding** Yellowknife (Northwest Territories), Iqaluit (Nunavut)

THE FINE PRINT

Children who are traveling to Canada without both parents need authorization from the nonaccompanying parent. Sometimes this is enforced and other times not but to play it safe you're better off with a notarized letter. Divorced parents should carry copies of legal custody documents.

Critters of the Great North

➡ **Moose** Nearly everywhere but especially Algonquin National Park (Eastern Ontario), Gros Morne National Park (Newfoundland) and Kananaskis (Alberta)

➡ **Polar Bears** Churchill (Manitoba)

➡ **Whales & Orcas** Vancouver Islands (British Columbia), Bay of Fundy (New Brunswick & Nova Scotia), Newfoundland

➡ **Bald Eagles** Brackendale (British Columbia), southern Vancouver Island (British Columbia) and Cape Breton Island (Nova Scotia)

Wet & Wild

➡ **Beaches** Prince Edward Island and British Columbia

➡ **Surfing** Lawrencetown Beach (Nova Scotia), Tofino (British Columbia)

➡ **Kayaking** Salt Spring (British Columbia), Georgian Bay (Ontario),

➡ **Canoeing** Algonquin National Park (Ontario), Bowron Lakes (British Columbia), Kejimkujik National Park (Nova Scotia)

➡ **Fishing** Lunenburg, Nova Scotia (lobster), Point Prim, Prince Edward Island (clams), Northern Saskatchewan (freshwater fish), Maritime Provinces (deep-sea fish)

Urban Adventures

➡ **Vancouver's outside action** Capilano Suspension Bridge, Stanley Park

➡ **Ottawa's museum mission** Canada Agricultural Museum, Museum of Nature, Science & Technology Museum, Museum of Civilization

➡ **Toronto's heights & depths** CN Tower to the subterranean corridors connecting downtown

➡ **Montréal's culture infusion** Old Montréal, Little Italy

➡ **Halifax's pirates & the Titanic** Maritime Museum of the Atlantic, *Titanic* graveyards

Theme Park Delights

➡ **Canada's Wonderland** (www.canadaswonderland.com) Amusement and water park, Toronto

➡ **Galaxy Land** (www.galaxyland.com) World's largest indoor amusement park, Edmonton

➡ **La Ronde** (www.laronde.com) Amusement park, Montréal

➡ **Calaway Park** (www.calawaypark.com) Amusement park and campground, Calgary

➡ **Playland** (www.pne.ca/playland) Oldest amusement park in Canada, Vancouver

Planning

Traveling around Canada with the tots can be child's play. Lonely Planet's *Travel with Children* offers a wealth of tips and tricks. The website **Travel For Kids** (www.travelforkids.com) is another good, general resource.

When to Go

Festivals fill Canadian calendars year-round and most are very family-oriented. Summer is the most festival-heavy time, with lots of outdoor get-togethers from jazz festivals to rodeos. Fall is a lovely time to visit Canada if you can arrange it around your children's school schedule. At this time the trees are changing colors, daytime temperatures are still manageably warm and most of the crowds have gone.

The best time for fresh snow and snow sports is January to April. Santa Claus parades usually kick off the holiday season in November and early December. Around the same time or just after, come the festivals of light where you can expect fireworks, parades and Christmas tree lightings.

Accommodations

Hotels and motels commonly have rooms with two double beds. Even those that don't have enough beds may bring in rollaways or cots, usually for a small extra charge. Some properties offer 'kids stay free' promotions, while others (particularly B&Bs) may not accept children. Ask when booking.

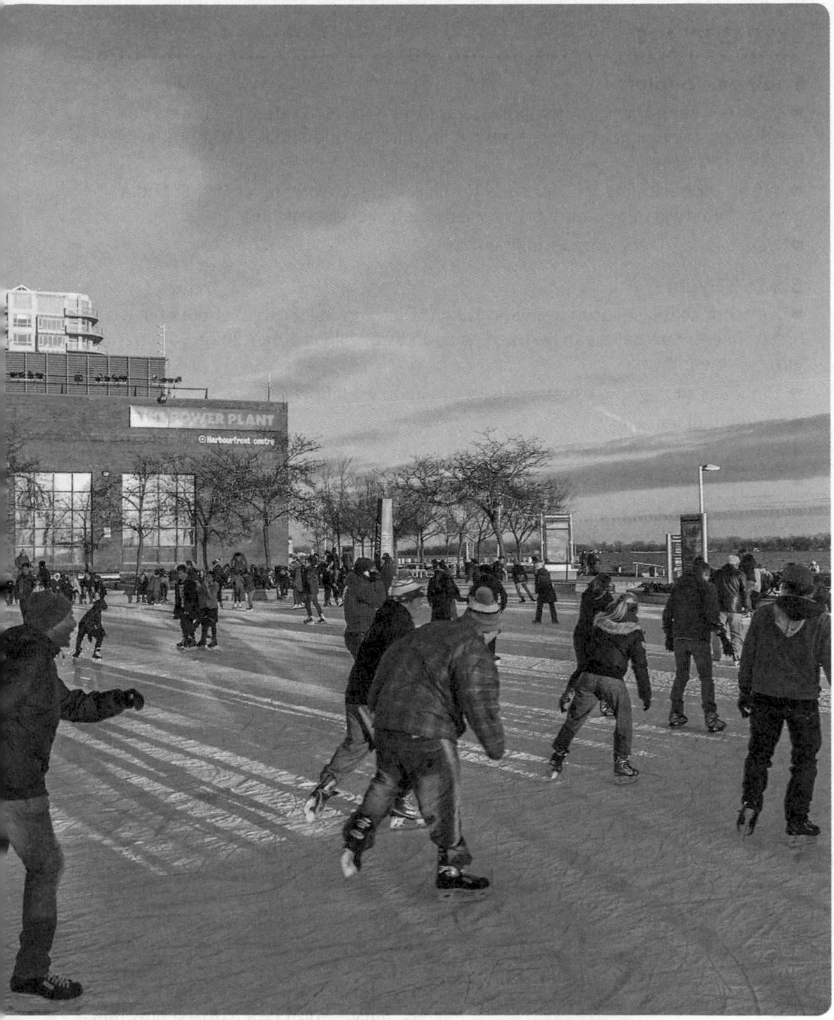

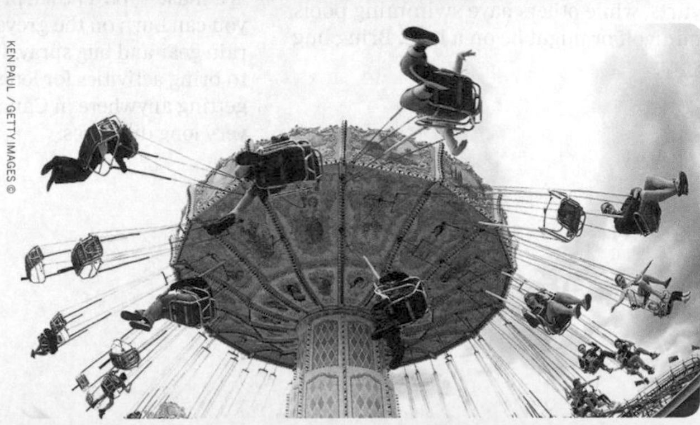

Top: Ice-skating at Harbourfront Centre (p70), Toronto
Bottom: Playland, Vancouver

KEN PAUL / GETTY IMAGES ©

EXTRAS BY AGE

Babies & Toddlers

- Kids' car seats: car-hire companies rent them for high rates; in Canada babies need a rear-facing infant safety seat, while children under 18kg (40lb) must be in a forward-facing seat.
- A front or back sling for baby and toddler if you're planning on hiking and a stroller for city jaunts (nearly everywhere is stroller-accessible).
- Sandcastle- or snowman-making tools.

Six to 12 years

- Kids' car seats: children between 18kg (40lb) and 36kg (80lb) should have a booster seat. Seatbelts can be used as soon as a child is either 36kg, 145cm (4ft 9in) tall or eight years old.
- Binoculars for young explorers to zoom in on wildlife.
- A bear bell for hikes.
- Field guides about Canada's flora and fauna.
- A camera to inject newfound fun into 'boring' grown-up sights and walks.
- Kite (for beaches).

Teens

- Canada-related iPhone or Android apps.
- Canada-related novels (find a list of Young Adult Canadian Book Award winners at www.cla.ca).
- French-Canadian phrasebook.

Another good option are cabins, which are usually rented out by the week and come with kitchens, any number of bedrooms, and other perks like barbecues. You can find full listings with each province's visitors guides online and in print (order them for free at each province's tourism website).

Camping is huge in Canada and many campgrounds also offer rustic cabins (bring your own bedding) that sometimes have kitchens, fire pits or barbecues. Some grounds offer exotic options like tipis or yurts, while others have swimming pools, minigolf or might be on a lake. Bring bug spray.

What to Pack

Canada is very family friendly so anything you forget can probably be purchased in-country. Breastfeeding in public is legal and tolerated, although most women are discreet about it. Most facilities can accommodate a child's needs; public toilets usually have diaper-changing tables.

What you will need is layered clothing for everyone, as it can get spontaneously cool even during the summer months. Sunscreen is a must – you'd be surprised how much you can burn on the greyest of days – as are rain gear and bug spray. It's also a good idea to bring activities for lengthy car rides since getting anywhere in Canada can involve very long distances.

Regions at a Glance

You can't go wrong in Canada. Each region has eye-popping landscapes and a slew of activities to match. Ontario, Québec and British Columbia (BC) – the most populated provinces – are the ones with the most going on. In addition to outdoor action, they hold Canada's largest cities – Toronto, Montréal and Vancouver – with multicultural museums, sophisticated eateries and wee-hours nightlife. Alberta booms in the Rockies with parks and oil-rich towns. Manitoba and Saskatchewan in the Plains hold big wildlife and arty surprises. The salty Atlantic provinces are tops for seafood munching and whale-watching. And the far north is the place to lose the crowds (and roads) and get well off the beaten path.

Ontario

Cuisine
Parks
Culture

Farms & Vineyards

At a geological and climactic nexus, Ontario is ripe with agriculture and viticulture. The province's wines are internationally recognized, pairing well with the delicious farm-to-table fare.

Fresh Air

If you're looking for a simple stroll, a multiday backpacking trip or some time on the water, Ontario supplies everything from green city spaces to massive provincial parks. This is the place to bring your binoculars and break in your hiking boots.

Museums

From tiny sports-memorabilia shrines to world-class collections of ancient artifacts and geological remnants, Ontario is a museum mecca.

p62

Québec

Cuisine
Winter Sports
Architecture

Joie de Vivre

Imagine sipping a *café au lait* and eating a buttery croissant on a sidewalk terrace while the murmurs of French waft through the air. It's easy to be swept away by the Québécois zest for life when fine wines and foods are so accessible.

Snow

The undulating Laurentians offer skiing and snowboarding opportunities, but it's the French panache of Mont-Tremblant that draws the international crowds.

Historic Style

Nowhere are the vestiges of Canada's colonial past more apparent than in the cobbled streets and grandiose facades of Old Montréal and within the fortified city walls of Québec City's Old Town.

p225

Nova Scotia

Culture
Activities
History

Cultural Mishmash

Tartan shops, French-speaking villages and First Nations communities are all within kilometers of each other, rendering the province one big cultural mosaic.

Coves, Cliffs & Tides

Coastal coves rich in flora and fauna beg you to go paddling. Cape Breton Island's vertiginous cliffs and the Fundy Coast with its mega-high tides are also gorgeous areas for adventure and wildlife.

Time Warp

Nova Scotians don't just preserve their historical vestiges, they get in period costume and reenact old-time activities from lace making to blacksmithing, letting you experience the scene as it was hundreds of years ago.

p330

New Brunswick

Canoeing
Fishing
Wildlife

You in a Canoe

From the tranquil Nictau and Nepisiguit chains of lakes to the quicksilver Tobique River, New Brunswick is absolutely tops for canoeing, surely the most Canadian of activities. You can even meet the artisans who make canoes.

Tie your Flies

New Brunswick's famed rivers are the kind anglers dream of – where they flycast into the current and within minutes reel in a fat silvery salmon or speckled trout.

Puffin Lovin'

Whether you're a hardcore birdwatcher or you just want to glimpse a moose, New Brunswick's got plenty of animal action to go around. Your best bet: observing rare Atlantic puffin on desolate Machias Seal Island.

p391

Prince Edward Island

Culture
Cuisine
Beaches

It's All About Anne

Personified by the redheaded star of LM Montgomery's *Anne of Green Gables* series, PEI is as pretty as it's portrayed in the books. Anne's hair mimics red sands, while white picket fences paint the real-life backdrop.

Lobsters & Spuds

The province vies with Idaho as potato capital of the Americas. Seek out town halls serving super-sized suppers of the island's famous lobster – alongside PEI spud salad!

White & Pink Beaches

PEI showcases sienna beach flats topped by red-and-white lighthouses, cream-colored dunes and stretches of white sand that 'sing' when you walk on them.

p433

Newfoundland & Labrador

Seascapes
Culture
History

Great Big Sea

'There's one!' someone shouts, and sure enough, a big humpback steams through the water, backdropped by a vista of hulking icebergs. Whether you're hiking along-shore or out in a boat, Newfoundland's sea delivers.

Strange Brew

The brogue is vaguely Irish and the slang indecipherable. Plates arrive with cod tongues, bakeapple jam and figgy duff. This place is so offbeat it even has its own time zone: a *half* hour ahead of the mainland.

Viking Vestiges

Feel the Vikings' edge-of-the-world isolation at L'Anse aux Meadows, Leif Eriksson's 1000-year-old settlement set on a bare, forlorn sweep of land.

p459

Manitoba

Wildlife
Open Spaces
Culture

Polar Bears & Whales

Polar bears prowling the icc: that's what sub-arctic Churchill is all about. The hemisphere's biggest predators turn up by the hundreds in the fall. Out on the water in summer, expect to see scores of shockingly white beluga whales.

Muskeg & Wheat

Drive through the south and you'll be mesmerized by kilometer after kilometer of wheat, punctuated by giant grain elevators. In the subarctic north, a year-round evergreen swath grows in the rich muskeg – think marshy soil from eons of plants.

Oh Winnipeg!

This surprising oasis of great dining, fun nightlife and hip culture rises up from the prairies around it.

p513

Saskatchewan

Wildlife
History
Culture

Moose & Critters

Although remote, the web of backroads that stretch across this huge province are not empty. Saskatchewan is alive with Canada's iconic critters, especially moose, which love roadside salt pools.

Revolution Rocks

In 1885 Louis Riel fought the law and, while the law won, he and a band of followers almost beat the army at Batoche, an Aboriginal town that declared independence after the national government broke treaties.

Cities on the Rise

Regina and Saskatoon both offer plenty to do after dark. Inventive restaurants using the province's produce combine with pubs serving regional microbrews.

p536

Alberta

Hiking
Winter Sports
Festivals

Banff & Jasper

These two parks are filled with wildlife, glacial lakes and hundreds of miles of trails. If you're ever going to fulfill your latent hiking ambitions, this protected wilderness is the place to do it.

Cross-country Skiing

While Alberta's downhill resorts heave with skiers, the backcountry is so quiet you can almost hear the snowflakes fall. There's nothing like breaking trail in Jasper's roadless Tonquin Valley on a pair of cross-country skis.

Edmonton Fringe Festival

Edinburgh invented it, but Edmonton has taken the concept of 'alternative theater' and given it a Canadian twist. At the International Fringe Festival, performers offer comedy, satire and weirdness.

p558

British Columbia

Landscapes
Cuisine
Wildlife

Breathtaking Views

From jaw-dropping mountains and multifjorded coastlines to dense old-growth forest and lush islands, BC is a vista-packed idyll for landscape-lovers.

Dine-around Delights

Local flavors are a foodie focus here, from North America's best Asian dining scene to a cornucopia of regional seafood and produce – accompanied, of course, by a BC wine or microbrewery beer.

Wildlife Wonderland

The Inside Passage is alive. Hop a ferry along the coast and stay glued to the deck for orca, whale, seal and birdlife sightings. Ashore, the entire cast of animal characters is here, especially huge grizzlies in the north.

p632

Yukon Territory

Wildlife
Parks
History

Bears, Oh My!

The Alaska Hwy cuts across the lower Yukon on its twisting journey to its namesake state. But stop to admire the wildlife and you may not bother reaching your destination. Keep your eyes peeled for bear, moose, bison, wolf and elk.

Unimaginable Beauty

Kluane National Park is a Unesco-recognized wilderness of glaciers cleaving through granite peaks. You'll feel minute surrounded by all this giant beauty.

Gold!

The Klondike gold rush of 1898 still shapes the Yukon with its spirited sense of adventure. Paddle your way to Dawson City, a time capsule town that's as lively now as then.

p770

Northwest Territories

Northern Lights
Kayaking
Winter Sports

Aurora Borealis

Fantastically remote and light-pollution-free, NWT is prime for seeing the green-draped flickerings. Outfitters take you far into the night, with heated viewing areas to fend off the chill.

Nahanni National Park Reserve

Nahanni National Park Reserve is a Unesco World Heritage site that offers some of the most spectacular river kayaking in Canada. With no road access, it is a true back-of-beyond adventure.

Dogsledding

With zero ski resorts, NWT specializes in more esoteric winter activities such as dogsledding. This traditional form of arctic transportation is a thrilling way to travel.

p793

Nunavut

Wildlife
Culture
Parks

Arctic Outfitters

Yes, animals live up here, it's just that they're not easy to spot. Hook up with a professional arctic outfitter for rare viewings of polar bear, caribou, walrus, narwhals and beluga whales.

Aboriginal Art

Shopping is the last thing on most Nunavut travelers' minds, but genuine Inuit art is one of the region's biggest draws. Unlikely souvenir outlets can be found in Cape Dorset, Pangnirtung and Iqaluit.

Untamed Wilderness

With each of them having annual visitation numbers that rarely hit three figures, Nunavut's four national parks guarantee an extreme wilderness experience. Sky-high costs are tempered by the moonlike emptiness of the incredible terrain.

p813

On the Road

Yukon
Territory
p770
Northwest
Territories
p793
Nunavut
p813
British
Columbia
p632
Alberta
p558
Saskatchewan
p536
Manitoba
p513
Ontario
p62
Québec
p225
Newfoundland
& Labrador
p459
Prince Edward
Island
p433
New
Brunswick
p391
Nova
Scotia
p330

Ontario

Includes ➡

Best Places to Eat

- ➡ Lee (p100)
- ➡ ND Sushi (p101)
- ➡ Beckta Dining & Wine Bar (p220)
- ➡ Buoys (p166)
- ➡ Pan Chancho (p201)
- ➡ Tomlin (p180)

Best Places to Sleep

- ➡ Clarence Park (p94)
- ➡ Drake Hotel (p97)
- ➡ Taboo Resort (p155)
- ➡ Three Houses Bed & Breakfast (p141)
- ➡ Fairmont Château Laurier (p218)
- ➡ Planet Travelers Hostel (p97)

Why Go?

The breathtaking four-seasonal palette of Ontario's vast wilderness, endless forests and abundant wildlife awaits. Around 40% of Canada's population lives here for good reason: Ontario is larger than France and Spain combined. Over 250,000 lakes, including the Great Lakes bordering the US, contain a fifth of the planet's fresh water.

Most Ontarians call behemoth Toronto or Ottawa, the nation's cosmopolitan capital, home. Foodies, fashionistas and funsters converge on Toronto's vibrant multicultural neighborhoods, where immigrants from far and wide live in hockey-following harmony. Both cities have hopping arts and entertainment scenes, kept current by the neighborly influences of New York and Montréal.

Whether you want to reconnect with nature or lose yourself in the excitement of the most multiculturally diverse and socially cohesive region on Earth, you've come to the right place.

When to Go

Toronto

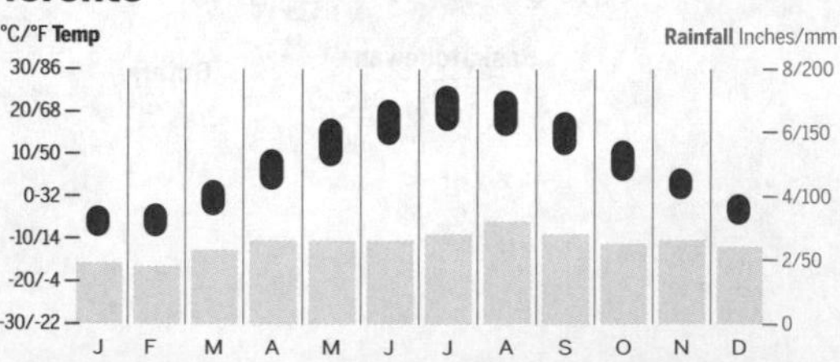

May–Jun Celebrate spring and marvel at moose, trilliums and loons in Ontario's parks.

Jul–Sep Join the frenzy of Toronto's festival mania or savor summer in cottage country.

Oct–Nov Unleash your inner artist as fall colors the leaves throughout the province.

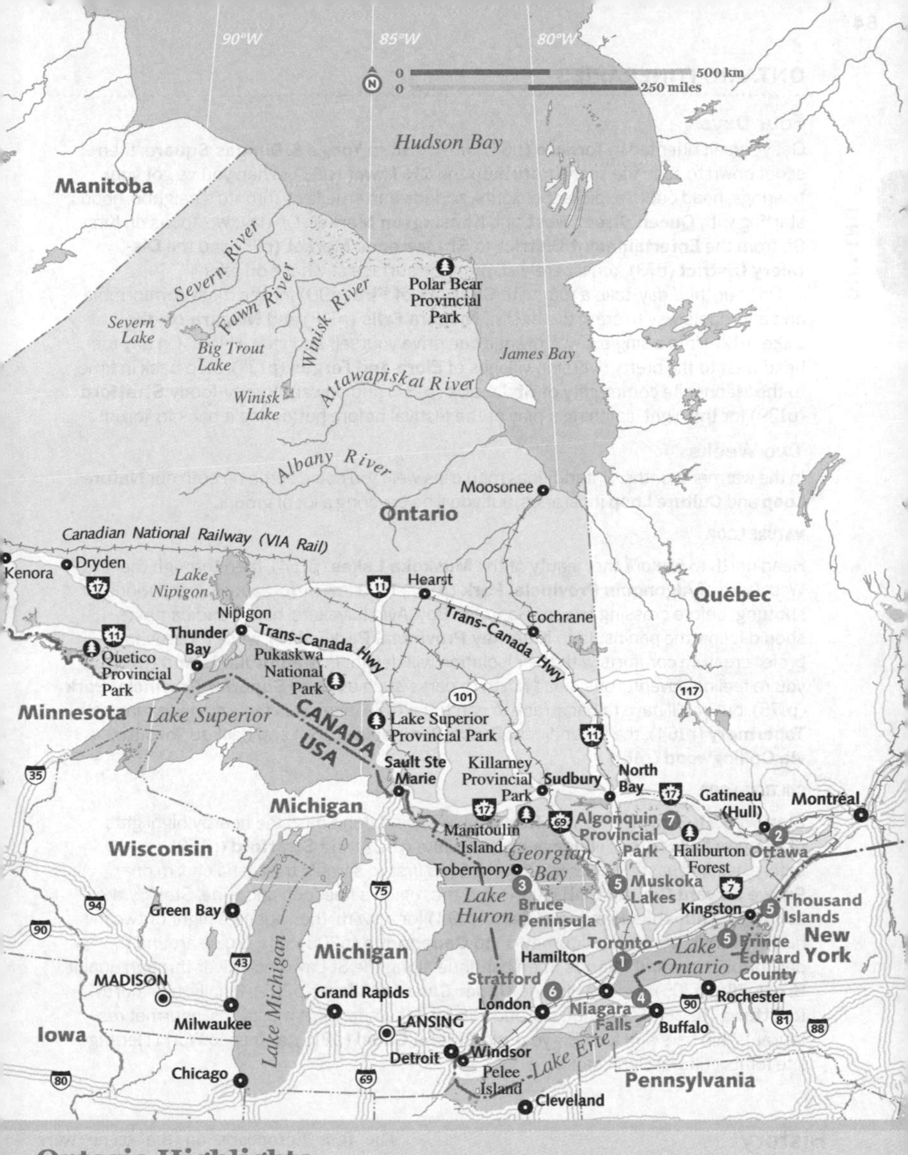

Ontario Highlights

❶ **Toronto** (p67)
Discovering what fashionistas and foodies adore about the city's diverse neighborhoods.

❷ **Ottawa** (p208) Getting cultured in the capital, with its French flavors and world-class museums.

❸ **Bruce Peninsula** (p162)
Exploring beautiful Tobermory, then catching the ferry to Manitoulin Island.

❹ **Niagara Falls** (p118)
Marveling at the sheer power of the border-straddling falls aboard a cruise boat.

❺ **Cottage Country** (p202) Drooling over cottages and rocky island retreats as you cruise around the Thousand Islands, Muskoka Lakes and Prince Edward County.

❻ **Stratford** (p139)
Heading back in time in this cultured town, with its festival celebrating Shakespeare and the arts.

❼ **Algonquin Provincial Park** (p187) Hiking or canoeing into this 7600-sq-km wilderness, one of many impressive northern provincial parks.

ONTARIO ITINERARIES

Four Days

Get yourself oriented in **Toronto** (p67) with a visit to **Yonge & Dundas Square**, then scoot down to scan the scene from atop the **CN Tower** (p69). When you've got your bearings, head out to explore the sights, sounds and smells of Toronto's neighborhoods, starting with **Queen Street West** and **Kensington Market.** On day two, focus on King St: from the **Entertainment District** to **St Lawrence Market (**p75) and the **Distillery District** (p73). You'll barely scratch the surface of what's on offer.

On your third day, take a tour with **Chariots of Fire** (p90) for the most comfortable and affordable way to cram the best of **Niagara Falls** (p118) and **Niagara-on-the-Lake** (p127) into a single day. Or rent a car, drive yourself and stay a night. On day four, head west to the pretty riverside villages of **Elora and Fergus** (p137), step back in time to the Mennonite community of **St Jacobs** (p137) and onward to arty-foody **Stratford** (p139) for the night, catching a play at the festival before hotfooting it back to Toronto.

Two Weeks

In the warmer months, Ontario does road trips well. You could combine both our **Nature Loop** and **Culture Loop** itineraries, but you'll be covering a lot of ground.

NATURE LOOP

Head north to explore the beauty of the **Muskoka Lakes** (p154), then through the West Gate of **Algonquin Provincial Park** (p187) for a few days' canoeing and moose spotting, before crossing toward Georgian Bay. Avid kayakers, hikers and campers should follow the peninsula to **Killarney Provincial Park** (p167), while those who prefer creature comforts with their isolation will delight in **Manitoulin Island** (p165). If you're feeling adventurous, head north to parks such as **Lake Superior Provincial Park** (p175), but you'll have to backtrack to catch the Chi-Cheemaun ferry down to magical **Tobermory** (p164), the magnificent **Bruce Peninsula** (p162) and back to **Toronto, via Collingwood** (p161).

CULTURE LOOP

Start with a few days in vibrant **Toronto** (p67), and don't miss the nearby highlights of **Niagara Falls** (p118), **Niagara-on-the-Lake** (p127) and **Stratford** (p139), before heading east along Lake Ontario. Stop first to sample the rustic charm of a **Prince Edward County B&B** (p194) and the region's fine food and wine. Stop by the county's **Sandbanks Provincial Park** (p194) for a swim, then spend a night or two in historic **Kingston** (p197). Journey on to **Gananoque** (p203) for a cruise around the delightful **Thousand Islands**, then continue along the St Lawrence River through quaint **Brockville** (p205) and the historic **Upper Canada Village** (p207). Finally, turn north to **Ottawa** (p208), the nation's proud capital, for a bounty of museums, gourmet restaurants, hip bars and the 185-year-old **Rideau Canal** (p215), a Unesco World Heritage site for its cultural significance.

History

When Europeans first stumbled through the snow into Ontario, several Aboriginal nations already called the region home. The Algonquin and Huron tribes had long occupied the southern portion of the province, but by the time European colonization took hold in the early 18th century, the Iroquois Confederacy (aka the Five Nations) held sway in the lands south of Georgian Bay and east to Québec. The Ojibwe occupied the lands north of the Great Lakes and west to Cree territory on the prairies (today's Alberta and Saskatchewan).

The first Europeans on the scene were 17th-century French fur traders, who established basic forts to facilitate trade links with the Mississippi River. With the arrival of the British Loyalists around 1775, large-scale settlement began. After the War of 1812, British immigrants arrived in larger numbers, and by the end of the 19th century Ontario's farms, industries and cities were rapidly developing. In the aftermath of both world wars, immigration from Europe boomed – Toronto has since evolved into one of the world's most multicultural cities.

An industrial and manufacturing powerhouse, Ontario is home to around 40% of Canada's population. Despite boom times in Alberta, Ontario remains the first choice of immigrants from across the globe, with solid employment prospects and Toronto's well-established immigrant support services proving a powerful draw.

FAST FACTS

- Population: 13,505,900
- Area: 1,076,395 sq km
- Capital: Toronto
- Quirky fact: There are actually 1864 islands in the Thousand Islands archipelago.

Local Culture

There's something for everyone in Toronto. Torontonians love their city and seem somewhat blinded to its flaws: bitter winters, expensive housing, congested roads and inadequate public transit. They smile through gritted teeth as if it were their duty to defend the city against criticism. Toronto's ethnocultural makeup is so diverse that it defies attempts to define or resist it: people just get along. You'll find all walks of life and all colors, flavors and traditions of the world represented here.

Outside cosmopolitan Toronto and Ottawa, rural Ontario is generally homogenous and unassuming, although communities have French, Belgian, German, Chinese, Finnish and Aboriginal roots and influences and there's a strong immigrant labor force. Farmers are practical, no-fuss folk who work hard, value things for their functionality and don't get too involved with life beyond the farm. Most Ontarians are mild-mannered folk who enjoy a good to high standard of living, but don't feel the need to boast about it.

More than any other province, Ontario is hockey-mad – this is the birthplace of Wayne 'The Great One' Gretzky – though less violent winter sports such as curling still have a following. One thing is universal: when the weather is fine, city and country folk all head for the sunshine and the water, where they commune with nature and their families; food, wine, good friends, healthy conversation and debate are all valued here.

Land & Climate

Ontario is big. Its longest north–south span is 1730km, and 1568km separate east from west. Unlike Canada's rugged west, the landscape is largely flat, with some mountainous regions and more lakes than you could skim stones across in a year: four of the five Great Lakes have shoreline in Ontario. Fifty percent of Ontario's area (around 50 million hectares) is part of the boreal forest (aka 'Amazon of the North') which transverses Canada. It's one of the world's largest storehouses of carbon, begins around the 50th parallel, between Lake Superior and Hudson Bay, and extends across the province in an east–west band up to 1000km wide.

In southern Ontario, cold air from the north collides with warm air from the Great Lakes, causing plenty of rain, humid summers and milder winters. The entire province gets blanketed with heavy snowfalls, but towns in the snowbelt, such as Parry Sound, Barrie and London (from Georgian Bay to Lake Huron) are generally hardest hit. Lake Ontario often spares downtown Toronto from the brunt of the snowfall, but winter storms have been known to shut down the city. January averages around -4°C on the Niagara Peninsula and -18°C in the north.

As summer draws closer, southwestern Ontario and the Niagara Peninsula get increasingly hot and sticky. It can feel oppressively humid in Toronto, where pollution can be stifling, and Ottawa. Summer storms are common along the Niagara Escarpment and conditions sometimes produce tornadoes. July averages around 23°C here and 15°C in the north. Late spring and early fall are the best times to visit, when temperatures are mild, days long and sunny.

National & Provincial Parks

Ontario contains six of Canada's national parks: Georgian Bay Islands National Park, Bruce Peninsula National Park (p164), Fathom Five National Marine Park (p164), Point Pelee National Park (p152) (the southernmost point of the Canadian mainland), Pukaskwa National Park (p177) and Thousand Islands National Park (p203). There are also more than 330 provincial parks here, many of which offer hiking and camping facilities. Campsites for up to six people cost between $35 and $52 per night. They range from basic sites without showers or electricity to well-located powered plots with showers. Make reservations with **Ontario Parks** (☎800-668-2746; www.ontarioparks.com).

ONTARIO AT A GLANCE

Don't Miss

The **Niagara Peninsula** (p118) is *the* day trip out of Toronto's hustle and bustle, but stay a few days if you can. Once you've experienced the awe-inspiring power of the world-famous falls and maxed out on gaudy tourist attractions, head up the road to the photogenic township of **Niagara-on-the-Lake** (p127) and its many wineries, galleries, boutiques and bistros. There's no shortage of delicious rooms in which to lay your weary head.

Consider scooting east to **Prince Edward County** (p194), Ontario's preeminent culinary destination, where vineyards and organic farms dot the landscape. Here you'll also find **Sandbanks Provincial Park** (p194), with some of Lake Ontario's best swimming beaches.

Hungry for more? For a quaint riverside romp within an hour and a half of Toronto, try the neighboring historical villages of **Elora and Fergus** (p137). Get your Puck on at the Shakespeare-crazy **Stratford Festival** (p140). If you really want to get away, head north to **Thunder Bay** (p178) and the wild shores of **Lake Superior** (p173); or to the magnificent scenery of the **Bruce Peninsula** (p162), flanked by Lake Huron's sandy beaches and warmer waters to the west and the stunning azure of **Georgian Bay** (p158) to the east.

What to Expect

Ontario is Canada's breadbasket, with excellent restaurants from Ottawa to Thunder Bay. When you're ready to burn off all those calories, why not hit a stretch of the many thousands of kilometers of scenic cycling trails? Of course, you may need to be adaptable and have a

ℹ Getting There & Around

AIR

Most Canadian airlines and major international carriers arrive at **Toronto Pearson International Airport** (p116). From here, **Air Canada** (www.aircanada.com) and **WestJet** (www.westjet.com) operate extensive services within the province and beyond. From the downtown **Billy Bishop Toronto City Airport** (p116), **Porter Airlines** (☎888-619-8622; www.flyporter.com) services Northern Ontario as well as Ottawa, Montréal, Chicago, New York, Boston, Washington and more.

The **John C Munro Hamilton International Airport** (YHM; ☎905-679-1999; www.flyhi.ca; 9300 Airport Rd, Mt Hope) is an alternative for budget US flights if Toronto is booked out. Distant Northern Ontario (p167) has a useful network of airports, including Moosonee, North Bay, Sault Ste Marie, Sudbury, Timmins and Thunder Bay.

Useful services from the small **Ottawa MacDonald-Cartier International Airport** (https://yow.ca/en) include flights to Iqaluit (Nunavut) and Yellowknife (Northwest Territories), operated by **Canadian North** (☎800-661-1505; www.canadiannorth.com), **First Air** (firstair.ca) and **Air North** (www.flyairnorth.com), with connections throughout the far north.

BUS

As a general rule, **Greyhound Canada** (www.greyhound.ca) covers southwestern Ontario and Ottawa, from Toronto; **Ontario Northland** (www.ontarionorthland.ca) takes care of Northern Ontario; and **Megabus** (☎866-488-4452; ca.megabus.com) offers dirt-cheap services from Toronto along the eastern corridor to Montréal, as well as to Niagara Falls and over the border to Buffalo, NY. With the latter, booking tickets well in advance can get huge discounts. If one carrier doesn't service the route you need, check the others.

Go Transit (www.gotransit.com) is a bus service that takes you to places near Toronto, such as Hamilton and London. **Parkbus** (☎800-928-7101; www.parkbus.ca) offers limited seasonal departures to Ontario's best national and provincial parks. Check the website for details.

CAR & MOTORCYCLE

Outside Toronto, Ontario's roads are in good shape and offer a pleasant driving experience (once you're off busy Hwy 401). When driving in Ontario, you can turn right on a red light after first having made a full stop. It's illegal to text or talk on a mobile device while driving. Try to observe speed limits in the north, despite the temptation to gun it down those empty roads, as fines exceed $100 even for minor infractions.

Car rental is practically essential if you want to enjoy the province, but not for exploring Toronto – driving and parking downtown is painful enough for residents who know their way around, but could really mess up your day as a visitor. Instead, use the TTC (Toronto Tranist Commission) in the city and pick up your rental on the day you're leaving: there is no shortage of car-rental companies.

sense of humor in the face of temperamental weather, whatever the season. And remember, wildlife abounds – bring your binoculars to spot birds and beavers, moose, otter and deer.

For indoorsy days, almost every significant town sports a museum – Ottawa's and Toronto's are some of the world's best. Make sure you pack your patience – Toronto transit and traffic frequently grinds to a halt. You've got lots of ground to cover, so allow yourself time to explore and prepare to be surprised!

Planning

Ontario is alive with activity during the long days of the short summer, when there's always a festival or something fun happening from Toronto to Thunder Bay. Be sure to book your accommodations in advance.

Ontario weather can change rapidly. If you're camping, or planning outdoor pursuits, pack for variations in temperature and remember the bug spray.

Resources

Ontario Travel Information Centres (☎800-668-2746; www.ontariotravel.net) Useful website and offices throughout the province.

Tourism Toronto (Map p78; ☎416-203-2500; www.seetorontonow.com; 207 Queens Quay W; ⏱8:30am-6pm Mon-Fri; Ⓢ Union) The website is a handy resource for planning your visit to the city.

Ottawa Tourism (p224) A comprehensive online look at the nation's capital.

Lonely Planet (www.lonelyplanet.com/canada/ontario) Destination information, hotel bookings, traveller forum and more.

Rental is cheaper in Toronto than anywhere else, including Ottawa.

The two main highways are the Trans-Canada (Hwy 17) from Ottawa northwest to the Manitoba border (just west of Kenora); and the 401, which runs southwest from the Ontario–Québec border to Windsor and the US border with Detroit.

TRAIN

VIA Rail (☎888-842-7245; www.viarail.ca) trains service the busy Ontario–Québec corridor, from Windsor in the southwest, all the way to Montréal. VIA Rail also operates Trans-Canada services which stop in Northern Ontario en route to Manitoba and beyond.

Toronto's GO Transit operates irregularly scheduled commuter trains, sometimes servicing Hamilton, Niagara Falls, Barrie, Kitchener and Guelph.

For a northern adventure, board the **Polar Bear Express** (p182) from Cochrane to even more remote Moosone, gateway to James Bay and Moose Factory island.

TORONTO

POP 6.1 MILLION

Welcome to Toronto, the most multiculturally diverse city on the planet: over 140 languages are spoken. It's estimated that over half of Toronto's residents were born outside Canada, and despite its complex makeup, Torontonians generally get along. When the weather is fine, Toronto is a blast: a vibrant, big-time city abuzz with activity. Some of the world's finest restaurants are found here, alongside happening bars and clubs and eclectic festivals.

Yes, winter in Toronto can be a real drag. Things get messy on the congested highways and archaic public transit system. But come with patience, an open mind and during the delightfully temperate and colorful spring or fall, and you're bound to have a great time.

There is a fresh international buzz about Toronto. Perhaps it's the influx of flush new residents from across the globe; or was it the Pan-Am Games that shone a spotlight on Toronto? Either way, this is a city that is waking up to its own greatness.

History

In the 17th century, present-day Toronto was Seneca Aboriginal land. Frenchman Étienne Brûlé was the first European here, in 1615, but unwelcoming locals impeded French invasion until 1720 when the French established a fur-trading post in what's now the west end. In 1763 the British took over and John Simcoe, lieutenant governor of the new Upper Canada, moved the capital from Niagara-on-the-Lake and founded the town of York. On April 27, 1813, during the War of 1812, American forces looted and razed York, but were only

Greater Toronto Area (GTA)

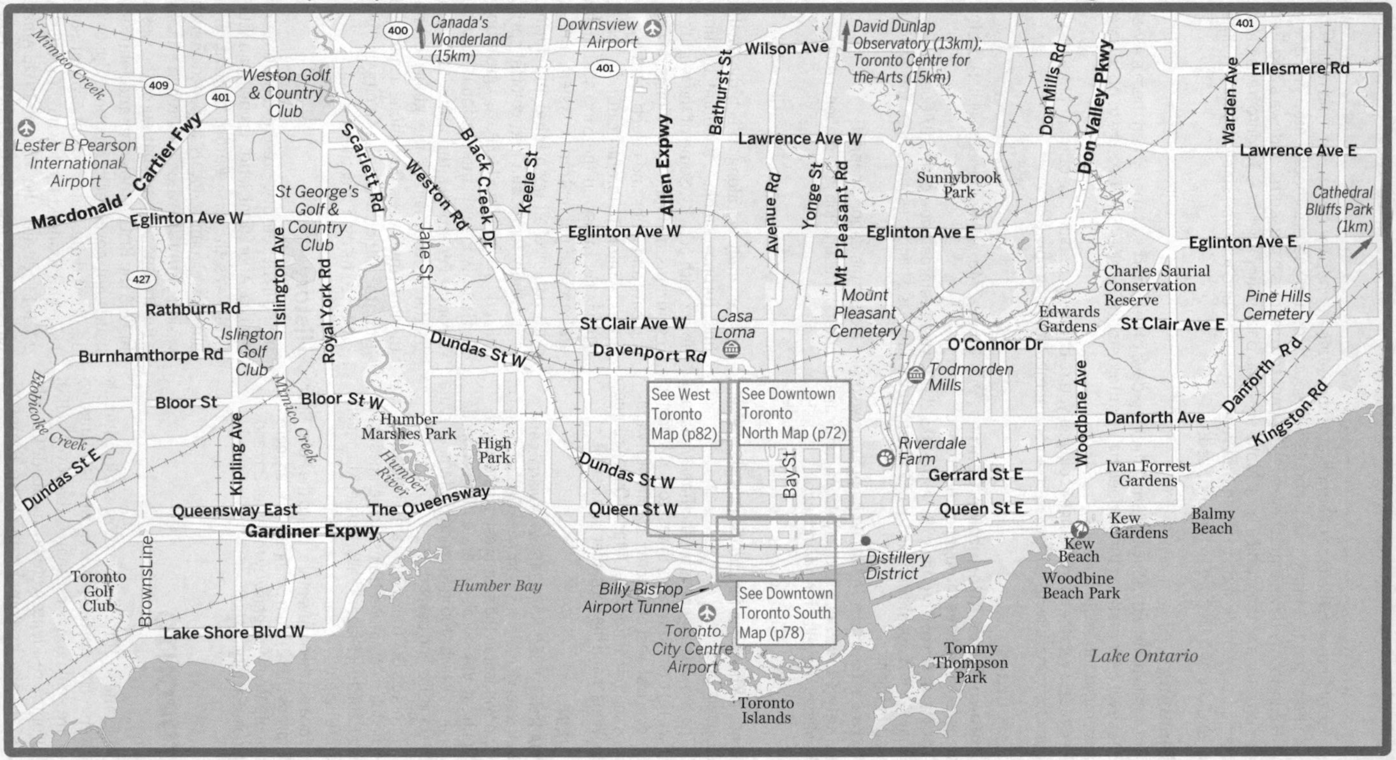

0 5 km
0 2.5 miles

Canada's Wonderland (15km)
Downsview Airport
David Dunlap Observatory (13km); Toronto Centre for the Arts (15km)
Wilson Ave
Ellesmere Rd
Weston Golf & Country Club
Lester B Pearson International Airport
Macdonald - Cartier Fwy
Bathurst St
Lawrence Ave W
Lawrence Ave E
Warden Ave
Don Mills Rd
Don Valley Pkwy
Sunnybrook Park
Cathedral Bluffs Park (1km)
St George's Golf & Country Club
Scarlett Rd
Weston Rd
Black Creek Dr
Keele St
Allen Expwy
Avenue Rd
Yonge St
Mt Pleasant Rd
Eglinton Ave W
Eglinton Ave E
Jane St
Islington Ave
Royal York Rd
Charles Saurial Conservation Reserve
Pine Hills Cemetery
Rathburn Rd
Islington Golf Club
St Clair Ave W
Casa Loma
Mount Pleasant Cemetery
Edwards Gardens
St Clair Ave E
Burnhamthorpe Rd
Dundas St W
Davenport Rd
O'Connor Dr
Danforth Rd
Todmorden Mills
Mimico Creek
Bloor St
Bloor St W
See West Toronto Map (p82)
See Downtown Toronto North Map (p72)
Woodbine Ave
Danforth Ave
Etobicoke Creek
Humber Marshes Park
High Park
Riverdale Farm
Kingston Rd
Dundas St E
Kipling Ave
Humber River
Bay St
Gerrard St E
Ivan Forrest Gardens
Queensway East
The Queensway
Queen St W
Queen St E
Kew Gardens
Balmy Beach
Gardiner Expwy
Kew Beach
Distillery District
Toronto Golf Club
BrownsLine
Humber Bay
Billy Bishop Airport Tunnel
See Downtown Toronto South Map (p78)
Woodbine Beach Park
Lake Shore Blvd W
Toronto City Centre Airport
Tommy Thompson Park
Lake Ontario
Toronto Islands

able to hold sway for six days before Canadian troops hounded them back to Washington.

Toronto was born in 1834, when Mayor William Lyon Mackenzie renamed the town from an aboriginal name meaning 'gathering place.' The Victorian city, controlled by conservative politicians, became known as 'Toronto the Good.' Religious restraints and strong antivice laws were such that on Sundays it was illegal to hire a horse, the curtains of department-store windows were drawn (window-shopping was sinful!) and film screenings prohibited.

In 1904, Toronto had a great fire, burning about 5 hectares of the inner city and leveling 122 buildings. Amazingly, no one was killed, and by the 1920s Bay St was booming, in part due to gold, silver and uranium discoveries in Northern Ontario.

Prior to WWII, 80% of the population was Anglo-Celtic. After the war, then Prime Minister Lester B Pearson introduced the world's first points-based immigration system. Since then Toronto has welcomed millions of skilled immigrants and refugees from all corners of the globe. The Anglo-Celtic figure is now closer to 50%. In 1998, five sprawling Toronto suburbs – York, East York, North York, Etobicoke and Scarborough – fused to become the Greater Toronto Area (GTA). As the fifth-largest city in North America, contemporary Toronto is booming – a million miles from its beginnings as 'Muddy York,' Ontario's second-choice town.

Sights

Downtown Toronto is an easy-to-navigate grid, bounded by a hodgepodge of bohemian, ethnic and historic neighborhoods. Yonge St, the world's longest, dissects the city: any downtown street with an East or West designation refers to its position relative to Yonge. Unlike New York, there is no distinction between the directions of avenues and streets: Spadina Ave runs north–south, but Danforth Ave runs east–west. There's also a street called Avenue Road. Go figure!

Most tourist sights hug the Harbourfront, Entertainment and Financial Districts at the southern end of downtown. The CN Tower, Rogers Centre stadium, Harbourfront Centre, Union Station and Theatre District are all here. South of the lakeshore, locals retreat to the Toronto Islands for solace and the hands-down best views of Toronto's gargantuan skyline – well worth the half-day roundtrip. Back on the mainland, east of Yonge and west of the Don Valley Pkwy, the former Old York area is home to some of Toronto's oldest and most well-preserved neighborhoods. That said, you're not likely to be seduced by Toronto's beauty, so we recommend you get a taste of its charm and character: you'll find both a little further afield.

Many argue that West is best: The Annex, Kensington Market and Queen West are all here. The East has a completely different feel: as full of flavor, but a little more grounded. Leslieville, everbody-loves-to-eat Greektown (aka the Danforth) and The Beaches, slightly San Franciscan in their sensibilities, are the main draws.

We suggest using the TTC (Toronto Transit Commission) to get around – driving in Toronto is an art that many locals have not yet mastered, the cost of parking is extortionate and roads are congested. Avoid the morning and evening rush hours when subways and streetcars are packed and services are frequently late.

Harbourfront

At the foot of Yonge and York Sts on Lake Ontario is the redeveloped Harbourfront area. Once a run-down district of warehouses, factories and docklands, the area now teems with folk milling about the restaurants, theaters, galleries, artists' workshops, stores, condos and parklands along Queens Quay. Ferries for the Toronto Islands dock here.

★CN Tower TOWER

(La Tour CN; Map p78; ☎416-868-6937; www.cntower.ca; 301 Front St W; Tower Experience adult/child $35/25; ⌚9am-10:30pm; Ⓢ Union) Toronto's iconic CN Tower, a marvel of 1970s engineering, looks like a giant concrete hypodermic needle. Its function as a communications tower takes a backseat to relieving tourists of as much cash possible – riding those glass elevators up the once-highest freestanding structure in the world (553m) is one of those things you just *have* to do in Toronto. Even if you don't, you're bound to catch a glimpse of the tower at night, when the entire structure puts on a brilliant free light show year-round.

On a clear day, the views from the top are astounding; if it's hazy (often) you won't see a thing. Queues for the elevator can be up to two hours long in each direction. Buying tickets online saves 15%. There's an obligatory revolving restaurant (called 360°): it's expensive, but the elevator price is waived for diners. Cashed-up daredevils (13 years plus) can

TORONTO IN...

Two Days

Quick weekend? Take a rocket-ride up the **CN Tower** (p69) – as high as Torontonians get without wings or drugs. Lunch at **St Lawrence Market** (p75), then head up to **Bloor-Yorkville** to window shop. Once inspired, max out your style-to-value ratio in **Kensington Market** followed by a thrifty dinner of dumplings in **Chinatown**.

Start early on day two and check out the amazing **Royal Ontario Museum** (p79), intriguing **Casa Loma** (p80) or the **Art Gallery of Ontario** (p77) – then take a long lunch in **Baldwin Village**. Afterwards, ride the ferry to the **Toronto Islands** (p85) and bike until the sun sets. Back on the mainland, relax with a pint at the **Mill Street Brewery** (p107) in the atmospheric **Distillery District** (p73).

Four Days

Begin with a loop on a **double-decker sightseeing tour** (p90) to get your bearings, then explore **The Annex** (p80) and have dinner in **Little Italy** (p81). Take our neighborhood **walking tour** (p86), or head east for brunch in **Leslieville** to up your energy for **The Beaches** (p85). Pick a patio for dinner and drinks before catching a show or hitting the dancefloor in the **Entertainment District** or **Church-Wellesley Village**.

Devote a whole day...or two...to exploring the boutiques, bars and eateries along **Queen West**, **Trinity Bellwoods** and **West Queen West**. Head to **High Park** (p85) for a picnic, or, if you're more about hot-dogs-and-beer, catch some baseball at the **Rogers Centre** (p71), hockey at the **Air Canada Centre** (p113), or all three for half the price at **Gretzky's** (p108).

One Week

Go beyond the downtown core: explore **Scarborough Bluffs** (p87), the **Sharon Temple** (p88) or the **McMichael Canadian Art Collection** (p88). Take a day trip to **Niagara Falls** (p118) and **Niagara-on-the-Lake** (p127).

now opt for the EdgeWalk ($175), a 20-minute outdoor walk around the unbounded perimeter of the main pod (356m). Not for the faint-hearted. For an even loftier, though indoor, view, opt for the SkyPod (447m; an extra $12).

The best street-level vantage of the tower is at the intersection of McCaul St and Queen St W, due north of the tower.

Harbourfront Centre LANDMARK

(Map p78; ☎416-973-4000; www.harbourfrontcentre.com; York Quay, 235 Queens Quay W; ⊙box office 1-6pm Tue-Sat, show nights to 8pm; P 👪; 🚊509, 510) The 4-hectare not-for-profit Harbourfront Centre exists to educate and entertain Toronto's community through a variety of year-round events, including Sunday family events and free outdoor summer concerts in the Toronto Music Garden and on the Concert Stage. There's also a lakeside ice-skating rink where you can slice up the winter ice. Don't miss the free galleries, including the **Photo Passage** and the functioning **Craft Studio**. Arriving at **Ontario Square** from Queens Quay, head to **Canada Square** with its dawn redwood trees, peering across Lake Ontario.

A 15-minute walk west, delicately strung along the western harborfront, the **Toronto Music Garden** was designed in collaboration with cellist Yo-Yo Ma. It expresses Bach's Suite No 1 for Unaccompanied Cello through landscape, with an arc-shaped grove of conifers, a swirling path through a wildflower meadow and a grass-stepped amphitheater where free concerts are held.

Power Plant Contemporary Art Gallery GALLERY

(Map p78; ☎416-973-4949; www.thepowerplant.org; 231 Queens Quay W; ⊙10am-5pm Tue & Wed, to 8pm Thu, to 6pm Fri-Sun; 🚊509, 510) FREE Easily recognized by its painted smokestack, the Power Plant gallery is at the Harbourfront Centre and is just that – a former power plant transformed into Toronto's premier gallery of contemporary Canadian art. Best of all, it's free and exhibitions change regularly.

Steam Whistle Brewing BREWERY

(Map p78; www.steamwhistle.ca; 255 Bremner Blvd; 45min tours $10; ⊙noon-6pm Mon-Thu, 11am-6pm Fri & Sat, to 5pm Sun; P; S Union, 🚊509, 510) 🌿 'Do one thing really really well,' is the motto of Steam Whistle Brewing, a microbrewery that makes only a crisp European-style pilsner. Bubbling away in a 1929 train depot, Steam Whistle continually works on being environmentally friendly, in part by using renewable energy, steam heating, all-natural (and often local) ingredients, and supercool ginger ale bottles that can be reused up to 40 times. Tours depart half-hourly from 1pm to 5pm and include tastings.

Rogers Centre STADIUM

(Map p78; ☎416-341-2770; www.rogerscentre.com; 1 Blue Jays Way; 1hr tours adult/child $16/10; S Union) Technically awe-inspiring, the Rogers Centre sports stadium opened in 1989 with the world's first fully retractable dome roof and seating for up to 55,000 people. Tours include a brain-scrambling video-wall screening footage of past sporting glories, concerts and events; a sprint through a box suite; a locker-room detour (sans athletes); and a memorabilia museum. A budget seat at a Blue Jays baseball or Argonauts football game is the cheapest way to see the center.

Fort York National Historic Site HISTORIC SITE

(☎416-392-6907; www.fortyork.ca; 250 Fort York Blvd; adult/child $9/4.25; ⏱10am-5pm Jun-Dec, to 4pm Mon-Fri Jan-May; P; 🚋509, 511) Established by the British in 1793 to defend the then town of York, Fort York was almost entirely destroyed during the War of 1812 when a small band of Ojibwe warriors and British troops were unable to defeat their US attackers. A handful of the original log, stone and brick buildings have been restored. From May to September, men decked out in 19th-century British military uniforms carry out marches and drills, firing musket volleys into the sky.

The fort is open year-round; check the homepage for special events and tour details.

Spadina Quay Wetlands PARK

(Map p78; ☎416-392-1111; www.toronto.ca; 479 Queens Quay W; ⏱dawn-dusk; 🚋509, 510) A former lakeside parking lot has been transformed into the 2800-sq-meter Spadina Quay Wetlands, a thriving, sustainable ecosystem full of frogs, birds, fish and butterflies. When lakeside fishers noticed that northern pike were spawning here each spring, the city took it upon itself to create this new habitat. Complete with flowering heath plants, poplar trees and a birdhouse, it's a little gem that led the way in the Harbourfront redevelopment.

Ripley's Aquarium of Canada AQUARIUM

(Map p78; ☎647-351-3474; www.ripleysaquariumofcanada.com; 288 Bremner Blvd; adult/child $30/20; ⏱9am-11pm; S Union) Toronto's newest attraction for young and old. Expect over 15,000 aquatic animals, 5.7 million liters of water in the combined tanks, as well as sleepovers, touch tanks and educational dive presentations. It opens 365 days a year, but sometimes closes earlier than regular hours for special events.

Exhibition Place NOTABLE BUILDING

(☎416-263-3600; www.explace.on.ca; off Lake Shore Blvd W, btwn Strachan Ave & Dufferin St; P; 🚋509, 511) Every August, historic Exhibition Place is revived for its original purpose, the Canadian National Exhibition (p92). Millions of visitors flood the midway for carnival rides, lumberjack competitions and more good, honest, homegrown fun than a Sunday-school picnic.

The beaux-arts *Victory* statue over Princes' Gate has stood proud since Canada's 60th birthday in 1927. Other events held at Exhibition Place include the Honda Indy Toronto (p91) in July and a slew of spectator sports and indie design shows. At other times the grounds are often spookily bereft of visitors.

Financial District

Union Station is Canada's busiest transport hub, serving 250,000 passengers daily. An extensive revitalization project is starting to come together handsomely, but the station, subway area and surrounding streetscape will still suffer from construction until 2018. The area just north of the station, on King and Adelaide and east to Bay St, equates to Toronto's 'Wall St' – the nicest of the skyscrapers are here, where the 'Bay St Boys' do their darndest to convince themselves this is actually New York.

Hockey Hall of Fame MUSEUM

(Map p78; ☎416-360-7765; www.hhof.com; Brookfield Pl, 30 Yonge St; adult/child $18/12; ⏱9:30am-6pm Mon-Sat, 10am-6pm Sun; S Union) Inside an ornate rococo gray-stone Bank of Montreal building (c 1885), the Hockey Hall of Fame is a Canadian institution. Even those unfamiliar with the superfast ultraviolent sport are likely to be impressed by this, the largest collection of hockey memorabilia in the world. Check out the collection of *Texas Chainsaw Massacre*–esque goalkeeping masks or go head to head with the great Wayne Gretzky, virtual-reality style.

Downtown Toronto North

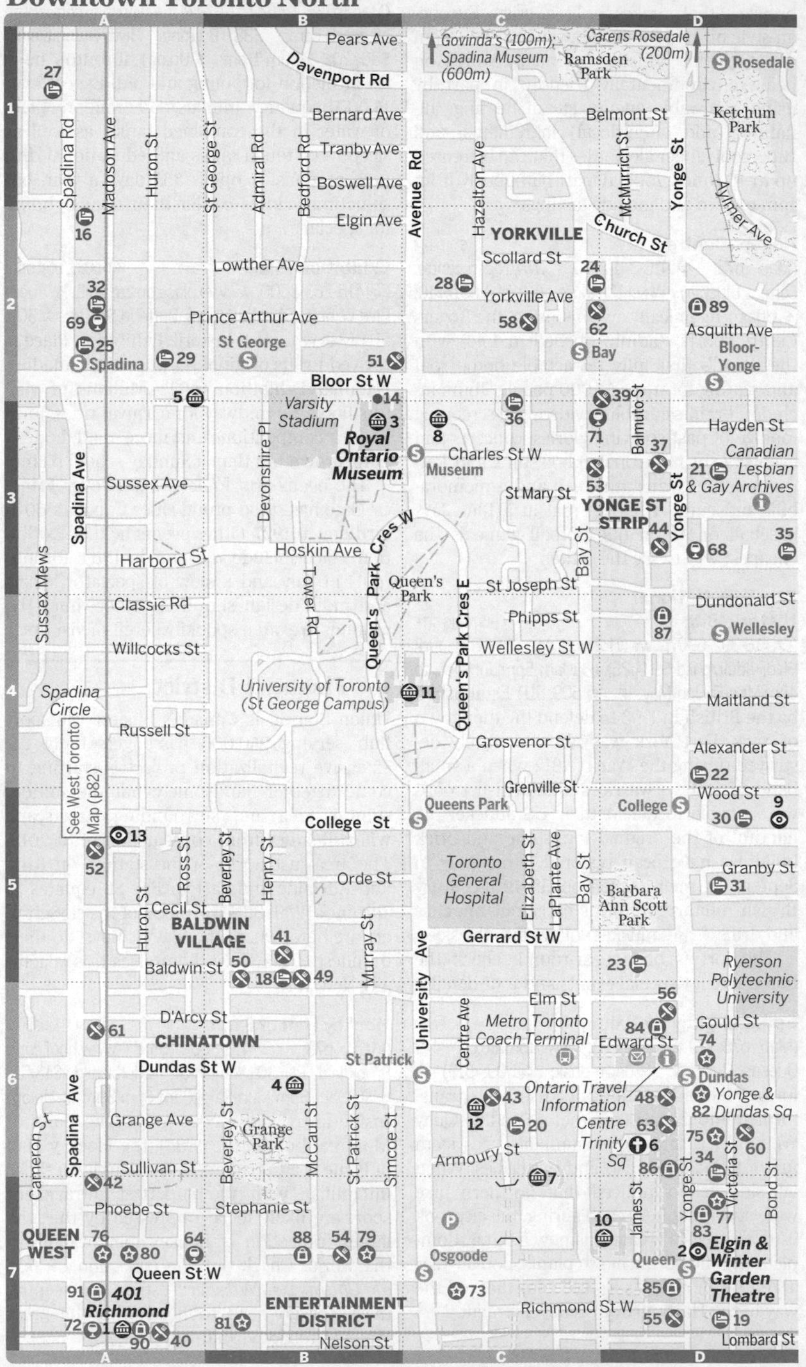

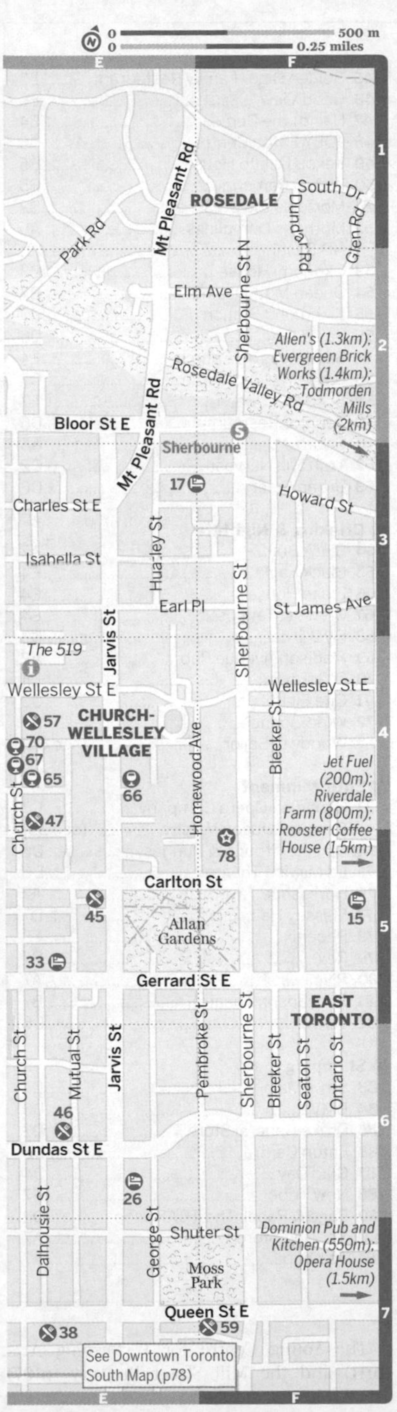

Cloud Gardens Conservatory GARDENS

(Bay Adelaide Park; Map p78; ☎416-392-7288; 14 Temperance St; ⏲10am-2:30pm Mon-Fri; Ⓢ Queen) FREE An unexpected sanctuary with its own waterfall, the steamy Cloud Gardens Conservatory is crowded with enormous jungle leaves, vines and palms. Information plaques answer the question 'What Are Rainforests?' The greenhouse is a great place to warm up during winter, but avoid the area after dark – the adjacent park attracts some shady characters.

TD Gallery of Inuit Art MUSEUM

(Map p78; ☎416-982-8473; https://art.td.com/visit; 79 Wellington St W, ground fl & mezzanine, TD Centre; ⏲8am-6pm Mon-Fri, 10am-4pm Sat & Sun; Ⓢ St Andrew) FREE A quiet pause in the bustle of the Financial District, the Toronto Dominion Gallery of Inuit Art provides an exceptional insight into Inuit culture. Inside the Toronto-Dominion Centre, a succession of glass cases displays otters, bears, eagles and carved Inuit figures in day-to-day scenes.

Design Exchange MUSEUM

(DX; Map p78; ☎416-363-6121; www.dx.org; 234 Bay St; adult/child $10/8; ⏲9am-5pm Tue-Fri, noon-4:30pm Sat & Sun; Ⓢ King) The original Toronto Stock Exchange now houses eye-catching industrial design exhibits. The permanent collection includes more than 1000 Canadian pieces that span six decades in a rather tiny museum. Prices for special exhibitions vary.

Old York

Historically speaking, the old town of York comprises just 10 square blocks. But today the neighborhood extends east of Yonge St all the way to the Don River, and from Queen St south to the waterfront esplanade. The ghosts of Toronto's past are around every corner.

★Distillery District AREA

(☎416-364-1177; www.thedistillerydistrict.com; 9 Trinity St; ⏲10am-7pm Mon-Wed, to 8pm Thu-Sat, 11am-5pm Sun; 🚊503, 504) Centered on the 1832 Gooderham and Worts distillery – once the British Empire's largest – the 5-hectare Distillery District is one of Toronto's best downtown attractions. Its Victorian industrial warehouses have been converted into soaring galleries, artists studios, design boutiques, cafes and eateries. On weekends, newlyweds pose before a backdrop of red brick and cobblestone, young families walk their dogs and the fashionable elite shop for art beneath

Downtown Toronto North

Top Sights
1 401 Richmond ... A7
2 Elgin & Winter Garden Theatre ... D7
3 Royal Ontario Museum ... B3

Sights
4 Art Gallery of Ontario ... B6
5 Bata Shoe Museum ... A2
6 Church of the Holy Trinity ... D6
7 City Hall ... C7
8 Gardiner Museum ... C3
9 Maple Leaf Gardens ... D5
10 Old City Hall ... D7
11 Provincial Legislature ... C4
12 Textile Museum of Canada ... C6
13 Toronto Public Library – Lillian H Smith Branch ... A5

Activities, Courses & Tours
14 ROMBus ... B2

Sleeping
15 Amsterdam Guesthouse ... F5
16 Annex Quest House ... A2
17 Au Petit Paris ... E3
18 Baldwin Village Inn ... B5
19 Cambridge Suites ... D7
20 Chestnut Residence ... C6
21 Comfort Hotel ... D3
22 Courtyard Toronto Downtown ... D4
23 Eaton Chelsea ... D5
24 Four Seasons ... C2
25 Global Guesthouse ... A2
26 Grand Hotel & Suites ... E6
27 Havinn ... A1
28 Hazelton ... C2
29 Holiday Inn Toronto Bloor-Yorkville ... A2
30 Holiday Inn Toronto Downtown Centre ... D5
31 Les Amis Bed & Breakfast ... D5
32 Madison Manor ... A2
33 Neill-Wycik College Hotel ... E5
34 Pantages ... D6
35 Victoria's Mansion Inn & Guesthouse ... D3
36 Windsor Arms ... C3

Eating
37 7 West Café ... D3
38 B Espresso Bar ... E7
39 Bloor Street Diner ... D2
40 Burrito Bandidos ... A7
41 Cafe la Gaffe ... B5
42 Dark Horse Espresso ... A7
43 Eat Fresh Be Healthy ... C6
44 Ethiopian House ... D3
45 Golden Diner Family Restaurant ... E5
46 Good View ... E6
47 Hair of the Dog ... E4
48 JOEY Eaton Centre ... D6
49 Kekou Gelato House ... B5
50 Kinton Ramen ... B5
51 Morton's the Steakhouse ... B2
52 Mother's Dumplings ... A5
ND Sushi ... (see 49)
53 Okonomi House ... C3
54 Queen Mother Café ... B7
55 Richmond Station ... D7
56 Salad King ... D6
57 Sambucas on Church ... E4
58 Sassafraz ... C2
59 Schnitzel Queen ... F7
60 Senator Restaurant ... D6
61 Swatow ... A6
62 Trattoria Nervosa ... C2
63 Urban Eatery ... D6

Drinking & Nightlife
64 Black Bull ... A7
65 Black Eagle ... E4
66 Blake House ... E4
67 Crews & Tangos ... E4
68 Fly 2.0 ... D3
69 Madison Avenue Pub ... A2
70 O'Grady's ... E4
71 One Eighty ... C3
72 Wide Open ... A7
Woody's/Sailor ... (see 65)

Entertainment
73 Canadian Opera Company ... C7
Cineplex Odeon Varsity ... (see 39)
74 Cineplex Yonge & Dundas ... D6
75 Ed Mirvish Theatre ... D6
76 Horseshoe Tavern ... A7
77 Massey Hall ... D7
78 Phoenix ... F5
79 Rex ... B7
80 Rivoli ... A7
81 Scotiabank Theatre ... B7
82 TO Tix ... D6

Shopping
83 8th + Main ... D7
84 BMV ... D6
85 Drake General Store ... D7
86 Eaton Centre ... D6
87 Glad Day ... D4
88 New Tribe ... B7
89 Page & Panel: The TCAF shop ... D2
90 Spacing Store ... A7
91 Te Koop ... A7

charmingly decrepit gables and gantries. In summer, expect live jazz, activities, exhibitions and foodie events.

The Young Centre for Performing Arts (p111) and the Mill Street Brewery (p107) are also here.

★ St Lawrence Market MARKET

(Map p78; ☎416-392-7129; www.stlawrencemarket.com; 92-95 Front St E; ⏲8am-6pm Tue-Thu, to 7pm Fri, 5am-5pm Sat; P; 🚋503, 504) Old York's sensational St Lawrence Market has been a neighborhood meeting place for over two centuries. The restored, high-trussed 1845 **South Market** houses more than 50 specialty food stalls: cheese vendors, fishmongers, butchers, bakers and pasta makers. The **Carousel Bakery** is famed for its peameal bacon sandwiches and **St Urbain** for its authentic Montréal-style bagels.

Inside the old council chambers upstairs, the **Market Gallery** (Map p78; ☎416-392-0572; www.toronto.ca/marketgallery; 95 Front St E; ⏲10am-6pm Tue-Thu, to 7pm Fri, 9am-5pm Sat, 10am-4pm Sun; 🚋503, 504) FREE has rotating displays of paintings, photographs, documents and historical relics.

On the opposite side of Front St, the North Market hosts a Saturday farmers market from 5am and a fantastic Sunday antique market – get in early for the best stuff. In 2010, the winners of a design competition to transform the North Market building were announced, but there's no sign of construction yet. A few steps further north, the glorious St Lawrence Hall (1849) is topped by a mansard roof and a copper-clad clock tower.

Entertainment District & King Street West

West of the Financial District, on King St, between University and Spadina Aves, Toronto's Entertainment District is home to theaters and performance halls, preshow bars and the acclaimed TIFF Bell Lightbox (p112) theater. The whole area as far west as Spadina is nightclub central. East on King, toward the Distillery District (p73), you'll find high-end furniture and design stores, good for window shopping, and some fine historic architecture.

★ 401 Richmond GALLERY

(Map p72; www.401richmond.net; 401 Richmond St W; ⏲9am-7pm Mon-Fri, to 6pm Sat; 🚋510) FREE Inside an early-20th-century lithographer's warehouse, restored in 1994, this 18,500-meter-sq New York–style artist collective hums with the creative vibes of 130 diverse contemporary galleries showcasing works in almost any artistic medium you can think of. Grab a snack and a latte at the ground-floor cafe and enjoy it on the expansive roof garden: a little-known oasis in the summer.

Canadian Broadcasting Centre MUSEUM

(CBC; Map p78; ☎416-205-5574; www.cbc.ca/museum; 250 Front St W; ⏲9am-5pm Mon-Fri; S Union, 🚋504) FREE Toronto's enormous CBC is the headquarters for English-language radio and TV across Canada. You can peek at the radio newsrooms anytime or attend a concert in the world-class Glenn Gould Studio (p110). Be sure to check out the **CBC Museum**, with its fantastic collection of antique microphones and broadcasting memorabilia. Next door, the **Graham Spry Theatre** screens ever-changing CBC programming. Best of all, it's free!

Downtown Yonge

Heading north on Yonge St, Yonge & Dundas Sq, Toronto's homage to New York's Times Square, is regarded as the center of the downtown core. It's an oddly positioned public space that neither looks good nor really delivers. There's usually something going on here, but it's as frequently about commercial exploits as community-building. Across the street, the landmark Eaton Centre mall, which sprawls between Dundas and Queen Sts, is the primary draw along with some historic theaters and Ryerson University. The mixed-bag continues north on Yonge, skirting past the colorful Church-Wellesley gay village, into chichi Yorkville at the intersection with Bloor St.

★ Elgin & Winter Garden Theatre THEATER

(Map p72; ☎416-314-2871; www.heritagetrust.on.ca/ewg; 189 Yonge St; tours adult/student $12/10; S Queen) This restored masterpiece is the world's last operating Edwardian double-decker theater. Celebrating its centennial in 2013, the Winter Garden was built as the flagship for a vaudeville chain that never really took off, while the downstairs Elgin was converted into a movie house in the 1920s.

Saved from demolition in 1981, the theaters received a $29-million face-lift: bread dough was used to uncover original rose-garden frescoes, the Belgian company that made the original carpet was contacted for fresh rugs, and the floral Winter Garden ceiling was replaced, leaf by painstaking leaf.

City Hall HISTORIC BUILDING

(Map p72; ☎416-392-2489, 311; www.toronto.ca; 100 Queen St W; ⏲8:30am-4:30pm Mon-Fri; P; S Queen) FREE Much-maligned City Hall was Toronto's bold leap of faith into architectural modernity. Its twin clamshell towers, central 'flying saucer,' ramps and mosaics were completed in 1965 to Finnish architect Viljo Revell's award-winning design. An irritable Frank Lloyd Wright compared it to a gravestone; Revell died before construction was finished.

Out front is **Nathan Phillips Square** (though most just call it City Hall too), a magnet for skaters, demonstrators, fast-food trucks, and tourists taking selfies with the lit-up 'Toronto' letters day and night. In summer, check out the Fresh Wednesdays farmers market, free concerts, special events and office workers on their lunch breaks, up the ramp on the green roof. Look for a tourist information pop-up on the corner of Bay and Queen. The fountain pool becomes a fun-filled ice-skating rink in winter.

Old City Hall HISTORIC BUILDING

(Map p72; ☎416-327-5614; www.toronto.ca/old_cityhall; 60 Queen St W; ⏰8:30am-4:30pm Mon-Fri; Ⓢ Queen) FREE Across Bay St from the current City Hall (p75) is the 1899 definitive work of Toronto architect EJ Lennox. Now housing legal courtrooms, the hall has an off-center bell tower, interesting murals and grimacing gargoyles.

Church of the Holy Trinity CHURCH

(Map p72; ☎416-598-4521; www.holytrinitytoronto.org; 10 Trinity Sq; ⏰11am-3pm Mon-Fri, services 12:15pm Wed, 10:30am & 2pm Sun; Ⓢ Dundas) Tucked away behind the west side of the gargantuan Eaton Centre is the oasis-like Trinity Sq, named after the welcoming Anglican Church of the Holy Trinity. When it opened in 1847, it was the first church in Toronto not to charge parishioners for pews. Today, it's notable for welcoming same-sex marriage ceremonies and is a cross between a house of worship, a small concert venue and a community drop-in center – everything a downtown church should be!

Textile Museum of Canada MUSEUM

(Map p72; ☎416-599-5321; www.textilemuseum.ca; 55 Centre Ave; adult/child $15/6, by donation 5-8pm Wed; ⏰11am-5pm Thu-Tue, to 8pm Wed, tours 2pm Sun; Ⓢ St Patrick) Obscurely located at the bottom of a condo tower, this museum has exhibits drawing on a permanent collection of 10,000 items from Latin America, Africa, Europe, Southeast Asia and India, as well as contemporary Canada. Workshops teach batik making, weaving, knitting and all manner of needle-stuff.

TORONTO FOR CHILDREN

Toronto is a kid-friendly city: there are plenty of things to see and do when traveling with little ones in tow.

➡ The **Harbourfront Centre** (p70) produces ongoing events through HarbourKIDS. The **Canadian National Exhibition** (p92) also has events in August.

➡ Inquisitive minds will love the **CN Tower** (p69), **Ontario Science Centre** (p87), **Royal Ontario Museum** (p79) and **LEGOLAND Discovery Centre** (p87).

➡ Arty and creative kids might enjoy the clay classes at the **Gardiner Museum** (p80), dropping in for story time at the **Toronto Public Library – Lillian H Smith Branch** (Map p72; ☎416-393-7746; www.torontopubliclibrary.ca; 239 College St; ⏰9am-8:30pm Mon-Thu, to 6pm Fri, to 5pm Sat, 1:30-5pm Sun; 👪; 🚋506, 510) FREE or catching a show at the **Young People's Theatre** (p112).

➡ The environmental custodians and animal doctors of the next generation will want you to take them to **Ripley's Aquarium** (p71), **Riverdale Farm** (p83), **High Park** (p85), **Spadina Quay Wetlands** (p71) and **Tommy Thompson Park** (p84).

➡ If they've got ants in their pants, they won't have after a trip to **Canada's Wonderland** (p87) or, for a way tamer version, the **Centreville Amusement Park** (p85). Teenagers will also enjoy the **Eaton Centre** (p101) and **Kensington Market** (p81).

➡ Roomier digs for families that shouldn't break the bank are at the **Eaton Chelsea** (p95), with its massive water slide, **Courtyard Toronto Downtown** (p96), the **Grand Hotel and Suites** (p95) and **Cambridge Suites** (p95).

➡ A handy online resource for parents is www.helpwevegotkids.com, which lists everything child-related in Toronto, including babysitters and day-care options.

The **3Pass** (www.3pass.ca) gets you admission into the Bata Shoe Museum (p80), Gardiner Museum (p80), and Textile Museum of Canada for $30 (tax included).

Chinatown & Baldwin Village

Toronto's grotty Chinatown occupies a chunk of downtown from University Ave to Spadina Ave between College and Queen Sts; a vermilion twin dragon gate marks the epicenter. Between Beverley and McCaul Sts, on Baldwin St, leafy Baldwin Village is a pretty strip of cheap eats and good vibes tucked away from the maddening crowds. The village has Jewish roots, but today's bohemian air stems from counterculture US exiles who decamped here during the Vietnam War.

Art Gallery of Ontario GALLERY
(AGO; Map p72; ☎416-979-6648; www.ago.net; 317 Dundas St W; adult/under 18yr $19.50/11; ⊙10:30am-5pm Tue & Thu, to 9pm Wed & Fri, to 5:30pm Sat & Sun; 🚋505) The AGO houses art collections both excellent and extensive (bring your stamina). Renovations of the facade, designed by the great Frank Gehry and completed in 2008, fail to impress at street level: perhaps because of a drab downtown location. Fortunately, everything changes once you step inside. Highlights of the permanent collection include rare Québecois religious statuary, First Nations and Inuit carvings, stunningly presented works by Canadian greats, the Group of Seven, the Henry Moore sculpture pavilion and a restored Georgian house, The Grange.

Church-Wellesley Village

North of Yonge & Dundas Sq along Yonge St, toward College St and Bloor St, you'll find Ryerson University and a smattering of cheap eats, sex shops and strip clubs, straight and gay. Toronto's gay village, known as 'Church & Wellesley' or 'the Village,' starts on the corner of Church and College and is centered a few blocks north on the intersection of Church and Wellesley Sts. Every summer, around the Canada Day long weekend, over a million shiny happy people descend on the streets for Toronto's massive Pride Parade (p91) – at the end of the Pride Month festival – a celebration of sexuality, diversity and freedom.

Maple Leaf Gardens STADIUM
(Mattamy Athletic Centre and Loblaws; Map p72; ☎416-598-5966; www.mattamyathleticcentre.ca; 50-60 Carlton St; **S** College) This hallowed hockey arena was built in an astounding five months during the Great Depression, and was home to the Toronto Maple Leafs for over 50 years until they relocated to the Air Canada Centre (p113) in 1999. In its heyday, Elvis, Sinatra and the Beatles all belted out tunes here. After a monumental redevelopment project, the facility is now home to Ryerson University's Athletic Centre.

TORONTO BY NUMBERS

- Canadian immigrants who settle in Toronto: one in four
- Residents of Toronto who were born outside of Canada: one in two
- Estimated number of visitors during Pride Week: 1 million
- Pint of local brew: $5
- TTC subway ride: $3
- Percentage of the US population within a day's drive of Toronto: 50%
- Height of the CN Tower: 553m
- Cheap seat at a Blue Jays game: $13
- Parkland as a percentage of Toronto's area: 18%
- Months in the year when parks are green and leafy: six
- Last time the Maple Leafs won the Stanley Cup: 1967
- Minutes per day the average Torontonian spends commuting: 82

Bloor-Yorkville

Once Toronto's version of New York's Greenwich Village or San Francisco's Haight-Ashbury, this formerly countercultural leopard has changed its spots to become the downtown home of Toronto's rich, famous, glam and fabulous. Yorkville's main drag is the stretch of Bloor St W to Avenue Rd, otherwise known as the Mink Mile: the place to go if high-end brand label shopping is your thing. The Holt Renfrew department store is here, along with Gucci, Prada, D&G and Louis Vuitton. There are some lovely boutiques and cafes in the streets north of Bloor to Davenport Rd and east of Avenue Rd. Hollywood celebrities are frequently spotted in Yorkville bars when the Toronto International Film Festival is in town.

Downtown Toronto South

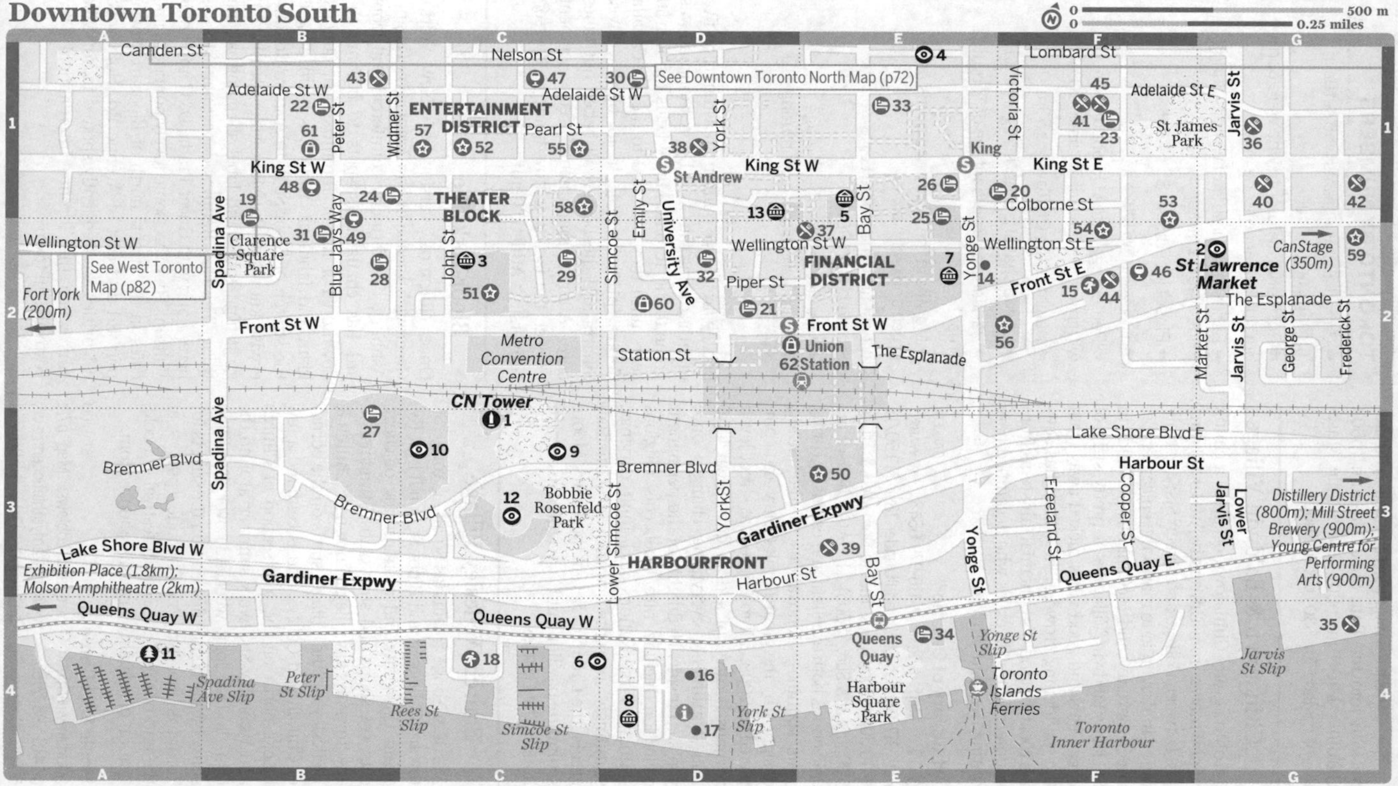

0 — 500 m
0 — 0.25 miles

A B C D E F G
1 2 3 4

Camden St
Nelson St
Lombard St
Adelaide St W
Adelaide St E
See Downtown Toronto North Map (p72)
See West Toronto Map (p82)
ENTERTAINMENT DISTRICT
THEATER BLOCK
FINANCIAL DISTRICT
HARBOURFRONT
Pearl St
King St W
King St E
King
St Andrew
Wellington St W
Wellington St E
Colborne St
Front St W
Front St E
Piper St
Station St
The Esplanade
Union Station
Spadina Ave
Peter St
Widmer St
Blue Jays Way
John St
Simcoe St
Emily St
University Ave
York St
Bay St
Yonge St
Victoria St
Jarvis St
Market St
George St
Frederick St
Clarence Square Park
St James Park
St Lawrence Market
Metro Convention Centre
CN Tower
Bobbie Rosenfeld Park
Bremner Blvd
Lake Shore Blvd W
Lake Shore Blvd E
Gardiner Expwy
Harbour St
Freeland St
Cooper St
Lower Jarvis St
Lower Simcoe St
Queens Quay W
Queens Quay E
Queens Quay
Harbour Square Park
Toronto Islands Ferries
Toronto Inner Harbour
Spadina Ave Slip
Peter St Slip
Rees St Slip
Simcoe St Slip
York St Slip
Yonge St Slip
Jarvis St Slip
Fort York (200m)
Exhibition Place (1.8km); Molson Amphitheatre (2km)
CanStage (350m)
Distillery District (800m); Mill Street Brewery (900m); Young Centre for Performing Arts (900m)

1 2 3 4 5 6 7 8 9 10 11 12 13 14 15 16 17 18 19 20 21 22 23 24 25 26 27 28 29 30 31 32 33 34 35 36 37 38 39 40 41 42 43 44 45 46 47 48 49 50 51 52 53 54 55 56 57 58 59 60 61 62

Downtown Toronto South

Top Sights

1 CN Tower ... C3
2 St Lawrence Market ... G2

Sights

3 Canadian Broadcasting Centre ... C2
4 Cloud Gardens Conservatory ... E1
5 Design Exchange ... E1
6 Harbourfront Centre ... C4
7 Hockey Hall of Fame ... E2
Market Gallery ... (see 2)
8 Power Plant Contemporary Art Gallery ... D4
9 Ripley's Aquarium of Canada ... C3
10 Rogers Centre ... C3
11 Spadina Quay Wetlands ... A4
12 Steam Whistle Brewing ... C3
13 TD Gallery of Inuit Art ... D1

Activities, Courses & Tours

14 Chariots of Fire ... E2
15 Europe Bound Outfitters ... F2
16 Mariposa Cruises ... D4
17 Tall Ship Kajama ... D4
18 Wheel Excitement ... C4

Sleeping

19 Clarence Park ... B1
20 Cosmopolitan ... F1
21 Fairmont Royal York ... D2
22 Hilton Garden Inn Toronto Downtown ... B1
23 Hostelling International Toronto ... F1
24 Hôtel Le Germain ... B1
25 Hotel Victoria ... E1
26 One King West ... E1
27 Renaissance Toronto ... B3
28 Residence Inn Toronto Downtown ... B2
29 Ritz Carlton ... C2
30 Shangri-La Hotel ... D1
31 Soho Metropolitan Hotel ... B2
32 Strathcona Hotel ... D2
33 Trump Toronto ... E1
34 Westin Harbour Castle ... E4

Eating

35 Against the Grain Urban Tavern ... G4
36 Bombay Palace ... G1
37 Bymark ... E2
38 Earl's ... D1
39 Harbour Sixty Steakhouse ... E3
40 Hiro Sushi ... G1
41 Nami ... F1
42 Patrician Grill ... G1
43 Ravi Soups ... B1
44 Sultan's Tent & Café Maroc ... F2
45 Terroni ... F1

Drinking & Nightlife

46 C'est What ... F2
47 Crocodile Rock ... C1
48 Underground Garage ... B1
49 Wayne Gretzky's ... B2

Entertainment

50 Air Canada Centre ... E3
51 Glenn Gould Studio ... C2
52 Princess of Wales Theatre ... C1
53 Rainbow Cinemas ... F1
54 Reservoir Lounge ... F2
55 Royal Alexandra Theatre ... C1
56 Sony Centre for the Performing Arts ... F2
57 TIFF Bell Lightbox ... C1
58 Toronto Symphony Orchestra ... C1
59 Young People's Theatre ... G2

Shopping

60 Bay of Spirits Gallery ... D2
61 MEC ... B1
62 Union Summer ... D2

★**Royal Ontario Museum** MUSEUM

(ROM; Map p72; 416-586-8000; www.rom.on.ca; 100 Queen's Park; adult/child $15/12; 10am-5:30pm Sat-Thu, to 8:30pm Fri; Museum) Celebrating its centennial in 2014, the multidisciplinary ROM is Canada's biggest natural history museum and one of the largest museums in North America. You'll either love or loathe the synergy between the original heritage buildings at the main entrance on Bloor St and the 2007 addition of 'the Crystal,' which appears to pierce the original structure and juts out into the street like a massive shard.

Inside, the permanent collection features over 6 million specimens and artifacts, divided between two main galleries: the Natural History Galleries (all on the 2nd floor) and the World Culture Galleries (on floors 1, 3 and 4). The Chinese temple sculptures, Gallery of Korean Art, and costumes and textile collections are some of the best in the world. Kids rush to the dinosaur rooms, Egyptian mummies and Jamaican bat-cave replica. The cedar crest poles carved by First Nations tribes in British Columbia are wonderful.

Each year, the ROM hosts a variety of big temporary exhibits from around the world (special exhibit surcharges apply). The on-site Institute of Contemporary Culture explores current issues through art, architecture, lectures and moving images. There are free museum tours daily. Keep an eye out for the Friday Night Live programs in spring and fall when the museum opens its doors, stocks its bars and calls in the DJs for a makeshift disco. ROM Summer Fridays from July to September have discounted admission from 4:30pm.

Bata Shoe Museum MUSEUM
(Map p72; ☎416-979-7799; www.batashoemuseum.ca; 327 Bloor St W; adult/child $14/5, 5-8pm Thu suggested donation $5; ⊙10am-5pm Mon-Wed, Fri & Sat, to 8pm Thu, noon-5pm Sun; S St George) It's important in life to be well shod, a stance the Bata Shoe Museum takes seriously. Impressively designed by architect Raymond Moriyama to resemble a stylized shoe box, the museum displays 10,000 'pedi-artifacts' from around the globe. Peruse 19th-century French chestnut-crushing clogs, Canadian aboriginal polar boots or famous modern pairs worn by Elton John, Indira Gandhi and Pablo Picasso.

The **3Pass** (www.3pass.ca) gets you admission into the Bata Shoe Museum, Gardiner Museum and Textile Museum of Canada (p76) for $30 (tax included).

Gardiner Museum MUSEUM
(Map p72; ☎416-586-8080; www.gardinermuseum.on.ca; 111 Queen's Park; adult/child $15/free, half-price 4-9pm Fri; ⊙10am-6pm Mon-Thu, to 9pm Fri, to 5pm Sat & Sun; S Museum) Opposite the Royal Ontario Museum, the Gardiner Museum was founded by philanthropists to house their ceramics. Spread over three floors, collections cover several millennia; various rooms focus on 17th- and 18th-century English tavern ware, Italian Renaissance majolica, ancient American earthenware and blue-and-white Chinese porcelain. There are free guided tours daily at 2pm.

The **3Pass** (www.3pass.ca) gets you admission into the Gardiner Museum, Bata Shoe Museum, and Textile Museum of Canada (p76) for $30 (tax included).

University of Toronto & The Annex

Founded in 1827, the prestigious University of Toronto (U of T) is Canada's largest, with close to 80,000 students and 18,000 employees. Feel free to stroll through the central St George campus to admire its collection of stately Victorian and Romanesque buildings. West and north of U of T lies The Annex, Toronto's largest downtown residential neighborhood, favored by students and academics. The number of pubs, organic grocery stores, world eats and spiritual venues here comes as no surprise. Some of Toronto's most majestic architecture is here, too.

★**Casa Loma** HISTORIC BUILDING
(☎416-923-1171; www.casaloma.org; 1 Austin Tce; adult/child $18/10; ⊙9:30am-5pm, last entry 4pm; P; 127, S Dupont) Toronto's only castle may have never housed royalty, but it certainly has grandeur, lording over The Annex from a cliff that was once the shoreline of the glacial Lake Iroquois, from which Lake Ontario derived. A variety of themed guided tours are available. If you're in Toronto around Christmas, a visit is a must. Check the website for details. To reach the *casa*, climb the 27m **Baldwin Steps** up the slope from Spadina Ave, north of Davenport Rd.

The 98-room mansion – an architectural orgasm of castellations, chimneys, flagpoles, turrets and Rapunzel balconies – was built between 1911 and 1914 for Sir Henry Pellat, a wealthy financier who made bags of cash from his contract to provide Toronto with electricity. He later lost everything in land speculation, the resultant foreclosure forcing Hank and his wife to downsize.

★**Spadina Museum** MUSEUM
(☎416-392-6910; www.toronto.ca/museums; 285 Spadina Rd; tours adult/child $8/5, grounds free; ⊙noon-4pm Tue-Sun; P; S Dupont) Atop the Baldwin Steps, this gracious home and its Victorian-Edwardian gardens were built in 1866 as a country estate for financier James Austin and his family. Donated to the city in 1978, it became a museum in 1984 and was recently painstakingly transformed to evoke the heady age of the 1920s and '30s: highly recommended.

Provincial Legislature HISTORIC BUILDING
(Map p72; www.ontla.on.ca; Queen's Park; ⊙8:30am-6pm Mon-Fri; S Queens Park) FREE The seat of Ontario's Provincial Legislature resides in an ornate 1893 sandstone building, north of College St in Queen's Park. For some homegrown entertainment, head for the visitors gallery when the adversarial legislative assembly is in session (Monday, Tuesday and Thursday, March to June and September to December). Viewing is free, but security regulations are in full force.

Wychwood Park PARK
(cnr Davenport Rd & Bathurst St; S Dupont) Formerly a gated artists colony, Wychwood Park, established in the late 19th century, showcases some of Toronto's most beautiful and fascinating heritage architecture. It's a great place for a stroll. Note that Wychwood is an actual residential community where people go about their daily lives: please be respectful.

KENSINGTON MARKET & LITTLE ITALY

Tattered around the edges, elegantly wasted **Kensington Market** is multicultural Toronto at its most interesting. It's not a constrained market as much as a working residential neighborhood. Eating here is a cheap and cheery trip around the flavors and aromas of the world – nowadays with foodie nods. Shopping too is a blast, with the biggest and best proliferation of vintage and secondhand clothing, books and bric-a-brac in the city. You'll find dreadlocked urban hippies, tattooed punks, potheads and dealers, bikers, goths, musos, artists and anarchists, generally behaving well and getting along fine. Hooch and Hendrix tinge the air. On weekends, it can feel like a small festival, especially on Pedestrian Sundays, when bipeds rule. It's more chilled on weekdays, when that extra personal space makes it easier to browse.

To get here, take the College streetcar to Spadina Ave or Augusta Ave and follow the activity. Augusta Ave between College and Dundas is the main strip, but the little stretch of Nassau St between Augusta and Bellevue has some wonderful cafes and can be a welcome oasis from the crowds.

Further along College St, **Little Italy** is what you expect – a tasty slice of the homeland. There's a long-established strip of outdoor cafes, bars and stylish restaurants that frequently change hands – affluent clientele are notoriously fickle. The further west you go on College, the more traditional things become, with aromatic bakeries, sidewalk gelaterias and rootsy ristoranti.

Native Canadian Centre of Toronto CULTURAL

(Map p82; ☎416-964-9087; www.ncct.on.ca; 16 Spadina Rd; ⌚9am-8pm Mon-Thu, to 6pm Fri, 10am-4pm Sat; Ⓢ Spadina) This community center hosts Thursday-night drum socials, seasonal powwows and elders' cultural events that promote harmony and conversation between tribal members and non–First Nations peoples. You can also sign up for workshops and craft classes, such as beading and dancing.

Queen West & Trinity Bellwoods

Although Queen West isn't home to any significant attractions, a trip to Toronto's best known 'hood is a must. Any self-respecting 20-to-40-something with an interest in popular culture will want to make this hip strip their first port of call.

To do Queen St justice, make a day of it: start at the corner of Yonge St and head west, although nothing really happens until the Osgoode subway station at the intersection of Queen St W and University Ave. The Queen West district begins here and continues for about 1.5km to Bathurst St. The first few blocks over to Spadina are a wonderful mix of mainstream retailers, bars and an eclectic bunch of boutiques, but it's really from Spadina to Bathurst where the wild things are. Infinitely more grungy, here you'll find all manner of cheap and delicious eats slotted between furniture, art and music stores. There's plenty of cafes and bars in which to glean inspiration and lose track of time.

West of Bathurst, past Trinity Bellwoods Park, for about 2km over to Dufferin St, is known as West Queen West. The first bit between Bathurst and happening Ossington Ave, south of Bloor, all the way down to Queen, is one of Toronto's best strips for food, drink and people-watching. This is the Trinity Bellwoods neighborhood – *the* place to live if you're a hipster, designhead, scenester or nonmainstream gay. (Yes, Toronto's neighborhoods can be this transparent.) The proliferation of excellent food and beverage joints on and around Ossington arose when high rents pushed many businesses further west. What emerged is a revitalised strip of Queen St, infinitely more trendy than the original. The quieter far west extremity of Queen is a hub of designer furniture stores.

Streetcars run the length of Queen St W, before it becomes the Queensway: nice to know if your feet get tired or you're loaded up with too many bags after a hard day hipsterising your wardrobe – it's a long walk back downtown.

Museum of Contemporary Art_Toronto_Canada MUSEUM

(Map p82; http://museumofcontemporaryart.ca; Queen St W; 🚋501) In May 2017 MoCA will transform into the Museum of Contemporary Art_Toronto_Canada, across the road.

West Toronto

West Toronto

Sights

1 Museum of Contemporary Art Toronto Canada A6

Activities, Courses & Tours

2 Community Bicycle Network C6
3 Native Canadian Centre of Toronto D2

Sleeping

4 Planet Travelers Hostel D4
5 Thompson Toronto C7

Eating

6 Aunties & Uncles C4
7 Avenue Open Kitchen D7
8 Bar Italia B4
9 Burger's Priest D6
10 By the Way D2
11 Caplansky's Deli D4
12 Chabichou C3
13 Chippy's B6
14 Country Style Hungarian Restaurant C2
15 Jumbo Empanadas D5
16 Kalendar B4
17 Khao San Road B6
18 Kupfert & Kim D7
19 Lee C7
20 Moonbean Coffee Company D5
21 Mr Tonkatsu C2
22 New York Subs & Burritos C6
23 Nguyen Huong D5
24 Patria D7
25 Pho Hu'ng D5
26 Pizzeria Libretto A5
27 Rose and Sons Swan A6
Thompson Diner .... (see 5)
28 Union A6
29 Urban Herbivore D4
30 Wvrst C7

Drinking & Nightlife

31 BarChef D6
32 Clinton's B2
33 El Convento Rico A4
34 Handlebar D5
35 Java House D6
Mod Club .... (see 33)
36 Ossington A6
37 Red Room D4
38 Sneaky Dee's C4
39 Sweaty Betty's A6
40 Uniun D7

Entertainment

41 Cameron House D6
42 Cineforum C4
43 Dakota Tavern A5
44 Factory Theatre C7
Hot Docs Ted Rogers Cinema .... (see 21)
45 Lee's Palace C2
46 Theatre Passe Muraille C6

Shopping

47 Beguiling C2
48 BMV D2
49 Come as You Are C6
50 Courage My Love D5

At Queen and Ossington, in the heart of West Queen West's design and arts precinct, MoCA's mandate had been to exhibit innovative works by Canadian and international artists that address themes of contemporary relevance. The new, larger museum will create a digital archive of work and interpret the modern world through art. Check the website for hours and details.

East End

The area east of Parliament St to the Don River was settled by Irish immigrants fleeing the potato famine of 1841. Because the area's sandy soil proved cabbage-conducive, it became known as Cabbagetown. Predominantly residential and officially designated a Heritage Conservation District, it has one of the largest concentrations of domestic Victorian architecture in North America, making for a pleasant stroll.

It's nice to walk across Riverdale Park, north on Broadview Ave, then east on Danforth Ave where you'll find yourself in Greektown/The Danforth. Further east on Gerrard St E you'll come to Little India. Both are heavenly haunts for the food-focused. Dropping south to Queen St E, discover Leslieville. Favored by lesbians and armies of young cashed-up moms, it's Toronto's antithesis to Queen West: chichi, sanitized and a lovely spot for a fancy brunch. Since 2005, when the *New York Times* pronounced the then up-and-coming Leslieville as Toronto's *'it'* neighborhood, real estate prices and interest in the area have soared.

★ Riverdale Farm MUSEUM

(416-392-6794; www.toronto.ca/riverdalefarm; 201 Winchester St; 9am-5pm; P; 506) FREE

On the former site of the Riverdale Zoo, where from 1888 to 1974 prairie wolves howled at night and spooked the Cabbagetown kids,

GAY & LESBIAN TORONTO

To say Toronto is LGBTI-friendly is an understatement. That it embraces diversity more fully than most other centers of its size is closer to the mark. In 2003 Toronto became the first city in North America to legalize same-sex marriage. Just over a year later, an Ontario Court also recognized the first legal same-sex divorce, as if to remind us that marriage can be hard work, whatever your orientation!

Toronto's LGBTI **Pride festival** (p91) is one of the largest in the world. On Parade day, the streets around Church and Wellesley swell with over a million happy homosexuals and their friends and families. If Pride is your bag, be sure to book accommodations well in advance as beds fill fast. At other times of the year, the Church St strip of the Village draws everyone from biker bears to lipstick lesbians to its modest smattering of sunny patios, pubs, cafes and restaurants for much promenading and people-watching. After dark it's all about the dancing: whether cabaret or drag, thumping top-40 and R & B or queer alterna-punk, late-night revelers spill onto the streets, especially on weekends.

Other gay-friendly neighborhoods include the Annex, Kensington, Queen West, Cabbagetown and Leslieville (aka 'Lesbianville'). Gay nightlife venues are abundant and although men's bars and clubs vastly outnumber lesbian venues, Toronto is also home to drag kings, women-only bathhouse nights and lesbian reading series.

Toronto is a great place to be gay or to explore your sexuality. Head to the *Daily Xtra* (www.dailyxtra.com) internet magazine for the latest scoop on LGBTI issues in the Village. There are also plenty of fantastic free community resources and support groups available:

The 519 (Church St Community Centre; Map p72; ☎416-392-6874; www.the519.org; 519 Church St; ⏲8:30am-10pm Mon-Fri, 9am-10pm Sat, 10am-5pm Sun; Ⓢ Wellesley) For over 35 years, the 519 has been the hub of the LGBTI community in Toronto, providing a variety of programs, services and support, from counseling to free anonymous HIV testing. Drop by and say hello!

Canadian Lesbian & Gay Archives (Map p72; ☎416-777-2755; www.clga.ca; 34 Isabella St; ⏲6:30-9pm Tue-Thu, 1-5pm Fri; Ⓢ Wellesley) Celebrating its 40th anniversary in 2013, the CLGA maintains an archive of anything of potential interest to LGBTI research in Canada – the largest of its kind in the world. Check out the exhibition schedule for its 2nd-floor gallery online, or just drop in.

Hassle Free Clinic (p115) Provides anonymous free HIV (by appointment only) and STI testing, and reproductive- and sexual-health services.

Queer West (www.queerwest.org) For those who appreciate things a little less mainstream. Check out the website for info on west Toronto's LGBTI scene, the Toronto Queer Arts Festival, Queer West Film Festival and the Smash Words Festival.

Riverdale Farm is a rural oasis in the downtown. Now a working-farm museum, it has two barns, a summer wading pool and pens of feathered and furry friends. Kids follow the farmer around as they do their daily chores, including milking the cows at 10:30am. There's a farmers market on Tuesdays (3pm to 7pm May to October).

Tommy Thompson Park PARK

(☎416-661-6600; www.tommythompsonpark.ca; Leslie St, off Lake Shore Blvd E; ⏲9am-6pm Sat & Sun Apr-Oct, to 4:30pm Nov-Mar; 🚌83 Jones S, 🚋501) A 5km-long artificial peninsula between the Harbourfront and The Beaches, Tommy Thompson Park reaches further into Lake Ontario than the Toronto Islands. This 'accidental wilderness' – constructed from Outer Harbour dredgings and fill from downtown building sites – has become a phenomenal wildlife success. It's one of the world's largest nesting places for ring-billed gulls, and is a haven for terns, black-crowned night herons, turtles, owls, foxes and even coyotes.

Open to the public on weekends and holidays; vehicles and pets are prohibited. Summer schedules offer interpretive programs and guided walks, usually with an ecological theme. At the end of the park there's a lighthouse and great city views. To get here, take any streetcar along Queen St E to Leslie St, then walk 800m south to the gates, or follow the Martin Goodman Trail.

The Beaches

Say The Beaches to locals and they picture the wealthy, professional neighborhood by the lake. To everyone else, it means the neighborhood, as well as the beaches themselves and the parklands along Lake Ontario. Of all the beaches, **Kew Beach** (416-392-8186; www.toronto.ca/parks/beaches/beaches; dawn-dusk; 501) is the most popular; its boardwalk runs east to **Balmy Beach** and west to **Woodbine Beach**.

Adjacent **Kew Gardens** has restrooms, snack bars, a skating rink, lawn bowls and tennis courts; at the western end there's an Olympic-size public swimming pool. For cyclists and in-line skaters, the **Martin Goodman Trail** leads past Ashbridge's Bay Park. Off Queen St E, with its restaurants, the sunken **Ivan Forrest Gardens** leads to Glen Stewart Ravine, a wilder patch of green running north to Kingston Rd.

RC Harris Filtration Plant NOTABLE BUILDING
(416-392-2934; www.toronto.ca; 2701 Queen St E; P; 501) Commanding heavenly views of the lakefront from a priceless slab of real estate, the elegantly proportioned RC Harris Filtration Plant is an art-deco masterpiece that has appeared in countless movies and TV shows. Originally disparagingly dubbed the 'Palace of Purification,' due to hefty construction costs during the Great Depression, the fully operational plant is rarely open to the public – try during Doors Open (p91) – but it makes a great photographic subject.

Toronto Islands

Once upon a time there were no Toronto Islands, just an immense sandbar stretching 9km into the lake. On April 13, 1858, a hurricane blasted through the sandbar and created the gap now known as the Eastern Channel. Toronto's jewel-like islands were born – nearly two-dozen isles covering 240 hectares and home to close-knit, 800-strong communities on **Algonquin Island** and **Ward's Island**. The islands are only accessible by ferry (15 minutes, adult/child $7.50/3.65). To get to the ferry docks from Union Station, take the 509 Harbourfront or the 510 Spadina streetcar south to the Bay and Queens Quay stop.

Centreville Amusement Park AMUSEMENT PARK
(416-203-0405; www.centreisland.ca; all-day ride passes adult/child/family $40/28.50/122; 10:30am-8pm May-Sep; Centre Island) From Centre Island ferry terminal, wander past the information booth to quaint Centreville's antique carousel, goofy golf course, miniature train and sky gondola. **Far Enough Farm** zoo presents kids with plenty of opportunities to cuddle something furry and step in something sticky. There's no admission fee to the park, but you need to purchase a pass to use the rides.

Hanlan's Point PARK
(Lakeshore Ave; Hanlan's Point) At the west end of Centre Island is Hanlan's Point, named after world-champion sculler 'Ned' Hanlan (1855–1904), a member of the first family to permanently settle here. Babe Ruth hit his first professional home run here in 1914 while playing minor-league baseball – the ball drowned in Lake Ontario, the ultimate souvenir lost forever!

Ward's Island ISLAND
(www.torontoisland.com; Ward's Island) The most residential of Toronto's islands. At the western end of Ward's Island is an 18-hole **Frisbee Golf Course** (www.discgolfontario.com; Ward's Island; dawn-dusk) FREE. An old-fashioned boardwalk runs the length of the south shore of the island, starting at Ward's Island beach and passing the back gate of the year-round Rectory Café (p107), with its delightful lakeside patio.

Greater Toronto Area (GTA)

Further afield, in outlying areas of the Greater Toronto Area (GTA), where Toronto's neighborhoods start to become suburbs and begin to look the same, there are a number of worthy attractions. The downside is they can be frustrating to get to by public transport, and even with a car.

★ **High Park** PARK
(www.toronto.ca/parks; 1873 Bloor St W; dawn-dusk; P; S High Park, 501, 506, 508) Toronto's favorite and best-known park is a wonderful place to unfurl a picnic blanket, swim, play tennis, bike around, skate on the **Grenadier Pond** in the winter, or in the spring meander through the groves of cherry blossoms donated to the park by the Japanese ambassador in 1959. There's also a theatrical stage, a small children's zoo and Colborne Lodge, built in 1836 by the Howard family, who donated much of High Park to the city in 1873.

Bus 30B picks up at High Park subway station, then loops through the park, on weekends and holidays from mid-June to early

City Walk
Subterranean Toronto Blues

START UNION STATION
FINISH TRINITY SQ
LENGTH 3KM; THREE TO FIVE HOURS

When it's just too cold to be outside, duck into Toronto's underground **PATH** (www.toronto.ca/path) system, a 28km (and growing) labyrinth of subterranean corridors connecting downtown sights, skyscrapers and shops. You'll be surprised at how much is interconnected. Allow yourself a full day if you want to try to do all of the below.

From **1 Union Station** (p116), you can head southeast to the **2 Air Canada Centre** (p113) or follow the tubular SkyWalk over the railroad tracks, emerging outdoors to the iconic **3 CN Tower** (p69), next to the **4 Rogers Centre** (p71). The tower is a must-see, even if just from the outside.

Back at Union Station PATH, cross beneath Front St and up the staircase into **5 Fairmont Royal York** (p93). From here, follow the color-coded arrows to **6 Brookfield Place** and the **7 Hockey Hall of Fame** (p71). Wander through Commerce Court to the **8 TD Centre**. Beyond the digital stock-market displays, go left and emerge at the **9 Design Exchange** (p73).

From back beneath TD Centre follow signs for the TD Waterhouse Tower to the **10 Toronto-Dominion Gallery of Inuit Art** (p73).

Next, head toward the Standard Life Centre, the Exchange Tower and then the Richmond-Adelaide complex. You will pass the Sheraton Centre to reach **11 City Hall** (p75) and Nathan Phillips Sq.

From City Hall you can head back underground and follow the signs for **12 The Bay** (Canada's oldest department store) and shop till you drop; or pass The Bay, diverting right and up some stairs to Temperance St and the **13 Cloud Gardens Conservatory** (p73).

The PATH continues to the **14 Eaton Centre** (p101), whose large atrium plazas bring the feeling of outside in. From here, it's easy to reach Trinity Sq in the shadows of the **15 Church of the Holy Trinity** (p76) or pick up the subway at Dundas station for your onward journey.

September. Otherwise it's a 200m walk from the subway station to the north gates. The 506 High Park streetcar drops off on the east side of the park. If you exit the park by Colborne Lodge at the south gates, walk down to Lake Shore Blvd W and catch any eastbound streetcar to downtown.

Evergreen Brick Works PARK

(☎416-596-7670; ebw.evergreen.ca; 550 Bayview Ave; ⏰9am-5pm Mon-Fri, 8am-5pm Sat, 10am-5pm Sun; P; 🚌28A, S Broadview) FREE Famed for the wonderful transformation of its once deteriorating heritage buildings into a prime location for all things geotourism, this dynamic LEED-certified community environmental center and park hosts interactive workshops and community festivals around the themes of ecology, technology and the environment. There's a garden market and lots of nature trails.

Todmorden Mills HISTORIC SITE

(☎416-396-2819; www.toronto.ca/todmordenmills; 67 Pottery Rd; adult/child $6.19/2.65, gallery free; ⏰10am-4:30pm Mon-Fri, noon-5pm Sat & Sun Apr-Dec; P; S Broadview) In an idyllic setting by the Don River, Todmorden Mills is a late-18th-century gristmill-turned-sawmill, then brewery and distillery, then paper mill. Historical relics are on display inside. Guides show visitors around old millers' houses and the petite Don train station. To get here, take the subway to Broadview station then board any bus. Alight at Mortimer/Pottery Rd (Dairy Queen), turn left and walk down Pottery Rd.

The renovated **Papermill Theatre and Gallery** showcases local and emerging artists. Nature paths start near the bridge and wind back to the secluded Todmorden Mills Wildflower **Preserve** (www.hopscotch.ca/tmwp), 9 hectares of wildflowers growing on former industrial wasteland, complete with boardwalks and viewing platforms.

Ontario Science Centre MUSEUM

(☎416-696-1000; www.ontariosciencecentre.ca; 770 Don Mills Rd; science center adult/child $22/13, Omnimax $13/9, combined ticket $28/19; ⏰10am-5pm Sun-Fri, to 8pm Sat; P 👪; 🚌34, 25) Climb a rock wall, journey to the center of a human heart, catch a criminal with DNA fingerprinting and race an Olympic bobsled at the excellent, interactive Ontario Science Centre. Over 800 high-tech exhibits and live demonstrations wow the kids (and the adults feigning interest at the back). There's also the giant domed Omnimax cinema.

Scarborough Bluffs PARK

(☎416-392-1111; www.toronto.ca; Scarborough; ⏰dawn-dusk; P; 🚌12, S Victoria Park) Atop this 14km stretch of glacial lakeshore cliffs, enjoy stunning views across Lake Ontario. Erosion has created cathedral spire formations, exposing evidence of five different glacial periods. Without wheels, getting to the bluffs can be a drag. Take the subway to Victoria Park, then bus 12 along Kingston Rd to Cathedral Bluffs Dr, east of the St Clair Ave E intersection.

If you're driving, from Kingston Rd (Hwy 2), turn south at Cathedral Bluffs Dr to reach the highest section of the bluffs, **Cathedral Bluffs Park** (65m). You can also access the shore at Galloway Rd further east. About 6km further east, you'll come to **Guildwood Park**, one of Toronto's most fascinating sites, filled with architectural relics and sculptures collected from the 1950s to 1970s by the forward-thinking Rosa and Spencer Clark.

David Dunlap Observatory OBSERVATORY

(☎905-883-0174; www.theddo.ca; 123 Hillsview Dr, Richmond Hill; $10; ⏰9pm Sat Jun-Oct, also 9pm Fri Jul-Aug; P; 🚌91, S Finch) North of the Toronto city limits, the David Dunlap Observatory houses Canada's largest optical telescope (the reflector measures 1.9m). On Saturday evenings, the observatory presents introductory talks on modern astronomy, followed by some interplanetary voyeurism. Check that weather conditions are favorable and book months ahead for limited tickets, though some ticketless drop-in events are also available. Some events don't allow children under 12.

LEGOLAND Discovery Centre AMUSEMENT PARK

(☎1-855-356-2150; www.legolanddiscoverycentre.ca/toronto; 1 Bass Pro Mills Dr, Vaughan; adult/child $22/18; ⏰10am-9pm Mon-Sat, 11am-7pm Sun; S Yorkdale) It may not be a full-fledged Legoland theme park but it's loved by kids and big kids alike, delighting with its collection of hands-on, educational Lego-centric attractions including an earthquake table, 4D cinema and Lego factory. It's in the sprawling Vaughan Mills shopping center; take the subway to Yorkdale station and transfer onto the 360 YRT Maple Express bus to Vaughan Mills. Note that it's not a Legoland, but a smaller version.

Canada's Wonderland AMUSEMENT PARK

(☎905-832-8131; www.canadaswonderland.com; 9580 Jane St, Vaughan; day passes adult/child $63/52; ⏰10am-10pm Jun-Aug, Sat & Sun only with earlier closing May & Sep; P; S York Mills)

LAKE ONTARIO

Unlike nearby Chicago, a city of similar size, population and lake frontage, Toronto has neglected its waterfront. Where Chicago has 29km of contiguous loved-by-locals lakefront trails, parks and beaches, Toronto has the toxic Gardiner Expwy, Lake Shore Blvd and a wall of waterfront condos obscuring the lake from general view. Lakeshore access has only opened up in recent decades and projects are ever so slowly trying to revitalize the shoreline. Updates can be found at www.toronto.ca/waterfront, and info on Toronto's section of a much bigger lakeshore trail project at www.waterfronttrail.org.

Chemicals, sewage and fertilizer runoff have traditionally fouled the waters of Lake Ontario, although the situation is improving. Many locals now seem content to swim in Toronto's eight blue-flag sanctioned **beaches**: www.toronto.ca/parks/beaches. For most citizens though, Lake Ontario is simply a big, gray, cold thing that stops the Americans from driving up Yonge St.

Lake Ontario is the 14th-largest lake in the world and the smallest and most easterly of the five Great Lakes: 311km long, 85km wide and 244m deep. The name 'Ontario' derives from *Skanadario,* an Iroquois word meaning 'sparkling water.' The name rings true; despite what lurks beneath, it still sparkles. Visit the Toronto Islands or Tommy Thompson Park to see the lake for what it really is – stoic, powerful and very beautiful.

Amusement park lovers will want to trek to this, Canada's largest, featuring over 60 rides including the mammoth Leviathan, with a peak height of 93m! There's also an exploding volcano, 20-hectare Splash Works water park and white-water canyon. Queues can be lengthy; most rides operate rain or shine and tickets are cheaper online. From York Mills subway, catch the 60 GO Bus (additional fee).

McMichael Canadian Art Collection GALLERY

(☎905-893-1121; www.mcmichael.com; 10365 Islington Ave, Kleinburg; adult/child $18/free; ⏲10am-5pm; P; 🚌13) Handcrafted wooden buildings (which include painter Tom Thomson's cabin, moved from its original location), set amid 40 hectares of conservation trails, contain works by Canada's best-known landscape painters, the Group of Seven, as well as First Nations, Inuit and other acclaimed Canadian artists. It's a 34km, 45-minute drive from Toronto: be sure to use a GPS. Tours are included with admission and parking is $5.

Sharon Temple HISTORIC BUILDING

(☎905-478-2389; www.sharontemple.ca; 18974 Leslie St, East Gwillimbury; adult/child $5/free; ⏲10am-4:30pm Thu-Sun May-Oct) A national historic site and one of the oldest museums in Canada, this quaint and fascinating temple was built in 1832 by a Quaker sect called the Children of the Peace, to a unique architectural style. Lovingly restored in 2011, the simple museum tells the story of its founders and makes a wonderful day trip out of Toronto. It's about 55km north of downtown.

Activities

They're often mummified in winter layers, but Torontonians still like to keep fit. Outdoor activities abound: folks bike, blade and run along the lakeshore and hike up the city's ravines. Ice-skating and hockey are winter faves.

Cycling & In-Line Skating

For cyclists and in-line skaters, the **Martin Goodman Trail**, a paved recreational trail from The Beaches through Harbourfront to the Humber River in the west, is the place to go. Head for the lake and you'll find it. On the way you can connect to the Don Valley mountain-bike trails at Cherry St. On the **Toronto Islands**, the south-shore boardwalk and the interconnecting paved paths are car free. For a longer trek, the Martin Goodman Trail is part of the **Lake Ontario Waterfront Trail** (www.waterfronttrail.org), stretching 450km from way east of Toronto to Niagara-on-the-Lake.

If you choose to explore Toronto by bike, stick to marked cycling trails when possible. Although many locals cycle to work, downtown is fraught with perils: aggressive drivers, streetcars and phone-blinded pedestrians. Cyclists do get hit by car doors, and rider accidents from connecting with streetcar tracks aren't uncommon. It's not a legal requirement to wear a helmet in Ontario.

Essential information for cyclists can be found at www.toronto.ca/cycling/map. Folks with smartphones should go to www.ridethecity.com for real-time route planning.

★ **Bike Share Toronto** CYCLING
(☎855-898-2378; www.bikesharetoronto.com; 1-/3-day passes $7/15) Bike Share Toronto is a service that allows unlimited 30-minute bike rides for one or three days. Collect and return a shared bicycle from any of over 200 docking stations dotted around the city – great for visitors. A $101 security deposit is frozen on your credit card on joining. Transit App lets you buy passes, locate stations and get ride codes to unlock bikes.

If you don't get a day pass, the first 30 minutes rental is free. A second 30-minute block is $1.50, then $4 for the next, and $7 per each additional 30-minute period.

Toronto Islands Bicycle Rental CYCLING
(☎416-203-0009; www.torontoislandbicyclerental.com; Centre Island; per hr bicycles/tandems $8/15, 2-/4-seat quadricycles $17/30; ⏰10:30am-6pm May-Sep; ⛴Centre Island) One of the best ways to explore Centre Island is by bicycle. Rent bikes here, beside Outlook Pier.

Toronto Bicycling Network CYCLING
(TBN; www.tbn.ca; rides for nonmembers $5) This recreational cycling club welcomes nonmembers to organized rides for a $5 fee.

Wheel Excitement OUTDOORS
(Map p78; ☎416-260-9000; www.wheelexcitement.ca; 249 Queens Quay W; bicycles & in-line skates per hr/day $15/35; ⏰10am-6pm; 🚊509, 510) Close to the ferries for Toronto Islands; day rentals here are cheaper than hiring on Centre Island and give you the freedom to explore further afield.

Community Bicycle Network CYCLING
(Map p82; ☎416-504-2918; www.communitybicyclenetwork.org; 761 Queen St W; rental 1st day/weekend/week $25/35/65; ⏰noon-6pm Tue-Fri, 10am-6pm Sat; 🚊501) 🍃 Celebrating 20 years championing sustainable transportation, CBN offers rentals, repairs, workshops and events.

Hiking

Feel like stretching your legs? Delve into Toronto's city parks, nature reserves or ravines. Alternatively, hook up with a group such as **Hike Ontario** (☎905-277-4453; www.hikeontario.com) or **Toronto Bruce Trail Club** (www.torontobrucetrailclub.org) for hardy day hikes.

Ice Skating

Locals love to skate. When the weather is freezing and the snow falling lightly, downtown Toronto's outdoor ice rinks come alive. The best-known rinks are at **Nathan Phillips Square** outside City Hall and at the Harbourfront Centre (p70). These artificial rinks are open daily (weather permitting) from 10am to 10pm mid-November to March. Admission is free; skate rental costs adult/child $10/5. Toronto Parks & Recreation (www.toronto.ca/parks) has info on other rinks around town, including those at **Kew Gardens** near Kew Beach and **Trinity Bellwoods Park** in West Toronto. If it's been *really* cold, you can skate on **Grenadier Pond** in High Park. Beginners might prefer the lesser-known **Ryerson Rink**, tucked away just north of Yonge & Dundas Sq at 25 Gould St.

Swimming

Torontonians generally avoid swimming in Lake Ontario, despite the presence of a dozen city beaches tended by lifeguards from July to August, eight of which are Blue Flag certified. Before taking the plunge, check with the **Beach Water Quality Hotline** (app.toronto.ca/tpha/beaches.html), as water quality deteriorates after heavy rain and the presence of e.coli bacteria is a potential risk.

From June to September, the City of Toronto operates over 50 outdoor swimming pools, generally open from dawn to dusk. The complete list is found at www.toronto.ca.

☞ Tours

Boat

Between May and September cruise operators sail from the Harbourfront beside Queens Quay Terminal or York Quay Centre. Reservations are recommended for brunch and dinner cruises. Keep in mind that ferries to the Toronto Islands offer similar views for half the price.

Mariposa Cruises BOATING
(Map p78; ☎416-203-0178; www.mariposacruises.com; Queens Quay Terminal, 207 Queens Quay W; 1hr tours adult/child $22/15.50; ⏰May-Sep; 🚊509, 510) Narrated harbor and two-hour buffet lunch tours (adult/child $50/26). Sunday brunch and dinner-and-dance cruises, too.

Tall Ship Kajama BOATING
(Map p78; ☎416-203-2322; www.tallshipcruisestoronto.com; 249 Queens Quay W, Suite 111; 90min cruises adult/child $27/15; ⏰May-Oct; 🚊509, 510) The dashing black three-master *Kajama,* a 1930 German trading schooner, sails from the foot of Lower Simcoe St; there's usually a ticket kiosk beside Queens Quay Terminal. Reservations can be made online.

Bus

Toronto isn't exactly London, Paris or Rome, where it's easy to ooh and ahh at endless historic marvels from the comfort of a coach. If traveling on a budget, you might find better value in a TTC day pass, exploring for yourself.

★City Sightseeing Toronto BUS
(☎416-410-0536; www.citysightseeingtoronto.com; adult/child $38/20) Hop-on, hop-off sightseeing tours on an open-top double-decker London-style bus, around a 24-stop city loop. The route takes in most major sights with commentary and includes a free (seasonal) Lake Ontario cruise. Tickets are valid for 72 hours: good value if you plan to use the bus over three days and a great way to get oriented.

★Chariots of Fire BUS
(Map p78; ☎1-905-877-0855; www.tourniagarafalls.com; 33 Yonge St; day tours $77; Ⓢ King) Low-cost day tours from Toronto to Niagara Falls, including a *Hornblower Niagara* boat ride and free time at Niagara-on-the-Lake. These guys are highly organized and comfortably present the best of the Falls, from Toronto, for those who only have a day to experience it all.

ROMBus BUS
(Map p72; ☎416-586-8000; www.rom.on.ca/en/whats-on/rombus; 100 Queen's Park; full-day tours $125-155; Ⓢ Museum) Toronto's Royal Ontario Museum (p79) organizes irregular special events tours, with educated, informative guides, around historical, cultural and architectural themes. Full-day tours, although pricey, can be worth the expense if the subject matter falls within your sphere of interest.

Walking & Cycling

The easiest way to experience Toronto is on foot, though cycling tours allow you to cover a bit more territory.

★Heritage Toronto WALKING
(☎416-338-3886; www.heritagetoronto.org; 157 King St E; donations encouraged; ⏱Apr-Oct) A diverse offering of fascinating historical, cultural and nature walks, and bike and bus (TTC) tours, led by museum experts and neighborhood historical society members. Tours generally last one to three hours.

ROMWalks WALKING
(☎416-586-8000; www.rom.on.ca/en/whats-on/romwalks; free-$10; ⏱Wed & Sun May-Sep) Well-informed volunteers from the Royal Ontario Museum (p79) lead one- to two-hour historical and architectural walking tours, including some of the city's lesser-known but most interesting buildings and neighborhoods. Most walks are free with appreciated tips, but some cost up to $10.

A Taste of the World WALKING
(☎416-923-6813; www.torontowalksbikes.com; 2-3½hr tours $25-50) Quirky, well-qualified guides lead offbeat walking and cycling tours of Toronto's nooks and crannies, usually with a foodie focus, but also including ghost hunting. Reservations recommended.

Festivals & Events

What Toronto lacks in visual appeal it makes up for in activity: there's always fun and excitement to be had in this vibrant city and the Toronto festival scene is no exception. In the long balmy days and nights of the short summer (June to August) there's so much on that it's hard to choose what to do. At times, when events overlap, it's best just to get out there and leave it to fate.

January

Winterlicious FOOD & DRINK
(www.toronto.ca/winterlicious; ⏱Jan) For two weeks in January, a staggering array of restaurants lures residents out of their living rooms for a prix-fixe extravaganza of lunches and dinners, showcasing Toronto's culinary diversity. If you're visiting in winter, we strongly recommend taking advantage of these fantastic cheap eats at every possible opportunity!

Next Stage Festival THEATER
(http://fringetoronto.com/next-stage-festival; ⏱Jan) From the people behind the Toronto Fringe Festival. Next Stage showcases the work of 10 fringe artists at the Factory Theatre (p112), as a platform for future success. The January event has a heated beer tent where audiences can mingle with the cast and crew before and after performances.

February

Canadian International Auto Show MOTOR SHOW
(www.autoshow.ca; ⏱late Feb) Revheads from around the world converge on the Metro Toronto Convention Centre for all things cutting edge about cars, with a little bit of automotive history thrown in.

April

Hot Docs FILM
(Canadian International Documentary Festival; www.hotdocs.ca; 506 Bloor St W; ⏱late Apr) North America's largest documentary film festival

screens more than 100 docos from around the globe from its home at the Hot Docs Ted Rogers Cinema.

420 Rally CULTURAL

(Dundas Sq; 20 Apr) Lovers of weed emerge from their basements and converge on Yonge & Dundas Sq in their thousands for this public prolegalization smoke-out in the middle of Canada's largest city.

May

InsideOut FILM

(Toronto LGBT Film Festival; www.insideout.ca; late May–Jun) For over 25 years, the Toronto LGBT Film Festival has showcased a huge range of gay-themed/interest films from around the world, with some screenings at the fantastic TIFF Bell Lightbox (p112). The last week of May to the start of Pride Toronto in June.

Doors Open Toronto CULTURAL

(www.toronto.ca/doorsopen; May) FREE Over the fourth weekend of May, over 500 public and private buildings of architectural and historical significance creak open their doors, allowing you to sneak a free peek at what's hot and what's not in other peoples' digs. Book ahead for walking tours and big-name buildings such as City Hall.

June

Luminato CULTURAL

(www.luminatofestival.com; Jun) Luminato seeks to bring a broad selection of the world's most accomplished musicians, dancers, artists, writers, actors and filmmakers to venues across Toronto in a celebration of creativity that reflects the city's diversity. Many performances are free. Past performers have included Aretha Franklin, Joni Mitchell, kd lang and Rufus Wainwright.

North by Northeast PERFORMING ARTS

(NXNE; www.nxne.com; mid-Jun) Musos can safely write off an entire week in mid-June in order to sample the plethora of indie bands (around 1000), films, shows and booze to be had in all of Toronto's coolest venues. A variety of wristbands tailored to your tastes are exceptional value.

★Pride Toronto LGBT

(www.pridetoronto.com; Jun-Jul) Toronto's most flamboyant event celebrates the diversity of sexuality and gender identity, with a whole month (it was a week) of community events, workshops and gatherings, mostly free. The exploration climaxes with a Trans March, Dyke March and a Pride Parade at the start of July, when the streets of Church-Wellesley Village throb with the beat of over 1 million revelers, including Prime Minister Justin Trudeau in 2016.

National Aboriginal Day CULTURAL

(www.aadnc-aandc.gc.ca; Jun 21) Canada's heritage of First Nations, Inuit and Métis cultures is celebrated on the summer solstice (June 21), with events leading up to it the week before.

Toronto Jazz Festival MUSIC

(www.tojazz.com; late Jun-early Jul) Jazz, blues and world beats blaze in the city's streets, nightclubs and concert halls, alongside musical workshops, and film screenings.

Union Summer FOOD & DRINK

(Map p78; http://torontounion.ca; Union Station, 65 Front St W; 7am-dusk Mon-Fri, 11am-dusk Sat & Sun; ; S Union Station) Union Station's summer food market was such a hit in 2015 that it has become an ongoing fixture, with a daily market of over 20 gourmet food stalls, activities, free outdoor film screenings, live music and drinks from late June to early September.

July

Summerlicious FOOD & DRINK

(www.toronto.ca/summerlicious; Jul) Be sure to book your tables in advance for this culinary extravaganza held at almost 200 restaurants, bars and cafes across the city. Great-value prix-fixe menus in three price categories mean there's something to suit everyone's tastes and budget.

★Toronto Fringe Festival CULTURAL

(http://fringetoronto.com; early Jul) Celebrating over 25 years in the spotlight, Toronto's largest theater and performance festival hosts dozens of plays on as many stages over two weeks in early July. Ranging from utterly offbeat to seriously emotive and including a program of kids' plays, the festival aims to make theater accessible to the community.

Open Roof Festival FILM

(www.openrooffestival.com; Jul) This enthusiastic bunch of film and music lovers put together a season of rooftop/outdoor film screenings and bands in hip urban locations.

Honda Indy Toronto SPORTS

(www.hondaindytoronto.com; mid-Jul) Drivers from the international circuit compete in front of massive crowds, reaching speeds of up to 300km/h along Lake Shore Blvd and causing locals to flee the city for the sake of their continued ability to hear.

Beaches International Jazz Festival MUSIC
(www.beachesjazz.com; late Jul) FREE This free three-day jazz fest plays to stages at Woodbine Gardens, Kew Gardens and along the Beaches Boardwalk. The highlight is the two-day Streetfest where a 2km stretch of Queen St E is closed to traffic and opened to the sounds of more than 50 Canadian bands and thousands of pedestrian admirers.

August

Caribana CARNIVAL
(Toronto Caribbean Carnival; www.caribana.com; late Jul-early Aug) North America's largest Caribbean festival; the carnival parade, featuring florid and almost-not-there costumes, takes five hours to gyrate past.

Canadian National Exhibition AGRICULTURAL
(CNE; www.theex.com; late Aug-early Sep) Dating from 1879, 'The Ex' features over 700 exhibitors, agricultural shows, lumberjack competitions, outdoor concerts and carnivalia at Exhibition Place (p71) in the 18 days leading up to Labour Day (first Monday of September). The air show and Labour Day fireworks take the cake.

Toronto International Buskerfest MUSIC
(http://torontobuskerfest.com; late Aug) For three days in late August, a ragtag troupe of Canadian and international buskers descends upon downtown Yonge St in support of Epilepsy Toronto: expect sword-swallowers, jugglers and musicians of unpredictable merit.

September

★Toronto International Film Festival FILM
(TIFF; torontointernationalfilmfestival.ca; Sep) Since its inception in 1976, TIFF has grown to be the crowning jewel of the Toronto festival scene and a key player in the world film circuit. Attracting over 400,000 eager cine-philes to the red-carpet celebrity frenzy of its 10-day run, the festival has become an important forum for showcasing new films.

In 1990 the festival expanded operations to include the year-round TIFF Cinematheque program, showcasing works from around the world. Two decades later, the Bell Lightbox (p112), with its five stunning cinemas, funky restaurants and bar, opened its doors as the permanent home for the festival and organization.

If you're in town for TIFF, be sure to book ahead: tickets for screenings and events sell fast, while already elevated room rates go through the roof closer to showtime. Celebrities and paparazzi are in town and Torontonians come from far and wide to embrace the Hollywood spirit: catch a glimpse if you can!

October

Nuit Blanche CULTURAL
(http://nbto.com; 1st Sat in Oct) One night. Over 130 overnight urban art experiences, all over town. Contrived 'chance encounters,' interactive dance pieces, and an all-night street market are part of the (sometimes chaotic) fun on the first Saturday of October.

International Festival of Authors LITERATURE
(www.readings.org; mid-Oct) For 11 days in mid-October, this festival corrals acclaimed authors from Canada and beyond to the Harbourfront Centre (p70) for readings, discussions, lectures, awards and book signings. There are kid-friendly events, too.

November

Royal Agricultural Winter Fair AGRICULTURAL
(www.royalfair.org; Nov) Since 1922, the largest indoor agricultural and equestrian fair in the world has been warming up audiences at the Exhibition Place (p71) for 10 days in November.

Santa Claus Parade CHRISTMAS
(www.thesantaclausparade.ca; Nov;) A Toronto tradition since 1905, the annual Santa Claus Parade features exactly that: a bunch of old guys dressed as Santa stopping downtown traffic for hours and exciting children way too long before Christmas. The date varies each year – usually mid to late November.

December

Toronto Christmas Market CHRISTMAS MARKET
(www.torontochristmasmarket.com; Dec) FREE The Distillery District (p73) is at its festive best over the first two weeks in December for this European-style Christmas Market, showcasing hundreds of local handcrafted products.

Sleeping

Toronto has no shortage of accommodations, but it can get expensive, especially in summer when rooms sell quickly at up to double their regular rates. It's essential to book in advance for stays from mid-May to late September.

Remember, 13% HST (harmonized sales tax) is almost always applied on top of the quoted rate.

Avoid visiting in March if possible: the weather can be lousy and the enormous annual PDAC mining convention secures the majority of downtown beds.

Bed & Breakfast

Homes of Toronto ACCOMMODATION SERVICES $$
(416-363-6362; www.bbcanada.com/associations/toronto2) Anything from modest family homes to deluxe suites. The website lets you search specifically for LGBTI-friendly B&Bs (not to say that other B&Bs aren't LGBTI-friendly).

Downtown Toronto Association of Bed and Breakfast Guest Houses ACCOMMODATION SERVICES $$
(647-654-2959; www.bnbinfo.com) Rooms in various neighborhoods, mostly in renovated Victorian houses.

Harbourfront

Renaissance Toronto HOTEL $$
(Map p78; 416-341-7100; www.renaissancetoronto.com; 1 Blue Jays Way; d/ste from $199/289; P; S Union) Seventy suites here overlook the Rogers Centre playing field – be prepared for floodlights and hollering sports fans! If you'd rather use your room for sleeping, don't worry: the restaurant and bar also overlook the field.

Westin Harbour Castle HOTEL $$$
(Map p78; 416-869-1600; www.westinharbourcastletoronto.com; 1 Harbour Sq; d from $262; 509, 510) If this were a hamburger, it'd be with 'the works' – restaurants, shops, gym, conference center, pool, disabled-access suites etc. Staff are surprisingly chipper for such a big hotel. Maybe the lobby keeps them amused, with enough marble to rival any Hollywood mansion. Tasty lake views.

Financial District

Hotel Victoria BOUTIQUE HOTEL $$
(Map p78; 416-363-1666; www.hotelvictoria-toronto.com; 56 Yonge St; d from $244; ; S King) The early-20th-century Hotel Victoria retains a charming period lobby. Guest rooms are on the smaller side but have been simply and stylishly refurbished, plus there is a gym. Bathrooms have great tubs, but some might be disappointed by the lack of vanity space.

Strathcona Hotel HOTEL $$
(Map p78; 416-363-3321; www.thestrathconahotel.com; 60 York St; d from $157; ; S Union) This downtown hotel features compact, renovated rooms with decent bathrooms. The downstairs pub and cafe are convenient. Despite the lack of on-site parking, the proximity to Union Station is ideal, although some will find the long-term construction projects there an annoyance.

One King West HOTEL $$
(Map p78; 416-548-8100; www.onekingwest.com; 1 King St W; d incl breakfast from $224; P; S King) One of the handsomest buildings in the Toronto skyline, the sleek One King West tower soars above the historic former head office of the Toronto Dominion bank with an effortless synergy. Studio and one-bedroom apartments are large, stylish and in a prime downtown location, with subway and streetcars at your door.

Fairmont Royal York HOTEL $$$
(Map p78; 416-368-2511; www.fairmont.com/royalyork; 100 Front St W; d from $379; P; S Union) Since 1929 the eminent Royal York (a former grand dame of the Canadian Pacific Railway and Toronto icon) has accommodated everyone from Tina Turner to Henry Kissinger, not that it shows. The 1300-plus guest rooms have undergone significant renovation, with a matching price bump. Consider coming for high tea in the Library Bar and a chance to visit the lesser-known rooftop bee apiary.

Trump Toronto HOTEL $$$
(Map p78; 416-306-5800; www.trumphotelcollection.com/toronto/; 325 Bay St; d from $594; P; S King) Words to describe Trump Toronto's oversize, modern guest rooms: sumptuous, decadent, bold, indulgent. High ceilings and full-length windows add to the feeling of space and luxury. Expect only the most attentive service and finest Clefs d'Or concierges. If money is no obstacle, welcome home.

Old York

Hostelling International Toronto HOSTEL $
(Map p78; 416-971-4440; www.hostellingtoronto.com; 76 Church St; dm/d from $35/109; ; 504) This award-winning hostel doesn't look much from the outside, but gets votes for its rooftop deck and friendly staff. Most dorms have their own bathrooms, and deluxe rooms offer good-value private accommodations, including breakfast. The on-site Cavern Bar & Bistro has themed game nights to help you make friends.

Cosmopolitan BOUTIQUE HOTEL $$
(Map p78; ☎416-350-2000; www.cosmotoronto.com; 8 Colborne St; ste from $209; P ⊖ ❄ ; S King) This compact hotel is sleek and quiet, with only five rooms per floor. Entry level Zen suites are on the small side. Lotus and Tranquility suites are significantly larger and have kitchens; some also have lake views. All have balconies. Both the treatment spa and funky downstairs wine bar, Eight (with its $1 per oz Friday night special), add to the appeal.

Entertainment District & King Street West

★ **Clarence Park** HOSTEL $
(Map p78; ☎647-498-7070; www.theclarencepark.com; 7 Clarence Sq; dm $32-36, d $70-85; P @ ; S St Andrew) In a prime and picturesque downtown location, you'll find this budget gem with cozy clean dorms and fresh private rooms, some overlooking the leafy square: all have en suite bathrooms. There's free wi-fi, a fabulous, modern communal kitchen and huge rooftop deck with BBQ for those lazy summer afternoons in the city.

★ **Residence Inn Toronto Downtown** HOTEL $$
(Map p78; ☎416-581-1800; www.marriott.com; 255 Wellington St W; ste incl breakfast from $222; P ⊖ ❄ ; 504, 508) Perfect for longer stays or traveling with kids, this modern business/tourist hotel is in a prime location and has a variety of comfortable, functional room types, up to two-bedroom suites. All have fully equipped kitchens, pleasant decor and lots of light. The included full breakfast buffet makes for excellent value.

Hôtel Le Germain BOUTIQUE HOTEL $$
(Map p78; ☎416-345-9500; www.germaintoronto.com; 30 Mercer St; d/ste from $285/480; P ❄ @ ; 504) Hip and harmonious, Le Germain resides in a quiet Entertainment District side street. Clean lines, soothing spaces and Zen-inspired materials deliver the promised 'ocean of well-being.' Luxury bath amenities and in-room stereos, plus a rooftop terrace, are bonuses. Parking costs $35.

Hilton Garden Inn Toronto Downtown HOTEL $$
(Map p78; ☎416-593-9200; www.hiltongardeninn.com; 92 Peter St; d from $169; P ⊖ ❄ ; 501) Not to be confused with its sister property on Jarvis St, this Garden Inn is a great midrange option. Well located in the heart of the Entertainment District, near Queen St W, it's perfect for nocturnal explorations. It can get noisy on Friday and Saturday nights.

★ **Thompson Toronto** HOTEL $$$
(Map p82; ☎888-550-8368; www.thompsonhotels.com/toronto; 550 Wellington St W; d from $369; P ❄ ; 504, 508) Many love Thompson Toronto – it's just so LA. Hip, modern rooms will be favored by those with a penchant for design (check the website's snaps); the rooftop bar, patio and pool are easily Toronto's finest; and the two on-site dining options, Thompson Diner (p100) and Scarpetta, independently deserve mention. Add the brilliant location and exceptional service and it's definitely splurge worthy.

Soho Metropolitan Hotel BOUTIQUE HOTEL $$$
(Map p78; ☎416-599-8800; www.soho.metropolitan.com; 318 Wellington St W; d from $345; P ❄ ; 510) Luxury and style await in Soho Met's 92 guest rooms and suites, featuring beautiful maple woodwork, private dressing rooms, floor-to-ceiling opening windows and Italian linens. Exquisite marble bathrooms feature a deep soaker tub, separate shower and everybody-loves Molton Brown amenities.

Ritz Carlton HOTEL $$$
(Map p78; ☎416-585-2100; www.ritzcarlton.com/toronto; 181 Wellington St W; d from $465; P ❄ ; S St Andrew) Opened in 2011, as the first of Toronto's new batch of shiny five-star hotels, the Ritz Carlton name is loaded with connotations, but there's something about the modernity of the property that just doesn't fit with the old-world Ritz styling emulated in the guest rooms. Of course, expect exceptional service, a wealth of comforts and five-star 'tude. There are better options for the price.

Downtown Yonge

Baldwin Village Inn B&B $
(Map p72; ☎416-591-5359; www.baldwininn.com; 9 Baldwin St; d incl breakfast with shared bath $105-125; ⊖ ❄ @ ; 505, 506) In the pretty enclave of Baldwin Village, just a few blocks from the Art Gallery of Ontario, this yellow-painted B&B faces a leafy street filled with cheap, interesting eateries and cafes. The front courtyard is perfect for lounging about and watching the people. There are quieter garden-facing rooms, too.

Les Amis Bed & Breakfast B&B $
(Map p72; 416-928-0635; www.bbtoronto.com; 31 Granby St; s/d incl breakfast from $99/139; ; College) Run by a multilingual Parisian couple, this cheery B&B offers full, gourmet vegetarian breakfasts. Colorful rooms are adorned with the owners' art and the leafy back deck is a great spot to chill out.

★ **Cambridge Suites** HOTEL $$
(Map p72; 416-368-1990; www.cambridgesuitestoronto.com; 15 Richmond St E; ste from $227; ; Queen) An excellent mid-range choice, this all-suite hotel has spacious, good-looking rooms with separate living and kitchen facilities. Cityscape suites, on upper floors, are more luxuriously appointed and include continental breakfast in the restaurant. Three impressive penthouses are available.

Eaton Chelsea HOTEL $$
(Map p72; 416-595-1975; chelsea.eatonhotels.com; 33 Gerrard St W; d/ste from $225/365; ; College) Toronto's largest (almost 1600 rooms!) hotel caters to everyone, and is especially popular with families who appreciate the apartment-style suites and indoor water slide. Many rooms have balconies.

Pantages BOUTIQUE HOTEL $$
(Map p72; 416-362-1777; www.pantageshotel.com; 200 Victoria St; d incl breakfast from $209; ; Queen) A good choice for longer stays, each of the 89 rooms in this all-suite hotel, the closest to Yonge & Dundas Sq, Massey Hall and the Eaton Centre, have full bathrooms, kitchen and laundry facilities. It's in a residential building: once in the main doors, turn left for the hotel lobby.

Grand Hotel & Suites HOTEL $$
(Map p72; 416-863-9000; www.grandhoteltoronto.com; 225 Jarvis St; d/ste incl breakfast from $249/299; ; Dundas, 505) A somewhat grotty and slightly seedy location is the bane of this otherwise solid performer's existence, although all that will change in the next few years as nearby condo projects reach completion. A variety of room types up to two-bedroom suites all have free wi-fi, kitchenettes and marble bathrooms. A hearty breakfast buffet is included in the rate.

Shangri-La Hotel HOTEL $$$
(Map p78; 647-788-8888; www.shangri-la.com/toronto; 188 University Ave; d from $380; ; St Andrew) Five-star Shangri-La's spanking-new, elegant guest rooms strive to synthesize Asian simplicity with Western indulgence and are among Toronto's largest. Each has separate bath, shower and toilet room, opening floor-to-ceiling windows, espresso machines, smartphone docks and designer bathroom amenities. The University Ave location is fantastic.

Church-Wellesley Village

Victoria's Mansion Inn & Guesthouse INN $
(Map p72; 416-921-4625; www.victoriasmansion.com; 68 Gloucester St; s/d/studio from $79/99/139; ; Wellesley) Festooned with international flags, gay-friendly Victoria's Mansion accommodates travelers in a renovated 1880s redbrick heritage building with a lovely garden out front. All rooms have fridge, microwave and private bathrooms, making the smaller singles good downtown value.

Neill-Wycik College Hotel HOSTEL $
(Map p72; 416-977-2320; www.torontobackpackershotel.com; 96 Gerrard St E; s/tw/tr with shared bath incl breakfast $58/85/115; ; College) Pronounced 'Why-zik,' this budget travelers' favorite operates from early May to late August, when the students are out. Private bedrooms with telephones are inside apartment-style suites that share a kitchen/lounge and bathroom. There are laundry facilities, lockers, TV lounges, a student-run cafeteria and incredible sundeck views.

Amsterdam Guesthouse HOSTEL $
(Map p72; 416-921-9797; 209 Carlton St; d & tw $76; ; 506) No frills, and centrally located on the edge of downtown. Staff are a little cold, but beds are comfortable. It's clean enough and makes a good budget option near the College-Wellesley gay village. College and Yonge is a 15-minute walk away, or five minutes on the tram outside.

Holiday Inn Toronto Downtown Centre HOTEL $$
(Map p72; 416-977-6655; www.holidayinn.com; 30 Carlton St; d from $173; ; College) Funky renovated bedrooms and a great location, steps from College subway station and a variety of inexpensive shopping, dining and entertainment options, make this hulking Holiday Inn a good choice for most budgets. That said, there's really no view to speak of and standard rooms are quite compact.

Courtyard Toronto Downtown HOTEL **$$**
(Map p72; ☎416 924 0611; www.marriott.com; 475 Yonge St; d from $151; P ❄ 📶 ≋; S College) The closest major hotel to Church-Wellesley Village is also a good stock-standard choice for a midrange hotel, with a walk-to-everything location, gym, hot tub and pool. All rooms are of a decent size and have free ultra high-speed wi-fi, and some have balconies. Great rates can be found online, in advance.

Bloor-Yorkville

Holiday Inn Toronto Bloor-Yorkville HOTEL **$$**
(Map p72; ☎416-968-0010; www.holiday-inn.com/torontomidtown; 280 Bloor St W; d from $212; P ❄ 📶; S St George) The familiar green banners outside this high-rise, brick monolith do little to improve its aesthetics. Inside, generic guest rooms have comfy queen- or king-size beds and plenty of room. Price and location are everything: the subway is at your feet, and the University of Toronto, Royal Ontario Museum and Bloor St shopping are close by.

Comfort Hotel HOTEL **$$**
(Map p72; ☎416-924-1222; www.choicehotels.ca/cn228; 15 Charles St E; d & tw from $189; P ❄ 📶; S Bloor-Yonge) It's generic and by no means fancy, but this basic tourist hotel is near some excellent cafes and is a hop, skip and jump from the Bloor St strip, where you'll pay three times the price for a room.

★**Four Seasons** LUXURY HOTEL **$$$**
(Map p72; ☎416-964-0411; www.fourseasons.com/toronto; 60 Yorkville Ave; d from $555; S Bay) One of Toronto's most senior and well-respected high-end hotels, it's all about luxury, relaxation and enjoyment: crisp, clean, light-filled guest rooms with stunning views exude comfort, granite bathrooms are to die for and the exquisite lobby is beautiful.

If the rates don't shock, you won't flinch picking up the tab at Michelin-starred **Café Boulud** and should happily submit to body pampering and soul elevation at 'spa': it's up there with heaven.

★**Hazelton** BOUTIQUE HOTEL **$$$**
(Map p72; ☎416-963-6300; www.thehazeltonhotel.com; 118 Yorkville Ave; d from $446; P ❄ 📶 ≋ 🐾; S Bay) Competitors in the luxury hotel class have in recent years made it harder for the Hazelton to uphold its self-professed reputation as Toronto's most exclusive hotel: but try it will, and you'll only benefit from its efforts. Sophisticated, dramatic and sexy, this hotel is small enough (62 rooms, 15 suites) to make you feel like the someone special that we all know you are.

Design aficionados will be spoiled for things to appreciate here. When it comes to dining, 'ONE,' restaurant of Toronto culinary master Mark McEwan, might further decimate your wallet, but it is destined to delight your taste buds.

Windsor Arms BOUTIQUE HOTEL **$$$**
(Map p72; ☎416-971-9666; www.windsorarmshotel.com; 18 St Thomas St; ste from $396; P ❄ 📶 ≋ 🐾; S Bay) The Windsor Arms is an exquisite piece of Toronto history – stay the night or drop in for afternoon tea. It's a 1927 neo-Gothic mansion boasting a grand entryway, stained-glass windows, polished service and its own coat of arms. Luxurious, oversize suites have separate tub and shower, Molton Brown amenities, butler service and buffet breakfast. Creatives will love that each comes with its own musical instrument!

University of Toronto & The Annex

Havinn GUESTHOUSE **$**
(Map p72; ☎416-922-5220; www.havinn.com; 118 Spadina Rd; s/d with shared bath incl breakfast $69/84; P ⊖ ❄ @ 📶; S Dupont) Located on busy Spadina Rd, this small guesthouse has six basic rooms with shared bathrooms and a communal kitchen. A simple breakfast is included. The price is right: cheaper than most B&Bs and more private than a hostel.

Global Guesthouse INN **$**
(Map p72; ☎416-923-4004; http://globalguesthousetoronto.com; 9 Spadina Rd; s/d $84/94, with shared bath $74/84; P ⊖ ❄ 📶; S Spadina) Built in 1889 this old-fashioned redbrick Victorian has beautiful carved gables and sits just north of Bloor St, right on Spadina station. The hostel has 10 gaudy rooms, cable TV, shared kitchenette and paintings by the owner's wife. It could be cleaner, but the good value means it still fills up quickly.

Annex Quest House INN **$**
(Map p72; ☎416-922-1934; www.annexquesthouse.com; 83 Spadina Rd; d from $95; P ⊖ ❄; S Spadina) Engaging the principles of *vastu*, an Indian architectural science promoting tranquillity through natural materials and asymmetrical layouts (similar to feng shui), this glorified backpackers has quaint, simple rooms. Wooden floors, patterned bedspreads and crafted copper bowls highlight the spaces.

Madison Manor BOUTIQUE HOTEL $$
(Map p72; ☎416-922-5579; www.madisonmanorboutiquehotel.com; 20 Madison Ave; d incl breakfast $99-189; P ⊖ ❄; S Spadina) A refurbished Victorian home near the University of Toronto. Rooms have private bathrooms and are furnished in a traditional style; a few have a fireplace or balcony. Note that the Manor is sandwiched between a frat house and the Madison Avenue Pub (p108): readers have complained of noise on weekends.

Chestnut Residence HOTEL $$
(Map p72; ☎416-977-0707; www.chestnut.utoronto.ca; 89 Chestnut St; d & tw incl breakfast $157; ❄ 📶; S St Patrick) This towering University of Toronto residence witnesses a slew of students, so look past the worn rooms to really enjoy your downtown crash pad. You do get a good breakfast, and City Hall is practically next door. Beds are comfortable, rooms large and with desks (for studying, of course), while bathrooms are clean are include bathtubs.

Kensington Market & Little Italy

★**Planet Travelers Hostel** HOSTEL $
(Map p82; ☎416-599-6789; www.theplanettraveler.com; 357 College St; dm/d/tr $31/75/90; ⊖ ❄ 📶; 🚋506) The Planet has a long history of delighting guests with an awesome rooftop patio bar, great rates and commitment to being clean and green. It still has perks like in-locker chargers for your gadgets. With 94 dorm beds, 10 private rooms and shiny, slick communal areas, you'll have everything you need to make friends and enjoy hostel life.

Queen West & Trinity Bellwoods

★**Drake Hotel** BOUTIQUE HOTEL $$
(☎416-531-5042; www.thedrakehotel.ca; 1150 Queen St W; d/ste from $169/319; P ⊖ ❄ 📶; 🚋501) While other hotels have rooms, the Drake has 'crash pads, dens, salons' and a rockin' little suite, beckoning bohemians, artists and indie musicians with a little cash to burn. The crash pads are tiny yet ineffably stylish and functional. In fact, all the rooms are on the small side, but are impeccably furnished.

The attached **bar** (☎416-531-5042; www.thedrakehotel.ca; 1150 Queen St W; ⊙8am-11pm; 🚋501) and band room is one of Toronto's finest venues for live music, and in summer the Sky Yard rooftop patio goes off to DJ beats and icy buckets of Coronas.

★**Gladstone Hotel** BOUTIQUE HOTEL $$
(☎416-531-4635; www.gladstonehotel.com; 1214 Queen St W; d/ste from $229/375; P ⊖ ❄ 📶; 🚋501) The 37 artist-designed rooms at this trendsetting hotel could have leaped straight from a Taschen design book. Pick a room theme from the informative website, then when you arrive, take the hand-cranked birdcage elevator to your arty boudoir on the 3rd or 4th floor. Locally produced bathroom products and a green roof showcase the Gladstone's eco commitment.

Downstairs, the Melody Bar (p108) band room and cafe are integral to the Toronto indie scene, while the 2nd floor is dedicated to studio space and exhibitions for renting artists.

Bonnevue Manor B&B $$
(☎416-536-1455; www.bonnevuemanor.com; 33 Beaty Ave; d incl breakfast from $157; P ⊖ ❄ @; 🚋501, 504, 508) Tucked away on a side street between the furthest extents of Queen and King Sts W, this cozy place occupies a restored 1890s redbrick mansion with divine handcrafted architectural details. Six guest rooms exhibit warm-colored, floral interiors; all have bathrooms. Enjoy your cooked breakfast out on the grapevine-covered deck.

East End & The Beaches

★**Only Backpackers Inn** HOSTEL $
(☎855-463-3249; http://theonlyinn.com; 972 Danforth Ave; dm incl breakfast $26-30; ❄ @ 📶; S Donlands) There is much to love about the Only! Inspired by owner James' globetrotting adventures, it's everything you want a hostel to be: clean, intimate, near the subway, and in a perfect spot on The Danforth (though not downtown). There's waffles for brekky and two private patios. Downstairs in the cafe there's a large patio with 24 gourmet brews on tap.

Au Petit Paris B&B $
(Map p72; ☎416-928-1348; www.bbtoronto.com/aupetitparis; 3 Selby St; s/d/tr incl breakfast $105/145/175; ⊖ ❄ 📶; S Sherbourne) Hardwood floors blend with modern decor inside this exquisite bay-and-gable Cabbagetown Victorian. The pick of the four ensuite rooms are the skylighted Nomad's Suite and the Artist's Suite, with garden views and extra-large bathtubs. The lovely vegetarian breakfast includes crêpes, fruit and waffles, but you can skip it for discounted room rates.

Toronto's Islands

Smiley's B&B B&B $$
(☎416-203-8599; www.erelda.ca; 4 Dacotah Ave, Algonquin Island; r with shared bath $106, apt per night/week $257/1400; ; Ward's Island) Sleep the night away in 'Belvedere' – a sunny B&B room – and dine with the hosts, or hole up in the studio apartment (June to September only) with its own kitchen and bathroom. Either way, on the car-free islands, relaxation is sure to come easy. Smiley's is a 15-minute ferry ride from Bay St.

Eating

Nowhere is Toronto's multiculturalism more potent and thrilling than on the plates of its restaurants. Eating here is a delight – you'll find everything from Korean walnut cakes to sweat-inducing Thai curries, New York steaks and good ol' Canuck pancakes with peameal bacon and maple syrup. Fusion food is hot: traditional Western recipes spiked with handfuls of zingy Eastern ingredients and cooked with pan-Asian flare. British influences also linger – fizzy lunchtime pints and formal afternoon high teas are much-loved traditions.

Executive diners file into classy restaurants in the Financial District and Old York, while affordable eateries fill Baldwin Village, Kensington Market, Queen West, Ossington Ave and the Yonge St strip. More ethnically consistent are Little Italy, Greektown (The Danforth), Little India and Chinatown. Ponder your profoundest cravings, identify your neighborhood of choice, then dive right in.

Harbourfront

Against the Grain Urban Tavern PUB FOOD $$
(Map p78; ☎647-344-1562; corusquay.atgurbantavern.ca; 25 Dockside Dr; mains $14-26; 11am-9pm Sun-Tue, to 10pm Wed, to 11pm Thu, to midnight Fri & Sat; 509) The best feature of this glorified pub is its enormous lakefront patio (seasonal) with some of the best views of the Toronto Harbourfront. Come with a friend to enjoy the sun and a martini, share a plate of pork belly or spicy lobster tacos, or get messy with the signature pulled pork sandwich.

Harbour Sixty Steakhouse STEAK $$$
(Map p78; ☎416-777-2111; www.harboursixty.com; 60 Harbour St; mains $32-130; 11:30am-late Mon-Fri, 5pm-late Sat & Sun; 509, 510) Inside the Gothically isolated 1917 Toronto Harbour Commission building, this opulent baroque dining room glows with brass lamps and plush booths. Indulge yourself in an eminent variety of enormous steaks, salmon or seasonal Florida stone-crab claws and broiled Caribbean lobster tail. Side dishes are big enough for two. Prepare to burn a significant hole in your wallet. Reservations essential.

Financial District

B Espresso Bar CAFE $
(Map p72; ☎416-866-2111; bespressobar.com; 111 Queen St E; coffee $3-6; 7:30am-5pm Mon-Fri; 501) The coffee creed at Italian-bistro-style B is 'Steamy, rich, smooth, strong, fine, bold, delicious.' Hot damn, has coffee ever sounded so sexy? Almost as sexy as the staff with caffeine coursing through their veins.

★**Richmond Station** INTERNATIONAL $$
(Map p72; ☎647-748-1444; www.richmondstation.ca; 1 Richmond St W; mains $21-28; 11:30am-10:30pm Mon-Sat; S Queen) Reservations are strongly advised at this busy and uncomplicated restaurant, brainchild of celebrity *Top Chef Canada* winner, Carl Heinrich. Dishes are 'ingredient focused and technique driven.' Try the excellent chunky lobster cocktail and buttery mushroom fettuccine. The eclectic menu is simple but gratifying, priced right and complemented by a well-paired wine list and daily chalkboard specials.

Terroni ITALIAN $$
(Map p78; ☎416-203-3093; www.terroni.com; 57 Adelaide St E; mains $14-25; 9am-10pm Mon-Thu, to 11pm Fri & Sat, 5-10pm Sat; S King) The Adelaide St branch of this popular Italian eatery (there are multiple branches in Toronto, and more in LA) occupies a former courthouse with high vaulted ceilings and labyrinthine dining areas. It's open, cool and, despite the size, generally packed. Reasonably priced wood-fired pizzas, rich pastas and fresh panini would make the Godfather proud. Modifications to dishes are a no-no.

Nami JAPANESE $$
(Map p78; ☎416-362-7373; www.namirestaurant.ca; 55 Adelaide St E; lunch sets $18-24, dinner mains from $20, sukiyaki per person $33; 11:45am-2:30pm & 5:30-10pm Mon-Fri, 5:30-10pm Sat; S King) The name means 'wave' (as in tsunami) – the neon wave on the outside of the building is unmissable and cool. Bustling about the black lacquered interior are kimono-clad hostesses and intense sushi chefs, who make only small concessions to North American palates. *Robatayaki* grilling is a specialty, so this is *the* place to try home-style *sukiyaki* hotpot.

FESTIVAL FOOD

Look out for good-value, prix-fixe menus during the **Summerlicious** (p91) and **Winterlicious** (p90) food festivals, plus the **Union Summer** (p91) food market at Union Station in the warmer months. Food trucks serving a variety of flavors are popular in Toronto. Download an app to track down one nearby.

Bymark FUSION $$$
(Map p78; ☎416-777-1144; www.bymark.mcewangroup.ca; TD Centre, 66 Wellington St W; mains $28-65; ⏰11:30am-3pm Mon-Fri, 5pm-midnight Mon-Sat; Ⓢ St Andrew) Toronto culinary powerhouse Mark McEwan brings his sophisticated menu of continentally hewn cuisine to this hip, bi-level downtowner. His creative kitchen crew whips seasonal, regional ingredients (wild truffles, quail, soft-shell crab) into sensational combinations, each with suggested wine or beer pairings. It's on street level.

Old York

Patrician Grill DINER $
(Map p78; ☎416-366-4841; 219 King St E; meals $3.75-10.95; ⏰7am-4pm Mon-Fri, 8am-2pm Sat; Ⓢ King) Built in the 1950s, the Patrician has been run by the same family since 1967 and looks the part. Photographers will have a field day with the neon outside and the original decor inside. Burgers, BLTs, bacon and eggs (cooked to perfection) and home fries are the order of the day. Friday lunchtime meatloaf is a local institution and sells out quickly.

Bombay Palace INDIAN $
(Map p78; ☎416-368-8048; www.bombaypalacetoronto.com; 71 Jarvis St; lunch buffet $12.99; ⏰11:30am-2pm & 5-9:30pm; Ⓢ King) This welcoming Indian restaurant occupies the front half of a quirky old house. It has a fine dining atmosphere, polite, old-fashioned service and authentic, well-presented dishes. The à la carte dinner menu is a little pricey, but you can't go past the daily lunch and Sunday dinner buffets for excellent value.

Sultan's Tent & Café Maroc MIDDLE EASTERN $$$
(Map p78; ☎416-961-0601; www.thesultanstent.com; 49 Front St E; mains $24-37; ⏰noon-4pm Mon-Fri, 11:30am-4pm Sat; 🚊503, 504) Dark and atmospheric, replete with stained-glass lanterns, candles and fringed cushions, the Sultan's Tent serves traditional Moroccan cuisine. Try the couscous royale ($24) and for dessert the *keskesu* (sweet couscous, cinnamon, almonds, raisins and orange blossom water).

Hiro Sushi SUSHI $$$
(Map p78; ☎416-304-0550; www.hirosushi.ca; 171 King St E; lunch specials from $12, dinner $35-70; ⏰noon-2:30pm Tue-Sat & 5:30-10:30pm Sat; 🚊503, 504) If sushi is your thing, good-humored Hiro is your man. This authentic Japanese *sushi-ya* prefers to operate on the traditional principle of *omakase:* leave it to the chef. If you do, a tantalizing journey awaits. However, Hiro understands the particular sensibilities of Western diners and offers a limited à la carte menu, which varies according to the availability of produce and his mood.

Entertainment District & King Street West

Wvrst EUROPEAN $
(Map p82; ☎416-703-7775; www.wvrst.com; 609 King St W; sausages from $6; ⏰11:30am-11pm Sun-Wed, to midnight Thu, to 1am Fri & Sat; 🚊504, 508) Like sausage? If Wvrst's phenomenal success is any indication, then Toronto's hipsters do too. With more bangers and snags than you can poke a stick at, do yourself a favor and get some pork on your fork at this 'beer and sausage hall.' Will you have the duck fat or dirty fries with that?

Avenue Open Kitchen DINER $
(Map p82; ☎416-504-7131; 7 Camden St; sandwiches/burgers from $3/4.50; ⏰7am-4pm Mon-Fri, 8am-3pm Sat; 🚊504) This cozy little joint off Spadina Ave feels like it's been here forever, but it's spotlessly clean and great value. Go on, have a BLT with cheese and a side of fries and gravy for your lunch: we dare you. Breakfasts and burgers are truly old school and easy on the wallet. There's always a daily special.

Burrito Bandidos MEXICAN $
(Map p72; www.burritobandidos.com; 120 Peter St; burritos from $6.55; ⏰11:30am-11pm Mon-Thu, to 4am Fri & Sat, noon-9pm Sun; 🚊501, 502) Clubhounds who haven't got lucky pile into this basement booth to assuage their disappointment with a hefty injection of chili, sour cream and salsa, and perhaps spicy pulled pork. There's not enough room in here for both you and your burrito – grab one to go.

VEGETARIAN HAVENS

Meat- and/or dairy-free eating options in food-obsessed Toronto run the gamut from gourmet to passé. These are sure-fire hits:

Govinda's (p103)

Kekou Gelato House (p100)

Kupfert & Kim (p105)

Urban Herbivore (p104)

Ravi Soups INTERNATIONAL **$**

(Map p78; ☎647-435-8365; www.ravisoup.com; 322 Adelaide St W; soups $9.99; ⊙11am-10pm Mon-Sat, to 8pm Sun; 504, 508) This one is pretty simple: a small menu of seven soups (think corn chowder with blue crab, and porcini mushroom wild rice bisque) and six wraps (curried beef with roasted yams) that are done to perfection – all are delicious. There's a small eating area with a shared table which is usually jam-packed.

Thompson Diner DINER **$**

(Map p82; ☎416-601-3533; www.thompsondiner.com; 550 Wellington St W; breakfast from $10, mains from $14; ⊙24hr; 504, 511) The casual dining option at the sexy Thompson hotel (p94) is open 24 hours (all-day breakfast). Whatever time of day, there's likely good people-watching to be had: this is nightclub territory, remember. Comfort food is a sure thing in a classic diner with a modern twist.

Dark Horse Espresso CAFE **$**

(Map p72; ☎416-979-1200; www.darkhorseespresso.com; 215 Spadina Ave; coffee $3-6; ⊙7am-7pm Mon-Fri, 8am-7pm Sat & Sun; 510) Excellent coffee in a tall-ceilinged space, perfect for intensive writing or people-watching.

★Lee ASIAN **$$**

(Map p82; ☎416-504-7867; www.susur.com/lee; 601 King St W; mains $15-45; ⊙5:30-10:30pm Sun-Wed, to 11:30pm Thu-Sat; 504, 508) Truly a feast for the senses, dinner at acclaimed *cuisinier* Susur Lee's self-titled flagship restaurant is an experience best shared. Slick servers assist in navigating the artisan selection of east-meets-west Asian delights: you really want to get the pairings right. It's impossible to adequately convey the wonderful dance of flavors, textures and aromas one experiences in the signature Singaporean slaw, with...how many?? ingredients!

Khao San Road THAI **$$**

(Map p82; ☎647-352-5773; www.khaosanroad.ca; 785 Queen St W; mains $13-16; ⊙noon-2:30pm & 5-10pm Mon & Tue, noon-2:30pm Wed-Sat; ; 504, 508) There is usually a line-up here for some of Toronto's best Thai food. Granted, if you're a fan of Thai flavors, it can be worth the wait. Once inside, everything functions like a machine: orders are turned around fast and the food is delish. There's a vegan menu, too.

Patria SPANISH **$$**

(Map p82; ☎416-367-0505; www.patriatoronto.com; 480 King St W; small plates $5-18; ⊙5:30pm-late daily & 10:30am-2:30pm Sun; 504, 508) Everything works beautifully in this expansive, modern restaurant specializing in Spanish tapas and cuisine. Knowledgeable servers help navigate the mouthwatering menu of cheeses, meats and seafood. Tapas are meant to be shared: order plenty and don't bother coming alone. Sunday brunch is a delightful deviation from the usual suspects.

Chinatown & Baldwin Village

★Kekou Gelato House ICE CREAM **$**

(Map p72; ☎416-792-8858; http://kekou.ca; 13 Baldwin St; ⊙12:30-10:30pm Sun-Thu, to 11pm Fri & Sat; ; S Osgoode) Whiskey, black sesame or oolong tea. No not cocktails, but excellent, Asian-inspired ice creams. The delicious flavors are not overly sweet or artificial, and the ginger and dark chocolate dairy free is the punchiest vegan gelato in Toronto. On a villagey end of Baldwin, with another branch on Queen W near the corner with Spadina.

Pho Hu'ng VIETNAMESE **$**

(Map p82; ☎416-593-4274; http://phohung.ca; 350 Spadina Ave; mains $6-13; ⊙10am-10pm; 510) Clipped service and infernally busy tables are the price you pay for Pho Hu'ng's awesome Vietnamese soups – the other dishes are passable. A few *pho* may be a touch too authentic for some (pork intestines and blood) but the Viet coffee is spot-on.

Mother's Dumplings CHINESE **$**

(Map p72; ☎416-217-2008; www.mothersdumplings.com; 421 Spadina Ave; 10 dumplings from $8.50; ⊙11:30am-10pm; ; 506, 510) The cleanest and best located of Chinatown's dumpling houses prepares plump and juicy dumplings to authentic recipes passed on down generations. However you like them, steamed or pan-fried, pork, chicken, beef, shrimp or vegetarian, these dumplings will fill your tum and delight your wallet. Always busy.

Kinton Ramen NOODLES $

(Map p72; ☎647-748-8900; www.kintonramen.com; 51 Baldwin St; noodles from $9.50; ⊙11:30am-10:30pm Sun-Thu, to 11:30pm Fri & Sat; 🚊505, 506) Ramen noodles are practically a religion in Japan and they're becoming increasingly popular in Toronto. The cool brains behind this clever outfit leaped upon the bandwagon with their own distinct flavor: caramelized pork. There's even a version with cheese, if you can imagine. This branch oozes atmosphere – it's lively, noisy, steamy and beery, but classy.

Swatow CHINESE $

(Map p72; ☎416-977-0601; 309 Spadina Ave; mains $8-14; ⊙11am-2am; 🚊505, 510) Catering to a late-night crowd, the menu here covers cuisine from Swatow (a city now known as Shantou, on the coast of China's Guangdong province). The house noodles are fiery and cooked in a style nicknamed 'red cooking' for its potent splashings of fermented rice wine. Cash only; be prepared to queue.

★ND Sushi JAPANESE $$

(Map p72; ☎416-551-6362; www.ndsushiandgrill.com; 3 Baldwin St; mains $11-22; ⊙11:30am-3pm Mon-Fri & 5-10pm Mon-Sat; 🚊505, 506) From its pole position at the beginning of Baldwin St, this unassuming *shokudō* prepares favorite Japanese treats like *gyoza* (dumplings), tempura and mouthwatering sashimi with authenticity. Its specialty is sushi, including a variety of not-so-traditional Western *maki* rolls: the spicy rainbow roll is divine. You could pay a whole lot more for Japanese food of this caliber.

Cafe la Gaffe CAFE $$

(Map p72; ☎416-596-2397; www.cafelagaffe.com; 24 Baldwin St; mains $15-29; ⊙11:30am-10pm Mon-Fri, 10am-10pm Sat & Sun; 🚊505, 506) Stripy cotton tablecloths and fresh-cut flowers adorn the tables in this little cafe. There's a street patio and a leafy garden patio where you can dine on market salads, a filet mignon sandwich or the hand-tossed pizzas. A small-print wine list offers an extensive selection.

Downtown Yonge

Urban Eatery FOOD HALL $

(Map p72; 1 Dundas St W; ⊙10am-9pm Mon-Sat, to 7pm Sun; 📶✍; Ⓢ Dundas) More than just a food court, the Urban Eatery, in the basement level of the gargantuan **Eaton Centre** (Map p72; ☎416-598-8560; www.torontoeatoncentre.com; 220 Yonge St; ⊙10am-9pm Mon-Fri, to 7pm Sat, 11am-6pm Sun; 📶; Ⓢ Queen, Dundas), has 24 outlets from fast food to seated dining. If you're at a pinch for something to eat and tired of walking, you're bound to find something here; in fact, you'll be spoiled for choice. In winter, it's an underground haven connected to the PATH and subway system, too.

Salad King THAI $

(Map p72; ☎416-593-0333; www.saladking.com; 340 Yonge St; mains $8.50-10.50; ⊙11am-10pm Mon-Thu, 11am-11pm Fri, noon-11pm Sat, noon-9pm Sun; Ⓢ Dundas) An institution among students of neighboring Ryerson University, colorful and somewhat misleadingly named Salad King dispenses large bowls of standard Thai curries, noodle soups, rice and, yes, salads, for around $10. Long stainless-steel shared tables and cozy booths are usually full of hungry patrons. You can specify your desired level of spice on a scale of one to 20!

Senator Restaurant DINER $

(Map p72; ☎416-364-7517; www.thesenator.com; 249 Victoria St; mains $8.45-17.95; ⊙8am-2:30pm Sun & Mon, to 9pm Tue-Sat; Ⓢ Dundas) Art-deco buffs will delight in the Senator's curved glass windows, fluted aluminum counter-face and original booths. Meals are refreshingly simple and home style: we love the fish and chips, meatloaf and macaroni. Say no more?

OLD-SCHOOL DINERS

In a city where franchised everything is inescapable, where neighborhoods are in a constant state of flux and restaurants come and go, it's refreshing to know that some things never change. We've sniffed out some of Toronto's most classic diners, greasy spoons and cheap eats to transport you back to the golden age of vinyl and laminate booths, elbow grease and good ole' fashioned home cookin': cheap, oh-so tasty and not-so good for the waistline. Aren't you on vacation, anyway?

Patrician Grill (p99)

Avenue Open Kitchen (p99)

Golden Diner (p102)

Gale's Snack Bar (p106)

Senator Restaurant (p101)

Thompson Diner (p100).

Good View CHINESE $$

(Map p72; ☎416-861-0888; www.goodviewrestaurant.ca; 134 Dundas St E; mains $12-22; ⏰11:30am-10pm Mon-Thu, to 11pm Fri, 4:30-11pm Sat; Ⓢ Dundas) Delicious Cantonese cuisine is prepared fresh at this glorified Chinese takeout not far from Yonge & Dundas Sq. Lunch and dinner specials are great value to take back to your hotel, but the real delight is in eating in with a few friends and choosing a variety of dishes from the à la carte menu.

Eat Fresh Be Healthy INTERNATIONAL $$

(Map p72; ☎647-258-8808; www.eatfreshbehealthy.com; 185 Dundas St W; lunch/dinner from $11/14; ⏰11:30am-9pm Mon-Fri, 3-9pm Sat; ✎; 🚋505) Truly a case of 'don't judge a book by its cover,' the exterior of this wonderful restaurant on a rather drab strip of Dundas St is easy to pass by. Don't. Inside, healthy, home-style meals include fresh, filled sandwiches and lean pastas for lunch, and braised lamb and mustard-glazed pork chops for dinner.

JOEY Eaton Centre MODERN AMERICAN $$

(Map p72; ☎647-352-5639; www.joeyrestaurants.com; 1 Dundas St W; mains $14-35; ⏰11am-1am Sun-Wed, to 2am Thu-Sat; Ⓢ Dundas) The downtown Toronto branch of this upscale casual grill and lounge bar has decor to impress and a menu to match with a center-of-town location atop Dundas Station at the Eaton Centre. Favorite items include the Baja fish tacos, crispy chicken sandwiches and lobster grilled cheese. Variations can be made for gluten-free and vegetarian diners.

Church Wellesley Village

Jet Fuel CAFE $

(☎416-968-9982; www.jetfuelcoffee.com; 519 Parliament St; coffees $3.25-5; ⏰6am-8pm; 🚋506) So arty and cool, this hangout is for east-end gentrifiers, cyclists and literati who like to jeer at the beautiful people of Yorkville. The best coffee east of Yonge St.

Golden Diner Family Restaurant DINER $

(Map p72; ☎416-977-9898; 105 Carlton St; breakfast from $2.50; ⏰6:30am-10pm; Ⓢ College) This good old-fashioned basement-level Greek diner has some natty booths and one of the best-value all-day breakfasts in the city. The $6.95 breakfast includes eggs, crispy or peameal bacon, a mound of home fries and a bottomless cup of coffee. Pancakes are $2.50! A filling, if not the best, breakfast in town, to save you some coin for dinner.

PICK OF THE PATIOS

With such short summers, vitamin-D starved locals beeline for Toronto's patio bars and restaurants at the first available opportunity. Be prepared for stiff competition for the best tables…or just any table really! Here are some favorites:

Hair of the Dog (p102)

Earl's (Map p78; ☎416-916-0227; www.earls.ca; Suite 100, 150 King St W; mains $13-29; ⏰11:30am-late; Ⓢ St Andrew)

Queen Mother Café (p105)

Rectory Café (p107)

One Eighty (p107)

Java House (p107)

Allen's (p106)

Drake Hotel (p97)

Against the Grain Urban Tavern (p98)

Ethiopian House AFRICAN $

(Map p72; ☎416-923-5438; www.ethiopianhouse.com; 4 Irwin Ave; mains $10-14; ⏰noon-11pm; ✎; Ⓢ Wellesley) You won't find cutlery at this culturally authentic dining experience. Slather chunks of *sherro wot* (seasoned chickpeas) and *gored-gored* (spiced beef) onto wonderful moist *injera* (bread) and eat with your hands, then try the after-dinner coffee ceremony: it's widely regarded that coffee originated in the then Ethiopian kingdom of Kaffa. Numerous vegetarian dishes are available as well as a good $8 lunch.

Guu JAPANESE $

(☎647-351-1314; www.guu-izakaya.com/toronto; 1314 Queen St W; mains $8-14; ⏰5:30-11:30pm Wed-Mon; 🚋501) Hip young Japanese use the street-word *'guu'* for 'good' or 'cool.' This so-named reproduction of a Japanese *izakaya* just moved from a packed Church St location but promises to be as lively. Come with friends for beer, sake and a selection of mouth-watering small plates like spicy *negitoro* (fatty tuna), deep-fried brie with mango sauce, and banana tempura with coconut ice cream!

★ **Hair of the Dog** PUB FOOD $$

(Map p72; ☎416-964-2708; www.hairofdogpub.com; 425 Church St; share plates $8-14, mains $13-25; ⏰11:30am-late Mon-Fri, 10:30am-late Sat & Sun; Ⓢ College) At its best in the warmer months when two levels of shaded patios spring to life with a mixed gay/straight crowd, this chilled puppy is delightfully less mainstream than its Village neighbors a few blocks north. Equally tempting as a drinking venue, the Dog serves great sharing plates and salads, too. No nonvegetarian can possibly resist the butter-chicken grilled cheese.

Sambucas on Church ITALIAN **$$**
(Map p72; ☎416-966-3241; www.sambucas.ca/home; 489 Church St; mains $10-22; ⏲10:30am-10:30pm; Ⓢ Wellesley) Great for weekday lunches, weekend brunches and dinner anytime, Sambucas' Italian menu has some North American twists. Pastas are hearty, risottos creamy and the chicken dishes noteworthy. Try the $25 prix-fixe lunch with tasty seafood linguine. If you're lucky, you'll secure a window table to watch the Villagers walk by.

Bloor-Yorkville

★Trattoria Nervosa ITALIAN **$**
(Map p72; ☎416-961-4642; www.eatnervosa.com; 75 Yorkville Ave; mains $16-29; ⏲11:30am-11pm Mon-Wed, to midnight Thu-Sat, noon-10pm Sun; 📶; Ⓢ Bay) In the heart of the fancy-pants Yorkville area, this restaurant is an attitude-free Italian oasis. The patio is a good corner from which to people-watch Toronto's well-heeled while digging into simple, excellent pasta – the *mafalde al funghi* has incredibly deep mushroom flavors without being overly creamy.

Okonomi House JAPANESE **$**
(Map p72; ☎416-925-6176; 23 Charles St W; mains $6-12; ⏲11:30am-10pm Mon-Fri, noon-10pm Sat; Ⓢ Bloor-Yonge) Okonomi House is one of the only places in Toronto, and perhaps North America, dishing up authentic *okonomiyaki* (savory Japanese cabbage pancakes filled with meat, seafood or vegetables). A must for Japanophiles.

7 West Café CAFE **$$**
(Map p72; ☎416-928-9041; www.7westcafe.com; 7 Charles St W; mains $11.95-17.95; ⏲24hr; Ⓢ Bloor-Yonge) Three floors of moody lighting, textured jade paint, framed nudes, wooden church pews and jaunty ceiling angels set the scene for a dazzling selection of pizzas, pastas, sandwiches and 24-hour breakfasts. Make like a vampire sipping blood-red wine (by the glass or bottle) as the moon dapples shadows across the street. Cool.

Bloor Street Diner INTERNATIONAL **$$**
(Map p72; ☎416-928-3105; www.bloorstreetdiner.com; Manulife Centre, 55 Bloor St W; mains $18-33, brunch $34; ⏲noon-1am; Ⓢ Bloor-Yonge) Deceptively named, the swanky Bloor Street Diner has been a Toronto favorite for over 30 years, loved for its Parisian-style patio, distinguished wine list and impressive Sunday brunch buffet with chocolate fountain.

Morton's the Steakhouse STEAK **$$$**
(Map p72; ☎416-925-0648; www.mortons.com/toronto; 4 Avenue Rd; mains from $28; ⏲5:30-11pm Mon-Sat, to 10pm Sun; Ⓢ Bay) If you like steak and don't find what you get here absolutely to your liking, we'd be extremely surprised if they didn't rectify the situation quick smart. These people are serious about steak: your server will bring a trolley of shrink-wrapped cuts to your table, so you can see just what you're getting. Expect to drop a couple of hundred here on a dinner for two with wine, then slip into a food coma.

Sassafraz FUSION **$$$**
(Map p72; ☎416-964-2222; www.sassafraz.ca; 100 Cumberland St; mains $21-39; ⏲11:30am-2am Tue-Sat, to midnight Sun & Mon; Ⓢ Bay) Popular with visiting celebrities and the nouveau riche, Sassafraz' style epitomizes Yorkville. Jazz combos serenade weekend brunchers; sassy receptionists distribute clientele between the sun-drenched patio and leafy indoor courtyard. The food? Predictably good.

University of Toronto & The Annex

Govinda's VEGETARIAN **$**
(☎888-218-1040; www.govindas.ca; 243 Avenue Rd; meal platters adult/child $10/5; ⏲noon-3pm & 6-8pm Mon-Sat; 🌶; Ⓢ Rosedale) The Hare Krishna movement has been feeding budget travelers around the globe for decades. Toronto is no exception. Politely decline any offers of religious conversion and enjoy tasty, karma-free, Indian vegetarian fare that is on the whole good for body and soul.

Chabichou FRENCH **$**
(Map p82; ☎647-430-4942; 196 Borden St; snacks $6-25; ⏲9am-7pm; 🚋510) This French *traiteur* (delicatessan) has a mouthwatering selection of fine cheeses and pâté (try the duck and pistachio), filled sandwiches on freshly baked bread and daily specials such as pork-apple stew: simple, hearty, awesome. The small cafe is a delight, but the booty on offer cries 'put me in your picnic basket'!

Mr Tonkatsu JAPANESE $

(Map p82; www.mrtonkatsu.com; 530 Bloor St W; mains $11-15; 11:30am-2:30pm & 4:30-10pm Mon-Sat, to 9pm Sun; Bathurst) Asking you to grind up your own sesame-seed rice topping might just be a trick to show you how authentic the place is, but it works. The crumbed pork (or chicken) is authentically crispy outside while juicy inside, and Mr Tonkatsu has that nice but casual vibe you find in restaurants in Japan.

Carens Rosedale FUSION $$

(647-352-8111; www.carensrosedale.com; 1118 Yonge St; mains $16-34; 5pm-midnight Mon, 8am-midnight Tue-Fri, 10:30am-2am Sat, 10:30am-midnight Sun; Rosedale) The staff of this delightful, stately restaurant will happily recommend wine pairings for its amazing selection of world cheeses. The boardroom-style bistro is serious enough for a date or work meeting. The $49 prix fixe might include rich duck confit, or pick from French classics and local dishes such as Ontario rainbow trout.

★Country Style Hungarian Restaurant HUNGARIAN $$

(Map p82; 416-536-5966; 450 Bloor St W; schnitzels from $18; 11am-10pm; Bathurst) This delightful Hungarian diner, with its checkered tablecloths and friendly family staff, hasn't changed a bit in at least a generation. The variety of enormous breaded schnitzels, cooked to crunchy perfection, are the best in town, and the cucumber salad is a treat. Hopefully they never change a thing. Note that menu prices *include* tax!

By the Way MIDDLE EASTERN $$

(Map p82; 416-967-4295; www.bythewaycafe.com; 400 Bloor St W; mains $10-18; 9am-9pm Sun-Wed, to 10pm Thu, to 11pm Fri & Sat; ; Spadina) An Annex fixture, this cheerful corner bistro has a fusion menu that leans toward Middle Eastern. Although there's plenty of meat on the menu, vegetarians won't go hungry.

Kensington Market & Little Italy

Moonbean Coffee Company CAFE $

(Map p82; 416-595-0327; www.moonbeamcoffee.com; 30 St Andrews St; coffees $3-4.25; 7am-9pm; 510) 'Nothing here is just ordinary,' says the dude behind the counter, and that's true. Serving the best latte west of Yonge St, Moonbean has organic and fair-trade coffees, all-day breakfasts for around $6, and 'Bite Me' vegan cookies. Grind-your-own beans from $10 per lb.

Aunties & Uncles CAFE $

(Map p82; 416-324-1375; www.auntiesanduncles.ca; 74 Lippincott St; mains $4.25-9.25; 9am-3pm; 510) There's usually a line on the sidewalk outside the picket fence of this always-bustling brunch/lunch joint with a simple menu of cheap and cheery homemade favorites. Plop yourself down in one of the mismatched chairs and dig into dishes like grilled brie with pear chutney and walnuts on challah, banana oatmeal pancakes or grilled Canadian cheddar. Cash only.

Jumbo Empanadas CHILEAN $

(Map p82; 416-977-0056; www.jumboempanadas.ca; 245 Augusta Ave; empanadas from $4.50; 10am-8pm; 510) They're not kidding – chunky Chilean empanadas (toasted delights stuffed with beef, chicken, cheese or vegetables) and savory corn pie with beef, olives and eggs always sell out early. A mini empanada will only set you back $1.50. Bread and salsas are also homemade.

Nguyen Huong SANDWICHES $

(Map p82; 416-599-4625; www.nguyenhuong.ca; 322 Spadina Ave; sandwiches from $5; 8:30am-8:30pm; 510) Cheap and delicious filled Vietnamese sandwiches are the name of the day at the original precursor to Toronto's *banh-mi* (baguette filled with pâté, cilantro, pork and pickled veg) phenomenon.

Urban Herbivore VEGETARIAN $

(Map p82; 416-927-1231; www.herbivore.to; 64 Oxford St; mains $7-14; 9am-7pm; ; 510) This humble wholefoods joint specializes in vegetarian meals *sans* additives and preservatives, including salads, rice bowls, chunky soups and specialty vegan gluten-free baked goodies. There's now a branch at the Eaton Centre's Urban Eatery (p101).

Kalendar CAFE $$

(Map p82; 416-923-4138; www.kalendar.com; 546 College St; mains $12-18; 11:30am-late Mon-Fri, 10:30am-late Sat & Sun; 510) It feels like France in Little Italy, with dark wood, tiled floors and a dainty sidewalk patio. The menu funks things up with different types of scrolls (crepe-style roti topped with all sorts of veggies and sauces) and nannettes – naan topped with yummies such as pesto, artichoke hearts and Asiago cheese.

Bar Italia ITALIAN $$

(Map p82; 416-535-3621; www.bar-italia.ca; 582 College St; mains $13-26; 11am-11pm Mon-Wed, to midnight Thu, to 2am Fri & Sat, 10am-10pm Sun; ;

(506) Locals love Bar Italia, a place to see and be seen (especially from a vantage point on the coveted front patio). Grab a sandwich or an al dente pasta – with a lemon gelato and a rich coffee afterward – and while away the entire afternoon or evening.

Caplansky's Deli DINER $$
(Map p82; 416-500-3852; www.caplanskys.com; 356 College St; mains $7-18; 10am-10pm Mon-Thu, to 11pm Fri & Sat, 9am-10pm Sun; 510) All-day breakfasts and Montréal-style hot smoked-meat deli sandwiches are the claim to fame of this authentic Jewish deli, also serving rich meaty dinners and daily specials. The friendly folks won't make you feel like chopped liver, though you're more than welcome to order some if you wish ($15).

Queen West & Trinity Bellwoods

Kupfert & Kim VEGETARIAN $
(Map p82; 416-504-2206; www.kupfertandkim.com; 140 Spadina Ave; mains $10-12; 7:30am-10pm Mon-Fri, 10:30am-10pm Sat & Sun; ; Osgoode, 501) The Korean and Canadian couple behind these restaurants have remixed the Korean *bibimbap* into extremely satisfying meatless and wheatless superfood bowls. Pomegranate, goji, quinoa, rainbow radish and plenty of raw greens feature in the vegan dishes. A smash hit for young couples and individuals in gym gear.

Chippy's FISH & CHIPS $
(Map p82; 416-866-7474; www.chippys.ca; 893 Queen St W; fish/chips from $9.75/4; 11:30am-9pm, closed Mon Dec-Mar; 501) For a city as food-diverse as Toronto, there's a definite lack of good fish and chipperys. Chippy's is an exception: the fish is as fresh as you get in the big smoke, the chips are cut daily from Ontario and Prince Edward Island potatoes, and the batter has two bottles of Guinness added to every batch. Sit in Trinity Bellwoods Park, opposite, to enjoy your catch.

New York Subs & Burritos FAST FOOD $
(Map p82; 416-703-4496; 520 Queen St W; burritos from $3.49; 11:30am-midnight Mon-Fri, to 10pm Sat; 501) Odd, but awesome burrito creations (butter chicken anyone?) have drawn flocks of late-night punters here for years. The joint ain't fancy, but these things are cheap, delicious and filling. Mushroom lovers sticking to their instincts will be rewarded.

★**Queen Mother Café** FUSION $
(Map p72; 416-598-4719; www.queenmothercafe.ca; 208 Queen St W; mains $13-19; 11:30am-1am Mon-Sat, to 11pm Sun; Osgoode) A Queen St institution, the Queen Mother is beloved for its cozy, dark wooden booths and excellent pan-Asian menu. Canadian comfort food is also on offer – try the Queen Mum burger. Check out the display of old stuff they found in the walls the last time they renovated. The patio is hidden and one of the best in town.

Pizzeria Libretto ITALIAN $$
(Map p82; 416-532-8000; http://pizzerialibretto.com; 221 Ossington Ave; mains $10-17; 11:30am-11pm; 505) In Portugal Village, Pizza Libretto crafts what is arguably the best pizza in town. The secret? A wood-fired oven built by a third-generation pizza-oven builder with stones shipped from Italy. Besides certified Neapolitan pizza and other Naples staples, the menu also includes a prix-fixe weekday lunch (salad, pizza and gelato for $16) and an all-Italian wine list.

Burger's Priest BURGERS $$
(Map p82; 647-748-8108; www.theburgerspriest.com; 463 Queen St W; from $5.49; noon-9:30pm Mon-Sat, to 8pm Sun; ; 501) Some say Priest's simple burgers are the best in town: fresh ground beef, soft bun, grilled to perfection. A top choice: 'the Priest' (of course), crowned with a breaded portobello mushroom. Check the secret menu online, if you're brave. For dessert, don't shy from the Vatican on ice: an ice cream sandwiched between two grilled cheese sandwiches...it's an experience.

Rose and Sons Swan CAFE $$
(Map p82; 647-348-7926; www.roseandsons.ca; 892 Queen St W; mains $14-28; 9am-10pm Sun-Wed, to 11pm Thu-Sat; ; 501) Rose and Sons continues the Swan legacy of glammed-up diner classics in art-deco booths. The hummus eggs with fried cauliflower, honey butter hot sauce and pine nuts makes brunch special. Dinner goes international with fried chicken, rice and Cambodian coleslaw.

Julie's Cuban LATIN AMERICAN $$
(416-532-7397; www.juliescuban.com; 202 Dovercourt Rd; tapas $4-15, mains $16-22; 5:30-10pm Tue-Sun; 501) This West Queen West neighborhood joint serves traditional Cuban dishes like *ropa vieja* (shredded beef in spicy tomato sauce with ripe plantains, white rice and black beans). The restaurant was once a corner store, and every effort has been made to retain the vibe.

BEST COFFEE SHOPS?

Too early for beer? Sidestep the coffee chains for some *real* barista action:

Rooster Coffee House (☎416-995-1530; www.roostercoffeehouse.com; 479 Broadview Ave; snacks $3-11; ⏰7am-8pm; 🚋504, 505) Opposite Riverdale Park.

Dark Horse Espresso (p100) Fashion District/Chinatown.

B Espresso Bar (p98) Financial District/Corktown.

Moonbean Coffee Company (p104) Kensington Market.

Jet Fuel (p102) Cabbagetown.

Remarkable Bean (p106) The Beaches.

★Union FUSION **$$**

(Map p82; ☎416-850-0093; www.union72.ca; 72 Ossington Ave; mains $18-34; ⏰6-10pm Mon & Tue, noon-3pm & 6-11pm Wed-Sun; 🚋501) This dandy little hipster kitchen serves a delicious fusion of French- and Italian-inspired dishes which it touts as 'simple done right,' though you could argue that pickled swordfish with snow crab isn't simple. Fortunately, the food, decor and service are masterfully executed: steak, chicken, ribs and fish are staples. There's a delightful little patio out back.

East End & The Beaches

Gio Rana's Really Really Nice Restaurant ITALIAN **$**

(☎416-469-5225; 1220 Queen St E; mains $9-23; ⏰6-11pm Tue-Sat; 🚋501, 502, 503) There's no signage at this quirky, fun joint – just a massive Italianate nose on the exterior of an otherwise nondescript 1950s bank building. Locals come here for the atmosphere, good humor and old-fashioned Italian comfort food: enormous meatballs, hot sausage risotto, veal and 'sexy duck.'

Remarkable Bean CAFE **$**

(☎416-690-2420; 2242 Queen St E; snacks $3-10; ⏰7am-10pm; 🚋501) This Beaches favorite serves up shepherd's pie and still-in-the-pan homemade desserts to go with your latte or *maté* (South American 'tea of life'). Fight for a window seat alongside the well-heeled.

Schnitzel Queen EUROPEAN **$**

(Map p72; ☎416-504-1311; 211 Queen St E; schnitzels $6.50-14.50; ⏰11am-7pm Mon-Fri, 1-6pm Sat; 🚋301, 501, 502) This poky German takeout specializes in golden delicious breaded schnitzel sandwiches that make great picnic fodder. These mammoth creations are excellent value and usually good for two meals – the schnitzel is double the size of the bun. Purists should nab a bar stool and stay in for the authentic dinner plates with mushroom sauce, potato salad and sauerkraut ($9.99).

Gale's Snack Bar DINER **$**

(539 Eastern Ave; meals $3-4; ⏰10am-6pm Mon-Fri, noon-5pm Sat; 🚋501, 502, 503) Off the gentrified Leslieville strip, on a working-class corner with high-vehicular traffic, you'll find this gritty hole-in-the-wall. If you can get past the fact that it hasn't been updated in decades, you'll discover some of Toronto's cheapest greasy-spoon eats, such as sandwiches with salmon, turkey or bacon fillings.

Siddhartha INDIAN **$$**

(☎416-465-4095; 1450 Gerrard St E; mains $9-18; ⏰11:30am-10pm; 🚋506) In a neighborhood stuffed with excellent South Asian food, Siddhartha is a consistent favorite. Although it's popular for its all-you-can-eat lunch and dinner buffets ($14), don't be afraid to order off the menu. The naan is perfect, the curries are classic and the samosas are massive. Cool your burning tongue with a Kingfisher.

Pan on the Danforth GREEK **$$**

(☎416-466-8158; www.panonthedanforth.com; 516 Danforth Ave; mezes $8-15, mains $17-32; ⏰noon-11pm Sun-Thu, to midnight Fri & Sat; **S** Pape) As Greek as Greektown (aka The Danforth), colorful, casual Pan serves unpretentious fare with traditional Greek flavors, like calamari, moussaka, and Santorini chicken stuffed with spinach and feta, served with new potatoes and seared veggies. Finish with a sticky chocolate baklava.

★Allen's PUB FOOD **$$$**

(☎416-463-3086; www.allens.to/allens; 143 Danforth Ave; mains $12-36; ⏰11:30am-2am; **S** Broadview, 🚋504, 505) Featuring one of the city's nicest patio dining areas (in warmer months), Allen's is more than just a pub, although it is a great place for lovers of Irish music and dance. The seasonal menu has hearty, sophisticated Irish fare: cuts of hormone- and additive-free beef (including one of Toronto's best burgers), lamb and veal, ale-battered halibut and curries.

Toronto Islands

Rectory Café CAFE $$

(416-203-2152; therectorycafe.com; 102 Lakeshore Ave, Ward's Island; mains $13-21; 11am-9pm Sun-Thu, to 10pm Fri & Sat; Ward's Island) Propped up next to the boardwalk, this cozy gallery-cafe serves light meals, cups of tea and weekend brunch with views of Tommy Thompson Park. Reservations recommended for brunch and dinner; quick snacks and drinks are more casual. Try to nab a seat on the lakeside patio if the sun is shining.

Drinking & Nightlife

Bars & Pubs

The Toronto pub and bar scene embraces everything from sticky-carpet beer holes, cookie-cutter franchised 'Brit' pubs and Yankee-style sports bars to slick martini bars, rooftop patios, sky-high wine rooms and an effervescent smattering of gay and lesbian hangouts. Thirsty work! Strict bylaws prohibit smoking indoors in public spaces, although some outdoor patios are permissive. Taps start flowing around midday and last call hovers between 1am and 2am.

★BarChef COCKTAIL BAR

(Map p82; 416-868-4800; www.barcheftoronto.com; 472 Queen St W; cocktails $15-45; 6pm-1:30am Tue & Wed, to 2am Thu-Sat; S Osgoode) Take a date here and there will never be awkward silence. You'll hear 'oohs' and 'aahs' from other tables in the intimate, near-darkness as cocktails emerge alongside a bonsai tree, or under a bell jar of vanilla and hickory-wood smoke. Beyond novelty, drinks show incredible, enticing complexity without overwhelming some unique flavors – truffle snow, chamomile syrup, cedar air, and soil!

Handlebar BAR

(Map p82; 647-748-7433; 159 Augusta Ave; 7pm-2am; 505) A jolly little spot paying homage to the bicycle and its lovers, from owners with a fine pedigree. In a great spot south of Kensington Market, there's some wonderful retro styling and a nice mix of shiny happy punters. A calendar of quirky hip events makes it an easier bar to visit if you're traveling solo.

Clinton's BAR

(Map p82; www.clintons.ca; 693 Bloor St; 4pm-2am Mon-Fri, 11am-2am Sat & Sun; S Christie) Weekly themed DJ nights, live music and comedy are all part of the lineup at iconic Clinton's, attracting a fun, arty crowd. There's a pub at the front serving decent food and a wicked dance hall at back: the 'Girl & Boy 90s Dance Party' on Fridays is kick-ass.

One Eighty BAR

(Map p72; 416-967-0000; www.the51stfloor.com; 51st fl, Manulife Centre, 55 Bloor St W; 5pm-late Mon-Thu, noon-late Fri-Sun; S Bay) Swanky and priced to match, the city's highest licensed patio has arguably Toronto's best views outside the CN Tower. It's in the Manulife Centre building and, unlike the tower, there's no admission fee, though you'll be scoffed at if you don't drop some cash on a martini or a meal.

Mill Street Brewery BREWERY

(416-681-0338; www.millstreetbrewery.com; 55 Mill St, Bldg 63, Distillery District; 11:30am-midnight; 503, 504) With 13 specialty beers brewed on-site in the atmospheric Distillery District (p73), these guys are a leading light in local microbrewing. Order a sample platter so you can taste all the award-winning brews, including the Tankhouse Pale Ale, Stock Ale and Organic Lager. On a sunny afternoon, the courtyard is the place to be. Their brewery-fare pairings include burgers and wraps.

Ossington BAR

(Map p82; 416-850-0161; www.theossington.com; 61 Ossington Ave; cover $5; 6pm-2am; 501) With a moody candlelit front bar and a cavernous backroom hosting Friday and Saturday DJ nights, local fave the Ossington is a great mix of twenty-to-thirty-somethings who still have a little life left in them and choose to stray from the mainstream mania.

Crocodile Rock PUB

(Map p78; 416-599-9751; www.crocrock.ca; 240 Adelaide St W; 4pm-2am Wed-Fri, 7pm-2am Sat, 9pm-2am Sun; S St Andrew) Like a thorny island in the middle of clubland and entertainment central, Crocodile Rock caters to a slightly older crowd, particularly since the renovation to its excellent rooftop patio. Expect out-of-towners, after-work suits for $3 specials, and anyone who remembers the '80s and still likes to party.

Java House BAR

(Map p82; 416-504-3025; 537 Queen St W; 10am-2am Mon-Fri, 9am-2am Sat & Sun; 510) In the grungy heart of Queen W you'll find this even grungier haven for seriously well-priced drinks and eats, with a huge side patio that is mostly packed in the summer months.

Blake House PUB
(Map p72; ☎416-975-1867; www.theblakehouse.ca; 449 Jarvis St; ⊙11am-midnight Sun-Thu, to 1am Fri & Sat; S Wellesley) Just east of the Village, this historic 1891 mansion is a good all-round performer. Nicely renovated in dark tones, it's wonderfully cozy and inviting in winter, and has a great patio out front in the summer months. There's cold beer, great food and friendly servers. It's popular, but not crowded.

Gladstone Hotel BAR
(☎416-531-4635; www.gladstonehotel.com; 1214 Queen St W; ⊙8am-10pm; 🚋501) This historic hotel (p97) revels in Toronto's avant-garde arts scene. The Art Bar and Gladstone Ballroom sustain offbeat DJs, poetry slams, jazz, book readings, alt-country and blues, while the Melody Bar hosts karaoke and other musical ventures.

Black Bull PUB
(Map p72; ☎416-593-2766; www.blackbulltavern.ca; 298 Queen St W; ⊙noon-midnight; 📶; 🚋501) The Black Bull may have Toronto's most desired patio in that it seems to catch more sunlight than anywhere else. A prime drinking spot for when you need a rest from Queen St shopping.

C'est What PUB
(Map p78; ☎416-867-9499; www.cestwhat.com; 67 Front St E; ⊙11:30am-1am Sun & Mon, to 2am Tue-Sat; 🚋503, 504) Over 30 whiskeys and six dozen Canadian microbrews (mostly from Ontario) are on hand at this underground pub (look for a doorway). An in-house brewmaster tightly edits the all-natural, preservative-free beers on tap and good bar food which makes the most of fresh produce from St Lawrence Market (p75) next door.

Madison Avenue Pub PUB
(Map p72; ☎416-927-1722; www.madisonavenuepub.com; 14-18 Madison Ave; ⊙11am-2am Mon-Sat, to midnight Sun; S Spadina) Comprising three Victorian houses in The Annex, the rowdy 'Maddy' draws a late 20s U of T crowd. Think billiards, darts, a sports bar, polished brass, antique-y lamps lighting the curtained upper floors, *five* patios and lots of hormones colliding between the boys and the girls.

Underground Garage BAR
(Map p78; ☎416-688-8787; www.undergroundgarage.ca; 365 King St W; cover $7; ⊙10pm-2am Sun-Wed, 9pm-2am Thu-Sat; 🚋504, 510) Trying valiantly to keep it real in the otherwise skin-deep Entertainment District, this urban rock bar is down a steep staircase lined with Led Zeppelin, Willie Nelson and John Lennon posters. Wailing guitars, cold beer and good times – just as it should be.

Red Room PUB
(Map p82; ☎416-929-9964; 444 Spadina Ave; ⊙11am-2am; 🚋506, 510) The Red Room rules. Part pub, part diner, part vintagey lounge – this arty Kensington Market room is the place to drag your hungover bones for a recuperative pint of microbrew, an all-day breakfast and an earful of Brit pop. Sink into a dimly lit booth and forget your misdemeanors.

Sweaty Betty's BAR
(Map p82; ☎416-535-6861; 13 Ossington Ave; ⊙5pm-2:30am Mon-Thu, 3:30pm-2:30am Fri-Sun; 🚋501) In a city of infused vodkas and creative cocktails, Betty's refuses to mix anything with more than three ingredients. This no-nonsense approach pares a night out at the bar to the essentials: having a good time and chatting people up. The tiny place is packed with hipsters on the weekends, and the living room-ish setup feels college party-ish.

Sneaky Dee's BAR
(Map p82; ☎416-603-3090; www.sneaky-dees.com; 431 College St; ⊙11am-3am Mon-Fri, 9am-3am Sat & Sun; 🚋506, 511) Spangled with graffiti on the prominent Bathurst/College St corner, Sneaky Dee's downstairs bar is true grunge with battered booths and years of history: fill up on Tex-Mex (half-price fajitas on Tuesdays!) while downing cheap-ish beer. The upstairs band room is a darkened breeding ground for new local rock and roll, although Saturdays go off to '60s to '80s 'Shake-a-tail' club nights.

Wayne Gretzky's PUB
(Map p78; ☎416-348-0099; http://gretzkys.com; 99 Blue Jays Way; ⊙11:30am-late Mon-Fri, 10am-late Sat & Sun; 🚋503, 504) Once part owned by Canada's favorite hockey legend but now just sharing his name, Gretzky's is a sports bar, restaurant and awesome rooftop patio serving fairly innocuous modern American food. Sports fans come to view the hockey memorabilia, but it's otherwise a good downtown spot for a beer.

Wide Open BAR
(Map p72; ☎416-727-5411; www.wideopenbar.ca; 139a Spadina Ave; ⊙4pm-2am Mon-Fri, 7pm-2am Sat & Sun; 🚋510) If you blink you'll miss this grotty little nondescript hole-in-the-wall, but if you do find it, you'll also have tracked down some

of Toronto's cheapest booze: half-price and $10 pitchers on Mondays, and happy hour Thursday when *all drinks* are $2.50 (5pm to 8pm). There's a drink special every day.

Clubs

'Clubland' convenes around Richmond St W and Adelaide St W at John St. After dark, nondescript doorways creak open, thick-necked bouncers cordon off sidewalks and queues of scantily clad girls and awkward guys in their Sunday best begin to form. The air hangs heavy with hormones and excitement but a few hours later, things get messy: drunk girls stagger, guys swing apocalyptic fists and hot-dog cart owners struggle to maintain order among the condiments. Many clubs now offer/require 'bottle service,' where you pay through-the-nose prices to reserve a bottle of liquor and a table for your group. This also helps you skip queues. Most clubs open around 9pm or 10pm (but don't get swinging until later) and close around 4am.

Not your idea of a good time? Head to neighborhoods like Little Italy, Church-Wellesley, Queen West and The Annex for more intimate haunts and wider scope. Cover charges range from $5 to $15. Bars with band rooms or miniclubs out back open early and don't close until 2am or 3am.

Uniun CLUB
(Map p82; 416-603-9300; http://uniun.com; 473 Adelaide St W; 10pm-3am Fri-Sun; 504, 508) The entrance to this ultra-schmick, ultra-cool, bottle-service nightclub is off Portland St. Don't even try to get in unless you look and feel a million bucks and have the cash to back it up. There's an insane LED-lighting system encased in the walls and ceilings, room enough for 1500 and style to burn.

Mod Club CLUB
(Map p82; www.themodclub.com; 722 College St; 8pm-midnight Mon-Thu, 6pm-3am Fri & Sat; 506) Celebrating all things UK, this excellent Little Italy club plays electronic, indie and Brit pop, with occasional live acts like The Killers and Muse taking the stage. If you want to flaunt your hip-hop rhymes, look out for 'trap karaoke.'

Gay & Lesbian Venues

★Fly 2.0 CLUB
(Map p72; 416-925-6222; www.flyyyz.com; 6 Gloucester St; cover $3-12; 10:30pm-4am Sat; S Wellesley) This fun multilevel gay club, just outside the Village, off Yonge St, has the kind of monumental Saturdays thumping out electro dance that you might see on a TV drama. In fact, it was the set for Club Babylon in *Queer as Folk USA*. It's still one of the best LGBTI megaclubs in Toronto. Arrive early for cheaper cover.

El Convento Rico CLUB
(Map p82; 416-588-7800; www.elconventorico.com; 750 College St; cover $8-10; 9pm-3:30am Fri & Sat; 506) With a friendly mixed crowd, this Latino-themed LGBTI dance bar has free salsa lessons on Friday at 11:30pm, as well as drag shows Friday and Saturday.

Black Eagle GAY
(Map p72; 416-413-1219; www.blackeagletoronto.com; 457 Church St; 3pm-3am Mon-Sat, to midnight Sun; S Wellesley) Men-only Eagle lures leather-men, uniform fetishists and their admirers. The year-round rooftop patio is the perfect place to meet a Daddy: Sunday afternoon barbecues draw a strong crowd. There's a cruising area upstairs and a renovated dance area downstairs. While it's not for the fainthearted, the folks and staff here are generally as friendly as they come.

Woody's/Sailor BAR
(Map p72; 416-972-0887; www.woodystoronto.com; 465-7 Church St; noon-2am; S Wellesley) Toronto's most well-known gay bar is a sprawling complex with a grab bag of tricks, from drag shows, 'best ass' contests and billiards tables to nightly DJs. Sailor is a slick bar off to one side.

Crews & Tangos BAR
(Map p72; 416-972-1662; www.crewsandtangos.com; 508 Church St; 5pm-2am; S Wellesley) Sprawling bar by day (with an excellent rear patio) and crowded nightclub by night, featuring live drag and cabaret shows and DJs out back. Boys who like boys, girls who like girls, girlish boys and boyish girls and all their friends tend to make up the lively crowd in this welcoming space.

O'Grady's PUB
(Map p72; 416-323-2822; www.ogradyschurch.ca; 517 Church St; 11am-2am; S Wellesley) The Village's largest patio fills up quick as soon as the sun comes out, but in the colder months there's nothing particularly noteworthy about this fairly standard gay-friendly Irish pub.

☆ Entertainment

As you might have guessed, there's always something going on here, from jazz to art-house cinema, offbeat theater, opera, punk rock, hip-hop and hockey. In summer, free outdoor festivals and concerts are the norm, but Toronto's dance and live-music scene keeps grooving year-round. Gay life is also rich and open, with plenty of clubs, groups, bar nights and activities for the community.

For the latest club, alt-culture and live-music listings, look for Toronto's free street press in venues, by subway entrances or online: *Now* (nowtoronto.com), and *Daily Xtra* (www.dailyxtra.com) for LGBTI events.

In an effort to promote arts and culture, many venues and events operate a 'Pay What You Can' (PWYC) policy: admission is free or by donation – give what you think is reasonable. Otherwise, Ticketmaster (www.ticketmaster.ca) sells tickets for major concerts, sporting matches and events.

Live Music

Dust off your Iggy Pop T-shirt, don your Docs and hit the pit. Alt-rock, metal, ska, punk and funk – Toronto has a thriving live music scene. Bebop, smoky swamp blues and acoustic balladry provide some alternatives. Expect to pay anywhere from nothing to a few dollars on weeknights; up to $20 for weekend acts. Megatours play the Rogers Centre (p71), the Air Canada Centre (p113) and the Molson Canadian Amphitheatre.

★ Horseshoe Tavern LIVE MUSIC
(Map p72; ☎416-598-4753; www.horseshoetavern.com; 370 Queen St W; ⏲noon-2am; 🚋501, 510) Well past its 65th birthday, the legendary Horseshoe still plays a crucial role in the development of local indie rock. This place just oozes a history of good times and classic performances. Come for a beer and check it out.

Reservoir Lounge JAZZ
(Map p78; ☎416-955-0887; www.reservoirlounge.com; 52 Wellington St E; ⏲7:30pm-2am Tue-Sat; 🚋503, 504) Swing dancers, jazz singers and blues crooners call this cool basement lounge home, and it has hosted its fair share of musical greats over the years. Where else can you enjoy a martini while dipping strawberries into chocolate fondue during the show?

Opera House CONCERT VENUE
(☎416-466-0313; www.theoperahousetoronto.com; 735 Queen St E; 🚋501, 502, 503) The old Opera House is an early-1900s vaudeville hall. Over the years, rockers like The Black Crowes, Rage Against the Machine, Eminem, A Perfect Circle and Beck have all strutted out beneath the proscenium arch, and it has held a number of dance parties and performances.

Lee's Palace LIVE MUSIC
(Map p82; ☎416-532-1598; www.leespalace.com; 529 Bloor St W; ⏲9am-2:30am; Ⓢ Bathurst) Legendary Lee's Palace has set the stage over the years for Dinosaur Jr, Smashing Pumpkins and Queens of the Stone Age. Kurt Cobain started an infamous bottle-throwing incident when Nirvana played here in 1990. You can't miss it – look for the primary-colored mural that seems to scream out front.

Glenn Gould Studio CLASSICAL MUSIC
(Map p78; ☎416-205-5555; glenngouldstudio.com; Canadian Broadcasting Centre, 250 Front St W; tickets $15-40; ⏲box office 2-6:30pm Mon-Fri, to 8pm Sat; Ⓢ Union, 🚋504) Glenn Gould Studio's acoustics do the namesake famous pianist honor. Purchase advance tickets for evening concerts of classical and contemporary music by soloists, chamber groups, choirs and sinfonia between September and June. Young international artists are often featured.

Dakota Tavern LIVE MUSIC
(Map p82; ☎416-850-4579; www.thedakotatavern.com; 249 Ossington Ave; ⏲8pm-2am Mon-Fri, 10am-2am Sat & Sun; 🚌63, 🚋501) This basement tavern rocks with wooden-barrel stools and a small stage where you can catch some twang. You'll hear mostly country, blues and some rock. Saturday and Sunday bluegrass brunches ($15; 11am to 3pm) are a *big* hit – they're tasty, filling and fun, but you'll have to queue to get in.

Massey Hall CONCERT VENUE
(Map p72; ☎416-872-4255; www.masseyhall.com; 178 Victoria St; ⏲box office from show days noon; Ⓢ Queen) Few venues have hosted as diverse a range of performances as Massey Hall, with over 120 years in the business. Extensive back-of-house renovations are slated to bring the 2500-seat space into the next generation, while retaining its period charm.

Toronto Symphony Orchestra CLASSICAL MUSIC
(TSO; Map p78; ☎416-593-4828; www.tso.ca; Roy Thomson Hall, 60 Simcoe St; ⏲box office 10am-6pm Mon-Fri, noon-5pm Sat; Ⓢ St Andrew) A range of classics, Cole Porter–era pops and new music from around the world are presented by the TSO at Roy Thomson Hall (sometimes also at Massey Hall and the Toronto Centre for the

Arts). Consult the website for the answers to such questions as 'What if I need to cough?' and 'Should I clap yet?'.

Toronto Centre for the Arts CLASSICAL MUSIC
(☎416-733-9388; www.tocentre.com; 5040 Yonge St; ⊙box office 11am-6pm Mon, to 8pm Tue-Sat, noon-4pm Sun; Ⓢ North York Centre) Way north on Yonge St, the 1000-seat George Weston Recital Hall is home to the Toronto Symphony Orchestra. The 1700-seat Main Stage Theatre and intimate Studio Theatre also host ballet and theater.

Dominion Pub and Kitchen JAZZ
(☎416-366-5555; www.dominionpub.ca; 500 Queen St E; ⊙11am-late Mon-Fri, 10:30am-late Sat & Sun; 🚋501, 502, 503) This jazzy pub has had a recent refresh but maintains a rep for sassy vocalists, trios and sextets through to full-blown swing bands. Music starts nightly around 9pm. Beers have a crafty edge, and there's plenty of *vin rouge* to soothe your big-city heartbreak.

Cameron House JAZZ
(Map p82; ☎416-703-0811; www.thecameron.com; 408 Queen St W; ⊙4pm-late Mon-Sat, 6pm-late Sun; 🚋501, 510) Singer-songwriters, soul, jazz and country performers grace the stage; artists, musos, dreamers and slackers crowd both front and back rooms.

Phoenix CONCERT VENUE
(Map p72; ☎416-323-1251; www.libertygroup.com; 410 Sherbourne St; 🚋506) The 1000-capacity Phoenix has occupied the former Harmonie Club, a grand ol' room that has seen the harmonious rock of bands like The Tragically Hip.

Rivoli LIVE MUSIC
(Map p72; ☎416-596-1908; www.rivoli.ca; 334 Queen St W; ⊙11:30am-1am; 🚋501) Songbird Feist got her start here. Nightly live music (rock, indie and solo singer-songwriters), weekly stand-up comedy and monthly hip-hop nights are all part of the lineup. There's an awesome pool hall upstairs and great food.

Sound Academy CONCERT VENUE
(☎416-649-7437; www.sound-academy.com; 11 Polson St; 🚌72, 72A) This harborside venue can hold around 3000 for rock concerts and live shows. Past acts include Guns & Roses, The Killers and Fall Out Boy.

Rex JAZZ
(Map p72; ☎416-598-2475; www.therex.ca; 194 Queen St W; ⊙music 6:30pm & 9:30pm; 🚋501) The Rex has risen from its pugilistic, blue-collared past to become an outstanding jazz and blues venue. Over a dozen different Dixieland, experimental and other local and international acts knock over the joint each week.

Theater

Long winter months indoors are conducive to the creation and performance of theatrical works. This, and Toronto's relative proximity to Broadway and cosmopolitan Montréal, help sustain the city's reputation as a theater maker's playground. Broadway and off-Broadway musicals and plays pack theaters around the Theatre Block in the Entertainment District and Yonge & Dundas Sq. There are numerous smaller venues and vibrant young production companies around Harbourfront, in the Distillery District (p73) and Queen West. Check the free street press for listings. Tickets for major productions are sold through TicketKing. For last-minute discounted tickets, go to **TO Tix** (Map p72; www.totix.ca; Yonge & Dundas Sq, 5 Dundas St E; ⊙noon-6:30pm Tue-Sat; Ⓢ Dundas) or ask about 'rush' tickets at box offices.

Mirvish TicketKing BOOKING SERVICE
(☎416-872-1212; www.mirvish.com/ticketking) Mirvish TicketKing sells tickets for shows at Royal Alexandra (p112), Princess of Wales (p112), Ed Mirvish and Panasonic Theatres.

Ed Mirvish Theatre THEATER
(Map p72; ☎416-872-1212; www.mirvish.com; 244 Victoria St; Ⓢ Dundas) Formerly the Canon, the Ed Mirvish Theatre was renamed in 2011 in honor of the late Ed Mirvish, Toronto's well-loved businessman, philanthropist and patron of the arts. One of four Mirvish theaters, the 1920s-era vaudeville hall is a hot ticket for musical extravaganzas.

Sony Centre for the Performing Arts CONCERT VENUE
(Map p78; ☎416-872-7669; www.sonycentre.ca; 1 Front St E; ⊙box office 10am-5:30pm Mon-Fri, to 1pm Sat; Ⓢ Union) With an entry awning protruding over Front St like a hummingbird beak, this place is hard to miss. Phone or book online for shows.

Young Centre for Performing Arts THEATER
(☎416-866-8666; www.youngcentre.ca; 55 Mill St, Bldg 49; 🚋503, 504) The $14 million Young Centre houses four separate performance spaces, utilized by theatrical tenants including Soulpepper (p112) and **George Brown Theatre Co** (www.georgebrown.ca/theatre). There's an on-site bookstore and bar, too.

Princess of Wales Theatre THEATER
(Map p78; ☎416-872-1212; www.mirvish.com; 300 King St W; 🚋504) The POW is a 2000-seat playhouse showing big-ticket productions such as *Strictly Ballroom* and *The Book of Mormon*.

Canadian Opera Company OPERA
(Map p72; ☎416-363-8231; www.coc.ca; Four Seasons Centre for the Performing Arts, 145 Queen St W; ⏰box office 11am-7pm Mon-Sat, to 3pm Sun; Ⓢ Osgoode) Canada's national opera company has been warbling its pipes for over 50 years. Tickets sell out fast; the Richard Bradshaw Amphitheatre (in the fabulous Four Seasons Centre) holds free concerts from September through June, usually at noon. Check the website for specific days.

Theatre Passe Muraille THEATER
(Theater Beyond Walls; Map p82; ☎416-504-7529; www.passemuraille.on.ca; 16 Ryerson Ave; tickets $20-35, previews $16; ⏰shows 7:30pm Tue-Sat, matinees 2pm Sat; 🚋501) Theatre Passe Muraille is a theater in the old Nasmith's Bakery & Stables. Since the 1960s, it has focused on radical new plays with contemporary Canadian themes. Postperformance chats with cast and producers occur often. Saturday matinees are 'Pay What You Can.'

Factory Theatre THEATER
(Map p82; ☎416-504-9971; www.factorytheatre.ca; 125 Bathurst St; 🚋511) This innovative theater company – 'Home of the Canadian Playwright' – has been busy for over 35 years. Sunday matinees are 'Pay What You Can.'

Young People's Theatre THEATER
(Map p78; ☎416-862-2222; www.youngpeoplestheatre.ca; 165 Front St E; ⏰box office 9am-5pm; 👪; 🚋503, 504) Catch a show at this innovative theater (previously known as Lorraine Kimsa Theatre for Young People) delivering enlightening children's plays and drama camps.

CanStage THEATER
(Canadian Stage Company; ☎416-368-3110; www.canstage.com; 26 Berkeley St; ⏰box office 10am-6pm Mon-Sat, show days to 8pm; 🚋503, 504) Contemporary CanStage produces top-rated Canadian and international plays by the likes of David Mamet and Tony Kushner from its own Berkeley Street Theatre. It's also behind the wonderfully accessible (pay-what-you-can) midsummer productions of 'Shakespeare in the Park,' under the stars in High Park: bring a blanket and show up early.

Royal Alexandra Theatre THEATER
(Map p78; ☎416-872-1212; www.mirvish.com; 260 King St W; 🚋504) The 'Royal Alex,' as she is sometimes affectionately known, is one of the more impressive theaters in the city and home to splashy Broadway musicals.

Soulpepper THEATER
(www.soulpepper.ca) A theater company that encourages youth theater and using performance art to teach English as a second language.

Cinemas

Torontonians love going to the movies: it might have something to do with the weather. Tickets cost around $14 for adults. Tuesday is discount day, when you can expect to pay around half that.

★TIFF Bell Lightbox CINEMA
(Map p78; www.tiff.net; cnr 350 King St W; 🚋504) Home of Toronto International Film Festival (p92), this resplendent cinema complex is the hub of all the action when the festival is in town. Throughout the year, it's used primarily for TIFF Cinematheque, screening world cinema, independent films, directorial retrospectives and other special events. Try to see a film here if you can.

Scotiabank Theatre CINEMA
(Map p72; ☎416-368-5600; www.cineplex.com; 259 Richmond St W; Ⓢ Osgoode) Managed by Cineplex, this fun gargantuan multiplex in the heart of Queen West features the latest technology, including IMAX 3D. Buy tickets downstairs then take the gigantic escalator upstairs where you can buy pizza, poutine and popcorn for the show!

Polson Pier Drive-In Theatre CINEMA
(☎416-465-4653; www.polsonpier.com; 11 Polson St; ⏰from 8:30pm Fri-Sun Apr-Oct) The drive-in isn't dead – even downtown! First-run blockbusters and special features start around dusk, down by the lake. Summer only.

Rainbow Cinemas CINEMA
(Map p78; ☎416-491-9731; www.rainbowcinemas.ca; 80 Front St E; 🚋503, 504) Plays first-run movies at second-run prices, right in Market Sq. Tuesdays are still $5.

Cineforum CINEMA
(Map p82; ☎416-603-6643; www.cineforum.ca; 463 Bathurst St; over/under 24yr $20/10; ⏰screenings 7pm & 9pm Sat-Thu; 🚋506, 511) An off-the-wall experience awaits at Cineforum. Irascible Toronto character Reg Hartt wraps posters

around telephone poles advertising his cinema – the front room of his house where he showcases classic and avant-garde films. Animation retrospectives are his specialty, as are Salvador Dalí prints. Idiosyncratic lectures are designed to expand your consciousness (like 'What I Learned from LSD'). Seats 20; bring your own food and drink.

Hot Docs Ted Rogers Cinema CINEMA
(Bloor Hot Docs Cinema; Map p82; ☎416-637-3123; www.bloorcinema.com; 506 Bloor St W; Ⓢ Bathurst) This art-deco theater with a two-tiered balcony screens a wonderfully varied schedule of new releases, art-house flicks, shorts, documentaries and vintage films and is home to the mind-expanding Hot Docs (p90) international documentary festival.

Cineplex Odeon Varsity CINEMA
(Map p72; ☎416-961-6304; www.cineplex.com; Manulife Centre, 55 Bloor St W; ⏰noon-midnight; Ⓢ Bloor-Yonge) This state-of-the-art multiplex has VIP theaters and smaller screens.

Cineplex Yonge & Dundas CINEMA
(Map p72; ☎416-977-9262; www.cineplex.com; 10 Dundas St E; Ⓢ Dundas, 🚊505) At the heart of Yonge & Dundas Sq this enormous cinema complex has 24 huge screens with fabulous stadium seating, IMAX, a food court and direct subway access to the building, perfect for those supercheap Tuesdays or freezing winter Sundays.

Sports

Many Torontonians weep with joy at the very mention of their beloved sporting teams: the Blue Jays for professional baseball and the Argonauts for football through the summer; the Maple Leafs for ice hockey, Raptors for basketball and Toronto Rock for lacrosse through the winter. **Ticketmaster** (www.ticketmaster.ca) sells advance tickets, as do the box offices at the Air Canada Centre and Rogers Centre (p71). Ticket scalping is illegal, but that doesn't seem to stop anybody.

Toronto Maple Leafs ICE HOCKEY
(☎416-815-5982; www.mapleleafs.com; ⏰Oct-Apr) The 13-time Stanley Cup–winning Maple Leafs slap the puck around the Air Canada Centre in the National Hockey League (NHL). Every game sells out, but a limited number of same-day tickets go on sale through Ticketmaster at 10am and at the Air Canada Centre ticket window from 5pm.

You can also buy tickets via the website from season ticket holders who aren't attending – expect to pay around $80 and up.

Toronto Blue Jays BASEBALL
(☎416-341-1234; bluejays.com; ⏰Apr-Sep) Toronto's Major League Baseball team (an icon of Toronto and a source of pride) plays at the Rogers Centre (p71). Buy tickets through Ticketmaster or at the Rogers Centre box office near Gate 9. Try for seats along the lower (pricier) level baselines where you have a better chance of catching a fly ball (or wearing one in the side of the head).

Toronto Argonauts FOOTBALL
(☎416-341-2746; www.argonauts.ca; ⏰Jun-Oct) The Toronto Argonauts crack their Canadian Football League (CFL) helmets at the Rogers Centre (p71). The Argonauts have won the Grey Cup a record 16 times, most recently in 2012. Bring a jacket – the open-roof Rogers Centre cools off at night. Tickets through Ticketmaster or the Rogers Centre.

Toronto Raptors BASKETBALL
(☎416-815-5500; www.nba.com/raptors; ⏰Oct-Apr) During hockey season, Toronto's basketball team play at the Air Canada Centre. The 'Raps' have been around since 1995, but haven't yet caused much of a flap.

Air Canada Centre SPECTATOR SPORT
(ACC; Map p78; ☎416-815-5500; www.theaircanadacentre.com; 40 Bay St; Ⓢ Union) The 13-time Stanley Cup–winning Toronto Maple Leafs slap the puck around the Air Canada Centre in the NHL.

Toronto Rock SPECTATOR SPORT
(☎416-596-3075; www.torontorock.com; ⏰Jan-Apr) Lacrosse may not immediately spring to mind when someone mentions Canadian sports, but Toronto's team is red hot, having won the championship six times. Games at the Air Canada Centre; tickets through Ticketmaster.

Shopping

Shopping in Toronto is a big deal. When it's -20°C outside, you have to fill the gap between brunch and the movies with *something*, right? People like to update their wardrobes and redecorate their homes, or just walk zombie-like around warm sprawling malls like the Eaton Centre (p101). This habit continues through to summer, making boutique-hopping an excuse to hit the streets, or vice versa.

MEC SPORTS & OUTDOORS
(Mountain Equipment Co-op; Map p78; ☎416-340-2667; www.mec.ca; 400 King St W; ⏰9am-9pm Mon-Fri, to 6pm Sat & Sun; 📶; Ⓢ St Andrew) MEC is your mecca if you have a fetish for outdoor and adventure equipment. Multiple brands of backpacking, camping, hiking and travel gear line the walls of this storehouse downtown. The helpful staff are swamped on weekends so try midweek if you need advice. Sign up for lifetime membership ($5) on the spot to purchase from this Canadian store.

Te Koop FASHION & ACCESSORIES
(Map p72; ☎416-348-9485; www.te-koop.ca; 421 Queen St W; ⏰10am-9pm Mon-Sat, 11am-8pm Sun; Ⓢ Osgoode) This backpack and luggage store champions Canadian brands such as Herschel, as well as hip, boutique international labels. The bags aren't cheap but you're unlikely to find lower-priced elsewhere in Toronto.

New Tribe TATTOOS
(Map p72; ☎416-977-2786; www.newtribe.ca; 2nd fl, 232 Queen St W; tattooing minimum $80; ⏰noon-8pm Mon-Thu, to 9pm Fri & Sat, to 6pm Sun; 🚋501) Body art is almost mainstream in Toronto – you'd run out of body parts before running through the city's tattoo and piercing shops. This one, in the heart of Queen St W, is a favorite. Top tatts, plus standard and custom body jewelry.

Come as You Are ADULT
(Map p82; ☎416-504-7934; www.comeasyouare.com; 493 Queen St W; ⏰11am-7pm Tue-Wed, to 8pm Thu-Sat, noon-5pm Sun & Mon; 🚋501) Catering to all genders and orientations, Canada's pioneering co-op sex shop (the only one of its kind in the world) sells it all. Grab some vegan condoms and sign up for a workshop on erotic photography or Bondage 101.

Craft Ontario Shop GIFTS & SOUVENIRS
(☎416-921-1721; www.craftontario.com; 1106 Queen St W; ⏰10am-6pm Mon-Wed & Sat, to 7pm Thu & Fri, noon-5pm Sun; 🚋501) Craft Ontario has been promoting artisans for over 70 years. Ceramics, jewelry, glasswork, prints and carvings make up most of the displays at this new Queen St W location, but you could also catch a special exhibition of Pangnirtung weaving or Cape Dorset graphics.

Page & Panel: The TCAF shop COMICS
(Map p72; ☎416-323-9212; www.torontocomics.com/tcafshop; 789 Yonge St; ⏰10:30am-8:30pm Mon-Fri, to 5pm Sat, noon-5pm Sun; Ⓢ Bloor-Yonge) What started as a pop-up for the Toronto Comic Arts Festival (TCAF) has become a permanent comics hub. It's a curated store and particularly good at picking out the best Canadian and international graphic novels and designer gifts.

Drake General Store GIFTS & SOUVENIRS
(Map p72; ☎416-861-6009; www.drakegeneralstore.ca; 176 Yonge St, Lower Level; ⏰10am-9:30pm Mon-Sat, to 7pm Sun; Ⓢ Queen) At this Canadian shop, expect plenty of 'oh that's neat' gifts, such as you might find in a museum store. Designer Toronto souvenirs by local artists include actually tasteful Blue Jays tees. You'll find branches at the basement of Hudson's Bay stores, such as this one, and a pop-up on the Union Station platform of the UP Express airport train.

8th + Main FASHION & ACCESSORIES
(Map p72; ☎647-348-1222; 211 Yonge St; ⏰10am-9pm Mon-Sat, to 7pm Sun; Ⓢ Queen) Vancouver's boutique success story now struts its well-priced threads to the hip men and women of Toronto. The large warehouse-like space is easy to browse without feeling intimidated. The focus is on small, contemporary labels.

Glad Day BOOKS
(Map p72; ☎416-961-4161; www.gladdaybookshop.com; 598a Yonge St; ⏰11am-6pm Sun-Tue, to 7pm Wed-Fri, to 8pm Sat; Ⓢ Bloor-Yonge) It's the oldest surviving gay bookstore in the world, making it an LGBTI landmark. Glad Day has transformed from a space to defy censorship of LGBTI publications, into an event and gathering space to promote creativity and further free speech.

Toronto Designers Market DESIGN
(☎416-570-8773; www.torontodesignersmarket.com; 1605 Queen St W; ⏰11am-6pm Wed-Sun; 🚋501) In the neglected far west of Queen, over 30 small designers have set up mini studio-storefronts within a cavernous space. It's a mixed bag, but there are plenty of fresh ideas in the pop-ups selling jewelry, clothes and gifts such as beard combs.

Spacing Store GIFTS & SOUVENIRS
(Map p72; ☎416-644-1017; http://spacing.ca/toronto; 401 Richmond St W; ⏰11am-7pm Mon-Fri, noon-6pm Sat; Ⓢ Osgoode) Spacing is a magazine with a thing for Canadian cities. Its store is a celebration of urban living with T-shirts, vintage TTC posters and other gifts by local designers. Proudly wear your favorite neighborhood as a button and get the inside staff gossip about upcoming changes to Toronto's streets.

BMV BOOKS
(Map p72; Dundas Sq, 10 Edward St; ⏲10am-11pm Mon-Sat, noon-8pm Sun; S Dundas) The biggest (and most popular) secondhand bookstore in Toronto, with a second outlet on **Bloor Street** (Map p82; 471 Bloor St W; ⏲10am-11pm Mon-Wed, to midnight Thu-Sat, noon-9pm Sun; S Spadina).

Bay of Spirits Gallery GIFTS & SOUVENIRS
(Map p78; ☎416-971-5190; www.bayofspirits.com; 156 Front St W; ⏲10am-6pm Mon-Sat; S Union) The works of Norval Morrisseau – the first indigenous artist to have a solo exhibit at the National Gallery of Canada – are proudly on display in this atmospheric space, which carries aboriginal art from across Canada. Look for the Pacific West Coast totem poles (from miniature to over 4m tall), Inuit carvings and Inukshuk figurines.

Beguiling BOOKS
(Map p82; ☎416-533-9168; www.beguilingbooksandart.com; 601 Markham St; ⏲11am-7pm Mon, Tue, Thu & Sat, to 9pm Wed & Fri, noon-6pm Sun; S Bathurst) Need a comic book fix? The Beguiling is the kind of crowded, mixed-up place that Robert Crumb would drop by (in fact, he once did). Be mesmerized by original 'zines, indie comics, pop culture books, limited edition artworks and posters. Check the website for events.

Courage My Love CLOTHING
(Map p82; ☎416-979-1992; 14 Kensington Ave; ⏲11:30am-6pm Mon-Sat, 1-6pm Sun; 🚋505, 510) Vintage clothing stores have been around Kensington Market for decades, but Courage My Love amazes fashion mavens with its secondhand slip dresses, retro pants and white dress-shirts in a cornucopia of styles. The beads, buttons, leather goods and silver jewelry are handpicked.

ℹ Information

DANGERS & ANNOYANCES

➡ By North American standards, Toronto is a safe city in which to live and visit, but don't be complacent.

➡ It's not a brilliant idea for women to walk alone after dark around Parliament and Jarvis Sts at the intersections with Carlton, Dundas St E and Queen St E, particularly around Allan Gardens and George St – and probably not a good idea during the day, either.

➡ The Entertainment District can get messy with drunken fools after midnight.

EMERGENCY

Police (☎emergency only 911, nonemergency 416-808-2222; www.torontopolice.on.ca)

SOS Femmes (☎416-487-4794; www.sos-femmes.com) French-language crisis line for women.

Toronto Rape Crisis Centre (☎416-597-8808; www.sexualassaultsupport.ca)

MEDIA

Globe & Mail (www.theglobeandmail.com) Doyen among the national daily newspapers.

Metro (www.metronews.ca) Free daily rag with bite-size news, sports and entertainment (often left on subway seats).

NOW (www.nowtoronto.com) Alternative weekly (good for events and concerts) free every Thursday.

Toronto Life (www.torontolife.com) Upscale monthly mag: lifestyle, dining, arts and entertainment.

Toronto Star (www.thestar.com) Canada's largest newspaper; a comprehensive left-leaning daily.

Toronto Sun (www.torontosun.com) Sensationalist tabloid with predictably good sports coverage.

Where Toronto (www.where.ca/toronto) The most informative of the free glossy tourist magazines.

Daily Xtra (www.dailyxtra.com) Online LGBTI news and entertainment source with street-press roots.

MEDICAL SERVICES

Dental Emergency Services (☎416-485-7172; www.dentalemergencyservices.ca; 1650 Yonge St; ⏲8am-midnight; S St Clair) Immediate appointments available. English, Japanese, Filipino and French spoken.

Hassle Free Clinic (☎416-922-0566; www.hasslefreeclinic.org; 2nd fl, 66 Gerrard St E; ⏲women 10am-3pm Mon, Wed & Fri, 4-8pm Tue & Thu, men 4-8pm Mon & Wed, 10am-3pm Tue & Thu, 4-7pm Fri, 10am-2pm Sat; S College) Provides anonymous free HIV (by appointment only) and STI testing, and reproductive- and sexual-health services.

Mount Sinai Hospital (☎416-596-4200, emergency 416-586-5054; www.mountsinai.on.ca; 600 University Ave; ⏲24hr; S Queens Park)

St Michael's Hospital (☎416-360-4000; www.stmichaelshospital.com; 30 Bond St; ⏲24hr; S Queen, Dundas) The very competent emergency unit of this major teaching and research hospital is in the heart of downtown on the corner of Victoria and Shuter Sts, around the corner from the Eaton Centre.

Toronto General Hospital (☎emergency 416-340-3111; www.uhn.ca; 190 Elizabeth St; ⏲24hr; S Queens Park)

Women's College Hospital (416-323-6400; www.womenscollegehospital.ca; 76 Grenville St; 24hr; College) Nonemergency women's and family health.

MONEY

- It's easy to get money using overseas credit cards or debit cards; look for the Cirrus or Plus symbols on ATMs, which are on practically every street corner.
- Many convenience store ATMs charge an additional machine fee.
- **American Express** (905-474-0870; www.americanexpress.com/canada) branches in Toronto function as travel agencies and don't handle financial transactions. Instead, tackle the banks or try **Money Mart** (416-920-4146; www.moneymart.ca; 617 Yonge St; 24hr; Wellesley).

POST

Toronto no longer has a main post office. There are a number of outlets in Shopper's Drug Mart stores around town. The most central full service post offices are below.

Adelaide Street Post Office (800-267-1177; www.canadapost.ca; 31 Adelaide St E; 8am-5:30pm Sun-Fri; Queen)

Atrium on Bay Post Office (Map p72; 416-506-0911; www.canadapost.ca; 595 Bay St; 9:30am-5:30pm Sun-Fri; Dundas)

TOURIST INFORMATION

Ontario Travel Information Centre (Map p72; 416-314-5899; www.ontariotravel.net; Union Station, 65 Front St W; 8am-8pm Mon-Sat, 10am-6pm Sun; Union) This large branch at the west side of Union Station has knowledgeable, multilingual staff and overflowing racks of brochures that cover every nook and cranny of Ontario...almost. This is an easy and sensible first port of call when you get to town, especially as it's there as you get off the UP Express train from the airport.

Tourism Toronto (p67) Contact one of the telephone agents; after hours use the automated touch-tone information menu.

Getting There & Away

Toronto is well-served by international and domestic flights to its main airport. There are a few more options if arriving from the USA, including a smaller island airport and a couple of Amtrak trains from Buffalo and New York. You can make a land crossing into Ontario from the southwest at Detroit-Windsor.

AIR

Toronto Pearson International Airport (YYZ; Lester B Pearson International Airport; Terminal 3 416-776-5100, Terminals 1 & 2 416-247-7678; http://torontopearson.com; 6301 Silver Dart Dr, Mississauga) Most Canadian airlines and international carriers arrive at Canada's busiest airport, 27km northwest of downtown Toronto. Terminal assignments are subject to change; call ahead or check airport entrance signs.

Billy Bishop Toronto City Airport (YTZ; 416-203-6942; www.torontoport.com) On the Toronto Islands, this small airport is home to regional airlines, Porter Airlines, helicopter companies and private flyers. Air Canada Jazz flights from Ottawa land here rather than at Pearson.

BUS

- Long-distance buses operate from the art-deco **Metro Toronto Coach Terminal** (Map p72; 416-393-4636; 610 Bay St; Dundas).
- **Greyhound Canada** (greyhound.ca) has numerous routes from Toronto. Megabus (ca.megabus.com) has a smaller, and cheaper, selection of destinations. Advance tickets offer significant savings; online sales often close two hours before departure.
- **Union Station** (416-869-3000; www.viarail.com; 140 Bay St) downtown serves as the bus and train depot for **GO Transit** (www.gotransit.com), the commuter service of the GTA.
- **Parkbus** (p66) offers limited seasonal departures to the Bruce Peninsula, Algonquin and Killarney Provincial Parks, Georgian Bay Islands and Elora Gorge. The range and frequency of service keep expanding: check the website for latest details.

GREYHOUND BUS INFORMATION

DESTINATION	COST	DURATION	FREQUENCY
Hamilton	$9.50	1hr	2 daily
London	$35-39	2-4hr	11 daily
Montréal	$55	8-9hr	5 daily
Niagara Falls	$18	1½-2hr	6 daily
Ottawa	$64	5-7hr	7 daily
Sault Ste Marie	$112	11hr	1 daily
Sudbury	$73	5hr	1 daily
Thunder Bay	$227	21hr	1 daily

CAR & MOTORCYLE

- Toronto is wrapped in a mesh of multilane highways, frequently crippled by congestion. The Gardiner Expwy runs west along the lakeshore into Queen Elizabeth Way (QEW) to Niagara Falls. At the city's western border Hwy 427 runs north to the airport. Hwy 401 is the main east–west arterial and is regularly jammed. On the eastern side of the city, the Don Valley Pkwy connects Hwy 401 to the Gardiner Expwy. Hwys 400 and 404 run north from Toronto. A GPS is strongly recommended.
- All major car-rental agencies, such as **Avis** (800-230-4898; www.avis.ca) and **Enterprise** (800-261-7331; www.enterpriserentacar.ca), have desks at Pearson airport and offices downtown and throughout the city. Book in advance for best rates. Cars sell out on busy summer weekends.
- Smaller independent agencies offer lower rates, but may have fewer (and older) cars. **Wheels 4 Rent** (416-585-7782; www.wheels-4rent.ca; 77 Nassau St; 510) rents compact cars from around $39 per day excluding taxes.
- For long-distance trips, try **Auto Drive-Away Co** (416-225-7754; www.torontodriveaway.com; 5803 Yonge St; 9am-6pm Mon-Fri, to 3pm Sat; 97), a private vehicle relocation service for Canadian and US destinations.

TRAIN

- Grand Union Station downtown is Toronto's main rail hub, with currency-exchange booths and Traveller's Aid Society help desks. The station is under renovation (but still operational) with completion due between 2017 and 2018.
- **VIA Rail** (p67) plies the heavily trafficked Windsor–Montréal corridor and beyond.
- **Amtrak** (www.amtrak.com) trains link Toronto's Union Station with Buffalo ($57, 4½ hours, one daily) and New York City ($156, 13½ hours, one daily).
- **GO Transit** (www.gotransit.com) trains and buses also use the station with an ever-expanding network of destinations including Kitchener, Hamilton, Barrie and other Ontario locations, often with the cheapest rail fares.

Getting Around

TO/FROM THE AIRPORT

Union Pearson Express (UP Express; www.upexpress.com; one-way adult/child/family of 5 $12/free/25, one-way on PRESTO card $9; 5:30am-1am;) The fastest way to get downtown from Pearson Airport is the Union Pearson Express (or UP Express) rail link. The comfortable trains leave every 15 minutes, have free wi-fi and power points and take just 25 minutes to get to Union Station.

One-way rides for adults are $12, or $9 with a **PRESTO card** (www.prestocard.ca) – highly recommended as the $6 rechargeable card pays for itself with a return trip to the airport and is useful for local transport in Toronto and on GO Transit.

BOAT

- From April to September, **Toronto Islands Ferries** (Map p78; 416-392-8193; www.city.toronto.on.ca; Bay St; adult/child return $7.50/3.65; S Union Station) runs every 15 to 30 minutes from 8am to 11pm.
- From October to March, ferry services are slashed (to roughly hourly), only servicing Ward's Island, plus a couple per day to Hanlan's Point.
- The journey (to either Ward's Island or Hanlan's Point) takes only 15 minutes, but queues can be long on weekends and holidays – show up early, or book online (secure.toronto.ca/FerryTicketOnline) to skip the purchase queue.
- The Toronto Islands Ferry Terminal is at the foot of Bay St, off Queens Quay.
- A few water taxis are also available from the terminal; they can take you anywhere for about $10 per person (pay onboard), and depart when full.

CAR & MOTORCYCLE

Parking in Toronto is expensive, usually $3 to $4 per half-hour. Private lots offer reduced rate parking before 7am and after 6pm. Traffic is horrendous amid ongoing construction. We don't recommend driving downtown. If you do, you must stop for streetcars – behind the rear doors, when the streetcar is collecting or ejecting passengers – and for pedestrians at crosswalks when signals are flashing. Look out for cyclists in your blind spots.

VIA RAIL TRAIN INFORMATION

DESTINATION	COST	DURATION	FREQUENCY
Kingston	$90	2½hr	frequent
London	$69	2hr	7 daily
Montréal	$109	5¼hr	6 daily
Niagara Falls	$24	2hr	seasonal, infrequent
Ottawa	$108	4½hr	8 daily
Sudbury Junction	$96	7hr	1 daily
Vancouver	from $725	83hr	3 weekly

Hwy 407 (www.407etr.com), running east–west from Markham to Mississauga, is an electronic toll road. It can be a wonderful alternative to the congested 401. Cameras record your license plate and the time and distance traveled. Expect a bill in the mail (Canada, US or Zanzibar, they'll find you).

PUBLIC TRANSPORTATION

➡ Subway lines operate regular service from around 6am (9am Sunday) until 1:30am daily. The two main lines are the crosstown Bloor–Danforth line, and the U-shaped Yonge–University–Spadina line. Stations are generally very safe and have Designated Waiting Areas (DWAs) monitored by security cameras.

➡ Streetcars are notoriously slow during rush hours, stopping frequently. The main routes run east–west along St Clair Ave and College, Dundas, Queen and King Sts. North–south streetcars grind along Bathurst St and Spadina Ave. TTC buses generally serve suburban areas. For more far-flung travel, the TTC system connects with GO Transit's network to surrounding areas like Richmond Hill, Brampton and Hamilton.

TAXI

Metered fares start at $4, plus $1.75 per kilometer, depending on traffic.

Crown Taxi (☎416-240-0000; www.crowntaxi.com)

Diamond Taxicab (☎416-366-6868; www.diamondtaxi.ca)

Royal Taxi (☎416-777-9222; www.royaltaxi.ca)

NIAGARA PENINSULA

Jutting east from Hamilton and forming a natural divide between Lake Erie and Lake Ontario, the Niagara Peninsula is a legitimate tourist hot spot. Though many see only the falls and Clifton Hill on a day tour from Toronto, there is lots to explore here. Consider a several-day visit to fully experience the delights of the peninsula.

Water flows from Lake Erie, 100m higher than Lake Ontario, via two avenues: stepping down steadily through the locks along the Welland Canal, or surging over Niagara Falls in a reckless, swollen torrent. A steep limestone escarpment (p119) jags along the spine of the peninsula, generating a unique microclimate. Humid and often frost free, this is prime terrain for viticulture: a fact not lost on the award-winning wineries of Niagara-on-the-Lake.

Niagara Falls

POP 83,000

An unstoppable flow of rushing water surges over the arcing fault in the riverbed with thunderous force. Great plumes of icy mist rise for hundreds of meters as the waters collide, like an ethereal veil concealing the vast rift behind the torrent. Thousands of onlookers delight in this spectacle every day, drawn by the force of the current and the hypnotic mist.

Otherwise, Niagara might not be what you expect: the town feels like a tacky outdated amusement park. It has been a saucy honeymoon destination ever since Napoleon's brother brought his bride here – tags like 'For newlyweds and nearly deads' and 'Viagra Falls' are apt. A crass morass of casinos, sleazy motels, tourist traps and strip joints line Clifton Hill and Lundy's Lane – a Little Las Vegas! Love it or loathe it, there's nowhere quite like it.

Sights & Activities

Parking access for sights and activities around the falls and Clifton Hill is expensive and limited.

The Falls & Around

Niagara Falls forms a natural rift between Ontario and New York State. On the US side, Bridal Veil Falls (p119) and the adjacent American Falls crash onto mammoth fallen rocks. On the Canadian side, the grander, more powerful **Horseshoe Falls** (Map p120) FREE plunge into the cloudy **Maid of the Mist Pool**. The prime falls-watching spot is Table Rock (p119), poised just meters from the drop – arrive early to beat the crowds.

Niagara is not the tallest of waterfalls (it ranks a lowly 50th) but in terms of sheer volume, there's nothing like it – more than a million bathtubs of water plummet downward every second. By day or night, regardless of the season, the falls never fail to awe: 12 million visitors annually can't be wrong. Even in winter, when the flow is partially hidden and the edges freeze solid, the watery extravaganza is undiminished. Very occasionally the falls stop altogether. This first happened on Easter Sunday morning in 1848, when ice completely jammed the flow.

Tickets for the four falls attractions listed below can be purchased separately, but the online 30% discounted **Niagara Falls Adventure Pass** (www.niagaraparks.com, adult/child $55/37) is better value. It includes a ride on Hornblower Niagara Cruises and admission to the Journey Behind the Falls (p123), White Water Walk and Niagara's Fury, plus two days transportation on the WEGO bus system. Passes are also available from the Niagara Parks Commission (p124) at Table Rock Information Centre and most attractions.

Hornblower Niagara Cruises BOATING
(www.niagaracruises.com; 5920 River Rd; adult/child $20/12.25; ⏲9am-7:45pm Jun-Aug, to 4:45pm Apr, May, Sep & Oct) Hornblower is the newer boat company in town, taking over from the age-old Maid of the Mist (which still runs on the American side of the falls). Hornblower's 700-person catamarans sail up close to **Bridal Veil Falls** (American Falls; Map p120) and Horseshoe Falls (p118), among other thundering cascades. You are supplied flimsy raincoats but will still get doused (in a fun way).

Departures are every 15 minutes, weather permitting. Sunrise and evening fireworks cruises are being added to the schedule, so check for updates.

White Water Walk WALKING
(Map p120; ☎905-374-1221; 4330 Niagara Pkwy; adult/child $12.25/8; ⏲9am-7:30pm) At the northern end of town, next to Whirlpool Bridge, the White Water Walk is another way to get up close and personal with the falls, this time via an elevator down to a 325m boardwalk suspended above the rampaging torrents, just downstream from the falls.

Table Rock VIEWPOINT
(Map p120) FREE The prime falls-watching spot is Table Rock, poised just meters from the drop of Horseshoe Falls, the main attraction of the Niagara Falls – arrive early to beat the crowds, but you're unlikely to wait longer than a few minutes to get to the front anyway.

Whirlpool Aero Car CABLE CAR
(Niagara Spanish Aero Car; ☎905-354-5711; 3850 Niagara Pkwy; adult/child $14.25/9.25; ⏲9am-8pm Mar-Nov) Dangling above the Niagara River, 4.5km north of Horseshoe Falls, the Whirlpool Aero Car was designed by Spanish engineer Leonardo Torres Quevedo and has been operating since 1916 (but don't worry – it's still in good shape). The gondola travels 550m between two outcrops above a deadly whirlpool created by the falls – count the logs and tires spinning in the eddies below. No wheelchair access.

Niagara's Fury SIMULATOR
(Map p120; ☎905-358-3268; 6650 Niagara Pkwy; adult/child $14.25/9.25; ⏲every 30min 10:30am-4pm) On the upper level of Table Rock, the falls' latest Universal Studios–style attraction takes you into an interactive 360-degree cinema-simulation of how the falls were created. Expect lots of high-tech tricks to suspend disbelief, including getting splashed, snow and a rapid drop in temperature. It feels aimed solely at kids.

Floral Showhouse GARDENS
(Map p120; ☎905-354-1721; www.niagaraparks.com; 7145 Niagara Pkwy; adult/child $5/3.75; ⏲9:30am-8pm) Around 1km south of Horseshoe Falls, the Showhouse offers year-round floral displays and some warm respite on a chilly day. Opposite, lodged on rocks in the rapids, the **Old Scow** is a rusty steel barge that's been waiting to be washed over the falls since 1918 – a teetering symbol of Western imperialism, perhaps?

JAGGED EDGES

The **Niagara Escarpment**, a 725km-long land formation that creates Niagara Falls, is a designated Unesco World Biosphere Reserve. Sweeping from eastern Wisconsin and along the shore of northern Lake Michigan, down through Lake Huron and across Manitoulin Island, slicing through Ontario and then curving under Lake Ontario and ending in New York State, the escarpment is a long spine of brush-covered stone. A combination of what was originally lime bed and ancient sea floor, the dolomitic limestone that makes up the land formation is more resistant than the land around it, which has eroded and left the bulge of limestone slithering around the Great Lakes: look for the cliffs near Hamilton, Milton, Lion's Head and Tobermory.

Great waterfalls are just one result of the escarpment. Together with Lake Ontario, the geological formation has created a microclimate perfect for viticulture. The soil (a combination of limestone and clay) and the warmth created by Lake Ontario generate growing conditions very similar to those of France's Burgundy region.

Niagara Falls

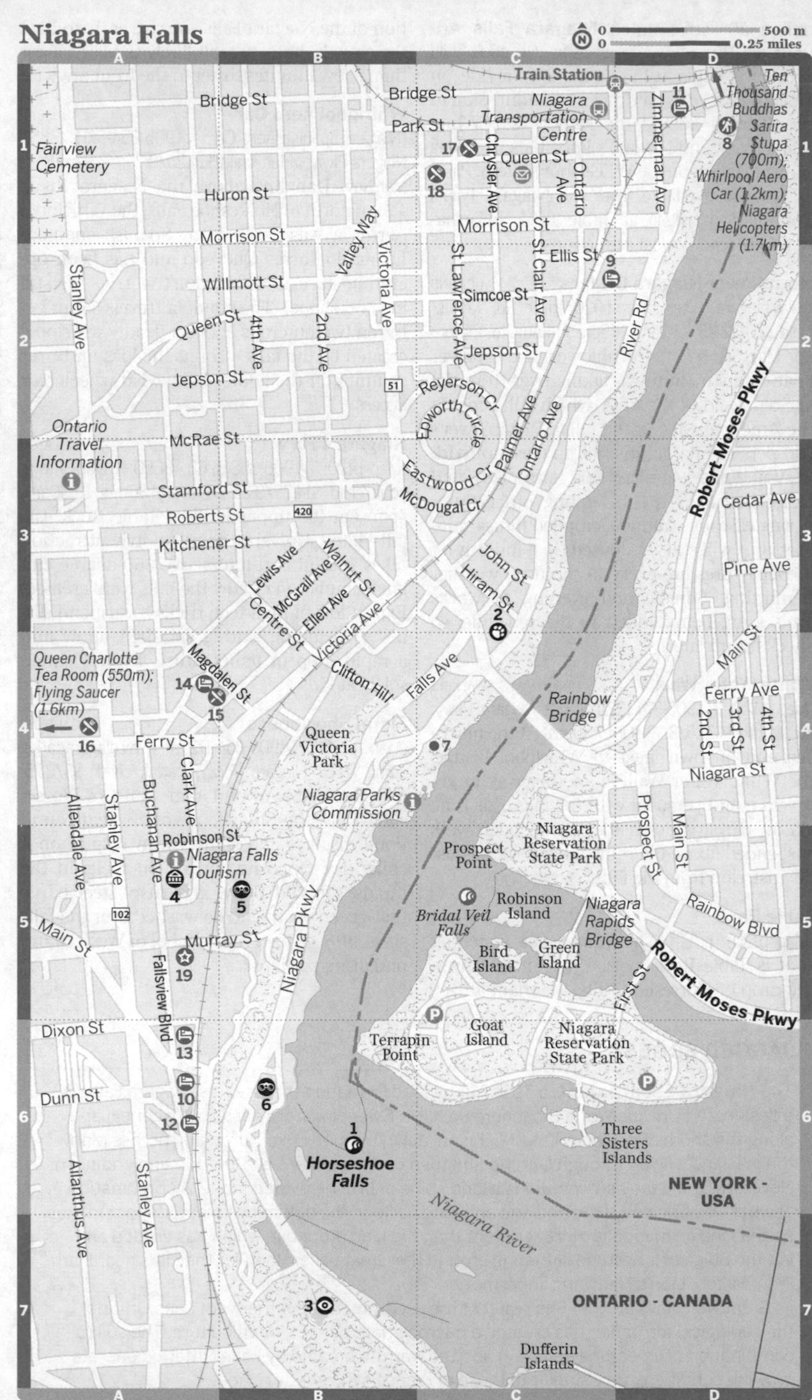

Niagara Falls

Top Sights
1 Horseshoe Falls...B6

Sights
2 Bird Kingdom...C3
3 Floral Showhouse...B7
4 IMAX Theatre & Daredevil Exhibit...A5
5 Skylon Tower...B5
6 Table Rock...B6

Activities, Courses & Tours
7 Double Deck Tours...C4
Journey Behind the Falls...(see 6)
Niagara's Fury...(see 6)
8 White Water Walk...D1

Sleeping
9 Always Inn Bed & Breakfast...C2
10 Embassy Suites...A6
11 Hostelling International Niagara Falls...D1
12 Marriott Niagara Falls...A6
13 Oakes Hotel...A6
14 Sterling Inn & Spa...A4

Eating
15 AG...A4
16 Napoli Ristorante Pizzeria...A4
17 Paris Crepes Cafe...C1
18 Taps on Queen Brewhouse & Grill...C1

Entertainment
19 Niagara Fallsview Casino...A5

Clifton Hill

Clifton Hill is a street name, but refers to a broader area near the falls occupied by a sensory bombardment of artificial enticements. You name it – House of Frankenstein, Louis Tussaud's Waxworks, Castle Dracula – they're all here. In most cases, paying the admission will leave you feeling like a sucker.

IMAX Theatre & Daredevil Exhibit MUSEUM
(Map p120; ☎905-358-3611; www.imaxniagara.com; 6170 Fallsview Blvd; Daredevil Gallery adult/child $8/6.50, movie prices vary; ⏱9am-9pm) The best reason to come here is for the Daredevil Exhibit attached to IMAX Niagara (which screens blockbusters and films about the falls; combo tickets are available). Scratch your head in amazement at the battered collection of barrels and padded bubbles in which people have ridden over the falls (see the boxed text, p125) – not all of them successfully. There's also a history of falls 'funambulism' (tightrope walking) here.

Bird Kingdom ZOO
(Map p120; ☎905-356-8888; www.birdkingdom.ca; 5651 River Rd; adult/child $17/12; ⏱9am-6:30pm; 👪) The jungly Bird Kingdom claims to be the world's largest indoor aviary, with 400 species of free-flying tropical birds from around the globe. You can also buddy-up with a boa constrictor in the Reptile Encounter Zone, and feed the birds. Discounted tickets on its website.

Ten Thousand Buddhas Sarira Stupa TEMPLE
(Cham Shan Temple; ☎905-371-2678; 4303 River Rd; ⏱9am-5pm, main temple Sat & Sun only) If the tourist bustle is messing with your yang, find some tranquillity at this out-of-context Buddhist temple. The modern building of Western construction is sterile. Visitors are welcome to wander the complex and view the various sculptures, bells and artworks.

Skylon Tower VIEWPOINT
(Map p120; ☎905-356-2651; www.skylon.com; 5200 Robinson St; adult/child $15/9; ⏱8am-10pm) The Skylon Tower is an ugly 158m spire with yellow elevators crawling like bugs up the exterior. The views from the indoor and outdoor observation decks are eye-poppers. There's also a revolving restaurant.

Around Niagara Falls

Niagara River Recreation Trail CYCLING
(www.niagaraparks.com) FREE The idyllic 3m-wide Niagara River Recreation Trail, for cycling, jogging and walking, runs parallel to the slow-roaming, leafy Niagara Pkwy. The trail can easily be divided into four chunks, each of which takes around two hours to pedal. The parkway meanders for 56km along the Niagara River, from Niagara-on-the-Lake past the falls all the way to Fort Erie.

Along the way you'll find parks, picnic areas and viewpoints. In season, fresh-fruit stands selling cold cherry cider adorn the side of the trail. Download a map online, or pick one up at a visitors center.

Niagara Glen Nature Reserve PARK
(☎905-371-0254; www.niagaraparks.com; Niagara Pkwy; ⏱dawn-dusk; P) About 8km north of the falls is this exceptional reserve, where you can get a sense of what the area was like pre-Europeans. There are 4km of walking

WELLAND CANAL AREA

Built between 1914 and 1932, the historic Welland Canal, running from Lake Erie into Lake Ontario, functions as a shipping bypass around Niagara Falls. It's part of the St Lawrence Seaway, allowing shipping between the industrial heart of North America and the Atlantic Ocean, with eight locks along the 42km-long canal overcoming the difference of about 100m in the lakes' water levels.

Before it shifted east to Port Weller, the original Welland Canal opened into Lake Ontario at Lakeside Park in Port Dalhousie. This rustic harbor area is a blend of old and new, with a reconstructed wooden lock and an 1835 lighthouse alongside bars, restaurants and ice-cream parlors.

Hikers and cyclists can stretch out along the 45km **Merritt Trail** (www.canadatrails.ca), an established track along the Welland Canal from Port Dalhousie to Port Colborne.

For an up-to-date look at the canal, the **Welland Canals Centre** (905-984-8880; www.stcatharineslock3museum.ca; 1932 Welland Canals Pkwy; 9am-5pm; P) FREE at Lock 3, just outside St Catharines, has a viewing platform close enough to almost let you touch the building-size ships as they wait for water levels to rise or fall. You can check the ships' schedules on the website and plan your visit accordingly. Also here is the **St Catharines Museum** (adult/child/concession $4.20/2.50/4), with displays on town history and canal construction, plus a lacrosse hall of fame.

Port Colborne, where Lake Erie empties into the canal, contains the 420m Lock 8 – one of the longest in the world. Check it out at **Lock 8 Park** (Mellanby St; 24hr), south of Main St.

trails winding down into a gorge, past huge boulders, cold caves, wildflowers and woods. The Niagara Parks Commission offers **guided nature walks** daily during the summer season for a nominal fee. Bring something to drink – the water in the Niagara River is far from clean.

Botanical Gardens and Butterfly Conservatory GARDENS

(905-356-8119; www.niagaraparks.com; 2565 Niagara Pkwy; butterfly conservatory adult/child $14.25/9.25, gardens free; 10am-4pm Mon-Fri, to 5pm Sat & Sun, 10am-7pm Jul & Aug; P) Entry to the 40 hectares of **Botanical Gardens** is free, but you'll need to pay to enter the **Butterfly Conservatory**, with its more than 50 species of butterflies (some as big as birds) flitting around 130 species of flowers and plants. This is also a breeding facility where you can see young butterflies released. Parking $5.

Queenston Heights Park HISTORIC SITE

(905-262-6759; www.niagaraparks.com; 14184 Niagara Pkwy, Queenston; dawn-dusk; P) FREE In Queenston village, a snoozy historic throwback north of the falls near the Lewiston Bridge to the US, is Queenston Heights Park, a national historic site. Here, the commanding **Brock Monument** honors Major General Sir Isaac Brock, 'Savior of Upper Canada.' Self-guided walking tours of the hillside recount the 1812 Battle of Queenston Heights and include a walk to the top for a magnificent view.

Mackenzie Printery & Newspaper Museum MUSEUM

(905-262-5676; www.mackenzieprintery.org; 1 Queenston St, Queenston; adult/child $6/4.75; 10am-5pm May-Sep; P) This ivy-covered museum was where the esteemed William Lyon Mackenzie once edited the hell-raising *Colonial Advocate*.

Tours

Double Deck Tours BUS

(Map p120; 905-374-7423; www.doubledecktours.com; cnr River Rd & Clifton Hill; tours adult/child from $80/52; 11am Apr-Oct) Offers a deluxe four-hour tour on a red double-decker bus. The price includes admission to the Whirlpool Aero Car (p119), Journey Behind the Falls and Hornblower Niagara Cruises (p119).

Niagara Helicopters SCENIC FLIGHTS

(905-357-5672; www.niagarahelicopters.com; 3731 Victoria Ave; 9min flights adult/child $140/87; 9am-sunset, weather permitting) A fantastic falls encounter, but pricey and not the most environmentally sensitive option.

Journey Behind the Falls WALKING

(Map p120; ☎905-354-1551; www.niagarafallstourism.com; 6650 Niagara Pkwy; adult/child Apr-Dec $16.75/10.95, Jan-Mar $11.25/7.30; ⏰9am-10pm) From Table Rock Information Centre you can don a very unsexy plastic poncho and traverse rock-cut tunnels halfway down the cliff – as close as you can get to the falls without hopping in a barrel. It's open year-round, but be prepared to queue. In winter, the lower deck is usually closed; hence the lower price.

Festivals & Events

Winter Festival of Lights LIGHT SHOW

(☎905-374-1616; www.wfol.com; ⏰late Nov–mid-Jan) A season of events from late November to mid-January, including more than 125 animated displays and 3 million tree and ground lights, the undisputed highlight of which is an over-the-top nocturnal light display along a 36km route. There are also concerts, fun runs and a cheerleading championship.

Sleeping

There are usually more beds than heads in Niagara Falls, but the town is sometimes completely booked up. Prices spike in summer, on weekends and during holidays. Cheap motels line Lundy's Lane. If you are coming from Toronto just for the falls, it really isn't necessary to stay overnight; a day trip is plenty.

Hostelling International Niagara Falls HOSTEL $

(Map p120; ☎905-357-0770; www.hostellingniagara.com; 4549 Cataract Ave; dm/d incl linen from $29/84; P ⊖ @ ☎) Quietly adrift in the old town, this homey, multicolored hostel sleeps around 90 people. The facilities, including a sizable kitchen, pool table, lockers and cool basement lounge, are in good shape; staff are friendly and ecofocused. It's close to the train and bus stations, and you can rent bicycles for $15 per day.

Always Inn Bed & Breakfast B&B $$

(Map p120; ☎905-371-0840; 4327 Simcoe St; d incl breakfast $130-180; P @ ☎) An old Victorian house with a spic-and-span interior is a pleasant surprise in these parts. The substantial communal breakfast is another. It's a pleasant 20-minute walk south along the Niagara Pkwy to the falls.

Niagara Parkway Court MOTEL $$

(☎905-295-3331; www.niagaraparkwaycourt.com; 3708 Main St; d incl breakfast from $109; P ❄ ☎) Elegant rooms in a variety of styles renovated twice in recent years, excellent customer service, flat-screens and transport to the falls from its pleasant spot just outside of town make this motel a great choice for lower-cost accommodations.

BRUCE TRAIL

For 800km the **Bruce Trail** (www.brucetrail.org) winds along the top of the Niagara Escarpment, from the Niagara Peninsula to the Bruce Peninsula. This wide, well-maintained path is excellent for hiking during summer months, while those armed with cross-country skis take it through its winter paces. Day hikes along the trail are an appealing way to spend a sunny afternoon.

Opened in 1967, it's the oldest hiking trail in Canada and the longest in Ontario. The trail winds through public and private land, as well as along roadways. Wander past wineries, farmlands and forests and marvel at Georgian Bay's shimmering azure from the escarpment's white cliffs. A multitude of campgrounds en route have budget accommodations for those on longer trips and trail towns offer B&Bs galore.

Embassy Suites HOTEL $$

(Map p120; ☎800-420-6980; www.embassysuitesniagara.com; 6700 Fallsview Blvd; ste from $195) This mammoth all-suite hotel by Hilton has a great position that makes you feel like you're almost on top of the Canadian falls. For that reason, its generic rooms get a lot of use. That said, they're spacious and a variety of suite types are available: most have great views. Breakfast and a welcome drink are included.

Sterling Inn & Spa BOUTIQUE HOTEL $$

(Map p120; ☎289-292-0000; www.sterlingniagara.com; 5195 Magdalen St; r from $135; ☎) The stylish rooms of this affordable boutique hotel (with either a Jacuzzi or steam shower) beckon you to relax and unwind with someone special, even if that someone is yourself. Quality furnishings, amenities and breakfast-in-bed baskets are the kind of touches to expect.

The on-site AG restaurant (p124) is fancy and delicious and there's a full-service treatment spa. Perfect for couples. Note that it is a low-rise property a little distance from the falls: no views.

Marriott Niagara Falls HOTEL $$
(Map p120; 888-501-8916; www.niagarafalls-marriott.com; 6740 Fallsview Blvd; r from $149) This sprawling giant is so close that you could almost touch the falls. A variety of room types are available, but many love the two-level loft suites with Jacuzzi, fireplace and awesome views from the floor-to-ceiling windows.

Oakes Hotel HOTEL $$
(Map p120; 905-356-4514; www.oakeshotel.com; 6546 Fallsview Blvd; d/ste from $109/159; P) A jaunty silver spire next to the Fallsview Casino, the Oakes has front-row-center views of the great cascades. Not all rooms have falls views; try for a terrace room if you can, though you'll likely pay extra. Suites have Jacuzzis and fireplaces.

Eating

The old downtown section of town has seen many failed revival attempts but it's worth checking out for new restaurants, if the other options aren't appealing. Fast food (and dressed-up, overpriced fast food) is abundant in the touristy strip, but the best eats can be found a little further afield. For cuisine a cut above, you're better off heading up the road to Niagara-on-the-Lake.

Flying Saucer FAST FOOD $
(905-356-4453; www.flyingsaucerrestaurant.com; 6768 Lundy's Lane; mains $8-27; 6am-3am Sun-Thu, to 4am Fri & Sat) For extraterrestrial fast food, you can't go past this iconic diner on the Lundy's Lane motel strip. Famous $1.99 early-bird breakfasts are served from 6am to 10am (eggs, fries and toast) with the purchase of a beverage. Heftier meals in the way of steaks, seafood, fajitas, burgers and hot dogs are also on board.

Queen Charlotte Tea Room BRITISH $
(905-371-1350; www.queencharlottetearoom.com; 5689 Main St; light meals $7-14, high tea $22; 9am-7pm Tue-Fri, 10am-7pm Sat & Sun) Expats craving a decent cuppa, cucumber sandwiches, steak and kidney or fish and chips with mushy peas should head straight to this quaint establishment on Main St, near the intersection with Lundy's Lane, for a spot of tiffin!

Napoli Ristorante Pizzeria ITALIAN $$
(Map p120; 905-356-3345; www.napoliristorante.ca; 5545 Ferry St; mains $14-32; 4-10:30pm) Head to Napoli for the best Italian in town, hands down. Delicious pizza, rich pasta, creamy risotto and veal parmigiana all feature on the familiar menu.

Taps on Queen Brewhouse & Grill INTERNATIONAL $$
(Map p120; www.tapsbeer.com; 4680 Queen St; mains $9-14; noon-10pm Mon, Tue & Sun, to midnight Wed-Sat;) Does a mix of stuff, from shepherd's pie to ancient grains curry (quinoa, couscous, adzuki beans, mung beans and veggies). All dishes are, naturally, best when paired with one of the brewery's tasty beers.

Paris Crepes Cafe FRENCH $$
(Map p120; 289-296-4218; www.pariscrepescafe.com; 4613 Queen St; mains $12-30; 10am-10pm Mon-Fri, 9am-10pm Sat & Sun) In the revitalized area of Queen St you'll find this quaint crêperie, a very long way from the streets of Paris: you can't miss the dark-red building. Sweet and savory crepe sensations are served among other continental delights from the wonderfully authentic Parisian menu.

AG CANADIAN $$$
(Map p120; 289-292-0005; www.agcuisine.com; 5195 Magdalen St; mains $18-36; 6-10:30pm Tue-Sun) Fine dining isn't something you find easily at the falls, which makes this fine restaurant at the Sterling Inn & Spa (p123) so refreshing. Service, decor, presentation and especially the quality of the food all rate highly. It has a seasonal menu featuring dishes like fennel pollen pickerel, roasted venison loin and crispy skinned trout, sourced locally.

Entertainment

Niagara Fallsview Casino CASINO
(Map p120; 905-371-7569; www.fallsviewcasinoresort.com; 6380 Fallsview Blvd; 24hr) This casino never closes. The building itself is worth a look – an amazing complex of commerce and crapshoots, with a fantastical fountain in the lobby. Corny old-timers like Kenny Rogers and Donny Osmond are regularly wheeled out to perform.

Information

Greater Niagara General Hospital (905-378-4647; www.niagarahealth.on.ca; 5546 Portage Rd; 24hr) Emergency room.

Ontario Travel Information (Map p120; 905-358-3221; www.ontariotravel.net; 5355 Stanley Ave; 8am-8pm) On the western outskirts of town; free tourist booklets containing maps and discount coupons.

Post Office (Map p120; www.canadapost.ca; 4500 Queen St; 8am-5pm Mon-Fri)

Niagara Parks Commission (Map p120; 905-371-0254; www.niagaraparks.com; 9am-11pm Jun-Aug) The falls' governing body.

DAREDEVILS

Surprisingly, more than a few people who have gone over Niagara Falls have actually lived to tell the tale. The first successful leap was in 1901, by a 63-year-old schoolteacher named Annie Taylor, who did it in a skirt, no less. This promoted a rash of barrel stunters that continued into the 1920s, including Bobby Leach, who survived the drop but met his untimely death after slipping on an orange peel and developing gangrene!

In 1984 Karl Soucek revived the tradition in a bright-red barrel. He made it, only to die six months later in another barrel stunt in Houston. Also during the 1980s two locals successfully took the plunge lying head to head in the same barrel.

A US citizen who tried to jet ski over the falls in 1995 might have made it – if his rocket-propelled parachute had opened. Another American, Kirk Jones, survived the trip over the falls unaided in 2003. After being charged by Canadian police with illegally performing a stunt, he joined the circus.

Only one accidental falls-faller has survived – a seven-year-old Tennessee boy who fell out of a boat upstream in 1960 and survived the drop without even breaking a bone.

Take the virtual plunge at **IMAX Niagara** (p121), and check out the over-the-falls barrels folks have used at the Daredevil Exhibit.

In addition to this office at Maid of the Mist Plaza, there's another at Table Rock Information Centre.

Niagara Falls Public Library (☎905-356-8080; www.nflibrary.ca; 4848 Victoria Ave; ⏲9am-8pm Mon & Tue, to 5:30pm Wed-Sat; 📶) Free internet and wi-fi access.

Niagara Falls Tourism (Map p120; ☎905-356-6061; www.niagarafallstourism.com; 5400 Robinson St; ⏲9am-5pm) On the Canadian side of the falls with information on the different neighborhoods and what's on. This office is located near the base of the Skylon Tower observation deck.

Getting There & Away

Niagara Falls is well serviced by buses from both Canada and the US. Parking is a nightmare, so leave the car behind.

BUS

➡ The **Niagara Transportation Centre** (Map p120; ☎905-357-2133; 4555 Erie Ave) is in the old part of town. Greyhound Canada buses depart for Toronto ($19, 1½ to two hours, five daily) and Buffalo, NY ($12, one to 1½ hours, six daily). GO Transit also operates services from Toronto (via Burlington) by combination of rail and bus and, in recent years, direct rail services on weekends (June to September). Check with www.gotransit.com.

➡ **Niagara Airbus** (☎905-374-8111; www.niagaraairbus.com) operates a door-to-door shared shuttle service between Niagara Falls and Toronto Pearson International Airport (one way/return $94/147, 1½ hours) or Buffalo International airport, NY ($95/156, 1½ hours).

➡ The **Fallsview Casino Resort** (p124) runs the **Safeway Tours** bus hourly from Toronto, making stops from Gerrard St E, to Carlton St and then Spadina Ave, finally arriving at the casino. Noncasino members pay the $20 return price on arrival, making it one of the cheapest ways to get to the falls, though no luggage is permitted and adult ID is required as it is a casino bus. Just turn up, or reserve on the website (safewaytours.net/casino-tours) as it can fill up.

TRAIN

Rail services from **Niagara Falls Train Station** (☎888-842-7245; www.viarail.ca; 4267 Bridge St) to Toronto operate only as a weekend summer service operated by GO Transit. You can, however, get to New York City ($151, 11½ hours, once daily).

Getting Around

BICYCLE

The Niagara region is perfect for cycling. The excellent **Zoom Leisure Bicycle Rentals** (☎866-811-6993; www.zoomleisure.com; 3850 River Rd, Niagara Falls) has offices in Niagara Falls and on the Niagara Pkwy, and will deliver to anywhere in the Niagara region. Riding from Niagara Falls to Niagara-on-the-Lake is a not-so-leisurely 90 minutes from the Niagara Falls Pkwy office. Excellent bike tours are also available.

CAR & MOTORCYCLE

Driving and parking around the center is an expensive headache. Park at the car park near the IMAX at the corner of Fallsview Blvd and Robinson St for just $5 for the whole day and walk, or follow the parking district signs and stash the car for the day (around $6 per 30 minutes, or $15 per day). The huge Rapidsview parking lot (also the WEGO depot) is 3km south of the falls off River Rd. See the website for all the locations: www.niagarafallstourism.com/plan/parking.

FORT ERIE

East of Port Colborne and south of Niagara Falls is the town of **Fort Erie** (☎905-871-0540; www.oldforterie.com; 350 Lakeshore Rd; adult/child $12.25/7.95; ⏰10am-5pm May-Nov; P), where the Niagara River leaks out of Lake Erie. Across from Buffalo, NY, it's connected to the US by the Peace Bridge. The main drawcard here is the historic, star-shaped Fort Erie, a key player in the War of 1812, and 'Canada's bloodiest battlefield.' Also known as the Old Stone Fort, it was first built in 1764. The US seized it in 1814 before retreating.

Inside there's a museum and immaculate, uniformed soldiers performing authentic military drills. Take the worthwhile guided tour (every 30 minutes) included in the admission fee.

PUBLIC TRANSPORTATION

➡ Cranking up and down the steep 50m slope between the falls and Fallsview Blvd is a quaint **Incline Railway** (www.niagaraparks.com; 6635 Niagara Pkwy; one way $2.75, day passes $7). It saves you a 10- to 20-minute walk around, and is best taken uphill.

➡ Formerly the seasonal Niagara Parks People Mover, **WEGO** (www.niagaraparks.com/wego; day passes adult/child $7.50/4.50) is an economical and efficient year-round transit system, geared for tourists. There are three lines: red, green and blue; between them, they've got all the major sights and accommodations covered. For areas further afield, locals use **Niagara Transit** (☎905-356-7521; www.niagarafalls.ca; one-way adult/student $2.75/2.50, day passes $7), though most have their own cars.

WALKING

Put on your sneakers and get t'steppin' – walking is the way to go! You'll only need wheels to visit outlying sights along the Niagara Pkwy or if you're staying on Lundy's Lane. There is very little shade along the falls vantage points.

Niagara Peninsula Wine Country

The Niagara Peninsula adheres to the 43rd parallel: a similar latitude as northern California and further south than Bordeaux, France. A primo vino location, the mineral-rich soils and a moderate microclimate are the perfect recipe for viticulture success. A visit to the area makes an indulgent day trip or lazy weekend, with haughty old vineyards and brash newcomers competing for your attention.

Touring the vineyards by car is the best way to go. There are two main areas to focus on: west of St Catharines around Vineland, and north of the Queen Elizabeth Way (QEW) around Niagara-on-the-Lake. Regional tourist offices stock wine-route maps and brochures, which are also available at winery tasting rooms.

Tours

Crush on Niagara WINE
(☎905-562-3373; www.crushtours.com; tours $90-120) Small-group morning and afternoon van tours departing from various pickup points in the Niagara region.

Niagara Airbus WINE
(☎905-374-8111; www.niagaraairbus.com; tours from Niagara Falls $49-129, from Toronto $129-190) Stops at well-known wineries; some itineraries include vineyard tours, lunch and shopping in Niagara-on-the-Lake.

Festivals & Events

There are three wine-related festivals (☎905-688-0212, www.niagarawinefestival.com) throughout the year: **Niagara New Vintage Festival**, celebrating Niagara's new-season vino and regional cuisine in late June; the main event, **Niagara Wine Festival**, a week-long event in mid-September celebrating the region's finest picks off the vine; and **Niagara Icewine Festival**, a 10-day winter festival held throughout the Niagara region during mid-January and showcasing Ontario's stickiest, sweetest ice wines.

Sleeping

Squirrel House Gardens B&B $$
(☎905-685-1608; www.squirrelhouseniagara.ca; 1819 5th St, St Catharines; ste incl breakfast $180; P ⊖ @ ≋) Stay in a massive suite in the old barn, built in 1850 as part of this country estate. Lovingly decorated, the room opens onto a massive garden and features brick and colored cement floors, original wood beams, and French doors that open onto a deck. The grounds have a swimming pool, patio and fire pit.

The delightful, arty owners are welcoming and friendly, and take as good care of you as they do of their impressive country garden.

Bonnybank B&B $$
(905-562-3746; www.bonnybank.ca; RR 1, Vineland Station; r incl breakfast $125-154; P) A stately Tudor-meets-Grimsby-sandstone house in an owl-filled wilderness setting. It's a little off the beaten track.

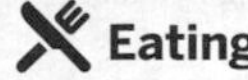

Eating

Pie Plate BAKERY $
(905-468-9743; www.thepieplate.com; 41516 Niagara Stone Rd, Virgil; sandwiches $7-11; 10am-6pm Tue-Sun) Simple, delicious lunches (it's easy to devour the pear and brie sandwich) at reasonable prices. It wouldn't be an Ontario bakery without butter tarts, but there are also thin-crust pizzas, meat pies, salads and a few beers on tap. A great place to fill up your belly while touring the wine country.

Peach Country Farm Market MARKET $
(905-562-5602; 4490 Victoria Ave, Vineland Station; items from $2; 9am-8pm Jun-Aug, to 6pm Sep & Oct) An open-fronted barn selling fresh fruit, jams, ice cream and fruit pies, all grown, picked and baked on-site by fourth-generation farmers – a roadside gem!

Peninsula Ridge FUSION $$$
(905-563-0900; peninsularidge.com; 5600 King St W, Beamsville; mains $24-34; noon-2:30pm & 5-9pm Wed-Sat, 11:30am-2:30pm Sun) Sit outside, upstairs or down in this high-Victorian 1885 manor at the **winery** (905-563-0900; peninsularidge.com; 5600 King St W, Beamsville; tours $5; 10am-5pm) of the same name, serving haute cuisine paired with local wines...of course.

Getting There & Away

The 100km drive from Toronto to the central peninsula takes around 1½ hours – take Hwy 403 then the QEW east from Hamilton toward Niagara Falls. The official Wine Route is signposted off the QEW, on rural highways and along backcountry roads.

Niagara-on-the-Lake

One of the best-preserved 19th-century towns in North America, affluent N-o-t-L is an undeniably gorgeous place, with tree-lined streets, lush parks and impeccably restored houses. Originally a neutral First Nations village, the town was founded by Loyalists from New York State after the American Revolution and later became the first capital of the colony of Upper Canada. Today, tour-bus stampedes overrun the streets, puffing Cuban cigars and dampening the charm; the town fountain is full of coins but there are no homeless people here to plunder it. Is this a *real* town, or just gingerbread? Is there a soul beneath the surface? Yes, after 5pm.

Lovely Queen St teems with shops of the ye olde variety selling antiques, Brit-style souvenirs and homemade fudge.

Sights

Lincoln & Welland Regimental Museum MUSEUM
(905-468-0888; www.lwmuseum.ca; cnr King & John Sts; adult/child $3/2; 10am-4pm Wed-Sun; P) Wonderfully aged displays of Canadian military regalia.

ICE, ICE BABY

Niagara's regional wineries burst onto the scene at Vinexpo 1991 in Bordeaux, France. In a blind taste test, judges awarded a coveted gold medal to an Ontario ice wine – international attendees' jaws hit the floor! These specialty vintages, with their arduous harvesting and sweet, multidimensional palate, continue to lure aficionados to the Niagara Peninsula.

To make ice wine, a certain percentage of grapes are left on the vines after the regular harvest is over. If birds, storms and mildew don't get to them, the grapes grow ever-more sugary and concentrated. Winemakers wait patiently until December or January when three days of consistent, low temperature (-8°C) freeze the grapes entirely.

In the predawn darkness (so the sun doesn't melt the ice and dilute the grape juice), the grapes are carefully harvested by hand, then pressed and aged in barrels for up to a year. After decanting, the smooth ice vintages taste intensely of apples, or even more exotic fruit, and pack a serious alcoholic punch.

Why are ice wines so expensive? It takes 10 times the usual number of grapes to make just one bottle. This, combined with labor-intensive production and the high risk of crop failure, often drives the price above $50 per 375mL bottle. Late-harvest wines picked earlier in the year may be less costly (and less sweet), but just as full-flavored and aromatic.

WINERY DRIVING TOUR

The following drive weaves through the best Niagara wineries. Besides tastings, most offer tours and dining. Parking is free at all vineyards.

Coming from Toronto, take Queen Elizabeth Way (QEW) exit 78 at Fifty Rd into Winona and **Puddicombe Estate Farms & Winery** (p132), a rustic farm specializing in fruit wines. Light lunches available.

Off QEW exit 74 is **Kittling Ridge Winery** (☎905-945-9225; www.kittlingridge.com; 297 South Service Rd, Grimsby; tastings & tours free; ⏲10am-6pm Mon-Sat, 11am-5pm Sun). It looks like a factory, but friendly staff and award-winning ice- and late-harvest wines will win you over.

Continue southeast on Main St W to King St; photogenic **Peninsula Ridge Estates Winery** (p127) is unmissable on a hilltop. The lofty timber tasting room, restaurant and hilltop setting are magic.

Turn right at Cherry Ave, about 10km further down the road, go up the hill, then turn left onto Moyer Rd for the stone buildings of **Vineland Estates Winery** (☎905-562-7088; www.vineland.com; 3620 Moyer Rd, Vineland; tours with tasting $12, with purchase $7; ⏲10am-6pm), the elder statesperson of Niagara viticulture. Almost all the wines here are excellent. The restaurant and accommodations are fabulous too.

Backtrack up to King St, to the intersection of King and Cherry, where you'll find a beloved hockey star's winery, **Wayne Gretzky Estate** (www.gretzkyestateswines.com; 3751 King St, Vineland; ⏲10am-8pm Mon-Sat, 11am-6pm Sun).

Follow King Rd east, turn right onto Victoria Ave, then left onto 7th Ave for friendly **Flat Rock Cellars** (☎905-562-8994; www.flatrockcellars.com; 2727 7th Ave, Jordan; tours with tasting $5-15; ⏲10am-5pm Mon-Sat, from 11am Sun). The hexagonal architecture and lake views here are almost as good as the wine.

Wander back toward the lake to 4th Ave and cheery **Creekside Estate Winery** (☎905-562-0035; www.creeksidewine.com; 2170 4th Ave, Jordan Station; tours free; ⏲10am-6pm), where you can tour the crush pad and underground cellars (book online).

From 7th Ave, scoot back onto the QEW and truck east into the Niagara-on-the-Lake region. Take exit 38 and head north onto Four Mile Creek Rd, which will take you to **Trius Winery at Hillebrand** (☎800-582-8412; www.hillebrand.com; 1249 Niagara Stone Rd; tastings $5-10; ⏲10am-9pm). Mass-market wines are the name of the game here. Hourly introductory tours and tasting-bar presentations are great for newcomers to the wine scene.

Further north, superiority emanates from elite **Konzelmann Estate Winery** (☎905-935-2866; www.konzelmann.ca; 1096 Lakeshore Rd; tours $5-15; ⏲10am-6pm, tours May-Sep), one of the oldest wineries in the region and the only one to take full advantage of the lakeside microclimate. Late-harvest vidal and ice wines are superb.

Next on the right is **Strewn** (p129), producing medal-winning vintages and home to a classy restaurant, and **Wine Country Cooking School** (p129), where one-day, weekend and week-long classes are a gastronomic delight.

Closer to Niagara-on-the-Lake, **Sunnybrook Farm Estate Winery** (☎905-468-1122; www.sunnybrookwine.com; 1425 Lakeshore Rd; tastings $1-3; ⏲10am-6pm) specializes in unique Niagara fruit and berry wines, and brews a mean 'hard' cider. It's only a little place, so tour buses usually don't stop here.

Stratus (☎905-468-1806; www.stratuswines.com; 2059 Niagara Stone Rd; ⏲11am-5pm), on Niagara Stone Rd, south of Niagara-on-the-Lake, was the first building in Canada to earn LEED (Leadership in Energy & Environmental Design) certification. The design addresses complex recycling, organic, energy-efficient and indigenous concerns.

Heading south down the Niagara Pkwy you'll find **Reif Estate Winery** (☎905-468-7738; www.reifwinery.com; 15608 Niagara Pkwy; tours $5-20; ⏲9am-6pm), pronounced 'Rife,' a well-established winery. Ice wines are what you're here for.

Complete your tour (if you're still standing) at **Inniskillin** (☎888-466-4754; www.inniskillin.com; 1499 Line 3, cnr Niagara Pkwy; tastings $1-20, tours $5-15; ⏲9am-6pm, tours hourly May-Oct), master of the ice-wine craft.

Niagara Historical Society Museum MUSEUM
(☎905-468-3912; www.niagarahistorical.museum; 43 Castlereagh St; adult/child $5/1; ⏰10am-5pm; P) A vast collection relating to the town's past, ranging from First Nations artifacts to Loyalist and War of 1812 collectibles (including the prized hat of Major General Sir Isaac Brock). South of Simcoe Park.

Fort George HISTORIC SITE
(☎905-468-6614; www.pc.gc.ca/fortgeorge; 51 Queens Pde; adult/child $11.70/5.80; ⏰10am-5pm May-Oct, Sat & Sun only Apr & Nov; P) On the town's southeastern fringe, restored Fort George dates from 1797. The fort saw some bloody battles during the War of 1812, changing hands between British and US forces a couple of times. Within the spiked battlements are officers' quarters, a working kitchen, a powder magazine and storage houses. Ghost tours, skills demonstrations, retro tank displays and battle re-enactments occur throughout the summer. Parking costs $6, but this is reimbursed with your ticket.

Tours

Grape Escape Wine Tours WINE
(☎866-935-4445; www.tourniagarawineries.com; tours $54-139) A range of wine-flavored regional tours, by bike, van or SUV. Tours include some kind of meal (cheese platters on cheaper tours through to full gourmet dinners). There's free hotel pickup/drop-off.

Niagara Wine Tours International FOOD & DRINK
(☎905-468-1300; www.niagaraworldwinetours.com; 443 Butler St; tours $65-165) Various bicycle and gourmet lunch and dinner tours around local wineries, including tastings.

Whirpool Jet Boat Tours BOATING
(☎905-468-4800; www.whirlpooljet.com; 61 Melville St; 45min tours adult/child $61/51; ⏰Apr-Oct) A wet and wild ride, full of fishtails and splashy stops – bring a change of clothes (and maybe underwear). Reservations required.

Wine Country Cooking School COOKING
(☎905-468-8304; www.winecountrycooking.com; 1339 Lakeshore Rd) The Wine Country Cooking School has one-day, weekend and week-long classes, which are all a gastronomic delight. They are held at the classy restaurant at **Strewn** (☎905-468-1229; www.strewnwinery.com; 1339 Lakeshore Rd; tours free; ⏰10am-6pm, tours 1:30pm), a winery that produces medal-winning vintages.

Festivals & Events

Fabulicious FOOD & DRINK
(www.niagaraonthelake.com) The Fabulicious food festival, held one week in late February or early March, highlights the food of the region with excellent-value lunch and dinner menus in a dozen restaurants or so.

Shaw Festival THEATER
(☎905-468-2172; www.shawfest.com; 10 Queens Pde; ⏰Apr-Oct, box office 10am-8pm) In 1962 a lawyer and passionate dramatist, Brian Doherty, led a group of residents in eight performances of George Bernard Shaw's *Candida* and 'Don Juan in Hell' from *Man and Superman*. Doherty's passionate first season blossomed into today's much-esteemed Shaw Festival. For 45 years the festival has lured global audiences, who haven't been shy about issuing praise.

Sleeping

Although there are over 300 B&Bs in town, accommodations are expensive and often booked out. When the Shaw Festival is running, lodging is even tighter. Plan ahead.

★**Historic Davy House B&B Inn** B&B $$
(☎888-314-9046; www.davyhouse.com; 230 Davy St; d incl breakfast $155-204; P 📶) This reasonably priced Historically Designated (for Canadian sites of historic significance) home built in 1842 has been beautifully restored to maintain its colonial charm and is meticulously maintained by expert hosts who've been in the hospitality biz for over 30 years. Guests are invited to enjoy the lush, landscaped grounds and rustic guest parlor. It's an excellent choice for comfortable, restful and authentic accommodations in this B&B-saturated area.

Charles Hotel HOTEL $$
(☎905-468-4588; www.niagarasfinest.com/charles; 209 Queen St; d incl breakfast from $195) This lovable romantic little hotel (c 1832) is by a golf course. Rooms of varying sizes are sumptuously decorated to a diverse range of styles.

White Oaks Resort & Spa HOTEL $$
(☎800-263-5766; www.whiteoaksresort.com; 234 Taylor Rd SS4; d from $159) This sprawling 220-room resort just off the QEW, 15km from Niagara-on-the-Lake, offers well-appointed rooms and resort-style service and facilities: there's a full-service spa and on-site restaurant. A variety of stay packages are available.

Britaly B&B B&B $$
(☎905-468-8778; www.britaly.com; 57 The Promenade; r incl breakfast $140-160; P ❄ ☎) This simple three-room B&B (choose from the English, Italian or Canadiana rooms) is extremely popular for its reasonable rates and wonderful hosts who maintain their lovely home and gardens to the highest standard.

Moffat INN $$
(☎905-468-4116; www.vintage-hotels.com/moffat; 60 Picton St; d from $189; ❄) Green trim and flower boxes lend an Irish pub feel to the outside of the Moffat, which bills itself as 'cottage chic.' Twenty-four rooms are tastefully decorated, and you'll probably find the word *charming* pop out of your mouth more than once while visiting.

Prince of Wales Hotel HOTEL $$$
(☎905-468-3246; www.vintage-hotels.com; 6 Picton St; d/ste from $299/439; P ❄ @) Prince of N-o-t-L, an elegant Victorian hotel, was knocked into shape around 1864 and retains much of its period primp: vaulted ceilings, timber-inlay floors, red-waistcoated bellhops. Frills and floral prints seem angled toward the elderly and honeymooners, but it's the perfect spot for anyone looking to splash out.

Eating

1875 Restaurant CANADIAN $$
(☎905-468-3424; www.notlgolf.com/restauranthome; 143 Front St; mains $11-28; ⊙8am-10pm) The restaurant at North America's oldest golf course was one of N-o-t-L's best-kept secrets, but no longer: its prime waterfront patio is incomparable, the vibe casual (for N-o-t-L) and service, friendly. The menu is refreshingly familiar: elevated crab cakes and fish and chips. Come for brunch, lunch, dinner or a drink and be pleasantly surprised.

Irish Harp Pub PUB FOOD $$
(☎905-468-4443; www.theirishharppub.com; 245 King St; mains $12-20; ⊙noon-11pm Mon-Thu, 11am-11pm Fri-Sun) Loved by locals throughout the Niagara region for its hearty pub meals (think Irish hot pot and steak and Guinness pie), some come just for the Irish 'craic' (fun and conversation) and of course, beer! There's Guinness on tap and Irish Harp lager, brewed locally from a traditional recipe. All told, plenty to wet your whistle and fill your tum.

Epicurean CAFE $$
(☎905-468-3408; 84 Queen St; mains $12-29; ⊙9am-9pm Wed-Sat, to 5:30pm Sun-Tue) By day this fare-thee-well cafeteria dishes up fresh, tasty sandwiches, salads, pies and quiches. The ambience ramps up at night with a bistro menu offering the likes of crispy-skin chicken with steamed rice, scallions and shiitake mushrooms in Thai coconut curry. The streetside patio is always full in warmer months.

Escabèche FUSION $$$
(☎905-468-3246; www.vintage-hotels.com; 6 Picton St; mains $27-48; ⊙7am-9pm) The fine-dining room at the opulent Prince of Wales Hotel takes its food seriously. The contemporary menu offers taste inventions like a tart of locally cured prosciutto, cacciatore sausage, tomato and mascarpone, followed by roast lamb with fine mustard, fingerling potatoes and baby amber turnips in ice-wine-braised shank jus. Leave room for dessert (you've been warned).

Information

Chamber of Commerce Visitors Information Centre (☎905-468-1950; www.niagaraonthelake.com; 26 Queen St; ⊙10am-7:30pm) A brochure-filled info center; staff can book accommodations for a $5 fee. Pick up the *Niagara-on-the-Lake Official Visitors' Guide* for maps and a self-guided walking tour.

Getting There & Away

Bus There are no direct buses between Toronto and Niagara-on-the-Lake, so head for St Catharines or Niagara Falls and then transfer.

Central Taxi (☎905-358-3232; www.centralniagara.com) shunts folks between Niagara Falls and Niagara-on-the-Lake. Call for pickup locations and times. A regular one-way taxi between the two towns costs around $48.

Cycling An ace way to explore the area. Rent a bike from (or have one delivered to you by) traveler-recommended **Zoom Leisure Bicycle Rentals** (☎905-468-2366; www.zoomleisure.com; 431 Mississagua St; rental per half-day/day/2 days $20/30/50; ⊙9am-7pm). Free delivery. Riding from Niagara Falls to Niagara-on-the-Lake is a lengthy 90 minutes from the Niagara Falls Pkwy office.

SOUTHWESTERN ONTARIO

Arcing around Lake Ontario are a number of the Greater Toronto Area's 'satellite' cities. Day trip the up-and-coming hip strip of Hamilton, or really escape Toronto's gravity in the delightful villages of Elora, Fergus and the unique Mennonite settlement of St Jacobs.

For more grit, stop in the thriving university centers of Guelph, Waterloo and London,

Southwestern Ontario

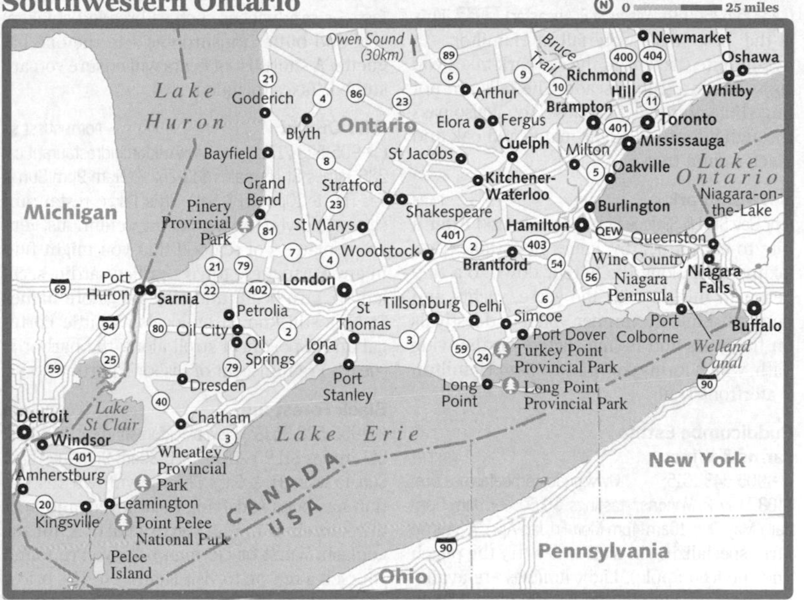

each with their own appeal if you dig deep. Nearby Stratford, birthplace of Justin Bieber and yet a remarkably cultured country town, is home to the penultimate festival of Shakespearean theater in honor of the bard's home in Stratford-upon-Avon, England.

From here, you can head northwest until the farmlands dissolve into the sandy shores of Lake Huron, or follow the dead-flat fields of gold – wheat, corn and everything-growing regions – until you reach the north shore of Lake Erie and quirky Pelee Island, Canada's southernmost point. The end (or beginning) of the road is in Windsor at the USA border.

Hamilton

☎519, 289, 905 / POP 519,949

Something special is happening in Hamilton. Once known as Canada's steel industry hub, skimmed through en route to the Niagara Peninsula, Hamilton's revitalized downtown has rebounded with unexpected hipness. A pocket of cosmopolitan life thrives with good eateries, quirky stores, independent galleries and cool bars. Yet the pace remains calm, with a haborside park, where you can clamber up a mansion for some sweeping harbor views, just a short stroll away.

Sights

Dundurn Castle MUSEUM

(☎905-546-2872; 610 York Blvd; adult/child 6-12yr $11.50/6; ⏲noon-4pm Tue-Sun; Ⓟ) Delightful and unexpected, this column-fronted, 36-room mansion once belonged to Sir Allan Napier McNab, Canadian prime minister from 1854 to 1856. It sits on a cliff overlooking the harbor amid lovely chestnut-studded grounds and is furnished in mid-19th-century style. Castle admission includes a one-hour tour (every 30 minutes) and entry into the Hamilton Military Museum.

Royal Botanical Gardens GARDENS

(☎1-800-694-4769; www.rbg.ca; 680 Plains Rd W, Burlington; admission incl shuttle bus adult/child 4-12yr $16/9; ⏲10am-8pm; Ⓟ) Northwest of Hamilton, Canada's largest and most spectacular botanic gardens comprise over a thousand hectares of trees, flowers and plants, including numerous rare species. There's also a rock garden, an arboretum and a wildlife sanctuary with trails traversing wetlands and wooded ravines. From June to October, thousands of delicate jewels bloom in the Centennial Rose Garden, and in spring over 125,000 flowering bulbs awaken in an explosion of color.

Tiffany Falls Conservation Area WATERFALL
(☎905-525-2181; Wilson St E, Ancaster) FREE This is the 'best value' waterfall in Hamilton – a five-minute stroll from the car park takes you right under a 21m cascade. The falls are not huge but you can get up close. You'll also pass through a forest of sugar maple, red oak and black walnut trees.

Bayfront Park PARK
(cnr Bay St N & Simcoe St W; ⏲dawn-dusk) After a bite to eat on nearby James St N, take a relaxing stroll along the harbor down to a tiny beach to mingle with the geese, yachts and people fishing. In summer, you'll find festivals on the grass and in-line skaters on the wide path, which forms part of the 7.5km Hamilton Waterfront Trail.

Puddicombe Estate Farms & Winery WINERY
(☎905-643-1015; www.puddicombefarms.com; 1468 Hwy 8, Winona; tastings $0.50; ⏲9am-5pm daily May-Dec, 10am-4pm Mon-Fri Jan-Apr) A rustic farm specializing in fruit wines (try the peach and the iced apple). Light lunches are available, and you can pick up freshly picked fruit, such as strawberries and peaches, depending on the season.

Sleeping & Eating

Hamilton Guesthouse GUESTHOUSE $
(☎289-440-8035; 158 Mary St; dm/d $25/46) If you are going to stay downtown near the restaurants of James St N, and the harbor, it may as well be in a converted 1855 mansion. The interior has mismatched furniture with spacious, quiet rooms, some with garden views. Free use of the laundry and a tea-filled kitchen add to the homeliness and value.

C Hotel by Carmen's HOTEL $$
(☎905-381-9898; http://carmenshotel.com; 1530 Stone Church Rd E; s & d from $150; P ⊖ ❄ ☎ ≋) You may be surprised that a hotel of this caliber is both a Best Western and in Hamilton. The handsome building pays an impressive tribute to art deco; its rooms and suites are both spacious and elegant. With an on-site Italian restaurant, indoor pool and all the comforts of home, you'll be more impressed by the good value.

Jack and Lois PUB FOOD $
(☎289-389-5647; www.jackandlois.com; 301 James St N; mains $10-13.50; ⏲9am-9pm Mon-Wed, to 10pm Thu, to 11pm Fri & Sat, to 8pm Sun) A hidden rear entrance adds to the cool factor of this pub-style diner. The patio is a relaxed spot to tackle unapologetically indulgent breakfasts or sandwiches such as breaded chicken, veal and butter mushrooms – in the one baguette. A short list of beers will ensure you are stuffed. Taxes included.

Wild Orchid PORTUGUESE $$
(☎905-528-7171; www.wildorchidrestaurant.ca; 286 James St N; mains $13-25; ⏲11am-9pm Sun & Tue-Thu, to 10pm Fri & Sat) This large restaurant serves (slowly) the kind of unpretentious, generous platters of seafood that you might find in any Portuguese town – grilled sardines, calamari, fava beans and olive oil galore. James St N is still known by locals as Little Portugal and a postmeal stroll along the harbor is (nearly) reminiscent of Lisbon's ports.

Black Forest Inn GERMAN $$
(☎905-528-3538; www.blackforestinn.ca; 255 King St E; mains $11.90-20.60; ⏲11:30am-9pm Tue-Thu & Sun, to 10pm Fri & Sat) This downtown institution has been satisfying meat lovers and beer drinkers since 1967. If you're a fan of schnitzel, goulash, wurst or German beer, you've found yourself a reason to visit Hamilton. The prices are great, so it's usually packed. In summer, the patio becomes a *biergarten* – perfect!

Entertainment

Zyla's Music and Menu LIVE MUSIC
(☎780-488-0970; http://zylas.ca; 199 James St N; ⏲6pm-midnight Wed-Thu, to 1am Fri & Sat) James St N does cute venues well and Zyla's is intimate enough for a real sense of the Hamilton vibe. Comedians and indie bands perform at beer-splashing distance from a young, cool crowd. If nothing's on, there are still good wraps and pub food, with plenty of vegan options.

Information

Tourism Hamilton (☎1-800-263-8590; www.tourismhamilton.com; 28 James St N; ⏲8:30am-4:30pm Mon-Fri) This downtown tourist office is keen to assist with all things Hamilton and surrounds; or just visit its impressive and up-to-date website.

Getting There & Away

GO Centre (www.gotransit.com; 36 Hunter St E; ⏲5am-11pm Mon-Fri, 6:15am-11pm Sat & Sun) Coach Canada, Greyhound Canada and Toronto-bound GO Transit commuter buses ($10.75, one to two hours, every 20 minutes) and trains ($10.75, one hour, three daily) roll out of the GO Centre, three blocks south of the center of Hamilton. There is nowhere to eat in the GO Centre or within a couple of blocks, so plan ahead.

Brantford

POP 93,650

Brantford is all about cultural sites. The Six Nations territory here has been a First Nations center for centuries, and gives you a look into the culture then and now. You can trace indigenous history, see contemporary art and visit an indigenous performance space. Captain Joseph Thayendanegea Brant led the Six Nations people here from upper New York State in 1784 and you can visit his tomb at the world's only Royal Indian Chapel. Then, for a bit more British-Canadian history, head to the former homestead of Alexander Graham Bell, who first patented the telephone.

There is little reason to stay overnight in Brantford when nearby Hamilton (and of course Toronto) has better sleeping and eating offerings.

Sights

Six Nations of the Grand River Territory AREA

(www.sixnations.ca) Southeast of Brantford is Six Nations of the Grand River Territory – the six nations being Mohawk, Oneida, Onondaga, Cayuga, Seneca and Tuscarora – and the village of **Ohsweken**, a well-known Aboriginal community. Established in the late 18th century, the territory gives visitors a glimpse of traditional and contemporary First Nations culture. The website sixnationstourism.ca lists events, craft stores and galleries in the area.

Bell Homestead National Historic Site HISTORIC SITE

(519-756-6220; www.bellhomestead.ca; 94 Tutela Heights Rd, Brantford; adult/child 7-12yr $6.50/4.50; 9:30am-4:30pm Tue-Sun; P) You might have known that Alexander Graham Bell, on July 26, 1874, shaped our futures by inventing the telephone (though the US Congress credits Italian Antonio Meucci). Did you know inspiration struck him in Brantford? Bell's first North American home has been lovingly restored to original condition.

Woodland Cultural Centre NOTABLE BUILDING

(519-759-2650; www.woodland-centre.on.ca; 184 Mohawk St; adult/child 5-18yr $7/5; 9am-4pm Mon-Fri, 10am-5pm Sat & Sun; P) An indigenous performance space, cultural museum and gallery. Exhibits follow a timeline from prehistoric Iroquoian and Algonquian exhibits through to contemporary indigenous art. The attached shop stocks basketry and jewelry, plus books, ceramics and paintings.

Her Majesty's Chapel of the Mohawks CHURCH

(519-756-0240; http://mohawkchapel.ca; 291 Mohawk St; $5; 10am-4pm Tue-Sun May-Sep, closed Oct-Apr; P) The tomb of Captain Brant, who led the Six Nations people to this area, is on the grounds of the tiny but exquisite Her Majesty's Chapel of the Mohawks, best visited on sunny afternoons when light streams through the gorgeous stained-glass windows. On the site of the original village, it's the oldest Protestant church in Ontario (1785) and the world's only Royal Indian Chapel.

Information

Brantford Visitors & Tourism Centre (519-751-9900; www.discoverbrantford.com; 399 Wayne Gretzky Pkwy; 9am-8pm Mon-Fri, to 9pm Sat, to 5pm Sun) Just north of Hwy 403, the sparkling tourism center is optimistic about Brantford's future, with plenty of brochures and helpful staff.

Six Nations Tourism (866-393-3001; www.sixnationstourism.ca; 2498 Chiefswood Rd; 9am-4:30pm Mon-Fri, 10am-3pm Sat & Sun) At the corner of Hwy 54 find this visitors center, with information on local sites, attractions and events in Six Nations.

Transport

Bus Greyhound Canada connects to Toronto ($24.70, 1½ to 2½ hours, two daily), London ($20.80, one to two hours, three daily) and (via Toronto and Hamilton) Niagara Falls ($30.10, five or seven hours, two daily) to the **Brantford Transit Terminal** (519-753-3847; www.brantford.ca/transit; 64 Darling St).

Train VIA Rail operates trains from Toronto ($41, one hour, five daily) and London ($72, one hour, seven daily) to the **Brantford Train Station** (519-752-0867; www.viarail.ca; 5 Wadsworth St).

Guelph

POP 121,700

Founded in 1827 by a Scottish novelist who planned the town's footprint in a European style, Guelph is best known for its popular university and…beer! Sleeman Breweries and two microbreweries call Guelph home. Strong manufacturing and education sectors contribute to Guelph's low unemployment rate, which fuels a vibrant youth scene: relaxed cafes, great food, rocking pubs and hip boutiques await. With a wealth of local history, a fantastic museum and lovely Victorian architecture, Guelph is worth a visit.

Sights & Activities

★Guelph Civic Museum MUSEUM

(519-836-1221; www.guelph.ca/museum; 52 Norfolk St; $5; 10am-5pm Tue-Sun; P) Housed in what was originally an 1854 sandstone convent and extensively transformed in 2012, this attractive LEED-certified museum offers exhibitions, programs and events digging up the history of the city (named after the British royal family's ancestors, the Guelphs). The 'Growing Up in Guelph' kids' exhibition makes a happy distraction.

Hours are extended and admission is free 5pm to 9pm on the fourth Friday of each month.

Basilica of Our Lady Immaculate CHURCH

(519-824-3951; www.churchofourlady.com; 28 Norfolk St; by donation; 7am-dusk; P) Lording over downtown Guelph is the dominant stone-faced bulk of this basilica and church in the Gothic Revival–style (think London, England's Houses of Parliament). It's hard to move around town without catching a glimpse of Our Lady's twin towers and elegantly proportioned rose window – no new buildings in town are allowed to be taller than the church. The basilica has awed parishioners since 1888, when it was a mere church. Pope Francis designated it a basilica in 2014.

University of Guelph Arboretum GARDENS

(519-824-4120; www.uoguelph.ca/arboretum; College Ave E; 8:30am-4:30pm Mon-Fri; P) FREE Modeled after the Arnold Arboretum of Harvard University, this stunning microcosm of flora and fauna has 8.2km of paths traversing 165 hectares of thoughtfully cultivated land. The variety of species represented here boggles the mind, and best of all, it's free! From June to August, the Wednesday Evening Walks (7pm) give guided tours for $2.

Macdonald Stewart Art Centre GALLERY

(519-837-0010; www.msac.ca; 358 Gordon St; suggested donation $3; noon-5pm Tue-Sun; P) Over 7000 works belong to the collection exhibited here in the Raymond Moriyama–designed galleries specializing in Inuit and Canadian art. The **Donald Forster Sculpture Park** is the largest at a public gallery in Canada and offers one hectare to explore: gravity-defying cubes, beached boats and cell phones spiked onto agricultural sickles.

Speed River Paddling KAYAKING

(www.fb.me/speedriverpaddling; 116 Gordon St; kayak/canoe rental per hr Mon-Fri $12/15, Sat & Sun $15/18; 10am-7pm Tue-Sun Jun-Aug) Get on the water then tackle the ice-cream store next door. This is also the starting point of a self-guided eco-heritage walk along the banks of the Speed and Eramosa Rivers, a 6km circuit with interpretive signs.

Festivals & Events

Hillside Festival PERFORMING ARTS

(519-763-6396; www.hillsidefestival.ca; Jul) For over 30 years, Hillside has delighted with an eclectic mix of furry and fuzzy, hippy and huggy performers from seasoned pros to the up-and-coming artists of tomorrow. Feel the love and jump on board for one short weekend in July. Consult the website for this year's lineup and details.

Sleeping

Comfort Inn MOTEL $

(519-763-1900; www.choicehotels.ca; 480 Silvercreek Pkwy; d incl breakfast from $90;) Tastefully renovated in 2012, this spotlessly maintained motel, about 5km north of the town center, offers great-value rooms including a light breakfast.

Norfolk Guest House B&B $$

(519-767-1095; www.norfolkguesthouse.ca; 102 Eramosa Rd; r incl breakfast $129-269; P) A central location and sumptuously furnished, themed bedrooms, most with en suite Jacuzzi, make the Norfolk – a delightfully restored Victorian home – the logical choice for luxury B&B accommodations in downtown Guelph.

Delta Guelph Hotel & Conference Centre HOTEL $$

(519-780-3700; www.deltahotels.com; 50 Stone Rd W; d/ste from $149/169; P) Conveniently located near the University of Guelph, 3km from downtown, this modern, tastefully furnished property has spacious standard rooms with dark woods and comfy beds. A variety of well-priced suites, some with fireplaces, kitchenettes and downy sofas, complete the package.

Eating

★Joint Cafe CAFE $

(519-265-8508; www.thejointcafe.com; 43 Cork St E; mains $11-14; 9am-3pm;) The Joint is a great brunch all-rounder. Come for coffee or drinks and you're bound to find something on the diverse and original menu that tickles your fancy – there's a definite emphasis on healthy comfort food and plenty of options for vegetarians.

Cornerstone CAFE $

(519-827-0145; www.fb.me/thecornerstoneguelph; 1 Wyndham St N; mains $6-10; 8am-midnight Mon-Fri, 9am-midnight Sat & Sun;) Thick stone walls plus scuffed wood floors equal serious comfiness at this well-loved vegetarian cafe. Go for coffee in the morning and return for a pint and some live music in the evening. If you're looking for a sandwich, consider the Taste of Downtown: avocado, brie, red peppers and garlic aioli ($8); or make a sweet beeline for the tofu cheesecake.

Miijidaa BISTRO $$

(519-821-9271; www.miijidaa.ca; 37 Quebec St; mains $15-25; 10am-11pm Mon-Thu, to midnight Fri & Sat, to 9pm Sun;) This spacious cafe-bistro is a casual spot for lunch, dinner or just a drink on the patio. Mains take modern twists on cuisines that have shaped Canada – mostly French and Portuguese. Try hay-smoked duck breast with kale, or a 'cured' pizza of wild salmon, gravlax and capers. There are also lots of salads, vegetarian options and a kids menu.

Bollywood Bistro INDIAN $$

(519-821-3999; www.thebollywoodbistro.com; 51 Cork St E; mains $10-17; 11:30am-2:30pm & 5-9pm Mon-Thu, to 10pm Fri & Sat, 5-9pm only Sun;) Guelph's favorite Indian restaurant uses a traditional tandoor oven to create well-known dishes with a contemporary twist, with influences from Nepal, Delhi and Mumbai. The creamy butter chicken ($15) is one of the best around, and there is a daily (except Sunday) lunch special.

Artisanale FRENCH $$$

(519-821-3359; www.artisanale.ca; 214 Woolwich St; mains $23-28; 11:30am-2:30pm & 5-9pm Tue-Sat) With an emphasis on fresh seasonal local produce, this French country kitchen has a wonderfully simple lunch menu and is popular for its Wednesday $35 prix-fixe dinners. Or create your own unfixed selection from irresistible hors d'oeuvres and sides, and hearty mains such as beef fricassee with carrot puree.

Drinking & Nightlife

★**Woolwich Arrow** PUB

(519-836-2875; www.woolwicharrow.ca; 176 Woolwich St; 11:30am-late) The 'Wooly,' as it's affectionately known, stands on its own two feet as a microbrewery but also ranks highly for delicious gourmet eat-with-beer munchies like longhorn beef chili poutine (small $5) and Lake Erie fish and chips ($17).

Manhattan's BAR

(519-767-2440; www.manhattans.ca; 951 Gordon St; 11am-late Mon-Fri, 4pm-late Sat & Sun;) The pizza here is hot and fresh like the smooth, smooth jazz: there's live music most nights. Check the website for details. No cover.

Entertainment

Bookshelf ARTS CENTER

(519-821-3311; www.bookshelf.ca; 41 Québec St; mains with movie $25; eBar 5pm-late Tue-Sat, bookstore 9am-9:30pm Mon-Sat, 10:30am-8pm Sun) Forty years young, Bookshelf is the pacemaker of Guelph's cultural heartbeat: part bookstore, cinema, cafe and music venue. Swing by to read the paper, catch an art-house flick or have a bite in the eBar. Regular salsa nights, poetry slams and flashback Fridays – there's something for everyone.

Information

Guelph Tourism Services (800-334-4519; www.visitguelphwellington.ca; 52 Norfolk St; 9am-4:30pm Mon-Sat) In the Civic Museum. Friendly staff are local experts.

Getting There & Away

All buses and trains depart from **Guelph Central Station** (Guelph Central GO Station; 888-842-7245; http://visitguelphwellington.ca; cnr Wyndham & Carden Sts; 6am-1pm & 4pm-midnight Mon-Fri, 9am-2pm & 4pm-midnight Sat & Sun).

Greyhound buses (greyhound.ca) go to Toronto ($24, 1½ hours, seven daily) and London ($30, two to four hours, three daily), with discounts online.

GO Transit (gotransit.com) has a mixed bus-train journey to Toronto ($14, two hours, every 30 minutes); and two early morning trains to Toronto ($14, 1½ hours) on the Kitchener line.

VIA Rail (viarail.ca) operates trains to Toronto ($30, 1½ hours, twice daily) and London ($37, 2¼ hours, twice daily).

Kitchener-Waterloo

519, 226 / POP 280,000

The adjacent cities of Kitchener (formerly called Berlin, due to its Germanic origins) and Waterloo are as different as they are alike. Although prettier 'uptown' Waterloo has some nice sandstone architecture, two universities and the largest community museum in Ontario, neither city is particularly exciting. The very best time to visit is festival time, when the twins come to life – Oktoberfest here is the second-largest after Munich, Germany! Otherwise, just pass through on your way to Elora and Fergus, St Jacobs or Stratford.

Sights & Activities

Waterloo Region Museum MUSEUM

(www.waterlooregionmuseum.com; 10 Huron Rd, Kitchener; adult/child $10/5; ⏲9:30am-5pm Mon-Fri, 11am-5pm Sat & Sun; P) Waterloo's most modern attraction is this primary-colored local history museum set on 24 hectares. It's the gateway to the **Doon Heritage Crossroads**, a recreated pioneer settlement where costumed volunteers do their best to help you time travel.

Joseph Schneider Haus HISTORIC SITE

(☎519-742-7752; http://josephschneiderhaus.com; 466 Queen St S, Kitchener; adult/child $6/4; ⏲10am-5pm Mon-Sat, 1-5pm Sun, closed Mon & Tue Sep-Jun; P) A national historic site, Joseph Schneider Haus was one of the first homes in the area, originally built for a prosperous Pennsylvanian Mennonite. It has been restored to full 19th-century splendor – the architecture is amazing, as are demonstrations of day-to-day 1800s chores and skills (everything from beadwork to making corn-husk dolls). There is a two-story washhouse and a schnitz house.

Waterloo Central Railway RAIL

(☎519-885-2297; www.waterloocentralrailway.com; 10 Father David Bauer Dr, Waterloo; from $16; ⏲Apr-Dec) This lovingly restored steam train shuttles between Waterloo and St Jacobs on Tuesdays, Thursdays and Saturdays in the warmer months: check the home page for schedules and ticket details.

Festivals & Events

Uptown Waterloo Jazz Festival MUSIC

(www.uptownwaterloojazz.ca; ⏲mid-Jul) FREE Big-time jazz, small-town environment; three days of free jazz around Waterloo.

Oktoberfest BEER

(☎519-570-4267; www.oktoberfest.ca; ⏲Oct) *Willkommen* to this nine-day beery Bavarian bash – the biggest of its kind in North America and possibly the largest outside of Germany. It's K-W's favorite event, bringing in about 500,000 people each year from early to mid-October for sauerkraut, oompah bands, *lederhosen* and *biergartens* galore.

Sleeping & Eating

Bingemans Camping Resort CAMPGROUND $

(☎519-744-1002; www.bingemans.com; 425 Bingemans Centre Dr, Kitchener; tent/RV sites $45/50, cabins from $75, reservations $10; P) South of Hwy 401, Bingemans is a combined water park and campground with enough pools, ponds and water slides to warrant 'Great Lake' status. The cabins are nothing spectacular, and sleep four. A wide range of camping and water-park packages are available.

Crowne Plaza Kitchener-Waterloo HOTEL $$

(☎519-744-4144; www.crowneplaza.com; 105 King St E, Kitchener; d from $144; P) The renovated Crowne Plaza has a futuristic lobby and 201 sparkling, modern guest rooms – these are the best digs for miles.

Walper Terrace Hotel HOTEL $$

(☎519-745-4321; www.walper.com; 1 King St W, Kitchener; r from $189; P) There's a rich sense of history at the Walper, a classy downtown player looking good for its age – the hotel was built in 1893 and renovated in 2011. All rooms have high ceilings and period features, flat-screen TVs and free wi-fi, but standard rooms are a tad cozy. Suites are more spacious.

Princess Cafe CAFE $

(☎519-886-0227; www.princesscafe.ca; 46 King St N, Waterloo; panini $8.50; ⏲11:30am-10:30pm) This quaint cafe next door to the cinema serves up coffee, toasted panini and other snacky delights. If you're a night owl, stop in for 'Cheeses Murphy': the ultimate drinking companion.

Concordia Club GERMAN $$

(www.concordiaclub.ca; 429 Ottawa St S, Kitchener; mains lunch $8-12, dinner $11-24; ⏲11:30am-11pm Mon-Sat, to 2pm Sun) Polish up your German verbs and fill up on schnitzel at Concordia, a Teutonic fave that's been around for decades. Dark wood, low ceilings, white linen and loud conversation complement the menu. There's red-hot polka action on Friday and Saturday nights, and a summer *biergarten*.

Information

City of Waterloo's Visitor and Heritage Information Centre (☎519-885-2297; www.explorewaterlooregion.com; 10 David Bauer Dr, Waterloo; ⏲9am-4pm Mon-Sat Apr-Dec) Friendly staff! At the terminus of the Waterloo Central Railway.

Kitchener Welcome Centre (☎519-745-3536; www.explorewaterlooregion.com; 200 King St W, Kitchener; ⏲8:30am-5pm Mon-Fri) Inside City Hall.

Getting There & Away

Air From **Waterloo International Airport** (☎519-648-2256; www.waterlooairport.ca; 4881 Fountain St N, Breslau), 7km east of town, there are flights to Calgary, Detroit and Chicago.

THE MENNONITES OF ST JACOBS & ELMIRA

The Mennonite story harks back to a 16th-century Swiss Protestant sect who moved around Europe due to religious disagreements. They ended up in the rural setting of what is now Pennsylvania, USA, where they were promised religious freedom and prosperity. Cheaper land and their unwillingness to fight under the American flag lured many Mennonites to southern Ontario in the late 19th century, where they remain today, upholding the same basic values of family, humility, simplicity, modesty and pacifism.

For a detailed history and information see www.mhsc.ca, or take a day trip to the quaint villages of St Jacobs, about 20 minutes' drive from Kitchener, and Elmira, 8km further north. Here, black buggies rattle past, the scent of cattle fills the air and bonnets, braces and buttons are de rigueur.

The quintessential **country market** (☎519-747-1830; www.stjacobs.com; cnr King & Weber Sts, St Jacobs; ⏰7am-3:30pm Thu & Sat year-round, also 8am-3pm Tue Jun-Aug), 3km south of St Jacobs, has an earthy soul. Folks come from miles for the farm-fresh produce, smoked meats, cheese, baked treats, arts and crafts. Pop in to the **visitors center** (☎519-664-3518; www.stjacobs.com; 1406 King St, St Jacobs; ⏰9am-5pm Mon-Sat) to see the Mennonite Story, an insightful exhibition on the Mennonites' history, culture and agricultural achievements. One of these is the production of maple syrup: learn about it at the **Maple Syrup Museum & Quilt Gallery** (☎800-265-3353; www.stjacobs.com; 1441 King St N, St Jacobs; ⏰10am-6pm Mon-Sat, noon-5:30pm Sun; P) FREE or sample the liquid gold at the **Maple Syrup Festival** (www.elmiramaplesyrup.com; ⏰early Apr). Round out the day with fresh fruit pie and some scones for the road from the **Stone Crock Bakery** (☎519-664-2286; 1402 King St N, St Jacobs; items $2-8; ⏰6:30am-6pm Mon-Sat, 11am-5:30pm Sun) and be on your way.

Bus Greyhound Canada operates from the **Charles Street Transit Terminal** (☎800-661-8747; www.greyhound.ca; 15 Charles St W, Kitchener), a five-minute walk from downtown. Buses run to Toronto ($23, 1½ to two hours, hourly) and London ($26, 1½ hours, one daily).

Train An easy walk north of downtown is **Kitchener Train Station** (☎888-842-7245; www.viarail.ca; cnr Victoria & Weber Sts, Kitchener). VIA Rail operates trains to Toronto ($24, 1½ hours, twice daily) and London ($34, two hours, twice daily). GO Transit operates commuter trains to Toronto ($17, two hours, twice daily).

Elora & Fergus

No longer one of Ontario's best-kept secrets, the delightful Wellington County riverside towns of Elora and Fergus, straddling the banks of the twisty Grand River, await your visit. Both have done a magnificent job preserving their heritage facades and streetscapes. Enticing Elora, with its gorge and swimming hole, is a wonderful place to escape the summer heat, while neighboring Fergus evokes nostalgia for a lost age and a distant northern kingdom...along with the desire to sample all of its cozy pubs.

Sights

Elora Gorge Conservation Area PARK

(www.grandriver.ca; Rte 21, 7400 Wellington County Rd, Elora; adult/child $6/3; ⏰8am-8pm late Apr–mid-Oct; P) About 2km south of Elora is this photo-worthy plunging limestone canyon through which the Grand River seethes. Easy walks extend to cliff views, caves and the Cascade waterfalls – a sheet of white water spilling over a stepped cliff. For a free gorge view from downtown Elora, head to the end of James St, off Metcalfe St.

Tubing (rental $25; ⏰9am to 5pm) is a lazy way to spend a warm afternoon at the gorge. You can also camp (p138) and zip-line here.

Elora Quarry Conservation Area NATURE RESERVE

(www.grandriver.ca; Rte 18, 319 Wellington County Rd, Elora; adult/child $6/3; ⏰11am-8pm Mon-Fri, 10am-8pm Sat & Sun Jun-Aug; P) A short walk east of Elora, this superb swimming hole offers possibly bottomless waters and 12m limestone cliffs. Hormone-fueled teens plummet from great heights, despite signs suggesting they don't.

Wellington County Museum MUSEUM
(☎519-846-0916; www.wcm.on.ca; Rte 18, Elora; by donation; ⏰9:30am-4:30pm Mon-Fri, 1-4pm Sat & Sun; Ⓟ) Midway between Fergus and Elora, an austere, red-roofed former 'Poor House' provided refuge for the aged and homeless for almost a century before becoming a museum in 1957. Historical and local modern-art exhibits extend through 12 galleries, displaying an obvious pride in local history and current culture. The centerpiece is the new 'If These Walls Could Speak' exhibit, which examines the lives of those who lived or worked there.

Tours

Elora Culinary Walking Tours WALKING
(☎226-384-7000; www.eloraculinarywalkingtour.com; 8 Mill St W; per person $25; ⏰2-4pm Sat May-Sep) Sample some of Elora's olive oils, gelato, coffee and pastries on this two-hour guided tour. Rain or shine, meet in front of the Village Olive Grove (8 Mill St W).

Festivals & Events

Elora Festival MUSIC
(www.elorafestival.com; Elora; ⏰mid-Jul–mid-Aug) A classical, jazz, folk and arts festival held from mid-July to mid-August, with concerts at the quarry and around town. Singers and musos from around the country crowd the schedule of Elora's premier event.

Fergus Scottish Festival & Highland Games CULTURAL
(www.fergusscottishfestival.com; Fergus; ⏰mid-Aug) If it's not Scottish, it doesn't count: tugs-of-war, caber tossing, bagpipes, Celtic dancing, kilts, haggis and Scotch nosing (aka tasting). Hoots! Held over two days in mid-August.

Sleeping

For a wide range of B&B options, try the **Fergus Elora Bed & Breakfast Association** (www.ferguselorahosts.com).

Elora Gorge Conservation Area Campground CAMPGROUND $
(☎519-846-9742; www.grandriver.ca; Rte 18, Elora; campsites $32-46, reservation fee $13; Ⓟ) More than 550 campsites in six distinct, riverside zones. They're overflowing during summer, especially on holiday weekends.

★**Stonehurst B&B** B&B $$
(☎519-843-8800; www.stonehurstbb.com; 265 St David St S, Fergus; s/d incl breakfast $123/140) This gorgeous country home, belonging to one of the wealthiest families in the area from 1853 to 1933, had a brief stint as a nursing home and newspaper office before adopting its best-suited fate as a B&B in 2001. Four comfortable rooms each have en suite bathrooms. Your welcoming hosts maintain the house, common areas and gardens magnificently.

Bredalbane INN $$
(☎519-843-4770; www.breadalbaneinn.com; 487 St Andrew St W, Fergus; ste incl breakfast from $185) Rooms at this compact inn are classically furnished without being tacky. Some have canopy beds and most have Jacuzzis. The annexed pub and bistro and prime main street location mean you won't need to venture far for entertainment, though it can sometimes get noisy.

Drew House INN $$
(☎519-846-2226; www.drewhouse.com; 120 Mill St E, Elora; r incl breakfast from $135; Ⓟ⊖❄) Drew House unites the old world with the new. On spacious grounds, the inn has both renovated stable suites (with private bathrooms) and guest rooms (with shared bathrooms) in the main house. Yard-thick stone walls whisper history as you drift into dreams before waking to a breakfast of fresh fruit, hot coffee, and bacon and eggs cooked how you love them.

Eating

Desert Rose Cafe VEGETARIAN $
(☎519-846-0433; 130 Metcalfe St, Elora; mains $11-13; ⏰11am-4pm Wed & Thu, to 7:30pm Fri & Sat, to 3pm Sun; 🖉) This seafood and vegetarian cafe, run by a long-time local, whips up tasty quiches, veg-filled salads, burgers, smoked-salmon bagels and burritos in a casual setting. The roasted eggplant moussaka is satisfying. Gluten-free options available.

Gorge Country Kitchen DINER $
(☎519-846-2636; 82 Wellington Rd, Elora; meals $8-22; ⏰7am-8pm Sun & Mon, to 8:30pm Tue-Thu, to 9pm Fri & Sat; 👪) The Gorge is usually hopping thanks to its family-friendly country-style cheap eats, especially the hearty breakfasts. There are daily specials.

Brewhouse PUB FOOD $$
(☎519-843-8871; www.brewhouseonthegrand.ca; 170 St David St S, Fergus; mains $10-22; ⏰11:30am-11pm Sun-Mon, to 1am Tue-Sat) Wave to the anglers on the Grand River from the shady Brewhouse patio as you weigh up the benefits of cheddar and ale soup, bangers and mash, or curried chicken enchilada. It sports a cozy bar, European beers on tap and live music to boot.

Cork EUROPEAN $$

(☎519-846-8880; www.eloracork.com; 146 Metcalfe St, Elora; mains $23-36; ⏰11:30am-9pm) Run by a mother and daughter team, Cork is a casual fine dining restaurant turning heads in Wellington County for its excellent service, delicious food and sunny patio. From the grilled beet and goat's cheese salad to the saffron lobster risotto, we think you'll be pleased with your investment.

Mill St Bakery & Bistro CAFE $$

(☎519-384-2277; www.millstreetbistro.com; 15 Mill St E, Elora; mains $14-18; ⏰9am-7pm Mon-Sat, 10am-7pm Sun) This busy breakfast-and-lunch joint has a fantastic river-view patio and serves sandwiches, your favorite comfort foods and a limited dinner menu.

Drinking & Nightlife

Goofie Newfie PUB

(☎519-843-4483; www.goofienewfie.ca; 105 Queen St W, Fergus; ⏰11:30am-late) Good food, cold booze, river views, live entertainment and happy patrons make the Goofie Newfie the jolly place it is.

Shepherd's Pub PUB

(8 Mill St W, Elora; ⏰noon-11pm Mon & Tue, to 1am Wed-Sat, to 10pm Sun) Pubby mains ($9 to $13) and cold pints of Guinness and Ontario craft beers by the river. All-day breakfast fry-ups, beer-battered fish and chips, and hearty beef pies will revive you if you spent too long here the night before.

Information

Elora Welcome Centre (☎519-846-2563; www.elora.info; 9 Mill St E, Elora; ⏰9am-5pm Mon-Fri, 10am-6pm Sat, to 5pm Sun) The staff are a font of knowledge for all things Wellington County.

Getting There & Away

Parkbus (parkbus.ca) runs from Carlton St, Toronto, to Elora Gorge for $49 return including admission. Coaches make the day trip once per weekend every fortnight or so from May to October; check the website for schedules and book ahead.

Greyhound and other coaches no longer run to Elora and Fergus, so you will need your own car for longer trips than the day trip offered by Parkbus. The 20-minute ride with **Green Taxi** (☎519-787-3700; 275 Gordon St, Fergus) from Guelph to Fergus is around $30, but call ahead to make sure they can come for you.

The 10-minute drive between Elora and Fergus is covered by **Green Taxi** (p139) for about $10.

Stratford

POP 30,890

Stratford is a success story: a wonderful country town that refuses to surrender to the depopulation plaguing rural centers worldwide. As the story goes, in 1952, upon hearing that the Canadian National Railways (the region's largest employer) was closing the doors of its Stratford facility, a young journalist by the name of Tom Patterson approached his council for a loan. His plan was to attract a troupe of actors to capitalize on the town's namesake: Shakespeare's birthplace. It worked. In 1953 the first performance of what has become the Stratford Festival (p140; the largest of its kind) was born, creating a whole new industry, which continues to support the town today.

Charming, cultured and classy, with a bunch of *other* festivals to boot, Stratford packs more punch than cities twice its size: there are plenty of great places to eat and stay. Whatever the season, you'll enjoy nature, arts and architecture, and the local welcome.

Sights

Gallery Stratford GALLERY

(☎519-271-5271; www.gallerystratford.on.ca; 54 Romeo St S; ⏰10am-5pm Tue-Sun Jun-Sep, to 3pm Oct-May; P) FREE In a wonderful renovated yellow-brick pump house (c 1880), Gallery Stratford exhibits innovative contemporary art with a Canadian emphasis. Regular art studios, movie nights and family days are held. It's very kid friendly.

Avon River RIVER

Stratford's swan-filled Avon River (what else were they going to call it?) flows slowly past the town, with plenty of riverbank lawns on which to chill out. Just west of Stratford Tourism on the riverbank, the **Shakespearean Gardens** occupy the site of an old wool mill. Parterre gardens, manicured box hedges,

SWANS ON PARADE

Stratford's beloved swans don't paddle around the Avon River all winter; instead, they are kept warm in winter pens. Come early April, the release of the birds to their summer home on the river is a Stratford celebration. The swans waddle down the street in parade formation, backed by bagpipe players marching in kilts.

herbs, roses and a bronze bust of Bill – pick up a brochure at **Stratford Tourism** (☎519-271-5140, 800-561-7926; www.visitstratford.ca; 47 Downie St; ⊙10am-2pm Sun & Mon, 9am-5pm Tue-Fri, 10am-6pm Sat).

Further along the river is **Queen's Park**, with paths leading from the Festival Theatre along the river past Orr Dam and an 1885 stone bridge to an **English flower garden**.

Stratford-Perth Museum MUSEUM
(☎519-393-5311; www.stratfordperthmuseum.ca; 4275 Huron Rd; suggested donation adult/child $7/5; ⊙9am-5pm May-Oct; P) The diverse and significant Stratford-Perth Museum collection includes artifacts and memorabilia from the early 1800s to the present day. Its mission is to celebrate and remember the community stories of Stratford and Perth County.

Tours

Boat Tours CRUISE
(☎519-271-7739; www.avonboatrentals.ca; 30 York St; tours from adult/child $8/5; ⊙9am-dusk May-Oct) Take in the parks, swans, riverbanks and grand gardens on Avon River. Tours depart below Stratford Tourism by the river. Canoes, kayaks ($16 per hour), paddleboats and bikes ($15 per hour) are available for rent.

Festivals & Events

Stratford Garden Festival GARDENS
(www.on.lung.ca/stratfordgardenfestival; $9; ⊙early Mar) A four-day horticultural extravaganza featuring flora from around the world, guest speakers and presentations.

Stratford Summer Music MUSIC
(☎519-271-2101; www.stratfordsummermusic.ca; tickets $10-45; ⊙mid-Jul–mid-Aug) Four weeks of classical, cabaret and theatrical music, with acclaimed musicians from around Canada tuning up and letting loose.

Savour Stratford Festival FOOD & DRINK
(☎519-271-7500; www.visitstratford.ca/savour-stratford; ⊙mid-Sep) Beer, wine and food tastings, workshops, farm tours and special dinners all highlight Perth County's abundance. Prices vary with the event.

Stratford Garlic Festival FOOD & DRINK
(www.stratfordgarlicfestival.com; $10; ⊙mid-Sep) A garlic-filled weekend of cooking, presentations and products. Bring your breath mints.

Sleeping

There's a plethora of accommodations in Stratford but savvy locals know how to make a buck: room rates can go through the roof during the Stratford Festival.

Stratford General Hospital Residence HOSTEL $
(SGH Residence; ☎519-271-5084; www.sgh.stratford.on.ca/residence; 130 Youngs St; s/d $65/80; P) These renovated nurses' quarters are the closest thing you'll find to a youth hostel in town: 360 rooms with shared bathrooms, kitchens and a heated pool. Cheap, clean and comfy, but not party central.

Parlour Historic Inn & Suites HOTEL $$
(☎519-271-2772; www.theparlour.ca; 101 Wellington St; d from $159) This handsome hotel occupies a heritage building in the center of town, near the Avon Theatre, and has been fully refitted to a high standard – most rooms are spacious and light filled. There's a pub downstairs with a lovely patio, but it doesn't get too rowdy.

THE STRATFORD FESTIVAL

Sir Alec Guinness played Richard III on opening night of this much-lauded **festival** (☎519-273-1600; www.stratfordfestival.ca; ⊙Apr-Nov), which began humbly in a tent at Queen's Park. With over 60 seasons under its belt, the festival has since achieved international acclaim. Far from its tented origins, today four theaters stage contemporary and period dramas, opera and, of course, works by the Bard, over a monster season lasting April to November. Actors from around the world prize festival residencies.

Aside from the plays, there's a peripheral schedule of interesting programs: post performance discussions, backstage tours, lectures, concerts and readings. Some are free.

Main-stage productions occur at the 1800-seat Festival Theatre and 1000-seat Avon Theatre. The Tom Patterson and Studio Theatres are more intimate. Tickets go on sale to the general public in early January. By showtime nearly every performance is sold out: book ahead! Spring previews and fall end-of-season shows are often discounted by 30%, with 50%-off 'rush' tickets, two hours before showtime.

Mercer Hall Inn BOUTIQUE HOTEL $$
(☎519-271-1888; www.mercerhallinn.com; 108 Ontario St; d $90-200; P ⊖ ❄ ☎) Downtown Mercer Hall Inn has more class than most: uniquely artistic rooms feature handcrafted furniture, kitchenettes and electric fireplaces. Some have Jacuzzis.

Swan Motel MOTEL $$
(☎519-271-6376; www.swanmotel.on.ca; 960 Downie St S; r $114-140; P ⊖ ❄ ☎ ≋) A fabulously maintained 1960s roadside motel 3km south of town, the Swan has spotless rooms with costume sketches and original artwork on the walls. Park-like grounds feature hammered-steel sculptures, fountains and a pool. The motel is closed from late October to early May.

Forest Motel and Woodland Retreat MOTEL $$
(☎519-271-4573; www.forestmotel.on.ca; 2941 Forest Rd/RR 4; d $99-235) Friendly hosts welcome you to this wonderful woody lakeside gem, secluded, but only 10 minutes from town and close to highway amenities. Comfy renovated rooms emphasize Conrad's carpentry skills. You'll feel more like you've stepped into a country cottage than a motel. All rooms have microwave, refrigerator and homely touches.

Festival Inn MOTEL $$
(☎519-273-1150; www.festivalinnstratford.com; 1144 Ontario St; d $119-189) This sprawling four-wing motel complex has over 160 pleasantly renovated rooms and suites in a variety of styles, offering good value during the festival period. On the highway near a bunch of amenities, it's a few minutes' drive to the festival and downtown attractions.

Acrylic Dreams B&B $$
(☎519-271-7874; www.acrylicdreams.com; 66 Bay St; r incl breakfast $140-175; P ⊖ ❄ ☎) Owned by a husband-and-wife team, this renovated 1879 B&B has polished wooden floorboards and spa amenities. Besides being artists (there are more than a few acrylic masterpieces on the walls) the owners also practice chair massage and reflexology, and can accommodate all diets.

Lofts at 99 BOUTIQUE HOTEL $$
(☎519-271-1121; 99 Ontario St; r $99-299; P ⊖ ❄ ☎) This modern, dark-wood furnished inn houses commodious bilevel suites and lofts. Skylights, kitchenettes and period furnishings are standard, the receptionists are friendly and the cafe/bar downstairs is always pumping (so this is one for heavy sleepers).

★**Three Houses Bed & Breakfast** B&B $$$
(☎519-272-0722; www.thethreehouses.com; 100 Brunswick St; ste incl breakfast $225-695; P ⊖ ❄ ☎ ≋) Two Edwardian townhouses, a garden carriage house and an 1870s Italianate house make up this meticulous, *almost* over-the-top 18-room inn. No detail has been spared in decorating these light-filled spaces – even the luggage racks match the quirky individual room designs. A saltwater pool and secret oasis garden add relaxing touches.

Eating

A local chef's school and surrounding farmland make Stratford a gourmet's delight. Reservations are recommended during festival time.

Boomer's Gourmet Fries FAST FOOD $
(☎519-275-3147; www.boomersgourmetfries.com; 26 Erie St; items $3-15; ⊙11:30am-7pm Tue-Fri, noon-7pm Sat) Crazy, weird, killer, delicious, amazing, irresistible, to die for: all have been used to describe the fries, poutines, burgers and fried creations that come out of this kooky and friendly little joint.

York Street Kitchen SANDWICHES $
(☎519-273-7041; www.yorkstreetkitchen.com; 24 Erie St; mains $7-16; ⊙8:30am-6pm Mon-Sat, to 3pm Sun) This cozy kitchen serves up showstopper sandwiches on homemade bread, brie fritters, salads, quiches and desserts. Try the 'Mennonite' sandwich: sausage, cheddar, corn relish, tomato, honey mustard, mayo and lettuce.

Mercer Hall EUROPEAN $$
(☎519-271-9202; www.mercerhall.com; 104 Ontario St; lunch $8-16, dinner $12-28; ⊙noon-8pm Sun & Mon, 11am-10pm Tue & Wed, to midnight Wed-Sat) This stylish artisanal eatery features a fantastic brunch menu and seasonal dinner delights such as beef brisket, aged bison and a delicious lentil and vegetable curry.

Raja INDIAN $$
(☎519-271-3271; www.rajaindiancuisine.ca; 10 George St W; mains $12-22; ⊙11:30am-2:30pm & 5-9pm; ✍) Challenging Stratford's demure Anglo tastes with funky lashings of chili and spice, Raja plates up super curries, soups, salads, breads, and vegetarian and tandoori dishes, and serves them on white linen. Staff are dapper and unfailingly polite.

★**Bijou** FRENCH $$$
(☎519-273-5000; www.bijourestaurant.com; 105 Erie St; lunch $9-19, dinner $48-54; ⊙11:30am-1pm Fri & Sat & 5-9pm Tue-Sat) Classy and delightful,

this French joint has a different prix-fixe menu written on the chalkboard each evening. The locally sourced meals might include quail, heirloom tomato salad or Lake Huron whitefish ceviche.

Information

Stratford Public Library (519-271-0220; www.stratford.library.on.ca; 19 St Andrew St; 1-9pm Mon, 10am-9pm Tue-Thu, 10am-5pm Fri & Sat) Free internet access.

Stratford Tourism (p140) Help with accommodations and all things 'festival.' The website is an excellent information source, with loads of tour options. This downtown office has one of Bieber's signed guitars (an endless source of fascination for giggling teen fans from around the world). There's even a self-guided Justin Bieber tour, where you can see where the tween star went on his first date, if you really have absolutely nothing better to do.

Getting There & Away

Stratford Direct (www.stratfordfestival.ca) is a shuttle service between Toronto and Stratford's four theaters during Festival season (performance days only, May to October) for only $25 round-trip! Buses pick up and drop off at Simcoe St, south of Front St, beside the Intercontinental Toronto. They may ask to see your theater ticket. You must purchase your shuttle ticket by 11pm the day before you travel, but they often sell out way before then, especially on days with cheap theater tickets. There are no stops between Toronto and Stratford, but there's wi-fi and a washroom onboard. Departure times vary; check the homepage for details and booking.

Stratford Airporter (519-273-0057; www.stratfordairporter.com; from $79) runs daily shuttles to **Pearson International Airport** (p116), departing Stratford from 4am to 7pm, and Toronto 7:30am to 11:30pm. It's cheaper if you're traveling with someone.

VIA Rail runs from **Stratford Train Station** (888-842-7245; www.viarail.ca; 101 Shakespeare St) to Toronto ($48, two hours, twice daily) and London ($30, one hour, twice daily).

Lake Huron Shoreline

Lake Huron has some of the cleanest waters of the Great Lakes and is wide enough that the sun sets on the waterline of its western shore: expect wonderful sunsets. If you've been lingering around Toronto and Lake Ontario, Lake Huron's 'blueness' will be both surprising and refreshing, as will its whitish sandy beaches.

Grand Bend

For most of the year, Grand Bend is a sleepy, shuttered town on the southeastern shore of Lake Huron, but from late May to late October the town heaves to life with sun-hungry university students from nearby London, Kitchener and Windsor. It's hard to imagine the transformation: the handful of year-round residents' peaceful lives interrupted by a mini Florida-style Spring Break on their doorsteps.

From a vantage point on the broad, sandy shoreline of the main beach, you can see how the town got its name: the coastline arcs dramatically from this point until it becomes almost a straight line, headed north. In early spring, it's quite a surreal experience to stand on the sandy shore in the sunshine and gaze out at the frozen, snow-covered lake, its edges whipped by the wind into frozen waves.

Sleeping & Eating

Pinery Provincial Park CAMPGROUND **$**

(info 519-243-2220, reservations 888-668-7275; www.reservations.ontarioparks.com; RR2; rates vary; 8am-10pm) South of Grand Bend is popular, picturesque Pinery Provincial Park, with 10km of wide sandy beaches and lots of trails winding through wooded sections and sand dunes (bike/canoe rental per day $45/40). There are hundreds of campsites and a number of yurts to choose from. Be sure to book in advance as spots fill fast.

Bonnie Doone Manor on the Beach INN **$$**

(519-238-2236; www.bonniedoone.ca; 16 Government Rd; d $160-255; P) Many love this ramshackle holiday motel – the only one on the beach – lovingly updated and maintained by the same family for over 50 years. Rooms are a time-warp with bright, colorful accents. Many face the water for unimaginably beautiful sunsets. There's also a quaint private cottage. It's the only lodging right on the beach and a hop-skip-and-jump from Main St.

Amber Hotel BOUTIQUE HOTEL **$$**

(519-238-2100; www.amberhotel.ca; 99 Ontario St S; d from $139) There are self-contained apartments here, but even the cheaper rooms at Amber feel like new condos with high-quality sheets, good air con, and extremely clean modern bathrooms. Black-out curtains and well sound-insulated walls make for deep sleeping. Just ignore the shopping plaza location and head to the nearish beach.

Riverbend Pizzeria PIZZA $
(☎519-238-6919; 26 Ontario St S; mains $10-18; ⊙3-10pm Mon, to 11pm Tue-Thu, 11am-midnight Fri & Sat, noon-8pm Sun) It may be a pizza restaurant by name, but regulars also come year-round to the Riverbend for huge portions of succulent hot chicken wings, karaoke nights and cold beer on the patio.

Schoolhouse Restaurant INTERNATIONAL $$
(☎519-238-5515; www.grandbendschoolhouse.ca; 1981 Crescent St; mains $11-26; ⊙9am-9pm Mon-Fri, 8am-9pm Sat & Sun; ✎) There's something for everyone at this foodie-friendly restaurant occupying, you guessed it, the former Grand Bend Public School. From tender roast chicken to succulent steak, ribs, lake-fresh seafood and a variety of A+ vegetarian options, you'll be delighted to find this alternative to Main St's touristy offerings.

Getting There & Away

There's no public transportation to Grand Bend. Rent a car from London if you want to avoid Toronto traffic.

Goderich

Previously awarded the title of Canada's prettiest town, charming Goderich's most recent and tragic claim to fame is for the EF-3 tornado which tore through it at 4:03pm on August 21, 2011. It was a Sunday and the crowded market square had just emptied. The twister formed over Lake Huron and followed a direct path across the town's distinctive octagonal town square, City Hall and beyond. Of the 97 century-old trees in the square, only three remained; hundreds of buildings were damaged or destroyed, scores injured and one life lost.

Several years on, the restoration and reconstruction work is now complete. As the trees set in and word spreads, visitors will be rewarded with a modern, grown-up version of a pretty town. The staff at Tourism Goderich will be delighted to provide you with a self-guided heritage walking tours brochure and field any questions you have about the town, tornado or otherwise.

Sights

Goderich has three sandy Lake Huron beaches, linked by kilometers of boardwalks. Don't miss a dusk stroll for swoon-worthy sunsets.

Huron County Museum MUSEUM
(☎519-524-2686; www.huroncountymuseum.ca; 110 North St; adult/child $5/3.50; ⊙10am-4:30pm Mon-Fri, 1-4:30pm Sat Jan-Apr, 10am-4:30pm Mon-Sat, 1-4:30pm Sun May-Dec) Walk the wooden floorboards for an informed look at local history, industry and transportation. Displays include everything from antique furniture and china to an old steam engine and a tank. Stays opens later, till 8pm, on Thursdays.

A combined ticket with Huron Historic Gaol is $7.50 for an adult, $5.50 for a child.

Huron Historic Gaol MUSEUM
(☎519-524-6971; www.huroncountymuseum.ca; 181 Victoria St N; adult/child $5/3.50; ⊙10am-4:30pm Mon-Sat, 1-4.30pm Sun May-late Oct, 10am-4:30pm Sat, 1-4pm Sun-Fri late Oct-Nov) Follow a creepy, prison-gray corridor into this octagonal fortress that served as courthouse and jail for almost 130 years (and was the site of Canada's last public hanging in 1869).

Festivals & Events

Celtic Roots Festival CULTURAL
(www.celticfestival.ca; ⊙Aug) The town fills up in early August for this, one of the largest celebrations of Celtic history and culture in North America.

Blyth Festival THEATER
(☎519-523-9300; www.blythfestival.com; ⊙Jun-Aug) The village of Blyth has the kind of main street Bruce Springsteen likes to sing about, and is home to the summer Blyth Festival. From June to August, primarily Canadian plays get an airing, from outdoor pioneer performances to indoor gut-busting comedies.

Performance days the box office is open from 9am to 9pm; nonperformance days it closes at 5pm.

Sleeping & Eating

Colborne B&B B&B $
(☎519-524-7400; www.colbornebandb.com; 72 Colborne St; d incl breakfast $95-130; P ❄ 📶) Formerly the manse for the Presbyterian Church, this handsome three-story property has four bright, smartly furnished guest bedrooms, each with en suite: two have whirlpools. Delicious gourmet breakfasts, served in the dining room, are a great way to start your day.

Benmiller Inn & Spa INN $$
(☎800-265-1711; www.benmiller.ca; 81175 Benmiller Line; d $172-289; P ❄ 📶 🏊) Just outside Goderich, riverside Benmiller is somewhere to treat yourself with a little old-fashioned luxury and country hospitality. There's a fantastic indoor swimming pool with river views, full-service Aveda treatment spa, the Ivey fine dining restaurant and 57 charming rooms.

Maple Leaf Motel MOTEL $$
(☎519-524-2302; www.themapleleafmotel.com; 54 Victoria St N; d from $159; P❄️📶) This central 11-room motel with quaint country decor is lovingly maintained to a high standard.

Culbert's Bakery BAKERY $
(☎519-524-7941; 49 West St; items from $2; ⏰8am-5:30pm Tue-Sat) Folks come from far and wide for this old-school bakery serving delicious and decadent cream puffs, muffins, tarts and fresh-from-the-oven loaves. The early bird catches the early calories.

West Street Willy's DINER $
(☎519-524-7777; 42 West St; items $8-18; ⏰7am-8pm Tue-Fri & Sun, to 9pm Sat) Hearty breakfasts and home-style faves await you at Willy's: pierogies, pizza, meatloaf and burgers are all on the menu.

Thyme on 21 INTERNATIONAL $$$
(☎519-524-4171; www.thymeon21.com; 80 Hamilton St; mains $20-38; ⏰11:30am-8pm Sun & Tue-Thu, to 9pm Fri, 5-9pm Sat) Goderich's only casual fine-dining establishment is good, despite the lack of competition. Global influences are present in the mouthwatering menu, with mains including lobster, veal, pad Thai and soufflé.

Information

Goderich Tourist Information Centre (☎519-524-6600; www.goderich.ca; 91 Hamilton St; ⏰9am-7pm) Grab the self-guided *4 Heritage Walking Tours* brochure or the *Visitor's Guide* to help you get your bearings.

Getting There & Around

There are no longer bus links to Goderich so you will need your own transport, at least to a larger town such as London.

Southampton & Around

Southampton has happily sequestered itself from the beaten path of rowdy summer holidays. The quaint colony's sandy beach feels almost undiscovered at times, and a stroll down the main streets reveals mom-and-pop shops and the piecemeal architecture of Queen Anne–styled homes.

To the south, neighboring **Port Elgin** is the year-round home to the bulk of shopping, dining and nightlife options for the region. It also has some of the better, more accessible (free parking) and lesser known beaches on this strip of Lake Huron.

About 20km north of Southampton, **Sauble Beach** has a delicious wide strip of white sand and warm, clear waters, but its huge popularity with holidaymakers and revelers and the high cost of car parking take some of the magic away. In winter, it's a ghost town.

Sights & Activities

Chantry Island ISLAND
Chantry Island, just 2km off the shoreline, is home to a lonely lighthouse and a sanctuary for migratory birds. The only way to reach the island is with Chantry Island Tours.

Bruce County Museum MUSEUM
(☎519-797-2080; www.brucemuseum.ca; 33 Victoria St N, Southampton; adult/child $8/4; ⏰10am-5pm Mon-Sat, 1-5pm Sun, to 8pm Wed Jun-Sep) This museum has an extensive collection of artifacts relating to shipwrecks in the region. There are also rotating summer exhibits for kids.

Saugeen-Paisley Rail Trail CYCLING
Cyclists will enjoy this 25km stretch of abandoned railway, which starts at the corner of Albert and Adelaide Sts and ends in the small town of Paisley.

Thorncrest Outfitters KAYAKING
(☎519-797-1608; www.thorncrestoutfitters.com; 193 High St, Southampton; canoe rental from $35) The Saugeen River, which flows into Lake Huron at Southampton, is one of the best-established routes for canoeing and kayaking in southern Ontario. Thorncrest Outfitters runs an extensive program of short self-guided and organized trips aimed at inexperienced paddlers.

Chantry Island Tours BOATING
(☎519-797-5862, 866-797-5862; www.chantryisland.com; per person $30; ⏰Jun-Sep) Informative outings led by the Marine Heritage Society provide fascinating insights into the region's nautical history as well as a chance to climb the blinking lighthouse. Book in advance as only nine people can be accommodated per tour.

Sleeping & Eating

Aunt Mabel's Inn MOTEL $
(☎866-868-2880; www.auntmabels.com; 5084 Hwy 21 S, Port Elgin; d from $80) These spotless, compact rooms have flat-screen TVs, refrigerators and microwaves and comfy beds. Some have soaker tubs. It's a few minutes' drive from some of the coast's best swimming beaches. Better still, Aunt Mabel's kitchen whips up the best home cookin' for miles (from 6am).

Southampton Inn INN $$
(☎519-797-5915; www.thesouthamptoninn.com; 118 High St, Southampton; r/ste $135/155; P ⊖ ❄ 📶) If the beachy blend of sand and wind isn't a good enough exfoliant, head downstairs for a full spa treatment. The upper level is dedicated to sprawling accommodations; each suite has a private sunny sitting room.

Chantry Breezes B&B $$
(☎519-797-1818; www.chantrybreezes.com; 107 High St, Southampton; r incl breakfast $139-189; P ⊖ 📶) This old Queen Anne manor, tucked gently behind gnarled evergreens, features seven rooms spread out among endearingly cluttered antiques and a private garden cottage. Made-to-order breakfasts are delightful to enjoy on the porch.

Elk and Finch CAFE $
(fb.me/ElkandFinch; 54 Albert St, Southampton; mains $8-24; ⊙10am-8pm Mon-Thu, to 9pm Fri, 8am-9pm Sat, 8am-8pm Sun) This 'coffee pub' serves more than caffeinated and alcoholic beverages: sandwiches, salads and thin-crust pizzas will fill you up. Sip your trendy brew in the wobbly house or park yourself at a table on the grassy lawn.

Armen's FUSION $
(224 High St, Southampton; mains $6-14.65; ⊙9am-4pm daily & 5-8pm Wed-Sat) Forget the local greasy spoons and say hi to chatty Armen as he prepares a tasty sandwich from the ever-changing menu. A rotating dinner menu in June, July and August highlights global cuisine; one night it's Canadian, another it's Moroccan. It keeps your taste buds on their toes. Sneak upstairs and enjoy your fresh eats on the sunny rooftop deck.

Information

Southampton Chamber of Commerce (☎519-797- 2215; 201 High St, Southampton; ⊙10am-4pm Mon-Sat, noon-4pm Sun) A small office in the town hall – the large brick building with a clock tower.

Saugeen Shores Chamber Office (☎519-832-2332; 559 Goderich St, Port Elgin; ⊙9am-5pm Mon-Fri, 10am-4pm Sat, noon-4pm Sun) In Port Elgin, 8km down the shoreline; offers a wider array of information about the region.

Sauble Beach Tourism (☎Jul-Aug 519-422-1262, Sep-Jun 519-422-2457; www.saublebeach.com; 672 Main St, Sauble Beach; ⊙9am-5pm) Check in for the lowdown on party town.

Getting There & Away

Passengers arriving at Lester B Pearson International Airport in Toronto can take the **Grey Bruce Airbus** (☎800-361-0393; www.greybruceairbus.com), which connects to Southampton and Port Elgin ($81, three hours, four daily). From Toronto Union bus terminal, **Can-ar** (☎800-387-7097; www.can-arcoach.com) operates a bus service to Port Elgin ($35 to $44, 4¾ hours, one daily), arriving at Ralph's Hi-way Shoppette in the center of town.

London

POP 366,000

Ontario's third-most populous city (after the GTA and Ottawa), midway between Toronto and Detroit, is London, aka the 'forest city.' It bears little resemblance to its English namesake, short of its substantial collection of fine Victorian homes, River Thames and a plethora of leafy parks and gardens. Aside from a smattering of beautiful art-deco buildings, London's downtown core is predictably turn-of-the-millennium, if not a little bit 1970s.

London is home to the University of Western Ontario in the city's north, favored by wealthy Toronto families as *the* spot to send their kids. The student population ensures a young, upbeat vibe.

There's plenty of accommodations in town, some good student-priced eateries and a handful of interesting tourist attractions: it's a great place to visit in the warmer months (it gets heavy snows in the winter) and a wonderful place to live. As Toronto continues to expand, eyes will be more focused on London in years to come.

Sights

Fanshawe Pioneer Village HISTORIC SITE
(☎519-457-1296; www.fanshawepioneervillage.ca; 1424 Clarke Rd; adult/child $7/free; ⊙10am-4:30pm Tue-Sun May-Oct; P) Explore London's history at this 30-building village on the eastern edge of town. Costumed blacksmiths, farmers and craftspeople carry out their duties in true 19th-century pioneer-village style. At the adjoining Fanshawe Conservation Area (p146) you can swim, walk and camp.

Eldon House HISTORIC BUILDING
(☎519-661-5169; www.eldonhouse.ca; 481 Ridout St N; adult/child $7/5; ⊙noon-5pm Tue-Sun) Built in 1834, London's oldest surviving house remains virtually unchanged since the last

century. Inside you'll find heirlooms and treasures belonging to the Harris family, a fascinating bunch, while outside you can enjoy the beautiful 19th-century garden.

Royal Canadian Regiment Museum MUSEUM
(☎519-660-5275; www.thercrmuseum.ca; 750 Elizabeth St; adult/child $5/3; ⏲10am-4pm Tue, Wed & Fri, to 8pm Thu, noon-4pm Sat & Sun; P) Inside the austere Wolseley Hall, this museum focuses on the oldest infantry regiment in Canada, with displays covering the North-West Rebellion of 1885 through both world wars to the Korean War.

Ska-Nah-Doht Village & Museum HISTORIC SITE
(☎519-264-2420; www.lowerthames-conservation.on.ca/Ska-Nah-Doht; Longwoods Rd Conservation Area; adult/child $3/free; ⏲9am-4:30pm; P) At this re-creation of a 1000-year-old Iroquois longhouse community, 32km west of London, village structures are encircled by a maze. The museum contains artifacts thousands of years old and recounts the area's history.

Museum of Ontario Archaeology MUSEUM
(☎519-473-1360; www.uwo.ca/museum; 1600 Attawandaron Rd; adult/child $5/3; ⏲10am-4:30pm; P) This educational and research facility affiliated with the University of Western Ontario displays materials and artifacts spanning 11,000 years of aboriginal history in Ontario. Next door is the **Lawson site**, an active excavation of a 500-year-old precontact Neutral Iroquoian village.

Museum London MUSEUM
(☎519-661-0333; www.museumlondon.ca; 421 Ridout St N; by donation; ⏲noon-5pm Tue-Wed & Fri-Sun, to 9pm Thu; P) Focusing on the visual arts and how they fit together with history, London's vibrant museum has 5000-plus works of art and 25,000-plus artifacts. Free tours run on Sundays at 2pm.

Festivals & Events

London Fringe Festival CULTURAL
(www.londonfringe.ca; ⏲mid-Jun) Eleven days of theater, spoken word, film and visual arts around downtown.

Sunfest MUSIC
(www.sunfest.on.ca; ⏲Jul) Canada's premier world-music festival.

Rock the Park MUSIC
(www.rockthepark.ca; ⏲Jul) For over a decade now, one weekend in July, riverside Harris Park swells with long-haireds and rockers for the likes of Whitesnake, Platinum Blonde and the Tragically Hip.

London Pride LGBT
(www.pridelondon.ca; ⏲Jul) London is big enough and gay enough to celebrate its very own pride festival.

Londonlicious FOOD & DRINK
(www.londonlicious.ca; ⏲Jul-Aug) A London homage to Toronto's hit Summerlicious (p91) festival brings cheap fancy eats to the peeps.

Sleeping

There's a bombardment of cheap, chain motels on the Wellington Rd approach from Hwy 401, but stay downtown if you can.

Woodfield Bed & Breakfast B&B $
(☎519-675-9632; www.woodfieldbb.com; 499 Dufferin Ave; s $90-100, d $95-125) In the heart of historic Woodfield, one of London's most attractive neighborhoods, you'll find this gorgeous B&B in a sprawling Victorian mansion. An alternative to London's generic tourist hotels, it's a great way to experience what this picturesque city has to offer.

StationPark All Suite Hotel HOTEL $
(☎800-561-4574; www.stationparkinn.ca; 242 Pall Mall St; ste from $119; P) This all-suite hotel has oversize bedrooms with separate living rooms. Granted, they could do with a makeover, but the service is excellent and the location near Richmond Row and Victoria Park can't be beat.

Holiday Inn Express & Suites HOTEL $
(☎519-661-0233; www.holidayinn.com/London; 374 Dundas St; d from $109; P) Centrally located, with some great restaurants nearby, this well-maintained property has bright rooms with comfy beds and good showers. Rooms have a refrigerator, microwave and large TV, and there's free internet and breakfast.

Fanshawe Conservation Area Campground CAMPGROUND $
(☎519-451-2800; www.fanshaweconservationarea.ca; 1424 Clarke Rd; campsites $37-47, reservations $13; ⏲May-Oct; P) Convenient camping within the city limits, across from Fanshawe Pioneer Village (p145). Also rents kayaks ($30 per four hours).

ST THOMAS: ALL ABOARD!

St Thomas is a low-key farming community 20km south of London, en route to Lake Erie. It has a well-maintained Victorian downtown and was once the center of rail travel in southern Canada. At its peak, over a hundred trains a day passed through: hard to imagine today, although some interesting relics from the time remain, inviting exploration.

You need to have your own transport to get here. From London, take Hwy 401 or Hwy 402 to the Kings Hwy 4.

North American Railway Hall of Fame (519-633-2535; 750 Talbot St; 8:30am-4:30pm Mon-Fri) From its home in the painstakingly restored Canada Southern Station, built in 1873, the North American Railway Hall of Fame operates a small free museum and oversees the ongoing restoration of this incredible building. Historical displays are presented in the waiting rooms, station board room and the ticket office. Rail buffs, drop in and say hello.

Elgin County Railway Museum (519-637-6284; www.ecrm5700.org; 225 Wellington St; adult/child $5/2; 10am-4pm Tue-Sun Jun-Sep; P) This brick rail shed full of red-hot locomotive action is a must for trainspotters and the kid in everyone. Special events such as comedy are held here.

★Metro BOUTIQUE HOTEL $$
(519-518-9000; www.hotelmetro.ca; 32 Covent Market Pl; d from $158) Rooms in this oh-so-cool boutique hotel in the heart of downtown have exposed-brick walls, rainfall showers, deep soaker tubs and plenty of interesting design elements to keep you entertained.

Delta Armouries HOTEL $$
(519-679-6111; www.deltahotels.com; 325 Dundas St; d from $169; P) The Armouries wing of London's premier hotel was originally a historic military training facility. Its period features remain to be enjoyed, though most rooms are in the tower wing. Expect comfortable, neutrally furnished accommodations, a central location and good-value rates.

Eating

★Covent Garden MARKET $
(519-439-3921; www.coventmarket.com; 130 King St; items from $2; 8am-6pm Mon-Thu & Sat, to 7:30pm Fri, 11am-4pm Sun) This humongous, barn-shaped market will whet and satisfy any appetite. There's a permanent collection of delis, bakeries, chocolate shops, fresh produce stalls and world cuisine eateries, plus seasonal vendors and a sunny, busker-fueled buzz on the patio.

Morrissey House PUB FOOD $
(519-204-9220; www.themorrisseyhouse.com; 359-361 Dundas St; mains $9-16; 11am-late) This centrally located 'grub-pub' offers classy, well-prepared menus and a relaxed vibe inside its Victorian manor rooms, or on the large sunny patio out front. Free wi-fi and great tunes are a bonus. Come for a meal, a few pints or both: everyone else is.

Early Bird DINER $
(519-439-6483; 355 Talbot St; mains $13-16; 9am-9pm Tue-Thu & Sun, to 11pm Fri & Sat) Delicious Early Bird delivers all-day breakfast, barbecue-and-beer Thursday nights, and its own take on from-scratch, home-style cooking. When we say unique, how about the Fat Elvis: smoked bacon, panko fried bananas, peanut butter and local honey sandwiched between French toast. Don't knock it till you've tried it.

Zen Gardens VEGETARIAN $
(519-433-6688; www.zen-garden.ca; 344 Dundas St; mains $10-15; 11:30am-9pm Mon-Sat, 5-9pm Sun) This Asian vegetarian restaurant downtown will impress vegetarians and their most hardened carnivorous mates alike. Tofu, mushrooms, and sauced-up soy and gluten meat feature heavily. Combinations, served in Japanese bento boxes and costing the same as a main, offer the best value.

★Budapest EUROPEAN $$
(519-439-3431; 348 Dundas St; mains $12-25; 11am-10pm Mon-Sat, 4-9pm Sun) If you've been in business for over 50 years, you've got to be doing something right. There is so much authenticity to owner Marika's humble establishment. Over the years, she's perfected her schnitzels, chicken paprikash and pierogies. Yum! Lunch specials are excellent value.

Thaifoon THAI $$
(☎519-850-1222; www.thaifoonrestaurant.com; 120 Dundas St; mains $14-22; ⏰11:30am-2pm Mon-Fri & 4:30-9pm daily) Classing Dundas St up a bit is Thaifoon. A calm, composed atmosphere and babbling water features provide relief from the mean streets, while chili-laden curries, stir-fries, soups and salads provide a kick in the pants.

Bertoldi's Trattoria ITALIAN $$
(☎519-438-4343; www.bertoldis.ca; 650 Richmond St; mains $14-28; ⏰11:30am-10pm Mon-Thu, to midnight Fri, 4pm-midnight Sat, to 10pm Sun) On Richmond Row, casual yet classy Bertoldi's does authentic Italian and has special regional menus and a substantial vino list. There's a nice patio for the warmer months.

Drinking & Entertainment

The vibrant student population ensures plenty of youthful, boozy entertainment. During the end of summer, before term begins, London's 'Richmond Row' (Richmond St from Oxford to Dundas) becomes party central.

Check out the local rag *Scene* (www.scenemagazine.com) for listings.

Barneys/CEEPS PUB
(671 Richmond St; ⏰11am-2am) Don't ask about the name – we don't get it either. Hands down London's largest and most hopping patio. Come for the bands and DJs, pool tables, shuffleboard, and local beers on tap. The original Richmond Row institution.

Call the Office LIVE MUSIC
(☎519-432-4433; www.calltheoffice.com; 216 York St; ⏰5pm-late) A grungy dive bar with cheap drinks and alt-rock live bands, sometimes pulling names like the Jon Spencer Blues Explosion.

London Music Club LIVE MUSIC
(☎519-640-6996; www.londonmusicclub.com; 470 Colborne St; ⏰7pm-late Wed-Sat) Touring blues and folk acts fall over themselves to play here, a rockin' room out the back of a cream-brick suburban house. Electric blues jam on Thursday nights; acoustic open mike on Fridays.

Information

London Public Library (www.londonpubliclibrary.ca; 251 Dundas St; ⏰9am-9pm Mon-Thu, to 6pm Fri, to 5pm Sat, 1-5pm Sun; 📶) A fabulous modern setting with a cafe, a reading garden, and free internet and wi-fi.

Post Office (☎800-267-1177; www.canadapost.ca; 515 Richmond St, at Dufferin St; ⏰9am-5pm Mon-Fri)

Tourism London (☎519-661-5000; www.londontourism.ca; 391 Wellington St; ⏰8:30am-4:30pm Mon-Fri, 10am-5pm Sat) Shares a building with the Canadian Medical Hall of Fame and its interesting/gory displays of brains, hearts and bones.

Getting There & Around

London International Airport (www.londonairport.on.ca; 1750 Crumlin Rd) is a regional base for Air Canada, WestJet and Delta with flights to Toronto, Detroit, and other limited Canadian and US destinations.

Greyhound Canada rolls out of **London Bus Station** (☎800-661-8747; www.greyhound.ca; 101 York St; ⏰6:30am-9pm) to Toronto ($35 to $39, two to four hours, 11 daily) and Windsor ($37, 2½ hours, four daily).

London Train Station (☎519-672-5722; www.viarail.ca; cnr York & Clarence Sts; ⏰5am-9:30pm Mon-Fri, 6:30am-9:30pm Sat & Sun) Has VIA (viarail.ca) trains to Toronto ($69, two hours, seven daily) and Windsor ($58, two hours, four daily).

London Transit (LTC; www.ltconline.ca; 150 Dundas St; ⏰7:30am-7pm Mon-Fri, 8:30am-6pm Sat) Provides extensive bus services around town ($2.75 a ride). At the time of writing, the new LTC smart card system was being rolled out, not without glitches and only for monthly passes...for now.

Windsor

POP 209,000

At the end of the highway on the southwestern tip of Ontario (across the river from Detroit, USA) this once booming center for trade and manufacturing has seen better days. That may change when the Gordie Howe International Bridge opens in 2020, increasing the volume of trade and speed of passage over the border.

For the moment, Windsor's empty facades bear the scars of decline. The upside? Cheap real estate, adjacency to the US and proximity to Lake Erie are slowly luring city slickers looking for a change of pace.

Not a showstopper, Windsor is an interesting urban curiosity for those who want to see a small multicultural town in flux. There's great Lebanese food east of downtown, and homely Italian cuisine a little further south, making a stopover a tasty journey before heading on to the US.

Sights

Visitors will enjoy walking along the Riverwalk, a multiuse path that extends from under the Ambassador Bridge for 5km along the riverfront. The historic Walkerville neighborhood is worth a look.

Dieppe Gardens GARDENS
(cnr Ouellette St & Riverside Dr) These beautiful gardens, on land once used by Detroit–Windsor ferries before the 1929 bridge and 1930 tunnel put them out of business, offer the best views of the smoke-and-mirrors Detroit skyline.

Walls Underground Railroad Museum MUSEUM
(☎ 519-727-6555; www.undergroundrailroadmuseum.org; 855 Puce Rd, Maidstone; $5; ⏲ 10am-4pm May-Oct; P) Some 20km east of Windsor, the 1846 log cabin built by John Freeman Walls, a fugitive slave from North Carolina, is the focal point of this site, which functioned as a safe terminal for others searching for freedom. Walls' descendants still run the museum.

Canadian Club Brands Centre DISTILLERY
(☎ 519-973-9503; www.canadianclubwhisky.com; 2072 Riverside Dr E; admission with tour $12; ⏲ Thu-Sat Jan-Apr, Wed-Sun May-Dec; P) Canadian Club has been sluicing here (formerly known as the Walkerville Distillery) since 1858. Tours (1½ hours at 11am, 1pm, 3pm and 5pm) explore the history of the ornate Italianate building and the distilling process, and offer a taste. Admission by tour only.

Art Gallery of Windsor GALLERY
(AGW; ☎ 519-977-0013; www.agw.ca; 401 Riverside Dr W; adult/child $10/5; ⏲ 11am-5pm Wed-Sun; P) FREE The jaunty glass-and-concrete prow of the AGW has an awesome permanent collection focused on contemporary Canadian sculpture and painting. A free tour (2pm Wednesday and Sunday) is included with admission.

Sleeping & Eating

University Place Accommodations HOTEL $
(☎ 519-254-1112; www.windsorexecutivestay.com; 3140 Peter St; r with shared bath from $39; P ❄ 🛜 🏊) Not affiliated with the university, this long- and short-term residence offers clean rooms with shared facilities including laundry. Rooms with en suites and bike rentals are available.

THE UNDERGROUND RAILROAD

Neither subterranean nor an actual railroad, the Underground Railroad refers to the secretive web of abolitionists and humanitarians – both black and white – who shepherded, sheltered, hid and transported escaped slaves north from the US to freedom in Canada. It's estimated that before the American Civil War 40,000 brave souls made the dangerous journey. This part of southwestern Ontario, so close to the US border, is rich with historic Underground Railroad sites. Many local towns have substantial populations descended from those African Americans who found sanctuary here.

Historical sights include the **Amherstburg Freedom Museum** (p151) and **Walls Underground Railroad Museum** (left). For more information visit www.blackhistorysociety.ca.

Kirk's B&B B&B $
(☎ 519-255-9346; www.kirksbandb.com; 406 Moy Ave; s/d from $75/89; P ⊖ ❄ 🛜) One block from the river, Kirk's is a three-story, old-fashioned brick affair, with a lush garden. Warm, tidy rooms have comfortable beds.

Holiday Inn Windsor Downtown HOTEL $$
(☎ 519-256-4656; www.holidayinn.com; 430 Ouellette Ave; d from $119; P ❄ 🛜 🏊) This generic Holiday Inn is looking a little dated, but has a great downtown position, comfy beds and spacious rooms. There's a full service restaurant on-site, a pool and plenty of parking.

Squirrel's Cage CAFE $
(☎ 519-252-2243; www.thesquirrelcage.ca; 1 Maiden Lane W; items $2-14; ⏲ 8:30am-8pm Mon-Thu & Sat, to 11pm Fri, 10am-3pm Sun) Former city slickers love their new life in Windsor and bring a taste of cosmopolitan Toronto to town in this stylish, upbeat licensed cafe. Expect coffees, soups, delicious filled panini and healthy salads daily, plus weekend brunches.

Cook's Shop ITALIAN $$
(☎ 519-254-3377; cooksshoprestaurant.wordpress.com; 683 Ouellette Ave; mains $15-24; ⏲ 5-10pm Tue-Sun) This reasonably priced fine dining establishment has been operating for over 35 years from its century-old premises. Specializing in seafood, pasta, lamb and beef.

Spago Trattoria e Pizzeria ITALIAN $$
(☎519-252-2233; www.spagos.ca; 690 Erie St E; mains $10-28; ⏲11:30am-10pm Mon-Sat, 1-9pm Sun) Windsor has a reputation for its Italian, and Spago's fits the bill. If you're not in the mood for delicious pasta, rest assured: staff also deliver outstanding wood-fired pizzas, seafood, salad and scaloppine.

Drinking & Entertainment

Manchester PUB
(☎519-977-8020; www.themanchester.ca; 546 Ouellette Ave; ⏲11:30am-late) Friendly staff, hearty British pub fare and a convenient downtown location make the Manchester a sensible choice for a casual relaxed meal and a couple of pints. There's plenty of North American munchies on the menu, too.

Caesar's Windsor CASINO
(☎800-991-7777; www.caesarswindsor.com; 377 Riverside Dr E; ⏲24hr) This provincially owned casino (affiliated with the Caesar's Las Vegas family) gives Windsor an economic boost, although crowds have declined with tighter border security and a strong Canadian dollar. Minimum age 19 years.

The annexed hotel has the best rooms in town – simple yet luxurious in neutral tones, some overlooking the riverfront trails of Windsor or Detroit. There is a pool for over 18s.

ℹ Information

Ontario Travel Information Centre (☎519-973-1338; www.ontariotravel.net; 110 Park St E; ⏲8:30am-8pm) Well stocked with brochures and helpful staff.

Tourism Windsor Essex (☎519-255-6530; www.visitwindsoressex.com; Suite 103, 333 Riverside Dr; ⏲8:30am-4:30pm Mon-Fri) Information on Windsor and the area; best accessed from Pitt St.

Getting There & Away

Detroit–Windsor is a major international border crossing, via either the famously expansive **Ambassador Bridge** (toll $6.25, US$5), or the **Detroit–Windsor Tunnel** (www.dwtunnel.com; toll $4.75-5.75, US$4.50-5) connecting the two downtowns.

Windsor Bus Station (☎519-254-7577; www.greyhound.ca; 300 Chatham St W; ⏲7am-9pm) runs buses to Toronto ($54, five hours, four daily) via London ($36, two hours, four daily). US-bound trips to Chicago ($79, seven to nine hours, four daily) transfer from Greyhound Canada to Greyhound in Detroit. Cheaper fares are available online, in advance. Also here is **Transit Windsor** (☎519-944-4111; www.dwtunnel.com), running Tunnel Bus buses to Detroit ($5, 30 minutes, every 30 minutes) – bring your passport.

Windsor Train Station (☎888-842-7245; www.viarail.ca; cnr Walker & Wyandotte Sts; ⏲5:15am-11:30pm), 3km east of downtown, has trains to Toronto ($124, four hours, four daily) via London ($56, two hours).

UNCLE TOM'S CABIN

About 100km northeast of Windsor, before Chatham, is **Uncle Tom's Cabin Historic Site** (☎519-683-2978; www.uncletomscabin.org; 29251 Uncle Tom's Rd, Dresden; adult/child/family $7/4.50/20; ⏲10am-4pm Mon-Sat, noon-4pm Sun May-Oct; P). Uncle Tom was the fictional protagonist and namesake of the book written by Harriet Beecher Stowe in 1852, based on real-life hero Reverend Josiah Henson. The 5-hectare site displays articles relating to the story and the Underground Railroad, as well as a theater, gallery and interpretive center. To get here, take exit 101 off the 401 and follow the signs.

Lake Erie Shoreline

From the Welland Canal near Niagara to the Detroit River at Windsor, the Lake Erie shoreline is a scenic, thinly populated strip of sandy beaches, small towns and peaceful parks. Many Ontarians have cottages here. Recent environmental efforts are such that you can swim in Lake Erie (the shallowest and warmest of the Great Lakes), but do check with the locals before you go in. If you really want to get away, try quirky Pelee Island, Canada's southernmost point. There's next to no public transport along the shoreline: the following listings assume you're driving between towns.

Amherstburg

War of 1812 and Underground Railroad buffs will find some enthralling diversions in historic Amherstburg, a small town south of Windsor, where the Detroit River flows into Lake Erie – although much more happened here in the past than of late.

Sights

Park House Museum MUSEUM
(519-736-2511; www.parkhousemuseum.com; 214 Dalhousie St; adult/child $4/2.50; 10am-5pm) The oldest house in town, and the only one not *from* town. It was built on the other side of the river, ferried across in 1799, and is now furnished in 1850s style.

Amherstburg Freedom Museum MUSEUM
(519-736-5433; www.amherstburgfreedom.org; 277 King St; adult/student $7.50/6.50; noon-5pm Tue-Fri, 1-5pm Sat & Sun; P) The main exhibition building documents the people escaping slavery in the US, and the black heritage of the region. The highlight here is the Nazrey African Methodist Episcopal Church, a National Historic Site, which was built by former slaves and played a role in the Underground Railroad (p149).

Fort Malden National Historic Site HISTORIC SITE
(519-736-5416; www.amherstburg.ca; 100 Laird Ave; adult/child $4/2; 10am-5pm May-Oct; P) This British fort was built on earthwork embankments along the river in 1840. Beginning with the arrival of the fur traders, the area saw a lot of friction between the French, First Nations and English and, later, the Americans. Here, during the War of 1812, British General Brock (together with his ally, Shawnee Chief Tecumseh) conspired to take Detroit.

Festivals & Events

Shores of Erie WINE
(www.soewinefestival.com; early Sep) Wine and entertainment are the name of the game in this late summer/early fall festival. Book accommodations in advance. Festivals have been canceled in the past, so check the website.

Sleeping & Eating

Bondy House B&B B&B
(519-736-9433; www.bondyhouse.com; 199 Dalhousie St; d with shared/private bath from $110/125; P) You can take a short stroll to the lake or just enjoy the large lily pond garden at this Victorian house. The suite and Captain's Room are the most stylish, but all five rooms are comfortable.

Lord Amherst Public House PUB FOOD $
(519-713-9165; www.lordamherst.ca; 273 Dalhousie St; mains $10-16; 11:30am-late Mon-Sun) Fancy, delicious pub meals and top-shelf beers make this quaint historic watering hole a lovely diversion from your heritage adventures.

Artisan Grill CANADIAN $$
(519-713-9009; www.artisangrill.ca; 269 Dalhousie St; meals $12-28; 11am-10pm Tue-Thu, to 11pm Fri & Sat) It's nice to know that a small town like Amherstburg has decent casual fine dining, as found here in the Artisan Grill: wraps, sandwiches, salads and steaks – even lobster – make the cut.

Information

Amherstburg Visitors Information Centre
(519-736-8320; www.amherstburg.ca; cnr Sandwich & William Sts; 10am-5pm Thu-Mon late May-Oct) This waterfront facility can point you in the right direction for your historical research.

Getting There & Away

You'll need your own wheels to get to Amherstburg. The newly reinstated (and only taxi service) **Amherstburg Taxi** (519-736-1761; www.amherstburgtaxi.ca) can take you to Windsor, the nearest larger town, for around $40.

Leamington & Pelee Island

Lakeside Leamington is the 'Tomato Capital of Ontario,' though most people come here just to get the ferry to Pelee Island. Southeast of town, Point Pelee National Park (the southernmost point of mainland Canada) is a pit stop for thousands of migratory birds during spring and fall.

Canada's southernmost outpost, Pelee Island is a surprising, sleepy oasis in the middle of Lake Erie. In 1788 the Ojibwe and Ottawa Nations leased it to Thomas McKee, though it remained undeveloped until William McCormick bought it in 1823. By 1900 Pelee had 800 residents, four churches and four schools. These days there are just 275 residents and not much else. Life revolves around a very relaxed and humble form of tourism. Green as green can be and surrounded by sandy beaches and shallow water, it's a place to get away from it all without leaving the province.

Sights

Pelee Island Heritage Centre MUSEUM
(519-724-2291; www.peleeislandmuseum.ca; 1073 West Shore Rd, Pelee Island; adult/child $3/2; 10am-5pm May-Oct; P) Near West Dock, the small Pelee Island Heritage Centre has one of the best natural history collections in Ontario. Engrossing displays cover early indigenous to 20th-century history, geology, wildlife, industry, sailing and shipwrecks.

Pelee Island Winery Wine Pavilion WINERY

(☎800-597-3533; www.peleeisland.com; 20 East-West Rd, Pelee Island; special tours adult/child $5/free; ⊙11am-4pm Oct-May, to 8pm Jun-Sep; P) Enjoy the fruits of island life. Regular tours are free at noon, 2pm and 4pm most days; special wine-and-cheese and wine-and-chocolate tours can be scheduled by calling.

Fish Point Nature Reserve PARK

(☎519-825-4659; www.ontarioparks.com/park/fishpoint; 1750 McCormick Rd, Pelee Island; ⊙dawn-dusk; P) This long sandy spit is absolutely the southernmost point of Canada. A 3.2km return forest walkway leads to the point, one of the island's best swimming spots. It's a bird-watcher's Eden, with black-crowned night herons and a multitude of shorebirds.

Point Pelee National Park PARK

(☎519-322-2365; www.pc.gc.ca; Point Pelee Dr, Leamington; adult/child $8/4; ⊙dawn-dusk; P) About 13km southeast of Leamington, this well-loved national park features nature trails, a marsh boardwalk, forests and lovely sandy beaches within the park. The fall migration of monarch butterflies is a spectacle of swirling black and orange.

Tours

Explore Pelee CYCLING

(☎519-325-8687; www.explorepelee.com; Pelee Island; from $40) Tours take you from the oldest home through to the canals, pump houses, lighthouse and island graveyard.

Sleeping & Eating

Stonehill Bed & Breakfast B&B $

(☎519-724-2193; www.stonehillbandb.com; 911 West Shore Rd, Pelee Island; s/d with shared bath $75/90; P ⊖) Built in 1875 with limestone from the quarry in back, this old farmhouse has waterfront views, a park-like setting and friendly hosts. Cozy bedrooms have patchwork quilts.

Wandering Pheasant Inn INN $$

(☎519-724-2270; www.thewanderingpheasantinn.com; 1060 E West Rd, Pelee Island; d incl breakfast $115-175) The most southern inn in Canada occupies one hectare on the island's eastern shore. With no streetlights in sight, it's easy to watch the magical fireflies. There are 15 simple rooms and a hot tub. No kids.

Anchor & Wheel Inn B&B $$

(☎519-724-2195; www.anchorwheelinn.com; 11 West Shore Rd, Pelee Island; unpowered/powered sites $25/40, d $90-115, cottages from $150; P ⊖ ❄) The effervescent Anchor & Wheel, in the northwest corner of Pelee, has a range of beds from grassy campsites through to air-conditioned guest rooms with Jacuzzis and a dockside cottage. There is also an on-site restaurant.

Conorlee's Bakery & Delicatessen BAKERY $

(☎519-724-2321; rickolte.wix.com/bakery; 5 North-shore Dr, Pelee Island; sandwiches $5-7; ⊙8:30am-4pm Mon-Wed, to 9pm Thu-Sun) Conorlee's bakes fresh breads, cakes, pizzas and pies, brews espresso and sells local honey. Grab a sandwich and eat it on the beach.

Drinking & Nightlife

Scudder Beach Bar & Grill BAR

(☎519-724-2902; www.scudderbeach.com; 325 North Shore Rd, Pelee Island; mains $8-16; ⊙noon-10pm May-Sep) This woody bar room serves wraps and sandwiches plus gallons of cold beer; there might even be a live band on Saturday night and a barbecue Saturday day.

Information

- There's an ATM at Scudder Beach Bar & Grill, but it can run out of money on busy weekends! Bring cash.
- For information on Leamington, go to www.tourismleamington.com or look for the Big Tomato on Talbot St.
- All there is to know about Pelee Island can be found at www.pelee.org. Book ferries and accommodations in advance. Services and amenities are limited, including internet access.

Getting There & Around

Access to Pelee Island is by a bumpy grassroots car ferry from April to December. At other times, you'll need a plane. Remember folks, it's an island: many of the roads are unpaved.

Ontario Ferries (☎519-326-2154; www.ontarioferries.com; adult/child/senior $7.50/3.75/6.25, car/bicycle/motorcycle $16.50/3.75/8.25; ⊙Apr–mid-Dec) services the island from Leamington (and sometimes Kingsville). Schedules depend on the day and season; reservations are essential. The trip takes 1½ hours each way.

Pelee Island Transportation (☎800-661-2220; www.ontarioferries.com) ferries also connect Pelee with Sandusky, OH. In winter, forget it.

Bicycles can be rented at **Comfortech Bicycle Rentals** (☎519-724-2828; www.peleebikerental.com; West Shore Rd, Pelee Island; per hr/day $10/25; ⊙May-Oct) near the West Dock.

Port Stanley

A working fishing village in a nook of Kettle Creek, **Port Stanley** (www.portstanley.net) has a pretty downtown and an agreeable, unpretentious atmosphere: it's the kind of place where people talk to you in the streets.

Rail buffs and the young at heart will enjoy **Port Stanley Terminal Rail** (877-244-4478; www.pstr.on.ca; 309 Bridge St; adult/child $15/9), a 14km section of the historic London–Port Stanley railroad. The schedule varies: check the website for details.

The **Port Stanley Festival Theatre** (519-782-4353; www.portstanleytheatre.ca; 302 Bridge St; adult/child from $32.50/19.50;) keeps and visitors amused over its summer season.

If the pace endears you, consider staying at **Inn on the Harbour** (519-782-7623; www.innontheharbour.ca; 202 Main St; d $189-299; P) where you can watch fishing boats come and go, offloading baskets of perch and pickerel, from this upmarket, maritime-hewn inn. In back, the **Little Inn** offers themed suites (think African Safari or Paris Boutique) for $259 per night.

Port Dover & Around

Port Dover is a summer-centric beach town with a sandy, laid-back vibe. Sunburned midlifers, bikini-ed teens and ice-cream-dripping kids patrol the main drag on summer vacation. Good bird-watching and swimming make it a hot spot for outdoor types; for those who like the wind in their flowing locks, there are also the massive, quirky Friday the 13th motorcycle meet ups every Black Friday when sleepy Port Dover turns noisy and social.

Sights

Long Point Provincial Park PARK
(519-586-2133; www.ontarioparks.com; 350 Erie Blvd, Port Rowan; admission per car $11; May-Oct; P) This excellent provincial park, on the coast to the southwest, occupies a sandy spit jagging into the lake, great for swimming.

Unpowered campsites are available for $28, powered for $33.

Turkey Point Provincial Park PARK
(519-426-3239; www.ontarioparks.com; 194 Turkey Point Rd, Turkey Point; admission per car $11; May-Oct; P) Southwest along the coast is this excellent provincial park. Its forests teem with bird nerds and nature lovers.

Unpowered campsites are available for $28, powered for $33.

Port Dover Harbour Museum MUSEUM
(519-583-2660; www.portdovermuseum.ca; 44 Harbour St; by donation; 11am-6pm) This reconstructed fishing shack focuses on the Lake Erie fishing industry and the exploits of local sea dog Captain Alexander McNeilledge ('Wear no specks, use no tobacco, take a wee dram as necessary').

SMOKE GETS IN YOUR EYES

The flat, sandy soils of northern Norfolk County between Port Dover and Port Stanley provide ideal growing conditions for alternate crops – what used to be a strictly tobacco-growing area now also supports hemp and ginseng fields. For a sniff of old 'baccy, take County Rd 45 one hour inland, northeast from Port Stanley, to the **Delhi Tobacco Museum & Heritage Centre** (519-582-0278; www.delhimuseum.ca; 200 Talbot Rd, Delhi; by donation; 10am-4:30pm Mon-Fri, 1-4pm Sat & Sun Jun-Aug; P), a wooden-crate, leaf-filled multicultural museum with displays on local history and tobacco production.

Festivals & Events

Friday the 13th CULTURAL
(www.pd13.com) The out of the ordinary but huge Friday the 13th motorcycle festival sees hundreds of Harley Davidson lovers converge on Port Dover each Black Friday. As one of the largest of its kind in the world, with up to 150,000 motorcycle enthusiasts converging from across North America, it's definitely a spectacle. Book accommodations in advance and expect inflated prices.

Sleeping

Erie Beach Hotel HOTEL $
(519-583-1391; www.eriebeachhotel.com; 19 Walker St, Port Dover; d $120; P) The most central beds in town are at the white-walled Erie Beach Hotel. The best rooms overlook impossibly perfect lawns, while the pubby dining rooms obsess over perch and shrimp (mains $10 to $20). Rooms are slightly cheaper October to May.

Information

Port Dover Visitors Centre (☎519-583-1314; www.portdover.ca; 19 Market St W, Port Dover; ⏰10am-5pm) Can help with accommodations and loan bicycles for free.

MUSKOKA LAKES

The city of Barrie marks the end of Toronto's suburban sprawl and the gateway to the Muskoka Lakes region, although pleasant, lakeside Barrie can feel like just another Toronto suburb at times.

The Muskoka Lakes (or just Muskoka) is a broader name for the region comprising Lakes Muskoka, Rosseau and Joseph, among many smaller others. Originally rich in lumber production and shipbuilding, the area is now at the heart of 'cottage country': a popular place for families to enjoy the water and, for many, to retire. Ontario's most extravagant cottages are here, many in the fabulous 'Millionaires' Row' on Lake Muskoka. Schedule a few days to explore the beauty and serenity of this forested, watery region, particularly delightful in the fall.

There's limited public transportation in the region, which is best explored by car: www.discovermuskoka.ca/suggested-driving-tours. Note that Friday northbound traffic (from Toronto) and southbound Sunday traffic on Hwy 400 can be a nightmare in the summer.

Ontario Northland (www.ontarionorthland.ca) do run buses that pass through each town, but infrequent services make it hard to spend less than two nights in one town.

It's worth stopping at the large **Ontario Travel Information Centre** (☎705-725-7280; www.ontariotravel.net; 21 Maple View Dr; ⏰8am-8pm), along Hwy 400 as you approach the lakes, to arm yourself with maps and brochures.

Orillia

Orillia proudly sits at the northern end of Lake Simcoe, which pours into Lake Couchiching. Neither are technically part of the Muskoka Lakes, but are major stops along the Trent-Severn Waterway. Triangular sails and motorboats clutter the harbor, while drivers turn off Hwy 11 for a stroll down time-warped Mississaga St, Orillia's main drag.

Sights & Activities

Coldwater Canadiana Heritage Museum MUSEUM
(☎705-955-1930; www.coldwatermuseum.com; 1474 Woodrow Rd, Coldwater; by donation; ⏰10am-4pm Mon-Sat late May-Oct) West of Orillia on Hwy 12 before it connects with Hwy 400, you'll find this charming riverside folk museum with its sweet collection of colonial buildings tracing the history of village life from 1830 to 1950.

Leacock Museum MUSEUM
(☎705-329-1908; www.leacockmuseum.com; 50 Museum Dr; ⏰10am-4pm) FREE In 1928 Canadian humorist Stephen Leacock built a lavish waterfront house that has since become the Leacock Museum. It is even easier to drop by now that admission is free and it's open daily. In July the museum hosts the Leacock Summer Festival, a well-regarded literary festival.

Island Princess CRUISE
(☎705-325-2628; www.obcruise.com; ⏰Jun-Oct) Orillia offers a variety of sightseeing cruises on the *Island Princess,* though Penetanguishene and Parry Sound have more picturesque cruising options. There are up to four cruises daily here in July and August. Lunch and dinner cruises require advance booking: check the website for cruise types, schedules and fares.

Sleeping & Eating

Stone Gate Inn HOTEL $$
(☎705-329-2535; www.stonegateinn.com; 437 Laclie St; r incl breakfast from $140; P❄📶🏊) It's the extra perks that set this modern inn apart from the rest: a swimming pool, full business center, hors d'oeuvres over the weekend and bathrobes in the rooms.

Cranberry House B&B $$
(☎705-326-6871; www.orillia.org/cranberryhouse; 25 Dalton Cres S; d incl breakfast from $140) This B&B sits on a quiet street that feels a lot like the set for the TV show *The Wonder Years.* Every house seems tidy and welcoming, and Cranberry House is no exception. Rooms have en suite bathrooms.

Mariposa Market MARKET $
(☎705-325-8885; www.mariposamarket.ca; 109 Mississaga St E; items from $2; ⏰7am-6pm Mon-Thu & Sat, to 8pm Fri, 8am-5:30pm Sun) This half-bakery, half-knickknack shack is a feast for the eyes and the taste buds. Try the assortment of savory pastries for a light lunch, grab a dessert, then shop for souvenirs.

Webers Hamburgers BURGERS $
(☎705-325-3696; www.webers.com; Hwy 11; hamburgers $4.25-6.25; ⌚10:30am-late) Just 12km north of Orillia on Hwy 11, this legendary charcoal-barbecued burger joint lures passers-by with cheap eats and a shmancy sky bridge to nab commuters on the other side. Endless lines of lip-lickers form, salivating over greasy treats.

Entertainment

Orillia Opera House PERFORMING ARTS
(☎705-326-8011; www.orilliaoperahouse.ca; 20 Mississaga St W) The turreted Orillia Opera House hosts a variety of productions including the likes of *Cats* and *Oklahoma!*

Casino Rama CASINO
(☎705-329-3325; www.casinorama.com; 5899 Rama Rd; ⌚24hr) Glitzy Casino Rama is also a main stage on the touring entertainment circuit.

Getting There & Away

Greyhound Canada (greyhound.ca) provides services between Orillia and Toronto ($32, 2¼ hours, six daily), as does **Ontario Northland** (www.ontarionorthland.ca; $31, 2¼ hours, five daily).

Gravenhurst

While nearby Bracebridge is favored among visitors, Gravenhurst is coming into its own. Check out Muskoka Wharf, a postmillennial waterfront development including shops, restaurants, condos, a farmers bazaar and a museum.

Sights

Bethune Memorial House HISTORIC BUILDING
(☎705-687-4261; www.pc.gc.ca/bethune; 297 John St N; adult/child $4/2; ⌚10am-4pm Jun-Oct) This small museum honors Canadian doctor Norman Bethune, who spent much of his life in China as a surgeon and educator. Bethune set up the world's first mobile blood-transfusion clinic while in Spain during the Spanish Revolution.

Muskoka Boat & Heritage Centre MUSEUM
(☎705-687-2115; www.realmuskoka.com; 275 Steamship Bay Rd; adult/child $7/2; ⌚10am-6pm Mon-Fri, to 4pm Sat & Sun) This museum tells the region's rich history of steamships and hoteliers with displays of over 20 wooden vessels. Also here, you'll find two ships: the *Segwun*, the oldest operating steamship in North America, and the *Wenonah II*, a modern cruiser with an old-school design. In a past life, the *Segwun* was a mail ship serving secluded Muskoka enclaves. A variety of cruises are available: check the website for details.

Festivals & Events

Music on the Barge MUSIC
(http://fb.me/musiconthebarge; Gull Lake Park; by donation; ⌚late Jun-late Aug) In summer, thousands flock to hear big-band numbers, jazz or country. Concerts start at 7:30pm each Sunday from late June to late August.

Sleeping & Eating

Residence Inn Muskoka Wharf HOTEL $$
(☎705-687-6600; www.marriott.com; 285 Steamship Bay Rd; d/ste from $125/160; P❄📶🏊) If you want to be by the water, it's hard to get closer than this hulking new property in the Muskoka Wharf complex offering large, freshly decorated studios and suites with full kitchens, separate living and sleeping areas and generous bathrooms. Some have balconies and lake views. Rates include buffet breakfast, and spike in peak periods.

★ **Taboo Resort** RESORT $$$
(☎705-687-2233; www.tabooresort.com; 1209 Muskoka Beach Rd; d from $199; P❄📶🏊) Finally, a boutique Ontario property with international appeal. Occupying a stunning lake frontage on a compact peninsula, Taboo's hotel rooms and suites have clean, minimalist lines, gray and maple woods, and slick bathrooms with designer bath products. Tri-level chalets are perfect if you're bringing the kids: they'll disappear into kids' clubs so you can enjoy a cocktail by the pool, a round of golf or the fabulous cuisine.

Pizza Station PIZZA $
(☎705-687-3111; 415 Bethune Dr N; small pizzas from $7; ⌚10am-10pm Mon-Sat) Locals swear by this nondescript pizza joint for its steaming-hot cheesy goodness with just the right amount of toppings and a crispy crunchy crust.

Blue Willow Tea Shop BRITISH $
(☎705-687-2597; www.bluewillowteashop.ca; 900 Bay St; high tea $24, mains $14-16; ⌚10am-4pm Mon-Thu, to 8pm Fri & Sat, to 3pm Sun) This lovely waterfront tearoom serves high tea daily from 2pm. There's a limited dinner menu with British staples like bangers and mash and fish and chips.

☆ Entertainment

Gravenhurst Opera House THEATER
(☎705-687-5550; www.gravenhurstoperahouse.com; 295 Muskoka Rd S) This charming heritage building presents a summer season of professional theater.

Information

Gravenhurst Chamber of Commerce (☎705-687-4432; www.gravenhurstchamber.com; 685 Muskoka Rd N; ⊙8:30am-5pm Mon-Fri, 9am-noon Sat) Located on the edge of town. Additional information can be found at www.gravenhurst.ca.

Getting There & Away

Ontario Northland (www.ontarionorthland.ca) runs buses between Toronto and Gravenhurst ($40, three hours, four to five daily) on the North Bay route, which pull in to the Gravenhurst Train Station. Trains have not served the region for years.

Bracebridge

Woodsy Bracebridge sits on the 45th parallel, halfway between the North Pole and the equator! This enchanting town reveals its natural charms throughout the year, with towering evergreens, gushing waterfalls and brilliant maples.

Sights

Bracebridge Falls WATERFALL
Near the visitors center you'll find the best known of Bracebridge's 22 waterfalls, Bracebridge Falls. Other favorites include Muskoka South Falls (33m), about 6km south of town, Wilson's Falls and High Falls, both to the north.

Muskoka Brewery BREWERY
(☎705-646-1266; www.muskokabrewery.com; 13 Taylor Rd; ⊙11am-5pm Mon-Sat, to 4pm Sun) Muskoka Brewery bottles some delicious flavors including a cream ale and a couple of lagers. In summer free taste-testing tours depart 12:30pm to 3:30pm on the half-hour, Thursday to Saturday.

Tours

Lady Muskoka BOATING
(☎705-646-2000; www.ladymuskoka.com; cruises adult/child from $32/16; ⊙May-Oct) Muskoka's largest cruise ship takes in the beauty of Lake Muskoka, including jaw-dropping 'Millionaires' Row,' where the other half relax. A variety of sailings, including brunch cruises, are available.

Festivals & Events

Muskoka Autumn Studio Tour CULTURAL
(www.muskokaautumnstudiotour.com) For over 35 years, each September local artists have opened their studio doors to the public.

Sleeping & Eating

Inn at the Falls HOTEL $$
(☎705-645-2245; www.innatthefalls.ca; 1 Dominion St; d $109-179; P ❄ 📶) Iron lanterns, antique candelabras, portraits and picket fences uphold the 1870s vibe of this local landmark, with its grand main building and six cottages. It's a popular wedding spot. Suites have charming decor and gargantuan beds that feel like boats. The on-site gourmet pub has a stunning patio surrounded by tiered gardens overlooking the bay. Rates lower Sunday to Thursday.

Wellington Motel MOTEL $$
(☎705-645-2238; www.wellingtonmotel.com; 265 Wellington St; d/ste $110/179; P ❄) This tidy, centrally located redbrick motel is retro but clean. Rooms have refrigerator, microwave and huge bathrooms. Suites come with full kitchens.

Old Station PUB FOOD $$
(☎705-645-9776; www.oldstation.ca; 88 Manitoba St; mains $13-30; ⊙11:30am-10pm Sun-Thu, to 11pm Fri & Sat) On summer evenings this is the most happening place in town. The patio overlooks the main drag – perfect for postkayak recovery sessions. Dig into a pulled pork sandwich and wash it back with a pint of Muskoka ale from the brewery just over the road.

Riverwalk Restaurant MEDITERRANEAN $$$
(☎705-646-0711; 1 Manitoba St; mains lunch $12-18, dinner $28-37; ⊙11:30am-2:30pm & 5:30-8:30pm Tue-Sun) Tear your eyes away from the view to focus on the menu, if you can. You'll need to choose between pork, chicken, duck, veal, beef, lamb or seafood. Reservations recommended.

Information

Bracebridge Visitors Centre (☎705-645-8121; www.bracebridge.ca; 1 Manitoba St; ⊙9am-5pm Mon-Fri, 10am-5pm Sat year-round, noon-4pm Sun Jun-Aug) Open year-round.

Getting There & Away

Ontario Northland (www.ontarionorthland.ca) buses connect Bracebridge with Toronto ($43, three hours, four to five daily) on the North Bay route.

Rosseau & Port Carling

You may pass through sleepy Rosseau on the way elsewhere. It's a quaint little village with a small beach, a historic library, a few antique shops and one or two cafes. It's your closest village if you choose to stay in Muskoka's luxury resort, the **Rosseau** (JW Marriott Resort & Spa; ☎705-765-1900; www.therosseau.com; 1050 Paignton House Rd, Minett; d/ste from $199/249;): ideal for couples with kids and/or money, it's the kind of place where Mom and Dad can swim by the pool while the youngsters ramble on guided nature walks. Dining is limited to the resort's expensive offerings. Suites have kitchens, but cost a small fortune. In short, it's huge, handsome and has it all, but isn't for everyone.

North of Bracebridge along Rte 118, in wealthy Port Carling, is a fantastic **mural** of an old ship. A closer glance reveals that the mural is actually a mosaic of vintage photographs: truly remarkable. Muskoka's majestic beauty serves as an inspiring backdrop for many other artists in the region. Contact **Muskoka Arts and Crafts** (muskokaartsandcrafts.com) for more information.

Huntsville

Pretty Huntsville, Muskoka's largest town, set among twisting lakes and furry pines, is the gateway to Algonquin Provincial Park in eastern Ontario. Base yourself here for day trips to the park, around Muskoka, or before setting off on an Algonquin adventure, although you'll need your own wheels.

Sights

Muskoka Heritage Place MUSEUM

(☎705-789-7576; www.muskokaheritageplace.org; 88 Brunel Rd; adult/child $17/12; May-Oct) Come here for a historical perspective of the region, which includes an authentic pioneer village, several informative museums and a working steam train from 1902 (departs several times per day; rides included in admission).

Festivals & Events

Festival of the Arts ART

(www.huntsvillefestival.on.ca) Music, films and general arts celebrations are held year-round.

Sleeping

Huntsville Inn MOTEL $

(☎866-222-8525; www.hunstvilleinn.com; 19 King William St; d from $55; P) In a prime location by the bridge, fully refurbished rooms with flat-screen TVs and free wi-fi offer excellent value.

Au Petit Dormeur INN $

(☎705-789-2552; www.aupetitdormeur.com; 22 Main St W; d $80-100; P) Set in a beautiful colonial home, rooms are stylish – there's even a fitness facility. Breakfast can be taken on the balcony overlooking the nearby lake.

Hidden Valley Resort RESORT $$

(☎705-789-2301; www.hvmuskoka.com; 1755 Valley Rd; d from $115;) Most of the well-proportioned, recently refurbished rooms in this '90s-style resort have a balcony with a wonderful vista of the lake and the expansive well-tended grounds. There's a restaurant with a fabulous patio, outdoor and indoor pools and even a small ski-hill nearby. It's 8km north of Huntsville.

Knights Inn Motel MOTEL $$

(☎705-789-4414; www.knightsinn.ca; 69 Main St W; d/tw $100/110; P) In a nice hillside spot across the road from the lake and a short walk to downtown, this quality motel includes breakfast in a sunny common room. There is also a picnic area, in-room microwave and children's play set.

Eating & Drinking

★**That Little Place by the Lights** ITALIAN $

(☎705-789-2536; www.thatlittleplacebythelights.ca; 76 Main St E; meals $6-14; 10am-9:30pm Mon-Sat) A local favorite, this little place by the lights is loved for its old-school pizzas, pastas and gelati. Excellent value.

Louis' Restaurant DINER $

(☎705-789-5704; www.eatatlouis.com; 24 Main St E; mains $9-18; 7am-9pm) This pleasant family diner is great for cheap breakfasts and cheery lunches like old-school BLTs, burgers and souvlaki. Daily specials.

Bo's Authentic Thai THAI $$
(☎705-789-8038; 79 Main St E; mains $12-19; ⊙11am-9pm; ☑) As the name suggests, authentic Thai dishes (although with only English names on the menu) are presented with flair in this joint by the water. Vegetarian options are available.

Mill on Main CANADIAN $$
(☎705-788-5150; www.themillonmain.ca; 50 Main St E; mains $12-20; ⊙11am-9pm Mon-Thu, to 1am Fri & Sat, to 8pm Sun) Try the famous cheese balls – you won't regret it. With a lovely covered patio offering glimpses of the water and some classy original twists on old favorites, the Mill is a good spot for a casual meal or a few drinks. There's sometimes live music on weekends.

On the Docks PUB
(☎705-789-7910; www.onthedockspub.com; 90 Main St E; items $6-14; ⊙11:30am-1am) Swing by for tasty wraps, appetizers and sandwiches on the fantastic multilevel water-view patio.

Information

Chamber of Commerce (☎705-789-1751; www.huntsville.ca; 8 West St N; ⊙9am-5pm Mon-Fri, 10am-3pm Sat) Loaded with local info.

Getting There & Away

Ontario Northland (www.ontarionorthland.ca) has buses from Toronto to Huntsville ($39.30, three hours, four to five daily), but there is no onward public transport to the park.

Parkbus (parkbus.ca) runs a good-value, seasonal service from Toronto to Algonquin Provincial Park ($88 return, three to four hours). It is infrequent and popular – book in advance on the website.

GEORGIAN BAY

A vast realm of blues and greens, Georgian Bay is a land of infinite dreaming. Summer breezes blow gently along sandy shores. Maples ignite in the fall and thick pines quiver at winter's frosty kiss. These ethereal landscapes inspired Canada's best-known painters and today the bay remains home to scores of thriving artistic communities.

In the bay's southern arc sits Wasaga Beach, the longest freshwater beach in the world. Neighboring Collingwood and Blue Mountain are home to the province's most popular winter skiing.

Heading north on its western shore from Owen Sound, the magnificent Bruce Peninsula is famed for its jagged limestone outcrops, shimmering cliffs and craggy beaches. It boasts tiny but impressive Tobermory, and Manitoulin Island. Linger here for a few days if you can.

This area's long distances require a set of wheels and a strong desire for a road trip. They also make the **Parkbus** (parkbus.ca) routes, particularly to Tobermory, an excellent and popular summer option, so book ahead.

Parry Sound

Formerly a busy shipping port, little Parry Sound is gently tucked behind hundreds of tiny islands in Georgian Bay. The atmosphere is laid-back and serene, despite the giant set of railroad tracks soaring through the sky near the docks.

Sights & Activities

Bobby Orr Hall of Fame MUSEUM
(☎877-746-4466; www.bobbyorrhalloffame.com; 2 Bay St; adult/child $9/6; ⊙10am-5pm Tue-Sat, 11am-5pm Sun) For the uninitiated, local legend and hockey hero Bobby Orr forever changed the role of defensemen with his awesome offensive prowess. At his huge modern shrine, fans can pretend to be a sports announcer or strap on goalie gear and confront an automated puck-firing machine.

MV Chippewa III CRUISE
(☎705-746-6064; www.spiritofthesound.ca; Seguin River Parkette, Bay St; ⊙Jun-Oct) Lunch and dinner cruises are among the variety of options aboard this tiny green tugboat. Check the website for fares and schedules.

Island Queen CRUISE
(☎800-506-2628; https://islandqueencruise.com; 9 Bay St; 2hr morning cruises adult/child $30/15, 3hr afternoon cruises $40/20; ⊙Jun-Oct) Cruise through the nearby 30,000 islands (that's right!) on the good ship *Island Queen*. A variety of sailings are available.

White Squall KAYAKING
(☎705-342-5324; www.whitesquall.com; 53 Carling Bay Rd, Nobel; rentals from $27, day tours from $129; ⊙9am-5:30pm Apr-Oct) Explore the area's waterways with rental kayaks and guided tours: friendly staff offer a range of programs. HQ is about 15km northwest of Parry Sound near Nobel, en route to Killbear Provincial Park.

Georgian Bay

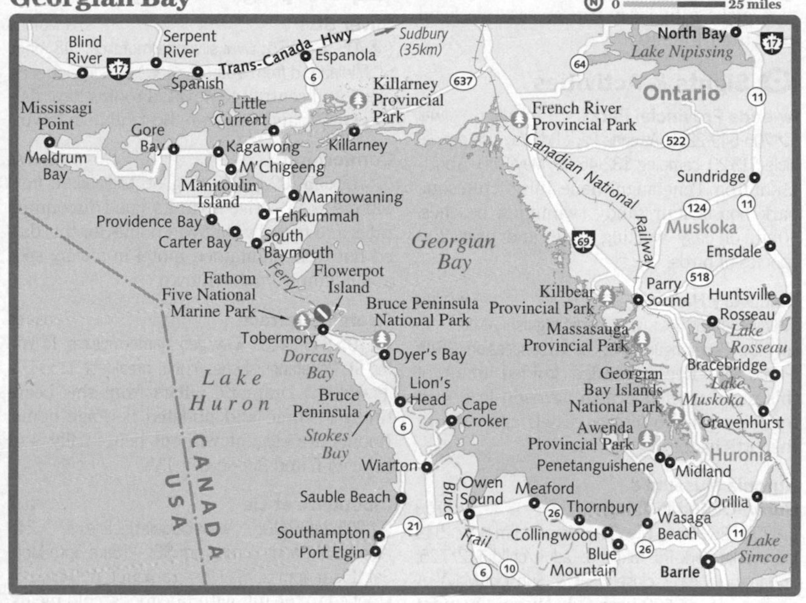

Festivals & Events

Festival of the Sound MUSIC
(www.festivalofthesound.ca; ⌚mid-Jul–mid-Aug) Parry Sound hosts a nationally renowned festival of classical music. Ticket prices vary.

Sleeping & Eating

Bayside Inn B&B **$$**
(☎705-746-7720; www.psbaysideinn.com; 10 Gibson St; r $108-148; P ⊖ ❄ @) Built in the 1880s as a luxurious private residence, this refurbished estate is full of pleasant surprises, including a twisting staircase behind the fireplace and 12 beautiful bedrooms with memory-foam mattresses. All rooms have en suite bathrooms.

Lill's Place CAFE **$**
(46 Seguin St; items $5-15; ⌚8am-3:30pm Wed-Sun) A mean eggs Benedict and good coffee are the stars of breakfast here. The friendly family owners help give it a local, unfussy vibe.

Wellington's PUB FOOD **$$**
(☎705-746-1333; www.wellingtonspubandgrill.com; 105 James St; mains $12-25; ⌚11am-10pm) Wellington's is the 'light beer' of pubs – it looks like a bar, but it's healthier for you. The menu has some calorie-conscious options like pecan chicken.

Information

Georgian Bay Country Visitors Centre (☎705-746-1287; www.gbcountry.com; 70 Church St; ⌚9am-5pm Mon-Fri) At the former train station.

Getting There & Away

Ontario Northland (www.ontarionorthland.ca) buses connect Parry Sound with Toronto ($57.20, three to four hours, three daily) on the Sudbury route.

Midland & Penetanguishene

The native Huron-Ouendat people first settled the region and developed a confederacy to encourage cooperation among neighboring Aboriginal tribes. This alliance attracted French explorers and Jesuit missionaries eager to save their souls. Much of Midland's fascinating history focuses on the bloody altercations between the Huron and the Christian stalwarts. Midland is also known for the more than 30 vibrant murals which have transformed downtown into an outdoor art/history lesson.

Less than 6km up the road Penetanguishene (pen-uh-*tang*-wa-sheen), a small town with a big name, makes a great base for exploring the 30,000 islands that are sprinkled around Georgian Bay. Together, they make a fine day trip or easy weekend away from Toronto.

Sights & Activities

Awenda Provincial Park PARK
(705-549-2231; Awenda Park Rd; day use per vehicle $12-20, camping $32-46; May-Oct) About 15km from Penetanguishene, this picturesque park boasts four sandy swimming beaches, 30km of easy walking trails and over 200 species of birds.

Discovery Harbour MUSEUM
(705-549-8064; www.penetanguishene.ca; 93 Jury Dr, Penetanguishene; adult/concession $8/7; May-Sep) Recommended guided tours of this reconstructed British garrison lead visitors through two replica vessels and recount the fort's history.

Huronia Museum & Huron-Ouendat Village MUSEUM
(705-526-2844; www.huroniamuseum.com; 549 Little Lake Park Rd, Midland; adult/child $12/7.25; 9am-5pm daily, closed Sat & Sun Oct-May) A replica of a 500-year-old Huron-Ouendat settlement. The museum houses a collection of almost a million pieces – not all are on display!

Ste-Marie among the Hurons HISTORIC SITE
(705-526-7838; www.saintemarieamongthe-hurons.on.ca; Hwy 12, Midland; adult/child $10/9; 10am-5pm Apr-Oct) Costumed staff members dote on visitors to this reconstruction 17th-century Jesuit mission, offering stories about hardship and torture with a cheerful smile.

Martyrs' Shrine MONUMENT
(www.martyrs-shrine.com; Hwy 12, Midland; adult/child $5/free; 8am-9pm May-Oct) This monument to six Jesuit missionaries who met their demise at the hands of the Iroquois features a large lawn strewn with crosses and the imposing cathedral-esque Shrine church. Each year, thousands make a pilgrimage here to pay homage to martyred St Jean de Brébeuf.

Tours

30,000 Island Tours BOATING
(705-549-3388; www.midlandtours.com; 177 King St, Midland; adult/child $30/16, with lunch $45/34; May-Oct) *Miss Midland* isn't a regional beauty pageant, but the name of a vessel: cruise on her daily at 2pm from Midland dock. Lunch and dinner cruises operate July to August.

Sleeping & Eating

Silver Star MOTEL $
(705-526-6571; www.silverstarmotel.ca; 748 Yonge St, Midland; d from $65; P) Cheap, cheery, clean and central! Renovated rooms have flat-screen TVs and free wi-fi. Best value in town.

Comfort Inn MOTEL $$
(705-526-2090; 980 King St, Midland; d from $105; P) Drive-up units, good discounted rates and friendly staff win points for this dated but well-maintained motel in a leafy spot about 3km from downtown.

Georgian Terrace B&B $$
(705-549-2440; www.georgianterrace.ca; 14 Water St, Penetanguishene; r incl breakfast $150-175; P) Dramatic pillars front this beautifully restored and updated heritage home. Rooms are elegant without being frilly, and have wi-fi and flat-screen TVs.

Ciboulette et cie DELI $
(705-245-0410; www.ciboulettetetcie.ca; 248 King St, Midland; items from $6; 8am-6pm Mon-Sat, 10am-4pm Sun) This gourmet deli/cafe is stocked to the hilt with fine foods, cold meats, cheeses, freshly made soups and sauces. The cafe serves great coffees and light meals, and there's a range of products to go.

★ **Captain Ken's Diner** FISH & CHIPS $$
(705-549-8691; www.captainkensdiner.com; 70 Main St, Penetanguishene; mains $12.50-30; 7am-9pm) Come say hello to Ken as he fries your lightly battered fresh lake pickerel to perfection. He got a part-time job here at 14 when it was a pool hall, bought the joint at 17 and over decades turned it into the smoothly operating fish, chips and sports-bar success story it is today. The food is as good as the story.

Explorer's Cafe INTERNATIONAL $$
(705-527-9199; www.theexplorerscafe.com; 345 King St, Midland; mains $21-30; 5-10pm Sun, Tue & Wed, noon-10pm Thu-Sat) This quirky restaurant remains a favorite: its walls are lined with booty from around the world. While meals are just as international, only local produce is used in their creation.

Cellarman's Ale House PUB FOOD $$
(705-526-8223; http://cellarmans.ca; 337 King St, Midland; mains $13-18; 11:30am-11pm Mon-Thu, to midnight Fri & Sat) This cozy pub has an intimate location, tucked away off King St. Hearty British fare keeps the locals strong during drafty winters: try a Scotch egg with your steak and mushroom pie. Mmm.

Entertainment

King's Wharf Theatre THEATER
(☎888-449-4463; www.kingswharftheatre.com; 93 Jury Dr, Penetanguishene; ⊙May-Sep) Hosts small-town productions of big-name musicals at its wonderful wooden lakeside theater.

Information

Southern Georgian Bay Chamber of Commerce (☎705-526-7884; http://southerngeorgianbay.ca; 208 King St, Midland; ⊙9am-5pm Mon-Fri) Produces the *Southern Georgian Bay Visitor Guidebook*: download it from the website.

Tourist Office (☎705-549-2232; 2 Main St, Penetanguishene; ⊙9am-5pm May-Oct) You can't miss this seasonal office on the docks.

Getting There & Away

There are no direct buses from Toronto to the area, but **Greyhound Canada** (greyhound.ca) runs a bus to Barrie. One hour later a bus runs from Barrie to Midland and Penetanguishene ($19, one hour, once daily). **Central Taxi Midland** (☎705-526-2626; www.centraltaximidland.ca) can take you between Midland and Penetanguishene if you don't have wheels.

WASAGA: WORLD'S LONGEST FRESHWATER BEACH

Wasaga has the distinct honor of being the longest freshwater beach in the world. It's also the closest full-fledged beach resort to Toronto, attracting thousands of visitors every summer. Most of the 14km-long expanse of soft sands and crashing waves belongs to **Wasaga Beach Provincial Park** (☎705-429-2516; www.wasagabeachpark.com; day use per vehicle $15; ⊙May-Oct); no camping. The beach receives so much hype during the summer, many people forget that Wasaga's pristine sand dunes transform into awesome cross-country skiing in the winter.

Greyhound Canada (greyhound.ca) operates services from Toronto to Wasaga Beach East ($35, three hours, once daily).

Collingwood & Blue Mountain

Pretty lakeside Collingwood and neighboring Blue Mountain, a handsome ski resort and summer playground, have become a year-round mecca for those who enjoy activity with their scenery. The area is called Blue Mountains; the resort is called Blue Mountain. If healthy outdoorsy pursuits aren't your thang, why not sink your teeth into the Apple Pie Trail, a delicious excuse to see Ontario's picturesque apple country (steamy lake air creates perfect growing conditions) while tasting one delicious apple pie after another.

Activities

★**Blue Mountain** SKIING
(☎705-445-0231; www.bluemountain.ca; 108 Jozo Weider Blvd, Blue Mountains; day & night lift tickets adult/child $20/19; ⊙9am-10pm) Hands down the best skiing and snowboarding in Ontario, from the folks who brought you Whistler and Mont-Tremblant: freestyle terrain, half-pipes, jump-on jump-off rails, 16 lifts and over 35 runs from beginner to double black diamond. The Blue Mountain Snow School offers a variety of lessons for all experience levels. Courses including day lift pass, rental and instruction start at $89.

In summer, activities abound, including mountain biking, sailing, climbing, hiking and windsurfing.

Scanidnave Spa SPA
(☎705-443-8484; www.scandinave.com/en/blue mountain; 152 Grey Rd 21, Blue Mountain; baths $55; ⊙10am-9pm) Indulge yourself silly in this fine Scandinavian-style treatment spa featuring hot baths, cold baths, waterfalls, snow-rolling (winter only) and saunas.

Free Spirit Tours ADVENTURE SPORTS
(☎705-444-3622, 519-599-2268; www.freespirit-tours.com; 236720 Grey Rd 13, Heathcote; activities from $55) Escape the crowds and enjoy a sensational day in the Georgian Bay region rock climbing, caving or kayaking (summer), or take a stab at snowshoeing in the winter.

Festivals & Events

Elvis Festival PERFORMING ARTS
(www.collingwoodelvisfestival.com; ⊙Jul) Since 1995, every July Collingwood becomes a sea of Elvises in this, one of the largest competitions for Elvis impersonators in the world.

Wakestock SPORTS
(www.wakestock.com; ⊙Aug) In August young wakeboarders descend on Collingwood with their expensive toys for this loud festival of action sports and music.

Sleeping & Eating

Mariner Motor Hotel MOTEL $$

(705-445-3330; www.marinermotorhotel.ca; 305 Hume St, Collingwood; d from $109; P) Who would have thought a piece of the great architect Frank Lloyd Wright's legacy would end up as a roadside motel in Collingwood. Basic, retro and even a little awkward; we just love the authenticity of this place.

Days Inn & Suites MOTEL $$

(705-444-1880; www.daysinncollingwood.com; 15 Cambridge St, Collingwood; d from $110) Midway between Collingwood and Blue Mountain, this 76-room chain motel is well maintained by professional staff. Neutrally furnished rooms have microwaves.

Blue Mountain Inn HOTEL $$

(705-445-0231; www.bluemountain.ca; 110 Jozo Weider Blvd, Blue Mountain; r $89-499; P@) Accommodations range from standard guest rooms to upscale mosaic three-bedroom suites, all of which have seen a face-lift in recent years. Check the website for the wide variety of options: rates vary dramatically.

★**Westin Trillium House** RESORT $$$

(705-443-8080; www.westinbluemountain.com; 220 Gord Canning Dr, Blue Mountain; d/ste from $199/249;) Couple-friendly, pet-friendly and family-friendly, this Westin upholds its brand's reputation for excellence in service. A wide range of guest rooms and suites are all luxuriously furnished and most overlook the Blue Mountain Village, pond or outdoor pools. Experiment with your dates for the best rates and packages.

Grandma Lambe's MARKET $

(Hwy 26; 8am-6pm Sat-Thu, to 7pm Fri) You won't regret the 35km trek to Grandma Lambe's (west on Hwy 26 between Thornbury and Meaford). The store is a delicious jumble of maple syrup vintages, butter tarts, bushels of vegetables and tables piled high with pies, buns and jellies.

Tremont Cafe EUROPEAN $$$

(705-293-6000; www.thetremontcafe.com; 80 Simcoe St, Collingwood; mains $16-34; 11am-3pm & 5:30-9:30pm Wed-Mon) Come for a mouth-watering weekend brunch or classic dinner at this delightful fine dining cafe in the historic Tremont building. Will you have the duck confit or Atlantic salmon after your lamb lollipops? Dinner menus change regularly.

Information

Georgian Triangle Tourism Association (705-445-7722; www.visitsouthgeorgianbay.ca; 45 St Paul St, Collingwood; 9am-5pm) Pop in to get inspired about the wonderful Georgian Bay region.

Getting There & Around

Greyhound Canada (greyhound.ca) has limited services from Toronto to Collingwood ($39, three hours, once daily) continuing to Owen Sound ($43, 4¼ hours, once daily).

Ace Cabs (705-445-3300; www.collingwoodtaxi.com) can drive you between Collingwood and Blue Mountain ($26, 15 minutes).

AUC Tours (416-741-5200; www.auctours.com) operates a shuttle ($21) from Toronto City Hall to Blue Mountain (from December to April). Refer to the website for online bookings.

Bruce Peninsula

The Bruce is a 100km limestone outcrop of craggy shorelines and green woodlands at the northern end of the Niagara Escarpment. The finger-like protrusion separates the cooler crystal waters of Georgian Bay from warmer Lake Huron. Owen Sound is the largest regional center, while delightful Tobermory is the reward at the tip of the peninsula.

Owen Sound

Owen Sound has a sordid past as a port rife with booze and prostitution. Things got so out of hand that alcohol was banned here for over 60 years – hard to believe, today. By the time the embargo was lifted in 1972, the town had transformed into a thriving artists' colony and remains so today: check out the Owen Sound Artist's Co-op when you're in town.

Sights

Tom Thomson Art Gallery MUSEUM

(519-376-1932; www.tomthomson.org; 840 1st Ave W; 10am-5pm Mon-Fri, noon-5pm Sat & Sun) FREE This gallery displays the work of Tom Thomson, granddaddy of modern Canadian landscape painting. His intimate and smoldering portrayal of nature is said to have inspired the formation of the Group of Seven painters. Thomson grew up near Owen Sound and many of his works were composed in nearby thickets. Especially worth popping by now that it's free.

Owen Sound Farmers Market MARKET
(114 8th St E; 8am-12:30pm Sat) This co-op of vendors is one of the oldest in Ontario. Expect the freshest produce, as well as maple syrup, soaps and baked goods.

Billy Bishop Heritage Museum MUSEUM
(519-371-3333; www.billybishop.org; 948 3rd Ave W; adult $5, child free with adult; 11am-5pm Tue-Fri, noon-5pm Sat & Sun, closed Sat & Sun Jan-Apr) Hometown hero William Avery ('Billy') Bishop, Canada's notorious WWI flying ace, is honored here at his childhood home. Now the Billy Bishop Heritage Museum, it celebrates Canada's aviation history.

Grey Roots Museum & Archives MUSEUM
(519-376-3690; www.greyroots.com; 102599 Grey Rd 18/RR 4; adult/child $8/4; 10am-5pm) This interesting museum highlights the region's rich pioneering history through displays about early settlers and local heroes. Interactive presentations focus on natural resources, climate and topography. Past exhibits have explored themes as diverse as Albertan dinosaurs and the history of the toilet.

Festivals & Events

Summerfolk Music Festival MUSIC
(www.summerfolk.org; mid-Aug) This epic three-day folk fest in mid-August draws world-class performers and artisans from far and wide.

Sleeping & Eating

Highland Manor B&B $$
(519-372-2699; www.highlandmanor.ca; 867 4th Ave A W; s/d $130/170; P) This magnificent Victorian mansion (c 1872) has been elegantly furnished by attentive hosts. Decadent, spacious suites all have their own bathrooms. Many have original fireplaces. Enjoy a glass of wine on the wraparound deck, or curl up by the fireplace. Highly recommended.

Diamond Motor Inn MOTEL $$
(519-371-2011; 713 9th Ave E; d $80-149; P) A pleasant, no-frills choice, this small motel contains bright rooms with wooden paneling and kitchenettes.

Shorty's Bar & Grill CANADIAN $$
(519-376-0044; www.shortysonline.com; 967 3rd Ave E; mains $20-34; 11:30am-late Mon-Sat) Locals love Shorty's and with good reason. Appetizers like escargots, crab cakes and calamari fail to disappoint seafood lovers, while mains range from burgers and steaks to chicken and seafood. And of course, there's plenty of cold beer and good conversation to boot.

Kathmandu Cafe FUSION $$
(519-376-2232; 941 2nd Ave E; mains $13-25; 11:30am-10pm Mon-Sat) The Nepalese owners are organic advocates serving up wild boar and Tibetan dumplings, with vegan and vegetarian options. You'll find plenty of south Asian flavors, especially delicious curries. Some locals still know Kathmandu by its previous name, Rocky Racoon Café.

Shopping

Owen Sound Artists' Co-op ARTS & CRAFTS
(artistscoop.ca; 279 10th St E; 9:30am-5:30pm Mon-Sat, noon-4pm Sun) Check out the arts and crafts handmade by 42 local artists. Everything is for sale.

Information

Owen Sound Visitors Information Centre
(519-371-9833; www.owensound.ca; 1155 1st Ave W; 9am-5pm Mon-Fri) Ask the friendly locals about the Bruce Peninsula's hidden gems.

Getting There & Away

Greyhound Canada (greyhound.ca) runs bus services to Toronto ($43, 4¼ hours, once daily) via Barrie ($35, 2½ hours, once daily). For Guelph ($35, nine hours, once daily) you have to transfer in Toronto.

First Student (519-376-5712) operates a limited bus schedule to Tobermory on Friday, Saturday and Sunday from July to early September ($34, 1½ hours, one daily).

Owen Sound to Tobermory

The 100km stretch of highway from Owen Sound to Tobermory is monotonous at best. Consider taking a side road or two to get a taste of the scenery that makes the Bruce so special.

From Owen Sound, follow Grey County Rd 1, which winds along the scenic shoreline of staggering pines between Owen Sound and the quaint village of Wiarton. Stop here to say hello to Wiarton Willy, Canada's version of Punxsutawney Phil, then continue on Hwy 6 to the sleepy and picturesque bay at Lion's Head, a great place to stop for lunch.

Heading further north on Hwy 6 for about 25km, you'll reach Dyer's Bay Rd. Turn right and maintain your heading for another 10km to the little village of Dyer's Bay, reminiscent of Cape Cod with its pretty clapboard houses and shoreline scenery. From here you must decide if you'll plow on for the further 11km to remote **Cabot Head Lighthouse** (by donation; May-Oct), which promises stunning views from the keeper's perch. It's wild and wonderful, but the windy unpaved road is slow going and there's only one way in and out...back to Hwy 6 and then north to Tobermory.

Tobermory

You've made it to the tip of the Bruce Peninsula: quite the trek from Toronto! Tiny Tobermory is a hippie, nature lover's paradise boasting some of Ontario's most stunning scenery and sunsets. The village centers on the harbor area known as Little Tub, which is bustling during ferry season (May to late October) and all but deserted in winter.

Some of the best wreck-diving in North America exists in these brilliant blue waters. Meander through 22 separate wrecks, some dating back to the 1800s, but note that the water is usually about one degree short of an ice bath. All divers must register in person at the Parks Canada Visitors Centre.

Sights & Activities

Fathom Five National Marine Park PARK
(☎519-596-2233; www.pc.gc.ca/fathomfive; adult/child $6/3) Established to protect the numerous shipwrecks and islands around Tobermory, this was the first park of its kind in Canada. Aside from the wrecks, the park is known for much loved Flowerpot Island with its top-heavy 'flowerpot' formations, eroded by waves.

Bruce Peninsula National Park NATIONAL PARK
(☎519-596-2233; www.pc.gc.ca/brucepeninsula; adult/child $6/3; ⊙May-Oct) Much of the area just south of Tobermory is protected by this national park, flaunting some of Ontario's finest assets: the Niagara Escarpment, 1000-year-old cedars, rare orchids and crystal-clear, limestone-refracted waters. Be sure to check in with the visitors center. Must-see locations include **Little Cove**, the **Grotto** and **Singing Sands**, on the other side of Hwy 6. The park remains stoic despite the recent spike in interest: be prepared to share the magic with tourist busloads during the short summer season.

Bruce Anchor Cruises CRUISE
(☎519-596-2555; http://bruceanchor.com; 7468 Hwy 6; adult/child from $28/19; ⊙May-Oct) Glass-bottom boat tours over the tops of rusty, barnacled shipwrecks and onward to Flowerpot Island depart from this private dock at the very end of Hwy 6 in Tobermory, also a brilliant spot to catch the sunset. Some sailings include shipwrecks, others go to Flowerpot direct: check online. Pay the surcharge to explore the island like Robinson Crusoe.

Diver's Den DIVING
(☎519-596-2363; www.diversden.ca; 3 Bay St S) These guys can hook you up with gear rentals, certification courses (open-water certification from $625) and walk-on dives from $50.

Thorncrest Outfitters KAYAKING
(☎519-596-8908; www.thorncrestoutfitters.com; Hwy 6; rentals from $40, day courses from $120) Choose from a variety of kayaking trips geared more toward intermediate paddlers. Independent paddlers can rent just about anything from this friendly outfitter.

Sleeping & Eating

Cyprus Lake Campground CAMPGROUND $
(☎519-596-2263; www.pc.gc.ca; Cyprus Lake Rd; sites/yurts from $23.50/120, reservations $13.50) Sites at the most central and substantial campground within the Bruce Peninsula National Park must be reserved through Parks Canada in advance (recommended) or at the visitors center. You can even glam it up in a yurt! Backcountry sites are available.

Peacock Villa MOTEL $
(☎519-596-2242; www.peacockvilla.com; 31 Legion St; d $50-174; P 📶) Six simple, pleasantly furnished motel rooms and four cozy cabins in a peaceful, woodsy setting a hop-skip-and-jump from downtown offer excellent value. Friendly owner Karen is a wealth of information about the town and surrounds.

Innisfree B&B $$
(☎519-596-8190; www.tobermoryaccommodations.com; 46 Bay St; r incl breakfast $95-170; ⊙May-Oct; P 🚭 📶) Whether it's due to the scent of fresh blueberry muffins, or the stunning harbor views from the sunroom and large deck, guests will adore this charming country home.

Big Tub Harbour Resort MOTEL $$
(☎519-596-2219; www.bigtubresort.ca; 236 Big Tub Rd; d from $155; P 📶) On the other side of Big Tub Harbour, a short drive or decent walk from the town and Little Tub, this calm motel has spacious, woody rooms (with the clunk of footfall on the lower level) and manicured gardens with a wonderful outlook. Both the isolation and on-site Bootlegger's Cove pub are wonderful. Water-sports rentals keep you occupied.

Blue Bay Motel MOTEL $$
(☎519-596-2392; www.bluebay-motel.com; 32 Bay St; d from $100;) Many of this centrally located motel's 16 bright and spacious guest rooms overlook Little Tub Harbour. Fresh and funky, each room is different: choose from double-double, queen and king beds. Some have fireplaces, soaker tubs and LCD TVs. Peek and choose on the website.

Craigie's Fish and Chips FAST FOOD $
(☎519-596-2867; 4 Bay St; mains $11-18; ⏲7am-7pm May-Oct) This white sea shanty has been serving fish and chips in Tobermory since 1932. Greasy breakfast specials are *the* way to start the day before an early morning ferry or hike into the wilderness. Cash only.

Bootlegger's Cove PUB FOOD $$
(☎519-596-2219; 236 Big Tub Rd; items $8-25; ⏲noon-8pm) Good service, tasty food and a stunning patio overlooking Big Tub Harbour make this joint the local secret that can't be kept. The fun menu includes wraps, quesadillas, pizzas and s'mores!

Drinking & Nightlife

Crows Nest Pub PUB
(☎519-596-2575; www.crowsnestpub.ca; 5 Bay St; ⏲11am-late Apr-Oct) The only pub in Little Tub, renovated Crows Nest has an elevated outdoor patio overlooking the town. Wraps, burgers and pizzas feature on the pub-style menu, which includes plenty of beers on tap.

Information

Parks Canada Visitors Centre (☎519-596-2233; www.pc.gc.ca/fathomfive; Alexander St; ⏲8am-8pm May-Oct) Has a fantastic interpretive center, exhibits, a movie theater, several hiking trails and a 20m viewing platform (112 steps). To get here by foot, follow the beaver signs from the Bruce Trail Monument opposite the LCBO. It's a 10-minute walk.

Tobermory Chamber of Commerce (☎519-596-2452; www.tobermory.org; Hwy 6; ⏲9am-9pm) As you pull into town (from the south) it's to your right: drop in for latest updates.

Getting There & Away

First Student (☎519-376-5712) operates a limited bus schedule from Owen Sound to Tobermory on Friday, Saturday and Sunday from July to early September ($34, 1½ hours, one daily). From Toronto, **Parkbus** (www.parkbus.ca) offers a limited schedule of express services ($89 return, five hours) with a number of downtown collection points. Check schedules and make bookings online.

Tobermory is not the end of the line: take the Chi-Cheemaun Ferry from the Bruce Peninsula across the mouth of Georgian Bay to Manitoulin Island. Operated by **Ontario Ferries** (☎800-265-3163; www.ontarioferries.com; adult/child/car $17/9/37; ⏲May-late Oct), the boat connects Tobermory with South Baymouth (two hours). There are four daily crossings from late June to early September, and two daily crossings during the rest of the season, with an additional voyage on Friday evenings. Reservations are highly recommended.

Manitoulin Island

Manitoulin (meaning 'Spirit Island' in the Ojibwe language) is a magical and remote place. There's a real sense of being 'away' up here. Expanses of white quartzite and granite outcrops lead to breathtaking vistas and hidden runes, but you'll need patience to find them: Manitoulin is the largest freshwater island in the world and its small communities, with names like Mindemoya, Sheguiandah and Wikwemikong, are many kilometers apart. Haweaters (people born on Manitoulin) will spot you a mile away as you fumble over six-syllable words. But don't let these syllabic setbacks deter you from visiting – a few days on Manitoulin is food for the soul.

Sights & Activities

Manitoulin isn't laden with historical sights as much as natural beauty. Take some time to drive around and explore its enclaves.

Bridal Veil Falls WATERFALL
(Kagawong) Just off Hwy 540 before Kagawong, there's a lovely picnic area at the top of this pretty waterfall. Walking trails lead down to the base where you can take a dip before continuing into the old town.

Ojibwe Cultural Foundation MUSEUM
(☎705-377-4902; www.ojibweculture.ca; cnr Hwys 540 & 551, M'Chigeeng; adult/child $7.50/free; ⏲9am-6pm Mon-Fri, 10am-4pm Sat, noon-4pm Sun) You're free to explore on your own, but guided tours of this insightful museum are highly recommended. Rotating exhibits reflect a rich history of legends and skilled craftwork.

Church of the Immaculate Conception CHURCH
(M'Chigeeng) This church in the round represents a tipi, a fire pit and the circle of life, and it welcomes aboriginal traditions and Catholic beliefs. Colorful paintings by local artists depict the stations of the cross, while magnificent carvings represent both Christ and the Great Spirit Kitche Manitou.

★Great Spirit Circle Trail CULTURAL

(☎877-710-3211; www.circletrail.com; 5905 Hwy 540; activities & tours from $30) The eight local First Nation communities have collaborated to form this consortium offering a wide variety of fun activities and cross-cultural day and overnight tours throughout the year: a wonderful way to get a sense of Manitoulin and its people.

Cup & Saucer Trail HIKING

From its origin near the junction of Hwy 540 and Bidwell Rd (18km southwest of Little Current) this 12km trail, with its 2km of dramatic 70m cliffs, leads to the highest point on the island (351m) with breathtaking views of the crinkled shoreline along the North Channel.

Festivals & Events

De-ba-jeh-mu-jig Theatre Group THEATER

(www.debaj.ca; ⏲Jul-Aug) Canada's foremost Aboriginal troupe, whose name appropriately means 'storytellers,' performs moving pieces of original work transcending various mediums. Check the website for the full story.

Wikwemikong Pow-wow CULTURAL

(☎705-859-2385; www.wikwemikongheritage.org; adult/child $10/2; ⏲Aug) The unceded First Nation of Wikwemikong (locals say 'Wiki') hosts a huge powwow on the first weekend in August. Expect vibrant and colorful displays of dancing, drumming and traditional games.

Sleeping & Eating

★My Friends Inn MOTEL $

(☎705-859-3115; www.myfriendsinn.com; 151 Queen St, Manitowaning; d from $85; P❄📶) First-time hotelier and former nurse Maureen Friend retired to Manitoulin with her husband to be closer to their daughter: they're doing a wonderful job. Rooms in this friendly little motel outside the pretty village of Manitowaning in central Manitoulin are smart and homely. Highly recommended.

Auberge Inn HOSTEL $

(☎705-377-4392; www.aubergeinn.ca; 71 McNevin St, Providence Bay; dm/d incl breakfast $40/97; P📶) Enthusiastic Auberge Inn is a hostel-plus. With one bunk room and one private room, the place isn't large, but it's comfortable and sociable with warm colors and custom cedar bunks. It's a short stroll to the beach. Small discounts for longer stays.

Queen's Inn B&B $$

(☎705-282-0665, 416-450-4866; www.thequeensinn.ca; 19 Water St, Gore Bay; s/d from $110/135; ⏲May-Dec; P) Like a pillared temple to remote elegance, this stately B&B peers over the silent cove of Gore Bay. Grab a book from the antique hutch library and idly thumb through it while relaxing on the white verandah among potted lilacs.

Southbay Gallery & Guesthouse B&B $$

(☎877-656-8324; www.southbayguesthouse.com; 15 Given Rd, South Baymouth; d incl breakfast $90-150; ⏲May-Sep; P❄📶🏊) A one-minute walk from the ferry docks you'll find this delightful melange of colorful guest rooms and summery cottages: friendly owner Brenda's breakfasts are overflowing. Check out the gallery of handcrafted works by talented local artisans.

Lake Huron Fish and Chips FISH & CHIPS $

(☎705-377-4500; 20 McNevin St, Providence Bay; fish & chips from $11; ⏲noon-8pm) You're going to crave it at some point, surrounded by all this water, and this is the place to go: golden fried fresh lake fish and crispy crunchy fries.

Garden Shed CAFE $

(10th Side Rd, Tehkummah; mains $3-10; ⏲9am-2pm) The Garden Shed takes rustic charm to a new level by placing you right inside a working greenhouse. Nibble among flats of greens, or sip your coffee in the light and airy shed. Breakfast from $2.99!

★Buoys SEAFOOD $$

(☎705-282-2869; www.buoyseatery.com; 1 Purvis Dr, Gore Bay; items $10-18; ⏲noon-8pm) This little joint by the Gore Bay beach and marina has it all: vibe, location, and food sourced from local providers and prepared fresh. The seasoned whitefish melts in your mouth, but if you're not feeling fishy, pizza, pasta and burgers also please. When you're done, linger with a beer on the sunny patio and feel a million miles from home.

Garden's Gate CAFE $$

(☎705-859-2088; www.manitoulin-island.com/gardensgate; Hwy 542, Tehkummah; mains $10-21; ⏲noon-8pm; P) Seriously good, home-style food can be found here, near the junction of Hwys 6 and 542. Rose, the owner, makes everything from scratch; she's always inventing desserts, which are regularly featured in the local newspaper.

Information

Manitoulin Tourism Association (705-368-3021; www.manitoulintourism.com; Hwy 6, Little Current; 8am-8pm May-Oct) Pamphlets and maps of the island can be found in the South Baymouth ferry terminal, as well as onboard the Chi-Cheemaun.

Getting There & Away

There are two ways on and off the island: a ferry to South Baymouth or across the swinging bridge in the north. There is no land-based public transportation to or around Manitoulin, so your own wheels are needed.

From Tobermory, take the Chi-Cheemaun vehicular ferry (two hours, two to four daily), operated by **Ontario Ferries** (p165), to the port of South Baymouth. Reservations recommended.

From here, Hwy 6 continues north for 65km to Little Current and a thin, swinging bridge that reconnects it to the mainland. In summer, the bridge closes for the first 15 minutes every hour to allow shipping traffic through the channel. Crossing the bridge leads to the Trans-Canada Hwy at Espanola, 50km further up the road

NORTHERN ONTARIO

'Big' is a theme in Northern Ontario. The area is so vast that it could fit six Englands and still have room for a Scotland or two. Industry is big here, too: most of the world's silver and nickel ore comes from local mines, while boundless forests have made the region a key timber producer. What's not so big is the local population; only Sudbury and Thunder Bay have over 100,000 citizens.

Two main highways weave an intersecting course across the province. Hwy 17 (the Trans-Canada) unveils the area's scenic pièce de résistance, the northern crest over Lake Superior. Between Sault Ste Marie and Thunder Bay, misty fjord-like passages hide isolated beaches among dense thickets of pine, cedar and birch.

Hwy 11 stretches deep into the north, where the Polar Bear Express connects Cochrane to Moose Factory island, an aboriginal reservation and former Hudson's Bay Company trading post near James Bay.

Ontario Northland's (705-472-4500; www.ontarionorthland.ca) bus network provides connections from Toronto to North Bay and Sudbury, continuing north to Temagami and Cochrane. Likewise, **Greyhound** (800-661-8747; www.greyhound.ca) buses connect Toronto and Ottawa to North Bay and Sudbury, then continue northwest along Lake Superior to Thunder Bay and on to Manitoba.

Parkbus (800-928-7101; www.parkbus.ca) is a useful shuttle from Toronto to Ontario's provincial parks including Killarney.

The legendary Polar Bear Express (p182) train runs north from Cochrane to the isolated outpost of Moosonee, gateway to Moose Factory island near James Bay. A **VIA Rail** (1-888-842-7245; www.viarail.ca) train heads northwest from Sudbury via Chapleau to White River. Sudbury Junction station, near Sudbury, is on VIA Rail's Canadian line between Toronto and Vancouver.

There are airports with connections to Toronto and beyond, and car rental companies, in North Bay, Sudbury, Sault Ste Marie, Thunder Bay and Timmins.

Killarney Provincial Park

The 645-sq-km Killarney Provincial Park covers vast expanses of Georgian Bay shoreline and is home to moose, black bears, beavers and deer, as well as over 100 bird species. The Group of Seven artists were instrumental in its 1964 establishment; today the park is considered to be one of the finest kayaking destinations in the world.

Sights & Activities

★**Killarney Provincial Park** OUTDOORS
(705-287-2900; www.ontarioparks.com/park/killarney; Hwy 637; day use per vehicle $11.25, campsite $37-45, backcountry camping adult/child under 18yr $12.50/6, yurt $98, cabin $142; year-round) Killarney is often called the crown jewel of the Ontario park system, and is considered to be one of the finest kayaking destinations in the world. Paddlers can spend from a day to a week exploring over 50 lakes, including two deep, clear gems on either side of the La Cloche ('the bell') Mountains.

The Group of Seven artists had a cabin near Hwy 6 (just west of the park) and persuaded the Ontario government to establish the park. In fact, the park's **La Cloche Silhouette Trail** is named after Franklin Carmichael's legendary painting of the range. The rugged 80km (seven- to 10-day) trek, geared toward experienced hikers, twists through a mountainous realm of sapphire lakes, thirsty birches, luscious pine forests and quartzite cliffs.

A network of shorter, less challenging hikes also offers glimpses of the terrain, including the **Cranberry Bog Trail** (a 4km loop) and the **Granite Ridge Trail** (a 2km loop).

Northern Ontario

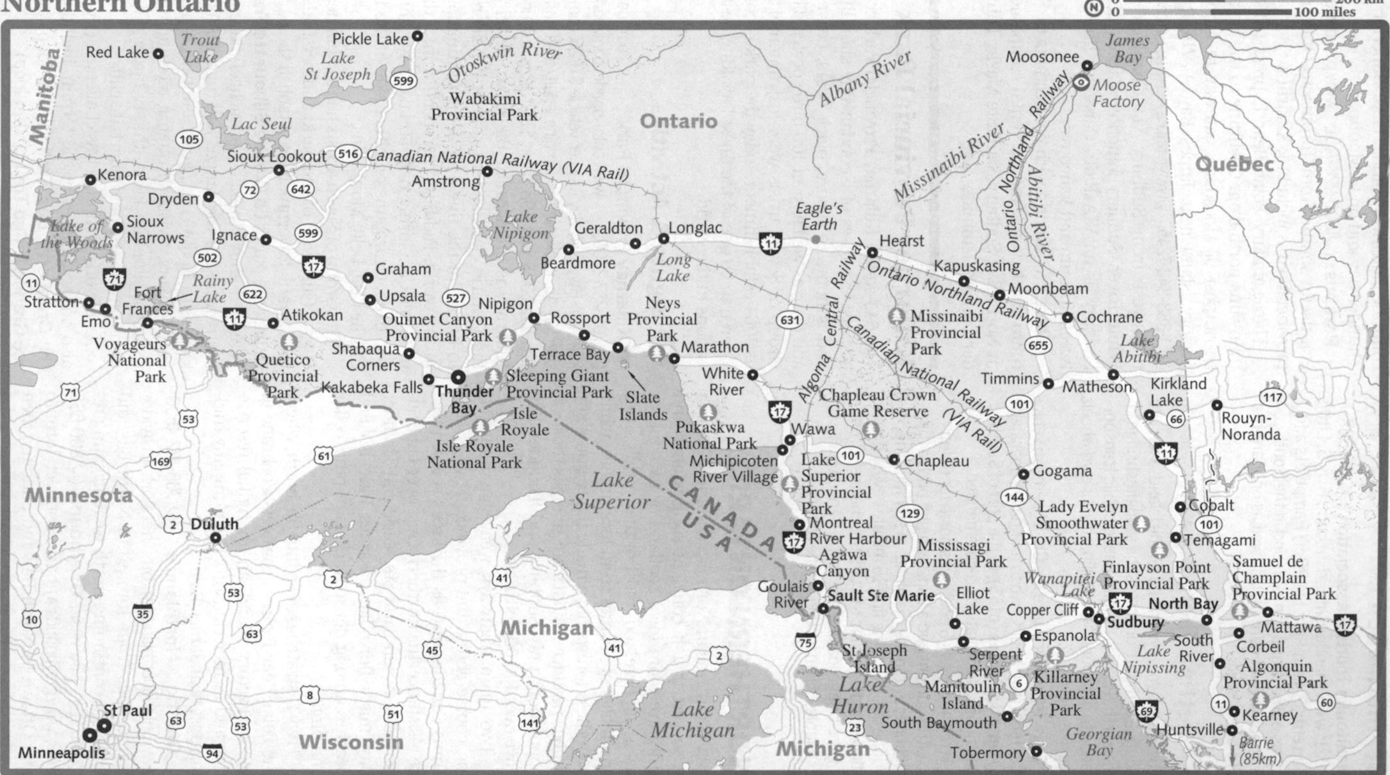

Killarney Kanoes (☎888-461-4446; www.killarneykanoes.com; 1611 Bell Lake Rd; canoe rental per day $25-40; ⌚8am-8pm May-Oct) provides canoe and kayak rentals, while **Killarney Outfitters** (☎705-287-2828; www.killarneyoutfitters.com; 1076 Hwy 637, Killarney; canoe & kayak rental per day $26-37, activities from $35) offers equipment rentals and fully outfitted packages (just bring your toothbrush!) for hiking, canoeing, kayaking and stand-up paddle boarding.

Sleeping & Eating

In Killarney village, **Killarney Mountain Lodge** (☎705-287-2242; www.killarney.com; 3 Commissioner St, Killarney; d/ste incl breakfast from $180/249; ⌚May-Oct;) is a sprawling holiday lodge with a bunch of facilities, woodsy lodge rooms and cabins – an excellent option for noncampers.

There are also several camping and accommodation options in the park (p167). The popular George Lake access point features an information center and limited campsites: none are powered. Contact Ontario Parks (www.ontarioparks.com) for reservations, and book well ahead in summer.

Stock up on food and firewood at **Grundy Lake Supply Post** (☎705-383-2251; www.grundylakesupplypost.com; cnr Hwys 69 & 522; ⌚9am-5pm mid-May–early Jul, 8am-9pm early Jul-early Sep), 40km south of the Killarney turnoff on Hwy 69.

There are a few lodge restaurants and a fish-and-chip shop in Killarney village, 10km west of the park on Hwy 637. Also in the village, Killarney Mountain Lodge's restaurant serves breakfast, lunch and dinner, and offers American plan (full board) and modified American plan (half board) packages.

Getting There & Away

Most people access the park from the Hwy 637 turnoff along Hwy 69, which terminates in the tiny village of Killarney.

Parkbus (p167) has limited summer services to the park (adult/student/child under 13yr $94/85/47, 5½ hours) from Toronto; otherwise, you'll need wheels.

Sudbury

Sudbury gets props for making something out of nothing. In the 1880s, it was but a desolate lumber camp called Ste-Anne-des-Pins. Then, when the Canadian Pacific Railway plowed through in 1883, the discovery of a mother lode of nickel-copper ore transformed the dreary region into the biggest nickel producer worldwide. By 1920, industrial toxicity and acid rain had killed the trees and fouled the soil, leaving Sudbury a bleak place of blackened boulders. So barren was the surrounding terrain that NASA came here to train in the 1960s.

Today, the story is more environmentally friendly: as part of the city's 'regreening' program, locals have planted over 12 million trees since 1980, although heavy industry and mining still rule. Sudbury has a university, two fantastic science museums, some cool haunts and chilled locals, but there's little reason to visit unless you're passing through.

Sights

If you're planning to visit both Science North and Dynamic Earth, save money with the 'Dynamic Duo Passport' (adult/child $50/41). Valid for three days, it includes admission to both attractions and their special exhibitions and movies.

★Science North MUSEUM
(☎705-522-3701; www.sciencenorth.ca; 100 Ramsey Lake Rd; adult/child from $26/22; ⌚9am-6pm Jul & Aug, 10am-4pm Sep-Jun) After passing through a tunnel dug deep within the 2.5-billion-year-old Canadian Shield, work your way down through the spiral of exciting hands-on activities in this fantastic museum. Wander through a living butterfly garden, stargaze in the digital planetarium or fly away on a bush-plane simulator. Visiting exhibits and IMAX films change regularly.

The 'Play All Day Passport,' which includes entrance to visiting exhibits, IMAX films and other extras, costs $37 (children $31).

Footpaths lead along the shore of Ramsey Lake from here.

Dynamic Earth MUSEUM
(☎705-522-3701; www.dynamicearth.ca; 122 Big Nickel Rd; adult/child $21/17, parking $5; ⌚9am-6pm Apr-Oct) Dynamic Earth's main attraction is the underground tour with simulated dynamite blast. Visitors stand to learn lots about geology and our planet from thought-provoking interactive exhibits. In summer, tours leave roughly every 30 minutes from 9:45am to 4:45pm. Be sure to take a snap in front of the Big Nickel, a 9m-high stainless steel replica of a 1951 Canadian nickel.

THE MAGNIFICENT SEVEN

Fired by an almost adolescent enthusiasm, the Group of Seven (aka the Algonquin School) were an all-male troupe of Canadian painters. They rampaged through the wilds of northern Ontario from 1920 to 1933, capturing the rugged Canadian wilderness through all its seasons, their joyful energy expressed in vibrant, light-filled canvases depicting mountains, lakes, forests and towns. From **Algonquin Provincial Park** (p187) to **Killarney Provincial Park** (p167) and on up Lake Superior, they immortalised northern Ontario in their expressive landscapes.

In 1917, before the group officially formed, their fellow painter and friend, Tom Thomson, drowned in Algonquin, just as he was producing his best work. The group – AY Jackson, Arthur Lismer, JEH MacDonald, Frank Johnston, Lawren Harris, Fred Varley and Franklin Carmichael – considered him their inspiration. Thomson's deep connection to the land is evident from his works hanging in Toronto's **AGO** (p77) and Ottawa's **National Gallery** (p209). His rustic cabin has been moved onto the grounds of Toronto's **McMichael Canadian Art Collection** (p88). Each has magnificent examples of the Group of Seven's profound talents.

Copper Cliff Museum HISTORIC BUILDING
(☎705-692-4448; 26 Balsam St, Copper Cliff; donations appreciated; ⏲10am-4pm Wed-Sun Jul & Aug) FREE This pioneer log cabin 6km west of downtown is filled with relics from an era when settlers first arrived to survey the land. The two-story 19th-century cabin was moved to this spot, where the first dwelling in Copper Cliff once stood, to make way for a nearby mine.

Sleeping & Eating

Radisson Sudbury BUSINESS HOTEL $$
(☎705-675-1123; www.radissonsudbury.com; 85 St Anne Rd; r from $116; P ❄ 🛜 ≋ 🐾) Offering 147 comfortable and restful rooms in a central location, Radisson's service and finish are a cut above its competitors. Facilities include a pool, hot tub, fitness center and guest laundry, while guests can wander into the adjoining Rainbow Centre mall for a food court and grocery store.

Holiday Inn BUSINESS HOTEL $$
(☎705-522-3000; www.holidayinn.com; 1696 Regent St; r from $114; P ❄ 🛜 ≋) Outside, this Holiday Inn looks frozen in 1972. Inside is what you'd expect: refurbished, generic rooms of a good size. There's an indoor pool, hot tub and fitness center. Bed and breakfast is an extra $10, or you can eat an à la carte breakfast in the restaurant.

Motley Kitchen CAFE $
(☎705-222-6685; www.themotleykitchen.com; 70 Young St; mains $12; ⏲11am-3pm Tue-Fri, 10am-2pm Sat & Sun) Sudbury's most popular brunch spot serves unlikely dishes such as breakfast burritos, Welsh rarebit, Croatian crêpes, and French toast stuffed with bananas and Nutella or strawberries and yogurt. Plates are garnished with home fries and fresh fruit, and weekday lunches of tacos, sandwiches and salads are served. The only drawback is the popularity can mean the food arrives slowly.

★**Respect is Burning** ITALIAN $$
(☎705-675-5777; www.ribsupperclub.com; 82 Durham St; lunch mains $10-15, dinner $17-32; ⏲4:30-10pm Mon-Thu, to 1am Fri & Sat; 🛜) This self-proclaimed supper club's focus is on rustic Tuscan cuisine but chefs aren't shy about getting experimental. The ever-shifting menu promises bursting flavors with every bite. Weekend evenings feature delectable sample platters and late-night drinks. The restaurant is living up to its name anew, having risen from the ashes after burning down in 2014.

Drinking & Entertainment

★**Laughing Buddha** BAR
(☎705-673-2112; www.laughingbuddhasudbury.com; 194 Elgin St; ⏲11am-2am Thu-Sat, to 11pm Sun-Tue, to midnight Wed) Sudbury's prime hangout for hipsters and slackers pulls off snobby sandwiches (such as the 'Brie LT'; $9) and pizzas ($13) while maintaining an uberchill vibe. In summer, slip out to the crimson-brick courtyard and enjoy your casual lunch or one of the 100-plus types of beer.

Kuppajo Espresso Bar COFFEE
(☎705-586-1298; 109 Larch St; ⏲7am-9pm Mon-Fri, 9am-5pm Sat & Sun; 🛜) This caffeine den is busy on weekdays and weekends alike, accompanying cups of black gold with pastries and paninis, as well as breakfast sandwiches ($8) and crab salad sandwiches.

Towne House Tavern LIVE MUSIC
(☎705-674-6883; www.thetownehouse.com; 206 Elgin St; ⏲11am-2am Mon-Sat, from noon Sun) This beloved grungy venue is all about Canadian indie from punk to gospel, and stages acts including local bands and big names from the south. Adding to the musical entertainment are a games room and a bar serving pub grub with outside seating.

ℹ Information

Greater Sudbury Development Corporation (☎1-866-451-8525; www.sudburytourism.ca; Tom Davies Square, 200 Brady St; ⏲8:30am-4:30pm Mon-Fri) Help and brochures are on hand in the city hall.

ℹ Getting There & Around

Greater Sudbury Airport (☎705-693-2514; www.flysudbury.ca; 5000 Air Terminal Dr) is about 25km northeast of downtown. Air Canada, Bearskin Airlines and **Porter Airlines** (p66) operate services to/from Toronto, Ottawa, Sault Ste Marie, Thunder Bay, Timmins, Kapuskasing and North Bay.

Several car-rental options are available at the airport and downtown, including **Enterprise** (☎705-693-9993; www.enterpriserentacar.ca).

Ontario Northland (p167) buses connect Sudbury to Toronto ($80, 5¾ hours, three daily). **Greyhound** (p167) connects Sudbury to Toronto ($81, five hours, one daily), Thunder Bay ($219, 14¼ hours, one daily) and Ottawa ($83, seven hours, one daily).

VIA Rail (p167) serves a small network of remote towns on its line between **Sudbury Train Station** (233 Elgin St) and White River (from $60, 8¼ hours) via Chapleau, departing three times a week. Sudbury Junction station, 10km northeast of downtown, is on VIA Rail's Canadian (p874) line between Toronto and Vancouver.

City buses roam the downtown region from the **transit terminal** (☎705-675-3333; www.greatersudbury.ca; Elm St). One-way fares are $3.10.

Elliot Lake

The tree-lined jaunt between Sudbury and Sault Ste Marie offers little more than forest views out the car window. Elliot Lake, the largest community in the area, is popular with retirees on a tight budget and, in winter, snowmobilers. Indeed, the region is a hub for outdoor activities year-round, including hiking, fishing, canoeing and cross-country skiing.

The little town made headlines in 2012 after an accident at the town mall, when a concrete section of its roof catastrophically collapsed, without warning. The slab fell three floors, taking the lives of two women and injuring 19.

Visit www.tourismelliotlake.com/en for more information about the town.

Mississagi Provincial Park PROVINCIAL PARK
(☎705-865-2021, Oct-May 705-862-1203; www.ontarioparks.com/park/mississagi; Hwy 639; day use per vehicle $11.25, campsites $37; ⏲late May-early Sep) Mississagi Provincial Park, 35km north of Elliot Lake, is a secluded expanse of hemlock forests, sandy beaches, trembling aspens and chirping birds. Hiking trails range from 0.8km along Flack Lake – revealing ripple rock, a geological feature formed by a billion years of wave action – to the multiday MacKenzie (22km) through the back country. Canoes can also be rented.

Mississagi is quiet and undeveloped: none of the campsites have electricity, and the limited facilities (the gatehouse and toilets), located just off Hwy 639 between Jim Christ and Semiwite Lakes, are solar-powered. There are also toilets and a picnic area at Flack Lake. Reserve your camping spot with **Ontario Parks** (www.ontarioparks.com).

ℹ Getting There & Away

Elliot Lake is on Hwy 108, 27km north of Hwy 17.

Greyhound (p167) buses connect the town with Sudbury ($48, 3¼ hours, one daily) and Sault Ste Marie ($57, 4½ hours, one daily).

Sault Ste Marie

POP 75,141

'The Soo,' as it's commonly known, quietly governs the narrow rapids between Lakes Huron and Superior. Perched alongside the US border and the St Lawrence Seaway, the sleepy city is the unofficial gateway to the far-flung regions of northwestern Ontario. Originally known as Baawitigong ('Place of the rapids'), it was a traditional gathering place for the Ojibwe and remains a strong First Nations area today. French fur traders changed the name to Sault Ste Marie *(soo-saynt muh-ree)* or 'St Mary's Falls,' but don't expect to see any waterfalls today: they've been tamed into a series of gargantuan locks.

Let's face it, Sault Ste Marie is not the prettiest city. Nonetheless, the Soo is a friendly place and a logical overnight stop on Trans-Canada itineraries. There's a US border crossing here, too.

Sights

Art Gallery of Algoma GALLERY

(705-949-9067; www.artgalleryofalgoma.com; 10 East St; adult/student/child under 12yr $7/5/free; 9am-5pm Tue & Thu-Sat, to 9pm Wed) Behind the library, this gallery has a permanent collection and seasonal exhibitions to inspire Group of Seven–themed trips along Lake Superior. Especially in summer, paintings by the group of local scenes are exhibited alongside the work of local First Nations artists.

Sault Ste Marie Canal National Historic Site HISTORIC SITE

(705-941-6205; parkscanada.gc.ca/sault; 1 Canal Dr; visitor center 10am-4pm Mon-Fri mid-May–early Oct) FREE On the Canadian side of St Mary's River, follow the 2.2km Attikamek walking trail around South St Mary's Island to see this canal dating to 1895, once the world's longest lock and the first to operate with electrical power. It was also novel in using an emergency swing dam to protect the lock in case of accident. The majority of freighter traffic occurs further afield in the American locks; the older Canadian lock is used for recreational vessels only.

Sault Ste Marie Museum MUSEUM

(705-759-7278; www.saultmuseum.com; 690 Queen St E; adult $8, seniors & students $6; 9:30am-5pm Tue-Sat;) Occupying the old post office dating to 1906, this three-story museum is a tribute to the early 1900s, detailing the town's history from several perspectives. The Discovery Gallery is geared toward children and the Skylight Gallery is a must-see. An interactive timeline from prehistory to the 1960s incorporates the local historical society's unique collection of preserved fossils and relics.

Canadian Bushplane Heritage Centre MUSEUM

(705-945-6242; www.bushplane.com; 50 Pim St; adult/child/student $12/3/7; 9am-6pm Jun-Sep, 10am-4pm Oct-May;) A visit to the Soo's most dynamic and kid-friendly museum is a great way to get a sense of how Northern Ontario works: bush planes are crucial to remote communities that are not accessible by road. Stroll among retired aircraft, housed in a former government hangar dating to 1924, to see how tiny these flyers really are. A flight simulator takes passengers on a spirited ride along sapphire lakes and towering pines.

SNOWMOBILING IN ONTARIO

Ontario has some 50,000km of recreational snowmobile trails, more than anywhere else in the world. Sudbury is one of the province's unofficial capitals of the snowy pastime. Many of Northern Ontario's motels and lodges cater to this subculture: it's not uncommon to see accommodations advertising snowmobile parking with video security or a secure enclosure. Visit the website of the **Ontario Federation of Snowmobile Clubs** (705-739-7669; www.ofsc.on.ca; 501 Welham Rd, Barrie) to learn what all the fuss is about.

Tours

Agawa Canyon Tour Train RAIL

(ACR; 800-242-9287; www.agawatrain.com; 129 Bay St; late Jun–mid-Oct) Constructed in 1899 to facilitate the transport of raw materials to Sault Ste Marie's industrial plants, the Algoma Central Railway is a 475km stretch of railroad from Sault Ste Marie due north to Hearst. Nowadays, it transports tour guests through unspoiled wilderness along the pristine lakes and jagged granite of the Canadian Shield.

The Agawa Canyon train offers day trips (adult/child $102/70) north to Agawa Canyon in the rugged Lake Superior hinterland once painted by the Group of Seven, leaving Sault Ste Marie at 8am and returning at 6pm. The best time to ride is from mid-September to mid-October, as the train twists its way through jaw-dropping blazing autumn foliage for as far as the eye can see.

Sleeping & Eating

The bulk of motels are found along Great Northern Rd, near Hwy 17, fast-food restaurants and malls. There are also several options scattered downtown, mostly on Bay St, where there's some scenic interest in the waterfront and the majority of attractions, but few amenities after dark.

★**Water Tower Inn** HOTEL $$

(800-461-0800; www.watertowerinn.com; 360 Great Northern Rd; d from $119;) Offering a resort for the price of a room, the Water Tower continues to stand out from the rest with its indoor and outdoor pools, grill-house bar-restaurant, pizza-slinging pub and treatment spa. The variety of room types includes family rooms and suites.

Sleep Inn MOTEL $$
(☎705-253-7533; choicehotels.ca/cn658; 727 Bay St; r incl breakfast from $109; P❄📶🐾) This tourist motel in a nice spot by the water has spacious and tidy rooms, an exercise room and sauna.

Muio's DINER $
(☎705-254-7105; www.muios.com; 685 Queen St E; lunch/dinner mains $10/18; ⏰7am-8pm) In a historic building dating to 1890, among pictures of the Soo of yore, 55-year-old Muio's continues to bask in anachronistic glory. Pretty much everything is homemade, including the pasta, and locals come for cuisine from burger-joint faves to more sophisticated steaks and seafood.

★**Arturo's Ristorante** ITALIAN $$$
(☎705-253-0002; www.arturoristorante.com; 515 Queen St E; mains $24-45; ⏰5-10pm Tue-Sat) A shimmering jewel in a dismal downtown strip, decades-old Arturo's is the kind of place you always remember. Atmospheric but unpretentious with soft lighting, starched white tablecloths and European scenes on the walls, the Italian mains such as veal marsala and chicken *piccata* (with lemon and capers) are tender and succulent, the sauces rich, and wines appropriately paired.

☆ Entertainment

LopLops LIVE MUSIC
(☎705-945-0754; www.loplops.com; 651 Queen St E; ⏰4pm-2am Wed-Sat) Grab a glass of *vino* or local craft beer from the glittering steel bar and enjoy an evening amid strumming guitars and the restless murmurs of tortured artists.

ℹ Information

Algoma Kinniwabi Travel Association (☎800-263-2546, 705-254-4293; www.algomacountry.com; 334 Bay St; ⏰8:30am-4:30pm Mon-Fri) Helpful office (and website) providing information and inspiration for travels along Lake Superior and into the hinterland.

Ontario Travel Information Centre (☎705-945-6941; www.ontariotravel.net; 261 Queen St W; ⏰8:30am-4:30pm) Sells permits for camping, fishing and hunting in the surrounding backcountry, and offers seasonal reports on where to catch the best fall colors, spring blossoms and snow. Near the International Bridge, it has a currency exchange.

Tourism Sault Ste Marie (☎705-759-5442; www.saulttourism.com; Level 1, Civic Centre, 99 Foster Dr; ⏰8:30am-4:30pm Mon-Fri) Stocks brochures and guides covering the Soo. In the Economic Development Corporation office.

ℹ Getting There & Around

Sault Ste Marie Airport (YAM; ☎705-779-3031; www.saultairport.com; 475 Airport Rd) is some 18km west of downtown. Take Second Line (Hwy 550) 13km west, then head south for 5km along Airport Rd (Hwy 565).

Flights to/from Toronto are available with Air Canada and Porter, and Bearskin Airlines offers direct services to Thunder Bay and Sudbury, with onward connections including Winnipeg, Timmins and North Bay.

Greyhound (☎800-661-8747; www.greyhound.ca) runs buses to Sudbury ($74, 4½ hours, one daily) and Thunder Bay ($148, 9½ hours, one daily) from the **bus stop** (☎705-541-9305; 503 Trunk Rd) outside the Howard Johnson Inn on Hwy 17, 5km east of downtown.

You can also get the **International Bridge Bus** (☎906-632-6882; www.saultstemarie.com/soo-area-and-great-waters-region/international-bridge; one-way $2; ⏰7am-7pm Mon-Fri, 9am-5pm Sat) over to sister Sault Ste Marie in Michigan. Buses depart the Canadian side at 20 minutes past every hour, from the bus stop near the Station Mall's front entrance on Bay St; and on the half-hour from the bus terminal on the corner of Queen St E and Dennis St, also downtown. Buses depart the US side on the hour. You must have your passport.

For a $2.50 bus ride (have the exact change ready), hop on the network of 11 city bus lines. Visit www.saultstemarie.ca for more information and route details.

Lake Superior Shoreline

Its name befitting its size and beauty, Lake Superior covers a surface area of 82,100 sq km: it's the largest freshwater lake on the planet, with its own ecosystem and microclimate. Much of its dazzling Canadian shoreline is hugged by the Trans-Canada Hwy (at this point Hwy 17), with the drive from Wawa to Sault Ste Marie regarded by some as one of the most picturesque on the highway's 8030km span. A 90km stretch of highway passes directly through Lake Superior Provincial Park.

The Great Lake freezes over for many months at a time and most businesses and parks here are seasonal (May to October). Keep an eye out for scraggly moose as you drive the highway, especially at dusk or dawn.

For inspiration on a motorbike trip around Lake Superior, taking in Ontario, Michigan, Wisconsin and Minnesota, visit www.ridelakesuperior.com and pick up a tourist map.

Sights & Activities

Harmony Beach BEACH

Heading north from Sault Ste Marie on Hwy 17 for about 40km, look for a left-hand turn to 'Harmony Beach Road,' to reach this popular summer swimming spot with views across the lake.

Chippewa Falls WATERFALL

These powerful waterfalls, 55km north of Sault Ste Marie on the side of Hwy 17, are at their best in spring when the volume of melting snow turns their otherwise steady flow into a thunderous roar. You will see them from the highway, and you can park on the south side of the bridge over the Chippewa River for a closer look.

Pancake Bay Provincial Park PROVINCIAL PARK

(☎1-888-668-7275, campsite reservations 705-882-2209; www.ontarioparks.com/park/pancakebay; Hwy 17; day use $14.50; ⏲late May–mid-Oct) It's been a long drive, but you've made it to one of Canada's finest stretches of white sandy beach and, if you time it right, you might have it all to yourself. In summer, that won't be the case, but you can find relative solitude on 3.5km- to 14km-long hiking trails. Be sure to reserve one of the 300-plus campsites in advance (tent site without hookup from $41.25), or just stop by for a swim.

Caribou Expeditions KAYAKING

(☎800-970-6662, 705-649-3540; www.caribou-expeditions.com; 1021 Goulais Mission Rd, Goulais River; courses from $75, day tours from $105) Join the team of experienced nature lovers (based about 34km north of Sault Ste Marie, on the quiet waters of Goulais Bay) for a variety of kayaking expeditions along the northern crest of Lake Superior. Canoe and kayak rentals are available.

Treetop Adventures ADVENTURE SPORTS

(☎705-649-5455; www.treetopadventures.ca; 6 Post Office Rd, Goulais River; admission from $40) This woodsy adventure park offers a variety of heart-pounding activities including a self-guided canopy tour, Tarzan style, and a moonlight version. It's open daily year-round by reservation; phone ahead.

Sleeping

Salzburgerhof Resort RESORT $

(☎705-882-2323; www.salzburgerhofresort.com; Corbeil Point Rd, Batchawana Bay; r from $91; ⏲early May-late Oct; 📶) Owned and run by an Austrian family since 1972, this little piece of the Tyrol looks right at home on the shores of Lake Superior. Rooms are predictably woodsy, European and a little bit retro, but that all just adds to the charm. There's a private beach and an Austrian restaurant. Take Hwy 563 south off Hwy 17 at Batchawana Bay.

The many accommodations options range from motel rooms and suites to two- and three-bedroom chalets.

Twilight Resort CAMPGROUND $

(☎705-882-2183; www.facebook.com/TwilightResort; Hwy 17, Montreal River Harbour; tent sites $30-40, cabins from $100; ⏲May-Oct) This wonderfully isolated spot, just south of the entrance to Lake Superior Provincial Park, was once a camp for Mennonite war objectors sent to work on the Trans-Canada Hwy. Today, it's a no-frills, back-in-time holiday spot with eight fishing cabins and plenty of campsites, all facing due west for jaw-dropping sunsets over Lake Superior.

Rossport Inn and Cabins INN $

(☎807-824-3213; 6 Bowman St, Rossport; cabins from $65; ⏲mid-Apr–mid-Oct; 📶🐾) The historic Rossport Inn has pleased passers-through since the Canadian Pacific Railway Company built it in 1884. Its kind owners have retired, but still rent their nine quaint cabins overlooking Rossport harbor. Facilities include a sauna and kayaks. Call in advance.

★ **Voyageur's Lodge** MOTEL $$

(☎705-882-2504; www.voyageurslodge.com; Hwy 17, Batchawana Bay; r $94-119, ste $145; ⏲Apr-late Oct; ❄📶) On the highway opposite Batchawana Bay's 4km of sandy beach, you'll find this roadside motel and **diner** (☎705-882-2504; www.voyageurslodge.com; Hwy 17, Batchawana Bay;

ST JOSEPH ISLAND

St Joseph Island, a quiet expanse of woodland about 60km southeast of Sault Ste Marie, sits alongside the US border in the northwest corner of Lake Huron. It's linked by bridge off Hwy 17. Here, the **Fort St Joseph National Historic Site** (☎705-246-2664; www.pc.gc.ca/fortstjoseph; Hwy 548; adult/child $4/2; ⏲10am-5pm Jul & Aug, Wed-Sun Jun & Sep) was once the most remote and westerly outpost of the British landholding in North America. The ruins of the 200-year-old fort are an archaeologist's dream.

mains $11-14; ⌚7am to 9pm Apr-late Oct). Clean and cozy woodsy rooms are perfect for a beach stop-off, with fridge, microwave and coffee maker. Two housekeeping suites have one bedroom, a lounge with fold-out couch and full kitchen. Also here are a general store selling alcohol and a gas station.

Lake Superior Provincial Park

Lake Superior Provincial Park (☎705-882-2026, 705-856-2284; www.lakesuperiorpark.ca; Hwy 17; day/2hr/4hr use per vehicle $14.50/5.25/7.50, campsites $41.25-46.90, backcountry tent sites adult/child $10.17/5.09; ⌚Agawa Bay Visitors Centre 9am-8pm Jun-Sep, to 5pm late May & early Oct) protects 1600 sq km of misty fjord-like passages, thick evergreen forest and tranquil sandy coves that feel like they've never known the touch of humankind. The best bits of the park require some level of hiking or canoeing to access, but if you're not so inclined or have limited time, there are numerous picture-perfect vistas just off the highway, which goes straight through the park. Sights and facilities generally open from May to October.

Your first stop should be the **Agawa Bay Visitors Centre**, 9km in from the park's southern boundary. The interactive museum and park experts will advise you well. There's a smaller information area at **Red Rock Lake**, 53km further north, if you're coming from the other direction. If you plan to stop in the park, you must buy a permit, but you do not need one if you will be driving straight through on Hwy 17.

Katherine Cove and Old Woman Bay picnic areas, both by the road, have panoramas of misty sand-strewn shores. Budding anthropologists will appreciate the **Agawa Rock Pictographs**: between 150 and 400 years old, the red-ocher images comprise a spiritual site for the Ojibwe, one of Canada's largest First Nations groups. A rugged 500m trail leads from near the visitors center to a rock ledge where, if the lake is calm, the mysterious pictographs can be seen. Park interpreters are on-site between 11am and 3pm in July and August, weather permitting.

Avid hikers will delight in the park's 11 exceptional trails. The signature hike is the 65km **Coastal Trail**, a steep, challenging route along craggy cliffs and pebble beaches (allow five to seven days total). There are six access points, allowing you to spend from a few hours to several days tackling a section of the trail. The **Nokomis Trail** (5km) loops around iconic **Old Woman Bay**, so named because it is said you can see the face of an old woman in the cliffs. Depending on the weather, wispy beard-like fog and shivering Arctic trees exude a distinctly primeval flavor. The diverse **Orphan Lake Trail** (8km) just north of Katherine Cove is a tasting plate of the park's ethereal features: isolated cobble beaches, majestic waterfalls, elevated lookouts and dense maple forests.

There's a burgeoning paddling culture here, with canoes available to rent in the park (per hour/day $10/30). Several charted inland routes range from the relatively mild 16km **Fenton-Treeby Loop** (with 11 short portages of 150m each max) to challenging routes accessible only via the Algoma Central Railway (p172), if it resumes its passenger services. Naturally Superior Adventures (p176) and Caribou Expeditions run extensive paddling programs in and around the park.

There are two campgrounds close to the highway: Agawa Bay, right on Lake Superior; and Rabbit Blanket Lake, next to an inland lake with less wind and higher temperatures but fewer coastal vistas. Booking through **Ontario Parks** (www.ontarioparks.com) is essential.

Wawa

In the middle of nowhere, enduring winters straight out of a Siberian nightmare, little Wawa is a tough bird. Literally. *Wawa* is an Ojibwe word meaning 'wild goose.' This resilient 1720s fur-trading post was so named because of the millions of geese that would rest by Lake Wawa during their seasonal migration. It's also the idea behind the 8.5m-tall gander that's been unapologetically luring travelers off the highway into town since the 1960s. And rightly so: Wawa is an obligatory Trans-Canada stop for many drivers and that's likely why you'll visit. It also makes a convenient base for Lake Superior explorations, with waterfalls, beaches and scenic viewpoints.

Sights & Activities

Magpie High Falls WATERFALL

(High Falls Rd) Also known as Scenic High Falls, this 23m-high, 38m-wide waterfall on the Magpie River is 5km southwest of town. There is an interpretive walking trail and a picnic shelter with barbecue. Ask at the Visitors Information Centre for details of the 3km riverside Voyageur Hiking Trail leading south from here to Silver Falls, where the Magpie meets the Michipicoten near Michipicoten River Village.

OFF THE BEATEN TRACK

CHAPLEAU

About 140km inland from Wawa, Little Chapleau (*chap*-loh) is the gateway to the world's largest crown game preserve, with nearly 1 million hectares of land: hunting is strictly prohibited. For information, check out www.chapleau.ca/en, or stop by the town's **Centennial Museum & Information Centre** (☎705-864-1330; www.chapleau.ca/en; 94 Monk St; ⏲9am-4pm May-Aug). Critters you might encounter include bald eagles, beavers, lynx, black bears, moose and more.

The Missinaibi River flows over 750km northeast from its source at Missinaibi Lake, 80km northwest of Chapleau, to James Bay, running through **Missinaibi Provincial Park** (☎705-864-3114, emergencies 705-234-2222; www.ontarioparks.com/park/missinaibi; day use per vehicle $11.25, campsites from $35, backcountry camping adult/child under 18yr $10.17/5.09; ⏲early May–mid-Sep), a 500km-long park in Chapleau Crown Game Preserve en route. Several outfits offer canoe rental and tours along the river, including **MHO Adventures** (☎855-226-6366; www.missinaibi.com; 41 Widjiitiwin Rd, Huntsville).

Sandy Beach BEACH

(Harbour Rd) Follow a gravel road and a path lined with dunes and fragile plants to this 1km white-sand beach on Michipicoten Bay, where Group of Seven member AY Jackson once painted. It's 6km southwest of town, accessed from Hwy 17 via Tremblay Rd (north of Wawa) or by heading toward Rock Island Lodge from Michipicoten River Village.

Wawa Goose MONUMENT

(26 Mission Rd) A trip through Wawa would be incomplete without posing for a photo with the Wawa Goose in front of the Visitors Information Centre, before it flies the coop: engineers say the 8.5m-tall goose is cooked, having rusted from the inside out, and it is set to be replaced by a $500,000 lookalike in 2017. There are two other big geese on the main road through town: see if you can spot them.

★**Naturally Superior Adventures** KAYAKING

(☎800-203-9092, 705-856-2939; www.naturallysuperior.com; 10 Government Dock Rd, Lake Superior; courses from $50, day trips from $137) Based 8km southwest of Wawa, the robust gang at Naturally Superior delight in guiding folks around the Lake Superior region by sea kayak, canoe, stand-up paddle board and hiking trail. Watery trips and courses range from day-long affairs to weekend and week-long expeditions, including beach camping. Self-guided paddle expeditions, guide-certification courses and photography workshops are also offered.

Sleeping

There's a glut of motels here from spick-and-span to cheap and nasty. Options are found both in town and on the approaches to Wawa; those on Hwy 17 are closer to the beaches and waterfalls around Lake Superior.

Parkway Motel MOTEL $

(☎705-856-7020; www.parkwaymotel.com; Hwy 17; r from $89; 📶) The Polish-owned Parkway's 13 appealing rooms feature microwave, fridge, coffee maker, LCD TV with cable, and the obligatory Group of Seven repros. The rooms also have a DVD player, with a library of complimentary movies in reception, and there's a boat-shaped picnic and barbecue deck on the front lawn. It's 5km south of Wawa along the highway.

Bristol Motel HOTEL $

(☎705-856-2241; www.bristolmotel.com; 170 Mission Rd; s/d/tr $75/85/95; ❄📶) The Bristol offers cheap and cheerful digs, with comfortable beds, functional wi-fi, fridge and TV in the rooms compensating for the worn carpets. Facilities also include a hot tub, picnic tables in the backyard and a microwave in the lobby, where free coffee and muffins fuel long-distance drivers from 5am.

★**Rock Island Lodge** LODGE $$

(☎705-856-2939; www.rockislandlodge.ca; 10 Government Dock Rd, Lake Superior; r/geo-dome incl breakfast $119/70, tent/tent site $37/20; ⏲May-Oct; 📶) Naturally Superior Adventures' (p176) lodge sits along Lake Superior between a craggy expanse of stone and smooth, sandy beach. The three basic rooms and one cabin are spotless and comfortable, and have en suite bathrooms and views of the evening sun as it gently melts into the lake. There's a beautiful guest kitchen and lounge, as well as wi-fi, but no TV.

Turn off Hwy 17 around 6.5km south of Wawa, toward Michipicoten River Village, to reach the lodge.

Eating

★Kinniwabi Pines INTERNATIONAL **$$**

(☎705-856-7226; Hwy 17; mains $18-32; ⏲9am-10pm May-Oct) What would you expect to find lurking behind the facade of a highway motel 7km south of Wawa? Food from Trinidad, mon! Add some spice to your trip and try the baked pork or the stewed catfish. European and Chinese dishes, and seafood including pickerel, are also available for those who don't care to dare their palate.

Shopping

Young's General Store FOOD, OUTDOORS

(☎705-856-2626; www.youngsgeneralstore.com; 111 Mission Rd; ⏲8am-9pm) Stock up for the long drive ahead at this delightfully old-fashioned store, established in 1971. Piled to the rafters and hanging from the ceiling are fresh local produce (sausage and fudge are specialties), fishing tackle, T-shirts and even the odd moose head.

Information

Visitors Information Centre (☎800 367-9292, 705-856-2244; www.experiencewawa.ca; 26 Mission Rd; ⏲8am-8pm Jul & Aug, 9am-5pm late May, Jun, Sep & early Oct; 📶) Drop in for info on Wawa, including an accommodations list and excellent tourist map, and the region's parks. Also here are a museum covering local history and a gallery exhibiting the town's arts and crafts.

Getting There & Away

Greyhound (p167) buses connect Wawa with Sault Ste Marie ($57, 2¾ hours, one daily) and Thunder Bay ($104, 6¾ hours, one daily).

Pukaskwa National Park

In Ontario's only wilderness **national park** (☎807-229-0801; www.parkscanada.gc.ca/pukaskwa; Hwy 627; day use adult/child $5.80/2.90, serviced campsite with hookup $30, unserviced campsite without hookup $26, backcountry tent sites $9.80; ⏲May-Oct), bear hugs are taken literally. The park has an intact predator-prey ecosystem, including a small herd of elusive caribou, and offers many of the same topographical features as Lake Superior Provincial Park. There are only 4km of roads in the 1878-sq-km wilderness, which visitors can explore on hiking trails and paddling routes.

Pukaskwa's frontcountry is based around its only general-use campground at **Hattie Cove**, near the park's entrance. Check in with the **visitors center** (☎807-229-0801; Hattie Cove; ⏲9am-4pm Jul-Aug) when you arrive: guided hikes and activities depart here most summer evenings.

Three short hiking trails begin at Hattie Cove, offering glimpses of the pristine setting. The popular **Southern Headland Trail** (2.2km) is a rocky, spear-shaped route that offers elevated photo-ops of the shoreline and craggy Canadian Shield. Look for the curious stunted trees, so formed by harsh winds blowing off the lake. The **Bimose Kinoomagewnan** (Walk of Teachings; 2.6km) loops around Halfway Lake, passing boards with stories and artwork from the Ojibwe. The **Beach Trail** (1.5km) winds along Horseshoe Bay and Lake Superior revealing sweeping vistas of crashing waves and undulating sand dunes.

The three trails can be combined for a 6.3km walk, while the **Manito Miikana** (Spirit Trail; 2km) follows a rocky ravine from the **Beach Trail**, to viewing decks overlooking the lake and Pic River dunes.

Pukaskwa's stunning backcountry is not for the fainthearted: the 1878 sq km of remote, untouched wilderness define isolation. The **Coastal Hiking Trail** (60km) is the main artery for hikers, dipping along the vast shoreline. For a taste of the backcountry, many fit hikers opt to traverse the first 7.8km of this trail, culminating at the 30m-long, 25m-high **White Water Suspension Bridge**. The trek is damp, arduous, and there's only one way in and out (15km total).

Paddlers can choose from three incredible multiday routes, including the acclaimed **White River Canoe Route** (72km; four to six days), which links Hattie Cove to **White Lake Provincial Park**. Check with the visitors center; part of the route was closed when we visited due to a hydroelectric project. Gentler paddles lead around the inlets and isles of Hattie Cove and Halfway Lake.

Do not attempt any of these hiking or water voyages without proper preparation and registration. If you need a water taxi, **McCuaig Marine Services** (☎705-206-2758; mccuaigmarine@shaw.ca) picks up and drops off anywhere along the coast, though fickle weather can delay the pick up service. If you're not a skilled independent hiker, Naturally Superior Adventures offers guided excursions through Pukaskwa's backcountry. It also runs multiday sea kayaking trips here, as does Caribou Expeditions (p174).

Marathon to Nipigon

The winding path over the northern crest of Lake Superior is a pleasant jaunt with several places that make a good excuse to stretch your legs. Rocky **Neys Provincial Park** (807-229-1624; www.ontarioparks.com/park/neys; day use per vehicle $11.25), 26km west of Marathon, has craggy beaches, furry caribou, short hiking trails, and long, lingering sunsets.

Drop by the town of **Terrace Bay** (www.terracebay.ca) and catch a boat 13km to the **Slate Islands** (807-825-3403; www.ontarioparks.com/park/slateislands). Possibly the remnants of an ancient meteorite, the archipelago is home to one of the world's largest herds of woodland caribou, as well as snowshoe hare and forested inlets for kayaking explorations. Naturally Superior Adventures (p176) runs kayaking expeditions here.

You can camp in Neys Provincial Park or spend the night in little Rossport, tucked between the grumbling railroad and one of Lake Superior's only natural harbors. The historic Rossport Inn and Cabins (p174) is a fabulous alternative if you perfer noncamping.

Sleeping Giant Provincial Park

Seen across the lake from Thunder Bay, the jagged Sleeping Giant Peninsula resembles a large reclining man. Its rugged, forested terrain has been considered a sacred realm for millennia. The **Sleeping Giant Provincial Park** (807-977-2526; www.ontarioparks.com/park/sleepinggiant; Hwy 587; day use per vehicle $11.25, campsites $37-42, cabins from $170, camping trailers $98-142) covers much of the craggy promontory, offering unforgettable views of Lake Superior.

The park is wild enough to offer backcountry camping and over 80km of hiking trails, yet compact enough for a fulfilling day trip from Thunder Bay, around 70km west. Contact **Ontario Parks** (www.ontarioparks.com) for reservations. On trails such as the 40km, multiday **Kabeyun**, which follows the peninsula's dramatic coastline, you might see moose, wolf, fox or lynx in the boreal forest. There are also short trails of 1km and up, and kayak and canoe rental.

At the tip of the peninsula, you'll find the remote community of **Silver Islet**. In the mid-1880s the town exploded with the world's richest silver mine, now abandoned, and was a Hollywood location of choice in the early 20th century.

Thunder Bay

POP 125,000

Thunder Bay is about as comfortably isolated as you can get – it's 706km west of Sault Ste Marie and 703km east of Winnipeg (Manitoba). If you're arriving by road, it's a welcome return to civilization: no matter how beautiful the forests and shoreline, they start to blur together after a few hundred kilometers. With a smattering of historical attractions, surrounding natural beauty, and creative restaurants and bars in its regenerated downtown Entertainment District, you might be pleasantly surprised that Thunder Bay hums along strong, in defiance and celebration of its long, dark winters. Maybe it has something to do with the fact that 10% of the population are of Finnish descent. If you're passing through, consider staying two nights to get a sense of the place.

Sights

★Fort William Historical Park MUSEUM

(807-473-2344; www.fwhp.ca; 1350 King Rd; adult/child $14/10; 10am-5pm mid-May–mid-Sep, tours every 45min) French voyageurs, Scottish gentlemen and Ojibwe scuttle about while re-enacting life in the early 1800s at this historical park. From 1803 to 1821, Fort William was the headquarters of the North West Company. Eventually the business was absorbed by the Hudson's Bay Company and the region's importance as a trading center declined. Today, the large heritage center offers 46 reconstructed historic buildings stuffed with entertaining and antiquated props such as muskets, pelts and birch-bark canoes.

Marina Park HARBOR

(www.thunderbay.ca/Living/recreation_and_parks; Sleeping Giant Pkwy) The focus of exciting development plans, Thunder Bay's marina area is a pedestrianized haven of parkland, fountains, footpaths, a skate park and public art. Pick up the free *Public Art Walking Tour Guide*, covering the many installations along the waterfront, from the tourist offices (or download it from www.thunderbay.ca/Living/culture_and_heritage/Public_Art.htm). Outdoor movies, concerts and festivals take place here in summer. The area is also known as Prince Arthur's Landing or just the plain old waterfront. Access it from downtown over the blue pedestrian bridge at the eastern end of Red River Rd, near the Pagoda Information Center.

Bay & Algoma Historical District AREA
Thunder Bay has a population of well over 10,000 Finnish Canadians, descended from immigrants who began arriving in the late 19th century. Locals happily honor this heritage by taking saunas and eating pancakes. In this historical Finnish district around the intersection of Bay and Algoma Sts, you will see Scandinavian shops and businesses and perhaps hear old people speaking Finnish.

David Thompson Astronomical Observatory OBSERVATORY
(807-473-2344; www.fwhp.ca; 1350 King Rd; adult/child $10/8; 10pm-midnight Thu-Sat May-Aug, 9-11pm Thu-Sat Sep-Oct, 7-9pm Thu-Sat Nov-Feb, 9:30-11:30pm Thu-Sat Mar-Apr) You too can peek at the stars through one of Canada's largest telescopes at the Fort William Historical Park's fantastic, accessible observatory. Check the website for the latest viewing conditions. Even if the weather is cloudy, join a Star Walk for a virtual tour of the night sky.

Thunder Bay Art Gallery GALLERY
(807-577-6427; www.theag.ca; 1080 Keewatin St, Confederation College; adult/student/child under 12yr $3/1.50/free; noon-8pm Tue-Thu, to 5pm Fri-Sun) Thunder Bay's premier gallery offers an eclectic assortment of contemporary art, including works by Aboriginal artists from northwestern Ontario and beyond. The Aboriginal painters' use of natural imagery, haunting masks and scorching primary colors will leave a lasting impression on visitors.

Thunder Bay Museum MUSEUM
(807-623-0801; www.thunderbaymuseum.com; 425 Donald St E; adult/child $3/1.50; 11am-5pm mid-Jun–early Sep, from 1pm Tue-Sun early Sep–mid-Jun) This century-old museum is engaging for adults and children alike. Displays about Ojibwe culture, fur trading, military history and recent developments incorporate well-presented artifacts to offer visitors a glimpse of the region's 10,000 years of human history.

Terry Fox Lookout & Memorial MONUMENT
(1000 Hwy 11/17) This memorial honors Terry Fox, a young cancer sufferer and amputee who began a trans-Canada walk on April 12, 1980 to raise money for cancer research. After traveling 5373km from St John's, Newfoundland, he arrived in Thunder Bay as his condition deteriorated. He never left. Today's memorial is erected close to where Terry ended his great 'Marathon of Hope.'

Mt McKay VIEWPOINT
(807-623-9543; www.fwfn.com; Mission Rd; per vehicle $5; 9am-10pm mid-May–early Oct) Mt McKay rises 350m over Thunder Bay, offering sweeping views of the region's patchwork of rugged pines and swollen rock formations. The lookout is part of the Fort William First Nation, and reveals its most majestic moments in the evening when the valley is but a sea of blinking lights. An easy walking trail ascends 175m from the viewing area to the top of the mountain. Watch your step while climbing – the shale rock can cause tumbles.

Amethyst Mine Panorama HISTORIC SITE
(807-622-6908; www.amethystmine.com; 500 Bass Lake Rd; adult/child under 5yr $8/free, amethyst per pound $3; 10am-5pm mid-May–mid-Oct) Visit this mine, 60km east of Thunder Bay, and pick your very own purple chunk of

WINNIE THE WHO?

The little logging town of **White River** (www.whiteriver.ca) lays claim to being the home of the original Winnie the Pooh.

As the story goes, back in 1914, a trapper returned to White River with an orphaned baby black bear cub. A veterinarian soldier named Harry Colebourn was on a rail layover in White River when he came across the trapper and fell in love with the cub, purchasing her for $20. He named her 'Winnipeg.' She boarded the Québec-bound troop train with Harry, en route to his native Britain.

When Harry was called to serve in France, he left Winnie in the care of the London Zoo, where she became an instant hit. One of the many hearts she won over belonged to a young Christopher Robin Milne, son of AA Milne. A frequent visitor to the zoo, young Christopher's pet name for the little bear was 'Winnie-the-Pooh.' In his 1926 first edition, AA Milne noted that his stories were about his son, the bear from the London Zoo, and Christopher's stuffed animals.

Eventually, Disney purchased Milne's tales of Winnie-the-Pooh and Christopher Robin, and…the rest is history. A monument to both bears, actual and fictional, stands in the park in White River, by the visitors center.

WORTH A TRIP

OUIMET CANYON PROVINCIAL PARK

Ouimet Canyon (807-977-2526; Ouimet Canyon Rd; donation $2; May-Oct), just 90km east of Thunder Bay, is a treacherous crevasse scoured out by ice and wind during the last Ice Age. A microclimate supporting a small collection of rare arctic-alpine plants has formed at the bottom, 150m below. A 1km loop hugs the jagged bluffs, offering views that will make your knees tremble. Camping is prohibited. The canyon is 12km from the turnoff on Hwy 17.

Nearby, **Eagle Canyon Adventures** (807-355-3064; www.eaglecanyonadventures.ca; 275 Valley Rd, Dorion; adult/child $20/10, zip line $50; 10am-6pm May–mid-Oct) has a 183m-long bridge over the deep canyon floor; it's the longest suspension footbridge in Canada. Additional superlatives – like the country's longest, highest and fastest zip line – will surely satisfy the adventurous all afternoon.

amethyst, Ontario's official gemstone, in the public digging area. While pulling into the parking lot, you may notice that the gravel has a faint indigo hue, a testament to the fact that the area is truly overflowing with these semiprecious pieces.

Activities

Sail Superior BOATING

(807-628-3333; www.sailsuperior.com; Pier 3, Sleeping Giant Pkwy) Sailboat tours on Lake Superior from Thunder Bay marina, including 1½-hour trips around the harbor (adult/child under 10 years $49/25, minimum four people).

Loch Lomond Ski Area SKIING

(807-475-7787; www.lochlomond.ca; 1800 Loch Lomond Rd; full-/half-day lift tickets from $46/34; Dec-Apr) With 17 runs, equally distributed between beginner, intermediate and advanced, this is a great hill to learn on and a wonderful place to ski with kids. Ski, snowboard and equipment rental and lessons are available. In summer, the slopes are open to hikers and mountain bikers.

Kangas SAUNA

(807-344-6761; www.kangassauna.ca; 379 Oliver Rd; sauna/hot tub hire from $17/15; 8am-10pm) Reflecting Thunder Bay's Finnish heritage, this local institution offers 1½-hour private rental of its saunas. Each accommodates up to six people, so go it alone, or grab a 'conference room' for you and your 'associates.' There's also a hot tub, and the cafe (mains $10) is popular for breakfast.

Chippewa Park SWIMMING

(www.chippewapark.ca; City Rd) This waterfront park is a great place to swim, frolic or picnic on a sunny day.

Eating

★Hoito Restaurant FINNISH $

(807-345-6323; www.314baystreet.com; 314 Bay St; mains $8-13; 7am-7:30pm Mon-Fri, from 8am Sat & Sun) You'll think you've stumbled into a staff cafeteria in Finland; indeed, that's how the Hoito started, over a century ago, providing affordable meals to Finnish workers. This Thunder Bay institution's all-day breakfast of flattened Finnish *lättyjä* pancakes is the only way to start the day here. It's in the basement of the historic Finnish Labour Temple, now a cultural center.

★Tomlin CANADIAN $$

(807-346-4447; www.tomlinrestaurant.com; 202 Red River Rd; mains $16-28, small plates $10-14, cocktails $10-14; 5-10pm Tue-Thu, to 11pm Fri & Sat) Locally lauded chef Steve Simpson's elevated comfort food uses seasonal local ingredients, with the regularly changing menu split between small plates (eg beef tartare and smoked cauliflower) and large (veal cavatelli, crab and scallop linguine, redfin trout). The wine list is 100% Ontario and includes ice wine.

Tokyo House ASIAN $$

(807-622-1169; www.tokyohouse.ca; 231 Arthur St W; lunch/dinner buffet from $15/24; noon-3pm & 4:30-10pm) There's nothing authentically Japanese about this shiny all-you-can-eat restaurant, but this is Thunder Bay and we're grateful Asian food is represented this far north at all! Most of your favorite Japanese dishes are here with a tonne of sushi options, all prepared to order.

Uptown Cut STEAK $$$

(807-344-4030; www.uptowncut.ca; 252 Algoma St S; mains from $25; noon-3pm Thu & Fri, 5pm-late Tue-Sat) Uptown Cut's tasting menu is focused on dry-aged and wagyu steaks, aiming to promote Ontario beef. So good are these cuts that a *New York Times* food critic proclaimed his wagyu the best steak of his life. Much creativity is also lavished on the uncarnivorous plates, making this a gourmet experience to remember.

Bight INTERNATIONAL **$$$**
(807-622-4448; bightrestaurant.ca; 2201 Sleeping Giant Pkwy; mains $15-35; 11:30am-10pm;) At this understated marina restaurant, chef Allan Rebelo has created a contemporary menu including charcuterie boards, pizza, fish tacos and shrimp and lobster pasta. Sit outside between giant teardrop sculptures, or in the black, white and metal interior.

Prospector Steakhouse STEAK **$$$**
(807-345-5833; www.prospectorsteakhouse.com; 27 Cumberland St S; mains $32; 5-9pm Sun-Thu, to 10pm Fri & Sat;) Appetites beware: you're about to be obliterated. In the historic Bank of Montreal building, hefty carnivorous portions are dished out amid black-and-white scenes of moose carts, animal heads, canoes and ranch-like curios. The infamous prime rib will give your arteries a workout. All mains come with the bottomless salad bar, soup and fresh bread buns.

Caribou Restaurant & Wine Bar FUSION **$$$**
(807-628-8588; www.caribourestaurant.com; 727 Hewitson St; lunch mains $15-18, dinner mains $17-48; 11:30am-2pm Thu & Fri, 5-9pm daily;) Between southern Thunder Bay's confusing haze of wide-set freeways and boxy mega-marts lies one of the town's best dining options. Caribou's facade is somewhat misleading, reeking of franchise banality; the inside is filled with attentive touches such as white-clothed tables and designer stemware. The menu ranges from wood-oven pizza to seafood in spicy Creole sauce and oven-baked Arctic char.

Bistro One INTERNATIONAL **$$$**
(807-622-2478; www.bistroone.ca; 555 Dunlop St; mains $27-42; 5-10pm Tue-Sat;) A diamond in the rough of a utilitarian area south of the city center, Bistro One sizzles with an innovative, ever-changing menu, sleek decor and a legendary wine list.

Giorg ITALIAN **$$$**
(807-623-8052; www.giorg.ca; 114 Syndicate Ave N; mains $15-47; 5:30-9pm Tue-Sat;) Despite its unprepossessing exterior, this charming Italian restaurant ranks as one of Thunder Bay's best, with scrumptious pastas made on-site. Heftier mains include pan-seared duck breast, aged beef tenderloin and sautéed shrimp with pancetta.

★ **Prime Gelato** ICE CREAM
(807-344-1185; 200 Red River Rd; cup $3.50-6.50, waffle cone $4.50-7.50; noon-10pm Tue-Sun) With ambitions to be a Ben & Jerry's of the north, Prime sells gelato and sorbet in creative flavors such as salted caramel, including alcoholic options made with Kenora's Lake of the Woods beer. The dozen or so gluten-free creations on offer frequently change, but most incorporate fresh local produce from maple syrup to strawberries.

Drinking & Nightlife

★ **Red Lion Smokehouse** CRAFT BEER
(807-286-0045; redlionsmokehouse.ca; 28 Cumberland St S; noon-midnight Tue-Thu, to 1am Fri, 3pm-1am Sat) Thunder Bay's new favorite hangout, a warehouse-style space with exposed pipes, seamlessly mixes industrial cool and coziness courtesy of board games, comfort food and the waitresses' cheery beer recommendations. There is a two-page beer menu, including locally brewed Sleeping Giant on tap, and home-smoked dishes ($12 to $29) such as burgers and pulled pork.

Sovereign Room BAR
(807-343-9277; www.sovereignroom.com; 220 Red River Rd; 4pm-2am Tue-Fri, from 11am Sat & Sun) From the chandelier behind the bar to the ornate olive wallpaper, dark woody booths and upward curling staircase by the storefront window, 'the Sov' is an atmospheric spot for a beer. There's live music, and the menu (mains $10 to $20) features staples and surprises such as duck poutine, stone-baked pizza, chicken wings and nachos.

The Foundry BAR
(807-285-3188; www.thefoundrypub.com; 242 Red River Rd; 11am-2am Mon-Sat) This long-standing local fave offers dozens of beers on tap and meals in a two-level venue. Dishes include scrumptious coconut curry soup, poutine with Thunder Bay gouda, and fish and chips featuring local Sleeping Giant beer in the batter. There's live music most nights.

St Paul Roastery COFFEE
(807-344-3900; 11 St Paul St; 7:30am-5pm Mon-Fri, from 9am Sat) Black gold is available on tap or in pour-over form at this hip temple to the bean, which doubles as a roastery and has an adjoining record shop.

Growing Season JUICE BAR
(807-344-6869; www.growingseason.ca; 201 Algoma St S; 11am-7pm Mon-Sat) Healthy blended juices and shakes are the name of the game at this 'juice collective.' There are also scrumptious dishes to accompany your smoothie, with ingredients supplied by a long list of local producers.

Madhouse Tavern Grill BAR
(807-344-6600; 295 Bay St; 11:30am-1am) Behind its unremarkable facade, this neighborhood hangout is a great place to relax and take a load off among warm, friendly chatter and cold beer. Overlooking the hubbub are swirly portraits of famous artists and writers from Frida Kahlo to Hunter S Thompson.

Information

Pagoda Information Center (807-684-3670; www.tourismthunderbay.com; cnr Red River Rd & Water St; 10am-6pm Tue-Sat Jul & Aug) Canada's oldest tourist information bureau, in a distinctive building dating to 1909, remains the city's most central source of visitor information.

Tourism Thunder Bay (807-983-2041; www.tourismthunderbay.com; 1000 Hwy 11/17; 9am-5pm) The city's largest tourist office is located 6km east of town at the Terry Fox Lookout & Memorial.

Getting There & Away

Thunder Bay Airport (YQT; 807-473-2600; www.tbairport.on.ca) is on the southwest side of the city, about 10km from downtown, at the junction of Arthur St W and Hwy 61. It is served by Air Canada, WestJet, Porter, Wasaya and Bearskin, with around 15 flights a day from Toronto ($120 one way). Other connections include Sudbury, Sault Ste Marie, Ottawa and Winnipeg.

Greyhound (p167) buses run to/from Sault Ste Marie ($148, 9½ hours, one daily) and Winnipeg ($126, 9½ hours, one daily). The Greyhound **bus depot** (807-345-2194; 815 Fort William Rd) is just off the Harbour Expwy near the Intercity mall.

Getting Around

Car-rental chains are well represented at the airport.

Thunder Bay Transit (807-684-3744; www.thunderbay.ca/transit) has the city covered. Buses run in every direction from central hub the **Waterfront Terminal** (Water St), including south to the airport, the Greyhound bus depot and the Fort William Historical Park. One-way trips cost $2.75.

Cochrane to Moose Factory & Moosonee

Time has not been kind to little Cochrane, whose raison d'être is the Polar Bear Express – the whistle-stop train shuttling passengers north to the remote recesses of James Bay. Cochrane doesn't pretend to be a dainty tourist destination and, in a way, that honesty is refreshing. Evidence of harsh, long winters is conspicuous in this windswept town, but despite the inhospitable winters, the largely Francophone population is warm and accommodating.

Moosonee and Moose Factory sit near the tundra line, and are as far north as most people ever get in eastern Canada. Expeditions further north will undoubtedly involve floatplanes, canoes, snowmobiles, dogsleds or snowshoes.

The railway reached Moosonee in 1932, about 30 years after it was established by Révillon Frères as a trading post. The neighboring island of Moose Factory is a small Cree settlement and the historic site of the Hudson's Bay Company trading hub founded in 1672.

Sights & Activities

Moosonee and Moose Factory could not be more different. Moosonee has a banal industrial vibe, while Moose Factory is a spirited reservation of friendly people and scores of smoke huts. The best way to experience the region is through a tour with the local Moose Cree.

Polar Bear Habitat & Heritage Village ZOO
(800-354-9948, toll-free 705-272-2327; www.polarbearhabitat.ca; 1 Drury Park Rd, Cochrane; adult/student/child 5-11yr $16/12/10; 9am-5pm late May–mid-Sep, 10am-4pm mid-Sep–late May;) Despite all the polar bear talk, there are no wild polar bears in the region. This center, the world's largest polar bear facility and the only one with access to a natural lake, is dedicated to the conservation, care and well-being of the furry giants. Current residents Ganuk and Henry may be joined by another bear soon. Visitors can interact with them and learn more at 'meet the keeper' sessions (daily in summer).

Polar Bear Express RAIL
(800-265-2356, toll-free 705-472-4500; www.ontarionorthland.ca; round-trip adult/child under 11yr $118.54/59.27; Sun-Fri late Jun-late Aug, Mon-Fri

WORTH A TRIP

THUNDER BAY TO MANITOBA

Decisions, decisions: if you're heading west from Lake Superior to Winnipeg, you have two choices. The **northern route** (Hwy 17) is faster and has more services along the way, but the scenic **southern route** (Hwy 11 and Hwy 71) offers some impressive diversions.

Leaving Thunder Bay, traffic and highway vistas thin out after **Kakabeka Falls** (☎807-473-9231; www.ontarioparks.com/park/kakabekafalls; Hwy 11-17; day use per vehicle $11.25). Then, at **Shabaqua Corners**, the highway forks: the northern route plows straight toward Winnipeg, while the southern route takes two extra hours as it ambles through more scenic countryside. Both routes shuttle you through prime fishing country, not least the idyllic **Lake of the Woods** region and its unofficial capital, **Kenora**.

Signs mark the beginning of a new time zone (you save an hour going west).

Northern Route

Ignace and the larger town of **Dryden**, respectively on Agimak Lake and Wabigoon Lake (no relation to Lake Wobegon, American novelist Garrison Keillor's fictional Minnesota town), are possible stop-offs. However, the biggest and best place to pause is **Kenora** (lakeofthewoods.com), the unofficial capital of the striking **Lake of the Woods** region and tourism hub for local summer cottages and fishing trips. Rambling across Ontario, Manitoba and Minnesota, Lake of the Woods is the local answer to Toronto's cottage country (p202) for weekending Winnipeggers.

M.S. Kenora (☎807-468-9124; www.mskenora.com; Bernier Dr; adult/child 3-10yr $29/15.50; ⏲May-Sep) offers daily 2¼-hour cruises around the northern section of Lake of the Woods, to see a little of the region's 100,000km of shoreline and 14,500 islands. Sunset dinner cruises are also offered.

The small **Lake of the Woods Museum** (☎807-467-2105; www.lakeofthewoodsmuseum.ca; 300 Main St S, Kenora; adult/student 6-17yr $4/3; ⏲10am-5pm Jul-Aug, Tue-Sat Sep-Jun) covers the aboriginal, industrial and gold-mining history of the area, with a particular focus on the last 100 years, when Kenora changed rapidly.

Southern Route

The longer southern route from Thunder Bay to Winnipeg has some spectacular distractions. The first major stop after the northern and southern highways diverge at Shabaqua Corners is the crusty mining town of **Atikokan** – a good base for a day trip to the stunning and secluded **Quetico Provincial Park** (☎807-597-2735; www.ontarioparks.com/park/quetico; Hwy 11; day use per vehicle $11.25, campsite with/without hookup $52/45, backcountry camping adult $12.50-21.50, child under 18yr $6-8.50, cabin $86). The endless waterlogged preserve has some of Canada's finest wilderness canoe and portage routes and hiking trails in its rugged backcountry. **Canoe Canada Outfitters** (☎807-597-6418; www.canoecanada.com; 300 O'Brien St, Atikokan) provides both self-guided and guided adventures through this dramatic wilderness.

Further west, **Fort Frances** sits right on the American border, with a bridge crossing to Minnesota. **Fort Frances Museum** (☎807-274-7891; www.fort-frances.com/museum; 259 Scott St, Fort Frances; adult/child 5-12yr $4/3; ⏲10am-5pm mid-May–early Sep, 11am-4pm Sep, 11am-4pm Tue-Sat Oct–mid-May) gives a historical introduction to the area. **Kay-Nah-Chi-Wah-Nung** (Manitou Mounds; ☎807-483-1163; www.manitoumounds.com; Shaw Rd, Stratton; admission $10; ⏲10am-6pm Wed-Sat May-Sep), 60km west (25km past Emo), is a sacred Ojibwe site containing the largest ancient ceremonial burial grounds in Canada.

Before linking back up with Hwy 17 near Kenora, consider stopping in the serene resort towns of **Nestor Falls** and **Sioux Narrows**, both on Hwy 71.

late Aug-late Jun) A northern legend since 1964, this whistle-stop train remains the most popular and affordable conduit to the remote communities of Moosonee and Moose Factory. It departs Cochrane at 9am, reaches Moosonee at 1:50pm, then returns south at 5pm, arriving in Cochrane at 9:42pm. The assortment of passengers is a sight in itself: locals, trappers, biologists, geologists, tourists, anglers and paddlers.

Moose Cree Outdoor Discoveries & Adventures OUTDOORS
(☎705-658-4619; www.moosecree.com/tourism/outdoordiscoveries.html; 22 Jonathan Cheechoo Dr, Moose Factory) Moose Cree First Nation's tourism department offers customized trips incorporating cultural activities (storytelling and traditional foods) with, for example, canoeing in summer and snowshoeing in winter. In tailoring your adventure, friendly staff will ask you exactly what you want to experience.

Tidewater Provincial Park PROVINCIAL PARK
(☎705-272-7107; www.ontarioparks.com/park/tidewater; day use per person $5, camping per person $10; ⏲late Jun-early Sep) Tidewater covers five islands in the Moose River estuary, with backcountry camping offered on Charles Island between Moose Factory and Moosonee. You might glimpse a seal or the milky white back of a beluga whale from your campsite. Access the island by water taxi from Moosonee; these waterways are only for experienced canoeists. Contact Moose Cree Outdoor Discoveries & Adventures for permits.

Cree Cultural Interpretive Centre MUSEUM
(☎705-658-4619; www.moosecree.com/tourism/ccic.html; Riverside Dr, Moose Factory; ⏲9am-5pm Sun-Fri Jun-Aug) Operated by Moose Cree First Nation, this center features indoor and outdoor exhibits of artifacts, including bone tools, traditional toys, reusable diapers and dwellings from the precontact era. You'll learn about *pashtamowin*, or 'what goes around, comes around' – the Cree's version of karma, if you will. It is best to explore the center with the aid of a guide, as they can relay fascinating details and personal anecdotes about the interesting displays.

Sleeping

There are a couple of lodging options in Moosonee, though we suggest staying on Moose Factory island. In addition to the ecolodge here, Moose Cree Outdoor Discoveries & Adventures (p184) can organize accommodations and camping on Moose Factory and neighbouring islands.

Cochrane has several options, including the **Best Western Swan Castle Inn** (☎705-272-5200; www.bestwestern.com; 189 Railway St, Cochrane; s/d incl breakfast from $145/155; ❄@📶) and **Commando Motel** (☎705-272-2700; t.cthomas@hotmail.com; 80 7th Ave, Cochrane; s/d $70/75; 📶) by the station – and of course the inn at the station itself.

Hudson's Bay Company Staff House GUESTHOUSE $
(☎705-658-4619; www.moosecree.com; 4 Front St, Moose Factory; r $75; 📶) This historic building doubles as a museum, with exhibits on the ground floor covering the fur-trading era when Hudson's Bay employees lodged here and the manager stayed next door. Managed by Moose Cree First Nation, the four pastel-painted rooms share a kitchen and ablutions.

Thriftlodge MOTEL $
(☎705-272-4281; www.travelodge.com; 50 Hwy 11 S, Cochrane; s $75-80, d $85-90; ❄@📶) One of the best deals in Cochrane, this chain motel offers 40 comfortable rooms with hair dryer, coffee maker and fridge, right next to the passable Terry's Steakhouse. The upstairs apartments are less pleasant and not recommended unless you are really counting the cents.

Cree Village Ecolodge LODGE $$
(☎705-658-6400; www.creevillage.com; 61 Hospital Dr, Moose Factory; r incl breakfast from $180; 📶) Cree Village is the northern hemisphere's first Aboriginal-owned and -operated lodge. With windows gazing at the tree-lined Moose River, the fascinating A-frame building was designed and furnished to reflect traditional Cree values. Its environmentally conscious design extends to the organic wool and cotton used in the carpets, blankets and bed linen, and organic soaps in every room.

Moose River Guesthouse GUESTHOUSE $$
(☎705-336-1555; www.mooseriverguesthouse.com; 51 Gardiner Rd, Moosonee; r $120, ste $135-185; 📶) On a quiet cul-de-sac about 300m from Moosonee train station, this cheerfully painted house and converted barn offers seven rooms and suites decorated in quaint country style. Each room shares a bathroom with one other, while suites have private facilities, and rates include continental breakfast.

Eating

Station Inn CANADIAN $
(200 Railway St, Cochrane; mains $8-15; ⏲7am-8pm Mon-Fri late Aug-late Jun, Sun-Fri late Jun-late Aug) Like the rest of the **Station Inn** (☎705-272-3500; www.ontarionorthland.ca; 200 Railway St, Cochrane; s/d $118/130; ❄📶), the restaurant is more functional than atmospheric, serving hefty meals and daily specials such as pork or veal cutlet, farmer's sausages, lasagne and burgers. Also on the menu are sandwiches and wraps, salads, and veggie options.

Polar Bear Restaurant DINER $
(☎705-272-5345; Fast Stop, Hwy 11 S, Cochrane; mains $7-18; ⊙6am-10pm) Francophone truck drivers hold court and the servers are always ready with a refill at this gas-station restaurant, which serves hearty breakfasts of pancakes or French toast piled with bacon and syrup. Lunch and dinner are snack-bar fare, such as 'polar bear's favorite' (fish burger) and 'polar bear poutine' (yes there's a theme here), plus some incongruous Greek specialties.

Kaylobs Kafe CAFE $
(☎705-272-4025; 282 8th Ave, Cochrane; mains $10-13, sandwiches $5; ⊙6am-7:45pm Mon-Fri, from 8am Sat, 8am-3:45pm Sun) This local cafe by Lake Commando serves burgers, poutine, breakfasts, daily specials and hearty home-style meals such as liver and onions.

Terry's Steakhouse STEAK $$
(☎705-272-4770; Hwy 11 S, Cochrane; mains $15-25; ⊙11am-9pm Mon-Fri, from 4pm Sat, from 10am Sun) With its red-and-black checkered tablecloths and chintzy chandeliers, Terry's is Cochrane's first choice for a steak. The likes of rib eye and filet mignon are charbroiled and accompanied by classic sauces such as peppercorn. Burgers, pasta, seafood, traditional favorites such as liver and onions, sandwiches and wraps are also on the menu.

Information

Cochrane Tourist Office (☎705-277-4926; www.cochraneontario.com; Hwy 11 S, Cochrane; ⊙9:30am-5pm Mon-Fri) This small office is next to the polar bear statue named Chimo (its name comes from the Cree word meaning 'be welcome'), at the intersection of Hwy 11 S (to North Bay) and Hwy 11 W (to Thunder Bay).

Cochrane Train Station (☎705-272-4228; 200 Railway St) The ticket desk at the train station is another useful source of northern knowledge.

Moose Cree Outdoor Discoveries & Adventures (p184) Information on accommodations and activities on Moose Factory.

Getting There & Around

Ontario Northland (p167) runs a bus between Cochrane and Timmins ($21.50, 1½ hours), to link in with the **Polar Bear Express** (p182) train. It departs Timmins at 6.25am on days the train operates, returning from Cochrane at 10:45pm. Timmins has an airport with flights to/from Toronto.

Ontario Northland buses also connect **Cochrane Train Station** (p185) to North Bay ($92.50, 6¼ hours, one daily) and Sudbury ($81.50, 6½ hours, one daily).

Moosonee, gateway to Moose Factory, is not accessible by car from the south. It can only be reached by the **Polar Bear Express** (p182). **Air Creebec** (☎705-336-2221; www.aircreebec.ca) from Cochrane or Air Creebec flights from Timmins ($442, one hour). Both the train and flights depart five to six days a week.

From Moosonee, water taxis shuttle passengers the 3km over to Moose Factory ($15, 15 minutes). Tell your driver if you are going to Cree Village Ecolodge, as it has a private dock north of the island's main docks. In winter the river becomes an ice bridge stable enough for cars and trucks (taxi $10). When the river is freezing in late fall and thawing in early spring, neither option is safe and you will have to take a **helicopter** (☎705-336-6063; www.expeditionhelicopters.com; Airport Rd, Moosonee; one-way flight $40).

Taxis from Moosonee train station to the docks, about 1km east, cost $6 per person.

Temagami

While god-fearing Egyptians were commissioning wondrous pyramids, this region of majestic old-growth pines and hushed lakes was a thriving network of trading routes. Evidence of these ancient trails exists today as hidden archaeological sites strewn throughout the region's provincial parks. Temagami's reputation for canoe and portage experiences of the untrameled Canadian wilderness has attracted adventurers such as British TV personality Ray Mears.

Check out Obabika River Park, or the vast Lady Evelyn Smoothwater Provincial Park, which has Ontario's highest point, Ishpatina Ridge (693m). There are no facilities, and campsites can only be reached by canoe. The easily accessible White Bear Forest has a soaring **fire tower** (O'Connor Rd; ⊙late May-early Oct) FREE at Caribou Mountain offering a bird's-eye view of the stocky trunks below. Pick up the *White Bear Forest Old Growth Trails* map from **Temagami Information Center** (☎705-569-3344; www.temagamiinformation.com; 7 Lakeshore Dr; ⊙9am-2pm Wed, 11am-5pm Thu-Mon late Jun-early Sep) for details of the 1km to 5km walks.

Sights & Activities

Even by Canadian standards, Temagami is a rugged, outdoorsy place. In summer, come for canoe trips through the wilderness, and plan to spend a few days – you need at least four to reach the unpopulated outback. In winter, come for snowmobile trails.

Finlayson Point Provincial Park PROVINCIAL PARK

(☎705-569-3205; www.ontarioparks.com/park/finlaysonpoint; Hwy 11; day use per vehicle $14.50, campsite with/without hookup $47/41.50; ⏲late May-Sep) This small peninsula on Lake Temagami offers canoeing, swimming and camping. Drop by the park office, just off Hwy 11 1km south of town, for information on the group of preserves surrounding Temagami.

Temagami Outfitting Co CANOEING

(☎705-569-2595; www.icanoe.ca; 6 Lakeshore Dr) The passionate guys at Temagami Outfitting Co offer fully outfitted wilderness canoe trips ($95 per person per day); you could turn up in a Hawaiian shirt and they would do the rest, from canoe and clothing to camping equipment. Guides cost an extra $150 per group per day. They also offer air shuttles all over the lakes, starting at $75.

Sleeping

Northland Paradise Lodge LODGE $

(☎705-569-3791; www.northland-paradise.com; 51 Stevens Rd; s/d $55/85, ste $150;) Right on the lake, Northland is a good old-fashioned fishing and hunting lodge with a games room, butchery and tackle-cleaning room. The motel-style rooms with kitchenette are perfect spots to crash after a day on the water, while the rustic housekeeping suites with lake-facing balconies are ideal for an outdoorsy break.

North Bay

POP 54,000

North Bay bills itself as 'just north enough to be perfect,' which begs the question: Perfect for what? It's just north enough to make visiting Torontonians feel like adventurers, and the lakeshore is lovely, but the city is not notably attractive. That said, its real appeal lies in its access to the lake and surrounding countryside, which is slowly becoming part of cottage country (p202) as weekend home-building city slickers pioneer north from oversubscribed Muskoka. To these charms, North Bay adds plenty of decent accommodations and some great restaurants by the water.

Ontario's two major highways (11 and 17) converge as they pass through town, making North Bay a logical layover for Trans-Canada tourists. The highways don't link up again until Nipigon (just before Thunder Bay), 1000km northwest.

Sights & Activities

Lake Nipissing Waterfront PARK

A walk along the scenic Lake Nipissing shoreline reveals several enjoyable activities. Shrubs, trees and perennials line the path, maintained by the North Bay Heritage Gardeners. At the marina are the Heritage Railway and Carousel, a restaurant on the *Chief Commanda* boat, Fun Rentals kayak hire, and lake cruises on the Chief Commanda II.

Fun Rentals KAYAKING

(☎705-471-4007; www.funrentals.ca; Memorial Dr; 1½hr kayak/canoe/stand-up paddle board $25/35/30, 3hr kayak/canoe/stand-up paddle board $40/50/50; ⏲11am-dusk Jul & Aug, from 4pm Fri, from 11am Sat & Sun May, Jun & Sep) Explore a little of Ontario's fourth-largest lake, Nipissing, in one of this outfit's kayaks, canoes or stand-up paddle boards. Take care and stay close to shore if the westerly wind is blowing, as it can be fierce. They also rent out 'unique bikes' (30 minutes/one hour/day from $15/20/60) for a family peddle along the waterfront.

Chief Commanda II CRUISE

(☎705-494-8167; www.chiefcommanda.com; King's Landing, 200 Memorial Dr; ⏲late May-early Oct) This jolly passenger liner cruises through Lake Nipissing's Manitou Islands (adult/child $27/14), along the French River ($44/24) on Sundays, and down to Callander Bay at sunset ($34/18). Dinner is available on the latter, and two-hour cruises to view the fall colors on the lake's north shore are a big hit. Book in advance.

Heritage Railway and Carousel AMUSEMENT PARK

(☎705-495-8412; www.heritagetrainandcarousel.weebly.com; 230 Memorial Dr; ride $2; ⏲10am-dusk late Jun-early Sep, Sat & Sun May, Jun, Sep, early Oct;) Ride a painted pony on this refurbished carousel dating to the 1890s, and travel on the mini-railway built by retired local rail workers.

Sleeping & Eating

Lincoln Inn MOTEL $

(☎705-472-3231; www.thelincolninn.ca; 594 Lakeshore Dr; r/apt from $69/130;) The Lincoln is a solid budget choice close to restaurants, with comfortable rooms and self-catering apartments, the latter featuring a bedroom with two beds plus lounge with sofa bed. Ask to see a few rooms as they vary in size and amenities; 117 is a good option. Rates include continental breakfast, and discounts are often available.

★**Sunset Inn** MOTEL $$

(☎705-472-8370; www.sunsetinn.ca; 641 Lakeshore Dr; r from $119;) This spotless waterfront option has its own private beach in a secluded cove off Lake Nipissing, which amply compensates for the odd lapse in taste in the decor. Numerous room types include luxurious suites with heart-shaped Jacuzzis and large flat-screen TVs, and two- and three-bedroom chalets with full kitchen. There's also a romantic beachfront cabin for two.

White Owl Bistro CANADIAN $$

(☎705-472-2662; www.thewhiteowlbistro.ca; 639 Lakeshore Dr; mains $25; 11am-9pm Mon-Sat, 10am-3pm & 5-9pm Sun;) Nestling among the lakefront motels, this lovely little bistro, built in 1934, serves a range of dishes including salads, pastas, venison burger, rainbow trout, pickerel and Sunday brunches, with seating inside and on the patio. The chicken and pork come from the owner-chefs' farm, Somewood. There are local beers on tap.

★**Churchill's** STEAK $$$

(☎705-476-7777; churchills.ca; 631 Lakeshore Dr; Churchill's/Winnie's Pub mains $36/16, tapas $10; 11am-10pm Mon-Sat, from 4pm Sun;) This low-lit bistro makes up for once being the first branch of mega-chain Tim Hortons by serving some of Canada's finest steaks and ribs, accompanied by homegrown produce and Ontario's largest wine selection north of Toronto. Ontario lamb and Atlantic salmon are also on the menu; alternatively, enjoy tapas at the bar or pub grub from the Winnie's Pub menu.

Information

North Bay Chamber of Commerce (☎705-472-8480; www.northbaychamber.com; 205 Main St E; 9am-4pm Mon-Fri) Has brochures and the helpful Sue is a fount of information.

Heritage Railway and Carousel (p186) The ticket office offers brochures, maps and information.

Transport

Ontario Northland (p167) buses connect Toronto and North Bay ($80, 5½ hours, four daily). **Greyhound** (p167) connects North Bay with Sudbury ($32, two hours, one daily) and Ottawa ($76, 5¼ hours, one daily). The terminus for services is the old train station, known as **the Station** (☎705-495-4200; 100 Station Rd).

Air Canada, Bearskin Airlines and Porter Airlines fly to the small **North Bay Jack Garland Airport** (☎705-474-3026; yyb.ca; 50 Terminal St), 10km northeast of town, from Toronto, Sudbury and Timmins.

EASTERN ONTARIO

Eastern Ontario encompasses the countryside east of Toronto as far as the Québec border. Within weekending distance of Toronto, Prince Edward County's fertile pastures support a long farming tradition and young wine industry. Travelers journeying on the busy Hwy 401 should detour through this scenic, culinary and historic realm.

For museums, history and urban vibes, head to Kingston, the first capital of modern-day Canada, and of course today's vibrant capital, Ottawa. East of Kingston is the Thousand Islands region, a foggy archipelago of lonely isles along the deep St Lawrence Seaway, where the towns of Gananoque and Brockville have a genteel Victorian feel.

Eastern Ontario's natural beauty extends to the interior, which overflows with scenic parks and preserves. Algonquin Provincial Park is the area's flagship domain, offering unparalleled canoeing and wildlife spotting among towering jack pines and lakes. Similar topography extends to the Haliburton Highlands, Kawarthas and Land O' Lakes.

Algonquin Provincial Park

Established in 1893, Ontario's oldest and second-largest park is a sight for city-sore eyes, with over 7600 sq km of thick pine forests, jagged cliffs, trickling crystal streams, mossy bogs and thousands (thousands!) of lakes. An easily accessible outdoor gem, this rugged expanse is a must-visit for canoeists and hikers.

Hwy 60 intersects a small portion of the park near its southern edge. Numerous campgrounds, lodges, attractions and short hiking trails are accessible from this well-trodden corridor. The vast, wooded interior of Algonquin is only accessible via over 2000km of charted canoe routes and strenuous hiking trails.

If you are stopping anywhere in the park, you must purchase a day permit ($17) at the gate. If you won't be stopping, you don't need a permit to cross Algonquin on Hwy 60.

Sights

Algonquin Visitors Centre MUSEUM

(☎613-637-2828; www.algonquinpark.on.ca; Km 43 on Hwy 60; 9am-5pm mid-May–mid-Jun & Oct, to 7pm mid-Jun–Sep, to 4pm Nov-Apr) At this world-class visitors center displays and dioramas illustrate the park's wildlife, history and geology. The center also has a bookstore, cafeteria, wi-fi and lookouts with spectacular views.

Eastern Ontario

Algonquin Art Centre GALLERY

(☎705-633-5555; www.algonquinartcentre.com; Km 20 on Hwy 60; ⏲10am-5pm Jun-Oct) FREE Exhibits an array of wilderness-themed art through several media including paintings, photography, carvings and sculpture. Outdoor interpretive panels are planned to mark the centenary in 2017 of Canadian artist Tom Thomson's death. Check the website for details of summer art classes and events.

Algonquin Logging Museum MUSEUM

(☎613-637-2828; Km 55 on Hwy 60; ⏲9am-5pm Jul-Oct) FREE This excellent museum has extensive exhibits dedicated to the park's logging heritage. The displays are spread along a 1.5km trail that remains open even when the reception area, bookstore and theater are closed.

Activities

Algonquin is famous for its wildlife-watching and scenic lookouts. During spring, you're almost certain to see moose along Hwy 60, as they escape the pesky black flies to lick the leftover salt from winter de-icing. Other creatures you may encounter include deer, beaver, otter, mink and many bird species. There's no limit to the breathtaking natural scenic beauty on offer.

Algonquin is also a great place to give canoeing or kayaking a whirl. Outfitters offer many opportunities for novice paddlers as well as advanced wilderness adventures for the experienced outdoors person. Canoe Lake on Hwy 60 is a popular starting point for beginners, although the launching dock is often crowded in summer.

Self-guided paddling trips are a popular option. A quota system governs the number of tourists at each backcountry camping spot; book ahead so you can canoe your preferred route.

★Portage Store CANOEING

(☎summer 705-633-5622, winter 705-789-3645; www.portagestore.com; Canoe Lake, Km 14 on Hwy 60; canoes per day from $30, 2-day complete outfitting packages from $92) Located 14km inside the park's West Gate on Canoe Lake at access point five, this sprawling complex has a restaurant, outfitters, grocery store and gift shop...oh, and North America's largest fleet of canoes. You can turn up in your least rugged Hawaiian shirt and staff will dispatch you to the wilderness complete with camping, canoeing and portage essentials and know-how.

★Opeongo Outfitters OUTDOORS

(☎613-637-5470, 800-790-1864; www.opeongooutfitters.com; 29902 Hwy 60, Whitney; canoes per day from $23) Algonquin's oldest outfitter is just outside the park's East Gate. It offers fully kitted canoeing and camping packages ($72 to $82 per person), and three- to five-day adventures, which transfer you by water taxi to a ready-made campsite in a remote location for camping, canoeing, fishing and moose spotting.

Voyageur Quest OUTDOORS

(☎800-794-9660, 416-486-3605; www.voyageurquest.com; Kawawaymog/Round Lake) Based at access point one, this 25-year-old operator offers popular paddling trips and log cabins.

Northern Edge Algonquin OUTDOORS

(☎888-383-8320; www.northernedgealgonquin.ca; 100 Ottawa Ave, South River) Offers paddling trips, women's getaways, yoga retreats, cabins and tailored programs in winter. En route to access point one (Kawawaymog/Round Lake) in the northwest of Algonquin.

Canoe Algonquin CANOEING

(☎800-818-1210, 705-636-5956; www.canoealgonquin.com; 1914 Hwy 518 E, Kearney; canoes per day from $28) North of Huntsville, this outfitter is the closest to access points two (Tim River), three (Magnetawan Lake) and four (Rain Lake) on the park's western side.

Algonquin Portage CANOEING

(☎613-735-1795; www.algonquinportage.com; 1352 Barron Canyon Rd, Pembroke; canoes per day from $25, r per adult/child under 13yr $30/20, camping per person $6) Rustic accommodations (BYO sleeping bag), shuttle service, camping gear, canoes, kayaks, mountain bikes, food and gas are all available here. It's east of the park's furthest eastern extent, on Rte 28.

Algonquin North Wilderness Outfitters CANOEING

(☎877-544-3544; www.algonquinnorth.com; Crooked Chute Lake, Hwy 17 & Hwy 630; canoes per day from $35) This outfitter is north of Algonquin Provincial Park at the junction of Hwy 17 and Hwy 630, about 18km west of Mattawa. From here, a paved road takes you 30km south to the Kioshkokwi Lake access point for secluded backcountry explorations. It offers both canoe rental and guided trips.

Algonquin Outfitters CANOEING

(☎800-469-4948; www.algonquinoutfitters.com; canoes per day from $23, day trips from $29) With stores in several locations, including a three-floor branch in Huntsville, another just outside the West Gate at Oxtongue Lake, and two further outlets within the Algonquin Provincial Park at Opeongo Lake and Brent, these guys have got the park covered. Guided trips are available, and water taxis can be reserved to whisk you across Opeongo Lake to wilder regions.

Sleeping

Algonquin is a nature preserve, which means that most noncamping accommodations are outside the park boundaries. Motels and lodges cluster outside the East Gate and West Gate, respectively in Whitney and along Hwy 60 to Huntsville.

TOP FIVE HIKES IN ALGONQUIN PROVINCIAL PARK

Whether you're visiting for a day or a month, sampling some of the over 140km of hiking trails, including many shorter jaunts accessible from Hwy 60, is a must. Hikes depart from various mileposts (actually kilometer-posts) along Hwy 60 between the West Gate (Km 0) and the East Gate (Km 56). You can buy a 50-cent hiking guide at the information centers and trailheads.

Mizzy Lake (moderate 11km loop) An excellent chance to see some diverse wildlife: all known species within the park have been witnessed here at some point. At Km 15.

Track & Tower (moderate 7.7km loop) A serene lakeside trail and an unusual elevated lookout point along an abandoned railway. At Km 25.

Booth's Rock (difficult 5km loop) Follow an abandoned railway for breathtaking views of the sweeping lakes and forests. To get there, follow the road 8km south from Km 40.

Centennial Ridges (difficult 10km loop) The best panoramas in the park, bar none. To get there, follow Rock Lake Road from Km 37.

Lookout Trail (moderate 2km loop) The busiest hike in Algonquin, but for good reason: a spectacular view of untouched nature awaits. At Km 40.

Ontario Parks Campgrounds CAMPGROUND $
(☎info 705-633-5572, reservations 888-668-7275; www.ontarioparks.com/park/algonquin; campsite with/without ablutions $45/40, yurt $98, backcountry camping adult/child under 18yr $13/6) There are 11 car-accessible developed campgrounds within the park, eight reached from Hwy 60, and some featuring yurts. Three sites in the north (Achray, Brent and Kiosk) are accessed via minor roads, reached along Hwy 17. The backcountry camping sites are only accessible by hiking or canoeing. In all cases, book well in advance, especially in summer.

West Gate

★**Wolf Den Nature Retreat** HOSTEL $
(☎705-635-9336, 866-271-9336; www.wolfdenbunkhouse.com; 4568 Hwy 60, Oxtongue Lake; dm/s/d without bathroom from $27/43/66) Located 10km outside the West Gate, this outdoorsy hostel-cum-resort offers lodging from dorms to gorgeous eco-cabins accommodating up to six. Guests can also choose between rustic '50s cabins, A-frame bunkhouses, and hostel rooms with shared bathrooms in the cozy central lodge, with its huge kitchen, stunning 2nd-floor lounge and cedar log sauna nearby.

Riverside Motel MOTEL $
(☎705-635-9021; www.riversidemoteldwight.com; Hwy 60, Dwight; r/f from $95/120;) Few roadside motels can claim a riverside plot with its own waterfall and swimming hole. Water gurgles under the footbridge leading to the small, neat 11-room motel, where picnic tables set among ponds on the expansive lawn complete the package.

Dwight Village Motel MOTEL $$
(☎705-635-2400; www.dwightvillagemotel.com; 2801 Hwy 60, Dwight; r $129;) You'll notice this excellent motel, with its wood-fronted rooms offering all the creature comforts, from the highway. There's a lovely outdoor picnic area with fire pits and plenty of room for kids to play. It's around 25km west of the West Gate, just past the village of Dwight.

Park Interior

In addition to the camping options, there are three upscale lodges within the park, all reached along Hwy 60. Arowhon Pines, Bartlett Lodge and Killarney Lodge operate between May and October. They mostly offer American plan (full-board) or modified American plan (half-board) accommodations.

Arowhon Pines LODGE $$$
(☎866-633-5661, 705-633-5661; www.arowhonpines.ca; Arowhon Rd, turnoff at Km 16 on Hwy 60; r per person $220-407, private cabins per person $373-520; ⏰late May-early Oct;) If you've ever wondered what an adult summer camp might be like, Arowhon Pines is the answer. The largest and most luxurious of Algonquin's all-inclusive lodges has canoes, kayaks, hiking and mountain-biking trails, tennis courts, a sauna and gourmet fine dining (BYOW – Bring Your Own Wine). It's blissfully secluded, 8km north of Hwy 60. Rates include American-plan (full-board) accommodation.

★**Killarney Lodge** LODGE $$$
(☎866-473-5551, 705-633-5551; www.killarneylodge.com; Lake of Two Rivers, turnoff at Km 33 on Hwy 60; cabin per person with full board from $280; ⏰mid-May–mid-Oct;) With 27 one- and two-bedroom lakeside cabins dating to the 1930s, Killarney recalls the innocent days when rustic cabins were synonymous with family vacations. On a peninsula in the lake, it's an idyllic place for a paddle or to relax on your private deck with a glass of wine (BYO). The delightful, log-cabin–style restaurant serves hearty and delicious meals.

Bartlett Lodge LODGE $$$
(☎866-614-5355, 705-633-5543; www.bartlettlodge.com; Cache Lake, turnoff at Km 24 on Hwy 60; luxury tent s/d $218/290, studio s/d $318/424; ⏰mid-May–Oct;) Running completely on solar power, the two-bedroom lakeside 'Sunrise' is perhaps Bartlett's most interesting cabin, but a variety of studio suites, cabins and glamping platform tents is available. All are accessed by boat, summoned using the telephone on the shore, from a point 24km inside the West Gate. The tents include breakfast; other accommodations also include dinner.

Couples Resort RESORT $$$
(☎866-202-1179; www.couplesresort.ca; 139 Galeairy Lake Rd, Whitney; r incl breakfast from $250;) Don't let the name fool you into thinking this smart resort is a naturalist swingers' den; it actually caters to couples on romantic getaways. The 46 rooms benefit from a lovely position on Galeairy Lake, just outside Algonquin's border, with a park pass lent to guests. All accommodations have a hot tub on the deck, king-size bed and fireplace.

The decadent, private (and slightly gaudy) lakeview 'chateaus' live up to the resort's motto, 'Valentine's every day,' with carved wood, comfy sofas, palatial bathroom, Jacuzzi, sauna and even a little conservatory. Couples who tire of each other can enjoy canoeing, kayaking, mountain biking, horse riding, swimming from the jetty, and the art gallery and spa. On summer Fridays, rates exceed $1000 for a chateau; Thursday and Sunday tend to be more competitive, as is the winter low season.

East Gate

Algonquin East Gate Motel MOTEL $
(☎613-637-2652; www.algonquineastgatemotel.com; Hwy 60, Whitney; s $67-75, d $73-82, cottage $125;) This cozy little motel just outside the park's East Gate has 11 comfortable rooms with small bathrooms and friendly, helpful staff. There's also a private housekeeping cottage out back. Breakfast ($6.50) is worth the outlay, with a menu extending to French toast. Canoe day trips ($25) can be arranged.

Information

Algonquin Provincial Park is accessible year-round. Drivers can pass through the park along Hwy 60; you must pay the day-use fee ($17 per vehicle) if you plan to stop and look around. The Hwy 60 corridor has limited cell-phone coverage in the park, and for several kilometers on each side. There are payphones.

Each kilometer of Hwy 60 within the park is tagged, starting at the West Gate (known as 'Km 0') and terminating at the East Gate ('Km 56'). Outfitters and accommodations use these markers when giving directions.

The **Algonquin Visitors Centre** (p187) has an information desk, bookstore and wi-fi.

There are information centers at the park's **West Gate** (☎admin 613-637-2780, info 705-633-5572; www.algonquinpark.on.ca; Km 0 on Hwy 60, West Gate; 8am-6pm May-Sep, 9am-4pm Oct-Apr) and **East Gate** (☎admin 613-637-2780, info 705-633-5572; www.algonquinpark.on.ca; Km 56 on Hwy 60, East Gate; 8am-6pm May-Sep, 9am-4pm Oct-Apr), respectively at Km 0 and Km 56 on Hwy 60.

Getting There & Away

Aside from the East Gate and West Gate on Hwy 60, Algonquin has 34 access points located around the periphery of the park and along the highway, for access to the park's backcountry.

The two large Muskoka towns of Huntsville and Bracebridge are within an hour's drive of the West Gate. Other small townships include Whitney, just outside the East Gate; Maynooth and Bancroft, respectively 40km and 65km south of the East Gate; and Mattawa, north of the park on Hwy 17.

Visiting is easiest with your own wheels, but **Parkbus** (☎800-928-7101; www.parkbus.ca) offers limited summer express departures from Toronto and Ottawa to several Algonquin accommodations and the West Gate (one way adult/child $63/32). Journey time from both cities is three to four hours. Check the website for the latest schedules, and book ahead to secure a spot on this popular service. Parkbus also offers packages including transport, canoe, equipment and food.

Otherwise, there are occasional **Greyhound** (☎1-800-661-8747; www.greyhound.ca) buses from southern Ontario to Maynooth, Huntsville and Bracebridge.

CRYING WOLF

Algonquin Provincial Park is active in wolf research, and public 'howls' are an incredible way to experience the presence of these furry beasts. Wolves will readily respond to human imitations of their howling, so the park's staff conducts communal howling sessions on the occasional summer evening. These events are highly organized: you could be one of 2000 people standing in the darkness waiting for the chilling wails. Wolf howls often take place on Thursdays in August and early September, but are only confirmed on the days they are actually held. Check park bulletin boards, www.algonquinpark.on.ca or phone the **information line** (☎613-637-2828) to be sure.

Haliburton Highlands

This rugged expanse of needleleaf trees feels like a southern extension of Algonquin Provincial Park. Over 300 sq km of the densely forested region is part of the Haliburton Forest, a privately owned woodland reserve offering activities such as hiking and mountain-biking. The area's main town is Bancroft, at the meeting of Hwy 62 and Hwy 28.

Tours

Haliburton Forest OUTDOORS
(☎705-754-2198, 800-631-2198; www.haliburtonforest.com; 1095 Redkenn Rd, Haliburton; day use spring, summer & fall $16, winter $49; main office 8am-5pm) This privately owned, 324-sq-km woodland can be accessed through its main office on Kennisis Lake, 30km north of Haliburton town. Numerous activities are available, including hiking and mountain-biking trails. The recommended four-hour canopy tour (adult/child $95/70) takes you on a

pulse-quickening adventure along a suspended boardwalk through the treetops, up to 20m above the forest floor.

The tour includes a lake crossing by canoe and a visit to the Wolf Centre, where visitors glimpse a pack of wolves from a safe distance as they meander through their 6-hectare enclosure. Thick pillows of snow in the winter encourage a thriving snowmobiling culture, and dogsledding (adult/child from $125/75 for a half-day tour) is a popular attraction as well.

South Algonquin Trails HORSE RIDING
(☎800-758-4801, 705-448-1751; www.southalgonquintrails.com; 4378 Elephant Lake Rd, Harcourt; 1hr ride $60;) Scenic horseback trail riding in the forests of the Haliburton Highlands and southern Algonquin Provincial Park.

Festivals & Events

Rockhound Gemboree CULTURAL
(www.rockhoundgemboree.ca; Jul) Canada's largest gem festival takes place in the small town of Bancroft, nestled in the York River Valley on the southern edge of the Canadian Shield. The town is well known for its mineral-rich soils and during the annual long weekend, geologists lead tours around nearby abandoned mines to scout out stones.

These 'rockhounding' adventures are usually quite successful: examples of over 80% of the minerals found in Canada are regularly dug up in the area.

Sleeping

Arlington Hotel & Pub HOSTEL $
(☎613-338-2080; www.thearlington.ca; 32990 Hwy 62, Maynooth; HI members dm/s/d/tr/q without bathroom $25/40/63/85/108, nonmembers dm/s/d/tr/q without bathroom $28/45/70/95/120; pub 7pm-1am Fri & Sat;) There's something about this towering century-old monster that makes you just want to disappear into it. In tiny Maynooth, the Arlington is a great place for artists, writers and lonely wanderers who want to escape into their craft for a while.

Peterborough & the Kawarthas

Peterborough, 140km northeast of Toronto in the heart of the wooded Kawarthas, is an excellent weekend getaway or launchpad for a journey through this sacred aboriginal land. Offering both cultural attractions and scenic nature preserves, it's a green university town with a bustling community, surrounded by thousands of private cottages dotted around the area's many lakes. Stoney Lake, one of the largest, has some of the most lavish and beautiful private homes in the area.

If you feel like hanging around, consider staying a night in pretty Lakefield, 14km north of town at the bottom of Katchewanooka Lake. Back in Peterborough, you'll find plenty of dining and shopping options and a quaint city center. Cruises and canoes ply the waterways to the Peterborough Lift Lock on the Trent-Severn Waterway, while cycle paths lead around town and over the Otonabee River. The Canadian Canoe Museum is a must-see.

Sights

★ **Canadian Canoe Museum** MUSEUM
(☎866-342-2663; www.canoemuseum.ca; 910 Monaghan Rd, Peterborough; adult/child $12/9.50, 5-8pm Thu free; 10am-5pm Mon-Wed, Fri & Sat, to 8pm Thu, from noon Sun;) Displaying the world's largest collection of canoes and kayaks, this museum is a must-visit. The phenomenal display of around 150 canoes (500 are stacked in the neighboring 'canoe cathedral' warehouse) details Canada's lengthy history of water navigation, from canoes' aboriginal origins through their use in exploration and fur trading to the period from 1870 to 1940, when this area was North America's canoe-building capital. After an hour at the center, you'll feel inspired to pick up a paddle.

A dynamic program of activities, tours and workshops offers more reasons to visit. The museum is set to move to shiny new premises in the Lift Lock area by 2020.

Whetung Ojibwa Centre GALLERY
(☎705-657-3661; www.whetung.com; 875 Mississauga St, Curve Lake Indian Reserve; 9am-5pm) FREE On a peninsula in the lakes, off Hwy 23 some 34km north of Peterborough, this gallery, shop and cultural center has a wonderful collection of aboriginal crafts from around the country, including the valued work of noted artist Norval Morrisseau.

Warsaw Caves Conservation Area PARK
(☎877-816-7604, 705-652-3161; www.warsawcaves.com; 289 Caves Rd; admission per vehicle $14; mid-May–mid-Oct;) Off Hwy 28, some 26km northeast of Peterborough, the Warsaw Caves Conservation Area offers hiking, swimming, camping, canoeing and spelunking in eroded limestone tunnels.

TRENT-SEVERN WATERWAY

This scenic **waterway** (www.trentsevern.com; May-Oct) cuts diagonally across eastern Ontario, linking the lakes and rivers of Simcoe County and the forested Kawarthas. The scenic hydro-highway starts at the Bay of Quinte, near Prince Edward County on Lake Ontario, and passes 45 locks before emptying into Lake Huron. A hundred years ago, this 386km-long aboriginal canoe route bustled with commercial vessels. Today, it's the province of houseboats, cruise vessels and canoes.

In Peterborough, head to the **Peterborough Lift Lock** near the city museum. It's the world's largest hydraulic lift and a source of great civic pride, with a dedicated visitors center. You can rent a canoe in town and paddle to the lock across Little Lake and along the canal.

Petroglyphs Provincial Park PARK
(705-877-2552; www.ontarioparks.com/park/petroglyphs; 2249 Northey's Bay Rd, Woodview; admission $11.50; 10am-5pm mid-May–mid-Oct) This day use–only park, 50km northeast of Peterborough, has Canada's largest collection of petroglyphs (ancient aboriginal rock carvings), depicting turtles, snakes, birds, humans and more. Rediscovered in 1954, this important spiritual site is home to over 900 icons (although only a small percentage are discernible) carved into limestone ridges overlooking bright blue-green McGinnis Lake. There are 5km to 7km hiking trails, and visitors will be pleased to find that the site isn't overrun with other tourists.

Sleeping & Eating

Lake Edge Cottages RESORT $$$
(705-652-9080; www.lakeedge.com; 45 Lake Edge Rd, Lakefield; cottages from $235;) This outdoorsy resort offers one- and two-bedroom rustic, but well-appointed lakefront cottages with deck and kitchen, on a secluded woody property. There's a wonderful swimming pool, while the cottages have barbecues and electric or gas fireplaces and most have a private hot tub.

Peterborough Farmers Market MARKET $
(Peterborough Memorial Centre, 151 Lansdowne St W, Peterborough; pizzas $12; 10am-2pm Wed) This community market is a great place to grab a coffee and stop at the C'est Chaud wood-fired pizza stand. It's mostly geared toward tasting and buying local produce, but stands sell bites such as vegan salads, Russian dishes and French toast. In summer, there's also a Wednesday outdoor market on Charlotte St between George and Aylmer Sts N.

Kawartha Dairy ICE CREAM $
(705-745-6437; www.kawarthadairy.com; Park Lane Plaza, 815 High St, Peterborough; small cone $4.20; 9am-9pm) This ice-cream parlor and drive-through sells flavors including the recommended Moose Tracks in cones, waffle cones, cups, milkshakes, smoothies and even choc-chip cookie sandwiches. The air-conditioned interior is welcome on a steamy summer day.

Information

Peterborough & The Kawarthas Visitors Centre (800-461-6424, 705-742-2201; www.thekawarthas.ca; 1400 Crawford Dr, Peterborough; 9am-5pm) This center should be your first stop: helpful staff will point you toward cultural attractions and scenic nature preserves.

Getting There & Away

Greyhound (p191) buses run to/from Toronto ($23, two hours, five daily).

Land O' Lakes

South of the Haliburton Highlands and east of the Kawarthas, the majestic **Land O' Lakes region** (www.travellandolakes.com) links the vast inland expanse of yawning lakes and bulky evergreens to the temperate pastures of the St Lawrence Seaway. Half of the region belongs to the Unesco-designated Frontenac Arch Biosphere (p206).

The region's crown jewel is the serene **Bon Echo Provincial Park** (613-336-2228; www.ontarioparks.com/park/bonecho; 16151 Hwy 41, Cloyne; day use per car $11.50, campsites with/without hookup $52/45, backcountry camping adult/child $10.50/5.50, yurt from $98, cabin from $142; mid-May–mid-Oct), which lures artists and adventurers alike with its untainted beauty and Mazinaw Rock, a sheer cliff covered in aboriginal pictographs. Closer to the St Lawrence, **Frontenac Provincial Park** (613-376-3489; www.ontarioparks.com/park/frontenac; Salmon Lake Rd, Sydenham; day use per car $11.50, backcountry camping adult/child $12.50/6) straddles the lowlands of southern Ontario and the rugged Canadian Shield, giving it a unique menagerie of wild plants and animals. Both parks offer hiking and canoeing adventures.

Tours

Frontenac Outfitters KAYAKING
(☎ 613-376-6220; www.frontenac-outfitters.com; 6674 Bedford Rd, Sydenham; kayak rental per day $50; ⊙ 9am-5pm Apr-Oct) Canoe, kayak and stand-up paddle board rentals near the entrance to Frontenac Provincial Park. It also offers Rideau Canal and Thousand Islands paddling tours.

Prince Edward County

Photographers will delight in Prince Edward County's sweeping expanses, dappled branches, undulating pastoral hills, rugged bluffs and windswept shorelines. Golden fields yield bountiful harvests in this region rich in farm-to-table cuisine, peppered with providers of the finest foods, inviting accommodations and up-and-coming wineries.

Small but active **Picton** is the unofficial capital of the affluent isthmus, a favorite getaway for Torontonians. Along the shores of Lake Ontario, Sandbanks Provincial Park's sandy beaches summon old-school holidaymakers to revel in the long hot days, summer storms and balmy nights around the campfire. In winter, it's a different story entirely.

The **Loyalist Parkway** (Hwy 33) unfurls 100km from Trenton, along Lake Ontario, to Kingston, retracing the steps of the British Loyalists who settled here after fleeing the American Revolution. There's a brief interruption to the road at Glenora, beneath the mystical Lake on the Mountain, where a car ferry whisks you across to Adolphustown.

Sights & Activities

Sandbanks Provincial Park PROVINCIAL PARK
(☎ 613-393-3319; www.ontarioparks.com/park/sandbanks; 3004 County Rd 12; day use per car $17; ⊙ 8am-8pm late Apr-early Oct) Offering some of the best sandy swimming beaches in Ontario, popular Sandbanks Provincial Park is divided into two sections: the **Outlet**, an irresistible strip of white sandy beach – one of Ontario's cleanest; and **Sandbanks**, with its impressive undulating dunes forming the world's largest bay-mouth barrier dune formation. A short trail leads through the dunes, which are unlike anywhere else in Ontario.

Lake on the Mountain Provincial Park PROVINCIAL PARK
(☎ 613-393-3319; www.ontarioparks.com/park/lakeonthemountain; 296 County Rd 7; ⊙ mid-May–mid-Oct) FREE Lake on the Mountain, near Glenora, is something of a mystery: 60m *above* adjacent Lake Ontario, it has a constant flow of clean, fresh water. Scientists are yet to confirm its source. The Mohawks offered gifts to its spirits and settlers thought it was bottomless. There's a delightful picnic ground with wonderful views of the Bay of Quinte on Lake Ontario.

BRIGHTON & PRESQU'ILE PROVINCIAL PARK

Just west of the county proper, pop off Hwy 401 at exit 509 to find quiet Brighton and **Presqu'ile Provincial Park** (☎ 613-475-4324; www.ontarioparks.com/park/presquile; 328 Presqu'ile Pkwy, Brighton; day use per car $14.50, campsites with/without hookup from $47/41.50; ⊙ day visits 7am-10pm), covering a curious boomerang-shaped peninsula in Lake Ontario. Relax on the beach, spot migrating birds in spring, or walk short trails including the Jobes Wood Trail; the 1km circular path is just rural enough to glimpse the diverse woodlands and wildlife. You can also drive 6km to the lighthouse at the peninsula's tip.

The **Friends of Presqu'ile** (www.friendsofpresquile.on.ca) provides all there is to know about local flora and fauna. Camping reservations (late April to early October) must be made through **Ontario Parks** (www.ontarioparks.com).

Bloomfield Bicycle CYCLING
(☎ 613-393-1060; www.bloomfieldbicycle.ca; 225 Bloomfield Main St, Bloomfield; half-/full-day rentals from $25/35; ⊙ 10am-6pm Apr-Oct) In little Bloomfield (en route to Sandbanks and Wellington from Picton), you can rent bicycles and gear to explore the surrounding countryside. In June, visitors can ride around picking luscious strawberries from the vine at numerous farms. Check out the website for a printable PDF cycling map of the area. Bikes can be delivered and picked up.

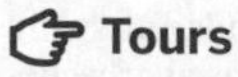

Tours

★ Taste Trail FOOD & DRINK
(www.tastetrail.ca) A great way to explore the wine and food producers of the county. Download a printable PDF of the self-guided tour, which takes in restaurants, farms, wineries and breweries, from the website. It's a gourmet adventure for the taste buds.

Arts Trail TOURS
(www.artstrail.ca) The Arts Trail is a self-guided tour leading to a few dozen studios and galleries across the county. Ceramics, glassworks, photography, jewelry and painting are some of the mediums you'll encounter. You can download a PDF map from the website.

Waupoos Estates Winery WINE
(☎613-476-8338; www.waupooswinery.com; 3016 County Rd 8; tour $5, tasting sample $1-2; ⊙10:30am-6pm May-Oct) White-gabled Waupoos winery, with its patio among the vines and scenic lake vistas, offers tours and tastings to discerning visitors. Tours run at 11am, 1pm and 3pm, lasting 30 to 45 minutes and including two wine samples. If the wine tickles your taste buds, why not stop for lunch? There's also a petting zoo for wine-indifferent kids.

Sleeping

Prince Edward County has a plethora of upscale B&Bs, boutique hotels and inns scattered among its three largest towns: Picton, Bloomfield and Wellington. Room rates are typically between $125 and $200 a night. Budget accommodations are in short supply, with more options to the north along Hwy 2 and Hwy 401, around more functional Belleville and Trenton.

Book ahead in summer. Picton's Chamber of Tourism & Commerce (p196) office has an accommodations list.

Sandbanks Provincial Park CAMPGROUND $
(☎613-393-3319; www.ontarioparks.com/park/sandbanks; 3004 County Rd 12; campsite without hookup from $45, cottage per night/week from $312/1400) Summer camping at Sandbanks is scenic and stress-free, but these lakeside sites get booked up to five months ahead. There are also two cottages, both requiring a minimum one-week stay in summer. They have two or four bedrooms, a working fireplace, satellite TV and a full kitchen. Bookings must be made through Ontario Parks.

Lake on the Mountain Resort INN $$
(☎613-476-1321; www.lakeonthemountain.com; 246 County Rd 7; cottages from $100, r from $130, ste from $250; ⊙late Apr-Oct; 📶) Comprising eight homey self-catering cottages and the 'House across the Road,' a beautiful Victorian with tastefully restored rooms and stunning views, this quaint country resort is the kind of secret you'll want to keep but just can't help sharing. Check the website for a taste of what's on offer, including what's cooking at the equally noteworthy restaurants and brewery.

Claramount Inn & Spa INN $$
(☎613-476-2709; www.claramountinn.com; 97 Bridge St, Picton; r $199-249; ❄📶🏊) 🌿 It's easy to be impressed by this opulent yellow mansion, now a luxurious spa retreat and fine dining restaurant. The individually themed rooms and suites are of generally grand proportions and include such features as Georgian period furniture, canopy beds, exotic fabrics, fireplaces and decadent bathrooms with separate soaker tubs and showers.

Red Barns B&B $$
(☎613-476-6808; www.theredbarns.com; 167 White Chapel Rd, Picton; r incl breakfast $125-140, ste $165; 📶) It's difficult to classify the Red Barns: part B&B, part artist's getaway, part craft center and school, this 6-hectare retreat is a creative hub of the county. Artists rent studio space (there's a glassblowing studio and a woodshop) or participate in pottery, glassblowing and wood-carving workshops, while guests can wander the gardens enjoying the outdoor art and general creativity.

Three B&B rooms are in the farmhouse, and there are two loft and coach-house suites.

Newsroom Suites GUESTHOUSE $$
(☎613-399-5182; www.newsroomsuites.ca; 269 Main St, Wellington; r $105-135; ❄📶) Upstairs from the working offices of the *Wellington Times* you'll find these two delightful and spacious private suites, furnished to a high standard of comfort and privacy.

Drake Devonshire Inn BOUTIQUE HOTEL $$$
(☎613-399-3338; www.drakedevonshire.ca; 24 Wharf St, Wellington; d from $250; ❄📶) From the folks behind Toronto's legendary Drake Hotel comes the Drake Devonshire, a historic foundry-turned-inn converted to a swooningly stylish and contemporary boutique hotel, hovering on Lake Ontario. Reopened in 2015 after a three-year renovation, the inn, its restaurant and cultural programming have quickly taken the county by storm.

Eating

Fifth Town Artisan Cheese Co CHEESE $
(☎416-984-4734; www.fifthtown ca; 4309 County Rd 8, Picton; cheese $7-18; ⊙11am-5pm Thu-Mon) 🌿 If you're assembling a picnic, pop into this funky, solar-powered dairy to pick up its handmade, Italian-inspired goat, cow and sheep cheeses. It also offers cheese and charcuterie boards to enjoy in the on-site pavilion, and for larger groups, tutored cheese and PEC wine tastings.

Miller House BRASSERIE $$
(613-476-1321; www.lakeonthemountain.com; 246 County Rd 7; platters $18; 11am-dusk) At Lake on the Mountain Resort (p195), you can't beat the sunset views from the patio of this restaurant occupying a converted late-18th-century miller's cottage. Charcuterie and cheese platters show off the best of the county's produce. No reservations.

County Canteen FUSION $$
(613-476-6663; www.thecountycanteen.com; 279 Main St W, Picton; mains $18; 11am-10pm;) This easygoing saloon offers a long list of craft beers and a global roster of eats, from bruschetta and quesadilla to Thai curry and Moroccan pita.

The Inn INTERNATIONAL $$
(613-476-1321; www.lakeonthemountain.com; 246 County Rd 7; mains $25; 11am-late) At Lake on the Mountain Resort (p195), this charming restaurant serves hearty meat and seafood dishes such as *tourtière* (a French Canadian beef and pork pie). Meals are prepared using only the finest local ingredients, and you can accompany them with a tasting of beers from the on-site brewery. A planned tap room will throw more focus on the brewery.

East & Main BISTRO $$
(613-399-5420; www.eastandmain.ca; 270 Main St, Wellington; lunch/dinner mains $12/25; noon-2:30pm & 5:30-9pm Wed-Sun) The meals at this fine bistro taste as good as they look: farm-fresh meats, vegetables and lake-fresh seafood form the basis of this treasure of epicurean delight, which pairs local wines beautifully with the chef's creations. Dinner features dishes such as *steak-frites*, while lunch is a more casual affair of quiches, sandwiches, stews and burgers.

County Cider Company CAFE $$
(613-476-1022; www.countycider.com; 657 Bongards Crossroad, Waupoos; mains $17; 11am-4pm May-Oct) Served on a hilltop patio surrounded by a vineyard and overlooking the lake, lunch here consists of pizzas, burgers, salads and wraps made from local ingredients, accompanied, of course, by a range of sparkling ciders. Stop in the tasting room to sample the products of their nearby orchards.

Blūmen Garden Bistro FUSION $$$
(613-476-6841; www.blumengardenbistro.com; 647 Hwy 49, Picton; mains $24-33; 5-10pm Wed-Mon) Enjoying Picton's best reputation since 2008, Blūmen is the work of Andreas Feller, a Swiss chef inspired by South American cuisine. With a relaxed, comfortable ambience, the bistro, true to its name, features a lovely garden where stepping stones lead to private, candlelit tables surrounded by fragrant flowers. The meat-dominated menu includes the signature braised rabbit and pan-seared pickerel. Reservations are recommended.

Drinking & Nightlife

Acoustic Grill BAR
(613-476-2887; www.theacousticgrill.ca; 172 Main St, Picton; mains $12-16; 11:30am-late) Acoustic folk, roots and blues acts can all be heard at this thigh-slappin' good-time bar and grill. The delicious bar menu is refreshingly down to earth for this foodie county, but still made fresh from local ingredients, and the music is live. Performances kick off at 7pm every Friday and Saturday, and on summer Wednesdays, Thursdays and Sundays.

Bean Counter Cafe CAFE
(613-476-1718; www.beancountercafe.com; 172 Main St, Picton; coffee/sandwiches $4/8; 7:30am-5pm;) Picton's favorite spot for a coffee, which is available in myriad forms, along with pastries, sandwiches, salads, bagels and smoothies. Local art and photography adorn the walls, and the seating out front allows you to watch Picton cruise past.

Entertainment

Regent Theatre THEATER
(613-476-8416; www.theregenttheatre.org; 224 Main St, Picton) Built in 1830 and continually upgraded (including a Hollywood-style update in 1931), the funky Regent Theatre hosts a diverse series of plays, concerts and readings. A new projector has expanded its repertoire to include movies from art house to mainstream.

Information

Check out Prince Edward County's inspirational tourism website at prince-edward-county.com.

Chamber of Tourism & Commerce (800-640-4717, 613-476-2421; www.pecchamber.com; 116 Main St, Picton; 9am-4:30pm Mon-Fri, from 10am Sat) Opposite the Bank of Montreal in Picton, this helpful office offers brochures, cycling maps, and lists of bike-rental outfits and short-term accommodations availability.

Getting There & Away

As the county's sights are spread out, you need your own wheels to appreciate the area. If you are heading along Hwy 33 to/from Kingston, a five-minute **car ferry** (6am-1:15am) crossing connects Glenora with Adolphustown.

Without a car, you can catch direct **VIA Rail** (p67) trains from Toronto, Kingston, Brockville and Ottawa to Belleville. From Belleville, take a **Deseronto Transit** (613-396-4008; deseronto.ca/departments/deseronto-transit) bus to Picton ($11, 45 minutes) via Bloomfield, with regular departures on weekdays only.

Kingston

POP 115,000

Modern-day Canada's first capital, albeit only for three years, Kingston was stripped of the title when Queen Victoria worried that it was too close to the American border and could not be properly defended. Today, the pretty city finds itself strategically placed as the perfect pit stop between Montréal or Ottawa and Toronto.

Often called the 'Limestone City,' Kingston is stocked with clunky halls of hand-cut stone and prim Victorian mansions. A noticeable lack of modern architecture helps to maintain the historical charm. Added to the slew of interesting museums and historical sites are the pretty waterfront location and vibrant, colorful gardens.

Founded in 1841, the same year as Kingston was proclaimed capital, Queen's University adds a dash of hot-blooded youthfulness to the mix. An assortment of great dining options, some with student-friendly prices, and a crankin' nightlife round out the package.

Sights

Conveniently, most sites are found around the central, historical downtown. If you plan to spend a day or more exploring Kingston, consider buying the **K-Pass** one- to three-day discount card (www.kpass.ca; from $78), which includes numerous sights and tours including Kingston 1000 Islands Cruises (p199) and Kingston Trolley Tours (p199).

Kingston Public Market MARKET

(Map p198; www.kingstonpublicmarket.ca; Springer Market Sq; 9am-6pm Tue, Thu & Sat Apr-Nov, Sun Apr-Oct) Canada's oldest continuous market takes place in the square behind City Hall. Stalls sell food, fresh produce, handicrafts, art and, on Sundays between April and October, antiques.

Fort Henry National Historic Site HISTORIC SITE

(613-542-7388; www.forthenry.com; Fort Henry Dr; adult/child under 6yr $18/free; 9:30am-5pm late May-early Sep, to 10pm Wed Jul & Aug) This restored British fortification, dating from 1832, overlooks Kingston from its hilltop perch. The postcard-perfect structure is brought to life by colorfully uniformed guards trained in military drills, artillery exercises and the fife-and-drum music of the 1860s. The soldiers put on displays throughout the day; don't miss the Garrison Parade (2:30pm late May to early September). Admission includes an optional guided tour of the fort's campus.

Check the website for details of the many special events throughout the year, including the ghostly Fort Fright in fall and Fort Frost in winter.

Bellevue House MUSEUM

(613-545-8666; www.parkscanada.gc.ca; 35 Centre St; adult/child 6-16yr $4/2; 10am-5pm Jul-Aug, Thu-Mon late May, Jun, Sep & early Oct) In the mid-19th century, this national historic site was briefly home to Sir John A Macdonald, Canada's first prime minister and a notorious alcoholic. Perhaps the architect also enjoyed a drop, as the Italianate mansion is wholly asymmetrical, a pompous use of bright color abounds and balconies twist off in various directions. There are also plenty of antiques and a sun-drenched garden, with staff in period costumes adding further kooky charm and intrigue. Children under six free.

Penitentiary Museum MUSEUM

(613-530-3122; www.penitentiarymuseum.ca; 555 King St W; admission by donation; 9am-4pm Mon-Fri, from 10am Sat & Sun May-Oct, to 7pm Tue-Sun late Jun-early Sep) The 'correctional service' is what Canadian bureaucrats call the nation's jail system, and this museum is a good way to enter that system without stealing a car. The museum, housed in the former warden's residence opposite the actual penitentiary, has a fascinating collection of weapons and tools confiscated from inmates during attempted escapes.

Visit www.kingstonpentour.com to organize a guided tour of the penitentiary itself, which closed in 2013.

City Hall NOTABLE BUILDING

(Map p198; 613-546-4291; www.cityofkingston.ca/city-hall; 216 Ontario St; 8:30am-4:30pm Mon-Fri, tours 10am-4pm Mon-Fri mid-May–mid-Oct, Sat & Sun late May-late Aug) FREE The grandiose City Hall is one of the country's finest classical

Kingston

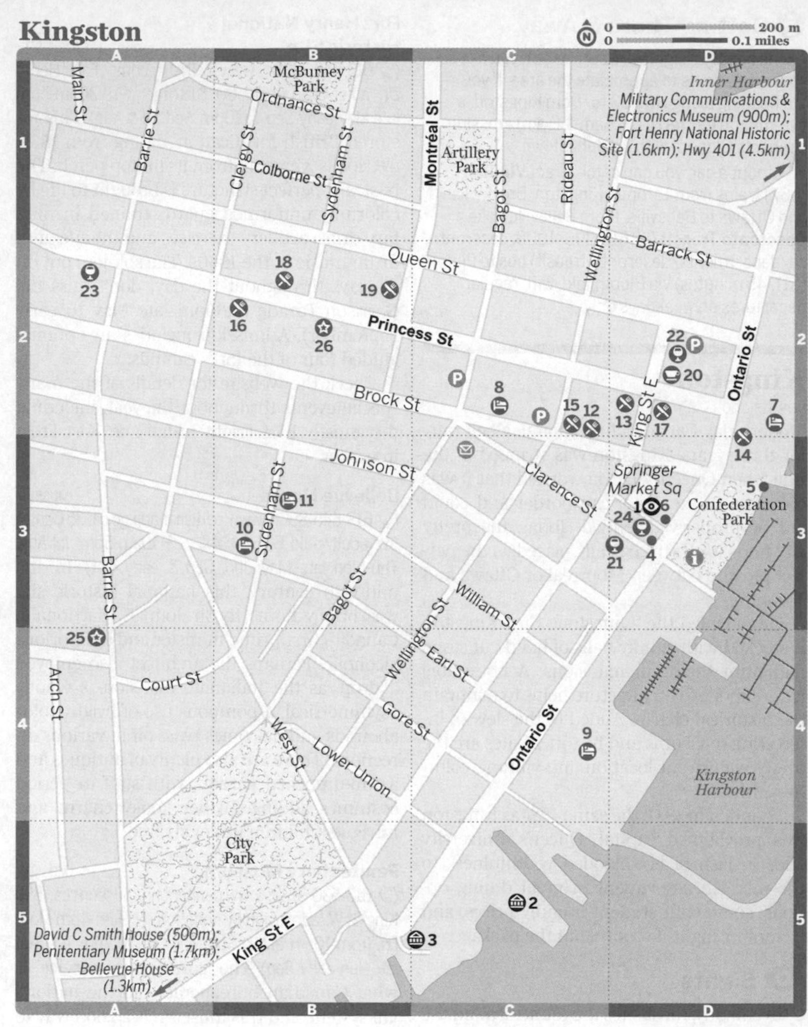

buildings and a relic from the time when Kingston was capital. Friendly volunteers conduct free tours during summer, revealing colorful stained glass, dozens of portraits, dusty jail cells and an ornate council chamber. You can also download a self-guided tour brochure from the website.

Pump House Steam Museum MUSEUM

(Map p198; ☎613-544-7867; www.steammuseum.ca; 23 Ontario St; adult/child $5/2; ⏰10am-5pm Tue-Sat, from noon Sun late May-early Sep, noon-4pm Thu, Fri & Sat Apr, May & Sep-late Nov; 👪) The one-of-a-kind, completely restored, steam-run pump house was used from 1849 to 1952. Today, the warehouse features all things steam-related, including two full-model train sets as well as the recently restored steamboat *Phoebe*. Also here are two late-19th-century steam-powered pumps, which supplied the city with water from Lake Ontario.

Marine Museum of the Great Lakes MUSEUM

(Map p198; ☎613-542-2261; www.marmuseum.ca; 55 Ontario St; adult/child $6.50/5; ⏰10am-5pm) Kingston was an important shipbuilding center from 1910 to 1960. This museum sits on

Kingston

Sights

1 City Hall D3
Kingston Public Market .... (see 1)
2 Marine Museum of the Great Lakes C5
3 Pump House Steam Museum C5

Activities, Courses & Tours

4 Haunted Walk D3
5 Kingston 1000 Islands Cruises D3
6 Kingston Trolley Tours D3

Sleeping

7 Holiday Inn Kingston Waterfront D2
8 Queen's Inn C2
9 Residence Inn by Marriott Kingston Water's Edge C4
10 Rosemount Inn B3
11 Secret Garden B3

Eating

12 Atomica C2
13 Chez Piggy D2
14 Curry Original D3
15 Le Chien Noir C2
16 Mlt Dwn B2
17 Pan Chancho D2
18 Stone City Ales B2
19 Wok Inn B2

Drinking & Nightlife

20 Coffee & Company D2
21 Kingston Brewing Company D3
22 Red House D2
23 Stages A2
24 Tir nan Og D3

Entertainment

25 Grad Club A4
26 Grand Theatre B2

the site of the old shipyard, offering a detailed history of the fascinating vessels constructed here and explaining shipping on the St Lawrence and Great Lakes today. Sadly, the museum was vacating its historic premises and looking for a new home in 2016. Check with Kingston Tourism (p202) for updates.

Military Communications & Electronics Museum MUSEUM
(☎613-541-4675; www.c-and-e-museum.org; 95 Craftsman Blvd; admission by donation; ⊙11am-5pm) Despite its dry name, this is a comprehensive and well-designed museum on Kingston's military base, offering chronological displays on communications technology and sundry military gadgets. Many of the voluntary guides are military veterans.

Tours

Haunted Walk TOURS
(Map p198; ☎613-549-6366; www.hauntedwalk.com; adult/child under 10yr $16/free) Tours featuring stories of hangings and grave robbers leave from the ticket office in the lobby of the Prince George Hotel (200 Ontario St). Check the website for details, but the 1½-hour tour starts at 8pm most evenings. A ghoulish nocturnal walk around Fort Henry and tamer time-travel adventure are also offered.

Kingston 1000 Islands Cruises BOATING
(Map p198; ☎613-549-5544; www.ktic.ca; Confederation Park; cruises from $29; ⊙May-early Oct) A variety of scenic cruises depart from the dock (and ticket office) at the northeastern corner of Confederation Park. A 1½-hour Kingston Harbour cruise and three-hour Thousand Islands cruise are offered, as well as lunch and dinner jaunts. Check the website for the latest rates and sailing times. It also operates the hop-on, hop-off Kingston Trolley Tours around the city.

Kingston Trolley Tours TOURS
(Map p198; ☎613-549-5544; www.kingstontrolley.ca; adult/child 4-12yr $26/12; ⊙late May-early Oct) A trackless mini-train departs every 30 to 45 minutes from outside City Hall, opposite the tourist office (p202), for 1¼-hour tours with cheery historical commentary. Hop on or off at nine stops including Bellevue House (p197). Ghost-themed evening tours also run. Kids three and under free.

Festivals & Events

From mid-June to early September, live music is staged in Confederation Park most lunchtimes, at 7pm on Thursdays and Fridays, and at 4pm on Saturdays. Movies, also free, show in Springer Market Sq on Thursdays at dusk. Visit www.downtownkingston.ca for more details, and check out tourism.kingstoncanada.com for a complete list of events throughout the year.

Limestone City Blues Festival MUSIC
(www.kingstonblues.com) All-star musicians gather for a four-day jam session in August.

Kingston Buskers Rendezvous MUSIC
(www.kingstonbuskers.com) Four days of tomfoolery in July.

Sleeping

Accommodations in Kingston are top-end heavy, with a larger confluence of pricier stays than budget options. Motels are strung along Hwy 2 (aka Princess St) on either side of town. The knowledgeable staff at the tourism office (p202) by Confederation Park can help you track down additional options. A few historic B&Bs are found on leafy Sydenham St; check out www.historicinnskingston.com for more.

David C Smith House HOSTEL $

(613-533-2223; queensu.ca/summeraccommodations; 222 Stuart St; s with/without bathroom $99/50, d $116; May-Aug; P ❄ @ ☎) Open to non-students when school's out for summer, these Queen's University digs offer affordable campus lodging about 20 minutes' walk from downtown. The spartan bedrooms and common rooms provide no-frills comfort and memories of halcyon student days. There is a basic cafe in reception and a branch of Tim Hortons coffee chain nearby. Two-bedroom, one-bathroom units are also available.

★ **Rosemount Inn** B&B $$

(Map p198; 888-871-8844, 613-531-8844; www.rosemountinn.com; 46 Sydenham St; r $175-229, ste $299; P ❄ ☎) Enjoy a decadent stay at this former dry-goods merchant's home in a historic district. Built in 1850, the massive stone Tuscan-style villa has been magnificently preserved in its 19th-century finery from the arched entrance to the ceiling roses. A small spa offers wine-based facials and chocolate body wraps, and rates include full breakfast and afternoon tea.

Secret Garden B&B $$

(Map p198; 877-723-1888, 613-531-9884; www.thesecretgardeninn.com; 73 Sydenham St; s $165-199, d $175-209; P ❄ @ ☎) Whether you recline in the stately salons with chandeliers overhead, or retreat upstairs to your canopied bed, you will have a comfortable stay at this Queen Anne–style Victorian home. Rates include breakfast; pay $10 less to 'hook the cook' and skip breakfast.

Queen's Inn BOUTIQUE HOTEL $$

(Map p198; 866-689-9177; www.queensinn.ca; 125 Brock St; r incl breakfast $120-160; ❄ ☎) Constructed in 1839, the Queen's Inn is one of the oldest hotels in the country. The outside has a stately limestone facade and some rooms have stone walls, skylights and leafy views. A downstairs pub and the downtown location make this a worthy option.

Holiday Inn Kingston Waterfront HOTEL $$

(Map p198; 613-549-8400; www.hikingstonwaterfront.com; 2 Princess St; d $169-290; P ❄ ☎ ≋ 🐾) You can't beat the location of this waterfront hotel. Its 197 spacious rooms have balcony, fridge, and microwave on request. Facilities include indoor and outdoor pools, and a harborside patio restaurant – Kingston's only eatery right on the water. Packages including breakfast and parking, which is $16 extra, are available.

Fireside Inn MOTEL $$

(613-549-2211; www.bestwesternkingston.ca; 1217 Princess St; r incl breakfast from $179; P ❄ ☎ ≋) The best things about this uptown motel are the gaudy but fun fantasy suites, evoking dream worlds from a Japanese love hotel to a moon base. Standard rooms have country decor with handmade pine furniture and a fireplace. There's an outdoor pool and two restaurants.

Residence Inn by Marriott Kingston Water's Edge HOTEL $$$

(Map p198; 613-544-4888; www.marriottresidenceinnkingston.com; 7 Earl St; r incl breakfast from $229; P ❄ ☎ ≋) Geared toward longer stays, this hulking new hotel offers 141 studios and apartments with king-size beds, kitchenettes and lounges with fold-out couch. It's in a prime spot on the water, near the university and a few minutes' walk from downtown. Facilities include an indoor saltwater pool and sauna.

Eating

★ **Stone City Ales** PUB FOOD $

(Map p198; 613-542-4222; www.stonecityales.com; 275 Princess St; mains $13; 11am-11pm) Beneath this hip brewery and restaurant's exposed pipes, staff bustle around changing the record on the turntable, serving charcuterie boards and guiding tasters through their flight (three 6oz beers $8). Choose between mainstays and special-release beers, accompanied by a menu of ribs, wings, chips, dips, cheese platters and more.

Mlt Dwn FAST FOOD $

(Map p198; 613-766-1881; www.mltdwn.com; 292 Princess St; sandwiches from $6; 11am-10pm Mon-Thu, to 3am Fri & Sat, to 9pm Sun) These *fromage*-loving fast-food-meisters have already expanded from this original branch to the Canadian capital and Québec. You won't be able to resist the calorific goodness oozing from just about every conceivable twist on the humble grilled cheese sandwich... especially if you're stumbling back from the pub. The menu also features less cheesy sandwiches and snacks from pulled pork to poutine.

Wok Inn ASIAN $
(Map p198; ☎613-549-5369; 30 Montréal St; dishes from $6.95; ⊙11:30am-2:30pm & 4:30-9pm Tue-Sat) Cambodian, Vietnamese and Thai dishes feature in this plain-Jane downtown eatery favored for takeout by starving university students.

★Pan Chancho FUSION $$
(Map p198; ☎613-544-7790; www.panchancho.com; 44 Princess St; mains $15; ⊙7am-4pm) This phenomenal bakery and cafe fuses unlikely ingredients into palate-pleasing dishes such as Vietnamese spring rolls and sesame tuna meatballs. The Moroccan-style, cumin-spiced lamb pita wrap with chickpeas is recommended. The all-day breakfast menu features dishes such as curried eggs. Kingstonians crowd the rear courtyard on summer days.

Atomica ITALIAN $$
(Map p198; ☎613-530-2118; www.atomica.ca; 71 Brock St; mains $18; ⊙11:30am-10pm;) This bustling downtown pizzeria and wine bar does all the classic pizzas with panache, as well as pastas, salads, daily specials, weekend brunches and a good dessert selection. Gluten-free options are offered, as is a cocktail happy hour from 2:30pm to 4:30pm.

Curry Original INDIAN $$
(Map p198; ☎613-531-9376; www.curryoriginal.ca; 253a Ontario St; mains $15; ⊙11:30am-2pm Tue-Sat & 5-9pm Tue-Sun) This smart outfit serves Kingston's finest Indian cuisine, including all the classic curries from butter chicken to vindaloo, korma to madras.

Le Chien Noir BISTRO $$$
(Map p198; ☎613-549-5635; www.lechiennoir.com; 69 Brock St; lunch/dinner mains $18/27; ⊙11:30am-9pm) It's a tad pricey but locals love this little taste of Paris with a hint of Québec in the Anglophone heart of Kingston: consider the gourmet poutine. Mains include lamb, duck, and the obligatory Prince Edward Island *moules* (mussels) or steak frites.

Brunch is served until 2:30pm at weekends, with live jazz on the terrace from midday on Sunday and happy hour from 2:30pm to 4:30pm daily.

Chez Piggy FUSION $$$
(Map p198; ☎613-549-7673; www.chezpiggy.com; 68r Princess St; dinner/lunch mains $35/15; ⊙11:30am-11pm Mon-Sat, from 10am Sun) Hidden in a flowery stone courtyard, the city's best-known restaurant has earned its reputation with an innovative menu and charming ambience. Dinner mains include marinated ostrich and confit of Muscovy duck leg, while the lunch menu is more casual. Reservations are recommended on weekends, when Sunday brunch is popular.

Drinking & Nightlife

Red House PUB
(Map p198; ☎613-767-2558; www.redhousekingston.com; 369 King St E; ⊙11:30am-2am) The ranch-raunchy pub has a killer selection of beers on tap and a fantastic bar menu ranging from comfort food (poutine, house burger) to smart dining (grilled trout, steak frites) – all in a casual pub setting. We love that there are roasted herbed potatoes cooked in duck fat as a side dish.

Kingston Brewing Company BREWERY
(Map p198; ☎613-542-4978; www.kingstonbrewing.ca; 34 Clarence St; mains $15; ⊙11am-2am) Chow down on burgers and sandwiches amid flickering Christmas lights and kitschy beer-themed paraphernalia, or grab a patio table outside. In summer they make beer using a recipe dating back to 1841, when Kingston was capital of the Province of Canada. Try the Dragon's Breath Pale Ale and White Tail Cream Ale, both so popular they're brewed and bottled off-site.

Tir nan Og PUB
(Map p198; ☎613-544-7474; www.facebook.com/kingston.tirnanog; 200 Ontario St; ⊙11am-late;) Set inside one of the oldest and most charming buildings along the waterfront, this Irish oasis serves up live music and overflowing pints, as well as a menu of pub grub, in its wood-lined interior. Beers come in 14oz or 18oz servings.

Coffee & Company COFFEE
(Map p198; ☎613-547-9211; www.facebook.com/coffeeandcompanykingston; 53 Princess St; ⊙7am-8pm;) Get your daily dose of barista-brewed coffee here with your daily shot of free wi-fi. Why not have a Godiva chocolate or White Mountain ice cream with that?

Stages CLUB
(Map p198; ☎613-547-5553; www.stages.ca; 393 Princess St; ⊙10pm-3am Mon & Thu-Sat) This is where young Kingston folk get their groove on and dance till they drop. The club hosts big nights for events such as Canada Day.

☆ Entertainment

Grad Club LIVE MUSIC
(Map p198; ☎613-546-3427; queensgradclub.wordpress.com; 162 Barrie St; ⏰11am-8pm Mon & Tue, to 1am Wed-Fri) Housed in an imposing Victorian mansion, this Queen's campus mainstay is one of the hottest venues for live music. It also hosts special events such as tastings of local craft beers.

Grand Theatre THEATER
(Map p198; ☎613-530-2050; www.kingstongrand.ca; 218 Princess St) Once an opera house, then a movie theater, the Grand is now the city's premier venue for theater, concerts and comedy. It has undergone extensive renovations since 1967, including a massive overhaul in 2008. The **Kingston Symphony orchestra** (www.kingstonsymphony.on.ca) regularly performs here.

ℹ Information

Post Office (Map p198; ☎866-607-6301; www.canadapost.ca; 120 Clarence St; ⏰8am-5:30pm Mon-Fri) Centrally located post office.

Kingston Tourism (Map p198; ☎888-855-4555, toll-free 613-548-4415; tourism.kingstoncanada.com; 209 Ontario St; ⏰10am-4pm) This useful information center has intelligent, friendly staff, well versed in the city's history. Across from City Hall, it has longer opening hours in summer.

ℹ Getting There & Away

The **Kingston Bus Terminal** (☎613-547-4916; 1175 John Counter Blvd) is 1km south of Hwy 401, just west of Division St. **Megabus** (p66) offers several daily services to Toronto (from $33, three hours) and Montréal ($26, 3¼ hours). **Greyhound** (p191) offers a daily bus to Ottawa ($35, 2¾ hours).

If you're arriving by car on Hwy 401, exits 611 to 623 will lead you downtown. Car rental chains in town include **Enterprise** (☎613-547-0755; www.enterprise.ca; 2244 Princess St).

Kingston train station (☎888-842-7245; www.viarail.ca; 1800 John Counter Blvd) is about 300m east of where Princess St and John Counter Blvd meet. Several daily trains run to Montréal ($87, 2¾ hours), Ottawa ($71, 2¼ hours) and Toronto ($90, 2½ hours).

For local bus schedules and fares, click to **Kingston Transit** (☎613-546-0000; www.cityofkingston.ca/residents/transit). A single journey costs $2.75 and you can pay on the bus. The **tourism office** (p202) sells day passes ($7.25).

Bus 16 connects the bus terminal and train station via the city center, generally departing both transport terminals at quarter past and quarter to the hour. Frequency is decreased to hourly on Sundays.

Cyclists will be happy to note that the Kingston area is generally flat, and both Hwys 2 and 5 have paved shoulders. Bikes are available at **Ahoy Rentals** (☎613-549-4277; www.ahoyrentals.com; 23 Ontario St; bike rental per hr/day $5/25).

Thousand Islands

The 'Thousand Islands' are a constellation of over 1800 rugged islands dotting the St Lawrence River from Kingston to Brockville. The lush archipelago offers loose tufts of fog, showers of trillium petals, quaking tide pools and opulent 19th-century summer mansions, whose turrets pierce the prevailing mist.

The narrow, slow-paced **Thousand Islands Parkway** dips south of Hwy 401 between Gananoque and Brockville, running along the river for 35km before rejoining the highway. The scenic journey winds along the pastoral strip of shoreline offering

COTTAGE COUNTRY

Much of Ontario, from the shores of Lake Erie to Muskoka, the Kawarthas, Haliburton Highlands and even the Thousand Islands, is cottage country – thousands of lakes dotted with rocky islands and forested shorelines offering dazzling sunsets: perfect for a weekend home. It won't be long after you arrive in Toronto that you're introduced to the slow pace and hospitality of someone's cottage, for that's what Ontario summers are all about – communing with friends, family and nature over cold beer, fine wine and good food.

Torontonians flock to the lakes as soon as the weather gets warm. Ramshackle fishing huts are prised open at the first available moment after the spring thaw, while sprawling waterfront mansions awake from their slumber. Flowerpots are replanted, freezers restocked and families begin their weekly pilgrimage from the city.

The common denominator of the cottage phenomenon is the sense of pride in one's place and the desire to be in the great outdoors. Canoes, kayaks, ski-boats and Sea-Doos all come out and the lazy days and wild nights begin, until winter, when the lakes freeze over, the snowmobiles appear and they do it all again.

picture-perfect vistas and dreamy picnic areas. The St Lawrence Bikeway bicycle path, part of the riverside Waterfront Trail between Niagara-on-the-Lake and Cornwall, extends the full length of the parkway.

★1000 Islands Tower VIEWPOINT
(☎613-659-2335; www.1000islandstower.com; 716 Hwy 137, Hill Island; adult/child $11/6; ⏰10am-6pm May-Sep) Just east of Ivy Lea, some 20km from Gananoque, a series of soaring bridges link Ontario to New York State, USA, over several islands. Halfway across, just before crossing the international border, this 130m-high observation tower offers fantastic views of the archipelago from two open decks, plus explanatory exhibits on a glass-enclosed deck. And yes, there's an elevator.

Thousand Islands National Park NATIONAL PARK
(☎613-923-5261; www.pc.gc.ca/pn-np/on/lawren/index.aspx; 2 County Rd 5, Mallorytown; parking $7, tent sites without hookup $16, Otentik camping $100-121; ⏰visitors center 10am-4pm Sat & Sun late May-Jun, daily Jul-Sep) On the Thousand Islands Pkwy south of Mallorytown, you'll find the Mallorytown Landing Visitors Centre for the Thousand Islands National Park, which preserves a gentle green archipelago of over 20 freckle-sized islands, scattered between Kingston and Brockville. A 2km walking trail and interpretive center allow visitors to learn more about the lush terrain and resident wildlife. Further hiking trails and canoe routes explore deeper into the park.

A dozen islands support backcountry camping (BYO boat). You can also stay in an Otentik luxurious roofed safari tent at the visitors center or on two of the islands.

Skywood Eco Adventure ADVENTURE SPORTS
(☎613-923-5120; www.parks.on.ca/attractions/skywood-eco-adventure-park; Thousand Islands Pkwy, Mallorytown; zip-line tour adult/youth 12-15yr $45/41; ⏰9am-5pm; 👪) East of Mallorytown, this fantastic new center is Canada's largest aerial adventure and zipline park, offering woodland fun from zip-lines to canopy tours and a large children's treehouse play area.

St Lawrence Bikeway CYCLING
(www.waterfronttrail.org) This bicycle path, part of the riverside Waterfront Trail between Niagara-on-the-Lake and Cornwall, extends the full length of the Thousand Islands Pkwy from Gananoque to Brockville.

Gananoque

Little Gananoque (gan-an-*awk*-way) is the perfect place to rest your eyes after a long day of squinting at the furry green islands on the misty St Lawrence. The dainty Victorian town, deep in the heart of the Thousand Islands region, teems with cruise-hungry tourists during summer and early fall. In spring and late fall, it's quiet as a mouse.

For some historical background to a stroll around this quaint town, pick up a heritage-themed self-guided walking tour map from the visitors center.

Sights & Activities

★Boldt Castle CASTLE
(☎800-847-5263, 315-482-9724; www.boldtcastle.com; Heart Island, Alexandria Bay, NY, USA; adult/child $9/6; ⏰10am-6:30pm May-late Sep, 11am-5pm late Sep–mid-Oct) This lavish turn-of-the-century island castle in the middle of the St Lawrence is only around 25km from Gananoque, but technically in the USA, so you'll need your passport to visit. It was built by George C Boldt, original proprietor of New York's famous Waldorf Astoria Hotel. Many Thousand Island cruise tours stop here, or you can drive 23km from Gananoque to Alexandria Bay, NY, USA, where 10-minute shuttles cross the 1km of water to the castle.

From the Thousand Islands Pkwy, Hwy 137/81 crosses the Thousand Islands Bridge (and the border) to Alexandria Bay. Canadian cruises depart from Gananoque for a five-hour tour (including the cruise and castle visit) and from Rockport for a 3½- or five-hour tour.

1000 Islands Kayaking KAYAKING
(☎613-329-6265; www.1000islandskayaking.com; 110 Kate St; half-day rentals/tours from $35/85) If you're feeling energetic, paddling is a great way to tour the islands. Choose from a multitude of packages including courses, half-day, full-day and sunset trips, and canoe-and-camp weekends.

Gananoque Boat Line CRUISE
(☎888-717-4837; www.ganboatline.com; 280 Main St; 1hr cruise adult/child 6-12yr from $25/13; ⏰May–mid-Oct) Several trip options, including one with a two-hour stopover at Boldt Castle, make this outfit a popular choice for cruising the Thousand Islands. The castle is technically in the USA, so be sure you have your passport (and possibly visa) if you are planning to visit. Cruises depart throughout the day and for special musical evenings.

DON'T MISS

WOLFE ISLAND

The largest island in the Thousand Islands chain, the 120-sq-km Wolfe Island divides the St Lawrence River from Lake Ontario. What was mostly undeveloped farmland is now home to hundreds of wind turbines – a little surreal. Getting to the island on the free **Wolfe Island car ferry** (613-548-7227; www.wolfeisland.com; hourly 6:15am-2am) FREE from Kingston is half the fun: the 25-minute trip affords views of the city, Fort Henry and islands.

The island is cycle-friendly, with four routes marked with colored signs. Download a map at www.wolfeisland.com. **Kingston Tourism** (p202) can give further advice on exploring the island, and you can hire a bike from **Ahoy Rentals** (p202) or on the island. On the Kingston side, the ferry terminal is at the intersection of Ontario and Barrack Sts. Check the website for the complete schedule.

In addition to the **Wolfe Island car ferry** linking the island to Kingston, **Horne's Ferry** (613-385-2402; www.hferry.com; passenger/bike/car $2/3/18; hourly 8am-7pm late Apr–mid-Oct) crosses the 11km between Alexandria Point on the island's southern side and Cape Vincent, New York, USA (10 minutes). You need your passport for this international crossing.

Sleeping

Misty Isles Lodge LODGE $$
(613-382-4232; www.mistyisles.ca; 25 River Rd, Lansdowne; r from $95, campsite with hookup $40;) Located about 5km east of Gananoque on the Thousand Islands Pkwy, you'll find this laid-back beachfront property boasting comfortable units with wicker furnishings. A variety of adventure outfitting is offered as well, including kayak rentals (half-day $35) and tours (half-day $75), and camping packages on some of the river's shrubby islands.

Gananoque Inn INN $$
(613-382-2165; www.gananoqueinn.com; 550 Stone St S; r $199-245;) Signature green shutters denote this stately inn at the junction of the Gananoque River and St Lawrence Seaway. The former carriage-works first opened its doors in 1896 and has retained much of its charm; the rooms are unremarkable but the waterside location is spectacular. Packages including accommodations and activities from spa treatments to helicopter flights are offered online.

Houseboat Holidays HOUSEBOAT $$$
(613-382-2842; www.houseboatholidays.ca; RR3, Gananoque; weekend/midweek/weekly rates from $550/750/1000) The only thing better than staying near the seaway is staying *on* the seaway! This experienced outfit just 4km west of Gananoque will set you up with your very own floating hotel and provide a brief instructional course for nautical newbies. They cover the whole Thousand Islands and Rideau Canal area, from Gananoque to Brockville and Kingston.

Eating

Socialist Pig CAFE $
(613-463-8800; www.thesocialistpiggananoque.com; 21 King St E; mains $14; 8am-8pm) With cool decor including a counter made of old books, Gananoque's favorite hangout serves tacos, burritos, Asian salads, sandwiches and weekend brunches – all featuring farm-fresh ingredients and cooked with love.

★ **Stonewater Pub** PUB FOOD $$
(613-382-2542; www.stonewaterbb.com; 490 Stone St S; mains $18; 11am-9pm Sun-Wed, to 1am Thu-Sat) Below a B&B, this homely little waterfront Irish pub and restaurant serves up hearty and delicious fare: the 'Irish tenderloin' (grilled, bacon-wrapped ground lamb and beef) and 'porky pig' (pork loin burger) are both must-tries for self-respecting carnivores. There's a bunch of creative salads, too. The vibe is straight out of *Moby Dick*, and especially delightful when there's live music.

Maple Leaf Restaurant CZECH $$
(Czech Schnitzel House; 613-382-7666; www.mapleleafrestaurant.ca; 65 King St E; mains $18; 11am-9:30pm Wed-Sun) As quintessentially Canadian as this old-school family diner can be, its name belies the European gems found inside: golden breaded schnitzel, goulash, borscht and beer. Burgers and poutine bring you back to terra Canadiana. There's a little patio out back, open in summer.

Ivy Restaurant MODERN CANADIAN $$$
(613-659-2486; www.ivyleaclub.ca; 61 Shipman's Lane, Lansdowne; mains $30; 11:30am-9pm Mon-Sat, from 10:30am Sun) In a charming waterfront

spot about 12km east of Gananoque, this beautifully refurbished restaurant belonging to the opulent Ivy Lea Club marina is open to the public. Casual patio lunches and Sunday brunches are more affordable ways to enjoy the stunning environment, but evening fine dining is available. If you fancy a half-chicken, go for the buttermilk-marinaded fried Cornwall hen.

Otherwise, just stop by for a look and a lick: there's an incredible ice-cream booth out front.

Drinking & Nightlife

Gananoque Brewing Co BREWERY

(613-463-9131; www.ganbeer.com; 9 King St E; 12oz beer/tasting flight $4.50/6.25; noon-9pm May-Oct, 1-8pm Thu-Sun Nov-Apr) Beneath the wooden beams of a converted 19th-century carriage-parts factory, try craft beers such as the Naughty Otter and Smuggler's Rush. Free brewery tours are also offered.

Entertainment

Thousand Islands Playhouse THEATER

(866-382-7020, 613-382-7020; www.1000islandsplayhouse.com; 185 South St) This delightful waterfront theater has presented a quality lineup of mainly light summer plays and musicals since 1982.

Shorelines Casino CASINO

(613-382-6800; shorelinescasinos.com/thousand-islands; 380 Hwy 2; 24hr) This small casino, often filled with senior citizens, can be a sad indictment of modern society, but the staff are friendly and for many punters, it's just good, clean fun. Minimum age 19.

Information

Visitor Services Centre (844-382-8044, 613-382-8044; www.travel1000islands.ca; 10 King St E; 9am-5pm mid-May–mid-Oct, 10am-4pm Tue-Sat mid-Oct–mid-May) The delightful staff at this immaculate visitors center are a font of information for all things Thousand Islands and beyond.

Getting There & Away

Gananoque is a short, 2km detour off Hwy 401 about 35km east of Kingston.

Gananoque Train Station (888-842-7245; www.viarail.ca; North Station Rd), 6km north of town, has direct services to/from Toronto ($94, three hours, one daily) and Ottawa ($101, 1¾ hours, one daily).

Brockville & Prescott

Attractive Brockville marks the eastern edge of the Thousand Islands region. The 'City of the Thousand Islands,' as it's known, has a cache of extravagant estates. Rows of Gothic spires twisting skyward make it easy to imagine the clip-clop of carriage horses that once rang through the streets. The riverfront parks and museums on the streets climbing sleepily inland make Brockville an appealing spot to while away a day.

Neighboring Prescott, 20km up the road, could be Brockville's younger brother: it's altogether smaller and scrappier, but offers accommodations and facilities. The 19th-century town is also just 6km from the International Bridge linking Johnstown, Ontario with Ogdensburg, New York State.

Sights

Fulford Place MUSEUM

(613-498-3003; www.heritagetrust.on.ca/Fulford-Place; 287 King St E, Brockville; adult/child $6/free; 10am-5pm late May-early Sep) This stunning 35-room Edwardian mansion was built in the early 1900s for quack-medicine millionaire George Taylor Fulford, the producer of the 'Pink Pills for Pale People.' Why not stop for a cup of tea on the verandah? Admission includes a guided tour.

Brockville Railway Tunnel HISTORIC SITE

(cnr Water St E & Block House Island Pkwy) In Armagh S Price Park, diagonally opposite the tourist office, look out for the entrance to Canada's oldest railway tunnel, dating to 1860. The tunnel is set to reopen by August 2017, allowing you to cross town following atmospheric feature lighting on the tracks.

Aquatarium MUSEUM

(613-342-6789; www.aquatarium.ca; Tall Ships Landing, 6 Broad St, Brockville; adult/child $20/10; 10am-5pm;) Opened in 2016, this all-singing all-dancing interactive center geared toward children brings to life the St Lawrence Seaway, its currents and shipwrecks.

Fort Wellington National Historic Site HISTORIC BUILDING

(613-925-2896; www.pc.gc.ca/eng/lhn-nhs/on/wellington/index.aspx; 370 Vankoughnet St, Prescott; adult/child $4/2; 10am-5pm Thu-Mon late May, Jun & early Sep-early Oct, daily Jul-early Sep) The original fort was built during the War of

FRONTENAC ARCH BIOSPHERE RESERVE

One of 18 Unesco-designated biosphere reserves in Canada, **Frontenac Arch** (☎613-659-4824; www.frontenacarchbiosphere.ca; 19 Reynolds Rd, Lansdowne; ⏲visitors center 9am-5pm May-Oct) encompasses an ancient granite land bridge from the Canadian Shield to Upstate New York's Adirondack Mountains. A towering mountain range has been weathered down to rolling hills and rugged cliffs: still dramatic after driving through flatlands. Archaeological finds in the area indicate that it was once part of a human migration route; knives from the Yellowknife region as well as shells from the Caribbean have been found in the area.

Five forests merge in the region, which is a natural conduit for flora and fauna, creating tremendous wildlife diversity. Incorporating 70% land and 30% water (in the Thousand Islands between Gananoque and Brockville), the 2700-sq-km reserve has ample recreation opportunities from biking and hiking to canoeing and diving. It's easily accessed from Hwy 401 and the Thousand Islands Pkwy between the aforementioned towns, and you'll find the visitors center just west of the turning for the 1000 Islands Tower. The excellent www.frontenacarchbiosphere.ca will guide you to further entry points.

1812 and was used again as a strategic locale in 1838, when an American invasion seemed imminent. Some original fortifications remain, as do the barracks, powder magazine and officer's quarters, all brought to life by costumed interpreters and exhibits. Renovations and improvements are ongoing.

Brockville Museum MUSEUM
(☎613-342-4397; www.brockvillemuseum.com; 5 Henry St, Brockville; admission by donation; ⏲10am-5pm Mon-Sat, 1-5pm Sun May-Oct, 10am-5pm Mon-Fri Nov-Apr) Take a look at the area's history here, where you'll find displays on Brockville's bygone car-building and hat-making industries among other community tidbits. The museum encompasses the Isaac Beecher House, built in the mid-19th century by a tanner of the same name and a good example of the homes built by loyalists fleeing the USA.

Afternoon and evening 1½-hour walking tours ($6) covering Brockville's criminal past leave from here on Fridays in July and August. Reserve with the museum.

Tours

1000 Islands Cruises BOATING
(☎800-353-3157, 613-345-7333; www.1000islandscruises.com; 30 Block House Island Pkwy, Brockville; cruises $24-50; ⏲May-Oct) Offers 1½- to two-hour sightseeing tours of the Thousand Islands on two vessels: a traditional sightseeing cruiser and the high-speed *Wildcat*. The latter features views of Boldt and Singer Castles, island châteaux just over the international border. Check the website for details, schedules and rates.

Sleeping

Brockville has plenty to satisfy, from historic B&Bs to chain motels, respectively found downtown and uptown around the junction of Hwy 401 and Stewart Blvd (Hwy 29). Prescott has some original accommodations options along the St Lawrence.

Dewar's Inn INN $
(☎613-925-3228, 877-433-9277; www.dewarsinn.com; 1649 County Rd 2, Prescott; r $84-87, cottage $91-115; 📶) These quaint riverside cottages, efficiency units and motel rooms are pleasantly furnished and spotlessly clean. The property is built on the site of an early-19th-century brewery, and scuba dives in the backyard have revealed sunken bottles of old brew. Decks along the river's edge have views of Ogdensburg, NY. Rates include breakfast. No pets or children under 12.

Green Door B&B $$
(☎613-341-9325; www.greendoorbb.com; 61 Buell St, Brockville; r incl breakfast $125; ⏲May-Oct; ❄📶) On an attractive residential street, this brick tabernacle dating to 1928 has found a new calling as a B&B. Crisp sunlight dances through the ample common space during the day.

Ship's Anchor Inn B&B $$
(☎613-925-3573; www.shipsanchorinn.com; 495 King St W, Prescott; s $79-125, d $99-145, apt $199; ❄📶) Once the beachside abode of a crusty sea captain, this 185-year-old hand-hewn stone manor is packed to the rafters with sea-shanty relics of bygone days: schools of taxidermic fish, anchors aplenty and models of wooden frigates.

Eating

Georgian Dragon Ale House PUB FOOD $
(☎613-865-8224; www.facebook.com/TheGeorgianDragonAleHouseAndPub; 72 King St W, Brockville; mains $14; ⊙11am-late Mon-Fri, from 9am Sat & Sun) This British ale house on the main drag has a good selection of beers on tap and tasty British pub favorites such as butter chicken and cottage pie.

The Mill ITALIAN $$
(☎613-345-7098; www.themillrestaurant.ca; 123 Water St W, Brockville; lunch/dinner mains $13/22; ⊙11:30am-2pm & 5-9pm Mon-Sat) There's a wonderful, romantic ambience to this quaint Italian restaurant located in a restored 1852 mill, with a stream trickling past its thick stone walls. The reasonably priced menu features tapas, pasta, seafood and veal, the latter in the recommended *vitello scallopini al marsala*.

Buell Street Bistro INTERNATIONAL $$
(☎613-345-2623; www.buellstreetbistro.com; 27 Buell St, Brockville; mains $13-32; ⊙11:30am-10pm Mon-Fri, from 5pm Sat & Sun) Three levels and a delectable patio break the space up at this local favorite. Seafood and pasta, steak frites and surf 'n turf mingle with curry dishes from further afield: there's enough variety to please the fussiest of palates, and there's a full gluten-free menu.

Entertainment

Brockville Arts Centre ARTS CENTER
(☎877-342-7122, 613-342-7122; www.brockvilleartscentre.com; 235 King St W, Brockville; ⊙box office 10am-5pm Mon-Fri, to 3pm Sat) Built in 1858 as Brockville's Town Hall, what is now the arts center has survived one fire and several incarnations. Today, the theater hosts performers from tribute bands to classical pianists, and the lobby gallery exhibits both local artists and biggish names.

Information

Brockville District Tourism (☎613-342-4357; www.brockvilletourism.com; 10 Market St W, Brockville; ⊙8am-6pm Mon-Sat, 10am-5pm Sun May-Oct, 9am-5pm Mon-Fri Nov-Apr) Open year-round and provides ample information about attractions all along the seaway.

Getting There & Away

VIA Rail trains leave Brockville's **train station** (☎888-842-7245; www.viarail.ca; 141 Perth St, Brockville), 1km north of the town center, for Toronto ($90, three hours, seven daily) and Ottawa ($35, 1¼ hours, five daily).

Megabus (☎866-488-4452; ca.megabus.com) runs daily buses to Toronto (from $22, four hours, three daily) and Montréal ($10, 2½ hours, three daily). Buses depart from the southwest corner of Stewart Blvd (Hwy 29) and Jefferson Dr, just off Hwy 401 and about 2km inland from downtown.

Merrickville

Tiny Merrickville can thank the Canadian Railroad for never laying tracks through town. Had the wee burg become a stop on the line, it would have swapped its stone structures for industrial eyesores. Instead, today's day-tripper from Ottawa can take a canal-side stroll back in time – to when the area was a Loyalist stronghold ready to defend the Crown against the rebellious Americans. Merrickville was such a desirable locale that Colonel By, master planner of the Rideau Canal, built his summer home here, and Benedict Arnold's sons were given land nearby in return for his betrayal of the Americans.

History buffs will enjoy the grand 19th-century buildings alongside the Rideau Canal, and boutique-browsers will love the numerous artisan workshops.

Blockhouse Museum HISTORIC BUILDING
(☎613-269-4791; www.merrickvillehistory.org; cnr Main & St Lawrence Sts; ⊙10am-5pm mid-Jun–early Sep, noon-4pm Sat & Sun late May–mid-Jun & early Sep–mid-Oct) FREE Explore this lockside fortification, one of the four built by the British in the early 1830s to defend the Rideau Canal. The displays inside cover the history of Merrickville and the canal, which brought the village much trade and wealth before the railways altered the picture and left Merrickville to its current slumber.

Merrickville is 85km south of Ottawa via Hwy 416. It's easiest to come by car, but the **County Shuttle** (☎613-552-0432; www.thecountryshuttle.com) links the village to Ottawa MacDonald-Cartier International Airport (from $57, one hour).

Visit www.realmerrickville.ca for more information on Merrickville.

Morrisburg

Little Morrisburg is known far and wide for its quality historic site, **Upper Canada Village** (☎613-543-4328; www.uppercanadavillage.com; 13740 County Rd 2, Morrisburg; adult/child $19/12; ⊙9:30am-5pm May-Sep, tours 10:30am, 1pm & 3pm early Sep-early Oct; 👪). Costume-clad interpreters animate this re-created town

EXPERIENCE AKWESASNE

Pop into this small **interpretive center** (☎613-575-2250; www.akwesasne.ca; Peace Tree Mall, 167 Akwesasne International Rd, Cornwall Island; ⏲8:30am-4:30pm Mon-Fri) FREE on **Cornwall Island**, between the bridge to the US border post and the bridge back to the Canadian mainland, to learn more about the Akwesasne Mohawk reservation, which sprawls across Ontario, Québec and New York. Explanatory panels, artworks and brochures are complemented by the helpful staff, who are happy to share stories from their community of over 12,000 people. The center is a hub for organizing cultural experiences and outdoor activities in the reservation.

Ask about visiting the nearby Native North American Travelling College, also on the island, which has exhibits on subjects such as basket making. Cars pay $3.50 to cross the bridge to Cornwall Island; in winter, phone ahead to check whether the center is open. The island is between the US and Canadian border posts; if you are returning to Cornwall afterwards, you will have to cross the Canadian border, explain that you were visiting the center and show your passport.

by emulating life in the 1860s. Around 6km east of Upper Canada Village on the riverside Hwy 2 (aka County Rd 2), the **Upper Canada Migratory Bird Sanctuary** (☎613-537-2024; www.uppercanadabirdsanctuary.com; 5591 County Rd 2, Ingleside; campsite with/without hookup from $45/35, cabins from $93; ⏲visitors center 9am-4:30pm Mon-Thu & Sun, to 9pm Fri & Sat mid-May–late Oct, hours vary late Oct–mid-May; 👪) FREE offers 8km of self-guided trails that meander through a variety of habitats.

If you are driving to/from Cornwall, be sure to take the Long Sault Pkwy, a scenic detour from Hwy 2 along a string of beach-fringed islands in the St Lawrence.

Megabus (☎866-488-4452; ca.megabus.com) will drop passengers on request at the entrance to Upper Canada Village, a 500m walk from the main site, on its run between Montréal and Toronto via Cornwall, Brockville and Kingston.

Ottawa

POP 951,727

Descriptions of Ottawa read like an appealing dating profile: dynamic, gregarious, bilingual, likes kids and long walks on the river. In person, the attractive capital fits the bill.

Canada's gargantuan Gothic Parliament buildings regally anchor the downtown core, an inspiring jumble of pulsing districts around the Rideau Canal. A few days' worth of world-class museums are architecturally inspiring homes to a variety of intriguing collections.

Parks, gardens and wide, open public spaces pay an accessible and year-round homage to all four seasons. Average temperatures are well below 0°C from December to March, but locals celebrate the city's longest-seeming season with a bunch of outdoor pursuits. Many skate to work or school on the frozen canal, while the Winterlude festival sees fantastical ice sculptures. As spring clicks to summer, auspicious tulips cheer the downtown, followed by vibrant fall leaves that line the streets with eye-popping reds and yellows.

History

Like many colonial capitals, Ottawa's birth was not an organic one. The site was chosen by Queen Victoria as a geographic compromise between Montréal and Toronto, and poof – the city was born. Canadians were initially baffled by her decision; Ottawa was far away from the main colonial strongholds. Many thought the region to be a desolate snowfield, when in fact the Ottawa area was long inhabited by Algonquin, who named the rolling river 'Kichissippi,' or 'Great River.'

For almost a century, Ottawa functioned as a quiet capital. Then, after WWII, Paris city planner Jacques Greber was tasked with giving Ottawa an urban face-lift. The master planner created a distinctive European feel, transforming the capital into the stunning cityscape of ample common and recreational spaces we see today.

Sights

Most of Ottawa's numerous world-class museums are within walking distance of each other. Some offer free general admissions on Thursday evenings, and many close a day or two weekly (normally Monday) in winter. Several may let you in for free if you arrive less than an hour before closing time, smiling politely; but you won't have much time to appreciate their extensive collections. The **Museums Passport** (www.museumspassport.ca; adult/family $45/99) is a better idea. If you plan to visit both the Museum of History and the War Museum, discounted tickets are available: inquire at either.

Out of town to the west are three interesting sights, the Diefenbunker (p214), Saunders Farm (p215) and Bonnechere Caves (p216).

★National Gallery of Canada MUSEUM

(Map p210; ☎613-990-1985, 800-319-2787; www.gallery.ca; 380 Sussex Dr; adult/child $12/6, 5pm-8pm Thu free; ⊙10am-6pm daily May-Sep, 10am-5pm Tue-Sun Oct-Apr, to 8pm Thu year-round) The National Gallery is a work of art in itself: its striking ensemble of pink granite and glass spires echoes the ornate copper-topped towers of nearby Parliament. Inside, vaulted galleries exhibit predominantly Canadian art, classic and contemporary, including an impressive collection of work by Inuit and other indigenous artists. It's the world's largest Canadian collection, although additional galleries of European and American treasures include several recognizable names and masterpieces. Interpretive panels guide visitors through the nation's history and cultural development.

Deep within the gallery's interior you'll find two smooth courtyards and the remarkable **Rideau Street Convent Chapel**. Built in 1888, the stunning wooden chapel was saved from demolition and rebuilt here 100 years later – quite extraordinary.

★Canadian Museum of History MUSEUM

(Map p210; ☎819-776-7000; www.historymuseum.ca; 100 Rue Laurier, Gatineau; adult/child 3-12yr $15/9, with Canadian War Museum $23/13; ⊙9:30am-5pm Fri-Wed, to 8pm Thu; 👪) Allow plenty of time to experience this high-tech, must-see museum across the river, in Hull, Québec. Documenting the history of Canada through a range of spectacular exhibits, it's an objective recounting of the nation's timeline from the perspectives of its Aboriginal peoples, its colonial beginnings and today's rich multicultural diversity. Entry includes admission to the **Canadian Children's Museum**, based around a theme of 'the Great Adventure': over 30 exhibition spaces whisk kids off on a journey around the world.

Outside, there are stunning views of Parliament Hill, across the river. The building's striking stone exterior has been sculpted into smooth ripples, like an undulating wave, to honor the aboriginal belief that evil dwells in angled nooks. A variety of visiting hands-on

OTTAWA IN...

One Day

If you're only here for a day, there's no time to waste! Get yourself to **Parliament Hill** (p212) for happy snaps with the Peace Tower and a quick tour of the lavish, Harry Potter-esque interior. Next, be seduced by the shimmering glass spires of the **National Gallery of Canada** (p209), with its carefully curated collection of Canadian and world art and the restored remains of a lovely wooden chapel. Pause for lunch at the **ByWard Market** (p221), where you'll uncover scores of vendors hawking farm-fresh produce around the maroon-brick market building, including several hundred local and international cheeses. Sample a fried dough beavertail and make tracks to the **Rideau Canal** (p215): in winter it becomes one of the world's largest ice-skating rinks (7.8km long).

Three Days

Cover the major sights flanking the **Ottawa Locks** (p212) on the first day, then gravitate toward the awe-inducing architecture, city views and fascinating exhibits of the **Canadian Museum of History** (p209). Ogle taxidermic megafauna at the **Canadian Museum of Nature** (p212) before heading for an inspired hike or swim in picturesque **Gatineau Park** (p215). Head back to town in time for tea, which could mean cocktails and tacos at **El Camino** (p220) or *plats du jour* at **Métropolitain Brasserie** (p220).

After a lazy brunch and morning stroll around **Confederation Park**, head to the quirky, Cold War marvel of the **Diefenbunker** (p214) and the pretty landscapes outside town. After another delicious dinner, round out your final day with a show at the **National Arts Centre** (p223) or rock out with some live music in the ByWard Market area's many venues.

Ottawa

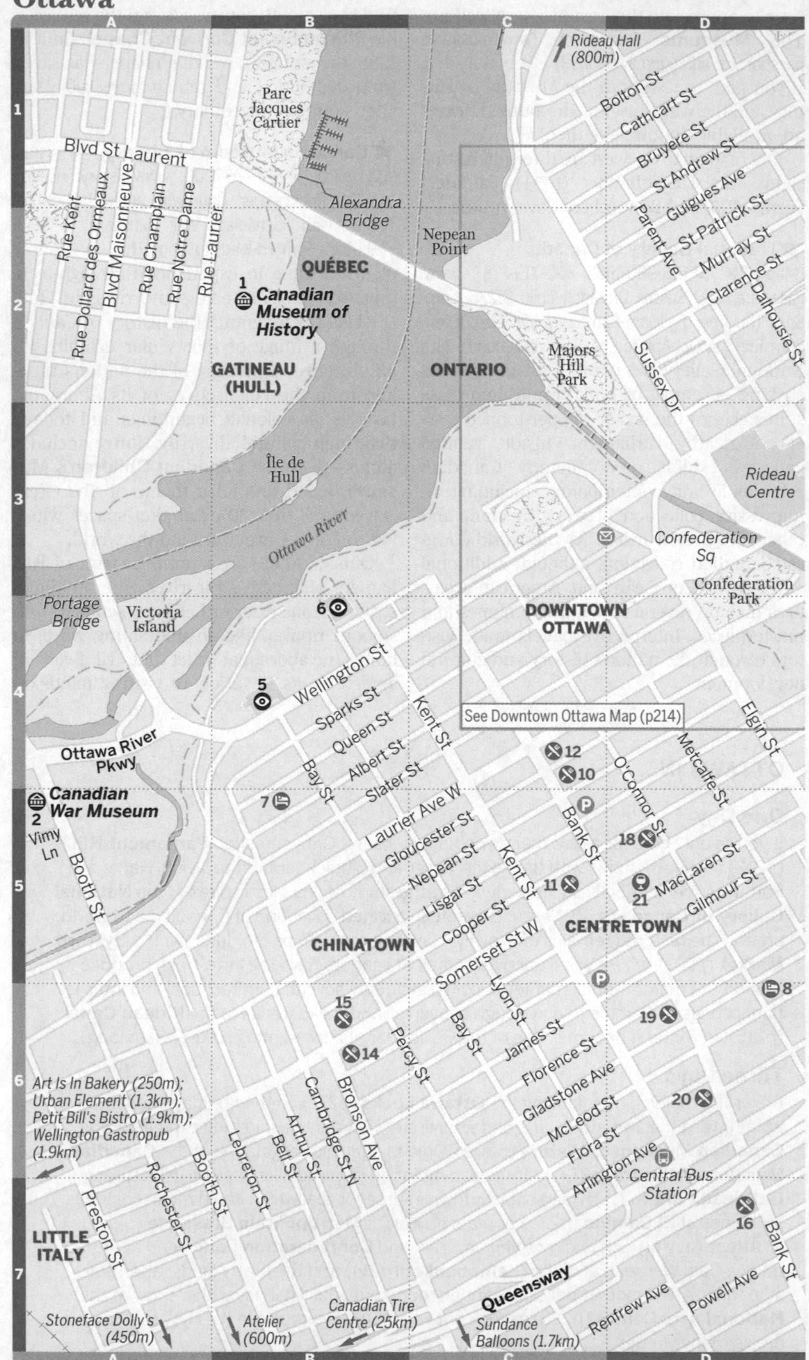

Rideau Hall (800m)
Parc Jacques Cartier
Blvd St Laurent
Rue Kent
Rue Dollard des Ormeaux
Blvd Maisonneuve
Rue Champlain
Rue Notre Dame
Rue Laurier
Alexandra Bridge
Nepean Point
QUÉBEC
1 Canadian Museum of History
GATINEAU (HULL)
ONTARIO
Majors Hill Park
Bolton St
Cathcart St
Bruyere St
St Andrew St
Guigues Ave
St Patrick St
Parent Ave
Murray St
Clarence St
Dalhousie St
Sussex Dr
Île de Hull
Ottawa River
Rideau Centre
Confederation Sq
Confederation Park
Portage Bridge
Victoria Island
DOWNTOWN OTTAWA
Wellington St
Sparks St
Queen St
Albert St
Slater St
Bay St
Kent St
See Downtown Ottawa Map (p214)
Ottawa River Pkwy
2 Canadian War Museum
Vimy Ln
Booth St
Laurier Ave W
Gloucester St
Nepean St
Lisgar St
Cooper St
Somerset St W
O'Connor St
Metcalfe St
Elgin St
Bank St
MacLaren St
Gilmour St
CENTRETOWN
CHINATOWN
Lyon St
Percy St
James St
Florence St
Gladstone Ave
McLeod St
Flora St
Arlington Ave
Central Bus Station
Bronson Ave
Cambridge St N
Arthur St
Bell St
Lebreton St
Rochester St
Preston St
Art Is In Bakery (250m); Urban Element (1.3km); Petit Bill's Bistro (1.9km); Wellington Gastropub (1.9km)
LITTLE ITALY
Queensway
Renfrew Ave
Powell Ave
Stoneface Dolly's (450m)
Atelier (600m)
Canadian Tire Centre (25km)
Sundance Balloons (1.7km)

Ottawa

Top Sights

1 Canadian Museum of History B2
2 Canadian War Museum........................A5

Sights

3 Canadian Museum of Nature E6
4 Laurier House National Historic Site..F2
5 Library & National Archives of Canada B4
6 Supreme Court of Canada................B4

Sleeping

7 Albert at Bay Suite Hotel B5
8 Best Western Plus Ottawa Downtown..D6
9 McGee's Inn E2

Eating

10 Bread & Sons Bakery C4
11 Ceylonta C5
12 Eggspectation C4
13 El Camino...E5
14 Saigon Boy Noodle House..................B6
15 Shanghai B6
16 The Works..D7
17 Town E5
18 Union Local 613..................................D5
19 Whalesbone Oyster House................ D6
20 Wilf & Ada's....................................... D6

Drinking & Nightlife

21 Centretown Pub D5
Manx .... (see 13)

Entertainment

22 ByTowne Cinema................................E2

exhibitions, events and state-of-the-art big-screen films maintain year-round appeal.

You can catch an **Aqua-Taxi** (Map p214; 819-329-2413; aufeeldeleau.ca; Canal Lane; one way $6) ferry there from Ottawa Locks.

★ Canadian War Museum MUSEUM

(Map p210; 819-776-8600; www.warmuseum.ca; 1 Vimy Pl; adult/child 3-12yr $15/9, with Canadian Museum of History $23/13; 9:30am-5pm Fri-Wed, to 8pm Thu) Fascinating displays twist through the labyrinthine interior of this sculpture-like, modern museum, tracing Canada's military history with the nation's most comprehensive collection of war-related artifacts. Many of the touching and thought-provoking exhibits are larger than life, including a replica of a WWI trench. Take a look at the facade in the evening, if you can: flickering lights pulse on and off spelling 'Lest We Forget' and 'CWM' in both English and French Morse code.

OTTAWA FOR CHILDREN

The **Canada Agriculture and Food Museum** (p213) is a fascinating experimental farm. Its rolling farmland is the perfect place for a scenic summer picnic, and in winter the grounds become a prime tobogganing locale. The farm can be reached on the city's network of cycling routes. Entry is free for kids under three years.

Just as farm-like, but without the animals, the hedge mazes and labyrinths at **Saunders Farm** (p215) will keep the kids going in circles for ages, so you can put your feet up! About 45 minutes' drive southwest of Ottawa, the farm also offers a waterpark, pedal carts, hay-wagon rides and much more seasonal fun.

Otherwise, most of Ottawa's museums have been designed with families in mind; several have entire wings devoted to child's play, like the **Canadian Museum of Nature**, the **Canada Science & Technology Museum** (reopening July 2017), and of course the **Canadian Museum of History's** (p209) interactive Canadian Children's Museum.

Family-friendly accommodations include the **Albert at Bay Suite Hotel** (p217), **Les Suites** (p219) and **Courtyard Ottawa East** (p217).

Ottawa Locks HISTORIC SITE

(Map p214) The series of steep, step-like locks between the Château Laurier and Parliament Hill marks the north end of the 200km Rideau Canal, which flows all the way down to Kingston. Colonel By, the canal's visionary engineer, set up headquarters here in 1826.

Parliament Hill HISTORIC BUILDING

(Map p214; ☎613-992-4793; www.parl.gc.ca/vis; 111 Wellington St; ⏲East Block tours 9:45am-4:45pm Jul-early Sep, Centre Block tours 9am-4:30pm Jul-early Sep, hours vary early Sep-Jun, sound-and-light show 10pm Jul, 9:30pm Aug, 9pm early Sep) FREE Vast, yawning archways, copper-topped turrets and Gothic revival gargoyles dominate the facade of the stunning lime and sandstone Parliament buildings. The main building, known as the Centre Block, supports the iconic Peace Tower. Completed in 1865, Canada's political core welcomes visitors year-round. Interesting from political and historical perspectives respectively, two free tours cover the Centre Block, home to the Senate, House of Commons and parliamentary library, and the East Block, the nerve center of Canada's government during its first century.

Notre Dame Cathedral-Basilica CHURCH

(Map p214; ☎613-241-7496; notredameottawa.com; 385 Sussex Dr; ⏲9am-6pm) Built in the 1840s, this shimmering tin-topped house of worship is the oldest church in all of Ottawa and the seat of the city's Roman Catholic archbishop. Pick up the small pamphlet at the entrance outlining the church's many idiosyncratic features, including elaborate wooden carvings and the dazzling indigo ceiling peppered with gleaming stars.

Laurier House National Historic Site HISTORIC SITE

(Map p210; ☎613-992-8142; www.parkscanada.gc.ca; 335 Laurier Ave East; adult/child $4/2; ⏲10am-5pm daily Jul & Aug, Thu-Mon late May, Jun, Sep & early Oct) This copper-roofed Victorian home built in 1878 was the residence of two notable prime ministers: Wilfrid Laurier and the eccentric Mackenzie King. The home is elegantly furnished, displaying treasured mementos and possessions from both politicos. Don't miss the study on the top floor.

Canadian Museum of Nature MUSEUM

(Map p210; ☎613-566-4700; www.nature.ca; 240 McLeod St; adult/child 3-12yr $13.50/9.50, 5-8pm Thu free; ⏲9am-5pm Wed & Fri-Sun, to 8pm Thu; 🚌1, 5, 6, 7, 14) This imposing baronial building houses one of the world's best natural history collections, which the vast museum brings to life with modern and interactive exhibits. There's an impressive collection of fossils, the full skeleton of a blue whale and an excellent stock of dinosaur skeletons and models. Everyone loves the realistic mammal and bird dioramas depicting Canadian wildlife – the taxidermic creatures are so lifelike, you'll be glad they're behind a sheet of glass.

General admission is free between 5pm and 8pm on Thursdays.

Rideau Hall NOTABLE BUILDING

(☎613-991-4422; www.gg.ca/rideauhall; 1 Sussex Dr; ⏰10am-4:30pm Jul-early Sep, noon-4pm Sat & Sun May, Jun, Sep & Oct) FREE Home of the Governor General, Rideau Hall was built in the 1830s with grand additions made by successive governors. There are free 45-minute walking tours of the fancy residence, featuring anecdotes about the various goings-on over the years. Otherwise, from 8am to one hour before sunset, the grounds are free to be enjoyed at your leisure (as is the building between 3pm and 4:30pm in July and August).

Canada Agriculture and Food Museum FARM

(☎613-991-3044; www.agriculture.technomuses.ca; 901 Prince of Wales Dr; adult/child 3-12yr $10/7; ⏰9am-5pm late Feb-Oct, Wed-Sun Nov-Feb) Nope, the Canada Agriculture and Food Museum isn't about the history of the pitchfork – it's a fascinating experimental farm. The government-owned property, southwest of downtown, includes about 500 hectares of gardens and ranches. Kids will love the livestock as they hoot and snort around the barn. The affable farmhands will even let the tots help out during feeding time.

Supreme Court of Canada NOTABLE BUILDING

(Map p210; ☎613-995-5361; www.scc-csc.ca; 301 Wellington St; ⏰9am-noon & 1-5pm daily May-Aug, Mon-Fri Sep-Apr) FREE This intimidating structure strikes an intriguing architectural balance with a modern concrete shell and a traditional copper roof. Visitors can stroll around the scenic grounds, grand entrance hall and dark oak-paneled courtroom. Between May and August, University of Ottawa law students conduct friendly and insightful 30-minute tours, starting on the hour. During the rest of the year, tours must be booked in advance.

RCMP Musical Ride Centre MUSEUM

(☎613-741-4285; www.rcmp-grc.gc.ca/en/ride-centre; 1 Sandridge Rd; ⏰9am-3:30pm May-Aug, 10am-1pm Tue & Thu Sep-Apr) FREE While the name sounds like Disney's newest attraction starring chipper red-vested policemen, the Musical Ride Centre is actually the stage where the Royal Canadian Mounted Police (aka the Mounties) perfect their pageant. The public are welcome to tour the stables, museum and riding school, and to meet the riders and their steeds when they are in town. They tour extensively between May and October; check their schedule on the website. It's about 7km northeast of Centretown.

Bytown Museum MUSEUM

(Map p214; ☎613-234-4570; www.bytownmuseum.ca; 1 Canal Lane; adult/child $6.50/3; ⏰10am-5pm Fri-Wed, 10am-8pm Thu Jun-Sep, 11am-4pm Thu-Mon Oct-May) Descend the stairs alongside the Ottawa Locks (p212) on Wellington St to find the Bytown Museum, sitting at the last lock before the artificial canal plunges into the waters of the Ottawa River. This well-curated collection of artifacts and documents about Ottawa's colonial past is displayed in the city's oldest stone building.

Canada Science & Technology Museum MUSEUM

(☎613-991-3044; www.sciencetech.technomuses.ca; 1867 St Laurent Blvd; adult/child $12/8; ⏰9:30am-5pm) Currently closed for renovations, expect ambient squeaks and boinks to fill the air of this hands-on museum when it reopens in summer 2017 as contented visitors gingerly turn knobs and push buttons, exploring the physical laws governing things like optical illusions and time. A walk through the 'Crazy Kitchen' is a blast: the lopsided galley makes you stumble from start to finish. There are trains out back to enlighten you on the science of coal and steam propulsion and a large display of space technology. Popular with adults and kids alike, it's informative and fun!

Canada Aviation and Space Museum MUSEUM

(☎613-991-3044; casmuseum.techno-science.ca; 11 Aviation Pkwy; adult/child 3-12yr $13/8; ⏰9am-5pm mid-May–Aug, from 10am Wed-Mon Sep–mid-May; 🚌129) With around 120 aircraft housed in this mammoth steel hangar about 5km northeast of downtown, you could be forgiven for thinking you were at the airport. Wander through the warehouse, try a flight simulator and get up close and personal with colorful planes ranging from the Silver Dart of 1909 to the first turbo-powered Viscount passenger jet.

Royal Canadian Mint NOTABLE BUILDING

(Map p214; ☎613-993-8990; www.mint.ca/tours; 320 Sussex Dr; guided tours adult/child $6/3, weekends $4.50/2.25; ⏰10am-5pm) Although Canada's circulation-coin mint is in Winnipeg, the royal mint holds its own by striking special pieces. The imposing stone building, which looks a bit like the Tower of London, has been refining gold and minting since 1908. Weekday tours of the coin-making process are highly recommended: visitors can glimpse the transformation as sheets of metal are spun into loads of coins. This doesn't happen on weekends, so the tour price is discounted.

Downtown Ottawa

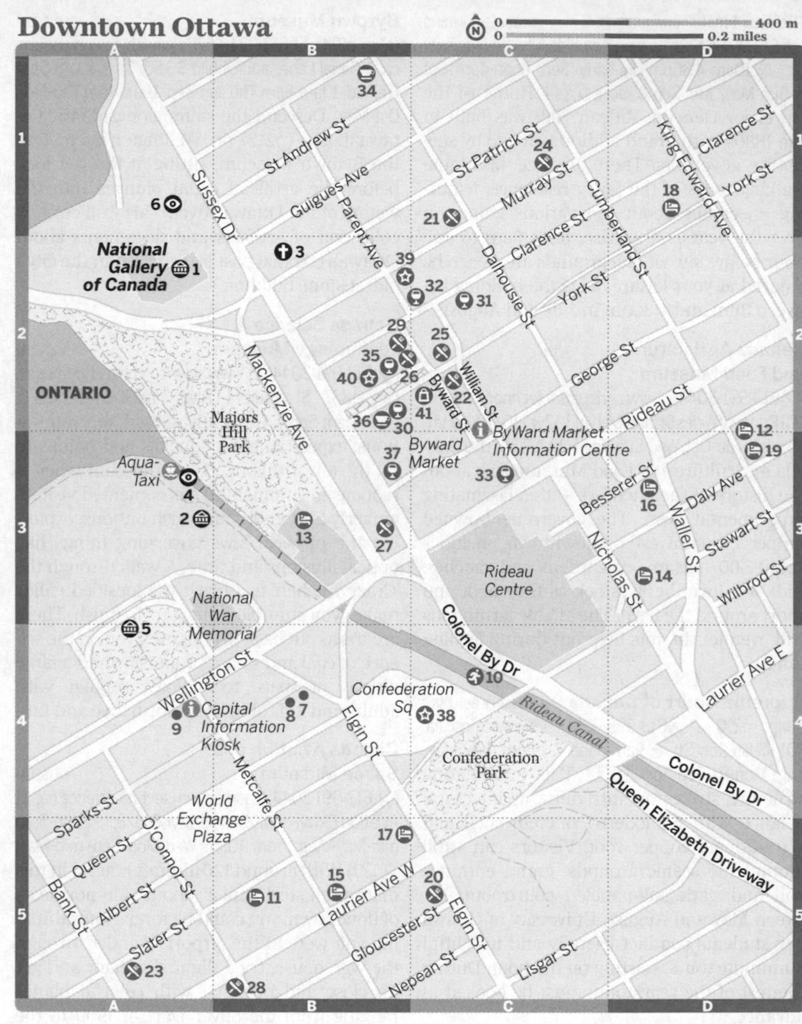

Library & National Archives of Canada NOTABLE BUILDING

(Map p210; ☎613-996-5115; www.collectionscanada.gc.ca; 395 Wellington St; ⏰6am-11pm Mon-Fri, 10am-6pm Sat & Sun) FREE The mandate of this monstrous concrete institution is to collect and preserve the documentation of Canada. Behind the tiny checkered windows lies a vast anthology of records, including paintings, maps, photographs, diaries, letters, posters and 60,000 cartoons and caricatures collected over the past two centuries. Rotating exhibits are displayed on the ground floor.

Diefenbunker HISTORIC BUILDING

(☎613-839-0007; www.diefenbunker.ca; 3929 Carp Rd, Carp; adult/child $14/8; ⏰11am-4pm daily Mar-Dec, 11am-3:30pm Tue-Sun Jan & Feb, ticket office 10:30am-3:30pm) During the Cold War, paranoid officials commissioned this gargantuan four-floored secret subterranean bunker, designed to allow the government to operate safely underground for 30 days during a nuclear attack. Descend over 20m to highlights including the prime minister's suite, the CBC radio studio and the Bank of Canada vault. Admission includes an optional one-hour

Downtown Ottawa

Top Sights

1 National Gallery of Canada ... A2

Sights

2 Bytown Museum ... A3
3 Notre Dame Cathedral-Basilica ... B2
4 Ottawa Locks ... A3
5 Parliament Hill ... A4
6 Royal Canadian Mint ... A1

Activities, Courses & Tours

7 Gray Line ... B4
8 Haunted Walk ... B4
Lady Dive ... (see 7)
9 Ottawa Walking Tours ... A4
Paul's Boat Line ... (see 4)
10 Rideau Canal ... C4

Sleeping

11 Arc ... B5
12 Barefoot Hostel ... D2
13 Fairmont Château Laurier ... B3
14 Hostelling International (HI) Ottawa Jail ... D3
15 Hotel Indigo ... B5
16 Les Suites ... D3
17 Lord Elgin Hotel ... B5
18 Ottawa Backpackers Inn ... D1
19 Swiss Hotel ... D3

Eating

20 Beckta Dining & Wine Bar ... C5
21 Benny's Bistro ... C1
22 Boulangerie Moulin de Provence ... C2
ByWard Market Square ... (see 41)
23 C'est Japon à Suisha ... A5
24 Chez Lucien ... C1
25 Lapointe ... C2
26 LUXE Bistro & Steakhouse ... B2
27 Métropolitain Brasserie ... B3
28 Tosca ... B5
29 Zak's Diner ... B2

Drinking & Nightlife

30 Château Lafayette ... B2
31 Clocktower Brew Pub ... C2
32 Heart & Crown ... C2
33 Highlander Pub ... C3
34 I Deal Coffee ... B1
35 Lookout Bar ... B2
36 Planet Coffee ... B2
37 Social ... B3

Entertainment

38 National Arts Centre ... C4
39 Rainbow Bistro ... B2
40 Zaphod Beeblebrox ... B2

Shopping

41 ByWard Market ... C2

audioguide; alternatively, guided tours leave at 11am and 2pm, with extra tours at noon and 1pm in July and August.

It's about 40km west of town, just off Hwy 417 in the village of Carp.

Saunders Farm PARK
(☎613-838-5440; www.saundersfarm.com; 7893 Bleeks Rd, Munster; admission $15; ⏰10am-5pm Tue-Sun Jul & Aug, Sat & Sun Jun & Sep; 👪) About 45 minutes' drive southwest of Ottawa, this family farm will easily fill a few hours with the world's largest collection of hedge mazes and labyrinths, a waterpark, pedal carts, haywagon rides and much more seasonal fun.

Activities

Residents of this city of long, harsh winters love to be outside, whatever the season.

The **Rideau Canal** (Map p214; www.ottawatourism.ca/ottawa-insider/rideau-canal-skateway), Ottawa's most famous outdoor attraction, doubles as one of the world's largest **ice-skating rinks**. The 7.8km of groomed ice is roughly the size of 90 Olympic-sized hockey rinks. Rest stops and changing stations are sprinkled throughout, but, more importantly, take note of the wooden kiosks dispensing scrumptious slabs of fried dough called beavertails. The three **skate and sled rental stations** are located at the steps of the National Arts Centre, Dow's Lake and 5th Ave.

Several nearby **ski resorts** offer a variety of alpine and cross-country trails. In the **Gatineau Hills**, about 20km from downtown, over 50 groomed slopes are available. **Camp Fortune** (☎819-827-1717; www.campfortune.com; 300 Chemin Dunlop, Chelsea) is a year-round adventure spot whose ski runs turn into a **mountain biking** and **zip-lining** paradise in summer. Popular ski resort **Mont Cascades** (☎819-827-0301; www.montcascades.ca; 448 Mont-des-Cascades Rd, Cantley) also flips its tricks in the summer, operating an expansive waterpark. **Mount Pakenham** (☎613-624-5290; www.mountpakenham.com; 577 Ski Hill Rd, Pakenham), 65km west of Ottawa, is a strictly winter affair. **Cross-country** skiers will love the trails in **Gatineau Park** (☎819-827-2020; 33 Scott Rd; ⏰9am-5pm May-Oct, 9am-4pm Mon-Fri, to 5pm Sat & Sun Nov-Apr).

OFF THE BEATEN TRACK

BONNECHERE CAVES

About 130km west of Ottawa en route to Algonquin Provincial Park, these **caves** (☎613-628-2283; www.bonnecherecaves.com; 1247 Fourth Chute Rd; tours adult/child $18/13; ⏲10am-4pm late May-early Oct) are some of the world's finest examples of solutional caves (dissolved out of solid rock by acidic waters). Formed 500 million years ago from the floor of a tropical sea, the dank passages feature a haunting collection of fossils including a prehistoric octopus. Learn about speleology (the study of caves) on the humorous tour, which details the site's quirky history.

Nimble guests will enjoy squeezing through a few extra-narrow, damp passages. The caves are signposted from Hwy 60 at Douglas and Eganville.

Tours

The **Capital Information Kiosk** (Map p214; ☎844-878-8333; canada.pch.gc.ca/eng/1446841663343; 90 Wellington St; ⏲9am-6pm mid-May–mid-Sep, to 5pm mid-Sep–mid-May) offers handy brochures for self-guided walking tours. You can also download a walking-tour app from www.canada.pch.gc.ca (search for 'capital app').

Sundance Balloons BALLOONING
(☎613-247-8277; www.sundanceballoons.ca; per person from $250; ⏲May-Oct) Hot-air ballooning has long been a popular leisure activity in the capital region. Sundance Balloons offers sunrise and sunset trips departing from Carleton University.

Gray Line TOURS
(Map p214; ☎613-562-9090; www.grayline.com/ottawa; cnr Sparks & Elgin Sts; ⏲Apr-Oct) Sightseeing tours including hop-on, hop-off bus services, bus-and-bike tours and Ottawa River cruises. Check the website or visit the sidewalk ticket booth for schedules and pricing. Bus tours depart from the booth, cruises from the Ottawa Locks.

Haunted Walk WALKING
(Map p214; ☎613-232-0344; www.hauntedwalk.com; 46 Sparks St; walks $16-19) Has several ghoulish walking tours including visits to the old county jail, now the HI hostel.

Ottawa Walking Tours WALKING
(Map p214; ☎613-799-1774; www.ottawawalkingtours.com; 90 Wellington St; adult/child under 11yr $15/free) These informative and fun two-hour tours with professional guides depart from the Terry Fox statue in front of the tourist office. Cash only.

Lady Dive BUS
(Map p214; ☎613-223-6211; www.ladydive.com; cnr Sparks & Elgin Sts; adult/child 3-12yr $32/22; ⏲May-early Oct; 👪) This one-hour tour on Lady Dive's 'amphibus' (half-bus half-boat) takes in Ottawa's favorite sights before plunging into the Ottawa River. Kids love it.

Paul's Boat Line BOATING
(Map p214; ☎613-225-6781; www.paulsboatcruises.com; Canal Lane; cruises from adult/child $25/15; ⏲May-Oct) Scenic 1½-hour cruises on the Ottawa River, departing from the Ottawa Locks.

Urban Element COOKING
(☎613-722-0885; www.theurbanelement.ca; 424 Parkdale Ave) 🌿 Housed in a converted fire station, this gustatory option wins on concept alone. Make a reservation at this kitchen-cum-classroom and cook your own full-course gourmet meal, with the help of a skilled cook, of course. The team of instructors includes a regular crew of chefs and several visiting professionals who work at the finest restaurants around town.

Festivals & Events

The capital is abuzz year-round with over 60 annual festivals and events. Visit www.ottawafestivals.ca for more information.

The history of both Ottawa and the country it represents will be celebrated by the **Ottawa 2017** (www.ottawa2017.ca) festivities, part of the nationwide party to mark 150 years since the Canadian Confederation formed modern Canada on July 1, 1867. Ottawa will host numerous events, its major museums and galleries will stage special exhibitions, and Canada Day 2017 promises to be a night to remember in the capital.

Winterlude FESTIVAL
(☎800-363-4465; www.canadascapital.gc.ca/winterlude; ⏲Feb) Three frosty weeks in early February celebrate Ottawa's winter, centering on the frozen canal, Confederation Park and Parc Jacques Cartier. Awe-inspiring ice sculptures abound, as well as the world's largest skating rink and snow playground.

Canadian Tulip Festival FESTIVAL
(800-668-8547; www.tulipfestival.ca; May) After the winter thaw, Ottawa explodes with color as beds of over 200 species of tulips come to life. Over 100,000 bulbs were gifted to the city in 1945 by the Dutch royal family in gratitude for Canada sheltering their Princess and her daughters during the war. Festivities include parades, regattas, car rallies, dances, concerts and fireworks.

Canada Day CULTURAL
(800-363-4465; canadaday.gc.ca; Jul 1) Ottawa is the best place in Canada to celebrate the nation's birthday on July 1. Huge crowds watch concerts and fireworks crackling and booming above the Parliament Buildings.

HOPE Volleyball Summerfest SPORTS
(613-742-4673; www.hopehelps.com; Jul) A giant volleyball tournament and rock festival in mid-July to raise money for local charities.

Ottawa Bluesfest MUSIC
(613-247-1188; www.ottawabluesfest.ca; Jul) One of the world's biggest blues festivals brings in the big names for 10 days of memorable concerts in mid-July.

Capital Pride LGBT
(613-680-3033; ottawacapitalpride.ca; Aug) A week's worth of rainbow celebrations culminating in a rowdy parade in mid-August.

Sleeping

Ottawa has an impressive array of accommodations in all price ranges. Reservations are recommended during summer and over festival times, especially Winterlude.

Downtown and, sprawling south to Queensway (Hwy 417), Centretown offer numerous options, including boutique hotels, suite hotels, and hostels around ByWard Market. South of the market, the Sandy Hill district has pleasant B&Bs among its stately heritage homes and international embassies – all within healthy walking distance of downtown.

Centretown

★Hostelling International (HI) Ottawa Jail HOSTEL $
(Map p214; 613-235-2595; www.hihostels.ca/ottawa; 75 Nicholas St; nonmembers dm $37-41, s/tw/d without bathroom $47/87/89, r $107; P ❄ @ ᯤ) This quirky hostel occupies nine floors of the 155-year-old former Ottawa Jail, considered to be one of the city's most haunted buildings. Guests can lock themselves away in a room or dorm in an actual cell, or opt for a more conventional four- to eight-bed dorm or ensuite room. Rates include a continental breakfast and HI members pay $5 less.

Check out the on-site gallows, where numerous criminals were hanged for their wretched crimes, in the eighth-floor 'death row' museum. The bar behind bars and free daily tours of the atmospheric building add to guests' experience of a night in the nick.

★Lord Elgin Hotel HISTORIC HOTEL $$
(Map p214; 613-235-3333; www.lordelginhotel.ca; 100 Elgin St; s/d from $169/179; P ❄ ᯤ ≋) In one of Ottawa's finest locations, the stately Lord Elgin was built in 1941 in a similar, but less grandiose style to Toronto's Fairmont Royal York. The 346 spacious, bright rooms are comfortably furnished with modern amenities including large flatscreen TVs. Many feature wonderful views over Confederation Park.

Best Western Plus Ottawa Downtown HOTEL $$
(Map p210; 613-567-7275; www.bestwesternottawa.com; 377 O'Connor St; r incl breakfast from $188; P @ ᯤ) Your loonies go a long way at this 128-room property in a delightful position near the Canadian Museum of Nature. The bright, airy suites have separate bedroom and lounge at executive and deluxe levels, and all have cable TV, writing desk, and kitchenette with fridge, microwave and coffee maker. Continental breakfast and an 8th-floor gym and sauna are also offered.

Albert at Bay Suite Hotel HOTEL $$
(Map p210; 800-267-6644; www.albertatbay.com; 435 Albert St; ste from $209; P ❄ ᯤ) This all-suite hotel is great for traveling families and those who prefer the comforts of home. Oversized multiroom one- and two-bedroom suites all have full kitchens and plush, comfortable furnishings. Many rooms have balconies. It's a little far west of the downtown action, but still offers excellent value.

Courtyard Ottawa East HOTEL $$
(613-741-9862; www.marriott.com; 200 Coventry Rd; r from $142; P ❄ ᯤ ≋) The closest hotel to Ottawa's not-so-central VIA Rail station is also a good choice if you're driving: free parking, and easy access from Hwy 417. It has spacious, functional rooms with contemporary furnishings. There's a rooftop indoor pool and on-site bar-restaurant. Consider elsewhere if you need to be very downtown, or if you're traveling in winter without a vehicle.

Hotel Indigo HOTEL $$

(Map p214; ☎613-369-5002; www.ottawadowntownhotel.com; 123 Metcalfe St; r $160-260; P ❄ 🛜 ≈) A prime downtown location helps score points for this 106-room, InterContinental-owned hotel with boutique ambitions. Quirks include an atrium lobby, floor-to-ceiling photographic murals in the rooms, iPad docking stations, and customer information written in haiku form, although some rooms are a little small and dark. It's a good bet if the price is right.

Arc BOUTIQUE HOTEL $$

(Map p214; ☎613-238-2888; www.arcthehotel.com; 140 Slater St; s/d from $119/129; P ❄ 🛜) Arc is a savvy boutique hotel with 112 minimal, yet elegant rooms and suites in a great location; call it low-key, muted and restfully hip. This mellow adult atmosphere continues through the chic lounge bar and restaurant. There's an extra charge for parking.

★Fairmont Château Laurier HISTORIC HOTEL $$$

(Map p214; ☎800-441-1414, 613-241-1414; www.fairmont.com/laurier; 1 Rideau St; d from $259; P ❄ @ 🛜 ≈) By the Ottawa Locks, the city's best-known hotel is a landmark in its own right. Built in 1912 to resemble a 16th-century French château, its 426 rooms and suites are predictably large and luxurious. Walking the opulent marble hallways, admiring the art and reclining on overstuffed chaises, guests and happy interlopers alike feel like the toast of the town. Parking is $30.

ByWard Market & Sandy Hill

Ottawa Backpackers Inn HOSTEL $

(Map p214; ☎613-241-3402; www.ottawahostel.com; 203 York St; dm/s/d/tr/q from $26/60/75/90/130, apt from $130; P @ 🛜) This laid-back hostel occupies a converted late-19th-century house boasting fresh-faced bathrooms, sun-drenched dorms and handy power outlets at every bed. Dorms are mixed or female-only with four to 10 beds and ensuite bathrooms in the larger options. There's a lounge and a rear terrace, and an apartment accommodating five.

Barefoot Hostel HOSTEL $

(Map p214; ☎613-237-0336; www.barefoothostel.com; 455 Cumberland St; dm $36; P ❄ @ 🛜) With just four mixed and single-sex four-bed dorms, Barefoot is a veritable 'boutique hostel' with a comfy lounge, small self-catering kitchen, two modern bathrooms and an outdoor patio.

Australis Guest House B&B $$

(☎613-235-8461; www.australisguesthouse.com; 89 Goulburn Ave; d with/without bath $129/109; P 🛜) Hosts Brian and Carol create a friendly atmosphere at this homely guesthouse in the green Sandy Hill neighborhood, between the Rideau River and the University of Ottawa. A good option for solo travelers and those wishing to get a local perspective on the capital.

Avalon B&B $$

(☎613-241-6403; www.avalonbedandbreakfast.com; 539 Besserer St; d $85-125; P 🛜) A refreshing departure from the usual antique-laden B&Bs, Avalon, on a street lined with grand houses and trees near the river, has a tasteful blend of modern furnishings. The four stylish rooms have ensuite bathrooms and pillow-top mattresses. Enormous healthy breakfasts are the norm.

★Swiss Hotel BOUTIQUE HOTEL $$

(Map p214; ☎613-237-0335; www.swisshotel.ca; 89 Daly Ave; r from $148; P ❄ @ 🛜) Owner Sabina's Swiss heritage is reflected in everything from the luxuriant buffet breakfast ($15) to the rooms' design-savvy stencil decor. The 22 stylish rooms all have appliances such as espresso machines and iPads; those featuring a queen-size bed with fireplace are a good option, while the Jacuzzi suite has real wow factor.

Benner's B&B B&B $$

(☎613-789-8320; www.bennersbnb.com; 541 Besserer St; r incl breakfast $95-130; P ❄ 🛜) Well appointed and spacious, this historic townhouse is a comfortable option in Sandy Hill, about 1.5km east of ByWard Market. The King Loft room is a great deal.

McGee's Inn B&B $$

(Map p210; ☎613-237-6089; www.mcgeesinn.com; 185 Daly Ave; r incl breakfast $109-198; P ❄ 🛜) Floral prints, embroidered chair caning, plush button-eyed teddy bears, varnished sewing machines and antique cuckoo clocks: this vast Victorian mansion has all the period trappings. A dozen rooms and suites take you back in time, including the elegant and atmospheric John McGee room. An excellent choice for those who love history and charm. Parking is $10.

Les Suites HOTEL $$

(Map p214; 613-232-3200; www.les-suites.com; 130 Besserer St; ste from $150;) Spacious suites in this downtown hotel at the edge of the ByWard Market district feature one or two bedrooms, full kitchens and in-suite laundries. Staff have a reputation for their customer service. Some suites have been refurbished more recently than others; clarify before you book. Parking is $22.

Eating

Ottawa's cultural diversity is reflected in its culinary prowess: its smorgasbord of gastronomic goodness rivals those of Toronto and Montréal, but is more accessible. The capital's compact footprint makes finding great food simple, with a plethora of excellent dining options catering to most tastes and budgets. Look forward to a dynamic mix of flavors and aromas from around the globe, prepared using fresh, local ingredients.

Centretown & Chinatown

★**Wilf & Ada's** DINER $

(Map p210; 613-231-7959; wilfandadas.com; 510 Bank St; mains $14; 7am-3pm Mon-Fri, from 8am Sat & Sun) This 'scratch diner' is one of Ottawa's hippest breakfast and lunch spots, with its retro art and everything made from scratch. Breakfast is all home-cured bacon, buttermilk French toast, 'homies' (home fries) and maple syrup, while chunky sandwiches, soup, salads and poutine are served for lunch. If it's full, head round the back to the affiliated cafe Arlington Five.

Art Is In Bakery BAKERY $

(613-695-1226; www.artisinbakery.com; 250 City Centre Ave; sandwiches $8-13; 7am-6pm Mon-Fri, 8am-5pm Sat, 9am-4pm Sun;) Start the day with a breakfast sandwich or croissant and excellent cappuccino at this buzzy bakery cafe, occupying a warehouse space on an industrial estate. The gourmet sandwiches have fillings such as pickle melt and Thai chicken, with gluten-free options and salads available.

Saigon Boy Noodle House VIETNAMESE $

(Map p210; 613-230-8080; 648 Somerset St W; mains $11; 11am-9pm) Locals rate Saigon Boy as the city's best choice for *pho*, a Vietnamese soup containing rice noodles with beef or chicken. Other dishes, such as grilled pork and rice, are also available.

> **LOCAL KNOWLEDGE**
>
> **EAT LOCAL**
>
> Check out **Savour Ottawa** (www.savourottawa.ca) and its Facebook page for listings of restaurants, market vendors and food festivals championing local produce.
>
> During weekday lunchtimes, food trucks across downtown sell everything from poutine to seafood to Ottawa's hungry workers. Plan your street-food odyssey around town by downloading the food-truck app from Streetfoodapp.com/ottawa. You can also find a map on the City of Ottawa website, Ottawa.ca.

Shanghai CHINESE $

(Map p210; 613-233-4001; shanghairestaurantottawa.com; 651 Somerset St W; mains $13; 4:30-10pm Wed-Fri, to 2am Sat, karaoke from 9pm Sat;) The first restaurant in Ottawa's Chinatown, Shanghai is now run by the artistic children of the original owners. The food is great – modern Chinese cuisine with lots of veggie options – but the real draw is the trendy decor, rotating art exhibits and fabulous weekend events (think 'Disco Bingo' and karaoke) hosted by the local diva tranny goddess China-Doll.

Ceylonta SRI LANKAN $

(Map p210; 613-237-7812; somerset.ceylonta.ca; 403 Somerset St W; mains $14; 11:30am-2pm Sun-Fri, 5-9pm daily) Locals recommend this friendly neighborhood Sri Lankan restaurant, serving fresh and zingy dishes. Go for the fish *thali* or the chicken or mutton *kothu rotti*.

Bread & Sons Bakery BAKERY $

(Map p210; 613-230-5302; breadandsons.com; 195 Bank St; pastries $2; 7am-5:30pm Mon-Fri) This bakery claims to do the best coffee on the block. It certainly makes wonderful pastries, cookies, scones, tarts, mini-quiches, pizza, and breakfast croissants.

★**Town** ITALIAN $$

(Map p210; 613-695-8696; www.townlovesyou.ca; 296 Elgin St; mains $20; 11:30am-2pm Wed-Fri, 5-10pm daily) Slick, smart and ineffably cool, this joint is always packed: arty-farty hipsters bump elbows with wealthy coiffured housewives. Ottawa foodies appreciate the use of local produce and northern Italian recipes, resulting in a short and seasonal menu of small and large plates, such as the mainstay ricotta-stuffed meatballs, with an abundance of Niagara wines to accompany.

★**Union Local 613** MODERN AMERICAN $$

(Map p210; ☎613-231-1010; www.union613.ca; 315 Somerset St W; mains $25; ⏲food served 11:30am-2pm Wed-Fri, from 10am Sat & Sun, 5:30-10pm Mon-Sat; 📶) Among low-lit decor of hummingbirds and hot-air balloons, drink the house beers and other local craft brews from screw-top jars. It's food with attitude, including southern-fried chicken and cornmeal-crusted catfish, and there's a 'speakeasy' behind a bookshelf in the basement (open 10:30pm to 2am Wednesday to Saturday).

Métropolitain Brasserie FRENCH $$

(Map p214; ☎613-562-1160; www.metropolitain-brasserie.com; 700 Sussex Dr; snacks $5-16, mains $18-35; ⏲9am-midnight) Métropolitain puts a modern spin on the typical brasserie with its swirling zinc countertop, flamboyant fixtures and Gallic soundtrack: you'll feel like you're dining on the set of *Moulin Rouge*. 'Hill Hour' (4pm to 7pm on weekdays, and from 9:30pm daily) buzzes with the spirited chatter of hot-blooded politicos as they down cheap *plats du jour*.

★**El Camino** MEXICAN $$

(Map p210; ☎613-422-2800; eatelcamino.com; 380 Elgin St; tacos $6; ⏲5:30pm-late Tue-Sun, takeout noon-2:30pm Tue-Fri) With a hip industrial aesthetic underscored by Day of the Dead references, El Camino is either praised as Ottawa's taco joint of the hour or derided as overpriced. Come for chorizo and crispy fish tacos, eaten at benches or taken out, and cocktails ($13) such as the sweet and spicy El Fuego – and book ahead.

Eggspectation BREAKFAST $$

(Map p210; ☎613-569-6505; www.eggspectation.ca; 171 Bank St; mains $9-23; ⏲7am-3pm) The downtown location of this breakfast (and more) franchise is so handy and the menu so *egg-citing* that we couldn't resist sharing. It's cheap, cheery and full of sunshine from its bright open windows. As the day wears on, *eggs-ecutive* burgers, *eggs-traordinary* pasta and more keep the puns coming and the punters happy.

The Works BURGERS $$

(Map p210; ☎613-235-0406; www.worksburger.com; 580 Bank St; burgers $15; ⏲11am-10pm) In a little over a decade this clever burger joint has flourished into a successful franchise. Build on your Canadian beef patty with myriad house and customized toppings, from fried eggs to brie cheese and peanut butter.

Tosca ITALIAN $$

(Map p214; ☎613-565-3933; www.tosca-ristorante.ca; 144 O'Connor St; mains $17-39; ⏲11:30am-10pm Mon-Fri, from 4pm Sat & Sun) In the heart of the downtown core, this upscale but accessible Italian *ristorante's* delicious, authentic food, extensive wine list and excellent service attract businesspeople and mums on shopping expeditions at lunchtime, when you can have soup and a main for under $20. The evening atmosphere is candlelit and serene, perfect for romancing or long conversations with old friends.

C'est Japon à Suisha JAPANESE $$

(Map p214; ☎613-236-9602; www.japaninottawa.com; 208 Slater St; sushi & sashimi from $6, mains $25; ⏲11:30am-2pm Mon-Fri, 5-9:30pm Mon-Sat) While strong in other culinary branches, Ottawa lacks a tonne of good Japanese restaurants. This long-running eatery is the exception: mouthwatering authentic dishes are delivered in a traditionally styled setting with sushi boats and private *washitsu* Japanese rooms. A wide variety of combinations and bento boxes are available from an extensive menu. Set lunch menus are around $18.

Lapointe SEAFOOD $$

(Map p214; ☎613-241-6221; www.lapointefish.ca; 55 York St; mains $17; ⏲11:30am-9:30pm) This fish market has served the community since 1867, offering a versatile array of dishes from cod tacos to old-school fish and chips. Sit on the front patio or inside on the ground floor or basement.

★**Beckta Dining & Wine Bar** MODERN CANADIAN $$$

(Map p214; ☎613-238-7063; www.beckta.com; 150 Elgin St; lunch mains $17-25, dinner menu $68; ⏲11:30am-3pm Mon-Fri, 5:30-10pm daily) 🍃 Book in advance for one of the hottest tables in the capital, if not the whole country. Beckta offers an upmarket dining experience with an original spin on regional cuisine. Lunch is à la carte, while dinner is a three-course menu or inspired five-course tasting menu ($95) – a great way to experience the bigger picture at work here, with a wine pairing offered.

LUXE Bistro & Steakhouse STEAK $$$

(Map p214; ☎613-241-8805; www.luxebistro.com; 47 York St; mains $17-49; ⏲11:30am-9:30pm Mon-Fri, 9am-2:30pm & 5-9:30pm Sat & Sun) If you like your steak a little French with a twist of New York, this smart ByWard Market bistro is bound to appeal. The decor is slick and the outdoor patio is a hit in the warmer months.

Whalesbone Oyster House SEAFOOD $$$
(Map p210; ☎613-231-8569; www.thewhalesbone.com; 430 Bank St; mains $25-40; ⊙11:30am-2pm Mon-Fri, 5-10pm daily) If the local chefs are purchasing their fish from Whalesbone's wholesale wing (or should we say 'fin'), then there's really no doubt that it's the best place in town for seafood. The on-site restaurant offers up a short list of fresh faves such as oysters, lobster and scallops ceviche on small plates. Book ahead.

ByWard Market & Sandy Hill

Boulangerie Moulin de Provence BAKERY $
(Map p214; ☎613-241-9152; www.moulindeprovence.com; 55 ByWard Market Sq; items from $2, mains $13; ⊙7am-10pm) Still riding on the buzz left by a visit from former US President Barack Obama, this bakery is packed to the hilt with sugary and savory goodness. The 'Obama Cookies' are a big hit, while others swear by the flaky croissants. With sandwiches, salads and ready-made meals in bains-marie, it's a good stop for a quick and affordable lunch.

Zak's Diner DINER $
(Map p214; ☎613-241-2401; www.zaksdiner.com; 14 ByWard Market Sq; mains $10-15; ⊙24hr) Shoo-bop along to the pop music that supplements the *Grease*-like atmosphere at this kitschy diner. The ByWard Market stalwart hosts families by day, but is at its best in the middle of the night, when the joint fills up for post-party munchies. Wraps, poutine and nachos are on offer, so it's not just a *Back to the Future* theme park.

★**ByWard Market Square** MARKET $
(Map p214; ☎613-244-4410; www.bywardmarketsquare.com; ByWard Market Sq; ⊙9:30am-6pm Mon-Wed & Fri, to 8pm Thu, to 5pm Sun) Anchoring the market district, this sturdy brick building is the perfect place to stop when hunger strikes. Aside from the fresh produce and cheese, an array of international takeaway joints offers falafel, spicy curries, flaky pastries, sushi…the list goes on. Look for the stand selling beavertails, Ottawa's signature sizzling flat-dough dish. Between William, Byward, George and York Sts.

There are also rich culinary pickings in the surrounding **outdoor market** (Map p214; ☎613-562-3325; www.byward-market.com; cnr York & ByWard Sts; ⊙6am-6pm), one of North America's largest outdoor farmers markets.

Fraser Cafe CAFE $$
(☎613-749-1444; www.frasercafe.ca; 7 Springfield Rd; mains brunch $10-17, lunch $14-18, dinner $27-32; ⊙11:30am-2pm Tue-Fri, from 10am Sat & Sun, 5:30-10pm daily) Take a little trek over to this smart cafe/restaurant across the Rideau River, northeast of ByWard Market, especially if you're in the mood for brunch (weekends only). True to its 'seasonal kitchen' subtitle, healthy, tasty, creative meals are prepared from the freshest ingredients.

Chez Lucien BISTRO $$
(Map p214; ☎613-241-3533; 137 Murray St; mains $17; ⊙11am-midnight) Exposed burgundy brick and classics on the free jukebox make this Gallic-accented gastropub one of Ottawa's favorite places to kick back in style. Numerous burgers, Dijon chicken and nachos are on the menu.

Signatures Restaurant FRENCH $$$
(☎613-236-2499; www.signaturesrestaurant.com; 453 Laurier Ave E; lunch mains/menu $24/34, dinner menu $68; ⊙11:30am-1:30pm Tue-Fri, 5:30-9pm Tue-Sat) Housed in the historic Tudor-style Munross Mansion, this restaurant affiliated with the prestigious Le Cordon Bleu culinary school focuses on modern French cuisine, under French executive chef Yannick Anton. The lengthy wine list looks more like an encyclopedia, and the regularly changing three-course lunch and dinner menus are rich seasonal banquets of dishes such as slow-cooked lamb's thigh.

Further Afield

White Horse Restaurant DINER $
(☎613-746-7767; www.thewhitehorserestaurant.com; 294 Tremblay Rd; mains $7; ⊙5:15am-7pm Mon-Fri, to 3pm Sat, 7am-4pm Sun) This wonderful little greasy spoon is the nearest place to get a meal from Ottawa train station, and boasts good old-fashioned home cooking and the cheapest breakfast in town.

Stoneface Dolly's FUSION $$
(☎613-564-2222; www.stonefacedollys.com; 416 Preston St; lunch/dinner mains $17/22; ⊙7:30am-2:30pm daily, 5-9pm Wed-Sun) Named for the owner's mother, who perfected the art of a stone-cold poker bluff, this popular joint is a great spot to taste local craft brews such as Beau's. There's food throughout the day, and it's popular for brunch. The eclectic and seasonal dishes range from South African cuisine to crab and porchetta fettuccine.

Benny's Bistro BISTRO $$

(Map p214; ☎613-789-7941; www.bennysbistro.ca; 119 Murray St; mains $19; ⏰11:30am-2:30pm Mon-Fri, from 10:30am Sat & Sun) The smell of freshly baked *pain au chocolat* (chocolate croissant) emanates from the French bakery at the front of this cool and arty bistro. Pastries are prepared using tried-and-true recipes from France. If you feel like lingering in the Gallic ambience, grab a table on Benny's black-and-white checkered floor and enjoy dishes such as salmon gravlax and lamb kofta.

Wellington Gastropub MODERN CANADIAN $$

(☎613-729-1315; www.thewellingtongastropub.com; 1325 Wellington St W; lunch/dinner mains $16/25; ⏰11:30am-2pm Mon-Fri, 5:30-9:30pm Mon-Sat) This gastropub is luring foodies to Ottawa's west end with its savvy selection of hearty mains, ranging from pulled pork ragout to east coast sea scallops. A dozen craft beers are available on tap, with many more from a bottle.

Atelier FUSION $$$

(☎613-321-3537; www.atelierrestaurant.ca; 540 Rochester St; menu $110; ⏰5:30-8:30pm Tue-Sat) The brainchild of celebrated chef and molecular gastronomy enthusiast Marc Lépine, Atelier is a white-walled laboratory dedicated to tickling the taste buds. There's no oven or stove – just Bunsen burners, liquid nitrogen and hot plates to create the unique 12-course tasting menu.

Drinking & Nightlife

From cheap-and-crusty beery dives to cheery local pubs and plush, see-and-be-seen lounges, Ottawa has it on tap. Head south on Bank or Elgin Sts for local hangouts, and to the buzzing ByWard Market area for out-and-out revelry. For something a little different, descend the stairs to Union Local 613's (p220) underground speakeasy. Many people cross the river to party on in Hull (Québec) when Ottawa winds down around 2am.

Heart & Crown IRISH PUB

(Map p214; ☎613-562-0674; www.heartandcrown.ca; 67 Clarence St; ⏰11am-2am) This ByWard Market stalwart is popular with young Ottawa folk for beers and pig platters of pub grub. Several rooms and patios sprawl into each other, incorporating four other pubs along the way, and big screens show soccer matches. There's music from live bands to acoustic sets seven days a week.

Highlander Pub PUB

(Map p214; ☎613-562-5678; www.thehighlanderpub.com; 115 Rideau St; ⏰11am-1am) Kilted servers, 17 taps and 200 single malt Scotches all add to the Scottish appeal of this ByWard Market area pub. The food is good too!

Clocktower Brew Pub BAR

(Map p214; ☎613-241-8783; www.clocktower.ca; 89 Clarence St; ⏰11:30am-11:45pm) Enjoy home-made brews such as Raspberry Wheat and Bytown Brown amid exposed brick and ByWard bustle. There are bar snacks aplenty and four additional locations around town.

Manx BAR

(Map p210; ☎613-231-2070; manxpub.com; 370 Elgin St; mains $13-15; ⏰11:30am-1am Mon-Wed, to 2am Thu & Fri, 10am-2am Sat) 'Ottawa's original sinkhole,' as this basement bar has called itself since Rideau St collapsed in 2016, offers a great selection of Canadian microbrews (including the beloved Creemore), served on copper-top tables.

I Deal Coffee COFFEE

(Map p214; ☎613-562-1775; www.idealcoffees.com; 176 Dalhousie St; coffee $3; ⏰7am-7pm Mon-Fri, from 8:30am Sat, 9am-6pm Sun) Ideal indeed; handcrafted blends are produced and roasted on-site. The decor is thin, with bins and sacks of 'light organic blend' and 'prince of darkness' stacked next to the roaster; it's all about rich, flavorful cups of joe (hot or iced). In the words of one happy customer, this might be Ottawa's best cappuccino.

Château Lafayette PUB

(Map p214; ☎613-241-4747; www.thelaff.ca; 42 York St; ⏰11am-2am) Dating to 1849, 'the Laff' is Ottawa's oldest bar and it retains its quirky charm – a run-down relic that captures ByWard's laid-back attitude.

Social BAR

(Map p214; ☎613-789-7355; www.social.ca; 537 Sussex Dr; lunch/dinner mains $20/30; ⏰11:30am-3pm Mon & Sun, 5pm-late Mon-Fri) This chic, flowing lounge with slick DJ beats, overstuffed furniture, cocktails and equally creative cuisine appeals to a trendy crowd. There's live jazz on the patio on Wednesday evenings, DJs on Friday and Saturday, and brunch on weekends.

Planet Coffee COFFEE

(Map p214; ☎613-789-6261; www.facebook.com/planetcoffeeott; 24a York St; ⏰7:30am-10pm Mon-Sat, 8am-8pm Sun) Recharge in this decades-old ByWard Market caffeine den's quiet courtyard. Sweetened ice coffees are a big hit.

Gay & Lesbian Bars

Ottawa has a small but thriving gay scene, although it's less happening than that of its neighbor Montréal, two hours up the road. Check out the Ottawa section of *Capital Xtra* (www.xtra.ca) for listings.

Centretown Pub GAY

(Map p210; 613-594-0233; centretownpub.blogspot.ca; 340 Somerset St W; 2pm-2am) A stalwart of the capital's gay scene for 30 years, this little neighborhood pub has a nondescript facade, but inside there's usually a party going on. There's pool on the ground level, a small rear patio, and an upper level that opens up for heaving club nights and events.

Lookout Bar GAY & LESBIAN

(Map p214; 613-789-1624; www.thelookoutbar.com; 41 York St; 2pm-2am Tue-Fri, to 10pm Sun & Mon) Keeping the ByWard Market crowds happy for 20 years, Lookout's nights range from karaoke on Tuesday and Wednesday to Saturday's drag show.

Entertainment

Ottawa has a variety of publications (print and web-based) that offer the latest scoop on the various goings-on around town. *Xpress* (www.ottawaxpress.ca) is the city's free entertainment weekly, found around town in cafes, bars and bookstores. Try www.ottawaentertainment.ca for more info and check out Thursday's *Ottawa Citizen* (ottawacitizen.com) for club and entertainment listings.

Live Music

Zaphod Beeblebrox LIVE MUSIC

(Map p214; 613-562-1010; www.zaphods.ca; 27 York St; 8pm-late) Taking its name from the *Hitchhiker's Guide to the Galaxy* alien, this space-obsessed 'nightclub at the edge of the universe' serves exotic cocktails such as its trademark Pan Galactic Gargle Blaster. For earthlings looking to forget the cares of terra firma, it's a kick-ass music venue and club with punky attitude.

Rainbow Bistro LIVE MUSIC

(Map p214; 613-241-5123; www.therainbow.ca; 76 Murray St) An oldie but a goodie: the best place in town to catch live blues. See live music here nightly in summer, with some sets starting as early as 3pm.

Irene's Pub LIVE MUSIC

(613-230-4474; www.irenespub.ca; 885 Bank St; 11:30am-2am) Friendly and funky, if a little grimy in the thick of a busy weekend, Irene's is the three-decade-old spiritual home for the Glebe neighborhood's artists and musicians. It offers live music, with a good line in Celtic, folk and blues, and other entertainment a few nights a week. Enjoy a great selection of whiskeys and local craft beers on tap.

Theater & Cinemas

National Arts Centre THEATER

(NAC; Map p214; 613-947-7000; www.nac-cna.ca; 53 Elgin St) The capital's premier performing arts complex delivers opera, drama, Broadway shows, and performances by its resident symphony orchestra. Freshly renovated, the modish complex stretches along the canal in Confederation Sq.

Mayfair Theatre CINEMA

(613-730-3403; www.mayfairtheatre.ca; 1074 Bank St; adult/child under 13yr $10/5) Check out this art-house cinema which hasn't changed much since the early '30s.

ByTowne Cinema CINEMA

(Map p210; 613-789-3456; www.bytowne.ca; 325 Rideau St) Ottawa's indie heart has been screening independent and international movies for 70 years.

Sports

Canadian Tire Centre SPECTATOR SPORT

(613-599-0100; www.canadiantirecentre.com; 1000 Palladium Dr, Kanata) Ottawa is a hard-core hockey town. It's worth getting tickets to a game even if you're not into hockey – the ballistic fans put on a show of their own. NHL team the Ottawa Senators play here, at their home ground, about 25km southwest of the center in Ottawa's west end. Big-ticket concerts also take place here.

TD Place Arena SPECTATOR SPORT

(613-232-6767; www.tdplace.ca; 1015 Bank St) You can watch the Ottawa 67's, a minor-league hockey team, at their home ground the TD Place Arena. You can also catch concerts, Ottawa Fury soccer club and the Ottawa Redblacks Canadian football team here.

Shopping

ByWard Market (p221) is the best place in town for one-stop shopping. Dalhousie St, a block east of the market, has been rising in popularity with a smattering of hipster boutiques and fashion houses.

The Glebe, a colorful neighborhood just south of the Queensway, bustles with quirky antique shops and charismatic cafes. Most of the action crowds along Bank St.

Information

Ottawa Tourism (www.ottawatourism.ca) Offers a comprehensive online look at the nation's capital, and can assist with planning itineraries and booking accommodations.

Capital Information Kiosk (p216) This helpful office is the city's hub for information and bookings.

ByWard Market Information Centre (Map p214; 613-244-4410; www.byward-market.com; ByWard & George Sts; 7:30am-6pm Jul & Aug, 8am-5pm Sep-Jun) Covers the whole city.

Ottawa Hospital (613-722-7000; www.ottawahospital.on.ca; 501 Smyth Rd; emergency 24hr) Southeast of downtown in Alta Vista; has an emergency department.

Central Post Office (Map p210; 866-607-6301; www.canadapost.ca; 59 Sparks St; 8:30am-5pm Mon-Fri) The main post office, occupying a historic building.

Accu-Rate Foreign Exchange (613-238-8454; www.accu-rate.ca; 1st fl, World Exchange Plaza, 111 Albert St; 9:15am-5:15pm Mon-Fri) Accommodates currency exchange, traveler's checks and EFTs.

Getting There & Away

AIR

The state-of-the-art **Ottawa MacDonald-Cartier International Airport** (YOW; 613-248-2125; yow.ca; 1000 Airport Pkwy) is 15km south of the city and, perhaps surprisingly, is very small. Almost all international flights require a transfer before arriving in the capital (normally in Toronto's Lester B Pearson International Airport). Nonetheless, numerous North American carriers serve the airport, including Air Canada, WestJet, Porter Airlines, United Airlines, Delta and American Airlines.

BUS

The **central bus station** (Map p210; 613-238-6668; 265 Catherine St) is just off Queensway (Hwy 417), near Kent St. Several companies operate bus services from the station, including **Greyhound** (p191) with services to Toronto (from $71, 5½ hours, six daily).

CAR & MOTORCYCLE

Major car-rental chains are represented at the airport and offer several locations downtown, on Catherine St and at the train station (both just off Hwy 417). You will likely get a better deal hiring a car in Toronto.

TRAIN

The **VIA Rail Station** (888-842-7245; www.viarail.ca; 200 Tremblay Rd) is 7km east of downtown, near the Hwy 19/Riverside Dr exit of Hwy 417. Trains run to Toronto ($108, 4½ hours, eight daily) via Brockville and Kingston, and to Québec City via Montréal ($62, two hours, six daily).

Getting Around

TO/FROM THE AIRPORT

The cheapest way to get to the airport is by city bus. Take bus 97 from Slater St between Elgin St and Bronson Ave (make sure you are heading in the 'South Keys & Airport' direction). The ride takes 40 minutes and costs $3.65.

Ottawa Shuttle Service (613-680-3313; www.ottawashuttleservice.com; 1 or 2 passengers $59; office 10am-10pm) offers private and shared shuttles from downtown hotels.

Blue Line Taxi (613-238-1111; www.bluelinetaxi.com) and **Capital Taxi** (613-744-3333; www.capitaltaxi.com) offer cab services; the fare to/from downtown is around $30.

BICYCLE

Right on the Rideau Canal bike path, the friendly staff at **Rent-A-Bike** (613-241-4140; www.rentabike.ca; East Arch Plaza Bridge, 2 Rideau St; rentals per hr from $10; 7am-7pm Apr-Oct) will set you up with a bike and offer tips about scenic trails. The **Capital Information Kiosk** (p216) has bike maps.

CAR & MOTORCYCLE

There is free parking in World Exchange Plaza on Albert St on weekends. Hourly metered parking can be found throughout downtown and in parking lots charging around $20 a day. There are lots charging around $10 a day dotted around Centretown, including on Somerset St W east of Lyon St N.

During winter, overnight on-street parking is prohibited if there has been (or is likely to be) more than 7cm of snow – to allow the snowplows to come through. Contact the **City of Ottawa** (613-580-2400; ottawa.ca) with additional parking queries.

PUBLIC TRANSPORTATION

OC Transpo (613-741-4390; www.octranspo.com) operates Ottawa's useful bus network and a light-rail system known as the O-train. Bus rides cost $3.65 ($1.90 for children under 13) and you can pay on the bus. Make sure you have the exact change on you. You can also purchase a day pass ($8.50) from the driver, and buy books of six tickets ($9.90) at convenience stores. Adults pay $5.15 on express routes. Be sure to take your ticket when boarding and paying; it allows you to transfer to other buses for a period of 90 minutes. The **Capital Information Kiosk** (p216) has bus maps.

The O-train does not currently stop downtown. It will become more useful when the Confederation Line is completed in 2018, providing a link between Parliament and the VIA Rail Station.

Ottawa and Hull/Gatineau operate separate bus systems. A transfer is valid from one system to the other, but may require an extra payment.

Québec

Includes ➡

Best Places to Eat

- ➡ L'Express (p249)
- ➡ Liverpool House (p248)
- ➡ Manoir Hovey (p268)
- ➡ Chez Boulay (p283)
- ➡ Vent du Large (p325)

Best Places to Sleep

- ➡ Auberge Saint-Antoine (p281)
- ➡ Hôtel Gault (p244)
- ➡ Maison Historique James Thompson (p279)
- ➡ Hôtel Le Germain (p246)
- ➡ Auberge Festive Sea Shack (p311)

Why Go?

Québec truly feels like a country within a country, an island of linguistic and cultural identity floating on the greater Canadian sea. Of course, this *is* Canada, with all the interplay of vast wilderness and cosmopolitanism implied, but Québec's embrace of *terroir*, its language, its passion for everything, from winter snow to wine to gastronomy, is something else, an 'else' that encompasses identities both distinctly North American and European.

Montréal and Québec City are bustling metropolises with a perfect mixture of sophistication and playfulness, and history-soaked preserved quarters tucked away around town. The rustic allurements of old Québec are scattered among the Eastern Townships, and produce from bucolic Charlevoix graces the tables of the region's stellar restaurants. Past these creature comforts is the raw outdoors: the jagged coasts of the unblemished Gaspé Peninsula, the vast taiga and tundra of the North Shore, and the windswept isolation of the Îles de la Madeleine.

When to Go

Montréal

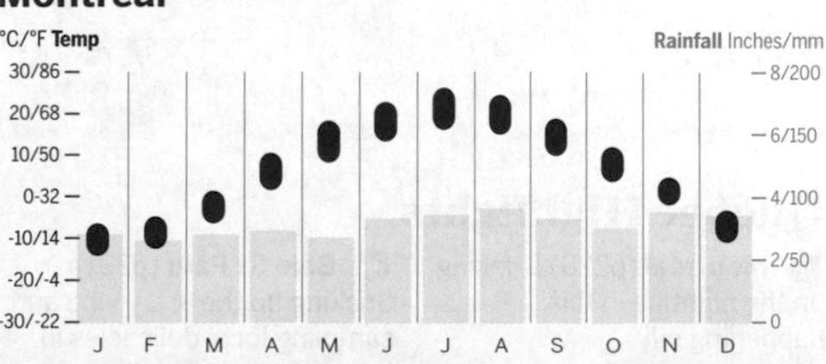

Dec & Jan Head to Mont-Tremblant – one of North America's best ski hills.

Feb Bundle up and join in the frigid festivities in Québec City's fete of the year, Carnaval.

Jul Montréal's summer-long party gets under way with the Festival International de Jazz.

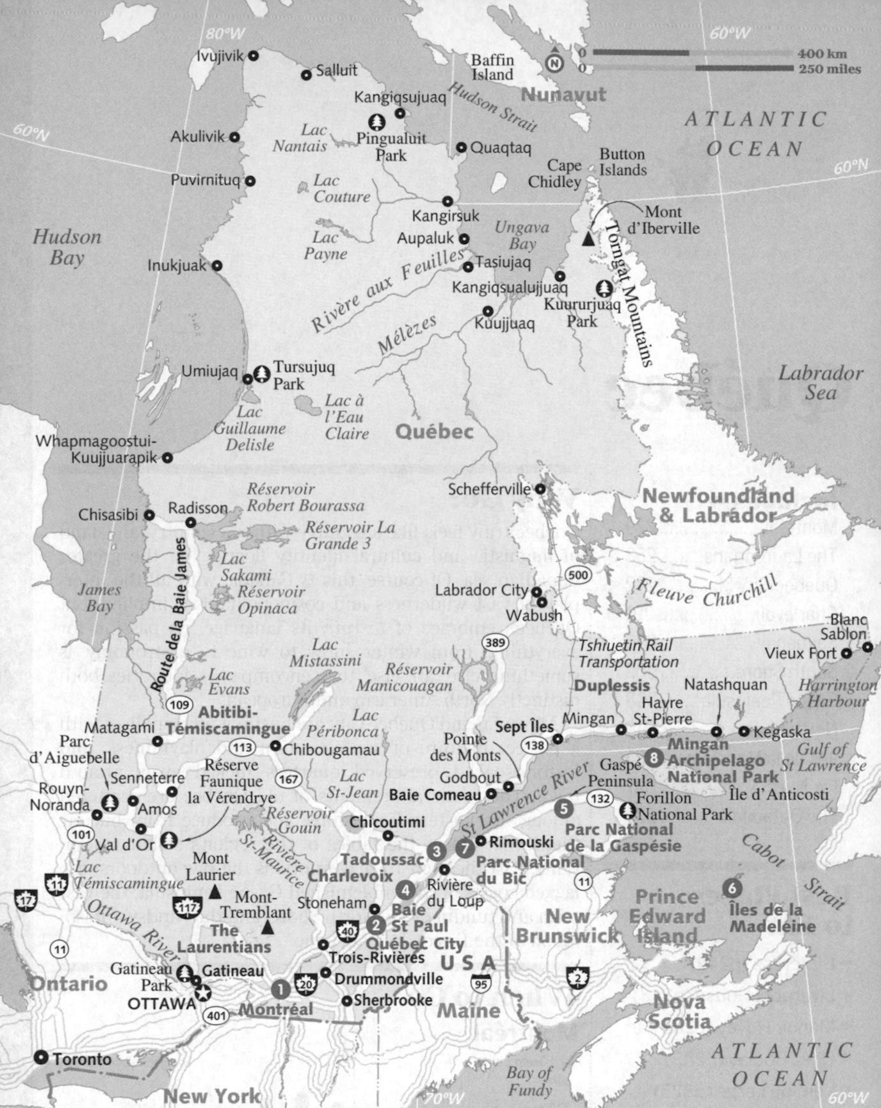

Québec Highlights

❶ **Montréal** (p229) Drinking up the nightlife in this happening city.

❷ **Québec City** (p272) Savoring the unparalleled culture, history and charm of this walled city.

❸ **Tadoussac** (p296) Getting sprayed by whales in the Saguenay River fjord.

❹ **Baie St Paul** (p291) Soaking up the artsy vibe and sampling local delicacies in this attractive, little town.

❺ **Parc National de la Gaspésie** (p312) Hiking the stunning peaks above the tree line in this pretty national park.

❻ **Îles de la Madeleine** (p324) Enjoying Acadian music and steaming fish pie in this stringy archipelago.

❼ **Parc National du Bic** (p306) Getting back to nature in this spectacular place.

❽ **Mingan Archipelago National Park** (p322) Sea kayaking amid these remote, sculpted islands.

History

Québec has had a tumultuous history and, by Canadian standards, a very long and complicated one.

At the time of European exploration, the entire region was fully settled and controlled by various Aboriginal groups, all of whom are resident today, including the Mohawks along the St Lawrence River, the Cree above them, the Innu still further north and east, and the Inuit in the remote far north. Relations between the Europeans and Aboriginal groups were tense at times but generally amicable, and the two groups forged a relationship based on commerce (specifically the fur trade), not politics.

French explorer Jacques Cartier landed in what is now Québec City and Montréal in 1535. Samuel de Champlain, also of France, first heard and recorded the word '*kebec*' (an Algonquian word meaning 'where the river narrows') when he founded a settlement at Québec City some 70 years later, in 1608.

Throughout the rest of the 17th century, the French and English skirmished over control of Canada, but where the British began settling large colonies across what would become the USA, the French Canadian population remained largely sparse. In 1759, the English, with a victory on the Plains of Abraham at Québec City, assumed a leadership role in the new colony of Canada. From that point onward, French political influence in the New World waned.

When thousands of British Loyalists fled the American Revolution in the 1770s, the new colony divided into Upper (today's Ontario) and Lower (now Québec) Canada; almost all the French settled in the latter region. Power struggles between the two groups continued through the 1800s, with Lower Canada joining the Canadian confederation as Québec in 1867.

The 20th century saw Québec change from a rural, agricultural society to an urban, industrialized one, but it continued to be educationally and culturally based upon the Catholic Church, which wielded immense power and still does (about 90% of the population today is Roman Catholic).

The tumultuous 1960s brought the so-called 'Quiet Revolution,' during which time all aspects of Francophone society were scrutinized and overhauled. Political systems were reorganized, massive secularization and unionization took place, and a welfare state was created. Intellectuals and extremists alike debated the prospect of independence from Canada, as Québécois began to assert their sense of nationhood.

Formed in 1968, the pro-independence Parti Québécois came to power in 1976, headed by the charismatic René Lévesque. Since then, two referendums have returned 'No' votes on the question of separating from Canada. In the new century, the notion of an independent Québec is less attractive to a younger generation with more global concerns.

FAST FACTS

- Population: 8,215,000
- Area: 1,540,687 sq km
- Capital: Québec City
- Quirky fact: the Château Frontenac in Québec City is the most photographed hotel in the world.

Local Culture

Québécois are a true hybrid of Europe and North America. In the cities, folks Instagram their dinners; in rural areas, they may drive a Ford F-350 with camo plates. But across the board, people take life a little slower, and take time to enjoy a coffee, beer or wine with their meals. In general, people here are friendly but not overbearing; there is a reserve to locals that feels both Continental European and rooted in the cold climate. The French language and its preservation is an issue near and dear to many Québécois, including those raised in more Anglophone-friendly Montréal.

Land & Climate

The Laurentians form a jagged, pine-clad arc of rugged highlands giving way to the windswept shores and forest-and-tundra vastness of the North Coast. Sheer cliffs plunge into the blue ocean off the Gaspé Peninsula, while in Charlevoix a patchwork of farms gives way to sweeping bays on the St Lawrence. Then there is the Far North – wild, barely populated, a land of lichen-studded tundra and wind-carved mountains.

In terms of temperature, the province is saddled with extremes. Montréal and Québec City can go from 40°C to -40°C in six months, and May could see a dump of snow. Generally, the summers are comfortably warm, although high humidity can make Montréal pretty steamy. Winters are very snowy, but usually bright, sunny and dry.

Parks

The province's protected areas are a highlight of any trip to Québec. In addition to preserving regions of remarkable beauty, they offer a host of invigorating activities, including canoeing, kayaking, rafting, hiking, cycling and camping in the wild. Forillon National Park and Saguenay, Bic, Mont-Tremblant and Gaspésie Provincial Parks are especially recommended.

Parks Canada (☎888-773-8888; www.pc.gc.ca) administers three national parks, 24 national historic sites and one National Marine Conservation Area in Québec. The historic sites are mostly day-use areas and reveal fascinating bits of history.

The **Société des Établissements de Plein Air du Québec** (Sépaq; ☎800-665-6527; www.sepaq.com) oversees Québec's 27 provincial parks and 15 wildlife reserves – confusingly, it refers to many provincial parks as 'national.' The parks, which range from beaches and bird sanctuaries to rugged gorges, provide some outstanding camping, wildlife-viewing, eco-adventures and other outdoor recreation. If there is no one staffing a provincial park entrance (often the case outside of summer), you are expected to pay the entrance fee and leave half of the receipt in a provided envelope. You retain the other half as proof of admission.

Réserve fauniques (wildlife reserves) conserve and protect the environment but also make these spaces publicly accessible. Hunters and fishers use the reserves (permits required), but more and more visitors are discovering them as less crowded alternatives to national and provincial parks.

Getting There & Around

Québec is easily accessible by air, bus, car and train. It shares borders with the US states of New York, Vermont, New Hampshire and Maine.

AIR

Québec's main airport is in Montréal, although Québec City is also busy. Carriers serving the province include Air Canada, Air Canada Express, Air France, Porter Airlines, Pascan and bargain airlines Air Transat and WestJet. Traveling to the Far North are **First Air** (☎800-267-1247; www.firstair.ca), **Air Inuit** (☎800-361-2965; www.airinuit.com) and **Air Creebec** (☎800-567-6567; www.aircreebec.ca). **Air Canada Express** (☎888-247-2262; www.aircanada.com) covers the North Shore and Îles de la Madeleine from Québec City and Montréal.

BOAT

There are numerous ferry services across the St Lawrence River, as well as to islands in the Gulf, such as the Îles de la Madeleine, and along the remote Lower North Shore toward Labrador.

BUS

Maritime Bus connects the province with Atlantic Canada, and Greyhound Canada and Megabus link Québec City and Montréal with Ontario. From the USA, Greyhound operates five daily bus services between Montréal and New York City. The province is particularly well served by bus lines.

Autobus Maheux (☎819-825-4767; www.autobusmaheux.qc.ca)

Galland (☎450-687-8666; www.galland-bus.com)

Greyhound Canada (☎800-661-8747; www.greyhound.ca)

Intercar (☎800-806-2167; www.intercar.qc.ca)

Limocar (☎866-692-8899; www.limocar.ca)

QUÉBEC ITINERARIES

One Day

Start with brunch in Montréal at **L'Express** (p249) and work the calories off on a hike up **Parc du Mont-Royal** (p239). Descend through **Mile End** (p238) or the **Plateau Mont-Royal** (p234), where you'll be spoiled for choice for dinner and drinks.

Three Days

Limit your time savoring Montréal's chilled-out vibe to one day, and then drive through the Laurentians to **Mont-Tremblant** (p260). Leave a day to stroll within **Québec City's walls** (p273) in the Old Upper Town, before searching for the ultimate *table d'hôte* in the **Old Lower Town** (p283).

One Week

Follow the three-day itinerary, then ramble through **Charlevoix** (p291) en route to the **Saguenay River** for two days. Stop for lunch in **Baie St Paul** (p291) or **La Malbaie** (p294). Spend the last two nights in welcoming **Tadoussac** (p296), whale-watching or cruising the fjord.

RESOURCES

Lonely Planet (www.lonelyplanet.com/canada/quebec) Destination information, hotel bookings, traveler forum and more.

Montréal Lifestyle (www.cultmontreal.com) Arts, culture and nightlife info for Montréal.

Tourism Montréal (www.tourisme-montreal.org) Official visitor gateway for Montréal.

Tourism Québec (www.quebecoriginal.com) This official tourism site is a great source for info on lodging and food.

Tourism Québec City (www.quebecregion.com) A good intro to Québec City and its environs.

Maritime Bus (☎ in New Brunswick 800-575-1807; www.maritimebus.com)
Megabus (☎ 866-488-4452; www.ca.megabus.com)
Orléans Express (☎ 888-999-3977; www.orleansexpress.com)

CAR & MOTORCYCLE

Continental US highways link directly with their Canadian counterparts at numerous border crossings. These roads connect to the Trans-Canada Hwy (Hwy 40 within Québec), which runs directly through Montréal and Québec City.

Highways throughout the province are good. In the far eastern and northern sections, however, slow, winding, even nonpaved sections are typical, and services may be few. For road conditions – a serious factor in winter – call ☎ 888-355-0511. Note that turning right at red lights is forbidden in some areas (always indicated by signage), especially on the island of Montréal and in Québec City.

The ride-share agency **Kangaride** (☎ 855-526-4274; www.kangaride.com) offers an inexpensive way to travel within Québec by linking up drivers and paying passengers headed the same way.

If you're visiting either Montréal or Québec City, consider leaving the car at home. Unlike other North American cities, Québec's metropolises are easily navigated on foot, with bustling sidewalks lined with outdoor cafes.

TRAIN

VIA Rail (☎ 888-842-7245, in Montréal ☎ 514-989-2626; www.viarail.ca) has fast and frequent services along the Québec City–Windsor corridor, via Montréal, and services the South Shore and Gaspésie. From the USA, **Amtrak** (☎ 800-872-7245; www.amtrak.com) trains run once daily between Montréal and New York City.

MONTRÉAL

POP 4.1 MILLION

Historically, Montréal – the only de facto bilingual city on the continent – has been torn right in half, the 'Main' (Blvd St-Laurent) being the dividing line between the east-end Francophones and the west-side Anglos. Today French pockets dot both sides of the map, a new wave of English-speaking Canadians have taken residence in some formerly French enclaves and thanks to constant waves of immigration, it's not uncommon for Montréalers to speak not one, or two, but three languages in their daily life. With the new generation concerned more with global issues (namely the environment), language battles have become so passé.

One thing not up for debate is what makes Montréal so irresistible. It's a secret blend of French-inspired joie de vivre and cosmopolitan dynamism that has come together to foster a flourishing arts scene, an indie rock explosion, a medley of world-renowned boutique hotels, the Plateau's extraordinary cache of swank eateries and a cool Parisian vibe that pervades every terrasse (patio) in the Quartier Latin. It's easy to imagine you've been transported to a distant locale, where hedonism is the national mandate. Only the stunning vista of a stereotypical North American skyline from Parc du Mont Royal's Kondiaronk Lookout will ground you.

History

In May 1642, a small fleet of boats sailed up the St Lawrence River. The few dozen missionaries aboard had survived a cold winter crossing the fierce Atlantic Ocean from their native France. Finally they had reached the spot their fellow countryman, explorer Jacques Cartier, had stumbled across over a century earlier. Led by Paul Chomedey de Maisonneuve, the pioneers went ashore and began building a small settlement they called Ville-Marie, the birthplace of Montréal.

Ville-Marie soon blossomed into a major fur-trading center and exploration base, despite fierce resistance from the local Iroquois. Skirmishes continued until the signing of a peace treaty in 1701. The city remained French until the 1763 Treaty of Paris, which saw France cede Canada to Great Britain. In 1775, American revolutionaries briefly occupied the city, but left after failing to convince the Québecois to join forces with them against the British.

Despite surrendering its pole position in the fur trade to Hudson Bay in the 1820s, Montréal boomed throughout the 19th century. Industrialization got seriously under way after the construction of the railway and the Canal de Lachine, which in turn attracted masses of immigrants.

After WWI the city sashayed through a period as 'Sin City' as hordes of Americans seeking fun flooded across the border to escape Prohibition. By the time mayor Jean Drapeau took the reins, Montréal was ripe for an extreme makeover. During his long tenure (1954–57 and 1960–86), the city gained the métro system, many of downtown's high-rise offices, the underground city and the Place des Arts. Drapeau also twice managed to firmly train the world's spotlight on Montréal: in 1967 for the World Expo and in 1976 for the Olympic Games.

Montréal has been enjoying a consistently positive growth rate for the past two decades, faring extremely well during the global economic recession thanks to a boom in the high-tech sector.

Sights

First on most itineraries is Old Montréal, where the heart of the city's history and grandeur can be chased through a labyrinth of winding lanes. Waterfront attractions in the Old Port have benefited immensely from recent rejuvenation, and across the water the attractions and trails of Parc Jean-Drapeau (p239) make a great summer escape from the urban jungle. Downtown encompasses stellar museums and universities, while the bohemian Mile End and Plateau Mont-Royal districts are perfect for meandering. The Village and Quartier Latin jolt awake at nighttime. Just outside the city, the Olympic Park and Lachine hold the greatest sightseeing appeal. From the panorama at Mont Royal it's possible to take it all in at once.

Old Montréal

The oldest section of the city is a warren of crooked cobblestone lanes flanked by colonial and Victorian stone houses filled with intimate restaurants, galleries and boutiques. A stroll around here will delight romantics and architecture fans, especially at night when the most beautiful facades are illuminated. And the waterfront is never far away.

Old Montréal is anchored by lively Place Jacques Cartier and dignified Place d'Armes, which are linked by busy Rue Notre-Dame. The southern end of Place Jacques Cartier gives way to Rue St-Paul, the district's prettiest and oldest street.

★**Basilique Notre-Dame** CHURCH
(Map p232; ☎514-842-2925; www.basiliquenddm.org; 110 Rue Notre-Dame Ouest; adult/child $5/4; ⏲8am-4:30pm Mon-Fri, to 4pm Sat, 12:30-4pm Sun)

MONTRÉAL IN...

One Day

Start your day in **Mile End** (p238), partaking in a local ritual – a long and leisurely brunch. Hike up **Mont Royal** (p239), stopping to catch your breath and snap the cityscape from the **Kondiaronk Lookout** (p239) before ending up in the **Plateau Mont-Royal** (p234) for dinner and evening entertainment.

Two Days

Follow the one-day itinerary, and on day two begin by exploring the cobblestone alleys of **Old Montréal**. Get a dose of history at **Musée d'Archéologie et d'Histoire Pointe-à-Callière** (p231) or soak up some culture at **Musée des Beaux-Arts** (p269). Head to **Little Italy** (p238) for dinner then sample the club scene in **The Village** (p236).

Four Days

Start day three at **Olympic Park** (p238). If the weather is behaving, follow up a visit to the **Biodôme** (p239) with a trip to the **Jardin Botanique** (p238) for a more fragrant affair.

On the last day, hit **Marché Atwater** (p234) for picnic supplies, then rent bicycles for a cruise along **Canal de Lachine** (p242) or take a jet boat ride on the **Lachine Rapids**.

After dinner at a big shot such as **Toqué!** (p247) or **L'Express** (p249), head to the glitzy **Casino de Montréal** (p241) to blow the last of your holiday money.

Montréal

Montréal's famous landmark, Notre-Dame Basilica, is a visually pleasing if slightly gaudy symphony of carved wood, paintings, gilded sculptures and stained-glass windows. Built in 1829 on the site of an older and smaller church, it also sports a famous Casavant organ and the **Gros Bourdon**, said to be the biggest bell in North America.

The basilica made headlines in 1994 when singer Céline Dion was married under its soaring ceiling, and again in 2000 when Jimmy Carter and Fidel Castro shared pall-bearing honors at the state funeral of former Canadian Prime Minister Pierre Trudeau.

A popular place for regular Montréalers to tie the knot is the much smaller **Chapelle du Sacré Coeur** behind the main altar. Rebuilt in a hodgepodge of historic and contemporary styles after a 1978 fire, its most eye-catching element is the floor-to-ceiling bronze altarpiece.

Place d'Armes HISTORIC SITE
(Map p232; Ⓜ Place-d'Armes) This open square is framed by some of the finest buildings in Old Montréal, including its oldest bank, first skyscraper and Basilique Notre-Dame. The square's name references the bloody battles that took place here as religious settlers and Aboriginal tribes clashed over control of what would become Montréal. At its center stands the **Monument Maisonneuve**, dedicated to city founder Paul de Chomedey, *sieur* de Maisonneuve.

Musée d'Archéologie et d'Histoire Pointe-à-Callière MUSEUM
(Museum of Archaeology & History; Map p232; ☎514-872-9150; www.pacmuseum.qc.ca; 350 Pl Royale; adult/child $20/8; ⏰10am-6pm Mon-Fri, 11am-6pm Sat & Sun; 👪; Ⓜ Place-d'Armes) One of Montréal's most fascinating sites, this museum takes visitors on a historical journey through the centuries, beginning with the early days of Montréal. Visitors should start

Old Montréal

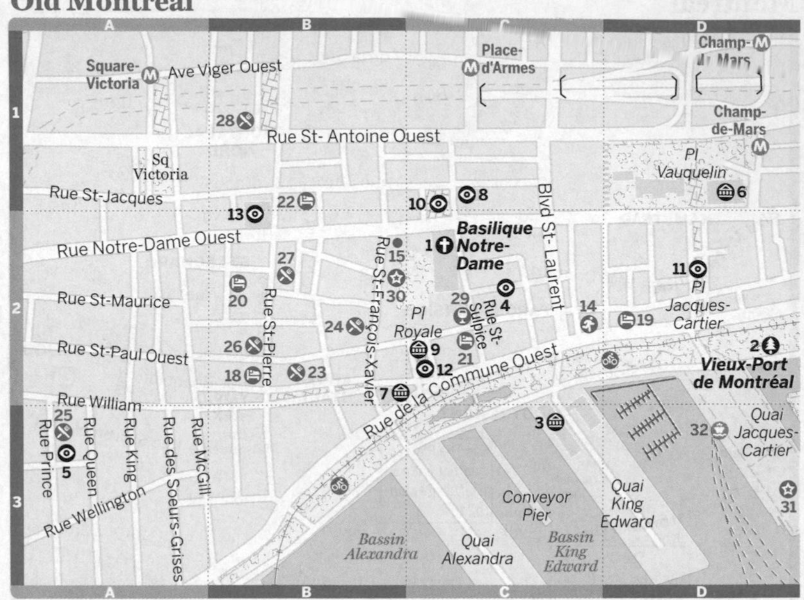

Old Montréal

Top Sights
1 Basilique Notre-Dame........ C2
2 Vieux-Port de Montréal........ D2

Sights
3 Centre des Sciences de Montréal........ C3
4 Cours Le Royer........ C2
5 Fonderie Darling........ A3
6 Hôtel de Ville........ D1
7 Musée d'Archéologie et d'Histoire Pointe-à-Callière........ B2
8 New York Life Building........ C1
9 Old Customs House........ C2
10 Place d'Armes........ C1
11 Place Jacques-Cartier........ D2
12 Place Royale........ C2
13 Royal Bank Tower........ B2

Activities, Courses & Tours
14 Ça Roule Montréal........ C2
15 Guidatour........ B2
Le Bateau Mouche........ (see 32)
Le Petit Navire........ (see 32)
16 MTL Zipline........ E2
17 Patinoire du Bassin Bonsecours........ E3

Sleeping
18 Auberge Alternative........ B2
19 Auberge du Vieux-Port........ D2
20 Hôtel Gault........ B2
21 Hôtel Nelligan........ C2
22 L Hotel........ B1
Lofts du Vieux-Port........ (see 19)

Eating
23 Barroco........ B2
24 Garde-Manger........ B2
25 Le Serpent........ A3
26 Olive + Gourmando........ B2
27 Titanic........ B2
28 Toqué!........ B1

Drinking & Nightlife
29 Philémon........ C2
Terrasse Nelligan........ (see 21)

Entertainment
30 Centaur Theatre........ B2
31 Cirque du Soleil........ D3

Transport
32 Ferries........ D3

with *Yours Truly, Montréal,* an 18-minute multimedia show that covers the arrival of the Amerindians, the founding of Montréal and other key moments. Afterward, head to the **archaeological crypt** where you can explore the remains of the city's ancient sewage and river system, and the foundations of its first buildings and public square.

Place Jacques-Cartier SQUARE
(Map p232; ; Champ-de-Mars) FREE The liveliest spot in Old Montréal, this gently inclined square hums with performance artists, street musicians and the animated chatter from terrace restaurants linings its borders. A public market was set up here after a château burned down in 1803. At its top end stands the **Colonne Nelson**, a monument erected to Admiral Lord Nelson after his defeat of Napoleon's fleet at Trafalgar.

Hôtel de Ville HISTORIC BUILDING
(City Hall; Map p232; 275 Rue Notre-Dame Est; 8:30am-5pm; Champ-de-Mars) FREE Montréal's handsome City Hall was built between 1872 and 1878, then rebuilt after a fire in 1926. Far from being a humdrum administrative center, it's actually steeped in local lore. Most famously, it's where French leader Charles de Gaulle took to the balcony in 1967 and yelled to the crowds outside *'Vive le Québec libre!'* ('Long live free Québec!'). Those four words fueled the fires of Québécois separatism and strained relations with Ottawa for years.

★ **Vieux-Port de Montréal** PARK
(Map p232;) Montréal's Old Port has morphed into a park and fun zone paralleling the mighty St Lawrence River for 2.5km and punctuated by four grand *quais*. Locals and visitors alike come here for strolling, cycling and in-line skating. Cruise boats, ferries, jet boats and speedboats all depart for tours from various docks. In winter, you can cut a fine figure on an outdoor ice-skating rink.

Centre des Sciences de Montréal MUSEUM
(Montréal Science Centre; Map p232; 514-496-4724; www.montrealsciencecentre.com; King Edward Pier; adult/teen/child $15/13/8.50, with IMAX 3D movie $23/19.50/14; 9am-4pm Mon-Fri, 10am-5pm Sat & Sun; ; Place-d'Armes) This sleek, glass-covered science center houses virtual and interactive games, technology exhibits and an 'immersion theater' that puts a video game on giant screens. Note that there is a huge range of different admission prices depending on which combinations of films and/or exhibits you want to take in. The center also has an IMAX cinema that shows vivid nature and science films.

Downtown

Montréal's modern downtown has a North American look, with wide thoroughfares chopping a forest of skyscrapers into a grid pattern. At street level you'll find some of the city's most beautiful churches, striking buildings, museums, green spaces and major shopping areas. You'll find that an almost Latin spirit pervades the cafes, restaurants and bars, especially along Rue Crescent.

★ **Musée des Beaux-Arts de Montréal** MUSEUM
(Museum of Fine Arts; Map p236; www.mbam.qc.ca; 1380 Rue Sherbrooke Ouest; permanent collection adult/under 13yr $12/free, special exhibitions $20/12; 10am-5pm, to 9pm Wed special exhibitions only; Guy-Concordia) A must for art lovers, the Museum of Fine Arts has amassed several millennia worth of paintings, sculpture, decorative arts, furniture, prints, drawings and photographs. European heavyweights include Rembrandt, Picasso and Monet, but the museum really shines when it comes to Canadian art. Highlights include works by Jean-Baptiste Roy-Audy and Paul Kane, landscapes by the Group of Seven and abstractions by Jean-Paul Riopelle.

There is also a fair amount of Inuit and aboriginal artifacts and lots of fancy decorative knickknacks, including Japanese incense boxes and Victorian chests.

Exhibits are spread across the classical, marble-clad Michal and Renata Hornstein Pavilion and the crisp, contemporary Jean-Noël Desmarais Pavilion across the street.

MONTRÉAL MUSEUM PASS

Custom-made for culture buffs, this handy **pass** (www.museesmontreal.org; $80) is the most cost-effective way to access 41 of Montréal's museums over a three-day period – the price includes unlimited public transportation during this time.

Chinatown AREA

(Map p236) Although this neighborhood, perfectly packed into a few easily navigable streets, has no sites per se, it's a nice area for lunch or for shopping for quirky knickknacks. The main thoroughfare, Rue de la Gauchetière, between Blvd St-Laurent and Rue Jeanne Mance, is enlivened with Taiwanese bubble-tea parlors, Hong Kong–style bakeries and Vietnamese soup restaurants. The public square, **Place Sun-Yat-Sen**, attracts crowds of elderly Chinese and the occasional gaggle of Falun Gong practitioners.

Centre Canadien d'Architecture MUSEUM

(CCA; Map p236; www.cca.qc.ca; 1920 Rue Baile; adult/child $10/free, 5:30-9pm Thu free; ⌚11am-6pm Wed-Sun, to 9pm Thu; Ⓜ Georgest-Vanier) A must for architecture fans, this center is equal parts museum and research institute. The building incorporates **Shaughnessy House**, a 19th-century gray limestone treasure. Highlights in this section include the conservatory and an ornate sitting room with intricate woodwork and a massive stone fireplace. The exhibition galleries focus on remarkable architectural works of both local and international scope, with a particular focus on urban design.

The CCA's **sculpture garden** is located on a grassy lot overlooking south Montréal. There's also a busy, well-stocked bookstore.

Musée McCord MUSEUM

(McCord Museum of Canadian History; Map p236; ☎514-398-7100; www.mccord-museum.qc.ca; 690 Rue Sherbrooke Ouest; adult/student/child $14/8/free, special exhibitions extra $5, after 5pm Wed free; ⌚10am-6pm Tue, Thu & Fri, to 9pm Wed, to 5pm Sat & Sun; Ⓜ McGill) With hardly an inch to spare in its cramped but welcoming galleries, the McCord Museum of Canadian History houses thousands of artifacts and documents illustrating Canada's social, cultural and archaeological history from the 18th century to the present day.

McGill University UNIVERSITY

(Map p236; ☎514-398-4455; www.mcgill.ca; 845 Rue Sherbrooke Ouest; Ⓜ McGill) Founded in 1828 by James McGill, a rich Scottish fur trader, McGill University is one of Canada's most prestigious learning institutions, with 39,000 students. The university's medical and engineering faculties have a fine reputation and many campus buildings are showcases of Victorian architecture. The campus, at the foot of Mont Royal, is rather nice for a stroll and also incorporates the **Musée Redpath** (Map p236; ☎514-398-4086; www.mcgill.ca/redpath/redpath-museum; 859 Rue Sherbrooke Ouest; by donation; ⌚9am-5pm Mon-Fri year-round, 1-5pm Sun summer, 11am-5pm Sun winter; Ⓜ McGill) FREE.

Musée d'Art Contemporain MUSEUM

(Map p240; ☎514-847-6226; www.macm.org; 185 Rue Ste-Catherine Ouest; adult/child $15/5, half-price 5-9pm Wed; ⌚11am-6pm Tue, to 9pm Wed-Fri, 10am-6pm Sat & Sun; Ⓜ Place-des-Arts) This showcase of modern Canadian and international art has eight galleries divided between past greats (since 1939) and exciting current developments. A weighty collection of 7600 permanent works includes Québécois legends Jean-Paul Riopelle, Paul-Émile Borduas and Geneviève Cadieux, but also temporary exhibitions of the latest trends in current art from Canadian and international artists. Forms range from traditional to new media, from painting, sculpture and prints to installation art, photography and video.

Marché Atwater MARKET

(☎514-937-7754; www.marchespublics-mtl.com; 138 Ave Atwater; ⌚7am-6pm Mon-Wed, to 7pm Thu, to 8pm Fri, to 5pm Sat & Sun; 👪; Ⓜ Atwater) Just off the Canal de Lachine (p242), this fantastic market has a mouthwatering assortment of fresh produce from local farms, excellent wines, crusty breads, fine cheeses and other delectable fare. The market's specialty shops operate year-round, while outdoor stalls open from March to October. It's all housed in a 1933 brick hall, topped with a clock tower, and little bouts of live music pop off with pleasing regularity. The grassy banks overlooking the canal are great for a picnic.

Plateau Mont-Royal

East of Parc du Mont-Royal, the Plateau is Montréal's youngest, liveliest and artiest neighborhood. Originally a working-class district, it changed its stripes in the 1960s and 70s, when writers, singers and other creative

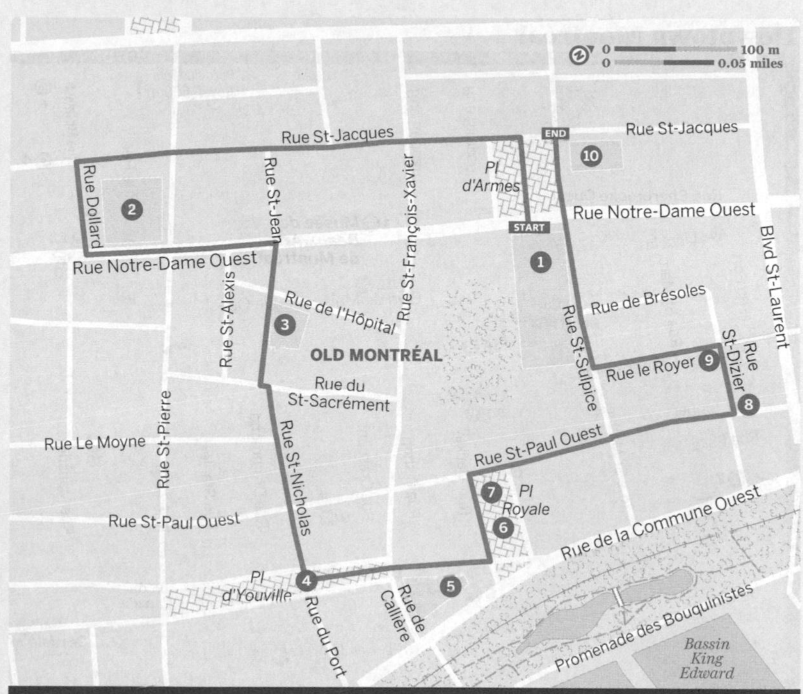

City Walk
Art & Architecture in Old Montréal

START BASILIQUE NOTRE-DAME
FINISH PLACE D'ARMES
LENGTH 2KM; TWO HOURS

On the southeast side of Place d'Armes is the city's most celebrated cathedral, magnificent **1 Basilique Notre-Dame** (p230). Inside is a spectacularly carved pulpit and richly hued stained-glass windows relating key events from the city's founding.

Head along Rue St-Jacques, once known as Canada's Wall St. Stop at the grand **2 Royal Bank Building**, Montréal's tallest edifice in 1928, to see its palatial interior.

Loop onto Rue Notre-Dame and down Rue St-Jean. On the corner of Rue de l'Hôpital, the **3 Lewis Building** has dragons and mischievous gargoyles on the facade. It was built for Cunard Shipping Lines, a steamship company founded in 1840.

A few blocks further is **4 Place d'Youville**, one of Old Montréal's prettiest squares. Some of the first Europeans settled here in 1642. An obelisk commemorates the city's founding.

Nearby is fascinating **5 Musée d'Archéologie et d'Histoire Pointe-à-Callière** (p231). Inside see the city's ancient foundations, or go to the top floor for fine views over the Old Port.

Across the road is the 1836 **6 Old Customs House**. It's in front of **7 Place Royale**, the early settlement's marketplace in the 17th and 18th centuries.

Walk down Rue St-Paul to see the 2006 bronze sculpture **8 Les Chuchoteuses** (the Whisperers), tucked in a corner near Rue St-Dizier. This was one of many projects to revitalize the old quarter.

Head up St-Dizier and turn left onto lovely **9 Cours Le Royer**, a tranquil pedestrian mall with fountains. On the north-side passageway is a stained-glass window of Jérôme Le Royer, one of Montréal's founders.

Turn right on Rue St-Sulpice and return to Place d'Armes. Note the **10 New York Life Building**, Montréal's first skyscraper (1888), eight stories tall.

Downtown Montréal

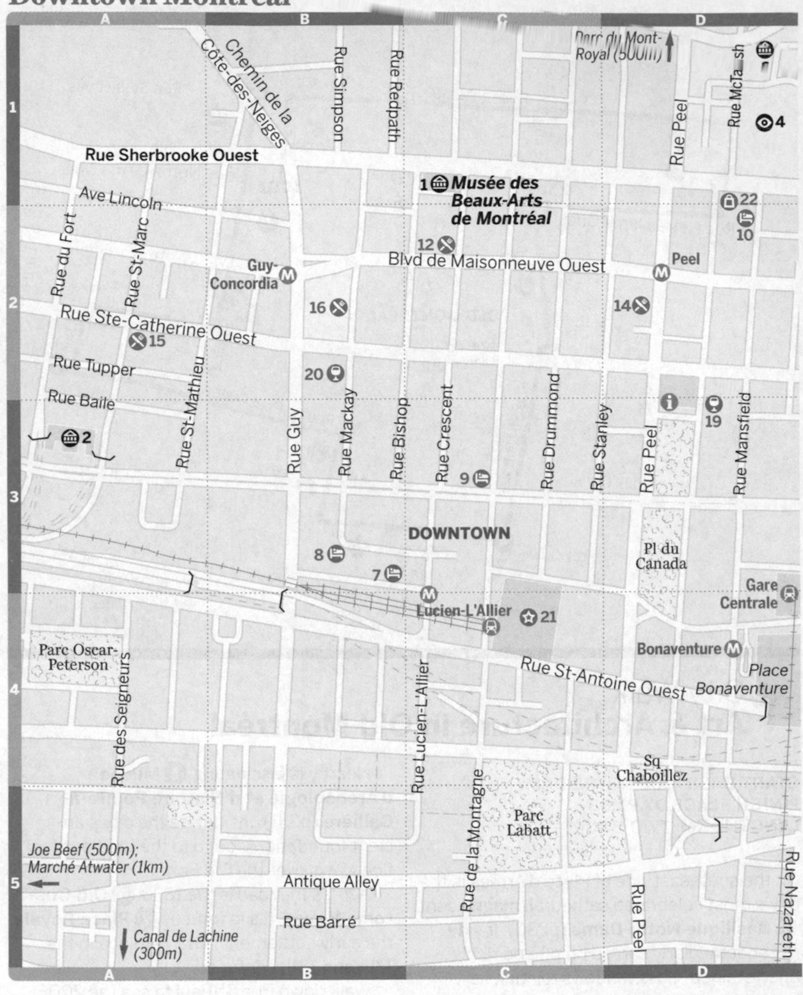

folk moved in. Among them was playwright Michel Tremblay, whose unvarnished look at some of the neighborhood's more colorful characters put the Plateau firmly on the path to hipdom.

These days, the Plateau is more gentrified than bohemian, but it's gentrified in a way that still *seems* pretty bohemian. As you stroll through its streets, admiring the signature streetscapes with their winding staircases, ornate wrought-iron balconies and Victorian roofs, you'll begin to understand why.

The Plateau is bordered roughly by Blvd St-Joseph to the north and Rue Sherbrooke to the south, Mont-Royal to the west and Ave de Lorimier to the east. The main drags are Blvd St-Laurent ('The Main'), Rue St-Denis and Ave du Mont-Royal, all lined with sidewalk cafes, restaurants, clubs and boutiques. Rue Prince Arthur, Montréal's quintessential hippie hangout in the 1960s, and Rue Duluth are alive with BYOW eateries.

Quartier Latin & The Village

The Quartier Latin is a boisterous neighborhood, a slightly grungy entertainment district made glitzy with an infusion of French

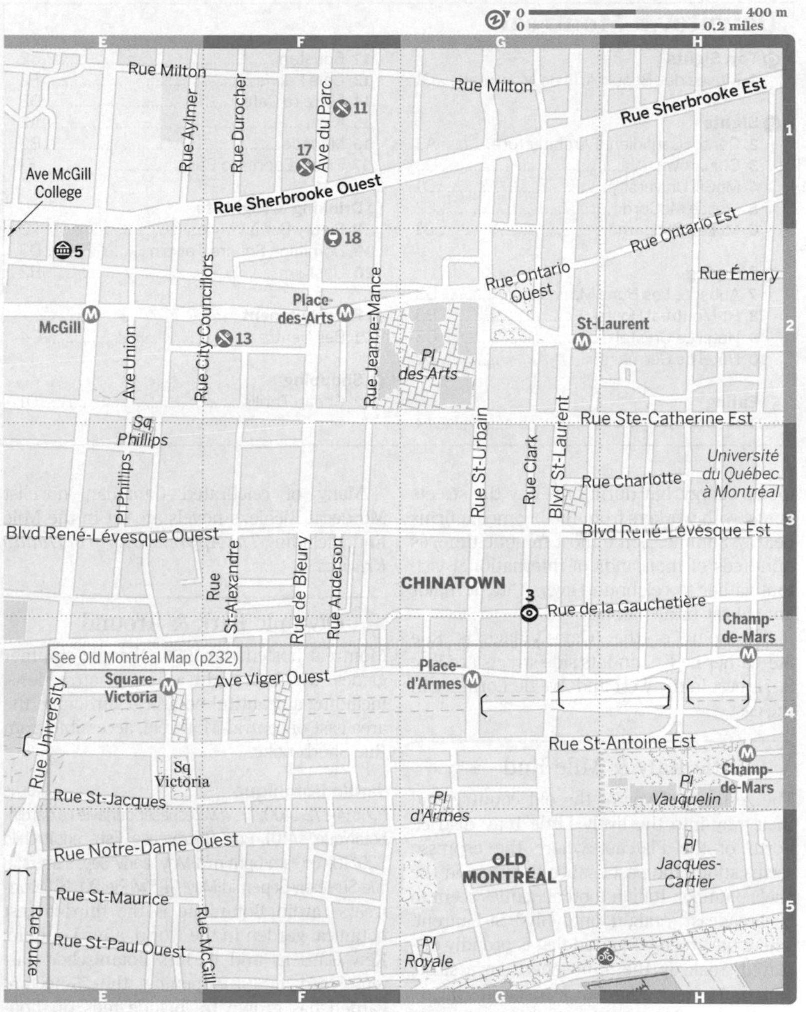

panache. The area blossomed with the arrival of the Université de Montréal in 1893, which drew several prestigious cultural institutions and the wealthy French bourgeoisie in its wake. Although it fell out of fashion after the university relocated to a larger campus north of Mont Royal and suffered from an influx of crime and neglect, things began looking up again when the Université du Québec was established in 1969.

A hotbed of activity, especially during the International Jazz Festival, Les FrancoFolies (p243) and Just for Laughs Festival (p243), the quarter bubbles 24 hours a day in its densely packed rows of bars, trendy bistros, music clubs and record shops. The Quartier Latin fits nicely within the borders of Rue Sanguinet, Rue Sherbrooke, Rue St-Hubert and Blvd René-Lévesque. Old Montréal is just south of here, best reached via Rue St-Denis.

Over the past decade or so, Montréal's gay community has breathed new life into The Village, a once poverty-stricken corner of the east end. Today, gay-friendly doesn't even begin to describe the neighborhood. People of all persuasions wander Rue Ste-Catherine and savor the joie de vivre in its cafes, bistros and discerning eateries. The nightlife is renowned

Downtown Montréal

Top Sights
1 Musée des Beaux-Arts de Montréal...... C1

Sights
2 Centre Canadien d'Architecture........... A3
3 Chinatown.. G3
4 McGill University.................................. D1
5 Musée McCord...................................... E2
6 Musée Redpath..................................... D1

Sleeping
7 Auberge Les Bons Matins..................... B3
8 HI-Montreal Hostel................................ B3
9 Hotel Le Crystal.................................... C3
10 Hôtel Le Germain................................ D2

Eating
11 Bistro Isakaya...................................... F1
12 Boustan.. C2
13 Café Parvis... F2
14 Ferreira Café.. D2
15 Kazu... A2
16 Myriade.. B2
17 Pikolo Espresso Bar............................. F1

Drinking & Nightlife
18 Bleury Bar à Vinyle............................... F2
19 Dominion Square Tavern...................... D3
20 Upstairs.. B2

Entertainment
21 Bell Centre... C4

Shopping
22 Cheap Thrills.. D1

for its energy, but during the day the streets bustle with workers from the big media firms nearby. Summer is the most frenetic time, as hundreds of thousands of international visitors gather to celebrate Divers/Cité, a major annual gay pride parade.

The spine of the (Gay) Village is Rue Ste-Catherine Est, and its side streets are Rue St-Hubert in the west and Ave de Lorimier in the east.

Little Italy & Mile End

The zest and flavor of the old country find their way into the lively Little Italy district, north of the Plateau, where the espresso seems stiffer, the pasta sauce thicker and the chefs plumper. Italian football games seem to be broadcast straight onto Blvd St-Laurent, where the green-white-red flag is proudly displayed. Soak up the atmosphere on a stroll, and don't miss Marché Jean-Talon (p256), which always hums with activity.

Dubbed the 'new Plateau' by the exodus of students and artists seeking a more affordable, less polished hangout, the Mile End district has all the coolness of its predecessor as well as two phenomenal bagel shops, upscale dining along Ave Laurier and tonnes of increasingly trendy hangouts at its epicenter: Rue St-Viateur and Blvd St-Laurent. The flavor here is multicultural – Hasidic Jews live side by side with immigrants from all over Europe – visible in the authentic Greek restaurants along Ave du Parc and Rue St-Urbain's neo-Byzantine Polish church, Église St-Michel.

Many of celebrated Canadian novelist Mordecai Richler's novels are set in the Mile End, including *The Apprenticeship of Duddy Kravitz*.

Olympic Park & Around

Montréal hosted the 1976 Olympic summer games, which brought a host of attractions, including a beautiful botanical garden, to the area east of central Montréal, accessible from Rue Sherbrooke.

Jardin Botanique GARDENS
(☎514-872-1400; www.espacepourlavie.ca/jardin-botanique; 4101 Rue Sherbrooke Est; adult/child $20/10; ⏲9am-6pm mid-May–early Sep, 9am-5pm Tue-Sun early Sep–mid-May; 👪; M Pie-IX) Montréal's Jardin Botanique is the third-largest botanical garden in the world, after London's Kew Gardens and Berlin's Botanischer Garten. Since its 1931 opening, the 75-hectare garden has grown to include tens of thousands of species in more than 20 thematic gardens, and its wealth of flowering plants is carefully managed to bloom in stages. The rose beds are a sight to behold in summertime. Climate-controlled greenhouses house cacti, banana trees and 1500 species of orchid. Bird-watchers should bring their binoculars.

A popular drawcard is the landscaped **Japanese Garden** with traditional pavilions, tearoom and art gallery; the bonsai 'forest' is the largest outside Asia. The twinning of Montréal with Shanghai gave impetus to plant a **Chinese Garden**. The ornamental penjing trees from Hong Kong are up to 100 years old. A Ming-dynasty garden is the feature around

Lac de Rêve (Dream Lake). In the northern part of the Jardin Botanique you'll find the **Frédérick Back Tree Pavilion**, a permanent exhibit on life in the 40-hectare arboretum. Displays include the yellow birch, part of Québec's official emblem. The **First Nations Garden** reveals the bonds between 11 Amerindian and Inuit nations and indigenous plants such as silver birches, maples, Labrador and tea. The **Orchidée Gift Shop** in the main building has a wonderful selection, including handmade jewelry and crafts, stuffed animals and beautifully illustrated books.

In fall (mid-September to early November) the Chinese Garden dons its most exquisite garb for the popular **Magic of Lanterns**, when hundreds of handmade silk lanterns sparkle at dusk.

Creepy-crawlies get top billing at the bug-shaped **Insectarium**. Most of the 250,000 specimens are mounted but live displays include bees and tarantulas.

The admission ticket includes the gardens, greenhouses and the Insectarium.

Biodôme MUSEUM

(514-868-3000; www.espacepourlavie.ca; 4777 Ave du Pierre de Coubertin; adult/child $20/10; 9am-6pm late Jun-Sep, 9am-5pm Tue-Sun rest of year; ; M Viau) At this captivating, kid-friendly exhibit you can amble through a rainforest, explore Antarctic islands, view rolling woodlands, take in aquatic life in the Gulf of St Lawrence, or wander along the raw Atlantic oceanfront – all without ever leaving the building. Be sure to dress in layers for the temperature swings. The five ecosystems house many thousands of animal and plant species; follow the self-guided circuit and you will see everything.

Planétarium LANDMARK

(514-868-3000; www.espacepourlavie.ca; 4801 Ave du Pierre de Coubertin; adult/child $20/10; 9am-5pm Sun, Tue & Wed, to 8pm Thu-Sat; M Viau) Opened in 2013, these futuristic metallic buildings bring a bit of the cosmos to Montréal, courtesy of two high-tech domed theaters and interactive exhibits on outer space. The round theaters have slightly different layouts and agendas: the Milky Way Theatre is more traditional, with comfy seats and films that give an eye-opening glimpse of what lies beyond earth, while the Chaos theater has bean bags and Adirondack chairs and takes a more philosophical look at the universe.

Parc Jean-Drapeau

Occupying the site of the hugely successful 1967 World's Fair, **Parc Jean-Drapeau** (www.parcjeandrapeau.com;) consists of two islands surrounded by the St Lawrence: Île Ste-Hélène and Île Notre-Dame. Although nature is the park's main appeal, it's also home to a Vegas-size casino, a Formula One racetrack and an old fort museum. In summer an **information kiosk** (514-872-6120; 8:30am-5pm Mon-Fri) opens near the Jean-Drapeau métro stop.

Drivers should take Pont (Bridge) Jacques Cartier for Île Ste-Hélène and Pont de la Concorde for Île Notre-Dame. Ferries (p257) shuttle pedestrians and bicycles to the park from the Old Port. Cyclists and in-line skaters can access the park by following the signs for Cité du Havre, then for Île Notre-Dame from the Canal de Lachine (p242) bike path.

Buses 777 (Casino) and 767/769 (La Ronde) run between the islands.

DON'T MISS

PARC DU MONT-ROYAL

Montréalers are proud of their 'mountain,' the work of New York Central Park designer Frederick Law Olmsted. **Parc du Mont-Royal** (514-843-8240; www.lemontroyal.qc.ca;) is a sprawling, leafy playground that's perfect for cycling, jogging, horseback riding, picnicking and, in winter, cross-country skiing and tobogganing. In fine weather, enjoy panoramic views from **Kondiaronk Lookout** near **Chalet du Mont-Royal**, a grand old stone villa that hosts big-band concerts in summer, or from **Observatoire de l'Est**, a favorite rendezvous for lovebirds.

It takes about 30 minutes to walk between the two. En route you'll spot the landmark 40m-high **Cross of Montréal** (1924), which is illuminated at night. It's there to commemorate city founder Maisonneuve, who single-handedly carried a wooden cross up the mountain in 1643 to give thanks to God for sparing his fledgling village from flooding.

The Plateau, Quartier Latin & The Village

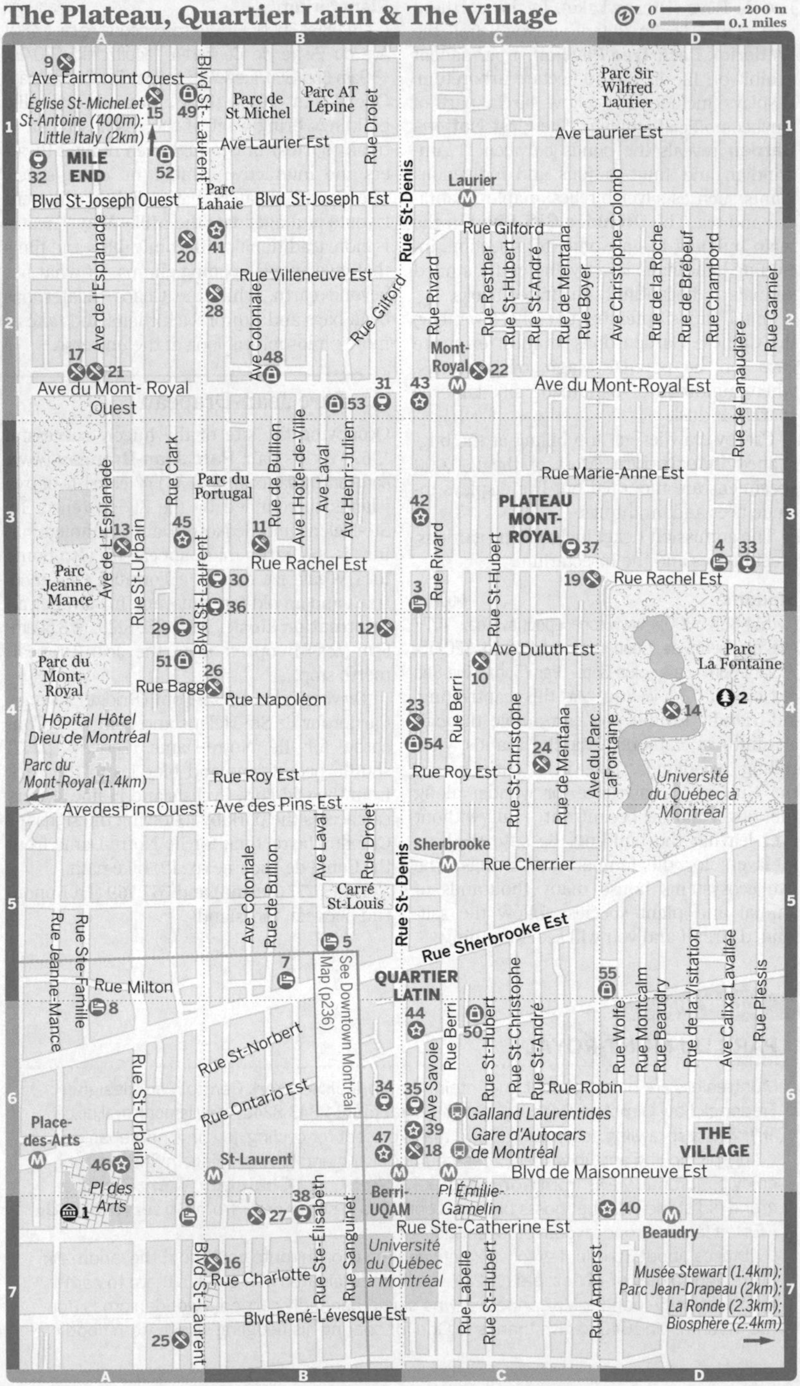

The Plateau, Quartier Latin & The Village

Sights
1 Musée d'Art Contemporain....A7
2 Parc La Fontaine....D4

Sleeping
3 Anne Ma Soeur Anne....C3
4 Auberge De La Fontaine....D3
5 Gingerbread Manor....B5
6 L'Abri du Voyageur....A7
7 Le Gîte du Plateau Mont-Royal....B5
8 Trylon Apartments....A6

Eating
9 Arts Cafe....A1
10 Au Pied de Cochon....C4
11 Cafe Névé....B3
12 ChuChai....B4
13 Crudessence....A3
14 Espace La Fontaine....D4
15 Fairmount Bagel....A1
16 Foodlab....B7
17 Hà....A2
18 Juliette et Chocolat....C6
19 La Banquise....C3
20 La Sala Rosa....A2
21 Le Filet....A2
22 Les Folies....C2
23 L'Express....C4
24 L'Gros Luxe....C4
25 Mai Xiang Yuan....A7
26 Moishe's....B4
27 Ong Ca Can....B7
28 Robin des Bois....B2

Drinking & Nightlife
29 Barfly....A4
30 Big in Japan....B3
31 Bily Kun....B2
32 La Buvette Chez Simone....A1
33 Le Lab....D3
34 Le Saint Sulpice....B6
35 L'Île Noire....C6
36 Majestique....B3
37 Pub Pit Caribou....C3
38 Pub Ste-Élisabeth....B7

Entertainment
39 Bistro à Jojo....C6
40 Cabaret Mado....D7
41 Casa del Popolo....B2
42 Dièse Onze....C3
Foufounes Électriques....(see 27)
43 La Rockette....C2
44 Le 4e Mur....C6
45 Le Divan Orange....A3
46 Orchestre Symphonique de Montréal....A6
47 Théâtre St-Denis....B6

Shopping
48 Artpop....B2
49 Au Papier Japonais....A1
50 Aux Quatre Points Cardinaux....C6
51 Friperie St-Laurent....A4
52 Jet-Setter....A1
53 Le Port de Tête....B2
54 Librairie Planète BD....C4
55 Marché St-Jacques....D5

La Ronde AMUSEMENT PARK
(☎514-397-2000; www.laronde.com; 22 Chemin Macdonald; adult/child $64/47; ⏱hours vary; P 👪) Québec's largest amusement park, La Ronde has a battery of impressive rides, including **Le Monstre**, the world's highest double wooden roller coaster, and **Le Vampire**, a corkscrew roller coaster with gut-wrenching turns. For a more peaceful experience, there's a Ferris wheel and a gentle minirail that offers views of the river and city.

Musée Stewart MUSEUM
(☎514-861-6701; www.stewart-museum.org; 20 Chemin du Tour de l'Île; adult/child $10/free; ⏱10am-5pm Tue-Sun; 👪) Inside the old Arsenal British garrison (where troops were stationed in the 19th century), this beautifully renovated museum displays relics from Canada's past in its permanent exhibition, History and Memory. In summer, there are military parades outside by actors in 18th-century uniforms; check the website for details.

Casino de Montréal CASINO
(☎514-392-2746; http://casinos.lotoquebec.com; 1 Ave du Casino; ⏱24hr; 📶; M Jean-Drapeau, then bus 777) Based in the former French pavilion from Expo '67, the Montréal Casino opened in 1993 and was so popular (and earned so much money) that expansion occurred almost instantly. It remains Canada's biggest casino, and has a sleek design, following a four-year, $300-million makeover completed in 2013.

Habitat 67 NOTABLE BUILDING
(www.habitat67.com; Ave Pierre Dupuy) The artificial peninsula **Cité-du-Havre** was created to protect the port from vicious currents and ice. Here, in 1967, architect Moshe Safdie designed a set of futuristic cube-like condominiums for Expo '67 when he was just 23 years old – from a distance, they resemble a microscopic zoom-in on table salt. This narrow spit of land connects Île Ste-Hélène with Old Montréal via the Pont de la Concorde.

Elsewhere in Montréal

The western suburb of Lachine is worth a visit for its history, architecture and general ambience. Not touristy, it reveals a little of Montréal's roots and culture. The side streets behind the impressive college St-Anne nunnery and City Hall, both along Blvd St-Joseph, make for good wandering.

Canal de Lachine CANAL

( ) FREE The Lachine Canal was built in 1825 as a means of bypassing the treacherous **Lachine Rapids** on the St Lawrence River. Today, it's a perfect marriage of urban infrastructure and green civic planing: a 14km-long cycling and pedestrian pathway, with picnic areas and outdoor spaces. Since the canal was reopened for navigation in 2002, flotillas of pleasure and sightseeing boats glide along its calm waters.

Fur Trade at Lachine National Historic Site HISTORIC SITE

(www.pc.gc.ca; 1255 Blvd St-Joseph; adult/child $4/2; 10am-5pm late-May–early Sep; 195, M Angrignon) This 1803 stone depot is now an engaging little museum telling the story of the fur trade in Canada. The Hudson Bay Company made Lachine the hub of its fur-trading operations because the rapids made further navigation impossible. Visitors can view the furs and old trappers' gear, and costumed interpreters show how the bales and canoes were schlepped by native trappers.

Activities

Cycling & In-Line Skating

Montréal is a cyclist's haven. With the recent unveiling of Bixi, a self-service, solar-powered bicycle rental system with more than 300 stations downtown, it's easy for anyone to reap the benefits of Montréal's more than 500km of bicycle and skating paths. If you're planning a longer cycling sojourn, you're better off visiting a rental shop for a greater selection of bikes and maps.

One popular route parallels the Canal de Lachine for 14.5km, starting in Old Montréal and passing a lot of history en route. Picnic tables are scattered along the way, so pick up some tasty victuals at the Marché Atwater.

The smooth **Circuit Gilles Villeneuve** on Île Notre-Dame is another cool track. It's open and free to all from mid-April to mid-November – except in mid-June when it hosts the Grand Prix du Canada Formula One car race.

Ça Roule Montréal CYCLING

(Map p232; 514-866-0633; www.caroulemontreal.com; 27 Rue de la Commune Est, Old Port; bikes per hour/day from $8/30, in-line skates 1st/additional hour $9/4; 9am-7pm, reduced hours winter; M Place-d'Armes) Near the Old Port, Ça Roule Montréal has a wide selection of bicycles, in-line skates, spare parts and a good repair shop. Each rental includes a lock, helmet, patch kit and cycling map. You can rent children's bikes, tandems and bike trailers for pulling the little ones along while you pedal.

Bixi CYCLING

(514-789-2494; http://montreal.bixi.com; basic fees per 30min/1 day $3/5; 24hr mid-Apr–Oct) Four-hundred-plus pickup and drop-off bike stations are located every few blocks and at every main attraction throughout the city.

Vélopiste Jacques-Cartier/Portneuf CYCLING

(418-337-7525; www.velopistejcp.com) Formerly a railway line linking St-Gabriel-de-Valcartier and Rivière-à-Pierre, this 68km cycling trail winds its way through verdant country scenery. It's linked to downtown Québec City by another rails-to-trails project, the 22km Corridor des Cheminots. (Incidentally, cyclists can also reach this trail by train from Montréal; VIA Rail offers thrice-weekly service from Montréal to Rivière-à-Pierre, the trail's western terminus.)

Ice Skating

Lac des Castors SKATING

(Parc du Mont-Royal; admission free, skate rentals per 2hr $8.50; 9am-9pm Sun-Thu, to 10pm Fri & Sat, weather permitting) An excellent place for outdoor skating – it's nestled in the woods near a large parking lot and pavilion.

Patinoire du Bassin Bonsecours SKATING

(Map p232; Parc du Bassin Bonsecours, Old Port; adult/child $7/4, skate rentals $9; 10am-9pm Mon-Wed, to 10pm Thu-Sat Dec-early Mar; 14, M Champ-de-Mars) This is one of Montréal's most popular outdoor-skating rinks, located on the shore of the St Lawrence River next to the Pavilion du Bassin Bonsecours.

Other Activities

MTL Zipline ADVENTURE SPORTS

(Map p232; 514-947-5463; https://mtlzipline.com/en; 363 Rue de la Commune Est; adult/child from $20/17; 11am-9pm May-Oct) This urban zip-line complex lets you soar over the Old Port – or see it rush toward your face at death-defying speeds via a 'Quick Jump' (basically, a bungee jump). You must be 12 or older.

Plage des Îles BEACH
(Île Notre-Dame; adult/child $9/4.50; ⌚10am-7pm daily mid-Jun–late-Aug, noon-7pm Sat-Mon late-Aug–early Sep; Ⓜ Jean-Drapeau, then bus 767) On warm summer days this artificial sandy beach can accommodate up to 5000 sunning and splashing souls. It's safe, clean and ideal for kids; picnic facilities and snack bars serving beer are on-site. There are also paddleboats, canoes and kayaks for rent.

Tours

Le Petit Navire BOATING
(Map p232; ☎514-602-1000; www.lepetitnavire.ca; Quai Jacques-Cartier; 45min tour per adult/child $20/9, 2hr tour $26/19; ⌚10am-7pm mid-May–mid-Oct; Ⓜ Champ-de-Mars) Aside from rowing a boat yourself, this outfit offers the most ecologically friendly boat tours in Montréal. The silent, electric-powered Le Petit Navire takes passengers on 45-minute tours departing hourly around the Old Port area. Equally intriguing are the 1½-hour cruises up the Canal de Lachine (departing Friday, Saturday and Sunday at 11:30am from Quai Jacques-Cartier and 2pm from Marché Atwater).

Le Bateau Mouche BOATING
(Map p232; ☎514-849-9952; www.bateaumouche.ca; 1hr tours adult/child $25/13, 1.5hr tours adult/child $29/15; ⌚60min tour 11am, 2:30pm, 4pm, 5:30pm May-Oct, 90min tour 12:30pm May-Oct; Ⓜ Champ-de-Mars) This comfortable, climate-controlled sightseeing boat with a glass roof offers narrated cruises of the Old Port and Parc Jean-Drapeau. Dinner cruises are also available. Phone ahead for reservations and make sure you board 15 minutes before departure.

Guidatour WALKING
(Map p232; ☎514-844-4021; www.guidatour.qc.ca; adult/child $25/14; ⌚scheduled tours Sat & Sun Apr-Nov & daily Jun-Oct, private tours year-round) In business for more than three decades, the experienced bilingual guides of Guidatour paint a picture of Old Montréal's eventful history with anecdotes and legends. They also offer culinary tours, plus a 'Christmas Secrets of Old Montréal' tour in December.

Festivals & Events

Fête des Neiges WINTER
(www.parcjeandrapeau.com; ⌚late Jan-early Feb) Montréal's Snow Festival features some ice-sculpting contests, dog-sled races, snow games and costumed characters such as mascot polar bear Boule de Neige. It's held over three consecutive weekends in late January and early February.

Montréal en Lumière CULTURAL
(www.montrealenlumiere.com; ⌚late Feb/early Mar) Created to help shake off the late-winter doldrums, Montréal en Lumière is a kind of wintry Mardi Gras with concerts, exhibitions and fireworks. Place des Arts becomes an illuminated fairground with a Ferris wheel and zip line. Most events happen downtown.

Les FrancoFolies CULTURAL
(www.francofolies.com; ⌚late Jun) This annual international showcase of French-language music and theater spotlights today's biggest stars and those on the rise. Held over 10 days.

Festival International de Jazz de Montréal MUSIC
(www.montrealjazzfest.com; ⌚late Jun-early Jul) For 11 days the heart of downtown explodes in jazz and blues during 650 concerts, most of them outdoors and free.

Just for Laughs Festival COMEDY
(www.hahaha.com; ⌚Jul) Everyone gets giddy for two weeks at this international comedy festival with hundreds of shows, including free ones in the Quartier Latin.

Montréal Pride LGBT
(☎514-903-6193; www.fiertemontrealpride.com) Montréal's Gay Pride Week, including the annual Montréal LGBTA Parade, attracts hundreds of thousands every August.

Black & Blue Festival LGBT
(☎514-875-7026; www.bbcm.org) This is one of Montréal's biggest gay events, with major dance parties, and cultural and art shows, all in the second week of October.

Sleeping

Montréal's accommodation scene is blessed with a tremendous variety of rooms and styles. Though rates aren't particularly cheap, they are reasonable by international standards – or even compared with Canadian cities such as Toronto or Vancouver. French- and Victorian-style inns and independent hotels cater to a variety of budgets.

Old Montréal

Auberge Alternative HOSTEL $
(Map p232; ☎514-282-8069; www.auberge-alternative.qc.ca; 358 Rue St-Pierre; dm incl tax $27-30, r $75-85; @ 📶; Ⓜ Square-Victoria) This laid-back hostel near the Old Port has a bohemian vibe with an inviting cafe-restaurant where you can mingle with other travelers or enjoy an organic breakfast ($5 extra). Guests

MONTRÉAL FOR CHILDREN

Montréal has many sights for young visitors. Depending on the season, you can go boating, cycling and skating, or get some amusement park or skydiving thrills. On warm days, Parc Mont-Royal and neighborhood parks are great places for picnics and free-spirited outdoor activity.

Kid-Friendly Museums

➡ Kids will love **Biodôme** (p239), a giant indoor zoo with forest, river and marine habitats.

➡ Check out Jardin Botanique's **Insectarium** (p238), with 250,000 specimens creeping, crawling or otherwise on display.

➡ Enjoy the **Planétarium** (p239), with domed theaters and interactive exhibits on outerspace.

➡ Take your tots on a virtual mission to Mars at **Cosmodôme** (☎450-978-3600; www.cosmodome.org; 2150 Autoroute des Laurentides; adult/family/student/child under 7yr $15/40/12/free; ⏲9am-5pm late Jun-early Sep, 10am-5pm rest of year; 🚌61 or 70, Ⓜ Montmorency), an engaging space center.

➡ At **Musée Ferroviaire Canadien** (☎450-632-2410; www.exporail.org; 110 Rue St-Pierre/Rte 209, St-Constant; adult/child $18/9; ⏲10am-6pm Jul-Sep, hours vary other times; 👪) there are trains of every kind – stationary, moving, new and old – that will thrill adults as much as children.

bunk in trim, colorfully painted dorms that accommodate anywhere from four to 20 people. There's a laundry and no curfew.

★ L Hotel BOUTIQUE HOTEL **$$**

(Map p232; ☎514-985-0019; www.lhotelmontreal.com; 262 Rue St-Jacques Ouest; d $170-280; P❄📶; Ⓜ Square-Victoria) Inside a grand 1870 building, L Hotel is a major draw for art lovers. Georges Marciano, founder of Guess jeans, opened the hotel in 2010, showering great artworks throughout the rooms and common areas. You might sleep in a room with an original piece by Andy Warhol, Roy Lichtenstein or Frank Stella, or one of scores of other famed artists.

★ Hôtel Nelligan BOUTIQUE HOTEL **$$$**

(Map p232; ☎514-788-2040, 877-788-2040; www.hotelnelligan.com; 106 Rue St-Paul Ouest; d from $238; P❄@📶; Ⓜ Place-d'Armes) Housed in two restored buildings and named in honor of Québec's famous and tragic poet, Émile Nelligan, this Old Montréal beauty has original details (such as exposed brick or stone) and luxurious fittings (down comforters, high-quality bath products, and Jacuzzis in some rooms). Verses, a plush bar and restaurant, is next door, with a magnificent roof patio, Terrasse Nelligan.

★ Hôtel Gault BOUTIQUE HOTEL **$$$**

(Map p232; ☎866-904-1616, 514-904-1616; www.hotelgault.com; 449 Rue Ste-Hélène; r from $230; P❄@📶; Ⓜ Square-Victoria) The Gault delivers beauty and comfort in its 30 spacious rooms. Lovely 19th-century architectural details figure in some rooms, with exposed brick or stone walls, though for the most part it boasts a fashion-forward, contemporary design. Rooms have extremely comfortable beds, ergonomic chairs, high ceilings, huge windows and spotless bathrooms (some with two-person bathtubs) with heated tile floors.

Auberge du Vieux-Port BOUTIQUE HOTEL **$$$**

(Map p232; ☎888-660-7678; www.aubergeduvieuxport.com; 97 Rue de la Commune E; r $200-430; P❄📶; Ⓜ Champ-de-Mars) Set in an 1882 warehouse, this is a stylish boutique hotel with exposed brick or stone walls, wooden beams, wrought-iron beds, high-quality furnishings (including occasional antiques) and big windows overlooking the waterfront. For more space and seclusion (a kitchen, multiple rooms), you can book one of its minimalist **lofts** (Map p232; ☎514-876-9119; www.loftsduvieuxport.com; apt $190-300; ❄) in a separate building around the corner.

➡ See oversized cannons, military parades and guides in period costumes inside an old British garrison at **Musée Stewart** (p241).

Outdoor Fun

➡ At Québec's largest amusement park, **La Ronde** (p241), kids will experience chills and thrills galore – plus fireworks on some nights.

➡ Enormous **Parc du Mont-Royal** (p239) in the heart of the city is especially fun for kids in winter, with tobogganing, skiing, snowshoeing and ice skating. **Parc La Fontaine** (Map p240; cnr Rue Sherbrooke Est & Ave du Parc La Fontaine; 6am-midnight; ; M Sherbrooke) is perfect for a casual, outdoor stroll, and sits at the edge of the bustling Plateau. Or try **Parc Nature du Cap-St-Jacques** (514-280-6871; 20099 Blvd Gouin Ouest, Pierrefonds; $9; 10am-6pm Jun-Aug, 10am-5pm Sep-May; P ; 69, M Henri-Bourassa), a verdant park with trails, a beach, a sugar shack and a working farm.

Live Performances

➡ World-renowned **Cirque du Soleil** (p254) combines dance, theater and circus in powerpacked summertime shows. It will thrill the kids, but is truly for all ages.

➡ For entertaining shows year-round, head to **TOHU** (888-376-8648, 514-376-8648; www.tohu.ca; 2345 Rue Jarry Est; guided tour $7; 9am-5pm Mon-Fri; M d'Iberville then bus 94), a circular theater in the St-Michel district.

Downtown

Trylon Apartments APARTMENT $
(Map p240; 877-843-3971, 514-843-3971; www.trylon.ca; 3463 Rue Ste-Famille; apt per day/week/month from $99/546/1560; P ; M Place-des-Arts) The modern high-rise Trylon Apartments are a plush alternative to top-end hotels at a fraction of the price. The small studios (36 sq meters) and one-bedroom apartments (51 sq meters) all have contemporary furnishings with kitchenettes, and guests can enjoy the indoor swimming pool, sauna, exercise room and rooftop terrace. Some rooms have balconies.

HI-Montreal Hostel HOSTEL $
(Map p236; 514-843-3317, 866-843-3317; www.hostellingmontreal.com; 1030 Rue Mackay; dm $30-45, r $55-110; @; M Lucien-L'Allier) This large, well-equipped HI hostel has bright, well-maintained dorm rooms (all with aircon) with four to 10 beds, and a handful of private en suite rooms. Rooms are small and, depending on your bunkmates, can feel cramped. Energetic staff organize daily activities and outings (pub crawls, bike tours, day trips), plus there's a lively cafe-bar on the ground floor.

Le Gîte du Plateau Mont-Royal HOSTEL $
(Map p240; 877-350-4483, 514-284-1276; www.hostelmontreal.com; 185 Rue Sherbrooke Est; dm/d/tr with shared bath from $20/62/84; @; M Sherbrooke) This popular youth hostel at the southern end of the Plateau (and the western edge of downtown) has all the expected hostel features (kitchen access, laundry room and lounge), though rooms and facilities are basic. Staff are friendly, and the rooftop terrace and communal lounge are fine places to meet other travelers.

Auberge Les Bons Matins BOUTIQUE HOTEL $$
(Map p236; 514-931-9167; www.bonsmatins.com; 1401 Ave Argyle; r $130-210; ; M Lucien-L'Allier) The Bons Matins has spacious rooms with gorgeous art, hardwood floors, brick walls and delicious breakfasts. The walk-up rooms are spread out over stately traditional town houses, and the entire affair is conveniently located at the edge of downtown.

L'Abri du Voyageur HOTEL $$
(Map p240; 866-302-2922, 514-849-2922; www.abri-voyageur.ca; 9 Rue Ste-Catherine Ouest; r $100-165; P ; M St-Laurent) It's on a seedy stretch of Rue Ste-Catherine but if you're not turned off by the nearby sex clubs (no pun intended), you can enjoy clean, cozy rooms with exposed brick walls, wood floors and comfortable furnishings.

★Hôtel Le Germain HOTEL $$$
(Map p236; ☎514-849-2050, 877-333-2050; www.germainmontreal.com; 2050 Rue Mansfield; r from $255; P ❄ 📶; M Peel) This stylish hotel boasts luxurious rooms with dark wood details (headboard, wood blinds), cream-colored walls, sheer curtains and artful lighting. You'll find all the creature comforts, such as goose-down duvets, iPod docks and rainfall showers; the bathrooms have a touch of the eccentric with one big window into the room. (Superior rooms have only a shower.)

Hotel Le Crystal BOUTIQUE HOTEL $$$
(Map p236; ☎514-861-5550; www.hotellecrystal.com; 1100 Rue de la Montagne; ste from $259; P ❄ 📶 🏊; M Bonaventure) This all-suite boutique hotel is a great spot for a sleeping splurge. The business-casual rooms have great views over the city and are arranged around a lobby decked out like a modern art exhibit. To round out the indulgence, hop into the pool and take in the city skyline.

Plateau Mont-Royal

Auberge De La Fontaine INN $$
(Map p240; ☎514-597-0166, 800-597-0597; www.aubergedelafontaine.com; 1301 Rue Rachel Est; r $122-197, ste from $237; P ❄ 📶; M Mont-Royal) A lovely inn on the edge of Parc La Fontaine (p245), this guesthouse has cheery rooms with comfy beds and touches of artwork. Standard rooms are small, while the best rooms have park views. The spacious suites also have in-room Jacuzzis. The snack refrigerator with free goodies is a nice touch. There's a wheelchair-accessible room available.

Gingerbread Manor B&B $$
(Map p240; ☎514-597-2804; www.gingerbreadmanor.com; 3445 Ave Laval; r without/with bath from $110/130; P 📶; M Sherbrooke) The hosts give a warm welcome at this charming B&B near leafy Carré St-Louis. The house itself is a stately three-story town house built in 1885 with bay windows, ornamental details and an attached carriage house. The elegant rooms – five in all – are uniquely furnished (only one has a private bath, the others share).

Anne Ma Soeur Anne HOTEL $$
(Map p240; ☎514-281-3187; www.annemasoeuranne.com; 4119 Rue St-Denis; r $87-220; P ❄ 📶; M Mont-Royal) These smart, fully equipped studios fill a valuable niche in the Plateau. They're suitable for short- or long-term stays; each unit has a 'microkitchen' with a microwave and stove, work space and Ikea-style furnishings built into the walls. The cheapest rooms are a little cramped with thin mattresses; others have private terraces, with some overlooking the shady backyard.

Croissants are delivered to your door for breakfast. Noise can be a problem: ask for a room on the garden side, rather than the street side.

Eating

Montréal is one of the great foodie destinations of the north. Here you'll find an outstanding assortment of classic French cuisine, hearty Québécois fare and countless ethnic restaurants from 80-odd nationalities. Today's *haute cuisine* is as likely to be conjured by talented young African, Japanese or Indian chefs as graduates from the Académie Culinaire du Québec.

Old Montréal

Titanic SANDWICHES $
(Map p232; ☎514-849-0894; www.titanicmontreal.com; 445 Rue St-Pierre; sandwiches around $10; ⊙8am-4pm Mon-Fri; 📶 🌿; M Square-Victoria) The sandwiches here have office workers scurrying to these cramped basement quarters from all over Old Montréal on their lunch breaks. The varieties are endless and can include grilled veggies with feta, smoked salmon with sweet roasted peppers or roast beef with horseradish. Excellent salads, soup, quiche and antipasto misto are popular takeouts.

Mai Xiang Yuan CHINESE $
(Map p240; ☎514-875-1888; 1082 Blvd St-Laurent; mains $6-10; ⊙11am-9pm; M Place-d'Armes) You'd be hard-pressed to find better dumplings in Montréal than the perfect little bits of heaven, pan-fried or steamed, that come out of the kitchen in this humble hole-in-the-wall. Each plate comes with 15 dumplings, and fillings include everything from lamb and onion to pork and leek, as well as tomato and egg for vegetarians.

★Olive + Gourmando CAFE $$
(Map p232; ☎514-350-1083; www.oliveetgourmando.com; 351 Rue St-Paul Ouest; mains $10-17; ⊙8am-5pm Tue-Sat; 🌿; M Square-Victoria) Named after the owners' two cats, this bakery-cafe is legendary in town for its hot panini, plump salads and flaky baked goods. Excellent choices include the melted goat's-cheese panini with caramelized onions, decadent mac 'n' cheese, and 'the Cubain' (a ham, roast pork and Gruyère sandwich).

Le Serpent ITALIAN $$

(Map p232; ☎514-316-4666; www.leserpent.ca; 257 Rue Prince; mains $13-35; ⏲5:45-10:30pm Mon-Wed, to 11pm Thu & Fri, 5-11pm Sat; Ⓜ Square-Victoria) Industrial style dominates at this renovated factory next to the **Fonderie Darling** (Map p232; ☎514-392-1554; www.fonderiedarling.org; 745 Rue Ottawa; $5, Thu free; ⏲noon-7pm Wed & Fri-Sun, to 10pm Thu; Ⓜ Square-Victoria) art space, which draws a creative tech-industry crowd. The menu features an interesting mix of risottos and pastas (such as bucatini with pork confit) and a handful of well-executed seafood and meat dishes (veal fillet with ricotta tortellini), plus a changing daily special.

★**Barroco** INTERNATIONAL $$$

(Map p232; ☎514-544-5800; www.barroco.ca; 312 Rue St-Paul Ouest; mains $28-41; ⏲6-10:30pm, to 11pm Fri & Sat; Ⓜ Square-Victoria) Small, cozy Barroco has stone walls, flickering candles and beautifully presented plates of roast duck, braised short ribs and grilled fish. The selection is small (just six or so mains and an equal number of appetizers), but you can't go wrong here – particularly if you opt for the outstanding seafood and chorizo paella.

Toqué! FRENCH $$$

(Map p232; ☎514-499-2084; www.restaurant-toque.com; 900 Pl Jean-Paul-Riopelle; mains $46-55; ⏲11:30am-1:45pm Tue-Fri, 5:30-10pm Tue-Thu, to 10:30pm Fri & Sat; Ⓜ Square-Victoria) Chef Normand Laprise has earned rave reviews for his innovative recipes based on products sourced from local farms. The bright, wide-open dining room has high ceilings accented by playful splashes of color, and a glass-enclosed wine cave with suspended bottles looming. The seven-course *menu dégustation* ($120) is the pinnacle of dining in Montréal – allow three hours for the feast.

Garde-Manger INTERNATIONAL $$$

(Map p232; ☎514-678-5044; www.crownsalts.com/gardemanger; 408 Rue St-François-Xavier; mains $34-40; ⏲5:30-11pm Tue-Sun; Ⓜ Place-d'Armes) The buzz surrounding Garde-Manger has barely let up since its opening back in 2006. This small, candlelit restaurant attracts a mix of local scenesters and *haute-cuisine*-loving out-of-towners who come for lobster risotto, short ribs, Cornish hen stuffed with foie gras and other changing chalkboard specials.

Downtown

Kazu JAPANESE $

(Map p236; ☎514-937-2333; http://kazumontreal.com; 1862 Rue Ste-Catherine Ouest; mains $10-17; ⏲noon-3pm Sun, Mon & Wed-Fri, 5:30-9:30pm Wed-Mon; Ⓜ Guy-Concordia) Kazuo Akutsu's frenetic hole-in-the-wall in the Concordia Chinatown draws long lines of people waiting for *gyoza* (dumplings), ramen noodle soup and awesome creations such as the 48-hour pork, attesting to its popularity. Be warned: it gets cramped inside.

Satay Brothers ASIAN $

(☎514-933-3507; www.sataybrothers.com; 3721 Rue Notre-Dame Ouest; mains $8-15; ⏲11am-11pm Wed-Sun; Ⓜ Lionel-Groulx) Amid red walls, hanging lamps and mismatched thrift-store furnishings, this lively and colorful spot serves some of the best 'street food' in Montréal. Crowds flock here to gorge on delicious chicken-satay sandwiches with peanut sauce served on grilled bread, tangy green papaya salad, braised pork (or tofu) buns, and *laksa lemak*, a rich and spicy coconut soup.

Ong Ca Can VIETNAMESE $

(Map p240; ☎514-844-7817; 79 Rue Ste-Catherine Est; mains $8-16; ⏲11am-3pm Mon, 11am-9pm Tue-Thu, to 10pm Fri, 5-10pm Sat; ✎) Despite its crisp white linens and intricate artwork, this bustling Vietnamese restaurant only looks pricey. The lemongrass rolls and anything with beef get especially high marks from loyal patrons.

Boustan LEBANESE $

(Map p236; ☎514-844-2999; http://boustan.ca; 2020 Rue Crescent; mains $5-10; ⏲11am-4am; ✎; Ⓜ Guy-Concordia) This friendly little Lebanese joint scores high in popularity on the city's *shwarma* circuit because of its delicious toasted pita sandwiches. Its late hours make it a favorite with pub crawlers in need of sustenance between bars.

★**Café Parvis** BISTRO $$

(Map p236; ☎514-764-3589; www.cafeparvis.com; 433 Rue Mayor; small plates $6-8; ⏲7am-11pm Mon-Wed, to midnight Thu & Fri, 10am-midnight Sat, to 10pm Sun; ✎; Ⓜ Place-des-Arts) Hidden away on a quiet downtown lane, Café Parvis is set with oversized windows, hanging plants, old wooden floorboards and vintage fixtures. Once part of the fur district, this cleverly repurposed room serves up delicious pizzas in inventive combinations.

MONTRÉAL'S THIRD WAVE

Like most North American cities, Montréal has been swept away by the so-called 'Third Wave' of cafes that have pushed coffee-drinkers away from the mass-produced, accessible-to-all coffee brands such as Folgers (first wave) to chains like Starbucks that focus on regional production and Italian espresso drinks (second wave), and toward a generation of artisanal, highly specialized coffee producers that practice direct-sourcing from single farms and in-house roasting.

Essentially the journey from bean to cup is a narrative, one that is just as important to the connoisseur as the taste of the coffee itself. Like the variety of grape to a winemaker, baristas and roasters at Third Wave establishments care about the flavor (the aromatics, tones, depth), the bean varietal, and the farm from which the bean was sourced, with 'single-origin' being most desirable. To fuel a long day of wandering and sightseeing and experience *haute* cafe culture at its finest, consider one of the following:

Cafe Falco (p250)

Cafe Névé (p249)

Myriade (Map p236; 514-939-1717; www.cafemyriade.com; 1432 Rue Mackay; baked goods around $7; 7:30am-8pm Mon-Fri, 9am-7pm Sat & Sun; M Guy-Concordia)

Pikolo Espresso Bar (Map p236; 514-508-6800; www.pikoloespresso.com; 3418b Ave du Parc; mains $6.50-9; 7:30am-7pm Mon-Fri, 9am-6pm Sat & Sun; ; M Place-des-Arts)

Foodlab INTERNATIONAL **$$**

(Map p240; 514-844-2033; www.sat.qc.ca/fr/foodlab; 3rd fl, 1201 Blvd St-Laurent; mains $15-25; 5-10pm Mon-Fri; M St-Laurent) On the upper floor of the arts center SAT, Foodlab is a creative culinary space, where the small menu changes every two weeks, and ranges across the globe. It's a casual but handsomely designed space, where patrons perch on bar stools, sipping creative cocktails and watching fast-moving chefs in the open kitchen.

Le Vin Papillon INTERNATIONAL **$$**

(www.vinpapillon.com; 2519 Rue Notre-Dame Ouest; small plates $7-17; 3pm-midnight Tue-Sat; ; M Lionel-Groulx) The folks behind Joe Beef continue the hit parade with this delightful wine bar and small-plate eatery next door to Liverpool House (another Joe Beef success). Creative, mouthwatering veggie dishes take top billing with favorites such as tomato and chickpea salad, sautéed chanterelles and smoked eggplant caviar, along with roasted cauliflower with chicken skin, guinea-fowl confit, and charcuterie and cheese platters.

Bistro Isakaya JAPANESE **$$**

(Map p236; 514-845-8226; www.bistroisakaya.com; 3469 Ave du Parc; mains $19-26; 11:30am-2pm Tue-Fri, 6-9:30pm Tue-Thu, 6-10:30pm Fri, 5:30-10pm Sat, 5:30-9pm Sun; M Place-des-Arts, then bus 80 or 129) This authentic, unpretentious Japanese restaurant has fairly simple decor but the fish is incredibly fresh. The owner is known for handpicking his seafood and preparing it in classic Japanese fashion.

★ Liverpool House QUÉBÉCOIS **$$$**

(514-313-6049; http://joebeef.ca; 2501 Rue Notre-Dame Ouest; mains $24-50; 5-11pm Tue-Sat;) The sister establishment (and neighbor) of Joe Beef, Liverpool House sets the standard so many Québec restaurants are racing for: an ambience that feels laid-back, like a friend's dinner party, where the food is sent from angels on high. Expect oysters, smoked trout, braised rabbit, lobster spaghetti and various other iterations of regional excellence.

Joe Beef QUÉBÉCOIS **$$$**

(514-935-6504; www.joebeef.ca; 2491 Rue Notre-Dame Ouest; mains $29-52; 6pm-late Tue-Sat; M Lionel-Groulx) In the heart of the Little Burgundy neighborhood, Joe Beef remains a darling of food critics for its unfussy, market-fresh fare. The rustic, country-kitsch setting is a great spot to linger over fresh oysters, braised rabbit, roasted scallops with smoked onions and a changing selection of hearty Québécois dishes.

Ferreira Café PORTUGUESE **$$$**

(Map p236; 514-848-0988; www.ferreiracafe.com; 1446 Rue Peel; mains $26-45; 11:45am-3pm Mon-Fri, 5:30-11pm Mon-Wed, 5:30pm-midnight Thu-Sat, 5-10pm Sun; M Peel) This warm and inviting restaurant serves some of Montréal's best Portuguese fare. The *cataplana* (a bouillabaisse-style seafood stew) is magnificent; tender morsels of grilled fish come to the table cooked to perfection, while meat lovers can feast on rack of lamb or spice-rubbed Angus rib-eye steak. Late diners can enjoy three-course, $24 meals from 10pm to close.

Plateau Mont-Royal

La Banquise QUÉBÉCOIS $

(Map p240; 514-525-2415; www.labanquise.com; 994 Rue Rachel Est; mains $8-15; 24hr; ; M Mont-Royal) A Montréal legend since 1968, La Banquise is probably the best place in town to sample poutine. More than 30 varieties are available, including a vegan poutine, the boogalou (with pulled pork) and straight-up classic poutine. There's an outdoor terrace, a full breakfast menu and a selection of microbrews, plus the kitchen never closes. Expect big lines on weekends.

Cafe Névé CAFE $

(Map p240; 514-903-9294; www.cafeneve.com; 151 Rue Rachel Est; sandwiches around $8; 8am-9pm Mon-Fri, from 9am Sat & Sun; ; M Mont-Royal) This much-loved neighborhood haunt serves excellent coffees, and the food selection goes far beyond the typical baked goods found in most cafes. Stop in for eggs Benedict or yogurt, granola and fresh fruit in the morning. For lunch, there are tasty sandwiches (including several vegetarian options) and French onion soup.

Espace La Fontaine BISTRO $

(Map p240; 514-280-2525; www.espacelafontaine.com; 3933 Ave du Parc La Fontaine; mains $10-16; 11am-8pm Tue-Fri, from 10am Sat, 10am-5pm Sun; ; M Sherbrooke) In a chalet perched above the water, Espace La Fontaine is a bright and cheery bistro that serves sandwiches and salads, as well as a good weekend brunch. It has a great outdoor terrace in summer, and in winter, there's ice skating just below the chalet.

★ L'Gros Luxe BISTRO $$

(Map p240; 514-447-2227; www.lgrosluxe.com; 3807 Rue St-André; small plates $5-10; 5-11:30pm Mon-Fri, from 11am Sat & Sun; ; M Sherbrooke) With its big windows, classy vintage decor and inexpensive comfort fare, L'Gros Luxe has obvious appeal. The small dining room is always packed with young Plateau residents who come for pork tacos, veggie burgers, and fish and chips. Plates are small, but nothing costs more than $10, and there's an extensive drinks menu (with much higher prices than the food).

★ L'Express FRENCH $$

(Map p240; 514-845-5333; http://restaurantlexpress.com; 3927 Rue St-Denis; mains $22-28; 8am-2am Mon-Fri, from 10am Sat & Sun; M Sherbrooke) L'Express has all the hallmarks of a Parisian bistro – black-and-white checkered floor, art-deco globe lights, papered tables and mirrored walls. High-end bistro fare completes the picture with excellent dishes such as grilled salmon, bone marrow with sea salt, roast duck with salad and beef tartare.

La Sala Rosa SPANISH $$

(Map p240; 514-844-4227; http://lasalarosa.com; 4848 Blvd St-Laurent; mains $13-17; 5-11pm Tue-Sun; ; M Laurier) A festive, local and often Spanish-speaking crowd comes to this little Iberian gem. Sala Rosa is best known for its five tasty varieties of paella (including vegetarian) as well as numerous tapas dishes and a changing lineup of Spanish specials. On Thursday nights (from 8:45pm) there's a live flamenco show and the place gets packed.

Hà VIETNAMESE $$

(Map p240; 514-848-0336; www.restaurantha.com; 243 Ave du Mont-Royal Ouest; mains $11-25; 11:45am-11pm Tue-Fri, from 3pm Sat & Sun; ; M Mont-Royal) Inspired by the street foods (and beers) of Vietnam, Chef Hong Hà Nguyen showcases simple but delectable recipes at this charmer near the foot of Mont-Royal. The menu is small, with highlights such as grilled beef with watercress salad, lemongrass pork ribs and spicy papaya salad.

Les Folies CANADIAN $$

(Map p240; 514-528-4343; www.restofolies.ca; 701 Ave du Mont-Royal Est; mains $14-20; 9am-midnight Sun-Wed, to 12:30am Thu, to 1am Fri & Sat; ; M Mont-Royal) Take a heaping spoonful of '50s retro vibe, mush it through the hipness of Montréal's Plateau, throw in some delicious poutine (with tender duck!) and burgers (chicken, goat's cheese and maple-syrup-caramelized onions) and you've got Les Folies. Breakfast is a true treat, so don't miss this spot in the mornings.

ChuChai THAI $$

(Map p240; 514-843-4194; www.chuchai.com; 4088 Rue St-Denis; mains $14-22; 11am-2pm & 5-10pm Tue-Fri, to 11pm Sat, 5-9pm Sun;) In Montréal's first vegetarian upscale eatery, zippy Thai-inspired stir-fries and coconut soups explore the potential of fragrant Kaffir lime, lemongrass and sweet basil. The fake duck could fool even the most discerning carnivore.

Robin des Bois FUSION $$

(Map p240; ☎514-288-1010; www.robindesbois.ca; 4653 Blvd St-Laurent; mains $13-23; ⏰11:30am-10pm Mon-Fri, 5-10pm Sat; Ⓜ St-Laurent, then bus 55) Montréal's own Robin Hood, restaurateur Judy Servay donates all profits and tips from this St-Laurent hot spot to local charities. Ever-changing dishes scribbled on the chalkboard could include a succulent braised pork roast, rich French onion soup or a creamy wild-mushroom risotto.

Crudessence VEGAN $$

(Map p240; ☎514-510-9299; www.crudessence.com; 105 Rue Rachel Ouest; mains $11-17; ⏰11am-9pm;) The raw, vegan *and* organic fare here is guaranteed to pique your interest. Start the day with a bowl of chia, granola and almond milk, or wait for lunch to experience unbaked lasagna with macadamia nut ricotta or olive-crust pizza with 'crumesan' (Brazil-nut Parmesan). The busy all-organic juice bar churns out smoothies and power shakes to flocks of Mile End locals.

Le Filet SEAFOOD $$$

(Map p240; ☎514-360-6060; www.lefilet.ca; 219 Ave du Mont-Royal Ouest; small plates $21-30; ⏰5:45-10:30pm Tue-Fri, from 5:30pm Sat; Ⓜ Mont-Royal) Le Filet presents masterfully crafted fish and seafood with Japanese touches in a low-lit setting facing Parc Jeanne-Mance. Plates are small and meant for sharing (two people typically order four to five dishes).

Au Pied de Cochon QUÉBÉCOIS $$$

(Map p240; ☎514-281-1114; www.aupieddecochon.ca; 536 Ave Duluth Est; mains $27-48; ⏰5pm-midnight Wed-Sun; Ⓜ Mont-Royal) One of Montréal's most respected restaurants features extravagant pork, duck and steak dishes, along with its signature foie gras plates. Irreverent, award-winning chef Martin Picard takes simple ingredients and transforms them into works of art. Dishes are rich and portions are large, so bring an appetite.

Moishe's STEAK $$$

(Map p240; ☎514-845-3509; www.moishes.ca; 3961 Blvd St-Laurent; mains $26-67; ⏰5:30-10pm Mon & Tue, to 11pm Wed, to midnight Thu & Fri, 5pm-midnight Sat, 5-10pm Sun; Ⓜ St-Laurent, then bus 55) Moishe's feels a bit like a social club, although guests from all backgrounds come to consume its legendary grilled meats and seafood. Closely set tables and old-fashioned hardwood paneling set the backdrop to the feasting. Skip the appetizers and launch straight into a gargantuan rib eye served with tasty fries or a Monte Carlo potato.

Quartier Latin & The Village

Juliette et Chocolat CAFE $

(Map p240; ☎514-287-3555; www.juliettetchocolat.com; 1615 Rue St-Denis; mains $8-15; ⏰11am-11pm Sun-Thu, to midnight Fri & Sat; ; Ⓜ Berri-UQAM) When the urge to devour something chocolaty arrives, make straight for Juliette et Chocolat, a bustling little cafe where chocolate is served in every shape and form – drizzled over crêpes, blended into creamy milkshakes and coffees, or straight up in a chocolate 'shot.' The setting is charming, but small and busy. For less hustle and bustle, visit the branch at 377 Ave Laurier Ouest.

Little Italy & Mile End

Fairmount Bagel BAKERY $

(Map p240; ☎514-272-0667; www.fairmountbagel.com; 74 Ave Fairmount Ouest; bagels 90¢; ⏰24hr; Ⓜ Laurier) One of Montréal's famed bagel places – people flood in here around the clock to scoop them up the minute they come out of the oven. Bagels are one thing Montréalers don't get too creative with. They stick to classic sesame or poppy seed varieties, though you can pick up anything from cinnamon to all-dressed here too.

Arts Cafe INTERNATIONAL $

(Map p240; ☎514-274-0919; www.artscafemontreal.com; 201 Ave Fairmount Ouest; mains $11-16; ⏰9am-10pm Mon-Fri, 10am-4pm Sat & Sun; ; Ⓜ Laurier) The Arts Cafe has instant appeal with its plank floors, white clapboard walls and sculptural knickknacks (a frenzy of light bulbs above the windows, vintage farmhouse relics) that adorn the space. But it's the food that warrants the most attention. Excellent brunches/breakfasts are served all day here.

Cafe Falco CAFE $

(☎514-272-7766; www.cafefalco.ca; 5605 Ave de Gaspé; mains $5-11; ⏰8am-5pm Mon-Thu, to 4pm Fri; Ⓜ Beaubien) Strong coffee, nice sandwiches and Japanese rice bowls – an incongruous mix, but a delicious one.

Porchetta SANDWICHES $

(☎514-278-7672; www.porchettamtl.ca; 6887 Blvd St-Laurent; mains $7-9; ⏰11am-8pm Mon & Tue, to 9pm Wed-Sun) We love Porchetta for its single-minded focus on, basically, one thing: beautiful Italian street food. The signature dishes are porchetta and mortadella sandwiches that are slow roasted to melting perfection; you'll want some napkins for all that delicious grease that soaks into the fresh bread.

La Croissanterie Figaro CAFE $
(☎514-278-6567; www.lacroissanteriefigaro.com; 5200 Rue Hutchison; sandwiches $9-13; ⏲7am-1am; Ⓜ Laurier) With its deco fixtures, wrought-iron marble-topped tables and lovely terrace, this charming neighborhood cafe has a Parisian vibe, and has long been a popular meeting spot for well-heeled locals. Stop in for warm, buttery croissants (among Montréal's best), baguette sandwiches or rich desserts. It's also a fine place to nurse a coffee or a cocktail.

Caffè Italia CAFE $
(☎514-495-0059; 6840 Blvd St-Laurent; sandwiches around $8, coffees $2-3; ⏲6am-11pm; Ⓜ De Castelnau) Calling this place old school is like calling the Sahara dry. 'Old school' isn't just a descriptor, but the essence of this little Italian espresso bar, where graybeards and guys unironically wearing flat caps seemingly step out of a time warp for a quick coffee on the Formica counter. Grab a panettone and an espresso, and live that *dolce vita*.

Comptoir 21 FISH & CHIPS $
(☎514-507-3474; www.comptoir21.com; 21 Rue St-Viateur Ouest; mains $8-14; ⏲11:30am-11pm Sun-Thu, to midnight Fri & Sat; Ⓜ Laurier) Slide onto a stool around the horseshoe-shaped wooden counter and feast on morsels of fish and chips, served on blue-and-white checked paper in pretty wooden baskets. Bonus points for the clever spray bottles of vinegar and the range of sauces available. It's a cozy space that draws a good cross-section of Montréal society.

Salmigondis QUÉBÉCOIS
(http://salmigondis.ca/en/; 6896 Rue St-Dominique; ⏲11:30am-2pm Thu & Fri, 6-11pm Wed-Sat, 10am-3pm Sat & Sun, 5-10pm Sun; 🖉; Ⓜ Castelnau) Young waitstaff traverse an airy space and a shaded back porch, bringing out plates topped with artful arrangements of *haute* Québécois cuisine: farm deer with arugula, arctic char ceviche and lobster risotto. The kitchen staff have carved a name for themselves in a competitive dining field; have a meal here and you'll see the reputation is justified.

Impasto ITALIAN $$$
(☎514-508-6508; www.impastomtl.ca; 48 Rue Dante; mains $29-36; ⏲11:30am-2pm Thu & Fri, 5-11pm Tue-Sat; Ⓜ De Castelnau) There's much buzz surrounding this polished Italian eatery – in no small part owing to the heavy-hitting foodies behind it: best-selling cookbook author Stefano Faita and celebrated chef Michele Forgione. Both have deep connections to Italian cooking, obvious in brilliant dishes such as braised beef cheeks with Savoy-style potatoes, arctic char with cauliflower puree and lentils, and housemade pastas like busiate with lobster.

Elsewhere in Montréal

Ludger FUSION $$
(☎438-383-3229; www.buvetteludger.com; 4001 Rue Notre-Dame Ouest; mains $17-28; ⏲5-11pm Mon-Sat, 10am-3pm Sun; Ⓜ Place-Saint-Henri) Hip French-Canadian fusion is the name of the game at this very modern, yet refreshingly laid-back restaurant that's turning heads across the city's southwest. Sunday brunch, which features a gorgeous pesto-chicken-Gruyère-egg sandwich, should not be missed.

Su TURKISH $$
(☎514-362-1818; www.restaurantsu.com; 5145 Rue Wellington; mains $18-26; ⏲5-10:30pm Tue-Sat, 10am-3pm Sat & Sun; Ⓜ Verdun) Chef Fisun Ercan takes her home-style but inventive Turkish cuisine beyond your expectations of kabobs and coffee. She prepares feather-light fried calamari, beef *manti* (dumplings) with garlic yogurt and spiced tomatoes, rich seafood rice (with shrimp, mussels and fish) and delicious *lokum* (Turkish delight). It's worth the trip to Verdun; be sure to reserve.

★Tuck Shop QUÉBÉCOIS $$$
(☎514-439-7432; www.tuckshop.ca; 4662 Rue Notre-Dame Ouest; mains $25-34; ⏲6-11pm Tue-Sat; 🖉; Ⓜ Place-Saint-Henri) Set in the heart of working-class St-Henri, Tuck Shop could have been plucked from London or New York if it weren't for its distinctly local menu, a delightful blend of market and *terroir* (locally sourced) offerings such as Kamouraska lamb shank, fish of the day with Jerusalem artichoke puree and a Québec cheese plate, all prepared by able chef Theo Lerikos.

Drinking & Nightlife

Montréalers love a good drink. Maybe it's the European influence: this is a town where it's perfectly acceptable, even expected, to begin cocktail hour after work and continue well into the night. On a sunny Friday afternoon, the *cinq-à-sept* (traditional 5pm to 7pm happy hour) often becomes 5-à-last-call. One caveat: many bars have a table service rule, which means that if you're not sitting at the bar, you have to be seated and waited on by waitstaff. This is an annoying policy – well intentioned it may be, but it seems to limit customers' ability to move and mingle.

★ **Whisky Café** LOUNGE
(☎514-278-2646; www.whiskycafe.com; 5800 Blvd St-Laurent; ⏰5pm-1am Mon-Wed, to 3am Thu & Fri, 6pm-3am Sat, 7pm-1am Sun; Ⓜ Place-des-Arts, then bus 80) Cuban cigars and fine whiskies are partners in crime at this classy 1930s-styled joint, hidden near the industrial sector of the Mile End. The well-ventilated cigar lounge is separated from the main bar, which stocks 150 Scotch whiskeys, plus wines, ports and tasting trios. Snacks range from duck rillettes to Belgian chocolates.

La Buvette Chez Simone WINE BAR
(Map p240; ☎514-750-6577; http://buvettechezsimone.com; 4869 Ave du Parc; ⏰4pm-3am; Ⓜ Laurier) An artsy-chic crowd of (mostly) Francophone bons vivants and professionals loves this cozy wine bar. The staff know their vino and the extensive list is complemented by a gourmet tapas menu. Weekends, the place is jammed from *cinc-à-sept* into the wee hours.

Bily Kun BAR
(Map p240; ☎514-845-5392; www.bilykun.com; 354 Ave du Mont-Royal Est; ⏰3pm-3am; Ⓜ Mont-Royal) One of the pioneers of 'tavern chic,' Bily Kun is a favorite local hangout for a chilled evening among friends. First-time visitors usually gawp at the ostrich heads that overlook the bar but soon settle into the music groove of live jazz (from 6pm to 8pm) and DJs (10pm onward).

Big in Japan COCKTAIL BAR
(Map p240; ☎438-380-5658; 4175 Blvd St-Laurent; ⏰5pm-3am; Ⓜ St-Laurent, then bus 55) Completely concealed from the street, Big in Japan always amazes first-timers. There you are walking along bustling St-Laurent, you find the unmarked door, walk down a rather unpromising corridor and emerge into a room lit with a thousand candles (or so it seems).

Barfly BAR
(Map p240; ☎514-284-6665; www.facebook.com/BarflyMtl; 4062 Blvd St-Laurent; ⏰4pm-2:30am; Ⓜ St-Laurent, then bus 55) Cheap, gritty, loud, fun and a little bit out of control – just the way we like our dive bars. Live bluegrass and rockabilly bands and bedraggled hipsters hold court alongside aging rockers at this St-Laurent hole-in-the-wall.

Majestique BAR
(Map p240; ☎514-439-1850; www.restobarmajestique.com; 4105 Blvd St-Laurent; ⏰4pm-3am daily, 11am-3pm Sun; Ⓜ St-Laurent, then bus 55) The Majestique manages to be both kitschy and classy at the same time, with wood-paneled walls, warm lighting and a buck's head presiding over the tables. The bartenders whip up some beautiful concoctions here, and the food menu is equally creative.

Dominion Square Tavern TAVERNA
(Map p236; ☎514-564-5056; www.dominiontavern.com; 1245 Rue Metcalfe; ⏰11:30am-midnight Mon-Fri, 4:30pm-midnight Sat & Sun; Ⓜ Peel) Once a down-and-out watering hole dating from the 1920s, this beautifully renovated tavern recalls a classic French bistro but with a long bar, English pub–style. Executive chef Éric Dupuis puts his own spin on pub grub, with mussels cooked with bacon, and smoked trout salad with curry dressing.

L'Île Noire PUB
(Map p240; ☎514-982-0866; www.ilenoire.com; 1649 Rue St-Denis; ⏰3pm-3am; Ⓜ Berri-UQAM) Roll into this slice of the Scottish Highlands in the heart of the Quartier Latin and sip from the selection of more than 140 scotches and whiskeys, as well as 15 varieties of beer on tap and several dozen wine choices.

Le Saint Sulpice PUB
(Map p240; ☎514-844-9458; www.lesaintsulpice.ca; 1680 Rue St-Denis; ⏰3:30pm-3:30am, closed Mon; Ⓜ Berri-UQAM) This student evergreen is spread over four levels in an old Victorian stone house – a cafe, several terraces, a disco and a sprawling back garden for drinks 'n' chats. The music changes with the DJ's mood, from hip-hop and ambient to mainstream rock and jazz.

Pub Pit Caribou MICROBREWERY
(Map p240; ☎514-522-9773; www.pitcaribou.com; 951 Rue Rachel Est; ⏰2pm-3am Mon-Sat, to midnight Sun; Ⓜ Mont-Royal) There are some awesome microbreweries in this province, and Pit Caribou is one of the greats. It has an outpost here in Montréal that serves its full line of hearty, sudsy goodness.

Le Lab COCKTAIL BAR
(Map p240; ☎514-544-1333; www.barlelab.com; 1351 Rue Rachel Est; ⏰5pm-3am; Ⓜ Mont-Royal) Home to some of Montréal's best cocktails, Le Lab prides itself on its wildly inventive elixirs and knowledgeable 'labtenders' who can whip up beautiful concoctions to suit your taste. The setting is classy, with a long solid-wood bar, vest- and tie-wearing staff, and old-fashioned decor, but it remains a fun, unpretentious place.

Upstairs BAR
(Map p236; ☎514-931-6808; www.upstairsjazz.com; 1254 Rue Mackay; ⏰11:30am-1am Mon-Thu, to 2am Fri, 5:30pm-2am Sat, 6:30pm-1am Sun; Ⓜ Guy-Concordia) This slick downtown bar hosts quality jazz and blues acts nightly, featuring both local and touring talent. The walled terrace behind the bar is enchanting at sunset, and the dinner menu features inventive salads and meals.

Pub Ste-Élisabeth PUB
(Map p240; ☎514-286-4302; www.ste-elisabeth.com; 1412 Rue Ste-Élisabeth; ⏰3pm-3am; Ⓜ Berri-UQAM) Tucked off a side street, this handsome pub is frequented by many for its heavenly vine-covered courtyard and drinks menu with a great selection of beers, whiskeys and ports. It has a respectable lineup of beers on tap, including imports and microbrewery fare.

Terrasse Nelligan BAR
(Map p232; ☎514-788-4021; www.terrassenelligan.com; 106 Rue St-Paul Ouest; ⏰11:30am-11:30pm summer; Ⓜ Place-d'Armes) Above heritage Hôtel Nelligan (p244), this delightful patio is the perfect spot to down a mojito while the sun sinks. There's a full menu for lunch and dinner, and splendid views over the St Lawrence River and the Old Port.

Bleury Bar à Vinyle BAR
(Map p236; ☎514-439-2033; www.vinylebleury.ca; 2109 Rue de Bleury; ⏰9pm-3am Tue, Wed, Fri & Sat, from 8pm Thu; Ⓜ Place-des-Arts) It's in a bit of a nightlife desert, but this cozy lounge-like space is well worth the trip if you're into music. A blend of DJs and live bands mixes things up, with a packed calendar of soul, funk, new-wave disco, world beats and house music.

Philémon CLUB
(Map p232; ☎514-289-3777; www.philemonbar.com; 111 Rue St-Paul Ouest; ⏰5pm-3am Mon-Wed, from 4pm Thu-Sat, from 6pm Sun; Ⓜ Place-d'Armes) A major stop for local scenesters rotating between watering holes in the old city, Philémon was carved out of stone, brick and wood with large windows looking out over Rue St-Paul. Twenty-somethings fill the space around a huge central bar sipping basic cocktails and nibbling on light fare (oysters, charcuterie plates, smoked-meat sandwiches), while a DJ spins house and hip-hop.

Burgundy Lion PUB
(☎514-934-0888; www.burgundylion.com; 2496 Rue Notre-Dame Ouest; ⏰11:30am-3am Mon-Fri, 9am-3am Sat & Sun; Ⓜ Lionel-Groulx) This trendy take on the English pub features pub fare, beers and whiskeys galore, and an attitude-free vibe where everyone (and their parents) feels welcome to drink, eat and be merry. Things get the good kind of crazy on late-night weekends.

☆ Entertainment

Montréal is Canada's unofficial arts capital, with both French and English theater, dance, classical and jazz music, and all sorts of interesting blends of the above on stage virtually every night of the week. The city's bilingualism makes it unique and encourages creative collaborations and cross-pollinations that light up the performing-arts scene.

Live Music

Le 4e Mur LIVE MUSIC
(Map p240; http://le4emur.com; 2021 Rue St-Denis; ⏰5pm-3am, from 7pm Sun; Ⓜ Sherbrooke) This bar is literally behind an unmarked door – look for a big intimidating bouncer or the beautiful folks walking past him. Follow on, into a basement bar where the cocktails are expertly mixed, live music pops off regularly, and burlesque is a regular fixture.

Le Divan Orange LIVE MUSIC
(Map p240; ☎514-840-9090; www.divanorange.org; 4234 Blvd St-Laurent; ⏰5pm-3am; Ⓜ St-Laurent, then bus 50) This space was launched as a kind of restaurant-entertainment venue co-op. There's a terrific artistic vibe here. On any given night there may be a DJ, world-music performer or record launch.

La Rockette LIVE MUSIC
(Rockette Bar; Map p240; ☎514-845-9010; 4479 Rue St-Denis; ⏰4pm-3am) Part bar, part concert venue, all grotty as hell, La Rockette is a grand, intimate (read: sometimes loud and cramped) spot to catch a show, and if a show isn't on, it's a good spot for a cheap beer.

Bistro à Jojo BLUES
(Map p240; ☎514-843-5015; www.bistroajojo.com; 1627 Rue St-Denis; ⏰noon-3am; Ⓜ Berri-UQAM) This brash venue in the Quartier Latin has been going strong since 1975. It's the nightly place for down 'n' dirty French- and English-language blues and rock groups. Sit close enough to see the band members sweat.

Dièse Onze LIVE MUSIC
(Map p240; ☎514-223-3543; www.dieseonze.com; 4115 Rue St-Denis; around $10; ⏰6pm-late; Ⓜ Mont-Royal) This downstairs jazz club has just the right vibe – with an intimate small stage so you can get close to the musicians.

GAY & LESBIAN MONTRÉAL

Montréal is a popular getaway for lesbian, gay and bisexual travelers. The gay community is centered in The Village, and it's huge business. The weeklong **Montréal Pride** (p243) attracts hundreds of thousands every August, while the **Black & Blue Festival** (p243) in early October features major dance parties along with cultural and arts events.

Gays and lesbians are well integrated into Montréal life. In neighborhoods such as the Plateau, for example, two men holding hands in public will scarcely raise an eyebrow.

The **Montréal Gay & Lesbian Community Centre & Library** (☎514-528-8424; www.ccglm.org; 2075 Rue Plessis; ⏰1-6pm Mon-Fri, to 8pm Wed; Ⓜ Beaudry) has been around since 1988 and provides an extensive library and loads of info on the city's gay and lesbian scene.

Fugues (www.fugues.com) is the free, French-language, authoritative monthly guide to the gay and lesbian scene for the province of Québec. It's an excellent place to find out about the latest clubs and gay-friendly accommodations.

There are shows most nights, with an eclectic lineup of artists. You can have a bite while the band plays, with good tapas options as well as a few heartier mains (goat's-cheese burger, mushroom risotto). Call for reservations.

Casa del Popolo LIVE MUSIC
(Map p240; ☎514-284-0122; www.casadelpopolo.com; 4873 Blvd St-Laurent; admission $5-15; ⏰noon-3am; Ⓜ Laurier) One of Montréal's most charming live venues, the 'House of the People' is also known for its vegetarian sandwiches and salads, its talented DJs and as a venue for art-house films and spoken-word performances. It's associated with the tapas bar La Sala Rosa (p249) and its concert venue La Sala Rossa.

Foufounes Électriques LIVE MUSIC
(Map p240; ☎514-844-5539; www.foufounes electriques.com; 87 Rue Ste-Catherine Est; ⏰3pm-3am; Ⓜ St-Laurent) A one-time bastion of the alternafreak, this cavernous quintessential punk venue still stages some wild music nights (rockabilly, ska, metal), plus the odd one-off (a night of pro-wrestling or an indoor skateboarding contest). The graffiti-covered walls and industrial charm should tip you off that 'Electric Buttocks' isn't exactly a mainstream kinda place.

Orchestre Symphonique de Montréal CLASSICAL MUSIC
(OSM; Map p240; ☎514-840-7400; www.osm.ca/en; 1600 Rue St-Urbain, Maison Symphonique, Pl des Arts; Ⓜ Place-des-Arts) This internationally renowned orchestra plays to packed audiences in its Place des Arts base, the Maison Symphonique de Montréal, a venue with spectacular acoustics that was inaugurated in 2011. The OSM's Christmas performance of *The Nutcracker* is legendary.

Rock-star conductor Kent Nagano, a Californian with a leonine mane and stellar credentials, took over as music director in 2006 and has proven very popular. Check for free concerts at the Basilique Notre-Dame (p230), the Olympic Stadium and in municipal parks in the Montréal area.

Theater & Dance

Cirque du Soleil THEATER
(Map p232; www.cirquedusoleil.com; Quai Jacques-Cartier; Ⓜ Champ-de-Mars) Globally famous Cirque du Soleil, one of the city's most famous exports, puts on a new production of acrobats and music in this marvelous tent complex roughly once every two years in summer. These shows rarely disappoint, so don't pass up a chance to see one on its home turf.

Cabaret Mado CABARET
(Map p240; ☎514-525-7566; www.mado.qc.ca; 1115 Rue Ste-Catherine Est; tickets $5-15; ⏰4pm-3am Tue-Sun; Ⓜ Beaudry) Mado is a flamboyant celebrity who has been featured in *Fugues*, the gay entertainment mag. Her cabaret is a local institution, with drag shows featuring an assortment of hilariously sarcastic performers in eye-popping costumes. Shows take place Tuesday, Thursday and weekend nights; check the website for details.

Théâtre St-Denis PERFORMING ARTS
(Map p240; ☎514-849-4211; www.theatrestdenis.com; 1594 Rue St-Denis; ⏰box office noon-6pm Mon-Sat; Ⓜ Berri-UQAM) This Montréal landmark and historic movie house hosts touring Broadway productions, rock concerts and various theatrical and musical performances. Its two halls are equipped with the latest sound and lighting gizmos and figure prominently in the Just for Laughs Festival (p243).

Centaur Theatre THEATER
(Map p232; ☎514-288-3161; www.centaurtheatre.com; 453 Rue St-François-Xavier; Ⓜ Place-d'Armes) Montréal's chief English-language theater presents everything from Shakespearean classics to works by experimental Canadian playwrights. It occupies Montréal's former stock exchange (1903), a striking building with classical columns.

Sports

Bell Centre STADIUM
(Map p236; ☎877-668-8269, 514-790-2525; www.centrebell.ca; 1909 Ave des Canadiens-de-Montréal) When it's not hosting matches of the city's beloved Montréal Canadiens hockey team, this 21,000-seat arena in downtown hosts all the big concerts. The likes of U2 and Céline Dion usually end up here when they're in town.

Montréal Alouettes FOOTBALL
(☎514-871-2255; www.montrealalouettes.com; Ave des Pins Ouest, Molson Stadium; tickets from $29; Ⓜ McGill) The Montréal Alouettes, a star franchise of the Canadian Football League, folded several times before going on to win the league's Grey Cup trophy in 2002, 2009 and 2010. Rules are a bit different from American football: the field is bigger and there are only three downs. Games are held at McGill University's Molson Stadium and sometimes at the Stade Olympique.

Shopping

Style is synonymous with Montréal living. The city itself is beautiful and locals live up to the standard it sets. Maybe it's that much touted European influence, but most Montréalers seem to instinctively lead stylish lives regardless of income level, enjoying aesthetic pleasures such as food, art and, of course, fashion.

Music, Books & Stationery

★ **Drawn & Quarterly** BOOKS
(☎514-279-2224; http://211blog.drawnandquarterly.com; 211 Rue Bernard Ouest; ⊙10am-9pm; Ⓜ Outremont) The flagship store of this cult independent comic-book and graphic-novel publisher has become something of a local literary haven. Cool book launches take place here, and the quaint little shop sells all sorts of reading matter including children's books, vintage Tintin comics, recent fiction and art books.

Librairie Planète BD COMICS
(Map p240; ☎514-759-9800; www.planetebd.ca; 3883 Rue St-Denis; ⊙10am-6pm Mon-Wed, Sat & Sun, to 9pm Thu & Fri; Ⓜ Sherbrooke) If you have a thing for comics and graphic novels – particularly French-language ones – this is a must-stop store. The owners have a passion for their beloved medium, and carry titles you'd be hard-pressed to find anywhere else.

Cheap Thrills MUSIC
(Map p236; ☎514-844-8988; www.cheapthrills.ca; 2044 Rue Metcalfe; ⊙11am-6pm Mon-Wed & Sat, to 9pm Thu & Fri, noon-5pm Sun) It's easy to lose track of time as you browse through this big selection of used books and music (CDs and some vinyl), both with a mainstream and off-beat bent and sold at bargain prices.

Le Port de Tête BOOKS
(Map p240; ☎514-678-9566; www.leportdetete.com; 262 Ave du Mont-Royal Est; ⊙10am-10pm Mon-Sat, to 8pm Sun; Ⓜ Mont-Royal) This is a wonderfully curated bookstore that often showcases up-and-coming work from dynamic small publishers. The selection is eclectic as hell: thousands of philosophy titles share space with plays, poetry and graphic novels.

Arts & Crafts

Artpop ARTS & CRAFTS
(Map p240; ☎514-843-3443; 129 Ave du Mont-Royal Est; ⊙10am-8pm Mon-Wed, to 9pm Thu & Fri, 10am-7pm Sat, from 11am Sun; Ⓜ Mont-oyal) Though tiny in size, Artpop is a real find when it comes to browsing for unique Montréal-themed gift ideas. You'll find graphic T-shirts, bags, pillow cases, iPhone covers and prints with iconic city signage.

Au Papier Japonais ARTS & CRAFTS
(Map p240; ☎514-276-6863; www.aupapierjaponais.com; 24 Ave Fairmount Ouest; ⊙10am-6pm Mon-Sat, noon-4pm Sun; Ⓜ Laurier) You might never guess how many guises Japanese paper can come in until you visit this gorgeous little shop, which stocks more than 800 varieties. Origami kits and art books make great gifts, as do the elegant tea pots, pottery and Buddha boards (where you can 'paint' ephemeral works with water).

Food

Le Marché des Saveurs du Québec FOOD & DRINKS
(☎514-271-3811; www.lemarchedessaveurs.com; 280 Pl du Marché-du-Nord; ⊙9am-6pm Sat-Wed, to 8pm Thu & Fri; Ⓜ Jean-Talon) Everything here is Québécois, from the food to the handmade soaps to one of the best collections of artisanal local beer, maple products, jams and cheeses in the city. The store was established so local producers could gain wider exposure for their regional products, and it's a joy to browse.

Marché St-Jacques MARKET
(Map p240; 514-418-6527; www.marchesaintjacques.com; 1125 Rue Ontario; 9am-7pm Mon-Fri, to 6pm Sat, to 5pm Sun; ; Beaudry) A market has stood here since 1879, making it one of the oldest public *marchés* in Canada. The current building dates from 1931 and boasts a lovely art-deco design. While the offerings are limited – especially compared to **Marché Jean-Talon** (514-937-7754; www.marchespublics-mtl.com; 7075 Ave Casgrain; 7am-6pm Mon-Wed & Sat, to 8pm Thu & Fri, to 5pm Sun; P ; Jean-Talon) and Marché Atwater (p234) – this is still a fine place to pick up a picnic or a quick bite while exploring The Village.

Clothing

Friperie St-Laurent FASHION & ACCESSORIES, VINTAGE
(Map p240; 514-842-3893; 3976 Blvd St-Laurent; 11am-6pm Mon-Wed, to 8pm Thu & Fri, to 5pm Sat, noon-5pm Sun; Sherbrooke) One of the Plateau's best-loved *friperies* (vintage shops) has a small but well-chosen selection of clothing from decades past. Fur-lined bomber jackets, elegant 1950s dresses, cowboy and motorcycle boots, tweed jackets and old college sweaters are all part of the treasure chest.

Other Specialties

★ **Monastiraki** VINTAGE
(www.monastiraki.blogspot.ca; 5478 Blvd St-Laurent; noon-6pm Wed, to 8pm Thu & Fri, to 5pm Sat & Sun; Laurier) This unclassifiable store named after a flea-market neighborhood in Athens calls itself a 'hybrid curiosity shop/art space,' but that doesn't do justice to what illustrator Billy Mavreas sells: 1960s comic books, contemporary zines (homemade magazines), silkscreen posters, and myriad antique and collectible knickknacks, as well as recent works mainly by local graphic artists.

Jet-Setter TRAVEL GOODS
(Map p240; 514-271-5058; www.jet-setter.ca; 66 Ave Laurier Ouest; 10am-6pm Mon-Wed, to 9pm Thu & Fri, to 5pm Sat, noon-5pm Sun; Laurier) An orgy of state-of-the-art luggage and clever travel gadgetry, Jet-Setter has inflatable sacks for wine bottles, pocket-sized T-shirts, 'dry-in-an-instant' underwear, silk sleep sacks, mini-irons and hairdryers, waterproof hats and loads of other items.

Aux Quatre Points Cardinaux MAPS
(Map p240; 514-843-8116; www.aqpc.com; 551 Rue Ontario Est; 10am-6pm Mon-Wed, to 9pm Thu & Fri, to 5pm Sat; Berri-UQAM) The globe-trotting folks at AQPC pack a range of goods for the seasoned traveler such as atlases, globes, maps, aerial photographs, and travel guides in English and French, including a good selection of Lonely Planet books.

Information

EMERGENCY

Montréal Police Station (emergencies 911, nonemergencies 514-280-2222)

MEDIA

Newspapers The *Montréal Gazette* is the main English-language daily newspaper with solid coverage of national affairs, politics and arts. The Saturday edition has useful what's-on listings.

Magazines The online alternative magazines *Cult* (www.cultmontreal.com) and *Hour Community* (www.hour.ca) are even better sources of what's-on listings.

Blogs *MTL Blog* (www.mtlblog.com) is great for up-to-date listings and lots of listicles.

MEDICAL SERVICES

CLSC (Centre Local de Services Communautaires; 514-934-0354; www.santemontreal.qc.ca/en; 1801 Blvd de Maisonneuve Ouest; 8am-8pm Mon-Fri; Guy-Concordia) Walk-in community health center for minor ailments.

Health Hotline (811) Call for non-urgent health services.

Montréal General Hospital (514-934-1934; www.muhc.ca/mgh; 1650 Ave Cedar; Guy-Concordia)

Pharmaprix Pharmacy (www.pharmaprix.ca; 1500 Rue Ste-Catherine Ouest; 8am-midnight; Guy-Concordia) This 'mega-chemist' also has a 24-hour location near **Mont Royal** (514-738-8464; 5122 Chemin de la Côte-des-Neiges).

Sexual Assault Center (in Montréal 514-398-8500, in Québec City 418-522-2120; www.sacomss.org/wp)

MONEY

Calforex (www.calforex.com; 1230 Rue Peel; 8:30am-9pm Mon-Sat, 10am-6pm Sun)

POST

Canada Post (Postes Canada; 866-607-6301, 416-979-3033; www.canadapost.ca) Canada's national postal system.

TOURIST INFORMATION

Centre Infotouriste Montréal (Map p236; 514-844-5400, 800-230-0001; www.tourisme-montreal.org; 1255 Rue Peel; 8:30am-7pm; Peel) Information about Montréal and all of Québec. Free hotel, tour and car reservations, plus currency exchange.

Tourisme Québec (in Canada 877-266-5687, worldwide 514-873-2015; www.tourisme.gouv.

qc.ca) Québec's province-wide tourist bureau, Tourisme Québec, operates tourist offices (known as Centres Infotouristes) in both Montréal and Québec City.

USEFUL WEBSITES

The Main MTL (www.themainmtl.com) Insider take on the latest in dining, drinking, music and the arts.

Ville de Montréal (www.ville.montreal.qc.ca) Useful travel info and events calendar from the city's official website.

Getting There & Away

AIR

Montréal is served by **Pierre Elliott Trudeau International Airport** (Trudeau YUL; www.admtl.com), known in French as Aéroport Montréal-Trudeau, or simply as Trudeau Airport. It's about 21km west of downtown and is the hub of most domestic, US and overseas flights. Trudeau Airport (still sometimes known by its old name, Dorval airport) has decent connections to the city by car and shuttle bus.

Autocars Skyport (☎514-631-1155; www.skyportinternational.com; one-way/return adult $98/165) Autocars Skyport runs express shuttles from Trudeau Airport to Mont-Tremblant ski resort in winter and summer.

BUS

Galland Laurentides (Map p240; ☎450-687-8666, 877-806-8666; www.galland-bus.com; 1717 Rue Berri; to Mont-Tremblant one-way/round trip $29/58) Provides bus service from Montréal to Mont-Tremblant and other destinations in the Laurentians.

Greyhound (www.greyhound.ca) Operates long-distance routes to Ottawa, Toronto, Vancouver, Boston, New York City and other points throughout Canada and the United States.

Limocar (www.limocar.ca) Offers bus service from Montréal to the Eastern Townships.

Moose Travel Network (www.moosenetwork.com) Popular with backpackers, this network operates several circuits around Canada, allowing travelers to jump on and jump off along the way. Pickup points are in Montréal, Québec City, Ottawa and Toronto, among other places. Destinations within Québec include Mont-Tremblant and the Gaspé Peninsula.

Orléans Express (www.orleansexpress.com) Makes the three-hour run between Montréal and Québec City.

CAR & MOTORCYCLE

All the major international car-rental companies have branches at the airport, main train station and elsewhere around town. **Auto Plateau** (☎514-281-5000; www.autoplateau.com; 3585 Rue Berri; M Sherbrooke) is a reputable local company.

Kangaride (p229) is a reliable online ride share agency. A sample fare is around $15 to Québec City.

TRAIN

Canada's trains are arguably the most enjoyable and romantic way to travel the country. Long-distance trips are quite a bit more expensive than those by bus, however, and reservations are crucial for weekend and holiday travel. A few days' notice can cut fares a lot.

Gare Centrale (Central Train Station; ☎arrivals & departures 888-842-7245, info & reservations ☎514-989-2626; www.viarail.ca; 895 Rue de la Gauchetière Ouest; M Bonaventure) The local hub of **VIA Rail** (☎514-989-2626; www.viarail.ca; M Bonaventure), Canada's vast rail network, which links Montréal with cities all across the country.

Amtrak (www.amtrak.com) Provides service between New York City and Montréal on its Adirondack line. The trip, though slow (11 hours), passes through lovely scenery along Lake Champlain and the Hudson River.

AMT (☎514-287-8726; www.amt.qc.ca/en) Commuter trains serve the suburbs of Montréal. Services from Gare Centrale are fast but infrequent, with two-hour waits between some trains.

FERRY

Ferries (Map p232; ☎514-281-8000; http://navettesmaritimes.com; Quai Jacques Cartier; one-way $4.25; ⊙mid-May–Oct) These ferries run between the Old Port and Parc Jean-Drapeau.

Getting Around

TO/FROM THE AIRPORT

Bus

Bus 747, the cheapest way to get into town, takes 45 to 60 minutes. Buses run round the clock, leaving from just outside the arrivals hall and dropping passengers downtown at the **Gare d'Autocars** (Map p240; ☎514-842-2281; www.gamtl.com; 1717 Rue Berri; M Berri-UQAM) and the Berri-UQAM metro station, in the Quartier Latin. The $10 fare can be paid by Visa, MasterCard or cash at vending machines in the international arrivals area, or tickets may be bought on board (coins only, exact change). Your ticket gives you unlimited travel on Montréal's bus and metro network for 24 hours.

Taxi

It takes at least 20 minutes to get downtown from the airport and the fixed fare is $40. Limousine services ($55 and up) are also available.

PUBLIC TRANSPORTATION

STM (Société de Transport de Montréal; ☎514-786-4636; www.stm.info) STM is the city's bus and metro (subway) operator. Schedules vary depending on the line, but trains generally run from 5:30am to midnight from Sunday to Friday, slightly later on Saturday night (to 1:30am at the latest).

A single bus or metro ticket costs $3.25. Two-ride tickets ($6) are also available in metro stations. If you're sticking around Montréal for longer, you'll save money by buying a rechargeable Opus card; the card costs $6 up front, but can be recharged at a discounted rate for 10 rides ($26.50), one day of unlimited rides ($10), three days ($18), a week ($25.50, Monday to Sunday) or a calendar month ($82).

Buses take tickets or cash but drivers won't give change. If transferring from the metro to a bus, use your original metro ticket as a free bus transfer. If you're switching between buses, or between bus and the metro, ask the driver for a free transfer slip (*correspondance* in French).

TAXI

Flag fall is a standard $3.45, plus another $1.70 per kilometer and 63¢ per minute spent waiting in traffic. Prices are posted on the windows inside taxis.

Taxi Co-Op (☎514-725-9885; www.taxi-coop.com) Provides taxi service in Montréal.

Taxi Champlain (☎514-273-1111; www.taxichamplain.qc.ca) Provides taxi service in Montréal.

THE LAURENTIANS

The Laurentians, or Les Laurentides in French, are perhaps the best-kept secret of Montréal day-trippers and are just an hour's drive from the city. Here you'll find gentle rolling mountains, crystal-blue lakes and meandering rivers peppered with towns and villages. A visit to this natural paradise is like putting your feet up after a long day.

Although sometimes criticized for being over-commercialized, Mont Tremblant offers outstanding skiing, rivaled only by Whistler in the whole of Canada. Speckling the Laurentians are many more lower-profile resort villages, whose miniature town centers deliver an air of the Alps, with breezy patios and exclusive, independent designer-clothing shops.

Expect higher prices and heavy crowds during high season, which includes the summer months and Christmas holidays. Check ahead for opening hours in winter.

ℹ Information

Tourisme Laurentides (☎800-561-6673, reservations 450-224-7007; www.laurentides.com; La Porte-du-Nord, Hwy 15, Exit 51; ⏲9am-8pm late Jun–early Sep, to 5pm rest of year) The regional tourist office can answer questions on the phone, make room bookings and mail out information. It operates a free room-reservation service, which specializes in lodgings along the **Parc Linéaire le P'tit Train du Nord** trail.

ℹ Getting There & Around

Galland Laurentides (p257) runs buses from Montréal's Central Bus Station to the Laurentians three times daily. Towns serviced include St-Jérôme, St-Sauveur, Val-David and Mont-Tremblant.

Nearly all towns in the Laurentians can be accessed via Hwy 15, the Autoroute des Laurentides. Old Rte 117, running parallel to it, is slow but considerably more scenic.

From mid-May to mid-October, **Autobus Le Petit Train du Nord** (☎888-893-8356, 450-569-5596; www.autobuslepetittraindunord.com; shuttle ticket $28-70, rental bike per day/week $25/126; ⏲mid-May–mid-Oct) runs two buses daily between St-Jérôme and Mont Laurier (tickets $28 to $70), stopping as needed. Bicycles are transported at no charge.

St-Jérôme

Some 43km north of Montréal, St-Jérôme is the official gateway to the Laurentians. Despite its administrative and industrial demeanor, it's worth a stop for the Roman-Byzantine-style **cathedral** (355 Pl du Curé-Labelle; ⏲8:30am-4:30pm Mon-Fri, to noon Sat & Sun; P) FREE. It's also the southern terminus of the **Parc Linéaire le P'tit Train du Nord** (☎450-745-0185; www.laurentides.com/parclineaire; ♿), a trail system built on top of old railway tracks. Less than an hour from Montréal, the nearby **Musée d'Art Contemporain des Laurentides** (☎450-432-7171; www.museelaurentides.ca; 101 Pl du Curé-Labelle; admission by donation; ⏲noon-5pm Tue-Sun, from 10am Sat; P), a contemporary-art museum, has small but superb exhibitions of work by regional artists.

St-Sauveur-des-Monts

St-Sauveur-des-Monts (or St-Sauveur, for short) is the busiest village in the Laurentians and is often deluged with day-trippers thanks to its proximity to Montréal (60km). A pretty church anchors Rue Principale, the attractive main street, which is flanked by restaurants, cafes and boutiques.

With about 100 runs for all levels of expertise crisscrossing five major ski hills, the downhill skiing is excellent in the region surrounding St-Sauveur. The biggest hill, Mont St-Sauveur, is famous for its night skiing. Thrill-seekers might also enjoy **Le Dragon**, a double zip line, and **Viking**, a scenic, dry 1.5 km-long toboggan ride through rugged mountain terrain; both are within the **St-Sauveur Valley Resort**, along with Mont St-Sauveur and Parc Aquatique. Cross-country skiers flock to the over 150km of interconnecting trails at Morin Heights.

St-Sauveur's Festival des Arts happens in late July.

Activities

Parc Aquatique WATER SPORTS
(Water Park; 450-227-4671; www.parcaquatique.com; 350 Rue St-Denis; adult/youth/child per day $37/30/17, half-day $28/27/15; 10am-7pm Jun-Aug, to 5pm Sep;) In summer, Mont St-Sauveur is transformed into the Parc Aquatique. Kids of all ages love getting wet in the wave pool, plunging down slides (some accessible by ski chairlift) or being pummeled on rafting rides.

Mont St-Sauveur SKIING
(450-227-4671, 514-871-0101; www.montsaintsauveur.com; 350 Ave St-Denis; lift ticket adult/youth/child $56/48/38; 9am-10pm Mon-Fri, 8:30am-10pm Sat & Sun Nov-Mar;) Mont St-Sauveur is one of the area's main ski centers. Hills are a bit tame but there's night skiing, a huge variety of runs and 100% snow coverage in season, thanks to snow blowers built into the slopes.

Festivals & Events

Festival des Arts PERFORMING ARTS
(450-227-0427; http://festivaldesarts.ca/en; late Jul) For eight days St-Sauveur's Festival des Arts brings dozens of international dance troupes to town. Many performances are free.

Sleeping & Eating

Le Petit Clocher B&B $$
(450-227-7576; www.lepetitclocher.com; 216 Rue de l'Église; s $165-215, d $185-235; P) A gorgeous inn occupying a converted monastery on a little hillside above town, Le Petit Clocher has seven rooms decorated in French Country style, many of which have lovely views.

Auberge Sous L'Edredon B&B $$
(450-227-3131; www.aubergesousledredon.com; 777 Rue Principale; r $139-199;) This Victorian inn, about 2km from the village center and close to a little lake, is overflowing with character. Some of the delightfully decorated rooms, which are more modern than the exterior suggests, have fireplaces and Jacuzzis.

La Brûlerie des Monts CAFE $
(450-227-6157; www.bruleriedesmonts.com; 197 Rue Principale; mains $5-13; 6am-7pm Mon Wed, to 8pm Thu, to 9pm Fri & Sat, 6:30am-7pm Sun;) *The* place in town for breakfast and sandwiches, with a great terrace. Coffee beans are roasted on-site.

Chez Bernard DELI $
(450-240-0000; www.chezbernard.com; 407 Rue Principale; dishes $6-15; 10am-6pm Mon-Thu, to 8pm Fri, 9am-6pm Sat, 10am-5pm Sun;) Superb deli with local specialties, some of which are homemade, plus full meals perfect for picnics.

Orange & Pamplemousse FUSION $$
(450-227-4330; www.orangepamplemousse.com; 120 Rue Principale; mains $14-32; 8am-2:30pm daily, plus 5-9pm Wed-Sun; P) Tranquil with the soft sounds of a Japanese bamboo water fountain, this restaurant is a great place to devour complex pasta dishes and extraordinary grilled fish. The breakfasts are also divine.

Le Rio BARBECUE $$
(www.riorestaurant.ca; 352 Rue Principale; mains $14-35; 4-10pm; P) It's a bit strange to imagine ordering a barbecue dinner in the mountains of rural Québec, but this classy diner (which, again, is a weird setting for barbecue) gets great reviews from American tourists and locals alike. Don't leave without at least a taste of the succulent, fall-off-the-bone baby back ribs.

Information

Tourist Office (450-227-2564; www.valleesaintsauveur.com; 30 Rue Fillion, Ste-Adèle) Friendly place providing information about guided tours and accommodations in the area.

Val-David

Tiny Val-David is the sort of village where, after a few hours enjoying great food, lovely wooded trails, strong coffee and views of the Rivière du Nord (running through the heart of everything), you start checking out real-estate listings. Its charms have made it a magnet for artists, whose studios and galleries line the main street, Rue de L'Église.

This was a major hippie mecca in the '60s, and there's more than a little New Age energy apparent today. This is balanced (and enhanced) by artisanal bakeries, jazz music in cafes on summer weekends and more than a few arts-and-crafts people. The town's tourist office, in a cute old train station, is handily located alongside the Parc Linéaire le P'tit Train du Nord (p258) recreation trail. Check out the **Val-David Farmers Market** (Marché d'Été; 9am-1pm Sat late May–mid-Oct) if you're in town on a Saturday morning.

Activities

The great outdoors is one of Val-David's main attractions. **Roc & Ride** (819-322-7978; www.rocnride.com; 2444 Rue de l'Église; cross-country skiing kit per half day/day $20/25; 9am-5pm Sat-Wed, to 6pm Thu & Fri) rents cross-country skis, snowshoes, skates, and in summer, bicycles. **À l'Abordage** (819-322-1234; www.activites-plein-air-laurentides.com; 2268 Rue de l'Église; 3hr kayak tours from $40; 9am-4:30pm Jun 23-Sep 5) rents bicycles, kayaks and canoes, and offers cycle-canoe packages and guided tours on the Rivière du Nord.

Rock climbing is to Val-David what skiing is to other Laurentian villages, with more than 500 routes – from easy walls to challenging cliffs.

A pedestrian and cycling path runs alongside **Chemin de la Rivière**, which in turn hugs the Rivière du Nord and winds through much of town. The well-maintained green way offers lovely views onto the water, especially around La Maison de Bavière, where a picturesque stone bridge crosses a rushing waterfall before linking up with a short footpath that leads to Chemin de l'Île.

Festivals & Events

1001 Pots Festival ART
(www.1001pots.com; mid-Jul–mid-Aug) This huge ceramic exhibit and sale with workshops brings around 100,000 people to town every summer.

Sleeping & Eating

★ **La Maison de Bavière** B&B $$
(819-322-3528; www.maisondebaviere.com; 1470 Chemin de la Rivière; r $115-165; P @) Fall asleep to the sound of Rivière du Nord outside the window. This inn has hand-painted Bavarian stencils and wooden beams giving it a European ski-chalet feel. Everything is geared toward a day of outdoors pursuits, from its location on the Parc Linéaire le P'tit Train du Nord (p258) trail to the energizing, full-gourmet breakfasts served each morning.

Le Mouton Noir FUSION $$
(819-322-1571; www.bistromoutonnoir.com; 2301 Rue de l'Église; 8am-9pm Mon-Wed, to 11pm Thu & Fri, 10am-11pm Sat, 10am-9pm Sun) This artsy spot attracts a very Val-Davidian crowd of beards – some hippie-esque, some hipster-esque, some lumberjack-y (female customers run the same gamut, sans the facial hair). Everyone enjoys some funky Canadian fusion: ever had poutine mixed with an Indian-style curry? It's pretty delicious. Live music keeps this black sheep rocking till late on weekends.

Bistro Des Artistes CANADIAN $$
(819-320-0899; www.bistroartistesvaldavid.com; 2489 Rue de l'Église; mains $13-28; 11am-9pm;) A seasonal, locally sourced menu serves up well-executed Canadian comfort food, from grilled local sausage and mash to perfect pizzas sent steaming from the oven. The wine list is pretty fantastic.

Drinking & Nightlife

Le Baril Roulant MICROBREWERY
(www.barilroulant.wordpress.com; 2434 Rue de l'Église; 3pm-midnight Mon-Thu, noon-1am Fri-Sun) Laid-back and brimming with local color, this artsy microbrewery complements its own creations with a plethora of other brews from the surrounding area. Chill on the outdoor deck in summer, or get cozy on multicolored chairs and couches in the brightly painted interior. Live bands and DJs provide regular entertainment, from jazz to psychedelia to electro-pop.

Information

Tourist Information Office (ext 4235 819-324-5678; www.valdavid.com; 2525 Rue de l'Église; 9am-5pm) This very helpful tourist office is located just off the town green, itself cut through by the Parc Linéaire du P'tit Train du Nord.

Ville de Mont-Tremblant

The Mont-Tremblant area is the crown jewel of the Laurentians, lorded over by the 968m-high eponymous mountain and dotted with pristine lakes and traversed by rivers. It's a hugely popular four-season playground, drawing ski bums from late October to mid-

April, and hikers, cyclists, golfers, water-sports fans and other outdoor enthusiasts the rest of the year.

The area of Ville de Mont-Tremblant is divided into three sections: Station Tremblant, the ski hill and pedestrianized tourist resort at the foot of the mountain; **Mont-Tremblant Village** (), a tiny cluster of homes and businesses about 4km southwest of here; and **St-Jovite**, the main town and commercial center off Rte 117, about 12km south of the mountain.

Sights & Activities

The southern mountain base spills over into a sparkling pedestrianized **tourist resort**, with big hotels, shops, restaurants and an amusement-park atmosphere. The cookie-cutter architecture doesn't quite exude the rustic European charm its planners sought to emulate, but this seems of little concern to the 2.5 million annual visitors milling along its cobbled lanes year after year.

Founded in 1938, **Mont-Tremblant Ski Resort** (514-764-7546, 888-738-1777; www.tremblant.ca; 1000 Chemin des Voyageurs; lift ticket adult/youth/child $87/60/50; 8:30am-4pm late Nov–mid-Apr;) is among the top-ranked international ski resorts in eastern North America according to *Ski* magazine and legions of loyal fans. The mountain has a vertical drop of 645m and is laced with 95 trails and three snow parks served by 14 lifts, including an express gondola. Ski rentals start at $32 per day.

Numerous kiosks in the **Station Tremblant** pedestrian village can arrange a variety of outdoor pursuits operated by the ski resort. These range from fishing to canoeing to horseback riding; ask for more information about the Scandinavian-style spa, dune-buggy trails, zip lines, hiking trails and literally dozens of other activities. During the summer you'll also see a **luge track** (819-681-3000; www.skylineluge.com/luge-canada/skyline-luge-mont-tremblant; 1/3/5 rides $15.50/23/32; May-Oct;) at the top of the incline on which the pedestrian village is set; the track snakes down the mountain for 1.4km.

Festivals & Events

Festival International du Blues MUSIC

(http://blues.tremblant.ca/en; early Jul) For 10 days the Station Tremblant resort is abuzz with music during the country's biggest blues festival.

Ironman SPORTS

(www.ironman.com; late Aug) Late August sees the annual Ironman North American Championship, which includes a 3.8km swim in Lac Tremblant, a 180km bike ride through surrounding forests and mountains, and a 42.2km run that follows the Parc Linéaire le P'tit Train du Nord (p258) trail and ends in the Station Tremblant pedestrian village. A shorter, less grueling Ironman 70.3 competition takes place here in late June.

Sleeping

HI Mont-Tremblant Hostel HOSTEL $

(819-425-6008, 866-425-6008; http://hostellingtremblant.com/en; 2213 Chemin du Village, Mont-Tremblant Village; dm $30, r $75-100;) This hostel right next to Lac Moore (free canoe rentals) has a big kitchen and large party room with bar, pool table and fireplace. The clean and spacious rooms often fill to capacity, especially in the ski season. Look for it along the main road, 1km east of Mont-Tremblant Village and 4km west of the slopes.

Homewood Suites HOTEL $$

(819-681-0808; www.homewoodsuites.com; 3035 Chemin de la Chapelle, Station Tremblant; ste from $160;) Smack dab in the middle of the pedestrian village, in the heart of all the action in both summer and winter (the ski gondola is 500m from the door), this homey chain has great-value suites with stunning mountain views, spiffy decor and basic hot breakfasts.

Auberge Le Lupin B&B $$

(819-425-5474, 877-425-5474; www.lelupin.com; 127 Rue Pinoteau, Mont-Tremblant Village; r $152-165;) This 1940s log house offers snug digs just 1km away from the ski station, with private beach access to the sparkling Lac Tremblant. The tasty breakfasts whipped up by host Pierre in his homey rustic kitchen are a perfect start to the day.

Hotel Quintessence BOUTIQUE HOTEL $$$

(866-425-3400; www.hotelquintessence.com; 3004 Chemin de la Chapelle, Mont-Tremblant Village; ste from $399;) This estate fuses Old World–style accents with North American nature, from wood fireplaces and private balconies overlooking Lac Tremblant to heated marble floors and plunge baths.

Eating

Creperie Catherine CREPERIE $
(www.creperiecatherine.ca; 977 Rue Labelle, Mont-Tremblant Village; mains $8-16; 7:30am-9pm Sun-Thu, to 10pm Fri & Sat;) This friendly little crêperie is beloved by locals and Québécois day-trippers coming in from the big city. There are over a dozen different crêpes on offer, many of which come swimming in béchamel sauce. Plus, the portions are enormous. Who needed that diet anyway?

Microbrasserie La Diable PUB FOOD $$
(819-681-4546; www.microladiable.com; 117 Chemin Kandahar, Station Tremblant; mains $13-28; 11:30am-2am) After a day of tearing down the mountain, the hearty sausages, burgers and pastas at this lively Station Tremblant tavern fill the belly nicely – although the real highlight here is the fine lineup of microbrews: blonde, red and Belgian trappist ales, wheat beer, double-black stout and rotating monthly specials.

sEb MODERN CANADIAN $$$
(819-429-6991; www.seblartisanculinaire.com; 444 Rue St-Georges, St-Jovite; mains $30-52, multicourse menu $49-90; 6-11pm Thu-Mon) Escape the mediocre and get a little taste of what culinary artisans can create with seasonal, sustainable local ingredients. A flexible, eager-to-please kitchen, an unforgettable menu and a never-ending wine list enhance the jovial atmosphere. sEb is best described as alpine chalet meets globetrotter (think African masks) meets Hollywood chic (Michael Douglas is a regular). Reservations essential.

Information

Centre Médical de St-Jovite (819-425-2728; 992 Rue de St-Jovite, St-Jovite; 8am-7pm Mon-Thu, to 5pm Fri) The local medical clinic.

Mont Tremblant Tourism (877-425-2434; https://mont-tremblant.ca/en; 5080 Montée Ryan, cnr Rte 327; 9am-6pm) The tourism office can help with national park and ski resort planning.

Getting There & Around

Galland Laurentides (p257) buses stop at 231 Rue de St-Jovite (in St-Jovite) and Montagne Chalet des Voyageurs, at the edge of the Station Tremblant tourist village.

A shuttle bus ($3) connects Station Tremblant, Mont-Tremblant Village and St-Jovite from 6am to 8pm Sunday to Thursday and 6am to 11pm on Friday and Saturday.

Parc National du Mont Tremblant

Nature puts on a terrific show in **Parc National du Mont Tremblant** (819-688-2281, reservations 800-665-6527; www.sepaq.com/pq/mot; Chemin du Lac Supérieur; adult/child $8.50/free;), the province's biggest and oldest park – it opened in 1895. Covering 1510 sq km of gorgeous Laurentian lakes, rivers, hills and woods, the park has rare vegetation (including silver maple and red oak), hiking and cycling trails, and canoe routes. It is home to fox, deer, moose and wolves, and is a habitat for more than 206 bird species, including a huge blue heron colony.

The park is divided into three sectors. The most developed area is the Diable sector, home to beautiful Lac Monroe. The main entrance is 28km northeast of Station Tremblant. The year-round service center, which also has equipment rentals, is another 11km from the entrance.

Diable's incredible trails range from an easy 20-minute stroll past waterfalls to day-long hikes that take in stunning views of majestic valleys. You can also take your bike out on some trails or rent canoes to travel down the serpentine Rivière du Diable. The gentle section between Lac Chat and La Vache Noire is perfect for families.

Further east, the Pimbina sector is a 10-minute drive from St-Donat. Here you'll find an information center, canoe and kayak rentals and campgrounds with some amenities. Activities include swimming at Lac Provost and hiking and biking trails nearby. A highlight is the **Carcan Trail**, a 14.4km route to the top of the park's second-highest peak (883m), which passes waterfalls and lush scenery on the way.

Further east is the L'Assomption sector, accessible via the town of St-Côme. It is the most untamed part of the park, with more trails, secluded cottages and remote camping options. In winter, you can't access this sector by car, as snow covers the roads.

The wilder interior and eastern sections are accessible by dirt roads, some of which are old logging routes. The off-the-beaten-track areas abound in wildlife. With some effort, it's possible to have whole lakes to yourself.

By late August, nights start getting cold and a couple of months later a blanket of snow adds a magic touch. That's when cross-country skiing and snowshoeing are popular activities in the Diable and Pimbina sectors.

Activities

Via Ferrata CLIMBING
(800-665-6527; www.sepaq.com/pq/mot/index.dot; adult/child from $42/31.50; mid-Jun–mid-Oct) A popular half-day guided climbing tour, Via Ferrata scales the rock face of **La Vache Noire** to take in a stunning vista of Rivière du Diable with the Laurentians behind. No rock-climbing experience is needed as guides cover the basics and supply the equipment. Reservations can be made through the park.

Sleeping

Campgrounds CAMPGROUND $
(800-665-6527; www.sepaq.com/pq/mot/tarifs.dot; campsites/yurts/cabins from $24/110/120) Camping ranges from rustic tent sites to four-person yurts to ready-to-camp Huttopia tent-cabin hybrids.

Cabins CABIN $$
(800-665-6527; www.sepaq.com/reservation/chalet.dot; cabins $124-250) Two- to ten-person cabin accommodations in Parc National du Mont Tremblant.

Information

Information Center (819-688-2281; mid-May–mid-Oct & mid-Dec–Mar)

MONTRÉAL TO QUÉBEC CITY

There's so much charm packed into the idyllic stretch of pastoral patchwork between Québec's two metropolises that it's bursting at the borders. Kick back and stay awhile to enjoy the picture-postcard scenery of the Eastern Townships and take in the unique bilingual atmosphere that constant American tourist traffic to this area has fostered. Alternatively, the Mauricie region – from Trois-Rivières north to Lac St Jean and following the flow of the mighty Rivière St-Maurice – has been known to enchant unsuspecting visitors in search of wild, unadulterated natural beauty.

The Trans-Canada Hwy (Hwy 20) cuts a straight path to Québec City from Montréal. The Eastern Townships are nestled between here and the Vermont border, mainly along Hwy 10; Mauricie falls to the north of Hwy 20 along Hwy 40.

Eastern Townships

Lush rolling hills, crystal-clear lakes and checkerboard farms fill the Eastern Townships, or the 'Cantons-des-l'Est' as it's known by French-speaking inhabitants. The region begins 80km southeast of Montréal and is squished between the labyrinth of minor highways that stretch all the way to the Vermont and New Hampshire borders. New Englanders will feel right at home: covered bridges and round barns dot the bumpy landscape, which is sculpted by the tail end of the US Appalachian mountain range.

A visit during spring is rewarding, as it's the season for 'sugaring off' – the tapping, boiling and preparation of maple syrup. In fall the foliage puts on a show of kaleidoscopic colors, to be toasted with freshly brewed apple cider, which is served in local pubs. The district is also home to a fast-growing wine region that produces some respectable whites and an excellent ice wine – a dessert wine made from frozen grapes.

Sights & Activities

Summer brings fishing and swimming in the region's numerous lakes, and cycling is also extremely popular in the warmer months, with nearly 500km of trails taking in sumptuous landscapes. Winter means excellent downhill skiing at the three main ski hills: Bromont, Mont Orford and Sutton.

Frelighsburg VILLAGE
A few kilometers from the Vermont border, this village makes a pleasant stop along the Eastern Townships Route des Vins (Wine Route). A cluster of stone and wood homes straddles the banks of the brook that runs through town, and the surrounding area is filled with apple orchards. Local eateries specialize in smoked fish and maple products; if you have a sweet tooth, don't miss the famous maple tarts at the old general store-cafe in the center of town.

Parc de la Gorge de Coaticook PARK
(819-849-2331, 888-524-6743; www.gorgedecoaticook.qc.ca; 400 Rue St-Marc, Coaticook; adult/child $7.50/4.50; year-round;) Straddling a lovely forested gorge outside the town of Coaticook, this scenic park is famous for having the world's longest pedestrian suspension bridge. Visitors come for hiking, mountain biking and horseback riding in summer,

Montréal to Québec City & Around

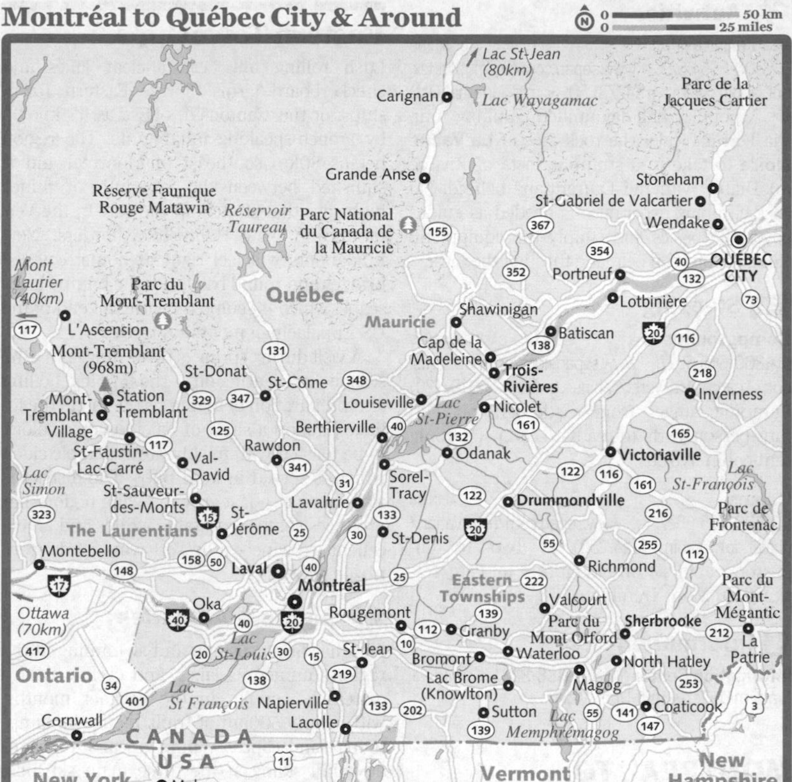

and snow-tubing and snowshoeing in winter. You can also camp or stay in one of the park's cabins. The surrounding area boasts some of the Eastern Townships' prettiest scenery, not to mention some wonderful cheese makers.

Route des Sommets SCENIC DRIVE

(Summit Drive; www.routedessommets.com) Off the beaten track, the Route des Sommets winds 193km along the high mountain slopes north of the New Hampshire border, passing a series of villages and scenic lookouts between La Patrie and St-Adrien. This is a great option for viewing the spectacular fall colors of the Eastern Townships.

Sleeping & Eating

Au Chant de l'Onde B&B $$

(450-298-5676; www.auchantdelonde.ca; 6 Rue de l'Église, Frelighsburg; r incl breakfast from $112;) In the heart of pretty Frelighsburg village, this peaceful three-room B&B enjoys a prime location along the banks of the Rivière aux Brochets. Guests have access to a lovely terrace and a spacious backyard within earshot of the river, as well as a library for relaxing, reading or playing board games.

Le Bocage B&B $$

(819-835-5653; www.lebocage.qc.ca; 200 Chemin Moe's River, Compton; d $100-125, ste $165-250, all incl breakfast; Tue-Sun;) From the welcome to the antiques, this Victorian gem of a B&B in the countryside between Coaticook and Sherbrooke is hard to fault. A multicourse meal is served nightly and can feature dishes such as guinea fowl stuffed with mushrooms, wild boar, red-deer medallions or other wild game. Discounts apply for multinight stays and reservations are essential.

Cabane du Pic-Bois QUÉBÉCOIS $$

(450-263-6060; www.cabanedupicbois.com; 1468 Chemin Gaspé, Brigham; adult/child $32/18; by reservation Fri-Sun Mar & Apr;) If you want to go all in, you can't do better than the all-you-can-eat spread at this traditional sugar shack. You get all the classics – omelettes, pork jowls, ham, maple sausage, beans and potatoes – plus cabbage salad dressed with Pic-Bois' famous maple vinegar. We'll gladly come back, even though they had to roll us out the door.

Information

Tourist Office (450-375-8774, 866-472-6292; www.easterntownships.org; 100 Rue du Tourisme, Hwy 10, exit 68, St-Alphonse-de-Granby; 8:30am-6pm Jun-Aug, 8:30am-4:30pm Mon-Fri, 9am-5pm Sat & Sun May, Sep & Oct) Just off Hwy 10, this is the most convenient branch of the Eastern Townships Tourist Office for travelers arriving by car from Montréal.

Getting There & Away

BUS

Transdev Limocar (514-842-2281; www.transdev.ca) operates bus services between Montréal's **Gare d'Autocars** (p257) and Bromont ($26, 2½ hours, 8:30am and 5:40pm), Lac Brome ($25, 1¾ hours, 8am – call ahead as this service is subject to passenger demand), Sutton ($26, 2½ hours, 4:30pm weekdays, four services Saturday, six Sunday), Magog ($32, 1½ to two hours, frequent) and Sherbrooke ($36, two to 2½ hours, frequent).

Orléans Express (p229) goes to Trois-Rivières in the Mauricie region.

CAR

Coming from Montréal, Hwy 10 will take you straight to the Eastern Townships to just east of Sherbrooke, where it continues as Rte 112. Coming from Québec City via Hwy 20, the fastest route is via Hwy 55, which you pick up near Drummondville.

Bromont

This town revolves around **Ski Bromont** (450-534-2200; www.skibromont.com; 150 Rue Champlain; full/half day $55/49), a year-round resort on the slopes of 533m-high Mt Brome. The mountain and its sister peaks dominate the surrounding landscape, which shifts from snowy pine woods in winter to green peaks in spring and summer to a riot of colors in the fall. Bromont is, in essence, beautiful all four seasons of the year.

On weekends from May to October, Bromont's other major attraction (in addition to its ski resort) is its giant **flea market** (Marché Aux Puces Bromont; 450-534-0440; www.mapbromont.com; 16 Rue Lafontaine; 9am-5pm Sat & Sun May-Oct; P) FREE, just off Hwy 10.

Lac Brome

Lac Brome is the name of seven amalgamated towns orbiting the eponymous lake, with Knowlton on the southern shore being the largest and most attractive. Although there is evidence of early habitation by Abenaki peoples, the area was first formally settled by Loyalists in 1802 and the town still retains an upmarket British flair and numerous 19th-century buildings. A stroll around its cute downtown, which teems with quality boutiques, art galleries, cafes and restaurants, is a fun way to spend an hour or two.

Sights

Musée Historique du Comté de Brome MUSEUM
(450-243-6782; www.bromemuseum.com; 130 Rue Lakeside; adult/child $8/2; 10am-5pm; P) The exhibits at this museum include a re-created general store and courthouse (Sunday only) and, incongruously, a WWI Fokker D-VII plane. An on-site, heavily interactive children's museum is nice for young kids.

Festivals & Events

Canard en Fête CULTURAL
(Brome Lake Duck Festival; www.canardenfete.ca; late Sep) Held on two weekends in late September, this festival celebrates Lac Brome's most famous bird. In addition to foie gras, duck pâté and other ducky treats, vendors sell local wine, cider, cheese and crafts.

Sleeping & Eating

Auberge Knowlton HISTORIC HOTEL $$
(450-242-6886; www.aubergeknowlton.ca; 286 Chemin Knowlton; d incl breakfast from $148;) Set in a landmark 1849 inn, this place features comfortable country-themed rooms and a sprinkling of antiques throughout the place. The on-site restaurant Le Relais serves regional specialties. Breakfast is à la carte.

Le Relais FRENCH $$
(450-242-2232; www.aubergeknowlton.ca/relais; 286 Chemin Knowlton; lunch $12-21, dinner $14-35; 11am-3pm & 5-10pm Mon-Fri, 8am-10pm Sat;) At Auberge Knowlton, this restaurant features juicy Lac Brome duck served many ways, such as duck ravioli in mushroom sauce, duck confit in orange sauce and duck livers with blackened butter.

Shopping

Brome Lake Duck Farm FOOD

(☎450-242-3825; www.canardsdulacbrome.com; 40 Chemin Centre; ⏲8am-5pm Mon-Wed, to 6pm Thu & Fri, 9:30am-6pm Sat, to 5:30pm Sun) Lac Brome is famous for its ducks, which have been bred here since 1912 on a special diet that includes soy and vitamins. Pick up pâté and other products at this shop; there's a second branch in Montréal.

Information

Tourist Office (☎450-243-1221; http://ville.lac-brome.qc.ca; 696 Chemin Lakeside; ⏲Jun-Aug) Helpful bilingual staff can set you up with accommodations and maps.

Sutton

Sutton is a little Loyalist town with a pretty main street where you can shop to your heart's content or let your hair down during après-ski partying (the ski area Mont Sutton is nearby). One of southern Québec's most attractive villages, Sutton is popular with artsy types, who come to appreciate the scenic beauty of the surrounding landscape, dominated by the northern Green Mountains. The downtown strip is filled with cafes, restaurants, inns and B&Bs, along with a helpful tourist office.

Sights & Activities

Chapelle Ste-Agnès WINERY

(☎450-538-0303; www.vindeglace.com; 2565 Chemin Scenic; guided visits incl tasting $20-30; ⏲guided visits 1:30pm Wed & Sun Jun-Oct, otherwise by arrangement; P) One of Québec's most renowned producers of ice wine, award-winning Chapelle Ste-Agnès is just north of the Vermont border near Sutton. In addition to the official guided visits, if you pop by between 10am and 5pm from June to October, you'll likely be given a 30-minute mini-tour.

Parc d'Environnement Naturel HIKING

(☎450-538-4085; www.parcsutton.com; adult/child $6/3; ⏲Jun-Oct; 👪) In summer, Sutton is prime hiking territory, especially in this conservation area, where 80km of trails have been carved through the thickly forested mountains. Backpackers can unfold their tents at three primitive campgrounds.

Mont Sutton SKIING

(☎450-538-2545; www.montsutton.com; 671 Chemin Maple; day tickets adult/youth/child $62/43/35; ⏲9am-4pm; 👪) Family-operated Mont Sutton, the ski area 5km east of Sutton, offers 60 downhill runs for all abilities and is especially well known for its glade skiing.

KIDS LOVE GRANBY

You'll score big with your kids if you take them to the **Granby Zoo** (☎450-372-9113; www.zoodegranby.com; 525 Rue St-Hubert, Granby; adult/child $39/26; ⏲10am-8pm late May-Aug, 10am-5pm Sat & Sun Sep & Oct; 👪). The tigers, kangaroos, elephants and some 170 other species of finned, feathered and furry friends rarely fail to enthrall the little ones. Tickets include admission to the **Parc Aquatique Amazoo**, a small water park with a churning wave pool and rides. Take exit 68 off Hwy 10.

Sleeping & Eating

★**Le Pleasant Hôtel & Café** HISTORIC HOTEL $$

(☎450-538-6188, 888-538-6188; www.lepleasant.com; 1 Rue Pleasant; r $140-220; ❄@📶) This luxurious inn is a great place for a weekend escape. Some of the sleek and modern rooms – well balanced by a classically historical facade – have views of Mont Sutton.

Le Cafetier CAFE $

(☎450-538-7333; 9 Rue Principale N; mains $8-15; ⏲7am-7pm; 📶👪) Locals flock to this stupidly cute, cheery cafe in the heart of Sutton for morning coffee, croissants, smoothies, omelettes and homemade muesli, but it's just as popular in the afternoon for salads, vegetarian chili, panini and croque monsieurs. Wine and beer, free wi-fi, decks of playing cards and toys for the kids encourage people of all ages to linger.

Auberge des Appalaches CANADIAN $$

(☎450-538-5799; http://auberge-appalaches.com; 234 Chemin Maple; mains $17-25; ⏲5-8pm Mon, 6-10pm Tue & Fri-Sun; ✍) Local produce and intense attention to detail characterize the cuisine at this inn. The seasonal menu is tough to predict, but may include seared calf's liver one evening, and elk tartare flavored with maple the next.

Information

Tourist Office (☎450-538-8455, 800-565-8455; https://tourismesutton.ca; 24a Rue Principale S; ⏲9am-5pm) Tourism info for the Sutton area.

Valcourt

Valcourt would be a mere blip on the radar were it not for local resident Joseph Armand Bombardier, the father of the Ski-Doo (snowmobile), whose invention is a great source of pride to Canadians. You can learn all about his creation at the **Musée J Armand Bombardier** (Museum of Ingenuity; www.bombardiermuseum.com; 1001 Ave J-A Bombardier; adult/child $12/8; 10am-5pm May-Aug, closed Mon Sep-Apr; P). Otherwise, Valcourt doesn't quite have the historical charms of its township neighbors, and feels largely like a sleepy residential burg.

Magog

Magog occupies a prime spot on the north shore of Lac Memphrémagog, a banana-shaped lake that stretches south for 44km, all the way across the US border, and the largest and best-known lake in the Eastern Townships, where most waterfront properties are privately owned. Magog is the biggest township on the lake, with a pretty main street and plenty of decent restaurants and hotels.

Sights & Activities

There's a **beach** in Magog, but in summer carving out space for your towel can be a tall order. The rest of the shore is largely in private hands, so the lake is best explored from the water with companies such as water-sports outfitter **Club de Voile** (819-847-3181; www.voilememphremagog.com; 155 Plage des Cantons) and **Croisières Escapades Memphrémagog** (819-843-7000; www.escapadesmemphremagog.com; adult $37-74, child $15-41; May-Oct;), which offers narrated cruises. Watch for Memphré, the feisty yet elusive creature that lives, Nessie-style, at the bottom of the lake!

Abbaye St-Benoît-du-Lac MONASTERY
(819-843-4080; www.st-benoit-du-lac.com; 1 Rue Principale, St-Benoît-du-Lac; church 5am-8:30pm, shop 9-10:45am & 11:45am-6pm Mon-Sat) This peaceful monastery sits on the western shore of Lac Memphrémagog, about 12km south of Magog. The complex is a blend of traditional and modern architecture, including a hallway awash in colorful tiles and a church with exposed structural beams and brick walls. If you can, visit at 7:30am, 11am or 5pm, when the monks practice Gregorian chanting, famous throughout Québec. Equally famous are the monks' apple cider and finely made cheeses.

Sleeping & Eating

Au Coq du Bonheur B&B $$
(866-643-6745; www.aucoqdubonheur.com; 79 Rue Bellevue; r $99-125;) This is simply an excellent B&B, all hardwood floors, natural light and funky art, mixed with warmth and hospitality and a lovely breakfast besides.

À L'Ancestrale B&B B&B $$
(819-847-5555; www.ancestrale.com; 200 Rue Abbott; r incl breakfast $99-160; @) Wake up to a five-course gourmet breakfast at this intimate retreat, whose five rooms are dressed in a romantic, countrified way and outfitted with refrigerators and coffee makers. It's central but on a quiet street.

Ô Bois Dormant B&B $$
(819-843-0450, 888-843-0450; www.oboisdormant.qc.ca; 205 Rue Abbott; r incl breakfast $110-145; @) Although only a short walk from the main street, the rambling back lawn at this towering Victorian feels like a secluded resort (the pool helps in this regard). Rooms are cozy, if a little chintzy.

Bistro Chez Sirano BISTRO $$
(819-769-4006; 362 Rue Principale W; mains $11-25; 5-9pm Tue, Thu & Sun, to 10pm Fri & Sat;) Chez Sirano is a down-to-earth breath of fresh air, a neighborhood bistro in the best sense of the word, all cozy, informal atmosphere and good food to boot, from classic steak frites to duck ravioli.

Fondissimo SWISS $$
(819-843-8999; www.fondissimo.ca; 276 Rue Principale E; mains $22-28; 5-11pm) With a name like Fondissimo, it's not hard to guess the specialty of this hip restaurant in an old renovated factory – there are eight varieties of Swiss fondue alone. Chinese fondue – meat, veggies and seafood, and a piping-hot vat of oil in which to cook it yourself – is also a popular choice.

Information

Tourist Office (819-843-2744; www.tourisme-memphremagog.com; 2911 Rue Milletta; 9am-5pm Sep-late Jun, to 6pm late Jun-Aug) Off Rte 115.

Parc National du Mont Orford

There's probably a better summer day than one spent in golden sunshine amid lush green foothills, cool blue lakes and spectacular viewpoints that take in all of the above, but we haven't found it yet. In the meantime, we'll happily show allegiance to **Parc National du Mont Orford** (☎819-843-9855; www.sepaq.com/pq/mor; 3321 Chemin du Parc, Orford; adult/child $8.50/free; ⊙year-round; P), home to snapping turtles, day-tripping families, countless bird species, and hiking, kayaking and canoeing opportunities. It's fairly compact, and often gets busy given its proximity to Magog.

Just outside the park boundaries, the **Orford Arts Centre** (Centre d'Arts Orford; ☎819-843-3981; www.arts-orford.org; 3165 Chemin du Parc, Orford) hosts the **Orford Festival**, a prestigious series of 40 to 50 classical concerts, from late June to mid-August.

Activities

Station de Ski Mont-Orford SKIING
(☎819-843-6548; www.orford.com; 4380 Chemin du Parc; lift tickets adult/child $62/35) Station de Ski Mont-Orford has a vertical drop of 589m and dozens of downhill ski slopes, mostly aimed at beginners and intermediate skiers. There's also a snow park with a half pipe and other fun features.

Sleeping

Auberge du Centre d'Arts Orford INN $
(☎819-843-3981; www.orford.mu/services-hoteliers; 3165 Chemin du Parc, Orford; r $60-90) This no-frills lodging offers 89 rooms without TV or telephone on 90 hectares at the edge of Parc National du Mont Orford. It's affiliated with the Orford Arts Centre, so rooms are unavailable during the center's summer music festival. However, come autumn, winter or spring, it's a lovely retreat where you can enjoy trails and mountain scenery right outside your door.

North Hatley

All of the Eastern Townships are cute, but even still, North Hatley is the geographic equivalent of a yawning puppy. It occupies an enchanting spot at the northern tip of the crystal-clear Lac Massawippi, about 17km east of Magog. This was a popular second home for wealthy US citizens who enjoyed the scenery – and the absence of Prohibition – during the 1920s. Many historic residences have been converted into inns and B&Bs. Popular summer activities include swimming, boating, admiring the lakeshore's natural beauty, and browsing the village's galleries, antique and craft shops.

Randonées Jacques Robidas HORSEBACK RIDING
(☎819-563-0166; www.equitationjacquesrobidas.com; 32 Chemin McFarland; riding from $65, two-day packages from $299; 👪) A great way to explore the rolling countryside surrounding North Hatley is on horseback with this professional outfit. Among its wide slate of horse trekking activities, there are classes for those who are new to the experience.

Sleeping & Eating

★**Manoir Hovey** RESORT $$$
(☎819-842-2421, 800-661-2421; www.manoirhovey.com; 575 Rue Hovey; d from $506, dinner & breakfast incl from $679; P❄@🛜≋) This lovely resort offers handsomely set rooms in a picturesque lakeside setting. You'll find expansive gardens, a heated pool and an ice rink (in winter), and you can arrange numerous outdoor activities – windsurfing, lake cruises and golfing. The award-winning restaurant **Le Hatley** is among the best in the Eastern Townships, with three-course meals highlighting refined Québécois fare ($75 for nonguests).

Pilsen PUB FOOD $$
(☎819-842-2971; www.pilsen.ca; 55 Rue Main; mains $12-27, set meals from $32; ⊙11:30am-3am) The liveliest restaurant in North Hatley is famous for its salmon, both grilled and smoked, and upmarket pub fare. There's a nice riverside terrace and another facing the lake.

★**Auberge Le Coeur d'Or** QUÉBÉCOIS $$$
(☎819-842-4363; www.aubergelecoeurdor.com; 85 Rue School; 4-course meal $42; ⊙6-9pm, closed Mon & Tue Nov-Apr) For a delightful night out, head to this charming farmhouse inn. The restaurant's four- to five-course dinners make abundant use of local ingredients, including cheeses from Sherbrooke, rabbit from Stanstead, duck from Orford and smoked trout from East Hereford. Save room for profiteroles, chocolate mousse cake, or the Coeur d'Or's trademark trio of crème brûlées.

Entertainment

Piggery Theatre THEATER
(☎819-842-2431; www.piggery.com; 215 Chemin Simard) This popular theater stages English-language dramas, concerts and comedy acts.

Information

Café North Hatley (819-842-4722; 90 Rue Main; 9am-5pm;) There is a small information center, free internet access and great coffee here, on the 2nd floor above the Passerose boutique.

Sherbrooke

Sherbrooke is the commercial center of the area, a bustling city that's perfect for refueling on modern conveniences before returning to the Eastern Townships. The historic center, 'Vieux Sherbrooke,' sits at the confluence of two rivers and is bisected by Rue Wellington and Rue King, the main commercial arteries. Highlights include the city's small but well-conceived Musée des Beaux-Arts, with works by Québécois and Canadian artists, and the 18km **Réseau Riverain** walking and cycling path along the Rivière Magog, which starts at Blanchard Park, west of downtown.

Sights

Lac des Nations LAKE
() South of all the sights, Rivière Magog flows into the pretty Lac des Nations, which is surrounded by a scenic paved trail perfect for walking, in-line skating and cycling (rentals available).

Bishop's University HISTORIC BUILDING
(www3.ubishops.ca/chapel; Rue du Collège; chapel 8:30am-6pm Mon-Sat, from noon Sun) FREE If you're interested in scholarly pursuits, head 5km south to Lennoxville to see the Anglican Bishop's University, founded in 1843 and modeled after Oxford and Cambridge in England. The campus' architectural highlight is **St Mark's Chapel**, richly decorated with carved pews and stained-glass windows.

Musée des Beaux-Arts MUSEUM
(619-821-2115; www.mbas.qc.ca; 241 Rue Dufferin; adult/student $10/7; 10am-5pm late Jun-Aug, noon-5pm Tue-Sun Sep-late Jun) This museum has a good permanent collection featuring works by regional artists; it also stages temporary exhibitions.

La Société d'Histoire de Sherbrooke MUSEUM
(819-821-5406; www.histoiresherbrooke.org; 275 Rue Dufferin; adult/child $7/4; 9am-noon & 1-5pm Tue-Fri, 1-5pm Sat & Sun) This center offers an engaging introduction to the town's history and includes exhibitions on the odd Loyalist-Francophone identity of the Eastern Townships region.

Sleeping & Eating

Hotel Le Floral HOTEL $$
(819-564-6812; www.hotellefloral.com/en; 1920 12e Avenue N; r from $109;) The best of the midrange bunch, Le Floral has modish, sleek, urban-chic rooms and friendly service.

Au Coin du Vietnam VIETNAMESE $$
(819-566-8383; www.aucoinduvietnam.com; 1530 Galt Ouest; set meals from $25; 11am-2:30pm Tue-Fri, 5-10pm daily) If you need a break from Canadian/Québécois cuisine, hit up Au Coin du Vietnam, which dishes out excellent, fresh Southeast Asian fare.

Drinking & Nightlife

Siboire MICROBREWERY
(819-565-3636; www.siboire.ca; 80 Rue du Dépôt; 6am-3am Mon-Fri, from 7:30am Sat & Sun) Sherbrooke's historic train depot houses this atmospheric microbrewery with nearly a dozen beers on tap, including Siboire's own IPA, wheat beer, oatmeal stout, Irish red ale and seasonal maple scotch ale. High ceilings, brick walls and a flower-fringed summer terrace create an inviting atmosphere for drinking everything in and enjoying some of the tastiest fish and chips in the Townships.

Information

ATMs are ubiquitous across the town center.

Banque Nationale (3075 Blvd Portland; 10am-3pm Mon-Wed, to 6pm Thu, to 4pm Fri)

Hospital Hôtel-Dieu (819-346-1110; www.chus.qc.ca; 580 Rue Bowen S; 24hr) Local hospital offering a wide range of services.

Tourism Eastern Townships (819-820-2020, 800-355-5755; www.easterntownships.org; 20 Rue Don-Bosco S; 8:30am-4:30pm Mon-Fri)

Tourist Office (Destination Sherbrooke; 819-821-1919; www.destinationsherbrooke.com; 785 Rue King W; 9am-5pm Mon-Sat, to 3pm Sun)

ZAP Sherbrooke (www.zapsherbrooke.org) Has a list of free wi-fi zones in Sherbrooke.

Getting There & Away

The **Transdev Limocar** (p265) bus terminal is at 80 Rue du Dépôt; there are frequent bus connections to Montréal. Sherbrooke lies along Hwy 10, about 25km northeast of Magog.

Parc National du Mont-Mégantic

Similar to many other provincial parks in Québec, Parc National du Mont-Mégantic is a lovely slice of preserved eastern Canadian woodlands and wilderness, an arcadian escape from the civilized world. Unlike many provincial parks, there's a heavy science component to Mont-Mégantic: this is the site of a major **astronomy observatory** (819-888-2941; http://astrolab-parc-national-mont-megantic.org/en; 189 Rte du Parc; adult/child from $18.50/free; noon-5pm late Jun-Aug, check website for other times), and was the world's first International Dark Sky Reserve. In scientific terms, that means the area possesses exceptional visibility under nocturnal conditions. In layman's terms: damn, the stars sure are pretty here.

Mauricie

Mauricie is one of Québec's lesser-known regions, despite being in a strategic spot halfway between Montréal and Québec City. Stretching 300km from Trois-Rivières north to Lac St Jean, it follows the flow of the mighty Rivière St-Maurice, which for centuries has been the backbone of the area's industrial heritage. Logs were being driven down the river to the pulp and paper mills until as recently as 1996. Centuries earlier, the region had given birth to the country's iron industry; the original forge is now a national historic site. Industry still dominates the lower region, but things get considerably more scenic after the river reaches the Parc National du Canada de la Mauricie.

Trois-Rivières

Founded in 1634, Trois-Rivières is North America's second-oldest city north of Mexico, but you'd never know it: a fire that swept through in 1908 left little of the city's historic looks. Still, the city center, right on the north shore of the St Lawrence River, is not without charms and some bona fide tourist attractions. A riverfront promenade leads to the oldest section of town along Rue des Ursulines.

The name, by the way, is a misnomer as there are only two, not three, streams here. There are, however, three branches of the Rivière St Maurice at its mouth, where islands split its flow into three channels.

Sights & Activities

La Domaine Joly de Lotbinière MUSEUM
(418-926-2462; www.domainejoly.com; Hwy 132, Rte de Pointe-Platon; adult/child/student $16/1/10; 10am-5pm late May-late Sep; P) This stately museum between Trois-Rivières and Québec City was built for Henri-Gustave Joly de Lotbinière (1849–1908), a premier of Québec. This is one of the most impressive manors built during the seignorial period of Québec and has been preserved in its late-19th-century state. The outbuildings and huge cultivated garden are a treat, and the cafe serves lunch and afternoon teas.

Musée Québécois de Culture Populaire MUSEUM
(819-372-0406; www.culturepop.qc.ca; 200 Rue Laviolette; adult/child $13/8; 10am-6pm Jun-Sep) One of the most interesting stops in the area, this museum's changing exhibits cover the gamut from folk art to pop culture, delving into the social and cultural life of the Québécois. Recent exhibits include a quirky show on the social significance of garage sales and woodcarvings of birds commonly sighted in the area.

Les Forges-du-St-Maurice MUSEUM
(www.pc.gc.ca; 10000 Blvd des Forges; adult/child $4/2; 10am-5pm mid-Jun–Sep; P) About 7km northwest of the center (take bus 4), Les Forges-du-St-Maurice is a National Historic Site preserving the 18th-century birthplace of the Canadian iron industry. Costumed guides take you around the grounds and into the blast furnace, while a sound-and-light show reveals the daily operations of Canada's first ironworks.

Musée des Ursulines MUSEUM
(418-694-0694; www.museedesursulines.com; 734 Rue des Ursulines; adult/child $8/free; 10am-5pm Tue-Sun) For a slice of the town's religious history, stop at this former hospital founded by Ursuline nuns in 1639. It forms a pretty backdrop for the fine collection of textiles, ceramics, books and prints related to religion that are on display. Beautiful frescoes adorn the chapel. Nearby, **Rue des Ursulines** is a pleasant place to stroll, with its picturesque homes (some now operating as B&Bs) and its unseen history, much of which is described on informational plaques throughout the neighborhood.

Vieille Prison MUSEUM
(819-372-0406; www.enprison.com; 200 Rue Laviolette; adult/child $15/10, incl museum $21/13; 10am-6pm Tue-Sun) Tour guides, including some former inmates, bring the harsh realities of the lock-up vividly to life during 90-minute tours that include a stop at dank underground cells known as 'the pit.' English tours run between 11:30am and 3:30pm from late June to the end of August, and by reservation the rest of the year. No children under 12!

Croisières AML BOATING
(☎866-856-6668; www.croisieresaml.com; adult/child $30/17; ⊙mid-Jun–early Sep;) For a different perspective on Trois-Rivières, take a 90-minute cruise along the St Lawrence River. Thrice-daily summer-only tours feature historical commentary about the town while traveling from the port to the Laviolette bridge, the **Notre-Dame-du-Cap** (www.sanctuaire-ndc.ca/en; 626 Rue Notre-Dame; ⊙8:30am-8pm; P) sanctuary, Île St-Quentin and the confluence of the St Lawrence and St Maurice Rivers.

Sleeping & Eating

Auberge Internationale de Trois-Rivières HOSTEL $
(☎819-378-8010; www.hihostels.ca; 497 Rue Radisson; dm/d $25/75; @) This wonderfully clean and friendly youth hostel is set in a two-story brick Georgian home, within easy walking distance of the bus station (p271), the riverfront and all the city's attractions. Dorms have four to eight beds each, and there are also reasonably priced private rooms. Bicycle rentals are available.

Le Gîte Loiselle B&B $$
(☎819-375-2121; www.giteloiselle.com; 836 Rue des Ursulines; r $95-135; P@) Local artwork, magnificent woodwork and tasteful antiques greet you at this Victorian redbrick one block from the river. Basic rooms with private toilets and shared shower put you right in the heart of the historic district. Congenial hosts Lisette and Mario, both avid cyclists and former restaurateurs, serve an ample breakfast to fuel you for the day's adventures.

Le Poivre Noir FUSION $$$
(☎819-378-5772; www.poivrenoir.com; 1300 Rue du Fleuve; mains $14-32; ⊙11:30am-2pm Wed-Fri, 5:30-10pm Tue-Sun;) At this upmarket place by the riverfront, chef José Pierre Durand's inspired, often daring blend of French, Québécois and international influences creates a memorable dining experience. Appetizers such as asparagus and blood-orange salad, or warm goat's-cheese 'snowballs' with tomatoes and pistachios are followed by equally delicious main dishes.

Drinking & Nightlife

Gambrinus BREWERY
(☎819-691-3371; www.gambrinus.qc.ca; 3160 Blvd des Forges; ⊙11am-1am Mon-Fri, 3pm-1am Sat) About 3km north of the riverfront, this decade-old brewery serves more than a dozen varieties of beer, including seasonal cranberry, raspberry and apple ales, an excellent IPA, and an unconventional hemp-and-honey blend called Miel d'Ange.

Information

Hôpital St-Joseph (☎819-370-2100; 731 Rue Ste-Julie) The local hospital.

Trois-Rivières Tourist Office (☎819-375-1122; www.tourismetroisrivieres.com; 1457 Rue Notre-Dame; ⊙9am-7pm Jul & Aug, 9am-5pm Mon-Fri, 10am-4pm Sat & Sun mid-May–Jun & Sep, 9am-5pm Mon-Fri Oct–mid-May) Extremely helpful tourist office.

Getting There & Away

Trois-Rivières lies about 150km northeast of Montréal and 130km southwest of Québec City and is easily accessible via Hwys 40 and 20 or Rtes 138 and 132.

The **Gare d'Autocars** (☎819-374-2944; 275 Rue St-Georges) bus station is behind the Hôtel Delta. **Orléans Express** (☎514-395-4000; www.orleansexpress.com) buses run to Montréal and Québec City.

Parc National du Canada de la Mauricie

Moose foraging by an idyllic lake, the plaintive cry of a loon gliding across the water, bear cubs romping beneath a potpourri of birch, poplar, maple and other trees waiting to put on a spectacular show of color in the fall – these are scenes you might possibly stumble across while visiting **La Mauricie National Park** (☎888-773-8888, 819-538-3232; www.pc.gc.ca/mauricie; adult/child $7.80/3.90; P). What may well be Québec's best-run and best-organized park is also among its most frequented. The arresting beauty of the nature here, whether seen from a canoe or a walking trail, is everyone's eye candy, but particularly suits those who don't want to feel completely disconnected from 'civilization.'

Activities

The numerous **walking trails**, which can take anywhere from half an hour to five days to complete, offer glimpses of the indigenous flora and fauna, brooks and waterfalls (the **Chutes Waber** in the park's western sector are particularly worth the hike), as well as panoramic views onto delicate valleys, lakes and streams.

The longest trail, **Le Sentier Laurentien**, stretches over 75km of rugged wilderness in the park's northern reaches. Backcountry campsites are spaced out every 7km to 10km. No more than 40 people are allowed on the trail at any time, making reservations essential. There's a fee of $46 and you must arrange for your own transportation to cover the 30km from the trail's end back to Rte Promenade. Topographic maps are for sale at the park.

The park is excellent for **canoeing**. Five canoe routes, ranging in length from 14km to 84km, can accommodate everyone from beginners to experts. Canoe and kayak rentals ($14/40 per hour/day) are available at three sites, the most popular being **Lac Wapizagonke**, which has sandy beaches, steep rocky cliffs and waterfalls. One popular day trip has you canoeing from the Wapizagonke campground to the west end of the lake, followed by a 7.5km loop hike to the Chutes Waber and back by canoe.

The most popular winter activity is cross-country skiing, with some 85km of groomed trails.

Sleeping

Camping at designated sites costs $25.50 without electricity and $29 with it; camping in the wild during canoe trips costs $15 without firewood, or $25 with firewood.

Outdoor Lodges LODGE **$**
(819-537-4555; www.info-nature.ca; per person per 2 nights adult/child $75/37; P) You can sleep in four- to 10-person dorms in one of two outdoor lodges. They are 3.5km from the nearest parking lots, so you must come in by foot, bike, canoe or skis.

Otentiks CABIN **$$**
(877-737-3783; cabins $120; P) Ideal for families, couples and groups (up to five people), part-cabin, part-tent Otentiks put you in a good spot in the Rivière-à-la-Pêche section in the east end of the park. Each one has a wood stove and dishes; you bring the linens, food and drinks.

Information

Information Center (888-773-8888; Hwy 55, exit 226, via St-Jean-des-Piles; 7am-9:30pm Jun-Sep, hours vary other times, closed late Oct-early May) Information and reception center for La Mauricie National Park.

QUÉBEC CITY

POP 542,045

Québec, North America's only walled city north of Mexico City, is the kind of place that crops up in trivia questions. Over the centuries, the lanes and squares of the Old Town – a World Heritage site – have seen the continent's first parish church, first museum, first stone church, first Anglican cathedral, first girls' school, first business district and first French-language university. Most of these institutions remain in some form. The historical superlatives are inescapable: flick through the *Québec Chronicle-Telegraph* and you're reading North America's oldest newspaper; if you have to visit L'Hôtel-Dieu de Québec, console yourself with the thought that it's the continent's oldest hospital.

Once past Le Château Frontenac, the most photographed hotel in the world, you'll find yourself torn between the various neighborhoods' diverse charms. In Old Upper Town, the historical hub, many excellent museums and restaurants hide among the tacky fleur-de-lis T-shirt stores. Old Lower Town, at the base of the steep cliffs, is a labyrinth, where it's a pleasure to get lost among street performers and cozy inns before emerging on the north shore of the St Lawrence. Leaving the walled town near the star-shaped Citadelle, hip St-Jean-Baptiste is one of the less historical but still interesting areas, and the epicenter of a vibrant nightlife.

History

A Huron village, 'Stadacona' – the kanata (settlement) referred to in Canada's name – stood on the site of Québec City when French explorer Jacques Cartier landed in 1535, on his second voyage to the New World. He returned in 1541 to establish a permanent post, but the plan failed, setting back France's colonial ambitions for 50 years. Explorer Samuel de Champlain finally founded the city for the French in 1608, calling it Kebec, from the Algonquian word meaning 'the river narrows here.' It was the first North American city to be founded as a permanent settlement, rather than a trading post.

The English successfully attacked in 1629, but Québec was returned to the French under a treaty three years later and became the center of New France. Repeated English attacks followed. In 1759, General Wolfe led the British to victory over Montcalm on the Plains

Québec City

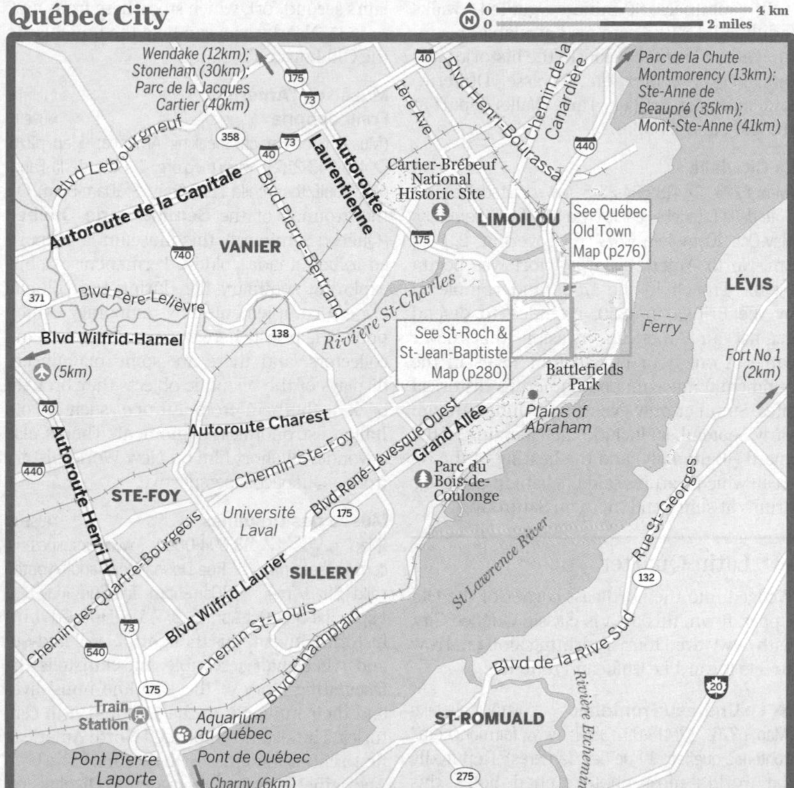

of Abraham. One of North America's most famous battles, it virtually ended the long-running conflict between Britain and France. In 1763, the Treaty of Paris gave Canada to Britain. In 1775, the American revolutionaries tried to capture Québec but were promptly pushed back. In 1864, meetings were held here that led to the formation of Canada in 1867. Québec became the provincial capital.

In the 19th century, the city lost its status and importance to Montréal. When the Great Depression burst Montréal's bubble in 1929, Québec regained some stature as a government center. Some business-savvy locals launched the now-famous Winter Carnival in the 1950s to incite a tourism boom. Obviously, it's still working.

In 2001, the city was the site of the Summit of the Americas, which exploded into mass demonstrations against globalization. In 2008, the city marked the 400th anniversary of Québec's founding.

Sights

Most of Québec City's sights are found within the compact cluster of Old Town walls, or just outside them, making this a dream destination for pedestrians.

Old Upper Town

Fortifications of Québec National Historic Site HISTORIC SITE

(Map p280; ☎418-648-7016; www.pc.gc.ca/eng/lhn-nhs/qc/fortifications/index.aspx; western entrance 2 Rue d'Auteuil, eastern entrance Frontenac Kiosk, Terrasse Dufferin; ⏱10am-5pm mid-May–mid-Oct, to 6pm Jul & Aug; 🚌3, 11) FREE These largely restored old walls are protected as a Canadian National Historic site and a Unesco World Heritage site. Walking the complete 4.6km circuit around the walls on your own is free of charge, and you'll enjoy fine vantage points on the city's historical buildings as you trace the perimeter of the Old Town.

In summer, 90-minute guided walks (adult/child $10/5) are also available, beginning at the Frontenac kiosk (the historic site's information center on Terrasse Dufferin) and ending at Artillery Park. Walks depart at 10:30am and 2:30pm.

La Citadelle FORT

(Map p276; ☎418-694-2815; www.lacitadelle.qc.ca; Côte de la Citadelle; adult/child $16/6; ⏰9am-5pm May-Oct, 10am-4pm Nov-Apr) Covering 2.3 sq km, North America's largest fort was begun by the French in the 1750s and completed by the British in 1850, intended to defend against an American invasion that never came. A one-hour guided tour takes in the regimental museum and numerous historical sites. Summer-only events (late June through early September) include the changing of the guard (10am daily) and the beating of the retreat, which features soldiers banging on their drums at shift's end (6pm on Saturdays).

Latin Quarter

Wedged into the northeast corner of the Old Upper Town, this area is classic Québec City, with dewy-eyed tourists drifting along narrow streets toward Le Château Frontenac.

★Le Château Frontenac HISTORIC BUILDING

(Map p276; ☎418-692-3861; www.fairmont.com/frontenac-quebec; 1 Rue des Carrières) Reputedly the world's most photographed hotel, this audaciously elegant structure was built in 1893 by the Canadian Pacific Railway as part of its chain of luxury hotels. Its fabulous turrets, winding hallways and imposing wings graciously complement its dramatic location atop Cap Diamant, a cliff that swoops into the St Lawrence River. Over the years, it's lured a never-ending line up of luminaries, including Alfred Hitchcock, who chose this setting for the opening scene of his 1953 mystery *I Confess*.

During WWII, Prime Minister MacKenzie King, Winston Churchill and Franklin Roosevelt planned D-Day here.

Terrasse Dufferin PARK

(Map p276) Perched on a clifftop 60m above the St Lawrence River, this 425m-long boardwalk is a marvelous setting for a stroll, with spectacular, sweeping views. In summer, it's peppered with street performers; in winter it hosts a dramatic toboggan run (p278). Near the statue of Samuel de Champlain, stairways descend to the recent excavations of Champlain's second fort, which stood here from 1620 to 1635. Nearby, you can take the funicular to the Old Lower Town.

Musée de l'Amérique Francophone MUSEUM

(Museum of French-Speaking America; Map p276; ☎418-643-2158; www.mcq.org; 2 Côte de la Fabrique; adult/teen/child $8/2/free; ⏰10am-5pm) On the grounds of the **Séminaire de Québec** (Québec Seminary), this museum is purported to be Canada's oldest. Permanent exhibits exploring seminary life during the colonial era are complemented by temporary exhibitions. The priests here were avid travelers and collectors, and there are some magnificent displays of the scientific objects they brought back with them from Europe, such as old Italian astronomical equipment. There's also a wonderful short film on New World history from a Québécois perspective.

Musée des Ursulines MUSEUM

(Map p276; ☎418-694-0694; www.ursulines-uc.com/musees.php; 12 Rue Donnacona; adult/youth/child $8/3/free; ⏰10am-5pm Tue-Sun May-Sep, 1-5pm Tue-Sun Oct-Apr; 🚌3, 7, 11) Housed in a historic convent, this thoughtful, well-laid-out and wheelchair-accessible museum tells the fascinating story of the Ursuline nuns' lives and their influence in the 17th and 18th centuries. The sisters established North America's first school for girls in 1641, educating both Aboriginal and French students. Displays on convent school life are enlivened by a vast array of historic artifacts, including examples of the Ursulines' expert embroidery. The adjoining chapel dates from 1902 but retains some interiors from 1723.

St-Louis Forts & Châteaux National Historic Site ARCHAEOLOGICAL SITE

(Map p276; www.pc.gc.ca/eng/lhn-nhs/qc/saintlouisforts/index.aspx; adult/child $4/2, incl guided tour $10/5; ⏰10am-6pm mid-May–Aug, to 5pm Sep–mid-Oct) 🍃 Hidden underneath Terrasse Dufferin are the ruins of four forts and two châteaus constructed by Samuel de Champlain and other early Québec residents between 1620 and 1694. These structures, excavated between 2005 and 2007, served as residences for the French and English governors of Québec for over 200 years before falling victim to bombardment, fire and neglect. In warm weather, Parks Canada offers twice-daily English-language tours of the archaeological site and the artifacts unearthed there.

QUÉBEC CITY FOR CHILDREN

Certainly, this town is about history, architecture and food. While much of the old city, including accommodations and restaurants, is geared toward adults, there are good things to do with younger ones in the central core, while around the edges are sights fully designed for kids' enjoyment.

In the historic area, walking the **Fortifications** (p273) suits all ages. **La Citadelle ceremonies** (p274), with uniformed soldiers, are winners too. **Terrasse Dufferin** (p274), with its river views and buskers, always delights children. Place d'Armes and Place-Royale are also good for street performers.

Choco-Musée Érico (p286) is a museum and store devoted to all things chocolaty. Get a history lesson, see the kitchen, sample a chunk and try to resist the shop.

Aquarium du Québec (418-659-5264, 866-659-5264; www.sepaq.com/ct/paq; 1675 Ave des Hôtels; adult/child $18.50/9.25; 9am-5pm Jun-Oct, 10am-4pm Nov-May;) has walrus, seals, polar bears and thousands of smaller species.

Children enjoy the 'bee safari' and adults enjoy the mead at **Musée de l'Abeille** (418-824-4411; www.musee-abeille.com; 8862 Blvd St-Anne; 9am-5pm May, Jun, Sep & Oct, to 6pm Jul & Aug;) FREE, a beekeeping *économusée* (workshop) 30km northeast of the city on Hwy 138.

Basilique-Cathédrale Notre-Dame-de-Québec CHURCH

(Map p276; 418-694-0665; http://holydoorquebec.ca/en; 16 Rue de Buade; guided tour $5; 8:45am-3:45pm Mon-Fri, to 4:45pm Sat & Sun, to 8:15pm daily summer) Québec's Roman Catholic basilica got its start as a small church in 1647. Despite frequent fires and battle damage over the ensuing years, especially during fighting between British and French armies in 1759, the church was repeatedly repaired and rebuilt, ultimately becoming the much larger cathedral you see today, which was completed in 1925. The interior is appropriately grandiose, though most of its treasures didn't survive the 1922 fire that left behind only the walls and foundations.

Old Lower Town

Sandwiched between the Upper Town and the waterfront, this area has the city's most intriguing museums, plus numerous plaques and statues and plenty of outdoor cafes and restaurants along its pedestrian-friendly streets. Street performers in period costume help recapture life in distant centuries.

Teeming Rue du Petit-Champlain is said to be, along with Rue Sous-le-Cap, one of the narrowest streets in North America, and it forms the heart of Quartier Petit-Champlain, the continent's oldest commercial district. Look for the incredible wall paintings that feature on the 17th- and 18th-century buildings.

Place-Royale has more than 400 years of history behind it. When Samuel de Champlain founded Québec, it was this bit of shoreline that was first settled. In 1690 cannons placed here held off the attacks of the English naval commander Phipps and his men. Today, the name 'Place-Royale' often generally refers to the district.

Built around the old harbor in the Old Lower Town northeast of Place-Royale, the Vieux-Port (Old Port) is being redeveloped as a multipurpose waterfront area.

From the Upper Town, you can reach the Lower Town in several ways. Walk down Côte de la Canoterie from Rue des Remparts to the Vieux-Port or edge down the charming and steep Rue Côte de la Montagne. About halfway down on the right there is a shortcut, the Escalier Casse-Cou (Break-Neck Stairs), which leads down to Rue du Petit-Champlain. You can also take the funicular.

★**Musée de la Civilisation** MUSEUM

(Museum of Civilization; Map p276; 418-643-2158; www.mcq.org; 85 Rue Dalhousie; adult/teen/child $16/5/free; 10am-5pm) This museum wows you even before you've clapped your eyes on the exhibitions. It is a fascinating mix of modern design that incorporates preexisting buildings with contemporary architecture. The permanent exhibits, such as the one on the cultures of Québec's Aboriginals and the one titled 'People of Québec: Then and Now,' are unique and well worth seeing, and many include clever interactive elements. At any given moment there's an outstanding variety of rotating shows.

Québec Old Town

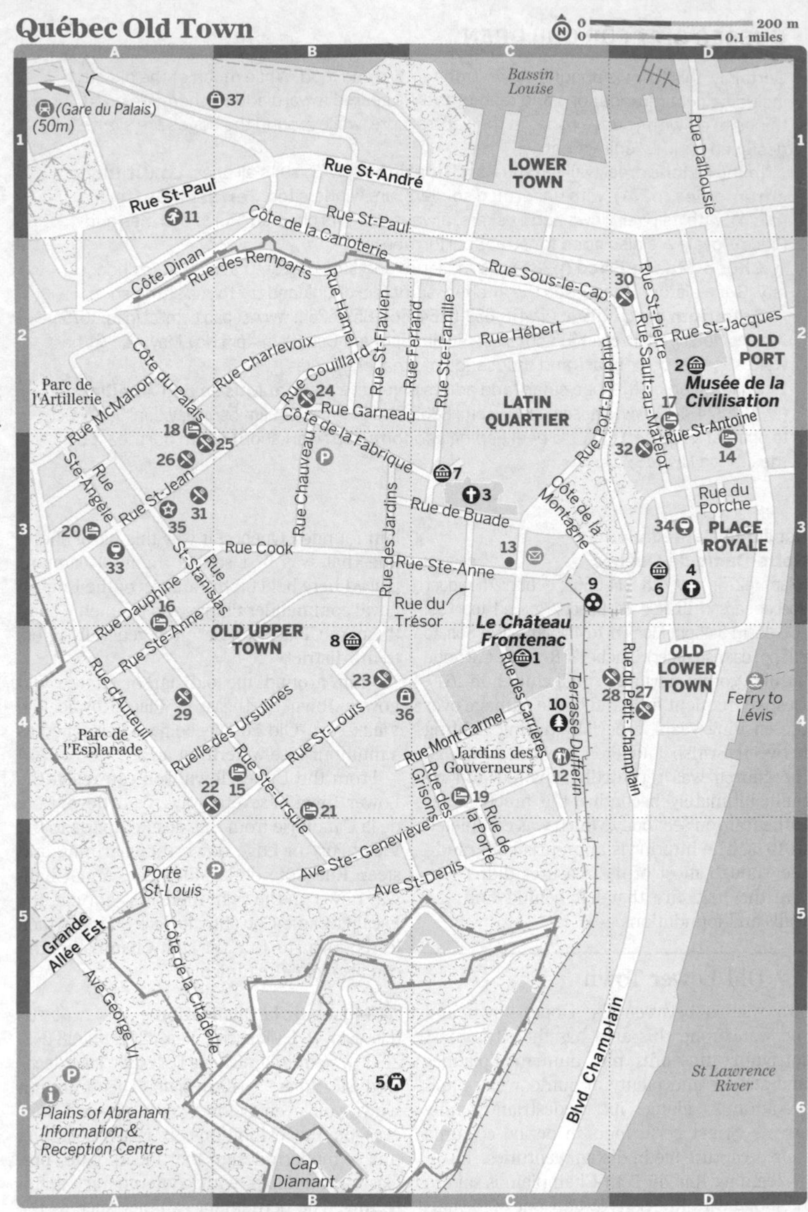

Musée de la Place-Royale MUSEUM

(Map p276; ☎418 646-3167; www.mqc.org; 27 Rue Notre-Dame; adult/teen/child $7/2/free; ⊙10am-5pm Tue-Sun; 👪) This interpretive center touts the Place-Royale neighborhood as the cradle of French history. The exhibits focus on the individual people, houses and challenges of setting up on the shores of the St Lawrence River. It goes a bit heavy on random artifacts, but it still includes some worthwhile displays that help illuminate what local life was like from the 1600s to the 20th century.

Québec Old Town

Top Sights
1 Le Château Frontenac C4
2 Musée de la Civilisation D2

Sights
3 Basilique-Cathédrale Notre-Dame-de-Québec C3
4 Église Notre-Dame-des-Victoires D3
5 La Citadelle B6
6 Musée de la Place-Royale D3
7 Musée de l'Amérique Francophone C3
8 Musée des Ursulines B4
9 St-Louis Forts & Châteaux National Historic Site C3
10 Terrasse Dufferin C4

Activities, Courses & Tours
11 Cyclo Services A1
12 Glissade de la Terrasse C4
13 Les Promenades Fantômes C3
Les Tours Voir Québec .... (see 13)

Sleeping
14 Auberge Saint-Antoine D3
15 Chez Hubert B4
Fairmont Le Château Frontenac .... (see 1)
16 HI Auberge Internationale de Québec A3
17 Hôtel 71 .... D2
18 Hotel Manoir Victoria A2
19 La Marquise de Bassano C4
20 Les Lofts 1048 .... A3
21 Maison Historique James Thompson B4

Eating
1608 .... (see 1)
22 Apsara A4
23 Aux Anciens Canadiens B4
24 Batinse B2
25 Chez Ashton A3
26 Chez Boulay A3
27 Le Cochon Dingue D4
28 Le Lapin Sauté D4
29 Le Saint-Amour A4
30 L'Échaudé D2
31 Paillard Café-Boulangerie A3
32 Toast! D3

Drinking & Nightlife
33 Bar Ste-Angèle A3
34 L'Oncle Antoine D3

Entertainment
35 Les Yeux Bleus A3

Shopping
36 Art Inuit Brousseau B4
37 Marché du Vieux-Port B1

Église Notre-Dame-des-Victoires CHURCH
(Our Lady of Victories Church; Map p276; ☎418-692-1650; 32 Rue Sous-le-Fort; ⏲9:30am-8:30pm late Jun-Aug, to 4:30pm late May-late Jun) Dating from 1688, and named for French victories over the British in 1690 and 1711, this is North America's oldest stone church. It stands on the spot where Champlain set up his 'Habitation,' a small stockade, 80 years prior to the church's arrival. Inside are copies of works by Rubens and Van Dyck. Hanging from the ceiling is a replica of a wooden ship, the *Brézé,* thought to be a good-luck charm for ocean crossings and battles with the Iroquois.

Outside the Walls

Most visitors venture through Porte St-Louis to take a peek at Québec City's most significant attraction outside the walls: Battlefields Park, site of the famous Plains of Abraham. Unfortunately, most then scuttle back to the safety of that fairy-tale land inside the walls. Some of the sights here are certainly more interesting than taking yet another snap of the Château – notably Hôtel du Parlement and Obsérvatoire de la Capitale. The St-Jean-Baptiste and St-Roch areas, which offer a taste of everyday Québec, are a depressurization chamber after the onslaught of historical tourism in the Old Town.

Hôtel du Parlement HISTORIC BUILDING
(Parliament Building; Map p280; ☎418-643-7239; www.assnat.qc.ca/en/visiteurs; 1045 Rue des Parlementaires; ⏲8:30am-4:30pm Mon-Fri, 9:30am-4:30pm Sat & Sun late Jun-Aug, 8am-5pm Mon-Fri Sep-late Jun) FREE Home to Québec's Provincial Legislature, the Parliament building is a Second Empire structure completed in 1886. Free 30-minute tours, offered in English and French year-round, get you into the **National Assembly Chamber**, the **Legislative Council Chamber** and the **Speakers' Gallery**. The facade is decorated with 23 bronze statues of significant provincial historical figures, including explorer Samuel de Champlain (1570–1635), early New France governor Louis de Buade Frontenac (1622–98) and the legendary generals James Wolfe (1727–59) and Louis-Joseph Montcalm (1712–59).

Obsérvatoire de la Capitale NOTABLE BUILDING
(Capital Observatory; Map p280; ☎418-644-9841, 888-497-4322; www.observatoirecapitale.org; 1037 Rue de la Chevrotière; adult/child $14/free; ⏰10am-5pm daily Feb–mid-Oct, closed Mon mid-Oct–Jan) Head 221m up to the 31st floor for great views of the Old Town, the St Lawrence River and (if it's clear enough) even the Laurentians. It all helps to get your bearings, while the information panels along the way will get you up to speed on some of the local history.

Battlefields Park HISTORIC SITE
(Parc des Champs de Bataille; ☎418-649-6157; www.ccbn-nbc.gc.ca/en; 835 Wilfrid-Laurier Ave; ⏰8:30am-5:30pm; 👪) One of Québec City's must-sees, this verdant clifftop park contains the **Plains of Abraham**, site of the infamous 1759 battle between British General James Wolfe and French General Louis-Joseph Montcalm that determined the fate of the North American continent. Packed with old cannons, monuments and commemorative plaques, it's a favorite local spot for picnicking, running, skating, skiing and snowshoeing, along with Winter Carnival festivities and open-air summer concerts. For information, visit the Plains of Abraham Information & Reception Centre (p287).

Musée National des Beaux-Arts du Québec MUSEUM
(☎418-643-2150; www.mnbaq.org; Battlefields Park; adult/youth/child $18/5/free; ⏰10am-5pm Tue-Sun Sep-May, 10am-6pm daily Jun-Aug, to 9pm Wed year-round) Carve out at least half a day to visit this excellent art museum, one of the province's best. Permanent exhibitions range from art in the early French colonies to Québec's abstract artists, with individual halls devoted entirely to 20th-century artistic giants such as Jean-Paul Lemieux and Jean-Paul Riopelle. Another highlight is the **Brousseau Inuit Art Collection**, a 2639-piece personal collection spanning 50 years.

St-Jean-Baptiste AREA
(Map p280) Strolling along **Rue St-Jean** is a great way to feel the pulse of this bohemian area. The first thing that strikes you, once you've recovered from crossing busy Ave Honoré Mercier, is the area's down-to-earth ambience. Good restaurants, hip cafes and bars, and interesting shops, some catering to a gay clientele, line the thoroughfare as far as Rue Racine. Take any side street and walk downhill (northwest) to the narrow residential streets such as Rue d'Aiguillon, Rue Richelieu and Rue St-Olivier.

St-Roch AREA
Traditionally a working-class district for factory and naval workers, St-Roch has been slowly gentrifying. On the main artery, **Rue St-Joseph**, spiffy new restaurants and bars have sprung up among the junk shops and secondhand clothes stores. Private art galleries are also found here and on **Rue St-Vallier Est**.

Walking down Côte Ste-Geneviève in St-Jean-Baptiste, you will come to a steep staircase, the Escalier de la Chapelle, which takes you down to St-Roch.

Activities

★Corridor du Littoral/Promenade Samuel-de-Champlain CYCLING, WALKING
(👪) Starting southwest of Québec City at Cap-Rouge and extending northeast via the Old Lower Town to Montmorency Falls, the Corridor du Littoral is a 48km multipurpose recreation path along the St Lawrence River, popular with cyclists, walkers and in-line skaters. The heart of the path is the Promenade Samuel-de-Champlain, an especially beautiful 2.5km section.

Glissade de la Terrasse SNOW SPORTS
(Map p276; ☎418-528-1884; www.au1884.ca; Terrasse Dufferin; per person $3; ⏰11am-5pm Sun-Thu, to 6pm Fri & Sat mid-Dec–mid-Mar; 👪; 🚌3, 11) Outside Le Château Frontenac (p274), the scenic Terrasse Dufferin (p274) on the riverfront stages this invigoratingly fast, triple-chute toboggan run all winter long, weather conditions permitting. Toboggans accommodating up to four people are available for rent at the bottom; buy tickets at the Au 1884 kiosk, then grab your toboggan, walk up to the top and let 'er rip.

Place d'Youville Skating Rink ICE SKATING
(Map p280; ☎418-641-6256; just outside Porte St-Jean; skating free, skate rentals $8; ⏰noon-10pm Mon-Thu, 10am-10pm Fri-Sun mid-Oct–mid-Mar; 👪) This improvised outdoor rink is one of the most scenic and popular places for ice skating once winter rolls around. It's a great place to mingle with locals, and you can also rent skates on-site.

Tours

Guided walking tours can pack a lot of specialized knowledge into a short time. For example, on one tour a cannonball wedged into a tree beside the sidewalk on Rue St-Louis is pointed out by a guide as strollers pass blindly by.

Cyclo Services CYCLING

(Map p276; ☎877-692-4050, 418-692-4052; www.cycloservices.net; 289 Rue St-Paul; rental per 2/24hr from $15/35; ⏱9am-5:30pm Mon-Fri, 10am-5pm Sat & Sun, variable hours Nov-Apr;) This outfit rents a wide variety of bikes (hybrid, city, tandem, road and kids' bikes) and organizes excellent cycling tours of the city and outskirts to places such as Wendake or Parc de la Chute Montmorency. The knowledgeable and fun guides frequently give tours in English. In winter, it rents snowshoes only, and hours are limited.

Les Tours Voir Québec WALKING

(Map p276; ☎418-694-2001, 866-694-2001; www.toursvoirquebec.com; 12 Rue Ste-Anne; tours from $23) This group offers excellent tours on the history, architecture and food of Québec City. The popular two-hour 'grand tour' takes in the Old City's highlights, while the food tour includes tastings of wines, cheeses, crêpes, chocolate, maple products and other Québécois specialties at a variety of shops and restaurants. Reserve ahead.

Les Promenades Fantômes WALKING

(Map p276; ☎418-692-0624; www.promenadesfantomes.com; 12 Rue Ste-Anne; adult/child $18.50/15.75; ⏱8pm May-Oct) Take a nocturnal trip by the light of a swinging lantern and learn about bygone Québec City's shadowy side.

Festivals & Events

Carnaval de Québec CARNIVAL

(Québec Winter Carnival; www.carnaval.qc.ca; ⏱Jan or Feb) This famous annual event is unique to Québec City. It bills itself as the biggest winter carnival in the world, with parades, ice sculptures, a snow slide, boat races, dances, music and lots of drinking. Activities take place all over town and the iconic slide is on the Terrasse Dufferin (p274) behind Le Château Frontenac (p274).

If you want to go, organize the trip early, as accommodations fill up fast, and don't forget to bring lots of warm clothes.

Fête Nationale du Québec CULTURAL

(Festival of John the Baptist; www.fetenationale.quebec; ⏱24 Jun) On this night, Québec City parties hard. Originally a holiday honoring John the Baptist, this day has evolved into a quasi-political event celebrating Québec's distinct culture and nationalistic leanings. Major festivities on the Plains of Abraham start around 8pm.

Festival d'Été MUSIC

(www.infofestival.com; ⏱Jul) This 11-day July festival attracts musicians from all over the world.

Fête Arc-en-Ciel LGBT

(☎418-809-3383; www.arcencielquebec.ca) This Gay Pride celebration rocks Québec City in September.

Sleeping

From old-fashioned B&Bs to stylish boutique hotels, Québec City has some fantastic options. The best choices are the numerous small European-style hotels and Victorian B&Bs scattered around the Old Town. As you'd expect in such a popular city, the top choices are often full, so make reservations well in advance, especially for weekends. It's unwise to show up in the city on a Saturday morning in summer or during holidays and expect to find a room for the same night.

Prices rise in the high-season summer months and during Winter Carnival. At other times of year, you can usually save 30% or so off the high-season prices.

Old Upper Town

HI Auberge Internationale de Québec HOSTEL $

(Map p276; ☎418-694-0755, 866-694-0950; www.aubergeinternationaledequebec.com; 19 Rue Ste-Ursule; dm $29-34, r without bath $72-84, with bath $100-125, all incl breakfast; ❄@📶) The frustrating labyrinth of corridors goes on forever, but this lively, well-located place heaves with energy year-round. It attracts a mix of independent travelers, families and groups. Staff are friendly but often harried just trying to keep up with all the comings and goings. It's usually full in summer, despite having almost 300 beds, so book ahead if you can.

★**Maison Historique James Thompson** B&B $$

(Map p276; ☎418-694-9042; www.bedandbreakfastquebec.com; 47 Rue Ste-Ursule; r $75-135; ❄📶) History buffs will get a real kick out of staying in the 18th-century former residence of James Thompson, a veteran of the Battle of the Plains of Abraham. The beautifully restored house comes complete with the original murder hole next to the front door. Rooms are spacious and brightly infused with host Guitta's cheerful artwork.

St-Roch & St-Jean-Baptiste

St-Roch & St-Jean-Baptiste

Sights

1 Fortifications of Québec National Historic Site D1
2 Hôtel du Parlement D3
3 Obsérvatoire de la Capitale C3
4 St-Jean-Baptiste C2

Activities, Courses & Tours

5 Place d'Youville Skating Rink D1

Sleeping

Auberge JA Moisan .... (see 15)
6 Hôtel Le Vincent A1

Eating

7 Le Hobbit C2

Drinking & Nightlife

8 Le Drague C2
9 Le Moine Échanson B2
10 Le Sacrilège B3

Entertainment

11 Bateau de Nuit A3
12 Fou-Bar B3
13 Scanner A1

Shopping

14 Érico B2
15 JA Moisan Épicier C2

★**La Marquise de Bassano** B&B **$$**
(Map p276; ☎418-692-0316, 877-692-0316; www.marquisedebassano.com; 15 Rue des Grisons; r incl breakfast $110-179; P@) The young, gregarious owners have done a beautiful job with this welcoming 19th-century Victorian family home, outfitting its five rooms with thoughtful touches, whether it's a canopy bed

or a claw-foot bathtub. It's peacefully placed on a low-traffic street surrounded by period homes, minutes from the important sights. Only two rooms have private baths; the other three share facilities.

Les Lofts 1048 APARTMENT **$$**

(Map p276; ☎418-657-9177; www.condovieuxquebec.ca; 1048 Rue St-Jean; apt $170-300; ❄📶) For a welcoming pied-à-terre in the heart of the Old Upper Town, try these gorgeously refurbished, bright, high-ceilinged apartments. Comfortable bedding, full kitchens, ultramodern bathrooms and laundry facilities make each loft a cozy home away from home.

Chez Hubert B&B **$$**

(Map p276; ☎418-692-0958; www.chezhubert.com; 66 Rue Ste-Ursule; r without bath incl breakfast $85-155; P@📶) This dependable family-run choice is in a Victorian town house with chandeliers, fireplace mantels, stained-glass windows, a lovely curved staircase and oriental rugs. The three tasteful, warm-hued rooms, two with a view of the Le Château Frontenac (p274), all share a pair of baths and come with a large buffet breakfast and free parking.

Fairmont Le Château Frontenac HOTEL **$$$**

(Map p276; ☎418-692-3861, 866-540-4460; www.fairmont.com/frontenac; 1 Rue des Carrières; r from $409; P❄📶) More than a hotel, the iconic Frontenac is one of Québec City's enduring symbols. Fresh off a 2014 makeover, its 611 rooms come in a dozen-plus categories. The coveted river-view rooms range in price from Deluxe units tucked under the 18th-floor eaves to the ultra-spacious Fairmont Gold Signature rooms, with concierge service, curved turret windows and vintage architectural details.

Hotel Manoir Victoria HOTEL **$$$**

(Map p276; ☎800-463-6283; www.manoir-victoria.com; 44 Côte du Palais; r $199-369, ste $329-550; P❄📶🏊) A historical, Old-World facade gives way to a modish chic lobby and lounge, modern rooms decked out with flat-screen TVs, and an indoor pool. An on-site spa and gym will keep you warm after walking through an Old Town winter.

Old Lower Town

★ **Auberge Saint-Antoine** BOUTIQUE HOTEL **$$$**

(Map p276; ☎418-692-2211, 888-692-2211; www.saint-antoine.com; 8 Rue St-Antoine; r $200-549, ste $600-1000; P❄@📶) This is one of Canada's finest hotels, with phenomenal service and endless amenities. The plush, spacious rooms come with high-end mattresses, goose-down duvets and luxury linens while the halls resemble an art gallery, filled with French colonial relics discovered during excavations to expand the hotel. **Panache**, the darling of Québec's fine-dining scene, is next door.

Hôtel 71 BOUTIQUE HOTEL **$$$**

(Map p276; ☎888-692-1171, 418-692-1171; www.hotel71.ca; 71 Rue St-Pierre; r/ste from $309/409; ❄@📶) Set in an imposing 19th-century greystone building, Hôtel 71 provides a boutique experience. Sleek, minimalist rooms offer unstinting comfort, with fantastic mattresses, plush down comforters, oversized TVs and dramatically lit baths. The penthouse suite, with its wraparound windows, commands some of Québec City's most astounding perspectives on Place-Royale, the St Lawrence River and the Château Frontenac (p274).

Outside the Walls

Prices are drastically lower and rooms bigger outside the walls, and for drivers, parking suddenly becomes a less complicated affair. All of the lodgings listed are within a 15-minute drive or walk from the Old Town.

Centre de Plein Air de Beauport CAMPGROUND **$**

(☎418-641-6112, 877-641-6113; www.centrepleinair-beauport.ca; 95 Rue de la Sérénité; campsites & RV sites from $38; ⏲Jun-early Sep; P) This excellent campground near Montmorency Falls is green, peaceful and just a 15-minute drive from the Old Town. To get there, take Hwy 40 toward Montmorency, get off at exit 321 and turn north.

Auberge JA Moisan B&B **$$**

(Map p280; ☎418-529-9764; www.jamoisan.com; 695 Rue St-Jean; s $130-150, d $140-160; P❄📶) This lovely top-floor B&B sits above the famous JA Moisan (p286) grocery store. Bedrooms are small and tucked under the eaves, while the floor below holds a cluster of common areas, including a parlor, tearoom, solarium, terrace and computer room. Gregarious host Clément St-Laurent makes guests feel right at home, and rates include breakfast, afternoon tea and free parking.

Grand Times HOTEL **$$**

(☎418-353-3333; www.grandtimeshotel.com; 5100 Blvd des Galeries; r $140-160, ste $240-410; P❄📶🏊) Alright, so the title seems to promise a lot, but the fact is this hotel, located a little ways out of town, offers designer chic

QUÉBEC'S COOLEST HOTEL

Visiting the **Ice Hotel** (Hôtel de Glace; ☎877-505-0423, 418-623-2888; www.hoteldeglace-canada.com; 1860 Valcartier Blvd; tour adult/youth/child $18/16/9; ⊙Jan-Mar; P) is like stepping into a wintry fairy tale. Nearly everything here is made of ice: the reception desk, the sink in your room, your bed – all ice.

Some 500 tonnes of ice and 15,000 tonnes of snow go into the five-week construction of this perishable hotel. First impressions are overwhelming – in the entrance hall, tall, sculpted columns of ice support a ceiling where a crystal chandelier hangs. To either side, carved sculptures, tables and chairs fill the labyrinth of corridors and guest rooms. Children will love the ice slides, while grown-ups gravitate to the ice bar, where stiff drinks are served in cocktail glasses made of ice (there's hot chocolate for the kids, too).

The Ice Hotel usually opens from January to March and offers packages starting at $380 per person (promo offers can knock around $100 off this price). Sleeping here is more about the adventure, and less about getting a good night's sleep, although thick sleeping bags laid on plush deer pelts do help keep things cozier than you might expect.

A better option for most people is to buy a day pass (adult/youth/child $18/16/9), which allows you to visit the guest rooms and all of the hotel's public spaces, including the ice bar and ice slides. The hotel is about 40 minutes northwest of Québec City off Rte 371.

accommodations for a midrange rate. The rooms all have that stripped-down loft-chic look going on, and there's a tonne of amenities on-site, from a spa to heated indoor pool.

Hôtel Le Vincent BOUTIQUE HOTEL **$$$**
(Map p280; ☎418-523-5000; www.hotellevincent.com; 295 Rue St-Vallier Est; r incl breakfast $179-279; P@≋) This hotel's nondescript brick facade may look unpromising, but things improve dramatically once you step inside. The lobby and adjacent stone-walled breakfast area, with their comfy furniture and pleasant fireside reading nook, are instantly inviting, while the rooms upstairs, especially corner suites are stylishly comfortable, with brick walls, tall windows, mod couches and sleek bathtubs.

Eating

Québec City's restaurant scene has never been better. While the capital has always excelled at classic French food, in recent years a number of new arrivals have put a trendy modern spin on the bistro experience. At the same time, some of the city's most famous chefs have begun embracing the concept of *cuisine boréale*, which emphasizes a return to indigenous northern ingredients such as wild game, seafood, mushrooms, apples, berries and root vegetables. Many of the better places can get a bit pricey, but don't write them off. Do what the locals do: a carefully chosen *table d'hôte* at lunchtime will give you exactly the same food for a more manageable price.

Old Upper Town

Paillard Café-Boulangerie BAKERY **$**
(Map p276; ☎418-692-4392; www.paillard.ca; 1097 Rue St-Jean; sandwiches $8-10; ⊙7am-9pm Sun-Thu, to 10pm Fri & Sat) At this bright, buzzy and high-ceilinged space, diners seated at long wooden tables tuck into tasty gourmet sandwiches, soups and salads. The attached bakery, with its alluring display cases, is downright irresistible – try the *tentation*, a delicious sweet pastry loaded with berries, or indulge in a savory *fougasse* (Provençal-style bread brushed with olive oil and studded with olives and herbs).

Chez Ashton FAST FOOD **$**
(Map p276; ☎418-692-3055; www.chez-ashton.com; 54 Côte du Palais; mains $4-10; ⊙11am-11:30pm Sun-Thu, to 4am Fri & Sat) For a break from fine dining, head to this Québec City fast-food institution with dozens of restaurants across town. On weekends, local revelers flock here in the wee hours of the morning to refuel with the classic Québécois comfort food, poutine (fries smothered in cheese curds and gravy).

Apsara CAMBODIAN **$**
(Map p276; ☎418-694-0232; http://restaurantapsara.com; 71 Rue d'Auteuil; mains $10-15; ⊙11:30am-2pm Mon-Fri, 5:30-11pm daily) Southeast Asian cuisine, from Thai to Vietnamese to Cambodian, all gets a little lumped together at this restaurant, but Cambodians are piloting the ship with delicious results, including thinly sliced beef stir-fry and pork-and-shrimp dumplings.

★Chez Boulay QUÉBÉCOIS $$
(Map p276; ☎418-380-8166; www.chezboulay.com; 1110 Rue St-Jean; lunch menus $17-26, dinner mains $20-34; ⏲11:30am-10pm Mon-Fri, 10am-10pm Sat & Sun) Renowned chef Jean-Luc Boulay's latest venture serves an ever-evolving menu inspired by seasonal Québécois staples such as venison, goose, wild mushrooms and Gaspé Peninsula seafood. Lunch specials and charcuterie platters for two (served 2pm to 5pm) offer an affordable afternoon pick-me-up, while the sleek, low-lit dining area makes a romantic setting for dinner.

Batinse QUÉBÉCOIS $$
(Map p276; ☎581-742-2555; http://batinse.com/home/; 1200 Rue St-Jean; mains $18-27; ⏲11am-11:45pm Mon-Fri, from 9am Sat & Sun) The kitchen staff here have fun, and it's hard not to smile along with their eclectic menu, which jukes from steak with a tea sauce to salmon pie topped with quail-egg béchamel to a divine shrimp and chorizo salad. Hip, locally sourced and not to be missed.

Le Saint-Amour FRENCH, QUÉBÉCOIS $$$
(Map p276; ☎418-694-0667; www.saint-amour.com; 48 Rue Ste-Ursule; mains $32-52, fixed-price menus $68-115; ⏲11:30am-2pm & 6-10pm Mon-Fri, 5:30-10pm Sat, 6-10pm Sun) One of Québec City's top-end darlings, Le Saint-Amour has earned a loyal following for its beautifully prepared grills and seafood. The soaring greenhouse-style ceiling trimmed with hanging plants creates a warm, inviting setting, and the midday *table d'hôte* ($25 to $33; available weekdays only) offers that rarest of Upper Town experiences – a world-class meal at an extremely reasonable price.

Aux Anciens Canadiens QUÉBÉCOIS $$$
(Map p276; ☎418-692-1627; www.auxanciens canadiens.qc.ca; 34 Rue St-Louis; mains $31-59, 3-course menu from $20; ⏲noon-9:30pm) Housed in the historic Jacquet House, which dates from 1676, this place is a well-worn tourist destination, specializing in robust country cooking and typical Québécois specialties served by waitstaff in historic garb. The *menu du jour*, offered from noon to 6pm, is by far the best deal at around $20 for three courses, including a glass of wine or beer.

Old Lower Town

Le Lapin Sauté FRENCH $$
(Map p276; ☎418-692-5325; www.lapinsaute.com; 52 Rue du Petit-Champlain; mains $16-26; ⏲11am-10pm Mon-Fri, 9am-10pm Sat & Sun) Naturally, *lapin* (rabbit) plays a starring role at this cozy, rustic restaurant near the foot of the funicular, in dishes like rabbit cassoulet or rabbit poutine. Other enticements include salads, French onion soup, charcuterie platters and an excellent value lunch menu (from $15). In good weather, sit on the flowery patio overlooking tiny Félix Leclerc park.

Le Cochon Dingue FRENCH $$
(Map p276; ☎418-692-2013; www.cochondingue.com; 46 Blvd Champlain; mains $15-34; ⏲7am-10pm Mon-Thu, to 11pm Fri, 8am-11pm Sat, to 10pm Sun;) Since 1979, this ever-popular choice has been serving visitors and locals straight-ahead French standbys, from café au lait *en bôl* (in a bowl) to croque monsieur, sandwiches, steak frites, salads, mussels or quiche.

1608 CHEESE $$
(Map p276; ☎418-692-3861; http://1608baravin.com; 1 Rue des Carrières; mains $22-34; ⏲4pm-midnight Mon-Thu, 2pm-1am Fri-Sun) At this wine-and-cheese bar you can either select some cheeses yourself or let the staff take you down a wine-and-cheese rabbit hole that's difficult to emerge from – without gaining a few kilos, anyway. Wine, *fromage* and a view of the St Lawrence by candlelight all make for a very romantic setting.

★Toast! BISTRO $$$
(Map p276; ☎418-692-1334; www.restauranttoast.com; 17 Rue Sault-au-Matelot; mains $25-38; ⏲6-10:30pm Sun-Thu, to 11pm Fri & Sat) Under the direction of Christian Lemelin (voted Québec's best chef in 2014 by a jury of his peers), Toast! is among the city's finest. The house's signature foie gras appetizer is followed by a sumptuous array of dishes and a superb wine list, with fiery red decor setting a romantic mood.

L'Échaudé FRENCH $$$
(Map p276; ☎418-692-1299; www.echaude.com; 73 Rue Sault-au-Matelot; lunch menus $15-28, dinner mains $24-36; ⏲11:30am-2:30pm & 5:30-11pm Mon-Fri, 10am-2pm & 5:30-11pm Sat, from 9am Sun;) Everything comes beautifully plated and bursting with flavor at this bistro, one of the rare Old Town eateries where locals regularly outnumber tourists. Classics such as duck confit, steak frites and salmon tartare share the menu with daily specials like fish and mussel stew in a lobster-and-wine broth. The terrific wine list favors bottles from France.

POUTINE, BIEN SÛR

Like all fast food, Québec's beloved poutine is perfect if you have a *gueule de bois* (hangover) after a night on the Boréale Blonde. In the calorie-packing culinary Frankenstein, the province's exemplary fries (fresh-cut, never frozen or served limp and greasy) are sprinkled with cheese curds and smothered in gravy. The dish was devised in the early 1980s and spread across Québec like a grease fire.

Poutine is a staple of the oft-seen roadside diners, *cantines* or *casse croûtes*, where you can sample embellished versions such as Italienne – with spaghetti. The eateries generally have their own top-secret recipe; for example, **Le Mouton Noir** (p260) in Val-David has a version loaded with Indian curry. As a general guide, these house specialties include mincemeat and green peppers. **Chez Ashton** (p282) in Québec City is a good place to take the poutine challenge.

Outside the Walls

Bügel Fabrique De Bagels CANADIAN **$**

(418-523-7666; http://bugel-fabrique.ca; 164 Rue Crémazie Ouest; mains $7-15; 7am-7pm Sun & Mon, to 9pm Tue-Sat) Don't be fooled by the title: there's more than bagels at this cute neighborhood nook. More accurately, imagine bagels and then some: served with Brie and pesto, or au gratin with ham and asparagus, or topped with smoked salmon. Ingredients are locally sourced.

Le Croquembouche BAKERY **$**

(www.lecroquembouche.com; 225 Rue St-Joseph Est; pastries from $2; 7am-6:30pm Tue-Sat, to 5pm Sun;) Widely hailed as Québec City's finest bakery, Croquembouche draws devoted locals from dawn to dusk. Among its seductive offerings are fluffy-as-a-cloud croissants, tantalizing cakes and éclairs, brioches brimming with raspberries, and gourmet sandwiches on fresh-baked bread. There's also a stellar array of *danoises* (Danish pastries), including orange and anise, cranberry, pistachio and chocolate, and lemon, ginger and poppy seed.

La Cuisine DINER **$**

(418-523-3387; www.barlautrecuisine.com; 205 Rue St-Vallier Est; mains $10; 11am-1am Mon-Wed, 11am-3am Thu & Fri, 2pm-3am Sat, 2pm-1am Sun) Retro decor and comfort food served till the wee hours are the hallmarks of this trendy, low-lit local hangout midway between St-Jean Baptiste and St-Roch. Formica tables, mismatched china and silverware, light fixtures made from colanders, a vintage Wurlitzer jukebox, and board games give the place a fun, relaxed feel. On weekend nights, DJs spin everything from electronica to soul.

Bati Bassak CAMBODIAN, THAI **$**

(418-522-4567; 125 Rue St-Joseph Est; mains $12-19; 11am-2pm Tue-Fri, 5-9:30pm Tue-Sun;) This bustling Thai-Cambodian eatery is a welcome change of pace, serving a menu full of tasty meat and fish dishes, along with several veggie offerings. Weekday lunch specials offer especially good value at $10 to $14 including appetizer, tea and dessert. No alcohol is served, but you're welcome to bring your own.

L'Affaire est Ketchup BISTRO **$$**

(418-529-9020; 46 Rue St-Joseph Est; mains $17-34; 6-11pm Tue-Sun) Book ahead for this quirky local favorite with only eight tables. Dressed in T-shirts and baseball caps, bantering relaxedly with one another as they cook on a pair of electric stoves, founders François and Olivier specialize in home cooking with a trendy modern twist. A good selection of wines and mixed drinks is available from the well-stocked bar.

Chez Victor BURGERS **$$**

(418-529-7702; www.chezvictorburger.com; 145 Rue St-Jean; mains $13-18; 11:30am-9pm Sun-Wed, to 10pm Thu-Sat;) One of Québec City's best-loved neighborhood eateries, Chez Victor specializes in juicy burgers, served with a hefty dash of creativity. Choose from deer, salmon, wild boar, straight-up beef or vegetarian, which you can then dress a number of ways (brie, smoked bacon, cream cheese etc). You'll find several other branches around town, including one down by the Vieux-Port.

Le Hobbit BISTRO **$$**

(Map p280; 418-647-2677; www.hobbitbistro.com; 700 Rue St-Jean; mains $16-29; 8am-10pm Mon-Fri, 9am-10pm Sat & Sun) This popular and inviting bistro has outdoor seating, a casual atmosphere and good-value lunch and dinner specials (check out the chalkboard). The classics are all nicely done, including juicy duck confit and steak frites. Various fresh pasta dishes and salads round out the menu, and there's a small but fairly priced wine list. Breakfast is served till 2:30pm on weekends.

Morena BISTRO $$

(☎418-529-3668; www.morena-food.com; 1038 Ave Cartier; mains $15-17; ⏲8am-7pm Mon-Wed, to 8pm Thu & Fri, to 6pm Sat & Sun) Tucked into a gourmet grocery-deli on tony Ave Cartier, this Italian-themed neighborhood bistro makes a lively but low-key lunch stop. Daily chalkboard specials are beautifully presented, with fresh veggies on the side and a soup or salad appetizer. After 3pm there's an à la carte snack menu.

Drinking & Nightlife

★Le Sacrilège BAR

(Map p280; ☎418-649-1985; www.lesacrilege.com; 447 Rue St-Jean; ⏲noon-3am) With its unmistakable sign of a laughing, dancing monk saucily flaunting his knickers, this bar has long been the watering hole of choice for Québec's night owls, who start or end their weekend revelry here. Even on Monday, it's standing-room only. There's a popular terrace out back; get to it through the bar or the tiny brick alley next door.

Le Moine Échanson WINE BAR

(Map p280; ☎418-524-7832; www.lemoineechanson.com; 585 Rue St-Jean; ⏲7:30am-10pm Mon-Thu, to 11pm Fri, 10am-11pm Sat & Sun) A darling of the city's wine connoisseurs, this convivial brick-walled bistro pours an enticing and ever-changing array of wines from all over the Mediterranean, by the glass and by the bottle, accompanied by hearty and homespun snacks and main dishes.

Les Salons d'Edgar BAR

(☎418-523-7811; www.lessalonsdedgar.com; 263 Rue St-Vallier Est; ⏲4:30pm-late Wed-Sat, 5:30pm-late Sun) At this unofficial 'official' hangout for the city's theater community, the eavesdropping is as much fun as the drinking – you'll be privy to chats on roles lost and roles gained.

La Revanche BAR

(☎418-263-5389; 585 Blvd Charest Est; ⏲5pm-midnight Mon, 4pm-1am Tue-Thu, to 2am Fri, noon-2am Sat, to midnight Sun) This eclectic bar-cafe is dedicated to table-top and board gaming. Seriously, there's a wall at Revanche that looks like it could have been plucked from a toy store. Staff are on hand to help you learn the ropes of any game.

Macfly Bar & Arcade BAR

(☎418-528-7000; 422 Rue Caron; ⏲4pm-3am) This bar's *Back to the Future*-ish title isn't an accident: the entire interior evokes the 1980s, or at least a specific idea of what the '80s were about – old-school arcade consoles, bright counter tops, and rows of pinball machines that await your wizardry. Not that it's easy to top your highest score after a couple of well-pulled beers…

La Barberie BREWERY

(☎418-522-4373; www.labarberie.com; 310 Rue St-Roch; ⏲noon-1am) This cooperative St-Roch microbrewery is beloved for its tree-shaded deck, its ever-evolving selection of eight home brews, and its unique BYO policy, which allows customers to bring snacks in from the outside. Seasonal offerings range from classic pale ales to quirkier options such as orange stout or hot pepper amber. Undecided? Sample 'em all in the popular eight-beer carousel!

Le Drague GAY

(Map p280; www.ledrague.com; 815 Rue St-Augustin; ⏲10am-3am) The star player on Québec City's tiny gay scene, Le Drague comprises a front outdoor terrace, a two-level disco where drag shows are held, and a more laid-back tavern.

Bar Ste-Angèle BAR

(Map p276; ☎418-692-2171; 26 Rue Ste-Angèle; ⏲8pm-3am) A low-lit, intimate hideaway, where the genial staff will help you navigate the list of cocktail pitchers and local and European bottled beers.

L'Oncle Antoine PUB

(Map p276; ☎418-694-9176; 29 Rue St-Pierre; ⏲11am-1am) Set clandestinely in the stone cave-cellar of one of the city's oldest surviving houses (dating from 1754), this great tavern pours out excellent Québec microbrews (try the Barberie Noir stout or the strong Belgian-style Fin du Monde), several drafts *(en fût)* and various European beers.

☆ Entertainment

The performing arts are in fine form in Québec City. The city boasts a symphony orchestra, L'Orchestre Symphonique de Québec, and an opera company, Opéra de Québec. Homegrown Québécois bands perform regularly, as do touring bands from across Canada, the US and Europe, especially during the Festival d'Été (p279) in July. Live performance venues abound, from concert halls to open-air amphitheaters, little jazz and rock clubs, and exuberant *boîtes à chanson* (Québec folk-music clubs), where generations of locals dance and sing with uncensored glee. French-language theater is also an interesting scene here, with tonnes of small companies producing a variety of shows.

★**Le Cercle** LIVE MUSIC
(418-948-8648; www.le-cercle.ca; 226½ Rue St-Joseph Est; 11:30am-1:30am Mon-Wed, 11:30am-3am Thu & Fri, 3pm-3am Sat, 10am-1:30am Sun) This very cool art space and show venue draws a hip crowd for its international DJs and underground bands, ranging from indie rock to electronica, blues to Cajun. It hosts numerous other events, including film, fashion and comic strip festivals, book- and album-release parties, wine tastings and more. Affordable tapas, weekend brunches and an atmospheric bar space sweeten the deal.

Fou-Bar LIVE MUSIC
(Map p280; 418-522-1987; www.foubar.ca; 525 Rue St-Jean; 2:30pm-3am) Laid-back and with an eclectic mix of bands, this bar is one of the town's classics for good live music. It's also popular for its reasonably priced food menu and its free *pique-assiettes* (appetizers) on Thursday and Friday evenings.

Scanner LIVE MUSIC
(Map p280; 418-523-1916; www.scannerbistro.com; 291 Rue St-Vallier Est; 3pm-3am Sat-Thu, 11:30am-3am Fri) Ask any local between the ages of 18 and 35 to suggest a cool place for a drink and this is where they might send you. DJs and live bands serve up a potent musical mix, from heavy metal to hard rock to punk to rockabilly. There's a terrace outside in summer, plus Foosball and pool inside year-round.

Les Yeux Bleus LIVE MUSIC
(Map p276; 418-694-9118; 1117 Rue St-Jean; 9pm-3am Mon, Tue & Thu, 8pm-3am Wed, 4pm-3am Fri-Sun) One of the city's better *boîtes á chanson* (live, informal singer/songwriter clubs), this is the place to catch newcomers, the occasional big-name Francophone concert and Québécois classics.

Bateau de Nuit LIVE MUSIC
(Map p280; 418-977-2626; 275 Rue St-Jean; 7pm-3am Mon & Tue, from 5pm Wed-Fri, from 8pm Sat & Sun) We really appreciate it when our dive bars come with a heavy dose of live music, which is exactly the case at this sweet little venue. The in-the-know bar staff can tell you about local musicians, or whoever carved their initials into the wall – the crowd here has likely played both roles, to be fair.

Shopping

While it may not have as many big international stores and high-end designer boutiques as some larger cities, Québec is a shopper's paradise in its own special way. Small, unique and authentic little boutiques are this touristy town's claim to retail fame, and the city's small size makes it ideal for strolling around and browsing for surprises. The best streets for aimless window-shopping include Rue du Petit-Champlain and Rue St-Paul in the Old Lower Town, Ave Cartier in Montcalm, Rue St-Joseph in St-Roch, and Rue St-Jean (both inside and outside the walls).

★**JA Moisan Épicier** FOOD
(Map p280; 418-522-0685; www.jamoisan.com; 695 Rue St-Jean; 8:30am-9pm Mon-Sat, 10am-7pm Sun) Established in 1871, this charming store bills itself as North America's oldest grocery. It's a browser's dream come true, packed with beautifully displayed edibles and kitchen and household items. Many products fall on the side of expensive, but you'll find items here you've never seen before, along with heaps of local goods and gift ideas.

Art Inuit Brousseau ARTS & CRAFTS
(Map p276; 418-694-1828; www.artinuit.ca; 35 Rue St-Louis; 9:30am-5:30pm) A stunning gallery selling soapstone, serpentine and basalt Inuit sculptures from Northern Québec. Prices range from $45 to several thousand dollars.

Marché du Vieux-Port FOOD & DRINKS
(Map p276; 418-692-2517; www.marchevieuxport.com; 160 Quai St André; 9am-6pm Mon-Fri, to 5pm Sat & Sun;) At this heaving local food market, you can buy fresh fruits and vegetables as well as dozens of local specialties, from Île d'Orléans blackcurrant wine to ciders, honeys, cheeses, sausages, chocolates, herbal hand creams and, of course, maple-syrup products. Weekends see huge crowds and more wine tastings than can be considered sensible.

Érico FOOD
(Map p280; 418-524-2122; www.ericochocolatier.com; 634 Rue St-Jean; 10:30am-6pm Mon-Wed & Sat, to 9pm Thu & Fri, 11am-6pm Sun, extended hours summer) The exotic smells and flavors here will send a chocolate lover into conniptions of joy. The main shop brims with truffles, chocolate-chip cookies, ice cream and seasonal chocolate treats, while the quirky museum next door has a dress made entirely of chocolate, old-fashioned gumball machines dispensing 25¢ samples, and a window where you can watch the chocolatiers at work.

Information

CLSC et Unité de Médecine Familiale de la Haute-Ville (☎ 418-641-2572; www.ciusss-capitalenationale.gouv.qc.ca/node/2023; 55 Chemin Ste-Foy; ⊙8am-8:30pm Mon-Fri, to 4pm Sat & Sun) Québec City's main health clinic for minor ailments.

Plains of Abraham Information & Reception Centre (Map p276; ☎ 855-649-6157, 418-649-6157; www.ccbn-nbc.gc.ca; 835 Ave Wilfrid-Laurier; ⊙8:30am-5:30pm Jul & Aug, 8:30am-5pm Mon-Fri, from 9am Sat & Sun Sep-Jun) Adjacent to the Musée des Plaines d'Abraham, at the main entrance to **Battlefields Park** (p278).

Post Office (Map p276; 5 Rue du Fort; ⊙8am-7:30pm Mon-Fri, 9:30am-5pm Sat) In the Old Upper Town.

Tourism Québec City (☎ 418-641-6290, 877-783-1608; www.quebecregion.com) Tourist information on Québec City.

Getting There & Away

AIR

Regular Air Canada flights (45 minutes) run from Montréal to Québec City's Jean Lesage Airport. There are also some direct flights from the United States and Europe.

Aéroport International Jean-Lesage de Québec (YQB; ☎ 418-640-3300, 418-640-2600; www.aeroportdequebec.com; 505 Rue Principal) Québec City's Aéroport International Jean-Lesage de Québec lies about 15km west of the center.

BOAT

Ferry (Map p276; ☎ 877-787-7483; www.traversiers.com; car & driver/adult/child one way $8.35/3.55/2.40) The 10-minute ferry from Québec City to Lévis.

BUS

Orléans Express (www.orleansexpress.com) runs daily services between Montréal's main bus station, **Gare d'Autocars** (p257), and Québec City's **Gare du Palais bus station** (p287). Prices for the journey (three to 3½ hours) start at $25/50 for a one-way/return ticket.

If you're coming from Montréal, your bus may first stop 10km west of the center at **Ste-Foy-Sillery Station** (p287), so ask before you get off.

Bus Station (☎ 418-525-3000; 320 Rue Abraham-Martin) Adjacent to the train station, with regular bus service to Montréal.

RTC (Réseau de Transport de la Capitale; ☎ 418-627-2511; www.rtcquebec.ca) Bus service within the city of Québec.

Ste-Foy-Sillery Station (☎ 418-650-0087; 3001 Chemin des Quatre Bourgeois)

Transport Accessible du Québec (☎ 418-641-8294; www.taq.qc.ca) Wheelchair-adapted vans available. Make reservations at least 24 hours in advance.

CAR & MOTORCYCLE

Québec City lies about 260km northeast of Montréal (three hours by car). The most common routes are Autoroute 40 along the north shore of the St Lawrence River, and Autoroute 20, on the south shore.

Avis (☎ 418-523-1075, airport 418-872-2861; 1100 Blvd René-Lévesque) Car rental.

Budget (☎ 418-523-1075, airport 418-872-8413; 1100 Blvd René-Lévesque E) Shares an office with Avis.

Discount (☎ 418-781-0847; www.discountquebec.com; 7300 Blvd Wilfrid-Hamel W) Car rental. There is also an office (☎ 418-652-7371) at 2300 Chemin Sainte-Foy.

Enterprise (☎ 418-523-6661, airport 418-861-8820; 690 Blvd René-Lévesque) Car rental.

Hertz (☎ 418-694-1224, airport 418-871-1571; 44 Côte du Palais) Car rental.

TRAIN

VIA Rail (www.viarail.ca) has several trains daily between Montréal's Gare Centrale and Québec City's **Gare du Palais** (☎ 888-842-7245; www.viarail.ca; 450 Rue de la Gare du Palais). Normal prices for the 3½-hour journey start at $98/196 for a one-way/return ticket, but we've seen promotional offers as low as $38 for a one-way seat.

Service is also good along the so-called Québec City–Windsor corridor that connects Québec City with Montréal, Ottawa, Kingston, Toronto and Niagara Falls.

Getting Around

TO/FROM THE AIRPORT

A taxi is your best option for travel between the airport and downtown Québec City, as there is no convenient public transportation along this route.

A taxi costs a flat fee of $34.25 to go into the city, or $15 if you're only going to the boroughs surrounding the airport. Returning to the airport, you'll pay the metered fare, which should be less than $30.

BICYCLE

Québec City has an extensive network of bike paths (some 70km in all), including a route along the St Lawrence that connects to paths along the Riviére St-Charles. Pick up a free map at the tourist office or at local bike shops.

Just across from Québec City's train station, **Cyclo Services** (p279) rents a wide variety of bikes, including hybrid, city, tandem, road and kids' models. It also organizes cycling tours in the Québec City region.

CAR & MOTORCYCLE

Compact Old Québec lends itself better to exploration on foot than by car. If you're driving up here, plan to park your vehicle for as much of your stay as possible.

Parking garages in and around the Old Town typically charge a day rate of $16 to $20 Monday to Friday, and $8 to $12 on weekends. In the Old Upper Town, the most central garage, and one of the cheapest, is underneath the Hôtel de Ville, just a couple of blocks from the Château Frontenac. In the Old Lower Town, there are a couple of convenient lots along Rue Dalhousie. Metered street parking is also widely available, but expensive ($2 per hour). Many guesthouses provide discount vouchers for nearby parking garages.

In winter, nighttime snow removal is scheduled on many streets between 11pm and 6:30am. Don't park during these hours on any street with a '*déneigement*' (snow removal) sign and a flashing red light, or you'll wake up to a towed vehicle and a hefty fine!

PUBLIC TRANSPORTATION

RTC (p287) offers efficient service all around town. Single rides on RTC buses cost $3.50; alternatively, purchase a day pass for $8.25, a five-day pass for $28.50 or unlimited weekend rides for $15. The most convenient hub for catching multiple buses is on Place d'Youville, just outside the Old Town walls. To get here from the Gare du Palais train station or long-distance bus station, take bus 21 or 800.

TAXI & CALÈCHE

Flag fall is a standard $3.45 plus another $1.70 per kilometer and 63¢ per minute spent waiting in traffic. Prices are posted on the windows inside taxis.

Taxis Coop (☎418-525-5191; www.taxiscoop-quebec.com) Provides taxi service in Québec City.

In Québec City, *calèches* cost $100 for a 40-minute tour for up to four passengers. You'll find them just inside the Porte St-Louis, in the Parc de l'Esplanade and near Le Château Frontenac.

AROUND QUÉBEC CITY

Québec City is surrounded by a quilt of rustic villages, day-tripper-friendly hamlets and suburbs that embrace the Euro-hybrid identity of the *ville*. Other than Lévis, the sights in this area are all on the north side of the river: Wendake, St Gabriel de Valcartier, Stoneham and Parc de la Jacques Cartier to the north of Québec City, and the rest to the northeast. The south side of the river is equally lovely.

Lévis

On the 1km ferry crossing to the town of Lévis, the best views are undoubtedly on the Québec City side of the vessel. The Citadelle (p274), Le Château Frontenac (p274) and the seminary dominate the clifftop cityscape. Once you disembark, riverside Lévis is a relaxing escape from the intensity of Québec City's Old Town.

Near the ferry landing, the **Terrasse de Lévis**, a lookout point inaugurated in 1939 by King George VI and (the then future) Queen Elizabeth II, offers excellent vistas of Québec and beyond from the top of the hill on Rue William-Tremblay.

In Old Lévis, the main shops and restaurants are on Ave Bégin. For more views of Québec, head south on the riverside path through Parc de l'Anse-Tibbits.

Sights & Activities

Fort No 1 FORT

(Lévis Forts National Historic Site; ☎418-835-5182; www.pc.gc.ca/eng/lhn-nhs/qc/levis/index.aspx; 41 Chemin du Gouvernement; adult/child $3.90/1.90; ⏲10am-5pm Jul & Aug, Sat & Sun only Sep-Jun; 👪) Between 1865 and 1872, the British built three forts on the south shore to protect Québec against an American invasion that never materialized. One, known as Fort No 1, has been restored and operates as a national historic site with guided tours. It's located amid suburban subdivisions, on the east side of Lévis, just off Rte 132/Blvd de la Rive Sud.

Éco-Parc de la Chaudière CYCLING

(https://levis.chaudiereappalaches.com; Hwy 73, Breakeyville exit) 🍃 This 5km trail runs along the picturesque Chaudière River and is a popular spot for walkers and cyclists.

Information

Tourisme Lévis (☎418-838-6026; 996 Rue de la Concorde; ⏲May-Oct) Tourism office at the ferry landing; has maps.

Wendake

Wendake, a relatively dynamic Aboriginal community, could be a town plucked from anywhere in the province, but for signs posted in the Huron-Ouendat language dotting the streets. In that language, the number eight is a letter, pronounced 'oua' (like the 'wh' in 'what'), which explains the curious name of **Onhoüa Chetek8e** (☎418-842-4308; www.huron-wendat.qc.ca; 575 Rue Chef Stanislas Koska; guided tour adult/youth/child $13.95/10.95/8.95; ⏲9am-4pm May-Oct, 10am-4pm Nov-Apr; 👪), the world's only reconstructed Huron village.

In 1960, Wendake became the first reserve with its own bank; today, it provides employment for other tribes. The town is very residential, even quiet, and beyond the reconstructed village, the main signs of life are day-to-day things: schools, churches and a few warehouses.

Wendake's major attraction is Onhoüa Chetek8e. Entry to the village is by a 45-minute tour. The tour guides are excellent (one is even a former land-claims negotiator), taking you around the village explaining Huron history, culture and daily life. It may be artificial, but visitors love this place and children go wild for the tipis, canoes and bow-and-arrow range.

Wendake is an easy 25-minute drive from Québec City via QC-175.

Contact **Tourisme Wendake** (☎418-847-1835; http://tourismewendake.ca) for information on shuttle services between Wendake and Québec.

St Gabriel de Valcartier

This suburb wouldn't particularly stand out if it wasn't for its enormous amusement park, Village Vacances, the source of many a nostalgic memory for folks from eastern Québec. If you're not into that sort of experience, there are also opportunities for outdoor exploration along the Jacques Cartier Rivière.

Announced by the 'pirate's den' slide overshadowing the packed car park, **Village Vacances** (☎418-844-2200; www.valcartier.com/en; 1860 Blvd Valcartier; summer adult/child $36/30; 10am-7pm Jun-Sep, see website for winter hours; P) is a water city that looms above the village like Jabba the Hutt next to Princess Leia. With 11 sections, each with slides, water games and heated pools, it's heaven on earth for children. During the winter (December to March), the park opens a Winter Playground.

For close-to-nature excitement less than an hour north of Québec City, head off on a guided rafting trip down the Jacques Cartier Rivière with **Expeditions Nouvelle Vague** (☎418-520-7238; www.expeditionsnouvellevague.com; 246 5e Ave; rafting trips $24-109, 1-/2-day kayaking course from $99/179;) . This outfit offers a broad range of rafting experiences, from the family friendly two-hour mini-rafting (ages three and up) – an ultra-low-key option – to full-on, adrenaline-packed three-to seven-hour white-water adventures in Class III, IV and (sometimes) V water.

Stoneham

Leaving Québec City's suburbs, Rte 371 winds along Rivière Jacques Cartier and through the hills. At Stoneham, the **Stoneham Mountain Resort** (☎800-463-6888; www.ski-stoneham.com/en; 600 Chemin du Hibou, Stoneham-et-Tewkesbury; lift ticket adult/youth/child $60/44/29; Dec–mid-Apr) offers an array of activities in a friendly resort atmosphere with lodgings and a restaurant. Stoneham is one of the province's main ski centers, switching to hiking, climbing, geocaching and kayaking in summer.

Aventures Nord-Bec (☎418-848-3732; www.traineaux-chiens.com; 4 Chemin des Anémones; camping $31, cabin $130) – where the main business is dogsledding, as the big huskies hanging around suggest – offers riverside camping, cabins and a restaurant. Want to try your hand at dogsledding? Winter training courses run $80/40 for adults/children.

Île d'Orléans

Before Jacques Cartier named Île d'Orléans in the Duke of Orleans' honor, it was known as L'Île de Bacchus for its wild vines. Four centuries later, Québécois troubadour Félix Leclerc, who died here in 1988, likened the island to France's famous Chartres cathedral. Today, there are no signs of Dionysian orgies on sleepy Île d'Orléans, which is 15km northeast of Québec City, but there is plenty to attract visitors. The island, still primarily a pastoral farming region, has emerged as the epicenter of Québec's agritourism movement. Foodies from all around flock to the local *économusées* (workshops) to watch culinary artisans at work.

One road (60km) circles it, with two more running north–south. Their edges are dotted with strawberry fields, orchards, cider producers, windmills, workshops and galleries. Some of the villages contain houses that are up to 300 years old, and there are wooden or stone cottages in the Normandy style.

Sights

La Forge à Pique-Assaut GALLERY
(☎418-828-9300; www.forge-pique-assaut.com; 2200 Chemin Royal, St-Laurent; 9am-5pm Jun-Sep, 9am-noon & 1:30-5pm Mon-Fri Oct-May; P) Artisan blacksmith Guy makes star railings and decorative objects at this *économusée* (workshop). There's a store attached.

Maison Drouin HISTORIC BUILDING
(☎418-829-0330; www.fondationfrancoislamy.org; 2958 Chemin Royal, Sainte-Famille; adult/child $6/free; 10am-6pm daily mid-Jun–Aug, noon-4pm Sat & Sun Sep–mid-Oct; P) This house was built in 1730 and is one of the most fascinating stops

on the island as it was never modernized (ie no electricity or running water) even though it was inhabited until 1984. Guides in period dress give tours of the house in summer.

Parc Maritime de Saint-Laurent MUSEUM
(☎418-828-9673; http://parcmaritime.ca/en; 120 Chemin de la Chalouperie, St-Laurent; adult/youth/child $5/3/free; ⏲10am-5pm Jun 11-Oct 10; P) This cozy little museum is an introduction to both the deep maritime heritage of the region and the rhythms of daily life on an estuarine island. Model ships, knot-tying workshops and enthusiastic guided tours are all part of the package.

ÉcoloCyclo CYCLING
(☎418-828-3070; www.ecolocyclo.net; 517 Chemin Royal, St-Laurent; ⏲10am-6pm Jun-Sep) Hires out traditional bikes (per hour/day $16/38) in addition to electric bikes ($30/63) and tandems ($27/72). It's near the bridge, around the corner from the tourist office (p291).

Sleeping & Eating

Camping Orléans CAMPGROUND $
(☎888-829-2953, 418-829-2953; www.camping orleans.com; 357 Chemin Royal, St-François; campsites $36-55; ⏲May 20-Oct 10;) This leafy site is at the water's edge at the far end of the island from the bridge. It's the only campsite left in the greater Québec City area. There's a swimming pool and pub on-site.

Auberge Restaurant Le Canard Huppé B&B $$
(☎418-828-2292; www.canardhuppe.com/en; 7326 Chemin Royal, St-Laurent; r $158-188; P) From the outside, this feels like a Brittany-esque rustic escape, but inside, rooms range from charmingly old-fashioned to comfortably modern. The real draw, however, is the cuisine – this auberge is deeply in touch with the island's locavore providers, and has the daily rotating menus to prove it.

Dans les Bras de Morphée B&B $$
(☎418-829-3792; www.danslesbrasdemorphee.com; 5474 Chemin Royal, St-Jean; r $138-174; P@) A locavore's dream, this stone mansion sits amid unspoiled gardens, streams and farms from which owners Marc and Louise source the ingredients for breakfast. It's no run-of-the-mill breakfast, either: Marc, a professional chef, constructs beautiful and tasty gourmet three-course affairs worthy of the front cover of *Bon Appétit*.

Au Toit Bleu B&B $$
(☎418-829-1078; 3879 Chemin Royal, Ste-Famille; r $87-120; P) Next to Le Mitan microbrewery, this B&B uses the decor gathered on the owner's travels to beautiful effect, with African, Indian, Indonesian and Japanese rooms. Choose between a shared bathroom or your own freestanding tub, then ponder the big questions in a hammock overlooking the river.

La Boulange BAKERY $
(☎418-829-3162; 2001 Chemin Royal, St-Jean; light meals $5-10; ⏲7:30am-5:30pm daily Jun-Sep, Thu-Sun May & Oct, Sat & Sun Nov-Apr) A memorable bakery with a small irresistible store, La Boulange is the perfect spot for a light lunch of sandwiches or pizza, or to gather picnic supplies. Devour to-die-for croissants while taking in views of the St Lawrence and an 18th-century parish church next door.

Le Moulin de St Laurent MEDITERRANEAN $$
(☎418-829-3888; www.moulinstlaurent.qc.ca; 754 Chemin Royal, St-Laurent; mains $18-35, meals $37-51; ⏲11:30am-2:30pm & 5:30-8:30pm May-Oct) You'd be hard-pressed to find a more agreeable place to dine than the terrace at the back of this early-19th-century flour mill, with tables inches from a waterfall. The well-prepared, diverse menu is continental with regional flourishes, such as trout and veal. Chalets (from $160) are also available.

Entertainment

Le Nouveau Théâtre de l'Île d'Orléans THEATER
(☎418-828-0967; http://nouveautheatredelile.com; 1721 Chemin Royal, St-Pierre) This enthusiastic theater brings a beloved dose of live drama to the Île d'Orléans cultural scene. Plays are, as you'd expect, in French.

Shopping

Chocolaterie de l'Île d'Orléans FOOD
(☎418-828-2252; www.chocolaterieorleans.com; 150 Chemin du Bout-de-Île, Ste-Pétronille; ⏲11am-7pm Mon-Thu, to 8pm Fri, 9:30am-8pm Sat, to 7pm Sun) Using cocoa beans from Belgium, the chocolatiers at this 200-year-old house churn out tasty concoctions, including almond bark and flavored truffles.

Domaine Steinbach FOOD
(☎418-828-0000; www.domainesteinbach.com; 2205 Chemin Royal, St-Pierre; ⏲10am-7pm May-Oct) This store stocks dozens of farm products, including seven ciders made using apples from the organic orchard, one with maple syrup. If

DON'T MISS

LE MASSIF

Outside of Petite-Rivière-St-François is **Le Massif** (☎877-536-2774; www.lemassif.com; 1350 Rue Principale, Petite-Rivière-St-François), perhaps the best little-known ski center in the country. It offers the highest vertical drop (770m) and most snow (600cm) east of the Rockies and has fabulous views over the St Lawrence. Hours change with the seasons; check the website or call for more information.

the generous tasting tickles your taste buds, tuck into a cheese or duck platter on the terrace overlooking the river.

Cassis Monna & Filles FOOD
(☎418-828-2525; www.cassismonna.com/en; 721 Chemin Royal, St-Pierre; ⊙10am-8pm late Jun-Sep) Learn all you ever wanted to know – and then some – about *cassis* (blackcurrant), also known as *gadelle noire* in Québécois, and pick up some treats to go, including jam (currant-onion is a popular pick), vinaigrette, mustard, wine and liquor. The on-site restaurant pairs the star of the show with light lunches.

Information

Île d'Orléans Tourist Office (☎866-941-9411, 418-828-9411; http://tourisme.iledorleans.com/en/; 490 Côte du Pont, St-Pierre; ⊙8:30am-6pm early Jun–early Sep, 9am-4:30pm rest of year) It's worth spending $1 on a brochure at the helpful tourist office, which you'll see soon after you cross the bridge.

Ste Anne de Beaupré

You may never pick up on how deep Québec's Catholic roots go in a city like Montréal, but here, in the province, that identity is strongly evident, and *here*, in Ste Anne de Beaupré, it's almost overwhelming. Approaching the town along Rte 138, the twin steeples of the 1920s **basilica** (☎418-827-3781; www.sanctuairesainteanne.org; 10018 Ave Royale; ⊙8am-5pm; P) FREE tower above the motels and *dépanneurs* (convenience stores). It's one of the few remaining mega-attractions in the province related not to nature or artificial diversions, but to faith. Since the mid-1600s, the village has been an important Christian site; the annual late-July pilgrimage draws thousands of visitors, who crowd every open space.

PLUMobile (☎418-827-8484, 866-824-1433) buses run between Place d'Youville and Gare du Palais (p287) in Québec City and the basilica. The comfortable buses have free wi-fi.

CHARLEVOIX

In winter, icy fog pours over snowcapped mountains into the rural valleys of Charlevoix, while in summer, the brilliant blue sky is matched by the deep azure of the St Lawrence. At all times of year, this is a stunning outdoors playground. For 200 years, this pastoral skein of streams and hills has been a summer retreat for the wealthy and privileged. Of late, it has become Québec City's preferred retreat from the stresses of city life.

Unesco has classified the entire area a World Biosphere Reserve, which has resulted in worthwhile restrictions on the types of permitted developments, and a palpable sense of pride among residents. There's also a lot to be proud of in the lovely local towns such as Baie St Paul, with *ateliers* (artists' studios), galleries and boutiques lining its few streets.

A driving route to consider taking is the 'River Drive' (Rte 362) one way, through Baie St Paul, Ste Irénée and La Malbaie. On the way back you can ride the ear-popping hills of the 'Mountain Drive' (Rte 138) inland and stop in at **Parc des Hautes Gorges de la Rivière Malbaie** (☎418-439-1227, reservations 800-665-6527; www.sepaq.com/pq/hgo; adult/child $8.50/free; ⊙visitor center 8am-9pm late June-late Aug, see website for other months;) for a hike en route.

Charlevoix is a center for the culinary arts. The Route des Saveurs (Route of Flavors) takes in 31 farms and eateries, and local menus generally read like inventories of Charlevoix produce.

Baie St Paul

Of all the little towns that lie within day-tripping distance of Québec City, this beautiful blend of the outdoors and the bohemian – this is Cirque du Soleil's hometown – may be the most attractive. Not that we recommend day-tripping: if you're coming to Baie St Paul, book a night in a historic house converted into a superb *gîte*, grab some local cuisine, have a glass of wine and set your watch to the estuarine rhythm of the St Lawrence and Gouffre Rivers as they flow in and out of Baie St Paul.

WORTH A TRIP

CHOO-CHOO CHARLEVOIX

If you're a rail junkie, or simply a lover of a more nostalgic means of getting around, consider the train. The **Train de Charlevoix** (☎418-240-4124; http://reseaucharlevoix.com/english; 50 Rue de la Ferme; Québec to La Malbaie one way/round trip from $49/70), to be exact, which chugs along 125km, connecting Québec City to La Malbaie via seven seaside settlements, taking in much of the natural beauty of Charlevoix in the process. The trip takes about 4½ hours in total one way, but if you'd like to get off the train, explore and re-board, that's cool – you're just not guaranteed a seat when the next train comes.

There's free wi-fi on the trains, but cellular service is pretty spotty. There's no full dining cart, but snacks that are often sourced from the area's many local agricultural producers are served. It's about as relaxing a way of seeing the spectacular Charlevoix countryside as you can imagine. Plus, the rail track passes areas that are completely separate from the road system; spaces you'd never discover unless you were a particularly avid hiker.

The main admin office for the train is in Baie St Paul and the main ticket offices are in that town, Québec City and La Malbaie, but you can purchase tickets on board the train or at small inter-station platforms that can be found all along the route.

Sights

Parc des Grands Jardins PROVINCIAL PARK
(☎418-439-1227; www.sepaq.com/pq/grj; adult/child $8.50/free;) This provincial park covers 310 sq km, much of it taiga. Excellent hiking and rugged topography are the lure at this gem. The hills frame well over 100 small lakes. Caribou may be spotted. The half-day trek up **Mont du Lac-des-Cygnes** (Swan Lake Mountain) is an exceptional short hike.

Musée d'Art Contemporain MUSEUM
(☎418-435-3681; www.macbsp.com; 23 Rue Ambroise-Fafard; adult/student/child $10/7/free; 10am-5pm mid-Jun–Aug, 11am-5pm Tue-Sun Sep–mid-Jun) This architecturally attention-grabbing gallery houses contemporary art by local artists and some photographic exhibits on loan from the National Gallery of Canada. The museum also organizes an international contemporary art symposium in August.

Activities

Randonnées Nature-Charlevoix OUTDOORS
(☎418-435-3864; www.randonneesnature.com; crater tour adult/child from $45/30) Nonprofit organization Randonnées Nature-Charlevoix runs two-hour French-language tours of a nearby meteor crater; group tours for English speakers can be arranged for $110.

Katabatik KAYAKING
(☎800-453-4850; www.katabatik.ca; 210 Rue Ste-Anne; half-day sea kayaking tours adult/youth $64/49, half-day canyoning adult/youth $89/69, paragliding $114; 8am-6:30pm Jul & Aug, 8:30am-5pm Sun-Fri, 8am-6pm Sat Jun, 9am-4pm Sun-Fri, 8:30am-5pm Sat Sep & Oct;) One of the most well-established outdoor/adventure tour companies in Charlevoix, Katabatik offers, among other services, sea-kayaking tours, canyoning and tandem paragliding.

Sleeping & Eating

Gite Fleury B&B $
(☎418-435-3668; http://gitefleury.com; 102 Rue St-Joseph; r low/high season $76/84;) François and Mario, the proprietors of this cute-as-a-kitten B&B, are simultaneously classy and hospitable, and cook up a mean breakfast to boot. They're happy to offer plenty of advice for those who want to tromp through the seaside villages and alpine highlands of Charlevoix, but you may be tempted to crash out in their cozy bedrooms.

Nature et Pinceaux B&B $$
(☎418-435-2366; www.natureetpinceaux.qc.ca; 33 Rue Nordet; r $110-145; Apr-Nov;) The views from the spacious rooms at this charming B&B, atop the mountain and peeking out over the river below, are surpassed only by the phenomenal three-course breakfasts cooked by host Mariette. The house is east of town, signposted off Rte 362.

L'Orange Bistro FRENCH $$
(☎418-240-1197; www.orangebistro.com; 29 Rue Ambroise-Fafard; mains $17-29; 11am-9pm) This central, colorful restaurant's terrace overlooks the main road into town, but it's easy to forget the cars when the food's this good. Local produce on offer includes organic chicken, spare ribs, veal, venison and mussels, while fresh herbs and organic vegetables edge the menu closer to perfection.

Le Mouton Noir FRENCH **$$$**
(☎418-240-3030; www.moutonnoirresto.com; 43 Rue Ste-Anne; set meals $36-41; ⊙11am-3pm & 5-11pm) Since 1978, the rustic-looking Black Sheep has been home to fine French cuisine. Fish – including walleye, the freshwater queen – is on offer when available, as are buffalo, caribou and steak, all enlivened by a deft touch that incorporates wild mushrooms and local produce. The outdoor terrace overlooks the Rivière du Gouffre. Reservations advised.

Information

Charlevoix Tourist Office (☎418-665-4454; www.tourisme-charlevoix.com; 444 Blvd Mgr-de-Laval; ⊙8:30am-7pm Jun 24-Aug) On Rte 138 just west of town.

Mont du Lac-des-Cygnes Visitors Kiosk (☎418-439-1227; www.sepaq.com/pq/grj; Rte 381; ⊙8:30am-8pm late Jun-late Aug, varies by season other times) Provides information and visitor services for those going to Parc des Grands Jardins.

Town Tourist Office (☎800-667-2276; 6 Rue St-Jean-Baptiste; ⊙9am-6pm summer)

Getting There & Away

The **bus station** (☎418-435-6569; https://intercar.ca; 50 Rue de la Ferme) is at Le Germain Hotel, about a 15-minute walk from downtown. Intercar buses go to Québec City thrice daily ($24, 1¼ hours), with two services on the weekend.

Île Aux Coudres

Quiet and rural, Île Aux Coudres feels remarkably remote. The hills of the north shore are never far from view, but this is nonetheless a place to forget the rest of the world. A 'coudriers,' by the way, is a small hazelnut tree, and the island is blanketed in bucolic woods. In the southwest corner, Anse de l'Église (Church Bight) is a small curve in the coastline fronted by a little village and Catholic church.

Sights & Activities

Les Moulins MUSEUM
(☎418-760-1065; www.lesmoulinsdelisleauxcoudres.com/home-visit; 36 Chemin du Moulin; adult/child $8.70/4; ⊙10am-5pm May 21-Oct 10) *Économusée* Les Moulins has two restored 19th-century mills and exhibits showing how wheat and buckwheat were once ground using grindstones.

Musée Maritime MUSEUM
(☎418-635-1131; www.museemaritime.com/en; 305 Rue de l'Église; adult/child $5/free; ⊙9am-5pm May-Oct) Before or after boarding the ferry in St-Joseph-de-la-Rive, drop into Musée Maritime. It details the schooner-building history of a region where it was common to see 20 different types of commercial boat on the St Lawrence. Visitors can climb aboard some beauties in the shipyard. There's also a display on the area's famous meteorite crater.

Centre Vélo-Coudres CYCLING
(☎418-438-2118; 2926 Chemin des Coudriers; bicycles per hour $4; ⊙8am-sunset Jul & Aug, to 5pm May, Jun, Sep & Oct) You can use the (free) climbing wall here, or rent bikes and bike equipment such as helmets and child carriers. It offers a free shuttle service from the ferry terminal if you call ahead.

Sleeping

Le Long Détour B&B **$$**
(☎418-438-1154; www.lelongdetour.com; 3101 Chemin des Coudriers; r $100-110; P 📶) You have two choices at this tastefully decorated B&B – the 'autumn' room or the 'spring' room. Both have DVD players and king-size beds. The hosts aim to please, with extravagant breakfasts that include dessert.

Information

Tourist Office (☎418-760-1066; www.tourismeisleauxcoudres.com; 1024 Chemin des Coudriers; ⊙9am-5pm Jul-Oct) Near the crossroads just beyond the port.

Getting There & Away

The MV *Joseph-Savard* and, during the summer, the MV *Radisson* run a free car and pedestrian **ferry** (☎information 877-787-7483, reservations 877-562-6560; www.traversiers.com/en/home; ⊙7am-11:30pm) from St-Joseph-de-la-Rive to the north shore of Île Aux Coudres. Departs every 30 minutes from 9am to 6pm, and every hour from 7am to 9am and 6pm to 11pm from May to October, less frequently at other times of the year.

Ste Irénée

With its cafes overlooking one of the area's best beaches, Ste Irénée is an inviting stop between Baie St Paul and La Malbaie.

Between June and August, the **Domaine Forget** (www.domaineforget.com) festival celebrates classical music, jazz and dance and attracts performers from around the world.

In a grand house built for an industrialist, **Hôtel Le Rustique** (☎418-452-8250; http://lerustique.charlevoix.qc.ca; 285 Rue Principale; s/d from $80/90) is one of Charlevoix' friendliest and most alluring B&Bs. With their pale colors and photos from owner Diane's travels, the rooms have the feel of an artist's seaside cottage. Three self-contained apartments are also available.

La Malbaie

Now encompassing five previously separate villages, La Malbaie was one of Canada's first holiday resorts. From the late 19th century, steamers run by the Richelieu and Ontario Navigation Company and Canada Steamship Lines docked here.

Arriving from the south on Rte 362 or the west on Rte 138, the first village you come to is **Pointe-au-Pic**. The village was a holiday destination for the wealthy at the beginning of the 20th century, drawing the elite from as far away as New York.

Ste-Agnès lies to the northwest, away from the St Lawrence. Adjoining Pointe-au-Pic (and technically merged with it) is **La Malbaie**, which begins west of the Malbaie River and continues to the other side. North of La Malbaie is **Rivière Malbaie**, while **St-Fidèle** and the ridiculously cute **Cap à l'Aigle** are east on Rte 138.

Sights

Les Jardins du Cap à l'Aigle GARDENS
(☎418-665-3747; 625 Rue St-Raphael, Cap à l'Aigle; adult/child $6/free; ⏲9am-5pm Jun-Oct) In Cap à l'Aigle, a little village 2km east of La Malbaie, are these gardens, where 800 types of lilac range up the hill between a waterfall, a footbridge and artists selling their daubs. When this spot is in full bloom it's a heavenly little detour.

Musée de Charlevoix MUSEUM
(☎418-665-4411; www.museedecharlevoix.qc.ca; 10 Chemin du Havre, Pointe-au-Pic; adult/student/child $8/6/free; ⏲9am-5pm; 👪) Part art gallery, part museum, this waterfront place portrays the life and times of Charlevoix through a variety of media.

Maison du Bootlegger HISTORIC BUILDING
(☎418-439-3711; www.maisondubootlegger.com; 110 Rang du Ruisseau-des-Frênes, Ste-Agnès; adult/child $10/5, meal, tour & entertainment from $40; ⏲10am-5pm daily late Jun-Sep, 10am-5pm Sat & Sun early Jun, Oct & Nov) This unexpected hostelry in a conventional-looking 19th-century farmhouse was surreptitiously modified by an American bootlegger during the Prohibition period. Tours reveal the marvel of secret doorways and hidden chambers intended to deter the morality squad. From 6pm, it turns into a party restaurant where meat feasts are accompanied by Al Capone beer in boot-shaped glasses and lots of boisterous entertainment.

Manoir Richelieu HISTORIC BUILDING
(☎418-665-3703; www.fairmont.com/richelieu-charlevoix; 181 Rue Richelieu, Pointe-au-Pic) The gray country cousin of Québec City's Château Frontenac (p274), this intimidating, palatial structure, owned by the Fairmont chain, looks like the headquarters of the last boss in an old Nintendo game. The sprawling, copper-roofed, castle-like structure, which was built in 1928, attests to the area's longtime prosperity. Wander the clifftop gardens, have a drink on the terrace and drop by the gallery displaying local art. Outside, coachloads of hopefuls stream into the much-advertised **Casino de Charlevoix**.

Sleeping

Parc des Hautes Gorges de la Rivière Malbaie Campsites CAMPGROUND $
(☎800-665-6527; www.sepaq.com/pq/hgo; campsites $23-35; P) Campsites that range from rustic to RV-accessible are scattered throughout the park.

Camping des Chutes Fraser CAMPGROUND $
(☎418-665-2151; www.campingchutesfraser.com; 500 Chemin de la Vallée, La Malbaie; tent & RV sites from $30, cottages from $95; ⏲camping May-Oct, cottages year-round) This campground with a waterfall, toward Mont Grand-Fonds park, is idyllic.

Auberge des Eaux Vives B&B $$
(☎418-665-4808; www.aubergedeseauxvives.com; 39 Rue de la Grève, Cap à l'Aigle; r $145-165) Sylvain and Johanne are the perfect hosts at this three-room B&B with breakfasts to write home about – think smoothies and a four-course extravaganza on a sunny terrace overlooking the St Lawrence. The decor is modern and chic, and there's a guest-only nook with a Nespresso machine, a full kitchen, two fireplaces and killer views.

Auberge des 3 Canards INN $$
(☎418-665-3761; www.auberge3canards.com; 115 Côte Bellevue, Pointe-au-Pic; r $145-225, ste $265; P❄📶🏊) With its 49 rooms sporting flat-screen TVs, vintage photos of the steamers,

WORTH A TRIP

PARC DES HAUTES GORGES DE LA RIVIÈRE MALBAIE

Work off all that Charlevoix produce with an invigorating hike in this 233-sq-km provincial park, which has several unique features, including the highest rock faces east of the Rockies. Sheer rock plummets (by as much as 800m) to the calm Rivière Malbaie, creating one of Québec's loveliest river valleys. The park is located about 40km northwest of La Malbaie.

There are trails of all levels, from ambles around the Barrage des Érables (Maple Dam) to vigorous hikes ascending from maple grove to permafrost.

A highlight is the **boat cruise** (800-665-6527; www.sepaq.com/pq/hgo; adult/child $35/free; late May-Oct;) up the river, squeezed between mountains. The river can also be seen from a canoe or kayak, which are available for hire, as are bikes. Boat tickets are available at the visitor center at the park entrance, and rentals 7km further on at the dam.

Many people make it a day trip from La Malbaie, but there are basic campsites (p294) available. Canoes can be used to reach the three riverside campgrounds. Bring all required supplies.

To reach the park from La Malbaie, head northwest on Rte 138 toward Baie St Paul, then take the turn for St-Aimé des Lacs and keep going for 30km.

local art and balconies overlooking the tennis court (with the St Lawrence behind), this 50-year-old institution is more special than it looks from Rte 138.

Les Terrasses Cap-à-L'Aigle RENTAL HOUSE **$$$**
(514-583-5720; www.terrassescapalaigle.com/en; 1 night/week from $850/1725;) These 10 cottages are all stunning examples of contemporary architecture; almost all feature sleek, geometric design accented by enormous glass details that let the natural light of Charlevoix spill into the living space. These homes are meant to be shared by groups – each residence can sleep four to 10 adults.

Eating

Café Chez-Nous CALIFORNIAN **$**
(418-665-3080; http://cafecheznous.com; 1075 Rue Richelieu, La Malbaie; mains $6-15; 7am-8pm Sun-Wed, to 9pm Thu-Sat;) This sunny little diner is stuffed with cutesy art and knickknacks, and serves up a menu that blends California, Italy and Québec. This is a good thing! Bagels with salmon share table space with Tuscan-style pizzas and mushroom ravioli.

Pains d'Exclamation BAKERY **$**
(418-665-4000; www.painsdexclamation.com; 398 Rue St-Étienne, La Malbaie; sandwiches $6-8; 6:30am-5:30pm Tue-Sat, to 5pm Sun & Mon) This bakery makes a good lunchtime stop, mainly for the grilled sandwich with Brie-like local cheese, Le Fleurmier, apples and walnuts.

Restaurant Bistro le Patriarche QUÉBÉCOIS **$$$**
(418-665-9692; www.bistrolepatriarche.com; 30 Rue du Quai, Pointe-au-Pic; set meals $34-64; 5-9pm Tue-Sun) This elegant, 10-table bistro in a house that dates to 1860 is quickly making a name for itself. Chef Michel churns out interestingly presented, impeccably executed French cuisine that often makes good use of the region's best ingredients.

Information

Regional Tourist Office (418-665-4454, 800-667-2276; www.tourisme-charlevoix.com; 495 Blvd de Comporté, La Malbaie; 8:30am-7pm Jun 24-Sep 24, hours vary other times) Located off Rte 362 and serves as the regional tourism office for all of Charlevoix.

St Siméon

A cozy fishing town perched on the St Lawrence, St Siméon is mainly known for Parc d'Aventure Les Palissades and **ferry** (418-862-5094; https://traverserdl.com/en/homepage; Rue du Quai; adult/child/car $19.20/12.80/45.50;) to Rivière du Loup. Otherwise, the road through town – and the quay road to the ferry – offers some great views of the headlands to the north.

Parc d'Aventure Les Palissades (418-647-4422; http://aventurex.net/palissades; 1000 Rte 170; zip line/via ferrata $13/50; 9am-5pm;) is an adventure sports center with multiple hiking trails, copious rock climbing (150-plus routes), a suspension bridge, rappelling and two *via ferrata* cliff walks with safety cables (no experience required). There's also a zip line. Accommodations range from camping and dorms to chalets; there's also a lakeside spa and sauna.

St Siméon is about 35km north of La Malbaie via Rte 138. Intercar (p228) runs one bus a day here, which leaves Québec City at 9:45am ($40, three hours) and La Malbaie around 11am ($10).

Baie Ste Catherine

This line of multicolored homes clings to the rocks and fronts the rough seas of the St Lawrence. It's an attractive, laid-back center for outdoor exploration.

Sights & Activities

Pointe Noire Observation Centre SCIENCE CENTER
(418-237-4383, 888-773-8888; www.pc.gc.ca/eng/amnc-nmca/qc/saguenay/natcul/natcul1.aspx; 141 Rte 138; adult/child $5.80/2.90; 10am-5pm daily Jun-Aug, Fri-Sun Sep & Oct) Up the hill from the ferry landing, this whale-study post, at the confluence of the Saguenay and St Lawrence Rivers, features an exhibit, a slide show and films, plus an observation deck with a telescope. From the boardwalk, you can often spy belugas in the Saguenay very close to shore, especially when the tide is coming in.

Pourvoirie Humanité BOATING
(418-638-5151; http://pourvoiriehumanite.com/en; off Chemin des Loisirs; kayaking $50;) Located about 10km outside of Baie Ste Catherine, the 'Humanity Lodge' is a outdoor-activity-center-cum-cabin collection. The main draw is kayaking in four icy blue lakes, but you can also do stand-up paddling, fishing for speckled trout, geocaching, moose observation and, in August, blueberry picking.

Croisières AML WHALE WATCHING
(418-237-4274, 800-563-4643; www.croisieresaml.com/en; 159 Rte 138; adult/child $70/40; 8am-6pm May-Oct, 8:30am-5pm Nov-Apr) Offers various whale-watching tours into the St Lawrence Seaway via large observation craft and smaller Zodiacs.

Sleeping

Gîte Entre Mer Et Monts B&B $
(877-337-4391, 418-237-4391; www.entre-mer-et-monts.com; 476 Rte 138; r from $70;) This friendly little B&B whips out some mean pancakes and brioche in the mornings, and offers some cozy, antique-chic rooms when you're worn out in the evening.

Getting There & Away

At the southern end of town, the free 10-minute ferry to Tadoussac runs across the Saguenay River. The 24-hour service departs every 20 minutes from 7am to 9pm from late April to October; at other times, it leaves every 40 minutes to one hour.

SAGUENAY

The roads snake north of Charlevoix, but they all spread into dozens of detours as they edge a deeply forested, craggy cleft that tears into the heart of this province: the Rivière Saguenay fjord. Overlooking its deep blue waters are windblown, lichen-and-pine studded cliffs that stretch some 500m high. Formed during the last Ice Age, the fjord is the most southerly one in the northern hemisphere. As deep as 270m in some places, the riverbed rises to a depth of only 20m at the fjord's mouth at Tadoussac.

This makes the relatively warm, fresh waters of the Saguenay jet out atop the frigid, salt waters of the St Lawrence, leading to massive volumes of krill, which in turn attract the visitor highlight of the region: whales. They and the entire waterway now enjoy protected status.

There are two main areas of the Saguenay region. The first hugs the Rivière Saguenay and consists of park and scenic villages along both sides. The second is the partially urban, industrialized section with midsize Chicoutimi as its pivot.

Tadoussac

For many visitors to Québec, Tadoussac is the one place in the province they visit outside Montréal and Québec City. What consistently draws the hordes to this spot is the whales. Not only do Zodiacs zip out in search of the behemoths, but smaller whales such as belugas and minkes can be glimpsed from the shore.

Added to that are activities such as sea kayaking, 'surfbiking,' exploring the fjord by boat or on foot, or simply wandering the dunes and headlands. Some of Tadoussac's vibrancy departs with the whales between November and May, but it remains a historic, bohemian town where the locals invariably have time for a chat.

History

Tadoussac became the first fur-trading post in European North America in 1600, eight years before the founding of Québec City. The word *tatouskak* in the Innu-aimun (Montagnais) language means breast, and refers to the two, rounded hills by the fjord and bay. When the Hudson's Bay Company closed its doors, Tadoussac was briefly abandoned, only to be revived as a resort with the building of Hotel Tadoussac in 1864, and as an important cog in the pulp and paper wheel.

Sights

Centre d'Interprétation des Mammifères Marins MUSEUM
(CIMM; 418-235-4701; http://gremm.org; 108 Rue de la Cale Sèche; adult/child $12/free; 9am-8pm May-Oct) The CIMM gives excellent background information on local sea creatures through multimedia exhibits.

Petite Chapelle HISTORIC SITE
(418-235-4324; www.chapelledetadoussac.com; 180 Rue du Bord de l'Eau; 10am-5pm Jun-early Oct) Built in 1747 by the Jesuits, Petite Chapelle is one of North America's oldest wooden churches. Also known as the Indian Chapel, it contains a small exhibition on missionary life.

Poste de Traite Chauvin HISTORIC SITE
(418-235-4657; 157 Rue du Bord de l'Eau; adult/child $4/2.50; 10am-7pm Jun-Oct) This replica of the continent's first fur-trading post offers some history on the first transactions between Aboriginals and Europeans.

Activities

Whale-Watching

From May to November, tourists flock to Tadoussac. The whale-watching is phenomenal, particularly between August and October, when blue whales are spotted. All over town, tickets are available for boat tours, from 12-person Zodiacs to the 600-person *Grand Fleuve*; check out the options carefully. Wait for a calm day, when the view won't be marred by waves and a rocking boat, and go out in the early morning or evening, when the whales are livelier and there are fewer vessels around. Zodiac passengers are given waterproofs; whatever trip you do, take lots of warm clothes.

Otis Excursions (418-235-4537; www.otisexcursions.com; 431 Rue du Bateau-Passeur; 2hr Zodiac trips $64, 3hr boat trips $74) is a local company that has been running for 35 years. Its Zodiacs get closest to the waves and offer the most exciting, if roughest, rides. Young children aren't permitted, however.

The Zodiac operated by **Croisières AML** (866-856-6668; www.croisieresaml.com; 177 Rue des Pionniers; Zodiac trips from $65, boat trips $70;) is twice the size of the others.

For the adventurous, sea-kayaking supremo **Mer et Monde** (418-232-6779; www.meretmonde.ca; 148 Rue du Bord de l'Eau; 3hr trips from $66; 8:30am-6:30pm) offers whale-watching expeditions and excursions up the fjord.

Hiking

There are four 1km paths in and around Tadoussac, marked on the map given out by the tourist office (p299). The lovely trails around Pointe de l'Islet, by the quay and, at the other end of the beach, Pointe Rouge are the best for spying whales from the shore.

Parc National du Fjord-du-Saguenay borders the fjord on both sides of the river. The provincial park has over 100km of splendid hiking trails, views down the fjord from atop 350m-plus cliffs, plus trailside refuges where you can spend the night. There are three refuges on the 43km trail from Tadoussac to Baie Ste-Marguerite, open May to October. Side note: what everyone calls 'dunes' in the area are actually marine terraces – formed by waves, not wind, as dunes are.

Overlapping with Parc National du Fjord-du-Saguenay, and extending to the Saguenay, Charlevoix and North Shore regions, with various entry points, **Parc Marin du Saguenay–St-Laurent** (418-235-4703; http://parcmarin.qc.ca;) was the first conservation project in Québec to be jointly administered by the federal and provincial governments. This park covers and protects 1138 sq km of the two rivers and their coastlines, from Gros Cap à l'Aigle to Les Escoumins and up the Saguenay as far as Cap à l'Est, near Ste-Fulgence.

Festivals & Events

Festival de la Chanson MUSIC
(Song Festival; 418-235-2002; www.chansontadoussac.com; Jun) Tadoussac's busy summer season begins with a vengeance at the 25-year-old Festival de la Chanson, a celebration of Francophone, mostly Québécois, music and a serious party. Stages spring up all over town and accommodations fill up for the long weekend.

Charlevoix, Saguenay & South Shore

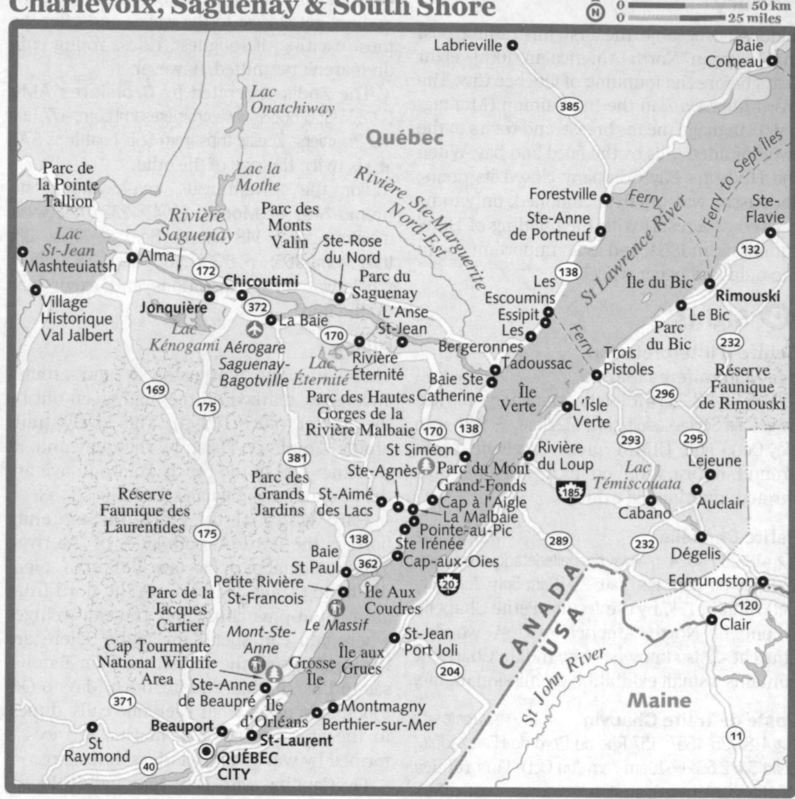

Sleeping

La Maison Harvey Lessard GUESTHOUSE $
(418-235-4802; www.harveylessard.com; r from $63; P ❄ 📶) Located just outside of town in a residential area, Harvey Lessard offers simple, comfortable rooms with excellent views of the fjord and the estuarine point of impact where the Saguenay hits the St Lawrence.

Domaine des Dunes CAMPGROUND $
(418-235-4843; www.domainedesdunes.com; 585 Chemin du Moulin à Baude; tent & RV sites $32, trailer or motorhome sites $45, chalet from $174; P 📶) This leafy campground is located about 3km from town. Self-catering chalets are also available; note that the rates given for chalets are for July and August, and that prices drop at other times of year.

Hôtel Tadoussac HOTEL $$
(418-235-4421, 800-561-0718; www.hoteltadoussac.com; 165 Rue du Bord de l'Eau; r from $165; P 📶 🏊) As locations go, this hotel, which commands the sweep of Tadoussac's bay, is winning, hands down. There's a sense of historic heritage as well; this is a hotel that's been hosting guests since 1870. Functional if not flashy rooms have plush carpets, ceiling fans and river views. Rates vary largely outside of the high season (July and August).

Auberge la Sainte Paix INN $$
(418-235-4803; www.aubergelasaintepaix.com; 102 Rue Saguenay; r $98-133; P ❄ 📶) Cheery host Marie is a ray of sunshine in the morning, as are her plentiful, fresh breakfasts. She's happy to help out with tour-planning and sightseeing, and can make good local recommendations. There are only seven rooms, so book well in advance.

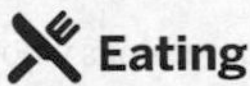

Eating

Chantmartin DINER $$
(☎418-235-4733; www.chantmartin.com/restaurant.html; 412 Rue du Bateau-Passeur; mains $12-26; ⏰6:30am-10pm summer, to 9:30pm other times; P) Despite its truck-stop-like appearance and attached line of generic motel rooms, Chantmartin is a good, rapid stop for everything from poutine and pizza to crab, prawns and roast chicken, and some damn fine truck-stop breakfast (eggs, sausages, bacon etc). Bonus: it's open year-round.

Café Bohème CAFE $$
(www.lecafeboheme.com/en; 239 Rue des Pionniers; set meals $14-26; ⏰7am-11pm Jul & Aug, 8am-10pm May, Jun, Sep & Oct;) The village's hangout of choice is a prime place for a breakfast of fruit and yogurt or a panino, or just to sip fair-trade coffee among the local intellectuals. Later in the day, choose between dishes such as duck confit salad and fresh pasta of the day.

Chez Mathilde FUSION $$$
(☎418-235-4443; 227 Rue des Pionniers; set meals from $31; ⏰10am-9pm Jun-Oct;) The stellar chef at this cute little house utilizes plenty of local produce in his creative, though limited, menu. The innovative dishes, cooked to perfection, are served up alongside a view of the port from an airy patio.

La Galouïne QUÉBÉCOIS $$$
(☎418-235-4380; http://lagalouine.com; 251 Rue des Pionniers; mains $22-34; ⏰7:30am-10pm May-Oct) Local ingredients dominate the table here, from fresh scallops out of the bay to venison caught from the woods. A rather extensive wine list makes it that much easier to enjoy your evening.

Information

Tourist Information Office (☎866-235-4744, 418-235-4744; www.tadoussac.com; 197 Rue des Pionniers; ⏰9am-5pm) Located in the middle of town, with very patient staff who can help with accommodations.

Getting There & Away

The 24-hour, 10-minute ferry from Baie Ste Catherine in Charlevoix is free. The terminal is at the end of Rue du Bateau-Passeur.

Tadoussac is off Rte 138. **Intercar** (p228) buses connect Tadoussac with Montréal ($106, eight hours) and Québec City ($53, four hours) twice a day and run as far northeast as Sept Îles. The bus stop is opposite Camping Tadoussac at the Petro-Canada garage.

Les Bergeronnes

The slow pace of the North Shore begins in Les Bergeronnes, which is pleasingly deserted. With a handful of attractions and an excellent campground, it's worth leaving nearby Tadoussac for.

Sights

Outside of Les Escoumins, 12km northeast of Les Bergeronnes on Rte 138, is **Essipit**, an Innu community. The Essipit Centre (p300) offers whale-watching cruises (Zodiac tours from $58); blue whales are more likely to be seen in this area.

Marine Environment Discovery Centre SCIENCE CENTER
(☎418-233-4414; 41 Rue des Pilotes; adult/child $7.80/3.90; ⏰9am-6pm Jun-Aug, 9am-5pm Fri-Sun Sep; P) Operated by Parks Canada, the Marine Environment Discovery Centre has sophisticated facilities such as interpretive exhibits and a video link with naturalist-divers foraging on the estuary floor. Staff help visitors observe marine mammals from the shore.

Cap de Bon Désir Interpretation Centre SCIENCE CENTER
(☎418-232-6751; 13 Chemin du Cap de Bon Désir; adult/child $7.80/3.90; ⏰9am-6pm Jun-Aug, 9am-5pm Wed-Sun Sep; P) Part science center, part park, this site consists of nature trails, observation platforms that look out onto the (hopefully) whale-studded St Lawrence, and a historic lighthouse. Call ahead to learn about different lectures and activities (and to check if they're available in English).

Archéo Topo SCIENCE CENTER
(☎418-232-6286; www.archeotopo.com; 498 Rue de la Mer; adult/child $6/3; ⏰8am-6pm Jun-Oct 15, to 8pm Jul & Aug; P) This research and exhibition center is dedicated to archaeological findings along the North Shore. Outside, trails lead down to the beach and offer some fantastic views over the sea cliffs of the North Shore.

Sleeping

Camping Paradis Marin CAMPGROUND $
(☎418-232-6237; www.campingparadismarin.com; 4 Chemin Émile Boulianne; campsites/chalets from $30/85; ⏰May-Oct; P) At Camping Paradis Marin, off Rte 138 northeast of Les Bergeronnes, you can hear whales breathing from your tent (or wigwam), rent kayaks ($9 per day) or arrange kayak tours ($62).

Essipit Centre ACCOMMODATION SERVICES **$$**
(☎888-868-6666, 418-233-2266; http://vacances essipit.com/en; 46 Rue de la Réserve, Essipit; camping/cottages/condos from $28/157/181; P ❄ ☎) The Essipit Centre can put you up in local campgrounds, cottages and comfortably appointed seaside condos. Rates drop outside of July and August.

L'Anse St Jean

First stop on the south side of the fjord is L'Anse St Jean, a little village with a lot going on in its ateliers. There's a pleasant mix of hippie-style self-exiles and families looking for a rustic escape out this way, not to mention a good crop of outdoor-activity infrastructure. If you drive on to the fjord, you'll find marvelous views at **L'Anse de Tabatière**.

Activities

Fjord en Kayak KAYAKING
(☎866-725-2925, 418-272-3024; www.fjord-en-kayak.ca; 359 Rue St-Jean-Baptiste; 3hr/1-day tours $58/134;) Offers well-regarded paddling excursions lasting from two hours to three days. Can also arrange bicycle rentals, whale-watching tours and sailing cruises.

Les Croisières du Fjord BOATING
(☎418-543-7630, 800-363-7248; www.croisieres-dufjord.com; 355 Rue St-Jean-Baptiste; fjord cruise adult/child from $56/29; ⌚Jul-Sep;) This well-organized, efficient tour company runs excellent trips up the Saguenay fjord, as well as a bicycle-friendly water taxi that connects L'Anse St Jean with Ste Rose du Nord, Rivière Éternité and Tadoussac. Rates vary depending on where you're going, but for $150 you can get a one-week 'Passe-Fjord,' which lets you hop on and off the boats at your leisure.

Centre Équestre des Plateaux HORSEBACK RIDING
(Equestrian Center; ☎418-272-3231; www.cedp.ca; 34 Chemin des Plateaux; 3hr tour $70) Has horses, ponies and even a horse-drawn sleigh for winter fun. It's signposted up the hill from Rue St-Jean-Baptiste.

Sleeping & Eating

L'Auberge du Boutdumonde INN **$**
(☎418-272-9979; www.boutdumonde.ca; 40 Chemin des Plateaux; dm/shared yurt/r $25/35/50; P ☎) It does indeed feel like it's at the end of the world, secluded on a steep hill (even by car it's a challenge). The former eco-commune was renovated by five twenty somethings who grew up here. Yoga classes, a cultural center, a lake, a herbal garden and forest are on the doorstep. Stock up on groceries before arriving. Cash only.

Auberge des Cévennes INN **$$**
(☎877-272-3180, 418-272-3180; www.auberge-des-cevennes.qc.ca; 294 Rue St-Jean-Baptiste; r incl breakfast $88-144; P ☎) You can hear the river gurgling across the street at this lovely inn, with a restaurant (set meal $30) overlooking the covered bridge. The interior is old-school, maybe even a little grandma's cottage-y, but the decor fits the location, and the owners are as friendly as anything.

Bistro de L'Anse PUB FOOD **$$**
(319 Rue St-Jean-Baptiste; mains $12-22; ⌚noon-1am late Jun-Aug, from 5pm Thu-Sat Sep-Oct 15) This is a popular local hub where you can catch live music on the weekends and tuck into sandwiches, salad and pasta on the verandah.

Getting There & Away

Transport Adapté du Fjord (☎418-272-1397; 213 Rte 170; one way/round trip from $4/8) in Chicoutimi runs a minibus that connects towns along the fjord; rates vary depending on where you're going. Reserve ahead and the bus will pick you up.

Buses (one way/return $7.50/15) leave L'Anse St Jean at 7:30am Monday to Friday (no service on Wednesday) and arrive at Chicoutimi around 9am; returning, buses leave Chicoutimi for L'Anse St Jean at 1:15pm Monday to Friday, arriving in L'Anse .St Jean at 2:30pm.

Rivière Éternité

This town is rather lacking in anything other than unlikely collections of religious art, but it is one of the main access points for both the Parc Marin du Saguenay–St-Laurent (p297) and Parc National du Fjord-du-Saguenay.

A four-hour-return hike, including a brutally long staircase, leads to an 8m-tall **statue of the Virgin Mary**. She stands on one of the fjord's highest cliffs, protecting the sailors and boats below. Charles Robitaille erected it in 1881, having narrowly escaped death the previous winter when his horse crashed through the ice on the river. Vowing to honor the Virgin Mary for saving his life, he commissioned the 3200kg statue, which took over a week to cart and assemble.

Back in town, the **church** has a renowned collection of 250 Christmas manger vignettes.

Nearby, over the wooden bridge off Rte 170, the **Halte des Artistes** is a free, drive-through park containing sculptures in little mangers.

Contact the Rivière Éternité–based park information **office** (Parc National du Fjord-du-Saguenay; ☎ 418-272-1556; www.sepaq.com/pq/sag; 91 Rue Notre Dame; ⏰ 8:30am-9pm Jun-Sep) about trips, trails, sea kayaking, sailing, Zodiac outings and numerous guided activities in Parc National du Fjord-du-Saguenay.

Chicoutimi

This regional center is a pleasant place to take care of chores before returning to the Saguenay wilds. The site of a 1676 fur-trading post, it was founded as late as 1842, and became a world pulp and paper capital in the early 20th century. It looks rather industrial from the approach roads, but downtown buzzes with students from the town's university and Cégep (pre-university college).

Sights

La Pulperie MUSEUM
(☎ 418-698-3100; www.pulperie.com; 300 Rue Dubuc; adult/child $14.50/7; ⏰ 9am-6pm daily Jun-Aug, 10am-4pm Wed-Sun Sep-May) This was once the world's biggest pulp mill. A guided tour and exhibitions explain the mill's history and its pivotal role in the development of a town that increased its population from 708 in 1899 to 4255 in 1929. The site also features the **House of Arthur Villeneuve**, now a museum. The barber-artist painted the entire building inside and out like a series of canvases in his bright, naive folk style.

Musee du Fjord MUSEUM
(☎ 418-697-5077; http://museedufjord.com; 3346 Blvd de la Grande-Baie Sud; adult/child $15/8.50; ⏰ 9am-6pm Jul-Sep, 9am-4:30pm Tue-Fri, 1-5pm Sat & Sun Oct-Jun; P 👪) Half museum, half aquarium, the Musee du Fjord helps visitors understand the unique ecosystem of the Saguenay fjord. It's a friendly, informative spot, but unless you have kids in tow, we recommend skipping the multimedia theater introduction.

Musée de la Petite Maison Blanche MUSEUM
(Little White House; ☎ 418-549-6600; www.petitemaisonblanche.com; 441 Rue Gédéon; adult/child $5/2.60; ⏰ 9am-9pm daily Jun-Aug, to 5pm Sep, to 5pm Sat & Sun only early Oct; P 👪) In the area known as 'the Basin' is this spindly museum. Built in 1900, the house withstood water with a force equivalent to Niagara Falls in a 1996 flood that caused $16 billion worth of damage to Chicoutimi. It's kind of a kitschy attic of stuff – historical bric-a-brac from the early 20th century, exhibits related to the aforementioned flood, even a few animatronic robots depicting old house residents – and has an odd appeal.

Sleeping & Eating

Auberge Racine B&B $$
(☎ 418-543-1919; www.aubergeracine.com; 334 Rue Racine E; s/d from $119/129; P 📶) In this 19th-century house, the delightful rooms have original details and are named after some of the first owner's three wives and 12 children.

★ **La Parizza** PIZZA $$
(☎ 418-973-9732; http://laparizza.com; 337 Rue Racine E; pizzas $12-28; ⏰ 10am-10pm Wed-Sun; 🖉) Pizza, objectively, is awesome. The Québec obsession with *terroir* ingredients is also awesome. When these two culinary concepts collide, you get La Parizza, which features such brilliant creations as margherita pizza served with a veritable charcuterie of local meats, pizza topped with truffle carpaccio and a pie containing spinach, goat's cheese, honey and walnuts.

Rouge Burger Bar BURGERS $$
(☎ 418-690-5029; http://rougeburgerbar.ca; 460 Rue Racine E; mains $16-25; ⏰ 5-10pm Tue & Wed, to 11pm Fri & Sat, to 9pm Sun & Mon) This build-your-own-burger bar has got a good thing going when it comes to meat on buns. There's a tonne of poutines and burger component options, from lamb to salmon to veg to good old beef, as well as a ridiculous beef tartare done with chorizo and truffle oil.

Information

Tourist Office (☎ 418-698-3157, 800-463-6565; http://tourisme.saguenay.ca; 295 Rue Racine E; ⏰ 8:30am-4:30pm Mon-Thu, to 8pm Fri, 10am-4pm Sat & Sun) Offers helpful bookings in the greater fjord region.

Getting There & Away

Located about 16km from downtown Chicoutimi, **Saguenay-Bagotville Airport** (YBG; ☎ 418-677-2651; http://aeroport.saguenay.ca; 7000 Chemin de l'Aéroport, Saguenay) offers connections to Montréal, Sept-Îles and Îles de la Madeleine via Air Canada Express, Air Transat and Pascan.

Intercar (☎ reservations 800-806-2167, station 418-543-1403; https://intercar.ca; 55 Rue Racine E) buses connect (four times daily) to Québec City ($48, 2½ hours), Montréal ($100, six hours) and Tadoussac ($26, 1½ hours).

Transport Adapté du Fjord (p300) runs a minibus down the Saguenay to L'Anse St Jean, hitting other towns along the way.

Lac St Jean

The open flats between Chicoutimi and Lac St Jean are not as immediately compelling as the cliff-straddled ruggedness of the nearby fjord, but upon reaching Lac St Jean's titular lake, you'll find a subtle beauty to this wide open space, where the meeting of sky and water is interrupted only by pale wooden houses and shining church spires. The area claims to be the province's blueberry and *tourtière* (meat pie) capital, as well as the heartland of Québec nationalism.

Sights & Activities

Musée Amérindien de Mashteuiatsh MUSEUM
(☎ 418-275-4842; www.museeilnu.ca; 1787 Rue Amishk, Mashteuiatsh; adult/child $12/7; ⏱ 10am-6pm; Ⓟ) North of Roberval on the lakeshore, one of the province's best-organized Aboriginal villages is home to this museum, featuring good exhibits on the area's Pekuakamiulnuatsh group.

Village Historique Val Jalbert HISTORIC SITE
(☎ 418-275-3132; www.valjalbert.com; 95 Rue St-Georges; adult/child $28/14; ⏱ 9am-6pm Jun-Sep) The Val Jalbert Historic Village is a ghost town that was inhabited from 1901 until a few years after the pulp mill closed in 1927. There's a trolleybus with running commentary from one of the zealous, costume-wearing guides, and a pleasant restaurant in the old mill by the dramatic waterfall. The peaceful spot also has a campground and cabins ($280).

Véloroute des Bleuets CYCLING
(Blueberry Bike Trail; www.veloroute-bleuets.qc.ca/en) The 272km of cycling trails around the lake combine to form the Blueberry Bike Trail, and nearly every town along the way has facilities to make the trip easier: rental and repair shops, B&Bs that cater to cyclists and rest areas. For maps, suggested itineraries and a list of helpful stops, visit the **Maison du Vélo** (Bicycle Tourism Information Center; ☎ 418-668-4541; www.veloroute-bleuets.qc.ca; 1692 Ave du Pont N, Alma; ⏱ 8:30am-6pm Jun-Sep) in Alma.

Sleeping

Auberge Île du Repos CAMPGROUND, HOSTEL $
(☎ 418-347-5649; www.iledurepos.com; 105 Rte Île du Repos; campsites/dm/r from $27/38/80) Taking up an entire little island off Péribonka and Parc de la Pointe Taillon, Auberge Île du Repos is a resort featuring dorms, kitchen facilities, private chalet rooms, camping, a cafe-bar, a beach, croquet and volleyball. With the closest Intercar terminal in Dolbeau-Mistassini, some 25km northwest, it can be a little ghostly despite its cheery pink facade.

Ste Rose du Nord

On the Saguenay River's less-frequented north side, Ste Rose du Nord is a member of the Association of the Most Beautiful Villages of Québec. Wander beneath the purple cliffs to the quay, with the fjord beyond, and it's easy to see why.

You can pitch your tent on a hill at **Camping Descente des Femmes** (☎ 418-675-2581; http://campingsaguenay.com; 154 Rue de la Montagne; campsites $22-30; ⏱ Jun-Sep; Ⓟ) and wake up to a breathtaking view over the village and onto the fjord. The showers and toilets are in a converted grange, and the owner's a hoot.

Signposted off Rte 172 between Ste-Fulgence and Ste-Anne du Rose, **Pourvoirie du Cap au Leste** (☎ 418-675-2000; www.capauleste.com; 551 Chemin du Cap à l'Est; r $115-150, ste $180-220; Ⓟ❄📶) is worth the bumpy 7km ride for its dramatic views over a large stretch of the fjord. The frugal but charming cabins have wood burners and balconies, and the restaurant serves superb regional cuisine. Hiking, canoeing, kayaking, climbing and mountain biking can be organized.

SOUTH SHORE

It's tempting to rush through the South Shore, which includes the Chaudière-Apalaches and Bas St-Laurent regions, en route to the Gaspé Peninsula. However, the area has a wonderfully eclectic mix of attractions, from haunting Grosse Île to refined Rivière du Loup. Other stops include a major woodcarving center, an island once used as a smugglers' stash, and museums devoted to a *Titanic*-like tragedy, Basque whalers and squeezeboxes.

Added to this are the spectacular views across the island-dotted St Lawrence to the undulating North Shore. Hwy 20 is fastest, but Rte 132 is more scenic and goes through the heart of numerous riverside villages.

Grosse Île

The first stop outside Québec City's urban sprawl is one of the region's most interesting. Grosse Île served as a major quarantine station for European immigrants in the 19th and early 20th centuries. A tour of the **Grosse Île National Historic Site** (☎418-234-8841, 888-773-8888; www.pc.gc.ca; adult/child $17.60/8.80; ⏲daily Jul & Aug, Wed-Sun May, Jun, Sep & Oct) sheds light on this little-known aspect of North American history. It is also possible to visit the 21-island **Île aux Grues** archipelago. For all trips, wear warm clothing and comfortable shoes.

Berthier-sur-Mer marina, 55km northeast of Québec City on Rte 132 (also accessible via Hwy 20) and 15km from Montmagny, is the closest departure point for the boat tours to Grosse Île.

Croisières AML (☎855-268-9090; www.croisieresaml.com; 110 Rue de la Marina, Berthier-sur-Mer; adult/child tours $65/35) offers a narrated return cruise to Grosse Île.

Montmagny

Montmagny, the first town of any size east of Lévis, exemplifies the laid-back, family-oriented attitude that seems to permeate the South Shore. Rue St-Jean-Baptiste E is as pretty a main street as you'll find anywhere in Québec.

Most tourists pass through Montmagny on their way to gently beautiful **Île aux Grues**. This 10km-long island, part of an otherwise uninhabited 21-island archipelago, has one of North America's largest unspoiled wetlands. Birders flock to the area in spring and autumn to spot migratory birds, including snow geese. The island has a couple of walking trails.

The **Musée de l'Accordéon** (Accordion Museum; ☎418-248-7927; www.accordeonmontmagny.com; 301 Blvd Taché E; adult/child $8/2; ⏲10am-4pm daily Jul & Aug, Mon-Fri Sep-Jun; 👪), North America's only one, gives an insight into this giant of the Gallic music scene. Squeezeboxes date back to 1820 and incorporate materials such as ivory and mother-of-pearl. In late August, the four-day Carrefour features performances by squeezebox aficionados from around the globe.

Orléans Express (p229) buses connect to Québec City and beyond; the bus stop is at 20 Blvd Taché E.

Ferries (☎877-562-6560; www.traversiers.com; ⏲Apr-Dec) FREE leave from Montmagny marina for the 30-minute crossing to Île aux Grues. There are two to four daily, April to December only. Other commercial excursions to the archipelago are also possible.

St Jean Port Joli

This exceptionally pretty town became known as a center of craftsmanship in the 1930s, a reputation it works hard to keep. Riverside Parc des Trois Berets, named after the three beret-wearing brothers who launched the town as a woodcarving capital, is the venue for an international **sculpture festival** in June.

There are scores of ateliers, boutiques and roadside pieces of art, covered by a free map available from the tourist office (p304).

Philippe Aubert de Gaspé, author of *Les Anciens Canadiens*, is buried in the 18th-century **church**.

Sights

Musée de la Mémoire Vivante MUSEUM
(Museum of Living Memory; ☎418-358-0518; www.memoirevivante.org; 710 Ave de Gaspé W; adult/child $8/free; ⏲9am-6pm Jul & Aug, 10am-5pm Jun & Sep, 10am-5pm Mon-Fri Oct-May; P) This fascinating museum explores the culture of Québec (particularly St Jean Port Joli) via exhibits sourced from thousands of community contributions and oral history interviews. Fair warning: the exhibitions were only presented in French when we visited.

Musée Maritime du Québec MUSEUM
(☎418-247-5001; www.mmq.qc.ca; 55 Chemin des Pionniers E, L'Islet; adult/child $12/8; ⏲9am-6pm Jul & Aug, 10am-5pm Jun, 10am-4pm Wed-Sun Mar-May & Sep-Nov; P 👪) This large, modern facility explores the deep historical and cultural ties this area has to shipbuilding and the sea. There's a life-sized ship to board, knot-tying classes and lots of interactivity that should please youngsters.

Musée des Anciens Canadiens MUSEUM
(☎418-598-3392; www.museedesancienscanadiens.com; 332 Rte 132 W; adult/child $8/3; ⏲8:30am-8pm Jul & Aug, 9am-5:30pm May, Jun, Sep & Oct) This museum has over 250 wood-carved figures from René Lévesque to Harry Potter, providing a good introduction to the work of the beret-clad Bourgaults and other local notables.

Sleeping & Eating

Au Boisé Joli B&B $

(418-598-6774; www.auboisejoli.com; 41 Ave de Gaspé E; s/d from $85/95;) This well-run little B&B occupies a modest residential home; the interior is alight in warm colors, hardwood floors and little artistic accents. Management can help you with bike rentals and general discovery of the area.

Camping de la Demi Lieue CAMPGROUND $

(418-598-6108, 800-463-9558; 598 Rte 132; campsites from $32, cottages from $120; May-Sep; @) Huge but well-equipped and closer to town than other campgrounds.

La Belle Époque B&B $$

(418-598-9905; www.auberge-labelleepoque.com; 63 Ave de Gaspé E; s/d from $105/120;) With its tasteful historical accents, art and general sense of lived-in coziness, the Belle Époque almost feels like a historic home (which is appropriate, given the name), but the service and amenities are modern and attentive.

La Coureuse des Grèves FRENCH $$

(418-598-9111; www.coureusedesgreves.com; 300 Rte de l'Église; mains $12-23; 8am-10pm Sun-Thu, to 11pm Fri & Sat;) This restaurant practically screams pleasant, but in an unhurried, rustic way. That's the vibe in this country cottage turned French restaurant, where the interior is all old-wood accents and the cuisine well-crafted classics.

La Boustifaille QUÉBÉCOIS $$

(418-598-3061; 547 Rte 132 E/Ave de Gaspé E; mains $15-25; 8am-9pm Jun-Sep; P) Renowned for huge portions of local classics such as pork ragout, *tourtière* (meat pie) and cheese quiche, and its adjacent theater.

Drinking & Nightlife

Microbrasserie Ras L'Bock MICROBREWERY

(418-358-0886; www.raslbock.com; 250 Rue du Quai; noon-3am Wed-Sun) Live music, strong beer, an outdoor garden where all the cool kids hang out and a laid-back vibe that's not afraid to throw down and party if the need arises – this beloved microbrewery is a winner.

Information

Tourist Office (418-598-3747; 20 Ave de Gaspé W; 9:30am-7:30pm late-Jun–Aug, 9am-5pm Wed-Sat, to 4pm Sun Sep–late-Jun) Provides maps of town and can connect you to local ateliers.

Getting There & Away

Orléans Express buses to/from Québec City stop in the center of town at Épicerie Régent Pelletier, 10 Rte 132.

Rivière du Loup

Its curious name (the Wolf River) either refers to seals (sea wolves), an Amerindian tribe or a 17th-century French ship, but one thing is certain: Rivière du Loup is a town of some distinction. Its key position on the fur and postal routes between the Maritimes and the St Lawrence made it the main town in eastern Québec during the 19th century. Formerly an English-speaking town, it was planned according to the British model, with open spaces in front of grand buildings such as the Gothic silver-roofed St Patrice. Having declined in the early 20th century, it's booming again, with one of the province's highest birthrates, as well as an influx of urban runaways and graduates returning to their beautiful birthplace.

Sights

Parc des Chutes PARK

(Sentier Parc des Chutes; P) Short trails make the most of the small but seductive Parc des Chutes, a few minutes' walk from downtown at the end of Rue Frontenac. If you get lost, just follow the sounds of the cars and the 30m waterfalls that power a small hydroelectric power station.

Parc de la Croix PARK

A short drive into the hilly part of town leads to tiny Parc de la Croix, where an illuminated cross guards a stunning view across town and the river. To get there from downtown, take Rue Lafontaine south to the underpass leading to Rue Témiscouata. Make a left on Chemin des Raymond, then turn left at Rue Alexandre, right at Rue Bernier and left at Rue Ste-Claire.

Musée du Bas St-Laurent MUSEUM

(418-862-7547; www.mbsl.qc.ca; 300 Rue St-Pierre; adult/student $7/5; 9am-5pm daily Jun & Aug, 1-5pm Wed-Sun Sep-May) The lively Musée du Bas St-Laurent has a collection of contemporary Québec art, but the main event is the 200,000 vintage photos of the local area, used in thematic, interactive exhibits that explore life on the St Lawrence.

Fraser Manor NOTABLE BUILDING

(☎ 418-867-3906; www.manoirfraser.com; 32 Rue Fraser; adult/child $7/4; ⏲ 9:30am-5pm Jul-Sep) Rivière du Loup was called Fraserville in the 19th century, named after the powerful Scottish dynasty that inhabited the grand Fraser Manor. Today, the Manor gives an insight into life in the upper echelons of the developing colony.

Activities

La Société Duvetnor CRUISE

(☎ 418-867-1660; www.duvetnor.com; 200 Rue Hayward) Offshore, a series of protected islands sport bird sanctuaries and provide habitat for other wildlife. The nonprofit group La Société Duvetnor offers bird-watching and nature excursions to the islands. Sighting belugas is common. There are 45km of trails on the largest island, **l'Île aux Lièvres**, and accommodations, including a campground.

Prices start at $25 for a 1½-hour cruise to Pot au l'Eau de Vie (the brandy pot), named for its use as a bootlegging way station during the Prohibition era.

Petit Témis Interprovincial Linear Park CYCLING, WALKING

(☎ 418-853-3593; www.petit-temis.ca) The Petit Témis Interprovincial Linear Park is a scenic bike and walking trail, mainly flat, which runs along an old train track for 135km to Edmundston, New Brunswick. The tourist office has maps, and Hobby Cycles rents bikes.

Croisières AML CRUISE

(☎ 866-856-6668; 200 Rue Hayward; 3½hr tours $70; ⏲ Jun-Aug) For whale-watching there's Croisières AML. If you're crossing the river to Tadoussac, save your trip for there.

Hobby Cycles CYCLING

(☎ 418-863-1112; www.hobbycycle.ca; 278 Rue Lafontaine; rental per day from $30; ⏲ 10am-5:30pm Tue & Wed, to 8pm Thu, to 6pm Fri, 10am-4pm Sat) Rents and fixes up bicycles and can direct you to some good trails.

Sleeping & Eating

Auberge Internationale HOSTEL $

(☎ 418-862-7566; www.aubergerdl.ca; 46 Blvd de l'Hôtel de Ville; dm/r incl breakfast from $28/60; P@) This excellent, central HI hostel in an old house has small dorms with attached bathrooms. The long-term staff create a placid, welcoming atmosphere, and there's a good communal vibe going on.

Auberge de la Pointe RESORT $$

(☎ 800-463-1222, 418-862-3514; www.aubergedelapointe.com; 10 Blvd Cartier; r $105-185, ste from $320; P) This enormous complex, located a little way out of town, consists of several pavilions overlooking a lovely bend of the St Lawrence. The rooms are brilliantly designed, achieving a nice balance between stripped-down-cool and warm coziness, and there's a spa, restaurant, bar and even a theater on the grounds.

Au Vieux Fanal MOTEL $$

(☎ 418-862-5255; www.motelauvieuxfanal.com; 170 Rue Fraser; r $70-125; ⏲ May-Nov) One of the best motels on this strip is multicolored Au Vieux Fanal, with great views of the river and a heated swimming pool.

★ **L'Innocent** CAFE $$

(☎ 418-862-1937; 460 Rue Lafontaine; mains $10-15; ⏲ 9am-10pm) The hippest cafe around serves great-value daily specials to a ska/indie/name-your-cool-music-genre-here soundtrack. It's the best place in town to meet locals; and if you're in a hurry, it serves coffee to go.

L'Estaminet PUB FOOD $$

(☎ 418-867-4517; www.restopubestaminet.com; 299 Rue Lafontaine; mains $15-32; ⏲ 7am-11pm Mon-Wed, to midnight Thu, to 1am Fri, 8am-1am Sat, 8am-11pm Sun) Feast on hearty pub grub and specials, including house-specialty mussels with fries, in this *bistro du monde* with 150 types of beer. Give the bison burger a whirl.

Chez Antoine FRENCH $$$

(☎ 418-862-6936; www.chezantoine.ca; 433 Rue Lafontaine; dinner mains $28-45; ⏲ 11am-2pm Mon-Fri, 5-9pm Mon-Sat) Long considered one of the best places to eat in town, Chez Antoine maintains its tradition. Specialties include Atlantic salmon, duBreton pork tenderloin and filet mignon, all served in an old white house with a classy dining room.

Information

Tourist Office (☎ 888-825-1981; www.tourismeriviereduloup.ca; 189 Blvd de l'Hôtel de Ville; ⏲ 8:30am-7:30pm Jul & Aug, 8:30am-4:30pm Mon-Fri, from 11am Sat Sep, 8:30am-4:30pm Mon-Fri Oct-Jun) Has internet access and a free Old Town walking map.

Getting There & Away

A **ferry** (☎ 418-862-5094; www.traverserdl.com; adult/child round-trip $24/16.30) runs between Rivière du Loup marina and St-Siméon.

Highway 20 (exit 503), Rte 132 and Hwy 85 lead directly into Rivière du Loup.

Orléans Express buses to Québec City and Rimouski stop at the **bus station** (317 Blvd de l'Hôtel de Ville).Transfer at Rimouski for New Brunswick.

Rivière du Loup is linked by **VIA Rail** (☎888-842-7245; www.viarail.ca; 615 Rue Lafontaine) every second day to Québec City and Halifax. The station is only open when the trains arrive, in the middle of the night.

Île Verte

For some respite from the road, which thins to one lane after Rivière du Loup but is busy as far as Rimouski, take the 15-minute ferry crossing to Île Verte.

Summer cottages have only recently begun creeping onto the 11km-long island, which has a permanent population of 45. It's popular for birding, cycling, whale-watching and, in the winter, ice-fishing.

The St Lawrence River's oldest **lighthouse** (1809) contains a museum. You can stay in the adjacent cottages at **Les Maisons du Phare** (☎418-898-2730; http://phareileverte.com; s/d incl breakfast $88/120; ⊙May-Oct;). This little hotel gets lots of natural light shining over colorful little rooms. The lodging is spread out over several cottages. If you're looking for something to eat, fresh eggs, soups and pastas, local cheeses and microbrewery beers all make an appearance at **Café d'Alphé** (mains $9-16; ⊙10am-10pm), a friendly little cafe.

Location de Bicyclettes Entre Deux Marées (☎418-860-7425; 4404 Chemin de l'Île; per day from $30) rents bicycles to those visiting the island. Call ahead to secure your rental; the office's opening hours coincide with ferry arrivals and departures.

Ferries (☎418-898-2843; www.traversiers.com; 1804 du Quai d'En Bas, Notre-Dame-des-Sept-Douleurs; one way adult/car/bicycle $6.70/40/1) run between the island and Notre-Dame-des-Sept-Douleurs about five times a day. In winter, during the freeze, access is by air or snowmobile only; call ☎418-898-3287 for details on how to cross, and call ahead anywhere on the island, as tourism infrastructure will likely be closed.

Trois Pistoles

You'll notice, upon entering this village, that Francophone Québec seems to have shifted to an outpost of Basque nationalism; every other business name seems to refer to local Basque heritage. Said demographic arrived via whalers, who were the first Europeans after the Vikings to navigate the St Lawrence, predating Jacques Cartier. The main reason for stopping here is exploration of the St Lawrence; the folks at **Kayak des Îles** (☎418-851-4637; www.kayaksdesiles.com; 60 Ave du Parc; 3/6hr tours $55/110) run good-value sea kayaking expeditions onto the water.

Sights

Île-aux-Basques ISLAND

(☎418-851-1202; www.provancher.qc.ca; adult/child $2/free; ⊙Jun-Aug) This wooded speck of Arcadian prettiness is dotted with 16th-century Basque ovens, has 2km of trails and is home to a bird refuge. Société Provancher offers guided tours during the summer – this is the only means of accessing the island.

Festivals & Events

Festival Rendez-vous des Grandes Gueules CULTURAL

(http://compagnonspatrimoine.com) The Festival Rendez-vous des Grandes Gueules, held on the first weekend of October, celebrates Francophone storytelling traditions from around the world.

Sleeping

La Rose des Vents B&B $

(☎418-851-4926; 80 2e Rang W; s/d incl breakfast $85/105; P@) This lovely old place is easily recognizable by its modified roofline. There's a breakfast room with huge windows gazing at the North Shore and simple rooms with big, soft beds for those who need a break from the road.

Camping & Motel des Flots Bleus Sur Mer CAMPGROUND $

(☎418-851-3583; Rte 132; tent & RV sites $25, r $60; ⊙May–mid-Oct; P) This small, quiet campground, located a little way out of Trois Pistoles, includes a very bare-bones motel.

Parc National du Bic

As you approach the Gaspé Peninsula, the cloud banks begin to roll in off the St Lawrence and percolate into a series of darkly forested inlets, islets and crescent bays. A 33-sq-km chunk of this land is protected and dubbed **Parc National du Bic** (☎418-736-5035; www.sepaq.com/pq/bic; 3382 Rte 132; adult/child $8.50/free; ⊙year-round). There's an excellent interpretation center here, and activities on offer, most of which can be organized by the helpful staff, include hiking, mountain biking, sea kayaking, guided walks and drives, wildlife observation by day and night, snowshoeing and Nordic skiing. The two-hour-return trail to **Champlain Peak** (346m) rewards with views across to Îlet au Flacon; the park runs a shuttle here.

Held in early August, **Festival Concerts aux Îles du Bic** (www.bicmusique.com/en; ⏲early Aug) is a chamber music festival set against the gorgeous backdrop of Parc National du Bic's forests and islands.

Located halfway between Parc National du Bic and Rimouski, **Theatre du Bic** (☎418-736-4141; http://theatredubic.com; 50 Rte du Golf-du-Bic) is known for assembling brilliant, original seasons that showcase a superb lineup of music, theater, dance and comedy acts.

Rimouski

Rimouski isn't as immediately charming as some of Québec's more postcard-perfect towns – it's a big oil distribution center – but it's prosperous, energetic and an important regional commercial hub. As such, there are some good restaurants, interesting museums and a healthy number of students. It's a great spot to wait for a ferry.

Sights & Activities

St-Barnabé Island ISLAND
(☎418-723-2280; www.ilestbarnabe.com; 50 Rue St-Germain W; adult/child $19/12.50; ⏲departures every 30min 9am-2:30pm, returns every 30min 10:15am-6:15pm Jun-Sep) About 20 minutes (and a world of activity) away from Rimouski, Île St-Barnabé is a quiet, forested chunk of sylvan loveliness, cut through with gentle trails, surrounded by lapping, stone-and-sand beaches and inhabited by blue herons and seals. Sturdy inflatable boats depart from the Rimouski marina.

Musée de la Mer MUSEUM
(☎418-724-6214; www.shmp.qc.ca; 1034 Rue du Phare; adult/child $15.75/9.25; ⏲9am-6pm Jun-Sep; P) Seven kilometers east of town, this museum narrates the *Empress of Ireland* tragedy, the worst disaster in maritime history after the *Titanic*. In the 14 minutes it took for the ship to disappear into the St Lawrence after colliding with a Norwegian collier, 1012 people lost their lives. The disaster was all but forgotten with the outbreak of WWI two months later.

Pointe au Père Lighthouse LIGHTHOUSE
(adult/child $4/3; ⏲9am-6pm) The tallest lighthouse in eastern Canada has a decent perch over the St Lawrence Seaway. It's part of the Musée de la Mer complex.

Musée Régional de Rimouski GALLERY
(☎418-724-2272; http://museerimouski.qc.ca; 35 Rue St-Germain W; adult/child $6/4; ⏲9:30am-6pm Jun-Aug, noon-5pm Wed & Fri-Sun, to 8pm Thu Sep-May; P) In a renovated stone church, this gallery has contemporary art exhibitions and regular events including film nights.

Le Canyon des Portes de l'Enfer HIKING
(☎418-735-6063; http://canyonportesenfer.qc.ca; 1280 Chemin Duchénier; adult/child $13/7; ⏲May-Oct) For hiking, mountain biking and a view of a canyon and waterfalls from the province's highest suspended bridge (62m), head to Le Canyon des Portes de l'Enfer (Hell's Gate Canyon), near St Narcisse de Rimouski, 30km south of town along Rte 232.

Sleeping & Eating

Auberge de l'Évêché INN $$
(☎866-623-5411, 418-723-5411; www.aubergedeleveche.com; 37 Rue de l'Évêché W; r incl breakfast $99-120; P) Above a *chocolaterie* opposite the town hall, the rooms here have TVs and are attractively decorated with vintage photos. There's a general aged-but-not-chintzy vibe.

Hôtel Rimouski HOTEL $$
(☎418-725-5000; www.hotelrimouski.com; 225 Blvd René-Lepage E; r from $125, ste from $163; P @) With a genteel elegance and a slightly faded regal demeanor, this grande dame of Rimouski has neat rooms, most with views of the boardwalk and water across the street. It's big with business travelers for the on-site convention center, and families for the super-fast, super-fun water slide and indoor pool.

★**La Brûlerie d'Ici** CAFE $
(☎418-723-3424; www.bruleriedici.com; 91 Rue St-Germain W; sandwiches $6; ⏲7am-11pm Mon-Wed, to 1am Thu & Fri, 8am-1am Sat, 8am-11pm Sun) A hip hangout offering Guatemalan and Ethiopian coffees, bites from bagels to banana bread, wi-fi and live music during the summer.

Les Complices QUÉBÉCOIS $$
(☎418-722-0505; www.lescomplices-resto.com; 108 Rue St-Germain E; mains $11-22; ⏲9am-10pm Mon-Sat, to 2pm Sun; P) The kitchen at Les Complices demonstrates lots of dedication and love for the fish, produce and livestock of

the wooded South Shore and Gaspé Peninsula. Salmon tartare mussels and *frites*, poutine in a *bourguignonne* (red wine) sauce – this is delicious local fare with not much pretension.

Le Crêpe Chignon CAFE $$
(☎418-724-0400; www.crepechignonrimouski.com; 140 Ave de la Cathédrale; mains $9-15; ⏱7-10pm Mon-Wed, to 11pm Thu & Fri, 8am-11pm Sat, to 10pm Sun; P 👪) This bright light on the Rimouski dining scene serves delicious savory and dessert crêpes. This is very much a favorite with locals and tourists, so expect a wait.

ℹ Information

Tourist Office (☎800-746-6875, 418-723-2322; http://tourismerimouski.com; 50 Rue St-Germain W; ⏱8:30am-7:30pm Jun-Aug, 8:30am-5:30pm Mon-Fri, 11am-4pm Sat & Sun Sep & Oct, 9am-noon & 1-4:30pm Mon-Fri Nov-May) On Place des Veterans, at the intersection of Rue St-Germain W and Ave de la Cathédrale.

ℹ Getting There & Away

BOAT

From May through September, a **ferry** (☎418-725-2725, 800-973-2725; https://ssl.pqm.net/cnmevolution; ⏱May-Sep) links Rimouski with Forestville on the North Shore (one way adult/child/car $24/15/48, 1¾ hours, two to four daily). Reservations are accepted.

The **Relais Nordik** (☎418-723-8787, 800-463-0680; www.relaisnordik.com; 17 Ave Lebrun; return to Natashquan $398; ⏱early Apr–mid-Jan) takes passengers on its weekly cargo ship to Sept Îles, Île d'Anticosti, Havre St-Pierre, Natashquan and the Lower North Shore. It departs Rimouski marina on Tuesday morning and gets to Blanc Sablon by Friday evening. One-way fares start at $640 for the full journey. Meals are available on board; mains run from $6 to $20. Cars can be taken, although it's extremely costly (fares are calculated according to the weight of the vehicle) and a bicycle is more convenient at the brief stopovers.

BUS

Orléans Express buses leave from the **bus station** (☎888-999-3977; www.orleansexpress.com; 90 Rue Léonidas) to Québec City ($58, four hours, three daily), Rivière du Loup ($32, 1½ hours, six daily) and Gaspé ($78, seven hours, five daily).

CAR

Ride-share agencies like **Kangaride** (p229) hook up drivers and passengers for locations including Québec City and Montréal.

TRAIN

For VIA Rail services, the **train station** (☎888-842-7245; 57 Rue de l'Évêché E) is only open when trains pull in, which is usually after midnight. Every second day, trains travel to/from Montréal.

GASPÉ PENINSULA

There's nowhere quite like 'La Gaspésie,' a peninsula of pine forests and looming cliffs that pokes into the chilly Gulf of St Lawrence. Somewhere on the road past Matane, the landscape becomes wilder, the cottages more colorful and precariously positioned along rockier promontories, the winds sharper and more scented with salt, and you realize you have entered, effectively, a Francophone version of the maritime provinces.

A silly amount of fantastic landscape is packed into this relatively small landmass. There's the famous pierced rock in Percé and endless beaches overshadowed by glacier-patterned cliffs. The mountainous, forested hinterlands, home to the breathtaking Parc de la Gaspésie, are crossed by few routes, among them the Matapédia Valley drive, the International Appalachian Trail and Rte 198, one of the province's quietest roads.

The tourist season runs from about June to mid-September. Outside those times, things seriously wind down.

History

Like the whales that can often be spotted spouting off in the distance, Normans, Bretons, Basques, Portuguese and Channel Islanders were attracted here by rich fishing grounds. English, Scottish and Irish fugitives from upheavals such as the Great Famine and American independence settled on the south shore, leaving isolated Anglophone communities. The Acadian red, white and blue flag dotted with a gold star can be seen fluttering above many homes strung along Rte 132.

Ste Flavie

The sense you're somewhere different becomes evident in Ste Flavie, where the road hugs the coast and...a crowd of odd figures can be seen marching in from the sea? More on this in a sec – just know that this is a relaxing place to pause before tackling the rocky landscape that soon rises above Rte 132.

👁 Sights

Centre d'Art Marcel Gagnon GALLERY
(☎866-775-2829, 418-775-2829; www.centredart.net; 564 Rte de la Mer; ⏱7:30am-9pm; P) FREE The star of the town's art trail is the Centre d'Art Marcel Gagnon. Outside, the extraordinary sculpture *Le Grand Rassemblement* (The Great Gathering) has more than 100 stone figures filing out of the St Lawrence.

Gaspé Peninsula

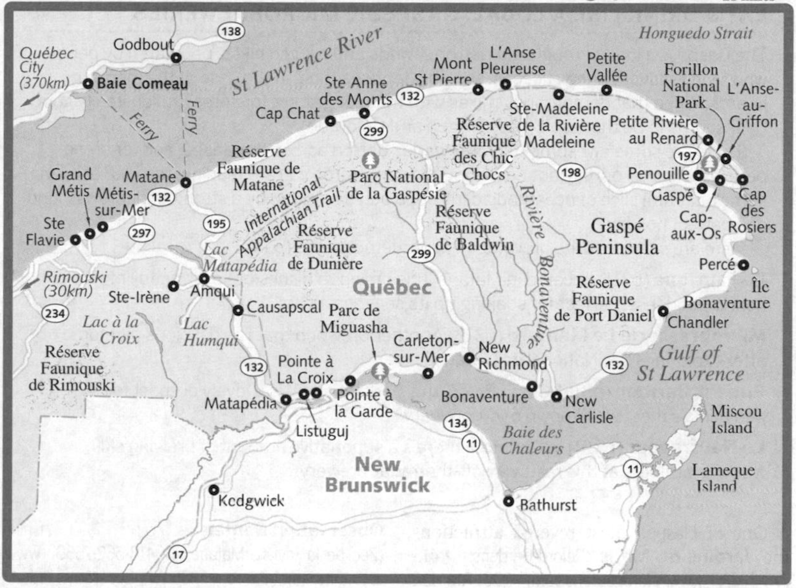

0 — 50 km
0 — 25 miles

Québec City (370km)
Godbout
Baie Comeau
Ferry
St Lawrence River
Honguedo Strait
Cap Chat
Ste Anne des Monts
Mont St Pierre
L'Anse Pleureuse
Petite Vallée
Ste-Madeleine de la Rivière Madeleine
Forillon National Park
L'Anse-au-Griffon
Petite Rivière au Renard
Penouille
Gaspé
Cap-aux-Os
Cap des Rosiers
Grand Métis
Métis-sur-Mer
Matane
Ste Flavie
Réserve Faunique de Matane
International Appalachian Trail
Parc National de la Gaspésie
Réserve Faunique des Chic Chocs
Réserve Faunique de Baldwin
Rivière Bonaventure
Gaspé Peninsula
Percé
Île Bonaventure
Réserve Faunique de Dunière
Lac Matapédia
Rimouski (30km)
Ste-Irène
Amqui
Causapscal
Québec
Parc de Miguasha
Réserve Faunique de Port Daniel
Chandler
Lac à la Croix
Lac Humqui
Réserve Faunique de Rimouski
Carleton-sur-Mer
New Richmond
Gulf of St Lawrence
Pointe à La Croix
Matapédia
Pointe à la Garde
Listuguj
Bonaventure
New Carlisle
Miscou Island
Baie des Chaleurs
New Brunswick
Lameque Island
Kedgwick
Bathurst
138, 132, 299, 197, 198, 297, 195, 234, 134, 11, 17

Unfortunately, the gallery, displaying work by Gagnon and his son, feels a little too commercial, with all manner of *Gathering* souvenirs for sale.

Vieux Moulin MUSEUM
(☎418-775-8383; http://vieuxmoulin.qc.ca/wp; 141 Rte de la Mer; museum $2.50; ⏲8am-9pm) This 19th-century windmill offers free tastings of Shakespeare's favorite tipple, mead, and has a small museum containing colonial and prehistoric aboriginal artifacts.

Sleeping

Centre d'Art Marcel Gagnon Auberge INN $$
(☎418-775-2829, 866-775-2829; www.centredart.net/chambres; 564 Rte de la Mer; r incl breakfast $95-135; P 📶) The *auberge* that hangs over the Centre d'Art Marcel Gagnon has understated artistic rooms with private bathrooms.

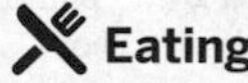

Eating

Centre d'Art Marcel Gagnon Restaurant PUB FOOD $$
(☎418-775-2829; 564 Rte de la Mer; mains $16-33; ⏲7:30am-9pm; P 👪) The restaurant at Centre d'Art Marcel Gagnon dishes up pizza, pasta and a plethora of seafood, with an emphasis on big, creamy sauces, all served with a great view.

Capitaine Homard SEAFOOD $$$
(☎418-775-8046; http://capitainehomard.com; 180 Rte de la Mer; mains $16-40; ⏲11am-10pm May-Aug; P 👪) Capitaine Homard ('Captain Lobster') has been the local 'kilometer 0' since 1968. It serves great seafood beneath a Davy Jones' Locker–like ceiling, and offers internet access, camping and chalets.

Information

Tourisme Gaspésie Office (☎418-775-2223, 800-463-0323; www.tourisme-gaspesie.com/en; 1020 Blvd Jacques-Cartier; ⏲8am-8pm) Just off the coastal road, Tourisme Gaspésie is Gaspé's main tourist office. If you're here in the off-season, pick up the pamphlet listing winter facilities.

Grand Métis

Grand Métis is a speck of a town that's primarily known for its landscaped gardens. As you drive northeast on Rte 132, the town effectively feels like an extension of Ste Flavie.

About 10km east of Grand Métis are the beach towns of **Métis Beach** and **Métis sur Mer**. With big lawns and British names on their street signs and mailboxes, they resemble American towns. Traditionally a retreat for the Anglophone bourgeoisie, the area has a predominantly native-English-speaking population.

LOCAL KNOWLEDGE

EAT & DRINK LIKE A LOCAL: GASPÉSIE MICROBREWERIES

The Gaspé is a land of rough seas, strong winds and rugged hikes, populated by people who tend to favor flannel, fleeces, sensible footwear and, in the case of the men, big beards. When that demography mixes with that geography, for some reason, really good beer seems to be the result (see: Oregon and Colorado).

There are some awesome microbreweries dotted across the Gaspé, and for some people, who may or may not be writing the very words you are reading, the idea of hiking some beautiful slice of ocean-adjacent Appalachia followed by a strong dark brew is kind of a perfect holiday.

Here are some favorite brewpubs encountered on the road.

La Fabrique (p311) Located in Matane, this brewpub dishes out a menu full of rich hearty goodness, perfect for soaking up its seasonal beers.

Microbrasserie Le Malbord (p312) Another brewpub that is a delicious pit stop after exploring Parc National de la Gaspésie.

Pub Pit Caribou (p316) Out in Percé, this dark little pub is a lovely outpost for the peninsula's most well-known microbrewery.

Le Naufrageur (p318) In Carleton, there's a superlative amount of brewing skill working wonders at this relatively off-the-radar brewery.

One of Gaspé's most revered attractions, the **Jardins de Métis** (Reford Gardens; ☎418-775-2222; www.refordgardens.com; 200 Rte 132; adult/child $20/free; ⏲8:30am-6pm May, Jun & Sep, to 8pm Jul & Aug; P) comprises more than 90 hectares of immaculately tended gardens boasting 3000 varieties of plants. Begun in 1910, the gardens are also known as the Reford Gardens – after Elsie Reford, who inherited the land from her uncle, Lord Mount Stephen, the founder of the Canadian Pacific Railway. His 37-room villa is now a **museum**. Also on-site: **ERE132**, a cunningly designed green home that's a little marvel of ecofriendly contemporary architecture.

Matane

This commercial fishing port isn't as postcard perfect as other villages on the peninsula, but it's friendly and useful for sampling some screamingly fresh local seafood.

Activities

Sentier International des Appalaches HIKING
(☎418-562-7885; www.sia-iat.com; 968 Ave du Phare W; 2-day, 2-night treks from $265; ⏲office 9am-5pm Mon-Fri) The International Appalachian Trail extends into the Gaspé, and this office organizes advanced and beginners' hikes on part of that route. Many of its treks cut through the wild, rugged Réserve Faunique de Matane.

Observation Center FISHING
(Zec de la Rivière Matane; ☎418-562-7560; www.zecsaumonmatane.com; 235 Ave St-Jérôme; adult/child $5/free; ⏲8am-7:45pm Jun-Sep; 👪) What are we observing? Fish. Big ones. Salmon weighing up to 19kg swim up the Rivière Matane to spawn in June, and if you'd like to see them, this observation center at the dam is worth a visit. It also sells permits to fish the 100km river starting right in town.

Sleeping & Eating

Camping Rivière CAMPGROUND $
(☎418-562-3414; www.campingmatane.com; 150 Rte Louis Félix Dionne; tent & RV sites from $27; 📶) Southwest of downtown, this campground has 124 secluded, private sites among the trees. From town, head south toward Amqui, on Rue Henri Dunant.

La Seigneurie INN $$
(☎418-562-0021, 877-783-4466; http://aubergelaseigneurie.com; 621 Ave St-Jérôme; r $89-119) This friendly B&B occupies a grand property dating from 1919 with attic rooms, a grand piano and a freestanding bath in the 'lovers' room.'

Hôtel Motel Belle Plage HOTEL $$
(☎418-562-2323, 888-244-2323; www.hotelbelleplage.com; 1310 Rue Matane sur Mer; r $114-195; P📶) You can order smoked salmon and white wine to your room and dine on the balcony. Pretty swish for a motel! It's close to the ferry terminal and away from the noise of Rte 132.

La Fabrique PUB FOOD $

(☎418-566-4020; www.publafabrique.com; 360 Ave St-Jérôme; mains $7-16; ⏰11:30am-1:30am; P) Thai shrimp, smoked ham, chipotle chicken and other locally sourced, internationally inspired variations on pub grub – including an awesome slate of creative takes on grilled-cheese sandwiches – grace the menu at this excellent microbrewery.

Shopping

Poissonnerie Boréalis FOOD

(☎418-562-7001; www.borealismatane.com; 985 Rte 132; ⏰8am-9pm) You like fish? Here's the shop for you. Our finned friends come in all varieties: sushi-ed, fresh, smoked and otherwise packaged for your consumption.

Information

Tourist Office (☎418-562-6734, 418-562-1065; www.tourismematane.com; 968 Ave du Phare W; ⏰8am-7pm Jul & Aug, 9am-6pm Jun & Sep) Based in a lighthouse alongside a maritime museum.

Getting There & Away

A **ferry** (☎877-562-6560, 418-562-2500; www.traversiers.com; 1410 Rue Matane sur Mer; adult/child/car $20/12/48) service runs between Matane, Baie Comeau and Godbout (adult/child/car $20/12/48, four to six daily). The ferry terminal is off Rte 132, about 2km west of the town center.

Buses (☎418-562-4085; www.orleansexpress.com; 521 Rte 132) arrive at and depart from the Irving gas station, 1.5km east of the town center. **Orléans Express** (p229) buses go to Gaspé ($38, five hours, two daily) and Rimouski ($26.25, 1½ hours, three daily).

Cap Chat

Cap Chat is a typical Gaspé village...apart from those 133 windmills beating above the white houses. This is Canada's largest wind farm and the world's most economical, producing 100 megawatts of electricity. Covering 100km, the dream-like structures perch on hilltops above the start of the St Lawrence Gulf. Dominating the gang is the world's largest vertical-axis windmill, which, alas, is no longer used.

If you'd like to take a one-hour tour of the area's windmills, contact **Éole Cap-Chat** (☎418-786-5719; www.eolecapchat.com; Rte 132; tours $10; ⏰9:30am-5:30pm Jul-Oct). Look for the signs on Rte 132 just west of Cap Chat. English-language tours are available.

Off Rte 132 east of the bridge at Cap Chat, **Camping au Bord de la Mer** (☎418-809-3675; http://campingauborddelamer.wix.com/campingmer; 173 Rue Notre Dame E; campsites $20-35) is a simple campground that offers river views and access to some windswept, pebbly beaches.

Ste Anne des Monts

As you travel along the north coast of the peninsula, the cliffs get rockier and the drops more sheer; there are houses in this town that look as precarious on the rocks as a herd of mountain goats. As a natural stopping point before heading into Parc National de la Gaspésie, Ste Anne des Monts is an ideal location to stock up before heading inland to the wilderness.

Sights

Exploramer AQUARIUM

(☎418-763-2500; www.exploramer.qc.ca; 1 Rue du Quai; adult/child $15/9.50; ⏰9am-5pm Jun-Oct; P 👪) This aquarium, which focuses on the marine life of the St Lawrence, is a great place for a pit stop on winding Rte 132. There are lots of tactile exhibits – in case you've ever wanted to touch a sea cucumber – and also a maritime museum, sea excursions and a peek into the process of sea harvesting. Little ones might prefer the nautically themed playground outside.

Sleeping & Eating

★ **Auberge Festive Sea Shack** HOSTEL $

(☎418-763-2999, 866-963-2999; www.aubergefestive.com; 292 Blvd Perron E; campsites $16, dm HI member/nonmember $26/30, cabins from $80; P @ 📶) A collection of chalets, cabins, tents and a huge bar and common area huddle behind the forested cliffs about 10km east of Ste Anne des Monts. This is the Sea Shack, the sort of hostel that gets people into backpacking in the first place. Bands play at the beach bar and water lovers take out kayaks or gaze at the St Lawrence from the outdoor Jacuzzi.

Auberge Château Lamontagne INN $$

(☎418-763-7666; www.chateaulamontagne.com; 170 1ère Ave E; r $95-140, ste from $175; P 📶) Perched on a hill overlooking the St Lawrence, this colorful inn boasts modern rooms with polished oak floors and a subtle, refined decor. The attached restaurant is an upscale, romantic nook for those seeking to sample local produce from land and sea.

La Seigneurie des Monts INN $$
(☎418-763-5308; www.bonjourgaspesie.com; 21 1ère Ave E; r $134-184) This lovably odd inn is all vintage weird (again, in a good way!): creaky floorboards, 'his and hers' dressing gowns, antiquarian books and chaise longues. The effect could feel artificial, but it doesn't, especially given the sincere and friendly owners who make it all the more appealing.

Microbrasserie Le Malbord PUB FOOD $$
(☎418-764-0022; www.lemalbord.com; 178 1ère Ave W; mains $8-17; ⏱11am-1am; P) Nothing warms you up after a long day of hiking in Parc National de la Gaspésie like a tall glass of red beer and some bacon and cheese melted over potatoes, or pizza with smoked salmon. All this – local beer, good grub – plus live-music.

Information

Tourist Bureau (Vacances Haute-Gaspésie; ☎418-763-0044; 464 Blvd Ste-Anne W; ⏱9am-8pm Jul & Aug, 10am-6pm Jun & Sep) Just off Rte 132, near the intersection of 28e Rue Ouest.

Parc National de la Gaspésie

After driving south from Ste Anne des Monts along Rte 299, you'd be forgiven for thinking you'd left the Atlantic coast and plunged into the heart of the Rocky Mountains. Except making that comparison isn't fair when describing Parc National de la Gaspésie, which has a raw, rugged beauty all its own, one as rooted in oceanic proximity (even in the Gaspé's interior) as mountainous soul.

After driving south from Ste Anne des Monts along Rte 299, you'd be forgiven for thinking you'd left the Atlantic coast and plunged into the heart of the Rocky Mountains. Except making that comparison isn't fair when describing **Parc National de la Gaspésie** (☎418-763-7494; www.sepaq.com/pq/gas; adult/child $8.50/free; ⏱year-round; P) , which has a raw, rugged beauty all its own, one as rooted in oceanic proximity (even in the Gaspé's interior) as mountainous soul. There are 802 sq km of spectacular scenery here, all dotted with lakes and two of Québec's most beautiful mountain ranges, the Chic Choc and McGerrigle, which together include 25 of the province's 40 highest summits. Some of Québec's most scenic camping spots can be found in the park, as well as 140km of hiking tracks, including one of the best sections of the International Appalachian Trail.

Be warned: even into May, there are trails here that will be inaccessible due to snowfall or ice. Welcome to Canada!

Activities

Québec's second-highest peak, **Mont Jacques Cartier** (1268m), is also its highest accessible summit. Hiking the mountain takes about 3½ hours return, passing through alpine scenery with fantastic views and a good chance of spying woodland caribou and moose.

Other fabulous walks include the strenuous trek to the top of **Mont Albert** (1151m) and the lesser-known, exhilarating half-day return trip up **Mont Xalibu** (1140m), with alpine scenery, mountain lakes and a waterfall on the way. **Mont Ernest Laforce** is good for moose, which also often feed at **Lac Paul** in the morning and evening.

The easiest walk in the park is a quick 1.7km round trip from the visitor center to **La Chute Ste-Anne**, an impressive waterfall. A longer waterfall trek that ascends through some stunning alpine scenery is the 7km hike to **La Chute du Diable**.

Sleeping

Park Campgrounds CAMPGROUND $
(tent & RV sites $24, huts/tents/cabins from $29/101/108; P) The park has four campgrounds. The busiest serviced grounds are near the Interpretation Center; try for a spot at the quietest – Lac Cascapédia. Two- to eight-person cabins, rustic huts and permanent tents are also available.

Gîte du Mont Albert INN $$
(☎418-763-2288, 866-727-2427; www.sepaq.com/pq/gma; r from $149; ⏱Jun-Oct & Jan-Mar;) This is a large, comfortable lodge next to the Interpretation Center for those who like their nature spliced with luxury. Facilities include a pool, sauna, first-class restaurant with mountain views through the floor-to-ceiling windows, and rooms with a surprisingly contemporary chic aesthetic.

Information

Interpretation Center (⏱8am-8pm daily Jul-Sep, reduced hours Oct-Jun;) Staff here are extraordinarily helpful in planning a schedule to match your time and budget. They also rent out hiking equipment.

Getting There & Away

A bus (round-trip adult/child $7.25/5.50) runs from the Ste Anne des Monts' Tourist Bureau to the **Interpretation Center**. It leaves at 8am daily from late June to the end of September, returning at 5pm.

Driving to Mont St Pierre from the Interpretation Center, taking Rte 299 and the coastal Rte 132, is faster, safer and more scenic than the tree-lined track through the park.

Mont St Pierre

The scenery on the Gaspé Peninsula becomes ever more spectacular east of Ste Anne des Monts. The North Shore, across the St Lawrence, disappears from view, and the road winds around rocky cliffs, every curve unveiling a stretch of mountains cascading to the sea.

Appearing after a dramatic bend in the road, Mont St Pierre takes its name from a 418m mountain with a cliff that's one of the continent's best spots for hang gliding and paragliding. At the end of July, the 10-day hang-gliding festival **Fête du Vol Libre** fills the sky with hundreds of sails. Near the eastern end of town and south of Camping Municipal, rough roads climb Mont St Pierre, where there are takeoff stations and excellent views. It takes about an hour to hoof it up the mountain.

Beneath the scree slopes of Mont St-Pierre, **Camping Municipal** (☎418-797-2250; www.mont-saint-pierre.ca; 103 Rte 2; campsites/RV sites $22/35; ⏰Jun-Sep; 🏊) 🍃 is a well-equipped campground that comes with laundry facilities, a pool and a tennis court.

East of Mont St Pierre

Here the land is all towering cliffs, pebbly beaches and telegraph poles protruding from mounds of scree. Next to the **lighthouse** (entry $2.50) at Ste-Madeleine de la Rivière Madeleine is a **museum** ($6 with lighthouse) about the local paper mill. Around the towering green valleys near **Grande Vallée**, there are more waves in the strata-lined cliff faces than in the bays on the other side of the road. **Petite Vallée** is a quaint waterfront village, particularly around the blue-and-white **Théâtre de Vieille Forge** (☎418-393-2222; 4 Rue de la Longue-Pointe, Petite Vallée), the venue for much of the **Festival en Chanson** (☎418-393-2592; http://festivalenchanson.com; Petite Vallée; ⏰late Jun-early Jul), one of Québec's most important folk-song festivals. Miniscule **St Yvon** is noteworthy for having been hit by a wayward torpedo in WWII. At **Cap-des-Rosiers**, the gateway to Forillon, the village's history of Irish, French and Channel Island settlers is described in the epitaphs in the clifftop **Cimetière des Ancêtres**. The **lighthouse** here is the highest in Canada.

Forillon National Park

The official land's end of the Gaspé Peninsula is simply gorgeous, and is encompassed by the boundaries of **Forillon National Park** (www.pc.gc.ca/forillon; adult/child $7.80/3.90; ⏰reception 9am-5pm Jun-Oct; P 👪) 🍃. Here you'll find treks that ascend into high tree lines over fields populated by porcupines and chipmunks, and views out to the ocean that would take your breath away, were it not for the winds blowing in some fresh sea air.

There are two main entrances with visitor centers where you can pick up maps: one at L'Anse au Griffon, east of Petite Rivière au Renard on Rte 132, and another on the south side of the park at Penouille.

Sights & Activities

The can't-miss trail here – and it is truly one of the great walks in the province – is the 8km round trip to **Land's End**. You'll cross an entire ecology textbook of biomes, from fields to forests to seaside cliffs, passing a fair few gorgeous coves scooped into the rocks along the way. At Cap-Gaspé, you'll find the terminus of the International Appalachian Trail, a solar powered lighthouse, and some of the freshest salt air this side of the Atlantic.

The north coast consists of steep limestone cliffs, some as high as 200m, and long pebble beaches, best seen at **Cap Bon Ami**. Keep a lookout through the telescope there for whales and seals, although if you're lucky, you'll spot them with your naked eye. In the **North Sector**, south of Cap-des-Rosiers, you'll find a great picnic area with a small, rocky beach.

The south coast (which includes the Land's End trail) features more beaches, some sandy, with small coves. **Penouille Beach** is said to have the warmest waters. The rare maritime ringlet butterfly flourishes in the salt marshes here, and the end of the curving peninsula is a prime sunset-watching spot. There's another wonderfully secluded beach at the bottom of the steps that lead away from the historic heritage site at **Grande-Grave**.

Parks Canada (p228) organizes activities (at least one a day in English), including a whale-watching cruise, sea kayaking, fishing and horseback riding.

CANADIAN APPALACHIAN

The 1034km Canadian segment of the 4574km **International Appalachian Trail** (IAT) was added to the American portion in 2001 and, though still not well known, it forced the 'International' prefix. Crossing the peaks and valleys of the Appalachian Mountains, one of the world's oldest chains, North America's longest continuous hiking trail stretches from Mt Springer, Georgia, USA, to Forillon National Park at the tip of the Gaspé Peninsula.

The Canadian section begins on the Maine/New Brunswick border, crosses New Brunswick, including the province's highest peak, Mt Carleton, and enters Québec at Matapédia. The 644km Québec part of the trail winds up the Matapédia Valley to Amqui, where it swings northeast for the highlight of this section, Parc National de la Gaspésie and the surrounding reserves. It then descends from the mountains to Mont St Pierre and follows the coast for 248km to its final destination, Cap Gaspé.

The trail is clearly marked and well maintained, apart from in the Matapédia Valley, and there are shelters and campgrounds along the way. Some portions should only be attempted by experienced hikers, and everyone should seek advice about matters such as black bears. More information and maps are available at tourist offices and park information offices in locations such as Matapédia, by calling ☎418-562-7885 and by visiting www.sia-iat.com.

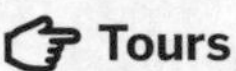

Tours

Cap Aventure KAYAKING
(☎877-792-5055; www.capaventure.net; 2052 Blvd Grande-Grève, Cap-aux-Os; half-day/full-day excursions from $75/130; ⏲May-early Oct) A lot of the most spectacular views within Forillon aren't visible from the land. You need to be at sea to see, as it were, some of the park's rawest juxtapositions of land and ocean – a good reason for organizing a kayaking tour through Cap Aventure.

Croisières Baie de Gaspé WHALE WATCHING
(Baleines Forillon; ☎418-892-5500; www.baleines-forillon.com; Quai de Grande-Grave; adult/child $75/40; ⏲Jun-early Oct;) Having a hard time spotting the whales from those Forillon cliffs? It's all good: on board the *Narval III*, you can get up close and personal with around seven different cetacean species.

Sleeping

Forillon Campgrounds CAMPGROUND $
(☎North America 877-737-3783, outside North America 519-826-5391; www.pccamping.ca; campsites from $25.50, tents from $100; ⏲Jun-Sep; P) The park contains over 350 campsites in three campgrounds, and it often fills to capacity. Petit-Gaspé is the most popular ground, as it is protected from sea breezes and has hot showers. Cap Bon Désir is the smallest, with 38 tent-only sites. Permanent basic tents with beds called 'Otentiks' can be found in and near Petit-Gaspé.

Auberge Internationale Forillon HOSTEL $
(☎877-892-5153; www.aubergeinternationaleforillon.com; 2095 Blvd Grande-Grève, Cap-aux-Os; dm/r $30/60; ⏲May-Nov; P) This hostel makes a great base for explorers, with friendly staff who dole out walking advice. The restaurant offers overpriced, average grub. The building can feel institutional, but the view across the bay is a redeeming feature. A *dépanneur* (convenience store) and bike and kayak rental are nearby.

Getting There & Around

Transportation is limited. **Orléans Express** (p229) buses between Rimouski and Gaspé stop in the park daily during the summer, at locations including Cap-des-Rosiers and Cap-aux-Os. A drawback is that this still leaves a walk along Rte 132 to the hiking trails and campgrounds, though the bus driver may drop passengers within the park.

Gaspé

The most scenic aspect of the peninsula's nominal capital is its view of Forillon, which can be spotted across the sweep of the Baie de Gaspé. This was where Jacques Cartier first landed in July 1534. After meeting the Iroquois of the region, he ignored their settlements, planted a wooden cross and claimed the land for the king of France. Today, Gaspé makes for a good refueling point; it's not as touristy as Percé, although it's not quite as picturesque either.

Sights

Musée de la Gaspésie MUSEUM

(☎418-368-1534; http://museedelagaspesie.ca/en; 80 Blvd Gaspé; adult/child $12.25/6; ⏰9am-5pm Jun-Oct, 10am-5pm Wed-Fri, 12:30-5pm Sat & Sun Nov-May; P ♿) Here you can get to grips with the peninsula's history, its maritime heritage evoked through artifacts such as a 17th-century hourglass. Most involving is the exhibition on Jacques Cartier, the former ship's boy who persuaded the French navy to back the voyages that laid the foundation for the European settlement of Québec. Outside, a bronze **monument** commemorates Cartier's landing.

Site d'Interpretation de la Culture Micmac de Gespeg MUSEUM

(☎418-368-7449; www.micmacgespeg.ca; 783 Blvd Pointe-Navarre; adult/student $11/8.50; ⏰9am-5pm Jun-Sep; P ♿) Northwest of town, next to the **Notre Dame des Douleurs** church, a Catholic pilgrimage site, is this center, which explains the culture and history of the local Mi'kmaq group through an exhibition, English- and French-language tours, a re-created village and workshops.

Sleeping & Eating

Auberge sous les Arbres INN $$

(☎418-360-0060; www.aubergesouslesarbres.com; 146 Rue de la Reine; r $120-140; P ❄ 📶) Book in advance to score a gilded room at this lovely old home, which has been converted into a stately country cottage-cum-inn. The interior decor has an early-20th-century summer-retreat vibe, while the central location gives guests easy access to town.

Bistro Bar Brise-Bise PUB FOOD $$

(☎418-368-1456; www.brisebise.ca; 135 Rue de la Reine; mains $12-28; ⏰11am-10pm, to late on show nights) Devour pizzas, burgers, mussels and fries, cod and lobster plucked fresh from the ocean while enjoying a nicely packed entertainment schedule here.

Getting There & Away

Daily Air Canada flights link the small **airport** (☎418-368-2104) 6.5km south of town with Îles de la Madeleine and Montréal via Québec City.

Orléans Express (p229) buses stop at **Motel Adams** (☎418-368-2244, 800-463-4242; http://moteladams.com/en) and link to the rest of the peninsula and beyond.

Percé

Gaspé's charms seem to lurk deep in its national parks rather than its towns, but then there's Percé and its famous Rocher Percé. One of Canada's best-known landmarks, the rock rears out of the sea near North America's largest migratory bird refuge, Île Bonaventure. Both sit in a patch of gulf that, from 1784, attracted schools of European cod fishers. Having stained a lobster bib, you can work off the fishy pounds with a hike in the hills, part of the Appalachians, that shelter the peninsula's most appealing town.

Sights & Activities

Rocher Percé LANDMARK

(Pierced Rock) This 88m-high, 475m-long chunk of multihued limestone has inspired descriptive entries in travel journals dating back to Samuel de Champlain's captain's log of 1603. The town's landmark attraction is only accessible from the mainland by cruise or boat. Île Bonaventure cruises always include a journey around the rock with commentary on its history and folklore.

Signs warning of falling rocks should be taken seriously: each year, some 150,000 tonnes of rock debris detach from the big rock. There used to be two holes in it, but one arch collapsed in 1845; in 2003, 100,000kg of debris fell at once.

Île Bonaventure ISLAND

Meeting the more than 100,000 gannets on green Île Bonaventure is an active antidote to gorging on Percé's tempting fish platters. Head toward the dock in Percé and you'll come across the tour operators' booths and touts selling tickets for cruises to the island. All of the boats circle Rocher Percé, get up close to the gannets on the side of the island, and then pull into the dock on Île Bonaventure's west side.

Hiking HIKING

Above town are some great hikes around southern Gaspé's most rugged, hilly area. Hike up the 3km path to **Mont Ste-Anne** (340m), beginning above the church, to enjoy the view and detour to **La Grotte** (the Cave). Another 3km trail leads to the **Great Crevasse**, a deep crevice in the mountain. The tourist office (p316) gives out a useful map.

Tours

Les Croisières Julien Cloutier BOATING
(☎418-782-5606, 877-782-2161; http://croisieres-julien-cloutier.com; 5 Rue du Quai; adult/child $30/14; ⊙May 15-Nov) One of the established tour companies that conducts excursions to Île Bonaventure and Rocher Percé. Also does whale-watching tours (adult/child $80/38).

Club Nautique de Percé WATER SPORTS
(☎418-782-5403; http://clubnautiqueperce.com/en; 199 Rte 132; sea kayaking to Rocher Percé/Île Bonaventure $55/85) Club Nautique de Percé offers kayak and scuba-diving tours and rentals; you can get PADI open water certified for $300.

Sleeping

Hôtel-Motel Rocher Percé B&B B&B $
(☎888-467-3723; www.hotelperce.com; 111 Rte 132 W; s/d from $59/75; P ❄ 📶) A decent breakfast and a homey vibe, plus local art decorating the walls, is what you get at this warm little bed and breakfast. The owner can point you in the direction of local hiking trails, and many rooms boast a good view of the rock.

Au Pic de l'Aurore CHALET $$
(☎418-782-2151, 866-882-2151; www.percechalet.com; 1 Rte 132 W; r $69-175, chalets $74-210; ⊙May-Oct; P ❄ @ 📶 🐾) Perched high on a cliff overlooking Percé, the sprawling grounds of the 'Peak of Dawn' offer something for everyone: chalets with or without kitchenettes, classy motel rooms and even a whole four-bedroom house to rent. Interiors have a cozy log-cabin feel with pine furniture, and there's a bar with outstanding views. Rates change by the week during high season.

Hôtel La Normandie HOTEL $$
(☎418-782-2112, 800-463-0820; www.normandie-perce.com; 221 Rte 132 W; r $99-249; ⊙May-Oct; P @ 📶) The classiest spot in town, the retreat-like Normandie has serious amenities: the beach, room balconies, a dining room for seafood and expansive lawns with panoramic views of the rock.

Gîte au Presbytère B&B $$
(☎418-782-5557, 866-782-5557; www.perce-gite.com; 47 Rue de l'Église; s/d incl breakfast $82/139; ⊙May-Oct; P @ 📶) With a well-tended garden by the massive church, this sizable, bright old rectory with gleaming hardwood floors is a nice option. Friendly and gracious host Michel is a wealth of local knowledge.

Eating & Drinking

Boulangerie Le Fournand CAFE $
(☎418-782-2211; www.boulangerielefournand.com; 194 Rte 132; snacks $4-13; ⊙7:30am-6:30pm May-Oct) For picnic breads, decent Italian coffee and mouthwatering French pastries and quiche, try this colorful bakery.

La Maison du Pêcheur SEAFOOD $$
(☎418-782-5331; 155 Pl du Quai; pizzas $13-23, set meals $18-50; ⊙11am-2:30pm & 5:30-9:30pm Jun-Oct; P 📶) In a former fishers' shack that became a commune in the 1960s (graffiti remains on the ceiling), this award-winning restaurant serves seafood, including lobster, and over a dozen types of pizza baked in a maple-wood-heated stove.

Restaurant La Maison Mathilde SEAFOOD $$$
(☎418-782-2349, 800-463-9700; www.auberge-lestroissoeurs.com; 77 Rte 132; set meals $24-49; ⊙7am-9pm; P) This cozy, down-to-earth spot serves up pretty stellar local seafood. This being the Gaspé, expect lots of flounder, cod and lobster, and expect it served after getting a rich treatment via melted butter and cream.

Pub Pit Caribou MICROBREWERY
(☎418-782-1444; www.pitcaribou.com/pub; 182 Rte 132 W; ⊙11am-1am) With its dark interior, dusty wooden walls and a cast of characters seemingly culled from a Hemingway novel, this is an excellent spot for trying one of the Gaspé's fabled microbrews, and on some nights, enjoying live music.

Information

Tourist Office (☎855-782-5448, 418-782-5448; 142 Rte 132; ⊙8am-9pm Jul & Aug, to 5pm Jun, Sep & Oct) Located in the middle of town.

Getting There & Away

Orléans Express (p229) buses stop at the tourist office en route to Gaspé ($14, 55 minutes, one daily), where you can transfer to Forillon National Park, and west to Rimouski ($77, eight hours, one daily).

New Carlisle

One of the main English towns on the peninsula, Loyalist-founded New Carlisle has New Brunswick–style clapboard houses and Protestant, Anglican and Presbyterian churches on grid-arranged streets. Incongruously, René Lévesque, that icon of Québécois Francophone identity politics, grew up here, at 16 Rue Mount Sorel.

The Palladian **Hamilton Manor** (☎418-752-6498; www.manoirhamilton.com; 115 Blvd Gérard Lévesque; tours $5; ⊙tours May-Dec) was built in 1852 by the town's first mayor. It's a wonderful portrait of colonial life – from the picture of Queen Victoria to the bread oven to the maids' attic quarters – and guest rooms are decked out in 19th-century decor. From Wednesday to Sunday between June and September, afternoon tea is served in porcelain cups and saucers. The *petit théâtre* screens classic films in the living room. Call ahead to arrange a tour.

Hamilton Manor (r incl breakfast $80; ⊙May-Dec; P ❄ @) also has lodgings. It's a little musty, but damn, this 19th-century hotel has character. It's not the best spot for fussy travelers, but if you don't mind the odd bit of tile grout, you'll love the quirky blend of history, chintzy decor and eccentric service.

If you need to grab a bite to eat while here, **Cafe Luna** (☎418-752-6693; 148 Blvd Gérard Lévesque; sandwiches $6-10; ⊙9am-9pm) feels like it was perfectly executed off some software program made to create the ultimate cute cafe. There's funky art, strong coffee, delicious panini, board games, tattered old books (even a few vintage Lonely Planets) and a general surfeit of bohemian bonhomie.

Bonaventure

Founded by Acadians in 1791, Bonaventure spreads out in skinny lines between Rte 132 and the water, eventually clustering into a very small town 'center' that's the nexus of local civic activity. The town is widely known as a major waypoint for the Acadians during their 'Great Upheaval,' and Acadian flags are a common sight throughout town.

Sights & Activities

Grotte de St Elzéar CAVE

(☎418-534-3905, 877-524-7688; https://lagrotte.ca; 136 Chemin Principal; adult/child $45/35; ⊙four tours daily 8am-3pm Jul & Aug; P) The almost 500,000-year-old Grotte de St Elzéar is one of Québec's oldest caves. You descend into the cool depths (bring warm clothes) and view the stalactites, stalagmites and moon milk (a mysterious, semi-liquid deposit found in caves). Book English tours in advance.

Musée Acadien MUSEUM

(☎418-534-4000; www.museeacadien.com; 95 Ave Port-Royal; adult/child $12/8; ⊙9am-5pm Jul-Oct, reduced hours Nov-Jun; P) The small Musée Acadien houses artistic interpretations of the Acadian plight, exile and eventual resettlement across North America. It hosts popular outdoor Acadian music concerts on Wednesday evenings during the summer.

Cime Aventure KAYAKING

(☎800-790-2463, 418-534-2333; www.cimeaventure.com; 200 Athanase-Arsenault; campsites/yurts/ecolodges/chalets from $33/115/159/300;) Dynamic Cime Aventure leads canoe/kayak trips lasting from 9km, or half a day (from $45), to three days ($665), with food and equipment, mostly on the scenic, tranquil Rivière Bonaventure. It also runs an excellent campground, with eight- or 12-person chalets, ecolodges reached by treetop walkways and a rustic resto-bar.

Eating

Boulangerie Artisanale La Pétrie CAFE $

(☎418-534-3445; www.boulangerieartisanalelapetrie.com; 128 Grand-Pré; mains $4-9; ⊙6am-6pm Mon-Fri, 7am-4:30pm Sat & Sun; P) This artsy cafe, bracketed by an enormous, colorful mural, serves up delicious hot sandwiches, slices of fluffy quiche and bowls of granola.

Café Acadien CAFE $$

(☎418-534-4276; http://cafeacadien.com; 168 Rue Beaubassin; mains $15-25; ⊙7:30am-9:30pm; P) Overlooking the marina, the boat-shed-like Café Acadien is great for breakfast crêpes and salmon, bacon and eggs. Bagels and Acadian, Cajun and Italian food are also on the menu. There are some small, colorful guest rooms upstairs (single/double including breakfast $70/80).

Information

Tourist Office (☎418-534-4014; 127 Ave de Louisbourg, off Rte 132; ⊙9am-noon & 1-4pm Mon-Fri Jun-Sep;) Has free wi-fi and computer access.

Carleton

A pleasant swath of mountainous coastline hugging the Baie-des-Chaleurs, Carleton-sur-Mer is much loved by Gaspésien day-trippers for its sandbars, bird-watching and walking trails.

Sights

From the quay, boats depart for fishing or sightseeing excursions. At the **bird observation tower** on the Banc de Carleton, beyond the marina, you can see herons, terns, plovers and other shorebirds along the sandbar. Walking paths and Rue de la Montagne climb to the blue, metal-roofed oratory on top of **Mont St-Joseph** (418-364-3723; www.montsaintjoseph.com; chapel tours adult/student $7/6; chapel 9am-7pm Jun-Aug, to 5pm Sep & Oct) (555m), which provides fine views over the bay to New Brunswick. You can also find stunning mosaics, stained-glass windows and art-deco marble finishes inside, plus an art gallery.

Sleeping & Eating

Camping de Carleton CAMPGROUND $
(418-364-3992; www.carletonsurmer.com; 319 Ave du Phare; campsites from $22; Jun-Sep; P) This campground occupies a spit of land between the Baie-des-Chaleurs and the calm inner bay, with access to kilometers of beach, which you can camp on.

Manoir Belle Plage HOTEL $$
(800-463-0780, 418-364-3388; www.manoirbelleplage.com; 474 Blvd Perron; r from $145; P) Modern rooms with luxurious linens await in this cheery hotel on the highway. There's an upscale restaurant on-site serving local specialties and a tasteful, whimsical nautical theme throughout the hotel – think strategically placed driftwood and marine poetry.

Brûlerie du Quai CAFE $
(418-364-6788; www.brulerieduquai.com; 200 Rte du Quai; coffees from $2; 7:30am-5pm) Locals flock to this lively roastery, store and coffee shop for out-of-this-world espresso drinks. There's a small patio overlooking the *quai* area, and you're welcome to bring lunch or picnic supplies – the nearby **La Mie Véritable** (418-364-6662; 578 Blvd Perron; baked goods $2-6; 7am-6pm; P) can help with that.

Le Marin d'Eau Douce SEAFOOD $$
(418-364-7602; www.marindeaudouce.com; 215 Rte du Quai; mains $16-30; noon-2pm & 5-10pm) An inviting dockside eatery right on the water that serves fresh seafood and other specialties using local ingredients. It has an upscale feel and friendly staff.

Restaurant La Seigneurie Hostellerie Baie Bleue QUÉBÉCOIS $$$
(418-364-3355; 482 Blvd Perron; mains $25-35; 7-11am Mon-Sat, to noon Sun, 6-9pm daily; P) If you're in need of some haute, locally sourced Gaspé goodness, look no further: here you'll find braised beef served with wild mushrooms and shrimp gnocchi cooked in goat's cheese sauce.

Drinking & Nightlife

Le Naufrageur MICROBREWERY
(418-364-5440; www.lenaufrageur.com; 586 Blvd Perron; 11am-midnight) With all due respect to the Irish, the St-Barnabé stout the folks at Naufrageur are putting out gives any black beer from the Emerald Isle a run for its money. Honestly, you can't go wrong with anything produced by the very talented staff at this microbrewery.

Information

Tourist Office (418-364-3544; 774 Blvd Perron; 8am-8pm Jun-Sep) In the Hôtel de Ville.

Getting There & Away

Orléans Express (p229) buses stop at 561 Blvd Perron; get tickets inside Restaurant Le Héron. Buses go to Rimouski ($56, three to four hours) and Gaspé ($37, four hours).

While there is a train station here, at the time of writing there was no regular service to Carleton.

Matapédia Valley

Driving through the Matapédia Valley, you'll get a taste of the terrain that challenges walkers on the International Appalachian Trail (p314). The trees covering the hillsides only stop for rivers, cliffs and lines of huge pylons charging through the wilderness. If it's raining, the mist-swathed pines look like they could have been plucked from a fantasy novel. The Rivière Matapédia, famous for its salmon fishing, attracted former US presidents Nixon and Carter.

Matapédia

The town of Matapédia is squaring up to Causapscal as a center for outdoor pursuits, with adventure companies such as **Nature-Aventure** (418-865-3554; www.matapediaaventure.com; Rue de l'Église, Matapédia; 2hr/4hr tour $45/65; mid-May–Sep) leading the charge.

It runs rugged paddles of varying difficulty along local rivers, including the Matapédia ('the accessible') and the Restigouche ('the magnificent'). Packages include two-hour tours, and excursions lasting one/two/three/four/five days ($95/270/340/480/600). It also rents canoes, wet suits and camping gear, and leads several different hiking excursions into the mountains. Camping can be arranged (sites from $20).

Causapscal

As its monolithic statue of 'the king of our rivers' suggests, Causapscal is crazy about salmon. The largest salmon caught here weighed over 16kg. Other outdoor activities on the town's doorstep include hiking, with trails meandering through the surrounding hills. The town itself has a beautiful stone church and many old houses with typical Québécois silver roofs, though odors from nearby sawmills sometimes spoil the picturesque scene.

Rivière Matapédia is the healthiest river for salmon; 13kg beauties are regularly netted there at the beginning of the season. There are covered bridges south of town and, in the center, a pedestrian-only **suspension bridge** across the Matapédia. Anglers go there to cast their lines where the Matapédia and Causapscal meet.

Head to **Matamajaw Historic Site** (☎418-756-5999; www.sitehistoriquematamajaw.com; 53 Rue St-Jacques; adult/child $8/free; ⌚9:30am-4:30pm Tue-Sun Jun-Sep) to see how the chaps in the old fishing club used to relax in wood-paneled luxury after a hard day on the river. On the other side of Rte 132 (which is Rue St-Jacques in town) is a **salmon pool**.

Appealingly old-fashioned **Auberge La Coulée Douce** (☎418-756-5720, 888-756-5270; www.lacouleedouce.com; 21 Rue Boudreau; r/chalet from $102/143; P❄📶) is perfect for fishers, and for those who simply want to sit in the comfortable dining room listening to ripping fishing yarns. The on-site restaurant is the best (well, OK, practically the only) spot in town for a home-cooked meal.

CGRMP (Corporation de Gestion des Rivières Matapédia et Patapédia; ☎418-756-6174; www.cgrmp.com; 1 Rue St-Jacques N; ⌚Jun-Sep) can arrange (expensive) fishing permits.

The **tourist office** (☎418-756-6048; www.causapscal.net; 5 Rue St-Jacques S; ⌚8am-8pm Jul & Aug) provides information on lodging, fishing and treks in the Matapédia Valley.

NORTH SHORE

As you drive (and drive, and drive) into the heart of the Côte Nord (North Shore), the feeling of frontier becomes ever more pronounced. At some point the patchwork of agriculture becomes endless kilometers of taiga, wide swaths of dark forest, tundra, and past that, the steel-gray St Lawrence, stretching to the Atlantic. There's just one way in and out – Rte 138 – evoking an eerie sense of isolation.

This enormous area comprises two regions: Manicouagan (stretching to Godbout) and Duplessis (east to the Labrador border). Statistics here are as overwhelming as the distances you have to drive to cross the areas. The two regions encompass an awesome 328,693 sq km (the size of New Zealand, Belgium and Switzerland combined). In this vast expanse live just over 100,000 hardy souls, mostly on the 1250km of coastline, making the area's population density just 0.3 persons per square kilometer.

Baie Comeau

This town owes its existence to Robert McCormick, former owner of the *Chicago Tribune*, who in 1936 decided to build a colossal pulp and paper factory here. This enterprise necessitated harnessing the hydroelectric power of the Manicouagan and Outardes Rivers, which in turn begat other hydro-dependent industries such as aluminum processing.

Today, it's the sort of industrial town that has decided things like locavore food and microbreweries should not merely be the province of places like Montréal, and as such, it's a pleasant enough place to stop for a day.

Sights

Baie Comeau is at the beginning of Rte 389, which runs north past the Manicouagan Reservoir, the fifth-largest meteorite crater in the world, to Labrador City and Wabush. Along the way is a fascinating landscape of lake-filled barrens, tundra and, about 120km north of the hydroelectric complex Manic Cinq, the Groulx Mountains, where the peaks reach as high as 1000m.

Sleeping & Eating

L'Hôtel Le Manoir HOTEL **$$**
(☎418-296-3391; www.manoirbc.com/en; 8 Ave Cabot; r from $140; P❄📶🏊) This hotel lives up to its name, at least externally – it looks like nothing less than a riverside château.

The interior is a little more modest, but the rooms are still comfortable and well-appointed for those who need some sleep.

Manoir du Café CAFE $
(418-294-6652; 5 Pl La Salle; mains $5-11; 7am-10pm Mon-Fri, from 7:30am Sat & Sun;) The spectrum of coffee here is pretty fantastic, and the staff brew it strong and tasty, served alongside a colorful menu of fresh sandwiches and homemade pizzas. All in all, an unexpectedly lovely spot for wi-fi and a filling meal.

Café Vieille France FRENCH $$$
(418-295-1234; 1050 Rue de Bretagne; set menu $26-38; 5:30-9:30pm) *Woah*. Where did this place come from? The exterior looks like a bomb shelter set across from a nondescript housing complex, but inside? Simply incredible French cuisine: rabbit draped in bacon cooked in local maple syrup, fresh cod in a rich butter sauce, and desserts to die for.

Drinking

Microbrasserie St-Pancrace MICROBREWERY
(418-296-0099; www.stpancrace.com; 55 Pl La Salle; 1pm-1am) Hey, if you're going to sink a beer in this town, let it be a local brew from this friendly little microbrewery. Also serves up some decent midrange pub grub for soaking up said suds.

Getting There & Away

A year-round **ferry** (877-562-6560; 14 Rte Maritime; per adult/child/car $19.70/12.15/48) makes the 2½-hour journey to Matane four times daily, providing the easternmost link to the South Shore. It's essential to make a reservation for vehicles, and advisable to reserve at least a day ahead for foot passengers.

Godbout

The principal activity in this sleepy village, which occupies a nicely dramatic bay, is the arrival of the ferry. If you feel like swimming, hit the beach below the Amérindien museum.

Musée Amérindien et Inuit (418-568-7306; 134 Rue Pascal Comeau; adult/child $5/2; 9am-10pm Jul-Sep; P) is more a gallery of Native American art and indigenous crafts – as you may guess from the name, there's a focus on Inuit objets d'art.

The **ferry** (877-562-6560; www.traversiers.com; 117 Rue Pascal Comeau; adult/child/car $19.70/12.15/48) links Godbout with Matane. Intercar (p228) bus services run to the ferry terminal, arriving around 6pm.

Pointe des Monts

This little promontory, buffeted by storms and sea breezes, marks the point where the coast veers north and the St Lawrence graduates from river to gulf.

Pointe des Monts Lighthouse (418-939-2400; http://pharedepointedesmonts.com; 1830 Chemin du Vieux Phare Casier; adult/child $6/free; 9am-5pm Jun-Sep; P) is a circa 1830 lighthouse, and one of Québec's oldest. It has lorded over dozens of shipwrecks, despite its function. Sitting on a picturesque spit of land, it has been converted into a museum explaining the lives of the keepers and their families.

Located next to the lighthouse, **Le Gîte du Phare de Pointe-des-Monts** (418-939-2332, 866-369-4083; www.pointe-des-monts.com; 1937 Chemin du Vieux Phare Casier; chalets per day/week from $88/580; May-Oct; P) is a collection of chalets and about the only accommodations game in town. The lodges are all comfortably decked out and boast nice views, and the host, Jean-Louis, is a treasure trove of local lore.

Baie Trinité

If you've developed a morbid interest in the St Lawrence's long history of shipwrecks, stop at **Centre National des Naufrages du St-Laurent** (National Shipwreck Center of the St Lawrence; 418-939-2231; 27 Rte 138; adult/child $8/6; 9am-6pm Jun-Sep; P), a small museum which is stuffed with relics plucked from the bed of the St Lawrence.

Sept Îles

Sept Îles feels a bit like the last city before civilization ends, which is not an entirely inaccurate impression, with all due respect to Havre St Pierre. So one would be forgiven for not expecting this frontier town to be as cool as it is. Of course, Sept Îles is one of the country's busiest ports, which helps explain why it's so refreshingly cosmopolitan. Exploring local museums, having a good meal and hitting up a neighborhood bar are perfect cures for the fatigue of long-distance driving.

Sights

Île Grande Basque ISLAND
(Jun-Sep) The largest island of the small archipelago off Sept Îles is a pretty spot to spend a day, walking on the 12km of trails or

picnicking on the coast. During the summer, Les Croisières du Capitaine runs regular 10-minute ferry crossings (adult/child from $25/15) between the island and Sept Îles port, as well as archipelago cruises. Tickets are available at the port, in the Parc du Vieux Quai (Old Docks).

Musée Régional de la Côte-Nord MUSEUM
(☎418-968-2070; http://museeregionalcotenord.ca/mrcn; 500 Blvd Laure; adult/child $7/free; ⏰10am-noon & 1-5pm Tue-Thu, 10am-5pm Fri, 1-5pm Sat & Sun; P ♿) This little museum tells the history of the North Shore and its 8000 years of human habitation through a mix of gadgets and artifacts such as 17th-century maps.

Le Vieux Poste HISTORIC SITE
(☎418-968-6237; http://vieuxposte.com; Blvd des Montagnais; adult/student $12/10; ⏰10am-6pm Tue-Sun, to 5pm Mon Jul & Aug) Seventeenth-century fur-trading post Le Vieux Poste has been reconstructed as a series of buildings showing the lifestyles of the hunters who called the forest home.

Musée Shaputuan MUSEUM
(☎418-962-4000; 290 Blvd des Montagnais; adult/child $5/free; ⏰8am-4:30pm Mon-Fri, 1-4pm Sat & Sun Jul & Aug, Mon-Fri Sep-Jun) This is the North Shore's best museum on aboriginal culture. The atmospheric circular exhibition hall, divided into four sections symbolizing the seasons, follows the Innu (Montagnais) people as they hunt caribou or navigate the treacherous spring rivers.

Tours

Les Croisières du Capitaine BOATING
(☎418-968-2173; http://lescroisieresducapitaine.com; Vieux Quai; adult/child from $25/15) Offers boat tours to Île Grande Basque.

Croisière Petit Pingouin BOATING
(☎418-968-9558; ⏰mid-Jun–mid-Sep) Does boat excursions to Île Grande Basque and leads various tours, including a three-hour razorbill-penguin-spotting excursion.

Sleeping & Eating

Le Tangon HOSTEL $
(☎418-962-8180; www.aubergeletangon.com; 555 Rue Cartier; dm/s/d $22/35/55; P @ 📶) The wooden balcony here is an uplifting sight after kilometers of Rte 138. Inside, this HI hostel has friendly faces in reception, power showers, small dorms and a homey lounge and kitchen.

Hôtel le Voyageur HOTEL $$
(☎418-962-2228; www.hotellevoyageur.com; 1415 Blvd Laure; r $99-231; P ❄ 📶) Cozy rooms with modern furniture betray the kitschy retro sign out front. Rooms are solidly midrange in quality, but that's the deal for most accommodations in this town.

Blanc Bistro QUÉBECOIS $$
(☎418-960-0960; http://blancbistro.ca; 14 Rue Père-Divet; mains $17-37; ⏰11:30am-2pm Tue-Fri, 5pm-1am Tue-Sat) With its deep crimson mood lighting, attractive, tattooed staff dressed up like lumberjacks, and open-kitchen plan, this spot feels like it's been plucked off St-Denis in Montréal. Braised duck thighs, fresh salmon and homemade sausages are some examples of the local produce, fish and fauna you might find parading across your plate.

Les Terrasses du Capitaine SEAFOOD $$$
(☎418-961-2535; 295 Ave Arnaud; set meals from $28; ⏰11am-1:30pm Mon-Fri, 4-9pm daily) Behind the fish market, this spot is famous across the North Coast as a spot for local seafood. It's unapologetically old school in decor and dining, and you won't walk away hungry after sampling the butter-soaked fish.

Drinking & Nightlife

Edgar Café Bar BAR
(☎418-968-6789; 490 Ave Arnaud; ⏰11am-midnight Tue-Fri, from 1pm Sat & Sun, from 4pm Mon) All the beauties flock to this bar for a deep beer selection and a decent sampling of spirits.

Information

Tourist Office (☎418-962-1238, 888-880-1238; www.tourismeseptiles.ca; 1401 Blvd Laure W; ⏰7:30am-9pm daily May-Sep, Mon-Fri Oct-Apr) On the highway west of town.

Getting There & Away

Sept Îles airport is 8km east of town; a taxi will cost about $12 to the center of town. **Air Labrador** (☎800-563-3042; www.airlabrador.com) serves the Lower North Shore, Labrador, Newfoundland, Québec City and Montréal.

The **Relais Nordik** (☎418-968-4707, 800-463-0680; www.relaisnordik.com) ferry travels to Île d'Anticosti and along the Lower North Shore (from Rimouski).

Intercar (☎418-627-9108; https://intercar.ca; 126 Rue Mgr Blanche) runs a daily bus to/from Baie Comeau ($41, four hours) and, Monday to Friday, another to/from Havre St Pierre ($40, 2¾ hours).

Mingan Archipelago National Park

Beyond Sept Îles, the landscape becomes primeval and sparse, with lichen-laced black bog stretching to a gray horizon, dotted by a few copses of wet pine trees huddled against the wind. The region's main attraction is **Mingan Archipelago National Park** (☎418-538-3331; www.pc.gc.ca/eng/pn-np/qc/mingan/index.aspx; adult/child $5.80/2.90; ⏲Jun-Sep; P) , a slice of Canadian wilderness wonderland that lies just past the reach of the mainland. You came a long way to get all the way here; now add a boat to your itinerary and engage in some North Coast island-hopping.

Sights & Activities

During the summer, tour companies operate out of the quays at Havre St Pierre and Longue-Pointe-de-Mingan, a small town that contains much of the administrative and tourism infrastructure for the archipelago. In general, the smaller the boat, the better the experience, but be aware of the weather, as rough seas will cause cancellations.

Cetacean Interpretation Center SCIENCE CENTER
(☎418-949-2845; www.rorqual.com; 378 Rue du Bord de la Mer, Longue-Pointe-de-Mingan; adult/child $8.50/4; ⏲9am-5:30pm Jun-Sep; P) Built by the researchers at Mingan Island Cetacean Study (MICS). It gives as much of an insight into the science of studying whales as it does the mysterious mammals themselves.

Research Day Trip OUTDOORS
(☎418-949-2845; www.rorqual.com; Rue du Bord de la Mer, Longue-Pointe-de-Mingan; per person incl equipment $140; ⏲Jun-Oct;) For a unique view of whales in their natural habitat, join a Mingan Island Cetacean Study scientist on a field-research day trip. During the roughly six-hour tour, you'll learn and practice the fieldwork techniques of marine biologists; this tour really hits the sweet spot between fun and educational. Boats depart the Mingan dock at 7:30am daily (weather permitting).

Sleeping

Camping CAMPGROUND $
(☎877-737-3783; https://reservation.pc.gc.ca/parkscanada; sites from $15.70, plus registration fee $5.80, permanent tents $120) Camping is allowed on some of the islands, but you must register at the Reception & Interpretation Center or the Havre St Pierre tourist information office. Mingan now offers permanent Otentik tent sites, which are good for families or those seeking a little more comfort.

Île aux Perroquets HERITAGE HOTEL $$$
(☎418-949-0005; www.ileauxperroquets.ca; s/d from $285/425; ⏲Jun-Sep;) Fancy a little historical heritage and quilted luxury during your visit to the Mingans? The lighthouse and lighthouse keeper's compound on Île aux Perroquets have been converted into a cozy, luxurious retreat. Rooms are decked out in art and crafts created on the North Shore, and packages include stays aimed at food lovers and bird-watchers. Transportation to the island is included.

Information

Reception & Interpretation Center (☎418-949-2126; 625 Du Centre St, Longue-Pointe-de-Mingan; ⏲8am-6:30pm mid-Jun–Aug) A clearing house of information on the park.

Getting There & Away

The park encompasses a huge swath of Hwy 138. Intercar runs buses between the park and Sept Îles or Havre St Pierre.

Croisières Anticosti (☎418-538-0911, 418-949-2095; www.croisieresanticosti.com; from $130; ⏲Jun-Sep) conducts the 50-minute crossing to Anticosti Island.

Havre St Pierre

This fishing town is worth a stop on the way northeast, mainly because it has the last garage for 124km.

The Havre St Pierre harbor is a nice spot to watch the boats come in; during the summer, dockside operators run tours out to the Mingan islands (around $65 for a three-hour tour). Be on the lookout for red, white and blue flags embellished with a gold star dotted around town – that's the symbol of the Acadians.

Auberge Boréale (☎418-538-3912; www.aubergeboreale.com; 1288 Rue Boréale; r $60; P) has nine cool, blue-and-white rooms and a pretty sea view. **Gîte Chez Françoise** (☎418-538-3778; www.gitechezfrancoise.qc.com; 1122 Rue Boréale; s/d from $68/95; P) is a friendly place that boasts artistically decorated rooms.

The **tourist information office** (☎418-538-2512; 1010 Promenade des Anciens; ⏲9am-9pm mid-Jun–mid-Sep) and **Variété Jomphe et Les Confections Minganie** (☎418-538-2035; 843 Rue de 'Escale; ⏲9am-4:30pm) are great hubs for information on tours.

Intercar (p228) buses pick up at 843 Rue de 'Escale daily at 5:30pm going to Sept Îles ($40, 2½ hours).

Île d'Anticosti

This 7943-sq-km island has only recently begun to unfold its beauty to a growing number of visitors. A French chocolate maker named Henri Menier (his empire became Nestlé) bought the island in 1895 to turn it into his own private hunting ground. With its thriving white-tailed deer and salmon populations, it has long been popular with hunters and fishers. Now wildlife reserves are attracting nature lovers to the heavily wooded, cliff-edged island with waterfalls, canyons, caves and rivers.

Though it's possible to reach and tour the island yourself, it requires much planning. Most visitors go with a small-group tour; **Sépaq** (www.sepaq.com) offers two- and seven-day packages with flights. It also offers shorter, half-day trips, if you arrive on the island on your own.

Sleeping

Auberge de la Pointe-Ouest CABIN $
(☎418-535-0335; www.anticosti.net/Auberge_Pointe_Ouest; r from $35) Kick back for a cozy night in these two lighthouse-keeper cabins, situated about 20km west of Port Menier. The owner can help arrange guided tours.

Information

Tourist Office (☎418-535-0250; www.ile-anticosti.com; 7 Chemin des Forestiers, Port Menier; ⊙Jun-Aug) Can help arrange accommodations and tours of Port Menier village.

Getting There & Around

Croisières Anticosti offers boat crossings from the mainland, as does **Relais Nordik**.

The island is also accessible by air, although flights are expensive. Contact the **tourist office** for more information.

One dirt road traverses the island. Visitors who come to Anticosti are almost always on package tours, so travel tends to be arranged beforehand. If you're traveling independently, you'll need to call ahead to organize transportation on the island; **Location Sauvageau** (☎866-728-8243, 418-535-0157; www.sauvageau.qc.ca; 5 Rue Panhard, Port Menier) can arrange 4WD rentals.

Natashquan

Wild, windswept and lonely, Natashquan is the end of the road. Well, OK, Kegashka, 50km east, is the actual end of Rte 138, but half the way out there is gravel track. What's here? A sweep of coast, some cottages huddled against the tundra breeze, damp taiga forest, scads of mist and views onto the stormy St Lawrence.

Sights

Les Galets HISTORIC SITE
Les Galets is a cluster of white huts with bright-red roofs, huddled together on a windblown peninsula; from a distance, they look like a textbook illustration for the concept of lonely isolation. Fishers used to salt and dry their catch here. Aside from enjoying the surrounding beaches, you can hike inland trails through isolated, peaceful woods full of waterfalls and lookouts and basically pick your nose with impunity. To get here, turn off Allée Les Galets off Rte 138.

Vieille École MUSEUM
(Old School; 24 Chemin d'En Haut; adult/child $5/2; ⊙10am-4pm Jul-Sep) This little one-room schoolhouse once educated Gilles Vigneault, the Natashquan native who would go on to become, effectively, Québec's national songwriter. Today, the schoolhouse has been converted into a museum that explores both Vigneault's songs and the history of Natashquan.

Sleeping & Eating

Auberge La Cache HOTEL $$
(☎418-726-3347; www.aubergelacache.ca; 183 Chemin d'En Haut; r from $150; P📶) This two-story inn offers clean, if slightly clinical rooms and dishes out a hearty breakfast.

John Débardeur CANADIAN $
(☎418-726-3333; 9 Rue du Pré; mains $8-13; ⊙11am-8pm; P) This convivial little diner dishes out stick-to-your-ribs fare – liver and onions, cod and rice and other meat-and-two-veg specialties that will keep you warm through those long North Shore nights.

Information

Tourist Information Office (☎418-726-3054; www.copactenatashquan.net; 24 Chemin d'En Haut; ⊙8:30am-5:30pm) Doubles as an interpretive center.

ÎLES DE LA MADELEINE

A salt-swept, gale-blown string of red-dirt islands crusted with fuzzy tufts of grass peppers the Gulf of St Lawrence, and they are a sight to behold. The Magdalen Islands, or Îles de la Madeleine, a stringy archipelago that resembles a Mandelbrot set on maps, are 105km north of Prince Edward Island. Between the islands' 350km of beach are iron-rich, red cliffs, molded by wind and sea into coves and caves just crying out to be explored by kayak.

As you circle above the crescent beaches on one of the tiny airplanes that fly here, you may wonder how anyone can traverse this windswept island chain; in fact, the six largest islands are connected by the 200km-long, classically named Rte 199. It takes a little over an hour to drive from one end of the archipelago to the other, assuming you don't stop to gawp at the views. Which you will.

Getting There & Away

AIR

The airport is on the northwest corner of Île du Havre aux Maisons. **Air Canada Express** (p228) offers daily flights from Montréal, Québec City and Gaspé; **Pascan** (☎888-313-8777; www.pascan.com) flies from the two cities and Bonaventure. In March 2016, former federal cabinet minister and journalist Jean Lapierre and six others, including his wife, sister and two brothers, were killed when their private plane crashed while approaching the islands. Since that tragedy, air traffic control officials have seemed particularly cautious with Îles de la Madeleine–bound flights, and delays and cancellations occur regularly when there is low visibility.

BOAT

The cheapest and most common arrival method is by ferry from Souris, Prince Edward Island, to Île du Cap aux Meules. **CTMA Ferries** (☎418-986-3278, 888-986-3278; www.ctma.ca; adult/child/bicycle/car $51.50/26/12.50/96) makes the five-hour cruise throughout the year. The large ferry, which can operate in most inclement weather, departs daily from July to early September; every day but Monday in May, June and September; and from October to April, around four times a week. In midsummer, reservations are strongly recommended if you're traveling by car (and are a safe bet even if you're on foot). There are discounts between mid-September and mid-June.

Between June and October, CTMA also operates a seven-day cruise from Montréal (one way/return from $434/1000), which stops in Chandler, on the Gaspé Peninsula. It's a great way of seeing the St Lawrence River, and you could always take your car ($305) and return by road.

Getting Around

Le Pédalier (☎418-986-2965; www.lepedalier.com; 545 Chemin Principale, Cap aux Meules; 1hr/4hr/1-week rental $6/18/85), in Cap aux Meules, rents bicycles. Hertz and local companies have airport car-rental outlets; book as far ahead as possible.

RéGÎM (☎877-521-0841, 418-986-6050; www.regim.info; in advance/on board $3/4; ⏲Mon-Fri) connects the islands via three bus routes, but it doesn't operate on weekends. Check the website for bus schedules and be at the bus stop five minutes before the scheduled arrival time; note that drivers do not carry change.

Île du Cap aux Meules

With more than half the archipelago's population, the islands' commercial center is quite developed compared with its neighbors. Nonetheless, it's still 100% Madelinot and, with its amenities, accommodations and lively nightlife – plus its central location – it makes an ideal base.

Sights

On the west side of the island, you can see the red cliffs in their glory. Their patterns of erosion can be glimpsed from the clifftop path between La Belle Anse and Fatima. Southwest, the lighthouse at **Cap du Phare** (Cap Hérissé) is a popular place to watch sunsets, and a cluster of bright boutiques and cafes overlooks a shipwreck at **Anse de l'Étang du Nord**. In the middle of the island, **Butte du Vent** offers views along the sandbanks running north and south.

Tours

Aerosport Carrefour d'Aventures KAYAKING
(☎418-986-6677; www.aerosport.ca; 1390 Chemin Lavernière, L'Étang-du-Nord; 3hr sea kayak tour $44; ⏲9am-6pm Jul-Sep) Young, enthusiastic thrill-seekers run this company, which offers kayak expeditions and cave visits that bring you face to face (well, paddle to water) with dramatic island scenery that is simply inaccessible from the shore. Wind-blown 'kite buggies' are also a blast.

MA Poirier BUS
(☎418-937-7067; 1027 Chemin du Grand-Ruisseau, Fatima; tours from $99) Runs several guided bus tours of the main sights throughout the islands.

Sleeping & Eating

Parc de Gros-Cap HOSTEL, CAMPGROUND $

(800-986-4505, 418-986-4505; www.parcdegroscap.ca; 74 Chemin du Camping, L'Étang-du-Nord; campsites from $24, dm/r from $34/72; Jun-Sep;) Situated on the Gros Cap peninsula overlooking a bay dotted with fishers in waders, this could be the HI network's most tranquil retreat. It has a communal atmosphere and is a good place to organize activities.

Pas Perdus INN $

(Not Lost; 418-986-5151; 169 Chemin Principal, Cap aux Meules; r from $75;) You can get a decent night's sleep in the bright bedrooms located just above the restaurant. We're not sure how thick the floors are, but even when it's buzzing downstairs, it's quiet upstairs.

Café d'Chez Nous CAFE $

(418-986-3939; 197 Chemin Principal, Cap aux Meules; mains $5-9; 7am-6pm Mon Fri, from 10am Sat & Sun;) As cute, bohemian and cozy a cafe as you please, this is a great spot for a strong coffee and a fresh croissant, or whatever other light sandwich, salad or baked good you so desire.

Pas Perdus FUSION $$

(418-986-5151; www.pasperdus.com; 169 Chemin Principal, Cap aux Meules; mains $15-28; 8am-11pm Jul-Sep;) Munching on a burger or lobster salad on the terrace at Pas Perdus, or in the red interior among curvy mirrors and thoughtfully curated local art, is a sure way to feel the islands' bohemian pulse.

Information

Main Tourist Office (877-624-4437, 418-986-2245; www.tourismeilesdelamadeleine.com; 128 Chemin Principal, Cap-aux-Meules; 7am-8pm Jul & Aug, 9am-5pm Jun & Sep, 9am-noon & 1-5pm Oct-May) A source of information about all the islands, located near the ferry terminal.

Getting There & Around

Cap aux Meules is the most centrally located of the islands, and provides easy access to both the airport and the **ferry terminal** (418-986-3278; www.traversierctma.ca; 70 Chemin du Débarcadère, Cap-aux-Meules).

Île du Havre Aubert

Heading south from Cap aux Meules to the archipelago's largest island, Rte 199 glides between dunes backed by the blue Atlantic and Baie-du-Havre-aux-Basques.

The liveliest area of Havre Aubert town is **La Grave**, which, with its small cottages, craft shops, beached boats and exterior laundry lines, perhaps exemplifies the rustic charm of a quintessential (or maybe clichéd) Madelinot fishing community. It takes about half an hour to drive a beautiful loop around the island via **Chemin du Bassin**.

Sights

Sandy Hook BEACH

(Plage de Havre-Aubert; accessible via Chemin du Sable, Havre Aubert;) This 12km stretch of windswept sand pretty much feels like the edge of the world (outside of a mid-August sand castle festival). Be careful swimming, as there are no lifeguards around.

Le Site d'Autrefois NOTABLE BUILDING

(418-937-5733; www.sitedautrefois.com; 3106 Chemin de la Montagne, Havre Aubert; adult/child $10/4; 9am-5pm Jun-Aug, 10am-4pm Sep;) Places like the Îles de la Madeleine tend to attract eccentric folks, and they don't get much more interesting than fisher Claude, who preserves Madelinot traditions through storytelling and singing at this model village.

Sleeping & Eating

Chez Denis à François INN $$

(418-937-2371; www.aubergechezdenis.ca; 404 Chemin d'en Haut, Havre Aubert; r incl breakfast $95-165;) This classic seaside retreat was built using lumber salvaged from a shipwreck. The spacious, Victorian-style rooms have ceiling fans, fridges, sofas and private bathrooms.

★**Vent du Large** QUÉBÉCOIS $$$

(514-919-9662; www.ventdularge.ca; 1009 Chemin de la Grave, Havre Aubert; tapas $6-16; 11am-11pm Mon-Fri, from 9am Sat & Sun;) Given the friendly owners who host frequent live-music nights, the free-flowing wine and beer, a terrace that overlooks the sea and a small-plates menu that jumps from scallops to seal sausage to fondue, it's hard not to fall in love with this place.

Shopping

Artisans du Sable ARTS & CRAFTS

(www.artisansdusable.com; 907 Rte 199, Havre Aubert; 10am-9pm) This gallery-shop sells chessboards, candlesticks and other souvenirs…all made of sand.

Information

Île du Havre Aubert is the southernmost island in the archipelago, and is about a 20-minute drive from Cap aux Meules.

Île du Havre aux Maisons

The home of the airport is one of the most populated islands but certainly doesn't feel it. The area to the east of Rte 199 is probably the most scenic, and is best seen from Chemin des Buttes, which winds between green hills and picture-perfect cottages.

A short climb from the car park on Chemin des Échoueries near Cap Alright, the cross-topped **Butte Ronde** has wonderful views of the lumpy coastline.

Sleeping

La Butte Ronde B&B **$$**
(☎866-969-2047, 418-969-2047; www.labutteronde.com; 70 Chemin des Buttes, Havre aux Maisons; r incl breakfast $100-165) With ticking clocks, classical music, beautiful rooms decorated with photos of Tuareg nomads, and a sea-facing conservatory, this grand home in a former schoolhouse has a calming, library-like air.

Domaine du Vieux Couvent HOTEL **$$$**
(☎418-969-2233; www.domaineduvieuxcouvent.com; 292 Rte 199, Havre aux Maisons; r incl breakfast $150-275; ⏲Mar-Dec, restaurant 5-9pm May-Dec; 🅿📶) Smack-dab in the middle of the archipelago, the Domaine is the swankiest digs in Îles de la Madeleine. Every room overlooks the ocean through a wall of windows, and the general level of service and elegance is a notch above the usual laid-back approach to life islanders tend to espouse.

Grosse Île

This island is home to most of the archipelago's English-speaking minority, their Newfoundland-like accents telling of their Celtic roots. The older Anglophone community long had an uneasy relationship with its Francophone neighbors; bar brawls and the like were not unheard of. Even today, many Anglophones cannot speak French, but intermarriage and bilingualism is becoming more common, and much of the tourism infrastructure on Grosse Île is run by Francophones.

Seacow Rd in Old Harry leads to the site where walrus were landed and slaughtered for their oil. Nearby, **St Peter's by the Sea**, built in 1916 using wood from shipwrecks, is bounded by graves of Clarkes and Clarks. The surname evolved as it was misspelt on formal documents.

Between Pointe de la Grosse Île and Old Harry, the wetlands of the 684-hectare East Point National Wildlife Reserve have the archipelago's most impressive beach, **Plage de la Grande Échouerie** (🐾) 🍃. The 10km sweep of pale sand extends northeast from Pointe Old Harry; there are car parks there and en route to Old Harry from East Cape.

The island is 40km north of Cap aux Meules, separated from the rest of the archipelago by a causeway buttressed by gently humping dunes.

Île de la Grande Entrée

Even by Madelinot standards, Grand Entry is a remote outpost, its homes seemingly outnumbered by the masts at the fishing port. This is quite literally the end of the road, which basically becomes the boat ramp that leads into the marina.

Sights

Seal Interpretation Center SCIENCE CENTER
(Centre d'Interprétation du Phoque; ☎418-985-2833; www.loup-marin.com; 377 Rte 199; adult/child $7.50/4; ⏲10am-6pm Jun-Sep, 10am-noon & 1-4pm Mon-Fri Oct-Dec) This museum delves into the biology and behavior of seals and explores their cultural significance to the islands, giving particular attention to the controversial act of seal clubbing.

Sleeping & Eating

La Salicorne CAMPGROUND **$**
(☎418-985-2833, 888-537-4537; www.salicorne.ca; 377 Rte 199; campsites from $22) This hotel/complex is a hive of activity, offering sea kayaking, windsurfing, caving, nature walks, archipelago tours, seafood tasting, fishers' storytelling and even mud baths. It has a campground and a ho-hum cafeteria (mains $13 to $25); the bedrooms are for multiday tour packages only.

Bistro Plongée Alpha SEAFOOD **$$**
(☎418-985-2422; 898 Rte 199; mains $10-24; ⏲11am-9pm Jul-Sep; 🅿📶) It's not every day you find a restaurant run by a guy who happens to be an Arctic and Antarctic diver/filmmaker, but hey, that's the Magdalen Islands. This seafood spot doles out lobster rolls, clam pizzas and hearty clam chowder.

FAR NORTH

This area truly represents the final frontier of Québec, where the province runs barren and eventually disappears into the depths of the Arctic Ocean. Here in the great Far North, remote villages, a strong Aboriginal presence and stunning geography entice those wanting to drop right off the tourist radar. The earth brims with valuable resources, such as silver, gold and copper, caribou run free and the waters teem with fish.

The North is an immense region, the most northerly sections of which are dotted with tiny Inuit and First Nations settlements accessible only by bush plane. The developed areas largely owe their existence to massive industrial operations – mining, forestry and hydroelectricity. While accessing the really far North (the Inuit communities in Nunavik) requires expensive flights, other areas of the Abitibi-Témiscamingue and James Bay regions can easily, with time, be reached by car and bus, and will provide a taste of Canada's true North.

Abitibi-Témiscamingue

The people barely outnumber the lakes in the over 65,140 sq km here. But despite the shortage of humans, this area occupies a special place in the Québécois imagination. The last area to be settled and developed on a major scale, it stands as a symbol of dreams and hardships.

The traditional land of the Algonquins, Abitibi-Témiscamingue is an amalgamation of two distinct areas, each named after different tribes. Témiscamingue, accessible via Northern Ontario or Rte 117 west from Val d'Or, sees few tourists. It's more diversified in its vegetation and landscape, with valleys and the grand Lac Témiscamingue. Most of Abitibi's slightly more visited terrain is flat, which makes the stunning valleys and cliffs of Parc d'Aiguebelle all the more striking.

This vast region of Québec retains an exotic air, partially due to its remoteness. Generally, visitors are seeking solitude in its parks or are en route to more epic northern destinations.

Réserve Faunique la Vérendrye

There's nothing better than breaking up kilometers of driving with a little bit of paddling, and in this vein, **Réserve Faunique la Vérendrye** (☎819-438-2017; www.sepaq.com/rf/lvy; Hwy 117; adult/child $8.50/free; ⏰May-Sep; P) 🍃, which encompasses a gorgeous series of lakes (4000 of them!), is practically perfect.

Camping, fishing, hunting and canoeing are the main attractions at the park. Even in a heat wave in midsummer, you may well have entire lakes virtually to yourself.

Camping sites (☎819-435-2331; www.sepaq.com/rf/lvy; campsites $21-47, chalets from $121) are peppered throughout the park.

The southern entryway to the park is via Hwy 117, at Km 276. **Southern Registration Center** (☎819-435-2216; Hwy 117, Lac Rapide; ⏰May-Sep) has more information.

Val d'Or

Born in 1933 around the Sigma gold mine, Val d'Or today looks like a mining boomtown of yesterday, with wide avenues and a main street (3e Ave) that retains its traditional rough edge – you can easily imagine how frenzied it would have been in the gold-rush days. The Sigma mine still operates, though it's no longer the city's economic engine.

Sights

Centre d'Exposition de Val-d'Or CULTURAL CENTRE
(☎819-825-0942; www.expovd.ca; 600 Rue 7e; ⏰1-7pm Mon & Tue, to 8:30pm Wed-Fri, 1-5pm Sat & Sun; P) Various traveling exhibits and works by local artists, some of them indigenous, can be found within this center. It's a good spot to visit, make conversation and get an idea of what's going on in Val d'Or.

La Cité de l'Or MUSEUM
(☎819-825-1274; www.citedelor.com; 90 Ave Perreault; audioguide tour adult/child $7/3, guided tour adult/child $25.25/12.25; ⏰tours 8:30am-5:30pm Jul & Aug, by appointment Sep-Jun; P) A restored gold mine has been converted into an interpretive historical site managed by La Cité de l'Or (The City of Gold). You get to don mining gear when you go underground – cool! Actually, it's more than cool – it can get downright chilly down there. You can also explore **Village Minier de Bourlamaque**, a restored mining village with 80 log houses.

Sleeping & Eating

Hôtel Forestel HOTEL $$
(☎819-825-5660; http://forestel.ca; 1001 3e Ave E; r from $135; P❄@🛜) With its big glass windows, smooth stone floors, industrial-design chic and geometric accents, this is a sleek and chic accommodations option out here in the hinterlands – and good value to boot.

Balthazar Café CAFE $
(☎819-874-3004; www.balthazarcafe.ca; 851 3e Ave; mains $6-12, buffets from $15; ⏰7am-5pm Mon-Fri, 10am-4pm Sat;) Equal parts cafe, bakery and deli, Balthazar does a line in delicious homemade sandwiches and hot and cold buffets and set meals that are excellent value for money. At the least, you'll be treated to a wide range of soups, salads and variations of delicious stuff on bread.

Microbrasserie Le Prospecteur PUB FOOD $$
(☎819-874-3377; www.microleprospecteur.ca; 585 3e Ave; mains $12-18; ⏰11am-3am Mon-Fri, from 4pm Sat) Duck poutine, elk burgers, bison sandwiches and quinoa salads all make an appearance alongside a nice hearty rack of home-brewed beers.

Information

Tourist Office (☎819-824-9646; http://tourismevaldor.com; 1070 3e Ave E; ⏰8:30am-6:30pm) On Hwy 117 at the eastern end of town.

Getting There & Away

Pascan (p324), **Air Canada Express** (p228) and **Air Creebec** (p228) all fly into Val d'Or from Montréal. **Autobus Maheux** (☎819-874-2200; www.autobusmaheux.qc.ca; 1420 4e Ave) buses go to Montréal ($106, seven hours, three times daily), Matagami ($66, 3½ hours, daily except Saturday) and Chibougamau via Senneterre ($90, six hours, daily).

Parc d'Aiguebelle

As the Abitibi landscape can be a tad on the dull side, the stunning scenery in **Parc d'Aiguebelle** (☎819-637-7322; www.sepaq.com/pq/aig; 12373 Rte d'Aiguebelle; adult/child $8.50/free; ⏰year-round; P) comes as a doubly pleasant surprise.

This lovely park is characterized by magnificent canyons and gorges, massive rocky cliffs with fascinating geological formations, and excellent, rugged hiking trails (some 60km worth) flanked by trees 200 years old. The small park (only 268 sq km) has two entrances – via Mont Brun (well marked on Hwy 117 west of Val d'Or; this is the closest to the suspended bridge) and Taschereau (south from Rte 111 between La Sarre and Amos).

Permanent Huttopia tents are available at the **campgrounds** (☎819-637-7322; www.sepaq.com/pq/aig; sites from $22, cabins from $124, Huttopia tents $100-120; ⏰Jun-Nov; P) from summer through fall.

James Bay

This area truly represents Québec's hinterland, where a seemingly endless forest of boreal spruces sprouts from the earth. On many evenings, the northern lights dye the sky a kaleidoscope of pinks and blues, which eventually give way to blazing orange sunsets. Only 42,000 people live here, in an area roughly the size of Germany. Almost half of them are Cree living on eight reserves separated by hundreds of kilometers.

The near mythic Rte de la Baie James ends at Radisson, a small village 1400km north of Montréal and 800km north of Amos. A 100km extension branches westward to Chisasibi, a Cree reserve near James Bay. This area is defined by the immense James Bay hydroelectric project, a series of hydroelectric stations that produces half of Québec's energy resources. Many visitors make the trek just to get a glimpse of these.

Matagami

After a lot of boreal forest, Matagami kind of pops out of nowhere and feels surprisingly busy. Since 1963, when the town was founded, it has been the site of a copper and zinc mine. It is also Québec's most northerly forestry center. Both of these industries are still going strong here, and shift workers are always coming and going. Plus, almost everyone driving through on Rte 109 on the way to Radisson stops here for the night.

Hôtel-Motel Matagami (☎819-739-2501, 877-739-2501; www.hotelmatagami.com; 99 Blvd Matagami; r from $107;) is considered the top place in town. It's decent enough and always seems to be crowded – mainly because of the restaurant (open 5am to 10pm).

Chisasibi

Near the point where Rivière La Grande meets James Bay, 100km west of Radisson, Chisasibi is a Cree village well worth visiting. The surrounding environment, windswept taiga doused by the arctic breezes from James Bay, is haunting.

The town as it looks now has existed only since 1981. Before this, the residents lived on the island of Fort George, 10km from town, where the Hudson's Bay Company had set up a fur-trading post in 1837. A vestige of the old-fashioned way of life survives in the many tipis seen in backyards, mainly used for smoking fish.

Contact **Cree Nation of Chisasibi** (819-855-3311, 819-855-2878; www.chisasibi.org; 9am-noon & 1-5pm Mon-Fri) for information on things to do and potential tours in and around Chisasibi.

Nunavik

This is Québec's northern limits, a land a tad smaller than France, yet only populated by around 13,000 people living in 14 villages. Hundreds of kilometers of tundra separate them from one another, and no roads join them. Almost 90% of the population is Inuit; the remainder includes Cree, Naskapis and white Québécois. This surreal territory stretches from the 55th to the 62nd parallel, bordered by Hudson Bay to the west, the Hudson Strait to the north and Ungava Bay and the Labrador border to the east.

Because Nunavik can only be accessed by plane, few casual tourists make the trip. Yet those willing to make their own local contacts can travel independently. Be prepared for high prices for goods and services. On average, food prices are close to double what they are in Québec City.

Getting There & Away

First Air (p228) provides service between Montréal and Kuujjuaq. **Air Inuit** (p228) flies the same route, as well as from Montréal to Puvirnituq. From there, flights go to other villages such as Whapmagoostui-Kuujjuarapik.

With **Air Creebec** (p228), you can go directly from Montréal to Whapmagoostui-Kuujjuarapik and Chisasibi. All of these flights will run over $1000; getting up here isn't cheap.

THE OUTAOUAIS

Across the river, after Hull, Québec, the Ottawa Valley becomes the Outaouais (pronounced as though you were saying 'Ottawa' with a French-Canadian accent). This large, mostly rural region extends from the Ottawa River north past Maniwaki, west past Fort Coulonge, and east to Montebello.

Gatineau

Gatineau is as much a twin city to Ottawa as it is a separate town. This urban continuation has more of an industrial feel than its Ontarian neighbor. In late 2001, 'Hull' was changed to 'Gatineau' as part of an administrative reshuffling, although the locals on both sides of the river still call the city by its old moniker. Gatineau is home to most of the area's French population, although you'll find Francophones on both sides of the river.

The most popular attraction on the Gatineau side of the river is the gorgeous **Canadian Museum of History** – an inspiring structure with rippling stone walls offering postcard-worthy views of the parade of parliament buildings.

Dining in Hull is largely influenced by French flavors; the city has two of the best and most acclaimed restaurants in the region, including **Le Baccara** (819-772-6210; Blvd du Casino; dinner mains $45-58; 5:30-9:30pm Wed, Thu & Sun, to 10:30pm Fri & Sat).

Information

The tourist office in Ottawa (p224) proper has heaps of information about the region.

Maison du Tourisme (819-778-2222; www.tourismeoutaouais.com; 103 Rue Laurier; 8:30am-6pm Mon-Sat Jun-Aug, 8:30am-4:30pm Mon-Fri, 10am-4pm Sat & Sun Sep-May) Situated in Gatineau just over the Alexandra Bridge.

Getting There & Away

The **Société de Transport de l'Outaouais** (819-773-2222; www.sto.ca; 111 Rue Jean-Proulx) has buses that operate along Rideau and Wellington Sts in Ottawa. From downtown, buses 8, 27 and 40 all go to the Promenade du Portage.

Gatineau Park

Gatineau Park is a deservedly popular 36,000-hectare area of woods and lakes in the Gatineau Hills of Québec. In summer, this green expanse of cedar and maple offers 150km of hiking trails and over 90km of cycling paths. Winters are just as crowded with dozens of alpine skiing hills. **Lac Lapêche**, **Lac Meech** and **Lac Philippe** have swimming beaches (including Lac Meech's nude gay beach), which lure the land-locked locals for a refreshing dip.

Also in the park is the **Mackenzie King Estate** (www.ncc-ccn.gc.ca/places-to-visit/mackenzie-king-estate; per car $10; 9am-7pm late May-Oct), the summer estate of a former Canadian prime minister. The **Fall Rhapsody** (819-827-2020; www.ncc-ccn.gc.ca/places-to-visit/gatineau-park/fall-rhapsody; early Oct) festival, celebrating the wonderful colors of fall, occurs in October.

Information

Gatineau Park Visitors Center (p215) Located 12km from Ottawa's Parliament Hill, off Hwy 5.

Nova Scotia

Includes ➡

Best Places to Eat

- Wild Caraway (p373)
- Le Caveau (p367)
- Black Spoon (p386)
- Lincoln Street Food (p353)
- 2 Doors Down (p342)
- Shanty Cafe (p359)

Best Places to Sleep

- Keltic Lodge at the Highlands (p382)
- Cabot Links (p378)
- Queen Anne Inn (p364)
- Roselawn Lodging (p366)
- Maple Inn (p371)
- Jumping Mouse Campground (p383)

Why Go?

If Nova Scotia were a film, its protagonists would be rugged yet kind-hearted, burnt by the wind and at one with the sea. It would be shot against a backdrop of rolling green fields and high sea-cliffs; its soundtrack would feature fiddles, drums and evocative piano scores; and its plot would be a spirited romp around themes of history, community and family.

Nova Scotia is the real deal. Its wild and wonderfully varied landscape is home to a diverse population of resourceful, hospitable folk, who love to sing and dance but who'd happily break you at dodgeball in a second.

Short-lived summers are a sheer delight, as the locals emerge from the cold to celebrate life: accommodations fill fast and prices hike. As difficult as the late spring and peak fall conditions are becoming to predict, these times afford spectacular scenery and a milder climate, while long, white winters are harsh but beautiful affairs.

When to Go

Halifax

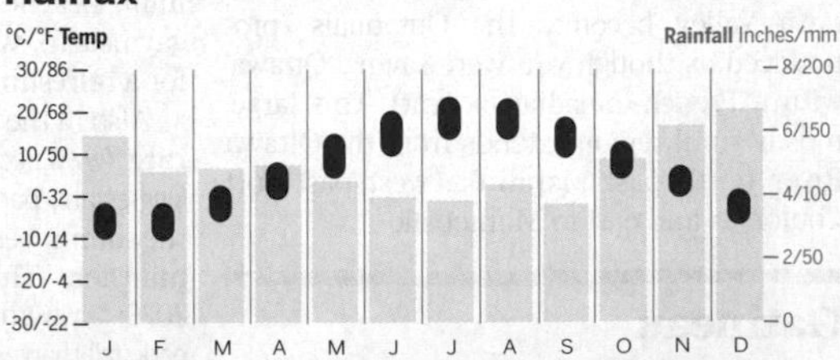

May & Jun Beat the summer price hike and feel like you have the province to yourself.

Jul & Aug Wildflowers bloom as temperatures and prices rise, while days go on forever.

Sep & Oct Locals make the most of stunning fall foliage before the long winter comes.

History

From time immemorial, the Mi'kmaq First Nation lived throughout present-day Nova Scotia. When the French established the first European settlement at Port Royal (today's Annapolis Royal) in 1605, Grand Chief Membertou offered them hospitality and became a frequent guest of Samuel de Champlain.

That close relationship with the French led to suspicions by the British after they gained control of Nova Scotia, and rewards were offered for Mi'kmaw scalps. Starting in 1755 most French-speaking Acadians were deported to Louisiana (where they became known as Cajuns) and elsewhere for refusing to swear allegiance to the British Crown.

Nova Scotia was repopulated by some 35,000 United Empire Loyalists retreating from the American Revolution, including a small number of African slaves owned by Loyalists and freed Black Loyalists. New England planters settled other communities and from 1773 waves of Highland Scots arrived.

Most Nova Scotians trace their ancestry to the British Isles, as a look at the lengthy 'Mac' and 'Mc' sections of the phone book easily confirms. Acadians who managed to return from Louisiana after 1764 found their lands in the Annapolis Valley occupied. They settled instead along the French Shore between Yarmouth and Digby, on Cape Breton Island around Chéticamp, and on Isle Madame. Today Acadians make up some 12% of the population, although not as many still identify French as their first language. African Nova Scotians make up about 5% of the population. Nova Scotia has close to 34,000 people of Aboriginal identity, of which around 22,000 are First Nations people, predominantly from 18 different Mi'kmaq communities.

Local Culture

With nearly 8000km of coastline, Nova Scotia has a culture that revolves around the sea. Historically, it has been a hard-working region of coal mines and fisheries. The current culture is still very blue-collar but, with the decline of the primary industries, many young Nova Scotians are forced to leave their province in search of work.

Perhaps because of the long winters and hard-working days, an enormous number of Nova Scotians play music. Family get-togethers, particularly Acadian and Scottish, consist of strumming, fiddling, foot-tapping and dancing.

FAST FACTS

- Population: 942,930
- Area: 55,284 sq km
- Capital: Halifax
- Quirky fact: Has the only tidal power plant in the western hemisphere

Getting There & Away

AIR

There are multiple flights daily between **Halifax Stanfield International Airport** (p346) and Toronto, Montréal, Ottawa, Saint John and Moncton, and less frequent flights to Boston and New York. In summer and fall there are direct flights to London and Iceland. Airlines covering these routes include Air Canada, Condor, Delta, Iceland Air, United and Westjet.

PAL Airlines (PB; ☎800-563-2800; www.palairlines.ca) can be useful for getting to Nova Scotia from regional locations in Quebec, New Brunswick and Newfoundland.

Air St-Pierre (PJ; ☎877-277-7765; www.airsaintpierre.com) also flies to the French territories of St Pierre and Miquelon from **Sydney JA Douglas McCurdy Airport** (YQY; ☎902-564-7720; www.sydneyairport.ca; 280 Silver Dart Way), which otherwise only services domestic routes.

BOAT

New Brunswick

Bay Ferries (☎877-762-7245; www.ferries.ca) operates boats from Digby to Saint John, NB (adult/child one-way from $36/20, from 2½ hours). Rates for vehicles start at $107 (including a fuel surcharge).

Newfoundland

Marine Atlantic (☎800-341-7981; www.marine-atlantic.ca) ferries ply the route between North Sydney and Port aux Basques, Newfoundland (adult/child one-way from $44/21, six to eight hours), year round. In summer, ferries also travel to Argentia (adult/child one-way from $116/65, 16 hours) on Newfoundland's east coast. Reservations are required for either trip.

Factor in an extra $114 to bring a standard-sized vehicle to Port aux Basques, and an extra $203 to Argentia.

Prince Edward Island

Bay Ferries cruises between Caribou, near Pictou, and Wood Islands on Prince Edward Island (PEI) up to nine times daily (adult/child from $19/free, 1¼ hours). A standard vehicle costs $81. No reservations are required, but it's wise to show up half an hour before departure.

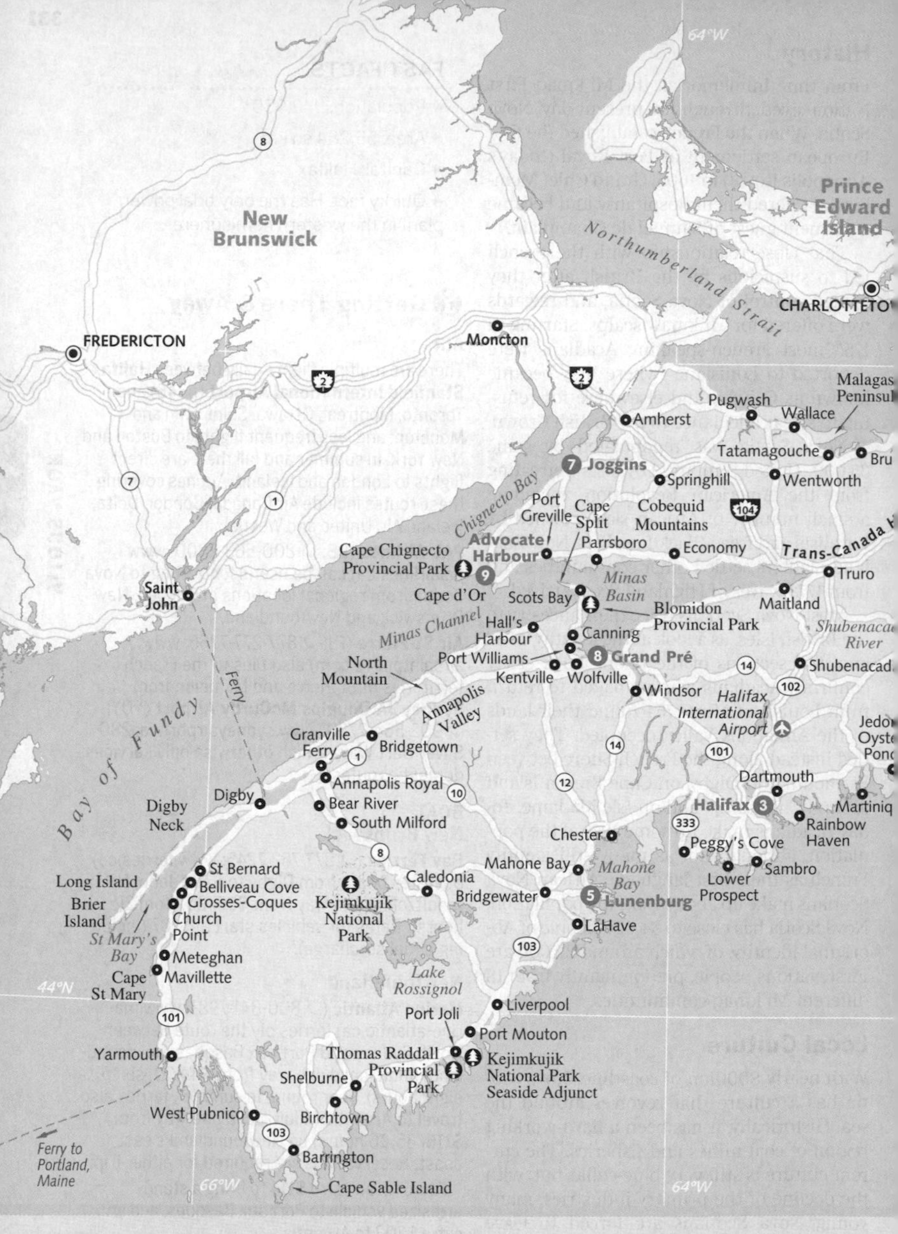

Nova Scotia Highlights

❶ **Cabot Trail** (p379) Driving Cape Breton Island's breathtaking twists and turns.

❷ **Louisbourg National Historic Site** (p388) Marveling at the province's long colonial history.

❸ **Canadian Museum of Immigration at Pier 21** (p335) Contemplating Canada's multicultural roots.

❹ **Memory Lane Heritage Village** (p388) Celebrating how a community has preserved its history at this re-created village in Lake Charlotte.

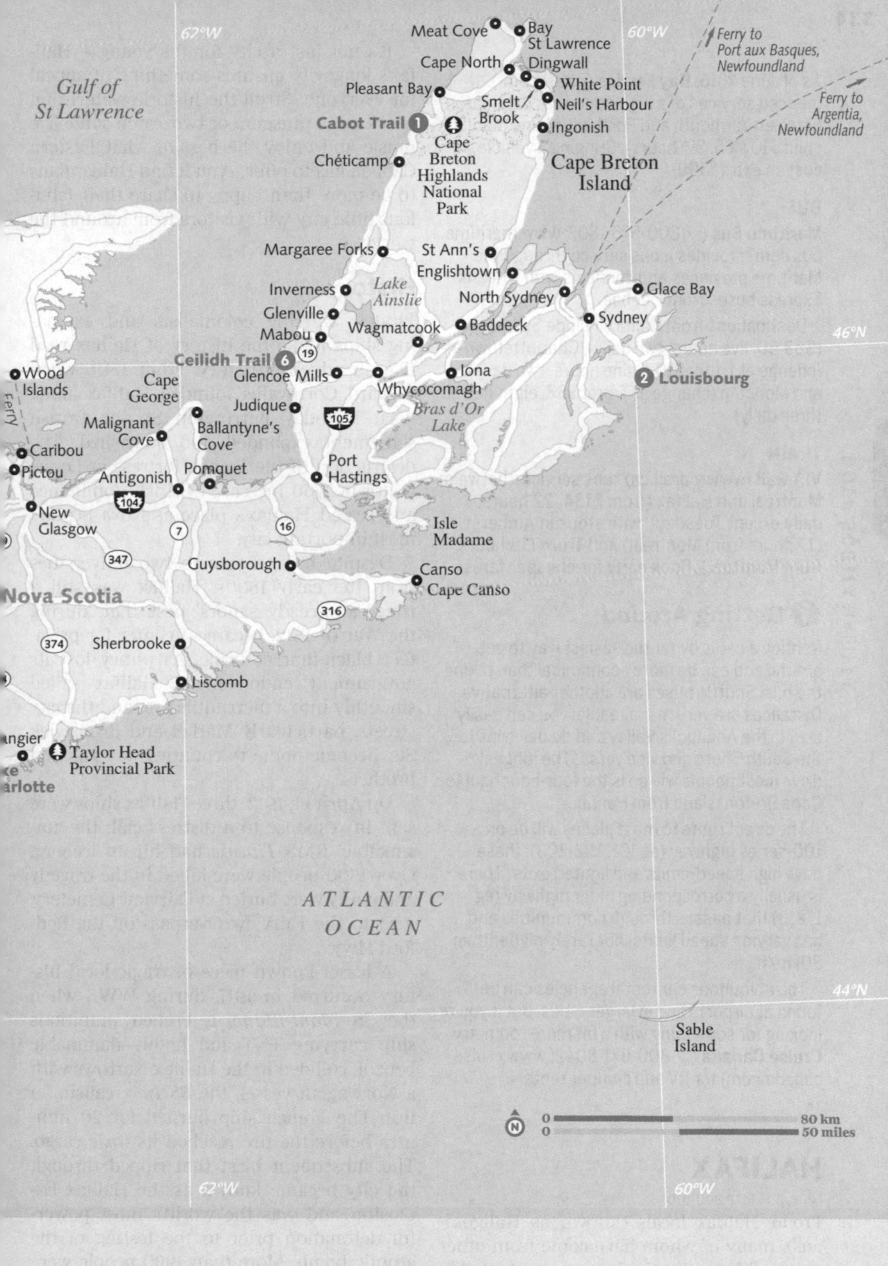

5 Ironworks Distillery (p351) Sampling a Bluenose Rum in World Heritage–listed Lunenburg.

6 Glenora Inn & Distillery (p377) Observing how a single malt is made at this distillery on the Ceilidh Trail.

7 Joggins Fossil Centre (p370) Contemplating evolution at these wondrous, well-preserved cliff faces.

8 Grand Pré National Historic Site (p365) Remembering the plight of the Acadians.

9 Cape d'Or Lighthouse (p372) Gawking at the view.

USA

As of June 2016, **Bay Ferries** (p331) commenced services of a high-speed car catamaran between Yarmouth and Portland, Maine (adult/child $107/65, 5½ hours). Bringing a vehicle will cost an extra $199.

BUS

Maritime Bus (☎800-575-1807; www.maritimebus.com) provides a bus service through the Maritime provinces and connects with Orleans Express buses from Québec.

Destinations from Halifax include Sydney ($63.50, five hours, two daily), Charlottetown (change at Truro; $103, nine hours, two daily) and Moncton (change at Truro; $83, eight hours, three daily).

TRAIN

VIA Rail (www.viarail.ca) runs services between Montréal and Halifax (from $134, 22 hours, daily except Tuesday), with stops in Amherst (17 hours from Montréal) and Truro (18 hours from Montréal). Book early for cheaper fares.

Getting Around

Renting a car is by far the easiest way to get around and can be more economical than taking the bus. Shuttle buses are another alternative. Distances are very manageable; you can easily stay in the Annapolis Valley and do day trips to the South Shore and vice versa. The longest drive most people will do is the four-hour haul to Cape Breton Island from Halifax.

The direct route to most places will be on a 100-series highway (eg 101, 102, 103); these have high speed-limits and limited exits. There is usually a corresponding older highway (eg 1, 2, 3) that passes through communities and has varying speed limits, but rarely higher than 80km/h.

The ubiquitous car rental agencies can be found at airports and in larger cities, but if you're looking for something with a bit more room, try **Cruise Canada** (☎800-671-8042; www.cruisecanada.com) for RV and camper rentals.

HALIFAX

☎902 / POP 390,100

Proud Halifax locals (known as Haligonians), many of whom have come from other parts of Nova Scotia, have a great quality of life: sea breezes keep the air clean; leafy, manicured parks and gardens nestle between heritage buildings; there's a thriving arts, theater and culinary scene; and the numerous pubs, with their craft-brew culture and love for bands, quite simply, go off.

It's not just a city for the young – Halifax's longevity ensures something of appeal for everyone. Stroll the historic waterfront, check out a museum or two, catch some live music and enjoy the best of what Eastern Canada has to offer – you'll find Haligonians to be more than happy to share their fabulous little city with visitors from around the world.

History

Pirates, warring colonialists and exploding ships make the history of Halifax read like an adventure story. From 1749, when Edward Cornwallis founded Halifax along what is today Barrington St, the British settlement expanded and flourished. The destruction of the French fortress at Louisbourg in 1760 increased British dominance and sealed Halifax's place as Nova Scotia's most important city.

Despite being home to two universities from the early 1800s, Halifax was still a rough-and-ready sailors' nest that, during the War of 1812, became a center for privateer black-market trade. As piracy lost its government endorsement, Halifax sailed smoothly into a mercantile era, and the city streets, particularly Market and Brunswick Sts, became home to countless taverns and brothels.

On April 14, 1912, three Halifax ships were sent in response to a distress call: the 'unsinkable' RMS *Titanic* had hit an iceberg. Over 1500 people were killed in the tragedy and many were buried at Fairview Cemetery, next to the Fairview Overpass on the Bedford Hwy.

A lesser-known piece of tragic local history occurred in 1917, during WWI, when the SS *Mont-Blanc,* a French munitions ship carrying TNT and highly flammable benzol, collided in the Halifax Narrows with a Norwegian vessel, the *SS Imo,* causing a fire. The French ship burned for 20 minutes before the fire reached its toxic cargo. The subsequent blast that ripped through the city became known as the Halifax Explosion and was the world's most powerful detonation prior to the testing of the atomic bomb. More than 1900 people were killed, and 9000 injured. The entire suburb of Richmond was leveled by the blast and First Nations Mi'kmaq communities along the shoreline were inundated by a resultant tsunami. The event remains the most significant disaster in Haligonian history.

Sights

Downtown

★Canadian Museum of Immigration at Pier 21 MUSEUM
(☎902-425-7770; www.pier21.ca; 1055 Marginal Rd; adult/child $11/7; ⏲9:30am-5:30pm May-Nov, reduced hours Dec-Apr) Pier 21 was to Canada what Ellis Island was to the USA. Between 1928 and 1971 over a million immigrants entered Canada here. Their stories and the historical context that led them to abandon their homelands form the basis of this brilliant museum, the compelling permanent exhibits of which include the recently renovated 'Pier 21 Story' and the new 'Canadian Immigration Story.' The collection, featuring firsthand testimonies and artifacts, is complemented by visiting exhibitions along related themes.

★Citadel Hill National Historic Site HISTORIC SITE
(☎902-426-5080; www.pc.gc.ca; 5425 Sackville St; adult/child $12/6; ⏲9am-5pm) Canada's most visited national historic site, the huge and arguably spooky Citadel is a star-shaped fort atop Halifax's central hill. Construction began in 1749 with the founding of Halifax; this version of the Citadel is the fourth, built from 1818 to 1861. Guided tours explain the fort's shape and history. The grounds inside the fort are open year-round, with free admission when the exhibits are closed.

From November to May, while the grounds remain open, visitor experience services are limited.

Art Gallery of Nova Scotia GALLERY
(☎902-424-5280; www.artgalleryofnovascotia.ca; 1723 Hollis St; adult/child $12/5, 5-9pm Thu free; ⏲10am-5pm Wed, Fri & Sat, to 9pm Thu, noon-5pm Sun) Don't miss the permanent, tear-jerking 'Maud Lewis Painted House' exhibit, which includes the tiny house (3m by 4m) that Lewis lived in most of her adult life. The main exhibit in the lower hall changes regularly, featuring anything from ancient art to the avant-garde. Free tours are given at 2pm Sunday year-round and daily during July and August.

Museum of Natural History MUSEUM
(☎902-424-7353; http://naturalhistory.novascotia.ca; 1747 Summer St; adult/child $6.30/5.25; ⏲9am-8pm Wed, to 5pm Thu-Tue mid-May–Oct, closed Mon Nov–mid-May; 👪) Daily summer programs introduce children to Gus the gopher tortoise and demonstrate the cooking of bugs. Exhibits on history and the natural world will keep parents engaged, too.

Halifax Public Gardens GARDENS
(www.halifaxpublicgardens.ca; 5665 Spring Garden Rd; ⏲sunrise-sunset) FREE Formally established in 1867 in celebration of Canada's Confederation, Halifax's delightful central public gardens are considered by many to be the finest Victorian city gardens in North America. Oldies bands perform off-key concerts in the gazebo on Sunday afternoons in summer, tai chi practitioners go through their paces, and anyone who brings checkers can play on outside tables.

St Paul's Church CHURCH
(☎902-429-2240; www.stpaulshalifax.org; 1749 Argyle St; ⏲9am-4pm Mon-Sat, Mass 10am Sun) The oldest surviving building in Halifax is also the oldest Protestant place of worship in Canada. Established in 1749 with the founding of Halifax, St Paul's Anglican Church once served parishioners from as far and wide as Newfoundland to Ontario. Drop in any time for a guided or self-directed tour of this fascinating building.

Alexander Keith's Nova Scotia Brewery BREWERY
(☎902-455-1474; www.keiths.ca; 1496 Lower Water St, Brewery Market; adult/child $26/12; ⏲11:30am-8pm Mon-Sat, to 6pm Sun) A tour of this brewery takes you to 19th-century Halifax via costumed thespians, quality brews and dark corridors. Finish your hour-long tour with a party in the basement pub, with beer on tap and ale-inspired yarns. Note that you'll need your ID. Kids are kept happy with lemonade. Multiple tours run daily from June to October, and from Friday to Sunday from November to May; check the website for tour times.

Maritime Museum of the Atlantic MUSEUM
(☎902-424-7490; http://maritimemuseum.novascotia.ca; 1675 Lower Water St; adult/child May-Oct $9.50/5, Nov-Apr $5/3; ⏲9:30am-5pm May-Oct, reduced hours Nov-Apr) Part of this popular waterfront museum used to be a chandlery, where all the gear needed to outfit a vessel was sold. You can smell the charred ropes, cured to protect them from saltwater. There's a range of permanent exhibits including displays on the RMS *Titanic* and the Halifax Explosion. Outside at the dock

Halifax

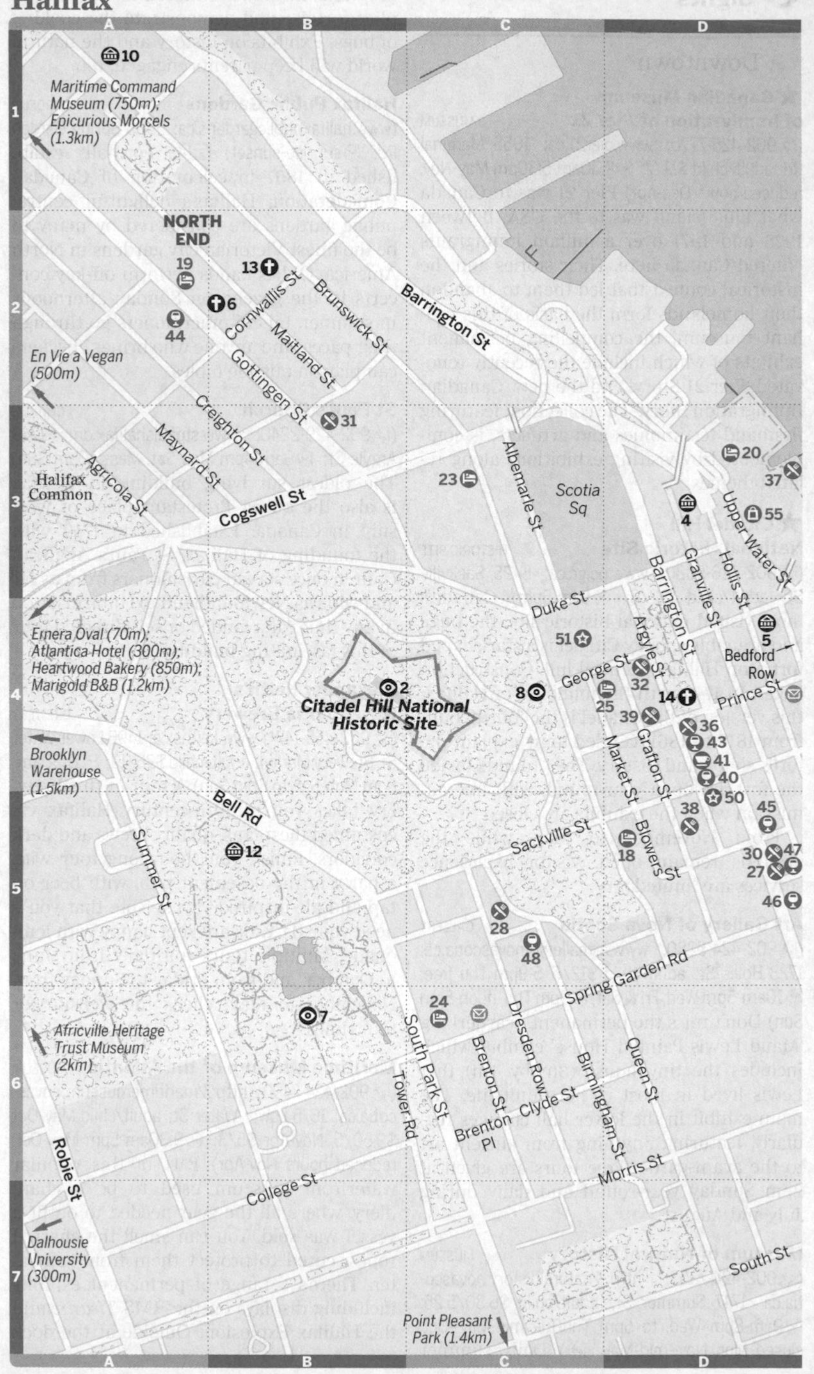

Maritime Command Museum (750m); Epicurious Morcels (1.3km)
NORTH END
En Vie a Vegan (500m)
Halifax Common
Emera Oval (70m); Atlantica Hotel (300m); Heartwood Bakery (850m); Marigold B&B (1.2km)
Brooklyn Warehouse (1.5km)
Africville Heritage Trust Museum (2km)
Dalhousie University (300m)
Point Pleasant Park (1.4km)
Citadel Hill National Historic Site
Scotia Sq
Bedford Row
Barrington St
Brunswick St
Cornwallis St
Maitland St
Gottingen St
Creighton St
Maynard St
Agricola St
Cogswell St
Albemarle St
Upper Water St
Hollis St
Granville St
Argyle St
Duke St
George St
Prince St
Market St
Grafton St
Blowers St
Sackville St
Bell Rd
Summer St
Spring Garden Rd
South Park St
Tower Rd
Brenton St
Brenton Pl
Dresden Row
Clyde St
Birmingham St
Queen St
Morris St
South St
College St
Robie St

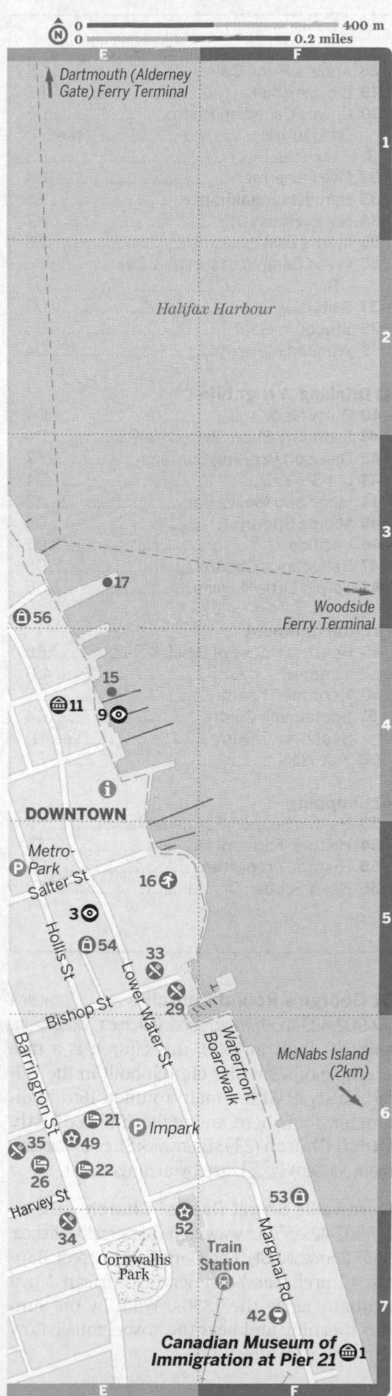

you can explore the CSS *Acadia,* a retired hydrographic vessel from England.

Canada's official Naval Memorial, the last WWII corvette, **HMCS Sackville** (☎902-429-2132; www.hmcssackville.ca; adult/child $3/2; ⏰10am-5pm Jun-Oct), is docked outside and staffed by the Canadian Navy.

Anna Leonowens Gallery GALLERY
(☎902-494-8223; http://alg.nscad.ca; 1891 Granville St; ⏰11am-5pm Tue-Fri, noon-4pm Sat) **FREE** Off the pedestrian area on Granville St, this gallery shows work by students and faculty of the Nova Scotia College of Art & Design. The gallery is named for the founder of the college, who was immortalized in *The King and I* for her relationship with the king of Siam.

Halifax Town Clock NOTABLE BUILDING
(Old Town Clock; Brunswick St) Atop Citadel Hill, Halifax's Palladian-styled town clock looks like it would be more at home in a Venetian lane, but has been faithfully keeping time here for over 200 years. The inner workings arrived in Halifax from London in 1803, after being ordered by Prince Edward, the Duke of Kent.

Fairview Lawn Cemetery HISTORIC SITE
(☎902-490-4883; 3720 Windsor St) When the RMS *Titanic* sank, the bodies not lost at sea were brought to Halifax. Among other sites, there are 19 graves at **Mt Olivet Catholic Cemetery** (7076 Mumford Rd) and 121 here at the Fairview Lawn Cemetery, including that of J Dawson, whose name was the basis for Leonardo DiCaprio's character in the film *Titanic*. Those with a keen eye will be able to locate the touching Celtic Cross and Unknown Child monuments.

North End

The North End has been a distinct neighborhood for almost as long as Halifax has existed. In the early 1750s the 'North Suburbs' area became popular and subsequently grew thanks to its larger building lots.

Africville Heritage Trust Museum MUSEUM
(www.africvillemuseum.org; 5795 Africville Rd; adult/child $4/2.30; ⏰10am-4pm Tue-Sun Jun-Aug, 10am-4pm Tue-Fri Sep-May) Learn the story of Africville, Halifax's predominantly African suburb, the residents of which were evicted and their homes razed in what became the local scandal of the 1960s. In 2010 Halifax's mayor issued a formal apology to the community. Poignantly, the museum is

Halifax

Top Sights

1 Canadian Museum of Immigration at Pier 21 .... F7
2 Citadel Hill National Historic Site B4

Sights

3 Alexander Keith's Nova Scotia Brewery E5
4 Anna Leonowens Gallery D3
5 Art Gallery of Nova Scotia D4
6 Cornwallis Street Baptist Church B2
7 Halifax Public Gardens B6
8 Halifax Town Clock C4
9 HMCS Sackville E4
10 Little Dutch Church A1
11 Maritime Museum of the Atlantic E4
12 Museum of Natural History B5
13 St George's Round Church B2
14 St Paul's Church D4

Activities, Courses & Tours

15 Bluenose II E4
16 I Heart Bikes E5
17 Murphy's the Cable Wharf E3
Tall Ship Silva .... (see 17)
Tattle Tours .... (see 8)

Sleeping

18 Cambridge Suites Halifax D5
19 Halifax Backpackers Hostel A2
20 Halifax Marriott Harbourfront D3
21 Halliburton E6
22 HI Nova Scotia E6
23 Homewood Suites by Hilton Halifax-Downtown C3
24 Lord Nelson Hotel & Suites C6
25 Prince George Hotel D4
26 Waverley Inn E6

Eating

27 2 Doors Down D5
28 Annie's Place Cafe C5
29 Bicycle Thief E5
30 Chives Canadian Bistro D5
Da Maurizio .... (see 54)
31 Edna B3
32 Five Fishermen D4
33 Hamachi Steakhouse E5
34 Henry House E7
35 Morris East E6
36 Press Gang Restaurant & Oyster Bar D4
37 Salty's D3
38 Stubborn Goat D5
39 Wooden Monkey D4

Drinking & Nightlife

40 Durty Nelly's D4
41 Economy Shoe Shop Cafe Bar D4
42 Garrison Brewing Company F7
43 Lot Six D4
44 Menz and Mollyz Bar A2
45 Middle Spoon D5
46 Pacifico D5
47 Reflections Cabaret D5
48 Tom's Little Havana C5

Entertainment

49 Bearly's House of Blues & Ribs E6
Carleton .... (see 43)
50 Neptune Theatre D5
51 Scotiabank Centre C4
Seahorse Tavern .... (see 41)
52 Yuk Yuks E7

Shopping

53 Halifax Seaport Farmers Market F6
54 Historic Farmers Market E5
55 Historic Properties D3
56 Nova Scotian Crystal E3

housed in a replica of the Seaview United Baptist Church that was once the center of the community.

Maritime Command Museum MUSEUM
(☎ 902-721-8250; www.psphalifax.ca/marcommuseum; 2725 Gottingen St; ⏲ 9am-3:30pm Mon-Fri) **FREE** The admiral of the British navy for all of North America was based in Halifax until 1819 and threw grand parties at Admiralty House, now the Maritime Command Museum. Apart from the beautiful Georgian architecture, the museum is worth a visit for its eclectic collections, including cigarette lighters, silverware and ship's bells, to name but a few.

St George's Round Church CHURCH
(☎ 902-423-1059; www.roundchurch.ca; 2222 Brunswick St) Built in 1800, this church is a rare example of a circular church built in the Palladian style, with a main rotunda 18m in diameter. Tours here, and of the affiliated **Little Dutch Church** (2393 Brunswick St; ⏲ by appointment Jul-Sep) **FREE**, are by arrangement.

Cornwallis Street Baptist Church CHURCH
(☎ 902-429-5573; www.cornwallisstreetbaptist.ca; 5457 Cornwallis St) The Cornwallis Street Baptist Church has been serving African Nova Scotians since the 1830s. Walk by on Sunday morning and hear the gospel music flow through its walls.

Outside the Centre

Crystal Crescent Beach Provincial Park STATE PARK

(http://parks.novascotia.ca/content/crystal-crescent-beach; 223 Sambro Creek Rd) Eighteen kilometers south of Halifax, near the village of Sambro, this gorgeous provincial park boasts three distinct beaches in separate coves; the third one out, toward the southwest, is clothing-optional and gay-friendly. An 8.5km **hiking trail** begins just inland and heads through barrens, bogs and boulders to **Pennant Point**.

Activities

Cycling is a great way to see sites on the outskirts of Halifax. You can take bikes on the ferries to Dartmouth or cycle over the MacDonald Bridge. In summer, there's usually a few outfitters renting out bikes along the waterfront around Bishop's Landing (at the end of Bishop St).

There are short and long hikes surprisingly close to downtown. **Hemlock Ravine** is an 80-hectare wooded area that has five trails, suitable for all levels. To get there, take the Bedford Hwy from central Halifax then turn left at Kent Ave; there's parking and a map of the trail at the end of this road. See www.novatrails.com for more detailed trail descriptions and directions to other trailheads.

McNabs Island HIKING

(www.mcnabsisland.ca) Fine sand and cobblestone shorelines, salt marshes, forests and abandoned military fortifications paint the landscape of this 400-hectare island in Halifax Harbour, where with a little imagination you could transport yourself back in time. Refer to the website for information on the various ways to get here, what to do (and what not to do) when here, and for a downloadable map.

Point Pleasant Park HIKING

(902-490-4700; 5718 Point Pleasant Dr; sunrise-sunset; 9) Some 39km of nature trails, picnic spots and a beautiful 18th-century **Martello Tower** are all found within this 75-hectare sanctuary, just 1.5km south of the city center. Trails around the perimeter of the park offer views of McNabs Island, the open ocean and the North West Arm.

I Heart Bikes CYCLING

(902-406-7774; www.iheartbikeshfx.com; 1507 Lower Water St; rentals per hour from $12) If you prefer two wheels to two legs, you'll heart these folks, too. Centrally located near the Halifax Waterfront, it's a great spot to pick up a chariot and start pedaling. Both rentals and cycling tours are available.

LOCAL KNOWLEDGE

FREE SKATING ON THE COMMON

Emera Oval (902-490-2347; www.halifax.ca/SkateHRM; 5775 Cogswell St; 7am-7pm) FREE on the Halifax Common serves as a speed-skating rink in winter and morphs into an in-line skating rink in summer. Skates, helmets and sledges (for use on the outside lane only) are free to borrow and there are even free lessons. Check the website and bring a valid photo ID.

Tours

Halifax Free Tours WALKING

(www.halifaxfreetours.wixsite.com/halifaxfreetours; 10am & 3pm Jun-Sep) FREE You can't beat the price of these free 1½-hour walking tours of downtown Halifax, led by friendly local guides. Send an email to reserve a spot and please remember to tip!

Adventure Canada ECOTOUR

(905-271-4000; www.adventurecanada.com) This provider of group eco- and adventure tours is one of the few companies permitted to operate on Sable Island (p340), with its population of wild horses and the world's largest breeding colony of grey seals.

Murphy's the Cable Wharf CRUISE

(902-420-1015; www.mtcw.ca; 1751 Lower Water St) This tourism giant runs a range of tours on Halifax Harbour, from deep-sea fishing and two-hour scenic cruises to the crowd-pleasing 55-minute Harbour Hopper Tours (adult/child $35/20) on an amphibious bus, and Theodore the Tugboat's Big Harbour Adventure tours ($20/10), wildly popular with youngsters.

Pedal & Sea Adventures CYCLING

(877-777-5699; www.pedalandseaadventures.com; bicycle rental per day/week from $35/149) Offers unique, all-inclusive cycling tours in Nova Scotia, as well as quality bike rentals, where they'll deliver the bike to you (for two-day rentals or longer), complete with helmet, lock and repair kit.

OFF THE BEATEN TRACK

SABLE ISLAND

This ever-shifting, 44km-long spit of sand lies some 300km southeast of Halifax and has caused more than 350 documented shipwrecks. But what makes Sable Island most famous is that it's home to one of the world's only truly wild horse populations, as well as the planet's largest breeding colony of grey seals.

The first 60 ancestors of today's Sable Island horses were shipped to the island in 1760 when Acadians were being deported from Nova Scotia by the British. The Acadians were forced to abandon their livestock and it appears that Boston merchant ship owner Thomas Hancock helped himself to their horses – then put them to pasture on Sable Island to keep it low-profile. The horses that survived became wild.

Today the island works as a research center: scientists come every year to study the horses and other wildlife, and to keep an eye on any impact from their neighbor, the ExxonMobil Sable Offshore Energy Project. Just 10km away, this site has been harvesting natural gas since 1999, although decommissioning plans are currently underway.

It's complicated and expensive – but not impossible – to visit Sable Island as a layperson; about 50 to 100 adventurous souls make it to the island each year. Contact **Sable Island Station** (902-426-1993; www.pc.gc.ca), in conjunction with Environment Canada, for information about how to get the necessary permissions and to independently arrange transport. Otherwise, Adventure Canada (p339) operates group tours.

Tall Ship Silva BOATING
(902-420-1015; www.tallshipsilva.com; 1751 Lower Water St; cruises adult/child $30/19) Lend a hand or sit back and relax while taking a 1½-hour daytime cruise or a two-hour evening party cruise on Halifax's square-masted tall ship. Check the website for sailing times.

Bluenose Sidecar Tours DRIVING
(902-579-7433; www.bluenosesidecartours.com; tours from $89) Enjoy free and breezy views from fun, old-school motorcycle sidecars on tours around Halifax or to Peggy's Cove, Lunenburg and the South Shore.

Bluenose II BOATING
(800-763-1963; www.bluenose.novascotia.ca; Lower Water St; 2hr cruises adult/child $20/10) This classic replica of the *Bluenose* racing schooner is sometimes in Halifax and sometimes in Lunenburg. Check the website for details.

Great Earth Expeditions ECOTOUR
(902-223-2409; www.greatearthexpeditions.com; tours from $90) Half- and full-day ecotours led from Halifax can include hiking, kayaking or historical themes, including a tour to McNabs Island in Halifax Harbour. Also offers longer four-day tours up the Cabot Trail (p379) and through Kejimkujik National Park (p354).

Local Tasting Tours FOOD & DRINK
(902-818-9055; www.localtastingtours.com; tours from $40) Eat your way around Halifax's burgeoning restaurant scene on these fun, foodie-themed tours, featuring up to six local restaurants per tour.

Tattle Tours WALKING
(902-494-0525; www.tattletours.ca; 7:30pm Wed-Sun) Lively two-hour tours depart from the Old Town Clock and are filled with local gossip, pirate tales and ghost stories. Walking tours are also available on demand. Rates vary depending on the number in your party.

East Coast Balloon Adventures BALLOONING
(902-306-0095; www.eastcoastballoonadventures.com; 45min flights $275) Float from Halifax over the patchwork fields of Annapolis Valley at sunrise or sunset for the ultimate, peaceful views of this stunning province. Minimum age for children is eight.

Festivals & Events

Halifax Pride Week LGBT
(www.halifaxpride.com; Jul) The largest LGBTI Pride festival east of Montreal paints the town pink and every other shade of the rainbow, with its massive grab-bag of fun, inclusive events and performances.

Nova Scotia Tattoo CULTURAL
(www.nstattoo.ca; tickets from $32; Jul) The world's 'largest annual indoor show' is a military-style event with lots of marching bands.

TD Halifax Jazz Festival MUSIC
(www.halifaxjazzfestival.ca; tickets from $28; Jul) Now in its fourth decade, Halifax's well-loved jazz festival boasts free outdoor jazz

concerts and evening performances ranging from world music to classic jazz trios.

Halifax International Busker Festival PERFORMING ARTS

(www.buskers.ca; ⏲ Aug) The oldest and largest festival of its kind in Canada draws comics, mimes, daredevils and musicians from around the world to the Halifax waterfront.

Atlantic Film Festival FILM

(www.atlanticfilm.com; tickets $10-16; ⏲ Sep) A week of great flicks from the Atlantic region and around the world.

Atlantic Fringe Festival THEATER

(www.atlanticfringe.ca; ⏲ Sep) The theater comes to town for ten days in September, showcasing offbeat and experimental works by emerging and established artists.

Halifax Pop Explosion MUSIC

(www.halifaxpopexplosion.com; day passes from $59; ⏲ Oct) Around 150 artists from genres as diverse as hip-hop, punk, indie rock and folk perform in 15 venues over a four-day period.

Sleeping

Marigold B&B B&B $

(☎902-423-4798; www.marigoldbedandbreakfast.com; 6318 Norwood St; s/d $75/85; P ⊖ ≋) Feel at home in this welcoming artist's nest full of bright floral paintings and fluffy cats, if that's your kind of vibe. Marigold is located in a tree-lined residential area in the North End, with easy public transport access.

Dalhousie University HOSTEL $

(☎902-494-8840; www.dal.ca/dept/summer-accommodations.html; 6230 Coburg Rd; s/d $49/69; ⏲ May-Aug; P ≋ ≈) Single and twin dorm rooms with shared bathrooms are clean but bland. Most are adjacent to all the included university amenities, a short walk from the Spring Garden Rd area.

HI Nova Scotia HOSTEL $

(☎902-422-3863; www.hihostels.ca; 1253 Barrington St; dm/r $30/68; ≋) Expect a dark and dormy night and a bright and cheery do-it-yourself breakfast at this exceptionally central 75-bed hostel. The staff are friendly, the shared kitchen is lively and the house is Victorian. Reserve ahead in summer. Slight rate reduction for HI members.

Halifax Backpackers Hostel HOSTEL $

(☎888-431-3170; www.halifaxbackpackers.com; 2193 Gottingen St; dm/d/tr $23/55/65; ≋) Coed dorms at this hip, 36-bed North End hostel hold no more than six beds. It draws a funky young crowd and everyone congregates at the downstairs cafe to swill strong coffee, eat cheap breakfasts and mingle with the eclectic local regulars. City buses stop right in front, but it's a slightly rough-edged neighborhood. Best suited for high-energy travelers who like to party and socialize.

★ **Cambridge Suites Halifax** HOTEL $$

(☎902-420-0555; www.cambridgesuiteshalifax.com; 1583 Brunswick St; d $149-209, ste $169-299; P ⊖ ❄ ≋) For those who value the comforts of home, this recently updated hotel features a wide range of studio rooms and suites featuring tasteful furnishings with dark woods and colorful, stylish accents. One-bedroom suites and above are oversized and have a fabulous, clever layout with windows that open. On top of all that, the location can't be beat. Free continental breakfast, wi-fi and local telephone calls are included in the rate.

★ **Prince George Hotel** HOTEL $$

(☎902-425-1986; www.princegeorgehotel.com; 1725 Market St; d $179-269; P ❄ @ ≈ 🐾) A suave and debonair gem, central Prince George has all the details covered. Garden patios are a great place to take a drink or a meal, or even work, as an alternative to indoor meeting areas. Guestrooms and suites are as classy as you'll find in Halifax and the hotel's common areas ooze urban-chic.

Homewood Suites by Hilton Halifax-Downtown HOTEL $$

(☎855-605-0320; www.hilton.com; 1960 Brunswick St; r/ste from $119/$159; P ⊖ ❄ ≋ ≈) As the brand name implies, this centrally located property is better suited for long-stay guests or traveling families who value the comforts of home; all suites, from studios to two-bedroom hospitality suites, feature full kitchens. Daily breakfast and an 'evening social' (Monday to Thursday) are included in the rates, which vary dramatically by season.

Pebble Bed & Breakfast B&B $$

(☎902-423-3369; www.thepebble.ca; 1839 Armview Tce; r $195-265; ⊖ ≋ 🐾) The two suites of this luxurious B&B feature plush, high beds, gorgeous bathrooms and a modern-meets-antique decor. Irish owner Elizabeth grew up with a pub-owning family and brings lively, joyous energy from the Emerald Isle to her delightful home in a posh, waterfront residential area, a stone's throw from downtown. There's a two-night minimum stay from June to October.

Atlantica Hotel HOTEL $$
(902-423-1161; www.atlanticahotelhalifax.com; 1980 Robie St; d $139-199;) Older hotels have solid bones and the Atlantica is no exception. Freshly updated in 2016, this well-located, privately owned hotel has everything in place to ensure a pleasant stay, from well-trained staff to a range of guestroom types, all generously proportioned and neutrally decorated. The on-site restaurant with room service and light-filled indoor pool add to the value proposition.

Waverley Inn INN $$
(902-423-9346; www.waverleyinn.com; 1266 Barrington St; d $135-235;) Every room in this historic inn is unique, furnished dramatically with bold antiques and luxurious linens. Both Oscar Wilde and PT Barnum once stayed here and probably would again today if they were still alive. On the downside, guestroom and bathroom dimensions aren't huge, but the location makes up for such shortfalls. One for those who value originality and flair.

Lord Nelson Hotel & Suites HOTEL $$
(902-423-5130; www.lordnelsonhotel.com; 1515 S Park St; d $159-239, ste $229-349;) The Lord Nelson has long had a reputation for being where the stars, like the Rolling Stones, stay when they come to town, but that doesn't mean it's Halifax's top hotel. Rooms vary in size from compact guest rooms to oversized suites dressed in an elegant (but not stuffy) style. It's a great choice for those who value history and individuality.

Halliburton INN $$
(902-420-0658; www.thehalliburton.com; 5184 Morris St; d $125-195, ste $235-305;) Class without fuss can be found at this comfortable and well-serviced historic hotel right in downtown. Colorful rooms with Keurig coffee machines and iPod docking stations range in size from compact 'petit rooms' to small suites with patios or four-poster beds.

Halifax Marriott Harbourfront HOTEL $$$
(902-421-1700; www.marriott.com; 1919 Upper Water St; d $229-369) The sprawling Marriott Harbourfront hotel occupies a prime location on, you guessed it, the Halifax waterfront. Plush rooms could do with a little more zing for the price, but the main draws are the property's impressive common areas, from the marble lobby to the bar and the fitness center.

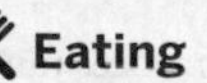

Eating

Heartwood Bakery VEGETARIAN $
(902-425-2808; www.iloveheartwood.ca; 6250 Quinpool Rd; mains $11-16; 11am-8pm;) Try the local organic salad bar or amazing baked goods, along with a cup of fair-trade coffee. Otherwise there's soup, sandwiches, pizza and veggie burgers.

Annie's Place Cafe BREAKFAST $
(www.anniesplacecafe.ca; 1592b Queen St; breakfasts $4-10; 7am-3pm Mon-Fri, 8am-2pm Sat) A slice of small town in the heart of Halifax, Annie welcomes you in and cooks up a hearty breakfast, including freshly baked bread and homemade chai. You'll have a whole new set of friends by the time you leave.

★ **En Vie a Vegan** VEGETARIAN $$
(902-492-4077; www.enviehalifax.com; 5775 Charles St; mains $11-18; 11am-9pm Tue-Fri, 10am-9pm Sat & Sun;) Finally, a restaurant focused on sustainable, organic, locally sourced plant-based eating that has universal appeal. There's nothing bland or boring about what's on offer here. Most menu items, from the coconut shrimp to the double-bacon cheeseburger, feature the original name of their non-vegan counterpart; there's no animal products in any of the dishes, but the ruse is highly convincing.

★ **2 Doors Down** MODERN CANADIAN $$
(902-422-4224; www.go2doorsdown.com; 1533 Barrington St; mains $10-20; 11am-10pm) Reservations aren't accepted at this food-lovers haunt that tempts with a welcome array of staples such as burgers, curries, and fish-and-chips, as well as more elevated offerings such as shrimp-and-snow-crab-stuffed shiitake caps and plenty of gluten-free goodness. The word is out about this cozy haunt, so be prepared for a short wait at busy times.

★ **Henry House** PUB FOOD $$
(902-423-5660; www.henryhouse.ca; 1222 Barrington St; mains $11-24; 11:30am-midnight) Jazz and classical music lilt above the din of respectably dressed diners chatting by the open fire in this handsome 1834 ironstone, serving upscale pub fare. When the gorgeous yet unpretentious Drawing Room upstairs is open (6pm to midnight, Friday and Saturday) you'll be able to dazzle your date with your extensive knowledge of the fine house whiskeys and smoked cocktails.

Brooklyn Warehouse CANADIAN **$$**
(☎902-446-8181; www.brooklynwarehouse.ca; 2795 Windsor St; mains lunch $10-18, dinner $16-30; ⏲11:30am-10pm Mon-Sat; ✎) This North End hot spot is loaded with vegetarian and vegan options – the eggplant moussaka stack is excellent. It has a huge beer and cocktail menu, and an atmosphere that feels like a hip, modern version of *Cheers* – but with way better food.

Wooden Monkey CANADIAN **$$**
(☎902-444-3844; www.thewoodenmonkey.ca; 1707 Grafton St; mains $15-30; ⏲11am-10pm; ✎) This dark, cozy nook with outdoor sidewalk seating on sunny days adamantly supports local organic farms and is a fab place to get superb gluten-free and vegan meals, as well as a selection of seafood and meat dishes prepared with conscience.

Salty's SEAFOOD **$$**
(☎902-423-6818; www.saltys.ca; 1869 Upper Water St; mains bar & grill $12-22, restaurant $25-30) Choose between the casual bar and grill downstairs or the upstairs dining room of this tourist-friendly waterfront seafood restaurant. Fortunately, hyped-up Salty's delivers tasty, well-presented seafood in a busy and thoroughly Halifax setting. Nightly specials are good value.

Stubborn Goat PUB FOOD **$$**
(☎902-405-4554; www.stubborngoat.ca; 1579 Grafton St; small plates $9-19, mains $16-29; ⏲11:30am-2am) Self-billed as a gastropub, the Goat goes beyond pub grub to serve fancy top-nosh small plates such as mouthwatering salmon-belly tartare and the always-popular 'balls' (meatballs stuffed with cheese). Mains such as lobster and smoked meatloaf are bound to tempt. You can also keep it simple with beer and a burger. Check the website for the location and hours of the Goat's seasonal waterfront beer garden.

Edna MODERN CANADIAN **$$**
(www.ednarestaurant.com; 2053 Gottingen St; brunch $12-20, mains $18-35; ⏲5-10pm Tue-Fri, 10am-2:30pm & 5-10pm Sat & Sun) From the Southern-fried rock hen to the filled-with-everything-good-from-the-sea Atlantic bouillabaisse, you'll find something to love here. You can dine at a big wooden table where guests from everywhere chat and mingle, at the bar for a little less socializing, or at a regular old table for two. It's a unique, vivacious, food-and-drink-loving atmosphere.

Hamachi Steakhouse JAPANESE **$$**
(☎902-425-1600; www.hamachirestaurants.com; 1477 Lower Water St; mains $12-28, teppanyaki $28-39; ⏲11:30am-10pm Mon-Sat, 4-10pm Sun) Watch the show grill-side while your chef slices, dices and sets the stove aflame to cook up the meats, seafood and veggies that make a crowd-pleasing Japanese teppanyaki. For a less theatrical experience, grab a table and enjoy the teppanyaki, sushi or Alberta steaks quietly, with a beautiful view of the harbor.

Morris East ITALIAN **$$**
(☎902-444-7663; www.morriseast.com; 5212 Morris St; pizzas $15-20; ⏲11:30am-9pm) At this cosmopolitan cafe, you'll find creative, wood-fired pizzas on your choice of white, whole-wheat or gluten-free ($3.50 extra) dough; try the peach, rosemary aioli and prosciutto pizza. There's also snazzy cocktails, such as a basil, lime and vodka punch.

Epicurious Morcels FUSION **$$**
(☎902-455-0955; www.epicuriousmorsels.com; 5529 Young St; mains $10-29; ⏲11:30am-2:30pm & 5-8:30pm Tue-Sun) The specialties on this diverse menu include smoked salmon, gravlax (dill-cured salmon) and a range of tasty, creative soups. There's something here for everyone.

★ **Bicycle Thief** ITALIAN **$$$**
(☎902-425-7993; www.bicyclethief.ca; 1475 Lower Water St; mains lunch $10-26, dinner $20-39; ⏲11.30am-late Mon-Fri, 5:30pm-late Sat) Named for the classic 1948 Italian film, this shabby-chic waterfront restaurant has won similar critical acclaim by local foodies – and with good reason. Start with regional oysters or polenta with wild mushroom ragout, then continue with dishes such as pistachio-honey-roasted salmon or pancetta-wrapped pork tenderloin. The wine and cocktail list is several pages longer than the food menu.

Press Gang Restaurant & Oyster Bar SEAFOOD **$$$**
(☎902-423-8816; www.thepressgang.ca; 5218 Prince St; single oysters $3.25, mains $36-40; ⏲5-10pm Sun-Wed, to midnight Thu-Sat) Order any number and combination of Nova Scotia and PEI oysters raw or baked – if you're a fan of the briny bivalves, you've found nirvana. Otherwise, choose from a short but impressive menu of delicious appetizers and mains and soak up the atmosphere of this slick and stylish outfit. Dress to impress.

Five Fishermen SEAFOOD $$$

(902-422-4421; www.fivefishermen.com; 1740 Argyle St; mains $29-39; noon-10pm Mon-Fri, 5-10pm Sat & Sun) This fabulous restaurant housed in what was once the John Snow funeral home that interred many of Halifax's 150 *Titanic* victims doesn't have to rely on this macabre and quirky fact to put bums on seats: thankfully, the seafood sells itself. Expect elevated oceanic delicacies, with lamb and steak thrown in for good measure.

Chives Canadian Bistro CANADIAN $$$

(902-420-9626; www.chives.ca; 1537 Barrington St; mains $24-35; 5-9:30pm) The menu changes with what's seasonally available and uses mostly local ingredients. The food is fine dining, while the low-lit cozy ambience is upscale casual.

Da Maurizio ITALIAN $$$

(902-423-0859; www.damaurizio.ca; 1496 Lower Water St; mains $28-39; 5-10pm Mon-Sat) Many locals cite this as their favorite Halifax restaurant, with exposed brick and clean lines bringing out all the flavors of the heritage brewery building. The cuisine is as fine as the ambience. Reservations are strongly recommended.

Drinking & Nightlife

★Lot Six COCKTAIL BAR

(902-428-7428; www.lotsix.ca; 1685 Argyle St; 4pm-2am) This slick bar and restaurant has a fabulous glass atrium that delivers extra atmosphere points, whatever the season. Score a cushy seat at the counter if you're flying solo or an extra-cute two-person booth if you're angling for *amour*.

Tom's Little Havana BAR

(902-423-8667; www.tomslittlehavana.wix.com/cafe; 1540 Birmingham St; 11:30am-2am) Craft beers, game nights, Scotch nights and a daily happy hour (5pm to 8pm) make Tom's feel like an extension of the living room at your best mate's place. There's a warm and friendly vibe here, which gets even warmer as the night wears on.

Durty Nelly's IRISH PUB

(902-406-7640; www.durtynellys.ca; cnr Argyle & Sackville Sts; 11:30am-1am) There are lots of reasons to come to Halifax's uberpopular Irish Pub, from open-mic and rib nights to regular live music, cold ales, great food and a fun and friendly atmosphere.

Middle Spoon COCKTAIL BAR

(902-407-4002; www.themiddlespoon.ca; 1559 Barrington St; 4-11pm Mon-Sat) What could be better than a place that serves only beer, wine, creative cocktails and decadent desserts? How about one with a super secret? (Should we even be writing this?) It has a speakeasy-inspired lounge downstairs that serves even better cocktails. Get the password by clicking on the >: symbol on the website and don't tell anyone we told you...

Economy Shoe Shop Cafe Bar CAFE

(902-423-8845; www.economyshoeshop.ca; 1663 Argyle St; 11:30am-midnight Mon-Thu, to 2am Fri-Sun) This has been the 'it' place to drink and people-watch in Halifax for well over a decade. On weekend nights, actors and journalists figure heavily in the crush. It's a pleasant place for afternoon drinks and the kitchen dishes out tapas until last call at 1:45am.

Pacifico CLUB

(902-422-3633; www.pacifico.ca; 1505 Barrington St; 9pm-2am Fri & Sat) Halifax's hottest hangout sprawls beneath Barrington and Salter Sts, with high-energy DJs, bottle service and party people.

Garrison Brewing Company BREWERY

(902-453-5343; www.garrisonbrewing.com; 1149 Marginal Rd; 10am-8pm Sun-Thu, to 10pm Fri & Sat) Not much beats a $2 taster glass of craft beer on a sunny patio, except maybe *five* varieties of tasters, which is how many the brewery serves on tap each day. Other bottled beers are sold in the shop but because they're not legally a bar (and Canada has complicated liquor laws), you can't drink them on the premises.

Gay & Lesbian

Reflections Cabaret GAY & LESBIAN

(902-422-2957; www.reflectionscabaret.com; 5187 Salter St; 10pm-3am Thu-Mon) If you're looking to get your glam on, this mainly gay disco attracts a mixed crowd. Nightly entertainment ranges from wrestling to drag shows to sensory stage shows. Check the website for events listings.

Menz and Mollyz Bar GAY & LESBIAN

(902-446-6969; www.facebook.com/menznmollyz; 2182 Gottingen St; 4pm-2:30am) Self-billed as Atlantic Canada's premier LGBTQI destination, Menz and Mollyz can be hit or miss, but that can be said for many community bars since the advent of phone-dating apps. Keep it friendly and rock up when there's an event on and you're bound to have a good time.

Entertainment

Check out the *Coast* (www.thecoast.ca) to see what's on. This free weekly publication, available around town, is the essential guide for music, theater, film and events.

Live Music

Halifax loves its music, with folk, hip-hop, alternative, country and rock gigs around town every weekend. Cover charges depend on the band.

Seahorse Tavern LIVE MUSIC
(902-423-7200; www.theseahorsetavern.ca; 1665 Argyle St) This joint hosts events that attract the crowds who are actually cool (not just faux-cool). Punk, indie, metal, funk, Motown, soul…and monthly themed dance parties. Check the website for what's on and when.

Bearly's House of Blues & Ribs LIVE MUSIC
(902-423-2526; www.bearlys.ca; 1269 Barrington St; 5pm-midnight) The best blues musicians in Atlantic Canada play here at incredibly low cover charges. Wednesday karaoke nights draw a crowd and some fine singers.

Carleton LIVE MUSIC
(902-422-6335; www.thecarleton.ca; 1685 Argyle St; noon-2am) Catch acoustic sets, then enjoy the meals, including a late-night menu.

Theatre

Shakespeare by the Sea THEATER
(902-422-0295; www.shakespearebythesea.ca; Point Pleasant Park; Jun-Sep) Fine performances of the Bard's works at the Cambridge Battery, an old fortification in the middle of Point Pleasant Park. Another reason to love Halifax! Check the website for a map and details.

Neptune Theatre THEATER
(902-429-7070; www.neptunetheatre.com; 1593 Argyle St) This downtown theater presents musicals and well-known plays on its main stage (from $35) and edgier stuff in the studio (from $15).

Yuk Yuks COMEDY
(902-429-9857; www.yukyuks.com/halifax; 1181 Hollis St) This is the place to go for local and international stand-up and improv gigs: check the website for what's on when.

Sports

Scotiabank Centre STADIUM
(902-451-1221; www.scotiabank-centre.com; 1800 Argyle St; box office 9am-5pm) Halifax's premier multipurpose indoor arena is smack-bang in the heart of downtown. The biggest matches, games and concerts to come to town are held here.

Shopping

★ **Halifax Seaport Farmers Market** MARKET
(902-492-4043; www.halifaxfarmersmarket.com; 1209 Marginal Rd; 10am-5pm Mon-Fri, 7am-3pm Sat, 9am-3pm Sun) Although it has operated in several locations since its inception in 1750, what's now known as the Halifax Seaport Farmers Market (in its present location since 2010) is North America's longest continuously operating market. With over 250 vendors from a province that prides itself on strong farm-to-table and maritime traditions, it's well worth a visit.

Historic Properties SHOPPING CENTRE
(www.historicproperties.ca; 1869 Upper Water St; store hours vary) The Historic Properties are a group of restored warehouse buildings on Upper Water St, built between 1800 and 1905, that have been converted into boutiques, restaurants and bars connected by waterfront boardwalks. The 1814 **Privateers Warehouse** was the former storehouse of government-sanctioned pirates and is the area's oldest stone building. Among the other vintage buildings are the wooden **Old Red Store**, and **Simon's Warehouse**, built in 1854.

Nova Scotian Crystal ARTS & CRAFTS
(888-977-2797; www.novascotiancrystal.com; 5080 George St; 9am-6pm Mon-Fri, 10am-5pm Sat & Sun) As much of a show as a place to shop – watch glass blowers form beautiful crystal glasses and vases, then pick the ones you want in the classy adjacent boutique.

Historic Farmers Market MARKET
(902-329-3276; www.historicfarmersmarket.ca; 1496 Lower Water St; 7am-1pm Sat) If you're in Halifax on a Saturday morning, pop by this grassroots, member-run, non-profit cooperative market, housed in a beautiful 1820s stone building.

Orientation

The downtown area, three universities and older residential neighborhoods are contained on a compact peninsula cut off from mainland Halifax by an inlet called the North West Arm. Almost all sights of interest to visitors are concentrated in this area, making walking the best way to get around. Point Pleasant Park is at the extreme southern end of the peninsula, and the lively and multicultural North End neighborhood – home to African Nova Scotians, art-school students and most of Halifax's gay bars – stretches from the midpoint to the northern extreme.

Two bridges span the harbor, connecting Halifax to Dartmouth and leading to highways north (for the airport) and east. The MacDonald Bridge at the eastern end of North St is closest to downtown.

Information

INTERNET ACCESS

Halifax Central Library (902-490-5700; www.halifaxcentrallibrary.ca; 5440 Spring Garden Rd; 9am-9pm Mon-Thu, to 6pm Fri & Sat, noon-6pm Sun;)

MEDICAL SERVICES

Family Focus (902-420-2038; www.thefamilyfocus.ca; 5991 Spring Garden Rd; 8:30am-9pm Mon-Fri, 11am-5pm Sat & Sun) Walk-in or same-day appointments.

Halifax Infirmary (Charles V Keating Emergency and Trauma Centre; 902-473-3383, 902-473-7605; www.cdha.nshealth.ca; 1796 Summer St; 24hr) For emergencies.

POST

Lawton's Drugs (902-429-0088; 5675 Spring Garden Rd; 8am-10pm Mon-Fri, 9am-9pm Sat, noon-8pm Sun) There's a post office in the rear of this pharmacy.

Main Post Office (902-494-4670; www.canadapost.ca; 1660 Bedford Row; 9am-5pm Mon-Fri)

TOURIST INFORMATION

Tourism Nova Scotia (800-565-0000, 902-425-5781; www.novascotia.com) Operates visitors information centers in Halifax and other locations within Nova Scotia province, plus a free booking service for accommodations, which is useful when rooms are scarce in midsummer. It publishes the *Doers & Dreamers Guide,* which lists places to stay, attractions and tour operators.

Visitor Information Centre (VIC; 902-424-4248; www.novascotia.com; 1655 Lower Water St; 9am-5pm) On the Halifax Waterfront, this official province-run plaza is a great place to start your wanderings of downtown Halifax; they'll load you up with maps and friendly advice. There is also an official VIC welcome center at the **airport** (902-873-1223; Halifax International Airport; 9am-9pm).

USEFUL WEBSITES

Destination Halifax (www.halifaxinfo.com)

Halifax Regional Municipality (www.halifax.ca)

Getting There & Away

AIR

Most air services in Nova Scotia go to/from Halifax and there are multiple daily flights to Toronto, Calgary and Vancouver.

International destinations serviced include Boston, New York and London.

Halifax Stanfield International Airport (YHZ; 902-873-4422; www.hiaa.ca; 1 Bell Blvd) is 32km northeast of town on Hwy 102, toward Truro.

BUS

The only province-wide (and beyond) bus company is **Maritime Bus** (p334), which services the main highways from Kentville to Halifax and up to Truro. From Truro the routes fork: toward North Sydney in one direction and toward Amherst and on to New Brunswick in the other.

Advance Shuttle (877-886-3322; www.advanceshuttle.ca) offers slow-going shuttle services from Halifax airport and downtown hotels to Prince Edward Island (from $69).

Cloud Nine Shuttle (902-742-3992; www.thecloudnineshuttle.com) can drop you at points along the South Shore as far as Yarmouth. Fares start at $75 and the journey takes about 3½ hours.

TRAIN

One of the few examples of monumental Canadian train station architecture left in the Maritimes is found at 1161 Hollis St. **VIA Rail** (www.viarail.ca) operates an overnight service to Montréal (from $134, 21 hours, daily except Tuesdays).

Getting Around

TO/FROM THE AIRPORT

The cheapest way to get to the airport is by Metro Transit public bus 320, which runs half-hourly to hourly between 5am and midnight from the Metro X bus stop on Albemarle St between Duke and Cogswell Sts.

If you arrive in the middle of the night, as many flights do, your only choice is a taxi, which costs $56 to downtown Halifax. There are often not enough taxis, so it's prudent to reserve one in advance. Try **Halifax Airport Taxi** (902-999-2434; www.halifaxairportlimotaxi.com), which has 24-hour airport service. The journey shouldn't take much longer than 30 minutes.

Maritime Bus (www.maritimebus.com) operates an airport shuttle ($22, 30 to 45 minutes) between May and October.

CAR & MOTORCYCLE

Pedestrians almost always have right of way in Halifax, so watch out for cars stopping suddenly.

Outside the downtown core, you can usually find free on-street parking for up to two hours. Halifax's parking meters are enforced from 8am to 6pm Monday to Friday.

All the major national car-rental chains are represented at the airport and in downtown Halifax. Some will let you pick up in town and drop off at the airport free of charge.

PUBLIC TRANSPORTATION

Halifax Transit (☎902-480-8000; www.halifax.ca/transit; single ride $2.50-3.50) runs the city bus system and the ferries to Dartmouth. Maps and schedules are available at the ferry terminals and at the information booth in Scotia Sq mall.

Bus 7 cuts through downtown and North End Halifax via Robie St and Gottingen St, passing both of Halifax's hostels. Bus 1 travels along Spring Garden Rd, Barrington St and the south part of Gottingen St before crossing the bridge to Dartmouth.

AROUND HALIFAX

Dartmouth

Founded in 1750, just one year after its counterpart across the harbor, working-class Dartmouth had long been regarded as Halifax's grubby little brother. In recent years, its proximity to Eastern Shore beaches, ease of access to downtown Halifax and a spate of waterfront redevelopment projects have rejuvenated Dartmouth's demographic and contributed to its growing popularity.

Sights

Dartmouth's compact, historic downtown is a pleasant place for a stroll and a pint: getting here on the ferry from Halifax – the oldest saltwater ferry system in North America – is half the fun, especially at sunset. Before you return, head west on Alderney Dr to climb the bluffs of **Dartmouth Commons** for excellent views across the harbor. Exercise the usual caution in the park after dark.

Quaker House HISTORIC BUILDING
(☎902-464-2300; www.dartmouthheritagemuseum.ns.ca; 59 Ochterloney St; $5; ⏱10am-5pm Tue-Sun Jun-Aug) Built in 1786 by Quaker whalers from Nantucket who fled the American Revolution, Quaker house is the oldest surviving house in the Halifax area. Admission includes entry into the Dartmouth Heritage Museum housed in nearby Evergreen House.

Dartmouth Heritage Museum MUSEUM
(☎902-464-2300; www.dartmouthheritagemuseum.ns.ca; 26 Newcastle St; $5; ⏱10am-5pm Tue-Sat) An eclectic collection of local historic artifacts is displayed here in **Evergreen House**, the former home of folklorist Helen Creighton, who traversed the province in the early 20th century, recording stories and songs. Tickets include same-day admission to the 1786 Quaker House.

Eating

Portland Street Creperie CREPERIE $
(☎902-466-7686; www.portlandstreetcreperie.com; 55 Portland St; crepes $4-9; ⏱8:30am-5pm Mon-Thu & Sat, to 7pm Fri, 10am-1pm Sun) There's a crepe for everyone at this local favorite. From the savory 'mushroom melt' to the sweet, sweet 'honeycomb,' drizzled with Nova Scotian honey and butter, these tempting treats are priced such that you mightn't be able to stop at just one.

Nena's All Day Breakfast DINER $
(☎902-406-0006; www.nenasbreakfast.com; 273 Wyse Rd; meals $6-16; ⏱7am-3pm) On a drab street corner surrounded by used-car lots and mechanic workshops you'll find this hopping, spotlessly clean breakfast joint, serving diner-style greasy faves. Breakfast is served all day, but there's a lunch menu also. If you're a fan of french fries (or home fries) and Canadian gravy, you're advised to stop by.

Two If By Sea BAKERY $
(☎902-469-0721; www.twoifbyseacafe.ca; 66 Ochterloney St; pastries $3-5; ⏱7am-6pm Mon-Fri, 8am-5pm Sat & Sun) Be warned...if you're wanting to gorge on the massive buttery chocolate croissants that TIBS are famous for, get in quick: they're often sold out by 1pm. Even sans pastries, it's a hip place to stop for coffee and people-watching on a sunny day, with a home-proud Dartmouth atmosphere.

Drinking & Nightlife

★**Battery Park Beer Bar & Eatery** MICROBREWERY
(☎902-446-2337; www.batterypark.ca; 62 Ochterloney St; ⏱2pm-midnight Wed-Mon) This local collaboration is the talk of the town for its small-batch specialty beers and out-of-this-world tasting menus, best shared. The aesthetic is wooden-industrial, the crowd is hip and the bacon fudge is addictive.

Celtic Corner PUB
(902-464-0764; www.celticcorner.ca; 69 Alderney Dr; 11am-midnight) Dartmouth's most popular and centrally located pub, with live music most nights and a wide variety of beers on tap and hearty pub food (mains $10 to $17).

Just Us! Coffee Roaster's Co-Op CAFE
(www.justuscoffee.com; 15 King's Wharf; 7am-5:30pm Mon-Thu, to 9pm Fri & Sat;) This bright yet cozy cafe serves up fair-trade, house-roasted coffee and baked goods made from locally sourced ingredients. What originally started in 1995 as Canada's first fair-trade coffee roaster now has a handful of outlets around the province, all with free wi-fi thrown in. Check the website for other locations.

Shopping

Alderney Landing MARKET
(902-461-4698; www.alderneylanding.com; 2 Ochterloney St; 9:30am-5pm Mon-Fri) This multipurpose venue houses a theater, market and a variety of cafes, restaurants and shops.

Getting There & Away

Halifax Transit (www.halifax.ca/transit) operates an extensive, easy-to-use network of buses and ferries. In Dartmouth, catch the ferry to Halifax ($2.50, 20 minutes) from the **Dartmouth Ferry Terminal** (replete with public-use piano) at Alderney Gate.

Peggy's Cove

Peggy's Cove is one of the most visited fishing villages in Canada, and for good reason: the rolling granite cove, highlighted by a perfect red-and-white lighthouse, exudes a dreamy seaside calm, even through the parading tour buses. Visit before 10am, after 6pm, or in the off-season to avoid the jam and to appreciate the true beauty and tranquility of the place.

If you're looking for the same kind of vibe without the mass of visitors, cute-as-a-button **Lower Prospect** is 30km to the east via Terrence Bay.

Sights

★ William E deGarthe Gallery & Monument GALLERY
(902-823-2256; 109 Peggy's Point Rd; $2; gallery 9am-5pm May-Oct) Finnish-born local artist William deGarthe (1907–83) sculpted the magnificent *Lasting Monument to Nova Scotian Fishermen* into a 30m granite outcropping behind his home. The sculpture depicts 32 fishermen, their wives and children, St Elmo with wings spread, and the legendary Peggy of her eponymous Cove. The homestead is now a gallery showcasing 65 of deGarthe's other works.

Swissair 111 Memorial MEMORIAL
(8250 Hwy 333) This moving memorial commemorates the 229 people who lost their lives on September 2, 1998, when Swissair Flight 111, bound for Geneva, Switzerland, plunged into the ocean 8km off the coast of Peggy's Cove.

Peggy's Point Lighthouse LIGHTHOUSE
(185 Peggys Point Rd; 9:30am-5:30pm May-Oct) The highlight of the cove is this picture-perfect lighthouse, which for many years was a working post office. Meander around the granite landscape that undulates much like the icy sea beyond.

Sleeping & Eating

Wayside Camping Park CAMPGROUND $
(902-823-2271; www.waysidecampground.com; 10295 Hwy 333, Glen Margaret; tent/RV sites $25/35; May-Oct;) About 10km north of Peggy's Cove and 36km from Halifax, this camping park has lots of shady sites on a hill. It gets crowded in midsummer.

Oceanstone Seaside Resort RESORT $$
(902-823-2160; www.oceanstoneresort.com; 8650 Peggy's Cove Rd, Indian Harbour; r $105-195, cottages $195-335;) Whimsically decorated cottages are a stone's throw from the beach and just a short drive from Peggy's Cove. Guests can use paddleboats to venture to small islands. **Rhubarb**, the inn's dining room, is considered one of the best seafood restaurants in the region.

Peggy's Cove Bed & Breakfast B&B $$
(902-823-2265; www.peggyscovebb.com; 17 Church Rd; d $155; Apr-Oct;) The only place to stay in the cove itself, this B&B has an enviable position with one of the best views in Nova Scotia, overlooking the fishing docks and the lighthouse; it was once owned by artist William deGarthe. You'll definitely need advance reservations.

Dee Dee's ICE CREAM $
(www.deedees.ca; 110 Peggy's Cove Rd; cones from $3.50; noon-6pm May-Sep) On hot days, explore the area while licking a delicious homemade-with-local-ingredients ice-cream cone from Dee Dee's. It's near the tourist information center.

Entertainment

Old Red Schoolhouse THEATER
(902-823-2099; www.beales.ns.ca; 126 Peggy's Point Rd; suggested donation $10) This performance venue puts on comedies and music performances through the high season. A few shows per season are serviced by shuttle vans that offer round-trips to Halifax hotels. Check the website for details.

Information

Visitor Information Centre (VIC; 902-823-2253; 109 Peggy's Cove Rd; 9am-7pm May-Oct) There's a free parking area with washrooms and a tourist information office as you enter the village. Free 45-minute **walking tours** are led from the tourist office daily from mid-June through August.

SOUTH SHORE

This is Nova Scotia's most visited coastline and it's here you'll find those quintessential lighthouses, forested coves with white beaches, and fishing villages turned tourist towns. The area from Halifax to Lunenburg is cottage country for the city's elite and ever-popular with day-trippers.

Chester

Established in 1759, the town of Chester has become a choice spot for well-to-do Americans and Haligonians to have a summer home. It's had a colorful history as the haunt of pirates and Prohibition-era bathtub-gin smugglers and it keeps its color today via the many artists' studios about town. It holds a large regatta in mid-August.

Sights

Tancook Island ISLAND
(www.tancookislandtourism.ca) This island (population 190) is a 45-minute ferry ride from Chester's government wharf (round-trip $5.50, four services daily Monday to Friday, two daily on weekends). Settled by Germans and French Huguenots in the early 19th century, the island is famous for its sauerkraut, and is crisscrossed with **walking trails**. The last ferry from Chester each day overnights in Tancook Island.

Lordly House Museum MUSEUM
(902-275-3842; 133 Central St; 10am-4pm Tue-Sat Jun-Sep) FREE A fine example of Georgian architecture from 1806, the Lordly House Museum has three period rooms illustrating 19th-century upper-class life and Chester history. The museum is also an artists' studio.

Sleeping & Eating

Graves Island Provincial Park CAMPGROUND $
(902-275-4425; www.parks.gov.ns.ca; campsites $24) An island in Mahone Bay connected by a causeway to the mainland has 64 wooded and open campsites. RVs usually park in the middle of the area, but some shady, isolated tent sites are tucked away on the flanks of the central plateau.

Mecklenburgh Inn B&B B&B $$
(902-275-4638; www.mecklenburghinn.ca; 78 Queen St; r $135-155; May-Dec;) This casual four-room inn, built in 1890, has a breezy 2nd-floor veranda. Some rooms have private adjacent balconies; most have private bathrooms. The owner is a Cordon Bleu chef, so expect an excellent breakfast.

Kiwi Café CAFE $
(902-275-1492; www.kiwicafechester.com; 19 Pleasant St; mains $9-16; 8am-4pm Sun-Wed, to 8pm Thu-Sat;) A New Zealand chef prepares excellent soups, salads, sandwiches and baked goods that you can eat in or take away. The walls are painted kiwi green and there's beer, wine and a relaxed atmosphere.

Rope Loft PUB
(902-275-3430; www.ropeloft.com; 36 Water St; 11:30am-11pm) You couldn't find a better setting for an ale than this bayside pub. Hearty pub food is served indoors or out.

Entertainment

Chester Playhouse THEATER
(902-275-3933; www.chesterplayhouse.ca; 22 Pleasant St; tickets around $25) This older theater space has great acoustics for live performances. Plays or dinner theater are presented most nights in July and August, with occasional concerts during spring and fall.

Information

Chester Visitor Information Centre (902-275-4616; www.vic.chesterchamber.ca; 20 Smith Rd; 9:30am-5:30pm) In the old train depot near the Chester turnoff, proud local staff are a font of knowledge.

Mahone Bay

The sun shines more often in Mahone Bay than anywhere else along the coast. With more than 100 islands in the bay, and less than 100km from Halifax, it's a great base for exploring this section of the South Shore. Take out a kayak or a bike or simply stroll down Main St, which skirts the harbor and is scattered with shops selling antiques, quilts, pottery and works by local painters.

Sights & Activities

Mahone Bay's seafront skyline is punctuated by three magnificent old **churches** that draw in many keen photographers and also host live classical music in the summer.

Mahone Bay Settlers' Museum MUSEUM
(902-624-6263; www.mahonebaymuseum.com; 578 Main St; 10am-4pm Jun–mid-Oct) FREE Exhibits on the area's architecture and its settlement by 'Foreign Protestants' in 1754.

Sweet Ride Cycling CYCLING
(902-531-3026; sweetridecycling.com; 523 Main St; half-/full-day rentals $20/30; 10am-5pm Mon-Sat, noon-5pm Sun) Pick up a sweet ride here and check in with the friendly staff for the best routes in the area.

Tours

South Shore Boat Tours CRUISE
(902-543-5107; www.southshoreboattours.com; tours from $45; Jun-Oct) Join Captain Chris for fascinating cruises around Mahone Bay, offering insight into the local wildlife and traditional fishing and boatbuilding industries.

Festivals & Events

Great Scarecrow Festival & Antiques Fair CULTURAL
(www.mahonebayscarecrowfestival.com; Oct) Locals make outlandish scarecrows and carve pumpkins to display outside their homes on the first weekend in October. Meanwhile, a popular antique fair rages on.

Sleeping & Eating

Kip & Kaboodle Backpackers Hostel HOSTEL $
(902-531-5494; www.kiwikaboodle.com; 9466 Hwy 3; dm/d/tr $30/69/105; Apr-Oct; P) This friendly nine-bed hostel is superbly located, 3km from the attractions of Mahone Bay and 7km from Lunenburg. Owners offer town pick-up, as well as economical tours, a shuttle service, barbecues and bonfires, and excellent area tips. There are also bike rentals and one private room.

Fisherman's Daughter B&B $$
(902-624-0483; www.fishermans-daughter.com; 97 Edgewater St; r $135-145;) Set on the bay by the three beautiful churches, this very old house (1840) has been meticulously remodeled for comfort, while retaining all the charm. Two rooms have views through sharply pitched Gothic-style windows, and all four rooms have good-sized attached bathrooms. It has all the friendly service you'd want from a top B&B.

Three Thistles B&B B&B $$
(902-624-0517; www.three-thistles.com; 389 W Main St; r $115-150; P) Owner Ama Phyllis uses environmentally conscious cleaning agents and cooks with organic foods. Rooms are sparkling-clean and there's a back garden that stretches to a wooded area. Yoga classes are available and the loft apartment is a real delight.

Biscuit Eater CAFE $
(902-624-2665; www.biscuiteater.ca; 16 Orchard St; mains $8-20; 9am-5pm Wed-Mon;) Dine on fabulous organic meals from soups to salads and sandwiches while surrounded by books. Or just stop for a fair-trade coffee and to Skype the folks back home.

LaHave Bakery DELI $
(902-624-1420; www.lahavebakery.com; 3 Edgewater; sandwiches $5-9.50; 8:30am-6:30pm;) This bakery is famous for its hearty bread. Sandwiches are made on thick slabs of it.

★ **Mateus Bistro** MODERN CANADIAN $$$
(902-531-3711; www.mateusbistro.com; 533 Main St; mains $22-35; 5-9pm Tue & Wed, 11:30am-9pm Thu-Mon) Tucked into a little gallery with an outdoor patio, this place may not have the sea views, but once you hit the cocktails, wine and food, you'll likely not care. The European-inspired menu changes with what's fresh locally, from oysters and Fundy scallops to duck and a rainbow of veggies.

Shopping

Amos Pewter ARTS & CRAFTS
(800-565-3369; www.amospewter.com; 589 Main St; 9am-7pm Mon-Sat, 10am-7pm Sun) Watch demonstrations in the art of pewter making, then buy wares in the attached store.

A PIRATE'S TREASURE

Oak Island, near Mahone Bay, is home to a so-called 'money pit' that has cost over $2 million in excavation expenses – and six lives. Few facts are known about what the pit is or what might be buried there, but if you're keen to find out more, *The Curse of Oak Island*, an ongoing reality TV series, seeks to expound all the theories – and maybe find some treasure!

The mystery began in 1795 when three inhabitants of the island came across a depression in the ground. Knowing that pirates had once frequented the area, they decided to dig and see what they could find. Just over half a meter down, they hit a layer of neatly placed flagstone; another 2.5m turned up one oak platform, then another. After digging to 9m, the men temporarily gave up, but returned eight years later with the Onslow Company, a professional crew.

The Onslow excavation made it down 27.5m; when the crew returned the next morning, the shaft had flooded and they were forced to halt the digging. A year later, the company returned to dig 33.5m down in a parallel shaft, which also flooded. It was confirmed in 1850 that the pit was booby-trapped via five box drains at Smith Cove, 150m from the pit. The beach was found to be artificial.

Ever since, people have come to seek their fortune from far and wide at the 'money pit.' Only a few links of gold chain, some parchment, a cement vault and an inscribed stone have been found.

Information

Mahone Bay (www.mahonebay.com) Links to restaurants and accommodations.

Mahone Bay Visitor Information Centre (902-624-6151; 165 Edgewater St; 9am-6pm May-Oct) Has do-it-yourself walking tour brochures.

Lunenburg

The largest of the South Shore fishing villages is historic Lunenburg, the region's only Unesco World Heritage site and the first British settlement outside Halifax. The town is at its most picturesque viewed from the sea around sunset, when the boxy, brightly painted old buildings literally glow behind the ship-filled port.

Lunenburg was settled largely by Germans, Swiss and Protestant French, who were first recruited by the British as a workforce for Halifax, then later became fishermen. Today Nova Scotia has been hard hit by dwindling fish stocks, but Lunenburg's burgeoning tourism trade has helped shore up the local economy.

Sights & Activities

Look out around town for the distinctive 'Lunenburg Bump,' a distinctive architectural feature of older buildings whereby a five-sided dormer window on the 2nd floor overhangs the 1st floor.

Ironworks Distillery DISTILLERY
(902-640-2424; www.ironworksdistillery.com; 2 Kempt St; noon-5pm Wed-Mon) Tastings are free but good luck getting out of this old ironworks building without buying a bottle of something. Local ingredients craft a changing selection of liqueurs, a strong apple brandy and a very quaffable black spiced rum.

Knaut-Rhuland House MUSEUM
(902-634-3498; 125 Pelham St; $3; 11am-5pm Tue-Sat, 1-5pm Sun Jun-Sep) Knaut-Rhuland House is considered the finest example of Georgian architecture in the province. This 1793 house has costumed guides who point out its features.

Fisheries Museum of the Atlantic MUSEUM
(902-634-4794; http://fisheriesmuseum.novascotia.ca; 68 Bluenose Dr; adult/child $10/3; 9:30am-5pm) The knowledgeable staff at the Fisheries Museum of the Atlantic includes a number of retired fisherfolk who can give firsthand explanations of the fishing industry. A cute aquarium on the 1st floor lets you get eye-to-eye with halibut, a 6kg lobster and other sea creatures. Film screenings and talks take place throughout the day.

Pleasant Paddling KAYAKING
(902-541-9233; www.pleasantpaddling.com; 221 The Point Rd; kayak rentals from $35, tours from $50; May-Oct) The knowledgeable folks at this beautiful place to paddle offer rentals and tours in single or double kayaks.

Lunenburg

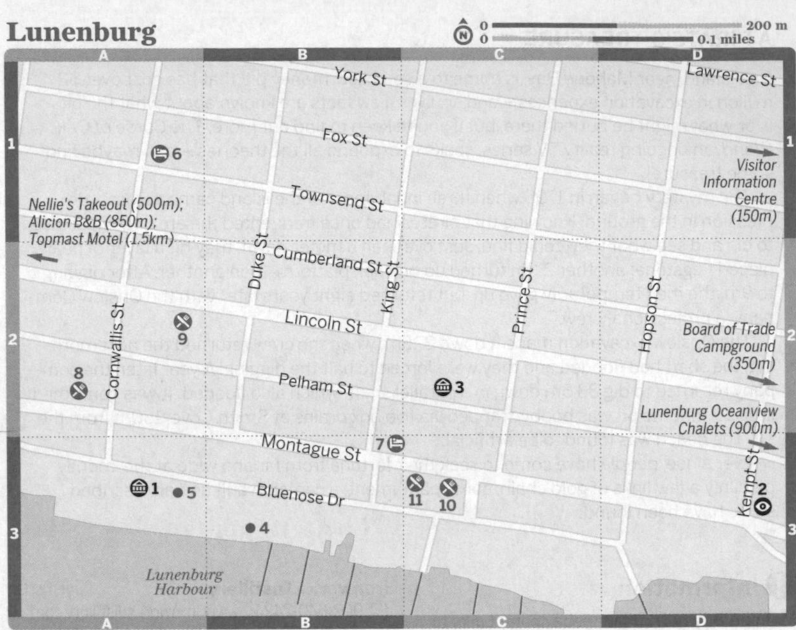

Lunenburg

Sights
1 Fisheries Museum of the Atlantic....... A3
2 Ironworks Distillery.......................... D3
3 Knaut-Rhuland House......................... C2

Activities, Courses & Tours
4 Bluenose II.. B3
5 Trot in Time A3

Sleeping
6 1775 Solomon House B&B.................. A1
7 Sail Inn B&B.. B3

Eating
8 Fleur de Sel.. A2
9 Lincoln Street Food A2
10 Magnolia's Grill................................. C3
11 Salt Shaker Deli................................. C3

Tours

Lunenburg Walking Tours WALKING
(☎902-521-6867; www.lunenburgwalkingtours.com; tours adult/child from $20/10) Enthusiastic and very experienced Sheila Allen and her team lead leisurely tours during the day or spooky lantern-lit ones at night.

Trot in Time TOURS
(☎902-634-8917; www.trotintime.ca; adult/child $20/10; ⏲Jun–mid-Oct) Take a half-hour tour of town in a horse-drawn cart. Leaves from outside the Fisheries Museum of the Atlantic.

Bluenose II BOATING
(☎902-634-1963; www.bluenose.novascotia.ca; 2hr cruises adult/child $20/10) This classic replica of the *Bluenose* racing schooner is sometimes in Halifax and sometimes in Lunenburg. Check the website for details.

Festivals & Events

Boxwood Festival MUSIC
(www.boxwood.org; festival pass $50; ⏲Jul) Flautists and pipers from around the world put on stellar public concerts.

Lunenburg Folk Harbour Festival MUSIC
(☎902-634-3180; www.folkharbour.com; ⏲Aug) Singer-songwriters from Canada and beyond, plus traditional music and gospel.

Nova Scotia Folk Art Festival ART
(www.nsfolkartfestival.com; ⏲Aug) Buffet dinner, artist talks and then a big art show and sale on the first Sunday in August.

Sleeping

Board of Trade Campground CAMPGROUND $
(☎902-634-8100; www.lunenburgns.com/campground; 11 Blockhouse Hill Rd; tent/RV sites $28/40; 📶) This campground perched on

the hill above Lunenburg has great views and a lot of gravel RV sites. Grassy tent sites are closely packed together and lack shade.

Sail Inn B&B B&B $$
(902-634-3537; www.sailinn.ca; 99 Montague St; r $110-180; P) Rooms have a view over the waterfront and are bright, airy and modern, with an antique twist. You get a free sail on the owner's 15m ketch with your stay. Don't miss the old well on the ground floor that has been turned into a lighted fish pond.

Alicion B&B B&B $$
(902-634-9358; www.alicionbb.com; 66 McDonald St; r $139-169; P) This classic 1911 B&B with its wraparound porch set on a leafy hill a healthy walk from downtown oozes Canadiana. Classic but not stuffy, the four airy, light-filled bedrooms make you want to kick back and read, if there just wasn't so much to see and do in town. Breakfasts are beautifully prepared and the owners are enviro aware.

Lunenburg Oceanview Chalets COTTAGE $$
(902-640-3344; www.lunenburgoceanview.com; 78 Old Blue Rocks Rd; cottages $139-179; P) For something a little different, these rustic log cabins with private decks atop a hill on the outskirts of Lunenburg might be just what the doctor ordered. They're fully self-contained, have wi-fi, log fires, ocean views (at a distance), and the refreshing sound of horses neighing in the meadows. Relaxing, romantic and reasonably priced. Two-night minimum stay June to September.

Topmast Motel MOTEL $$
(902-634-4661; www.topmastmotel.ca; 76 Masons Beach Rd; d $105-155) No other accommodation in town has the incredible view of Lunenburg across the harbor that rooms at this simple, bright and spotlessly clean motel enjoy. Its manager is one of the friendliest hosts you could hope to find. An excellent alternative if you're looking for the privacy and isolation that B&Bs sometimes lack.

1775 Solomon House B&B B&B $$
(902-634-3477; solomonhouse@ns.sympatico.ca; 69 Townsend St; d $135;) A wonderful place with undulating floors and low door frames, this B&B has an extraordinarily cordial and helpful owner. Rooms are cozy amid the aging walls and you'll be talking about the breakfasts for the rest of your trip. The only drawbacks are the minuscule bathrooms.

Salt Shaker Deli DELI $
(902-640-3434; www.saltshakerdeli.com; 124 Montague St; mains $9-17; 11am-9pm) With a clean-cut modern atmosphere, a waterfront deck and amazing food, it's no wonder this deli-restaurant is always packed. Try the thin-crust pizzas or a pound of mussels cooked in the style of your choosing.

Nellie's Takeout FAST FOOD $
(902-634-4574; www.facebook.com/nelliestakeout; 53 Falkland St; items $4-9; 11am-6pm Mon-Sat, noon-6pm Sun) Near the frequently overlooked chunk of the Berlin Wall (yes, it's legit), Nellie's food truck is a local favorite that not too many tourists have yet discovered. That could all be about to change. We're talking fish-and-chips, fried scallops, burgers and all sorts of greasy goodness at down-to-earth prices.

Magnolia's Grill DINER $
(902-634-3287; www.magnolias-grill.com; 128 Montague St; mains $9-17; 11am-9pm Mon-Sat) Try one of the many soups of the day at this diner-style locals' favorite. Seafood, including Solomon Gundy, and an extensive wine list are also available.

★ **Lincoln Street Food** CANADIAN $$$
(902-640-3002; www.lincolnstreetfood.ca; mains $24-29, 3-course prix fixe $45; 5-9pm Wed-Sat, 11am-2pm & 5-9pm Sun;) This spot is turning heads with its market-inspired fresh food that includes vegan, vegetarian and sustainable fish and meat options. The meals are complemented by a preservative-free wine list and an uber-chic interior that looks like it's straight out of NYC's Lower East Side.

Fleur de Sel FRENCH $$$
(902-640-2121; www.fleurdesel.net; 53 Montague St; mains $22-38; 11am-2pm & 5-10pm;) On sabbatical in 2016 after 12 years knocking the socks off diners from far and wide, owners Martin and Sylvie promise to return to the helm of their elegant establishment serving French-inspired dishes made from organic produce for the 2017 season. Check the website to hold them to their promise.

Information

Explore Lunenburg (www.explorelunenburg.ca) Local history and tourism information.

Visitor Information Centre (VIC; 902-634-8100; 11 Blockhouse Hill Rd; 9am-8pm May-Oct) Perched high above town, this helpful center has maps and will help with finding beds when accommodations are in short supply.

Lunenburg Public Library (902-634-8008; 19 Pelham St; 10am-6pm Tue, Wed & Fri, to 8pm Thu, to 5pm Sat;) Free internet access.

Getting There & Away

Lunenburg is just shy of 100km from Halifax on Hwy 103. There is currently no scheduled public bus service between Halifax and Lunenburg.

Liverpool

There is plenty to see and do in historic Liverpool, one of the South Shore's larger centers. It's a pretty town with some fine heritage architecture, and is well situated for exploring several gorgeous beaches, as well as Kejimkujik National Park (69km to the north) and its Seaside Adjunct (32km southwest), but lacks a little of the seaside charm found in villages to its north.

Sights

Rossignol Cultural Centre MUSEUM
(902-354-3067; www.rossignolculturalcentre.com; 205 Church St; adult/child $5/3; 10am-5:30pm Mon-Sat) Local character Sherman Hines' most fabulous endeavor is a must-see for anyone who enjoys the offbeat. There are halls of taxidermy animals, cases of gorgeous aboriginal beadwork, walls of Hines' beautiful photography (including from his Mongolian adventures), and a room dedicated to outhouses around the world.

Hank Snow Home Town Museum MUSEUM
(902-354-4675; www.hanksnow.com; 148 Bristol Ave; $4; 9am-5pm Mon-Sat, noon-5pm Sun) This museum sheds light on Nova Scotia's status as a northern Nashville. In the old train station, it captures the history of Snow, Wilf Carter and other crooners and yodelers.

Fort Point Lighthouse LIGHTHOUSE
(902-354-5260; 21 Fort Lane; 10am-6pm May-Oct) FREE At Fort Point a cairn marks the site where Frenchman Samuel de Champlain landed in 1604. You can blow the hand-pumped foghorn in the lighthouse at the end of Main St.

Queen's County Museum MUSEUM
(902-354-4058; www.queenscountymuseum.com; 109 Main St; $4; 9:30am-5:30pm Mon-Sat, 1-5:30pm Sun) This museum has First Nations artifacts and materials relating to town history, as well as some writings by early citizens.

Perkins House Museum MUSEUM
(902-354-4058; http://perkinshouse.novascotia.ca; 105 Main St; adult/child $4/2; 9:30am-5:30pm Mon-Sat, 1-5:30pm Sun Jun-Oct) Perkins House Museum displays articles and furniture from the colonial period. Built in 1766, it's the oldest house belonging to the Nova Scotia Museum.

Festivals & Events

Privateer Days CULTURAL
(www.privateerdays.ca; Jun) This three-day summer festival is a celebration of piracy and the town's history.

Sleeping & Eating

Geranium House B&B $
(902-354-4484; 87 Milton Rd; r $60; May-Sep) This B&B on a large wooded property next to the Mersey River has three rooms with shared bathroom – ideal for cyclists and families – and a fascinating host.

Lane's Privateer Inn INN $$
(902-354-3456; www.lanesprivateerinn.com; 27 Bristol Ave; d $135-190;) Originally the home of a swashbuckling privateer, this 200-year-old inn has all the modern updates and is a clean and pleasant place to stay. It's the center of action in summer, with live music on weekends and special events such as wine tastings. There's also an excellent dining room (mains $10 to $25, open 7am to 10pm).

Entertainment

Astor Theatre THEATER
(902-354-5250; www.astortheatre.ns.ca; 59 Gorham St) The Astor is the oldest continuously operating performance venue in the province. Built in 1902 as the Liverpool Opera House, it presents films, plays and live music.

Kejimkujik National Park

Some of Nova Scotia's most unique, magnificent and unspoiled terrain is found in the Kejimkujik National Park (shortened to 'Keji' by locals). The main park occupies 381 sq km in the center of the mainland, while its smaller Seaside Adjunct is located 107km to the south.

Less than 20% of Keji's wilderness is accessible by car; the rest is reached on foot or by canoe. Bird-watchers will be in their element, while wildlife ranges from porcupines to black bear. On a less joyful note, biting insects are rampant; watch out for eel-like leeches in the lakes and some seriously large mosquitoes.

The 'Keji Adjunct' protects landscapes of rolling low brush, wildflowers, white sandy coves and the granite outcrops spreading between Port Joli and Port Mouton Bay.

The Port Joli Basin contains the **Point Joli Migratory Bird Sanctuary**, with waterfowl and shorebirds in great numbers. It's only easily accessible by kayak.

Activities

September to early October is prime hiking time; the bugs in the spring would drive you mad. More than a dozen lakes are connected by a system of portages, allowing canoe trips of up to seven days. A topographical map ($10) should be acquired for ambitious multiday trips.

The main hiking loop in the main park, the **George Lake Trail** is a 60km trek that begins at the east end of George Lake and ends at the Big Dam Lake trailhead. A shorter loop, ideal for an overnight trek, is the 26km **Channel Lake Trail**, which begins and ends at Big Dam Lake.

In the adjunct section of the park, two mostly flat trails lead to the coast from the parking lot. **Harbour Rocks Trail** (5.2km return) follows an old cart road through mixed forest to a beach where seals are often seen. The **Port Joli Head Trail** is an 8.7km loop.

Rossignol Surf Shop SURFING
(☎902-354-7100; www.surfnovascotia.com; White Point Beach Resort, White Point; ⏰10am-5pm Jul-Aug) The Rossignol Surf Shop, 32km from Keji Adjunct, rents surfboards (half-/full-day rental $20/35) and offers two-hour surfing lessons ($85). The schedule is limited; check the website for details.

Keji Outfitters CANOEING
(☎902-682-2282; www.whynotadventure.ca; ⏰8am-9pm Jun-Sep) Rent canoes and other equipment in the park at Jakes Landing. One-/24-hour hire of a double kayak, canoe or bike is $15/40. One-week hire for any of these is $165. It's open during the off-season by appointment.

Sleeping

Jeremy's Bay Campground CAMPGROUND $
(☎877-737-3783; www.pc.gc.cax; tent/RV sites $26/30; ⏰May-Oct) Of the 360 campsites within the park, 30% are assigned on a first-come, first-served basis. It costs from $10 to reserve a site.

Caledonia Country Hostel HOSTEL $
(☎902-682-3266; www.caledoniacountryhostel.com; 9960 Hwy 8, Caledonia; dm/d $30/70; 📶) In the heart of Caledonia – the only town near the park that has an internet cafe, a gas station and a grocery store – this spotless hostel has beds on the 2nd floor of an adorable Victorian-style home. Cozy nooks with TV, books and old-style upholstered chairs abound. Tours and shuttle services available.

Raven Haven Hostel & Family Park HOSTEL $
(☎902-532-7320; www.hihostels.ca; 2239 Virginia Rd, South Milford; dm/cabins $24/72, tent/RV sites $20/24; ⏰Jun-Aug; P🚭📶) This HI hostel and campground is 25km south of Annapolis Royal and 27km north of Kejimkujik National Park. The four-bed hostel is in a cabin near the beach, and rustic two-bedroom cabins have equipped kitchens but no linens. There are 15 campsites, but the camping in the park is better. Canoes and paddleboats can be rented.

Mersey River Chalets CABIN $$
(☎902-682-2447; www.merseyriverchalets.ns.ca; 315 Mersey River Chalets Road E, Caledonia; tipis $90-115, cabins $175-195; 🚭📶) Comfy cabins have pine floors, wood-burning stoves and very private porches complete with barbecue; rooms in the lodge have private decks with lake views; and cozy tipis have fully equipped kitchens. Free canoes and kayaks are available for guests.

Thomas Raddall Provincial Park CAMPGROUND
(☎902-683-2664; http://parks.novascotia.ca/content/thomas-raddall; campsites $24; ⏰May-Oct) Thomas Raddall Provincial Park, across Port Joli Harbour from Keji Adjunct, has large, private campsites, eight of which are walk-in. The forested campground extends out onto awesome beaches.

Information

Kejimkujik National Park Visitor Centre
(☎902-682-2772; www.parkscanada.gc.ca/keji; 3005 Main Pkwy, Maitland Bridge; park entrance adult/child $6/3; ⏰8:30am-8pm Jul-Sep, to 4:30pm May, Jun & Oct) Get an entry permit and park maps and reserve backcountry sites here. If you're into birding, see if they have a copy of *Nova Scotia Birding on the Lighthouse Route*.

Getting There & Away

Entrance to the Kejimkujik National Park is through the visitor center on Hwy 8, which can be approached from Annapolis Royal, 49km to the northwest. From the east, the park is 69km from Liverpool, or 68km from Bridgewater, from where it's another 19km to Lunenburg.

The only access into Kejimkujik National Park Seaside Adjunct is via Hwy 103 and then along a 6.5km gravel road. The park is 47km east of Shelburne and 32km west of Liverpool. For GPS navigation systems, search for 1188 Saint Catherine's River Road, Port Joli.

Shelburne

Shelburne's historic waterfront bobs with sailboats and has 17 homes that were built pre-1800 – it feels like a historical re-creation. The wonderfully maintained, low-in-the-earth buildings once housed Loyalists who retreated here from the American Revolution. In 1783 Shelburne was the largest community in British North America, with 16,000 residents, many from the New York aristocracy, who exploited the labor of Black Loyalists living in nearby Birchtown. Shelburne's history is celebrated with **Founders' Days** over the last weekend of July.

Sights

From mid-June to mid-August Shelburne boasts a slew of daily demonstrations around town by folks in period costume, including old-style cooking, sewing, music, military exercises, carving and more; schedules change daily but start around 1pm. Check with the visitor information center for details.

> **BLACK LOYALIST BIRCHTOWN**
>
> Just as Shelburne was once the largest settlement in British North America, so Birchtown was once the largest settlement of freed African slaves in North America. After the American Revolution, about 3500 Black Loyalists were rewarded by the British with land for settlements near Shelburne, Halifax, Digby and Guysborough. Nine years later, in 1792, after barely surviving harsh winters and unequal treatment, 1200 of them boarded 15 ships bound for Sierra Leone, in West Africa, where they founded Freetown. An additional 2000 from the USA settled in the Maritimes after the War of 1812, and others came from the Caribbean in the 1890s to work in the Cape Breton Island coal mines.

Black Loyalist Heritage Centre MUSEUM
(902-875-1310; http://blackloyalist.novascotia.ca; 119 Old Birchtown Rd; adult/child $8/5; 10am-5pm) Birchtown's Black Loyalist Heritage Centre and museum was moved to its shiny new facility in 2015, 7km outside town, on the site of what was Canada's largest free African settlement in the 1780s. The museum offers a fascinating insight into this largely untold Canadian story. There's a **trail** for hiking or cycling the 6km to Birchtown across from Spencer's Garden Centre at the far south end of Main St.

Dory Shop Museum MUSEUM
(902-875-3219; http://doryshop.novascotia.ca; 11 Dock St; adult/child $4/free; 9:30am-5:30pm Jun–mid-Oct) Shelburne dories (small open boats once used for fishing from a mother schooner) are still made to order at the Dory Shop Museum for use as lifeboats.

Ross-Thomson House MUSEUM
(902-875-3141; http://rossthomson.novascotia.ca; 9 Charlotte Lane; adult/child $4/free; 9:30am-5:30pm Jun–mid-Oct) Built in 1784, Ross-Thomson House belonged to well-to-do Loyalist merchants who arrived in Shelburne from Cape Cod. Furniture, paintings and original goods from the store are on display. The house is surrounded by authentic period gardens. Admission is free on Sunday mornings.

Shelburne County Museum MUSEUM
(902-875-3219; www.shelburnemuseums.com; 20 Dock St; by appointment) FREE A c 1787 Loyalist house is now the Shelburne County Museum. It has a collection of Loyalist furnishings, displays on the history of the local fishery, and a small collection of Mi'kmaw artifacts.

Sleeping & Eating

Islands Provincial Park CAMPGROUND $
(902-875-4304; http://parks.novascotia.ca/content/islands; 183 Barracks Rd; campsites $24; Jun-Oct) Across the harbor from Shelburne are 65 campsites in mature forest and a beach for swimming.

★ **Cooper's Inn B&B** B&B $$
(902-875-4656; www.thecoopersinn.com; 36 Dock St; r $130-220;) Part of this waterfront building dates to 1784 and was brought here from Boston. Now it's a relatively modern but still charmingly heritage-style inn with six rooms. There's also a flower-filled garden, where you can drink your complimentary bottle of Jost wine at sunset.

Bean Dock CAFE $

(902-875-1302; sandwiches $3.50-7; 10am-4pm Mon, Tue & Thu-Sat, to 8pm Wed) Grab a wooden table overlooking the bay for coffee, grilled sandwiches and light mains, from fish cakes to sun-dried tomato pasta salad. The giant Adirondack chair out front is worth chatting about.

★ **Charlotte Lane** MODERN CANADIAN $$$

(902-875-3314; www.charlottelane.ca; 13 Charlotte Lane; mains $18-33; 11:30am-2:30pm & 5-8pm Tue-Sat) People drive from Halifax to eat here, and rave about it; evening reservations are highly recommended. Swiss chef Roland Glauser is constantly revising an extensive, annotated wine list to accompany his ever-changing menu of local seafood, meat and pasta dishes.

Information

Visitor Information Centre (VIC; 902-875-4547; 43 Dock St; 9am-4pm May-Sep) Has copies of an excellent self-guided historic district walking tour.

ACADIAN SHORES

Along the Acadian Shores (which include a smaller area known as the French Shore) you'll be regularly waved to by the Stella Maris, the single-starred, tricolored Acadian flag. With the exception of British-feeling Yarmouth – the largest town in the area, first settled by the Acadians but later a stronghold for the New Empire Loyalists – this region comprises small communities who proudly uphold their French-Acadian language and traditions. This is the place to admire elaborate Catholic churches, learn about the historical struggles of the resilient Acadian people and take a stroll along a fine sandy beach. If you stay longer, don't miss the chance to sample the region's foot-tapping music performances that take place in summer.

The Acadian Shores are located along an approximately 120km-long stretch of mostly coastal land between Digby to the north and the city of Yarmouth and the communities of the Pubnicos to the south. There's no public transport outside Yarmouth and, unless you're a spirited cyclist, the distances between communities make self-driving the only practical way of exploring the region.

French Shore

The villages of Church Point, Grosses-Coques, Belliveau Cove and St Bernard, on the mainland directly across St Mary's Bay from Digby Neck, make up the heart of the French Shore. This is where Acadians settled when, after trekking back to Nova Scotia following deportation, they found their homesteads in the Annapolis Valley already occupied. Now linked by Hwy 1 – pretty much the only road in each town – these are small fishing communities.

The best way to explore this fading but unique part of the province is to follow Hwy 1 as it hugs the shoreline, from Belliveau Cove to as far south as Mavilette Beach. It can be approached equally in the reverse direction.

Sights & Activities

Rendez-Vous de la Baie CULTURAL CENTER

(www.rendezvousdelabaie.com; 23 Lighthouse Road, Church Point; 7am-7pm Mon-Fri, 9am-5pm Sat & Sun) FREE If there's one essential stop along this coast, this is it. Learn about Acadian history and culture at the museum; check out local art at the gallery; watch musical performances and more at the theater; and get tourist tips at the information center. The center also runs Acadian-themed tours.

Smuggler's Cove Provincial Park STATE PARK

(http://parks.novascotia.ca; 7651 Hwy 1, Meteghan; mid-May–mid-Oct) Named for its popularity with 19th-century pirates, this park is today frequented by picnickers. A hundred wooden stairs take you down to a rocky beach. There are picnic sites with barbecue pits at the top of the stairs, and a view across St Mary's Bay to Brier Island.

Gilbert's Cove Lighthouse LIGHTHOUSE

(902-837-5584; www.gilbertscovelighthouse.com; 244 Lighthouse Rd, Gilbert's Cove; 10am-4pm Mon-Sat, noon-4pm Sun May-Sep) FREE Built in 1904, this gorgeous little lighthouse had only two light-keepers throughout its years of service. It was rescued in 1982 from vandalism and decay by the local historical society, who have turned it into a charming museum. There's a scenic picnic area and a great spot for beachcombing and swimming.

Église St Bernard CHURCH

(St Bernard's Church; 902-837-5687; 3623 Hwy 1, St Bernard; 9am-5pm May-Nov) St Bernard is known for its church, a huge granite structure built by locals who added one row of blocks each year between 1910 and 1942. It has incredible acoustics, showcased each summer in regular musical performances.

Belliveau Beach BEACH

Belliveau Beach, near the southern end of Belliveau Cove, is made up of masses of sea-polished stones broken up by small clumps of incredibly hardy fir trees. Just behind the beach, a **cemetery** and **monument** recall the struggles of the early Acadian settlers of the French Shore.

Hinterland Adventures & Gear KAYAKING

(902-837-4092; www.kayakingnovascotia.com; 54 Gates Lane, Weymouth; kayak rentals per 1hr/day $8/42, tours from $48) Running tours for over 15 years, this respected kayaking and canoeing outfit specializes in paddling tours of St Mary's Bay and the Sissiboo River.

Festivals & Events

Festival Acadien de Clare CULTURAL

(www.festivalacadiendeclare.ca; Aug) The largest and oldest of the annual Acadian cultural festivals is held over seven days in and around the village of Church Point.

Sleeping & Eating

À la Maison d'Amitié B&B B&B $$

(902-645-2601; www.houseoffriendship.ca; 169 Baseline Rd, Mavilette; r $185; Jun-Oct;) À la Maison d'Amitié B&B is perched dramatically on a cliff close to the beach on six private hectares. The huge, American-style home has cathedral ceilings and sky-high windows with views on all sides.

Roadside Grill ACADIAN $

(902-837-5047; 3334 Hwy 1, Belliveau Cove; mains $9-18; 8am-9pm) Try the steamed clams or the *rappie* pie at this pleasantly old-fashioned and long-running local restaurant. It also rents out three small cabins (singles/doubles $60/80) with cable TV and microwaves. There's live Acadian music Tuesday nights from 5:30pm to 7:30pm June through August.

La Cuisine Robicheau ACADIAN $$

(www.lacuisinerobicheau.ca; 9651 Hwy 1, Saulnierville; mains $10-25; 8am-9pm Tue-Sun) This is the most elevated of Acadian cuisine found on this coast. The *rappie* pie, seafood lasagna and chocolate pie are so good and affordable they may make you exclaim *'sacre bleu!'*. It's family-run, always busy, and there's often live music at suppertime during summer.

Yarmouth

Founded in 1761 by New Englanders from Massachusetts, Yarmouth reached the peak of its prosperity in the 1870s. It's still the biggest town in southern Nova Scotia due to the ferry that once linked the province to Bar Harbor (Maine, USA). When that service was terminated in 2010, Yarmouth had it tough, with locals lobbying unsuccessfully to get it back. What they did get, however, is in many people's eyes even better: a high-speed passenger and vehicle catamaran linking Yarmouth with Portland, Maine's largest city.

The **Collins Heritage Conservation District**, centered on Collins St, boasts some beautiful Victorian buildings to complement Yarmouth's handful of interesting attractions, but there's no compelling reason to stick around. That said, with its recent re-positioning as the gateway to exploring the quiet, gentle pleasures of the Acadian Shores and Annapolis Valley, the locals hope you will – stick around, that is.

Sights

★ Cape Forchu Lightstation LIGHTHOUSE

(Yarmouth Light; 902-742-4522; www.capeforchulight.com; Hwy 304; 9am-5pm Jun-Sep) FREE Resembling a giant red-and-white-striped candlestick, this local icon celebrated its 175th birthday in 2015. The lighthouse affords spectacular views and there's a tearoom below. The drive in and out is also a little bit magical.

Art Gallery of Nova Scotia GALLERY

(902-749-2248; www.artgalleryofnovascotia.ca; 341 Main St; adult/child $6/free, Thu after 5pm free; 10am-5pm Tue, Wed, Fri & Sat, to 9pm Thu, noon-5pm Sun) Practical Yarmouth is the unexpected home to this refreshingly cosmopolitan branch of the Art Gallery of Nova Scotia. The ultra-modern building houses well-selected works from mostly Maritime artists.

Yarmouth County Museum MUSEUM

(902-742-5539; www.yarmouthcountymuseum.ca; 22 Collins St; adult/student $5/2; 9am-5pm Mon-Sat Jun-Sep, 2-5pm Tue-Sat Oct-May) This museum in a former church contains five period rooms related to the sea. The ticket includes Pelton-Fuller House next door.

Pelton-Fuller House HISTORIC BUILDING

(902-742-5539; www.yarmouthcountymuseum.ca; 20 Collins St; adult/student $5/2; hours vary Jun-Sep) Step back in time in this 1892 wooden home built in the Victorian Italianate style, filled with antiques and memorabilia, and with a meticulously cared-for rose garden out back. Admission includes entry to the neighboring Yarmouth County Museum.

Sleeping & Eating

★MacKinnon-Cann House Historic Inn INN $$
(☎866-698-3142; www.mackinnoncanninn.com; 27 Willow St; r $169-239;) Each of the six rooms represents a decade, ranging from the Victorian 1900s to the groovy 1960s, depicting the era at its most stylish while managing to stay calming and comfortable. Two rooms can be joined to create a family suite.

Best Western Mermaid MOTEL $$
(☎902-742-7821; www.bwmermaid.com; 545 Main St; d $115-165;) Close to the ferry terminal, this chain motel is in good shape and has the important bits covered: clean rooms, good water pressure and comfy beds. There's also a pool the kids will love in the warmer months, plus free breakfast and wi-fi.

Lakelawn B&B Motel MOTEL $$
(☎902-742-3588; www.lakelawnmotel.com; 641 Main St; r $109-159;) This place is as cute and service-oriented as motels come. Rooms are clean and basic, and some of the better meals in town are available in the country-style dining area. Go even classier in the four B&B-style rooms in the central Victorian house.

★Shanty Cafe CAFE $
(☎902-742-5918; www.shantycafe.ca; 6b Central St; items $4-9; 7am-7pm Mon-Sat;) It's almost worth coming to Yarmouth just to start your day with something delicious and healthy from this proudly sparkling cafe, where you can tell it's a labor of love for all concerned. For lunch, Indian and Mexican flavors spice up Western favorites on a menu that's as inexpensive as it is diverse.

Rudder's Brew Pub PUB FOOD $
(☎902-742-7311; www.ruddersbrewpub.com; 96 Water St; pub menu $8-14, dinner mains $14-32; 11am-late) The 300 seats at this waterfront pub and restaurant fill fast. A mean ale is brewed on-site and there's a wide-ranging menu. Drinks are poured until the wee hours on busy summer nights.

Marco's Grill and Pasta House ITALIAN $$
(☎902-742-7716; www.marcosgrill.com; 624 Main St; mains $10-24; 11am-9pm) If you've been traveling around the province for a while, there'll come a day when the thought of eating another lobster or bucket of mussels will tip you over the edge. That's when Marco's fabulous, very Italian pastas will be the most comforting thing since mom's lasagna. Don't pass up the breaded mushrooms.

Stanley Lobster Pound SEAFOOD $$
(☎902-742-8291; www.stanleylobster.com; 1066 Overton Rd; market price varies; 3-8pm Wed-Sat) You can't get more authentic than choosing your own lobster and walking it home. Well, not really, but you can have your lobster two ways – live or cooked. It's a lot easier to have the little critter boiled up, so you can dine by campfire overlooking the Bay of Fundy. Down-home Nova Scotia atmosphere aplenty.

> WORTH A TRIP
>
> **ACADIAN VILLAGE**
>
> The 17-acre **Le Village historique acadien de la Nouvelle-Écosse** (Historical Acadian Village of Nova Scotia; ☎902-762-2530; http://levillage.novascotia.ca; 91 Old Church Rd, Lower West Pubnico; adult/child $7/3; 9am-5pm Jun-Oct) overlooking Pubnico Harbour re-creates an Acadian village, with vintage Acadian buildings and a cemetery. The village is located in West Pubnico, one of Nova Scotia's original Acadian communities (and not to be confused with all the other nearby Pubnicos), about a 40-minute drive southeast of Yarmouth.

Information

Visitors Information Centre (VIC; ☎902-742-5033; 228 Main St; 7:30am-9pm May-Oct) Ask for a local walking tour map.

Izaak Walton Killam Memorial Library (☎902-742-2486; 405 Main St; 10am-4pm Mon-Sat;) Has free internet access.

Getting There & Away

Yarmouth is 300km southwest of Halifax on Hwy 103, and 104km south of Digby on Hwy 101.

There are no scheduled bus services from Yarmouth to Halifax and beyond, but Cloud Nine Shuttle (p346) can get you to the capital or to Halifax International Airport.

As of June 2016, Yarmouth is once again connected to the USA by sea. The trip, operated by **Bay Ferries** (www.ferries.ca) travels to Portland, Maine (adult/child $107/65, 5½ hours). Bringing a vehicle will cost an extra $199.

Getting Around

You can rent bikes and surreys (four-wheeled covered bicycles) from **Wheelhouse** (☎902-307-7433; www.thewheelhouse.ca; 5 Collins Street; bikes per hour from $12; ⏰9am-5pm) for a fun way to explore Yarmouth.

ANNAPOLIS VALLEY

Historically, the fertile and sparsely populated Annapolis Valley was known as the breadbasket of colonial Canada. Today, the region still produces much of Nova Scotia's fresh produce, especially apples, but the real excitement surrounds the growth of the valley's viticulture industry. The wineries boast a similar latitude to Bordeaux, France, and have taken advantage of the sandy soil and reconnected with the area's French roots.

Regional highlights include the **Annapolis Valley Apple Blossom Festival** (www.appleblossom.com), visits to the Fundy coast at Annapolis Royal for tidal vistas over patchwork farmland, the vibrant and spirited town of Wolfville, and taking a moment to contemplate the past while gazing upon the World Heritage landscape of Grand Pré.

Getting There & Away

Hwy 101, which begins on the outskirts of Halifax, continues for 74km to Wolfville at the northern extent of the Annapolis Valley, then runs straight down to Digby in the south. Because of the distances between towns and the many and varied side-trips to discover, self-driving is the most practical and enjoyable way to explore the region.

At Digby, **Bay Ferries** (www.ferries.ca) links Nova Scotia to Saint John, NB, via car ferry. The journey takes approximately 2¼ hours in peak season and 2¾ hours during off season. Check the website for schedules.

Getting Around

The **Kings Transit** (www.kingstransit.ns.ca) bus line runs every other hour from 6am to around 7pm from Weymouth (just north of Church Point) to Bridgetown (just north of Annapolis Royal) and then as far as Wolfville, stopping in every little town along the way.

Long Island

The long and narrow strip of land that resembles a giraffe's neck craning out to take a peek into the Bay of Fundy is known as **Digby Neck**. At the far western end of this appendage, Long Island, and then Brier Island, are connected by ferry with the rest of the peninsula. The entire area is a haven for whale and seabird watchers.

Many people head straight to Brier Island, but Long Island is easier to get to and has a few more residents. At the northeastern edge of Long Island, **Tiverton** (population 300) is a tiny fishing community. Continuing along the main road for 15km, you'll reach the southwestern end of the island and the village of **Freeport** (population 250), central for exploring both Brier and Long Islands.

In the center of the island, **Central Grove Provincial Park** has a muddy, 2km-long hiking trail to the Bay of Fundy.

Sights & Activities

Island Museum MUSEUM
(☎902-839-2034; www.islandshistoricalsociety.com; 243 Hwy 217, Freeport; by donation; ⏰9:30am-4:30pm Jun-Sep) This local history museum has exhibits on island life and a tourist information desk.

★**Ocean Explorations Whale Cruises** WHALE WATCHING
(☎902-839-2417; www.oceanexplorations.ca; tours from $75; ⏰Jun-Oct) One of the best whale-watching tours in the province is led by biologist Tom Goodwin and has the adventurous approach of getting you down low to whale level in a Zodiac. Shimmy into an orange coastguard-approved flotation suit and hold on tight! Goodwin has been leading whale-watching tours since 1980 and regularly donates to wildlife conservation and environmental education organizations.

Eating

Lavena's Catch Café CAFE $
(☎902-839-2517; 15 Hwy 217, Freeport; mains $7-18; ⏰11:30am-8pm; 📶) Lavena's Catch Café is a country-style cafe directly above the wharf at Freeport; it's the perfect spot to enjoy a sunset and you might even see a whale from the balcony. There's occasional live music in the evenings.

Getting There & Away

Long island is connected to Digby Neck by a ferry (foot passenger/car free/$5), which runs from the aptly named East Ferry to Tiverton, every hour on the half-hour from 9:30am to 4:30pm, and returns on the hour.

Brier Island

Brier Island bills itself as a top ecotourism destination. The island was home to Joshua Slocum who, in 1895, became the first man to sail solo around the world. Westport, Brier Island's only permanent settlement, is a quaint fishing village and a good base for exploring the numerous excellent, if rugged and windy, hiking trails around the island. Columnar basalt rocks are seen all along the coast and agates can be found on the beaches.

Plankton stirred up by the strong Fundy tides attracts finback, minke and humpback whales, and this is the best place in the world to see the endangered North Atlantic right whale. Blue whales, the world's largest animal, are also sighted on occasion, plus you're almost certain to see plenty of seals.

Bring plenty of warm clothing (regardless of how hot it seems), sunblock and binoculars; motion-sickness pills are recommended.

Sights & Activities

Brier Island Lighthouse LIGHTHOUSE
(Western Light; 720 Lighthouse Rd) Originally built in 1809, this rugged outpost has seen many incarnations over the years. Its present form, a striking red-and-white-striped concrete tower standing 18.3m tall, was built in 1944 and has been automated since 1987.

Brier Island Whale & Seabird Cruises WHALE WATCHING
(902-839-2995; www.brierislandwhalewatch.com; adult/child from $50/28; Jun-Oct) You can book excellent whale-watching tours (2½ to five hours, depending on where the whales are) with this eco-conscious company.

Sleeping

Brier Island Lodge LODGE $$
(902-839-2300; www.brierisland.com; 557 Water Street, Westport; r $109-169; May-Oct) Atop cliffs 1km east of Westport, Brier Island Lodge has 37 rooms, many with ocean views. Its **restaurant** (mains $8 to $29) has views on two sides, friendly service and fabulously fresh seafood. Boxed lunches are available.

Getting There & Away

Brier Island is fairly remote, even by Canadian standards. It's just over 70km from Digby (itself a little removed from the rest of Nova Scotia) via Long Island and two car-ferry crossings. The best way to understand ferry timings is to check out www.brierisland.org/info.html. Needless to say, you'll need your own wheels.

Digby

Nestled in a protected inlet off the Bay of Fundy, Digby is known for its scallops, mild climate and daily ferry to Saint John, NB. Settled by United Empire Loyalists in 1783, it's now home to the largest fleet of scallop boats in the world.

Emigration in recent years has been hard on Digby, parts of which are looking a little rough around the edges. The town lacks the architectural charm of starlets such as Lunenburg, Wolfville and Annapolis Royal, but it remains a logical base for explorations of Digby Neck, Long and Brier Islands, and the French Shore.

If you're here in passing, the best things to do are to stroll the waterfront, watch the scallop draggers come and go, eat as much of their catch as you can, then squeeze in a sunset at **Point Prim**.

Sights

Admiral Digby Museum MUSEUM
(902-245-6322; www.admiraldigbymuseum.ca; 95 Montague Row; by donation; 9am-5pm Mon-Sat) The only real sight in town is the Admiral Digby Museum, a mid-19th-century Georgian home that contains exhibits of the town's marine history and early settlement.

Festivals & Events

Digby Scallop Days FOOD & DRINK
(www.digbyscallopdays.com; Aug) If you're around in summer, reserve even more space in your belly and itinerary for this delicious seafood festival.

Wharf Rat Rally MOTORCYCLE
(www.wharfratrally.com; late Aug–early Sep) Rev your engines for the Wharf Rat Rally at the end of August, where tens of thousands of bikers roar into town for motorcycle-oriented contests, tours and general mingling. Book your accommodations well in advance.

Sleeping & Eating

Digby Backpackers Inn HOSTEL $
(902-245-4573; www.digbyhostel.com; 168 Queen St; dm/r $30/65) Saskia and Claude keep the solid four-bed dorm rooms spotless and often spontaneously host barbecues or take the whole hostel out to see the sunset. The heritage house has plenty of communal areas, including a deck, and there's a welcoming vibe. Internet access, a light breakfast and towels are included in the price. Cash only.

Digby Pines Golf Resort & Spa RESORT $$
(902-245-2511; www.digbypines.ca; 103 Shore Rd; d/ste/cottage from $140/195/265; May-Oct;) Although standard rooms are elegantly furnished with dark woods and comfy bedding, they're small for the price, and the resort could do with some general TLC. That said, Digby Pines still offers the town's highest standard of accommodation, with attentive staff, an excellent restaurant and fabulous, family-friendly facilities, which include a world-class golf course, outdoor pool and day-spa.

Josie's Place DINER $
(902-245-2952; 88 Warwick St; mains $7-18; 7am-8pm) There's nothing fancy about Josie's – just good, old-fashioned, no-frills diner-style cooking, from fry-up breakfasts to meatloaf like your mom used to make, along with sandwiches, salads, and fish-and-chips. Cheap and cheery. There's a line out the door when the bikers are in town.

Shoreline Restaurant SEAFOOD $$
(902-245-6667; 88 Water St; mains $12-28; 11am-9pm) Walk through the gift store to the restaurant out back, where you can choose a table by the window or a booth on the deck overlooking a grassy lawn and the harbor beyond. Daily specials and all your seafood faves are on the menu (including bacon-wrapped scallops!), as well as steaks, burgers and salads.

Information

Western Counties Regional Library (902-245-2163; www.westerncounties.ca; 84 Warwick St; 12:30-5pm & 6-8pm Tue-Thu, 10am-5pm Fri, 10am-2pm Sat;) Free internet access.

Transport

Digby is 32km southwest of Annapolis Royal, just off Hwy 1. From Yarmouth, it's 104km along Hwy 101, heading northeast.

Kings Transit (902-628-7310; www.kingstransit.ns.ca; one-way fare adult/child $3.50/1.75) operates a local bus service that runs north as far as Wolfville, via Annapolis Royal.

Bay Ferries (www.ferries.ca) operates a daily car-ferry service to Saint John, NB, on the *Fundy Rose* (adult/child from $36/20, 2¼ to 2¾ hours). Rates for vehicles start at $107, including fuel surcharge.

Bear River

Bear River is a delightful riverside enclave popular with artists and those who moved here from larger centers for a 'tree change'. There's a strong Mi'kmaq presence mixed in with Scottish roots, giving Bear River a unique vibe. Some buildings near the river are on stilts, while other historic homes nestle on the steep hills of the valley. A few wineries are starting to pop up just out of town.

Sights

Bear River First Nation Heritage & Cultural Centre CULTURAL CENTER
(902-467-0301; 194 Reservation Rd; $3) Bear River First Nation is a five-minute drive from Bear River town: turn left after crossing the bridge, then take a left where the road forks. A 1km trail starts behind the center and highlights plants with traditional medicinal uses. The Heritage & Cultural Centre offers demonstrations of traditional crafts and hands-on workshops, but unfortunately it's open infrequently.

Annapolis Highland Vineyards WINERY
(902-467-0363; www.annapolishighlandvineyards.com; 2635 Clementsvale Rd; 10am-5pm Mon-Sat, noon-5pm Sun) Don't miss the gold-medal White Wedding dessert wine if you come in for a free tasting at this rather commercial winery. Delicious fruit wines are also available.

Bear River Winery WINERY
(902-467-4156; www.wine.travel; 133 Chute Rd; by appointment) All estate-produced, award-winning wines made at this adorable little winery are created using solar energy, biodiesel, wind power and the natural slope of the property. Stop by to take a free tour and tasting (July to September) or stay longer at friendly hosts Chris and Peggy's one-room **B&B** ($140 per night) to enjoy wine-making workshops and retreats.

Eating

Myrtle and Rosie's Cafe CAFE $
(902-467-0176; 1880 Clementsvale Rd; mains $7-14; 10am-5pm Tue-Sun) Stop in to chat with locals, have coffee over a slice of pie, or chow down on a delicious BLT or a juicy burger, and enjoy the view of Bear River.

Shopping

Flight of Fancy GIFTS & SOUVENIRS
(☎902-467-4171; www.theflight.ca; 1869 Clementsvale Rd; ⊙10am-6pm) This exquisitely curated craft store and gallery has work by close to 200 artists and craftspeople. If you want to buy just one treasure to take away from Nova Scotia, this is a good place to find it.

Annapolis Royal

The community's efforts to restore and promote their village as a tourist destination have made Annapolis Royal one of the most delightful places to visit in the region. At the time of writing, it remained one of the only well-trodden towns in the province without a ubiquitous Tim Horton's coffee and donut franchise.

As teeny-tiny as it feels, Annapolis Royal is dripping with historical significance: the area was the location of Canada's first permanent European settlement and was capital of Nova Scotia until the founding of Halifax in 1749. Formerly called Port Royal, it was founded by French explorer Samuel de Champlain in 1605. As the British and French battled, the settlement often changed hands. In 1710 the British had a decisive victory and changed the town's name to Annapolis Royal in honor of Queen Anne.

Sights

★Fort Anne National Historic Site HISTORIC SITE
(☎902-532-2397; www.parkscanada.gc.ca/fortanne; Upper St George St; adult/child $4/2; ⊙9am-5:30pm) This historic site in the town center preserves the memory of the early Acadian settlement, plus the remains of the 1635 French fort. Entry to the extensive grounds is free, but you'll also want to visit the museum, where artifacts are contained in various period rooms. An extraordinary four-panel tapestry, crafted in needlepoint by more than 100 volunteers, depicts 400 years of history.

Port Royal National Historic Site HISTORIC SITE
(☎902-532-2898; www.pc.gc.ca; 53 Historic Lane; adult/child $4/2; ⊙9am-6pm) Some 14km northwest of Annapolis Royal, Port Royal National Historic Site is the actual location of the first permanent European settlement north of Florida. The site is a replica of de Champlain's 1605 fur-trading habitation, where costumed workers help tell the story of this early settlement.

Annapolis Royal Historic Gardens GARDENS
(☎902-532-7018; www.historicgardens.com; 441 St George St; adult/child $14.50/6; ⊙9am-8pm Jul & Aug, to 5pm May, Jun, Sep & Oct) These gorgeous gardens cover a rambling 6.5 hectares with various themed areas such as an Acadian kitchen garden one might have seen in the late 1600s, and an innovative modern one. Munch on blueberries, ogle the vegetables and look for frogs. The **Secret Garden Café** offers lunches and German-style baked goods.

Activities

★Tour Annapolis Royal WALKING
(www.tourannapolisroyal.com; tours adult/child $9/5; ⊙Jul-Oct) This outfit runs several history-oriented tours. The best is a creepy tour of the Fort Anne graveyard led by an undertaker-garbed guide. Everyone carries a lantern and winds through the headstones to discover this town's history. Proceeds go to the local historical society. Hour-long tours begin at 9:30pm; check the website for dates.

Delap's Cove Wilderness Trail HIKING
Over the North Mountain from Annapolis Royal, Delap's Cove Wilderness Trail lets you get out on the Fundy shore. It consists of two loop trails connected by an old inland road that used to serve a Black Loyalist community. Today, only relics of old foundations and apple trees remain in the woods. Both the loop trails are a 9km round-trip.

Sleeping & Eating

Dunromin Campground CAMPGROUND $
(☎902-532-2808; www.dunromincampground.ca; 4618 Hwy 1, Granville Ferry; tent/RV sites from $30/45, cabins/caravans from $70/145; ⊙May-Oct; P 📶 🐾) This popular, offbeat campground has some secluded riverside sites, as well as nifty options such as a tipi for up to six people and a gypsy caravan. Canoes are available to rent ($10 per hour).

Croft House B&B B&B $
(☎902-532-0584; www.crofthouse.ca; 51 Riverview Lane; d from $85; P 📶 🐾) This farmhouse stands on approximately 40 hectares of land, about a five-minute drive from Annapolis Royal across the river. One of the enthusiastic owners is a chef and he whips up a fine breakfast with organic ingredients.

★Queen Anne Inn INN $$
(☎902-532-7850; www.queenanneinn.ns.ca; 494 Upper St George St; r $129-179, carriage house from $189; ⊙May-Oct; P❄📶) Arguably the most elegant property in Annapolis Royal, this B&B is the perfect balance of period decor and subtle grace. It's so beautiful, with the Tiffany lamp replicas, manicured grounds and sweeping staircases, that it might seem stuffy were it not for the friendly owners, who make you feel like you could (almost) kick your feet up on the antique coffee table.

Bailey House B&B B&B $$
(☎902-532-1285; www.baileyhouse.ca; 150 Lower St George St; r $145; P📶) The only B&B on the waterfront, Bailey House is also the oldest inn and one of the best in the area. The friendly owners have managed to keep the vintage charm (anyone over 6ft might hit their head on the doorways!), while adding all the modern comforts and conveniences.

★Cafe Restaurant Compose EUROPEAN $$
(☎902-532-1251; www.restaurantcompose.com; 235 St George St; mains lunch $11-18, dinner $18-34; ⊙5-8:30pm Wed, 11:30am-2:30pm & 5-8:30pm Thu-Tue; 📶) This cafe offers fine dining in a relaxed setting, with wonderful views of the Bay of Fundy. Dine alfresco (in season) to get even closer to the shore. With an emphasis on fresh seafood and local produce, the menu reads well and is executed beautifully, with something for everyone.

Bistro East BISTRO $$
(☎902-532-7992; www.bistroeast.com; 274 St George St; mains $12-28; ⊙11am-10pm) Great for lunch and dinner, Bistro East has been serving juicy steaks, fresh seafood and handmade pasta for almost a decade. Friday and Saturday nights feature live, good-for-the-ambience music from 8pm. This is one of those jovial little establishments where it's genuinely difficult to be disappointed.

German Bakery & Sachsen Cafe GERMAN $$
(☎902-532-1990; www.germanbakery.ca; 358 St George St; mains $9-20; ⊙9am-7pm) In an area where seafood is king, it's nice to find hearty German breads, schnitzels and desserts in this casual, although slightly overpriced, cafe.

🍷 Drinking & Entertainment

Ye Olde Pub PUB
(☎902-532-2244; 9 Church St; ⊙11am-11pm Mon-Sat, noon-8pm Sun) Rumored to be Nova Scotia's smallest pub, it's by no means the dullest. On sunny days drink beer and eat pub grub (mains $5 to $15) on the outdoor terrace; when it's cooler, slip into the dark and cozy old bar, which was once a bank.

King's Theatre THEATER
(☎902-532-7704; www.kingstheatre.ca; 209 St George St; movies $10, live shows from $15) Right on the waterfront, this nonprofit theater presents musicals, dramas and concerts most evenings in July and August, and occasionally during the rest of the year. Hollywood films are screened on most weekends and independent films most Tuesdays year-round.

 Shopping

Farmers & Traders Market MARKET
(www.annapolisroyalfarmersmarket.com; cnr St George & Church Sts; ⊙8am-noon Sat May-Oct, also 10am-2pm Wed Jul & Aug) Annapolis Royal's thriving community of artists and artisans offer their wares alongside local farm produce at this popular market. There's live entertainment most Saturday mornings.

 Information

Tourist Information Centre (☎902-532-5769; www.annapolisroyal.com; 236 Prince Albert Rd; ⊙10am-6pm May-Oct) At the Tidal Power Project; pick up a historic walking tour pamphlet.

Wolfville & Grand Pré

Visually arresting, Wolfville has a perfect blend of old-college-town culture, small-town homeyness and a culinary scene that has developed in concert with the surrounding wine industry. Combined with the town's permanent residents, the students and faculty of local Acadia University bump the town's residential population to over 7000, injecting a youthful vigor to this otherwise quiet district and making Wolfville one of the province's most livable and ethnically diverse towns.

Essentially just down the road, Grand Pré, Wolfville's bucolic neighbor, is a small bilingual community. In the 1750s, however, it was the site of one of the most tragic but compelling stories in eastern Canada's history, the Acadian deportation. In 2012, the marshland and polder farmland of Grand Pré were given Unesco World Heritage status.

Beyond the two towns, you'll find Acadian dikes, scenic drives and some of the best hiking along the Fundy Coast.

WOLFVILLE & GRAND PRÉ WINERIES

Most of Nova Scotia's best wineries and vineyards are found in the rolling hills and valleys around Wolfville and Grand Pré. Our pick of the bunch (so to speak):

Luckett Vineyards (902-542-2600; www.luckettvineyards.com; 1293 Grand Pré Rd, Wolfville; tastings from $5; 10am-5pm May-Oct) Palatial views over the vines and hillsides down to the Bay of Fundy cliffs. Sample the red, white, fruit and dessert wines, and the particularly good ice wine, then stay for lunch on the patio.

Gaspereau Vineyards (902-542-1455; www.gaspereauwine.com; 2239 White Rock Rd, Gaspereau; 10am-5pm May-Oct, tours noon, 2pm & 4pm) One of the province's best-known wineries, with award-winning ice wine, an elegant Estate Riesling, and super-friendly staff.

Domaine de Grand Pré (902-542-1753; www.grandprewines.ns.ca; 11611 Hwy 1, Grand Pré; tours $9; 10am-6pm, tours 11am, 3pm & 5pm) A great destination winery and one of the best known in the province. It features a delicious spicy muscat and a nice sparkling Champlain Brut.

L'Acadie Vineyards (902-542-8463; www.lacadievineyards.ca; 310 Slayter Rd, Wolfville; 10am-5pm May-Oct) Overlooking Gaspereau Valley, this geothermally powered winery grows certified-organic grapes to make traditional-method sparkling and dried-grape wines.

Blomidon Estate Winery (902-582-7565; www.blomidonwine.ca; 10318 Hwy 221, Canning; tastings from $5; 10am-6pm Jun-Sep) The friendly and laid-back winemaker comes out to chat with those tasting wines. The sparkling wines and Tidal Bay are probably the best, but the oaky red merits a try.

If you don't want to drive, hop on the **Wolfville Magic Winery Bus**, which runs from June through mid-October.

Sights

★Grand Pré National Historic Site — HISTORIC SITE

(902-542-3631; www.pc.gc.ca; 2205 Grand Pré Rd, Grand Pré; adult/child $8/4; 9am-6pm May-Oct) This interpretive center explains the historical context for the deportation of the French-Acadian people from Acadian, Mi'kmaw and British perspectives and traces the many routes Acadians took from, and back to, the Maritimes. Beside the center, a serene park contains gardens, an Acadian-style stone church, and a bust of American poet Henry Wadsworth Longfellow, who chronicled the Acadian saga in *Evangeline: A Tale of Acadie,* and a statue of his fictional Evangeline, now a romantic symbol of her people.

★Tangled Garden — GARDENS

(902-542-9811; www.tangledgardenherbs.ca; 11827 Hwy 1, Grand Pré; garden $5; 10am-6pm) These unique, sumptuous terraced gardens afford wonderful views of the surrounding countryside. A labor of love, the meticulous grounds are the perfect spot to wander, picnic or contemplate, especially when walking the meditative **labyrinth**. The gift shop is probably the best-smelling shopping experience in Nova Scotia. Be sure to pick up a jar of the phenomenal rosemary quince jelly.

Randall House Museum — MUSEUM

(902-542-9775; 171 Main St, Wolfville; by donation; 10am-5pm Mon-Sat, 2-5pm Sun Jun-Sep) Randall House Museum relates the history of the New England planters and colonists who replaced the expelled Acadians.

Waterfront Park — PARK

(cnr Gaspereau Ave & Front St, Wolfville) Waterfront Park offers a stunning view of the tidal mudflats, Minas Basin and the red cliffs of Cape Blomidon. Displays explain the tides, dikes, flora and fauna, and the history of the area. This is an easy spot to start a walk or cycle on top of the dikes.

Tours

Wolfville Magic Winery Bus — BUS

(902-542-4093; www.wolfvillemagicwinerybus.ca; hop-on/hop-off bus passes $30; Thu-Sun Jun-Oct) If you think you'd like to sample more than a few wines in the area's four amazing vineyards, best to have a local

WORTH A TRIP

CAPE BLOMIDON & THE UPPER ANNAPOLIS VALLEY

The North Mountain, which ends at the dramatic Cape Blomidon, defines one edge of the Annapolis Valley. On the other side of the mountain are fishing communities on the Bay of Fundy. The valley floor is crisscrossed with small highways lined with farms and orchards. It's a great place to get out your road map – or throw it away – and explore.

Around 3km from the village of Port Williams, the 1814 **Prescott House Museum** (902-542-3984; http://prescotthouse.novascotia.ca; 1633 Starr's Point Rd; adult/student $4/3; 10am-5pm Mon-Sat, 1-5pm Sun Jun-Sep) – considered to be one of the finest examples of Georgian architecture in Nova Scotia – was the former home of the horticulturalist who introduced many of the apple varieties grown in the Annapolis Valley.

In the quaint, historic town of Canning, stop for a fair-trade coffee (or an art class) at **Art Can Gallery & Café** (902-582-7071; www.artcan.com; 9850 Main St; mains $10-14; 9am-5pm;) or head just out of town to sample wines at Blomidon Estate Winery (p365).

North out of Canning, along Hwy 358, stop at the well-signposted Look-Off. About 200m above the Annapolis Valley, it's the perfect spot to view the farmlands below and, if you're lucky, bald eagles above: from November to March they number in the hundreds, attracted by local chicken farms.

Hwy 358 ends in Scots Bay, where the dramatic 14km **Cape Split hiking trail** (www.scottsbay.com/cape-split) leads to views of the Minas Basin and the Bay of Fundy. If you're not up for the hike, nearby **Blomidon Provincial Park** (902-582-7319; www.parks.gov.ns.ca; 3138 Pereau Rd, Canning) has a picnic area and plenty of easier walks.

For some lunch after all that fresh air, head to Centreville's **Hall's Harbour Lobster Pound** (902-679-5299; www.hallsharbourlobster.com; 1157 W Halls Harbour Rd; mains $13-24; noon-7pm May-Oct) and gorge yourself on ocean delicacies, straight from the source.

Round out your afternoon with a visit to Kentville, the county seat for the area, where you can rent a bike at **Valley Stove & Cycle** (902-542-7280; www.valleystoveandcycle.com; 353 Main St; bike rental half/full day $25/35) to admire the town's stately old homes, or check out the region's apple farming history at **Blair House Museum** (Kentville Agricultural Centre; 902-678-1093; 32 Main St; 8:30am-4:30pm Mon-Fri Jun-Sep) FREE or other local history and art at **Old King's County Museum** (902-678-6237; www.kingscountymuseum.ca; 37 Cornwallis Ave; 9am-4pm Mon-Sat Jun-Aug, closed Sat Apr, May & Sep–mid-Dec) FREE.

drive you around – on a classic British double-decker, no less! Check the website for updated schedules.

Festivals & Events

Canadian Deep Roots Festival MUSIC
(www.deeprootsmusic.ca; late Sep) If you're in Wolfville in early fall, rock out to modern roots music at this annual festival.

Sleeping

Garden House B&B B&B $
(902-542-1703; www.gardenhouse.ca; 220 Main St, Wolfville; r $85-120;) This antique house retains its old-time feel in the most comfortable way. Creaky floors, a rustic breakfast table decorated with wildflowers, and a lived-in vibe you instantly feel a part of (everyone is encouraged to take off their shoes). Bathrooms are shared.

★ **Olde Lantern Inn & Vineyard** INN $$
(902-542-1389; www.oldlanterninn.com; 11575 Hwy 1, Grand Pré; r $129-150;) Clean lines, a friendly welcome and attention to every comfort makes this a great place to stay. The vineyard grounds overlook Minas Basin, where you can watch the rise and fall of the Fundy tides and gaze over the World Heritage Grand Pré landscape.

★ **Blomidon Inn** INN $$
(800-565-2291; www.blomidon.ns.ca; 195 Main St, Wolfville; d $139-159, ste $179-269;) Grand Victorian architecture and old-world extravagance make this a very upper-crust-feeling inn. Set in 2.5 hectares of perfectly maintained gardens, with rooms just as well groomed. Check online for package deals.

★ **Roselawn Lodging** MOTEL $$
(902-542-3420; www.roselawnlodging.ca; 32 Main St, Wolfville; d $95-185;) This

wonderful little 1960s-style complex features a variety of motel-style rooms and freshly updated cute-as-a-button cottages with full kitchens, and makes a welcome alternative to Wolfville's lofty B&Bs. With a pool, tennis court and spacious grounds, it's easy to make this place your little home away from home.

Victoria's Historic Inn INN $$
(902-542-5744; www.victoriashistoricinn.com; 600 Main St, Wolfville; r $149-229) This elegant inn is directly opposite Acadia University. Each of its luxuriously appointed rooms vary in style, but all are decorated with excellent taste and attention to detail. Expect indulgences such as four-poster beds, period furnishings, fine linens, and memorable full breakfasts. Check the website to pick your favorite room; the Chase suite is hard to beat.

Gingerbread House Inn INN $$
(902-542-1458; www.gingerbreadhouse.ca; 8 Robie Tufts Dr, Wolfville; d $125, ste $185-210;) Although not in bad taste, the exterior of this unique, floral and frilly, B&B is like a big pink birthday cake with lacy white edging. All rooms have private external entrances.

Eating

Wolfville's proximity to local vineyards and growing reputation as *the* culinary hot spot outside Halifax means there's no shortage of great food to enjoy, from tasty student-priced eateries to fabulous fine dining.

Dining in Grand Pré is limited to the region's selection of higher-end winery cafes and restaurants.

Naked Crepe CREPERIE $
(902-542-0653; www.thenakedcrepebistro.ca; 402 Main St, Wolfville; crepes $3-12; 9am-11pm) Who doesn't enjoy a wafer-thin, flaky crepe filled with delicious sweet or savory goodness? Catering to both the breakfast crowd *and* the late-nighters, Naked Crepe boasts a huge range of inventive fillings. Excellent value.

Tin Pan CAFE $
(902-691-0020; 978 Main St, Port Williams; mains $6-14; 8am-8pm Mon-Sat) Only a blink away from Wolfville on Hwy 358 is the Tin Pan, a favorite for motorcyclists who head here on Saturday mornings for hearty breakfasts.

Troy MEDITERRANEAN $$
(902-542-4425; www.troyrestaurant.ca; 12 Elm Ave, Wolfville; mains $16-26; noon-8pm) It's refreshing to taste the spectacular flavors of healthy Mediterranean cuisine, presented in a modern and incredibly colorful restaurant, in otherwise mostly unadventurous, rural Nova Scotia. A range of light appetizers, which work equally well in a tapas-style presentation, is complemented by predominantly meat-based kebabs and mains, with some vegetarian and gluten-free options.

★ **Le Caveau** EUROPEAN $$$
(902-542-1753; www.grandprewines.ns.ca/restaurant; 11611 Hwy 1, Grand Pré; mains lunch $12-18, dinner $20-34; 11:30am-2pm & 5-9pm May-Oct) Considered to be the finest Northern European–style restaurant in the province, this Swiss restaurant is on the grounds of Domaine de Grand Pré (p365). The beautiful outdoor patio is paved with fieldstones and shaded with grapevines.

Privet House FUSION $$$
(902-542-7525; www.facebook.com/PrivetHouseRestaurant; 268 Main St, Wolfville; mains lunch $12-20, dinner $19-38; 11:30am-3pm & 5-9pm Tue-Sun) The finest dining in town serves up aged Atlantic beef, local seafood and game (all ingredients are Canadian) prepared with everything from European to Indian and Thai influences. Tablecloths are white, the wine list is long and the service is top-notch.

Drinking & Entertainment

Library Pub & Wine Tavern PUB
(902-542-4315; www.thelibrarypub.ca; 472 Main St, Wolfville; 11am-midnight) Wolfville's Main St drinking establishment is a jolly place in a quaint historic building. If you're flying solo and of an agreeable temperament, you're bound to make some new friends here.

Acadia Cinema's Al Whittle Theatre THEATER
(902-542-3344; www.alwhittletheatre.ca; 450 Main St, Wolfville) Operated by the volunteer-run Acadia Cinema Co-op, this fabulous historic building, a Wolfville cultural icon, functions as a multipurpose cinema, theater and performance space. Check the website for regular events listings and screening times and to learn about the theater's history.

Information

Wolfville Memorial Library (902-542-5760; 21 Elm Ave, Wolfville; 10am-5pm Tue-Sat, 1-5pm Sun;) Free internet access.

Tourist Information Centre (902-542-7000; www.wolfville.ca; 11 Willow Ave, Wolfville; 9am-9pm May-Oct)

Getting There & Away

Wolfville is linked to Halifax by Hwy 101; the journey takes an hour in good traffic.

Maritime Bus (www.maritimebus.com) services from Halifax stop at Acadia University in front of Wheelock Hall off Highland Ave. **Kings Transit** (www.kingstransit.ns.ca) buses run between Cornwallis (southwest of Annapolis Royal) and Wolfville, stopping at 209 Main St.

Windsor

Windsor was once the only British stronghold in this region, but today it's just a graying little town eking out an existence between the highway and the Avon River. Windsor is a place to enjoy bluegrass music – think lots of fast banjo picking.

While in town, check out **Haliburton House** (902-798-2915; http://haliburtonhouse.novascotia.ca; 414 Clifton Ave; adult/student $4/3; 10am-5pm Mon-Sat, 1-5pm Sun Jun-Oct), once home to Judge Thomas Chandler Haliburton (1796–1865), writer of the Sam Slick stories. Many of Haliburton's expressions, such as 'quick as a wink' and 'city slicker,' are still used. There's also a **blues festival** (www.smokinbluesfest.ca), Windsor's hottest ticket.

Stay the night at the **Clockmaker's Inn** (902-792-2573; www.theclockmakersinn.com; 1399 King St; d incl breakfast $99-179; P), a French-château-style mansion with curved bay windows, lots of stained glass and sweeping hardwood staircases. It's gay-friendly and afternoon tea is served daily.

CENTRAL NOVA SCOTIA

Hiking, rafting and rockhounding are the activities of choice around this pleasant and often overlooked region. For those traveling overland from the rest of Canada, the town of **Amherst**, geographic center of the Maritimes and a crossroads between New Brunswick, Prince Edward Island and Nova Scotia, will be your first taste of the province, if you swing off the Trans-Canada Hwy (Hwy 104 at this point).

From Amherst you can follow the 'Glooscap Trail' – named for the figure in Mi'kmaw legend who created the unique geography of the Bay of Fundy – as far as Wolfville in the Annapolis Valley, or take the road less traveled and hug the shoreline, visiting the World Heritage-listed Joggins Fossil Cliffs, the delightful hamlet of Advocate Harbour and the village of Parrsboro. This is the part of Nova Scotia famed for the legendary Fundy Tides and tidal bore rafting.

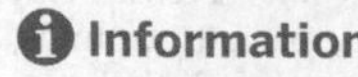

Information

Amherst Visitor Information Centre (VIC; 902-667-8429; Amherst; 8:30am-8pm) This massive visitor information center is at exit 1 off Hwy 104, just as you cross the border from New Brunswick.

Getting There & Away

Amherst is the gateway to Nova Scotia for visitors arriving by land, although the town itself is largely bypassed by the Trans-Canada Hwy (Hwy 104).

Maritime Bus (www.maritimebus.com) connects Amherst with Moncton, NB ($14, one hour, three daily), and Truro with Halifax ($25.50, 1½ hours, five daily).

Shubenacadie

Shubenacadie, or simply 'Shube,' 35km south of Truro off Hwy 2, is best known for the **Shubenacadie Provincial Wildlife Park** (902-758-2040; www.wildlifepark.novascotia.ca; 149 Creighton Rd; adult/child $5/3; 9am-6:30pm daily mid-May–mid-Oct, 9am-3pm Sat & Sun mid-Oct–mid-May). It's the place to commune with Nova Scotia's fauna. You can hand-feed the deer and, if you're lucky, pet a moose. The animals were either born in captivity or once kept as 'pets' and thus cannot be released into the wild – they live in large enclosures. Turn off Hwy 102 at exit 11 and follow Hwy 2 to the park entrance.

Maitland

Tiny Maitland is the place to go rafting on the white water that is created by the outflow of the Shubenacadie River meeting the blasting force of the incoming Fundy tides. It's also one of the oldest towns in Canada.

Wave heights are dependent on the phases of the moon; get information from your rafting company about the tides for your chosen day as your experience (either mild or exhilarating) will be dictated by them. Outboard-powered Zodiacs plunge right through the white water for the two to three hours that the rapids exist. Prepare to get very, very wet – no experience is needed.

Activities

★ Shubenacadie River Runners RAFTING
(902-261-2770; www.tidalborerafting.com; 8681 Hwy 215; half-day rafting $60-70) The region's largest rafting company is organized and professional in every way. Prices depend on how big the tide and waves are; refer to the website for the lowdown on how it all works.

Shubenacadie River Adventures RAFTING
(902-261-2222; www.shubie.com; 10061 Hwy 15; tours from $60) Besides the exciting tidal-bore-rafting day trips, mellow half-day river tours are also on offer. Check the website for tide times and the full details of what's available.

Sleeping

Cresthaven by the Sea B&B $$
(902-261-2001; www.cresthavenbythesea.com; r $139-149; May-Oct;) Stay here for what is possibly the best view over the Fundy tides. The immaculate white Victorian house sits on a bluff right over the point where the Shubenacadie River meets the bay. All the rooms have river views and the lower ones are wheelchair-accessible.

Tidal Life Guesthouse B&B $$
(902-261-2583; www.thetidallife.ca; 9568 Cedar St; dm/r $55/110; May-Oct;) This old beauty of a house has grand, airy rooms and large windows overlooking grassy fields. Artistically designed communal spaces are everywhere, including the back porch with requisite hammock. All accommodations include a big, healthy, locally sourced breakfast. Bathrooms are shared.

Truro

Several major highways converge here, along with a VIA Rail line, so it's no wonder Truro is known as the hub of Nova Scotia. While the town does look somewhat like an aging shopping mall, it's exceptionally well serviced and can make a good stop to pick up that nagging item you need or just to stock up on food.

Escape Truro's busy streets at **Victoria Park** (Park St, off Brunswick St), 400 hectares of green space in the very center of town that includes a deep gorge and two waterfalls. The park attracts dozens of bird species.

The best time to visit Truro is when Millbrook First Nation hosts its **annual powwow** (902-897-9199; www.millbrookfirstnation.net; Aug). Campsites and showers are available; drugs and alcohol are prohibited.

If you're looking for a place to stay in Truro, **Baker's Chest B&B** (902-893-4824; www.bakerschest.ca; 53 Farnham Rd; r $110-130;) is a newly restored classic older home with a fitness room, a pool and a hot tub. The famous **tearoom** is open from noon to 2pm on weekdays and is an adorable stop for soups, snacks and, of course, a nice cup of tea.

THE POWER OF THE BORE

The tidal bore phenomenon occurs when the first surge of the extreme Bay of Fundy tides flows upriver at high tide. Sometimes the advancing wave is only a ripple but, with the right phase of the moon, it can be a meter or so in height, giving the impression that the river is flowing backwards. You'll have to sit awhile to see the changes in the tide; a good place to watch is from the lookout on Tidal Bore Rd, off Hwy 236 just west of exit 14 from Hwy 102 on the northwest side of Truro.

Visit the **Environment Canada** website (www.tides.gc.ca/eng/find/zone/30) for the arrival time of the tidal bore at a variety of locations.

Information

Truro Welcome Centre (902-893-2922; 695 Prince St; 9am-5pm May-Oct;) Offers internet access and a guide to the tree sculptures around town, which were carved after the region was affected by Dutch elm disease more than 30 years ago.

Getting There & Away

Hwy 102 from Halifax (95km) and the Trans-Canada Hwy (Hwy 104) intersect in Truro, along with a number of other highways and secondary roads.

Maritime Bus (www.maritimebus.com) services from Halifax ($25.50, 1½ hours) stop in Truro en route to Amherst ($25.50, 1¼ hours).

Economy & Five Islands

Hwy 2 hugs the shore of the Minas Basin, the northeast arm of the Bay of Fundy. Economy is the first sizable community that you'll arrive at west of Truro, followed by the aptly named Five Islands. There's some great hiking and views in the area, as well as several interesting sights.

WORTH A TRIP

JOGGINS FOSSIL CLIFFS

The wealth of fossils in this 15km stretch of seaside cliffs, including rare land species, are preserved in their original setting. The site is said to be the penultimate location to see what life on earth was like in the late Carboniferous period – 300 million years ago!

The state-of-the-art **Joggins Fossil Centre** (www.jogginsfossilcliffs.net; 100 Main St, Joggins; tours from $10.50; ⏲10am-4pm mid-Apr–Oct, by appointment Nov–mid-Apr) is the place to start your visit, and explains through displays and film what you can see in the Unesco World Heritage–listed cliffs below. The best time to visit the cliffs is at low tide when all of the beaches can be accessed – otherwise you'll be cut off from some of the more interesting sites by high water. Check the website to understand the various tours available and the level of difficulty for each. Note that tours leave on an irregular schedule, depending on the tides, and can be reserved in advance.

Sights & Activities

Cobequid Interpretive Centre MUSEUM
(☎902-647-2600; www.cobequidinterpretivecentre.com; 2 River Philip Rd, Economy; by donation; ⏲9am-4:30pm Jun-Sep) Stop here for good exhibits on the region's ecology and history. Climb a WWII observation tower for a bird's-eye view of the surrounding area and pick up hiking information from the staff. The nearby **Thomas Cove Coastal Trail** is actually two 3.5km loops with great views across the Minas Basin and the Cobequid Mountains. The trails begin down Economy Point Rd, 500m east of the interpretive centre. Follow the signs to a parking area.

Five Islands Provincial Park STATE PARK
(☎902-254-2980; http://parks.novascotia.ca/content/five-islands) Just 7km west of Economy, are several hikes in this park. The 4.5km **Red Head Trail** is well developed, with lookouts, benches and great views.

Economy Falls HIKING
The most challenging hikes in the area are around Economy Falls. The **Devil's Bend Trail** begins 7km up River Phillip Rd toward the Cobequid Mountains. The 6.5km (one-way) trail follows the river to the falls. The 20km-loop **Kenomee Canyon Trail** begins at the top of the falls and twists up the river to a protected wilderness area.

Note that on the latter option, several streams have to be forded; there are designated campsites, making this a good two-day adventurous trek.

Sleeping & Eating

High Tide B&B B&B $
(☎902-647-2788; www.hightidebb.com; 2240 Hwy 2, Lower Economy; d $85-95;) This friendly, modern bungalow has great views. Janet, one of the owners, will have you down on the beach for a clam boil in no time.

Four Seasons Retreat RESORT $$
(☎902-647-2628; www.fourseasonsretreat.ns.ca; 320 Cove Rd, Upper Economy; cottages $120-255; P) Fully equipped cottages are surrounded by trees and face the Minas Basin. In summer, there's a hot tub near the pool; on a chilly night there are woodstoves.

That Dutchman's Cheese Farm CAFE $
(☎902-647-2751; www.facebook.com/ThatDutchmansCheeseFarm; 112 Brown Rd, Upper Economy; mains $8-13; ⏲11am-5pm Jul & Aug) The yummy cafe here offers sandwiches, soups and plates of the eccentric farmer's own Gouda. You can tour the farm for a small fee.

Parrsboro

Rock hounds come from far and wide to forage the shores of Parrsboro, the largest of the towns along the Minas Basin. The Fundy Geological Museum has wonderful exhibits and good programs that take you to the beach areas known as Nova Scotia's 'Jurassic Park.'

Sights

FORCE RESEARCH STATION
(Fundy Ocean Research Center for Energy; ☎902-254-2510; www.fundyforce.ca; 1156 West Bay Road, Black Rock; ⏲10am-5pm Thu-Mon Jun-Oct) FREE Science and environment buffs will get a kick from this fascinating leading research center for in-stream tidal energy, which welcomes visitors. It's best to phone ahead to express your interest.

Ottawa House Museum MUSEUM
(☎902-254-2376; 1155 Whitehall Rd; $2; ⏲10am-6pm) This 21-room mansion was once

the summer home of Sir Charles Tupper (1821–1915), who served as both premier of Nova Scotia and prime minister of Canada. The museum has exhibits on shipbuilding, rum-running and the former settlement on Partridge Island.

Fundy Geological Museum MUSEUM
(☎902-254-3814; http://fundygeological.novascotia.ca; 162 Two Islands Rd; adult/child $9/5; ⊙10am-5pm) This award-winning museum got a million-dollar makeover in 2010 and uses interactive exhibits to help its visitors 'time travel' to when the fossils littering Parrsboro's beaches were living creatures. You can see a lab where dinosaur bones are being cleaned and assembled. **Beach tours** are included in the admission price and focus on minerals or fossils; times, length and frequency are dependent on the tides.

Festivals & Events

Nova Scotia Gem & Mineral Show GEM SHOW
(http://fundygeological.novascotia.ca/gemshow; ⊙mid-Aug) This annual three-day event is the biggest in Parrsboro's calendar, when rock hounds from far and wide descend on the Fundy Shore in search of treasure.

Sleeping & Eating

Riverview Cottages COTTAGE $
(☎902-254-2388; www.riverviewcottages.ca; 3575 Eastern Ave; cottages $60-105; ⊙May-Nov; P) These rustic, country-cute, completely equipped cottages are a steal. You can canoe and fish on the bordering river and there's a big lawn perfect for a barbecue. It really is like going back in time to a 1960s holiday camp, but in an exceptionally well-maintained kind of way.

Mad Hatter Hostel HOSTEL $
(☎902-254-3167; www.madhatterhostel.webs.com; 16 Prince St; dm/s/d $20/35/50;) More like a few rooms and beds upstairs in an inviting home, this 'hostel' offers a ton of hospitality, kitchen use and a great location right in town.

★ **Sunshine Inn** MOTEL $$
(☎877-706-6835; www.thesunshineinn.net; 4487 Hwy 2; r $110, cottages $139-149; ⊙May-Nov; P) Let the Sunshine Inn! It certainly does on this bright, windswept address 3km north of Parrsboro. Choose between immaculately kept and beautifully updated 1970s-style motel rooms or a range of inviting self-contained cottages, equally well maintained and scattered about the beautiful property, which also boasts its own lake. Excellent-value good vibes all round.

★ **Maple Inn** B&B $$
(☎902-254-3735; www.mapleinn.ca; 2358 Western Ave; d $99-169; ⊙May-Oct; P) This elegant B&B in what was once the town's hospital is a true credit to its friendly owners. The wonderfully appointed rooms are filled with gorgeous antiques from Canada and Austria and updated unobtrusively with modern conveniences such as Jacuzzis, jet showers, wi-fi and flat-screen TVs. Delicious breakfasts kick-start the day.

Evangeline's Tower B&B B&B $$
(☎902-254-3383; www.evangelinestower.ca; 322 Main St; d $95-110; P) This elegantly decorated 1890s Victorian home has three rooms; two can be combined into a two-room suite for families. The generous, home-cooked breakfasts are delicious and cyclists are welcome.

★ **Black Rock Bistro** BISTRO $$
(☎902-728-3006; www.blackrockbistro.ca; 151 Main St; mains $14-24; ⊙noon-9pm May-Oct; P) Friendly, attentive service and beautifully executed meals – from delicate homemade pastas to fresh seafood (seared scallops, lobster lollipops!) and tender juicy steaks – are complemented by an excellent wine list and infrequent visiting musicians in the adjacent wine room. Be sure to leave room for the decadent desserts.

Harbour View Restaurant CANADIAN $$
(☎902-254-3507; 476 Pier Rd; mains $12-24; ⊙7am-8pm) Hang out with the local fishers devouring Parrsboro's best fish-and-chips, along with chowder, homemade pies and more at this casual, family-friendly restaurant, right on the water.

WORTH A TRIP

AGE OF SAIL

Stop for tea, baked goods and a tour at the **Age of Sail Heritage Centre** (☎902-348-2030; www.ageofsailmuseum.ca; 8334 Highway 209, Port Greville; $4; ⊙10am-6pm May-Oct) in Port Greville, about 20km to the west of Parrsboro on Rte 209. Capturing the area's shipbuilding heritage, the site also includes a restored 1857 Methodist church and a working blacksmith shop.

Entertainment

Ship's Company Theatre THEATER
(902-254-3000; www.shipscompanytheatre.com; 18 Lower Main St; tickets from $15; Jul-Sep) This innovative theater company performs new Canadian and Maritime works 'on board' the MV *Kipawo*, the last of the Minas Basin ferries, now integrated into a new theater. There's high-quality theater for kids, improv comedy, readings and concerts.

Shopping

Tysons' Fine Minerals ROCKS & MINERALS
(902-254-2376; www.tysonsfineminerals.com; 249 Whitehall Rd; 10am-4pm) This place is more like a museum than a shop, with some of the most sparkling, massive and colorful minerals on display you're likely to see anywhere. Sometimes Helen takes visitors in to see the Tysons' own private collection, which is even more breathtaking.

Advocate Harbour

Advocate Harbour is a breathtaking little place with a 5km-long beach piled high with driftwood that changes dramatically with the tides. Behind the beach, salt marshes – reclaimed with dikes by the Acadians – are now replete with birds.

Most visitors pass through here on the scenic route to Amherst or en route to the famous Unesco World Heritage fossil cliffs (p370) in Joggins, 32km south of Amherst.

Sights & Activities

★**Cape d'Or Lighthouse** LIGHTHOUSE
(902-670-0534; www.capedor.ca; 1 Cape d'Or Rd, Diligent River) This spectacular cape of sheer cliffs was misnamed Cape d'Or (Cape of Gold) by Samuel de Champlain in 1604 – the glittering veins he saw in the cliffs were actually made of copper. Mining took place between 1897 and 1905 and removed the sparkle. The present lighthouse was added in 1922. Access is by the partially unsealed side road off Hwy 209 to Cape d'Or, then hike down the dirt trail. If you can't bring yourself to leave, there's a guesthouse.

Cape Chignecto Provincial Park STATE PARK
(902-392-2085; http://parks.novascotia.ca/content/cape-chignecto; W Advocate Rd; hiking permits per day/year $5/25; May-Oct) This isolated wilderness park in the Bay of Fundy features vast sea cliffs, pristine coastline, sheltered bays, and rare flora and fauna. It's best known for the **Cape Chignecto Coastal Trail**, a rugged 60km, four-day hiking loop that showcases the park's natural beauty. All park visitors must register and leave an itinerary at the visitors center; camping in the backcountry requires reservations.

Easier overnight hikes include the **Mill Brook Canyon Trail** (15km), the hike to **Refugee Cove** (20km), and the **Eatonville Trail** (28km), sections of which can be tackled as a day trip. All trails require a good level of fitness.

Some hikers have tried to avoid the ups and downs of the trails by taking shortcuts along the beach at low tide and have been cut off by Bay of Fundy tides. Get a tide table and ask park staff about current conditions before setting out.

Nova Shores Adventures KAYAKING
(866-638-4118; www.novashores.com; 3838 Hwy 209; day tours from $100) Kayak through Cape Chignecto Provincial Park with Nova Shores Adventures. You'll often see seals and bears. Overnight tours include accommodations and food.

Sleeping & Eating

Cape d'Or Kitchen & Guest House INN $$
(902-670-0534; www.capedor.ca; 1 Cape d'Or Rd, Diligent River; r $80-110, whole house $340; May-Oct;) The original lighthouse keeper's residence is now a laid-back four-room guesthouse at what is perhaps one of the most perfect spots in Nova Scotia (even more so when the sun's out). Its cosmopolitan **restaurant** has views to die for and serves lunch (mains $7 to $15) and dinner (mains $12 to $30), including seafood, meat and vegetarian dishes. To get here, take the partly unsealed road off Hwy 209 signposted to Cape d'Or. From the car park, you need to walk about 150m down a steep dirt trail.

Cape Chignecto Provincial Park Campgrounds CAMPGROUND
(902-392-2085; http://parks.novascotia.ca/content/cape-chignecto; campsites $24; May-Oct) In addition to 51 wilderness campsites at six points along the coastal trail and 27 walk-in sites near the visitor center, there is also a bunkhouse and a wilderness cabin (both $55 for up to four people). There are no drive-up sites in the park. All campsite reservations can be made online.

★Wild Caraway Restaurant & Cafe CANADIAN $$
(☎902-392-2889; www.wildcaraway.com; 3721 Hwy 209; mains lunch $7-16, dinner $18-28; ⊙11am-8pm Thu-Mon; 📶) This gorgeous cafe-restaurant has some of the best locavore dining you'll find along this coast; it's also pretty as a postcard. Try the ploughman's lunch with house-smoked pork and cheese from That Dutchman's Cheese Farm (p370), or dine on applewood-smoked mackerel or a selection of seasonal specials.

SUNRISE TRAIL

It's claimed that the Northumberland Strait between Nova Scotia's north shore and PEI has some of the warmest waters north of the US Carolinas, with water temperatures averaging slightly over 20°C during summer. The Sunrise Trail is a prime area for beach-hopping, cycling and exploring friendly countryside towns.

Tatamagouche

The Malagash Peninsula, which juts out into protected Tatamagouche Bay, is a low-key, bucolic loop for a drive or bike ride. Taste local wines, go beachcombing or take a peek in some interesting museums found just inland. Tatamagouche is the largest town on the Northumberland Shore coast west of Pictou and makes a great base for exploring the region.

Sights

Balmoral Grist Mill HISTORIC SITE
(☎902-657-3016; http://balmoralgristmill.novascotia.ca; 544 Peter MacDonald Rd, Balmoral Mills; adult/child $4/3; ⊙9:30am-5:30pm Mon-Sat, 1-5:30pm Sun) In a gorgeous setting on the stream that once provided it with power, the Balmoral Grist Mill still grinds wheat in summer. From Tatamagouche, turn south on Hwy 311 (at the east edge of town) and then east on Hwy 256.

Jost Winery WINERY
(☎902-257-2636; www.devoniancoast.ca; 48 Vintage Ln, Malagash; tours $5; ⊙wine store 10am-5pm Mar-Dec, tours noon & 3pm Jun-Sep) Take a tour of the scenically located Jost Winery. While regular wine is free to taste, the ice wine costs $5. If you want to try all three ice wine varieties, ask to have three small glasses for the price of one large one. Winery signs direct you about 5km off Hwy 6.

Wallace Bay National Wildlife Area BIRD SANCTUARY
(☎800-668-6767; www.ec.gc.ca) About 30km northwest of town, this vast sanctuary protects 585 hectares, including tidal and freshwater wetlands. In the spring, keep your eyes peeled for bald eagles nesting near the parking lot, which is on the left just before the causeway.

Blue Sea Beach BEACH
(651 Blue Sea Rd, Malagash Point) Blue Sea Beach on the Malagash Peninsula has warm water and fine sand, and a marsh area just inland that's ideal for **bird-watching**. There are picnic tables and shelters to change in.

Rushton's Beach Provincial Park STATE PARK
(http://parks.novascotia.ca/content/rushtons-beach; 723 Hwy 6, Brule) Small cottages crowd around Rushton's Beach, just east of Tatamagouche in Brule. It's worth a visit to look for seals (turn left at the end of the boardwalk and walk toward the end of the beach) and birdlife in the adjoining salt marsh.

Sutherland Steam Mill HISTORIC SITE
(☎902-657-3365; http://sutherlandsteammill.novascotia.ca; 3169 Denmark Station Rd, Denmark; adult/child $4/3; ⊙9:30am-5:30pm Mon-Sat, 1-5:30pm Sun Jun-Oct) Built in 1894, the Sutherland Steam Mill produced lumber, carriages, wagons and windows until 1958. To get here from Tatamagouche, follow Hwy 6 for about 10km until the junction with Hwy 326, then drive south for 4km.

Wallace Museum MUSEUM
(☎902-257-2191; www.wallaceandareamuseum.com; 13440 Hwy 6; by donation; ⊙9am-5pm Mon-Fri Mar-Nov) The tourist information center is at the Wallace Museum. Collections of baskets woven by the Mi'kmaq, period dresses and shipbuilding memorabilia are displayed.

Festivals & Events

Oktoberfest BEER
(☎902-657-2380; www.nsoktoberfest.ca; tickets $10-20; ⊙Sep) The wildly popular Oktoberfest is held the last weekend in September – yes, September.

Sleeping & Eating

Wentworth Hostel HOSTEL $
(☎902-548-2379; www.hihostels.ca; 249 Wentworth Station Rd, Cumberland; dm/r $30/50; 📶) From Tatamagouche, follow Hwy 246 south for 26km until you reach Hwy 4. The 24-bed Wentworth Hostel is 1.3km west of Hwy 4

on Valley Rd, up steep, unsealed Wentworth Station Rd. The rambling farmhouse, built in 1866, has been used as a hostel for decades. It's a central base for both the Sunrise Trail and much of the Minas Basin shore.

Trails for hiking and mountain biking start just outside the door; the hostel gets particularly booked up in winter for the cross-country and downhill skiing nearby.

★Train Station Inn INN $$
(902-657-3222; www.tatatrainstation.com; 21 Station Rd; carriages $109-199; May-Nov;) It's a museum, it's a kooky gift shop, it's a restaurant, it's a hotel and…it's a stationary train. Each unique carriage suite is a train-spotter's dream, decorated with period train posters, toy trains and locomotive books.

The dreamer behind the inn, James LeFresne, grew up across the tracks and saved the train station from demolition. Dine on delicious seafood, meat and salads in the c 1928 dining car or have a blueberry pancake breakfast in the station house. Free self-guided tours are available from the gift shop.

Sugar Moon Farm CANADIAN $$
(902-657-3348; www.sugarmoon.ca; 221 Alex MacDonald Rd, Earltown; mains $12-30; 9am-4pm Jul & Aug, reduced hours Sep-Jun) The food – simple, delicious pancakes and locally made sausages served with maple syrup – is the highlight of this working maple farm and woodlot. Check online for special happenings. To reach the farm from Tatamagouche, simply follow Hwy 311 south for 25km, then follow the signs on Alex MacDonald Rd.

Shopping

Lismore Sheep Farm GIFTS & SOUVENIRS
(902-351-2889; www.lismoresheepfarmwoolshop.com; 1389 Louisville Rd, River John; 9am-5pm) A working farm with more than 300 sheep, this is a fun destination even if you don't buy a rug, a blanket or socks. From May to October, the barn is open for visitors to pat the lambs and learn all about producing wool. The farm is 19km east of Tatamagouche off Hwy 6.

Information

Fraser Cultural Centre (902-657-3285; www.fraserculturalcentre.org; 362 Main St; 10am-5pm Mon-Fri, to 4pm Sat, 11am-3pm Sun Jun-Sep;) Tourist information, internet access and local history displays.

Pictou

Many people stop in Pictou for a side trip or as a stopover via the ferry from Prince Edward Island, but it's also an enjoyable base for exploring Northumberland Strait. Water St, the main street, is lined with interesting shops and beautiful old stone buildings (but unfortunately the sea views are blighted by a giant smoking mill in the distance). The town is known as the 'Birthplace of New Scotland' because the first Scottish immigrants to Nova Scotia landed here in 1773.

Sights & Activities

Picnic and swim at **Caribou-Munroes Island Provincial Park**, a 10-minute drive from town.

Hector SHIP
(902-485-4371; www.shiphector.com; 33 Caladh Ave; adult/child $8/6; 10am-4pm Jun-Oct) A replica of the ship *Hector*, which carried the first 200 Highland Scots to Nova Scotia, is tied up for viewing. Descend into the large hull crammed with bunks to get a feel of how challenging the crossing would have been. The ticket includes admission to Hector Heritage Quay.

Hector Heritage Quay MUSEUM
(902-485-4371; 33 Caladh Ave; adult/child $8/6; 10am-4pm Jun-Oct) Ticket price also includes admission to the good ship *Hector*. The Quay has an interpretive center, a re-created blacksmith shop, a collection of shipbuilding artifacts, and displays about the *Hector* and its passengers.

Northumberland Fisheries Museum MUSEUM
(902-485-8925; 21 Caladh Ave; $5; 10am-6pm Mon-Sat) Located in the old train station, this museum explores the area's fishing heritage. Exhibits include strange sea creatures and the spiffy *Silver Bullet*, an early 1930s lobster boat.

Festivals & Events

Pictou Landing First Nation Powwow CULTURAL
(902-752-4912; www.plfn.ca/cultural-history/yearly-events/powwow; Jun) Across the Pictou Harbour (a 25-minute drive through New Glasgow), this annual powwow on the first weekend in June features sunrise ceremonies, drumming and craft demonstrations.

WORTH A TRIP

THE ROAD TO CAPE GEORGE POINT

The eastern arm of the Sunrise Trail, from New Glasgow to Antigonish has some gorgeous diversions – perfect for a half-day excursion when the weather is fine. Be sure to pack some snacks and remember your beach towel.

Perhaps start your day with a hands-on visit to the Museum of Industry (p376), especially if you have kids in tow, then head along the coast to pretty **Arisaig Provincial Park** (☎902-863-4513; 5704 Hwy 245), where you can take a dip or search for fossils. Continue on to **Malignant Cove**. From here, the 55km coastal stretch of Hwy 245 has been compared in beauty to parts of the Cabot Trail, although less mountainous and more accessible.

After a short drive east you'll reach **Cape George Point Lighthouse** (www.parl.ns.ca/lighthouse), the handsome jewel in the day's crown, where you can look out over the calm waters of St Georges Bay. If it's nearing lunch time, head just around the cape to the fish-and-chip truck near the **Ballantyne's Cove Tuna Interpretive Centre** (57 Ballantyne's Cove Wharf Rd), then work off the fried goodness with a dip or a stroll at Crystal Cliffs Beach (p377).

Just 15 minutes south, there's plenty to see and do in Antigonish (p376), or keep up the outdoorsy theme and round out the day with a roar, high above the trees at **Anchors Above Zipline Adventure** (☎902-922-3265; www.anchorsabovezipline.ca; 464 McGrath Mountain Rd, French River; 1 ride $30; ⏲10am-5pm), about 40km from Antigonish – watch for the signs on the Trans-Canada Hwy (Hwy 104).

Camping and food are available on-site; it's strictly alcohol- and drug-free.

Lobster Carnival FOOD & DRINK
(☎902-485-5150; www.pictoulobstercarnival.ca; ⏲Jul) Started in 1934 as the Carnival of the Fisherfolk, this four-day event now offers free entertainment, boat races and lots of chances to feast on lobster.

Sleeping

Caribou-Munroes Island Provincial Park CAMPGROUND $
(☎902-485-6134; www.parks.gov.ns.ca; 2119 Three Brooks Rd; campsites $24) Less than 10km from Pictou, this park is set on a gorgeous beach. Sites 1 to 22 abut the day-use area and are less private; sites 78 to 95 are gravel and suited for RVs. The rest are wooded and private.

★ **Pictou Lodge** RESORT $$
(☎902-485-4322; www.pictoulodge.com; 172 Lodge Rd; r $129-239, cottages $189-429; 📶🏊🐾) This atmospheric 1920s resort is on more than 60 hectares of wooded land between Caribou-Munroes Island Provincial Park and Pictou. Beautifully renovated oceanside log cabins have original stone fireplaces. Motel rooms are also available. There's a life-sized checkerboard, paddleboats, a private beach and the best **restaurant** in town.

Willow House Inn B&B $$
(☎902-485-5740; www.willowhouseinn.com; 11 Willow St; r $90-130; 📶🐾) This historic c 1840 home is a labyrinth of staircases and cozy, antique rooms. The owners whip up great breakfasts, as well as conversation and tips for what to do around town.

Customs House Inn INN $$
(☎902-485-4546; www.customshouseinn.ca; 38 Depot St; d $90-125; 📶) The tall stone walls here are at once imposingly chic and reassuringly solid. The chunky antique decor is as sturdy and elegant as the architecture, and many rooms have waterfront views. You'll be left pretty much to your own devices, including at the continental breakfast in the basement, which can be a nice break after days of B&B chitchat.

☆ Entertainment

deCoste Centre LIVE PERFORMANCE
(☎902-485-8848; https://decostecentre.ca; 91 Water St; tickets from $20; ⏲box office 11:30am-5pm Mon-Fri, 1-5pm Sat & Sun) Opposite the waterfront, this impressive performing arts center stages a range of live shows. Experience some top-notch Scottish music during a summer series of ceilidhs (*kay*-lees; adult/child $15/7). Check the website for performance dates and times.

Information

Eastern and Northumberland Shores Visitor Information Centre (☎902-485-8540; Pictou Rotary; ⏲9am-5pm) Large info center situated northwest of town to meet travelers arriving from the PEI ferry.

Town of Pictou (www.townofpictou.ca) Links to sights and festivals.

Pictou Public Library (☎902-485-5021; 40 Water St; ⏲noon-9pm Tue & Thu, to 5pm Wed, 10am-5pm Fri & Sat; 📶) Free internet access.

Getting There & Away

Bay Ferries (p331) services to PEI leave from a terminal a few kilometers from Pictou. New Glasgow, 17km south, is the nearest town of any size.

New Glasgow

The largest town on the Northumberland Shore, New Glasgow has always been an industrial hub; the first mine opened in neighboring Stellarton in 1807. Still, it's a pleasant town with plenty of aging architecture and a pretty river running through the center. The few major local attractions are in **Stellarton**, a 5km drive south.

Sights

Crombie House GALLERY
(☎902-755-4440; www.sobeyartfoundation.com; 1780 Granton Abercrombie Rd, Pictou; ⏲tours hourly 9-11am & 1-4pm Wed Jul & Aug) FREE A 10-minute drive north of town, in the personal residence of the founder of the Sobeys supermarket chain, this private gallery has an excellent collection of 19th- and early 20th-century Canadian art, including works by Cornelius Krieghoff and the Group of Seven.

Museum of Industry MUSEUM
(☎902-755-5425; http://museumofindustry.novascotia.ca; 147 N Foord St, Stellarton; adult/child $9/4; ⏲9am-5pm Mon-Sat, 10am-5pm Sun Jul-Oct; 👪) This is a wonderful place for kids. There's a hands-on water-power exhibit and an assembly line to try to keep up with.

Sleeping & Eating

Comfort Inn MOTEL $
(☎902-755-6450; www.newglasgowcomfortinn.com; 740 Westville Rd; d $79-139; 🅿📶) Our pick of the New Glasgow motels, the recently updated Comfort Inn has drive-up rooms and is well maintained. It's in a good location for cheap and easy eats.

The Bistro MODERN CANADIAN $$
(☎902-752-4988; www.thebistronewglasgow.com; 216 Archimedes St; mains $19-32; ⏲from 5pm Tue-Sat) The only constant on the Bistro menu is creativity in spicing and sauces. The menu changes daily according to what's available and in summer everything is organic. The local art on display is also for sale.

Hebel's INTERNATIONAL $$$
(☎902-695-5955; www.hebelsrestaurant.ca; 71 Stellarton Rd; mains lunch $10-14, dinner $18-36; ⏲11:30am-2pm Tue-Fri, 5-9pm Tue-Sat) Flavors from all over the world are mingled with fresh Nova Scotian ingredients at this bright and homey, fire-warmed spot in an elegant Victorian. Choices may include anything from seafood creole or beef Stroganoff to miso-glazed salmon on Japanese noodles.

Antigonish

Beautiful beaches and hiking possibilities north of town could easily keep you busy for a couple of days, but Antigonish town itself is lively enough and has some great places to eat. Catholic Scots settled and established St Francis Xavier University and today the university still dominates the ambience of the town. Antigonish is known for the Highland Games held here each July since 1861.

Sights

St Francis Xavier University UNIVERSITY
(www.stfx.ca) The attractive campus of this 125-year-old university makes for an interesting stroll. The **Hall of the Clans** is on the 3rd floor of the old wing of the Angus L MacDonald Library, just beyond the St Ninian's Cathedral parking lot. In the hall, crests of all the Scottish clans that settled this area are displayed. Those clans gather each July for the Antigonish Highland Games.

St Ninian's Cathedral CHURCH
(120 St Ninian St; ⏲7:30am-8pm) The area's Catholic cathedral, completed in 1874, is a fine example of Canadian Romanesque architecture.

Antigonish Heritage Museum MUSEUM
(☎902-863-6160; www.heritageantigonish.ca; 20 East Main St; ⏲10am-5pm Mon-Sat Jul & Aug, 10am-noon & 1-5pm Mon-Fri Sep-Jun; 🅿) FREE In the town's former railway station, this compact museum features displays devoted to remembering the history of Antigonish and its residents.

Activities

Crystal Cliffs Beach SWIMMING

(Crystal Cliffs Farm Rd) About 15km northeast of Antigonish, turn off Hwy 337 and head down Crystal Cliffs Farm Rd to this popular beach for swimming and beach walks.

Antigonish Landing HIKING

A 4km hiking and cycling trail to the nature reserve at Antigonish Landing begins just across the train tracks from the Antigonish Heritage Museum, then 400m down Adam St. The landing's estuary is a good **bird-watching** area where you might see eagles, ducks and ospreys.

Festivals & Events

Antigonish Highland Games CULTURAL

(www.antigonishhighlandgames.ca; Jul) An extravaganza of dancing, pipe-playing, and heavy-lifting events involving hewn logs and iron balls.

Eating

Gabrieau's Bistro MODERN CANADIAN $$

(902-863-1925; www.gabrieaus.com; 350 Main St; mains lunch $10-16, dinner $18-30; 10am-9pm Mon-Fri, 4-9:30pm Sat;) Dine on any of a number of imaginative vegetarian dishes, salads, meats and seafood for lunch or dinner. Locals credit chef Mark Gabrieau for setting the culinary high-water mark in Antigonish. Dishes such as Thai shrimp and lobster risotto make frequent appearances on the exotic menu.

Information

Antigonish Visitor Information Centre (902-863-4921; 145 Church St; 10am-8pm Jun-Sep;) Brochures, free local calls and free internet access. Located in the Antigonish Mall parking lot at the junction of Hwys 104 and 7.

Antigonish Public Library (902-863-4276; 274 Main St; 10am-9pm Tue & Thu, to 5pm Wed, Fri & Sat;) Free internet access. Enter off College St.

Getting There & Away

Antigonish is at the northern end of Hwy 7, 62km from Sherbrooke. New Glasgow is 57km to the west on the Trans-Canada Hwy (Hwy 104).

Maritime Bus (www.maritimebus.com) services to Halifax ($42, 3½ hours) and Sydney ($46, 3¼ hours) stop at Bloomfield Centre at St Francis Xavier University.

CAPE BRETON ISLAND

Floating over the rest of Nova Scotia like an island halo, Cape Breton Island is a heavenly, forested realm of bald eagles, migrating whales, palpable history and foot-tapping music. Starting up the Ceilidh Trail along the western coastline, Celtic music vibrates through the pubs and community centers, eventually morphing into more eclectic Acadian-style tunes around Chéticamp.

Linked to the rest of mainland Nova Scotia by a steel swing bridge, the island proudly claims the jewel in Nova Scotia's tourism crown: the 297km-long **Cabot Trail**, which twists and climbs its way through and around Cape Breton Highlands National Park. The trail traverses coastal mountains with glorious ocean views, passes plenty of loose moose on the roads (watch out!) and boasts dozens of challenging trails to bring you back to nature.

Most tourists visit in July and August, and many restaurants, accommodations and attractions are only open from June through October. **Celtic Colours** (www.celtic-colours.com; Oct), a popular roving music festival that attracts top musicians from countries with Celtic connections, helps extend the tourist season on Cape Breton Island into the fall, a superb time to visit.

Ceilidh Trail

From Port Hastings, the Ceilidh Trail (Hwy 19) snakes along the western coast of Cape Breton Island. This area was settled by Scots and is renowned for its ceilidh music performances, square dances and parties.

Mabou is the hot spot of Cape Breton's Celtic music scene, where you can hike away your days and dance away your nights with a little help from that single-malt whiskey from the distillery down the road.

The trail continues to the former coal mining town of **Inverness**, with its sandy beach and 1km-long boardwalk, and then twists north to **Margaree Forks**, where you can pick up the Cabot Trail.

Sights

★ **Glenora Inn & Distillery** DISTILLERY

(902-258-2662; www.glenoradistillery.com; 13727 Route 19, Glenville; guided tours incl tasting $7; tours hourly 9am-5pm Jun-Oct) Take a tour and taste the rocket fuel at the only distillery making single-malt whisky in Canada. Stay for an excellent meal at the gourmet pub (there are daily lunchtime and dinner ceilidhs) or even for the night. Cave-like rooms ($125 to $150) are perfect for sleeping it off if you've been drinking the local beverage; the chalets ($175 to $240) are a better choice if you want brighter surroundings.

Inverness County Centre for the Arts CULTURAL CENTER
(902-258-2533; www.invernessarts.ca; 16080 Hwy 19, Inverness; 10am-5pm) Inverness County Centre for the Arts is a beautiful establishment with several galleries and an upmarket gift shop featuring works by local and regional artists. It's also a music venue, with a floor built for dancing, of course.

Celtic Music Interpretive Centre MUSEUM
(902-787-2708; www.celticmusiccentre.com; 5473 Hwy 19, Judique; exhibit room $8; 10am-5pm Mon-Fri Jun-Aug) Offers a great introduction to local culture. Half-hour **tours** (which can be self-guided if you arrive when no guides are available) may include a fiddle lesson and a dance step or two. The location and times of local square dances are advertised around the admissions desk and ceilidhs are also held at the center; inquire for details.

Inverness Miners' Museum MUSEUM
(902-258-3822; 62 Lower Railway St, Inverness; by donation; 9am-5pm Mon-Fri, noon-5pm Sat & Sun Jun-Oct) In the old train station just back from the beach, the Inverness Miners' Museum presents local history.

Activities

Cape Mabou Highlands HIKING
Within the Cape Mabou Highlands, an extensive network of hiking trails extends between Mabou and Inverness toward the coast west of Hwy 19. The trails are sometimes closed when the fire danger is high; otherwise, hikes ranging from 4km to 12km start from three different trailheads. An excellent trail guide ($5) is available at the grocery store across the road from Mabou's Mull Café & Deli when the trails are open. Maps are also posted at the trailheads.

Sleeping & Eating

MacLeods Inn INN $$
(902-253-3360; www.macleods.com; 30 Broad Cove Marsh Rd, Inverness; r $160-180; Jun-Oct; P) MacLeods Inn is a high-end B&B about 5km north of Inverness. The house is big and modern, but the decoration is in keeping with Cape Breton heritage.

Duncreigan Country Inn INN $$
(902-945-2207; www.duncreigan.ca; 11411 Hwy 19, Mabou; r $145-220;) Nestled in oak trees on the banks of the river, this inn has private, spacious rooms, some with terraces and water views. Bikes are available to guests and there's a licensed **dining room** that serves breakfast to guests or dinner by reservation (mains $10 to $23).

Clayton Farm B&B B&B $$
(902-945-2719; 11247 Hwy 19, Mabou; s/d $80/105; May-Nov; @) This 1835 farmhouse sits on a working Red Angus ranch and is run by hardworking Isaac Smith. Paraphernalia of old Cape Breton life and of Isaac's family are casually scattered throughout the common areas and comfortable guest rooms. It's rustically perfect.

★Cabot Links RESORT $$$
(855-652-2268; www.cabotlinks.com; 15933 Central Ave, Inverness; r $295-435, villas from $975; May-Oct; P) Even if you don't play golf, you might want to consider this slick resort for a night or two of guaranteed luxury. Accommodations range from stylish hotel rooms in the main lodge to private villas overlooking the greens to truly indulgent (and expensive) multi-room residences. Expect to rub shoulders with a gentrified crowd.

★Red Shoe Pub PUB FOOD $$
(902-945-2996; www.redshoepub.com; 11533 Hwy 19, Mabou; mains $13-25; noon-11pm Sun-Wed, to 2am Thu-Sat) Straddling the spine of the Ceilidh Trail, this pub is the beating heart of Mabou. Listen to a local fiddle player (often from the Rankin family) while enjoying a pint and a superb meal. The desserts, including the gingerbread with rum-butterscotch sauce and fruit compote, are divine.

Shopping

Bear Paw BOOKS
(902-258-2528; 15788 Central Ave, Inverness; 9am-5pm Mon-Fri) This little book shop sells the works of local Canadian novelist Alistair MacLeod (1936–2014).

Information

Visitor Information Centre (VIC; 902-625-4201; 96 Hwy 4, Port Hastings; 9am-8pm) This big and busy visitor info center is on your right as you drive onto Cape Breton Island.

It's definitely worth a stop; there are few other information centers on the island, especially outside of July and August, and the staff are very well informed.

Cabot Trail

Driving the Cabot Trail is Nova Scotia's most famous recreational activity, taking you along winding roads, by serene lakes, beneath soaring eagles and on to cliff-top vistas that are sure to make your jaw drop.

Along the way, artists' workshops dot the southeastern flank of the trail like Easter eggs, from Englishtown to St Ann's Bay. Seize this treasure: drop in to a studio or two to meet an interesting mishmash of characters. You'll find pottery, leather, glass and pewter workers, painters and sculptors, and discover living remnants of Mi'kmaw and Acadian culture.

The most breathtaking scenery is found on the island's northwestern shore as the trail slopes down to Pleasant Bay and Chéticamp. Keep your eyes on the circuitous road, as tempting as the views become: there are plenty of places to stop, look and hike through a tapestry of terrain for boundless vistas over the endless, icy ocean.

Accommodations around the 298km trail are limited. If you intend to drive the trail in one or two days, plan to base yourself at Baddeck or Ingonish on its eastern flank, or Chéticamp or Pleasant Bay on its west. In the peak times of July and August, be sure to make bookings well in advance.

If you're looking for an ecofriendly stay, consider spending a night at **Chanterelle Country Inn & Cottages** (902-929-2263; www.chanterelleinn.com; 48678 Cabot Trail, North River; r from $145; May-Nov;) overlooking 60 hectares of rolling pastures and bucolic bliss, about 35km north of Baddeck. Meals (a separate cost) are served on the screened-in porch of the main inn.

Predictably, dining options on the trail are limited and seafood is king. If you have dietary restrictions or an aversion to crustaceans, it's pertinent to research your options in advance. Settle on some accommodations and then inquire with your innkeeper about what will be best for you. Locals are generally super-friendly and more than happy to help.

At **Dancing Goat** (902-248-2727; www.facebook.com/DancingGoatCafe; 6289 Cabot Trail, Margaree Valley; items $5-13; 8am-5pm Sat-Thu, to 8pm Fri;) everything is homemade, most ingredients are local, and hearty breakfasts are as good as you'll get on Cape Breton. Big sandwiches and salads can be eaten in or taken away for hiking. It's also one of the few establishments open year-round.

Chéticamp

Chéticamp is not only the western gateway to Cape Breton Highlands National Park, it's more importantly Nova Scotia's most vibrant and thriving Acadian community, owing much of its cultural preservation to its geographical isolation – the road didn't make it this far until 1949. Upon entering the town from either direction you'll immediately feel like you've arrived in a little French village, although the landscape is decidedly reminiscent of the rugged Scottish highlands.

In the warmer months, there's always something going on, with plenty of opportunities to observe and experience Acadian culture, from interesting museums to sampling folk crafts (Chéticamp is famed for its hooked rugs) and toe-tapping live-music performances.

Sights

Le Centre de la Mi-Carême MUSEUM
(902-224-1016; www.micareme.ca; 51 Old Cabot Trail Rd, Grand Étang; adult/child $5/4; 10am-4pm Jun-Oct) Mi-Carême, celebrated in the middle of Lent, is Chéticamp's answer to Mardi Gras. Locals wear masks and disguises and visit houses, trying to get people to guess who they are. This museum covers the history of the celebration and displays traditional masks.

Les Trois Pignons MUSEUM
(902-224-2642; www.lestroispignons.com; 15584 Cabot Trail; adult/child $5/4; 9am-4pm May-Oct) This excellent museum explains how rug hooking went from being a home-based activity to an international business. Artifacts, including hooked rugs, illustrate early life and artisanship in Chéticamp. Almost everything here – from bottles to rugs – was collected by one eccentric local resident.

Église St Pierre CHURCH
(St Peter's Church; 902-224-2064; 5 Aucoin Rd) The unique and photogenic 1893 Église St Pierre dominates the town with its silver spire and colorful frescoes.

Tours

Love Boat Whale Cruises WHALE WATCHING
(902-224-2899; www.loveboatwhalecruises.ca; Quai Mathieu; tours from $40; Jun-Oct) Friendly captains and regular sailings make this operator of whale-watching tours one of the better choices in Chéticamp. A minimum of six passengers is required for a sailing. Tours last from 2½ to three hours, and though there are no guarantees that whales will be sighted, guest reports are good.

Sleeping

Albert's Motel MOTEL $
(902-224-2077; 15086 Cabot Trail; d $79-129; May-Oct; P) This quaint motel has four cozy rooms with delightful patchwork quilts, mini-fridges, microwaves and large TVs, plus a communal deck overlooking the harbor. The place is spotlessly clean and the hosts are as friendly as they come.

★**Maison Fiset House** B&B $$
(902-224-1794; www.maisonfisethouse.com; 15050 Cabot Trail; d/ste $169/219; P) A little luxury in Chéticamp is found in this grand old 1895 home. If you're in a suite, lounge in your Jacuzzi tub and enjoy the ocean views. Most importantly, experience the fully fledged Acadian hospitality from your host. Inquire about the rental units at the rear of the property. Open year-round.

Cornerstone Motel MOTEL $$
(902-224-3232; www.cornerstonemotel.com; 16537 Cabot Trail; d $99-169; May-Oct; P) The local 1950s motels always look fabulous with a coat of paint and a few updates. This one, at the very edge of Cape Breton Highlands National Park, 7km from town, fits that bill. All the standard features are here, with comfy bedding and hot showers, a fire pit, and a lovely outlook, perfect for that real road-trip vibe. Bikers welcome.

Eating

La Boulangerie Aucoin BAKERY $
(902-224-3220; www.aucoinbakery.com; 14 Lapointe Rd; items $3.50-9; 7am-5pm Mon-Sat;) This is the place to go for fresh-baked French- and American-style loaves, pastries, cakes, pies and ready-made sandwiches perfect for that picnic on the Cabot Trail. Family-owned and operated since 1959.

Harbour Restaurant CANADIAN $$
(902-224-1144; www.baywindsuites.com; 15299 Cabot Trail; mains $14-30) At the Harbour Restaurant, local harbor-front dining at its best includes a range of Canadian and Acadian meals, not limited to oceanic treats. That said, the mushroom-topped scallops and Acadian *morue en cabane* (slow-cooked cod with pork and chives) are a great combination to share if you're dining with a companion.

All Aboard CANADIAN $$
(902-224-2288; www.facebook.com/AllAboardRestaurant; 14925 Cabot Trail; mains $10-24; noon-9pm Wed-Mon;) This family-friendly restaurant serving seafood (including lobster, haddock and local salmon), steaks, burgers, pasta and salad is fast becoming an area favorite. Delicious and great value.

Drinking & Nightlife

Doryman Pub & Grill PUB
(902-224-9909; www.doryman.ca; 15528 Cabot Trail) This is the joint to swing by for live fiddler and piano sessions every Saturday (2pm to 6pm). Live entertainment most weeknights.

Information

Tourist Information Centre (902-224-2642; www.lestroispignons.com/visitor-information; 15584 Cabot Trail; 8:30am-5pm May-Oct) Housed in the same building as Le Trois Pignons cultural center.

Cape Breton Highlands National Park

The **Cape Breton Highlands National Park** (902-224-2306; www.pc.gc.ca; adult/child/vehicle & passengers $8/4/20) offers visitors some of Eastern Canada's most dramatic scenery. It's accessible via the famous Cabot Trail, one-third of which runs through the park. Here you'll find expanses of woodland, tundra and bog, and startling sea views. Established in 1936 and encompassing 20% of Cape Breton's landmass, it's the fancy feather in Nova Scotia's island cap.

There are two park entrances, one at Chéticamp and one at Ingonish Beach; purchase an entry permit at either. A one-day pass is good until noon the next day. Wheelchair-accessible trails are indicated on the free map available at either entrance.

THE ACADIANS

When the French first settled the area around the Minas Basin, they called the region Arcadia, a Greek and Roman term for 'pastoral paradise.' This became Acadia and, by the 18th century, the Acadians felt more connection with the land here than with the distant Loire Valley they'd come from.

To the English, however, they would always be French, with whom rivalry and suspicion was constant. Considering it an affront to their Catholic faith, the Acadians refused to take an oath of allegiance to the English king after the Treaty of Utrecht granted Nova Scotia to the British. When hard-line lieutenant governor Charles Lawrence was appointed in 1754, he became fed up with the Acadians and ordered their deportation. The English burned many villages and forced some 14,000 Acadians onto ships.

Many Acadians headed for Louisiana and New Orleans; others went to various Maritime points, New England, Martinique in the Caribbean, Santo Domingo in the Dominican Republic, or back to Europe. Some hid out and remained in Acadia. In later years many of the deported people returned but found their lands occupied. In Nova Scotia, Acadians resettled the Chéticamp area on Cape Breton Island and the French Shore north of Yarmouth.

Activities

Hiking

Two trails on the west coast of the park have spectacular ocean views. **Fishing Cove Trail** gently descends 330m over 8km to the mouth of rugged Fishing Cove River. You can opt for a steeper and shorter hike of 2.8km from a second trailhead about 5km north of the first. Double the distances if you plan to return the same day. Otherwise, you must preregister for one of eight backcountry sites ($10) at the Chéticamp Information Centre. Reviews of trails in and near the park are available at www.cabottrail.com.

Most other trails are shorter and close to the road, many leading to ridge tops for impressive views of the coast. The best of these is the **Skyline Trail**, a 7km loop that puts you on the edge of a headland cliff right above the water. The trailhead is about 5.5km north of Corney Brook Campground.

Just south of Neil's Harbour, on the eastern coast of the park, the **Coastal Trail** runs 11km round-trip and traverses more gentle coastline.

Cycling

Don't make this your inaugural trip: the riding is tough, there are no shoulders in many sections and you must be comfortable sharing the incredible scenery with RVs. Alternatively, you can mountain bike on four inland trails in the park; only Branch Pond Lookoff Trail offers ocean views.

Sea Spray Outdoor Adventures CYCLING
(☎902-383-2552; www.cabot-trail-outdoors.com; 299 Shore Rd, Dingwall; bicycle rental per day/week from $45/160; ⏲9am-5pm Jun-Oct) In Smelt Brook near Dingwall, this outfitter rents bikes and does emergency repairs. It also offers help planning trips and leads organized cycling, kayaking and hiking tours.

Sleeping

Cape Breton Highlands National Park Campgrounds CAMPGROUND
(tent sites/RV sites/oTENTiks from $18/30/100) Cape Breton Highlands National Park has six drive-in campgrounds. Most sites are first-come, first-served, but wheelchair-accessible sites, group campsites and backcountry sites can be reserved for $9.80. In the smaller campgrounds further from the park entrances, just pick a site and self-register. To camp at any of the three larger ones near the park entrances, register at an information center.

Chéticamp and Broad Cove campgrounds now have ready-made tent sites (oTENTiks), which are wildly popular.

From late October to early May, you can camp at the Chéticamp and Ingonish Campgrounds for $22, including firewood. In truly inclement weather, tenters can take refuge in cooking shelters with wood stoves.

Information

Chéticamp Information Centre (☎902-224-2306; www.parkscanada.gc.ca; 16646 Cabot Trail; ⏲8:30am-7pm) Has displays and a relief map of the park, plus a bookstore. Ask the staff for advice on hiking or camping.

Ingonish Beach Information Centre (☎902-285-2535; 37677 Cabot Trail; ⏲8am-8pm May-Oct) On the eastern edge of the park, with displays, maps and friendly bilingual staff.

Pleasant Bay

A perfect base for exploring the Cape Breton Highlands National Park, Pleasant Bay is a carved-out bit of civilization hemmed in on all sides by wilderness. It's also an active fishing harbor known for its whale-watching tours and for its Tibetan monastery.

Sights & Activities

Gampo Abbey MONASTERY

(902-224-2752; www.gampoabbey.org; 1533 Pleasant Bay Rd; tours 1:30-3:30pm Mon-Fri Jun-Sep) This abbey, 8km north of Pleasant Bay past the village of Red River, is a monastery for followers of Tibetan Buddhism. Ane Pema Chödrön is the founding director of the abbey and a noted Buddhist author, but you aren't likely to see her here as she is often on the road. You can visit the grounds any time during the day, but you'll get a more authentic experience with an escorted tour.

Whale Interpretive Centre MUSEUM

(902-224-1411; 104 Harbour Rd; adult/child $5/4; 9am-5pm Jun-Oct) Stop here before taking a whale-watching tour from the adjacent wharf. Park entrance permits are for sale, and internet access is available downstairs.

Captain Mark's Whale & Seal Cruise WHALE WATCHING

(902-224-1316; www.whaleandsealcruise.com; adult/child $55/35; May-Sep) Depending on the season, two to five tours depart, either in the lower-priced *Double Hookup* motorboat (adult/child $45/20) or closer to the action in a Zodiac. Captain Mark promises not only guaranteed whale sightings, but also time to see seabirds and seals, as well as Gampo Abbey. Tours leave from the wharf next to the Whale Interpretive Centre.

Pollett's Cove HIKING

The popular, challenging, 20km round-trip hiking trail to Pollett's Cove begins at the end of the road to Gampo Abbey. There are great views along the way and perfect spots to camp when you arrive at the abandoned fishing community. This is not a Parks Canada trail, so it can be rough underfoot.

Sleeping

HI-Cabot Trail Hostel HOSTEL $

(902-224-1976; www.cabottrailhostel.com; 23349 Cabot Trail; dm/r $28/68; @) Bright and basic, this very friendly 18-bed hostel has a common kitchen and barbecue area.

Ingonish

At the eastern entrance to Cape Breton Highlands National Park are Ingonish and Ingonish Beach (along with Ingonish Ferry, Ingonish Harbour and Ingonish Centre), small towns lost in the background of motels and cottages. This is a long-standing and popular tourist destination, but there are few real attractions. There are several hiking trails and an information center nearby in the national park.

Sights & Activities

Ingonish Beach BEACH

This long, wide strip of sand is tucked in a bay surrounded by green hills.

Highlands Links Golf Course GOLF

(902-285-2600; 275 Keltic Inn Rd; green fees from $60; 6am-6pm May-Oct) Avid golfers in the know report that this 18-hole, par-72 course, designed by world-renowned Stanley Thompson, is one of the most beautiful and challenging in Canada.

Sleeping & Eating

Driftwood Lodge INN $

(902-285-2558; www.driftwoodlodge.ca; 36125 Cabot Trail, North Ingonish; d/ste from $55/80; May-Nov; P) Located 8km north of the Ingonish park entrance, this funky cabin-meets-hotel establishment is a steal. The owner works at the national park and is a mine of info about hiking and activities. There's a fine-sand beach just below the lodge.

Maven Gypsy B&B & Cottages B&B $$

(902-929-2246; www.themavengypsy.com; 41682 Cabot Trail, Wreck Cove; r $105-135; Jun-Nov) With fresh-baked goods for breakfast and friendly hosts, this adorable butter-yellow cottage is only three minutes' walk to the beach.

★ **Keltic Lodge at the Highlands** LODGE $$$

(902-285-2880; www.kelticlodge.ca; Ingonish Beach; r $155-285, cottages $329-589; May-Oct) Extensively renovated in 2016, the finest digs in the area are scattered around this clifftop Tudor-style resort erected in 1940, sharing Middle Head Peninsula with its eponymous golf course. A range of room types, from guestrooms to apartments to gorgeous rustic cottages, are available; check the website for details. The day-spa and pool are like no other in Nova Scotia.

Clucking Hen Deli & Bakery CAFE $
(☎902-929-2501; 45073 Cabot Trail; mains $7-18; ⌚7am-7pm May-Oct) Listen to the locals cluck away while you eat a delicious meal of home-made breads, soup and salad.

★ **Main Street Restaurant & Bakery** CANADIAN $$
(☎902-285-2225; www.mainstreetrestaurantandbakery.ca; 37764 Cabot Trail, Ingonish Beach; mains $10-24; ⌚7am-9pm Tue-Sat) By far the best breakfast stop near Cape Breton Highlands National Park and also a great stop for lunch and dinner. Sandwiches and French toast are made with thick, fresh bread, and the seafood plates are immense. Try the lobster angel-hair pasta with crab and mussels in a brandy cream sauce: you won't be disappointed.

The Far North

North of Ingonish, the first village outside Cape Breton Highlands National Park is **Neil's Harbour**, the nicest of the area's remote outposts. Continue on via New Haven Road to come to **White Point**. Both are simple, hard-working communities where fishing boats outnumber houses. If neither village floats your boat, follow twisty, windswept White Point Rd to get back onto the Cabot Trail.

If you're determined to get to the top of Nova Scotia, follow Bay St Lawrence Rd to take a look at the pretty, eponymous settlement. From here on, the road gets rougher and the scenery gets wilder. The last 7km of the 13km stretch of hectic, slow-going road between **Bay St Lawrence** and the unfortunately named **Meat Cove** is gravel. If you're not an avid camper/hiker, Meat Cove might not be your cup of tea.

Sights & Activities

Cabots Landing Provincial Park STATE PARK
(☎902-662-3030; http://parks.novascotia.ca) Stop in this wonderful provincial park, 10km north of the Cabot Trail en route to Bay St Lawrence, to enjoy Aspy Bay and its spectacular beach.

Grassy Point HIKING
You can't beat the views over the coast from Grassy Point, accessible via a small foot trail (about 40 minutes round-trip) that starts just past the Meat Cove Campground. Sit for a while at the point to look for whales and nesting bald eagles.

Cape St Lawrence Lighthouse HIKING
From Meat Cove, a 16km hiking trail heads west to Cape St Lawrence lighthouse and **Lowland Cove**. Spend an hour gazing over the ocean and you're guaranteed to see pods of pilot whales. They frolic here all spring and summer and into the fall. Carry a compass and refrain from exploring side paths; locals have gotten lost in this area.

Captain Cox's Whale Watch WHALE WATCHING
(☎902-383-2981; www.whalewatching-novascotia.com; 578 Meat Cove Rd, St Margaret Village; adult/child $45/25) Captain Cox has been taking people to see whales aboard the 35ft *Northern Gannet* since 1986. He offers trips at 10:30am, 1:30pm and 4:30pm in July and August. Call for spring and fall schedules.

Sleeping & Eating

★ **Jumping Mouse Campground** CAMPGROUND $
(☎902-383-2914; www.ecocamping.ca; 3360 Bay St Lawrence Rd, Bay St Lawrence; tent sites/cabin $30/60; ⌚Jun-Sep) This ecofriendly campground is the best reason to get off the Cabot Trail, with 10 magical oceanfront sites and a beautifully built four-bunk cabin. There are hot showers, pit toilets, a cooking shelter and frequent whale sightings, and the whole place is nearly bug-free.

Two Tittle B&B $
(☎902-383-2817; www.twotittle.com; 2119 White Point Rd, White Point; r $60-100; P 📶) Stay the night at homey Two Tittle, which smells like supper. Don't miss the short but gorgeous walk out back to the Two Tittle Islands the B&B is named for – and look out for whales and eagles.

Hine's Ocean View Lodge LODGE $
(☎902-383-2512; www.hinesoceanviewlodge.ca; Meat Cove; r $60, whole house $200; 📶 🐾) This isolated spot, high up its own road (signposted off Meat Cove Rd), has plain, almost-dormitory style rooms and a shared kitchen. The views are truly breathtaking, but it's not for those who don't like the feeling of being isolated. Cash only.

Meat Cove Campground CAMPGROUND $
(☎902-383-2379; www.meatcovecampground.ca; 2475 Meat Cove Rd, Capstick; tent sites/cabins from $30/60; ⌚Jun-Nov; 📶) This remote campground is in an undoubtedly spectacular spot, perched on a grassy bluff high above the ocean in the middle of nowhere. Four cabins with no electricity or plumbing

share the view; bring your own bedding. Note: there are no protective railings and campers have fallen to their death here. Not great for kids. Be prepared for high winds.

Chowder House SEAFOOD $$
(902-336-2463; 90 Lighthouse Rd, Neil's Harbour; chowder $7-12, mains $14-24; 11am-8pm May-Oct) This establishment, out beyond the lighthouse at Neil's Harbour, is the perfect stop for lunch or dinner. It's famous for its chowder, but also serves great-value suppers of snow crab, lobster, mussels and more. There are plenty of dining locals, who like to chat with folks from far away while they splatter themselves with seafood juice.

Information

Meat Cove Welcome Center (902-383-2284; 2296 Meat Cove Rd, Meat Cove; 8am-8:30pm Jul-Sep;) Stop by to get excellent info on hiking trails, check email, and grab a bite to eat (from sandwiches to lobster suppers). Leave your car here if there's no room at the trailhead.

Baddeck

The highlands meet the lowlands in Baddeck, an aging resort town in a pastoral setting on the northern shore of Bras d'Or Lake – a veritable inland saltwater sea, where eagles nest and puffins play. At 1099 sq km, the lake is the biggest in Nova Scotia and all but cleaves Cape Breton Island in two. Just south of Baddeck, **Wagmatcook First Nation** (www.wagmatcook.com) is composed of two Mi'kmaq communities.

Sights

★Alexander Graham Bell National Historic Site MUSEUM
(902-295-2069; www.pc.gc.ca; 559 Chebucto St; adult/child $8/4; 9am-6pm May-Oct) The inventor of the telephone is buried near his summer home, **Beinn Bhreagh**, which is visible across the bay from Baddeck. The excellent museum of the Alexander Graham Bell National Historic Site, at the eastern edge of town, covers all aspects of his inventions and innovations. Although nothing looks spectacular at first glance, it's the story of the man that will hook you. See medical and electrical devices, telegraphs, telephones, kites and seaplanes, and then learn how they all work.

Great Hall of the Clans Museum MUSEUM
(902-295-3411; www.gaeliccollege.edu/great-hall-of-the-clans; 51779 Cabot Trail, Englishtown; adult/child $8/6; 9am-5pm Mon-Fri Jun-Oct) This museum at the Gaelic College of Celtic Arts & Crafts, about 20km north of Baddeck, traces Celtic history from ancient times to the Highland clearances.

Wagmatcook Culture & Heritage Centre MUSEUM
(902-295-2999; www.wagmatcookcentre.com; Hwy 105, Wagmatcook; 9am-8pm May-Oct, reduced hours Nov-Apr) Stop in the Mi'kmaw community of Wagmatcook just west of Baddeck to visit the Wagmatcook Culture & Heritage Centre. This somewhat empty cultural attraction offers an entryway into Mi'kmaw culture and history.

Tours

Amoeba CRUISE
(902-295-7780; www.amoebasailingtours.com; 2hr tours adult/child $25/10; Jun-Oct) Classic schooner sailing tours on the Bras d'Or Lake bring you past Alexander Graham Bell's grand Beinn Bhreagh mansion and under soaring bald eagles.

Sleeping

Bear on the Lake Guesthouse HOSTEL $
(866-718-5253; www.bearonthelake.com; 10705 Hwy 105, Aberdeen; dm/r $32/78;) Bear on the Lake Guesthouse, between Wagmatcook and the next town of Whycocomagh, is a fun place overlooking the lake. Dorm and private rooms are available, plus there's inviting communal areas and a large sunny deck. Backpackers should note that, without a vehicle, the location is quite isolated, with no facilities or transport nearby.

★Silver Dart Lodge LODGE $$
(902-295-2340; www.maritimeinns.com; 257 Shore Road; r/chalet from $150/180;) The Silver Dart boasts recently and thoroughly renovated rooms, ranging from quaint chalets with kitchenettes at the rear of the property to motel-style units. McCurdy's Dining Room, the on-site bar-restaurant, has good food and lovely views. There's even a decent-sized pool for those hot summer days.

Dunlop Inn B&B $$
(902-295-1100; www.dunlopinn.com; 552 Chebucto St; d $120-170;) This quaint,

historic B&B offers an unrivaled position with immediate water-frontage on Bras d'Or Lake. Subsequently, water views abound. Its five self-contained rooms are tastefully decorated, and the self-service breakfast kitchen is fresh from renovation.

Lynwood Inn INN $$
(902-295-1995; www.lynwoodinn.com; 441 Shore Rd; d from $100;) Rooms in this enormous inn go far beyond the hotel standard, with Victorian wooden beds, muted color schemes and airy living spaces. There's a family-style restaurant downstairs that serves breakfast, lunch and dinner; breakfast is not included in room rates.

Broadwater Inn & Cottages INN $$
(902-295-1101; www.broadwaterinn.com; 975 Bay Rd; r $129-159, cottages $149-289; May-Nov;) In a tranquil spot 2km northeast of Baddeck, this c 1830 home once belonged to JAD McCurdy, who worked with Alexander Graham Bell on early aircraft designs. The rooms in the inn are full of character, have bay views and are decorated with subtle prints and lots of flair. Modern cottages are set in the woods and are great for families.

Eating & Drinking

Herring Choker Deli DELI $
(902-295-2275; www.herringchokerdeli.com; 1958 Hwy 105; items $6-15; 9am-6pm May-Oct;) On Hwy 105, 12km southwest of Baddeck, this deli is one of the region's best pit stops for gourmet sandwiches, soups and salads.

High Wheeler Cafe CAFE $
(902-295-3006; 486 Chebucto St; sandwiches $9; 6am-8pm May-Oct;) This place bakes great bread and goodies (some gluten-free) and makes big, tasty sandwiches, quesadillas, soups and more. Finish off on the sunny deck licking an ice-cream cone. Box lunches for hikers also available.

★**Baddeck Lobster Suppers** SEAFOOD $$$
(902-925-3307; www.baddecklobstersuppers.ca; 17 Ross St; mains $22-28; 4-9pm Jun-Oct) In the former legion hall, this institution offers your choice of lobster, salmon, snow crab or strip-loin with all-you-can-eat mussels, chowder and dessert for $38. Feast on delicacies without the fuss of fancy fine-dining.

Big Spruce Brewing MICROBREWERY
(902-295-2537; www.bigspruce.ca; 64 Yankee Line Rd, Nyanza; noon-7pm) Pop into this farmyard brewery, about 14km southwest of Baddeck, to grab yourself a growler of unfiltered, unpasteurized, 'unbelievably good,' locally brewed beer.

Entertainment

Baddeck Gathering Ceilidhs LIVE MUSIC
(902-295-0971; www.baddeckgathering.com; 8 Old Margaree Rd, St Michael's Parish Hall; adult/child from $10/5; 7:30pm Jul & Aug) Nightly fiddling and dancing. The parish hall is just opposite the tourist information center in the middle of town.

Information

Visit Baddeck (www.visitbaddeck.com) Has maps, plus info on tour operators, golf courses and more.

Tourist Information Centre (902-295-1911; 454 Chebucto St; 10am-4pm Jun-Oct)

Getting There & Away

Baddeck is located on the Trans-Canada Hwy (Hwy 105), 78km southwest of Sydney.

Maritime Bus (www.maritimebus.com) has one or two services daily to Sydney ($21, 1½ hours) and Halifax ($64, 5½ hours).

North Sydney

North Sydney is a small and friendly industrial town, although there's not much to see or do here. The main reason you'll be passing through is if you're heading to the Cabot Trail from Sydney, or heading to or from Newfoundland on the ferry.

Sleeping & Eating

A Boat to Sea B&B $$
(902-794-8326; www.aboattosea.com; 61 Queen St; r $100-110;) Right on the waterfront and surrounded by beautiful gardens (look for bald eagles), this grand home is decorated with stained glass and a quirky antiques collection. Relax on the waterfront patio and enjoy hearty breakfasts. There are only three rooms, so book ahead in high season, when there's a two-night minimum stay.

Heritage Home B&B B&B $$
(902-794-4815; www.bedandbreakfastnorthsydney.com; 110 Queen St; r $110-120;) This exceptionally well decorated and maintained Victorian home is an extremely elegant place to stay for the price. Breakfasts are home-cooked and most rooms have private bathrooms.

Bette's Kitchen SEAFOOD $
(☎902-794-4452; 138 Queen St; mains $9-18; ⏰noon-8pm) This is *the* place on Cape Breton Island for a good ole-fashioned fry-up. Fried scallops, tender battered fish and golden, crunchy fries… It's *all* good, but perhaps not so good for you. Run with the adage: you only live once.

★**Black Spoon** MODERN CANADIAN $$
(☎902-241-3300; www.blackspoonbistro.com; 320 Commercial St; mains $12-19; ⏰11am-8pm Mon-Thu, to 9pm Fri & Sat) At this hip black-and-beige restaurant, dine on local faves with a delectable twist such as breaded haddock with mango salsa or the colorful grilled vegetable salad with goat's cheese. There's also espresso drinks, cocktails and a reasonable wine list.

Lobster Pound & Moore SEAFOOD $$$
(☎902-794-2992; 161 Queen St; mains $24-38; ⏰noon-8pm Tue-Sun) With the standard lobster here weighing in at almost a kilo (2lb), show up hungry because portions are massive. But big quantity doesn't affect the freshness, high quality and all around deliciousness of the food. Try Korean grilled steaks, seafood stew, or the ravioli stuffed with fresh lobster and topped with even more. Decor is chic bistro meets seafood shack.

Getting There & Away

North Sydney is 21km from Sydney, and 48km from the Cabot Trail at Indian Brook via the 24-hour vehicular Englishtown ferry ($7, five minutes).

The town is the boarding point for **Marine Atlantic ferry** (☎800-341-7981; www.marine-atlantic.ca) services to Port-aux-Basques, NL (one-way adult/child $44/21, six to eight hours), and Argentia, NL (one-way adult/child $116/65, 16 hours). It costs an extra $114 to bring a standard-sized vehicle to Port-aux-Basques and an extra $203 to Argentia.

Sydney

☎902 / POP 31,600

The second-biggest city in Nova Scotia and the only real city on Cape Breton Island, Sydney is the embattled core of the island's collapsed industrial belt. The now-closed steel mill and coal mines were the region's largest employers and now the city feels a bit empty, but there are some lovely older houses, especially in the North End residential areas where most of the B&Bs are found. Overall, the city is well serviced and you get more bang for your buck staying here as a base to explore Louisbourg and the Cabot Trail than you would in more scenic areas.

Sights

Downtown, Charlotte St is lined with stores and restaurants and there's a pleasant **boardwalk** along Esplanade.

The North End historic district has a gritty charm. There are eight buildings older than 1802 in a two-block radius in North End. Three are open to the public.

★**Cape Breton Miners' Museum** MUSEUM
(☎902-849-4522; www.minersmuseum.com; 42 Birkley St, Glace Bay; tour & mine visit adult/child $15/13; ⏰10am-6pm) Glace Bay, 6km northeast of Sydney, would be just another fading coal town were it not for this exceptional museum, the highlight of which is the 'Men of the Deeps' adventure under the seafloor to visit decommissioned mines with a retired miner as a guide – not for the claustrophobic. The museum's restaurant (11am to 8pm) is highly recommended, and offers seafood, sandwiches and burgers (mains $13 to $28); there's a daily lunch buffet from noon to 2pm.

Jost Heritage House HISTORIC BUILDING
(☎902-539-0366; 54 Charlotte St; $3; ⏰9am-5pm Mon-Sat, 1-5:30pm Sun) Jost Heritage House features a collection of model ships and an assortment of medicines used by an early 20th-century apothecary.

Cape Breton Centre for Heritage & Science MUSEUM
(☎902-539-1572; 225 George St; $2; ⏰9am-4pm Mon-Sat) This humble local history center explores the social and natural history of Cape Breton Island.

St Patrick's Church Museum HISTORIC BUILDING
(☎902-562-8237; 87 Esplanade; $2; ⏰9am-5pm Mon-Sat Jun-Oct) Built in 1828 in the Pioneer Gothic style, St Patrick's Church is the oldest Catholic church on Cape Breton Island and now houses a museum recounting Sydney's religious past.

Cossit House HISTORIC BUILDING
(☎902-539-7973; http://cossithouse.novascotia.ca; 75 Charlotte St; adult/concession $2/1; ⏰9am-5pm Mon-Sat, 1-5pm Sun Jun-Oct) Built in 1787, this is the oldest house in Sydney and one of the oldest surviving buildings in Nova Scotia.

Tours

Ghosts & Legends of Historic Sydney WALKING
(☎902-539-1572; www.oldsydney.com; tours $13; ⏰6:30pm Thu Jul & Aug) This walking tour, designed to scare the pants off you, leaves from St Patrick's Church Museum, does a loop of historic buildings and finishes with tea and scones.

Sleeping & Eating

Sydney has some solid chain-hotel choices and, unlike much of the rest of the island, most properties here are open year-round.

★**Colby House** B&B $$
(☎902-539-4095; www.colbyhousebb.com; 10 Park St; r $100-125; 📶) It's worth staying in Sydney for the affordable luxury of this exceptional B&B. The owner used to travel around Canada for work and decided to offer everything she wished she'd had on the road. The result is a mix of heritage and modern design, the softest sheets you can imagine, guest bathrobes, and too many other comfort-giving details to list.

Hampton Inn by Hilton HOTEL $$
(☎855-605-0317; www.hilton.com; 60 Maillard St; d $149-269; P ⊖ ❄ 📶 ≋) A little way from the action of Sydney's waterfront area, this impressive tourist hotel is particularly popular with families. Oversized, stylish and comfortable rooms exceed brand standards, and the hotel staff are excellent.

Cambridge Suites Sydney HOTEL $$
(☎902-562-6500; www.cambridgesuitessydney.com; 380 Esplanade; d $139-239; P ❄ 📶) This smart hotel in a hard-to-beat, downtown location has comfortable, nicely renovated rooms in a variety of configurations, many with water views. Rates include a decent serve-yourself breakfast spread and free wi-fi.

Gathering House B&B B&B $$
(☎902-539-7172; kmp38@msn.com; 148 Crescent St; r $85-125; P ⊖ ❄ 📶 🐾) This welcoming, ramshackle Victorian home is close to the heart of town. Staying here makes you feel like you're part of a big, lively family.

Governors Pub & Eatery PUB FOOD $$
(☎902-562-7646; www.governorseatery.com; 233 Esplanade; mains $9-22; ⏰11am-11pm) Easily the most popular place in Sydney. Stop in to mingle with the after-work crowd for drinks, dine on gourmet pub grub made with local ingredients, and stay for live-music events such as the Wednesday-night Irish jam sessions. Check the website for what's on.

Flavor on the Water MODERN CANADIAN $$
(☎902-567-1043; www.cbflavor.com/flavor; 60 Esplanade; mains $11-28; ⏰11am-8pm; 🖉) Sydney's swankiest restaurant on the Esplanade offers artfully presented dishes made from local ingredients, from salads, sandwiches and burgers for lunch to fish, chicken and steak for dinner. The restaurant itself, with its high ceilings and waterfront location, is both stylish and impressive. Check the website to learn about its humble origins and other local branches.

Entertainment

Fiddlers and other traditional musicians from the west coast of the island and a lot of touring bands perform in the area.

Savoy Theatre THEATER
(☎902-842-1577; www.savoytheatre.com; 116 Commercial St, Glace Bay) Six kilometres from Sydney, Glace Bay's grand 1920 Savoy Theatre is the region's premier entertainment venue.

Casino Nova Scotia CASINO
(☎902-563-7777; www.sydney.casinonovascotia.com; 525 George St; ⏰11am-3am) This popular casino (there's not a great deal else to do in town) has hundreds of slot machines, blackjack and poker tables and live entertainment.

Information

Sydney Port Tourist Information (☎902-539-9876; 74 Esplanade; ⏰8:30am-6pm) Offers maps and brochures on Sydney and Cape Breton.

Getting There & Away

Sydney is 403km by road from Halifax. **Maritime Bus** (www.maritimebus.com) travels from Sydney to Halifax ($72.50, seven hours) and Truro ($63.50, five hours) from where you can connect to services bound for New Brunswick and Prince Edward Island.

If you're able to book in advance and they have a driver available, **Bay Luxury Shuttle** (☎855-673-8083; www.capebretonshuttle.ca) runs from Glace Bay to Halifax (one-way from $65) via North Sydney, Sydney and Hwy 105.

Both Air Canada and Westjet offer direct services to Halifax and Toronto from Sydney's compact **JA Douglas McCurdy Airport** (p331), which is 13km from downtown.

Air St-Pierre (☎877-277-7765; www.airsaint-pierre.com) offers less frequent, seasonal flights to the French territory of St-Pierre and Miquelon.

Louisbourg

Louisbourg, 35km southeast of Sydney, is famous for its historic fortress. The town itself, with its working fishing docks, old-timers and friendly vibe, has plenty of soul.

Sights

★Louisbourg National Historic Site HISTORIC SITE
(902-733-3552; www.fortressoflouisbourg.ca; 58 Wolfe St; adult/child $18/9; 9:30am-5pm) You'll need at least a few hours to fully explore this extraordinary historic site that faithfully re-creates the Louisbourg Fortress as it was in 1744, right down to the people – costumed thespians take their characters and run with them. Free guided tours around the site are offered throughout the day. Travelers with mobility problems can ask for a pass to drive their car up to the site.

Built to protect French interests in the region, the fortress was also a base for cod fishing and an administrative capital. Louisbourg was worked on continually from 1719 to about 1745. The British took it in a 46-day siege in 1745, but it would change hands twice more. In 1760, after British troops under the command of General James Wolfe took Québec City, the walls of Louisbourg were destroyed and the city burned to the ground.

In 1961, with the closing of many Cape Breton Island coal mines, the federal government funded the largest historical reconstruction in Canadian history as a way to generate employment.

WORTH A TRIP

MEMORY LANE HERITAGE VILLAGE

A 20-minute drive from Tangier, this outstanding example of how a community can work together to preserve its history re-creates a 1940s Eastern Shore **village** (877-287-0697; www.heritagevillage.ca; 5435 Clam Harbour Rd, Lake Charlotte; 11am-4pm Jun-Sep) in a series of lovingly relocated and restored buildings, chock full of hands-on antiques, as if frozen in time. You'll find vintage cars, a farmstead with animals (great for kids), a schoolhouse, a church, a miner's hut, a blacksmith, shipbuilding shops and so much more. A must for history buffs of any kind.

Though the scale of the reconstruction is massive, three-quarters of Louisbourg is still in ruins. The 2.5km **Ruins Walk** guides you through the untouched terrain. A short interpretive walk discusses the relationship between the French and the Mi'kmaq.

Louisbourg Lighthouse LIGHTHOUSE
(555 Havenside Rd) Canada's first lighthouse was built on this wild, rugged and extremely scenic site in 1734. The present lighthouse was opened in 1923. You can't go in, but it's worth a visit to explore the site and the rugged 6km **trail** that follows the coast over bogs and Precambrian polished granite.

Sleeping & Eating

★Cranberry Cove Inn INN $$
(902-733-2171; www.cranberrycoveinn.com; 12 Wolfe St; r $105-160; May-Nov;) From the dark-pink facade to the period-perfect interior, you'll be transported back in time through rose-colored glasses at this stunning B&B. Each room is different, and several have Jacuzzis and fireplaces.

Point of View Suites INN $$
(888-374-8439; www.louisbourgpointofview.com; 15 Commercial St Extension; r $125-265;) If B&Bs aren't your thing, your best bet in town is this inn comprising a range of accommodation types, from motel-style rooms to self-contained apartments with full kitchens. Most have wonderful views over the harbor.

Grubstake CANADIAN $$
(902-733-2308; www.grubstake.ca; 7499 Main St; mains lunch $8-18, dinner $16-35; 11am-8pm) This informal restaurant is the best place to eat in town. The menu features burger platters at lunch and pastas and fresh seafood for dinner.

Beggar's Banquet SEAFOOD $$$
(888-374-8439; www.louisbourgpointofview.com; 15 Commercial St Extension; meals $38; 6-8pm Jul-Sep) Finally, here's a chance for you to get into period costume and gorge on a feast of local seafood in a replicated 18th-century tavern. There's a choice of four delicious and copious mains, including crab and lobster.

Entertainment

Louisbourg Playhouse THEATER
(902-733-2996; www.louisbourgplayhouse.ca; 11 Lower Warren St; tickets from $15; 8pm-late Jun-Aug) A cast of young local musicians entertain in this 17th-century-style theater.

Information

Tourist Information Office (902-733-2720; 7495 Main St; 9am-7pm) Operated by the Destination Cape Breton Association; located in the center of town.

EASTERN SHORE

If you want to escape into the fog, away from summer crowds, this pristine region is the place to explore. Running from the outskirts of Dartmouth, across the harbor from Halifax, to Cape Canso at the extreme eastern tip of the mainland, the Eastern Shore has no large towns and the main road is almost as convoluted as the rugged shoreline it follows. For those seeking wildlife and barely touched wilderness, and opportunities to enjoy hiking, kayaking or fishing, this is your heaven.

Historically, villages in the region were linked only by boat, then by rail, which was later taken away. Spirited and resilient, these close-knit communities have maintained their traditions for decade upon decade.

Sights & Activities

There are beautiful, long, white-sand beaches all along the Eastern Shore, although the water never gets very warm. The closest and busiest of the Eastern Shore beaches, 1km-long **Rainbow Haven** has washrooms, showers, a canteen and a boardwalk with wheelchair access to the beach. Lifeguards supervise a swimming area.

The most popular surf destination, cobblestone **Lawrencetown Beach** faces directly south and often gets big waves, compliments of hurricanes or tropical storms hundreds of kilometers away. It boasts a supervised swimming area, washrooms and a canteen. If you want to try surfing, but don't have a board or don't know what to do, **East Coast Surf School** (902-449-9488; www.ecsurfschool.com; 4348 Lawrencetown Rd, East Lawrencetown; lessons from $75) will get you vertical on the water.

The longest swimming beach in Nova Scotia and the prettiest in the area, with more than 3km of grass-backed white sand, is **Martinique Beach**. Even if you find the water too cold for a swim, it's a beautiful place to walk, watch birds or play Frisbee.

Sleeping & Eating

Liscombe Lodge Resort RESORT **$$**
(902-779-2307; www.liscombelodge.ca; 2884 Nova Scotia Trunk 7, Marie Joseph; r $149-199, chalet $175-285; May-Oct) A nature lover's dream, this rambling country lodge comprises 30 spacious, nicely decorated riverside rooms in the main lodge, a rustic three-bedroom Canadian-style cottage and 17 sweeter-than-sweet chalets with fireplaces and decks overlooking the woodsy grounds and river.

Dobbit Bakehouse BAKERY **$**
(902-889-2919; 7896 Hwy 7, Musquodoboit Harbour; baked goods $2-6; 8am-5pm;) Come chat with the friendly baker, a font of local knowledge, at this wonderful country bakery, which boasts rustic fresh breads and baked goods free from preservatives and using only seasonal local ingredients wherever possible. The selection changes daily. Free wi-fi.

Guysborough

Sleepy Guysborough was settled by United Empire Loyalists after the American Revolution. Despite such a long history, the town has become another particularly scenic yet economically challenged Eastern Shore community. Some degree of investment over recent years, however, has seen a flicker of renewed tourist appeal.

Sights & Activities

The 26km **Guysborough Trail**, part of the Trans Canada Trail (TCT), is great for biking and hiking, and the region's sheltered coves and bays beg to be kayaked.

Old Court House Museum MUSEUM
(902-533-4008; 106 Church St; 9am-5pm Mon-Fri, 10am-4pm Sat & Sun) FREE The Old Court House Museum displays artifacts related to early farming and housekeeping. It also offers tourist information and guides to hiking trails.

Sleeping & Eating

Boylston Provincial Park CAMPGROUND **$**
(902-533-3326; www.parks.gov.ns.ca; off Hwy 16; campsites $18) The 36 shaded sites are never all taken. From the picnic area on the highway below the campground, a foot bridge leads to a small island off the coast about 12km north of Guysborough.

Desbarres Manor INN **$$**
(902-533-2099; www.desbarresmanor.com; 90 Church St; r $189-259;) This tastefully renovated 1830 grand mansion with opulent rooms, some with water glimpses, is a good choice if you're spending a night in town.

DON'T MISS

TAYLOR HEAD PROVINCIAL PARK

A little-known scenic highlight of Nova Scotia, this spectacular **park** (☎902-772-2218; http://parks.novascotia.ca/content/taylor-head; 20140 Hwy 7, Spry Bay) encompasses a peninsula jutting 6.5km into the Atlantic. On one side is a long, very fine, sandy beach fronting a protected bay. Some 17km of hiking trails cut through the spruce and fir forests. The **Headland Trail** is the longest at 8km round-trip and follows the rugged coastline to scenic views at **Taylor Head**. The shorter **Bob Bluff Trail** is a 3km round-trip hike to a bluff with good views.

Rare Bird Pub PUB FOOD $$
(☎902-533-2128; www.rarebirdpub.com; 80 Main St; mains $12-18; ⏰11:30am-8pm May-Oct) The Bird is a logical stop for a swig of local ale, a pot of mussels, some East Coast music on the weekend, and occasional fiddlers on the wharf. Check the website for schedules.

Canso

One of North America's oldest seaports, Canso today stands as a lonely cluster of boxy fishers' homes on a treeless bank of Chedabucto Bay. Long dependent on the fishery, Canso has been decimated by emigration and unemployment since the northern cod stocks collapsed around 1990.

Sights & Activities

Grassy Island National Historic Site HISTORIC SITE
(☎902-366-3136; www.pc.gc.ca; 1465 Union Street; suggested donation $3.50; ⏰10am-6pm Jun-Sep) An interpretive center on the waterfront tells the story of Grassy Island National Historic Site, which lies just offshore and can be visited by boat until 4pm. In 1720 the British built a small fort to offset the French, who had their headquarters in Louisbourg, but it was totally destroyed in 1744. Among the ruins today, there's a self-guided **hiking trail** with eight interpretive stops explaining the history of the area. The boat to Grassy Island departs from the center upon demand, weather permitting.

Whitman House Museum MUSEUM
(☎902-366-2170; 1297 Union St; ⏰9am-5pm Jun-Sep) FREE The 1885 Whitman House Museum holds reminders of the town's history and offers a wonderful view from the widow's walk on the roof. The museum also serves as Canso's unoffical tourist information office.

Chapel Gully Trail HIKING
This 10km boardwalk and hiking trail along an estuary and out to the coast begins near the lighthouse on the hill behind the hospital at the eastern end of Canso.

Festivals & Events

★ **Stan Rogers Folk Festival** MUSIC
(www.stanfest.com; ⏰Jul) Most people who come to Canso come for the Stan Rogers Folk Festival, the biggest festival in Nova Scotia. It quadruples the town's population, with six stages showcasing folk, blues and traditional musicians from around the world.

Sleeping

Last Port Motel MOTEL $$
(☎902-366-2400; www.lastportmotel.ca; 10 Hwy 16; r $80-100; P📶) The only place to stay in Canso is this basic though spotlessly clean and super-friendly motel, just outside town.

Tangier

About 10km southwest of Taylor Head Provincial Park, Tangier is one of the best settings for **kayaking** in the Maritimes.

Highly recommended **Coastal Adventures Sea Kayaking** (☎902-772-2774; www.coastaladventures.com; off Hwy 7; tours from $75, single/double kayak rental from $50/70; ⏰Jun-Sep) offers introductory sea-kayaking trips, extended guided tours and kayak rentals, and has cosy rooms if you choose to stick around.

Unless you're camping or hanging with your kayaking crew, the nearest accommodations are in Dartmouth. Be sure to bring your own food if you plan on spending any time paddling around the area's coves and bays. Services in the area are limited. **Murphy's Camping on the Ocean** (☎902-772-2700; www.murphyscamping.ca; 291 Murphy's Rd; tent/RV sites $27/39; ⏰May-Oct; 📶🐾) gets you out of your tent and into the water to collect mussels; you eat your labors at a beach barbecue to the music of yarns told by Brian, the owner. There are RV sites, RV rentals, secluded tent sites and a very rudimentary room above the dock that can sleep four people.

New Brunswick

Includes ➡

Best Places to Eat

- Rossmount Inn Restaurant (p405)
- Port City Royal (p415)
- Naru (p397)
- Inn at Whale Cove (p411)
- Manuka (p423)

Best Places to Sleep

- Quartermain House B&B (p396)
- Algonquin Resort (p405)
- Mahogany Manor (p414)
- Hotel Paulin (p430)
- Treadwell Inn (p405)

Why Go?

In the early 20th century, New Brunswick was a very big deal. Millionaire businesspeople, major-league baseball players and US presidents journeyed here to fish salmon from its silver rivers and camp at rustic lodges in its deep primeval forests. But over the decades, New Brunswick slipped back into relative obscurity. Today some joke that it's the 'drive-through province,' as vacationers tend to hotfoot it to its better-known neighbors Prince Edward Island (PEI) and Nova Scotia.

But the unspoiled wilderness is still here. There are rivers and coastal islands for kayaking, snowy mountains for skiing and quaint Acadian villages for exploring. So do yourself a favor, and don't just drive through. PEI will still be there when you're done, we promise.

When to Go

Fredericton

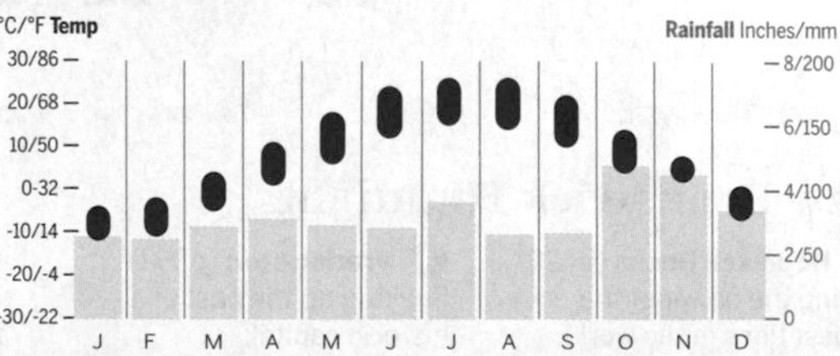

Jul–Sep St Andrews By-The-Sea bustles with crowds of whale-watchers.

Aug Acadians unleash their Franco-Canadian spirit for the Festival Acadien in Caraquet.

Nov–Mar Cross-country skiers hit the groomed trails of Fundy National Park.

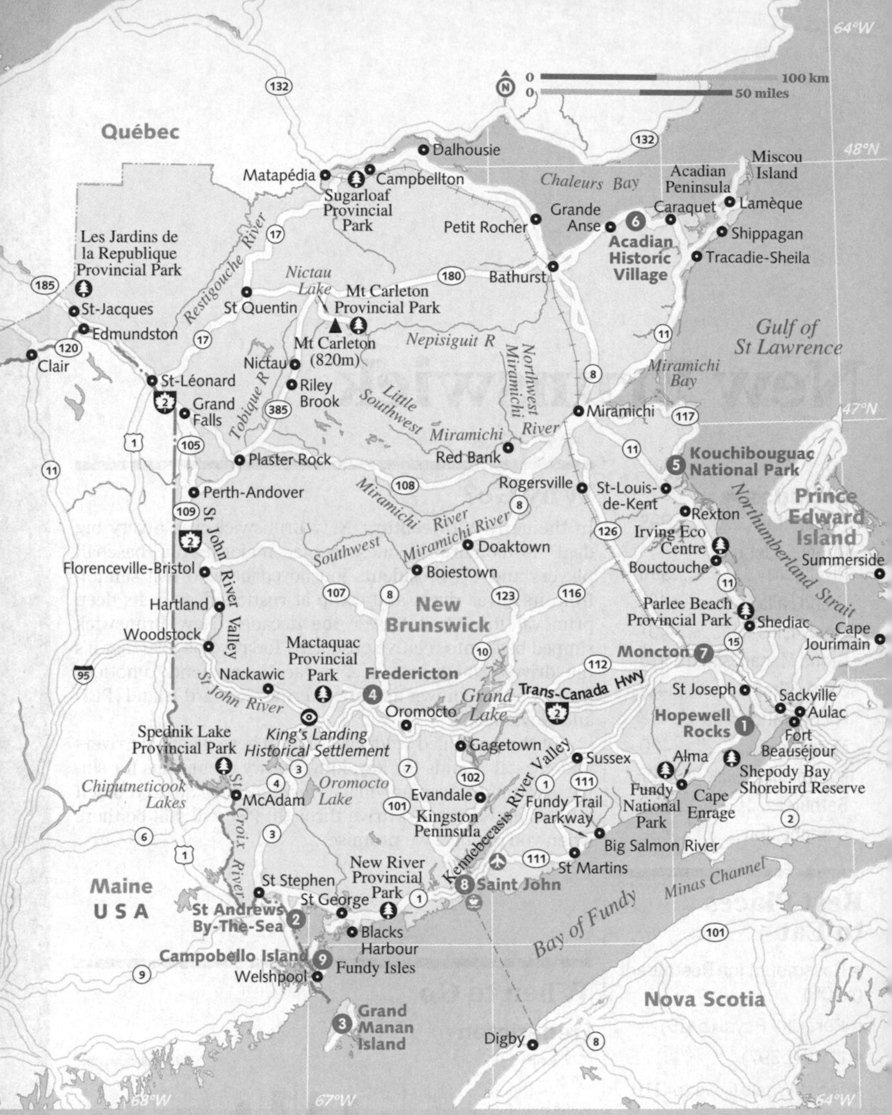

New Brunswick Highlights

1 Hopewell Rocks (p422) Feeling the power of the highest tides in the world.

2 St Andrews By-The-Sea (p404) Discovering this picturesque seaside town.

3 Grand Manan Island (p410) Breathing in the fresh sea air and unwinding on the peaceful, isolated island.

4 Fredericton (p393) Soaking up the past of a historic capital.

5 Kouchibouguac National Park (p426) Stretching out on the sandy beach or splashing in the lagoon.

6 Acadian Historic Village (p429) Living Acadian history at this reconstructed scene.

7 Moncton (p422) Tasting delicacies at the city's local markets.

8 Saint John (p412) Sipping on a local brew before hitting the hipster foodie scene.

9 Campobello Island (p409) Filling the shoes of Franklin D Roosevelt at his favorite holiday retreat.

History

What is now New Brunswick was originally the land of the Mi'kmaq and, in the western and southern areas, the Maliseet Aboriginals. Many places still bear their aboriginal names, although the Aboriginal people (who today number around 17,000) are now concentrated on small pockets of land.

Following in the wake of explorer Samuel de Champlain, French colonists arrived in the 1600s. The Acadians, as they came to be known, farmed the area around the Bay of Fundy. In 1755 they were expelled by the English, many returning to settle along the Bay of Chaleur. In the years following, the outbreak of the American Revolution brought an influx of British Loyalists from Boston and New York seeking refuge in the wilds of New Brunswick. These refugees settled the valleys of the Saint John and St Croix Rivers, established the city of Saint John and bolstered the garrison town at Fredericton.

Through the 1800s, lumbering and shipbuilding boomed, and by the start of the 20th century, other industries, including fishing, had developed. That era of prosperity ended with the Great Depression. Today, pulp and paper, oil refining and potato farming are the major industries.

Land & Climate

The province encompasses a varied geography of moist, rocky coastal areas, temperate inland river valleys and a heavily forested and mountainous interior. Summers are generally mild with occasional hot days. The Fundy shore is prone to fog, particularly in the spring and early summer. The primary tourist season lasts from late June to early September. Many tourist facilities (beaches, organized tours and some accommodations in resort areas) shut down for the remainder of the year.

Language

New Brunswick is Canada's only officially bilingual province; one-third speak French as their first language. You'll rarely have a problem being understood in English or French.

Getting There & Away

AIR

Air Canada has several daily flights from Halifax, Montréal, Ottawa and Toronto into Moncton, Saint John, Fredericton and Bathurst. Moncton has WestJet services from Toronto. WestJet also flies into Fredericton.

NEW BUNSWICK FAST FACTS

- Population: 756,800
- Area: 73,400 sq km
- Capital: Fredericton
- Quirky fact: Home to the world's biggest fake lobster (Shediac), axe (Nackawic) and fiddlehead (Plaster Rock).

BOAT

The **Bay Ferries** (877-762-7245; www.bayferries.com; adult/child/senior $46/31/36, car/bicycle $92/10) sails between Saint John and Digby, Nova Scotia, year-round. The three-hour crossing can save a lot of driving.

Free government ferries service Deer Island and White Head Island; **East Coast Ferries** (506-747-2159; www.eastcoastferries.nb.ca; car & driver $16, additional passenger $3; 9am-7pm) runs between Campobello Island and Deer Island. Another private ferry company also serves Grand Manan Island. Reserve ahead.

BUS

Maritime Bus (800-575-1807; www.maritimebus.com) services the major transportation routes in New Brunswick, with service to Nova Scotia, PEI and into Québec as far as Rivière-du-Loup, where buses connect with **Orléans Express** (888-999-3977; www.orleansexpress.com) services to points west.

CAR & MOTORCYCLE

For drivers, the main access points into New Brunswick are the cities of Edmundston and Houlton, and can be accessed from Nova Scotia and PEI, as well as Maine (USA). If you're going to PEI, there's no charge to use the Confederation Bridge eastbound from Cape Jourmain – you pay on the way back. Traffic is generally light, although crossing the Maine border usually means a delay at customs.

TRAIN

VIA Rail (888-842-7245; www.viarail.ca) operates passenger services between Montréal and Halifax, with stops in Campbellton, Bathurst, Miramichi and Moncton.

FREDERICTON

POP 56,000

This gorgeous provincial capital does quaint very well. The Saint John River curves lazily through Fredericton, past the stately government buildings on the waterfront and the university on the hill. Its neatly mowed, tree-lined banks are dotted with fountains, walking paths and playing fields. On warm weekends, 'The Green,' as it's known, looks like something out of a watercolor painting – families strolling, kids kicking soccer balls, couples picnicking.

On a flat, broad curve in the riverbank, the small downtown commercial district is a neat grid of redbrick storefronts. Surrounding it are residential streets lined with tall, graceful elms shading beautifully maintained Georgian and Victorian houses and abundant flower beds. A canopy of trees spreads over the downtown, pierced here and there by church spires.

Sights

The two-block strip along Queen St between York and Regent Sts is known as the Historic Garrison District. It comprises Barracks Square (p394) and Officers' Square (p394). In 1875 Fredericton became the capital of the newly formed province of New Brunswick, and the garrison housed British soldiers for much of the late 18th and early 19th centuries. It's now a lively multiuse area with impressive stone architecture.

★Beaverbrook Art Gallery — MUSEUM

(www.beaverbrookartgallery.org; 703 Queen St; adult/child $10/free; ⌚10am-5pm Mon-Wed, Fri & Sat, to 9pm Thu, noon-5pm Sun) This excellent gallery was a gift to the town from Lord Beaverbrook (see Beaverbrook House, p427). The exceptional collection includes works by international heavyweights and is well worth an hour or so. Among others you will see Dalí, Freud, Gainsborough and Turner, Canadian artists Tom Thompson, Emily Carr and Cornelius Kreighoff, as well as changing contemporary exhibits of Atlantic art.

At the time of writing it was undergoing a multi-million-dollar expansion to be completed in 2017.

Barracks Square — SQUARE

(497 Queen St) Part of the Garrison District (two city blocks and an important national historic site), Barracks Square is framed by the Soldiers' Barracks and the Guard House. You can see how the common soldier lived in the 1820s (lousy food, too much drink). When a guard was not on his beat, he could rest at the Guard House, built in 1828, on a bed made of hard planks. Conditions (especially for those in the cells) were nasty at best.

Loyalist Village — HISTORIC SITE

(☎506-363-4999; www.kingslanding.nb.ca; 5804 Rte 102, Prince William; adult/child/family $18/12.50/42; ⌚10am-5pm mid-Jun–Oct) One of the province's best sites is this re-creation of an early-19th-century Loyalist village, 36km west of Fredericton. A community of costumed staff create a living museum by role-playing in houses, a school, church, store and sawmill typical of those used a century ago, providing a glimpse and taste of pioneer life in the Maritime provinces. Demonstrations and events are staged throughout the day and horse-drawn carts shunt visitors around. It offers excellent children's programs and special events occur regularly.

The King's Head Inn, a mid-1800s pub, serves traditional food and beverages by candlelight. It's not hard to while away a good half-day or more. The prosperous Loyalist life reflected here can be tellingly compared to that at the Acadian Historic Village (p429) in Caraquet.

Old Loyalist Burial Ground — CEMETERY

(Brunswick St; ⌚8am-9pm) This Loyalist cemetery, dating back to 1784, is an atmospheric, thought-provoking history lesson of its own, revealing large families and kids dying tragically young. The Loyalists arrived from the 13 colonies after the American Revolution of 1776.

Christ Church Cathedral — CHURCH

(http://cccath.ca/wp; 168 Church St) Built in 1853, this cathedral is a fine early example of 19th-century Gothic Revival style and has exquisite stained glass. It was modeled after St Mary's in Snettisham, Norfolk.

Government House — HISTORIC BUILDING

(www.gnb.ca/lg/ogh; 51 Woodstock Rd; ⌚10am-4pm Mon-Sat, noon-4pm Sun) FREE This magnificent sandstone palace was erected for the British governor in 1826. The representative of the queen moved out in 1893 after the province refused to continue paying his expenses, and during most of the 20th century the complex was a Royal Canadian Mounted Police (RCMP) headquarters. It now evocatively captures a moment in time with tours led by staff in period costume.

Officers' Square — HISTORIC SITE

(www.historicgarrisondistrict.ca; btwn Carleton & Regent Sts; ⌚ceremonies 11am & 4pm daily, plus 7pm Tue & Thu Jul & Aug) Once the military parade ground, the Garrison District's

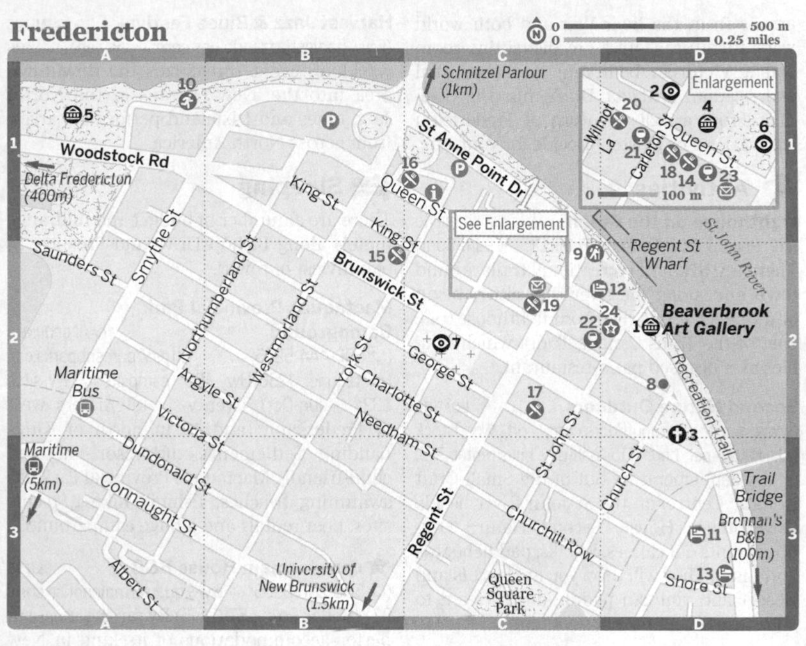

Fredericton

Top Sights
1 Beaverbrook Art Gallery D2

Sights
2 Barracks Square D1
3 Christ Church Cathedral D2
4 Fredericton Region Museum D1
5 Government House A1
6 Officers' Square D1
7 Old Loyalist Burial Ground C2

Activities, Courses & Tours
Haunted Hikes .... (see 8)
8 Heritage Walking Tours D2
9 Lighthouse on the Green C2
10 Second Nature Outdoors A1

Sleeping
11 Carriage House Inn D3
12 Crowne Plaza Lord Beaverbrook C2
13 Quartermain House B&B D3

Eating
14 540 Kitchen & Bar D1
15 Caribbean Flavas B2
16 Chess Piece Patisserie & Cafe C1
17 Fredericton Boyce Farmers Market C2
18 Naru D1
19 Ten Resto C2
20 The Palate D1

Drinking & Nightlife
21 Boom! Nightclub D1
22 Lunar Rogue Pub C2
23 Red Rover Ciderhouse D1

Entertainment
24 Playhouse D2

Officers' Sq now hosts a full-uniform changing-of-the-guard ceremony in summertime. Also in summer the Calithumpians Outdoor Summer Theatre performs daily at 12:15pm weekdays and 2pm weekends; the free historical skits are laced with humor. Summer evenings bring jazz, Celtic and rock concerts, see the website for schedules.

Fredericton Region Museum MUSEUM
(☎506-455-6041; www.frederictonregionmuseum.com; Officers' Sq; adult/student $5/2; ⏰10am-5pm Jul & Aug, to 4pm Apr-Jun & Sep-Nov, by appointment Dec-Mar) Housed in the 19th-century officers' quarters on the western side of Officers' Sq, this museum's collection preserves the city's past. Displays feature military pieces used by local regiments and by British and German

armies from the Boer War and both world wars; furniture from a Loyalist sitting room and a Victorian bedroom; and aboriginal and Acadian artifacts. Don't miss the Coleman Frog, a 42lb creature of Fredericton legend. Real or plaster? Decide for yourself.

Activities

Lighthouse on the Green HIKING, BIKING
(cnr Regent St & St Anne Point Dr; 9am-6pm) There are 87km of recreational trails around town and along the river that either begin or intersect at this riverfront lighthouse (one part of the Trans Canada Trail), which doubles as a licensed patio-restaurant.

Second Nature Outdoors BOATING
(www.secondnatureoutdoors.com; off Woodstock Rd; kayak per hour $15, half-day bike rental $15; May-Sep) Operating out of the Small Craft Aquatic Centre, on the St John River beside Government House, Second Nature Outdoors rents out canoes, kayaks, paddleboards and bikes. They will drop you at Heart Island Resort and you can paddle downstream to your heart's and muscle's content…

Haunted Hikes WALKING
(506-457-1975; www.calithumpians.com; 796a Queen St; adult/child $14/9; 9pm Mon-Sat Jul & Aug) Actors from the university masquerading as ghoulish thespians run entertaining Fredericton ghost tours.

Heritage Walking Tours WALKING
(506 457 1975; 796 Queen St; 10am, 2:30pm & 5pm daily Jul & Aug, 4pm Jun, Sep & Oct) FREE Enthusiastic young people wearing historic costumes lead good, free hour-long tours of the river, the government district or the Historic Garrison District, departing from City Hall.

Festivals & Events

New Brunswick Highland Games Festival CULTURAL
(late Jul) Kilts, clans and all things positively Celtic are exposed at this fun highlands games extravaganza held annually on the grounds of Government House. Competitors and visitors are drawn to its celebration of all things Scottish culture: dancing, caber toss competitions, whisky tastings, piped music and more.

Silver Wave Film Festival FILM
(www.swfilmfest.com; early Nov) Three days of New Brunswick, Canadian and international films and lectures organized by the NB Filmmakers' Cooperative.

Harvest Jazz & Blues Festival MUSIC
(www.harvestjazzandblues.com; Sep) This weeklong event transforms the downtown area into the 'New Orleans of the North.' Jazz, blues and Dixieland performers arrive from across North America.

Sleeping

There are a number of budget and midrange motels along Bishop Drive and Prospect St (southwest of town).

Mactaquac Provincial Park Campground CAMPGROUND $
(506-444-5205; https://parcsnbparks.ca/Mactaquac; 1256 Hwy 105; campsites & RV sites $32; Jun-Oct) Twenty-six kilometers west of Fredericton (and 10km north of Kings Landing Settlement), the resort-like and child-friendly Mactaquac Provincial Park has swimming beaches, fishing, hiking, picnic sites, boat rentals and a huge campground.

★ **Quartermain House B&B** B&B $$
(506-206-5255; www.quartermainhouse.com; 92 Waterloo Row; r $110-145) By far the most superior accommodations of its kind in New Brunswick, Quartermain ticks all the right boxes: delightful period home on Fredericton's exclusive Waterloo Row; warm, professional host; and incredible breakfasts. The price is ridiculous in comparison to other places in the region, but if you're going to splurge anywhere, this is the place.

Delta Fredericton BUSINESS HOTEL $$
(506-457-7000; www.marriott.com; 225 Woodstock Rd; r from $159; P) For a 'predictable' chain-hotel experience, this one surprises. Its location on the banks of Saint John River and a river trail is ideal. And recent renovations have brought a sleek, sharp focus: large and very pleasant rooms, plus trimmings (pools, restaurants and gym). Breakfast is not included in the price. The hotel is within walking distance of the center.

University of New Brunswick UNIVERSITY ACCOMMODATIONS $$
(506-447-3227; http://stay.unb.ca; 20 Bairley Dr; s/d/tr with private bath $54/84/115; s/d with shared bath $40/62.50; 7am-11pm May–mid-Aug; P) Fredericton's only budget accommodations is located at the university. It's a great deal, but the catch is, rooms are available in summer only. Traditional rooms have shared bathrooms but a light continental breakfast is offered. The 'suites' have private bathrooms and kitchenettes. Rooms may be a bit

sparse, but it's a lovely campus with views over Fredericton and the Saint John River.

Brennan's B&B B&B $$
(☎506-455-7346; www.bbcanada.com/3892.html; 146 Waterloo Row; s $115-195, d $125-210, incl breakfast; P ⊖ ❄ @) Built for a wealthy wood-merchant family in 1885, this turreted white riverfront mansion is now a handsome six-room B&B; three of the rooms boast water views and two have kitchenettes. There's stunning original fretwork throughout.

Carriage House Inn B&B $$
(☎506-452-9924; www.carriagehouse-inn.net; 230 University Ave; r incl breakfast $129-149; P ⊖ ❄ ᯤ) In a shady Victorian neighborhood near the Green, this 1875 Queen Anne was built for a lumber baron and former Fredericton mayor. The grand common room has polished hardwood floors, antiques, comfy sofas, fireplaces and a grand piano. Upstairs, things deteriorate. Although charming, rooms are faded, their high ceilings, floral wallpapers and vintage artwork showing age (and little upkeep). There is a deep verandah for lounging.

Crowne Plaza Lord Beaverbrook HOTEL $$$
(☎506-455-3371; www.cpfredericton.com; 659 Queen St; r $120-270; P ❄ ᯤ ≋) Always bustling with weddings, conventions and business travelers, this 1948 downtown hotel is another one of Lord Beaverbrook's legacies to the city. The beaver mosaics on the facade are wonderful and the lobby has a touch of vintage glamour, but the 168 rooms, if comfortable, are showing signs of wear. Check online for specials.

Eating

Chess Piece Patisserie & Cafe CAFE $
(www.chesspiece.ca; 361 Queen St; snacks $3-8; ⏲7am-9pm Mon-Fri, 8am-9pm Sat, 10am-4pm Sun) A wonderful new addition to the local scene, this little laid-back cafe has an in-house patisserie bakery. Although it's one of Fredericton's best places for coffee and soup, the things to devour are the generously proportioned cakes and pastries, made on the premises using quality ingredients. And oh so sweet to both the eye and the taste buds.

Fredericton Boyce Farmers Market MARKET $
(www.frederictonfarmersmarket.ca; 665 George St; ⏲6am-1pm Sat) This Fredericton institution is great for picking up fresh fruit, vegetables, meat, cheese, handicrafts, dessert and flowers. Many of the 150 or so stalls recall the city's European heritage, with everything from German-style sausages to French duck pâtés to British marmalade. There is also an eatery where Frederictonians queue to chat and people-watch.

★ **Ten Resto** INTERNATIONAL $$
(☎506-206-3951; www.facebook.com/tenresto; 87 Regent St; mains $19-30; ⏲5-9pm Tue-Sat; ✎) Coming here is a bit of an unorthodox numbers game. This pleasant locale has 10 tables and a choice of 10 dishes per sitting (and 10 menu changes a year). This means that you can be in an empty or very full restaurant, depending on the reservation timings. The reasons? Owners Keith and Shelley like you to feel at home.

★ **Naru** JAPANESE $$
(536 Queen St; mains $12-15; ⏲11am-9pm Mon-Thu & Sat, to 10pm Fri; ✎) A word of warning for purists of Japanese cuisine: this top-quality Japanese restaurant incorporates local Canadian produce and ideas into its recipes. But, given the high-quality Canadian seafood and produce, and the delicate presentation, the results are sublime. The sashimi, *maki* and tempura selections are fabulous; but look no further than the grilled scallop roll, topped with Parmesan cheese and *tobiko*. Good range of vegetarian options too.

The Palate INTERNATIONAL $$
(www.thepalate.com; 462 Queen St; mains $19-22; ⏲11am-3pm & 5-9pm Mon-Fri, 10am-3pm & 5-9pm Sat) This modest, family-friendly place has an Italian-bistro feel and stands out because it doesn't blow its own trumpet. It has stood the test of time among Fredericton's thriving gastropub scene, doing what it does best for 16 years: preparing unpretentious but enjoyable seafood, chicken and pasta dishes with fresh produce, including some from its own gardens.

540 Kitchen & Bar INTERNATIONAL $$
(540 Queen St; mains $14-32; ⏲11:30am-9pm Mon & Tue, to 10pm Wed & Thu, to 11pm Fri & Sat; ✎) A fabulous gastropub that sticks to its mantra: locally sourced produce, everything made from scratch, seasonal menu. Wash down the likes of pork belly or rack of Spring lamb with a choice of beer. There are 10 taps that represent local micro-breweries. Good veggie options too. Get here early or reserve; it's popular.

Caribbean Flavas CARIBBEAN $$
(www.caribbeanflavas.ca; 123 York St; mains $15-30; ⌚11:30am-2:30pm Tue-Fri, plus 4:30-8pm Tue-Sat) A bright nook dishing up the tastes and colors of the Caribbean. Great for a casual, flavorful meal and a fruit-based drink (read: this place is alcohol-free).

Schnitzel Parlour GERMAN $$
(☎506-450-2520; www.theschnitzelparlour.com; 304 Union St; mains $15-21; ⌚5:30-8pm Tue-Sat) Specializing in hearty, old-fashioned German fare, this cozy countryside restaurant on the northern side of the river has richly spiced goulash (the secret ingredient is chocolate), wild-boar stew and nine kinds of schnitzel on homemade spätzle (soft egg noodles). BYOB. The on-site Chocolaterie Fackleman (with the same hours as the restaurant) sells truffles and traditional Central European tortes.

Drinking & Nightlife

In the evenings the bars, pubs and rooftop patios of King and Queen Sts come alive. Craft beer (and a great ciderhouse) are the rage here. Younger things hit the one-stop (drinking) shop quadrant known as The Tannery.

Red Rover Ciderhouse BAR
(www.facebook.com/redroverbrew; 546 Queen St; ⌚5-9pm Mon, noon-9pm Tue-Thu, noon-10pm Fri & Sat) If you're up to your esophagus with craft beer, or you prefer wine or cocktails, you're in a win:win situation at this convivial, industrial chic ciderhouse. It serves craft cider made by New Brunswick's first (and very passionate) cider producers. They're constantly perfecting their brews and flavors (14 to date) using Canadian apples. And they're receiving awards for their efforts.

Lunar Rogue Pub PUB
(www.lunarrogue.com; 625 King St; ⌚11am-late Mon-Sat, to 10pm Sun) Named a 'great whisky bar of the world' for good reason: this jolly locals' joint has a fine assortment of single malts, part of the 500-plus whiskey collection. Work your way through the drams on the outdoor patio; it's wildly popular during the warmer weather.

Soak up the intake with a mighty fine breakfast or a selection from the bar menu (mains $8 to $14).

Boom! Nightclub CLUB
(www.boomnightclub.ca; 474 Queen St; cover charge $5-8; ⌚8pm-late Wed-Sun) A hip gay bar and dance club welcoming folks of all stripes.

✪ Entertainment

In summer downtown venues from Officers' Sq to the Lighthouse on the Green feature **outdoor summer concerts** (www.tourismfredericton.ca) with ranging from highland bagpipes and drums to country and blues. Check the website for schedules.

Playhouse THEATER
(☎866-884-5800; www.theplayhouse.nb.ca; 686 Queen St) Stages concerts, theater, ballet and shows throughout the year.

ℹ Information

The entire CBD is wired for free internet access. Otherwise, **Fredericton Public Library** (12 Carleton St; ⌚10am-5pm Mon, Tue & Thu, to 9pm Wed & Fri) has free internet access on a first-come, first-served basis.

Dr Everett Chalmers Hospital (☎506-452-5400; 700 Priestman St) Located 2km south of the city center.

Main post office (☎506-444-8602; 570 Queen St; ⌚8am-5pm Mon-Fri)

Visitor Information Centre (☎506-460-2129; www.tourismfredericton.ca; City Hall, 397 Queen St; ⌚10am-8pm Jul & Aug, to 5pm Jun & Sep, to 4.30pm May & Oct) Provides free city parking passes. A secondary office opens in summer at Kings Landing (42 Prince William Rd, Prince William; ⌚10:30am-5:30pm Jun-Oct).

ℹ Getting There & Away

AIR

Fredericton International Airport (YFC; ☎506-460-0920; www.frederictonairport.ca) is on Hwy 102, 14km southeast of town. AirCanada has flights between Fredericton and the US, including New York City and Orlando (via other Canadian cities), as well flights to London, UK. Fredericton is also part of a good network of domestic flights.

BUS

The **Maritime Bus** (☎506-455-2049; www.maritimebus.com; 105 Dundonald St; ⌚8am-8pm Mon-Fri, 10am-8pm Sat & Sun) terminal is a few kilometers southwest of downtown. Some useful destinations include Moncton ($44, 2¼ hours, two daily); Charlottetown, PEI ($69, 5½ hours, two daily); Bangor, ME ($58, 7½ hours, one daily); and Saint John ($31, 1½ hours, two daily).

CAR & MOTORCYCLE

Cars with out-of-province license plates are eligible for a free three-day parking pass for downtown Fredericton May to October, available at the **visitor center** (p398) at City Hall. In-province visitors can get a one-day pass. The major car-rental agencies all have desks at the airport.

Getting Around

A taxi to the airport costs $18 to $22.

The city has a decent bus system; tickets cost $3 and include free transfers. Service runs Monday through Saturday from 6:15am to 11pm. Most city bus routes begin at King's Place Mall, on King St between York and Carleton.

Bicycle rentals are available at **Radical Edge** (506-459-3478; www.radicaledge.ca; 386 Queen St; rental per day $25).

UPPER ST JOHN RIVER VALLEY

The St John River winds along the western border of the province past forests and lush farmland. It drifts through Fredericton between tree-lined banks and around flat islands between rolling hills before emptying into the Bay of Fundy 700km later. The river is the province's dominant feature and for centuries has been its major thoroughfare. The valley's eye-pleasing landscape makes for scenic touring by car, or by bicycle on the Trans Canada Trail (TCT), which follows the river for most of its length.

Two automobile routes carve through the valley: the quicker Trans-Canada Hwy (Hwy 2), mostly on the western side of the river, and the more scenic old Hwy 105 on the eastern side, which meanders through many villages. Branching off from the valley are Hwy 17 (at St-Léonard) and Rte 385 (at Perth-Andover), which cut northeast through the Appalachian highlands and lead to rugged Mt Carleton Provincial Park.

Mt Carleton Provincial Park & the Tobique Valley

The 17,427-hectare provincial park is one of the region's best-kept secrets. It offers visitors a wilderness of mountains, valleys, rivers and wildlife including moose, deer and bear. The park's main feature is a series of rounded glaciated peaks and ridges, including Mt Carleton (820m). This range is an extension of the Appalachian Mountains, which begin in Georgia, USA, and end in Québec. Mt Carleton is little known and relatively unvisited, even in midsummer.

The park is open from mid-May to October. All roads are gravel-surfaced. The nearest towns are Riley Brook, 40km to the south, and St Quentin, 42km to the north, so bring all food and a full tank of gas.

Activities

Canoeing

The Mt Carleton area boasts superb wilderness canoeing. In the park itself, the Nictau and Nepisiguit chains of lakes offer easy day-tripping through a landscape of tree-clad mountains. For experienced canoeists, the shallow and swift Little Tobique River rises at Big Nictau Lake, winding in tight curls through dense woods until it joins the Tobique itself at Nictau. The more remote Nepisiguit River flows out of the Nepisiguit Lakes through the wilderness until it empties into the Bay of Chaleur at Bathurst, over 100km away.

The lower reaches of the Tobique, from Nictau, through minute Riley Brook and down to Plaster Rock is a straight, easy paddle through forest and meadow that gives way to farmland as the valley broadens, with a couple of waterfront campgrounds along the way. The easy 10km between Nictau and the Bear's Lair landing in Riley Brook makes for a relaxing afternoon paddle.

Bill Miller CANOEING
(506-356-2409; www.millercanoes.com; 4160 Rte 385, Nictau) Bill Miller welcomes visitors to his cluttered canoe-making workshop in Nictau (population roughly 8), on the forested banks of the Tobique River at the foot of Mt Carleton, where he and his father and grandfather before him have handcrafted wooden canoes since 1922.

Guildo Martel WATER SPORTS
(506-235-0286; kayak & canoe per day $40; Jun-Sep) Guildo Martel rents canoes and kayaks for the day and will deliver them where required. He's located 4km from the park toward St Quentin. He will guide for a total of $100 on top of rental prices (for up to six people).

Bear's Lair KAYAKING
(506-356-8351; www.bearslairhunting.com; 3349 Rte 385, Riley Brook; kayak/canoe rental per day $35/50) Owners will drop you off upriver so you can paddle and float your way downstream and back to home base, Bear's Lair, the cozy lodge.

Hiking

The best way to explore Mt Carleton is on foot. The park has nearly 70km network of trails: most of them are loops winding to the handful of rocky knobs that are the peaks. The **International Appalachian Trail** (IAT) passes through here.

DON'T MISS

FLORENCEVILLE-BRISTOL

The tidy and green riverside village of Florenceville-Bristol is ground zero of the global french-fry industry. It's home to the McCain Foods frozen-foods empire, which is sustained by the thousands of hectares of potato farms that surround it in every direction. Started by the McCain brothers in 1957, the company produces one-third of the world's french-fry supply at its Florenceville factory. That adds up to 453,600kg of chips churned out every hour and $5.8 billion in annual net sales. To get your head around the spud industry, head to **Potato World** (www.potatoworld.ca; Rte 110; tours adult/family $5/16, experiential tours $10/32; ⏲9am-6pm Mon-Fri, to 5pm Sat & Sun Jun-Aug, 9am-5pm Mon-Fri Sep–mid-Oct), a tasteful, top-class interactive exposition of the history of the humble potato in these parts.

The easiest peak to climb is **Mt Bailey**; a 7.5km loop trail to the 564m hillock begins near the day-use area. Most hikers can walk this route in three hours. The highest peak is reached via the **Mt Carleton Trail**, a 10km route that skirts over the 820m knob, where there's a fire tower. Plan on five hours for the trek and pack your parka; the wind above the tree line can be brutal.

The most challenging hike (and the most rewarding for the views) is the **Sagamook Trail**, a 6km loop to a 777m peak with superlative vistas of Nictau Lake and the highlands area to the north of it; allow four hours for this trek. The **Mountain Head Trail** connects the Mt Carleton and Sagamook Trails (the latter being part of the Appalachian Trail), making a long transit of the range possible.

All hikers intending to follow any long trails must register at the visitors center (p401) before hitting the trail. Outside the camping season (mid-May to mid-September), you should call ahead to make sure the main gate will be open, as the Mt Carleton trailhead is 13.5km from the park entrance. Otherwise, park your car at the entrance and walk in – the Mt Bailey trailhead is only 2.5km from the gate.

Festivals & Events

World Pond Hockey Tournament SPORTS
(www.worldpondhockey.com; Rte 109, Plaster Rock; admission free; ⏲Feb) The forest town of Plaster Rock (population 1200), 84km from Mt Carleton, hosts the World Pond Hockey Tournament. Over 20 rinks are plowed on Roulston Lake, which is ringed by tall evergreens, hot-chocolate stands and straw-bale seating for the thousands of spectators drawn to the four-day event. Over 120 amateur four-person teams come from around the world.

If you want to play, register early. If you want to watch, pack your long johns and a *toque* (wool hat) and book your accommodations early. The organizers keep a list of local folks willing to billet out-of-towners in their homes.

Fiddles on the Tobique MUSIC
(☎506-356-2409; ⏲late Jun) This weekend festival is held annually in Nictau and Riley Brook. It is a magical idea: a round of community-hall suppers, jam sessions and concerts culminating in a Sunday-afternoon floating concert down the Tobique River from Nictau to Riley Brook. Upward of 800 canoes and kayaks join the flotilla each year – some stocked with musicians, some just with paddlers – and 8000 spectators line the riverbanks to watch. By some accounts, the event has been damaged by its own popularity, devolving into a boisterous booze cruise. Others call it a grand party and good fun.

Sleeping

Heritage Cottages COTTAGE $
(☎506-235-0793; www.nbparks.ca; Mt Carleton Provincial Park; d $60-90) Eleven delightful, restored cottages (the originals date from the late 1800s) sit on Bathurst Lakes and at Little Nictau. You must bring everything, including bedding, pots and pans. Some share facilities; others have their own kitchens and bathrooms.

Armstrong Brook Campground CAMPGROUND $
(☎506-235-0793; www.nbparks.ca; campsites/RV sites $28/28; ⏲May-Oct) The park's largest campground has 88 sites nestled among the spruce on the northern side of Nictau Lake, 3km from the entrance. It has toilets, showers and a kitchen shelter, but no sites with hookups. Recreational vehicle (RV) drivers often have their noisy generators running, so tenters should check out the eight tent-only sites on the northern side of the campground.

Bear's Lair INN $
(☎506-356-8351; www.bearslairhunting.com; 3349 Rte 385, Riley Brook; r from $65; ⊙May-Sep; P ⊜) If any place in the province captures the essence of life in the north woods, this is it. A cozy log hunting lodge set on the banks of the Tobique River, it is busiest during fall hunting season – the high-ceilinged main lodge is adorned with numerous taxidermied specimens – but is also a relaxing base for outdoor enthusiasts year-round.

Information

Visitors center (☎506-235-0793; www.nbparks.ca; off Rte 385; per vehicle $10; ⊙8am-8pm May-Sep, to 6pm Oct) At the entrance to the park. Has maps and information. Park entry is paid here.

Grand Falls

With a drop of around 25m and a 1.6km-long gorge with walls as high as 80m, these falls merit a stop in this otherwise-unscenic town. The Grand Falls are best when the dam gates are open (often after rain) – in summer much of the water is diverted for generating hydroelectricity – yet the gorge is appealing any time.

Activities

Open Sky Adventures ADVENTURE SPORTS
(☎506-477-9799; 16087 Rte 105, Drummond; ⊙Jun-Oct) Gorge yourself silly on Open Sky Adventures' activities. A one-hour boat trip costs $25 ($15 per child), plus there's dee-pelling (apparently that's face-forward rappelling; $100), zip-lining ($35) and kayaking (from $30 per day).

La Rochelle OUTDOORS
(1 Chapel St; tours adult/child $5/2; ⊙Jul & Aug) A 401-step stairway down into the gorge begins at La Rochelle, across the bridge from the Malabeam Reception & Interpretation Centre and left on Victoria St.

Sleeping & Eating

Falls & Gorge Campground CAMPGROUND $
(☎506-475-7769; 120 Manse St; campsites/RV sites $25/35; ⊙Jun-Sep) If you do decide to spend the night in Grand Falls, there are dramatically situated tent and RV sites here.

Le Grand Saut AMERICAN $$
(www.legrandsautristorante.com; 155 Broadway Blvd; mains $11-20; ⊙10:30am-10pm) For a half reasonable feed, Le Grand Saut, a popular, two-tiered spot with an inviting deck out front, serves up generous portions of salads, pastas, pizzas and steaks.

Information

Malabeam Tourist & Interpretation Centre (☎506-475-7788; www.grandfalls.com; 25 Madawaska Rd; admission free; ⊙10am-6pm May & Jun, 9:30am-6pm Jul & Aug, 10am-5pm Sep & Oct) In the middle of town, overlooking the falls, the Malabeam Reception & Interpretation Centre doubles as a tourist office. Among the displays is a scale model of the gorge showing its extensive trail system. The newer interpretation wing affords fabulous views of the falls.

Getting There & Away

Maritime Bus (☎506-473-4862; www.maritimebus.com; 555 Madawaska Rd; ⊙noon-midnight) services stop at the Esso station, just west of downtown.

Hwy 108 (known locally as the Renous Hwy) cuts across the province through Plaster Rock to the East Coast, slicing through forest for nearly its entirety. It is tedious, but fast. Watch out for deer and moose.

Edmundston & Around

Working-class Edmundston has a large paper mill, a utilitarian town center and a mainly bilingual French citizenry. There's few sights, but it makes a convenient stopover for those traveling east from Québec.

Sights

Petis Témis Interprovincial Linear Park PARK
(Edmundston) Edmundston is the eastern terminus of the Petis Témis Interprovincial Linear Park, a 134km cycling and hiking trail between Edmundston and Rivière-du-Loup, Québec. It follows an old railbed along the Madawaska River and the shores of Lake Témiscouata, passing by several small villages and campgrounds along the way. Mountain bikers can hit the 45km of single mountain-bike trails in the surrounding Appalachian mountain range.

New Brunswick Botanical Garden GARDENS
(www.jardinnbgarden.com; off Rte 2, St-Jacques; adult/child $14/7; ⊙9am-5pm May, Jun & Sep, to 8pm Jul & Aug) Halfway between the Québec border and Edmundston in the small community of St-Jacques is the New Brunswick

Botanical Garden. Here there are 80,000 plants, a herb pavilion and 3D flower sculptures to brighten your day, all accompanied by classical music. Kids might prefer the neat temporary exhibitions, such as a butterfly garden.

Sleeping & Eating

Look out for the *ploye,* a kind of buckwheat pancake and an important part of history and tradition for the Madawaska Valley. It's often eaten with butter, sugar or maple syrup.

Local restaurants that use and promote local products are listed at www.acadiegourmet.ca; for a complete list of eateries, see the tourist office website.

Auberge Les Jardins INN $$
(☎506-739-5514; www.lesjardinsinn.com; 60 Rue Principale, St-Jacques; r $119-175; P 📶 🏊) Get out of gritty Edmundston and sleep next to the botanical gardens at Auberge Les Jardins, a gracious inn with 17 rooms that are each decorated with a different Canadian flower or tree theme. There's also a modern motel in back, and a wood-and-stained-glass dining room that's considered one of the best restaurants in the province (check out the fabulous wine list).

Restaurant le Patrimoine PIZZA $$
(http://pizzalepatrimoine.com; 115 Chemin Rivière-à-la-Truite, St-Jacques; pizzas $12-20; ⏲4-9pm Wed & Sun, to 10pm Thu, to 11pm Fri & Sat) Housed in a former golf clubhouse, this is way above par with its quality pizzas. It strikes the sweet spot every time with white- and whole-crust pizzas with gourmet toppings served up direct from its wood-fired oven. *Squisito* (delicious)!

Information

Edmunston Visitor Information Centre (www.tourismedmundston.com; 121 Victoria St; ⏲9am-7pm Jun-Aug, to 5pm Mon-Fri Sep-May) Has information on Edmunston and the locale.

Saint Jacques Provincial Visitor Information Centre (www.tourismnewbrunswick.ca; 17412 Rte 2, Saint Jacques; ⏲9:30am-6:30pm May, Jun & Sep, to 7:30pm Jul & Aug) This regional tourist office, about 20km north at the Québec border, has information on New Brunswick.

Getting There & Away

The **Maritime Bus** (☎506-739-8309; www.maritimebus.com; 191 Victoria St, Edmundston; ⏲5am-midnight) network stops in Edmunston and heads south to Fredericton ($53.25, 3½ hours, one or two daily) and beyond, or westward into Rivière-du-Loup ($29.50, 30 minutes, one or two daily), from where you can catch connections into Québec.

WESTERN FUNDY SHORE

Almost the entire southern edge of New Brunswick is presided over by the constantly rising and falling waters of the Bay of Fundy.

The resort town of St Andrews By-The-Sea, the serene Fundy Isles, fine seaside scenery and rich history make this easily one of the most appealing regions of the province. Whale-watching is a thrilling area activity. Most commonly seen are the fin, humpback and minke; less so, the increasingly rare right whale. Porpoises and dolphins are plentiful. And let's not overlook the seafood – it's bountiful and delicious.

St Stephen

Right on the US border across the river from Calais, ME, St Stephen is a busy entry point with small-town charm and one tasty attraction. It is home to Ganong, a family-run chocolate business operating since 1873; its products are known around eastern Canada. The 5¢ chocolate nut bar was invented by the Ganong brothers in 1910, and they can also be credited with developing the heart-shaped box of chocolates seen everywhere on Valentine's Day.

Sights & Tours

Chocolate Museum MUSEUM
(☎506-466-7848; www.chocolatemuseum.ca; 73 Milltown Blvd; adult/student/family $10/8.50/30; ⏲10am-4pm Mon-Fri, 11am-3pm Sat & Sun Apr-Nov) The Chocolate Museum has tasteful (and tasty) interactive displays of everything from antique chocolate boxes to manufacturing equipment.

Chocolate Museum Guided Heritage Walking Tour WALKING
(adult/child $15/13.50; ⏲Jul & Aug) In summer the museum (p402) arranges guided heritage walking tours of St Stephen, led by local students.

Festivals & Events

Chocolate Fest FOOD & DRINK
(www.chocolate-fest.ca; ⏲early Aug) It's all things cocoa and sugar at St Stephen's Chocolate

WORTH A TRIP

SCENIC DRIVE: LOWER SAINT JOHN RIVER VALLEY

The main highway (Rte 7) between the capital and the port city of Saint John barrels south through a vast expanse of trees, trees and more trees. A far more scenic route (albeit about twice as long) follows the gentle, meandering Saint John River through rolling farmland and a couple of historic villages down to the Fundy coast.

Start on the north side of the river in Fredericton, and follow Rte 105 south through Maugerville to Jemseg. Follow the new bridge across Hwy 2 West. (This is in place of the Gagetown ferry which stopped operating in 2015; locals are protesting against its closure. Check to see if it's open.)

Head to the pretty 18th-century village of **Gagetown** – well worth a look-see. Front St is lined with craft studios and shops and a couple of inviting cafes. Stop into the excellent **Queen's County Museum** (16 Court House Rd, Gagetown; adult/child $3/free; ⏲10am-5pm mid-Jun–mid-Sep), the town's first court as well as the **Tilley House** (69 Front St, Gagetown; adult/child $3/free; ⏲10am-5pm mid-Jun–mid-Sep), Sir Leonard Tilley's childhood home. The top-notch staff will show you through the exhibits spanning pre-Colonial aboriginal history in the area, 18th-century settler life, and up to WWII.

From Gagetown, head south on Rte 102, known locally as 'the **Old River Road**,' denoting its status as the major thoroughfare up the valley in the kinder, simpler era between the decline of the river steamboats and the construction of the modern, divided highway. The grand old farmhouses and weathered hay barns dotted at intervals along the valley belong to that earlier age. The hilly 42km piece of road between Gagetown and the **Evandale ferry landing** (⏲24hr year-round) is especially picturesque, with glorious panoramic views of fields full of wildflowers, white farmhouses and clots of green and gold islands set in the intensely blue water of the river.

A hundred years ago, tiny Evandale was a bustling little place, where a dance band would entertain riverboat passengers. Across the water, Rte 124 takes you the short distance to the **Belleisle ferry** (⏲24hr year-round) which deposits you on the rural Kingston Peninsula, where you can cross the peninsula to catch the **Gondola Point Ferry** (p419) and head directly into Saint John.

Fest, when the town celebrates all things chocolate with a parade, tours of the local Ganong factory and unlimited sampling of the goods (yes, really!), and games for the kids.

Sleeping & Eating

Blair House INN $$
(☎506-466-2233; www.blairhouseheritageinn.com; 38 Prince William St; r incl breakfast from $100; P⊝❄☜) The five eclectic but comfortable rooms are complemented by a quiet garden at this fabulous Victorian home. Affable David serves up a generous cooked breakfast. You can walk to the main street easily from here.

Something's Brewing CAFE $
(www.somethingsbrewingcafe.ca; 140 Milltown Blvd; snacks $4-10; ⏲7am-8pm, to 10pm Fri) A lovely little local cafe and just the spot for a coffee – a range of fair-trade and organic coffees, in fact (if you count soy chai latte, which a purist definitely wouldn't). In any case, there are also great teas and wonderful home-baked cakes and pastries.

Carman's Diner DINER $
(☎506-466-3528; 164 King St; mains $4-16; ⏲7am-10pm) Home cooking is served up at this 1960s throwback with counter stools and your own mini (and working) jukeboxes at the tables. There's everything from burgers to sandwiches, but the homemade pies are the things to go for. It's only convenient if you have a car, as it's not in the center of town.

Shopping

Chocolate Museum Shop FOOD
(www.chocolatemuseum.ca; 73 Milltown Blvd; ⏲9am-5pm) The Chocolate Museum shop sells boxes of Ganong hand-dipped chocolates and is free to visit. Try the iconic chicken bone (chocolate-filled cinnamon sticks) or the old-fashioned Pal-O-Mine candy bar.

Information

Tourist office (www.tourismnewbrunswick.ca; Rte 170, Unit 4; ⏲9am-6pm May & Jun, Sep & Oct, to 7pm Jul & Aug) This new office in the Circle K Irving Complex at the junction as you enter town has information on the province.

Getting There & Away

Across the border in Calais, ME, **West's Coastal Connection** (☎800-596-2823; www.westbus-service.com) buses head to Bangor (one-way ticket $27, four hours, one daily). In Bangor, buses use the Greyhound terminal and connect to Bangor airport.

St Andrews By-The-Sea

St Andrews is a genteel summer resort town. Blessed with a fine climate and picturesque beauty, it also has a colorful history. Founded by Loyalists in 1783, it's one of the oldest towns in the province. It's busy with holiday-makers and summer residents in July and August, but the rest of the year there are more seagulls than people.

The town sits on a peninsula pointing southward into the Bay of Fundy. Its main drag, Water St, is lined with restaurants and several craft shops.

Sights

Minister's Island ISLAND

(☎506-529-5081; www.ministersisland.ca; adult/child under 8yr $10/free; ⏰May-Oct) This picturesque tidal island was once used as a retreat by William Cornelius Van Horne, builder of the Canadian Pacific Railway and one of Canada's wealthiest men. As well as touring the island on foot along four marked trails of varying lengths, you can visit **Covenhoven**, his splendid 50-room Edwardian cottage, plus the towerlike stone bathhouse, tidal swimming pool and château-like barn (the largest freestanding wooden structure in Canada).

Important: the island can be visited at low tide, when you can drive (or walk, or bike) on the hard-packed sea floor. A few hours later it's 3m under water, so be careful. During high tide, a ferry departs from Bar Rd. To get to Minister's Island from downtown St Andrews, follow Rte 127 northeast for about 1km and then turn right on Bar Rd.

Wild Salmon Nature Centre MUSEUM, AQUARIUM

(☎506-529-1384; http://wildsalmonnaturecentre.ca; Chamcook Lake No 1 Rd, off Rte 127; adult/student/child $6/4/3; ⏰9am-5pm Mon-Sat, noon-5pm Sun May-Aug) This handsome lodge has an in-stream aquarium, guided tours and displays devoted to the life and trials of the endangered wild Atlantic salmon.

Sheriff Andrew House HISTORIC BUILDING

(☎506-529-5080; cnr King & Queen Sts; admission by donation; ⏰9:30am-4:30pm Tue-Sun mid-Jun–Sep) This 1820 neoclassical house has been restored to look like a middle-class home in the 1800s, and it's attended by lively and informative costumed guides.

St Andrews Blockhouse HISTORIC BUILDING

(Joe's Point Rd; ⏰10am-6pm Jun-Aug) FREE The restored wooden Blockhouse Historic Site is the only one left of several that were built here for protection in the War of 1812. If the tide is out, there's a path that extends from the blockhouse out across the tidal flats.

Kingsbrae Garden GARDENS

(☎506-529-3335; www.kingsbraegarden.com; 220 King St; adult/student/family $16/12/38, tours per person $3; ⏰9am-6pm May-Oct, to 8pm Jul & Aug) Extensive, multihued Kingsbrae Garden is considered one of the best horticultural displays in Canada. Check out the wollemi pine, one of the world's oldest and rarest trees.

Fundy Discovery Aquarium AQUARIUM

(www.huntsmanmarine.com/aquarium; 1 Lower Campus Rd; adult/child $14.25/10; ⏰10am-5pm) This aquatic center focuses on the local marine ecology; a 20,000-sq-ft aquarium has most specimens that are found in Bay of Fundy waters, including seals (feedings at 11am and 4pm), seahorses (feedings at 10.15am and 3.30pm), salmon (feedings at 10.35am and 3pm), lobsters and sturgeon. Kids (and parents) love the touch pool reserved just for slippery skates.

Activities

Numerous companies offering boat trips and whale-watching cruises have offices by the wharf at the foot of King St. They're open from mid-June to early September. The cruises (around $60) take in the lovely coast. Seabirds are commonplace and seeing whales is the norm. The ideal waters for watching these beasts are further out in the bay, however, so if you're heading for the Fundy Isles, do your trip there.

Two Meadows Walking Trail WALKING

The 800m Two Meadows Walking Trail, a boardwalk and footpath through fields and woodlands, begins opposite 165 Joe's Point Rd beyond the blockhouse.

Eastern Outdoors CYCLING, KAYAKING

(☎506-529-4662; www.easternoutdoors.com; 165 Water St; mountain bikes per hour/day $20/30, kayaks per day $60; ⏰May-Oct) This St Andrews-based outfitter offers a variety of trips, including a three-hour trip around nearby

Navy Island ($60), and full-day trips to Passamaquody Bay ($125) and Deer Island ($125).

Quoddy Link Marine BOATING
(☎506-529-2600; http://quoddylinkmarine.com/; adult/child $58/28; ⊙mid-Jun–Oct) Serious whale-watchers should hop aboard this catamaran, staffed by trained marine biologists. There are one to three tours daily.

Jolly Breeze BOATING
(☎506-529-8116; www.jollybreeze.com; adult/child $60/40; ⊙tours 9am, 12:45pm & 4:30pm Jun-Oct) This antique-style tall ship sails around Passamaquoddy Bay looking for seals and whales as well as porpoises and eagles.

Sleeping

Kiwanis Oceanfront Camping CAMPGROUND $
(☎877-393-7070; www.kiwanisoceanfrontcamping.com; 550 Water St; campsites/RV sites $31/39; ⊙Apr-Oct) After the green and quaintness of St Andrews, this unattractive place – mostly a gravel parking area for trailers – comes as a shock. There's a few spaces for tents if you can squeeze in. It's situated at the far eastern end of town on Indian Point.

Picket Fence Motel MOTEL $
(☎506-529-8985; www.picketfencenb.com; 102 Reed Ave; r $85-110; P ❄ ☎) They're neat-as-a-pin, if dated motel-style rooms on approach into town but within walking distance of the main drag. It's among the cheapest you'll find in St Andrews, and while management is ultrafriendly, we're not convinced by its price-to-quality ratio.

★ **Treadwell Inn** B&B $$
(☎506-529-1011, 888-529-1011; www.treadwellinn.com; 129 Water St; r incl breakfast $179-229; ⊙May-Sep; ⊗ ❄ ☎) Big, light, airy handsome rooms in an 1820 ship chandler's house. Each of the four rooms has private decks and ocean views. Delightful Tom keeps things shipshape. Breakfast is buffet continental.

Garden Gate B&B $$
(☎506-529-4453; www.bbgardengate.com; 364 Montague St; r $150; P ☎) Sunlight pours through the three spotless rooms in this handsome home several blocks behind the ocean. Excellent cooked breakfasts and small touches such as tea and cookies make for a pleasant experience.

Rossmount Inn INN $$
(☎506-529-3351; www.rossmountinn.com; 4599 Rte 127; r $129-138; ⊙Apr-Dec; P ❄ ☎ ≋) Flags flap in the breeze in front of this stately yellow summer cottage, perched atop a manicured slope overlooking Passamaquoddy Bay. Inside, the 18 rooms have a stylish mix of antiques and modern decor, with hand-carved wooden furniture and snowy white linens. It's about 4.5km north of downtown St Andrews on Rte 127.

Breakfast costs $6 (continental style) or $9 (full). The hotel restaurant is not only the town's best – we'd extend that to New Brunswick.

★ **Algonquin Resort** HOTEL $$$
(☎855-529-8693, 506-529-8823; www.algonquinresort.com; 184 Adolphus St; r from $229; P ❄ ☎ ≋) The doyenne of New Brunswick hotels, this Tudor-style 'Castle-by-the-Sea' has sat on a hill overlooking town since 1889 and was given a makeover in 2015. With its elegant verandah, gardens, rooftop terrace, golf course, tennis courts and indoor pool with water slides, it's worth a look even if you're not spending the night. Prices vary according to seasons and demand.

Eating

Clam Digger SEAFOOD $
(4468 Hwy 127, Chamcook; mains $6-15; ⊙11:30am-3pm & 5-9pm Apr-Sep) Cars park three-deep outside this teeny red-and-white seafood shack that's a summertime tradition in these parts. In short: locals go nuts for it. Order your clam platter or dripping (yes, that would be the grease) cheeseburger, and claim one of the red-painted picnic tables. It's 3.5km north of the visitor center.

Honeybeans CAFE $
(157a Water St; snacks $3-6; ⊙7.30am-5pm Wed-Mon, 10am-5pm Sun) Listen to the gossip (it's a magnet for the locals) over a cup of good espresso-based coffee and a freshly baked treat.

★ **Rossmount Inn Restaurant** MODERN CANADIAN $$
(☎506-529-3351; www.rossmountinn.com; 4599 Rte 127; mains $18-30; ⊙5-9:30pm) The Swiss chef-owner makes wonderful use of local bounty in this warm, art-filled dining room. The ever-changing menu might include foraged goose-tongue greens and wild mushrooms, periwinkles or New Brunswick lobster. They each play a part in complex, exquisite dishes – say, lobster with nasturtium-flower dumplings and vanilla bisque, or foie gras with cacao nibs and bee balm–poached peach.

St Andrews By-The-Sea

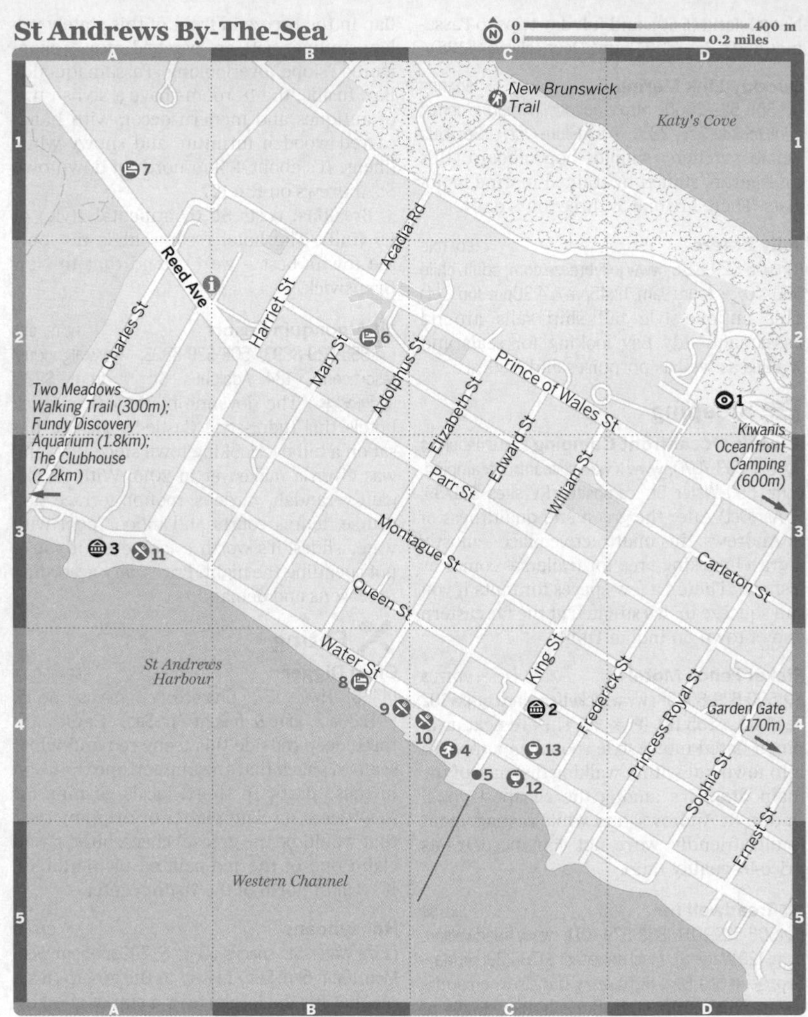

Gables SEAFOOD $$
(☎506-529-3440; 143 Water St; mains $10-20; ⊙11am-10pm) Seafood and views of Navy Island through a row of tall windows dominate this comfortable place. To enter, head down the alley onto a gardenlike patio on the water's edge.

Kingsbrae Garden Cafe CAFE $$
(www.kingsbraegarden.com; 220 King St; mains $10-18; ⊙10am-5pm May-Oct, to 7pm Jul & Aug) At the beautiful Kingsbrae Garden, the terrace cafe serves sandwiches and salads for lunch with a glass of wine or local ale. Excellent brunches include salmon and scrambled eggs ($15).

Niger Reef Tea House CANADIAN
(www.nigerreefteahouse.com; 1 Joes Point Rd; mains $12-29; ⊙11am-9pm May-Oct) Located in a historic building near the blockhouse overlooking the water, its interior murals date from the 1920s. Owner-chef David blends fresh, local ingredients (whatever is going that day) to create some beautiful salads, and the likes of curry lamb ragout and fiddlehead soup.

St Andrews By-The-Sea

Sights

1 Kingsbrae Garden....D2
2 Sheriff Andrew House.... C4
3 St Andrews Blockhouse....A3

Activities, Courses & Tours

4 Eastern Outdoors.... C4
5 Jolly Breeze.... C4
Quoddy Link Marine....(see 5)

Sleeping

6 Algonquin Resort....B2
7 Picket Fence Motel....A1
8 Treadwell Inn....B4

Eating

9 Gables....B4
10 Honeybeans.... C4
Kingsbrae Garden Cafe....(see 1)
11 Niger Reef....A3

Drinking & Nightlife

12 Red Herring Pub.... C4
13 Shiretown Pub.... C4

Drinking & Nightlife

The Clubhouse BAR

(http://algonquinresort.com; 465 Brandy Cove Rd; 7am-9pm May-Oct) Kick back with a beer, wine or cocktail at the '19th tee' and watch as the punters come up the 18th hole of this stunning golf course. The Clubhouse's inviting terrace has one of the region's best vistas.

Red Herring Pub PUB

(211 Water St; noon-2am Mar-Jan) A fun, slightly divey downtown watering hole with pool tables, live music and frosty Canadian beers.

Shiretown Pub PUB

(www.kennedyinn.ca; 218 Water St; 11am-2am) On the ground floor of the delightfully creaky Kennedy Inn, this extremely old-school English pub draws a mixed-age crowd of partiers. Early afternoons mean sipping New Brunswick–brewed Picaroons bitter on the porch, while late nights bring live music and raucous karaoke.

Information

Tourist office (www.townofstandrews.ca; 46 Reed Ave; 9am-7pm Jul & Aug, to 5pm May, Jun, Sep & Oct;) This well organized office has free walking-tour brochures that include a map and brief description of some of the most noteworthy places. It also has free internet access.

New River Provincial Park

Just off Hwy 1, about 35km west of Saint John on the way to St Stephen, this large **park** (506-755-4046; https://parcsnbparks.ca) has one of the best beaches along the Fundy shore, a wide stretch of sand bordered on one side by the rugged coastline of Barnaby Head. During camping season the park charges a $10 fee per vehicle for day use, which includes parking at the beach and Barnaby Head trailhead.

You can spend an enjoyable few hours hiking Barnaby Head along a 5km network of nature trails. The **Chittick's Beach Trail** leads through coastal forest and past four coves, where you can check the catch in a herring weir or examine tidal pools for marine life. Extending from this loop is the 2.5km **Barnaby Head Trail**, which hugs the shoreline most of the way and rises to the edge of a cliff 15m above the Bay of Fundy.

The park's **campground** (506-755-4046; https://parcsnbparks.ca; 78 New River Beach Rd; campsites/RV sites $28/31; May-Sep) is across the road from the beach and features 100 secluded sites, both rustic and with hookups, in a wooded setting. Drawbacks are the gravel emplacements and traffic noise.

FUNDY ISLES

The thinly populated, unspoiled Fundy Isles are ideal for a tranquil, nature-based escape. With grand scenery, colorful fishing wharves tucked into coves, supreme whale-watching, uncluttered walking trails and steaming dishes of seafood, the islands will make your everyday stresses fade away and your blood pressure ease. The three main islands each have a distinct personality and offer a memorable, gradually absorbed peace. Outside of the summer season, all are nearly devoid of visitors and most services are shut.

Deer Island

Deer Island, the closest of the three main Fundy Isles, is a modest fishing settlement with a lived-in look. The 16km-by-5km island has been inhabited since 1770, and 1000 people live here year-round. It's well forested, and deer are still plentiful. Lobster is the main catch and there are half a dozen wharves around the island.

Fundy Isles

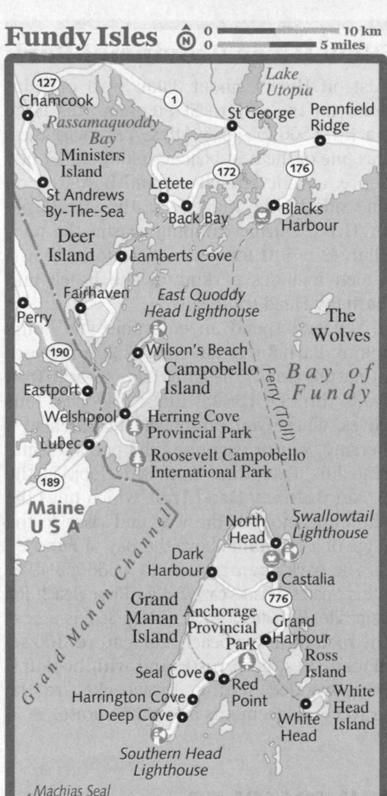

Deer Island can be easily explored on a day trip. Narrow, winding roads run south down each side toward Campobello Island and the ferry.

Sights

At the end of Cranberry Head Rd is a deserted beach. Most land on the island is privately owned, so there are no hiking trails.

Lobster Pound VIEWPOINT

(Lamberts Cove) At Lamberts Cove is a huge lobster pound used to hold live lobster (it could well be the world's largest). Another massive pound squirms at Northern Harbor.

Old Sow Whirlpool WATERFRONT

(Deer Island Point Park) From the shores of the pretty, community-run 16-hectare Deer Island Point Park, Old Sow, the world's second-largest natural tidal whirlpool, is seen offshore a few hours before high tide. Whales pass occasionally too.

Tours

Whales usually arrive in mid-June and stay until October. You can be lucky enough to spot these offshore; for a closer look, head out on a kayak tour with **Seascape Kayak Tours** (☎506-747-1884; www.seascapekayaktours.com; 40 NW Harbour Branch Rd, Richardson, Deer Island; half-/full-day trips $85/150; ⏲mid-May–mid-Sep).

Sleeping & Eating

Deer Island Inn GUESTHOUSE $

(☎506-747-1998; www.deerislandinn.com; 272 Route 772, Lord's Cove; r incl breakfast $85-105; ⏲May–mid-Oct) If island-stays are your thing, this excellent-value, conveniently located home brings a touch of Deer Island heritage and has five pleasantly appointed rooms. Excellent full breakfasts set you up for taking on the local sights.

Deer Island Point Park CAMPGROUND $

(☎506-747-2423; www.deerislandpointpark.com; 195 Deer Island Point Rd; campsites $25-30; ⏲Jun-Sep) Set up your tent on the high bluff and spend an evening watching the Old Sow whirlpool. The campground is directly above the Campobello ferry landing.

The Pilgrim's Rest FAST FOOD $

(18 Cooks Lane, Lord's Cove; snacks $4-12, lobster rolls $11.50; ⏲noon-8pm Sat & Sun May–mid-Jun, noon-8pm Tue-Sun mid-Jun–late Sep) An apt name for an apt spot. The Pilgrim's Rest is a simple, hole-in-the-wall eatery and is the place to get your fill of seafood (much of it fried) plus great lobster rolls to enjoy on the small patio or to take out for a picnic.

Information

Tourist information (☎506-747-0119; www.deerisland.nb.ca; 193 Rte 772, Lords Cove; ⏲10am-5pm Jul-Sep) This helpful place run by local volunteers out of the community centre.

Getting There & Away

A free government-run ferry (25 minutes) runs to Deer Island from Letete, which is 14.5km south of St George on Hwy 172 via Back Bay. The ferries run year-round every half-hour from 6am to 7pm, and hourly from 7pm to 10pm. Get in line early on a busy day.

In summer **East Coast Ferries** (☎506-747-2159; www.eastcoastferries.nb.ca; car & driver $20, additional passenger $4; ⏲8:30am-6:30pm late Jun–mid-Sep) services Campobello Island.

Campobello Island

The wealthy have long been enjoying Campobello, a gentle and prosperous island, as a summer retreat. Due to the island's accessibility to New England, it feels as much a part of the USA as of Canada, and most of the tourists here are Americans.

Like many moneyed families, the Roosevelts bought property in this peaceful coastal area at the end of the 1800s. The southern half of Campobello is almost all park, and a golf course occupies still more.

Come to the island prepared. The island's biggest community, Wilson's Beach, 10km north of Roosevelt Park, has just a grocery store and post office. An ATM is at Welshpool. The island has no gas station – the 1000 residents of the 16km-long Campobello must cross the bridge to Lubec, ME, to fill their tanks.

Sights

★Roosevelt Campobello International Park PARK
(506-752-2922; www.fdr.net; Hwy 774) FREE The southernmost green area of Campobello Island is this 1100-hectare park. Its biggest visitor attraction is the **Roosevelt Cottage**, the 34-room lodge where Franklin D Roosevelt grew up (between 1905 and 1921) and visited periodically throughout his time as US president (1933–45). The arts-and-crafts-style structure is furnished with original Roosevelt furniture and artifacts. Adjacent **Hubbard House**, built in 1891, is also open to visitors.

The park is just 2.5km from the Lubec bridge, and from the Roosevelt mansion's front porch you can look directly across to Eastport, ME. You'd hardly know you were in Canada.

Unlike the manicured museum area, most of the international park has been left in its natural state to preserve the flora and fauna that Roosevelt appreciated so much. A couple of gravel roads meander through it, leading to beaches and 7.5km of nature trails. It's a surprisingly wild, little-visited part of Campobello Island. Deer, moose and coyotes call it home, and seals can sometimes be seen offshore on the ledges near Lower Duck Pond, 6km from the visitor center. Look for eagles, ospreys and loons.

Herring Cove Provincial Park PARK
FREE Along the northern boundary of Roosevelt Campobello International Park is Herring Cove Provincial Park. This park has 10km of walking trails as well as a campground and a picnic area on an arching 1.5km beach. It makes a fine, picturesque place for lunch.

East Quoddy Head Lighthouse LIGHTHOUSE
Four kilometers north of Wilson's Beach is East Quoddy Head Lighthouse. Whales browse offshore and many people sit along the rocky shoreline with binoculars enjoying the sea breezes.

Tours

Island Cruises CRUISE
(506-752-1107; www.bayoffundywhales.com; 62 Harbour Head Rd, Wilson's Beach; adult/child $50/40; Jul-Oct) Offers 2½-hour whale-watching cruises.

Sleeping & Eating

Herring Cove Provincial Park CAMPGROUND $
(506-752-7010; www.campobello.com/cmpgrd-fe.html; 136 Herring Cove Rd; campsites/RV sites $22/24; Jun-Sep) This 76-site park on the eastern side of the island, 3km from the Deer Island ferry, has some nice secluded sites in a forest setting, plus there's a sandy beach and ample hiking.

Owen House B&B B&B $$
(506-752-2977; www.owenhouse.ca; 11 Welshpool St, Welshpool; d incl breakfast private/shared bath from $115/104; P) A classic seaside vacation home of yesteryear, complete with antique spool beds made up with quilts, cozy reading nooks and lots of windows on the ocean.

Pollock Cove Cottages COTTAGE $$
(506-328-7932; pollockcove@gmail.com; 2455 Rte 774, Wilson's Beach; cottages $75-175; P @) Simple, clean one- and two-bedroom cottages with million-dollar views. All have kitchens.

Fireside Restaurant MODERN AMERICAN $$
(506-752-6055; www.fdr.net; Roosevelt Park; luncheon special $12-18, mains $12-28; noon-5pm Sun-Wed, to 9pm Thu-Sat late May–mid-Oct) Housed in a former summer residence of the Adams family (Mrs Adams was a cousin of President Roosevelt), this lovely spot has a daily luncheon special, salads, pastas and, of course, lobster rolls (price varies according to the lobster market).

Family Fisheries Restaurant SEAFOOD $$
(www.familyfisheries.com; 1977 Rte 774, Wilson's Beach; mains $9-25; 11:30am-9pm Apr-Sep) Part of a fresh-fish market, this ultracasual seafood shack specializes in fish-and-chips

(all the seafood is caught by family members), plus lip-smacking chowders and lobster rolls.

Information

Visitors Center (506-752-2922; www.fdr.net; Hwy 774; 10am-5pm) Principally an information center for the Roosevelt Campobello International Park, but can point you in the right direction to elsewhere on the island.

Getting There & Away

East Coast Ferries (p393) Connects Deer Island to Welshpool (25 minutes, half-hourly) on Campobello Island.

Grand Manan Island

Grand Manan is a peaceful, unspoiled place. There are no fast-food restaurants, no trendy coffeehouses or nightclubs, no traffic lights and no traffic. Just a ruggedly beautiful coastline of high cliffs and sandy coves interspersed with spruce forest and fields of long grass. Wonderful lighthouses, including the famous Swallowtail Lighthouse, stand guard above cliffs. Along the eastern shore and joined by a meandering coastal road sit a string of pretty and prosperous fishing villages. There is plenty of fresh sea air and that rare and precious commodity in the modern world: silence, broken only by the rhythmic ocean surf. Some people make it a day trip, but lingering is recommended.

Sights

Grand Manan Art Gallery GALLERY
(506-662-3662; www.grandmananartgallery.com; 21 Cedar St, Castalia; $2; noon-6pm Mon-Sat, 1pm-5pm Sun mid-Jun–late Sep) This lovely, not-for-profit local gallery showcases local, seasonal and regional artists, as well as well-known historic and emerging figures. Definitely worth checking out.

Fishing Weirs LANDMARK
Those round contraptions comprising wooden posts that you see dotting the waters around Grand Manan are based on the design of ancient fishing traps; some of those you see date back to the 19th century, though, sadly, only a few remain these days. They were formerly labelled with names such as 'Ruin,' 'Winner,' 'Outside Chance' and 'Spite,' evoking the heartbreak of relying on an indifferent sea for a living.

Seal Cove HISTORIC SITE
Seal Cove is the island's prettiest village. Much of its charm comes from the fishing boats, wharves and herring-smoking sheds clustered around the tidal creek mouth. For a century, smoked herring was king on Grand Manan. A thousand men and women worked splitting, stringing and drying fish in 300 smokehouses up and down the island. The last smokehouse shut down in 1996. Although herrings are still big business around here, they're now processed at a modern cannery.

Grand Manan Historical Museum MUSEUM
(506-662-3524; www.grandmananmuseum.ca; 1141 Rte 776, Grand Harbour; adult/student & senior $5/3; 9am-5pm Mon-Fri Jun-Sep, plus Sat Jul & Aug) This museum makes a good destination on a foggy day. Its diverse collection of local artifacts provides a quick primer on island history. You can see a display on shipwreck lore and the original kerosene lamp from nearby Gannet Rock lighthouse (1904). There is also a room stuffed with 200-plus taxidermied birds (including the now-extinct passenger pigeon).

Swallowtail Lighthouse LIGHTHOUSE
(www.tourismnewbrunswick.ca; adult/under 12yr $5/free; Jul & Aug) Whitewashed Swallowtail Lighthouse (1860) is the island's signature vista, cleaving to a rocky promontory about 1km north of the ferry wharf. Access is via steep stairs and a wooden footbridge. Since the light was automated in 1986, the site has been left to the elements. Nevertheless, the grassy bluff is a stupendous setting for a picnic. You can explore the lighthouse on your own (for a fee); even when it's closed it's illuminating, set where it is and all.

Activities

Around 70km of hiking trails crisscross and circle the island. Grab the comprehensive guide *Heritage Trails and Footpaths on Grand Manan* ($5), available at most island shops. Stay well away from the cliff edges as unstable, undercut ground can give way beneath your feet.

For an easy hike, try the 1.6km shoreline (boardwalk) path from Long Pond to Red Point (about one hour round-trip; suitable for children). In Whale Cove, the Hole-in-the-Wall is an often photographed natural arch jutting into the sea. It's a short hike from the parking area.

Sea Watch Tours BIRDWATCHING
(☎877-662-8552, 506-662-8552; www.seawatch-tours.com; Seal Cove Fisherman's Wharf; adult/child $115/56; ⏱Mon-Sat Jul & Aug) Make the pilgrimage out to isolated **Machias Seal Island** to see the Atlantic puffins waddle and play on their home turf. Access is limited to 15 visitors a day, so reserve well in advance. Getting onto the island can be tricky, as the waves are high and the rocks slippery. Wear sturdy shoes.

Whales-n-Sails Adventures BOATING
(☎888-994-4044, 506-662-1999; www.whales-n-sails.com; North Head Fisherman's Wharf; adult/child $66/46; ⏱Jul-Sep) A marine biologist narrates these exhilarating whale-watching tours aboard the sailboat *Elsie Menota*. You'll often see puffins, razorbills, murre and other seabirds.

Adventure High KAYAKING, CYCLING
(☎506-662-3563; www.adventurehigh.com; 83 Rte 776, North Head; day tours $45-110, bicycles per half day/day/week $18/25/125; ⏱May-Oct) This outfitter offers tours of the Grand Manan coastline ranging from lovely two-hour sunset paddles to multiday Bay of Fundy adventures. Excellent educational information along the way.

Sleeping

You'll need to reserve ahead in summer to stay on Grand Manan.

Hole-in-the-Wall Campground CAMPGROUND $
(☎506-662-3152; www.grandmanancamping.com; 42 Old Airport Rd, North Head; campsites/cabins $28/42; ⏱May-Oct) These spectacular cliff-top campsites are secluded among the rocks and trees, with fire pits, picnic tables and breathtaking views. Choose an inland site if you sleepwalk or suffer from vertigo. Showers and laundry facilities are available, as well as a couple of spotless, simple cabins (linen provided).

Anchorage Camping CAMPGROUND $
(☎506-662-7022; Rte 776, Anchorage; campsites/RV sites $24/26; ⏱May-Sep) Family-friendly camping in a large field surrounded by tall evergreens, a former provincial park, located at Anchorage, between Grand Harbour and Seal Cove. There's a kitchen shelter for rainy days, a playground, laundry and a long pebbly beach. Get down by the trees to block the wind. The areas adjoins marshes, which comprise a migratory bird sanctuary, and there are several short hiking trails.

Inn at Whale Cove INN $$
(☎506-662-3181; www.whalecovecottages.ca; Whistle Rd, North Head; s/d incl breakfast $145/155; ⏱May-Oct; P ❄) 'Serving rusticators since 1910', including writer Willa Cather, who wrote several of her novels here in the 1920s and '30s. The main lodge (built in 1816) and six shingled cottages (two with fully equipped kitchens) retain the charm of that earlier era. They are fitted with polished pine floors and stone fireplaces, antiques, chintz curtains and well-stocked bookshelves.

They're pricey for singles, but head here for the holistic experience. Trails lead to Whale Cove and the area is full of wildflowers.

McLaughlin's GUESTHOUSE $$
(☎506-662-3672; www.mclaughlinswharfinn.ca; 1863 Rte 776, Seal Cove; r $109) If it were any closer to the historic smoke shacks you'd be smoked yourselves. Perched on a wharf in Seal Cove is this atmospheric and very homely B&B with quilted beds and unique outlooks.

Compass Rose B&B $$
(☎506-662-3563; www.compassroseinn.com; 65 Rte 776, North Head; r incl breakfast $99-165; P ❄ ⓦ) It's hard to go wrong at this neat little spot, which has had a recent makeover and features airy and comfortable guest rooms, all with harbor views. It's within walking distance of the ferry dock, and has one of the island's most atmospheric restaurants attached. Handily, the owner, Kevin, runs the local kayaking company.

Eating

The island's scant options are nearly nonexistent in the off-season. For the few decent places that are open for dinner, reservations are essential. Be sure to try dulse, a dark purple seaweed harvested locally and eaten like crisps (chips) by locals. Chefs use it as a seasoning. You might even see a 'DLT sandwich' (yep, that's dulse instead of bacon).

★**Inn at Whale Cove** MODERN CANADIAN $$$
(☎506-662-3181; www.whalecovecottages.ca; Whistle Rd, North Head; mains $22-28; ⏱5-7pm) Wonderful food in a relaxed country setting on Whale Cove. The menu changes daily, but includes mouth-watering meals such as pulled pork and tagliatelle, seafood bouillabaise and a to-die-for hazelnut crème caramel for dessert. Come early and have a cocktail by the fire in the cozy, old-fashioned parlor.

Be on time (or risk the owner's wrath – all in the name of protecting the tranquillity of her inn guests, however).

Food for Thought CAFE
(922 Rte 776; snacks $4.25-7; ⏲6:30am-5pm Mon & Tue, to 6pm Wed & Thu, to 8pm Fri, 7am-3pm Sat Apr-Dec) This welcome relative newcomer to Grand Manan may not look like much from the outside, but step over the threshold and you'll find a cozy spot that churns out fresh and fabulous made-on-the-premises items, from excellent rolls and salads for picnics to hearty soups. The cookies and pastries are worth coming for alone (don't miss the cinnamon buns!) The owner is a caterer, and it's easy to see why.

Shopping

Roland's Sea Vegetables MARKET
(174 Hill Rd; ⏲9am-5pm) This is the spot in the world to learn about dulse. Grand Manan is one of the few remaining producers of dulse, a type of seaweed that is used as a snack food or seasoning in Atlantic Canada and around the world. Dulse gatherers wade among the rocks at low tide to pick the seaweed, then lay it out on beds of rocks to dry, just as they've been doing for hundreds of years.

Information

Tourist Information Office (☎506-662-3442; www.grandmanannb.com; 130 Rte 776, North Head; ⏲mid-Jun–late Aug) Locally run tourist organization that has maps, brochures and ferry schedules.

Getting There & Away

The only way to get from Blacks Harbour on the mainland to North Head on Grand Manan is by a private ferry company, **Coastal Transport** (☎506-662-3724; http://grandmanan.coastaltransport.ca; adult/child/car/bicycle $12/6/36/4.10). The crossing takes 1½ hours, and there are around three to four daily departures from each port in summer. Reserve and pay in advance as it gets busy. It's best to pay for a return trip, rather than one way, so you don't get stuck on the island. Watch for harbor porpoises and whales en route.

The ferry dock is within walking distance of several hotels, restaurants, shops and tour operators. To explore the whole of the island, bring your own car, as there is no rental company on Grand Manan.

Getting Around

The ferry disembarks at the village of North Head at the northern end of the island. The main road, Rte 776, runs 28.5km down the length of the island along the eastern shore. It connects all of Grand Manan's settlements en route to the lighthouse, which is perched atop a bluff at South Head. You can drive from end to end in about 45 minutes. The western side of Grand Manan is uninhabited and more or less impenetrable: a sheer rock wall rising out the sea, backed by dense forest and bog, broken only at Dark Harbour where a steep road drops down to the water's edge. Hiking trails provides access to this wilderness.

Adventure High (p411) rents out bicycles. Be aware, though, that the roads are winding and high season is busy. At other times, keen cyclists can enjoy the undulating routes.

SAINT JOHN

POP 70,100

Saint John is the economic engine room of the province, a gritty port city with a dynamism that's missing from the demure capital. The setting is impressive – a ring of rocky bluffs, sheer cliffs, coves and peninsulas surrounding a deep natural harbor where the mighty Saint John and Kennebecasis Rivers empty into the Bay of Fundy. It can take a bit of imagination to appreciate this natural beauty, obscured as it is by the smokestacks of a pulp mill, oil refinery and garden-variety urban blight. But those who push their way through all this to the historic core are rewarded with beautifully preserved redbrick and sandstone 19th-century architecture and glimpses of the sea down steep, narrow side streets.

Originally a French colony, the city was incorporated by British Loyalists in 1785 to become Canada's first legal city. Thousands of Irish immigrants arrived during the potato famine of the mid-1800s and helped build the city into a prosperous industrial town, important particularly for its wooden shipbuilding. Today, a large percentage of the population works in heavy industry, including pulp mills, refineries and the Moosehead Brewery. There is also a large IT knowledge cluster.

Sights

The Bay of Fundy tides and their effects are a predominant regional characteristic. The rapids here on the Saint John River are part

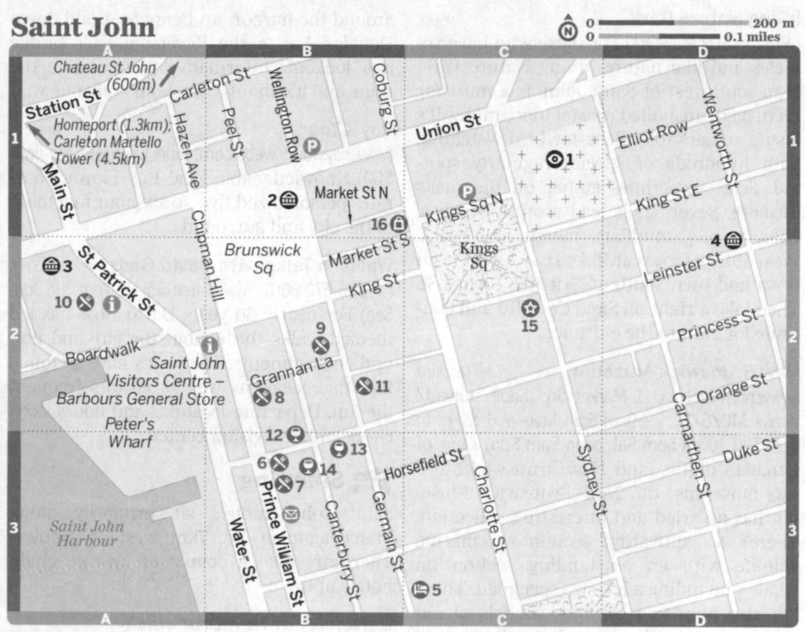

Saint John

Sights

1 Loyalist Burial Ground C1
2 Loyalist House B1
3 New Brunswick Museum A2
4 Saint John Jewish Historical Museum D2

Sleeping

5 Mahogany Manor C3

Eating

Billy's Seafood Company ..... (see 16)
6 Britt's Pub & Eatery B3
7 East Coast Bistro B3
8 Java Moose B2
9 Port City Royal B2
10 Saint John Ale House A2
11 Taco Pica B2

Drinking & Nightlife

12 Big Tide Brewing Company B3
13 Happinez Wine Bar B3
14 O'Leary's B3

Entertainment

15 Imperial Theatre C2

Shopping

16 Old City Market B1

of that and are one of the best-known sites in the province. Known as 'reversing rapids', the name is a bit of a misnomer. When the high tides at Bay of Fundy rise, the current in the river reverses, causing the water to flow upstream. When the tides go down (up to 8.5m), the water flows in the normal way. Generally, it looks like rapids.

Saint John Visitors Centre – Reversing Rapids (p417), next to the bridge over the river, can supply a tides table that explains where in the cycle you are.

Loyalist Burial Ground CEMETERY

This solemn cemetery, with tombstones from as early as 1784, is just off Kings Sq in a park-style setting in the center of town.

Saint John Jewish Historical Museum MUSEUM

(91 Leinster St; admission by donation; ⏲10am-4pm Mon-Fri Jun-Oct, plus 1-4pm Sun Jul & Aug) This modest museum traces the history of Saint John's once-thriving Jewish community, whose members included Louis B Mayer of Metro-Goldwyn-Mayer (MGM) Hollywood fame.

Irving Nature Park PARK

(⏲8am-dusk May-Oct) For those who have vehicles and like nature, Irving Nature Park, 9km southwest of Saint John, is a must for its rugged, unspoiled coastal topography. It's also a remarkable place for bird-watching, with hundreds of species regularly spotted. Seals sometimes gather on the rocks offshore. Seven trails lead around beaches, cliffs, woods, mudflats, marsh and rocks. Wear sturdy footwear. Take Hwy 1 west from town and turn south at Exit 107, Bleury St. Then take a right on Sand Cove Rd and continue for 2km to the entrance.

New Brunswick Museum MUSEUM

(www.nbm-mnb.ca; 1 Market Sq; adult/student/family $10/6/22; ⏲9am-5pm Mon-Wed & Fri, to 9pm Thu, 10am-5pm Sat, noon-5pm Sun) One of Canada's oldest (and New Brunswick's finest) museums, the New Brunswick Museum has a varied and interesting collection. There's a captivating section on marine wildlife with an outstanding section on whales, including a life-size specimen. There are also hands-on exhibits, models of old sailing ships and a stunning collection of Canadian and international artwork on the top floor. Well worth a visit.

Carleton Martello Tower HISTORIC BUILDING

(454 Whipple St; adult/child $3.90/1.90; ⏲10am-5:30pm late Jun-Sep) Built during the War of 1812 for defence purposes, this round stone fort features a restored barracks and other historical displays, but the real reason to go is the panoramic view over Saint John and the Bay of Fundy from the hilltop locale.

Loyalist House HISTORIC BUILDING

(☎506-652-3590; www.loyalisthouse.com; 120 Union St; adult/child/family $5/2/7; ⏲10am-5pm late May-Sep) Dating from 1810, the Georgian-style Loyalist House is one of the city's oldest unchanged buildings. It's now a museum, depicting the Loyalist period, and contains some fine carpentry.

Activities & Tours

As a popular stop for cruise-ship travelers, Saint John has a large range of tour options. Whale-watching, unfortunately, is not an attraction in Saint John, save for the very occasional, very wayward minke.

Harbour Passage WALKING

Beginning on a boardwalk at Market Sq (behind the Hilton Hotel), Harbour Passage is a red-paved walk and cycle trail that leads around the harbor, up Bennett St and down Douglas Ave to the Reversing Falls bridge and lookout. Informative plaques line the route and it's about a one-hour walk one way.

Roy's Tour DRIVING

(www.roystours.webs.com; tours per group per hour $60) Knowledgeable local Roy Flowers narrates personalized five- to six-hour taxi tours of the city and surrounds.

Walks 'n Talks with David Goss WALKING

(☎506-672-8601; walks free-$5; ⏲7pm Tue Jun-Sep) For nearly 30 years David Goss has led themed walks throughout the city and natural environments. The walks have so much flair that locals as well as visitors frequent the fun. Departure locations and hours vary; check with the visitor center.

Sleeping

Saint John motels sit primarily along Manawagonish Rd, 7km west of uptown. There are also a couple of upscale chain hotels uptown.

University of New Brunswick Summer Residences RESIDENCE HALL $

(☎506-648-5755; www.unbsj.ca; off Sandy Point Rd, near Rockwood Park; s/d/ste $40/50/80; wifi) From May to August, the University of New Brunswick's Saint John campus offers simple rooms and rather spartan kitchenette suites in two residence halls. The university is 6km north of the city center. Take a bus from Kings Sq; for the correct number, look for 'University' on the schedules.

Rockwood Park CAMPGROUND $

(☎506-652-4050; www.rockwoodparkcampground.com; Lake Dr S; campsites/RV sites $29/39; ⏲May-Sep; wifi) A couple of kilometers north of the downtown area is huge Rockwood Park, with small lakes, a woodland crisscrossed by walking paths, and a campground in a small open field.

★Mahogany Manor B&B $$

(☎506-636-8000; www.sjnow.com/mm; 220 Germain St; d incl breakfast from $110; P non-smoking wifi) On the loveliest street in Saint John, this gay-friendly, antique-filled Victorian is a wonderful place to temporarily call home. Five light and airy rooms are a comfy mix of antiques and plush, modern bedding. The upbeat owners know more about the city than you'll be able to absorb – even which meal to order at which restaurant!

DON'T MISS

SCENIC DRIVE: FUNDY TRAIL

This magnificent **trail** (www.fundytrailparkway.com; adult/child/family $7.50/5/23; ⏲6am-8pm May-Oct) is not one track, per se, but comprises a network of roads, trails and footpaths along the Bay of Fundy coast. The main auto-parkway traverses a rugged section of what has been called the only remaining coastal wilderness between Florida and Newfoundland. The 19km-long parkway to Long Beach (opened in 2016) via Salmon River put an end to the unspoiled wilderness part, but it's still beautiful; off here are numerous viewpoints (lookouts), picnic areas and parking places. In 2018, the parkway will extend to Fundy National Park (30.5km total).

Running parallel to the parkway is a separate 11km-long multiuse trail for walkers and cyclists. In the off-season, the main gate is closed, but you can park at the entrance and hike or pedal in.

At Big Salmon River visit the **Big Salmon River Interpretative Center** (⏲8:30am-8pm mid-May–mid-Oct), which has exhibits from when a logging community lived here. Near there, a suspension bridge leads to a vast wilderness hiking area beyond the end of the road. This is known as the **Fundy Footpath**, but this is for hard-core hikers only – it's a solid five-day trek from Big Salmon River to Goose River in Fundy National Park. Think wilderness, rocky scree, tidal crossings and a rope ladder or two. You must register at either end.

Chateau Saint John BUSINESS HOTEL **$$**
(☎506-644-4444; www.chateausaintjohn.ca; 369 Rockland Rd; r from $155; P❄📶) Despite its behemoth appearance, situated on a main road on the edge of the CBD, Chateau Saint John surprises with large, spacious rooms and city views. Professional service and the price to quality ratio make this a good choice. It's a 15-minute walk into town and there's ample parking on-site. It's popular with groups and business people.

Homeport B&B **$$**
(☎888-678-7678, 506-672-7255; www.homeport.nb.ca; 60 Douglas Ave; r incl breakfast $109-175; P⊖❄📶) Perched above once-grand Douglas Ave, this imposing Italianate-style B&B was once two separate mansions belonging to shipbuilder brothers. It has a boutique-hotel vibe, with a stately parlor, a full bar and 10 elegant old-world guest rooms (try to snag one with a claw-foot bathtub). It's about 1km west of the uptown peninsula.

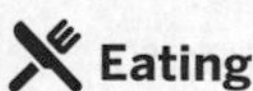

Eating

Java Moose CAFE **$**
(www.javamoose.com; 84 Prince William St; snacks $3-6; ⏲8am-6pm; 📶) Get your caffeine fix (fab or otherwise depending on your local or international taste buds) at this homegrown coffeehouse.

Taco Pica MEXICAN, GUATEMALAN **$**
(www.tacopica.ca; 96 Germain St; mains $14-24; ⏲10am-10pm Mon-Sat) A fusion of authentic Guatemalan and Mexican fare is served in this colorful cantina and is a welcome alternative to standard fare. An economical introduction to the cuisine is Taco Pica's *pepian* – a simple but spicy beef stew that is as good as you'll find in any Guatemalan household. The hardworking Guatemalan owner has been here for years. Live music is also often on the menu.

★ **Port City Royal** INTERNATIONAL **$$**
(☎506-631-3714; www.portcityroyal.com; 45 Grannan St; share plates $12-14; ⏲11:30am-late Tue-Fri, 2pm-late Sat) Owner-chef Jacob heads up this revered spot, housed in a renovated historic building. He declares that 'the menu is constantly in a state of evolution and never quite finished'. He loves experimenting with local produce, using whole animals (and their every last scrap for pâtés, soups and sausages) and his dishes (mainly share plates) are ever changing.

★ **East Coast Bistro** INTERNATIONAL **$$**
(☎506-696-3278; www.eastcoastbistro.com; 60 Prince William St; mains $20-31; ⏲11am-4pm Mon, to 9pm Tue-Thu, to 11pm Fri, to 10pm Sat) East Coast Bistro is one of the standout restaurants in Saint John, offering top-notch cuisine at digestible prices. Sustainable, local cuisine is the real deal here – it even makes its own bread. The menu changes seasonally, but braised Atlantic beef-cheek agnolotti and seafood sauté are just two of the luscious dishes whipped up in this casual space.

Britt's Pub & Eatery MODERN AMERICAN **$$**
(www.brittspub.ca; 42 Princess St; mains $14-24; 7:30am-1am Mon-Wed, to 2am Thu & Fri, 9am-2am Sat, 9am-midnight Sun) This cheery spot is one of the more affordable eating places around so it attracts a crowd. It's meant to emulate a British pub (though we're not so sure it does that), but it has good, modern fare and drinks. Good for single travelers who can enjoy the experience without standing out like a Union Jack–waving Brit in a Canadian pub.

Saint John Ale House MODERN AMERICAN **$$$**
(www.sjah.ca; 1 Market Sq; mains $18-40; 11am-late Mon-Fri, 10:30am-late Sat & Sun) On the lips of most locals who suggest the ale house for a great selection of beers, both craft and on tap (served in a pub downstairs) as well as its sleek, sprawling bistro and hearty meals based on the 'eat local and forage' mantra (menu changes daily). It offers a great brunch menu too, from the likes of pulled pork and eggs to frittata.

Billy's Seafood Company SEAFOOD **$$$**
(www.billysseafood.com; 49 Charlotte St; mains $25-32; 11am-10pm Mon-Sat, 4-10pm Sun) Since we are on the East Coast after all… This popular casual restaurant at the top of the City Market does reasonable seafood dishes. It's one of the few eateries open on Sunday evening.

Kingston Farmers Market MARKET
(Rte 845, Kingston; 8am-1pm Sat) A favorite (and fun) Saturday-morning activity for Saint Johners, head here for your fix of fresh fruits and vegetables and various ethnic foods.

THE TIDES OF FUNDY

The tides of the Bay of Fundy are the highest in the world. A Mi'kmaq legend explains the tide as the effect of a whale's thrashing tail sending the water forever sloshing back and forth. A more prosaic explanation is in the length, depth and gradual funnel shape of the bay itself.

The contrasts between the high and ebb tide are most pronounced at the eastern end of the bay and around the Minas Basin, with tides of 10m to 15m twice daily 12½ hours apart. The highest tide ever recorded anywhere was 16.6m, the height of a four-story building, at Burncoat Head near Noel, Nova Scotia.

Drinking & Entertainment

O'Leary's PUB
(www.olearyspub.com; 46 Princess St; 11:30am-11pm Mon & Tue, to 2am Wed-Fri, 3pm-2am Sat) Shoot the breeze with local barflies at this divey but friendly downtown institution.

Happinez Wine Bar BAR
(www.happinezwinebar.com; 42 Princess St; 4pm-midnight Wed & Thu, to 1am Fri, 5pm-1am Sat) For a quiet tipple in a sleek urban environment, duck into this intimate little wine bar. Cellar wines by the bottle come with a hefty price tag, but wines by the glass are available too.

Big Tide Brewing Company BREWERY
(www.bigtidebrew.com; 47 Princess St; 11am-midnight Mon-Sat, 3-9pm Sun) This subterranean brewpub is a cozy spot for a pint (try the Confederation Cream Ale or the Whistlepig Stout), a selection from the pub menu or a friendly game of trivia. All tap beer is brewed on the premises.

Imperial Theatre THEATER
(506-674-4100; www.imperialtheatre.nb.ca; 24 Kings Sq S) Now restored to its original 1913 splendor, this is the city's premier venue for performances ranging from classical music to live theater.

Shopping

Old City Market MARKET
(658 2820; 47 Charlotte St; 7:30-6pm Mon-Fri, to 5pm Sat) Wedged between North and South Market Sts, this sense-stunning food hall has been home to wheeling and dealing since 1876. The interior of the impressive brick building is packed with produce stalls, bakeries, fishmongers and butcher shops, as well as numerous counters selling a range of delectable prepared meals. Locals head to the lunch counter at Slocum and Ferris.

Information

Main post office (126 Prince William St)

Saint John Library (1 Market Sq; 9am-5pm Mon & Tue, 10am-9pm Wed & Thu, 10am-5pm Fri-Sun) Free internet access.

Saint John Regional Hospital (506-648-6000; 400 University Ave; 24hr) Northwest of the town center.

Saint John Visitors Centre – Barbours General Store (St Andrew's Bicentennial Green; 10am-6pm mid-May–Sep) Conveniently located in the old-fashioned Barbours General Store, at the central St Andrew's Bicentennial Green.

Saint John Visitors Centre – Reversing Rapids (450 Bridge Rd; ⏲9am-6pm mid-May–Sep, to 7pm Jul & Aug)

Visitor & Convention Bureau (☎506-658-2990; www.discoversaintjohn.com; City Hall, 15 Market Sq; ⏲9am-6pm mid-May–mid-Oct, to 7pm Jul & Aug) Knowledgeable, friendly staff. Ask for the self-guided walking-tour pamphlets.

 Getting There & Away

AIR

The airport is 5km east of town on Loch Lomond Rd toward St Martins. Air Canada runs daily flights to Toronto, Montréal and Halifax.

BOAT

The **Bay Ferries** (p393) sails daily between Saint John and Digby, Nova Scotia, year-round. The three-hour crossing can save a lot of driving.

Arrive early or call ahead for vehicle reservations, as the ferry is very busy in July and August. Even with a reservation, arrive an hour before departure. Walk-ons and cyclists should be OK any time. There's a restaurant and a bar.

BUS

Long-haul bus services are operated by **Maritime Bus** (☎506-672-2055; www.maritimebus.com; 125 Station St; ⏲8am-8pm Mon-Fri, 9am-8pm Sat & Sun). Routes include Fredericton ($25.50, 1½ hours) and Moncton ($34, two to four hours).

 Getting Around

Downtown (known as Uptown) Saint John sits on a square, hilly peninsula between the mouth of the Saint John River and Courtenay Bay. Kings Sq marks the nucleus of town, and its pathways duplicate the pattern of the Union Jack.

West over the Harbour Bridge is Saint John West. Many of the street names in this section of the city are identical to those of Saint John proper, and to avoid confusion, they end in a west designation, such as Charlotte St W. Saint John West has the ferries to Digby, Nova Scotia.

EASTERN FUNDY SHORE

Much of the rugged, unspoiled Eastern Fundy Shore from Saint John to Hopewell Cape has been incorporated into the Fundy Trail Parkway, both a 19km-long road and parallel 10km trail that will soon link up with the Fundy National Park. Indeed, hikers, cyclists, kayakers and all nature-lovers will be enchanted by this marvelous coast, edged by dramatic cliffs and tides. Since it's not yet possible to drive directly along the coastline from St Martins to Fundy National Park, a detour inland by Sussex is necessary.

St Martins

A 40km drive east of Saint John, St Martins is a winsome seaside hamlet surrounded by steep cliffs and flower-studded pastureland. Once a major wooden shipbuilding center, this (now sedate) spot springs to life in the summer. Hikers, bikers and scenic-drivers flock to the 19km Fundy Trail Parkway (p415), which starts east of the village and winds along a jaw-dropping stretch of coastline. In town, check out the impressive red sandstone sea caves of Mac's Beach, accessible by foot when the tide is low. The village's twin covered bridges are a popular photo op, so bring your camera.

 Tours

Red Rock Adventure KAYAKING, WALKING
(☎506-833-2231; www.redrockadventure.ca; 415 Main St; per person walking tours $30-50, kayaking trips $125) Located opposite the St Martins Wharf and its pretty covered bridge, Red Rock Adventures offers walking tours, including one of historic St Martins, and kayaking adventures.

River Bay Adventures KAYAKING
(☎506-663-9530; www.riverbayadventures.com; tours from $65) Runs two- to three-hour guided sea-kayaking trips to the caves and islands along the coast.

Sleeping & Eating

Salmon River B&B B&B $$
(☎506-833-1110; www.salmonriverbandb.com; 4 Snows Lane; r $105-125; ⏲mid-May–mid-Oct) Eight plain but pleasant rooms above Fiori's restaurant, run by the same folk. It's in a handy location bang in the middle of town.

The Caves RESTAURANT $
(82 Bayview Rd; mains $10-27; ⏲11am-7pm May-Oct, to 8:30pm Jul & Aug) One of two seaside spots known for their creamy chowder sitting side by side on Mac's Beach. Also serves salads, burgers and sandwiches.

Seaside Restaurant & Take Out SEAFOOD $$
(80 Big Salmon River Rd; mains $10-20; ⏲11am-8pm Mar-Nov) Right on Mac's Beach, the spacious but simple Seaside Restaurant serves fish-and-chips, scallops, chowder and more. Now you know you are on holiday.

Fundy National Park

Fundy National Park (www.pc.gc.ca/eng/pn-np/nb/fundy; daily permit adult/child/family $7.80/3.90/19.60; ⏲May-Oct) is the region's most popular. Highlights include the world's highest tides, the irregularly eroded sandstone cliffs and the wide beach at low tide that makes exploring the shore for small marine life and debris such a treat. The park is delightfully wooded and lush and features an extensive network of impressive hiking trails.

Activities

Cycling

Mountain biking is permitted on six trails: Goose River, Marven Lake, Black Hole, East Branch, Bennett Brook (partially open) and Maple Grove. Surprisingly, at last report there were no bicycle rentals in Fundy National Park or in nearby Alma. Contact the visitor centers to find current information on this.

Hiking

Fundy features 120km of walking trails, where it's possible to enjoy anything from a short stroll to a three-day trek. Several trails require hikers to ford rivers, so be prepared.

The most popular backpacking route is the **Fundy Circuit**, a three-day trek of 45km through the heart of the park. Hikers generally spend their first night at Tracy Lake and their second at Bruin Lake, returning via the Upper Salmon River. You must reserve your wilderness campsites online ($10 per night).

Enjoyable day hikes in Fundy National Park include the **Matthews Head Loop**, a 4.5km stretch with the nicest coastal views of the park (ranked moderate to difficult); and the **Third Vault Falls Trail**, a challenging one-way hike of 3.7km to the park's tallest falls. Alternatively, a short and pleasant stroll along a boardwalk takes you to **Dickson Falls**.

For serious, experienced hikers, the most popular one-night backcountry trek is the **Goose River Trail**. It joins the **Fundy Footpath** (not to be confused with Fundy Circuit). The Fundy Footpath is an undeveloped five-day wilderness trek and one of the most difficult in the province. While you can cycle to Goose River, the trail beyond can only be done on foot.

In summer rangers lead a variety of family-friendly educational programs, including night hikes.

Swimming

The ocean is pretty bracing here. A heated saltwater **swimming pool** (⏲11am-6:30pm Jul & Aug), located near the park's southern entrance, is currently being renovated. It, along with a splash pad, is due to reopen in 2017.

Sleeping

Point Wolfe Campground CAMPGROUND $
(☎877-737-3783; http://reservation.pc.gc.ca; campsites $26) This lovely campground (with 146 sites and 10 Otentiks), 8km southwest of the visitor center, is a little more secluded than the park's other mainstream campgrounds; it's the closest of all the campgrounds to the water. Twelve sites have water and electricity; this means that you may encounter RVs.

Chignecto North CAMPGROUND $
(☎877-737-3783; http://reservation.pc.gc.ca; campsites/RV sites $26/36) This beautifully wooded campground (with 251 sites in total) is popular with families as it has playgrounds and good facilities. Sites are secluded and private, despite its generous size, and it's a 4km drive from the beach. Also has yurts and Otentiks (both $100).

Headquarters Campground CAMPGROUND $
(☎877-737-3783; http://reservation.pc.gc.ca; campsites/RV sites $26/37, Otentiks/yurts $100/115) Of all the campsites in Fundy National Park, this is the most mainstream, and the only one close to both the beach and Alma village. It has 101 sites and offers yurts and Otentiks for those who don't have their own camping gear. It's not entirely wooded but the tent sites are grassy.

★ **Fundy Highlands Motel & Chalets** CABIN, MOTEL $$
(☎888-883-8639, 506-887-2930; www.fundyhighlands.com; 8714 Hwy 114; r $99, cabins from $125; ⏲May-Oct) The only private accommodations in Fundy National Park, this spot has charming little cabins, all with decks, kitchenettes and superlative views. On the same premises is a small, well-kept motel that offers rooms with kitchenettes. While not luxurious, it's got an appealing touch of retro and the delightful owners and staff ensure happy guests.

WORTH A TRIP

SCENIC DRIVE: KENNEBECASIS RIVER VALLEY

On a Saturday in summer, do what loads of Saint Johners do and take the **Gondola Point Ferry** (signposted off Hwy 1 at Exit 141) to the bucolic Kingston Peninsula, then follow Rte 845 east to the Kingston Farmers Market (p416). Sample the fresh fruits and vegetables and various ethnic foods on offer, or stop for lunch at the restored **1810 Carter House Tea Room** (www.facebook.com/1810CarterHouse; 874 Rte 845, Kingston; cakes & teas $5-9; ⏲9am-4pm Tue-Sat Jun-Aug), which is, of course, haunted – by a ghost who likes to tidy up and rearrange the books.

Leave the city folk behind, continuing on Rte 845 into the bustling community of Hampton, where you pick up Rte 121, which follows the northern side of the Kennebecasis River through farm country and the villages of Norton and Apohaqui into **Sussex** (population 4200).

Sussex is a working farming community nestled in a green valley dotted with dairy farms. The old-fashioned main street could be a movie set for a heartwarming 1950s coming-of-age story (but please, enough with the outdoor murals!). The well-preserved railway station houses the tourist information center, a small museum devoted to the area's military regiment, and an ice-cream parlour.

Gasthof Old Bavarian (☎506-433-4735; www.oldbavarian.ca; 1130 Knightville Rd, Studholm; mains $10-24; ⏲noon-10pm Fri-Sun) is the place for a truly memorable meal in the countryside. On a country road in a quiet valley settled by German and Dutch farmers, this place could have been transported – beer steins and all – from the Black Forest. Despite being more or less in the middle of nowhere, this place is always packed for dinner, so reservations are recommended. It's cash only.

Hang a left out of Gasthof's back onto the Knightville Rd, then left again onto Country View Rd at Anagance Ridge, then right onto Rte 890 into Petitcodiac. This stretch of road affords breathtaking vistas of rolling green countryside that will make you want to sell up, move here and raise chickens. If you can work up an appetite, stroll through the greenhouses and have a healthy organic lunch or tea and cake at **Cornhill Nursery & Cedar Cafe** (www.cornhillnursery.com; 2700 Rte 890, Cornhill; mains $9-15; ⏲10am-4pm Sun-Thu, to 9pm Fri & Sat May-Oct). From Petitcodiac you can rejoin Hwy 1, heading east to Moncton or west back to Fundy Park and Saint John. The views of the valley from Hwy 1 between Hampton and Sussex are also lovely.

Information

Headquarters Visitors Centre (☎506-887-6000; ⏲10am-6pm May-Oct, to 8pm Jun & Jul) At the park's southern entrance.

Getting There & Away

If heading east, it's yet not possible to drive directly along the coastline from St Martins to Fundy National Park; instead, a detour inland by Sussex is necessary. There's no public transport in the area.

Alma

The tiny, fully fledged fishing village of Alma is a useful supply center for Fundy National Park. It has accommodations, restaurants, a small gas station, grocery store, liquor outlet and laundry. Most facilities close in winter, when it becomes a ghost town, all except for the presence of Molly Kool (okay, statue of), the first female sea captain on the continent.

Fresh Air Adventure (☎800-545-0020, 506-887-2249; www.freshairadventure.com; 16 Fundy View Dr; tours from $69; ⏲Jun-Sep) offers myriad kayaking tours, from two-hour trips to multiday excursions, in and around Fundy.

Sleeping & Eating

Parkland Village Inn INN $$
(☎506-887-2313; www.parklandvillageinn.com; 8601 Hwy 114; r $125-165) Parkland Village Inn is a busy 60-year-old inn with comfy, renovated rooms, some with killer Bay of Fundy views. Breakfast is only included out of high season.

The Beach House B&B B&B
(☎506-887-9880; http://thebeachhousebedandbreakfastalma.com; 24 Foster Rd; r $100; ⏲May-Oct; P 📶) Run by friendly British expats, Lynn and Jeff, this modest, comfortable spot offers two spacious and neat rooms,

conveniently located yet off the busy main drag. Lynn supplies a generous breakfast and there's satellite TV.

Octopus's Garden Café CAFE $
(8561 Main St; snacks $4-12, mains $18; ⏲7am-10pm June-Oct; 📶) A welcome addition to Alma's seafood-oriented food scene, the Octopus's tentacles extend as far as Italy. It serves up fabulous homemade pasta and sauces, good panini and, joy of joy, dishes such as muesli and yogurt. And, wait for it, there's an espresso machine. And yes, staff seem to know how to use it (a rarity in these parts).

Kelly's Bake Shop BAKERY $
(www.facebook.com/homeofthestickybun; 8587 Main St; snacks from $2.50; ⏲7am-6pm) Sweet-lovers from far and wide flock here for one thing: the cinnamon sticky buns. Follow their lead.

Cape Enrage & Mary's Point

The 150-year-old lightstation at windblown and suitably named **Cape Enrage** (www.capeenrage.ca; off Rte 905; adult/child $6/5; ⏲10am-5pm mid-May–Oct, to 8pm Jul & Aug) is, these days, a not-for-profit organisation that earns its keep through the admission entry and adventure activities: **rappelling** off the steep rock faces and a zip line. Or you can simply wander the beach looking for fossils (low tide only!). Its lighthouse was one of the first 12 built in New Brunswick and still operates, albeit with an automated light.

At Mary's Point, 22km east of Cape Enrage, is the **Shepody Bay Shorebird Reserve** (Mary's Point Rd, off Hwy 915) FREE. From mid-July to mid-August hundreds of thousands of shorebirds, primarily sandpipers, gather here, at Mary's Point. Nature trails and boardwalks lead through the dikes and marsh. The interpretive center is open from late June to early September, but you can use the 6.5km of trails any time.

When all that activity gets you hungry, head to the **Cape House Restaurant** (www.facebook.com/CapeHouseRestaurant; mains $14-33; ⏲11:30am-11pm) in the original lighthouse-keeper's house, where you can enjoy the dramatic view while dining on pan-seared local scallops, hearty steaks and lobster chowder.

SOUTHEASTERN NEW BRUNSWICK

The southeastern corner of New Brunswick province is a flat coastal plain sliced by tidal rivers and salt marshes. Moncton, known as 'Hub City,' is a major crossroads with two well-known attractions where nature appears to defy gravity. Southeast, toward Nova Scotia, are significant historical and birdlife attractions.

Moncton

Once a major wooden shipbuilding port, Moncton is now the fastest-growing city in the Maritime provinces, with an economy built on transportation and call centers drawn here by the bilingual workforce. It's a pleasant, suburban city, with a small red-brick downtown along the muddy banks of the Petitcodiac River. There are some decent restaurants and bars, a bustling Acadian farmers market and an interesting museum at the Resurgo Place complex. Apart from that, there is little to detain the visitor.

Sights

Moncton Museum & Transport Discovery Centre MUSEUM
(☎506-856-4383; http://resurgo.ca/monctonmuseum; 20 Mountain Rd; adult/child/youth $10/5/7; ⏲10am-5pm Mon-Sat, noon-5pm Sun, closed Mon Sep-May) A visit to these interesting exhibitions will teach you about Moncton and its growth through artefacts and photographs that cover information on the Mi'kmaqs to the present day, plus Acadian history and agriculture and shipbuilding industries. The neighbouring Transport Discovery Centre, with its interactive displays relating to anything that moves, will appeal to kids especially. Check out the traveling exhibitions as well.

Magnetic Hill AMUSEMENT PARK
(cnr Mountain Rd & Hwy 2; admission per car $5; ⏲8am-8pm May-Sep) At Magnetic Hill, one of Canada's best-known (though not best-loved) attractions, gravity appears to work in reverse. Start at the bottom of the hill in a car, and you'll drift upward. You figure it out. After hours and out of season, admission is free. It's a goofy novelty, worth the head-scratching laugh, but all the money-

Moncton

Moncton

Sleeping

1 Auberge au Bois Dormant Inn............A1
2 C'mon Inn............B2
L'Hotel St James............(see 8)

Eating

3 Cafe Archibald............B1
4 Cafe C'est la Vie............C3
5 Calactus............C2
6 Manuka............C1
7 Pump House............D2

Drinking & Nightlife

8 Saint James' Gate............C3
9 Tide & Boar............C3

Entertainment

10 Capitol Theatre............C3

Shopping

11 Moncton Market............C3

generating, spin-off hoopla now surrounding the hill is a bit much. The family-oriented attractions include a zoo, a faux village hawking ice cream and souvenirs, and a water park. Magnetic Hill is located about 10km northwest of downtown off Mountain Rd.

Tours

Roads to Sea BUS

(506-850-7623; www.roadstosea.com; per person $173; May-Oct) Roads to Sea offers nine-hour bus tours to Hopewell Rocks (p422) and the Bay of Fundy (including the Fundy National Park and Cape Enrage, plus

WORTH A TRIP

HOPEWELL ROCKS

At Hopewell Cape, where the Petitcodiac River empties into Shepody Bay, are the **Hopewell Rocks** (www.thehopewellrocks.ca; off Hwy 114; adult/child/family $10/7.25/25.50, shuttle per person $2; ⌚9am-5pm May-Oct, longer hours summer; 🚻). The 'rocks' are bizarre sandstone erosion formations known as 'flowerpots,' which rise from the ocean floor. They resemble giant arches, stone mushrooms and ice-cream cones. Visitors marvel at their Dr Seussian look, making the rocks New Brunswick's top attraction (and certainly one of its most crowded). You can only walk amid the rocks at low tide – check the tide tables at any tourist office or area hotel. At high tide, the rock towers are still visible from the well-trafficked trails that wind through the woods above. For a different perspective, **Baymount Outdoor Adventures** (p422) offers two-hour kayaking tours around the rocks.

The park features a large interpretive center with educational displays, two cafes and picnic areas (stock up and take your own). In high season there are traffic jams and a lot of people (on the staircases). Despite tourist buses being available, Hopewell Rocks is easiest visited with your own wheels. There is a massive car park, though this gets packed in summer.

lighthouses and covered bridges). The company's unique marketing pitch is that you get to see extreme high and low tides in the same day. The bus seats 12 people.

Baymount Outdoor Adventures KAYAKING
(☎877-601-2660; www.baymountadventures.com; tours adult/child $69/59; ⌚Jun-Sep) Offers two-hour paddling tours in kayaks around the Hopewell Rocks.

Sleeping

Reservations are a good idea as the city is a major conference destination and often gets packed solid. Most chain hotels are clustered around Magnetic Hill and on Main St.

C'mon Inn HOSTEL $
(☎506-530-0905, 506-854-8155; www.monctonhostel.ca; 47 Fleet St; dm $37, r $78-83; P@📶) One of Moncton's two hostels is housed in a rambling Victorian two blocks from the bus station. Two small dorms (one female only) and private doubles with shared bathroom are nothing fancy, but they are clean and comfortable. There is a kitchen for guest use and lots of space for lounging on the verandahs. The owner, Monique, is very helpful.

Auberge au Bois Dormant Inn B&B $$
(☎506-855-6767; www.auberge-auboisdormant.com; 67 John St; s $85-140, d $95-150; 🚭❄📶) A gracious Victorian renovated with crisp modern flair. This gay-friendly establishment is on a quiet, tree-lined residential street and an excellent breakfast is served. Some of the rooms have access to balconies and the attic room is lovely.

L'Hotel St James BOUTIQUE HOTEL $$$
(☎888-782-1414; www.stjamesgatecanada.com; 14 Church St; r $169-289; P❄📶) On the 2nd floor of a 19th-century brick shop building, this downtown boutique hotel has 10 stylish urban-chic guest rooms that wouldn't look a bit out of place in Montréal or New York. Swank design touches include mod tile walls, crisp white linens, huge flat-screen TVs and iPod docks. Downstairs there's a popular pub (p423) and restaurant.

Eating

Two excellent markets, the **Dieppe Farmers Market** (www.marchedieppemarket.com; cnr Acadie Ave & Gauvin Rd, Dieppe; ⌚7am-1:30pm Sat) and **Moncton Market** (www.marchemonctonmarket.ca; 120 Westmoreland St; ⌚7am-2pm), are the places to buy fresh produce, baked goods and all kinds of ethnic dishes.

Calactus VEGETARIAN $
(☎506-388-4833; www.calactus.ca; 125 Church St; mains $11-17; ⌚11am-10pm; 🌿) Shangri-la for vegetarians! Enjoy the freedom to order anything off the globally inspired menu, which includes falafel plates, tofu cheese pizza and fried Indian *pakoras*. The natural wood, warm earth colors and burbling fountain create a soothing atmosphere. Wonderful service further heightens the experience.

Cafe C'est la Vie CAFE $
(www.cafecestlavie.ca; 75 Main St; snacks $6.50-7.50, bibimbap $10; ⌚7:30am-6pm Mon-Wed, to 8pm Thu & Fri, 9am-6pm Sat & Sun) A useful spot for a quick and easy filling lunch, such as good sandwiches, panini and salads. The

Korean owners serve up great *bibimbap* (Korean mixed rice dish) options.

Cafe Archibald FRENCH, CANADIAN $
(221 Mountain Rd; mains $8-13; ⏰9am-11pm Mon-Thu, to midnight Fri, 8:30am-midnight Sat & Sun) The bistro looks a bit tired but the cuisine is good. Crepes are the house specialty, whipped up in the open kitchen and served at redwood banquettes or on the screened-in porch. Alternatively, feast on the smoked salmon and mozzarella pizza with a leafy salad.

★ **Manuka** INTERNATIONAL $$
(☎506-851-5540; www.facebook.com/restomanuka; 184 Alma St; lunch mains $12-14, 3-course dinner menu $25; ⏰11am-2pm Tue-Fri, 5-9pm Wed-Sat) Housed incongruously in a yellow clapboard home, Belgian-owned Manuka is a bit like going to a friend's house for dinner...only the friend happens to be a very good cook. It's a fine-dining experience and one of the town's best gourmet options, where the chefs make everything from scratch.

Pump House BREWERY $$
(www.pumphousebrewery.ca; 5 Orange Lane; mains $12-15; ⏰11am-late Mon-Sat, noon-midnight Sun) The Pump is where the locals unwind and you can get a good burger, steak-based meal or wood-fired pizza. Of the brews made on the premises, the blueberry ale is popular and the Muddy River stout is tasty – or better still, try the beer sampling tray.

Little Louis' MODERN CANADIAN $$$
(☎506-855-2022; www.littlelouis.ca; 245 Collishaw St; mains $24-36; ⏰5-10pm) The odd location of this nouvelle cuisine bistro – upstairs in a faceless industrial strip mall – only adds to its speakeasy vibe. The atmosphere is cozy, with low lights, white tablecloths and jazzy live music. Local foodies rave about dishes like pan-seared scallop, fried beef, roasted cauliflower and beluga lentils.

Drinking & Entertainment

Saint James' Gate BAR
(www.stjamesgate.ca; 14 Church St; ⏰11am-2am Mon-Fri, 10am-2am Sat & Sun) An upmarket tavern with a hum that reverberates off its interior Moorish-style arches. The bar, with its faux-leather-and-studded seats, is a pleasant place to prop yourself up, while a small outdoor patio brings in the summer cocktail crowd. Also serves up fancy food (mains $18 to $33). Upstairs is the boutique hotel L'Hotel St James (p422).

Tide & Boar PUB
(☎506-857-9118; www.tideandboar.com; 700 Main St; ⏰11am-midnight Mon-Wed, to 2am Thu-Sat, noon-midnight Sun) A classy gastro pub that serves an interesting selection of beer (types you wouldn't find elsewhere), plus wines and quirky cocktails. Serves up a positive vibe and has music on weekends.

Capitol Theatre THEATER
(www.capitol.nb.ca; 811 Main St) You can sip a glass of wine during the interval at the grand Capitol Theatre, a 1922 vaudeville house that has been restored to its original glory. It's the venue for concerts and live theater throughout the year.

Information

Moncton Hospital (☎506-857-5111; 135 MacBeath Ave) Emergency room.

Moncton Public Library (https://monctonpubliclibrary.ca; 644 Main St; ⏰10am-5pm Thu-Mon, to 9pm Tue & Wed; 📶) Free internet access.

Visitors Information Centre (20 Mountain Rd, Resurgo Pl; ⏰10am-5pm Mon-Sat, noon-5pm Sun) This new center is in the recently opened Moncton Museum.

Getting There & Away

AIR

Greater Moncton International Airport (YQM; ☎506-856-5444; www.gmia.ca) is about 6km east of Champlain Place Shopping Centre via Champlain St. Air Canada runs daily flights to Toronto and Montréal.

BUS

Maritime Bus (☎506-854-2023; www.maritimebus.com; 1240 Main St) services Fredericton ($41.75, 2½ hours); Saint John ($33.75, two hours); Charlottetown, PEI ($41.75, three hours); and Halifax ($53.25, four hours).

CAR & MOTORCYCLE

There are six municipal parking lots around town, plus several private lots. Public parking meters cost $1 to $2.50 per hour. The municipal parking lot at Moncton Market on Westmorland St is free on Saturday, Sunday and evenings after 6pm. The city uses HotSpot Parking, a mobile payment service where you can pay for parking (and top up your metered space parking time) with your cell phone. Rates and maps can be found at www.moncton.ca.

TRAIN

With **VIA Rail** (☎506-857-9830; www.viarail.ca; 1240 Main St), the Ocean line (Montreal–Halifax) goes through northern New Brunswick, including Miramichi and Campbellton, and into Québec, on its way to Montréal. The train to Halifax (from $39) departs three days a week.

Getting Around

The airport is served by bus 20 from Champlain Pl nine times a day on weekdays. A taxi to the center of town costs about $15 to $20.

Codiac Transit (www.codiactranspo.ca) is the local bus system, with 40 wi-fi-equipped buses going all over town.

If you need wheels, there are car-rental desks at the airport, or try **Discount Car Rentals** (506-857-2309; www.discountcar.com; 470 Mountain Rd, cnr High St; 7:30am-5.30pm Mon-Fri, 8am-midday Sat) in town.

Sackville

Sackville is a small, very quaint university town that's in the right place for a pit stop – for birds and people (when in town, students double the population). The Sackville Waterfowl Park is on a major bird migration route.

Sackville Waterfowl Park BIRD SANCTUARY
(24hr) FREE The Sackville Waterfowl Park, across the road from the university off East Main St, is on a major bird migration route. It's worth taking a quick stroll around the boardwalk trail. Interpretive signs explain a little about the area.

The Black Duck CAFE $
(www.theblackduck.ca; 19 Bridge St; meals $6.50-8; 7am-9pm) Popular among university students for its contemporary vibe and offerings, this bakery and cafe whips up wonderful baked goods on the premises. Excellent grilled sandwiches, bagels and reasonable coffee are on the menu here; perfect for the full gamut of meals.

Mel's Tea Room DINER $
(17 Bridge St; mains $5-11; 8:30am-8:30pm) Take a fun trip down memory lane at Mel's Tea Room. It's been operating in the center of town since 1919, now with the charm of a 1950s diner – with a jukebox and prices to match. Serves up good breakfast egg dishes, plus milkshakes and ice cream.

Coy Wolf Bistro INTERNATIONAL $$
(506-536-8084; www.coywolfbistro.ca; 19 Bridge St; mains $20-30; 5-9pm Wed-Sun) This cutting-edge eatery should howl its menu from the rooftops, so to speak. It follows the 'eat sustainable and local' philosophy and whips up creative dishes and a constantly evolving menu. Think the likes of Northumberland clam chowder or the wolf burger, a local beef with gourmet filling. Funky decor without being try-hard cool is a bonus too.

Information

Sackville Visitor Information Centre (https://sackville.com/explore-sackville/visitor-information; 34 Mallard Drive; 9am-5pm May-Oct, to 8pm Jul & Aug)

Getting There & Away

Buses run between Sackville and Moncton ($14.25, 45 minutes, three daily).

NORTHUMBERLAND SHORE

New Brunswick's Northumberland Shore stretches from the Confederation Bridge to Kouchibouguac National Park and is dotted with fishing villages and summer cottages. Shediac, on all lobster-lovers' itineraries, is a popular resort town in a strip of summer seaside and beach playgrounds. A good part of the population here is French-speaking, and Bouctouche is an Acadian stronghold. Further north, Kouchibouguac National Park protects a swath of scenic coastal ecosystems.

Cape Jourimain

Set on the Northumberland Strait, the 675-hectare **Cape Jourimain Nature Centre** (506-538-2220; www.capejourimain.ca; Rte 16; admission free; 8am-7pm May-Oct) has 13km of walking trails, a museum with information on the area and a restaurant. A four-storey tower affords great views of the Confederation Bridge (that crosses to PEI) and the Cape Jourimain Lighthouse that was built in 1869. It's a twitcher's favorite for the migratory birds.

Shediac

Shediac, a self-proclaimed lobster capital, is a busy summer beach town and home of the annual July lobster fest. Have your picture taken with the 'World's Largest Lobster' sculpture – you can't miss it! (If the big claw doesn't grab your attention, it's handily located near the helpful tourist office).

It seems on any hot weekend that half the province is flaked out on the sand at **Parlee Beach**. South at Cap-Pelé are vast stretches of more sandy shorelines. Terrific **Aboiteau Beach** comprises over 5km of unsupervised sand, while others have all amenities and lifeguards.

Popular **Shediac Bay Cruises** (☎888-894-2002, 506-532-2175; www.lobstertales.ca; Pointe-du-Chene wharf; adult/child/family $70/48/204) takes passengers out on the water, pulls up lobster traps, then shows you how to cook and eat (that is, crack!) 'em.

After dinner, catch a flick at wonderfully retro **Neptune Drive-In** (www.neptunedrivein.ca; 691 Main St; per person/carload $10/20; ⊙Jun-Sep).

Sleeping & Eating

Auberge Gabriele Inn INN $$
(☎506-532-8007; www.aubergegabrieleinn.com; 296 Main St; r $125-170; P ⊖ ❄ ☎) One of the better options in Shediac, this attractive yellow building gets an extra tick for its good on-site restaurant. Rooms above are pleasant, if slightly dated, and offer a homey mix of antiques and modern.

Maison Tait INN $$
(☎506-532-4233; www.maisontaithouse.com; 293 Main St; r incl breakfast from $149; ☎) Lodgings at Maison Tait, a luxurious 1911 mansion, consist of nine sun-drenched rooms. Despite the fact they are outdated, they are upscale enough to enjoy.

Captain Dan's SEAFOOD $$
(www.captaindans.ca; Pointe-du-Chêne wharf; mains $11-28; ⊙11am-10pm Jun-Sep) Grab fresh seafood and strawberry daiquiris at always-packed Captain Dan's at the busy Pointe-du-Chêne wharf.

Paturel's Shore House SEAFOOD $$
(☎506-532-4774; www.paturelrestaurant.ca; 2 Cap Bimet Rd, Grand-Barachois; mains $17-33; ⊙4-10pm Tue-Sun late May–mid-Sep) Tops for dining out on fresh seafood is this simple place that resembles a large white house, located near to the shore. It's 7km east of Shediac; turn off Main St, direction north on Cap Bimet Road.

Information

Visitors Information Centre (☎506-533-7925; www.shediac.ca; 229 Main St; ⊙9am-5pm May-Sep, to 9pm Jul & Aug) Provides excellent information on New Brunswick and maps of Shediac and surrounds.

Getting There & Away

Maritime Bus (www.maritimebus.com) Runs from Shediac to Moncton ($12.25, 30 minutes, one daily) and Fredericton ($46, three hours, one daily); you must reserve 24 hours in advance. Buses also run from Shediac to Halifax, Nova Scotia.

Bouctouche

This small, surprisingly busy waterside town is an Acadian cultural focal point with several unique attractions. The visitors information center at the town's south entrance features an impressive boardwalk that extends over the salt marsh.

Sights & Activities

Irving Eco Centre PARK
(www.irvingecocentre.com; 1932 Rte 475, St-Édouard-de-Kent; ⊙interpretive center 10am-6pm late May-late Sep) On the coast 9km northeast of Bouctouche, this nature center protects and makes accessible 'La Dune de Bouctouche,' a beautiful, long sandspit jutting into the strait. The interpretive center has displays on the flora and fauna, but the highlight is the **boardwalk** that snakes above the sea grass along the dunes for 1km. The peninsula itself is 12km long, taking four to six hours to hike over the loose sand and back. There's a 12km hiking/cycling trail through mixed forest to Bouctouche town, which begins at the Eco Centre parking lot.

Le Pays de la Sagouine PARK
(☎506-743-1400; www.sagouine.com; 57 Acadie St; adult/student/family $20/15/45; ⊙10am-5:30pm Jul & Aug) Sitting on a small island in the Bouctouche River, this reconstructed Acadian village has daily programs in English and French. There are interactive cooking and craft demos, historical-house tours and live music, as well as several cafes in which to sample old-fashioned Acadian cuisine. In July and August there are regular supper theater performances (tickets from $20).

Olivier Soapery MUSEUM
(www.oliviersoaps.com; 831 Rte 505, Ste-Anne-de-Kent; ⊙9am-7pm Jun-Aug, 8:30am-4.30pm Mon-Fri Sep-May) An old-fashioned soap factory that promotes its 'museum'. It's really more of a store, with tons of luscious-smelling hand-molded soaps, but it does have regular scheduled talks on the soap-making process and a few interesting historical displays.

MR BIG

Kenneth Colin (KC) Irving was born in Bouctouche in 1899. From a modest beginning selling cars, he built up a business Goliath spanning oil refining, shipyards, mass media, transportation, pulp and paper, gas stations, convenience stores and more. The Irving name is everywhere. At least 8% of the province's workforce is employed by an Irving endeavor. KC died in 1992, leaving his three sons to carry on the vast Irving Group empire.

Sleeping & Eating

Chez les Maury CAMPGROUND $
(506-743-5347; www.fermemaury.com; 2021 Rte 475, St-Édouard-de-Kent; campsites $25-30; May-early Oct) On the grounds of a family-run vineyard, 200m from the Irving Eco Centre, this small, basic campground has toilets, showers and a tiny private beach across the way. A bell rings at 6.30pm for the 7pm free sampling of its wares – we're talking the likes of elderberry and strawberry wines (and they're good).

Le Vieux Presbytère INN $$
(506-743-5568; www.vieuxpresbytere.nb.ca; 157 Chemin du Couvent; apt $160;) This former priest's residence was once a popular religious retreat for Acadians from across the province. Several unpretentious but lovely apartments with high molded ceilings and delightfully sunny decor are up for grabs. All have kitchen and garden and water outlooks. There is a three-night minimum stay.

SCKS Société culturelle Kent-Sud CAFE $
(www.sckentsud.com; 5 Blvd Irving; snacks $9-11; 8am-3pm Tue-Sat Sep-May, to 5pm daily Jun-Aug) A little not-for-profit cafe and a pleasant place to stop for coffee (read: espresso machine) and simple French-style snack lunches using, where possible, local produce.

Restaurant La Sagouine ACADIAN $
(www.sagouine.nb.ca; 43 Blvd Irving; mains $8-18; 6am-10pm) Fried clams or a traditional Acadian dinner are on offer at this simple, old-fashioned spot that has (understandably) a slightly fuggy aroma of cooked seafood. In summer there are seats on the outdoor patio.

Information

Visitors Information Center (506-743-8811; www.tourismnewbrunswick.ca; 14 Acadie St; 10am-3pm late May-late Sep, longer hours summer)

Kouchibouguac National Park

Beaches, lagoons and offshore sand dunes extend for 25km here, inviting strolling, bird-watching and clam-digging. The **park** (www.pc.gc.ca; adult/child $7.80/3.90; 8am-dusk year-round) encompasses hectares of forest and salt marshes, crisscrossed or skirted by bike paths, hiking trails and groomed cross-country ski tracks. Kouchibouguac (*koosh*-e-boo-gwack), a Mi'kmaq word meaning 'River of Long Tides,' also has moose, deer and sometimes black bear.

Activities

Kouchibouguac has 60km of bikeways, crushed gravel paths that wind through the park's backcountry.

The calm, shallow water between the shore and the dunes, which run for 25km north and south, makes for a serene morning paddle. **Voyageur Canoe** (506-876-2443; per person $29.40) offers a must-do activity, especially for nonhikers. You paddle a four- or eight-person Canadian canoe to the sandy barrier islands, learning about the Mi'kmaq way of life plus viewing birds. The highlight is observing the grey seals; between 300 to 600 return to these feeding grounds each summer.

The park has 10 trails, mostly short and flat. The excellent **Bog Trail** (1.9km) is a boardwalk beyond the observation tower, and only the first few hundred meters are crushed gravel. The **Cedars Trail** (1.3km) is a lovely boardwalk trail with interpretation boards. The **Osprey Trail** (5.1km) is a loop trail through the forest. **Kelly's Beach Boardwalk** (600m one way) floats above the grass-covered dunes. When you reach the beach, turn right and hike around 6km to the end of the dune (the limits vary according to the location of the piping plover's nesting grounds). Take drinking water.

For swimmers, the lagoon area is shallow, warm and safe for children, while adults will find the deep water on the ocean side invigorating.

Sleeping

Kouchibouguac has two drive-in campgrounds and three primitive camping areas totaling 360 sites. The camping season is from mid-May to mid-October, and the park is very busy throughout July and August, especially on weekends. Camping reservations are necessary for the majority of the sites. The park entry fee is extra.

The three primitive campgrounds cost $10 per person per night; they have only vault (pump) toilets. You should take your own water to both Sipu and Petit-Large. Pointe-a-Maxime is the most difficult to get to (access by water only), but this does not translate into remote seclusion. There is a constant stream of passing motorized boat traffic from the fishing wharf nearby.

Cote-a-Fabien CAMPGROUND $
(☎877-737-3783; www.pccamping.ca; campsites drivein/walk-in $21/11) On the northern side of Kouchibouguac River, this is the best choice for those seeking a bit of peace and privacy. There is water and vault toilets, but no showers. Some sites are on the shore, others nestled among the trees, with a dozen walk-in sites (100m; wheelbarrows provided for luggage) for those who want a car-free environment. The Osprey hiking trail starts here.

South Kouchibouguac CAMPGROUND $
(☎877-737-3783; www.pccamping.ca; campsites/Otentiks $28/15) South Kouchibouguac is the largest campground. It's 13km inside the park near the beaches in a large open field ringed by trees, with Otentiks (a type of yurt), plus sites for tents and RVs, showers and a kitchen shelter.

Information

Visitors Center (☎506-876-2443; www.pc.gc.ca/kouchibouguac; 186 Rte 117; ⌚8am-4:30pm Oct-May, to 8pm Jul-Sep) Has maps and helpful staff with good information and maps. If the center is closed, visit the administration office opposite, which is open all year.

Getting There & Around

It's difficult to get to and around the park without a car or bicycle. From the park gate it's at least 10km to the campgrounds and beaches.

The nearest bus stop is in Rexton, 16km south of the park, where **Maritime** (☎800-575-1807; www.maritimebus.com; 126 Main St) buses stop at the Irving Circle K gas station. Daily buses head south to Moncton ($20.25) and head north to Miramichi ($14.25).

MIRAMICHI RIVER VALLEY AREA

In New Brunswick, the word Miramichi refers to both the city and the river, but it connotes even more: an intangible, captivating mystique. The spell the region casts emanates partially from the Acadian and Irish mix of folklore, legends, superstitions and tales of ghosts. It also seeps from the dense forests and wilderness of the area and from the character of the residents, who wrestle a livelihood from these natural resources. The fabled river adds its serpentine cross-country course, crystal tributaries and salmon fishing. The region produces some wonderful rootsy music and inspires artists, including noted writer David Adams Richards, whose work skillfully mines the temper of the region.

Miramichi

The working-class mill town of Miramichi (formerly Newcastle) is an amalgam of the towns of Chatham, Newcastle, Douglastown, Loggieville, Nelson and several others for a 12km stretch on both sides of the Miramichi River. Miramichi – with its First Nations plus Irish, Scottish and French background – is an English-speaking enclave in the middle of a predominantly French-speaking region.

Traditional folk-music enthusiasts might want to visit here for the **Irish Festival** (www.canadasirishfest.com; ⌚mid-Jul) and the **Miramichi Folksong Festival** (www.miramichifolksongfestival.com; ⌚early Aug), the oldest of its kind in North America.

Sights

Beaverbrook House MUSEUM
(www.beaverbrookhouse.com; 518 King George Hwy; ⌚9am-5pm Mon-Sat, 1-5pm Sun Jun-Sep) FREE In the central square of Miramichi is a statue to Lord Beaverbrook (1879–1964), one of the most powerful press barons in British history and a major benefactor of his home province. His ashes lie under the statue presented as a memorial to him by the town. The 1877 Beaverbrook House, Beaverbrook's boyhood home, is now a museum.

Sleeping & Eating

Enclosure Campground CAMPGROUND $
(☎506-622-0680; http://enclosurecampground.com; 8 Enclosure Rd, Derby Junction; campsites/

OFF THE BEATEN TRACK

HISTORICAL MUSEUM OF TRACADIE

Unmasking a little-known but gripping story, the **Historical Museum of Tracadie** (Rue du Couvent; adult/child $5/free; ⏲9am-5pm Mon-Fri, noon-5pm Sat & Sun mid-Jun–early Sep) focuses on the leprosy colony based here from 1849 to as late as 1965. It's the only place in Canada providing details on a leprosarium. The nearby cemetery has the graves of 59 victims of Hansen's Disease (leprosy). Tracadie-Sheila is 77km northeast of Miramichi.

RV sites $31/36; ⏲May-Oct) Southwest of Newcastle off Hwy 8, this former provincial park has a beautiful wooded area with spacious quasi-wilderness sites for tenters. Despite the website promoting a restaurant, this no longer operates.

Rodd Miramichi River HOTEL **$$**
(☎506-773-3111; www.roddmiramichi.com; 1809 Water St; r from $200; P❄🛜🏊) One of Miramichi's more upmarket hotels, the massive Rodd sprawls along the waterfront on the southern side of the river. It has all the mod cons of a business hotel, but with a resort-like feel. Check online for specials.

Governor's Mansion B&B **$$**
(☎506-622-3036; www.governorsmansion.ca; 62 St Patrick's Dr; r incl breakfast $89-159; P❄🛜) On the southern side of the river overlooking Beaubears Island is the creaky, but elegant, antique-filled Victorian Governor's Mansion (1860), onetime home of the first Irish lieutenant governor of the province. Rooms are lovely, if ever so tired, but it provides a cozy place to rest your head.

Bistro 140 INTERNATIONAL **$$**
(www.facebook.com/Bistro140; 295 Pleasant St; mains $15-25; ⏲11:30am-9pm Mon-Thu, 4-10pm Fri & Sat) It's referred to by locals as Miramichi's 'fine-dining option', and while that might be taking it a bit far, it's a friendly bistro and serves up decent food with surprising quirks and an emphasis on local (seasonal fiddleheads as a vegetable side). The entrance is through an office-style building.

Getting There & Away

Maritime Bus (☎506-773-5515; www.maritimebus.com; 186 King St) services depart from the Best Value Inn. Daily buses leave for Fredericton ($63.50, five hours), Saint John ($65.05, five hours) and Campbellton ($38.75, three hours).

The **VIA Rail station** (www.viarail.ca; 251 Station St, cnr George St) is in Newcastle. Trains from Montréal and Halifax stop here.

Miramichi River Valley

The Miramichi is actually a complex web of rivers and tributaries draining much of central New Brunswick. The main branch, the 217km-long Southwest Miramichi River, flows from near Hartland through forest to Miramichi where it meets the other main fork, the Northwest Miramichi.

For over a hundred years, the entire system has inspired reverent awe for its tranquil beauty and incredible Atlantic salmon fly-fishing. Famous business tycoons, international politicians, sports and entertainment stars and Prince Charles have all wet lines here. Even Marilyn Monroe is said to have dipped her toes in the water.

The legendary fishery has had some ups and downs with overfishing, poaching and unknown causes (perhaps global warming) affecting stocks, and there is ongoing debate as to the best way of sustaining levels: to introduce stocks or let nature take its course. While sportfishing is on the wane, the area is beautiful all the same.

Sights

Metepenagiag Heritage Park HISTORIC SITE
(☎506-836-6118; www.metpark.ca; 2156 Micmac Rd, Red Bank; adult/child $8/6; ⏲10am-5pm May-Oct) Forty kilometers northwest of Miramichi, on the Esk River, the Metepenagiag Heritage Park has interpretive tours of Mi'kmaq culture and history on a 3000-year-old archaeological site.

Atlantic Salmon Museum MUSEUM
(www.atlanticsalmonmuseum.com; 263 Main St, Doaktown; adult/child $5/3; ⏲9am-5pm Mon-Sat, noon-5pm Sun Jun-Oct) Learn about historic Doaktown's storied fishing history, plus wonderful artworks and anthropological gems at this lodgelike museum. Doaktown is 90km southwest of Miramichi.

Activities

The **Miramichi Trail**, a walking and cycling path along an abandoned rail line, is now partially complete, with 75km of the projected 200km usable.

At McNamee, 15km southwest of Doaktown, the pedestrian Priceville Suspension Bridge spans the river. It's a popular put-in spot for **canoeists and kayakers** spending half a day paddling downriver to Doaktown. Ask around about equipment rentals, shuttle services and guided trips for leisurely canoe, kayak or even tubing trips along the river.

Sportfishing is not something you come and do in a day. It's a multiday activity and, as such, few travellers take it up spontaneously. For those who do fish, it's tightly controlled for conservation. Licenses are required and all anglers must employ a registered guide. A three-day license for nonresidents is $60. All fish must be released. (Most of the salmon served up in the province is, in fact, salmon farmed in the Bay of Fundy.)

Sleeping

Beautiful rustic lodges and camps abound, many replicating the halcyon days of the 1930s and '40s. Check out www.miramichirivertourism.com for more accommodations and fishing outfitters.

Storeytown Cottages COTTAGE **$$**
(506-365-7636; www.facebook.com/storeytowncottages; 439 Storeytown Rd, Doaktown; cottages from $129) Run by a dynamic young couple, this place has simple but cozy log cabins on the riverbank. Outdoor activities include tubing ($10), kayaking ($35), canoeing ($40) and stand-up paddleboarding ($35). For $5, they'll shuttle you upriver so you can float or paddle back down. Bring mosquito repellent.

Shopping

WW Doak & Sons SPORTS & OUTDOORS
(www.doak.com; 331 Main St, Doaktown; 8am-5pm Mon-Sat) WW Doak & Sons is one of Canada's best fly-fishing shops.

Information

Visitor Information Centre (www.doaktown.com; 263 Main St, Doaktown; 9am-5pm Mon-Sat, noon-5pm Sun Jun-Oct) The tourist office is in the Salmon Museum in Doaktown, the center of most valley activity.

NORTHEASTERN NEW BRUNSWICK

The North Shore, as it is known to New Brunswickers, is the heartland of Acadian culture in the province. The region was settled 250 years ago by French farmers and fishers, starting from scratch again after the upheaval of the Expulsion (when the British deported some 14,000 Acadians from the region), frequently intermarrying with the original Mi'kmaq inhabitants. The coastal road north from Miramichi, around the Acadian Peninsula and along Chaleurs Bay to Campbellton passes through small fishing settlements and peaceful ocean vistas. At Sugarloaf Provincial Park, the Appalachian Mountain Range comes down to the edge of the sea. Behind it, stretching hundreds of kilometers into the interior of the province, is a vast, trackless wilderness of rivers and dense forest, rarely explored.

Caraquet

The oldest of the Acadian villages, Caraquet was founded in 1757 by refugees from forcibly abandoned homesteads further south. It's now the quiet, working-class center of the peninsula's French community. Caraquet's colorful, bustling fishing port, off Blvd St-Pierre Est, has an assortment of moored vessels splashing at the dock. East and West Blvd St-Pierre are divided at Rue le Portage.

It's a self-proclaimed 'cultural capital of Acadia'; each August the town is the proud host of the massive **Festival Acadien** (www.festivalacadien.ca; Aug), a historic occasion that celebrates their survival. It draws 100,000 visitors, and more than 200 performers including singers, musicians, actors, and dancers from Acadia and other French regions (some from overseas).

Sights

Acadian Historic Village PARK
(www.villagehistoriqueacadien.com; 14311 Hwy 11; adult/student/family $20/16/45; 10am-6pm Jun-Sep) Acadian Historic Village, 15km west of Caraquet, is a major historical reconstruction set up like a village of old. Thirty-three original buildings have been relocated to the site, and animators in period costumes reflect life from 1780 to 1880. Several hours are required to have a good look, and then you'll definitely want to eat. For that, there

are old-fashioned sit-down Acadian meals at La Table des Ancêtres, the 1910 historical menu at the Château Albert dining room and several snack bars.

The village has a program for kids ($35), which provides them with a costume and seven hours of supervised historical activities.

Sleeping & Eating

★Maison Touristique Dugas INN, CAMPGROUND $
(506-727-3195; www.maisontouristiquedugas.ca; 683 Blvd St-Pierre W; campsites/r from $25/89, cabins $119) Five generations of the ultrafriendly Dugas family have run this rambling, something-for-everyone property, 8km west of Caraquet. The homey, antique-filled 1926 house has 11 rooms, four with shared bathrooms. There are five clean, cozy cabins with private bathrooms and cooking facilities, a small field for RVs beyond that, and a quiet, tree-shaded campground with access to the water for tenters.

★Hotel Paulin HOTEL $$
(506-727-9981, 866-727-9981; www.hotelpaulin.com; 143 Blvd St-Pierre W; r incl breakfast $149-289; P) Scrimp elsewhere and splurge on a night at the exquisite Hotel Paulin. This vintage seaside hotel overlooking the bay was built in 1891 and has been run by the Paulin family since 1905. Good old-fashioned service remains and the rooms are sunny and polished, done up in crisp white linens, lace and quality antiques.

Château Albert INN $$$
(506-726-2600; www.villagehistoriqueacadien.com/chateauanglais.htm; Acadian Historic Village; d incl dinner & site visit $150; P) For complete immersion in the Acadian Historic Village, spend the night in early 20th-century style – no TV and no phone, just a charming, quiet room restored to its original 1909 splendor (with a modern bath). The original Albert stood on the main street in Caraquet until it was destroyed by fire in 1955. Packages are available that include breakfast and a site visit.

Mitchan Sushi JAPANESE $$
(www.mitchansushi.com; 114 Blvd St-Pierre West; sushi $6-10, mains $8-14; 5-8pm Wed-Sat) A tasteful, ordered experience where beautifully concocted Japanese morsels comprise fresh local seafood. Unfortunately, it's not open daily; check hours.

Le Caraquette CANADIAN $$
(89 Blvd St-Pierre Est; mains $8-15; 6-9pm Mon-Sat, 7-9pm Sun) Overlooking the harbor, this no-fuss, family diner-style restaurant serves Maritime provinces standards including fried clams and mayonnaise shrimp salad, along with French Canadian specialties like poutine and smoked-meat sandwiches.

Information

Visitor Information Centre (202-726-2676; www.caraquet.ca/en/tourism/discover-caraquet; 39 Blvd St-Pierre West; 9am-5pm Jun-Sep) Information on all things local, and the Acadian Historic Village.

Getting There & Away

Public transportation around this part of the province is very limited, as Maritime Bus services don't pass this way. Local residents wishing to connect with the bus or train in Miramichi or Bathurst use a couple of van shuttles; ask for details at the **visitor information centre**.

Bathurst

A former mining town, the tranquil, pretty city of Bathurst is situated on Bathurst Harbour, and enclosed by two peninsulas: Carron Point and Alston Point. The town itself is joined by a bridge that spans the harbor, with most things of interest for the tourist on the southern side.

Several historic buildings were damaged by fire in 2015, but the streets still are a pleasant place for a stroll and to stretch your legs. The revamped harborfront is where you'll find the tourist office and a couple of restaurants. There's not a lot to do here, but it's a good jumping-off point to nature-based activities around the town and wider Chaleur Bay area: Youghall Beach (near Alston Point), the lovely Daly Point Nature Reserve, and the Pabineau Falls.

Bathurst's original name was Nepisiquit, a Mi'qmaq word meaning 'Rough Waters'.

Sights

Point Daly Reserve NATURE RESERVE
(Carron Dr) Located 5.5km east of Bathurst, this lovely nature reserve has various marked trails, all courtesy of a former mining company. In fall you can see the Canada geese on their migratory voyage. There are also eagles, osprey and lovely trees and shrubs. Informative boards are located throughout the trails.

Bathurst Heritage Museum MUSEUM
(☎506-546-9449; 360 Douglas Ave; ⏲8:30am-4:30pm late Jun–mid-Aug) Bathurst's history is proudly displayed here with artifacts galore, from photos to documents.

Sleeping & Eating

Auberge & Bistro l'Anjou B&B $$
(http://aubergedanjou.com; 587 Principale St, Petit Rocher; r $89-108) Located 30km northwest of Bathurst in the small village of Petit-Rocher, this is the perfect spot for anyone wishing to stay in the region. It's both a comfortable B&B and smart bistro in one. Locals rave about its cuisine (with instructions not to miss the sugar pie). The bistro is open are Wednesday to Sunday; check website for hours.

L'Étoile du Havre B&B B&B $$
(☎506-545-6238; www.etoileduhavre.com; 405 Youghall Dr; r $125; P ❄ 📶) Situated in a tranquil location opposite a golf course, and en route to Youghall Beach, this designer-sleek, open-plan, ultracontemporary B&B with six rooms looks like it's out of the pages of an LA showroom magazine. Cooked breakfasts (the likes of pancakes) are served to all in the massive open-plan kitchen-lounge room. It's gay friendly.

Pabineau Seafood Restaurant SEAFOOD $
(☎506-546-5150; www.facebook.com/pabineauseafood; 1295 Pabineau Falls Rd, Pabineau First Nation; mains $8-20; ⏲11am-8pm Thu-Sun May-Sep) Located near the site of the **Pabineau Falls** (Pabineau Falls Rd, Pabineau First Nation), this small eatery, run by the local First Nations group, is the spot to pick up your picnic supplies before heading to the rapids. Lobster rolls and fried shrimp, scallops and clams are on the menu. Call ahead to check it's open.

Nectar INTERNATIONAL $$$
(www.facebook.com/nectarcuisineinternationale; 50 Douglas Ave; mains $26-36; ⏲9am-8pm Mon-Sat) Perched over the Bathurst Harbour, Nectar caters to everyone from cafe-goers (downstairs) to those after a light lunch to heftier (and pricier) fine-dining options (upstairs). The ambitious menu includes everything from lobster sandwiches to salmon dishes and a variety of salads. A smart martini lounge is on the premises too. Popular among the local businesspeople and a safe option.

Information

Tourist office (☎506-548-0412; www.bathurst.ca; Bathurst Harbor; ⏲9am-4pm Mon-Fri Sep-Apr, to 5pm May, to 8pm Jun-Aug) This helpful office will direct you to nature-based activities around Bathurst.

Getting There & Away

Maritime Bus (www.maritimebus.com) services Bathurst. Handy links include Fredericton ($68.50, six hours, one daily), Campbellton ($25.50, 1½ hours, one daily), Saint John ($63.50, 6¼ hours, one daily) and Moncton ($46, 3¼ hours, one daily). Note: for Shediac ($41.75, 2¾ hours, one daily) you must book 24 hours ahead. See the website for services to Sydney, Nova Scotia.

WORTH A TRIP

SCENIC DRIVE: THE ACADIAN PENINSULA

Take a run out to the very northeastern tip of the province – a chain of low, flat islands pointing across the Gulf of St Lawrence to Labrador. Rte 113 cuts across salt marsh and scrub arriving first in **Shippagan**, home of the province's largest fishing fleet, where crab is king. Hop the bridge to **Lamèque**, a tidy fishing village that has hosted the **Lamèque International Baroque Festival** (☎506-344-5846; www.festivalbaroque.com; ⏲late Jul) for over 30 years. Note the red, white and blue Acadian flags flying from nearly every porch. Grab a light lunch at the excellent **Aloha Café-Boutique** (41 Rue Principale, Lamèque; mains $7-9; ⏲7am-4pm Mon-Thu, to 9pm Fri, 8:30am-4pm Sat & Sun; 📶). Rte 113 continues north to **Miscou Island**. The road dead-ends at a beautiful lighthouse. On the way back, just before you cross the bridge, at the quay, gorge yourself on lobster and seafood at **La Terrasse à Steve** (Rte 113, Quai de Miscou, Miscou Island; mains from $20, seafood platter $130; ⏲8am-8pm May-Sep). The good news? Fresh fish and not a skerrick of frying.

Campbellton

Campbellton is a pleasant but unremarkable mill town on the Québec border. The lengthy Restigouche River, which winds through northern New Brunswick and then forms the border with Québec, empties to the sea here. The Bay of Chaleur is on one side and dramatic rolling hills surround the town on the remaining sides. Across the border is Matapédia and Hwy 132 leading to Mont Joli, 148km into Québec.

The last naval engagement of the Seven Years' War was fought in the waters off its coast in 1760. The Battle of Restigouche marked the conclusion of the long struggle for Canada by Britain and France.

These days, there are really only two reasons to come here: to transit to/from Québec, or to hike, ski and camp at **Sugarloaf Provincial Park** (www.parcsugarloafpark.ca; 596 Val d'Amours Rd, Atholville). Dominated by Sugarloaf Mountain, which rises nearly 400m above sea level and looks vaguely like one of its other namesakes in Rio, the park is off Hwy 11 at Exit 415. From the base, it's just a half-hour walk to the top – well worth the extensive views of the town and part of the Restigouche River. Another trail leads for 4.2km around the bottom of the hill.

Sleeping

Campbellton Lighthouse Hostel HOSTEL $
(☎506-759-7044; www.hihostels.com/hostels/hi-campbellton; 1 Ritchie St; dm $16.50; ⏲Jun-Aug; 📶) The Campbellton Lighthouse Hostel, a converted lighthouse by the Restigouche River, makes for an illuminatingly novel stay. Dorms are clean and separate male and female arrangements apply. It's near the Maritime bus stop and Campbellton's 8.5m salmon sculpture.

Dans les Draps de Morphée B&B $
(☎506-329-0274; www.drapsdemorphee.com; 7 Ritchie St; r $75-100) A spotless B&B with four rooms (plus loft apartment) in a pleasant house and in a central location near the lighthouse. The hearty cooked breakfast is served in the owners' kitchen.

Sugarloaf Provincial Park CAMPGROUND $
(☎506-789-2366; www.parcsugarloafpark.ca; 596 Val d'Amours Rd; campsites/RV sites $28/36, yurts $43; ⏲end May-end Sep) Four kilometers from downtown Campbellton, Sugarloaf Provincial Park has 76 campsites in one of the most beautiful nonwild camping areas around. RVs have separate areas, though you may still hear generator noise. If you don't have a tent you can opt for a yurt. The communal kitchen has a wood stove for baking.

Maison McKenzie House B&B B&B $$
(☎506-753-3133; www.bbcanada.com/4384.html; 31 Andrew St; r with shared bath incl breakfast $75-100; P🚭📶) Maison McKenzie House B&B is a homey 1910 house handy to downtown. For $60, the folks here will rent you a kayak and drop you off upriver.

Information

Provincial tourist office (☎506-789-2367; www.tourismnewbrunswick.ca; 56 Salmon Blvd; ⏲9am-5:30pm May & Jun, 9am-7pm Jul & Aug, 9:30am-6pm Sep & Oct) This helpful office is next to City Centre Mall and near the 8.5m giant salmon feature.

Getting There & Away

Maritime Bus (☎506-753-6714; www.maritimebus.com; 157 Roseberry St; ⏲6am-9pm) services stop at the Pik-Quik convenience store, near Prince William St. Buses departs daily for Fredericton ($82, 7½ hours) and Moncton ($59, five hours). Twice a day (morning and afternoon), an **Orléans Express** (www.orleansexpress.com) bus leaves from the Pik-Quik for Gaspé ($41, six hours) and Québec City ($91, seven hours).

The **VIA Rail station** (www.viarail.ca; 99c Roseberry St) is conveniently central. Trains depart three times weekly to Québec City ($95 including tax, eight hours).

Prince Edward Island

Includes ➡

Best Places to Eat

- Inn at Bay Fortune (FireWorks) (p447)
- New Glasgow Lobster Supper (p453)
- Landmark Café (p448)
- Harbourview Restaurant (p444)
- Water Prince Corner Shop & Lobster Pound (p442)

Best Places to Sleep

- Fairholm National Historic Inn (p440)
- Dalvay by the Sea (p449)
- Barachois Inn (p452)
- Great George (p440)
- Around the Sea (p452)

Why Go?

Prince Edward Island (PEI) is as pretty as a storybook: Lucy Maud Montgomery's classic *Anne of Green Gables*, to be exact. Like Anne Shirley, the book's heroine, loved the world over, the island too is a redhead – from coast to coast, rich, sienna-colored soil nourishes luminous green pastures and shores are lined with rose and golden sand. Anne's beloved landscape, a patchwork of lush rolling fields, tidy gabled farmhouses and seaside villages has barely changed.

The island is, as far as islands go, largely self-sufficient and has gained a reputation as a farm- and ocean-to-table culinary destination. Its size makes it easy to explore by car or bike – the island's Confederation Trail is one of the world's best cycling destinations. And, like the rest of the Maritime provinces, its people are warm and inviting.

When to Go

Charlottetown

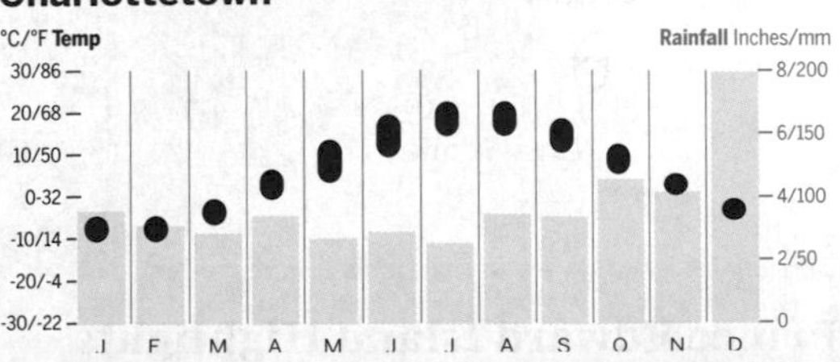

Jun Enjoy the spring calm and blooming wildflowers before the crowds hit.

Jul & Aug The entire island is in festival mode with live music and Lobster Suppers nightly.

Sep Traditional music and a bevy of food events mark PEI's Fall Flavours Festival.

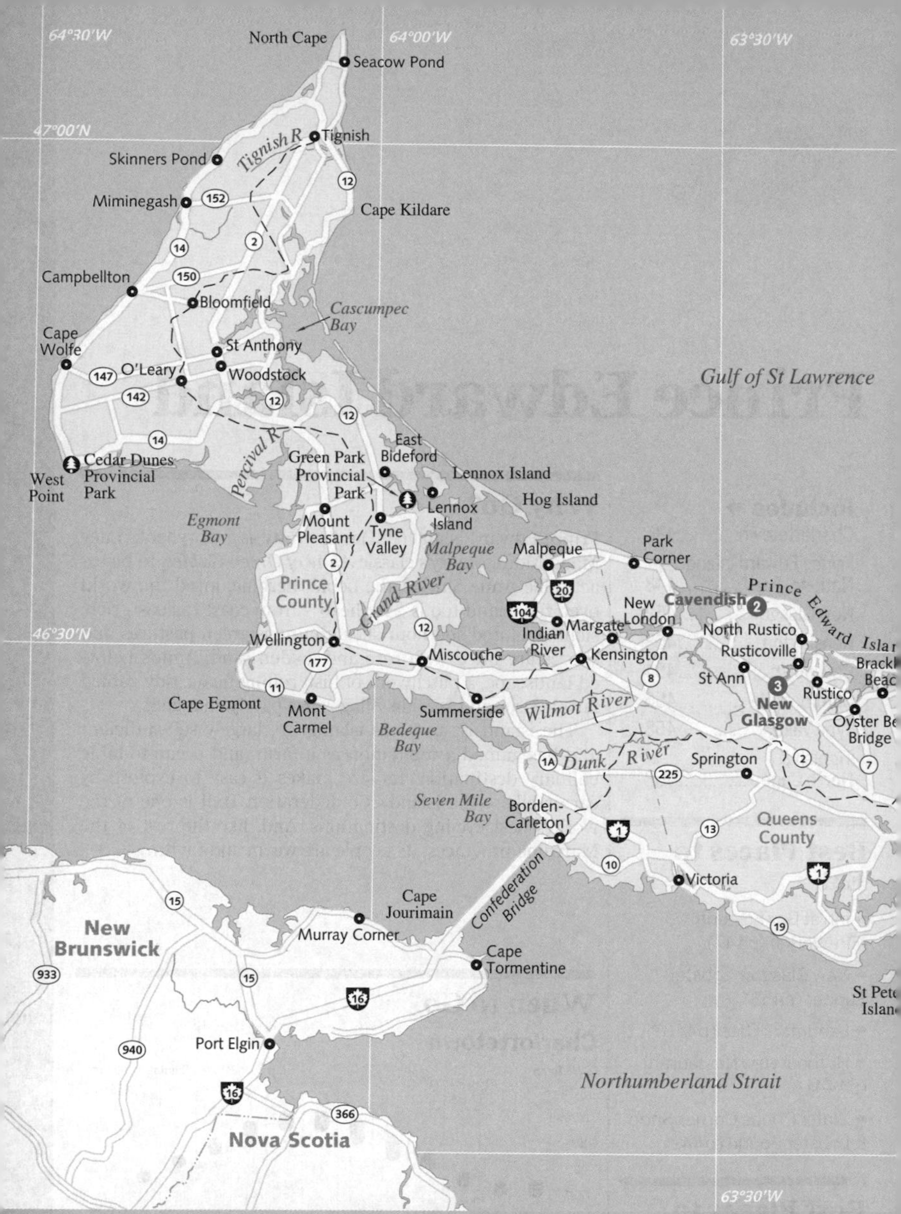

Prince Edward Island Highlights

❶ **Charlottetown** (p436) Staying in a heritage B&B, walking the scenic waterfront and enjoying fine dining.

❷ **Green Gables Heritage Place** (p454) Finding yourself among the pages of *Anne of Green Gables*, in Cavendish.

❸ **New Glasgow Lobster Supper** (p453) Gorging yourself on lobster at PEI's original crustacean extravaganza.

❹ **Greenwich Interpretation Centre** (p447) Walking the floating boardwalk into the undulating dunes.

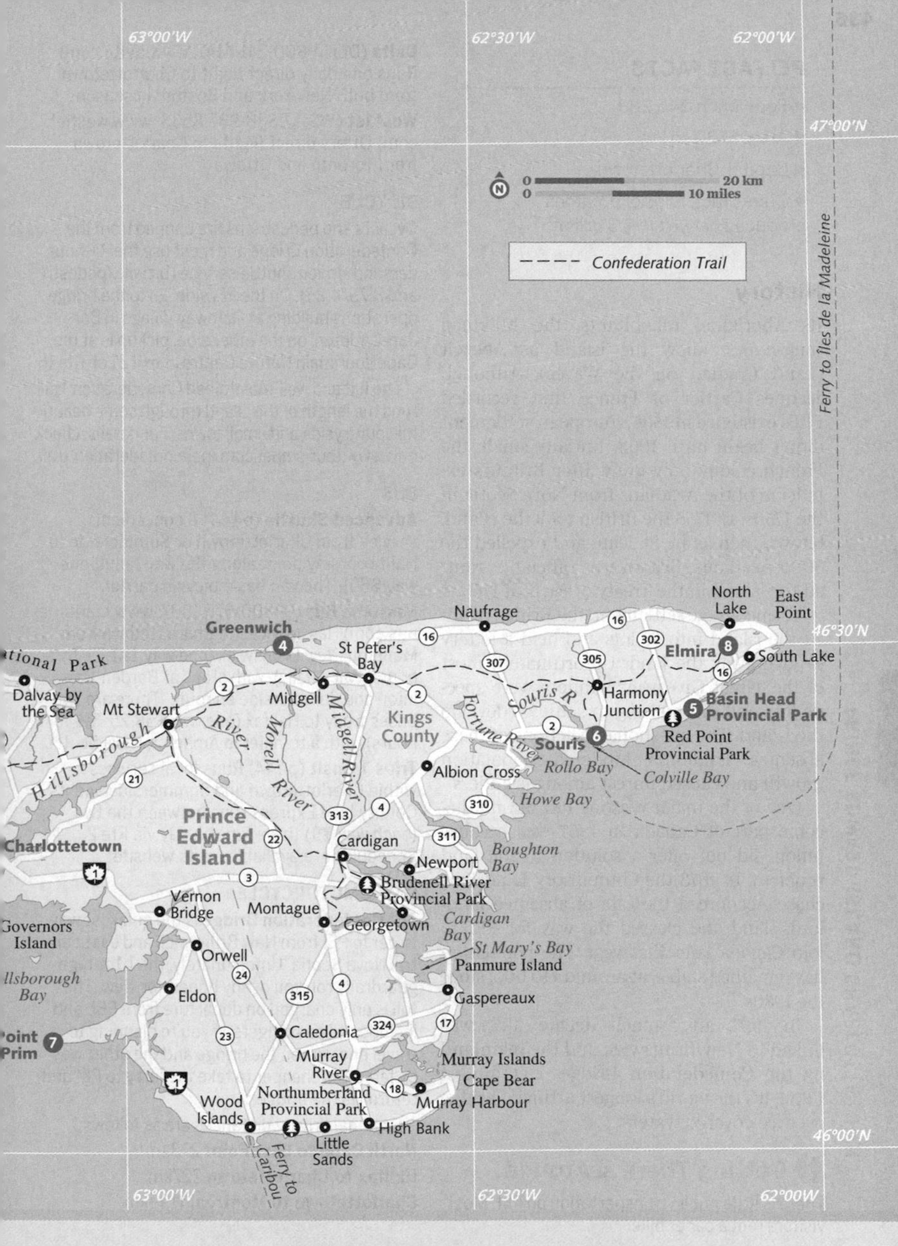

5 Basin Head Provincial Park (p446) Listening to the sounds of the singing sands beneath your feet before taking a dip.

6 Inn at Bay Fortune (p447) Indulging in this dining sensation, near Souris.

7 Point Prim Lighthouse (p441) Imagining yourself as a lonely lighthouse keeper from another time.

8 Elmira Railway Museum (p446) Reliving childhood and taking ownership of your inner train-spotter.

PEI FAST FACTS

- Population: 146,283
- Area: 5700 sq km
- Capital: Charlottetown
- Quirky fact: Kilos of potatoes produced per year – 1.3 billion

History

Its Aboriginal inhabitants, the Mi'kmaq (mig-*maw*), knew the island as Abegeit (Land Cradled on the Waves). Although Jacques Cartier of France first recorded PEI's existence in 1534, European settlement didn't begin until 1603. Initially small, the French colony only grew after Britain's expulsion of the Acadians from Nova Scotia in the 1750s. In 1758 the British took the island, known then as Île St Jean, and expelled the 3000 Acadians. Britain was officially granted the island in the Treaty of Paris of 1763.

To encourage settlement, the British divided the island into 67 lots and held a lottery to give away the land. Unfortunately, most of the 'Great Giveaway' winners were speculators and did nothing to settle or develop the island. The questionable actions of these absentee landlords hindered population growth and caused unrest among islanders.

One of the major reasons PEI did not become part of Canada in 1867 was because union did not offer a solution to the land problem. In 1873 the Compulsory Land Purchase Act forced the sale of absentee landlords' land and cleared the way for PEI to join Canada later that year. The population has remained stable, at around 140,000, since the 1930s.

In 1997, after much debate, PEI was linked to New Brunswick and the mainland by the Confederation Bridge – at almost 13km, it's the world's longest artificial bridge over ice-covered waters.

Getting There & Around

There is little public transportation on PEI. Most visitors rent a car or bike.

AIR

Charlottetown Airport (p444) Located 8km from town and serves all flights entering and leaving the province.

Air Canada (AC; ☎888-247-2262; www.aircanada.com) Has daily flights to Charlottetown from Halifax and Toronto, and from Montréal in the high season (June to September).

Delta (DL; ☎800-241-4141; www.delta.com) Runs one daily direct flight to Charlottetown from both New York and Boston, in season.

WestJet (WS; ☎888-937-8538; www.westjet.com) Offers direct flights to Charlottetown from Toronto and Ottawa.

BICYCLE

Cyclists and pedestrians are banned from the Confederation Bridge and must use the 24-hour, demand-driven shuttle service (bicycle/pedestrian $8.75/4.25). On the PEI side, go to the bridge operations building at Gateway Village in Borden-Carleton; on the other side, pickup is at the Cape Jourimain Nature Centre at exit 51 on Rte 16.

The flat and well-maintained Confederation Trail runs the length of the island through some beautiful countryside and small towns. For details, check out: www.tourismpei.com/pei-confederation-trail.

BUS

Advanced Shuttle (p444) A convenient service from Charlottetown or Summerside to Halifax or any point along the way (adult one-way $69). The van has a bicycle carrier.

Maritime Bus (☎800-575-1807; www.maritimebus.com) Has services to Charlottetown from Moncton, New Brunswick (one way $41.75, three hours, twice daily), with stops at Borden-Carleton and Summerside en route. There are two buses a day to Halifax (one way $58.25, 5½ hours), with a transfer in Amherst, Nova Scotia.

Trius Transit (p444) Runs local services within Charlottetown and Summerside and its County Line Express runs between the two (each way $9) three times a day via Rte 2. Schedules are available on its website.

CAR & MOTORCYCLE

The **Confederation Bridge** is the quickest way to get to PEI from New Brunswick and east central Nova Scotia. Unfortunately, the 1.1m-high guardrails rob you of any hoped-for view. The toll is only charged on departure from PEI, and includes all passengers. If you're planning to travel one way on the bridge and the other way by ferry, it's cheaper to take the ferry to PEI and return via the bridge.

Regional driving distances are as follows:

North Cape to East Point 273km
Halifax to Charlottetown 227km
Charlottetown to Montréal 1199km

CHARLOTTETOWN

POP 34,562 / ☎902

If it weren't for its isolation and inhospitable winters, charming Charlottetown might just be one of the loveliest, affordable places to live, anywhere. Failing that, a visit is recommended. This little city is the perfect size with big-city benefits minus the unpleasant stuff like overcrowding, pollution and the need for public transportation.

Historically, in 1864, it was here that the Confederation Conference set in motion a series of events that led to the birth of the nation of Canada.

There is, however, a burgeoning restaurant scene capitalizing on the island's abundant seafood and fresh produce, combined with its wealth of talented graduates from the Culinary Institute of Canada. Add a lively cultural scene and you have a capital city oozing small-town feel and appeal.

History

Charlottetown is named after the exotic consort of King George III. Her African roots, dating back to Margarita de Castro Y Sousa and the Portuguese royal house, are as legendary as they are controversial.

While many believe the city's splendid harbor was the reason Charlottetown became the capital, the reality was less glamorous. In 1765 the surveyor-general decided on Charlottetown because he thought it prudent to bestow the poor side of the island with some privileges. Thanks to the celebrated 1864 Confederation Conference, however, Charlottetown is etched in Canadian history as the country's birthplace.

Sights

Charlottetown isn't top-heavy on sights. That said, think of the whole of the downtown area (known as Old Charlottetown), with its beautifully preserved and colorful colonial buildings, and the wealth of boutiques, bistros and bars they contain, as the main event.

★Victoria Park — PARK

(www.city.charlottetown.pe.ca/victoriapark.php) Dedicated in 1873, Charlottetown's most popular and beautiful waterfront green space has 16 hectares of loveliness for you to enjoy on a fine day.

COWS Creamery — FACTORY

(902-566-5558; www.cowscreamery.ca/tours; 397 Capital Dr; 10am-6pm) FREE Who doesn't love a self-guided, buttery, *fromagerie* and ice-creamery tour that spits you out in the mecca retail store that is this PEI institution's award-winning dairy heaven, hmm?

St Dunstan's Basilica — NOTABLE BUILDING

(902-894-3486; www.stdunstanspei.com; 45 Great George St; 9am-5pm) FREE Rising from the ashes of a 1913 fire, the three towering stone spires of this Catholic, neo-Gothic basilica are now a Charlottetown landmark. The marble floors, Italianate carvings and decoratively embossed ribbed ceiling are surprisingly ornate.

Government House — NOTABLE BUILDING

(902-368-5480; 165 Richmond St; 10am-4pm Mon-Fri Jul & Aug) FREE This striking colonial mansion, with its grand hall, Palladian window and Doric columns, has been home to PEI's lieutenant governors since 1835. As it is a private residence, the house is not open to the public outside the months of July and August when guided tours are conducted.

Beaconsfield Historic House — NOTABLE BUILDING

(902-368-6603; www.peimuseum.com; 2 Kent St; adult/student/family $5/4/14; 10am-5pm) With its crowning belvedere, intricate gingerbread trim and elegant 19th-century furnishings, Beaconsfield House is the finest Victorian mansion in Charlottetown. Have a wander or sit on the verandah and be stunned by the view.

Tours

Self-guided walking-tour booklets are available at the visitor center (p443).

★Happy Clammers — FISHING

(866-887-3238; www.experiencepei.ca/happy-clammers; Rte 1, Pinette; adult/child $100/25, minimum 4 people; Mon-Sat Jul-Oct , times vary with tides) Many folks come out this way to dig razor, soft-shell, bar and quahog clams. Once you've filled your buckets, go home to Gilbert and Goldie's house to steam up your catch and dine on other treats cooked up by this charming local family.

★Confederation Players Walking Tours — WALKING

(800-565-0278; www.confederationcentre.com; 6 Prince St; adult/child $15/8; daily Jul-Aug) There is no better way to tour Charlottetown. Playing the fathers and ladies of Confederation, actors garbed in 19th-century dress educate and entertain through the town's historic streets. Tours leave from Founders' Hall, with a variety of themes and itineraries to choose from.

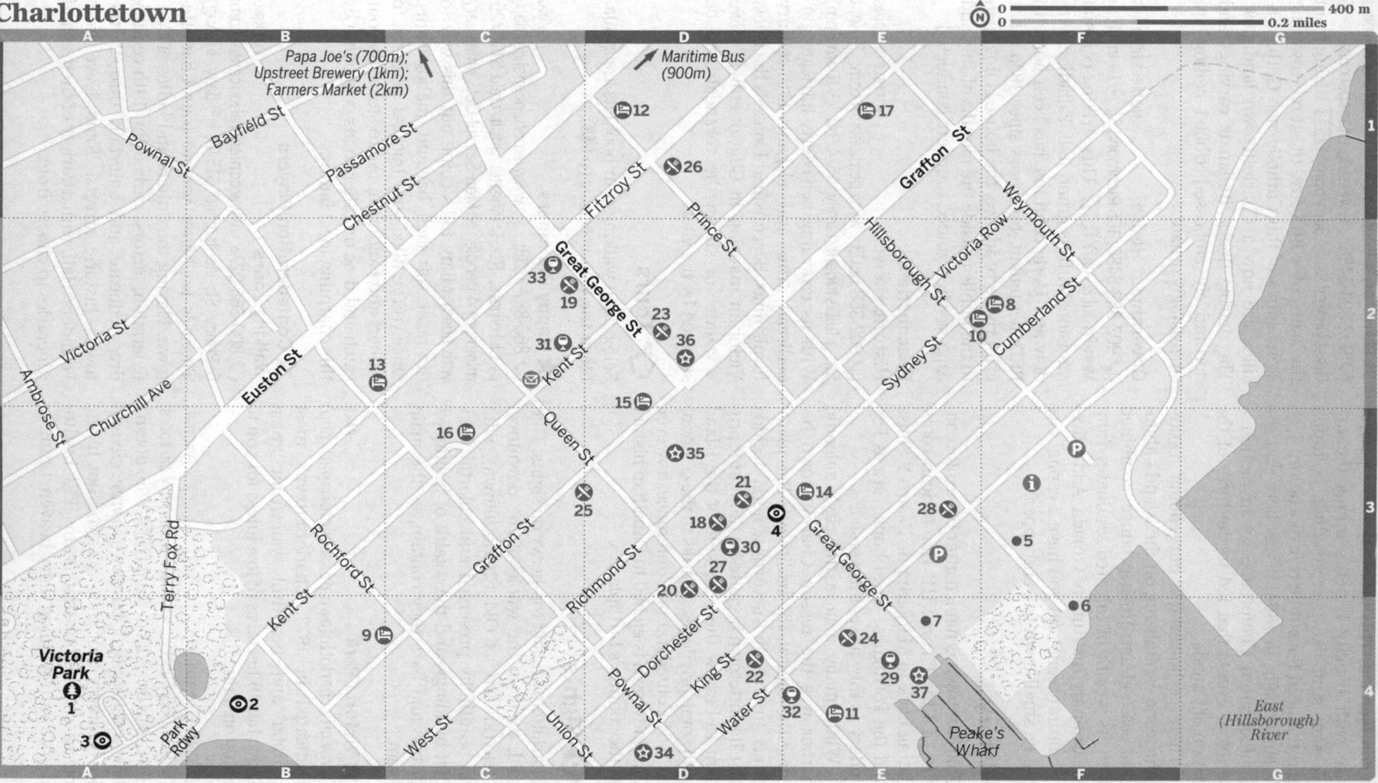
Charlottetown
0
0
400 m
0.2 miles
Papa Joe's (700m); Upstreet Brewery (1km); Farmers Market (2km)
Maritime Bus (900m)
Pownal St
Bayfield St
Passamore St
Chestnut St
Fitzroy St
Prince St
Grafton St
Weymouth St
Victoria Row
Hillsborough St
Cumberland St
Sydney St
Great George St
Kent St
Victoria St
Euston St
Ambrose St
Churchill Ave
Queen St
Terry Fox Rd
Rochford St
Grafton St
Richmond St
Great George St
Kent St
Dorchester St
King St
Pownal St
Water St
Union St
West St
Park Rdwy
Victoria Park
Peake's Wharf
East (Hillsborough) River

Charlottetown

Top Sights
1 Victoria Park A4

Sights
2 Beaconsfield Historic House B4
3 Government House A4
4 St Dunstan's Basilica D3

Activities, Courses & Tours
5 Confederation Players Walking Tours F3
6 Harbour Hippo Hippopotabus F4
7 Peake's Wharf Boat Cruises E4

Sleeping
8 Aloha Tourist Home F2
9 Charlotte's Rose Inn B4
10 Charlottetown Backpackers Inn E2
11 Delta Prince Edward E4
12 Fairholm National Historic Inn D1
13 Fitzroy Hall B&B B2
14 Great George E3
15 Holman Grand Hotel D2
16 Rodd Charlottetown C3
17 Spillett House B&B E1

Eating
18 Brickhouse Kitchen & Bar D3
19 Cedar's C2
20 Churchill Arms D3
21 Claddagh Oyster House D3
22 Kettle Black D4
23 Leonhard's D2
24 Local 343 .... E4
25 Pilot House C3
26 Splendid Essence D1
27 Terre Rouge D3
28 Water Prince Corner Shop & Lobster Pound E3

Drinking & Nightlife
29 Brakish E4
30 Gahan House D3
31 Hopyard C2
Marc's Studio .... (see 18)
32 Merchantman E4
33 Old Triangle C2

Entertainment
Baba's Lounge .... (see 19)
34 City Cinema D4
35 Confederation Centre of the Arts D3
36 Mack D2
Olde Dublin Pub .... (see 21)
37 Peake's Quay E4

Peake's Wharf Boat Cruises CRUISE
(☎902-566-4458; www.charlottetownboattours.com; 1 Great George St; tours from $34; ⊙2:30pm, 6:30pm & 8pm Jun-Aug) Observe sea life, hear interesting stories and witness a wonderfully different perspective of Charlottetown from the waters of its harbor aboard the 45ft good ship *Fairview*. A variety of itineraries of varying durations is available.

Harbour Hippo Hippopotabus TOURS
(☎902-628-8687; www.harbourhippo.com; 2 Prince St; 1hr tour adult/child $26/19) Want to explore historic Charlottetown but afraid the kids will get bored? Hop on this amphibious bus that takes you to all the sights on land, then floats in the water.

Festivals & Events

PEI Burger Love FOOD & DRINK
(www.peiburgerlove.ca; ⊙Mar) This monthlong celebration of the humble burger has gained cultlike status in the restaurants of Charlottetown, which try to outdo each other for the title of PEI's most-loved burger.

Festival of Small Halls MUSIC
(www.smallhalls.com; ⊙mid-Jun) Island musicians, dancers and storytellers who have 'made it' out of the province return to their homeland to perform in rural community halls around PEI during this popular festival.

Charlottetown Festival PERFORMING ARTS
(☎800-565-0278; www.confederationcentre.com; ⊙Jun-Sep) This long-running festival organized by the Confederation Centre of the Arts (p443) features free outdoor performances, a children's theater and dance programs.

Old Home Week CULTURAL
(☎902-629-6623; www.oldhomeweekpei.com; ⊙mid-Aug) Held at the Provincial Exhibition grounds, this 10-day event features carnival rides, musical entertainment, games of chance, harness racing and livestock shows.

Fall Flavours FOOD & DRINK
(☎866-960-9912; www.fallflavours.ca; ⊙Sep) Now one of the island's largest festivals, this massive, monthlong kitchen party merges traditional music with incredible cuisine. Don't miss the oyster-shucking championships or the chowder challenge.

Sleeping

Old Charlottetown's charms and proximity to major sights and restaurants makes it the most enviable area to rest your head. During summer, Charlottetown hums with activity, so it's wise to book ahead. In the off-season, accommodations are plentiful and most places reduce their rates. Parking is freely available at, or close to, all accommodations.

Charlottetown Backpackers Inn HOSTEL $
(902-367-5749; www.charlottetownbackpackers.com; 60 Hillsborough St; dm/r incl breakfast $33/80;) Impossible to miss with its bright red-and-white paint job and happy hostellers milling about on the lawn, this superbly happening backpackers has cozy single-sex or mixed dorms, a good kitchen, and a quirky common room with a turntable and a rather epic vinyl collection. Be prepared for spontaneous barbecues and pub outings.

Spillett House B&B B&B $
(902-892-5494; www.spilletthouse.pe.ca; 157 Weymouth St; d from $70;) This lovely heritage home is scrupulously clean, with polished hardwood floors and antique furnishings, homemade quilts on the beds and lace curtains on the windows. Kids are welcome and there are storage facilities for bicycles. Shared bathrooms.

Aloha Tourist Home B&B $
(902-892-5642; www.alohaamigo.com; 234 Sydney St; d/ste from $65/140;) A central, welcoming choice that's really a heritage B&B complete with antiques and comfy beds, but without the hefty price tag: three of the six rooms have shared bathrooms and there's a two-bedroom family suite. Breakfast is a tasty serve-yourself affair.

Holman Grand Hotel HOTEL $$
(877-455-4726; www.theholmangrand.com; 123 Grafton St; d/ste from $119/189) This modern, minimalist private hotel has a neat selection of simple, stylish rooms incorporating some unique features like sun-drenched terraces and lofty nooks. The indoor-pool and gym area is one you might actually want to use!

Great George BOUTIQUE HOTEL $$
(902-892-0606; www.thegreatgeorge.com; 58 Great George St; d/ste from $179/219;) This colorful collage of celebrated buildings along Charlottetown's most famous street has rooms ranging from plush and historic to bold and contemporary – but all are simply stunning. It's both gay- and family-friendly. A babysitting service is available, as is a fitness room.

Rodd Charlottetown HISTORIC HOTEL $$
(902-894-7371; 75 Kent St; d from $149;) Built by Canadian Pacific Railways in 1931, this once-grand hotel hasn't changed much over the years. Many would say it's due for a revamp, but others will love the gently jaded rooms, antique bathrooms, solid doors and opening windows. It's age and the competition in town means bargain rates can be found if you keep your eyes peeled.

Fitzroy Hall B&B B&B $$
(866-627-9766; www.fitzroyhall.com; 45 Fitzroy St; d/ste from $165/219;) A perfect blend of elegance and comfort, this house is as grand as they come, while the welcome is warm and down to earth. The innkeepers have put serious thought into how to make their guests comfortable, with refined antiques, muted color schemes, and details like hidden alcoves with fridges to keep cold drinks and hot pots to make tea.

Charlotte's Rose Inn INN $$
(902-892-3699; www.charlottesrose.ca; 11 Grafton St; apt from $150, d from $165;) Miss Marple must be around here somewhere. This decadent Victorian has true English flair with bodacious rose-printed wallpaper, lace canopies, big fluffy beds and grand bathrooms. There's a fire in the parlor for guests to enjoy along with complimentary tea and cakes. A modern loft apartment can accommodate five and has its own private rooftop deck. Two-night minimum stay.

★**Fairholm National Historic Inn** INN $$$
(902-892-5022; www.fairholminn.com; 230 Prince St; d/ste from $129/289;) This historic inn was built in 1838 and its rooms feature luxurious fabrics, beautiful local art and grand antiques. Out back are brilliantly designed, well-appointed, self-contained apartments. At the time of writing, the inn's fabulously intelligent, resourceful and friendly owner was expanding his empire to his equally beautiful neighboring properties. Be sure to check the website for the full scoop.

★**Delta Prince Edward** HOTEL $$$
(902-566-2222; www.marriott.com; 18 Queen St; d/ste from $169/269;) You can't beat the Delta's prime waterfront location in the heart of Old Charlottetown's vibrant restaurant district. It's also hard to fault its selection of comfy, freshly updated rooms with their crisp, clean lines, modern styling and (for many) harbor views. Wi-fi is free when you book direct.

WORTH A TRIP

ORWELL CORNER & POINT PRIM

If you're looking for a sweet, kid-friendly, half-day trip from Charlottetown and have had your fill of Anne of Green Gables action, head east on Rte 1. After about 30km, you'll come to **Orwell Corner Historic Village** (☎902-651-8510; www.peimuseum.com; Resource Rd 2, Vernon Bridge; adult/child $9/4.50; ⏰9am-4:30pm Jul-Sep, 9:30am-4:30pm Mon-Fri Jun & Sep-Nov), a recreation of a rustic 19th-century farming community with animals, antiques and costumed locals. Further down the road, the **Sir Andrew MacPhail Homestead** (☎902-651-2789; www.macphailhomestead.ca; 271 MacPhail Park Rd, Vernon Bridge; ⏰10am-5pm Wed-Sun Jul-Sep) is open for tea on summer afternoons.

The real delight of the excursion is found continuing south on Rte 1 for a further 11km, where you'll come to signs for Point Prim. This skinny bucolic spit of land is covered in wild rose, Queen Anne's lace and wheat fields through summer and has views of red sand shores on either side. At the tip is the **Point Prim Lighthouse** (☎902-659-2768; www.pointprimlighthouse.com; 2147 Point Prim Rd, Belfast; adult/child $3.50/2; ⏰10am-6pm Jul & Aug, 10am-6pm Wed-Sun Jun & Sep): the province's oldest and, we think, prettiest. If you're lucky, you'll be able to climb to the top to pump the foghorn.

If you need more to do, get in touch with the friendly folks at **Happy Clammers** (p437), who'll take you searching for soft-shell, bar and quahog clams, then take you home and show you how to turn your briny catch into a fantastic feast.

Round out your day with a cup of chowder by the ocean at **Point Prim Chowder House** (☎902-659-2187; www.chowderhousepei.com; 2150 Point Prim Rd, Belfast; mains $8-25; ⏰11am-7pm Jun-Oct), then head back to Charlottetown, or continue south to Wood Islands (30km) for your ferry to Nova Scotia.

Eating

Thanks largely to the Culinary Institute of Canada, which keeps churning out talented chefs, the city has a heaped helping of fine eateries. During summer, Victoria Row's pedestrian mall and the waterfront are hot spots for diners and drinkers. Pubs are also a great place to go for good-value eating.

Cedar's LEBANESE $
(☎902-892-7377; 181 Great George St; mains $10-25; ⏰11am-11pm Mon-Sat, to 4pm Sun; 🖉) Cedar's has been serving the home-style flavors of Lebanon to the people of Charlottetown since 1979 and it still rates as one of the best places for a cheap, tasty and healthy feed in town. Nightly specials every day.

Leonhard's CAFE $
(www.leonhards.ca; 142 Great George St; sandwiches from $8; ⏰9am-5pm Tue-Sat) Find absolute comfort in this little cafe full of cushioned seating and soothing country-style muted hues. Treat yourself to excellent German pastries, salads and creative sandwiches, as well as all-day breakfasts made with free-range eggs, a great cheese selection and cold cuts like Black Forest ham. Wash it down with farmers-market teas and espresso.

Splendid Essence TAIWANESE $
(☎902-566-4991; www.splendidessence.com; 186 Prince St; mains $7-14; ⏰11:30am-3pm & 5-8pm; 🖉) Savory Taiwanese vegetarian dishes are served in this cozy Victorian, fitted out with warm wood paneling and intimate booths upholstered in red, green and gold and accented with Chinese art. Recommended are the spicy vegetables and fried rice chased with a steaming mug of hot almond milk.

Maid Marian's DINER $
(☎902-566-4641; 7 Ellis Rd; meals $5-9; ⏰7am-8pm) This old-school local hot spot is always hopping. It's not downtown, but it is a great spot to stop for a quick, cheap breakfast on your way to the airport. There's nothing fancy here: just awesome 1980s green-vinyl booths, PEI people watching, nightly specials including scallop dinners, and plenty of basic, hearty meals for under $10.

Papa Joe's CANADIAN $
(☎902-566-5070; www.papajoespei.ca; 345 University Ave; mains $10-18; ⏰11am-9pm) This family-style restaurant is super popular with locals. Here all pretensions are checked at the door as you dine on bacon-wrapped meatloaf, turkey pot pie or a steak sandwich. Wednesdays go exotic with Indian cuisine served all day.

Kettle Black CAFE $
(☎902-370-0776; 45 Queen St; light lunches $9; ⏰7am-7pm) A cozy bakery and cafe that feels like a mix between a rural farmhouse and an urban art gallery. Enjoy great coffee, breakfasts and light lunches.

★**Water Prince Corner Shop & Lobster Pound** SEAFOOD $$
(☎902-368-3212; http://waterprincelobster.ca; 141 Water St; mains $12-36; ⏰9:30am-8pm) When locals want seafood they head to this inconspicuous, sea-blue eatery near the wharf. It is deservedly famous for its scallop burgers, but it's also the best place in town for fresh lobster. You'll probably have to line up for a seat, otherwise order take-out lobster, which gets you a significant discount.

★**Claddagh Oyster House** SEAFOOD $$
(☎902-892-6992; http://claddaghoysterhouse.com; 131 Sydney St; mains $13-32; ⏰5-9pm) Locals herald the Claddagh Room as one of the best seafood restaurants in Charlottetown. Trust 'em! The Irish-inspired Galway Bay Delight features a coating of fresh cream and seasonings over scallops and shrimp that have been sautéed with mushrooms and onions, then flambéed with Irish Mist liqueur.

Terre Rouge CANADIAN $$
(☎902-892-4032; www.terrerougepei.ca; 72 Queen St; mains $12-32; ⏰11am-3pm & 5-10pm Tue-Sun) Self billed as a craft kitchen, Terre Rouge is the place where healthy eating meats comfort and fun. Only the most boring of eaters will struggle to find something on the menu to get excited about: beet salad, fish cakes, chowder, lentil burgers and tacos are all presented here in happy, hipster-friendly environs.

Local 343 CAFE $$
(☎902-569-9343; 98 Water St; ⏰11:30am-8pm; 🌶) This fabulous deli-cum-cafe was a local secret until we let the cat out of the bag. Swing by for tasty home-style soups, salads, sandwiches, quiches, meatloaf, crab cakes... you get the gist. There's plenty you can order and go for those perfect PEI picnic days, or if you're feeling like laying low and enjoying the comforts of your swanky digs.

Brickhouse Kitchen & Bar MODERN CANADIAN $$
(☎902-566-4620; http://brickhousepei.com; 125 Sydney St; mains $16-36; ⏰11am-10pm) The chic ambience of this heritage brick building is matched by creative dishes inspired by island culture and made with local ingredients. Try the lobster poutine, seafood bouillabaisse, Thai curry chicken or just a good PEI beef burger. Don't leave without enjoying a cocktail or dessert in the upstairs lounge.

Churchill Arms PUB FOOD $$
(☎902-367-3450; www.churchillarms.ca; 75 Queen St; mains $10-22; ⏰11:30am-9pm Mon-Sat) Equally worthy as a standalone drinking haunt, this lively, quintessentially British pub makes the grade for heavy, authentic Brit-pub food: curries, shepherd's pies, bangers and mash, killer fish-and-chips (sourced locally) and bubble and squeak, for those times when, well, nothing else will do.

Pilot House MODERN CANADIAN $$$
(☎902-894-4800; http://thepilothouse.ca; 70 Grafton St; mains $24-39; ⏰11am-10pm Mon-Sat) The oversized wood beams and brick columns of the historic Roger's Hardware building provide a bold setting for fine dining or light pub fare. A loyal clientele tucks into lobster-stuffed chicken, vegetarian pizza or seafood torte. Lunch specials start at $10.

🍷 Drinking & Nightlife

Charlottetown has an established and burgeoning drinking scene. Historic pubs dot the old part of town. Most bars and pubs have a small cover charge (about $5) on weekends, or when there is live music. People spill into the streets at 2am when things wrap up.

★**Gahan House** PUB
(☎902-626-2337; http://charlottetown.gahan.ca; 126 Sydney St; ⏰11am-midnight) Within these homey, historic walls the pub owners brew PEI homegrown ales. Sir John A's Honey Wheat Ale is well worth introducing to your insides, as is the medium- to full-bodied Sydney Street Stout. The food here is also great – enjoy with friends old and new.

Hopyard BAR
(☎902-367-2599; 131 Kent St; ⏰11am-midnight) Beer, food and vinyl: that's the promise of these newcomers to the growing Charlottetown bar scene...and the locals are loving it!

Upstreet Brewery BREWERY
(☎902-894-0543; www.upstreetcraftbrewing.com; 41 Allen St; ⏰noon-midnight) This original craft brewer is fast becoming Charlottetown's favourite drinking haunt with a fun vibe and great beer.

Old Triangle IRISH PUB
(☎902-892-5200; www.oldtrianglecharlottetown.com; 189 Great George St; ⊙11am-10pm) This lively Irish Pub has regular live music and the Guinness just keeps on flowing.

Merchantman BAR
(☎902-892-9150; www.merchantman.ca; 23 Queen St; ⊙11am-9pm) Merchantman wears many hats; it's a bar, it's a restaurant, it's a takeout. In summer months, the patio tables are a great place to soak up the sun and enjoy a drink while you work up your appetite for fresh PEI oysters, seafood or all manner of upscale pub grub.

Brakish BAR
(☎902-894-1112; www.brakish.com; 2 Lower Water St; ⊙noon-11pm) This joint comes alive in the summer months when it's known for having Charlottetown's best waterfront patio, perfect for drinking the long sunny days away, but if you must stop to eat, there's plenty of fresh local seafood on the menu.

Marc's Studio BAR
(☎902-566-4620; http://brickhousepei.com/marcs-studio.html; 125 Sydney St; ⊙4:30pm-midnight) Climb the stairs for a cocktail or a nightcap. Think plenty of art by the late, local artist Marc Gallant (who restored this building in the 1980s) and cozily grouped sofas set against exposed brick walls. It usually closes around midnight, but will stay open until the crowd thins out.

☆ Entertainment

Charlottetown serves up a great mix of theater, music, island culture and fun. Throughout the city, various venues host traditional ceilidhs (kay-lees), sometimes referred to as 'kitchen parties.' These lively community gatherings almost always feature gleeful Celtic music and dance. The Friday edition of the *Guardian* newspaper and the free monthly *Buzz* list times and locations of upcoming ceilidhs, along with other details of what's on when and where.

★Confederation Centre of the Arts THEATER
(☎902-566-1267; www.confederationcentre.com; 145 Richmond St) This modern complex's large theater and outdoor amphitheater host concerts, comedic performances and elaborate musicals. *Anne of Green Gables – The Musical* has been entertaining audiences here as part of the Charlottetown Festival since 1964, making it Canada's longest-running musical. You'll enjoy it, and your friends will never have to know.

Peake's Quay LIVE MUSIC
(☎902-368-1330; www.peakesquay.com; 11 Great George St; ⊙noon-midnight) It's actually more of a bar-restaurant (with the largest patio on the island) but this venue is the closest thing to a nightclub Charlottetown has to offer, with guest DJs and special events.

Mack THEATER
(128 Great George St) An intimate venue where guests sit at round tables for predominantly comedy gigs.

City Cinema CINEMA
(☎902-368-3669; http://citycinema.net; 64 King St) A small independent theater featuring Canadian and foreign-language films.

Benevolent Irish Society LIVE MUSIC
(☎902-963-3156; 582 North River Rd; $10; ⊙8pm Fri) On the north side of town, this is a great place to catch a ceilidh. Come early, as seating is limited.

Olde Dublin Pub LIVE MUSIC
(☎902-892-6992; 131 Sydney St; $8) A traditional Irish pub with a jovial spirit and live entertainment nightly during the summer months. Celtic bands and local notables take to the stage and make for an engaging night out.

Baba's Lounge LIVE MUSIC
(☎902-892-7377; 81 University Ave; ⊙noon-midnight) Located above Cedar's Eatery, this welcoming, intimate venue hosts great local bands playing their own tunes. Occasionally there are poetry readings.

Shopping

Farmers Market MARKET
(☎902-626-3373; http://charlottetownfarmersmarket.weebly.com; 100 Belvedere Ave; ⊙9am-2pm Sat, also Wed Jul & Aug) Come hungry and empty-handed. Enjoy some prepared island foods or peruse the cornucopia of fresh organic fruit and vegetables. The market is north of the town center off University Ave.

Information

Charlottetown Visitor Information Centre
(☎902-368-4444; 178 Water St; ⊙9am-5pm May-Oct) The island's main tourist office has all the answers, a plethora of brochures and maps, and free internet access.

Main Post Office (☎902-628-4400; 101 Kent St; ⊙9am-5pm Mon-Fri.) Central post office.

Polyclinic Professional Centre (☎902-629-8810; polyclinic· online.com; 199 Grafton St; ⊙5:30-8pm Mon-Fri, 9:30am-noon Sat) Charlottetown's after-hours, walk-in medical clinic.

Queen Elizabeth Hospital (☎902-894-2111; 60 Riverside Dr; ⊙24hr) Emergency room.

Royal Canadian Mounted Police (☎902-368-9300; 450 University Ave) Nonemergencies only.

Getting There & Around

Charlottetown Airport (YYG; ☎902-566-7997; www.flypei.com; 250 Maple Hills Ave) is 8km north of the city center. A taxi to/from town costs $12, plus $3.50 for each additional person.

Rental cars, available from a variety of providers with city and airport depots, are the preferred method of transportation. During summer cars are in short supply, so be sure to book ahead.

Limited public transportation is provided by **Trius Transit** (T3 Transit; ☎902-566-9962; www.triustransit.ca/), but walking or renting a bike are both great ways to get around this compact city.

Advanced Shuttle (☎877-886-3322; www.advancedshuttle.ca) Offers shuttle services between PEI and Nova Scotia.

City Taxi (☎902-892-6567; www.citytaxipei.com) Operates taxi services.

MacQueen's Bicycles (☎902-368-2453; www.macqueens.com; 430 Queen St; rental per day/week $25/125) Rents a variety of quality bikes. Children's models half price.

Smooth Cycle (☎902-566-5530; www.smoothcycle.com; 330 University Ave; rental per day/week $26/115) Offers well-priced bike rentals and sales.

Yellow Cab PEI (☎902-566-6666; www.yellowcabpei.com)

EASTERN PRINCE EDWARD ISLAND

You can make your own tracks across Kings County, the eastern third of the province and PEI's most under-touristed region. From stretches of neatly tended homesteads to the sinuous eastern shore with its protected harbors, sweeping beaches and country inns, majestic tree canopies seem to stretch endlessly over the scenic heritage roads. The 338km Points East Coastal Drive winds along the shore, hitting the highlights.

Wood Islands

Wood Islands is the jumping-off point for ferries to Nova Scotia.

If you'll be waiting a while at the terminal, **Wood Islands Provincial Park** and its 1876 lighthouse are well worth the short walk.

From Wood Islands, Rte 4 heads east along the Northumberland Strait, veering inland at High Bank toward the lively and surprisingly artsy fishing settlement of **Murray River**. The coastal road becomes Rte 18, keeping the sea in view as it rounds Cape Bear, passing the lighthouse before looping back through the village of Murray Harbour and into Murray River. This stretch of flat, empty road offers superbly serene scenery and excellent cycling possibilities. Cyclists can follow the coastal road from Murray River, then loop back on the extension of the Confederation Trail at Wood Islands.

Sights

Newman Estate Winery — WINERY

(☎902-962-4223; www.newmanestatewinery.com; 9404 Gladstone Rd, Gladstone; ⊙by appointment) Head toward the coast from Murray River along Rte 348 (Gladstone Rd) to find Newman Estate Winery. This lovely place specializes in blueberry wines, but has recently begun making white wine from grapes.

Rossignol Estate Winery — WINERY

(☎902-962-4193; www.rossignolwinery.com; 11147 Shore Rd, Murray River; ⊙10am-5pm Mon-Sat, 1-5pm Sun May-Oct) For wine tasting on a grand scale, cruise over to Little Sands, 9km from the Wood Islands Ferry, where Rossignol Estate Winery has free tastings and specializes in fruit wines. The divine Blackberry Mead has won a string of gold medals and the Wild Rose Liquor made from rose hips is also well worth a try; call ahead for winter hours.

Eating

Crabby's Seafood — SEAFOOD $

(☎902-962-3228; 84 Lighthouse Rd, Wood Islands; items from $5; ⊙noon-6pm Jun-Sep) Munch on a rock-crab sandwich or a lobster roll at Crabby's Seafood near the ferry terminal.

★**Harbourview Restaurant** — CANADIAN $$

(☎902-962-3141; www.harbourviewrestaurant.ca; 7 Mariners Lane, Murray Harbour; mains $8-24; ⊙8am-9pm Mon-Sat, 11am-9pm Sun) When the owners of this popular restaurant formerly known as Brehaut's retired, some of the staff decided they'd step up and take over, renaming it and keeping tried-and-true local favorites alongside new items. Dine in cozy, country-cute booths on the island's best chowder and other casual eats. They make a mean milkshake too! Murray Harbour is 21km east of Wood Islands.

Information

Wood Islands Visitor Information Centre
(902-962-7411; 13054 Shore Rd; 10:30am-9pm) This is the main visitor center for those arriving on PEI by ferry.

Getting There & Away

Wood Islands is 51km southeast of Charlottetown and the boarding point for **Bay Ferries** (p331) services to Caribou, Nova Scotia (adult/child $19/free, 1¼ hours). A standard vehicle costs $81.

Montague & Georgetown

The fact that Montague isn't flat gives it a unique, inland feel. Perched on either side of the Montague River, the busy little town is the service center for Kings County; its streets lead from the breezy, heritage marina area to modern shopping malls, supermarkets and fast-food outlets.

Around the peninsula, the many heritage buildings in Georgetown are testament to the town's importance as a shipbuilding center in the Victorian era. Today it's a sleepy village cum tourist spot thanks to its great places to eat and waterfront setting.

Sights & Activities

Panmure Head Lighthouse LIGHTHOUSE
(902-838-3568; 62 Lighthouse Rd, Panmure Island; tours $5; 9:30am-5pm Jul & Aug, hours vary Jun & Sep) Needing a little TLC, this is the island's first octagonal and oldest wooden lighthouse.

Garden of the Gulf Museum MUSEUM
(902-838-2467; www.montaguemuseumpei.com; 564 Main St, Montague; adult/child under 12yr $3/free; 9am-5pm Mon-Fri Jun-Sep) On the southern side of the river, the statuesque former post office and customs house (1888) overlooks the marina, and houses the Garden of the Gulf Museum. Inside are several artifacts illustrating local history.

Tranquility Cove Adventures FISHING
(902-969-7184; www.tranquilitycoveadventures.com; Fisherman's Wharf, 1 Kent St, Georgetown; half-/full-day tours from $60/100) Tranquility Cove Adventures leads excellent fishing and clamming trips, as well as kundalini yoga on a deserted island. Check the website for details on other packages.

Brudenell Riding Stables HORSEBACK RIDING
(902-652-2396; www.brudenellridingstables.com; 1hr ride $35; Jun-Sep) You can take a one-hour horseback trail ride through the sun-dappled forest and onto the beach with Brudenell Riding Stables.

Festivals & Events

Panmure Island Powwow CULTURAL
(902-892-5314; mid-Aug) There's a powwow held each year with drumming, crafts and a sweat tent – it attracts around 5000 visitors, so don't expect any secluded beaches!

Sleeping

★ **Maplehurst** B&D $$
(902-838-3959; www.maplehurstproperties.com; 1220 Route 347; d from $145; May-Nov;) For luxury, stay at the grand Maplehurst B&B. Marsha Leftwich has mustered every glimmer of her native Southern hospitality to create this exceptional B&B illuminated by gorgeous chandeliers and furnished with the utmost attention to detail.

Georgetown Inn & Dining Room INN $$
(902-652-2511; www.peigeorgetownhistoricinn.com; 62 Richmond St, Georgetown; d from $105;) Right in the center of Georgetown, this place is as equally well known for its PEI-themed rooms (including a Green Gables room) as for its fine casual island-fare dining.

Brudenell River Provincial Park CAMPGROUND
(902-652-8966; www.tourismpei.com/provincial-park/brudenell-river; off Rte 3, Cardigan; tent sites $21, RV sites $24-28; May-Oct) Just north of town, development meets nature at Brudenell River Provincial Park, which is a park and resort complex. Tent and RV sites are available, as well as cottages and motel-style accommodation. Activities range from kayaking to nature walks and golf on two championship courses.

Panmure Island Provincial Park CAMPGROUND
(902-838-0668; www.tourismpei.com/provincial-park/panmure-island; Hwy 347; tent & RV sites from $27; Jun-Sep) Bring a picnic for the supervised beach at Panmure Island Provincial Park. The park campground has every amenity for its 44 sites (most unserviced) tucked under the trees and along the shore.

Eating

Cardigan Lobster Suppers SEAFOOD $$
(902-583-2020; www.peicardiganlobstersuppers.com; 4557 Wharf Rd, Cardigan; adult/child $39/26; 5-9pm Jun-Oct) In tiny Cardigan, enjoy a five-course Lobster Supper in a heritage building on Cardigan Harbor.

Famous Peppers PIZZA $$
(902-361-6161; www.famouspeppers.ca; 3 Rink St, Montague; pizzas from $10) Quite simply, the best pizza in town – not that there's much competition.

Clamdigger's Beach House & Restaurant SEAFOOD $$
(902-652-2466; 7 West St, Georgetown; mains $12-37; 11am-9pm) Some claim this place serves PEI's best chowder, but no matter what your opinion, you can't help but ooh and aah about the water view from the deck or through the dining room's giant windows.

Windows on the Water Café MODERN CANADIAN $$
(902-838-2080; cnr Sackville & Main Sts; mains $9-17; 11:30am-9:30pm May-Oct) Enjoy a flavorful array of seafood, chicken and vegetarian dishes on the deck overlooking the water and, sort of, the road. Try the lobster quiche and leave room for a freshly baked dessert.

Information

Island Welcome Center (902-838-0670; cnr Rtes 3 & 4; 9am-6pm May-Oct) In the old train station on the riverbank there's an Island Welcome Center, which is a font of knowledge about this corner of the island.

Souris

Wrapped around the waters of Colville Bay is the bustling fishing community of Souris (*sur*-rey). It owes its name to the French Acadians and the gluttonous mice who repeatedly ravaged their crops. It's now known more for its joyous annual music festival than for the hungry field rodents of old.

This is a working town that's a friendly jumping-off point for cycling the coastal road (Rte 16) and the Confederation Trail, which comes into town. Souris is also the launching point for ferries to the Îles de la Madeleine in Québec. The wooded coast and lilting accents along this stretch of coastline offer some welcome variety from the patchwork of farms found inland. Giant white windmills march across the landscape. North Lake and Naufrage harbors are intriguing places to stop and, if you feel so inclined, join a charter boat in search of a monster 450kg tuna.

DON'T MISS

BASIN HEAD PROVINCIAL PARK

The star attraction of **Basin Head Provincial Park** (www.tourismpei.com/provincial-park/basin-head; Basin Head) is the sweeping sand of golden **Basin Head Beach**. Many islanders rank this as their favorite beach and we have to agree. The sand is also famous for its singing – well, squeaking – when you walk on it. Unfortunately, the sand only performs when dry, so if it's been raining, it's no show. Five minutes of joyous 'musical' footsteps south from the museum and you have secluded bliss – enjoy!

Sights

Elmira Railway Museum MUSEUM
(902-357-7234; Rte 16A; adult/student/family $5/4/10; 10am-6pm Jun-Sep) The railway museum in Elmira includes a quirky miniature train ride (adult/student/family $6/4/15) that winds through the surrounding forest. The station marks the eastern end of the Confederation Trail.

East Point Lighthouse LIGHTHOUSE
(902-357-2106; adult/child $4/2; 10am-6pm Jun-Aug) Built the same year Canada was unified, the East Point Lighthouse still stands guard over the northeastern shore of PEI. After being blamed for the 1882 wreck of the *British Phoenix*, the lighthouse was moved closer to shore. The eroding shoreline is now chasing it back. There's a gift shop and a little cafe next to the lighthouse that serves lobster rolls ($9.50), chowder and sandwiches.

Basin Head Fisheries Museum MUSEUM
(902-357-7233; adult/student $4.50/2; 9am-6pm Jun-Sep) This small museum explores the history of the fishing industry in PEI.

Festivals & Events

PEI Bluegrass & Old Time Music Festival MUSIC
(902-569-3153; http://peibluegrass.tripod.com; early Jul) Draws acts from as far away as Nashville. Come for just a day, or camp out for all three.

Sleeping & Eating

Johnson Shore Inn INN $$

(902-687-1340; www.jspei.com; 9984 Northside Rd, Hermanville; r from $175; May-Feb;) Treat yourself to a little luxury at this impeccably managed inn blessed with a stunning setting on a red bluff that looks over endless sea.

★**Inn at Bay Fortune** INN $$$

(902-687-3745; www.innatbayfortune.com; 758 Rte 310, Bay Fortune; r from $225;) Returning to the inn where he spent seven formative years of his training, celebrated chef Michael Smith and his wife Chastity have returned to their roots and reimagined this fabulous property and its restaurant, **FireWorks**, to be one of Canada's hottest culinary destinations. You come for the epic interactive dining experience 'The Feast' (from $95) then enjoy the inn.

21 Breakwater CANADIAN $$

(902-687-2556; 21 Breakwater St; mains $12-28; 11:30am-8pm Mon-Sat) Patrons come for casual fine dining in this historic mansion overlooking the industrial waterfront. The menu focuses on the usual suspects, such as burgers, pasta with scallops, steamed mussels or chowder, but the preparation is top notch, as is the service.

Getting There & Away

Souris is 72km east of Charlottetown and located in the northeast corner of the island. Souris is also the boarding point for the **CTMA Ferr** (traversierctma.ca/en)y to Quebec's Îles de la Madeleine (from $52, five hours).

Saint Peter's Bay to Mt Stewart

The area between the villages of St Peter's Bay and Mt Stewart is a hotbed for cycling. The section of the Confederation Trail closest to Saint Peter's Bay flirts with the shoreline and rewards riders with an eyeful of the coast. In Mt Stewart three riverside sections of the Confederation Trail converge, giving riders and hikers plenty of attractive options

Sights

Greenwich Interpretation Centre NATURE RESERVE

(902-961-2514; Rte 13; 9:30am-7pm Jul & Aug, to 4:30pm May, Jun, Sep & Oct) Avant-garde meets barn at the Greenwich Interpretation Centre, where an innovative audiovisual presentation details the ecology of the dune system and the archaeological history of the site. The highlight, though, is getting out into the tree-eating dunes. Four walking trails traverse the park; the Greenwich Dunes Trail (4.5km return, 1½ hours) is especially scenic.

Sleeping & Eating

There are only a handful of accommodations in the area, mostly centered around the Confederation Trail. Dining in both St Peter's Bay and Mt Stewart is of the casual takeout and diner variety at best. Nearby Souris has a better selection for food-lovers.

Inn at St Peters Village INN $$$

(902-961-2135, 800-818-0925; www.innatstpeters.com; 1168 Greenwich Rd; d $125-265;) Even with its large, comfortable rooms and stunning water views, the main reason to come to this inn is to dine on some of PEI's finest fare at the sunset-facing restaurant (lunch/dinner mains from $17/22). Rooms are simply and elegantly decorated with antique furniture, but if you don't stay here, we still highly recommend stopping in for a meal (even you, sweaty bikers).

★**Trailside Cafe & Inn** CAFE $$

(902-628-7833; www.trailside.ca; 109 Main St, Mt Stewart; mains $12-17; r $89) It's a cafe, it's a music venue, it's an inn. In all ways this place exudes the best of PEI. Grab a pot of mussels or a taster plate of local cheeses and a beer and let the live local music tingle your spine. Check the website for showtimes and tickets.

Information

Provincial Tourist Office (902-961-3540; Rte 2; 8am-7pm Jul & Aug, 9am-4:30pm Jun, Sep & Oct) Both the Confederation Trail and a tourist office are found next to the bridge in St Peter's.

WORTH A TRIP

GREENWICH

Massive, dramatic and ever-shifting sand dunes epitomize the amazing area west of Greenwich. These rare parabolic giants are fronted by an awesome, often empty beach – a visit here is a must. Preserved by Parks Canada in 1998, this 6km section of shore is now part of Prince Edward Island National Park. Learn about it all in the Greenwich Interpretation Centre.

CENTRAL PRINCE EDWARD ISLAND

Central PEI contains a bit of all that's best about the island: verdant fields, quaint villages and forests undulating north to the dramatic sand-dune-backed beaches of Prince Edward Island National Park. Anne of Green Gables, the engaging heroine of Lucy Maud Montgomery's 1908 novel, has spawned a huge global industry focused on the formerly bucolic hamlet of Cavendish. However, this being PEI, even its most savagely developed patch of tourist traps and commercial detritus is almost quaint – freshly painted bedecked with flowers.

For those entering central PEI via the Confederation Bridge, it's worth stopping at the **Gateway Village Visitors Information Centre** (902-437-8570; Hwy 1; 8:30am-8pm), just off the bridge on the PEI side, for its free maps, brochures, restrooms and an excellent introductory exhibit called 'Our Island Home' (open May to November). Staff can point you to the Confederation Trail, which starts nearby.

Victoria

A place to wander and experience more than 'see,' the shaded, tree-laden lanes of this lovely little fishing village scream character and charm. The entire village still fits neatly in the four blocks laid out when the town was formed in 1819. Colorful clapboard and shingled houses are home to more than one visitor who was so enthralled by the place they decided to stay. There's a profusion of art, cafes and eateries, as well as an excellent summer theater festival.

Sights & Activities

Victoria Seaport Lighthouse Museum MUSEUM
(Water St; entry by donation; 9am-5:30pm Jun-Aug) This museum has an interesting exhibit on local history. If it's closed, get the key from the shop across the road.

By the Sea Kayaking KAYAKING
(902-658-2572; www.bytheseakayaking.ca; 1 Water St; kayak rentals per hour/day from $25/50) Paddle round on your own or on a guided tour, then take a dip at the beach, where change rooms are available. The outfit also operates popular 'I Dig Therefore I Clam' expeditions ($8) and offers bike rentals (per hour $15).

Sleeping & Eating

Orient Hotel B&B B&B $$
(902-658-2503; www.theorienthotel.com; 34 Main St; d/ste from $95/135;) A delightful Victorian confection of buttercup yellow, red and blue, this historic inn is a perfect jewel.

★ **Landmark Café** CAFE $$
(902-658-2286; www.landmarkcafe.ca; 12 Main St; mains $12-28; 11:30am-10pm May-Sep) Diners come from miles around for the imaginative food at this family-run cafe. Prepared with wholesome ingredients, every colorful menu item from lasagnas and homemade soups to Cajun stir-fries and feta-stuffed vine leaves is a winner.

Drinking & Entertainment

Lobster Barn Pub and Eatery PUB
(902-658-2722; 19 Main St; noon-10pm) This gorgeous little pub in an old barn is a great place for a beer, but the food's pretty special too – and yes, there's lobster on the menu!

Victoria Playhouse THEATER
(902-658-2025; www.victoriaplayhouse.com; 20 Howard St; ticket prices vary; 8pm Jun-Sep) This ornate theater presents a series of plays over summer, and concerts from some of the region's finest musicians on Monday nights.

Prince Edward Island National Park

Heaving dunes and red sandstone bluffs provide startling backdrops for some of the island's finest stretches of sand; welcome to **Prince Edward Island National Park** (902-672-6350; www.pc.gc.ca; day pass adult/child $7.80/3.90). This dramatic coast, and the narrow sections of wetland and forests behind it, is home to diverse plants, animals and birdlife, including the red fox and endangered piping plover.

The park is open year-round, but most services only operate between mid-May and mid-October, with full services operational for the months of July and August. Entrance fees (charged when the picnic grounds and beaches are open, from mid-June to mid-September) admit you to all park sites, except Green Gables Heritage Place (p454). If you're planning to stay longer than five days, look into a seasonal pass. The park maintains an information desk at the Cavendish Visitor Information Centre (p455).

WORTH A TRIP

DISTILLERIES

Two distinctly different distilleries operate on PEI, echoing the province's fame for bootlegging during Prohibition. Even today many families distill their own moonshine (which is technically illegal) which is often mixed in punch and cocktails at weddings and parties.

Prince Edward Distillery (902-687-2586; www.princeedwarddistillery.com; Rte 16, Hermanville; 11am-6pm) specializes in potato vodka that, even in its first year of production, has turned international heads (some calling it among the finest of its class). Stop in for tours of the immaculate distillery and to taste the different vodkas (potato, grain and blueberry) as well as the newer products, such as bourbon, rum, whiskey, pastis, and a very interesting and aromatic gin.

Myriad View Distillery (902-687-1281; www.straitshine.com; 1336 Rte 2, Rollo Bay; 11am-6pm Mon-Sat, 1-5pm Sun) produces Canada's first and only legal moonshine. The hard-core Straight Lightning Shine is 75% alcohol and so potent it feels like liquid heat before it evaporates on your tongue. Take our advice and start with a micro-sip! A gulp could knock the wind out of you. The 50% alcohol Straight Shine lets you enjoy the flavor a bit more. Tours and tastings are free and the owner is happy to answer any questions.

It's about a 10-minute drive on Rte 307 between the two places.

Sights & Activities

Beaches lined with marram grasses and wild rose span almost the entire length of the park's 42km coastline. In most Canadians' minds, the park is almost synonymous with these strips of sand. **Dalvay Beach** sits to the east, and has some short hiking trails through the woods. The landscape flattens and the sand sprawls outward at **Stanhope Beach**. Here, a boardwalk leads from the campground to the shore. Backed by dunes, and slightly west, is the expansive and popular **Brackley Beach**. On the western side of the park, the sheer size of **Cavendish Beach** makes it the granddaddy of them all. During summer this beach sees copious numbers of visitors beneath its hefty dunes. If crowds aren't your thing, there are always the pristine sections of sand to the east. Lifeguards are on duty at Cavendish, Brackley and Stanhope beaches in midsummer. A beautiful bike lane runs all the way along this coast.

Sleeping

Parks Canada operates three highly sought-after **campgrounds** (800-414-6765; www.pc.gc.ca/eng/pn-np/pe/pei-ipe/visit.aspx; tent/RV sites $28/36; Jun-Aug), which are spread along the park's length. Reservations can be made online. You can request a campground, but not a specific site; you must accept whatever is available when you arrive. While 80% of sites can be booked in advance, the remaining sites are first-come, first-served, so it's wise to arrive early.

Stanhope Campground (Gulfshore East Pkwy) is nestled nicely in the woods behind the beach of the same name. There is a well-stocked store on-site. Located at the end of Brackley Point, **Robinsons Island Campground** (Gulfshore East Pkwy) is the most isolated of the three campgrounds. It's not too much fun if the wind gets up. The proximity of **Cavendish Campground**, off Rte 6, to the sights makes it the most popular. It has exposed oceanfront sites as well as sites within the shelter and shade of the trees. Don't be lured by the view – it's nice, but sleep is better.

Andy's Surfside Inn INN $
(902-963-2405; 469 Gulfshore Pkwy W; d from $50;) Inside Prince Edward Island National Park, 2.7km toward Orby Head from North Rustico, is this very rambling, ramshackle house overlooking beautiful Doyle's Cove. It has been a salty-dog inn since the 1930s. Sit back on the porch, put your feet up and thank your lucky stars. Basic accommodations with shared bathroom.

★**Dalvay by the Sea** HISTORIC HOTEL $$$
(902-672-2048; www.dalvaybythesea.com; 16 Cottage Cres, Dalvay; d/cottages from $199/379; May-Oct;) Overlooking its eponymous beach, this majestic 1895 historic mansion has a fascinating history. Aside from the main inn with its gorgeous woods and country-lodge luxury, a range of high-end cabins are dotted around the grounds. The drawing-room bar is a wonderful place for a beverage or casual eats, while the public dining room is a fancy affair.

Around PEI National Park

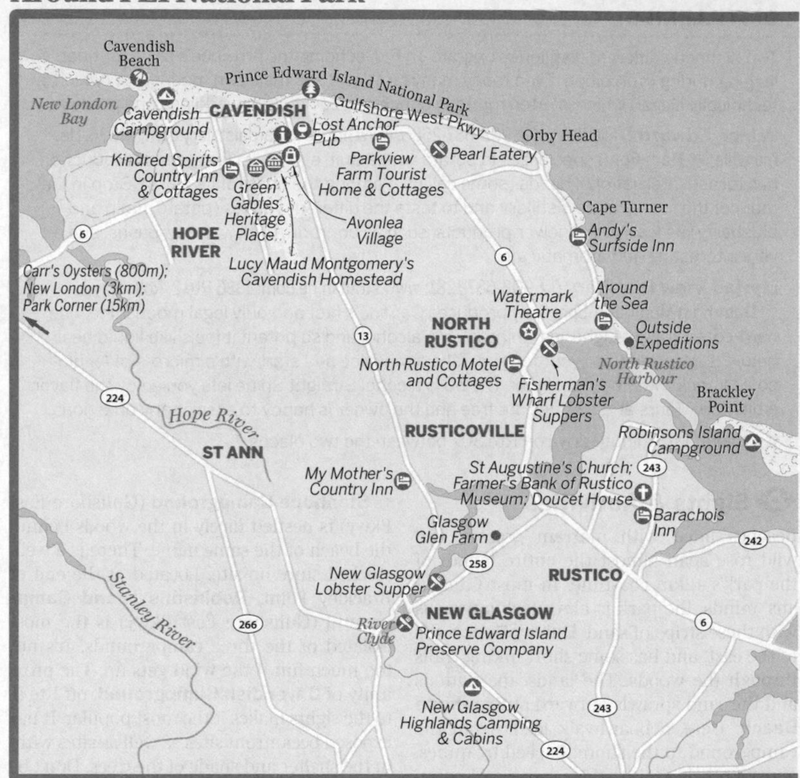

Brackley Beach

Brackley Beach isn't so much a town as a rural area, with a few scattered amenities and the main beach access to the central eastern beaches of Prince Edward Island National Park.

Sleeping & Eating

Brackley Beach Hostel HOSTEL $
(902-672-1900; www.brackleybeachhostel.com; 37 Britain Shore Rd; dm/q from $27/59;) For near-the-beach budget digs you won't find better than this clean and super-friendly hostel housed in a big barn about 2km from the shoreline. There are several eight-bed dorm rooms and a few quads, as well as plenty of showers and an equipped kitchen.

Shaw's Hotel & Cottages COTTAGE $$
(902-672-2022; www.shawshotel.ca; 99 Apple Tree Rd; d/cottages from $95/175;) Shaw's Hotel & Cottages, open since 1860, is Canada's oldest family-operated inn. The hotel occupies 30 hectares of the family farm, with a private lane leading to Brackley Beach, a 600m walk away. Rooms in the inn have old-fashioned simplicity. One- to four-bedroom cottages, ranging from rustic to modern, are scattered around the property.

The dining room is open to outside guests (mains $18 to $28); reservations are recommended for the popular Sunday-evening buffet ($45; held in July and August).

Dunes Café & Gallery FUSION $$
(902-672-2586; www.dunesgallery.com; 3622 Brackley Point Rd; dinner mains $16-28; 11:30am-10pm) While over-the-top springs to mind, Dunes Café & Gallery is a nice change of pace. Where else on the island can you enjoy Vietnamese rice-noodle salad in the shade of a giant Buddha? Come for coffee, a meal or to roam the eclectic mix of Asian and island art in the sprawling glass gallery and garden.

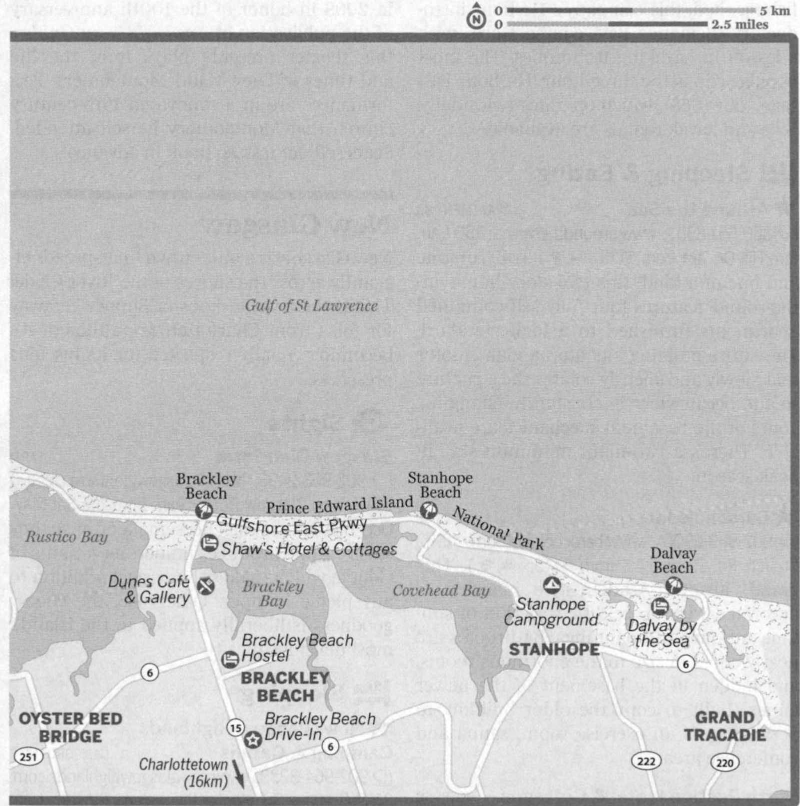

Entertainment

Brackley Drive-In Theatre CINEMA

(902-672-3333; www.drivein.ca; 3164 Brackley Point Rd; adult/child from $9/6; May-Sep) It's fun to catch a movie at this long-standing drive-in. Check the website for what's on.

Rustico & North Rustico

The seafront Acadian settlement at Rustico dates back to 1700, and several fine historic buildings speak of this tiny village's former importance.

Just 5km further along Rte 6, North Rustico feels less like a tourist town with its rickety, boxy fisher's houses painted in navies, brick reds and beiges. A walk east from the pier along the boardwalk is a great way to take this atmospheric little village and its busy harbor packed with fishing boats.

Sights & Activities

If your idea of ocean activity is reeling in a big one, look for the plethora of deep-sea fishing operators along Harbourview Dr. Expect to pay around $50 per person.

Farmer's Bank of Rustico Museum MUSEUM

(902-963-2194; www.farmersbank.ca; Church Rd, Rustico; adult/student $4/2; 9:30am-5:30pm Mon-Sat, 1-5pm Sun) The solid redstone Farmer's Bank of Rustico operated here between 1864 and 1894. Nextdoor is **Doucet House**, an old Acadian dwelling that was relocated here. This museum describing the settlement of the community and the establishment of the bank is now housed in the two secular buildings.

Outside Expeditions OUTDOORS

(902-963-3366; www.getoutside.com; 374 Harbourview Dr; tours from $45; May-Oct) Situated at the far end of the harbor in a bright-yellow fishing shed, this company's 1½-hour introductory 'Beginner Bay' course starts with a lesson in kayaking techniques. The most popular trip is the three-hour 'Harbour Passage' tour ($65), which operates twice daily. Bike and kayak rentals are available.

Sleeping & Eating

★Around the Sea APARTMENT $$
(☎866-557-8383; www.aroundthesea.ca; 130 Lantern Hill Dr; apt from $125;) Truly unique and one of a kind, this two-story home 'in-the-round' features four fully self-contained apartments furnished to a high standard. The entire building sits atop a giant motor that slowly and silently rotates the structure so the ocean view is constantly changing. Tours of the basement mechanics are available. There's a two-night minimum stay in peak season.

★Barachois Inn B&B $$
(☎902-963-2906; www.barachoisinn.com; 2193 Church Rd, Rustico; r from $145;) This grand, historic Acadian-style mansion is decorated with an eclectic selection of sublime antiques and paintings. Bathrooms are nearly equal in size to the enormous rooms, and hidden in the basement of the newer annex (built to copy the older building to perfection) is an exercise room, sauna and conference area.

North Rustico Motel & Cottages MOTEL $$
(☎902-963-2253; www.cottages-pei.ca; 7103 Cavendish Rd; r/cottages from $89/125) The best feature of this updated 1980s-style vacation property with a variety of accommodation types is its charming, wood-paneled, self-contained cottages scattered about the leafy grounds.

Fisherman's Wharf Lobster Suppers SEAFOOD $$$
(☎902-963-2669; http://fishermanswharf.ca; 7230 Rustico Rd; lobster dinners from $32; ⏲noon-9pm) During the dinner rush in July and August this huge place has lines of people out the door. Come hungry, as there are copious servings of chowder, tasty local mussels, rolls and a variety of desserts to go with your pound of messy crustacean. If things go your way, you may get a table with an ocean view.

Entertainment

Watermark Theatre THEATER
(☎902-963-3963; www.watermarktheatre.com; North Rustico Village; ticket prices vary) Opened in 2008 in honor of the 100th anniversary of the publication of *Anne of Green Gables*, this theater presents plays from the life and times of Lucy Maud Montgomery. Performances are in a renovated 19th-century church that Montgomery herself attended. Seats sell out fast, so book in advance!

New Glasgow

New Glasgow is a quiet town that spreads elegantly across the shores of the River Clyde. This is the favorite Lobster Supper getaway for folks from Charlottetown, although it's becoming equally respected for its luscious preserves.

Sights

Glasgow Glen Farm FARM
(☎902-963-2496; http://glasgowglenfarm.ca; 190 Lower New Glasgow Rd; ⏲9am-5pm Tue-Sat May-Oct) Blessed are the cheesemakers, or so they say. This one produces numerous variants of Gouda, which makes the perfect addition to any picnic hamper. Otherwise, the cheesy goodness is liberally applied to the island's most delicious pizzas.

Sleeping

★New Glasgow Highlands Camping & Cabins CAMPGROUND $
(☎902-964-3232; www.newglasgowhighlands.com; 2499 Glasgow Rd, Hunter River; tent/RV sites from $36/42, cabins from $65; ⏲Apr-Nov;) In Hunter River, 7km south of New Glasgow, you'll find this lovely campground with well-spaced sites that each have a fire pit. For rainy days there are simple cooking facilities in the lodge. There are also bright cabins, each with two bunks, a double bed, a sofa and a picnic table, but no linen or pillows; bathrooms are shared. Be sure to book ahead and don't even think about making late-night noise. It's all about peace and quiet. There's a laundry, a small store and a mystifying absence of bugs.

My Mother's Country Inn B&B $$
(☎902-964-2508; www.mymotherscountryinn.com; 6123 Hwy 13; r/cottages from $110/135;) An oasis within 20 hectares of rolling hills, brisk streams and enchanting woodlands, this is a pure, rural delight. The house is the essence of country style with sea-green and ochre painted walls, bright pastel quilts, wood floors and plenty of light. A big red barn just begs to be photographed beside a storybook brook.

Eating

Tucking in to one of New Glasgow's spectacular Lobster Suppers is something you must do when you come to PEI. You're in for a real treat if you've not experienced this Maritime way of dining before.

Their popularity with visitors has given rise to a nice bunch of locavore dining establishments in the surrounding area, catering to those who aren't so keen on these communal crustacean cook-offs.

★New Glasgow Lobster Supper SEAFOOD $$
(902-964-2870; http://peilobstersuppers.com; 604 Rte 258; lobster dinners from $35; 4-8pm Jun-Oct) You can make a right mess with the lobster here at the home of the original PEI Lobster Suppers (since 1958), while also gorging on an endless supply of great chowder, mussels, salads, breads and homemade desserts. Finish the feast with a mile-high lemon pie...if you possibly can.

★Prince Edward Island Preserve Company CAFE $$
(902-964-4300; http://preservecompany.com; 2841 New Glasgow Rd; mains $12-26; 9am-8pm;) Try free samples of delicious, though pricey, local preserves (such as raspberry champagne and orange ginger) before enjoying a casual meal overlooking the River Clyde. Hopefully your arrival won't coincide with a tour bus, which can take the edge off the serenity a little. Vegetarians are well catered for and the house specialty, raspberry cream cheese pie, is the bomb.

New London

New London is Green Gables country, with strong ties to Lucy Maud Montgomery. Of course, the town remains forever entwined with all things Anne.

Sights

Lucy Maud Montgomery Birthplace MUSEUM
(902-886-2099; www.lmmontgomerybirthplace.ca; cnr Rtes 6 & 20; $4; 9am-5pm) This house is now a museum that contains some of Lucy Maud's personal belongings, including her wedding dress.

Anne of Green Gables Museum MUSEUM
(902-886-2884; www.annemuseum.com; 4542 Rte 20; adult/child $5/1; 9am-6pm May-Oct) Surrounded by a luscious 44-hectare property, this is the charming home Lucy Maud called Silver Bush. It was always dear to her and she chose the parlor for her 1911 wedding. The museum contains such items as her writing desk and autographed 1st-edition books.

Courses

★Table COOKING
(902-314-9666; thetablepei.com; 4295 Graham's Rd; 2hr course from $65) Formerly the extremely popular Annie's Table, this unique outfit continues to operate in a similar vein under the new tutelage of Chef Derrick. Learn the secrets of local lavender, discover how to make PEI spuds spectacular and wrangle seafood into deliciousness at a cookery course in this gorgeous historic church that has been remodeled into a chef's kitchen.

Eating & Drinking

★Blue Winds Tea Room TEAHOUSE $$
(902-886-2860; http://bluewindstearoom.blogspot.com; 10746 Rte 6, New London; meals $10-14; 11am-6pm Mon-Thu, to 8pm Fri-Sun) This most charming place to stop for a bite and a cup of tea is surrounded by English gardens. Like everything else in this region, the fare can be very 'Anne'-centric. Order a raspberry cordial or some New Moon Pudding – both recipes have been taken from Lucy Maud's journals.

Sou'west Bar and Grill BAR
(902-886-3000; http://souwestbargrill.com; 6457 Rte 20; noon-11pm May-Oct) This modern joint with its sunny waterfront beer deck, sports on the big screen and weekly live music looks a little out of place in the bucolic countryside.

Shopping

★Village Pottery CERAMICS
(902-886-2473; www.villagepottery.ca; 10567 Rte 6; 10am-5pm) PEI's longest-running pottery studio is a family affair and a labor of love. Come in and meet Suzzane (she's tops!) for a chat or demonstration. We doubt you'll be able to leave without taking home one of the beautiful and colorful original works, which make great souvenirs.

Kensington

Kensington is a busy market town about halfway between Cavendish and Summerside. It's a good place to replenish supplies and the closest service center for those attending the popular Indian River Festival.

Tours

Malpeque Bay Kayak Tour Ltd KAYAKING
(☎866-582-3383; www.peikayak.ca; 3hr kayak tour $55) Just 15km from Kensington, this outfitter will kit you up and get you on the water above those famous oysters. Both kayak and stand-up paddleboard tours are available.

Festivals & Events

Indian River Festival MUSIC
(www.indianriverfestival.com; ⏲Jul-Sep) The Indian River Festival features a full season of performances by some of Canada's finest musicians (from Celtic to choral) in the wonderfully acoustic St Mary's Church.

Sleeping & Eating

Home Place Inn & Restaurant INN $
(☎902-836-5686; www.thehomeplace.ca; 21 Victoria St E; d/ste from $89/149; ⏲May-Oct; 📶) Home Place Inn & Restaurant exudes country elegance at its finest. In the morning you may be awakened with scents of freshly baking cinnamon rolls, and there's a licensed pub and restaurant on the premises.

★**Malpeque Oyster Barn** SEAFOOD $$
(☎902-836-3999; King St, Malpeque Bay; 6 oysters $14; ⏲11am-9pm Mon-Sat, noon-9pm Sun) The hamlet of Malpeque Bay is where PEI's famous eponymous oysters come from, renowned for their briny taste that's perfect with a beer. This atmospheric cafe sits in the top of a fisher's barn overlooking the bay.

Shipwright's Café MODERN CANADIAN $$$
(☎902-836-3403; http://shipwrightspei.com; 11869 Hwy 6, Margate; mains $18-28; ⏲11:30am-8:30pm Mon-Fri, from 5pm Sat & Sun) In Margate, 5km from Kensington, the Shipwright's Café is housed in an 1880s farmhouse overlooking rolling fields and flower gardens. It earns rave reviews for its seafood dishes and vegetarian fare concocted from organic herbs and vegetables from the gardens.

Cavendish

Anyone familiar with *Anne of Green Gables* might have lofty ideas of finding Cavendish as a quaint village bedecked in flowers and country charm; guess again. While the Anne and Lucy Maud Montgomery sites are right out of the imagination-inspiring book pages, Cavendish itself is a mishmash of manufactured attractions with no particular center.

The junction of Rtes 6 and 13 is the tourist center and the area's commercial hub. When you see the service station, wax museum, church, cemetery and assorted restaurants, you know you're there. This is the most-visited community on PEI outside of Charlottetown and, although an eyesore in this scenic region, it is a kiddie wonderland.

Sights

Green Gables Heritage Place HISTORIC SITE
(☎902-672-7874; www.pc.gc.ca/eng/lhn-nhs/pe/greengables/visit.aspx; 8619 Hwy 6; adult/child $8/4; ⏲10am-5pm Mon-Sat) Cavendish is the home town of Lucy Maud Montgomery (1874–1942), author of *Anne of Green Gables*. Here she is simply known as Lucy Maud or LM. Owned by her grandfather's cousins, the now-famous House of Green Gables and its Victorian surrounds inspired the setting for her fictional tale. A variety of combination tickets and packages are available.

In 1937 the house became part of the national park and it's now administered as a national heritage site, celebrating Lucy Maud and Anne with exhibits and audiovisual displays.

Cavendish Beach BEACH
(http://cavendishbeachpei.com) Beautiful Cavendish Beach gets crowded during summer months, but with perfect sand and a warm (ish) ocean in front, you won't really care

Lucy Maud Montgomery's Cavendish Homestead HISTORIC SITE
(☎902-963-2231; www.peisland.com/lmm; 8523 Cavendish Rd; adult/child $3/1; ⏲9am-5pm) This is considered hallowed ground to Anne fans Raised by her grandparents, Lucy Maud lived in this house from 1876 to 1911 and it is here that she wrote *Anne of Green Gables*. You'll find the old foundation of the house, many interpretive panels about Lucy Maud, a small on-site museum and a bookshop.

Festivals & Events

Cavendish Beach Music Festival MUSIC
(www.cavendishbeachmusic.com; ⏲early Jul) This hugely popular weekend festival attracts the biggest names in the US country scene and revelers from across the Maritime provinces.

Sleeping & Eating

While accommodations are numerous, remember that this is the busiest and most expensive area you can stay. There are more

WALKING LUCY MAUD MONTGOMERY'S CAVENDISH

If you haven't read the 1908 novel, this is the place to do it – not just to enjoy it, but to try and understand all the hype. The story revolves around Anne Shirley, a spirited 11-year-old orphan with red pigtails and a creative wit, who was mistakenly sent from Nova Scotia to Prince Edward Island. The aging Cuthberts (who were brother and sister) were expecting a strapping boy to help them with farm chores. In the end, Anne's strength of character wins over everyone in her path.

To really get a feel for the *Anne of Green Gables* scenery, get out and walk the green, gentle creek-crossed woods that Lucy Maud herself knew like the back of her hand. The best way is to start at the Lucy Maud Montgomery's Cavendish Homestead, then walk the 1.1km return trail to the Green Gables Heritage Place through the 'Haunted Wood.' In this way you arrive to a magical view from below the house rather than via a big parking lot and modern entrance. Once you're at the House of Green Gables you can enjoy the site plus many other surrounding trails, including 'Lover's Lane,' before hoofing it back to the Homestead.

bargains and more bucolic settings east, toward North Rustico, or just stay in Charlottetown (37km) and visit as a day trip.

Parkview Farms Tourist Home & Cottages GUESTHOUSE $
(902-963-2027; www.parkviewfarms.com; 8214 Cavendish Rd; r/cottages from $65/170;) This fine choice is set on a working dairy farm, 2km east of Cavendish. Ocean views, bathrooms and flowered wallpaper and frills abound in this comfortable and roomy tourist home. Each of the seven cottages contains a kitchen and a barbecue, plus a balcony to catch the dramatic comings and goings of the sun. The cottages are available May to mid-October; the B&B is open year-round.

Kindred Spirits Country Inn & Cottages INN $$
(902-963-2434; www.kindredspirits.ca; 46 Memory Lane; r/cottages from $95/120;) A huge, immaculate complex, this place has something for everyone from a storybook-quality inn-style B&B to deluxe suites. Rooms are every Anne fan's dream, with dotty floral prints, glossy wood floors and fluffy, comfy beds. Downstairs the lounge has a fireplace that will make you wish it would snow.

Carr's Oysters SEAFOOD $$
(902-886-3355; www.carrspei.ca; 32 Campbellton Rd, Stanley Bridge; mains $14-32; 10am-7pm) Dine on oysters straight from Malpeque Bay, or lobster, mussels and seafood you've never even heard of, like quahogs. There is also plenty of fish on offer, from salmon to trout. The setting is sociable and bright, and there's also an on-site seafood market.

★ Pearl Eatery MODERN CANADIAN $$$
(902-963-2111; http://pearleatery.com; 7792 Cavendish Rd, North Rustico; brunch $8-12, mains $22-32; from 4:30pm daily, 10am 2pm Sun) This shingled house just outside Cavendish is surrounded by flowers and is an absolutely lovely place to eat. There are plenty of unusual and seasonally changing options like ice-wine-infused chicken-liver pâté on a Gouda brioche and locally inspired mains, such as delicious butter-poached scallops.

Drinking & Nightlife

Lost Anchor Pub PUB
(902-388-0118; 8572 Cavendish Rd; noon-9pm) If all this talk of Anne is driving you to drink, here's where to come. Simple but hearty pub meals are available.

Shopping

Avonlea Village MALL
(902-963-3050; www.avonlea.ca; Rte 6; adult/family $19/70; 10am-5pm Jun-Sep) What was once a theme park has wound down into a glorified shopping mall. Still, costumed actors portray characters from the book and perform dramatic moments and scenes from its chapters. You might see a cow being milked, or ride on a wagon.

Information

Cavendish Visitor Information Centre (902-963-7830; cnr Rte 6 & Hwy 13; 9am-5pm) Anne fans will want to chat with the friendly staff who really know their stuff about all things PEI.

WESTERN PRINCE EDWARD ISLAND

Malpeque and Bedeque Bays converge to almost separate the western third of PEI from the rest of the province. This region sits entirely within the larger Prince County, and it combines the sparse pastoral scenery of Kings County's interior with some of Queens County's rugged coastal beauty.

The cultural history here stands out more than elsewhere on the island. On Lennox Island a proud Mi'kmaq community is working to foster knowledge of its past, while French Acadians are doing the same in the south, along Egmont and Bedeque Bays.

PEI's second-largest city, Summerside, is located on the region's southern shore.

Summerside

902 / POP 14,751

While it lacks the elegance and cosmopolitan vibe of Charlottetown, Summerside is a simpler, seaside-oriented place with everything you need in one small, tidy package. Recessed deep within Bedeque Bay and PEI's second-largest 'city,' this tiny seaside village possesses a modern waterfront and quiet streets lined with leafy trees and grand old homes. The two largest economic booms in the province's history, shipbuilding and fox breeding, shaped the city's development in the 19th and early 20th centuries. Like Charlottetown, its outskirts are plagued by unsightly development – you'll find most of Summerside's interesting bits along, or near to, Water St, which runs parallel to the waterfront.

Sights

Acadian Museum MUSEUM
(902-432-2880; http://museeacadien.org; 23 Maine Dr E, Miscouche; $5; 9:30am-7pm) The very worthwhile Acadian Museum, in Miscouche, uses 18th-century Acadian artifacts, texts, visuals and music to enlighten visitors about the tragic and compelling history of the Acadians on PEI since 1720. The introspective video introduces a fascinating theory that the brutal treatment of the Acadians by the British may have backhandedly helped preserve a vestige of Acadian culture on PEI.

Bottle Houses ARCHITECTURE
(902-854-2987; Rte 11, Cape Egmont; adult/child $5/2; 9am-8pm) The artful and monumental recycling project of Edouard Arsenault, this islander favorite features over 25,000 bottles of all shapes and sizes, stacked in white cement to create a handful of buildings with light-filled mosaic walls.

Spinnaker's Landing WATERFRONT
This redeveloped waterfront is the highlight of Summerside. A continually expanding boardwalk allows you to wander and enjoy the harbor and its scenic surrounds. There are some very nice eateries, a stage for live music in the summer and numerous shops. A mock lighthouse provides an attractive lookout and some local information, while a large model ship is a dream playground for kids.

Eptek Exhibition Centre GALLERY
(902-888-8373; 130 Harbour Dr; entry by donation; 10am-4pm) The modern Eptek Exhibition Centre features local and traveling art exhibitions.

Sleeping & Eating

Cedar Dunes Provincial Park CAMPGROUND $
(902-859-8785; www.tourismpei.com/provincial-park/cedar-dunes; tent sites $23-25, RV sites $26-27) Has tent space in an open grassy field adjacent to West Point Lighthouse. Its red-sand beach is an island gem.

Willowgreen Farm B&B $
(902-436-4420; www.willowgreenfarm.com; 117 Bishop Dr; r from $65;) With the Confederation Trail at its back door, this rambling farmhouse is an incredibly great-value place to stay; you feel like you're in the country, but actually you're in central Summerside. Rooms are bright, and the bold country interior is a refreshing change from busy period decors. Read beside the woodstove, or check out some of the interesting farm animals.

Summerside Bed & Breakfast B&B $$
(902-620-4993; www.summersideinnbandb.com; 98 Summer St; r from $115;) Poetically located on the corner of Summer and Winter Sts, the room you should obviously angle for is the bright and spacious Spring Room. This fine heritage building has been home to two Canadian premiers and boasts plenty of sitting areas and charm. Your friendly hosts prepare delicious hot breakfasts.

Five Eleven West CANADIAN $$
(http://fiveelevenwest.com; 511 Notre Dame St; mains $12-24; 11:30am-2pm Mon-Fri, 5-8pm daily) Summerside's most modern eatery is tucked into a very unlikely corner of the town's multipurpose sports complex. Once you find it (to the left of the snack bar) be

Summerside

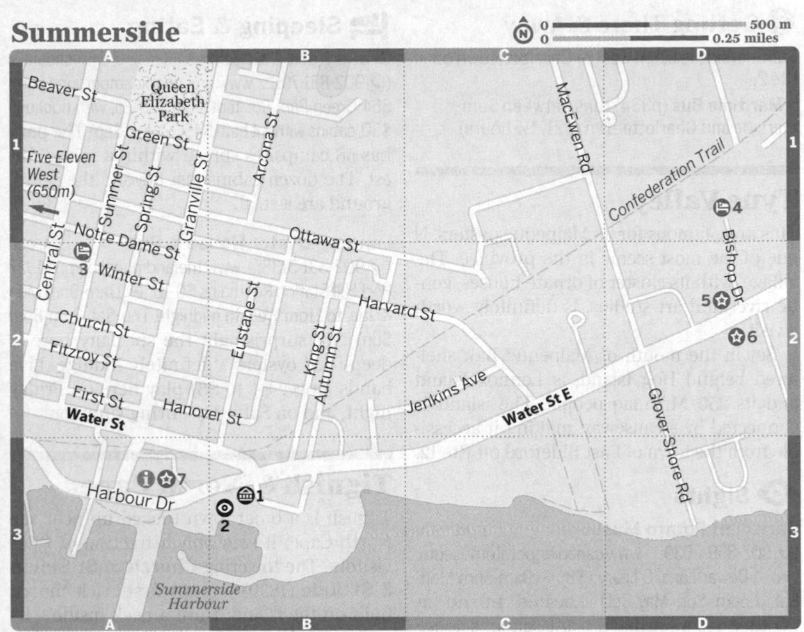

Summerside	
Sights	
1 Eptek Exhibition Centre	B3
2 Spinnaker's Landing	B3
Sleeping	
3 Summerside Bed & Breakfast	A2
4 Willowgreen Farm	D1
Entertainment	
5 College of Piping & Celtic Performing Arts	D2
6 Feast Dinner Theatres	D2
7 Harbourfront Theatre	A3

prepared to be impressed. Everything from the massive portion of beer-battered fish-and-chips to Madras chicken over rice, steamed mussels and prime rib is beautifully prepared, and the ambience is chic.

Entertainment

College of Piping & Celtic Performing Arts LIVE MUSIC
(902-436-5377; http://collegeofpiping.com; 619 Water St E; ceilidhs adult/student $12/7; 9am-9pm, ceilidhs 7pm) In celebration of Celtic dance and music, this school provides visitors with free 20-minute miniconcerts from Monday to Friday at 11:30am, 1:30pm and 3:30pm – expect bagpipes, singing and dancing. Inspired? Then get yourself out to the 'Highland Storm,' a Celtic music and dance extravaganza with a cast of 30 of the island's best performers. It's performed three days a week through summer.

Feast Dinner Theatres THEATER
(902-888-2200; http://feastdinnertheatres.com; 618 Water St E; dinner & show from $40; 6:30pm Mon-Sat Jun-Dec) Most locals giggle when they speak of their last time at Feast Dinner Theatres, the longest-running theater restaurant in Atlantic Canada. Music, script and improvisation combine with audience participation to make for a truly memorable evening. And the food's not too shabby either.

Harbourfront Theatre THEATER
(902-888-2500; www.harbourfronttheatre.com; 124 Harbour Dr) This modern theater is the venue for a changing series of plays, comedy and more.

Information

Visitor Information Centre (902-888-8364; 124 Harbour Dr; 9am-7pm Jul & Aug, reduced hours May, Jun, Sep & Oct) Pick up a copy of the useful walking-tour pamphlet, which details the town's finer 19th-century buildings.

Getting There & Away

Summerside is 61km west of Charlottetown on Rte 2.

Maritime Bus (p334) runs between Summerside and Charlottetown ($21, 1½ hours).

Tyne Valley

This area, famous for its Malpeque oysters, is one of the most scenic in the province. The village, with its cluster of ornate houses, gentle river and art studios, is definitely worth a visit.

Set in the mouth of Malpeque Bay, sheltered behind Hog Island, is Lennox Island and its 250 Mi'kmaq people. The island is connected by a causeway, making it accessible from the town of East Bideford off Rte 12.

Sights

Canadian Potato Museum MUSEUM
(902-859-2039; www.canadianpotatomuseum.info; 1 Dewar Lane, O'Leary; $8; 9am-5pm Mon-Sat, 1-5pm Sun May-Oct) Located inland at O'Leary. It's a bit like a giant school science fair project with hallways of information panels and pictures on the walls.

Lennox Island Aboriginal Ecotourism Complex NOTABLE BUILDING
(866-831-2702; 2 Eagle Feather Trail, Lennox Island; adult/student $4/3; 10am-6pm Mon-Sat Jun-Sep) Small, changing exhibits and information about the two excellent interpretive trails around the island. These trails consist of two loops, forming a total of 13km, with the shorter one (3km) being accessible to people in wheelchairs – if you're lucky and someone's around, a local will guide you for a small fee. Also ask at the information desk if anything else is on offer, as the complex's program changes frequently

Green Park Shipbuilding Museum MUSEUM
(902-831-7947; 360 Green Park Rd; adult $5; 9am-5pm) This museum and restored Victorian home, **Historic Yeo House**, along with a recreated shipyard and partially constructed 200-tonne brigantine, combine to tell the story of the booming shipbuilding industry in the 19th century.

Festivals & Events

Tyne Valley Oyster Festival FOOD & DRINK
(www.tvoysterfest.ca; Aug) Four days of shucking and slurping slimy oysters. Not for everyone. A must for lovers of the bivalve.

Sleeping & Eating

Green Park Campsites CAMPGROUND $
(902-831-7912; www.greenparkcampground.com; 364 Green Park Rd; tent sites $23-25, with hookups $30, cabins without bath $45; Jun-Sep) The park has 58 campsites spread within a mixed forest. The dozen cabins just beyond the campground are a steal.

Landing Oyster House & Pub SEAFOOD
(902-831-3138; www.thelandingpei.com; 1327 Port Hill Station Rd; mains $9-16; 11am-9pm Mon & Tue, to 11pm Wed, to midnight Thu-Sat, 8am-8pm Sun) Not surprisingly, the specialty here is deep-fried oysters – definitely indulge. Live bands (cover $4 to $8) play here on Friday night, and on Saturday during summer.

Tignish & North Cape

Tignish is a quiet town tucked up near the North Cape; it sees only a fraction of PEI's visitors. The towering **Church of St Simon & St Jude** (1859) was the first brick church built on the island. Have a peek inside – its ceiling has been restored to its gorgeous but humble beginnings, and the organ (1882) is of gargantuan proportions.

The narrow, windblown North Cape home to the Atlantic Wind Test, and to the longest natural rock reef on the continent. At low tide, it's possible to walk out 800m to explore tide pools and search for seals.

Tignish Cultural Centre NOTABLE BUILDING
(902-882-1999; 305 School St, Tignish; 8am-4pm Mon-Fri) FREE The Confederation Trail begins two blocks south of the church on School St. The Tignish Cultural Centre, near the church, has a good exhibition of old maps and photos and tourist information.

Interpretive Center MUSEUM
(902-882-2991; Rte 12, North Cape; $6; 9:30am-8pm) Provides high-tech displays dedicated to wind energy, and informative displays on the history of the area. The aquarium is always a hit with kids. The Black Marsh Nature Trail (2.7km) leaves the interpretive center and takes you to the west side of the cape – at sunset these crimson cliffs simply glow against the deep-blue waters.

Wind & Reef Restaurant & Lounge SEAFOOD
(902-882-3535; mains $9-29; noon-9pm) The menu and view are equally vast and pleasing at this atmospheric restaurant, lcoated above the Interpretive Center.

Newfoundland & Labrador

Includes ➡

Best Places to Eat

- ➡ Merchant Tavern (p470)
- ➡ Bonavista Social Club (p483)
- ➡ Chafe's Landing (p475)
- ➡ Norseman Restaurant (p497)
- ➡ Adelaide Oyster House (p469)

Best Places to Sleep

- ➡ Fogo Island Inn (p490)
- ➡ Tuckamore Lodge (p498)
- ➡ Artisan Inn (p481)
- ➡ Skerwink Hostel (p481)
- ➡ Quirpon Lighthouse Inn (p497)

Why Go?

With rocky crags, drifting icebergs and puffins flapping by, Canada's easternmost province – and historically its most rebellious floats in a stunning world of its own. The island that has long moved to its own beat maintains its own time zone (a half-hour ahead of the mainland) and lilting old-world dialect (the *Dictionary of Newfoundland English* provides translation).

St John's, with its buoyant music, modern dining scene and steep, foggy streets, abounds with entertainment. Outside of the good-time capital, wee fishing villages freckle the coast and isolated outer isles. Here the natural world is your oyster. Set off for woodland hikes, berry picking and sea kayaking with glittering views. Don't miss the Viking vestiges, plates of cod tongue and partridgeberry pie, or the rum-soaked tales that color this remote hunk of northern rock.

When to Go

St John's

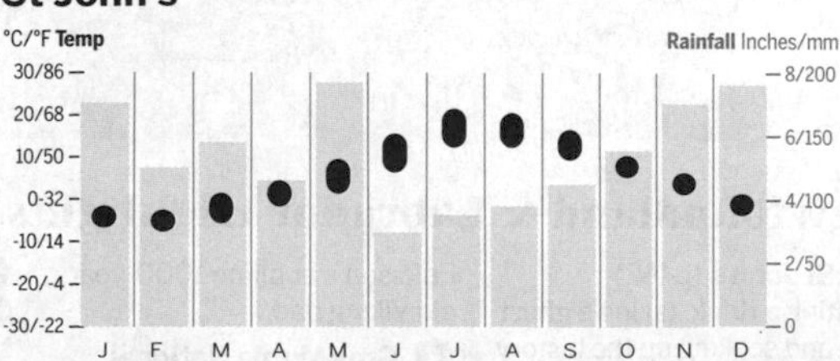

Jun Icebergs glisten offshore, though the weather can be wet and foggy.

Jul & Aug Whales cavort, festivals rock the weekends, and the province is at its sunniest.

Dec & Jan Skiers hit the slopes as Marble Mountain receives most of its 5m of snow.

54°W
52°W
0 100 km
0 50 miles
Labrador
Port Hope Simpson
Mary's Harbour
Belle Isle
Strait of Belle Isle
Red Bay 8
Québec
L'Anse aux Meadows National Historic Site
Cape Onion 3
Quirpon Island
St Lunaire-Griquet
St Anthony
Pinware
Forteau
Old Fort Bay
Blanc Sablon
Hare Bay
St Barbe
Main Brook
Plum Point
Conche
Grey Islands
Roddickton
Port au Choix
Northern Peninsula
Hawke's Bay
ATLANTIC OCEAN
52°N
Gulf of St Lawrence
50°N
The Arches
Cow Head
Sally's Cove
Gros Morne National Park 4
Rocky Harbour
Norris Point
Trout River
Woody Point
Glenburnie
Fleur de Lys
Baie Verte
Baie Verte Peninsula
La Scie
Notre Dame Bay
Twillingate Island 6
Change Islands
5 Fogo Island
Springdale
Moreton's Harbour
Farewell
Boyd's Cove
Lewisporte
Deer Lake
Grand Lake
York Harbour
Corner Brook
Marble Mountain
Grand Falls-Windsor
Gander
Bonavista Bay
Port au Port Peninsula
Lourdes
Stephenville
Port au Port West
Red Indian Lake
Newfoundland
Terra Nova National Park
Burnside
Salvage
Bonavista
Elliston
Trinity
Port Rexton
Bay de Verde Peninsula
Bonavista Peninsula
Trans-Canada Hwy
Barachois Pond Provincial Park
Maelpaeg Lake
St George's Bay
Bay du Nord Wilderness Reserve
Head of Bay d'Espoir
Clarenville
Trinity Bay
Conception Bay
48°N
Cape Anguille
Isle aux Morts
Rose Blanche
Cape Ray
Port aux Basques
St Alban's
Heart's Content
Heart's Delight
Harbour Grace
St John's 1
Cupids
Burgeo
Grey River
McCallum
François
Pool's Cove
Dildo
Brigus
Petty Harbour
Sandbanks Provincial Park
Ramea
Hermitage
Harbour Breton
Avalon Peninsula
Burin Peninsula
Argentia
Witless Bay Ecological Reserve 2
Placentia
La Manche PP
South Coast Outports Ferry
Fortune Bay
Grand Bank
Marystown
Cape St Mary's Ecological Reserve
St Mary's
Ferryland
Avalon Wilderness Reserve
Île de Miquelon
Fortune
Burin
St Lawrence
St-Pierre & Miquelon (FRANCE)
7 Île St-Pierre
Chance Cove PP
St Vincent's
Mistaken Point Ecological Reserve
Port aux Basques-North Sydney (NS) Ferry
Cabot Strait
Argentia-North Sydney (NS) Ferry
58°W
56°W
54°W
52°W

Newfoundland & Labrador Highlights

1 **St John's** (p462) Hoisting a drink, taking a ghost tour and soaking up the history of North America's oldest city.

2 **Witless Bay Ecological Reserve** (p475) Sharing the waves with whales and puffins.

3 **L'Anse aux Meadows National Historic Site** (p496) Exploring Leif Eriksson's sublime 1000-year-old Viking pad.

4 **Gros Morne National Park** (p492) Hiking the ridges and kayaking the fjord-like lakes.

5 **Fogo** (p490) Trying out the modern outport life.

6 **Twillingate** (p488) Ogling icebergs, hiking and sipping Moose Joose.

7 **St-Pierre** (p484) Getting your French fix – wine, éclairs and baguettes.

8 **Red Bay** (p509) Learning Basque whaling history then walking alongside ancient whale bones.

History

The Paleo-Indians walked into Labrador 9000 years ago. They hunted seals, fished for salmon and tried to stay warm. The Vikings, led by Leif Eriksson, washed ashore further south at L'Anse aux Meadows in Newfoundland in AD 1000 and established North America's first European settlement.

John Cabot (Italian-born Giovanni Caboto) sailed around the shores of Newfoundland next. It was 1497, and he was employed by England's Henry VII. Cabot's stories of cod stocks so prolific that one could nearly walk on water spread throughout Europe. Soon the French, Portuguese, Spanish and Basques were also fishing off Newfoundland's coast.

The 1713 Treaty of Utrecht ceded all of Newfoundland to England. The land remained a British colony for most of the next two centuries, with life revolving around the booming fishing industry. Newfoundland's Aboriginal people, the Beothuk, did not fare well after settlement began. Diseases and land conflicts contributed to their demise by 1829.

Ever true to its independent spirit, Newfoundland was the last province to join Canada, doing so in 1949. While Labrador was always part of the package, it wasn't until 2001 that it became part of the provincial name.

Language

Two hundred years ago, coastal fishing families from Ireland and England made up almost the entire population. Since then, as a result of living in isolated outposts, their language has evolved into almost 60 different dialects. Strong, lilting inflections, unique slang and colorful idioms pepper the language, sometimes confounding even residents.

The authoritative source is the *Dictionary of Newfoundland English* (www.heritage.nf.ca/dictionary).

Land & Climate

They don't call it the Rock for nothing. Glaciers tore through, leaving behind a rugged landscape of boulders, lakes and bogs. Newfoundland's interior remains barren, while the island's cities and towns congregate at its edges near the sea.

Labrador is sparser than Newfoundland, puddled and tundra-like, with mountains thrown in for good measure.

Temperatures peak in July and August, when daytime highs average 20°C. These are also the driest months; it rains or snows about 15 out of every 30 days. Wintertime temperatures hover at 0°C. Fog and wind plague the coast much of the year (which makes for a lot of canceled flights).

Parks & Wildlife

Whales, moose and puffins are Newfoundland's wildlife stars, and most visitors see them all. Whale-watching tours depart from all around the province and will take you close to the sea mammals (usually humpback and minke). Puffins – the funny-looking love child of the penguin and parrot – flap around Witless Bay and Elliston. Moose nibble shrubs near roadsides throughout the province, so keep an eye out while driving. Some visitors also glimpse caribou near the Avalon Wilderness Reserve, which is special because usually these beasts can only be seen in the High Arctic. Caribou herds also roam in Labrador, though their numbers have been declining sharply in recent years.

PLANNING YOUR TRIP

- Book ahead for rental cars and accommodations. If you're arriving during the mid-July to early August peak, secure a car by April or May and don't wait much longer to book a room. **Newfoundland & Labrador Tourism** (☎800-563-6353; www.newfoundlandlabrador.com) has listings.
- Driving distances are lengthy so have realistic expectations of what you can cover. For instance, it's 708km between St John's and Gros Morne National Park. The **Road Distance Database** (www.stats.gov.nl.ca/DataTools/RoadDB/Distance) is a good reference.
- Know the seasons for puffins (May to August) and whales (July to August). Icebergs (June to early July) can be tricky to predict. Check **Iceberg Finder** (www.icebergfinder.com) to get the drift.

Getting There & Around

AIR

St John's International Airport (p473) is the main hub for the region, though **Deer Lake Airport** (p492) is an excellent option for visitors focusing on the Northern Peninsula. Airlines flying in include **Air Canada** (☎888-247-2262; www.aircanada.com), **PAL Airlines** (☎709-576-1666; www.palairlines.ca), **Porter** (☎888-619-8622; www.flyporter.com) and **United** (☎800-864-8331; www.united.com).

NEWFOUNDLAND ITINERARIES

Five Days

Start in **St John's** by visiting **Signal Hill** (p463) and **Cape Spear** (p474). Both are historic sites, but they also offer walking trails and views where you just may see an iceberg, a whale or both. At night sample St John's eateries, funky shops and music-filled pubs.

After a couple of days of 'big city' life, move onward through the **Avalon Peninsula**. Cruise to see whales and puffins at **Witless Bay Ecological Reserve** (p475), plan a picnic in **Ferryland** (p476) or visit the birds at **Cape St Mary's Ecological Reserve** (p479). Spend the last day or two soaking up the historic eastern communities of **Trinity** (p480) and **Bonavista** (p482) and the cliffside hikes in between.

Ten Days

Do the five-day itinerary and then go west, possibly via a quick flight to **Deer Lake** (p492), and reap the reward of viewing the mighty fjords of **Gros Morne National Park** (p492) and the monumental Viking history at **L'Anse aux Meadows National Historic Site** (p496). With a few extra days you could sail across the **Strait of Belle Isle** and slow way down among the wee towns and bold granite cliffs of the **Labrador Straits** (p506).

BOAT

Marine Atlantic (☎800-341-7981; www.marine-atlantic.ca) operates two massive car/passenger ferries between North Sydney (NS) and Newfoundland. There's a daily, six-hour crossing to Port aux Basques (western Newfoundland) year-round, and a thrice-weekly, 14-hour crossing to Argentia (on the Avalon Peninsula) in summer. Reservations are recommended, especially to Argentia.

Provincial Ferry Service (www.gov.nl.ca/ferryservices) runs the smaller boats that travel within the province to various islands and coastal towns. Each service has its own phone number with up-to-the-minute information; it's wise to call before embarking.

BUS

DRL (☎709-263-2171; www.drl-lr.com) sends one bus daily each way between St John's and Port aux Basques (13½ hours), making 25 stops en route. Other than DRL, public transportation consists of small, regional shuttle vans that connect with one or more major towns. Although not extensive, the system works pretty well and will get most people where they want to go.

CAR & MOTORCYCLE

The Trans-Canada Hwy (Hwy 1) is the main cross-island roadway. Driving distances are deceptive, as travel is often slow going on heavily contorted, single-lane roads. Watch out for moose, especially at dusk.

Be warned: rental-car fleets are small (thanks to the island's remoteness and short tourist season), which means loads of visitors vie for limited vehicles in midsummer. Costs can rack up to $100 per day (including taxes and mileage fees). Reserve well in advance – April or May is recommended if you're traveling during the mid-July-to-early-August peak – and confirm the booking before you arrive.

Driving distances include the following:

St John's to Port aux Basques 905km
St John's to Gros Morne 708km
Gros Morne to St Anthony 372km

ST JOHN'S

POP 106,200

North America's oldest city sits on the steep slopes of a snug and sheltered harbor. With jelly-bean-colored row houses lining the hilly streets, the city begs comparisons to San Francisco – though in miniature. It too is home to artists, musicians, cutting-edge eateries, inflated real estate and young, iPhone-using denizens. Yet the vibe of Newfoundland's largest city and capital remains refreshingly small-town.

Highlights include a jaunt up Signal Hill, with its sweeping views of the harbor, and listening to live music and hoisting a pint (or shot of rum) in pubs along George St. Many visitors take advantage of the city's excellent dining and lodging options by making St John's their base camp for exploring the Avalon Peninsula. Cape Spear, Witless Bay Ecological Reserve and Ferryland are among the easy day trips.

History

St John's excellent natural harbor, leading out to what were once seething seas of cod, prompted the first European settlement here in 1528. During the late 1600s and much of the 1700s, St John's was razed and taken over several times as the French, English and Dutch fought for it. Britain won the ultimate victory on Signal Hill in 1762.

The harbor steadfastly maintained its position as the center of world trade for salted cod well into the 20th century. By midcentury, warehouses lined Water St, and the merchants who owned them made a fortune. Come the early 1960s, St John's had more millionaires per capita than any other city in North America.

Today the city's wharves still act as service stations to fishing vessels from around the world and the occasional cruise ship, though the cod industry suffered mightily after a 1992 fishing moratorium. The offshore oil industry now drives the economy.

Sights

Most sights are downtown or within a few kilometers, though be prepared for some serious uphill walking.

★Rooms MUSEUM

(☎709-757-8000; www.therooms.ca; 9 Bonaventure Ave; adult/child $7.50/4, 6-9pm Wed free; ⊙10am-5pm Mon, Tue & Thu-Sat, to 9pm Wed, noon-5pm Sun) Not many museums offer the chance to see a giant squid, hear avant-garde sound sculptures and peruse ancient weaponry all under one roof. But that's the Rooms, the province's all-in-one historical museum, art gallery and archives. The building itself, a massive stone-and-glass complex, is impressive to look at, with views that lord it over the city. Has an on-site cafe and excellent restaurant.

Quidi Vidi HISTORIC SITE

Over Signal Hill, away from town, is the tiny picturesque village of Quidi Vidi. Check out the 18th-century battery and the lakeside regatta museum, but make your first stop Quidi Vidi Brewery (p466). The fee includes ample tastings and a bottle to sip while touring. Be sure to try the Iceberg brand, made with water from the big hunks.

Nearby you'll find the oldest cottage in North America, the 1750s-era Mallard Cottage (p470). At press time it was being converted into a restaurant serving Newfoundland comfort foods.

The 1762 **Quidi Vidi Battery**, atop the hill end of Cuckhold's Cove Rd, was built by the French after they took St John's. The British quickly claimed it, and it remained in military service into the 1800s.

Inland from the village, **Quidi Vidi Lake** is the site of the city-stopping St John's Regatta. The **Royal St John's Regatta Museum** (☎709-576-8921; cnr Lakeview Ave & Clancy Dr, off Forest Rd; ⊙by appointment) FREE is on the 2nd floor of the boathouse. A popular walking trail leads around the lake.

Quidi Vidi is about 2km from the northeast edge of downtown. Take Plymouth Rd, go left on Quidi Vidi Rd, then right on Forest Rd (which becomes Quidi Vidi Village Rd). For the brewery, bear right onto Barrows Rd. For the battery, veer off on Cuckold's Cove Rd. For the regatta museum, take a left off Forest Rd onto Lakeview Ave. You can also walk from Signal Hill via the Cuckold's Cove Trail, which takes about 30 minutes.

Signal Hill National Historic Site HISTORIC SITE

(☎709-772-5367; www.pc.gc.ca/signalhill; ⊙grounds 24hr) The city's most famous landmark is worth it for the glorious view alone, though there's much more to see. The tiny castle atop the hill is **Cabot Tower** (⊙8:30am-5pm Apr-Nov) FREE, built in 1900 to honor both John Cabot's arrival in 1497 and Queen Victoria's Diamond Jubilee. In midsummer soldiers dressed as the 19th-century Royal Newfoundland Company perform a tattoo (p472) and fire cannons.

The Signal Hill Visitor Centre (p466) features interactive displays on the site's history. The last North American battle of the Seven Years' War took place here in 1762, and Britain's victory ended France's renewed aspirations for control of eastern North America. The tattoo takes place next to the center at O'Flaherty Field.

You can see cannons and the remains of the late 18th-century British battery at **Queen's Battery & Barracks** further up the hill. Inside Cabot Tower, educational displays relay how Italian inventor Guglielmo Marconi received the first wireless transatlantic

NEWFOUNDLAND FAST FACTS

- Population: 527,000
- Area: 405,212 sq km
- Capital: St John's
- Quirky fact: Newfoundland has 82 places called Long Pond, 42 called White Point and one called Jerry's Nose

St John's

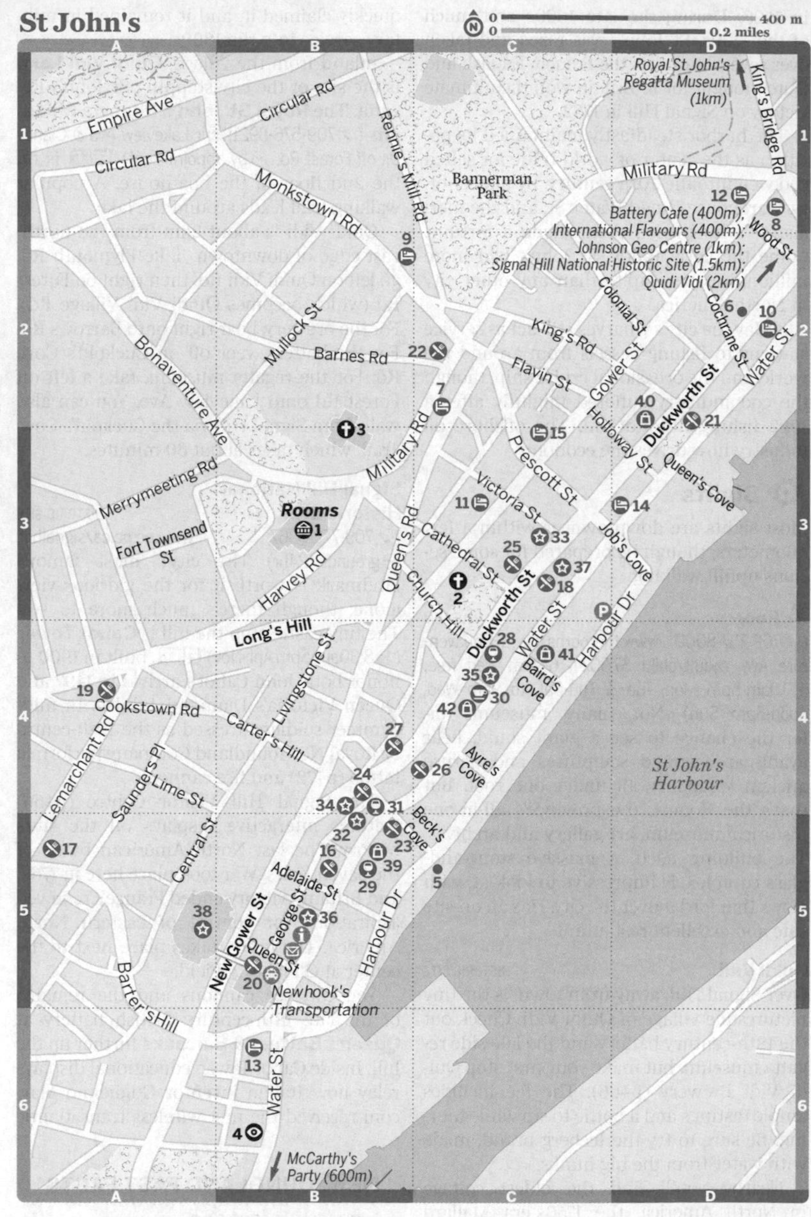

message from Cornwall, England at the site in 1901. An amateur radio society operates a station in the tower in July and August.

Signal Hill also offers guided tours around the grounds, Thursday lunches where you eat like an 18th-century soldier and sunset concerts. Check the website's 'Activities' section for details and costs.

An awesome way to return to downtown is along the 1.7km North Head Trail (p467).

The site sits 1.5km from downtown, up Signal Hill Rd.

St John's

CA Pippy Park PARK

(www.pippypark.com) Full of features, 1343-hectare CA Pippy Park coats downtown's northwestern edge. Recreational facilities include walking trails, picnic areas, playgrounds, a golf course and a campground. **Memorial University**, the province's only university, is here too. The university's botanical garden (p466) is at Oxen Pond, at the park's western edge off Mt Scio Rd.

Cultivated areas and a nature reserve fill the botanical landscape. Together, these and the park's **Long Pond** marsh give visitors an excellent introduction to Newfoundland's flora, habitats (including boreal forest and bogs) and animals (look for birds at Long Pond and the occasional moose). Take the 3km **Long Pond Walk** for the full effect.

The **Fluvarium** (709-754-3474; www.fluvarium.ca; 5 Nagle's Pl; adult/child/family $8/6/25; 9am-5pm Mon-Fri, from 10am Sat & Sun Jul & Aug, reduced hours Sep-Jun), a glass-sided cross-section of a 'living' river, is located across the street from the campground. Viewers can peer through large windows to observe the undisturbed goings-on beneath the surface of Nagle's Hill Brook. Numerous brown trout and the occasional eel can be seen. If there has been substantial rain or high winds, all visible life is completely lost in the murkiness.

To get here from downtown, take Bonaventure Ave north to Allandale Rd and follow the signs; it's about 2km.

Johnson Geo Centre MUSEUM

(709-737-7880; www.geocentre.ca; 175 Signal Hill Rd; adult/child $12/6; 9:30am-5pm) Nowhere in the world can geo-history, going back to the birth of the earth, be accessed so easily as in Newfoundland, and the Geo Centre does a grand job of making snore-worthy geological information perk up with appeal via its underground, interactive displays.

The center also has an exhibit on the *Titanic,* and how human error and omission, not just an iceberg, caused the tragedy. For instance, the ship's owners didn't supply her with enough lifeboats so as not to 'clutter the deck,' and the crew ignored myriad ice warnings. What any of this has to do with geology remains unclear, but who cares? It's fascinating.

Trails with interpretive panels wind around outside. The Geo Centre is up Signal Hill Rd, about 1km beyond downtown.

Memorial University Botanical Garden GARDENS

(☎709-737-8590; www.mun.ca/botgarden; adult/child $8/3; ⏰10am-5pm May-Aug, reduced hours Sep-Apr) The premier botanical garden of the province, with nature trails, a large cultivated garden and a greenhouse within a 100-acre nature reserve.

Newman Wine Vaults HISTORIC SITE

(☎709-739-7870; www.seethesites.ca; 436 Water St; admission by donation; ⏰by appointment) Dating from the 1780s, these dark, cool wine vaults are where the Newman company aged its port until 1996 (when EU regulations forced the process back to Portugal). Guides used to give tours, but at press time they were on hold. The vaults often host music, literary and foodie events.

Quidi Vidi Brewery BREWERY

(☎709-738-4040; www.quidividibrewery.ca; 35 Barrows Rd; tasting or tour $10; ⏰10am-4pm) Quidi Vidi Brewing is a microbrewery located in an old fish-processing plant on the tiny wharf. It's a swell place to slake one's thirst. By car, take Forest Rd from the city and follow it past the lake until it turns into Quidi Vidi Village Rd. Locals prefer you to park on the outskirts of town and walk in.

Anglican Cathedral of St John the Baptist CHURCH

(☎709-726-5677; www.stjohnsanglicancathedral.org; 16 Church Hill; high tea $9; ⏰9:30am-4pm) Serving Canada's oldest parish (1699), the Anglican cathedral is one of the finest examples of ecclesiastical Gothic architecture in North America. Although originally built in the 1830s, all but its exterior walls were reduced to ashes by the Great Fire of 1892. Rebuilt in 1905, its Gothic ribbed ceiling, graceful stone arches and long stained-glass windows are timeless marvels. **High tea** is offered in the crypt on weekday afternoons in July and August.

Harbourside Park PARK

With iconic statues of a Newfoundland dog and a Labrador retriever, this park hosts the City of St John's free Music at Harbourside lunchtime concert series, on Fridays at 12:30pm throughout the summer.

Bowring Park PARK

(www.bowringpark.com; Waterford Bridge Rd) A beautiful 200-acre city park with a duck pond, tennis courts, swimming pool and playground.

Signal Hill Visitor Centre MUSEUM

(adult/child $3.90/1.90; ⏰10am-6pm May-Oct) Features interactive displays on the site's history. The last North American battle of the Seven Years' War took place here in 1762, and Britain's victory ended France's renewed aspirations for control of eastern North America.

Basilica of St John the Baptist CHURCH

(☎709-754-2170; www.thebasilica.ca; 200 Military Rd; ⏰9:30am-5pm) Built in 1855, the soaring twin spires of the basilica pierce the sky and are visible all the way from Signal Hill. Its design marks the revival of classical architecture in North America. Inside, 65 stained-glass windows illuminate the remarkable polychromatic Italianate ceiling and its gold-leaf highlights.

ST JOHN'S FOR CHILDREN

St John's will keep the wee ones entertained, rain or shine.

Boat Tours (right) The various boat tours are also a great bet, but inquire if there are icebergs and whales in the area first.

Bowring Park (p466) The ever-hungry ducks at the pond love company.

CA Pippy Park (p465) A kids' haven, with a huge playground, lots of trails and, of course, the Fluvarium.

Johnson Geo Centre (p465) While geology may not initially spark their interest, the fact that this center is underground may do the trick.

Ocean Sciences Centre (p506) Check out the sea creatures.

Signal Hill Tattoo (p472) Just knowing a cannon will blast at the end of the tattoo should keep kids riveted.

St John's Haunted Hike (p467) Older kids will enjoy the ghostly tales.

Activities

★North Head Trail — WALKING

An awesome way to return to downtown from Signal Hill is along the North Head Trail (1.7km) that connects Cabot Tower with the harborfront Battery neighborhood. The walk departs from the tower's parking lot and traces the cliffs, imparting tremendous sea views and sometimes whale spouts. Because much of the trail runs along the bluff's sheer edge, it isn't something to attempt in icy, foggy or dark conditions.

Grand Concourse — WALKING

(www.grandconcourse.ca) The Grand Concourse is an ambitious 160km-long network of trails all over town and linking St John's with nearby Mt Pearl and Paradise via downtown sidewalks, trails, river corridors and old railway beds.

Tours

★St John's Haunted Hike — WALKING

(www.hauntedhike.com; adult/child $10/5; 9:30pm Sun-Thu Jun-Sep) The black-caped Reverend Thomas Wyckham Jarvis Esq leads these super-popular explorations of the city's dark corners. He'll spook you with tales of headless captains, murderers and other ghosts. Departure is from the Anglican Cathedral's west entrance. On midsummer Fridays and Saturdays, the spine-tingling action moves to Signal Hill for a seated, indoor show of ghost stories (8pm, tickets $15).

Outfitters — KAYAKING

(709-579-4453; www.theoutfitters.nf.ca; 220 Water St; half-/full-day tour $69/169; 10am-6pm Mon-Wed, to 9pm Thu & Fri, 10am-6pm Sat, noon-5pm Sun) Popular kayak tours at Bay Bulls, with shuttle service (round-trip $30) from Outfitters' store downtown. It also rents outdoor equipment and has good information on the East Coast Trail (p474).

McCarthy's Party — BUS

(709-579-4480; www.mccarthysparty.com; 566 Water St; 3hr tour $55) A seasoned tour company with wonderful guides that will give you a true sense of local culture. Offerings range from half-day tours of St John's and Cape Spear to 12-day trips around the island.

Iceberg Quest — BOATING

(709-722-1888; www.icebergquest.com; Pier 6; 2hr tour adult/child $65/28) Departs from St John's harbor and makes a run down to Cape Spear in search of icebergs in June and whales in July and August. There are multiple departures daily in a new 100-person boat.

O'Brien's — BOATING

(709-753-4850; www.obriensboattours.com; 126 Duckworth St; 2hr tour adult/child $58/30) See whales, puffins and icebergs at Witless Bay. Boats launch from Bay Bulls 31km south, but O'Brien's has a shuttle service (round-trip $25) that picks up from hotels throughout St John's. Buy tickets at the O'Brien's shop.

Legend Tours — BUS

(709-753-1497; www.legendtours.ca; 3hr tour $59-69) This award-winning operator covers St John's, Cape Spear and the northeast Avalon Peninsula. The commentary is richly woven with humor and historical tidbits. Call to reserve; they'll pick you up at your hotel or B&B.

Festivals & Events

Sound Symposium — PERFORMING ARTS

(www.soundsymposium.com; tickets from $10; early Jul) Held in even-numbered years, it's a big, avant-garde week of concerts, workshops, dance, theater and film experiments.

Shakespeare by the Sea Festival — THEATER

(709-722-7287; www.shakespearebythesea festival.com; tickets $20-25; early Jul–mid-Aug) Live outdoor productions are presented at Signal Hill, local parks and other venues. Buy all tickets on-site; cash only. Some performances are free.

George Street Festival — MUSIC

(www.georgestreetlive.ca; tickets from $20; late Jul/early Aug) The mighty George St becomes one big nightclub for a fabulous week of daytime and nighttime musical performances.

Downtown Busker Festival — CARNIVAL

(www.downtownstjohns.com; early Aug) Jugglers, magicians, acrobats, comedians and more take their performances to the streets for a long weekend.

Newfoundland & Labrador Folk Festival — MUSIC

(www.nlfolk.com; early Aug) This three-day event celebrates traditional Newfoundland music, dancing and storytelling. It's held the weekend after the regatta.

Royal St John's Regatta — SPORTS

(www.stjohnsregatta.org; 1st Wed Aug) The streets are empty, the stores are closed and everyone migrates to the shores of Quidi Vidi Lake. This rowing regatta officially began in 1825 and is now the oldest continuously held sporting event in North America. Postponed if the rowing conditions are poor.

Doors Open CULTURAL
(www.doorsopendays.com; ⊙early Sep) Every year in the second week of September, normally private businesses and buildings open their doors to the public for an inside look. Venues change, but have featured warehouses, churches and old museums.

Sleeping

Scores of B&Bs offer a place to rest your head in the heart of St John's; they're usually better value than the hotels and motels. They fill fast, so book ahead. Many have a two-night minimum-stay requirement. The ones listed here all serve a hot breakfast. The city's 17% tax is not included in prices listed here. Parking is available at or near all accommodations.

Memorial University Rooms ACCOMMODATION SERVICES $
(☎877-730-7657; www.mun.ca/conferences; r with shared bath $59-72; ⊙late Jun-Aug;) One of the best deals in town, the local university offers summer accommodations in its dormitory housing with shared washroom facilities. There's the option of twin or double beds in modern, pleasant rooms. Guests have access to kitchen facilities, a pool and fitness center. There are no TVs, and it's BYO toiletries.

HI St John's HOSTEL $
(☎709-754-4789; www.hihostels.ca; 8 Gower St; dm $38, r 89-103;) It's everything a good hostel should be: well located near the action, spick-and-span facilities, not too big (16 beds in all), and helpful. Doubles are less of a deal, with rooms that seem pretty worn out for the price. A whiteboard lists everything of interest happening in town each day. The hostel also books reasonably priced tours.

JAG BOUTIQUE HOTEL $$
(☎709-738-1524; www.steelehotels.com; 115 George St W; r from $236;) What's not to like about a hotel that blasts the Stones or Dylan in the lobby? This rock-and-roll-themed boutique hotel occupies a tall multistory building with harbor views. Spacious rooms have a sleek look of muted colors with pleated leather headboards and oversized windows (double-paned with blackout curtains specially made for rock stars). The on-site restaurant and bar are excellent.

Cabot House B&B $$
(☎709-754-0058; www.abbainn.com; 26 Monkstown Rd; s/d $209/219;) A stunning 1904 Queen Anne revival mansion, this sprawling house full of antiques and stained-glass windows makes for a subdued stay. Gorgeous, spacious rooms are mostly restored to their original layout, with the addition of bathrooms and a Jacuzzi suite. With no on-site host, the experience is more hotel-like.

Leaside Manor B&B $$
(☎709-722-0387; www.leasidemanor.com; 39 Topsail Rd; r $179-229;) The higher-end rooms in this old merchant's home have a canopied bed, fireplace and Jacuzzi, which explains why the *Globe and Mail* designated Leaside one of Canada's 'most romantic destinations.' It's about a half-hour walk from downtown; to be closer, inquire about the downtown apartments.

Gower House B&B $$
(☎709-754-0058; www.abbainn.com; 180 Gower St; s/d $149/159;) Gower House is more like a boarding house than a frilly B&B. Rooms are small, but with restful bedding, a flat-screen TV and amenity-laden en suite bathroom. An on-site manager cooks the egg-filled breakfast.

At Wit's Inn B&B $$
(☎709-739-7420; www.atwitsinn.ca; 3 Gower St; r $160;) Polished floorboards, plasterwork ceilings, ornate fireplaces, brightly colored walls, and beds you'll have trouble leaving make this B&B memorable. The living and dining rooms are as swank as they are comfy. It's also in a convenient location.

RESOURCES

City of St John's (www.stjohns.ca) The 'Visiting Our City' category has descriptions of and links to attractions, accommodations, eateries and events.

Downhome (www.downhomelife.com) A folksy, *Reader's Digest*–style monthly for the region.

The Overcast (www.theovercast.ca) Free alternative newspaper covering local arts and politics.

St John's Telegram (www.thetelegram.com) The city's daily newspaper.

SCRUNCHEONS, TOUTONS & FLIPPER PIE: A GASTRONOMIC GUIDE

Get ready for a whole new culinary vocabulary when you enter Newfoundland. Lesson number one: having a 'scoff' is local parlance for eating a big meal.

Two of Newfoundland's favorite dishes are fish 'n' brewis and Jiggs dinner. Fish 'n' brewis is a blend of salted fish, onions, scruncheons (aka fried pork fat) and a near-boiled bread. Jiggs dinner is a right feast comprising a roast (turkey or possibly moose) along with boiled potatoes, carrots, cabbage, salted beef and pea-and-bread pudding. A touton is fried dough that you dip in gooey molasses.

Cod tongues are the tender, fleshy bits between the lower jaws served battered and fried, while cod cheeks are just that: cheeks from the fish. Fishcakes are a blend of cod, potato and onion mashed together and fried – delicious. Seal flipper pie, on the other hand, is for the brave; the strong flavor of seal meat is definitely an acquired taste.

To finish off your meal, try figgy duff, a thick fig pudding boiled in a cloth bag.

Balmoral House B&B **$$**

(☎709-754-5721; www.balmoralhouse.com; 38 Queen's Rd; r $149-199;) While the Balmoral is a typical B&B in many ways (cherub statues, long wooden antique tables), its owners live off-site and breakfast is self-serve, so it's more relaxed and private than many B&Bs. The beds have super-comfy mattresses.

Abba Inn B&B **$$**

(☎709-754-0058; www.abbainn.com; 36 Queen's Rd; s/d $159/169;) The Abba shares a building with Balmoral House (p469), and both B&Bs have similar amenities and ambience. If Abba is full, the owner also has nearby Gower House and Cabot House. There's often no on-site host; guests let themselves in with a lock code.

Narrows B&B B&B **$$**

(☎709-739-4850; www.thenarrowsbb.com; 146 Gower St; s/d $135/170;) Warm colors mix with elegant trims and large wooden beds in the rooms of this welcoming B&B. Some rooms are on the slim side. There are modern amenities throughout and a gorgeous sitting room and balcony where guests can mingle and swap whale stories.

Courtyard St John's HOTEL **$$**

(☎709-722-6636; www.marriott.com/yytcy; 131 Duckworth St; r $189-244;) It's the Marriott chain's typical property, with comfy beds. Some rooms have harbor views (about $20 extra).

★Luxus BOUTIQUE HOTEL **$$$**

(☎844-722-8899; www.theluxus.ca; 128 Water St; r $379-579;) Opened by a businessman originally from the area, the Luxus' amenities read like a wishlist of those who travel for a living. Bose speakers, check. Dual jet shower and freestanding tub, check. Electronic Japanese toilet, check. All six luxurious rooms boast harbor views, minibar and a whopping 70-inch (178cm) flat-screen TV. Don't miss happy hour at the ambient cocktail bar. Parking is off-site in a garage.

Eating

★Adelaide Oyster House INTERNATIONAL **$**

(☎709-722-7222; 334 Water St; small plates $8-17; 5-10pm) For a boisterous, busy happy hour it would be hard to do better than the Adelaide, a stylish sliver of a bar and restaurant in the thick of things. Its specialty is small plates such as fish tacos, Kobe beef lettuce wraps topped with spicy kimchi, and, of course, fresh oysters from both coasts. With lovely cocktails. It's good for singles too.

★Battery Cafe CAFE **$**

(☎709-722-9167; 1 Duckworth St; snacks $3-9; 6:30am-6:30pm Mon-Fri, 7:30am-6:30pm Sat & Sun) This Aussie-run espresso bar and cafe brews the finest cup in town; there are also good sandwiches and baked goods. Has outdoor picnic-table seating in good weather.

Piatto PIZZA **$**

(☎709-726-0709; www.piattopizzeria.com; 377 Duckworth St; mains $12-19; 11:30am-10pm Mon-Thu, to 11pm Fri & Sat, to 9pm Sun) Offering a great night out without breaking the bank, cozy brick Piatto wood-fires pizza like nobody's business. Go trad or try a thin-crust pie topped with proscuitto, figs and balsamic. It's all good. There are nice fresh salads too, wine and Italian cocktails.

Fixed Coffee & Baking CAFE **$**

(www.fixedcoffee.com; 183 Duckworth St; baked goods $3-8; 7am-6pm Mon-Fri, from 9am Sat & Sun;) Hipster haven Fixed pours the city's best hot chocolate and mighty fine coffee and chai, plus it's cheaper than elsewhere. Housemade bagels and breads add to the divine aroma.

Rocket Bakery BAKERY $
(www.rocketfood.ca; 272 Water St; mains $3-10; ⏲7:30am-9pm Mon-Sat, to 6pm Sun;) Cheery Rocket is the perfect spot for a cup o' joe, groovy sandwich or sweet treat. Try the hummus on crusty homemade multigrain bread, or maybe a croissant with lemon curd. The fish cakes also win raves. Order at the counter, then take your goodies to the tables in the adjoining room.

Hungry Heart CAFE $
(☎709-738-6164; www.hungryheartcafe.ca; 142 Military Rd; mains $13-16; ⏲10am-2pm Mon-Sat) Eat in this warm-toned cafe and you're helping abused women and others in need to train in food service. Try the curry mango chicken or pulled-pork sandwiches. Saturday brunch brings out the cheese scones with crisp, house-cured bacon and cherry bread pudding. Lots of baked goodies too. Attentive service.

Sprout VEGETARIAN $
(☎709-579-5485; www.thesproutrestaurant.com; 364 Duckworth St; mains $10-15; ⏲11:30am-9pm Mon-Fri, from 10am Sat;) Full-on vegetarian food is almost unheard of in Newfoundland. Sprout offers both vegan and gluten-free options. So take a seat in this small cafe and savor your marinated tofu burger, walnut-pesto-melt sandwich and brown rice poutine (fries served under miso gravy) before leaving town. Sandwiches feature thick slices of homemade bread.

International Flavours PAKISTANI $
(☎709-738-4636; 4 Quidi Vidi Rd; mains $11-14; ⏲noon-7pm Tue-Sat;) A popular choice for locals on their lunch break, this Middle Eastern restaurant provides a welcome respite from fish-and-chips. Pakistani owner Talat ladles out a whopping spicy plateful of dal or curry with basmati rice for her daily set meal, also available vegetarian. It's in a small room at the bottom of Signal Hill Rd.

Ches's FAST FOOD $
(☎709-726-2373; www.chessfishandchips.ca; 9 Freshwater Rd; mains $8-15; ⏲11am-2am Sun-Thu, to 3am Fri & Sat) Ches's and its fish-and-chips are an institution in Newfoundland. No frills, just cod that will melt in your mouth.

★**Merchant Tavern** CANADIAN $$$
(☎709-722-5050; http://themerchanttavern.ca; 291 Water St; mains $15-45; ⏲11:30am-2pm & 5:30pm-midnight Tue-Thu, to 2am Fri, 10:30am-2am Sat, 10:30am-3pm Sun) An elegant tavern housed in a former bank building, Merchant shares its chef with Canadian top-tier restaurant Raymond's, but without the $400 price tag. Gorgeous seafood stews, grilled local lamb sausage and cod with smoked bacon near perfection. For happy endings, the salted-caramel soft serve is a must. Some seating faces the open-view kitchen – good for chatting with the cooks.

Chinched MODERN CANADIAN $$$
(☎709-722-3100; www.chinchedbistro.com; 7 Queen St; mains $14-35; ⏲5:30-9:30pm Mon-Sat) Quality dishes without the white-tablecloth pretense – think octopus tacos or Newfoundland wild mushroom risotto served in a warm, dark-wood room. On an ever-changing menu, meat figures prominently – don't skip the charcuterie boards or homemade pickles. The young chefs' creativity extends to the singular desserts (say, wild-nettle ice cream) and spirits (partridgeberry vodka) made in-house.

Reluctant Chef MODERN CANADIAN $$$
(☎709-754-6011; www.thereluctantchef.ca; 281 Duckworth St; set menu $60; ⏲5-9:30pm Tue-Sun) The reluctant-but-passionate Jonathan Schwartz creates lovingly prepared, five-course meals for an intimate room. The dishes always vary, but may include originals like duck in dandelion broth or a rhubarb and sorrel dessert. There's also weekend brunch ($18). Check the Facebook page menu and reserve ahead. Then plan on a three-hour flavorgasm. Those with special dietary needs should advise ahead.

Bacalao MODERN CANADIAN $$$
(☎709-579-6565; www.bacalaocuisine.ca; 65 Lemarchant Rd; mains $26-36; ⏲noon-2:30pm Tue-Fri, from 11am Sat & Sun, 6-10pm Tue-Sun) Cozy Bacalao sources local, sustainable ingredients for its 'nouvelle Newfoundland cuisine.' Dishes include salt cod du jour and caribou in partridgeberry sauce, washed down by local beer and wines. It's located 1.5km west of downtown; take Water St south to Waldegrave St, then Barters Hill Rd.

Mallard Cottage CANADIAN $$$
(☎709-237-7314; www.mallardcottage.ca; 2 Barrows Rd; mains $19-35; ⏲10am-2pm Wed-Sat, 5:30-9pm Tue-Sat, 10am-5pm Sun) A lot of res-

taurants give lip service to local and sustainable, but this one is spot on and devilishly good. The blackboard menu changes daily. Think turnips with yogurt and crispy shallots or brined duck with spaetzle and fried rosemary. The adorable Mallard Cottage, which dates from the 1750s, is a historic site.

Basho SUSHI $$$

(☎709-576-4600; www.bashorestaurant.com; 283 Duckworth St; mains $22-36; ⏰6pm-late Mon-Sat) This trendy newcomer is St John's best bet for high-grade, traditional sushi, Nobu-style sashimi and crisp tempura with sea salt. Basho is also known for exceptional cocktails. The popular lounge opens up an hour before dinner on Fridays.

Drinking & Nightlife

George St is the city's famous party lane. Water and Duckworth Sts also have plenty of places to drink, but the scene is slightly more sedate. Bars stay open until 2am (3am on weekends). Expect many places to charge a small cover (about $5) on weekends or when there's live music. Don't forget to try the local Screech rum.

★**Duke of Duckworth** PUB

(www.dukeofduckworth.com; McMurdo's Lane, 325 Duckworth St; ⏰noon-late; 📶) 'The Duke,' as it's known, is an unpretentious English-style pub that represents all that's great about Newfoundland and Newfoundlanders. Stop in on a Friday night and you'll see a mix of blue-collar and white-collar workers, young and old, and perhaps even band members from Great Big Sea plunked down on the well-worn, red-velour bar stools.

Mochanopoly CAFE

(☎709-576-3657; 204 Water St; per hour boardgames $2.50; ⏰noon-midnight Mon-Thu, to 1am Fri & Sat, to 11pm Sun) Welcome to Newfoundland's first boardgame cafe. Inspired by counterparts in South Korea, young brothers and game gurus Erich and Leon opened this welcoming branch with over 300 games, ranging from classics like Battleship to Pandemic and Exploding Kittens. It's usually packed after 7pm. It also serves small bites and coffee drinks. Kids under six can play free.

Yellow Belly Brewery PUB

(☎709-757-3784; www.yellowbellybrewery.com; 288 Water St; ⏰11:30am-2am Mon-Fri, to 3am Sat & Sun) Refreshing brews crafted on-site are front and center at this casual meeting spot, a brick behemoth dating back to 1725. Everyone's having a good time and there's decent pub grub to soak up the brews. For extra ambience descend to the underbelly – a dark basement bar with a speakeasy feel.

Velvet CLUB, GAY & LESBIAN

(http://twitter.com/Velvetniteclub; 208 Water St; ⏰11pm-3am Fri & Sat) This is the premier gay dance bar in Newfoundland. Straights are equally welcome to soak up the fun energy. Located above Rose & Thistle; the entrance is via McMurdo's Lane.

Gypsy Tea Room BAR

(☎709-739-4766; www.gypsytearoom.ca; 315 Water St; ⏰11:30am-3pm & 5:30-11pm Mon-Fri, from 11am Sat & Sun) It holds a well-regarded Mediterranean restaurant and chic lounge, but the courtyard is where you want to be, sipping wine, cocktails and other refreshing beverages under the stars.

Entertainment

The Overcast (www.theovercast.ca) has the daily lowdown. Perhaps because this is such an intimate city, word of mouth and flyers slapped on light poles are also major vehicles for entertainment information. Venues are close together – have a wander and enjoy.

GETTING SCREECHED IN

Within a few days of your arrival in St John's, you'll undoubtedly be asked by everyone if you've been 'screeched in,' or in traditional Newfoundland slang, 'Is you a screecher?' It's not as painful as it sounds, and is, in fact, locals' playful way of welcoming visitors.

Screeching derives from the 1940s when new arrivals were given their rites of passage, and from pranks played on sealers heading to the ice for the first time. Today the ceremony takes place in local pubs, where you'll gulp a shot of rum (there's actually a local brand called Screech), recite an unpronounceable verse in the local lingo, kiss a stuffed codfish and then receive a certificate declaring you an 'Honorary Newfoundlander.' Sure it's touristy, but it's also good fun. The more the merrier, so try to get screeched in with a crowd.

Cover charges for live music range from $5 to $10. Mighty Pop (www.mightypop.ca) lists cool upcoming shows.

Ship Pub LIVE MUSIC
(☎709-753-3870; 265 Duckworth St; ⊙noon-late) Attitudes and ages are checked at the door of this little pub, tucked down Solomon's Lane. You'll hear everything from jazz to indie, and even the odd poetry reading. Wednesday is folk-music night.

Shamrock City LIVE MUSIC
(www.shamrockcity.ca; 340 Water St; ⊙noon-late) Bands, most playing Irish and Newfoundland-style music, take the stage nightly at this all-ages pub.

Rose & Thistle LIVE MUSIC
(☎709-579-6662; 208 Water St; ⊙9am-late) Pub where well-known local folk musicians strum.

Fat Cat BLUES
(www.fatcatbluesbar.com; George St; ⊙8pm-late Tue-Sun) Blues radiates from the cozy Fat Cat nightly during the summer months.

Rock House LIVE MUSIC
(☎709-579-6832; 8 George St) When indie bands visit town, they plug in here.

Signal Hill Tattoo MILITARY PERFORMANCE
(www.rnchs.ca/tattoo; $10; ⊙11am & 3pm Wed-Thu, Sat & Sun Jul & Aug) An award-winning historical animation program that brings back British 19th-century military might with cannon fire, mortars and muskets backed by a fife and drum band. It's set atop Signal Hill.

Resource Centre for the Arts PERFORMING ARTS
(☎709-753-4531; www.rca.nf.ca; 3 Victoria St) Sponsors indie theater, dance and film by Newfoundland artists, all of which play downtown in the former longshoremen's union hall (aka LSPU Hall). Box office is on the website.

St John's IceCaps HOCKEY
(www.stjohnsicecaps.com; 50 New Gower St; ⊙Oct-May) The popular IceCaps, part of the American Hockey League, slap the puck at Mile One Centre.

Shopping

You'll find traditional music, berry jams and local art in the nooks and crannies of Water and Duckworth Sts.

Outfitters SPORTS & OUTDOORS
(☎709-579-4453; www.theoutfitters.nf.ca; 220 Water St; ⊙10am-6pm Mon-Wed & Sat, to 9pm Thu & Fri, noon-5pm Sun) A camping and gear shop where you can get the local outdoorsy low-down (check the bulletin board) and good rentals. For hikers, it sells East Coast Trail (p474) maps and butane canisters.

Fred's MUSIC
(☎709-753-9191; www.fredsrecords.com; 198 Duckworth St; ⊙9:30am-9pm Mon-Fri, to 6pm Sat, noon-5pm Sun) This is the premier music shop in St John's. It features local music such as Hey Rosetta, Buddy Wasisname, Ron Hynes, Amelia Curran, The Navigators and Great Big Sea.

Living Planet GIFTS & SOUVENIRS
(☎709-739-6810; www.livingplanet.ca; 181 Water St; ⊙10am-5pm Mon-Sat, noon-5pm Sun) For quirky tourist T-shirts and buttons even locals are proud to wear.

Downhome GIFTS & SOUVENIRS
(☎709-722-2070; 303 Water St; ⊙10am-5:30pm Mon-Sat, noon-5pm Sun) It's touristy, but it does have a fine selection of local goods such as jams, woolen wear, moose cookbooks and the coveted *How to Play the Musical Spoons* CD.

Information

MEDICAL SERVICES

Health Sciences Complex (☎709-777-6300; 300 Prince Phillip Dr; ⊙24hr) A 24-hour emergency room.

MONEY

Banks stack up near the Water St and Ayre's Cove intersection.

CIBC (215 Water St; ⊙9:30am-5pm Mon-Fri)

Scotia Bank (245 Water St; ⊙10am-5pm Mon-Fri)

POST

Central Post Office (☎709-758-1003; 354 Water St)

TOURIST INFORMATION

Quidi Vidi Visitors Centre (☎709-570-2038; tourism@stjohns.ca; 10 Maple View Pl, Quidi Vidi Village Plantation; ⊙11am-5pm Tue-Sun) An outpost of the St John's visitor center, with good information on local happenings. Open year-round.

Visitors Centre (☎709-576-8106; www.stjohns.ca; 348 Water St; ⊙10am-4:30pm May-early Oct) Excellent resource with free provincial and city road maps, and staff to answer questions and help with bookings.

Getting There & Away

AIR

St John's International Airport (YYT; ☎709-758-8500; www.stjohnsairport.com; 100 World Pkwy;) is 6km north of the city on Portugal Cove Rd (Rte 40).

Air Canada offers a daily direct flight to and from London, WestJet goes direct to Dublin and Gatwick. **United Airlines** (p461) flies to the USA.

The main carriers:

Air Canada (p461)

PAL Airlines (p461)

Porter Airlines (p461)

WestJet (☎888-937-8538; www.westjet.com)

BUS

DRL (p462) sends one bus daily each way between St John's and Port aux Basques ($126, cash only, 13½ hours) via the 905km-long Hwy 1, making 25 stops en route. It leaves at 7:30am from Memorial University's Student Centre, in CA Pippy Park.

CAR & MOTORCYCLE

Avis, Budget, Enterprise, Hertz, National and Thrifty have offices at the airport. Rent RVs and motorhomes from **Islander RV** (☎709-364-7368; www.islanderrv.com; Paddy's Pond, Exit 40, Trans Canada Hwy).

SHARE TAXIS

These large vans typically seat 15 and allow you to jump on or off at any point along their routes. You must call in advance to reserve. They pick up and drop off at your hotel. Cash only.

Foote's Taxi (☎709-832-0491) Travels daily down the Burin Peninsula as far as Fortune ($45, 4½ hours).

Newhook's Transportation (☎709-682-4877, in Placentia 709-227-2552) Travels down the southwestern Avalon Peninsula to Placentia ($35, two hours), in sync with the Argentia ferry schedule.

Shirran's Taxi (☎709-468-7741) Plies the Bonavista Peninsula daily, making stops at Trinity ($50, 3½ hours) and Bonavista ($40, four hours), among others.

Getting Around

BUS

The **Metrobus** (☎709-722-9400; www.metrobus.com; 25 Messenger Dr) system covers most of the city (fare $2.25). Maps and schedules are online and in the visitor center. Bus 3 is useful; it circles town via Military Rd and Water St before heading to the university. The new 'trolley line' (it's actually a bus) loops around the main tourist sights, including Signal Hill. It costs $5/20 per person/family per day.

CAR & MOTORCYCLE

The city's one-way streets and unique intersections can be confounding. Thankfully, citizens are incredibly patient. The parking meters that line Water and Duckworth Sts cost $1.50 per hour. **Sonco Parking Garage** (☎709-754-1489; cnr Baird's Cove & Harbour Dr; ⊙6:30am-11pm) is central, but there are several others; most charge around $2 per hour.

TAXI

Except for the trip from the airport, all taxis operate on meters. A trip within town should cost around $8. **Jiffy Cabs** (☎709-722-2222; www.jiffycab.com) provides dependable service.

AVALON PENINSULA

The landscape along the coastline's twisting roads is vintage fishing-village Newfoundland. Many visitors make day trips to the peninsula's sights from St John's, which is easily doable, but there's something to be said for burrowing under the quilt at night, with the sea sparkling outside your window, in Cupids or Branch. Four of the province's six seabird ecological reserves are in the region, as are 28 of its 41 national historic sites.

Much of the East Coast Trail (p474) runs through the area. The ferry to Nova Scotia leaves from Argentia.

Southeastern Avalon Peninsula

This area, sometimes called the South Shore, is known for its wildlife, archaeology, boat and kayak tours, and unrelenting fog. Scenic Rtes 10 and 90, aka the Irish Loop (p477), lasso the region. For a quick taste, visit the Cape Spear Lighthouse and the fishing village of Petty Harbour, though sites further south are well worth exploring. Highlights include watching the puffins and whales in Witless Bay, exploring La Manche Provincial Park and hiking the East Coast Trail.

Cape Spear

A 15km drive southeast of St John's leads you to the most easterly point in North America, with spectacular coastal scenery and whale-watching during much of the summer. A **trail** leads along the edge of the headland cliffs, past 'the most easterly point' observation deck and up to the lighthouse. You can continue all the way to Maddox Cove and

Petty Harbour along the East Coast Trail; even walking it a short way is tremendously worthwhile.

Heed all signs warning visitors off the coastal rocks, as rogue waves have knocked people into the water.

Sights & Activities

★ Cape Spear Lighthouse LIGHTHOUSE
(entry incl with Cape Spear National Historic Site; ⏲10am-6pm Jun-Aug, reduced hours May, Sep & Oct) Constructed in 1835, the oldest surviving lighthouse in the province sits on the dramatic headlands of the continent's most easterly point.

Cape Spear Interpretive Center MUSEUM
(entry incl with Cape Spear National Historic Site; ⏲10am-6pm May-Oct) Offers exhibits on lighthouse technology and its changes throughout time.

Cape Spear National Historic Site HISTORIC SITE
(☎709-772-5367; www.pc.gc.ca/capespear; Blackhead Rd; adult/child $3.90/1.90; ⏲grounds year-round) In a stunning windswept setting, Cape Spear National Historic Site includes an interpretive center, the refurbished 1835 lighthouse and the heavy gun batteries and magazines built in 1941 to protect the harbor during WWII. Hikers can also join up with the East Coast Trail here.

Getting There & Away

Many St John's day tours include Cape Spear. Otherwise, it's possible to come by private vehicle or taxi from St John's.

You reach the cape from Water St by crossing the Waterford River south of town and then following Blackhead Rd for 11km.

Goulds & Petty Harbour

Backed against steep slopes, beautiful, pocket-sized Petty Harbour shelters weathered boats in an active port filled with wharves and sheds. It has a lively sense of community and plenty to do. Nearby Goulds is a useful stop for groceries.

Sights & Activities

Petty Harbour Mini Aquarium AQUARIUM
(☎709-330-3474; www.miniaqua.org; Main Rd, Petty Harbour; adult/child $8/5; ⏲10am-6pm Jun-Oct) This small attraction is perfect for kids, who will love the touch tanks filled with sea life. Animals are re-released into the ocean at season's end. The big attractions are the wolf fish and golden lobster.

★ Fishing for Success FISHING
(www.islandrooms.org; 10d Main Rd, Petty Harbour; adult/child $99/50) Run by Kimberly and Leo, a local fishing family, this new nonprofit organization seeks to rescue the local fishing traditions by teaching them to local kids and visitors. Dory trips include rowing lessons in traditional wood boats and cod jigging. For $50 extra they can cook up your catch and serve it to you Newfoundland-style right on the pier. There's also a full-day option that includes net-knitting, rope work and a historical wharf tour.

North Atlantic Zip Lines ADVENTURE SPORTS
(☎709-368-8681; www.zipthenorthatlantic.com; 62 Main Rd, Petty Harbour; adult/child $130/95) Canada's longest zip-line course has 10 zip lines at its family adventure center ranging from 300ft to 2200ft in length. Tours run at 11am, 3pm and 6pm.

HIKING THE EAST COAST TRAIL

Skirting gaping cliffs, fairy-tale forests and fields of edible berries, the world-class **East Coast Trail** (☎709-738-4453; www.eastcoasttrail.ca) is a through-hiker's delight. It stretches 265km from Cape St Francis (north of St John's) south to Cappahayden with an additional 275km still underway.

Its 26 sections range in difficulty from easy to challenging, but most make good day hikes. For a sample, try the scenic 9.3km path between Cape Spear and Maddox Cove (near Petty Harbour), it should take between four and six hours.

For seasoned hikers, the ECT can also be walked as a through-hike, combining camping with lodging in villages along the way. Campsites generally feature pit toilets and a good water source nearby. Fires are prohibited. A local taxi service operates at the trailheads and can bring you to nearby lodging or your vehicle.

Topographical maps are available in St John's at Outfitters (p467) or Downhome (p472). Visit the trail website for detailed information and the lowdown on guided hikes.

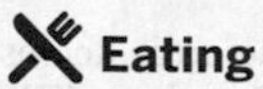

Eating

WaterShed CAFE $
(☎709-747-0500; 24a Main Rd, Petty Harbour; ⏲10am-4pm Jun-Sep, Sat & Sun only in winter;) Joy is here: real espresso drinks at a refurbished waterfront shed. Owner Karen loves talking local lore, she also makes a mean hiker cookie, packed with seeds. It also has great baked treats and sandwiches. If you have an extra few hours to chill out, spend them on the deck.

★**Chafe's Landing** SEAFOOD $$
(☎709-747-0802; www.chafeslanding.com; 11 Main Rd, Petty Harbour; mains $9-19; ⏲11am-8pm Mon-Thu, to 9pm Fri & Sat, 2-9pm Sun) Most folks here day trip from St John's specifically for these fish-and-chips, the freshest you can find. Lines get long and parking might be impossible, but it's worth it. It also serves locally made moose sausage, beer-steamed mussels, and salads.

Shopping

Bidgood's FOOD
(www.bidgoods.ca; Bidgood's Plaza, Goulds; ⏲9am-7pm Mon-Sat, 10am-5pm Sun) Just a normal supermarket, except for the fresh seal flipper (in pies, jars or jerky-like strips) and caribou steak. Partridgeberry and bakeapple jams are the other Newfoundland specialties on hand. In Goulds, at the junction of Rte 10 and the road to Petty Harbour.

Witless Bay Ecological Reserve & Around

This is a prime area for whale-, iceberg- and puffin-watching, and several boat tours will take you to see them from the towns of **Bay Bulls** (31km south of St John's) and **Mobile** (10km south of Bay Bulls). Midway between the towns, there's lodging in **Witless Bay**.

Four islands off Witless Bay and southward are preserved as the **Witless Bay Ecological Reserve** (www.env.gov.nl.ca/parks) and represent one of the top seabird breeding areas in eastern North America. The reserve is North America's largest Atlantic puffin colony, with over 260,000 pairs nesting here during the late spring and summer. In fact, every summer, more than a million pairs of birds gather here, including puffins, kittiwakes, storm petrels and the penguin-like murres. Tour boats sail to the islands, hugging the shore beneath sheer cliffs and giving you a shrieking earful as well as an eyeful.

The best months for trips are late June and July, when the humpback and minke whales arrive to join the birds' capelin (a type of fish) feeding frenzy. If you really hit the jackpot, in early summer an iceberg might be thrown in too.

Tours

Tours from Bay Bulls visit Gull Island, which has the highest concentration of birds in the Witless Bay Ecological Reserve. Tours that depart to the south around Bauline East head to nearby Great Island, home to the largest puffin colony. Bauline East is closer to the reserve, so less time is spent en route, but you see the same types of wildlife on all of the tours.

Also popular, kayaking provides a special perspective on wildlife. After all, you don't just see a whale while paddling, you feel its presence.

You can't miss the boat operators – just look for signs off Rte 10. Sometimes the smaller companies cancel tours if there aren't enough passengers; it's best to call ahead to reserve and avoid such surprises. They operate from mid-May through mid-September. Most depart several times daily between 9:30am and 5pm.

★**Captain Wayne's** WHALE-WATCHING
(☎709-763-8687; www.captwaynes.com; Northside Rd, Bay Bulls; tour $80) Descended from generations of Newfoundland fishers, Captain Wayne really knows his coast and his enthusiasm proves contagious. Best of all, he only does small, 12-person tours in his custom boat. The three-hour tour includes puffin- and whale-watching. There are several departures daily, but photographers should go at 5pm for best light.

Molly Bawn Tours BOATING
(☎709-334-2621; www.mollybawn.com; Rte 10, Mobile; 1hr tour adult/child $45/40) These popular tours cruise over the waves on a small, 35ft boat. Mobile is halfway between Bay Bulls and Bauline East.

Outfitters KAYAKING
(☎709-579-4453; www.theoutfitters.nf.ca; Bay Bulls; half-/full-day tour $69/169) Popular half-day kayak tours leave at 9am and 2pm; full-day tours depart at 9:30am and travel beyond the inner bay of Bay Bulls to the top of the eco reserve. There is a shuttle service (round-trip $25) from St John's that leaves from Outfitters at 220 Water St.

DON'T MISS

RUNNING THE GOAT

This active **printing press** (709-334-3239; http://runningthegoat.com; Cove Rd, Tors Cove; 10:30am-5:30pm Thu-Tue mid-May–Oct) is a bibliophile's dream. Owner Marnie Parsons gives tours of her presses, one from 1830s London. In addition to handmade poetry chapbooks and manifestos, there's a wonderful selection of local artists' prints and good books for adults and children authored by Newfoundlanders.

O'Brien's BOATING

(709-753-4850; www.obriensboattours.com; 2hr tour adult/child $55/25) O'Brien's, on the south side of Bay Bulls, is the granddaddy of tours and includes storytelling, music and more on its nice, big boat. A more expensive but exhilarating option is the two-hour tour in a high-speed Zodiac ($85). There's a shuttle service from St John's (round-trip $25).

Gatherall's BOATING

(800-419-4253; www.gatheralls.com; Northside Rd, Bay Bulls; 1½hr tour adult/child $57/38) A large, fast catamaran. A good choice for people prone to seasickness.

Sleeping

Armstrong's Suites MOTEL $

(709-334-2201; 236 Main Hwy, Witless Bay; r $80) Though this is just your run-of-the-mill roadside motel, it's unlikely that even your own grandmother could better receive your visit. The kind owner thinks nothing of going the extra mile, providing extra cots and towels and breakfast fixings to East Coast Trail through-hikers.

Bread & Cheese B&B $$

(709-334-3994; 22a Bread & Cheese Rd, Bay Bulls; r incl breakfast $149;) This gorgeous country house with a wraparound porch and sprawling lawn is a sight for sore feet, located a short stroll from the East Coast Trail. Rooms are smart and modern, with one handicapped-accessible option. Our only wish is for a cheerier welcome.

Bears Cove Inn B&B $$

(709-334-3909; www.bearscoveinn.com; 15 Bears Cove Rd, Witless Bay; d with ocean/forest view $149/129;) A pleasant place to stay, this seven-room B&B has all the amenities you could want, including water views and a lovely garden and barbecue area. Rooms feature country decor and flat-screen TVs. The helpful owners also run a local pub and speak French.

La Manche Provincial Park

Diverse birdlife, along with beavers, moose and snowshoe hare, can be seen in this lush **park** (www.env.gov.nl.ca) FREE only 53km south of St John's. A highlight is the 1.25km trail to the remains of La Manche, a fishing village that was destroyed in 1966 by a fierce winter storm. Upon arrival, you'll see the beautiful newly built suspension bridge dangling over the narrows – it's part of the East Coast Trail (p474). The trailhead is situated at the park's fire-exit road, past the main entrance.

There is excellent camping at **La Manche Provincial Park Camping** (709-685-1823; www.nlcamping.ca; Rte 10; campsites $18-26, per vehicle $5; May-Sep). Lovely and shaded, it has 83 campsites, picnic tables, fire pits, water taps and pit toilets. Firewood is available at the checkpoint.

Ferryland

Ferryland, one of North America's earliest settlements, dates to 1621, when Sir George Calvert established the Colony of Avalon. A few Newfoundland winters later he was scurrying for warmer parts. He settled in Maryland and eventually became the first Lord Baltimore. Other English families arrived later and maintained the colony despite it being razed by the Dutch in 1673 and by the French in 1696.

For gorgeous windswept panoramas, don't miss the 2km walk out to the lighthouse.

Sights

Colony of Avalon ARCHAEOLOGICAL SITE

(709-432-3207, 709-432-3200; www.colonyofavalon.ca; Rte 10; adult/child $12.70/10.20; 10am-6pm Jun-Sep) The seaside surrounds of the Colony of Avalon archaeological site only add to the rich atmosphere, where you'll see archaeologists unearthing everything from axes to bowls. The worthwhile interpretation center houses beautiful displays and many of the artifacts that have been recovered. Guided 45-minute tours are offered upon request.

Historic Ferryland Museum MUSEUM

(709-432-2711; www.manl.nf.ca/ferrylandmuseum; Baltimore Dr; $3; 10am-4pm Mon-Sat,

1-4pm Sun Jun-Aug) The village's former courthouse is now the small Historic Ferryland Museum. The towering hill behind the museum was where settlers climbed to watch for approaching warships, or to escape the Dutch and French incursions. After seeing the view, you'll understand why the settlers named the hill 'the Gaze.'

Tours

Stan Cook Adventures ADVENTURE

(☎709-579-6353; www.wildnfld.ca; Harbour Rd, Cape Broyle; 2½hr kayak tour from $59) Located near Ferryland, this company offers great guided kayak tours for beginners and advanced paddlers as well as mountain biking and hiking options.

Eating

★**Lighthouse Picnics** SANDWICHES $$

(☎709-363-7456; www.lighthousepicnics.ca; Lighthouse Rd; per person $26; ⊙11:30am-4:30pm Wed-Sun Jun-Sep; 🐾) Lighthouse Picnics has hit upon a winning concept: it provides a blanket and organic picnic meal (say, a curried chicken sandwich, mixed-green salad and lemonade from a Mason jar) that visitors wolf down while sitting in a field overlooking explosive ocean views. It's at Ferryland's old lighthouse, off Rte 10; you have to park and hike 2km to reach it, but ooh is it worth it. Reserve in advance.

Mistaken Point Ecological Reserve

Designated a World Heritage site in 2016, this **ecological reserve** (www.env.gov.nl.ca/parks) FREE protects 575-million-year-old multi-celled marine fossils – the oldest in the world. The only way to reach it is via a free, ranger-guided, 45-minute hike from the **Edge of Avalon Interpretive Centre** (☎709-438-1100; www.edgeofavalon.ca; Rte 10; adult/child $8/5; ⊙10am-6pm mid-May–Oct) in Portugal Cove South. This center offers information and interesting exhibits on the reserve's history.

You can also drive the bumpy gravel road between here and Cape Race. At the end, a lighthouse rises up beside an artifact-filled, replica 1904 Marconi wireless station. It was the folks here who received the fateful last message from the *Titanic*.

The 'Mistaken Point' name, by the way, comes from the blinding fog that blankets the area and has caused many ships to lose their way over the years.

Along Route 90

The area from St Vincent's to St Mary's provides an excellent chance of seeing whales, particularly humpbacks, which feed close to shore. The best viewing is from **St Vincent's beach**. Halfway between the two villages is **Point La Haye Natural Scenic Attraction**, a dramatic arm of fine pebbles stretching across the mouth of St Mary's Bay – it's perfect for a walk.

Salmonier National Park (☎709-229-7189; www.env.gov.nl.ca/snp; Rte 90; ⊙10am-5pm Jun-Aug, to 3pm Sep & Oct) FREE is an animal rehabilitation center for injured and orphaned animals with an interpretive center and touch displays for children. A 2.5km trail through pine woods takes you past indigenous fauna and natural enclosures with moose, caribou and cavorting river otters. The park is on Rte 90, 12km south of the junction with Hwy 1.

Settled by Irish, scenic Rte 90 makes up part of the aptly named **Irish Loop** (www.theirishloop.com), a lovely driving route in the Avalon Peninsula.

Baccalieu Trail

The Bay de Verde Peninsula has a scenic driving route known as the Baccalieu Trail. Fishing villages and pirate haunts stretch endlessly along Conception Bay's scenic western shore, a mere 80km from St John's. Highlights include Brigus, in all its Englishy, rock-walled glory combined with North Pole history, and Cupids, a 1610 settlement complete with an archaeological dig to explore.

OFF THE BEATEN TRACK

AVALON WILDERNESS RESERVE

Dominating the interior of the region is the 1070-sq-km Avalon Wilderness Reserve. Illegal hunting dropped the region's caribou population to around 100 in the 1980s. Thirty years later, a couple of thousand now roam the area. Permits for hiking, canoeing and bird-watching in the reserve are available at La Manche Provincial Park.

Even if you don't trek into the wilds, you still might see caribou along Rte 10 between Chance Cove Provincial Park and St Stevens.

Brigus

Resting on the water and surrounded by rock bluffs is the heavenly village of Brigus. Its idyllic stone-walled streams meander slowly past old buildings and colorful gardens before emptying into the serene Harbour Pond.

During WWI, American painter Rockwell Kent lived here, before his eccentric behavior got him deported on suspicion of spying for the Germans in 1915. The path toward his old cottage makes a great walk.

Captain Robert Bartlett, the town's most famous son, is renowned as one of the foremost Arctic explorers of the 20th century. His house, **Hawthorne Cottage** (☎709-753-9262; www.pc.gc.ca/hawthornecottage; cnr Irishtown Rd & South St; adult/child $4/2; ⏲10am-6pm Jul & Aug, Wed-Sun Jun), is a national historic site and museum.

On the waterfront, below the church, **Brigus Tunnel** was cut through rock in 1860 so Robert Bartlett could easily access his ship in the deep cove on the other side.

Every perfect village needs a perfect eatery. At **North St Cafe** (☎709-528-1350; 29 North St; light meals $6-14; ⏲11am-6pm May-Oct), quiche, fish cakes, scones and afternoon tea are all on order.

Cupids

This atmospheric village is imbued with rich history. Merchant John Guy sailed here in 1610 and staked out England's first colony in Canada, now **Cupids Cove Plantation Provincial Historic Site** (☎709-528-3500; www.seethesites.ca; Seaforest Dr; adult/child $6/3; ⏲9:30am-5pm May-Oct). It features an ongoing archaeological dig that's worth touring. A stone's throw down the road is the **Cupids Legacy Centre** (www.cupidslegacycentre.ca; Seaforest Dr; adult/child $8/4; ⏲9:30am-5pm Jun-Oct), with fascinating exhibits.

Afterward, head to the town's northern edge and hike the **Burnt Head Trail**. Climb to the rocky headlands, past blueberry thickets and stone walls that once fenced settlers' gardens, and look out over the same sea-buffeted coast that drew Guy. The trail departs from **Cupid's Haven B&B and Tea Room** (☎709-528-1555; www.cupidshaven.ca; 169 Burnt Head Loop; r $119-169; 🚭📶), an old Anglican church that has been converted into a divine B&B. Each of the four rooms has a private bathroom, vaulted ceilings and Gothic arched windows that let light stream in.

Harbour Grace & Around

Notable historic figures have paraded through Harbour Grace over the past 500 years, including the pirate Peter Easton and aviator Amelia Earhart. Their stories are told at **Conception Bay Museum** (☎709-596-5465; www.hrgrace.ca; Water St; adult/child $3/2; ⏲10am-6pm Jun-Aug). Nearby **Harbour Grace Airfield** (www.hrgrace.ca/air.html; Earhart Rd) is the site where Earhart launched her historic solo Atlantic flight from in 1932.

It's hard to miss the large ship beached at the mouth of the harbor. This is the **SS Kyle** (1913), wrecked during a 1967 storm. Locals liked the look of it so much they paid to have it restored instead of removed.

Clinging to cliffs at the northern end of the peninsula are the remote and striking villages of Bay de Verde and Grates Cove. Hundreds of 500-year-old **rock walls** line the hills around Grates Cove and have been declared a national historic site.

Further offshore, in the distance, is the inaccessible **Baccalieu Island Ecological Reserve**, which is host to three million pairs of Leach's storm petrel, making it the largest such colony in the world.

Heart's Content

The **Cable Station Provincial Historic Site** (☎709-583-2160; www.seethesites.ca; Rte 80; adult/child $6/3; ⏲10:30am-5:30pm May-Oct) tells the story of the first permanent transatlantic cable that was laid here in 1866. The word 'permanent' is significant, because the first successful cable (connected in 1858 to Bull Arm, on Trinity Bay) failed shortly after Queen Victoria and US President James Buchanan christened the line with their congratulatory messages.

Dildo

Oh, go on – take the obligatory sign photo. For the record, no one knows definitively how the name came about; some say it's from the phallic shape of the bay, others think it named for an oar pin. Nevertheless, proud and stalwart locals have denied several campaigns to change the town name.

Joking aside, Dildo is a lovely village and its shore is a good spot for whale-watching.

The **Dildo Interpretation Centre** (☎709-582-3339; Front Rd; adult/child $2/1; ⏲10am-4:30pm Jun-Sep) features a whale skeleton and exhibits on the ongoing Dorset Eskimo archaeological dig on Dildo Island. It's not terribly exciting, but outside are excellent photo opportunities with Captain Dildo and a giant squid.

The many 'Dildo' logoed items sold at **Kountry Kravins 'n' Krafts** (☎709-582-3888; ⏰9am-8pm Mon-Sat, 10am-6pm Sun Jun-Sep) may be a fine souvenir for folks back home.

Cape Shore

The ferry, French history and lots of birds fly forth from the Avalon Peninsula's southwesterly leg.

Argentia

Formerly a US Naval Station during WWII, Argentia's main purpose today is to play host to the ferry from Nova Scotia.

A provincial **Visitors Centre** (☎709-227-5272; Rte 100) is 3km from the ferry on Rte 100. Its opening hours vary to coincide with ferry sailings.

The **Marine Atlantic ferry** (☎800-341-7981; www.marine-atlantic.ca; adult/child $115/54, car/motorcycle $225/113; ⏰mid-Jun–late Sep) links Argentia with North Sydney in Nova Scotia, a 14-hour trip. It's 134km to St John's.

Placentia

In the early 1800s, Placentia – then Plaisance – was the French capital of Newfoundland, and the French attacks on the British at St John's were launched from here. Today it's a useful hub for those sailing to Nova Scotia on the ferry.

Sights

Near town, lording over the shores, is **Castle Hill National Historic Site** (☎709-227-2401; www.pc.gc.ca/castlehill; adult/child $3.90/1.90; ⏰10am-6pm Jun-Aug), where remains of French and British fortifications from the 17th and 18th centuries provide panoramic views over the town.

The fascinating **graveyard** next to the Anglican church holds the remains of people of every nationality who have settled here since the 1670s. For local history, visit **O'Reilly House Museum** (☎709-227-5568; 48 Orcan Dr; adult/child $5/2; ⏰9am-5pm Jun-Aug) and other notable buildings, including the Roman Catholic church and the stone convent. A boardwalk runs along the stone-skipper's delight of a beach.

Sleeping & Eating

Rosedale Manor B&B — B&B $$
(☎877-999-3613; www.rosedalemanor.ca; 40 Orcan Dr; r $109-139; 🚭📶) A beautiful heritage B&B that has flower gardens and romantic rooms with claw-foot tubs.

Philip's Cafe — CAFE $
(170 Jerseyside Hill; mains $3-12; ⏰7:30am-3:30pm Tue-Sat; 📶) A must pre- or post-ferry ride for yummy baked goods and creative sandwiches like apple and sharp cheddar on molasses-raisin bread. The breakfasts are well known; come early and skip the wait.

Three Sisters — PUB FOOD $$
(☎709-227-0124; 2 Orcan Dr; mains $8-30; ⏰8am-9pm Mon-Fri, 10am-9pm Sat & Sun) Lovely pub grub and chilly pints of beer are served in this atmospheric Placentia house. It's usually busy.

Cape St Mary's Ecological Reserve & Around

At the southwestern tip of the peninsula is Cape St Mary's Ecological Reserve, one of the most accessible bird colonies on the continent, with 70,000 specimens, including gannets, kittiwakes, murres and razorbills. Birders swoon over it, and it's impressive even for those who aren't bird crazy.

There's food and lodging in the wee town of Branch 22km away.

Sights

Stop at the Interpretive Centre (p480) for directions for the 1km trail to Bird Rock.

Bird Rock — VIEWPOINT
Bird Rock is reached by an easy footpath through fields of sheep and blue irises, and then suddenly you're at the cliff's edge facing a massive, near-vertical rock swarmed by squawking birds.

Cape St Mary's Ecological Reserve — PARK
(☎709-277-1666; www.env.gov.nl.ca/parks) FREE A major seabird colony, with breeding-season populations of tens of thousands of northern gannet, black-legged kittiwake and common murre. Viewing is easy, with land sightings as close as 10m. There are also thick-billed murres, razorbills, black guillemots, double-crested and great cormorants, and northern fulmars. Call ahead to reserve a free guided tour.

Interpretive Centre MUSEUM
(☎709-277-1666; ⊙9am-5pm May-Oct) With information on nesting seabirds and displays on local ecology.

Sleeping & Eating

Driftwood Cottage COTTAGE $$
(☎709-338-2133; www.driftwoodcottagebranch.com; Branch; r incl breakfast $120;) A wonderful little spot to stay near the reserve. It's well-kept and painted in brilliant, happy tones with a deck overlooking the water.

Loft SEAFOOD $
(☎709-338-2090; Main Rd, Branch; mains $10-12; ⊙11am-8pm) Overlooking the water (on the 2nd floor of a convenience store), this little spot has great fresh fish and moose burgers.

EASTERN NEWFOUNDLAND

Two peninsulas stretched out from the heartland comprise the sliver of eastern Newfoundland. The beloved, well-touristed Bonavista Peninsula projects northward. Historic fishing villages freckle its shores, and windblown walking trails swipe its coast. Clarenville (www.clarenville.net) is the Bonavista Peninsula's access point and service center, though there's not much for sightseers.

To the south juts the massive but less-traveled Burin Peninsula, with fishing villages struggling to find their way in the post-cod world. You will need your passport to hop the ferry from Fortune to the nearby French islands of St-Pierre and Miquelon, a regional highlight complete with wine, éclairs and Brie.

Trinity

Let's set the record straight: Trinity is the Bonavista Peninsula's most popular stop, a historic town of crooked seaside lanes, storybook heritage houses and gardens with white picket fences. Trinity Bight, however, is the name given to the 12 communities in the vicinity, including Trinity, Port Rexton and New Bonaventure.

If it all looks familiar, it may be because *The Shipping News* was partly filmed here. While the excitement has faded, there are still historic buildings, stunning hiking and theater along with whale-watching.

First visited by Portuguese explorer Miguel Corte-Real in 1500 and established as a town in 1580, Trinity is one of the oldest settlements on the continent.

Sights

Trinity's Historic Buildings HISTORIC SITE
(7-site admission adult/child $20/free; ⊙9:30am to 5pm, May to mid-October) One admission ticket lets you gorge on seven buildings scattered throughout the village of Trinity. They are run by both the **Trinity Historical Society** and the provincial government (www.seethesites.ca).

➡ **Interpretation Centre**
(☎709-464-2064; www.seethesites.ca; West St) Worth a stop if you're interested in a comprehensive history of Trinity.

➡ **Lester Garland Premises**
(☎709-464-2064; www.seethesites.ca; West St) Lester Garland Premises depicts an 1820s general store with costumed interpreters.

➡ **Trinity Museum**
(www.trinityhistoricalsociety.com; Church Rd) Displays more than 2000 pieces of historical relics, including North America's second-oldest fire wagon.

➡ **Cooperage**
(☎709-464-3599; www.trinityhistoricalsociety.com; West St) A historical site used for fisheries and shipping-related activities. First a seasonal 'fishing room' for drying codfish, it later housed an expanding mercantile business, with a real live barrel-maker.

➡ **Hiscock House**
(☎709-464-2064; www.seethesites.ca; Church Rd) A restored merchant's home from 1910.

➡ **Green Family Forge**
(☎709-464-3599; www.trinityhistoricalsociety.com; West St) An iron-tool-filled blacksmith museum.

➡ **Lester Garland House**
(☎709-464-3599; www.trinityhistoricalsociety.com; West St) This historic home was rebuilt to celebrate cultural links between Trinity and Dorset, England – major trading partners in the 17th, 18th and 19th centuries.

Fort Point HISTORIC SITE
FREE At Fort Point (aka Admiral's Point) there's a pretty lighthouse and four cannons, the remains of the British fortification from 1745. There are 10 more British cannons in the water, all compliments of the French in

1762. An interpretive center and trail tell the tale. It's accessible from Dunfield, a few kilometers south on Rte 239.

Activities

★ Skerwink Trail HIKING
(www.theskerwinktrail.com) This 5km loop is well worth the effort, with dramatic coastal vistas of sea stacks, early summer icebergs and a lighthouse. Be on guard for moose. The trailhead is near the church in Trinity East, off Rte 230.

Tours

Rugged Beauty Tours WILDLIFE
(☎709-464-3856; www.ruggedbeautyboattours.net; 3hr tour adult/child $90/60; ⏲10am & 2pm May-Oct) Unique trips with Captain Bruce, who takes you to abandoned outports and makes their history come alive. You might even see an eagle along the way.

Sea of Whales BOATING
(☎709-464-2200; www.seaofwhales.com; 1 Ash's Lane; 3hr tour adult/child $80/50) Zodiac boats head out in search of whales three times per day.

Trinity Historical Walking Tours WALKING
(☎709-464-3723; www.trinityhistoricalwalkingtours.com; Clinch's Lane; adult/child $15/free; ⏲10am Mon-Sat Jul & Aug) These entertaining and educational tours start behind Hiscock House.

Sleeping & Eating

There are numerous fine inns and B&Bs. Space gets tight in summer, so book ahead.

★ Skerwink Hostel HOSTEL $
(☎709-436-3033; www.skerwinkhostel.com; dm/r $34/69; ⏲May-Oct; 📶) Travelers of all ages stay at homey, community-oriented Skerwink. With two six-bed dorms (with squishy, plastic-coated mattresses) and two private rooms, it's part of Hostelling International. Lots of locals drop by to chat and play guitar with the staff. Fresh bread and weak coffee are included for breakfast, and the fabulous Skerwink Trail (p481) is across the street.

It's off Rte 230, about 500m from the Skerwink Trail.

★ Artisan Inn & Campbell House INN $$
(☎709-464-3377; www.trinityvacations.com; 57 High St; r incl breakfast $125-179; ⏲mid-May–Oct; 🚭📶) A fantasy coastal getaway, these gorgeous properties are adjacent to each other and managed by the same group. Both have ocean vistas. The three-room inn hovers over the sea on stilts; set further back, Campbell House has lush gardens.

Fishers' Loft INN $$
(☎709-464-3240; http://fishersloft.com; Port Rexton; r incl breakfast $145-218; 📶) Featuring traditional 19th-century local architecture, this colonial is a favorite of return travelers. Rooms and suites are bright and spacious with fluffy duvets and down pillows; the treetop rooms offer stunning views of the bay. It's kitted out perfectly, with iPod docks, hiking poles and binoculars.

Eriksen Premises B&B $$
(☎709-464-3698; www.newfoundlandexperience.com; 8 West St; r $130-190; ⏲mid-May–mid Oct; 🚭📶) This 19th-century merchant home offers elegance in accommodations and dining (mains $20 to $30, open lunch and dinner). It also books two nearby B&Bs: Kelly's Landing (four rooms) and Bishop White Manor (nine rooms).

Trinity Mercantile CAFE $
(www.trinitymercantile.ca; 24 West St; mains $6-15; ⏲8am-6pm; 📶) Grab coffee and a bagel topped with salmon smoked on-site and eavesdrop on the local gossip mill. There are also baked goods, sandwiches, chowder, salt cod and beer.

★ Twine Loft CANADIAN $$$
(☎709-728-1805; 57 High St; prix-fixe $46) The upscale restaurant of the Artisan Inn serves a three-course, prix-fixe meal of local specialties, with wonderful seafood and wine selections guided by an in-house sommelier. Reservations are necessary, but you can also stop by for a sunset drink on the deck. Check the daily menu posted out front.

Drinking & Entertainment

Two Whales Cafe COFFEE
(☎709-464-3928; http://twowhales.com; 99 Main Rd, Port Rexton; ⏲10am-6pm) An adorable coffee shop serving the full-octane variety and lemon blueberry cake that's off the charts. It also does good vegetarian fare and organic salads.

Trinity Pageant THEATER
(adult/child $27/free; ⏲2pm Wed & Sat) An entertaining outdoor drama on Trinity's history held at the Rising Tide Theatre.

Rising Tide Theatre THEATER
(☎709-464-3232; www.risingtidetheatre.com; Water St; ⊙Jun-Sep) Alongside the Lester Garland Premises is the celebrated Rising Tide Theatre, which hosts the 'Seasons in the Bight' festival and the Trinity Pageant.

Rocky's Place Lounge LIVE MUSIC
(☎709-464-3400; High St; ⊙from 7pm) Rocky's hosts bands from time to time, but even if the mikes are quiet, it's a friendly place to hoist a brew.

Information

The town website (www.townoftrinity.com) has tourism information.

RBC Royal Bank (West St; ⊙10:30am-2pm Mon-Thu, to 5pm Fri) No ATM.

Getting There & Away

Trinity is 259km from St John's and is reached via Rte 230 off Hwy 1. **Shirran's Taxi** (☎709-468-7741) offers a daily taxi service to St John's.

Bonavista

'O buona vista!' (Oh, happy sight!), shouted John Cabot upon spying the New World from his boat on June 24, 1497. Or so the story goes. From all accounts, this pretty spot is where he first set foot in the Americas. Today Bonavista's shoreline, with its lighthouse, puffins and chasms, continues to rouse emotions.

Sights

Cape Bonavista Lighthouse LIGHTHOUSE
(☎709-468-7444; www.seethesites.ca; Rte 230; adult/child $6/3; ⊙9:30am-5pm May-Oct) A brilliant red-and-white-striped lighthouse dating from 1843. The interior has been restored to the 1870s, and it is now a provincial historic site. A puffin colony lives just offshore; the birds put on quite a show around sunset.

Dungeon Park PARK
(Cape Shore Rd, off Rte 230) Nowhere is the power of water more evident than at the Dungeon, a deep chasm 90m in circumference that was created by the collapse of two sea caves, through which thunderous waves now slam the coast.

Ye Matthew Legacy HISTORIC SITE
(☎709-468-1493; www.matthewlegacy.com; Roper St; adult/child $7.25/3; ⊙9:30am-4:45pm Jun-Sep) A 15th-century replica of *The Matthew*, which Cabot sailed into Bonavista.

Ryan Premises National Historic Site HISTORIC SITE
(☎709-468-1600; www.pc.gc.ca/ryanpremises; Ryans Hill Rd; adult/child $3.90/1.90; ⊙10am-6pm Jun-Sep) Ryan Premises National Historic Site is a restored 19th-century saltfish mercantile complex. The slew of white clapboard buildings honors five centuries of fishing in Newfoundland via multimedia displays and interpretive programs.

Sleeping

The cute town options fill up in high season. Check www.bonavista.net for other lodgings.

White's B&B B&B $
(☎709-468-7018; www.bbcanada.com/3821.htm; 21 Windlass Dr; s/d $95/100; @) Low-key White's has three rooms to choose from, all with either private bathroom or en suite. Enjoy the bike rentals, barbecue use and ocean view.

HI Bonavista HOSTEL $
(☎709-468-7741; www.hihostels.ca; 40 Cabot Dr; dm $26-30, r $79-120; @) This tidy white-clapboard hostel offers four private rooms, two shared dorm rooms, free bike use, and kitchen and laundry facilities. It's a short walk from the center.

Harbourview B&B B&B $$
(☎709-468-2572; www.harbourviewgetaway.com; 21 Ryans Hill Rd; r $115; ⊙Jun-Sep;) The name doesn't lie: you get a sweet view at this simple, four-room B&B, plus an evening snack (crab legs) with owners Florence and Albert. Breakfast has a gluten-free option.

Eating

Bonavista has one of the best restaurant scenes in the province.

Boreal Diner CAFE $
(☎709-476-2330; 61 Church St; mains $6-15; ⊙11am-7pm Tue-Sat;) In a bright-red colonial house, this mom-and-pop cafe offers great alternative eats. Crab pot stickers, cod in tarragon sauce, and burgers with toasted buns are some of the scrumptious offerings. It also does vegan and gluten free. Real espresso drinks keep you wired.

Neil's Yard CAFE $
(www.neilsyard.org; Mockbeggar Plantation, Mockbeggar Rd; mains $5-12; ⊙10am-8pm May-Oct;) Get comfortable. Here, the gregarious English owner will set you up with a steaming mug of exotic tea, while his wife cooks

WORTH A TRIP

ELLISTON: ROOT CELLARS & PUFFINS

The Root Cellar Capital of the World, aka Elliston, lies 6km south of Bonavista on Rte 238. The teeny town was struggling until it hit upon the idea to market its 135 subterranean veggie storage vaults, and then presto – visitors came a knockin'. Actually, what's most impressive is the **puffin colony** just offshore and swarming with thousands of chubby-cheeked, orange-billed birds from mid-May to mid-August. A quick and easy path over the cliffside brings you quite close to them and also provides whale and iceberg views.

Stop at the **Elliston Visitors Centre** (709-468-7117; www.townofelliston.ca; Main St; 10am-5pm) as you enter town, and the kindly folks will give you directions to the site along with a map of the cellars (which you're welcome to peek inside).

Work up an appetite while you're here, because **Nanny's Root Cellar Kitchen** (709-468-7998; Orange Hall; mains $7-15; 8am-10pm) in historic Orange Hall cooks a mighty fine lobster, Jiggs dinner (roast meat with boiled potatoes, carrots, cabbage, salted beef and pea-and-bread pudding) and other traditional foods, plus she's licensed.

The **Roots, Rants and Roars Festival** (www.rootsrantsandroars.ca; mid-Sep) celebrates the province's top chefs, who prepare outdoor feasts in a dramatic setting.

From the adjoining hamlet of **Maberly** a gorgeous 17km coastal hiking trail winds over the landscape to Little Catalina.

up buckwheat crepes, carrot ginger soup, cheesecake with local berries and other healthy fare. Service can be slow, but there's plenty to look at in the attached craft shop.

Walkham's Gate CAFE $

(709-468-7004; www.walkhamsgatepub.ca; mains $5-12; 24hr;) One side is a coffee shop with whopping pies and hearty soups, the other side a congenial pub tended by music-lover Harvey. Located in the town center, near the courthouse.

★ **Bonavista Social Club** MODERN CANADIAN $$

(709-445-5556; www.bonavistasocialclub.com; Upper Amherst Cove; mains $12-23; 11am-8pm Tue-Sun) Social Club's innovative meals are sourced on-site and served with a view. From incredible wood-fired breads and pizzas to rhubarb lemonade and local moose burgers with partridgeberry ketchup, the kitchen churns out satisfying fare. Tables are few for the demand. The goats roaming the grounds provide milk for cheese, while the chickens lay the eggs. Reserve ahead.

The rustic restaurant is about 15 minutes from Bonavista via Rte 235 (turn left when you see the sign for Upper Amherst Cove). The chef's dad carved all the beautiful wood decor in his workshop next door.

☆ Entertainment

Garrick Theatre THEATER

(www.garricktheatre.ca; 18 Church St) The artfully restored Garrick shows mainstream and indie films and hosts live-music performances.

Information

MONEY

There's several bank branches, including **Scotiabank** (709-468-1070; 1 Church St; 9:30am-4pm Mon-Thu), in town.

MEDICAL SERVICES

Bonavista Community Health Centre (709-468-7881; Hospital Rd)

TOURIST INFORMATION

The town website (www.townofbonavista.com) has tourism information.

Getting There & Away

Bonavista is a scenic 50km drive north of Trinity along Rte 230. **Shirran's** (709-468-7741; $40) offers a daily shuttle service from St John's.

Burin Peninsula

It's not exactly lively on the Burin Peninsula, due to the effects of the besieged fishing economy. Still, the coastal walks inspire, and the region is a low-key place to spend a day or two before embarking toward the baguettes of France (aka St-Pierre).

Marystown is the peninsula's largest town; it's jammed with big-box retailers but not much else. **Burin** is the area's most attractive town, with a gorgeous elevated boardwalk over the waters of its rocky shoreline. **St Lawrence** is known for fluorite mining and scenic coastal hikes. In **Grand Bank**, there's an interesting self-guided walk through the historic buildings and along the waterfront. Just south is fossil-rich **Fortune**, the jump-off point for St-Pierre.

Sights

Fortune Head Ecological Reserve PARK
(www.env.gov.nl.ca/parks; off Rte 220; 24hr) The reserve protects fossils dating from the planet's most important period of evolution, when life on earth progressed from simple organisms to complex animals some 550 million years ago. The reserve is about 3km west of Rte 220, by the Fortune Head Lighthouse.

Fortune Head Geology Centre MUSEUM
(709-832-3031; www.fortunehead.com; Bunker Hill Rd, Fortune; adult/child $7.50/5; 8am-8pm Jun-Aug) New exhibits examine the geology of the Burin Peninsula, minerals and rocks, the 1929 Grand Banks tsunami and prehistoric animals. Kids will appreciate this interactive center with fossils to touch from Fortune Head Ecological Reserve; it's in town by the St-Pierre ferry dock. It also offers children's day camp with a daily rate. Daily tours go to the reserve ($25).

Burin Heritage Museums MUSEUM
(709-891-2217; Seaview Dr, Burin; 9am-6pm Mon-Fri, 10:30am-6pm Sat & Sun Apr-Sep) FREE Displays in two historic homes tell of life's highs and lows in remote outports.

Provincial Seamen's Museum MUSEUM
(709-832-1484; www.therooms.ca/museum; Marine Dr, Grand Bank; $2.50; 9:30am-4:45pm May-Oct) The impressive-looking Seamen's Museum depicts both the era of the banking schooner and the changes in the fishery over the years.

Activities

Ask at the Burin Heritage Museum about locating the **Cook's Lookout** trailhead. It's a 20-minute walk from town to the panoramic view. Off Pollux Cres in St Lawrence, the rugged, breath-draining **Cape Trail** (4km) and **Chamber Cove Trail** (4km) shadow the cliff edges and offer amazing vistas to rocky shores and some famous WWII shipwrecks. Another good (and easier) trail is the **Marine Hike** (7km), which traces Admiral's Beach near Grand Bank. It leaves from Christian's Rd off Rte 220.

Sleeping & Eating

Options are spread thinly. For those heading to St-Pierre, Grand Bank and Fortune are the best bases. Grand Bank has better lodging, but at 8km from the ferry dock it's further from St-Pierre. Fortune has a sweet bakery by its dock. For more choices check the Heritage Run (www.theheritagerun.com).

Thorndyke B&B B&B $$
(709-832-0820; www.thethorndyke.ca; 33 Water St, Grand Bank; r $130; May-Oct;) This handsome old captain's home overlooks the harbor. Antique wood furnishings fill the four light and airy rooms (each with private bathroom). The hosts will provide dinner with advance notice.

Fortune Harbourview B&B B&B $$
(709-832-7666; www.fortuneharbourview.com; 74 Eldon St, Fortune; r $119-159;) The five rooms aren't fancy, and they're perched on top of a beauty salon, but they're tidy and, best of all, located near the ferry to St-Pierre. It's a serve-yourself, continental-style breakfast.

Stage Head Cafe CAFE $
(709-832-5796; 18 Bayview St, Fortune; mains $6-14;) Attached to the ferry office in Fortune, this small restaurant does a bustling business in quick breakfasts, lunch sandwiches and fish-and-chips. The set dinners ($30) with fresh-caught seafood are well worth it.

Sharon's Nook & the Tea Room CAFE $
(709-832-0618; 12 Water St, Grand Bank; mains $7-12; 7:30am-9pm Mon-Sat, 11am-7:30pm Sun) This kitschy and countrified eatery serves up lasagna, chili, sandwiches and over a dozen varieties of heavenly cheesecake.

Getting There & Away

The Burin Peninsula is accessed via Rte 210 off Hwy 1. The drive from St John's to Grand Bank is 359km and takes just over four hours. Several shuttle services, including **Foote's Taxi** (709-832-0491) and **Matthew's Taxi** (709-832-4633), go from St John's down the peninsula as far as Fortune.

ST-PIERRE & MIQUELON

POP 6100

Twenty-five kilometers offshore from the Burin Peninsula floats a little piece of France. The islands of St-Pierre and Miquelon aren't just French-like with their berets, baguettes and Bordeaux, they *are* France, governed and financed by the *tricolore*.

Locals kiss their hellos and pay in euros, while sweet smells waft from the myriad pastry shops, and French cars crowd the tiny one-way streets. It's a world away from Newfoundland.

St-Pierre is the more populated and developed island, with most of its 5500 residents living in the town of St-Pierre. Miquelon is larger geographically but has only 600 residents overall.

Jacques Cartier claimed the islands for France in 1536, after they were discovered by the Portuguese in 1520. At the end of the Seven Years' War in 1763, the islands were turned over to Britain, only to be given back to France in 1816. And French they've remained ever since.

Sights

Miquelon & Langlade ISLAND

(adult/child 3hr tour €35/18; Jun-Sep) The island of Miquelon is less visited and less developed than St-Pierre. The village of **Miquelon**, centered on the church, is at the northern tip of the island. From nearby **l'Étang de Mirande** a walking trail leads to a lookout and waterfall. From the bridge in town, a scenic 25km road leads across the isthmus to the wild and uninhabited island of Langlade. There are some wild horses, and around the rocky coast you'll see seals and birds. Tours are operated by the Comite Regional de Tourisme.

Île aux Marins HISTORIC BUILDING

(3hr tour adult/child €24/16; 9am & 1:30pm May-Sep) The magical Île aux Marins is a beautiful abandoned village on an island out in the St-Pierre harbor. A bilingual guide will walk you through colorful homes, a small schoolhouse museum and the grand church (1874). Book tours at the visitor center. You can also go over on the boat (€6) sans guide, but be aware most signage is in French. Outside of July and August boats must be pre-arranged (see the tourism office).

Les Salines AREA

(Rue Boursaint & the waterfront) Old-timers hang out around this scenic cluster of multihued fishing shacks.

L'Arche Museum MUSEUM

(508-410-435; www.arche-musee-et-archives.net; Rue du 11 Novembre; adult/child €5/3; 10am-noon & 2-6pm Tue-Sun Jun-Sep) The well-done exhibits cover the islands' history, including Prohibition times. The showstopper is the **guillotine** – the only one to slice in North America. Islanders dropped the 'timbers of justice' just once, in 1889, on a murderer. The museum also offers bilingual **architectural walking tours** (€7).

Activities

In St-Pierre, the best thing to do is just walk around and soak it up – when you're not eating, that is. Pop into stores and sample goods you'd usually have to cross an ocean for. Or conduct research as to the best chocolate-croissant maker. A couple of **walking trails** leave from the edge of town near the power station and loop between the far coast and inland lakes.

Zodiac Tours BOATING

(adult/child €41/35) Full-day, bilingual tours by Zodiac cover both Miquelon and Langlade. Book at the visitor center. Rates include snack.

Fronton PELOTE

(Rues Maître Georges Lefèvre & Gloanec) Watch locals play the Basque game of *pelote* (a type of handball) at the outdoor court here.

Festivals & Events

From mid-July to the end of August, folk dances are often held in St-Pierre's square.

Basque Festival CULTURAL

(mid-Aug) A weeklong festival with music, marching and invigorating street fun.

Bastille Day CULTURAL

(Jul 14) The largest holiday of the year.

Sleeping

There are about a dozen accommodations on St-Pierre; most include continental breakfast. Book ahead in summer.

Auberge Quatre Temps B&B B&B $

(508-414-301; www.quatretemps.com; s/d €78/82; @) Quatre Temps is a 15-minute schlep from the ferry dock, but don't let that deter you. All six rooms have their own bathroom. There's a fine terrace where you can buy drinks and sip alfresco. The owner also runs the Saveurs des Îles restaurant.

Bernard Dodeman B&B B&B $

(508-413-060; www.pensiondodeman.com; 15 Rue Paul Bert; r €55; @) The Dodeman's three simple rooms share two bathrooms and a communal TV parlor. It's a 15-minute walk from the ferry, on a hill above town.

★**Auberge St Pierre** B&B **$$**
(☎508-414-086; www.aubergesaintpierre.fr; 16 Rue Georges Daguerre; d €88-176; 📶) Guests rave about the warm service and lovely atmosphere of this family-run island B&B. Arrive to chilled wine and cheese. Remodeled rooms feature flat-screen TVs and hydromassage showers; they're also stocked with robes and extra towels. Transportation to and from the ferry and island tours included.

Nuits St-Pierre B&B **$$**
(☎508-412-720; www.nuits-saint-pierre.com; 10 Rue du Général Leclerc; r €130-175; 🚭📶) An upscale lodging aimed at the honeymoon crowd. The five rooms, each with private bathroom and blissful, downy beds, are named after famous French authors. There's free pickup from the airport or ferry. The attached tea salon is open every afternoon from 2pm to 6pm and is a must for a restorative beverage and slice of cake. It also boasts a fitness center.

Hotel Robert HOTEL **$$**
(☎508-412-419; www.hotelrobert.com; 2 Rue du 11 Novembre; d €90-118; 📶) Most visitors end up in this decent-value hotel, the largest on the island. Rooms are pleasant, with crisp white sheets and powerful showers. Some are dated. A downstairs restaurant serves breakfast (not included) but be warned: there's only one waiter serving two clamoring, hungry rooms. It's within close walking distance of the ferry.

Eating

The few island restaurants can barely meet demand in summer, so be sure to make dinner reservations well in advance if you plan on eating out. It's not unusual for all restaurants to be fully booked.

★**Guillard Gourmandises** BAKERY **$**
(31 Rue Boursaint; pastries €1-3; ⏰7am-noon & 2-5:30pm Tue-Sat, to 4:30pm Sun) It's worth memorizing the complicated schedule to make good on this slice of *la belle* France. After all, these cream-plumped chocolate éclairs, macarons, piping-hot pastries and gateaux are the reason you came, right?

Le Cafe du Chat Luthier SUSHI, PIZZA **$$**
(www.lecafeduchatluthier.com; 6 Rue Amiral Muselier; mains €9-22; ⏰noon-1:30pm Tue-Fri, 6-10pm Tue-Sun) An apt response to everything St-Pierre lacks, this amicable hipster hideout serves wonderful sushi rolls, crisp, wood-fired, wafer-thin pizzas and gourmet burgers. If you are stuck without a dinner reservation, the takeout is a godsend. Offers set lunches on weekdays.

L'Atelier Gourmand FRENCH **$$$**
(☎508-415-300; www.lateliergourmandspm.com; 12 Rue du 11 Novembre; mains €18-25; ⏰noon-2pm & 6-10:30pm; 📶) Crowds of diners tuck into classic French fare at this cozy restaurant with a streetfront patio. Yet the prix-fixe menu can be hit or miss and service is painfully slow. However, you can't go wrong with a heaping bowl of mussels served with a nice vintage and topped off with white chocolate crème brûlée.

Information

Americans, EU citizens and all visitors except Canadians need a passport for entry. Those staying longer than 30 days also need a visa. Other nationalities should confirm with their French embassy if a visa is needed prior to arrival. Canadians can enter with a driver's license.

BUSINESS HOURS

Most shops and businesses close between noon and 1:30pm. Some stores also close on Saturday afternoons, and most are closed on Sunday.

ST-PIERRE'S BOOZY BACKSTORY

When Prohibition dried out the USA's kegs in the 1920s, Al Capone decided to slake his thirst – and that of the nation – by setting up shop in St-Pierre.

He and his mates transformed the sleepy fishing harbor into a booming port crowded with warehouses filled with imported booze. Bottles were removed from their crates, placed in smaller carrying sacks and taken secretly to the US coast by rum runners. The piles of Cutty Sark whiskey crates were so high on the docks that clever locals used the wood both to build and heat houses. At least one house remains today and is known as the 'Cutty Sark cottage'; most bus tours drive by.

The tourist information center offers a special two-hour Prohibition tour (adult/child €20/10) that covers sites related to the theme. If nothing else, drop by the Hotel Robert near the tourist information center and check out Al Capone's hat; it hangs in the gift shop.

CUSTOMS

To merit the duty-free waiver on alcohol, you must stay on the islands at least 48 hours.

LANGUAGE

French is the language, but many people also speak English.

MONEY

Most vendors accept credit cards. Some accept the loonie, though they return change in euros. If you're staying more than an afternoon, it's probably easiest to get euros from the local ATMs.

TELEPHONE

Calling the islands is an international call, meaning you must dial ☎011 in front of the local number. Phone service links in to the French system, so beware of roaming charges on your mobile.

TIME

Half an hour ahead of Newfoundland Time.

TOURIST INFORMATION

The **visitor center** (www.st-pierre-et-miquelon.com; 8:30am-6:30pm;), near the ferry dock, has a map showing all the banks, restaurants etc. Staff also provides info on the islands' hotels and tours and makes bookings for free.

Getting There & Away

AIR

Air St-Pierre (www.airsaintpierre.com; round-trip $353) flies to St John's, Montréal and Halifax. There are two to three flights weekly to each city. Taxis to/from the airport cost around €5.

BOAT

From Fortune on Newfoundland, the **St-Pierre Ferry** (☎709-832-3455; www.saintpierreferry.ca; 14 Bayview St, Fortune; adult/child return $93/58) makes the hour-long trip to and from the island once daily (twice on Wednesdays) in July and August. It runs less often the rest of the year. Departure times vary, so check the website. Boats carry foot passengers only, though there are plans for two car ferries. Staff coordinate Fortune parking in lots near the dock (per day $10). Buy tickets in advance and arrive 30 minutes early or one hour before departure if you need to leave a car.

Getting Around

Much can be seen on foot. Roads are steep, so prepare to huff and puff. Car-rental agencies are resistant to renting to tourists, who admittedly have difficulty navigating the unsignposted, narrow, one-way streets.

The visitor center rents bicycles (per day €13) and there are also motorized bicycles for rent. Local ferries head to Miquelon and Langlade; check with the visitor center for schedules and costs.

CENTRAL NEWFOUNDLAND

Central Newfoundland elicits fewer wows per square kilometer than the rest of the province, but that's because huge chunks of the region are pure bog land and trees. The islands of Notre Dame Bay – particularly Twillingate, when icebergs glide by – are the exceptions.

Terra Nova National Park

Backed by lakes, bogs and hilly woods, and fronted by the salty waters of Clode and Newman Sounds, Terra Nova National Park is spliced by Hwy 1 running through its interior.

Sights

Burnside Archaeology Centre MUSEUM

(☎709-677-2474; www.digthequarry.com; Main St; adult/child $3/1; 9am-6pm Jul-Oct) About 15km from the western gate of Terra Nova National Park, the Burnside Archaeology Centre catalogs artifacts found at local Beothuk sites.

Terra Nova National Park PARK

(☎709-533-2801; www.pc.gc.ca/terranova; adult/child/family per day $5.80/2.90/14.70) Though not nearly as dramatic as the province's other national parks, it does offer moose, bears, beavers and bald eagles, as well as relaxed hiking, paddling, camping and boat tours.

Activities

Terra Nova's 14 hiking trails total almost 100km; pick up maps at the Visitors Centre (p488). Highly recommended is the **Malady Head Trail** (5km), which climaxes at the edge of a headland cliff offering stunning views of Southwest Arm and Broad Cove. **Sandy Pond Trail** (3km) is an easy loop around the pond – your best place to spot a beaver. The area is also a favorite for **swimming**, with a beach, change rooms and picnic tables. In winter the park grooms trails here for cross-country skiing.

The epic **Outport Trail** (48km) provides access to backcountry campgrounds and abandoned settlements along Newman Sound. The loop in its entirety is rewarding, but be warned: parts are unmarked, not to mention mucky. A compass, a topographical map and ranger advice are prerequisites for this serious route.

Kayak rentals are available at the kiosk by the visitor center. Inquire about the **Sandy Pond–Dunphy's Pond Route** (10km), a great paddle with only one small portage.

Also in the region is **Salvage**, a photogenic fishing village with well-marked walking trails. It's near the park's north end on Rte 310, about 26km from Hwy 1.

Tours

Boat Tours BOATING
(per adult/child $45/30) Interesting boat tours reach the more far-flung settlements. Ask at the Terra Nova National Park Visitors Centre or the Burnside Archaeology Centre for information.

Coastal Connections BOATING
(709-533-2196; www.coastalconnections.ca; 2½hr tours adult/child $85/35; 10am & 2pm May-Oct) Climb aboard for a trip through Newman Sound, where you'll pull lobster pots, examine plankton under a microscope and engage in other hands-on activities. It's common to see eagles, less so whales.

Sleeping

Camping is the only option within the park itself. Those with aspirations of a bed should head to Eastport; it's near the park's north end on Rte 310, about 16km from Hwy 1. For camping reservations (recommended on summer weekends), call **Parks Canada** (877-737-3783; www.pccamping.ca; reservation fee $10.80) or go online.

Backcountry Camping CAMPGROUND $
(free permit required, tent sites $16) There are several backcountry sites around the Outport Trail, Beachy Pond, Dunphy's Island and Dunphy's Pond, reached by paddling, hiking or both. Register at the visitor center.

Newman Sound Campground CAMPGROUND $
(campsites $26-30) This is the park's main (noisier) campground, with 343 sites, a grocery store and a laundromat. It has electricity, toilets and showers. It's open for winter camping too.

Information

Make your first stop the **Terra Nova National Park Visitors Centre** (709-533-2942; Hwy 1; 10am-6pm Jul & Aug, to 4pm May, Jun & Sep), which has oodles of park information, ranger-guided programs and marine displays with touch tanks and underwater cameras. It's 1km off Hwy 1 at Salton's Day-Use Area, 80km east of Gander.

Gander

Gander sprawls across the juncture of Hwy 1 and Rte 330, which leads to Notre Dame Bay. It is a convenient stopping point and offers a couple of sights for aviation buffs. Big-box retailers are everywhere, as this is the region's main town. If you need to stock up on anything, do it here.

For aviation fanatics, the **North Atlantic Aviation Museum** (709-256-2923; www.northatlanticaviationmuseum.com; Hwy 1; adult/child $6/5; 9am-7pm Jul & Aug, to 4pm Mon-Fri Sep-Jun) is a drawcard. Just east on Hwy 1 is the sobering **Silent Witness Monument**, a tribute to 248 US soldiers whose plane crashed here in December 1985.

Though expensive for the location, the hotel rooms at **Sinbad's Hotel & Suites** (709-651-2678; www.steelehotels.com; Bennett Dr; r $129-147) in the center of Gander are clean and welcoming for a rest from highway driving.

There is a **Visitors Centre** (www.gandercanada.com; 8am-8pm Jun-Sep, 8:30am-5pm Oct-May) on Hwy 1 at the central entry into town.

The **Gander Airport** (YQX; 709-256-6666; www.ganderairport.com) gets a fair bit of traffic. **DRL** (709-263-2171; www.drl-lr.com) buses stop at the airport en route to St John's (four hours) and Port aux Basques (nine hours).

Twillingate Island & New World Island

This area of Notre Dame Bay gets ample attention thanks to an influx of whales and icebergs every summer. Twillingate (comprised of two barely separated islands, North and South Twillingate) sits just north of New World Island. The islands are reached from the mainland via short causeways. On a summer day it can be touristy, though stunning. Every turn of the road reveals new ocean vistas, fishing wharves or outcrops of tidy pastel houses.

Sights

★**Prime Berth Fishing Museum** MUSEUM
(709-884-2485; www.primeberth.com; Main Tickle Causeway; $5, tour $8; 10am-5pm Jul & Aug) Make this your first stop. Run by an engaging fisherman, the private museum, with its imaginative and deceptively simple

concepts (a cod splitting show!), is brilliant, and fun for mature scholars and schoolkids alike. It's the first place you see as you cross to Twillingate.

Long Point Lighthouse LIGHTHOUSE
(☎709-884-2247; ⏰10am-6pm) FREE Long Point provides dramatic views of the coastal cliffs. Travel up the winding steps, worn from lighthouse-keepers' footsteps since 1876, and gawk at the 360-degree view. Located at the tip of the north island, it's an ideal vantage point for spotting icebergs in May and June.

Auk Island Winery WINERY
(☎709-884-2707; www.aukislandwinery.com; 29 Durrell St; tastings $3, with tour $5; ⏰9am-9pm Jul & Aug, reduced hour Sep-Jun) Visit the grounds that produce Moose Joose (blueberry-partridgeberry), Funky Puffin (blueberry-rhubarb) and other fruity flavors using iceberg water and local berries. There's also ice cream made from iceberg water.

Little Harbour WATERFRONT
In Little Harbour, en route to the town of Twillingate, a 5km trail leads past the vestiges of a resettled community and rock arch to secluded, picturesque **Jone's Cove**.

Twillingate Museum MUSEUM
(☎709-884-2825; www.tmacs.ca; admission by donation; ⏰9am-5pm May-Sep) Housed in a former Anglican rectory off Main St, the museum tells the island's history since the first British settlers arrived in the mid-1700s. One room delves into the seal hunt and its controversy. There's a historic **church** next door.

Durrell Museum MUSEUM
(☎709-884-2780; Museum St; adult/child $3/1.50; ⏰9am-5pm Jun-Sep) Don't neglect to see scenic Durrell and its museum, dwelling off Durrell St atop Old Maid Hill. The polar bear is a bonus. Bring your lunch; there are a couple of picnic tables and a spectacular view.

Tours

Fun two-hour tours to view icebergs and whales depart daily from mid-May to early September.

Iceberg Man Tours BOATING
(☎800-611-2374; www.icebergtours.ca; Southside; adult/child $50/25) Captain Cecil's popular two-hour tour departs at 9:30am, 1pm and 4pm. Guests rave about the service.

Twillingate Adventure Tours BOATING
(☎888-447-8687; http://twillingateadventuretours.com) Depart from Twillingate's wharf off Main St at 10am, 1pm and 4pm (and sometimes 7pm).

Festivals & Events

Fish, Fun & Folk Festival MUSIC
(www.fishfunfolkfestival.com; ⏰late Jul) Traditional music and dance, some of which goes back to the 16th century, merrily take over Twillingate during this weeklong festival.

Sleeping & Eating

Despite having about 20 lodging options, Twillingate gets very busy in the summer. Book early.

Paradise B&B B&B $
(☎709-884-5683; www.capturegaia.com/paradiseb&b.html; 192 Main St; r incl breakfast $90 110; ⏰May-Sep;) Set on a bluff overlooking Twillingate's harbor, Paradise offers the best view in town. You can wander down to the beach below, or relax on a lawn chair and soak it all up. Oh, the three rooms are comfy too. Angle for room 1. Cash only.

Anchor Inn Hotel HOTEL $$
(☎709-884-2777; www.anchorinntwillingate.com; 3 Path End; r $135-165; ⏰Mar-Dec;) The waterfront Anchor has rooms with deliciously soft beds. Amenities include the hotel's view-worthy deck and the barbecue grill for do-it-yourself types. There's also an excellent on-site restaurant.

Captain's Legacy B&B B&B $$
(☎709-884-5648; www.captainslegacy.com; Hart's Cove; r $110-140; ⏰May-Oct;) A real captain named Peter Troake once owned this historic 'outport mansion,' now a gracious four-room B&B overlooking the harbor.

R&J Restaurant SEAFOOD $
(☎709-884-2212; 110 Main St; mains $8-14; ⏰8am-11pm) A greasy spoon popular with families – probably because it serves pizza and burgers alongside fish 'n' brewis (a blend of salted fish, onions, fried pork fat and a near-boiled bread).

★**Doyle Sansome & Sons** SEAFOOD $$
(www.sansomeslobsterpool.com; 25 Sansome's Place, Hillgrade; mains $8-24; ⏰10am-9pm) It's well worth veering out of your way for this classic fish shack serving crisp cod, fish cakes with rhubarb relish and fresh lobster. If it's a nice day, the dock seating provides a fine

view. Don't be fooled by the name – a slew of friendly women cook here. The village of Hillgrade is 17km before Twilingate on the left.

Entertainment

Twillingate/NWI Dinner Theatre THEATER (709-884-2300; Crow Head; adult/child $32/16; 5:30pm Mon-Sat Jun-Sep) Six of Newfoundland's best will not only cook you a traditional meal, they'll also leave you in stitches with their talented performances. It's just south of the Long Point Lighthouse.

Fogo Island & Change Islands

POP 2400

Settled in the 1680s, Fogo is an intriguing and rugged island to poke around. Keep an eye on this place: it has embarked on an ambitious, arts-oriented sustainable tourism plan that's quite progressive for the region. The rare Newfoundland pony roams the Change Islands, which float to the west.

Sights & Activities

On Fogo, the village of **Joe Batt's Arm**, backed by rocky hills, is a flashback to centuries past – though it now has a mod twist thanks to the luxe new Fogo Island Inn. A **farmers market** takes place at the ice rink on Saturday mornings.

Nearby **Tilting** is perhaps the most engaging village on the island. Irish roots run deep here and so do the accents. The inland harbor is surrounded by picturesque fishing stages and flakes, held above the incoming tides by weary stilts. There's also the great coastal **Turpin's Trail** (9km), which leaves from Tilting, near the beach at **Sandy Cove**.

On the opposite end of the island is the village of **Fogo** and the indomitable **Brimstone Head**. After you take in the mystical rock's view, do another great hike in town: the **Lion's Den Trail** (5km), which visits a Marconi radio site. Keep an eye out for the small group of caribou that roams the island.

As part of the development plan, the island has built **art studios** along its walking trails, and invites painters, filmmakers and photographers from around the world for residencies.

The Change Islands are home to the **Newfoundland Pony Sanctuary** (709-621-6381; www.nlponysanctuary.com; 12 Bowns Rd; admission by donation; by appointment), established to increase numbers of the native, endangered Newfoundland pony. Less than 100 registered beasts of breeding age remain in the province.

Festivals & Events

Brimstone Head Folk Festival MUSIC (www.brimstoneheadfestival.com; mid-Aug) A three-day hootenanny; Irish and Newfoundland music.

Great Fogo Island Punt Race CULTURAL (www.fogoislandregatta.com; late Jul) Locals row traditionally built wooden boats (called punts) 16km across open sea to the Change Islands and back.

Sleeping & Eating

Accommodations range from B&Bs to the most exclusive hotel in Newfoundland. Reserve ahead as Fogo is wildly popular in summer.

★ **Tilting Harbour B&B** B&B $ (709-658-7288; www.tiltingharbourbnb.ca; 10a Kelley's Island Rd, Tilting; r $98-110;) Outstanding in hospitality, this traditional, 100-year-old home has four spotless rooms with renovated bathrooms. While angles are sharp, it's comfortable and cozy. Best of all, the owner Tom is an accomplished chef who offers wonderful, social dinners ($35) with fresh local seafood. Breakfast scones are also a big hit.

Peg's B&B B&B $ (709-266-2392; www.pegsbb.com; 60 Main St, Fogo; r $85-105; May-Oct;) In the heart of Fogo village, Peg's four-room place offers up a friendly atmosphere and harbor views.

Quintal House INN $$ (www.quintalhouse.ca; 153 Main Rd, Joe Batt's Arm; d $130-150;) Open year-round, this colorful heritage house has just three guest rooms adorned with works from local artisans. Guests have kitchen and laundry access. If there's a disadvantage, it's being right on the main road close to traffic. Reservations only.

★ **Fogo Island Inn** INN $$$ (709-658-3444; www.fogoislandinn.ca; Joe Batt's Arm; 2-night stay incl meals $1775-2875;) With modern, minimalist design and sterling service, this 29-room inn is an architectural wonder clasping the edge of the world. Canada's Prime Minister Justin Trudeau vacations here. Rooms have king-sized beds draped with quilts, plus binoculars and phenomenal sea views. The chef sources ingredients from island forages. In July nonguests can tour the ecofriendly facilities daily at 11am and 2:30pm.

Growler's ICE CREAM $
(Joe Batt's Arm; cones $5; ⏲12:30-7pm Wed-Sun) It would be a pity to miss this seaside stop, serving homemade partridgeberry-pie ice cream flecked with cinnamon and salty crumbs of crust.

Nicole's Cafe CAFE $$
(☎709-658-3663; www.nicolescafe.ca; 159 Main Rd, Joe Batt's Arm; mains $16-22; ⏲10:30am-8pm Mon-Sat) Nicole uses ingredients from the island – sustainably caught seafood, root vegetables and wild berries – for her contemporary take on dishes like Jiggs dinner, caribou pâté and the daily vegetarian plate. It's a sunny spot with big wood tables and local artwork and quilts on the walls.

Fogo Island Inn Restaurant CANADIAN $$$
(☎709-658-3444; www.fogoislandinn.ca; Joe Batt's Arm; lunch mains $20-45, prix-fixe dinner $115; ⏲7-10am, noon-3pm & 6-9pm, by reservation only) With sparkling sea views, this tiny gourmet eatery dishes up innovative three-course dinners sourced as locally as possible. The menu changes daily. Think delicate preparations of snow crab with sea salt, Prince Edward Island grass-fed beef and rye ice cream with nettles. Drinks extra. Nonguests should reserve at least three days ahead and park roadside, a five-minute walk from the inn.

Getting There & Away

Rte 335 takes you to the town of Farewell, where the ferry sails to the Change Islands (20 minutes) and then onward to Fogo (45 minutes). Demand is heavy in summer – it is worth arriving two hours before your departure to ensure a spot for your vehicle.

Five boats leave between 7:45am and 8:30pm. Schedules vary, so check with **Provincial Ferry Services** (☎709-627-3492; www.gov.nl.ca/ferryservices; round-trip Fogo vehicle/passenger $18/6). Note it is about 25km from Fogo's ferry terminal to Joe Batt's Arm.

Grand Falls-Windsor

POP 13,700

The sprawl of two small pulp-and-paper towns has met and now comprises the community of Grand Falls-Windsor. The historic Grand Falls portion, south of Hwy 1 and near the Exploits River, is more interesting for visitors.

Sights

Mary March Provincial Museum MUSEUM
(☎709-292-4522; http://manl.nf.ca; 24 St Catherine St; adult/child $2.50/free; ⏲9am-4:30pm Mon-Sat, from noon Sun May-Oct) Worth visiting with exhibits on the recent and past histories of Aboriginal peoples in the area, including the extinct Beothuk tribe. Take exit 18A south to get here. Admission includes the loggers' museum.

Salmonid Interpretation Centre PARK
(☎709-489-7350; www.exploitsriver.ca; adult/child $6.50/3; ⏲8am-8pm Jun-Sep) Watch Atlantic salmon start their mighty struggle upstream to spawn. Unfortunately, they do so under the pulp mill's shadow. To get there, cross the river south of High St and follow the signs.

Festivals & Events

Salmon Festival MUSIC
(www.evsalmonfestival.com; ⏲mid-Jul) The five-day Salmon Festival rocks with big-name Canadian bands.

Sleeping & Eating

Hill Road Manor B&B B&B $$
(☎709-489-5451; www.hillroadmanor.com; 1 Hill Rd; r $119-129; 📶) Elegant furnishings, cushiony beds that will have you gladly oversleeping and a vibrant sunroom combine for a stylish stay. Kids are welcome.

Kelly's Pub BURGERS $
(☎709-489-9893; 18 Hill Rd; mains $8-14; ⏲9am-2am) Hidden neatly behind the smoky pub is this great countrified spot. It makes the best burgers in town and the stir-fries are not too shabby either.

Getting There & Away

DRL (☎709-263-2171; www.drl-lr.com) has its bus stop at the Highliner Inn on the Hwy 1 service road. Buses go 430km to St John's ($72) and to 477km Port aux Basques ($124).

Central South Coast

Rte 360 runs 130km through the center of the province to the south coast. It's a long way down to the first settlements at the end of **Bay d'Espoir**, a gentle fjord. Note there is no gas station on the route, so fill up on Hwy 1. **St Alban's** is on the west side of the fjord. You'll find a few motels with dining rooms and lounges around the end of the bay.

Further south is a concentration of small fishing villages. The scenery along Rte 364 to **Hermitage** is particularly impressive, as are the landscapes around **Harbour Breton**. The largest town (population 1700) in the region, it huddles around the ridge of a gentle inland bay.

Sleeping & Eating

Southern Port Hotel HOTEL $$
(709-885-2283; www.southernporthotel.ca; Rte 360, Harbour Breton; r $110-129;) Provides spacious, standard-furnished rooms; even-numbered ones have harbor views.

Scott's Snackbar BURGERS $
(709-885-2406; Harbour Breton; mains $7-15; 10:30am-11pm Sun-Thu, to 1am Fri & Sat) Near lodgings, Scott's Snackbar serves burgers and home-cooked dishes; it's licensed.

Getting There & Away

To access this remote area it's best to go by private vehicle, though **Thornhill Taxi Service** (709-885-2144) also runs between Grand Falls and Harbour Breton. **Provincial Ferry Services** (709-292-4302; www.tw.gov.nl.ca/ferryservices) serve Hermitage, making the western south-coast outports accessible from here.

NORTHERN PENINSULA

The Northern Peninsula points upward from the body of Newfoundland like an extended index finger, and you almost get the feeling it's wagging at you saying, 'Don't you dare leave this province without coming up here.'

Heed the advice. Two of the province's World Heritage–listed sites are here: Gros Morne National Park, with its fjord-like lakes and geological oddities, rests at the peninsula's base, while the sublime, 1000-year-old Viking settlement at L'Anse aux Meadows stares out from the peninsula's tip. Connecting these two famous sites is the **Viking Trail** (www.vikingtrail.org), aka Rte 430, an attraction in its own right that holds close to the sea as it heads resolutely north past the ancient burial grounds of Port au Choix and the ferry jump-off point to big, brooding Labrador.

The region continues to gain in tourism, yet the crowds are nowhere near what you'd get at Yellowstone or Banff, for example.

Deer Lake

There's little in Deer Lake for the visitor, but it's an excellent place to fly into for trips up the Northern Peninsula and around the west coast.

For B&B comfort, hunker down at plain-and-simple **Auntie M's Lucas House** (709-635-3622; www.lucashouse.net; 22 Old Bonne Bay Rd; r $75-85; May-Sep;); it's a five-minute ride from the airport.

The **visitors center** (709-635-2202; dlvic@gov.nl.ca; Hwy 1; 9am-7pm) and the **DRL** (709-263-2171; www.drl-lr.com) bus stop at the Irving gas station sit beside each other on Hwy 1. A taxi from the airport to any of these spots costs about $10.

Visitors to Gros Morne National Park usually fly into the **Deer Lake Airport** (YDF; 709-635-3601; www.deerlakeairport.com; 1 Airport Rd;). Long-distance DRL buses transit the Trans Canada Hwy.

Gros Morne National Park

The stunning flat-top mountains and deeply incised waterways of this **national park** (709-458-2417; www.pc.gc.ca/grosmorne; per day adult/child/family $9.80/4.90/19.60) are simply supernatural playgrounds. Designated a World Heritage Site in 1987, the park offers special significance to geologists as a blueprint for the planet. The bronze-colored Tablelands feature rock from deep within the earth's crust, supplying evidence for theories such as plate tectonics. Nowhere else in the world is such material as easily accessed as it is in Gros Morne.

Several small fishing villages dot the shoreline and provide amenities. Bonne Bay swings in and divides the area: to the south is Rte 431 and the towns of **Glenburnie**, **Woody Point** and **Trout River**; to the north is Rte 430 and **Norris Point**, **Rocky Harbour**, **Sally's Cove** and **Cow Head**. Centrally located Rocky Harbour is the largest village and most popular place to stay. Nearby Norris Point and further-flung Woody Point also make good bases.

Sights

The park is quite widespread – it's 133km from Trout River at the south end to Cow Head in the north – so it takes a while to get from sight to sight. Don't forget to stop at the park's visitor centers, which have interpretive programs and guided walks.

THE SEAL HUNT DEBATE

Nothing ignites a more passionate debate than Canada's annual seal hunt, which occurs in March and April off Newfoundland's northeast coast and in the Gulf of St Lawrence around the Îles de la Madeleine and Prince Edward Island. The debate pits animal-rights activists against sealers (typically local fishers who hunt in the off-season). The main issues revolve around the following questions.

Are baby seals being killed? Yes and no. Whitecoats are newborn harp seals, and these are the creatures that have been seen in horrifying images. But it has been illegal to hunt them for decades. After seals lose their white coats at 12 to 14 days old, they're considered fair game.

Are the animals killed humanely? Sealers say yes, that their guns and/or clubs kill the seals humanely. Animal activists dispute this, saying seals are injured and left on the ice to suffer until the sealers come back later and finish the job.

Is the seal population sustainable? The Canadian government says yes, and sets the yearly quota based on the total seal population in the area (estimated at 7.3 million). For 2015, the harp-seal quota was 468,000, despite market decline.

Is the seal hunt really an important part of the local economy? Activists say no, that it represents a fraction of Newfoundland's income. The province disagrees, saying for some sealers it represents up to one-third of their annual income. And in a province with unemployment near 12%, that's significant.

In 2009 the EU banned the sale of seal products, which hurt the industry considerably. For more on the two perspectives, see the Canadian Sealers Association (www.sealharvest.ca) and the Humane Society of the United States (www.protectseals.org).

Tablelands GEOLOGICAL FEATURE

Dominating the southwest corner of the park, near Trout River, are the unconquerable and eerie Tablelands. This huge flat-topped massif was part of the earth's mantle before tectonics raised it from the depths and planted it squarely on the continent. Its rock is so unusual that plants can't even grow on it. You can view the barren golden phenomenon up close on Rte 431, or catch it from a distance at the stunning photography lookout above Norris Point. West of the Tablelands, dramatic volcanic sea stacks and caves mark the coast at **Green Gardens**.

Bonne Bay Marine Station AQUARIUM

(☎709-458-2550; www.bonnebay.ca; Rte 430, Norris Point; adult/child/family $6.25/5/15; ⏲9am-5pm Jun-Aug) At the wharf in Norris Point is this research facility, which is part of Memorial University. Every half-hour there are interactive tours, and the aquariums display the marine ecological habitats in Bonne Bay. For children, there are touch tanks and a rare blue lobster lurking around.

Arches Provincial Park PARK

These scenic arched rocks on Rte 430 north of Parsons Pond are formed by pounding waves and worth a look-see.

Shallow Bay BEACH

This gentle, safe, sand-duned beach seems out of place, as if transported from the Caribbean. The water, however, provides a chilling dose of reality, rarely getting above 15°C.

Broom Point Fishing Camp HISTORIC SITE

(Rte 430, Broom Point; ⏲10am-5:30pm May-Oct) FREE This restored fishing camp sits a short distance north of Western Brook Pond. The three Mudge brothers and their families fished here from 1941 until 1975, when they sold the entire camp, including boats, lobster traps and nets, to the national park. It's staffed by guides.

SS Ethie SHIPWRECK

(Rte 430, past Sally's Cove) Follow the sign off the highway to where waves batter the rusty and tangled remains of the SS *Ethie*. The story of this 1919 wreck, and the subsequent rescue, was inspiration for a famous folk song.

Activities

Hiking

Twenty maintained trails of varying difficulty snake through 100km of the park's most scenic landscapes. The gem is the 16km **Gros Morne Mountain Trail** to the peak of Gros Morne, the highest point at 806m. A good alternative in poor weather, the 16km **Green Gardens Trail** is almost as scenic and challenging.

Shorter scenic hikes are **Tablelands Trail** (4km), which extends to Winterhouse Brook Canyon; **Lookout Trail** (5km), which starts behind the Discovery Centre and loops to the site of an old fire tower above the tree line; **Lobster Cove Head Trail** (2km), which loops through tidal pools; and **Western Brook Pond Trail** (Rte 430), the most popular path.

The granddaddies of the trails are the **Long Range Traverse** (35km) and **North Rim Traverse** (27km), serious multiday treks over the mountains. Permits and advice from park rangers are required.

If you plan to do several trails, invest $20 in a copy of the *Gros Morne National Park Trail Guide*, a waterproof map with trail descriptions on the back, which is usually available at the visitor centers.

Kayaking & Boating

Kayaking in the shadow of the Tablelands and through the spray of whales is truly something to be experienced.

★Western Brook Pond Boat Tour BOATING
(2hr trip per adult $58-65, child $26-30) With dramatic views second to none, this acclaimed tour is run by Bon's Tours. Prices are cheapest for morning tours. It's about a 25-minute drive from Bon's office to the trailhead. The dock is a 3km walk from Rte 430 via the easy Western Brook Pond Trail.

Gros Morne Adventures TOURS
(☎709-458-2722; www.grosmorneadventures.com; Norris Point wharf; 2hr kayak tour adult/child $55/45) A great way to experience Bonne Bay is through this outfitter's daily sea-kayak tours. It also offers full-day and multiday kayak trips and various hiking tours. Also provides kayak rentals (single/double per day $55/65) for experienced paddlers.

Bon Tours BOATING
(☎709-458-2016; www.bontours.ca; Ocean View Motel, Main St, Rocky Harbour) Bon runs the phenomenal Western Brook Pond boat tour every hour between 10am and 5pm and boat tours of Bonne Bay. If you haven't purchased a park pass, you must do so before embarking. Reserve in advance, either online or at Bon's office in the Ocean View Hotel.

Bonne Bay Boat Tours BOATING
(2hr trip adult/child $45/19) Bonne Bay boat tours depart from Norris Point wharf, as does a water taxi (adult/child $14/10 round-trip, foot passengers and bikes only) from Norris Point to Woody Point. Both taxi and tour are run by Bon Tours.

Skiing

Many trails in the park's impressive 55km cross-country ski-trail system were designed by Canadian Olympic champion Pierre Harvey. Contact the Main Visitor Centre (p495) for trail information and reservations for backcountry huts.

Cycling

The Corner Brook–based **Cycle Solutions** (☎709-634-7100; www.cyclesolutions.ca; Rte 430, Rocky Harbour) offers mountain biking and cycling tours through Gros Morne, from easy half-day rides to hard-core, multiday trips. Prices vary. The office is next to Rocky Harbour's town information center.

Festivals & Events

Writers at Woody Point Festival LITERATURE
(☎709-453-2900; www.writersatwoodypoint.com; tickets from $20; ⏲mid-Aug) Authors from across Newfoundland, Canada and the world converge at the Woody Point Heritage Theatre for readings. There's also live-music

Gros Morne Theatre Festival THEATER
(☎709-243-2899; www.theatrenewfoundland.com; tickets $15-35; ⏲late May–mid-Sep) Eight productions of Newfoundland plays, staged both indoors and outdoors at various locations throughout the summer.

Sleeping

Rocky Harbour has the most options. Woody Point and Norris Point are also good bets. Places fill fast in July and August.

For backcountry campsites reachable by hiking, inquire at the Main Visitor Centre (p495). Four developed **campgrounds** (☎877-737-3783; www.pccamping.ca) lie within the park: Berry Hill (campsites $19-26, oTENTik per night $120, reservation fee $11; ⏲Jun-Sep), Lomond (campsites $19-26, reservation fee $11; ⏲Jun-Oct), Trout River (campsites $19-26, reservation fee $11; ⏲Jun-Sep) and Shallow Bay (campsites $19-26, oTENTik per night $120, reservation fee $11; ⏲Jun-Sep).

Gros Morne Accommodations & Hostel HOSTEL $
(☎709-458-3396; www.grosmorneaccommodationsandhostel.com; 8 Kin Pl, Rocky Harbour; dm/r $30/70;) At this well-kept, newish hostel,

dorms have pincwood bunk beds with thin plastic-covered mattresses. It offers cable TV, a shared kitchen and towels for a small fee. There's no reception on-site. Check in at the Gros Morne Wildlife Museum at 76 Main St, which is a bit of a walk if you're without a car.

Aunt Jane's B&B B&B $

(☎709-453-2485; www.grosmorneescapes.com; Water St, Woody Point; d $70-90; ⊙May-Oct; ⊖) This historic house oozes character. Cheaper rooms share a bathroom. It sits beachside, so you may be woken early in the morning by the heavy breathing of whales.

Gros Morne Cabins CABIN $$

(☎709-458-2020; www.grosmornecabins.ca; Main St, Rocky Harbour; cabins $149-209; ⓦ) While backed by tarmac, most of these beautiful log cabins are fronted by nothing but ocean (ask when booking to ensure a view). Each has a full kitchen, TV and pullout sofa for children. Bookings can be made next door at Endicott's variety store.

Anchor Down B&B B&B $$

(☎709-458-2901; www.theanchordown.com; Pond Rd, Rocky Harbour; r $100-110; ⊖@) The home and its five rooms are pretty simple, but guests have raved about excellent hospitality and cooking from the friendly hosts. Rooms with the higher rate have a Jacuzzi tub.

Middle Brook Cottages CABIN $$

(☎709-453-2332; www.middlebrookcottages.com; off Rte 431, Glenburnie; cabins $99-149; ⊙Mar-Nov; ⊖ⓦ) These all-pinewood, spick-and-span cottages are both perfectly romantic and perfectly kid friendly. They have kitchens and TVs, and you can splash around in the swimming hole and waterfalls behind the property.

Eating

Java Jack's CAFE $

(☎709-458-3004; www.javajacks.ca; Main St, Rocky Harbour; mains $9-19; ⊙7:30am-8:30pm Wed-Mon May-Sep; ✎) To escape the tyranny of fried food, head to Jack's. This popular artsy outpost offers Gros Morne's best coffees, wraps and soups by day. By night, the upstairs dining room fills hungry, post-hike bellies with fine seafood, caribou and vegetarian fare. Greens come fresh from the property's organic garden.

Earle's CANADIAN $

(☎709-458-2577; Main St, Rocky Harbour; mains $8-14; ⊙9am-11pm) Earle is an institution in Rocky Harbour. Besides selling groceries and renting DVDs, he has great ice cream, pizza, moose burgers and traditional Newfoundland fare that you can chomp on the patio.

Old Loft SEAFOOD $$

(☎709-453-2294; www.theoldloft.com; Water St, Woody Point; mains $10-21; ⊙11:30am-9pm Jul & Aug, to 7pm May, Jun & Sep) Set on the water in Woody Point, this tiny place is popular for its traditional Newfoundland meals and seafood. Try the crisp onion rings.

Information

Park admission includes the trails, the Discovery Centre and all day-use areas.

Discovery Centre (☎709-453-2490; Rte 431, Woody Point; ⊙9am-6pm May-Oct) Has interactive exhibits and a multimedia theater explaining the area's ecology and geology. There's also an information desk with maps, daily interpretive activities and a small cafe.

Main Visitor Centre (☎709-458-2066; Rte 430; ⊙8am-8pm May-Oct) As well as issuing day and backcountry permits, it has maps, books, Viking Trail materials and an impressive interpretive area.

Park Entrance Kiosk (Rte 430; ⊙10am-6pm May-Oct) Near Wiltondale.

Rocky Harbour (www.rockyharbour.ca) Online information about lodging, restaurants and attractions in Rocky Harbor.

Western Newfoundland Tourism (www.gowesternnewfoundland.com)

Getting There & Away

Deer Lake Airport is 71km south of Rocky Harbour. There are shuttle-bus services (p502) from the airport to Rocky Harbour, Woody Point and Trout River.

Port au Choix

Port au Choix, dangling on a stark peninsula 13km off the Viking Trail, houses a large fishing fleet, a quirky museum and a worthy archaeological site that delves into ancient burial grounds.

Sights

Port au Choix National Historic Site HISTORIC SITE

(☎709-861-3522; www.pc.gc.ca/portauchoix; Point Riche Rd; adult/child $3.90/1.90; ⊙9am-6pm Jun-Sep) These ancient burial grounds of three different Aboriginal groups date back 5500 years. The modern **visitors center** tells of these groups' creative survival in the area and of one group's unexplained disappearance 3200 years ago. Several good trails around the park let you explore further. Reached by walking, **Phillip's Garden**, a site with vestiges of Paleo-Eskimo houses, is a highlight.

Two trails go to Phillip's Garden. One is the **Phillip's Garden Coastal Trail** (4km), which leaves from Phillip Dr at the end of town. From here you hopscotch your way over the jigsaw of skeletal rock to the site 1km away.

If you continue, it's another 3km to the **Point Riche Lighthouse** (1871), also accessible via the visitors-center road.

Another way to Phillip's Garden is the **Dorset Trail** (8km). It leaves the visitors center and winds across the barrens past stunted trees, passing a Dorset Paleo-Eskimo **burial cave** before finally reaching the site and linking to the Coastal Trail.

Ben's Studio GALLERY

(☎709-861-3280; www.bensstudio.ca; 24 Fisher St; ⏰9am-5pm Mon-Fri, 9am-5pm every other weekend Jun-Sep) FREE At the edge of town is Ben Ploughman's capricious studio of folk art. Pieces like *Crucifixion of the Cod* are classic and the artist himself welcomes conversation.

Sleeping & Eating

Jeannie's Sunrise B&B B&B $

(☎709-861-2254; www.jeanniessunrisebb.com; Fisher St; r $79-99;) Jeannie radiates hospitality through her spacious rooms, bright reading nook and demeanor as sweet as her muffins. Guests rave about the big breakfasts with homemade jam. Rooms at the lower end of the price spectrum share a bathroom.

Anchor Cafe SEAFOOD $

(☎709-861-3665; Fisher St; mains $12-18; ⏰11am-9pm) You can't miss this place – the front half is the bow of a boat – and don't, because it has great service and the best meals in town. Perfect fries and cod, rich moose stew and original salads are served in cozy leather booths. Lunch specials offer good value and the dinner menu features a wide array of seafood.

St Barbe to L'Anse aux Meadows

As the Viking Trail nears St Barbe, the waters of the gulf quickly narrow and give visitors their first opportunity to see the desolate shores of Labrador. Ferries take advantage of this convergence and ply the route between St Barbe and the Labrador Straits. At Eddies Cove, the road leaves the coast and heads inland.

As you approach the northern tip of the peninsula, Rte 430 veers off toward St Anthony, and two new roads take over leading to several diminutive fishing villages that provide perfect bases for your visit to L'Anse aux Meadows National Historic Site. Route 436 hugs the eastern shore and passes through (from south to north) St Lunaire-Griquet, Gunners Cove, Straitsview and L'Anse aux Meadows village.

L'Anse aux Meadows has a stunning end-of-the-road ambience, surrounded by gemstone isles and bergs. Route 437 heads in a more westerly direction through Pistolet Bay, Raleigh and Cape Onion.

Sights

★L'Anse aux Meadows National Historic Site HISTORIC SITE

(☎709-623-2608; www.pc.gc.ca/lanseauxmeadows; Rte 436; adult/child/family $11.70/5.80/29.40; ⏰9am-6pm Jun-Sep) Leif Eriksson and his Viking friends lived here circa AD 1000. Visitors can see the remains of their waterside

THE VIKINGS

Christopher Columbus gets the credit for 'discovering' North America, but the Vikings were actually the first Europeans to walk upon the continent. Led by Leif Eriksson, they sailed over from Scandinavia and Greenland some 500 years before Columbus and landed at L'Anse aux Meadows. They settled, constructed houses, fed themselves and even smelted iron out of the bog to forge nails, attesting to their ingenuity and fortitude. That it was all accomplished by a group of young-pup twenty-somethings is even more impressive.

Norse folklore had mentioned a site called 'Vinland' for centuries. But no one could ever prove its existence – until 1968, when archaeologists found a small cloak pin on the ground at L'Anse aux Meadows. Archaeologists now believe the site was a base camp, and that the Vikings ranged much further along the coast.

settlement: eight wood-and-sod buildings, now just vague outlines left in the spongy ground, plus three replica buildings inhabited by costumed docents. The latter have names such as 'Thora' and 'Bjorn' and simulate Viking chores such as spinning fleece and forging nails. Allow two or three hours to walk around and absorb the ambience.

The premise may seem dull – visiting a bog in the middle of nowhere and staring at the spot where a couple of old sod houses once stood – but somehow this site lying in a forlorn sweep of land turns out to be one of Newfoundland's most stirring attractions.

Be sure to browse the interpretive center and watch the introductory film, which tells the captivating story of Norwegian explorer Helge Ingstad, who rediscovered the site. Also worthwhile is the 3km trail that winds through the barren terrain and along the coast surrounding the interpretive center.

Norstead HISTORIC SITE
(709-623-2828; www.norstead.com; Rte 436; adult/child/family $10/6.50/30; 9:30am-5:30pm Jun-Sep) Can't get enough of the long-bearded Viking lifestyle? Stop by Norstead, just beyond the turnoff to the national historic site. This re-created Viking village features costumed interpreters smelting, weaving, baking and telling stories around real fires throughout four buildings. Sounds cheesy, but they pull it off with class. There's also a large-scale replica of a Viking ship on hand.

Activities

★Quirpon Lighthouse Inn ADVENTURE SPORTS
(709-634-2285; www.linkumtours.com; Main Rd; per person package incl boat transfer $250-400; May-Sep) Whales and icebergs skim by this deserted island located 9km west of L'Anse aux Meadows. As remote getaways go, it would be hard to beat this 10-room inn, close by a working lighthouse with an indoor whale-watching station. Package stays include hiking, Zodiac tours and guided kayaking.

Sleeping & Eating

Hillsview B&B B&B $
(709-623-2424; Gunner's Cove; r from $80;) Ina Hill hosts this lovely B&B set in a large modern home with bay views. Rooms have granny-style charm, with comfortable quilt-covered beds. Breakfast features homemade jams.

Viking Village B&B B&B $
(709-623-2238; www.vikingvillage.ca; Hay Cove, L'Anse aux Meadows village; s/d from $65/88;) A timbered home with ocean views, Viking Village offers comfy, quilted rooms just 1km from the Viking site. Ask for one of the rooms with balcony access and watch the sun rise.

Valhalla Lodge B&B B&B $$
(709-623-2018; www.valhalla-lodge.com; Rte 436, Gunners Cove; r $95-115; May-Sep;) Sea views from this hilltop location inspired Pulitzer Prize–winning author E Annie Proulx, who penned *The Shipping News* here. Sleep in a simple cottage or in the more modern main lodge with a cozy living-room fireplace and a deck to watch icebergs in comfort. The five-room Valhalla is only 8km from the Viking site.

Snorri Cabins CABIN $$
(709-623-2241; www.snorricabins.com; Rte 436, Straitsview; cabins $119; Jun-Sep;) These modern cabins offer simple comfort and great value. They're perfect for families, with a full kitchen, sitting room and a pullout sofa. There's a convenience store on-site.

Northern Delight SEAFOOD $
(709-623-2220; Rte 436, Gunners Cove; mains $10-16; 8am-9pm) Dine on local favorites such as turbot cheeks and pan-fried cod, fresh lobster and mussels, or just have a 'Newfie Mug-up' (bread, molasses and a strong cup of tea). There's live music on some evenings.

Daily Catch SEAFOOD $$
(709-623-2295; 112 Main St, St Lunaire-Griquet; mains $10-26; 11am-9pm) A stylish little restaurant serving finely prepared seafood and wine. The basil-buttered salmon gets kudos. Fish cakes, crab au gratin and cod burgers also please the palate.

★Norseman Restaurant & Art Gallery SEAFOOD $$$
(709-623-2018; www.valhalla-lodge.com; Rte 436, L'Anse aux Meadows village; mains $20-38; noon-9pm May-Sep) This lovely waterfront outpost ranks among Newfoundland's best. Emphasizing local products and creative preparations, the menu will have you wavering between tantalizing options. Relish a kale Caesar salad with Arctic char, seared scallops or tender Labrador caribou tenderloin. Espresso drinks are served and cocktails come chilled with iceberg ice.

WORTH A TRIP

ROUTE 432 & THE FRENCH SHORE

Surprises await along lonely Rte 432. Follow the moose to **Tuckamore Lodge** (☎709-865-6361; www.tuckamorelodge.com; Main Brook; r incl breakfast $150-180;), a wood-hewn, lakeside retreat with heavenly beds and home-cooked meals, located smack in the middle of nowhere. Owner Barb Genge arranges fishing, bird-watching, hunting and photography classes with first-rate guides.

The little towns along the coast are known as the French Shore (www.frenchshore.com) for the French fishers who lived in the area from 1504 to 1904. Top of the heap is **Conche** with its intriguing sights: a **WWII airplane** that crashed in town in 1942, the seaside **Captain Coupelongue walking trail** past old French grave markers, and a crazy-huge **tapestry** in the local interpretation center.

A woman named Delight runs the sunny **Bits-n-Pieces Cafe** (☎709-622-5400; 9 Stage Cove Rd, Conche; mains $10-15; ⏲8am-8pm, to 9pm Thu-Sat), ladling out cod cakes, Thai chicken and other satisfying fare. It's about 68km from Tuckamore Lodge; take Rte 433 to unpaved Rte 434.

Getting There & Away

The road to the Northern Peninsula is narrow and potholed. Travel extra slow in the rain. Access by private vehicle.

A ferry travels between St Barbe and Blanc Sablon, Québec (near the Labrador border) daily. The two-hour trip across the Strait of Belle Isle is run by **Labrador Marine** (☎866-535-2567; www.labradormarine.com; adult/child/vehicle $8.25/6.60/25); see the website for schedules.

St Anthony

Congratulations. You've made it to the end of the road, your windshield has culled the insect population and you have seen two World Heritage Sites. After such grandeur, St Anthony may be a little anticlimactic. Though not pretty, it possesses a rough-hewn charm and inspiring hiking and whale- and iceberg-watching.

Grenfell is a big name around here. Sir Wilfred Grenfell was a local legend and, by all accounts, quite a man. This English-born and educated doctor first came to Newfoundland in 1892 and, for the next 40 years, traveling by dogsled and boat, built hospitals and nursing stations and organized much-needed fishing cooperatives along the coast of Labrador and around St Anthony.

Sights

Fishing Point Park PARK

The main road through town ends at Fishing Point Park, where a lighthouse and towering headland cliffs overlook the sea. The **Iceberg Alley Trail** and **Whale Watchers Trail** both lead to cliff-top observation platforms – the names say it all.

There's also a visitor center–cafe and an adjacent craft shop; in the side room there's a polar bear display. Creatures like this guy have been known to roam St Anthony from time to time as pack ice melts in the spring.

Grenfell Interpretation Centre HISTORIC BUILDING

(www.grenfell-properties.com; West St; multi-site admission adult/child/family $10/3/22; ⏲8am-5pm Jun-Sep) A number of local sites pertaining to pioneering doctor Wilfred Grenfell are subsumed under Grenfell Historic Properties. The Interpretation Centre, opposite the hospital, is a modern exhibit recounting the historic and sometimes dramatic life of Grenfell. Its **handicraft shop** has some high-quality carvings and artwork, as well as embroidered parkas made by locals – proceeds go to maintenance of the historic properties.

Grenfell Museum MUSEUM

(www.grenfell-properties.com; multi-site admission adult/child/family $10/3/22; ⏲9am-6pm Jun-Sep) Admission to the Grenfell Historic Properties also includes Grenfell's beautiful mansion, now the Grenfell Museum. It's behind the hospital, about a five-minute walk from the waterfront. Dyed burlap walls and antique furnishings envelop memorabilia, including a polar-bear rug and, if rumors are correct, the ghost of Mrs Grenfell.

Tours

Northland Discovery Tours BOATING

(☎709-454-3092; www.discovernorthland.com; 2½hr tour adult/child $60/32; ⏲9am, 1pm & 4pm

Jun-Sep) Northland offers highly recommended cruises for whale- or iceberg-viewing that leave from the dock behind the Grenfell Interpretation Centre on West St. If you tend to get seasick, medicate before this one.

Sleeping & Eating

Fishing Point B&B B&B **$$**
(☎709-454-3117; www.bbcanada.com/6529.html; Fishing Point Rd; r $110;) This teensy place clings to the rocks en route to the lighthouse and offers the best harbor view in St Anthony. Get up early, enjoy a bountiful breakfast and watch the boats head out to sea. The three rooms each have their own bathroom.

Lightkeeper's Seafood Restaurant SEAFOOD **$$**
(☎709-454-4900; Fishing Point Park; mains $12-20; 11:30am-8pm Jun-Sep) Smack in the shadow of the lighthouse, this restaurant gazes out on icebergs and whales. Unfortunately, you're shelling out for the view, not the rather ordinary food. Fat fish burgers with fries beat out the bland cod and mashed potato dinner.

Getting There & Away

The St Anthony Airport is 22 miles northwest of town. **PAL Airlines** (☎800-563-2800; www.provincialairlines.ca; St Anthony Airport) makes the trip from St John's daily.

If you're leaving St Anthony by car, you have two options: backtrack entirely along Rte 430, or take the long way via Rte 432 along the east coast and Hare Bay. This will meet up with Rte 430 near Plum Point, between St Barbe and Port aux Choix.

WESTERN NEWFOUNDLAND

Western Newfoundland presents many visitors with their first view of the Rock, thanks to the ferry landing at Port aux Basques. It's big, cliffy, even a bit forbidding with all those wood houses clinging to the jagged shoreline against the roaring wind. From Port aux Basques, poky fishing villages cast lines to the east, while Newfoundland's second-largest town, Corner Brook, raises its wintry head (via its ski mountain) to the northeast.

Corner Brook

POP 19,900

Newfoundland's number-two town is pretty sleepy, though skiers, hikers and anglers will find plenty of action. The handsome Humber Valley, about 10km east, is where it's going on. Centered on the Marble Mountain ski resort, the area experienced a huge development boom until the bottom fell out of the international economy. But now the area is heating up again. The valley offers adventure-sport junkies places to play, while the city itself sprawls with big-box retailers and a smoke-belching pulp and paper mill.

Sights

Captain James Cook Monument MONUMENT
(Crow Hill Rd) While this cliff-top monument is admirable – a tribute to James Cook for his work in surveying the region in the mid-1760s – it's the panoramic view over the Bay of Islands that is the real payoff.

Railway Society of Newfoundland MUSEUM
(☎709-634-2720; Station Rd, off Humber Rd; admission $3; 9am-8pm Jun-Aug) Within historic Humbermouth Station, it has a good-looking steam locomotive and some narrow-gauge rolling stock that chugged across the province from 1921 to 1939.

Activities

Marble Mountain SKIING
(☎709-637-7616; www.skimarble.com; Hwy 1; day pass adult/child $60/35; 10am-4:30pm Sat-Thu, 9am-9:30pm Fri Dec-Apr) Marble Mountain is the lofty reason most visitors come to Corner Brook. With 35 trails, four lifts, a 488m vertical drop and annual snowfall of 5m, it offers Atlantic Canada's best skiing. There are snowboarding and tubing parks, as well as night skiing on Friday, plus there's Oh My Jesus (you'll say it when you see the slope).

When the white stuff has departed, the **Steady Brook Falls Trail** (500m) leads from the ski area's rear parking lot, behind the Tim Hortons, to a cascade of water that tumbles more than 30m.

Cycle Solutions CYCLING
(☎709-634-7100; www.cyclesolutions.ca; 35 West St; 9am-6pm Mon-Wed & Sat, to 8:30pm Thu & Fri) This sweet bike shop runs local cycling and caving tours; it's attached to the Brewed Awakening coffee shop.

Corner Brook

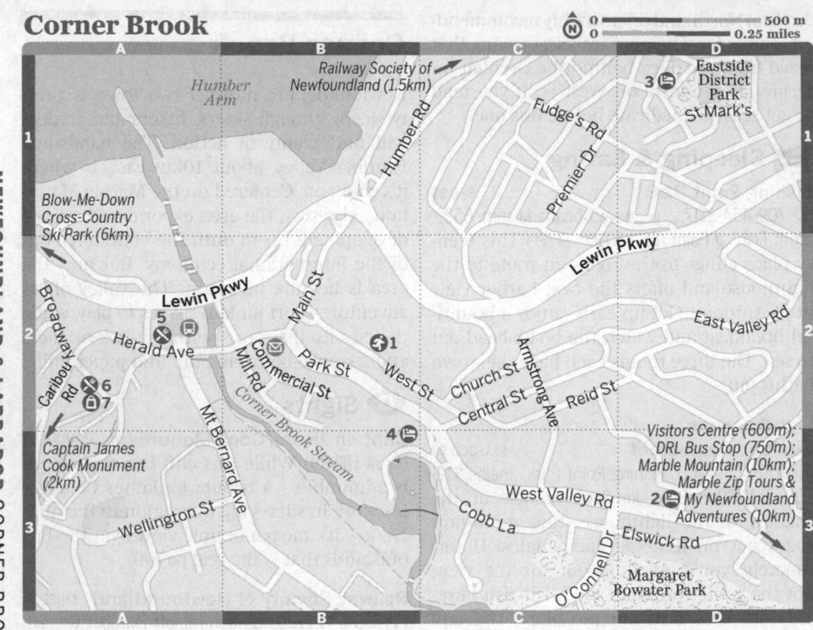

Corner Brook

Activities, Courses & Tours
1 Cycle Solutions B2

Sleeping
2 Brookfield Inn D3
3 Garden Hill Inn D1
4 Glynmill Inn B3

Eating
Brewed Awakening .... (see 1)
5 Gitano's A2
6 Taste of Jamaica A2
Thistle's Place .... (see 5)

Shopping
7 Newfoundland Emporium A2

Blow-Me-Down Cross-Country Ski Park SKIING
(☎709-639-2754; www.blowmedown.ca; Lundigran Dr; day pass $20; ⊙sunrise-9pm Dec-Apr) It has 50km of groomed trails; ski rentals (per day $15) are available. It's about 6km southwest of downtown.

Marble Zip Tours ADVENTURE SPORTS
(☎709-632-5463; www.marbleziptours.com; Thistle Dr; 2hr tour adult/child $99/89) It's the highest zip line in eastern Canada. Strap in near the mountaintop, and zigzag platform to platform down a gorge traversing Steady Brook Falls. It'll take your breath away. Tours depart four to five times daily. The office is past Marble Mountain's lodge.

My Newfoundland Adventures ADVENTURE SPORTS
(☎709-638-0110; www.mynewfoundland.ca) If skiing doesn't get the adrenaline flowing, you must try snow-kiting (a windsurfing-meets-snowboarding endeavor). Or there's snowshoeing, ice fishing and even ice climbing. Canoeing, salmon fishing and caving all take place in the warmer seasons. Pretty much anything is possible with these patient folks; no experience is required. The office is at Marble Mountain's base by the Tim Hortons.

Sleeping & Eating

Brookfield Inn B&B $
(☎709-639-3111; brookfieldinn@gmail.com; 2 Brookfield Ave; r $60-90;) A cool couple runs this B&B. The white-frame house has homey rooms, with hardwood floors and plump beds. In the morning make your own breakfast from the eggs, bacon, cheeses and breads in the well-stocked kitchen. In the

evening watch the sun set from the deck. The house dogs will amble up for a scratch if you want.

Glynmill Inn HOTEL $$
(709-634-5181; www.steelehotels.com; 1 Cobb Lane; r incl breakfast $135-165;) Lawns and gardens surround the gracious Tudor-style Glynmill. It was built originally for the engineers supervising the pulp mill's construction in the 1920s, at that time the largest project in the history of paper making. The inn retains an elegant if somewhat faded ambience.

Garden Hill Inn B&B $$
(709-634-1150; www.gardenhillinn.ca; 2 Ford's Rd; r $95-120;) Gordon Bell's rambling green house tops a hill that's a 15-minute walk from downtown. The eight smallish, comfy rooms all have private bathroom; rooms 1 and 4 have harbor views. Breakfast includes coffee, fruit and blueberry pancakes.

★ **Taste of Jamaica** JAMAICAN $
(www.tasteofjamaica.ca; 33 Broadway; mains $8-16; 11:30am-10pm Tue-Sun) Get instantly transported to the Caribbean with these mouth-watering preparations of jerk chicken, stuffed avocados and spiced kabobs. Chef Kirk Myers, a native islander, does his best with the local selection of produce.

Brewed Awakening COFFEE $
(www.brewedawakening.ca; 35 West St; baked goods $3-7; 7am-9pm Mon-Fri, 8am-9pm Sat, 9am-6pm Sun;) This small, funky, art-on-the-wall coffee shop pours fair-trade, organic java done right. It's attached to the groovy bike shop Cycle Solutions.

Thistle's Place CAFE $
(709-634-4389; www.thistledownflorist.com; Millbrook Mall, Herald Ave; sandwiches $6-11; 9am-5pm Mon-Sat;) Walk through the front flower shop to reach the smoked meat, curried chicken and whole-wheat vegetable wraps at the wee cafe out the back.

Gitano's MEDITERRANEAN $$
(709-634-5000; www.gitanos.ca; Millbrook Mall, Herald Ave; tapas $8-14, mains $22-45; 11:30am-2pm Mon-Fri, 5-9pm Sun-Thu, to 10pm Fri & Sat;) Behind Thistle's Place and owned by the same family, Gitano's dishes up *estofado* (stewed sweet potatoes, chickpeas and figs over couscous), pastas and locally sourced tapas (try the saltfish cakes). Live jazz wafts through the supper-club-esque room on weekends.

Shopping

Newfoundland Emporium GIFTS & SOUVENIRS
(709-634-9376; 11 Broadway; 9am-5pm Mon-Sat) A trove of local crafts, music, antiques and books.

Information

CIBC Bank (709-637-1700; 9 Main St; 10am-5pm Mon-Fri)

Post Office (14 Main St; 9am-5pm Mon-Fri)

Visitors Centre (709-639-9792; www.cornerbrook.com; 15 Confederation Dr; 9am-5pm) Just off Hwy 1 at Exit 5. Has a craft shop.

Western Memorial Regional Hospital (709-637-5000; 1 Brookfield Ave)

Getting There & Away

Corner Brook is a major hub for bus services in Newfoundland. **DRL** (709-263-2171; www.drl-lr.com; Confederation Dr) stops on the outskirts of town at the Irving Gas Station, just off Hwy 1 at exit 5 across from the visitor center.

All other operators use the **bus station** (709-634-7777; Herald Ave, Millbrook Mall) in the Millbrook Mall building. The following are shuttle vans. Prices are one way. You must make reservations.

Burgeo Bus (709-634-7777, reservations 709-886-6162; bus station, Millbrook Mall) Runs to Burgeo ($40 cash only, two hours) departing at 3pm Monday through Friday. Leaves Burgeo between 8am and 9am.

Deer Lake Airport Shuttle (709-634-4343) Picks up from various hotels en route to Deer Lake Airport ($22, 45 minutes) three to five times daily.

Eddy's (709-643-2134; bus station, Millbrook Mall) Travels to/from Stephenville ($25, 1¼ hours) twice daily on weekdays, once daily on weekends.

Gateway (709-695-9700; bus station, Millbrook Mall) Runs to Port aux Basques ($40,

OFF THE BEATEN TRACK

STEPHENVILLE ON STAGE

As the drive into town past deserted hangars, piles of rusted pipes and tract housing portends, Stephenville is hardly a tourism hub. Yet it's well worth a detour for the **Stephenville Theatre Festival** (709-643-4553; www.stephenvilletheatrefestival.com; Stephenville; Jul & Aug). Featuring cutting-edge Newfoundland plays, it also stirs the pot with a good dose of the Bard and Broadway.

three hours) on weekdays at 3:45pm. Departs Port aux Basques at 7:45am.

Martin's (☎709-453-2207, 709-458-7845; bus station, Millbrook Mall) Operates weekdays, departing for Woody Point ($18, 1½ hours) and Trout River ($20, two hours) at 4:30pm. Returns from Trout River at 9am.

Pittman's (☎709-458-2486; bus station, Millbrook Mall) Runs to Rocky Harbour ($35, two hours) via Deer Lake on weekdays at 4:30pm. Departs Rocky Harbour at noon.

Blomidon Mountains

The Blomidon Mountains (aka Blow Me Down Mountains), heaved skyward from a collision with Europe around 500 million years ago, run along the south side of the Humber Arm, west of Corner Brook. They're tantalizing for hikers, providing many sea vistas and glimpses of the resident caribou population. Some of the trails, especially ones up on the barrens, are not well marked, so topographical maps and a compass are essential for all hikers. Further on, Blow Me Down Provincial Park has beaches and scenery.

Activities

Many trails are signposted off Rte 450, which runs west from Corner Brook along the water for 60km.

Copper Mine Trail HIKING
(York Harbour) This moderately difficult 7km trail by York Harbour provides awesome views of the Bay of Islands and also links to the International Appalachian Trail (IAT).

Blow Me Down Brook Trail HIKING
(Frenchman's Cove) One of the easiest and most popular trails in the Blomidon range, this 5km trail begins west of Frenchman's Cove at a parking lot. The trail can be followed for an hour or so; for more avid hikers it continues well into the mountains, where it becomes part of the IAT.

APPALACHIAN TRAIL

Think the **International Appalachian Trail** ends in Québec? Think again. It picks up in Newfoundland, where another 1200km of trail swipes the west coast from Port aux Basques to L'Anse aux Meadows. The province has linked existing trails, logging roads and old rail lines through the Long Range Mountains, part of the Appalachian chain. It's a work in progress, but some of the most complete sections are around Corner Brook and the Blomidon Mountains. See www.iatnl.com for trail details.

Sleeping

The only accommodations is a provincial-park campground.

Blow Me Down Provincial Park CAMPGROUND $
(☎709-681-2430; www.nlcamping.ca; Rte 450; campsites $18, per vehicle $5; ⊙Jun-Aug) Nice campsites in a beach setting.

Port au Port Peninsula

The large peninsula west of Stephenville is a French-speaking area, a legacy of the Basque, French and Acadians who settled the coast starting in the 1700s. Today, the culture is strongest along the western shore between **Cape St George** and **Lourdes**. Here children go to French school, preserving their dialect, which is now distinct from the language spoken in either France or Québec.

In Port au Port West, near Stephenville, the gorgeous Gravels Trail (3km) leads along the shore, passing secluded beach after secluded beach. Nearby in Felix Cove, stop at **Alpacas of Newfoundland** (www.alpacasofnfld.ca; Rte 460, Felix Cove; ⊙9am-6pm) FREE for an entertaining farm tour.

Port Aux Basques

POP 4170

Traditional wood houses painted aqua, scarlet and sea green clasp the stony hills, but it's all about the ferry in Port aux Basques. Most visitors come here to jump onto the Rock from Nova Scotia, or jump off for the return trip. That doesn't mean the town isn't a perfectly decent place to spend a day or night. Laundry blows on the clotheslines, boats moor in backyard inlets and locals never fail to wave hello to newcomers.

Port aux Basques (occasionally called Channel-Port aux Basques) was named in the early 16th century by Basque fishers and whalers who came to work the waters of the Strait of Belle Isle. The town is a convenient place to stock up on food, fuel and money before journeying onward.

Port aux Basques

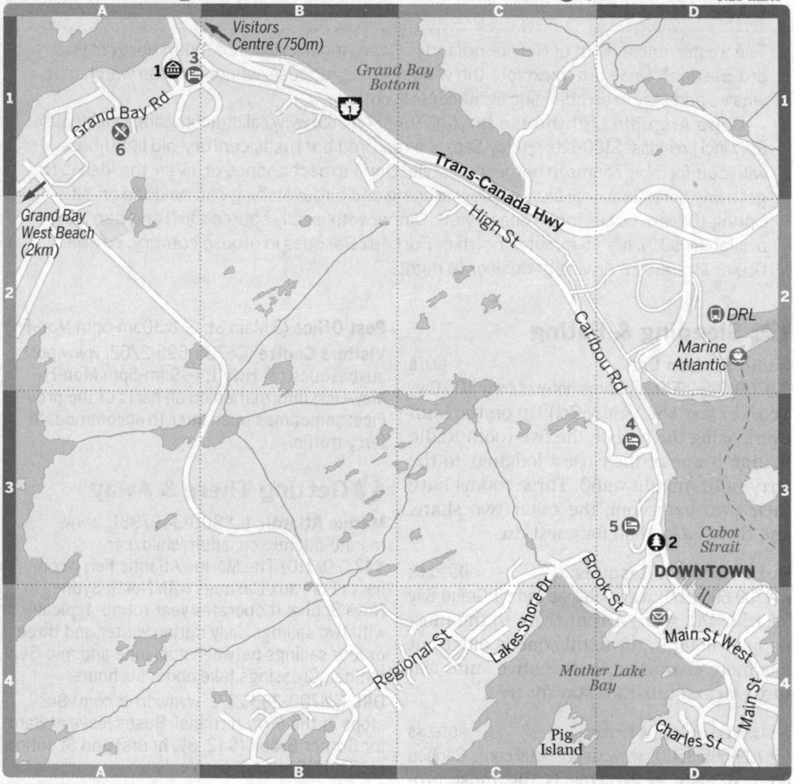

Visitors Centre (750m)
Grand Bay Bottom
Grand Bay Rd
Grand Bay West Beach (2km)
Trans-Canada Hwy
High St
Caribou Rd
DRL
Marine Atlantic
Cabot Strait
DOWNTOWN
Brook St
Lakes Shore Dr
Regional St
Main St West
Mother Lake Bay
Main St
Charles St
Pig Island

Sights

Several scenic fishing villages lie to the east.

Grand Bay West Beach BEACH
(Kyle Lane) Located a short distance west of town, the long shore is backed by grassy dunes, which are breeding grounds for the endangered piping plover. The **Grand Bay West Trail** leaves from here and flirts with the coast for 10km.

Railway Heritage Centre MUSEUM
(☎709-695-5775; off Hwy 1; museum $2, railcars $5; ⏰10am-8pm Jul & Aug) The center has two things going on. One is a museum stuffed with shipwreck artifacts. Its showpiece is the astrolabe, a striking brass navigational instrument made in Portugal in 1628. The device is in remarkable condition and is one of only about three dozen that exist in the world. Restored railway cars are the center's other drawcard.

Port aux Basques

Sights

1	Railway Heritage Centre	A1
2	Scott's Cove Park	D3

Sleeping

3	Hotel Port aux Basques	A1
4	Radio Station Inn	D3
5	St Christopher's Hotel	D3

Eating

6	Alma's	A1
	Captain's Room	(see 5)

Scott's Cove Park PARK
(Caribou Rd) This park, with its restored boardwalk, candy-colored snack shacks and boat-shaped amphitheater, is the place to mingle with townsfolk and listen to live music.

WORTH A TRIP

CAPE ANGUILLE

The westernmost point of Newfoundland is Cape Anguille, located 58km north of Port aux Basques. Drive out to explore the windswept lighthouse, where you can watch blue whales and stay in an adjoining lightkeeper's cottage.

Cape Anguille Lighthouse Inn (709-634-2285; www.linkumtours.com; 1 Lighthouse Rd; r incl breakfast $100-120; May-Sep) is a restored but rustic century-old lighthouse with comfortable rooms in homespun style. Don't expect phones or TVs – the idea is to get away here. Seasonal blue-whale-watching and bird-watching can be done on-site. Spring 10 extra bucks for an ocean view. Dinner with locally sourced fish and berries is available ($30). It's 45 minutes north of Port aux Basques in moose country; pay particular attention if driving at dusk or at night.

Sleeping & Eating

Radio Station Inn B&B $
(709-695-2906; jggillam@hotmail.com; 100 Caribou Rd; r from $69; May-Oct) Up on the bluff overlooking the harbor, the five-room Radio Station is one of the closest lodgings to the ferry (a 10-minute walk). Three rooms have their own bathroom, the other two share, and there's a kitchen for guest use.

Hotel Port aux Basques HOTEL $$
(709-695-2171; www.hotelpab.com; 1 Grand Bay Rd; r $85-170;) A runner-up to the most popular hotel in town, this one is older but has more character. An executive suite features Jacuzzi tub. Kids stay for free.

St Christopher's Hotel HOTEL $$
(709-695-3500; www.stchrishotel.com; Caribou Rd; r $121-146;) This is the most professional digs in town, with a small fitness room and a seafood restaurant called the Captain's Room (p504). Odd-numbered rooms have harbor views.

Alma's CANADIAN $
(709-695-3813; Mall, Grand Bay Rd; mains $7-15; 8am-8pm Mon-Sat) Follow the locals into this no-frills family diner for heaping portions of cod, scallops, fish cakes and berry pies. Your best bet for a good meal in town, it serves breakfasts, burgers and sandwiches too.

Captain's Room SEAFOOD $
(709-695-3500; St Christophers Hotel, Caribou Rd; mains $10-17; 7am-1:30pm & 5-10pm) A mixed bag for fine dining with a nautical theme. Think seafood and moose burgers. The authentic potato skins beat the fries.

Information

Bank of Montréal (83 Main St; 10am-5pm Mon-Fri)
Hospital (709-695-2175; Grand Bay Rd)
Post Office (3 Main St; 8:30am-5pm Mon-Fri)
Visitors Centre (709-695-2262; www.portauxbasques.ca; Hwy 1; 9am-5pm Mon-Fri May-Oct) Information on all parts of the province; sometimes open later to accommodate ferry traffic.

Getting There & Away

Marine Atlantic (800-341-7981; www.marine-atlantic.ca; adult/child/car $42/20/110) The Marine Atlantic Ferry connects Port aux Basques with North Sydney in Nova Scotia. It operates year-round, typically with two sailings daily during winter and three or four sailings between mid-June and mid-September. Crossings take about six hours.
DRL (709-263-2171; www.drl-lr.com) Bus stops at the ferry terminal. Buses leave at 8am for Corner Brook ($42, 3½ hours) and St John's ($124, 13½ hours); cash only.

Cape Ray

Adjacent to John T Cheeseman Provincial Park and 19km north of Port aux Basques is Cape Ray. The coastal scenery is engaging, and the road leads up to the windblown **Cape Ray Lighthouse** (8am-8pm Tue-Sun Jul & Aug) FREE. After the original 1871 lighthouse was struck by lightning and burned in 1885, it was replaced by the current version. This area is the southernmost known Dorset Paleo-Eskimo site, dating from 400 BC to AD 400. Thousands of artifacts have been found here and some dwelling sites can be seen.

John T Cheeseman Provincial Park (www.env.gov.nl.ca/env/parks; Rte 408) rests next to the beach and has top-notch facilities.

There are some fine hikes in the area. **Table Mountain Trail** (Hwy 1) is more like a rugged road (but don't even think about driving up it) and begins on Hwy 1 opposite the exit to Cape Ray. The hike leads to a

518m plateau, where there are ruins from a secret US radar site and airstrip from WWII. It's not a hard hike, but it's 12km long so allow three or four hours.

If you're looking for somewhere to camp, **John T Cheeseman Provincial Park Campground** (709-695-7222; www.nlcamping.ca; Rte 408; campsites $18-28, per vehicle $5; Jun-Sep) has 92 campsites featuring picnic table and fire pit. Water and pit toilets are available.

South Coast

Visitors often ignore Rte 470, and that's a shame because it's a beauty. Heading east out of Port aux Basques for 45km and edging along the shore, the road rises and falls over the eroded, windswept terrain, looking as though it's following a glacier that plowed through yesterday.

Isle aux Morts (Island of the Dead) got its label compliments of the many shipwrecks that occurred just offshore over some 400 years. Named after a family famous for daring shipwreck rescues, the **Harvey Trail** (7km) twists along the rugged shore and makes a stirring walk. Look for the signs in town.

Another highlight is the last settlement along the road, **Rose Blanche**, an absolutely splendid, traditional-looking village nestled in a cove with a fine natural harbor – a perfect example of the classic Newfoundland fishing community. From here follow the signs to the restored **Rose Blanche Lighthouse** (709-956-2052; www.roseblanchelighthouse.ca; admission $6; 9am-9pm May-Oct). Built in 1873, it's the last remaining granite lighthouse on the Atlantic seaboard.

If you think Rose Blanche is too pretty to leave, stay the night at the **Rose Sea Guest House** (709-956-2872; www.roseblanche.ca; r $95-110; Jun-Oct). It offers five rooms in a recently refurbished traditional home right on the water. It also offers workshops on craft-making or geology.

KILLICK COAST

The peninsula just north and west of St John's is known as the Killick Coast, a 55km one-way journey that makes a good day trip. About 8km north of St John's, Memorial University's Ocean Sciences Centre (p506) has outdoor exhibits in summer. Secluded and rocky, **Middle Cove** and **Outer Cove** are a bit further north on Rte 30 – they're perfect for a beach picnic.

North at the head of **Torbay Bight** is the enjoyably short **Father Troy Path**, which hugs the shoreline. The view from **Cape St Francis** is worth the bumpy gravel road from Pouch Cove. There's an old battery and you may see a whale or two.

OFF THE BEATEN TRACK

SOUTH COAST OUTPORTS

If you have the time and patience, a trip across the south coast with its wee fishing villages – called outports – is the best way to witness Newfoundland's unique culture. These little communities are some of the most remote settlements in North America, reachable only by boat as they cling to the convoluted shore. An anomaly is Burgeo (population 1460), connected by an easy road trip; it has an unspoiled, isolated feel, yet good amenities for travelers. **Ramea** (population 525) is another uncomplicated option. It's an island just offshore from **Burgeo** with lodging and activities.

When the sun is out and the sea shimmers between endless inlets and islands, Burgeo is a dream. Climb the stairs to Maiden Tea Hill and look out in admiration. The 7km of white-sand beaches at Sandbanks Provincial Park may be the best in the entire province (at least the piping plover who dawdle there think so).

Author Farley Mowat lived in Burgeo for several years, until he penned *A Whale for the Killing* and irked the locals. The book tells the story of how Burgeo's townsfolk treated an 80-tonne fin whale trapped in a nearby lagoon. Let's just say the outcome was not a happy one for the whale. Locals can point out the lagoon and Mowat's old house, though expect to get an earful about it.

Ramea Retreat (709-625-2522; www.easternoutdoors.com; 2 Main St, Ramea; dm/r $39/89; May-Nov;) is an adventure lodge with 10 hostel beds and options for kayaking, bird-watching, hiking and fishing tours. In addition, the lodge owners rent rooms in various vintage clapboard houses scattered around Ramea.

West of St John's on Topsail Rd (Rte 60), just past Paradise, is **Topsail Beach**, with picnic tables, a walking trail and panoramic views of Conception Bay and its islands.

To reach Bell Island, go 14km northwest from St John's to Portugal Cove and the ferry.

Sights

Bell Island Community Museum MUSEUM
(☎709-488-2880; adult/child $12/5; ⊙11am-6pm Jun-Sep) Miners here used to work in shafts under the sea at the world's largest submarine iron mine. Conditions were grim: the museum tells tales of adolescents working 10-hour days by candlelight. Visitors can also go underground; dress warmly.

Ocean Sciences Centre AQUARIUM
(☎709-864-2459; www.mun.ca/osc; ⊙10am-5pm Jun-Aug) FREE Right out of *20,000 Leagues Under the Sea*, this university center examines the salmon life cycle, seal navigation, ocean currents and life in cold oceanic regions. The outdoor visitors area consists of local sea life in touch tanks. It's about 8km north of St John's, just before Logy Bay.

From the city, take Logy Bay Rd (Rte 30), then follow Marine Dr to Marine Lab Rd and take it to the end.

Bell Island ISLAND
(www.tourismbellisland.com) The largest of Conception Bay's little landmasses makes an interesting day trip from St John's. It was the only place on the continent hit by German forces in WWII. U-boats torpedoed the pier and 80,000 tonnes of iron ore in 1942. At low tide, you can still see the aftermath. The island sports a pleasant mélange of beaches, coastal vistas, lighthouses and trails.

Getting There & Away

Visitors will need a car to explore the Killick Coast. The **Bell Island Ferry** (☎709-895-6931; www.tw.gov.nl.ca; per passenger/car $2.50/7; ⊙hourly 6am-10:30pm) provides quick transit between Portugal Cove and the island.

LABRADOR

POP 26,700

Undulating, rocky, puddled expanses form the sparse, primeval landscape of Labrador. Home to Inuit and Innu, its 293,000 sq km sprawl toward the Arctic Circle. If you ever wanted to imagine the world before humans, this is the place.

Inuit and Innu have occupied Labrador for thousands of years. Until the 1960s they were the sole inhabitants, alongside a few longtime European descendants known as 'liveyers,' who eked out an existence by fishing and hunting from tiny villages that freckled the coast. The interior was virgin wilderness.

The simplest way to take a bite of the Big Land is via the Labrador Straits region, which connects to Newfoundland via a daily ferry. From there, a solitary road connects the interior's main towns. The aboriginal-influenced northern coast is accessible only by plane or supply ferry. Here, the newly designated Torngat Mountains National Park offers a privileged glimpse into ultra-remote wilderness.

Labrador is cold, wet and windy, and its bugs are murderous. Facilities are few and far between throughout the behemoth region, so planning ahead is essential.

Labrador Straits

And you thought the Northern Peninsula was commanding? Sail the 28km across the Strait of Belle Isle and behold a landscape even more windswept and black-rocked. Clouds rip across aqua-and-gray skies, and the water that slaps the shore is so cold it's purplish. Unlike the rest of remote Labrador, the Straits region is easy to reach and exalted with sights such as Red Bay and a slew of great walking trails that meander past shipwreck fragments and old whale bones. 'Labrador Straits' is the colloquial name for the communities that make up the southern coastal region of Labrador.

Blanc Sablon to L'Anse au Clair

After arriving by ferry or plane in Blanc Sablon, Québec, and driving 6km northeast on Rte 510 you come to Labrador and the gateway town of L'Anse au Clair. The town makes a good pre-ferry base, with sleeping and basic dining options and a useful visitor center.

Sleeping & Eating

Northern Light Inn HOTEL $$
(☎709-931-2332; www.northernlightinn.com; 56 Main St, L'Anse au Clair; campsites $25-35, d $115-129; ❄📶) The modern, well-kept Northern Light Inn is a tour-bus favorite, with a dining room that serves the best meals in town. Even-numbered rooms have harbor views. The campground has showers and laundry.

Labrador

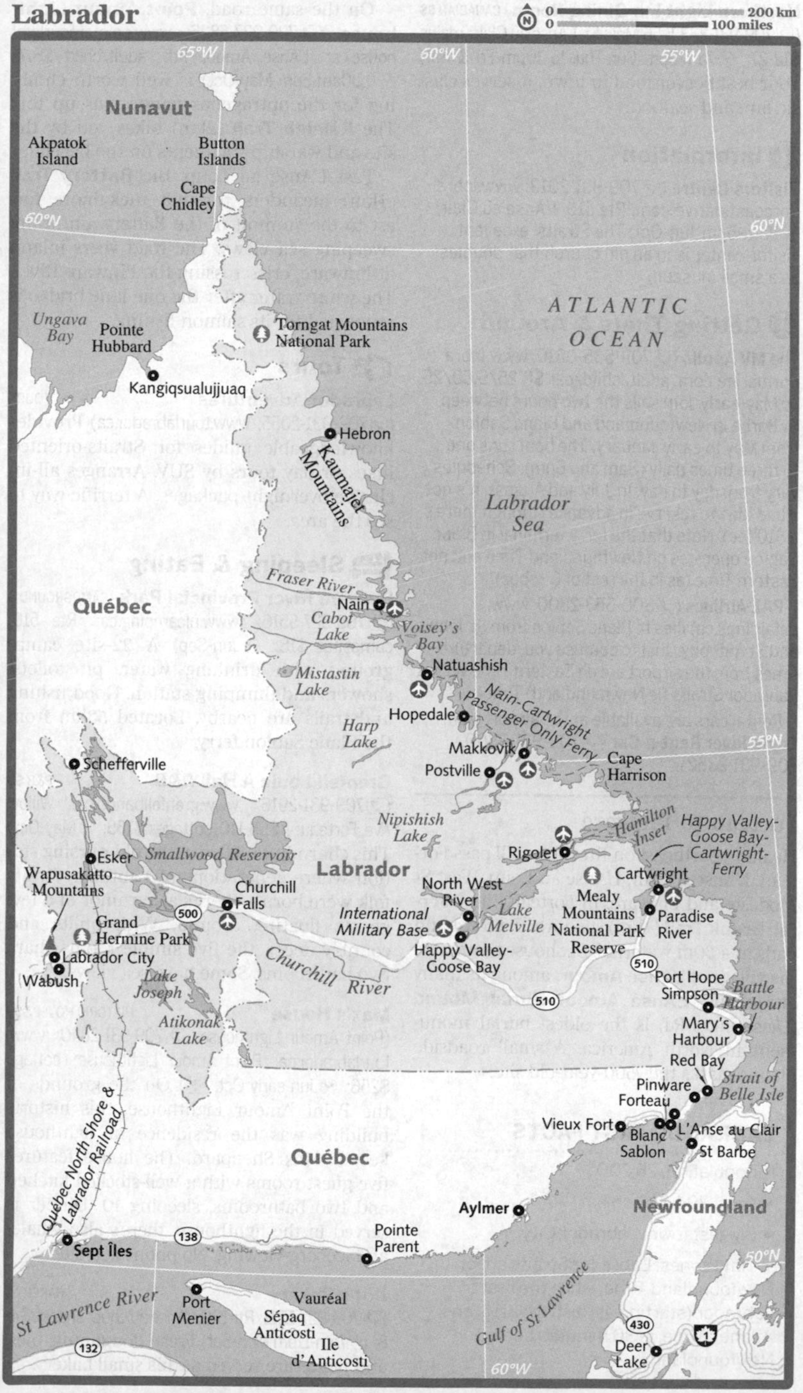

0 200 km
0 100 miles

65°W
60°W
55°W
60°N
55°N
50°N
Nunavut
Akpatok Island
Button Islands
Cape Chidley
Ungava Bay
Pointe Hubbard
Kangiqsualujjuaq
Torngat Mountains National Park
ATLANTIC OCEAN
Hebron
Kaumajet Mountains
Labrador Sea
Fraser River
Québec
Nain
Cabot Lake
Voisey's Bay
Mistastin Lake
Natuashish
Hopedale
Nain-Cartwright Passenger Only Ferry
Harp Lake
Makkovik
Postville
Cape Harrison
Schefferville
Nipishish Lake
Hamilton Inset
Happy Valley-Goose Bay-Cartwright-Ferry
Rigolet
Esker
Smallwood Reservoir
Labrador
Cartwright
Wapusakatto Mountains
Churchill Falls
North West River
Mealy Mountains National Park Reserve
Paradise River
500
International Military Base
Lake Melville
Grand Hermine Park
Happy Valley-Goose Bay
Labrador City
Churchill River
510
Wabush
Lake Joseph
Port Hope Simpson
Battle Harbour
510
Atikonak Lake
Mary's Harbour
Red Bay
Strait of Belle Isle
Pinware
Forteau
Vieux Fort
Blanc Sablon
L'Anse au Clair
St Barbe
Québec North Shore & Labrador Railroad
Québec
Newfoundland
Aylmer
Pointe Parent
138
Sept Îles
St Lawrence River
Port Menier
Vauréal
Sépaq Anticosti
Ile d'Anticosti
Gulf of St Lawrence
430
1
Deer Lake
132
60°W

Northern Light Inn Dining Room CANADIAN $$
(709-931-2332; 56 Main St, L'Anse au Clair; mains $12-27; 7am-9pm Sun-Thu, to 10pm Fri & Sat) Your best bet for food in town, it serves classic fare and seafood.

Information

Visitors Centre (709-931-2013; www.labradorcoastaldrive.com; Rte 510, L'Anse au Clair; 9am-5pm Jun-Oct) The Straits' excellent visitor center is in an old church that doubles as a small museum.

Getting There & Around

The **MV Apollo** (709-535-0810; www.labradormarine.com; adult/child/car $8.25/6.60/25; May-early Jan) sails the two hours between St Barbe in Newfoundland and Blanc Sablon from May to early January. The boat runs one to three times daily (8am and 6pm). Schedules vary from day to day. In July and August, it's not a bad idea to reserve in advance (though there's a $10 fee). Note that the ferry terminal in Blanc Sablon operates on Newfoundland Time and not Eastern Time (as in the rest of Québec).

PAL Airlines (800-563-2800; www.palairlines.ca) flies to Blanc Sablon from St John's and St Anthony. Just to confuse you, departure times from the airport are on Eastern Time versus Labrador Straits (ie Newfoundland) Time.

Rental cars are available at the airport from **Eagle River Rent-a-Car** (709-931-3300, 709-931-2352).

Forteau to Pinware

Heading northeast on Rte 510 you'll pass Forteau, L'Anse Amour, L'Anse au Loup, West St Modeste and Pinware. In Forteau, the **Overfall Brook Trail** (4km) shadows the coast and ends at a 30m waterfall. Six houses comprise the village of **L'Anse Amour**; among its many attractions, **L'Anse Amour Burial Mound** (L'Anse Amour Rd) is the oldest burial monument in North America. A small roadside plaque marks the 7500-year-old site.

LABRADOR FAST FACTS

- Population: 26,700
- Area: 294,330 sq km
- Biggest town: Labrador City
- Time zones: Labrador Straits are on Newfoundland Time, while the rest of Labrador (starting at Cartwright) is on Atlantic Time, ie 30 minutes behind Newfoundland.

On the same road, **Point Amour Lighthouse** (709-927-5825; www.pointamourlighthouse.ca; L'Anse Amour Rd; adult/child $6/4; 9:30am-5pm May-Oct) is well worth climbing for the outrageous panoramas up top. The **Raleigh Trail** (2km) takes you by the site and warship fragments on the beach.

Past L'Anse au Loup, the **Battery Trail** (4km) meanders through tuckamore forest to the summit of the Battery, unfurling sweeping sea views. The road veers inland at Pinware, crisscrossing the Pinware River. The white water after the one-lane bridge is renowned for its salmon fishing.

Tours

Labrador Adventures TOURS
(709-931-2055; www.tourlabrador.ca) Provides knowledgeable guides for Straits-oriented hikes or day tours by SUV. Arranges all-inclusive overnight packages. A terrific way to see the area.

Sleeping & Eating

Pinware River Provincial Park CAMPGROUND $
(709-927-5516; www.nlcamping.ca; Rte 510; campsites $18; Jun-Sep) A 22-site campground with drinking water, pit toilets, showers and dumping station. Good fishing and trails are nearby. Located 53km from the Blanc Sablon ferry.

Grenfell Louie A Hall B&B B&B $$
(709-931-2916; www.grenfellbandb.ca; Willow Ave, Forteau; r $95-110, cottages $165; May-Oct) This charming B&B is in the old nursing station where generations of Labrador Straits folk were born – there's also rumor of a few ghosts floating around. With quilts and country decor, the five simple rooms share two bathrooms. Some have sea views.

Max's House HISTORIC HOTEL $$$
(Point Amour Lighthouse; 709-931-2840; www.tourlabrador.ca; Point Amour Lighthouse; cottage $256; Jun-early Oct;) On the grounds of the Point Amour Lighthouse, this historic building was the residence of lighthouse keeper Max Sheppard. The house features five guest rooms with a well-stocked kitchen and two bathrooms, sleeping 10. Dinner is served in the lighthouse, there's also whale- and iceberg-viewing. No phones on-site.

Dot's Bakery BAKERY $
(709-927-5311; Rte 510, L'Anse au Loup; snacks $4-8; 7am-11pm Mon-Sat) Fresh doughnuts, pies, and pizzas are served at this small bakery.

OFF THE BEATEN TRACK

TORNGAT MOUNTAINS NATIONAL PARK

With otherworldly scenery of spindle peaks and rocky headlands that plunge to a turquoise river basin, **Torngat Mountains National Park** (709-922-1290; www.pc.gc.ca/torngat) is nature at its wildest. It's also an important area for scientific research, with some of the world's oldest rock (3.9 billion years) and a rare population of seals in a freshwater lake habitat. The **Kaumajet Mountains**, south of the park, also make for an out-of-this-world hiking experience.

Sitting at Labrador's wintry tip, access is by charter flight, private vessel or cruise ship only. Healthy polar-bear numbers means that armed bear guards are required for visitors. The Inuit-run Torngat Mountains Base Camp and Research Station (p510) offers package tours. The park headquarters is in Nain, where staff can direct you to local Inuit guides.

Seaview Restaurant CANADIAN $$
(Rte 510, Forteau; mains $10-25; 11am-9pm) Enjoy some fresh seafood or chow down on the famous fried chicken and tender caribou. A grocery store and jam factory are also on-site.

Red Bay

Spread between two venues, Red Bay National Historic Site (declared a Unesco World Heritage site in 2013) chronicles the discovery of three 16th-century Basque whaling galleons on the seabed here. Well preserved in the ice-cold waters, the vestiges of the ships tell a remarkable story of what life was like here some four centuries ago.

In the 16th century Red Bay was the largest whaling port in the world, with more than 2000 residents. Have a look at the reconstructed *chalupa* (a small Basque dingy used for whale hunting) and some of the other relics in the museum. Then hop in a small boat ($2) to nearby **Saddle Island**, where there is a self-guided interpretive trail around the excavated land sites. Allow at least two or three hours for the museum and island.

Sights & Activities

Across the bay, the amazing **Boney Shore Trail** (2km) skirts along the coast and passes ancient whale bones (they pretty much look like rocks) scattered along it. **The Tracey Hill Trail** climbs a boardwalk and 670 steps to the top of American Rockyman Hill for a bird's-eye view of the harbor; it takes about 20 minutes each way.

Red Bay National Historic Site HISTORIC SITE
(709-920-2051; www.pc.gc.ca/redbay; Rte 510; adult/child/family $7.80/3.90/19.60; 9am-5pm Jun-Sep) In the mid-16th century, Basque whalers came to the Strait of Belle Isle to hunt large numbers of right and bowhead whales and harvest their oil to light lamps all around Europe. The major whaling port of Red Bay is now a national historic site and World Heritage Site. View the original Basque artifacts, remains, and a restored *chalupa* (whaling boat) on-site.

Selma Barkham Town Centre MUSEUM
($2; 9am-5pm Jul-Sep) Selma Barkham was a tireless investigator of local history. Check out the stories she uncovered in this pleasant museum, which also features a 15m, 400-year-old North Atlantic right whale skeleton.

Sleeping & Eating

Basinview B&B B&B $
(709-920-2002; blancheearle@hotmail.com; 145 Main St; s/d with shared bath $60/70, d $90) Basinview B&B is a simple four-room, shared bathroom home right on the water.

Whaler's Station INN $$
(709-920-2156; www.redbaywhalers.ca; 72-76 West Harbour Dr; r $95-135) Divided between several buildings, these rustic but comfortable lodgings provide a central base for visits to the historic site. Some rooms offer water views. They all have private bathrooms, TV, a microwave and refrigerator. There's also an on-site restaurant.

Whaler's SEAFOOD $$
(mains $9-20; 8am-8pm) For fish-and-chips with partridgeberry pie, look no further than this friendly restaurant, a focal point for visitors to the bay. It also serves substantial breakfasts, and picnickers can order boxed lunches.

Battle Harbour

Sitting on an island in the Labrador Sea is the elaborately restored village and saltfish premises of Battle Harbour. Now a national historic district, it used to be the unofficial 'capital' of Labrador during the early 19th century, when fishing schooners lined its docks. Another claim to fame: Robert E Peary gave his first news conference here after reaching the North Pole in 1909.

★Battle Harbour Heritage Properties INN $$
(☎709-921-6325; http://battleharbour.com; r $75-245, package with 3 meals, tour & transport from $545; ⏰Jun-Sep; 📶) In addition to a classic inn, there are adorable heritage homes and cottages throughout the settlement. Think decks with sea views and little distraction: there are no cars, cell signal or TVs on the island. Instead you will find hiking trails with good berry-picking prospects and boat rides. Wi-fi is available in a common lounge area of the inn, which also serves meals.

Battle Harbour Dining Room CANADIAN $$
(Battle Harbour Inn; meals incl with lodgings; ⏰8am-6pm) Gourmet dining with set serving times; it's part of a package deal with lodging on the island.

Getting There & Away

Battle Harbour is accessed by boat from Mary's Harbour (departure at 11am, one hour). The passenger ferry is included with accommodations.

Northern Coast

North of Cartwright up to Ungava Bay there are a half-dozen small, semitraditional Inuit communities accessible only by sea or air along the rugged, largely unspoiled mountainous coast. Torngat Mountains National Park is the (literal) high point.

In 1993, geologists discovered copper, cobalt and large quantities of nickel on the shores of Voisey's Bay near Nain. Mining could pump billions into the provincial economy over the next few decades, but it also compromises both the environment and the way of life of native Innu and Inuit people.

Sights

The first port of call on the northern coast is **Makkovik**, an early fur-trading post and a traditional fishing and hunting community. Both new and old-style crafts are sold here.

Further north in **Hopedale** visitors can look at the old wooden Moravian mission church (1782). This **national historic site** (☎709-933-3864; $5; ⏰8:30am-7pm Jul-Oct) also includes a store, residence, some huts and a museum collection.

Natuashish is a new town that was formed when the troubled village of Utshimassit (Davis Inlet) was relocated to the mainland in 2002. The move was made after a 2000 study showed that 154 of 169 youths surveyed had abused solvents (ie sniffed gasoline) and that 60 of them did it on a daily basis.

The last stop on the ferry is **Nain**. Fishing has historically been the town's main industry, but this is changing due to the Voisey's Bay nickel deposit. It's the last town of any size as you go northward.

Sleeping

Most travelers use the ferry as a floating hotel. For those wishing to get off and wait until the next boat, it usually means winging it for a room, as only Postville, Hopedale and Nain have official lodging.

Amaguk Inn HOTEL $$
(☎709-933-3750; www.amagukinn.ca; 3 Harbour Dr, Hopedale; s/d $130/155; 📶) This 18-room inn also has a dining room (meals $15 to $20), and a lounge where you can get a cold beer. Airport transfers are also available.

Atsanik Lodge HOTEL $$
(☎709-922-2910; atsaniklabrador@msn.com; Sand Banks Rd, Nain; r $125-180; 📶) This large, 25-room lodge and its restaurant (meals $15 to $22) are your best bet in Nain.

★Torngat Mountains Base Camp & Research Station LODGE $$$
(☎855-867-6428; www.thetorngats.com; Torngat Mountains National Park; 4-night all-inclusive packages from $5200; ⏰Jul & Aug) The only way to enjoy Torngat Mountains National Park overnight is at this well-heeled base camp in the park. Guests sleep in comfortable yurts or more luxuriant dome tents with heat and electricity. There are also showers and chef-made meals. At camp, activities include hiking, boating and heli-tour options. An electrified fence keeps out polar bears.

Getting There & Away

Daily flights to North Coast communities leave from Happy Valley-Goose Bay with air carriers **Air Labrador** (☎800-563-3042; www.airlabrador.com) and **PAL Airlines** (Provincial Airlines; ☎800-563-2800; www.palairlines.ca).

The passenger-only **MV Northern Ranger** (www.labradorferry.ca; 1-way adult/child $157/78) plies this section of coast from mid-June to mid-November. It leaves once per week, making the three-day (one way) journey between Happy Valley-Goose Bay and Nain, stopping in Makkovik, Hopedale and Natuashish along the way. Check online for the ever-evolving schedule and fares.

Central Labrador

Making up the territorial bulk of Labrador, the central portion is an immense, sparsely populated and ancient wilderness. Paradoxically, it also has the largest town in Labrador, Happy Valley-Goose Bay, home to a military base. The town (population 7600) has all the usual services, but unless you're an angler or hunter, there isn't much to see or do.

Goose Bay was established during WWII as a staging point for planes on their way to Europe. The airport is also an official NASA alternate landing site for the space shuttle.

Sights

Labrador Interpretation Centre MUSEUM
(709-497-8566; www.therooms.ca/exhibits/regional-museums; 2 Portage Rd, North West River; 9am-4:30pm Mon-Sat, 1-4:30pm Sun) FREE This is the provincial museum, which holds some of Labrador's finest works of art. It's in North West River, via Rte 520.

Northern Lights Building MUSEUM
(709-896-5939; 170 Hamilton River Rd, Happy Valley-Goose Bay; 10am-5:30pm Tue-Sat) FREE Hosts a military museum, interesting lifelike nature scenes and simulated northern lights.

Sleeping & Eating

Big Land B&B B&B $
(709-896-2082; http://biglandbedandbreakfast.com; 34b Palliser Cres, Happy Valley-Goose Bay; r $85;) Friendly family-run B&B that also welcomes pets. Rooms are well-equipped and continental breakfasts with homemade bread and regional jam are served.

Royal Inn & Suites HOTEL $$
(709-896-2456; www.royalinnandsuites.ca; 5 Royal Ave, Happy Valley-Goose Bay; s/d/ste from $120/130/150;) The Royal has a variety of rooms to choose from; many have kitchens. It also loans out satellite phones to drivers through the region-wide safety program.

Davis' B&B B&B $$
(709-896-5077; valleybb5077@gmail.com; 14 Cabot Cres, Happy Valley-Goose Bay; s/d $100/120;) Family atmosphere and caribou sausages await you at Davis' four-room home.

El Greco PIZZA $
(709-896-3473; 133 Hamilton River Rd, Happy Valley-Goose Bay; mains $9-18; 4pm-1am Sun-Wed, to 3am Thu-Sat) Popular for pizzas and takeout, El Greco also serves pasta and Greek-style kabobs. It's near the Royal Inn.

Mariner's Galley SEAFOOD $$
(709-896-9301; 25 Loring Dr, Happy Valley-Goose Bay; mains $7-24; 6am-9pm) Come here for fried cod tongues with scruncheons (pork rind) or crab cocktail. Visitors rave about the friendly service and buffet options.

Information

Visitor Information Centre (www.tourismlabrador.com; 6 Hillcrest Rd, Happy Valley-Goose Bay; 8:30am-8pm Mon-Fri, 9am-5pm Sat & Sun;) Provides information on Central Labrador, plus brochures and maps. Events are announced on the Facebook page. There's also a useful town website (www.happyvalley-goosebay.com).

Getting There & Away

AIR

Daily flights are available to Happy Valley-Goose Bay from St John's via Deer Lake and Halifax. Montréal has daily flights to Wabush. The following offer services:

Air Canada (888-247-2262; www.aircanada.com)

PAL Airlines (Provincial Airlines; 800-563-2800; www.palairlines.ca)

BOAT

You can reach Happy Valley-Goose Bay by the seasonal passenger-only ferry **MV Northern Ranger** (709-896-2262; www.labradorferry.ca; adult/child to Nain $157/78; Jul-Aug).

CAR & MOTORCYCLE

From Happy Valley-Goose Bay you can take the mostly gravel Rte 500 west to Churchill Falls and then on to Labrador City. The drive to Labrador City takes about seven hours. There are no services until Churchill Falls, so stock up. The Royal Inn & Suites has free satellite phones you can take on the road (part of a region-wide safety program).

The partially paved Rte 510 heads toward Cartwright (383km) and L'Anse au Clair (623km).

Before leaving, contact the Department of Transportation & Works (www.roads.gov.nl.ca) for the latest conditions. Many rental-car agreements prohibit driving on the Trans Labrador Hwy or will not provide insurance, some have vehicles specifically designated for the route. You can hire cars from **National** (709-896-5575), among others.

Labrador West

Just 5km apart and 15km from Québec, the twin mining towns of Labrador City (population 9400) and Wabush (population 1900) are referred to collectively as Labrador West, and this is where the western region's population is concentrated. The largest open-pit iron ore mine in the world is in Labrador City, though the nearby Wabush mine closed in 2014 due to a slump in steel demand. The landscape is massive and the celestial polychromatic artwork can expand throughout the entire night sky.

Sights & Activities

Grande Hermine Park PARK
(☎709-282-5369; ⊙Jun-Sep) From Wabush, 39km east on Rte 500 is Grande Hermine Park, which has a beach and some fine scenery. The **Menihek hiking trail** (15km) goes through wooded areas with waterfalls and open tundra. Outfitters can take anglers to excellent fishing waters.

Gateway Labrador MUSEUM
(☎709-944-5399; 1365 Rte 500; ⊙9am-4pm Mon-Fri, 10am-5pm Sat) FREE In the same building as the visitor center is Gateway Labrador and its Montague Exhibit Hall, where 3500 years of human history and culture, including the fur trade, are represented with intriguing artifacts and displays.

Activities

The Wapusakatto Mountains are 5km from town, popping up off the vast landscape interspersed with flat northern tundra. A good, cold dry snow falls from late October to late April, so the ski season here is much longer than anywhere else in Canada.

Menihek Nordic Ski Club SKIING
(☎709-944-5842; www.meniheknordicski.ca; day pass adult/child $20/15) Offers 30km of trails with world-class cross-country skiing. The Canadian national team trains here, but novices are also welcome. There are lessons, skate skiing, night skiing options and rentals for skis and snowshoes.

Smokey Mountain Ski Club SKIING
(☎709-944-2129; www.smokeymountain.ca; Smokey Mountain Rd; ⊙Nov-Apr) There's still some steeps at this small snow-sports resort with 845m of vertical. It's serviced by a double chairlift and poma lift with a quad chairlift in the works. It's 5km from Labrador City.

Sleeping & Eating

Ptarmigan's Nest B&B $
(☎709-944-3040; theptarmigansnest@gmail.com; 28 Snow's Dr; r $98;) A lakeside retreat located in a quiet area 10 minutes from Labrador City with elegant, classic decor. Includes continental breakfast.

Wabush Hotel HOTEL $$
(☎709-282-3221; www.wabushhotel.com; 9 Grenville Dr, Wabush; r $165-175;) Centrally located in Wabush, this chalet-style 68-room hotel has spacious and comfortable rooms. The dining room has a popular buffet. Also the place to get free satellite phones on loan for driving the remote regions of the province.

Carol Inn MOTEL $$
(☎709-944-7736; www.carolinn.ca; 215 Drake Ave, Labrador City; s/d $140/165;) All 20 rooms here have a kitchenette. There's also a dining room with proper meals and a pub.

Sushi Lab SUSHI $
(☎709-944-4179; 118 Humphrey Rd, Labrador City; mains $6-16; ⊙11am-2pm & 5-11pm Mon-Fri, 5-11pm Sat & Sun) This pleasant dining experience is nouveau-Labrador all the way. Order from a selection of dozens of sushi rolls with an iPad, and you will be pleasantly rewarded. For less adventurous diners, there's also Chinese food or pizza.

Information

Destination Labrador (www.destinationlabrador.com) is comprehensive tourism website with special events, services and tips, and there's a **visitors centre** (☎709-944-5399; www.labradorwest.com; 1365 Rte 500) just west of Labrador City, in the Gateway Labrador building.

Getting There & Away

AIR

Air Canada (☎888-247-2262; www.aircanada.com), **PAL Airlines** (Provincial Airlines; ☎800-563-2800; www.palairlines.ca), **Air Inuit** (☎800-361-2965; www.airinuit.com) and **Air Labrador** (p510) fly into Happy Valley-Goose Bay and Wabush, with some other destinations.

CAR & MOTORCYCLE

Fifteen kilometers west from Labrador City along Rte 500 is Fermont, Québec. From there, Rte 389 is mainly paved (with some fine gravel sections) and continues south 581km to Baie Comeau.

Happy Valley-Goose Bay is a seven-hour drive east on Rte 500, considered a good gravel road. **Budget** (☎709-282-1234) has an office at the airport; rental cars may not be driven on Rte 50

Manitoba

Includes ➜

Best Places to Eat

- ➜ Deer + Almond (p523)
- ➜ Lazy Bear Cafe (p535)
- ➜ Forks Market (p523)
- ➜ Gypsy's Bakery (p535)
- ➜ Segovia (p524)
- ➜ Marion Street Eatery (p523)

Best Places to Sleep

- ➜ Beechmount B&B (p522)
- ➜ Blue Sky Bed & Sled (p534)
- ➜ Lazy Bear Lodge (p534)
- ➜ Inn at the Forks (p522)
- ➜ Mere Hotel (p522)
- ➜ Solmundson Gesta Hus Bed & Breakfast (p528)

Why Go?

The two prominent stars of Manitoba are Winnipeg, with its big-city sophistication, and Churchill, wlth its profusion of natural wonders. But it's what lies between that truly defines this often misunderstood prairie province. Open spaces seem to stretch forever – gently rolling fields of grain and sunflowers and wildflowers reach all the way north to Arctic tundra.

The magnitude of this land is only fully appreciated while standing on the edge of a vivid yellow canola field counting three different storms on the horizon, or on the edge of Hudson Bay's rugged coastline counting polar bears while belugas play in the distance. Wander its empty roads, stop in its evocative little towns, find the subtle dramas in the land and expect surprises, whether it's a moose looming in front of you on the road or a future pop legend performing on stage.

When to Go

Winnipeg

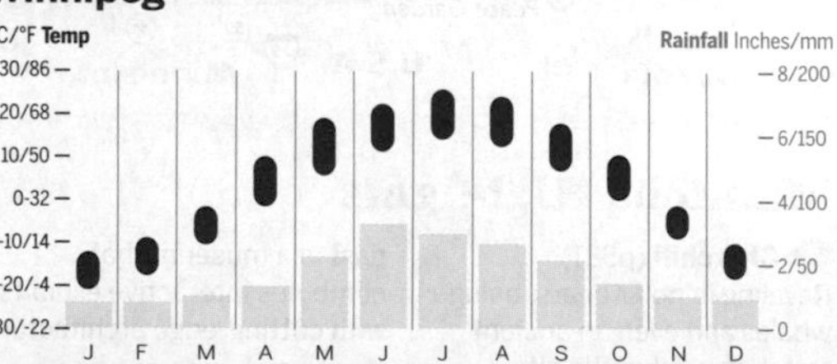

May Wildflowers spring up along the roads and signal the end of a long winter.

Jun–Aug Days *can* be balmy but cool nights rule; at Churchill, 18°C is considered hot.

Oct & Nov The best time to see polar bears around Churchill.

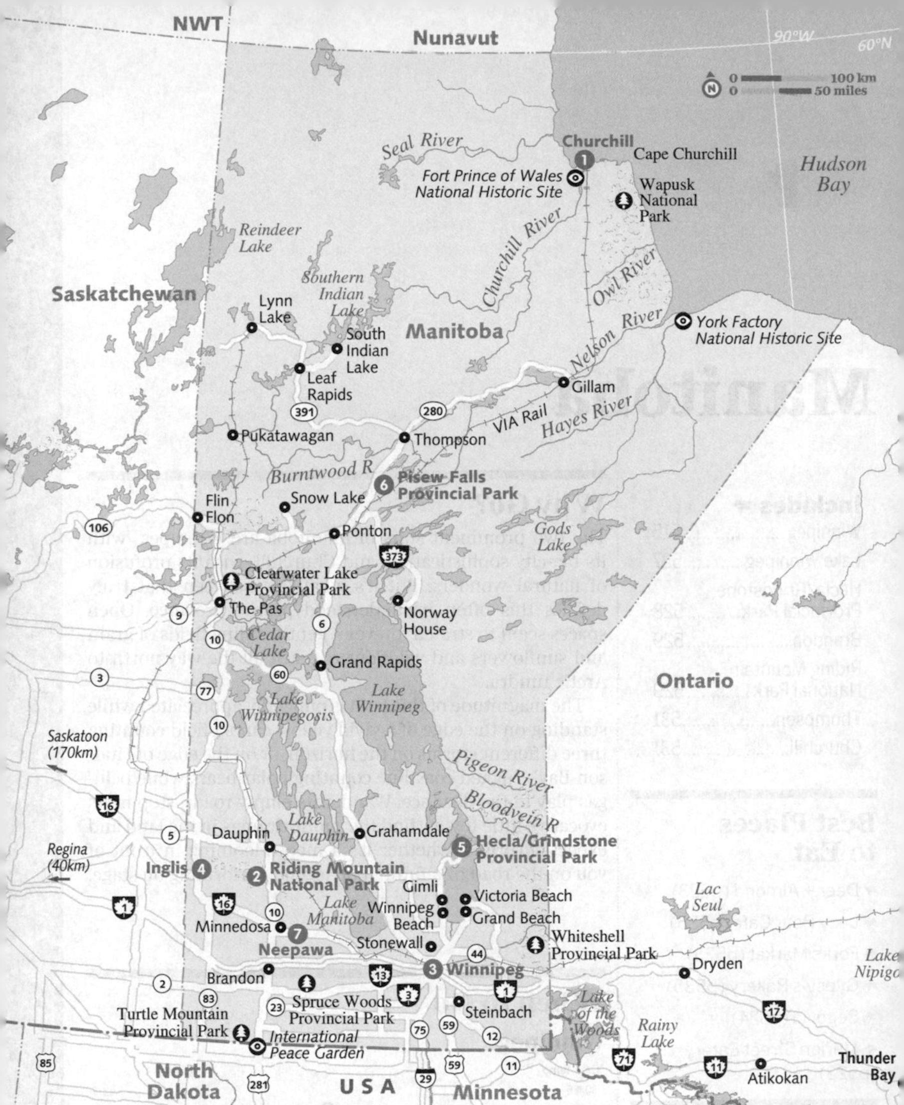

Manitoba Highlights

1. **Churchill** (p531) Reveling in polar bears, beluga whales and even an ancient fort in this subarctic city.
2. **Riding Mountain National Park** (p529) Hiking and paddling Manitoba's best natural setting.
3. **Canadian Museum for Human Rights** (p517) Delving deep into Canada's past in a museum that combines interactive exhibits with cutting-edge architecture.
4. **Inglis Grain Elevators National Historic Site** (p530) Seeking out the monumental sentinels of the prairie from bygone days.
5. **Hecla/Grindstone Provincial Park** (p528) Contemplating nature virtually surrounded by Lake Winnipeg.
6. **Pisew Falls Provincial Park** (p530) Driving lonely roads and stopping
7. **Neepawa** (p529) Discovering small-town gems, where time seems to stand still in some past idyllic era.

History

Tired of being labeled soft, early European explorers shunned the more hospitable south and braved the cold, rugged north coast of Hudson Bay. Indigenous Dene got involved in the fur trade soon after Hudson's Bay Company (HBC) established trading posts here in the 17th century.

British agricultural settlers moved to the future site of Winnipeg in 1811, creating constant friction with existing Métis over land rights. When HBC sold part of the land to the federal government, Métis leader Louis Riel launched a rebellion and formed a provisional government. Negotiations between Riel and the federal government resulted in Manitoba joining the federation as Canada's fifth province in 1870, though Riel himself was executed for treason.

Land & Climate

Manitoba's geography is as wide-ranging as you'll find anywhere in the country. Southern agricultural flatlands blend into green woodlands embracing Canada's largest lakes. Glacial footprints of potholed lakes, stubby vegetation and scraped-bare lands of the Canadian Shield characterize the north. Everywhere you go, the skies are massive.

The climate is just as variable and totally unpredictable. Average northern temperatures range from -50°C to summer highs of 20°C. Southern summers average 25°C dropping to -15°C during winter. Notoriously strong winds all year create summer dust storms, even the occasional tornado, and winter blizzards where wind chills make it feel 30 degrees colder than it is. Spring flooding is common in southern areas, and there is nothing like an intense prairie summertime thunderstorm.

Parks & Wildlife

It can't be overstated: every kind of popular Canadian animal can be seen here. Moose, beavers, bears, lynx, deer, caribou, foxes, rabbits and so on. And, of course, the real stars: Churchill's polar bears.

Riding Mountain National Park is a microcosm of Manitoba ecology, while Wapusk National Park defines raw wilderness.

Manitoba Provincial Parks Guide, published by Manitoba Parks (www.manitobaparks.com), is available at visitor information centers. Reserve ahead online, as campgrounds often fill up.

MANITOBA FAST FACTS

- Population: 1,282,000
- Area: 647,797 sq km
- Capital: Winnipeg
- Quirky fact: Manitobans are the highest per-capita consumers of 7-Eleven slurpees in the world

Getting There & Away

Major airlines connect Winnipeg with the main Canadian cities and US Midwest hubs. **Calm Air** (800-839-2256; www.calmair.com) serves northern communities in Nunavut as well as Churchill.

Manitoba shares more than a dozen US–Canada vehicle border crossings with North Dakota and Minnesota. There are several routes into Saskatchewan, but only the Trans-Canada Hwy (Hwy 1) leads into Ontario. Southern Manitoba's extensive road network disappears heading north, where Hwy 10 or Hwy 6 are the only options and services are few (watch your gas gauge).

VIA Rail's *Canadian* passes through Winnipeg and southern communities two or three times a week. Also out of Winnipeg, the two- or three-times-a-week service to subarctic Churchill.

WINNIPEG

POP 663,615

Winnipeg surprises. Rising above the prairie, it's a metropolis where you least expect it. Cultured, confident and captivating, it's more than just a pit stop on the Trans-Canada haul, but a destination in its own right, with a couple of world-class museums and a wonderfully diverse dining scene. Wander its historic neighborhoods and lap up a vibe that enjoys being the butt of a *Simpsons* joke ('That's it! Back to Winnipeg!') and revels in one of the world's best fringe theater festivals.

History

An aboriginal hub for 6000 years and center of the 19th-century fur-trade rivalry between HBC and North West Company, the confluence of the Assiniboine and Red Rivers had little choice in any other official name than the Europeanized *win nipee* (Cree for 'muddy waters').

Greater Winnipeg

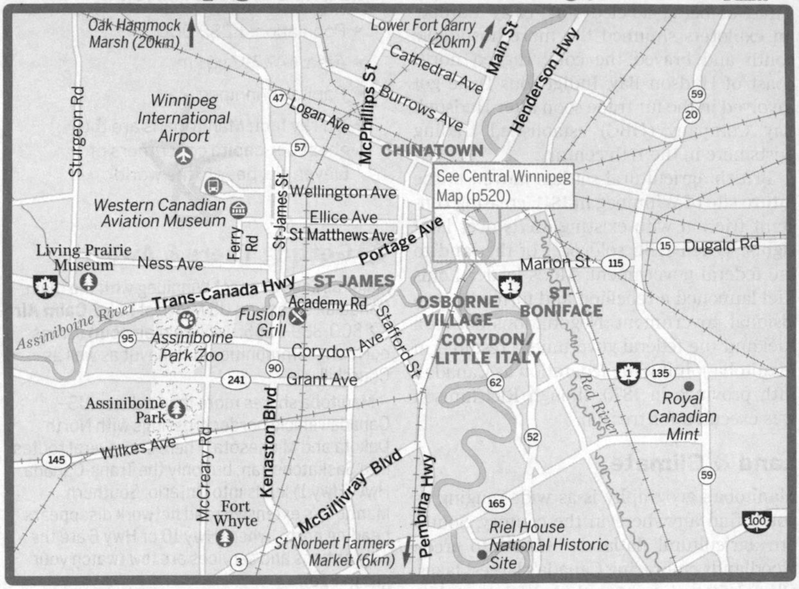

0 — 4 km
0 — 2 miles

See Central Winnipeg Map (p520)

French settlers established the neighborhood of St-Boniface, birthplace of the controversial Métis leader Louis Riel.

The railroad's arrival in 1886 solidified Winnipeg's commercial importance, later rendered moot by the opening of the Panama Canal. Winnipeg subsequently stagnated, although a landmark general strike in 1919 helped raise union recognition across Canada. Today it has a diverse economy and modest growth. Its most notable brand is familiar to anyone with the munchies: Old Dutch, the potato-chip maker.

Sights

Winnipeg is mostly concentrated around the walkable downtown area; other sights are reached most easily by vehicle.

'Portage and Main' marks the center of downtown and is famous for incredibly strong winds and frigid temperatures – Randy Bachman and Neil Young wrote a song about it, 'Prairie Town,' with the chorus repeating the line 'Portage and Main, 50 below.'

To the north, 1900s limestone architecture marks the warehouse-and-arts Exchange District. South of downtown is the Forks and across the Red River is the French neighborhood of St-Boniface; west of there is the very strollable Osborne Village and Corydon Ave. A short drive west of the city center is Assiniboine Park with its terrific zoo. Other attractions are found on the outskirts of the city in all directions.

Downtown

★Winnipeg Art Gallery GALLERY

(WAG; ☎204-786-6641; www.wag.ca; 300 Memorial Blvd; adult/child $12/6; ⏱11am-5pm Tue, Wed & Fri-Sun, to 9pm Thu) This ship-shaped gallery plots a course for contemporary Manitoban and Canadian artists, including the world's largest collection of Inuit work, alongside a permanent collection of European Renaissance art. Temporary exhibits include artworks by Chagall and Karel Funk, and serpentinite carvings by internationally successful Inuit carver Oviloo Tunnillie.

Manitoba Legislative Building NOTABLE BUILDING

(Map p520; ☎204-945-5813; www.gov.mb.ca/legtour; 450 Broadway Ave; ⏱8am-8pm, tours hourly 9am-6pm Jul & Aug) FREE Designed during Winnipeg's optimistic boom of the early 20th century, this 1920 building flaunts neoclassical beaux-arts design, limestone construction and governmental importance above the Red River. Surrounded by impeccable lawns and gardens, ancient gods and contemporary heroes are immortalized, including the Louis Riel monument facing St-Boniface. *Eternal Youth and the Spirit of Enterprise* – aka Golden Boy – shines his 23½-carat-gold-covered splendor atop the oxidized copper dome.

Upper Fort Garry Heritage Provincial Park HISTORIC SITE
(Map p520; www.upperfortgarry.com; 130 Main St) FREE Original 1830s oak, stone and mortar walls stand where four different forts have stood since 1738. The entire site – known as Winnipeg's birthplace and formerly a trading center for a chunk of Canada larger than Eastern Europe – has had a drastic revamp and reopened in 2015 as a rather lavish urban park, complete with trellises showing the course of some of the old walls. An interpretive center is set to open in 2017.

Plug In Institute of Contemporary Art GALLERY
(204-942-1043; www.plugin.org; 460 Portage Ave; noon 6pm Tue, Wed & Fri, to 8pm Thu, 9am-5pm Sat & Sun) FREE Contemporary art rules at this gallery with changing exhibitions from local and international artists.

The Forks

Strategically important and historically significant, the meeting place of the muddy and small Assiniboine River and the muddy and large Red River has been drawing people for millennia.

It's the focus for many visitors and combines several distinct areas. Parks Canada runs a historic site amid beautifully landscaped parks. Nearby, old railway shops have been converted into the **Forks** (204-957-7618; www.theforks.com), a touristy collection of shops, cafes and restaurants in renovated old buildings.

★Canadian Museum for Human Rights MUSEUM
(Map p520; 204-289-2000; www.humanrightsmuseum.ca; Waterfront Dr & Provencher Blvd; adult/7-17yr/student $18/9/14; 10am-5pm Thu-Tue, to 9pm Wed) Housed in a stunning contemporary building designed by American architect Antoine Predock, this terrific museum explores human rights issues as they relate to Canada, its culture and the rest of the world through the medium of striking interactive displays, videos, art and more. Exhibits don't shy away from sensitive subjects, such as the internment of Canadian-Japanese during WWII and Aboriginal children forced into residential schools as recently as the 1990s, and the Holocaust and Holodomor are given sensitive treatment.

> **MANITOBA TOURIST INFO**
>
> **Travel Manitoba** (800-665-0040; www.travelmanitoba.com) is an invaluable resource. In addition to seasonal booths (open 9am to 7pm) at major highway entrances into the province, it also operates the Explore Manitoba Centre in Winnipeg.
>
> **Bed & Breakfast of Manitoba** (www.bedandbreakfast.mb.ca) lists dozens of B&Bs.

★Forks National Historic Site HISTORIC SITE
(Map p520; 204-957-7618; www.theforks.com;) In a beautiful riverside setting, modern amenities for performances and interpretive exhibits in this park outline the area's history as the meeting place of Aboriginal people for centuries.

The rivers routinely overflow during spring runoff and flooded pathways are not uncommon, an event as exciting as it is dangerous. Follow the waterways with a canoe from Splash Dash (p519). Kids can go nuts in the heritage-themed playground, the **Variety Heritage Adventure Park**.

Winnipeg Railway Museum MUSEUM
(Map p520; 204-942-4632; www.wpgrailwaymuseum.com; 123 Main St; adult/child $5/3; 10am-4pm daily Apr-Oct, 9am-1pm Mon & Thu, 11am-4pm Sat & Sun rest of year;) Winnipeg's imposing and underused Union Station (opened in 1911 and designed by the same firm that did New York's Grand Central Terminal) houses a small but thorough museum on the history of Canadian railways. Highlights include an impressive model railway, the *Countess of Dufferin* locomotive and a collection of historic Canadian railway cars that you can climb inside.

Exchange District

Restored century-old brick buildings are the backdrop to the Exchange District, Winnipeg's most vibrant neighborhood downtown. Hipsters, tourists and vagrants congregate amid heritage buildings housing restaurants, clubs, boutiques and art galleries. It's been

WINNIPEG FOR CHILDREN

Right in the Forks, kids learn by doing at **Manitoba Children's Museum** (Map p520; ☎204-924-4000; www.childrensmuseum.com; 45 Forks Market Rd; $11; ⏲9:30am-4:30pm Sun-Thu, to 6pm Fri & Sat; 👪), where 'hands off' is not part of the program. The colorful, interactive exhibits encourage tykes to act as train conductors, astronauts and empire builders. It has outdoor programs in summer.

Also in the Forks, the much-heralded Manitoba Theatre for Young People (p525) uses colorful sets for enthusiastic performances for kids without being too treacly for adults.

Over 2000 animals populate Assiniboine Park Zoo (p519), which specializes in animals that are indigenous to harsh climates. The new International Polar Bear Conservation Centre has exhibits on its namesake critters and often cares for orphaned cubs. It's part of the zoo's huge, excellent **Journey to Churchill**, which combines exhibits and live animals, such as musk oxen and wolves. From bogs to Arctic beaches, the province's ecology is covered.

Kids get the chance to play pilot or air traffic controller at the **Western Canadian Aviation Museum** (☎204-786-5503; www.wcam.mb.ca; 958 Ferry Rd; adult/3-12yr $7.50/3; ⏲9:30am-4:30pm Mon-Fri, 10am-5pm Sat, noon-5pm Sun) amid planes from the past 90 years.

For old-fashioned thrills, **Tinkertown Family Fun Park** (☎204-257-8095; www.tinkertown.mb.ca; 621 Murdock Rd; unlimited ride ticket $17; ⏲noon-5pm, until 7pm some days May-Sep; 👪) has rides and games in a carnival setting. Play mini-golf and then have a miniature doughnut.

Kids also love the critters and activities at Fort Whyte (p519); while the Science Gallery at Manitoba Museum (p518) has kid-friendly fun, including a lab where you build a race car.

declared a national historic site; walking tours provide context.

The grassy haven of **Old Market Square** is the neighborhood focal point. There's regular live music in summer at the controversially modern **Cube** (Map p520; Old Market Sq).

★ Manitoba Museum MUSEUM

(Map p520; ☎204-956-2830; www.manitobamuseum.ca; 190 Rupert Ave; adult/child from $11/9; ⏲10am-5pm late May-Sep, reduced hours rest of year; 👪) Nature trips through the subarctic, history trips into 1920s Winnipeg, cultural journeys covering the past 12,000 years – if it happened in Manitoba, it's here. Amid the superb displays are a planetarium and an engaging science gallery. One exhibit shows what Churchill was like as a tropical jungle, a mere 450 million years ago, while a replica of the *Nonsuch*, the 17th-century ship that opened up the Canadian west to trade, is another highlight.

Outworks Art Gallery GALLERY

(Map p520; ☎204-479-4804; www.outworksgallery.com; 290 McDermot Ave; ⏲noon-4pm Thu-Sat) FREE Collective of Winnipeg-based artists showcasing their paintings, photography, ceramics and more.

Urban Shaman Contemporary Aboriginal Art GALLERY

(Map p520; ☎204-942-2674; www.urbanshaman.org; 290 McDermot Ave; ⏲noon-5pm Tue-Sat) Artist-run gallery displaying contemporary Canadian aboriginal art, from paintings to installations.

St-Boniface

Canada's oldest French community outside of Québec sits just across the Red River from the Forks.

Visitor information centers have an excellent historical self-guided walking map. **Taché Promenade** follows the Red River along Ave Taché, past many of St-Boniface's historical sites.

★ St-Boniface Museum MUSEUM

(Map p520; ☎204-237-4500; http://msbm.mb.ca; 494 Ave Taché; adult/6-17yr/student $6/4.50/5.50; ⏲10am-4pm Mon-Fri, noon-4pm Sat & Sun) A mid-19th-century convent is Winnipeg's oldest building and the largest oak-log construction on the continent. The museum inside focuses on the establishment of St-Boniface, the birth of the Métis nation, and the 3000km journey of the first of the

Grey Nuns, who arrived here by canoe from Montréal. Artifacts include pioneer furniture and tools, First Nations' beadwork and weaponry, and the coffin used to transport the body of Louis Riel after his execution.

Fort Gibraltar PARK
(Map p520; ☎204-237-7692; www.fortgibraltar.com; 866 Rue St Joseph; adult/6-17yr $8/5; ⏰10am-6pm Wed & Thu, to 4pm Fri & Sat) Behind wooden walls sits this re-created fur-trade fort. Along with inspired interpreters, real clothes, tools, furs, bunks, and bannock and blacksmith shops give a sense of 1810-era life at the Forks, the fort's original location.

St-Boniface Basilica HISTORIC SITE
(Map p520; 151 Ave de la Cathédrale) Mostly destroyed by fire in 1968, the original white-stone facade still stands as a 100-year, imposing reminder of the basilica that once stood here. A more current structure was rebuilt on the ruins and Manitoba founder Louis Riel rests in a modest grave in the cemetery.

Greater Winnipeg

★Assiniboine Park PARK
(www.assiniboinepark.ca; 2355 Corydon Ave; ⏰24hr) FREE Winnipeg's emerald jewel, this 4.5-sq-km urban park is easily worth at least a half-day's frolic. Besides the top-notch **zoo** (☎204-927-6000; www.assiniboineparkzoo.ca; 460 Assiniboine Park Dr; adult/child $19.75/17.50; ⏰9am-6pm), there are playgrounds, gardens, a conservatory and much more.

Royal Canadian Mint NOTABLE BUILDING
(☎204-257-3359; www.mint.ca; 520 Blvd Lagimodière; tours adult/under 17yr $6/3; ⏰9am-4pm Tue-Sat) Producing loonies to the tune of billions of dollars, this high-tech mint produces money for Canada and 60 other nations. Tour the pyramid-shaped glass facility to see how money is made (the greatest action occurs on weekdays). It is 9km southeast of the city center. Entry is cheaper on weekends.

Riel House National Historic Site HISTORIC SITE
(☎204-257-1783; www.parkscanada.ca/riel; 330 River Rd; adult/child $4/2; ⏰10am-5pm Jul & Aug) After Louis Riel's 1885 execution for treason, his body was brought to his family home before being buried in St-Boniface Basilica. Riel grew up on this farm in a cabin by the river; the 1880s house now on display housed his descendants as recently as the 1960s. Now surrounded by subdivisions, the house is 9km south of the city center.

Living Prairie Museum PARK
(☎204-832-0167; www.winnipegmuseums.org; 2795 Ness Ave; ⏰10am-5pm Jul & Aug, Sun only May, Jun, Sep & Oct) FREE Protects 12 hectares of original, unplowed, now-scarce, tall prairie grass. Self-guided tours from the nature center show the seasons of wildflowers in what was once an ocean of color across the prairie provinces and which supported millions of bison. Free nature hikes at 10am on Wednesdays between mid-July and mid-August; book ahead.

Fort Whyte PARK
(☎204-989-8355; www.fortwhyte.org; 1961 McCreary Rd; adult/child $8/6; ⏰9am-5pm Mon-Fri, 10am-5pm Sat & Sun) A vast, trail-laced natural site with an eco-focus; here you can spot bison, deer and other wildlife. Learn about sod houses and rent seasonal activity gear like snowshoes and canoes for modest rates. Even better, in winter, toboggans are free. It's 13km southwest of the city center.

Tours

★SquarePeg Tours WALKING
(☎204-898-4678; www.squarepegtours.ca; adult/child from $12/8) Numerous entertaining and historically themed walking tours – including the popular 'Murder, Mystery & Mayhem' and 'Pestilence, Shamans & Doctors' – depart on regular schedules all summer. 'Symbols, Secrets & Sacrifices Under the Golden Boy' is a much-acclaimed look at the hidden meanings in the capital, while the 'Naughty Bawdy Tour' of the Exchange District is for over-18s only.

★Historic Exchange District Walking Tours WALKING
(Map p520; ☎204-942-6716; www.exchangedistrict.org; Old Market Sq; adult/child $10/free; ⏰9am-4:30pm Mon-Sat early May-Aug) Entertaining themed and history tours departing from Old Market Sq. Book in advance.

Splash Dash BOATING
(Map p520; ☎204-783-6633; www.splashdash.ca; adult/child $11/9; ⏰10am-sunset May-Oct) Runs 30-minute, insightful tours of the river from the Forks.

Routes on the Red TOURS
(www.routesonthered.ca) Offers thorough, downloadable tours of Winnipeg for walkers, cyclists, drivers and skiers.

Central Winnipeg

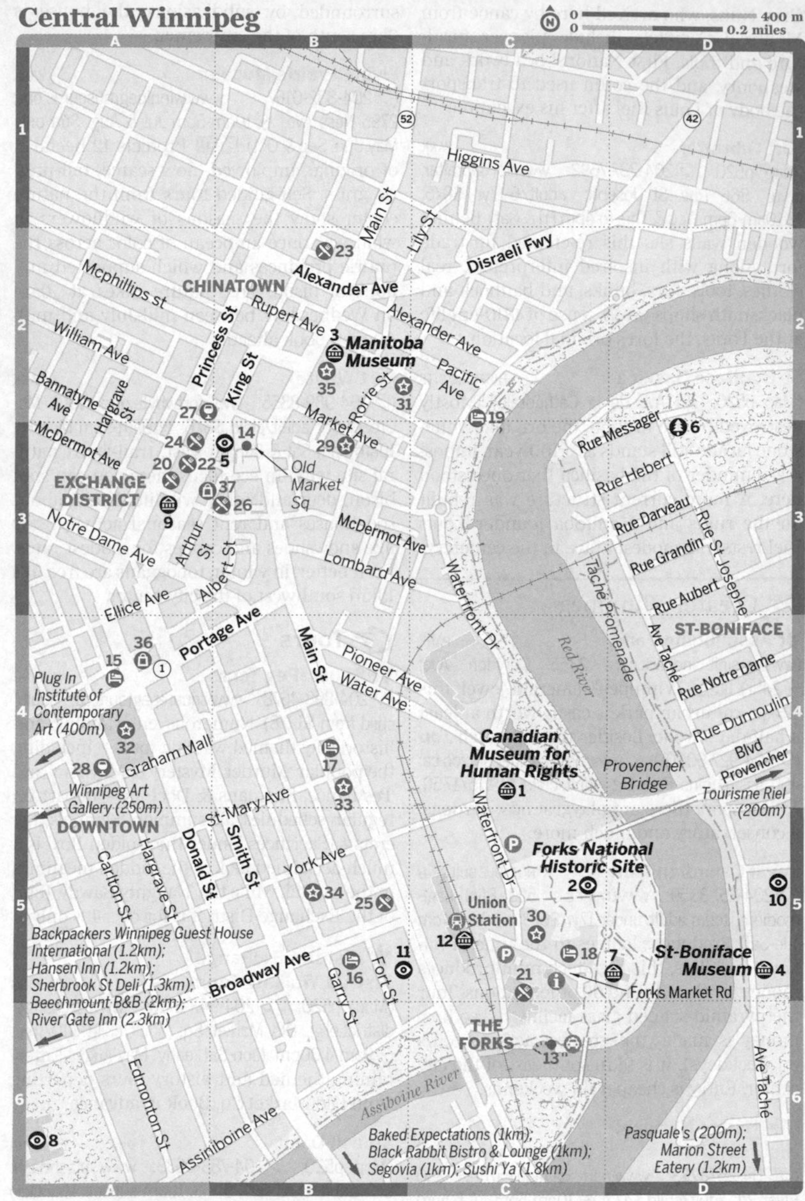

Festivals & Events

Festival du Voyageur CULTURAL

(http://festivalvoyageur.mb.ca; Fort Gibraltar; ⏰mid-Feb) Winnipeg's signature event. Everyone gets involved in the 10-day winter festival celebrating fur traders and French voyageurs. Centered around Fort Gibraltar; enjoy concerts, dogsled races, a torch-lit procession and joie de vivre.

Central Winnipeg

Pride Winnipeg LGBT
(www.pridewinnipeg.com; ⌚late May) Nine-day LBGT celebration with a great parade, music and other events.

★**Winnipeg Folk Festival** MUSIC
(☎204-231-0096; www.winnipegfolkfestival.ca; ⌚early Jul) More than 100 concerts on seven stages over three days in Birds Hill Provincial Park.

★**Winnipeg Fringe Theatre Festival** PERFORMING ARTS
(☎204-943-7464; www.winnipegfringe.com; ⌚mid-Jul) North America's second-largest fringe fest; the comedy, drama, music and cabaret are often wildly creative, raw and great fun. Held over 10 days in the Exchange District.

Folklorama CULTURAL
(☎204-982-6230; www.folklorama.ca; ⌚early Aug) Longest-running multicultural event of its kind in the world. Performances, storytelling and more in pavilions representing various cultures across town.

Manito Ahbee CULTURAL
(☎204-956-1849; www.manitoahbee.com; ⌚late Aug) A huge celebration of aboriginal culture, involving music, arts, crafts and dance, that draws participants from across the globe.

Sleeping

You'll find plenty of chain motels on main routes around Winnipeg and near the airport. Downtown hotels are the city's priciest options but convenient for exploring on foot. Sherbrook St and around has a good clutch of guesthouses in a quiet, residential location, but is within easy walking distance to downtown.

Hansen Inn GUESTHOUSE $
(☎204-960-6516; www.hanseninn.com; 150 Sherbrook St; r $79-89; ❄📶) This quiet residential house comprises several fan-cooled rooms (most of them en suite), studios and apartments, all with kitchen access, fridge and fast wi-fi. Within easy reach of downtown and the airport, and with several good restaurants just steps away.

Backpackers Winnipeg Guest House International HOSTEL $
(204-772-1272; www.backpackerswinnipeg.com; 168 Maryland St; dm/r $30/60; P ❄ @) This creaky-floored Victorian house turned hostel lives on a quiet, tree-lined street west of the city center. The musty basement has a crowded games room and small showers, and the rooms could be cleaner. Still, pubs, restaurants and shops are nearby.

★**Beechmount B&B** B&B $$
(866-797-0905; www.beechmount.ca; 134 W Gate; d $108-130, f $216;) The rich history of this beautifully restored 19th-century heritage home is intertwined with that of Winnipeg. Its three sumptuous rooms are presided over by the affable Christine and Giovanni, and the excellent cooked breakfast comes with Italian touches. Your hosts are happy to share their local knowledge.

★**Mere Hotel** BOUTIQUE HOTEL $$
(Map p520; 204-594-0333; www.merehotel.com; 333 Waterfront Dr; r from $149; ❄) Besides the winning riverside location, there's a lot going for this quiet boutique hotel: the helpful staff, the compact, contemporary rooms (comfortable if sparsely furnished), the rain showerheads in the bathrooms, the bold splashes of color... Get here early, since parking spaces are scarce.

★**Inn at the Forks** BOUTIQUE HOTEL $$
(Map p520; 204-942-6555; www.innforks.com; 75 Forks Market Rd; r $148-259; P ❄ @) This funky boutique hotel has a lot going for it: a quiet, green location in the Forks, eco-credentials, supermodern bathrooms, splashes of contemporary art and solid colors in 117 spacious rooms, a great new restaurant that makes the most of locally sourced ingredients... Enjoy river views and the services of a high-end spa, too.

River Gate Inn B&B $$
(204-489-5817; www.rivergateinn.biz; 186 W Gate; r $129-149; P ❄) With its mock-Tudor facade and creaky floors, this mansion-cum-B&B sits on a tree-lined street overlooking the river, and is one of the more characterful places to stay in Winnipeg. Hosts Bob and Mavis cook excellent breakfasts to order, and there's an honor bar for guests who wish to stay up and socialise.

Alt Hotel Winnipeg BUSINESS HOTEL $$
(Map p520; 431-800-4279; www.althotels.com; 310 Donald St; r $149; P ❄) Sleek, shiny and right in the middle of the Exchange District, this is a welcome newbie on the accommodations scene. Rooms are stylish, with particular attention to creature comforts (fantastic beds, spa-style showers). The decor is minimalist, all whites and charcoals, with the exception of some eye-bending color in the gym.

Humphry Inn HOTEL $$
(Map p520; 204-942-4222; www.humphryinn.com; 260 Main St; r $139-169; P ❄ @) This modern, six-story hotel is well located downtown. Rooms are large and nicely appointed with fridges and microwaves; get one facing east for good views. The free breakfast buffet is extensive, but parking is not; get here early to secure an on-site space.

Fort Garry Hotel HOTEL $$
(Map p520; 204-942-8251; www.fortgarryhotel.com; 222 Broadway Ave; r $118-209; P ❄ @) Winnipeg history radiates from this locally owned 1913 limestone legacy. Built as one of Canada's chateau-style railway stopovers, the grand foyer embodies the hotel's spirit: look for historical photographs lining the walls and lament that they really don't make them like this any more. Extensive breakfast and an excellent spa, too, but the rooms are dated, thin-walled and need refurbishing.

Eating

Winnipeg is an excellent place to dine, with a diverse choice of cuisines, from Ethiopian to cutting-edge fusion. The Exchange District, St-Boniface, Osborne Village and the Corydon Ave strip are all loaded with options. A 15-minute walk west of the city center, the delis and diners of Sherbrook St are also worth a mention.

Downtown

VJ's Drive-In FAST FOOD $
(Map p520; 204-943-2655; 170 Main St; mains $6-11; 10am-midnight) Across from Union Station, VJ's is a fave for take-out fixes. There may be a line at lunchtime, but overstuffed chili dogs, greasy cheeseburgers and bronze-hued fries consistently voted the best in Winnipeg won't disappoint. Seating is limited to outdoor picnic tables. Staff won't win any congeniality awards.

The Forks

The commercial area of the Forks has a number of indifferent restaurants aimed at tourists, but the market building offers great redemption, with a plethora of terrific lunch spots under one roof.

★Forks Market MARKET $
(Map p520; www.theforks.com; 1 Forks Market Rd; mains $5-12; 9:30am-6pm Mon-Thu & Sat, to 9pm Fri;) Gourmet food specialists, vendors selling prepared foods and an array of ethnic food stalls, running the gamut from Japanese tapas, Caribbean and Chilean to hearty Polish and Sri Lankan, are the unbeatable draw here. Enjoy the bounty at tables scattered about inside or picnic by the river outside.

Tall Grass Prairie BAKERY $
(Map p520; 204-957-5097; www.tallgrassbakery.ca; 1 Forks Market Rd; mains from $4; 7am-9pm Mon-Sat, to 6:30pm Sun) Spread over two stalls in the Forks Market, this local legend uses organic Manitoba fare to create lovely baked goods, sandwiches and prepared meals. The coffee's good, too.

Peasant Cookery BISTRO $$
(Map p520; 204-989-7700; www.peasantcookery.com; 100-283 Bannatyne Ave; mains $10-28; 11am-2pm Mon-Fri & 5-9pm daily) In a high-ceilinged, high-profile corner space in a 1907 warehouse, this inviting bistro has a menu with ingredients drawn right from the fertile central Canada countryside. Meats and vegetables are offered seasonally, and favourites include clam and bacon pasta, and beef brisket. Lunch leans toward pastrami sandwiches and burgers.

Exchange District & Around

On a summer evening, sitting outside at a funky place on the lively, historic streets of the Exchange District is a treat. Some of Winnipeg's most imaginative restaurants are found here, along with the Chinese flavors of Winnipeg's small Chinatown.

★King + Bannatyne SANDWICHES $
(Map p520; 204-691-9757; www.kingandbannatyne.com; 100 King St; mains from $9; 11am-9pm Mon-Sat) The hand-cut meat sandwiches at this brisk, casual spot verge on sublime. There are only five to choose from (brisket, smoked chicken, slow-roast pork...) with one sole delicious concession to the noncarnivorous: the roast portobello with melted provolone. Get yours with a house pickle, soup of the day or salt-roasted caramel corn. Perfect.

Winnipeg Free Press News Cafe CAFE $
(Map p520; 204-943-0682; www.winnipegfreepress.com/cafe; 237 McDermot Ave; mains $7-12; 8am-6pm Sat-Thu, to 10pm Fri;) This great corner cafe is run by Winnipeg's major daily newspaper, the *Free Press*. Besides great breakfasts (homemade granola) and lunches that include a famous pulled-pork sandwich, there's a definite newsy vibe. Reporters can be spotted doing interviews at some tables, and there is regular programming featuring talks on local issues and performances by neighborhood musicians.

★Deer + Almond FUSION $$
(Map p520; 204-504-8562; www.deerandalmond.com; 85 Princess St; mains $12-25; 11am-3pm & 5-11pm Mon-Sat) At the most innovative restaurant in the Exchange District, with an ever-changing menu, chef Mandel's daring pairing of ingredients marks him as some kind of mad genius. And yet it all comes together: the wild sockeye and cherries, the Cornish hen and maple chutney...The cocktails and beers don't disappoint either, and you shouldn't leave without trying one of the unusual desserts.

Kum-Koon Garden CHINESE $$
(Map p520; 204-943-4655; www.kumkoongarden.com; 257 King St; mains $4-20; 11:30am-10pm) Decent dim sum pushed around on traditional trolleys draws legions of loyal fans to this Chinatown anchor. Service can be as abrupt as the whack of the blade on a duck in the kitchen but you'll barely notice as you navigate the huge menu. Mains are big enough for several people – the reason you see everybody leave with bags of little boxes.

St-Boniface

The charming old neighborhood of St-Boniface has some fine little restaurants, which, not surprisingly, reflect the local French accent and specialise in comfort food. None are more than a 20-minute walk over the river from the city center.

★Marion Street Eatery CANADIAN $
(204-233-2843; www.marionstreeteatery.com; 393 Marion St; mains $12-15; 11am-8pm Mon & Tue, 7am-8pm Wed-Sat, 9am-2pm Sun;) With its industrial-chic decor and plenty of room around the horseshoe bar for solo

diners, this bustling spot is all about eating well. It specialises in comfort food, from apple whiskey pancake stack for breakfast to the chunky extreme BLT and quite possibly the best mac 'n' cheese in Manitoba.

Pasquale's ITALIAN $$
(☎204-231-1403; www.pasqualesrest.com; 109 Marion St; mains $14-29; ⏲11am-10pm Mon-Fri, from 4pm Sat) Classic red-sauce Italian fare keeps this family eatery packed. The mussels and the thin-crust pizza are standouts, although the cannelloni is a quiet contender. Portions are bounteous. When weather allows, head straight to a table on the rooftop patio and bathe in the twinkle of the prairie's stars.

Osborne Village & Corydon Ave

Some of Winnipeg's trendiest restaurants are in Osborne Village, close to the city center; a number double as excellent drinking venues.

All manner of places line the genteel climes of Corydon Ave, which runs through one of Winnipeg's oldest and nicest neighborhoods. Near the middle is a string of cafes that comprise Little Italy, most with terraces perfect for having a cup of strong coffee.

Baked Expectations CAFE $
(☎204-452-5176; www.bakedexpectations.ca; 161 Osborne St; mains $9-19; ⏲11:30am-midnight Sun-Thu, to 1am Fri & Sat;) A delightful cafe specializing in all sorts of decadent baked goodies and light meals.

Sherbrook Street Deli KOSHER $
(☎204-615-3354; www.sherbrookstreetdeli.com; 102 Sherbrook St; mains $6-11; ⏲10am-8pm;) This established kosher deli re-creates a New-York-style deli vibe with Manitoba ingredients and a rock soundtrack. The matzah ball soup is the ultimate comfort food and the sandwiches really shine, from the smoked meat and mustard on rye to lox and cream cheese and pickled herring with sour cream.

★**Segovia** MEDITERRANEAN $$
(☎204-477-6500; www.segoviatapasbar.com; 484 Stradbrook Ave; tapas $5-16; ⏲5-11pm Wed-Mon) Set in a stylishly renovated old home in a quiet spot just off noisy Osborne St, Segovia has a long list of wines and cocktails you can savor on the patio while enjoying – and sharing – tapas such as seared scallops with gremolata and tuna tostadas with chipotle aioli.

Black Rabbit Bistro & Lounge FUSION $$
(☎204-615-1130; www.blackrabbit.menu; 135 Osborne St; mains from $15; ⏲11:30am-2am;) Is it a sports bar? Is it a sophisticated bistro? Black Rabbit takes a decent stab at fulfilling both roles, with a solid list of Canadian beers and wines that span the world, big screens for watching the game, bison tartare, seafood ceviche and other tasty small plates, as well as imaginative thin-crust pizzas.

Sushi Ya SUSHI $$
(☎204-452-3916; 659 Corydon Ave; mains $13-22; ⏲11:30am-10pm Mon-Fri, noon-9pm Sat & Sun;) Typical of the vibrant storefronts along Corydon Ave, this sushi spot packs in locals for its classic rolls and other fare. The fried tofu wins plaudits and there's a taste of Korean, courtesy of the piquant kimchi.

Drinking & Nightlife

The greatest concentration of decent places is found in Osborne Village and the Exchange District. Look for the local Fort Garry and Half Pints microbrews.

★**King's Head Pub** PUB
(Map p520; ☎204-957-7710; www.kingshead.ca; 120 King St; ⏲11am-2am;) Vaguely British, the gregarious sidewalk tables are the place to be in the Exchange District on a balmy evening. Inside, it's all rough and tumble wood and it can get seriously loud (hint: this is not the venue for a romantic date).

Tavern United BAR
(Map p520; ☎204-944-0022; 345 Graham Ave; ⏲noon-late) The rooftop patio is massive, with views across to the MTS Centre. It bustles with a sports-bar vibe and rocks for Jets home games.

Entertainment

After hockey, Winnipeg's impressive arts and cultural scene earns well-deserved applause – not bad for the town that produced Neil Young.

Live Music

★**Times Chang(d)**
High & Lonesome Club LIVE MUSIC
(Map p520; ☎204-957-0982; www.highandlonesomeclub.ca; 234 Main St; ⏲7pm-late) Honky-tonk/country/rock/blues weekend bands jam while beer and whiskey flow at this small, rough, raunchy and real throwback. Don't miss the Sunday-night jam.

JETS FLY HOME

In 1996 the hearts of Winnipeg's hockey fans (basically everybody in town) were broken when the beloved local National Hockey League (NHL) franchise, the Winnipeg Jets, headed south, not just for the winter, but for good. In search of TV revenues, the franchise moved to Phoenix and was renamed the Coyotes.

Meanwhile, fans across Manitoba prayed, begged, hoped and schemed for a new team called the Jets. In 2011, a collective roar was heard around Winnipeg and the province when True North Sports & Entertainment bought the failing Atlanta NHL franchise, the glottal-stop-challenged Thrashers, and moved it to Winnipeg. As operators of the huge arena, MTS Centre, True North had good reason to buy a team guaranteed to sell tickets in hockey-mad Winnipeg. And what was barely a gamble paid off as season tickets for the newly reborn Jets sold out in record time.

Although success on the ice was elusive during the reborn Jets' early seasons, ticket sales are strong and Winnipeg is alive with excitement on any day there's a home game. A fan favorite is the mascot, Mick E Moose, a holdover from the minor-league team the Manitoba Moose, who played in Winnipeg during the Jet-less years. His costume now includes a vintage aviator helmet.

Another tradition, the 'White Out,' in which fans wear all white when the Jets are in the playoffs, will require the Jets to actually make the playoffs.

Windsor Hotel LIVE MUSIC
(Map p520; ☎204-942-7528; 187 Garry St; ⏰7pm-late) The well-worn Windsor is Winnipeg's definitive live blues bar. There's open stage some nights; bands perform at weekends. The local color that hangs out here is either a boon or a bane, depending on what you're into.

Performing Arts

Winnipeg Symphony Orchestra CLASSICAL MUSIC
(Map p520; ☎204-949-3999; www.wso.ca; Centennial Concert Hall, 555 Main St; tickets $20-60; ⏰Sep-May) Classical-music performances, as well as appearances by the likes of Jann Arden and Sheena Easton.

Royal Winnipeg Ballet BALLET
(Map p520; ☎204-956-2792; www.rwb.org; Centennial Concert Hall, 555 Main St) An excellent international reputation means performances at Centennial Concert Hall are popular.

Manitoba Opera OPERA
(Map p520; ☎204-942-7479; www.manitobaopera.mb.ca; Centennial Concert Hall, 555 Main St; tickets $35-115; ⏰Nov-Apr) From classics, such as *The Marriage of Figaro*, to premieres, such as *Massenet Werther*.

Manitoba Theatre Centre THEATER
(Map p520; ☎204-942-6537; www.mtc.mb.ca; 174 Market Ave) This company produces popular shows on the main stage and more-daring works at the MTC Warehouse.

MTC Warehouse THEATER
(Map p520; ☎204-956-1340; www.mtc.mb.ca; 140 Rupert Ave) Cutting-edge drama performances.

Manitoba Theatre for Young People THEATER
(Map p520; ☎204-942-8898; www.mtyp.ca; 2 Forks Market Rd; tickets $20; ⏰Oct-Apr) The much-heralded Manitoba Theatre for Young People uses colorful sets for enthusiastic performances for kids without being too yawn-inducing for adults.

Sports

★**Winnipeg Jets** ICE HOCKEY
(☎204-987-7825; www.nhl.com/jets; MTS Centre, 260 Hargrave St; ⏰Sep-Apr) There's Manitoba mania for the Jets who play at the MTS Centre. The ice-hockey games are raucous and often sold out; ask around for tickets.

MTS Centre STADIUM
(Map p520; ☎204-987-7825; www.mtscentre.ca; 260 Hargrave St) Modern downtown arena that hosts concerts and sports.

Shopping

The Exchange District groans with art galleries and funky stores. Osborne Village and Corydon Ave are excellent places to browse (especially around Lilac St along the latter). Academy Rd has top-end boutiques.

Red River Books BOOKS
(Map p520; ☎943-956-2195; 92 Arthur St; ⊙10am-5pm Sat-Tue, to 7pm Wed-Fri) Literally piles of secondhand books, collectors' comics and more; a treasure trove of literature.

Mountain Equipment Co-Op SPORTS & OUTDOORS
(MEC; Map p520; ☎204-943-4202; www.mec.ca; 303 Portage Ave; ⊙10am-9pm) Canada's favorite outdoor store rents gear for hiking and camping, plus kayaks, snowshoes and more.

Information

Explore Manitoba Centre (Map p520; ☎204-945-3777; 25 Forks Market Rd; ⊙10am-6pm) Provincial information center at the Forks; has plenty of info on Winnipeg and the rest of Manitoba.

Millennium Library (☎204-986-6450; http://wpl.winnipeg.ca/library; 251 Donald St; ⊙10am-9pm Mon-Thu, to 6pm Fri & Sat;) Free wi-fi and internet computers.

Tourisme Riel (☎204-233-8343; www.tourismeriel.com; 219 Blvd Provencher; ⊙9am-5pm) St-Boniface visitor information center that specializes in Francophone attractions.

Getting There & Away

AIR

Winnipeg International Airport (YWG; www.waa.ca; 2000 Wellington Ave) has a flash terminal a convenient 10km west of downtown. It has service to cities across Canada, such as Toronto, Montréal, Calgary and Vancouver, and to major hubs in the US. Regional carriers handle remote destinations, including Churchill.

BUS

Greyhound buses stop at a **terminal** (☎204-949-7777; www.greyhound.ca; 2015 Wellington Ave) at Winnipeg International Airport.

TRAIN

VIA Rail's transcontinental *Canadian* departs **Union Station** (123 Main St) three times weekly in each direction. The painfully slow *Hudson Bay* service to Churchill runs twice a week via Thompson.

Getting Around

Walking is easy and enjoyable from downtown to any of the surrounding neighborhoods. In poor weather, under- and above-ground walkways connect some downtown buildings.

BUS

Winnipeg Transit (☎204-986-5700; www.winnipegtransit.com; adult/child $2.65/2) runs extensive bus routes around the area, most converging on Fort St. Get a transfer and use exact change. Its free *Downtown Spirit* runs three daily routes, connecting the Forks with Portage Ave, the Exchange District and Chinatown.

CAR & MOTORCYCLE

Downtown street parking (free after 6pm) and parking lots are plentiful. Break ins are common at Union Station, so enclosed lots downtown are a better option if you're taking the train.

If transiting Winnipeg by road, the slow Trans-Canada Hwy (Hwy 1) goes right through downtown. You can bypass this on looping Hwy 100, although suburban roads west, east and south of the city are often jammed.

WATER TAXI

See the city from a new perspective on the water bus run by **River Spirit** (Map p520; ☎204-783-6633; www.splashdash.ca; one way/day pass $3.50/20; ⊙noon-9pm Mon-Wed, to 11pm Thu-Sun Jul & Aug) between the Forks, the Legislature Building, Osborne Village, St-Boniface and the Exchange District.

AROUND WINNIPEG

Lower Fort Garry

Huge stone walls on the banks of the Red River bank surround the only stone **fort** (☎204-785-6050; www.parkscanada.ca/garry; 5925 Hwy 9; buildings adult/6-16yr $8/4; ⊙buildings 9.30am-5pm daily May-Sep, grounds open year-round) still intact from the fur-trading days. The walls are surprisingly low, making you wonder how they kept invaders out. It's impeccably restored and reflective of the mid-19th century, with costumed tour guides adding color. The lovely parklike site is 32km northeast of Winnipeg.

Oak Hammock Marsh

Smack in the middle of southern Manitoba's wetlands is **Oak Hammock Marsh** (☎204-467-3300; www.oakhammockmarsh.ca; Rte 200, at Hwy 67; adult/3-17yr $8/6; ⊙10am-4.30pm), home and migratory stopping point for hundreds of thousands of birds and one of the best sanctuaries around. Springtime has diversity and autumn sees up to 400,000 geese. The admission fee is for the visitor center and floating boardwalk only; access to the network of short trails is free. Leave your car keys at reception in exchange for a pair of binoculars.

SPIRIT OF PRAIRIE: LOUIS RIEL

Born in 1844 on the Red River near today's Winnipeg, Louis Riel became a leader of the Métis, like him people of mixed Aboriginal and European backgrounds. He battled for their rights, and helped lead the Red River Rebellion, which gave the Métis political power but led to his exile in the US. Riel eventually returned to Canada; in 1885 he was tried for treason and hanged.

The third Monday of February is a provincial holiday in Riel's honor. You can find numerous Riel legacies in Manitoba and Saskatchewan. Riel House (p519) is his birthplace and the family house where he was taken after his execution, and his grave is at St-Boniface Basilica (p519).

Try to catch a performance of the seasonal play, Trial of Louis Riel (p543), which dramatizes his trial for treason. Meanwhile, Batoche (p556) is the haunting site of his last battle.

LAKE WINNIPEG

The southern end of Canada's fifth-largest lake has been a resort destination since the 1920s. Sandy white beaches, constant sunshine and the ocean-like size of the lake made a visit like 'going to the coast' for all Winnipeggers. It's a tremendously popular summer destination; in winter, when snowy white beaches line the frozen lake, it's virtually deserted. The most appealing of the southern beach towns is Gimli, while nearby Hecla is a living example of 1920s Icelandic heritage.

There is good birding and animal-watching at the Hecla/Grindstone Provincial Park, and decent hiking in **Grand Beach Provincial Park** (☎204-754-2212; Hwy 12), where hundreds of species of birds use the lagoon behind the beach and the nearby dunes reach 12m. It's also one of Manitoba's busiest campgrounds (tent sites $12 to $24, RV sites $16 to $29), meaning it can get loud.

Most land around and between Lake Winnipeg and Lakes Manitoba and Winnipegosis, aka Interlake, is privately owned and cottage rentals are possible. Plenty of small towns and villages are lived in year-round so standard motels and B&Bs can be found everywhere.

Gimli

On the surface it could be another clichéd tourist trap, but beneath the kitsch and tackiness is historic Gimli (Icelandic for 'Home of the Gods'). Settled by around 1000 emigrants from Iceland as part of 'New Iceland' in 1875, this neat little town has retained its fascinating heritage.

The **New Iceland Heritage Museum** (☎204-642-4001; www.nihm.ca; 94 1st Ave; adult/child $7/6; ⏰10am-4pm Jun-Aug) is packed with history and artifacts telling the story of an unlikely people settling an unlikelier part of Canada. Look for the huge **Viking statue** by the lake – a symbol of Gimli's Icelandic heritage.

The general store, **HP Tergesen & Sons** (☎204-642-5958; 82 1st Ave; ⏰10am-6pm Mon-Sat), has been around since 1899 and the building is a hefty slice of local history.

Festivals & Events

Islendingadagurinn CULTURAL
(www.icelandicfestival.com; ⏰early Aug) It's all Iceland during Islendingadagurinn, a provincially popular fest including Islendingadance (Icelanders Dance), Icelandic games, live music (no Björk), Viking battles, fireworks and, of course, an Iceland-themed parade with a lot of blonde people.

Sleeping & Eating

Lakeview Resort HOTEL $$
(☎204-642-8565; www.lakeviewhotels.com; 10 Centre St; r $130-170; P ❄ 📶 ✉) Its balconies catching the lake breeze, this large hotel offers spacious, if impersonal, rooms with satellite TV and coffeemakers. Not likely to make your social media posts, but comfortable and right by the lake.

Autumnwood Motel & RV Resort MOTEL $$
(☎204-642-8565; www.autumnwoodresort.com; 19150 Gimli Park Rd; r $100-160; P ⊖ ❄ 📶) Just outside of town, this motel has 17 standard rooms with polychromatic decor nestled in a quiet location among trees.

Eating & Drinking

Ship and Plough PUB FOOD $$
(204-642-5276; 42 Centre St; mains $13-26; noon-11pm Mon-Thu, to 2am Fri & Sat;) This cozy pub serves the likes of homemade meatloaf, fish-and-chips, ribs and fish tacos to the accompaniment of live music on weekends. There's no drinks list but it serves reliable classic cocktails, as well as beergaritas and a few local brews.

★**Flatland Coffee Roasters** COFFEE
(204-651-0169; 40 Centre St; coffee from $2.50; 7am-5pm) Almost too cool for tiny Gimli, the sign above the cafe states: 'We are the coffee shop.' And they are. Whether you're craving an espresso, latte or frappuccino, they'll do it perfectly, with Ethiopia Worka, Colombia Nodier Anerade or other exotic beans. One for connoisseurs.

Hecla/Grindstone Provincial Park

On an island away from the tacky hustle of Lake Winnipeg's beaches sits a natural oasis featuring Manitoba the way it's meant to be seen. The islands, marshes and forests are full of deer, moose, beavers and bears. Stop at **Grassy Narrows Marsh**, which has bird-watching trails close to the park's entrance leading to shelters and towers perfect for habitat-viewing. The small **interpretative centre** (www.manitobaparks.com; Village Rd, Hecla School; 2-4pm Sat, 11am-3pm Sun Jul & Aug) is inside the Hecla School and provides information for visitors.

Picturesque **Hecla Heritage Historic Village** (Village Rd; driving permit $5) has been a lived-in Icelandic settlement since 1876. You can go on a 1km self-guided tour of the old lakefront buildings, most still in use, and check out the pelicans haunting the fishers on the lakeshore. Ask at Hecla School about the Hecla Island Heritage Home Museum – a re-created 1920s Icelandic home.

Apart from Hecla Village itself, there are various hiking trails around Hecla Island. Hecla/Grindstone Provincial Park Interpretative Centre has the details. There is a driving permit charge for entering Hecla Island.

Solmundson Gesta Hus Bed & Breakfast (204-279-2088; www.hecla.ca; Village Rd; r $95-110;) is a beautiful historic home with a hot tub surrounded by manicured gardens. It is found along the lakeshore, just north of the church.

SOUTHEASTERN MANITOBA

Heading east from Winnipeg, the flat expanse typical of the prairies blends with forests and lakes typical of the Great Lakes region. While most visitors speed through toward Kenora and beyond, the eastern region of Manitoba has the same rugged woodland terrain as neighboring Ontario.

Whiteshell Provincial Park

Foreshadowing the green forests, clear lakes and Canadian Shield of northern Ontario, pine-covered hills erupt from the plains immediately inside this **park** (www.manitobaparks.com).

The park is fairly commercialized; resorts and stores are found every few kilometers and larger centers have park offices. However, there is still a sense of spirituality and you can get away via hiking trails of varying lengths – the longest being the six-day, 60km Mantario – and canoe routes, the most popular being the tunnels of **Caddy Lake**.

There are hundreds of campsites throughout the park. The large, well-equipped and tree-lined **Falcon Lakeshore Campground** (204-948-3333; www.gov.mb.ca; tent sites $12-24, RV sites $16-29) is only a short walk from the lake's beaches. **Big Whiteshell Lodge** (204-348-7623; www.bigwhiteshelllodge.com; Hwy 309; cottages $175-250) has deluxe cottages for two to six people each in a quiet, woodsy location on the shores of Big Whiteshell Lake at the end of Rte 309.

WESTERN MANITOBA

Between Winnipeg and Saskatchewan, Manitoba is a seemingly endless sea of agriculture until you decide to make a few detours here and there to often-overlooked natural delights, such as unexpected sand dunes, and the atmospheric early 20th-century train elevators found in Inglis and along Hwy 16.

The dense woodland and lakes of Riding Mountain National Park make it an ideal summer destination for hiking, biking and canoeing, and there are bison to be spotted, too.

Brandon

POP 46,061

Manitoba's second-largest center is an attractive residential city with a historic downtown bisected by the Assiniboine River.

Start your riverside walks from the **Riverbank Discovery Centre** (204-729-2141; www.brandontourism.com; 545 Conservation Dr; 8:30am-8pm), which is also a good source of visitor information.

The **Royal Canadian Artillery Museum** (204-765-3000; www.rcamuseum.com; Hwy 340, Shilo; adult/student $6/4; 10am-5pm) is worth seeking out to the east of Brandon for its weaponry displays through the centuries.

Though it won't win any architectural awards, **Redwood Motor Inn** (204-813-6998; www.redwoodmotorinn.ca; 345 18th St N; d $72; P ❄) is clean, comfortable and good value, and rooms come with flat-screen TV and private bath. Ideal for breaking up long road trips.

Toward the west end of Brandon, **Chilli Chutney** (204-573-9310; www.thechillichutney.ca; 555 34th St; mains $12-15; 11:30am-9pm Mon-Fri, noon-10pm Sat, 4:30-9:30pm Sun; P ❄) is an unpretentious restaurant that makes up in authentic East Indian flavours what it lacks in atmosphere. The Goan prawn curry is a wonderful balance of flavours with kick, the naan bread is perfect and the buffet (lunch/dinner $14/17) is excellent value.

Brandon is 214km west of Winnipeg along the Trans-Canada Hwy. One **Greyhound** (204-727-0643; 141 6th St) bus passes through daily in each direction from Winnipeg to Regina.

Riding Mountain National Park

Rising like a vision above the plains, **Riding Mountain National Park** (204-848-7275; www.parkscanada.ca/riding; adult/child $8/4) is more than 3000 sq km of boreal forest, deep valleys, lofty hills and alpine lakes. It rewards those with an hour or a week. The unpaved Rte 354 runs west from Onandole (30 minutes) to the **Bison Enclosure**, where you can spot these giants from the road or lookout point. Elsewhere, you might even see a bear or a moose.

Most of the park is wilderness; **Wasagaming**, on the south shore of eponymously named Clear Lake, is almost a cliché in its perfection as a little summer town.

Activities

Hwy 10 cuts a 53km course down the middle of the park, with numerous walking, cycling and horseback-riding trails branching off. Hikes range from the 1km-long Lakeshore Trail to a 17km trek through forest and meadows to a cabin used by naturalist Grey Owl.

FLOWERS OF THE PRAIRIE: SMALL-TOWN MANITOBA

Manitoba's welter of rural roads is ideal for random explorations. Many lead to small towns that make the journey worthwhile. Here are a few of our favorites:

Carman Gorgeous river setting an hour southwest of Winnipeg with a 5km walking trail.

Minnedosa Perfect little Main St with Dairy Isle ice-cream stand and a bowling alley.

Morden Southern town with brick buildings, a grain elevator, the Canadian Fossil Discovery Centre and the Manitoba Baseball Hall of Fame; enough said.

Neepawa Tree-lined streets and old houses mean this town is often voted Manitoba's prettiest. Look for U-pick berry farms here.

Norway House A large Cree community steeped in history on Lake Winnipeg's isolated northern shore.

Snow Lake Fun little town on the shores of Snow Lake, just north of Hwy 10, with mining museum and roadside bear crap.

Stonewall Hanging baskets, peaceful atmosphere and limestone-quarry swimming hole, an hour north of Winnipeg.

Victoria Beach Greenest village ever. Cottage-centric with limited vehicle access (walk or bike) and Lake Winnipeg's sandiest beaches, located on the eastern shore.

Stand-up paddleboarding and kayaking are excellent and offer shoreline glimpses of wildlife. Rentals are available from **Clear Lake Marina** (204-848-1770; www.theclearlakemarina.com; Wasagaming Pier; per hour from $19; May-Sep).

Elkhorn Riding Adventures (204-848-4583; www.elkhornresort.mb.ca; trail rides from $45) beside Elkhorn Resort offers a chance to honor the park's name atop a horse.

Sleeping & Eating

Backcountry camping is possible; check with the visitor center. Motels and cabins are plentiful in Wasagaming; some open year-round.

There are 600 campgrounds in the park: Wasagaming Campground is the most popular; Lake Audy has abundant wildlife; and Whirlpool Lake has lakeside walk-in sites within thick forest a 50m hike from the parking lot.

Idylwylde Cabins LODGE $$
(204-848-2383; www.idylwylde.ca; 136 Wasagaming Dr, Wasagaming; cabins $105-245;) These cute, self-contained cabins range from compact and rustic to lavish and Jacuzzi-endowed.

Elkhorn Resort LODGE $$
(204-848-2802; www.elkhornresort.mb.ca; Mooswa Dr W, Wasagaming; r $144-259;) For wood-shingled private cabins, motel-style rooms, activity-filled grounds and an excellent steak restaurant, Elkhorn Resort fits the bill.

Whitehouse Bakery BAKERY $
(204-848-7700; www.whitehousebakeryclearlake.ca; 104 Buffalo Dr, Wasagaming; snacks from $3; 8am-4pm May-Sep) From sticky cinnamon buns to wraps, panini and salads, this is the place to stock up on picnic supplies.

Information

Visitor Center (204-848-7275; Wasagaming Rd; 9:30am-8pm Jul & Aug, to 5pm May, Jun, Sep & Oct) This beautiful 1930s visitor center contains impressive dioramas, the invaluable *Visitor Guide* and backcountry permits.

NORTHERN MANITOBA

'North of 53' (the 53rd parallel), convenience takes a backseat to rugged beauty as lake-filled timberland dissolves into the treeless tundra of the far north. The ample wildlife around Churchill is justifiably the big draw and reason enough for the journey north, with Thompson now playing 'Wolf Capital' to Churchill's 'Polar Bear Capital.' Around 80km southwest of Thompson along Hwy 6, **Pisew Falls Provincial Park** (www.manitobaparks.ca; Hwy 6) is a great place to stop and get drenched by the spray from the waterfall that roars through a gorge.

The Pas

A traditional meeting place of Aboriginal and European fur traders, the Pas (pronounced 'pah') is a useful stop for services on northern trips.

GRAIN ELEVATORS

Barn-red, brilliant white, midnight-black or tractor-green; striking yet simple; function and form: characterizing prairie landscapes like the wheat they hold, grain elevators were once flagships of prairie architecture.

Introduced in 1880, more than 7000 of the vertical wooden warehouses lined Canadian train tracks by 1930. Their importance was invaluable, as the prairies became 'the breadbasket of the world', and they were built next to the railway lines, which revolutionized the loading and sorting of grain. Also, their stoic simplicity inspired Canadian painters, photographers and writers who gave them life.

Today's concrete replacements are as generic as their fast-food-chain neighbors. For a glimpse of the vanishing past, make the detour to **Inglis Grain Elevators National Historic Site** (204-821-6131, 204-563-2412; www.ingliselevators.com; 10am-6pm Mon-Sat, noon-6pm Sun Jun-Aug) FREE. A stunning row of five elevators is in the process of being restored to its original splendor. Inside the creaky interior of the Paterson elevator, exhibits capture the thin lives where success or failure rested with the whims of commodity brokers.

Inglis is 20km north of the Yellowhead Hwy (Hwy 16) near the Saskatchewan border.

Clearwater Lake Provincial Park (☎20 4-624-5525; www.gov.mb.ca), near the airport, is a pelican haven and there's a picturesque walking trail.

The **Northern Manitoba Trappers' Festival** (☎204-623-2912; www.trappersfestival.com; ⊙mid-Feb) celebrates local heritage in raucous winter celebrations.

Motels are strung out along Hwy 10. **Andersen Inn & Suites** (☎204-623-1888; www.andersoninn.com; 1717 Gordon Ave; r $129; P 🛜 ≋ 🐾) may not make your social-media posts and soundproofing between rooms could be improved, but it's clean, comfortable and comes with a pool. With a trapper's-cabin ambience, **Miss the Pass** (☎204-623-3130; 158 Edwards St; mains from $8; ⊙7am-7pm Mon-Sat) has the kind of tasty, hearty fare that will ready you for adventure.

The Pas is 140km from Flin Flon and 392km from Thompson.

VIA Rail's sluggish train stops at the **train station** (380 Hazelwood Ave) on its way south to Winnipeg and north to Churchill via Thompson.

Thompson

Carved out of the boreal forest by mining interests in the 1950s, Thompson is a rather charmless town that travelers pass through en route to Churchill. Charmless, that is, except for two exceptions. Its relatively new fame as 'Wolf Capital of the World' and a **Boreal Discovery Centre** (www.borealdiscoverycentre.org) that allows visitors to learn all about this predator, common in the wilderness around town, as well as other denizens of the boreal forest. A newly designed **Spirit Way** (www.thompsonspiritway.ca) connects the town's important landmarks, from the **Heritage North Museum** (☎204-677-2216; www.heritagenorthmuseum.ca; 162 Princeton Dr; ⊙9am-5pm Mon-Fri) FREE to the immense wolf mural, **wolf statues** (www.thompsonspiritway.ca) and the Norseman floatplane.

McCreedy Campground (☎204-778-8810; 114 Manasan Dr; tent & RV sites from $22; ⊙May-Sep) is set up for RVs and has a few campsites in the trees; it's just north of the river. Centrally located, **Lakeview Inn & Suites** (☎20 4-778-8879; www.lakeviewhotels.com; 70 Thompson Dr N; r $125-135; P ❄ 🛜) has motel-style rooms with bathtubs. Staff are helpful and happy to offer early check-ins to travellers who've just rolled off the bus/train.

Attached to Burntwood Inn, **Holy Spice** (☎204-939-3435; 146 Selkirk Ave; mains from $11, lunch buffet $14; ⊙6am-9pm; 🌶) is a casual stop for Canadian breakfasts and reasonably authentic Indian food, including a plethora of vegetarian dishes. If you like it spicy, be quite emphatic in letting the staff know. The lunchtime buffet and the *thalis* are excellent value. Confusingly, the sign still says 'Grapes.'

Calm Air (p515) flies throughout Manitoba including Winnipeg and Churchill to/from **Thompson Airport** (YTH; ☎204-778-5212; www.thompsonairport.ca), 10km north of town.

From the **bus station** (☎204-677-0360; 81 Berens Rd), one overnight Greyhound bus runs to/from Winnipeg ($108, nine hours). Other Hwy 6 destinations use the bus station near the tourist information center within Heritage North Museum.

Thompson is the end of paved roads; the lethargic VIA Rail train runs north to Churchill (5pm Monday, Wednesday and Friday, 16 hours) and south to Winnipeg (2pm Wednesday, Friday, Sunday, 45 hours) via the Pas (the Wednesday train terminates at the Pas). The **train station** (☎204-677-2241; 1310 Station Rd), in an industrial area 1km from town, is not a safe spot to leave your vehicle. McReedy Campground offers vehicle storage and shuttles to the train (per night/week $8/40).

Churchill

POP 820

The 'Polar Bear Capital of the World,' Churchill lures people to the shores of Hudson Bay for its majestic predators, beluga whales, a huge old stone fort and endless subarctic majesty. But while the highly accessible wildlife is enough for Churchill to be on any itinerary, there's something less tangible that makes people stay longer and keeps them coming back: a hearty seductive spirit that makes the rest of the world seem – thankfully – even further away than it really is.

Prime times to visit are July and August and then again during the peak polar-bear-viewing period of mid-October to November. At other times Churchill is often frozen and desolate, which has its own appeal.

History

Permafrost springs upwards about 2.5cm per millennia, chronicling old shorelines and leaving nearby evidence of aboriginal settlements up to 3000 years old. In European exploration, Churchill is one of the oldest places in Canada. The first outpost of HBC (said to stand for 'Here Before Christ') was built here in 1717. It was a stop in attempts to find the fabled Northwest Passage by explorers such as Samuel Hearne and Lord Churchill, former HBC governor and the town's namesake.

Churchill's strategic location ensured a military presence over centuries. The railway's arrival and opening of the huge port in 1929 have made the town a vital international grain-shipping point for the prairie provinces.

Sights

The town itself is an assemblage of tattered Northern structures. Wander the streets, stop and peruse the beach (!) and its *inukshuk* (Inuit stone monument), visit the excellent museum, and then get out onto the land and water for nature at its most magnificent.

★Itsanitaq Museum MUSEUM

(Eskimo Museum; ☎204-675-2030; 242 La Verendrye Ave; by donation; ⏲1-5pm Mon, 9am-noon & 1-5pm Tue-Sat) This one-room museum showcases an exceptional collection of Inuit carvings made of whalebone, soapstone and caribou antler, as well as millenia-old harpoon heads and bone carvings of shamans and bears left over from the pre-Inuit Thule and Dorset cultures of the Igloolik region. The place really sucks you in and you can spend hours here.

★Cape Merry HISTORIC SITE

A lone cannon behind a crumbling wall is all that's left of the battery built at Cape Merry, 2km northwest of town. It's an incredibly beautiful location in its own right and, during summer, belugas can be seen from the shore. It's included in cultural tours of Churchill.

Fort Prince of Wales National Historic Site HISTORIC SITE

It took 40 years to build, its cannons were never used, but the star-shaped, stone Fort Prince of Wales has been standing prominently on rocky Eskimo Point across the Churchill River since the 1770s. As English-French tensions mounted in the 1720s, HBC selected the site for presence and strategy, but surrendered during the first French attack in 1782, making it an Anglo-Maginot Line forerunner. It's a lonely, buggy place, with a real sense that duty here was best avoided.

The fort is one of three sites in the area documenting Churchill's varied history, administered by **Parks Canada** (☎204-675-8863; ⏲8am-noon & 1-4pm Mon-Fri). Transportation to the sites across the water is handled by licensed tour operators and the entry fee is included in tour costs.

Four kilometers south of the fort, **Sloop's Cove** was a harbor for European vessels during Churchill's harsh winters. The only indications of early explorers are simple yet profound: names such as Samuel Hearne, local 18th-century governor and first to make an overland trip to the Arctic Ocean, are carved into the seaside rocks.

Wapusk National Park PARK

(☎204-675-8863; www.parkscanada.ca/wapusk) Established primarily to protect polar bear maternity denning sites (*wapusk* is Cree for 'white bear') and critical habitats for waterfowl and shore birds, this remote park extends along Hudson Bay's shores 45km southeast of Churchill. Its location between boreal forests and Arctic tundra gives it importance for monitoring the effects of climate change. Visits center on polar bears and are only possible through licensed operators.

York Factory National Historic Site HISTORIC SITE

(www.parkscanada.ca/yorkfactory; ⏲Jun-Sep) Around 250km southeast of Churchill and impossibly remote, this HBC trading post, near Hayes River, was an important gateway to the interior and active for 273 years until 1957. The stark-white buildings are an amazing sight contrasting with their barren setting. It's accessible only by air or boat.

POLAR BEAR JAIL

Located in a former aircraft hangar near the airport, this secure facility serves as holding center for problem polar bears who repeatedly turn up in Churchill and pose a danger to its residents. With the exception of family groups, bears are held for at least 30 days before being released. Repeat offenders may be relocated by helicopter.

Miss Piggy LANDMARK

Out toward the airport lies the wreck of a Curtiss C-46 freight plane that crashed here in 1979 after developing engine trouble, but without a single fatality. It's called Miss Piggy because freight planes were typically overloaded (and it once carried a cargo of pigs).

Fort Churchill HISTORIC SITE

Amid the undulating rocks, late-season ice and scraggy trees looms a Cold War relic. Spotted long before you complete the 20km drive east from the airport, Fort Churchill was Canada's Cape Kennedy. Starting in 1954, over 3500 small rockets were launched from here on military and scientific missions.

Courses

Churchill Northern Studies Centre WILDLIFE WATCHING

(CNSC; ☎204-675-2307; www.churchillscience.ca; Launch Rd; courses from $1425) Located at Fort Churchill 23km east of town, CNSC is an active base for researchers. Learning vacations feature all-inclusive (dorms, meals and local transportation) multiday courses with scientists working on projects involving belugas, wildflowers, birds and polar bears. There are also courses in winter survival, northern lights and astronomy.

Tours

Independent exploration is not encouraged in Churchill, not just for reasons of safety but primarily due to expertise. Local guides have a wealth of knowledge that guide you to wildlife and provide vital context for exploring the area.

Polar-Bear Tours

Polar bears overshadow Churchill's other draws. In summer you may see them as part of other tours on land and even swimming in the river and Hudson Bay. Later in the year, however, is the main event. Special lightweight vehicles riding high on huge tires to protect the tundra venture out on day trips (about $400 per person). Heated cabins and open-air porches allow you to get good views of the marauding bears.

★Lazy Bear Lodge WILDLIFE

(☎204-663-9377; www.lazybearlodge.com; 2-night summer tour from $420) Has live-aboard tundra coaches and also runs multiday beluga- and polar-bear-spotting adventures in the summer, based out of its lodge. Excellent day outings include kayaking and snorkeling with belugas, tundra vehicle ventures, full-day whale-watching boat tours on Hudson Bay, and cultural tours of Churchill and its environs.

Great White Bear Tours WILDLIFE

(☎204-487-7633; www.greatwhitebeartours.com; 266 Kelsey Blvd; per day from $473) Uses tundra coaches but only operates day tours; guests sleep in town. Daily outings in October and November; occasional outings in summer.

Tundra Buggy Adventure WILDLIFE

(☎204-949-2050; www.tundrabuggy.com; 124 Kelsey Blvd; tours $189-469; ⏲Jun-Nov & Feb-Mar) The pioneers of tundra-buggy polar-bear-viewing run six-hour tundra tours in summer and all-day tours in search of polar bears and other tundra wildlife in October and November. In February and March the tundra buggies are used for aurora-viewing.

CHURCHILL'S FIVE SEASONS

In climatological terms, Churchill has three seasons: July, August and winter. For visitors, it has five: bird, wildflower, beluga whale, polar bear and northern lights.

Bird (peak season: mid-May to September) Two hundred-plus species use Churchill as nesting grounds, including rare Ross's gulls, or as a stopover on their way further north. Granary Ponds by the port, Cape Merry or Bird Cove are good viewing spots.

Wildflower (June to August) As the ice melts and the sun hits the soil for the first time in months, Churchill explodes in colors and aromas.

Beluga whale (mid-June to August) Curious as dolphins and as voluble as the label 'sea canaries' implies, about 3000 of these glossy white, 4m-long creatures summer in Churchill River. Go snorkeling (from early July), kayaking or view them from a boat.

Polar bear (September to early November) Peak season is late October to late November, but sightings can begin in July.

Northern lights (October to March) The aqua-turquoise-yellow dance of the aurora borealis is nothing short of spectacular.

Land & Sea Tours

Several outfits offer land tours of the area in summer. These typically take in Cape Merry, Churchill Northern Studies Centre (CNSC) and the disused missile site, plus novelties such as a crashed plane and a grounded ship. The cost averages $85 for several hours and you may well see a bear or two.

Sea tours typically center around whale-watching, snorkelling with belugas and kayaking with belugas. Those concerned with the welfare of whales should be aware that swimming with whales in the wild is considered by some to be disruptive to the habitat and behaviour of the animals.

There are dogsledding outings available in summer and winter, as well as scenic flights.

★Sea North Tours ADVENTURE
(☎204-675-2195; www.seanorthtours.com; 39 Franklin St; tours from $105; ⊙Jul & Aug) Summer beluga-whale tours use a custom viewing boat and Zodiac inflatables; visits to Fort Prince of Wales are often included. Floe-ice tours in early June are terrific bird-watching opportunities, while snorkeling with the curious belugas in July is another available tour option. Kayaking and stand-up paddleboarding excursions also run in July.

★Nature 1st WALKING
(☎204-675-2147; www.nature1sttours.ca; tours from $95; ⊙Jun-Aug) Hiking, trekking and birding are combined in half- and full-day nature tours that explore the four distinct ecosystems around Churchill.

Blue Sky Mushing DOGSLEDDING
(www.blueskymush.com; per person $95) Entertaining, safety-conscious dogsledding in winter and dog-carting in summer around a forested loop. Outings end with a slide show and freshly baked bannock.

Wapusk Adventures DOGSLEDDING
(☎204-675-2887; www.wapuskadventures.com; per person $95) Métis dog whisperer Dave lets you meet his exuberant huskies, explains the workings of a dog team, and takes you for a ride in a dogsled or dog-cart along the 'Iditamile' loop track in the forest.

Churchill Wild ADVENTURE
(☎204-377-5090; www.churchillwild.com; multiday tours from $9295; ⊙Jul-Oct) This outfit has remote lodges you reach from Churchill by floatplane and boat. The highlight is its safaris that get close to bears, and the remote location, ideal for uninterrupted viewing of the northern lights.

Sleeping

Rates rise dramatically in polar-bear season when demand is high and people book up to a year in advance. There's a good selection of motel-style hotels, a lodge, several guesthouses/B&Bs and a couple of cheapies. All places are walkable and central. Camping is generally not possible as there are rules against feeding yourself to the bears. Most places close between December and June.

★Blue Sky Bed & Sled B&B $$
(☎204-675-2001; www.blueskymush.com; 100 Button St; r $120, 3-night package for 2 with dogsled ride $400;) Right on the edge of the tundra, Churchill's loveliest B&B is run by Gerald, who takes his guests husky-sledding, and his indefatigable wife, Jenifar, who cooks up the best breakfast in town and whose cookies are the stuff of local legend. The four snug rooms are decorated with northern-themed prints, fold-out beds accommodate kids and there are friendly huskies underfoot.

Polar Bear B&B B&B $$
(☎204-675-2819; http://polarbearbandb.web.fc2.com; 26 Hearne St; s/d $55/110; ⊙closed Dec-Apr;) A much-needed addition to Churchill's accommodations scene, this is the closest the town has to a hostel. The three rooms (for up to four people each) are a cheery yellow with polar-bear-patterned bedding, there are free bicycles for guests and the helpful owner can arrange ultralight flights. Lack of bug netting on the windows is an issue in summer.

Polar Inn & Suites MOTEL $$
(☎204-675-8878; www.polarinn.com; 153 Kelsey Blvd; s/d from $145/165, bear season s & d from $200;) Basic motel-style units come with fridges inside an appealing log-cabin setting. There are also studios with small kitchens and full apartments, which tend to get booked up first. Owned by Sea North and popular with tour groups.

★Lazy Bear Lodge LODGE $$$
(☎866-687-2327; www.lazybearlodge.com; 313 Kelsey Blvd; s/d $200/240;) Making great use of a natural disaster, Churchill's coziest lodge is built entirely of reclaimed forest-fire-singed tree trunks. The common spaces are welcoming, particularly the dining room with its massive stone fireplace. The rooms are compact and wood-panelled, the bathrooms come with tubs, and the service is friendly and helpful. Group packages take precedence, but independent travelers welcomed.

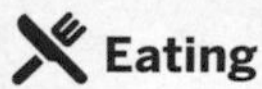

Eating

Look out for wild items on menus, such as elk and bison. Seek out Arctic char, a delicious local fish that is like a cross between salmon and trout. Out of a half-dozen places to eat in town, three restaurants are particularly good.

★ Lazy Bear Cafe CANADIAN $$
(☎204-675-2969; www.lazybearlodge.com; 313 Kelsey Blvd; mains $18-25; ⏰7am-9pm; 📶✏) Serving elk, Arctic char and bison, augmented with local berries and mushrooms, this restaurant acquaints you with the best of Manitoba's wild ingredients. Creative vegetarian specials make a daily appearance and this is the only place in town with an espresso machine (and coffee drinks named after staff).

★ Gypsy's Bakery CANADIAN $$
(☎204-675-2322; 253 Kelsey Blvd; mains $8-30; ⏰7am-9pm; 📶) One of the best places to eat in Churchill. Luscious baked goods await in display cases and you can order from a full cafeteria-style menu. The breakfasts, sandwiches, gyros with Greek salad and pasta dishes are tops. Departing by train? Load up on take-out vittles here in lieu of the VIA Rail offerings.

Tundra Inn Lounge CANADIAN $$
(☎204-675-8831; 32 Franklin St; mains $15-25; ⏰4pm-late Tue-Sat; 📶✏) Combining innovative dishes with the town's most popular watering hole, this place is onto a winner here. The wild rice/bean/vegetable Borealis Burger and vegetable curry are veggie-pleasers, while more carnivorous diners can tuck into elk meatloaf, ribs and wings.

Shopping

Arctic Trading Company ARTS & CRAFTS
(☎204-675-8804; www.arctictradingco.com; 141 Kelsey Blvd; ⏰10am-6pm Mon-Sat, 2-4pm Sun) Has locally made antler carvings, Inuit stone sculpture, clothing, psychedelic paintings by a local artist, bone jewelry, and plenty of beaded moccasins and mukluks.

Information

In summer, it's war with the swarms of mosquitoes and black flies. Pack bug repellent with *at least* 30% DEET. Always have warm clothing handy as it can get cold fast in summer. Heed all polar-bear warnings.

Both www.churchill.ca and www.everythingchurchill.com are particularly useful websites.

Chamber of Commerce (☎204-675-2022; 211 Kelsey Blvd; ⏰11am-3pm Mon-Sat Jul-Nov) Near the train station.

Parks Canada (p532) An essential first stop, but opening hours are variable.

Royal Bank (☎204-675-8894; La Verendrye Ave) One of several local ATMs.

Getting There & Away

There is no road to Churchill; access is by plane or train only. A popular option is exploring Manitoba to Thompson and then catching a train or plane from there.

AIR

Calm Air (p515) serves Thompson and Winnipeg, as well as Nunavut destinations north of Churchill. Airfares can feel like the bite of a polar bear: a return fare from Winnipeg averages $1400, Thompson $660. On a few days each month the airline offers some seats slightly cheaper, while on many days the seats cost much more.

TRAIN

Via Rail's **Churchill train** is slow. It runs to Winnipeg (seat/berth/private cabin $220/573/979, 45½ hours) at 7:30pm on Thursdays and Saturdays via Thompson (seat/berth/private cabin $70/284/483, 15½ hours) and the Pas (seat/berth/private cabin $120/415/711, 28 hours); Tuesday departures terminate at the Pas. That said, there is a mesmerizing quality to the journey, as you fall asleep amid boreal forest and wake up to an endless vista of muskeg and stunted trees, or vice versa. You could take the train up and fly back.

Getting Around

Churchill Airport (YYQ; ☎204-675-8868) is 11km east of town. Arrange airport drop-off/pickup with your lodging, otherwise you'll need to call a **taxi** (☎204-675-2517). Airport to town costs $25.

Most locals walk or cycle around the compact town but you should be bear aware. **Polar Inn** (☎204-675-8878; 15 Franklin St; per day $20) and **Polar Bear B&B** rent bicycles for $20 a day. **Tamarack Rentals** (☎204-675-2192; www.tamarackrentals.ca; 299 Kelsey Blvd; ⏰8:30am-5pm) rents battered pickup trucks and SUVs, and can meet you at the airport. Prices are $75 to $150 per day.

Saskatchewan

Includes ➡

Best Places to Eat

➡ Truffles Bistro (p554)

➡ Ayden Kitchen and Bar (p554)

➡ Flip Eatery & Drink (p542)

➡ Willow on Wascana (p542)

➡ Blue Bird Cafe (p549)

Best Places to Sleep

➡ James (p553)

➡ Delta Bessborough (p553)

➡ Hotel Saskatchewan (p541)

➡ Sturgeon River Ranch (p557)

Why Go?

To paraphrase an old line, there are no boring parts of Saskatchewan, just boring visitors. Yes, the terrain lacks drama, there's not a lot of people here, the two major towns define the vaguely complimentary 'nice,' and so on. But that simply means that the savvy visitor can dig deep to discover the province's inherent appeal.

Start with all that flat: those rippling oceans of grain have a mesmerizing poetry to their movement, the songbirds and crickets providing accents to the endlessly rustling wind. If you're ready for the sheer tranquility of solitude, pick any unpaved road and set off across the country – and delight when you find water-dappled coulees and tree-covered hills.

And don't forget the province's people. Not just the plain-spoken residents of today, but also the people who populate Saskatchewan's story, whether eking out a living off the land, fomenting revolution or taming a frontier.

When to Go

Saskatoon

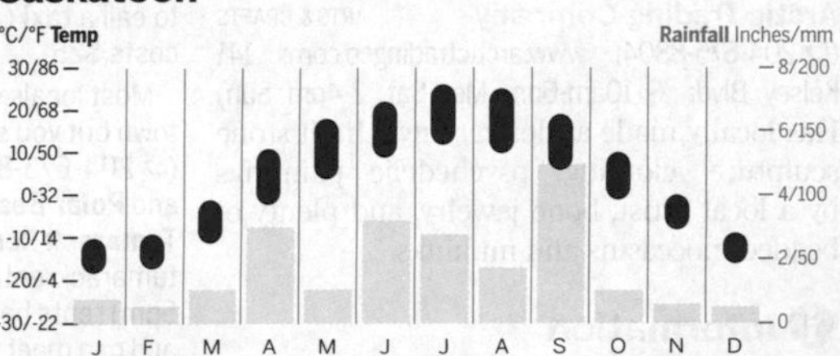

May Spring wildflowers paint the landscape and birdsong fills the air as life, post-winter, returns.

Jun–Aug Long sunny days draw happy locals to lakes, parks and patios.

Sep Crisp air, endless skies and dramatic fall colors herald the year's final harvests.

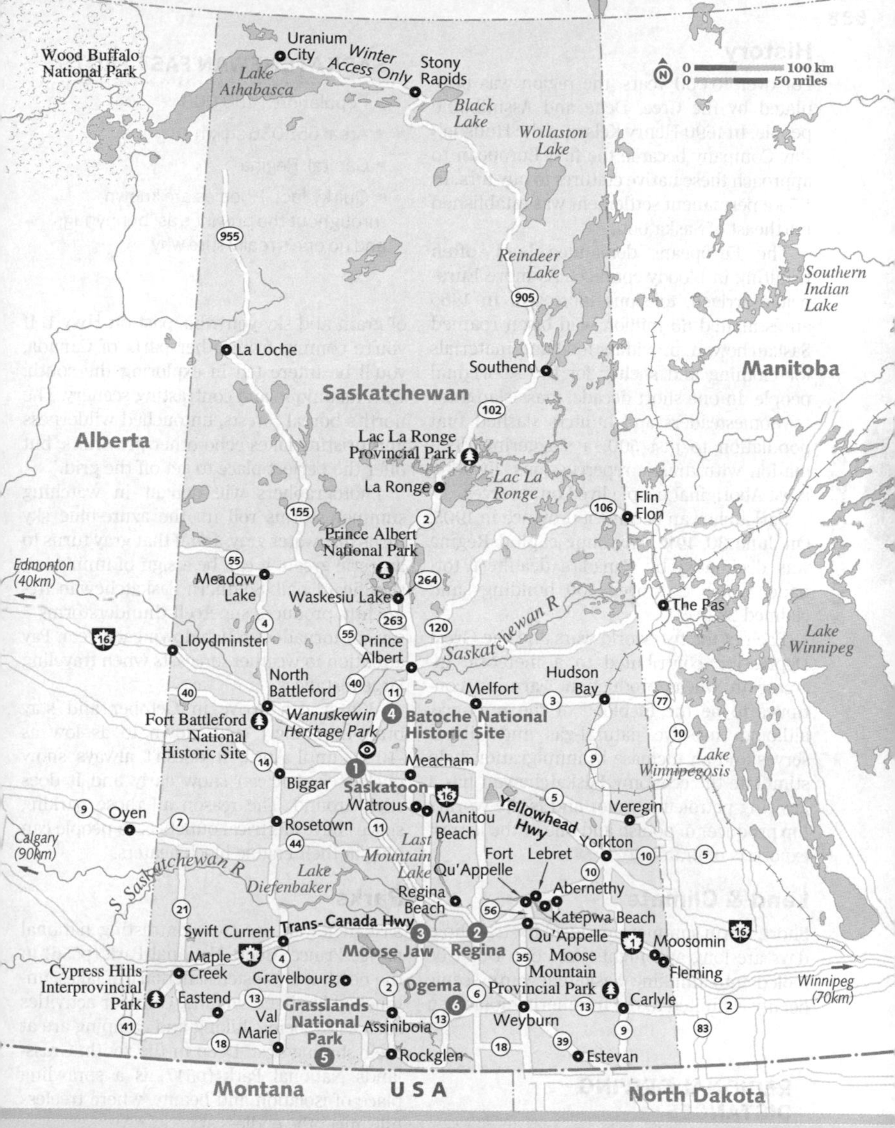

Saskatchewan Highlights

1. **Saskatoon** (p550) Enjoying the urban pleasures – especially the food and drink – of the Paris of the Prairies.

2. **Regina** Donning a watermelon hat at a Roughriders game (p543) with some of Canadian football's most ardent fans.

3. **Moose Jaw** (p544) Digging deep to experience the town's underground past from the days of Al Capone.

4. **Batoche National Historic Site** (p556) Remembering the Métis revolutionaries in the place where Louis Riel almost changed the course of Canadian history.

5. **Grasslands National Park** (p547) Hearing the rustling of the long grass and the thunder of the bison (if you can find them).

6. **Ogema** (p545) Stepping back in time aboard the Southern Prairie Railway and in the one-of-a-kind Deep South Pioneer Museum.

History

For over 10,000 years, the region was populated by the Cree, Dene and Assiniboine people. In 1690 Henry Kelsey of the Hudson's Bay Company became the first European to approach these native cultures to buy furs. In 1774 a permanent settlement was established northeast of Saskatoon.

The Europeans demanded land, often resulting in bloody conflicts. As more Europeans arrived, tensions increased. In 1865 an estimated 60 million wild bison roamed Saskatchewan, providing food and materials for clothing and shelter for the Aboriginal people. In one short decade, mass slaughter by homesteaders and hunters slashed that population to just 500: a staggering decimation with drastic repercussions. By 1890 most Aboriginal people lived on reserves.

Saskatchewan became a province in 1905. On June 30, 1912, its young capital Regina was decimated by Canada's deadliest tornado, which destroyed 500 buildings and claimed 28 lives.

Each of the two world wars and the Great Depression contributed to a meteoric increase in wheat production. Farming continues to be the lifeblood of the province, although massive natural-gas and oil reserves and an increase in immigration help stimulate the economy. Saskatchewan has a growing petroleum sector and is the world's top producer of potash and one of the largest exporters of uranium.

SASKATCHEWAN FAST FACTS

- Population: 1,130,000
- Area: 651,036 sq km
- Capital: Regina
- Quirky fact: Hoodies are known throughout the province as 'bunnyhugs' and no one's really sure why.

Land & Climate

Short, warm summers are ideal for traveling: days are long and nights are cool. Don't be fooled into thinking Saskatchewan's scenic beauty is limited to the mesmerizing tableau of grain and sky you whiz past on Hwy 1. If you're coming from other parts of Canada, you'll be interested in exploring the south, with its unique and contrasting scenery. The north's boreal forests, untouched wilderness and pristine lakes echo other provinces, but offer the perfect place to get off the grid.

Photographers will delight in watching summer storms roll in: the azure-blue sky turns dishwater gray, and if that gray turns to an eerie green, it can be a sign of imminent, significant hail. Southern Saskatchewan frequently produces supercell thunderstorms – several tornadoes touch down each year. Pay attention to weather forecasts when traveling large distances.

Winter can arrive in October and stay brain-numbingly cold (down to as low as -40°C) until April; it doesn't always snow buckets, but it can snow early and it does stick around. The reason all those parking spaces have electrical outlets is so people can plug in their engine-block heaters.

REGIONAL DRIVING DISTANCES

Saskatoon to Prince Albert National Park 230km

Saskatoon to Regina 260km

Regina to Cypress Hills Interprovincial Park 415km

Cypress Hills to Grasslands National Park 225km

Parks

Saskatchewan has two contrasting national parks. Prince Albert National Park (p556) in the north is a forested sanctuary of lakes, untouched land and wildlife. Outdoor activities such as canoeing, hiking and camping are at their shining best. Deep in the south, Grasslands National Park (p547) is a sprawling place of isolation and beauty, where treeless hills meet the endless sky.

There are also numerous provincial parks. Cypress Hills Interprovincial Park (p547), jointly managed with Alberta, has spectacular vistas, abundant wildlife and a unique microclimate.

Camping is available in most parks, and some have backcountry sites. Go to www.saskparks.net for information and bookings.

Getting There & Away

It's almost impossible to get to know Saskatchewan without the freedom of four wheels, but if you are without your own vehicle, Greyhound Canada operates bus services into Alberta, Manitoba and beyond, and Via Rail's Toronto to Vancouver *Canadian* serves Saskatoon.

If you are driving, Hwy 1 runs across the south from Alberta to Manitoba, passing through Regina, Moose Jaw and Swift Current; Hwy 16 cuts diagonally across the province, through Saskatoon; and a number of roads cross into Montana and North Dakota in the USA.

John G Diefenbaker International Airport in Saskatoon and Regina International airport both have frequent air services to/from major Canadian destinations.

Getting Around

To properly explore the deepest wilds, renting a 4WD or SUV is useful, although you can still traverse rural backwaters in a regular car. Many provincial roads are unpaved and major highways can be riddled with potholes after the winter melt; pay attention to these potential hazards and that of wild deer, elk and moose. Be sure to have enough fuel, music and munchies before you set out; townships are small and separated by significant distances.

Within the province, **Saskatchewan Transportation Company** (800-663-7181; www.stcbus.com) buses serve close to 300 communities. Frequent rider cards save 20% on regular fares.

REGINA

POP 193,100

Bisected by the Trans-Canada Hwy (Victoria Ave, at this point), the provincial capital is by default the primary destination of visitors to Saskatchewan. There's heady rivalry with Saskatoon, the attractive city 230km to the north, ever since it was a hunting ground for the Cree, who called Regina Wascana (Pile of Bones).

Leafy parks make the capital a pleasant place to be: the Wascana Centre and Victoria Park are great spots to sit and ponder. Other highlights include the gentrified Cathedral Village and the up-and-coming Regina Warehouse District, although on game days, the town's sole focus is on the Roughriders football team.

Regina has good restaurants, bars and comfortable accommodations. These, combined with its location, make Regina a good base from which to explore southern Saskatchewan, and an appropriate place for a sojourn as you cross the Canadian interior.

Sights & Activities

★ Provincial Legislature NOTABLE BUILDING

(306-787-2376; www.legassembly.sk.ca; Legislative Dr; 8am-9pm Jun-Aug, to 5pm Sep-May; P) FREE Escaping significant damage from the devastating tornado in its year of completion (1912), the arresting 'Leg,' nestled in Wascana Centre's leafy embrace, stands as a proud symbol to the people of Regina. Ponder the rich marble and ornate carvings of this lavish example of beaux arts architecture on free half-hourly tours or just play Frisbee out front on the Great Lawn.

Wascana Centre PARK

(Map p540; P) The geographic and cultural center of Regina, this sprawling public nature haven has miles of lakeside walking trails and is home to the Royal Saskatchewan Museum, Saskatchewan War Memorial and Saskatchewan Science Centre. Public events and celebrations are held by Wascana Lake's clear waters, which mirror such vistas as the stunning Provincial Legislature building and the Spruce Island bird sanctuary. Park residents include mink, hare, beavers and the occasional moose.

Royal Saskatchewan Museum MUSEUM

(Map p540; 306-787-2667; www.royalsaskmuseum.ca; 2445 Albert St; suggested donation adult/child $6/3; 9:30am-5pm; P) The Royal provides a great insight into the people and geography that make up Saskatchewan. Three galleries focus on earth and life sciences and aboriginal history. Prairie dioramas tell the story of the native flora, fauna and cultures that lived off the harsh land. Tipis, dinosaurs and deer all make an appearance. Don't miss Megamunch, a robotic Tyrannosaurus rex.

RCMP Heritage Centre MUSEUM

(306-522-7333; www.rcmpheritagecentre.com; 5907 Dewdney Ave W; adult/child $10/6; 11am-5pm; P) Exhibits chart the past, present and future of the iconic Canadian Mounties (you even get to dress up like one). This is also part of the Royal Canadian Mounted Police (RCMP) training center: check out the jutting jaws at the Sergeant Major's Parade.

Regina

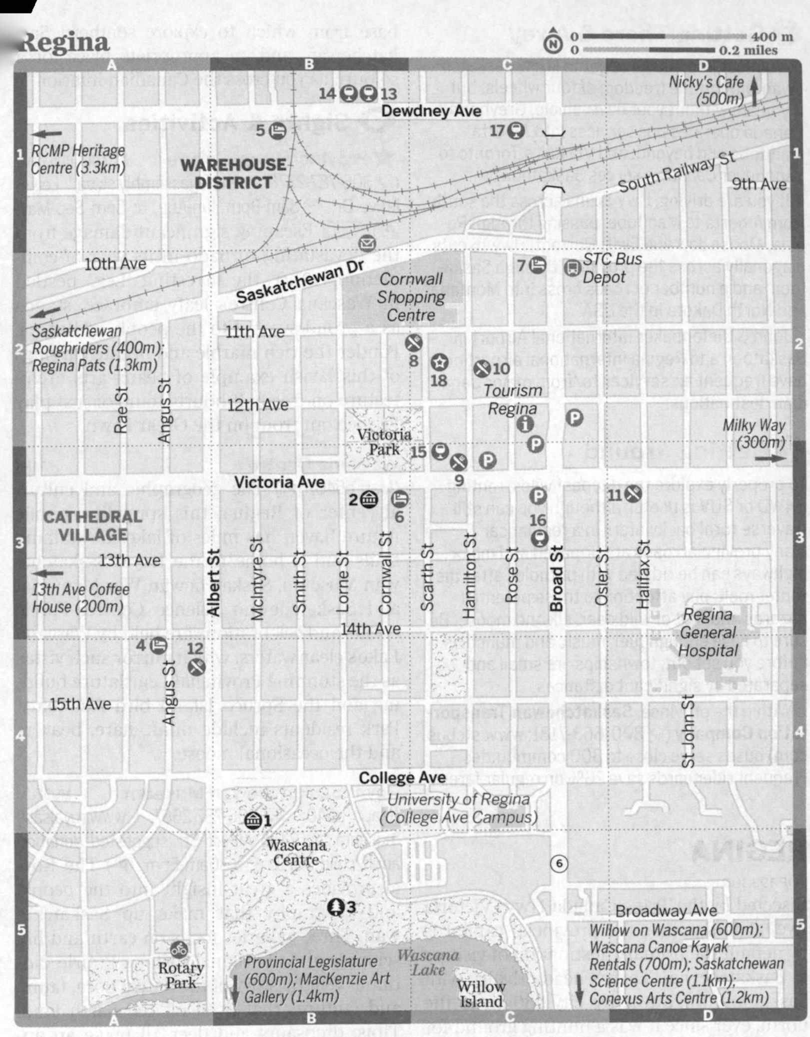

Saskatchewan Science Centre MUSEUM

(☎306-522-4629; www.sasksciencecentre.com; 2903 Powerhouse Dr; adult/child $10/8, with IMAX feature $18/14; ⏰9am-6pm Mon-Fri, 11am-6pm Sat & Sun; P) Science class was never this much fun! Try your hand at scoring a goal against a virtual goalkeeper, blow bubbles the size of a car or discover the secret to burping. With over 180 hands-on exhibits, it's a hit with kids; the center also has an IMAX theater and an observatory.

MacKenzie Art Gallery GALLERY

(☎306-584-4250; www.mackenzieartgallery.ca; 3475 Albert St; ⏰10am-5:30pm Mon & Wed-Sat, noon-5:30pm Sun; P) FREE This gallery features a permanent outdoor sculpture garden, grazed by Joe Fafard's famed bronzed cows, and keeps things fresh with rotating and special exhibitions primarily concerned with historical and contemporary Canadian art.

Regina

Sights
1 Royal Saskatchewan Museum B4
2 Saskatchewan Sports Hall of Fame B3
3 Wascana Centre B5

Sleeping
4 Dragon's Nest B&B A4
5 Four Points by Sheraton B1
6 Hotel Saskatchewan B3
7 Wingate by Wyndham C2

Eating
8 Beer Bros. Gastropub & Deli C2
9 Flip Eatery & Drink C3
10 Green Spot Cafe C2
11 Italian Star Deli D3
12 La Bodega A4

Drinking & Nightlife
13 Bushwakker Brewpub B1
14 McNally's Tavern B1
15 O'Hanlon's C3
16 Q Nightclub and Lounge C3
17 Rebellion Brewing C1

Entertainment
18 Globe Theatre C2
Trial of Louis Riel .... (see 1)

Saskatchewan Sports Hall of Fame MUSEUM
(Map p540; 306-780-9232; www.sasksportshalloffame.com; 2205 Victoria Ave; adult/child $5/2; 10am-4:30pm Mon-Fri, noon-5pm Sat; P) With an emphasis on grassroots athletes, this museum tells the story of over 480 of the province's sporting heroes.

Wascana Canoe Kayak Rentals WATER SPORTS
(Marina Rentals; 306-757-2628; 3000 Wascana Dr; canoe/kayak/pedal boat rentals per hour $15/10/15; noon-7pm May-Sep) In the grounds of Wascana Centre at the Wascana Marina you'll find this seasonal provider of canoes, kayaks and pedal boats for use on Wascana Lake.

Festivals & Events

Regina comes alive during the long days of the short summer. For a listing of events, go to www.tourismregina.com.

First Nations University of Canada Pow Wow CULTURAL
(www.fnuniv.ca/powwow; Apr) Held over a weekend in spring, dancers from around North America converge for this, the largest and longest running celebration of First Nations' culture in the province.

Queen City Ex FIESTA
(306-781-9200; www.thequeencityex.com; Jul/early Aug) Saskatchewan's favorite festival; people dress up in pioneer garb for six days of concerts, pancake breakfasts, amusement-park rides, a beard-growing contest and parades. Dates vary year to year.

Sleeping

There's plenty of decent accommodations in Regina. Victoria Ave (Hwy 1) east of town has no shortage of chain motels.

★ **Hotel Saskatchewan** HISTORIC HOTEL $$
(Map p540; 306-522-7691; www.hotelsask.com; 2125 Victoria Ave; r $100-250; P) Overlooking Victoria Park, this 1927 former grand dame of the Canadian National Railroad maintains a lofty presence. There's a degree of wow-factor upon entry. The 224 rooms come in sizes from compact to grand and feature luxe, period decor.

Four Points by Sheraton HOTEL $$
(Map p540; 306-789-8008; www.starwoodhotels.com; 2415 Dewdney Ave; r $95-160; P) Just north across the tracks from downtown, this new hotel is in walking distance for Roughriders games and for the nightlife of the Warehouse District. The 127 rooms are large and have fridges and microwaves. The pool is indoors.

Homesuites by d3h MOTEL $$
(306-522-4434; www.homesuites.ca; 3841 Eastgate Dr; r incl breakfast $100-200; P) Practicality and good design are the hallmark of this above-average property on the Hwy 1 motel strip outside town. The 60 roomy suites include kitchenettes and have access to a spa.

Wingate by Wyndham HOTEL $$
(Map p540; 306-584-7400; www.wingatebywyndhamregina.com; 1700 Broad St; r $90-160; P) The central Wingate offers 118 good-value, large and comfortable guest rooms in a modern seven-story building. Rooms have fridges and microwaves.

Dragon's Nest B&B B&B $$
(Map p540; 306-525-2109; www.dragonsnestbb.com; 2200 Angus St; s/d incl breakfast from $100/125, with shared bathroom $70/85;) This stylish six-room B&B is run by a feng shui consultant, so it's all lined up for optimum comfort. Included breakfasts are country fresh and hearty. The house dates to 1912.

Eating

Regina has a good share of interesting and inventive restaurants in the center and in nearby neighborhoods.

Milky Way ICE CREAM $
(306-352-7920; www.milkywayicecream.com; 910 Victoria Ave; snacks from $2; 11am-10pm Mar-Oct) Regina's taste of summer is flavored by fun. Six types of soft-serve ice cream are the basis for shakes, sundaes, cones and myriad more treats. Balance out your meal with a burger, hot dog or chili.

Italian Star Deli DELI $
(Map p540; 306-757-6733; www.italianstardeli.com; 1611 Victoria Ave; sandwiches $5-8; 9am-5pm Tue-Sat) Since 1966, this authentic Italian deli has brought the flavors of Europe to the prairies. Folks flock for the delicious panini and you're well advised to follow suit – they're great value and bursting with freshness. Perfect for your picnic basket.

13th Ave Coffee House CAFE $
(306-522-3111; www.13thavecoffee.com; 3136 13th Ave; mains $6-15; 7:30am-9pm Tue-Sat;) 'Healthy, fresh and local' is the mantra of this Cathedral Village anchor. Come for your fix of locally roasted, fair-trade java and get your daily dose of quinoa, antioxidants and vitamins as well. Carnivores aren't excluded, but vegetarians will feel right at home.

Green Spot Cafe VEGETARIAN $
(Map p540; 306-757-7899; www.greenspotcafe.ca; 1838 Hamilton St; snacks from $4; 7am-5pm Mon-Fri, 8am-3pm Sat;) This 100% vegetarian cafe features a downtown location and a menu of healthy treats chock-full of good karma.

★**Willow on Wascana** CANADIAN $$
(306-585-3663; www.willowonwascana; 3000 Wascana Dr; mains lunch $12-25, dinner $20-30; 11:30am-11pm Mon-Sat, to 1:30pm Sun) Views over Wascana Lake are one of Regina's upscale pleasures. The menu here changes seasonally and is a classic example of farm-to-table creativity. Dishes are kept simple to let the flavors come through. Sample the kitchen's best with a six-course tasting menu. Long wine list.

★**Flip Eatery & Drink** MODERN CANADIAN $$
(Map p540; 306-205-8345; www.fliprestaurant.ca; 1970 Hamilton St; mains $16-30; 11am-11pm Mon-Thu, to 2am Fri & Sat, 10am-3pm Sun) Seasonal fare from Saskatchewan is the basis for this inventive restaurant with an ever-changing menu. Although there is an Asian bent to some dishes, expect an eclectic menu. The lounge is popular until late; the beer and wine lists are well-curated, while the cocktails match the kitchen's creativity.

Nicky's Cafe CANADIAN $$
(306-757-3222; www.nickys.ca; 1005 8th Av; mains $8-25; 7am-9pm;) Comfort food doesn't get more comfy – or tasty – than this. Breakfasts feature famous hash browns, superb omelets and winter-insulating pancakes. Later in the day, burgers come in a dozen variations or you can go for seafood or ribs. Portions are large and quality is high.

Beer Bros. Gastropub & Deli PUB FOOD $$
(Map p540; 306-586-2337; www.beerbros.ca; 1821 Scarth St; mains $12-20; 11:30am-11pm Sun-Thu, to 1am Fri & Sat) It's hard not to love this downtown pub in the heritage Northern Bank building. Think hearty – sandwiches, burgers, cheese plates – but with a gourmet twist. As you'd expect from the name, the beer list is long and has an excellent range of Canadian microbrews.

La Bodega TAPAS $$
(Map p540; 306-546-3660; www.labodegaregina.com; 2228 Albert St; tapas $10-15, mains $12-30; 4pm-midnight Tue-Sun) Ambience is the word of the day at this restaurant, situated in a leafy residential area. It has a fantastic tri-level patio wraps around a huge tree. The food has many Spanish classics but Canadian faves are served as well, including fish-and-chips and lobster poutine. Good wine list.

Drinking & Nightlife

There are good bars and breweries in and around downtown and the nearby Warehouse **District** (www.warehousedistrict.ca). In summer people flock to the many patios.

★**Rebellion Brewing** MICROBREWERY
(Map p540; 306-522-4666; www.rebellionbrewing.ca; 1901 Dewdney Ave; 11:30am-10pm) Hard by the old train tracks, Saskatchewan's best microbrewery has a tap room with

excellent burgers and pizza. There's a modern corrugated metal aesthetic and hop-shaped fixtures. Reserve in advance for tours on Saturdays (2pm). The beer list is long and changing, but don't miss the Sour Rye.

Bushwakker Brewpub PUB
(Map p540; ☎306-359-7276; www.bushwakker.com; 2206 Dewdney Ave; ⏲11am-late Mon-Sat) In a 1913 warehouse, Bushwakker is reason enough to cross the tracks to the Warehouse District. There's live music many nights, but the real draw is the beer: over a dozen house brews on rotating taps.

Q Nightclub and Lounge GAY
(Map p540; ☎306-569-1995; www.qlcrclub.ca; 2070 Broad St; ⏲5pm-3am) Occupying a former church building, this gay bar/club is a welcoming, straight-friendly affair, run by a members co-op. The awesome rough-around-the-edges, multilevel space has an outdoor patio. There are DJs many nights.

O'Hanlon's PUB
(Map p540; ☎306-566-4094; www.ohanlons.ca; 1947 Scarth St; ⏲11:30am-late) O'Hanlon's has a grungy Irish pub feel and sidewalk tables overlooking Victoria Park and the Hotel Saskatchewan. It's the kind of place where you can find yourself eating, drinking and babbling on until the wee hours. Great beer list.

McNally's Tavern LOUNGE
(Map p540; ☎306-522-4774; 2226 Dewdney Ave; ⏲4pm-late) Warehouse District pub with a bare-brick vibe; there are bands, karaoke and open-mike and jam sessions most nights.

☆ Entertainment

★Saskatchewan Roughriders FOOTBALL
(☎888-474-3377, 306-525-2181; www.riderville.com; Mosaic Stadium, Elphinstone St; ⏲Jun-Nov) The Green Riders, as they're known to legions of rabid locals, have achieved cult status within the Canadian Football League (CFL). Don't underestimate how crazy things get in this town, for this team. A new venue, **Mosaic Stadium** (www.newmosaicstadium.com), was due to open in 2017 and will seat 33,000, over one-quarter of the local population!

★Trial of Louis Riel THEATER
(Map p540; ☎306-728-5728; www.rielcoproductions.com; 2445 Albert St, Royal Saskatchewan Museum; adult/child $20/10; ⏲Jul & Aug) Actual transcripts from Riel's 1885 trial – which resulted in his hanging – are the basis of this, Canada's second-longest-running play, first performed in 1967. Performances take pl[ace] in the Royal Saskatchewan Museum (p53[…]) over three weeks each summer.

Regina Pats HOCKEY
(☎306-543-7800; www.reginapats.com; Brandt Centre, 1700 Elphinstone St; $13-23; ⏲Sep-Mar) The younger, tougher, more eager players of the Western Hockey League (WHL) make for an exciting brand of hockey. The stadium is about 3km west of the center.

Conexus Arts Centre THEATER
(☎306-565-4500; www.conexusartscentre.ca; 200a Lakeshore Dr) Home of the symphony orchestra and venue of choice for touring musicians and shows, the Arts Centre vaguely resembles vintage Saskatchewan grain elevators.

Globe Theatre THEATER
(Map p540; ☎306-525-6400; www.globetheatrelive.com; 1801 Scarth St; ticket prices vary) Contemporary theatrical presentations in the round are part of a schedule that includes live music and other performances.

ℹ Information

Free wi-fi is available throughout much of the downtown and Cathedral Village areas.

Regina Public Library (☎306-777-6000; 2311 12th Ave; ⏲9:30am-9pm Mon-Thu, to 6pm Fri, to 5pm Sat, 1:30-5pm Sun; 📶) Free internet access.

Main Post Office (Map p540; ☎866-607-6301; 2200 Saskatchewan Dr; ⏲9am-5pm Mon-Fri)

Regina General Hospital (☎306-766-4444; www.rqhealth.ca; 1440 14th Ave; ⏲24hr) Emergency room.

Prairie Dog (www.prairiedogmag.com) Feisty and free biweekly newspaper with good entertainment and restaurant listings.

Tourism Regina (Map p540; ☎306-789-5099, 1-800-661-5099; www.tourismregina.com; 1925 Rose St; ⏲9am-5pm Mon-Fri) A few local guides and maps.

ℹ Getting There & Away

Regina International Airport (YQR; ☎306-761-7555; www.yqr.ca; 5200 Regina Ave), 5km west of downtown, has services to major Canadian destinations.

Greyhound Canada (www.greyhound.ca) runs east to Winnipeg ($105, 9½ hours, one daily) and west to Calgary ($77, 11 hours, one daily). **STC** (☎306-787-3340; www.stcbus.com) runs buses in all directions, including to Saskatoon ($51, 2¾ to four hours, three daily). All depart from the **STC Bus Depot** (Map p540; 1717 Saskatchewan Dr).

Getting Around

…e airport is a 10-minute cab ride ($15) from …owntown; there is no public transit service.

Regina Transit (☎306-777-7433; www.regina transit.com; adult/child $3/2.50, day pass $9) operates city buses, most of which converge on 11th St downtown.

Regina Cabs (☎306-543-3333; www.reginacabs.com) comes when you call.

SOUTHERN SASKATCHEWAN

Along the Trans-Canada Hwy (Hwy 1) is iconic Saskatchewan, the sort of wide open prairie that country songs are written about. As you explore the rabbit warren of unpaved, lonely back roads, it's easy to feel divorced from modern life. It's not hard to imagine thousands of bison charging over a nearby hill, aboriginal villages in the valley or the North West Mounted Police (NWMP) patrolling the prairie on horseback. There is diversity among this immensity, though, with rolling grasslands, short sharp hills and badlands befitting a classic Western.

Moose Jaw

POP 33,280

Moose Jaw is a welcome island in a prairie sea, a rough diamond with surprising charm. From grassroots beginnings as a Canadian Pacific Railway outpost, the town grew steadily in size and infamy, earning a reputation for rebellion, corruption, brushes with the Ku Klux Klan and even slavery. In the days of US Prohibition, it was a haven for Al Capone and his gang, who used it as a base for smuggling whiskey across the border on Soo Line trains to Chicago. (Ironically, the grand old train station is now a liquor store.)

Today's Moose Jaw bears little resemblance to its wild past, although it has done well to memorialize the fascinating stories of less respectable days. It's also known as 'Little Chicago' for its well preserved art-deco buildings, colorful murals and lurid past.

Sights

Main St and the historic downtown should be your focus. Expect to spend a couple of hours wandering about. Over 45 **murals** capturing tamer moments in Moose Jaw's history adorn walls around town.

★Tunnels of Moose Jaw TUNNEL
(☎306-693-5261; www.tunnelsofmoosejaw.com; 18 Main St; tours adult/child from $15/8.50; ⊙open year-round, hours vary) Buried deep under the town's streets is a series of passages that have a tragic and fascinating history. Take a tour and learn about the hardship and discrimination heaped upon Chinese workers on their 'Passage to Fortune.' Fast-forward a few decades to make the 'Chicago Connection.' Al Capone is rumored to have visited Moose Jaw in the 1920s to oversee his bootlegging operation, masterminded in these very tunnels.

Yvette Moore Gallery GALLERY
(☎306-693-7600; www.yvettemoore.com; 76 Fairford St W; ⊙10am-5pm Mon-Sat) FREE Just west of Main St in a proud heritage building, this renowned local artist displays her evocative and hyper-realistic works portraying Saskatchewan and its people. It has a simple but good cafe serving lunch.

Western Development Museum MUSEUM
(WDM; ☎306-693-5989; www.wdm.ca; 50 Diefenbaker Dr; adult/child $10/4; ⊙9am-5pm; P) If you can drive it, fly it, pedal it or paddle it, odds are you'll find an example of it at this branch of the WDM. Dedicated to transport within Saskatchewan, it has planes, trains, automobiles and even the odd wagon. It's by the bypass, north of the center.

Activities

Download walking maps from www.tourismmoosejaw.ca.

Temple Gardens Mineral Spa SPA
(☎306-694-5055; www.templegardens.sk.ca; 24 Fairford St E; adult/child Mon-Thu $8/7, Fri-Sun $16/11; ⊙10am-late) This modern complex houses the locally famous indoor-outdoor pool filled with steaming mineral water from deep below the prairie. A long list of treatments are available. The annexed resort accommodations are less inspiring.

Moose Jaw Trolley Company BUS
(☎306-693-8537; www.tourismmoosejaw.ca; adult/child $13/7; ⊙Jun-Aug) Enjoy a tour of the town's murals and historic buildings aboard a fake trolley. Departures from the visitors centre (p545).

Sleeping & Eating

Grant Hall Hotel HISTORIC HOTEL $$
(☎844-885-4255; www.granthall.ca; 401 Main St N; r $80-140; P❄🛜) Small-town luxe describes this vintage (1928) hotel in the center. Opulently restored in 2001, the hotel's public spaces are grand. The 28 rooms offer traditional comforts. The terrace is a good place to relax in the sun and enjoy park views.

Wakamow Heights Bed & Breakfast B&B $$
(☎306-693-9963; www.wakamowheights.com; 690 Aldersgate St; r incl breakfast $100-120; P🛜) In an elevated spot on the outskirts of town, this historical B&B has lush gardens and a variety of deliciously furnished rooms of differing color schemes.

Déjà Vu Cafe DINER $
(☎306-692-6066; www.dejavucafe.ca; 23 High St E; mains $8-15; ⏲11am-9pm) Plethora – that's the theme at this legendary diner located downtown. Milkshakes come in 80 flavors, and there are dozens of dipping sauces for the various fried treats (chicken tenders, fries, onion rings) on offer. Yes, it's a simple menu but everything on it is superb.

Bobby's Place Olde World Tavern PUB FOOD $
(☎306-692-3058; 63 High St E; mains $9-13; ⏲11am-late Mon-Sat) Bobby's place is always busy and has been for years. Come for a beer on the patio or, as everyone else does, for the fabulous home-cooked meals. The home-breaded chicken fingers are tender, juicy and always popular.

Information

Visitors Centre (☎866-693-8097; www.tourismmoosejaw.ca; Thatcher Dr E, at Hwy 1; ⏲9am-5pm mid-May–Aug, 9:30am-noon & 1-4:30pm Sep–mid-May) Look for the huge anatomically correct moose statue near the bypass.

Getting There & Away

STC (www.stcbus.com) runs buses to Regina ($19, one hour, two to three daily) from the downtown **bus station** (☎306-692-2345; 63 High St E).

Ogema

In this desolate part of the province's deep south, two extraordinary attractions are worthy draws to this tiny hamlet with huge community spirit.

Ogema's **Southern Prairie Railway** (☎306-459-7808; www.southernprairierailway.com; 401 Railway Ave; tours adult/child from $47/32; ⏲Sat & Sun Jun-Sep) has been turning heads since its maiden voyage for the town's centenary in 2012. The informative 1½- to three-hour tours chug across the prairie to explore an abandoned grain elevator among other sights. Special tours are held throughout the year including the occasional stargazing expedition.

Formed as early as 1977 from a desire to preserve the memories, stories and possessions of Ogema's forefathers, the unexpected **Deep South Pioneer Museum** (☎306-459-7909; www.ogema.ca; 510 Government Rd; adult/child $5/2; ⏲10am-5pm Sat & Sun May-Sep) is an astounding collection of over 30 preserved buildings, along with farming equipment, scores of vehicles and a huge volume of historic artifacts. Townsfolk young and old have contributed to the creation and maintenance of this unique memorial site. The authenticity of its lovingly preserved buildings and the openness with which they are presented is extraordinary.

Gravelbourg

About 190km southwest of Regina, delightful Fransaskois Gravelbourg is one of the last places you'd expect to find a taste of Europe, adrift on a vast sea of prairie. Lavish buildings designed to lure French settlers date to the early 1900s.

Palatial buildings are scattered along 1st Ave, including the tiny community's elementary school, **École Élémentaire de Gravelbourg**.

Sights & Activities

The best way to explore this surprising destination is to do the **Heritage Walking Tour** found at www.gravelbourg.ca.

Our Lady of the Assumption Co-Cathedral CHURCH
(La Co-Cathédrale Notre Dame de l'Assomption; ☎306-648-3322; www.gravelbourgcocathedral.com; 1st Ave; P) FREE The undisputed centerpiece of this *très jolie* little town is the disproportionately large and beautiful Our Lady of the Assumption Co-Cathedral, built in 1919 in a Romanesque and Italianate style. It was designated a national historic site in 1995. Enter if it's open and crane your neck to marvel at the Sistine Chapel–esque frescoes.

Monsignor Maillard, who not only designed the chapel's interior and presided over the parish, painted the frescoes himself, from 1921 to 1931 – an astonishing feat.

Gravelbourg & District Museum MUSEUM
(☎306-648-2332; 300 Main St; $5; ⊙10am-5:30pm Tue-Sat) Learn about Gravelbourg's rich cultural traditions at this museum, two blocks south of the cathedral.

Sleeping & Eating

Bishop's Residence B&B $
(☎888-648-2321; www.bishopsresidencebandb.com; 112 1st Ave W; r incl breakfast $60-100; P) The handsome yellow-brick former bishop's residence has been turned into a unique B&B with nine rooms, some with private bathrooms and balconies.

Gravelbourg Inn MOTEL $
(☎306-648-3182; cnr Hwys 43 & 58; r $60-80; P ❄ 📶) For simple style, this motel has tidy rooms on the eastern approach to town.

Café Paris CAFE $
(☎306-648-2223; 306 Main St; mains $6-12; ⊙9am-6pm Mon-Sat) Pop in to see the friendly folks at the Café Paris for a light lunch and a delicious milkshake. It's right downtown; vintage details include a pressed-tin ceiling.

Swift Current

Swift Current's main claim to fame is as a travelers' oasis on Hwy 1. The downtown area is about 3km south of the highway strip – follow the signs.

Sights

Mennonite Heritage Village MUSEUM
(☎306-773-7685; www.mennoniteheritagevillage.ca; 17th Ave SE; by donation; ⊙1-6pm Fri-Sun Jul & Aug) This 1900s heritage village depicts a way of life unfamiliar to most. Many Mennonite and Hutterite communities still exist in the area. There's an annual summer watermelon festival.

Swift Current Museum and Visitors Centre MUSEUM
(☎306-778-9174; www.tourismswiftcurrent.ca; 44 Robert St W; ⊙9am-5pm Mon-Fri) FREE You'll want to make a stop to check out the massive woolly bison in this little museum inside the Swift Current visitor center.

Sleeping & Eating

Safari Inn Motel MOTEL $
(☎306-773-4608; www.safariinn.ca; 810 S Service Rd E; r $65-100; P 📶) A non-chain alternative on the motel strip, the Safari beckons with a throwback neon sign. The owners can't do enough to please, and the rooms have all the amenities: fridges, microwaves, even Netflix. It's far from flashy, but it compensates with spirit.

Home Inn & Suites MOTEL $$
(☎306-778-7788; www.homeinnswiftcurrent.ca; 1411 Battleford Trail E; r incl breakfast from $120-180; P ❄ 📶 ≋) Modern, tastefully decorated suites in this chain motel have kitchenettes, comfortable beds and room to move. There's an indoor pool with waterslide and a little day spa so you can relieve those tired driving muscles.

★ **Russell Up Some Grub** DINER $$
(☎306-778-4782; 12a 1081 Central Ave N; mains $8-20; ⊙6am-3pm Mon-Wed & Sat, to 8pm Thu & Fri) Homestyle Mennonite meals such as cheddar pierogi in sausage gravy, cranberry chicken, and a great selection of sandwiches, burgers, local fish and salads are reason enough to pull off the highway. A gluten-free menu, friendly staff, and a spotlessly clean, bright dining room complete the picture.

Akropol Family Restaurant GREEK $$
(☎306-773-5454; 133 Central Ave N; mains $9-20; ⊙11am-late Mon-Sat) This Greek restaurant serves up traditional favorites such as gyros, calamari and spanakopita. There's a lovely outdoor patio and it has locally brewed Black Bridge beers. The lounge is popular and there is often live music.

Miso House ASIAN $$
(☎306-778-4411; 285 N Service Rd W; mains $6-20; ⊙11am-10pm Tue-Sun) Miso House has done a great job of bringing tasty sushi, Korean delights and Japanese bento boxes to the prairies. It's on the motel strip.

☆ Entertainment

Lyric Theatre THEATER
(☎306-773-6292; www.lyrictheatre.ca; 227 Central Ave N) Saskatchewan's oldest running theater was founded in 1912. Ongoing renovations to restore it to its former glory mix with weekly open-stage nights, improv performances and more.

Getting There & Away

Hwy 1 passes directly through Swift Current, about 170km east of the Alberta border. Greyhound buses on the Trans-Canada pass through once each day. **STC** (www.stcbus.com) buses run a daily service to Saskatoon ($54, 3¾ hours).

Val Marie & Grasslands National Park

Val Marie, at the gateway to Grasslands National Park, is tiny, rough around the edges and endearing. The **park** (877-345-2257; www.parkscanada.ca/grasslands) contains thousands of hectares of grasses, undulating hills, wildflower accents and oodles of solitude. Virtually absent of trees, it's a splendid place to appreciate the bigger picture. The **visitor center** (306-298-2257; cnr Hwy 4 & Centre St, Val Marie; 9am-5pm daily Jul & Aug, Thu-Mon mid-May–Jun & Sep–mid-Oct) is an essential port of call for advice on where to camp and how best to experience the full majesty of the park. Prepare well for expeditions and BYO shade – Grasslands is wild and lonely; there's the potential for rattlesnake encounters. If you're lucky you might catch a glimpse of the resident herd of bison. Park accommodations include primitive campsites ($16) and tipis ($45).

For a holier-than-thou sleeping experience, the **Convent Inn** (306-298-4515; www.convent.ca; Hwy 4; r incl breakfast $75-95; P) offers beds amid classic brickwork and beautiful hardwood floors. Built in 1935, this former residential school has 10 beautifully restored rooms, a labyrinth of staircases and even a confessional (in case you break a vow or two during the night). It has lovely patios for chilling with the view.

Eastend

Isolated in southwest Saskatchewan, Eastend is tumbleweed quiet but not without charm. Nestled into a small valley, the town's few streets are lined with older buildings dating from its founding in 1914.

Eastend's claim to fame was for the 1994 discovery of one of the most complete Tyrannosaurus rex skeletons ever found. The **T-Rex Discovery Centre** (306-295-4009; www.trexcentre.ca; T-Rex Dr; by donation; 10am-6pm Jun-Aug; P) is a glitzy working lab carved into the hillside. Various tours are available, along with dinosaur dig options.

The **Eastend Historical Museum and Visitor Information** (306-295-4144; www.eastendhistoricalmuseum.com; cnr Red Coat Dr & Elm Ave S; 10am-5pm May-Sep) FREE has more fossils and bones on display. There's also a 1905 log cabin next door.

Maple Creek

Founded in 1883, this small town right on the railroad main line has an attractive center and makes a good stop off the Trans-Canada Hwy (Hwy 1). Jasper St, one of the town's main shopping strips, makes for a nice stroll. The town is a gateway to Cypress Hills Provincial Park and has activities and services.

If you choose to stay the night, **Maple Creek Commercial Hotel** (306-662-2988; www.maplecreekcommercialhotel.ca; 26 Pacific Ave; r $75-135;) is a nicely restored 1885 hotel with very comfortable, modernized rooms. The dining room has good lunches and dinners, while the lounge and patio are pleasant places to relax.

Daily Grind (306-662-3133; 132 Jasper St; snacks $3-6; 8am-5pm), a cute storefront on the main drag, has excellent coffees and fine baked goods that promise a shot of joy during the day.

Cypress Hills Interprovincial Park

The contrasts within this isolated **interprovincial park** (306-662-4411; www.cypresshills.com; P) straddling the Alberta–Saskatchewan border are arresting: endless prairies turn to undulating hills forested with cypress, harboring inland lakes. Elk, deer, moose and birdlife flourish in this fertile sanctuary. Each of the two sections has a distinctly different feel. We recommend exploring both to get the full perspective.

The small town of Maple Creek is a gateway to the park. It has a historic main street and good cafes, plus activities and services.

Sights

Centre Block

This is the most accessible part of the park. There are numerous hiking trails, and for some adrenaline action, various activity operators offer excitement. Some are based in Maple Creek.

Be sure to follow Bald Butte Rd from the park entrance to **Lookout Point** and **Bald Butte**. These are some of the highest elevations between the Rockies and Labrador and offer literally breathtaking views (if you run excitedly to the top) over the sea of prairies.

Western Block & Cypress Hills

More remote than the Centre Block, the Western Block spills over into Alberta's Cypress Hills. The major site is Fort Walsh, otherwise much of the park is remote and not easily accessed. The Saskatchewan side of the Western Block is serene and backcountry. At Elkwater in Alberta, take a leisurely stroll around the lake and surrounding park – you might encounter elk as they feed at dusk. Outside of summer high season, the silence will only be interrupted by light birdsong and the sound of your thoughts.

★ Fort Walsh National Historic Site HISTORIC SITE
(306-662-3590; www.parkscanada.ca/fortwalsh; off Hwy 271, Cypress Hills Interprovincial Park; adult/child $10/5; 9:30am-5:30pm daily Jul & Aug, Tue-Sat Jun & Sep; P) Amid rolling prairies is this interesting historic site. Established in 1875 and operational for eight years, this outpost had a small yet significant role in the history of the west. After the battle of Custer's Last Stand, Chief Sitting Bull and 5000 of his followers arrived in the area. The local mounties moved their headquarters to Fort Walsh and maintained peaceful relations with the Sioux while they remained in Canada.

Activities

Cypress Hills Eco-Adventures ADVENTURE SPORTS
(306-662-4466; www.ecoadventures.ca; off Hwy 21 S; adventures from $55; 10am-6pm) The friendly outdoorsy folks at Cypress Hills Eco-Adventures will have you whizzing above the forest floor on Saskatchewan's only zipline canopy tour in next to no time. A bunch of other adrenaline-fueled activities including slacklining, rock-wall climbing and, our fave, the treetop free fall, are available. Reservations recommended.

Sleeping

Cypress Hills Campgrounds CAMPGROUND $
(Centre Block reservations 855-737-7275; www.cypresshills.com; tent & RV sites $16-36; P) The popular Cypress Hills Centre Block campgrounds fill up over weekends and on holidays: five campgrounds accommodate over 600 campsites with a range of services and hookups. It's best to reserve ahead in summer at www.saskparks.net. The Western Block has over 350 sites near Elkwater.

Resort at Cypress Hills RESORT $$
(306-662-4477; www.resortatcypresshills.ca; off Hwy 21 S; r $105-200; P) Surrounded by a dense thicket of cypress, this sprawling woody resort has a bunch of comfortable motel rooms, cabins (great value) and town houses. There's an on-site restaurant and a plethora of fun activities to enjoy within the park.

Elkwater Lake Lodge & Resort RESORT $$
(403-893-3811; www.elkwaterlakelodge.com; 401 4th St, Elkwater, Alberta; r $140-200, cabins from $190; P) Occupying a lakeside spot on the Alberta side of Cypress Hills Interprovincial Park, a few minutes from the picturesque township of Elkwater Lake, this quiet resort offers a wide variety of comfortable, modern rooms and suites, some with Jacuzzis and fireplaces. All are decorated in a style befitting the woodsy location.

Information

Cypress Hills Interprovincial Park Visitors Centre (306-662-5411; www.cypresshills.com; off Hwy 221, Centre Block; hours vary) Near the main entrance to the park's Centre Block, this is an essential stop.

Qu'Appelle Valley

The Qu'Appelle Valley's wide river and gently rolling hills highlight Saskatchewan's remarkable contrasts.

Heading northeast from Regina on Hwy 10, don't be afraid to get off the main road and explore. After 70km, pass through **Fort Qu'Appelle** and turn right on Hwy 56 toward the village of **Lebret** and the beautiful fieldstone **Sacred Heart Church**, completed in 1925. Spin around and ponder the ominous **Stations of the Cross** and **Chapel on the Hill**. You can walk up there if you feel inspired.

WORTH A TRIP

LITTLE BEACHES ON THE PRAIRIE

Regina Beach

Kids play by Last Mountain Lake and picnickers enjoy the shady waterfront park at this idyllic summer spot 50km northwest of Regina.

The **Blue Bird Cafe** (☎306-729-2385; 108 Centre St; mains $8-15; ⏰10am-8pm May-Sep) is an old-time classic with wooden floors and creaky screen doors. The fish and chips are legendary: lighter-than-air crispy batter on tender white fish. Follow that with an ice cream and you're set.

Manitou Beach

Near the town of Watrous, Manitou Lake has Dead Sea–style waters full of minerals and salt. Right on the water, the village of Manitou Beach feels like a throwback to a simpler time.

Soak in the reputedly healing waters at the **Manitou Springs Resort & Mineral Spa** (☎306-946-2233, 800-667-7672; www.manitousprings.ca; cnr Lake Ave & Watrous St; pool day pass adult/child $18/12). A stop at nearby **Danceland** (☎306-946-2743; www.danceland.ca; 511 Lake Ave; ⏰Jun-Oct), an amazing dance hall caught in a vortex immune to the passing of time. Locals have been treading the boards here for over 80 years, and they tell us Elvis, Buddy Holly, Glen Miller and Duke Ellington all played here during its heyday.

Take Hwy 22 off Hwy 10 for the tiny village of **Abernethy** and the nearby historic park.

Katepwa Beach is a small waterfront village on scenic Hwy 56. There's a lovely grassy campground and swimming spot with walking trails, picnic areas and shady trees.

Sights

Motherwell Homestead National Historic Site HISTORIC SITE
(☎306-333-2116; www.parkscanada.gc.ca/motherwell; Hwy 22, Abernethy; adult/child $4/2; ⏰10am-4pm daily Jul & Aug, Mon-Fri Jun; 🅿) Some 3km south of Abernethy, Motherwell Homestead National Historic Site is a fascinating early Saskatchewan farm where you can make hay with huge draft horses and meet characters dressed up in period costume. A small cafe serves homemade lunches.

Sleeping & Eating

Sunday's Log Cabins CABIN $$
(☎306-621-3900; www.sundayslogcabins.com; off Hwy 56, Katepwa Beach; cabins $130-200; ⏰May-Oct; 🅿) These four handsome, well-maintained log cabins offer all the comforts of home in an almost beachfront setting. Follow Hwy 56 until you come to Katepwa Point Provincial Park, turn south to get to the park beach; the cabins are across the street, next to the store.

Main Beach Bar and Grill PUB FOOD $$
(☎306-332-4696; www.katepwahotel.com; Hwy 56, Katepwa Beach; mains $9-21; ⏰noon-9pm) If it's a sunny day, linger awhile here. It's open year-round, serving cold beer and the best (and only) pub grub in town. There's a fantastic large patio overlooking the park and the lake.

EASTERN SASKATCHEWAN

Yorkton

Yorkton is a typical prairie town. It's a no-nonsense place that makes a good pit stop as you pass through on any one of the many converging roads. Out on the plains, look for old Orthodox churches amid the amber waves of grain, especially on Hwy 16 heading northwest.

Yorkton honors its strong Eastern European and Ukrainian roots at its large branch of the **Western Development Museum** (WDM; ☎306-783-8361; www.wdm.ca; Hwy 16 W; adult/child $10/4; ⏰9am-5pm daily mid-Jun–mid-Aug, reduced hours rest of year). Indoor and outdoor displays tell the stories of settlers from over 50 countries who carved an existence out of the rough landscape.

The 16m-high dome at **St Mary's Ukrainian Catholic Church** (306-783-4549; 155 Catherine St) is a breathtaking work of art, painted from 1939 to 1941 by Stephen Meush.

Canadian filmmakers and producers compete for Canada's Golden Sheaf Awards at the acclaimed **Yorkton Film Festival** (306-782-7077; www.goldensheafawards.com; late May). It honors Canadian films that are less than an hour in length.

Veregin

A century ago in mother Russia lived a group of people called the Doukhobors. Oppressed because of their pacifist leanings and opposition to the Orthodox church, 7500 Doukhobors immigrated to Canada in 1899. Their benefactor? Leo *'War and Peace'* Tolstoy. Today, this tiny hamlet is a withering outpost from that era.

Learn the story of Veregin's Russian roots at the **National Doukhobor Heritage Village** (306-542-4441; www.ndhv.ca; Hwy 5; adult/child $5/1; 10am-6pm mid-May–mid-Sep), a living artifact of provincial life in the early 1900s. Against a backdrop of historic grain elevators, a compound of buildings furnished in period style are open to the public. If you're lucky, there'll be bread baking.

Veregin is about 70km northeast of Yorkton.

SASKATOON

POP 223,500

Saskatoon is full of hidden treasures. Don't be misled by first appearances – head into the downtown core and inner neighborhoods to get a sense of this vibrant city. The majestic South Saskatchewan River winds through downtown, offering beautiful, natural diversions.

Leafy parks and rambling riverside walks help you make the most out of long, sunny summer days, and there are plenty of great spots to stop for a refreshing drink and a chat with locals.

Despite the town's legacy as an 1883 settlement by the 'Temperance Colonization Society' (Ontario's bunch of anti-funsters), Saskatoon knows how to heat up cold winter days and short summer nights, with a proud heritage of local rock and country music and a vibrant live-music scene. Indeed, if you only have time for one Saskatchewan stop, make it Saskatoon.

Sights

The river is crossed by a gaggle of attractive bridges including the rickety 1907 **Victoria Bridge** and the soaring 1908 **Canadian Pacific Railway Bridge**. The banks are lined with walking and cycling paths that link serene parks throughout the center including **Kiwanis Memorial Park** and **River Landing**.

Just west of the center, **Riversdale** is an old and gentrifying neighborhood with creative boutiques and eateries. South of the river, **Nutana** is a great place to wander for a day of food, drinks and music.

★ Meewasin Valley — NATURE RESERVE

(www.meewasin.com) The Meewasin Valley, formed by the South Saskatchewan's wide swath through the center of town, is named for the Cree word for 'beautiful'. Mature trees populate the riverbanks, while sections of the 60km **Meewasin Trail**, extend from downtown paths, winding through forests and along the riverbank. Popular with walkers, cyclists and wandering travelers, picnic areas line the trails. Further north, **Mendel Island** is home to abundant wildlife.

★ Western Development Museum — MUSEUM

(WDM; 306-931-1910; www.wdm.ca; 2610 Lorne Ave S; adult/child $10/4; 9am-5pm; P) The flagship Saskatoon branch of the province's Western Development Museum is a faithful re-creation of Saskatoon the boom town, c 1910. Inside Canada's longest indoor street, you can roam through the town's many buildings, from a dentist's office straight out of a horror film to the pharmacy, the walls of which are lined with hundreds of vintage concoctions. There are trains, tractors, buggies, sleighs and a jail. It's about 4km south of downtown.

Wanuskewin Heritage Park — PARK

(306-931-6767; www.wanuskewin.com; Penner Rd, off Hwy 11; adult/child $8.50/4; 9am-4:30pm; P) Devoted to the history of the province's first inhabitants, this riverside heritage park 17km northeast of Saskatoon interprets a 7000-year history. At Wanuskewin (wah-nus-*kay*-win; Cree for 'seeking peace of mind') you can wander interpretive trails through the 116 hectares of grassy hills and valley meadows, discovering some of the 19 pre-contact sites. Invisible from the surrounding prairie, the untouched Opamihaw Valley is a spiritual and sacred place. Cultural dance performances take place on summer afternoons.

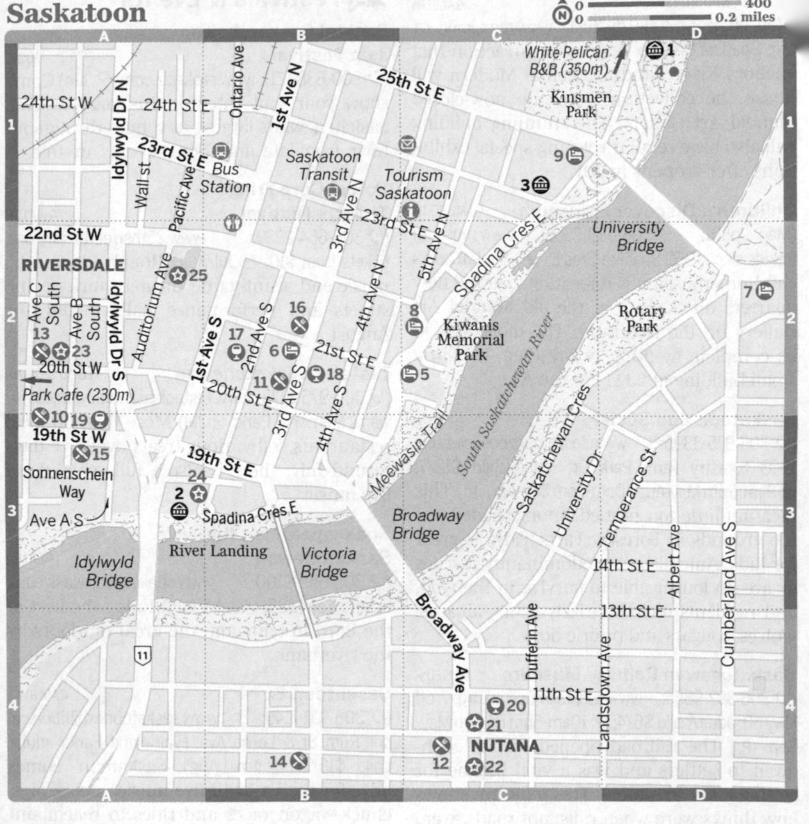

Saskatoon

Sights

1 Children's Discovery Museum D1
2 Remai Modern A3
3 Ukrainian Museum of Canada C1

Activities, Courses & Tours

4 Shearwater Boat Cruises D1

Sleeping

5 Delta Bessborough C2
6 Hotel Senator B2
7 Inn on College D2
8 James C2
9 Park Town Hotel C1

Eating

10 Asian Hut A3
11 Ayden Kitchen and Bar B2
Calories Bakery & Restaurant .... (see 21)
12 Christie's Il Secondo Bakery & Pizzeria C4
13 Grazing Goat A2
14 Homestead Ice Cream B4
15 Saskatoon Farmers Market A3
16 Truffles Bistro B2

Drinking & Nightlife

17 Congress Beer House B2
18 Diva's Nightclub B2
19 Drift Sidewalk Cafe & Vista Lounge A3
20 Hose and Hydrant C4
Winston's English Pub & Grill .... (see 6)

Entertainment

21 Broadway Theatre C4
22 Buds on Broadway C4
23 Gordon Tootoosis Nīkānīwin Theatre A2
24 Persephone Theatre A3
25 TCU Place A2

Remai Modern GALLERY

(Map p551; ☎306-975-7610; www.remaimodern.org; Spadina Cres) A huge new attraction that anchors River Landing, Remai Modern will house the collection from the now-closed Mandel Art Gallery. The stunning building will also have regular rotating special exhibitions after it opens in 2017.

Children's Discovery Museum MUSEUM

(Map p551; ☎306-683-2555; www.museumforkids.sk.ca; 950 Spadina Cres E;) Saskatoon's children's museum is relocating to grand new quarters on the site of the old Mandel Art Gallery on the riverfront. The move should be complete by 2018; before then, it is in a small building at 2325 Preston Ave.

Saskatoon Zoo Society ZOO

(☎306-975-3395; www.saskatoonzoosociety.ca; 1903 Forestry Farm Park Dr; adult/child $12/7; 9am-9pm May-Aug, 10am-4pm Sep-Apr; P) This pleasant little zoo, nestled among shaded picnic grounds in Forestry Farm Park, is great for kids. Animals are predominantly rescues or are no longer able to survive in the wild, and residents include grizzly bears, alpacas, wolves, cougars and prairie dogs.

Saskatchewan Railway Museum MUSEUM

(☎306-382-9855; www.saskrailmuseum.org; off Hwy 60; adult/child $6/4; 10am-5pm Fri-Sun May-Sep; P) The railroad opened up Saskatchewan to settlers and was a vital lifeline for getting grain to market. This museum shows how things were when rails, not roads, were the most important links in the province. It's west of the center on Hwy 7, then 2km south on Hwy 60.

Ukrainian Museum of Canada MUSEUM

(Map p551; ☎306-244-3800; www.umc.sk.ca; 910 Spadina Cres E; adult/child $6/4; 10am-5pm Tue-Sat, 1-5pm Sun; P) This museum tells the story of Ukrainian immigration to Canada. With an emphasis on traditional clothing and contemporary artwork, it provides a good insight into the world of Ukrainian Canadians.

Tours

Shearwater Boat Cruises BOATING

(Map p551; ☎888-747-7572; www.shearwatertours.com; Spadina Cres E; adult/child from $24/15; Tue-Sun May-Sep) Open-top boats cruise the river all summer long. Ponder the bridges while enjoying a cool drink from the bar; Friday sunset cruises are popular. The dock is near the University Bridge.

Festivals & Events

Sasktel Saskatchewan Jazz Festival MUSIC

(☎800-638-1211; www.saskjazz.com; Jun) Come show your soul patch at this jazzy festival, Saskatchewan's largest, at venues throughout town from late June. Some events are free.

PotashCorp Fringe Theatre Festival THEATER

(☎306-664-2239; www.25thstreettheatre.org; tickets from $10; Jul/Aug) Rough-edged acts, music and avant-garde theater quirk up the streets and performance halls in July or August.

Taste of Saskatchewan FOOD & DRINK

(☎306-975-3175; www.tasteofsaskatchewan.ca; Kiwanis Memorial Park; Jul) More than 30 local restaurants sell various treats over five days in mid-July; there is also a full schedule of live music.

Shakespeare on the Saskatchewan THEATER

(☎306-652-9100; www.shakespearesask.com; tickets from $25; Jul & Aug) Enjoy the best of the Bard in tents and the great outdoors by the riverbank.

Saskatoon Ex CARNIVAL

(☎306-931-7149; www.saskatoonexhibition.ca; cnr Ruth St & Lorne Ave, Prairieland Park; adult/child $16/12; mid-Aug) Saskatoon comes alive for the Ex, with live music, racing pigs, chuck-wagon races and rides to reacquaint you with your fairy floss. Children under 11 are free when accompanied by an adult.

Sleeping

White Pelican B&B B&B $

(☎306-249-2645; www.saskatoon.ca; 912 Queen St; r $80-100;) This three-room B&B is in a comfy 100-year-old house close to the river and the downtown parks. Two rooms share a bathroom. Promisingly, the owners have written a breakfast cookbook.

Inn on College GUESTHOUSE $

(Map p551; ☎306-665-9111; www.innoncollege.com; 1020 College Dr; r $60-100; P) Saskatoon's best-value digs, this home-style property has clean, compact rooms and a communal kitchen. It's a satisfying 15-minute walk across the bridge to the center.

Gordon Howe Campground CAMPGROUND $
(306-975-3328; www.saskatoon.ca; 1640 Ave P S; tent/RV sites $21/35; mid-Apr–mid-Oct; P wi-fi) How cool to have a campground just 2km southwest of downtown! There are enough trees amid the large 135 RV sites and 12 tent sites to give you a bit of privacy.

★ **James** BOUTIQUE HOTEL $$
(Map p551; 306-244-6446; www.thejameshotel.ca; 620 Spadina Cres E; r from $160; P air-con wi-fi) Attentive service at the James begins with your welcome to the property. From the minimalist yet sumptuous rooms featuring marble bathrooms, balconies and top-notch bedding to the stylish cocktail bar, the James gets it right. It's close to the riverfront parks; try for a room with a view.

★ **Hotel Senator** HISTORIC HOTEL $$
(Map p551; 306-244-6141; www.hotelsenator.ca; 243 21st St E; r $90-150; P air-con @ wi-fi) Dating from 1908, this well-maintained and updated hotel is creaky but cool. You can get a sense of the ornate past in the compact lobby. The pub is a good place to while away the night, and you can't beat the location – everything is a short walk away.

★ **Delta Bessborough** HERITAGE HOTEL $$
(Map p551; 306-244-5521, 800-268-1133; www.deltahotels.com; 601 Spadina Cres E; r from $130; P air-con @ wi-fi pool) In the grand tradition of the famed Canadian railway hotels, the Bessborough lives up to the castle standard; it is the architectural exclamation point on the Saskatoon skyline. The refurbished interior blends modern pastel styling with grand post-deco architecture. Rooms and suites come in many shapes and sizes. Relax in the lush public gardens.

Park Town Hotel HOTEL $$
(Map p551; 306-244-5564; www.parktownhotel.com; 924 Spadina Cres E; r $100-160; P air-con @ wi-fi pool) This hotel occupies prime real estate with park and river frontage. Ask for a river view from your choice of 172 rooms.

Eating

A rich tradition of farm-to-table cuisine is evident in Saskatoon's many restaurants. Graze your way around downtown, Riversdale and Nutana.

Homestead Ice Cream ICE CREAM $
(Map p551; 306-653-5588; www.homesteadicecream.ca; 822 Victoria Ave; treats $2-7; 1-8:30pm) A red-and-white vision of fun, this old-style ice-cream parlor is in a residential neighborhood close to Nutana. The list of flavors is endless; enjoy them outside under a pine tree.

Asian Hut ASIAN $
(Map p551; 306-954-0188; www.facebook.com/asianhutrestaurant; 320 Ave C S; mains $7-12; 11am-2pm & 5-9pm Tue-Fri, 11am-9pm Sat & Sun) There's a down-at-the-heels hipster vibe at this Riversdale outpost for cheap and cheerful Asian food. People line up for the fresh and tasty Chinese, Vietnamese and Thai fare.

Saskatoon Farmers Market MARKET $
(Map p551; 306-384-6262; www.saskatoonfarmersmarket.com; 414 Ave B S; market 10am-3pm Wed & Sun, 8am-2pm Sat, cafes 10am-3pm Tue-Sun) In the River Landing area, this market has a indoor area with cafes and stalls open through the year, but the main action is outside on market days in summer.

Park Cafe CAFE $
(306-652-6781; www.parkcafe.ca; 515 20th St W; mains $8-14; 8am-4pm) For breakfasts to fuel your adventures, this unassuming Riversdale joint serves up legendary morning platters: the hash browns are works of art, as are the onion rings.

Grazing Goat FUSION $$
(Map p551; 306-952-1136; www.thegrazinggoatgoodeats.com; 210 20th St W; mains lunch $11-15, dinner $18-28; 11:30am-2pm & 5pm-midnight Tue-Sat) A funky and creative bare-brick restaurant and lounge on the revitalized 20th St strip in Riversdale. The eclectic menu personifies a farm-to-table ethos. There are numerous small-plate and sharing choices that go well with the long (and superb) cocktail and beer list.

Berry Barn CAFE $$
(306-978-9797; www.berrybarn.ca; 830 Valley Rd; mains $12-20; 10am-8pm Apr–mid-Dec) The highly commercial Berry Barn, 15km south of town, has the expected over-cluttered gift shop as well as a popular cafe. Enjoy the riverside setting, and in summer pick some juicy Saskatoon berries – plump dark blue numbers that are like sweet boysenberries. Feast on hearty fare and all manner of berry-laced drinks, mains and desserts.

Calories Bakery & Restaurant MODERN CANADIAN $$
(Map p551; 306-665-7991; www.caloriesrestaurant.ca; 721 Broadway Ave; mains lunch $12-15, dinner $20-26; 11am-2:30pm & 5-9pm Mon-Sat, 10am-3pm Sun) Menus change every six weeks or so at this classy yet casual affair, proud of its commitment to using local, organic ingredients in its creative cuisine. With an extensive wine list, a Sunday brunch menu to look forward to and a dessert counter that will make you drool, you can't go wrong.

Christie's Il Secondo Bakery & Pizzeria CAFE $$
(Map p551; 306-384-0509; 802c Broadway Ave; mains $15-25; 8am-8pm Tue-Sat) Fresh pizzas, daily-baked bread specials and delicious Italian-style filled sandwiches are popular at this Nutana institution. Tables inside and out are always busy.

★ **Ayden Kitchen & Bar** MODERN CANADIAN $$$
(Map p551; 306-954-2590; www.aydenkitchenandbar.com; 265 3rd Ave S; mains $20-40; 11:30am-2pm & 5:30-10pm Mon-Fri, 5:30-10pm Sat) Saskatoon's restaurant-of-the-moment works magic with local produce and other seasonal specialties. Chef Dale MacKay and his co-chef and butcher Natan Guggenheimer are stars on the Canadian food scene. You never know what surprises they have in store at this unpretentious downtown bistro. Book ahead.

★ **Truffles Bistro** MODERN CANADIAN $$$
(Map p551; 306-373-7779; www.trufflesbistro.ca; 230 21st St E; mains $24-32; 5-10pm Mon-Fri, 10am-2:30pm & 5-10pm Sat, 10am-2pm Sun) Smooth jazz sets up the classic ambience of this modern bistro. Fine wines accompany beautifully presented, delightfully simple preparations of *steak frites* (steak and fries), pork tenderloin and local Lake Diefenbaker trout. The menu changes with the seasons. Excellent desserts.

Drinking & Nightlife

Downtown and Nutana reward carousers and bar-hoppers. Look for locally brewed Great Western beers.

★ **Congress Beer House** PUB
(Map p551; 306-974-6717; www.congressbeerhouse.com; 215 2nd Ave S; 11am-1am) This huge pub has a bit of a ski-lodge vibe. Seating is at tables and in comfy leather booths. As you'd surmise, the beer list is the best in the province, with numerous choices of hard-to-get brews. The food options are excellent, with creative takes on burgers and other pub faves.

Drift Sidewalk Cafe & Vista Lounge LOUNGE
(Map p551; 306-653-2256; www.driftcafe.ca; 339 Ave A S; 8am-10pm Sun-Thu, to midnight Fri & Sat) Split personalities mark this hip Riversdale spot. The cafe serves crêpes, sandwiches and a long list of varied snacks through the day; enjoy a coffee at a table outside. The lounge is sleeker and has a fun cocktail list, many with house-made libations. It also serves mid-priced international dishes.

Winston's English Pub & Grill PUB
(Map p551; 306-374-7468; www.winstonspub.ca; 243 21st St E; 11am-2am) A huge and popular pub with 72 taps. Besides a predictable domestic and imported lineup, the beer list includes a rotating array of excellent local microbrews. The food is solid: fish-and-chips, burgers and the like (mains $12 to $16).

Diva's Nightclub GAY & LESBIAN
(Map p551; 306-665-0100; www.divasclub.ca; 220 3rd Ave S; 9pm-late Wed-Sat) Gay or straight, you don't have to be a diva to get your groove on at this straight-friendly gay bar. Enter through the alley.

Hose and Hydrant PUB
(Map p551; 306-477-3473; www.hoseandhydrant.com; 612 11th St E; 11:30am-11pm) A fun pub in a converted fire station. Enjoy tables on a patio and deck with mellow side-street outlooks.

Entertainment

Buds on Broadway LIVE MUSIC
(Map p551; 306-244-4155; http://buds.dudaone.com; 817 Broadway Ave; 11:30am-late) Classic blues and old-time rock and roll are the standards here in this beer-swilling joint.

Saskatoon Symphony CLASSICAL MUSIC
(306-665-6414; www.saskatoonsymphony.org; tickets $15-60) The Saskatoon Symphony plays regularly at TCU Place.

Persephone Theatre THEATER
(Map p551; 306-384-7727; www.persephonetheatre.org; 100 Spadina Cres E; ticket prices vary) This perennial theatrical standout has excellent new quarters in the Remai Arts Centre at River Landing. Comedy, drama and musicals are all regulars.

WORTH A TRIP

MEACHAM

Some 68km due east of Saskatoon you'll find the village of Meacham, where free-thinking, multidisciplinary artists and salt-of-the-earth farmers find themselves in quiet, harmonious coexistence. It's a great spot to get a sense of the silent golden prairies. The wonderful **Hand Wave Gallery** (306-376-2221; www.handwave.ca; 409 3rd Ave; 11am-6pm Thu-Mon May-Sep, 1-6pm Thu-Mon Oct-Dec) represents a talented range of artists.

Stroll the tumble-down center and look for the tiny by-appointment **museum** and the professional **Dancing Sky Theatre** (306-376-4445; www.dancingskytheatre.com; 201 Queen St), which has been producing rural Canadian plays since 1997. There's also an original Pool Saskatchewan **grain elevator**.

Meacham is an easy trip from Saskatoon or an easy detour en route along Hwy 16.

Gordon Tootoosis Nīkānīwin Theatre THEATER
(GTNT; Map p551; 306-933-2262; www.gtnt.ca; 914 20th St W; Feb-Jun) Contemporary stage productions by Canadian First Nations, Métis and Inuit artists highlight cultural issues through comedy and drama.

Broadway Theatre CINEMA
(Map p551; 306-652-6556; www.broadwaytheatre.ca; 715 Broadway Ave; adult/child $10/5) This historic Nutana cinema shows cult classics, art-house films and occasional local live performances. Regularly screens *South Park:Bigger, Longer and Uncut;* sing along with 'Blame Canada'!

TCU Place THEATER
(Map p551; 306-975-7777; www.tcuplace.com; 35 22nd St E) Saskatoon's Arts and Convention Centre offers a variety of concerts, lectures, dance performances and plays through the year, as well as regularly hosting the Saskatoon Symphony.

Saskatoon Blades HOCKEY
(306-975-8844; www.saskatoonblades.com; 3535 Thatcher Ave, SaskTel Centre; adult/child from $23/13; Sep-Mar) This WHL team plays a fast, rough and sharp style of hockey.

Information

Main Post Office (Map p551; 800-267-1177; www.canadapost.ca; 309 4th Ave N; 8am-5pm Mon-Fri)

Saskatoon City Hospital (306-655-8000; www.saskatoonhealthregion.ca; 701 Queen St; 24hr)

Planet S (www.planetsmag.com) Irreverent and free biweekly newspaper with good entertainment listings.

Tourism Saskatoon (Map p551; 306-242-1206, 800-567-2444; www.tourismsaskatoon.com; 202 4th Ave N; 8:30am-5pm Mon-Fri) Has local and regional info.

Getting There & Away

AIR

John G Diefenbaker International Airport (YXE; 306-975-8900; www.yxe.ca; 2625 Airport Dr) is 5km northeast of the city, off Idylwyld Dr and Hwy 16. WestJet and Air Canada have services to major Canadian cities.

BUS

STC (www.stcbus.com) covers the province extensively from the **bus station** (Map p551; 306-933-8000; 50 23rd St E); buses head south to Regina ($51, 2¾ to four hours, three daily) and north to Prince Albert ($31, two hours, three daily). **Greyhound Canada** (www.greyhound.ca) runs buses to Winnipeg ($134, 12½ hours, one daily) and Edmonton ($71, seven hours, two daily).

TRAIN

Saskatoon's **train station** (Chappell Dr) is 8km southwest from downtown; the thrice-weekly VIA Rail *Canadian* stops here on its Vancouver–Toronto run.

Getting Around

A taxi to the airport or train station costs about $20. **Blueline Taxi** (306-653-3333; www.unitedgroup.ca) is easily reached.

Bike Doctor (306-664-8555; www.bikedoctor.ca; 623 Main St; rentals per day from $60) rents bikes.

Saskatoon Transit (Map p551; 360-975-7500; www.transit.saskatoon.ca; adult/child $3/2.25) runs city buses, which converge on the transit hub of 23rd St E (between 2nd and 3rd Aves N).

NORTHERN SASKATCHEWAN

North of Saskatoon, driving options funnel into one northern route as the scenery changes around you. Gone are the vast wheat fields of the south, replaced by rugged boreal forests and myriad lakes. There is a cultural shift up here too: an independent spirit that carved a life out of the rugged landscape.

The Battlefords

Linked by bridge across the North Saskatchewan River, Battleford and its larger sibling North Battleford seem only slightly removed from a century ago when they embodied the hardscrabble existence of early prairie settlers.

The re-created town at North Battleford's branch of the **Western Development Museum** (WDM; ☎306-445-8083; www.wdm.ca; Hwy 16, at Hwy 40, North Battleford; adult/child $10/4; ⏲9am-5pm daily Apr-Dec, Tue-Sun Jan-Mar, outdoor village closed Oct-May) is an insight into the immense amount of labor required by the pioneers to convert prairie to farmland. Walking along the boardwalk-covered streets and through the preserved houses, it's easy to imagine how hard life would have been. At the **Fort Battleford National Historic Site** (☎306-937-2621; www.parkscanada.ca/battleford; off Hwy 4, Battleford; adult/child $4/2; ⏲10am-4pm daily Jul & Aug, Mon-Fri Jun), costumed guides and cannon firings give life to the NWMP fort, built in 1876.

Art lovers will be enthralled by the **Allen Sapp Gallery** (☎306-445-1760; www.allensapp.com; 1 Railway Ave E, North Battleford; by donation; ⏲11am-5pm daily Jun-Sep, noon-4pm Wed-Sun Oct-May) right on Hwy 16. Sapp's work, depicting his Cree heritage, is a breathtaking mix of landscapes and portraits.

Prince Albert National Park

Prince Albert National Park is a jewel in the wild. Just when you thought the vast prairie would never end, the trees begin, signaling the start of the vast boreal forest. This national park is one of those special places that will give you the feeling that you are truly on the edge of the known world.

The quaint village of **Waskesiu Lake** is your base for exploration within the park.

Sights & Activities

Prince Albert National Park PARK
(☎306-663-4522; www.parkscanada.ca/princealbert; adult/child $8/4) A forested sanctuary of lakes, untouched land and wildlife, this park puts the 'wild' back into 'wilderness.' Outdoor activities such as canoeing, hiking and camping are at their shining best. Indeed, there is a multitude of potential adventures to be had here, whether it be the unforgettable 20km trek to **Grey Owl's Cabin**, a canoe trip or even just chilling out on a beach.

Waskesiu Marina MARINA
(☎306-663-1999; www.waskesiumarina.com; Waskesiu Lake; kayaks per hour from $17) Waskesiu Marina rents canoes, kayaks and motorboats. It has guided boat trips to Grey Owl's Cabin.

DON'T MISS

BATOCHE NATIONAL HISTORIC SITE

A virtual civil war was fought here in 1885 when Louis Riel led the Métis in defending their land from the government. The children of French fur traders and Aboriginal mothers, the Métis were forced from Manitoba in the mid-1800s and many made their home in Batoche. Frustrated by the government's continual betrayal of treaties, the Métis and a number of Cree declared their independence from Canada: an announcement met by military force, led by Major General Frederick Middleton. Although outnumbered by 800 to 200, the Métis fought for four days and almost won, but Riel was captured (and later hung for treason).

Once-prosperous Batoche was devastated and within a few years almost nothing was left except for the church you see today. The **historic site** (☎306-423-6227; www.parkscanada.ca/batoche; Rte 225, Wakaw; adult/child $8/4; ⏲9am-5pm daily Jul & Aug, Mon-Fri Jun & Sep) is an auspicious place to contemplate the events of 1885, as silent waves of prairie grass bend in the wind.

Batoche is 70km north of Saskatoon, east of Hwy 11.

Canoeski Discovery CANOEING
(☎306-653-5693; www.canoeski.com; canoe rental per day from $45) With a large variety of multiday paddling trips in the local area and beyond, Canoeski is a great way to see the countryside and learn to canoe at the same time.

Sleeping

★ **Sturgeon River Ranch** RANCH $$
(☎306-469-2356; www.sturgeonriverranch.com; off Hwy 55, Big River; camping expeditions per person from $500) Outside the western border of the park, Sturgeon River Ranch is regarded for its nature focus and horseback rides (from $125 per person) into the wilderness.

Flora Bora Forest Lodging YURT $$
(☎877-763-5672; www.florabora.ca; off Hwy 263, Emma Lake; yurts $165-200; P) Yurt it up in the delightful Flora Bora Forest Lodging, between Emma and Christopher Lakes. These wilderness huts have decks and are removed from the parking area.

Elk Ridge Resort RESORT $$
(☎306-663-4653; www.elkridgeresort.com; off Hwy 264, Waskesiu Lake; r from $120; P ☎) For a little bit of luxury, consider this sprawling resort, which has its own small lake, golf course and more.

Information

The **Waskesiu Chamber of Commerce** (☎306-663-5410; www.waskesiulake.ca; 35 Montreal Dr, Waskesiu Lake; ⏱9am-5pm Jul & Aug, reduced hours Sep-Jun) and park **visitor center** (☎306-663-4522; 969 Lakeview Dr, Waskesiu Lake; ⏱8am-8pm Jun-Aug) can help with accommodations and park info.

La Ronge & the Far North

La Ronge is the southern hub of the far north – your last chance for supplies before heading off the grid. It's a rough, basic town, popular with anglers, hunters and folks on the run.

It's hard to believe that almost half of Saskatchewan still lies further north. This is frontier territory, the end of the paved road. If you're not skittish about extreme isolation and you're outfitted appropriately, then this is it! You'll discover tiny burgs such as **Southend**, and pass the vast **Reindeer Lake**, before arriving at the winter-only section at **Stony Rapids**, some 12 hours north of La Ronge. Self sufficiency here is key: make sure you maintain your vehicle, have plenty of fuel, gear and supplies, and keep your head together.

Lac La Ronge Provincial Park (☎306-425-4234; www.saskparks.net/laclaronge; Hwy 2; ⏱May-Sep) surrounds huge, island-filled Lac La Ronge, great for fishing, canoeing and hikes among stubby pines. There are over 100 more lakes and over 1000 islands. The park has five year-round campgrounds and endless backcountry camping.

Robertson's Trading Post (☎306-425-2080; 308 La Ronge Ave, La Ronge; ⏱8am-5pm Mon-Sat) is the place to go if you're in the market for a bear trap, wolf hide or case of baked beans. You can buy pretty much anything you'd ever need here and some stuff that you never would.

Alberta

Includes ➡

Best Places to Eat

- ➡ Packrat Louie Kitchen & Bar (p568)
- ➡ Market (p582)
- ➡ 49° North Pizza (p629)
- ➡ Trough (p590)
- ➡ Other Paw Bakery (p612)
- ➡ Al Forno Cafe & Bakery (p581)

Best Places to Sleep

- ➡ Deer Lodge (p605)
- ➡ Tekarra Lodge (p611)
- ➡ Mt Engadine Lodge (p588)
- ➡ Varscona (p566)
- ➡ Heartwood Inn & Spa (p623)
- ➡ Prince of Wales Hotel (p629)

Why Go?

Alberta does lakes and mountains like Rome does cathedrals and chapels, but without the penance. For proof head west to Jasper and Banff, two of the world's oldest national parks; despite their wild and rugged terrain, they remain untrammeled and easily accessible. No one should leave this mortal coil without first laying eyes on Lake Louise and the Columbia Icefield – and think twice about dying before you've traveled east to the dinosaur-encrusted badlands around Drumheller, south to the Crypt Lake trail in Waterton Lakes National Park, and north to spot bison in the vast northern parklands.

In the center of the province, the wheat blows and the cattle roam; here you'll find historic ranches, sacred native sights and the eerie landscape of the hoodoos. What Alberta's cities lack in history they make up for with their spirit: Calgary has become unexpectedly cool, with top museums and cocktail bars, while Edmonton's fringe theater festival is the world's second largest.

When to Go

Edmonton

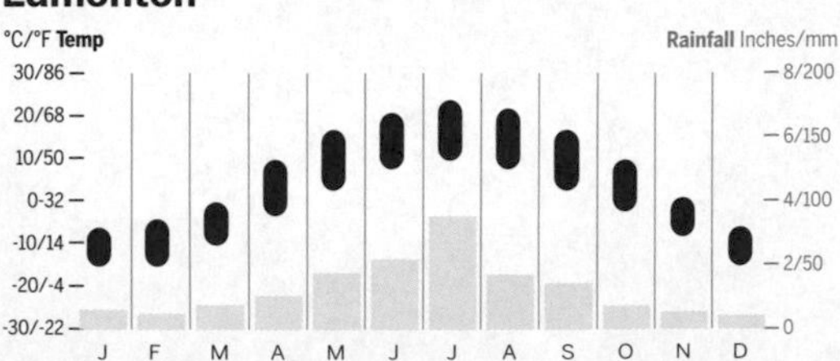

Jul Prime time for festivals, with Edmonton's Street Performers and the Calgary Stampede.

Jul–Sep Banff and Jasper's trails are snow-free, making a full range of hikes available.

Dec–Feb Winter-sports season in the Rocky Mountains.

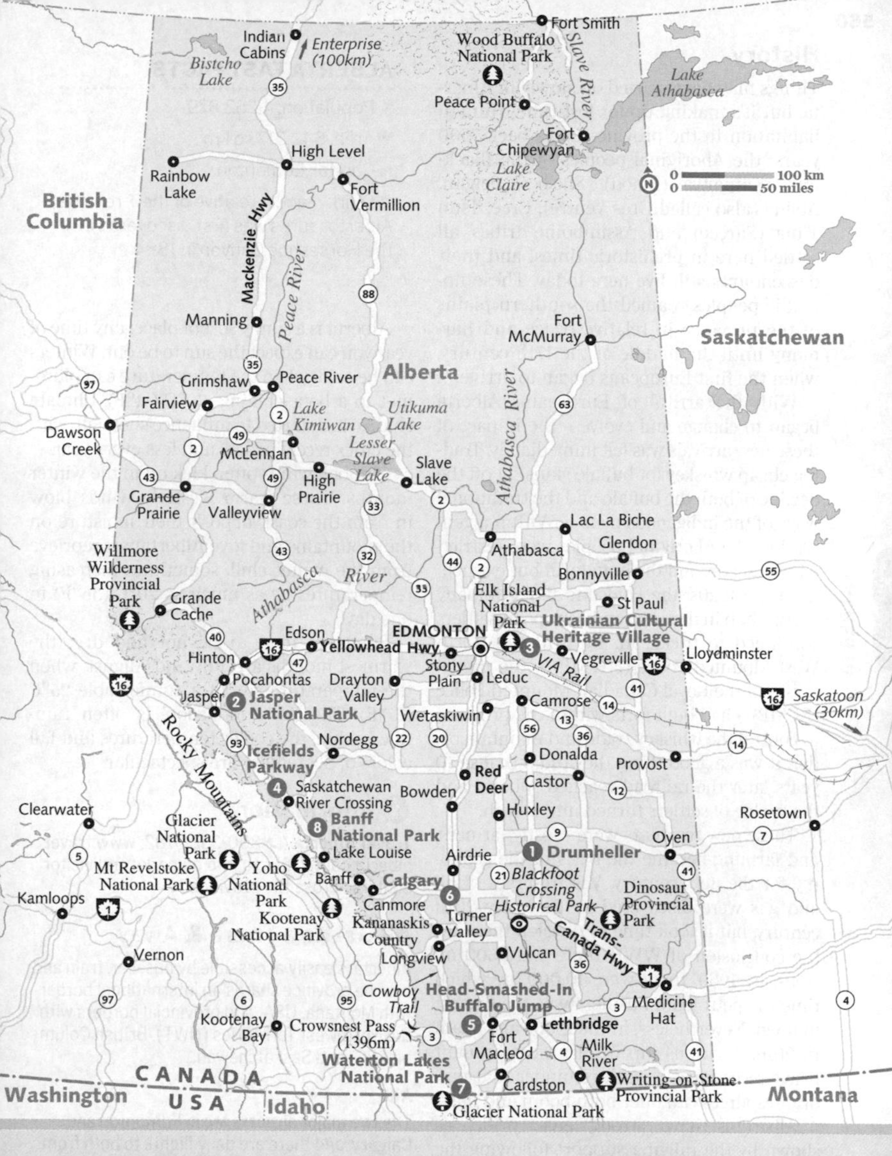

Alberta Highlights

1 Royal Tyrrell Museum of Palaeontology (p614) Exploring the Jurassic remnants of Drumheller.

2 Miette Hot Springs (p606) Soaking beaneath the mountain peaks of Jasper National Park.

3 Ukrainian Cultural Heritage Village (p571) Stepping back in time to experience new immigrant life at the turn of the century.

4 Icefields Parkway (p591) Driving between towering mountains, a bevy of bears and scenic viewpoints.

5 Head-Smashed-In Buffalo Jump (p624) Delving into the fascinating history of First Nations culture.

6 National Music Centre (p575) Living out your rock-and-roll fantasies at Calgary's newest and coolest museum.

7 Waterton Lakes National Park (p627) Kayaking surrounded by fairy-tale scenery.

8 Lake Agnes Teahouse (p605) Enjoying glacial-water tea high above Lake Louise.

History

Things may have started off slowly in Alberta, but it's making up for lost time. Human habitation in the province dates back 7500 years: the Aboriginal peoples of the Blackfoot, Kainaiwa (Blood), Siksika, Peigan, Atsina (also called Gros Ventre), Cree, Tsuu T'ina (Sarcee) and Assiniboine tribes all settled here in prehistoric times, and their descendants still live here today. These nomadic peoples roamed the southern plains of the province in relative peace and harmony until the middle of the 17th century, when the first Europeans began to arrive.

With the arrival of Europeans, Alberta began to change and evolve – the impact of these new arrivals was felt immediately. Trading cheap whiskey for buffalo skins set off the decline of both the buffalo and the traditional ways of the indigenous people. Within a generation, the Aboriginal peoples were restricted to reserves and the buffalo all but extinct.

In the 1820s, the Hudson's Bay Company set up shop in the area, and European settlers continued to trickle in. By 1870 the North West Mounted Police (NWMP) – the predecessor of the Royal Canadian Mounted Police (RCMP) – had built forts within the province to control the whiskey trade and maintain order. It was a good thing they did, because 10 years later the railroad reached Alberta and the trickle of settlers turned into a gush.

These new residents were mostly farmers, and farming became the basis of the economy for the next century. Vast reserves of oil and gas were discovered in the early 20th century, but it took time to develop them. At the conclusion of WWII there were 500 oil wells; by 1960, there were 10,000, by which time the petroleum business was the biggest in town. Nevertheless, in the 1980s and again in 2016, a serious dip in oil prices brought heavy recession – a stark reminder that natural resources can offer both boom and bust.

Albertans have strong civic pride, as shown by the rallying support following the 2013 floods in Calgary and the 2016 wildfires in Fort McMurray. With their can-do attitude, there's little doubt they'll pull through.

Land & Climate

The prairies that cover the eastern and southern parts of Alberta give way to the towering Rocky Mountains that form the western edge of the province. That mountainous spine forms the iconic scenery for which Alberta is known.

ALBERTA FAST FACTS

- Population: 4,252,879
- Area: 642,317 sq km
- Capital: Edmonton
- Quirky fact: A relative of the T-rex, the Albertosaurus was first discovered in the Horseshoe Canyon in 1884.

Alberta is a sunny sort of place; any time of year you can expect the sun to be out. Winters can be cold, when the temperature can plummet to a bone-chilling -20°C (-4°F). Climate change has started to influence snowfall, with the cities receiving less and less every year.

Chinook winds often kick up in the winter months. These warm westerly winds blow in from the coast, deposit their moisture on the mountains and give Albertans a reprieve from the winter chill, sometimes increasing temperatures by as much as 20°C (36°F) in one day!

Summers tend to be hot and dry; the warmest months are July and August, when the temperature sits at a comfortable 25°C (77°F). The 'June Monsoon' is often rain-filled, while the cooler temperatures and fall colors of September are spectacular.

Information

Travel Alberta (800-252-3782; www.travelalberta.com) Links to info on parks and visitor centers across the province.

Getting There & Away

Alberta is easily accessible by bus, car, train and air. The province shares an international border with Montana, USA, and provincial borders with the Northwest Territories (NWT), British Columbia (BC) and Saskatchewan.

AIR

The two major airports are in Edmonton and Calgary, and there are daily flights to both from major hubs across the world. Carriers serving the province include Air Canada, American Airlines, British Airways, Delta, Horizon Air, KLM, United Airlines and WestJet.

BUS

Greyhound Canada (customer service 877-463-6446, fares & schedules 800-661-8747; www.greyhound.ca) has bus services to Alberta from neighboring provinces, and Greyhound has services from the USA. Times can vary greatly, based upon connections, and fares can be reduced by booking in advance.

Useful destinations, with one-way fares, from Edmonton:

Prince George ($100, 10 hours, daily)
Vancouver ($150, 17 hours, five daily)
Whitehorse ($240, 29 hours, one daily)
Winnipeg ($170, 20 hours, three daily)

Destinations from Calgary:

Kamloops ($95, 10 hours, four daily)
Regina ($85, 10 hours, two daily)
Saskatoon ($78, nine hours, four daily)
Vancouver ($99, 15 hours, five daily)
Winnipeg ($175, 20 hours, daily)

Moose Travel Network (☎604-297-0255; www.moosenetwork.com) runs a variety of trips in western Canada. Tours start in Vancouver or Banff and along the way hit the highlights of the mountain parks and other Alberta must-sees. In winter it operates ski-focused tours that are a great option for car-less ski bums. Trips depart daily during the summer months and a few times per week in the winter season.

CAR & MOTORCYCLE

Alberta was designed with the car (and an unlimited supply of oil) in mind. There are high-quality, well-maintained highways and a network of back roads to explore. Towns will for the most part have services, regardless of the population.

Be aware that in more remote areas, especially in the north, those services could be a large distance apart. Fill up your gas tank wherever possible and be prepared for possible emergencies with things like warm clothes and water.

TRAIN

Despite years of hard labor, countless work-related deaths and a reputation for being one of the great feats of 19th-century engineering, Alberta's contemporary rail network has been whittled down to just two regular passenger train services. **VIA Rail** (☎888-842-7245; www.via.ca) runs the *Canadian* from Vancouver to Toronto two or three times per week, passing through Jasper and Edmonton in both directions. Edmonton to Vancouver costs $225 and takes 27 hours; Edmonton to Toronto costs $405 and takes 55 hours. The Toronto-bound train stops in Saskatoon, Saskatchewan; Winnipeg, Manitoba; and Sudbury Junction, Ontario. VIA Rail also operates the train from Jasper to Prince Rupert, BC ($117, 32 hours, three weekly).

ALBERTA ITINERARIES

One Week

Spend the day in **Calgary** exploring the **Glenbow Museum** (p575) and the **National Music Centre** (p575), then grab a meal on trendy 17th Ave or wander through the artsy neighborhoods of Kensington and Inglewood. The next day, get into dino mode by taking a day trip to **Drumheller** and visiting the **Royal Tyrrell Museum of Palaeontology** (p614). Back in Calgary, head east to spot wild bison at **Elk Island National Park** (p573) and step back in time at the authentic **Ukrainian Cultural Heritage Village** (p571).

Wake early and head west. Have fresh bagels for breakfast in **Canmore** and then carry on to into **Banff National Park** and check out the **Whyte Museum of the Canadian Rockies** (p594).

After a stay in Banff, follow the scenic Bow Valley Pkwy to **Lake Louise**, finding time for the short, steep hike to the **Lake Agnes Teahouse** (p605) and a trip up the **Lake Louise Gondola** (p604) to spot grizzly bears. Head out on the spectacular **Icefields Parkway** to the **Columbia Icefield** (p592).

Roll into **Jasper** and check into **Tekarra Lodge** (p611) for some much-needed R & R. Drive out to **Maligne Lake** (p607), where a short hike might let you spot a bear or a moose. Carry on north to **Miette Hot Springs** (p606) for a fabulous soak amid mountain scenery. Escape the mountains and head to **Edmonton**, diving into the Old Strathcona neighborhood, and finishing your Alberta adventure with a gourmet meal at **Packrat Louie Kitchen & Bar** (p568).

The Complete Rockies

Follow the One Week itinerary, but before reaching Canmore, head south down Hwy 5, known as the **Cowboy Trail**, to take in **Bar U Ranch** (p625). Continue south to **Waterton Lakes National Park** (p627), experiencing this less-visited mountain paradise. Return north through Kananaskis Country, stopping for tea or an overnight stay at **Mt Engadine Lodge** (p588). Then carry on north to **Canmore**.

Rocky Mountaineer (☎604-606-7245; www.rockymountaineer.com; 5 days from $2650; ⏲May-Oct) tours chug east from Vancouver through the Rockies via Kamloops to Jasper or Banff, or north from Vancouver to Jasper via Whistler and northern BC. These luxury trains have been transporting tourists on multiday journeys for a quarter century.

EDMONTON

POP 899, 447

Modern, spread out and frigidly cold for much of the year, Alberta's second-largest city and capital is a government town that you're more likely to read about in the business pages than the travel supplements. Edmonton is often a stopover en route to Jasper National Park, which is four hours' drive west, or for explorations into the vast and empty landscape to the north.

Downtown is for the moneyed and the down-and-out. There's hope that the much-lauded Rogers Place will breathe life into it, but this seems like a tall order. For the soul of the city, head south of the river to the university district and happy-go-lucky Whyte Ave, home to small theaters, diners and a spirited Friday-night mood. Edmonton also has a few decent museums, an annual fringe festival second only to Edinburgh's, and some top nearby sights like the Ukrainian Cultural Village and Elk Island National Park.

History

The Cree and Blackfoot tribes can trace their ancestry to the Edmonton area for 5000 years. It wasn't until the late 18th century that Europeans first arrived in the area. A trade outpost was built by the Hudson's Bay Company in 1795, which was dubbed Fort Edmonton.

Trappers, traders and adventurers frequented the fort, but it wasn't until 1870, when the government purchased Fort Ed and opened up the area to pioneers, that Edmonton saw its first real growth in population. When the railway arrived in Calgary in 1891, growth really started to speed up.

Meanwhile, the Aboriginal tribes had been severely weakened by disease and the near extinction of their primary food source, the bison. Increasingly vulnerable, they signed away most of their land rights to the Canadian government in a series of treaties between 1871 and 1921 in return for money, reservation lands and hunting rights.

Gold was the first big boom for the area – not gold found in Alberta, but gold in the Yukon. Edmonton was the last stop in civilization before dreamers headed north to the Klondike. Some made their fortunes, most did not; some settled in Edmonton, and the town grew.

In the 1940s, WWII precipitated the construction of the Alaska Hwy, and the influx of workers further increased the population. Ukrainians and other Eastern European immigrants came to Edmonton in search of work and enriched the city.

Edmonton is again the hub for those looking to earn their fortune in the north. But it isn't gold or roads this time – it's oil.

Sights & Activities

★Art Gallery of Alberta — GALLERY

(Map p566; ☎780-422-6223; www.youraga.ca; 2 Sir Winston Churchill Sq; adult/child $12.50/8.50; ⏲11am-5pm Tue-Sun, to 9pm Wed) With the opening of this maverick art gallery in 2010, Edmonton at last gained a modern signature building to counter the ubiquitous boxy skyscrapers with a giant glass-and-metal space helmet. Its collection comprises 6000 pieces of historical and contemporary art, many of which have strong Canadian bias, that rotate through eight galleries. Numerous worthwhile temporary shows also pass through, and you'll find a shop, theater and restaurant on-site.

★Fort Edmonton Park — HISTORIC SITE

(☎780-496-8787; www.fortedmontonpark.ca; cnr Fox & Whitemud Drs; adult/child/family $26.20/20.90/95; ⏲10am-5pm Jul & Aug, 10am-3pm Mon-Fri, 10am-5pm Sat & Sun May-Jun, 11am-5pm Sat & Sun Sep & holidays; 👪) The riverside reconstruction of Hudson's Bay Company's log fort gives you a glimpse into life in a trading post in the 1840s, right down to the smell of tanned hides. To reach it, pass by a 1920s midway and farm, and a few blocks of Edmonton in the 1920s, 1905 and 1885. Hop on a street car or horse carriage, chat with 'locals' (employees dressed up from the relevant era), do some yesteryear shopping or try the penny arcade.

Muttart Conservatory — GARDENS

(Map p564; ☎780-496-8755; www.muttartconservatory.ca; 9626 96A St; adult/child/family $12.50/6.50/37; ⏲10am-5pm Fri-Wed, to 9pm Thu) Looking like some sort of pyramid-shaped, glass bomb shelter, the Muttart Conservatory is actually a botanical garden that sits south of the river off James MacDonald Bridge. Each of the four pyramids holds a different climate region and corresponding foliage. It's an interesting place to wander about, especially for gardeners, plant fans and those in the mood for something low-key. The excellent on-site cafe uses locally sourced ingredients and fresh greens from the greenhouse.

Royal Alberta Museum MUSEUM
(Map p564; ☎780-453-9100; www.royalalbertamuseum.ca; ⊙9am-5pm) Since getting its 'royal' prefix in 2005 when Queen Liz II dropped by, Edmonton's leading museum has successfully received funding – a cool $340 million – for a new downtown home, which should be complete by late 2017. The new museum (103A Ave) will be the largest in western Canada, with an enormous collection of Alberta's natural and cultural history. Until then, the museum is closed.

Alberta Railway Museum MUSEUM
(☎780-472-6229; www.albertarailwaymuseum.com; 24215 34th St; adult/child $7/3.50; ⊙10am-5pm Sat & Sun May-Aug) This museum, on the northeast edge of the city, has a collection of more than 75 railcars, including steam and diesel locomotives and rolling stock, built and used between 1877 and 1950. On weekends, volunteers fire up some of the old engines, and you can hop on the diesel locomotives on Sundays or the 1913 steam locomotive on holiday weekends.

Ukrainian Museum of Canada MUSEUM
(www.umcalberta.org; 10611 110th Ave; by donation; ⊙10am-4pm May-Aug) FREE With a huge Ukrainian population and a long history of immigration, this museum is surprisingly small. While it continues to search for bigger digs, it shows a tiny collection of traditional costumes, toys and artwork. The cultural center in the same building hosts pierogi suppers on the last of Friday of each month ($15). Check its website (www.uocc-stjohn.ca) for details.

Telus World of Science MUSEUM
(☎780-451-3344; www.edmontonscience.com; 11211 142nd St; adult/child $28/20; ⊙9am-6pm Sun-Wed, to 10pm Thu, to 8pm Fri & Sat; 👪) With an emphasis on interactive displays, this science museum has a million things to do, all under one roof. Fight crime with the latest technology, see what living on a spacecraft is all about, go on a dinosaur dig and explore what makes the human body tick. The center also includes an IMAX theater (extra cost) and an observatory with telescopes (no extra cost).

Valley Zoo ZOO
(Map p564; ☎780-496-8787; www.valleyzoo.ca; 13315 Buena Vista Rd; adult/child/family $14/8.75/45.50; ⊙9am-6pm; 👪) The Valley Zoo has more than 100 exotic, endangered and native animals. Kids will enjoy the petting zoo, camel and pony rides, miniature train, carousel and paddleboats. If you want to brave the zoo in the frigid winter, admission costs are reduced.

North Saskatchewan River Valley PARK
Edmonton has more designated urban parkland than any other city in North America, most of it contained within an interconnected riverside green belt that effectively cuts the metropolis in half. The green zone is flecked with lakes, bridges, wild areas, golf courses, ravines, and approximately 160km worth of cycling and walking trails. It is easily accessed from downtown.

Sir Winston Churchill Square SQUARE
(Map p566) With huge umbrellas, a splashing fountain, and tables and chairs, this public square is a good place to catch your breath in the summer. A giant chess board on the ground, Ping-Pong tables and daily classes in everything from Zumba to lightsaber training are all here. It's also worth checking out the awesome gift shop in Tix on the square, with work from local artists.

Alberta Government House HISTORIC BUILDING
(Map p564; ☎780-427-2281; 12845 102nd Ave; ⊙11am-4:30pm Sun & holidays mid-Feb–Nov) FREE This opulent mansion was the former residence of the lieutenant governor but is now used for government conferences and receptions. It is steeped in history and immaculately preserved – you'd never guess it's over 100 years old. The artwork alone is worth visiting: the walls are lined with stunning works by Canadian artists.

☞ Tours

Quirky free walking tours of downtown are offered in the summer months by students on vacation and employed by the Downtown Business Association. They leave weekdays at 1pm from the corner of 104th St and 101st Ave.

Edmonton

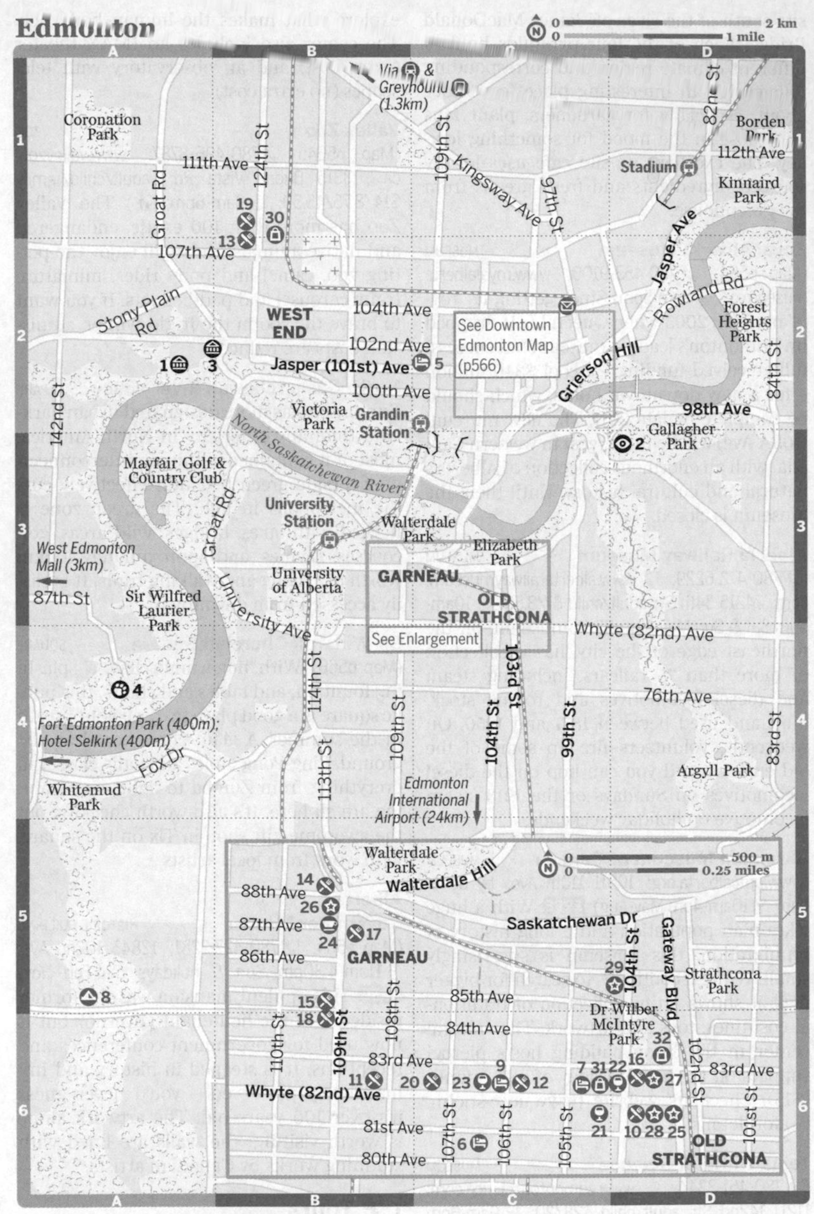

★ **Cobblestone Freeway** CULTURAL

(☎780-436-7482; cobblestonefreeway.ca; day tours from C$89) With knowledgeable guides who have strong links to the local Ukrainian community, on these tours you can experience traditional dance performances, authentic Ukrainian food and heritage sights, as well neighboring Ukrainian communities. They can also get you to the city's must-see sights or as far afield as Jasper. Especially great at tailoring tours to traveler's interests, service is both personable and professional.

Edmonton

Sights
1 Alberta Government House A2
2 Muttart Conservatory D3
3 Royal Alberta Museum........................ A2
4 Valley Zoo A4

Sleeping
5 Canterra Suites Hotel.......................... C2
6 HI-Edmonton Hostel............................. C6
7 Metterra Hotel on Whyte C6
8 Rainbow Valley Campground & RV Park... A5
9 Varscona... C6

Eating
10 Block 1912 .... D6
11 Café Mosaics B6
12 Da-De-O C6
13 Duchess Bake Shop B2
14 High Level Diner................................. B5
15 Noorish.. B5
16 Packrat Louie Kitchen & Bar D6
17 Remedy Cafe....................................... B5
18 Three Boars Eatery B6
19 Tiramisu Bistro B1
20 Tokyo Noodle Shop.............................. C6

Drinking & Nightlife
21 Black Dog Freehouse........................... C6
22 Next Act... D6
23 O'Byrne's C6
24 Transcend Coffee................................. B5

Entertainment
25 Blues on Whyte..................................... D6
26 Garneau Theatre B5
27 New Varscona Theatre.......................... D6
28 Princess Theatre D6
29 Roxy Theatre.. D5

Shopping
30 124 Grand Market.................................. B1
31 Junque Cellar C6
32 Old Strathcona Farmers Market.......... D6

Edmonton Ghost Tours WALKING
(www.edmontonghosttours.com; tours per person $10; 9pm Mon-Thu Jul & Aug) Spooky walking tours led by storytellers recounting the ghostly history of Edmonton. Tours cover various neighborhoods; check the website to see where to meet. No booking is required, just turn up 15 minutes early. Cash only.

Festivals & Events

International Street Performers Festival THEATER
(www.edmontonstreetfest.com; 2nd week Jul) Sometimes the best theater is outside. International performers perform alfresco in this busker bonanza. Performers are curated and most strut their stuff in Sir Winston Churchill Sq.

K-Days CARNIVAL
(www.k-days.com; late Jul) For years, Capital Ex (Klondike Days) was the big summer festival in Edmonton. Since 2012, it has been known as K-Days, with less focus on gold-rush history and more on contemporary fun. Big names in music grace two stages, the midway has adrenaline charged rides and you'll still find a nugget's worth of olden-days fun.

Edmonton International Fringe Festival THEATER
(www.fringetheatre.ca; tickets $13; mid-Aug) The ultimate Edmonton experience is an 11-day program of live alternative theater on outdoor stages, in the parks, and in small theaters and venues. It's second in size only to the Edinburgh Fringe Festival. Many shows are free and no ticket costs more than $15. There's no booking – you choose a theater and stand in line. The festival draws half a million people each year to Old Strathcona.

Sleeping

While many hotels in the city are banking on visitors traveling on an expense account, Edmonton has a decent range of independent accommodations, including some with some character. If you are in town mainly to visit the West Edmonton Mall, then staying in or near it is feasible, but the digs there are definitely leaning toward the touristy side of the spectrum.

HI-Edmonton Hostel HOSTEL $
(Map p564; 780-988-6836; www.hihostels.ca; 10647 81st Ave; d $85, dm/d with shared bath $31/69; P @) Situated in the heart of Old Strathcona, this busy hostel is a safe bet. Many of the rooms are a bit jam-packed with bunks and it feels somewhat like a converted old people's home (it used to be a convent), but recent renovations have brightened things up and produced a fantastic outdoor patio. The location and price are hard to beat.

Downtown Edmonton

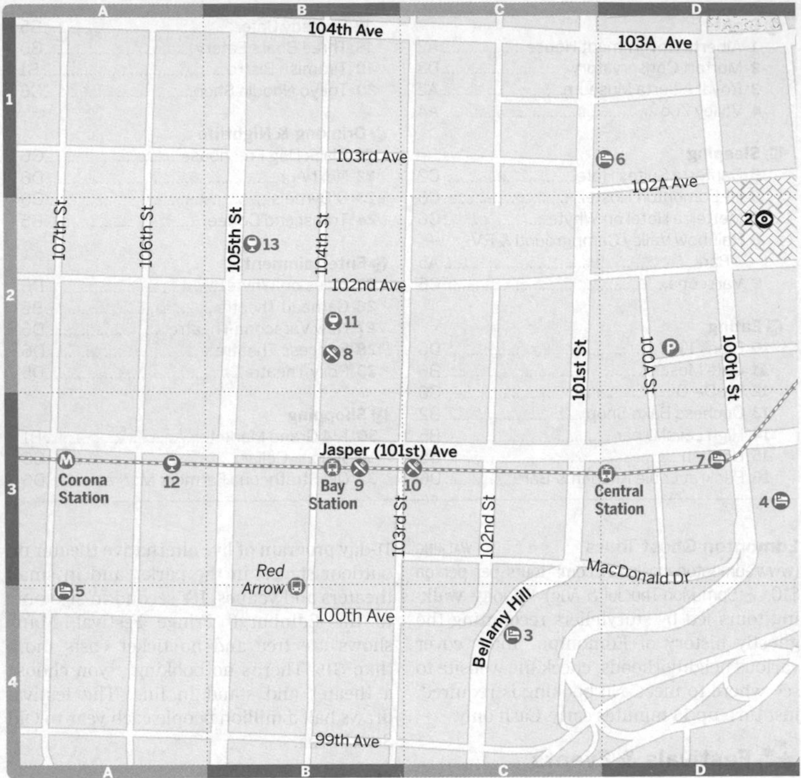

Rainbow Valley Campground & RV Park CAMPGROUND $
(Map p564; ☎780-434-5531; www.rainbow-valley.com; 13204 45th Ave; tent/RV sites $37/42; ⊙Apr-Oct; P) For an inner-city camping spot, this one is pretty good. It's in a good location to get to 'The Mall' and keep some distance from it at the same time. There are lots of trees, a playground, cookhouse, showers and wood-burning stoves. Rates are reduced out of peak season (late May to early September).

★**Matrix** BOUTIQUE HOTEL $$
(Map p566; ☎780-429-2861; www.matrixedmonton.com; 10001 107th St; r from $150; P@) Modern and slick, the lobby here could be James Bond's living room, complete with low leather furniture and a large glassed-in fireplace. Rooms are similarly stylish with plenty of up-to-date gadgets. Service is stellar and genuine, breakfasts are mammoth, there's free wine and cheese in the evening, and a shuttle downtown.

★**Varscona** BOUTIQUE HOTEL $$
(Map p564; ☎780-434-6111; www.varscona.com; 8208 106th St, cnr Whyte Ave; r incl breakfast from $140; P@) This charming hotel is elegant but not too hoity-toity, suggesting you can roll up in a tracksuit or a business suit – or some kind of combination of the two. Recently renovated rooms have splashes of color and lots of comfort, and Edmonton's coolest neighborhood is on the doorstep. Parking, and evening wine and cheese sweeten the deal.

Metterra Hotel on Whyte BOUTIQUE HOTEL $$
(Map p564; ☎780-465-8150; www.metterra.com; 10454 Whyte Ave; r from $150; P@) Sleek and regularly updated, this small hotel has a prime location on Whyte Ave. Earthy tones, cloud-like beds and splashes of Indonesian art give rooms a luxurious feel. The friendly

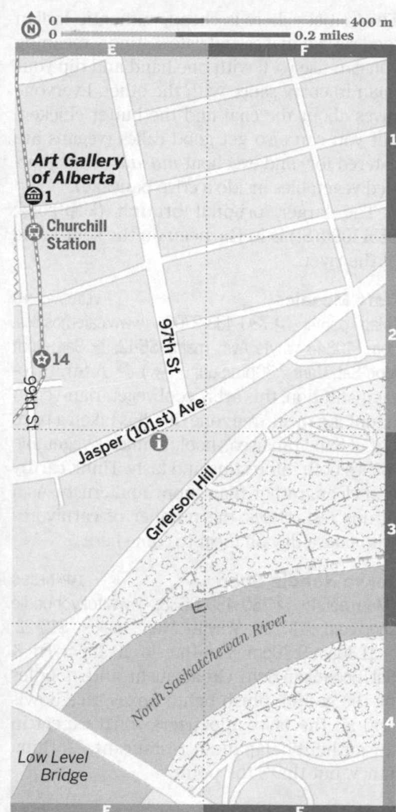

Downtown Edmonton

staff can fill you in on what's happening in the neighborhood.

Hotel Selkirk HOTEL $$
(780-496-7227; www.fortedmontonpark.ca/hotel-selkirk/; 7000 143rd St, Fort Edmonton Park; r/ste from $149/169; P ❄ ☎) If you're into the idea of visiting the past at Fort Edmonton, why not take it to the next level and spend the night? This historic hotel has simple period-decorated rooms from the roaring 1920s, and staying here gives you free entry into the fort and its surrounds. There's an on-site restaurant and English high tea ($20) on offer during the summer. Once the park closes, it's quiet – very, very quiet.

Chateau Lacombe HOTEL $$
(Map p566; 780-428-6611; www.chateaulacombe.com; 10111 Bellamy Hill; r from $120; P ❄ @ ☎) Going defiantly against the grain, the spectacular Chateau was a chain hotel that, in 2013, was bought out by local private investors. This riverside behemoth has 24 floors, wonderful views and a revolving restaurant. It's not exactly swish but with an opulent lobby, fitness center and club-ish bar, it remains regally plush – and now at a bargain price!

Canterra Suites Hotel HOTEL $$
(Map p564; 780-421-1212; www.canterrasuites.com; 11010 Jasper Ave; ste from $199; ❄ ☎) Catering to traveling businesspeople, the Canterra has large, comfortable suites equipped with modern kitchenettes. It's close to downtown and right next to a supermarket. Ideal for long- or short-term stays.

★**Union Bank Inn** BOUTIQUE HOTEL $$$
(Map p566; 780-423-3600; www.unionbankinn.com; 10053 Jasper Ave; r from $220; P ❄ @ ☎) This posh boutique hotel on Jasper Ave, in a former bank building dating from 1910, is an upmarket masterpiece. With just 34 rooms, the staff will be at your beck and call, and the in-room fireplaces make even Edmonton's frigid winters almost bearable. There's an equally fancy restaurant – Madison's Grill (p569) – on the ground floor.

Fairmont Hotel Macdonald HOTEL $$$
(Map p566; 780-424-5181; www.fairmont.com; 10065 100th St; r from $210; P @ ☎ ≋) Stealing

the best nook in town (as Fairmont always does), Edmonton's historic Fairmont Hotel exhibits the usual array of intricate stucco, Italian marble, ornate chandeliers and lush carpets. In the early 20th century it was one in a luxurious chain of railway hotels that dotted the cross-continental line from east to west.

Sutton Place Hotel HOTEL **$$$**
(Map p566; ☎780-428-7111; www.suttonplace.com; 10235 101st St; r from $230; P @ ≋) Silk papered walls, thick carpets and plush linen are some of the luxuries you'll enjoy at the Sutton. You may not get the intimacy you find in smaller hotels but there's a beautiful pool, great restaurants and a cocktail lounge that's full of glitz and glamour. Look out for room-rate specials.

Eating

Edmonton's food scene reflects its multiculturalism and if you're willing to hunt around, you can get a quality meal at any price. The most varied and economical place to eat is on or around Whyte Ave, while the best downtown nexus is Jasper Ave or the rejuvenated warehouse district north of Jasper Ave on 104th St.

★**Duchess Bake Shop** BAKERY, CAFE **$**
(Map p564; ☎780-488-4999; www.duchessbakeshop.com; 10720 124th St; baked goods from $2, breakfast & lunch $6-13; ⏲9am-8pm Tue-Fri, 10am-6pm Sat, to 5pm Sun) Duchess is a destination. You'd cross town to eat here – barefoot in snow if necessary. Feeling like it dropped straight from France, complete with Louis XV–style chairs, the Duchess' French-press coffee and huge array of fresh baking leave you spoiled for choice. Mocha meringues, cream-cheese-and-leek croissants, and cherry basil eclairs are just the tip of the iceberg.

★**Block 1912** CAFE **$**
(Map p564; www.block1912.com; 10361 Whyte Ave; snacks $5-12; ⏲9am-midnight Mon-Sat, 10am-11pm Sun) A regal attempt at a genuine Torinese coffee bar, this inviting place allows you to recline on European-style sofas and armchairs and enjoy your coffee, beer or wine beneath twinkly lights. Grab a snack or something more substantial like coffee-crusted steak or Thai chicken. Gelato comes in fab flavors like root-beer float or crème caramel and desserts are drool worthy.

Remedy Cafe INDIAN **$**
(Map p566; ☎780-433-3096; www.remedycafe.ca; 10279 Jasper Ave; mains $8-10; ⏲8am-midnight;) The 'remedy' here is cheap, authentic Indian food served in a casual cafe setting – meaning you can use wi-fi with one hand and dip your naan in curry sauce with the other. Everyone raves about the chai and the butter chicken, but you can also get good cakes (vegans are catered for) and excellent *masala dosas* (curried vegetables inside a crisp pancake).

The larger, original **branch** (Map p564; 8631 109th St) is in Garneau on the south side of the river.

Café Mosaics VEGETARIAN **$**
(Map p564; ☎780-433-9702; www.cafemosaics.com; 10844 Whyte Ave; mains $6-12; ⏲9am-9pm Mon-Sat, 11am-2:30pm Sun;) A Strathcona institution, this artsy, cool vegetarian-vegan haunt is a meat-free zone that has taken a page out of San Francisco's book: it makes vegetable dishes both interesting and tasty. Think earthy and clean, rather than hippy and crusty. As a litmus test, check the number of carnivores who take a day off meat to come here.

Tokyo Noodle Shop JAPANESE **$**
(Map p564; ☎780-430-0838; www.tokyonoodleshop.com; 10736 Whyte Ave; mains $10-22; ⏲11:30am-9:30pm Mon-Thu, to 10:30pm Fri & Sat, noon-9pm Sun) Great sushi and noodles by the gallon, plush bento boxes, rice bowls and all the tasty appetizers you'd expect in an authentic Japanese restaurant. Nothing fancy, but that's the point.

High Level Diner DINER **$**
(Map p564; ☎780-433-1317; www.highleveldiner.com; 10912 88th Ave; mains $6-15; ⏲8am-10pm Mon-Thu, to 11pm Fri & Sat, 9am-9pm Sun;) Popular for its weekend brunch and sticky cinnamon buns, this cheerful diner is frequented by students, neighbors in the know and the odd hipster. Specials like Ukrainian Thursdays and Short Rib Saturdays keep things lively, and there are some great vegetarian options like black bean chili and spinach pie. And the ketchup is made in-house!

★**Packrat Louie Kitchen & Bar** CANADIAN **$$**
(Map p564; ☎780-433-0123; www.packratlouie.com; 10335 83rd Ave NW; lunch $14-18, dinner $17-35; ⏲11.30am-10pm Mon-Sat) Tucked off Whyte Ave in a converted brick building, Louie's is truly gourmet. Mains like black-olive-crusted cod, housemade chorizo fritters, or pork tenderloin with spätzle and wild mushroom wine sauce have graced the ever-changing menu that's always impressive. Pizzas are taken to a new level and even the lunchtime sandwiches are orgasmic. Reservations recommended.

Three Boars Eatery TAPAS $$
(Map p564; ☎780-757-2600; www.threeboars.ca; 8424 109th St; small plates $13-21; ⏱4pm-late) Three Boars is part of the burgeoning farm-to-table food movement, using local suppliers to create gourmet food. It specializes in small plates, fine Edmonton microbrews on draught and divinely crafted cocktails. If you have an appetite for a large Alberta steak, this isn't your bag. If you're up for tasting pork terrine and smoked quail, it definitely is.

Tiramisu Bistro ITALIAN $$
(Map p564; ☎780-452-3393; www.cafetiramisu.ca; 10750 124th St; pastas $12-15; ⏱9am-8pm Mon, to 9pm Tue-Thu, to 10pm Fri & Sat;) This bistro serves fresh salads, wraps, panini and pasta, but its risottos are the coup – try saffron with duck confit, or beet, lime, goat's cheese and Pinot Grigio. Mornings bring breakfast pizzas and crepes with fillings like elk cherry sausage. It also has an awesome kids menu that assumes children like food beyond chicken strips.

Blue Plate Diner VEGETARIAN $$
(Map p566; ☎780-429-0740; www.blueplatediner.ca; 10145 104th St; mains $12-18; ⏱7:30am-9pm Mon-Thur, to 10pm Fri, 9am-10pm Sat, 9am-9pm Sun;) In one of the redbrick buildings in Edmonton's warehouse district, this vegetarian-biased diner serves healthy food in hearty portions. And there's style too. Cool colored lighting and exposed brickwork mean you can eat locally grown veggies without feeling as if you've joined a hippy commune. The creative menu is well executed, there's an excellent kids menu, and the desserts? Mmm…

Da-De-O CAJUN $$
(Map p564; ☎780-433-0930; www.dadeo.ca; 10548a Whyte Ave; mains $15-26; ⏱11:30am-10pm Mon, Tue & Thu, to 11pm Fri & Sat, noon-10pm Sun) An unexpected summoning up of the Big Easy in the frozen north, this retro diner – complete with red vinyl chairs, chrome kitchen tables and a jukebox – whips up Cajun calamari, oysters, jambalaya and southern fried chicken. Plucked straight out of Louisiana legend are the spice-dusted sweet-potato fries and the ginormous po'boys (especially the blackened catfish). No minors allowed.

Noorish VEGETARIAN $$
(Map p564; ☎780-756-6880; www.noorish.ca; 8440 109th St; mains $10-20; ⏱11am-10pm Tue-Sun;) Noorish takes healthy eating to a whole new level. Walnut-zucchini meat and coconut bacon might sound odd, but it packs in the diners. Dig into full-flavored pad Thai or truffle mac 'n' cheese and you'll see why. Raw food, gluten-free and vegan options are available, and you can head downstairs to the yoga room to feed your soul afterwards.

Corso 32 ITALIAN $$$
(Map p566; ☎780-421-4622; www.corso32.com; 10345 Jasper Ave; mains $24-40; ⏱5-11pm Tue-Sun) Chef and owner, Daniel Costa, delivers the best of Italy. Classy, small and candlelit, with a narrow interior and minimalist decor, the evolving menu features dishes with ingredients like homemade goat ricotta, rabbit and pancetta ragu or black truffle honey. The pasta is all handmade and the wine list is the best in Edmonton (if you're Italian).

Madison's Grill FUSION $$$
(Map p566; ☎780-401-2222; www.unionbankinn.com; 10053 Jasper Ave; mains $34-45; ⏱8am-10pm Mon-Thu, to 11pm Fri & Sat, to 8pm Sun) Located in the posh Union Bank Inn, Madison's has no problem keeping up with its high standards of service and quality. Its delicate dishes are beautifully presented; try pork-cheek pierogi with saskatoon berries, seared halibut with basil gnocchi, or fig- and brie-stuffed chicken roulade wrapped in prosciutto. The three-course meal with wine pairing for $100 is well worth it.

LOCAL KNOWLEDGE

EDMONTON'S WEST END

While Edmonton's downtown struggles to forge a collective personality, a small neighborhood 3km to the west, centered on 124th St, exhibits enough charisma to be referred to as the 'West End.' Acting as a kind of quirky antidote to West Edmonton Mall, 124th St between Jasper Ave and 111th Ave is home to an abundance of small art galleries linked by occasional art walks, along with some interesting locally owned restaurants, the cutting-edge Roxy Theatre and two of the best European bakery-cafes this side of Winnipeg: Duchess Bake Shop (p568) and Tiramisu Bistro (p569). A small street market has also taken root: 124 Grand Market (p572) plies organic wares sold by local producers. It's a classic case of local businesses and businesspeople claiming back their community.

Drinking & Nightlife

The best nightlife scene has traditionally centered on or around Whyte Ave in Old Strathcona. Clubs open and close in a blink; bars tend to stay longer.

Transcend Coffee COFFEE

(Map p564; www.transcendcoffee.ca/garneau; 8708 109th St; 7:30am-9pm Mon-Sat, to 5pm Sun;) In a city where cafes producing their own microroasted coffee beans are few, Transcend should be treated like gold dust. Expert baristas on first-name terms with their Guatemalan farmer-producers concoct cups of their own roasted coffee with enough precision to satisfy a severely decaffeinated Seattleite. In a renovated theater, this spot is hip but not remotely pretentious.

Yellowhead Brewery BREWERY

(Map p566; www.yellowheadbrewery.com; 10229 105th St NW; 11am-6pm Mon-Fri) First things first. This isn't a pub. It's a tasting room next door to a brewery where you can sup on Yellowhead's one and only offering: Yellowhead amber ale – a light, not unpleasant lager, brewed in the big vats visible through a glass partition. It also serves small snacks and offers brewery tours if you book in advance.

Cavern WINE BAR

(Map p566; 780-455-1336; www.thecavern.ca; 10169 104th St NW; 7am-8pm Mon-Thu, to 11pm Fri, 8am-11pm Sat, 10am-5pm Sun) Once a commerical warehouse, this industrial and candlelit small cafe is an underground bastion of good taste in vogue 104th St, particularly in the deli department (plates $6 to $16). You can browse the glass cabinet filled with divine cheese before you choose and wash it down with a glass of wine.

Next Act PUB

(Map p564; www.nextactpub.com; 8224 104th St NW; 11am-1am Sun-Thu, to 2am Fri & Sat) Theater-district pub just off Whyte Ave with a good quotient of arty types. There are well-selected ales, including local stalwarts Yellowhead and Alley Kat, plus a long list of imports. Decent burgers and mac 'n' cheese are here to soak up the beer.

Black Dog Freehouse PUB

(Map p564; 780-439-1089; www.blackdog.ca; 10425 Whyte Ave; 2pm-2am) Insanely popular with all types, the Black Dog is essentially a pub with a couple of hidden extras: a rooftop patio, known as the 'wooftop patio,' a traditional ground-floor bar (normally packed cheek to jowl on weekday nights), and a basement that features live music, DJs and occasional parties. The sum of the three parts has become a rollicking Edmonton institution.

O'Byrne's PUB

(Map p564; 780-414-6766; www.obyrnes.com; 10616 Whyte Ave; 11:30am-2am) Get lost in the labyrinth of rooms in this popular Irish pub – Edmonton's oldest. There's a variety of beers on tap, including the obligatory stout. Live music (from 8:30pm) keeps the place lively and the big patio is most often packed.

Pub 1905 PUB

(Map p566; 780-428-4711; 10525 Jasper Ave; 11am-midnight) A popular local watering hole with a happening happy hour, billiards and plates of smoked chicken drumsticks or riblets to snack on. The plethora of TVs is usually tuned in to the latest Oilers game.

Entertainment

Theater! Don't leave Edmonton without trying some. *See* and *Vue* are free local alternative weekly papers with extensive arts and entertainment listings. For daily listings, see the *Edmonton Journal* newspaper.

Roxy Theatre THEATER

(Map p564; 780-453-2440; www.theatrenetwork.ca; 8529 Gateway Blvd) This theatre opened after Theatre Network's beloved 1940's Roxy theater burned down. Nevertheless, it keeps things eclectic, showing burlesque, live bands and comedy.

Garneau Theatre CINEMA

(Map p564; www.metrocinema.org; 8712 109th St NW) Edmonton's only surviving art-deco-era cinema has operated under various guises since 1940, changing hands most recently in 2011. It's affectionately described as 'vintage,' meaning the seats could be more comfortable, but who cares when you roll in for a *Trainspotting* matinee and the concession stand is open for beer?

New Varscona Theatre THEATER

(Map p564; www.varsconatheatre.com; 10329 83rd Ave; tickets from $14) There are only 176 precious seats at the Varscona, a cornerstone of the Old Strathcona theater district that puts on 350 performances annually of edgy plays, late-night comedy and morning kids' shows.

Princess Theatre CINEMA

(Map p564; 780-433-0728; www.princesstheatre.ca; 10337 Whyte Ave; tickets adult/student & child

LOCAL KNOWLEDGE

EDMONTON'S UKRAINIAN COMMUNITIES

If you've been in Edmonton for any length of time, you may well be wondering, 'Why all the perogies?' Between the 19th and early 20th century, around 250,000 Ukrainians immigrated to Canada, settling in farming communities on the prairies where the landscape reminded them of the snowy steppes of home. Today the Ukrainian population in Canada is second only to that in Russia and Ukraine itself, and many famous Canadians trace their roots back to the Ukraine, including Wayne Gretzky and Randy Bachman. The largest number of Ukrainian-Canadians live in and around Edmonton and, with 16% of the city's population claiming Ukrainian heritage, the cultural influence extends far beyond perogies.

Vincent Rees has a Masters in Ukrainian Culture, is a professional Ukrainian dancer, and runs cultural tours in both Edmonton and Ukraine. A resident of Edmonton for more than two decades, if anyone knows where to experience Ukrainian culture in the region, it's him.

'I think you would find it difficult not to feel the presence of Ukrainians in Edmonton. There are stores and restaurants, dance groups and choirs, and domes decorating the skyline. The culture is very alive and very present. One of the most interesting ways to experience it is to explore the **Ukrainian Cultural Heritage Village** (☎780-662-3640; www.history.alberta.ca/ukrainianvillage; adult/child/family $15/10/40; ⏲10am-5pm May-Sep) with its character role players acting out what life in a rural Ukrainian-Canadian community would have been like.' He also suggests checking out the small Ukrainian towns east of the city, including Vegreville, with the world's largest Easter egg; Mundare, with a giant Ukrainian sausage; and Glendon, with the biggest – you guessed it – perogy.

But today's Ukrainian-Canadian culture isn't just grandmas pushing perogies; many young Edmontonians are full of Ukrainian pride. 'The Ukrainian bilingual school program is popular and there are over a dozen Ukrainian dance groups within the city alone and a Ukrainian studies program at the University of Alberta.' Nevertheless, those grannies are pretty persuasive. 'There are many Ukrainian specialty restaurants and the churches often have special perogy nights and sell bulk perogies to take home for emergencies. In Edmonton, you're never very far from a perogy.'

To experience Ukrainian culture firsthand, check out Cobblestone Freeway (p564), which runs both city and regional tours.

$10/8) The Princess is a grand old theater that defiantly sticks her finger up at the multiplexes that are dominant elsewhere. Dating from the pre-talkie days (1915), it screens first-run, art-house and cult classics. Tickets for Mondays and weekend matinees are reduced.

Blues on Whyte LIVE MUSIC
(Map p564; ☎780-439-981; www.bluesonwhyte.ca; 10329 Whyte Ave) This is the sort of place your mother warned you about: dirty, rough, but still somehow cool. It's a great place to check out some live music; blues and rock are the standards.

Edmonton Eskimos SPECTATOR SPORT
(www.esks.com; adult/child from $43/21.50) The Eskimos take part in the Canadian Football League (CFL) from July to October at **Commonwealth Stadium** (11000 Stadium Rd).

Edmonton Oilers SPECTATOR SPORT
(www.edmontonoilers.com; tickets from $38.50) To avoid any embarrassing situations, wise up on the Oilers before you arrive in Edmonton. The local National Hockey League (NHL) team dominated the game in the 1980s thanks to a certain player named Wayne Gretzky – aka 'The Great One' – but haven't won much since. The season runs from October to April.

The team will likely have moved downtown to the new Rogers Place by the time you read this.

Edmonton Opera OPERA
(☎780-424-4040; www.edmontonopera.com; tickets from $24; ⏲Oct-Apr) Since its beginning in 1963, Edmonton Opera has been getting rave reviews from opera lovers, and breathing new life into classics like *Carmen* and *The Barber of Seville*. Performances are infrequent but worth seeing if you're in town.

Citadel Theatre THEATER
(Map p566; www.citadeltheatre.com; 9828 101A Ave; tickets from $45; ⏲Sep-May) Edmonton's foremost company is based in downtown's Winston Churchill Sq. Expect glowing performances of Shakespeare and Stoppard, Dickens adaptations and the odd Sondheim musical.

Shopping

Old Strathcona is the best area for unique independent stores – vintage magazines, old vinyl, retro furnishings and the like. If you're in search of the opposite – ie big chains selling familiar brands – sift through the 800-plus stores in West Edmonton Mall.

★Old Strathcona Farmers Market FOOD
(Map p564; ☎780-439-1844; osfm.ca; 10310 83rd Ave, at 103rd St; ⊙noon-5pm Tue, 8am-3pm Sat Jul & Aug) Since it began in 1983, the market's motto has been 'We Make it! We Bake it! We Grow it! We Sell it!' Inside the city's old bus garage, it offers everything from organic food to arts and crafts, and hosts some 130 vendors. Everyone comes here on Saturday morning. You'd be wise to do the same.

124 Grand Market MARKET
(Map p564; www.124grandmarket.com; 108th Ave, btwn 123rd & 124th Sts; ⊙4-8pm Thu) Plenty of food trucks, artisans and produce to keep your belly and your shopping bag well satiated.

Junque Cellar FASHION & ACCESSORIES
(Map p564; 10442 Whyte Ave; ⊙10am-9pm Mon-Sat, to 6pm Sun) What is plain old junk to some is retro-cool to others. Sift through the typewriters, lava lamps, old phones, comics, clothes and other flashbacks of erstwhile pop culture.

West Edmonton Mall SHOPPING MALL
(www.westedmontonmall.com; 170th St; ⊙10am-9pm Mon-Fri, to 6pm Sat, noon-6pm Sun;) Kitsch-lovers who can't afford the trip to Vegas might just be enchanted with West Edmonton Mall, while those less enamored by plastic plants and phony re-creations of 15th-century galleons will hate it. Edmonton's urban behemoth has waterslides, an indoor wave pool, an amusement park, a skating rink, minigolf courses, a fake reef with a real seal lion and a penguin swimming around, a petting zoo, a hotel and 800 retail stores thrown in as a bonus.

Information

Custom House Global Foreign Exchange (10104 103rd Ave) Foreign currency exchange.

Edmonton Tourism (Map p566; exploreedmonton.com/visitor-centre; 9797 Jasper Ave; ⊙8am-5pm) Friendly place with tons of flyers and brochures.

Main post office (Map p564; 9808 103A Ave; ⊙8am-5:45pm Mon-Fri)

Royal Alexandra Hospital (☎780-477-4111; 10240 Kingsway Ave) Has a 24-hour trauma center. Located 1km north of the downtown core.

Getting There & Away

AIR

Edmonton International Airport (YEG; www.flyeia.com) is about 30km south of the city along the Calgary Trail, about a 45-minute drive from downtown.

BUS

The large **Greyhound bus station** (12360 121st St) has services to numerous destinations, including Jasper ($74, 4½ hours, four daily) and Calgary ($50, from 3½ hours, from 10 daily).

Red Arrow (Map p566; www.redarrow.ca) buses stop downtown at the Holiday Inn Express and serve Calgary ($70, 3½ hours, six daily) and Fort McMurray ($87, six hours, three daily). The buses are a step up, with wi-fi, sockets for your laptop, single or double seats, a free minibar and hot coffee.

CAR & MOTORCYLE

All the major car-rental firms have offices at the airport and around town. **Driving Force** (www.thedrivingforce.com; 11025 184th St) will rent, lease or sell you a car. Check the website; it often has some good deals.

TRAIN

The small **VIA Rail station** (www.viarail.ca; 12360 121st St) is rather inconveniently situated 5km northwest of the city center near Edmonton City Centre Airport. The *Canadian* travels three times a week east to Saskatoon ($105, eight hours), Winnipeg ($220, 20 hours) and Toronto ($480, 55 hours), and west to Jasper ($143, 5½ hours), Kamloops ($207, 16½ hours) and Vancouver ($268, 27 hours). At Jasper, you can connect to Prince George and Prince Rupert.

Getting Around

TO/FROM THE AIRPORT

Bus 747 leaves from outside the arrivals hall every 30 to 60 minutes and goes to Century Park ($5), the southernmost stop on Edmonton's Light Rail. From here regular trains connect to Strathcona and downtown.

Sky Shuttle Airport Service (☎780-465-8515; www.edmontonskyshuttle.com; adult/child $18/10) runs three different routes that service hotels in most areas of town, including downtown and the Strathcona area. The office is by carousel 12. Journey time is approximately 45 minutes. If you're looking for a lift to the airport, reserve at least 24 hours in advance.

Cab fare from the airport to downtown costs about $50.

CAR & MOTORCYCLE

There is metered parking throughout the city. Most hotels in Old Strathcona offer complimentary parking to guests. Visitors can park their car for the day and explore the neighborhood easily on foot. Edmonton also has public parking lots, which cost about $12 per day or $1.50 per half-hour; after 6pm you can park for a flat fee of about $2.

PUBLIC TRANSPORTATION

City buses and a 16-stop Light Rail Transit (LRT) system cover most of the city. The fare is $3.20. Buses operate at 30-minute intervals between 5:30am and 1:30am. Check out the excellent transit planning resources at www.edmonton.ca. Daytime travel between Churchill and Grandin stations on the LRT is free.

Between mid-May and early September you can cross the High Level Bridge on a streetcar ($5 round-trip, every 30 minutes between 11am and 10pm). The vintage streetcars are a great way to travel to the Old Strathcona Market (103rd St at 94th Ave), where the line stops. Or go from Old Strathcona to the downtown stop, next to the Grandin LRT Station (109th St between 98th and 99th Aves).

TAXI

Two of the many taxi companies are **Yellow Cab** (780-462-3456) and **Alberta Co-Op Taxi** (780-425-2525; co-optaxi.com). The fare from downtown to the West Edmonton Mall is about $25. Flag fall is $3.60, then it's 20¢ for every 150m. Most cab companies offer a flat rate to the airport calculated from your destination.

AROUND EDMONTON

West of Edmonton

Heading west from Edmonton toward Jasper, Hwy 16 is a long and fairly monotonous drive through rolling wooded hills and past ranches with what appear to be a bazillion cows. **Hinton** is a small, rough-around-the-edges town carved from the bush. It's here that you'll get your first true view of the Rockies. The pervasive logging industry keeps the majority of the town's population gainfully employed.

Just northwest of Hinton lies the settlement of **Grande Cache**. There's little of interest in this small industry town – only a few overpriced hotels aimed at expense-account-wielding natural-resources workers. However, the drive along **Highway 40** between Hinton and Grande Cache is spectacular, with rolling forested foothills, lakes and wildlife.

Activities

There's some good **mountain biking** to be found here; the **visitor info center** (780-865-2777; Hwy 16, Hinton; 9am-7pm) has information on trails, including the 3km bike park and longer routes of varying difficulty beyond the park. You can rent your ride from **Vicious Bikes** (780-865-7787; www.viciouscanada.com; 106 Park St, Hinton; bikes per day from $35; 10am-6pm Mon-Sat, 11am-5pm Sun).

WORTH A TRIP

ELK ISLAND NATIONAL PARK

In case you hadn't noticed, there are five national parks in Alberta, and three of them *aren't* Jasper or Banff. Overshadowed by the Gothic Rockies, tiny **Elk Island National Park** (www.pc.gc.ca/elkisland; adult/6-16yr/senior $7.80/3.90/6.80, campsites & RV sites $25.50, campfire permits $8.80; dawn-dusk) attracts just 5% of Banff's annual visitor count despite its location only 50km east of Edmonton. Not that this detracts from its attractions. The park – the only one in Canada that is entirely fenced – contains the highest density of wild hoofed animals in the world after the Serengeti. If you come here, plan on seeing the 'big six' – plains bison, wood bison, mule deer, white-tailed deer, elk and the more elusive moose. The wood bison live entirely in the quieter southern portion of the park (which is cut in two by Hwy 16), while the plains bison inhabit the north. Most of the infrastructure lies in the north, too, around **Astotin Lake**. Here you'll find a campground, a nine-hole golf course (with a clubhouse containing a restaurant), a beach and a boat launch. Four of the park's 11 trails lead out from the lakeshore through trademark northern Albertan aspen parkland – a kind of natural intermingling of the prairies and the boreal forests.

Public transportation to the park is nonexistent. Either hire a car or join a guided tour from Edmonton with **Watchable Wildlife Tours Group** (780-405-4880; www.birdsandbackcountry.com; per person $95), led by wildlife expert Wayne Millar. It's a lovely way to watch the sunset surrounded by animals on a long summer evening.

While you're in Hinton, it's also worth heading out to the **Beaver Boardwalk** at nearby Maxwell Lake. There are 5kms of lovely trails here and – you guessed it – beavers!

Athabasca Lookout Nordic Centre SKIING, CYCLING
(www.hintonnordic.ca; William A Switzer Park, Hwy 40; day pass $10) When there's snow on the ground, the Athabasca Lookout Nordic Centre offers winter visitors beautifully groomed cross-country ski trails up to 25km long. There's also illuminated night skiing on a 1.5km trail, plus a 1km luge run. In summer you can cycle here, too. For more information, contact the Hinton Visitor Information Centre (p573), off Hwy 16.

Getting There & Away

Greyhound (p560) has a daily service from Edmonton to Hinton (three hours and 40 minutes, $57) and on to Jasper Town (five hours, $71).
Sundog (Map p610; www.sundogtours.com; 414 Connaught Dr, Jasper Town; ⏲8am-8pm) also services this route between Edmonton airport and Jasper Town ($99), with stops along the way.

CALGARY

POP 1,097,000

Calgary will surprise you with its beauty, cool eateries, nightlife beyond honky-tonk and long, worthwhile to-do list. Calgarians aren't known for their modesty; it's their self-love and can-do attitude that got them through disastrous flooding in 2013 and, in 2016, saw them helping residents of wildfire-stricken Fort McMurray with unquestioning generosity. We mustn't forget – Calgary also hosted the highly successful 1988 Winter Olympics, elected North America's first Muslim mayor, and throws one of Canada's biggest parties, the Calgary Stampede.

Calgary was once known to forsake quality for quantity, but this trend is changing with fantastic results. Community activists in emerging neighborhoods like Inglewood and Kensington are finally waking up and smelling the single-origin home-roasted coffee, with new bars, boutiques, restaurants and entertainment venues exhibiting more color and experimentation. The city that to non-Calgarians long served as a somewhat bland business center or a functional springboard has actually become – ahem – cool.

History

From humble and relatively recent beginnings, Calgary has been transformed into a cosmopolitan modern city that has hosted an Olympics and continues to wield huge economic clout. Before the growth explosion, the Blackfoot people called the area home for centuries. Eventually they were joined by the Sarcee and Stoney tribes on the banks of the Bow and Elbow Rivers.

In 1875, the North-West Mounted Police (NWMP) built a fort and called it Fort Calgary after Calgary Bay on Scotland's Isle of Mull. The railroad followed a few years later and, buoyed by the promise of free land, settlers started the trek west to make Calgary their home. The Blackfoot, Sarcee and Stoney Aboriginals signed Treaty 7 with the British Crown in 1877 that ushered them into designated tribal reservations and took away their wider land rights.

Long a center for ranching, the cowboy culture was set to become forever intertwined with the city. In the early 20th century, Calgary simmered along, growing slowly. Then, in the 1960s, everything changed. Overnight, ranching was seen as a thing of the past, and oil was the new favorite child. With the 'black gold' seeming to bubble up from the ground nearly everywhere in Alberta, Calgary became the natural choice of place to set up headquarters.

The population exploded, and the city began to grow at an alarming rate. As the price of oil continued to skyrocket, it was good times for the people of Cowtown. The 1970s boom stopped dead at the '80s bust. Things slowed and the city diversified.

The 21st century began with an even bigger boom. House prices have gone through the roof, there is almost zero unemployment and the economy is growing 40% faster than the rest of Canada. Not bad for a bunch of cowboys.

Sights

Calgary's downtown has the Glenbow Museum and the new National Music Centre, but it's the surrounding neighborhoods that hold more allure. **Uptown 17th Avenue** has some of the top restaurants and bars and is a hive of activity in the evening. **Inglewood**, just east of downtown, is the city's hippest neighborhood, with antique shops, indie boutiques and some esoteric eating options. **Kensington**, north of the Bow River, has some good coffee bars and a tangible community spirit.

★National Music Centre MUSEUM
(Map p576; ☎403-543-5115; http://studiobell.ca; 850 4 St SE; adult/child $18/11; ⏱10am-5pm Wed-Sun) Looking like a whimsical copper castle, this fabulous new museum is entirely entertaining, taking you on a ride through Canada's musical history with cool artifacts (like the guitar Guess Who used to record 'American Woman') and interactive displays. Test your skill at the drums, electric guitar or in a sound-recording room and even create your own instruments. Don't miss the Body Phonic room or the solar-powered Skywalk with its repurposed pianos destroyed in the 2013 flood.

★Glenbow Museum MUSEUM
(Map p576; ☎403-777-5506; www.glenbow.org; 130 9th Ave SE; adult/child/family $16/10/40; ⏱9am-5pm Mon-Sat, noon-5pm Sun, closed Mon Oct-Jun) With an extensive permanent collection and an ever-changing array of traveling exhibitions, the impressive Glenbow has plenty for the history buff, art lover and pop-culture fiend to ponder. Temporary exhibits are often daring, covering contemporary art and culture. Permanent exhibits bring the past to life with strong historic personalities and lots of voice recordings. Hang out in a tipi, visit a trading post and walk through the rail car of a train.

Bow Habitat Station AQUARIUM
(☎403-297-6561; aep.alberta.ca; 1440 17A St SE; adult/child $10/6; ⏱10am-4pm Tue-Sat, tours noon & 2pm) Raising and releasing up to 1.5 million trout each year, this working hatchery is a favorite with kids for its aquariums, hands-on exhibits and chance to fish in the pond (May to October). Look down over the hatchery pools or get up close and feed the juvenile fish on a tour.

Esker Foundation Contemporary Art Gallery MUSEUM
(eskerfoundation.com; 1011 9th Ave SE, Inglewood; ⏱10am-6pm Tue-Sun) FREE This small, private art gallery hosts fabulous temporary exhibitions in its beautiful 4th-floor location. Past exhibitions have considered everything from immigration to the Northwest Passage. Check the website for workshops and be sure to check out the very cool boardroom nest.

Prince's Island Park PARK
(Map p576) For a little slice of Central Park in the heart of Cowtown, take the bridge over to this island, with grassy fields made for tossing Frisbees, bike paths and ample space to stretch out. During the summer months, you can catch a Shakespeare production in the park's natural grass amphitheater or check out the Folk Music Festival in July. You'll also find the upscale River Island restaurant here.

Heritage Park Historical Village HISTORIC SITE
(☎403-259-1900; www.heritagepark.ab.ca; 1900 Heritage Dr SW, at 14th St SW; adult/child $26.25/13.50; ⏱9.30am-5pm daily May-Aug, Sat & Sun Sep & Oct) Want to see what Calgary used to look like? Head down to this historical park where all the buildings are from 1915 or earlier. There are 10 hectares of re-created town to explore, with a fort, grain mill, church and school. Go for a hay ride, visit the antique midway or hop on a train. Costumed interpreters are on hand to answer any questions.

Calgary Tower NOTABLE BUILDING
(Map p576; ☎403-266-7171; www.calgarytower.com; 101 9th Ave SW; adult/youth $18/9; ⏱observation gallery 9am-9pm Sep-Jun, to 10pm Jul-Aug) This 1968 landmark tower is an iconic feature of the Calgary skyline, though it has now been usurped by numerous taller buildings and is in danger of being lost in a forest of skyscrapers. There is little doubt that the aesthetics of this once-proud concrete structure have passed into the realm of kitsch, but, love it or hate it, the slightly phallic 191m structure is a fixture of the downtown area.

Contemporary Calgary GALLERY
(Map p576; ☎403-770-1350; www.contemporarycalgary.com; 117 8th Ave SW; ⏱noon-6pm Wed-Sun) FREE This small, inspiring modern-art gallery has four floors of temporary exhibits that change every four months. The gallery has plans to move to the former Centennial Planetarium in the southwest; renovations are due to be completed in 2018. With much more exhibition space, great things are expected.

Calgary Zoo ZOO
(☎403-232-9300; www.calgaryzoo.com; 1300 Zoo Rd NE; adult/child $25/17; ⏱9am-5pm; 👪) More than 1000 animals from around the world, many in enclosures simulating their natural habitats, make Calgary's zoo one of the top rated in North America. The zoo's well-regarded conservation team study, reintroduce and protect endangered animals in Canada.

Calgary

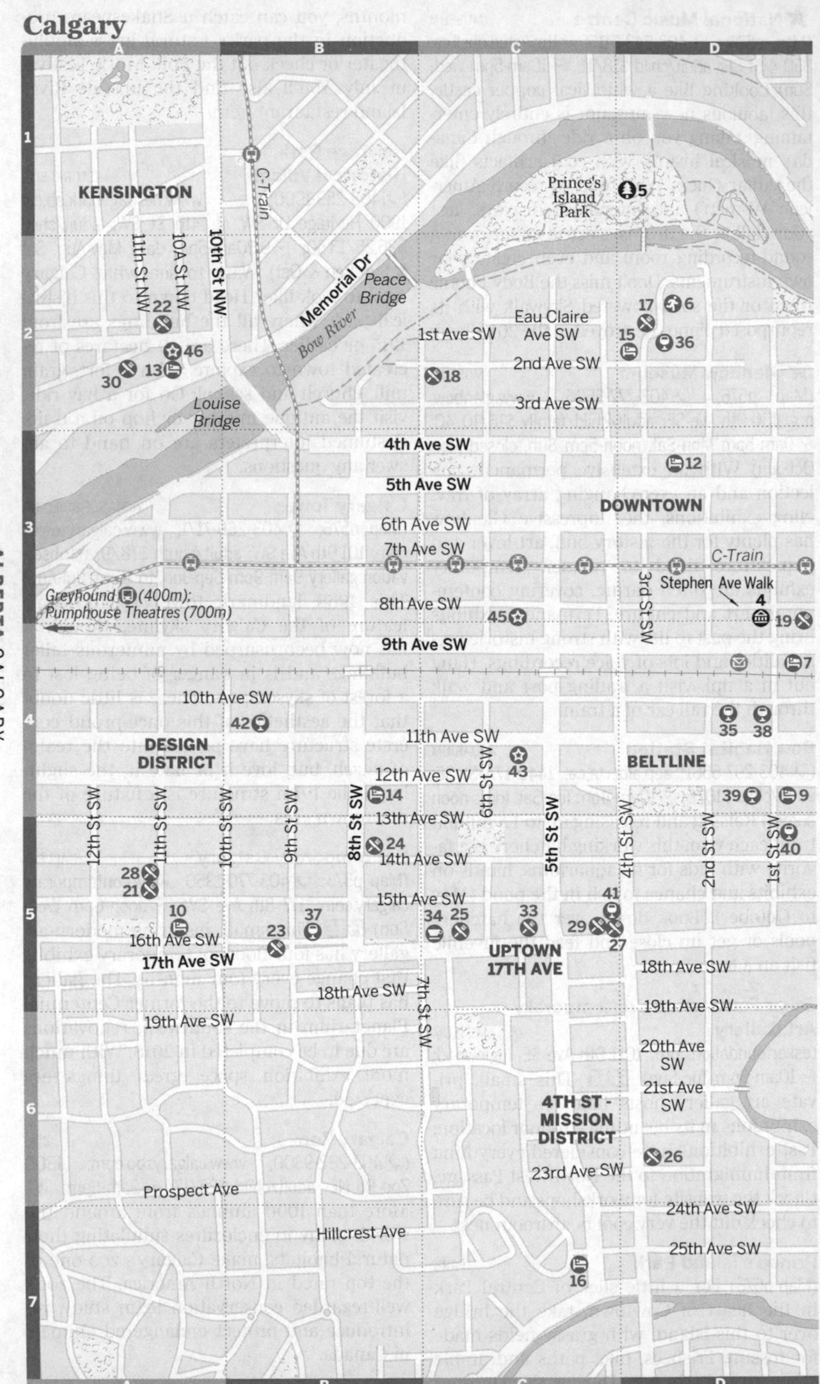
KENSINGTON
11th St NW
10A St NW
10th St NW
C-Train
Memorial Dr
Peace Bridge
Bow River
Louise Bridge
Prince's Island Park
Eau Claire Ave SW
1st Ave SW
2nd Ave SW
3rd Ave SW
4th Ave SW
5th Ave SW
6th Ave SW
7th Ave SW
8th Ave SW
9th Ave SW
10th Ave SW
11th Ave SW
12th Ave SW
13th Ave SW
14th Ave SW
15th Ave SW
16th Ave SW
17th Ave SW
18th Ave SW
19th Ave SW
20th Ave SW
21st Ave SW
23rd Ave SW
24th Ave SW
25th Ave SW
DOWNTOWN
Stephen Ave Walk
Greyhound (400m); Pumphouse Theatres (700m)
DESIGN DISTRICT
BELTLINE
UPTOWN 17TH AVE
4TH ST - MISSION DISTRICT
12th St SW
11th St SW
10th St SW
9th St SW
8th St SW
7th St SW
6th St SW
5th St SW
4th St SW
3rd St SW
2nd St SW
1st St SW
Prospect Ave
Hillcrest Ave
ALBERTA CALGARY

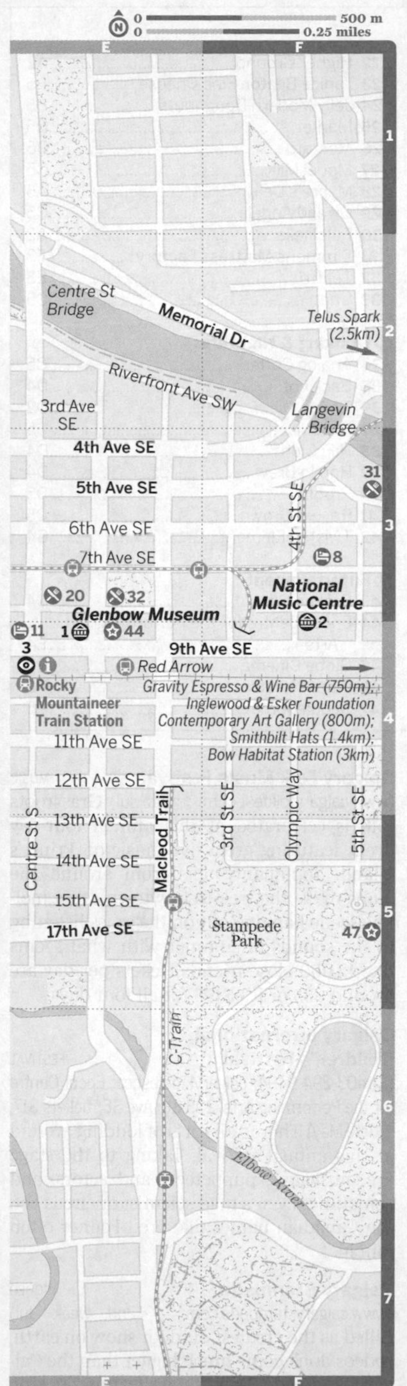

Telus Spark — SCIENCE CENTER

(☎403-817-6800; www.sparkscience.ca; 220 St George's Dr NE; adult/child $20/13; ⏰10am-5pm; 👪) You'll wish science class was as fun as the Telus World of Science. Kids get a big bang out of this user-friendly and very interactive science center. There is a giant dome, where light shows depicting the cosmos are projected.

Fish Creek Provincial Park — PARK

(☎403-297-5293; www.albertaparks.ca; ⏰8am-dusk) Cradling the southwest edge of Calgary, this huge park is a sanctuary of wilderness hidden within the city limits. Countless trails intertwine to form a labyrinth, to the delight of walkers, mountain bikers and the many animals who call the park home.

Calaway Park — AMUSEMENT PARK

(☎403-240-3822; www.calawaypark.com; adult/child/family $38/31/120; ⏰10am-7pm Jul-early Sep, 11am-6pm Sat & Sun early Sep-early Oct, 5-9pm Fri, 10am-7pm Sat & Sun late May-Jul) Children of all ages will enjoy Calaway Park, western Canada's largest outdoor family amusement park. It features 30 rides from wild to mild, live stage entertainment, 22 food vendors, 28 different carnival games, a trout-fishing pond and an interactive maze. The youngsters will love camping at the amusement park, close enough to town to be not too far to drive.

Inglewood Bird Sanctuary — NATURE RESERVE

(☎403-268-2489; 2425 9th Ave SE; sanctuary & interpretive center free, donations appreciated; ⏰dawn-dusk, interpretive center 10am-4pm) Get the flock over here. With more than 260 bird species calling the sanctuary home, you're assured of meeting some feathered friends. It's a peaceful place, with walking paths and benches to observe the residents.

Activities

Rapid Rent — CYCLING

(Map p576; www.outlawsports.ca; Barclay Pde SW; bikes/rollerblades/helmet per day from $30/15/5; ⏰10am-7pm Mon-Fri, to 6pm Sat, to 5pm Sun) Rents bikes, child trailers and rollerblades.

Olympic Oval — ICE SKATING

(☎403-220-7954; www.ucalgary.ca/oval; University of Calgary; adult/child/family $7/5/18.50; ⏰Jul-mid Mar) Get the Olympic spirit at the University of Calgary, where you can go for a skate on Olympic Oval. Used for the speed-skating events at the Olympics, it offers public skating on the long track and has skates available to rent, as well as mandatory helmets. See the website for current schedules.

Calgary

Top Sights
1 Glenbow Museum ... E4
2 National Music Centre ... F4

Sights
3 Calgary Tower ... E4
4 Contemporary Calgary ... D3
5 Prince's Island Park ... D1

Activities, Courses & Tours
6 Rapid Rent ... D2

Sleeping
7 Fairmont Palliser ... D4
8 HI-Calgary ... F3
9 Hotel Arts ... D4
10 Hotel Elan ... A5
11 Hotel Le Germain ... E4
12 International Hotel ... D3
13 Kensington Riverside Inn ... A2
14 Nuvo Hotel Suites ... B4
15 Sheraton Suites Calgary Eau Claire ... D2
16 Twin Gables B&B ... C7

Eating
17 1886 Buffalo Cafe ... D2
18 Al Forno Cafe & Bakery ... C2
19 Blink ... D4
20 Catch ... E3
21 Galaxie Diner ... A5
22 Higher Ground ... A2
23 Janice Beaton Fine Cheese ... B5
24 Jelly Modern Doughnuts ... B5
25 Market ... C5
26 Mercato ... D6
27 Model Milk ... C5
28 Myhre's Deli ... A5
29 Ox and Angela ... C5
30 Pulcinella ... A2
31 Simmons Mattress Factory ... F3
32 Teatro ... E3
33 Una ... C5

Drinking & Nightlife
34 Analog Coffee ... C5
35 Back Lot ... D4
36 Barley Mill ... D2
37 Cru Juice ... B5
38 HiFi Club ... D4
39 Hop In Brew ... D4
40 Proof ... D5
41 Rose & Crown ... C5
42 Twisted Element ... B4

Entertainment
43 Broken City ... C4
44 Epcor Centre for the Performing Arts ... E4
45 Globe Cinema ... C3
46 Plaza Theatre ... A2
47 Saddledome ... F5

Canada Olympic Park ADVENTURE SPORTS
(☎403-247-5452; www.canadaolympicpark.ca; 88 Canada Olympic Rd SW; mountain biking hill tickets/lessons $22/99; ⏰9am-9pm Mon-Fri, 10am-5pm Sat & Sun) In 1988 the Winter Olympics came to Canada for the first time. Calgary played host, and many of the events were contested at Canada Olympic Park. It's near the western edge of town along Hwy 1 – you can't miss the distinctive 70m and 90m ski jumps crowning the skyline.

Calgary Walking Tours CULTURAL
(☎855-620-6520; www.calgarywalks.com; adult/youth/under 7yr $18/15/free) Join the two-hour Core City tour to learn about the architecture, history and culture of various buildings, sculptures, gardens and hidden nooks.

Festivals & Events

For a year-round list of the city's events, go to www.visitcalgary.com/things-to-do/events-calendar. The big festival in Calgary is the annual Calgary Stampede; however, there are many other smaller festivals, markets and exhibitions throughout the year.

Calgary Folk Music Festival MUSIC
(www.calgaryfolkfest.com; ⏰late Jul) Grassroots folk is celebrated at this annual four-day event featuring great live music on Prince's Island. Top-quality acts from around the globe make the trek to Cowtown. It's a mellow scene hanging out on the grass listening to the sounds of summer with what seems like 12,000 close friends.Tickets per day are around $85 or it's $195 for all four days.

Calgary International Children's Festival FESTIVAL
(☎403-294-9494; calgarykidsfest.ca; Epcor Centre for the Performing Arts, 205 8th Ave SE; tickets $17; ⏰late May) There's all sorts of kidding around at this annual festival. Taking to the stage are musicians, puppeteers and actors, and sometimes even a mad scientist or circus act. Big Canadian names like Fred Penner often join in.

Calgary Stampede RODEO
(www.calgarystampede.com; ⏰2nd week Jul) Billed as the greatest outdoor show on earth, rodeos don't come much bigger than the Calgary Stampede. Daily shows feature bucking

broncos, steer wrestling, chuckwagon races, a midway and a sensational grandstand show. Civic spirits soar, with free pancake breakfasts and a cowboy hat on every head in the city. All of this is strongly tempered by animal rights issues.

Each year, numerous animals are put down after suffering injuries at the stampede. Humane societies and animal rights activists strongly oppose endangering animals for entertainment and spotlight calf roping and chuckwagon races as two of the most dangerous activities at the Stampede.

Sleeping

Calgary has recently found its independent spirit and established a range of boutique hotels across different price ranges.

Downtown hotels are notoriously expensive, although many run frequent specials. Business-oriented hotels are often cheaper over weekends. Near the city's western edge (next to the Banff Trail C-Train station), you'll find every chain hotel you can think of.

During the Calgary Stampede (early July), rates rise and availability plummets. Book ahead.

Calgary West Campground CAMPGROUND $
(403-288-0411; www.calgarycampground.com; Hwy 1; tent/RV sites $36/44; mid-Apr–mid-Oct; P @) Featuring terraced grounds with views across the city, this campground has 320 sites with great facilities, including a heated outdoor pool, nature trails, mini-golf and free wi-fi. Situated west of downtown Calgary on the Trans-Canada Hwy (Hwy 1), it's a quick trip into the city.

HI-Calgary HOSTEL $
(Map p576; 403-269-8239; www.hostellingintl.ca/Alberta; 520 7th Ave SE; dm/d from $33/100; @) Clean and comfortable, if not particularly homey, this pleasant hostel is one of the only options for budget-minded travelers in Calgary, with fairly standard bunk rooms and a few doubles. It has a kitchen, laundry, pool table and internet facilities, as well as a patio with a barbecue. It's a popular crossroads for travelers and a good place to organize rides and share recommendations.

★Kensington Riverside Inn BOUTIQUE HOTEL $$
(Map p576; 403-228-4442; www.kensingtonriversideinn.com; 1126 Memorial Dr NW; r from $199; P) This small inn has impeccable service and rooms to match. Soaker tubs, fireplaces, balconies, Geneva sound systems, French doors and fine linens are all to be found. It's a short trip over the bridge to downtown and the hotel restaurant is top-notch.

Hotel Alma BOUTIQUE HOTEL $$
(403-220-3203; www.hotelalma.ca; 169 University Gate NW; r from $129, apt $180;) Cleverly tucked away on the university campus, this fashionable boutique establishment has a definite hip vibe. Super modern Euro-style rooms are small but cozy rather than cramped. The city suites have one bedroom and are lovely right down to their Piero Lissoni sofas and hand-embroidered cushions. Guests have access to on-campus facilities, including a fitness center, pool and fine lobby bistro.

Hotel Elan BOUTIQUE HOTEL $$
(Map p576; 403-229-2040; www.hotelelan.ca; 1122 16th Ave SW; r weekday/weekend from $249/160;) Stylish and modern, Hotel Elan is popular with business travelers. The rooms are a splendid surprise after the more-functional-than-fancy lobby. Heated bathroom floors and pillow-top mattresses are among the creature comforts, along with rain shower heads and gourmet coffee pods. Away from downtown, it's an easy walk to the happening scene on 17th Ave.

Nuvo Hotel Suites HOTEL $$
(Map p576; 403-452-6789; www.nuvohotelsuites.com; 827 12th Ave SW; ste from $150;) Your hip home away from home, the Nuvo has large, stylish studio apartments with full kitchens, including washing machines, all for an excellent price in the Beltline neighborhood. Handy for downtown and Uptown 17th action.

Centro Motel MOTEL $$
(403-288-6658; www.centromotel.com; 4540 16th Ave NW; r incl breakfast from $114; P @) A 'boutique motel' sounds like an oxymoron until you descend on the misleadingly named Centro, an old motel building that has been transformed with modern features. The indie owners have left no detail missing, from light fittings to bathrobes, wooden floors and walk-in spa showers. You'll find it 7km northwest of downtown on the Trans-Canada Hwy (Hwy 1).

International Hotel HOTEL $$
(Map p576; 403-265-9600; www.internationalhotel.ca; 220 4th Ave SW; d from $109; P @) Even the standard rooms here are suites

LOCAL KNOWLEDGE

CARLESS IN CALGARY

As the main operations center for Canada's oil industry, Calgary has a reputation for big, unsubtle automobiles plying endless low-rise suburbs on a network of busy highways. But, hidden from the ubiquitous petrol heads is a parallel universe of urban parkways (712km of 'em!) dedicated to walkers, cyclists and skaters, and many of them hug the banks of the city's two mighty rivers, the Bow and the Elbow. Even better, this non-car-traffic network is propped up by a cheap, efficient light-rail system: the C-Train was significantly expanded in 2012 and carries a number of daily riders comparable to the Amsterdam metro. Yes, dear reader, Calgary without a car is not an impossible – or even unpleasant – experience.

Not surprisingly, the best trails hug the riverbanks. The Bow River through downtown and over into Prince's Island is eternally popular, with the new pedestrian-only Peace Bridge providing a vital link. If you're feeling strong, you can follow the river path 20km south to Fish Creek Provincial Park and plenty more roadless action. Nose Creek Parkway is the main pedestrian artery to and from the north of the city, while the leafy Elbow River Pathway runs from Inglewood to Mission in the south.

Abutting the downtown Bow River Pathway is Rapid Rent (p577), an outlet of Outlaw Sports located next to the Eau Claire shopping center.

The city publishes an official *Calgary Pathways and Bikeways* map available from any local leisure center or downloadable from the City of Calgary website (www.calgary.ca). There's also a mobile app at www.calgary.ca/mobileapps.

with great city views and cloud-comfy beds. Decor is fairly neutral but service is not. There's a level for women only and another for gentlemen with tailored (if slightly stereotypical) conveniences.

Carriage House Inn INN $$

(☎403-253-1101; www.carriagehouse.net; 9030 Macleod Trail S; r $159-189; P ❄ @ ≋) When you arrive here, the boxlike exterior is less than inspiring, but things brighten inside. Recently renovated rooms are classy with modern interiors. Feather beds are hard to get out of, but there are lots of eating and shopping options nearby. The inn is 8km south of downtown Calgary on the arterial MacLeod Trail.

Twin Gables B&B B&B $$

(Map p576; ☎403-271-7754; www.twingables.ca; 611 25th Ave SW; ste $99-175; P @) This could be your grandma's house – if you were visiting her in 1910. Featuring hardwood floors, stained-glass windows, Tiffany lamps and antique furnishings, this B&B is a little fussy but entirely comfortable. With just three rooms, it's located in a historic house across from the Elbow River, meaning walking trails are at the ready.

★ **Hotel Le Germain** BOUTIQUE HOTEL $$$

(Map p576; ☎403-264-8990; www.germain-calgary.com; 899 Centre St SW; d from $309; P ❄ @ ≈) A posh boutique hotel to counteract the bland assortment of franchise inns that service downtown Calgary. Part of a small French-Canadian chain, the style verges on opulent. Rooms are elegant, while the 24-hour gym, in-room massage, complimentary newspapers and Jetson-style lounge add luxury touches.

Hotel Arts BOUTIQUE HOTEL $$$

(Map p576; ☎403-266-4611; www.hotelarts.ca; 119 12th Ave SW; ste from $269; P ❄ @ ≈ ≋) This boutique hotel plays hard on the fact that it's not part of an international chain. Aimed at the traveler with an aesthetic eye, there are hardwood floors, thread counts Egyptians would be envious of and art on the walls that could be in a gallery. Standard king rooms are small but well designed with rain shower heads and blackout curtains.

Fairmont Palliser HOTEL $$$

(Map p576; ☎403-262-1234; www.fairmont.com/palliser; 133 9th Ave SW; r from $319; P @ ≈ ≋) All satin, velvet and crystal, with marble columns and golden ceiling domes, the Fairmont is palatial. Cut from the same elegant cloth as other Fairmont hotels, the Palliser has a deep regal feel to it, unlike anything else that lies within the city limits. All 407 rooms are newly renovated and elegant. Classic, beautiful and worth every penny.

Sheraton Suites Calgary Eau Claire HOTEL $$$
(Map p576; ☎403-266-7200; www.sheraton.com; 255 Barclay Pde SW; ste from $379; P ❄ @ ☜ ≋) With a great location and overflowing with amenities, this business-oriented all-suite hotel is comfortable without being plush. The staff go the extra mile, and valet parking and a pool top it all off.

Eating

In Calgary, the restaurant scene isn't just fast-moving – it's supersonic, with ever-better quality and greater variety. Where solitary cows once roamed, vegetables and herbs now prosper, meaning that trusty old stalwart, Alberta beef, is no longer the only thing propping up the menu.

You'll find good eat streets in Kensington, Inglewood, Uptown 17th Ave and downtown on Stephen St.

★Al Forno Cafe & Bakery CAFE $
(Map p576; ☎403-454-0308; alforno.ca; 222 7th St SW; mains $8-15; ⏰7am-9pm Mon-Fri, 8am-9pm Sat & Sun) This ultra-modern, super-comfortable cafe is the kind of place you'll want to hang out all day. Beer on tap, carafes of wine and excellent coffee won't discourage you from lingering, nor will magazines, comfy sofas or window seats. With pastas, flatbreads, salads, soups and panini, all homemade, it's difficult to leave room for the amazing cakes, tarts and biscuits.

★1886 Buffalo Cafe BREAKFAST $
(Map p576; 187 Barclay Pde SW; ⏰6am-3pm Mon-Fri, from 7am Sat & Sun) This is a true salt-of-the-earth diner in the high-rise-dominated city center. Built in 1911 and the only surviving building from the lumber yard once here, the interior feels fairly authentic with family photos and antique clocks. This is a ketchup on the table, unlimited coffee refills kind of place famous for its brunches and especially its huevos rancheros.

Myhre's Deli DELI $
(Map p576; 1411 11th St SW; mains $5-13; ⏰11am-4pm) Satisfying meat cravings for 15 years, this deli's mahogany interior and vintage signs are restored from the Palace of Eats, a Stephen Ave institution from 1918 to 1964. Well-filled smoked Montreal meat sandwiches are made fresh, and all beef hot dogs, including the steamed Ruben dog with sauerkraut, are embellished with your choice of seven mustards. Everything is topped with a pickle.

Janice Beaton Fine Cheese CHEESE $
(Map p576; ☎403-229-0900; janicebeaton.com/shop; 1017 16th Ave SW; cheese $3-15; ⏰10am-6pm Sat-Thu, to 7pm Fri) Selling cheeses to Calgarians for 15 years, this shop is a serious find for any cheese-lover. Eat your way from Switzerland to Salt Spring; whether you're into blue cheese or cheddar, there's something here to fill your belly. It all goes down perfectly with a bag of homemade flatbread. And Janice Beaton? This woman knows her cheeses.

Jelly Modern Doughnuts BAKERY $
(Map p576; ☎403-453-2053; www.jellymoderndoughnuts.com; 1414 8th St SW; doughnuts from $2; ⏰7am-6pm Mon-Fri, 9am-6pm Sat, to 5pm Sun) Bright pink and sugary-smelling, Jelly Modern has grabbed the initiative on weird doughnut flavors. The maple and bacon or bourbon vanilla varieties won't help ward off any impending heart attacks, but they'll make every other doughnut you've ever tasted seem positively bland by comparison.

Gravity Espresso & Wine Bar CAFE $
(www.cafegravity.com; 909 10th St SE; light lunches $6-12; ⏰8am-6pm Sun & Mon, to 10pm Tue-Thu, to midnight Fri & Sat) 🍃 This hybrid cafe-bar, which alters its personality depending on the clientele and the time of day, is a thoughtful, community-led business. The crux of the operation is the locally roasted Phil & Sebastian coffee beans, but that's just an overture for loads of other stuff, including live acoustic music, curry nights, home-baked snacks and fund-raisers.

Galaxie Diner BREAKFAST $
(Map p576; ☎403-228-0001; www.galaxiediner.com; 1413 11th St SW; mains $9-15; ⏰7am-3pm Mon-Fri, to 4pm Sat & Sun) Looking more authentic than themed, this classic, no-nonsense 1950s diner serves all-day breakfasts, burgers and milkshakes. Squeeze into a booth, grab a pew at the bar or (more likely) join the queue at the door.

Higher Ground CAFE $
(Map p576; ☎403-270-3780; www.highergroundcafe.ca; 1126 Kensington Rd NW; snacks $5-8; ⏰7am-11pm Mon-Thu, 8am-midnight Fri-Sun) 🍃 Giving Calgary's indie coffee-bar scene the shot of home-roasted caffeine it needs, Higher Ground is a delicious mix of art gallery, gossip shop, public theater and community resource. It is also where you come for lunch-size panini and a damned fine cup of coffee.

Peter's Drive-In BURGERS $

(☎403-277-2747; www.petersdrivein.com; 219 16th Ave NE; mains $2.50-5; ⏱9am-midnight) In 1962 Peter's opened its doors and locals have been flocking here ever since to a largely unchanged menu of super thick shakes, burgers off the grill and fries that make no pretense of being healthy. It's a true drive-in, so either bring the car along or be happy to eat on the lawn out front.

★Market CANADIAN $$

(Map p576; ☎403-474-4414; marketcalgary.ca; 718 17th Ave SW; mains lunch $12-17, dinner $8-20; ⏱11.30am-late) With an earthy yet futuristic feel, award-winning Market has gone a step further in the fresh-local trend. Not only does it bake its own bread, it butchers and cures meat, makes cheese and grows 16 varieties of heirloom seeds year-round. As if that weren't enough, it's then all whipped into meals that are scrumptious and entirely satisfying.

Simmons Mattress Factory CANADIAN $$

(Map p576; www.evexperience.com/simmons; 618 Confluence Way SE; bakery $7-12, restaurant mains $12-25; ⏱bakery items 8am-6pm, restaurant 11.30am-10pm, cafe 7.30am-9pm) This old brick factory is breathing new life into Inglewood, where you can have all of your culinary cravings satisfied: Charbar's upstairs and rooftop restaurant serves incredible meals straight from the fire pit, Sidewalk Citizen Bakery can fill your belly with salads, sandwiches and yummy treats, and Phil & Sebastian Coffee Roasters makes a damn fine cup of joe.

Without Papers PIZZA $$

(☎403-457-1154; wopizza.ca; 1216 9th Ave SE; pizzas $16-22; ⏱11am-10pm Mon-Thu, to 11pm Fri & Sat, 4-9pm Sun) These authentic pizzas are baked in an Italian pizza oven that was lowered through the ceiling. The busy pizzeria's name is a nod to early Italian immigrants, while its pizzas and calzones are fresh and creative. The walls are covered in old movie posters and the tables are filled with happy pizza eaters.

Una PIZZA $$

(Map p576; ☎403-453-1183; www.unapizzeria.com; 618 17th Ave SW; pizzas $17-22; ⏱11.30am-1am) There's often a line out the door but nobody seems to mind waiting – that's how good these thin-crust pizzas are. Toppings like double smoked bacon and *fior di latte* mozzarella could quite possibly be addictive. There's plenty of good house wine, too.

Ox and Angela TAPAS $$

(Map p576; ☎403-457-1432; www.oxandangela.com; 528 17th Ave SW; tapas $4-14; ⏱11:30am-late) Re-creating Spain in modern Calgary isn't an obvious go-to but Ox and Angela has somehow managed it with colorful tiles and delicious tapas. Order piecemeal from a menu of Manchego cheese, tortilla (Spanish omelette) and cured *jamón serrano*.

Mercato ITALIAN $$

(Map p576; ☎403-263-5535; www.mercatogourmet.com; 2224 4th St SW; mains $16-22; ⏱11:30am-11pm) Attached to an open-plan Italian market-deli that sells everything from coffee to salami, Mercato is one of those local restaurants that gets everything right. Decor, service, atmosphere, food and price all hit the spot in a modern but authentic take on la dolce vita in the endearing Mission neighborhood.

Pulcinella ITALIAN $$

(Map p576; ☎403-283-1166; www.pulcinella.ca; 1147 Kensington Cres NW; pizzas $15-20; ⏱11:30am-11pm) With an authentic pizza oven, Pulcinella specializes in amazing thin crispy Neapolitan pizzas with purposefully simple toppings. You won't want to leave without trying the homemade gelato with flavors like black cherry and pistachio.

Blink FUSION $$

(Map p576; ☎403-263-5330; www.blinkcalgary.com; 111 8th Ave SW; mains from $20; ⏱11am-2pm Mon-Fri, 5-10pm Mon-Sat) 🍃 It's true, you could miss this small oasis tucked along a busy street and that would be a shame. Inside this trendy gastro haven, an acclaimed chef oversees an ever-evolving menu of fine dishes like smoked ricotta ravioli with walnuts and truffle vinaigrette or grilled striploin with caramelized shallots and red-wine sauce. Food is fresh and, wherever possible, locally sourced.

Catch SEAFOOD $$

(Map p576; ☎403-206-0000; www.catchrestaurant.ca; 100 8th Ave SW; mains $17-27; ⏱11:30am-2pm Mon-Fri, 5-10pm Mon-Sat) The problem for any saltwater fish restaurant in landlocked Calgary is that if you're calling it fresh, it can't be local. Overcoming the conundrum, the lively, ever-popular Catch, situated in an old bank building on Stephen Ave Walk, flies its 'fresh catch' in daily from both coasts (British Columbia and the Maritimes).

Teatro ITALIAN $$$

(Map p576; ☎403-290-1012; www.teatro.ca; 200 8th Ave SE; mains lunch $18-20, dinner $28-50; ⊙noon-4pm Mon-Fri, 5-10pm daily) In a regal bank building next to the Epcor Centre of Performing Arts, Teatro has an art nouveau touch with its marble bar top, swirling metalwork and high-backed curved sofas. Dishes are works of art and fuse Italian influences, French nouvelle cuisine and a bit of traditional Alberta.

Model Milk CANADIAN $$$

(Map p576; ☎403-265-7343; www.modelmilk.ca; 108 17th Ave SW; mains $19-32; ⊙5pm-1am) Model Milk's revolving menu changes before the ink's even dry, but your choices are always great at the former dairy turned hip restaurant. Look for favorites like grits and sausage or chicken with buttermilk waffles and peanut coleslaw. More certain is the excellent service and the cool ambience that comes with an open kitchen and communal seating.

Rouge FUSION $$$

(☎403-531-2767; www.rougecalgary.com; 1240 8th Ave SE; mains lunch $16-20, dinner $30-46; ⊙11:30am-1:30pm Mon-Fri, 5-10pm Mon-Sat) One of the city's most celebrated restaurants, Rouge is located in a historic 1891 mansion in Inglewood. It's to hard to get a table, but once inside, enjoy the inspired, sustainable food and exceptional fit-for-a-king service. The menu evolves weekly but you'll find dishes like duck and pistachio terrine, beef bolognaise with hand-cut noodles or rockfish with curry coconut broth.

Drinking & Nightlife

Hit 17th Ave NW for a slew of martini lounges and crowded pubs, and 4th St SW for a lively after-work scene. Other notable areas include Kensington Rd NW and Stephen Ave. Evenings bring out stretch limos and noisy stag nights in corporate bars. For Calgary's gay and lesbian nightlife, pick up a copy of *Outlooks* (www.outlooks.ca).

★Proof COCKTAIL BAR

(Map p576; ☎403-246-2414; www.proofyyc.com; 1302 1st St SW; ⊙4pm-1am) This place might be small but the bar is big enough to require a library ladder. Big leather chairs and lots of metal and wood highlight craftsmanship – as do the expertly created cocktails. The menu itself is a beautiful thing to behold and the drinks look so stunning, you almost don't want to drink them. Almost.

Cru Juice JUICE BAR

(Map p576; ☎403-452-2159; www.crujuice.com; 816 16th Ave SW; juice $7-12) Cold-pressed juice is the latest craze in Calgary. Like a meal in a bottle, it can be found in trendy cafes or at this flagship store. Some flavors are super tasty, like The Pixie (watermelon, pink grapefruit, strawberry, lime and mint), while others are a little more challenging – take the Dirty Lemonade (lemon, honey, clay and charcoal).

Analog Coffee COFFEE

(Map p576; www.fratellocoffee.com; 740 17th Ave SW; coffees $2-5; ⊙7am-10pm) The third-wave coffee scene is stirring in Calgary, led by companies like Fratello, which runs this narrow, overflowing hipster-ish 17th Ave cafe, which displays the beans of the day on a clipboard and has rows of retro vinyl spread along the back wall.

Barley Mill PUB

(Map p576; ☎403-290-1500; www.barleymillcalgary.com; 201 Barclay Pde SW; ⊙11am-late) Built in a 1900s style, with the original distillery's lumber used for the top floor and an actual waterwheel churning outside, the Barley Mill draws crowds for its pub grub, long lineup of draught beers and a well-stocked bar. Two patios for when it's warm and a big stone fireplace for when it's not keeps it busy in every season.

Back Lot GAY

(Map p576; thebacklotbar.com; 209 10th Ave SW; ⊙9pm-2:30am) Calgary's oldest gay bar is West Hollywood–style – as in rough around the edges. Drinks are cheap and it often has live bands or karaoke.

Twisted Element GAY & LESBIAN

(Map p576; www.twistedelement.ca; 1006 11th Ave SW; ⊙9pm-late Wed-Sun) Consistently voted the best gay dance venue by the local community, this club has weekly drag shows, karaoke nights and DJs spinning nightly. Its tagline reads: Coming out was hard enough; going out shouldn't be.

HiFi Club CLUB

(Map p576; www.hificlub.ca; 219 10th Ave SW; ⊙9pm-2:30am Wed-Sun) The HiFi is a hybrid. Rap, soul, house, electro, funk – the dance floor swells nightly to the sounds of live DJs who specialize in making you sweat.

Rose & Crown PUB

(Map p576; ☎403-244-7757; www.roseandcrowncalgary.ca; 1503 4th St SW; ⊙11am-late) Originally a funeral home in the 1920s and believed by many to be haunted, this popular, multilevel British-style pub is a popular place for a pint. Upstairs you'll find vintage wallpaper and possibly a ghost or two.

Hop In Brew PUB
(Map p576; ☎403-266-2595; 213 12th Ave SW; ⏲4pm-late) Without the hand-printed Pub sign in the window, this would just look like the old arts-and-crafts-style house that it is, clinging on for dear life amid the spanking new condos. Downscale and snug, the Hop continues to be listed in Calgary's top pub lists with good tunes and plenty of beers on tap.

☆ Entertainment

For complete entertainment guides, pick up a copy of *ffwd* (www.ffwdweekly.com), the city's largest entertainment weekly. The paper is free and found in numerous coffee bars, restaurants and street boxes in Calgary, Banff and Canmore.

Ironwood Stage & Grill LIVE MUSIC
(www.ironwoodstage.ca; 1229 9th Ave SE, Inglewood; ⏲shows 8pm Sun-Thu, 9pm Fri & Sat) Cross over into the hip universe of Inglewood to find the grassroots of Calgary's music scene. Local bands alternate with bigger touring acts for nightly music in the welcoming, woody confines of Ironwood. Country and folk are the staples. Events are all ages.

Calgary Flames SPECTATOR SPORT
(☎403-777-0000; flames.nhl.com) Archrival of the Edmonton Oilers, the Calgary Flames play ice hockey from October to April at the **Saddledome** (Map p576; Stampede Park). Make sure you wear red to the game and head down to 17th Ave afterwards, or the 'Red Mile,' as they call it during play-offs.

Loose Moose Theatre Company THEATER
(☎403-265-5682; www.loosemoose.com; 1235 26th Ave SE) Guaranteed to be a fun night out, Loose Moose has digs near the Inglewood neighborhood. It specializes in improv comedy and, at times, audience participation. (You've been warned.) You'll also find kids' theater.

Epcor Centre for the Performing Arts THEATER
(Map p576; www.epcorcentre.org; 205 8th Ave SE) This is the hub for live theater in Calgary. With four theaters and one of the best concert halls in North America, here you can see everything from ballet to Bollywood.

Globe Cinema CINEMA
(Map p576; www.globecinema.ca; 617 8th Ave SW) This art-house theater specializes in foreign films and Canadian cinema – both often hard to find in mainstream movie houses. Look for discounts on Tuesdays and matinees on the weekend.

Plaza Theatre CINEMA
(Map p576; ☎403-283-3636; 1113 Kensington Rd NW) Built in the 1920s as a garage but turned into a neighbourhood theatre during the 1930s depression, the Plaza is the last operating neighborhood theater in Calgary. Right in the heart of Kensington, it shows art-house flicks and cult classics. Call the 24-hour movie line for what's on.

Broken City LIVE MUSIC
(Map p576; ☎403-262-9976; www.brokencity.ca; 613 11th Ave SW; ⏲11am-2am) There's something on stage here most nights – everything from jazz jams to hip-hop, along with comedy and quiz nights. The rooftop patio is ace in the summer, and the small but well-curated menu keeps you happy whether you're after a steak sandwich or vegan cauliflower wings.

Calgary Stampeders SPECTATOR SPORT
(☎403-289-0258; www.stampeders.com) The Calgary Stampeders, part of the CFL, play from July to September at **McMahon Stadium** (1817 Crowchild Trail NW) in the University District, located 6km northwest of downtown.

Pumphouse Theatres THEATER
(www.pumphousetheatres.ca; 2140 Pumphouse Ave SW) Set in what used to be, you guessed it, the pumphouse, this theater company puts on avant-garde, edgy productions like *One Man Star Wars Trilogy*.

🛍 Shopping

Calgary has several hot shopping spots, but these districts are reasonably far apart. The Kensington area and 17th Ave SW have a good selection of interesting, fashionable clothing shops and funky trinket outlets. Stephen Ave Walk is a pedestrian mall with shops, bookstores and atmosphere. Inglewood is good for antiques, junk, apothocaries, and secondhand books and vinyl.

Tea Trader TEA
(☎403-264-0728; www.teatrader.com; 1228a 9th Ave SE; ⏲10am-5pm Tue-Sat, noon-4pm Sun) Canadians are Canadians and even in Calgary they drink tea. This little shop is up a set of stairs and very easy to miss but also worth

searching out. Teas from all over the world line the shelves, as well as some local flavors: try Calgary Welsh Breakfast or the Alberta Clipper.

Smithbilt Hats CLOTHING
(☎403-244-9131; www.smithbilthats.com; 1103 12th St SE; ⏰9am-5pm Mon-Thu, 8am-4:30pm Fri) Ever wondered how a cowboy hat is made? Well, here is your chance to find out. Smithbilt has been shaping hats in the traditional way since you parked your horse out front. You can pick up one made of straw or beaver felt and priced accordingly.

Alberta Boot Co SHOES
(☎403-263-4605; www.albertaboot.com; 50 50th Ave SE; ⏰9am-6pm Mon-Sat) Visit the factory and store run by the province's only Western boot manufacturer and pick up a pair of your choice made of kangaroo, bullhide or boring old cowhide. Over 200 hours of labor go into each boot, which can be custom-designed. Prices range from $375 to $2100.

Information

Main post office (Map p576; 207 9th Ave SW; ⏰8am-5:45pm Mon-Fri)

Tourism Calgary (Map p576; www.tourismcalgary.com; 101 9th Ave SW; ⏰8am-5pm) Has a visitor center in the base of the Calgary Tower. The staff will help you find accommodations. Information booths are also available at both the arrivals and departures levels of the airport.

Getting There & Away

AIR

Calgary International Airport (YYC; www.ycc.com) is about 15km northeast of the center off Barlow Trail, a 25-minute drive away.

BUS

Greyhound Canada (☎bus station 403-263-1234, ticket purchase 800-661-8747; www.greyhound.ca; 850 16th St SW) has services to Banff ($29, 1¾ hours), Edmonton ($52, 3½ hours), Drumheller ($38, 1¾ hours) and Lethbridge ($46, 2½ hours). Note that discounts are available online.

For a more comfortable experience, go with the super-luxurious **Red Arrow** (Map p576; www.redarrow.pwt.ca; 205 9th Ave SE) buses to Edmonton ($71, 3½ hours, six daily) and Lethbridge ($49, 2½ hours, one daily).

Canmore and Banff ($65, 2¼ hours, eight daily) are served by the legendary Brewster (www.brewster.ca).

Red Arrow picks up downtown on the corner of 9th Ave SE and 1st Ave SE. Brewster buses pick up at various downtown hotels. Inquire when booking.

WORTH A TRIP

TURNER VALLEY

As you head south on the Cowboy Trail (Hwy 22), you'll pass through Turner Valley. At first glance it looks like many of the small towns…until you put your nose to the air and get a waft of the aroma-imbued air. It's definitely worth stopping here to fill both your belly and your liquor cabinet.

Chuck Wagon Cafe (www.chuckwagoncafe.ca; 105 Sunset Blvd, Turner Valley; mains $15-30; ⏰8am-2:30pm Mon-Fri, to 3:30pm Sat & Sun) Housed in a tiny red barn, this legendary cafe feels much like the homestead kitchen it is – it draws hungry diners from miles around. The enormous, all-day breakfast of smoked hash, triple-A steak and eggs Benedict will have you shouting, "Yeehaw!" This is ranch cooking at its best.

Eau Claire Distillery (www.eauclairedistillery.ca; tasting $6.50, tasting & tour $12, cocktails $17-20; ⏰11am-6pm Mon-Thu, 10am-8pm Fri & Sat, 10am-6pm Sun, tours noon, 2pm & 4pm) Next door to the cafe, this is the province's first craft distillery, using Alberta grain and custom-crafted German stills. Having taken over the town's original movie theater and built on the site of the neighboring brothel, this award-winning place pours tastings of gin, vodka and EquineOx – a barley-based spirit – infused with natural flavors like prickly pear and lemon, as well as single-malt whiskey. Take a tour and sit yourself down at the bar for a cocktail.

CAR & MOTORCYCLE

All the major car-rental firms are represented at the airport and downtown.

TRAIN

Inexplicably, Calgary welcomes no passenger trains (which bypass the city in favor of Edmonton and Jasper). You have to find other transport from those destinations.

Getting Around

TO/FROM THE AIRPORT

Sundog Tours (☎403-291-9617; www.sundogtours.com; adult/child one-way $15/8) runs every half-hour from around 8:30am to 9:45pm between all the major downtown hotels and the airport.

You can also go between the airport and downtown on public transportation. From the airport, take bus 57 to the Whitehorn stop (northeast of the city center) and transfer to the C-Train; reverse that process coming from downtown. You can also take bus 300 from the city center all the way to the airport. Either way, the trip costs only $3, and takes between 45 minutes and an hour.

A taxi to the airport costs about $35 from downtown.

CAR & MOTORCYCLE

Parking in downtown Calgary is an expensive nightmare – a policy designed to push people to use public transportation. Luckily, downtown hotels generally have garages. Private lots charge about $20 per day. There is also some metered parking. Outside the downtown core, parking is free and easy to find.

Calgary has the largest fleet of car2go smart cars (www.car2go.com), making it a super convenient way to get around town and even to the airport.

PUBLIC TRANSPORTATION

Calgary Transit (www.calgarytransit.com) is efficient and clean. You can choose from the Light Rapid Transit (LRT) rail system, aka the C-Train, and ordinary buses. One fare ($3) entitles you to transfer to other buses or C-Trains. The C-Train is free in the downtown area along 7th Ave between 10th St SW and 3rd St SE. If you're going further or need a transfer, buy your ticket from a machine on the C-Train platform. Most buses run at 15- to 30-minute intervals daily. There is no late-night service.

TAXI

For a cab, call **Checker Cabs** (☎403-299-9999; www.thecheckergroup.com) or **Calgary Cabs** (☎403-777-1111). Fares are $3 for the first 150m, then 20¢ for each additional 150m.

BANFF & JASPER NATIONAL PARKS

With the Rocky Mountains stretched across them, Banff and Jasper National Parks are filled with dramatic, untamed wilderness. Rugged mountaintops scrape the skyline while enormous glaciers cling to their precipices. Glassy lakes flash emerald, turquoise and sapphire, filled by waterfalls tumbling down cliff faces and thundering through bottomless canyons. Deep forests blanket wide valleys and lofty alpine meadows explode with vibrant flowers. It's the scenery that you only expect to see on postcards, right here at your fingertips. And through it wander a cast of elusive wildlife characters such as bears, elk, moose, wolves and bighorn sheep.

Of the thousands of national parks scattered around the world today, Banff, created in 1885, is the third oldest and Canada's first, while adjacent Jasper was only 22 years behind. Situated on the eastern side of the Canadian Rockies, the two bordering parks were designated Unesco World Heritage sites in 1984. In contrast to some of North America's more remote parks, they both support small towns that lure from two to five million visitors each year.

Despite the throngs who come for the parks' more famous sites, like Lake Louise and Miette Hot Springs, it's by no means difficult to escape to a more tranquil experience of this sublime wonderland. However you choose to experience the parks, be it through hiking, backcountry skiing, paddling or simply sitting at a lake's edge beneath towering, castle-like mountains, the intensity and scale of these parks will bowl over even the most seasoned traveler. The more you see, the more you'll come to appreciate these parks' magic – and the more you'll want to discover.

Kananaskis Country

Kananaskis, or K-Country as the locals call it, is a mountainous Shangri-la, with all the natural highlights of Banff National Park, but with almost no clamor. With less traffic and no fencing, you are very likely to encounter plenty of wildlife here. Kananaskis abuts Banff National Park in the southeast, and at an impressive 4000 sq km, it's a hefty tract of landscape to try and take in. Luckily, there's a network of hiking trails to get you into the backcountry and away from the roads. Hikers,

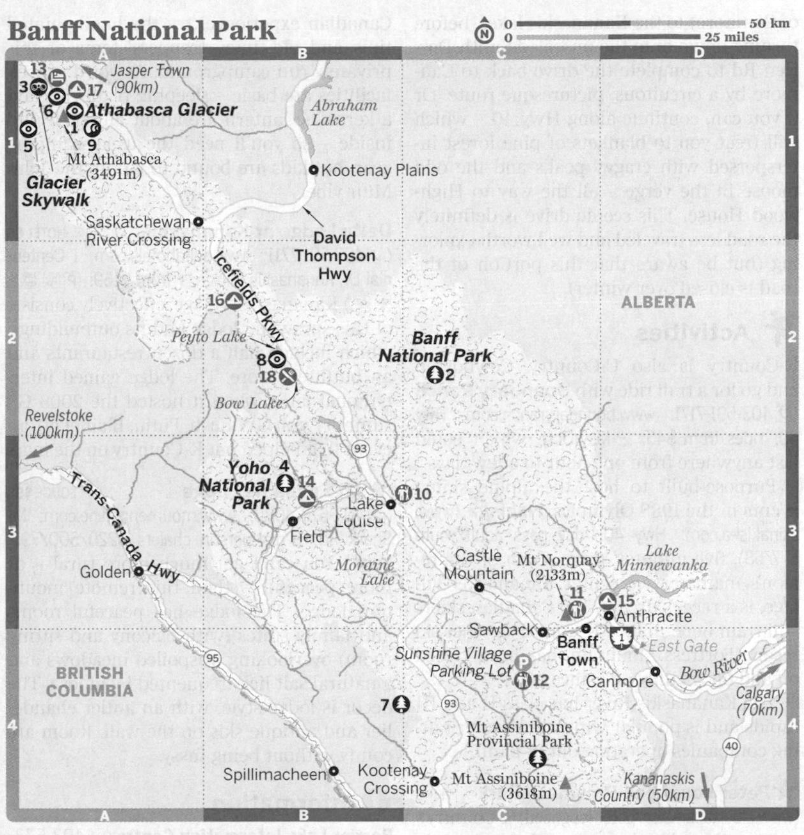

Banff National Park

Top Sights

1 Athabasca Glacier A1
2 Banff National Park C2
3 Glacier Skywalk A1
4 Yoho National Park B3

Sights

5 Columbia Icefield A1
6 Columbia Icefield Discovery Centre A1
7 Kootenay National Park B4
8 Peyto Lake B2
9 Weeping Wall A1

Activities, Courses & Tours

Athabasca Glacier Icewalks .... (see 13)
Glacier Adventure .... (see 6)
10 Lake Louise Ski Area C3
11 Mt Norquay C3
12 Sunshine Village C4

Sleeping

13 Glacier View Inn A1
14 Kicking Horse Campground B3
15 Two Jack Lakeside D3
16 Waterfowl Lakes Campground B2
17 Wilcox Creek Campground A1

Eating

18 Num-Ti-Jah Lodge B2

cross-country skiers, cyclists and climbers – mainly in-the-know Albertans – all lust over these hills, which are the perfect combination of wild, accessible, unspoiled and inviting. If you recognize anything, it's probably because you've seen it in one of a score of films made here, including *Brokeback Mountain*.

On the eastern edge of the mountains you can drive the scenic and sparsely trafficked Hwy 40 (south off Hwy 1, 20km east of Canmore) to the Kananaskis lakes, before turning down onto the unsealed Smith Dorrien Rd to complete the drive back to Canmore by a circuitous, picturesque route. Or if you can, continue along Hwy 40 – which will treat you to blankets of pine forest interspersed with craggy peaks and the odd moose in the verge – all the way to Highwood House. This scenic drive is definitely the road less traveled and well worth exploring (but be aware that this portion of the road is closed over winter).

Activities

K-Country is also C-Country. Cowboy-up and go for a trail ride with **Boundary Ranch** (403-591-7171; www.boundaryranch.com; Hwy 40; rides from $46; May-Oct), which could last anywhere from one hour to a few days.

Purpose-built to host the alpine skiing events in the 1988 Olympics, **Nakiska** (www.skinakiska.com; Hwy 40; day pass adult/youth $77/58), five minutes' drive south of the region's main service center Kananaskis Village, is a racer's dream. Top Canadian skiers still train here, in fact. K-Country's other ski resort, Fortress Mountain, has been closed on and off (mainly off) since 2004.

The Kananaskis River has class II and III rapids and is popular with white-water rafting companies operating out of Banff.

★**Peter Lougheed Provincial Park** HIKING
(www.albertaparks.ca/peter-lougheed) K-Country's quiet trails and backcountry offer superb hiking, especially around this 304-sq-km park on the west side of Kananaskis Valley, which includes the **Upper** and **Lower Kananaskis Lakes** and the **Highwood Pass**, the highest navigable road pass in Canada (2350m; usually open from June to October). It's an excellent area for wildlife-spotting: watch for foxes, wolves, bears, lynx and coyotes.

Kananaskis Outfitters ADVENTURE SPORTS
(www.kananaskisoutfitters.com; Kananaskis Village; bike/ski rental per day $45/25; 10am-6pm) Outfitter in Kananaskis Village that rents bikes, cross-country skis and fat bikes for winter rides. It also runs canoe tours in the summer on Barrier Lake and winter bike tours over frozen waterfalls.

Sleeping

★**Sundance Lodges** CAMPGROUND $
(403-591-7122; www.sundancelodges.com; Kananaskis Trail; campsites $32, tipis $65-90, trappers' tents $90; mid-May–Oct) For that authentic Canadian experience, try the hand-painted tipis and old-timey trappers' tents at this privately run campground. As you'd expect, facilities are basic – sleeping platforms and a kerosene lantern are about all you'll find inside – so you'll need the usual camping gear, but kids are bound to lap up the John Muir vibe.

Delta Lodge at Kananaskis HOTEL $$
(403-591-7711; www.deltahotels.com; 1 Centennial Dr, Kananaskis Village; r from $169; P ❄ @ 🛜 ≋) Kananaskis 'village' effectively consists of this sprawling lodge and its outbuildings, which include half a dozen restaurants and an outfitters store. The lodge gained international fame when it hosted the 2008 G8 summit (with GW Bush, Putin, Blair et al), an event that helped put K-Country on the map.

★**Mt Engadine Lodge** LODGE $$$
(403-678-4080; www.mountengadine.com; Mt Shark Rd; s/d/4-person chalets $220/500/795; P 🛜) You can't get much more rural – or more peaceful – than this remote mountain lodge. The lodge has peaceful rooms and family suites (with balcony and sitting room) overlooking unspoiled meadows and a natural salt lick frequented by moose. The decor is lodge-style, with an antler chandelier and antique skis on the wall. Room are comfy without being fussy.

Information

Barrier Lake Information Centre (403-673-3985; www.albertaparks.ca; Hwy 40; 9am-5pm) Has info and sells backcountry camping permits ($12); located on Hwy 40, about 8km from Hwy 1.

Elbow Valley Visitor Centre (403-949-2461; www.albertaparks.ca; 10:30am-2pm & 3-6pm Fri, 9am-12:30pm & 1:30-4:30pm Sat & Sun May-Oct) Just west of Bragg Creek.

Peter Lougheed Information Centre (403-591-6322; www.albertaparks.ca/peter-lougheed; Kananaskis Lakes Rd; 9am-9pm Jul & Aug, 9:30am-4pm Apr-Jun, Sep & Oct, closed Nov-Mar) Near the junction with Hwy 742, north of Kananaskis Lakes.

Getting There & Away

Brewster (403-762-6750; www.brewster.ca; 100 Gopher St, Banff Town) runs two or three buses between the Delta Lodge in Kananaskis Village to Calgary's airport (adult/youth $60/30). You can also sometimes get a shuttle from the Delta to Nakoda Resort on Hwy 1, where you can meet up with Brewster buses to Banff or Jasper.

It's best to have your own wheels. Be sure to double-check your policy if you're driving a rental; the Smith Dorrien Rd is unsealed so not all rental insurance will cover it. Also be aware that there is virtually no cell-phone service along that route, and no gas stations.

Canmore

POP 12,288

A former coal-mining town, Canmore was once the quiet alternative to the mass tourism of Banff. But after one too many 'best-kept secret' travel articles, everybody started coming here for a little peace and quiet. Despite the commotion, the soul of the town has remained intact, and Canmore, although not national-park protected, has been developed sensibly and sustainably – so far. At just 26km from Banff and on the cusp of Kananaskis Country, it's at the crossroads of some of the most magnificent scenery you will ever see. For those seeking a mountain holiday with slightly less glitz – with more of a rugged feel and less pretension – Canmore can still cut it.

Sights

Canmore Museum & Geoscience Centre MUSEUM
(www.cmags.org; 907 7th Ave, Canmore; adult/youth/child $7/5/free; noon-5pm Mon-Fri, 11am-5pm Sat & Sun May-Sep, 1-4pm Fri-Mon Oct-Apr) Completely renovated in 2016 following flood damage from three years previous, this small but well-curated museum is worth a visit. Exhibits cover the region's coal-mining past and the community's survival following the mine closure in 1979. Check out the 160-million-year-old petrified cypress stump and the stunning images taken by local photographer Craig Richards.

North West Mounted Police Barracks MUSEUM
(www.cmags.org; 601 8th St; 1-4pm Mon & Tue, 10am-5pm Wed-Sun summer, 1-4pm Fri-Mon winter) FREE The oldest surviving barracks in western Canada was built in 1893 and used by the Royal Canadian Mounted Police (RCMP) until 1929. Today this itty-bitty wooden building is home to a small display of Mountie-themed memorabilia and a quaint tearoom.

Activities

Canmore excels in three mountain activities: cross-country skiing, mountain biking and rock climbing.

★**Canmore Nordic Centre** MOUNTAIN BIKING, SKIING
(www.canmorenordiccentre.ca; Olympic Way) Nestled in the hills to the west of town on the way to the Spray Lakes Reservoir, this huge trail center was originally developed for the Nordic events of the 1988 Winter Olympics. It's now one of the best mountain-bike parks in western Canada, with over 65 km (40 miles) of groomed trails developed by some of the nation's top trail designers. In winter, trails are open to cross-country skiers (day pass $15), with 6.5km lit for night skiing.

Yamnuska Mountain Adventures CLIMBING
(403-678-4164; www.yamnuska.com; Suite 200, Summit Centre, 50 Lincoln Park; 9am-5pm Mon-Fri, to 4pm Sat) This well-regarded company offers instruction courses in both rock and ice climbing, for beginner, intermediate or advanced climbers. From Tuesday to Saturday in July and August there's a daily climb for $140 per person, including gear and transport. Just show up at Bow Falls (p594) in Banff at 8:30am.

Canmore Cave Tours ADVENTURE
(403-678-8819; www.canmorecavetours.com) Buried deep beneath the Grotto Mountain near Canmore is a system of deep caves known as the **Rat's Nest**. Canmore Cave Tours runs guided trips into the maze of twisting passageways and claustrophobic caverns.

Snowy Owl Tours DOG SLEDDING
(403-678-9588; www.snowyowltours.com; 829 10th St; 2hr tour adult/child $160/85) Dog sledding has been a traditional mode of travel in the Canadian Rockies for centuries, and it's a wonderful way to see the wilderness. Snowy Owl Tours offers sled trips on custom-built sleighs pulled by your own well-cared-for team of Siberian and Alaskan huskies.

Sleeping

Staying in Canmore is often seen as a cheaper, more relaxed alternative to Banff. Nevertheless, the good selection of hotels and B&Bs has made it popular in its own right so it's wise to book ahead.

Canmore Clubhouse HOSTEL $
(403-678-3200; www.alpineclubofcanada.ca; Indian Flats Rd; dm from $40; P) Steeped in climbing history and mountain mystique, the Alpine Club of Canada's beautiful hostel sits on a rise overlooking the valley,

LOCAL KNOWLEDGE

THE LEGACY TRAIL

It's not often that getting from point A to B involves dazzling scenery, the possibility of spotting a moose and a huge dose of mountain air. The Legacy Trail is a 26.8km paved route that connects cyclists, pedestrians and skaters with Canmore and Banff Town. Shadowing Hwy 1 and gaining 30m elevation, the trail takes most peddlers two or three hours round-trip. For those not up to cycling/walking in both directions, **Bike 'n' Hike Shuttle** (☎403-762-2282; www.bikeandhikeshuttle.com; $10-20; ⏱May-Oct) offer a handy bus service between the trailheads to get you back to your starting point.

Banff and Canmore are linked by two additional trails, the rugged **Rundle Riverside Trail** (for experienced off-road cyclists) and the easier **Goat Creek Trail**. Check with **Parks Canada** (www.pc.gc.ca) for current conditions.

with views through big picture windows. There's all of the usual hostel amenities here, along with a sauna. It's a great place to find climbing partners or just soak up the spirit of adventure. It is located 5km south of town.

Lady Macdonald Country Inn GUESTHOUSE **$$**
(☎800-567-3919; www.ladymacdonald.com; 1201 Bow Valley Trail; r $125-199, ste $200-250; P Wi-Fi) This quaint little inn wouldn't look out of place in small-town Connecticut, with its elegant verandahs, turrets and wooden cladding. Rooms are petite, with wrought-iron beds, cushions and some floral print for good measure. Each is unique so it's worth checking out a few.

Blackstone Mountain Lodge HOTEL **$$**
(☎888-830-8883; www.blackstonecanmore.ca; 170 Kananaskis Way; d/ste from $160/200; P ❄ Wi-Fi pool) The pick of several Bellstar properties around Canmore, the Blackstone is located a quick drive out of town on the Bow Valley Trail. Traditional rooms have plush linens while suites come with their own fully equipped kitchen (complete with oven, dishwasher and washing machine), making them ideal for families. All in all, it's a bit of a steal.

Paintbox Lodge B&B **$$**
(☎403-609-0482; www.paintboxlodge.com; 629 10th St, Canmore; r $150-280; P Wi-Fi) Run by ex-Olympic skiers Thomas Grandi and Sarah Renner, this B&B takes Canadian decor to a new level, right down to the tartan carpet. Its five unique suites offer a mix of country chic and luxury comfort. For maximum space ask for the Loft Suite, which sleeps four people and features beamed ceilings, mountain-view balcony and sexy corner tub.

Eating

★Communitea CAFE **$**
(www.thecommunitea.com; 1001 6th Ave; lunch mains $12-15; ⏱9am-5pm; Wi-Fi family) Locally run, ethically aware and all organic, this community cafe somehow manages to sidestep any crusty hippy vibe with a warm, relaxed feel and simple style. Food is ultra fresh and an explosion of flavor: think noodles, rice bowls, wraps, salads and burgers. Slurp fresh-pressed juices, well-executed coffee and, of course, every type of tea you can conceive of.

Rocky Mountain Bagel CAFE **$**
(☎403-678-9978; www.thebagel.ca; 829 8th St; bagels $6-8; ⏱6am-6pm; Wi-Fi) Is there anything better in life than sitting under the flower baskets at Rocky Mountain Bagel, studying the morning shadows on the Three Sisters peaks while enjoying a toasted maple bagel and a latte? Possibly not. Bagelwiches, pizza bagels, breakfast bagels or a bag of bagels to go. Rocky Mountain Bagels has got it covered.

Grizzly Paw PUB FOOD **$$**
(☎403-678-9983; www.thegrizzlypaw.com; 622 8th St; mains $13-20; ⏱11am-midnight) Alberta's best microbrewery (offering six year-round beers) is hiding in the mountains of Canmore. With beer and food pairings, big burgers, hand-crafted sodas and a view-filled patio, it's a popular spot. The veterans of Raspberry Ale and Grumpy Bear beer have a nearby brewery and microdistillery where tours and tasters are available.

★Trough CANADIAN **$$$**
(☎403-678-2820; www.thetrough.ca; 725 9th St; mains $32-38; ⏱5:30pm-late Tue-Sun) Canmore's slinkiest bistro is a bit tucked away on 9th St, but it's absolutely worth the effort

to find. It regularly features in the Rockies' top restaurant lists, and with good reason. The mother-son team here create amazing dishes like Prince Edward Island (PEI) mussels with house-smoked tomatoes, Moroccan-spiced Alberta lamb chops, and BC halibut with mango and sweet peppers. With just nine tables, it's wise to book ahead.

Information

Alberta Visitor Information Centre (403-678-5277; www.travelalberta.com; 2801 Bow Valley Trail; 8am-8pm May-Oct, to 6pm Nov-Apr) Regional visitor center just off the Trans-Canada Hwy northwest of town.

Canmore Visitors Information Centre (www.tourismcanmore.com; 907a 7th Ave; 9am-5pm)

Getting There & Away

Canmore is easily accessible from Banff Town and Calgary from Hwy 1. The **Banff Airporter** (403-762-3330; www.banffairporter.com) runs up to 10 buses a day to/from Calgary Airport ($59). **Brewster** (866-606-6700; www.brewster.ca) has connections with the airport and downtown Calgary for roughly the same price.

Greyhound (www.greyhound.ca) has multiple daily trips to Calgary ($27, 75 minutes) and Banff ($6, 25 minutes). **Roam** (403-762-0606; www.roamtransit.com; 6am-10pm) buses run every hour to Banff ($6, 20 minutes). Buses stop downtown on 9th St near 7th Ave.

Icefields Parkway

As the highest and most spectacular road in North America, the **Icefields Parkway** (www.icefieldsparkway.ca; Hwy 93) takes you about as close as you're going to get to the Rockies' craggy summits in your vehicle; if you get out and follow one of the many trailheads en route, you'll feel like you're on top of the world within a matter of hours. Numerous roadside stops give you the chance to take in the parkway's brilliantly colored glacial lakes, gushing waterfalls and exquisite viewpoints. While you can cover the 230km route between Lake Louise and Jasper within a few hours, it's worth spending a few days exploring the region.

Much of the route followed by the parkway was established in the 1800s by Aboriginal people and fur traders. An early road was built during the 1930s as part of a work project for the unemployed, and the present highway was opened in the early 1960s. These days it's used almost entirely by tourists, with the exception of the occasional elk, coyote or bighorn sheep meandering along its perimeter. It can get busy in July and August, particularly with large recreational vehicles (RVs). Many also tackle it on a bike – the road is wide and sprinkled with plenty of strategically spaced campgrounds, hostels and hotels.

Sights & Activities

There are two types of sights here: static (lakes, glaciers and mountains) and moving (elk, bears, moose etc). If you don't see at least one wild animal (look out for the inevitable 'bear jams') you'll be very unlucky.

★ Athabasca Glacier — GLACIER

(Map p587) The tongue of the Athabasca Glacier runs from the Columbia Icefield to within walking distance of the road opposite the Icefield Centre. It can be visited on foot or in a Snocoach bus. It has retreated about 2km since 1844, when it reached the rock moraine on the north side side of the road. To reach its toe (bottom edge), walk from the Icefield Centre along the 1.8km **Forefield Trail**, then join the 1km **Toe of the Athabasca Glacier Trail**.

You can also park at the start of the latter trail. While it is permitted to stand on a small roped section of the ice, do not attempt to cross the warning tape – many do, but the glacier is riddled with crevasses and there have been fatalities.

To walk safely on the Columbia Icefield, you'll need to enlist the help of **Athabasca Glacier Icewalks** (Map p587; 780-852-5595; www.icewalks.com; Icefield Centre, Icefields Pkwy; 3hr tour adult/child $95/50, 6hr tour adult/child $120/60; Jun-Oct), which supplies all the gear you'll need and a guide to show you the ropes. Its basic tour is three hours; there's a six-hour option for those wanting to venture further out on the glacier. Hikers must be at least seven years of age.

The other, far easier (and more popular) way to get on the glacier is via a **Snocoach** (Map p587; www.columbiaicefield.com; Snocoach & Skywalk tour adult/child $85/43; 9am-6pm Apr-Oct) ice tour offered by Brewster in conjunction with its **Skywalk** (Map p587; www.brewster.ca; skywalk adult/child $32/16; 10am-5pm Apr-Oct) tour. For many people this is the defining experience of their Columbia Icefield visit. The large hybrid bus-truck grinds a track onto the ice, where it stops to allow you to go for a wander on the glacier. Dress warmly, wear good shoes and bring a water bottle to try some freshly melted glacial water. Tickets

CYCLING THE ICEFIELDS PARKWAY

With its ancient geology, landscape-altering glaciers, and lakes bluer than Picasso paintings from his blue period, the 230km-long Icefields Parkway is one of the world's most spectacular roads, and, by definition, one of the world's most spectacular bicycle rides – if your legs and lungs are up to it. Aside from the distance, there are several long uphill drags, occasional stiff headwinds and two major passes to contend with, namely Bow Summit (2088m) and Sunwapta Pass (2035m). Notwithstanding these issues, the route is highly popular in July and August (don't even think about doing it in the winter), with aspiring cyclists lapping up its bicycle-friendly features. No commercial trucks are allowed on the parkway, there's a generous shoulder throughout, two-wheeled company is virtually guaranteed, and accommodations along the route (both campgrounds and hostels/hotels) is plentiful and strategically placed. Some ply the parkway as part of an organized tour (with back-up vehicles), others do it solo over two to five days. There's a choice of six HI hostels and four lodge/motel accommodations en route. Book ahead. Basic provisions can be procured at Saskatchewan River Crossing, 83km north of Lake Louise.

It's considered slightly easier to cycle from north to south, starting in Jasper and finishing in Lake Louise, but the differences aren't great. Some people tack on the extra 60km between Banff and Lake Louise at the start or finish, proceeding along the quiet Bow Valley Parkway and avoiding the busy Trans-Canada (Hwy 1).

Sturdy road bikes can be rented from **Wilson Mountain Sports** (www.wmsll.com; Samson Mall, Lake Louise village; ⌚9am-7pm) in Lake Louise village. Brewster buses can sometimes transport bicycles, but always check ahead. **Backroads** (☎510-527-1555; www.backroads.com; 7-day tour from $2800) runs a Canadian Rockies Bike Tour, a six-day organized trip that incorporates cycling along the parkway.

can be bought at the Icefield Centre or online; tours depart every 15 to 30 minutes.

Weeping Wall WATERFALL

(Map p587) This towering rock wall sits just above the east side of the highway. In the summer months it is a sea of waterfalls, with tears of liquid pouring from the top, creating a veil of moisture. Come winter, it's a whole different story: the water freezes up solid to form an enormous sheet of ice. The vertical ice field is a popular playground for ice climbers, who travel from around the globe to test their mettle here.

Mt Edith Cavell MOUNTAIN

(Map p608) Rising like a snowy sentinel over Jasper Town, Mt Edith Cavell (3363m) is one of the park's most distinctive and physically arresting peaks. What it lacks in height it makes up for in stark, ethereal beauty. Accessed via a winding, precipitous road that branches off the Icefields Pkwy 6km south of Jasper, the mountain is famous for its flower meadows and its wing-shaped **Angel Glacier**.

Columbia Icefield GLACIER

(Map p587) About halfway between Lake Louise village and Jasper Town, you'll glimpse the vast Columbia Icefield, covering an area the size of Vancouver and feeding eight glaciers. This remnant of the last ice age is up to 350m thick in places and stretches across the plateau between **Mt Columbia** (3747m) and **Mt Athabasca** (3491m). For serious hikers and climbers, this is also the only accessible area of the icefield. For information and conditions, visit Parks Canada at the Columbia Icefield Discovery Centre (p592).

Peyto Lake LAKE

(Map p587) You'll have already seen the indescribable blue of Peyto Lake in a thousand publicity shots, but there's nothing like gazing at the real thing – especially since the viewing point for this lake is from a lofty vantage point several hundred feet above the water. The lake is best visited in early morning, between the time the sun first illuminates the water and the first tour bus arrives.

Columbia Icefield Discovery Centre CENTER

(Map p587; www.brewster.ca; Icefields Pkwy; ⌚10am-5pm May-Oct) FREE Situated on the Icefields Pkwy, close to the toe of the Athabasca Glacier, the green-roofed Icefield Centre is a bit of a zoo in the summer, with tour coaches cramming the car park. Decamp here to purchase tickets and board buses for the Snocoaches and Glacier Skywalk. You'll also find a hotel, cafeteria, restaurant, gift shop and Parks Canada information desk.

Athabasca Glacier to Jasper Town SCENIC DRIVE

As you snake your way through the mountains on your way to Jasper, there are a few places worth stopping at. **Sunwapta Falls** (Map p608) and **Athabasca Falls** (Map p608), closer to Jasper, are both worth a stop. The latter is the more voluminous and is at its most ferocious in the summer, when it's stoked with glacial meltwater.

A less visited spot is idyllic, blue-green Horseshoe Lake (p606), revered by ill-advised cliff divers. Don't be tempted to join them.

At Athabasca Falls, Hwy 93A quietly sneaks off to the left. Take it. Literally the road less traveled, this old route into Jasper offers a blissfully traffic-free experience as it slips serenely through deep, dark woods and past small, placid lakes and meadows.

Sleeping & Eating

The Icefields Parkway is punctuated by several well-camouflaged hostels. Most are close to the highway in scenic locations. More substantial hotels/lodges are available at Bow Lake, Saskatchewan Crossing, Columbia Icefield and Sunwapta Falls.

There are also numerous primitive campgrounds in the area. Good options are **Honeymoon Lake** (Map p608; Icefields Pkwy; tent & RV sites $16; Jun-Sep), **Jonas Creek** (Map p608; Icefields Pkwy; tent & RV sites $16; May-Sep), **Mt Kerkeslin** (Map p608; Icefields Pkwy; tent & RV sites $16; Jun-Sep), **Waterfowl Lakes** (Map p587; Icefields Pkwy; tent & RV sites $22; Jun-Sep) and **Wilcox Creek** (Map p587; Icefields Pkwy; tent & RV sites winter/summer $10/16) campgrounds. These campsites are nonreservable.

Mt Edith Cavell International Hostel HOSTEL $

(Map p608; 780-852-3215; www.hihostels.ca; Cavell Rd; dm $26; mid-May–mid-Oct) Sitting in the foothills of one of the Rockies' most sublime mountain peaks, this hostel enjoys phenomenal views from the deck and outdoor firepit. The kitchen and common room have wooden beams and homey touches. There's solar electricity but no flush toilets, showers, phone or wi-fi. It's located directly across the road from the trailhead for the Tonquin Valley.

There's a manager here from June to October but the hostel is open for cross-country skiers from February to May on a key-collect system. Guests have use of showers at the main hostel in Jasper (p611).

Athabasca Falls International Hostel HOSTEL $

(Map p608; 780-852-3215; www.hihostels.ca; Icefields Pkwy; dm/d $30/72; May-Sep) A super-friendly hostel in the woods with an ingenious watering-can shower (summer only); a big, alpine-style kitchen–sitting area; table tennis; and heated dorms in separate wooden cabins. There's no running water (just an outdoor pump) and the toilets are in outhouses, earning the place a 'rustic' tag.

Sunwapta Falls Resort HOTEL $$

(Map p608; 888-828-5777; www.sunwapta.com; Icefields Pkwy; r from $225; P @) A handy Icefields rest stop 53km south of Jasper Town, Sunwapta offers a comfortable mix of suites and lodge rooms, each with a fireplace or wood-burning stove and cocooned in pleasant natural surroundings. Clean and comfortable but not fancy, it's close to the falls and plenty of hiking. There's also a home-style restaurant on-site that's popular with the tour-bus crowd.

Glacier View Inn HOTEL $$$

(Map p587; 877-423-7433; Icefield Centre, Icefields Pkwy; r with mountain/glacier view $269/289; May-Oct; P) Panoramic views of the glacier are unbelievable at this chalet, found in the same complex as the Icefield Centre. At times it can feel like staying in a shopping mall, but once the buses go away you're left in one of the most spectacular places around. Rooms aren't luxurious but are very comfortable.

★ **Num-Ti-Jah Lodge** CANADIAN $$$

(Map p587; 403-522-2167; www.num-ti-jah.com; Icefields Pkwy; mains $32-45; 5-10pm May-Oct) Rustic yet elegant, the Num-Ti-Jah's historic Elkhorn Dining Room lets you step back in time to a Simpson's 1940s hunting lodge, complete with stone fireplace and majestic views. Dine on braised bison short rib or mushroom pappardelle beneath the watchful eye of moose, wolverines and other hunting trophies. Guests get seating priority; if you're staying elsewhere make sure you reserve ahead.

Information

Columbia Icefield Discovery Centre (p592) Parks Canada has a desk here where they dole out information about Jasper, Banff and the

Icefields Parkway. Check in here for current hiking conditions.

South Gate The entrance to the parkway north of Lake Louise, where you can purchase your park pass and pick up a map and brochures.

Getting There & Away

Brewster (www.brewster.ca) has buses plying the parkway between Banff, Lake Louise and Jasper, with stops at Saskatchewan Crossing, Columbia Icefield Discovery Centre and Sunwapta Falls.

If you're driving, start out with a full tank of gas. It's fairly pricey to fill up at Saskatchewan Crossing, the only gas station on the parkway.

Banff Town

POP 7584

A resort town with boutique shops, nightclubs and fancy restaurants is not something any national-park purist would want to claim credit for. But Banff is no ordinary town. It developed not as a residential district, but as a service center for the park that surrounds it. Today it brings busloads of tourists keen to convene with shops as much as nature, as well as artists and writers who are drawn to Banff.

Nevertheless, wander 15 minutes in any direction and you're in wild country, a primeval food chain of bears, elk and wolves. Banff civilized? It's just a rumor.

Sights

★Banff National Park NATIONAL PARK

(Map p587; www.pc.gc.ca/banff; day pass adult/youth/family $9.80/4.90/19.60) Towering like giant castles in the sky, the mountains and valleys of Banff provide endless opportunities for wildlife-watching, hiking, boating, climbing, mountain biking, skiing or simply convening with nature. Lush canyons compete for your attention with lofty fields of alpine wildflowers, while tranquil waterways meander past and dense emerald forests bid you to delve inside. Created in 1885 and ranging over 6641 sq km, Banff is the world's third-oldest national park – and was Canada's first.

★Whyte Museum of the Canadian Rockies MUSEUM

(Map p596; www.whyte.org; 111 Bear St; adult/student/child $10/4/free; ⏲10am-5pm) Founded by local artists Catharine and Peter Whyte, the century-old Whyte Museum is more than just a rainy-day option. It boasts a beautiful, ever-changing gallery displaying art from 1800 to present, by both regional, Canadian and international artists, many with a focus on the Rockies. Watch for work by the Group of Seven (aka the Algonquin School). There's also a permanent collection telling the story of Banff and the hardy men and women who forged a home among the mountains.

Banff Gondola CABLE CAR

(☎403-762-2523; Mountain Ave; adult/child $45/23, after 6pm $37/16; ⏲8am-6pm May, 9am-9pm Jun, 8am-10pm Jul-Oct) In summer or winter, you can summit a peak near Banff thanks to the Banff Gondola, with four-person enclosed cars that glide up to the top of Sulphur Mountain in less than 10 minutes. Named for the thermal springs that emanate from its base, this peak is a perfect viewing point and a tick-box Banff attraction.

Upper Hot Springs Pool HOT SPRINGS

(www.hotsprings.ca; Mountain Ave; adult/child/family $7.30/6.30/22.50; ⏲9am-11pm mid-May–mid-Oct, 10am-10pm Sun-Thu, to 11pm Fri & Sat mid-Oct–mid-May) Banff quite literally wouldn't be Banff if it weren't for its hot springs, which gush out from 2.5km beneath **Sulphur Mountain** at a constant temperature of between 32°C (90°F) and 46°C (116°F) – it was the springs that drew the first tourists to Banff. You can still sample the soothing mineral waters at the Upper Hot Springs Pool, near the Banff Gondola.

Vermilion Lakes NATURE RESERVE

Northwest of town, this trio of tranquil lakes is a great place for **wildlife-spotting**: elk, beavers, bald eagles and ospreys can often be seen around the lakeshore, especially at dawn and dusk. A paved driveway – part of the **Legacy bike trail** – runs along the lake's southern side for 4.5km, but the proximity of the Trans-Canada Hwy means that it's not as peaceful as it could be.

Bow Falls WATERFALL

About 500m south of town, just before the junction with Spray River, the Bow River plunges into a churning melee of white water at Bow Falls. Though the drop is relatively small – just 9m at its highest point – Bow Falls is a dramatic sight, especially in spring following heavy snowmelt.

Banff Park Museum MUSEUM

(Map p596; ☎403-762-1558; 93 Banff Ave; adult/child $3.90/1.90; ⏲10am-5pm) Occupying an old wooden Canadian Pacific Railway building dating from 1903, this museum is a national historic site. Its exhibits – a taxidermic collection of local animals, including grizzly and black bears, plus a tree carved with graffiti dating from 1841 – was curated by Norman Sanson, who ran the museum and Banff weather station until 1932. Much-needed restorations were done in the early 2000s.

Cave & Basin National Historic Site HISTORIC SITE
(☎403-762-1557; Cave Ave; adult/child $3.90/1.90; ⊙10am-5pm mid-May–mid-Oct, noon-4pm Wed-Sun mid-Oct–mid-May) The Canadian National Park system was effectively born at these hot springs, discovered accidentally by three Canadian Pacific Railway employees on their day off in 1883 (though known to Aboriginals for 10,000 years). The springs quickly became a bun fight for private businesses offering facilities for bathers to enjoy the then-trendy thermal treatments.To avert an environmental catastrophe, the government stepped in, declaring Banff Canada's first national park in order to preserve the springs.

Activities

Canoeing & Kayaking

Despite a modern penchant for big cars, canoe travel is still very much a quintessential Canadian method of transportation. The best options near Banff Town are **Lake Minnewanka** and nearby **Two Jack Lake**, both to the northeast, or – closer to the town itself – the **Vermilion Lakes**. Unless you have your own canoe, you'll need to rent one; try **Banff Canoe Club** (Map p596; ☎403-762-5005; www.banffcanoeclub.com; cnr Wolf St & Bow Ave; canoe & kayak rental per first/additional hour $36/20; ⊙10am-6pm mid-May–mid-Sep).

Cycling

There are lots of riding options around Banff, both on the road and on selected trails. Popular routes around Banff Town include **Sundance** (7.4km round-trip) and **Spray River Loop** (12.5km); either is good for families. **Spray River & Goat Creek** (19km one way) and **Rundle Riverside** (14km one way) are both A-to-Bs with start/finish points near Canmore. The former is pretty straightforward; the latter is more challenging, with ups and downs and potential for thrills and spills.

Serious road cyclists should check out Hwy 1A between Banff and Lake Louise; the rolling hills and quiet road here are a roadie's dream. Parks Canada publishes the brochure *Mountain Biking & Cycling Guide – Banff National Park,* which describes trails and regulations. Pick it up at the Banff Visitor Centre (p602).

Snowtips/Bactrax (Map p596; ☎403-762-8177; www.snowtips-bactrax.com; 225 Bear St; bike rental per hour/day from $12/42; ⊙8am-8pm) has a barn full of town and trail bikes to rent (from $12/42 per hour/day) and will deliver them to your hotel. Ask about shuttles to trailheads.

Hiking

Hiking is Banff's tour de force and the main focus of many travelers' visit to the area. The trails are easy to find, well signposted and maintained enough to be comfortable to walk on, yet rugged enough to still get a wilderness experience.

In general, the closer to Banff Town you are, the more people you can expect to see and the more developed the trail will be. But regardless of where in the park you go walking, you are assured to be rewarded for your efforts.

Before you head out, check at the Banff Visitor Centre (p602) for trail conditions and possible closures. Keep in mind that trails are often snow-covered much later into the summer season than you might realize, and trail closures due to bears are a possibility, especially in berry season (June to September).

One of the best hikes from the town center is the **Bow River Falls & The Hoodoos Trail**, which starts by the Bow River Bridge and tracks past the falls to the Hoodoos – weird-looking rock spires caused by wind and water erosion. The trail plies its way around the back of Tunnel Mountain through forest and some river meadows (10.2km round-trip).

You can track the north shore of Lake Minnewanka for kilometers on a multi-use trail that is sometimes closed due to bear activity. The classic hike is to walk as far as the **Alymer Lookout**, just shy of 10km one way. Less taxing is the 5.6km round-trip hike to **Stewart Canyon**, where you can clamber down rocks and boulders to the Cascade River.

Some of the best multiday hikes start at the Sunshine Village parking lot (where skiers grab the gondola in winter). From here you can plan two- to four-day sorties up over **Healy Pass** and down to **Egypt Lake**, or else get a bus up to **Sunshine Village** (Map p587; www.skibanff.com; day ski pass adult/youth $95/73), where you can cross the border into

Banff Town

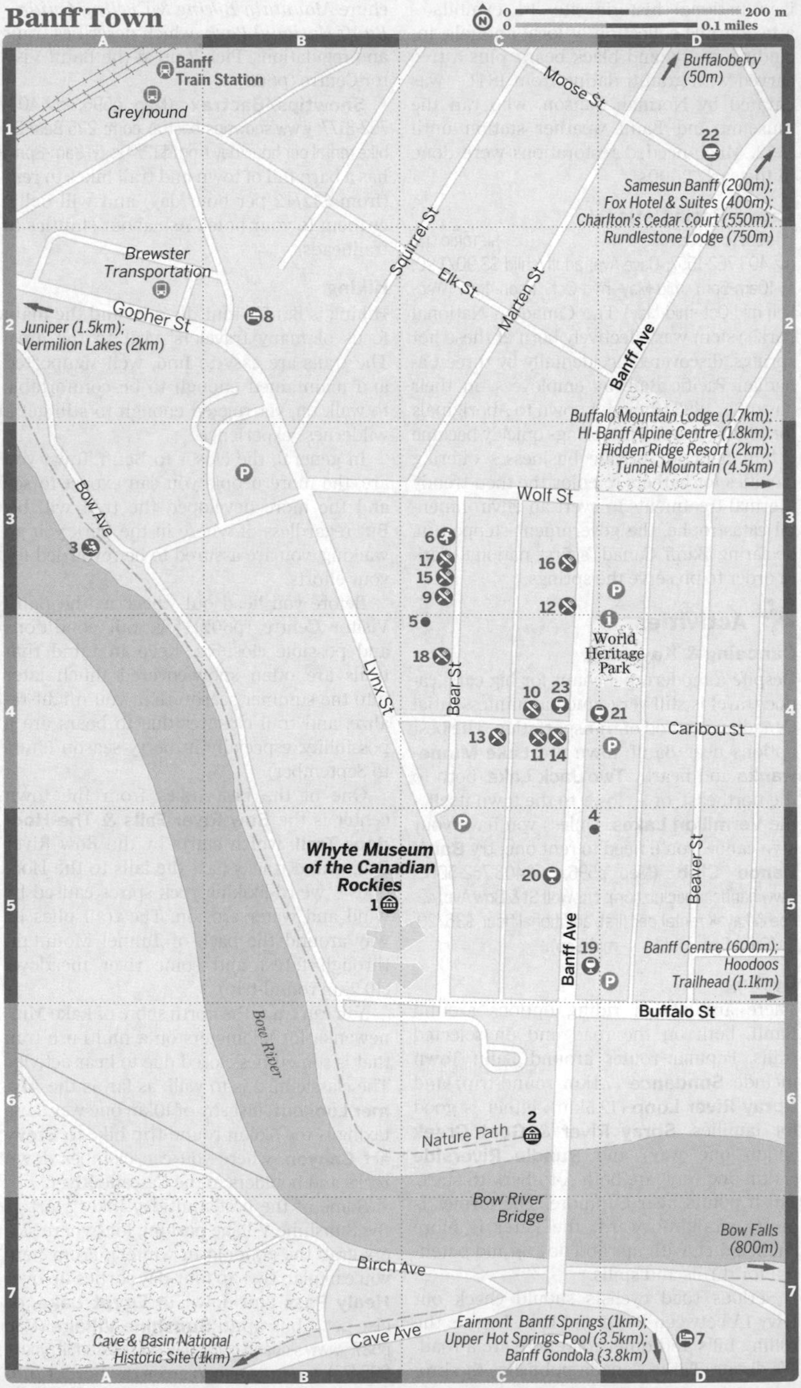

0 200 m
0 0.1 miles
A
B
C
D
1
2
3
4
5
6
7
Banff Train Station
Greyhound
Moose St
Buffaloberry (50m)
22
Samesun Banff (200m);
Fox Hotel & Suites (400m);
Charlton's Cedar Court (550m);
Rundlestone Lodge (750m)
Brewster Transportation
Squirrel St
Elk St
Marten St
Gopher St
8
Juniper (1.5km);
Vermilion Lakes (2km)
Banff Ave
Buffalo Mountain Lodge (1.7km);
HI-Banff Alpine Centre (1.8km);
Hidden Ridge Resort (2km);
Tunnel Mountain (4.5km)
Bow Ave
Wolf St
6
17
15
9
16
12
3
5
World Heritage Park
18
Lynx St
Bear St
10
23
21
Caribou St
13
11
14
4
Whyte Museum of the Canadian Rockies
1
20
Beaver St
19
Banff Centre (600m);
Hoodoos Trailhead (1.1km)
Buffalo St
Bow River
2
Nature Path
Bow River Bridge
Bow Falls (800m)
Birch Ave
Cave Ave
Fairmont Banff Springs (1km);
Upper Hot Springs Pool (3.5km);
Banff Gondola (3.8km)
7
Cave & Basin National Historic Site (1km)

Banff Town

Top Sights
1 Whyte Museum of the Canadian Rockies ... B5

Sights
2 Banff Park Museum ... C6

Activities, Courses & Tours
3 Banff Canoe Club ... A3
4 Banff Trail Riders ... C5
Discover Banff Tours ... (see 12)
GyPSy Guide ... (see 12)
5 Hydra River Guides ... C4
6 Snowtips/Bactrax ... C3

Sleeping
7 Banff Y Mountain Lodge ... D7
8 Poplar Inn ... B2

Eating
9 Bear St Tavern ... C3
Bison Restaurant & Terrace ... (see 9)
10 Block Kitchen & Bar ... C4
11 Eddie Burger & Bar ... C4
12 Evelyn's Coffee Bar ... C3
13 Magpie & Stump ... C4
14 Maple Leaf Grille ... C4
15 Nourish ... C3
16 Park ... C3
17 Saltlik ... C3
18 Wild Flour ... C4

Drinking & Nightlife
19 Banff Ave Brewing Co ... C5
20 Elk & Oarsman ... C5
21 Rose & Crown ... D4
22 Whitebark Cafe ... D1
23 Wild Bill's Legendary Saloon ... C4

BC and head out across Sunshine Meadows and **Mt Assiniboine Provincial Park**.

The best backcountry experience is arguably the **Sawback Trail**, which travels from Banff up to Lake Louise the back way – it's over 74km, with six primitive campsites and three spectacular mountain passes.

Check out Lonely Planet's *Banff, Jasper & Glacier National Parks* guide for more details about more single-day and multiday hikes.

Horseback Riding

Banff's first European explorers – fur traders and railway engineers – penetrated the region primarily on horseback. You can re-create their pioneering spirit on guided rides with **Warner Guiding & Outfitting** (Map p596; 403-762-4551; www.horseback.com; 132 Banff Ave; guided rides per person $54-139; 9am-6pm), which will fit you out with a trusty steed and lead you along narrow trails for part of the day. Instruction and guiding are included; a sore backside is more or less mandatory for beginners. Grin and bear it.

If you're really into it, Warner's six-day Wildlife Monitoring Adventure Expeditions will take you out to limited-access areas, accompanied by a Parks Canada researcher.

Skiing & Snowboarding

Strange though it may seem, there are three ski areas in the national park, two of them located in the vicinity of Banff Town. Large, snowy Sunshine Village is considered world-class. Tiny Norquay, situated a mere 5km from the center, is your half-day, family-friendly option.

Sunshine Village (p595) straddles the Alberta–BC border. Though slightly smaller than Lake Louise in terms of skiable terrain it gets much bigger dumpings of snow, or 'Champagne powder' as Albertans like to call it (up to 9m annually). Aficionados laud Sunshine's advanced runs and lengthy ski season, which lingers until Victoria Day weekend in late May. A high-speed gondola whisks skiers up in 17 minutes to the village, which sports Banff's only ski-in hotel, the Sunshine Mountain Lodge.

Ski Banff@Norquay (Map p587; 403-762-4421; www.banffnorquay.com; Mt Norquay Rd; day ski pass adult/youth/child $65/50/25;), just 6km north of downtown Banff, has a long history of entertaining Banff visitors. The smallest and least visited of the three local hills, this is a good place to body-swerve the major show-offs and hit the slopes for a succinct half-day.

Local buses shuttle riders from Banff hotels to both resorts (and Lake Louise) every 30 minutes during the season.

White-Water Rafting

The best rafting is outside the park (and province) on the **Kicking Horse River** in Yoho National Park, BC. There are class IV rapids here, meaning big waves, swirling holes and a guaranteed soaking. Lesser rapids are found on the **Kananaskis River** and the Horseshoe Canyon section of the **Bow**

River. The Bow River around Banff is better suited to mellower float trips.

Several rafting companies are located in the park. They offer tours starting at around $80. (Factor in $15 more for a Banff pickup.)

Tours

Hydra River Guides RAFTING
(Map p596; ☎403-762-4554; www.raftbanff.com; 211 Bear St; ⊙9am-7pm) This well-regarded company has been running rafting trips for three decades. The most popular is the 20km Kicking Horse Classic ($125), with varied rapids (up to class IV) and a BBQ lunch. Hardier rafters can try the full-day trip ($179); for novices and families there's a sedate float trip ($55). The Flast Blast ($90) is for those short on time.

Discover Banff Tours TOURS
(Map p596; ☎403-760-5007; www.banfftours.com; Sundance Mall, 215 Banff Ave) Discover Banff has a great selection of tours to choose from, including three-hour Banff Town tours, sunrise and evening wildlife tours, Columbia Icefield day trips and even a 10-hour grizzly-bear tour, taking in a grizzly-bear refuge.

GyPSy Guide DRIVING
(Map p596; ☎403-760-8200; www.gypsyguide.com/canada; per day $39) Offers downloadable tours of the area with lively running commentary about local highlights and history and recommending places to stop. Tours run from 1½ hours to three to five days and range from $3 to $15, covering Banff, Lake Louise, Columbia Icefield, Jasper and Calgary. Best of all, if you tire of the tour guide, just turn it off.

Sleeping

Compared with elsewhere in the province, accommodations in Banff Town are fairly costly and, in summer, often hard to find. The old adage of the early bird catching the worm really holds true here, and booking ahead is strongly recommended.

The Banff/Lake Louise Tourism Bureau tracks vacancies on a daily basis; check the listings at the Banff Visitor Centre (p602). You might also try **Enjoy Banff** (☎888-313-6161; www.enjoybanff.com), which books rooms for more than 75 different lodgings.

Camping in Banff National Park is popular and easily accessible. There are 13 campgrounds to choose from, most along the Bow Valley Parkway or near Banff Town.

Two Jack Lakeside CAMPGROUND $
(Map p587; Minnewanka Loop Dr; tent & RV sites $28; ⊙May-Oct; P) Right on Two Jack Lake, and the most scenic of the Banff-area campgrounds, Lakeside fills its 74 nonreservable sites quickly. You can now 'glamp' at Two Jack in one of 10 'oTENTiks' – fully serviced A-frame 'tents' with hot showers and electricity. They sleep up to six people and cost a thoroughly reasonable $120 per night.

HI-Banff Alpine Centre HOSTEL $
(☎403-762-4122; www.hihostels.ca; 801 Hidden Ridge Way; dm from $32, d with shared/private bath from $85/104, private cabins from $124; P @) Near the top of Tunnel Mountain, Banff's best hostel is well away from the madness of Banff Ave. Buildings are classic mountain-lodge style without classic mountain-lodge prices. Rooms are spic-n-span; choose from dorms, private doubles and cabins. Common areas are open and comfortable, with fireplaces and good views. The public bus runs right by the front door; passes are complimentary.

Samesun Banff HOSTEL $
(☎403-762-5521; www.banffhostel.com; 433 Banff Ave; dm incl breakfast from $60; P @) The Samesun is zanier, edgier and a little cheaper than other local budget digs, and features a large central courtyard with barbecue, an on-site bar, plenty of activities and 100 dorm beds spread across modern, compact six- to 14-person rooms with en suites (some with fireplaces); DIY breakfast included. The clientele is international, backpacker and young (at least at heart).

Banff Y Mountain Lodge HOSTEL $
(Map p596; ☎403-762-3560; www.ymountainlodge.com; 102 Spray Ave; s/d $109/129, with shared bath $99/109; P @) The YWCA is Banff's swankiest hostel option, offering dorm rooms along with private family-oriented accommodations down by the river. Spacious, wheelchair-accessible buildings with fireplaces and big decks create an alpine – if not exactly homey – atmosphere. There's a kitchen, sauna and family room and activities galore. Rates drop significantly in the winter.

Tunnel Mountain CAMPGROUND $
(Tunnel Mountain Dr; tent & RV sites $28-39; ⊙kiosk 7am-midnight) Banff's massive campground is split over three separate 'villages' halfway up the slope of Tunnel Mountain, offering 1000 sites. It fills to capacity in summer thanks

SASQUATCH

In the untamed land between Banff and Jasper, you may well expect to encounter a little wildlife. However, if you're anticipating elk or even a grizzly, what lurks beyond that next bend might surprise you.

That's what happened to David Thompson. In 1811, as a young surveyor forging across the Rocky Mountains en route to Jasper, he became the first European to encounter was what known as the Monster Bear. He had stumbled upon tracks near the Athabasca River that measured a staggering 36cm x 20cm.

Around Saskatchewan River, the Stoney people had been catching glimpses of Monster Bears throughout the previous century. It was known to them as 'M-s-napeo' – today it's more commonly called Sasquatch or Bigfoot. Big, hairy and supposedly preceded by a foul smell, sightings continue to be reported by locals and visitors around Banff and Jasper National Parks right into the present decade. Keep your eyes – and nose – on the lookout!

to its convenient location just a quick drive from downtown Banff. With its many trees, it's not as grim as it sounds but if you're truly after tranquillity, you might want to look elsewhere.

Poplar Inn B&B **$$**
(Map p596; ☎403-760-8688; www.thepoplarinn.ca; 316 Lynx St; d $185; P) Two lovely rooms in a beautiful heritage home just steps from Banff Ave offer a home away from home. Both have luxury touches such as Egyptian cotton sheets and sliding doors onto private garden patios. Breakfast of muffins, croissants and homemade granola is served in one of the house's turrets.

Juniper HOTEL **$$**
(☎403-762-2281; www.thejuniper.com; 1 Juniper Way; r $229-460; P❄📶🐾) Perched beneath Mt Norquay, the modern, pet-friendly Juniper has comfortable rooms, and suites with Jacuzzis and fireplaces. Staff are friendly and welcome many hikers, skiers and cyclists. The bistro has a creative menu, awesome views and a big patio. Not far from the highway, the hotel gets some traffic noise.

Charlton's Cedar Court MOTEL **$$**
(☎403-762-4485; www.charltonsbanff.com; 513 Banff Ave; r from $219; P❄📶🏊) Yes, it's a bit old-fashioned, but this motel complex on Banff Ave has some of the most consistent rates in town. Cheaper rooms are dowdy, so better to opt for one of the larger, split-level suites, some of which have kitchenettes and mezzanine sleeping areas. Luxury it ain't, but it's a reasonable downtown base.

Rundlestone Lodge HOTEL **$$**
(☎403-762-2201; www.rundlestone.com; 537 Banff Ave; d/ste from $209/274; P📶🏊) This place is filled with pseudo 'old English' charm, complete with *Masterpiece Theater*-style chairs in the lobby. The standard rooms are fairly, well...standard, but family and honeymoon suites come with a kitchen, fireplace and loft.

★ **Buffalo Mountain Lodge** HOTEL **$$$**
(☎800-661-1367; www.crmr.com/buffalo; 700 Tunnel Mountain Dr; r $339-379; 📶) Three hectares of private forested grounds make this lodge on Tunnel Mountain one of Banff's most pleasant mountain retreats. Rooms have plush rustic charm, with timber beams, clawfoot tubs, fieldstone log fires and underfloor heating in the bathrooms. Dine at the in-house restaurant Cilantro or wander 15 minutes by foot into town.

★ **Fox Hotel & Suites** HOTEL **$$$**
(☎800-760-8500; www.bestofbanff.com; 461 Banff Ave; d from $329; P@📶🏊) Aesthetically, the Fox is a step above its neighbors. Its forest-like lobby is instantly calming. Centered around a courtyard, rooms aren't overly plush but have a Canadian feel to them, right down to the wallpaper. The highlight is the Cave & Basin–inspired hot tub, with an opening in the roof that gives out to the sky. Service is attentive.

Buffaloberry B&B **$$$**
(☎403-762-3750; www.buffaloberry.com; 417 Marten St; r $385; P❄📶) This purpose-built B&B makes a comfortable place to stay. The four bedrooms are each unique and heavy on homey charm, and the underfloor heating and nightly turn-down treats keep the pamper factor high. With an ever-changing menu (such as baked Camembert egg custard, homemade granola and buttermilk pancakes), the breakfast is divine.

Hidden Ridge Resort RESORT $$$

(☎403-762-3544; www.bestofbanff.com; 901 Coyote Dr; condos $319-629; P ❄ 📶 🐾) Half hotel, half self-catering resort, the Hidden Ridge is a great option for families, with modern condos and A-frame chalets. The basic chalets boast wood-burning stoves, galley kitchens and mountain-view porches; at the top end you can get Jacuzzis and cozy loft bedrooms for the kids. There's even a forest hot tub if you can brave the mountain air.

Fairmont Banff Springs HOTEL $$$

(☎403-762-2211; www.fairmont.com/banffsprings; 405 Spray Ave; r from $559; P @ 📶 🏊) Rising like a Gaelic Balmoral above the trees at the base of Sulphur Mountain and visible from miles away, the Banff Springs is a wonder of early 1920s revivalist architecture and one of Canada's most iconic buildings. Wandering through its grand lobby and elegant lounge, wine bar and restaurant, it's easy to forget that it's also a hotel.

Eating

Banff dining is more than just hiker food. Sushi and foie gras have long embellished the restaurants of Banff Ave, and some of the more elegant places will inspire grubby hikers to return to their hotel rooms and take a shower before pulling up a chair. Many of Banff's hotels also have their own excellent on-site restaurants, which welcome nonguests. AAA Alberta beef makes an appearance on even the most exotic à la carte menu.

Wild Flour CAFE $

(Map p596; ☎403-760-5074; www.wildflourbakery.ca; 211 Bear St; mains $5-10; ⏰7am-7pm; 📶 ✍) 🌿 If you're in a need of a relatively guilt-free treat, come here for cheesecake, dark-chocolate torte or – well, 'and' really – macaroons. These, along with breakfasts, well-stuffed sandwiches on homemade bread, and soups, are all organic. Not surprisingly, it's busy; so much so that a smaller version with the bare necessities (coffee and pastries) is opening on Banff Ave.

Evelyn's Coffee Bar CAFE $

(Map p596; ☎403-762-0352; www.evelynscoffeebar.com; 215 Banff Ave; mains $6-10; ⏰6:30am-11pm; 📶) Pushing Starbucks onto the periphery, Evelyn's parades two downtown locations, both on Banff Ave. Dive in to either one of them for wraps, pies and – best of all – its own selection of giant homemade cookies, the saviour of many an exhausted hiker. The second branch is a block further south at 119 Banff Ave.

★**Saltlik** STEAK $$

(Map p596; ☎403-762-2467; www.saltlik.com; 221 Bear St; mains $18-29; ⏰11am-late Mon-Fri, 11:30am-late Sat & Sun) With rib eye in citrus-rosemary butter and peppercorn New York strip loin on the menu, Saltlik is clearly no plain-Jane steakhouse knocking out flavorless T-bones. No, this polished dining room abounds with rustic elegance and a list of steaks the length of many establishments' entire menu. In a town not short on steak providers, this could be number one.

★**Bear St Tavern** PUB FOOD $$

(Map p596; www.bearstreettavern.ca; 211 Bear St; mains $15-19; ⏰11:30am-late) This gastro-pub hits a double whammy: ingeniously flavored pizzas washed down with locally brewed pints. Banffites head here in droves for a plate of pulled-pork nachos or a bison-and-onion pizza, accompanied by pitchers of hoppy ale. The patio overlooking Bison Courtyard is the best place to linger if the weather cooperates.

Block Kitchen & Bar TAPAS $$

(Map p596; ☎403-985-2887; www.banffblock.com; 201 Banff Ave; tapas $7-26; ⏰11am-1am; ✍) This casual bar serves up tapas with heavy Asian and Mediterranean influences – or 'Mediterrasian,' as they call it. The small but creative tapas plates might not satisfy truly ravenous post-hiking appetites, but there are plenty of vegan and gluten-free options and it continues to serve until 1am. Decorated with bird cages and copper, it's got a quirky, welcoming edge.

Nourish VEGETARIAN $$

(Map p596; ☎403-760-3933; www.nourishbistro.com; 215 Bear St; mains $12-29; ⏰11:30am-10pm; ✍) Confronted by a huge and strangely beautiful papier-mâché tree when you walk in the door, you instantly know this vegetarian bistro is not average. With locally sourced dishes like bourbon-glazed stuffed mushrooms and gluten-free beer-batter onion rings, Nourish has carved out a gourmet following in Banff. Dinner is served as shareable platters (think giant tapas).

Eddie Burger & Bar BURGERS $$

(Map p596; ☎403-762-2230; www.eddieburgerbar.ca; 6/137 Banff Ave,; burgers $13-19; ⏰11am-2am) Eddie's are not your average burgers.

His love for the patty has inspired him to create large, crave-worthy burgers, from the usual classics to specialties like the elk burger with avocado and Gouda. Add to this a hearty helping of poutine and a shaken Caesar garnished with a chicken wing, and you're set – for the next week.

Magpie & Stump MEXICAN $$

(Map p596; ☎403-762-4067; www.magpieandstump.ca; 203 Caribou St; mains $9-21; ⊙11:30am-2am) A classic, lively cantina full of Sol-swigging snowboarders. It has ramped up somc of the classics, like the Three Pig Queso Quesadilla with pulled pork, smoky bacon *and* chorizo, or the Popcorn Shrimp Tacos with mango salsa. The Build-Your-Own nacho menu is just asking for trouble. It's difficult to save room for the key lime pie in a jar.

Park MODERN AMERICAN $$$

(Map p596; ☎403-762-5114; www.parkdistillery.com; 219 Banff Ave; mains $17-44; ⊙11am-late) Banff gets hip with a microdistillery to complement its microbrewery, plying spirits (gin, vodka and whiskey) and beer made from Alberta's foothills' grain. It all goes down perfectly with a mesquite beef hoagie, fish tacos or anything off the excellent appetizer menu.

Bison Restaurant & Terrace CANADIAN, FUSION $$$

(Map p596; ☎403-762-5550; www.thebison.ca; 211 Bear St; mains $16-45; ⊙5pm-late) Rustically elegant, the Bison is often full of trendy, well-off Calgarians dressed in expensive hiking gear, drawn by its regionally sourced, meat-heavy menu. Appetizers like seafood waffles and escargot in a bone, followed up with Peking-style duck or cider-braised pork belly, fill the creative, seasonal menu. You'll find the more casual Bear St Tavern (p600) on the terrace below.

Maple Leaf Grille CANADIAN $$$

(Map p596; ☎403-762-7680; www.banffmapleleaf.com; 137 Banff Ave; mains $25-55; ⊙11am-10pm) With plenty of local and foreign plaudits, the classy Maple Leaf eschews all other pretensions in favor of one defining word: 'Canadian.' The menu is anchored by Albertan beef, along with BC salmon, East Coast cod and Okanagan Wine Country salad. Not surprisingly, the interior is all wood and stone, with local artwork.

🍷 Drinking & Nightlife

Throw a stone in Banff Ave and you're more likely to hit a gap-year traveller than a local. This makes for a lively, if rather young, drinking scene. Many of the local watering holes also have live music. Have a look through the listings in the 'Summit Up' section of the weekly newspaper *Banff Crag & Canyon*.

★ Wild Bill's Legendary Saloon BAR

(Map p596; ☎403-762-0333; www.wildbillsbanff.com; 201 Banff Ave; ⊙11am-late) Forget swanky wine bars and cafes – you haven't really been to Banff if you miss Wild Bill's. Hang out with real live cowboys and get an eyeful of two-stepping, bull riding, karaoke and live music of the twangy Willie Nelson variety. The grub is exactly what you'd expect: big portions of barbecued pork rinds, crispy corn fritters, burgers and chili.

Elk & Oarsman PUB

(Map p596; www.elkandoarsman.com; 119 Banff Ave; ⊙11am-1am) Located upstairs with a crow's-nest view of Banff Ave, this is the town's most refined sports pub, with a decent lineup of beers on tap and live music; the kitchen will fix you up with some good food if you so desire. The rooftop patio is prime real estate in the summer.

Whitebark Cafe COFFEE

(Map p596; ☎403-760-7298; www.whitebarkcafe.com; 401 Banff Ave; ⊙6:30am-7pm) Coffee in Banff recently got a wake-up call thanks to this new cafe in the Aspen Lodge on Banff Ave. What it lacks in indoor seating space, the Whitebark makes up for in the excellence of its java, expertly confected by a team of friendly baristas. Snacks and sandwiches provide added fuel, but it's primarily about the high-quality brews.

Banff Ave Brewing Co MICROBREWERY

(Map p596; www.banffavebrewingco.ca; 110 Banff Ave; ⊙11:30am-2am) Feeling like a prairie beer hall, this place has plenty of craft brews, created on the premises and infused with Saskatoon berries and the like. It also has soft pretzels, bratwurst, burgers and salads, although the service often gives you plenty of time to savor your drink before the food arrives.

Rose & Crown PUB

(Map p596; ☎403-762-2121; www.roseandcrown.ca; 202 Banff Ave, Banff Town; ⊙11am-2am) Banff's oldest pub (since 1985!) is a fairly standard

British-style boozer with pool tables and a rooftop patio. Out of all of the town's drinking houses, it's best known for its live music, which raises the rafters seven nights a week – everything from communal sing-alongs to Seattle grunge.

Information

Banff Visitor Centre (Map p596; ☎403-762-1550; www.pc.gc.ca/banff; 224 Banff Ave, Banff Town; ⏰9am-7pm mid-Jun–Aug, to 5pm Sep–mid-Jun) The Parks Canada office doles out info and maps. This is where you can find current trail conditions and weather forecasts, and register for backcountry hiking and camping.

Friends of Banff (Map p596; ☎403-760-5331; www.friendsofbanff.com; 224 Banff Ave) Charitable organization that runs educational programs, including walking tours and junior naturalist workshops. It also runs Park Radio 101.1FM, offering weather and trail reports, local history and info. It runs a gift shop and has an info booth inside the Banff Visitor Centre.

Mineral Springs Hospital (☎403-762-2222; 305 Lynx St; ⏰24hr) For emergency medical treatment.

Getting There & Away

AIR

The nearest airport is **Calgary International Airport** (p585). Over 20 shuttle buses a day operate year-round between the airport and Banff. Buses are less frequent in the spring and fall. Companies include Brewster Transportation (p588) and **Banff Airporter** (☎403-762-3330; www.banffairporter.com). The adult fare for each is around $55 to $65 each way.

BUS

Greyhound Canada (Map p596; ☎800-661-8747; www.greyhound.ca; 327 Railway Ave) operates buses to Calgary ($28, one hour 40 minutes, four daily), Vancouver ($104, 13 hours, four daily) and points in between.

Brewster Transportation (p588) will pick you up from your hotel. It services Calgary ($65, one hour 15 minutes), Jasper ($100, five hours, daily) and Lake Louise ($30, one hour, several daily).

SunDog (www.sundogtours.com) also runs transport between Banff and Jasper (adult/child $69/39, five hours, daily) and Lake Louise ($20, one hour, daily).

CAR & MOTORCYCLE

All of the major car-rental companies (Avis, Budget, Enterprise) have branches in Banff Town. During summer all vehicles might be reserved in advance, so call ahead. If you're flying into Calgary, reserving a car at the airport (where the fleets are huge) may yield a better deal than waiting to pick up a car when you reach Banff Town.

Getting Around

Banff Transit (☎403-762-1215; www.banff.ca) runs four hybrid 'Roam' buses on two main routes. Stops include Tunnel Mountain, the Rimrock Resort Hotel, Banff Upper Hot Springs, Fairmont Banff Springs and all the hotels along Banff Ave. Route maps are printed on all bus stops. Buses start running at 6:30am and finish at 11pm; the fare is adult/child $2/1 (or $5 for a day pass).

Taxis (which are metered) can easily be hailed on the street, especially on Banff Ave. Otherwise call **Banff Taxi** (☎403-762-4444).

Lake Louise

POP 1175

Lake Louise is what makes Banff National Park the phenomenon it is, an awe-inspiring natural feature that is impossible to describe without resorting to shameless clichés. Standing next to the serene, implausibly turquoise lake, the natural world feels (and is) tantalizingly close, with a surrounding amphitheater of finely chiseled mountains that hoist Victoria Glacier up for all to see. Famous for its teahouses, grizzly bears and hiking trails, it's also well-known for its much-commented-on 'crowds,' plus a strangely congruous (or incongruous – depending on your viewpoint) lump of towering concrete known as Chateau Lake Louise. But, frankly, who cares? You don't come to Lake Louise to dodge other tourists. You come to share in one of the most spectacular sights in the Rockies, one that has captured the imaginations of mountaineers, artists and visitors for more than a century.

When you're done with gawping on the shimmering lakeshore, try hiking up into the beckoning mountains beyond. Lake Louise also has a widely lauded ski resort and some equally enticing cross-country options. Thirteen kilometers to the southeast along a winding seasonal road is Moraine Lake, another spectacularly located body of water; it may not have the dazzling color of its famous sibling, but has an equally beguiling backdrop in the Valley of Ten Peaks and the jaw-dropping Tower of Babel, which ascends solidly skyward. In summer, this narrow road is sometimes shut to new visitors for short periods to empty out the traffic.

The village of Lake Louise, just off Hwy 1, is little more than an outdoor shopping mall, a gas station and a handful of hotels. The object of all your yearnings is 5km away by car or an equitable distance on foot along

Lake Louise Area

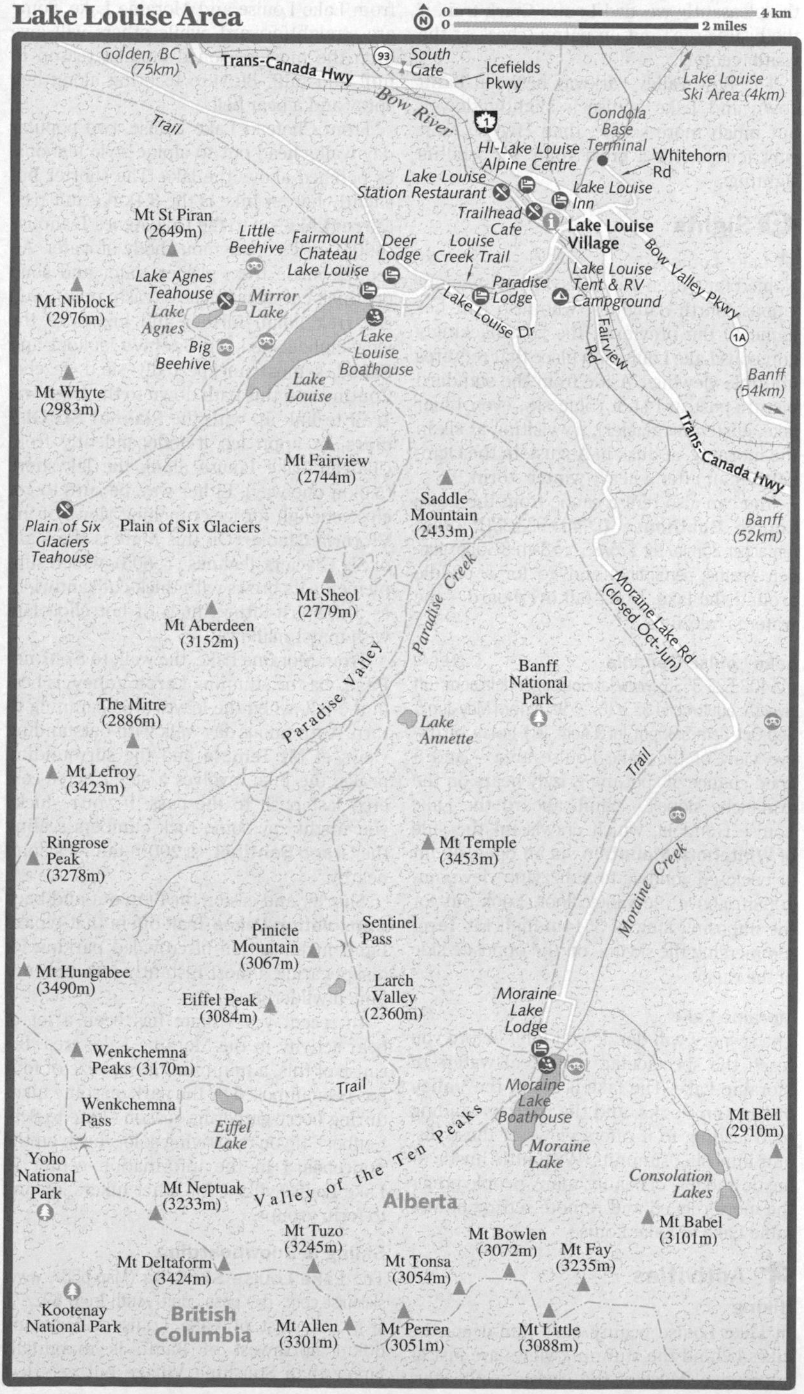

0 4 km
0 2 miles

Golden, BC (75km)
Trans-Canada Hwy
South Gate
Icefields Pkwy
Bow River
Lake Louise Ski Area (4km)
Gondola Base Terminal
Whitehorn Rd
HI-Lake Louise Alpine Centre
Lake Louise Station Restaurant
Lake Louise Inn
Trailhead Cafe
Lake Louise Village
Trail
Mt St Piran (2649m)
Little Beehive
Fairmount Chateau Lake Louise
Deer Lodge
Louise Creek Trail
Bow Valley Pkwy
Lake Agnes Teahouse
Mt Niblock (2976m)
Mirror Lake
Lake Agnes
Paradise Lodge
Lake Louise Tent & RV Campground
Lake Louise Dr
Big Beehive
Lake Louise Boathouse
Fairview Rd
Mt Whyte (2983m)
Lake Louise
Banff (54km)
Trans-Canada Hwy
Mt Fairview (2744m)
Saddle Mountain (2433m)
Plain of Six Glaciers Teahouse
Plain of Six Glaciers
Banff (52km)
Mt Sheol (2779m)
Paradise Creek
Moraine Lake Rd (closed Oct-Jun)
Mt Aberdeen (3152m)
Paradise Valley
Banff National Park
The Mitre (2886m)
Lake Annette
Mt Lefroy (3423m)
Trail
Ringrose Peak (3278m)
Mt Temple (3453m)
Moraine Creek
Pinicle Mountain (3067m)
Sentinel Pass
Mt Hungabee (3490m)
Larch Valley (2360m)
Eiffel Peak (3084m)
Moraine Lake Lodge
Wenkchemna Peaks (3170m)
Trail
Moraine Lake Boathouse
Wenkchemna Pass
Eiffel Lake
Valley of the Ten Peaks
Mt Bell (2910m)
Moraine Lake
Yoho National Park
Consolation Lakes
Mt Neptuak (3233m)
Alberta
Mt Babel (3101m)
Mt Tuzo (3245m)
Mt Bowlen (3072m)
Mt Fay (3235m)
Mt Deltaform (3424m)
Mt Tonsa (3054m)
Kootenay National Park
British Columbia
Mt Allen (3301m)
Mt Perren (3051m)
Mt Little (3088m)

the pleasantly wooded Louise Creek trail, if the bears aren't out on patrol (check at the visitor center).

The Bow Valley Parkway between Banff Town and Lake Louise is slightly slower, but much more scenic, than Hwy 1. As it isn't fenced, it's a great route for wildlife sightings.

Sights

★Lake Louise LAKE

Named for Queen Victoria's otherwise anonymous fourth daughter (who also lent her name to the province), the gobsmackingly gorgeous Lake Louise is a place that requires multiple viewings. Aside from the standard picture-postcard shot (blue sky, even bluer lake, glistening glacier), try visiting at six in the morning, at dusk in August, in the October rain or after a heavy winter storm.

You can also rent a canoe from the **Lake Louise Boathouse** (☎403-522-3511; canoe rental per 30min/1hr $75/85; ⊙8am-8:30pm Jun-Sep, weather permitting) and go for a paddle around the lake. Don't fall overboard – the water is freezing.

Lake Louise Gondola CABLE CAR

(☎403-522-3555; www.lakelouisegondola.com; off Hwy 1A; adult/child $33/16; ⊙9am-4pm May-Jun & Sep-Oct, 8am-5:30pm Jul & Aug;) For a bird's-eye view of the Lake Louise area – and a good chance of spotting grizzly bears on the avalanche slopes – climb aboard the Lake Louise Gondola, which crawls up the side of **Whitehorn Mountain** via an open ski lift or enclosed gondola to a dizzying viewpoint 2088m above the valley floor. Look out for the imposing fang of 3544m-high **Mt Temple** piercing the skyline on the opposite side of the valley.

Moraine Lake LAKE

The scenery will dazzle you long before you reach the spectacular, deep teal waters of Moraine Lake. The lake is set in the **Valley of the Ten Peaks**, and the narrow winding road leading to it offers views of these distant imposing summits. With little hustle or bustle and lots of beauty, many people prefer the more rugged and remote setting of Moraine Lake to Lake Louise.

Activities

Hiking

In Lake Louise beauty isn't skin-deep: the hikes behind the stunning views are just as impressive. Most of the classic walks start from Lake Louise and Moraine Lake. Some are straightforward, while others will give even the most seasoned alpinist reason to huff and puff. Be sure to bring along bug spray and a bear bell.

From Chateau Lake Louise, two popular day walks head out to alpine-style teahouses perched above the lake. The shorter but slightly harder hike is the 3.4km grunt past **Mirror Lake**, up to the Lake Agnes Teahouse (p605) on its eponymous body of water. After tea made from glacier water and soup or thick-cut sandwiches (cash only), you can trek 1.6km further and higher to the view-embellished **Big Beehive** lookout and Canada's most unexpectedly sited gazebo. Continue on this path down to the **Highline Trail** to link up with the **Plain of Six Glaciers**, or approach it independently from Chateau Lake Louise along the lakeshore (5.6km one-way). Either way, be sure to get close enough for ice-crunching views of the **Victoria Glacier**. On this route is the Plain of Six Glaciers Teahouse (p605), which supplements its brews with thick-cut sandwiches and spirit-lifting mugs of hot chocolate with marshmallows.

From Moraine Lake, the walk to **Sentinel Pass**, via the stunning **Larch Valley**, is best in the fall, when the leaves are beginning to turn. A strenuous day walk with outstanding views of **Mt Temple** and the surrounding peaks, the hike involves a steep, scree-covered last push to the pass. If you're lucky you might spy some rock climbers scaling the **Grand Sentinel** – a 200m-tall rock spire nearby.

Shorter and easier, the 6km out-and-back **Consolation Lakes Trail** offers that typical Banff juxtaposition of crowded parking lot disappearing almost instantly into raw, untamed wilderness.

In recent years there has been a lot of bear activity in the Moraine Lake area. Because of this, a minimum group size of four has been imposed by the park on some hikes during berry-gathering season (June to September). If you're arriving solo, check on the noticeboard in the information center in Lake Louise village for other hikers looking to form groups.

Skiing & Snowboarding

The **Lake Louise Ski Area** (Map p587; www.skilouise.com; day pass adult/youth from $92/72;), 3km east of Lake Louise village and 60km northwest of Banff, is marginally larger than Sunshine Village but gets less natural snow. The ample runs, containing plenty of beginner and intermediate terrain, are on four separate mountains, so it's closer to a European ski experience than anything else on offer in Canada. The front side is a good place to get your ski legs back with a good selection of simpler stuff and fantastic views. On the far side there are some great challenges, from the knee-pulverizing moguls of Paradise Bowl to the high-speed cruising of the Larch area. Make sure you grab a deck burger at the Temple Lodge – it's part of the whole experience.

Sleeping

Other than a very popular hostel and a fantastic campground, Lake Louise doesn't have much in the way of budget accommodations options.

Lake Louise Tent & RV Campground CAMPGROUND $
(www.reservation.parkscanada.gc.ca; Lake Louise village; tent/RV sites $28/33; tent park May-Sep, RV park year-round) Near the village, this efficient, wooded campground is divided into two, with RVs on one side of the river and all tents and soft-sided vehicles on the other, protected from bears behind an electric fence. Many tent sites have fire pits ($9). Choose a site away from the railway tracks to enjoy views of Mt Temple in relative peace.

HI-Lake Louise Alpine Centre HOSTEL $
(403-522-2201; www.hihostels.ca; Village Rd, Lake Louise village; dm/d from $42/115; P) This is what a hostel should be: clean, friendly, affordable and full of interesting travelers. With raw timber and stone, the rustic, comfortable building fits in well with Rockies architecture. Dorm rooms are fairly standard and the private rooms are small and a bit overpriced, but this as close as you'll get to budget in Lake Louise.

★ **Deer Lodge** HOTEL $$$
(403-410-7417; www.crmr.com; 109 Lake Louise Dr; r from $250; P) Tucked demurely behind Chateau Lake Louise, historic Deer Lodge dates from the 1920s and has managed to keep its genuine alpine feel intact. The rustic exterior and maze of corridors can't have changed much since the days of bobbed hair and F Scott Fitzgerald. Lodge rooms are fairly tiny but quaint, while spacious Heritage rooms have smart, boutique-like furnishings.

★ **Moraine Lake Lodge** HOTEL $$$
(800-522-2777; www.morainelakelodge.com; d $400-700; Jun-Sep; P) The experience here is intimate, personal and private, and the service is famously good. While billed as rustic (ie no TVs), the rooms and cabins offer mountain-inspired luxury with big picture windows, wood-burning or antique gas fireplaces, soaking tubs, feather comforters and balconies overlooking the lake. The fine-dining restaurant on-site wins equal plaudits. Canoe use is free for guests.

Paradise Lodge CABIN $$$
(403-522-3595; www.paradiselodge.com; r $260-340; May-Sep) Cozy and well restored, these 1930s log cabins are surrounded by woods and only moments from Lake Louise's shore. Each is unique, but look for huge comfy beds, cast-iron stoves and claw-foot soaking tubs. The newer lodge rooms are hotel-style, and the surrounding lawns provide plenty of lounging opportunities beneath the forest's trees.

Fairmont Chateau Lake Louise HOTEL $$$
(403-522-3511; www.fairmont.com/lake-louise; Lake Louise Dr; d from $470; P@) The opulent Fairmont enjoys one of the world's most enviable locations on the shores of Lake Louise. Built in the 1890s and added to in 1925 and 2004, the hotel and its plastered exterior does little to fit in with its surroundings. Nevertheless, the giant interloper's facilities, service and fork-dropping views are undeniably luxurious.

Eating

★ **Lake Agnes Teahouse** CAFE $
(lunch $7-13; 9am-6pm Jun-Aug, 10am-5:30pm Sep & Oct) The 3.4km view-filled hike from Lake Louise to Lake Agnes is one of the area's most popular – surely because it ends here, at this fabulously rustic alpine teahouse that seems to hang in the clouds beside the ethereal lake and its adjacent waterfall. Homemade bread, soup, thick-cut sandwiches and lake-water tea offer fuel for the jaunt back down. Cash only.

Plain of Six Glaciers Teahouse CAFE $
(snacks $6-14; 8am-6pm Jun–mid-Oct) Constructed in 1927 as a way station for Swiss mountaineering guides leading clients up to the summit of Mt Victoria, this twin-level log chalet looks like something out of the pages of *Heidi*. Nestled in a quiet glade, it dishes up homemade sandwiches, cakes,

gourmet teas and hot chocolates to a steady stream of puffed-out hikers.

Bill Peyto's Café CAFE $

(☎ 403-522-2201; www.hihostels.ca; HI-Lake Louise Alpine Centre, Village Rd, Lake Louise village; mains $5-12; ⏰ 7am-10pm May-Sep, to 9pm Oct-Apr) Lively Peyto's is a popular hangout, with live music and a decent bar. The menu's not fancy but the food is consistently good. Fill up on homemade granola or a burrito *huevo* for breakfast; try seafood chili or mac 'n' cheese at dinner. The patio is nice when the sun (or moon) is shining. Expect queues when the hostel's full.

★ Lake Louise Station Restaurant CANADIAN $$

(☎ 403-522-2600; www.lakelouisestation.com; 200 Sentinel Rd; mains $20-45; ⏰ 11am-4pm & 5-9pm) Dine in the station's great hall or one of the dining cars, which are nothing short of elegant. Details like stacks of turn-of-the-century luggage and the stationmaster's desk take you back to 1910, when the station was first built. Dig into the first-class Rocky Mountain sausage plate, maple salmon or bison burger and soak up the almost palpable atmosphere. Reservations recommended.

Information

Lake Louise Visitors Centre (Samson Mall, Lake Louise village; ⏰ 9am-7pm mid-Jun–Aug, to 5pm May–mid-Jun & Sep–mid-Oct, 9am-4:30pm Thu-Sun mid-Oct–Apr) Come here for Parks Canada info on Banff and Jasper and to register for backcountry hikes. You'll also find some good geological displays, a local tourist information desk and a small film theater.

Getting There & Away

Brewster (p591) runs bus service here from Banff and Jasper; the bus terminal is a marked stop at Samson Mall.

The easiest way to get here from Banff is by car.

Jasper Town & Around

Take Banff, halve the annual visitor count, increase the total land area by 40% and multiply the number of bears, elk, moose and caribou by three. The result: Jasper, a larger, less trammeled, more wildlife-rich version of the other Rocky Mountains parks. Its rugged backcountry wins admiring plaudits for its deep river canyons, rampart-like mountain ranges and delicate ecosystems.

Most people enter Jasper Town from the south via the magnificently Gothic Icefields Parkway that meanders up from Lake Louise amid foaming waterfalls and glacier-sculpted mountains, including iconic Mt Edith Cavell, easily visible from the town. Another option is to take a legendary VIA Rail train (from either Edmonton or BC) through foothills imbued with fur-trading and Aboriginal history.

Stacked up against Canada's other national parks, Jasper scores high marks for its hiking, pioneering history, easy-to-view wildlife and hut-to-hut backcountry skiing possibilities. Similarly, bike enthusiasts consistently laud it as having one of the best single-track cycling networks in North America.

Sights

★ Jasper National Park NATIONAL PARK

(Map p608; www.pc.gc.ca/jasper; day pass adult/youth/family $9.80/4.90/19.60) Mountain lions, wolves, caribou, beaver and bear roam freely; glaciers stretch out between mountain peaks; waterfalls thunder over slopes; and valleys are wide and lush, with rivers charging turbulently through them – this is Jasper National Park, covering a diverse 10878sq km. Jasper is far from built up: while activities like hiking and mountain biking are well established and deservedly popular, it's still easy to experience the solitude and remoteness that abound in this park.

★ Miette Hot Springs HOT SPRINGS

(Map p608; www.pc.gc.ca/hotsprings; Miette Rd; adult/child/family $6/5/18.50; ⏰ 8:30am-10:30pm) More remote than Banff's historic springs, Miette Hot Springs ('discovered' in 1909) are 61km northeast of Jasper off Hwy 16, near the park boundary. The soothing waters, kept at a pleasant 40°C (104°F), are surrounded by peaks and are especially enjoyable when the fall snow is drifting down and steam envelops the crowd. Raining summer evenings also make for stunning, misty conditions.

Horseshoe Lake LAKE

(Map p608) This idyllic, blue-green, horseshoe-shaped lake just off the Icefields Pkwy is missed by many visitors, making a stopover here all the more alluring. A choice spot for a bracing summer swim or a short stroll around the perimeter, the lake is surrounded by steep cliffs and is frequented by cliff divers. It's probably safer to watch than join in.

Maligne Lake LAKE
(Map p608) Almost 50km from Jasper at the end of a stunning road that bears its name, 22km-long Maligne Lake is the recipient of a lot of hype. It is billed as one of the most beautiful lakes within the park and there's no denying its appeal: the baby-blue water and a craning circle of rocky, photogenic peaks are a feast for the eyes.

Maligne Canyon CANYON
(Map p608) A steep, narrow gorge shaped by a river flowing at its base, this canyon at its narrowest is only a few meters wide and drops a stomach-turning 50m beneath your feet. Crossed by six bridges, it has various **trails** leading out from the parking area on Maligne Lake Rd, where there's also a quaint, basic teahouse. In the winter, waterfalls freeze solid into sheets of white ice and are popular with ice climbers.

Jasper Skytram CABLE CAR
(Map p608; ☎780-852-3093; www.jaspertramway.com; Whistlers Mountain Rd; adult/child/family $40/20/100; ⏰9am-8pm Apr-Oct) If the average, boring views from Jasper just aren't blowing your hair back, go for a ride on this sightseeing gondola. The journey zips up through various mountain life zones to the high barren slopes of the Whistlers, where there's a small, pricey cafe. From the top of the gondola you can take the steep 1.5km hike to the mountain's true summit, where views stretch for 75km.

Medicine Lake LAKE
(Map p608) A geological rarity, Medicine Lake is perhaps best described as a sinking lake that has holes in the bottom and functions rather like a bathtub without a plug. In summer, when the run-off is high, the lake fills more quickly than it can drain away, and the body of water appears deep and expansive. In winter, as the run-off slows, the water empties, causing the lake to shrink to the size of a small stream.

Lakes Annette & Edith LAKE
(Map p608) On the opposite side of the highway to the town, Lakes Annette and Edith are popular for water activities in the summer; both have small beach areas and a number of picnic spots. If you're brave and it's very hot, Annette is good for a quick summer dip – just remember that the water was in a glacier not too long ago! Edith is frequented more by kayakers and boaters.

Patricia & Pyramid Lakes LAKE
(Map p608) These two lakes, less than 10km (6.2 miles) from town, offer abundant water activities. Patricia Lake contains the wreck of a WWII ice-based aircraft carrier called *Habbakuk,* sunk after a secret wartime mission to create the unsinkable ship. Experienced divers can examine it close up with **Jasper Dive Adventures** (☎780-852-3560; www.jasperdiveadventures.com; dives $75; ⏰May-Sep). Pyramid Lake, overlooked by a resort, is popular with canoers and kayakers in summer and ice-skaters in winter. It has a lovely island, popular with nighttime stargazers, that's accessible by a bridge.

Activities

Cycling

Jasper tops Banff for single-track mountain biking; in fact, it's one of the best places in Canada for the sport. Many routes are within striking distance of the town. Flatter, on-road options include the long-distance grunt along the Icefields Parkway. The holy grail for experienced off-road cyclists is the **Valley of the Five Lakes** – it's varied and scenic, with plenty of places where you can let rip. For more information, get a copy of *Mountain Biking Guide, Jasper National Park* from the Jasper Information Centre (p613).

Vicious Cycle (Map p610; ☎780-852-1111; www.viciouscanada.com; 630 Connaught Dr, Jasper Town; bike rental per hour/day from $8/32; ⏰9am-6pm) can sort out bike rentals and offer additional trail tips.

Hiking

Even when judged against other Canadian national parks, Jasper's trail network is mighty, and with comparatively fewer people than its sister park to the south, you've a better chance of seeing more wildlife and fewer humans.

Initiate yourself on the interpretative **Discovery Trail**, an 8km easy hike that encircles the town and highlights its natural, historical and railway heritage.

Other short trails include the 3.2km **Mary Schäffer Loop** by Maligne Lake, named for one of the earliest European visitors to the area; the 3.5km **Old Fort Loop** to the site of an old fur-trading post; and the 9km **Mina and Riley Lakes Loop** that leads out directly from the town.

Further away and slightly harder, the famous 9.1km **Path of the Glacier Trail** runs below the impressive face of Mt Edith Cavell

Jasper National Park

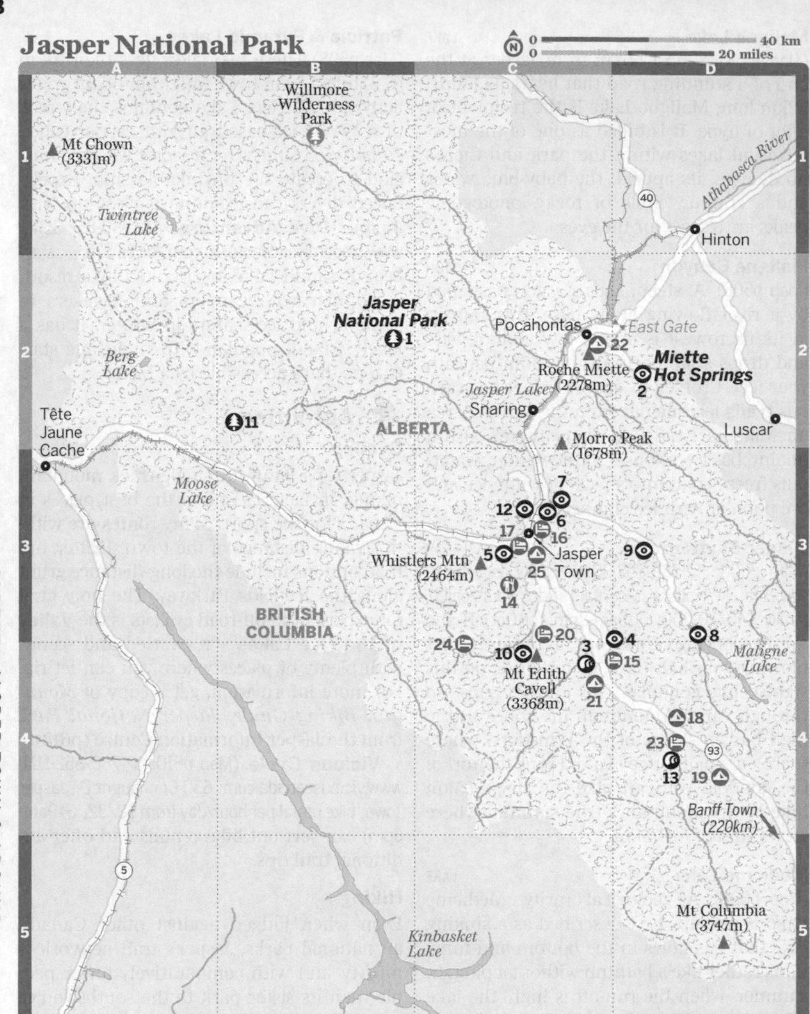

and takes you to the foot of the Angel Glacier through the flower-scattered Cavell meadows.

The blue-ribbon multiday hike is the **Skyline Trail** – unusual in that almost all of its 46km are on or above the tree line, affording amazing cross-park views. The hike is usually split over two days, starting at Maligne Lake and emerging near Maligne Canyon on Maligne Lake Rd. You can pitch your tent in a campground or stay in the historic Shovel Pass Lodge (p611).

The leaflet *Day-Hikers' Guide to Jasper National Park* has descriptions of most of the park's easy walks, while the backcountry visitor guide *Jasper National Park* details longer trails and backcountry campsites, with suggested itineraries for hikes of two to 10 days. If you're hiking overnight, you must obtain a backcountry permit (per person per night $10; a season pass is $69) from Parks Canada in the Jasper Information Centre (p613).

Horseback Riding

Incredible, fully guided summer pack-trips head into the roadless **Tonquin Valley**, where you are bivouacked in the backcountry (but comfortable) Tonquin Amethyst Lake Lodge (p611). The trips are run by **Tonquin Valley**

Jasper National Park

Top Sights
1 Jasper National Park........................B2
2 Miette Hot Springs...........................D2

Sights
3 Athabasca Falls................................C4
4 Horseshoe Lake.................................D3
5 Jasper Skytram..................................C3
6 Lakes Annette & Edith........................C3
7 Maligne Canyon..................................C3
8 Maligne Lake......................................D3
9 Medicine Lake.....................................D3
10 Mt Edith Cavell.................................C4
11 Mt Robson Provincial Park.................B2
12 Patricia & Pyramid Lakes...................C3
13 Sunwapta Falls..................................D4

Activities, Courses & Tours
14 Marmot Basin.....................................C3

Sleeping
15 Athabasca Falls International Hostel.......D4
16 Fairmont Jasper Park Lodge..............C3
17 HI-Jasper Hostel...............................C3
18 Honeymoon Lake Campground...........D4
19 Jonas Creek Campground..................D4
Miette Hot Springs Resort..........(see 2)
20 Mt Edith Cavell International Hostel.......C3
21 Mt Kerkeslin Campground.................C4
22 Pocahontas Campground...................C2
23 Sunwapta Falls Resort.......................D4
24 Tonquin Amethyst Lake Lodge.........C4
25 Wapiti Campground...........................C3

Adventures (780-852-1188; www.tonquinadventures.com; 3-/4-day trips $895/1195) and include accommodations, meals and complimentary fishing trips on Amethyst Lake.

Skiing & Snowboarding

Jasper National Park's only downhill ski area is **Marmot Basin** (Map p608; www.skimarmot.com; Marmot Basin Rd; day pass adult/child $89/71), which lies 19km southwest of town off Hwy 93A. Though not legendary, the presence of 86 runs and the longest high-speed quad chairlift in the Rockies mean Marmot is no pushover – and its relative isolation compared to the trio of ski areas in Banff means shorter lift lines.

On-site are some cross-country trails and a predictably expensive day lodge, but no overnight accommodations. Regular shuttles link to Jasper Town in season. Seriously cold weather can drift in suddenly off the mountains, so dress appropriately.

White-Water Rafting

There's nothing like a glacial splashdown to fight the summer heat. The Jasper area has lots of good rafting opportunities, from raging to relaxed, on the **Maligne**, **Sunwapta** and **Athabasca Rivers**. The season runs from May to September.

Tours

Jasper Walks & Talks HIKING
(Map p610; 780-852-4994; www.walksntalks.com; 626 Connaught Dr, Jasper Town; adult/child $90/50; Jun-Oct) A local resident and former Parks Canada guide leads small groups on breathtaking five- to six-hour tours that can take in Mt Edith Cavell Meadows, Maligne Canyon or the Valley of Five Lakes. Bring a picnic lunch, good walking shoes, your camera and lots of questions for your very knowledgeable guide. Tours depart at 9:30am from June to October.

Rockaboo Adventures CLIMBING
(Map p610; 780-820-0092; www.rockaboo.ca; 807 Tonquin St, Jasper Town;) Jasper's most comprehensive year-round climbing guides offer everything from a four-hour Experience Rock Climbing course ($125), suitable for kids aged six and up, to strenuous ascents of lofty Mt Edith Cavell. They also arrange rappelling ($79).

Festivals & Events

Dark Sky Festival SCIENCE
(tickets $45-100; late Oct) Two weeks are filled with events celebrating space and the night sky. Hear talks by astronauts and celebrities like Bill Nye, listen to the symphony under the stars, see the aurora borealis reflected in a glacial lake and gaze through a telescope into the great beyond. There are some free events but the big hitters sell out months in advance.

Sleeping

Despite its reputation as a quiet antidote to Banff, Jasper Town still gets busy in the summer. Book ahead or consider visiting in the less crowded late winter/early spring shoulder season, when the deserted mountainous landscapes (best accessed on cross-country skis) take on a whole new dimension. There are considerable winter discounts to be found.

Accommodations in Jasper are generally cheaper than Banff, but that's not really saying much. Several places outside the town proper offer bungalows (usually wooden

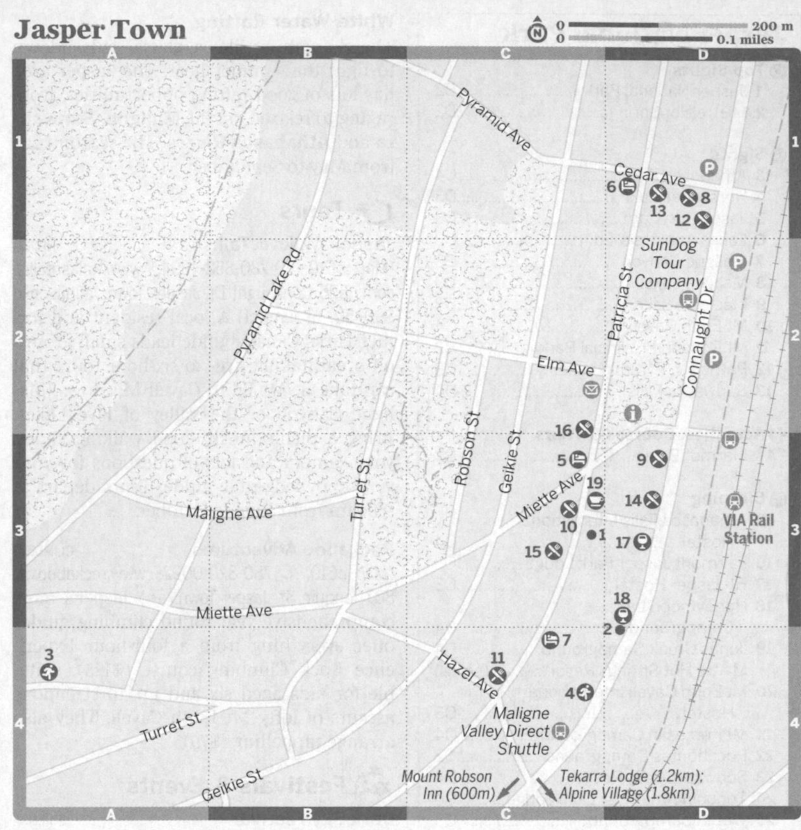

Jasper Town

Activities, Courses & Tours

1 Jasper Adventure Centre C3
2 Jasper Walks & Talks D4
3 Rockaboo Adventures A4
4 Vicious Cycle C4

Sleeping

5 Athabasca Hotel C3
6 Jasper Downtown Hostel D1
7 Park Place Inn C4

Eating

8 Bear's Paw Bakery D1
9 Cassio's Trattoria D3
10 Coco's Cafe C3
11 Evil Dave's Grill C4
12 Jasper Pizza Place D1
13 Olive Bistro D1
14 Other Paw Bakery D3
15 Patricia Street Deli C3
16 Raven Bistro C2

Drinking & Nightlife

17 Downstream Bar D3
18 Jasper Brewing Co D3
19 SnowDome Coffee Bar C3

cabins) that are open only in summer. Jasper's 10 park campgrounds are open from mid-May to September/October. One (Wapiti) is partly open year-round; four of them take reservations. For information, contact Parks Canada at the Jasper Information Centre (p613).

★ **Jasper Downtown Hostel** HOSTEL $
(Map p610; ☎780-852-2000; www.jasperdowntownhostel.ca; 400 Patricia St, Jasper Town; dm/d $40/126; 📶) Stay right downtown for a song? Yes! Rooms in this former residence have been remodeled to create simple, modern two- to eight-bed dorms, along with comfortable pri-

vate rooms for up to five. Upstairs rooms are brighter, with wooden floors, and many rooms have private baths. There is no kitchen or common area, but town is on your doorstep.

Pocahontas Campground CAMPGROUND $
(Map p608; www.reservation.parkscanada.gc.ca; Miette Hot Springs Rd; tent & RV sites $21.50; ⏲May-Sep) As spacious and densely wooded as it is, you'd never know this place has 140 sites. Facilities are minimal, albeit with flush toilets and wheelchair-accessible sites, but it's very well maintained.

Wapiti Campground CAMPGROUND $
(Map p608; www.reservation.parkscanada.gc.ca; Hwy 93; tent/RV sites $28/33) Jasper's second-biggest campground (362 sites) is located close to its largest (the Whistlers), with a handy bike/hike trail linking them and continuing on to Jasper Town (5km). Clean and well-maintained shower and toilet blocks are a given here, but Wapiti's main draw is its location on the banks of the Athabasca River.

HI-Jasper Hostel HOSTEL $
(Map p608; ☎780-852-3215; www.hihostels.ca; Whistlers Mountain Rd; dm/d $30/80; P @) It would be easy to not like this hostel. With dorm rooms that sleep upward of 40 people, meaning you're pretty much guaranteed some midnight snoring, and a location just far enough from town that the walk is a killer, it's already two strikes down. Despite all of this, though, it's a great place to stay.

★Tekarra Lodge HOTEL $$
(☎780-852-3058; www.tekarralodge.com; Hwy 93A; lodge/cabins from $199/240; ⏲May-Oct; P) The most atmospheric cabins in the park are set next to the Athabasca River amid tall trees and splendid tranquillity. Hardwood floors, wood-paneled walls plus stone fireplaces and kitchenettes inspire coziness. It's only 1km from town, but has a distinct backcountry feel. The on-site restaurant is fine dining by Jasper standards.

★Park Place Inn BOUTIQUE HOTEL $$
(Map p610; ☎780-852-9970; www.parkplaceinn.com; 623 Patricia St, Jasper Town; r $229-269; @) Its ordinary exterior among a parade of downtown shops gives nothing away, but the Park Place is a head-turner as soon as you ascend the stairs to its plush open lobby. Parks Canada offices until 2002, the 14 renovated heritage rooms are elegant, with gleaming wooden floors, claw-foot or Jacuzzi tubs and a general air of refinement and luxury.

Shovel Pass Lodge LODGE $$
(☎780-852-4215; www.skylinetrail.com; r per person incl meals $199; ⏲Jun-Sep) Built in 1921 and rebuilt in 1991, the Shovel Pass Lodge is situated halfway along the emblematic Skyline Trail. The seven guest cabins are basic, with log bed frames, fresh linen, propane lights and hot water delivered daily. Two hearty meals and a packed lunch are included, as are some of the most phenomenal views around.

Athabasca Hotel HOTEL $$
(Map p610; ☎780-852-3386; www.athabascahotel.com; 510 Patricia St, Jasper Town; r without/with bath $139/199; P @) A taxidermist's dream, the Atha-B (as it's known) has small, clean rooms with wooden and brass furnishings and thick, wine-colored carpets. Many of the rooms share a bathroom; there's no elevator. Dated but not worn, it feels like you're staying at Grandma's (if Grandma liked to hunt). Service is fickle and the bar downstairs can get noisy. Around since 1929, this is the best bargain in town. Expect significant discounts in winter.

Miette Hot Springs Resort MOTEL, CABIN $$
(Map p608; ☎780-866-3750; www.mhresort.com; Miette Hot Springs Rd; r/chalets/cabins $99/127/187; P) This low-key 'resort' at the hot springs is a collection of old-fashioned but charming log cabins and motel rooms dating from 1938 and chalets from the 1970s. Cabins sleep up to six and have kitchenettes and stone fireplaces (some of the 17 motel rooms also have kitchenettes). The restaurant has reasonably priced standard meals. Bears regularly meander through the grounds.

Alpine Village CABIN $$$
(☎780-852-3285; www.alpinevillagejasper.com; 2-/4-person cabins from $210/420; ⏲May-Oct; P) Characterful log cabins with modern, renovated bathrooms are a cut above the competition, with an ace location flush against the Athabasca River. Enjoy the tranquillity – you're just outside the hubbub of town, but close enough to walk. The cabins have plush, country-style decor, with mezzanine bedrooms and stone fireplaces. The nearest neighbors are usually elk.

Tonquin Amethyst Lake Lodge LODGE $$$
(Map p608; ☎780-852-1188; www.tonquinadventures.com; r per person incl meals $195) Rustic accommodations in historic cabins with views of Amethyst Lake and the towering mountains of The Ramparts range, approximately

JASPER IN WINTER

Half of Jasper shuts down in the winter; the other half just adapts and metamorphoses into something just as good (if not better) than its summertime self. Lakes become skating rinks, hiking and biking routes (and some roads) become cross-country skiing trails, waterfalls become ice climbs, and – last but by no means least – prices become far more reasonable.

The best natural outdoor skating rink is on **Lac Beauvert** in front of the Fairmont Jasper Park Lodge, an area that is floodlit after dark. More skating can be found 6km northeast of the town on **Pyramid Lake**.

The park has an incredible 200km of cross-country skiing trails. Routes less prone to an early snow melt are the **Pyramid Lake Fire Road**, the **Meeting of the Waters** (along a closed section of Hwy 93A), the **Moab Lake Trail** and the **Mt Edith Cavell Road**. Relatively safe, but dramatic, backcountry skiing can be found in the **Tonquin Valley**; however, these routes are sometimes closed due to caribou conservation (see www.tonquinvalley.com for more details).

Slightly less athletic is the three-hour **Maligne Canyon Ice Walk** offered by **Jasper Adventure Centre** (Map p610; ☎780-852-5595; www.jasperadventurecentre.com; 611 Patricia St, Jasper Town; adult/child $65/29), a walk through frozen waterfalls viewable from December to April. Extremists tackle these slippery behemoths with rappels and ice axes.

24km from the nearest road. You can hike in on your own or join one of the lodge's multiday **horseback-riding treks** (three/four days $895/1195) in summer, while in winter you can arrive via cross-country skis. Reservations are required.

Mount Robson Inn MOTEL $$$
(☎780-852-3327; www.mountrobsoninn.com; 902 Connaught Dr, Jasper Town; r incl breakfast from $260; P ❄ @ 📶) A plush and newly renovated place laid out motel-style on the edge of Jasper Town that offers hot tubs, an on-site restaurant and a substantial complimentary breakfast. With everything from sleek queen rooms to family and Jacuzzi suites, you'd be hard-pressed to find something you didn't like.

Fairmont Jasper Park Lodge HOTEL $$$
(Map p608; ☎780-852-3301; www.fairmont.com/jasper; 1 Old Lodge Rd, Jasper Town; r from $480; P @ 📶) Sitting on the shore of Lac Beauvert and surrounded by manicured grounds and mountain peaks, this classic old lodge can't quite match the panache of the Banff and Lake Louise Fairmonts, although you'll bump into fewer afternoon-tea-seeking tourists. With a country-club-meets-1950s-holiday-camp air, the amenity-filled cabins and chalets are a throwback to a more opulent era.

Eating

★Other Paw Bakery CAFE, BAKERY $
(Map p610; 610 Connaught Dr, Jasper Town; snacks $2-6; ⏲7am-6pm) An offshoot of the Bear's Paw, a larger cafe around the corner, the Other Paw offers the same insanely addictive mix of breads, pastries, muffins and coffee, along with tasty soups and well-stuffed wraps. This one stays open later, too.

Patricia Street Deli SANDWICHES $
(Map p610; 610 Patricia St, Jasper Town; sandwiches $7-9; ⏲10am-5pm Mon-Fri, to 6pm Sat & Sun) Come to the Patricia Street Deli hungry – really hungry. Homemade bread is made into generously filled sandwiches by people who are just as generous with their hiking tips. Choose from a huge list of fillings, including various pestos, chutneys, veggies and meat cuts. Join the queue and satiate your ravenous backcountry appetite.

Bear's Paw Bakery BAKERY, CAFE $
(Map p610; www.bearspawbakery.com; 4 Cedar Ave, Jasper Town; pastries $3-5; ⏲6am-6pm) One of the best bakery-cafes west of Winnipeg. Thank your lucky stars the Bear Paw is situated here, just where you need it most at the end of an energy-sapping hike/bike/ski. Try any of the insanely addictive scones, cookies, muffins, focaccia-like breads and wraps. The coffee is equally gratifying.

Coco's Cafe CAFE $
(Map p610; ☎780-852-4550; 608 Patricia St, Jasper Town; mains $5-12; ⏲8am-4pm; 🖉) If you're looking for breakfast, you can't go wrong at Coco's. There's not much room inside, but many are happy to cram in to plan hikes and trade bear sightings. There's plenty of locally sourced, vegan, veggie and celiac-friendly fare on the menu, while

carnivores are kept happy with Montreal smoked meat, pulled pork and lox.

For lunch, try the grown-up grilled cheese sandwich with apple and onion chutney.

Olive Bistro MEDITERRANEAN $$
(Map p610; ☎780-852-5222; www.olivebistro.ca; 401 Patricia St, Jasper Town; mains $16-25; ⏲5-11pm; ✍) This casual restaurant with big booths has a classy menu. Choose from main dishes like whiskey barbecue ribs, bison lasagna or wild-mushroom risotto, or opt for sharing plates like white-truffle scallops or a charcuterie plate of local smoked meats. The cocktails are excellent and there's often mellow live music.

Cassio's Trattoria ITALIAN $$
(Map p610; 602 Connaught Dr, Jasper Town; mains $14-30; ⏲7:30am-11pm; 👪) In the long-standing Whistlers Inn, the Cassio family concentrates on presenting *real* Italian fare: gnocchi, meatballs, veal marsala, pasta marinara and a well-stuffed antipasto plate. There's not a lot of atmosphere, but you won't care once you dive in to the food.

Jasper Pizza Place PIZZA $$
(Map p610; ☎780-852-3225; 402 Connaught Dr, Jasper Town; pizzas $13-20; ⏲noon-10pm) Baked in a traditional wood-burning oven, the much-sought-after pizzas here are rather good. Build your own from a long list of toppings and sauces or choose one of their crafty creations. This place can get packed, with a long line out the door. Inside it's casual, with sports on the TVs and beer on tap.

Raven Bistro MEDITERRANEAN $$$
(Map p610; ☎780-852-5151; www.theravenbistro.com; 504 Patricia St, Jasper Town; mains $24-32; ⏲5-10pm; ✍) This small, tastefully designed bistro offers vegetarian dishes, encourages shared plates and wouldn't be out of place in a small Spanish city. Creative offerings like pomegranate-braised lamb shank and Kaffir lime–coconut seafood pot grace the menu. In summer, brunch is available on weekends from 9am to 1pm.

Evil Dave's Grill CANADIAN, FUSION $$$
(Map p610; ☎780-852-3323; www.evildaves.com; 622 Patricia St, Jasper Town; mains $22-35; ⏲5-11pm Mon-Fri, 4-11pm Sat & Sun) There's nothing evil about Dave's, other than its attempts to bury Jasper's image as a bastion of family-friendly, post-hiking grub that fills stomachs rather than excites taste buds. The excellent fusion food comes from all over the map, with Caribbean, Middle Eastern and Japanese influences lighting up the fish and beef. Save room for the deadly desserts.

Drinking & Nightlife

SnowDome Coffee Bar COFFEE
(Map p610; www.607patricia.com; 607 Patricia St, Jasper Town; ⏲7:45am-8pm) Some of the best damn coffee in Jasper is – no lie! – served out of a launderette. Patricia St's Coin Clean Laundry is no ordinary washing place – as well as being surgically clean, it also serves as an art gallery, shower facility, internet cafe and all-round community resource. Sanitize your dirty hiking socks and savor a latte.

Downstream Bar BAR
(Map p610; 620 Connaught Dr, Jasper Town; ⏲4pm-late) This is likely the most well-stocked bar in town, with a wide array of whiskeys, vodkas and other alcoholic indulgences – and a bar staff who know how to use them. There's some awesome food to keep your head above water and, often, live music.

Jasper Brewing Co BREWERY
(Map p610; ☎780-852-4111; www.jasperbrewing.co.ca; 624 Connaught Dr, Jasper Town; ⏲11:30am-1am) 🌿 This brewpub was the first of its type in a Canadian national park, using glacial water to make its fine ales, including the signature Rockhopper IPA and the slightly more adventurous Rocket Ridge Raspberry Ale. It's a sit-down affair, with TVs and a good food menu.

Information

Jasper Information Centre (Map p610; ☎780-852-6176; www.pc.gc.ca/jasper; 500 Connaught Dr, Jasper Town; ⏲9am-7pm May-Oct, 10am-5pm Nov-Apr) This wonderful information center is housed in Jasper's oldest building, dating from 1913. You'll find a Parks Canada desk and the local tourist information stand, plus an excellent gift shop.

Post office (Map p610; 502 Patricia St; ⏲9am-5pm Mon-Fri)

Seton General Hospital (☎780-852-3344; 518 Robson St)

Getting There & Away

BUS

The **bus station** (Map p610; 607 Connaught Dr, Jasper Town) is at the train station. **Greyhound** (☎800-661-8747; www.greyhound.ca) buses have daily services to Edmonton ($70, from five hours), Prince George ($70, six hours),

Kamloops ($78, six hours) and Vancouver ($148, from 12 hours).

Brewster Transportation (☎403-762-6700; www.brewster.ca), departing from the same station, operates express buses to Lake Louise village ($75, four hours, at least one daily) and Banff Town ($100, five hours, at least one daily). SunDog (p574) also has daily services from May to October to Edmonton airport ($50), Lake Louise ($59), Banff ($69) and Calgary airport ($119).

TRAIN

VIA Rail (☎888-842-7245; www.viarail.ca) offers tri-weekly train services west to Vancouver ($242, 20 hours) and east to Toronto ($516, 62 hours). In addition, there is a tri-weekly service to Prince Rupert, BC ($205, 33 hours). Call or check in at the **train station** (607 Connaught Dr, Jasper Town) for exact schedule and fare details.

Getting Around

Maligne Valley Shuttle (Map p610; ☎780-852-3331; www.maligneadventures.com; adult one-way/round-trip $30/60, youth one-way/round-trip $14/30) Runs a 9am daily shuttle from outside the Jasper Information Centre to Maligne Lake, with stops at trailheads along the way. Shuttles return from the lake at 10:15am, 2pm and 5pm.

Jasper Taxi (☎780-852-3600) Has metered cabs.

SOUTHERN ALBERTA

Alberta's national parks and cities grab most of the headlines, leaving the expansive south largely forgotten. This is true cowboy land, where the ghosts of herders like John Ware and the Sundance Kid are woven through the history of endless ranch land. It's often interrupted by deep, dramatic canyons carved in the last ice age, as well as towering hoodoos – funky, Dr Seuss–like rock sculptures. History abounds at Head-Smashed-In Buffalo Jump and Dinosaur Provincial Park, two Unesco World Heritage areas that preserve the region's past.

Picture-perfect landscapes are plentiful here. The dusty badlands around Drumheller open up into wide open prairies that stretch east all the way to the Cyprus Hills of western Saskatchewan. To the west lies Waterton Lakes National Park, with some of the most spectacular scenery in the Rockies – utterly different from Banff and Jasper yet still under the radar of most visitors.

Drumheller & Around

As you approach Drumheller, the road dips down dramatically into the Red Deer Valley, looking like a big layered cake. This community was founded on coal but now thrives on another subterranean resource – dinosaur bones. A small town set amid Alberta's enigmatic badlands, it acts as the nexus of the so-called **Dinosaur Trail**. Paleontology is a serious business here (the nearby fantastic Royal Tyrrell Museum is as much research center as tourist site), and downtown the cartoon dino statues on most street corners add some color and character to an otherwise average town (though the dino-related prefixes to business names is sometimes pushing it a little). And then there's the large matter of the 26m-high fiberglass *Tyrannosaurus rex* that haunts a large tract of downtown. But don't let the paleontological civic pride deter you: there's enough to do around here (dinosaur-related and otherwise) to keep you from dwelling on the kitsch. Add in the museums in nearby East Coulee and the ghosts of Wayne, and you've got a full itinerary.

The summers are hot, and the deep-cut river valley in which Drumheller sits provides a much-needed break to the monotony of the prairies. Hoodoos dominate this badlands landscape, which has featured in many a movie (mainly Westerns).

Sights & Activities

★**Royal Tyrrell Museum of Palaeontology** MUSEUM
(☎403-823-7707; www.tyrrellmuseum.com; 1500 North Dinosaur Trail, Midlands Provincial Park, Drumheller; adult/child $18/10; ⏲9am-9pm mid-May–Aug, 10am-5pm Sep, 10am-5pm Tue-Sun Oct–mid-May; 👪) This fantastic museum is one of the preeminent dinosaur museums on the planet. Even if you have no interest in dinos, you'll come out feeling like you missed your calling as a paleontologist. The exhibits are nothing short of mind-blowing. Look for the skeleton of 'Hell-Boy', a new dinosaur discovered in 2005, and 'Black Beauty', a 67-million-year-old *T rex* rearing its head into the sky. You can learn how they're extracted and even peer into the fossil lab.

Rosedale Suspension Bridge BRIDGE
(Hwy 56, Rosedale) This suspension bridge isn't very long or high, but it's definitely not for the faint of heart. Made of see-through wire mesh,

(*Continued on page 623*)

National Parks

If there's one thing that Canada excels at in the global pecking order (other than hockey), it's national parks. An early pioneer in ecological management in the late 1800s, the nation now flaunts more than 40 national parks, from groundbreaking, user-friendly Banff to the vast, empty wildernesses of the Arctic.

Contents

Above Moraine Lake (p604), Banff National Park, Alberta

GLOWING EARTH PHOTOGRAPHY / LONELY PLANET IMAGES ©

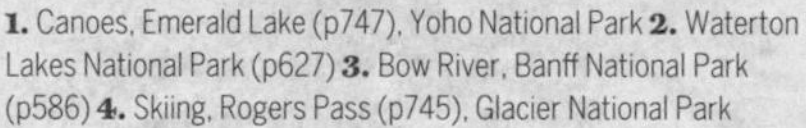
1. Canoes, Emerald Lake (p747), Yoho National Park **2.** Waterton Lakes National Park (p627) **3.** Bow River, Banff National Park (p586) **4.** Skiing, Rogers Pass (p745), Glacier National Park

3

2

BGSMITH / SHUTTERSTOCK ©

4

The Early Western Parks

The Canadian National Parks system has its roots in the imposing Gothic spires of the Rocky Mountains. Galvanized by the formation of Banff in 1885, the early parks were directly linked to the development of the cross-continental railway, which toted rich and curious tourists into previously unexplored wilderness areas.

Banff

Predated only by Yellowstone in the USA and Royal National Park in Australia, Banff's history is entwined with the history of the national park movement and the pioneering Canadian Pacific Railway that helped pave its way.

Yoho

Named for the ancient Cree word for 'wonder' and 'awe', Yoho is one of the geological highlights of the Rocky Mountain parks, with its Burgess Shale fossil deposits exhibiting 120 marine species over a 500-million-year trajectory.

Waterton Lakes

The Canadian Rockies' forgotten corner is a continuation of the Glacier National Park (USA) to the south and is notable for its easily accessible high-alpine day hikes. Its trademark Prince of Wales hotel is linked by historic red buses to Amtrak's Seattle–Chicago *Empire Builder* train.

Jasper

Once a nexus for fur traders, Jasper welcomed two railroads in the 1910s. They are both still in operation, running passenger services to Prince Rupert and Vancouver and allowing easy access to this larger, quieter, more fauna-packed northern neighbor of Banff.

Glacier

Established just one year after Banff in 1886, Glacier was another 'railroad park,' these days better known for its legendary dumpings of powdery snow ideal for heli-skiing and backcountry excursions.

Expanding East

With the formation of the world's first coherent national parks service – Parks Canada – in 1911, the park network spread east as the age of the motorcar brought Canada's spectacular natural beauty to the masses. While environmental protective measures were always important, the early national parks were tailored more to a first-class 'visitor experience.'

Prince Edward Island

PEI, a park since 1937, enhances its diminutive stature with dune-backed beaches, narrow wetlands and a gigantic literary legacy enshrined in the old farm 'Green Gables,' the inspiration for the 1908 novel *Anne of Green Gables* by Lucy Maud Montgomery.

Riding Mountain

A huge array of trails – more than 400km worth – pepper this forested Unesco Biosphere Reserve that sits like a wooded island amid fertile agricultural land in southern Manitoba. In winter, many trails are groomed for cross-country skiing.

Point Pelee

Geographically tiny but vital to birds (and birdwatchers), Point Pelee in Ontario on Canada's most southerly tip overlooking Lake Erie, is an important fly-through area for over 360 feathered species.

Cape Breton Highlands

The font of Nova Scotia's once distinct French-Acadian culture, Cape Breton – made a park in 1936 – is best accessed via 25 moderate day hikes that contour the coast near the Cabot Trail scenic highway.

Gros Morne

A spectacular jumble of fjords, headlands, sheer cliffs and waterfalls on the Newfoundland coast, Gros Morne came late to the Parks Canada fold in 1973. It has since been listed by Unesco for its importance in understanding the processes of continental drift.

1

3

1. Lighthouse in New London (p453), Prince Edward Island
2. Horseback riding in Riding Mountain National Park (p529)
3. Point Pelee National Park (p152) **4.** Cape Breton Highlands National Park (p380)

CHRIS HILL / SHUTTERSTOCK ©

MIKE GRANDMAISON / GETTY IMAGES ©

DON JOHNSTON / GETTY IMAGES ©

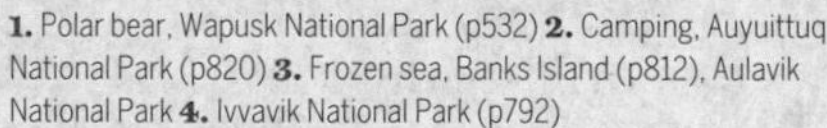

1. Polar bear, Wapusk National Park (p532) **2.** Camping, Auyuittuq National Park (p820) **3.** Frozen sea, Banks Island (p812), Aulavik National Park **4.** Ivvavik National Park (p792)

MANUEL LACOSTE / SHUTTERSTOCK ©

Northern Exposure

By the 1980s, the national parks service had shifted its philosophy from a purely visitor-centric view of park management to a position that prioritized ecological integrity. Vast wildernesses in the north of Canada were gradually taken under the parks umbrella, often with the cooperation of local Aboriginal peoples.

Aulavik

More people have visited the moon than drop by Aulavik annually (official annual tourist numbers rarely exceed a dozen). Situated on arctic Banks Island, this land of musk oxen and 24 hour summer sunlight is the true 'back of beyond'.

Wapusk

Polar bears are Wapusk's *raison d'être* (the name means 'white bear' in Cree) and the best place in the world to see these animals in the wild. Book a guided tour and head for Churchill, Manitoba.

Auyuittuq

A name few Canadians will recognize (or be able to pronounce), Auyuittuq ('the land that never melts') is another leave-your-car-at-home kind of park. Situated on Baffin Island it is ideal for ski touring, climbing or backcountry camping.

Ivvavik

No services, no facilities, just miles of untamed tundra. Save some money, hone your backcountry survival skills, and live out your expedition fantasies.

Nahanni National Park Reserve (p808

Young Parks

Parks Canada has always been an open-ended project with a long-term roll-out plan, and parks continue to be formed. Eight have gained federal approval since 2000 and the network now covers an impressive 3% of Canada's total land mass – roughly the size of Italy.

Nahanni

Nahanni National Park Reserve in the Northwest Territories became a national park in the 1970s and had the honour of being made Unesco's first natural World Heritage site in 1978. After years of negotiations, it was significantly expanded in 2011. It is now Canada's third-largest national park covering an area the size of Belgium.

Torngat Mountains

A stark mélange of glaciated mountains and roaming caribou on the wild coast of Labrador; created in 2005 as Canada's 42nd national park.

Nááts'ihch'oh

This park, inaugurated in 2012, abuts the expanded Nahanni National Park Reserve and has a strong spiritual significance to the Métis and Dene First Nations who played a role in the legal negotiations. It is also a northern roaming ground for grizzly bears, caribou and Dall sheep.

Sable Island

A sinuous sand spit 300km off Nova Scotia, grassy Sable Island is home to hundreds of feral horses thought to be left over from the Great Acadian Expulsion in the 1750s. More than 350 ships have met their watery end on this hard-to-reach outpost. It became Canada's newest national park in 2013.

(Continued from page 614)

it sways like a river reed in the wind. The bridge was used by miners from 1931 to 1957; on the far side of the Red Deer river, you can see the now-closed mines. Despite previous use of rowboats and aerial cable cars, it was the bridge that was considered dangerous due to high winds and floods.

Horseshoe Canyon CANYON

(Hwy 9) The baddest of the badlands can be seen at Horseshoe Canyon, a spectacular chasm cut into the otherwise flat prairie located 17km west of Drumheller on Hwy 9. A large sign in the parking lot explains the geology of the area; **hiking trails** lead down into the canyon, where striated colored rock reveals millions of years of geological history. (Beware: trails are very slippery when wet.)

World's Largest Dinosaur LANDMARK

(60 1st Ave W, Drumheller; $3; 10am-6pm;) In a town filled with dinosaurs, this *T rex* is the king of them all. Standing 26m high above a parking lot, it dominates the Drumheller skyline (and is featured in the *Guinness Book of Records*). It's worth climbing the 106 steps to the top for the novelty of standing in the dino's toothy jaws – plus the views are mighty good. Ironically, the dinosaur isn't technically very accurate: at 46m long, it's about 4.5 times bigger than its extinct counterpart.

Dinosaur Trail & Hoodoo Drive SCENIC DRIVE

Drumheller is on the Dinosaur Trail, a 48km loop that runs northwest from town and includes Hwys 837 and 838. The scenery is stunning and worth the drive – badlands and river views await you at every turn.

The loop takes you past **Midland Provincial Park** (no camping), where you can take a self-guided hike, and the past the vast **Horsethief Canyon** and its picturesque views. Glide peacefully across the Red Deer River on the free, cable-operated **Bleriot Ferry**, which has been running since 1913; watch for beavers, who have a dam here. This area is also frequented by moose, lynx and cougars. On the west side of the valley, pause at **Orkney Viewpoint**, which overlooks the area's impressive canyons.

The 25km Hoodoo Drive starts about 18km southeast of Drumheller on Hwy 10; the route is usually done as an out-and-back with Wayne as the turnaround point. Along this drive you'll find the best examples of **hoodoos** – weird, eroded, mushroom-like columns of sandstone rock – between Rosedale and Lehigh; there's also an interpretive trail.

This area was once the site of a prosperous coal-mining community; the historic **Atlas Coal Mine** (403-822-2220; www.atlascoalmine.ab.ca; East Coulee; $10, tours $20-25; 9:45am-5pm Sep-Jun, to 7:30pm Jul-Aug) and **East Coulee School Museum** (403-822-3970; www.ecsmuseum.ca; 359 2nd Ave, East Coulee; 10am-5pm) are both worth a stop. Take the side trip on Hwy 10X (which includes 11 bridges within 6km) from Rosedale to the small community of **Wayne** (population 27) with its famous and supposedly haunted saloon.

Sleeping

River Grove Campground & Cabins CAMPGROUND $

(403-823-6655; www.camprivergrove.com; 25 Poplar St, Drumheller; campsites/RV sites/tipis/cabins from $35/41/67/125; May-Sep;) Right in town and close to the big *T rex*, this shaded campground next to the river has lots of amenities. You can even rent a tipi for the night, although it's not an entirely faithful re-creation (the Stoney people likely didn't have concrete floors in theirs).

★ **Heartwood Inn & Spa** INN $$

(403-823-6495; www.innsatheartwood.com; 320 N Railway Ave E, Drumheller; d $155-190;) This lovely country inn is full of character and reason enough to visit Drumheller. The rooms are luxurious and each uniquely decorated; some have Jacuzzis and fireplaces and all have beautiful touches. There's a deck, a small garden and an on-site spa. The friendly owners are founts of local knowledge.

Taste the Past B&B B&B $$

(403-823-5889; 281 2nd St W, Drumheller; s/d $115/140;) This converted turn-of-the-century house has evolved into a cozy downtown B&B. All rooms have a private bathroom, and there is a communal living room that could have been airlifted straight from your Grandma's house. With only three rooms, a stay here feels more like visiting with friends.

Eating & Drinking

Ivy's Awesome Kitchen & Bistro BISTRO $

(www.ivysawesomekitchen.com; 35 3rd Ave West, Drumheller; mains $8-12; 8am-5pm;) With good, home-style cooking that won't clot your arteries, Ivy's offers breakfasts, panini, burgers, fresh soups and beautiful salads. You'll find dishes that cater to vegans, vegetarians and gluten-free diets. Chilled and friendly, it's a great place to have lunch. Save room for the homemade desserts: the chocolate lava cake and sticky toffee pudding are difficult to resist.

Bernie and the Boys Bistro DINER $
(☎403-823-3318; www.bernieandtheboys.com; 305 4th St W, Drumheller; burgers $6-8; ⏰11am-8:30pm Tue-Sat) Bistro it isn't, but Bernie's is a small-town, family-run diner that replenishes appetites with hearty gourmet burgers and legendary milkshakes. Join the queue.

★ **Last Chance Saloon** BAR
(☎403-823-9189; www.visitlastchancesaloon.com; Hwy 10X, Wayne; ⏰11am-11pm) Last Chance is the real thing – a Western saloon from 1913, complete with bear skins, old kerosene lamps, antique photos and bullet holes in the wall. Since its original heyday, Wayne's population has dwindled from 2500 to 33, many of whom you'll find in this lively, eclectic place. Meat pies, maple-bacon burgers and chicken dinners go well with the beer.

ℹ Information

Tourist information center (☎403-823-1331; www.traveldrumheller.com; 60 1st Ave W, Drumheller; ⏰9am-9pm) At the foot of the *T rex*. The entrance to the body of the beast is in the same building.

ℹ Getting There & Away

Greyhound (p560) runs buses from the bus station (308 Centre St, Drumheller) to Calgary ($38, two hours, two daily) and Edmonton ($69, seven hours, two daily).

Hammerhead Tours (www.hammerheadtours.com) runs a full-day tour ($124) from Calgary to the Drumheller badlands and the Royal Tyrrell Museum.

Dinosaur Provincial Park

In no other place on earth has such a large number of dinosaur bones been found in such a small area – over 40 species and 400 skeletons. Set where *The Lost World* meets *Little House on the Prairie*, **Dinosaur Provincial Park** (☎403-378-4344; www.dinosaurpark.ca; off Hwy 544; ⏰8:30am-5pm Sun-Thu, to 7pm Fri & Sat) FREE – a Unesco World Heritage site – comes at you by surprise, deep in a chasm that opens before your feet from the grassy plain. A dehydrated fantasy landscape, there are hoodoos, colorful rock formations and dinosaurs aplenty.

The 81-sq-km park begs to be explored, with wildflowers, the odd rattler in the rocks and, if you're lucky, maybe even a *T rex*. This isn't just a tourist attraction, but a hotbed for science: paleontologists have uncovered countless skeletons here, which now reside in many of the finest museums around the globe.

There are five short interpretive **hiking trails** to choose from and a driving loop runs through part of the park, giving you the chance to see a number of dinosaur skeletons in their death posts. To preserve the fossils, access to 70% of the park is restricted and may be seen only on guided hikes or **bus tours** (adult/child $15/8), which operate from late May to October. (The hikes and tours are popular, so be sure to reserve a place.)

The park's **Dinosaur Visitors Centre** (☎403-378-4342; www.albertaparks.ca; adult/child $6/3; ⏰8:30am-5pm) is a field station of the Royal Tyrrell Museum (p614) in Drumheller and has a small, yet excellent, series of dino displays, as well as exhibits on the realities of paleontology.

In a hollow by a small creek sits the park's **Dinosaur Campground** (☎403-378-4342; www.albertaparks.ca; campsites/RV sites $28/35, comfort camping $105-130, reservations $12; ⏰year-round; Ⓟ). The ample tree cover is a welcome reprieve from the volcanic sun. Laundry facilities and hot showers are available, as are a small shop and cafe. This is a popular place, especially with the RV set, so phone ahead.

Though 75 million years ago dinosaurs cruised around a tropical landscape, it's now a hot and barren place – make sure you dress for the weather, with sunscreen and water at the ready. It's halfway between Calgary and Medicine Hat, and some 48km northeast of Brooks. From Hwy 1, take Secondary Hwy 873 to Hwy 544.

Head-Smashed-In Buffalo Jump

The story behind the place with the strangest name of any attraction in Alberta is one of ingenuity and resourcefulness – and is key to the First Nations' (and Canada's) cultural heritage. For thousands of years, the Blackfoot people used the cliffs near the town of Fort Macleod to hunt buffalo. **Head-Smashed-In Buffalo Jump** (☎403-553-2731; www.head-smashed-in.com; Secondary Hwy 785; adult/child $15/10; ⏰9am-5pm mid-May–Sep, 10am-5pm Sep–mid-May)

WORTH A TRIP

BAR U RANCH & THE COWBOY TRAIL

Cowboy culture is woven into the cultural fabric of southern Alberta, but to experience it in its rustic purity you have to exit Calgary and its Stetson-wearing oil entrepreneurs and head south through the province's verdant rolling foothills on Hwy 22, aka the Cowboy Trail. What is today a smooth asphalt road frequented by shiny SUVs was once a dirt track used by dust-encrusted cow herders driving their cattle north to the Canadian Pacific Railway in Calgary. Unperturbed by the modern oil rush, these rolling foothills are still punctuated by giant ranches, one of which, **Bar U Ranch** (www.friendsofthebaru.ca; Hwy 22, Longview; adult/child/family $7.80/3.90/19.60; ⏲10am-5pm Jun-Oct), has been converted into a historic site by Parks Canada.

Founded in 1882, Bar U was once one of the largest commercial ranches in the world, covering 160,000 acres. John Ware, a freed African American slave and, allegedly, Alberta's first cowboy, was an early visitor. A decade later, the ranch's horses were trained by Harry Longabaugh (known to history and Hollywood as the Sundance Kid), a dapper cowboy who worked at the ranch in 1891 before taking up a more lucrative career holding up banks with the Wild Bunch. The next visitor was more regal but no less notorious: the Prince of Wales, later King Edward VIII, passed through in 1919 and was so taken with the place that he bought the EP Ranch next door. Edward visited the region five times, including twice after his abdication; the EP was managed in his name until 1962.

Wander back in time through the Bar U's two dozen buildings – including a cookhouse, post office, corral, smithy and slaughterhouse – which have been preserved in their Sundance Kid–era glory. Costumed interpreters demonstrate ranch skills while telling stories of the past. Visitors can hop on a wagon ride, saddle up horses, try to rope a steer and gather with the ranch hands beneath the cottonwood trees for a campfire and cowboy coffee. The on-site restaurant dishes up ranch-style food like hamburger soup and bison black-bean chili.

Bar U Ranch is just off Hwy 22, 13km south of the town of Longview.

was a marvel of simple ingenuity. The well-presented displays and films at the interpretive center built cleverly into the hillside are definitely worth the excursion from Calgary or Lethbridge.

You can walk along the cliff trail to the end of the drive land, the spot where the buffalo plummeted. The site, about 18km northwest of Fort Macleod and 16km west of Hwy 2, also has a cafe and a shop staffed by Blackfoot First Nations.

Lethbridge

Right in the heart of southern Alberta farming country sits the former coal-mining city of Lethbridge, divided by the distinctive coulees of the Oldman River. Though there isn't a lot to bring you to the city, copious parkland and a few good historical sites and museums will help you to easily fill a day. The downtown area, like many North American downtowns, has made a good stab at preserving its not-so-ancient history. To the east, less inspiring Mayor Magrath Dr (Hwy 5) is a chain-store-infested main drag that could be Anywhere, North America.

Sights & Acivities

There are ample hiking opportunities in the **Oldman River Valley**, a 100m-deep coulee bisected by the proverbial Eiffel Tower of steel railway bridges, and the largest of its kind in the world.

Galt Museum & Archives MUSEUM
(www.galtmuseum.com; 320 Galt St; adult/child $6/3; ⏲10am-5pm Mon-Sat, to 9pm Thu, 1-5pm Sun) The story of Lethbridge is told at the Sir Alexander Galt Museum, encased in an old hospital building (1910) on the bluff high above the river. Interactive kid-oriented displays let you sit in a streetcar and watch historical footage, set print at the *Herald* newsroom and try to put out a (virtual) fire; a small gallery with contemporary and historical art will interest bigger kids. The view from the lobby out onto the coulee is great – and free.

Southern Alberta Art Gallery MUSEUM
(☎403-327-8770; www.saag.ca; 601 3rd Ave S; adult/child $5/free, Sun free; ⏲10am-5pm Tue-Sat, to 7pm Thu, 1-5pm Sun) With new temporary exhibits every three months, this small gallery focuses on contemporary art. Past

exhibitions have included local artists as well as national and international ones, with everything from photography to installation art. The space itself is open and bright and the gift shop is ace.

Helen Schuler Nature Centre & Lethbridge Nature Reserve NATURE RESERVE
(www.lethbridge.ca; Indian Battle Rd; by donation; ⏲10am-4pm Tue-Sun Apr-May & Sep-Nov, 10am-6pm Jun-Aug, 1-4pm Tue-Sun Dec-Mar) Permanent displays tell the story of the river valley and coulee, while temporary exhibits focus on bats, bees and the like. Check out Sophie the gopher snake and say hello to Taco Charlie, the tiger salamander. The surrounding trails give you the opportunity to see long-eared and great horned owls and plenty of porcupines sleeping in the trees.

Nikka Yuko Japanese Garden GARDENS
(www.nikkayuko.com; cnr Mayor Magrath Dr & 9th Ave S; adult/child $9/4; ⏲9am-6pm mid-May–mid-Oct) The Nikka Yuko Japanese Garden is the perfect antidote to the stresses of the road. These immaculate grounds, interspersed with ponds, flowing water, bridges, bonsai trees and rock gardens, form an oasis of calm amid the bustle of everyday life. Authentic Japanese structures sit among the grassy mounds.

Fort Whoop-Up FORT, MUSEUM
(☎403-329-0444; www.fortwhoopup.ca; 200 Indian Battle Park Rd; ⏲May-Sep) Inside expansive Indian Battle Park, bizarrely named Fort Whoop-Up is a replica of Alberta's first and most notorious illegal-whiskey trading post. Around 25 of these outposts were set up in the province between 1869 and 1874 for trading whiskey, guns, ammunition and blankets for buffalo hides and furs from the Blackfoot tribes. At the time of writing, it was closed and new management was being sought. Check the website to see if it has reopened.

Sleeping & Eating

Lethbridge Lodge HOTEL $$
(☎403-328-1123; www.lethbridgelodge.com; 320 Scenic Dr S; r from $99; P@) Rooms here are clean and bright, if a little unmemorable; the atrium, on the other hand, is something else, making this a great deal. All of the rooms look down into the fake-foliage-filled tropical interior, complete with winding brick pathways, a kidney-shaped pool and water features.

WORTH A TRIP

VULCAN

Originally named by a railway surveyor after the Roman god of fire, the 1990s saw Vulcan boldly go where no Canadian town had gone before and proclaim itself Canada's *Star Trek* headquarters – an unlikely title for this tiny prairie town but one made official by the Canadian Broadcasting Corporation (CBC) in 2010.

Your first encounter will be the **Vulcan Tourism & Trek Station** (☎403-485-2994; www.vulcantourism.com; 115 Centre Street E; ⏲9am-6pm May-Sep, 10am-5pm Oct-Apr), built like a space station and crammed full of memorabilia. You can look up local info on the control center that's been signed by the *Star Trek: Next Generation* cast and dress up and snap photos with their cardboard counterparts. You can also stock up on Mr Spock T-shirts and other Trekker goodies.

Outside, a replica starship *Enterprise* is poised on the edge of town, a beacon to hundreds of *Star Trek* fans who flock here in costume from all corners of the world for the annual Spock Days and Vul-Con Conventions. Previous guests have included Leonard Nimoy and other stars from the show.

As you wander down the main street, passing busts of the crew, wall-sized murals and businesses with names like Latinum Loonie and Starfleet Supplies, it becomes clear that this town is in deep. While some Vulcans are tired of it – 'I'm not even a *Star Trek* fan,' one local whispered to us – there's no denying that this out-there bid for tourism has put an otherwise missable town on the map and added an unlikely but very welcome economic opportunity. It's certainly the only place in Canada where you can buy Vulcan ears in the grocery store and enter the local pub wielding a phaser without getting a second glance. It appears Vulcan won't go the way of its nearly-ghost-town neighbors but will, in fact, live long and prosper.

To reach Vulcan from Lethbridge, follow Hwy 23 north for 92km.

★Telegraph Tap House PUB $
(☎403-942-4136; 310 6th Street S; mains $10-16; ⏲11:30am-late) So this is where cool Lethbridgians go. Park yourself at the bar with a craft brew and pulled-pork sliders or chili-cheese fries. Feeling brave? Take on the Dead Albertan burger, a 6oz beef patty between two grilled cheese sandwiches. Is the stack of antique suitcases left over from others who dared it and didn't make it out the door?

The walls are lined with B&W images of Letherbridge from yesteryear, and popular TV shows are often shown on the big screen.

Bread Milk & Honey CAFE $
(☎403-381-8605; www.breadmilkhoney.ca; 427 5th St S; menu items $6-12; ⏲7:30am-7pm Mon-Fri, 9am-3pm Sat; 📶) With excellent coffee and everything from oatmeal loaded with banana, cinnamon and almond to a bacon burrito, this is *the* place to come for breakfast. The interior is all exposed brick and wood; if Lethbridge had hipsters, they'd hang out here, devouring a grilled turkey and Brie wrap or a freshly baked scone.

ℹ Information

Chinook Country Tourist Association (☎403-320-1222; www.chinookcountry.com; 2805 Scenic Dr S; ⏲9am-5pm)

ℹ Getting There & Away

The **Lethbridge airport** (☎403-329-4474; www.lethbridgeairport.ca; 417 Stubb Ross Rd), a short drive south on Hwy 5, is served by commuter affiliates of Air Canada. Six or seven flights per day go to Calgary.

Greyhound Canada (☎403-327-1551; www.greyhound.ca; 411 5th St S) goes to Calgary ($46, three hours, five daily) and Regina ($117, 16½ hours, two daily). Luxurious **Red Arrow** (☎800-232-1958; www.redarrow.ca; 449 Mayor Magrath Dr S) buses connect once daily with Calgary ($55, three hours) and Fort MacLeod ($34, 45 minutes)

Writing-on-Stone Provincial Park

Perhaps the best thing about the **Writing-on-Stone Provincial Park** (☎403-647-2364; www.albertaparks.ca) FREE is that it really isn't on the way to anywhere. For those willing to get off the main thoroughfare, all efforts will be rewarded. It's named for the extensive carvings and paintings made by the Plains First Nations on the sandstone cliffs along the banks of Milk River – more than 3000 years ago. There is an excellent, self-guided **interpretive trail** that takes you to some of the more spectacular viewpoints and accessible pictographs.

You must stay on the trails to prevent damage to the hoodoos. Many visitors feel the need to add their own marks to the hoodoos – don't be one of them. Not only are you vandalizing a piece of history, you're also desecrating a sacred First Nations site.

The best art is found in a restricted area (to protect it from vandalism), which you can visit only on a **guided tour** (10am, 2pm and 6pm daily in summer; adult/youth/child $18/8/5) with the park ranger. Other activities possible here include **canoeing** and **swimming** in the river in summer and **cross-country skiing** in winter. Park wildlife is ample, and the visitor center, built in the shape of a traditional tipi, blends perfectly with the region's natural and cultural heritage. Beware: it can get exceedingly hot in the summer and you must have close-toed shoes. (This is rattlesnake country!)

The park's riverside campground has 64 sites, running water, showers and flush toilets. It's popular on weekends.

The park is southeast of Lethbridge and close to the US border; the Sweetgrass Hills of northern Montana are visible to the south. To get to the park, take Hwy 501 east for 42km from the town of Milk River, on Hwy 4.

Waterton Lakes National Park

Here flat prairies collide dramatically with the Rockies, with a sparkling lake and a hilltop castle that may make you wonder if you've fallen into a fairy tale. Sadly, **Waterton Lakes National Park** (www.pc.gc.ca/waterton; adult/child per day $7.80/3.90) is rarely known to outside visitors. While Banff and Jasper, its siblings to the north, hemorrhage with tourists and weekend warriors, Waterton is a pocket of sublime tranquillity.

Established in 1895 and now part of a Unesco World Heritage site, Unesco Biosphere Reserve and International Peace Park (with the USA's Glacier National Park), this 525-sq-km reserve lies in Alberta's southwestern corner. The park is a sanctuary for numerous iconic animals – grizzlies, elk, deer and cougar – along with 800-odd wildflower species.

WORTH A TRIP

BLACKFOOT CROSSING HISTORICAL PARK

Standing stoically in the center of a First Nations reserve, **Blackfoot Crossing Historical Park** (☎403-734-5171; www.blackfootcrossing.ca; Hwy 842; adult/child $12/8; ⏲9am-5pm Mon-Fri) celebrates and embraces authentic Siksika (Blackfoot) culture and is entirely worth exploring.

The history of southern Alberta pre-1880 belongs to the Blackfoot confederacy, an amalgamation of the Peigan, Blood and Montana-based Blackfeet tribes. Blackfoot Crossing, long an important tribal nexus, was unique in that it was the only place where nomadic First Nations tribes built a semi-permanent settlement. It was here that the notorious Treaty 7 was signed by Chief Crowfoot in 1877, ceding land to the British crown and establishing the Siksika reservation. After a visit from Prince Charles in 1977, the idea for a historical site was hatched; after 30 years of planning, the park finally opened in 2007.

It's anchored by an architecturally stunning, ecofriendly main building that incorporates elements of tipis and feathered headdresses into its creative design. Within its walls lie a 100-seat theater showcasing cultural dances, a set of exhibits chronicling Blackfoot history and guided tours with local Siksika interpreters and storytellers. Outside, you can enjoy various trails, prairie viewpoints, and a tipi village where traditional crafts are practiced and taught.

To get here, head 100km east of Calgary on Hwy 1 and then 7km south on Hwy 842. The historical park hasn't yet made it onto the mainstream tourist track and remains curiously light on visitors.

The town of **Waterton**, a charming alpine village with a winter population of about 40, provides a marked contrast to larger, flashier Banff. Its 1920s-era Prince of Wales Hotel stands regally above town on the lakefront.

Sights

★Red Rock Canyon CANYON

FREE The clear waters of Blakiston Creek rush through the startlingly crimson Red Rock Canyon. Follow a 0.7km interpretive **loop trail** along the cliffs to learn a little geology and see jaw-dropping scenery. Amazingly, half the beauty is in getting here: the 15km trip along **Red Rock Parkway** through Blakiston Valley offers spectacular views of grassy plains crashing into looming mountains, with bears and wildflowers aplenty.

Cameron Lake LAKE

Backed by the sheer-sided slopes of Mt Custer, placid Cameron Lake is tucked tantalizingly beneath the Continental Divide at the three-way meeting point of Montana, Alberta and British Columbia. Poised at the end of the 16km (10-mile) **Akamina Parkway**, this is where day-trippers stop to picnic, hike and rent boats. From foam flowers to fireweed, copious wildflower species thrive here, while grizzly bears are known to frequent the lake's isolated southern shores.

Cameron Falls WATERFALL

(Cameron Falls Dr) Located at the west end of Cameron Falls Dr (a short hop from the center of town) is this dramatically poised torrent of foaming water, notable among geologists for harboring the oldest exposed Precambrian rocks in the Canadian Rockies. Estimates suggest they are 1.5 billion years old, give or take the odd millennium. The lookout here is paved for wheelchair access and the falls are rather fetchingly lit up at night.

Activities

Hiking

Those looking to stretch their legs are in luck – Waterton is a hiker's haven. With over 225km of walking tracks, you'll run out of time before you run out of trails. The trails are shared with bikes and horses (where permitted); once the snow lands, cross-country skis will get you to the same places. The 17km walk to **Crypt Lake** is a standout: there's a 20m tunnel, a stream that materializes out of the ground and a ladder to negotiate. The only way to get to the trailhead is by boat. **Waterton Shoreline Cruises** (☎403-859-2362; www.watertoncruise.com; adult/youth/child $47/24/16; ⏲May-Oct) leave the town's marina in the morning and pick up the weary at the **Crypt Lake trailhead** in the afternoon (adult/child $24/12).

Another example of Waterton's 'small is beautiful' persona is the 19km **Carthew–Alderson Trail**, often listed as one of the best high-alpine day hikes in North America. **Tamarack Outdoor Outfitters** (☎403-859-2378; www.hikewaterton.com; 214 Mt View Rd; ⊙8am-8pm May-Sep) runs a shuttle every morning in summer to the trailhead by Cameron Lake (reservations recommended). From here you'll hike back over the mountains to town.

Tamarack also offers shuttles to many other trailheads, including free shuttles to all of the hikes on the Akamina Pkwy.

Lake Cruises

A highlight for many visitors here is a boat ride with Waterton Shoreline Cruises (p628) across the shimmering waters of Upper Waterton Lake to the far shore of Goat Haunt, Montana (USA). The two-hour trip is scenic, with a lively commentary as you go. Grab your passport before you jump on the (often rather full) boats, as they dock in the USA for about 30 minutes.

Sleeping

The park has three vehicle-accessible Parks Canada campgrounds, with one right in the town of Waterton. Regular campsites can be reserved online or by phone, but backcountry campsites are limited and should be reserved through the visitor center (p630).

Crandell Mountain Campground CAMPGROUND $
(☎403-859-5133; Red Rock Pkwy; tent & RV sites $22; ⊙June-early Sep; P) For big, wide-open views, head out to this secluded camping spot a few minutes' drive up Red Rock Pkwy. Some of the loops, especially H and L, offer beautiful mountain views and direct access to Blakiston Brook. Evening ranger talks are held in a charming amphitheater. There are no services, toilets but no showers, and no reservations.

★Northland Lodge B&B $$
(☎403-859-2353; www.northlandlodgecanada.com; 408 Evergreen Ave; r $169-209; ⊙mid-May–mid-Oct;) Located on the edge of town within earshot of gushing Cameron Falls is this cozy house that Louis Hill (the genius behind the Prince of Wales Hotel) built for himself. A B&B with a wide range of quaint rooms (some with shared bath) and a creaking staircase, it's steeped in character. The welcoming host's freshly baked breakfast is fabulous.

Crandell Mountain Lodge HOTEL $$
(☎403-859-2288; www.crandellmountainlodge.com; 102 Mt View Rd; r from $130;) With homemade cookies in the lobby, this 1940s lodge is doing a good impersonation of a Tudor cottage plucked from a quiet English village. The Crandell has old-fashioned rooms with quilts like Grandma used to make, fireplaces and a front deck facing Emerald Bay across the street. Service is very welcoming.

Bear Mountain Motel MOTEL $$
(☎403-859-2366; www.bearmountainmotel.com; 208 Mt View Rd; r $115-135; ⊙mid-May–Sep; P) Upfront about its offerings, Bear Mountain is a standard, retro-style motel with immaculate rooms and friendly service. There are barbecues and picnic tables; some rooms are pet friendly and some have kitchenettes. This is about as 'budget' as you get in Waterton.

Aspen Village Inn HOTEL $$
(☎403-859-2255; www.aspenvillageinn.com; 111 Windflower Ave; r $129-269; ⊙May–mid-Oct; P) These standard, motel-style rooms are a favorite with families, with an on-site kids playground and resident deer finding shade in the grounds. Barbecues and picnic tables offer ambience on warm summer nights, while satellite TV can take the chill out of a damp autumn evening. Many rooms have kitchenettes.

★Prince of Wales Hotel HISTORIC HOTEL $$$
(☎403-859-2231; www.princeofwaleswaterton.com; Prince of Wales Rd; r from $249; ⊙May-Sep; P) With a Hogwarts-like setting on a bluff overlooking Upper Waterton Lake, the grand Prince of Wales blends Swiss-style architecture with the atmosphere of a Scottish castle. The old-world charms extend to serving staff in kilts and high tea in the main lounge – very civilized. The large lake-facing windows show the raw wilderness that awaits.

Eating & Drinking

★49° North Pizza PIZZA $
(☎403-859-3000; www.49degreesnorthpizza.com; 303 Windflower Ave; pizzas $10-20; ⊙noon-10pm May-Sep) Seriously satisfying pizza with all of the expected renditions, plus some creative gourmet options such as bison and Saskatoon berries. Service is top-notch and there's a good beer selection; if the handful of tables and patio are full, you can get takeout. Need we say more?

Wieners of Waterton HOT DOGS $
(www.wienersofwaterton.com; 301 Windflower Ave; hot dogs $6-8; ⏲11am-11pm;) Not all wieners are made equal and those served here approach the gourmet level, including locally smoked and breakfast-dog varieties. Get 'em with a side of sweet-potato fries. Rightfully popular, it commonly sees lines out the door in the summer months.

Waterton Bagel & Coffee Co CAFE $
(☎403-859-2466; 309 Windflower Ave; bagels from $5; ⏲10am-10pm) A godsend if you've just staggered out of the wilderness, this tiny caffeine stop has a handful of window stools, life-saving peanut-butter-and-jam bagels and refreshing blended coffee drinks.

Thirsty Bear Saloon PUB
(☎403-859-2211; 111 Waterton Ave; ⏲4pm-2am Mon-Sat mid-May–Sep) It may look like a dark, sketchy hall from the outside but it's worth crossing the threshold. Inside, this large, friendly, barnlike pub is where wild nights happen in the wilderness, aided by live music, pool tables and good beer.

ℹ Information

My Waterton (www.mywaterton.ca) Waterton Lakes' Chamber of Commerce website with up-to-date visitor information, including a listing of monthly events.

Parks Canada Visitor Centre (☎403-859-2378; www.pc.gc.ca/waterton; ⏲8am-7pm May-Sep) The central stop for information on everything from trail conditions to hotels. Across the street from the Prince of Wales Hotel.

ℹ Getting There & Away

Waterton lies in Alberta's southwestern corner, 130km from Lethbridge and 156km from Calgary. The one road entrance into the park is in its northeastern corner, along Hwy 5. Most visitors coming from Glacier and the USA reach the junction with Hwy 5 via Hwy 6 (Chief Mountain International Hwy) from the southeast. From Calgary, to the north, Hwy 2 shoots south toward Hwy 5 into the park. From the east, Hwy 5, through Cardston, heads west and then south into the park.

There is no public transportation from Canadian cities outside the park. However, a shuttle service (adult/child US$50/25) operated by **Glacier Park Inc** (☎reservations 866-435-1605; www.glacierparkinc.com) offers daily transport from the Prince of Wales Hotel to the Glacier Park Lodge in Montana (USA) from May to September. From here you can link up with the Amtrak train network for travel elsewhere in the US.

ℹ Getting Around

Tamarack Outdoor Outfitters (p629) offers shuttles to many trailheads, including Chief Mountain ($20) and Tamarack ($30). It also offers free shuttles to all hikes on the Akamina Pkwy. Book your seat online or at the kiosk inside the shop.

Crowsnest Pass

West of Fort Macleod the Crowsnest Hwy (Hwy 3) heads through the prairies and into the Rocky Mountains to Crowsnest Pass (1396m) and the British Columbian border. The Pass, as it's known, is a string of small communities just to the east of the BC border. Of note is the story of the town of **Frank**. In 1903, Frank was almost completely buried when 30 million cubic meters (some 82 million tonnes' worth) of nearby Turtle Mountain collapsed and killed around 70 people. Some believe the coal mine dug into the base of the mountain was to blame. But the mining didn't stop; this black gold was the ticket to fortune for the entire region some hundred years ago. Eventually the demand for coal decreased, and after yet more cave-ins and fear of a second slide, the mines shut down for good.

★Frank Slide Interpretive Centre MUSEUM
(www.frankslide.org; Hwy 3; adult/child $13/9; ⏲9am-6pm July-Aug, 10am-5pm Sep-Jun;) This excellent museum overlooks the Crowsnest Valley and helps put a human face on the tragedy of the Frank landslide. Displays bring mining, the railroad and the early days of this area to life; kids will enjoy having things to pull, push and jump on, as well as puzzles and other interactive activities. There's also a fantastic film dramatizing the tragic events of 1903. Trails from the museum take you out over the slide site itself.

NORTHERN ALBERTA

Despite the presence of its increasingly infamous oil sands, the top half of Alberta is little visited and even less known. Once you travel north of Edmonton, the population drops off to Siberian levels. The sense of remoteness here is almost eerie.

If it's solitude you seek, then this is paradise found. Endless stretches of pine forests seem to go on forever, nighttime brings aurora borealis displays that are better than any chemical hallucinogens, and it's here you can still see herds of buffalo roaming.

The Cree, Slavey and Dene were the first peoples to inhabit the region, and many of them still depend on fishing, hunting and trapping for survival. The northeast has virtually no roads and is dominated by Wood Buffalo National Park, the Athabasca River and Lake Athabasca. The northwest is more accessible, with a network of highways connecting Alberta with northern BC and the NWT.

Peace River & Around

Heading northwest along Hwy 43 leads to the town of Dawson Creek, BC, and mile zero of the Alaska Hwy. Dawson is a whopping 590km from Edmonton, so it's a long way to go to check out this isolated section of northern Alberta. Along the way you'll pass through **Grande Prairie**, the base of operations for the local agricultural industry and home to chuckwagon-racing legend Kelly Sutherland.

Peace River is so named because the warring Cree and Beaver Indians made peace along its banks. The town of **Peace River** sits at the confluence of the Heart, Peace and Smoky Rivers. West out of town, Hwy 2 leads to the Mackenzie Hwy.

Mackenzie Highway

The small town of **Grimshaw** is the official starting point of the Mackenzie Hwy (Hwy 35) north to the NWT. There's not much here except for the mile-zero sign and a few shops. The relatively flat and straight road is mostly paved, though there are stretches of loose gravel where the road is being reconstructed.

The mainly agricultural landscape between Grimshaw and Manning gives way to endless stretches of spruce and pine forest. Come prepared – this is frontier territory: services become fewer (and more expensive) as you head northward through the wilderness. Make sure you fill your tank any time you see a gas station from here on.

High Level, the last settlement of any size before the NWT border, is a timber-industry center. Workers often stay in its motels during the week. The only service station between High Level and Enterprise (in the NWT) is at Indian Cabins.

Lake District

From St Paul, more than 200km northeast of Edmonton, to the NWT border lies Alberta's immense lake district. As you cross over the North Saskatchewan River, the land turns to rolling forested hills, peppered with abandoned farms and eerily beautiful dilapidated houses and barns. Fishing is popular (even in winter, when there is ice fishing), but many of the lakes, especially further north, have no road access and you have to fly in.

St Paul is the place to go if you are looking for little green people. Its **flying-saucer landing pad** – which is still awaiting its first customer – is open for business. Residents built the 12m-high circular landing pad in 1967 as part of a Canadian Centennial project, declaring the land underneath the pad international (and, one can assume, intergalactic). It's billed as the world's largest, and only, UFO landing pad and UFO enthusiasts have been visiting ever since. Check out the **UFO Data Center** (☎780-645-6800, UFO hotline 888-733-8367; www.town.stpaul.ab.ca/Tourist-Information; 50 Avenue, St Paul; ⊙10am-6pm May-Sep) with its space-themed gift shop and book of 137 recorded local sightings, along with images and accounts of local cattle mutilations, abductions and crop circles. There's also a UFO hotline for people to report new sightings.

Hwy 63 is the main route into the province's northeastern wilderness interior. The highway, with a few small settlements and campgrounds on the way, leads to **Fort McMurray**, 439km northeast of Edmonton. Originally a fur-trading outpost, it's now home to the Athabasca Oil Sands, the world's largest single oil deposit and Alberta's economic bread and butter. The history of oil sands and the story of how crude oil is extracted from them is told through interactive displays at the **Oil Sands Discovery Centre** (☎780-743-7167; http://history.alberta.ca/oilsands; 515 MacKenzie Blvd, Fort McMurray; adult/child/family $11/7/29; ⊙9am-5pm mid-May–mid-Sep, 10am-4pm Tue-Sun mid-Sep–mid-May). The town itself isn't particularly interesting; non–oil workers who do visit come to see the aurora borealis (northern lights). The town hit the world press in 2016 when a massive wildfire swept through; all residents were evacuated for months and many, sadly, didn't have a home to return to.

British Columbia

Includes ➡

Best Places to Eat

- Bistro 694 (p702)
- Pilgrimme (p720)
- Vij's (p656)
- Ask for Luigi (p654)
- Nova Kitchen (p678)

Best Places to Sleep

- Free Spirit Spheres (p702)
- Wickaninnish Inn (p706)
- Shades of Jade Inn & Spa (p679)
- Skwachays Lodge (p650)
- Old Courthouse Inn (p680)

Why Go?

Visitors to Canada's westernmost province should pack a long list of superlatives to deploy here; the words 'wow,' 'amazing' and 'spectacular' will only go so far. Luckily, it's not too hard to wax lyrical about the mighty mountains, deep forests and dramatic coastlines here that instantly lower heart rates to tranquil levels.

There's much more to British Columbia (BC) than nature-hugging dioramas, though. Vancouver fuses cuisines and cultures from Asia and beyond, while mid-sized cities such as Victoria and Kelowna are creating their own vibrant scenes. It's also hard to beat the welcoming, sometimes quirky character of smaller communities – from Cumberland to Powell River and to Salt Spring – that are the beating heart of BC.

Wherever you head, the great outdoors will always call. Don't just point your camera at it: BC is unbeatable for skiing, kayaking and hiking experiences that can make this the trip of a lifetime.

When to Go

Vancouver, BC

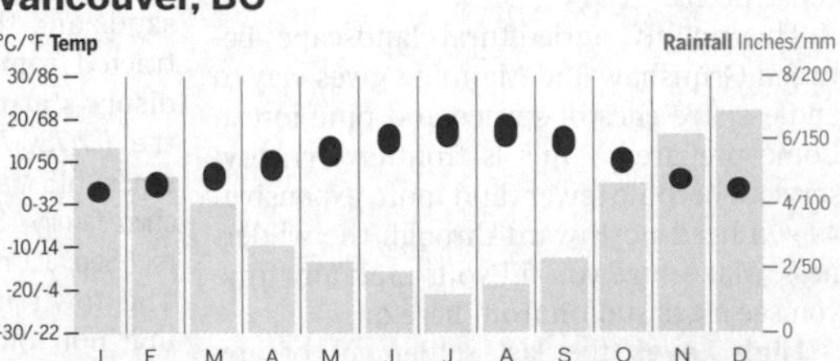

Dec–Mar Best powder action on the slopes of Whistler and Blackcomb mountains.

Jul & Aug Beaches, patios and a plethora of outdoor festivals in sun-dappled Vancouver.

Sep & Oct Dramatic surfing and the start of storm-watching season in beachy Tofino.

Parks & Wildlife

BC's national parks include snowcapped **Glacier** and the Unesco World Heritage sites of **Kootenay** and **Yoho**. The newer **Gulf Islands National Park Reserve** protects a fragile coastal region. Visit the website of **Parks Canada** (www.pc.gc.ca) for information.

The region's almost 1000 provincial parks offer 3000km of hiking trails. Notables include **Strathcona** and remote **Cape Scott**, as well as the Cariboo's canoe-friendly **Bowron Lake** and the Kootenays' Matterhorn-like **Mt Assiniboine**. Check the website of **BC Parks** (www.bcparks.ca) for information.

Expect to spot some amazing wildlife. Land mammals – including elk, moose, wolves, grizzlies and black bears – will have most visitors scrambling for their cameras, and there are around 500 bird varieties, including blue herons and bald eagles galore. Ocean visitors should keep an eye out for orcas.

Getting Around

The sheer size of BC can overwhelm some visitors: it's a scary-sounding 1508km drive from Vancouver to Prince Rupert, for example. While it's tempting to simply stick around Vancouver – the main point of entry for most BC-bound visitors – you won't really have experienced the province unless you head out of town.

Despite the distances, driving remains the most popular method of movement in BC. Plan your routes via the handy **DriveBC website** (www.drivebc.ca) and check out the dozens of services offered by the extensive **BC Ferries** (☎888-223-3779; www.bcferries.com) system.

VIA Rail (www.viarail.com) operates two BC train services. One trundles across the north from the coastline to Jasper. Pick up the second in Jasper for a ride back to Vancouver. A third line on Vancouver Island may also reopen in the coming years.

VANCOUVER

POP 604, 778

Walkable neighborhoods, drink-and-dine delights and memorable cultural and outdoor activities framed by dramatic vistas – there's a glassful of great reasons to love this lotusland metropolis.

Downtown is just the start of Vancouver. Walk or hop public transit and within minutes you'll be hanging with the locals in one of the city's many diverse and distinctive 'hoods. Whether discovering the coffee shops of Commercial Dr or the hipster haunts of Main St, the indie bars and restaurants of Gastown or the heritage-house beachfronts and browsable stores of Kitsilano, you'll find this city perfect for easy-access urban exploration. Just be sure to chat to the locals wherever you go: they might seem shy or aloof at first, but Vancouverites love talking up their town.

BC FAST FACTS

- Population: 4.7 million
- Area: 944,735 sq km
- Capital: Victoria
- Fact: BC is North America's third-largest film and TV production center.

History

The First Nations lived in this area for up to 16,000 years before Spanish explorers arrived in the late 1500s. When Captain George Vancouver of the British Royal Navy sailed up to these shores in 1792, he met a couple of Spanish captains who informed him of their country's land claim (the beach they met on is now called Spanish Banks). But by the early 1800s, as European settlers began arriving, the British crown had gained an increasing stranglehold.

Fur trading and a feverish gold rush soon redefined the region as a resource-filled Aladdin's cave. By the 1850s, thousands of fortune seekers had arrived, prompting the Brits to officially claim the area as a colony. Local entrepreneur 'Gassy' Jack Deighton seized the initiative in 1867 by opening a bar on the forested shoreline of Burrard Inlet. This triggered a rash of development – nicknamed Gastown – that became the forerunner of modern-day Vancouver.

But not everything went to plan. While Vancouver rapidly reached a population of 1000, its buildings were almost completely destroyed in an 1886 blaze (quickly dubbed the Great Fire, even though it only lasted 20 minutes). A prompt rebuild followed and the new downtown core soon took shape. Buildings from this era still survive, as does Stanley Park. Originally the town's military reserve, it was opened as a public recreation area in 1888.

Relying on its port, the growing city became a hub of industry, importing thousands of immigrant workers to fuel economic development. The Chinatown built at

British Columbia Highlights

1 Stanley Park (p636) Stretching your legs on the breathtaking 8.8km seawall stroll.

2 Tofino (p704) Surfing up a storm (or just watching a storm) on Vancouver Island's wild west coast.

3 Okanagan Valley (p724) Slurping some celebrated tipples on an ever-winding winery tour.

4 Whistler (p670) Skiing the Olympian slopes, then enjoying a warming après-ski beverage in the village.

5 Gwaii Haanas National Park Reserve (p762) Exploring the ancient and ethereal rainforest and kayaking the coastline for a bird's-eye view of the region.

6 Salt Spring Island (p716) Puttering around the lively Saturday Market and scoffing more than a few treats.

7 Alert Bay (p713) Walking the waterfront boardwalk and exploring evocative First Nations arts and culture.

8 Sea to Sky Gondola (p668) Hopping on the new gondola near Squamish for panoramic up-top views of the shimmering region.

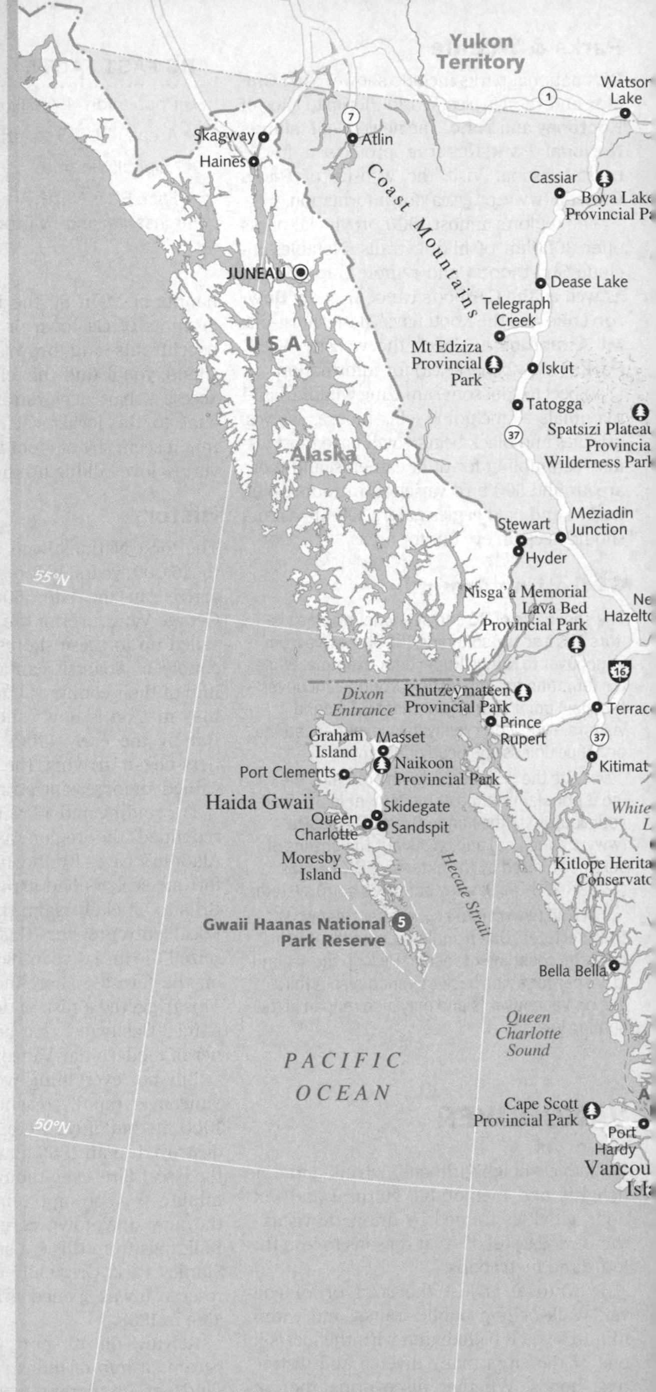

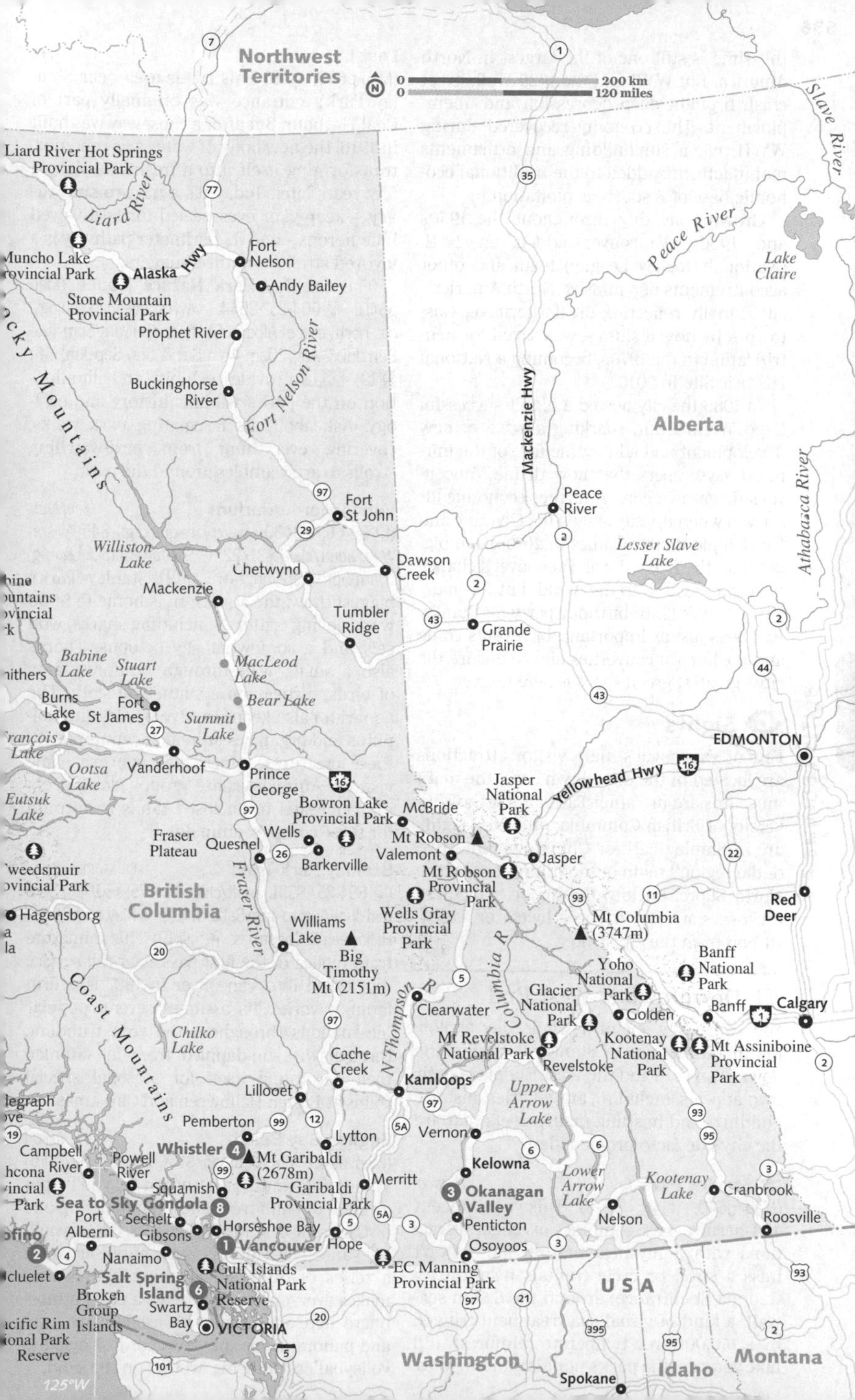

Northwest Territories
0 200 km
0 120 miles
Liard River Hot Springs Provincial Park
Liard River
Muncho Lake Provincial Park
Alaska Hwy
Fort Nelson
Andy Bailey
Stone Mountain Provincial Park
Prophet River
Buckinghorse River
Fort Nelson River
Rocky Mountains
Fort St John
Williston Lake
Chetwynd
Dawson Creek
Mackenzie
Tumbler Ridge
Babine Lake
Stuart Lake
MacLeod Lake
Smithers
Burns Lake
Fort St James
Bear Lake
Summit Lake
François Lake
Vanderhoof
Ootsa Lake
Prince George
Eutsuk Lake
Bowron Lake Provincial Park
McBride
Wells
Fraser Plateau
Quesnel
Barkerville
Mt Robson
Valemont
Mt Robson Provincial Park
Tweedsmuir Provincial Park
Hagensborg
British Columbia
Fraser River
Wells Gray Provincial Park
Williams Lake
Big Timothy Mt (2151m)
Coast Mountains
N Thompson R
Clearwater
Chilko Lake
Cache Creek
Lillooet
Kamloops
Pemberton
Lytton
Whistler
Mt Garibaldi (2678m)
Campbell River
Powell River
Strathcona Provincial Park
Squamish
Garibaldi Provincial Park
Merritt
Sea to Sky Gondola
Port Alberni
Sechelt
Gibsons
Horseshoe Bay
Tofino
Vancouver
Hope
Nanaimo
Ucluelet
Salt Spring Island
Gulf Islands National Park Reserve
Broken Group Islands
Swartz Bay
Pacific Rim National Park Reserve
VICTORIA
125°W
Peace River
Mackenzie Hwy
Slave River
Lake Claire
Alberta
Athabasca River
Lesser Slave Lake
Grande Prairie
EDMONTON
Jasper National Park
Yellowhead Hwy
Jasper
Red Deer
Mt Columbia (3747m)
Columbia R
Yoho National Park
Banff National Park
Glacier National Park
Golden
Banff
Calgary
Mt Revelstoke National Park
Revelstoke
Kootenay National Park
Mt Assiniboine Provincial Park
Upper Arrow Lake
Vernon
Kelowna
Okanagan Valley
Lower Arrow Lake
Kootenay Lake
Cranbrook
Penticton
Nelson
Roosville
Osoyoos
EC Manning Provincial Park
USA
Washington
Spokane
Idaho
Montana

this time is still one of the largest in North America. But WWI and the 1929 Wall Street crash brought deep depression and unemployment. The economy recovered during WWII, when shipbuilding and armaments manufacturing added to the traditional economic base of resource exploitation.

Growing steadily throughout the 1950s and 1960s, Vancouver added an NHL (National Hockey League) team and other accoutrements of a midsize North American city. Finally reflecting on its heritage, Gastown – by now a slum – was saved for gentrification in the 1970s, becoming a National Historic Site in 2010.

In 1986 the city hosted a highly successful Expo World's Fair, sparking a wave of new development and adding the first of the mirrored skyscrapers that now define Vancouver's downtown core. A further economic lift arrived when the city staged the Olympic and Paralympic Winter Games in 2010. Even bigger than the Expo, it was Vancouver's chance to showcase itself to the world. But for many locals, 2013's 125th birthday party for Stanley Park was just as important: big events come and go, but Vancouverites aim to ensure the city's greatest green space is here forever.

Sights

Few of Vancouver's main visitor attractions are located in the downtown core: the main museums are in Vanier Park and at the University of British Columbia, other top sights are in Stanley Park or Chinatown, and two of the region's main outdoor lures are on the North Shore. Luckily, the majority of these must-sees are easy to reach by car or a transit hop from the city center.

Downtown & West End

You can easily spend a whole day exploring the attractions of Stanley Park. But the downtown core and the West End have their own appeals, including art galleries, historic buildings and bustling main streets that are the city's de facto promenades.

★Stanley Park PARK
(Map p640; P; 19) This magnificent 404-hectare park combines excellent attractions with a mystical natural aura. Don't miss a stroll or cycle (rentals near the W Georgia St entrance) around the 8.8km seawall: a kind of visual spa treatment fringed by a 150,000-tree temperate rainforest, it'll take you past the park's popular totem poles.

Lost Lagoon LAKE
(Map p640; 19) This rustic area near Stanley Park's entrance was originally part of Coal Harbour. But after a causeway was built in 1916, the new body of water was renamed, transforming itself into a freshwater lake a few years later. Today it's a **nature sanctuary** – keep your eyes peeled for beady-eyed blue herons – and its perimeter pathway is a favored stroll for nature-huggers.

The **Stanley Park Nature House** (Map p640; 604-257-8544; www.stanleyparkecology.ca; north end of Alberni St; free; 10am-5pm Tue-Sun Jul & Aug, 10am-4pm Sat & Sun Sep-Jun; ; 19) FREE provides exhibits and illumination on the park's wildlife, history and ecology. Ask about its fascinating park walks, covering everything from bird-watching strolls to artsy ambles around the park.

Vancouver Aquarium AQUARIUM
(604-659-3400; www.vanaqua.org; 845 Avison Way; adult/child $31/22; 9:30am-6pm Jul & Aug, 10am-5pm Sep-Jun; ; 19) Stanley Park's biggest draw, the aquarium is home to 9000 water-loving critters – including sharks, wolf eels and a somewhat shy octopus. There's also a small, walk-through rainforest area of birds, turtles and a statue-still sloth. The aquarium also keeps captive whales and dolphins and organizes animal encounters with these creatures, which may concern some visitors. Animal-welfare groups claim keeping cetaceans in enclosed tanks is harmful for these complex animals.

Stanley Park Train MINIATURE RAILWAY
(604-257-8531; adult/child $6/4.75; 10am-5pm mid-Jun–Aug, to 4pm Sat & Sun Apr & May, plus Easter, Halloween & Christmas; ; 19) This miniature train replica of the first passenger-rail service that rolled into Vancouver in 1887 is a firm family favorite. Its assumes several popular incarnations throughout the year, trundling through the sun-dappled trees in summer, then decorating itself for seasonal special trains at Easter, Halloween and Christmas.

English Bay Beach BEACH
(Map p640; cnr Denman St & Beach Ave; 5) Wandering south on Denman St, you'll spot a clutch of palm trees ahead announcing one of Canada's best urban beaches. Then you'll see Vancouver's most popular public artwork: a series of oversized laughing figures that makes everyone smile. There's a party atmosphere here in summer as locals catch rays and panoramic ocean views…or just ogle the volleyballers prancing around on the sand.

Vancouver

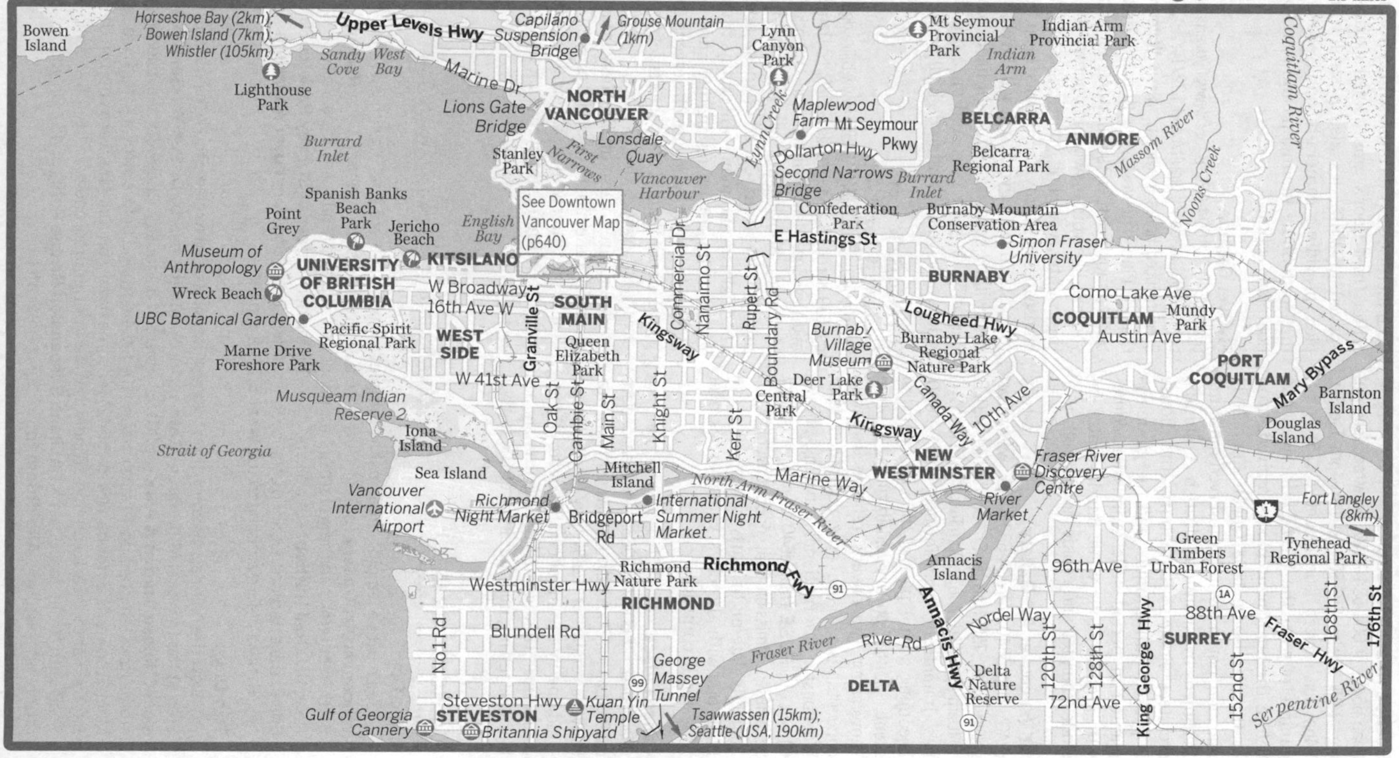

0 5 km
0 2.5 miles

Bowen Island
Horseshoe Bay (2km); Bowen Island (7km); Whistler (105km)
Upper Levels Hwy
Capilano Suspension Bridge
Grouse Mountain (1km)
Lynn Canyon Park
Mt Seymour Provincial Park
Indian Arm Provincial Park
Indian Arm
Coquitlam River
Sandy Cove
West Bay
Lighthouse Park
Marine Dr
Lions Gate Bridge
NORTH VANCOUVER
Maplewood Farm
Mt Seymour Pkwy
BELCARRA
ANMORE
Massom River
Noons Creek
Lynn Creek
Burrard Inlet
Stanley Park
First Narrows
Lonsdale Quay
Dollarton Hwy
Belcarra Regional Park
Vancouver Harbour
Second Narrows Bridge
Burrard Inlet
Spanish Banks Beach Park
Point Grey
Jericho Beach
English Bay
See Downtown Vancouver Map (p640)
Confederation Park
Burnaby Mountain Conservation Area
E Hastings St
Simon Fraser University
Museum of Anthropology
UNIVERSITY OF BRITISH COLUMBIA
KITSILANO
Wreck Beach
W Broadway
16th Ave W
Granville St
SOUTH MAIN
Commercial Dr
Nanaimo St
Rupert St
Boundary Rd
BURNABY
Como Lake Ave
COQUITLAM
Mundy Park
Austin Ave
Lougheed Hwy
UBC Botanical Garden
Pacific Spirit Regional Park
WEST SIDE
Queen Elizabeth Park
Kingsway
Burnaby Village Museum
Burnaby Lake Regional Nature Park
PORT COQUITLAM
Mary Bypass
Marne Drive Foreshore Park
W 41st Ave
Oak St
Cambie St
Main St
Knight St
Kerr St
Central Park
Deer Lake Park
Canada Way
10th Ave
Barnston Island
Douglas Island
Musqueam Indian Reserve 2
Iona Island
Strait of Georgia
Kingsway
NEW WESTMINSTER
Fraser River Discovery Centre
Sea Island
Mitchell Island
North Arm Fraser River
Marine Way
River Market
Fort Langley (8km)
Vancouver International Airport
Richmond Night Market
Bridgeport Rd
International Summer Night Market
Green Timbers Urban Forest
Tynehead Regional Park
Richmond Nature Park
Richmond Fwy
Annacis Island
96th Ave
Westminster Hwy
RICHMOND
Annacis Hwy
88th Ave
Nordel Way
SURREY
Fraser Hwy
168th St
176th St
No1 Rd
Blundell Rd
Fraser River
River Rd
120th St
128th St
King George Hwy
152nd St
George Massey Tunnel
DELTA
Delta Nature Reserve
72nd Ave
Serpentine River
Steveston Hwy
Kuan Yin Temple
Gulf of Georgia Cannery
STEVESTON
Britannia Shipyard
Tsawwassen (15km); Seattle (USA, 190km)

Roedde House Museum MUSEUM
(Map p640; ☎604-684-7040; www.roeddehouse.org; 1415 Barclay St; $5; ⊙11am-4pm Tue-Sat, 1-4pm Sun, reduced hours in winter; 🚌5) For a glimpse of what the West End looked like before the apartment blocks arrived, drop by this handsome 1893 Queen Anne–style mansion, now a lovingly preserved museum. Designed by infamous British Columbia architect Francis Rattenbury, the house is packed with antiques and the garden is planted in period style. Admission comes with a guided tour while Sunday entry includes tour, tea and cookies for just $8.

★**Vancouver Art Gallery** GALLERY
(VAG; Map p640; ☎604-662-4700; www.vanartgallery.bc.ca; 750 Hornby St; adult/child $20/6; ⊙10am-5pm Wed-Mon, to 9pm Tue; 🚌5) The VAG has dramatically transformed since 2000, becoming a vital part of the city's cultural scene. Contemporary exhibitions – often showcasing Vancouver's renowned photoconceptualists – are now combined with blockbuster international traveling shows. Check out **FUSE** (Map p640; www.vanartgallery.bc.ca/fuse; admission $24; ⊙8pm-midnight), a quarterly late-night party where you can hang out with the city's young arties over wine and live music.

Canada Place LANDMARK
(Map p640; ☎604-775-7063; www.canadaplace.ca; 999 Canada Place Way; Ⓟ; Ⓢ Waterfront) Vancouver's version of the Sydney Opera House, – judging by the number of postcards it appears on –, this iconic landmark is shaped like sails jutting into the sky over the harbor. Both a cruise-ship terminal and convention center (next door's grass-roofed expansion opened in 2010), it's also a stroll-worthy pier, providing camera-hugging views of the North Shore mountains and some busy floatplane action.

FlyOver Canada THEATER
(Map p640; ☎604-620-8455; www.flyovercanada.com; 999 Canada Pl; adult/child $22/14; ⊙10am-9pm, reduced hours in winter; 👪; Ⓢ Waterfront) Canada Place's newest attraction, this breathtaking movie-screen simulator ride makes you feel like you're swooping across the entire country, waggling your legs over grand landscapes and city landmarks from coast to coast. En route, your seat will lurch, your face will be sprayed and you'll likely have a big smile on your face. And once the short ride is over, you'll want to do it all again.

Bill Reid Gallery of Northwest Coast Art GALLERY
(Map p640; ☎604-682-3455; www.billreidgallery.ca; 639 Hornby St; adult/child $10/5; ⊙11am-5pm mid-May–Sep, 11am-5pm Wed-Sun Oct–mid-May; Ⓢ Burrard) Showcasing carvings, paintings and jewelry from Canada's most revered Haida artists and many others, this tranquil gallery is lined with fascinating and exquisite works – plus handy touch-screens to tell you all about them. The space centers on the Great Hall, where there's often a carver at work. Be sure to also hit the mezzanine level: you'll come face to face with an 8.5m-long bronze of intertwined magical creatures, complete with impressively long tongues.

VANCOUVER IN...

One Day

Begin with a heaping breakfast at **Templeton** (p650) before strolling south to the **Vancouver Art Gallery** (p638). Next, take a window-shopping wander along **Robson St**, then cut down to the waterfront for panoramic sea and mountain vistas. Walk west along the **Coal Harbour** seawall and make for the dense trees of **Stanley Park** (p636). Spend the afternoon exploring the beaches, totem poles and **Vancouver Aquarium** (p636) here before ambling to the **West End** for dinner.

Two Days

Follow the one-day itinerary, then the next morning head to clamorous Chinatown. Stop at the towering **Millennium Gate** and duck into the nearby **Dr Sun Yat-Sen Classical Chinese Garden & Park** (p639) for a taste of tranquility. Check out the colorful stores (and tempting pork buns) around the neighborhood before strolling south along Main St towards **Science World** (p642) for some hands-on fun. Afterwards hop on the SkyTrain at the nearby station, trundle to Waterfront Station, and then take the scenic SeaBus to North Vancouver's **Capilano Suspension Bridge Park** (p645). On your return, hit Gastown's **Alibi Room** (p657) for some craft beers.

Gastown & Chinatown

Just wandering the historic, sometimes cobbled streets of Gastown and Chinatown on foot is the best way to spend a few hours in this part of the city. But there are also a couple of unique, must-see attractions worth stopping off at.

Vancouver Police Museum MUSEUM
(Map p640; ☎604-665-3346; www.vancouverpolicemuseum.ca; 240 E Cordova St; adult/child $12/8; ⏰9am-5pm Tue-Sat; 🚌4) Illuminating the crime-and-vice-addled history of the region, this quirky museum is lined with confiscated weapons and counterfeit currency. It also has a former mortuary room where the walls are studded with preserved slivers of human tissue – spot the bullet-damaged brain slices. Consider adding a **walking tour** ($20) to learn all about the area's salacious olden days. And buy a toe tag T-shirt in the gift shop.

Dr Sun Yat-Sen Classical Chinese Garden & Park GARDENS
(Map p640; ☎604-662-3207; www.vancouverchinesegarden.com; 578 Carrall St; adult/child $14/10; ⏰9:30am-7pm mid-Jun–Aug, 10am-6pm Sep & May–mid-Jun, 10am-4:30pm Oct-Apr; Ⓢ Stadium-Chinatown) A tranquil break from clamorous Chinatown, this intimate 'garden of ease' reflects Taoist principles of balance and harmony. Entry includes a 45-minute guided tour, where you'll learn about the symbolism behind the placement of the gnarled pine trees, winding covered pathways and ancient limestone formations. Look out for the lazy turtles bobbing in the jade-colored water.

Steam Clock LANDMARK
(Map p640; cnr Water & Cambie Sts; Ⓢ Waterfront) Halfway along Water St, this oddly popular tourist magnet lures the cameras with its tooting steam whistle. Built in 1977, the clock's mechanism is actually driven by electricity; only the pipes on top are fueled by steam (reveal it to the patiently waiting tourists and you might cause a riot). It sounds every 15 minutes, and marks each hour with little whistling symphonies.

Chinatown Millennium Gate LANDMARK
(Map p640; cnr W Pender & Taylor Sts; Ⓢ Stadium-Chinatown) Inaugurated by Canadian prime minister Jean Chretien in 2002, Chinatown's towering entrance is the landmark most visitors look for. Stand well back, since the decoration is mostly on its lofty upper reaches, an elaborately painted section topped with a terracotta-tiled roof. The characters inscribed on its eastern front implore you to 'Remember the past and look forward to the future.'

BEST MUSEUMS

- Museum of Anthropology (p644)
- Museum of Vancouver (p644)
- Vancouver Police Museum (p639)
- Roedde House Museum (p638)
- Beaty Biodiversity Museum (p644)
- Vancouver Maritime Museum (p645)

Yaletown & Granville Island

Granville Island is a self-guided sight unto itself – and it's not just about the market. Add a miniferry hop across False Creek and you can include some history- and sport-themed attractions from Yaletown on your grand day out.

★ **Granville Island Public Market** MARKET
(Map p640; ☎604-666-6655; www.granvilleisland.com/public-market; Johnston St; ⏰9am-7pm; 🚌50, ⛴miniferries) Granville Island's highlight is the covered Public Market, a multisensory smorgasbord of fish, cheese, fruit and bakery treats. Pick up some fixings for a picnic at nearby Vanier Park or hit the international food court (dine off-peak and you're more likely to snag a table). From June to September, there's also an alfresco **farmers market** outside where, depending on the harvest, you'll find BC cherries, peaches and blueberries.

Engine 374 Pavilion MUSEUM
(Map p640; www.roundhouse.ca; Roundhouse Community Arts & Recreation Centre, 181 Roundhouse Mews; ⏰10am-4pm, reduced hours off-season; 👪; Ⓢ Yaletown-Roundhouse) FREE May 23, 1887 was an auspicious date for Vancouver. That's when Engine 374 pulled the very first transcontinental passenger train into the fledgling city, symbolically linking the country and kick-starting the eventual metropolis. Retired in 1945, the engine was, after many years of neglect, restored and placed in this splendid pavilion. The friendly volunteers here will show you the best angle for snapping the perfect photo of the engine.

BC Sports Hall of Fame & Museum MUSEUM
(Map p640; ☎604-687-5520; www.bcsportshalloffame.com; Gate A, BC Place Stadium, 777 Pacific Blvd;

Downtown Vancouver

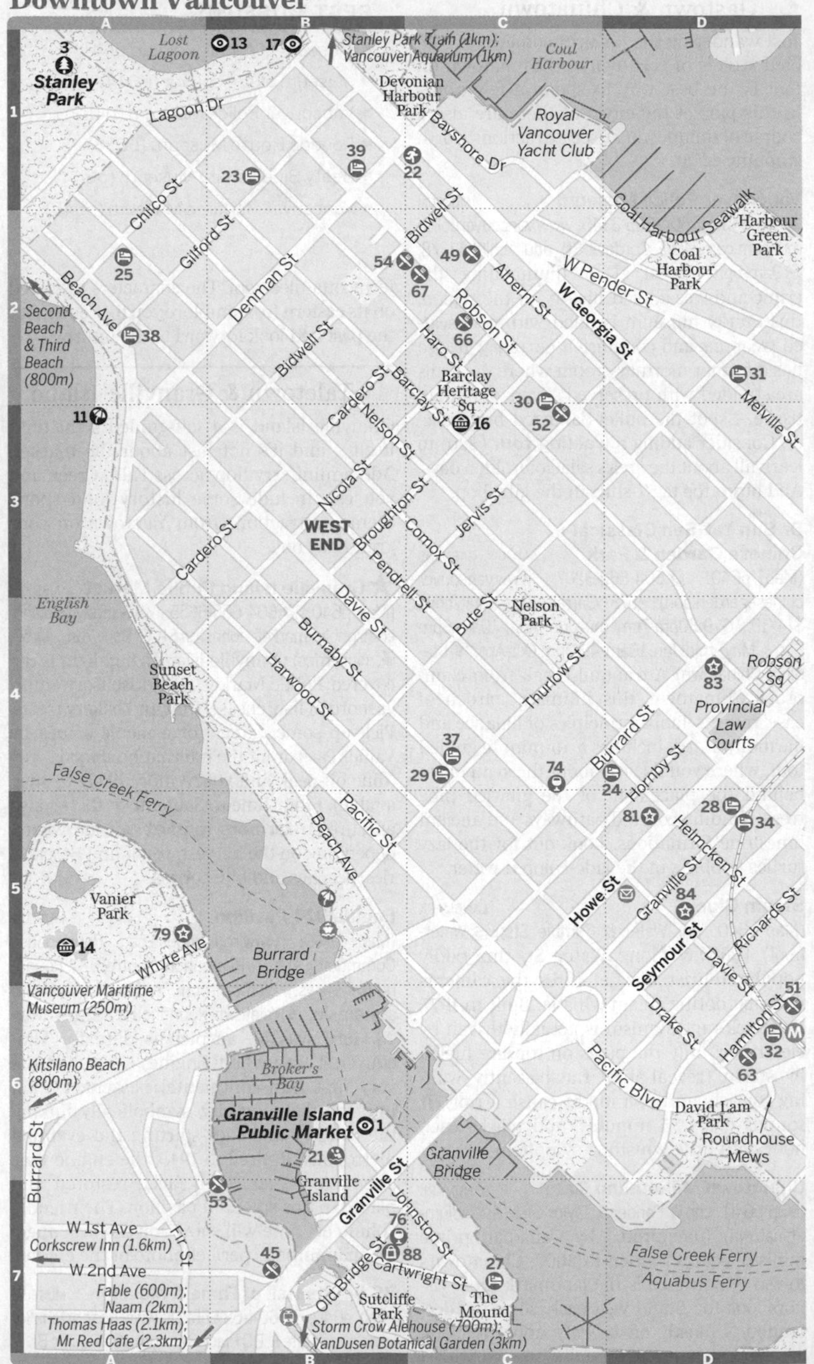

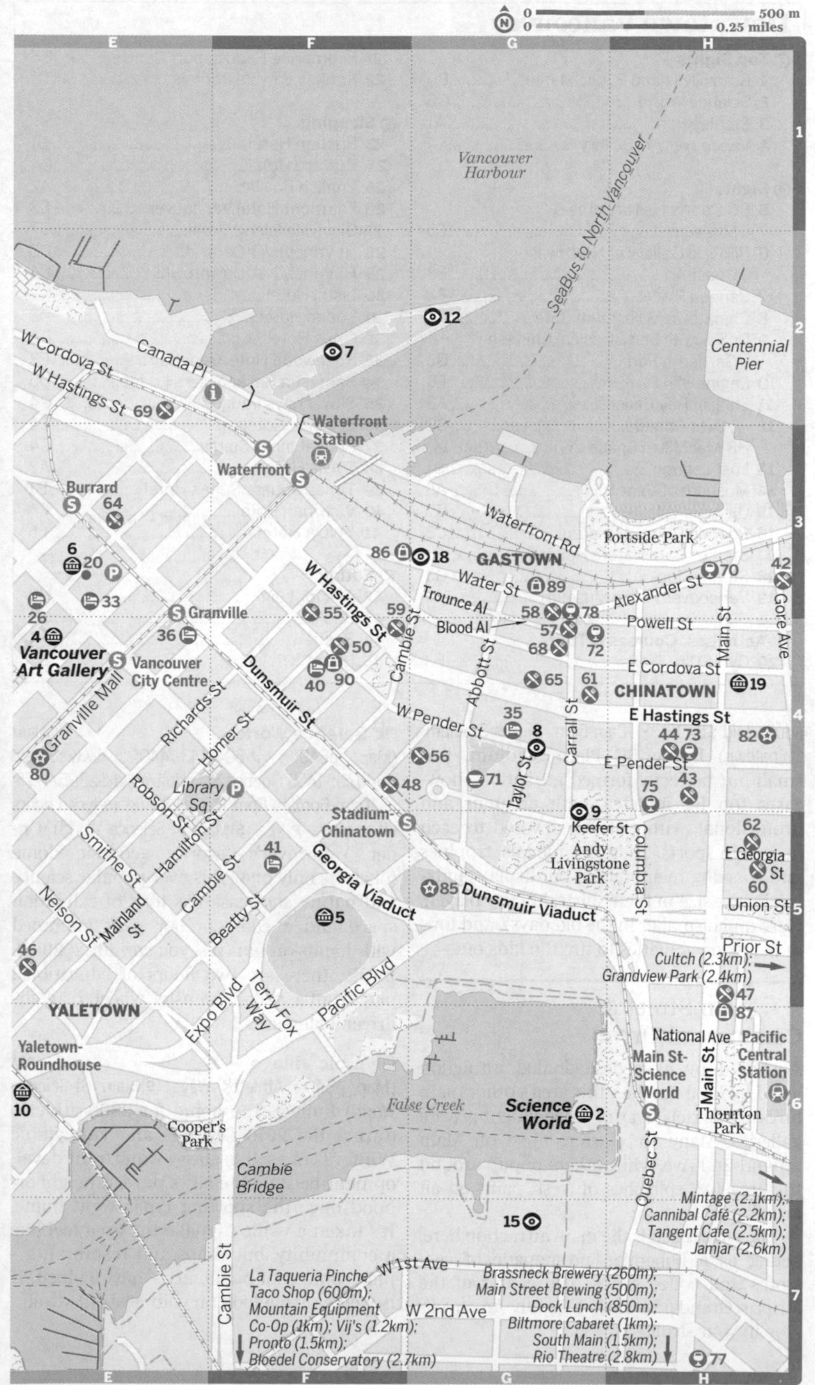
0 500 m
0 0.25 miles
Vancouver Harbour
SeaBus to North Vancouver
Centennial Pier
W Cordova St
Canada Pl
W Hastings St
69
12
7
Waterfront Station
Waterfront
Burrard
64
Waterfront Rd
Portside Park
GASTOWN
86
18
6
20
33
26
W Hastings St
Water St
89
Alexander St
70
42
Gore Ave
Trounce Al
Blood Al
58
78
Powell St
Main St
55
59
Cambie St
57
72
Granville
36
4
Vancouver Art Gallery
Vancouver City Centre
50
40
90
68
65
61
E Cordova St
CHINATOWN
19
Dunsmuir St
Abbott St
Carrall St
Granville Mall
Richards St
W Pender St
35
8
E Hastings St
44
73
82
Homer St
56
Taylor St
E Pender St
80
Library Sq
48
71
75
43
Robson St
Hamilton St
Stadium-Chinatown
9
Keefer St
Columbia St
62
Smithe St
41
Andy Livingstone Park
E Georgia St
60
Cambie St
Georgia Viaduct
85
Dunsmuir Viaduct
Union St
Nelson St
Mainland St
Beatty St
5
Prior St
46
Cultch (2.3km);
Grandview Park (2.4km)
Expo Blvd
Terry Fox Way
Pacific Blvd
47
87
YALETOWN
Yaletown-Roundhouse
National Ave
Main St-Science World
Main St
Pacific Central Station
10
False Creek
Science World
2
Thornton Park
Cooper's Park
Cambie Bridge
Quebec St
Mintage (2.1km);
Cannibal Café (2.2km);
Tangent Cafe (2.5km);
Jamjar (2.6km)
15
Cambie St
W 1st Ave
La Taqueria Pinche Taco Shop (600m);
Mountain Equipment Co-Op (1km); Vij's (1.2km);
Pronto (1.5km);
Bloedel Conservatory (2.7km)
W 2nd Ave
Brassneck Brewery (260m);
Main Street Brewing (500m);
Dock Lunch (850m);
Biltmore Cabaret (1km);
South Main (1.5km);
Rio Theatre (2.8km)
77
BRITISH COLUMBIA

Downtown Vancouver

Top Sights
1 Granville Island Public Market B6
2 Science World G6
3 Stanley Park A1
4 Vancouver Art Gallery E4

Sights
5 BC Sports Hall of Fame & Museum F5
6 Bill Reid Gallery of Northwest Coast Art E3
7 Canada Place F2
8 Chinatown Millennium Gate G4
9 Dr Sun Yat-Sen Classical Chinese Garden & Park G5
10 Engine 374 Pavilion E6
11 English Bay Beach A3
12 FlyOver Canada G2
HR MacMillan Space Centre .... (see 14)
13 Lost Lagoon B1
14 Museum of Vancouver A5
15 Olympic Village G7
16 Roedde House Museum C3
17 Stanley Park Nature House B1
18 Steam Clock G3
19 Vancouver Police Museum H4

Activities, Courses & Tours
20 Cycle City Tours E3
21 Ecomarine Paddlesport Centres B6
22 Spokes Bicycle Rentals C1

Sleeping
23 Buchan Hotel B1
24 Burrard Hotel D4
25 English Bay Inn A2
26 Fairmont Hotel Vancouver E3
27 Granville Island Hotel C7
28 HI Vancouver Central D5
29 HI Vancouver Downtown C4
30 Listel Hotel C2
31 Loden Hotel D2
32 Opus Hotel D6
33 Rosewood Hotel Georgia E3
34 Samesun Backpackers Lodge D5
35 Skwachays Lodge G4
36 St Regis Hotel E4
37 Sunset Inn & Suites C4
38 Sylvia Hotel A2
39 Times Square Suites Hotel B1
40 Victorian Hotel F4
41 YWCA Hotel F5

Eating
42 Ask for Luigi H3
43 Bao Bei H4
44 Bestie H4
45 Bistro 101 .... B7

adult/child $15/12; 10am-5pm; ; Stadium-Chinatown) Inside BC Place Stadium, this small but perfectly formed attraction showcases top BC athletes, both amateur and professional, with galleries devoted to each decade in sports. There are medals, trophies and sporting memorabilia on display (judging by the size of their shirts, hockey players were much smaller in the old days), and tons of hands-on activities to tire the kids out.

Main Street & Commercial Drive

Anchored by a geodesic-domed attraction loved by local families, this area's other main lures are its rich array of independent private galleries. Many are clustered just off Main around 2nd Ave, while others popup around the area like splotches of fresh paint on an artist's palette.

The Drive itself is the main attraction here, acting as a bohemian promenade of cool stores and coffee shops. The center of the strip is Grandview Park, a handy green pitstop in your stroll.

★ Science World MUSEUM

(Map p640; 604-443-7440; www.scienceworld.ca; 1455 Quebec St; adult/child $25.75/17.75; 10am-6pm, to 8pm Thu Jul & Aug, reduced hours off-season; P; Main St-Science World) Under Vancouver's favorite geodesic dome (okay, its only one), this ever-popular science and nature showcase has tons of exhibition space and a cool outdoor park crammed with hands-on fun (yes, you *can* lift 2028kg). Inside, there are two floors of educational play, from a walk-in hamster wheel to an air-driven ball maze.

Olympic Village AREA

(Map p640; Athletes Way; Main St-Science World) Built as the home for 2800 athletes during the 2010 Olympic and Paralympic Winter Games, this glassy waterfront development became the city's newest neighborhood once the sporting types went home. It's taken a while to make the area feel like a community, but shops and restaurants – plus some cool public art – have helped. It is well worth a look on your seawall stroll.

46	Blue Water Cafe	E5
47	Bodega	H5
48	Chambar	F4
49	Fat Badger	C2
50	Finch's	F4
51	Flying Pig	D6
52	Forage	C3
53	Go Fish	B7
54	Guu with Garlic	B2
55	Indigo Age Cafe	F3
56	Jam Cafe	G4
57	L'Abattoir	G4
58	MeeT in Gastown	G3
59	Nuba	F4
60	Phnom Penh	H5
61	Purebread	G4
62	Ramen Butcher	H5
63	Rodney's Oyster House	D6
64	Royal Dinette	E3
65	Save On Meats	G4
66	Sura Korean Cuisine	C2
67	Sushi Itoga	C2
68	Tacofino	G4
	Timber	(see 52)
69	Tractor	E2

Drinking & Nightlife

70	Alibi Room	H3
71	Catfe	G4
72	Diamond	G4
73	Fortune Sound Club	H4
74	Fountainhead Pub	C4
75	Keefer Bar	H4
76	Liberty Distillery	B7
77	Narrow Lounge	H7
78	Six Acres	G3

Entertainment

79	Bard on the Beach	A5
	BC Lions	(see 5)
80	Commodore Ballroom	E4
	FUSE	(see 4)
81	Pacific Cinémathèque	D5
82	Rickshaw Theatre	H4
83	Scotiabank Theatre	D4
84	Vancity Theatre	D5
85	Vancouver Canucks	G5
	Vancouver Whitecaps	(see 5)

Shopping

86	Coastal Peoples Fine Arts Gallery	F3
87	Eastside Flea	H6
88	Gallery of BC Ceramics	B7
89	John Fluevog Shoes	G3
90	Paper Hound	F4

Grandview Park PARK
(Commercial Dr, btwn Charles & William Sts; 20) The Drive's alfresco neighborhood hangout is named after the smashing views peeking between its trees: to the north are the North Shore mountains, while to the west is a cityscape vista of twinkling towers. Teeming with buskers, dreadlocked drummers and impromptu sidewalk sales, the park is a big summertime lure for nearby locals.

Fairview & South Granville

Parks and botanical attractions are the main visitor sights in this area and they're easily accessible via transit along Cambie St and Oak St.

VanDusen Botanical Garden GARDENS
(604-257-8335; www.vandusengarden.org; 5251 Oak St; adult/child Apr-Sep $12.25/5.75, reduced off-season; 9am-8:30pm Jun-Aug, reduced hours off-season; P; 17) The city's favorite green-thumbed tranquility break, this 22-hectare, 255,000-plant idyll is a web of paths weaving through many small, specialized gardens: the **Rhododendron Walk** blazes with color in spring, while the **Korean Pavilion** is a focal point for a fascinating Asian collection. Save time to get lost in the maze and look out for the herons and turtles that call the ponds here home. Check the online calendar for tours and events.

★**Bloedel Conservatory** GARDENS
(604-257-8584; www.vandusengarden.org; Queen Elizabeth Park, 4600 Cambie St; adult/child $6.75/3.25; 9am-8pm Mon-Fri, 10am-8pm Sat & Sun May-Aug, 10am-5pm daily Sep-Apr; P; 15) Cresting the hill in Queen Elizabeth Park, this balmy, triodetic-domed conservatory is an ideal rainy-day warm-up spot, as well as Vancouver's best-value attraction. For little more than the price of a latte, you'll find tropical trees and plants bristling with hundreds of free-flying, bright-plumaged birds. Look for the resident parrots but also keep your eyes peeled for rainbow-hued Gouldian finches, shimmering African superb starlings and maybe even a sparkling Lady Amherst pheasant, snaking through the undergrowth. The attendants might even let you feed the smaller birds from a bowl.

Kitsilano & University of British Columbia

Kitsilano's Vanier Park is home to a triumvirate of museums, with some of the city's best beaches stretching from here along the shoreline to the University of BC. The campus itself has more than enough attractions of its own to justify an alternative day out from the city center.

★Museum of Anthropology MUSEUM
(☎604-822-5087; www.moa.ubc.ca; 6393 NW Marine Dr; adult/child $18/16; ⊙10am-5pm Wed-Sun, to 9pm Tue; P; 🚌99B-Line) Vancouver's best museum is studded with spectacular First Nations totem poles and breathtaking carvings – but it's also teeming with artifacts from cultures around the world, from Polynesian instruments to Cantonese opera costumes. Take one of the free daily **tours** (check ahead for times) for some context, but give yourself at least a couple of hours to explore on your own. It's easy to immerse yourself here.

Museum of Vancouver MUSEUM
(Map p640; ☎604-736-4431; www.museumofvancouver.ca; 1100 Chestnut St; adult/child $15/5; ⊙10am-5pm, to 8pm Thu; P 👪; 🚌22) The MOV has hugely improved in recent years with cool temporary exhibitions and evening events aimed at culturally minded adults. It hasn't changed everything, though. There are still evocative displays on local 1950s pop culture and 1960s hippie counterculture – a reminder that 'Kits' was once the grass-smoking center of Vancouver's flower-power movement – plus a shimmering gallery of vintage neon signs from around the city.

SAVE YOUR DOUGH

The **Vanier Park Explore Pass** costs adult/child $36/30 and covers entry to the Museum of Vancouver, Vancouver Maritime Museum and HR MacMillan Space Centre. It's available at each of the three attractions and can save you around $10 on individual adult entry. You can also save with the **UBC Museums and Gardens Pass**. It costs adult/child $33/28 and includes entry to the Museum of Anthropology, Botanical Garden, Nitobe Memorial Garden and Beatty Biodiversity Museum. Available at any of these attractions, it also includes discounts for the Greenheart TreeWalk, plus deals on campus parking, dining and shopping.

Kitsilano Beach BEACH
(cnr Cornwall Ave & Arbutus St; 🚌22) Facing English Bay, Kits Beach is one of Vancouver's favorite summertime hangouts. The wide, sandy expanse attracts buff Frisbee tossers and giggling volleyball players, and those who just like to preen while catching the rays. The ocean is fine for a dip, though serious swimmers should consider the heated **Kitsilano Pool** (☎604-731-0011; www.vancouverparks.ca; 2305 Cornwall Ave; adult/child $5.86/2.95; ⊙7am-evening mid-Jun–mid-Sep), one of the world's largest outdoor saltwater pools.

UBC Botanical Garden GARDENS
(www.botanicalgarden.ubc.ca; 6804 SW Marine Dr; adult/child $9/5; ⊙9:30am-4:30pm, to 8pm Thu mid-Mar–Oct, 9:30am-4pm Nov–mid-Mar; P; 🚌99 B-Line, then C20) You'll find a giant collection of rhododendrons, a fascinating apothecary plot and a winter green space of off-season bloomers in this 28-hectare complex of themed gardens. Save time for the attraction's **Greenheart TreeWalk** (☎604-822-4208; adult/child $20/10; ⊙10am-4:30pm daily , to 7:30pm Thu Apr-Oct; 👪), which lifts visitors 17m above the forest floor on a 308m guided eco tour. A combined botanical garden and walkway ticket costs $20.

Beaty Biodiversity Museum MUSEUM
(☎604-827-4955; www.beatymuseum.ubc.ca; 2212 Main Mall; adult/child $12/10; ⊙10am-5pm Tue-Sun; 👪; 🚌99B-Line) UBC's newest museum is also its most family-friendly. Showcasing two million natural history specimens that have never before been available for public viewing, the museum features fossil, fish and herbarium displays. The highlight is the 25m blue whale skeleton, artfully displayed in the museum's two-story main entrance, plus the first display case, which is crammed with tooth-and-claw taxidermy. Check the schedule for free tours and kids' activities.

HR MacMillan Space Centre MUSEUM
(Map p640; ☎604-738-7827; www.spacecentre.ca; 1100 Chestnut St; adult/child $18/13; ⊙10am-5pm Jul-Aug, 10am-3pm Mon-Fri, 10am-5pm Sat & noon-5pm Sun Sep-Jun; P 👪; 🚌22) Popular with schoolkids – expect to have to elbow them out of the way to push the flashing buttons – this slightly dated science center illuminates the world of space. There's plenty of fun to be had battling aliens, designing spacecraft

or strapping yourself in for a simulator ride to Mars – as well as with movie presentations on all manner of spacey themes.

Vancouver Maritime Museum MUSEUM
(www.vancouvermaritimemuseum.com; 1905 Ogden Ave; adult/child $11/8.50; ⏲10am-5pm, to 8pm Thu, reduced hours off-season; P; 🚌22) Combining dozens of intricate models, detailed re-created ship sections and some historic boats, the prize exhibit in this waterfront A-frame museum is the *St Roch*, a 1928 Royal Canadian Mounted Police Arctic patrol vessel that was the first to navigate the legendary Northwest Passage in both directions. On a budget? Thursday entry (after 5pm) is by donation.

North Shore

The North Shore is home to some of Metro Vancouver's favorite outdoor attractions. But North Van, in particular, is also starting to buzz as an urban visitor lure, especially at the shoreline end of Lonsdale Ave. Save some time to wander along the waterfront here, where gritty shipyard spaces are being reclaimed for market halls and public art. This is also the home of the striking new **Polygon Gallery**, which was under construction during our visit; see www.presentationhousegallery.org for updates.

Grouse Mountain OUTDOORS
(☎604-980-9311; www.grousemountain.com; 6400 Nancy Greene Way, North Vancouver; Skyride adult/child $44/15; ⏲9am-10pm; P 👪; 🚌236) The self-proclaimed 'Peak of Vancouver,' this mountaintop playground offers smashing views of downtown glittering in the water below. In summer, Skyride gondola tickets include access to lumberjack shows, alpine hiking, bird of prey displays and a grizzly bear refuge. Pay extra for **ziplining** and Eye of the Wind, a 20-story, elevator-accessed turbine tower with a panoramic viewing pod that will have your camera itching for action.

Capilano Suspension Bridge Park PARK
(☎604-985-7474; www.capbridge.com; 3735 Capilano Rd, North Vancouver; adult/child $40/12, reduced off-season; ⏲8:30am-8pm Jun-Aug, reduced off-season; P 👪; 🚌236) As you walk gingerly onto one of the world's longest (140m) and highest (70m) suspension bridges, swaying gently over the roiling Capilano Canyon, remember that its thick steel cables are embedded in concrete. That should steady your feet – unless there are teenagers stamping across. Added park attractions include a glass-bottomed **cliffside walkway** and an elevated **canopy trail** through the trees.

Maplewood Farm FARM
(☎604-929-5610; www.maplewoodfarm.bc.ca; 405 Seymour River Pl, North Vancouver; adult/child $7.80/4.70; ⏲10am-4pm Apr-Oct, closed Mon Nov-Mar; 👪; 🚌239 from Lonsdale Quay, then C15) This popular farmyard attraction includes plenty of hands-on displays, plus more than 200 birds and domestic animals. Your wide-eyed kids can pet some critters, watch the milking demonstration and feed some squawking, ever-hungry ducks and chickens. The highlight is the daily round-up (3:30pm), when hungry critters streak back into their barn for dinner.

Mt Seymour Provincial Park OUTDOORS
(www.bcparks.ca; 1700 Mt Seymour Rd, North Vancouver; ⏲dawn-dusk) A popular rustic retreat from the downtown clamor, this giant, tree-lined park is suffused with summertime **hiking trails** that suit walkers of most abilities (the easiest path is the 2km Goldie Lake Trail). Many trails wind past lakes and centuries-old Douglas firs. This is also one of the city's main winter playgrounds.

RESOURCES

Destination British Columbia (www.hellobc.com) Official trip-planning website for the region.

BC Explorer (www.bcexplorer.com) Inspirational Instagram photo feed, curated by Destination British Columbia.

Mountain Biking BC (www.mountainbikingbc.ca) Introduction to the province's amazing off-road cycling scene.

Van Dop Arts & Cultural Guide (www.art-bc.com) Art-scene and gallery-location information for BC.

British Columbia Beer Guide (www.bcbeer.ca) Discover beers and breweries to try around the region.

Wines of British Columbia (www.winebc.com) Handy site exploring BC's wine regions.

Lonely Planet (www.lonelyplanet.com/canada/british-columbia) Destination information, hotel bookings, traveler forum and more.

LOCAL KNOWLEDGE

IT'S OFFICIAL

BC's provincial bird is the Steller's jay; its official mammal is the Kermode bear, a black bear with white fur.

The park is a great spot for **mountain biking** and has many dedicated trails. It's around 30 minutes from downtown Vancouver by car; drivers can take Hwy 1 to the Mt Seymour Parkway (near the Second Narrows Bridge) and follow it east to Mt Seymour Rd.

Lynn Canyon Park PARK
(www.lynncanyon.ca; Park Rd, North Vancouver; 7am-9pm; ; 229) Amid a dense bristling of ancient trees, the main feature of this popular park is its **suspension bridge**, a free alternative to Capilano. Not quite as big as its tourist-magnet rival, it nevertheless provokes the same jelly-legged reaction as you sway over the river that runs 50m below – and it's always far less crowded. **Hiking trails**, swimming areas and picnic spots will keep you busy here as well.

The park's **Ecology Centre** (www.lynncanyonecologycentre.ca; 3663 Park Rd, North Vancouver; entry by suggested $2 donation; 10am-5pm Jun-Sep, 10am-5pm Mon-Fri & noon-4pm Sat & Sun Oct-May; ; 227) houses interesting displays, including dioramas and video presentations, on the area's rich biodiversity. It stages talks and events for kids, especially in summer.

Activities

Vancouver's variety of outdoorsy activities is a huge hook: you can ski in the morning and hit the beach in the afternoon; hike or bike scenic forests; windsurf along the coastline; or kayak to your heart's content – and it will be content, with grand mountain views as your backdrop. There's also a full menu of spectator sports to catch here.

Ecomarine Paddlesport Centres KAYAKING
(Map p640; 604-689-7575; www.ecomarine.com; 1668 Duranleau St; kayak/paddleboard rental per 2hrs $39/29; 9am-9pm Jun & Jul, to 8pm Aug, 10am-6pm Sep-May; 50) Headquartered on Granville Island, the friendly folks at Ecomarine offer kayak and stand-up paddle board (SUP) rentals, as well as popular guided tours around the area. At the center's **Jericho Beach branch** (1300 Discovery St, Jericho Sailing Centre; 10am-dusk Mon-Fri, 9am-dusk Jun-Aug; 4), events and seminars are organized where you can rub shoulders with local paddle nuts. Fancy exploring further? They also arrange multiday tours around some of BC's most magical marine regions.

Spokes Bicycle Rentals CYCLING
(Map p640; 604-688-5141; www.spokesbicyclerentals.com; 1798 W Georgia St; adult bicycle rental per hour/day from $6.67/26.67; 8am-9pm, reduced hours off-season; 5) On the corner of W Georgia and Denman Sts, this is the biggest of the bike shops servicing the Stanley Park cycling trade. It can kit you and your family out with all manner of bikes, from cruisers to kiddie one-speeds. Ask for tips on riding the Seawall; it extends far beyond Stanley Park.

Grouse Mountain SNOW SPORTS
(604-980-9311; www.grousemountain.com; 6400 Nancy Greene Way, North Vancouver; winter adult/child $58/25; 9am-10pm mid-Nov–mid-Apr; ; 236) Vancouver's favorite winter hangout, family-friendly Grouse offers 26 ski and snowboard runs (including 14 night runs). There are classes and lessons available for beginners and beyond, and the area's forested snowshoe trails are magical. There are also a couple of dining options if you just want to relax and watch the snow with hot chocolate in hand.

Cypress Mountain SNOW SPORTS
(604-926-5612; www.cypressmountain.com; Cypress Bowl Rd, West Vancouver; lift ticket adult/youth/child $71/57/38; 9am-10pm mid-Dec–Mar, 9am-4pm mid-Nov–mid-Dec & Apr) Around 8km north of West Van via Hwy 99, Cypress Provincial Park transforms into Cypress Mountain resort in winter, attracting well-insulated locals with its 53 runs, 11km of snowshoe trails, cross-country ski access and a family-friendly six-chute snowtubing course. Upgraded for the 2010 Winter Olympics, the resort's newer facilities include an expanded lodge and upgrades to several runs.

Tours

★ **Forbidden Vancouver** WALKING
(604-227-7570; www.forbiddenvancouver.ca; adult/senior/student $22/19/19) This quirky company offers highly entertaining tours: a delve into Prohibition-era Vancouver and a poke around the seedy underbelly of historic Gastown. Not recommended for kids. Every few months, it also offers an excellent behind-the-scenes history tour of the infamous

Penthouse nightclub, a strip joint that has a rich, somewhat glamorous and sometimes seedy past. Check the website for details.

Talaysay Tours WALKING
(☎604-628-8555; www.talaysay.com) Providing a range of authentic First Nations–led tours, including a signature Stanley Park walking option, this operator can also arrange guided kayak jaunts around the region.

Sewell's Marina BOATING
(☎604-921-3474; www.sewellsmarina.com; 6409 Bay St, Horseshoe Bay; adult/child $87/57; ⏲Apr-Oct; ; 250) West Vancouver's Horseshoe Bay is the departure point for Sewell's two-hour marine-wildlife-watching boat tours. Orcas are always a highlight but even if they're not around, you'll almost certainly spot harbor seals lolling on the rocks and pretending to ignore you. Seabirds and bald eagles are also big stars of the show.

Cycle City Tours TOURS
(Map p640; ☎604-618-8626; www.cyclevancouver.com; 648 Hornby St; tours from $59, bicycle rental per hour/day $8.50/34; ⏲9am-6pm, reduced hours in winter; S Burrard) Striped with an ever-increasing number of dedicated bike lanes, Vancouver is a good city for two-wheeled exploring. But if you're not great at navigating, consider a guided tour with this friendly operator. If you're a beer fan, aim for the Craft Beer Tour ($90), with nine tasty samples included. Alternatively, go it alone with a rental; there's a bike lane right outside.

Festivals & Events

Chinese New Year CULTURAL
(www.vancouver-chinatown.com; ⏲Jan or Feb) Festive kaleidoscope of dancing, parades and great food held in January or February.

Winterruption CULTURAL
(www.granvilleisland.com; ⏲mid-Feb) Granville Island brushes off the winter blues with tours, music and performances.

Vancouver International Wine Festival WINE
(www.vanwinefest.ca; ⏲late Feb) The city's oldest and best annual wine celebration, with a different regional focus every year.

Vancouver Craft Beer Week BEER
(www.vancouvercraftbeerweek.com; ⏲late May) A taste-tripping showcase for BC's amazing craft beer scene, with dozens of events around the city.

Vancouver International Children's Festival PERFORMING ARTS
(www.childrensfestival.ca; ⏲late May;) Storytelling, performance and activities around Granville island.

Vancouver International Jazz Festival MUSIC
(www.coastaljazz.ca; ⏲Jun & Jul) City-wide cornucopia of superstar shows and free outdoor events from mid-June.

Celebration of Light FIREWORKS
(www.hondacelebrationoflight.com; ⏲late Jul) FREE Three-night international fireworks extravaganza in English Bay.

Pride Week CARNIVAL, PARADE
(www.vancouverpride.ca; ⏲late Jul) Parties, concerts and fashion shows, as well as the city's biggest street parade.

Pacific National Exhibition CULTURAL
(www.pne.ca; Hastings Park; ⏲mid-Aug–Sep;) Family-friendly shows, music concerts and fairground fun (plus lots of naughty things to eat).

Vancouver International Film Festival FILM
(www.viff.org; ⏲late Sep) Popular two-week showcase of Canadian and international movies. Book ahead; tickets are hot items here.

Eastside Culture Crawl ART
(www.culturecrawl.ca; ⏲mid-Nov) Vancouver's best visual-arts festival: a four-day gallery and studio open house with hundreds of participants.

DON'T MISS

MAIN'S BEST FEST

If you make it to June's annual **Car Free Day** (www.carfreevancouver.org; ⏲mid-Jun) – staged along Main St, south of the Broadway intersection, for at least 30 blocks – you'll realize there's much more diversity to this area than you thought. Taking over the streets for this family-friendly community fest are live music, craft stalls, steaming food stands and a highly convivial atmosphere that makes for a party-like afternoon with the locals. And if you miss it? Consider checking out September's **Autumn Shift Festival** as well. It's just as much fun and has a sustainability theme.

FAMILY ATTRACTIONS

Vancouver has a wide of range of inviting sights to keep your kids happy, from a popular **aquarium** (p636) to an excellent **science center** (p642) – both of which are easily worth half-day visits. And if they want to get close to some local critters, there's a great city **farm** (p645) on the North Shore. Wherever you take them, be sure to go by train: the SkyTrain system here is popular with younger children, especially if they head to the front and pretend to drive. They can compare the experience to a more traditional journey via a ride on Stanley Park's **miniature train** (p636).

Santa Claus Parade CHRISTMAS
(www.rogerssantaclausparade.com; early Dec;) The city's main Christmas procession, centered on West Georgia St, complete with the great man himself.

Sleeping

Metro Vancouver is home to more than 25,000 hotel, B&B and hostel rooms – many in or around the downtown core. The city is packed with visitors in summer, so book ahead...unless you fancy sleeping against a damp log in Stanley Park. Rates peak in July and August, but there are good spring and fall deals, when you can also expect some accompanying 'Wet Coast' rainfall.

Downtown & West End

Samesun Backpackers Lodge HOSTEL $
(Map p640; 604-682-8226; www.samesun.com; 1018 Granville St; dm/r incl breakfast $35/100; ; 10) Vancouver's party hostel, the popular Samesun is right on the city's nightlife strip. Ask for a back room if you fancy a few hours of sleep or just head down to the large on-site bar (provocatively called the Beaver) to join the beery throng. Dorms are comfortably small, and there's a large kitchen. Continental breakfast is included.

HI Vancouver Central HOSTEL $
(Map p640; 604-685-5335; www.hihostels.ca/vancouver; 1025 Granville St; dm/r incl breakfast $40/100; ; 10) On the Granville Strip, this warren-like hostel is more of a party joint than its **HI Downtown** (Map p640; 604-684-4565; 1114 Burnaby St; dm/r incl breakfast $40/100; ; 6) sibling. Some of the benefits of its past hotel incarnation remain, including air-conditioning and small rooms, some of which are now private, with the rest converted to dorm rooms with up to four beds. There are dozens of two-bed dorms (some en suite) for privacy fans.

★ **St Regis Hotel** BOUTIQUE HOTEL $$
(Map p640; 604-681-1135; www.stregishotel.com; 602 Dunsmuir St; d incl breakfast $299; ; S Granville) Transformed in recent years, this is now an art-lined boutique sleepover in a 1913 heritage shell. Befitting its age, almost all the rooms seem to be a different size, and they exhibit a loungey élan with leather-look wallpaper, earth-toned bedspreads, flatscreen TVs and multimedia hubs. Rates include value-added flourishes like cooked breakfasts, access to the nearby gym and free international phone calling.

Times Square Suites Hotel APARTMENT $$
(Map p640; 604-684-2223; www.timessquaresuites.com; 1821 Robson St; d $225; P; 5) Superbly located a short walk from Stanley Park, this West End hidden gem (even the entrance can be hard to spot) is the perfect apartment-style Vancouver sleepover. Rooms are mostly one-bedroom suites and are spacious, with tubs, laundry facilities, full kitchens and well-maintained (if slightly 1980s) decor. Rates include nearby gym access.

Burrard Hotel HOTEL $$
(Map p640; 604-681-2331; www.theburrard.com; 1100 Burrard St; d from $229; P; 22) A groovy makeover has transformed this 1950s downtown motel into a knowingly cool sleepover with a tongue-in-cheek retro-cool feel. The mostly quite compact rooms have been spruced up with mod flourishes and contemporary amenities such as fridges, flatscreens and Nespresso coffee machines. But not everything has changed: the hidden interior courtyard of Florida-style palm trees is *très* cool.

Victorian Hotel HOTEL $$
(Map p640; 604-681-6369; www.victorianhotel.ca; 514 Homer St; d incl breakfast from $145; ; S Granville) The high-ceilinged rooms at this popular Euro-style, heritage-building hotel combine glossy hardwood floors, a sprinkling of antiques, an occasional bay window and plenty of historical charm. The best rooms are in the renovated extension, where raindrop showers, marble bathroom floors and flatscreen TVs add a slice of luxe. Rates

include continental breakfast, and rooms are provided with fans in summer.

Buchan Hotel HOTEL $$

(Map p640; ☎604-685-5354; www.buchanhotel.com; 1906 Haro St; d with/without bathroom $149/109; P ⊖ @ ≋; 🚌5) The great-value 1926-built Buchan has bags of charm and is just steps from Stanley Park. Along corridors lined with prints of yesteryear Vancouver, its pension-style budget rooms – most with shared bathrooms – are clean, cozy and well maintained, although some furnishings have seen better days. The pricier rooms are correspondingly prettier, while the eastside rooms are brighter. The front desk is friendly.

Sylvia Hotel HOTEL $$

(Map p640; ☎604-681-9321; www.sylviahotel.com; 1154 Gilford St; d $199; P ⊖ ≋ 🐾; 🚌5) This ivy-covered 1912 charmer enjoys a prime location overlooking English Bay. Generations of guests keep coming back – many requesting the same room every year – for a dollop of old-world ambience, plus a side order of first-name service. The rooms, some with older furnishings, have a wide array of comfortable configurations, but the best are the large suites, which have kitchens and waterfront views.

Sunset Inn & Suites HOTEL $$

(Map p640; ☎604-688-2474; www.sunsetinn.com; 1111 Burnaby St; d incl breakfast $220; P ❄ @ ≋; 🚌6) A good-value cut above most of Vancouver's self-catering suite hotels, the popular Sunset Inn offers larger-than-average rooms with full kitchens. Each has a balcony, and some – particularly those on south-facing higher floors – have partial views of English Bay. Rates include continental breakfast and, rare for Vancouver, gratis parking. The attentive staff is among the best in the city.

Listel Hotel BOUTIQUE HOTEL $$

(Map p640; ☎604-684-8461; www.thelistelhotel.com; 1300 Robson St; d $265; ⊖ ❄ @ ≋; 🚌5) A sophisticated, self-described 'art hotel,' the Listel attracts grown-ups through its on-site installations and package deals with local galleries. Many rooms display original artworks and all have a relaxing, mood-lit West Coast feel. Artsy types should check out the lobby sculptures for selfie opportunities, while the property's on-site bar and restaurant are arguably the best hotel drink and dine options in the city.

Loden Hotel BOUTIQUE HOTEL $$$

(Map p640; ☎604-669-5060; www.theloden.com; 1177 Melville St; d $449; P ❄ @ ≋ 🐾; M Burrard) The stylish Loden is the real designer deal, and one of the first boutique properties in years to give Yaletown's Opus (p650) a run for its money. The chic, mocha-hued rooms have a contemporary feel, with luxe accoutrements such as marble-lined bathrooms and those oh-so-civilized heated floors. Service is top-notch; try the lobby resto-bar as well as the complimentary London taxicab limo service.

Rosewood Hotel Georgia HOTEL $$$

(Map p640; ☎604-682-5566; www.rosewoodhotels.com; 801 W Georgia St; d $520; ⊖ ❄ @ ≋ ≈ 🐾; S Vancouver City Centre) Vancouver's current 'It' hotel underwent a spectacular renovation a few years back that brought the 1927-built landmark back to its golden-age glory. Despite the abstract modern art lining its public areas, the hotel's rooms take a classic, elegant approach with warming earth and coffee tones, pampering treats such as deep soaker tubs and (in some rooms) sparkling downtown cityscape views.

Fairmont Hotel Vancouver HOTEL $$$

(Map p640; ☎604-684-3131; www.fairmont.com/hotelvancouver; 900 W Georgia St; d $399; P ❄ @ ≋ ≈ 🐾; S Vancouver City Centre) Opened in 1939 by visiting UK royals, this sparkling grand dame is a Vancouver landmark. Despite the provenance, the hotel carefully balances comfort with elegance: the lobby is bedecked with crystal chandeliers but the rooms have an understated business-hotel feel. If you have the budget, check in to the Gold Floor for a raft of pampering extras.

English Bay Inn B&B $$$

(Map p640; ☎604-683-8002; www.englishbayinn.com; 1968 Comox St; d incl breakfast from $260; P ⊖ ≋; 🚌6) Each of the six antique-lined rooms in this Tudoresque B&B near Stanley Park has a private bathroom, and some have sumptuous four-poster beds. You'll think you've arrived in Victoria, BC's determinedly Olde English capital, by mistake. Rates include a lovely three-course breakfast – arrive in the dining room early for the alcove table. There's also a canopy-shaded garden for hanging out in summer.

Gastown & Chinatown

★Skwachays Lodge BOUTIQUE HOTEL $$
(Map p640; ☎604-687-3589; www.skwachays.com; 29 W Pender St; d from $220; ❄📶; Ⓢ Stadium-Chinatown) The 18 rooms at this First Nations art hotel include the captivating Forest Spirits Suite, with floor-to-ceiling birch branches, and the sleek Longhouse Suite, with its illuminated metalwork frieze. Deluxe trappings, from plasma TVs to eco-friendly toiletries, are standard and there's an on-site gallery for purchasing one-of-a-kind artworks to take home.

Yaletown & Granville Island

★YWCA Hotel BUDGET HOTEL $
(Map p640; ☎604-895-5830; www.ywcahotel.com; 733 Beatty St; s/d/tr without bath $93/138/160; P⊖❄@📶; Ⓢ Stadium-Chinatown) A good-value, well-located option offering nicely maintained (if spartan) rooms of the student accommodation variety. There's a wide range of configurations, from singles to five-bed rooms, plus shared, semi private or private bathrooms. Each room has a minifridge and guests can use the three large communal kitchens. Rates include access to the YWCA Health & Fitness Centre, a 10-minute walk away.

Opus Hotel BOUTIQUE HOTEL $$$
(Map p640; ☎604-642-6787; www.opushotel.com; 322 Davie St; d $390; P❄📶🐾; Ⓢ Yaletown-Roundhouse) The Opus kick-started Vancouver's boutique hotel scene and, with regular revamps, it's remained one of the city's top sleepover options. The designer rooms have contemporary-chic interiors with bold colors, mod furnishings and feng-shui bed placements, while many of the luxe bathrooms have clear windows overlooking the streets (visiting exhibitionists take note).

Granville Island Hotel BOUTIQUE HOTEL $$$
(Map p640; ☎604-683-7373; www.granvilleislandhotel.com; 1253 Johnston St; d $375; P⊖@📶🐾; 🚌50) This gracious boutique property hugs Granville Island's quiet southeastern tip, enjoying tranquil views across False Creek to Yaletown's mirrored towers. You'll be a stroll from the Public Market, with shopping and theater options on your doorstep. Rooms have a West Coast feel with some exposed wood flourishes. There's also a rooftop Jacuzzi, while the on-site brewpub-restaurant has one of the city's best patios.

Kitsilano & University of British Columbia

HI Vancouver Jericho Beach HOSTEL $
(☎604-224-3208; www.hihostels.ca/vancouver; 1515 Discovery St; dm/d $34/80; ⊙May-Oct; P@📶; 🚌4) One of Canada's largest hostels looks like a Victorian hospital but has a scenic, near-the-beach location. Basic rooms make this the least palatial Vancouver HI hostel, but it has a large kitchen, bike rentals and a recently revamped, licensed cafe. Dorms are also larger here. Book ahead for the popular, budget-hotel-style private rooms, which come in both shared and private bathroom options.

Corkscrew Inn B&B $$
(☎604-733-7276; www.corkscrewinn.com; 2735 W 2nd Ave; d incl breakfast from $215; P📶; 🚌4) This immaculate, gable-roofed property appears to have a drinking problem: it houses a little museum, available only to guests, that's lined with quirky corkscrews and antique vineyard tools. Aside from the boozy paraphernalia, this lovely century-old Craftsman home has five artsy, wood-floored rooms (we like the Art Deco room) and is just a short walk from the beach. Sumptuous breakfast included.

Eating

Vancouver has an amazing array of generally great-value dine-out options: top-drawer sushi joints, clamorous Chinese restaurants, inviting indie eateries, tempting food trucks and a fresh-picked farm-to-table scene are all on the menu. You don't have to be a local to indulge: just follow your tastebuds and dinner will become the most talked-about highlight of your Vancouver visit.

Downtown & West End

Templeton DINER $$
(☎604-685-4612; www.thetempleton.ca; 1087 Granville St; mains $10-16; ⊙9am-11pm Mon-Wed, to 1am Thu-Sun; 🌶👪; 🚌10) A chrome-and-vinyl '50s-look diner with a twist, Templeton serves up plus-sized organic burgers, addictive fries, vegetarian quesadillas and perhaps the best hangover cure in town – the 'Big Ass Breakfast.' Sadly, the mini jukeboxes on the tables don't work, but you can console yourself with a waistline-busting chocolate ice-cream float. Avoid weekend peak times or you'll be queuing for ages.

Finch's CAFE $

(Map p640; ☎604-899-4040; www.finchteahouse.com; 353 W Pender St; mains $5-10; ⏲9am-5pm Mon-Fri, 11am-4pm Sat; ✎; 🚌4) For a coveted seat at one of the dinged old tables, arrive off-peak at this sunny corner cafe that has a 'granny-chic' look combining creaky wooden floors and junk-shop bric-a-brac. You'll be joining in-the-know hipsters and creative types who've been calling this their local for years. They come mainly for the freshly prepared baguette sandwiches (pear, Brie, prosciutto and roasted walnuts recommended).

Tractor CANADIAN $

(Map p640; ☎604-979-0550; www.tractorfoods.com; Marine Building, 335 Burrard St; ⏲7am-9:30pm Mon-Fri, 11am-9:30pm Sat & Sun; ✎; S Waterfront) A healthy fast-food cafeteria tucked into the base of the Marine Building. Step up to the counter and choose from 10 or so hearty mixed salads, then add a half or whole grilled sandwich. Wholesome and satisfying, housemade soups and stews are also available but make sure you add a lemonade as well – there's usually a tempting flavor or two.

Sushi Itoga JAPANESE $

(Map p640; ☎604-687-2422; www.itoga.com; 1686 Robson St; sushi combos $8-18; ⏲11:30am-2pm & 5-8pm Mon-Sat, 5-8pm Sun; 🚌5) You'll be rubbing shoulders with other diners at the large communal dining table here, one of the best spots in town for a superfresh sushi feast in a casual setting. Check the ever-changing blackboard showing what's available and then tuck into expertly prepared and well-priced shareable platters of all your fave *nigiri*, *maki* and sashimi treats. Udon dishes are also available.

★**Forage** CANADIAN $$

(Map p640; ☎604-661-1400; www.foragevancouver.com; 1300 Robson St; mains $16-29; ⏲6:30-10am & 5pm-midnight Mon-Fri, 7am-2pm & 5pm-midnight Sat & Sun; 🚌5) A champion of the local farm-to-table scene, this sustainability-hugging restaurant is the perfect way to sample the flavors of the region. Brunch has become a firm local favorite (turkey-sausage hash recommended), and for dinner the idea is to sample an array of tasting plates. The menu is innovative and highly seasonal, but look out for the seafood chowder with quail's egg.

BEST VANCOUVER FOOD BLOGS

Sherman's Food Adventures (www.shermansfoodadventures.com)

Vancouver Foodster (www.vancouverfoodster.com)

Food Gays (www.foodgays.com)

Van Foodies (www.vanfoodies.com)

Follow Me Foodie (www.followmefoodie.com)

★**Guu with Garlic** JAPANESE $$

(Map p640; ☎604-685-8678; www.guu-izakaya.com; 1698 Robson St; small plates $4-9, mains $8-16; ⏲11:30am-2:30pm & 5:30pm-12:30am Mon-Sat, 11:30am-2:30pm & 5:30pm-midnight Sun; 🚌5) One of the Vancouver's best *izakayas*, this welcoming, wood-lined joint is a cultural immersion. Hotpots and noodle bowls are available but it's best to experiment with some Japanese bar tapas, including black cod with miso mayo, deep-fried egg and pumpkin balls or finger-lickin' *tori-karaage* fried chicken. Garlic is liberally used in most dishes. It's best to arrive before opening time for a seat.

Royal Dinette INTERNATIONAL $$

(Map p640; ☎604-974-8077; www.royaldinette.ca; 905 Dunsmuir St; mains $15-34; ⏲11:30am-2pm & 5-10pm; S Burrard) Seasonal and regional are the foundations of this smashing downtown restaurant, but add friendly, unpretentious service and it becomes a winner. The lunchtime two- or three-course prix fixe ($30 or $35) is a good way to try the place out, but dinner is all about a lingering opportunity to savor international influences combined with local ingredients: the squid-ink spaghetti is our favorite.

Jam Cafe BREAKFAST $$

(Map p640; ☎778-379-1992; www.jamcafes.com; 556 Beatty St; mains $11-16; ⏲8am-3pm; 📶✎; S Stadium-Chinatown) The Vancouver outpost of Victoria's wildly popular breakfast and brunch superstar hit the ground running soon after opening here. It's typically packed, so you'll have to wait for a table (reservations not accepted) unless you're smart enough to dine very off-peak. You'll find a white-walled room studded with Canadian knick-knacks and a huge array of satisfying options, from chicken and waffles to red-velvet pancakes.

Timber PUB FOOD $$

(Map p640; ☎604-661-2166; www.timbervancouver.com; 1300 Robson St; mains $10-19; ⏰11am-1pm Mon-Thu, 10am-1pm Fri & Sat, 10am-midnight Sun; 🚌5) One of two good dining options attached to the Listel Hotel, this resto-pub combines a great BC-focused craft beer menu along with a tongue-in-cheek array of Canadian comfort food. Snap some photos with the taxidermied beaver and Canada goose, then dive into bison burgers, ketchup-flavored potato chips (Canada's fave flavor) and deep-fried cheese curds. It's like a crash course in calorific Canadian grub.

Sura Korean Cuisine KOREAN $$

(Map p640; ☎604-687-7872; www.surakoreancuisine.com; 1518 Robson St; mains $10-20; ⏰11am-4pm & 5-10:30pm; P; 🚌5) From the 1400-block of Robson St on and around onto Denman and Davie Sts, you'll find a smorgasbord of authentic Korean and Japanese eateries. A cut above its ESL-student-luring siblings, slick Sura offers awesome Korean comfort dishes in a cosy, bistro-like setting. Try the spicy beef soup, kimchi pancakes and excellent *bibimbap*: beef, veggies and a still-cooking egg in a hot stone bowl.

Indigo Age Cafe VEGAN $$

(Map p640; ☎604-622-1797; www.indigoagecafe.com; 436 Richards St; mains $10-13; ⏰10am-8pm Mon-Thu, to 9pm Fri & Sat; 📶✏; 🚌14) 🌿 A cozy subterranean spot beloved of in-the-know Vancouver vegans and raw-food fans. Snag a log-slice table here and dive into a hearty array of house-made dishes. Pierogies, cabbage rolls and pizza have their fans here but we recommend the delicious zucchini pasta with Portobello mushroom 'steak.'

Fat Badger BRITISH $$$

(Map p640; ☎604-336-5577; www.fatbadger.ca; 1616 Alberni St; mains $20-38; ⏰5-11pm Tue-Sun; 🚌5) A gourmet reinvention of a British pub in a gabled heritage-listed building, the atmospheric dark-wood interior here is the ideal setting for hunkering in a corner on a rainy night and stuffing yourself with Scotch eggs, lamb-and-Guinness pie and the kind of sticky toffee pudding that might make you propose marriage to your dessert (again).

Chambar EUROPEAN $$$

(Map p640; ☎604-879-7119; www.chambar.com; 562 Beatty St; mains $27-34; ⏰8am-3pm & 5-10pm; P; S Stadium-Chinatown) This giant, brick-lined cave is a great place for a romantic night out. The sophisticated Belgian-esque menu includes perfectly delectable *moules et frites* (mussels and fries) and a braised lamb shank with figs that's a local dining legend. An impressive wine and cocktail list (try a blue-fig martini) is also coupled with a great Belgian beer menu dripping with *tripels* and *lambics*.

Gastown & Chinatown

★Tacofino MEXICAN $

(Map p640; ☎604-899-7907; www.tacofino.com; 15 W Cordova St; tacos $6-12; 🚌14) Food-truck favorite Tacofino made an instant splash with this huge, handsome dining room (think stylish geometric-patterned floors and hive-like lampshades). The simple menu focuses on a handful of taco options (six at lunch, more at dinner), plus nachos, soups and a boozy selection of beer, agave and naughty tequila flights. Fish tacos are the top seller, but we love the super-tender lamb *birria* (stew).

★Purebread BAKERY

(Map p640; ☎604-563-8060; www.purebread.ca; 159 W Hastings St; baked goods $3-6; ⏰8:30am-5:30pm; 📶; 🚌14) When Whistler's favorite bakery opened here, salivating Vancouverites began flocking in en masse. Expect to stand slack-jawed in front of the glass panels as you try to choose from a cornucopia of cakes, pastries and bars. Cake-wise, we love the coconut buttermilk loaf, but make sure you also pick up a crack bar or salted caramel bar to go (or preferably both).

Bestie GERMAN

(Map p640; ☎604-620-1175; www.bestie.ca; 105 E Pender St; mains $4-11; ⏰11:30am-10pm Sun-Thu, to midnight Fri & Sat; 📶; 🚌3) Like a food truck with a permanent home, this white-walled hole-in-the-wall specializes in Berlin-style currywursts – hearty sausages slathered in curry sauce, served with crunchy fries. It's popular with passing hipsters, so arrive off-peak for a chance of snagging the little cubby-hole window table, the best in the house. There's always a small but well curated array of local craft beers to add to the fun.

FOOD-TRUCK FRENZY

Keen to emulate the legendary street-food scenes of Portland and Austin, Vancouver jumped on the kitchen-equipped bandwagon in 2011, launching a pilot scheme with 17 food carts. Things took off quickly and there are now dozens dotted around the city, serving everything from halibut tacos to Korean sliders, pulled-pork sandwiches to French crepes. Prices are typically $8-12 per entree.

While there are a number of experimental fusion trucks, several have quickly risen to the top; look out for local favorites Le Tigre, Kaboom Box, TacoFino, Soho Road, Mom's Grilled Cheese and Vij's Railway Express – plus Johnny's Pops artisan ice lollies. Locating the trucks can sometimes be challenging; there are usually a couple outside the Vancouver City Centre Canada Line station and on busy stretches of downtown arteries like Georgia, Robson and around the Vancouver Art Gallery perimeter. Also look out for the trucks at city farmers markets and outside some microbreweries (you're allowed to eat your truck takeout in the brewery tasting rooms).

For listings, opening hours and locations, the handy www.streetfoodapp.com/vancouver website tells you excatly where to go. Alternatively, **Vancouver Foodie Tours** (☎604-295-8844; www.foodietours.ca; tours from $50) offers a tasty guided walk that includes samples at four trucks. But if you're keen to loosen your belt and sample as many as you can in one belly-busting afternoon, check out August's three-day-long **YVR Food Fest** (www.yvrfoodfest.com; Olympic Village; S Main St-Science World), where dozens of food carts congregate to lure the deeply ravenous. And if you fancy an easy trip from town, August's one-day **Columbia StrEat Food Truck Fest** in New Westminster (easily reached via SkyTrain) is also well-worth checking out, with its 70+ trucks. See www.downtownnewwest.ca for details.

Ramen Butcher RAMEN **$**
(Map p640; ☎604-806-4646; www.theramenbutcher.com; 223 E Georgia St; mains $10-12; ⊙11am-3pm & 5-10pm Tue-Thu, 11am-10pm Fri-Sun; 🚌3) One of several new Asian-themed restaurants arriving in Chinatown in recent years, this is the first North American foray of a well-known Japanese ramen franchise. The signature thin noodles come in several broth-bowl varieties with slabs of slow-cooked pork; we recommend the garlicky Red Ramen. Still have some soup in your bowl? They'll toss in a second serving of noodles for free.

Save On Meats DINER **$**
(Map p640; ☎604-569-3568; www.saveonmeats.ca; 43 W Hastings St; mains $5-15; ⊙7am-10pm Mon-Thu, 8am-10pm Fri & Sat, 8am-7pm Sun; 👪; 🚌14) A former old-school butcher shop, Save On Meats has been transformed into a popular hipster diner. But it's not just about looking cool. Slide into a booth or take a perch at the long counter and tuck into comfort dishes, including a good-value $5 all-day breakfast, plus a menu of basic faves such as shepherd's pie, and mac and cheese.

MeeT in Gastown VEGAN **$$**
(Map p640; ☎604-688-3399; www.eatmeet.ca; 12 Water St; mains $7-15; ⊙11am-11pm Sun-Thu, to 1am Fri & Sat; 🌿; M Waterfront) Bringing great vegan comfort dishes to locals without the rabbit-food approach, this wildly popular spot can be clamorously busy at times. But it's worth the wait for a wide-ranging array of herbivore- and carnivore-pleasing dishes, from rice bowls and mac 'n' cheese (made from vegan nut 'cheese') to Portobello mushroom burgers and poutine-like fries slathered in cashew gravy (our recommendation).

Bodega SPANISH **$$**
(Map p640; ☎604-565-8815; www.bodegaonmain.com; 1014 Main St; small plates $7-20; ⊙11am-midnight Mon-Fri, 4:30pm-midnight Sat & Sun; 🚌3) The newest of several recently arrived restaurants in this once-sketchy Main St stretch is actually the relocated reincarnation of one of Vancouver's oldest Spanish eateries. A downtown mainstay for decades, the new Bodega is a sumptuous room of bordello-red seats and paintings evoking the old country, plus a menu of lovely tapas favorites like meatballs, grilled octopus and slow-roasted rabbit.

Phnom Penh VIETNAMESE, CAMBODIAN **$$**
(Map p640; ☎603-682-5777; 244 E Georgia St; mains $8-18; ⊙10am-9pm Mon-Thu, to 11pm Fri-Sun; 🚌3) The dishes at this bustling joint are

split between Cambodian and Vietnamese soul-food classics. It's the highly addictive chicken wings and their lovely pepper sauce that keep regulars loyal. Once you've piled up the bones, dive back in for round two: papaya salad, butter beef and spring rolls show just how good a street-food-inspired Asian menu can be.

Nuba MIDDLE EASTERN **$$**

(Map p640; ☎604-688-1655; www.nuba.ca; 207 W Hastings St; mains $9-30; ⏰11:30am-10pm Mon-Fri, noon-10pm Sat, 5-10pm Sun; 🌿; 🚌14) Tucked under the landmark Dominion Building, this Lebanese restaurant attracts budget noshers and cool hipsters in equal measure. If you're not sure what to go for, split some tasty, surprisingly filling mezze dishes, including excellent hummus and falafel, or just dive straight into a shareable La Feast for two ($38) that covers all the bases (including the inevitable doggie-bag takeout).

Bao Bei CHINESE **$$**

(Map p640; ☎604-688-0876; www.bao-bei.ca; 163 Keefer St; small plates $5-19; ⏰5:30pm-midnight Mon-Sat, 5:30-11pm Sun; 🌿; 🚌3) Reinterpreting a Chinatown heritage-building interior with hipster-esque flourishes, this Chinese brasserie is the area's most seductive dinner destination. Bringing a contemporary edge to Asian cuisine are, tapas-sized, MSG-free dishes such as *shao bing* (stuffed Chinese flatbread), duck salad and steamed pork belly buns: there's also an inventive cocktail array to keep you occupied if you have to wait at the bar for your table.

★Ask for Luigi ITALIAN **$$$**

(Map p640; ☎604-428-2544; www.askforluigi.com; 305 Alexander St; mains $22-24; ⏰11:30am-2:30pm & 5:30-10:30pm Tue-Fri, 9:30am-2:30pm & 5:30-11pm Sat, 9:30am-2:30pm & 5:30-9:30pm Sun; 🚌4) Consider an off-peak lunch if you don't want to wait too long for a table at this white-clapboard, shack-look little charmer (reservations are not accepted). Inside, you'll find a checkerboard floor and teak-lined interior crammed with tables and delighted diners tucking into (and sharing) plates of scratch-made pasta that mama never used to make; think bison tagliatelle and borage-and-ricotta ravioli.

L'Abattoir FRENCH **$$$**

(Map p640; ☎604-568-1701; www.labattoir.ca; 217 Carrall St; mains $35-44; ⏰5:30-10pm Sun-Thu, to 10:30pm Fri & Sat, brunch 10am-2pm Sat & Sun; 🚌4) Gastown's most romantic top-end restaurant, this candlelit, brick-lined spot makes an art of attending to every detail. Be careful not to fill up on the warm bread before you tuck into a menu of French-influenced West Coast dishes. We recommend the lamb leg with spicy *merguez* sausage. Reservations are suggested: ask for a table in the delightful, window-walled back room.

> **GUILT-FREE FISH & CHIPS**
>
> Seafood is BC's main dining choice. Support the sustainability of the region's aquatic larder by frequenting restaurants operating under the Ocean Wise banner; see www.oceanwise.ca.

Yaletown & Granville Island

Go Fish SEAFOOD **$**

(Map p640; ☎604-730-5040; 1505 W 1st Ave; mains $8-14; ⏰11:30am-6:30pm Mon-Fri, noon-6:30pm Sat & Sun; 🚌50) A short stroll westwards along the seawall from the Granville Island entrance, this almost-too-popular seafood stand is one the city's fave fish-and-chip joints, offering halibut, salmon and cod encased in crispy golden batter. The smashing (and lighter) fish tacos are also recommended, while ever-changing daily specials – brought in by the nearby fishing boats – often include scallop burgers or ahi tuna sandwiches.

★Bistro 101 CANADIAN **$$**

(Map p640; ☎604-724-4488; www.picachef.com; 1505 W 2nd Ave; ⏰11:30am-2pm & 6-9pm Mon-Fri; 🚌50) Vancouver's best-value gourmet dining option, the training restaurant of the **Pacific Institute of Culinary Arts** is popular with in-the-know locals, especially at lunchtime, when $22 gets you a delicious three-course meal (typically three options for each course) plus service that's earnestly solicitous. The dinner option costs $8 more and there's a buffet offering on the first Friday of the month. Reservations recommended.

Rodney's Oyster House SEAFOOD **$$**

(Map p640; ☎604-609-0080; www.rohvan.com; 1228 Hamilton St; mains $16-32; ⏰11:30am-11pm; Ⓢ Yaletown-Roundhouse) Vancouver's favorite oyster eatery, Rodney's always has a buzz. And it's not just because of the convivial room with its nautical flourishes: these folks really know how to do seafood. While the fresh-shucked oysters with a huge array of sauces (try the spicy vodka) never fail to impress, there's also everything from sweet mussels to superb Atlantic lobster available here.

Flying Pig CANADIAN **$$**
(Map p640; ☎604-568-1344; www.theflyingpigvan.com; 1168 Hamilton St; mains $19-27; ⏲11am-midnight Mon-Fri, 10am-midnight Sat, 10am-11pm Sun; **S** Yaletown-Roundhouse) Yaletown's best midrange restaurant is a warm, woodsy bistro that has mastered the art of friendly service and saliva-triggering, gourmet comfort food. Dishes focus on seasonal local ingredients and are virtually guaranteed to make your belly smile. Wine-braised short ribs and roast chicken served with buttermilk mash top our to-eat list but it's best to arrive off-peak to avoid the crowds.

Blue Water Cafe SEAFOOD **$$$**
(Map p640; ☎604-688-8078; www.bluewatercafe.net; 1095 Hamilton St; mains $29-48; ⏲5-11pm; **S** Yaletown-Roundhouse) Under celebrated executive chef Frank Pabst, this is one of Vancouver's best high-concept seafood restaurants. Gentle music fills the brick-lined, blue-hued interior, while top-notch char, sablefish and butter-soft scallops grace the tables inside and on the patio. Not a seafood fan? There's also a small array of meaty 'principal plates' to sate your carnivorous appetite, including Wagyu beef.

Commercial Drive

★Jamjar LEBANESE **$**
(☎604-252-3957; www.jamjaronthedrive.com; 2280 Commercial Dr; small plates $6-12; mains $17-22; ⏲11:30am-10pm; ; 20) This super-friendly, cafe-style joint has a rustic-chic interior and a folky Lebanese menu of ethically sourced ingredients and lots of vegetarian options. You don't have to be a veggie to love the crispy falafel balls or the utterly irresistible deep-fried cauliflower stalks – which will have you fighting for the last morsel if you made the mistake of ordering to share.

★Cannibal Café BURGERS **$**
(☎604-558-4199; www.cannibalcafe.ca; 1818 Commercial Dr; mains $11-16; ⏲11:30am-10pm Mon-Thu, 11:30am-midnight Fri, 10am-midnight Sat, 10am-10pm Sun; 20) This is a punk-tastic diner for fans of seriously real burgers made with love. You'll find an inventive array from classics to the recommended Korean BBQ burger. Top-notch ingredients will ensure you never slink into a fast-food chain again. Check the board outside for daily specials and keep in mind there are happy hour deals from 3pm to 6pm weekdays.

Tangent Cafe DINER **$**
(☎604-558-4641; www.tangentcafe.ca; 2095 Commercial Dr; mains $11-14; ⏲8am-3pm Mon & Tue, to midnight Wed & Thu, to 1am Fri & Sat, to 10pm Sun; ; 20) Lined with 1970s-style wood-paneling, this popular hangout combines comfort-classic BLTs and burgers with several Malaysian curry options. But breakfast (served until mid-afternoon) is when most locals roll in, often to cure hangovers founded right here the night before. A great craft beer menu (check the corner chalkboard) and live music (mostly jazz) three nights a week makes this a popular nighttime haunt.

Main Street

Hawkers Delight ASIAN **$**
(☎604-709-8188; 4127 Main St; mains $4-10; ⏲noon-9pm Mon-Sat; ; 3) It's easy to miss this cash-only hole-in-the-wall, but it's worth retracing your steps for authentic Malaysian and Singaporean street food, made from scratch at this family-run favorite. Prices are temptingly low, so order to share – from spicy *mee pok* to noodle-heavy *mee goreng* and prawn-packed *laksa*. Check the counter when ordering for the addictive veggie fritters – they're just $1 for two.

Slickity Jim's Chat 'N' Chew DINER **$**
(☎604-873-6760; www.skinnyfatjack.com; 3475 Main St; mains $8-14; ⏲8:30am-4pm Mon & Tue, to 8pm Wed, Thur & Sun, to midnight Fri & Sat; ; 3) This local favorite gets jam-packed with bleary-eyed locals soothing their hangovers, but it's worth the wait for a quirky, darkened room lined with the kind of oddball art David Lynch probably favors in his house. Menu-wise, they've nailed breakfast here, with traditional as well as inventive (and heaping) plates enlivened with quirky names like the Breakfast of Broken Dreams.

★Dock Lunch INTERNATIONAL **$$**
(☎604-879-3625; 152 E 11th Ave; mains $10-14; ⏲11:30am-5pm Mon-Fri, 11am-3pm Sat & Sun) Like dining in a cool hippie's home, this utterly charming room in a side-street house serves a daily-changing menu of one or two soul-food mains (think spicy tacos or heaping weekend brunches). Arrive early and aim for one of the two window seats and you'll soon be chatting with the locals or browsing the cookbooks and Huxley novels on the shelves.

DON'T MISS

UBC'S APPLETASTIC FOOD FESTIVAL

From Salish to Aurora Golden Gala and from Gravensteins to Cox's Orange Pippins, fans of the real king of fruit have plenty to bite into at the autumnal, weekend-long **UBC Apple Festival** (www.ubcbotanicalgarden.org/events; adult/child $4/free; ⏲mid-Oct). Staged every October at the **UBC Botanical Garden** (p644), it's one of Vancouver's most popular community events. Along with live music and demonstrations on grafting and cider-making, there are lots of smile-triggering children's activities. But the event's main lure is the chance to nibble on a vast array of around 40,000 pounds of BC-grown treats that make most supermarket apples taste like hockey pucks.

The best way to sample as many as possible is to pay an extra $5 and dive into the **Tasting Tent**. Here, 60 locally grown heritage and more recent varieties are available for considered scoffing, including rarities such as Crestons and Oaken Pins. Before you leave, follow your nose to the sweet aroma of perhaps the best apple pie you'll ever taste. A highlight of the festival, the deep-dish, golden-crusted slices for sale here are an indulgence you could happily eat until you explode – with an apple-flavored smile on your face.

Fairview & South Granville

★La Taqueria Pinche Taco Shop MEXICAN $

(☎604-558-2549; www.lataqueria.ca; 2549 Cambie St, Fairview; 4 tacos $8.50-10.50; ⏲11am-8:30pm Mon-Sat, noon-6pm Sun; 🌿; Ⓢ Broadway-City Hall) This popular taco spot expanded from its tiny Hastings St location (which is still there) with this larger storefront. It's just as crowded but luckily many of the visitors are going the take-out route. Snag a brightly painted table, then order at the counter from a dozen or so meat or veggie soft tacos (take your pick or ask for a selection).

★Pronto ITALIAN $$

(☎604-722-9331; www.prontocaffe.ca; 3473 Cambie St, Cambie Village; mains $14-22; ⏲11:30am-9pm Sun, Tue & Wed, to 10pm Thu-Sat; 🚌15) A delightful neighborhood eatery, this charming Cambie Village trattoria combines woodsy candlelit booths, perfectly prepared house-made pasta and the kind of welcoming service few restaurants manage to provide. Drop by for a lunchtime *porchetta* sandwich, or head here for dinner, when the intimate, wood-floored space feels deliciously relaxed. Check the blackboard specials or head straight for the gnocchi with pesto and pancetta.

★Vij's INDIAN $$$

(☎604-736-6664; www.vijsrestaurant.ca; 3106 Cambie St, Cambie Village; mains $19-27; ⏲5:30-10pm; 🌿; 🚌15) A sparkling (and far larger) new location for Canada's favorite East Indian chef delivers a warmly sumptuous lounge coupled with a cavernous dining area and cool rooftop patio. The menu, a high-water mark of contemporary Indian cuisine, fuses BC ingredients, global flourishes and classic ethnic flavors to produce many inventive dishes. Results range from signature 'lamb popsicles' to flavorful meals like sablefish in yogurt-tomato broth.

Kitsilano & University of British Columbia

Kitsilano's two main arteries – West 4th Ave and Broadway – offer a healthy mix of eateries: it's well worth the trek here to lounge on a beach or stroll the shopping areas, then end your day with a rewarding meal. The neighborhood's hippie past has left a legacy of vegetarian-friendly restaurants, but Kits' more recent wealth means there are also some top-notch high-end options well worth a splurge. If you're at UBC, there are some dining options available; alternatively, hop on a bus to nearby Kitsilano for a far superior selection.

★Mr Red Cafe VIETNAMESE $

(☎604-559-6878; 2680 W Broadway; mains $6-14; ⏲11am-9pm; 🌿; 🚌9) Serving authentic northern Vietnamese homestyle dishes that look and taste like there's a lovely old lady making them out back. Reservations are not accepted; dine off-peak to avoid waiting for the handful of tables, then dive into shareable gems like pork baguette sandwiches, *cha ca han oi* (spicy grilled fish) and the ravishing pyramidical rice dumpling, stuffed with pork and a boiled quail's egg.

★ Fable CANADIAN $$

(☎604-732-1322; www.fablekitchen.ca; 1944 W 4th Ave; mains $19-31; ⏲11:30am-2pm Mon-Fri, 5:30-10pm Mon-Sat, brunch 10:30am-2pm Sat & Sun; 🚌4) One of Vancouver's favorite farm-to-table restaurants is a lovely rustic-chic room of exposed brick, wood beams and prominently displayed red rooster logos. But looks are just part of the appeal. Expect perfectly prepared bistro dishes showcasing local seasonal ingredients, such as duck, lamb and halibut. It's great gourmet comfort food with little pretension – hence the packed room most nights. Reservations recommended.

Naam VEGETARIAN $$

(☎604-738-7151; www.thenaam.com; 2724 W 4th Ave; mains $9-16; ⏲24hr; 🖉; 🚌4) An evocative relic of Kitsilano's hippie past, this vegetarian restaurant has the feel of a comfy farmhouse. It's not unusual to have to wait for a table at peak times, but it's worth it for the huge menu of hearty stir-fries, nightly curry specials, bulging quesadillas and ever-popular fries with miso gravy. It's the kind of veggie spot where carnivores delightedly dine.

Drinking & Nightlife

Vancouverites spend a lot of time drinking. And while British Columbia (BC) has a tasty wine sector and is undergoing an artisanal distilling surge, it's the regional craft beer scene that keeps many quaffers merry. For a night out with locally made libations as your side dish, join savvy drinkers supping in the bars of Gastown, Main St and around Commercial Dr.

★ Alibi Room PUB

(Map p640; ☎604-623-3383; www.alibi.ca; 157 Alexander St; ⏲5-11:30pm Mon-Thu, 5pm-12:30am Fri, 10am-12:30am Sat, 10am-11:30pm Sun; 📶; 🚌4) Vancouver's best craft beer tavern has an exposed brick bar that stocks a roster of around 50 drafts, mostly from celebrated BC breweries such as Driftwood, Four Winds and Yellow Dog. Adventurous taste-trippers – hipsters and veteran beer fans alike – enjoy the $11.50 'frat bat' of four samples: choose your own or ask to be surprised. Check the board for ever-changing guest casks.

★ Storm Crow Alehouse PUB

(☎604-428-9670; www.stormcrowalehouse.com; 1619 W Broadway, South Granville; ⏲11am-1am Mon-Thu, 11am-2am Fri, 9am-2am Sat, 9am-1am Sun; 🚌9) This large, nerdy pub welcomes everyone from the Borg to beardy *Lord of the Rings* dwarfs. They come to peruse the memorabilia-studded walls (think Millennium Falcon models and a Tardis washroom door), play the board games and dive into apposite refreshments including Romulan Ale and Pangalactic Gargleblasters. Hungry? Miss the chunky chickpea fries at your peril.

★ Brassneck Brewery MICROBREWERY

(☎604-259-7686; 2184 Main St; ⏲2-11pm Mon-Fri, noon-11pm Sat & Sun; 🚌3) Vancouver's favourite microbrewery concocted more than 50 different beers in its first six months of operating and continues to win new fans with an ever-changing chalkboard of intriguing libations with names like Bivouac Bitter, Stockholm Syndrome and Magician's Assistant. Our recommendation? The delicious Passive Aggressive dry-hopped pale ale. Arrive early for a seat in the small tasting bar, especially on weekends.

★ Catfe CAFE

(Map p640; ☎778-379-0060; www.catfe.ca; International Village Mall, 88 Pender St; with/without cafe purchase $5/8; ⏲11am-9pm Fri- Wed; 👪; Ⓢ Stadium-Chinatown) Vancouver's only cat cafe; book online for your time slot (walk-ins may also be available), buy a coffee and then meet the moggies in the large feline play room, where at least a dozen whiskered wonders await. All the cats come from the SPCA (Society for the Prevention of Cruelty to Animals) and are available for adoption via their usual procedures.

★ Shameful Tiki Room BAR

(www.shamefultikiroom.com; 4362 Main St; ⏲5pm-midnight Sun-Thu, to 1am Fri & Sat; 🚌3) This windowless snug instantly transports you to a Polynesian beach. The lighting – including glowing puffer-fish lampshades – is permanently set to dusk and the walls are lined with tiki masks and rattan coverings under a straw-shrouded ceiling. But it's the drinks that rock: seriously well-crafted classics from Zombies to Mai Tais to a four-person Volcano Bowl.

Narrow Lounge BAR

(Map p640; www.narrowlounge.com; 1898 Main St; ⏲5pm-1am Mon-Fri, to 2am Sat & Sun; 🚌3) Enter through the doorway on 3rd Ave – the red light tells you if it's open or not – then descend the graffiti-lined stairway into Vancouver's coolest small bar. Little bigger than a train carriage and lined with moth-eaten taxidermy and junk-shop pictures, it's an atmospheric nook that always feels like midnight. In summer, try the hidden alfresco bar out back.

Fountainhead Pub GAY

(Map p640; ☎604-687-2222; www.thefountainheadpub.com; 1025 Davie St; ⏰11am-1am Sun-Thu, to 2am Fri & Sat; 🚌6) The area's loudest and proudest gay neighborhood pub, this friendly joint is all about the patio, which spills onto Davie St like an overturned wine glass. Take part in the ongoing summer-evening pastime of ogling passing locals or retreat to a quieter spot inside for a few lagers or a naughty cocktail: anyone for a Porn Star or a Red Stag Sour?

Main Street Brewing MICROBREWERY

(☎604-336-7711; www.mainstreetbeer.ca; 261 E 7th Ave; ⏰2-11pm Mon-Thu, noon-11pm Fri-Sun; 🚌3) Tucked into an historic old brewery building, Main Street Brewing has a great, industrial-chic little tasting room and a booze roster divided into regular beers and casks. Start with a four-flight tasting sampler then dive in with a larger order. The Westminster Brown Ale is our favorite but there's usually an IPA or two worth quaffing here as well.

Diamond COCKTAIL BAR

(Map p640; www.di6mond.com; 6 Powell St; ⏰5:30pm-1am Mon-Thu, to 2am Fri & Sat, to midnight Sun; 🚌4) Head upstairs via the unassuming entrance and you'll find yourself in one of Vancouver's warmest little cocktail bars. A renovated heritage room studded with sash windows – try for a view seat – it's popular with local coolsters but is rarely pretentious. A list of perfectly nailed premium cocktails helps, coupled with a tapas menu that includes lots of Japanese-influenced options.

Fortune Sound Club CLUB

(Map p640; ☎604-569-1758; www.fortunesoundclub.com; 147 E Pender St; ⏰9:30pm-3am Fri & Sat, plus special events; 🚌3) Vancouver's best club has transformed a tired Chinatown spot into a slick space with the kind of genuine staff and younger, hipster-cool crowd rarely seen in Vancouver venues. Slide inside and you'll find a giant dance floor popping with party-loving locals just out for a good time. Expect weekend queues, and check out Happy Ending Fridays, when you'll possibly dance your ass off.

Keefer Bar COCKTAIL BAR

(Map p640; ☎604-688-1961; www.thekeeferbar.com; 135 Keefer St; ⏰5pm-midnight Mon, to 1am Tue-Thu & Sun, to 2am Fri & Sat; Ⓜ Stadium-Chinatown) A dark, narrow and atmospheric Chinatown bar that's been claimed by local cocktail-loving coolsters from day one. Drop in for a full evening of liquid taste-tripping and you'll have a blast. From perfectly prepared rosemary gimlets and Siamese slippers to an excellent whiskey menu and some tasty tapas, it offers up a great night out.

★Liberty Distillery DISTILLERY

(Map p640; ☎604-558-1998; www.thelibertydistillery.com; 1494 Old Bridge St; ⏰11am-8pm; 🚌50) Vancouver's most attractive craft distillery has a saloon-like tasting room where you can gaze through windows at the shiny, steampunk-like booze-making equipment beyond. It's not all about looks, though. During happy hour (Monday to Thursday, 3pm to 6pm), sample house-made gin, vodka and white whiskey plus great cocktails for just $6 a pop. Tours are available ($10; Saturdays and Sundays; 11:30am and 1:30pm).

Six Acres BAR

(Map p640; ☎604-488-0110; www.sixacres.ca; 203 Carrall St; ⏰11:30am-11:30pm Sun-Thu, to 12:30am Fri & Sat; 📶; 🚌4) Gastown's coziest tavern; you can cover all the necessary food groups via the carefully chosen draft- and bottled-beer list here. There's a small, animated summer patio out front but inside (especially upstairs) is great for hiding in a chatty, candlelit corner and working your way through the brews – plus a shared small plate or three.

RAISE A GLASS: BC'S TOP BEERS

Fat Tug IPA Driftwood Brewery (www.driftwoodbeer.com)

Dive Bomb Porter Powell Street Craft Brewery (www.powellbeer.com)

Four Winds IPA Four Winds Brewing (www.fourwindsbrewing.ca)

Persephone Pale Ale Persephone Brewing Company (www.persephonebrewing.com)

Zunga Blonde Ale Townsite Brewing (www.townsitebrewing.com)

Red Racer India Red Ale Central City Brewers & Distillers (www.centralcitybrewing.com)

Father John's Winter Ale Howe Sound Brewing (www.howesound.com)

✩ Entertainment

You'll never run out of options if you're looking for a good time here. Vancouver is packed with activities from high- to low-brow, perfect for those craving a play one night, a soccer match the next, and a rocking live music show to follow. Ask the locals for tips and they'll likely point out grassroots happenings you never knew existed.

Live Music

★Commodore Ballroom LIVE MUSIC
(Map p640; ☎604-739-4550; www.commodoreballroom.com; 868 Granville St; 🚌10) Local bands know they've made it when they play Vancouver's best mid-sized venue, a restored art deco ballroom that still has the city's bounciest dance floor – courtesy of tires placed under its floorboards. If you need a break from your moshing, collapse at one of the tables lining the perimeter, catch your breath with a bottled Stella and then plunge back in.

Rickshaw Theatre LIVE MUSIC
(Map p640; ☎604-681-8915; www.liveatrickshaw.com; 254 E Hastings St; 🚌14) Revamped from its grungy 1970s incarnation, the funky Rickshaw shows that Eastside gentrification can be positive. The stage of choice for many punk and indie acts, it's an excellent place to see a band. There's a huge mosh area near the stage and rows of theater-style seats at the back.

Biltmore Cabaret LIVE MUSIC
(☎604-676-0541; www.biltmorecabaret.com; 2755 Prince Edward St; 🚌9) One of Vancouver's best alt venues, the Biltmore is a firm favorite on the local indie scene. A low-ceilinged, good-vibe spot to mosh to local and touring musicians, there are also regular event nights: check the online calendar for upcoming happenings, including the hugely popular **Kitty Nights Burlesque shows** (www.kittynights.com), which end with a full-on DJ dance party.

Cinemas

★Pacific Cinémathèque CINEMA
(Map p640; ☎604-688-3456; www.thecinematheque.ca; 1131 Howe St; tickets $11, double bills $16; 🚌10) This beloved cinema operates like an ongoing film festival with a daily-changing program of movies. A $3 annual membership is required – organize it at the door – before you can skulk in the dark with other chin-stroking movie buffs who probably named their children (or pets) after Fellini and Bergman.

Rio Theatre CINEMA, THEATER
(☎604-879-3456; www.riotheatre.ca; 1660 E Broadway; Ⓢ Commercial-Broadway) Vancouver's most eclectic cinema, this restored 1980s movie house is like a community rep theater, staging everything from blockbuster and art-house movies to live music (there's an excellent sound system), improv comedy and saucy burlesque nights. Check the calendar to see what's on: the Gentlemen Heckler narrated movie screenings are recommended.

Vancity Theatre CINEMA
(Map p640; ☎604-683-3456; www.viff.org/theatre; 1181 Seymour St; tickets $12, double bills $18; 🚌10) The state-of-the-art headquarters of the Vancouver International Film Festival (p647) screens a wide array of movies throughout the year in the kind of auditorium that cinephiles dream of: generous legroom, wide armrests and great sight lines from each of its 175 seats. It's a place where you can watch a four-hour subtitled epic about a dripping tap and still feel comfortable.

Scotiabank Theatre CINEMA
(Map p640; www.cineplex.com; 900 Burrard St; 🚌2) Downtown's shiny multiplex is big enough to have its own corporate sponsor and it's the most likely theater to be screening the latest must-see blockbuster. In contrast, it also shows occasional live broadcast performances from major cultural institutions such as London's National Theatre and New York's Metropolitan Opera. Drop by on Tuesdays for discounted admission.

Theater & Classical Music

★Bard on the Beach PERFORMING ARTS
(Map p640; ☎604-739-0559; www.bardonthebeach.org; Vanier Park, 1695 Whyte Ave; tickets from $20-57; ⊙Jun-Sep; 🚌22) Watching Shakespeare performed while the sun sets against the mountains beyond the tented stage is a Vancouver summertime highlight. There are usually three of Shakespeare's plays, plus one Bard-related work (*Rosencrantz and Guildenstern are Dead,* for example), to choose from during the run. Q&A talks are staged after Tuesday-night performances, along with regular opera, fireworks and wine-tasting nights throughout the season.

★Cultch THEATER
(Vancouver East Cultural Centre; ☎604-251-1363; www.thecultch.com; 1895 Venables St; 🚌20) This once-abandoned church has been a

gathering place for performers and audiences since being officially designated as a cultural space in 1973. Following comprehensive renovations a few years back, the beloved Cultch (as everyone calls it) is now one of Vancouver's entertainment jewels, with a busy roster of local, fringe and visiting theatrical shows staging everything from spoken word to touring Ibsen productions.

Arts Club Theatre Company THEATER
(☎604-687-1644; www.artsclub.com) Vancouver's largest, most popular and most prolific theater company, the Arts Club stages shows at three theaters around the city.

Vancouver Symphony Orchestra PERFORMING ARTS
(☎604-876-3434; www.vancouversymphony.ca) The city's orchestra plays classical and popular music concerts (think movie music) around the city and beyond. Venues range from the palatial Orpheum Theatre to large outdoor spaces in Stanley Park.

Sports

Vancouver Canucks HOCKEY
(Map p640; ☎604-899-7400; canucks.nhl.com; Rogers Arena, 800 Griffiths Way; S Stadium-Chinatown) Vancouver's National Hockey League (NHL) team toyed with fans in 2011's Stanley Cup finals before losing Game 7 to the Boston Bruins, triggering riots across the city. But love runs deep and 'go Canucks, go!' is still boomed out from a packed Rogers Arena at most games. Book your seat early or just head to a local bar for some raucous game-night atmosphere.

Vancouver Whitecaps SOCCER
(Map p640; ☎604-669-9283; www.whitecapsfc.com; BC Place Stadium, 777 Pacific Blvd; tickets $30-150; ⏱Mar-Oct; 👪; S Stadium-Chinatown) Using BC Place Stadium as its home, Vancouver's professional soccer team plays in North America's top-tier Major League Soccer (MLS). They've struggled a little since being promoted to the league in 2011, but have been finding their feet (useful for soccer players) in recent seasons. Save time to buy a souvenir soccer shirt to impress everyone back home.

BC Lions FOOTBALL
(Map p640; ☎604-589-7627; www.bclions.com; BC Place Stadium, 777 Pacific Blvd; tickets from $35; ⏱Jun-Nov; 👪; S Stadium-Chinatown) The Lions are Vancouver's team in the Canadian Football League (CFL), which is arguably more exciting than its US counterpart, the NFL. They've had some decent showings in recent years but they haven't won the all-important Grey Cup championship since 2011. Tickets are easy to come by – unless the boys are laying into their arch enemies, the Calgary Stampeders.

Shopping

Vancouver's retail scene has developed dramatically in recent years. Hit Robson St's mainstream chains, then discover the hip, independent shops of Gastown, Main St and Commercial Dr. Granville Island is stuffed with artsy stores and studios, while South Granville and Kitsilano's 4th Ave serve up a wide range of ever-tempting boutiques.

★Regional Assembly of Text ARTS & CRAFTS
(☎604-877-2247; www.assemblyoftext.com; 3934 Main St; ⏱11am-6pm Mon-Sat, noon-5pm Sun; 🚌3) This ironic antidote to the digital age lures ink-stained locals with its journals, handmade pencil boxes and T-shirts printed with typewriter motifs. Check out the tiny under-the-stairs gallery showcasing zines from around the world, and don't miss the monthly **Letter Writing Club** (7pm, first Thursday of every month), where you can hammer on vintage typewriters, crafting erudite missives to your far-away loved one.

★Paper Hound BOOKS
(Map p640; ☎604-428-1344; www.paperhound.ca; 344 W Pender St; ⏱10am-7pm Sun-Thu, to 8pm Fri & Sat; 🚌14) Proving the printed word is alive and kicking, this small but perfectly curated bookstore opened a couple of years ago and has already become a dog-eared favorite among locals. A perfect spot for browsing your day away, you'll find tempting tomes (mostly used but some new) on everything from nature to poetry to chaos theory. Ask for recommendations: they really know their stuff here.

★Mintage VINTAGE
(☎604-646-8243; www.mintagevintage.com; 1714 Commercial Dr; ⏱10am-7pm Mon-Sat, 11am-6pm Sun; 🚌20) Where Drive hipsters add a little vintage glam to their look. There's a Western-saloon feel to the interior here, but don't be fooled – this is one of the city's most kaleidoscopically eclectic stores. Ladieswear dominates – you'll find everything from saris to tutus – while the menswear at the back is ideal for finding a velour leisure suit with 'matching' Kenny Rogers T-shirt.

★Mountain Equipment Co-Op SPORTS & OUTDOORS
(☎604-872-7858; www.mec.ca; 130 W Broadway; ⏲10am-9pm Mon-Fri, 9am-6pm Sat, 10am-6pm Sun, reduced hours off-season; 🚌9) Grown hikers weep at the amazing selection of clothing, kayaks, sleeping bags and clever camping gadgets at this cavernous outdoors store: MEC has been encouraging fully fledged outdoor enthusiasts for years. You'll have to be a member to buy, but that's easy to arrange for just $5. Equipment – canoes, kayaks, camping gear etc – can be rented here.

Eastside Flea MARKET
(Map p640; www.eastsideflea.com; Ellis Building, 1014 Main St; $3; ⏲6-10pm Fri, 11am-5pm Sat & Sun, third weekend of the month; 🚌3) Running for years at halls around the city, the monthly Flea's new Ellis Building location means 50 new and vintage vendors, plus food trucks, live music and a highly inviting atmosphere. Arrive early so you can buy a top hat and swan around like the ironic out-of-time Victorian gentleman you've always wanted to be (bring your own waxed mustache).

John Fluevog Shoes SHOES
(Map p640; ☎604-688-6228; www.fluevog.com; 65 Water St; ⏲10am-7pm Mon-Wed & Sat, to 8pm Thu & Fri, noon-6pm Sun; Ⓢ Waterfront) Like an art gallery for shoes, this alluringly cavernous store showcases the famed footwear of local designer Fluevog, whose men's and women's boots and brogues are what Doc Martens would have become if they'd stayed interesting and cutting-edge. Pick up that pair of thigh-hugging dominatrix boots you've always wanted or settle on some designer loafers that would make anyone walk tall.

Smoking Lily CLOTHING
(☎604-873-5459; www.smokinglily.com; 3634 Main St; ⏲11am-6pm Mon-Sat, noon-5pm Sun; 🚌3) Art-school-cool rules at this mostly womenswear boutique, with skirts, belts and halter-tops whimsically accented with prints of insects, narwhals and the periodic table. Anatomically correct heart motifs are also popular, appearing on shirts, jewelry and cushion covers. And there's a great array of accessories, including quirky purses and shoulder bags beloved of the local pale-and-interesting set.

★Gallery of BC Ceramics ARTS & CRAFTS
(Map p640; ☎604-669-3606; www.bcpotters.com; 1359 Cartwright St; ⏲10:30am-5:30pm; 🚌50) The star of Granville Island's arts-and-crafts shops and the public face of the Potters Guild of BC, this excellent spot exhibits and sells the striking works of its member artists. You can pick up one-of-a-kind ceramic tankards or swirly-painted soup bowls; the hot items are the cool ramen-noodle cups, complete with holes for chopsticks. It's well-priced art for everyone.

Coastal Peoples Fine Arts Gallery ARTS & CRAFTS
(Map p640; ☎604-684-9222; www.coastalpeoples.com; 312 Water St; ⏲10am-7pm mid-Apr–mid-Oct, to 6pm mid-Oct–mid-Apr; Ⓢ Waterfront) This museum-like store showcases an excellent array of Inuit and Northwest Coast aboriginal jewelry, carvings and prints. On the high-art side of things, the exquisite items here are ideal if you're looking for a very special souvenir for someone back home. Don't worry: they can ship the totem poles if you can't fit them in your suitcase.

Thomas Haas FOOD
(☎604-736-1848; www.thomashaas.com; 2539 W Broadway; ⏲8am-5:30pm Tue-Sat; 🚌9) This independent chocolatier is often bursting with locals purchasing its regular supplies of gourmet treats, such as caramel-pecan squares and chili-suffused bon-bons. But the stars of the glass cabinet are the choc-encased fruit jellies (raspberry ganache recommended). A good spot for Vancouver-made souvenirs like chunky chai and espresso chocolate bars.

Red Cat Records MUSIC
(☎604-708-9422; www.redcat.ca; 4332 Main St; ⏲11am-7pm Mon-Thu, to 8pm Fri & Sat, to 6pm Sun; 🚌3) The ideal destination to hang out on a Main St rainy day, Red Cat's wooden racks are home to a well-curated collection of new and used CDs and vinyl records in what is one of the coolest record stores in the city. It helps that it's co-owned by musicians; ask them for tips on whom to see live on the local scene.

Front & Company CLOTHING, ACCESSORIES
(☎604-879-8431; www.frontandcompany.ca; 3772 Main St; ⏲11am-6:30pm; 🚌3) A triple-fronted store where you could easily spend a couple of hours; the largest section here contains trendy consignment clothing (where else can you find that vintage velvet smoking jacket?). Next door houses new, knowingly cool housewares, while the third area includes must-have gifts and accessories such as manga figures, peace-sign ice trays and nihilist chewing gum (flavorless, of course).

Information

MEDICAL SERVICES

St Paul's Hospital (604-682-2344; 1081 Burrard St; 22) Downtown hospital for accidents and emergencies.

Shoppers Drug Mart (604-669-2424; 1125 Davie St; 24hr; 6) Pharmacy chain.

Ultima Medicentre (604-683-8138; www.ultimamedicentre.ca; Plaza Level, Bentall Centre, 1055 Dunsmuir St; 8am-5pm Mon-Fri; S Burrard) Appointments not necessary.

MONEY

Vancouver Bullion & Currency Exchange (604-685-1008; www.vbce.ca; 800 W Pender St; 9am-5pm Mon-Fri; S Granville) Aside from the banks, try Vancouver Bullion & Currency Exchange for currency exchange. It often has a wider range of currencies and competitive rates.

POST

Howe St Postal Outlet (Map p640; 604-688-2068; 732 Davie St; 9am-7pm Mon-Fri, 10am-5pm Sat; 6)

TOURIST INFORMATION

The **Tourism Vancouver Visitor Centre** (Map p640; 604-683-2000; www.tourismvancouver.com; 200 Burrard St; 8:30am-5pm; S Waterfront) is a large repository of resources for visitors, with a staff of helpful advisers ready to assist in planning your trip. Services and info available here include free maps, visitor guides, half-priced theater tickets, accommodation and tour bookings, plus a host of glossy brochures on the city and the wider BC region.

Getting There & Away

AIR

Canada's second-busiest airport, **Vancouver International Airport** (YVR; 604-207-7077; www.yvr.ca;), lies 13km south of downtown in the city of Richmond. There are two main terminals – international (including flights to the US) and domestic – just a short indoor stroll apart. A third (and much smaller) South Terminal is located a quick drive away; free shuttle-bus links are provided. This terminal services floatplanes, helicopters and smaller aircraft traveling on lower-capacity routes to small communities in BC and beyond. In addition, short-hop floatplane (p679) and helicopter services (p693) to and from Vancouver Island and beyond also depart from the city's downtown waterfront, near Canada Place.

The main airport has shops, food courts, currency-exchange booths and a tourist information desk. It's also dotted with handsome aboriginal artworks. Baggage carts are free (no deposit required) and there is also free wi-fi.

BOAT

BC Ferries (250-386-3431; www.bcferries.com) services arrive at Tsawwassen, an hour south of Vancouver, and at Horseshoe Bay, 30 minutes from downtown in West Vancouver. The company operates one of the world's largest ferry networks, including some spectacular routes throughout the province.

Main services to Tsawwassen arrive from Vancouver Island's Swartz Bay, near Victoria, and Duke Point, near Nanaimo. Services also arrive from the Southern Gulf Islands.

Services to Horseshoe Bay arrive from Nanaimo's Departure Bay. Services also arrive here from Bowen Island and from Langdale on the Sunshine Coast.

To depart Tsawwassen via transit, take bus 620 (adult/child $5.50/3.50) to Bridgeport Station and transfer to the Canada Line. It takes about 40 minutes to reach downtown.

From Horseshoe Bay to downtown, take bus 257 (adult/child $4/2.75, 45 minutes), which is faster than bus 250. It takes about 35 minutes.

Cruise ships, big business here from May to September, dock at downtown's Canada Place or at Ballantyne Pier, just to the east.

BUS

- Most intercity nontransit buses trundle to a halt at Vancouver's neon-signed **Pacific Central Station** (1150 Station St; S Main St-Science World). It's the main arrival point for cross-Canada and transborder **Greyhound buses** (www.greyhound.com; www.greyhound.ca); cross-border budget bus services on **Bolt Bus** (www.boltbus.com); and services from Seattle and Seattle's Sea-Tac International Airport on **Quick Shuttle** (www.quickcoach.com).
- The station has a ticket office and left-luggage lockers, and is also the city's trans-Canada and cross-border train terminal.
- The Main St-Science World SkyTrain station is just across the street for connections to downtown and the suburbs.
- There are car-rental desks in the station and cabs are available just outside.

CAR & MOTORCYCLE

If you've rented a car in the US and are driving it into Canada, bring a copy of the rental agreement to save any possible hassles with border officials.

Gas is generally cheaper in the US, so be sure to fill up before you cross into Canada.

TRAIN

- **Pacific Central Station** (p662) is the city's main terminus for long-distance trains from across Canada on **VIA Rail** (www.viarail.com), and from Seattle (just south of the border) and beyond on **Amtrak** (www.amtrak.com). It's also the main arrival point for major intercity, including cross-border, bus services.

➡ The Main St-Science World SkyTrain station is just across the street for connections to downtown and beyond.

➡ There are car-rental desks in the station and cabs are also available just outside the building.

Getting Around

TO/FROM THE AIRPORT

Taxi

➡ Follow the signs from inside the airport terminal to the cab stand just outside. The fare to downtown, around 30 minutes away, will usually cost between $35 and $45, plus tip (15% is the norm).

➡ Alternatively, limo-car services are also available close to the main taxi stand. Expect to pay around $20 more for your ride to the city if you want to arrive in style.

Train

SkyTrain's 16-station **Canada Line** (see the route maps at www.translink.ca) operates a rapid-transit train service from the airport to downtown. Trains run every few minutes from early morning until after midnight and take around 25 minutes to reach downtown's Waterfront Station. The airport station is located just outside, between the domestic and international terminals. Follow the signs from inside either terminal and buy your ticket from the platform vending machines. These accept cash, and credit and debit cards – look for green-jacketed Canada Line staff if you're bleary-eyed and need assistance after your long-haul flight. Fares from the airport cost between $7.75 and $10.50, depending on your destination and the time of day.

BICYCLE

➡ Vancouver is a relatively good cycling city, with more than 300km of designated routes crisscrossing the region.

➡ Cyclists can take their bikes for free on SkyTrains, SeaBuses and transit buses, which are all now fitted with bike racks. Cyclists are required by law to wear helmets.

➡ In recent years, dedicated bike lanes have been created downtown and, in 2016, a new public bike-share scheme called **Mobi** (www.mobibikes.ca) was introduced.

➡ Pick up a free *Metro Vancouver Cycling Map* for details on area routes and bike-friendly contacts and resources – or download it via the TransLink website.

➡ If you're traveling sans bike, you can also rent wheels (often including inline skates) from businesses around the city, especially on Denman St near Stanley Park – home of Vancouver's most popular scenic cycling route.

BOAT

Operators offer day passes ($10 to $15) as well as discounted books of tickets for those making multiple water hops. Single trips cost from $3.50.

Aquabus Ferries (☎604-689-5858; www.theaquabus.com; adult/child from $3.50/1.75) Runs frequent minivessels (some big enough to carry bikes) between the foot of Hornby St and Granville Island. It also services several additional spots along the False Creek waterfront, as far as Science World.

False Creek Ferries (Map p640; ☎604-684-7781; www.granvilleislandferries.bc.ca; adult/child from $3.25/2) Operates a similar Granville Island service from Sunset Beach, and has additional ports of call around False Creek.

CAR & MOTORCYCLE

For sightseeing in the city, you'll be fine without a car (the city center is especially easy to explore on foot and transit routes are extensive). For visits that incorporate the wider region's mountains and communities, however, a vehicle makes life much simpler: the further you travel from downtown, the more limited your transit options become.

PUBLIC TRANSPORTATION

Bus

➡ Vancouver's **TransLink** (www.translink.ca) bus network is extensive. All vehicles are equipped with bike racks and all are wheelchair accessible. Exact change (or more) is required; buses use fare machines and change is not given. Fares cost adult/child $2.75/1.75 and are valid for up to 90 minutes of transfer travel. While Vancouver's transit system covers three geographic fare zones, all bus trips are regarded as one-zone fares.

➡ Bus services operate from early morning to after midnight in central areas. There is also a handy night-bus system that runs every 30 minutes between 1:30am and 4am. The last night-bus leaves downtown Vancouver at 3:09am. Look for night-bus signs at designated stops.

SeaBus

➡ The iconic SeaBus shuttle is part of the TransLink transit system (regular transit fares apply) and it operates throughout the day, taking 12 minutes to cross Burrard Inlet between Waterfront Station and Lonsdale Quay in North Vancouver. At Lonsdale you can then connect to buses servicing North Vancouver and West Vancouver; this is where you pick up bus 236 to both Capilano Suspension Bridge and Grouse Mountain.

➡ SeaBus services leave from Waterfront Station between 6:16am and 1:22am, Monday to Saturday (8:16am to 11:16pm on Sunday). Vessels are wheelchair accessible and bike-friendly.

- Tickets must be purchased from vending machines on either side of the route before boarding. The machines take credit and debit cards and also give change up to $20 for cash transactions.

SkyTrain

- TransLink's SkyTrain rapid-transit network currently consists of three routes and is a great way to move around the region, especially beyond the city center. A fourth route, the Evergreen Line, is scheduled to begin operations in 2017 and will link the suburban communities of Burnaby, Coquitlam and Port Moody.
- Compass tickets for SkyTrain trips can be purchased from station vending machines (change is given; machines also accept debit and credit cards) prior to boarding.
- SkyTrain journeys cost $2.75 to $5.50 (plus $5 more if you are traveling from the airport), depending on how far you are journeying.

TAXI

Vancouver currently does not allow Uber-type services. Try the following long-established taxi companies:

Black Top & Checker Cabs (604-731-1111; www.btccabs.ca;)

Vancouver Taxi (604-871-1111; www.vancouvertaxi.cab)

Yellow Cab (604-681-1111; www.yellowcabonline.com;)

LOWER MAINLAND

Stretching from coastal Horseshoe Bay as far inland as the verdant Fraser Valley, this region encompasses the towns and suburbs within an hour or two by car or transit from downtown Vancouver, including those communities immediately adjoining the city that together are known as Metro Vancouver. Ideal for day-tripping, the area is striped with looming mountains, forested coastal parks, wildlife sanctuaries and historic attractions.

Burnaby

Immediately east of Vancouver and accessible via SkyTrain from the city center, Burnaby is a quiet residential suburb with a half-day's worth of attractions. For information on the area, visit the **Tourism Burnaby** (604-419-0377; www.tourismburnaby.com) website.

The pathways of tranquil **Deer Lake Park** (6450 Deer Lake Park Ave) crisscross meadows and woodlands, circling a lake where birds and other wildlife hang out. In summer, it's home to the annual **Burnaby Blues + Roots Festival** (www.burnabybluesfestival.com; Aug). The adjoining **Burnaby Village Museum** (www.burnabyvillagemuseum.ca; 6501 Deer Lake Ave; 11am-4:30pm Tue-Sun May-Aug;) FREE colorfully re-creates a pioneer town, complete with replica homes, businesses and a handsome 1912 carousel. To get directly there by car, take the Sperling Ave exit off Hwy 1 and follow the museum signs.

Topping Burnaby Mountain, 50-year-old **Simon Fraser University** (www.sfu.ca; 8888 University Dr; 135) is the Lower Mainland's second-biggest campus community. Small visitor attractions here include the **SFU Gallery** (778-782-4266; www.sfu.ca/galleries; noon-5pm Tue-Fri) FREE and the **Museum of Archaeology & Ethnology** (778-782-3135; www.sfu.ca/archaeology/museum.html; 10am-noon & 1-4pm Mon-Fri) FREE.

Getting There & Away

TransLink's (604-953-3333; www.translink.ca) SkyTrain Expo and Millennium lines trundle from Vancouver into Burnaby every few minutes throughout the day. It's a two-zone transit hop between the two cities (two-zone fare $4).

Fort Langley

Little Fort Langley's tree-lined streets and 19th-century storefronts make it one of the Lower Mainland's most picturesque historic villages, ideal for an afternoon jaunt from Vancouver. Aside from the fort itself, cafes, boutiques and ice-cream-scoffing opportunities abound.

The highlight of a visit here is **Fort Langley National Historic Site** (604-513-4777; www.parkscanada.gc.ca/fortlangley; adult/child $7.80/3.90; 10am-5pm;), the region's most important and evocative old-school landmark.

A fortified trading post built in 1827, it's where James Douglas announced the creation of British Columbia in 1858, giving the site a legitimate claim to being the province's birthplace. With costumed reenactors, re-created artisan workshops and a gold-panning area that's a kid-friendly must-do (they also enjoy charging around the wooden battlements), it's an ideal destination for families aiming to add a little education to their trips.

If you need an introduction before you start wading into the buildings, there's a surprisingly entertaining time-travel-themed movie presentation on offer. Also check the website before arriving: there's a wide array of interpretive events and activities that bring the past to life here, including blacksmithing workshops (book ahead).

You won't go hungry in Fort Langley, where there are several enticing eateries a short stroll from the fort. But if you want to hang with the locals, drop into **Wendel's Bookstore & Cafe** (604-513-2238; www.wendelsonline.com; 9233 Glove Rd; dishes $8-14; 7:30am-10pm;).

New Westminster

A short SkyTrain ride from downtown Vancouver, 'New West' is one of BC's most historic communities – it was briefly the capital of the new Colony of British Columbia in 1859. Its star faded during much of the last century but recent years have seen attempts at revival. It's easily worth a couple of hours of your time if you're looking for an accessible excursion from Vancouver.

Hop off at the New Westminster SkyTrain station and stroll downhill towards the Fraser River, where the **Waterfront Esplanade Boardwalk** includes a shoreline stroll studded with artsy flourishes and shimmering river views (looks for seals, herons and log-towing boats here).

The adjoining indoor **River Market** (604-520-3881; www.rivermarket.ca; 810 Quayside Dr; 10am-6pm) is a good lunch stop, and you'll also spot what claims to be **the world's largest tin soldier** looming over the shoreline. If you have time, nip into the **Fraser River Discovery Centre** (604-521-8401; www.fraserriverdiscovery.org; 788 Quayside Dr; suggested donation $6; 10am-4pm Jun-Aug, 10am-4pm Wed-Sat Sep-May;) for the story of the mighty river flowing alongside. Then turn your back on the water and hit nearby Columbia St for the shops and historic buildings.

Information

For more information on the area, connect with **Tourism New Westminster** (604-526-1905; www.tourismnewwestminster.com; 777 Columbia St; 10am-5pm Mon-Sat Jun-Sep, 10am-4pm Oct-May).

Getting There & Away

Frequent **TransLink** (604-953-3333; www.translink.ca) SkyTrain services from downtown Vancouver take about 25 minutes to whisk you to New West. It's a two-zone fare ($4).

Richmond & Steveston

The region's modern-day Chinatown is easy to reach via Canada Line SkyTrain from Vancouver, making for an accessible half-day of Asian shopping malls followed by a taste-trip through Chinese, Japanese and Vietnamese restaurants. And don't miss the city's historic waterfront Steveston village – a popular destination for sunset-viewing locals with a penchant for great fish and chips, it also has a couple of great museums.

Sights

Gulf of Georgia Cannery MUSEUM

(604-664-9009; www.gulfofgeorgiacannery.org; 12138 4th Ave, Steveston; adult/child $10.20/6.30; 10am-5pm; ; M Richmond-Brighouse, then bus 401) British Columbia's best 'industrial museum' illuminates the sights and sounds of the region's bygone era of labor-intensive fish processing. Most of the machinery remains and there's an evocative focus on the people who used to work here; you'll hear recorded testimonies from old employees percolating through the air like ghosts, bringing to life the days they spent immersed in entrails as thousands of cans rolled down the production line. Take one of the guided tours for the full story.

Britannia Shipyard MUSEUM

(640-718-8038; www.britanniashipyard.ca; 5180 Westwater Dr, Steveston; 10am-5pm Fri-Wed, to 8pm Thu May-Sep, noon-5pm Sat & Sun Oct-Apr; M Richmond-Brighouse, then bus 410) FREE A riverfront complex of historic sheds housing dusty tools, boats and reminders of the region's maritime past, this is one of the most evocative, fancy-free historic sites in the region. Check out the preserved **Murakami House**, where a large Japanese family lived before being unceremoniously interned during the war. Ask the volunteers plenty of questions: they have some great stories to tell.

Richmond Night Market MARKET

(604-244-8448; www.richmondnightmarket.com; 8351 River Rd, Richmond; adult/child $3.25/free; 7pm-midnight Fri & Sat, to 11pm Sun mid-May–mid-Oct; S Bridgeport) The larger of Richmond's two Asian-flavored night markets and the easiest to reach via transit; expect to line-up for entry at this wildly popular summer tradition. Inside, you'll find the usual rows of blingy trinkets plus live entertainment and dozens of steaming, hunger-abating food stalls. Fans of fish balls, deep-fried squid and bubble tea? This is the place for you.

Panda Market MARKET
(☎604-278-8000; www.pandamarket.ca; 12631 Vulcan Way, Richmond; ⏲7pm-midnight Fri & Sat, to 11pm Sun May–mid-Sep; 🚌407) FREE Originally known as the International Summer Night Market, thousands of hungry locals are lured here every weekend to check out the tacky vendor stands and – more importantly – the dozens of hawker food stalls. Don't eat before arriving and you can taste-trip through steaming Korean, Japanese and Chinese treats. Do not miss the spiral fried potatoes on sticks.

Richmond Olympic Oval STADIUM
(☎778-296-1409; www.richmondoval.ca; 611 River Rd, Richmond; ⏲6am-11pm; skytrain, 🚌Brighouse, then 🚌C94) The biggest new venue built for the 2010 Winter Olympics (it hosted long-track speed skating), this riverfront behemoth has since become a community sports facility shared by locals around the region. The five rings haven't been forgotten, though: the on-site **Richmond Olympic Experience** (www.therox.ca) offers a host of simulator experiences enabling you to pretend you won your own medal.

International Buddhist Temple BUDDHIST TEMPLE
(☎604-274-2822; www.buddhisttemple.ca; 9160 Steveston Hwy, Richmond; ⏲9:30am-5:30pm; 🚌403, S Richmond-Brighouse) FREE The highlight of this classical Chinese temple complex is the sumptuous Gracious Hall, complete with deep-red exterior walls and a gently flaring porcelain roof. Check out the colorful 100m Buddha mural and the golden, multi-armed Bodhisattva figure. The landscaped garden, with sculptures and bonsai trees, is another highlight. You don't have to be a Buddhist to visit and the monks are highly welcoming if you're keen to have a look around.

Eating

★**Pajo's** SEAFOOD $
(☎604-272-1588; www.pajos.com; The Wharf, Steveston; mains $9-16; ⏲11am-7pm; skytrain, 🚌Richmond-Brighouse, then 🚌401) There's no better spot to enjoy fish and chips than Steveston's boat-bobbing wharf. Follow your nose and descend the ramp to the little ordering hatch here and you'll be greeted by a friendly face and a menu more extensive than your average chippy. Go the traditional fresh fried cod, salmon or halibut route (with secret-recipe tartar sauce), adding mushy peas for the full effect.

Parker Place FOOD COURT $
(☎604-273-0276; www.parkerplace.com; 4380 No 3 Rd, Richmond; mains $5-10; ⏲11am-7pm Sun-Thu, to 9pm Fri & Sat; 📶; S Aberdeen) There are several popular Asian shopping malls in Richmond, but while Aberdeen Centre and Lansdowne Centre are bigger, Parker Place has an authentic-feeling food court that evokes a Singaporean hawker market. It's beloved of Asian-Canadian locals. Dive in for good-value noodle, fish-ball and dragon's-beard candy dishes; buy a few plates and share 'em at your table.

Shibuyatei RAMEN $
(☎778-297-1777; 2971 Sexsmith Rd, Richmond; mains $7-14; ⏲11:30am-2pm & 5pm-9pm Mon-Sat) Inauspiciously located next to a car wash, this tiny, local-favorite hole-in-the-wall serves sushi but it's really all about great ramen bowls (with no MSG) and tasty Japanese curries, served with chicken or pork *katsu* (deep-fried). It's a one-man operation so avoid peak times if you don't want to wait too long.

Shanghai River Restaurant CHINESE $$
(☎604-233-8885; 7381 Westminster Hwy, Richmond; mains $10-22; ⏲11am-3pm & 5:30-10pm; S Richmond-Brighouse) Grab a seat at the kitchen window at this cavernous northern Chinese eatery and you'll be mesmerized by the handiwork that goes into folding some of the area's best dim-sum dumplings. Order plates to share – one dish per person is the usual ratio – and be careful not to squirt everyone with the juicy pork or shrimp dumplings.

Sushi Hachi SUSHI $$
(☎604-207-2882; 8888 Odlin Cres, Richmond; rmains $8-22; ⏲6pm-9pm Mon-Sat; S Aberdeen) An authentic, fancy-free mom-and-pop operation serving top-notch *nigiri* (raw fish or seafood on a rice ball) and sashimi to in-the-know locals, this place isn't like the hundreds of other similar-sized sushi joints in the region. Call ahead for a reservation and you'll soon be tucking into delectable flounder, octopus and jack mackerel. Add some sake for the full effect.

Shopping

Daiso DEPARTMENT STORE
(604-295-6601; www.daisocanada.com; 4151 Hazelbridge Way, Aberdeen Centre; 9:30am-9pm; Aberdeen) Canada's first (and so far only) branch of Japan's favorite discount store has a cult-like following in Metro Vancouver. A visit to the large, two-floor store is as much a cultural exploration as a chance to buy temptingly low-priced stationery, rice bowls and Ultraman-type action figures, plus oddball plastic items that seem unfathomable, some of them adorned with hilarious 'Japanese English' slogans.

YVR Thirft Store THRIFT STORE
(www.yvrchaplain.com/thrift-store; 4871 Miller Rd, Vancouver International Airport; noon-5pm Fri; YVR-Airport) If you're at Vancouver International Airport with a spare hour, it's a 10-minute stroll from the terminal to this unusual thrift store. Wondering what happens to those scissors and nail clippers confiscated at airport security – not to mention the books and sweaters (and a stroller, on our visit) passengers leave behind before jetting in or out? This is their final resting place.

Information

For information on both areas, drop into the **Tourism Richmond Visitor Centre** (604-271-8280; www.tourismrichmond.com; 3811 Moncton St, Steveston; 9:30am-6pm Jul-Aug, 9:30-5pm Mon-Sat & noon-4pm Sun Sep-Jun; 402).

Getting There & Away

TransLink's (604-953-3333; www.translink.ca) Canada Line SkyTrains trundle in from Vancouver every few minutes throughout the day. The service splits at Bridgeport Station, with some trains heading to the airport and others winding further into Richmond; make sure you're on the right one. Transit buses (including those to Steveston) connect to the Canada Line at Bridgeport and other stations.

BOWEN ISLAND

One of the best days out you can have from Vancouver – it's just a 20-minute boat hop from Horseshoe Bay but it feels a million miles from downtown – Bowen is like British Columbia in miniature. That means a sigh-triggering ferry ride to **Snug Cove**, a cute, village-like settlement with lots of quirky locals and lashings of outdoorsy appeal.

Stroll the Snug Cove boardwalks and drink-in the old-school ambience of dozens of wooden cottages and Tudor-look buildings. On weekends throughout July and August, there's an arts, crafts and food **market** to keep things lively. If you miss it, climb the fairly steep hill to **Artisan Square** for a loop of clapboard galleries and boutique shops – including **Cocoa West Chocolatier** (604-947-2996; www.cocoawest.com; 581C Artisan Ln; 10am-5pm May-Sep, reduced hours off-season).

Visitors used to roll in here by steamship in the 1920s and 1930s; you can hear all about these halcyon days on a fascinating excursion with **Bowen Island Tours** (604-812-5041; www.bowenislandtours.com; tours from adult/child $25/12). Alternatively, explore the breathtaking woodland trails of **Crippen Regional Park** and **Killarney Lake** – see www.bowentrails.ca for tips. Look out for Opa, the island's grandest old-growth tree, said to be centuries old, or hit the water with **Bowen Island Sea Kayaking** (604-947-9266; www.bowenislandkayaking.com; Bowen Island Marina, Snug Cove; rentals/tours from $45/$75; Apr-Sep).

Plans for a hotel have been under discussion for years but there are several cool accommodation options on Bowen. Chocolate fans should consider the swish suite at Cocoa West Chocolatier, complete with a tasty welcome pack on your pillow. Alternatively, some of the old **Union Steamship Marina** (604-947-0707; www.ussc.ca; Snug Cove; d from $180;) cottages and buildings have been renovated as unique sleepovers; see their website for options.

A short stroll from the ferry, you'll find **Doc Morgan's Restaurant & Pub** (604-947-0808; 437 Bowen Island Trunk Rd; mains $16-22; noon-11pm Sun-Fri, 10-1am Sat).

Information

Drop into the **visitors center** (604-200-2399; www.tourismbowenisland.com; 432 Cardena Rd; 9am-4pm mid-May–Sep), just steps from the ferry dock, for insider tips.

Getting There & Away

Take a **TransLink** (604-953-3333; www.translink.ca) transit bus from downtown Vancouver – the 257 express bus is best – and you'll be at the Horseshoe Bay **BC Ferries** (250-386-3431; www.bcferries.com) terminal in around 40 minutes. Ferry services depart from here to Bowen Island's Snug Cove throughout the day (adult/child/car $12.35/6.20/34.85, 20 minutes, 12 daily).

SEA TO SKY HIGHWAY

Otherwise known as Hwy 99, this breathtakingly picturesque cliffside roadway links a string of communities between West Vancouver and Lillooet and is the main route to Squamish and Whistler from Metro Vancouver. Upgraded in recent years, the winding road has several worthwhile stops – especially if you're an outdoor activity fan, history buff or lover of British Columbia's eye-poppingly scenic vistas.

Getting There & Away

Most travelers visiting this area from Vancouver are driving via Hwy 99, which handily links the city to Squamish, Whistler and beyond. Intercity bus services ply the same route, including **Greyhound Canada** (www.greyhoundcanada.ca) and **Pacific Coach Lines** (☎604-662-7575; www.pacificcoach.com). If you're driving, tune into Mountain Radio (107.1FM) for handy traffic and road-condition updates.

Squamish & Around

An hour north of Vancouver and another hour to Whistler, Squamish sits at the meeting point of ocean, river and alpine forest. Originally just a grungy logging town, it's now a popular base for outdoor activities and is also a hub for top attractions nearby.

Sights

Sea to Sky Gondola GONDOLA

(☎604-892-2551; www.seatoskygondola.com; 36800 Hwy 99, Squamish; adult/child $40/14; ⏰10am-6pm daily May-Oct, to 8pm Fri & Sat May-Sep, reduced hours in winter) The biggest new Squamish-area attraction to open in years, this popular eco lure whisks visitors up the tree-studded mountainside then serves up a rich slab of breathtaking BC scenery from its summit viewing platforms. Once you've depleted your camera batteries snapping the Howe Sound vistas, shimmy over the lofty suspension bridge and check out the bird-lined forest trails and view-hugging restaurant. There are free **nature tours** in summer while winter visitors can access activities from **snow tubing** to backcountry snowshoeing.

Britannia Mine Museum MUSEUM

(☎604-896-2260; www.britanniaminemuseum.ca; Hwy 99, Britannia Beach; adult/child $29/18.50; ⏰9am-5pm; 👪) Once the British Empire's largest copper mine, this giant and superbly restored industrial museum is just 10 minutes before Squamish on Hwy 99. The rattling underground train tour is highly recommended (included with entry) and there are plenty of kid-friendly exhibits, including hands-on gold panning. You'll never moan about your boss again as you discover just how grim it was to work a *real* job back in the day. Save time for the gift shop and a sparkly pyrite souvenir.

West Coast Railway Heritage Park MUSEUM

(☎604-898-9336; www.wcra.org; 39645 Government Rd, Squamish; adult/child $18/13; ⏰10am-5pm; 👪) Train nuts should continue just past central Squamish to this large, mostly alfresco museum that's lined with clapboard buildings and dozens of historic locomotives and carriages – including BC's legendary Royal Hudson steam engine, housed in the purpose-built Roundhouse. Spend time chatting to the volunteers – many are retired railway operators with lots of stories to share – and don't miss the old walk-through mail train. Check ahead for kid-friendly special events, particularly during Christmas and school holidays.

Garibaldi Provincial Park PARK

(www.bcparks.ca; Hwy 99) Outdoorsy types should make a beeline for this 1950 sq km park, justly renowned for hiking trails colored by diverse flora, abundant wildlife and panoramic wilderness vistas. Summer hikers seem magnetically drawn here but the trails also double as cross-country ski routes in winter. There are five main trail areas – directions to each are marked by the blue-and-white signs you'll see off Hwy 99. Among the park's most popular trails, the **Cheakamus Lake hike** (3km) is relatively easy, with minimal elevation.

Stawamus Chief Provincial Park PARK

(www.bcparks.ca; Hwy 99, Squamish) On the way into Squamish from Vancouver, you'll see a sheer, 652m-high granite rock face looming ahead. Attracting hardy climbers, it's called the 'Chief' and it's the highlight of Stawamus Chief Provincial Park. You don't have to gear up to experience the summit's breathtaking vistas: there are hiking routes up the back for anyone who wants to have a go. Consider Squamish Rock Guides (p669) for climbing assistance or lessons.

Shannon Falls Provincial Park WATERFALL

(www.bcparks.ca; Hwy 99, Squamish) About 4km before you reach Squamish, you'll hear the rushing waters of Shannon Falls Provincial Park. Pull into the parking lot and stroll the short trail to BC's third-highest waterfall, where water cascades down a 335m drop. A few picnic tables make this a lovely spot for an alfresco lunch.

Gillespie's Fine Spirits DISTILLERY
(☎604-390-1122; www.gillespiesfinespirits.com; 38918 Progress Way, Squamish; ⊙noon-6pm Fri-Sun, Mon-Thu by appointment) Fiendishly well-hidden in an industrial area, this friendly little micro-distillery is worth the search. Drop by for Saturday or Sunday tours (2pm) or roll up to the tasting bar and grab one of their housemade gin, vodka and liqueurs – served in mismatched thrift-store glasses (3 samples for $5). Check their Facebook feed for evening lounge openings and bookable cocktail classes.

Brandywine Falls Provincial Park PARK
(www.bcparks.ca; Hwy 99) A few kilometers north of Squamish and adjacent to Hwy 99, the focus of this tree-lined 143-hectare park is its spectacular 70m waterfall. A short stroll through the forest leads to a leg-jellying platform overlooking the top of the falls, where water drops suddenly out of the trees like a giant faucet. A 7km looped trail leads further through the dense forest and ancient lava beds to **Cal-Cheak Suspension Bridge**.

Activities

Sea to Sky Air SCENIC FLIGHTS
(☎604-898-1975; www.seatoskyair.ca; Squamish Airport, Squamish; from $109; ⊙9am-6pm Apr-Oct, to 5pm Thu-Sun & Tue Nov-Mar) Running a series of small airplane tours from the town's forest-fringed little airport, the friendly folk here will soon have you snapping photos over snow-peaked valleys and glittering glacier-fed lakes. But the best option is the Introductory Flight Experience ($199), where you'll start with a runway plane inspection, shimmy up into the sky alongside the pilot and then take the controls.

Squamish Spit OUTDOORS
(Squamish) If you prefer to travel under your own steam, the Squamish Spit is a popular kiteboarding (and windsurfing) hot spot; the season runs from May to October. The **Squamish Windsports Society** (www.squamishwindsports.com) is your first point of contact for weather and water conditions and information on access to the spit.

WORTH A TRIP

KAOHAM SHUTTLE

One of British Columbia's smallest trains trundles locals and visitors through arguably the province's most scenic short rail journey. Call ahead to book your spot on the two-car **Kaoham Shuttle** (☎250-259-8300; www.tsalalh.net/shuttle.html; round-trip $10), especially in summer when the 30 seats fill up quickly. Aim for the Friday service, which is more feasible for day tripping. Then drive on Hwy 99 past Pemberton to Lillooet Station to hop abroad. It's less than two hours to **Seton Portage** and back but on the way you'll be immersed in spectacular lake and mountain views and frequent opportunities for wildlife-watching, often including bears, bighorn sheep and grouse skittering across the tracks ahead. The best part? It costs just $10 round-trip.

Squamish Rock Guides CLIMBING
(☎604-892-7816; www.squamishrockguides.com; guided rock climbs half-day/day from $85/135) This outfit provides guided climbs and lessons for the Stawamus Chief Provincial Park (p668).

Sleeping & Eating

Alice Lake Provincial Park CAMPGROUND $
(www.discovercamping.ca; Hwy 99, Brackendale; campsites $35) This large, family-friendly campground, 13km north of Squamish, has more than 100 sites. There are two shower buildings with flush toilets, and campers often indulge in activities like swimming, hiking and biking (rentals available). Consider an interpretive ranger tour through the woods (July and August only). Reserve far ahead; this is one of BC's most popular campgrounds.

Sunwolf CABIN $$
(☎604-898-1537; www.sunwolf.net; 70002 Squamish Valley Rd, Brackendale; d $150;) This idyllic place – with a clutch of 10 comfortable, well-maintained riverside cabins along a forested riverbank – is the perfect tranquility break from the city. Bald eagles flying overhead are common, while additional attractions include popular rafting excursions and a gabled on-site cafe that lures in-the-know locals – sit outside under a tree and feast on the area's best breakfast or brunch.

Howe Sound Inn INN $$
(☎604-892-2603; www.howesoundinn.com; 37801 Cleveland Ave, Squamish; d $129;) Quality rustic

is the approach at this comfortable inn-style accommodation, where the rooms are warm and inviting with plenty of woodsy touches. Recover from your climbing escapades at the Stawamus Chief via the property's popular sauna – or just head to the downstairs **brewpub**. It serves some of BC's best house-made beers; inn guests can request free brewery tours.

Even if you're not staying, it's worth stopping in at the restaurant here for great pub grub with a gourmet twist.

Galileo Coffee Company CAFE $
(☎604-896-0272; www.galileocoffee.com; 173 Hwy 99; baked goods from $4; ⏲6am-3pm Mon-Fri, 7am-3pm Sat & Sun) Across from the entrance to Britannia Mine Museum (p668), Galileo Coffee is everyone's favorite java pit stop en route to Whistler.

Information

Head to the slick visitors center, named the **Squamish Adventure Centre** (☎604-815-5084; www.exploresquamish.com; 38551 Loggers Lane, Squamish; ⏲8am-8pm; 📶), to see what's on offer. It's crammed with good info on hiking and biking trails in the area.

Getting There & Away

Greyhound Canada (www.greyhound.ca) buses arrive in Squamish from Vancouver ($16, 65 minutes, two daily) and Whistler ($12, 70 minutes, two daily). The more salubrious **Pacific Coach Lines** (☎604-661-1725; www.pacificcoach.com) buses also arrive here from downtown Vancouver ($60, 70 minutes, up to six daily). But ask the locals and they'll tell you they take the comfortable **Squamish Connector** (☎604-802-2119; www.squamishconnector.com) minibus shuttle between here and Vancouver ($25, one hour, two daily).

WHISTLER

POP 10,300

Named for the furry marmots that populate the area and whistle like deflating balloons, this gabled alpine village and 2010 Olympics venue is one of the world's most popular ski resorts. Nestled in the formidable shadow of the Whistler and Blackcomb Mountains, the village has a frosted, Christmas-card look in winter. But summer visitors now outnumber their ski-season equivalents, with many lured by the area's scenic hiking, biking and thrill-popping outdoor adventures. It's surprisingly easy to get lost walking around the labyrinthine little village but you're unlikely to find yourself too far from your destination once you turn around the next corner.

Sights

★**Audain Art Museum** GALLERY
(Map p672; ☎604-962-0413; www.audainartmuseum.com; 4350 Blackcomb Way; adult/child $18/free; ⏲10am-5pm Sat-Mon & Wed, to 9pm Thu & Fri) BC's finest new art museum is housed in a dramatic angular building that's a landmark in itself. But inside is even better. The rooms display a jaw-dropping array of historic First Nations carvings followed by iconic paintings of the region by leading artists from Emily Carr to EJ Hughes. There's also a strong commitment to contemporary work, with sparkling photoconceptualist images by Jeff Wall, Rodney Graham et al. The final rooms showcase eye-popping modern First Nations works to great effect.

Peak 2 Peak Gondola GONDOLA
(☎604-967-8950; www.whistlerblackcomb.com/discover/360-experience; 4545 Blackcomb Way; adult/teen/child $57/50/29; ⏲10am-4:45pm) Built to link the area's two main mountaintops, this record-breaking engineering marvel gently eases goggle-eyed passengers along a lofty 4.4km gondola ride that takes around 11 minutes to complete. En route, you'll be mesmerized by the unfolding panorama of forest-snow-and-peak vistas – especially if you snag one of the two glass-bottomed cars. Equally popular in summer and winter.

Whistler Museum & Archives MUSEUM
(Map p672; ☎604-932-2019; www.whistlermuseum.org; 4333 Main St; suggested donation $5; ⏲11am-5pm, to 9pm Thu) Tucked into an anonymous green shed behind the library building and tracing Whistler development from wilderness outpost to Olympic resort, this great little museum has quirky exhibits that include an original 1965 ski lift gondola and a 2010 Olympic torch. New exhibitions were being planned in mid-2016, as well as a hoped-for larger venue. Check ahead for events and add one of their area walking tours in summer (by donation; 1pm daily, from June to August).

Squamish Lil'wat Cultural Centre MUSEUM
(☎604-964-0990; www.slcc.ca; 4584 Blackcomb Way; adult/child $18/8; ⏲9:30am-5pm Apr-Sep, 10am-5pm Tue-Sun Oct-Mar) This handsome, wood-beamed facility showcases two quite different First Nations groups – one coastal

and one interior-based. Take a tour for the vital context behind the museum-like exhibits and keep your eyes open for on-site artist demonstrations during the summer, when there are also Tuesday-night barbecue dinners. If you miss it, the on-site cafe serves tasty bannock tacos while the recently-expanded gift shop offers an excellent array of BC-made arts and crafts.

Activities

Skiing & Snowboarding

Comprising 37 lifts and crisscrossed with over 200 runs, the **Whistler-Blackcomb** (☎604-967-8950; www.whistlerblackcomb.com; 2-day winter lift ticket adult/child $258/129) sister mountains are also physically linked by the resort's mammoth 4.4km Peak 2 Peak Gondola (p670). It takes just 11 minutes to shuttle wide-eyed powder hogs between the two high-alpine areas, so you can hit the slopes on both mountains on the same day.

More than half the resort's runs are aimed at intermediate-level skiers, and the season typically runs from late November to April on Whistler and November to June on Blackcomb – December to February is the peak for both.

You can beat the crowds with an early-morning (upload is between 7:15am and 8am) Fresh Tracks ticket ($20), available in advance at Whistler Village Gondola Guest Relations. Coupled with your regular lift ticket, it gets you an extra hour on the slopes and the ticket includes buffet breakfast at the Roundhouse Lodge up top.

Snowboard fans should also check out the freestyle terrain parks, mostly located on Blackcomb, including the **Snow Cross** and the **Big Easy Terrain Garden**. There's also the popular **Habitat Terrain Park** on Whistler.

If you didn't bring you own gear, **Mountain Adventure Centres** (☎604-967-8950; www.whistlerblackcomb.com/rentals; ⊙8am-5pm) has several equipment rental outlets around town. It offers online reservations – choose your favorite gear before you arrive – as well as lessons for ski and snowboard first-timers.

Cross-country Skiing & Snowshoeing

A pleasant stroll or free shuttle bus away from the village, **Lost Lake** (☎604-905-0071; www.crosscountryconnection.ca; day pass adult/child $20/10; ⊙8am-8pm mid-Dec–Mar) is the hub for 25km of wooded cross-country ski trails, suitable for novices and experts alike. Around 4km of the trail is lit for additional nighttime skiing and there's a handy 'warming hut' providing lessons and equipment rentals. Snowshoers are also well served in this area: you can stomp off on your own on 15km of trails or rent equipment and guides.

Southwest of the village via Hwy 99, **Whistler Olympic Park** (☎604-964-0060; www.whistlersportlegacies.com; 5 Callaghan Valley Rd, Callaghan Valley; park access per vehicle weekdays/weekends $10/15) is a pristine, snow-swathed venue that hosted several 2010 Olympic Nordic events. Now perfect for visiting (and local) snowshoers and cross-country skiers, it has more than 130km of marked trails. In summer, it's also popular with hikers and bikers.

Mountain Biking

Colonizing the melted ski slopes in summer and accessed via lifts at the village's south end, **Whistler Mountain Bike Park** (☎604-967-8950; http://bike.whistlerblackcomb.com; 1-day lift ticket adult/child $59/35; ⊙May-Oct) offers barreling downhill runs and an orgy of jumps and bridges twisting through well-maintained forested trails. Luckily, you don't have to be a bike courier to stand the knee-buckling pace: easier routes are marked in green, while blue intermediate trails and black-diamond advanced paths are offered if you want to **Crank It Up** – the name of one of the most popular routes.

Outside the park area, regional trails include **Comfortably Numb** (a tough 26km with steep climbs and bridges); **A River Runs Through It** (suitable for all skill levels, it has teeter-totters and log obstacles); and the gentle **Valley Trail**, an easy 14km loop that encircles the village and its lake, meadow and mountain chateau surroundings – this is recommended for first-timers.

Hiking

With more than 40km of flower-and-forest alpine trails, most accessed via the Whistler Village Gondola, the region is ideal for those who like nature of the strollable variety. Favorite routes include the **High Note Trail** (8km), which traverses pristine meadows and has stunning views of the blue-green waters of Cheakamus Lake. Free route maps are available at the Whistler Visitors Centre (p677). Guided hikes are also offered by the friendly folk at **Mountain Skills Academy & Adventures** (Map p672; ☎604-938-9242; www.mountainskillsacademy.com; 4368 Main St; ⊙8am-7pm reduced hrs off-season), who can also help with rock-climbing excursions.

Whistler

Rafting

Tumbling waterfalls, dense forests and a menagerie of wildlife are some of what you might see as you lurch along the roiling stretches of local rivers on an adrenaline-charged rafting trip. **Wedge Rafting** (Map p672; 604-932-7171; www.wedgerafting.com; 4293 Mountain Sq; tours adult/child from $99/69;) offers paddle-like-crazy excursions, plus more gentler jaunts that are popular with kids.

Whistler

Festivals & Events

Winterpride LGBT
(www.gaywhistler.com; Jan) A week of gay-friendly snow action and late-night partying.

World Ski & Snowboard Festival SPORTS
(www.wssf.com; Apr) A multi-day showcase of pro ski and snowboard competitions, plus partying.

Crankworx SPORTS
(www.crankworx.com; Aug) An adrenaline-filled celebration of bike stunts, speed contests and mud-splattered shenanigans.

Cornucopia FOOD & DRINK
(www.whistlercornucopia.com; Nov) Bacchanalian food and wine fest crammed with parties.

Sleeping

Winter, especially December and January, is the peak for prices, but last-minute deals are still possible if you're planning an impromptu overnight from Vancouver – check the website of **Tourism Whistler** (www.whistler.com) for room sales and packages. Most hotels extort parking fees of up to $40 daily and some also slap on resort fees, so confirm these before you book.

HI Whistler Hostel HOSTEL $
(604-962-0025; www.hihostels.ca/whistler; 1035 Legacy Way; dm/r $37/97;) Built as athlete accommodation for the 2010 Winter Olympics, this sparkling hostel is 7km south of the village, near Function Junction. Transit buses to/from town stop right outside. Book ahead for private rooms (with ensuite bathrooms and TVs) or save by staying in a small dorm. Eschewing the sometimes institutionalized HI hostel feel, this one has IKEA-style furnishings, art-lined walls and a licensed cafe.

Riverside Resort CAMPGROUND, CABIN $$
(604-905-5533; www.whistlercamping.com; 8018 Mons Rd; campsites/yurts/cabins $35/119/219;) Just a few minutes past Whistler on Hwy 99, this facility-packed, family-friendly campground and RV park has elevated itself in recent years by adding cozy cabin and yurt options. The yurts come with basic furnishings, electricity and bedding provided, and are especially recommended. The resort's on-site Riverside Junction Cafe serves great breakfasts. Yurts and cabins have a two-night minimum stay.

Whistler Peak Lodge HOTEL $$
(Map p672; 604-938-0878; www.whistlerpeaklodge.com; 4295 Blackcomb Way; d from $240;) Brilliantly located in the heart of the village, this former Holiday Inn has been upgraded but still has some of the best rates in town (if you book far enough ahead). There's a wide array of rooms available but full kitchen or kitchenette facilities are standard – you're steps from many restaurants if you're feeling too lazy to cook.

Bear Tracks Whistler Chalet B&B $$
(604-932-4187; www.beartrackswhistler.ca; 7461 Ambassador Crs; d from $130;) A short walk from the village, this Bavarian-look B&B has several bright and sunny rooms – think pine furnishings and crisp white duvets – plus a garden that's ideal for a spot of

OFF THE BEATEN TRACK

FUNCTION JUNCTION

Take bus number 1 southbound from the village and within 20 minutes you'll be in the heart of a favorite locals' neighborhood. **Function Junction** started life as a hidden-among-the-trees area where industrial businesses carried on without affecting the village's Christmas-card visuals. But things have changed in recent years and many of its industrial units have given way to galleries and cafes.

The are a couple of streets to explore, but the best is **Millar Creek Rd**. Start with some bakery treats at **Purebread** (☎604-983-3013; www.purebread.ca; 1040 Millar Creek Rd; baked goods $3-6; ⏲8:30am-5pm), then nip across to **Whistler Brewing Company** (☎604-962-8889; www.whistlerbeer.com; 1045 Millar Creek Rd; tours $16; ⏲1-8pm Mon-Thu, to 10pm Fri, noon-7pm Sat & Sun). The area's very own beer maker is responsible for challenging the choke hold of factory-made suds at bars in the village. You can take a tour of the facilities and try a few brews in the taproom; with any luck, the sought-after Chestnut Ale will be available. For more options and information, visit the handy www.shopfunction.ca website.

evening wine quaffing. Or you can just hop in the hot tub and dream about the large breakfast coming your way in the morning.

Pinnacle Hotel Whistler HOTEL $$
(Map p672; ☎604-938-3218; www.whistlerpinnacle.com; 4319 Main St; d from $240;) Just across the street from the museum, this friendly, well-established, adult-oriented lodge has the perfect extra in almost every room: a large, jetted soaker tub that dominates proceedings. Balconies and full kitchens are also de rigueur and there's an on-site restaurant if it's too cold to stray far from your room.

Adara Hotel BOUTIQUE HOTEL $$
(Map p672; ☎604-905-4009; www.adarahotel.com; 4122 Village Green; r from $209;) Unlike all those lodges now claiming to be boutique hotels, the sophisticated and very centrally located Adara is the real deal. Studded with designer details, including a mod circular sofa in the lobby, it offers accommodations with spa-like bathrooms and fireplaces that look like TVs. Despite the ultra-cool aesthetics, service is warm and relaxed. Check ahead for packages and off-season deals.

Whistler Village Inn & Suites HOTEL $$
(Map p672; ☎604-932-4004; www.whistlervillageinnandsuites.com; 4429 Sundial Pl; d $189;) Superbly located in the heart of the village action, just a few steps from the Whistler Village Gondola, this comfy 1980s-stye hotel has been renovated in recent years and now offers a wide range of accommodation options. The studios and standard rooms are fine, but the loft suites are the way to go with their contemporary furnishings and handy kitchenettes.

Nita Lake Lodge BOUTIQUE HOTEL $$$
(☎604-966-5700; www.nitalakelodge.com; 2135 Lake Placid Rd; d from $240;) Adjoining the handsome Creekside railway station, this swanky timber-framed lodge is perfect for a pampering retreat. Hugging the lakeside, the chic but cozy rooms feature individual patios, rock fireplaces and bathrooms with heated floors and large tubs; some also have handy kitchens. Creekside lifts are a walkable few minutes away and there's an on-site spa to soothe your aching muscles.

The hotel also has an excellent West Coast restaurant but a free shuttle can whisk you to the village if you want to dine further afield.

Pan Pacific Whistler Mountainside HOTEL $$$
(Map p672; ☎604-905-2999; www.panpacific.com; 4320 Sundial Cres; d from $240;) One of Whistler's two Pan Pacifics, the Mountainside wins for its slope-hugging views of the skiers swishing down to the base of Whistler Mountain. Rooms are apartment-style and comfortable with full kitchens and cozy fireplaces, but for many the (heated) outdoor swimming pool, with its surrounding vista of snow-capped peaks, is a key lure.

Eating

★Purebread BAKERY $
(Map p672; ☎604-962-1182; www.purebread.ca; 4338 Main St; baked goods $3-6; ⏲8:30am-5:30pm) When this Function Junction legend finally opened a village branch, the locals came running and they've been

queuing ever since. They're here for the cornucopia of drool-worthy bakery treats, including salted caramel bars, sour-cherry choc-chip cookies and the amazing Crack, a naughtily gooey shortbread cookie bar. There's savory here, too; go for the hearty homity or pudgie pie.

Peaked Pies AUSTRALIAN **$**
(Map p672; ☎604-962-4115; www.peakedpies.com; 4369 Main St; mains $7-13; ⏰8am-9pm) A chatty little nook that's very busy at mealtimes (takeout recommended), this is the place to dive into Australia's age-old pie infatuation. Check the glass cabinet for the day's available offerings – kangaroo is included but the butter chicken is our favorite – and 'peak it' with added toppings of mashed potato, mushy peas and gravy. Add a lamington cake dessert for the full Aussie effect.

La Cantina Urban Taco Bar MEXICAN **$**
(Map p672; ☎604-962-9950; www.tacoslacantina.ca; 4340 Lorimer Rd; mains $8-14; ⏰11am-9pm) A busy corner eatery where you order at the counter and then grab a perch (the high stools down the side usually have some empty spots), aim for a selection of $3 tacos or dive into a bulging burrito if you're really hungry. This place gets jam-packed at peak times so consider a takeout rather than resorting to fisticuffs to find a seat.

Gone Village Eatery CAFE **$**
(Map p672; ☎604-938-1990; www.gonevillageeatery.com; 4205 Village Sq; mains $10-12; ⏰6:30am-9pm; 📶🖉) This well-hidden locals' fave (just behind the store Armchair Books) serves a wide range of hearty, good-value comfort grub of the chili, pad Thai and salmon burger variety. This is where many fuel up for a day on the slopes and have a Marsbar coffee when they return. There's a patio out back for summer evening basking.

Add a Howe Sound Brewing beer to the mix – just $5.50 for a real pint. There are also lots of options here for vegetarians.

Mount Currie Coffee Co CAFE **$**
(Map p672; ☎604-962-2288; www.mountcurriecoffee.com; 4369 Main St; mains $5-9; ⏰7am-6pm; 📶) One of Whistler's favorite independent coffee pit stops, this outpost of the popular Pemberton company also offers plenty of baked treats to tempt you from your java-only diet (carrot cake recommended). Croissants and panini are also popular at lunchtimes.

Sachi Sushi JAPANESE **$$**
(Map p672; ☎604-935-5649; www.sachisushi.com; 106-4359 Main St; mains $7-32; ⏰noon-2pm Tue-Fri, & 5pm-late daily) This popular Japanese spot is a sushi specialist but they also serve everything from pork gyoza to spicy hotpots and stomach-warming udon noodle bowls – the tempura noodle bowl is best. A relaxing après-ski hangout, it's great for a glass of hot sake on a cold winter's day.

Red Door Bistro FRENCH **$$$**
(☎604-962-6262; www.reddoorbistro.ca; 2129 Lake Placid Rd; $22-38; ⏰5pm-late) As soon as you know you're coming to Whistler, call for a reservation at this hot little Creekside eatery that delighted locals love as much as in-the-know visitors. Taking a French bistro approach to fine, mostly West Coast ingredients means mouthwatering lamb and seafood dishes plus a highly-recommended cassoulet that's brimming with everything from duck to smoked pork.

Bar Oso SPANISH **$$$**
(Map p672; ☎604-962-4540; www.baroso.ca; 4222 Village Square; small plates $7-27; ⏰3pm-late) Taking a Spanish approach ('oso' translates as 'bear') to BC's cornucopia of great ingredients, the top-notch small plates (don't miss the lamb meatballs) and housemade charcuterie plates are a taste-tripping delight here – especially if you're able to snag a seat at the dramatic swirly-stone bar and add a cocktail or two to the proceedings.

Christine's on Blackcomb INTERNATIONAL **$$$**
(☎604-938-7437; Rendezvous Lodge, Blackcomb Mountain; mains $28-32) A viewtastic gondola-accessed mountaintop restaurant where the swish menu combines with diners dressed in ski gear, Christine's is the best place to eat during your skiing or hiking day out. Book ahead (or try to avoid the lunch rush) then dive into the smashing Keralan fish curry. Can't get a table? The adjoining cafeteria serves everything from burgers to burritos and ramen bowls.

Araxi Restaurant & Bar CANADIAN **$$$**
(Map p672; ☎604-932-4540; www.araxi.com; 4222 Village Sq; mains $28-48; ⏰dinner from 5pm daily) Whistler's best splurge restaurant, Araxi cooks up an inventive and exquisite Pacific Northwest menu and has charming and courteous service. Try the seared wild scallops and drain the 15,000-bottle wine selection but save room for dessert: a regional cheese plate or the amazing chocolate ganache tart…or both.

WORTH A TRIP

DETOUR TO COWBOY COUNTRY

If you're craving an alternative to bustling Whistler Village (but you don't want to head into the wilderness like Grizzly Adams on a day out), the next community north along Hwy 99 is **Pemberton**. Founded as a farming and cowboy town, it still has a distant-outpost feel, with enough to keep you occupied for a half-day. You can get the 99 Pemberton Commuter transit bus here from Whistler ($4.50, 40 minutes, four times daily) but a car will enable you to explore much more effectively. Plan ahead via www.tourismpemberton.com.

Start with coffee and a giant cinnamon bun at the woodsy little **Blackbird Bakery** (☎604-894-6226; www.blackbirdbread.com; 7424 Frontier St; baked goods & sandwiches $3-8; ⏰6am-8pm Mon-Sat, 7am-8pm Sun) in the former train station, then head over to **Pemberton Museum** (☎604-894-5504; www.pembertonmuseum.org; 7455 Prospect St; ⏰10am-5pm May-Oct) for the lowdown on how this quirky little town started. Ask them about the Pemberton mascot, a neckerchief-wearing potato dressed like a cowboy.

Next, drive over to **Pemberton Distillery** (☎604-894-0222; www.pembertondistillery.ca; 1954 Venture Pl; ⏰noon-5pm Wed & Thu, to 6pm Fri & Sat Jun–early Sep, reduced hours in winter). A pioneer of BC's latter-day artisan booze movement, they have tours and a tasting room. And while they started with silky potato vodka, they've expanded production to include top-selling gin and a seductive whiskey and wild-honey liqueur. Next – with designated driver at the wheel – trundle 20 minutes out of town and uphill to **Joffre Lakes**. There's a lovely two-hour hike from the trailhead here or you can just snap some breathtaking glacier photos from the parking lot.

Finally, when dinner beckons, weave back into town and find a table at the rustic, red-walled **Pony** (☎604-894-5700; www.thepony.ca; 1392 Portage Rd; mains $9-18; ⏰6:30am-late; 🖉). The town's main dining hangout, it serves an elevated comfort-food menu (pizzas recommended) and some choice BC craft beers.

Here in July? Book ahead for the mountain-framed **Pemberton Music Festival** (www.pembertonmusicfestival.com), one of the best and biggest in BC.

Drinking & Nightlife

Merlin's Bar & Grill PUB
(☎604-938-7700; 4553 Blackcomb Way; ⏰11am-1am) If you must drink fizzy Kokanee beer this is the place to do it. A cavernous party pub with a huge patio at the base of Blackcomb, the log-lined walls, ceiling-mounted lift cars and bra-draped moose head add to the casual ambience. Food covers the pub-grub classics (there's also better beer than Kokanee available) and there's often live music during peak season.

Garibaldi Lift Company PUB
(Map p672; ☎604-905-2220; 4165 Springs Lane, Whistler Village Gondola; ⏰11am-1am) The closest bar to the slopes, you can smell the sweat of the skiers or mountain bikers hurtling past the patio at this cavernous bar that's known by every local as the GLC. The furnishings have the scuffs and dings of a well-worn pub, and the best time to come is when DJs or bands turn the place into a clubbish mosh pit.

Dubh Linn Gate PUB
(Map p672; ☎604-905-4047; www.dubhlinngate.com; 4320 Sundial Cres; ⏰8am-1am Mon-Fri, 7am-1am Sat & Sun) Whistler's favorite Irish pub, this dark, wood-lined joint would feel just like an authentic Galway watering hole if not for the obligatory heated patio facing the slopes. Tuck yourself into a shady corner table inside and revive your inner leprechaun with a stout – there's Guinness as well as Murphy's. Even better is the slightly pricey BC-craft-brew menu and regular live music, often of the trad Irish variety.

Moejoe's CLUB
(Map p672; ☎604-935-1152; www.moejoes.com; 4155 Golfer's Approach; ⏰9pm-2am) Popular with the kind of party-hard international under-30s that work in Whistler shops and coffeehouses so they can ski the slopes as much as possible, this is the best place in town if you like dancing yourself into a drooling heap. Locals will tell you that Fridays are the best nights.

Longhorn Saloon & Grill PUB
(Map p672; ☎604-932-5999; www.longhornsaloon.ca; 4284 Mountain Sq; ⏰9am-1am) Across from lifts at the base of Whistler Mountain, the sprawling patio here sometimes threatens to take over the village (especially with

its pumping party soundtrack). Popular with twentysomethings, it's all about downing jugs of fizzy lager and eyeing up potential partners from your chair. The food is nothing special, but it's hard to beat the atmosphere on hopping winter evenings.

Information

Post Office (Map p672; www.canadapost.ca; 4360 Lorimer Rd; 8am-5pm Mon-Fri, to noon Sat)

Whistler Visitors Centre (Map p672; 604-935-3357; www.whistler.com; 4230 Gateway Dr; 8am-8pm Sun-Wed, 8am-10pm Thu-Sat Jun-Aug, reduced hours off-peak) Flyer-lined visitors center with friendly staff.

Public Library (604-935-8433; www.whistlerlibrary.ca; 4329 Main St; 11am-7pm Mon-Thu, 10am-6pm Fri, 11am-5pm Sat & Sun;) Free wi-fi plus internet-accessible computers on-site (free for up to one hour per person per day).

Northlands Medical Clinic (604-932-8362; www.northlandsclinic.com; 4359 Main St; 9am-5:30pm) Walk-in medical center.

Getting There & Away

While most visitors arrive by car from Vancouver via Hwy 99, **Greyhound Canada** (www.greyhound.ca) buses also service the route, arriving at Creekside and Whistler Village from the city ($26, 2½ hours, four daily). Buses are equipped with free wi-fi.

Pacific Coach Lines (604-662-7575; www.pacificcoach.com) services also arrive from Vancouver ($55, two hours, six daily) and Vancouver International Airport and drop off at Whistler hotels. **Snowbus** (604-451-1130; www.snowbus.com) operates a wintertime service from Vancouver (adult $38, up to three hours, up to three daily).

Whistler Transit System (www.bctransit.com/whistler) buses (single fare/one-day pass $2.50/$7) are equipped with ski and bike racks. In summer, there's a free service from the village to Lost Lake.

SUNSHINE COAST

Fringing the forested coastline for 139km from Langdale in the south to Lund in the north, the Sunshine Coast – separated from the Lower Mainland by the Coast Mountains and the Strait of Georgia – has an independent, island-like mentality that belies the fact it's just a short hop by ferry or plane from Metro Vancouver. Hwy 101 handily strings together the key communities of Gibsons, Roberts Creek, Sechelt and Powell River, making this an easy and leisurely region to explore. Popular with hikers, kayakers and mountain bikers, there's also a lively and welcoming arts scene. Peruse the website of **Sunshine Coast Tourism** (www.sunshinecoastcanada.com) for information and pick up the *Recreation Map & Activity Guide* – available in upper and lower region versions – for outdoorsy suggestions throughout the area.

Gibsons

POP 4500

If you're arriving on the Sunshine Coast via BC Ferries from Horseshoe Bay, your first port of call after docking in Langdale and driving or busing into town will be the pretty waterfront strip called Gibsons Landing. A rainbow of painted wooden buildings overlooking the marina, its streets are lined with browsable boutiques and tempting eateries while its wharf is a summer-hugging promenade for languid boat watching.

Transformation was coming to the Gibsons Landing waterfront on our visit, with a new hotel breaking ground and a handsome public market building being renovated nearby. Drop into the **visitor centre** (604-886-2374; www.gibsonsvisitorinfo.com; 417 Marine Dr; 10am-4pm Wed-Sat & Mon, 10am-3pm Sun) for the latest news.

Eavesdrop on locals gossiping about the changes to the town at **Gibsons Public Art Gallery** (604-886-0531; www.gpag.ca; 431 Marine Dr; 11am-4pm Thu-Mon) FREE, where new shows pop-up monthly.

Need to hit the water? Book a rental or guided tour via the friendly folk at **Sunshine Kayaking** (604-886-9760; www.sunshinekayaking.com; Molly's Lane; kayak rentals 2hr/24hr $35/85; 9am-7pm, call ahead for reservations).

Accommodation-wise, the lovely **Bonniebrook Lodge** (604-886-2887; www.bonniebrook.com; 1532 Ocean Beach Esplanade; d from $199;) is an historic wood-built inn overlooking a quiet waterfront stretch. The area also abounds with B&Bs, including the homely, family-friendly **Arcturus Retreat Bed & Breakfast** (604-886-1940; www.arcturusretreat.ca; 160 Pike Rd; d from $160;), handily located just up the hill from the ferry dock. They can also point you to the nearby **Sprockids Mountain Bike Park**.

LOCAL KNOWLEDGE

SUNSHINE COAST GALLERY CRAWL

Pick up the free *Purple Banner* flyer at area visitor centers for the location of dozens of studios and galleries throughout the region. Many are open for drop-in visitors (especially in summer) – look out for the purple flags along the road on your travels – and they're a great way to meet the locals and find unique souvenirs. For further information, see www.suncoastarts.com. Also, if you're here in October, don't miss the three-day **Sunshine Coast Art Crawl** (www.sunshinecoastartcrawl.com), a party-like showcase of local studios, galleries and events.

If you're thirsty for Sunshine Coast beer, head to **Persephone Brewing Company** (☎778-462-3007; www.persephonebrewing.com; 1053 Stewart Rd; ⊙11am-7pm Tue-Thu & Sun, 10am-9pm Fri & Sat, reduced hours in winter) – especially on summer weekends, when its rustic tasting lounge spills outside for growler supping at log tables; there's also live music and a pizza food truck. Don't miss their delicious Pale Ale but look out for intriguing seasonals as well.

Eating

Smoke on the Water BBQ Shack BARBECUE $
(☎604-840-0004; www.smokeonthewaterbbq.ca; 611 School Rd; $10-16; ⊙11am-6:30pm, Apr-Oct) Follow your nose along the wharf for this shingle-sided gourmet barbecue shack, like a food truck with a permanent (albeit seasonal) location. Brisket or pulled-pork sandwiches are staples but look out for the occasional barbecued salmon special – it disappears quickly. If you miss it, console yourself with their amazing meat-lovers poutine (your calorie intake for the week).

Smitty's Oyster House SEAFOOD $$
(☎604-886-4665; www.smittysoysterhouse.com; 643 School Rd Wharf; mains $12-24; ⊙noon-late Tue-Sat, to 8pm Sun, reduced hours in winter) The best spot for seafood in Gibsons (especially if you snag a seat at the communal long table alongside the marina boardwalk), Smitty's sparked a renaissance in local dining when it opened a few years back. It's still as popular as ever, especially on summer evenings when this is the perfect place to scoff a pile of fresh-shucked bivalves.

The Nova Kitchen BISTRO $$$
(☎604-886-5858; www.thenovakitchen.com; 546 Gibsons Way; $19-30; ⊙4:30pm-9pm Tue-Thu, to 9:30pm Fri & Sat) While the steep climb to get here seems off-putting, it's worth it for this smashing little farm-to-table bistro – especially if you snag a patio table with its dramatic views over Gibsons Landing and the shoreline panorama. The seasonal menu can include BC-sourced treats like Chilliwack pork or Yarrow Meadow duck, lovingly prepared and served with delicious sides and super-warm service.

Getting There & Away

BC Ferries (☎250-386-3431; www.bcferries.com) services arrive at Langdale, 6km northeast of Gibsons, from West Vancouver's Horseshoe Bay (passenger/vehicle $16.15/54, 40 minutes, nine daily).

Pacific Ferries (☎778-866-5107; www.pacificferries.ca) runs passenger-only services between Gibsons Landing and Horseshoe Bay ($15, 30 minutes, two daily).

Regular **Sunshine Coast Regional Transit System** (www.busonline.ca) buses arrive in Gibsons from the Langdale ferry terminal and other Sunshine Coast communities (adult/child $2.25/1.75).

Roberts Creek

Just off Hwy 101 via Roberts Creek Rd, the funky 'downtown' here looks like a little hobbit community, if hobbits had gone through a hippie phase. Poke around the wood-built, shack-like stores and eateries and then wander downhill to the beach, checking out the huge, ever-changing **Community Mandala** painted on the ground.

Join the locals for coffee and baked goodies (including excellent pizza) at the wood-floored **Gumboot Cafe** (1057 Roberts Creek Rd; mains $8-11; ⊙7am-6pm Mon-Fri, 8am-6pm Sat & Sun; ☎). But save yourself for dinner at the nearby **Gumboot Restaurant** (☎604-885-4216; www.gumbootrestaurant.com; 1041 Roberts Creek Rd; mains $14-27; ⊙10am-8:30pm Mon-Thu, 9am-9pm Fri & Sat, 9am-8:30pm Sun), which serves lovingly-prepared, often organic West Coast dishes from lamb to seafood.

Sleeping

Up the Creek Backpackers B&B HOSTEL $
(☎604-837-5943; www.upthecreek.ca; 1261 Roberts Creek Rd; dm/r $28/80; ☎) The Sunshine

Coast's best hostel includes small dorms plus private rooms aimed at couples and families – the back garden cabin is a cozy delight. Tent pitches are available ($14) and they'll even rent you a two-person tent if you've left yours at home ($28). The small shared kitchen is well-equipped and there's an active eco approach including rigorous recycling.

Shades of Jade Inn & Spa B&B **$$**
(604-885-3211; www.shadesofjade.ca; 1489 Henderson Rd; d from $189;) Aimed at tranquility-craving adults, this luxe two-unit B&B – with its Asian–West Coast fusion decor approach – couldn't be more relaxing. Each spacious room (we love the upstairs one with its hidden little deck) is equipped with a kitchen and steam shower while there's an outdoor hot tub plus on-site spa treatments to provide you with multiple reasons to never leave.

Getting There & Away

Regular **Sunshine Coast Regional Transit System** (www.busonline.ca) buses run from the ferry terminal at Langdale into Roberts Creek and beyond (adult/child $2.25/1.75).

Sechelt

POP 9775

Not quite as alluring as Gibsons, Roberts Creek or Powell River, Sechelt is nevertheless a good stop-off on your Sunshine Coast jaunt: there are tasty places to fuel up plus access to some cool outdoor activities – including a camera-triggering stroll along the town's waterfront.

With a good kayak launch site and a sandy beach, fir-and-cedar-forested **Porpoise Bay Provincial Park** (www.bcparks.ca; Hwy 101) is 4km north of Sechelt along East Porpoise Bay Rd. There are trails throughout the park and a large **campground** (www.discovercamping.ca; campsites $29) with handy hot showers.

For visiting paddlers, **Pedals & Paddles** (604-885-6440; www.pedalspaddles.com; 7425 Sechelt Inlet Rd; kayak rentals 2/24hr $37/95) organizes kayak rentals and can also take you on kayak, Zodiac or SUP tours of the inlet's wonderfully tranquil waters. Alternatively, dive in (not literally) with a First Nations interpretive kayak or hiking tour organized by **Talaysay Tours** (604-628-8555; www.talaysay.com; Porpoise Bay Provincial Park; tours from $59; Apr-Sep).

If you like secluded waterfront retreats, check out the cottage and two spacious suites at **Beachside by the Bay** (604-741-0771; www.beachsidebythebay.com; 5005 Sunshine Coast Hwy; d from $199;). You'll be waking up to spectacular Davis Bay panoramas. Alternatively, continue on Hwy 101 for 30 minutes past Sechelt to lovely **Halfmoon Bay** for a night overlooking the water from your spacious villa at **Painted Boat Resort Spa & Marina** (604-883-2122; www.paintedboat.com; 12849 Lagoon Rd; d from $385;) – units have full kitchens and there's a handy supermarket nearby (plus a celebrated on-site restaurant).

Back in Sechelt, drop into downtown's hip **Basted Baker** (604-885-1368; bastedbaker.com; 5685 Cowrie St; $9-12; 8:30am-5pm Mon-Fri, 9:30am-4pm Sat & Sun;) for a bulging biscuit sandwich (check the specials before ordering) along with a housemade sweet treat to go. Alternatively, aim for a heartier meal at local favorite **Ty's Fine Foods & Bistro** (604-740-9818; www.tysfinefoods.com; 5500 Trail Ave; $12-18; 11am-5pm Mon-Fri, 11am-3pm Sat), where tapas, soups and sandwiches are prepared with care.

Information

For more information, drop by the **Sechelt Visitor Centre** (604-885-1036; www.sechelt visitorcentre.com; 5790 Teredo St; 9am-5pm Jul & Aug, 9am-5pm Mon-Sat Jun & Sep, reduced hours in winter).

Getting There & Away

Regular **Sunshine Coast Regional Transit System** (www.busonline.ca) buses arrive in Sechelt from the Langdale ferry terminal and other Sunshine Coast communities (adult/child $2.25/1.75).

Harbour Air Seaplanes (604-885-2111; www.harbourair.com) flies floatplanes from downtown Vancouver to Sechelt three times a day ($118, 20 minutes).

Powell River

POP 12,900

An historic paper mill town founded more than a century ago, this upper Sunshine Coast community has been busy reinventing itself in recent years. The result is an increasingly hip town – especially in the historic Townsite area – that's also a gateway to splendid outdoor activities.

DON'T MISS

THE OTHER WEST COAST TRAIL

Vancouver Island's West Coast Trail is so popular it's hard not to run into other hikers en route. But the Sunshine Coast offers its own under-the-radar version that many BC locals have only just started discovering. Running from Sarah Point to Saltery Bay, the 180km-long **Sunshine Coast Trail** is a wilderness paradise of ancient forests, eagle-dotted waterfronts and breathtaking snowcapped vistas. Unlike the West Coast Trail, this one is free and reservations are not required – there are also 12 free-use sleeping huts dotted along the route. For more information, visit www.sunshinecoasttrail.com.

Sights & Activities

Pick up a free walking tour flyer from the visitors centre (p680) and wander the Townsite's heritage buildings, including many carefully restored arts-and-crafts constructions. Highlights include **Dr Henderson's House** (6211 Walnut Ave) and the lovely **Patricia Theatre** (604-483-9345; www.patriciatheatre.com; 5848 Ash Ave), Canada's oldest continually operating cinema. Step inside to peruse its mural-painted interior. Also touch base with the **Townsite Heritage Society** (604-483-3901; www.powellrivertownsite.com; 6211 Walnut Ave, Dr Henderson's House; $5), which often runs guided tours of the historic neighborhood in summer.

Conclude your wander with a free tour at **Townsite Brewing** (604-483-2111; www.townsitebrewing.com; 5824 Ash Ave; 11am-7pm Apr-Oct, 11am-7pm Tue-Sat Nov-Mar) (Saturdays year-round plus Thursdays in summer) in the old post office building. For $8, you'll get a tasty, four-beer sample flight – don't miss the lip-smacking Suncoast Pale Ale, which is only available here. Need some booze for your Sunshine Coast Trail hike? Buy one of their sought-after steel growlers to go (don't forget to fill it).

If you need to blow away a few cobwebs, hit the water for a refreshing paddle with **Powell River Sea Kayak** (604-483-2160; www.bcseakayak.com; 10676 Crowther Rd; 3/12hr rental $35/44).

Sleeping & Eating

When it's time to rest your weary noggin, it's hard to beat the highly welcoming **Old Courthouse Inn** (604-483-4000; www.oldcourthouseinn.ca; 6243 Walnut St; d from $129;), an immaculately restored Tudoresque antique-lined hotel. Each room, individualized with its own knickknacks, feels like a cozy home-away-from-home decorated by a nostalgic aunt with artistic appreciation. Rates include cooked breakfast in the lovely **Edie Rae's Diner** (homemade biscuits recommended), where there's also a great Monday-night dinner deal offered every week.

Need a mid-morning coffee? **Base Camp** (604-485-5826; www.basecamp-coffee.com; 4548 Marine Dr; mains $8-16; 7am-7pm Sun-Thu, 7am-9pm Fri & Sat;) serves every local in town at some point during the day. And when lunch beckons, drop in for tacos at the tiny, brightly painted **Costa del Sol** (604-485-2227; www.costadelsollatincuisine.com; 4578 Marine Ave; mains $10-16; 11:30am-late, Wed-Mon;) nearby. Alternatively, hit the view-tastic deck for craft beers and comfort food – chicken-and-waffle sandwich recommended – at **Coastal Cookery** (604-485-5568; www.coastalcookery.com; 4553 Marine Ave; mains $12-28; 11:30am-late Mon-Sat, 4pm-late Sun) across the street. The menu changes seasonally and there's a tasty commitment to BC-sourced ingredients (and top-flight beer).

Information

Visitors Centre (604-485-4701; www.powellriver.info; 4670 Joyce Ave; 9am-6pm Jul & Aug, to 5pm Mon-Sat Sep-Jun)

Getting There & Away

If you're driving here from the lower Sunshine Coast, you'll hop the **BC Ferries** (250-386-3431; www.bcferries.com) service between Earls Cove and Saltery Bay en route (passenger/vehicle $15.85/52.60, 50 minutes, up to 7 daily). From there, it's a 40-minute drive to Powell River. The company also operates Powell River services to and from Texada Island (passenger/vehicle $11.45/26.95, 35 minutes, up to 9 daily) and Vancouver Island's Comox (passenger/vehicle $15.90/45.70, 90 minutes, up to 5 daily).

Pacific Coastal Airlines (604-273-8666; www.pacificcoastal.com) flies into Powell River from the South Terminal of Vancouver International Airport four times daily (from $106, 35 minutes).

VANCOUVER ISLAND

The largest populated landmass between western North America and New Zealand – around 500km long and 100km wide – Vancouver Island is studded with colorful, quirky communities, many founded on logging or fishing and featuring the word 'Port' in their name.

The locals are a friendly bunch, proud of their region and its distinct differences. You'll find a wide range of attractions, experiences and activities that feel many miles from the bustle of mainland Vancouver. Which reminds us: to make a good impression, don't mistakenly refer to the place as 'Victoria Island.'

While the history-wrapped BC capital Victoria is the arrival point for many, it shouldn't be the only place you visit here. Food and wine fans will love the Cowichan Valley farm region; outdoor-activity enthusiasts shouldn't miss the surf-loving wild west coast radiating from Tofino; and visitors venturing north will find an uncrowded region of independent communities fringed by rugged wilderness.

Information

For an introduction to the island, contact **Tourism Vancouver Island** (250-754-3500; www.vancouverisland.travel) for listings and resources.

Victoria

POP 85,000

With a wider metro population approaching 380,000, this picture-postcard provincial capital was long-touted as North America's most English city. Thankfully, the tired theme-park version of old-fashioned England is no more. Fueled by an increasingly younger demographic, a quiet revolution has seen lame tourist pubs, eateries and stores transformed into the kind of brightly painted bohemian shops, coffee bars and innovative restaurants that would make any city proud. It's worth seeking out these enclaves on foot, but activity fans should also hop on their bikes: Victoria has more cycle routes than any other Canadian city. Once you've finished pedaling, there's BC's best museum, a park fringed by a windswept seafront and outdoor activities from kayaking to whale-watching.

Sights

★Miniature World MUSEUM

(Map p686; 250-385-9731; www.miniatureworld.com; 649 Humboldt St; adult/child $15/10; 9am-9pm mid-May–mid-Sep, to 5pm mid-Sep–mid-May; ; 70) Tucked along the side of the Empress Hotel, this old-school hidden gem is a must-see, especially if you appreciate the craft of extremely intricate model-making. Lined with dozens of diminutive diorama scenes, divided into themes from Camelot to space and from fairyland to Olde England, there's plenty of push-button action, several trundling trains and the chance to see yourself on a miniature movie theater screen. An immaculately maintained reminder of innocent yesteryear attractions.

★Craigdarroch Castle MUSEUM

(250-592-5323; www.thecastle.ca; 1050 Joan Cres; adult/child $14/5; 9am-7pm mid-Jun–Aug, 10am-4:30pm Sep–mid-Jun; P; 14) One of Canada's finest stately home attractions, this elegant turreted mansion illuminates the lives of the city's Victorian-era super-rich. Lined with sumptuous wood paneling and stained-glass windows, the rooms are teeming with period antiques, giving the impression the residents have just stepped away from their chairs. Climb the tower's 87 steps for distant views of the Olympic Mountains. Save time to read up on the often tragic story behind the family that lived here.

Royal BC Museum MUSEUM

(Map p686; 250-356-7226; www.royalbcmuseum.bc.ca; 675 Belleville St; adult/child from $16/11; 10am-5pm daily, to 10pm Fri & Sat mid-May–Sep; ; 70) Start in the natural history gallery of BC's best museum and say hello to the hulking woolly mammoth exhibit. From there, wander alongside evocative dioramas, then head up to the First Peoples exhibit with its fascinating mask gallery – complete with a ferret-faced white man. The museum's highlight, though, is the walk-through colonial street with its chatty Chinatown and detailed storefronts.

Beacon Hill Park PARK

(www.beaconhillpark.ca; Douglas St; P; 3) Fringed by crashing ocean, this waterfront park is ideal for feeling the breeze in your hair – check out the windswept trees along the clifftop. You'll also find a gigantic totem pole, Victorian cricket pitch and

Vancouver Island

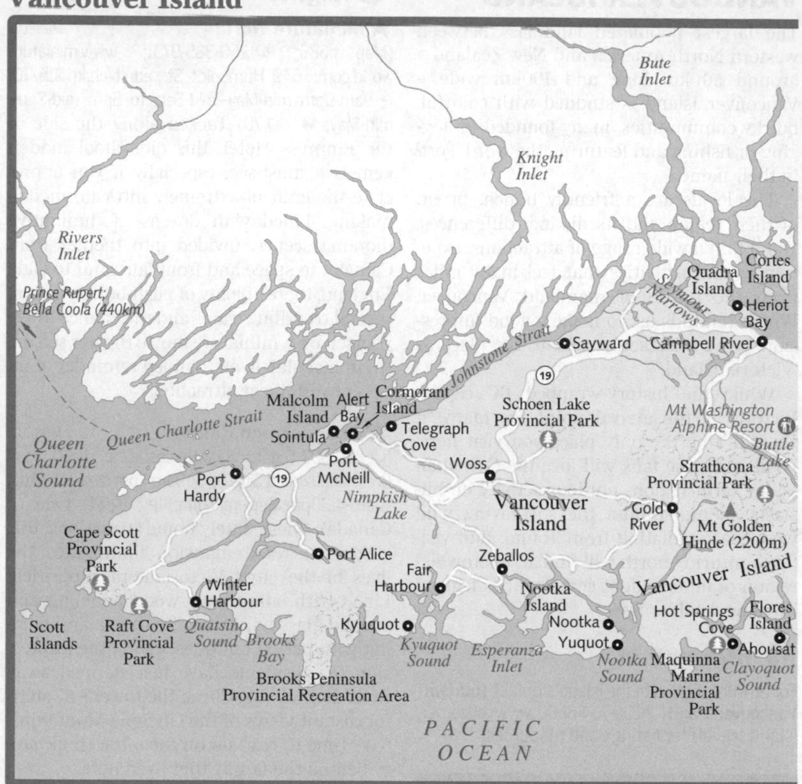

a marker for Mile 0 of Hwy 1, alongside a statue of Canadian legend Terry Fox. If you're here with kids, you should consider the popular **children's farm** (www.beaconhillchildrensfarm.ca) as well.

Victoria Bug Zoo ZOO

(Map p686; ☎250-384-2847; www.victoriabugzoo.com; 631 Courtney St; adult/child $12/8; ⏰10am-5pm Mon-Fri, to 6pm Sat & Sun, reduced hours off-season; 👪; 🚌70) The most fun any kid can have in Victoria without realizing it's educational. Step inside the brightly painted main room for a cornucopia of show-and-tell insect encounters. New owners have spruced the place up with more tanks but it's still all about the enthusiasm of the young guides who are great at firing up your enthusiasm for atlas beetles, dragon-headed crickets and thorny devils. There are plenty of chances to snap shots of your kids handling the goods (under supervision).

Parliament Buildings HISTORIC BUILDING

(Map p686; ☎250-387-3046; www.leg.bc.ca; 501 Belleville St; ⏰tours 9am-5pm mid-May–Aug, 9am-5pm Mon-Fri Sep–mid-May; 🚌70) FREE This dramatically handsome confection of turrets, domes and stained glass is the province's working legislature and is also open to history-loving visitors. Peek behind the facade on a colorful (and free) 45-minute guided tour then stop for lunch at the 'secret' politicians' restaurant inside. Return in the evening when the elegant exterior is illuminated like a Christmas tree.

Robert Bateman Centre GALLERY

(Map p686; ☎250-940-3630; www.batemancentre.org; 470 Belleville St; adult/child $12.50/6; ⏰10am-5pm daily, to 9pm Fri & Sat Jun-Aug; 🚌70) Colonizing part of the Inner Harbour's landmark old Steamship Terminal building, this gallery showcases the photo realistic work of Canada's most popular nature painter, along with a revolving roster of works by other art-

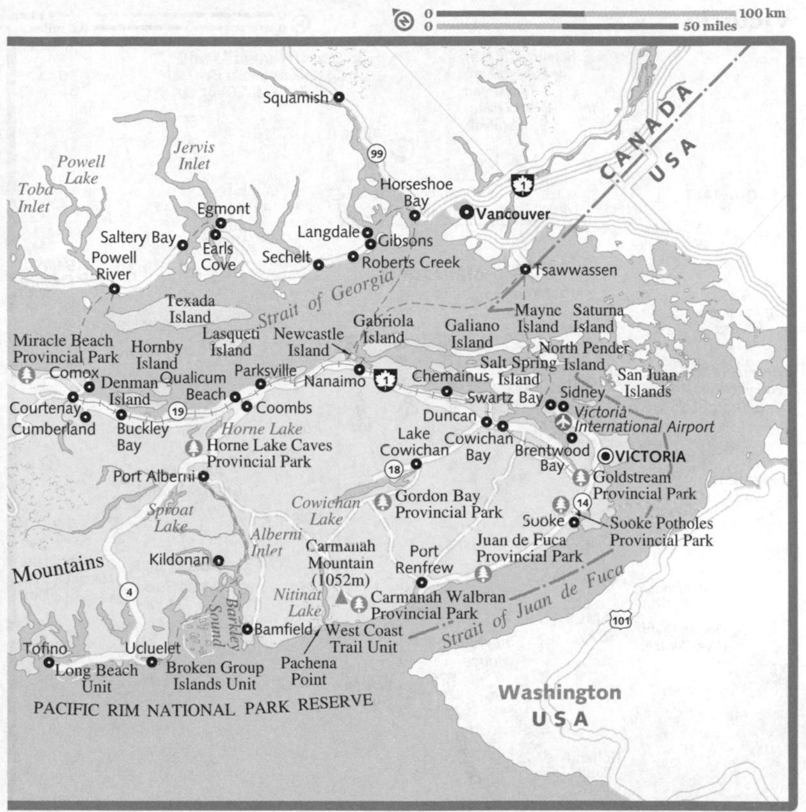

ists. Start with the five-minute intro movie, then check out the dozens of achingly beautiful paintings showing animals in their natural surroundings in BC and beyond.

Art Gallery of Greater Victoria GALLERY
(☎250-384-4171; www.aggv.ca; 1040 Moss St; adult/child $13/2.50; ⏲10am-5pm Mon-Sat, noon-5pm Sun, closed Mon mid-Sep–mid-May; 🚌14) Head east of downtown on Fort St and follow the gallery street signs to one of Canada's best Emily Carr collections. Aside from Carr's swirling nature canvases, you'll find an immersive array of Asian art and an ever-changing menu of temporary exhibitions. Check online for events, including lectures and frequent guided tours. Admission is by donation on the first Tuesday of every month.

Emily Carr House MUSEUM
(☎250-383-5843; www.emilycarr.com; 207 Government St; adult/child $6.75/4.50; ⏲11am-4pm Tue-Sat May-Sep; P; 🚌3) The birthplace of BC's best-known painter, this bright-yellow gingerbread-style house has plenty of period rooms, plus displays on the artist's life and work. There's an ever-changing array of local contemporary works on display, but head to the Art Gallery of Greater Victoria if you want to see more of Carr's paintings. On your visit here, look out for the friendly house cats.

Activities

Whale-watching

Raincoat-clad tourists head out by the boatload throughout the May to October viewing season. The whales don't always show, so most excursions also visit the local haunts of lolling sea lions and portly elephant seals.

Eagle Wing Tours WHALE WATCHING
(☎250-999-0502; www.eaglewingtours.ca; 12 Erie St, Fisherman's Wharf; adult/child $125/95; ⏲Mar-Oct) Long-established whale-watching boat tour operator, based at Fisherman's Wharf.

Victoria

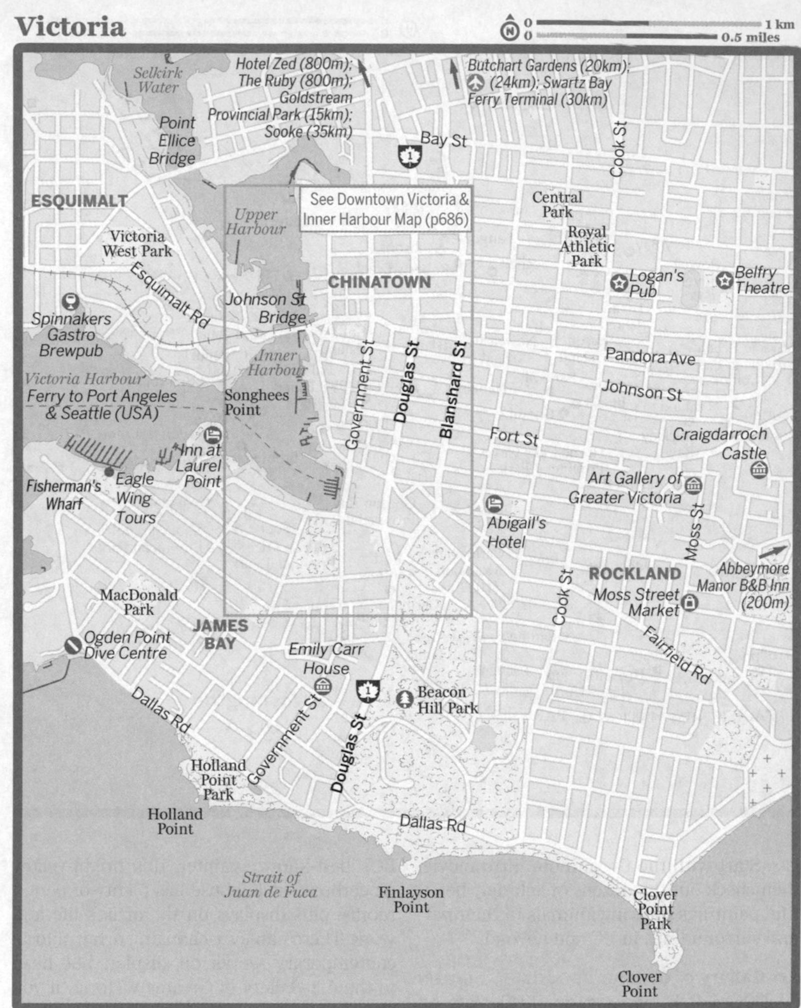

Prince of Whales WHALE WATCHING
(Map p686; ☎250-383-4884; www.princeofwhales.com; 812 Wharf St; adult/child from $120/95;) Long-established local operator offering several ways to check out the local whales and marine life from the water.

Springtide Charters WHALE WATCHING
(Map p686; ☎250-384-4444; www.springtidecharters.com; 1119 Wharf St; adult/child $105/85; ⏰8am-10pm, reduced hours off-season) This experienced operator has been offering local whale-watching tours for more than two decades and is one of the city's most popular marine excursion companies.

Water Sports

Paddling around the coastline is the perfect way to see this region, especially if you spot soaring eagles and starfish-studded beaches. If you like what you see on the surface, consider a dive below.

Ocean River Sports KAYAKING
(Map p686; ☎250-381-4233; www.oceanriver.com; 1824 Store St; rental per 2hr $40, tours from $75; ⏰9:30am-6pm Mon-Fri, to 6pm Sat, 10am-5pm Sun) Rentals and popular kayak day tours in the area (including evening options). Stand-up paddling and multi-day tours also available.

Ogden Point Dive Centre DIVING
(☎250-380-9119; www.divevictoria.com; 199 Dallas Rd; ⏲9am-6pm) Dive courses and rentals a few minutes from the Inner Harbour.

Tours

Harbour Air SCENIC FLIGHTS
(Map p686; ☎250-384-2215; www.harbourair.com; Inner Harbour; tours from $109) For a bird's-eye Victoria view, these breathtaking floatplane tours from the Inner Harbour are fab, especially when they dive-bomb the water on landing.

Pedaler CYCLING
(Map p686; ☎778-265-7433; www.thepedaler.ca; 719 Douglas St; tours from $49, rentals from $10; ⏲9am-6pm, reduced hours off-season) Offering bike rentals and several guided two-wheeled tours around the city, including the Hoppy Hour Ride with its craft-beer-sampling focus.

Hike Victoria HIKING
(☎250-889-3008; www.hikevictoria.com; tours from $65) Guided nature hikes (they pick you up from your hotel) on the outskirts of Victoria, with a focus on taking great scenic photos.

Big Bus Victoria BUS
(☎250-389-2229; www.bigbusvictoria.com; 1 day adult/child $36/21; ⏲May-Oct) Handy hop-on hop-off bus service that covers most of Victoria major attractions: one-day and two-day options are available.

Festivals & Events

Victoria Day Parade PARADE
(www.gvfs.ca; ⏲mid-May) Street fiesta, with dancers, marching bands and 50,000-plus spectators.

Victoria Ska & Reggae Fest MUSIC
(www.victoriaskafest.ca; ⏲mid-Jun) The largest music festival of its kind in Canada.

Victoria International JazzFest MUSIC
(www.jazzvictoria.ca; ⏲late Jun) Toe-tapping jazz shows over 10 days.

Victoria International Buskers Festival PERFORMING ARTS
(www.victoriabuskers.com; ⏲mid-Jul) Ten days of street performing action from local and international artists.

Victoria Fringe Theater Festival THEATER
(www.victoriafringe.com; ⏲late Aug) Two weeks of quirky short plays and stand-up performances throughout the city.

Rifflandia MUSIC
(www.rifflandia.com; ⏲Sep) Victoria's coolest music festival sees indie bands playing around the city.

Sleeping

From heritage B&Bs to cool boutiques and high-end options, Victoria is stuffed with accommodation for all budgets. Off-season sees great deals. Tourism Victoria's **room reservation service** (☎250-953-2033, 800-663-3883; www.tourismvictoria.com/hotels) can show you what's available. Keep in mind that most downtown accommodation also charge for parking.

Ocean Island Inn HOSTEL $
(Map p686; ☎250-385-1789; www.oceanisland.com; 791 Pandora Ave; dm/d $28/96; @📶; 🚌70) This brightly painted hostel combines a labyrinth of small dorms with three en suite pension-style private rooms adorned with Indonesian craft flourishes and with their own TVs and fridges. Dorms also have fridges and sleep a maximum of six, while there are plenty of private bathrooms on each floor. A simple breakfast is included and there's a busy events roster (including weekly pub crawls).

HI Victoria Hostel HOSTEL $
(Map p686; ☎250-385-4511; www.hihostels.ca/victoria; 516 Yates St; dm/d $33/80; @📶; 🚌70) This quiet downtown hostel situated in a high-ceilinged heritage building has two large single-sex dorms, three small coeds and a couple of private rooms. A games room and a book-lined reading area keep guests busy but you're also in the heart of the action if you want to do your own thing. Free city tours are also regularly scheduled. Free breakfast, tea and coffee included.

Hotel Zed MOTEL $$
(☎250-388-4345; www.hotelzed.com; 3110 Douglas St; d from $175; P📶≋🐾; 🚌70) Accommodation Austin Powers would love, this motel has been given a tongue-in-cheek retro makeover, complete with rainbow paintwork and free VW van rides to downtown (a 10-minute walk away). The rooms are also fun: 1970s phones, bathroom comic books and brightly painted walls. Loaner bikes and free coffee are provided via the front desk and there's also a great diner if you're hungry.

Downtown Victoria & Inner Harbour

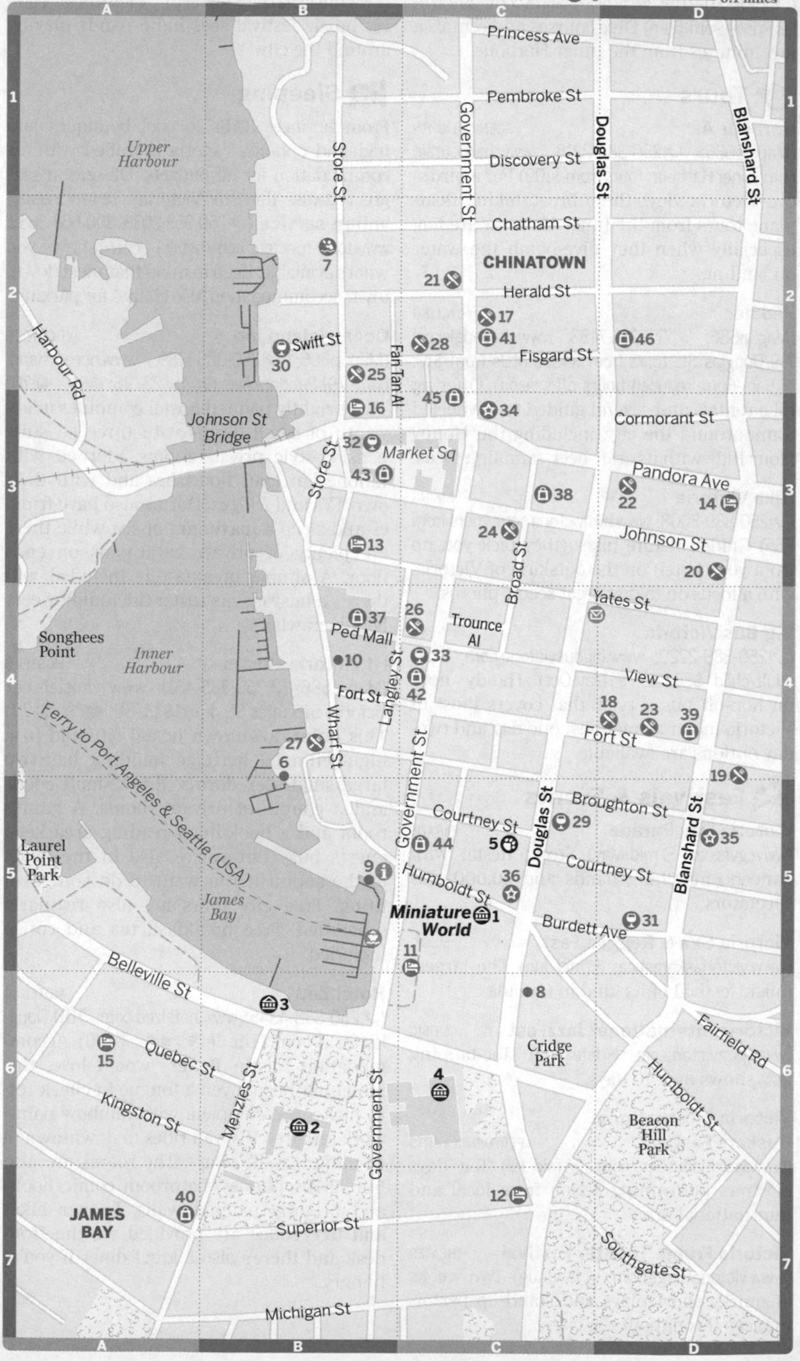

0 200 m
0 0.1 miles

A B C D
1 2 3 4 5 6 7

Princess Ave
Pembroke St
Discovery St
Chatham St
Herald St
Fisgard St
Cormorant St
Pandora Ave
Johnson St
Yates St
View St
Fort St
Broughton St
Courtney St
Burdett Ave
Humboldt St
Fairfield Rd
Southgate St
Superior St
Michigan St
Belleville St
Quebec St
Kingston St
Menzies St
Government St
Douglas St
Blanshard St
Store St
Fan Tan Al
Broad St
Trounce Al
Langley St
Wharf St
Harbour Rd
Johnson St Bridge
Market Sq
Ped Mall
CHINATOWN
JAMES BAY
Upper Harbour
Inner Harbour
James Bay
Songhees Point
Laurel Point Park
Cridge Park
Beacon Hill Park
Miniature World
Ferry to Port Angeles & Seattle (USA)

1 2 3 4 5 6 7 8 9 10 11 12 13 14 15 16 17 18 19 20 21 22 23 24 25 26 27 28 29 30 31 32 33 34 35 36 37 38 39 40 41 42 43 44 45 46

Downtown Victoria & Inner Harbour

Top Sights
1 Miniature World C5

Sights
2 Parliament Buildings B6
3 Robert Bateman Centre B6
4 Royal BC Museum C6
5 Victoria Bug Zoo C5

Activities, Courses & Tours
6 Harbour Air B4
7 Ocean River Sports B2
8 Pedaler C6
9 Prince of Whales B5
10 Springtide Charters B4

Sleeping
11 Fairmont Empress Hotel C5
12 Helm's Inn C7
13 HI Victoria Hostel B3
14 Ocean Island Inn D3
15 Royal Scot Hotel & Suites A6
16 Swans Suite Hotel B3

Eating
17 Brasserie L'École C2
18 Crust Bakery D4
19 Fishhook D4
20 Foo Asian Street Food D3
21 Jam Cafe C2
22 John's Place D3
23 La Taqueria D4
Legislative Dining Room .... (see 2)
24 Lotus Pond Vegetarian Restaurant C3
25 Olo B2
26 ReBar C4
27 Red Fish Blue Fish B4
28 Venus Sophia C2

Drinking & Nightlife
29 Big Bad John's C5
30 Canoe Brewpub B2
31 Clive's Classic Lounge D5
32 Drake B3
33 Garrick's Head Pub C4

Entertainment
34 McPherson Playhouse C3
35 Royal Theatre D5
36 Vic Theatre C5

Shopping
37 Bastion Square Public Market B4
38 Cherry Bomb Toys C3
39 Ditch Records D4
40 James Bay Market A7
41 Milkman's Daughter C2
42 Munro's Books C4
43 Regional Assembly of Text B3
44 Rogers' Chocolates C5
45 Silk Road C3
46 Victoria Public Market D2

Helm's Inn HOTEL $$
(Map p686; ☎250-385-5767; www.helmsinn.com; 600 Douglas St; d from $140; P @ 🛜; 🚌70) One of downtown's best value hotels (you're also just a couple of blocks away from the Inner Harbour), the 42 well-maintained rooms at this three-building, motel-style property all have handy kitchen facilities (either full kitchens or fridges and microwaves). Family-run for three decades, coin laundry is also available and the front-desk staff has plenty of suggestions for how to enjoy your stay in the city.

Swans Suite Hotel BOUTIQUE HOTEL $$
(Map p686; ☎250-361-3310; www.swanshotel.com; 506 Pandora Ave; d from $145; 🛜 🐾; 🚌70) This former brick-built warehouse has been transformed into an art-lined boutique hotel. Most rooms are spacious loft suites where you climb upstairs to bed in a gabled nook, and each is decorated with a comfy combination of wood beams, rustic chic furniture and deep leather sofas. The full kitchens are handy but there's also a brewpub downstairs for liquid sustenance.

Royal Scot Hotel & Suites HOTEL $$
(Map p686; ☎250-388-5463; www.royalscot.com; 425 Quebec St; d from $230; P 🛜 🏊 🐾; 🚌70) The best of several midrange options crowding the banks of the Inner Harbour near the Parliament Buildings, rooms at the Royal Scot are spotlessly maintained. Expect a friendly welcome and lots of cruise-ship seniors in the lobby. Rooms come in a variety of configurations, some with full kitchens. A free local shuttle service is available.

Inn at Laurel Point HOTEL $$$
(☎250-386-8721; www.laurelpoint.com; 680 Montreal St; d from $260; ❄ @ 🛜 🏊 🐾; 🚌70) Tucked along the Inner Harbour a short seaside stroll from the downtown action, this friendly, art-lined and ever-comfortable hotel is all about the views across the waterfront. Spacious rooms come with private balconies for drinking in the mesmerizing sunsets. Still owned by a local family, with a resort-like level of calm relaxation. In-room spa treatments and bike rentals are also available.

Fairmont Empress Hotel HOTEL $$$
(Map p686; ☎250-384-8111; www.fairmont.com/empress-victoria; 721 Government St; d from $340; P❄@🛜≋; 🚌70) Undergoing an upgrade on our visit (including the removal of the Bengal Lounge bar), this century-old Inner Harbour landmark is Victoria's favorite hotel. Aim for a room overlooking the water and expect classic decor and effortlessly solicitous service. Add a sumptuous high tea on the lobby level and, even if you're not staying here, stroll through and soak up the Old World charm.

Abbeymoore Manor B&B Inn B&B $$$
(☎250-370-1470; www.abbeymoore.com; 1470 Rockland Ave; d from $199; P@🛜; 🚌14) A romantic 1912 arts-and-crafts mansion, Abbeymoore's handsome colonial exterior hides seven antique-lined rooms furnished with Victorian knickknacks. Some units have kitchens and jetted tubs and the hearty breakfast will fuel you up for a day of exploring: Craigdarroch Castle (p681) and the Art Gallery of Greater Victoria (p683) are nearby.

Abigail's Hotel B&B $$$
(☎250-388-5363; www.abigailshotel.com; 906 McClure St; d from $249; P@🛜; 🚌7) One of Victoria's most romantic sleeping options, this sumptuous guest house is a short walk from the Inner Harbour. Behind its Tudoresque facade, accommodations range from flowery standard rooms to antique-lined, gable-ceilinged suites with canopy beds, marble fireplaces and Jacuzzi tubs. Whatever their price bracket, all guests enjoy a great breakfast: a three-course belt-buster of regionally sourced ingredients. Adults only.

STROLLABLE 'HOODS

Start your exploration of Canada's oldest, and possibly smallest, **Chinatown** at the handsome gate near the corner of Government and Fisgard Sts. From here, Fisgard is studded with neon signs and traditional grocery stores, while **Fan Tan Alley**, a narrow passageway between Fisgard St and Pandora Ave, is a small warren of traditional and trendy stores hawking cheap and cheerful trinkets, cool used records and funky artworks. If you crave company, consider a guided Chinatown amble with **Discover the Past** (☎250-384-6698; www.discoverthepast.com; adult/child $15/13; ⏰10:30am Sat year-round, plus Tue & Thu Jun-Aug).

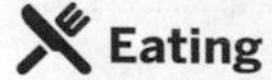

Eating

Victoria's dining scene has been radically upgraded in recent years. Pick up the free *Eat Magazine* to check out the latest foodie happenings. Looking for browsable options? Check out downtown's Fort St, the city'sde factodining row.

Crust Bakery BAKERY $
(Map p686; ☎250-978-2253; www.crustbakery.ca; 730 Fort St; baked goods $3-6; ⏰8am-5:30pm; 🚌14) Arrive early for the best selection at Victoria's favorite new bakery. A fresh-baked egg, bacon and rosemary Danish should start you off nicely but be sure to fill your backpack with tartlets and top-selling cronuts, as well as chocolate and coconut bread and butter pudding; you may be able to trade them on the streets for ten times their face value.

La Taqueria MEXICAN $
(Map p686; ☎778-265-6255; www.lataqueria.com; 766 Fort St; tacos up to $3 each; ⏰11am-8:30pm Sun-Thu, to 11pm Fri & Sat; ✎; 🚌14) The huge, aquamarine-painted satellite of Vancouver's popular and authentic Mexican joint, this ultra-friendly spot specializes in offering a wide array of soft taco options (choose four for $10.50, less for vegetarian options), including different specials every day. Quesadillas are also available and you can wash everything down with margaritas, Mexican beer or mezcal – or all three.

Red Fish Blue Fish SEAFOOD $
(Map p686; ☎250-298-6877; www.redfish-bluefish.com; 1006 Wharf St; mains $6-16; ⏰11am-7pm; 🚌70) 🍃 On the waterfront boardwalk at the foot of Broughton St, this freight-container takeout shack serves fresh-made, finger-licking sustainable seafood. Highlights like jerk fish poutine, amazing chowder and tempura-battered oysters (you can also get traditional fish and chips, of course). Expanded new seating has added to the appeal but watch out for hovering gull mobsters as you try eat.

Foo Asian Street Food ASIAN $
(Map p686; ☎250-383-3111; www.foofood.ca; 769 Yates St; mains $9-14; ⏰11:30am-10pm Mon-Sat, to 9pm Sun; P; 🚌70) Like a permanent food truck tucked inauspiciously in a parking lot, this locals' fave food shack focuses

on hearty dishes inspired by Asian hawker stalls. Grab a perch inside or out, check the specials board and dive into fresh-cooked, good-value options, from saag paneer to octopus salad. Beer-wise, there's a love for local-made brews from the likes of Hoyne and Driftwood.

Jam Cafe BREAKFAST $

(Map p686; ☎778-440-4489; www.jamcafevictoria.com; 542 Herald St; mains $9-16; ⏰8am-3pm; 📶✎) The locals won't tell you anything about this slightly off-the-beaten-path place. But that's not because they don't know about it – it's because they don't want you to increase the lineups for Victoria's best breakfast. The wide array of Benedict varieties is ever popular, but we also recommend the amazing, and very naughty, chicken French toast. Arrive early or off-peak; there are no reservations.

Fishhook SEAFOOD $$

(Map p686; ☎250-477-0470; www.fishhookvic.com; 805 Fort St; mains $13-24; ⏰11am-9pm) 🍃 Don't miss the smokey, coconutty chowder at this Indian-and-French influenced seafood gem but make sure you add a tartine open-faced sandwich: it's the house specialty. If you still have room (and you're reluctant to give up your perch at the communal table) split a seafood *biryani* platter with your dining partner. Focused on local and sustainable fish supplies.

Venus Sophia VEGETARIAN $$

(Map p686; ☎250-590-3953; www.venussophia.com; 540 Fisgard St; mains $10-19; ⏰10am-6pm Jul & Aug, 11am-6pm Wed-Sun Sep-Jun; ✎; 🚌70) A delightful cream-walled tearoom combining traditional tea service (including a lovely afternoon tea) with beautifully presented vegetarian lunches, this is a uniquely tranquil respite from Chinatown's sometimes busy streets. Try the blue-cheese-and-pear panino and add an organic tea (served in mismatched vintage cups) from the wide selection. Our favorite? The delicious cream Earl Grey.

John's Place DINER $$

(Map p686; ☎250-389-0711; www.johnsplace.ca; 723 Pandora Ave; mains $9-17; ⏰7am-9pm Mon-Fri, 8am-4pm & 5-9pm Sat & Sun; 📶✎; 🚌70) This ever-friendly, wood-floored hangout is lined with quirky memorabilia, while its enormous menu is a cut above standard diner fare. They'll start you off with a basket of addictive housemade bread, but save room for heaping pasta dishes, piled-high salad mains or a pancake or Tex-Mex brunch. A near-perfect breakfast spot; save time to peruse the signed celebrity photos on the walls.

The Ruby DINER $$

(☎250-507-1325; www.therubyvictoria.com; 3110 Douglas St; mains $13-18; ⏰8am-9pm; 🅿📶) The Hotel Zed's upmarket diner lures locals (arrive off-peak to avoid the crush) with its breakfast tacos and eggs Benedict platters (Mexi Benny recommended) but the rest of the day is all finger-licking comfort dishes, typically including succulent rotisserie chicken. Local ingredients are key and extras like meat rubs and hot sauce are made from scratch. Check out the serious vinyl record collection.

Lotus Pond Vegetarian Restaurant CHINESE, VEGETARIAN $$

(Map p686; ☎250-380-9293; www.lotuspond1998.ca; 617 Johnson St; mains $9-17; ⏰11:30am-3pm & 5-9pm Tue-Sat, noon-3pm & 5-8pm Sun; ✎; 🚌70) This no-frills downtown spot was satisfying local vegetarians long before meat-free diets became fashionable. Superior to most Chinese eateries and with a menu that easily pleases carnivores as well as veggie types, the best time to come is lunch, when the busy buffet lures everyone in the vicinity. Don't miss the turnip cakes, a house specialty.

Legislative Dining Room CANADIAN $$

(Map p686; ☎250-387-3959; www.leg.bc.ca; 501 Belleville St, Parliament Buildings; mains $9-18; ⏰hours vary Mon-Fri; 🚌70) One of Victoria's best-kept dining secrets, the Parliament Buildings has its own subsidized, old-school restaurant where both MLAs and the public can drop by for a silver-service menu of regional dishes, ranging from salmon salads to velvety steaks and a BC-only wine list. Entry is via the security desk just inside the building's main entrance; photo ID is required.

ReBar VEGETARIAN, FUSION $$

(Map p686; ☎250-361-9223; www.rebarmodernfood.com; 50 Bastion Sq; mains $9-17; ⏰11:30am-9pm Mon-Fri, 9:30am-9pm Sat & Sun; ✎; 🚌70) A beloved local fave with new monochrome-painted exterior (although the same riotously colorful tablecloths inside), this is the best place in town for vegetarians and carnivores to dine together without one side feeling cheated. The signature almond burger is one of many excellent veggie options, while meaty-types will find lots of fish and chicken options. Also a popular weekend brunch spot.

WORTH A TRIP

HIT THE TRAILS

Easily accessed along the Island Hwy just 16km from Victoria, **Goldstream Provincial Park** (☎250-478-9414; www.goldstreampark.com; 2930 Trans-Canada Hwy; P), at the base of Malahat Mountain, makes for a restorative nature-themed day trip from the city. Dripping with ancient, moss-covered cedar trees and a moist carpet of plant life, it's known for its chum-salmon spawning season from late October to December. Hungry bald eagles are attracted to the fish and bird-watchers come ready with their cameras. Head to the park's **Freeman King Visitors Centre** (☎250-478-9414; 2390 Trans-Canada Hwy; ⊙9am-4:30pm) for area info and natural history exhibits.

Aside from nature watching, you'll also find great hiking: marked trails range from tough to easy and some are wheelchair accessible. Recommended treks include the hike to 47.5m-high **Niagara Falls** (not *that* one) and the steep, strenuous route to the top of **Mt Finlayson**, one of the region's highest promontories. The visitors center can advise on trails and will also tell you how to find the park's forested **campground** (www.discovercamping.ca; campsites $35; P) if you feel like staying over.

Olo CANADIAN **$$$**
(Map p686; ☎250-590-8795; www.olorestaurant.com; 509 Fisgard St; mains $24-30; ⊙5pm-midnight Sun-Thu, to 1am Fri & Sat; ✎) Slightly confusingly re-invented from the Ulla restaurant that used to be here, version 2.0 ploughs the farm-to-table furrow even deeper. The sophisticated seasonal menu can include anything from Quadra Island scallops to local smoked duck breast, but the multicourse, family-style tasting menu is the way to go if you're feeling flush (from $45 per person).

Brasserie L'École FRENCH **$$$**
(Map p686; ☎250-475-6260; www.lecole.ca; 1715 Government St; mains $18-50; ⊙5:30-11pm Tue-Sat; 🚌70) Preparing West Coast ingredients with French-bistro flare, this warm and ever-popular spot is perfect for an intimate night out. The dishes constantly change to reflect seasonal highlights, like figs, salmonberries and heirloom tomatoes, but we recommend any seafood you find on the menu, or the ever-available *steak frites* (steak and fries) with a red-wine and shallot sauce.

🍷 Drinking & Nightlife

Victoria is one of BC's best beer towns; look out for local-made craft brews at pubs around the city. Rest assured: repeated first-hand research was undertaken for this section.

★Drake BAR
(Map p686; ☎250-590-9075; www.drakeeatery.com; 517 Pandora Ave; ⊙11:30am-midnight; 📶; 🚌70) Victoria's best taphouse, this hangout has more than 30 amazing craft drafts, including revered BC producers like Townsite, Driftwood and Four Winds. Arrive on a rainy afternoon and you'll find yourself still here several hours later. Food-wise, the smoked tuna club is a top-seller but the cheese and charcuterie plates are ideal for grazing.

Spinnakers Gastro Brewpub PUB
(☎250-386-2739; www.spinnakers.com; 308 Catherine St; ⊙11am-11pm; 📶; 🚌15) One of Canada's first craft brewers, this wood-floored smasher is a short hop from downtown via Harbour Ferry. Sail in for copper-colored Nut Brown Ale and the lip-smacking Lion's Head Cascadia Dark Ale and check out the daily casks to see what's on special. Save room to eat: the menu here is true gourmet gastropub grub.

Garrick's Head Pub PUB
(Map p686; ☎250-384-6835; www.garrickshead.com; 66 Bastion Sq; ⊙11am-late; 🚌70) Great spot to dive into BC's brilliant craft beer scene. Pull up a perch at the long bar and you'll be faced with 55-plus taps serving a comprehensive menu of beers from Driftwood, Phillips, Hoyne and beyond. There are always 10 rotating lines with intriguing tipples (ask for samples) plus a comfort-grub menu of burgers et al to line your boozy stomach.

Clive's Classic Lounge LOUNGE
(Map p686; ☎250-361-5684; www.clivesclassiclounge.com; 740 Burdett Ave; ⊙4pm-midnight Mon-Thu, 4pm-1am Fri, 5pm-1am Sat, 5pm-midnight Sun; 🚌70) Tucked into the lobby level of the Chateau Victoria Hotel, this is the best spot in town for perfectly prepared cocktails. Completely lacking the snobbishness of big-city cocktail haunts, this ever-cozy spot is totally dedicated to its mixed-drinks menu, which means timeless classic cocktails, as well as cool-ass fusion tipples that are a revelation.

Canoe Brewpub PUB
(Map p686; ☎250-361-1940; www.canoebrewpub.com; 450 Swift St; ⊙11:30am-11pm Sun-Wed, to midnight Thu, to 1am Fri & Sat; 🚌70) The cavernous brick-lined interior is great on rainy days, but the patio is also the best in the city with its usually sunny views over the harbor. Indulge in on-site-brewed treats, like the hoppy lager and the summer-friendly honey wheat ale. Grub is also high on the menu, with the mussels recommended.

Big Bad John's PUB
(Map p686; ☎250-383-7137; www.strathconahotel.com; 919 Douglas St; ⊙noon-2am; 🚌70) Easily missed from the outside, this dark little hillbilly-themed bar feels like you've stepped into the backwoods. But rather than some dodgy banjo players with mismatched ears, you'll find good-time locals enjoying the cave-like ambience of peanut-shell-covered floors and a ceiling dotted with old bras. A good spot to say you've been to, at least once.

Entertainment

Check the weekly freebie *Monday Magazine* for the lowdown on local happenings. Entertainment resources online include **Live Victoria** (www.livevictoria.com) and **Play in Victoria** (www.playinvictoria.net).

Logan's Pub LIVE MUSIC
(☎250-360-2711; www.loganspub.com; 1821 Cook St; ⊙3pm-1am Mon-Fri, 10am-1am Sat, 10am-midnight Sun; 🚌6) A 10-minute walk from downtown, this no-nonsense pub looks like nothing special from the outside, but its roster of shows is a fixture on the local indie scene. Fridays and Saturdays are your best bet for performances; check the online calendar to see what's coming up.

Vic Theatre CINEMA
(Map p686; ☎250-389-0440; www.thevic.ca; 808 Douglas St; 🚌70) Screening arthouse and festival movies in the heart of downtown. A $2 membership is required alongside your ticket admission here.

Belfry Theatre THEATER
(☎250-385-6815; www.belfry.bc.ca; 1291 Gladstone Ave; 🚌22) A 20-minute stroll from downtown, the celebrated Belfry Theatre showcases contemporary plays in its lovely former-church-building venue.

Royal Theatre THEATER
(Map p686; ☎888-717-6121, 250-386-6121; www.rmts.bc.ca; 805 Broughton St; 🚌70) With a rococo interior, the Royal Theatre hosts mainstream theater productions, and is home to the Victoria Symphony and Pacific Opera Victoria.

McPherson Playhouse THEATER
(Map p686; ☎888-717-6121, 250-386-6121; www.rmts.bc.ca; 3 Centennial Sq; 🚌70) One of Victoria's main stages, McPherson Playhouse offers mainstream visiting shows and performances.

Shopping

While Government St is a souvenir shopping magnet, those looking for more original purchases should head to the Johnson St stretch between Store and Government, which is lined with cool independent stores.

Regional Assembly of Text STATIONERY
(Map p686; ☎778-265-6067; www.assemblyoftext.com; 560 Johnson St; ⊙11am-6pm Mon-Sat, noon-5pm Sun; 🚌70) The satellite of Vancouver's charming hipster stationery store is socked into a quirky space resembling a hotel lobby from 1968. You'll find the same clever greeting cards and cool journals, plus the best Victoria postcards you'll ever find; postage is available. Add the button-making

DON'T MISS

TO MARKET, TO MARKET

On rainy days, **Victoria Public Market** (Map p686; ☎778-433-2787; www.victoriapublicmarket.com; 1701 Douglas St; ⊙10am-6pm Mon-Sat, 11am-5pm Sun; 🚌4) serves up a couple of dozen food-focused vendors – from artisan tea to chocolate and cheese – in its downtown heritage building location. But if the weather's fine, slap on the suntan lotion and head outside.

Bastion Square Public Market (Map p686; www.bastionsquare.ca; Bastion Sq; ⊙11am-4:30pm Thu-Sat, 11am-4pm Sun May-Sep; 🚌70) offers art-and-craft stalls all summer, while **James Bay Market** (Map p686; www.jamesbaymarket.com; 494 Superior St; ⊙9am-3pm Sat mid-May–mid-Sep; 🚌27) and the large **Moss Street Market** (www.mossstreetmarket.com; 1330 Fairfield Rd; ⊙10am-2pm Sat May-Oct; 🚌7) offer a community-focused combo of both arts and food. Come hungry: there is plenty to eat at these two.

table, typewriter stations and a *Mister Mitten* chapbook purchase and you'll be happier than a shiny new paper clip.

Munro's Books BOOKS
(Map p686; ☎250-382-2464; www.munrobooks.com; 1108 Government St; ⏰9am-6pm Mon-Wed, 9am-9pm Thu-Sat, 9:30am-6pm Sun; 🚌70) Like a cathedral to reading, this high-ceilinged bookstore lures legions of locals and visitors who love communing with the written word. There's a good array of local-interest tomes, as well as a fairly extensive travel section at the back on the left. Check out the piles of bargain books, too – they're not all copies of *How to Eat String, Volume II* from 1974.

Silk Road TEA
(Map p686; ☎250-704-2688; www.silkroadtea.com; 1624 Government St; ⏰10am-6pm Mon-Sat, 11am-5pm Sun; 🚌70) A pilgrimage spot for regular and exotic tea fans where you can pick up all manner of leafy paraphernalia. Alternatively, sidle up to the tasting bar to quaff some adventurous brews. There's also a small on-site spa, where you can indulge in oil treatments and aromatherapy.

Milkman's Daughter CLOTHING, GIFTS
(Map p686; www.themilkmansdaughter.ca; 1713 Government St; ⏰10am-6:30pm Mon-Thu & Sat, 10am-8pm Fri, noon-5pm Sun; 🚌70) This shop is a hipster's dream, with an array of clothing as well as must-have artisan creations from both locals and those from further afield, mostly from the West Coast. It's an eclectic mix, from jewelry to pottery and from buttons to notebooks, but it's easy to find something to fall in love with.

ON YER BIKE

Take your bike across on the ferry from the mainland to Swartz Bay, Vancouver Island, from where you can hop onto the easily accessible and well-marked **Lochside Regional Trail**. The 29km, mostly flat route to downtown Victoria is not challenging – there are only a couple of overpasses – and it's an idyllic, predominantly paved ride through small urban areas, waterfront stretches, rolling farmland and forested countryside. You'll find several spots to pick up lunch en route and, if you adopt a leisurely pace, you'll be in town within four hours or so.

Rogers' Chocolates FOOD
(Map p686; ☎250-881-8771; www.rogerschocolates.com; 913 Government St; ⏰9:30am-7pm; 🚌70) This charming, museum-like confectioner serves the best ice-cream bars, but repeat offenders usually spend their time hitting the menu of rich Victoria Creams, one of which is usually enough to substitute for lunch. Varieties range from peppermint to seasonal specialties and they're good souvenirs, so long as you don't scoff them all before you get home (which you will).

Ditch Records MUSIC
(Map p686; ☎250-386-5874; 784 Fort St; ⏰10am-6pm Mon-Sat, 11am-5pm Sun; 🚌14) A fave record store among the locals, Ditch is lined with tempting vinyl, plenty of CDs and many furtive musos perusing releases by acts like Frazey Ford and Nightmares on Wax. An ideal rainy-day hangout; if it suddenly feels like time to socialize, you can book gig tickets here, too.

Cherry Bomb Toys TOYS
(Map p686; ☎250-385-8697; www.cherrybombtoys.com; 1410 Broad St; ⏰10am-6pm Mon-Sat, noon-5pm Sun; 👪; 🚌70) The nostalgically inclined will love this large toy emporium of collectibles, especially if they head upstairs to the mezzanine-level **toy museum**. It's crammed with everything from vintage GI Joes to antique Lego plus old computer game consoles that will likely trigger Proustian flashbacks. They encourage donations if you want to visit the museum but it's free if you buy anything downstairs.

ℹ Information

Downtown Medical Centre (☎250-380-2210; 622 Courtney St; ⏰8:30am-5pm Mon-Fri; 🚌70) Handy walk-in clinic.

Main Post Office (Map p686; 709 Yates St; ⏰9am-5pm Mon-Fri; 🚌70) Near the corner of Yates and Douglas Sts.

Tourism Victoria Visitor Centre (Map p686; ☎250-953-2033; www.tourismvictoria.com; 812 Wharf St; ⏰8:30am-8:30pm mid-May–Aug, 9am-5pm Sep-May; 🚌70) Busy, flyer-lined visitors center overlooking the Inner Harbour.

ℹ Getting There & Away

AIR

Victoria International Airport (☎250-953-7500; www.victoriaairport.com) is 26km north of the city via Hwy 17. Frequent **Air Canada** (www.aircanada.com) services arrive from Vancouver ($169, 25 minutes), while **Westjet**

(www.westjet.com) flights arrive from Calgary ($265, 1½ hours). Both offer cross-Canada connections.

YYJ Airport Shuttle (☎778-351-4995; www.yyjairportshuttle.com) buses run between the airport and downtown Victoria ($25, 30 minutes). In contrast, a taxi to downtown costs around $50.

Harbour Air (☎250-384-2215; www.harbourair.com) flies into the Inner Harbour from downtown Vancouver ($205, 30 minutes) throughout the day. Similar **Helijet** (www.helijet.com) helicopter services arrive from Vancouver ($245, 35 minutes).

BUS

Buses rolling into the city include **Greyhound Canada** (www.greyhound.ca) services from Nanaimo ($26, two hours, up to six daily) and **Tofino Bus** (☎250-725-2871; www.tofinobus.com) services from points across the rest of the island. Frequent **BC Ferries Connector** (☎778-265-9474; www.bcfconnector.com) services, via the ferry, arrive from Vancouver (from $45, 3½ hours) and Vancouver International Airport ($50, four hours).

BOAT

BC Ferries (☎250-386-3431; www.bcferries.com) arrive from mainland Tsawwassen (adult/vehicle $17/56, 1½ hours) at Swartz Bay, 27km north of Victoria via Hwy 17. Services arrive frequently throughout the day in summer, less often off-season.

Victoria Clipper (☎250-382-8100; www.clippervacations.com) services arrive in the Inner Harbour from Seattle (adult/child US $109/54, three hours, up to twice daily). **Black Ball Transport** (☎250-386-2202; www.ferrytovictoria.com) boats also arrive here from Port Angeles (adult/child/vehicle US$18.50/9.25/64, 1½ hours, up to four daily).

Getting Around

BICYCLE

Victoria is a great cycling capital, with routes crisscrossing the city and beyond. Check the website of the **Greater Victoria Cycling Coalition** (www.gvcc.bc.ca) for local resources. Bike rentals are offered by **Cycle BC Rentals** (☎250-380-2453; www.cyclebc.ca; 685 Humboldt St; 🚌1).

BOAT

Victoria Harbour Ferry (Map p686; ☎250-708-0201; www.victoriaharbourferry.com; fares from $6) covers the Inner Harbour and beyond with its colorful armada of little boats.

BUS

Victoria Regional Transit (www.bctransit.com/victoria) buses (fare/day pass $2.50/5) cover a wide area from Sidney to Sooke, with some routes served by modern-day double-deckers. Children under five travel free.

TAXI

Yellow Cab (☎250-381-2222; www.yellowcabvictoria.com)

BlueBird Cabs (☎250-382-2222; www.taxicab.com)

Southern Vancouver Island

Not far from Victoria's madding crowds, southern Vancouver Island is a laid-back region of quirky little towns that are never far from tree-lined cycle routes, waterfront hiking trails and rocky outcrops bristling with gnarly Garry oaks. The wildlife here is abundant and you'll likely spot bald eagles swooping overhead, sea otters cavorting on the beaches and perhaps the occasional orca sliding silently by just off the coast.

Saanich Peninsula & Around

Home to Vancouver Island's main airport and busiest ferry terminal, this peninsula north of Victoria has plenty to offer day-trippers looking to escape from the city.

SIDNEY

At the peninsula's northern end, seafront Sidney is a pleasant afternoon diversion, with a walkable waterfront, strollable shops (especially bookstores) and laid-back places to eat.

The popular **Shaw Ocean Discovery Centre** (☎250-665-7511; www.oceandiscovery.ca; 9811 Seaport Pl; adult/child $15/8; ⊙10am-4:30pm) is Sidney's kid-luring highlight. Enter through a dramatic Disney-style entrance – it makes you think you're descending below the waves – then step into a gallery of aquatic exhibits, including alien-like jellyfish, a large touch tank with purple starfish and an octopus that likes to unscrew a glass jar to snag its fresh crab dinner. Continue your marine education aboard a whale-watching boat trek with **Sidney Whale Watching** (☎250-656-7599; www.sidneywhalewatching.com; 2537 Beacon Ave; adult/child $115/89; ⊙Mar-Oct), located a few steps away.

If you decide to stick around, the swish **Sidney Pier Hotel & Spa** (☎250-655-9445; www.sidneypier.com; 9805 Seaport Pl; d from $209; @📶🐾) situated on the waterfront fuses West Coast lounge – cool with beach pastel colors.

DON'T MISS

BOOKSTORE CENTRAL

Beacon Avenue is lined with shops and there are more than half a dozen bookstores here if that's what you're into. **Tanner's Books** (☎250-656-2345; www.tannersbooks.com; 2436 Beacon Ave; ⏰8am-9pm) is a cavernous corner shop with a large array of magazines and a comprehensive travel-book section. They also organize evening book readings, typically at the Red Brick Cafe across the street – check their website for listings. Also, save time for **Beacon Books** (☎250-655-4447; 2372 Beacon Ave; ⏰10am-5:30pm Mon-Sat, noon-4pm Sun). It's a multi-room shop piled high with used tomes guarded by a house-cat who may or may not let you stroke her (probably not). Look out for the collection of vintage postcards, then send one home, pretending you're vacationing in 1942.

If it's time to eat, check out **Sabhai Thai** (☎250-655-4085; www.sabhai.ca; 2493 Beacon Ave; mains $12-18; ⏰11:30am-2pm & 5-9pm), a cozy locals' favorite with a bonus patio and a good line in authentic curry and *phad* dishes. The lunch combos (around the $10 mark) are good value and include rice and spring rolls.

Serving the best coffee in Sidney, **Toast Cafe** (☎250-665-6234; 2400 Bevan Ave; mains $6-12; ⏰6:30am-4pm Mon-Sat; 📶) is a wood-floored, just-off-the-main-drag corner joint that makes great breakfast wraps and thick-cut, superbly satisfying, salad-accompanied sandwiches. On sunny days, aim for a perch at the communal table outside and fill your belly – check the daily special on the chalkboard inside before you order, though.

BRENTWOOD BAY

A 30-minute drive from Victoria, this countryside swath has some attractions of its own, including one of BC's most popular visitor destinations.

The rolling farmlands of Brentwood Bay are home to the immaculate, green-thumbed **Butchart Gardens** (☎250-652-5256; www.butchartgardens.com; 800 Benvenuto Ave; adult/teen/child $32.10/16.05/3; ⏰9am-10pm, reduced hours off-season; 🚌75), Vancouver Island's most visited attraction. It's divided into separate gardens where there's always something in bloom; the tour buses roll in relentlessly throughout the summer here but Saturday-night fireworks in July and August make it all worthwhile. Tea fans take note: the **Dining Room Restaurant** serves a smashing afternoon tea; leave your diet at the door. Also ask about November's fascinating behind-the-scenes **greenhouse tours**.

If you have time, also consider nearby **Victoria Butterfly Gardens** (☎250-652-3822; www.butterflygardens.com; 1461 Benvenuto Ave; adult/child $16/5; ⏰10am-4pm mid-Mar–Oct, 10am-3pm Oct–mid-Mar), which offers a kaleidoscope of thousands of fluttering critters, from around 75 species, in a free-flying environment. As well as watching them flit about and land on your head, you can learn about ecosystem life cycles, and eyeball exotic fish, plants and birds. Look out for Spike, the long-beaked puna ibis, who struts around the trails as if he owns the place.

Sooke & Around

Rounding Vancouver Island's rustic southern tip towards Sooke, a 45-minute drive from Victoria, Hwy 14 is lined with twisted Garry oaks and unkempt hedgerows, while the houses – often artisan workshops or homely B&Bs – seem spookily hidden in the forest shadows.

Sights & Activities

Sharing the same building and hours as the visitors center, the fascinating **Sooke Region Museum** (☎250-642-6351; www.sookeregionmuseum.com; 2070 Phillips Rd; ⏰9am-5pm mid-May–mid-Oct, closed Mondays mid-Oct–mid-May) FREE illuminates the area's rugged pioneer days. Check out Moss Cottage in the museum grounds: built in 1869, it's the oldest residence west of Victoria.

If you're craving some thrills, find your inner screamer on the forested zip-line tours operated by **Adrena LINE** (☎250-642-1933; www.adrenalinezip.com; 5128 Sooke Rd; adult/child from $80/70; ⏰9am-5pm Mar-Oct). Its full-moon zips are the most fun (book ahead) and, if you don't have your own transport, they can also shuttle you to and from Victoria for an extra $15.

A more relaxed way to encounter the natural world is the **Sooke Potholes Provincial Park** (☎250-474-1336; www.bcparks.ca; Sooke River Rd), a 5km drive from Hwy 14 (the turnoff is east of Sooke). With rock pools and potholes carved into the river base during the last ice age, it's ideal for summertime swimming and tube floating.

Juan de Fuca Marine Trail HIKING (www.juandefucamarinetrail.com) The 47km Juan de Fuca Marine Trail in **Juan de Fuca Provincial Park** (250-474-1336; www.bcparks.ca; Hwy 14) rivals the West Coast Trail as a must-do trek. From east to west, its trailhead access points are China Beach, Sombrio Beach, Parkinson Creek and Botanical Beach. It takes around four days to complete the route, but you don't have to go the whole hog if you want to take things easier.

Be aware that some sections are often muddy and difficult to hike, while bear sightings and swift weather changes are not uncommon. The most difficult stretch is between Bear Beach and China Beach. The route has several basic backcountry campsites and you can pay your camping fee ($10 per adult) at any of the trailheads. The most popular spot to pitch your tent is the more salubrious, family-friendly **China Beach Campground** (800-689-9025, 519-826-6850; www.discovercamping.ca; campsites $20; mid-May–mid-Sep), which has pit toilets and cold-water taps but no showers. There's a waterfall at the western end of the beach and booking ahead in summer is essential.

Booking ahead is also required on the **West Coast Trail Express** (888-999-2288, 250-477-8700; www.trailbus.com; fares from $30; May-Sep) minibus that runs between Victoria, the trailheads and Port Renfrew.

Sleeping & Eating

You'll find B&Bs dotted along the route here but, for one of the province's most delightful and splurge-worthy options, head to Whiffen Spit's **Sooke Harbour House** (250-642-3421; www.sookeharbourhouse.com; 1528 Whiffen Spit Rd; d from $329;). The restaurant is also a great place for fine West Coast dining, whether or not you're staying here.

Located between Sooke and Jordan River, the rustic, locally beloved **Shirley Delicious Cafe** (250-528-2888; 2794 Sheringham Point Rd; mains $4-10; 8am-5pm) is bristling with home-baked treats, bulging sandwiches and hearty soups.

Port Renfrew

Conveniently nestled between the Juan de Fuca and West Coast Trails, delightfully remote Port Renfrew is a great access point for either route. There are several places to rest your weary head and also fuel up with great grub here.

If you've had enough of your sleeping bag, **Wild Renfrew** (250-647-5541; www.wildrenfrew.com; 17310 Parkinson Rd; lodge d from $139, cabin from $249;) has woodland cabins and lodge rooms that have all been upgraded in recent years. There are many ways to unplug from the city and sink into the retreat-like feel of the rainforest here. The woodsy seaside cottages are best and each includes a kitchen for preparing your alfresco balcony breakfast in the morning – there's also a pub nearby if you're feeling lazy.

For a respite from campground pasta, **Coastal Kitchen Cafe** (250-647-5545; 17245 Parkinson Rd; mains $8-16; 7am-9pm) is a laid-back, locally loved hangout that serves hearty comfort grub from breakfast to dinner (add a glass of BC craft beer to the latter). The dish to have here? Miss the halibut and chips at your peril.

Tacked onto the historic Port Renfrew Hotel, summer drinking at **Renfrew Pub** (250-647-5541; 17310 Parkinson Rd; $12-24; noon-8pm Mon-Fri, 8am-8pm Sat, 8am-7pm Sun) is all about snagging a spot on the patio alongside the wharf. On lazy days, it's hard to peel yourself away from the shimmering shoreline views, especially if you've had a huge bowl of seafood chowder and a round or two of BC craft ale.

Cowichan Valley

A swift Hwy 1 drive northwest of Victoria, the farm-filled Cowichan Valley region is ripe for discovery, especially if you're a traveling foodie or an outdoor activity nut.

Contact **Cowichan Regional Visitor Centre** (250-746-4636; www.tourismcowichan.com; 2896 Drinkwater Rd; 9am-5pm Sun-Tue, to 6pm Wed-Sat Jun-Aug, reduced hours in winter) for more information.

Duncan

Developed as a logging industry railroad stop, Duncan is the valley's main community. A useful base for regional exploration, it's known for its dozens of totem poles, which dot downtown like sentinels.

If your First Nations curiosity is piqued, head to the **Quw'utsun' Cultural & Conference Centre** (250-746-8119; www.quwutsun.ca; 200 Cowichan Way; adult/child $15/8; 10am-4pm Mon-Sat Jun-Sep) to learn about carving and traditional salmon runs. Its on-site **Riverwalk Cafe** serves First Nations–inspired cuisine.

Save time during your Duncan visit for a selfie with the **World's Largest Hockey Stick**, a 62-meter-long behemoth attached to the **Island Savings Centre** on James St.

Also, drive 3km north of town to the **BC Forest Discovery Centre** (250-715-1113; www.bcforestdiscoverycentre.com; 2892 Drinkwater Rd; adult/child $16/11; 10am-4:30pm Jun-Aug, reduced hours off-season;), complete with pioneer-era buildings, logging machinery and a working **steam train** you can hop aboard for a trundle (check website for the schedule).

Eating & Drinking

Duncan Garage Cafe & Bakery CAFE $
(250-748-6223; 3330 Duncan St; mains $7-12; 7am-6pm Mon-Sat, 8:30am-5pm Sun;) This always-busy and ever-chatty hangout is the main attraction in the red-painted Duncan Garage heritage building across from the old train station (there's also a bookstore and food shop here). The entirely vegetarian chalkboard menu is crammed with tempting breakfast, lunch and bakery treats but aim for the rice bowls or poutine if you're feeling especially hungry.

Old Firehouse Wine Bar WEST COAST $$
(250-597-3473; www.theoldfirehouse.ca; 40 Ingram St; mains $13-22; 11:30am-11pm Tue-Sat, reduced hours off-season) Divided into several rooms, this surprisingly large, dark-painted resto-bar is a popular spot for evening cocktails in the center of town. But it's also a great dining option with a well-executed menu of seasonally changing dishes – the flatbreads are menu mainstays (try the fig and prosciutto).

Hudson's on First WEST COAST $$
(250-597-0066; www.hudsonsonfirst.ca; 163 First St; mains $12-32; 11am-2pm Tue, 11am-late Wed-Fri, 10am-late Sat, 10am-2pm Sun) In an immaculately restored heritage building, the ever-changing seasonal menu here fuses local ingredients with subtle European influences. For lunch, go for the gourmet fish and chips (add the housemade soup) or drop by for an excellent eggs Benedict brunch on the weekend. But if you come for dinner, start with a cocktail in the tin-ceilinged bar.

Craig Street Brew Pub PUB FOOD $$
(250-737-2337; www.craigstreet.ca; 25 Craig St; mains $8-18; 11am-11pm Mon-Thu, to midnight Fri & Sat, to 10pm Sun;) An inviting, multi-floor locals' hangout (aim for the top-floor patio in summer), this dark-wood boozer offers a huge menu of elevated pub grub, from taco salads to finger-licking pizzas (a favorite among diners). They also make their own beer. Go for a five-glass sampler ($12) and make sure it includes a seasonal plus the top-selling pilsner-style Cow Bay Lager.

WORTH A TRIP

CANADA'S ONLY TEA FARM

Hidden in bucolic farmland 8km north of Duncan you'll find one of Canada's rarest agricultural operations. Tucked into the hillside, the oasis-like **Teafarm** (www.teafarm.ca; 8530 Richards Trail, North Cowichan; 10am-5pm Wed-Sun) has been growing its own tea plants for several years. The main harvest is coming soon, but until that time its contemporary, winery-like tasting room – or, better still, its flower-framed outdoor seating area – is the perfect spot to indulge in one of dozens of excellent tea blends (Sweet Morocco recommended), along with some decadent sweet treats. The tea is served in lovely pottery teapots made by owner Margit, while husband and tea guru Victor will be on hand to tell you about the operation. One of the most relaxing and surprisingly good-value ways to spend an hour or two in the region. It's not well signposted, so deploy your GPS.

Getting There & Away

Greyhound Services (www.greyhound.ca) trundle in from Nanaimo (up to six times daily, one hour, $20) and Victoria (up to three times daily, one hour, $19.40).

Cowichan Bay

'Cow Bay' to the locals, the region's most attractive pit stop is a colorful string of wooden buildings perched over a mountain-framed ocean inlet. It's well worth an afternoon of your time, although it might take that long to find parking on a busy summer day.

Start your visit with a fresh-baked snack at **True Grain Bread** (250-746-7664; www.truegrain.ca; 1725 Cowichan Bay Rd; 8am-6pm, closed Mon Nov-Feb) then duck into the **Maritime Centre** (250-746-4955; www.classicboats.org; 1761 Cowichan Bay Rd; suggested donation $5; dawn-dusk May-Sep, reduced hours in winter) to peruse the salty boat-building exhibits and intricate models. Next, strol

VANCOUVER ISLAND BOOZE TRAIL

Vancouver Island's blossoming local food movement has spread to booze in recent years, with wineries, breweries, cideries and distilleries popping up across the region, giving visitors plenty of reason to appoint a designated driver. But unless you know where to go, many of these artisan operators can be hard to find. Here are some thirst-slaking recommendations for visitors.

In the Comox Valley, **Cumberland Brewing** (p710) is one of the island's tastiest new beer makers – don't miss their Red Tape Pale Ale. A weave around the Cowichan region delivers **Cherry Point Vineyards** (250-743-1272; www.cherrypointvineyards.com; 840 Cherry Point Rd, Cobble Hill; 10am-5pm), with its lip-smacking blackberry port; **Averill Creek** (250-709-9986; www.averillcreek.ca; 6552 North Rd, Duncan; 11am-5pm), with its patio views and lovely pinot noirs; and the rustic-chic **Merridale Estate Cidery** (250-743-4293; www.merridalecider.com; 1230 Merridale Rd, Cobble Hill; 11am-5pm, reduced hours off-season), an inviting apple-cider producer that also makes brandy and has a great patio bistro.

Further south in Saanich – just a short drive from Victoria – organic apples are also on the taste-tripping menu at **Sea Cider** (250-544-4824; www.seacider.ca; 2487 Mt St Michael Rd, Saanichton; 11am-4pm Jun-Sep, 11am-4pm Wed-Sun Oct-May). Booze of a stronger hue is the approach at Sidney's **Victoria Distillers** (250-544-8218; www.victoriadistillers.com; 9891 Seaport Pl; tours $7; 10am-5pm Sat & Sun Apr-Sep), where the lovely Oaken Gin is recommended. Both offer tours and tastings.

the shoreline to **Cowichan Estuary Nature Centre** (250-597-2288; www.cowichanestuary.ca; 1845 Cowichan Bay Rd; suggested donation $2;) for illuminating displays on the region's flora and fauna, including an aquarium touch tank.

This region is filled with welcoming B&B options, including the delightful **Ambraden Pond B&B** (250-743-2562; www.ambraden.com; 971 Aros Rd, Cobble Hill; d from $175;), with its secluded natural setting, two spacious rooms (plus self-catering carriage house suite) and Lulu, the welcoming house dog. It's a 10-minute drive from Cow Bay.

When you're ready for a lunchtime fuel-up, hook a waterfront table at **Rock Cod Cafe** (250-746-1550; www.rockcodcafe.com; 1759 Cowichan Bay Rd; mains $10-18; 11am-9pm Jul & Aug, 11am-7pm Sun-Thu, to 8pm Fri & Sat Sep-Jun;) for fish and chips or a bowl of chowder, but save some belly space for an elongated dinner on the waterfront deck at the charming **Masthead Restaurant** (250-748-3714; www.themastheadrestaurant.com; 1705 Cowichan Bay Rd; mains $26-35; 5-10pm). The three-course tasting menu is surprisingly good value and you can add a bottle of local wine to keep things lively.

Chemainus

After the last sawmill shut down in 1983, tiny Chemainus became the model for BC communities dealing with declining resource jobs. Instead of submitting to a slow death, town officials commissioned a giant wall mural depicting local history. More than 45 artworks were later added and a tourism industry was born.

Stroll the Chemainus streets (expect a permanent aroma of fresh-cut logs from the nearby sawmill) on a mural hunt and you'll pass artsy boutiques and tempting ice-cream shops, some housed in heritage buildings, others in attractive faux-historic piles. In the evening, the surprisingly large **Chemainus Theatre** (www.chemainustheatrefestival.ca; 9737 Chemainus Rd; tickets from $25) stages professional productions, mostly popular plays and musicals, to keep you occupied.

Nearby, the town's **Chemainus Inn** (250-246-4181; www.chemainushotel.com; 9573 Chemainus Rd; d from $169;) is like a midrange business hotel transplanted from a much larger town; the rooms here are slick and comfortable and many include kitchen facilities. Rates include breakfast.

Drop by the handsome yellow heritage building housing **Willow Street Café** (250-246-2434; www.willowstreetcafe.com; 9749 Willow St; mains $13-15; 8am-5pm;). With a menu founded on wraps, sandwiches and quesadillas, this cafe in the heart of town has a popular summertime patio out front. Save room for a slab of cheesecake then jog around the building a dozen times to work it off.

Check in at the **visitors center** (250-246-3944; www.visitchemainus.ca; 9799 Waterwheel Cres; 9:30am-5pm mid-Jun–Aug, reduced hours in winter) for mural maps and further information, plus the little community museum in the same building.

Nanaimo

POP 85,000

Vancouver Island's 'second metropolis,' Nanaimo will never have the allure of tourist-magnet Victoria but the Harbour City has undergone some quiet upgrades since the 1990s with the emergence, especially on Commercial St, of some good shops and eateries, plus a good museum. With dedicated ferry services from the mainland, the city is also a handy hub for exploring the rest of the island.

Sights

Nanaimo Museum MUSEUM

(Map p699; 250-753-1821; www.nanaimomuseum.ca; 100 Museum Way; adult/child $2/75¢; 10am-5pm daily, closed Sun Sep–mid-May) Just off the Commercial St main drag, this popular museum showcases the region's heritage, from First Nations to colonial, maritime, sporting and beyond. Highlights of the eclectic collection include exhibits on Nanaimo bars and bathtub racing plus a carved golden beaver from an 1890s tugboat. Ask at the front desk about the museum's guided walking tour program as well as summertime entry to the nearby **Bastion**, an 1853 wooden tower fortification.

Newcastle Island Marine Provincial Park PARK

(www.newcastleisland.ca) Nanaimo's rustic outdoor gem offers 22km of **hiking** and **biking** trails, plus beaches and wildlife spotting. Traditional Coast Salish land, it was the site of shipyards and coal mines before becoming a popular summer excursion for locals in the 1930s when a tea pavilion was added. Accessed by a 10-minute ferry hop from the harbor (adult/child return $9/5), there's a seasonal eatery and regular First Nations dancing displays.

Wild Play Element Parks AMUSEMENT PARK

(250-716-7874; www.wildplay.com; 35 Nanaimo River Rd; adult/child $35/20; 10am-6pm mid-May–Sep, reduced hours off-season;) The perfect spot to tire your kids out, this tree-lined adventure playground is packed with adrenaline-pumping fun, from bungee jumping to scream-triggering zip-lining. Along with its fun obstacle courses, there's plenty of action to keep the family occupied, from walking trails to busy volleyball courts.

Old City Quarter AREA

(Map p699; www.oldcityquarter.com; cnr Fitzwilliam & Wesley Sts) A steep hike uphill from the waterfront on Bastion and Fitzwilliam Sts delivers you to a strollable heritage hood of independent stores, galleries and eateries in brightly painted old buildings. Highlights include McLeans Specialty Foods; A Wee Cupcakery; and Taphouse Restaurant, a large pub that has taken over the town's old train station. Look out for the heritage plaques on buildings in this area.

Sleeping

Painted Turtle Guesthouse HOSTEL $

(Map p699; 250-753-4432; www.paintedturtle.ca; 121 Bastion St; dm/r $38/99;) New owners have not diminished the quality at this top-notch, well-maintained HI-affiliated hostel where small dorms combine with 10 hotel-style private rooms (there are also two family rooms). The hardwood floors and IKEA-style furnishings line a large and welcoming kitchen-lounge combo and you can book tours from the front desk if you've had enough of strumming the hostel's guitar.

Buccaneer Inn MOTEL $$

(250-753-1246; www.buccaneerinn.com; 1577 Stewart Ave; d/ste from $100/160;) Handy for the Departure Bay ferry terminal, this friendly, family-run motel has a gleaming white exterior that makes it hard to pass by. It's worth staying in as the neat-and-tidy approach is carried over into the maritime-themed rooms, most of which have kitchen facilities. Splurge on a spacious suite and you'll have a fireplace, full kitchen and flatscreen TV.

Coast Bastion Hotel HOTEL $$

(Map p699; 250-753-6601; www.coasthotels.com; 11 Bastion St; d from $175;) Downtown's best hotel has an unbeatable location overlooking the harbor, with most guests enjoying waterfront views. Rooms have been well refurbished with a lounge-modern élan in recent years, adding flatscreen TVs and, in most rooms, small fridges. The lobby restaurant-bar is a popular hangout and there's a spa if you want to chillax.

Nanaimo

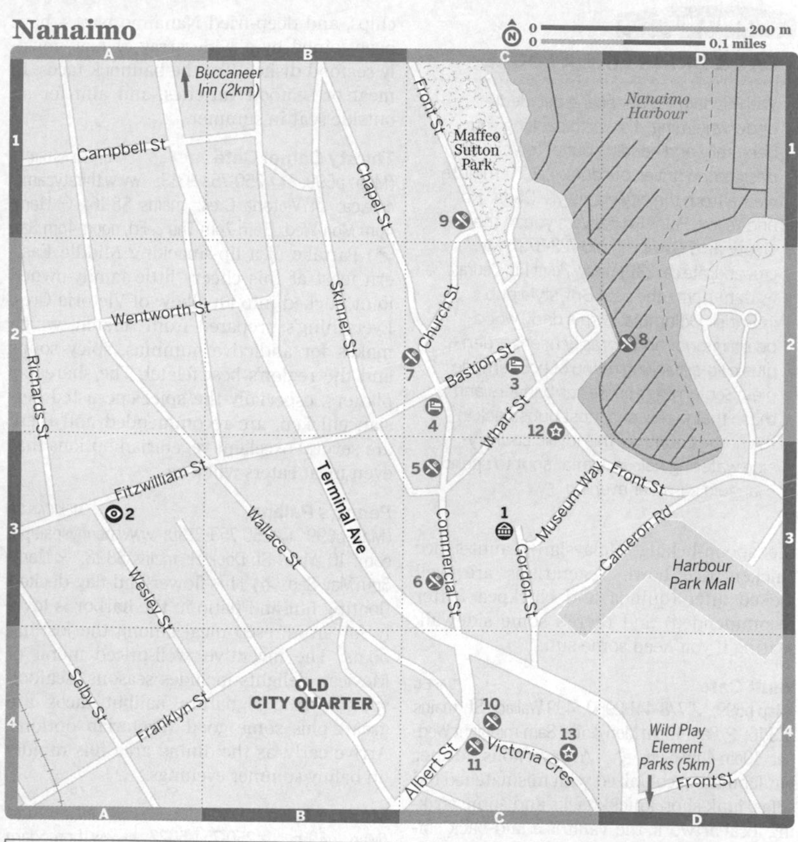

Nanaimo

Sights
1 Nanaimo Museum C3
2 Old City Quarter A3

Sleeping
3 Coast Bastion Hotel C2
4 Painted Turtle Guesthouse C2

Eating
5 2 Chefs Affair C3
6 Gabriel's Gourmet Café C3
7 Modern Cafe C2
8 Penny's Palapa D2
9 Pirate Chips C1
10 Thirsty Camel Café C4
11 Vault Cafe C4

Entertainment
12 Port Theatre C2
13 Queen's Hotel C4

Inn on Long Lake HOTEL $$
(250-758-1144; www.innonlonglake.com; 4700 Island Hwy; d from $160;) This family-owned motel property is handily located just off the highway. But don't worry about noise: all the rooms face the tranquil lake. A large-scale renovation has transformed rooms with kitchen facilities and new bathrooms, and rates include a good continental-breakfast buffet.

Eating

★ **Gabriel's Gourmet Café** INTERNATIONAL $
(Map p699; 250-714-0271; www.gabrielscafe.ca; 39 Commercial St; mains $9-13; 8am-7pm;) An expanded new location for Nanaimo's best farm-to-table eatery (check out the tables made from old bowling-alley wood) means a larger menu of international-influenced comfort dishes. But some things never change, including favorites like

DON'T MISS

EAT & DRINK LIKE A LOCAL

With Nanaimo's bar scene decidedly underwhelming, it's worth packing your beer belly and heading out of town (with a designated driver, of course). A 20-minute weave from the city via Hwy 1, Cedar Rd and Yellow Point Rd delivers you to the **Crow and Gate** (☎250-722-3731; www.crowandgate.ca; 2313 Yellow Point Rd, Cedra; ⊙11am-11pm), the best Brit-style pub in British Columbia. With a dark, wood-beam interior and a grassy beer garden – plus a lip-smacking menu of housemade pies, Scotch eggs as well as bangers and mash that far exceed most pubs back in the home country – this idyllic countryside watering hole is a great spot to spend a languid summer evening.

the spoon-licking Malaysian-peanut-sauce chicken rice bowl. Vegetarians are well looked after (quinoa and chickpea fritter recommended) and there's some sidewalk seating if you need some sun.

Vault Cafe CAFE $

(Map p699; ☎778-441-2950; 499 Wallace St; mains $13-16; ⊙8am-10pm Mon & Tue, 8am-midnight Wed-Sat, 10am-4pm Sun; 📶) A cavernous former bank building colonized with mismatched old sofas, junk-shop knickknacks and some striking local artwork, the Vault is a laid-back coffeehouse and lunch spot (with bulging toasted sandwiches) by day and a bohemian hangout by night, when there are often bands, open-mic events or film screenings.

2 Chefs Affair DINER $

(Map p699; ☎250-591-4656; www.twochefsaffair.com; 123b Commercial St; mains $13-15; ⊙8am-3pm; 📶) Focused on great comfort food at great prices, with a fresh, made-from-scatch approach, this highly welcoming locals' haunt in the heart of downtown is a great spot for breakfast – go the eggs Benedict route. Lunch is arguably even more enticing: ask for the 'Cheating Heart' sandwich and you won't be disappointed.

Pirate Chips FAST FOOD $

(Map p699; ☎250-753-2447; www.pirate-chips.com; 75 Front St; mains $10-18; ⊙11am-9pm Tue-Thu, to 10pm Fri & Sat, to 8pm Sun) A sparkling new location for this former Nanaimo hole-in-the-wall means the old faves – fish and chips, and deep-fried Nanaimo bars – have been joined by a wide array of new, mostly seafood dishes. Try the bannock tacos, in meat or seafood varieties, and aim for an outside seat in summer.

Thirsty Camel Café MIDDLE EASTERN $

(Map p699; ☎250-753-9313; www.thirstycamelcafe.ca; 14 Victoria Cres; mains $8-16; ⊙11am-4pm Mon-Wed, 11am-7pm Thu & Fri, noon-4pm Sat; 🌱) Partake of a lip-smacking Middle Eastern feast at this cheery little family-owned joint, tucked into an elbow of Victoria Cres. Everything's prepared from scratch, which makes for addictive hummus, spicy soups and the region's best felafel. The shareable platters, especially the spice-encrusted Persian chicken, are recommended and there are several excellent vegetarian options that even meat eaters will love.

Penny's Palapa MEXICAN $$

(Map p699; ☎250-753-2150; www.pennyspalapa.com; 10 Wharf St, Dock H; mains $8-18; ⊙11am-8pm May-Sep; 🌱) This flower-and-flag-decked floating hut and patio in the harbor is lovely for an alfresco meal among the jostling boats. The inventive, well-priced menu of Mexican delights includes seasonal seafood specials (the signature halibut tacos are great) plus some good vegetarian options. Arrive early, as the dining area fills rapidly on balmy summer evenings.

Modern Cafe INTERNATIONAL $$

(Map p699; ☎250-754-5022; www.themoderncafe.ca; 221 Commercial St; mains $12-22; ⊙11am-11pm Mon-Wed, 11am-midnight Thu-Sat, 10am-11pm Sun) This reinvented old coffee shop has cool, loungy interiors combining exposed brick and comfy booths and, for when it's sunny, a ray-warmed street-side patio. The menu includes some great gourmet comfort food – go for the lobster ravioli – and the weekend brunch draws the locals.

☆ Entertainment

Port Theatre THEATER

(Map p699; ☎250-754-8550; www.porttheatre.com; 125 Front St) Presenting local and touring live theater shows.

Queen's Hotel LIVE MUSIC

(Map p699; ☎250-754-6751; www.thequeens.ca; 34 Victoria Cres) The city's best live music and dance spot, hosting an eclectic roster of performances and club nights, ranging from indie to jazz and country.

Information

For tourist information, drop into the main **Nanaimo Visitor Centre** (250-751-1556; www.tourismnanaimo.com; 2450 Northfield Rd; 9am-6pm, reduced hours off-season) or, in summer, hit the satellite branch located at the Bastion historic site on the waterfront.

Getting There & Away

AIR

Nanaimo Airport (250-924-2157; www.nanaimoairport.com) is 18km south of town via Hwy 1. Frequent **Air Canada** (www.aircanada.com) flights arrive here from Vancouver (from $150, 25 minutes) throughout the day.

Frequent and convenient **Harbour Air** (250-714-0900; www.harbourair.com) floatplane services also arrive in the inner harbor from downtown Vancouver ($100, 20 minutes).

BOAT

BC Ferries (250-386-3431; www.bcferries.com) from Tsawwassen (passenger/vehicle $17/56, two hours) arrive at Duke Point, 14km south of Nanaimo. Services from West Vancouver's Horseshoe Bay (passenger/vehicle $17/56, 95 minutes) arrive at Departure Bay, 3km north of the city center via Hwy 1.

BUS

Greyhound Canada (www.greyhound.ca) buses arrive from Victoria ($28, two hours, up to 6 daily).

Getting Around

Downtown Nanaimo, around the harbor, is highly walkable, but after that the city spreads out and a car or strong bike legs are required. Be aware that taxis are expensive here.

Nanaimo Regional Transit (www.bctransit.com; single trip/day pass $2.50/6.25) Buses stop along Gordon St, west of Harbour Park Mall. Bus 2 goes to the Departure Bay ferry terminal. No city buses run to Duke Point.

Nanaimo Airporter (www.nanaimoairporter.com; from $26) Provides door-to-door service to downtown from both ferry terminals, as well as handy airport drop-off and pick-up.

Parksville & Qualicum

This popular mid-island seaside region, which also includes rustic Coombs, has been a traditional destination for vacationing families for decades – hence the water parks and miniature golf attractions. It's a great spot to take a breather on your trip up or down island.

Sights & Activities

Morningstar Farm FARM

(250-954-3931; www.morningstarfarm.ca; 403 Lowry's Rd, Parksville; 9am-5pm;) FREE Check out the region's 'locavore' credentials at this delightful and highly welcoming working farmstead. Let your kids run wild – most will quickly fall in love with the rabbits – then hunt down some samples from the on-site Little Qualicum Cheeseworks and Mooberry Winery: Bleu Claire cheese is recommended, along with a bottle of velvety blueberry wine to go.

Coombs Old Country Market MARKET

(250-248-6272; www.oldcountrymarket.com; 2326 Alberni Hwy, Coombs; 9am-7pm) The mother of all pit stops, this sprawling, ever-expanding indoor food and crafts menagerie is stuffed with bakery and produce delectables. It attracts huge numbers of visitors on summer days, when cameras are pointed at the grassy roof, where a herd of goats spend the season. Nip inside for giant ice-cream cones, heaping pizzas and the deli makings of a great picnic. Souvenir required? Grab a Billy Gruff chocolate bar.

Save some time to explore the attendant store and attractions around the site, from clothing emporiums to an Italian trattoria.

Horne Lake Caves & Outdoor Centre PARK

(250-248-7829; www.hornelake.com; tours from $24; 10am-5pm) A 45-minute drive from Parksville delivers you to BC's best spelunking. Some caves are open to the public for self-exploration, though the excellent guided tours are recommended, from family-friendly to extreme; book ahead for these. To get there, take Hwy 19 towards Courtenay, then exit 75 and proceed for 12km on the gravel road; if you get lost en route give them a call.

Milner Gardens & Woodland GARDENS

(250-752-6153; www.milnergardens.org; 2179 W Island Hwy, Qualicum Beach; adult/youth/child $11/$6.50/free; 10am-5pm mid-Apr–Aug, 10am-5pm Thu-Sun Sep–mid-Oct) This idyllic outdoor attraction combines rambling forest trails shaded by centuries-old trees with flower-packed gardens planted with magnificent trilliums and rhododendrons. Meander down to the 1930s **tearoom** on a stunning bluff overlooking the water. Then tuck into a full afternoon tea ($21) on the porch and drink in views of the bird-lined shore and snowcapped peaks shimmering on the horizon.

Sleeping & Eating

★Free Spirit Spheres CABIN $$

(☎250-757-9445; www.freespiritspheres.com; 420 Horne Lake Rd, Qualicum Beach; cabins from $175) These unique, spherical tree houses enable guests to cocoon themselves in the forest canopy. Compact inside, 'Eve' is small and basic, while 'Eryn' and 'Melody' are lined with built-in cabinets. It's all about communing with nature (TVs are replaced by books) and guests receive snacks for their stay on arrival. There's also a ground-level facilities block with sauna, BBQ and hotel-quality showers.

Blue Willow Guest House B&B $$

(☎250-752-9052; www.bluewillowguesthouse.com; 524 Quatna Rd, Qualicum Beach; d from $140) A surprisingly spacious, delightfully tranquil Victorian-style cottage, this lovely B&B has a book-lined lounge, exposed beams and a fragrant country garden. The two rooms and one self-contained suite are lined with antiques and each is extremely homey. The attention to detail carries over to the gourmet breakfast: served in the conservatory, it's accompanied by finger-licking home-baked treats.

Crown Mansion BOUTIQUE HOTEL $$

(☎250-752-5776; www.crownmansion.com; 292 E Crescent Rd, Qualicum Beach; d from $209;) A sumptuous family home built in 1912, this handsome, white-painted mansion has been restored to its former glory and opened as a unique hotel. Recall past guests Bing Crosby and John Wayne as you check out the family crest in the library fireplace, then retire to your elegant room. Rates include continental breakfast; arrive early to snag the window table.

Bistro 694 CANADIAN $$

(☎250-752-0301; www.bistro694.com; 694 Memorial Ave, Qualicum Beach; mains $21-30; ⏲4pm-9pm Wed-Sun) Ask the locals and they'll tell you to cancel your dinner plans and head straight here. You'll find an intimate, candlelit dining room little bigger than a train carriage and a big-city menu fusing top-notch regional ingredients with knowing international nods. We favor the seafood route, especially if the Balinese prawn curry or highly addictive seafood crepes are available. Reserve ahead.

Fish Tales Café SEAFOOD $$

(☎250-752-6053; www.fishtalescafe.com; 3336 Island Hwy W, Qualicum Beach; mains $12-25; ⏲11:30am-9pm Tue-Fri, 8am-9pm Sat & Sun) This Tudoresque landmark has the look of an old English tea shop, but it's been reeling in visitors with its perfect fish and chips for years. It's worth exploring the non-deep-fried dishes; the grilled salmon dinner is recommended. If you arrive early enough, grab a table in the flower-studded, fairy-lighted garden.

Information

For more information on the area, visit www.parksvillequalicumbeach.com.

Getting There & Away

Tofino Bus services arrive in Parksville from Victoria ($35, two to three hours, three daily) and Nanaimo ($17, 30 minutes, three daily) among others.

Port Alberni

With resource jobs declining, Alberni – located on Hwy 4 between the island's east and west coasts – has been dipping its toe into tourism in recent years. And while the downtown core is a little run-down, there are some good historical attractions and outdoorsy activities to consider before you drive through.

Sights & Activities

Cathedral Grove PARK

(www.bcparks.ca; MacMillan Provincial Park) Between Parksville and Port Alberni, this spiritual home of tree huggers is the mystical highlight of **MacMillan Provincial Park**. It's often overrun with summer visitors – try not to knock them down as they scamper across the highway in front of you. The accessible forest trails wind through a dense, breathtaking canopy of vegetation, offering glimpses of some of BC's oldest trees, including centuries-old Douglas firs more than 3m in diameter. Try hugging that.

Alberni Valley Museum MUSEUM

(☎250-723-2181; www.alberniheritage.com; 4255 Wallace St; by donation; ⏲10am-5pm Tue-Sat, to 8pm Thu) Don't be put off by the unassuming concrete exterior: this is one of Vancouver Island's best community museums. Studded with fascinating First Nations displays – plus an eclectic array of vintage exhibits ranging from bottle caps to dresses and old-school toys – it's worth an hour of anyone's time. History buffs should also hop aboard the summertime **Alberni Pacific Railway steam train** (www.albernisteamtrain.ca) for a trundle to McLean Mill; it's a National Hiistoric Site.

MV Frances Barkley CRUISE
(☎250-723-8313; www.ladyrosemarine.com; 5425 Argyle St; round-trip $60-82) This historic boat service is a vital link for the region's remote communities, ferrying freight, supplies and passengers between Alberni and Bamfield thrice weekly. In summer, with its route extended to Ucluelet and the beautiful Broken Group Islands, it lures kayakers and mountain bikers, but it's also open for those who just fancy an day cruise up Barkley Sound.

The company recently purchased a decommissioned BC Ferries vessel which they'll also be deploying on the route.

Sleeping & Eating

Hummingbird Guesthouse B&B $$
(☎250-720-2111; www.hummingbirdguesthouse.com; 5769 River Rd; ste from $140;) With four large suites and a huge deck with its own hot tub, this modern B&B has a home-away-from-home feel. There's a shared kitchen on each of the two floors and each suite has satellite TV; one has its own sauna. For families, there's a teen-friendly games room out back.

All Mex'd Up MEXICAN $
(☎250-723-8226; 5440 Argyle St; mains $4-10; ⏰11am-4pm Sun-Fri, 9am-4pm Sat) A funky and highly colorful Mexican eatery near the waterfront, this fairy-lighted little spot makes everything from scratch and focuses on local ingredients as much as possible. Tuck into a classic array of made-with-love tacos, quesadillas and big-ass burritos and you'll be full for your day of exploring, especially if you add a side of nachos with spicy *pico de gallo* (salsa).

Bare Bones Fish & Chips FISH & CHIPS $$
(☎250-720-0900; 4824 Johnston Rd; mains $9-21; ⏰11:30am-7:30pm Sun-Thu, to 8pm Fri & Sat) Colonizing a decommissioned wooden church, this smashing fry-joint serves cod, salmon and halibut in three different styles (beer-battered recommended), adding a tangle of delicious chips and their own lemon-dill dip. Arrive off-peak to avoid the rush (this place is a true local favorite) and add a prawn side dish if you're still hungry (you won't be).

Information

For more on what to do in the region, visit www.albernivalleytourism.com

Getting There & Away

Tofino Bus services arrive here from Victoria ($46, four hours, three daily) and Tofino ($29, two hours, three daily) among others.

Pacific Rim National Park Reserve

Dramatic, wave-whipped beaches and mist-licked forests make the **Pacific Rim National Park Reserve** (☎250-726-3500; www.pc.gc.ca/pacificrim; 2040 Pacific Rim Hwy; park day-pass adult/child $7.80/3.90) a must-see for anyone interested in encountering BC's raw West Coast wilderness. The 500-sq-km park comprises the northern Long Beach Unit, between Tofino and Ucluelet; the Broken Group Islands Unit in Barkley Sound; and, to the south, the ever-popular West Coast Trail Unit. If you're stopping in the park, you'll need to pay and display a pass, available from the visitors center or from the yellow dispensers dotted along the highway.

Long Beach Unit

Attracting the lion's share of park visitors, Long Beach Unit is easily accessible by car along the Pacific Rim Hwy. Wide sandy beaches, untamed surf, lots of beachcombing nooks, plus a living museum of dense, old-growth rainforest, are the main reasons for the summer tourist clamor. **Cox Bay Beach** alone is an ideal hangout for surfers and families. Seabirds, sand dollars, and purple and orange starfish abound.

For an introduction to the area's natural history and First Nations heritage, visit the **Kwisitis Visitor Centre** (Wick Rd; ⏰10am-5pm Jun-Oct, 11am-3pm Fri-Sun Nov-May) FREE overlooking Wickaninnish Beach. If you're suddenly inspired to plunge in for a stroll, try one of the following **walking trails**, keeping your eyes peeled for swooping bald eagles and giant banana slugs. Safety precautions apply: tread carefully over slippery surfaces and never turn your back on the mischievous surf.

➡ **Long Beach** Great scenery along the sandy shore (1.2km; easy).

➡ **Rainforest Trail** Two interpretive loops through old-growth forest (1km; moderate).

➡ **Schooner Trail** Through old- and second-growth forests with beach access (1km; moderate).

➡ **Shorepine Bog** Loops around a moss-layered bog (800m; easy and wheelchair accessible).

West Coast Trail Unit

The 75km West Coast Trail is BC's best-known hiking route. It's also one of the toughest, not for the uninitiated. There are two things you'll need to know before tackling it: it will hurt and you'll want to do it again next year.

The trail winds along the wave-licked rainforest shoreline between trailhead information centers at Pachena Bay, 5km south of Bamfield on the north end, and Gordon River, 5km north of Port Renfrew on the southern tip. The entire stretch takes between six and seven days to complete. Alternatively, a mid-point entrance at Nitinat Lake, operated by the **Ditidaht First Nation** (☎250-745-3999; www.westcoasttrail.com), can cut your visit to a two-or three-day adventure. Check their website for packages.

Open from May to the end of September, access to the route is limited to 60 overnight backpackers each day and **reservations** (☎519-826-5391, 877-737-3783; www.reservation.pc.gc.ca; nonrefundable reservation fee $11) are required. Book as far ahead as you can – reservations open in January every year. All overnighters must pay a trail-user fee ($127.50), plus a per-person reservation fee ($24.50) and the price of the short ferry crossings along the length of the route. All overnighters must attend a detailed orientation session before departing. If you don't have a reservation on the day you arrive, your name can be added to a standby list for any remaining spots (don't count on this, though, especially during the summer peak).

If you don't want to go the whole hog (you wimp), you can do a day hike or hike half the trail from Pachena Bay, considered the easier end of the route. Overnight hikers who only hike this end of the trail can exit from Nitinat Lake. Day hikers are exempt from the pricey trail-user fee, but they need to get a day-use permit at one of the trailheads.

West Coast Trail walkers must be able to manage rough, slippery terrain, stream crossings and adverse, suddenly changing weather. There are more than 100 little, and some not-so-little, bridges and 70 ladders. Be prepared to treat or boil all water and cook on a lightweight camping stove; you'll be bringing in all your own food. Hikers can rest their weary muscles at any of the basic campsites along the route, most of which have solar-composting outhouses. It's recommended that you set out from a trailhead at least five hours before sundown to ensure you reach a campsite before nightfall – stumbling around in the dark is the prime cause of accidents on this route.

West Coast Trail Express (☎250-477-8700; www.trailbus.com; from $60; ⏰daily mid-Jun–mid-Sep, odd-numbered days May–mid-Jun & last two weeks of Sep) runs a handy shuttle service to and from the trailheads. Book ahead.

Broken Group Island Unit

Comprising some 300 islands and rocks scattered across 80 sq km around the entrance to Barkley Sound, this serene natural wilderness is beloved of visiting kayakers – especially those who enjoy close-up views of whales, porpoises and multitudinous birdlife. Compasses are required for navigating here, unless you fancy paddling to Hawaii.

If you're up for a trek, **Lady Rose Marine Services** (☎250-723-8313; www.ladyrosemarine.com) will ship you and your kayak from Port Alberni to its Sechart Lodge three hours away in Barkley Sound. The lodge rents kayaks if you'd rather travel light and it also offers accommodations (single/double $164/263, including meals).

From there, popular paddle destinations include **Gibraltar Island**, one hour away, with its sheltered campground and explorable beaches and tidal pools. **Willis Island** (1½ hours from Sechart) is also popular. It has a campground and, at low tide, you can walk to the surrounding islands. Remote **Benson Island** (four hours from Sechart) has a campground, grazing deer and a blowhole.

Camping fees are $9.80 per night, payable at Sechart or to the boat-based staff who patrol the region – they can collect additional fees from you if you decide to stay longer. The campgrounds are predictably basic and have solar composting toilets, but you must carry out all your garbage. Bring your own drinking water since island creeks are often dry in summer.

Tofino

POP 2050

Transforming from resource outpost to hippie enclave and now a resort town, Tofino is Vancouver Island's favorite outdoorsy retreat. It's not surprising that surf fans, families and city-escaping Vancouverites keep coming: packed with activities and blessed with spectacular local beaches, it sits on Clayoquot Sound, where forested mounds rise from roiling, ever-dramatic waves.

Sights

Tofino Botanical Gardens GARDENS
(☎250-725-1220; www.tbgf.org; 1084 Pacific Rim Hwy; 3-day admission adult/child $12/free; ⏲8am-dusk Jun-Aug, reduced hours off-season) Explore what coastal temperate rainforests are all about by checking out the frog pond, forest boardwalk, native plants and educational workshops at this smashing, bird-packed attraction. New sculptures have been added to the garden in recent years, many by local artists. Pick up a self-guided field guide from the front desk to illuminate your exploration.There's a $1 discount on admission if you arrive car-free.

Tofino Brewing Company BREWERY
(☎250-725-2899; www.tofinobrewingco.com; 681 Industrial Way; ⏲11am-10pm Jun-Aug, reduced hours off-season) Hidden around the back of an unassuming industrial building, this smashing little brewery makes islanders very merry, which is why its brews are in restaurants around town and beyond. Roll up to the tasting bar and check out a few samples (four-glass flights are $6). Always ask for the seasonal offerings and check out the excellent Kelp Stout and Tuff Session Ale.

Maquinna Marine Provincial Park PARK
(www.bcparks.ca) One of the most popular day trips from Tofino, the highlight here is **Hot Spring Cove**. Tranquility-minded trekkers travel to the park by Zodiac boat or seaplane, watching for whales and other sea critters en route. From the boat landing, 2km of boardwalks lead to the natural **hot pools**.

Eagle Aerie Gallery GALLERY
(☎250-725-3235; royhenryvickers.com; 350 Campbell St; ⏲10am-5pm) Showcasing the work of First Nations artist Roy Henry Vickers, this dramatic, longhouse-style building is a downtown landmark. Inside you'll find beautifully presented paintings and carvings as well as occasional opportunities to meet the man himself.

Ahousat PARK
(www.wildsidetrail.com) Situated on remote Flores Island and accessed by tour boat or kayak, Ahousat is the mystical location of the spectacular **Wild Side Heritage Trail**, a moderately difficult path that traverses 11km of forests, beaches and headlands between Ahousat and Cow Bay. There's a natural warm spring on the island and it's also home to a First Nations band. A popular destination for kayakers, camping (no facilities) is allowed.

Meares Island PARK
Visible through the mist and accessible via kayak or tour boat from the Tofino waterfront, Meares Island is home to the **Big Tree Trail**, a 400m boardwalk through old-growth forest that includes a stunning 1500-year-old red cedar. The island was the site of the key 1984 Clayoquot Sound anti-logging protest that kicked off the region's latter-day environmental movement.

Activities

Surf Sister SURFING
(☎250-725-4456; www.surfsister.com; 625 Campbell St; lessons $79) Introductory lessons for kids, families and beginner adults.

T'ashii Paddle School CANOEING
(☎250-266-3787; www.tofinopaddle.com; 1258 Pacific Rim Hwy; tour from $65) Tour the regional waters in a canoe (you'll also be doing the paddling) with a First Nations guide who provides an evocative interpretive narration. Walking tours also available.

Ocean Outfitters BOATING
(☎250-725-2866; www.oceanoutfitters.bc.ca; 368 Main St; adult/child $99/79) Whale-watching tours, with bear and hot-springs treks as well as fishing charters also offered.

STORMING TOFINO

Started as a clever marketing ploy to lure off-season visitors, **storm watching** has become a popular reason to visit the island's wild west coast between November and March. View spectacularly crashing winter waves, then scamper back inside for hot chocolate with a face freckled by sea salt. There are usually good off-peak deals to be had in area accommodations during storm-watching season and many hotels can supply you with loaner 'Tofino tuxedos,' otherwise known as waterproof gear. The best spots to catch a few crashing spectacles are Cox Bay, Chesterman Beach, Long Beach, Second Bay and Wickaninnish Beach. Just remember not to get too close or turn your back on the waves: these gigantic swells will have you in the water within seconds given half the chance.

DON'T MISS

PACIFIC RIM PIT STOP

Don't drive too fast in your rush to get to end-of-the-highway Tofino or you'll miss the locals' favorite stomping ground. Ostensibly known as the **Beaches Shopping Centre** area, 1180 Pacific Rim Hwy is home to dozens of cool little wood-built businesses where you could easily spend a happy half-day. Start with a java at **Tofitian** (1180 Pacific Rim Hwy; 7:30am-5pm Jun-Aug, reduced hours off-season;) then add some chocolate and maybe an ice-cream at **Chocolate Tofino** just around the corner (salted caramels recommended). When lunch beckons, join the line-up at **Tacofino** (250-726-8288; www.tacofino.com; 1184 Pacific Rim Hwy; mains $5-13; 11am-7pm, reduced hours off-season) (or call your order in like the locals do) or avoid queuing completely by heading to **Wildside Grill** (250-725-9453; www.wildsidegrill.com; 1180 Pacific Rim Hwy; mains $6-18; 9am-9pm, reduced hours off-season) for panko-fried prawns.

Jamie's Whaling Station BOATING
(250-725-3919; www.jamies.com; 606 Campbell St; adult/child $109/79) Spot whales, bears and sea lions on Jamie's boat jaunts. Short or multiday kayak tours are also available.

Sleeping

Whalers on the Point Guesthouse HOSTEL $
(250-725-3443; www.hihostels.ca; 81 West St; dm/r $45/129;) Close to the action, but with a secluded waterfront location, this excellent HI hostel is a comfy, wood-lined retreat. Dorms are mercifully small (the female-only one has the best waterfront views) and there are some highly sought-after private rooms. Facilities include a BBQ patio, games room and a wet sauna. Reservations are essential in summer. Bike rentals are available ($35 for 24 hours).

Tofino Inlet Cottages CABIN $$
(250-725-3441; www.tofinoinletcottages.com; 350 Olsen Rd; ste from $130;) Located in a pocket of tranquility just off the highway, this hidden gem is perfect for waking up to glassy-calm waterfront views. It consists of two 1960s-built A-frame cottages, divided into suites, and a spacious woodsy house, which has a lovely circular hearth and is ideal for families.

Ecolodge HOSTEL $$
(250-725-1220; www.tbgf.org; 1084 Pacific Rim Hwy; r from $159;) In the grounds of the botanical gardens, this quiet, wood-built education center has a selection of rooms, a large kitchen and an on-site laundry. Popular with families and groups, there's a bunk room that's around $40 each per night in summer for groups of four. Rates include garden entry and there's a copy of Darwin's *The Origin of Species* in every room.

Ocean Village Beach Resort CABIN $$$
(250-725-3755; www.oceanvillageresort.com; 555 Hellesen Dr; ste from $229;) This immaculate beachside resort of beehive-shaped cedar cabins – hence the woodsy aroma when you step in the door – is a family favorite, with a Scandinavian look. Each unit faces the nearby shoreline and all have handy kitchens. If your kids tire of the beach, there's a saltwater pool and lots of loaner board games to keep them occupied. No in-room TVs.

Pacific Sands Beach Resort RESORT $$$
(250-725-3322; www.pacificsands.com; 1421 Pacific Rim Hwy; d from $350;) Combining comfortable lodge rooms, all with full kitchens, plus spectacular three-level beach houses, this family-friendly resort hugs dramatic Cox Bay Beach. Wherever you stay, you'll be lulled to sleep by the sound of the nearby rolling surf. The spacious, contemporary-furnished beach houses are ideal for groups and have stone fireplaces and top-floor bathtubs with views. Free summertime kids' camps.

Wickaninnish Inn HOTEL $$$
(250-725-3100; www.wickinn.com; Chesterman Beach; d from $420;) Cornering the market in luxury winter-storm-watching packages, 'the Wick' is worth a stay any time of year. Embodying nature with its recycled-wood furnishings, natural stone tiles and the ambience of a place grown rather than constructed, the sumptuous guest rooms have push-button gas fireplaces, two-person hot tubs and floor-to-ceiling windows. It's one of BC's most romantic hotels.

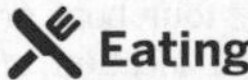

Eating

Common Loaf Bake Shop BAKERY $
(250-725-3915; 1801 First St; menu items $8-12; 8am-6pm) The locals' favorite bakery hangout, this red-painted back street hangout is lined with local art and has a little community library box outside if you

need something to read over your java and croissant. Lunch-hungry visitors should head down the grilled cheese sandwich route, while apposite egg-based sandwiches are also available for breakfasters. Cash only.

Schooner SEAFOOD **$$**
(☎250-725-3444; www.schoonerrestaurant.ca; 331 Campbell St; mains $18-32; ⌚9am-10pm) A Tofino fixture for almost 70 years, this local legend has never rested on its laurels. Start your evening with a cocktail, then launch your voyage into the region's seafood bounty; the giant, two-person Admiral's Plate blowout of local salmon, scallops et al is the way to go. Come back the next morning for a crab Benedict brunch.

Sobo CANADIAN **$$**
(☎250-725-2341; www.sobo.ca; 311 Neill St; mains $14-33; ⌚11:30am-9:30pm) This local favorite launched as a food truck but has been a popular sit-down eatery for years. The focus at Sobo – meaning Sophisticated Bohemian – is seasonal West Coast ingredients prepared with international influences. A brilliant place to dive into fresh-catch seafood, there's a hearty, well-priced lunch menu if you need an early fill-up; chowder, fish tacos and gourmet pizzas are recommended.

Wolf in the Fog CANADIAN **$$$**
(☎250-725-9653; www.wolfinthefog.com; 150 Fourth St; mains $15-45; ⌚9am-late, dinner from 5pm) Reserve ahead for your table at this sparkling regional- and seasonal-focused restaurant that's won awards as Canada's best new restaurant in recent years. The larger plates to share are the best way to go (expect anything from Fraser Valley duck to delectable shellfish) but make sure you also add a taste-bud-popping cedar-sour cocktail.

ℹ Information

Tourism Tofino Visitor Centre (☎250-725-3414; www.tourismtofino.com; 1426 Pacific Rim Hwy; ⌚9am-8pm Jun-Aug, reduced hours off-season) A short drive south of town, the visitors center has detailed information on area accommodations, hiking trails and hot surf spots. There's also a kiosk in the town center in summer that dispenses advice to out-of-towners.

ℹ Getting There & Away

Orca Airways (☎604-270-6722; www.flyorcaair.com) Flights arrive at Tofino Airport from Vancouver International Airport's South Terminal ($217, one hour, up to five daily).

Tofino Bus (www.tofinobus.com) Services arrive from Port Alberni ($29, two hours), Nanaimo ($46, three to four hours), Victoria ($69, six to seven hours) and beyond. Their 'Beach Bus' service rolls in along Hwy 4 from Ucluelet ($17, 40 minutes).

Ucluelet

POP 1,500

Threading along Hwy 4 through the mountains to the west coast, you'll arrive at a junction sign proclaiming that Tofino is 33km to your right, while just 8km to your left is Ucluelet. Sadly, most still take the right-hand turn, which is a shame, since sleepier 'Ukee' has more than a few charms of its own (especially in the culinary department) and is a good reminder of what Tofino was like before tourism arrived.

👁 Sights & Activities

Ucluelet Aquarium AQUARIUM
(☎250-726-2782; www.uclueletaquarium.org; Main Street Waterfront Promenade; adult/child $14/7; ⌚10am-5pm mid-Mar–Nov) This excellent catch-and-release facility on the waterfront focuses on illuminating the marine critters found in the region's local waters, which can mean anything from alien-looking sea cucumbers to a squirming, and frankly mesmerizing, Pacific octopus or two. But it's the enthusiasm of the young staff that sets this place apart, along with the ability to educate on issues of conservation without browbeating. A great kid-friendly facility – you can expect to walk away with renewed excitement about the wonders of ocean wildlife.

Wild Pacific Trail HIKING
(www.wildpacifictrail.com) This 10km nature trail provides smashing, easy-access views of the wave-whipped shoreline. From the intersection of Peninsula and Coast Guard Rds, it winds around the cliffs past the lighthouse (get your camera out) and along the craggy shore fringing the town. Seabirds are abundant and it's a good storm-watching spot; stick to the trail or the waves might pluck you from the cliffs.

Subtidal Adeventures WILDLIFE
(☎250-726-7336; www.subtidaladventures.com; 1950 Peninsula Rd; adult/child $99/79) A long-established local company offering popular Zodiac boat tours that illuminate the regional wildlife scene, with options including a summer favorite that often includes sightings

of bears, several types of whales, lots of seabirds and maybe a sea otter (if you're lucky).

Relic Surf Shop SURFING
(☎250-726-4421; www.relicsurfshop.com; 1998 Peninsula Rd; rentals from $35) The perfect place if you want to practice the ways of the surf – rentals, lessons and stand-up paddle boarding included.

Sleeping

Surfs Inn Guesthouse CABIN, HOSTEL $
(☎250-726-4426; www.surfsinn.ca; 1874 Peninsula Rd; dm/cottages from $28/139;) It's hard to miss this blue-painted house near the center of town, with its small, recently upgraded dorm rooms. But the real find is hidden out back: two cute cabins ideal for groups and families. One is larger and self-contained while the other is divided into two suites with kitchenettes. Each has a BBQ. Ask about surf packages if you fancy hitting the waves.

C&N Backpackers HOSTEL $
(☎250-726-7416; www.cnnbackpackers.com; 2081 Peninsula Rd; dm/r $28/70; Apr-Oct;) Take your shoes off at the door and slide into this large, woodsy hostel, where the gigantic outback garden is the best place to hang (in a hammock) on lazy evenings. A spacious downstairs kitchen and recently renovated bathrooms add to the appeal, while the dorms are joined by three sought-after private rooms.

Whiskey Landing Lodge HOTEL $$
(☎855-726-2270; www.whiskeylanding.com; 1645 Cedar Rd; d from $219;) Right on the harbor (expect to wake to honking seals), this wood-beamed, apartment-style hotel is steps from Ukee's main restaurants. But since each of its 15 studios and suites also has its own kitchen, you can chef up your own meals as well (there's a supermarket up the hill). Don't forget to say hello to Pebbles, the lodge dog.

Eating

Zoe's Bakery & Cafe BAKERY $
(☎250-726-2253; 250 Main St; sandwiches $8-10; 7am-4pm Tue-Sun, reduced hours off-season) Most locals visit this sunny, centrally located bakery at least once a day, dropping by for coffee, Black Magic Bars or the lunchtime soup and sandwich special. Local, organic ingredients are deployed wherever possible and if you're here early enough you can scoop up a slice of our favorite breakfast: a finger-licking savory bread-pudding egg bake.

Ravenlady SEAFOOD $$
(www.ravenlady.ca; 1801 Bay St; mains $15-18; noon-2pm & 5-8pm Fri-Tue) The sole exponent of Ucluelet's food-truck scene is far superior to many bricks-and-mortar seafood restaurants. Specializing in fresh-shucked regional oysters, there are also gourmet delights from octopus linguini to baguette po'boys stuffed to the gills with albacore tuna or *panko*-fried oysters. You can also order these *panko* delights separately ($5), while snagging a picnic table seat in the sun.

Howler's PUB FOOD $$
(☎250-726-2211; 1992 Peninsula Rd; mains $14-18; noon-midnight;) The place to meet the locals, this family-friendly, pub-style restaurant covers a lot of bases: heaping plates of pasta, wraps and burgers (go for the elk), craft beers from Tofino Brewing, a four-lane bowling alley and a backroom of billiard tables and arcade games. Complete with friendly service, it's the kind of place you can easily hang out all evening.

Norwoods CANADIAN $$$
(☎250-726-7001; www.norwoods.ca; 1714 Peninsula Rd; mains $24-38; 5-10pm) Showing how far Ucluelet's dining scene has elevated itself in recent years, this lovely candlelit room would easily be at home in Tofino. The ever-changing menu focuses on seasonal regional ingredients; think halibut and duck breast. All are prepared with a sophisticated international approach, plus there's a full menu of BC (and beyond) wines, many offered by the glass.

Information

Ucluelet Visitors Centre (www.ucluelet.ca; 1604 Peninsula Rd; 9am-5pm Jun-Aug, 9:30am-4:30pm Mon-Fri Sep-May) For a few good reasons to stick around in Ukee, including a dining scene that finally has some great options, make for the handy downtown visitors center for tips.

Getting There & Away

Tofino Bus (www.tofinobus.com) services arrive from Port Alberni (from $26, 1½ hours, three daily), Nanaimo (from $46, three to four hours, three daily) and Victoria (from $34, six hours, four daily), among others. Their 'Beach Bus' comes into town along Hwy 4 from Tofino ($17, 40 minutes, up to three daily).

Denman & Hornby Islands

The main Northern Gulf Islands, Denman and Hornby share laid-back attitudes, artistic flair and some tranquil outdoor activities. You'll arrive by ferry at Denman first from Buckley Bay on Vancouver Island, then hop from Denman across to Hornby. Stop at **Denman Village**, near the first ferry dock, and pick up a free map and attractions guide for both islands.

Denman has three provincial parks: **Fillongley**, with easy hiking and beachcombing; **Boyle Point**, with a beautiful walk to the lighthouse; and **Sandy Island**, only accessible by water from north Denman.

Among Hornby's provincial parks, **Tribune Bay** features a long sandy beach with safe swimming, while **Helliwell** offers notable hiking. **Ford's Cove**, on Hornby's south coast, offers the chance for divers to swim with six-gilled sharks. The island's large **Mt Geoffrey Regional Park** is crisscrossed with hiking and mountain-biking trails.

If you fancy hitting the water, **Denman Hornby Canoes & Kayaks** (☎250-335-0079; www.denmanpaddling.ca; 4005 East Rd, Denman Island; rental/tour from $50/120) offers rentals and guided tours.

Sleeping & Eating

Blue Owl B&B **$$**
(☎250-335-3440; www.blueowlondenman.ca; 8850 Owl Cres, Denman Island; d $140;) An idyllically rustic retreat for those craving an escape from city life, this woodsy little cottage is a short walk from the ocean. Loaner bikes are freely available if you fancy exploring (there's a swimmable lake nearby), but you might want to just cozy up for a night in. There's a two-night minimum stay policy.

Sea Breeze Lodge HOTEL **$$**
(☎250-335-2321; www.seabreezelodge.com; 5205 Fowler Rd, Hornby Island; adult/child $200/70) This 12-acre retreat, with 16 cottages overlooking the ocean, is a popular island fixture. Rooms are comfortable rather than palatial and some have fireplaces and full kitchens. You can swim, kayak and fish or just flop lazily around in the cliffside hot tub. Rates are per person.

Cardboard House Bakery BAKERY **$**
(☎250-335-0733; www.thecardboardhousebakery.com; 2205 Central Rd, Hornby Island; mains $5-10; 8:30am-9pm Tue-Sun, to 4pm Mon, reduced hours off-season) It's easy to lose track of time at this old shingle-sided farmhouse that combines a hearty bakery and cozy cafe. It's impossible not to stock up on a bag full of oven-fresh muffins, cookies and croissants for the road. Stick around for an alfresco crepe lunch in the adjoining orchard, which also stages live music Wednesday and Sunday evenings in summer.

Island Time Café CAFE **$**
(3464 Denman Rd, Denman Island; mains $7-12) This village hangout specializes in fresh-from-the-oven bakery treats, like muffins and scones, plus organic coffee, as well as bulging breakfast wraps and hearty house-made soups. The pizza is particularly recommended, and is served with a side order of gossip from the locals. If the sun is cooperating, you can sit outside and catch some rays.

Information

For more information on the islands, see www.visitdenmanisland.ca and www.hornbyisland.com.

Getting There & Away

BC Ferries (☎250-386-3431; www.bcferries.com) Services arrive throughout the day at Denman from Buckley Bay (passenger/vehicle $10.50/24.35, 10 minutes). Hornby Island is accessed by ferry from Denman (passenger/vehicle $10.50/24.35, 10 minutes).

Comox Valley

Comprising the towns of Comox and Courtenay as well as the hipster-favorite village of Cumberland, this is a region of rolling mountains, alpine meadows and colorful communities. A good outdoor adventure base and a hotbed for mountain biking, its activity highlight is Mt Washington.

Sights & Actvities

Courtenay and District Museum & Palaeontology Centre MUSEUM
(☎250-334-0686; www.courtenaymuseum.ca; 207 4th St, Courtenay; by donation; 10am-5pm Mon-Sat, noon-4pm Sun, closed Mon & Sun in winter;) With its life-sized replica of an elasmosaur (a prehistoric marine reptile first discovered in the area) this excellent small museum also houses pioneer and First Nations exhibits. Pick up a dino-themed chocolate bar from the gift shop: the perfect edible souvenir.

Cumberland Museum MUSEUM
(☎250-336-2445; www.cumberlandmuseum.ca; 2680 Dunsmuir Ave, Cumberland; adult/child $5/4; ⏰10am-5pm Jun-Aug, 10am-5pm Wed-Sun Sep-May) A wonderfully quirky museum located on a row of clapboard buildings that looks like a Dodge City movie set, there are evocative exhibits on the area's pioneer past and Japanese and Chinese communities here. There's also a walk-through mine tunnel that offers a glimpse of just how tough the job would have been (the frightening iron lung exhibited upstairs does the same).

Mt Washington Alpine Resort OUTDOORS
(☎250-338-1386; www.mountwashington.ca; winter lift ticket adult/child $85/43) The main reason for winter visits, this has long been the island's skiing and snowboarding spot, with dozens of runs, plus snowshoeing and tubing options. But there are also great summer activities, including some of the region's best hiking and biking trails.

Sleeping

★Riding Fool Hostel HOSTEL $
(☎250-336-8250; www.ridingfool.com; 2705 Dunsmuir Ave, Cumberland; dm/r $28/60; @ 📶) One of BC's finest hostels colonizes a restored Cumberland heritage building with its rustic wooden interiors, large kitchen and lounge areas and, along with small dorms, the kind of immaculate family and private rooms often found in midrange hotels. Bicycle rentals are available (this is a great hostel to meet mountain bikers) but you'll need to book ahead for the summer peak.

Cona Hostel HOSTEL $
(☎250-331-0991; www.theconahostel.com; 440 Anderton Ave, Courtenay; dm/r $26/65; @ 📶) It's hard to miss this orange riverside hostel, popular along mountain-bikers gearing up for the area's multitudinous trails. The friendly folks at the front desk have plenty of other suggestions for what to explore, but you might want to just stay indoors as there's a large kitchen, foosball table and beer growlers you can fill up for cheap at a nearby microbrewery.

Old House Village Hotel & Spa HOTEL $$
(☎250-703-0202; www.oldhousevillage.com; 1730 Riverside Ln, Courtenay; d from $149; 📶 🏊) Neither an old house nor in a village, this superior lodge-look apartment-style hotel has full kitchens, heated bathroom floors and excellent front-desk staff are ready with helpful suggestions for area sightseeing and dining. There's also an on-site restaurant as well as a spa if you don't fancy straying too far from the building.

Eating & Drinking

Waverley Hotel Pub BURGERS $$
(☎250-336-8322; www.waverleyhotel.ca; 2692 Dunsmuir Ave, Cumberland; mains $13-18; ⏰11am-10:30pm Sun-Thu, 11am-late Fri & Sat; 📶 🍴) Hit this historic, antler-studded saloon for a pub-grub dinner while you flick through a copy of glossy local magazine *CV Collective*. There are a dozen or so craft drafts to keep you company, while the menu ranges from the recommended Thai green curry to some excellent burgers (the Big Wave is the locals' fave). Check ahead for live music.

Mad Chef Café CANADIAN, FUSION $$
(☎250-871-7622; www.madchefcafe.ca; 444 Fifth St, Courtenay; mains $13-16; ⏰11am-8pm Mon-Thu, to 9pm Fri & Sat; 🍴) A large new location for this super-friendly neighborhood favorite hasn't changed the approach. There's still a great selection of made-from-scratch pizzas, wraps and gigantic salads (seafood bowl recommended). Whatever you choose, be sure to add a bowl of the signature Miso Yummy soup, unless you're having the mammoth Death by Bacon Burger, in which case you won't be able to eat anything else.

Atlas Café FUSION $$
(☎250-338-9838; www.atlascafe.ca; 250 6th St, Courtenay; mains $12-18; ⏰8:30am-9:30pm Tue-Thu, to 10pm Fri & Sat, to 3:30pm Sun; 🍴) One of Courtenay's favorite dining options has a pleasing modern bistro feel with a global menu that fuses Asian, Mexican and Mediterranean flourishes. Check out the gourmet fish tacos, plus ever-changing seasonal treats. Good vegetarian options, too. Looking for weekend breakfast? Aim for the blue-crab Benedict.

Cumberland Brewing BREWERY
(☎250-400-2739; www.cumberlandbrewing.com; 2732 Dunsmuir Ave, Cumberland; ⏰noon-9pm Sun, Tue, & Wed, noon-9pm Thu-Sat) A microbrewery that's mastered the neighborhood-pub vibe, this tasty spot combines a woodsy little tasting room with a larger outdoor seating area striped with communal tables. Dive into a tasting flight of four beers; make sure it includes the Red Tape Pale Ale.

BRITISH COLUMBIA COMOX VALLEY

Gladstone Brewing Company BREWERY
(www.gladstonebrewing.ca; 244 4th St, Courtanay; ⏰10am-late) Order a pizza at the adjoining servery and grab a parasol table outside this excellent addition to the region's drinking scene. Check the chalkboard for the current roster of brews then order a four-glass tasting flight ($8). The porter is a favorite but there are usually some intriguing Belgian-influenced beers to whet your whistle as well.

Information

Vancouver Island Visitors Centre (☎885-400-2882; www.discovercomoxvalley.com; 3607 Small Rd, Cumberland; ⏰9am-5pm) Drop by the slick visitors center for tips on exploring the area.

Getting There & Away

The area's three main communities are linked by easy-to-explore highway routes, while **Tofino Bus** (☎250-725-2871; www.tofinobus.com) services trundle into Courtenay at least twice a day from communities across the island.

If you're flying in from the mainland, **Pacific Coastal Airlines** (☎604-273-8666; www.pacificcoastal.com) services arrive at **Comox Valley Airport** (☎250-890-0829; www.comoxairport.com) from Vancouver's South Terminal ($132, 55 minutes, up to nine daily).

Campbell River

POP 33,400

Southerners will tell you this marks the end of civilization on Vancouver Island, but Campbell River is a handy drop-off point for wilderness tourism in **Strathcona Provincial Park** and is large enough to have plenty of attractions and services of its own. Head to the waterfront for seal and boat-bobbing marina views or wander the shops and restaurants on Pier St.

Sights

Discovery Passage Aquarium AQUARIUM
(☎250-914-5500; www.discoverypassageaquarium.ca; 705 Island Hwy; adult/child $8/5; ⏰10am-5pm May-Sep; 👪) Repurposing the old blue shed aquarium that was moved here from Ucluelet, this smashing little marine-critter attraction can be found at the entrance to the Discovery Pier. A showcase of local aquatic life: look out for starfish, eel grass beds and (if you're lucky) an octopus or two. Great spot for kids on a rainy day.

Museum at Campbell River MUSEUM
(☎250-287-3103; www.crmuseum.ca; 470 Island Hwy; adult/child $8/5; ⏰10am-5pm mid-May–Sep, noon-5pm Tue-Sun Oct–mid-May) This fascinating museum is worth an hour of anyone's time. Its diverse collection showcases aboriginal masks, an 1890s pioneer cabin and video footage of the world's largest artificial, non-nuclear blast (an underwater mountain in Seymour Narrows that caused dozens of shipwrecks before it was blown apart in a controlled explosion in 1958).

Discovery Pier LANDMARK
Since locals claim the town as the 'Salmon Capital of the World,' you should wet your line off the downtown Discovery Pier (rental rods available) or just stroll along with the crowds and see what everyone else has caught. Much easier than catching your own lunch: you can also buy fish and chips here.

Sleeping & Eating

Heron's Landing Hotel HOTEL $$
(☎250-923-2848; www.heronslandinghotel.com; 492 S Island Hwy; d from $130; @📶🐾) Superior motel-style accommodation with renovated rooms, including large loft suites ideal for families. Rates include breakfast but rooms also have their own kitchens if you need to chef up your own eggs-and-bacon special. There are also handy coin-operated laundry facilities on-site.

Dick's Fish & Chips FISH & CHIPS $
(☎250-287-3336; www.dicksfishandchips.com; 660 Island Hwy; mains $7-16; ⏰10:30am-dusk) The locals' favorite fish and chip shop, this gable-roofed restaurant a short walk from the Discover Pier is often busy, so consider an off-peak visit. Alongside the usual golden-battered meals, you'll find popular salmon, oyster and halibut burgers, as well as house-made mushy peas that some Vancouver Islanders just can't live without.

Getting There & Away

Pacific Coastal Airlines (☎604-273-8666; www.pacificcoastal.com) Flights from Vancouver ($132, 45 minutes, up to six daily) arrive throughout the day.

Campbell River Transit (☎250-287-7433; www.bctransit.com; adult/child $2/1.75) Operates buses throughout the area and beyond.

Tofino Bus (☎250-725-2871; www.tofinobus.com) Services roll in from points around Vancouver Island, including Nanaimo, Victoria and Port Hardy.

WORTH A TRIP

QUADRA ISLAND HOP

For a day out with a difference, take your bike on the 10-minute **BC Ferries** (p701) trip from Campbell River to rustic **Quadra Island**. There's an extensive network of trails across the island; maps are sold in local stores. Many of the forested trails are former logging routes, and the local community has spent a lot of time building and maintaining the trails for mountain bikers of all skill levels. If you don't have your wheels, you can rent a bike on the island or in Campbell River. For more information on visiting the island, see www.quadraisland.ca.

Quadra's fascinating **Nuyumbalees Cultural Centre** (www.nuyumbalees.com; 34 Weway Rd; adult/child $10/5; ⌚10am-5pm May-Sep) illuminates the heritage and traditions of the local Kwakwaka'wakw First Nations people, showcasing carvings and artifacts and staging traditional dance performances. But if you just want to chill out with the locals, head to **Spirit Sq**, where performers entertain in summer.

If you decide to stick around for dinner, head for the waterfront pub or restaurant at the handsome **Heriot Bay Inn & Marina** (☎250-285-3322; www.heriotbayinn.com; Heriot Bay; d/cabins from $109/229) where, if you have a few too many drinks, you might also choose to stay the night. The hotel has motel-style rooms and charming rustic cabins.

Strathcona Provincial Park

Centered on Mt Golden Hinde (2200m), the island's highest point, **Strathcona Provincial Park** (☎250-474-1336; www.bcparks.ca) is a magnificent pristine wilderness crisscrossed with enticing trail systems. Give yourself plenty of time and you'll soon be communing with waterfalls, alpine meadows, glacial lakes and mountain crags.

On arrival at the park's main entrance, get your bearings at **Strathcona Park Lodge & Outdoor Education Centre**. A one-stop shop for park activities, including kayaking, zip-lining, guided treks and rock climbing, this is a great place to rub shoulders with outdoorsy types. All-in adventure packages are available, some aimed specifically at families. Head to the **Whale Room** or **Myrna's** eateries for a fuel-up before you get too active.

Notable park hiking trails include **Paradise Meadows Loop** (2.2km), an easy amble in a delicate wildflower and evergreen ecosystem; and **Mt Becher** (5km), with its great views over the Comox Valley and mountain-lined Strait of Georgia. Around Buttle Lake, easier walks include **Lady Falls** (900m) and the trail along **Karst Creek** (2km), which winds past sinkholes, percolating streams and tumbling waterfalls.

The park's **lodge** (☎250-286-3122; www.strathconaparklodge.com/escape/accommodation; 41040 Gold River Hwy; r/cabin from $139/250; 🐾) offers good accommodations, ranging from rooms in the main building to secluded timber-framed cottages. If you are a true back-to-nature fan, there are also several campsites available in the park. Consider pitching your tent at **Buttle Lake Campground** (☎519-826-6850, 800-689-9025; www.discovercamping.ca; campsites $20; ⌚Apr-Oct); the swimming area and playground alone make it a great choice for families.

North Vancouver Island

Down-islanders, meaning anyone south of Campbell River, will tell you, 'There's nothing up there worth seeing,' while locals here will respond, 'They would say that, wouldn't they?' Parochial rivalries aside, what this giant region, covering nearly half the island, lacks in towns, infrastructure and population, it more than makes up for in character and natural beauty. Despite the remoteness, some areas are remarkably accessible to hardy hikers, especially along the North Coast Trail.

Port McNeill

Barreling down the hill almost into the harbor, Port McNeill is a useful pit stop for those heading to Port Hardy or craving a coffee before boarding the ferry to delightful (and highly recommended) Alert Bay.

Check out the **museum** (351 Shelley Cres; ⌚10am-5pm Jul-Sep, 1pm-4pm Sat & Sun Oct-Jun) for the region's backstory and don't miss the **World's Biggest Burl** as you stroll towards the entrance. A giant warty outgrowth from a huge tree, it's the best selfie opportunity in the area. If you fancy communing further with the local wilderness, book a backcountry guided hike with **North Island Daytrippers** (☎800-956-2411; www.islanddaytrippers.com).

More a superior motel than a resort, the hilltop **Black Bear Resort** (☎250-956-4900; www.port-mcneill-accommodation.com; 1812 Campbell Way; d/cabin incl breakfast from $162/212;) overlooks the town and is located across from the shops and restaurants. Standard rooms are small but clean and include microwaves and fridges; full-kitchen units are also available and a string of roadside cabins was added a few years back.

For a perfect coffee stop before boarding the Alert Bay ferry, check out **Mugz** (☎250-956-3466; 1597 Beach Dr; pastries & sandwiches $3-11; 7am-8pm Mon-Sat, 7am-7pm Sun;). There's also ice cream and a lunch panini to tempt you at this popular locals hangout. In summer, snag a perch on the patio.

Drop into the gabled **visitors center** (☎250-956-3881; www.town.portmcneill.bc.ca; 1594 Beach Dr; 8:30am-5:30pm May-Sep, reduced hours in winter) for regional insights.

Tofino Bus (☎250-287-7151; www.tofinobus.com) services roll in from places including Port Hardy ($17, 50 minutes, daily) and Campbell River ($44, two to three hours, daily).

Alert Bay

Hop the 45-minute BC Ferries service from Port McNeil for one of the region's best days out. Located on Cormorant Island and radiating from the ferry dock along easily strolled waterfront boardwalks, Alert Bay's brightly painted shacks and houses-on-piles are highly photogenic – even the ones that are crumbling into the briny. Home to the Namgis First Nation, there are lots of ways to experience indigenous culture here, plus some cozy spots to eat or sleep. Expect eagles and ravens to be whirling overhead.

Sights & Activities

This area is highly explorable on foot, so poke along the waterfront boardwalk from the ferry; head right for the breathtaking **Original Namgis Burial Grounds**, with its incredible totem poles, or left for the **Culture Shock Interactive Gallery** (☎250-974-2484; www.cultureshockgallery.ca; 10 Front St; 9:30am-6pm Jul-Sep, closed Sun May, Jun & Oct, reduced hours in winter), a store crammed with contemporary First Nations crafts, T-shirts and jewelry. There's a coffee shack alongside the gallery plus a summer program of cultural experiences for visitors ranging from storytelling to salmon barbecues; check the website to see what's coming up.

Also, don't miss the **U'mista Cultural Centre** (☎250-974-5403; www.umista.ca; 1 Front St; adult/child $12/5; 9am-5pm Jul & Aug, 9am-5pm Tue-Sat Sep-May), a longhouse-like facility proudly displaying dozens of culturally priceless indigenous artifacts confiscated when potlatch ceremonies were outlawed in Canada. These were distributed to museums and collections around the world, but the Centre has been slowly negotiating their return and the main gallery here is a spine-tingling celebration of these efforts. Summer programs include book readings and cedar-bark weaving demonstrations (check the Facebook page for events) while the gift shop is a treasure trove of ethically sourced First Nations art.

And if the ocean is calling, **Seasmoke Whale Watching** (☎250-974-5225; www.seasmokewhalewatching.com; adult/child $120/95; tours mid-May–Sep) offers five-hour marine wildlife-spotting voyages on its yacht, including afternoon tea.

Sleeping & Eating

There are some B&Bs and woodsy cabins available here if you're looking to stay. Contact the **visitors center** (☎250-974-5024; www.alertbay.ca; 118 Fir St; 9am-5pm Jul & Aug, 9am-5pm Mon-Fri Jun, Sep & Oct) for suggestions, especially in summer, when availability is limited. Aim for a secluded sleepover with **Alert Bay Cabins** (☎604-974-5457; www.alertbaycabins.net; 390 Poplar Rd; d from $135).

There are several homestyle eateries along the boardwalk but the best of the bunch is **Pass 'n Thyme** (☎250-974-2670; www.passnthyme.com; 4 Maple Rd; mains $13-21; 11am-8pm Tue-Thu & Sat, 11am-9pm Fri).

Getting There & Away

BC Ferries (☎250-386-3431; www.bcferries.com) arrive in Alert Bay from Port McNeil (adult/vehicle $12.35/28.40, 45 minutes, up to six daily).

Telegraph Cove

Built as a one-shack telegraph station, this charming destination has since expanded into one of the north's main visitor lures. Its pioneer-outpost feel is enhanced by the dozens of brightly painted wooden buildings perched around the marina on stilts. Be aware that it can get very crowded with summer day trippers.

Sights & Activities

Head first along the boardwalk to the smashing **Whale Interpretive Centre** (☎250-928-3129; www.killerwhalecentre.org; by donation adult/child $5/3; ⏰9am-5pm mid-May–Oct), bristling with hands-on artifacts and artfully displayed skeletons of cougars and sea otters. But the main lure at this unique, rustic-barn-like museum are the whale skeletons, mostly hanging from the ceiling. Minke, grey, fin and pygmy are part of the menagerie; give yourself plenty of time to peruse everything carefully.

You can also see whales of the live variety just offshore: this is one of the island's top marine-life viewing regions and **Stubbs Island Whale Watching** (☎250-928-3185; www.stubbs-island.com; adult/child $99/84; ⏰May-Oct) will get you up close with the orcas on a boat trek; you might also see humpbacks, dolphins and sea lions. Mid-July to mid-September is prime time for orca-viewing.

For a bear-tastic alternative, **Tide Rip Grizzly Tours** (☎250-339-5320; www.tiderip.com; tours $299-340; ⏰May-Sep) leads full-day trips to local beaches and inlets in search of the area's furry locals.

Sleeping & Eating

The well-established **Telegraph Cove Resorts** (☎250-928-3131; www.telegraphcoveresort.com; campsites/cabins from $32/150) provides accommodations in forested tent spaces and a string of rustic cabins, while the nearby **Dockside 29** (☎250-928-3163; www.telegraphcove.ca; d from $185; 📶) is a good, motel-style alternative.

Seahorse Cafe CAFE $

(☎250-527-1001; www.seahorsecafe.org; mains $9; ⏰8:30am-7pm May-Sep) This popular dockside cafe has plenty of outdoor picnic tables for you to relax at while digging into barbecued Bavarian smokies, bison burgers, salmon burgers and home-cut fries.

Killer Whale Café BISTRO $$

(☎250-928-3155; mains $14-18; ⏰mid-May–mid-October) Killer Whale Café is the cove's best eatery – the salmon, mussel and prawn linguine is recommended. Aim for a window seat in this creaky-floored heritage building so you can gaze over the marina.

Getting There & Away

Telegraph Cove is a winding but well-signposted turnoff drive from Hwy 19.

Port Hardy

A handy hub for exploring the north's many rugged outdoor experiences, this is also the spot for catching your breath before hopping aboard the breathtaking BC Ferries Inside Passage route.

Sights & Activities

North Island Lanes BOWLING ALLEY

(☎250-949-6307; 7210 Market St; per game incl shoes $6; ⏰1pm-3pm Tue, 5pm-9:30pm Wed-Sun, to 10pm Fri & Sat) With old-school bowling alleys tumbling like knocked-over pins across BC, this immaculately preserved six-lane hangout is a must-see even if you don't want to play. Like stepping into the 1970s, the yellow-painted walls with retro-cool back lights is like a living museum. But rather than being a mothballed old exhibit, it's also one of the friendliest and liveliest evening hangouts in town, especially on Fridays and Saturdays when 'cosmic bowling' takes over.

Quatse Salmon Stewardship Centre FARM

(☎250-949-9022; www.thesalmoncentre.org; 8400 Byng Rd; ⏰10am-5pm Wed-Sun mid-May–Sep; 👪) Bring your kids and they'll learn all about the salmon life-cycle at this off-the-beaten-path hatchery attraction. Besides lots of hands-on action (as well as a cylindrical fish tank you can pop your head into) there are also hatchery tours for a more in-depth education.

Nakwakto Rapids Tours BOATING

(☎250-230-3574; www.nakwaktorapidstours.com; 154 Tsulquate Reserve; tour $100; ⏰by appointment) There's more to this four-hour boat tour than experiencing the roiling waters of 'the world's fastest tidal surge.' Your First Nations guides also provide a rich interpretive narration as well as taking you to some of the region's most scenically remote areas.

Sleeping & Eating

North Coast Trail Backpackers Hostel HOSTEL $

(☎250-949-9441; www.northcoasthostel.com; 8635 Granville St; dm/r $29/64; @📶) This spacious, homey hostel is a warren of small and larger dorms, overseen by friendly owners with plenty of tips on how to encounter the region. The hostel's hub is a large rec room and, while the kitchen is small, the adjoining mural-painted cafe can keep you well fueled. Pension-style private rooms are available and traveling families are also welcomed.

Pier Side Landing HOTEL **$$**
(☎250-949-7437; www.piersidelanding.com; 8600 Granville St; d from $120; 📶) It's hard to beat the location of this elevated motel-style property that has recently been fully renovated: in the center of town, on the waterfront and (if you get an 'ocean view' rather than a 'mountain view' room) offering smashing vistas along a shoreline bristling with bald eagles. Rooms are spacious (not all have balconies, though) and the in-room fridges are handy.

Café Guido CAFE **$**
(☎250-949-9808; www.cafeguido.com; 7135 Market St; mains $6-8; ⏰7am-6pm Mon-Fri, 8am-6pm Sat, 8am-5pm Sun; 📶) You'll easily end up sticking around for an hour at this friendly locals' hangout, especially if you also purchase a tome to read from the bookstore downstairs. The grilled 'Gladiator' pesto flatbread sandwich is ever-popular at lunchtime but save room for the raspberry-lemon scones. Say hi to resident pooch Lucy, who's usually hanging out in the upstairs craft store.

Sporty Bar & Grill PUB FOOD **$$**
(☎250-949-7811; www.sportybar.ca; 8700 Hastings St; mains $11-24; ⏰11:30am-11pm; 📶) Great service and pub grub push this neighborhood bar to the top of the Port Hardy dine-out tree. Sporty's offers hearty burgers, pizzas and fish and chips but there's also a great-value Cobb salad ($13) that's well worth faceplanting into. Beer-wise, eschew the Lucky Lager (the north's traditional favorite) and go for Victoria-brewed Hermann's Dark Lager.

ℹ Information

Port Hardy Visitor Information Centre
(☎250-949-7622; www.visitporthardy.com; 7250 Market St; ⏰9am-6pm Jun-Sep, 8am-4pm Mon-Fri Oct-May) Lined with flyers and staffed by locals who can help you plan your visit in town and beyond, this your first port of call. They're especially adept with area hiking tips.

ℹ Getting There & Away

Pacific Coastal Airlines (www.pacific-coastal.com) Services arrive from Vancouver ($209, 65 minutes, up to four daily).

BC Ferries (☎250-386-3431; www.bcferries.com) Services arrive from Prince Rupert (passenger/vehicle $206/469, 16 hours, schedules vary) via the scenically splendid Inside Passage.

Tofino Bus (☎250-725-2871; www.tofinobus.com) Services roll in from southern destinations, including Port McNeil ($17, 50 minutes, daily).

North Island Transportation (☎250-949-6300; shuttle $8) Operates a handy shuttle to/from the ferry and area hotels.

Cape Scott Provincial Park

It's more than 550km from Victoria to the nature-hugging trailhead of this remote park on the island's crenulated northern tip. This should be your number-one destination if you really want to experience the raw, ravishing beauty of BC, especially its unkempt shorelines, breeze-licked rainforests and stunning sandy bays animated with tumbling waves and beady-eyed seabirds.

Hike the park's well-maintained 2.5km **San Josef Bay Trail** and you'll stroll from the shady confines of the trees right onto one of the best beaches in BC, a breathtaking, windswept expanse of roiling water, forested crags and the kind of age-old caves that could easily harbor lost smugglers. You can camp right here on the beach or just admire the passing ospreys before plunging back into the trees.

One of the area's shortest trails (2km), in adjoining **Raft Cove Provincial Park** (www.bcparks.ca), brings you to the wide, crescent beach and beautiful lagoons of Raft Cove. You're likely to have the entire 1.3km expanse to yourself, although the locals also like to surf here – it's their secret, so don't tell anyone.

If you really like a challenge, consider the 55km **North Coast Trail**, which typically takes up to seven days. You'll be passing sandy coves, deserted beaches and dense, wind-whipped rainforest woodland, as well as a couple of river crossings on little cable cars. The trail is muddy and swampy in places, so there are boardwalks to make things easier. The area is home to elk, deer, cougars, wolves and black bears; make sure you know how to handle an encounter before you set off. The trail is for experienced and well-equipped hikers only. There are backcountry campsites at Nissen Bight, Laura Creek and Shuttleworth Bight.

ℹ Getting There & Away

If you're aiming to tackle the North Coast Trail, take an early morning **Cape Scott Water Taxi** (☎250-949-6541; www.capescottwatertaxi.ca; 6555 Port Hardy Bay Rd) service to Shushartie Bay and, after your hike, hop the **North Coast Trail Shuttle** (☎250-949-6541; www.northcoasttrailshuttle.com) minibus back to Port Hardy. Book ahead for both services.

SOUTHERN GULF ISLANDS

Stressed Vancouverites love escaping into the restorative arms of these laid-back islands, strung like a shimmering necklace between the mainland and Vancouver Island. Formerly colonized by hippies and US draft dodgers, Salt Spring, Galiano, Mayne, Saturna, and North and South Pender deliver on their promise of rustic, sigh-triggering getaways. For additional visitor information, see www.sgislands.com.

Salt Spring Island

POP 10,500

The busiest and most developed of the islands, Salt Spring has a reputation for palatial vacation homes, but it's also lined with artist studios and artisan food and drink producers who welcome visitors. Well worth a long weekend visit, the heart of the community is Ganges, home of Salt Spring's awesome summer market.

Sights & Activities

★Saturday Market MARKET
(www.saltspringmarket.com; Centennial Park, Ganges; 9am-4pm Sat Apr-Oct) The best market in British Columbia, this gigantic cornucopia of produce, edible goodies and locally made artworks lures everyone like a magnet on summer Saturdays. Arrive in the morning; it can be oppressively jam-packed at times. Alternatively, join the locals at the smaller, produce-only Tuesday market.

Salt Spring Island Cheese FARM
(250-653-2300; www.saltspringcheese.com; 285 Reynolds Rd; 11am-5pm May-Sep, to 4pm Oct-Apr;) A family-friendly farmstead with a strollable garden, wandering chickens and a winery-like tasting room and shop, this must-see spot produces goat and sheep milk chèvres, feta and Camembert styles; the soft-goat cheese rounds in several flavors (the garlic one is recommended) are the farm's specialty. You can watch the handmade production through special windows but look out for glimpses of the farm's gamboling goats.

Saltspring Island Ales BREWERY
(250-653-2383; www.saltspringislandales.com; 270 Furness Rd; noon-5pm) Colonizing a rustic, cedar-built shack between the trees, this microbrewery's woodsy little tasting room offers a roster of all-organic brews, from malty Extra Special Bitter to smooth Heatherdale Ale. There are always intriguing seasonal beers to try as well; growlers are available if you need a takeout.

Mistaken Identity Vineyards WINERY
(250-538-9463; www.mistakenidentityvineyards.com; 164 Norton Rd; 11am-6pm) If you're on a picnic-gathering push and need an accompanying libation, consider an exploratory tasting visit (with designated driver) to this locals'-favorite vineyard. The lovely Bliss rosé is recommended.

Ruckle Provincial Park PARK
(www.bcparks.ca) A southeast gem with ragged shorelines and gnarly arbutus forests: there are trails for all skill levels here, with **Yeo Point** making an ideal pit stop.

Salt Spring Adventure Co KAYAKING
(250-537-2764; www.saltspringadventures.com; 126 Upper Ganges Rd, Ganges; rentals/tours from $30/55; 8:30am-6pm Jun-Sep) When it's time to hit the water, touch base with this well-established local operator. They can kit you out for a bobbling kayak tour around Ganges Harbour, but they also serve the stand-up paddleboard crowd. Bike rentals and extended kayak tours around the region are also on the menu.

Salt Spring Studio Tour TOURS
(www.saltspringstudiotour.com) Art fans should hit the trail on Salt Spring by checking out gallery and studio locations via the free downloadable *Studio Tour Map*. Highlights include **Blue Horse Folk Art Gallery** (250-537-0754; www.bluehorse.ca; 175 North View Dr; 10am-5pm Sun-Fri Mar-Dec) and **Duthie Gallery** (250-537-9606; www.duthiegallery.com; 125 Churchill Rd, Ganges; 11am-5pm Thu-Mon, reduced hours off-season).

Sleeping & Eating

Oceanside Cottages COTTAGE $$
(250-653-0007; www.oceansidecottages.com; 521 Isabella Point Rd; d from 135) These four unique cottages are nooks of bliss. Each is exceedingly private and filled with eclectic artwork and creative flourishes. We especially love the groovy little Love Shack, with its retro, Austin Powers vibe.

Salt Spring Inn HOTEL $$
(250-537-9339; www.saltspringinn.com; 132 Lower Ganges Rd, Ganges; d from $90;) In the heart of Ganges and located above a popular bar, the small but well-maintained rooms at

Southern Gulf Islands

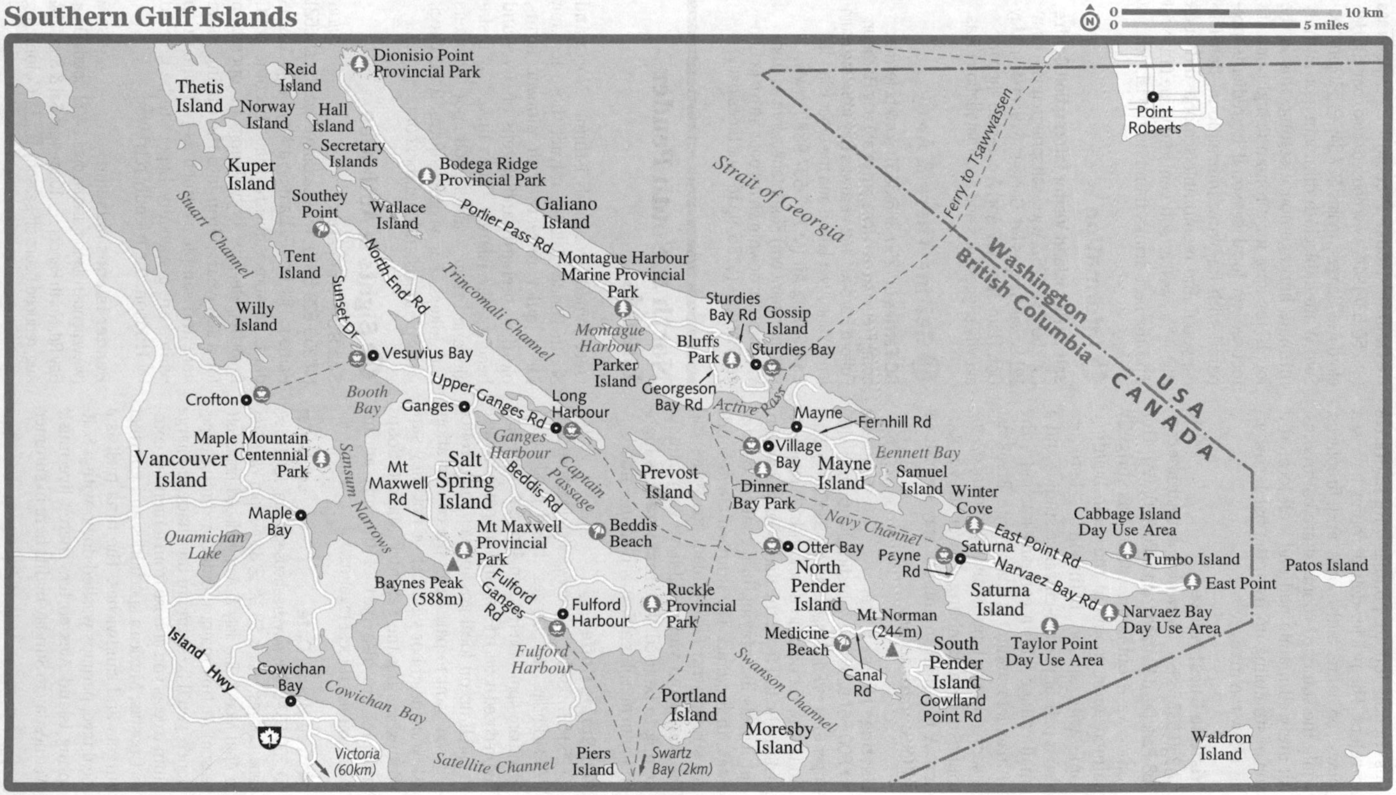

this friendly inn are popular with midrange travelers. The pricier deluxe rooms have sea views, en suite bathrooms and fireplaces, while the standard rooms share bathrooms. All are well maintained and well located if you're stumbling up from the bar below after a few too many.

Wisteria Guest House B&B $$
(☎250-537-5899; www.wisteriaguesthouse.com; 268 Park Dr; d/cottage from $120/180; 📶) This home-away-from-home B&B has brightly painted guest rooms in the main building, some with shared bathrooms. There are also a pair of private-entrance studios and a small cottage with a compact kitchen – the immaculate studio 1 is our favorite. Breakfast is served in the large communal lounge, surrounded by a rambling, flower-strewn garden. A two-night minimum stay sometimes applies; check ahead.

Hastings House Hotel HOTEL $$$
(☎800-661-9255; www.hastingshouse.com; 160 Upper Ganges Rd, Ganges; d from $350; 📶) This smashing rustic-chic hotel with 17 rooms is just up the hill from the main Ganges action, but it feels like staying in a country cottage estate in England. The immaculate grounds are strewn with locally made artworks and the waterfront views will have your camera itching to be used. The **restaurant** is high-end gourmet; breakfast is recommended.

Salt Spring Coffee CAFE $
(☎250-537-0825; www.saltspringcoffee.com; 109 McPhillips Ave, Ganges; baked goods $3-8; ⏲6:30am-4pm Mon-Fri, 7am-4pm Sat, 8am-4pm Sun, reduced hours off-season) The perfect place to catch up on local gossip over some coffee – if you want to partake of the conservation, ask your neighbor whether or not they support expanding the Saturday Market. Soups and pies are also part of the mix at this ever-animated local legend.

★ **Tree House Café** CANADIAN $$
(☎250-537-5379; www.treehousecafe.ca; 106 Purvis Lane, Ganges; mains $8-17; ⏲8am-10pm Wed-Sun, to 4pm Mon & Tue July & Aug, reduced hours off-season) At this magical outdoor dining experience, you'll be sitting in the shade of a large plum tree as you choose from a menu of comfort pastas, Mexican specialties and gourmet burgers and sandwiches. The tuna melt is a local fave, perhaps washed down with a Saltspring Island Ales porter. There's live music Wednesday to Sunday nights here in summer.

Restaurant House Piccolo CANADIAN $$$
(☎250-537-1844; www.housepiccolo.com; 108 Hereford Ave, Ganges; mains $27-34; ⏲5-10pm Wed-Sun) White-tablecloth dining in a beautifully intimate heritage-house setting, this is the locals' top spot for a romantic night out. It's focused on local seasonal ingredients prepared with knowing international flourishes; you'll find memorable seafood and duck dishes, as well as soft venison. Wine fans will find the best drinks menu on the island.

ℹ Information

Salt Spring Island Visitor Information Centre (☎250-537-5252; www.saltspringtourism.com; 121 Lower Ganges Rd, Ganges; ⏲9am-4pm May-Oct, 11am-3pm Nov-Apr) A one-stop shop for activity suggestions and accommodation ideas.

ℹ Getting There & Away

BC Ferries (☎250-386-3431; www.bcferries.com) Frequent services arrive at Long Harbour, Fulford Harbour and Vesuvius Bay from the mainland, Vancouver Island and the other islands.

Salt Spring Air (☎250-537-9880; www.saltspringair.com) Floatplane services from Vancouver's downtown harbour arrive in Ganges Harbour ($135, up to four times daily)

North & South Pender Islands

POP 2250

Once joined by a sandy isthmus, North and South Pender Islands attract those looking for a quiet retreat. With pioneer farms, old-time orchards and dozens of coves and beaches, the islands – now linked by a single-lane bridge – are a good spot for bikers and hikers. For visitor information, check www.penderislandchamber.com.

Sights & Activities

Sea Star Vineyards WINERY
(☎250-629-6960; www.seastarvineyards.ca; 6621 Harbour Hill Dr; ⏲11am-5pm May-Sep) A verdant, 26-acre vineyard that's become a BC favorite, despite only being in operation for a few years; drop into the tasting room here and sample as much as you can. Crisp whites are a specialty. Expect to be greeted by Hudson, the friendly retriever.

Pender Islands Museum MUSEUM
(www.penderislandmuseum.org; 2408 South Otter Bay Rd, North Pender; ⏲10am-4pm Sat & Sun Jul & Aug, reduced hours off-season) FREE Colonizing

WORTH A TRIP

THE NORTH'S BEST BREAKFAST

Whether you're driving up or down island, look for road signs to Sayward and you'll soon find yourself double-taking at the quirkiest streetside diner you've ever seen. The **Cable Cook House Cafe** (250-282-3433; Sayward Rd; mains $8-14;) is completely enveloped in 2500 meters of thick steel cable (it took three months to coil it around the building) and it's a beloved local landmark to those in the know. Once you've perused the menagerie of rusting logging machinery dotted around the grounds (and the painted outhouses out back), head inside for a traditional breakfast and a few giant cinnamon buns to go. But don't miss the murals at the back of the room. Painted by Len Whelan in the 1970s, these humorous folk-art masterpieces depict scenes from the area's logging camps. Look out for an endless logging truck winding around a mountain and a man having coffee poured over his head.

an historic white-clapboard farmhouse, this community museum includes an eclectic array of exhibits tracing the human heritage of the area, including thousands of years of First Nations history. Look out for some evocative photos of the early pioneer days.

Pender Island Arts TOURS
(www.penderarts.com) Many artists call Pender home and you can find them via the handy listings on Pender Island Arts website. Most are on North Pender, where you can visit several within easy walking distance of each other. If you're here in mid-July, don't miss the annual **Art Off The Fence** event, where you'll likely meet every creative in the area.

Pender Island Kayak Adventures KAYAKING
(250-629-6939; www.kayakpenderisland.com; 4605 Oak Rd, North Pender Island; rentals/tours from $59/35) Hit the water with a paddle (and hopefully a boat) via the friendly folks here. They also rent stand-up paddleboards as well as bicycles, and run popular guided kayak tours; the sunset tour is especially recommended. They also run multi-day tours around the region – great if you want to go in-depth (while still remaining in your kayak).

Sleeping & Eating

Woods on Pender CABIN $$
(250-629-3353; www.woodsonpender.com; 4709 Canal Rd, North Pender; d/cabin/Airstream from $100/200/200;) With lodge rooms and rustic cabins also available, the stars here are the six self-catering Airstream caravans, each with their own barbecue-equipped decks. The tree-lined site also includes hot tubs, outdoor games (bocce included) and a restaurant serving comfort grub and dozens of board games. There's a three-night minimum stay for cabins and Airstreams in summer.

Poet's Cove Resort & Spa HOTEL $$$
(250-629-2100; www.poetscove.com; 9801 Spalding Rd, Bedwell Harbour, South Pender; d from $350;) This luxurious harbor-front lodge has arts-and-crafts-accented rooms, most with great views across the glassy water. Extras include an activity center that books eco-tours and fishing excursions, and an elegant West Coast restaurant, Aurora, where you can dine in style. The resort also offers kayak treks plus a full-treatment spa, complete with that all-important steam cave.

Pender Island Bakery Cafe CAFE $
(4605 Bedwell Harbour Rd, Driftwood Centre, North Pender; mains $6-20; 7am-5pm;) At the locals' fave coffeehouse, the coffee is organic, as are many of the bakery treats, including cinnamon buns, which will have you wrestling an islander for the last one. This is a good spot to stock up on croissants for breakfast; see if you can hang on until morning or end up scoffing one in the middle of the night.

Cafe at Hope Bay CANADIAN $$
(250-629-2090; www.thecafeathopebay.com; 4301 Bedwell Harbour Rd, North Pender; mains $10-23; 11am-8:30pm Mon-Sun) West Coast ingredients with international influences rule at this bistro-style spot just a few minutes from the Otter Bay ferry dock, closely followed by the sterling views across Plumper Sound. The fish and chips is predictably good, but dig deeper into the menu for less-expected treats, like the lip-smacking coconut-curried mussels and prawns.

Getting There & Away

BC Ferries (p718) Frequent services arrive from Tsawwassen (adult/child/car $19.80/9.90/72.80), Swartz Bay (adult/child/car $13.45/6.75/41.90) and other islands.

Seair Seaplanes (☎604-273-8900; www.seairseaplanes.com) Services arrive on North Pender from Vancouver International Airport ($119, three times a day)

Pender has a cool **'community transit' system**, where car-driving locals pick people up at designated stops across the islands.

Galiano Island

POP 1150

With the most ecological diversity of the Southern Gulf Islands, this skinny landmass – named after a 1790s Spanish explorer – offers activities for marine enthusiasts and landlubbers alike.

The Sturdies Bay ferry end is busier than the rest of the island (with restaurants and shops to match) while the island becomes ever more forested and tranquil as you drive away from the dock.

Sights & Activities

Once you've got your bearings – that is, driven off the ferry – head for **Montague Harbour Marine Provincial Park** for trails to beaches, meadows and a cliff carved by glaciers. In contrast, **Bodega Ridge Provincial Park** is renowned for eagle and cormorant birdlife plus spectacular vistas.

The protected waters of **Trincomali Channel** and the more chaotic waters of Active Pass satisfy paddlers of all skill levels. **Galiano Kayaks** (☎250-539-2442; www.seakayak.ca; 3451 Montague Rd; 2hr/day rental from $35/60, tours from $60) can help with rentals and guided tours. If you fancy exploring on land, rent a moped from **Galiano Adventure Company** (☎250-593-3443; www.galianoadventures.com; Montague Harbour Marina; rental per hour from $20; ⏲May-Sep).

Sleeping & Eating

Among the island's sleeping options, sophisticates will enjoy **Galiano Inn** (☎250-539-3388; www.galianoinn.com; 134 Madrona Dr; d from $249;), close to the Sturdies Bay ferry dock. Those craving a nature retreat should head to **Bodega Ridge** (☎250-539-2677; www.bodegaridge.com; 120 Manastee Rd; cabins $275;), a tranquil woodland clutch of cedar cabins at the other end of the island.

Fuel up on breakfast, treats and local gossip at **Sturdies Bay Bakery** (☎250-539-2004; 2450 Sturdies Bay Rd; mains $6-12; ⏲7am-3pm Mon-Thu, to 5pm Fri-Sun;). Once you're done exploring the island, drop in for beer and fish and chips at the venerable, forest-fringed **Hummingbird Pub** (☎250-539-5472; www.hummingbirdpub.com; 47 Sturdies Bay Rd; mains $12-17). But make time for dinner at **Pilgrimme** (☎250-539-5392; www.pilgrimme.ca; 2806 Montague Rd; mains $16-30; ⏲5pm-10pm Wed-Mon), an innovative, top-notch eatery that would still be massively popular in a far bigger community. Seasonal, regional and often locally foraged, the regular menu features highlights including duck and Pacific octopus.

Information

Drop into the **visitors info booth** (www.galianoisland.com; 2590 Sturdies Bay Rd; ⏲10am-5pm Mon-Sat, Jun-Aug, reduced hours off-season) before you leave the ferry area. If it's closed, nearby **Galiano Island Books** (☎250-539-3340; www.galianoislandbooks.com; 76 Mardona Dr; ⏲10am-5:30pm Sun-Fri, 9:30am-5:30pm Sat) has a great selection and friendly staffers who can point you in the right direction.

Getting There & Away

BC Ferries (p718) Frequent services arrive at the Sturdies Bay dock from Tsawwassen (adult/child/car $19.80/9.90/72.80), Swartz Bay (adult/child/car $13.45/6.75/41.90) and other islands.

Seair Seaplanes (p720) Flights from Vancouver International Airport arrive at Montague Harbour ($119, twice daily).

Saturna Island

POP 350

Suffused with tranquility, tiny Saturna is a natural retreat remote enough to deter casual visitors. Almost half the island, laced with curving bays, stunning rock bluffs and towering arbutus trees, is part of the **Gulf Islands National Park Reserve** and the only crowds you'll see are feral goats that have called this munchable area home. If you've had enough of civilization, this is the place to be.

On the north side of the island, **Winter Cove** has a white-sand beach that's popular for swimming, boating and fishing. Great for a hike is **Mt Warburton Pike** (497m), where you'll spot wild goats, soaring eagles and panoramic views of the surrounding islands: focus your binoculars and you might spy a whale or two sailing quietly along the coast.

If you're here on Canada Day (July 1), join the locals at the annual **Lamb Barbecue** (www.saturnalambbarbeque.com; adult/child $23/12). It's the biggest party on the island.

Alongside campsites and B&Bs, you'll find a small selection of other sleeping options. Aim for **Saturna Lodge** (☎250-539-2254; www.saturna.ca; 130 Payne Rd; d from $145;), a peaceful respite surrounded by a garden.

Dining is generally of the rustic variety here. Not far from the ferry dock, **Wild Thyme Coffee House** (☎250-539-5589; www.wildthymecoffeehouse.com; 109 East Point Rd; mains $6-10; 5:45am-4:30pm Mon-Fri, 8am-4:30pm Sat & Sun;) is a delightful converted double-decker bus (seats and tables inside and out) serving wholesome breakfasts, soup and sandwich lunches, and baked treats, all made with foodie love. There's a focus on local ingredients and fair-trade coffee.

Information

Saturna Island Tourism Association (www.saturnatourism.com) Visit the Saturna Island Tourism Association website for more information.

Getting There & Away

BC Ferries (p718) Services dock at Lyall Harbour on the west of the island from Tsawwassen (adult/child/car $19.80/9.90/72.80), Swartz Bay (adult/child/car $13.45/6.75/41.90) and other islands.

Seair Seaplane (p720) Services arrive Lyall Harbour from Vancouver International Airport ($119, three times daily)

Mayne Island

POP 1,100

Once a stopover for gold-rush miners, who nicknamed it 'Little Hell,' Mayne is the region's most historic island. Long past its importance as a commercial hub, it now houses a colorful clutch of resident artists. For further visitor information, see www.mayneislandchamber.ca.

The heritage **Agricultural Hall** in Miners Bay hosts the lively **Farmers Market** (☎250-222-0034; 430 Fernhill Rd, Agricultural Hall; 10am-1pm Sat May-Oct) of local crafts and produce. But if it's time to explore, the south shore's **Dinner Bay Park** (Dinner Point Rd) has a lovely sandy beach, as well as an immaculate **Japanese Garden**, built by locals to commemorate early-20th-century Japanese residents. If you're feeling active, **Bennett Bay Kayaking** (☎250-539-0864; www.bennettbaykayaking.com; 494 Arbutus Dr; kayak rentals/tours from $37/66; Apr-Oct) can help kayakers and stand-up paddleboarders get out on the water via rentals and tours.

If you're just too tired to head back to the mainland, **Mayne Island Resort** (☎250-539-3122; www.mayneislandresort.com; 494 Arbutus Dr; d from $159;) combines ocean-view rooms in a century-old inn with swanky luxe beach cottages. There's also a spa and large restaurant-bar. Alternatively, go the heritage B&B route at the charming **Fairview Farm** (☎604-539-5582; www.fairviewonmayne.com; 601 Bell Bay Rd; d from $125).

If it's time for treats, head to **Sunny Mayne Bakery Cafe** (☎250-539-2323; www.sunnymaynebakery.com; 472 Village Bay Rd; mains $4-10; 6am-6pm) – don't miss the sausage rolls. But when dinner is required, aim for a water-view seat at **Bennett Bay Bistro** (☎250-539-3122; www.bennettbaybistro.com; 494 Arbutus Dr; mains $12-22; 11:30am-8:30pm).

Getting There & Away

BC Ferries (p718) Frequent services arrive at Village Bay from Tsawwassen (adult/child/car $19.80/9.90/72.80), Swartz Bay (adult/child/car $13.45/6.75/41.90) and other islands.

Seair Seaplanes (p720) Flights arrive from Vancouver International Airport at Miners Bay ($119, twice daily).

FRASER & THOMPSON VALLEYS

Those looking for an inland escape from Vancouver can shoot east on Hwy 1 through the fertile plains of places such as Abbotsford. Mostly people just whiz past this farmland, and you should too, unless you have a hankering to see a turnip in the rough. That said, the Fraser Canyon thrills with stunning river-gorge beauty and the Thompson River looks little changed in decades.

Information

About 150km east of Vancouver, Hope has a good **visitors center** (☎604-869-2021; www.hopebc.ca; 919 Water Ave; 9am-5pm) with plenty of information about the local provincial parks and the region.

EC Manning Provincial Park

This 708-sq-km **provincial park** (☎604-795-6169; www.bcparks.ca; P), 30km southeast of Hope, is a hint of bigger – much bigger – things to come as you head east,

Fraser & Thompson Valleys

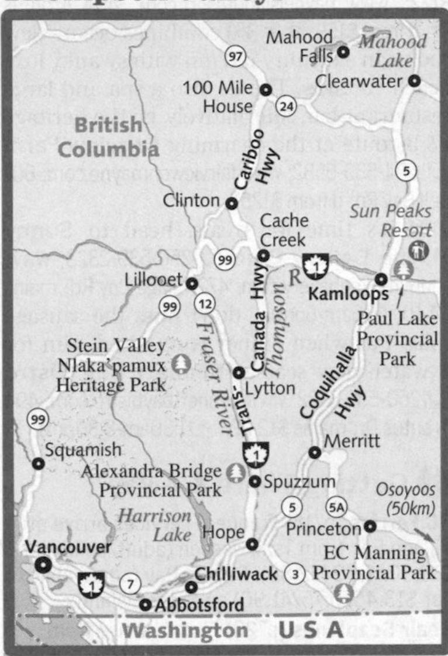

away from the farmlands of the Lower Mainland, towards the Rocky Mountains. It packs in a lot: dry valleys dark; mountainous forests; roiling rivers and alpine meadows. The park makes a good pause along Hwy 3, but don't expect solitude, as there are scores of folk from the burgs west seeking the same thing.

Sights & Activities

Manning is a four-seasons playground. Manning Park Resort (p722) has winter sports. In summer boat rentals are available on Lightning Lake, and you can enjoy the alpine splendor on day hikes.

The following walks are easily reached from Hwy 3:

- **Dry Ridge Trail** Crosses from the dry interior into an alpine climate; excellent views and wildflowers (3km round-trip, one hour).
- **Canyon Nature Trail** Nice loop trail with a river crossing on a bridge (2km, 45 minutes).
- **Lightning Lake Loop** The perfect intro: a level loop around this central lake (9km, two hours). Look for critters in the evening.

Sleeping

Lightning Lake Campground CAMPGROUND $
(reservations 800-689-9025; www.discovercamping.ca; EC Manning Provincial Park; campsites $35) A popular campground that accepts advance reservations.

Manning Park Resort RESORT $$
(800-330-3321, 250-840-8822; www.manningpark.com; 7500 Hwy 3; dm from $35, r from $120; P) Manning Park Resort has the only indoor accommodations in the park. The 73 rooms are housed in the lodge and cabins. All provide use of a hot tub, requisite after a day of downhill **skiing** and **snowboarding** (adult/child day pass $53/33). It also has 100km of groomed trails for cross-country skiing and snowshoeing.

Information

The park's **visitor center** (604-668-5953; Hwy 3; 9am-6pm mid-Jun–mid-Sep) is 30km inside the western boundary. It has detailed hiking descriptions, and a relief model of the park and nearby beaver ponds.

Getting There & Away

The park is east of Hope on Hwy 3. **Greyhound Canada** (800-661-8747; www.greyhound.ca) has buses from Hope ($20, one hour, one daily).

Fraser River Canyon

The name alone makes **Spuzzum** a fun stop along Hwy 1 on its way to Cache Creek, 85km west of Kamloops. The road shadows the swiftly flowing Fraser River through the eponymous canyon and, as you'd expect, white-water rafting is huge here. Grand scenery and several good provincial parks make this a winning trip.

North from Spuzzum, **Stein Valley Nlaka'pamux Heritage Park** (250-371-6200; www.bcparks.ca; Stein Valley Rd, Lytton; P) is an ecologically diverse park that is managed together with the Lytton First Nation. It offers some excellent long-distance **hiking** through dry valleys and snow-clad peaks amid one of the best-preserved watersheds in lower BC.

Two kilometers north of Spuzzum, **Alexandra Bridge Provincial Park** (604-795-6169; www.bcparks.ca; off Hwy 1; P) makes for a scenic stop, where you can picnic while gazing up at the bridge's historic 1926 span.

White-water rafting down the Fraser and its tributaries' fast-flowing rapids is popular and **Fraser River Raft Expeditions** (☎604-863-2336; www.fraserraft.com; 30950 Hwy 1, Yale; trips from $160) covers all the main waterways in the area. **Kumsheen Rafting Resort** (☎800-663-6667; www.kumsheen.com; Hwy 1, 5km east of Lytton; campsites/tipis from $35/130; P) also offers a variety of trips and funky accommodations.

Kamloops

POP 89,500

If you've opted to follow Hwy 1 from Vancouver east to the Rockies and Banff, Kamloops makes a useful break in the journey. Motels abound, and there's a walkable heritage center. Historically, the Shuswap First Nation found the area's many rivers and lakes useful for transportation and salmon fishing. Traders set up camp for fur hunting in 1811.

The focus of the downtown area is tree-lined Victoria St, which is a lively place on sunny days; very busy train tracks separate the wide Thompson River from downtown. Franchises and malls line the highlands along Hwy 1.

The 2017 *Power Rangers* movie was filmed here.

Sights

Using Victoria St as your anchor, stroll downtown, stopping at the art gallery and museum. Pick up the *Downtown Cultural Heritage Walking Tour* brochure from the visitor center (p724).

Look for **back-alley art**, a series of murals in the alley between Victoria and Seymour Sts east of 2nd Ave.

Kamloops Heritage Railway HISTORIC RAILWAY
(☎250-374-2141; www.kamrail.com; 510 Lorne St; adult/child from $25/12; ⏲Aug; P) Across the train tracks from downtown, the Kamloops Heritage Railway runs steam-engine-powered excursions. Confirm the schedule in advance.

Kamloops Art Gallery GALLERY
(☎250-377-2400; www.kag.bc.ca; 465 Victoria St; adult/child $5/3; ⏲10am-5pm Mon-Sat, to 9pm Thu) Suitably loft-like in feel, this gallery has an emphasis on contemporary Western and aboriginal works by regional artists.

WORTH A TRIP

BC'S PARK GEM

From Kamloops, Hwy 5 runs north toward the Alberta border and Jasper National Park, 440km from Kamloops. Along the way, it passes near **Wells Gray Provincial Park** (p757), 125km from Kamloops, one of BC's finest and a haven for those who really want to get away from civilization.

Kamloops Museum & Archives MUSEUM
(☎250-828-3576; www.kamloops.ca/museum; cnr Seymour St & 2nd Ave; adult/child $3/1; ⏲9:30am-4:30pm Tue-Sat;) Kamloops Museum is in a vintage building and has a suitably fitting collection of historic photographs. Come here for the scoop on river-namesake David Thompson, and an entire floor dedicated to exhibits for kids.

Paul Lake Provincial Park PARK
(☎250-819-7376; www.bcparks.ca; Pinantan Rd; P) On the often-hot summer days, the beach at Paul Lake Provincial Park beckons and you may spot falcons and coyotes. There is a 20km **mountain-biking loop**, and campsites ($18). It's 24km northeast of Kamloops, via Hwy 5.

Sleeping

Older and shabbier motels can be found along a stretch of Hwy 1 east of downtown. Columbia St, from the center up to Hwy 1 above town, has another gaggle of chain and older indie motels, some with sweeping views. The nearby parks have good camping.

★**Plaza Hotel** HOTEL $$
(☎877-977-5292, 250-377-8075; www.plazaheritagehotel.com; 405 Victoria St; r $75-200; P) In a town of bland modernity as far as lodgings go, the Plaza reeks of character. This 67-room, six-story classic has changed little on the outside since its opening in 1928. Rooms are nicely redone in a chic heritage style, though, and the included breakfast is excellent.

Scott's Inn MOTEL $$
(☎250-372-8221; www.scottsinn.com; 551 11th Ave; r from $100; P@) Unlike many of its competitors, Scott's is close to the center and very well run. The 51 rooms are nicely furnished for a motel, and extras include an indoor pool, hot tub, cafe and rooftop sun deck.

South Thompson Inn Guest Ranch LODGE $$
(☎250-573-3777; www.stigr.com; 3438 Shuswap Rd E; r $160-260; P❄📶🏊) Some 20km west of town via Hwy 1, this luxe waterfront lodge is perched on the banks of the South Thompson River and set amid rolling grasslands. Its 57 rooms are spread between the wood-framed main building, a small manor house and some converted stables.

Eating & Drinking

Art We Are CAFE $
(www.theartweare.com; 246 Victoria St; mains from $8; ⏰9am-9pm Mon-Sat; 📶✍) Tea joint, local artist venue, hangout, bakery and more – this funky cafe is a great place to let some Kamloops hours slip by. The organic menu changes daily. Saturday night has live rock or blues.

Hello Toast CAFE $
(☎250-372-9322; www.facebook.com/hellodouble; 428 Victoria St; mains $5-12; ⏰7:30am-3pm; ✍) 🌿 As opposed to Good Morning Croissant, this veggie-friendly, organic cafe offers whole grains for some, and fried combos of bacon and eggs or burgers for others. Nice open front and sidewalk tables.

★**Noble Pig** PUB FOOD $$
(☎778-471-5999; www.thenoblepig.ca; 650 Victoria St; mains $12-20; ⏰11:30am-11pm Mon-Wed, to midnight Thu-Sat, 3-10pm Sun) This large and slick microbrewery has a rotating lineup of seven of its own beers (its excellent IPA is always on tap) plus other top BC brews. The food is equally good and includes salads, burgers, pizza and various specials. Try the fries. The inside is warm and welcoming; in summer you can't beat the huge patio.

Commodore PUB
(☎250-851-3100; www.commodorekamloops.com; 369 Victoria St; ⏰11am-late Mon-Sat) An old-style pub with a long menu that highlights burgers and fondue (mains from $12), the Com is the place on Friday nights for live jazz and funk. Other nights, DJs spin pretty much anything. Enjoy the sidewalk seating.

Information

The **visitor center** (☎250-374-3377, 800-662-1994; www.tourismkamloops.com; 1290 W Hwy 1, exit 368; ⏰8am-6pm; 📶) is just off Hwy 1, overlooking town.

Getting There & Away

Greyhound Canada (p722) is about 1km southwest of the center off Columbia St W. Destinations include the following:

Jasper $70, 5½ hours, one daily
Kelowna $37, 2½ hours, two daily
Prince George $89, seven hours, one daily
Vancouver $59, five hours, six daily

VIA Rail (p633) serves Kamloops North Station, 11km from town off Hwy 5, with the tri-weekly *Canadian* on its run from Vancouver (9½ hours) to Jasper (another 9½ hours) and beyond. Fares vary greatly by season and class of service.

Getting Around

Kamloops Transit System (☎250-376-1216; www.bctransit.com/kamloops; fares $2) runs local buses.

Sun Peaks

The hills looming northeast of Kamloops are home to the **Sun Peaks Resort** (☎800-807-3257; www.sunpeaksresort.com; 1280 Alpine Rd; lift tickets adult/child $92/46, mountain biking $45/27). This ever-growing resort boasts 135 ski runs (including some 8km-long powder trails), 12 lifts and a pleasant base-area village. In summer, lifts provide access to more than two dozen mountain-bike trails.

Sun Peaks has many lodges, B&Bs and luxury condos. **Sun Peaks Hostel** (☎250-578-0057; www.sunpeakshostel.com; 1140 Sun Peaks Rd; dm/d from $27/75; 📶) has a mix of dorms and private rooms in a woodsy lodge setting.

Sun Peaks is 50km northeast of Kamloops via Hwy 5. In winter there are shuttles from Kamloops ($15).

OKANAGAN VALLEY

It's hard to know which harvest is growing faster in this fertile and beautiful valley midway between Vancouver and Alberta: tourists or fruit. The 180km-long Okanagan Valley is home to orchards of peaches and apricots, and scores of excellent wineries whose vines spread across the terraced hills, soaking up some of Canada's sunniest weather. The valley has provided a summertime escape for generations of Canadians, who frolic in the string of lakes linking the Okanagan's towns.

Okanagan Valley

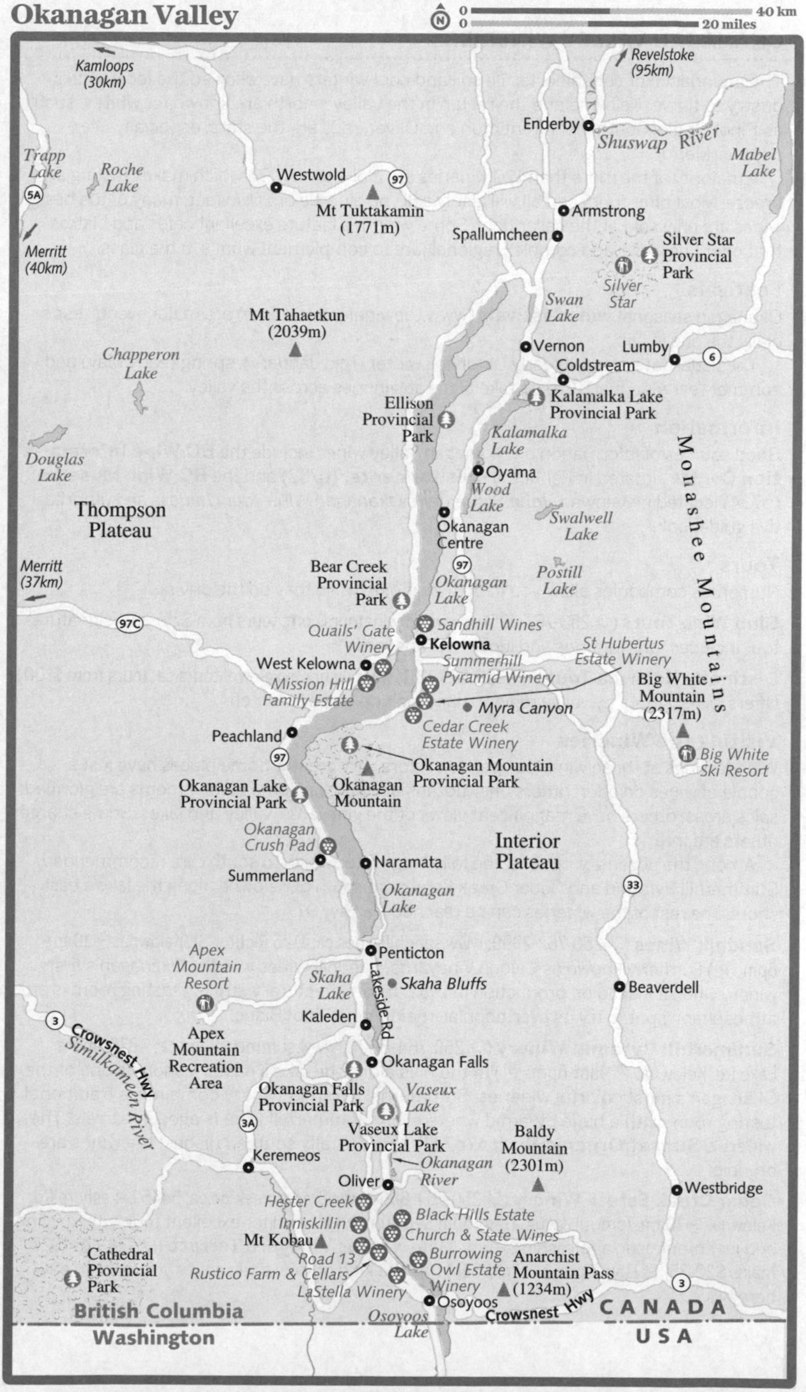

0 40 km
0 20 miles

Kamloops (30km)
Revelstoke (95km)
Enderby
Shuswap River
Trapp Lake
Roche Lake
Mabel Lake
5A
Westwold
97
Mt Tuktakamin (1771m)
Armstrong
Spallumcheen
Silver Star Provincial Park
Merritt (40km)
Silver Star
Swan Lake
Mt Tahaetkun (2039m)
Vernon
Lumby
6
Coldstream
Chapperon Lake
Kalamalka Lake Provincial Park
Ellison Provincial Park
Kalamalka Lake
Monashee Mountains
Douglas Lake
Oyama
Wood Lake
Thompson Plateau
Okanagan Centre
Swalwell Lake
97
Merritt (37km)
Bear Creek Provincial Park
Okanagan Lake
Postill Lake
97C
Sandhill Wines
Quails' Gate Winery
Kelowna
St Hubertus Estate Winery
West Kelowna
Summerhill Pyramid Winery
Mission Hill Family Estate
Big White Mountain (2317m)
Myra Canyon
Cedar Creek Estate Winery
Peachland
97
Okanagan Mountain Provincial Park
Big White Ski Resort
Okanagan Lake Provincial Park
Okanagan Mountain
Okanagan Crush Pad
Interior Plateau
Naramata
Summerland
33
Okanagan Lake
Penticton
Apex Mountain Resort
Skaha Lake
Lakeside Rd
Skaha Bluffs
Beaverdell
3
Kaleden
Crowsnest Hwy
Similkameen River
Apex Mountain Recreation Area
Okanagan Falls
Okanagan Falls Provincial Park
Vaseux Lake
3A
Vaseux Lake Provincial Park
Baldy Mountain (2301m)
Keremeos
Okanagan River
Oliver
Westbridge
Hester Creek
Black Hills Estate
Inniskillin
Church & State Wines
Mt Kobau
Cathedral Provincial Park
Road 13
Burrowing Owl Estate Winery
Anarchist Mountain Pass (1234m)
Rustico Farm & Cellars
3
LaStella Winery
Osoyoos
Crowsnest Hwy
British Columbia
CANADA
Osoyoos Lake
Washington
USA

OKANAGAN VALLEY WINERIES

The abundance of sunshine, fertile soil and cool winters have allowed the local wine industry to thrive. Kelowna and the region in the valley's north are known for whites, such as Pinot Grigio. South, near Penticton and Oliver, reds are the stars, especially ever-popular Merlot.

A majority of the more than 120 wineries are close to Hwy 97, which makes tasting a breeze. Most offer tours and all will gladly sell you a bottle or 20; in fact, many of the best wines are only sold at the cellar door. Some wineries feature excellent cafes and bistros that offer fine views and complex regional fare to complement what's in the glass.

Festivals

Okanagan seasonal **wine festivals** (www.thewinefestivals.com) are major events, especially the one in fall.

The usual dates are fall (early October), winter (mid-January), spring (early May) and summer (early August). Events take place at wineries across the valley.

Information

Good sources of information on Okanagan Valley wines include the **BC Wine Information Centre** situated in Penticton's **visitor center** (p733) and the **BC Wine Museum** (p734) located in Kelowna. *John Schreiner's Okanagan Wine Tour Guide* is an authoritative guidebook.

Tours

Numerous companies allow you to do the sipping while they do the driving.

Club Wine Tours (☎250-762-9951; www.clubwinetours.com; tours from $75) The 'signature' tour includes four wineries and lunch in a vineyard.

Distinctly Kelowna Tours (☎250-979-1211; www.distinctlykelownatours.ca; tours from $100) Offers winery tours by valley region; many include stops for lunch.

Visiting the Wineries

Wine tastings at those wineries open to visitors vary greatly. Some places have just a couple of wines on offer; others offer dozens of vintages. Some tasting rooms are glorified sales areas; others have magnificent views of the vineyards, valley and lakes. Some charge; others are free.

Among the dozens of options, the following (listed north to south) are recommended. Summerhill Pyramid and Cedar Creek Estate are south of Kelowna along the lake's east shore. The rest of the wineries can be reached via Hwy 97.

Sandhill Wines (☎250-762-2999; www.sandhillwines.ca; 1125 Richter St, Kelowna; ⊙10am-6pm; P) Formerly known as Calona Vineyards, Sandhill Wines was the Okanagan's first winery when it kicked off production in 1932. Its architecturally striking tasting room is an atmospheric spot to try its ever-popular, melon-note Pinot Blanc.

Summerhill Pyramid Winery (☎250-764-8000; www.summerhill.bc.ca; 4870 Chute Lake Rd, Kelowna; ⊙9am-6pm; P) In the hills along the lake's eastern shore is one of the Okanagan's most colorful wineries. Summerhill Pyramid Winery combines a traditional tasting room with a huge pyramid where every Summerhill wine is aged in barrels. The winery's **Sunset Organic Bistro** (p737) offers locally sourced dishes; the wines are organic.

Cedar Creek Estate Winery (☎250-764-8866; www.cedarcreek.bc.ca; 5445 Lakeshore Rd, Kelowna; ⊙10am-7pm Jul & Aug, 11am-5pm Sep-Jun; P) Known for excellent tours, its Riesling and its Ehrenfelser, a refreshing fruity white wine. Its **Vineyard Terrace** (☎778-738-1027; mains $20-35; ⊙11am-9pm Jun–mid-Sep) has the kind of view that makes you want to eat here twice.

Quails' Gate Winery (☎250-769-2501; www.quailsgate.com; 3303 Boucherie Rd, West Kelowna; ⏱10am-8pm; P) A small winery with a huge reputation; it's known for its Pinot Noir, Chardonnay and Chenin Blanc. The **Old Vines Restaurant** (☎250-769-4451; mains $20-35; ⏱11:30am-2pm & 5-9pm) is among the best.

Mission Hill Family Estate (☎250-768-7611; www.missionhillwinery.com; 1730 Mission Hill Rd, West Kelowna; ⏱10am-6pm; P) As if it were a Tuscan hill town, this winery's architecture wows. Go for a taste of one of the blended reds (try the Bordeaux) or the excellent Syrah. **Terrace** (p734) is one of the valley's best restaurants and sources fine foods locally; book ahead.

Okanagan Crush Pad (☎250-494-4445; www.okanagancrushpad.com; 16576 Fosbery Rd, Summerland; ⏱10:30am-5:30pm; P) Ages many of its wines in concrete tanks, reviving a centuries-old practice that largely died out when the industry shifted to stainless steel. Tastings range across more than 20 varieties from the multiple labels that are produced here.

Hester Creek (☎250-498-4435; www.hestercreek.com; 877 Road 8, Oliver; ⏱10am-7pm; P) Has a sweeping location, a great new tasting room and is known for its reds, especially its richly flavored Cabernet Franc. **Terrafina** (p730) has a Med accent.

Inniskillin (☎250-498-4500; www.inniskillin.com; 7857 Tucelnuit Dr, Oliver; ⏱10am-5pm; P) BC's first producer of Zinfandel is also home to the elixirs known as ice wines, which are harvested when the grapes are frozen on the vine; go for the golden-hued Riesling.

Road 13 (☎250-498-8330; www.road13vineyards.com; 799 Ponderosa Rd, Road 13, Oliver; ⏱10am-5:30pm May-Oct, 11am-4pm Mon-Sat Nov-Apr; P) Its very drinkable reds (Pinot Noir) and whites (Chenin Blanc) win plaudits. The no-frills vibe extends to its picnic tables with gorgeous views and the motto 'It's all about dirt.' The attractive lounge has views of the grapes.

Rustico Farm & Cellars (☎250-498-3276; www.rusticowinery.com; 4444 Golden Mile Dr, Oliver; ⏱10am-6pm Apr-Oct; P) Who says winemaking is serious? For Bruce Fuller, it's a hoot. Set in a 19th-century bunk house now covered in vines, this winery produces fine reds and whites such as the Bonanza Old Vine Zinfandel. There is an Old West feel here, helped along by the cowboy-hat-wearing Fuller.

Black Hills Estate (☎250-498-0666; www.blackhillswinery.com; 4190 Black Sage Rd, Oliver; guided tastings $10-30; ⏱10am-5pm Apr-Nov; P) The tasting room here is an arresting vision of glass and metal, with deeply shaded patios for sunset tippling. Besides vintages such as Viognier, there are many blends, including Alibi, a blend of Sauvignon Blanc and Semillon. It offers a sunset happy hour with local transport in summer from 4pm to 7pm.

Church & State Wines (☎250-498-2700; www.churchandstatewines.com; 4516 Ryegrass Rd, Oliver; ⏱11am-6pm; P) Making a big splash at its Coyote Bowl vineyards, especially with its full-bodied, luscious Syrahs. Also home to the Lost Inhibitions label, which produces popularly priced wines with names such as Chill the F*uck Out and I Freakin' Love You.

Burrowing Owl Estate Winery (☎250-498-0620; www.burrowingowlwine.ca; 500 Burrowing Owl Pl, Oliver; ⏱10am-6pm mid-Fed–mid-Dec; P) Wine with an eco-accent that includes organic farm techniques; try the Syrah. Other award-winners include the Cabernet Franc and Meritage. This Golden Mile landmark includes a hotel and the excellent **Sonora Room** (p730) restaurant.

LaStella Winery (p728) A beautiful vision of Italy rises up near Osoyoos Lake. Terracotta roof tiles and floors and granite touches combine for one of the valley's most beautiful wineries. The Cabernet Sauvignon–based Maestoso is highly regarded.

Osoyoos, near the US border, is almost arid, but things become greener heading north. Central Kelowna is a fast-growing city that's a heady mix of lakeside beauty and fun.

In July and August the entire valley is as overburdened as a grapevine before harvest; the best times to visit are in the late spring and early fall, when the crowds lessen. Snowy winters also make nearby Big White resort an attraction for skiers and snowboarders.

Osoyoos

POP 5100

Once-modest Osoyoos has embraced an upscale future. The town takes its name from the First Nations word *soyoos*, which means 'sand bar across'; even if the translation is a bit rough, the definition is not: much of the town is indeed on a narrow spit of land that divides Osoyoos Lake. It is ringed with beaches, and the waters irrigate the lush farms, orchards and vineyards that line Hwy 97 going north out of town.

Nature's bounty aside, this is the arid end of the Okanagan Valley and locals like to say that the town marks the northern end of Mexico's Sonoran Desert; much of the town is done up in a style that loses something across borders. From the cactus-speckled sands to the town's cheesy faux-tile-and-stucco architecture, it's a big change from the BC image of pine trees and mountains found in both directions on Hwy 3.

Sights & Activities

Osoyoos Lake is one of the warmest in the country. That, together with Osoyoos' sandy beaches, means great swimming, a huge relief when the summer temp hits 42°C (108°F). Many lakeside motels and campgrounds hire out kayaks, canoes and small boats.

Osoyoos Desert Centre PARK
(250-495-2470; www.desert.org; off Hwy 97; adult/child $7/6; 9:30am-4:30pm mid-May–mid-Sep, shorter hours mid-Sep–mid-May; P) Hear the rattle of a snake and the songs of birds at the Osoyoos Desert Centre, 3km north of town, where interpretive kiosks along raised boardwalks meander through the dry land. The nonprofit center offers 90-minute **guided tours**. Special gardens focus on delights such as delicate wildflowers.

Nk'Mip Desert & Heritage Centre MUSEUM
(250-495-7901; www.nkmipdesert.com; 1000 Rancher Creek Rd; adult/child $14/10; 9:30am-5:30pm May-Sep, shorter hours Oct-Apr; P) Part of a First Nations empire, the Nk'Mip Desert & Heritage Centre features cultural demonstrations and tours of the arid ecology. Located off 45th St north of Hwy 3, it also has a desert **golf course**, the noted winery **Nk'Mip Cellars**, a resort and more.

LaStella Winery WINERY
(250-495-8180; www.lastella.ca; 8123 148 Ave, Osoyoos; 10:30am-6:30pm Apr-Oct; P) A beautiful vision of Italy rises up near Osoyoos Lake. Terra-cotta roof tiles and floors and granite touches combine for one of the valley's most beautiful wineries. The Cabernet Sauvignon–based Maestoso is highly regarded.

Cathedral Provincial Park PARK
(604-795-6169; www.bcparks.ca; Ashnola Rd; P) About 30km west of Keremeos, Cathedral Provincial Park is a 330-sq-km mountain wilderness that's a playground for the truly adventurous. The park offers excellent backcountry camping ($13) and **hiking** around wildflower-dappled alpine expanses and turquoise waters.

ATB Watersports WATER SPORTS
(250-498-9044; www.atbwatersports.com; 5815 Oleander Dr, Safari Beach Resort; SUP rental per hour from $25; Jun-Sep) Osoyoos Lake is mirror-flat, perfect for paddleboarding hijinks. Rent or take lessons. Also available: kayaks and canoes.

Sleeping & Eating

The eastern edge of the lake is lined with campgrounds. More than a dozen modest motels line the narrow strip of land that splits Osoyoos Lake, but beware of shabby older properties. Many cluster around Hwy 3 and there's another clump on the southwest shore near the border. Chains can be found at the junction.

Nk'Mip Campground & RV Resort CAMPGROUND $
(250-495-7279; www.campingosoyoos.com; 8000 45th St; campsites/RV sites from $35/48, cabins from $170; P) Choose from more than 300 sites at this year-round lakeside resort off Hwy 3. Now offers large cabins as well.

Avalon Inn MOTEL $$
(☎250-495-6334; www.avaloninn.ca; 9106 Main St; r $90-180; P ❄ 📶) Away from the lake but close to good restaurants, this 20-unit indie motel has large rooms and gardens that get more ornate by the year. Some rooms have kitchens.

Walnut Beach Resort RESORT $$$
(☎250-495-5400; www.walnutbeachresort.com; 4200 Lakeshore Dr; r $150-350; P ❄ 📶 🏊) This large resort is an upscale addition to the east shore of the southern half of the lake. There are 112 large suites (some with two bedrooms) and a vast terrace surrounding a pool.

Roberto's Gelato GELATERIA $
(☎250-495-5425; www.robertosgelato.com; 15 Park Dr, Watermark Beach Resort; gelato from $3; ⏲noon-10pm Jun-Sep, shorter hours Oct-May) Located downtown near the lake, Roberto's always offers at least 24 house-made flavors.

★**Dolci Socialhaus** CAFE $$
(☎250-495 6807; www.dolcideli.com; 8710 Main St; mains $14-25; ⏲11:30am-9pm Tue-Sat) Tucked into a small storefront mid-block, this cafe is easy to miss – but to do so would be a mistake. The simple fare is transcendent thanks to a passionate flair for food provenance – even the bacon is smoked in-house. Go for a table on the terrace and graze the farm board.

Information

The large **visitor center** (☎250-495-5070; www.destinationosoyoos.com; cnr Hwys 3 & 97; ⏲9am-6pm; 📶) has info, maps and books, and it can book bus tickets and accommodations for you.

Getting There & Away

Greyhound Canada (p722) runs to Vancouver ($77, seven hours, one daily), departing from outside the visitor center. One bus runs north up the valley daily, including to Penticton ($20, 70 minutes).

Oliver

POP 5200

Oliver has emerged as a hub of excellent wineries and other natural bounty. Over the 20km drive between Oliver and Osoyoos, Hwy 97 plunges through orchard after orchard laden with lush fruits, earning it the moniker 'The Golden Mile.' Roadside stands display the ripe bounty and many places will let you pick your own.

IT'S TIME FOR FRUIT

Roadside stands and farms where you can buy and even pick your own fruit line Hwy 97 between Osoyoos and Penticton. Major Okanagan Valley crops and their harvest times:

Cherries Mid-June to late July

Apricots Mid-July to mid-August

Peaches Mid-July to mid-September

Pears Mid-August to late September

Apples Early September to late October

Table Grapes Early September to late October

Sights & Actvities

The small roads through the vineyards around Oliver are made for exploring by bike. Local walking and biking routes include the excellent 18.4km **International Bike Trail**.

Pick up the heritage walking-tour brochure from the tourist office to fully appreciate this traditional orchard town.

Double O Bikes CYCLING
(☎250-535-0577; www.doubleobikes.com; 6246 Main St; bicycle rental per day from adult/child $24/20; ⏲9:30am-5pm) Bike rental and good route advice. Has another store that is located in Osoyoos.

Sleeping & Eating

Mount View Motel MOTEL $$
(☎250-498-3446; www.mountviewmotel.com; 5856 Main St; r $80-120; P ❄ 📶) Close to the center of town, seven units sunbathe around a flower-bedecked vintage motor court. All have kitchens – and corkscrews. The decor features new wood floors and a contemporary style.

★**Burrowing Owl Guest House** BOUTIQUE HOTEL $$$
(☎250-498-0620; www.burrowingowlwine.ca; 500 Burrowing Owl Pl, off Black Sage Rd; r $170-350; ⏲May-Oct, reduced hours Nov-Apr; P ❄ 📶 🏊) What is one of the Okanagan's best wineries has 10 rooms with patios facing southwest over the vineyards. There's a big pool, a hot tub, king-size beds and corporate mission-style decor. The Sonora Room (p730) is noted for its fusion cuisine. It's 13km south of Oliver, off Hwy 97.

Hester Creek INN $$$
(☎250-498-4435; www.hestercreek.com; 877 Road 8; r $200-300; P ❄ 📶) One of the valley's top wineries, Hester Creek has six suites in a Mediterranean-style villa with a sweeping view over the vineyards. The trappings are plush, with fireplaces, soaking tubs and more. Onsite Terrafina (p730) serves excellent Tuscan-accented fare using foods from the region.

Medici's Gelateria GELATERIA $
(☎250-498-2228; www.medicisgelateria.ca; 9932 350th Ave/Fairview Rd; treats from $3; ⏰10am-5pm) Frozen delights so good you'll worship them – appropriate, given the setting in an old church. Also serves good coffee, plus soups, panini and more, all made with local produce. It's just west of Hwy 97.

Farmers Market MARKET $
(Lion's Park, Hwy 97; ⏰8am-1pm Sat & 5-8pm Wed summer) A vibrant market that celebrates the region's bounty.

★Terrafina ITALIAN $$$
(☎250-495-3278; www.terrafinarestaurant.com; 887 Road 8, Oliver; mains $20-35; ⏰11:30am-9pm daily Jun-Sep, Wed-Sun Oct-May) This intimate restaurant at Hester Creek Estate Winery serves up exquisite Tuscan-flavored dishes. Its outdoor terrace is one of the valley's finest.

Sonora Room FUSION $$$
(☎250-498-0620; www.burrowingowlwine.ca; 500 Burrowing Owl Pl, Burrowing Owl Estate; mains $20-35; ⏰11:30am-9pm May–mid-Oct, shorter hours mid-Oct–Apr) Fresh fare with light Italian and French touches is the hallmark at this very attractive Tuscan-style restaurant in one of the valley's warmest corners. It offers transport to/from the resorts in Osoyoos for $25.

Information

The **visitor center** (☎778-439-2363; www.winecapitalofcanada.com; 6431 Station St; ⏰9am-5pm) has affable staff and is located in the old train station near the center of town. It has regional info, and walking and biking maps.

Vaseaux Lake

About 10km north of Oliver on Hwy 97, nature reasserts itself at this lake – an azure gem, framed by sheer granite cliffs.

If you're not in a hurry, the small roads on the east side of **Skaha Lake** between Okanagan Falls and Penticton are more interesting for their wineries and views than Hwy 97.

Vaseux Lake Provincial Park (www.bcparks.ca; Hwy 97) has a 300m boardwalk for viewing oodles of birds, bighorn sheep, mountain goats and some of the 14 species of bat. You can also hike to the **Bighorn National Wildlife Area** and the **Vaseux Lake National Migratory Bird Sanctuary**, which has more than 160 bird species.

Penticton

Penticton combines the idle pleasures of a beach resort with its own edgy vibe. It's long been a final stop in life for Canadian retirees, which adds a certain spin to its Salish-derived name Pen-Tak-Tin, meaning 'place to stay forever.' The town today is growing fast, along with the rest of the Okanagan Valley.

Penticton makes a good base for your valley pleasures. There are plenty of activities and diversions to fill your days, even if you don't travel further afield. Ditch Hwy 97, which runs west of the center, for Main St and the attractively walkable downtown area, which extends about 10 blocks southward from the picture-perfect lakefront; avert your eyes from the long stretch of strip malls and high-rise condos further south.

Sights

Okanagan Beach boasts about 1300m of sand, with average summer water temperatures of about 22°C (72°F). If things are jammed, quieter shores are often found at 1.5km-long **Skaha Beach**, south of the center.

★SS Sicamous Inland Marine Museum HISTORIC SITE
(☎250-492-0405; www.sssicamous.ca; 1099 Lakeshore Dr W; adult/child $6/3; ⏰10am-5:30pm) Back when the best way to get around inland BC was by boat, the SS *Sicamous* hauled passengers and freight on Okanagan Lake from 1914 to 1936. Now the boat has been restored and permanently moored; a tour is an evocative self-guided ramble.

Skaha Bluffs Provincial Park PARK
(www.bcparks.ca; Smythe Dr; ⏰Mar-Nov) Propelled by the dry weather and compact gneiss rock, climbers from all over the world come to this park to enjoy **climbing** on more than 400 bolted routes. The local climbing group has comprehensive info on the bluffs (see www.skaha.org), which are off Lakeside Rd on the east side of Skaha Lake.

Penticton Museum MUSEUM
(☎250-490-2451; www.pentictonmuseum.com; 785 Main St; by donation; ⏰10am-5pm Tue-Sat) Inside the library, the Penticton Museum has delightfully eclectic displays, including the de rigueur natural-history exhibit with stuffed animals and birds, and everything you'd want to know about the juicy fruits of the Peach Festival (p732).

Art Gallery of Southern Okanagan GALLERY
(☎250-493-2928; www.pentictonartgallery.com; 199 Marina Way; adult/child $2/free; ⏰10am-5pm Tue-Fri, 11am-4pm Sat & Sun) The beachfront Art Gallery of Southern Okanagan displays a diverse collection of regional, provincial and national artists.

Activities

Aquatic fun abounds, and classic, cheesy resort diversions such as miniature golf await at the west end of Okanagan Beach.

Water Sports

Okanagan and Skaha Lakes both enjoy some of the best sailboarding, boating and paddling conditions in the Okanagan Valley.

There are several water-sports rental places on Okanagan Lake.

The paved **Okanagan River Channel Biking & Jogging Path** follows the rather arid channel linking Okanagan Lake to Skaha Lake. But why pound the pavement when you can float on the water?

★Coyote Cruises WATER SPORTS
(☎250-492-2115; www.coyotecruises.ca; 215 Riverside Dr; rentals & shuttle $12; ⏰10am-5pm mid-Jun–Sep) Coyote Cruises rents out inner tubes that you can float on to a midway point on the Okanagan River Channel. It then buses you back to the start near Okanagan Lake. If you have your own floatable, it's $5 for the bus ride.

Pier Water Sports WATER SPORTS
(☎250-493-8864; www.pierwatersports.com; Rotary Park, Lakeshore Dr W; party barges per 2hr from $275, SUP rentals 1hr/$20, kayak rentals 1hr/$15; ⏰9am-7pm May-Sep) Rents several types of boats as well as kayaks, SUPs and pretty much anything else that floats.

Penticton Cruises BOATING
(☎250-215-2779; www.pentictoncruises.com; Penticton Marina, 293 Marina Way; adult/child $25/12.50; ⏰May-Sep) Stimulate your inner seafarer with a one-hour, open-air lake tour on a faux stern wheeler. There are multiple daily sailings at summer's peak.

Mountain Biking & Cycling

Long dry days and rolling hills add up to perfect conditions for mountain biking. Get to popular rides by heading east out of town, toward Naramata. Follow signs to the city dump and **Campbell's Mountain**, where you'll find a single-track and dual-slalom course, both of which aren't too technical. Once you get there, the riding is mostly on the right-hand side, but once you pass the cattle guard, it opens up and you can ride anywhere.

Cyclists can try the route through Naramata and onto the Kettle Valley Rail Trail (p738). Other good options include the small, winery-lined roads south of town and east of Skaha Lake.

Freedom – The Bike Shop CYCLING
(☎250-493-0686; www.freedombikeshop.com; 533 Main St; bicycle rental per day from $40; ⏰9am-5:30pm Mon-Sat) Rents bikes and offers a wealth of information. Can arrange transport to/from the Kettle Valley Rail Trail.

Rock Climbing

Propelled by the dry weather and compact gneiss rock, climbers from all over the world come to Skaha Bluffs Provincial Park (p730) to enjoy climbing on more than 400 bolted routes. The local climbing group's website www.skaha.org has comprehensive info on the bluffs, which are off Lakeside Rd on the east side of Skaha Lake.

★Skaha Rock Adventures CLIMBING
(☎250-493-1765; www.skaharockclimbing.com; 437 Martin St; 1-day intros from $160; ⏰by appointment) Skaha Rock Adventures offers advanced technical instruction, as well as introductory courses for anyone venturing into a harness for the first time.

Snow Sports

Apex Mountain Resort SKIING
(☎877-777-2739, condition report 250-487-4848; www.apexresort.com; off Green Mountain Rd; lift tickets adult/child $78/48) One of Canada's best small ski resorts is 37km west of Penticton. It has more than 68 downhill runs for all ability levels, but the mountain is known for its plethora of double-black-diamond and technical runs; the drop is more than 600m. It is usually quieter than nearby Big White.

Festivals & Events

Elvis Festival
MUSIC

(www.pentictonelvisfestival.ca; late Jun) Dozens of Elvis impersonators could be your idea of heaven or hound-dog hell, especially on the afternoon of open-microphone singalongs.

Peach Festival
CULTURAL

(250-487-9709; www.peachfest.com; early Aug) The city's premier event is basically a party that has taken place since 1948, loosely centered on the ripe succulent orbs and the crowning of a Peach Queen.

Pentastic Jazz Festival
MUSIC

(250-770-3494; www.pentasticjazz.com; early Sep) More than a dozen bands perform at five venues over three days.

Sleeping

HI Penticton Hostel
HOSTEL $

(250-492-3992, reservations 866-782-9736; www.hihostels.ca; 464 Ellis St; dm/r from $35/76;) This 47-bed hostel is near the center in a heavily worn 1908 house. Arranges activities, including wine tours.

Bowmont Motel
MOTEL $$

(800-811-1377; www.bowmontmotel.com; 80 Riverside Dr; r $80-180;) Look past the dubious faux-Southwestern facade and you'll find an excellent indie motel near the lake. The 45 rooms are immaculate and all share terraces or balconies. Each has a full kitchen and there is a gas barbecue near the pool.

Tiki Shores Beach Resort
MOTEL $$

(250-492-8769; www.tikishores.com; 914 Lakeshore Dr W; condos $150-300;) This lively resort across from the beach has 40 condo-style units with kitchens, most with separate bedrooms. Rooms have a light color scheme that seems ideal for a freshwater lakeside holiday.

Quidni Estate Winery Guest Rooms
APARTMENT $$$

(250-490-5251; www.quidniwine.com; 1465 Naramata Rd; r from $350;) Three plush suites await at this winery on the lovely Naramata Rd, 5km from Penticton. Views open up across the vineyards and down to the lake. Bathrooms feature marble and the soft furnishings are luxe. Cyclists enjoying the many local routes are well catered for here (spare tire tubes available etc). Enjoy tastings of the winery's products.

Crooked Tree Bed & Breakfast
B&B $$$

(250-490-8022; www.crooked-tree.com; 1278 Spiller Rd; suite $175-215;) All of Okanagan Lake glistens below you from this mountainside retreat that's 9km east of downtown Penticton. The three large apartments each have multiple decks amid this woodsy aerie and are well stocked with luxuries. Minimum stay two nights.

Eating & Drinking

★ Burger 55
BURGERS $

(778-476-5529; www.burger55.com; 52 Front St; mains $9-15; 11am-9pm) Best burger in Canada? It's your own fault if it isn't, as you have myriad ways to customize at this downtown restaurant. Six kinds of buns, 10 kinds of cheese, and toppings that include roasted garlic and *pico de gallo* are just some of the options. Sides, such as fries, are equally excellent. There's a fine patio and a good beer list.

★ Penticton Farmers Market
MARKET

(250-583-9933; www.pentictonfarmersmarket.org; 100 Main St; 8:30am-1pm Sat May-Oct) Penticton definitely has its share of good eats. The farmers market, based at Gyro Park on Main St, has large numbers of local organic producers.

Bench Market
CAFE $

(250-492-2222; www.thebenchmarket.com; 368 Vancouver Ave; meals $9-12; 7am-5pm) Always buzzing – and not just because of the excellent organic coffee – this neighborhood fave is consistently busy. The patio is where locals meet and exchange gossip. Egg dishes star at breakfast; lunch is about sandwiches and salads. Great baked goods and other deli items are sold through the day.

Il Vecchio Deli
DELI $

(250-492-7610; 317 Robinson St; sandwiches $6; 9am-5pm Mon-Sat) The smell that greets you as you enter confirms your choice. The best lunch sandwiches in town can be consumed at a couple of tables in this atmospheric deli, but will taste better on a picnic. Choices are many; we like the sandwich with garlic salami and marinated eggplant.

Theo's
GREEK $$

(250-492-4019; www.eatsquid.com; 687 Main St; mains $10-25; 11am-10pm) The place for dating locals. Serves up authentic Greek-island cuisine in the atmospheric, fire-lit interior or out on the patio. The *garithes uvetsi* is a starter symphony of shrimp.

Dream Cafe FUSION $$
(☎ 250-490-9012; www.thedreamcafe.ca; 67 Front St; mains $11-25; ⏰ 11am-9pm Tue-Sun;) The heady aroma of spices hits as you enter this pillow-bedecked, upscale-yet-funky bistro. Asian and Indian flavors mix on the menu, which has numerous veggie options. There's live acoustic music by touring pros on many nights; tables outside hum all summer long.

Hooded Merganser PUB FOOD $$
(☎ 250-493-8221; www.hoodedmerganser.ca; Penticton Lakeside Resort, 21 Lakeshore Dr; mains $12-30; ⏰ 7am-midnight) Named for a small breed of duck noted for its vibrant plumage, this huge lakeside pub attracts plenty of birds of a similar feather. On a summer afternoon its waterfront terrace literally heaves. Food is designed for sharing, with some steaks and burgers tossed into the mix.

Hillside Bistro BISTRO $$$
(☎ 250-493-6274; www.hillsidewinery.ca; 1350 Naramata Rd; mains $16-35; ⏰ 11:30am-2pm & 5-9pm mid-Jun–Sep) Beautifully set among its namesake vineyards about 5km from Penticton, this casual eatery has great lakeside views from its various open-air decks. The menu includes upscale versions of burgers, pasta and other dishes made from ingredients sourced locally. Enjoy a glass of Mosaic, the house Bordeaux-style blended red.

★ **Mile Zero Wine Bar** WINE BAR
(☎ 250-488-7944; www.milezerowinebar.ca; 200 Ellis St; ⏰ 3pm-midnight) Long overdue! This sleek, industrial-edged wine bar is right in the center and is a magnificent place to sample the region's wine bounty. There are always 10 varieties on tap and dozens more available by the glass. Enjoy live jazzy tunes on Friday nights; note that this is where the local vintners like to party.

Information

The **visitor center** (☎ 250-276-2170; www.visitpenticton.com; 553 Vees St, off Hwy 97; ⏰ 9am-6pm;) has a full range of info on area activities and wine.

Getting There & Away

Greyhound Canada (p722) Has services to Vancouver ($69, six hours, one daily) and Kelowna ($20, one hour, four daily).

Penticton Transit (☎ 250-492-5602; www.bctransit.com; single trips/day pass $2/4) Runs between both waterfronts.

DON'T MISS

SCENIC DRIVE TO NARAMATA

On all but the busiest summer weekends, you can escape many of Penticton's mobs by taking the road less traveled, 18km north from town along the east shore of Okanagan Lake. The route through the **Naramata Bench** (www.naramatabench.com) is lined with more than 30 wineries, as well as farms producing organic lavender and the like. This is a good route for cycling and at several points you can access the Kettle Valley Rail Trail (p738). There are numerous places to hike, picnic, bird-watch or do whatever else occurs to you in beautiful and often secluded surroundings. Naramata itself is a cute little village.

Penticton to Kelowna

Lakeside resort town **Summerland**, 18km north of Penticton on Hwy 97, features some fine 19th-century heritage buildings on the hillside above the ever-widening and busy highway. There are some good wineries here, too.

Hugging the lake below Hwy 97, some 25km south of Kelowna, the little town of **Peachland** is good for a quick, breezy stroll along the water amid parks and interesting shops.

Between Peachland and Kelowna, urban sprawl becomes unavoidable, especially through the billboard-lined nightmare of **West Kelowna** (aka Westbank).

Sights & Activities

Zipzone Peachland ADVENTURE SPORTS
(☎ 855-947-9663; www.zipzone.ca; Princeton Ave, Peachland; adult/child from $110/80; ⏰ 9am-5pm May-Oct) Zoom along Canada's highest zip lines at Zipzone Peachland, where you can sail high over Deep Creek Canyon.

Kettle Valley Steam Railway RAIL
(☎ 877-494-8424; www.kettlevalleyrail.org; 18404 Bathville Rd, Summerland; adult/child $25/16; ⏰ May-Oct) The Kettle Valley Steam Railway is an operating, 16km remnant of the famous tracks. Ride behind an old steam locomotive in open-air cars and enjoy orchard views.

Sleeping & Eating

A View of the Lake B&B $$
(☎250-769-7854; www.aviewofthelake.com; 1877 Horizon Dr, West Kelowna; r $120-185; P ❄ ☜) Set on the west side of Okanagan Lake, this B&B offers privacy and magnificent views. Book the Grandview Suite for a lake vista that extends even to the air-jet bathtub. Rooms are peaceful; beds are comfy; and the three-course breakfast on the deck is gourmet.

★**Peach Pit** MARKET $
(☎778-516-7003; cnr Hwy 97 & Jones Flat Rd, Summerland; treats from $3; ⊙9am-6pm May-Oct) Amid oodles of competition, this roadside stand on Hwy 97 on the north side of Summerland stands out. The owners have an orchard right behind the market. They also have deals with some of the valley's very best producers (the $3 tub of raspberries will have you checking local real-estate prices) and they create wonderful baked goods.

★**Terrace** MODERN AMERICAN $$$
(☎250-768-6467; www.missionhillwinery.com; 1730 Mission Hill Rd, Mission Hill Family Estate, West Kelowna; mains $25-35; ⊙11am-9pm Jun-Oct) A suitably impressive restaurant to go with a very impressive winery. Terrace (yes, there are views) exemplifies farm-to-table with its fresh and inventive menu.

Kelowna

POP 123,500

A kayaker paddles past scores of new tract houses on a hillside: it's an iconic image for ever-growing Kelowna, the unofficial 'capital' of the Okanagan and the sprawling center of all that's good and not-so-good with the region.

Entering from the north, the ever-lengthening urban sprawl of tree-lined Hwy 97/Harvey Ave seems to go on forever. Once past the ceaseless waves of chains and strip malls, the downtown is a welcome respite. Museums, culture, nightlife and the park-lined lakefront feature. You can spend a day strolling here. About 2km south of the center is **Pandosy Village**, a charming and upscale lakeside enclave.

Sights

The focal point of the city's shoreline, the immaculate downtown **Kelowna City Park** (Map p736) is home to manicured gardens, water features and **Hot Sands Beach** (Map p736), where the water is a respite from the hot summer air.

Restaurants and pubs take advantage of the uninterrupted views of the lake and forested shore opposite. North of the marina, **Waterfront Park** (Map p736; Lakefront) has a variegated shoreline and a popular open-air stage.

Among the many outdoor statues near the lake, look for the one of the **Ogopogo** (Map p736; Kelowna City Park), the lake's mythical – and hokey – monster. More prosaic is **Bear** (Map p736; Water St), a huge, lacy confection in metal. The visitor center has a lavish public art guide.

Be sure to pick up the **Cultural District** walking-tour brochures at the visitor center (p738) and visit www.kelownamuseums.ca for exhibitions info.

BC Orchard Industry Museum MUSEUM
(Map p736; ☎250-763-0433; www.kelownamuseums.ca; 1304 Ellis St; by donation; ⊙10am-5pm Mon-Sat, 11am-4pm Sun) Located in the historic Laurel Packing House, the BC Orchard Industry Museum recounts the Okanagan Valley from its ranchland past, grazed by cows, to its present, grazed by tourists. The old fruit-packing-crate labels are works of art.

Carmelis Goat Cheese Artisan FARM
(☎250-764-9033; www.carmelisgoatcheese.com; 170 Timberline Rd; tours $5; ⊙10am-6pm May-Sep, 11am-5pm Mar, Apr & Oct, closed Nov-Feb; P 👪) Call ahead to book a tour of the dairy, milking station and cellar. Even without the tour, you can sample soft-ripened cheeses with names such as Moonlight and Heavenly, or the hard-ripened Smoked Carmel or Goatgonzola. For those with a milder palate, there are super-soft unripened versions, such as feta and yogurt cheese. And then there's the goat's-milk gelato!

BC Wine Museum MUSEUM
(Map p736; ☎250-763-2417; www.kelownamuseums.ca; 1304 Ellis St; by donation; ⊙10am-5pm Mon-Sat, 11am-4pm Sun) Housed in the historic Laurel Packinghouse and newly expanded in 2016, the museum offers a look at celebrated bottles, labels and equipment, along with an overview of winemaking in the region.

Okanagan Lavender Farm FARM
(☎250-764-7795; www.okanaganlavender.com; 4380 Takla Rd; tours $5-15; ⊙10am-6pm, tours 10:30am Jun-Aug; P 👪) Visiting Okanagan Lavender Farm is a heady experience. Rows

and rows of more than 60 types of lavender waft in the breeze against a backdrop of the Okanagan Lake. Enjoy a guided or self-guided tour of the aromatic acres, and pop into the shop for everything from bath products to lavender lemonade. Your wine-soaked palate will be well and truly cleansed. The farm is 9km south of the center.

Okanagan Heritage Museum MUSEUM
(Map p736; ☎250-763-2417; www.kelownamuseums.ca; 470 Queensway Ave; by donation; ⊙10am-5pm Mon-Sat) The Okanagan Heritage Museum looks at centuries of local culture in an engaging manner that includes a First Nations pit house, a Chinese grocery and a Pandosy-era trading post.

Kelowna Art Gallery GALLERY
(Map p736; ☎250-979-0888; www.kelownaartgallery.com; 1315 Water St; $5; ⊙10am-5pm Tue, Wed, Fri & Sat, to 9pm Thu, 1-4pm Sun) The airy Kelowna Art Gallery features works by Canadian artists.

Activities

The balmy weather makes Kelowna ideal for fresh-air fun, whether on the lake or in the surrounding hills.

You'll find great **hiking** and **mountain biking** opportunities all around town. The 17km **Mission Creek Greenway** is a meandering, wooded path following the creek along the south edge of town. The western half is a wide and easy expanse, but to the east the route becomes sinuous as it climbs into the hills.

Knox Mountain, which sits at the northern end of the city, is another good place to hike or ride. Populated with bobcats and snakes, the 235-hectare park has well-maintained trails and rewards visitors with excellent views from the top.

Cycling on the Kettle Valley Rail Trail (p738) and amid the vineyards is popular.

★ **Monashee Adventure Tours** CYCLING
(☎250-762-9253; www.monasheeadventuretours.com; bicycle rental per day from $30) Offers scores of biking and hiking tours of the Okanagan Valley, its parks, Kettle Valley Rail Trail (from $120) and wineries. Many tours are accompanied by entertaining local guides. Prices usually include bike hire, lunch and a shuttle to the route. Shuttles can also be used by independent riders looking for one-way transport. Offers snowshoe tours in winter.

Myra Canyon Bike Rentals CYCLING
(☎250-878-8763; www.myracanyonrental.com; Myra Canyon; bicycle rental per half-day from adult/child $40/30, bike tours from $70; ⊙9am-5:30pm mid-May–mid-Oct) Offers bike rentals and tours at the Kettle Valley Rail Trail (p738) head.

Okanagan Rent A Boat BOATING
(Map p736; ☎250-862-2469; www.lakefrontsports.com; 1310 Water St, Delta Grand Okanagan Resort; kayak rental per 2hr $40; ⊙May-Sep) Rent speedboats (starting at $145 per hour), canoes, kayaks, wakeboards, pedal boats and much more from this seasonal booth on the lakefront.

Sleeping

Kelowna Samesun International Hostel HOSTEL $
(Map p736; ☎250-763-9814; www.samesun.com; 245 Harvey Ave; dm/r from $33/100; P ❄ @ 📶) Near the center and the lake, this purpose-built hostel has 88 dorm beds in four- and eight-bed dorms, plus private rooms. There is a hot tub; activities include various group outings.

Kelowna International Hostel HOSTEL $
(☎250-763-6024; www.kelowna-hostel.bc.ca; 2343 Pandosy St; dm/r from $25/60; @ 📶) About 1km south of City Park, this small hostel is in a '50s home on a tree-lined residential street. Neighbors no doubt enjoy the regular keg parties, free bongo drums and other social events that keep the cheery place hopping. Ask for Greyhound pickup.

Willow Creek Family Campground CAMPGROUND $
(☎250-762-6302; www.willowcreekcampground.ca; 3316 Lakeshore Rd; campsites/RV sites from $30/42; P 📶) South of the center, close to Pandosy Village and a beach, this 82-site facility has a laundry. Tent sites are on a grassy verge.

Hotel Zed MOTEL $$
(Map p736; ☎250-763-7771; www.hotelzed.com; 1627 Abbott St; r $90-180; P ❄ 📶 🏊) An old Travelodge has been reborn as this throwback to a 1960s that never existed. The 52 rooms come in many shapes and sizes; all are in cheery colors. Extras such as free bike rentals, ping-pong, hot tub, comic books in the bathrooms and much more are way cool. It's located downtown and across from City Park.

Accent Inns Kelowna MOTEL $$
(☎250-862-8888; www.accentinns.com; 1140 Harvey Ave; r $90-180; P ❄ 📶) Best of the chain motels near the center, this three-storey property

Kelowna

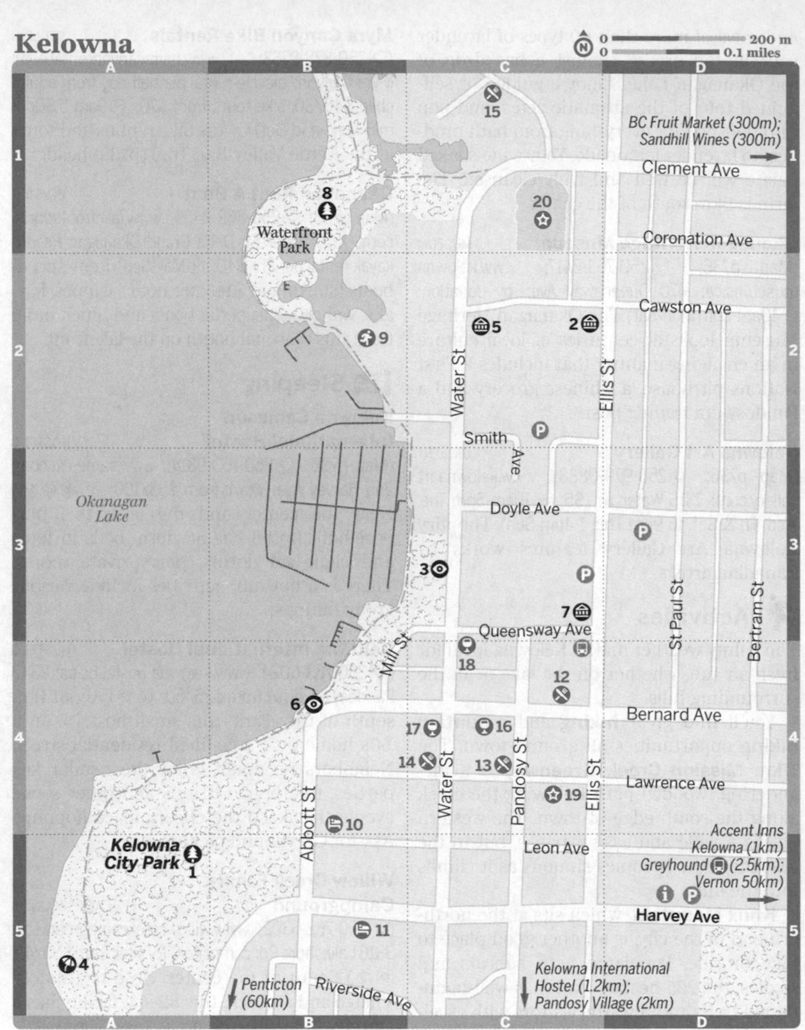

is a 10-minute walk from the lake. The 102 rooms are roomy and have many thoughtful extras, such as office supplies in the desks, plus fridges and microwaves. Flowers adorn the walkways, and the staff are charmers.

Lakeshore Bed & Breakfast B&B $$
(250-764-4375; www.lakeshorebb.ca; 4186 Lakeshore Rd; r $115-175;) This bright, two-room B&B has a prime lakefront location, 6km south of the center, complete with its own tiny strip of sand. The larger of the two rooms is a real deal, with broad water views and a private outdoor sitting area. Furnishings are modern and upscale.

★ **Hotel Eldorado** HOTEL $$$
(250-763-7500; www.hoteleldoradokelowna.com; 500 Cook Rd; r $180-400;) This historic lakeshore retreat, south of Pandosy Village, has 19 heritage rooms where you can bask in antique-filled luxury. A modern, low-key wing has 30 more rooms and six opulent waterfront suites. It's classy, artful and funky all at once. Definitely the choice spot for a luxurious getaway.

Eating

Little Hobo CAFE $

(Map p736; ☎778-478-0411; www.thelittlehobo.com; 438 Lawrence Ave; mains $7-12; ⊙10am-2pm Mon-Fri) This unadorned sandwich shop is hugely popular and for good reason: the food is excellent. Custom sandwiches are good, but the daily specials really shine (meatloaf, pasta, pierogi etc) and the variety of soups is simply superb.

Kelowna Farmers Market MARKET $

(☎250-878-5029; cnr Springfield Rd & Dilworth Dr; ⊙8am-1pm Wed & Sat Apr-Oct) The farmers market has more than 150 vendors, including many with prepared foods. Local artisans also display their wares. It's located off Hwy 97.

BC Tree Fruits Market MARKET $

(☎250-763-8872; www.bctree.com; 826 Vaughan Ave; fruit from $1; ⊙9am-5pm Mon-Sat) Run by the local fruit-packing cooperative, BC Tree Fruits Market has dozens upon dozens of the Okanagan's best fruits on display and available for tasting. Prices are half of that in supermarkets. An adjoining tasting room sells locally produced ciders.

Pulp Fiction Coffee House CAFE $

(Map p736; ☎778-484-7444; www.pulpfictioncoffeehouse.com; 1598 Pandosy St; coffee $2; ⊙7am-10pm) Baked goods, paninis and soups go with your excellent coffee or tea at this sharp, category-busting cafe right downtown. It includes an antiques and rare-book store.

★ **RauDZ Regional Table** FUSION $$

(Map p736; ☎250-868-8805; www.raudz.com; 1560 Water St; mains $12-30; ⊙5-10pm) Noted chef Rod Butters has defined the farm-to-table movement with his casual bistro that's a temple to Okanagan produce and wine. The dining room is as airy and open as the kitchen. The seasonal menu takes global inspiration for its Mediterranean-infused dishes, which are good for sharing, and serves steaks and seafood. Suppliers include locally renowned Carmelis goat's cheese.

Sunset Organic Bistro BISTRO $$

(☎250-764-8000; www.summerhill.bc.ca; 4870 Chute Lake Rd, Summerhill Pyramid Winery, Kelowna; mains $15-30; ⊙11am-9pm) Acclaimed chef Alex Lavroff has created excellent locally sourced and organic menus for lunch and dinner. In between, there is an exquisite selection of small dishes, which go well with an afternoon of organic wine tasting.

Waterfront Restaurant & Wine Bar BISTRO $$$

(Map p736; ☎250-979-1222; http://waterfrontrestaurant.ca; 1180 Sunset Dr; mains $25-38; ⊙5-10pm) Chef and sommelier Mark Filatow has created his vision for a farm-to-table restaurant in Kelowna that celebrates the bounty of the region, both on the plate and in a glass. The tapas menu is long and encourages sharing. Many local wines are available by the glass. The atmosphere is sleek and contemporary.

Drinking & Nightlife

The local microbrewer, Tree Brewing, has an excellent range of beers that are sold around town. Downtown Kelowna's clubs are mostly at the west end of Leon and Lawrence Aves.

Micro PUB
(Map p736; ☎778-484-3500; www.microkelowna.com; 1500 Water St; ⏲11:30am-3pm Thu-Sun, 3pm-late daily) This great small bar from the team behind local bistro RauDZ is hard to leave. Craft beers, local wines and fine cocktails are served. Small bites are fresh and inventive, good for sharing – or for lunch. Gather at the wood-block bar or at a sidewalk table.

Sturgeon Hall PUB
(Map p736; ☎250-860-3055; 1481 Water St; ⏲11am-late Mon-Sat) Fanatical fans of the Kelowna Rockets hockey team feast on excellent burgers and thin-crust pizza (mains from $10 to $20) while quaffing brews at the bar or outside at sidewalk tables. In season, this Kelowna institution shows hockey on every TV.

Doc Willoughby's PUB
(Map p736; ☎250-868-8288; 353 Bernard Ave; ⏲11:30am-2am) Right downtown, this pub boasts a vaulted interior lined with wood, as well as tables on the street. Perfect for a drink or a meal; the fish and chips are good (mains cost $10 to $20). The beer selection is excellent, including brews from Tree Brewing and Penticton's Cannery Brewing.

Entertainment

Blue Gator LIVE MUSIC
(Map p736; ☎250-860-1529; www.bluegator.net; 441 Lawrence Ave; ⏲3pm-late Tue-Sun) Head for blues, rock, acoustic jam and more at the valley's sweaty dive for live music and cold beer.

Kelowna Rockets HOCKEY
(Map p736; ☎250-860-7825; www.kelownarockets.com; tickets from $25; ⏲Sep-Mar) The much-beloved local WHL hockey team is a perennial contender, playing in the 6000-seat stadium **Prospera Place** (Map p736; ☎250-979-0888; www.prosperaplace.com; cnr Water St & Cawston Ave). Home games see the local pubs fill before and after the match.

Information

Kelowna Visitor Center (Map p736; ☎250-861-1515; www.tourismkelowna.com; 544 Harvey Ave; ⏲9am-6pm) Near the corner of Ellis St and Hwy 97; a good source for free maps and tour info.

DON'T MISS

KETTLE VALLEY RAIL TRAIL

The famous **Kettle Valley Rail Trail** vies with wine-drinking and peach-picking as the attraction of choice for the region's visitors – smart ones do all three.

Once stretching 525km in curving, meandering length, the railway was built so that silver ore could be transported from the southern Kootenays to Vancouver. Finished in 1916, it remains one of the most expensive railways ever built, on a per-kilometer basis. It was entirely shut by 1989, but it wasn't long before its easy grades (never more than 2.2%) and dozens of bridges were incorporated into the **Trans Canada Trail (TCT)**.

Of the entire Kettle Valley Rail Trail, the most spectacular stretch is close to Kelowna. The 24km section through the **Myra Canyon** has fantastic views of the sinuous canyon from **18 trestles** that span the gorge for the cliff-hugging path. That you can enjoy the route at all is something of a miracle, as 12 of the wooden trestles were destroyed by fire in 2003. All have been rebuilt; much credit goes to the **Myra Canyon Trestle Restoration Society** (www.myra-trestles.com), the website of which has downloadable maps and info. The broad views sweep down to Kelowna and the lake, more than 900m below. You can see alpine meadows reclaiming the fire-cleared landscape.

To reach the area closest to the most spectacular trestles from Kelowna, follow Harvey Ave (Hwy 97) east to Gordon Dr. Turn south and then go east 2.6km on KLO Rd and then join McCulloch Rd for 7.4km after the junction. Look for the Myra Forest Service Rd; turn south and make a winding 8.7km climb on a car-friendly gravel road to the parking lot. It's about a 40-minute drive from Kelowna's center.

Myra Canyon is just part of an overall 174km network of trails in the Okanagan that follow the old railway through tunnels, past Naramata and as far south as Penticton and beyond. You can easily access the trail at many points, or book hiking and cycling tours. **Myra Canyon Bike Rentals** (p735) offers bike rentals and tours at the main trail head.

Getting There & Away

From **Kelowna International Airport** (www.kelownaairport.com; 5533 Airport Way, off Hwy 97), Westjet serves major cities in Canada. Air Canada Jazz serves Vancouver and Calgary. Alaska Air serves Seattle. The airport is 20km north of the center on Hwy 97.

Greyhound Canada (250-860-2364; www.greyhound.ca; 2366 Leckie Rd) is inconveniently located east of the downtown area, off Hwy 97. City buses 9 and 10 make the run from downtown (every 30 minutes between 6:30am and 9:45pm). Routes include: Golden ($67, 5½ hours, one daily), Kamloops ($37, three hours, two daily), Penticton ($20, one hour, four daily) and Vancouver ($69, six hours, four daily).

Getting Around

Kelowna Regional Transit System (250-860-8121; www.transitbc.com; single fare/day pass $2.50/6.50) runs local bus services. All downtown buses pass through **Queensway Station** (Map p736; Queensway Ave, btwn Pandosy & Ellis Sts). Bus 97 serves West Kelowna.

All major car-rental companies are found at **Kelowna International Airport**. Taxi companies include **Kelowna Cabs** (250-762-4444, 250-762-2222; www.kelownacabs.ca).

Vernon

POP 38,900

The Okanagan glitz starts to fade before you reach Vernon. Maybe it's the weather. Winters have more of the traditional inland BC bite here and wineries are few, but that doesn't mean the area is without its charms. The orchard-scented valley is surrounded by three lakes – Kalamalka, Okanagan and Swan – that attract fun-seekers all summer long.

Downtown life is found along 30th Ave, known as Main St. Confusingly, 30th Ave is intersected by 30th St in the middle of downtown, so mind your streets and avenues. The north side of town is a mess of strip malls.

Sights & Activities

Davison Orchards FARM

(250-549-3266; www.davisonorchards.ca; 3111 Davison Rd; 8am-8pm Apr-Oct; P) FREE Has tractor rides, homemade ice cream, fresh apple juice, winsome barnyard animals and more. Follow 25th Ave west, turn north briefly on 41st St, then go west on Bella Vista Rd and watch for signs.

Planet Bee FARM

(250-542-8088; www.planetbee.com; 5011 Bella Vista Rd; 8am-6pm; P) FREE Planet Bee is a working honey farm where you can learn all the sweet secrets of the golden nectar and see a working hive up close. Follow 25th Ave west, turn north briefly on 41st St, then go west on Bella Vista Rd and watch for signs. It's near Davison Orchards.

Kalamalka Lake Provincial Park PARK

(250-545-1560; www.bcparks.ca; off Hwy 6; P) The beautiful 9-sq-km Kalamalka Lake Provincial Park lies south of town on the eastern side of the warm, shallow lake. The park offers great swimming at Jade and Kalamalka Beaches, good fishing and a network of mountain-biking and hiking trails. Innerspace Watersports operates a seasonal booth in the park.

Innerspace Watersports WATER SPORTS

(250-549-2040; www.innerspacewatersports.com; 3006 32nd St; canoe rental per hour $25; 10am-5:30pm Mon-Sat) Offers canoe and stand-up paddleboard rentals at Kalamalka Lake Provincial Park; has a full-service store located in town, which has scuba gear. Park location open mid-June to August.

BIG WHITE SKI RESORT

Perfect powder is the big deal at **Big White Ski Resort** (250-765-8888, snow report 250-765-7669; www.bigwhite.com; off Hwy 33; 1-day lift pass adult/child $91/51), located 56km east of Kelowna off Hwy 33. With a vertical drop of 777m, it features 15 lifts and 118 runs that offer excellent downhill and backcountry skiing, while deep gullies make for killer snowboarding. Because of Big White's isolation, most people stay up here on-site. The resort includes numerous restaurants, bars, hotels, condos, rental homes and a hostel. The website has lodging info and details of the ski-season shuttle to Kelowna.

Sleeping & Eating

Ellison Provincial Park CAMPGROUND $

(info 250-494-6500, reservations 800-689-9025; www.discovercamping.ca; Okanagan Landing Rd; campsites $32; Apr-Oct; P) Some 16km southwest of Vernon, this is a great tree-shaded, 219-acre place near the lake. The 71 campsites fill up early, so reserve in advance.

Tiki Village Motel MOTEL **$$**
(☎250-503-5566; www.tikivillagevernon.com; 2408 34th St; r $70-150; P ❄ 📶 🏊) An ode to the glory days of decorative concrete blocks, the Tiki has suitably expansive plantings and 30 rooms with a vaguely Asian minimalist theme. All rooms have fridges; some have kitchenettes.

Beaver Lake Mountain Resort LODGE **$$**
(☎250-762-2225; www.beaverlakeresort.com; 6350 Beaver Lake Rd; campsites from $29, cabins $85-180; P @) Set high in the hills east of Hwy 97, about midway between Vernon and Kelowna, this postcard-perfect lakeside resort has a range of rustic log cabins and some more-luxurious cabins that sleep up to six people.

Little Italy ITALIAN **$**
(☎778-475-5898; http://littleitalymarketdeli.foodpages.ca; 3105 35th Ave; mains $10-20; ⏰9am-5pm Mon-Sat; 📶) Order a cup of authentic Italian coffee and enjoy it on the porch at this cute little market and deli just east of Hwy 97.

Vernon Farmers Market MARKET
(☎250-351-5188; www.vernonfarmersmarket.ca; 3445 43rd Ave, Kal Tire Place; ⏰8am-1pm Mon & Thu) The market draws more than 150 vendors. It's just west of Hwy 97.

★**Bamboo Beach Fusion Grille** FUSION **$$**
(☎250-542-7701; www.facebook.com/BambooBeachFusionGrille; 3313 30th Ave; mains $12-25; ⏰noon-9pm; 🍷) Flavors from across Asia season popular local foods at this sprightly restaurant. Look for Japanese, Korean and Thai influences in the halibut curry, the fish and chips, and much more. The curry soba noodles show the talent of the Japanese-trained chef.

ℹ Information

The **visitor center** (☎250-542-1415; www.tourismvernon.com; 3004 39th Ave; ⏰9am-6pm; 📶) is near the town center.

BC MASCOTS

Some BC towns have their own quirky mascots, which sometimes appear at community events. On your travels, look out for **Knuckles** the grey whale in Ucluelet; **Peter Pine** the tree in Princeton; **Mr PG** in Prince George; and, our favorite, **Potato Jack** in Pemberton – a jaunty tuber dressed as a cowboy, complete with spurs and a neckerchief.

ℹ Getting There & Away

Greyhound Canada (☎800-661-8747; www.greyhound.ca; 3102 30th St, cnr 31st Ave) Services from Vernon include Kelowna ($17, 45 minutes, four daily) and Revelstoke ($31, 2½ hours, one daily).

Vernon Regional Transit System (☎250-545-7221; www.transitbc.com; fares from $2) Buses leave downtown from the bus stop at the corner of 31st St and 30th Ave. For Kalamalka Lake, catch bus 1; for Okanagan Lake, bus 7.

North of Vernon

Just north of Vernon, beautiful Hwy 97 heads northwest to Kamloops via tree-clad valleys punctuated by lakes. **Armstrong**, 23km north of Vernon, is a cute little village. Attractions are few in this area, which is more notable for its major highway connections.

Home to the O'Keefe family between 1867 and 1977, the **O'Keefe Ranch** (www.okeeferanch.ca; 9380 Hwy 97N; adult/child $14/9; ⏰10am-5pm May, Jun & Sep, to 6pm Jul & Aug) retains its original log cabin, and has lots of live displays of old ranching techniques. Before orchards – and later grapes – covered the valley, ranching as portrayed here was the typical way of life. The ranch is 12km north of Vernon, 4km after Hwy 97 splits from Hwy 97A, which continues northeast to Sicamous and Hwy 1.

Silver Star

Classic inland BC dry powder makes **Silver Star** (☎250-542-0224, snow report 250-542-1745; www.skisilverstar.com; 123 Shortt St, Silver Star Mountain; 1-day lift ticket adult/child $92/48) a very popular ski resort.

The ski resort has all types of accommodations, from hostels to condos. **Samesun Lodge** (☎250-545-8933; www.samesun.com; 9898 Pinnacles Rd, Silver Star; dm/r from $32/80; P @ 📶) runs a very popular and almost posh backpacker hostel.

To reach Silver Star, take 48th Ave off Hwy 97. The resort is 22km northeast of Vernon. Check with your accommodations for various seasonal van and bus services to the resort.

Shuswap Region

Rorschach-test-like **Shuswap Lake** anchors a somewhat bland but pleasing region of green, wooded hills, some farms and two small towns, **Sicamous** and **Salmon Arm**. The former has a lakefront park that's good for picnics, just northwest of Hwy 1.

The entire area is home to several lake-based provincial parks and is a popular destination for families looking for outdoor fun. Many explore the lakes via houseboats.

The main attraction here is the annual spawning of sockeye salmon at **Roderick Haig-Brown Provincial Park** (☎250-851-3000; www.bcparks.ca; off Hwy 1, Saquilax). The 10.59-sq-km park protects both sides of the Adams River between Shuswap Lake and **Adams Lake**, a natural bottleneck for the bright-red sockeye when they run upriver every October. The fish population peaks every four years, when as many as four million salmon crowd the Adams' shallow riverbed. The next big spawn is due in 2018.

Meet the cows, then lick the ice cream at **D Dutchmen Dairy** (☎250-836-4304; www.dutchmendairy.ca; 1321 Maeir Rd; treats from $3; ⏲8am-9pm Jun-Sep), an off-beat dairy close to Hwy 1. There are dozens of flavors of traditional frozen treats.

THE KOOTENAYS & THE ROCKIES

You can't help sighing as you ponder the plethora of snow-covered peaks in the Kootenay Region of BC. Deep river valleys cleaved by white-water rivers, impossibly sheer rock faces, alpine meadows and a sawtooth of white-dappled mountains stretching across the horizon inspire awe, action and even mere contemplation.

Coming from the west, the mountain majesty builds as if choreographed. The roughly parallel ranges of the Monashees and the Selkirks striate the West Kootenays, with the Arrow Lakes adding texture. Appealing towns such as Revelstoke and Nelson nestle against the mountains and are centers of year-round outdoor fun. The East Kootenays cover the Purcell Mountains region below Golden, taking in Radium Hot Springs and Fernie.

BC's Rocky Mountains national parks (Mt Revelstoke, Glacier, Yoho and Kootenay) don't have the profile of Banff and Jasper National Parks over the border, but for many that's an advantage: each has its own spectacular qualities, often relatively unexploited by the Banff-bound hordes.

Revelstoke

POP 7700

Gateway to serious mountains, Revelstoke doesn't need to toot its own horn – the ceaseless procession of trains through the center does that. Built as an important point on the Canadian Pacific transcontinental railroad that first linked Eastern and Western Canada, Revelstoke echoes not just with whistles but with history. The compact center is lined with heritage buildings, yet it's more than a museum piece. There's a vibrant local arts community, and most locals take full advantage of the boundless opportunities for hiking, kayaking and, most of all, skiing.

It's more than worth a long pause as you pass on Hwy 1, which bypasses the town center to the northeast. The main streets include 1st St and Mackenzie Ave.

Sights

Grizzly Plaza, between Mackenzie and Orton Aves, is a pedestrian precinct and the heart of downtown, where free live-music performances take place every evening in July and August.

While outdoor activities are Revelstoke's real drawcard, a stroll of the center and a moment spent at the museums is a must. Pick up the *Public Art* and *Heritage* walking-tour brochures at the tourist office.

★Mt Revelstoke National Park PARK

(www.pc.gc.ca/revelstoke; off Hwy 1; adult/child incl Glacier National Park $8/4) Grand in beauty if not in size, this 260-sq-km national park, just northeast of its namesake town, is a vision of peaks and valleys – many of which are all but untrodden.

There are several good **hiking trails** from the summit. To overnight in the wild, you must have a Wilderness Pass camping permit ($10, in addition to your park pass), which is available from the **Parks Canada Revelstoke Office** (☎250-837-7500; revglacier.reception@pc.gc.ca; 301 3rd St, Revelstoke; ⏲8am-4:30pm Mon-Fri) or from the Rogers Pass Centre (p745) inside Glacier National Park (p745). Both centers also have excellent hiking info on trails long and short; don't miss the 30-minute **Skunk Cabbage Trail**.

Revelstoke Railway Museum MUSEUM

(☎250-837-6060; www.railwaymuseum.com; 719 Track St W; adult/child $10/2; ⏲9am-5pm May-Sep,

The Kootenays & The Rockies

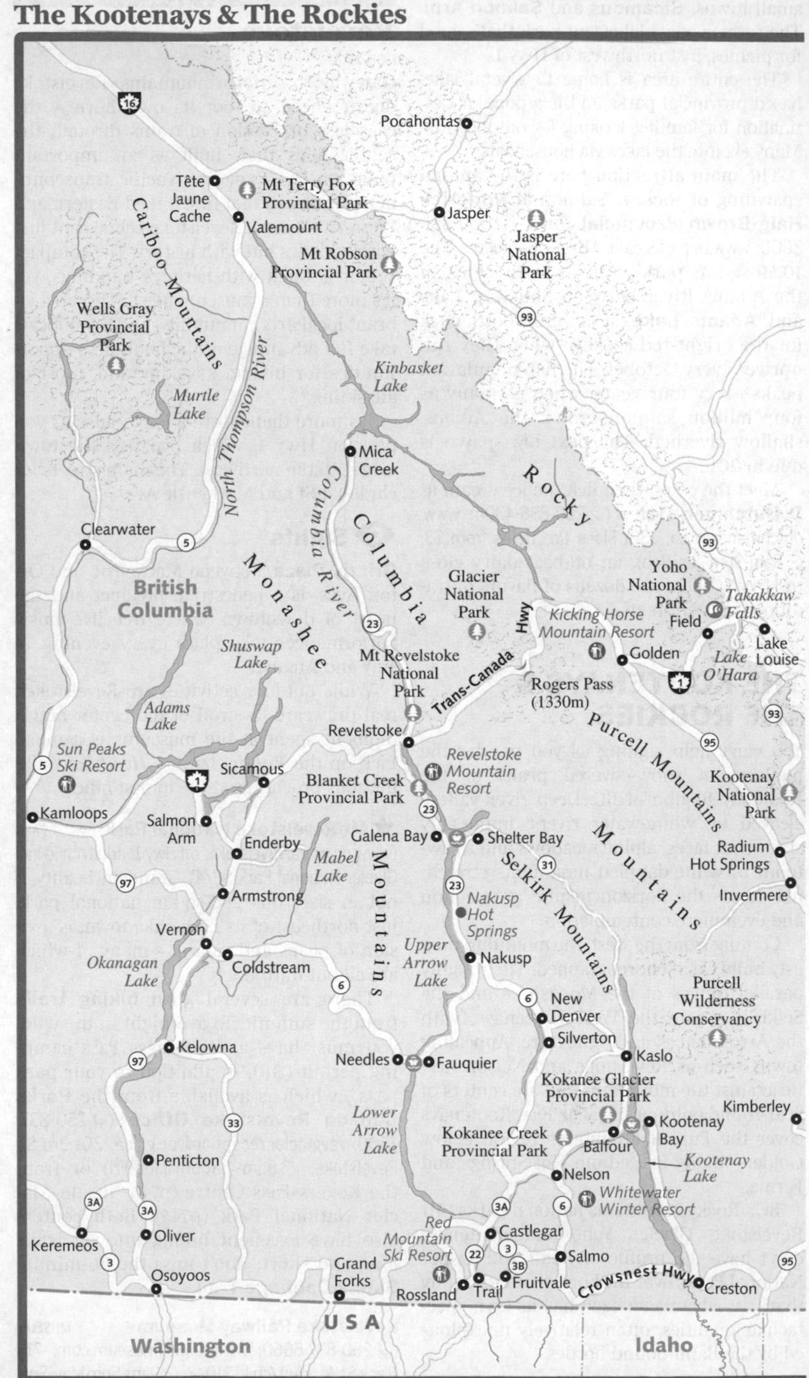

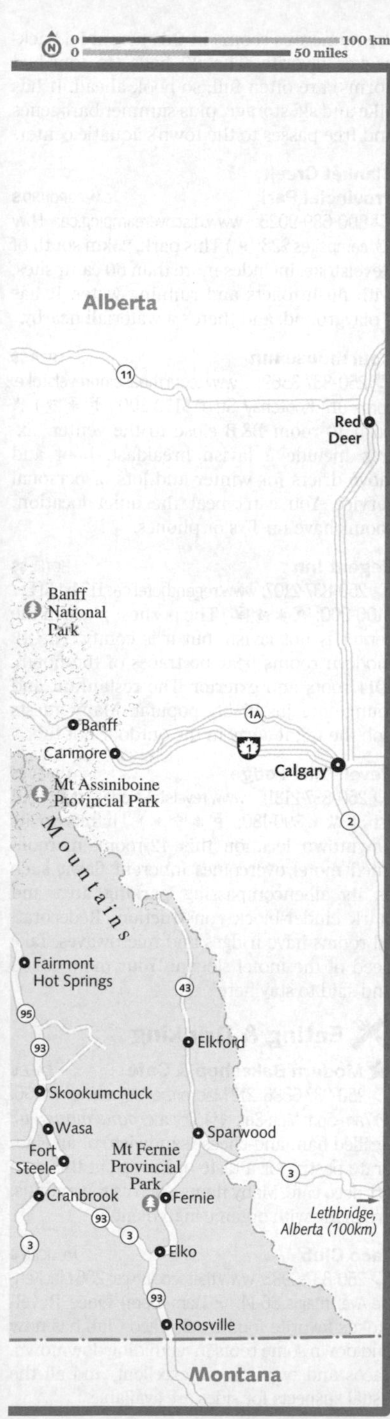

shorter hours Oct-Apr; P) In an attractive building across the tracks from the town center, Revelstoke Railway Museum contains restored steam locomotives, including one of the largest steam engines ever used on Canadian Pacific Railway (CPR) lines. Photographs and artifacts document the construction of the CPR, which was instrumental – actually, essential – in linking Eastern and Western Canada.

Revelstoke Museum MUSEUM

(☎250-837-3067; www.revelstokemuseum.ca; 315 1st St W; adult/child $5/free; ⊙10am-6pm Mon-Sat year-round, 11am-5pm Sun Jul & Aug) Furniture and historical odds and ends – including mining, logging and railway artifacts that date back to the town's establishment in the 1880s – line the rooms. The local skiing history displays are worthwhile.

Activities

Sandwiched between the vast but relatively unknown Selkirk and Monashee mountain ranges, Revelstoke draws serious snow buffs looking for vast landscapes of crowd-free powder. It's where North America's first ski jump was built, in 1915.

For **cross-country skiing**, head to the 22km of groomed trails at Mt MacPherson Ski Area, 7km south of town on Hwy 23; see www.revelstokenordic.org for information.

All that white snow turns into white water come spring and **rafting** is big here. **Mountain biking** is also huge; pick up trail maps from the visitor center.

Revelstoke Mountain Resort SKIING

(☎888-837-2188; www.revelstokemountainresort.com; Camozzi Rd; 1-day lift ticket adult/child $86/26) Just 6km southeast of town, the Revelstoke Mountain Resort has ambitions to become the biggest ski resort this side of the Alps. It has seemingly endless virgin slopes and 65 runs. In one run you can ski both 700m of bowl and 700m of trees. At 1713m, the vertical drop is the greatest in North America.

Apex Rafting Co RAFTING

(☎250-837-6376; www.apexrafting.com; 112 1st St E; adult/child $95/80; ⊙Jun-Aug;) Runs kid-friendly two-hour guided trips on the Illecillewaet River in spring and summer.

Wandering Wheels CYCLING

(☎250-814-7609; www.wanderingwheels.ca; lessons per hour from $35, tours from $60; ⊙Jun-Oct) Offers bike shuttle services, lessons and tours.

AVALANCHE WARNING

The Kootenays are the heart of avalanche country. Such events kill more people in BC each year than any other natural phenomenon. The toll is stubbornly high every year.

Avalanches can occur at any time, even on terrain that seems relatively flat. Roughly half the people caught in one don't survive. It's vital that people venturing out onto the snow make inquiries about conditions first; if an area is closed, don't go there. Whether you're backcountry ski touring or simply hiking in the alpine region, you'll want to rent a homing beacon; most outdoor shops can supply one.

In Revelstoke, **Avalanche Canada** (250-837-2141; www.avalanche.ca) tracks avalanche reports and offers forecasts for BC and the Canadian Rockies. It has a vital website and a phone app.

Revelstoke Dogsled Adventures ADVENTURE SPORTS
(250-814-3720; www.revelstokedogsledadventures.ca; from $200; winter) Thrill at winter wonders while a team of huskies pulls you through the Kootenay wilderness.

Skookum Cycle & Ski CYCLING
(250-814-0090; www.skookumrevelstoke.com; 118 Mackenzie Ave; mountain bike rental per day from $40; 10am-5pm) Pick up trail maps and rent bikes in summer, skis in winter.

Natural Escapes Kayaking KAYAKING
(250-837-7883; www.naturalescapes.ca; rental per 4hr from $60, tours from $70; Jun-Sep) Has tours, lessons and rents kayaks and canoes.

Free Spirit Sports SNOW SPORTS, WATER SPORTS
(FSS; 250-837-9453; www.freespiritsports.com; 203 1st St W; SUP rental per day $50; 10am-5pm Mon-Sat) Rents a wide variety of summer and winter gear, including essential avalanche equipment for skiers.

Mica Heliskiing SKIING
(877-837-6191; www.micaheli.com; 207 Mackenzie Ave; per day from $1500; Dec-Apr) Mica Heliskiing offers trips to remote bowls accessible by helicopter.

Sleeping

Samesun Backpacker Lodge HOSTEL $
(250-837-4050; www.samesun.ca; 400 2nd St W; dm/r from $30/80; P @) Ramble though the numerous rooms in this perennial backpacker favorite. The 80 beds (in four-bed dorms) are often full, so book ahead. It has bike and ski storage, plus summer barbecues and free passes to the town's aquatic center.

Blanket Creek Provincial Park CAMPGROUND $
(800-689-9025; www.discovercamping.ca; Hwy 23; campsites $28; P) This park, 25km south of Revelstoke, includes more than 60 campsites, with flush toilets and running water. It has a playground, and there's a waterfall nearby.

Courthouse Inn B&B $$
(250-837-3369; www.courthouseinnrevelstoke.com; 312 Kootenay St; r $130-200; P) A posh 10-room B&B close to the center. Extras include a lavish breakfast, boot and glove driers for winter and lots of personal service. You can't beat the quiet location; rooms have no TVs or phones.

Regent Inn HOTEL $$
(250-837-2107; www.regenthotel.ca; 112 1st St E; r $100-200; P) The poshest place in the center is not lavish, but it is comfy. The 42 modern rooms bear no traces of the hotel's 1914 roots and exterior. The restaurant and lounge are justifiably popular. Many guests bob the night away in the outdoor hot tub.

Revelstoke Lodge MOTEL $$
(250-837-2181; www.revelstokelodge.com; 601 1st St W; r $90-180; P) Thanks to its downtown location this 42-room, maroon-hued motel overcomes inherent flaws, such as its all-encompassing parking area and stark cinder-block construction. Redecorated rooms have fridges and microwaves. Take heed of the motel slogan: 'Your mom called and said to stay here.'

Eating & Drinking

★**Modern Bakeshop & Café** CAFE $
(250-837-6886; 212 Mackenzie Ave; mains from $6; 7am-5pm Mon-Sat;) Try a *croque monsieur* (grilled ham-and-cheese sandwich) or an elaborate pastry for a taste of Europe at this cute art-deco cafe. Many items, such as the muffins, are made with organic ingredients.

Taco Club MEXICAN $
(250-837-0988; www.thetacoclub.ca; 206 MacKenzie Ave; mains $6-14; 11am-10pm) Once Revelstoke's favorite food truck, Taco Club has now laid down some roots in a building downtown. Tacos and burritos are excellent, and all the usual suspects for sides are available.

Farmers Market MARKET $
(Grizzly Plaza; ⏲8:30am-1pm Sat May-Oct) The farmers market sprawls across Grizzly Plaza.

★ **Woolsey Creek** FUSION $$
(☎250-837-5500; www.woolseycreekbistro.ca; 604 2nd St W; mains $20-30; ⏲5-10pm;) The food at this lively and fun place is both artistic and locally sourced. There are global influences across the menu, which features meat, fish and a fine wine list.

Cabin BAR
(☎250-837-2144; www.cometothecabin.com; 200 1st St E; ⏲5pm-midnight Tue-Sat) Bowling alley, bar, outdoor-gear store and gallery: it's a cool spot serving a few snacks to go with the beers.

Information

The **visitor center** (☎250-837-5345; www.seerevelstoke.com; 301 Victoria Rd; ⏲9am-6pm) is an excellent source for hiking and mountain-biking info and maps.

Getting There & Away

Greyhound Canada (☎250-837-5874; www.greyhound.ca; 122 Hwy 23 N; ⏲9am-6pm) is located west of town, just off Hwy 1; it has storage lockers. Buses go east to Calgary ($63, six hours, four daily) via Golden and Banff, and west to Kelowna ($49, 3½ hours, one daily). In winter there are various shuttles to Kelowna's international **airport** (p739) and up to the ski resort. Check with the visitor center for details.

Revelstoke to Golden

Keep your eyes on the road or, better yet, let someone else drive as you traverse the Trans-Canada Hwy (Hwy 1) for 148km between Revelstoke and Golden. Stunning mountain peaks follow one after another as you go.

Glacier National Park (www.pc.gc.ca/glacier; adult/child incl Mt Revelstoke National Park $8/4) should be called '430 Glaciers National Park'. The annual snowfall can be as much as 23m, and due to the sheer mountain slopes, this is one of the world's most active avalanche areas. For this reason, skiing, caving and mountaineering are regulated; you must register with park wardens before venturing into the backcountry. Check the weather and get an avalanche report (p744) in season. **Rogers Pass** ranks as one of the most beautiful mountain passes you'll ever traverse. Be sure to pause at the **Hemlock Grove Trail**, 54km east of Revelstoke, where a 400m boardwalk winds through an ancient hemlock rainforest.

Not far from Rogers Pass are Glacier National Park's three **campgrounds** (Rogers Pass, off Hwy 1; campsites $16-22; ⏲late Jun–early Sep): Illecillewaet, Mount Sir Donald and Loop Brook. Sites are available on a first-come, first-served basis.

Rogers Pass Centre (☎250-814-5233; off Hwy 1; ⏲8am-7pm mid-Jun–early Sep, shorter hours mid-Sep–mid-Jun) displays Canadian Pacific Railway (CPR) dioramas, 72km east of Revelstoke and 76km west of Golden. Shows films about Glacier National Park and organizes guided walks in summer. Has an excellent bookstore run by the Friends of Mt Revelstoke & Glacier.

Golden

POP 3850

Golden is well situated for national-park explorations – there are six nearby. White-water rafting excitement lies even closer, where the Kicking Horse River converges with the Columbia.

Don't just breeze past the strip of franchised yuck on Hwy 1 or you'll miss the tidy town center down by the tumbling river.

Sights & Activities

Golden is the center for **white-water rafting** trips on the turbulent and chilly Kicking Horse River. Along with the powerful grade III and IV rapids, the breathtaking scenery along the sheer walls of the Kicking Horse Valley makes this rafting experience one of North America's best.

Note that access to the lower canyon, where the best rapids are located, is threatened by the Canadian National Railway, which at random times has cut off vital access across its tracks.

★ **Alpine Rafting** RAFTING
(☎250-344-6778; www.alpinerafting.com; 101 Golden Donald Upper Rd; raft trips $25-180; ⏲Jun-Sep;) Offers several good family rafting options, including a white-water run for kids aged four years and over, right up to the more extreme class IV+ 'Kicking Horse Challenge'.

WATCH YOUR GAS

The closure of services at **Rogers Pass** means that there is no gas (petrol) available along the 148km stretch between Revelstoke and Golden on Hwy 1.

DON'T MISS

TWO PERFECT WALKS

Easily accessible, **Skunk Cabbage Trail**, 28km east of Revelstoke on Hwy 1, is a 1.2km boardwalk along the Illecillewaet River that's lined with its huge namesakes. Another 4km east, the **Giant Cedars Boardwalk** winds a 500m course up and down and all around a grove of huge old-growth cedars.

Northern Lights Wolf Centre PARK
(☎250-344-6798; www.northernlightswildlife.com; 1745 Short Rd; adult/child $12/6; ⏰9am-7pm Jul & Aug, 10am-6pm May, Jun & Sep, noon-5pm Oct-Apr; P) This small wildlife center houses a small pack of gray wolves and wolf-husky crosses, all born and bred in captivity. Visits include an introduction to the resident wolves – although most of the viewing is done through wire-frame pens.

Kicking Horse Mountain Resort SKIING, MOUNTAIN BIKING
(☎866-754-5425, 403-254-7669; www.kickinghorseresort.com; Kicking Horse Trail; 1-day lift ticket adult/child winter $90/36, summer $41/21) Some 60% of the 120 ski runs at Kicking Horse Mountain Resort are rated advanced or expert. With a 1260m (4133ft) vertical drop and a snowy position between the Rockies and the Purcells, the resort's popularity grows each year. It's renowned for its summer mountain biking, which includes the longest cycling descent in Canada.

Sleeping & Eating

There are scores of chain motels along busy, charmless Hwy 1.

★**Dreamcatcher Hostel** HOSTEL $
(☎250-439-1090; www.dreamcatcherhostel.com; 528 9th Ave N; dm/r from $35/90; P📶) Run by two veteran travelers, this centrally located hostel has everything a budget traveler could hope for. There are 33 beds across eight rooms, as well as a vast kitchen and a comfy common room with a stone fireplace. Outside there's a garden and a barbecue.

Golden Eco-Adventure Ranch CAMPGROUND $
(☎250-344-6825; www.goldenadventurepark.com; 872 MacBeath Rd; tent & RV sites $35, yurts $52; ⏰early Apr–late Sep) Spread over 160 hectares (395 acres) of mountain meadow 5km south of Golden on Hwy 95, this great campground-cum–outdoors center feels a world away from the cramped confines of municipal camping. Sites are spacious; there are full RV hookups; and you can even sleep in a Mongolian yurt if you're tired of your tent.

Mary's Motel MOTEL $$
(☎250-344-7111; www.marysmotel.com; 603 8th Ave N; r $80-150; P❄📶🏊) In town, right on the roaring river, Mary's has 81 rooms spread across several buildings; get one with a patio. There's a large outdoor pool, plus an indoor one and two hot tubs. It's an easy walk to nightlife.

Kicking Horse Canyon B&B GUESTHOUSE $$
(☎250-344-6848; www.kickinghorsecanyonbb.com; 644 Lapp Rd; d $125-145; P📶) Hidden away among the hills to the east of Golden (phone for directions), this endearingly offbeat B&B takes you into the bosom of the family the minute you cross the threshold. Run by genial host Jeannie Cook and her husband, Jerry, it's a real alpine home-away-from-home, surrounded by private grassy grounds with views across the mountains.

Canyon Ridge Lodge GUESTHOUSE $$
(☎250-344-9876; www.canyonridgelodge.com; 1392 Pine Dr; d $109-125; P📶) Three white rooms and a smart, high-ceilinged studio suite are on offer at this lovely timber-framed home, 1km from Golden's visitor center just off Golden Donald Upper Rd. It's nicely finished (underfloor heating, slate-tiled private bathrooms) and there's a communal hot tub.

Bacchus Cafe CAFE $
(☎250-344-5600; www.bacchusbooks.ca; 409 9th Ave N; mains $6-12; ⏰9am-5:30pm Mon-Sat, 10am-4pm Sun) This bohemian hideaway at the end of 8th St is a favorite haunt for Golden's artsy crowd. Browse for books (new and secondhand) in the downstairs bookstore, then head upstairs to find a table for tea among the higgledy-piggledy shelves. Sandwiches, salads and cakes are all made on the premises, and the coffee is as good as you'll find in Golden.

★**Wolf's Den** PUB FOOD $$
(☎250-344-9863; www.thewolfsdengolden.ca; 1105 9th St; mains $10-20; ⏰4-10pm) An excellent pub with live music on Sundays. It's popular with locals, who love the burgers and hearty fare, which is way above average. The beer menu includes some of BC's best on tap. It's south of the river from downtown.

Eleven22 FUSION $$

(☎250-344-2443; www.eleven22.ca; 1122 10th Ave S; mains $12-26; ⊙5-10pm) A cross between a restaurant and a home dinner party, this appealing option has art on the walls of the dining rooms and all the stars you can count out on the patio. Watch the kitchen action from the lounge area while sharing small plates.

Information

The **visitor center** (☎250-344-7125; www.tourismgolden.com; 500 N 10th Ave; ⊙9am-5pm daily May-Sep, to 4pm Tue-Fri Oct-Apr) is 1km east on Hwy 1 from the Hwy 95 turnoff into Golden.

Getting There & Away

Delays may offset improvements on Hwy 1 east of Golden as the road is reconstructed from scratch; see www.kickinghorsecanyon.ca.

Greyhound Canada (p722) Serves Vancouver ($128, nine to 13 hours, five daily) and Calgary ($48, 3½ hours, five daily) via Banff.

Sun City Coachlines (☎250-417-3117; www.suncity.bc.ca) Runs one daily bus each way on Hwy 95 between Golden and Cranbrook ($70, four hours).

Yoho National Park

The surging waters of glacier-fed, ice-blue Kicking Horse River that plow through a valley of the same name are an apt image for dramatic Yoho National Park. This spectacular park is home to looming peaks, pounding waterfalls, glacial lakes and patches of pretty meadows.

Sights & Activities

★ **Burgess Shale Fossil Beds** NATIONAL PARK

This World Heritage site protects the amazing Cambrian-age fossil beds on Mt Stephen and Mt Field. These 515-million-year-old fossils preserve the remains of marine creatures that were some of the earliest forms of life on earth. You can only get to the fossil beds by guided hikes, which are led by naturalists from the **Burgess Shale Geoscience Foundation** (☎800-343-3006; www.burgess-shale.bc.ca; 200 Kicking Horse Ave, Field; tours adult/child from $95/65; ⊙mid-Jun–mid-Sep). Reservations are essential.

Kicking Horse Pass & Spiral Tunnels VIEWPOINT

The historic Kicking Horse Pass between Banff and Yoho National Parks is one of the most important passes in the Canadian Rockies. It was discovered in 1858 by the Palliser Expedition, which was tasked with discovering a possible route across the Rockies for the Canadian Pacific Railway. Accessible 8km east of Field from the west-bound lanes of Hwy 1, the viewing area is often closed and the view obscured by vegetation.

Takakkaw Falls WATERFALL

A thundering torrent of water tumbles from its source in the nearby Daly Glacier over a sheer cliff face for 255m, making it the second-highest waterfall in Canada. At the end of the road, a trail leads for around 800m from the Takakkaw parking lot to the base of the falls. The road is open from late June to early October.

Emerald Lake LAKE

For most visitors, this vividly colored lake is Yoho's most unmissable sight. Ringed by forest and silhouetted by impressive mountains, including the iconic profile of **Mt Burgess** to the southeast, it's a truly beautiful – if incredibly busy – spot. Escape the mobs in a rental canoe. The lake road is signed off Hwy 1 just to the southwest of Field and continues for 10km (6.2 miles) to the lake shore.

Twin Falls & the Whaleback HIKING

This moderate 8.2km route from Takakkaw Falls parking lot through pine forest takes in four waterfalls: the **Angel's Staircase**, **Point Lace Falls**, **Laughing Falls** and the double-tiered Twin Falls.

Yoho Lake & Wapta Highline HIKING

This strenuous route ranks among the finest (and hardest) day hikes in the Rockies. The route starts at the Whiskey Jack trailhead near Takakkaw Falls, and climbs to Yoho Lake before ascending onto the sky-top flanks of Wapta Mountain.

Sleeping

The four campgrounds within Yoho all close from mid-October to mid-May. In addition to a couple of lodges in the park, you can find a range of lodgings in Field.

HI-Yoho National Park HOSTEL $

(Whiskey Jack Hostel; ☎403-670-7580; www.hihostels.ca; Yoho Valley Rd, Yoho National Park; dm from $28; ⊙Jul-Sep) Yoho National Park's Takakkaw Falls are so close you can see them from the hostel's timber deck. Three nine-bed dorms and a basic kitchen comprise the rudimentary facilities; it's usually booked out in summer.

Kicking Horse Campground CAMPGROUND $
(Map p587; Yoho Valley Rd; tent & RV sites $28; May-Oct; wifi) This is probably the most popular campground in Yoho. It's in a nice forested location, with plenty of space between the 88 sites, and there are showers. Riverside sites (especially 68 to 74) are the pick of the bunch.

Takakkaw Falls Campground CAMPGROUND $
(Yoho Valley Rd; campsites $18; Jul-Oct) This appealing campground, 13km along a gravel road, has 35 walk-in (200m) campsites for tents only.

Emerald Lake Lodge LODGE $$$
(403-410-7417; www.crmr.com/emerald; Emerald Lake Rd, Yoho National Park; r $250-450; P wifi) Commanding a picture-perfect five-hectare site accessed by a bridge and situated right beside the tranquil shores of Emerald Lake, this lodge couldn't have a better position. The interiors are disappointingly old-fashioned, however, so sit back on the porch and enjoy the lake view.

Information

Yoho National Park Information Centre
(250-343-6783; off Hwy 1, Field; 9am-7pm May-Oct) provides maps and trail descriptions; however, this vital resource is often closed due to budget cuts. Rangers can advise on itineraries and conditions. Alberta Tourism staffs a desk here in summer.

Lake O'Hara

Perched high in the mountains, Lake O'Hara is an encapsulation of the Rockies region, and worth the significant hassle to reach it. Compact wooded hillsides, alpine meadows, snow-covered passes, mountain vistas and glaciers wrap around the stunning lake. A day trip is rewarding, but if you stay overnight in the backcountry you'll be able to access many **hiking trails** – some quite difficult, and all quite spectacular. The **Alpine Circuit** (12km) has a bit of everything.

Sleeping

You can camp or stay in Lake O'Hara Lodge, but reserve well in advance and prepare to jump through hoops to secure a spot.

Lake O'Hara Campground CAMPGROUND $
(reservations 250-343-6433; Yoho National Park; tent sites $10, reservation fee $12; Apr-Oct) Reserve three months in advance to snare one of 30 campsites. Available spots are often taken in the first hour that reservation phone lines are open (from 8am Mountain time). If you don't have advance reservations, three to five campsites are set aside for 'standby' users; call at 8am the day before you wish to stay.

★ **Lake O'Hara Lodge** LODGE $$$
(250-343-6418; www.lakeohara.com; Yoho National Park; s/d from $500/665, cabins $940; Jan-Apr & Jun-Oct) Leaving guests slack-jawed for more than 80 years, the lodge is the only place to stay at the lake if you're not traveling with a tent. It's luxurious in a rustic way, and its environmental practices are lauded. Food comes from BC producers and is excellent. There's a two-night minimum stay.

Getting There & Away

To reach the lake, take the **shuttle bus** (reservations 877-737-3783; adult/child return $15/8, reservation fee $12; mid-Jun–Sep) from the Lake O'Hara parking lot, 15km east of Field on Hwy 1. A quota system governs bus access to the lake. Given the lake's popularity, reservations are basically mandatory, unless you want to walk. That said, if you don't have advance reservations, six day-use seats on the bus are set aside for 'standby' users. Call at 8am the day before and think 'lucky'.

You can freely walk the 11km from the parking area, but no bikes are allowed. The area around Lake O'Hara usually remains covered with snow or else stays very muddy until mid-July.

Field

Right off xHwy 1, this historic railroad town is worth a stop for its dramatic overlook of the river and quaint yet unfussy atmosphere. Many buildings date from the early days of the railways, when the town was the Canadian Pacific Railway's headquarters for exploration and, later, for strategic planning, when engineers were working on the problem of moving trains over Kicking Horse Pass.

Sleeping & Eating

Fireweed Hostel HOSTEL $
(250-343-6999; www.fireweedhostel.com; 313 Stephen Ave; dm/r from $40/125; wifi) This four-room hostel in Field is a real find, beautifully finished in rustic pine. Dorms are small but smart; each room has two pine bunk beds and a shared bathroom off the hallway, and all have full use of a kitchen and sitting room.

Canadian Rockies Inn GUESTHOUSE **$$**
(☎250-343-6046; www.canadianrockiesinn.com; Stephen Ave; r $125-190; P 📶) Spotless rooms and enormous beds are the main attractions. All rooms have microwaves, kettles and fridges.

Truffle Pigs FUSION **$$$**
(☎250-343-6303; www.trufflepigs.com; 100 Centre St; mains $12-30; ⏱11am-3pm & 5-9pm Mon-Fri, 8am-3pm & 5-9pm Sat & Sun; 📶) 🌿 A legendary cafe serving inventive, high-concept bistro fare that's locally sourced and usually organic. The menu changes seasonally.

Kootenay National Park

Kootenay is the the only national park in Canada to contain both glaciers and cacti. From BC you can create a fine driving loop via Kootenay and Yoho National Parks; many of the top sights are easily reached by car.

The very remote **Mt Assiniboine Provincial Park** (www.bcparks.ca) offers true adventurers a remarkable wilderness experience.

Sights

Kootenay National Park NATIONAL PARK
(Map p587; ☎250-347-9505; www.pc.gc.ca/kootenay; Hwy 93; adult/child $10/5, campsites $22-39; ⏱camping May-Oct) Shaped like a lightning bolt, Kootenay National Park is centered on a long, wide, tree-covered valley shadowed by cold, gray peaks. Encompassing 1406 sq km, Kootenay has a more moderate climate than other Rocky Mountains parks and, in the southern regions especially, summers can be hot and dry, which is a factor in the frequent fires.

The interpretive **Fireweed Trail** (500m or 2km) loops through the surrounding forest at the north end of Hwy 93. Panels explain how nature is recovering from a 1968 fire. Some 7km further on, **Marble Canyon** has a pounding creek flowing through a nascent forest. Another 3km south on the main road you'll find the easy 2km trail through forest to ochre pools known as the **Paint Pots**. Panels describe both the mining history of this rusty earth and its importance to Aboriginal people.

Learn how the park's appearance has changed over time at the **Kootenay Valley Viewpoint**, where informative panels vie with the view. Just 3km south, **Olive Lake** makes a perfect picnic or rest stop. A 500m lakeside interpretive trail describes some of the visitors who've come before you.

> **CHECK YOUR WATCH**
>
> It is a constant source of confusion that the East Kootenays lie in the Mountain time zone, along with Alberta, unlike the rest of BC, which falls within the Pacific time zone. West on Hwy 1 from Golden, the time changes at the east gate of Glacier National Park. Going west on Hwy 3, the time changes between Cranbrook and Creston. Mountain time is one hour later than Pacific time.

Sleeping

Kootenay National Park has a few lodges and campgrounds inside its border, and nearby Radium Hot Springs has a huge number of lodgings. Mt Assiniboine Provincial Park is limited to wilderness camping, a few huts and a remote lodge.

Marble Canyon Campground CAMPGROUND **$**
(off Hwy 93, Kootenay National Park; campsites $22; ⏱Jul-Sep) This high-country 61-pitch campground is situated near the Marble Canyon trail, and has flush toilets but no showers. Most sites have tree cover to shelter from the wind. The eastern side has the best views.

McLeod Meadows Campground CAMPGROUND **$**
(off Hwy 93, Kootenay National Park; campsites $22; ⏱Jun-Sep) An 80-pitch campground located on the banks of the Kootenay River just a 2.6km walk to the shores of pretty Dog Lake. There are plentiful trees and spacious, grassy sites.

Kootenay Park Lodge CABIN **$$**
(☎403-762-9196; www.kootenayparklodge.com; Hwy 93, Vermilion Crossing, Kootenay National Park; d cabins $135-200; ⏱mid-May–late Sep; P) The pick of the few places to stay inside the park, this lodge has a range of cute log cabins complete with verandas, fridges and hot plates. Think rustic charm.

Information

The main **Kootenay National Park visitor center** (p750) is in Radium Hot Springs. It has excellent resources for hikers.

Radium Hot Springs

Lying just outside the southwest corner of Kootenay National Park, Radium Hot Springs is a major gateway to the entire Rocky Mountains national park area.

Radium boasts a large resident population of bighorn sheep, which often wander through town, but the big attraction is the namesake hot springs, 3km north of town.

The **hot springs'** (250-347-9485; www.pc.gc.ca/hotsprings; off Hwy 93; adult/child $7/6; 9am-11pm) pools are quite modern and can get very busy in summer. The water comes from the ground at 44°C, enters the first pool at 39°C and hits the final one at 29°C.

Radium glows with lodging. **Cedar Motel** (250-347-9463; www.cedarmotel.ca; 7593 Main St W; r $85-100; P) is clean, cheap and (as its name suggests) cedar-clad. This Swiss-run place is one of the more attractive motels in Radium. The rooms are boxy but bright, with large beds and Technicolor bedspreads. Some have teeny kitchenettes.

Village Country Inn (250-347-9392; www.villagecountryinn.bc.ca; 7557 Canyon Ave; r $120-175; P) is a cute gabled house just off the main drag, with rooms decked out in country fashion. The same folksy feel runs into the downstairs tea room, where afternoon tea is served on bone china and frilly doilies.

An ideal road-trip breaker is **Meet on Higher Ground Coffee House** (250-347-6567; www.meetonhigherground.com; 7527 Main St; snacks $3-10; 6am-5pm;), where you can refuel with coffee and a cinnamon bun or something more savory.

Parks Canada rangers and the Radium tourism people share space at the **Kootenay National Park & Radium Hot Springs Visitors Centre** (250-347-9331; www.radiumhotsprings.com; 7556 Main St E, Hwy 93/95; visitor center 9am-5pm year-round, Parks Canada May-Oct;), and they provide excellent local hiking info. There are some good displays on the park.

Sun City Coachlines (p747) runs one daily bus each way on Hwy 95 to Golden ($27, one hour) and Cranbrook ($43, three hours).

Radium Hot Springs to Fernie

South from Radium Hot Springs, Hwy 93/95 follows the wide Columbia River valley between the Purcell and Rocky Mountains. It's not especially interesting, unless you're into the area's industry (ski resort construction), agriculture (golf courses) or wild game (condo buyers).

South of Skookumchuck on Hwy 93/95, the road forks. Go left on Hwy 95 and you'll come to **Fort Steele Heritage Town** (250-426-7342; www.fortsteele.ca; 9851 Hwy 93/95; adult/child $12/5; 9:30am-6pm mid-Jun–Aug, shorter hours winter), a re-created 1880s town that's less irritating than many of similar ilk. In summer there are all manner of activities and re-creations, which taper off to nothing in winter, although the site stays open.

From Fort Steele it's 95km to Fernie along Hwys 93 and 3.

Fernie

POP 4800

Surrounded by mountains on four sides – that's the sheer granite Lizard Range you see looking west – Fernie defines cool. Once devoted solely to lumber and coal, the town has used its sensational setting to branch out. Skiers love the 8m-plus of dry powder that annually blankets the runs seen from town. In summer, this same dramatic setting lures scores of hikers and mountain bikers.

Despite the town's discovery by pleasure seekers, it still retains a down-to-earth, vintage-brick vibe, best felt in the cafes, bars, shops and galleries along Victoria (2nd) Ave in the historic center, three blocks south of Hwy 3 (7th Ave).

Sights & Activities

One of many disasters suffered, Fernie experienced a devastating fire in 1908, which resulted in a brick-and-stone building code. Today you'll see numerous fine **early 20th-century buildings**, many of which were built out of local yellow brick, giving the town an appearance unique in the East Kootenays. Get a copy of *Heritage Walking Tour* ($5), a superb booklet produced by the **Fernie Museum** (250-423-7016; www.ferniemuseum.com; 491 2nd Ave; adult/child $5/free; 10am-5:30pm).

★Fernie Alpine Resort SKIING

(250-423-4655; www.skifernie.com; 5339 Ski Area Rd; 1-day pass adult/child $90/36) In fall, all eyes turn to the mountains for more than just their beauty: they're looking for snow. A five-minute drive from downtown, fast-growing Fernie Alpine Resort boasts 142 runs, five bowls and almost endless dumps of powder. Most hotels run shuttles here daily.

Mt Fernie Provincial Park PARK
(250-422-3003; www.bcparks.ca; Mt Fernie Park Rd, off Hwy 3) Mountain biking is popular at Mt Fernie Provincial Park, which is just 3km south of town. It also offers hikes for all skills and interests, plus camping.

Fernie Bike Guides CYCLING
(250-423-3650; www.ferniebikeguides.ca; guiding per hr $30) Raise your mountain-biking game with expert coaching, and let them show you the far reaches of the Elk Valley.

Mountain High River Adventures RAFTING
(250-423-5008; www.raftfernie.com; 100 Riverside Way, Standford Resort; trips adult/child from $140/100; May-Sep) The Elk River is a classic white-water river, with three grade IV rapids and 11 grade III rapids. In addition to rafting, Mountain High offers kayaking, floats, rentals and more on the surging waters.

Ski & Bike Base SKIING, CYCLING
(250-423-6464; www.skibase.com; 432 2nd Ave; bicycle rental per day from $45; 10am-6pm Mon-Sat year-round, 11am-5pm Sun Jun-Aug) One of several excellent all-season gear-sales and -rental shops on 2nd Ave.

Sleeping

Being a big ski town, Fernie's high season is winter. You'll have the most fun staying in the center.

Fernie Central Reservations (250-423-2077; www.ferniecentralreservations.com) can book you a room at the ski resort.

HI Raging Elk Hostel HOSTEL $
(250-423-6811; www.ragingelk.com; 892 6th Ave; dm/r from $30/76;) Wide decks allow plenty of inspirational mountain-gazing at this well-run central hostel. Raging Elk has good advice for those hoping to mix time on the slopes or trails with seasonal work. The pub (open from 4pm to 11pm) is a hoot (and offers cheap beer).

Mt Fernie Provincial Park CAMPGROUND $
(800-689-9025; www.discovercamping.ca; Mt Fernie Park Rd, off Hwy 3; campsites $30; May-Sep) Only 3km south of town, this campground has 41 sites, flush toilets, waterfalls and access to mountain-bike trails.

Park Place Lodge HOTEL $$
(250-423-6871; www.parkplacelodge.com; 742 Hwy 3; r $130-240;) The nicest lodging close to the center, Park Place offers 64 comfortable rooms with fridges and microwaves and access to an indoor pool and hot tub. Some have balconies and views.

Snow Valley Motel & RV Park MOTEL $$
(250-423-4421; www.snowvalleymotel.com; 1041 7th Ave, Hwy 3; RV campsites $35, r $65-140;) Great value in the middle of town. The 20 motel units are large and come equipped with microwaves and fridges; some have full kitchens. Nothing is fancy here, but there is a barbecue deck with a hot tub and views.

Eating & Drinking

Blue Toque Diner CAFE $
(250-423-4637; 601 1st Ave; mains from $12; 9am-2:30pm Thu-Mon;) Part of the Arts Station community gallery, this is *the* place for breakfast. The menu features lots of seasonal and organic vegetarian specials.

Big Bang Bagel BAKERY $
(250-423-7778; www.bigbangbagels.com; 502 2 Ave; mains $4-10; 7am-5pm) The wooden floors creak in accompaniment to the anticipatory growls of your stomach at this popular corner bakery. Everything from bagels to sandwiches to lunch mains are good. Excellent coffee.

★**Yamagoya** JAPANESE $$
(250-430-0090; www.yamagoya.ca; 741 7th Ave, Hwy 3; small dishes $4-8, mains $11-30; 5-10pm) As compact as a California roll, this gem of a sushi place serves up a wide range of classics, from sashimi to tempura. The miso soup is good, especially after a day of skiing. In addition to sake, there's a great beer selection. Also has outdoor seating.

Bridge Bistro CANADIAN $$
(250-423-3002; 301 Hwy 3; mains $11-25; 11am-10pm) Enjoy the views of the Elk River and surrounding peaks from the deck, but save some attention for the long menu of tasty burgers, steaks, salads and pizza.

Royal Hotel PUB
(250-946-5395; www.facebook.com/RoyalFernie; 501 1st Ave; 9pm-2am Mon-Sat) A local institution. This old brick bar has live music many nights, from blues to punk. On any night, it's good for a drink and a chat.

Information

The **visitor center** (250-423-6868; www.ferniechamber.com; 102 Commerce Rd; 9am-5pm Mon-Fri Sep-Jun, daily Jul & Aug) is east of town off Hwy 3, just past the Elk River crossing.

It includes the **Fernie Nature Centre**, which has displays on local critters. The **Fernie Museum** (p750) also has tourist info.

Getting There & Away

Shuttles operate between town and the ski resort. **Greyhound Canada** (250-423-5577; www.greyhound.ca; 1561 9th Ave) runs buses west to Kelowna ($108, 11 hours, one daily) and Nelson ($62, five hours, one daily), and east to Calgary ($63, 6½ hours, one daily). The stop is near Hwy 3, just north of the center.

Kimberley

When big mining left Kimberley in 1973, a plan was hatched to transform the little mountain village at 1113m altitude into a tourist destination with a Bavarian theme. The center became a pedestrian zone named the Platzl; locals were encouraged to prance about in lederhosen and dirndl; and sausage was added to many a menu. Now, more than three decades later, that shtick is long-gone. There's still a bit of fake half-timbering here and there, but for the most part Kimberley is a diverse place that makes a worthwhile detour off Hwy 95 between Cranbrook and Radium Hot Springs.

Take a 15km ride on **Kimberley's Underground Mining Railway** (250-427-7365; www.kimberleysundergroundminingrailway.ca; Gerry Sorensen Way; adult/child $25/10; tours 11am-3pm May-Sep, trains to resort 10am Sat & Sun), where the tiny train putters through the steep-walled Mark Creek Valley toward some sweeping mountain vistas.

At the end of the Underground Mining Railway, a chair lift takes you up to the **Kimberley Alpine Resort** (250-427-4881; www.skikimberley.com; 301 N Star Blvd; 1-day lift pass adult/child $73/29). (You can also drive up if you wish.) In winter, the resort has more than 700 hectares of skiable terrain, including 80 runs, and mild weather.

Information

The **visitor center** (778-481-1891; www.tourismkimberley.com; 270 Kimberley Ave; 10am-5pm daily Jul & Aug, closed Sun Sep-Jun) sits in the large parking area behind the Platzl.

Cranbrook

The region's main center, 31km southeast of Kimberley, Cranbrook is a modest crossroads. Hwy 3/95 bisects the town, which is a charmless array of strip malls.

The one great reason for stopping in Cranbrook? The **Cranbrook History Centre** (250-489-3918; www.cranbrookhistorycentre.com; 57 Van Horne St S, Hwy 3/95; from $15; 10am-5pm daily Jun-Aug, Tue-Sat Sep-May), which includes the **Canadian Museum of Rail Travel**. It has some fine examples of classic Canadian trains, including the luxurious 1929 edition of the **Trans-Canada Limited**, a legendary train that ran from Montréal to Vancouver.

Cranbrook to Rossland

Hwy 3 twists and turns its way 300km from Cranbrook to Osoyoos at the south end of the Okanagan Valley. Along the way it hugs the hills close to the US border and passes eight border crossings.

Creston, 123km west of Cranbrook, is known for its orchards and as the home of Columbia Brewing Co's Kokanee True Ale. Hwy 3A heads north from here for a scenic 80km to the free **Kootenay Lake Ferry**, which connects to Nelson.

Some 85km west of Creston, **Salmo** is notable mostly as the junction with Hwy 6, which runs north for a bland 40km to Nelson. The Crowsnest Hwy splits 10km to the west. Hwy 3 bumps north through **Castlegar**, notable for the closest large airport to Nelson and a very large pulp mill. Hwy 3B dips down through the cute cafe-filled town of **Fruitvale** and industrial **Trail**.

Sights

Columbia Brewery BREWERY

(250-428-9344; www.columbiabrewery.ca; 1220 Erikson St; tours $5; 9:30am-3pm Jul & Aug, 9:30am-2:30pm Mon-Fri mid-May–Jun & Sep–mid-Oct) This is the home of the Columbia Brewery, creators of the Kokanee and Kootenay brands. The brewery offers tours (four to six daily) and visits to the sample room.

Creston Valley Wildlife Management Area WILDLIFE RESERVE

(250-402-6900; www.crestonwildlife.ca; 1760 West Creston Rd; dawn-dusk) This wildlife spot 11km west of Creston is a good place to spot oodles of birds, including blue herons, from the 1km boardwalk.

Sleeping & Eating

Valley View Motel MOTEL $

(250-428-2336; www.valleyviewmotel.info; 216 Valley View Dr, Creston; r from $90;) In the motel-ville of Creston, this could be your best bet. On a view-splayed hillside, it's clean, comfortable and quiet.

Retro Cafe FRENCH $
(☎250-428-2726; www.retrocafe.ca; 1431 NW Blvd, Creston; mains from $6; ⏰7am-5pm Mon-Fri, to 3pm Sat) A French mirage in Creston, 'retro' will probably be the last thing on your mind as you scour the hand-scrawled blackboard and tuck into *très délicieux* crepes.

Rossland

Rossland is a world apart. High in the Southern Monashee Mountains (1023m), this old mining village is one of Canada's best places for **mountain biking**. A long history of mining has left the hills crisscrossed with old trails and abandoned rail lines, all of which are perfect for riding.

Free-riding is all the rage as the ridgelines are easily accessed and there are lots of rocky paths for plunging downhill. The **Seven Summits & Dewdney Trail** is a 35.8km single track along the crest of the Rossland Range. The **Kootenay Columbia Trails Society** (www.kcts.ca) has good maps online.

Red Mountain Ski Resort (☎250-362-7384, snow report 250-362-5500; www.redresort.com; Hwy 3B; 1-day lift pass adult/child $84/42) draws mountain bikers in summer and plenty of ski enthusiasts in winter. Red, as it's called, includes the 1590m-high Red Mountain, the 2075m-high Granite Mountain and the 2048m-high Grey Mountain, for a total of 1670 hectares of challenging, powdery terrain and 110 runs.

Information

The **visitor center** (☎250-362-7722; www.rossland.com; 1100 Hwy 3B, Rossland Museum; ⏰9am-5pm May-Sep) is located in the Rossland Museum building, at the junction of Hwy 22 (coming from the US border) and Hwy 3B.

Nelson

POP 11,100

Nelson is an excellent reason to visit the Kootenays and should feature on any itinerary in the region. Tidy brick buildings climb the side of a hill overlooking the west arm of deep-blue Kootenay Lake, and the waterfront is lined with parks and beaches. The thriving cafe, culture and nightlife scene is a bonus. However, what really propels Nelson is its personality: a funky mix of hippies, creative types and rugged individualists. You can find all these along Baker St, the pedestrian-friendly main drag where wafts of patchouli mingle with hints of fresh-roasted coffee.

Born as a mining town in the late 1800s, Nelson embarked on a decades-long heritage-preservation project in 1977. Today there are more than 350 carefully preserved and restored period buildings. The town is also an excellent base for hiking, skiing and kayaking the nearby lakes and hills.

Sights

Almost a third of Nelson's **historic buildings** have been restored to their high- and late-Victorian architectural splendor. Pick up the superb *Heritage Walking Tour* from the visitor center. It gives details of more than 30 buildings in the center and offers a good lesson in Victorian architecture.

Lakeside Park PARK
(Lakeside Dr; P) By the iconic Nelson Bridge, Lakeside Park is a flower-filled, shady park and a beach, and has a great summer cafe.

Touchstones Nelson MUSEUM
(☎250-352-9813; www.touchstonesnelson.ca; 502 Vernon St; adult/child $8/4; ⏰10am-5pm Mon-Wed, Fri & Sat, to 8pm Thu, 10am-4pm Sun Jun-Aug, closed Mon Sep-May) An enormous renovation transformed what was once a baronial old city hall (1902) into Touchstones Nelson, a museum of local history and art. Every month brings new exhibitions, many of which celebrate local artists. The history displays are engaging and interactive, banishing images of musty piles of poorly labeled artifacts.

Activities

From the center, follow the **Waterfront Pathway**, which runs along the length of the shore – its western extremity passes the airport and has a remote river vantage. You might choose to walk to Lakeside Park and then ride **Streetcar 23** (☎250-352-7672; www.nelsonstreetcar.org; Waterfront Pathway; adult/child $3/2; ⏰11am-4:30pm mid-May–mid-Nov) back along the 2km track from the park to the wharf at Hall St.

★**Kokanee Glacier Provincial Park** HIKING
(☎trail conditions 250-825-3500; www.bcparks.ca; Kokanee Glacier Rd) This park boasts 85km of some of the area's most superb hiking trails. The fantastic summer-only 2.5km (two hour) round-trip hike to **Kokanee Lake** on a well-marked trail can be continued to the

treeless, boulder-strewn expanse around the glacier. Turn off Hwy 3A 20.5km northeast of Nelson, then head another 16km on Kokanee Glacier Rd.

Kootenay Kayak Company KAYAKING
(250-505-4549; www.kootenaykayak.com; kayak rentals per day $40-50, tours from $55) Rents kayaks and has a variety of guided kayak tours.

Sacred Ride MOUNTAIN BIKING
(250-354-3831; www.sacredride.ca; 213b Baker St; bicycle rental per day $45-100; 9am-5:30pm Mon-Sat) Sacred Ride has a wide variety of rentals. Also sells *Your Ticket to Ride,* an extensive trail map.

Pulpit Rock HIKING
(www.pulpitrocknelson.com) The two-hour climb to Pulpit Rock, just across the lake, affords fine views of Nelson and Kootenay Lake. The trailhead starts at the parking lot on Johnstone Rd.

Great Northern Rail Trail HIKING
Extending 42km from Nelson to Salmo along an old rail line, this trail has stunning views amid thick forest. Turn back whenever you want, but the first 6km have many highlights. The trailhead is at the corner of Cherry and Gore Streets.

Whitewater Winter Resort SKIING
(250-354-4944, snow report 250-352-7669; www.skiwhitewater.com; off Hwy 6; 1-day lift ticket adult/child $76/38) Known for its heavy powdery snowfall, this laid-back resort 12km south of Nelson off Hwy 6 has a small-town charm. Lifts are few, but so are the crowds, who enjoy a drop of 623m on 81 runs. There are 11 groomed Nordic trails.

Sleeping

★HI Dancing Bear Inn HOSTEL $
(250-352-7573; www.dancingbearinn.com; 171 Baker St; dm/r from $28/59;) The brilliant management here offers advice and smooths the stay of guests in the 14 shared and private rooms, all of which share bathrooms. There's a gourmet kitchen, a library, patio and a laundry.

City Tourist Park CAMPGROUND $
(250-352-7618; campnels@telus.net; 90 High St; campsites from $25; May-Sep;) Just a five-minute walk from central Baker St, this small municipal campground has 43 shady sites, showers, a kitchen and a laundry.

★Hume Hotel HOTEL $$
(250-352-5331; www.humehotel.com; 422 Vernon St; r incl breakfast $100-200;) This 1898 classic hotel maintains its period grandeur. The 43 rooms vary greatly in shape and size; ask for the huge corner rooms with views of the hills and lake. Rates include a delicious breakfast. It has several appealing nightlife venues.

Adventure Hotel HOTEL $$
(250-352-7211; www.adventurehotel.ca; 616 Vernon St; r $80-160;) Rooms come in three flavors at this renovated hotel: budget (tiny, two bunk beds, shower down the hall), economy (full private bath) and deluxe (a choice of beds). Common areas include a lounge, patio, a gym and a rooftop sauna. The decor is IKEA-basic, in warm hues.

Victoria Falls Guest House INN $$
(250-505-3563; www.victoriafallsguesthouse.com; cnr Victoria & Falls Sts; r $85-165;) The wide porch wraps right around this festive, yellow, renovated Victorian. The five suites have sitting areas and cooking facilities. Decor ranges from cozy antiques to family-friendly bunk beds. There is a barbecue.

Cloudside Inn B&B $$
(250-352-3226; www.cloudside.ca; 408 Victoria St; r $125-215;) Live like a silver baron at this vintage mansion, where the seven rooms are named after trees. Luxuries abound, and a fine patio looks over the terraced gardens and the town. Most rooms have private bathrooms.

Mountain Hound Inn GUESTHOUSE $$
(250-352-6490; www.mountainhound.com; 621 Baker St; r $80-140;) The 19 rooms are small, but have an industrial edge – to go with the cement-block walls. It's ideally located in the center and is a good-value, no-frills choice. There's a public laundry right next door.

Eating & Drinking

★Cottonwood Community Market MARKET $
(www.ecosociety.ca; 199 Carbonate St, Cottonwood Falls Park; 9:30am-3pm Sat mid-May–Oct) Close to downtown and next to the surging Cottonwood waterfall, this market encapsulates Nelson. There's great organic produce; fine baked goods, many with heretofore-unheard-of grains; and various craft items with artistic roots in tie-dyeing. A second event, the Downtown Market, is less colorful.

Full Circle Cafe DINER $
(☎250-354-4458; 402 Baker S; mains $8-15; ⏲6:30am-2:30pm) A downtown diner beloved for its omelettes, the Full Circle will have you doing just that as you return for skillfully made breakfast classics, such as eggs Benedict. It gets popular on weekends, so prepare for a wait.

Downtown Market MARKET $
(400 block Baker St; ⏲9:30am-3pm Wed mid-Jun–Sep) Nelson's mid-week market.

Cantina del Centro MEXICAN $$
(☎250-352-3737; 561 Baker St; small plates $6-10; ⏲11am-late) Bright and vibrant, Cantina del Centro gets jammed with diners. The tacos and other small plates reflect the vivid colors of the Mexican tile floor. You can watch your meal being grilled behind the counter while you chill with a margarita. Opt for the buzz of an outdoor table.

Bibo FUSION $$
(☎250-352-2744; www.bibonelson.ca; 518 Hall St; mains $18-30; ⏲5pm-late) Bibo is all about exposed brick inside, while outside tables on the hillside terrace overlook the lake and mountains beyond. Small plates celebrate local produce: enjoy tapas or a cheese and charcuterie plate accompanied by flights of wine. The short list of upscale mains includes burgers and seafood.

★**All Seasons Cafe** FUSION $$$
(☎250-352-0101; www.allseasonscafe.com; 620 Herridge Lane; mains $23-36; ⏲5-10pm) Sitting on the patio here beneath little lights twinkling in the huge maple above you is a Nelson highlight; in winter, candles inside provide the same romantic flair. The eclectic menu changes with the seasons but always celebrates BC foods. Presentations are artful; service is gracious.

Royal BAR
(☎250-354-7014; www.royalgrillnelson.com; 330 Baker St; ⏲5pm-2am Tue-Sat) This gritty old pub on Baker gets some of the region's best music acts. It has a whole section of tables outside on the street and serves decent pub food.

Oso Negro CAFE
(☎250-532-7761; www.osonegrocoffee.com; 604 Ward St; coffee from $2; ⏲7am-5pm; 📶) This local favorite corner cafe roasts its own coffee in 20 blends. Outside there are tables in a garden that burbles with water features amid statues. Enjoy baked goods and other snacks.

Shopping

★**Still Eagle** HOMEWARES
(☎250-352-3844; www.stilleagle.com; 476 Baker St; ⏲10am-8pm Mon-Sat, 11am-7pm Sun) Fair-trade and Kootenay-produced clothing, kitchen goods and products for the home are sold in this large store, which has a deep environmental commitment. Many products are made from recycled materials.

Otter Books BOOKS
(☎250-352-7525; 398 Baker St; ⏲9:30am-5:30pm Mon-Sat, 11am-4pm Sun) A good local indie with books and maps.

Information

The **visitor center** (☎250-352-3433; www.discovernelson.com; 91 Baker St; ⏲8:30am-6pm daily May-Oct, to 5pm Mon-Fri Nov-Apr) is housed in the beautifully restored train station. It offers excellent brochures detailing driving and walking tours.

Listen to the Nelson beat on **Kootenay Co-Op Radio** (93.5FM).

Getting There & Away

Castlegar Airport (www.wkrairport.ca; Hwy 3A) The closest airport to Nelson is 42km southwest.

Greyhound Canada (☎250-352-3939; 1128 Lakeside Dr, Chahko-Mika Mall) Buses serve Fernie ($69, 4¾ hours, one daily) and Kelowna ($62, 5¼ hours, one daily).

Queen City Shuttle (☎250-352-9829; www.kootenayshuttle.com; one-way adult/child $25/10) Links with Castlegar Airport (one hour); reserve in advance.

West Kootenay Transit System (☎855-993-3100; www.bctransit.com; fares $2) Buses 2 and 10 serve Chahko-Mika Mall and Lakeside Park. The main stop is at the corner of Ward and Baker Sts.

Nelson to Revelstoke

Heading north from Nelson to Revelstoke, there are two options, both scenic. Hwy 6 heads west for 16km before turning north at **South Slocan**. The road eventually runs alongside pretty Slocan Lake for about 30km before reaching New Denver, 97km from Nelson.

Going north and east from Nelson on Hwy 3A is the most interesting route. Head 34km northeast to Balfour, where the free **Kootenay Lake Ferry** (☎250-229-4215; www2.gov.bc.ca/gov/content/transportation/passenger-travel) connects to Kootenay Bay (35 minutes). The ferry's a worthwhile side trip for its long lake vistas of blue mountains rising sharply from the water. From Kootenay Bay, Hwy 3A heads 80km south to Creston. Continuing north from the ferry at Balfour, the road becomes Hwy 31 and follows the lake 34km to Kaslo, passing cute towns along the way. From Kaslo to New Denver is spectacular. North of there you pass the village of Nakusp and another ferry before reaching Revelstoke. This is a great all-day trip.

Kaslo

A cute little town, Kaslo is an underrated gem with a beautiful lakeside setting.

Don't miss the restored 1898 lake steamer **SS Moyie** (☎250-353-2525; http://klhs.bc.ca; 324 Front St; adult/child $10/4; ⏰10am-5pm mid-May–mid-Oct). It also has tourist info on the myriad ways to kayak and canoe the sparkling-blue waters.

There's a range of acommodations in and around town, including the appealing downtown **Kaslo Hotel** (☎250-353-7714; www.kaslohotel.com; 430 Front St; r $150-220; ❄📶), a veteran hotel (1896) which has lake views and a good pub. Rooms have balconies and porches.

New Denver

Wild mountain streams are just some of the spectacular highlights on Hwy 31A, which goes up and over some rugged hills west of Kaslo. At the end of this twisting 47km road, you reach New Denver, which seems about five years away from ghost-town status. But that's not necessarily bad, as this historic little gem slumbers away peacefully right on the clear waters of Slocan Lake. The equally sleepy old mining town of **Silverton** is just south.

Housed in the 1897 Bank of Montreal building, the **Silvery Slocan Museum** (☎250-358-2201; www.newdenver.ca; 202 6th Ave; adult/child $5/free; ⏰9am-4pm Jun-Aug) features well-done displays from the booming mining days, a tiny vault and an untouched tin ceiling. It also has visitor info.

Nakusp

Situated right on Upper Arrow Lake, Nakusp was forever changed by BC's orgy of dam building in the 1950s and 1960s. The water level here was raised and the town was relocated to its current spot, which is why it has a 1960s-era look. It has some attractive cafes and a tiny museum.

The **Nakusp Hot Springs** (☎250-265-4528; www.nakusphotsprings.com; 8500 Hot Springs Rd; adult/child $10/9; ⏰9:30am-9:30pm), 12km northeast of Nakusp off Hwy 23, feel a bit artificial after receiving a revamp. However, you'll forget this as you soak away your cares amid an amphitheater of trees.

CARIBOO, CHILCOTIN & THE COAST

This vast and beautiful region covers a huge swath of BC north of Whistler. It comprises three very distinct areas. The Cariboo region includes numerous ranches, and terrain that's little changed from the 1850s, when the 'Gold Rush Trail' passed through from Lillooet to Barkerville.

Populated with more moose than people, the Chilcotin lies to the west of Hwy 97, the region's north–south spine. Its mostly wild, rolling landscape has a few ranches and some Aboriginal villages. Traveling west along Hwy 20 from Williams Lake leads you to the Bella Coola Valley, a spectacular bear-and-wildlife-filled inlet along the coast.

Much of the region can be reached via Hwy 97, enabling you to build a circle itinerary to other parts of BC via Prince George in the north. The Bella Coola Valley is served by ferry from Port Hardy on Vancouver Island, which makes for even cooler circle-routes.

ℹ Getting There & Away

Hwy 97 forms the spine of the region; it's a good-quality road that continues to be improved. A twice-daily **Greyhound Canada** (p722) service runs along Hwy 97; Cache Creek to Prince George takes six hours.

Williams Lake to Prince George

Cattle and lumber have shaped **Williams Lake**, the hub for the region. Some 206km north of the junction of Hwys 1 and 97, this small town has a pair of **museums**.

In the tiny town center, sprightly **New World Café** (☎778-412-5282; www.newworld-coffee.ca; 72 Oliver St, Wiliams Lake; mains $7-15; ⏰8am-5pm Mon-Wed, to 8pm Thu-Sat) has a bakery and excellent coffee. Get a sandwich to go, or eat in to enjoy the menu of soups, salads, hot specials and more.

Quesnel, 124km north of Williams Lake on Hwy 97, is all about logging. From Quesnel, Hwy 26 leads east to the area's main attractions, **Barkerville Historic Park** and **Bowron Lake Provincial Park**. North of Quesnel it's 116km on Hwy 97 to Prince George.

Information

Williams Lake has a superb **visitor center** (250-392-5025; www.williamslake.ca; 1660 Broadway S, off Hwy 97; 9am-5pm) in a huge log building. It has full regional info and gives the lowdown for trips west to the coast on Hwy 20.

Barkerville & Around

In 1862 Billy Barker, previously of Cornwall, struck gold deep in the Cariboo. **Barkerville** soon sprung up, populated by the usual fly-by-night crowds of prostitutes, tricksters and just plain prospectors. Today it's a compelling attraction, a time capsule of the Old West.

You can visit more than 125 restored heritage buildings in **Barkerville Historic Town** (888-994-3332; www.barkerville.ca; Hwy 26; adult/child $14.50/4.75; reception 8am-8pm mid-Jun–Aug, 8:30am-4pm mid-May–mid-Jun & Sep), which also has shops, cafes and a couple of B&Bs. In summer, people dressed in period garb roam through town and, if you can tune out the crowds, it feels more authentic than forced. At other times of the year, you can wander the town for free, but don't expect to find much open.

Barkerville lies 82km east of Quesnel along Hwy 26. Historic **Cottonwood House**, a park-like area, makes an atmospheric stop on the way. Nearby **Wells** is an offbeat town.

Information

The **visitor center** (250-994-2323, 877-451-9355; www.wellsbc.com; 4120 Pooley St; 9am-5pm May-Sep) has regional info and a small museum.

Bowron Lake

The place heaven-bound canoeists go when they die, **Bowron Lake Provincial Park** (778-373-6107; www.bowronlakecanoe.com; off Hwy 26; May-Sep; P) is a fantasyland of 10 lakes surrounded by snowcapped peaks.

Forming a natural circle with sections of the Isaac, Cariboo and Bowron Rivers, Bowron Lake Provincial Park's 116km **canoe circuit** (permits $30 to $60) is one of the world's finest. There are eight portages, with the longest (2km) over well-defined trails. The park website has maps, and details everything you'll need to know for planning your trip, including mandatory reservations, which sometimes book up in advance. Campsites cost $18. You can rent, canoes, kayaks and carriers at the park.

The whole canoe circuit takes between six and 10 days, and you'll need to be completely self-sufficient. September is a good time to visit, both for the bold colors of changing leaves and the lack of summertime crowds.

Whitegold Adventures (866-994-2345; www.whitegold.ca; Hwy 26, Wells; 8-day canoe circuit from $1620) offers four- to eight-day guided paddles of Bowron Lake. There is also a one-day paddle trip ($120).

For accommodations, **Bowron Lake Lodge** (800-519-3399, 250-992-2733; www.bowronlakelodge.com; Bowron Lake; campsites $35, r from $100; May-Sep) is picture-perfect and right on the lake. It has simple cabins and motel rooms, and rents canoes, kayaks and gear.

Wells Gray Provincial Park

Plunging 141m onto rocks below, **Helmcken Falls** may only be Canada's fourth-highest waterfall but it is one of the undiscovered facets of Wells Gray Provincial Park, itself an under-appreciated gem.

Clearwater, the town near the park entrance, has everything you'll need for a visit.

Sights & Activities

Wells Gray Provincial Park PARK
(250-587-2090; www.bcparks.ca; Wells Gray Rd) BC's fourth-largest park is bounded by the Clearwater River and its tributaries, which define the park's boundaries. Highlights for visitors include five major lakes, two large river systems, scores of waterfalls such as **Helmcken Falls** and most every kind of BC land-based wildlife. Many hiking trails and sights, such as Helmcken Falls, are accessible off the main park road, which ends at **Clearwater Lake**.

You'll find opportunities for **hiking**, **cross-country skiing** and **horseback riding** along more than 20 trails of varying lengths. Rustic backcountry campgrounds dot the area around four of the lakes.

Clearwater Lake Tours WATERSPORTS
(☎250-674-2121; www.clearwaterlaketours.com; canoe/kayak rental per day from $55) Rents canoes and kayaks, and also leads tours of the park.

Sleeping

In addition to camping in the park, you'll find all manner of holiday accommodations outside the park around Clearwater.

Wells Grey Provincial Park Campgrounds CAMPGROUND $
(☎reservations 800-689-9025; www.discovercamping.ca; Wells Grey Provincial Park; campsites $20-23) There are three vehicle-accessible yet simple campgrounds in the park. Woodsy **Pyramid Campground** is just 5km north of the park's south entrance and is close to Helmcken Falls. There's also plenty of **backcountry camping** ($5).

Dutch Lake Resort LODGE $$
(☎888-884-4424, 250-674-3351; www.dutchlake.com; 361 Ridge Dr, Clearwater; campsites $31-44, cabins $140-210) This family-friendly waterfront resort has cabins and 65 campsites. Rent a canoe and practice for more fun in the park.

Wells Gray Guest Ranch LODGE $$
(☎250-674-2792, 866-467-4346; www.wellsgrayranch.com; Clearwater Valley Rd; campsites from $25, r $175-290) Wells Gray Guest Ranch has cabins and cozy rooms in the main lodge building. It's inside the park, 27km north of Clearwater. There are horse rides and many more activities.

Information

Clearwater's **visitor center** (☎250-674-3334; www.wellsgraypark.info; 416 Eden Rd, off Hwy 5, Clearwater; ⏰9am-6:30pm May-Oct; 📶) is a vital info stop for the park. It books rooms and fun-filled white-water-rafting trips.

Chilcotin & Highway 20

Meandering over the lonely hills west of the Chilcotin, Hwy 20 runs 450km from Williams Lake to the Bella Coola Valley. You'll come across a few aboriginal villages, as well as gravel roads that lead off to the odd provincial park and deserted lake.

Long spoken about by drivers in hushed and concerned tones, Hwy 20 has received steady improvement and is now more than 90% paved. However, the unpaved section remains a doozy: **The Hill** is a 30km stretch of gravel that's 386km west of Williams Lake. It descends 1524m from Heckman's Pass to the valley, which is nearly at sea level, through a series of sharp switchbacks and 11% grades. But by taking your time and using low gear, you'll actually enjoy the stunning views. It's safe for all vehicles – visitors in rented SUVs will be humbled when a local in a Ford beater zips past.

Bella Coola Valley

The verdant Bella Coola Valley is at the heart of Great Bear Rainforest, a lush land of huge stands of trees, surging white water and lots of bears. It's a spiritual place: Nuxalk First Nation artists are active here and, for many creative types from elsewhere, this is literally the end of the road. The valley lies west of the dry expanses of the Chilcotin.

The valley stretches 53km to the shores of the **North Bentinck Arm**, a deep, glacier-fed fjord that runs 40km inland from the Pacific Ocean. The two main towns, **Bella Coola** on the water and **Hagensborg** 15km east, almost seem as one, with most places of interest in or between the two.

Sights & Activities

There's really no limit to activities here. You can hike into the hills and valleys, accessible from roads (consider **Odegaard Falls**) or at points only reachable by boat along the craggy coast.

Walk amid 500-year-old cedars just west of Hagensborg at **Walker Island Park**, on the edge of the wide and rocky Bella Coola River floodplain.

Tweedsmuir Provincial Park PARK
(☎250-398-4414; www.bcparks.ca; off Hwy 20) Spanning the Chilcotin and the east end of the valley, the southern portion of Tweedsmuir Provincial Park is the second-largest provincial park in BC. It's a seemingly barely charted place, perfect for challenging backcountry adventures. Day hikes off Hwy 20 in the valley follow trails into lush and untouched coastal rainforest. Campsites $20.

★**Kynoch Adventures** ADVENTURE, WILDLIFE
(☎250-982-2298; www.bcmountainlodge.com; 1900 Hwy 20, Hagensborg; tours from adult/child $90/45) Specializes in critter-spotting trips down local rivers and wilderness hikes. Highly recommended float trips to spot the valley's renowned **grizzly bear** population run from late August into October ($150 per person).

Sleeping

There are B&Bs and small inns along Hwy 20.

Rip Rap Camp CAMPGROUND $
(☎250-982-2752; www.riprapcamp.com; 1854 Hwy 20, Hagensborg; campsites $20-28, cabins $60-125; ⊙May-Oct; P 📶) A much-lauded campground, Rip Rap has plenty of services and a great viewing deck overlooking the river.

Tallheo Cannery GUESTHOUSE $$
(☎604-992-1424; www.bellacoolacannery.com; campsites $15, r incl transport $125) One of BC's most unusual places to stay is 3km across the inlet from Bella Coola in an old cannery. The adventurous will find that the views (stunning), explorations (it's an entire village with its own beach) and mystery (abandoned detritus of an old cannery) make this a fascinating stay. Transport for campers is $10; tours for day-trippers cost $50.

Bella Coola Mountain Lodge INN $$
(☎250-982-2298; www.bcmountainlodge.com; 1900 Hwy 20, Hagenshorg; r $100-160; P @ 📶) The 14 rooms, many with kitchen facilities, are huge and there's an excellent espresso bar. The owners also run Kynoch Adventures (p758), which offers river tours and wilderness hikes.

Information

The volunteer-run **Bella Coola Valley Tourism visitor center** (☎250-799-5202; www.bellacoola.ca; 442 MacKenzie St, Copper Sun Art Gallery, Bella Coola; ⊙10am-6pm Jun-Sep) has oodles of info and advice, including trail guides. The visitor center in Williams Lake is also a good resource.

The Bella Coola visitor center and your accommodations will point you to guides and gear for skiing, mountain biking, fishing, rafting and much more. Car repair, ATMs, laundry and groceries are available. Most tourist services are closed October to April.

Getting There & Away

BC Ferries (☎888-223-3779; www.bcferries.com) links to Bella Coola. The route to reach Port Hardy or Prince Rupert (adult/child $200/100, car from $400) requires a transfer in Bella Bella, a small Inside Passage town – a major inconvenience. Schedules allow a trip every few days in summer (much less often in winter) and it can take 18 or more hours to reach the final port.

There are no buses along Hwy 20 from Williams Lake, but you can go by charter plane. **Pacific Coastal Airlines** (☎800-663-2872; www.pacificcoastal.com) has daily one-hour flights from Vancouver.

NORTHERN BRITISH COLUMBIA

Northern British Columbia is where you'll truly feel that you've crossed that ethereal border into some place different. Nowhere else are the rich cultures of Canada's Aboriginal people so keenly felt, from the Haida on Haida Gwaii to the Tsimshian on the mainland. Nowhere else does land so exude mystery, whether it's the storm-shrouded coast and islands or the silent majesty of glaciers carving passages through entire mountain ranges. And nowhere else is so alive with fabled fauna, from orcas to moose to grizzlies.

It's also a region of promise. Highways such as the fabled Alaska or the awe-inspiring Stewart-Cassiar encourage adventure, discovery or even a new life. Here, your place next to nature will never be in doubt; you'll revel in your own insignificance.

Prince Rupert

POP 12,700

People are always 'discovering' Prince Rupert, and realising what a find it is. This intriguing city with a gorgeous harbor is not just a transportation hub for ferries heading south to Vancouver Island, west to Haida Gwaii and north to Alaska: it's a destination in its own right. It has two excellent museums, fine restaurants and a culture that draws much from its aboriginal heritage. Yet the city struggles to attract the huge cruise ships plying the Inside Passage.

It may rain 220 days a year, but that doesn't stop the drip-dry locals enjoying activities in the misty mountains and waterways. Originally the dream of Charles Hays, who built the railroad here before going to a watery grave on the *Titanic*, Rupert always seems one step behind a bright future. But its ship may finally have come in, or at least anchored offshore: the city's expanding container port speeds cheap tat from China to the US.

Sights

A short walk from the center, **Cow Bay** is a delightful place for a stroll. The eponymous spotted decor is everywhere, but somehow avoids seeming clichéd. There are shops, cafes and a good view of the waterfront, especially from the cruise ship docks at the Atlin Terminal.

You'll see **totem poles** all around town; two flank the statue of Charlie Hays beside City Hall on 3rd Ave. Also watch around town for more than 30 huge **murals** adorning buildings. Noted artist Jeff King paints history and nature.

★North Pacific Cannery National Historic Site HISTORIC SITE
(☎250-628-3538; www.northpacificcannery.ca; 1889 Skeena Dr; adult/child $12/8; ⏲10am-5pm daily Jul & Aug, Tue-Sun May, Jun & Sep) Explore the history of fishing and canning along the Skeena River. This fascinating all-wood complex was used from 1889 to 1968; exhibits document the miserable conditions of the workers, and tours cover the industrial process or cannery life. Prince Rupert Transit has bus service to the site. Situated about 20km south of Prince Rupert, near the town of Port Edward.

★Museum of Northern BC MUSEUM
(☎250-624-3207; www.museumofnorthernbc.com; 100 1st Ave W; adult/child $6/2; ⏲9am-5pm daily Jun-Aug, Tue-Sat Sep-May) Residing in a building styled after an aboriginal longhouse, this museum is a don't-miss. It shows how local civilizations enjoyed sustainable cultures that lasted for thousands of years – you might say they were ahead of their time. The displays include a wealth of excellent Haida, Gitksan and Tsimshian art and plenty of info on totem poles. The bookshop is excellent.

Activities

Among the many local walks, a good place to start is the **Butze Rapids Trail**, a 4.5km loop beginning 3km south of town. It has interpretive signs.

Further afield, **Khutzeymateen Grizzly Bear Sanctuary** is a natural area home to more than 50 of the giants; it can be visited through **Prince Rupert Adventure Tours** (☎250-627-9166; www.adventuretours.net; 210 Cow Bay Rd, Atlin Terminal; bear tours $225, whale tours $115).

Skeena Kayaking KAYAKING
(☎250-624-1921; www.skeenakayaking.ca; kayak rentals from $50) Offers both kayak rentals and custom tours of the area, which has a seemingly infinite variety of places to put in the water.

Sleeping

Rupert has a range of accommodations, including more than a dozen B&Bs. When all of the three ferries are docked, competition gets fierce, so book ahead.

Black Rooster Guesthouse GUESTHOUSE $
(☎250-627-5337; www.blackrooster.ca; 501 6th Ave W; dm $35, r $65-150; P@📶) This renovated house just 400m up the hill from the center has a patio and a bright common room. Rooms range from spartan singles to large apartments.

Pioneer Hostel HOSTEL $
(☎250-624-2334; www.pioneerhostel.com; 167 3rd Ave E; dm $30-40, r $60-95; P@📶) Located between Cow Bay and downtown, Pioneer Hostel has spotless, compact rooms accented with vibrant colors. There's a small kitchen and barbecue facilities out back.

Prince Rupert RV Campground CAMPGROUND $
(☎250-624-5861; www.princerupertrv.com; 1750 Park Ave; campsites from $21, RV sites $33-48; P📶) Located near the ferry terminal, this somewhat barren campground has 77 sites, hot showers, laundry facilities and a small playground.

★Crest Hotel HOTEL $$
(☎250-624-6771; www.cresthotel.bc.ca; 222 1st Ave W; r $130-300; P📶) Prince Rupert's premier hotel has harbor-view rooms that are worth every penny, right down to the built-in bay-window seats with loaner binoculars. Avoid the smallish rooms overlooking the parking lot. Suites are opulent.

Inn on the Harbour MOTEL $$
(☎250-624-9107; www.innontheharbour.com; 720 1st Ave W; r incl breakfast $110-260; P📶) Sunsets may dazzle you to the point that you don't notice the humdrum exterior at this modern harbor-view motel. The 49 rooms have a plush, contemporary look.

Eagle Bluff B&B B&B $$
(☎250-627-4955; www.eaglebluff.ca; 201 Cow Bay Rd; r $85-155; @📶) In an ideal location on Cow Bay, this pier-side B&B is in a heritage building that has a striking red-and-white paint job. Inside, the seven rooms have harbor views – some quite spectacular; two share bathrooms.

Eating

Cowpuccino's CAFE $
(☎250-627-1395; 25 Cow Bay Rd; coffee $2; ⏲7am-9pm; 📶) This woodsy local cafe will make you forget the rain with its coffee and fine selection of baked goods (great cookies) and sandwiches. Good for picnics or eating in.

★Charley's Lounge PUB FOOD $$
(☎250-624-6771; www.cresthotel.bc.ca; 222 1st Ave W, Crest Hotel; mains $12-25; ⏲noon-10pm) Locals flock to trade gossip while gazing out over the harbor from the heated patio. The food matches the view: the pub menu features some of Rupert's best seafood.

Fukasaku JAPANESE $$
(☎250-627-7874; www.fukasaku.ca; 215 Cow Bay Rd; mains $15-30; ⏲5-8:30pm) This excellent sushi place has a menu crafted with certified sustainability in mind. Enjoy uber-fresh seafood in rolls, sashimi, *donburi* etc. The dining area is properly minimalist.

Smiles Seafood SEAFOOD $$
(☎250-624-3072; www.smilesseafoodcafe.ca; 113 Cow Bay Rd; mains $8-30; ⏲9am-9pm) Since 1934 Smiles has served classic, casual seafood meals. Slide into a vinyl booth and enjoy a shrimp club sandwich or a fresh halibut steak. Also has fine diner-style breakfasts.

Cow Bay Café ITALIAN $$
(☎250-627-1212; www.cowbaycafe.com; 205 Cow Bay Rd; mains $16-25; ⏲11:30am-2pm & 5-9pm Tue-Sat, 1-8pm Sun) This bistro is right in Cow Bay and has wraparound water views. Serves a menu that's heavy on red sauce.

Waterfront Restaurant FUSION $$$
(☎250-624-6771; www.cresthotel.bc.ca; 222 1st Ave W, Crest Hotel; mains $15-40; ⏲6:30am-9pm Mon-Fri, 7am-9pm Sat & Sun) Nab a table with a fantastic waterfront view and dig into delicious, fresh ingredients used with color and flair.

ℹ Information

Prince Rupert Visitor Center (☎250-624-5637; www.visitprincerupert.com; 215 Cow Bay Rd, Atlin Terminal; ⏲9am-5pm) Has regional info. Located next to a display promoting the ever-growing port.

ℹ Getting There & Away

The ferry and train terminals are 3km southwest of the center.

AIR

Prince Rupert Airport (☎250-622-2222; www.ypr.ca) Located on Digby Island, across the harbor from town. The trip involves a bus and ferry; pickup is at the Highliner Hotel (815 1st Ave) about two hours before flight time. Confirm all the details with your airline or the airport.

Air Canada Jazz (☎888-247-2262; www.aircanada.com) Flies to Vancouver.

BOAT

Alaska Marine Highway System (☎250-627-1744, 800-642-0066; www.ferryalaska.com) One or two ferries each week ply the spectacular Inside Passage to the Yukon gateways of Haines and Skagway in Alaska.

BC Ferries (☎250-386-3431; www.bcferries.com) Sails the Inside Passage run to Port Hardy, hailed for its amazing scenery. There are three services per week in summer and one per week in winter on the *Northern Expedition*.

BUS

Greyhound Canada (p722) Buses depart for Prince George ($142, 10½ hours) once a day in summer, less often other times. Check to see if a mooted **BC Transit bus** (www.bctransit.com) is also running on this route.

TRAIN

VIA Rail (p633) Operates tri-weekly services to Prince George (12½ hours) and, after an overnight stop, Jasper in the Rockies. Much of the run is spectacular, especially between Rupert and Smithers.

Haida Gwaii

Haida Gwaii forms a dagger-shaped archipelago of some 450 islands lying 80km west of the BC coast, and offers a magical trip for those who make the effort. The number-one attraction here is remote Gwaii Haanas National Park, which makes up the bottom third of the archipelago. Attention has long focused on the many unique species of flora and fauna to the extent that 'Canada's Galápagos' is a popular moniker. But each year it becomes more apparent that the real soul of the islands is the Haida culture itself.

Haida reverence for the environment is protecting the last stands of superb old-growth rainforests, where the spruce and cedars are some of the world's largest. Amid this sparsely populated, wild and rainy place are bald eagles, bears and much more wildlife. Offshore in marine-protected waters, sea lions, whales and orcas abound, and once-rare right whales and sea otters have been spotted.

👁 Sights

The Haida Gwaii portion of the **Yellowhead Hwy** (Hwy 16) heads 110km north from Queen Charlotte (known as QCC) past Skidegate, Tlell and Port Clements. The last was where a golden spruce tree, famous for its colour, that stood on the banks of the Yakoun River was cut down by a demented forester in 1997. The incident is detailed in the best-selling *The Golden Spruce* by John Vaillant, an excellent book on the islands and Haida culture.

All along the road to **Masset**, look for seaside pullouts, oddball boutiques and cafes that are typical of the islands' character.

★Gwaii Haanas National Park Reserve, National Marine Conservation Area Reserve & Haida Heritage Site NATIONAL PARK
(☎250-559-8818; www.parkscanada.ca/gwaiihaanas; Haida Gwaii) This huge Unesco World Heritage site with a name that's a mouthful encompasses Moresby and 137 smaller islands at its southern end. It combines a time-capsule look at abandoned Haida villages with hot springs, amazing natural beauty and some of the continent's best kayaking.

Access to the park is by boat or plane only. A visit demands a decent amount of advance planning and usually requires several days. From May to September, you must obtain a reservation, unless you're with a tour operator.

Archaeological finds have documented more than 500 ancient Haida sites, including villages and burial caves throughout the islands. The most famous village is **SGang Gwaay** (Ninstints) on Anthony Island, where rows of weathered totem poles stare eerily out to sea. Other major sights include the ancient village of **Skedans**, on Louise Island, and **Hotspring Island**, whose natural hot springs are back on after being disrupted by earthquakes in 2012. The sites are protected by Haida Gwaii caretakers, who live on the islands in summer.

In 2013 the **Gwaii Haanas Legacy Pole** was raised at Windy Bay, the first new pole in the protected area in 130 years.

Contact Parks Canada (p764) with questions. The website has links to the essential annual trip planner. Any visitor not on a guided tour must attend a free orientation at the park office. All visitors must register.

The number of daily reservations is limited: plan well in advance. User fees apply (adult/child $20/10 per day). Fees are waived if you have a Parks Canada Season Excursion Pass. A few much-coveted standby spaces are made available daily: call Parks Canada.

The easiest way to get into the park is with a tour company. Parks Canada can provide you with lists of operators; tours last from one day to two weeks. Many can also set you up with rental kayaks (average per day/week $60/300) and gear for independent travel.

★Haida Heritage Centre at Kay Llnagaay MUSEUM
(☎250-559-7885; www.haidaheritagecentre.com; Hwy 16, Skidegate; adult/child $16/5; ⏲10am-6pm Mon-Wed, to 8pm Thu-Sun Jun-Aug, 10am-5pm Tue-Sat Sep-May) One of the top attractions in the north is this marvelous cultural center. With exhibits on history, wildlife and culture, it would be enough reason to visit the islands just by itself. The rich traditions of the Haida are fully explored in galleries, programs and work areas, where contemporary artists create works such as the totem poles lining the shore. Look for the remarkable model of Skidegate before colonial times.

In summer there are worthwhile free tours of the collection. There are also frequent talks and walks by Parks Canada rangers.

Naikoon Provincial Park PARK
(☎250-626-5115; www.bcparks.ca; off Hwy 16) Much of the island's northeastern side is devoted to the beautiful 726-sq-km Naikoon Provincial Park, which combines sand dunes and low sphagnum bogs, surrounded by stunted and gnarled lodgepole pine, and red and yellow cedar. The starkly beautiful **beaches** on the north coast feature strong winds, pounding surf and flotsam from across the Pacific. They can be reached via the stunning 26km-long Tow Hill Rd, east of Masset.

Dixon Entrance Maritime Museum MUSEUM
(☎250-626-6066; 2182 Collinson Ave; adult/child $3/free; ⏲1-6pm daily Jun-Aug, 2-4pm Sat & Sun Sep-May) Housed in what was once the local hospital, the museum features exhibits on the history of this seafaring community, with displays on shipbuilding, medical pioneers, military history, and nearby clam and crab canneries.

Port Clements Museum MUSEUM
(☎250-557-4576; www.portclementsmuseum.ca; 45 Bayview Dr; adult/child $3/free; ⏲10am-4pm Jun–mid-Sep, 2-4pm Sat & Sun mid-Sep–May) Learn about early logging practices and check out toys and tools from pioneering days. Nearby is the fenced-in cutting of the famous but felled **Golden Spruce**. It's alive but rather shrub-like.

Activities

Away from the park, Haida Gwaii has myriad other natural places to explore on land and sea.

Yakoun Lake HIKING

(☎250-557-6810) Hike 20 minutes through ancient stands of spruce and cedar to pristine **Yakoun Lake**, a large wilderness lake towards the west side of Graham Island. A small beach near the trail is shaded by gnarly Sitka alders. Dare to take a dip in the bracing waters, or just enjoy the sweeping views.

The trailhead is at the end of a rough track off a branch from the main dirt-and-gravel logging road between Queen Charlotte (QCC) and Port Clements – watch for signs for the lake, about 20km north of QCC. It runs for 70km. On weekdays, phone for info on active logging trucks. This is 4WD country.

★**Moresby Explorers** ADVENTURE

(☎800-806-7633, 250-637-2215; www.moresbyexplorers.com; Sandspit; 1-day tours from $215) Offers one-day Zodiac tours, including the Louise Island trip that takes in the town of Skedans and its important totem poles, as well as much longer trips (the four-day trip is highly recommended). Also rents kayaks and gear, and provides logistics.

Archipelago Ventures KAYAKING

(☎250-652-4913, 888-559-8317; www.tourhaidagwaii.com; 6-day tours from $2350) Runs multiday kayak trips that fully explore the Gwaii Haanas National Park Reserve. Guests are housed on the mothership MV *Island Bay*, and emphasis is placed on building a cohesive group, eg chores are shared, etc. Itineraries are flexible and the guides take care to see that guests' desires are met.

Haida Style Expeditions CULTURAL

(☎250-637-1151; www.haidastyle.com; tours $275-375; ⊙May–mid-Sep) Buzz through the Gwaii Haanas National Park Reserve in a large inflatable boat. This Haida-run outfit runs four different one-day tours (eight to 12 hours) that together take in the most important sights in the park.

Sleeping

Small inns and B&Bs are mostly found on Graham Island. There are numerous choices in Queen Charlotte (QCC) and Masset, with many in between and along the spectacular north coast. Naikoon Provincial Park has two campgrounds, including a dramatic, windswept one on deserted Agate Beach, 23km east of Masset.

Agate Beach Campground CAMPGROUND $

(☎250-557-4390; www.env.gov.bc.ca/bcparks; Tow Hill Rd, North Shore, Naikoon Provincial Park; campsites $18; P) This stunning, wind-whipped campground is right on the beach on the north shore. Frolic on the sand, hunt for its namesake rocks and see if you can snare some flotsam.

★**Premier Creek Lodging** INN $$

(☎250-559-8415, 888-322-3388; www.qcislands.net/premier; 3101 3rd Ave, QCC; dm from $30, r $50-160; P Wi-Fi) Dating from 1910, this friendly Queen Charlotte lodge run by Lenore has eight beds in a hostel building out back, and 12 rooms in the main building that range from tiny but great-value singles to spacious rooms with views, kitchens and porches.

THE GREAT BEAR RAINFOREST

It's the last major tract of coastal temperate rainforest left on the planet. The Great Bear Rainforest is a wild region of islands, fjords and towering peaks. Covering 64,000 sq km (7% of British Columbia), it stretches south from Alaska along the BC coast and Haida Gwaii to roughly Campbell River on Vancouver Island (which isn't itself part of the forest). The forests and waters are remarkably rich in life: whales, salmon, eagles, elk, otters and more thrive. Remote river valleys are lined with forests of old Sitka spruce, Pacific silver fir and various cedars that are often 100m tall and 1500 years old.

In 2016, BC's provincial government announced that 85% of the Great Bear Rainforest region would be permanently protected from industrial logging. However, the area is still under threat from a proposed Northern Gateway Pipelines project. For an introduction to the campaign to save the area, head to www.savethegreatbear.org.

From Bella Coola you can arrange boat trips and treks to magical places in the Great Bear, including hidden rivers where you might see a rare **Kermode bear**, a white-furred offshoot of the black bear known in tribal legend as the 'spirit bear' and the namesake of the rainforest.

HAIDA HISTORY

Haida Gwaii, which means 'Islands of the People,' is home to the Haida, one of the most advanced and powerful First Nations. The people suffered terribly after Westerners arrived; however, their culture is resurgent and can be found across the islands in myriad ways beyond their iconic totem poles, and contributes greatly to the protection of the islands' spectacular natural environment.

Haida Gwaii was formerly known as Queen Charlotte Islands, which name was officially dropped as a name in 2010.

North Beach Cabins CABIN **$$**
(250-557-2415; www.northbeachcabins.com; Km 16, Tow Hill Rd, North Shore; cabins $100-175; P) Tucked into the dunes of beautiful North Beach are six cozy escapes. You're totally off the grid, but thanks to propane you can cook, which will be about the only diversion from the fabulous views and endless sandy strolls.

All The Beach You Can Eat CABIN **$$**
(250-626-9091; www.allthebeachyoucaneat.com; Km 15, Tow Hill Rd, North Shore; cabins $100-190; P) On beautiful North Beach, five cabins are perched in the dunes, back from the wide swath of sand that runs for miles east and west. One, the lovely little Sweety Pie, has views that seem to reach to Japan. Similar to other properties with rental cabins out here, there is no electricity; cooking and lighting are fueled by propane. It's off the grid and out of this world.

Copper Beech House B&B **$$**
(250-626-5441; www.copperbeechhouse.com; 1590 Delkatla Rd, Masset; r $100-160; P) This legendary B&B in a rambling old house on Masset Harbor is owned by poet Susan Musgrave. It has five unique rooms, and there's always something amazing cooking in the kitchen.

Eating

The best selection of restaurants is in Queen Charlotte (QCC), and there are also a few in Skidegate and Masset. Ask at the visitor centers about local Haida feasts, where you'll enjoy the best salmon and blueberries you've ever had. Good supermarkets are found in QCC and Masset.

Moon Over Naikoon BAKERY **$**
(250-626-5064; 16443 Tow Hill Rd, Masset; snacks from $3; 8am-5pm Jun-Aug) Embodying the spirit of its location, on a road to the end of everything, this tiny community center-cum-bakery is housed in an old school bus in a clearing about 6km from Masset. The baked goods and coffee are brilliant.

Queen B's CAFE **$**
(250-559-4463; 3201 Wharf St, QCC; mains $3-10; 9am-5pm) This funky place in Queen Charlotte excels at baked goods, which emerge from the oven all day long. There are tables with water views outside, and lots of local art inside.

★**Charters Restaurant** SEAFOOD **$$**
(250-626-3377; 1650 Delkatla Rd, Masset; mains $15-30; 5-9pm Wed-Sun) The numbers are small: six tables, three entrees. But the pleasure is great: simply delicious food, such as seafood fettuccine and fresh local halibut. The changing menu also features burgers, ribs, salads and more. The attention to detail is extraordinary: the greens used to ornament plates are grown under lights in the kitchen. Reserve ahead.

Haida House SEAFOOD **$$**
(855-557-4600; www.haidahouse.com; 2087 Beitush Rd, Tlell; mains $20-30; 5-7:30pm Tue-Sun mid-May–mid-Sep) This Haida-run restaurant has excellent, creative seafood and other dishes with island accents, such as Haida favorites with berries. Also rents plush rooms.

Information

Download, browse online or pick up a free copy of the encyclopedic annual *Haida Gwaii Visitors Guide* (www.gohaidagwaii.ca).

Parks Canada (250-559-8818, reservations 877-559-8818; www.parkscanada.ca/gwaiihaanas; Haida Heritage Centre at Kay Llnagaay, Skidegate; office 8:30am-noon & 1-4:30pm Mon-Fri) Has a lot of information online.

QCC Visitor Centre (250-559-8316; www.queencharlottevisitorcentre.com; 3220 Wharf St, QCC; 9am-8pm Mon-Sat, noon-8pm Sun May-Sep, shorter hours other times) Handy visitor center that can make advance excursion bookings by phone.

Sandspit Airport Visitor Center (250-637-5362; Sandspit Airport; 9:30-11:30am & 1-4pm) Useful visitor center.

Getting There & Away

The main airport for Haida Gwaii is at Sandspit on Moresby Island, 12km east of the ferry landing at Aliford Bay. Note that reaching the airport from Graham Island is time-consuming: eg if your flight is at 3:30pm, you'll need to line up at the car ferry at Skidegate Landing at 12:30pm (earlier in summer). There's also a small airport at Masset.

Air Canada (www.aircanada.com) flies daily between Sandspit and Vancouver.

The **BC Ferries** (250-386-3431; www.bcferries.com) service is the most popular way to reach the islands. Mainland ferries dock at Skidegate Landing on Graham Island, which houses 80% of residents. Services run between Prince Rupert and Skidegate Landing five times a week in summer and three times a week in winter on the *Northern Adventure*. Travel time is six to seven hours; fares cost adults $39 to $48, children half-price, and for cars $139 to $169. Cabins are useful for overnight schedules (from $90).

Getting Around

The main road on Graham Island is Hwy 16, which is fully paved. It links Skidegate with Masset, 101km north, passing the small towns of Tlell and Port Clements. The principal town is Queen Charlotte (previously Queen Charlotte City and still known by its old QCC acronym), 7km west of Skidegate. Off paved Hwy 16, most roads are gravel or worse. There is no public transit.

BC Ferries link Graham and Moresby Islands at Skidegate Landing and Alliford Bay (adult/child $11/5.50, cars from $25, 20 minutes, every two hours from 7am to 10pm). Schedules seem designed to inconvenience air passengers.

Eagle Transit (250-559-4461, 877-747-4461; www.eagletransit.net; airport shuttle adult/child $30/22) buses meet Sandspit flights and serve Skidegate and QCC.

Renting a car can cost roughly the same ($60 to $100 per day) as bringing one over on the ferry. Local companies include **Budget** (250-637-5688; www.budget.com; Sandspit Airport). There are several small, locally owned firms.

You can rent bikes at the small **Sandspit Airport Visitor Center** (p764) for $30 per day and take them across to Graham Island on the ferry.

Prince Rupert to Prince George

You can cover the 725km on Hwy 16 between BC's Princes in a day or a week. There's nothing that's an absolute must-see, but there's much to divert and cause you to pause if so inclined. With the notable exception of Skeena River, the scenery along much of the road won't fill your memory card, but it is a pleasing mix of mountains and rivers.

Prince Rupert to Smithers

For the first 150km out of Prince Rupert, Hwy 16 hugs the wide and wild **Skeena River**. This is four-star scenic driving and you'll see glaciers and jagged peaks across the waters.

Tatty **Terrace** is nobody's idea of a reward at the end of the stretch. From Terrace, Hwy 16 continues 93km east to Kitwanga, where the **Stewart-Cassiar Hwy** (Hwy 37) strikes north towards the Yukon and Alaska.

Just east of Kitwanga is the **Hazelton** area, comprising New Hazelton, Hazelton and South Hazelton. It's the center of some interesting aboriginal sites, including **'Ksan Historical Village & Museum** (250-842-5544; www.ksan.org; off Hwy 16, Hazelton; from $2; 10am-9pm Jun-Aug, shorter hours Sep-Jul). The re-created site of the Gitksan people features longhouses, a museum, various outbuildings and totem poles. The narrated tour ($10) is a must.

Smithers

Smithers is a largish town with a cute old downtown, roughly halfway between Prince Rupert and Prince George. It's the hub of the vibrant Bulkley Valley cultural scene.

Great hiking is found at **Babine Mountains Provincial Park** (250-847-7329; www.bcparks.ca; Old Babine Lake Rd) nearby. It's a 324-sq-km park with trails to glacier-fed lakes and subalpine meadows. Backcountry cabins cost $5 to $10 per person.

You can't beat the location of **Stork Nest Inn** (250-847-3831; www.storknestinn.com; 1485 Main St; r $90-110; P ❄ 📶), right across Hwy 16 from the center. The 23 rooms are large, and a good full breakfast is included. The owners offer great area advice.

All sorts of joy emerges from **Caravan** (778-210-1074; www.facebook.com/caravanhwy16; cnr Main St & Broadway Ave; mains $8-14; 11am-3pm Tue-Sat), an excellent food truck that draws up in a small park in the heart of town. The menu changes daily and uses what's fresh from the many local suppliers. If the steak sandwich with onion rings is on, order it!

Named after the Mountain Pine Beetle, the **Bugwood Bean** (250-877-3505; www.bugwoodbean.com; 2nd & Main Sts; coffee $2; 7:30am-4:30pm; 📶) has homemade baked goods and great organic, fresh-roasted coffee.

Smithers to Prince George

Heading south and then east from Smithers along Hwy 16 for 146km will have you passing through **Burns Lake**, the center of a popular fishing district. Continue another 128km towards **Vanderhoof**, where you can either detour north or carry on along Hwy 16 for 100km toward Prince George. The highway passes through a region filled with dead trees typical of those seen across the north. These dark-grey specimens are victims of mountain pine beetles, whose explosive population growth is linked to comparatively milder winters due to climate change. Note the many sawmills processing the dead trees.

From Vanderhoof, Hwy 27 heads 66km north to **Fort St James National Historic Site** (250-996-7191; www.pc.gc.ca; Kwah Rd; adult/child $8/4; 9am-5pm Jun-Sep). The former Hudson's Bay Company trading post that's on the tranquil southeastern shore of Stuart Lake has been restored to its 1896 glory.

Prince George

POP 72,700

In First Nations times, before outsiders arrived, Prince George was called Lheidli T'Enneh, which means 'people of the confluence,' an appropriate name given that the Nechako and Fraser Rivers converge here. Today the name would be just as fitting, although it's the confluence of highways that matters most. A mill town since 1807, it is a vital BC crossroads, and you're unlikely to visit the north without passing through at least once.

Hwy 97 from the south cuts through the center of town on its way north to Dawson Creek (360km) and the Alaska Hwy. Hwy 16 becomes Victoria St as it runs through town westward to Prince Rupert (724km), and east to Jasper (380km) and Edmonton. The downtown, no beauty-contest winner, is compact and has some good restaurants.

Sights

Prince George Railway & Forestry Museum MUSEUM
(250-563-7351; www.pgrfm.bc.ca; 850 River Rd, Cottonwood Island Nature Park; adult/child $8/5; 10am-5pm daily Jun-Aug, 11am-4pm Tue-Sat Sep-May) This museum honors trains, the beaver and local lore. It's located in **Cottonwood Island Nature Park**, which has sylvan walks alongside the river.

Exploration Place MUSEUM
(250-562-1612; www.theexplorationplace.com; 333 Becott Pl, Fort George Park; adult/child $11/8; 9am-5pm) Southeast of downtown (follow 20th Ave east of Gorse St), Exploration Place has various kid-friendly galleries devoted to science, and natural and cultural history.

Sleeping

Hwy 97 (Central St) makes an arc around the center, where you'll find legions of modest motels.

97 Motor Inn MOTEL $
(250-562-6010; www.97motorinn.ca; 2713 Spruce St; r $70-100; P) This modern motel is located on – yes, you guessed it – Hwy 97, near the junction with Hwy 16. Some of the 19 basic rooms have balconies and kitchens.

Economy Inn MOTEL $
(250-563-7106; www.economyinn.ca; 1915 3rd Ave; r $65-95; P) Close to the center, this simple blue-and-white motel has 30 rooms with fridges, microwaves and a spa bath. Celebrate your savings on accommodation with a Dairy Queen dip cone from across the street.

Bee Lazee Campground CAMPGROUND $
(250-963-7263; www.beelazee.ca; 15910 Hwy 97 S; campsites $25-32; May-Sep; P) About 15km south of town, this RV-centric place features full facilities, including (free) hot showers, fire pits and laundry.

Coast Inn of the North HOTEL $$
(250-563-0121; www.coasthotels.com; 770 Brunswick St; r $100-160; P) One of the nicest stays in a town with few options, the Coast is a high-rise with 153 very comfy rooms, some with balconies. There's an indoor pool, which is handy during the long months of cold temperatures. It's close to the center and its nightlife.

Eating

★**Nancy O's** PUB FOOD $$
(250-562-8066; www.nancyos.ca; 1261 3rd Ave; mains $10-25; 11am-late Mon-Fri, from 10am Sat & Sun) Nancy O's may make you want to spend two nights in Prince George. Locally sourced ingredients are combined to create fabulous food: burgers, veggie specials,

NORTH TO THE YUKON

There are three main ways to go north from BC by vehicle. All are good routes, so you have several ways of creating a circle itinerary to the Yukon, and even Alaska.

Alaska Highway

Proposed for many years but not constructed until WWII, this historic and epic route starts in Dawson Creek (364km northeast of Prince George) and weaves through northeast BC to Watson Lake (944km). It's most convenient for those coming from Edmonton and the east.

Stewart-Cassiar Highway

The Stewart-Cassiar (Hwy 37) runs 700km through wild scenery from the junction with Hwy 16, 240km east of Prince Rupert and 468km west of Prince George. A side trip to the incomparable glaciers around Stewart is essential and easy. This route is convenient for people coming from most areas of BC, Alberta and the western US. It ends at the Alaska Hwy, near Watson Lake, in the Yukon.

Alaska Marine Highway System

We love Alaska's **car ferries** (www.ferryalaska.com) that sail the Inside Passage. Free of frills, they let you simply relax and view one of the world's great shows of marine life while enjoying the same scenery that cruise-ship passengers spend thousands to see. You can take a three-day ride on boats heading from Bellingham (north of Seattle), in Washington, US, to Haines and Skagway in southeast Alaska, on the Yukon border. Or catch ferries in Prince Rupert for service to those same two Alaskan towns. The ferries, especially cabins, fill up fast in summer, so reserve.

a great avocado salad and a truly amazing *steak frites*. The bottled beer selection is fab (Belgian and BC), and there's live music and DJs many nights. The vibe is hipster-comfy.

Cimo MEDITERRANEAN **$$**
(☎250-564-7975; www.cimo.ca; 601 Victoria St; mains $12-30; ⏲11:30am-2pm & 5-9:30pm Mon-Sat) The authentic Mediterranean dishes never disappoint here. Dine or simply enjoy a glass of BC wine in the stylish interior or outside on the patio. Much of the produce comes from Cimo's kitchen garden. Great BC wine list and specials.

Information

Prince George Visitor Center (☎250-562-3700; www.tourismpg.com; 1300 1st Ave, VIA Rail Station; ⏲8am-6pm Jun-Aug, shorter hours other times; 📶) This excellent visitor center can make bookings, such as ferry tickets. Loans out free (!) bikes and fishing rods.

Getting There & Away

Prince George Airport (☎250-963-2400; www.pgairport.ca; 4141 Airport Rd) is off Hwy 97. **Air Canada Jazz** (☎888-247-2262; www.aircanada.com) and **Westjet** (☎888-937-8538; www.westjet.com) serve Vancouver.

Greyhound Canada (☎800-661-8747; www.greyhound.ca; 1566 12th Ave) Bus services may run less than daily in winter. Services include Dawson Creek ($85, six hours), Jasper ($70, 5½ hours), Prince Rupert ($142, 10½ hours) and Vancouver ($93, 11 hours).

VIA Rail (www.viarail.ca; 1300 1st Ave) Trains head west three times a week to Prince Rupert (12½ hours) and east three times a week to Jasper (7½ hours). Through passengers from either direction must overnight in Prince George.

Prince George to Alberta

Look for lots of wildlife as well as some good parks along the 380km stretch of Hwy 16 that links Prince George with Jasper, just over the Alberta border. **McBride** is good for a pause.

About 113km east of Prince George is the site of BC's newest park, **Ancient Forest/ Chun T'oh Whudujut Park** (www.ancientcedar.ca; off Hwy 16). The Ancient Forest Trail leads 1km to some real behemoths of the temperate inland rainforest: old-growth red cedars and hemlocks that reach heights of 60m, are more than 1000 years old and are 16m in circumference. Short trails, including a 500m boardwalk, access the trees.

WORTH A TRIP

STEWART & HYDER

Awesome. Yes, the word is almost an automatic cliché, but when you gaze upon the **Salmon Glacier**, you'll understand why it was coined in the first place. This horizon-spanning expanse of ice is more than enough reason to make the 67km detour off Hwy 37; the turnoff is 158km north of Meziadin Junction. In fact, your first confirmation comes when you encounter the iridescent blue expanse of the **Bear Glacier** looming over Hwy 37A.

The sibling border towns of **Stewart** and **Hyder**, Alaska, perch on the coast at the head of the Portland Canal. Stewart, the much more businesslike of the pair, has excellent places to stay and eat.

Among several campgrounds and motels, Stewart's real star is **Ripley Creek Inn**.

Hyder ekes out an existence as a 'ghost town.' Some 40,000 tourists come through every summer, avoiding any border hassle from US customs officers (because there aren't any), although going back to Stewart you'll pass through beady-eyed Canadian customs. It has muddy streets and two businesses of note: the **Glacier Inn**, a bar you'll enjoy if you ignore the touristy 'get Hyderized' shot-swilling shtick; and the **Seafood Express**.

The enormous, horizon-filling Salmon Glacier is 33km beyond Hyder, up a winding dirt road that's OK for cars when it's dry. Some 3km into the drive, you'll pass the **Fish Creek viewpoint**, an area alive with bears and doomed salmon in late summer.

Northern BC's major mountain attraction abuts Jasper National Park, but on the BC side of the border. Uncrowded **Mt Robson Provincial Park** (Map p608; ☎250-964-2243; www.bcparks.ca; off Hwy 16) has steep glaciers, prolific wildlife and backcountry hiking that is overshadowed by its famous neighbor. Campsites are available ($22 to $28).

Stewart-Cassiar Highway

The 700km Stewart-Cassiar Hwy (Hwy 37) is a viable and ever-more-popular route between BC and the Yukon and Alaska. But it's more than just a means to get from Hwy 16 (via Meziadin Junction) in BC to the Alaska Hwy in the Yukon (7km west of Watson Lake) – it's a window onto one of the largest remaining wild and woolly parts of the province. It's also the road to Stewart (p768), a near-mandatory detour to glaciers, and more.

Gitanyow, a mere 15km north of Hwy 16, has an unparalleled collection of totem poles and you can often see carvers creating another.

Boya Lake Provincial Park (☎250-771-4591; www.bcparks.ca; off Hwy 37), a serene little park less than 90km south of the Yukon border, surrounds Boya Lake, which seems to glow turquoise. You can camp on the shore (campsites $20).

Sleeping & Eating

There's camping along the highway and a motel in Dease Lake. Otherwise stay in Smithers, Stewart or Watson Lake.

Ripley Creek Inn GUESTHOUSE **$$**
(☎250-636-2344; www.ripleycreekinn.com; 306 5th Ave, Stewart; r $60-150; P 📶) The 40 rooms in various heritage buildings are decorated with new and old items; decor varies greatly. There's a huge collection of vintage toasters.

Seafood Express SEAFOOD **$$**
(☎250-636-9011; Hyder, Alaska; mains $12-25; ⏲noon-8pm Jun-Sep) Serves the tastiest seafood ever cooked in a school bus.

Glacier Inn BAR
(☎250-636-9248; International St, Hyder, Alaska; ⏲noon-late) You'll enjoy this grizzled, old bar if you ignore the touristy 'get Hyderized' shot-swilling shtick and settle in with the crusty but affable locals.

Getting There & Away

All major roads linking to the Stewart-Cassiar Hwy are in excellent condition. Except for areas of construction, the highway is sealed and suitable for all vehicles. At any point, you should not be surprised to see bears, moose and other large mammals. Note that the region's untouched status is waning as projects such as the invasive Northwest Transmission Line are carved across the wilderness.

There's never a distance greater than 150km between gas stations. BC provides **road condition reports** (☎800-550-4997; www.drivebc.ca). When it's dry in summer, people drive from Stewart to Whitehorse (1043km) or from Smithers to Watson Lake (854km) in a single day, taking advantage of the long hours of daylight. But this a real haul, so prepare.

Alaska Highway

Even in Prince George you can start to smell the Alaska Hwy. As you travel north along Hwy 97, the mountains and forests give way to gentle rolling hills and farmland. Nearing Dawson Creek (360km), the landscape resembles the prairies of Alberta. There's no need to dawdle.

From **Chetwynd** you can take Hwy 29 along the wide vistas of the Peace River valley north via Hudson's Hope to join the Alaska Hwy north of Fort St John.

Dawson Creek is *the* starting point (Mile 0) for the Alaska Hwy and it capitalizes on this at the **Alaska Highway House** (☎250-782-4714; 10201 10th St, Dawson Creek; by donation; ⏲9am-5pm), an engaging museum in a vintage building overlooking the milepost. The nearby downtown blocks make a good stroll and have free wi-fi, and there's a **walking tour** of the old buildings. The **visitor center** (☎866-645-3022, 250-782-9595; www.tourismdawsoncreek.com; 900 Alaska Ave, Dawson Creek; ⏲8am-5:30pm mid-May–Sep, shorter hours other times; 📶) is housed in the old train station and has lots of Alaska Hwy info. Note that this corner of BC stays on Mountain Standard Time year-round. So in winter, the time is the same as Alberta, one hour later than BC. In summer, the time is the same as Vancouver.

Now begins the big drive. Heading northwest from Dawson Creek, Fort St John is a stop best not made. In fact, the entire 430km to **Fort Nelson** gives little hint of the wonders to come.

Fort Nelson has seen boom and bust in recent years with the fluctuation of oil prices. This is the last place of any size on the Alaska Hwy until Whitehorse in the Yukon – most 'towns' along the route are little more than a gas station and motel or two.

Around 140km west of Fort Nelson, **Stone Mountain Provincial Park** (☎250-427-5452; www.bcparks.ca; off Hwy 97) has hiking trails, with backcountry camping and a campground. The stretches of road often have dense concentrations of wildlife: moose, bears, bison, wolves, elk and much more. From here, the Alaska Hwy rewards whatever effort it took getting this far.

A further 75km brings you to **Muncho Lake Provincial Park** (www.bcparks.ca; off Hwy 97), centered on the emerald-green lake of the same name and boasting spruce forests, vast rolling mountains and some truly breathtaking scenery. There are two campgrounds by the lake, plus a few lodges scattered along the highway.

Finally, **Liard River Hot Springs Provincial Park** (☎250-427-5452; www.bcparks.ca; off Hwy 97; adult/child $5/3) has a steamy ecosystem that allows a whopping 250 species of plants to thrive. After a long day in the car, you'll thrive, too, in the soothing waters. From here it's 220km to Watson Lake and the Yukon.

Yukon Territory

Includes ➡

Best Places to Eat

- ➡ Drunken Goat Taverna (p790)
- ➡ Klondike Kate's (p790)
- ➡ Klondike Rib & Salmon (p777)
- ➡ Antoinette's (p777)

Best Places to Sleep

- ➡ Coast High Country Inn (p776)
- ➡ Robert Service Campground (p776)
- ➡ Bombay Peggy's (p789)
- ➡ Klondike Kate's (p789)
- ➡ Kathleen Lake Campground (p782)

Why Go?

This vast and thinly populated wilderness, where most four-legged species far outnumber humans, has a grandeur and beauty only appreciated by experience. Few places in the world today have been so unchanged over the course of time. Aboriginal people, having eked out survival for thousands of years, hunt and trap as they always have. The Klondike Gold Rush of 1898 was the Yukon's high point of population, yet even its heritage is ephemeral, easily erased by time.

Any visit will mean much time outdoors: Canada's five tallest mountains and the world's largest ice fields below the Arctic are all within Kluane National Park, while canoe expeditions down the Yukon River are epic. And don't forget the people: get set to appreciate the offbeat vibe of Dawson City and the bustle of Whitehorse, and join the growing numbers of people who've discovered the Yukon thanks to TV shows such as *Yukon Gold* and *Dr Oakley: Yukon Vet*.

When to Go

Dawson City

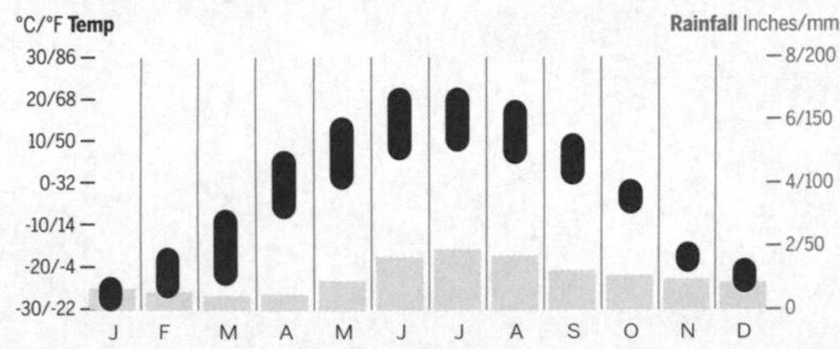

Nov–Apr Days of snowy winter solitude end when the river ice breaks up.

Jun–Aug Summers are short but warm, with long hours of daylight.

Sep You can feel the north winds coming. Trees erupt in color, crowds thin and places close.

Yukon Territory Highlights

1. **Dawson City** (p785) Getting caught up in the modern vibe of Canada's funkiest historic town.
2. **Whitehorse** (p773) Spending an extra day in this surprising city filled with culture.
3. **Klondike Hwy** (p783) Counting moose and bears along this stunning road – they may outnumber cars.
4. **Yukon River** (p775) Living the dream of kayakers and canoeists on this legendary river.
5. **Tombstone Territorial Park** (p785) Losing yourself in this vast park, where the grandeur of the north envelops you.
6. **Kluane National Park** (p781) Finding and naming one of the 100 unnamed glaciers in this untamed Unesco-listed park.
7. **White Pass & Yukon Route** (p778) Sitting back and enjoying the ride on the fabled Gold Rush railroad.

History

There's evidence that humans were eating animals in the Yukon some 15,000 to 30,000 years ago, depending on your carbon-dating method of choice. However, it's widely agreed that these people were descended from those who crossed over from today's Siberia while the land bridge was in place. There's little recorded history otherwise, although it's known that a volcanic eruption in AD 800 covered much of the southern Yukon in ash. Similarities to the Athapaskan people of the southwest United States have suggested that these groups may have left the Yukon after the volcano ruined hunting and fishing.

In the 1840s Robert Campbell, a Hudson's Bay Company explorer, was the first European to travel the district. Fur traders, prospectors, whalers and missionaries all followed. In 1870 the region became part of the Northwest Territories (NWT). But it was in 1896 when the Yukon literally hit the map, after gold was found in a tributary of the Klondike River, near what was to become Dawson City. The ensuing gold rush attracted upward of 40,000 hopefuls from around the world. Towns sprouted overnight to support the numerous wealth-seekers, who were quite unprepared for the ensuing depravities.

In 1898 the Yukon became a separate territory, with Dawson City as its capital. Building the Alaska Hwy (Hwy 1) in 1942 opened up the territory to development. In 1953 Whitehorse became the capital, because it had the railway and the highway. Mining continues to be the main industry, followed by tourism, which accounts for over 330,000 visitors a year.

EXTREME YUKON

Tough conditions spawn tough contests:

Yukon Quest (www.yukonquest.com; ⏲Feb) This legendary 1600km dogsled race goes from Whitehorse to Fairbanks, AK, braving winter darkness and -50°C temperatures. Record time: eight days, 14 hours, 21 minutes, set in 2014.

Yukon River Quest (www.yukonriverquest.com; ⏲late Jun) The world's premier canoe and kayak race, which covers the classic 742km run of the Yukon River from Whitehorse to Dawson City. Record times include team canoe (39 hours, 32 minutes) and solo kayak (42 hours, 49 minutes).

Klondike Trail of '98 Road Relay (www.klondikeroadrelay.com; ⏲early Sep) Some 100 running teams of 10 athletes each complete the overnight course from Skagway to Whitehorse.

Local Culture

The 33,000-plus hardy souls who live in the Yukon Territory take the phrase 'rugged individualist' to heart. It's safe to say that the average Yukoner enjoys the outdoors (in all weather conditions!), relishes eating meats seldom found on menus to the south and has a crack in their truck's windshield (caused by one of the many dodgy roads).

More than 70% of the territory's annual revenue each year comes from the federal government, and it has been used to fund all manner of services at relatively comfortable levels. Whitehorse, for instance, has a range of cultural and recreational facilities that are the envy of southern Canadian communities many times its size. More than 5000 people have government jobs.

Thanks to the Yukon's long isolation before WWII, the 14 First Nations groups have maintained their relationship with the land and their traditional culture, compared to groups forced to assimilate in other parts of Canada. They can be found across the territory and in isolated places such as Old Crow, living lives not fundamentally changed in centuries. It's not uncommon to hear various aboriginal dialects spoken by elders.

Light – or the lack thereof – does play an important role in local life. Many people adjust to the radical variations in daylight through the year, but others do not. Every year you hear of longtime residents and newcomers alike who one day (often in February) announce enough is enough and move south for good.

Parks

The Yukon has a major Unesco World Heritage site in raw and forbidding Kluane National Park, which sits solidly within the Yukon abutting Tatshenshini-Alsek Provincial Park in British Columbia. Glacier Bay and Wrangell-St Elias National Parks are found in adjoining Alaska.

The Yukon has a dozen parks and protected areas (www.yukonparks.ca), but much of the territory itself is parklike and government campgrounds can be found throughout.

Tombstone Territorial Park is remote, yet accessible via the Dempster Hwy, so you can absorb the horizon-sweeping beauty of the tundra and majesty of vast mountain ranges.

Information

There are excellent visitor information centers (VICs) covering every entry point in the Yukon: Beaver Creek, Carcross, Dawson City, Haines Junction, Watson Lake and Whitehorse.

The Yukon government produces enough literature and information to supply a holiday's worth of reading. Among the highlights are *Camping on Yukon Time, Art Adventures on Yukon Time,* the very useful *Yukon Wildlife Viewing Guide* and lavish walking guides to pretty much every town with a population greater than 50. Start your collection at the various visitors centers online (www.travelyukon.com). Another good internet resource is www.yukoninfo.com.

Getting There & Around

Whitehorse is linked by air to Vancouver, Kelowna, Calgary and Edmonton. There are even flights nonstop to Germany during summer. Dawson City has flights to Whitehorse, and to Inuvik in the Northwest Territories.

There are three major ways to reach the Yukon by road: first by ferry to the entry points of Skagway and Haines, AK; by the Alaska Hwy from Dawson Creek, British Columbia (BC); and by the Stewart-Cassiar Hwy from northwest BC that joins the Alaska Hwy near Watson Lake.

You can reach Whitehorse from British Columbia by bus. From there a patchwork of companies provides links to Alaska and Dawson. Rental cars (and Recreational Vehicles) are expensive and only available in Whitehorse. The Alaska Hwy and Klondike Hwy are paved and have services every 100km to 200km.

To check the territory's road conditions, contact **511Yukon** (☎511; www.511yukon.ca).

WHITEHORSE

POP 26,500

The capital city of the Yukon Territory (since 1953, to the continuing regret of much smaller and isolated Dawson City), Whitehorse will likely have a prominent role in your journey. The territory's two great highways, the Alaska and the Klondike, cross here; it's a hub for transportation (it was a terminus for the White Pass & Yukon Route railway from Skagway in the early 1900s, and during WWII was a major center for work on the Alaska Hwy). You'll find all manner of outfitters and services for explorations across the territory.

YUKON TERRITORY FAST FACTS

- Population: 34,300
- Area: 482,443 sq km
- Capital: Whitehorse
- Quirky fact: Home to Robert Service, the poet who immortalized the Yukon through works such as *The Shooting of Dan McGrew* and *The Cremation of Sam McGee*.

Not immediately appealing, Whitehorse rewards the curious. It has a well-funded arts community (with an especially vibrant visual arts community), good restaurants and a range of motels. Exploring the sights within earshot of the rushing Yukon River can easily take a day or more. Look past the bland commercial buildings and you'll see many heritage ones awaiting discovery.

Sights

You can explore Whitehorse's main sights in a day, mostly on foot.

★MacBride Museum MUSEUM
(Map p774; ☎867-667-2709; www.macbridemuseum.com; cnr 1st Ave & Wood St; adult/child $10/5; ⏲9:30am-5pm) The Yukon's attic covers the gold rush, First Nations, intrepid Mounties and much more. Old photos vie with old stuffed critters, and daily demonstrations, such as gold-panning, are good fun. Various buildings colorfully re-create the Yukon's past; don't miss the stuffed albino moose.

★SS Klondike HISTORIC SITE
(Map p774; ☎867-667-4511; www.parkscanada.ca; cnr South Access Rd & 2nd Ave; ⏲9:30am-5pm May-Aug) FREE Carefully restored, this was one of the largest stern-wheelers used on the Yukon River. Built in 1937, it made its final run upriver to Dawson in 1955 and is now a national historic site.

Whitehorse Waterfront AREA
One look at the surging Yukon River and you'll want to spend time strolling its bank. The beautiful **White Pass & Yukon Route Station** (Map p774; 1109 1st Ave) has been restored and anchors an area that's in the midst of a revitalization. **Rotary Peace Park** (Map p774; off 2nd Ave) at the southern end is a great picnic spot, the Kwanlin Dün

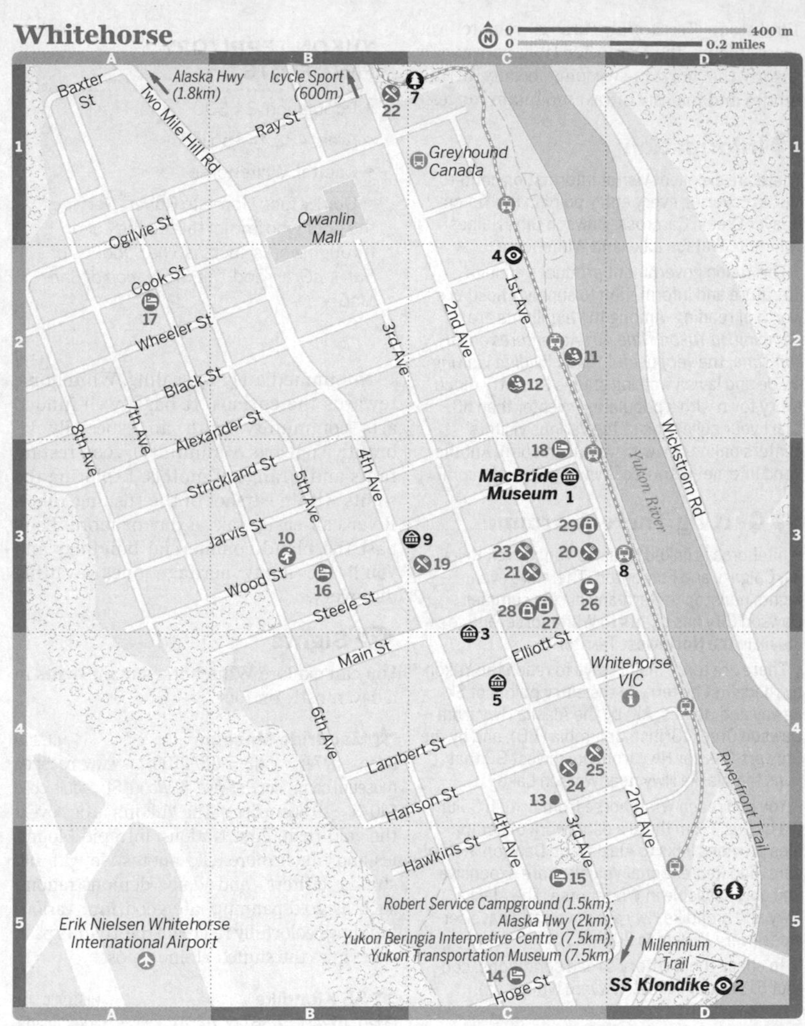

Cultural Centre is a dramatic addition in the middle, and **Shipyards Park** (Map p774; off 2nd Ave) at the northern end has a growing collection of historic structures moved here from other parts of the Yukon.

Linking it all is a cute little **waterfront trolley** (☎867-667-6355; www.yukonrails.com; one-way $3; ⏱10am-6pm Jun-Aug).

Arts Underground GALLERY
(Map p774; ☎867-667-4080; 305 Main St, Hougen Centre lower level; ⏱10am-5pm Tue-Sat) Operated by the Yukon Arts Society. There are carefully selected and well-curated rotating exhibits.

Whitehorse Fishway LANDMARK
(☎867-633-5965; Nisutlin Dr; by donation; ⏱9am-5pm Jun-Aug) Stare down a salmon at the Whitehorse Fishway, a 366m wooden fish ladder (the world's longest) past the hydroelectric plant south of town. Large viewing windows let you see chinook salmon swim past starting in late July (before that it's grayling).

The fishway is easily reached on foot via the Millennium Trail.

Whitehorse

Top Sights
1 MacBride Museum C3
2 SS Klondike D5

Sights
3 Arts Underground C4
4 Kwanlin Dün Cultural Centre C2
5 Old Log Church C4
6 Rotary Peace Park D5
7 Shipyards Park C1
8 White Pass & Yukon Route Station D3
9 Yukon Artists@Work C3

Activities, Courses & Tours
10 Cadence Cycle B3
11 Kanoe People C2
12 Up North Adventures C2
13 Yukon Conservation Society C4

Sleeping
14 Beez Kneez Bakpakers C5
15 Coast High Country Inn C5
16 Historical House B&B B3
17 Midnight Sun Inn A2
18 River View Hotel C3

Eating
19 Antoinette's C3
20 Baked Café & Bakery C3
21 Burnt Toast C3
22 Fireweed Community Market B1
23 Klondike Rib & Salmon C3
24 Sanchez Cantina C4
25 Yukon Meat & Sausage C4

Drinking & Nightlife
26 Dirty Northern Public House C3

Shopping
27 Mac's Fireweed Books C3
28 Midnight Sun Emporium C3
29 North End Gallery C3

Yukon Transportation Museum MUSEUM
(867-668-4792; www.goytm.ca; 30 Electra Cres; adult/child $10/5; 10am-8pm Tue, to 6pm Wed-Mon mid-May–Aug, noon-5pm Sun & Mon Sep–mid-May) Find out what the Alaska Hwy was really like back in the day; let's just say mud was a dirty word. Exhibits cover planes, trains and dogsleds. The museum is near the Beringia Centre. Look for the iconic **DC-3 weather vane** (yes, it spins!) out front.

Yukon Beringia Interpretive Centre MUSEUM
(867-667-8855; www.beringia.com; Km 1473 Alaska Hwy; adult/child $6/4; 9am-6pm) This place focuses on Beringia, a mostly ice-free area that encompassed the Yukon, Alaska and eastern Siberia during the last ice age. Engaging exhibits re-create the era, right down to the actual skeleton of a 3m-long giant ground sloth – although some prefer the giant beaver.

Kwanlin Dün Cultural Centre CULTURAL CENTER
(Map p774; 867-456-5322; www.kwanlindunculturalcentre.com; 1171 1st Ave; by donation; 9am-5pm Mon-Fri, 10am-4pm Sat & Sun) Opened in 2012, the striking Kwanlin Dün Cultural Centre has changing exhibits and a permanent collection of First Nations art.

Yukon Artists@Work GALLERY
(Map p774; 867-393-4848; www.yaaw.com; 4129 4th Ave; 11am-6pm Tue-Sat, to 4pm Sun) Operated by local artists, some of whom may be busily creating when you visit.

Old Log Church HISTORIC BUILDING
(Map p774; 867-668-2555; www.oldlogchurchmuseum.ca; 303 Elliott St; adult/child $6/5; 10am-6pm May-Aug) The only log-cabin-style cathedral in the world is a 1900 downtown gem. Displays include the compelling story of Rev Isaac Stringer, who boiled and ate his boots while lost in the wilderness for 51 days. Fittingly, all that's left is his sole. There are summer guided tours.

Activities

The VIC (p778) can guide you to numerous local hikes and activities year-round. Otherwise, Whitehorse is a major outfitting center for adventures on Yukon waterways.

Canoeing & Kayaking

Whitehorse is the starting place for popular canoeing and kayaking trips to Carmacks or on to Dawson City. It takes an average of eight days to the former and 16 days to the latter. Outfitters offer gear of all kinds (canoes and kayaks are about $40 to $50 per day), guides, tours, lessons and planning services, and can arrange transportation back to Whitehorse. Most paddlers use the map *The Yukon River: Marsh Lake to Dawson City*; available at www.yukonbooks.com.

Kanoe People CANOEING
(Map p774; 867-668-4899; www.kanoepeople.com; cnr 1st Ave & Strickland St; 1-day Yukon River paddle tour $95) At the river's edge. Can

arrange any type of trip including paddles down Teslin and Big Salmon Rivers. Gear, maps and guides for sale, bikes for rent.

Up North Adventures CANOEING
(Map p774; 867-667-7035; www.upnorthadventures.com; 103 Strickland St; 19-day Yukon River canoe trip for beginners $3000; 9am-7pm) Offers guided tours, rentals and transportation on the major rivers. Also paddling lessons, guided mountain-bike trips and winter sports.

Cycling

Whitehorse has scores of bike trails along the Yukon River and into the surrounding hills. The VIC has maps.

Cadence Cycle CYCLING
(Map p774; 867-633-5600; www.cadencecycle.squarespace.com; 508 Wood St; bike/electric bike rental per day from $35/45; 10am-6pm Mon-Sat) Sells and rents good used mountain bikes and does repairs.

Icycle Sport CYCLING
(867-668-7559; www.icyclesport.com; 9002 Quartz Rd; bike rental per day from $45; 10am-6pm Mon-Sat, noon-6pm Sun) Rents top-end mountain bikes, plus skis in winter.

Walking & Hiking

You can walk a scenic 5km loop around Whitehorse's waters that includes a stop at the fishway. From the SS *Klondike* go south on the **Millennium Trail** until you reach the Robert Service Campground and the **Rotary Centennial Footbridge** over the river. The fishway is just south. Head north along the water and cross the Robert Campbell Bridge and you are back in the town center.

Yukon Conservation Society HIKING
(Map p774; 867-668-5678; www.yukonconservation.org; 302 Hawkins St; Tue-Sat Jun-Aug) FREE Discover the natural beauty all around Whitehorse with a free Yukon Conservation Society nature hike. There are various itineraries ranging from easy to hard. Many focus on the drama of Miles Canyon.

Sleeping

Whitehorse can get almost full during the peak of summer, so book ahead. Whitehorse has a lot of midrange motels that earn the sobriquet 'veteran.' Check a room first before you commit.

★**Robert Service Campground** CAMPGROUND $
(867-668-3721; www.robertservicecampground.com; 120 Robert Service Way; tent sites $20; mid-May–Sep;) It's a pretty 15-minute walk from town on the Millennium Trail to the 70 sites at this tents-only campground on the river 1km south of town. Sites have picnic tables and fire pits. The on-site cafe has excellent coffee, baked goods and ice cream.

Hi Country RV Park CAMPGROUND $
(867-667-7445; www.hicountryrv.com; 91374 Alaska Hwy; campsites $22-42; May-Sep; P) At the top of Robert Service Way, this woodsy 130-site campground offers hookups, showers, laundry and a playground.

Beez Kneez Bakpakers HOSTEL $
(Map p774; 867-456-2333; www.bzkneez.com; 408 Hoge St; dm/r $35/70;) Like the home you've left behind, this cheery hostel has a garden, deck, grill and bikes. Two simple cabins are much in demand.

Boréale Ranch GUESTHOUSE $$
(888-488-8489; www.be-yukon.com; Klondike Hwy; r $100-200; P) A lodge with an emphasis on cycling, 30 minutes' drive south of Whitehorse. There are four rooms in the appealingly minimalist main building. Outside there's a hot tub. Guests can use fat-tire bikes for free and there are numerous cycling programs. There are also summer-only yurts and tents with hardwood floors. The food wins plaudits.

Midnight Sun Inn B&B $$
(Map p774; 867-667-2255; www.midnightsunbb.com; 6188 6th Ave; r $115-155; P) A modern B&B in a sort of overgrown suburban-style house with six rooms – some with themes, some sharing bathrooms. The Sun has a loyal following, is downtown, and serves big breakfasts.

★**Coast High Country Inn** HOTEL $$
(Map p774; 800-554-4471; www.highcountryinn.yk.ca; 4051 4th Ave; r $110-220; P) Towering over Whitehorse (four stories!), the High Country is popular with business travelers and groups. The 84 rooms are large – some have huge whirlpools right in the room. The pub is popular.

Historical House B&B B&B $$
(Map p774; 867-668-2526; www.yukongold.com; cnr 5th Ave & Wood St; r $105-130;) A classic wooden home from 1907 with three

guest rooms. Top-floor rooms have individual bathrooms one floor down and angled ceilings. A larger unit has a huge kitchen. Rooms have high-speed internet, and there's a nice garden.

River View Hotel MOTEL $$
(Canada's Best Value Inn; Map p774; ☎888-315-2378; www.riverviewhotel.ca; 102 Wood St; r $100-170; P@☎) The floors sound hollow here, but many of the 53 rooms have the views implied by the name (ask for one) and all are very large. It's close to everything, yet on a quiet street. Plus your car can bunk up almost as well as you: there's heated indoor parking in winter.

Eating & Drinking

Ignore the influx of chain eateries and enjoy one of Whitehorse's excellent downtown restaurants. There's a great range; look for fresh Yukon salmon in season.

Baked Café & Bakery CAFE $
(Map p774; ☎867-633-6291; www.facebook.com/bakedcafewhitehorse; 100 Main St; mains from $6; ⊙7am-7pm; ☎) In summer, the outdoor tables at this buzzing cafe are packed. Smoothies, soups, daily lunch specials, baked goods and more. Don't miss the raspberry pecan scones and take-out sandwiches.

Yukon Meat & Sausage DELI $
(Map p774; ☎867-667-6077; 203 Hanson St; sandwiches from $7; ⊙8:30am-5:30pm Mon-Sat) The smell of smoked meat wafts out to the street and you walk right in; there's a huge selection of prepared items and custom-made sandwiches. Great for picnics, or dine in the simple table area.

★Klondike Rib & Salmon CANADIAN $$
(Map p774; ☎867-667-7554; www.klondikerib.com; 2116 2nd Ave; mains $12-25; ⊙11am-9pm May-Sep) It looks touristy and it seems touristy and it *is* touristy, but the food is excellent at this sprawling casual place with two decks. Besides the namesakes (the salmon kabobs are tops), there are other local faves.

Burnt Toast BISTRO $$
(Map p774; ☎867-393-2605; www.burnttoastcafe.ca; 2112 2nd Ave; mains $8-25; ⊙8am-9pm Mon-Sat, 9:30am-2pm Sun) The food is far better than the coy name suggests! Brunch is excellent at this inviting bistro (try the French toast) and lunch and dinner specials abound. Food is local and seasonal; consult the blackboard. Good salads, sandwiches and Yukon meats.

Sanchez Cantina MEXICAN $$
(Map p774; ☎867-668-5858; 211 Hanson St; mains $14-25; ⊙11:30am-3pm & 5-9:30pm Mon-Sat) You have to head south across two borders to find Mexican this authentic. Burritos are the thing – get them with the spicy mix of red and green sauces. Settle in for what may be a wait on the broad patio.

★Antoinette's FUSION $$$
(Map p774; ☎867-668-3505; www.antoinettesfoodcache.ca; 4121 4th Ave; dinner mains $20-35; ⊙11am-2pm & 4:30-9pm Mon-Fri, 4:30-9pm Sat) Antoinette Oliphant runs one of the most creative kitchens in the Yukon. Her eponymous restaurant has an ever-changing, locally sourced menu. Many dishes have a Caribbean flair. There is often live bluesy, loungey music on weekends.

Fireweed Community Market MARKET
(Map p774; www.fireweedmarket.ca; Shipyards Park; ⊙3-8pm Thu mid-May–early Sep) The Fireweed Community Market draws vendors from the region; the berries are fabulous. There is a second, smaller market midday summer Saturdays near the White Pass & Yukon Route Station on the river.

★Dirty Northern Public House PUB
(Map p774; ☎867-633-3305; www.facebook.com/dirtynorthernpublichouse; 103 Main St; ⊙3pm-late) There are hints of style at this upscale pub, which has a great draft-beer selection and makes excellent mixed drinks. Grab a booth and chase the booze with a wood-fired pizza. Top local acts perform many nights.

Shopping

★Mac's Fireweed Books BOOKS
(Map p774; ☎867-668-2434; www.macsbooks.ca; 203 Main St; ⊙8am-8pm Mon-Sat, to 6pm Sun) Mac's has an unrivaled selection of Yukon titles. It also stocks topographical maps, road maps and periodicals.

North End Gallery ARTS & CRAFTS
(Map p774; ☎867-393-3590; www.yukonart.ca; 1116 1st Ave; ⊙9am-7pm Mon-Sat, to 5pm Sun) High-end Canadian art featuring top Yukon artists.

Midnight Sun Emporium ARTS & CRAFTS
(Map p774; ☎867-668-4350; www.midnightsunemporium.com; 205c Main St; ⊙9am-7pm Mon-Sat) Has a good selection of Yukon arts, crafts and products.

Information

Among local newspapers, the *Yukon News* (www.yukon-news.com) is feisty.

VIC (Map p774; ☎867-667-3084; www.travelyukon.com; 100 Hanson St; ⊙8am-8pm) An essential stop with vast amounts of territory-wide information.

Whitehorse General Hospital (☎867-393-8700; www.yukonhospitals.ca; 5 Hospital Rd; ⊙24hr) The top hospital in the territory.

Getting There & Away

AIR

Erik Nielsen Whitehorse International Airport (YXY; Map p774; ☎867-667-8440; www.gov.yk.ca/yxy; off Alaska Hwy;) is five minutes west of downtown. Air Canada and Westjet serve Vancouver. Locally owned Air North (www.flyairnorth.com) serves Dawson City (with flights on to Inuvik, NWT, and Old Crow), plus Vancouver, Kelowna, Edmonton and Calgary. Condor (www.condor.com) has weekly summer flights to/from Frankfurt.

BUS

Check the latest bus service information with the VIC.

Alaska/Yukon Trails (☎907-479-2277; www.alaskashuttle.com) Serves Fairbanks, AK (US$385, thrice weekly June to mid-September), via Dawson City.

Greyhound Canada (Map p774; ☎867-667-2223; www.greyhound.ca; 2191 2nd Ave) Runs south along the Alaska Hwy to Dawson Creek ($285, 20 hours, thrice weekly); connects with buses for the rest of BC and Canada.

Husky Bus (☎867-993-3821; www.huskybus.ca) Serves Dawson City ($110, thrice weekly) and makes all stops along the Klondike Hwy. Departures are from the VIC. It will do pickups of paddlers and canoes along the Klondike Hwy with advance arrangement.

White Pass & Yukon Route (☎867-633-5710; www.wpyr.com; 1109 1st Ave; adult/child one-way $130/65; ⊙ticket office 9am-5pm Mon-Sat mid-May–mid-Sep) Offers a jaw-droppingly scenic daily 10-hour rail and bus connection to/from Skagway, AK, via Fraser, BC in season. On some days the bus meets the train in Carcross, which maximizes the beautiful train ride (this is the preferred option).

Getting Around

TO/FROM THE AIRPORT

A **Yellow Cab** (☎867-668-4811) taxi to the center (10 minutes) will cost around $22.

BUS

Whitehorse Transit System (☎867-668-7433; $2.50; ⊙Mon-Sat) runs through the center. Route 3 serves the airport, Route 5 passes the Robert Service Campground.

CAR & RECREATIONAL VEHICLE

Check your rental rate very carefully as it's common for a mileage charge to be added after the first 100km, which will not get you far in the Yukon. Also understand your insurance coverage and ask whether damage from Yukon's rugged roads is included.

Budget (☎867-667-6200; www.budget.com; Erik Nielsen Whitehorse International Airport)

Fraserway RV Rentals (☎867-668-3438; www.fraserwayrvrentals.com; 9039 Quartz Rd) Rents all shapes and sizes of RV from $200 per day depending on size (it matters) and season. Mileage extra; rates can quickly add up.

Whitehorse Subaru (☎867-393-6550; www.whitehorsesubaru.com; 17 Chilkoot Way) Has good rates; most cars have manual transmissions.

ALASKA HIGHWAY

It may be called the Alaska Hwy, but given that its longest stretch (958km) is in the Yukon, perhaps another name is in order...

Roughly 2450km in length from Dawson Creek, BC, to Delta Junction, far inside Alaska, the Alaska Hwy has a meaning well beyond just a road; it's also a badge, an honor, an accomplishment. Even though today it's a modern thoroughfare, the very name still evokes images of big adventure and getting away from it all.

As you drive the Alaska Hwy in the Yukon, you're on the most scenic and varied part of the road. From little villages to the city of Whitehorse, from meandering rivers to the upthrust drama of the St Elias Mountains, the scenery will overwhelm you.

British Columbia to Whitehorse

You'll never be far from an excuse to stop on this stretch of the highway. Towns, small parks and various roadside attractions appear at regular intervals. None are a massive draw, but overall it's a pretty drive made compelling by the locale.

Watson Lake

Originally named after Frank Watson, a British trapper, Watson Lake is the first town in the Yukon on the Alaska Hwy and is just over the border from British Columbia (BC). It's mostly just a good rest stop, except for the superb **VIC** (☎867-536-7469; www.travelyukon.com; off Alaska Hwy; ⏰8am-8pm May-Sep), which has a good museum about the highway and a passel of territory-wide info.

The town is famous for its **Sign Post Forest** just outside the VIC. The first signpost, 'Danville, Illinois,' was nailed up in 1942. Others were added and now there are 72,000 signs, many purloined late at night from municipalities worldwide.

Some 136km west on the Alaska Hwy, past the 1112 Km marker, look for the **Rancheria Falls Recreation Site**. A boardwalk leads to powerful twin waterfalls. It's an excellent stop.

For accommodations, the **Air Force Lodge** (☎867-536-2890; www.airforcelodge.com; off Alaska Hwy; s/d $85/95; P 📶) has spotless rooms with shared bathrooms in a historic 1942 barracks for pilots. Just west of the junction with the Stewart-Cassiar Hwy (Hwy 37), family-run **Nugget City** (☎867-536-2307; www.nuggetcity.com; Alaska Hwy; campsites from $25, r $65-130; P 📶) has accommodations and food that are three cuts above the Alaska Hwy norm. Stop just for the baked goods, especially the berry pie. Choose from a variety of cabins and suites.

Teslin

Teslin, on the long, narrow lake of the same name, is 260km west of Watson Lake. It's long been a home to the Tlingits (lin-*kits*), and the Alaska Hwy brought both prosperity and rapid change to this aboriginal population.

This engrossing **George Johnston Museum** (☎867-390-2550; www.gjmuseum.yk.net; Alaska Hwy; adult/child $5/2.50; ⏰9am-6pm May-Aug) details the life and culture of a 20th-century Tlingits leader through photographs, displays and artifacts.

Johnson's Crossing

Some 50km northwest of Teslin is Johnson's Crossing, at the junction of the Alaska Hwy and Canol Rd (Hwy 6). During WWII the US army built the Canol pipeline at tremendous human and financial expense to pump oil from Norman Wells in the NWT to Whitehorse. It was abandoned after countless hundreds of millions of dollars (in 1943 money, no less) were spent.

The Teslin River Bridge offers sweeping views.

WORTH A TRIP

ROBERT CAMPBELL HIGHWAY

To get right off the beaten path, consider this lonely gravel road (Hwy 4), which runs 585km from Watson Lake north and west to Carmacks, where you can join the Klondike Hwy (Hwy 2) for Dawson City. Along its length, the highway parallels various rivers and lakes. Wilderness campers will be thrilled.

Around 360km from Watson Lake, at the junction with Canol Rd (Hwy 6) is **Ross River**, home to the Kaska First Nation and a supply center for the local mining industry. There are campgrounds and motels in town.

Whitehorse to Alaska

For long segments west of Whitehorse, the Alaska Hwy has been modernized to the point of blandness. Fortunately, this ends abruptly in Haines Junction. From here the road parallels legendary Kluane National Park and the St Elias Mountains. The 300km to Beaver Creek is the most scenic part of the entire highway.

Haines Junction

It's goodbye flatlands when you reach Haines Junction and see the sweep of imposing peaks looming over town. You've reached the stunning Kluane National Park and this is the gateway. The town makes an excellent base for exploring the park or for staging a serious four-star mountaineering, backcountry or river adventure.

The magnificent Haines Hwy heads south from here to Alaska. The four-hour drive to Haines, traversing raw alpine splendor, is one of the north's most beautiful.

Oh, and that thing that looks like an acid-trip cupcake at the main junction? It's a **sculpture** that's meant to be a winsome tableau of local characters and critters.

SPRUCE BEETLES

Even as beetles wreak havoc on forests across British Columbia and the Rockies, the forests of the Yukon are recovering. The millions upon millions of trees killed by the spruce beetle since 1994 have shed their brown needles and are now a ghostly gray. Meanwhile, fast-growing opportunists are adding a bright green hue to the tableaux.

Many reasons for the tree deaths center on climate change, including warmer winters, allowing far more beetles than usual to survive from one year to the next. In recent years, however, several factors have been working against the beetles: dead trees mean less food, a very cold winter killed many beetles and there is now a population explosion of beetle-eaters. Meanwhile, nature has opened the door to other trees, including birch and alder, which grow relatively quickly.

To get a sense of the devastation caused by beetles in the last two decades stop at the short **Spruce Beetle Loop**, 17km northwest of Haines Junction, just off the highway. It has interpretive signs.

Sights & Activities

Although Kluane National Park will most likely be your focus, there are some good activities locally. For a hike after hours of driving, there's a pretty 5.5km **nature walk** along Dezadeash River where Hwy 3 crosses it at the southern end of town.

Da Kų Cultural Centre CULTURAL CENTER
(☎867-634-4200; www.cafn.ca/da-ku-cultural-centre; 280 Alaska Hwy; ⏱8:30am-6pm mid-May–Aug) FREE This large and impressive facility has a variety of exhibit areas that showcase the culture and history of the Champagne and Aishihik people. It has a picnic area.

★**Kluane Glacier Air Tours** SCENIC FLIGHTS
(☎867-634-2916; www.kluaneglacierairtours.com; off Alaska Hwy, Haines Junction Airport; tours from $250) Kluane Glacier Air Tours offers flight-seeing of Kluane and its glaciers that will leave you limp with amazement. Options begin with a one-hour tour. There are several other air-tour outfits at the airport.

Tatshenshini Expediting RAFTING
(☎867-393-3661; www.tatshenshiniyukon.com; rafting trip from $135, kayak rental per day $35; ⏱May-Sep) Tatshenshini Expediting leads white-water rafting trips on the nearby Tatshenshini River, which has rapids from grade II to grade IV. Trips leave from Haines Junction and Whitehorse. It also arranges custom river trips and rents gear.

Sleeping & Eating

There's a cluster of motels and RV parks in Haines Junction. There's a beach and shade at Pine Lake, a territorial campground 6km east of town on the Alaska Hwy.

Wanderer's Inn HOSTEL $
(☎867-634-5321; www.wanderersinn.ca; 191 Backe St; campsite/dm/r $25/40/90; ⏱May-Sep, by reservation Oct-Apr; P 📶) This modern house is right in the center of town amid a grove of trees. It has a kitchen and a common deck.

Alcan Motor Inn MOTEL $$
(☎867-634-2371; www.alcanmotorinn.com; cnr Alaska & Haines Hwys; r $110-180; P ❄ 📶) The modern two-story Alcan has 23 large rooms with great views of the jagged Auriol Range; some rooms have full kitchens. The on-site Northern Lights cafe has hearty fare.

★**Village Bakery & Deli** BAKERY $
(☎867-634-2867; cnr Kluane & Logan Sts; mains $6-12; ⏱7am-7pm May-Sep; 📶) The bakery here turns out excellent goods all day, while the deli counter has tasty sandwiches you can enjoy on the large deck. On Friday night there's a popular barbecue with live folk music. It has milk and other very basic groceries.

Frosty's Freeze BURGERS $
(☎867-634-7070; Alaska Hwy; mains $7-11; ⏱11am-9pm May-Sep) What looks like a humdrum fast-food joint is several orders of magnitude better. The shakes are made with real ice cream, the sundaes feature fresh berries, and the burgers (try the mushroom-Swiss number) are huge and juicy.

Information

The **VIC** (☎867-634-2345; www.travelyukon.com; 280 Alaska Hwy, Da Kų Cultural Centre; ⏱8am-8pm May-Sep) has Yukon-wide info.

Parks Canada (☎867-634-7250; www.parkscanada.gc.ca/kluane; 280 Alaska Hwy, Da Kų Cultural Centre; ⌚9am-7pm) has full Kluane details, including hiking info. Both share space in the First Nations' Da Kų Cultural Centre (p780). There are excellent films about the park, as well as engrossing exhibits on the park and aboriginal life.

For local info beyond the VIC, see www.hainesjunctionyukon.com.

Getting There & Away

Haines Junction is a hub of highways: the Haines Hwy (Hwy 3) and the Alaska Hwy (Hwy 1) meet here.

Who What Where Tours (☎867-333-0475; www.whitehorsetours.com) offers the only public service between Whitehorse and Haines Junction (one way $73, twice weekly June to September).

Kluane National Park & Reserve

Unesco-recognized as an 'empire of mountains and ice,' Kluane National Park and Reserve looms south of the Alaska Hwy much of the way to the Alaska border. This rugged and magnificent wilderness covers 22,015 sq km of the southwest corner of the territory. Kluane (kloo-wah-neee) gets its far-too-modest name from the Southern Tutchone word for 'Lake with Many Fish.'

With British Columbia's Tatshenshini-Alsek Provincial Park to the south and Alaska's Wrangell-St Elias National Park to the west, this is one of the largest protected wilderness areas in the world. Deep beyond the mountains you see from the Alaska Hwy are over 100 named glaciers and as many unnamed ones.

Winters are long and harsh. Summers are short, making mid-June to early September the best time to visit. Note that wintery conditions can occur at any time, especially in the backcountry.

Sights

The park consists primarily of the **St Elias Mountains** and the world's largest nonpolar **ice fields**. Two-thirds of the park is glacier interspersed with valleys, glacial lakes, alpine forest, meadows and tundra. The **Kluane Ranges** (averaging a height of 2500m) are seen along the western edge of the Alaska Hwy. A greenbelt wraps around the base of these mountains, where most of the animals and vegetation live. Turquoise **Kluane Lake** is the Yukon's largest. Hidden are the immense ice fields and towering peaks, including **Mt Logan** (5959m), Canada's highest mountain, and **Mt St Elias** (5489m), the second highest. Partial glimpses of the interior peaks can be found at the Km 1622 **viewpoint** on the Alaska Hwy and also around the **Donjek River Bridge**, but the best views are from the air.

In Haines Junction, Kluane Glacier Air Tours (p780) offers highly recommended flight-seeing of Kluane and its glaciers.

Activities

There's excellent hiking in the forested lands at the base of the mountains, along either marked trails or less defined routes. There are about a dozen in each category, some following old mining roads, others traditional aboriginal paths. Detailed trail guides and topographical maps are available at the information centers. Talk to the rangers before setting out. They will help select a hike and can provide updates on areas that may be closed due to bear activity. Overnight hikes require backcountry permits ($10 per person per night).

A good pause during an Alaska Hwy drive is the **Soldier's Summit Trail**, an easy 1km hike up from the Tachal Dhal information center. It has views across the park and plaques commemorating the inauguration of the Alaska Hwy at this point on November 20, 1942. You can listen to the original CBC broadcast of the opening.

The Tachal Dhal information center is also the starting point for **Ä'äy Chù (Slim's West)**, a popular 45km round-trip trek to **Kaskawulsh Glacier** – one of the few that can be reached on foot. This is a difficult route that takes from two to four days to complete and includes sweeping views from Observation Mountain (2114m).

An easy overnight trip is the 15km **Auriol loop**, which goes from spruce forest to subalpine barrens and includes a wilderness campground. It's 7km south of Haines Junction.

> **READING THE YUKON**
>
> A great way to get a feel for the Yukon and its larger-than-life stories is to read some of the vast body of Yukon novels. Start with Jack London – *Call of the Wild* is free online at www.online-literature.com.

Fishing is good and wildlife-watching plentiful. Most noteworthy are the thousands of Dall sheep that can be seen on **Sheep Mountain** in June and September. There's a large and diverse population of grizzly bear, as well as black bears, moose, caribou, goats and 150 varieties of birds, among them eagles and the rare peregrine falcon.

Many park visitors enjoy skiing or snowshoeing, beginning in February.

Sleeping

★Kathleen Lake Campground CAMPGROUND **$**
(www.parkscanada.gc.ca/kluane; off Haines Hwy; campsites $16) Cerulean waters highlight Kathleen Lake, which has a Parks Canada campground and is 24km south of Haines Junction off the highway. The lake is a good stop by day and there are frequent ranger tours and programs in summer.

Information

Parks Canada has two information centers. One is in Haines Junction (p781) and the other is at T**achal Dhal** (Sheep Mountain; Alaska Hwy; 9am-4pm mid-May–Aug), 130km west of Haines Junction, which has excellent resources and views of Sheep Mountain. Rangers have wildlife and hiking info.

At both, get a copy of the park guide, which shows the scope of the park (and how little is actually easily accessible). The map shows hikes ranging from 10 minutes to 10 days.

Destruction Bay

This small village on the shore of huge Kluane Lake is 106km northwest of Haines Junction. It was given its evocative name after a storm tore through the area during construction of the highway during WWII. Most of the residents are First Nations, who live off the land through the year.

Stop in at the local motel, or head 17km east of town on the Alaska Hwy to **Congdon Creek**, which has an 81-site territorial campground and a fine lakeside setting.

Burwash Landing

Burwash Landing boasts a spectacular setting, with Kluane National Park on one side and Kluane Lake on the other. It's a good place to stretch those legs and visit the excellent museum. The town was established by fur traders in 1909.

Commune with an enormous, albeit stuffed, moose at the **Kluane Museum** (867-841-5561; www.kluanemuseum.ca; Alaska Hwy; adult/child $5/3; 9am-6:30pm mid-May–mid-Sep). Enjoy intriguing wildlife exhibits and displays on natural and aboriginal history.

Beaver Creek

Wide-spot-in-the-road Beaver Creek is a beacon for sleepy travelers or those who want to get gas – certainly its lackluster eateries will ensure the latter. The Canadian border checkpoint is just north of town; the US border checkpoint is 27km further west. Both are open 24 hours.

A strange **sculpture garden** just north tempts the silly (or intoxicated) into unnatural acts.

Of the four motels in town, the **1202 Motor Inn** (867-862-7600; www.1202motorinn.ca; 1202 Alaska Hwy; r $90-100; 8am-11pm; P ❄) is the most appealing. The 30 rooms are basic and functional. Get one away from the idling trucks.

The **VIC** (867-862-7321; www.travelyukon.com; Km 1202 Alaska Hwy; 8am-8pm May-Sep) has information on all of the Yukon.

HAINES HIGHWAY

If you're doing only a short loop between Haines and Skagway in Alaska via Whitehorse, this 259km road might be the highlight of your trip. In fact, no matter what length your Yukon adventure, the Haines Hwy (Hwy 3) might be the high point. In a relatively short distance you'll see glaciers, looming snow-clad peaks, lush and wild river valleys, windswept alpine meadows and a river delta dotted with the shadows of bald eagles.

Heading south of Haines Junction, look west for a close-up of the St Elias Mountains, those glaciers glimpsed at the top stretch all the way to the Pacific Ocean. About 80km south, look for the **Tatshenshini River viewpoint**. This white-water river flows through protected bear country and a valley that seems timeless.

About 10km further, you'll come to **Million Dollar Falls**. For once the sight lives up to the billing, as water thunders through a narrow chasm. As you drive, watch for glacier views.

The highway crosses into British Columbia for a mere 70km, but you'll hope for more as you traverse high and barren alpine

YUKON IS MELTING, MELTING...

The Yukon could serve as exhibit one in the case confirming climate change. Every corner of the territory is experiencing rapid changes in the environment because it's getting warmer a lot quicker than anybody ever imagined. In the far north, Herschel Island is literally dissolving as the permafrost thaws. One gruesome sign: long-buried coffins floating to the surface of the melting earth. Unesco has listed it as one of the world's most threatened historic sites.

In Dawson City, locals have for decades bet on the day each spring when the Yukon River suddenly breaks up and begins flowing. Detailed records show that the mean date for this has moved one week earlier in the last century to May 5, with the pace accelerating.

Preparing the Yukon for a radically different and warmer future is now a major political topic, even if nobody yet has the answers.

wilderness, where sudden snow squalls happen year-round. At the 1070m **Chilkat Pass**, an ancient aboriginal route into the Yukon, the road suddenly plunges down for a steep descent into Alaska. The US border is 72km north of Haines, along the wide Chilkat River Delta.

The delta is home to scores of bald eagles year-round; the handsome birds flock like pigeons each fall when they mass in the trees overlooking the rivers, drawn by the comparatively mild weather and steady supply of fish. Pullouts line the Haines Hwy (Hwy 7 in Alaska), especially between mileposts 19 and 26. Take your time driving and find a place to park. Just a few feet from the road it's quiet, and when you see a small tree covered with 20 pensive – and sizable – bald eagles, you can enjoy your own raptor version of *The Birds*.

Note that the weather can turn nasty any time of the year on the road's higher reaches. Otherwise it is smooth and very well-maintained.

KLONDIKE HIGHWAY

Beginning seaside in Skagway, AK, the 716km Klondike Hwy climbs high to the forbidding Chilkoot Pass before crossing into stunning alpine scenery on the way to Carcross. For much of its length, the road generally follows the **Gold Rush Trail**, the route of the Klondike prospectors. You'll have a much easier time of it than they did.

North of Whitehorse, the road passes through often-gentle terrain that has been scorched by wildfires through the years. Signs showing the dates let you chart nature's recovery.

Carcross

Long a forgotten gold-rush town, cute little Carcross, 73km south of Whitehorse, is an evocative stop. There are four trains weekly in summer from Skagway to Carcross (and vice versa) on the **White Pass & Yukon Route** (☎800-343-7373; www.wpyr.com; one-way from Skagway adult/child $165/82.50; ⏱Jun-Aug). These five-hour rides over White Pass access a lot of remote scenery that the shorter regular trips to Bennett don't cover. There are packages that include bus transport in one direction to allow Skagway-based day trips. Some old buildings are being restored and the site on Lake Bennett is superb. (Although Klondike prospectors who had to build boats here to cross the lake didn't think so.)

The old **train station** has good displays on local history.

Carcross Desert, often considered the world's smallest desert, is the exposed sandy bed of a glacial lake. It's 2km north of town.

VIC (☎867-821-4431; www.travelyukon.com; ⏱8am-8pm May-Sep) In a modern complex with seasonal shops and cafes. Get the excellent walking-tour brochure.

Carmacks

This small village sits right on the Yukon River and is named for one of the discoverers of gold in 1896, George Washington Carmack. A rogue seaman wandering the Yukon, it was almost by luck that Carmack (with Robert Henderson, Tagish Charlie and Keish – aka Skookum Jim Mason) made their claim on Bonanza Creek. Soon he was living the high life and it wasn't long before he abandoned his First Nations family and

WORTH A TRIP

CHILKOOT TRAIL

Arduous at best, and deadly at its worst in 1898, the Chilkoot Trail was the route most prospectors took to get over the 1110m Chilkoot Pass from Skagway and into the Yukon. Today, hikers reserve spots months in advance to travel the same route.

The well-marked 53km trail begins near **Dyea**, 14km northwest of Skagway, and heads northeast over the pass. It then follows the Taiya River to Lake Bennett in British Columbia (BC), and takes three to five days to hike. It's a hard route in good weather and often treacherous in bad. You must be in good physical condition and come fully equipped. Layers of warm clothes and rain gear are essential.

Hardware, tools and supplies dumped by the prospectors still litter the trail. At several places there are wooden shacks where you can put up for the night, but these are usually full, so a tent and sleeping bag are required. There are 10 designated campgrounds along the route, each with bear caches.

At the Canadian end you can either take the White Pass & Yukon Route train from Bennett back to Skagway or further up the line to Fraser in BC, where you can connect with a bus for Whitehorse.

The Chilkoot Trail is a primary feature of the **Klondike Gold Rush National Historical Park** (www.nps.gov/klgo), a series of sites managed by both Parks Canada and the US National Park Service that stretches from Seattle, WA, to Dawson City. Each Chilkoot hiker must obtain one of the 50 permits available for each day in summer; reserve well in advance. Parks Canada/US National Park Service charge $55 for a permit plus $12 for a reservation. Each day eight permits are issued on a first-come, first-served basis. For information, contact the **Chilkoot Trail Centre** (cnr Broadway & 2nd Ave; ⏲8am-5pm Jun-Aug) in Skagway or go online to the park's website. Necessary preplanning includes determining which campsites you'll use each night.

headed south to the US. Given his record as a husband and father, it's fitting that Carmack be honored by this uninspired collection of gas stations and places to stay. Like elsewhere in the territory, residents here are keenly attuned to the land, which supplies them with game and fish throughout the year. A pretty 15-minute **interpretive walk** by the river provides a glimmer of insight into this life.

The main reason to stop off for a visit to Carmacks is the excellent **Tagé Cho Hudän Interpretive Centre** (☎867-863-5831; off Hwy 2; by donation; ⏲9am-6pm May-Sep), where volunteers explain aboriginal life past and present.

Besides the interpretive center, there are things to see on the Klondike Hwy north and south of Carmacks.

About 25km north of Carmacks, the **Five Finger Rapids Recreation Site** has excellent views of the treacherous stretch of the rapids that once tested the wits of riverboat captains traveling between Whitehorse and Dawson. There's a steep 1.5km walk down to the rapids.

Heading out on the road south, there are a series of water features starting with **Twin Lakes**, located 23km from Carmacks, followed by **Fox Lake**. Situated another 24km south, you can't miss serene **Lake Laberge**. The final 40km to Whitehorse is marked by low trees and a few cattle ranches.

Minto

Easily missed (unless you're toting a canoe or kayak), Minto is where the Klondike Hwy leaves the route of the Gold Rush Trail. This is a popular place to put in for the four- to five-day trip down the Yukon River to Dawson City. It's about 75km north of Carmacks.

Stewart Crossing

Another popular place to get your canoe wet, Stewart Crossing is on the Stewart River, which affords a narrow and somewhat more rugged experience before it joins the Yukon to the west for the trip to Dawson.

Otherwise unexceptional, the village is situated at the junction of the Klondike Hwy (Hwy 2) and the **Silver Trail** (Hwy 11), which makes a 225km round-trip to the nearly abandoned town of **Keno City** and the tiny village of **Mayo**.

DAWSON CITY

POP 1400

If you didn't know its history, Dawson City would be an atmospheric place to pause for a while, with a seductive, funky vibe. That it's one of the most historic and evocative towns in Canada is like gold dust on a cake: unnecessary but damn nice.

Set on a narrow shelf at the confluence of the Yukon and Klondike Rivers, a mere 240km south of the Arctic Circle, Dawson was the center of the Klondike Gold Rush. Today, you can wander the dirt streets of town, passing old buildings with dubious permafrost foundations, and discover Dawson's rich cultural life (that person passing by may be a dancer, filmmaker, painter or miner).

Dawson can be busy in the summer, especially during its festivals. But by September the days are getting short, the seasonal workers have fled south and the 1400 year-round residents are settling in for another long, dark winter.

History

In 1898 more than 30,000 prospectors milled the streets of Dawson – a few newly rich, but most without prospects and at odds with themselves and the world. Shops, bars and prostitutes relieved these hordes of what money they had, but Dawson's fortunes were tied to the gold miners and, as the boom ended, the town began a decades-long slow fade.

The territorial capital was moved to Whitehorse in 1952 and the town lingered on, surviving on the low-key but ongoing gold-mining industry. By 1970 the population was under 900. But then a funny thing happened on the way to Dawson's demise: it was rediscovered. Improvements to the Klondike Hwy and links to Alaska allowed the first major influx of summertime tourists, who found a charmingly moldering time capsule from the gold rush. Parks Canada designated much of the town as historic and began restorations.

Sights

Dawson is small enough to walk around in a few hours, but you can easily fill three or more days with the many local things to see and do. If the summertime hordes get you down, head uphill for a few blocks to find timeless old houses and streets.

After draconian government budget cuts during the Harper era, Parks Canada is now enjoying greatly increased budgets, which mean programs and restorations are showing new vigor in Dawson. Check out the pass options, good for the many Parks Canada sites.

★Klondike National Historic Sites — HISTORIC SITE

(☎867-993-7210; www.pc.gc.ca/dawson; Parks Canada passes adult $7-31) It's easy to relive the gold rush at myriad preserved and restored places. Parks Canada runs walking tours (p788) through the day that allow access into various examples of the 26 restored buildings. Take several tours so you can see a wide variety. Outside of tours, various buildings such as the **Palace Grand Theatre** (Map p786; King St) are open for free on a rotating basis, usually 4:30pm to 5:30pm.

★Bonanza Creek Discovery Site — HISTORIC SITE

(Bonanza Rd) FREE Some 1.5km up the valley from Dredge No 4, this national historic site is roughly where gold was first found in 1896. It's a quiet site today with a little water burbling through the rubble. A fascinating 500m-long walk passes interpretive displays. Pick up a guide ($2.50) at the VIC (p773).

★Dredge No 4 — LANDMARK

(☎867-993-5023; Bonanza Creek Rd; adult/child $20/10, return transport from Dawson $10; ⏲10am-4pm May-Sep, tour times vary) The

WORTH A TRIP

TOMBSTONE DETOUR

Tombstone Territorial Park (☎867-667-5648; www.yukonparks.ca; Dempster Hwy), which lies along Dempster Hwy for about 50km, is an easy day trip from Dawson City. Shades of green and charcoal color the wide valleys here and steep ridges are dotted with small glaciers and alpine lakes. Summer feels tentative but makes its statement with a burst of purple wildflowers in July. Clouds sweep across the tundra, bringing squalls punctuated by brilliant sun. Stand amid this and you'll know the meaning of the sound of silence.

The park's excellent **Interpretive Centre** (Dempster Hwy; ⏲9am-7pm Jun-early Sep), which offers walks and talks, is 71km from the start of Hwy 5.

Dawson City

scarred valleys around Dawson speak to the vast amounts of toil that went into the gold hunt. Most emblematic is Bonanza Creek, where gold was first found and which still yields some today. Dredge No 4, 13km off the Klondike Hwy, is a massive dredging machine that tore up the Klondike Valley and left the tailings, which remain as a blight on the landscape. Tours of this Parks Canada site are run by Goldbottom Tours (p788).

Learn about this huge machine, which worked something like a freakish giant worm in a science-fiction novel.

★Jack London Interpretive Centre

MUSEUM

(Map p786; ☎867-993-5575; Firth St; adult/child $5/free; ⏲11am-6pm May-Aug) In 1898 Jack London lived in the Yukon, the setting for his most popular stories, including *Call of the Wild* and *White Fang*. At the writer's cabin there are excellent daily interpretive talks. A labor of love by the late historian Dick North, Dawne Mitchell and others, this place is a treasure trove of stories – including the search for the original cabin.

Dawson City

Crocus Bluff VIEWPOINT

(off Mary McLeod Rd) Near Dawson's cemeteries, there's a short path out to pretty Crocus Bluff, which has excellent views of Dawson and the Klondike and Yukon Rivers. If driving, take New Dome Rd and turn at Mary McLeod Rd (ignoring the 'No Exit' signs). It is a short walk up King St from town. You can also take the 400m **Crocus Bluff Connector** path off the **Ninth Avenue Trail**, which intersects with numerous streets along its 2.5km.

Fortymile Gold Workshop/Studio GALLERY

(Map p786; 867-993-5690; 3rd Ave, btwn York & King Sts; 9am-6pm May-Sep) Watch as jewelry is made from local refined gold, which is silky and has a rich yellow color, as opposed to the bling you see peddled on late-night TV. Examples of gold from various local claims and locations shows how old miners could tell where gold originated.

Midnight Dome VIEWPOINT

(New Dome Rd) The slide-scarred face of this hill overlooks the town to the north, but to reach the top you must travel south of town about 1km, turn left off the Klondike Hwy onto New Dome Rd, and continue for about 7km. The Midnight Dome, at 880m above sea level, offers great views of the Klondike Valley, Yukon River and Dawson City. There's also a steep **trail** that takes 90 minutes from Judge St in town; maps are available at the VIC (p773).

Robert Service Cabin HISTORIC SITE

(Map p786; cnr 8th Ave & Hanson St; Parks Canada admission $7; several events daily May-Aug) The 'Bard of the Yukon,' poet and writer Robert W Service, lived in this typical gold rush cabin from 1909 to 1912. Each day in season there are dramatic readings, guided walks and tours.

Harrington's Store MUSEUM

(Map p786; cnr 3rd Ave & Princess St; 9:30am-8:30pm) FREE This restored old shop has historic photos from Dawson's heyday.

Commissioner's Residence HISTORIC BUILDING

(Map p786; Front St; Parks Canada admission $7; 1:30-4:30pm May-Sep) Built in 1901 to house the territorial commissioner, this proud building was designed to give potential civic investors confidence in the city. The building was the longtime home of Martha Black, who came to the Yukon in 1898, owned a lumberyard and was elected to the Canadian Parliament at age 70. (*Martha Black* by Flo Whyard is a great book about this remarkable woman.)

SS Keno HISTORIC SITE

(Map p786; cnr Front & Queen Sts; Parks Canada admission $7; noon-4pm May-Aug) The SS *Keno* was one of a fleet of paddle wheelers that worked the Yukon's rivers for more than half a century. Grounded along the waterfront, the boat re-creates a time before any highways.

Dawson City Museum MUSEUM
(Map p786; ☎867-993-5291; 5th Ave; adult/child $9/7; ⏰10am-6pm May-Aug) Make your own discoveries among the 25,000 gold-rush artifacts at this museum. Engaging exhibits walk you through the grim lives of the miners. The museum is housed in the landmark 1901 Old Territorial Administration building.

Cemeteries CEMETERY
(Mary McLeod Rd) A 15-minute walk up King St and Mary McCloud Rd near town leads to 10 cemeteries that are literally filled with characters. Among them is Joe Vogler, who fought to have Alaska secede from the US. He was buried here in 1993, having vowed never to be buried in an Alaska that wasn't free. Todd Palin (husband of Sarah) is among his acolytes.

Dänojà Zho Cultural Centre NOTABLE BUILDING
(Map p786; ☎867-993-6768; www.trondekheritage.com; Front St; adult/child $7/free; ⏰10am-5pm Mon-Sat Jun-Sep) Inside this impressive riverfront wood building there are displays and interpretative talks on the Tr'ondëk Hwëch'in (River People) First Nations. The collection includes traditional artifacts and a re-creation of a 19th-century fishing camp.

Klondike Institute for Art & Culture NOTABLE BUILDING
(KIAC; Map p786; ☎867-993-5005; www.kiac.org; cnr 3rd Ave & Queen St) The Klondike Institute for Art & Culture is part of Dawson's thriving arts community. It has an impressive studio building, galleries and educational programs.

ODD Gallery GALLERY
(Map p786; ☎867-993-5005; www.kiac.ca/oddgallery; cnr 2nd Ave & Princess St; ⏰hours vary) The exhibition space of the Klondike Institute for Art & Culture, this gallery has regular shows.

Activities

Besides arriving by canoe or kayak, many people also exit Dawson City via the Yukon River. A popular trip good for novices goes from Dawson for three days and 168km downstream to Eagle, AK.

A three-hour hike to **Moosehide**, an old First Nations village, is popular. The trail follows hillsides above the river north of town. Be sure to get a map at the VIC.

You can explore much of the Dawson area by bike, including the 33km **Ridge Road Heritage Trail**, which winds through the gold fields south of town.

Dawson City River Hostel CANOEING, CYCLING
(www.yukonhostels.com; bike rental per day from $25; ⏰May-Sep) Arranges all manner of canoe rentals, trips and transportation from Whitehorse and points further downstream to Dawson and from Dawson to the Alaskan towns of Eagle and Circle.

Dawson Trading Post CANOEING
(Map p786; ☎867-993-5316; Front St; canoe rental per day from $40; ⏰9am-5pm Jun-Aug) Rents out canoes and can arrange trips.

Tours

★**Parks Canada Walking Tours** WALKING
(single tour $7, unlimited tours $31; ⏰May-Aug) Parks Canada docents, often in period garb, lead excellent walking tours. On each tour, learn about a few of the 26 restored buildings and the many characters that walked the streets (many of whom could be called 'streetwalkers'). There are also self-guided 90-minute audio tours (adult $7, 9am to 5pm).

★**Goldbottom Tours** HISTORY
(Map p786; ☎867-993-5750; www.goldbottom.com; tours with/without transport from Dawson $55/45; ⏰May-Sep) Run by the legendary Millar mining family. Tour their placer mine 15km up Hunker Creek Rd, which meets Hwy 2 just north of the airport. The three-hour tours include a gold-panning lesson; you get to keep what you find. You can also just pan for gold on their site for $20. The ticket office is on Front St.

Klondike Experience BUS
(Map p786; ☎867-993-3821; www.klondikeexperience.com; 954 2nd Ave; tours $25-120; ⏰May-Aug) Runs various tours that include Midnight Dome (75 minutes), the Goldfields (three hours) and Tombstone Park (7½ hours). The latter is highly recommended.

Klondike Spirit BOATING
(Map p786; ☎867-993-5323; www.klondikespirit.com; tours $50-65; ⏰May-Sep) This faux old stern-wheeler cruises the river on various tours. Purchase tickets from the Triple J Hotel on the corner of 5th Avenue and Queen St.

Festivals & Events

Dawson City Music Festival MUSIC
(☎867-993-5384; www.dcmf.com; ⏰mid-Jul) Popular – tickets sell out months in advance and the city fills up; reservations are essential.

THE KLONDIKE GOLD RUSH

The Klondike Gold Rush continues to be the defining moment for the Yukon. Certainly it was the population high point. Around 40,000 gold seekers washed ashore (some literally) in Skagway, hoping to strike it rich in the gold fields of Dawson City, some 700km north.

To say that most were ill-prepared for the enterprise is an understatement. Although some were veterans of other gold rushes, a high percentage were American men looking for adventure. Clerks, lawyers and waiters were among those who thought they'd just pop up North and get rich. The reality was different. Landing in Skagway, they were set upon by all manner of flimflam artists, most working for the incorrigible Soapy Smith. Next came dozens of trips hefting their 1000lb of required supplies over the frozen Chilkoot Pass. Then they had to build boats from scratch and make their way across lakes and the Yukon River to Dawson. Scores died trying.

Besides more scamsters, there was another harsh reality awaiting in Dawson: by the summer of 1897 when the first ships reached the West Coast of the US with news of the discoveries on Dawson's Bonanza Creek, the best sites had all been claimed. The Klondike gold-rush mobs were mostly too late to the action by at least a year. Sick and broke, the survivors glumly made their way back to the US. Few found any gold and most sold their gear for pennies to merchants who in turn resold it to incoming gold seekers for top dollar. Several family fortunes in the Yukon today can be traced to this trade.

Today, even the hardiest folk seem like couch potatoes when compared to the protagonists of these harrowing stories. The deprivation, disease and heartbreak of these 'dudes' of the day make for fascinating reading. Among the many books about the Klondike Gold Rush, the following are recommended (and easily found in the Yukon):

- *The Klondike Fever* by Pierre Berton is the classic on the gold rush.
- *Sailor on Snowshoes* by Dick North traces Jack London's time in the Yukon and the hunt for his cabin. London's stories of the gold rush made his name as a writer.
- *The Floor of Heaven* by Howard Blum is a fabulous read. It details the lives of George Carmack, who was a gold discoverer; Soapy Smith, a legendary Skagway-based con man; and Charlie Siringo, a private cop who saved Carmack from Soapy.

★Discovery Days CULTURAL
(www.dawsoncity.ca; 3rd Mon in Aug) Celebrates the you-know-what of 1896 with parades and picnics. Events begin days before, including an excellent art show. It's a hoot!

Sleeping

Reservations are a good idea in July and August, although the VIC can help. Many places will pick you up at the airport; ask in advance.

Dawson City River Hostel HOTEL $
(867-993-6823; www.yukonhostels.com; dm $22, r from $48; May-Sep) This delightfully eccentric hostel is across the river from town and five minutes up the hill from the ferry landing. It has good views, cabins, platforms for tents, and a communal bathhouse. Tent sites are $14. Owner Dieter Reinmuth is a noted Yukon author and all-around character.

Yukon River Campground CAMPGROUND $
(campsites $12; May-Sep; P) On the western side of the river about 250m up the road to the right after you get off the ferry; has 98 shady sites.

★Bombay Peggy's INN $$
(Map p786; 867-993-6969; www.bombaypeggys.com; cnr 2nd Ave & Princess St; r $95-220; Mar-Nov) A renovated former brothel with alluring period furnishings and spunky attitude. Budget 'snug' rooms share bathrooms. Rooms are plush in a way that will make you want to wear a garter.

★Klondike Kate's LODGE $$
(Map p786; 867-993-6527; www.klondikekates.ca; cnr King St & 3rd Ave; cabins $140-200; Apr-Sep; P) The 15 cabins behind the restaurant of the same name are rustic without the rusticisms. Some units have microwaves and fridges. All have porches, perfect for decompressing. Green practices are many.

Aurora Inn INN $$
(Map p786; ☎867-993-6860; www.aurorainn.ca; 5th Ave; r $110-210; P 📶) All 20 rooms in this European-style inn are large and comfortable. And if there's such a thing as old-world cleanliness, it's here: the admonishments to remove your (invariably) muddy shoes start at the entrance.

Triple J Hotel HOTEL $$
(Map p786; ☎867-993-5323; www.triplejhotel.com; cnr 5th Ave & Queen St; r $100-180; P 📶) The 47 rooms in this modern motel with a throwback look are in a modern (retro-looking) wing, in the renovated main building or in a cabin. It's a good mainstream choice.

Eating

Alchemy Cafe CAFE $
(Map p786; ☎867-993-3831; www.alchemycafe.ca; 878 3rd Ave; mains $8-15; ⏰8:30am-5pm Tue-Fri, 9:30am-5pm Sat & Sun; 📶) Groovy in the best sense of the word, Alchemy combines fantastic vegetarian food with a life-affirming green ethos. The coffees are way cool (in a hot sort of way) and special events include music, talks and, yes, rap sessions. The newly built vintage-style building has an alluring porch.

Cheechako's Bake Shop BAKERY $
(Map p786; ☎867-993-5303; cnr Front & Princess Sts; mains $4-9; ⏰7am-4pm Mon-Sat) A real bakery and a good one, on the main strip. Muffins, cookies and treats vie for your attention with sandwiches made on homemade bread.

Farmers Market MARKET $
(Map p786; Front St; ⏰11am-5pm Sat May-Sep) A farmers market thrives by the iconic waterfront gazebo. The sweet-as-candy carrots are the product of very cold nights. Try some birch syrup.

★**Klondike Kate's** CANADIAN $$
(Map p786; ☎867-993-6527; www.klondikekates.ca; cnr King St & 3rd Ave; mains $8-25; ⏰4-9pm Mon-Sat, 8am-3pm & 4-9pm Sun Apr-Oct) Two ways to know spring has arrived: the river cracks up and Kate's reopens. Locals in the know prefer the latter. The long and inventive menu has fine sandwiches, pastas and fresh Yukon fish. Look for great specials. Excellent list of Canadian craft brews.

> **STREET NUMBERS & OPENING HOURS**
>
> Street numbers are a rarity in Dawson and, unless noted otherwise, sights, attractions and many businesses are closed outside of the summer high season.

★**Drunken Goat Taverna** GREEK $$
(Map p786; ☎867-993-5800; www.drunkengoattaverna.com; 2nd Ave; mains $14-28; ⏰noon-9pm) Follow your eyes to the flowers, your ears to the Aegean music and your nose to the excellent Greek food, run year-round by the legendary Tony Dovas. A new terrace out back is a fine place to while away an evening.

Drinking & Nightlife

The spirit(s) of the prospectors lives on in several saloons. On summer nights the action goes on until dawn, which would mean something if it weren't light all night.

★**Bombay Peggy's** PUB
(Map p786; ☎867-993-6969; www.bombaypeggys.com; cnr 2nd Ave & Princess St; ⏰11am-11pm Mar-Nov) There's always a hint of pleasures to come swirling around the tables of Dawson's most inviting bar. Enjoy good beers, wines and mixed drinks inside or out.

Billy Goat PUB
(Map p786; ☎867-993-5800; 2nd Ave; ⏰5pm-late) Not a branch of the famed Chicago original, but a friendly lounge from Tony of Drunken Goat fame. Serves food from the Drunken Goat menu until late. Note the murals on the walls.

Downtown Hotel PUB
(Map p786; ☎867-993-5346; www.downtownhotel.ca; cnr Queen St & 2nd Ave; ⏰11am-late) This unremarkable bar comes to life at 9pm in summer for what can best be called the 'Sourtoe Schtick.' Tourists line up to drink a shot of booze ($10) that has a pickled human toe floating in it.

It's a long-running gag that's delightfully chronicled in Dieter Reinmuth's *The Saga of the Sourtoe*. (That the toe – it is real – looks much like a bit of beef jerky should give pause to anyone used to late-night Slim Jim jonesing...) And if you swallow it, the fee is $2500.

Bars at Westminster Hotel BAR
(Map p786; ☎867-993-5339; 3rd Ave; ⏰noon-late) These two legendary bars carry the mostly affectionate monikers 'Snakepit,' 'Armpit' or simply 'Pit.' Theses are places for serious drinkers, with live music many nights.

WORTH A TRIP

DAWSON CITY TO ALASKA

From Dawson City, the free ferry crosses the Yukon River to the scenic **Top of the World Hwy** (Hwy 9). Only open in summer, the mostly paved 106km-long ridgetop road to the US border has superb vistas across the region.

You'll continue to feel on top of the world as you cross the border. The land is barren alpine meadows with jutting rocks and often grazing caribou. The border crossing (open 9am to 9pm Yukon time/8am to 8pm Alaska time 15 May to 15 September) has strict hours – if you're late you'll have to wait until the next day.

On the US side, Alaska shows its xenophobic side, as the 19km connection to the Taylor Hwy (Hwy 5) is mostly dirt and often impassable after storms (expect to get dirt in parts of your vehicle and person you didn't think possible). The old gold-mining town of Eagle on the Yukon River is 105km north. Some 47km south over somewhat better roads, you encounter **Chicken**, a delightful place of free thinkers happy to sell you a stupid T-shirt at one of the gas-station cafes or offer their views regarding government bureaucrats. Another 124km south and you reach the Alaska Hwy, where a turn east takes you to the Yukon. Just a tick west, **Tok** has services and motels. Alaska time is one hour earlier than the Yukon.

☆ Entertainment

★Diamond Tooth Gertie's Gambling Hall CASINO
(Map p786; ☎867-993-5575; cnr Queen St & 4th Ave; $10; ⊙7pm-2am Mon-Fri, 2pm-2am Sat & Sun May-Sep) This popular re-creation of an 1898 saloon is complete with small-time gambling, a honky-tonk piano and dancing girls. The casino helps promote the town and fund culture. Each night there are three different floor shows with singing and dancing, which are often surprisingly contemporary.

ℹ Information

Much of Dawson is closed October to May. The biweekly, volunteer-run *Klondike Sun* (www.klondikesun.com) covers special events and activities.

CIBC ATM (2nd Ave; ⊙24hr) Near Queen St.

Northwest Territories Information Centre (Map p786; ☎867-993-6167; www.spectacularnwt.com; Front St; ⊙9am-7pm May-Sep) Has maps and information on the NWT and the Dempster Hwy.

VIC (Map p786; ☎867-993-5566; www.travelyukon.com; cnr Front & King Sts; ⊙8am-8pm May-Sep) Combines tourist and Parks Canada information (buy activity tickets and passes here). It also has essential schedules of events and activities.

ℹ Getting There & Away

Dawson City is 527km from Whitehorse. Public transportation to/from Whitehorse is often in flux. Should you fly in, there are no rental cars.

Dawson City Airport is 19km east of Dawson.

Air North (☎800-661-0407; www.flyairnorth.com) serves Whitehorse and Old Crow, and Inuvik in the NWT.

Alaska/Yukon Trails (☎907-479-2277; www.alaskashuttle.com) Runs buses to Fairbanks, AK ($285, thrice weekly June to mid-September).

Husky Bus (Map p786; ☎867-993-3821; www.huskybus.ca) Serves Whitehorse ($110, thrice weekly) and makes all stops along the Klondike Hwy. Departures are from the VIC. Husky will do pickups of paddlers and canoes along the Klondike Hwy with advance arrangement . Uses the Klondike Experience (p788) office.

DEMPSTER HIGHWAY

Rather than name this road for an obscure Mountie (William Dempster), this road should be named the Michelin Hwy or the Goodyear Hwy for the number of tires it's sent to an explosive demise. This 736km thrill ride is one of North America's great adventure roads, winding through stark mountains and emerald valleys, across huge tracts of tundra, and passing through Tombstone Territorial Park (p785).

The Dempster (Hwy 5 in the Yukon, Hwy 8 in the NWT) starts 40km southeast of Dawson City off the Klondike Hwy and heads north over the Ogilvie and Richardson Mountains beyond the Arctic Circle and on to Inuvik in the NWT, near the shores of the Beaufort Sea.

Road Conditions

Built on a thick base of gravel to insulate the permafrost underneath (which would otherwise melt, causing the road to sink without a trace), the Dempster is open most of the year, but the best time to travel is between June and early September, when the ferries over the Peel and Mackenzie Rivers operate. In winter, ice forms a natural bridge over the rivers, which become ice roads. The Dempster is closed during the spring thaw and the winter freeze-up; the timing of these vary by the year and can occur from mid-April to June and mid-October to December, respectively.

Check road conditions in the Yukon (p773) and the **NWT** (☎800-661-0750; www.dot.gov.nt.ca); the Northwest Territories Information Centre (p791) in Dawson City is a good resource. It takes 10 to 12 hours to drive to Inuvik without stopping for a break. (Given that William Dempster regularly made 700km dogsled journeys in subzero weather, this rugged and challenging road is properly named after all.)

Sleeping & Eating

Accommodations and vehicle services along the route are few. The Yukon government has three campgrounds: at **Tombstone** (with the interpretive centre, 71km from the start of the highway), **Engineer Creek** (194km) and **Rock River** (447km). There's also a NWT government campground at **Nitainlaii Territorial Park**, 9km south of Fort McPherson. Sites at these campgrounds are $12.

The Eagle Plains Hotel (☎867-993-2453; eagleplains@northwestel.net; Dempster Hwy; r $100-160; P @) is open year-round and offers 32 rooms in a low-rise building in a stark setting. The next service station is 180km further north at Fort McPherson in the NWT.

ARCTIC PARKS

North of the Arctic Circle, the Yukon's population numbers a few hundred. It's a lonely land with little evidence of humans and only the hardiest venture here during the short summers.

The 280-person village of **Old Crow** is home to the Vuntut Gwitch'in First Nations and is unreachable by vehicle. Residents subsist on caribou from the legendary 130,000-strong Porcupine herd, which migrates each year between the Arctic National Wildlife Refuge (ANWR) in Alaska and the Yukon.

On the Yukon side of this vast flat arctic tundra, a large swath of land is now protected in the adjoining **Vuntut National Park** and **Ivvavik National Park**. Information on both can be obtained from the Parks Canada office (p781) in Inuvik, NWT, where you can get information on the very limited options for organizing visits to the parks. There are no facilities of any kind in the parks.

The aboriginal name **Herschel Island-Qikiqtaruk Territorial Park** (☎867-777-4058; www.yukonparks.ca) means 'It is Island' and indeed it is. Barely rising above the waters of Mackenzie Bay on the Beaufort Sea, the park has a long tradition of human habitation. In the late 1800s American whalers set up shop at Pauline Cove. Abandoned in 1907, Pauline Cove has several surviving wooden buildings left behind by the whalers. Summer visits to Herschel Island are possible via tours from Inuvik.

Today, Inuvialuit families use the island for traditional hunting, although climate change is causing the island to dissolve into the sea.

Northwest Territories

Includes ➡

Best Places to Eat

➡ Woodyard Brewhouse & Eatery (p802)

➡ Alestine's (p811)

➡ Yellowknife Farmers' Market (p801)

➡ Bullocks Bistro (p801)

➡ Zehabesha (p801)

➡ Anna's Home Cooking (p806)

Best Places to Sleep

➡ Sean's Guesthouse & Aurora Tours (p800)

➡ Blachford Lake Lodge (p800)

➡ Mackenzie Rest Inn (p808)

➡ Whooping Crane Guest House (p806)

➡ Arctic Chalet (p811)

Why Go?

On a planet containing seven billion people, it's difficult to imagine that there are still places as empty as the Northwest Territories (NWT). A vast swath of boreal forest and Arctic tundra five times the size of the UK, it has a population of a small provincial town. In the 19th century, gold prospectors passed it over as too remote; modern Canadians, if they head north at all, prefer to romanticize about iconic Nunavut or the grandiose Yukon. More people orbit the earth each year than visit lonely Aulavik, one of the territory's four national parks.

What they're missing is something unique: a potent combo of epic, remarkably beautiful, accessible terrain, singular aboriginal culture and a vibrant, cosmopolitan regional capital. With one of the world's greatest waterfalls and North America's deepest lake, it has enough brutal wilderness to keep a modern-day David Livingstone happy for a couple of lifetimes.

When to Go

Yellowknife

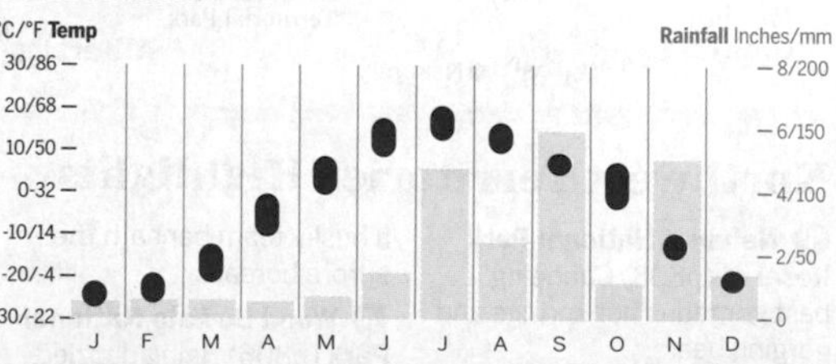

Jun See the midnight sun and go hiking before the horseflies hatch.

Jul & Aug Hyperactive summer, good for fishing and canoeing. Aurora sightings in late August.

Mar Best winter visits, with aurora viewing, husky mushing and Yellowknife's Snowking festival.

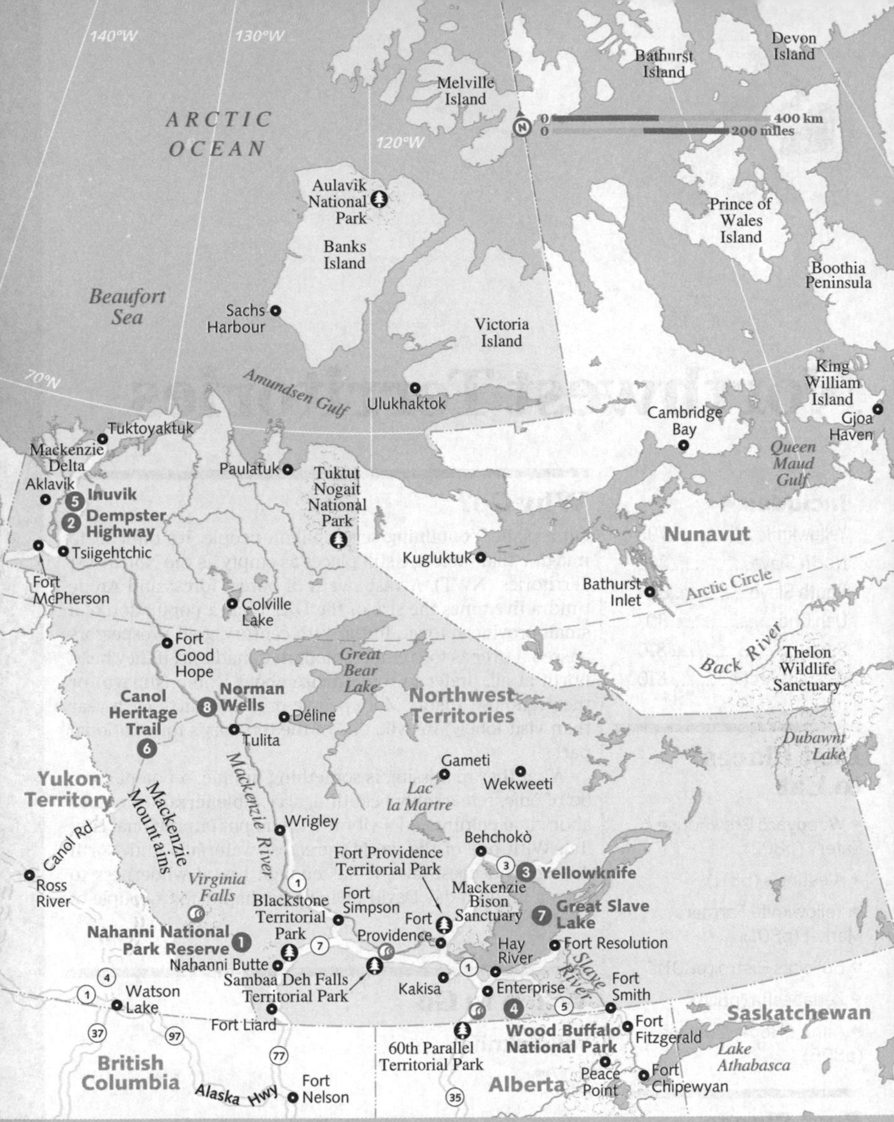

Northwest Territories Highlights

❶ **Nahanni National Park Reserve** (p808) Canoeing past gorgeous hot springs and gorging bears.

❷ **Dempster Highway** (p811) Packing two spare tires and a camera for this gob-smacking highway.

❸ **Yellowknife** (p796) Driving your own sled with a husky team beneath the aurora borealis.

❹ **Wood Buffalo National Park** (p806) Being dazzled by herds of bison, vast salt plains, vanishing rivers and the brilliant night sky.

❺ **Inuvik** (p810) Visiting the Western Arctic's remotest communities and dipping your toe in the Arctic Ocean.

❻ **Canol Heritage Trail** (p810) Hiking where few have hiked before.

❼ **Great Slave Lake** (p797) Paddling past buzzing floatplanes and bobbing houseboats.

❽ **Norman Wells** (p810) Embarking on a canoeing adventure down the mighty Mackenzie.

History

The first NWT residents, ancestors of today's Dene, tramped here from Asia about 14,000 years ago. The Inuvialuit (Western Canadian Inuit), who migrated from Alaska, showed up more recently. Fur-hunting Europeans, followed by missionaries, penetrated the area in the 18th and 19th centuries. After oil turned up near Tulita in the 1920s, a territorial government was formed. In the '30s, gold near Yellowknife and radium near Great Bear Lake brought a population influx. In 1999 the territory was cut in half with the formation of Nunavut: NWT is now evenly divided between Aboriginals and non-Aboriginals. The latter group, and to a smaller extent the former, have benefited from oil, gas and diamond development.

Land & Climate

The NWT is a supersized wilderness reaching poleward from the 60th parallel. The south is evergreen flatlands, the east is the boulder-filled landscape of the Canadian Shield, and toothy mountains rear up from the west. Canada's biggest river, the Mackenzie, bisects the territory, draining two gargantuan lakes, Great Slave and Great Bear.

Summers have been warm recently but can bring anything. One sure thing is daylight: from May through July there's no end of it. June's the driest summer month, but lake ice can linger until the month's end. Most visitors come in July, when much of the region is plagued with horseflies and mosquitoes.

Winters are long and punishing. In January, lows in Yellowknife collapse to -40°C (-40°F) and daylight is feeble. If you're keen on a winter visit, try March or April, when the sun climbs and the mercury follows suit.

Art & Music

The NWT has a rich tradition of aboriginal art and music. The Dene, Inuvialuit, Slavey, Gwich'in and Métis communities keep traditional music and dance alive and it's worth catching the music festivals in Yellowknife, Fort Simpson and Fort Smith. In Inuvik traditional dance is showcased on Aboriginal Day.

The territories are also known for their art and traditional crafts. Look out for birch-bark baskets, decorated with colorfully dyed porcupine quills and traditionally tanned moose and caribou hides made into beaded moccasins, mukluks and crow boots, as well as mittens and jackets. Northern motifs of drum dancers, shamans, hunters, fishermen, bears and musk ox are reflected in carvings and sculptures made of soapstone, caribou antler, whalebone and musk-ox horn, and found in Inuvik and its surrounding communities, as well as Yellowknife.

Examples of Northern art particularly worth seeking out are Holman (Ulukhaktok) prints. In 1957 stonecut printmaking was introduced to the remote hamlet of Holman (now Ulukhaktok); ever since, Inuvialuit artists have been producing limited editions of 50 prints per design, featuring vibrantly colored Northern imagery.

NORTHWEST TERRITORIES FAST FACTS

- Population: 44,340
- Area: 1,141,000 sq km
- Capital: Yellowknife
- Quirky fact: The world's first 'grolar bear' (grizzly and polar bear hybrid) was discovered in the wild here in 2006.

Getting There & Away

AIR

Edmonton is the main gateway. **First Air** (867-669-6600; www.firstair.ca), **Canadian North** (867-669-4000; www.canadiannorth.com), **Air Canada** (888-247-2262; www.aircanada.com), **Northwestern Air** (877-872-2216; www.nwal.ca) and **WestJet** (888-937-8538; www.westjet.com) fly Edmonton–Yellowknife, starting around $427 return. Canadian North also flies from Edmonton direct to Inuvik ($2333 return) and Norman Wells ($1854). Northwestern Air serves Hay River and Fort Smith direct from Edmonton ($990 to $1120 return).

Air Canada also serves Yellowknife from Calgary ($475 return).

From Whitehorse, Yukon, **Air North** (867-668-2228; www.flyairnorth.com) goes via Dawson City to Inuvik ($725 return).

From Iqaluit, Nunavut, First Air and Canadian North depart for Yellowknife ($3400 return).

BUS

At the time of writing, there was no bus link into the NWT.

CAR & MOTORCYCLE

There are two overland routes to the southern NWT. From Edmonton, a 924km drive up Hwy 35 brings you to the NWT border, 84km shy of Enterprise. From Fort Nelson, British Columbia (BC), the Liard Trail runs 137km to the border. Fort Liard is another 38km north.

NORTHWEST TERRITORIES INFORMATION

Northwest Territories Tourism (www.spectacularnwt.com) has a detailed website and distributes excellent material via mail or download, including the annual *NWT Explorers' Guide*.

A great resource is the wonderful **Up Here** (www.uphere.ca) magazine. It lists up-to-date info and features interesting articles on all aspects of Northern life.

If you're heading up to the Mackenzie Delta, you can set out from Dawson City, Yukon, on the shockingly scenic but challenging Dempster Hwy, which reaches the NWT border after 465km.

Getting Around

AIR

Yellowknife is the region's hub. Half of the NWT's 32 communities are fly-in only, accessed from Yellowknife with **Air Tindi** (☎888-545-6794; www.airtindi.com), Norman Wells with **North-Wright Air** (☎867-587-2288; www.north-wrightairways.com) and Inuvik with **Aklak Air** (☎867-777-3555; www.aklakair.ca).

BUS

Frontier Coachlines (☎867-874-2566; www.frontiercoachlinesnwtltd.ca) runs between Hay River and Yellowknife (5½ hours, three times a week), and Fort Smith (three hours, twice a week).

CAR & MOTORCYCLE

To best appreciate the NWT, you need wheels. Automobiles can be rented in all major communities.

The territory has two highway networks: a southern system, linking most communities in the North Slave, South Slave and Deh Cho regions; and the Dempster Hwy, which winds through the Mackenzie Delta. Getting to the Delta from southern NWT requires a two-day detour through BC and the Yukon. Roads are either sealed or are gravel roads.

In summer free ferries cross several rivers; in winter vehicles drive across on 4ft-thick ice. Travel is interrupted for several weeks during 'breakup' (April and May) and 'freeze-up' (November). High river levels can interrupt ferry services on the Dempster for days. Check www.dot.gov.nt.ca for current conditions.

If traveling by yourself, make a trip plan and share it with someone responsible. Bring the right gear for the season and extra food, water and a sleeping bag in case you break down. If you do break down, stay with your vehicle. There is no phone reception along most of the Dempster Hwy and along some other remote roads; consider taking a satellite phone.

YELLOWKNIFE

POP 19,234

Amid the droning bush planes and picturesque houseboats of Yellowknife's Old Town, it's still possible to detect a palpable frontier spirit. It's as if you're standing on the edge of a large, undiscovered and barely comprehensible wilderness – and you *are*. Draw a line north from Yellowknife to the Arctic Ocean and you won't cross a single road.

Friendly, multicultural, subarctic Yellowknife supports 50% of the NWT population and is a blend of Dene and Métis from across the territory; Inuit and Inuvialuit from further north; grizzled non-Aboriginal pioneers; get-rich-quick newcomers from southern Canada; and a sizable selection of more recent immigrants from different parts of the world.

Named Somba K'e (Place of Money) in the local Tlicho language, the city, a mining hub and surprisingly artsy place, has been the territorial capital since 1967.

History

When the first Europeans reached Great Slave Lake in 1771, the north shore was home to the Tetsot'ine, who were dubbed the Yellowknives due to their penchant for copper blades. Wars and disease eradicated them, but the moniker remained.

Over a century later, Klondike-bound prospectors on Yellowknife Bay unearthed gold. By the mid-1930s, bush planes had made the area accessible to commercial mining. Yellowknife became a boomtown.

In 1967, when Ottawa devolved management of the NWT, Yellowknife became the capital. Though gold mining ceased in the early 21st century, diamonds were discovered nearby in 1991, with subsequent diamond mines fueling a new boom, and turning Yellowknife into the cosmopolitan place it now is. Though plans for more diamond exploration are afoot, locals are wondering what's next when the stones run low in a decade or so.

Sights

Uphill from the Old Town, Yellowknife's less characterful downtown was built – quite literally – on gold in the 1940s and '50s.

★Prince of Wales Northern Heritage Centre MUSEUM
(Map p798; ☎867-873-7551; www.pwnhc.ca; ⊙10:30am-5pm; P ♿) FREE Acting as NWT's historical and cultural archive, this well-laid-out museum overlooks Frame Lake. Expertly

assembled displays address natural history, European exploration, Northern aviation, diamond mining and, especially, Dene and Inuit history and culture. Temporary exhibits include exceptional soapstone and whalebone sculpture by Inuvialuit artist Abraham Anghik Ruben. There's a cafe with leafy perspectives and a good zone for younger kids.

Yellowknife Cultural Crossroads PUBLIC ART
(Map p798; Franklin Ave) On a huge boulder by the road there's a striking work of art: a soaring eagle, a whirl of colorful handprints and the skeletal outline of a tipi. In front there's a bronze replica sculpture of the one found inside the Legislative Assembly, and another stone sculpture. This work is a collaboration between Métis, Dene, Inuvialuit, French-Canadian and English-Canadian artists.

NWT Diamond Centre NOTABLE BUILDING
(Map p798; ☎867-920-7108; 5105 49th St; ⏲10am-6pm Mon-Sat) Not just a place to buy your diamond bling, this gallery provides a good overview of diamond mining in Canada's frigid north. The accompanying video explains the difference between different diamond types and why they truly are forever. Diamond-polishing sessions are held from 2:30pm to 3:30pm.

Bush Pilot's Monument MONUMENT
(Map p798) Perched atop 'The Rock,' a large outcrop in the middle of the Old Town, this simple needle pays homage to the gutsy bush pilots who opened up the NWT a century ago. Climb the stairs to the viewpoint to watch modern floatplane traffic and envy the people on polychromatic houseboats in the bay.

Legislative Assembly NOTABLE BUILDING
(Map p798; ☎867-669-2230; www.assembly.gov.nt.ca; 4570 48th St; ⏲9am-6pm Mon-Fri year-round, tours 10:30am, 1:30pm & 3:30pm Mon-Fri & 1:30pm Sun Jun-Aug)  In the impressive, igloo-shaped Legislative Assembly, you can learn about the territory's aboriginal-style government by joining a free hour-long tour. There's Northern art throughout, you get to peek into the chamber where debates happen, and you learn the story of the Speaker's Mace, the symbol of authority engraved with the slogan 'One land, many voices.'

Activities

In popular **Fred Henne Territorial Park** (www.nwtparks.ca) there's chilly swimming at **Long Lake Beach**.

With clear skies in August and for much of winter, Yellowknife is considered to be one of the best places in the world to view the **northern lights**.

There are various hikes around town. Longest and best is the 9km Frame Lake Trail. Start downtown in Capital Area Park; spurs connect to the 1.2km Range Lake Trail and precipitous Jackfish Lake Trail. There's also the 3.2km Prospector Trail, in Fred Henne Territorial Park.

Yellowknife Outdoor Adventures OUTDOORS
(Map p798; ☎867-444-8320; www.yellowknifeoutdooradventures.com; 3603 Franklin Ave; 1hr snowmobiling $125, half-day pike fishing $145) These guys organize top-notch pike fishing, birding and floatplane flightseeing tours in summer and snowmobile day tours and aurora borealis-viewing packages in winter.

NORTHWEST TERRITORIES IN...

One Week

Fly to **Yellowknife** and spend the first day at the **Prince of Wales Northern Heritage Centre**, ambling around the **Old Town** (Map p798), and getting out on the lake among floatplanes and houseboats. In the evening, sip beer, eat lake fish and (in summer) watch the sun not set.

Then rent a car and head south. Car-camp along the Waterfalls Route, then drive to **Fort Smith** (p805) to snap the woolly behemoths that inhabit **Wood Buffalo National Park** (p806). Backtrack to **Fort Simpson** (p807) and join a flightseeing tour into **Nahanni National Park Reserve** (p808).

Two Weeks

Spend two days exploring Yellowknife, then fly to to Fort Simpson, meet your outfitter and spend 10 days paddling the paradisiacal **South Nahanni River** (p808).

Or...stop in **Norman Wells** (p810) en route to Inuvik for a couple of days' paddling on the Mackenzie River, and then drive the scenic, challenging **Dempster Highway** (p811) from Inuvik and back. And then follow the one-week trip south from Yellowknife.

Yellowknife

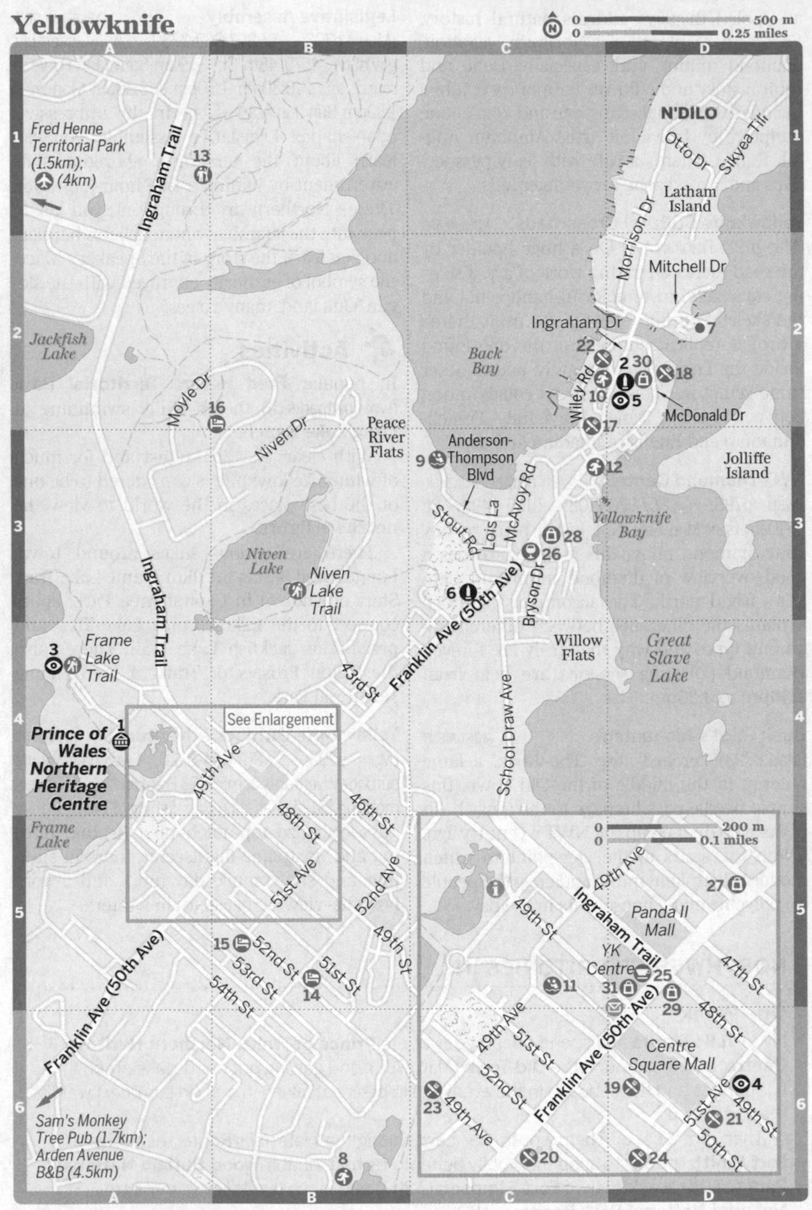

Old Town Paddle & Co WATER SPORTS
(Map p798; ☎867-447-4927; www.oldtownpaddle.com; 3506 Racine Rd; daily rental $50; ⊙Wed & Fri-Sun) Rent your stand-up paddleboard (SUP) here to explore the vast wateriness of Great Slave Lake. Courses ($85) available; check website for dates.

Overlander Sports KAYAKING, SKIING
(Map p798; ☎867-873-2474; www.overlandersports.com; 4909 50th St; kayak rental per day/week $45/200, ski/snowshoe rental per day $25/18; ⊙9:30am-6pm Mon-Fri, to 5pm Sat) Yellowknife's main outfitter store rents canoes and kayaks in summer and cross-country skis in winter.

Yellowknife

Top Sights
1 Prince of Wales Northern Heritage Centre ... A4

Sights
2 Bush Pilot's Monument ... D2
3 Legislative Assembly ... A4
4 NWT Diamond Centre ... D6
5 Old Town ... D2
6 Yellowknife Cultural Crossroads ... C3

Activities, Courses & Tours
7 Air Tindi ... D2
8 My Backyard Tours ... B6
9 Narwal Northern Adventures ... C3
10 Old Town Paddle & Co ... C2
11 Overlander Sports ... C5
12 Yellowknife Outdoor Adventures ... C3
13 Yellowknife Ski Club ... A1

Sleeping
Bayside B&B ... (see 18)
14 Embleton House B&B ... B5
15 Jenny's B&B ... B5
16 Sean's Guesthouse & Aurora Tours ... B2

Eating
17 Bullocks Bistro ... C2
18 Dancing Moose Café ... D2
19 Fat Fox ... D6
20 Javaroma ... C6
21 Korea House ... D6
22 Wildcat Café ... C2
23 Yellowknife Farmers' Market ... C6
24 Zehabesha ... D6

Drinking & Nightlife
25 Gourmet Cup ... D5
26 Woodyard Brewhouse & Eatery ... C3

Shopping
27 Erasmus Apparel ... D5
28 Gallery of the Midnight Sun ... C3
29 Northern Images ... D5
30 Old Town Glassworks ... D2
31 Yellowknife Book Cellar ... D5

Narwal Northern Adventures KAYAKING
(Map p798; ☎867-873-6443; www.narwal.ca; 4702 Anderson-Thompson Blvd; kayak rental per day $45) Run out of a B&B on Back Bay (part of Great Slave Lake), it rents canoes, SUPs and kayaks, and also offers entertaining floating dinner-theater tours, multiday kayaking along the North Arm of the lake and lessons.

Yellowknife Ski Club SNOW SPORTS
(Map p798; ☎867-669-9754; www.skiyellowknife.com; Ingraham Trail; day-pass individual/family $10/25) The nexus for cross-country ski activities is on Hwy 4 near the Hwy 3 intersection. There are 14km of trails, some lit.

Tours

Dogsledding, a Dene fish barbecue, overnighting in a trapper's tent, sightseeing from a bush plane: Yellowknife offers plenty of 'only in the NWT' experiences.

★ **Strong Interpretation** TOURS
(☎867-873-5546; www.experienceyellowknife.com; 3hr history tour $80) With over two decades of guiding experience, local resident Rosie puts together fantastic walking tours, from historical tours of Yellowknife to rambles in the boreal forest in search of edible and medicinal plants. Custom-made tours arranged on request, depending on whether you're interested in local art, Northern culture, mining heritage or more.

★ **North Star Adventures** OUTDOORS
(☎867-446-2900; www.northstaradventures.ca) This aboriginal-run company offers excellent Dene cultural tours ($89), boat tours ($79), fishing trips ($109), aurora-viewing trips ($109) and snowmobiling on Great Slave Lake (2½ hours, $158).

★ **Air Tindi** SCENIC FLIGHTS
(Map p798; ☎867-669-8218; www.airtindi.com; 23 Mitchell Dr; 30min/1hr/4hr tour per person $140/245/569) Offers excellent 30-minute tours over the city, Ingraham Trail and Yellowknife Bay. There's also a dramatic four-hour tour to Great Slave Lake's cliff-flanked East Arm, with an hour-long stop for hiking. Five-person minimum. Very occasionally, it runs an 11-hour scenic flight trip to Nahanni National Park ($1449 per person, seven-person minimum).

Borealis Bike Tours Unlimited CYCLING
(www.borealisbiketours-unlimited.com; tours $84; ⏲tours 6pm Tue-Fri, 10am, 2pm & 6:30pm Sat & Sun) Want to cycle on snow? Then go for one of the three-hour fat-bike tours run by an enthusiastic Ontario expat. Book in advance via email.

My Backyard Tours OUTDOORS
(Map p798; ☎867-920-4654; www.mybackyardtours.com; 65 Rycon Dr; city tour $60, half-day northern-lights tour $118) Recommended city walking tours and artists'-studio tours in

summer and northern-lights tour packages in winter. Can also organize multiday Arctic photography workshops and trout fishing at Point Lake.

B Dene Adventures CULTURAL

(☎867-444-0451; www.bdene.com) These recommended summer and winter tours have a focus on Northern experiences and, particularly, Dene cultural tours that guide you through the N'diloh and Dettah communities (from $75 per person). The base for activities is a lakeside camp.

Beck's Kennels ADVENTURE

(☎867-873-5603; www.beckskennels.com; 124 Curry Dr) In winter take an 8km guided dogsled tour ($65), learn to drive your own team ($75) or chase the northern lights ($140). Multiday adventures cost $400 per day. In summer the dogs pull ATVs: fun but not the same.

Aurora Village ADVENTURE

(☎867-669-0006; www.auroravillage.com) Specialists in aurora-viewing trips on special heated seats ($120 including transport, drinks and snacks), it also offers dogsledding ($95), snowmobiling ($95) and snowshoeing ($95). The lodge and the viewing areas are located just off the first section of the Ingraham Trail.

Festivals & Events

★Snowking Winter Festival PERFORMING ARTS

(www.snowking.ca; Mar) The Snowking, a grizzled houseboater, organizes this great winter event, hosting concerts, theatrical performances and hockey games right through March at a giant ice castle he builds on Yellowknife Bay.

Folk on the Rocks MUSIC

(www.folkontherocks.com; day/weekend pass $90/130; mid-Jul) This stellar two-day event on Long Lake features everything from hip-hop and rock to Dene drumming. It draws musicians from throughout Canada.

Old Town Ramble & Ride CULTURAL

(www.oldtownyk.com; end Jul–early Aug) This lively weeklong cultural fest culminates in a three-day weekend of bike rallies, crafts demonstrations, art shows, floatplane tours and live music.

Sleeping

Jenny's B&B B&B $

(Map p798; ☎867-765-5456; ayk5102@gmail.com; 5102 52 St; r $85;) A block away from the main street, friendly, helpful Jenny presides over a clutch of tidy, compact rooms. The walls are quite thin, so you may feel like you're in bed with your neighbors. Breakfast ingredients await in the shared kitchen.

Fred Henne Territorial Park CAMPGROUND $

(☎867-920-2472; www.nwtparks.ca; Hwy 3; tent/RV sites $22.50/32; May-Sep;) This is the closest campground to town with full facilities for Recreational Vehicles (RVs), tent pads and plenty of lake beachfront. You can walk to downtown in 40 minutes via trails.

★Sean's Guesthouse & Aurora Tours GUESTHOUSE $$

(Map p798; ☎867-444-1211; www.seansguesthouse.com; 133b Moyle Dr; s/d $95/110;) Travelers are raving about Sean and his cozy, immaculate Scandi-style home, set in the quiet residential neighborhood by Niven Lake. It's like staying with a good friend (who's a great cook to boot); Sean is happy to share his knowledge of

WORTH A TRIP

A FLYING VISIT

The excellent **Blachford Lake Lodge** (☎867-873-3303; www.blachfordlakelodge.com; 2 nights cottage/lodge per 2 adults incl transport & meals $2225/3378;) sits on a pristine lake a half-hour floatplane flight from Yellowknife. It's a stunning spot to get away from it all, offering numerous summer and winter activities. You can stay either in rustic wood cabins or in the lodge itself, where smart, colorful rooms give you the chance to see the aurora from under the covers.

Sociable common areas include lounges, decks, the dining room and an outdoor Jacuzzi. There are skis, skates, snowshoes, kayaks, canoes, hiking paths and more at your disposal and fishing, snowmobiling and husky-sledding excursions are easily arranged. Prince William and Kate made headlines when they went for a paddle on the lake here in 2011.

It's a friendly, relaxed place and it's often looking for volunteer staff, including wwoofers for the organic vegetable garden.

Yellowknife. Every evening (August to April), he also does outings into the countryside to chase the northern lights ($100 per person).

Bayside B&B B&B $$

(Map p798; ☎867-669-8844; www.baysidenorth.com; 3505 McDonald Dr; s/d from $95/105;) There are not many lodgings in Yellowknife where you can watch floatplanes take off from your bedroom window, but this cute guesthouse with a shingled turret is one of them. There are just four snug rooms, two with their own bathrooms; cooked breakfast in the cafe downstairs includes such delights as eggs with Arctic char.

Embleton House B&B B&B $$

(Map p798; ☎867-873-2892; www.embletonhouse.com; 5203 52nd St; s/d with shared bath $105/126, with private bath $163/184;) This well-kitted-out downtown B&B offers two options: compact, cozy rooms with shared bathroom and kitchen, or fabulous decorative themed suites with private whirlpool baths, robes and well-equipped kitchenettes. In both, ingredients are supplied for you to make your own breakfast.

Eating

★Fat Fox CAFE $

(Map p798; 5008 50th St; mains $8-14; 7am-7pm Mon-Fri, 9am-7pm Sat;) This is Yellowknife's top cafe: think mismatched furniture, twinkling fairy lights, cozy nook at the back, sofas and armchairs you can spend all day in, a book exchange as well as an interesting tea and coffee selection. Daily lunchtime specials include the likes of lentil curry and baked potato with chili. Great cakes, too.

Korea House KOREAN $

(Map p798; ☎867-669-0188; 5103 50th St; mains $8-17; 11am-8pm Mon-Sat;) What this place lacks in atmosphere – it's a brightly lit, canteen-style setup – it makes up for with authentic Korean flavors. The spicy tofu stew is a fantastic cold-weather warmer, the *bibimbap* (mixed rice bowl) comes with lots of fresh veggies, and the *bulgogi* (grilled beef) and the veggie dumplings hit the spot, too.

Javaroma CAFE $

(Map p798; www.javaroma.ca; 5201 Franklin Ave; light meals $6-10; 7am-10pm Mon-Fri, 8am-10pm Sat, 9am-10pm Sun;) This main-drag joint offers some of the best coffee in town, accompanied by sandwiches, soups, tasty muffins and bubble teas. There's outdoor seating, albeit on the busy road, and occasional acoustic live music in the evenings.

★Zehabesha ETHIOPIAN $$

(Map p798; ☎867-873-6400; 5030 51st St; mains $9-19; 11am-9pm Mon-Sat;) Authentic Ethiopian food? In northern Canada? As unexpected as it is welcome, this unpretentious restaurant has earned itself a loyal clientele with generous portions of curried goat, *doro wot* (chicken stew) and other flavorful offerings. The *mahiberawi* combination is a great way to try a little of each dish with *injera* (spongy sourdough flatbread).

Dancing Moose Café CAFE $$

(Map p798; ☎867-669-8842; www.dancingmoosecafe.ca; 3505 McDonald Dr; mains $13-21; 8am-3pm Tue-Sun;) Watch floatplanes taking off as you kick back in the backyard of this pleasant cafe. The interior gets busy at lunchtime, with soups, salads and sandwich specials. It's also a good breakfast choice, with ingredients often locally sourced.

Wildcat Café CANADIAN $$

(Map p798; ☎867-873-8850; cnr Wiley Rd & Doornbos Lane; mains $17-42; 7am-10pm Jun-Sep) A beloved local landmark, this refurbished Old Town log cabin has been churning out food since 1937, though today's fare is more sophisticated, ranging from pickerel tempura tacos and smoked Arctic char bagel to bison rib eyes and epic burgers.

★Bullocks Bistro SEAFOOD $$$

(Map p798; ☎867-873-3474; 3534 Weaver Dr; mains $25-40; 11:30am-9pm Mon-Sat, 4-9pm Sun) This legendary shack, brimful of bumper stickers, happy diners, diners' graffiti, and mix-and-match furniture, is a sassy, humorous place specializing in huge portions of fish. It comes pan-fried, grilled or deep-fried with chips, salad and a very hefty price tag. Slabs of grilled arctic char are superb, as is the blue-cheese dressing.

★Yellowknife Farmers' Market MARKET

(Map p798; www.yellowknifefarmersmarket.ca; Somba K'e Civic Plaza; 5:15-7:30pm Tue Jun 7-Sep 20;) If you're in Yellowknife on a Tuesday, you're in for a treat. The farmers' market is a great place to hang out, catch up on local gossip and try everything from authentic Indian, Japanese and Vietnamese home cooking to Russian *pelmeni* (dumplings) and borscht, Filipino-Taiwanese fusion, awesome sandwiches, and cakes and quiches by a Cordon Bleu–trained chef.

Drinking & Nightlife

★ Woodyard Brewhouse & Eatery MICROBREWERY
(Map p798; ☎867-873-2337; www.nwtbrewingco.com; 3905 Franklin Ave; beer from $6; ⏰5-11pm Mon, 11:30am-11pm Tue-Thu, 11:30am-1am Fri & Sat; wi-fi) This award-winning microbrewery is a fantastic new addition to Yellowknife's dining scene. Consistently packed with locals and visitors, it does many things right: the food (thin-crust pizza, mac 'n' cheese) is great, the friendly service is prompt, the decor is industrial-meets-hunter's-cabin and there's an outdoor patio for kicking back with a pint of one of its seven beers. Does get noisy, though.

Gourmet Cup COFFEE
(Map p798; ☎867-873-8782; www.gourmetcupyellowknife.ca; Franklin Ave, basement of the YK Centre; ⏰7:30am-6pm Mon-Fri, 9am-6pm Sat; wi-fi) Filled to the brim with loose-leaf teas and bags of gourmet coffee beans, this basement coffee shop is a good place to join laptop-wielding locals for a caffeine fix.

Shopping

★ Northern Images ARTS & CRAFTS
(Map p798; ☎867-873-5944; www.northernimages.ca; 4801 Franklin Ave; ⏰10am-6pm Mon-Sat, noon-6pm Sun) Owned by aboriginal art-and-crafts cooperatives, this excellent place carries the famed Inuit prints and lithographs from Cape Dorset, Pangnirtung and Ulukhaktok, along with splendid soapstone sculptures, Dene birch-bark baskets and moccasins and art by Yukon artists. Prices are very fair and it can arrange shipping.

★ Erasmus Apparel CLOTHING
(Map p798; ☎867-444-0307; www.erasmusapparel.com; 4602 Franklin Ave; ⏰10am-6pm Mon-Sat) Come here for colorful, locally designed hoodies, T-shirts, tops, Dene mittens, hats and cool shades that double as bottle openers.

★ Yellowknife Book Cellar BOOKS
(Map p798; www.yellowknifebooks.com; 4923 49th St; ⏰9:30am-8pm Mon-Fri, to 6pm Sat, noon-5pm Sun) This bookstore stocks a great selection of Northern and aboriginal titles; it also sells maps.

Old Town Glassworks GLASS
(Map p798; ☎867-669-7654; www.oldtownglassworks.com; 3510 McDonald Dr; workshops $54; ⏰10am-6pm Mon-Fri, noon-5pm Sat & Sun) This Old Town shop makes exquisite Northern-themed glasses and vases from old bottles. Want to do one to your exact specifications? Take one of the entertaining workshop classes (two to four daily; two hours). Also rents bicycles.

Gallery of the Midnight Sun GIFTS & SOUVENIRS
(Map p798; ☎867-873-8064; www.gallerymidnightsun.com; Franklin Ave; ⏰10am-6pm Mon-Sat, noon-5pm Sun) Has an ample supply of aboriginal art, including ornately decorated Dene moccasins and jackets, soapstone sculpture by Inuvialuit artists and striking musk-ox-horn and bison-horn jewelry. Also stocks prints and souvenirs.

Information

You'll find the big banks downtown on Franklin Ave.

Ambulance & Fire (☎867-873-2222) Note that ☎911 is not the emergency number in the NWT.

Police (☎emergencies 867-669-1111, nonemergencies ☎867-669-5100; 5010 49th Ave)

Northern Frontier Visitors Centre (Map p798; ☎867-873-4262; www.visityellowknife.com; 4807 49th St; ⏰9:30am-5:30pm Mon-Fri, noon-5pm Sat & Sun; wi-fi) This place has reams of maps and brochures, plus the indispensable annual *Explorers' Guide*. Inside are good exhibits on the NWT environment, a decent souvenir selection and free wi-fi. To explore town, grab a free bike.

Yellowknike Old Town Soundwalk (www.yellowknifesoundwalk.ca) An excellent downloadable app that takes you on a guided tour of Old Town.

Post office (Map p798; www.canadapost.ca; 4902 Franklin Ave; ⏰9am-5:30pm Mon-Fri)

Stanton Territorial Hospital (☎867-669-4111; www.stha.ca; 550 Byrne Rd; ⏰24hr)

Yellowknife Public Library (2nd fl, Centre Square Mall; ⏰9:30am-8:30pm Mon-Thu, 10am-6pm Fri, 10am-5pm Sat) Northern books, free internet, rowdy youth.

Getting There & Away

AIR

Yellowknife is the NWT's air hub. Prices given here are all one way. First Air serves Hay River ($236, 45 minutes) and Fort Simpson ($705, one hour), as well as Cambridge Bay ($1165) and Iqaluit ($1758) via Rankin Inlet ($1243). Both First Air and Canadian North fly to Inuvik ($900, 2½ hours) via Norman Wells ($731, one hour); the latter is also served by the comparably priced **North-Wright Airways** (☎867-587-2288; www.north-wrightairways.com), which flies Monday to Saturday. Smaller airlines sometimes offer good specials.

Northwestern Air hits Fort Smith ($417 or $199 standby, one hour, Sunday to Friday); **Buffalo Airways** (☎867-873-6112; www.buffaloairways.com), Hay River ($205, 45 minutes, Sunday to Friday); and **Air Tindi** (☎867-669-8200; www.airtindi.com), Fort Simpson ($485, 80 minutes).

BUS

Frontier Coachlines (p796) depart 5pm Monday, Wednesday and Friday from the Shell gas station on Range Lake Rd, stopping in Fort Providence and Enterprise en route to Hay River ($118, 5½ hours).

CAR

Car rental is expensive. A small car typically costs about $80/500 per day/week, *plus* 35¢ per kilometer, with 250 free kilometers thrown in with weekly rentals only. If you're doing major miles, consider renting in Edmonton and driving up. Big-name agencies are at the airport.

The cheapest is **Rent-a-Relic** (Royal Rent-a-Car; ☎867-873-3400; xferrier@ssimicro.com; 356 Old Airport Rd; per day/week $50/325, 50km free per day then 30¢ per km). Expect a battered but serviceable vehicle and a laissez-faire attitude. It does airport pick ups.

Getting Around

TO/FROM AIRPORT

Yellowknife's airport is a couple of kilometers west of downtown. Taxis charge about $15. A free shuttle bus runs to the Explorer Hotel and Yellowknife Inn, among other central hotels.

BICYCLE

From early June until early September, free bikes are available from the visitor center.

BUS

Yellowknife City Transit (☎867-920-5600; www.yellowknife.ca; ticket adult/child over 5yr $3/2) runs three bus routes. Route A serves Old Airport Rd and downtown. Route B circles the Range Lake community and runs downtown. Route C connects downtown and Old Town. Buses run every half-hour, roughly 7:15am to 7pm Monday to Saturday.

TAXI

Cabs are plentiful. Try **City Cab** (☎867-873-4444).

AROUND YELLOWKNIFE

Ingraham Trail

The Ingraham Trail (Hwy 4), 69km east of Yellowknife, is where locals go to play. The partly sealed route reveals scenic, lake-dotted, pine-covered Canadian Shield topography, and offers good fishing, hiking, camping, paddling and, in winter, skiing and snowmobiling.

Prelude Lake ($5.25 per day), 28km from Yellowknife, is a family-oriented spot with a vast **campground** (www.campingnwt.ca; tent/RV sites $15/22.50; ⌚May-Sep; 🐾), boat launch (rentals available) and two nature trails.

At **Hidden Lake Territorial Park** FREE, 46km from Yellowknife, a 1.2km trail leads to popular **Cameron Falls**. Cross the footbridge and crawl to the brink of this marvelous cascade. Another 9km down the Ingraham Trail, a 400m trail goes to Cameron River Ramparts, the falls' smaller cousin.

At **Reid Lake** FREE, 61km from Yellowknife, you can canoe or fish for pike, whitefish and trout. The friendly **campground** (www.campingnwt.ca; tent & RV sites $22.50; ⌚May-Sep; 🐾) has a good beach and walking trail, plus ridgetop campsites with lake views.

In summer, the Ingraham Trail ends at pretty **Tibbitt Lake**, 70km from town.

NORTH SLAVE

The North Slave region, between Great Slave and Great Bear Lakes, is rocky, densely forested, lake-strewn and rich in minerals. Save for the people in Yellowknife, most people here are Tlicho, living traditional (and non-tourist-oriented) lives. This is a true land o' lakes – a wonderland for canoeists, kayakers, fishers and nature lovers.

Highway 3

From Yellowknife, Hwy 3 runs northwest, rounds the North Arm of Great Slave Lake, and dives to Fort Providence (314km).

The first stretch winds through bogs, taiga and pinkish outcrops of the Canadian Shield. Watch out for roller-coaster bumps, caused by the road's heat, which melts the permafrost in summer. **Behchokò** (pop 1926), 10km north of Hwy 3 on an access road, is the largest of NWT's First Nations, with a gas station, lodgings and indigenous art for sale.

Later, the land becomes flat boreal forest, ubiquitous in the southern NWT. The **Mackenzie Bison Sanctuary**, home to Canada's northernmost population of around 4000 free-ranging wood bison, flanks the road for around 150km. The animals outweigh your car and have tempers, so give them space.

South of here, a 5km access road leads to Fort Providence. A few kilometers further, the **Deh Cho Bridge** spans the Mackenzie River.

SOUTH SLAVE

The South Slave region, encompassing the area south of Great Slave Lake, is mostly flat forestland. It's cut through by big rivers and numerous waterfalls, and is home to mighty herds of bison and the historic fur-trading outposts of Hay River and Fort Smith.

Mackenzie Highway

From the Hwy 3 junction, 23km south of the Mackenzie River, the Mackenzie Hwy (Hwy 1) branches west into the Dehcho region and southeast into the South Slave. The Alberta-bound latter branch is dubbed the **Waterfalls Route**.

First up is **Lady Evelyn Falls Territorial Park** (Hwy 1, Km 167) FREE, 7km down the access road to **Kakisa**. There's a short path to the 17m falls, which pour over an ancient, crescent-shaped coral reef, and a **campground** (www.nwtparks.ca; tent & RV sites $28; May-Sep;).

From here, it's 83km to **Enterprise**, a crossroads settlement.

South of Enterprise, the Mackenzie Hwy parallels impressive **Twin Falls Gorge Territorial Park** (Hwy 1, Km 72) FREE. A 2km forested trail links the tiered, 15m **Louise Falls** on the Hay River with splendid Alexandra Falls (33m). There's also a **campground** (www.nwtparks.ca; tent & RV sites $28; May-Sep;) here.

At the Alberta border, 72km south, is the **60th Parallel Territorial Park**. The **visitor center** (867-984-3811; Hwy 1; 8:30am-8:30pm mid-May–mid-Sep;) displays aboriginal crafts; there's a small **campground** (www.campingnwt.ca; tent & RV sites $22.50; May-Sep;) as well.

Hay River

POP 3606

Blue-collar Hay River, settled as a fur-trading post in 1868, is the territory's second-largest town and an important rail terminus, lake harbor and freight-distribution nexus. It's a useful service center rather than a drawcard in itself. The nicest part of town is the original settled area, Vale Island, with a picturesque beach on the impossibly large Great Slave Lake. There's good fishing, boating and dogsledding available. Downtown is dominated by the highway and an out-of-place residential tower. Across the river is a Dene reserve.

Sights & Activities

Vale Island ISLAND

At the mouth of the Hay River on vast Great Slave Lake, this island, linked to the mainland by a bridge, is the oldest and nicest part of town. It's an ensemble of rickety wooden buildings, rusting boats, freight trains and the driftwood-strewn town beach, 7km by road from downtown.

Hay River Heritage Centre MUSEUM

(867-874-3872; cnr Mackenzie Dr & 102nd Ave, Vale Island; 1-5pm Jun-Oct) FREE In the town's old Hudson's Bay Company trading post on Vale Island, this is an enthusiastically run local-history museum, with an absorbing collection of Hay River photos through the ages, period objects and fossils.

Kiwanis Nature Trail WALKING

This interpretive trail starts in Riverview Dr and runs for 5km along the Hay River and the West Channel of Great Slave Lake.

2 Seasons Adventures BOATING

(867-875-7112; www.2seasons.ca; Lagoon Rd; Jun-Sep) runs boat trips to Louise Falls and rents out canoes, kayak and paddleboards. The visitor center can provide information on hiking, flightseeing, fishing, and canoe rentals.

Sleeping

Paradise Garden & Campground CAMPGROUND $

(867-875-4430; www.paradisegardencampground.com; 82 Paradise Rd; tent/RV sites $21/31.50;) Between Enterprise and Hay River on a small organic farm, this friendly, idyllically located place has electrical hookups for RVs and offers berry-picking.

Hay River Territorial Park CAMPGROUND $

(867-874-3772; www.nwtparks.ca; 104th St, Vale Island; tent/RV sites $15/28; May-Sep;) A Frisbee throw from the beach, this densely wooded campground has hot showers, a barbecue area and a children's playground.

Harbour House B&B $$

(867-874-2233; www.greenwayaccommodations.ca; 2 Lakeshore Dr, Vale Island; s/d $85/110;) In a lovely, peaceful setting on Vale Island right next to the beach, this sunny, nautical-feeling B&B sits on flood-cheating pilings. There's a kitchen, a great deck to kick back on, and a good continental breakfast.

Ptarmigan Inn HOTEL $$
(☎867-874-6781; www.ptarmiganinn.com; 10 J Gagnier St; s/d/ste $163/167/207;) In the heart of downtown, Hay River's only true hotel has clean, spacious, well-appointed rooms, a pub, a restaurant and a fitness center with Jacuzzi.

Eating

She Takes The Cake Cafe CAFE $
(☎867-874-3330; 2-4 Courtoreille St; cakes from $4; ⏲8:30am-4pm Mon-Fri, noon-4pm Sat) Right in the heart of town, this cafe serves good coffee, freshly baked sticky cinnamon buns, bagels, muffins, sandwiches and daily lunch specials.

Back Eddy SEAFOOD $$
(☎867-874-6680; 6 Courtoreille St; mains $15-25; ⏲11am-2pm & 5pm-late Mon-Sat;) This low-lit bar and dining room (enter on Capital Dr) is a reliable local favorite. The dinner menu features fresh-caught Great Slave Lake fish, including pan-fried whitefish topped with scallops and shrimp.

Information

Library (www.nwtpls.gov.nt.ca; 75 Woodland Dr; ⏲10am-5pm & 7-9pm Mon-Thu, 1-5pm Fri-Sun;) Free internet in the heart of town.

Visitor Information Center (☎867-874-3180; www.hayriver.com; cnr Mackenzie Hwy & McBryan Dr; ⏲9am-9pm May-Sep) On the highway in the center of town. Off-season, stop by the town hall, a block north on Commercial Dr.

Getting There & Away

AIR

Legendary **Buffalo Airways** (p803) and **First Air** (p795) fly to Yellowknife for $205 (45 minutes) and $236, respectively. **Northwestern Air** (www.nwal.ca) serves Edmonton ($607, 2¼ hours) and Fort Smith ($234, 40 minutes). Fares listed here are one-way.

BUS

Frontier Coachlines (p796) goes from the downtown Rooster convenience store to Yellowknife ($118, six hours) via Fort Providence at 9am on Monday, Wednesday, and Friday; and to Fort Smith ($87, three hours) at 9am on Tuesday and Thursday.

CAR & MOTORCYCLE

By road, it's a paved 38km to Enterprise. About 5km out of town is the turnoff to partially paved Hwy 5, leading 267km to Fort Smith.

TRAIN

Hay River is famously Canada's northernmost rail terminus, but it's freight only.

Fort Smith

POP 2093

On a high bluff above the Slave River, friendly Fort Smith has been the gateway to the North for years, situated at the end of a portage route around the Slave River rapids. The Hudson's Bay Company set up shop here in 1874 and, until Yellowknife became the territorial capital in 1967, it was the administrative center for most of Canada's northern territories. Today it remains a government hub and headquarters of Wood Buffalo National Park, Canada's largest protected area. Two-thirds of the residents are Cree, Chipewyan or Métis.

Sights

Northern Life Museum MUSEUM
(☎867-872-2859; cnr King St & McDougal Rd; ⏲10am-5pm Mon-Sat) FREE This museum has intriguing displays on local history, from the first Dene arrivals 10,000 years ago to the founding of the 19th-century fur-trapping post. Look out for the re-created fur-trapper home and store, plus the taxidermied body of Canus, a whooping-crane sire whose sexual efforts helped save his species from extinction.

Fort Smith Mission Historic Park PARK
(cnr Breynat St & Mercredi Ave; ⏲May-Sep) FREE This park commemorates the days when Fort Smith was Catholicism's beachhead into the North. Self-guided tour maps are available from the visitor center.

Activities

The rapids here are famous among hard-core paddlers and are also the northernmost nesting colony of white pelicans. The Rapids of the Drowned, in front of town, are accessible off Wolf Ave. Upriver, you can hike the Trans Canada Trail, bike from town or walk from the Fort Fitzgerald road to view the Mountain, Pelican and Cassette Rapids.

★ **Pelican Rapids** RIVER
Twelve kilometers south of Fort Smith, an old roadway leads east towards the river, with a footpath dipping down to a creek and ascending a bluff overlooking the tumultuous river. There are not that many pelicans here, but you can wander out onto the great slabs of pink granite rising from the water.

★ **Rapids of the Drowned** RIVER
Named after a fatal 19th-century boat accident, these turbulent rapids are the northernmost pelican nesting site in the world.

Walk ten minutes from the top of Portage St to observe the birds snatching fish out of the swirling waters. Keep your distance to avoid disturbing them.

Festivals & Events

Slave River Paddlefest SPORTS
(www.slaveriverpaddlefest.ca; Aug) Held on the first weekend in August, this wet 'n' wild river festival involves paddling the Slave River, encompassing everything from flat-water canoeing to serious white water. Instructional clinics, Dene traditional games and white-water events are part of the fun.

★ **Dark Sky Festival** LIGHT SHOW
(www.tawbas.ca; mid-Aug) The Thebacha & Wood Buffalo Astronomical Society in Fort Smith runs a weekend full of events around mid-August, when the nights are dark and clear and there's tremendous potential for spotting the northern lights and viewing the stars through a telescope in Wood Buffalo National Park.

Sleeping & Eating

Queen Elizabeth Territorial Park CAMPGROUND $
(867-872-2607; www.campingnwt.ca; tent/RV sites $15/28; May-Sep;) At the end of Tipi Trail, 4km west of town, this lovely underused campground with showers and firewood lies near the river bluff.

★ **Whooping Crane Guest House** B&B $$
(867-872-3426; www.whoopingcraneguesthouse.com; 13 Cassette Crescent; r from $120;) Luxurious, stylish and welcoming, this B&B occupies an intriguing octagonal wooden building down a very quiet street off Calder Ave. Boons include helpful hosts, delicious breakfasts, artistic quilting on the walls, and an abundance of books, bikes and hammocks. One spacious suite has a kitchen and dining area, while two enchantingly decorated rooms boast magnificent private (exterior) bathrooms.

★ **Anna's Home Cooking** CAFE $
(867-872-2582; 338 Calder Ave; lunch $6-11, mains $13-27; 8am-8pm Mon-Fri;) Home cooking prepared with care is the key here, with a range of mighty breakfasts, delicious salads, panini, tasty fresh juices, stone-baked pizzas and lunchtime specials such as chili. Dinner is burgers and more substantial barbecue mains. It's a casual, cozy place with a yoga-healing vibe (massages and more available) and outdoor seating.

Shopping

Rusty Raven ARTS & CRAFTS
(867-872-2606; 66 Portage Ave; 8am-5:30pm Mon-Fri, 9am-5:30pm Sat, 9am-5pm Sun) This sweet place sells some Dene beadwork, local art, books on local attractions and ESPE faux-leather handbags.

Information

Library (170 McDougal Rd; 2:30-5:30pm & 7-9pm Mon-Thu, 2:30-5:30pm Fri, 2-5pm Sat & Sun) Closed Sundays July to September.

Town of Fort Smith (www.fortsmith.ca) A good resource for local information.

Wood Buffalo National Park Information Centre (867-872-7960; www.pc.gc.ca; 149 McDougal Rd; 9am-6pm;) Located in Fort Smith, this national park information point also doubles as the town visitor center. It has an interesting exhibition on local ecology, as well as inspiring audiovisual displays of the park. It runs guided walks in the park in summer.

Getting There & Away

Northwestern Air (867-872-2216; www.nwal.ca) serves Yellowknife ($397 one way, one hour), Hay River ($224 one way, 45 minutes) and Edmonton ($680 one-way, two hours), as well as Fort McMurray and Fort Chipewyan.

Frontier Coachlines (p796) has services to Hay River ($87, three hours, Tue & Thu at 1pm). In winter, an ice road runs to Fort McMurray, Alberta.

Wood Buffalo National Park

Straddling the Alberta–NWT border is one of the world's largest national parks (44,000 sq km): a vast expanse of taiga forest, karstic formations and enormous freshwater systems.

The park was established in 1922 to protect a large, dark and distinctly Northern subspecies of bison. Thousands inhabit the region and you'll likely see them grazing along roadsides. Their interaction with wolves here was memorably filmed in the BBC's *Frozen Planet* and David Suzuki's *The Nature of Things*.

Also protected is the last wild migratory flock of whooping cranes on earth. These birds nearly disappeared, but are now rebounding. They, along with millions of ducks and geese, avail themselves of the wetlands including the Peace-Athabasca Delta, among the world's largest freshwater deltas. Moose, caribou, bears and lynx are also residents, along with, in summer, countless mosquitoes and horseflies.

Sights & Activities

Salt Plains Lookout VIEWPOINT
Some 25km west of Fort Smith along the road to Hay River, an 11km access road branches off toward a viewpoint overlooking the great salt-encrusted expanse of the Salt Plains, punctuated by salt mounds. Steps lead down to the plains so that you can investigate further; visitors are requested to walk barefoot to preserve the fragile ecology.

★Highway 5 SCENIC DRIVE
Approaching from the west, points of interest include the enormous **Angus Sinkhole** (Angus Fire Tower), disappearing **Nyarling River**, and **Little Buffalo River Falls**, which has an unstaffed campground and 2km nature trail. Further on, there's an 11km side road to Salt Plains Lookout; a short trail leads down to a vast white field formed by saltwater burbling from an ancient seabed.

Peace Point Road SCENIC DRIVE
Between Fort Smith and Peace Point is **Salt River Day-Use Area**, home to a snake hibernaculum (they only have group sex in late April), and the trailhead for excellent day hikes to salt flats and sinkholes. About 60km from Fort Smith, at popular Pine Lake Campground, you can bask on white-sand beaches and swim in the aquamarine water.

Canoeing CANOEING
An adventurous option is to canoe from Peace Point, then hike 13km in to the Sweetgrass area, where there are vast grasslands and old bison corrals. Here you'll see herds of bison and possibly wolves.

Hiking HIKING
There are eight walking trails in the park, ranging from easy to moderate and varying in length from 500m to 13km. Particularly rewarding are the North Loop (7.5km) and South Loop (9km) at Salt River. The former for its sinkholes, the latter for its salt meadows and salt flats at Grosbeak Lake.

Sleeping

Little Buffalo River Falls Territorial Park CAMPGROUND $
(867-872-2602; www.campingnwt.ca; tent/RV sites $15/22.50; May-Sep) Just off the road to Hay River, near Fort Smith, this small campground with six nonpowered campsites sits near the picturesque Little Buffalo River Falls.

Pine Lake Campground CAMPGROUND $
(www.pc.gc.ca; tent & RV sites $15.70; May-Sep;) This peaceful campground is 60km from Fort Smith along Pine Lake Rd. Sites come with picnic tables and firepits. Bug repellent is essential.

Information

Wood Buffalo National Park Information Center is in Fort Smith.

DEH CHO

Dehcho means 'big river' in the local tongue, and this southwestern region is awash in waterways, most notably the Mackenzie, Liard and Nahanni. The area is also blessed with one of Canada's most spectacular national parks, bisected by the Mackenzie Mountains, warmer temperatures and rich Dene culture.

Fort Simpson

POP 1238

In the local tongue, Fort Simpson is *Liídlii Kue,* meaning 'Where Two Rivers Meet' – the voluminous Liard and Mackenzie Rivers being the waterways in question. For centuries, the Dene used to gather here to trade, before the Hudson Bay Company established a fur-trading post in 1822, followed by the priests and the gold-seekers. Today, with an easygoing blend of Dene, Métis and European cultures, it's the regional hub, has all services and is the gateway to nearby Nahanni National Park Reserve.

Sights & Activities

Historic **MacPherson House** (cnr 93rd Ave & MacKenzie Dr) and the **cabin** (MacKenzie Dr) of eccentric gold prospector Albert Faille, who never struck it lucky, are located along the Mackenzie riverfront. **Elevate** (www.openskycreativesociety.com; early Jul), held around Canada Day, is a three-day music-and-arts event. The organizers have a **gallery** (867-695-3005; www.openskycreativesociety.com; 100th St; 1-4pm Mon-Fri) in the library building in town displaying contemporary and traditional Dehcho art.

Flightseeing excursions or canoeing trips to the Nahanni are the reason most people are in town: air companies are located on Antoine Dr near the in-town airstrip. If you want to paddle the Liard and the Mackenzie on your lonesome, Simpson Air rents canoes for $25 per day.

Sleeping

Fort Simpson Territorial Campground CAMPGROUND $
(867-695-2321; www.nwtparks.ca; tent/RV sites $22.50/28; May-Sep;) Centrally located in woods near the river, the campground has showers, pit toilets and 32 pleasant campsites.

★ **Mackenzie Rest Inn** B&B $$
(867-695-2357; www.mackenzierest.ca; 10518 99th St; s/d with shared bath $150/180;) A sweet, charming, well-furnished B&B in a land of floatplanes and giant rivers. Faultless hospitality is matched with very cute, stylish rooms in a characterful, nobly furnished house with great river views, books and magazines on Canada's North, and relaxing deck spaces. Rooms are all different – the top one is our favorite – and share modern bathrooms.

Willows Inn MOTEL $$
(867-695-2077; www.janor.ca; cnr of 103 Ave & Antoine Dr; s/d $170/195;) This spotless new motel comprises six self-sufficient, spacious rooms geared toward all seasons, with air-con and in-floor heating, and all with coffeemakers, fridges and microwaves. There's also a fully equipped guest kitchen and appealing patio with deck chairs and a barbecue.

Janor Guest House B&B $$
(867-695-2077; www.janor.ca; cnr 99B Ave & 100th St; s/d $150/175;) This homey guesthouse, run by the welcoming Leah and Colin, has six snug bedrooms (two of them en suite) and guests have full use of the sunny living room and fully equipped kitchen. They can also help themselves to the vegetables in the garden, have a barbecue or use the small gym.

Information

Fort Simpson visitor center (867-695-3182; www.fortsimpson.com; 8am-8pm Mon-Fri, 10am-8pm Sat & Sun May-Sep) has brochures on Fort Simpson and the NWT.

Nahanni National Park Reserve visitor center (867-695-7750; www.parkscanada.gc.ca/nahanni; cnr 100 St & 100 Ave; 8:30am-noon & 1-5pm Jul & Aug, shorter hr Sep-Jun) provides information on the Nahanni National Park Reserve.

Getting There & Around

Air Tindi (p803) serves Yellowknife ($485 one-way, 80 minutes, daily except Sun). **First Air** (p795) does nonstop flights to Yellowknife ($704) and connecting flights to Edmonton, Hay River, Inuvik and Ottawa. There's no bus service.

If you're driving south, this is your last chance to fuel up for hundreds of kilometers.

Nahanni National Park Reserve

To many, Nahanni means wilderness. Situated in the southwestern NWT near the Yukon border, this 30,000-sq-km park embraces its namesake, the epic **South Nahanni River**. This untamed river tumbles more than 500km through the jagged Mackenzie Mountains. It's a dream destination for canoeing and one of Canada's most spectacular places.

Appropriately, the Nahanni is a Canadian Heritage river, and the park is a Unesco World Heritage site. In 2009, the federal government and Dehcho First Nations signed an agreement increasing the park's size more than sixfold.

Sights

★ **Virginia Falls** WATERFALL
Yes, there is a higher set of falls in British Columbia, but for the sheer gushing power of two mighty torrents of water, falling from a height of 96m (twice the height of Niagara Falls), and for the remote, spectacular setting, Virginia Falls is the most impressive waterfall in Canada.

Glacier Lake LAKE
Flanked by the Britnell Glacier in the northwest reaches of the park, this spectacular lake is surrounded by the granite mountains of the Ragged Range and is the gateway to the climbers' mecca known as the Cirque of the Unclimbables.

Activities

White-Water Rafting & Canoeing

Raft and canoe trips can be arranged with a licensed outfitter. Prices range from $4900 to $8120, depending on distance and number of days. Try to book months in advance. Canoes require some basic experience; rafts, steered by a guide, are relaxing and suitable for all.

Most trips begin at Moose Ponds, Rabbitkettle Lake or Virginia Falls, because those are where floatplanes can land. From Moose Ponds to Rabbitkettle is about 160km, much of it Class III white water. For the 118km from Rabbitkettle to the falls, the river meanders placidly through broad valleys. Once the falls are portaged, it's another 252km to Blackstone Territorial Park, first through steep-sided, turbulent canyons, and then along the broad Liard River. The lower-river trip requires seven to 10 days. From Rabbitkettle it's around 14 days, while from Moose Ponds it's 21.

★Black Feather KAYAKING, CANOEING
(☎705-746-1372; www.blackfeather.com) This operator's offerings include special family and women-only trips. Kayaking in the Canadian Arctic and canoeing the Nahanni are on offer; a 10-day Nahanni Getaway costs $5150.

Nahanni River Adventures CANOEING, RAFTING
(☎867-668-3180; www.nahanni.com) Highly rated, Yukon-based adventure travel company with top-notch guides. Offers canoeing and rafting trips along 20 Canadian and Alaskan rivers, including the South Nahanni, Tatshenshini-Alsek and Firth. Nahanni trips range from eight ($5220) to 21 ($8120) days.

Nahanni Wilderness Adventures CANOEING, RAFTING
(☎403-678-3374; www.nahanniwild.com) Eco-conscious operator committed to minimizing carbon footprint through shorter charter flights. David has been paddling the South Nahanni River since 1989 and arranges trips ranging from eight ($4950) to 22 ($6250) days.

Hiking & Climbing

There is also some excellent hiking in the Nahanni River Valley, from the boardwalk leading to the waterfall lookout to the full-day hike to the peak of **Sunblood Mountain**, across the river from Virginia Falls campground. The **Ragged Range** around Glacier Lake offers days of hiking and challenging rock-climbing routes.

Cirque of the Unclimbables CLIMBING
There's world-class rock climbing in the granite peaks around Glacier Lake. The Lotus Flower Tower, an 18-pitch 5.11 monolith known as one of the most beautiful big-wall routes in the world, throws down the gauntlet to experienced climbers.

Hot Springs

There are two sets of hot springs in the park: **Rabbitkettle Hot Springs**, surrounded by the largest tufa mounds in the northern world, and the smaller, smellier, sulfur-rich **Kraus Hot Springs**. You can soak in both.

Flightseeing

Wolverine Air SCENIC FLIGHTS
(☎867-695-2263; www.wolverineair.com; Antoine Dr) Friendly operator offering flights to Nahanni National Park Reserve; some with landings at Virginia Falls (from $570 per person) and Glacier Lake (from $720 per person). Call them as they don't answer emails.

★Simpson Air SCENIC FLIGHTS
(☎867-695-2505; www.simpsonair.ca; Antoine Dr) Excellent operator that handles most flightseeing excursions to Nahanni National Park, including Virginia Falls ($494 per person) and Glacier Lake ($646 per person). There's a three-person minimum or else you charter the whole plane. Flyovers without landing are cheaper. Pilot owner Ted runs the remote fly-in Nahanni Mountain Lodge on Little Doctor Lake.

Sleeping

★Nahanni Mountain Lodge LODGE $$$
(☎867-695-2505; www.simpsonair.ca; 4-night stay for 4 guests incl Virginia Falls tour per person $1351) Sitting on the shore of the picture-perfect Little Doctor Lake, right outside the national-park boundary, this rustic lodge accommodates up to 20 people (single group or family) in four wooden cabins. It's just you and the wilderness, with nothing to do but swim, fish or float. Lodge stays, combined with Nahanni Park visits, need to be booked through Simpson Air.

Information

You can obtain park information and permits in Fort Simpson at Nahanni National Park Reserve visitor center visitor center. The day-use fee is $24.50; the Backcountry Pass, valid for a year, costs $147.20. Nahanni National Park Reserve is open to fly-in visitors between mid-June and mid-September.

Getting There & Away

The park is only accessible by floatplane.

Liard Trail

The gravel Liard Trail (Hwy 7) branches off the Mackenzie Hwy (Hwy 1) and heads south through the Liard Valley, with the Mackenzie Mountains appearing to the west. Black bear and bison abound. The only gas is at Fort Simpson and Fort Liard. Halfway between Checkpoint and Fort Liard is Blackstone Territorial Park, with interpretive displays, a visitor center, an appealing **campground** (www.nwtparks.ca; tent/RV sites $15/22.50; ⏲May-Sep; 🐾) shaded by birch and spruce forest, short hiking trails and terrific views over mountains and the Liard-Nahanni confluence. Most South Nahanni canoeing trips end here.

SAHTU

Mountain-studded Sahtu, centered on the Great Bear Lake, is accesible by plane year-round and by ice road in winter. The Mackenzie, swollen by water draining from one-fifth of Canada, cuts its way through here, in places more than 3km wide. Either side, bald-headed peaks arise, guarding some of the wildest country – and best hiking and paddling – left in the world.

Norman Wells

POP 727

This historic oil town springs from the boreal frontier, halfway between Fort Simpson and Inuvik. It's a launchpad for canoeists, hikers tackling the Canol Heritage Trail, adventurers heading into the Mackenzie Mountains and fisherfolk heading for Great Bear Lake.

Sights & Activities

Norman Wells Historical Centre MUSEUM
(☎867-587-2415; www.normanwellsmuseum.com; Mackenzie Dr; ⊙10am-5:30pm Mon-Fri, 10am-4pm Sat, noon-4pm Sun) FREE A labor of love, this small museum showcases regional history, geology, arts and crafts, and has information on the rivers and the Canol Heritage Trail.

★**Canol Heritage Trail** HIKING
The wild, challenging Canol Heritage Trail leads 358km southwest to the Yukon border, traversing peaks, canyons and barrens. Wildlife is abundant and there are numerous deep river crossings. The only shelter is provided by old Quonset huts. Hiking the whole length takes three to four weeks and most people arrange food drops. Contact **Northwest Territories Tourism** (www.gov.nt.ca/services/visitors) for outfitters.

★**Canoe North Adventures** CANOEING, HIKING
(☎May-Sep 867-587-4440, Oct-Apr 519-941-6654; www.canoenorthadventures.com; Beaver Lane; ⊙mid-May–mid-Sep) This excellent setup has decades of experience organizing rugged canoeing trips on the Nahanni, Mountain, Keele and other mighty rivers. They also arrange hiking excursions on the Canol Heritage Trail. At their base at the North-Wright floatplane dock they hire out all necessary equipment for self-guided trips and offer accommodation in private and bunk rooms with cooking facilities.

Sleeping

★**Canoe North Lodge B&B** B&B $$
(☎867-587-4440; www.canoenorthadventures.com; 8 Beaver Ln; s/d $115/200; @) Right at their floatbase, this canoeing/hiking outfitter has a cozy lodge for active travelers. You have a choice of private rooms and cheaper bunkrooms; ample breakfasts are thrown in and lunch ($20) and dinner ($40) can be arranged. In between bouts of canoeing, hang out in the common areas or use the kitchen for meals.

Heritage Hotel HOTEL $$$
(☎867-587-5000; www.heritagehotelnwt.com; 27 Mackenzie Dr; r incl breakfast $300;) This clean, minimalist, rather posh hotel seems out of place in working-class Wells. Many of the rooms have river views, plus there's a spa, an adjacent small golf course and the Ventures dining room, which, with dishes like Thai-marinated steak, is the best eatery in town – no contest.

Getting There & Away

North-Wright Airways (p802), **Canadian North** (www.canadiannorth.com) and **First Air** (p795) serve Yellowknife and Inuvik.

In winter, an ice road runs 333km from Wrigley to Norman Wells and goes north as far as Colville Lake.

WESTERN ARCTIC

Comprising the Mackenzie Delta, the Richardson Mountains and several High Arctic islands, this is the NWT's most diverse region. Several remote national parks are here, plus aboriginal hamlets whose residents still maintain a largely traditional lifestyle of whaling, trapping and hunting. The region's 'metropolis' is prefabricated Inuvik, reached via the heart-wrenchingly beautiful Dempster Hwy.

Inuvik

POP 3396

Inuvik, a few dozen kilometers from the mouth of the Mackenzie River, was founded in 1955 as an administrative post to replace the inconveniently located Aklavik. With its rainbow-colored rows of houses and warren of above-ground heated pipes, this close-knit community still feels like a work in progress. During the summer's constant daylight, lots of visitors arrive in search of Arctic adventure via the rugged, awesome 737km Dempster Hwy from the Yukon.

Sights & Activities

Our Lady of Victory Church CHURCH
(☎867-777-2236; 174 Mackenzie Rd; donation $5; ⊙tours 6:30pm Mon, Wed, Fri & Sat, noon Sun) The town landmark is the wooden Our Lady of Victory Church, also called the Igloo Church, designed to reflect the local Inuvialuit culture. It has a resplendent gleaming dome and its appealing interior is decorated with scenes from the Rapture, painted by Inuvialuit artist Mona Thresher.

★**Dempster Highway** SCENIC DRIVE
The 737km road that leads south into Yukon is the notorious Dempster Hwy, a most worthy contender for Canada's most scenic and challenging drive. It passes through dense boreal forest and bare tundra, and rises gently between snow-tipped mountains. It's an unpaved, partially potholed road with treacherous muddy sections, potential delays at ferry crossings and no phone signal. Likely wildlife sightings.

Tours

For most visitors, Inuvik is the gateway to the Arctic Ocean. Popular tours involve flights over the braided Mackenzie Delta and the weather-beaten Arctic coast – where trees peter out and the landscape becomes riddled with pingos (ice-cored hills that erupt from the tundra) – with a tour of the whaling village of Tuktoyaktuk. Photographers should try for a seat at the rear of the plane. Once the road to Tuktoyaktuk is completed, the focus will shift toward MacKenzie Delta boat tours, scenic flights to remoter destinations, husky sledding, and Dempster Hwy scenic drives.

Tundra North Tours ADVENTURE
(☎800-420-9652; http://tundranorthtours.com; 185 Mackenzie Rd) This professional operator offers flights to Tuktoyaktuk on the Arctic coast ($549 per person) to view pingos and the town itself, boat-flight combos to Tuktoyaktuk ($599), scenic flights to remote Herschel Island ($1199 per person), summer boating in the Mackenzie Delta ($299 per person) and drives along the Dempster. Winter guests get the opportunity to herd reindeer.

Arctic Adventures ADVENTURE
(White Huskies; ☎867-777-3535; www.whitehuskies.com; 25 Carn St) Highly recommended excursions include year-round chauffeured runs on the Dempster Hwy, summer flights to Tuktoyaktuk ($550 per person) and tours with excellent Inuvialuit guide, opportunities to meet their beautiful snow-white huskies ($55) and, in winter, daily dogsled tours (from $158) and snowmobiling outings. They also rent vehicles and canoes.

Sleeping & Eating

Jàk Park Campground CAMPGROUND $
(☎867-777-3613; www.campingnwt.ca; tent & RV sites $22.50; ⊙Jun-Aug; 🐾) This pretty government-operated campground, about 6km south of town on the Dempster Hwy, provides hot showers and firewood. There's a good view of the delta, an observation tower for bird-watching and the breeze keeps the mosquitoes at bay a bit. There's another campground downtown.

★**Andre's Place** B&B $$
(☎867-777-3177; www.facebook.com/Andresplaceinuvik; 55 Wolverine Rd; s/d $195/225; 📶) Run by an affable French-Chilean couple, this B&B consists of a single bedroom with an adjoining immaculate bathroom. Guests get the benefit of Andre's fantastic cooked breakfasts and the hosts are happy to share their insight into life in the far north.

★**Arctic Chalet** GUESTHOUSE $$
(☎867-777-3535; www.arcticchalet.com; 25 Carn St; r $125-150, cabin $185-200; 📶🐾) In a boreal glade 3km from town, the main house showcases local fauna in the form of animal skins and piles of antlers. Satellite cabins have simple kitchen facilities. Some rooms are en suite. Wi-fi is restricted to a small daily allowance. The affable owners rent canoes, kayaks and cars, and run dogsledding tours.

★**Alestine's** CANADIAN $$
(48 Franklin Rd; mains $11-22; ⊙noon-2pm & 5-8pm Mon-Fri, 4-8pm Sat & Sun) This fantastic mom-and-pop place has single-handedly elevated Inuvik's dining scene. The menu is succinct and makes the most of fresh local produce. Feast on whitefish tacos, grilled salmon and reindeer chili on the upstairs deck or inside the cube-like interior, decked out with local prints.

★**Andre's Place** FRENCH $$$
(☎867-777-3177; 55 Wolverine Rd; 4-course menu $75; ⊙6:30pm Wed & Fri) Andre is a classically trained chef who learned his craft in Paris and he shares his culinary skills every Wednesday and Friday. Expect fine dining in an intimate setting; the menu changes weekly (see the updated menu at the visitor center), but may include the likes of rack of lamb with Provençal sauce and tarte tatin.

Information

Parks Canada (867-777-8800; www.pc.gc.ca; 81 Kingmingya Rd) Has info on Tuktut Nogait, Ivvavik and Aulavik National Parks. Park visitors must register and deregister here. Staff organize multiday trips into Ivvavik and Tuktut Nogait.

Western Arctic Regional Visitors Centre (p812) Has tourism literature, eager staff and a nature display.

Western Arctic Regional Visitor Center (867-777-4727, info off-season 867-777-7237; www.inuvik.ca; 284 Mackenzie Rd; 9am-8pm Mon-Fri, 10am-7pm Sat & Sun May-Sep) Excellent tourist office, run by enthusiastic staff. Pick up the printout on things to do, places to eat and shopping in Inuvik, as well as the Dempster Hwy passport. Check out the thorough nature display and the whiteboard for events.

Getting There & Around

AIR

Air North (p795) flies to Dawson City, Old Crow and Whitehorse. **Aklak Air** (867-777-3555; www.aklakair.ca) hits Tuktoyaktuk, Paulatuk and Sachs Harbour and provides charters to the national parks.

The airport is 14km south of town. Town Cab and Delta Cab charge $30/36 for one/two people to downtown.

CAR

Driving Force (867-777-2346; www.drivingforce.ca; 60 King Rd; 8am-noon & 1-5pm Mon-Fri) and **Arctic Chalet Car Rental** (867-777-3535; www.arcticchalet.com; 25 Carn St) rent vehicles and have airport counters. If you are driving, it's vital that you check Dempster Hwy road and ferry **conditions** (800-661-0750; www.dot.gov.nt.ca, www.511yukon.ca); the road is closed during the initial fall freeze and spring thaw. The recently completed gravel road north to Tuktoyaktuk (124km) is due to open to the public in 2017. Petrol is by far the most expensive in the NWT; if driving south, it's worth refueling at Fort McPherson instead.

Tuktoyaktuk

POP 854

About 140km northeast of Inuvik on the Arctic coast is Tuktoyaktuk (Place Resembling Caribou), long home of the whale-hunting Inuvialuit, and now also a land base for Beaufort Sea gas explorations.

Pods of belugas may be seen in summer. Visible year-round are pingos, of which the Tuk Peninsula has the Western Arctic's highest concentration. Some 1400 of these huge mounds of earth and ice dot the land; the largest two have been designated the Pingo Canadian Landmark.

In Tuk, notable buildings include two replica **sod houses** (www.inuvialuitsodhouse.ca) – traditional Inuvialuit dwellings, and the **Icehouse** – a natural freezer dug into the permafrost where villagers keep their catch. Near the two is the beautifully restored **Our Lady of Lourdes** schooner; it delivered supplies to far-flung Catholic missions in the Arctic in the 1930s and '40s.

For tours of the area, check out **Arctic Ocean Tuk Tours** (867-977-2406; eileenjacobson@hotmail.com) run by Eileen Jacobson who is an excellent local guide. She offers detailed insights into traditional Inuvialuit life, especially since she still lives it herself. She also lives off the land, hunting, trapping and fishing, and her cultural tours include a visit to her home where you can taste smoked whale meat, musk ox and dried fish. Eileen collaborates with Arctic Adventures (p811) in Inuvik.

Information

Hamlet office (867-977-2286; www.tuk.ca) Can provide more information on services.

Getting There & Away

There are at least two daily flights to Tuktoyaktuk with **Aklak Air**. Most visitors come either with aerial or boat tours from Inuvik.

Once the newly built road from Inuvik opens to the public in 2017, it will be possible to drive North America's only road to the Arctic Ocean in around two hours.

Banks Island

Adrift in the Arctic Ocean, Banks Island has abundant wildlife by polar standards, and is one of the world's best places to see musk oxen. The island has two bird sanctuaries with summer flocks of snow geese and seabirds. **Sachs Harbour**, a small hunting, fishing and trapping Inuvialuit community on the south coast, is the only settlement. On the north end of the island, seldom-visited **Aulavik National Park** covers 12,275 sq km. It has the world's largest concentration of musk oxen, as well as badlands, tundra and archaeological sites.

Visit the Parks Canada office in Inuvik for information on Aulavik National Park. Aklak Air fly three times weekly from Inuvik to Sachs Harbour. Aulavik National Park can be reached only by private charter plane.

Nunavut

Includes ➡

Best for Art

- West Baffin Eskimo Cooperative (p821)
- Uqqurmiut Centre for Arts & Crafts (p820)
- Carvings Nunavut (p819)
- Rankin Inlet (p823)
- Cambridge Bay (p824)

Best Places to Sleep

- Dorset Suites (p821)
- Accommodations by the Sea (p817)
- Discovery (p817)
- Arctic Circle Paws & Paddles B&B (p824)
- Nanuq Lodge (p823)
- Nunattaq Suites (p817)

Why Go?

Picture a treeless, ice-encrusted wilderness lashed by unrelenting weather with a population density that makes Greenland seem claustrophobic. Add polar bears, narwhals, beluga whales and a scattered Inuit population who have successfully mastered a landscape so harsh that foreigners could not colonize it.

Nunavut is Canada's largest and most lightly populated subdivision, a mythical assortment of uninhabited islands and frigid ocean that exists on the planet's climatic and geographic extremes. Visitors here face multiple obstacles, not least perennial blizzards, no roads and massive travel costs. But those that do get through have the benefit of welcoming communities and awe-inspiring natural wonders, as well as the privilege of joining a small band of intrepid trailblazers, safe in the knowledge that they are setting foot where few have trodden before.

When to Go

Iqaluit

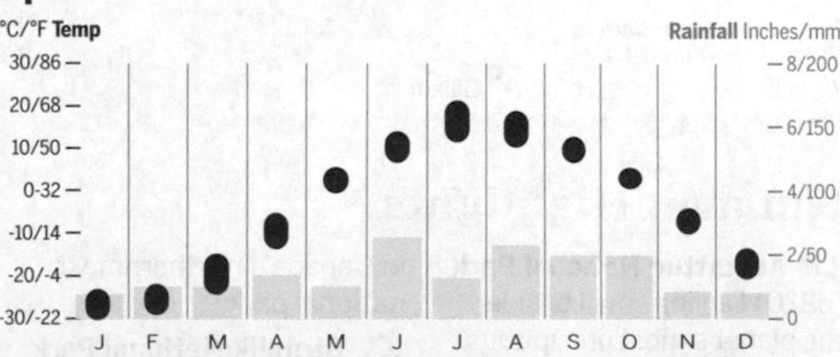

Aug & Sep Prime visiting time during the short hyperactive summer season.

Apr & May The ideal time for dogsledding and other snow sports and activities.

Jun The midnight sun coincides with Iqaluit's Alianait Arts Festival.

Nunavut Highlights

1 **Auyuittuq National Park** (p820) Feeling small beside the planet's most precipitous cliffs.

2 **Cape Dorset** (p821) Encountering serpentine polar bears and colourful Inuit prints.

3 **Quttinirpaaq National Park** (p822) Going on a musk-ox-watching adventure in Canada's northernmost national park.

4 **Sirmilik National Park** (p821) Hitting Pond Inlet for wildlife-watching and scuba diving beneath the ice.

5 **Iqaluit** (p815) Chomping char, caribou and musk ox at eateries in Canada's most curious capital.

6 **Resolute** (p822) Moonwalking across this awesomely lunar place.

7 **Katannilik Territorial Park** (p822) Canoeing amid cascades and caribou on the Edenic Soper River.

8 **Ukkusiksalik National Park** (p824) Seeing polar bears from the safety of a boat.

History

Nunavut has been populated for over 4000 years, first by the Dorset people, who were gradually pushed out by the Thule, the ancestors of the Inuit, who arrived from the west just a millennium ago. Supremely adapted to survive in the harshest of climates, they lived nomadic lifestyles, hunting whale, narwhal and seal.

Vikings likely visited Baffin Island (Helluland in the sagas); later, in 1576, Martin Frobisher came seeking the Northwest Passage. Over the centuries came more explorers (including Sir John Franklin, who disappeared here in 1845), and Roald Amundsen, who finally traversed the Passage between 1903 and 1906, with whalers, traders and missionaries hot on their heels.

After WWII, Canada finally recognized the Arctic's strategic importance. In the 1950s and '60s Inuit were settled into villages, while the northernmost communities of Resolute Bay and Grise Fjord were created when a number of Inuit families were relocated there by deceit, to bolster national sovereignty.

In the 1960s and '70s rising political awareness inspired dreams of Inuit self-government. In 1994 the Inuit won a landmark case against the Canadian government when the deception of the 1950s made its way through court, and compensation was paid to survivors of the relocated families. Nunavut split from the Northwest Territories in 1999 to become a separate territory.

Land & Climate

Gargantuan Nunavut sprawls across Canada's northeast. About half – the mainland – is the 'Barrenlands,' an expanse of undulating rock and tundra cut through by major rivers. Even more barren is the Arctic archipelago, scattering north to Ellesmere Island, just shy of the Pole, and east to enormous Baffin Island, home to skyscraping mountains. At over 2 million sq km, Nunavut is larger than many of the world's most populous nations including Mexico and Indonesia. If it were a country, it would rank 14th in size.

The territory's 26 communities are incredibly isolated and rely on air transport and the July 'sealift,' when ships bring a year's worth of supplies to otherwise inaccessible harbors. Houses sit on stilts to negate ferocious winds. Water is rationed and delivered daily from a central village deposit by truck.

NUNAVUT FAST FACTS

Population 36,919

Area 2,038,722 sq km

Capital Iqaluit

Quirky fact There are almost as many polar bears (around 17,000) as men (19,000) or women (17,900) in Nunavut.

Getting There & Around

Nunavut is essentially roadless; the only way to get here and around is via (extremely pricey) flights. Iqaluit is served from Montréal, Ottawa and Yellowknife. Cambridge Bay is linked to Yellowknife, and Rankin Inlet to Yellowknife and Winnipeg. Smaller communities are reached from those three hubs. Flights are operated by **Canadian North** (www.canadiannorth.com), **Calm Air** (www.calmair.com) and **First Air** (www.firstair.ca); Iqaluit-based **Kenn Borek Air** (867-979-0040; www.borekair.com) offers charter flights.

Flying standby halves the price of normal flights. In winter medical staff and fish get priority and there are lots of weather-induced cancellations (also the case in July fog), but in summer (if you're flexible), you've a chance of saving some money.

Cruise ships ply the Northwest Passage, calling at communities such as Cambridge Bay, Gjoa Haven and Kimmirut.

IQALUIT

867 / POP 6699

Nunavut's capital, Iqaluit (ee-*kal*-oo-eet), feels like a different country. All the signs are in Inuktitut and you'll hear it widely spoken in the street. The dusty townscape, with its spectacular natural setting and its moon-base buildings, houses a fascinating mixture of Inuit professionals, politicians and dropouts, Johnny-come-latelies from around Canada (and beyond) drawn by high salaries, enormous SUVs with elaborately courteous drivers limited by a few short kilometers of road, and barking dogs contesting territory with huge bossy ravens. It's surprisingly cosmopolitan and has good places to stay and eat, as well as some wilderness-lite to explore on the outskirts of town.

History

For centuries, nomadic Inuit trekked to the Sylvia Grinnell River to spear char in the roiling summer waters. They called the area Iqaluit (Place of Fish).

In 1576 English captain Martin Frobisher showed up seeking the Northwest Passage. He unearthed glittering yellow ore and sailed home with a million pounds of worthless fool's gold. Local Inuit kept fishing, interrupted occasionally by whalers, explorers and missionaries. During WWII, an American airbase was established here. After the war, Canadian forces stayed on, and the outpost, named Frobisher Bay, became the administrative center of the eastern Arctic.

In 1995 voters picked Iqaluit – now officially named as such – as Nunavut's capital. Since then the population has more than doubled.

Sights & Activities

Despite spongy, ankle-bending terrain, the wide-open landscapes around Iqaluit make hiking a delight. Trails are few, but no trees means it's difficult to get lost.

★ Nunatta Sunakkutaangit Museum MUSEUM, GALLERY
(☎867-979-5537; Sinaa St; ⏲1-5pm Tue-Sun) FREE This friendly little museum in an old Hudson's Bay Company building hosts high-quality temporary exhibitions of contemporary artists, though the permanent collection of traditional Inuit clothing, tools, weaponry and splendid carvings is particularly interesting. The gift shop stocks carvings, jewelry, *ulus* (Inuit women's knives) and tiny watercolours by a local artist.

★ Legislative Assembly NOTABLE BUILDING
(☎867-975-5000; www.assembly.nu.ca; Federal Rd; ⏲9am-5pm Mon-Fri, tours 1:30pm Jun-Aug or by appointment) FREE It's well worth taking an entertaining free tour of the prefab parliament to learn about all manner of Inuit art, as well as about the chamber, with its aboriginal touches, such as the igloo-like interior, sealskin benches and seats for community elders.

Sculpture Garden SCULPTURE
There's an extensive range of mostly stone sculpture by local artists right near the post office, with northern themes well represented. Our favourite? A thuggish-looking Sedna (sea goddess) with raised fist and a raven made of scrap metal.

Qaummaarviit Territorial Park ISLAND
(www.nunavutparks.ca) This tiny bay island is a 12km boat ride from Iqaluit and preserves a 750-year-old Inuit (Thule) winter camp. You can see well-preserved sod houses and a grave site. It's a great half-day trip; to get there, contact Iqaluit outfitters.

Apex AREA
Iqaluit's beach suburb, 5km from downtown, was where nomadic Inuit began to settle when modern Iqaluit was an airbase. On the shore is the photogenic Hudson Bay Trading Post complex. It's a beautiful 30-minute walk along the waterfront from downtown; the trail starts at the cemetery. At low tide continue past Apex to explore Tarr Inlet.

Sylvia Grinnell Territorial Park PARK
(www.nunavutparks.ca; Iqaluit Rd; P 🐾) The viewpoint at this bleakly beautiful park, 2km southwest of town, overlooks the rapids that Arctic char swim up and the snow-flecked tundra. Various short paths (25 to 45 minutes one way) lead to a waterfall and escarpments.

Igloo Cathedral CHURCH
(☎867-979-5595; Mattaq Cres) This igloo-shaped Anglican cathedral was designed to reflect Inuit culture. This recent incarnation was built in 2012 to replace the original, burnt down in a 2005 arson fire.

Tours

Consult the Nunavut Tourism website (www.nunavuttourism.com) or the visitor center (p819) for available tours and outfitters. Reserve early.

Arctic Kingdom OUTDOORS
(☎867-979-1900, 867-222-3995; www.arctickingdom.com; Hotel Arctic, Bldg 923, Federal Rd) This professional setup can organize everything from half-day hiking, boating, ATV, kayaking or snowmobiling trips around Iqaluit to multiday wildlife-watching adventures throughout Nunavut. The best bet for something at short notice.

Inukpak Outfitting OUTDOORS
(☎867-222-6489; www.inukpakoutfitting.ca; Niaqunngusiariaq St) Rents inflatable canoes, camping equipment, satellite phones and polar clothing. Also runs winter dogsledding (half-day $200), snowmobiling, and igloo-building, and summer hiking, canoeing (day trip $170 per person) and sea-kayaking.

Northwinds Arctic Adventures ADVENTURE
(☎867-979-0551; www.northwinds-arctic.com) These seasoned pros lead Arctic expeditions (including to Quttinirpaaq National Park) and dogsledding programs, and have worked with everyone from the BBC's *Top Gear* to *Canadian Geographic*.

ARCTIC PACKAGES

Independent travel offers the chance for trailblazing, saving cash and seeing the reality. Except, perhaps, in Nunavut. Here you should consider a package tour: only groups can achieve the economies of scale that make the Arctic affordable.

Cruises, especially, let you visit several Nunavut communities and offer excellent opportunities for wildlife-spotting. Sure, a $8000 cruise is costly, but you'll spend as much on a do-it-yourself trip of similar duration. The **Great Canadian Adventure Company** (780-414-1676; www.adventures.ca) offers good-value trips; Inuit-operated **Adventure Canada** (905-271-4000; www.adventurecanada.com) also has lots of options.

Tours are numerous, ranging from guided national-park hiking (check for special deals with Parks Canada) to wildlife-spotting safaris, Arctic diving trips and stays in middle-of-nowhere wilderness lodges used as bases for wildlife-watching. See the website of Nunavut Tourism (p824) for more information.

Festivals & Events

★ Alianait Arts Festival CULTURAL
(www.alianait.ca; late Jun-early Jul) A midsummer celebration of Inuit culture with art, music, film, storytelling, food and a circus.

Sleeping

Iqaluit has the best range of accommodations in Nunavut, but that's not saying a great deal. Camping is the only cheap option. For hotel accommodations, book ahead and hemorrhage cash. Hotels offer free airport pickup. There are a couple of AirBnb options, but they're not cheap either.

Sylvia Grinnell Territorial Park CAMPGROUND $
(Iqaluit Rd; campsites free; P) There are no facilities at this scenic campground except pit toilets. Take the road to the right after entering, rather than continuing up to the hut on the hill. It's a 30-minute walk from town.

★ Nunattaq Suites B&B $$
(867-975-2745; www.nunattaqsuites.com; Bldg 4141, Imiqtarviminiq Rd; r $198; P) This spotless, large, well-equipped grey-blue house overlooks a lake, a 15-minute walk from town. The suite with the claw-foot tub has the best lake views; all four rooms come with excellent modern bathrooms. Guests also have the run of the kitchen, laundry facilities and a lounge-balcony area with BBQ. The friendly host stops by daily and makes you very welcome.

★ Accommodations by the Sea B&B $$
(867-979-0131; www.accommodationsbythesea.ca; Bldg 2536, Paurngaq Cr; r with breakfast $149-229; P@) A half-hour walk from downtown, this end-of-the-road spot has a lovely bay outlook. It's comfortable, modern and decked out in ski-chalet style. Guests have use of a kitchen with breakfast supplies, and a great lounge with DVDs. Cheaper rooms share a bathroom. Airport pickup available. Often booked for airline crew, so call ahead.

Beaches B&B B&B $$
(867-979-3034; www.iqaluitbeaches.ca; 114 Sinaa St; r $168-210;) Overlooking the waterfront, near the visitor center, this is the only Inuit-owned lodging in town and the only budget-ish central option. In inclement weather travelers gather in the small lounge with kitchenette. The friendly hosts can organize tours.

Arctic Hotel BUSINESS HOTEL $$
(867-979-6684; www.hotelarctic.ca; Bldg 923, Federal Rd; r $224-274, ste $330; P) As central as it gets, this smart business hotel gets top marks for its super-comfortable beds, friendly staff, gym and good restaurant. Cons? Walls are thin and sound travels. The lively on-site bar is either a boon or a bane, depending on how much you enjoy residing at the epicenter of Iqaluit's nightlife.

★ Discovery BOUTIQUE HOTEL $$$
(867-979-4433; www.thediscoveryiqaluit.com; Bldg 1056, Mivvik St; s/d/ste $250/295/350; P) Located between the airport and the center, the fresh decor of this well-run place stands out. Big TVs, cozy bathrooms, lots of hanging space, and the town's best restaurant make this an appealing stay. Little details like free laundry and chaise longues in the business suites seal the deal.

Eating & Drinking

The best eateries are in the hotels. Expect big portions at hugely inflated prices (most stuff is flown in). Arctic specials like char and musk ox are widely available. If you're in town during an Inuit feast, you may get to try seal meat, dried Arctic char and other local specialties.

Most crimes and suicides in Iqaluit are linked to drinking, so alcohol is served only at hotel bars and the Royal Canadian Legion.

Caribrew Café CAFE $

(www.frobisherinn.com; Astro Hill Tce; light meals $8-11; ⏲7am-6pm Mon-Fri, 9am-4pm Sat & Sun) This appealing place with a slate fireplace occupies a widened corridor in the Frobisher Inn, offering a warm refuge from the wind and reasonable value for coffee, banana bread, salads, quiches, panini and sandwiches.

Big Racks Barbecue BARBECUE $$

(☎867-979-5555; 810 Aviq St; mains $17-35; ⏲11am-9pm) The carnivore-pleasing menu of ribs, wings, country fried chicken, burgers, beef brisket and pulled-pork sandwiches has quickly endeared itself to locals at this buzzing new spot. The vibe? Brisk cafeteria. Portion sizes? Enormous. Takeout available.

Yummy Shawarma & Pizza KEBAB $$

(☎867-979-1515; Bldg 1085E, Mivvik St; shawarmas $10-15, pizzas $24-33; ⏲11am-10pm Mon-Sat, to 7:30pm Sun) Nunavut now has its first kebab joint, with a pleasant, Lebanese-themed dining area. Delivery available.

Grind & Brew CAFE $$

(☎867-979-0606; Sinaa St; mains $22-28, pizzas $19-31; ⏲6am-6pm, delivery until later) Iqaluit's friendly beachfront coffee shop, down the road from the museum, offers basic joe and delicious greasy breakfast sandwiches.

★Granite Room FRENCH, FUSION $$$

(☎867-979-4433; www.thediscoveryiqaluit.com; Bldg 1056, Mivvik St; mains $54-63; ⏲6:30-9am, noon-2pm & 6-9pm) Nunavut's top restaurant at the Discovery hotel is consistently better and more imaginative than the competition. The French-influenced fare includes specials to complement à la carte dishes that incorporate arctic char and caribou. Homemade desserts are excellent. The all-you-can-eat buffet Sunday brunch ($44) is terrific value.

Gallery CANADIAN $$$

(☎867-979-2222; Astro Hill Tce; mains $18-56; ⏲7-10:30am, 11:30am-1:30pm & 5-8:30pm Mon-Fri, from 8am Sat & Sun) The popular upmarket restaurant at the Frobisher Inn offers arctic char wraps, pad Thai, paella and musk-ox burgers at lunchtime. Dinner is more refined; prime ribs, bison steak and arctic char dominate. Try to get a window seat.

Storehouse Bar & Grill BAR

(Astro Hill Tce; ⏲5pm-12:30am Mon-Sat) As befits the main genteel drinkery in town, this watering hole in the Frobisher Inn is a little bit of everything: pub, pool hall, sports bar and disco. The food (pizza, burgers, ribs; mains $12 to $24) is also good, but don't expect beer out of anything other than a can.

★Royal Canadian Legion CLUB

(☎867-979-6215; Queen Elizabeth Way; ⏲7pm-late Fri & Sat) 'But it's a Legion!,' you might say. Yes, and it doubles as a club and karaoke joint on weekends and becomes the most hopping place in Iqaluit, with a mixed crowd of party-goers. To get in, either get a member to sign you in or call ahead for a visitor's pass (use for entry before 9pm).

INUIT CULTURE & LANGUAGE

Most Nunavut residents are Inuit (singular: Inuk), whose transition from an isolated, nomadic culture to a settled population has been very swift: many living Inuit ('Eskimo' is considered insensitive and embarrassingly archaic, although, confusingly, it's the preferred term of Alaskan Inuit) elders grew up moving between hunting grounds, living in sealskin tents and igloos. The rapid change hasn't been without problems. Alcohol abuse, drugs, lack of opportunities, obesity, crime and suicide are all prevalent; in much of Nunavut, alcohol is either restricted or banned. Nevertheless, Nunavut still buzzes with optimism and can be the friendliest of places.

The population is concentrated almost wholly in settlements. Inuit remain at heart rural hunter-gatherers: though the tools have changed, nature and its rhythms still hold sway. Harvesting animals remains a holy sacrament and it is the legal right of the Inuit to hunt game, even within national-park boundaries.

Around 70% of Nunavummiut speak one of two Inuktut dialects (Inuktitut or Inuvialuktun) as their primary tongue; for some, it's the only language. Inuktitut is written in syllabics, while Inuvialuktun uses Latin characters.

Shopping

Inuit prints, carvings and tapestries are world renowned, and in Iqaluit, you'll find a great selection of art, particularly from around Baffin Island – at a price. You'll also be approached on the street and in hotel restaurants by locals hawking less-refined wares.

★ **Carvings Nunavut** ARTS & CRAFTS
(www.carvingsnunavut.com; Bldg 626, Queen Elizabeth Way; ⏲10am-6pm Mon-Sat, to 3pm Sun) Inside the Tumiit Plaza building, this place has an excellent, fairly priced collection of Inuit soapstone and whalebone sculpture for sale, as well as prints by Nunavut's artists.

Piruvik ARTS & CRAFTS
(☎867-222-8355; Bldg 611, Queen Elizabeth Way; ⏲10am-6pm Mon-Fri, 11am-4pm Sat) This cheerful little store next to the post office sells Inuit music CDs, Northern-themed T-shirts and earrings, sealskin purses and a selection of small stone carvings.

Arctic Survival Store SPORTS & OUTDOORS
(☎867-979-1984; Bldg 170, Nipisa St; ⏲9am-9pm) Your one-stop shop for bug jackets, bug repellent, fishing equipment, and a selection of outdoor clothing.

Rannva CLOTHING
(☎867-979-3183; www.rannva.com; cnr Pitsi Lane & Mattaq Cres; ⏲11am-6pm Mon-Sat) In a bright-purple studio, Faroese designer Rannva Erlingsdóttir Simonsen sews together the ancient and the chic, generating beautiful fur and sealskin garments. Located on the same street as the Igloo Cathedral.

Information

Note that 911 is not the emergency number in Nunavut; see below for ambulance, fire and police.

Ambulance & Fire (☎867-979-4422)

Iqaluit Centennial Library (www.publiclibraries.nu.ca; Sinaa St; ⏲1-6pm Mon, Wed & Fri, 3-8pm Tue & Thu, 1-4pm Sat & Sun) Free internet in the visitor center building.

Parks Canada (☎867-975-4673; www.pg.gc.ca; 1104b Qamaniqtuaq St; ⏲9am-noon & 1-5pm Mon-Fri) Has info on all of Nunavut's national parks. Find it in on the ground floor of the green apartment building behind Yummy Shawarma.

Police (☎867-979-1111)

Qikiqtani Hospital (☎867-979-7300; Niaqunngusiaq Rd; ⏲24hr)

Royal Bank of Canada (cnr Queen Elizabeth Way & Niaqunngusiaq Rd)

Unikkaarvik Visitor Centre (☎867-979-4636; Sinaa St; ⏲9am-6pm Mon-Fri, to 6pm Sat, often closed noon-1pm) Has pamphlets, a museum and nature display, plus a reference collection of Nunavut books and videos. Arctic-themed movie screenings on Thursday at 7.30pm.

POLAR BEARS

Nanuq (the Inuit name for a polar bear) is an inveterate wanderer and can turn up just about anywhere, at any time of year. Worse, unlike grizzlies and black bears, they actively prey on people. Enquire about sightings before trudging out of town or venturing into national parks, or use a local guide.

Getting There & Around

Canadian North (p815) and First Air (p815) have direct flights to a number of Nunavut communities from Iqaluit, as well as Ottawa, Ontario and Yellowknife, Northwest Territories. Kenn Borek Air (p815) offers charter flights.

Central Iqaluit is walkable; even the airport is a 10-minute stroll from downtown. All cabs charge $7 per person to anywhere. Hail them on the street even if they've got passengers and expect to share. Try **Pai-Pa Taxi** (☎867-979-5222).

BAFFIN REGION

Comprising Nunavut's eastern and High Arctic islands, this region reaches from the swampy, forested isles of James Bay to the glaciers and jagged peaks of Ellesmere Island, 3000km north. It encompasses four of Nunavut's five remarkable national parks and offers unparalleled opportunities for viewing Arctic wildlife and wilderness trekking.

Pangnirtung

POP 1425

Among Nunavut's outlying communities, Pangnirtung, or 'Pang,' has a thriving artistic scene and outdoor opportunities galore. Located 40km south of the Arctic Circle, Pang's natural beauty is stunning. It's also the main gateway to even more spectacular scenery at Auyuittuq National Park.

Sights & Activities

Stroll the picturesque waterfront admiring the handsome buildings of the old Hudson Bay Company blubber station. Hiking options include a trail up Mt Duval – a stiff climb rewarded by staggering views.

★**Uqqurmiut Centre for Arts & Crafts** GALLERY
(☎867-473-8669; www.uqqurmiut.ca; ⏲9am-noon & 1-5pm Mon-Fri) Pang is famous for its lithographs, prints and tapestries, and this extraordinary place brings it all together. Artists create prints via a variety of techniques in the adjacent workshop, and there's a stunning collection available to browse and buy. Crocheted hats are another highlight, as are stone carvings and toasty-warm scarves.

Kekerten Historic Park HISTORIC SITE
About 50km south of town is this old island whaling station. A heritage trail leads past the remains of 19th-century houses, tools and graves. Outfitters offer day trips for around $250 per person (minimum three people).

Tours

★**PEO Services** OUTDOORS
(☎867-473-4060; www.kilabukoutfitting.com) From July to October, Peter, former speaker of Nunavut Legislative Assembly, offers trips to Auyuittuq National Park and Kekerten Historic Park, wildlife-spotting boat trips on Cumberland Sound and fishing trips.

Alivaktuk Outfitting Services OUTDOORS
(☎867-473-8721; www.alivaktukoutfitting.ca) Can set you up with wildlife-spotting boat trips, fishing camps, igloo-building, day trips to Kekerten Historic Park and excursions to Auyuittuq National Park.

Sleeping

Territorial Campground CAMPGROUND $
(☎867-473-8737; tent sites $5; P 🐾) Picturesquely situated by the rushing Duval River, this campground has wooden shelter platforms to help with the howling wind, barbecues, pit toilets and great views; watch out for theft. Pay at the Angmarlik Visitor Center.

Auyuittuq Lodge HOTEL $$$
(☎867-473-8955; www.pangnirtunghotel.com; per person with/without bath $260/240; 📶) An enterprising, charismatic manager runs this as a one-man show and makes it a great place to stay and eat. En suite rooms outclass the older ones; some have a marvelous view. Sharing is a possibility when busy. Meals (lunch/dinner $25/39) are tasty, sociable affairs.

Information

Angmarlik Visitor Center (☎867-473-8737; oarnaqaq1@gov.nu.ca; ⏲8:30am-8pm) This enthusiastically run place has great views as well as interesting displays on Inuit and whaling history and info on local outfitters. Elders congregate here thrice weekly. Make sure staff explain the game of seal flipperbone Monopoly.

Parks Canada (☎867-473-2500; www.parkscanada.gc.ca; ⏲8:30am-noon & 1-5pm) Good info about Auyuittuq National Park next to the Angmarlik Visitor Center. Register and de-register here and pay the park fee if you're going.

Qimiruvik Library (☎867-473-8678; www.publiclibraries.nu.ca; ⏲6-9pm Mon, 3-6pm Tue-Fri, 3-5pm Sat) In Angmarlik Visitor Center. Free internet.

Auyuittuq National Park

Among the globe's most flabbergasting places and Nunavut's most accessible national park, Auyuittuq (ah-you-ee-tuk) means 'the Land That Never Melts.' Appropriately, there are plenty of glaciers in this 19,500-sq-km park, plus jagged peaks, vertiginous cliffs and deep valleys. Hikers trek the 97km Akshayuk Pass (crossing the Arctic Circle) in summer, when it's snow-free. Nearby, experienced climbers and base jumpers scale Mt Thor (1500m), the earth's highest sheer cliff, and twin-peaked Mt Asgard (2015m), famed for the parachute scene from *The Spy Who Loved Me*.

The biggest draw for visitors is the exceptional hiking. **Akshayuk Pass** is best hiked in late July, August or September; allow 10 days for the hike. The pass can be crossed in fewer days, but you have to allow extra time for river crossings, as you may have to wait for water levels to go down. You need to be an experienced wilderness operator, and fit. Polar bears can be seen most seasons, but generally not inland. A guide makes sense: speak to outfitters in Pangnirtung or book a package with **Black Feather** (☎888-849-7668; www.blackfeather.com). Another multiday hike heads 20km each way to Summit Lake. Skiing excursions into the park are possible from March to early May.

Even if you're not hiking, it's worth taking a boat into the park for a day trip – the boat ride is awe-inspiring, and hiking this wilderness, if only for a few hours, is memorable.

Register at Parks Canada in Pangnirtung and pay the fee (day/overnight/maximum $12/24.50/147.20). Maps ($20) are sold here. You must de-register after leaving the park.

Getting There & Away

The park is accessed along the fjords by boat ($130 per person each way) or snow machine (depending on the season), either from Pangnirtung

(28km) or Qikiqtarjuaq (34km). During breakup (late June to mid-July) and winter freeze-up the park is inaccessible. For about $250 per person, through-hikers can arrange to be picked up at the other end of the pass by a local outfitter.

Tour operators in Pangnirtung offer boat transfers. In Qikiqtarjuaq, hikers should contact the **Hamlet office** (867-927-8832; 9am-5pm Mon-Fri) for local operators.

Cape Dorset

POP 1363

On a small rocky island just off Baffin Island's Foxe Peninsula, this is the epicenter of Inuit art. In the late 1950s residents pioneered modern Arctic carving and printmaking, marketing it to the world with remarkable success. A number of Dorset's artists, such as Pudlo Pudlat, Pitseolak Ashoona and Kenojuak Ashevak, have achieved international recognition.

Sights & Activities

★**West Baffin Eskimo Cooperative** GALLERY
(Kinngait Arts; 867-897-8965; www.dorsetfinearts.com; 9am-5pm Mon-Fri) Though many Inuit communities now generate world-class artworks, Cape Dorset's remain the most revered. This cooperative has workshops where you can watch artists work.

Mallikjuaq Historic Park ARCHAEOLOGICAL SITE
(www.nunavutparks.ca) Features ruins of thousand-year-old Thule stone houses, hiking trails, wildlife and tundra flowers. You can hike here at low tide (45 minutes), or Huit Huit Tours can take you by boat (10 minutes).

Huit Huit Tours CULTURAL
(867-897-8806; www.capedorsettours.com; 4-day tour per person $1500) Based at Cape Dorset Suites, Huit Huit offers four- and seven-day summertime excursions focusing on Inuit art and culture. Prices are inclusive of accommodation at Dorset Suites.

Sleeping & Eating

All three hotels have restaurants; Dorset Suites is the best of the three. There's also a fast-food joint and a bakery.

Kingnait Inn BUSINESS HOTEL $$
(867-897-8863; r per person $240;) With bay views and easy access to the town, this friendly place gives visitors a free tour of town on arrival and offers solid meals and plain but commodious rooms.

★**Dorset Suites** BOUTIQUE HOTEL $$$
(867-897-8806; www.dorsetsuites.com; r from $300;) This excellent place is Nunavut's most appealing hotel. Spacious suites with balconies have warm wood furnishings and some have kitchenettes. The restaurant (open to nonguests for lunch weekdays and dinner Thursday and Friday; lunch mains $16 to $29, dinner mains $49 to $58) serves delicious and generous meals.

Pond Inlet

POP 1549

Sitting on the perpetually icy Lancaster Sound, against a backdrop of snow-covered mountains, Pond Inlet is the gateway to **Sirmilik National Park** (www.pc.gc.ca; per night $24.50, max $147.20), breeding ground for countless seabirds. The 22,200-sq km park encompasses Bylot Island, a glacier-draped bird sanctuary; Oliver Sound, a fjord with exciting canoeing; Lancaster Sound, home to walrus and several species of seal and whale, and Borden Peninsula with its striking hoodoos (eroded red sandstone towers).

The vast majority of visitors come as part of organized multiday adventures with the highly recommended **Polar Sea Adventures** (613-237-6401; www.polarseaadventures.com; 12-day hiking trip per person $5395, 4-person minimum) . This eco-conscious, long-standing outfit employs Inuit guides and offers the only scheduled hiking expeditions to Sirmilik National Park. A week at the floe edge, the biologically rich area where sea ice meets open water, is around $7600. Black Feather also run trips here.

The helpful **Sirmilik National Park Administration & Visitor Center** (867-899-8092; www.pc.gc.ca; 8:30am-noon & 1-5pm Mon-Fri) has a local wildlife exhibition and handles park registration. Contact it in advance for recommendations on licensed operators that run trips to Sirmilik.

Operated by an aboriginal cooperative, **Sauniq Inn** (867-899-6500; www.pondinlethotel.com; r per person $280;) offers the usual cozy, slightly austere facilities typical of the Inns North chain. Airport pick-up is included and staff can contact outfitters.

Information

Nattinnak Centre (867-899-8225; www.pondinlet.ca; 10am-noon & 1-5pm Tue, Thu & Fri, 1-5pm & 7-9pm Wed, 2-4pm Sun) Has information on activities and outfitters, plus a

OFF THE BEATEN TRACK

QAUSUITTUQ NATIONAL PARK

Spanning over 11,000 sq km of pristine arctic wilderness, Canada's newest national park encompasses a cluster of frozen islands and most of the northern half of Bathurst Island. Its Inuit name means 'Where the Sun Doesn't Rise' – appropriate for a location that sees several months of total darkness each year. The park, jointly managed by the Inuit community of Resolute, is home to the endangered Peary caribou, polar bears and other wildlife.

fine mini-museum with displays on wildlife and local culture. Check out the life-size dioramas and the fish-skin baskets.

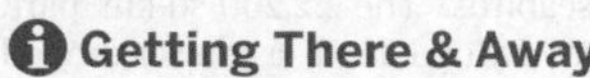

Getting There & Away

First Air and Canadian North fly from Iqaluit (2½ hours, daily).

Kimmirut

POP 455

Baffin Island's southernmost community sits at the mouth of Soper River, overlooking Glasgow Inlet. The area has been continuously inhabited by the ancestors of the Inuit for around 4000 years. The hamlet is a stop on cruise ship routes and the gateway to **Katannilik Territorial Park**. Near Iqaluit and one of Nunavut's finest parks, Katannilik means 'Place of Waterfalls'. A Canadian Heritage waterway, aquamarine **Soper River** splashes 50 navigable kilometers through a deep, fertile valley, past cascades, caribou, gemstone deposits and dwarf-willow forest to Kimmirut, attracting paddlers. Hikers and skiers take the **Itijjagiaq Trail**, a traditional 120km route (one week) over the tablelands of the Meta Incognita Peninsula and through the Soper valley to the Frobisher Bay trailhead, 10km west of Iqaluit.

Most paddlers charter a plane from Iqaluit to the riverside airstrip at Mt Joy, float three to five days from the put-in to Kimmirut, and then fly back to Iqaluit. Kenn Borek Air (p815) does charters. Iqaluit outfitters can take hikers to the trailhead by boat.

You can bed down at the overpriced but friendly **Kimik Hotel** (867-939-2093; r $250; wifi) or camp out at the simple **Taqaiqsirvik Territorial Park Campground** (tent sites $5), which has fire pits and pit toilets. Kimik Hotel is the only place to dine out in Kimmirut.

Before entering Katannilik Territorial Park, you have to register either at the visitor center (p819) in Iqaluit (which stocks the invaluable *The Itijjagiaq Trail*) or the **Katannilik Park Center** (867-939-2416; www.nunavutparks.com; 9am-5pm Mon-Fri) in Kimmirut.

Getting There & Away

First Air links Kimmirut and Iqaluit four times weekly ($418 one way).

Resolute

POP 214

A clutch of minuscule homes in a wind-lashed gravel desert on Cornwallis Island (known as Quasuittuq, 'Place with no Dawn') is Canada's worst-climate community. It was founded in 1953, when several Inuit families were lured here from Pond Inlet, as well as Inukjuak, Québec, with false promises of a better life. Visitors pass through heading for the North Pole, Quttinirpaaq National Park or scenic Grise Fiord.

Seek marine fossils at **Tupirvik Territorial Park** or fly to National Historic Site **Beechey Island**, where the ill-fated Franklin expedition wintered in 1845–46 before vanishing.

Given the likelihood of being 'weathered in,' it's fortuitous there are good hotels. **Qausuittuq Inns North** (867-252-3900; www.resolutebay.com; r $280; P @ wifi) is a delightful family-style place with good home cooking (full board available). It's the starting point for many North Pole expeditions. **South Camp Inn** (867-252-3737; www.southcampinn.com; s/d $300/400; P @ wifi), Resolute's nerve center, is friendly, and comes with a gym and spacious rooms. Full board is available.

Quttinirpaaq National Park

The northernmost, remotest and most mountainous of Nunavut's national parks, 37,775-sq-km **Quttinirpaaq** is Canada's second largest, way up on Ellesmere Island (next stop: North Pole). Fossil finds up here suggest that four million years ago, when camels roamed the forests, the place was tropical. Now the mass of frozen crags, topped with age-old ice caps, deep fjords, vast glaciers and sheltered valleys boast one of the world's most inhospitable climates, tolerated only by musk ox, wolverine and Peary caribou.

Highlights include 24-hour daylight, 6ºC summers, Mt Barbeau (2616m), eastern North America's highest peak, and Lake Hazen Basin, a thermal oasis where animals, unfamiliar with humans, are strangely tame. Wilderness expertise is crucial. The best time to visit is late May to mid-August.

Hikers explore the park from the drop-off points at Tanquary Fjord or Lake Hazen, or do the 11- to 12-day hike between the two. Ski touring in April and May is also possible, but you have to be completely self-sufficient.

Parks Canada's **Tanquary Fjord base camp** (www.pg.gc.ca; 8:30am-noon & 1-5pm Mon-Fri May-Aug) is staffed during the summer season. Visitors must register and undergo orientation training on arrival, and de-register upon leaving.

KIVALLIQ REGION

This region, a flat, windswept area, cut through by wild rivers and a refuge of caribou and waterfowl, takes in the Hudson Bay coast and the Barrenlands to the west. Ukkusiksalik National Park, reachable from Rankin Inlet or recently renamed Naujaat (formerly Repulse Bay), is the prize here, with its cornucopia of wildlife and one of the world's greatest concentrations of polar bears.

Rankin Inlet

POP 2266

Muddy, dusty and busy, Rankin Inlet grew up around nickel mining in the late '50s and is the Kivalliq region's largest community. New gold mines and mineral exploration means it's still an important center. It's also an arty place and a base for accessing Kivalliq, and there's good char and grayling fishing close to town. The town's other claim to fame is that it's the home of Jordin Tootoo, the only Inuk player in the National Hockey League.

Sights

★ Matchbox Gallery GALLERY

(867-645-2674; www.matchboxgallery.com; hours vary) This small space is famed for having pioneered Inuit ceramic art. Watch artists at work, and browse and buy a wide range of beautiful handicrafts.

Marble Island HISTORIC SITE

(www.marbleisland.ca) In Hudson Bay, 50km east of town, this is a graveyard for James Knight and his crew, who sought the Northwest Passage in the 18th century. Some wrecks of 19th-century whalers are there too, and you may spot whales, seals and seabirds en route. Ask at the visitor center for outfitters to take you there.

Iqalugaarjuup Nunanga Territorial Park NATURE RESERVE

(www.nunavutparks.com) This tongue twister of a park is located 5km from town and is popular for hiking and berry-picking. Near the Meliadine River's mouth are archaeological sites where the pre-Inuit Dorset people dwelled, as well as a re-creation of a traditional sod dwelling.

Sleeping & Eating

★ Nanuq Lodge B&B $$

(867-645-2650; www.nanuqlodge.com; 1 Atausiq St; s/d $150/200; P @) This big, friendly, sunny B&B is the region's best place to stay. It rents kayaks, loans bicycles and arranges tours, especially dogsledding. Enjoy comfortable en suite rooms. Its alternative accommodation, Nanuq Suites, has upmarket doubles.

Katimavik Suites BUSINESS HOTEL $$$

(867-857-2752; www.katimaviksuites.com; Tupirvik Ave; r $260; P) Rankin Inlet's newest (and most comfortable) hotel has spacious suites with kitchenettes and splashes of bright colours. Continental breakfast is thrown in, and the helpful management can arrange car rental.

Wild Wolf Restaurant CANADIAN, THAI $$

(867-645-4499; 1270 Nuvua St; mains $20-30; 11:30am-7pm Mon-Sat;) As unexpected as it is welcome, the restaurant inside the Wild Wolf serves reasonably authentic Thai food, conjured up with ingredients imported from Thailand. The Wolf Burger with double meat patty and oodles of toppings should sate a carnivore's appetite.

Information

There's a **visitor centre** (867-645-3838; kivalliqtourism@qiniq.com; 8:30am-7pm Mon-Fri) at the airport. For more information see www.rankininlet.ca.

Getting There & Away

Canadian North (p815) and **First Air** (p815) fly from Yellowknife ($1243 one way) and Iqaluit ($1300 one way); First Air and **Calm Air** (p815) serve Churchill ($747 one way) and Winnipeg ($1052 one way).

OFF THE BEATEN TRACK

THELON RIVER

Among the big Barrenland rivers, the most notable is the legendary Thelon. A Canadian Heritage river, it wends 1000km through utterly wild country. Caribou, grizzly bears, wolves, musk oxen and gyrfalcons abound. Ancient Inuit campsites flank the riverbanks.

Canoeing the river doesn't require remarkable paddling skills, but it *does* demand you to be wilderness savvy. Most opt to paddle just a portion and charter a plane to drop-off and pickup. A simpler option is to sign on with an outfitter such as **Canoe Arctic** (☎867-872-2308; www.canoearctic.com).

Ukkusiksalik National Park

Surrounding the great inland sea of Wager Bay, a large inlet off Hudson Bay, Ukkusiksalik National Park comprises 20,885 sq km of bleak uninhabited tundra interspersed with myriad lakes. This is one of the world's best places to observe polar bears, as here five different populations of bears overlap, as well as caribou and ample sealife. July and early August are the best times to visit.

Highlights include abundant animals and birds, great hiking and boating, and a spectacular reversing waterfall, caused by the bay's high tides. This is a truly wild place; hiring an Inuit guide is highly recommended.

Visitors to the park are required to register and de-register at the nearest **Parks Canada** (☎867-462-4500; ⊙8:30am-noon & 1-5pm Mon-Fri) office in Naujaat, pay park fees and receive mandatory wilderness orientation. Contact **Nunavut Tourism** (☎866-686-2888; www.nunavuttourism.com) in advance for recommendations on local outfitters; **Arctic Kingdom** (☎416-322-7066, toll-free in US & Canada 888-737-6818; www.arctickingdom.com) and Black Feather (p820) can organize custom-made trips.

Naujaat

POP 945

Appropriately named 'the Resting Place of Seagulls', the cliffs around Naujaat (formerly Repulse Bay; www.repulsebay.ca) are important nesting places for thousands of seagulls, snowbirds and other winged creatures. This small community on the Arctic Circle is the gateway to Ukkusiksalik National Park and is an excellent place to fish for Arctic char.

Accommodations-wise, you can choose between the standard business-inclined **Naujat Hotel** (☎867-462-4304; www.innsnorth.com; r $199-295; 🚭📶) and the homey **Arctic Circle Paws & Paddles B&B** (☎867-462-4482; http://arcticcirclepawsandpaddles.weebly.com; r per person incl breakfast $200), which can organize dogsledding and kayaking excursions.

KITIKMEOT REGION

Nunavut's least populated region occupies the mainland's Arctic coast and the islands north of there. Between them runs the fabled Northwest Passage, plied by cruise ships during the summer season.

Cambridge Bay

POP 1608

Wind-wracked Cambridge Bay (www.cambridgebay.ca) on Victoria Island is the regional center and stop for cruise ships navigating the Northwest Passage. The federal Canadian High Arctic Research Station (CHARS) is due to open here in 2017, attracting scientists worldwide to monitor climate change. The Inuinnaqtun dialect is spoken here and Cambridge Bay is known for its crafts, including clothing made out of *qiviut* (supremely warm musk-ox down).

Explorers seeking the Northwest Passage often sheltered here; the remains of Roald Amundsen's schooner *Maud* lie in the harbor.

South across the Northwest Passage is **Queen Maud Bird Sanctuary**, the world's largest migratory bird refuge, home to snow geese and tundra swans. **Ovayok Territorial Park**, accessible via a rough road or 15km hike, is a prime place to see musk ox and offers good views from Mt Pelly (200m). It has walking trails and camping spots.

Green Row Executive Suites (☎867-983-3456; apt per person $235; P🚭📶) is Cambridge Bay's plushest setup. A solid addition to Cambridge Bay's limited dining scene is **Saxifrage Resto-Cafe** (☎867-983-3111; 21 Mitik St; mains from $20; ⊙11am-1:30pm & 5-7pm Mon-Sat).

Arctic Coast Visitor Center (☎867-983-2224; Omingmak St; ⊙8:30am-5pm Mon-Fri, 10am-5pm Sat, 1-4pm Sun) supplies information and can help organize tours. Canadian North and First Air fly from Yellowknife.

Understand Canada

Canada Today

In 2015 Canada got a major facelift with Liberal prime minister Justin Trudeau. Suddenly the world saw photographs of a young leader surfing, hiking, marching in gay pride parades and championing women's rights. There was a collective sigh of relief as Canada became cool again. But with oil prices plummeting and the not-too-quiet whisper of recession in the air, the future isn't looking rose-tinted for everyone; tension between natural resources and a carbon-free economy runs high.

Best on Film

Room (Lenny Abrahamson; 2015) Canadian-Irish film about a mother and son finally released after years of captivity.

Sleeping Giant (Andrew Cividino; 2015) Teens surviving summer in an isolated Ontario cottage community.

Bon Cop, Bad Cop (Eric Canuel; 2006) An Anglophone and Francophone join forces; one of Canada's top-grossing films.

C.R.A.Z.Y. (Jean-Marc Vallée; 2005) A gay teen growing up in a large Catholic family in 1970s Montréal does his best to fit in.

Best in Print

The Illegal (Lawrence Hill; 2015) A marathoner in a fictional land running from the law; takes on race and immigration.

Indian Horse (Richard Wagamese; 2012) An Ojibwe man in rehab recalls his life as a hockey star, touching on Ojibwe rituals and spirituality.

Dear Life (Alice Munro; 2012) Most recent collection of short stories by the 2013 Nobel Prize laureate.

Alias Grace (Margaret Atwood; 1996) A fictional drama set around the notorious real-life 1843 murders of a gentleman and his housekeeper.

Economy

Compared to its international brethren, Canada weathered the global financial crisis pretty well. Yes, the economy dropped into a recession, and Ottawa posted its first fiscal deficit in 2009 after 12 years of surplus. But six years later, Canada clawed its way out and was only one of the seven major industrialized democracies to return to surplus in 2015. The Conservative government of the time focused on federal job cuts that impacted many departments, including Parks Canada and Aboriginal Affairs. In their first full year back in office, the Liberals planned for a $30 billion deficit in 2016–17, claiming investment in job creation, support for the middle class and infrastructure would build a brighter, more sustainable future.

Oil Between Neighbors

Voltaire may have written off Canada as 'a few acres of snow' back in the mid-18th century, but those few acres have yielded vast amounts of oil, timber and other natural resources, and propelled Canada to an enviable standard of living.

Extracting and developing the resources have, however, come with an ecological price. Oil, in particular, is a conundrum. Northern Alberta's Athabasca Oil Sands are the world's second-biggest oil reserves, and they've done an excellent job boosting the economy. They also produce 5% of Canada's greenhouse gas emissions, according to Environment Canada. The pro-industry camp says improvements are being made and, when compared to other oil producers such as Saudi Arabia and Venezuela, the oil sands measure up, especially when human-rights issues and decreased transportation distances are factored in (most of Canada's oil goes to the USA).

The controversial Keystone XL pipeline played into these themes. Aimed to funnel Alberta's crude oil to refineries on the Texas and Louisiana coast, much of it was already built when the US State Department refused approval for the pipeline's completion in late 2015, saying Canada could be doing more to curb carbon emissions. The project was also contentious within Canada, with environmentalists and Aboriginal communities vocal about their concerns regarding damage to sacred sites and water contamination. Interestingly, the US rejection did little to antagonize relations between the new Canadian Liberal government and the US Democrats, but instead brought strong disapproval of the Liberals from oil-industry communities in Canada. Many believe the pipeline could return to the table.

Table Talk

The nation's much-cherished but ailing universal health-care system sparks serious table talk. Although no one will admit it, a two-tiered system is in place, and those with deep pockets can access additional, often quicker care in private facilities. Still, a free, portable health-care system that's available to everyone is quite a feat. To many citizens, it's at the very root of what makes Canada great. So are progressive views on same-sex marriage, immigration and marijuana use.

With wildfires, oil leaks and flooding making headlines, climate change is another hot topic. A 2016 poll showed only 61% of Canadians believe climate change is caused by human activity; it revealed those in Alberta and Saskatchewan were least likely to believe this, while residents of British Columbia, Ontario and Québec were most likely to.

Politics

After being under Conservative rule for almost 10 years, Canada went to the polls in record numbers in 2015 in an election that strongly divided the population. Resource-based communities backed the Conservatives, while many others felt the party had sold out to big business and was being short-sighted in supporting industry over the environment. Many also feared that a split in votes between the leftist New Democratic Party (NDP) and the Liberals would return the Conservatives to power.

The Liberals took back the reigns with a majority leadership headed by the young Justin Trudeau. Son of Pierre Trudeau, the country's 15th prime minister, Justin is a media magnet much like his father, and Canada is witnessing a return to the Trudeau-mania of the 1970s and '80s. Just 43 when he took office, Justin's forthright support of women, children, immigrants, same-sex marriage, marijuana legalization and environmentalism has been welcomed by many Canadians disheartened by Conservative rule. For them, Trudeau embodies much of what it means to be Canadian. Meanwhile, industry-based communities are less than enamored.

POPULATION: **36.3 MILLION**

AREA: **9,984,670 SQ KM**

GDP: **US$1.5 TRILLION**

GDP GROWTH: **1.1%**

INFLATION: **1.5%**

UNEMPLOYMENT: **6.9%**

if Canada were 100 people

28 would be of British Isles origin
23 would be of French origin
15 would be of European origin
34 would be of other origin

belief systems

(% of population)

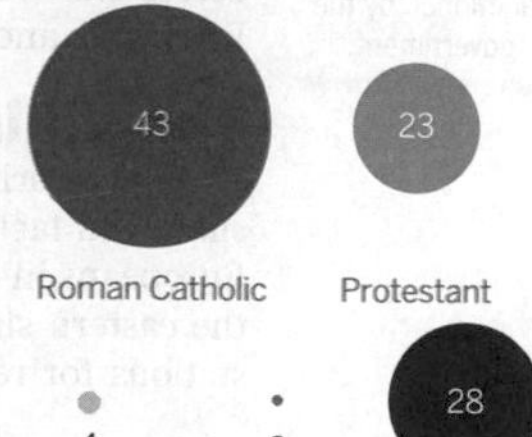

population per sq km

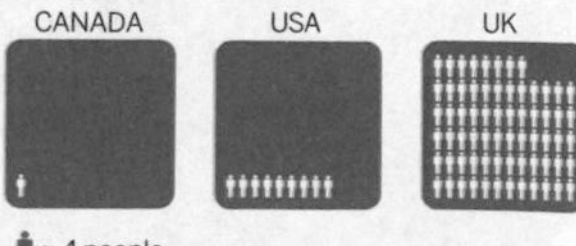

History

The human story of Canada begins around 15,000 years ago, when Aboriginal locals began carving thriving communities from the abundant wilderness. Everything changed, though, when the Europeans rolled in from the late 15th century onward, staking claims that triggered rumbling conflicts and eventually shaped a vast new nation. Much of this colorful heritage is accessible to visitors, with more than 950 national historic sites covering everything from forts to battlefields to famous homes.

Atlantic Canada had a notorious history of pirates. Peter Easton was the first in 1602, plundering around Newfoundland. Black Bart, aka Bartholomew Roberts, was another, c 1720. He disliked booze and gambling and encouraged prayer among his employees. In Halifax pirates were called 'privateers' and were sanctioned by the government.

The First Inhabitants

Canada's first inhabitants were most likely hunter-nomads who, in hungry pursuit of caribou, elk and bison, crossed over from Asia on the land bridge that once linked Siberia and Alaska. As the earth warmed and the glaciers retreated, these immigrants began to trickle across the Americas.

About 4500 years ago, a second major wave of migration from Siberia brought the ancestors of the Inuit to Canada. The new arrivals took one look at the North, sized it up as a tasty icebox filled with fish-and-seal dinners, and decided to hang around. These early Inuit were members of the Dorset Culture, named after Cape Dorset on Baffin Island, where its remains were first unearthed. Around AD 1000 a separate Inuit culture, the whale-hunting Thule of northern Alaska, began making its way east through the Canadian Arctic. As these people spread, they overtook the Dorset Culture. The Thule are the direct ancestors of the modern Inuit.

By the late 15th century, when the first Europeans arrived, Aboriginal peoples had spread beyond the Arctic into four other major locations across Canada: the Pacific, the Plains, the southern Ontario/St Lawrence River area and the Northeast woodlands.

The Vikings & European Explorers

Viking celebrity Leif Eriksson was the first European to reach Canada's shores. In fact, he and his tribe of Scandinavian seafarers were the first Europeans in all of North America. Around AD 1000 they poked around the eastern shores of Canada, establishing winter settlements and way stations for repairing ships and restocking supplies, such as at L'Anse

TIMELINE

c 70 million BC

Dinosaurs enjoy the warm, coastal climate that exists in southern Alberta (the hefty creatures think of it like today's Victoria).

c 25,000 BC

Hot on the hoofs of juicy caribou and bison, the first humans arrive in Canada by crossing the land bridge that once connected Siberia to North America.

1000 BC

After hanging around for a few thousand years, the Maritime Archaic Indians, known for their ceremonial burials at sites like Port aux Choix, inexplicably disappear.

aux Meadows in Newfoundland. The local tribes didn't exactly roll out the welcome mat for these intruders, who eventually tired of the hostilities and went home. There would be no more visits from the outside for another 300 to 400 years.

The action heated up again in the late 15th century. In 1492, backed by the Spanish crown, Christopher Columbus went searching for a western sea route to Asia and instead stumbled upon some small islands in the Bahamas. Other European monarchs, excited by his 'discovery,' quickly sponsored expeditions of their own. In 1497, Giovanni Caboto, better known as John Cabot, sailed under a British flag as far west as Newfoundland and Cape Breton.

Cabot didn't find a passage to China, but he did find cod, a much-coveted commodity in Europe at the time. In short order, hundreds of boats were shuttling between Europe and the fertile new fishing grounds. Basque whalers from northern Spain soon followed. Several were based at Red Bay in Labrador, which became the biggest whaling port in the world during the 16th century.

King François I of France looked over the fence at his neighbors, stroked his beard, then snapped his fingers and ordered Jacques Cartier to appear before him. By this time, the hunt was on not only for the Northwest Passage but also for gold, given the findings by Spanish conquistadors among the Aztec and Inca civilizations. François hoped for similar riches in the frosty North.

Upon arrival in Labrador, Cartier found only 'stones and horrible rugged rocks,' as he wrote in his journal in 1534. He dutifully kept exploring and soon went ashore on Québec's Gaspé Peninsula to claim the land for France. The local Iroquois thought Cartier a good neighbor, until he kidnapped two of the chief's sons and took them back to Europe. To his credit, Cartier returned them a year later when sailing up the St Lawrence River to Stadacona (present-day Québec City) and Hochelaga (today's Montréal). Here he got wind of a land called Saguenay that was full of gold and silver. The rumor prompted Cartier's third voyage, in 1541, but alas, the mythical riches remained elusive.

France retains a token of its early exploits in Canada: St-Pierre and Miquelon, two small islands off Newfoundland's coast, remain staunchly French to this day.

Explorer Jacques Cartier bestowed Canada with its name. Scholars say it comes from *kanata*, a Huron-Iroquois word for 'village' or 'settlement,' which was written in Cartier's journal and later transformed by mapmakers to 'Canada.'

Fur Trade Ignites

François I became bored with his distant colony, which wasn't producing the wealth he wanted. But his interest perked up a few decades later when fur hats became all the rage. Everyone who was anyone was wearing one and, as the fashion mavens knew, there was no finer *chapeau* than one made from beaver pelts. With beavers pretty much extinct in the Old World, the demand for a fresh supply was strong.

In 1588, the French crown granted the first trading monopoly in Canada, only to have other merchants promptly challenge the claim. And so

AD 1000

Viking Leif Eriksson and crew wash up at L'Anse aux Meadows, where they build sod houses. They're the first Europeans in North America, beating Columbus by 500 years.

1497

John Cabot sails over from Britain and finds Newfoundland instead of China. It's not a bad trade-off because the waters are filled with fat, delicious codfish.

1528

St John's, Newfoundland, bobs up as North America's first town. It belongs to no nation; rather it serves fishing fleets from all over Europe.

1534

Jacques Cartier sails into what is now Québec. He searches for gold and precious metals, but finds only chilled rocks. He claims the land for France anyway.

the race for control of the fur trade was officially on. The economic value of this enterprise and, by extension, its role in shaping Canadian history, cannot be underestimated. It was the main reason behind the country's European settlement, at the root of the struggle for dominance between the French and the British, and the source of strife and division between Aboriginal groups. All because of a hat.

The Canadian Military History Gateway (www.cmhg.gc.ca) provides access to digitized resources on Canada's military history, including audio links to old CBC war broadcasts.

In order to gain control of the distant lands, the first order of business was to put European bodies on the ground. In the summer of 1604, a group of French pioneers established a tentative foothold on Île Ste-Croix (a tiny islet in the river on the present US border with Maine). They moved to Port Royal (today's Annapolis Royal) in Nova Scotia the following spring. Exposed and difficult to defend, neither site made a good base for controlling the inland fur trade. As the would-be colonists moved up the St Lawrence River, they finally came upon a spot their leader, Samuel de Champlain, considered prime real estate – where today's Québec City stands. It was 1608 and 'New France' had become a reality.

French vs English

The French enjoyed their plush fur monopoly for several decades, but in 1670 the British mounted a formidable challenge. They caught a lucky break when a pair of disillusioned French explorers, Radisson and Des Groseilliers, confided that the best fur country actually lay to the north and west of Lake Superior, which was easily accessible via Hudson Bay. King Charles II quickly formed the Hudson's Bay Company and granted it a trade monopoly over all the lands whose rivers and streams drained into the bay. This vast territory, called Rupert's Land, encompassed about 40% of present-day Canada, including Labrador, western Québec, northwestern Ontario, Manitoba, most of Saskatchewan and Alberta, and part of the Northwest Territories.

Top Historical Sites: West

- *Klondike sites, Yukon*
- *Batoche, Saskatchewan*
- *Head-Smashed-In Buffalo Jump, Alberta*
- *Fort Edmonton, Alberta*

The English infuriated the French with such moves, and so the French kept right on galling the English by settling further inland. Both countries had claims to the land, but each wanted regional dominance. They skirmished back and forth in hostilities that mirrored those in Europe, where wars raged throughout the first half of the 18th century.

Things came to a head with the Treaty of Utrecht, which ended Queen Anne's War (1701–13) overseas. Under its provisions, the French had to officially recognize British claims to Hudson Bay and Newfoundland, and give up all of Nova Scotia (then called Acadia) except for Cape Breton Island.

The conflict simmered for a few decades, then ramped up to a new level in 1754 when the two countries battled each other in the French and Indian Wars (also known as the Seven Years' War). The tide soon turned in the Brits' favor with the capture of the Louisbourg fortress, giving them control of a strategically important entrance to the St Lawrence River.

1608

After four years of moving around, Samuel de Champlain finds his dream-home site, putting down stakes at Québec City and giving New France its first permanent settlement.

1610

The British take their turn: merchant John Guy builds a plantation at Cupids, Newfoundland. It's England's first colony in Canada (and second in the New World after Jamestown).

1670

King Charles II creates the Hudson's Bay Company to shore up the local fur trade for the Brits. Years later, the company morphs into the Bay department store chain.

1755

The English deport some 14,000 French Acadians from the Bay of Fundy region. They're forced onto ships during the Great Expulsion; many head to Louisiana in the USA.

In 1759 the British besieged Québec, scaling the cliffs in a surprise attack and quickly defeating the stunned French; it was one of Canada's bloodiest and most famous battles, and left both commanding generals dead. At the Treaty of Paris (1763), France handed Canada over to Britain.

Growing Pains

Managing the newly acquired territory presented quite a challenge for the British. First, they had to quell uprisings by the Aboriginal tribes, such as the attack on Detroit by Ottawa Chief Pontiac. The British government issued the Royal Proclamation of 1763, which prevented colonists from settling west of the Appalachian Mountains and regulated purchases of aboriginal land. Though well-intentioned, the proclamation was largely ignored.

The French Canadians caused the next headache. Tensions arose when the new rulers imposed British law that heavily restricted the rights of Roman Catholics (the religion of the French), including the rights to vote and hold office. The British hoped their discriminatory policy would launch a mass exodus and make it easier to anglicize the remaining settlers. The plan didn't work – the French just crossed their arms and further dug in their heels.

As if the tribes and French weren't problems enough, the American colonies started making revolutionary rumbles to the south. The British governor, Guy Carleton, wisely reasoned that winning the French settlers' political allegiance was more valuable than turning them into tea drinkers. This led to the passage of the Québec Act of 1774. The act confirmed French Canadians' right to their religion, allowed them to assume political office and restored the use of French civil law. Indeed, during the American Revolution (1775–83) most French Canadians refused to take up arms for the American cause, although not many willingly defended the British either.

Top Historical Sites: East

L'Anse aux Meadows, Newfoundland

Fortifications of Québec, Québec City

Louisbourg, Nova Scotia

Province House, Prince Edward Island

The USA has invaded Canada twice – in 1775 and 1812 – both times to no avail.

THE MAPLE LEAF SYMBOL

It's on the penny, on Air Canada planes, on Toronto hockey-team jerseys – you can't escape the maple leaf. The leaf has been considered a national symbol for almost two centuries. In 1836, *Le Canadien* newspaper, published in Lower Canada, wrote about it as a suitable emblem for the nation. Ontario and Québec both were using it on their coat of arms by 1868. The Canadian Armed Forces used it during the world wars. And finally, after much wrangling over the design (one leaf? three leaves? 13 points?), the current 11-point leaf was granted national-symbol status and went on the flag in 1965.

1759

Canada's most famous battle, between the French and English, happens on the Plains of Abraham at Québec City. It lasts less than an hour. France loses.

1763

The Treaty of Paris boots France out of Canada after France loses the Seven Years' War. Thus, Canada ceases to ping-pong between power-mongering France and Britain.

1775

American rebels invade Canada and try to entice Québec to join the revolt against the British in the American Revolution, but the locals refuse.

1793

Explorer Alexander Mackenzie makes the first transcontinental journey across the land. He scrawls 'from Canada by land' on a rock near Bella Coola, BC.

After the revolution, the English-speaking population exploded when some 50,000 settlers from the newly independent US migrated northward. Called United Empire Loyalists due to their presumed allegiance to Britain, many settlers were motivated more by cheap land than by love of king and crown. The majority ended up in Nova Scotia and New Brunswick, while a smaller group settled along the northern shore of Lake Ontario and in the Ottawa River Valley (forming the nucleus of what became Ontario). About 8000 people moved to Québec, creating the first sizeable Anglophone community in the French-speaking bastion.

It was Newfoundland's Beothuk Aboriginals and their ceremonially ocher-coated faces who were dubbed 'red men' by arriving Europeans, a name soon applied to all of North America's indigenous groups. Tragically, the Beothuk died out by 1829.

The Nation Splits: Upper & Lower Canada

Partly in order to accommodate the interests of Loyalist settlers, the British government passed the Constitutional Act of 1791, which divided the colony into Upper Canada (today's southern Ontario) and Lower Canada (now southern Québec). Lower Canada retained French civil laws, but both provinces were governed by the British criminal code.

The British crown installed a governor to direct each colony. The governor in turn appointed the members of his 'cabinet,' then called the Executive Council. The legislative branch consisted of an appointed Legislative Council and an elected Assembly, which ostensibly represented the interests of the colonists. In reality, though, the Assembly held very little power, since the governor could veto its decisions. Not surprisingly, this was a recipe for friction and resentment. This was especially the case in Lower Canada, where an English governor and an English-dominated Council held sway over a French-dominated Assembly.

Rampant cronyism made matters even worse. Members of the conservative British merchant elite dominated the Executive and Legislative Councils and showed little interest in French-Canadian matters. Called the Family Compact in Upper Canada and the Château Clique in Lower Canada, their ranks included brewer John Molson and university founder James McGill. The group's influence grew especially strong after the War of 1812, an ultimately futile attempt by the US to take over its northern neighbor.

In 1837, frustration over these entrenched elites reached a boiling point. Parti Canadien leader Louis-Joseph Papineau and his Upper Canadian counterpart, Reform Party leader William Lyon Mackenzie, launched open rebellions against the government. Although both uprisings were quickly crushed, the incident signaled to the British that the status quo wasn't going to cut it any longer.

Best Historic Neighborhoods

- *Gastown, Vancouver*
- *Québec City, Québec*
- *Old Montréal, Montréal*
- *Downtown Halifax, Nova Scotia*

1818

The USA and Britain hash out the Treaty of 1818. The upshot: Canada's border is defined as the 49th Parallel from Lake of the Woods to the Rocky Mountains.

1858

Yee-haw! Prospectors discover gold along the Fraser River in BC, spurring thousands of get-rich-quick dreamers to move north and start panning. Most remain poor.

1864

The Fathers of the Confederation meet in Charlottetown, PEI, and mold a new country called Canada from the group of loosely knit colonies that now comprise the land.

1867

It's official: the British North America Act unites the colonies under the Dominion of Canada, a card-carrying member of the British Empire. Queen Victoria celebrates with Canadian bacon for breakfast.

Cautious Reunion

The British dispatched John Lambton, the Earl of Durham, to investigate the causes of the rebellions. He correctly identified ethnic tensions as the root of the problem, calling the French and British 'two nations warring in the bosom of a single state.' He then earned the nickname 'Radical Jack' by asserting that French culture and society were inferior and obstacles to expansion and greatness – only assimilation of British laws, language and institutions would quash French nationalism and bring long-lasting peace to the colonies. These ideas were adopted into the Union Act of 1840.

Upper and Lower Canada soon merged into the Province of Canada and became governed by a single legislature, the new Parliament of Canada. Each ex-colony had the same number of representatives, which wasn't exactly fair to Lower Canada (ie Québec), where the population was much larger. On the plus side, the new system brought responsible government that restricted the governor's powers and eliminated nepotism.

While most British Canadians welcomed the new system, the French were less than thrilled. If anything, the union's underlying objective of destroying French culture, language and identity made Francophones cling together even more tenaciously. The provisions of the act left deep wounds that still haven't fully healed.

Thus the united province was built on slippery ground. The decade or so following unification was marked by political instability as one government replaced another in fairly rapid succession. Meanwhile, the USA had grown into a self-confident economic powerhouse, while British North America was still a loose patchwork of independent colonies. The American Civil War (1861–65) and the USA's purchase of Alaska from Russia in 1867 raised fears of annexation. It became clear that only a less volatile political system would stave off these challenges, and the movement toward federal union gained momentum.

Best History Museums

Maritime Museum of the Atlantic, Halifax

Canadian War Museum, Ottawa

Musée d'Archéologie et d'Histoire de Pointe-à-Callière, Montréal

Royal BC Museum, Victoria

Ukrainian Cultural Heritage Village, Alberta

Confederation

In 1864, Charlottetown, Prince Edward Island (PEI), served as the birthing room for modern Canada. At the town's Province House, the 'Fathers of Confederation' – a group of representatives from Nova Scotia, New Brunswick, PEI, Ontario and Québec – got together and hammered out the framework for a new nation. It took two more meetings before Parliament passed the British North America Act in 1867. And so began the modern, self-governing state of Canada, originally known as the Dominion of Canada. The day the act became official, July 1, is celebrated as Canada's national holiday; it was called Dominion Day until it was renamed Canada Day in 1982.

Delegates to the Charlottetown Conference in 1864 had to sleep on their steamships because the circus was in town and all the inns were fully booked.

1885

Canada's first national park opens in Banff, Alberta; meanwhile, in Craigellachie, BC, workers drive in the spike that completes the Canadian Pacific Railway.

1893

The Montréal AAA hockey team accepts the first Stanley Cup (donated by one Lord Stanley of Preston). It's now the oldest trophy North American pro sports teams compete for.

1896

Prospectors find more of the shiny stuff, this time in the Yukon. The Klondike Gold Rush is on, with 40,000 hopefuls bringing their picks and pans to Dawson City.

1913

Immigration to Canada crests, with more than 400,000 people embracing the maple leaf. Most are Americans and Eastern Europeans, who can't resist the call of the nation's fertile prairies.

How the West was Won

Task one on the infant dominion's to-do list was to bring the remaining land and colonies into the confederation. Under its first prime minister, John A Macdonald, the government acquired vast Rupert's Land in 1869 for the paltry sum of £300,000 (about $11.5 million in today's money) from the Hudson's Bay Company. Now called the Northwest Territories (NWT), the land was only sparsely populated, mostly by Plains First Nations and several thousand Métis (may-*tee*), a racial blend of Cree, Ojibwe or Saulteaux and French-Canadian or Scottish fur traders, who spoke French as their main language. Their biggest settlement was the Red River Colony around Fort Garry (today's Winnipeg).

Manual laborers from China built much of the Canadian Pacific Railway's western stretch. They earned $0.75 to $1.25 per day, and often were given the most dangerous, explosive-laden jobs.

The Canadian government immediately clashed with the Métis people over land-use rights, causing the latter to form a provisional government led by the charismatic Louis Riel. He sent the Ottawa-appointed governor packing and, in November 1869, seized control of Upper Fort Garry, thereby forcing Ottawa to the negotiating table. However, with his delegation already en route, Riel impulsively executed a Canadian prisoner he was holding at the fort. Although the murder caused widespread uproar in Canada, the government was so keen to bring the west into the fold it agreed to most of Riel's demands, including special language and religious protections for the Métis. As a result, the then-pint-sized province of Manitoba was carved out of the NWT and entered the dominion in July 1870. Macdonald sent troops after Riel but he narrowly managed to escape to the USA. He was formally exiled for five years in 1875.

Gold Diggers (2010), by Charlotte Gray, tells of the last great gold rush in history. Between 1896 and 1899 Dawson City, in the Yukon, boomed from 400 people to 30,000 people. The author uses letters and newspaper articles by resident journalists, bankers, prostitutes, priests and lawmen to depict the era.

British Columbia (BC), created in 1866 by merging the colonies of New Caledonia and Vancouver Island, was the next frontier. The discovery of gold along the Fraser River in 1858 and in the Cariboo region in 1862 had brought an enormous influx of settlers to such gold-mine boom towns as Williams Lake and Barkerville. Once the gold mines petered out, though, BC was plunged into poverty. In 1871 it joined the dominion in exchange for the Canadian government assuming all its debt and promising to link it with the east within 10 years via a transcontinental railroad.

The construction of the Canadian Pacific Railway is one of the most impressive chapters in Canadian history. Macdonald rightly regarded the railroad as crucial in unifying the country, spurring immigration and stimulating business and manufacturing. It was a costly proposition, made even more challenging by the rough and rugged terrain the tracks had to traverse. To entice investors, the government offered major benefits, including vast land grants in western Canada. Workers drove the final spike into the track at Craigellachie, BC, on November 7, 1885.

To bring law and order to the 'wild west,' the government created the North-West Mounted Police (NWMP) in 1873, which later became the

1917

Canada introduces the draft to replenish forces fighting for England in WWI. French Canadians, in particular, oppose the call-up, foreshadowing tensions to come.

1931

The residential school system peaks. Aboriginal, Inuit and Métis children are removed from their communities and forced to attend schools (most operated by churches) far from home to 'assimilate.'

1933

Three out of 10 people are out of work, as Canada feels the effects of the Great Depression. The prairies are especially hard hit by the drought-induced Dust Bowl.

1942

Newfoundland becomes the only North American site directly attacked by German forces during WWII, when a U-boat launches a torpedo that strikes inland at Bell Island.

EXTREME MAKEOVER: THE IMAGE OF LOUIS RIEL

Rebel, murderer, traitor – Métis leader Louis Riel was called many things, and not many of them were compliments, when he was hanged for treason in 1885. But today a growing number of Canadians see him as a hero who defended the rights of the oppressed against an unjust government. Statues of Riel stand on Parliament Hill in Ottawa and outside the Manitoba Legislature in Winnipeg, where his boyhood home and grave have become places of pilgrimage. The government's 1998 Statement of Reconciliation to Canada's Aboriginal peoples even included an apology for Riel's execution.

Royal Canadian Mounted Police (RCMP). Nicknamed 'Mounties,' they still serve as Canada's national police force today. Although they were effective, the NWMP couldn't prevent trouble from brewing on the prairies, where the Plains First Nations had been forced to sign various treaties relegating them to reserves. It wasn't long before these groups began to challenge their status.

Meanwhile, many Métis had moved to Saskatchewan and settled around Batoche. As in Manitoba, they quickly clashed with government surveyors over land issues. In 1884, after their repeated appeals to Ottawa had been ignored, they coaxed Louis Riel out of exile to represent their cause. Rebuffed, Riel responded the only way he knew: by forming a provisional government and leading the Métis in revolt. Riel had the backing of the Cree, but times had changed: with the railroad nearly complete, government troops arrived within days. Riel surrendered in May and was hanged for treason later that year.

The Nova Scotia government maintains a website (http://titanic.gov.ns.ca) of all things *Titanic*, including a list of passengers buried in local graveyards and artifacts housed in local museums. The province played a vital role in the tragedy, as ships from Halifax were sent out to recover victims.

Cutting Ties to England

Canada rang in the 20th century on a high note. Industrialization was in full swing, prospectors had discovered gold in the Yukon, and Canadian resources – from wheat to lumber – were increasingly in demand. In addition, the new railroad opened the floodgates to immigration.

Between 1885 and 1914 about 4.5 million people arrived in Canada. This included large groups of Americans and Eastern Europeans, especially Ukrainians, who went to work cultivating the prairies. Optimism reigned: a buoyant Prime Minister Wilfrid Laurier said 'The 19th century was the century of the United States. I think we can claim that it is Canada that shall fill the 20th century.' It was only natural that this new-found self-confidence would put the country on track to autonomy from Britain. The issue took on even greater urgency when WWI broke out in 1914.

Canada – as a member of the British Empire – found itself automatically drawn into the conflict. In the war's first years, more than 300,000 volunteers went off to European battlefields. As the war dragged on and

early 1960s

It's a time of change: the Quiet Revolution modernizes, secularizes and liberalizes Québec, while Aboriginal peoples are finally granted citizenship nationwide.

1961

The kind and neighborly folks of Saskatchewan introduce the first universal health-care plan, an idea that soon spreads to the rest of Canada.

1962

Canada becomes the third nation in space, after the Soviet Union and the USA, when it launches the *Alouette* satellite into the stratosphere.

1963

After smoothing a whole lot of concrete, workers lay the final touches on the Trans-Canada Hwy, spanning 7821km from St John's, Newfoundland, to Victoria, BC.

thousands of soldiers returned in coffins, recruitment ground to a halt. The government, intent on replenishing its depleted forces, introduced the draft in 1917. It proved to be a very unpopular move, to say the least, especially among French Canadians. Animosity toward Ottawa was already at an all-time high since the government had recently abolished bilingual schools in Manitoba and restricted the use of French in Ontario's schools. The conscription issue fanned the flames of nationalism even more. Thousands of Québecois took to the streets in protest, and the issue left Canada divided and Canadians distrustful of their government.

More than one million Canadians served in the armed forces during WWII from a population of approximately 11.5 million; 42,000 died.

By the time the guns of WWI fell silent in 1918, most Canadians were fed up with sending their sons and husbands to fight in distant wars for Britain. Under the government of William Lyon Mackenzie King, an eccentric fellow who communicated with spirits and worshiped his dead mother, Canada began asserting its independence. Mackenzie King made it clear that Britain could no longer automatically draw upon the Canadian military, started signing treaties without British approval, and sent a Canadian ambassador to Washington. This forcefulness led to the Statute of Westminster, passed by the British Parliament in 1931. The statute formalized the independence of Canada and other Commonwealth nations, although Britain retained the right to pass amendments to those countries' constitutions.

Oddly, that right remained on the books for another half century. It was removed only with the 1982 Canada Act, which Queen Elizabeth II signed into law on Parliament Hill in Ottawa on April 17. Today, Canada is a constitutional monarchy with a parliament consisting of an appointed upper house, or Senate, and an elected lower house, the House of Commons. The British monarch remains Canada's head of state, although this is predominantly a ceremonial role and does not diminish the country's sovereignty. Within Canada, the appointed governor general is the monarch's representative.

Searching for your Cajun roots? The Acadian Genealogy Homepage (www.acadian.org) has compiled census reports harking back to 1671, plus maps and histories of local Acadian communities.

Modern-Day Canada

The period after WWII brought another wave of economic expansion and immigration, especially from Europe.

Newfoundland finally joined Canada in 1949. Joey Smallwood, the politician who persuaded the island to sign up, claimed it would bring economic prosperity. Once he became Newfoundland's premier, he helped this prosperity along by forcing a resettlement program upon citizens. People living in small, isolated fishing communities (aka outports) were strongly encouraged to pack up and move inland where the government could deliver schools, health care and other services more economically. One method for 'encouraging' villagers was to cut ferry services to their communities, thus making them inaccessible since there were no roads.

1964

Tim Hortons, started by the eponymous ice-hockey defenseman, serves its first doughnut and cup of coffee in Hamilton, Ontario. It's now Canada's largest restaurant franchise.

1967

The Great Canadian Oil Sands plant opens at Fort McMurray, Alberta, and starts pumping out black gold. It's reputed to hold more oil than all of Saudi Arabia.

1982

Queen Elizabeth II signs the Canada Act, giving Canada complete sovereignty. However, she retains the right to keep her face on the money and to appoint a governor general.

1990

The Oka Crisis, a violent standoff between the government and a band of Mohawk activists near Montréal, is sparked by a land claim over a golf course. One person dies.

QUÉBEC'S SEPARATIST MOVEMENT

Québec's separatist movement began in earnest in 1968, when René Lévesque founded the sovereigntist Parti Québecois (PQ).

The issue intensified quickly. In October 1970, the most radical wing of the movement, the Front de Libération du Québec (FLQ; Québec Liberation Front), kidnapped Québec's labor minister Pierre Laporte and a British trade official in an attempt to force the independence issue. Prime Minister Pierre Trudeau declared a state of emergency and called in the army to protect government officials. Two weeks later, Laporte's body was found in the trunk of a car. The murder discredited the FLQ in the eyes of many erstwhile supporters and the movement quickly faded.

Still, Lévesque's PQ won the 1976 Québec provincial election and quickly pushed through a bill that made French the province's sole official language. His 1980 referendum on secession, however, was resoundingly defeated, with almost 60% voting *non*. The issue was put on the back burner for much of the 1980s.

Lévesque's successor, Robert Bourassa, agreed to a constitution-led solution – but only if Québec was recognized as a 'distinct society' with special rights. In 1987 Prime Minister Brian Mulroney unveiled an accord that met most of Québec's demands. To take effect, the so-called Meech Lake Accord needed to be ratified by all 10 provinces and both houses of parliament by 1990. Dissenting premiers in three provinces eventually pledged their support but, incredibly, the accord collapsed when a single member of Manitoba's legislature refused to sign. Mulroney and Bourassa drafted a new, expanded accord, but the separatists picked it apart and it too was trounced.

Relations between Anglos and Francophones hit new lows, and support for independence was rekindled. Only one year after returning to power in 1994, the PQ, under Premier Lucien Bouchard, launched a second referendum. This was a cliff-hanger: Québecois decided by 52,000 votes – a majority of less than 1% – to remain within Canada.

The issue lost some of its luster in the years that followed, though the PQ remained a viable force. In 2012, the PQ won 32% of the vote in Québec's elections, enough to form a minority government. But by 2013, the party was losing ground again after its controversial proposal that public workers be banned from wearing religious headgear.

The only province truly left behind during the 1950s boom years was Québec. For a quarter century, it remained in the grip of ultra-conservative Maurice Duplessis and his Union Nationale party, with support from the Catholic Church and various business interests. Only after Duplessis' death did the province finally start getting up to speed during the 'Quiet Revolution' of the 1960s. Advances included expanding the public sector, investing in public education and nationalizing the provincial hydroelectric companies. Still, progress wasn't swift enough for radical nationalists who

1992
The government imposes the Atlantic cod moratorium, and thousands of fisherfolk lose their livelihoods. The ban was supposed to be lifted within a few years, but depleted stocks never rebounded.

1999
Nunavut, Canada's newest province, is chiseled from the icy eastern Arctic, giving about one-fifth of Canadian soil to the 28,000 Inuit who live there.

2003
Canada becomes the world's third-largest diamond producer (after Botswana and Russia), thanks to riches discovered in the NWT. The baubles spark a modern-day boom similar to gold-rush times.

2005
Canada legalizes gay marriage throughout the country. Most provinces and territories had permitted it, but now hold-outs Alberta, PEI, Nunavut and the NWT join the ranks.

claimed independence was the only way to ensure Francophone rights. Québec has spent the ensuing years flirting with separatism.

In 1960, Canada's Aboriginal peoples were finally granted Canadian citizenship. Issues involving land rights and discrimination played out in the decades that followed. In 1990, Aboriginal frustration reached boiling point with the Oka Crisis, a standoff between the government and a group of Mohawk activists near Montréal. The conflict was set off by a land claim: the town of Oka was planning to expand a golf course onto land that the Mohawk considered sacred. A 78-day clash ensued, and one policeman died of gunshot wounds. The event shook Canada.

In *Canadian History for Dummies*, best-selling author Will Ferguson uses his irreverent, opinionated and energetic style to take you on an entertaining cruise through his country's wild and wacky past.

In the aftermath of Oka, a Royal Commission on Aboriginal Peoples issued a report recommending a complete overhaul of relations between the government and indigenous peoples. In 1998 the Ministry of Indian and Northern Affairs issued an official Statement of Reconciliation that accepted responsibility for past injustices toward Aboriginal peoples. In 1999, the government resolved its biggest land claim, creating the new territory of Nunavut and handing it over to the Inuit people who have long lived in the northern region. Recent disputes have focused on renaming landmarks, such as Mt Douglas near Victoria, BC, which First Nations people want returned to its original name of Pkols.

In 1985, Canada became the first country in the world to pass a national multicultural act. Today, more than 20% of Canada's population is foreign-born. BC has a long history of welcoming Japanese, Chinese and South Asian immigrants. The prairie provinces have traditionally been the destination of large numbers of Ukrainians, and Ontario, which has sizable Caribbean and Russian populations, is also home to 60% of Canada's Muslims.

The new millennium has been kind to Canada. The loonie took off around 2003 – thanks to the oil, diamonds and other natural resources fueling the economy – and tolerance marches onward, with medical marijuana and gay marriage both legalized. The country showed off its abundant assets to the world when it successfully hosted the 2010 Winter Olympics in Vancouver.

Canadian Inventions

foghorn (1854)

basketball (1892)

Insulin (1922)

peanut butter (1884)

egg carton (c 1911)

IMAX (1967)

2006

The census shows almost 20% of the population is foreign-born – the highest proportion in 75 years. Immigrants from Asia (including the Middle East) make up the largest proportion of newcomers.

2010

Vancouver and Whistler showcase the west coast's gorgeous mountains and cool urbanity when they host the 2010 Winter Olympics. Team Canada wins the gold medal for hockey.

2013

Calgary is hit by epic floods; four people die and 100,000 others are forced from their homes. It's the costliest natural disaster in Canadian history.

2016

Fort McMurray and the surrounding area succumbs to wildfires, with 80,000 evacuated and an area larger than PEI razed.

Aboriginal Cultures

Canada's original inhabitants began living on the land more than 15,000 years ago. The term 'Aboriginal' refers to the descendants of these earliest residents, which now comprise three groups: First Nations (those of North American Indian descent), Métis (those with 'mixed blood' ancestry) and Inuit (those in the Arctic). Together they make up 4.3% of Canada's total population. The growing popularity of aboriginal tourism is an indicator of native people's determination to retain or regain their traditional cultural roots.

The People

First Nations

This broad term applies to all Aboriginal groups except the Métis and Inuit. Almost 852,000 First Nations people live in Canada (about 2.5% of the total population), comprising more than 600 communities (sometimes called bands). British Columbia (BC) is home to the most First Nations (198 groups), while Ontario is second (126 groups).

Pacific

Historically, the people along the Pacific Coast built cedar-plank houses and carved elaborate totem poles and canoes. The potlatch, a ritual feast where the host gives away lavish gifts and possessions, is a renowned facet of many local cultures. The Canadian government banned the practice from 1885 to 1951 for being 'uncivilized.'

The Haida of Haida Gwaii, a group of islands off BC's northern shore, are perhaps the region's best-known First Nations group. Their artistic traditions are extraordinary, and they're famed for their wood carvings, totem poles and stylized prints of animals. Many other groups along the coast have similar art forms.

Plains

The Plains First Nations, which traditionally included the Sioux, Cree and Blackfoot, occupied the prairies from Lake Winnipeg to the Rocky Mountain foothills. Primarily buffalo hunters, they cunningly killed their prey by driving them over cliffs, such as at Head-Smashed-In Buffalo Jump in southern Alberta.

The Plains today still have a strong First Nations (and Métis) presence. Winnipeg has the largest number of First Nations people in Canada, with Edmonton not far behind. In Regina, **First Nations University of Canada** (www.fnuniv.ca) is the only First Nations–run institution of higher learning in the country.

Great Lakes & St Lawrence River Area

Present-day southern Ontario and the area along the St Lawrence River are the time-honored home of the Iroquoian-speaking peoples, who were once divided into the Five Nations (including the Mohawk, Oneida and Seneca), the Huron, the Erie and the Neutral confederacies. Although often at war with one another, they were relatively modern societies who

Urban Aboriginal Populations

- Winnipeg *68,380*
- Edmonton *52,100*
- Vancouver *40,310*
- Calgary *26,575*
- Toronto *26,575*
- Saskatoon *21,535*
- Ottawa *20,590*
- Montréal *17,865*
- Regina *17,105*

ABORIGINAL ARTISTS

There was little outside recognition of the art produced by Aboriginal communities until the 20th century. But over the last 50 years or so, there's been a strong and growing appreciation of this body of work, led initially by the paintings, sculptures and carvings of revered Haida artist Bill Reid (1920–1998), whose work appears on the back of the $20 bill. Roy Henry Vickers is well known for his prints; check out his gallery in Tofino, BC. Also look out for colorful paintings by Norval Morriseau; mixed-media works by Saskatchewan-born Edward Poitras; and challenging younger artists like Marianne Nicolson and Brian Jungen, who explore political and environmental themes in their art.

lived in large farming communities, built sturdy longhouses and traded with other tribes.

Today Manitoulin Island, floating in Lake Huron, preserves Ojibwe culture through its several reserves, where visitors can attend powwows and follow the **Great Spirit Circle Trail** (www.circletrail.com).

Aboriginal Population Percentages

Nunavut	*86%*
Northwest Territories	*52%*
Yukon Territory	*23%*
Manitoba	17%
Saskatchewan	16%
Alberta	*6%*
BC	*5%*
Ontario	*2%*

Maritime Provinces

The Mi'kmaqs and Maliseets are the main First Nations in the Maritimes, accounting for just over 1% of the total population there. Traditionally they fished the shores in summer, and moved inland to hunt moose and caribou in winter.

In New Brunswick, the Maliseets (renowned basket-makers) live in the upper St John River valley in the west, while the Mi'kmaqs live to the east. In Nova Scotia, the Mi'kmaqs live in 14 communities, mostly around Bras d'Or Lake on Cape Breton and near Truro. A small group also lives on Prince Edward Island (PEI).

The Maritimes have experienced a revival of traditional song and dance, language programs, and healing and ritual ceremonies. Public powwows often take place, especially around Truro.

Northeastern Québec & Labrador

The Innu are the long-time inhabitants of the cold boreal forest stretching across the north of Québec and Labrador. The Innu are often confused with the Inuit, but they are not related. Rather, two First Nations – the Naskapi and the Montagnais – make up the Innu. In the past, they were fairly nomadic, and survived by hunting caribou and moose for food and skins.

About 80% of Innu live in Québec, with 20% in Labrador.

'Eskimo' was the term given to Inuit by European explorers. It's now rarely used in Canada. It derives from an Algonquian term meaning 'raw meat eaters,' and many find it offensive.

Northern Ontario, Manitoba & Saskatchewan

The Cree dominate this chilly landscape. As one of Canada's largest First Nations, they also extend west into the Plains and east into Québec. There's a well-known reserve in Ontario at Moose Factory (a former Hudson Bay fur-trading post), which built the hemisphere's first aboriginal ecolodge. Many Cree also live in polar-bear-epicenter Churchill, Manitoba, where they make up about one-third of the local population; it's not uncommon to hear people speaking Cree in Churchill. The Cree have a reputation for being gifted healers.

Yukon & Northwest Territories

The Dene were the first people to settle in what is now the Northwest Territories. Today many live in Yellowknife, as well as villages throughout the Mackenzie Delta, west into the Yukon and Alaska, east toward Nunavut and south into the prairies. Traditionally they're hunters, fishers and trappers and known for their birch-bark basket weaving.

The Gwich'in First Nations people live farther north and rely on caribou for a major part of their diet and lifestyle. They've actively protested drilling in the Arctic National Wildlife Refuge, saying it will deplete the caribou herd there that they depend on for food. The economy of their communities is based mostly on hunting and fishing.

Métis

Métis is the French word for 'mixed blood.' Historically, the term was applied to the children of French fur traders and Cree women in the prairies, and English and Scottish traders and Dene women in the north. Today the term is used broadly to describe people with mixed First Nations and European ancestry.

Métis account for about one-third of the overall Aboriginal population. They are largely based in western Canada. Winnipeg and Edmonton are the cities with the highest number of Métis.

Louis Riel (1844–1885) is the culture's most famous individual. He battled for the rights of Métis, who were often trampled during Canada's westward expansion. Riel led two resistance movements against the government, the last at Batoche, Saskatchewan, in 1885. He was caught and convicted of treason, though today he's considered a hero by most Canadians.

Unlike First Nations people, Métis were never placed on reserves.

Inuit

The Inuit are native to arctic Canada. Today they number 59,000 (4% of the overall Aboriginal population) and are spread throughout four Arctic regions: Nunavut, the Inuvialuit area in the Northwest Territories, Nunavik (northern Québec) and Nunatsiavut (Labrador). All in all, they cover one-third of Canada.

Inuit have never been placed on reserves as their frozen territory was not carved up in the same way. Instead they live in small communities: 38% of their villages have a population of less than 500 people. About 29% have between 500 and 999 people, while 33% have 1000 or more residents.

Traditionally, Inuit hunted whales and big game, traveled by kayak and dog sled, and spent winters in igloos. Snowmobiles and houses have replaced the sleds and igloos these days, but subsistence hunting is still a big part of the economy, as is traditional soapstone carving and printmaking.

The Inuit language is Inuktitut, a system of syllabics versus letters.

Recent History

Canada never experienced the all-out massacres that marred the European–Native American clashes in the USA. Nevertheless, Canada's Aboriginal population still suffered massive discrimination, loss of territory and serious civil rights violations throughout the country's history.

In 1993 Canada's biggest land claim was settled when Prime Minister Brian Mulroney signed into existence the new territory of Nunavut, which took effect in 1999, giving the Inuit self-government after more

Aboriginal Peoples

Pacific: Haida, Tsimshians, Tlingit

Plains: Sioux, Cree, Blackfoot

Great Lakes/St Lawrence: Ojibwe, Huron

Maritimes: Mi'kmaq, Maliseet

Québec, Labrador: Innu

Northern Ontario, Manitoba, Saskatchewan: Cree

Yukon, NWT: Dene, Gwich'in

Arctic: Inuit

Top First Nations Cultural Centers

Museum of Northern British Columbia

Haida Heritage Centre, BC

Squamish Lil'wat Cultural Centre, BC

Dänojà Zho Centre, Yukon

Wanuskewin Heritage Park, Saskatchewan

ABORIGINAL MEDIA

First Nations Drum (www.firstnationsdrum.com) National newspaper.

CBC Aboriginal (www.cbc.ca/aboriginal) The broadcaster's online site devoted to aboriginal news and culture, with links to regional programming in native languages.

Aboriginal Peoples Television Network (www.aptn.ca) National cable/satellite network that produces and airs aboriginal programming.

than 20 years of negotiations. The 28,000 people of the far north now have control over about one-fifth of Canadian soil.

Following this, in 2010 the government formally apologized for the relocation of Inuit families to the high Arctic during the 1950s. At the time, the government promised the families a better life by moving to the region, but it didn't follow through in providing them with necessary supports like adequate shelter and supplies. As a result, the families struggled greatly to survive. Many have argued the government moved the families not to help them, as stated, but to establish Canada's Arctic sovereignty during the Cold War. The apology was a follow-up to a 1996 settlement, in which the government agreed to pay $10 million into a trust fund to compensate the families.

Apology and compensation was also given to the 150,000 First Nations people, Métis and Inuit who were forced into Residential Schools from 1880 until the last closed in 1996. Taken from their homes and not allowed to speak their languages or practice their culture, the students were often subjected to abuse and severe mistreatment (over 6000 died while attending). In 2007, the federal government granted a $1.9 billion compensation pack and an official apology the following year.

Top Museums for Aboriginal Arts

Art Gallery of Ontario, Toronto

Museum of Civilization, Gatineau

National Gallery, Ottawa

UBC Museum of Anthropology, Vancouver

Aboriginal Tourism

From learning to paddle a traditional canoe in Tofino, BC, to sampling bannock bread in a Mi'kmaq cafe on PEI's Lennox Island to perusing the Great Northern Arts Festival in Inuvik in the Northwest Territories, there are many opportunities to immerse yourself in aboriginal culture.

The further north in Canada you head, the more your travel dollars benefit Aboriginal communities. **First Air** (www.firstair.ca) and **Air Creebec** (www.aircreebec.ca) are Aboriginal-owned, as are **Inns North hotels** (www.innsnorth.com), located in several communities throughout Nunavut and the Northwest Territories.

A good website with links to aboriginal tourism opportunities nationwide is https://aboriginalcanada.ca. BC has its own **Aboriginal Tourism Association** (www.aboriginalbc.com), with the lowdown on Aboriginal-owned businesses in the province.

Outdoor Activities

While the great Canadian outdoors is undeniably postcard pretty, the wilderness here has more than good looks, with activities ranging from hiking and kayaking to biking and climbing. There are countless operators across the country that can help you gear up and get out there.

Skiing & Snowboarding

It seems like almost everyone in Canada was born to ski. Visitors will find some of the world's most renowned resorts here – British Columbia (BC), Alberta and Québec host the premier ones – but it's also worth asking the locals where they like to hit the slopes: for every big-time swanky resort, there are several smaller spots where the terrain and the welcome can be even better.

Québec boasts some big slopes – Le Massif, near Québec City, has a vertical drop of 770m (2526ft) – located handily close to the cities. Most of these lower-elevation resorts, such as Mont-Tremblant, are a day's drive from Toronto and less than an hour from Québec City and Montréal. Ski areas in Québec's Eastern Townships offer renowned gladed runs that weave through a thinned forest.

Head west and you'll hit the big mountains and vast alpine terrains. Glide down gargantuan slopes at Whistler-Blackcomb, which has North America's highest vertical drop and most impressive terrain variation. You'll also slide through stunning postcard landscapes in the Canadian Rockies, especially at Sunshine in Banff National Park.

In BC's Okanagan Valley, resorts like Apex and Big White boast good snow year after year. Snowpack ranges from 2m to 6m-plus, depending on how close the resort is to the Pacific Ocean. The deepest, driest snow in the world piles up in BC's Kootenay Region. Ski it at Nelson's Whitewater, Rossland's Red Mountain or Fernie's Alpine Resort.

For cross-country skiing, **Canmore** (www.canmorenordic.com) in Alberta offers popular trails that were part of that other Canadian Winter Olympics, Calgary in 1988.

For further information and resources covering the national scene, check the website of the **Canadian Ski Council** (www.skicanada.org).

Sweetest Slopes

- Whistler-Blackcomb, Whistler, BC
- Le Massif, Baie St-Paul, Québec
- Sunshine Village, Banff, Alberta
- Big White, Kelowna, BC
- Fernie Alpine Resort, Fernie, BC

Hiking

You don't have to be a hiker to hike in Canada. While there are plenty of multiday jaunts for those who like tramping through the wilderness equipped only with a Swiss Army knife, there are also innumerable opportunities for those who prefer a gentle stroll around a lake with a pub visit at the end.

The country's hiking capital is Banff National Park, crisscrossed with stupefying vistas accessible to both hard and soft eco-adventurers. At Lake Louise, for example, you can march through dense spruce and pine forests, then ascend into alpine meadows carpeted with wildflowers and surrounded by rugged glaciers and azure lakes.

Top Day Hikes

- Lake Louise, Banff, Alberta
- Skyline Trail, Cape Breton Highlands, Nova Scotia
- Stanley Park, Vancouver, BC
- Bruce Trail, Ontario

HOCKEY: THE NATIONAL PASTIME

Canadians aren't fooling around when it comes to hockey. They play hard and well and if they're not playing, they cheer and catcall like they mean it.

Grassroots hockey, aka pond hockey, takes place in communities across the country every night on a frozen surface. All you need is a puck, a hockey stick and a few friends to live the dream.

If you'd rather watch than play, Vancouver, Edmonton, Calgary, Toronto, Ottawa, Winnipeg and Montréal all have **NHL** (www.nhl.com) teams who skate tough and lose the odd tooth. Minor pro teams and junior hockey clubs fill many more arenas with rabid fans; check the **Canadian Hockey League** (www.chl.ca) and **American Hockey League** (www.theahl.com) for local stick wielders.

In BC's provincial **parks system** (www.bcparks.ca), you'll have a choice of more than 100 parks, each with distinct landscapes to hike through: check out Garibaldi Park's landscape of ancient volcanoes (not far from Whistler) and Mt Robson Park's popular Berg Lake alpine trail. Vancouver's North Shore is home to the Grouse Grind, a steep forest hike that's also known as 'Mother Nature's Stairmaster.' Across the water in Vancouver Island's Pacific Rim Park, the lush 75km **West Coast Trail** (www.westcoasttrail.com) is undoutedly one of the country's most breathtaking, combining traditional First Nations trails and life-saving routes used by shipwreck survivors.

Out east, awe-inspiring trails pattern the landscape. In southern Ontario, the **Bruce Trail** (www.brucetrail.org) tracks from Niagara Falls to Tobermory. It's the oldest and longest continuous footpath in Canada and spans more than 850km. Though portions are near cities like Hamilton and Toronto, it's surprisingly serene. Cape Breton Highlands National Park offers exquisite hiking over stark, dramatic coastline. Newfoundland's trails make for fantastic shoreline hiking and often provide whale views. The **East Coast Trail** (www.eastcoasttrail.ca) on the Avalon Peninsula is particularly renowned for its vistas.

And don't forget the cities. Canada's major metropolises offer some great urban hikes, an ideal way to get to know the communities you're visiting. Slip into your runners for a stroll (or a jog) with the locals in Montréal's Parc du Mont Royal or in Vancouver's gemlike Stanley Park, where the idyllic seawall winds alongside towering trees and lapping ocean.

Kayaking & Canoeing

Top Places to Paddle

- *South Nahanni River, Northwest Territories*
- *Witless Bay, Newfoundland*
- *Gwaii Haanas National Park Reserve, BC*

The Canadian Arctic, kayaking's motherland, still remains one of its special places: cruise the polar fjords of Ellesmere Island and watch narwhals and walruses during the fuse-short summer. Further south, slide silently past ancient forests and totem poles in BC's Gwaii Haanas National Park Reserve, or in the province's Johnstone Strait and watch orcas breaching. The east coast has sea kayaking galore. Paddlers in Witless Bay or Gros Morne, Newfoundland, often glide alongside whales.

If you're on a tight schedule and don't have time for multiday odysseys, there are plenty of more accessible ways to get your kayaking fix. Big cities like BC's Vancouver and Victoria offer tours and lessons near town, while the province's Sunshine Coast and Salt Spring Island offer crenulated coastlines combined with tranquil sea inlets.

As old as kayaking, and equally as Canadian, is the canoe. Experienced paddlers can strike out on one of 33 **Canadian Heritage Rivers** (www.chrs.ca). Some of the best include the Northwest Territories' South Nahanni River (near Fort Simpson) and Ontario's French River (near Sudbury).

Mountain Biking & Cycling

Mountain biking is a big deal in Canada. While cycling enthusiasts in Europe might be into trundling around town or along a gentle riverside trail, in Canada you're more likely to find them hurtling down a mountainside covered in mud. Given the landscape, of course, it was just a matter of time before the wheels went off-road here.

If you need to ease yourself in, start gently with BC's **Kettle Valley Rail Trail** (www.kettlevalleyrailway.ca), near Kelowna. This dramatic segment of converted railway barrels across picturesque wooden trestle bridges and through canyon tunnels.

Looking for more of an adrenaline rush? In Vancouver's North Shore area, you'll be riding on much narrower and steeper trestles. Birthplace of freeride mountain biking (which combines downhill and dirt jumping), this area offers some unique innovations: elevated bridges, log rides and skinny planks that loft over the wet undergrowth. It's a similar story up at Whistler where the melted ski slopes are transformed into a summertime bike park that draws thousands every year – especially during the annual **Crankworx Mountain Bike Festival** (www.crankworx.com/whistler) in July.

For road touring, Canada's east coast, with more small towns and less emptiness, is a fantastic place to pedal, either as a single-day road ride or a multiday trip. Circle Québec's Lac St-Jean; try any part of the 4000km **Route Verte** (www.routeverte.com), the longest network of bicycle paths in the Americas; or follow Prince Edward Island's bucolic red roads and its **Confederation Trail** (www.tourismpei.com/pei-cycling).

Best Biking

- *Confederation Trail, PEI*
- *Kettle Valley Rail Trail, Kelowna, BC*
- *North Shore, Vancouver, BC*
- *Route Verte, Québec*

Climbing

All those inviting crags you've spotted on your trip are an indication that Canada is a major climbing capital, ideal for both short sport climbs or epic big-wall ascents.

BC's Squamish region, located between Vancouver and Whistler, is a climbing center, with dozens of accessible (and not so accessible) cracks, faces, arêtes and overhangs. Tap into the scene via **Squamish Rock Guides** (www.squamishrockguides.com). Canmore, near Banff, is another ideal destination for rock climbers, no matter what your skill level. For the adventure of a lifetime, the Northwest Territories' Cirque of the Unclimbables is certainly near the top of the list. If your trip takes you out east instead, Ontario's favorite climbing havens dot the Bruce Peninsula.

If mountaineering is more your thing, the Rockies are the recommended first stop. **Yamnuska** (www.yamnuska.com) is one company that offers ice climbing, ski mountaineering and avalanche training in the region. The Matterhorn of Canada is BC's Mt Assiniboine, located between the Kootenay and Banff National Parks. Other western classics include Alberta's Mt Edith Cavell, in Jasper; BC's Mt Robson and Sir Donald in the Rockies; and Garibaldi Peak, in Garibaldi Provincial Park, near Whistler. If you need a guide, check in with the excellent **Alpine Club of Canada** (www.alpineclubofcanada.ca).

Top Climbs

- *The Chief, Squamish, BC*
- *Canmore, Alberta*
- *Pont-Rouge, Québec*
- *Skaha Bluffs, Okanagan Valley, BC*
- *Bugaboo Spire, near Golden, BC*

FISHING

Built on its aboriginal and pioneer past, Canada has a strong tradition of fishing and you can expect to come across plenty of opportunities to hook walleye, pike, rainbow or lake trout on your travels. Among the best fishing holes to head for are Lunenburg in Nova Scotia and the Miramichi River in New Brunswick. And while salmon are the usual draw on the Pacific coastline, hopping aboard a local vessel for some sea fishing off Haida Gwaii can deliver the kind of giant catches you'll be bragging about for years to come.

RESOURCES

Parks Canada (www.pc.gc.ca) National park action.

Alpine Club of Canada (www.alpineclubofcanada.ca) Climbing and mountaineering.

Canada Trails (www.canadatrails.ca) Hiking, biking and cross-country skiing.

Canadian Ski Council (www.skicanada.org) Skiing and snowboarding.

Paddling Canada (www.paddlingcanada.com) Kayaking and canoeing.

Surfing & Windsurfing

If you're aiming to become a temporary beach bum on your Canada trip, head to the wild west coast of BC's Vancouver Island and hang out on the beaches around Tofino. Surfing schools and gear rental operations stud this region and you'll have an awesome time riding the swells (or just watching everyone else as you stretch out on the sand). Backed by verdant rainforest, it's an idyllic spot to spend some time.

June to September is the height of the season here, but serious surfers also like to drop by in winter to face down the lashing waves. Check **Surfing Vancouver Island** (www.surfingvancouverisland.com) for a taste of what to expect.

Some 6000km away, the east coast of Nova Scotia can also dish out some formidable swells. The US south coast's hurricane season (August to November) brings Canadians steep fast breaks, snappy right and left point breaks, and offshore reef and shoal breaks in areas like Lawrencetown, just outside Halifax, as well as across the entire South Shore region. There are also a couple of surf schools here. **Scotia Surfer** (www.scotiasurfer.com) has the lowdown.

Windsurfers set their sails for Howe Sound in Squamish, BC, and for Québec's Magdalen Islands, a small chain in the Gulf of St Lawrence.

Top Places to Surf & Windsurf

Tofino, Vancouver Island, BC

Lawrencetown, Nova Scotia

Nitinat Lake, Vancouver Island, BC

Magdalen Islands, Québec

Howe Sound, Squamish, BC

Wildlife

On land, in the water and in the air, Canada is teeming with the kind of camera-worthy critters that make visitors wonder if they haven't stepped into a safari park by mistake. And when we say 'critters,' we're not talking small fry: this is the home of grizzlies, polar bears, moose and bald eagles, and offers perfect coastal viewing spots for a roll call of huge whales. Extra camera batteries are heartily recommended.

Grizzly Bears & Black Bears

Grizzly bears – *Ursus arctos horribilis* to all you Latin scholars out there – are most commonly found in the Rocky Mountain regions of British Columbia (BC) and Alberta. Standing up to 3m tall, you'll know them by their distinctive shoulder hump and labrador-like snout. Solitary animals with no natural enemies (except humans), they enjoy crunching on elk, moose and caribou, but they're usually content to fill their bellies with berries and, if available, fresh salmon. Keep in mind that you should never approach any bear. And in remote areas, be sure to travel in groups.

In 1994, coastal BC's Khutzeymateen Grizzly Bear Sanctuary (near the northern town of Prince Rupert) was officially designated with protected status. Over 50 grizzlies currently live on this 45,000-hectare refuge. A few ecotour operators have permits for viewing the animals.

Just to confuse you, grizzlies can be brown or black, while their smaller, more prevalent relative, the black bear, is commonly brown. Canada is home to around half a million black bears and they're spread out across the country, except for Prince Edward Island, southern Alberta and southern Saskatchewan. In regions such as northern BC, as well as in Banff and Jasper National Parks, seeing black bears feasting on berries or dandelions as you drive past on the highway is surprisingly common.

The world's only white-colored black bears roam in northern BC. Born with a recessive gene, there are approximately 400 of these 'spirit bears' living in mostly coastal areas.

Best Bear-Spotting

Churchill, Manitoba – polar bears

Khutzeymateen Grizzly Bear Sanctuary, Prince Rupert, BC – grizzlies

Icefields Parkway, Alberta – black bears

Lake Louise Gondola – grizzlies

Polar Bears

Weighing less than a kilogram at birth, the fiercest member of the bear clan is not quite so cute when it grows up to be a hulking 600kg. But these mesmerizing animals still pack a huge visual punch for visitors. If your visit to Canada won't be complete until you've seen one, there's really only one place to go: Churchill, Manitoba, on the shores of Hudson Bay (late September to early November is the viewing season). About 900 of the planet's roughly 20,000 white-furred beasts prowl the tundra here.

Just remember: the carnivorous, ever-watchful predators are not cuddly cartoon critters. Unlike grizzlies and black bears, polar bears actively prey on people.

ROBERTA OLENICK / GETTY IMAGES ©

Top Bull elk, Jasper National Park (p586)

Bottom Grizzly bear, British Columbia

Moose

Canada's iconic shrub-nibbler, the moose is a massive member of the deer family that owes its popularity to its distinctively odd appearance: skinny legs supporting a humongous body and a cartoonish face that looks permanently inquisitive and clueless at the same time. And then there are the antlers: males grow a spectacular rack every summer, only to discard them come November.

Adding to their *Rocky and Bullwinkle Show* appeal, a moose can move at more than 50km per hour and easily outswim two adults paddling a canoe – all on a vegetarian diet comprised mostly of tasty leaves and twigs.

You'll spot moose foraging for food near lakes, muskegs and streams, as well as in the forests of the western mountain ranges in the Rockies and the Yukon. Newfoundland is perhaps the moosiest place of all. In 1904, the province imported and released four beasts into the wild. They enjoyed the good life of shrub-eating and hot sex, ultimately spawning the 120,000 inhabitants that now roam the woods.

During mating season (September), the males can become belligerent, as can a mother with her calves, so keep your distance.

Best Moose-Viewing

- *Northern Peninsula, Newfoundland*
- *Cape Breton Highlands National Park, Nova Scotia*
- *Algonquin Provincial Park, Ontario*
- *Maligne Lake, Jasper National Park, Alberta*
- *Kananaskis, Alberta*

Elk, Deer & Caribou

Moose are not the only animals that can exhibit a Mr Hyde personality change during rutting season. Usually placid, male elk have been known to charge vehicles in Jasper National Park, believing their reflection in the shiny paintwork to be a rival for their harem of eligible females. It's rare, though, and Jasper is generally one of the best places in Canada to see this large deer species wandering around attracting camera-toting travelers on the edge of town.

White-tailed deer can be found anywhere from Nova Scotia's Cape Breton to the Northwest Territories' Great Slave Lake. Its bigger relative, the caribou, is unusual in that both males and females sport enormous antlers. Barren-ground caribou feed on lichen and spend most of the year on the tundra from Baffin Island to Alaska. Woodland caribou roam further south, with some of the biggest herds trekking across northern Québec and Labrador. These beasts, which have a reputation for not being especially smart, also show up in the mountain parks of BC, Alberta and Newfoundland, which is where many visitors see them. In 2009, the small herd in Banff National Park set off an avalanche that ultimately wiped out the population. Also known as reindeer, the caribou is on the Canadian 25-cent quarter.

Whales

More than 22 species of whale and porpoise lurk offshore in Atlantic Canada, including superstars like the humpback whale, which averages 15m and 36 tons; the North Atlantic right whale, the world's most endangered leviathan, with an estimated population of just 350; and the mighty blue whale, the largest animal on earth at 25m and around 100 tons. Then there's the little guy, the minke, which grows to 10m and often approaches boats, delighting passengers with acrobatics as it shows off. Whale-watching tours are very popular throughout the region.

You can also spot humpbacks and gray whales off the west coast. But it's the orca that dominates viewing here. Their aerodynamic bodies, signature black-and-white coloration and incredible speed (up to 40km/h) make them the Ferraris of the aquatic world, and their diet includes seals, belugas and other whales (hence the killer whale nickname). The waters around Vancouver Island, particularly in the Strait of Juan de Fuca, teem with orcas every summer. Whale-watching tours depart from

Whale Hot Spots

- *Witless Bay, Newfoundland*
- *Digby Neck, Nova Scotia*
- *Victoria, BC*
- *Tofino, BC*
- *Tadoussac, Québec*
- *Cabot Trail, Nova Scotia*

points throughout the region; Tofino and Victoria are particular hot spots for operators. It's also not uncommon to see them from the decks of the BC ferries.

Belugas glide in Arctic waters to the north. These ghostly white whales are one of the smallest members of the whale family, typically measuring no more than 4m and weighing about 1 ton. They are chatty fellows who squeak, groan and peep while traveling in closely knit family pods. Churchill, Manitoba, is a good place to view them, as is Tadoussac, Québec (the only population outside the Arctic resides here).

Birds

Best Birding

- *Cape St Mary's, Newfoundland*
- *Point Pelee National Park, Ontario*
- *Witless Bay, Newfoundland*
- *Grand Manan Island, New Brunswick*
- *Brackendale, BC*

Canada's wide skies are home to 462 bird species, with BC and Ontario boasting the greatest diversity. The most famous feathered resident is the common loon, Canada's national bird – if you don't spot one in the wild, you'll see it on the back of the $1 coin. Rivaling it in the ubiquity stakes are Canada geese, a hardy fowl that can fly up to 1000km per day and seems to have successfully colonized parks throughout the world.

The most visually arresting of Canada's birds are its eagles, especially the bald variety, whose wingspan can reach up to 2m. Good viewing sites include Brackendale, between Vancouver and Whistler in BC, where up to 4000 eagles nest in winter. Also train your binoculars on Bras d'Or Lake on Cape Breton Island, Nova Scotia and on Vancouver Island's southern and western shorelines.

Seabirds flock to Atlantic Canada to breed. Think razorbills, kittiwakes, Arctic terns, common murres and, yes, puffins. Everyone loves these cute little guys, a sort of waddling penguin-meets-parrot, with black-and-white feathers and an orange beak. They nest around Newfoundland in particular. The preeminent places to get feathered are New Brunswick's Grand Manan Island and Newfoundland's Witless Bay and Cape St Mary's (both on the Avalon Peninsula near St John's). The best time is May through August, before the birds fly away for the winter.

Cuisines of Canada

Canadian cuisine is nothing if not eclectic, a casserole of food cultures blended together from centuries of immigration. Poutine, Montréal-style bagels, salmon jerky and pierogi jostle for comfort-food attention. For something more refined, Montréal, Toronto and Vancouver have well-seasoned fine-dining scenes, while regions across the country have rediscovered the unique ingredients grown, foraged and produced on their doorsteps – bringing distinctive seafood, artisan cheeses and lip-smacking produce to menus.

Local Flavors

If you're starting from the east, the main dish of the Maritime provinces is lobster – boiled in the pot and served with a little butter – and the best place to sample it is a community hall 'kitchen party' on Prince Edward Island. Dip into some chunky potato salad and hearty seafood chowder while waiting for your crustacean to arrive, but don't eat too much; you'll need room for the mountainous fruit pie coming your way afterwards.

Next door, Nova Scotia visitors should save their appetites for butter-soft Digby scallops and rustic Lunenberg sausage, while the favored food of nearby Newfoundland and Labrador often combines rib-sticking dishes of cod cheeks and sweet snow crab. If you're feeling really ravenous, gnaw on a slice of seal flipper pie – a dish you're unlikely to forget in a hurry.

Québec is the world's largest maple syrup producer, processing around 6.5 million gallons of the sweet pancake accompaniment every year. In this French-influenced province, fine food seems to be a lifeblood for the locals, who will happily sit down for four-hour dinners where accompanying wine and conversation flow in equal measures.

The province's cosmopolitan Montréal has long claimed to be the nation's fine-dining capital, but there's an appreciation of food here at all levels that also includes hearty pea soups, exquisite cheeses and tasty pâtés sold at bustling markets. In addition, there's also that national dish, poutine, waiting to clog your arteries plus smoked-meat deli sandwiches so large you'll have to dislocate your jaw to fit them in your mouth.

Ontario – especially Toronto – is a microcosm of Canada's melting pot of cuisines. Like Québec, maple syrup is a super-sweet flavoring of choice here, and it's found in decadent desserts such as beavertails (fried, sugared dough) and on breakfast pancakes the size of Frisbees. Head south to the Niagara Peninsula wine region and you'll also discover restaurants fusing contemporary approaches and traditional local ingredients, such as fish from the Great Lakes.

Far north from here, Nunavut in the Arctic Circle is Canada's newest territory, but it has a long history of Inuit food, offering a real culinary adventure for extreme-cuisine travelers. Served in some restaurants (but more often in family homes – make friends with locals and they may invite you in for a feast), regional specialties include boiled seal, raw frozen char and *maktaaq* – whale skin cut into small pieces and swallowed whole.

Festivals

International Shellfish Festival, Prince Edward Island (www.peishellfish.com)

Shediac Lobster Festival, New Brunswick (www.shediaclobsterfestival.ca)

Feast Tofino, British Columbia (www.feasttofino.com)

Ribfest, Ontario (www.canadaslargestribfest.com)

Festival des Fromages Fins, Québec (www.festivaldesfromages.qc.ca)

In contrast, the central provinces of Manitoba, Saskatchewan and Alberta have their own deep-seated culinary ways. The latter, Canada's cowboy country, is the nation's beef capital – you'll find top-notch Alberta steak on menus at leading restaurants across the country. If you're offered 'prairie oysters' here, though, you might want to know (or maybe you'd prefer not to) that they're bull's testicles prepared in a variety of ways designed to take your mind off their origin. In the Rockies things get wilder – try elk, bison and even moose.

There's an old Eastern European influence over the border in Manitoba, where immigrant Ukrainians have added comfort food staples such as pierogi and thick, spicy sausages. Head next door to prairie-land Saskatchewan for dessert. The province's heaping fruit pies are its most striking culinary contribution, especially when prepared with tart Saskatoon berries.

In the far west, British Columbians have traditionally fed themselves from the sea and the fertile farmlands of the interior. Okanagan Valley peaches, cherries and blueberries – best purchased from seasonal roadside stands throughout the region – are the staple of many summer diets. But it's the seafood that attracts the lion's share of culinary fans. Tuck into succulent wild salmon, juicy Fanny Bay oysters and velvet-soft scallops and you may decide you've stumbled on foodie nirvana.

Foodie Books

- *Sugar Shack Au Pied de Cochon* (Martin Picard; 2012)
- *On The Flavour Trail* (Christabel Padmore; 2013)
- *Modern Native Feasts* (Andrew George Jr; 2013)
- *The SoBo Cookbook* (Lisa Ahier and Andrew Morrison; 2014)
- *Duchess Bake Shop* (Giselle Courteau; 2015)

Top City Dining

Ask anyone in Toronto, Montréal or Vancouver to name Canada's leading foodie city and they'll likely inform you that you've just found it. But while each of the big three claims to be at the top table when it comes to dining, their strengths are so diverse they're more accurately defined as complementary courses in one great meal.

First dish on the table is Montréal, which was Canada's sole dine-out capital long before the upstarts threw off their fried-meat-and-mashed-potato shackles. Renowned for bringing North America's finest French-influenced cuisine to local palates, it hasn't given up its crown lightly. Chefs here are often treated like rock stars as they challenge old-world conventions with daring, even artistic, approaches – expect clever, fusion-esque gastronomy. You should also expect a great restaurant experience: Montréalers have a bacchanalian love for eating out, with lively rooms ranging from cozy old-town restaurants to the animated patios of Rue Prince Arthur and the sophisticated, often funky eateries of the Plateau.

If Montréal serves as an ideal starter, that makes Toronto the main course – although that's a reflection of its recent elevation rather than its prominence. Fusion is also the default approach in Canada's largest city, although it's been taken even further here with a wave of contemporary immigration adding modern influences from Asia to a foundation of European cuisines. With a bewildering 7000 restaurants to choose from, though, it can be a tough choice figuring out where to unleash your top-end dining budget. The best approach is to hit the neighborhoods: both the Financial District and Old York areas are studded with classy, high-end joints.

And while that appears to make Vancouver the dessert, it could be argued this glass-towered, west-coast metropolis is the best of the bunch. In recent years, some of the country's most innovative chefs have set up shop here, inspired by the twin influences of an abundant local larder and Canada's most cosmopolitan population. Fusion is the starting point here in fine-dining districts like Yaletown and Kitsilano. But there's also a high level of authenticity in top-notch Asian dining: the best sushi bars and *izakayas* outside Japan jostle for attention with superb Vietnamese and Korean eateries.

Tasty Blogs

- National Nosh (www.thenationalnosh.blogspot.com)
- Dinner With Julie (www.dinnerwithjulie.com)
- Seasonal Ontario Food (www.seasonalontariofood.blogspot.com)
- Vancouver Foodster (www.vancouverfoodster.com)

Wine Regions

While many international visitors – especially those who think Canadians live under a permanent blanket of snow – are surprised to learn that wine is produced here, their suspicion is always tempered after a drink or two. Canada's wines have gained ever-greater kudos in recent years and while their small-scale production and the industry dominance of other wine regions mean they will never be global market leaders, these wines could definitely hold their own in an international taste-off.

Regional Wine List

Depending on how thirsty you are, you're rarely too far from a wine region in Canada. Which means that most visitors can easily add a mini taste-tripping tour to their visit if they'd like to meet a few producers and sample some intriguing local flavors. Here's a rundown of the best areas, including the magnum-sized larger regions and the thimble-sized smaller locales – why not stay all summer and visit them all?

Okanagan Valley, British Columbia

The rolling hills of this lakeside region are well worth the five-hour drive from Vancouver. Studded among the vine-striped slopes are more than 100 wineries enjoying a diverse climate that fosters both crisp whites and bold reds. With varietals including pinot noir, pinot gris, pinot blanc, merlot and chardonnay, there's a wine here to suit almost every palate. Most visitors base themselves in Kelowna, the Okanagan's wine capital, before fanning out to well-known blockbuster wineries like Mission Hill, Quail's Gate, Cedar Creek and Summerhill Pyramid Winery (yes, it has a pyramid). Many of them also have excellent restaurants.

Find out more about BC's wine regions and annual festivals and download free touring maps at www.winebc.com.

Niagara Peninsula, Ontario

This picture-perfect region of country inns and charming old towns offers more than 60 wineries and grows more than three-quarters of Canada's grapes. Neatly divided between the low-lying Niagara-on-the-Lake area and the higher Niagara Escarpment, its complex mix of soils and climates – often likened to the Loire Valley – is ideal for chardonnay, riesling, pinot noir and cabernet-franc varietals. This is also the production center for Canadian ice wine, that potently sweet dessert libation. Home to some of Canada's biggest wineries, including Inniskillin, Jackson-Triggs and Peller Estates, don't miss smaller pit-stops like Magnotta and Cave Spring Cellars.

Prince Edward County, Ontario

Proving that not all Ontario's wineries are clustered in Niagara, this comparatively new grape-growing region – located in the province's southeastern corner – is a charming alternative if you want to avoid the tour buses winding through the main wine area. A long-established fruit-growing district with generally lower temperatures than Niagara,

Wine Reads

Okanagan Wine Tour Guide (John Schreiner; 2012)

Crush on Niagara: (Andrew Brooks; 2010)

Wine Lover's Guide to Atlantic Canada (Moira Peters & Craig Pinhey; 2016)

Island Wineries of British Columbia (Gary Hynes; 2013)

Explore Ontario further by downloading a free map and wine country visitor guide from www.winesofontario.org.

cooler-climate wines are favored here, including chardonnay and pinot noir. The most intriguing wineries include Closson Chase, Black Prince Winery and Grange of Prince Edward. If your taste buds are piqued, consider checking out other Ontario wine regions like Pelee Island and Lake Erie North Shore.

Hundreds of Canadian wineries are sampled at the Wines of Canada website (www.winesofcanada.com).

Eastern Townships, Québec

Starting around 80km southeast of Montréal, this idyllic farmland region is studded with quiet villages, leafy woodlands, crystal-clear lakes and winding country roads. A rising tide of wineries has joined the traditional farm operations here in recent years, with rieslings and chardonnays particularly suited to the area's cool climate and soil conditions. But it's the local ice wines, dessert wines and fruit wines that are the area's main specialties, so make sure you come with a sweet tooth. Wineries to perk up your taste buds here include Domaine Félibre, Vignoble de L'Orpailleur and Vignoble Le Cep d'Argent.

The dominant player in Québec's wider Eastern Townships is Montérégie, a bumpy and bucolic area packed with vineyards and orchards (not to mention a surfeit of maple groves). As a major fruit-farming region – this is an ideal spot to try ciders and flavor-packed fruit wines – growers here are happy to try just about any red or white varietal, but it's their rosés that are particularly memorable. Recommended wineries include Domaine St-Jacques, Les Petits Cailloux and Vignoble des Pins; and keep in mind that Québecois restaurants often encourage diners to bring their own bottles, so fill your car as you explore the region.

Find out more about Nova Scotia's wine region, including information on courses and festivals, at www.winesofnovascotia.ca.

Nova Scotia

Divided into six boutique wine-producing regions – from the warm shoreline of Northumberland Strait to the verdant Annapolis Valley – Nova Scotia's two-dozen wineries are mostly just a couple of hours drive from Halifax. One of the world's coldest grape-growing areas, cool-climate whites are a staple here, including a unique varietal known as l'Acadie Blanc. Innovative sparkling wines are a Nova Scotia specialty and they tend to dominate the drops on offer at the popular stops such as the excellent Benjamin Bridge Vineyards. Other highly recommended destinations include Gaspereau Vineyards, Jost Vineyards and Domaine de Grand Pré.

Festivals

Canada is dripping with palate-pleasing wine events, which makes it especially important to check the dates of your trip: raising a few glasses with celebratory locals is one of the best ways to encounter the country.

If you're in BC, it's hard to miss one of the Okanagan's three main festivals – see www.thewinefestivals.com for dates. If you prefer not to leave the big city, check out March's Vancouver International Wine Festival (www.vanwinefest.ca).

Across the country in Ontario, Niagara also stages more than one annual event to celebrate its winey wealth, including June's New Vintage Festival and September's giant Niagara Wine Festival. For information, visit www.niagarawinefestival.com.

Québec-bound oenophiles should drop into the annual Montréal Passion Vin (www.montrealpassionvin.ca), a swish two-day charity fundraiser focused on unique and rare vintages. For regional food as well as wine, the Eastern Townships' Magog-Orford area hosts the multiday Fête des Vendanges (www.fetedesvendanges.com) in September.

Visitors to the east coast are not left out. Nova Scotia hosts a 50-event Fall Wine Festival (www.mynslc.com) in mid-September.

Wine Online

John Schreiner on Wine (www.johnschreiner.blogspot.com)

Dr Vino (www.drvino.com)

Girl on Wine (www.girlonwine.com)

Survival Guide

Directory A–Z

Accommodations

Seasons

- Peak season is summer, basically June through August, when prices are highest.
- It's best to book ahead during summer, as well as during ski season at winter resorts, and during holidays and major events, as rooms can be scarce.
- Some properties close down altogether in the off-season.

Amenities

- At many budget properties (campgrounds, hostels, simple B&Bs) bathrooms are shared.
- Midrange accommodations, such as most B&Bs, inns (*auberges* in French), motels and some hotels, generally offer the best value for money. Expect a private bathroom, cable TV and, in some cases, free breakfast.
- Top-end accommodations offer an international standard of amenities, with fitness and business centers and on-site dining.
- Most properties offer in-room wi-fi. It's typically free in budget and midrange lodgings, while top-end hotels often charge a fee.
- Many smaller properties, especially B&Bs, ban smoking. Marriott and Westin brand hotels are 100% smoke-free. Other properties have rooms set aside for nonsmokers.
- Air-conditioning is not a standard amenity at most budget and midrange places. If you want it, be sure to ask about it when you book.

Discounts

- In winter, prices can plummet by as much as 50%.
- Membership in the American Automobile Association (AAA) or an associated automobile association, American Association of Retired Persons (AARP) or other organizations also yields modest savings (usually 10%).

B&Bs

- **Bed & Breakfast Online** (www.bbcanada.com) is the main booking agency for properties nationwide.
- In Canada, B&Bs (*gîtes* in French) are essentially converted or purpose-built private homes whose owners live on-site. People who like privacy may find B&Bs too intimate, as walls are rarely soundproof and it's usual to mingle with your hosts and other guests.
- Standards vary widely, sometimes even within a single B&B. The cheapest rooms tend to be small, with few amenities and a shared bathroom. Nicer ones have added features such as a balcony, a fireplace and an en suite bathroom. Breakfast is always included in the rates (though it might be continental instead of a full cooked affair).
- Not all B&Bs accept children.
- Minimum stays (usually two nights) are common, and many B&Bs are only open seasonally.

Camping

- Canada is filled with campgrounds – some federal or provincial, others privately owned.
- The official season runs from May to September, but exact dates vary by location.
- Facilities vary widely. Backcountry sites offer little more than pit toilets and fire rings, and have no potable

BOOK YOUR STAY ONLINE

For more accommodations reviews by Lonely Planet authors, check out http://lonelyplanet.com/canada/hotels/ You'll find independent reviews, as well as recommendations on the best places to stay. Best of all, you can book online.

water. Unserviced (tent) campgrounds come with access to drinking water and a washroom with toilets and sometimes showers. The best-equipped sites feature flush toilets and hot showers, and water, electrical and sewer hookups for recreational vehicles (RVs).

➡ Private campgrounds sometimes cater only to trailers (caravans) and RVs, and may feature convenience stores, playgrounds and swimming pools. It is a good idea to phone ahead to make sure the size of sites and the services provided at a particular campground are suitable for your vehicle.

➡ Most government-run sites are available on a first-come, first-served basis and fill up quickly, especially in July and August. Several national parks participate in Parks Canada's **camping reservation program** (☎877-737-3783; www.pccamping.ca; reservation fee online/call center $11/13.50), which is a convenient way to make sure you get a spot.

➡ Nightly camping fees in national and provincial parks range from $25 to $35 (a bit more for full-hookup sites); fire permits often cost a few dollars extra. Backcountry camping costs about $10 per night. Private campgrounds tend to be a bit pricier. British Columbia's parks, in particular, have seen a hefty rate increase in recent years.

➡ Some campgrounds remain open for maintenance year-round and may let you camp at a reduced rate in the off-season. This can be great in late autumn or early spring when there's hardly a soul about. Winter camping, though, is only for the hardy.

Homestays

How do you feel about staying on the couch of a perfect stranger? If it's not a problem, consider joining an organization that arranges homestays. The groups following charge no fees to become a member, and the stay itself is also free.

Couch Surfing (www.couchsurfing.org)

Hospitality Club (www.hospitalityclub.org)

Hostels

Canada has independent hostels as well as those affiliated with Hostelling International (HI). All have dorms ($25 to $40 per person on average), which can sleep from two to 10 people, and many have private rooms (from $70) for couples and families. Rooms in HI hostels are often gender-segregated. Nonmembers pay a surcharge of about $4 per night.

Bathrooms are usually shared, and facilities include a kitchen, lockers, free wi-fi, internet access, laundry room and a shared TV room. Many also include a free continental breakfast. Some hostels allow alcohol, others don't; smoking is prohibited.

Most hostels, especially those in the big cities, are open 24 hours a day. If they are not, ask if you can make special arrangements if you are arriving late.

Backpackers Hostels Canada (www.backpackers.ca) Independent hostels.

Hostelling International Canada (www.hihostels.ca)

Hostels.com (www.hostels.com) Includes independent and HI hostels.

Hotels & Motels

Most hotels are part of international chains, and the newer ones are designed for either the luxury market or businesspeople. Rooms have cable TV and wi-fi; many also have swimming pools and fitness and business centers. Rooms with two double or queen-sized beds sleep up to four people, although there is usually a small surcharge for the third and fourth person. Many places advertise 'kids stay free,' but sometimes you have to pay extra for a crib or a rollaway (portable bed).

In Canada, like the USA (both lands of the automobile), motels are ubiquitous. They dot the highways and cluster in groups on the outskirts of towns and cities. Although most motel rooms won't win any style awards, they're usually clean and comfortable and offer good value for travelers. Many regional motels remain typical mom-and-pop operations, but plenty of North American chains have also opened up across the country.

University Accommodations

In the lecture-free summer months, some universities and colleges rent beds in their student dormitories to travelers of all ages. Most rooms are quite basic, with rates ranging from $25 to $40 per night, and often including breakfast. Students can usually qualify for small discounts.

SLEEPING PRICE RANGES

The following price ranges refer to a double room with private bathroom in high season, unless stated otherwise. Tax (which can be up to 17%) is not included in the prices listed.

$ less than $100

$$ $100–250

$$$ $250

Customs Regulations

The **Canada Border Services Agency** (www.cbsa.gc.ca) website has the customs lowdown. A few regulations to note:

Alcohol You can bring in 1.5L of wine, 1.14L of liquor or 24 355mL beers duty-free.

Gifts You can bring in gifts totaling up to $60.

Money You can bring in/take out up to $10,000; larger amounts must be reported to customs.

Personal effects Camping gear, sports equipment, cameras and laptop computers can be brought in without much trouble. Declaring these to customs as you cross the border might save you some hassle when you leave, especially if you'll be crossing the US–Canadian border multiple times.

Pets You must carry a signed and dated certificate from a veterinarian to prove your dog or cat has had a rabies shot in the past 36 months.

Prescription drugs You can bring in/take out a 90-day supply for personal use (though if you're taking it to the USA, know it's technically illegal, but overlooked for individuals).

Tobacco You can bring in 200 cigarettes, 50 cigars, 200g of tobacco and 200 tobacco sticks duty-free.

Discount Cards

Discounts are commonly offered for seniors, children, families and people with disabilities, though no special cards are issued (you get the savings on-site when you pay). AAA and other automobile association members can also receive various travel-related discounts.

International Student Identity Card (www.isic.org) Provides students with discounts on travel insurance and admission to museums and other sights. There are also cards for those who are under 26 but not students, and for full-time teachers.

Montréal Museum Pass (www.museesmontreal.org; $75)

Ottawa Museums Passport (www.museumspassport.ca; adult/family $45/99)

Parks Canada Discovery Pass (adult/child/family $68/33/136; www.pc.gc.ca) Provides access to more than 100 national parks and historic sites for a year. Can pay for itself in as few as seven visits over daily entry fees; also provides quicker entry into sites. Note that in 2017, all Parks Canada sites will be free in celebration of the country's 150th birthday.

Many cities have discount cards for local attractions, such as:

Vanier Park Explore Pass (Vancouver; www.spacecentre.ca/explore-pass; adult/child $36/30)

Electricity

Embassies & Consulates

All countries have their embassies in Ottawa, including those listed here, and maintain consulates in such cities as Montréal, Vancouver, Calgary and Toronto. Contact the relevant embassy to find out which consulate is closest to you.

Australian High Commission (☎613-236-0841; www.canada.embassy.gov.au; Suite 710, 50 O'Connor St)

British High Commission (☎613-237-1530; www.gov.uk/government/world/canada; 80 Elgin St)

French Embassy (☎613-789-1795; www.ambafrance-ca.org; 42 Sussex Dr)

German Embassy (☎613-232-1101; www.ottawa.diplo.de; 1 Waverley St)

Irish Embassy (☎613-233-6281; www.embassyofireland.ca; 130 Albert St, Suite 1105, 11th fl)

Italian Embassy (☎613-232-2401; www.ambottawa.esteri.it; 21st fl, 275 Slater St)

Japanese Embassy (613-241-8541; www.ca.emb-japan.go.jp; 255 Sussex Dr)

Mexican Embassy (613-233-8988; http://embamex.sre.gob.mx/canada_eng/; World Exchange Plaza, 45 O'Connor St, Suite 1000)

Netherlands Embassy (613-237-5031; http://ottawa.the-netherlands.org; Suite 2020, 350 Albert St)

New Zealand High Commission (613-238-5991; www.nzembassy.com/canada; Suite 1401, 150 Elgin St)

US Embassy (613-688-5335; http://canada.usembassy.gov; 490 Sussex Dr)

Etiquette

Canadians are a fairly relaxed crowd and don't offend easily; however, some rules of etiquette do apply.

➡ **Politeness** Canadians value their please and thank-yous. Bumping into someone without apologizing or not thanking someone for holding the door will earned shocked looks.

➡ **Patriotism** Commenting that Canadians and Americans aren't much different is considered highly offensive.

➡ **Language** In French-speaking areas, always attempt to speak French before English (regardless of how poor your French is).

➡ **Lining up** While Canadians usually tut rather than speak out, jumping ahead in line is an exception and can cause a full-blown argument.

Food & Drink

It's worth booking ahead for popular places, especially on the weekend (which, in the restaurant world, includes Thursdays). Most cafes or budget restaurants don't accept reservations.

EATING PRICE RANGES

The following price ranges are for main dishes:

$ less than $15

$$ $15–25

$$$ more than $25

➡ **Restaurants** Range from steakhouses to vegan raw food joints and everything in between. Many are family-friendly and casual; some are not.

➡ **Cafes** Not just for coffee; you can often get sandwiches, soups and baked goods. Often have counter service.

➡ **Bistros** Small and often classy, with home-cooked food.

➡ **Delis** Choose your food, have it wrapped and take it with you. Usually have sandwiches and wraps.

➡ **Diners** Brunches and lunches; often very family-friendly.

➡ **Pubs** Home-cooked fish and chips, burgers and salads.

LGBTI Travelers

Canada is tolerant when it comes to gays and lesbians, though this outlook is more common in the big cities than in rural areas. Same-sex marriage is legal throughout the country (Canada is one of only 21 nations worldwide that permits this).

Montréal, Toronto and Vancouver are by far Canada's gayest cities, each with a humming nightlife scene, publications and lots of associations and support groups. All have sizeable Pride celebrations, too, which attract big crowds.

Attitudes remain more conservative in the northern regions. Throughout Nunavut, and to a lesser extent in the aboriginal communities of the Northwest Territories, there are some retrogressive attitudes toward homosexuality. The Yukon, in contrast, is more like British Columbia, with a live-and-let-live West Coast attitude.

The following are good resources for LGBTI travel; they include Canadian information, though not all are exclusive to the region:

Damron (www.damron.com) Publishes several travel guides, including *Men's Travel Guide, Women's Traveller* and *Damron Accommodations;* gay-friendly tour operators are listed on the website, too.

Gay Canada (www.gaycanada.com) Search by province or city for queer-friendly businesses and resources.

Out Traveler (www.outtraveler.com) Gay travel magazine.

Purple Roofs (www.purpleroofs.com) Website listing queer accommodations, travel agencies and tours worldwide.

Queer Canada (www.queercanada.ca) A general resource.

Xtra (www.xtra.ca) Source for gay and lesbian news nationwide.

Health

Before You Go

HEALTH INSURANCE

Canada offers some of the finest health care in the world. However, unless you are a Canadian citizen, it can be prohibitively expensive. It's essential to purchase travel health insurance if your regular policy doesn't cover you when you're abroad. Check www.lonelyplanet.com/travel-insurance for supplemental insurance information.

Bring medications you may need clearly labeled in their original containers. A signed, dated letter from your physician that describes your medical conditions and medications, including generic names, is also a good idea.

MEDICAL CHECKLIST

- acetaminophen (eg Tylenol) or aspirin
- anti-inflammatory drugs (eg ibuprofen)
- antihistamines (for hay fever and allergic reactions)
- antibacterial ointment (eg Neosporin) for cuts and abrasions
- steroid cream or cortisone (for poison ivy and other allergic rashes)
- bandages, gauze, gauze rolls
- adhesive or paper tape
- safety pins, tweezers
- thermometer
- insect repellent
- permethrin-containing insect spray for clothing, tents and bed nets
- sunblock
- motion-sickness medication

RECOMMENDED VACCINATIONS

No special vaccines are required or recommended for travel to Canada. All travelers should be up to date on routine immunizations.

WEBSITES

Government travel-health websites are available for **Australia** (www.smarttraveller.gov.au), the **United Kingdom** (www.nhs.uk/healthcareabroad) and the **United States** (www.cdc.gov/travel).

MD Travel Health (www.mdtravelhealth.com) General health resources.

Public Health Agency of Canada (www.phac-aspc.gc.ca) Canadian health resources.

World Health Organization (www.who.int) General health resources.

In Canada

AVAILABILITY & COST OF HEALTH CARE

Medical services are widely available. For emergencies, the best bet is to find the nearest hospital and go to its emergency room. If the problem isn't urgent, call a nearby hospital and ask for a referral to a local physician, which is usually cheaper than a trip to the emergency room (where costs can be $500 or so before any treatment).

Pharmacies are abundant, but prescriptions can be expensive without insurance. However, Americans may find Canadian prescription drugs to be cheaper than drugs at home. You're allowed to take out a 90-day supply for personal use (it's technically illegal to bring them into the USA, but overlooked for individuals).

ENVIRONMENTAL HAZARDS

Cold exposure This can be a significant problem, especially in the northern regions. Keep all body surfaces covered, including the head and neck. Watch out for the 'Umbles' – stumbles, mumbles, fumbles and grumbles – which are signs of impending hypothermia.

Heat exhaustion Dehydration is the main contributor. Symptoms include feeling weak, headache, nausea and sweaty skin. Lay the victim flat with their legs raised; apply cool, wet cloths to the skin; and rehydrate.

INFECTIOUS DISEASES

Most are acquired by mosquito or tick bites, or environmental exposure. The **Public Health Agency of Canada** (www.phac-aspc.gc.ca) has details on all listed below.

Giardiasis Intestinal infection. Avoid drinking directly from lakes, ponds, streams and rivers.

Lyme Disease Occurs mostly in southern Canada. Transmitted by deer ticks in late spring and summer. Perform a tick check after you've been outdoors.

Severe Acute Respiratory Syndrome (SARS) At the time of writing, SARS had been brought under control in Canada.

West Nile Virus Mosquito-transmitted in late summer and early fall. Prevent by keeping covered (wear long sleeves, long pants, hats, and shoes rather than sandals) and apply a good insect repellent, preferably one containing DEET, to exposed skin and clothing.

Insurance

Make sure you have adequate travel insurance, whatever the length of your trip. At a minimum, you need coverage for medical emergencies and treatment, including hospital stays and an emergency flight home. Medical treatment for non-Canadians is very expensive.

Also consider insurance for luggage theft or loss. If you already have a homeowners or renters policy, check what it will cover and get only supplemental insurance to protect against the rest. If you have prepaid a large portion of your vacation, trip cancellation insurance is worthwhile.

Worldwide travel insurance is available at www.lonelyplanet.com/travel-insurance. You can buy, extend and claim online at anytime – even if you're already on the road. Also check the following providers:

Insure.com (www.insure.com)

Travel Guard (www.travelguard.com)

Travelex (www.travelexinsurance.com)

Internet Access

- It's easy to find internet access. Libraries and community agencies in practically every town provide free wi-fi and computers for public use. The only downsides are that usage time is limited (usually 30 minutes), and some facilities have erratic hours.

- Internet cafes are limited to the main tourist areas; access generally starts around $2 per hour.
- Wi-fi is widely available. Most lodgings have it (in-room, with good speed), as do many restaurants, bars and Tim Hortons coffee shops.
- For a list of wi-fi hot spots around Canada, visit **Wi-Fi Free Spot** (www.wififreespot.com).

PRACTICALITIES

Newspapers The most widely available newspaper is the Toronto-based *Globe and Mail*. Other principal dailies are the *Montréal Gazette*, *Ottawa Citizen*, *Toronto Star* and *Vancouver Sun*. *Maclean's* is Canada's weekly news magazine.

Radio & TV The Canadian Broadcasting Corporation (CBC) is the dominant nationwide network for both radio and TV. The CTV Television Network is its major competition.

Weights & Measures Canada officially uses the metric system, but imperial measurements are used for many day-to-day purposes.

Smoking Banned in all restaurants, bars and other public venues nationwide.

Legal Matters

Police

If you are arrested or charged with an offense, you have the right to keep your mouth shut and to hire any lawyer you wish (contact your embassy for a referral, if necessary). If you cannot afford one, ask to be represented by public counsel. There is a presumption of innocence.

Drugs & Alcohol

- The blood-alcohol limit is 0.08% and driving cars, motorcycles, boats and snowmobiles while drunk is a criminal offense. If you are caught, you may face stiff fines, license suspension and other nasty consequences.
- Consuming alcohol anywhere other than at a residence or licensed premises is also a no-no, which puts parks, beaches and the rest of the great outdoors off-limits.
- Avoid illegal drugs, as penalties may entail heavy fines, possible jail time and a criminal record. The only exception is the use of marijuana for medical purposes, which became legal in 2001. Meanwhile, the decriminalization of pot possession for personal use remains a subject of ongoing debate among the general public and in Parliament.

Other

- Abortion is legal.
- Travelers should note that they can be prosecuted under the law of their home country regarding age of consent, even when abroad.

Maps

- Most tourist offices distribute free provincial road maps.
- For extended hikes or multiday backcountry treks, it's a good idea to carry a topographic map. The best are the series of 1:50,000 scale maps published by the government's **Centre for Topographic Information**. These are sold by bookstores and parks around the country.
- You can also download and print maps from **GeoBase** (http://geogratis.gc.ca).

Money

- All prices quoted are in Canadian dollars ($), unless stated otherwise.
- Canadian coins come in 5¢ (nickel), 10¢ (dime), 25¢ (quarter), $1 (loonie) and $2 (toonie or twoonie) denominations. The gold-colored loonie features the loon, a common Canadian waterbird, while the two-toned toonie is decorated with a polar bear. Canada phased out its 1¢ (penny) coin in 2012.
- Paper currency comes in $5 (blue), $10 (purple), $20 (green) and $50 (red) denominations. The $100 (brown) and larger bills are less common. The newest bills in circulation – which have enhanced security features – are actually a polymer-based material; they feel more like plastic than paper.
- The Canadian dollar has seen fluctuations over the last decade, though since 2007 it has tracked quite closely to the US dollar.
- For changing money in the larger cities, currency exchange offices may offer better conditions than banks.

ATMs

- Many grocery and convenience stores, airports, and bus, train and ferry stations have ATMs. Most are linked to international networks, the most common being Cirrus, Plus, Star and Maestro.
- Most ATMs also spit out cash if you use a major credit card. This method tends to be more expensive because, in addition to a service fee, you'll be charged interest

immediately (in other words, there's no interest-free period as with purchases). For exact fees, check with your own bank or credit card company.

➡ Visitors heading to Canada's more remote regions (such as Newfoundland) won't find an abundance of ATMs, so it is wise to cash up beforehand.

➡ Scotiabank, common throughout Canada, is part of the Global ATM Alliance. If your home bank is a member, fees may be less if you withdraw from Scotiabank ATMs.

Cash

Most Canadians don't carry large amounts of cash for everyday use, relying instead on credit and debit cards. Still, carrying some cash, say $100 or less, comes in handy when making small purchases. In some cases, cash is necessary to pay for rural B&Bs and shuttle vans; inquire in advance to avoid surprises. Shops and businesses rarely accept personal checks.

Credit Cards

Major credit cards such as MasterCard, Visa and American Express are widely accepted in Canada, except in remote, rural communities, where cash is king. You'll find it difficult or impossible to rent a car, book a room or order tickets over the phone without having a piece of plastic. Note that some credit card companies charge a 'transaction fee' (around 3% of whatever you purchased); check with your provider to avoid surprises.

For lost or stolen cards, these numbers operate 24 hours:

American Express (☎800-869-3016; www.americanexpress.com)

MasterCard (☎800-622-7747; www.mastercard.com)

Visa (☎800-847-2911; www.visa.com)

Taxes & Refunds

Canada's federal goods and services tax (GST), variously known as the 'gouge and screw' or 'grab and steal' tax, adds 5% to just about every transaction. Most provinces also charge a provincial sales tax (PST) on top of it. Several provinces have combined the GST and PST into a harmonized sales tax (HST). Whatever the methodology, expect to pay 10% to 15% in most cases. Unless otherwise stated, taxes are not included in prices given.

You might be eligible for a rebate on some of the taxes. If you've booked your accommodations in conjunction with a rental car, plane ticket or other service (ie if it all appears on the same bill from a 'tour operator'), you should be eligible to get 50% of the tax refunded from your accommodations. Fill out the GST/HST Refund Application for Tour Packages form, available from the **Canada Revenue Agency** (www.cra-arc.gc.ca).

Tipping

Tipping is a standard practice. Generally you can expect to tip:

➡ **Restaurant waitstaff** 15% to 20%

➡ **Bar staff** $1 per drink

➡ **Hotel bellhop** $1 to $2 per bag

➡ **Hotel room cleaners** From $2 per day (depending on room size and messiness)

➡ **Taxis** 10% to 15%

Traveler's Checks

Traveler's checks are becoming more and more obsolete. Traveler's checks issued in Canadian dollars are generally treated like cash by businesses; those in most other currencies must be exchanged for Canadian dollars at a bank or foreign currency office. The most common issuers are American Express, MasterCard and Visa.

Opening Hours

Opening hours vary throughout the year. We've provided high-season opening hours; hours will generally decrease in the shoulder and low seasons.

Banks 10am–5pm Monday to Friday; some open 9am–noon Saturday

TAX RATES BY PROVINCE

Percentages represent federal and provincial taxes combined:

PROVINCES & TERRITORIES	TAX RATE
Alberta	5%
British Columbia	12%
Manitoba	13%
New Brunswick	15%
Newfoundland & Labrador	15%
Northwest Territories	5%
Nova Scotia	15%
Nunavut	5%
Ontario	13%
Prince Edward Island	14%
Québec	15%
Saskatchewan	10%
Yukon Territory	5%

Restaurants breakfast 8–11am, lunch 11:30am–2:30pm Monday to Friday, dinner 5–9:30pm daily; some open for brunch 8am to 1pm Saturday and Sunday

Bars 5pm–2am daily

Clubs 9pm–2am Wednesday to Saturday

Shops 10am–6pm Monday to Saturday, noon–5pm Sunday; some open to 8pm or 9pm Thursday and/or Friday

Supermarkets 9am–8pm; some open 24 hours

Post

➡ Canada's national postal service, **Canada Post/ Postes Canada** (www.canadapost.ca), is neither quick nor cheap, but it is reliable. Stamps are available at post offices, drugstores, convenience stores and hotels.

➡ Postcards or standard letters cost $1 within Canada, $1.20 to the USA and $2.50 to all other countries.

➡ Travelers often find they have to pay high duties on items sent to them while in Canada, so beware.

Public Holidays

Canada observes 10 national public holidays and more at the provincial level. Banks, schools and government offices close on these days.

National Holidays

New Year's Day January 1

Good Friday March or April

Easter Monday March or April

Victoria Day Monday before May 25

Canada Day July 1; called Memorial Day in Newfoundland

Labour Day First Monday of September

Thanksgiving Second Monday of October

Remembrance Day November 11

Christmas Day December 25

Boxing Day December 26

POSTAL ABBREVIATIONS

PROVINCES & TERRITORIES	ABBREVIATION
Alberta	AB
British Columbia	BC
Manitoba	MB
New Brunswick	NB
Newfoundland & Labrador	NL
Northwest Territories	NT
Nova Scotia	NS
Nunavut	NU
Ontario	ON
Prince Edward Island	PE
Québec	QC
Saskatchewan	SK
Yukon Territory	YT

Provincial Holidays

Some provinces also observe local holidays, with Newfoundland leading the pack.

Family Day Third Monday of February in Alberta, Ontario, Saskatchewan and Manitoba (second Monday in British Columbia); known as Louis Riel Day in Manitoba

St Patrick's Day Monday nearest to March 17

St George's Day Monday nearest to April 23

National Day Monday nearest to June 24 in Newfoundland; June 24 in Québec (aka St-Jean-Baptiste Day)

Orangemen's Day Monday nearest to July 12 in Newfoundland

Civic Holiday First Monday of August everywhere except Newfoundland, Québec and Yukon Territory

Discovery Day Third Monday of August in Yukon Territory

School Holidays

Kids break for summer holidays in late June and don't return to school until early September. University students get even more time off, usually from May to early or mid-September. Most people take their big annual vacation during these months.

Telephone

Canada's phone system is almost identical to the USA's system.

Domestic & International Dialing

➡ Canadian phone numbers consist of a three-digit area code followed by a seven-digit local number. In many parts of Canada, you must dial all 10 digits preceded by ☎1, even if you're calling across the street. In other parts of the country, when you're calling within the same area code, you can dial the seven-digit number only, but this is slowly changing.

➡ For direct international calls, dial ☎011 + country code + area code + local phone number. The country code for Canada is ☎1 (the same as for the USA, although international rates still apply for all calls made between the two countries).

➡ Toll-free numbers begin with ☎800, 877, 866 or 855 and must be preceded by 1. Some of these numbers are good throughout Canada and the USA, others only work within Canada, and some work in just one province.

Emergency Numbers

Dial ☎911. This is *not* the emergency number in the Yukon, Northwest Territories or Nunavut.

Cell Phones

Local SIM cards can be used in unlocked GSM 850/1900 compatible phones. Other phones must be set to roaming.

➡ If you have an unlocked GSM phone, you should be able to buy a SIM card from local providers such as **Telus** (www.telus.com), **Rogers** (www.rogers.com) or **Bell** (www.bell.ca). Bell has the best data coverage.

➡ US residents can often upgrade their domestic cell phone plan to extend to Canada. **Verizon** (www.verizonwireless.com) provides good results.

➡ Reception is poor and often nonexistent in rural areas no matter who your service provider is.

Public Phones

Coin-operated public pay phones are fairly plentiful. Local calls cost 50¢; many phones also accept prepaid phonecards and credit cards. Dialing the operator (☎0) or directory assistance (☎411 for local calls, ☎1 + area code + 555-1212 for long-distance calls) is free of charge from public phones; it may incur a charge from private phones.

Phonecards

➡ Prepaid phonecards usually offer the best per-minute rates for long-distance and international calling. They come in denominations of $5, $10 or $20 and are widely sold in drugstores, supermarkets and convenience stores. Beware of cards with hidden charges, such as 'activation fees' or a per-call connection fee.

➡ A surcharge ranging from 30¢ to 85¢ for calls made from public pay phones is common.

Time

➡ Canada spans six of the world's 24 time zones. The Eastern zone in Newfoundland is unusual in that it's only 30 minutes different from the adjacent zone. The time difference from coast to coast is 4½ hours.

➡ Canada observes daylight saving time, which comes into effect on the second Sunday in March, when clocks are put forward one hour, and ends on the first Sunday in November. Saskatchewan and small pockets of Québec, Ontario and BC are the only areas that do not switch to daylight saving time.

➡ In Québec especially, times for shop hours, train schedules, film screenings etc are usually indicated by the 24-hour clock.

TIME DIFFERENCE BETWEEN CITIES

When it's 3pm in Vancouver, it's:

➡ 6pm in Montréal and Toronto

➡ 6pm in New York City

➡ 7:30pm in St John's (Newfoundland)

➡ 11pm in London

Tourist Information

➡ The **Canadian Tourism Commission** (www.canada.travel) is loaded with general information, packages and links.

➡ All provincial tourist offices maintain comprehensive websites packed with information helpful in planning your trip. Staff also field telephone inquiries and, on request, will mail out free maps and directories about accommodations, attractions and events. Some offices can also help with making hotel, tour or other reservations.

➡ For detailed information about a specific area, contact the local tourist office, aka visitors center. Just about every city and town has at least a seasonal branch with helpful staff, racks of free pamphlets and books and maps for sale. Provincial tourist offices:

Newfoundland & Labrador Tourism (www.newfoundlandlabrador.com)

Northwest Territories Tourism (www.spectacularnwt.com)

Nunavut Tourism (www.nunavuttourism.com)

Ontario Tourism (www.ontariotravel.net)

Prince Edward Island Tourism (www.tourismpei.com)

Tourism British Columbia (www.hellobc.com)

Tourism New Brunswick (www.tourismnewbrunswick.ca)

Tourism Nova Scotia (www.novascotia.com)

Tourism Saskatchewan (www.sasktourism.com)

Tourisme Québec (www.quebecoriginal.com/en)

Travel Alberta (www.travelalberta.com)

Travel Manitoba (www.travelmanitoba.com)

Yukon Department of Tourism (www.travelyukon.com)

Travelers with Disabilities

Canada is making progress when it comes to easing the everyday challenges facing people with disabilities, especially the mobility-impaired.

➡ Many public buildings, including museums, tourist offices, train stations, shopping malls and cinemas, have access ramps and/or lifts. Most public restrooms feature extra-wide stalls equipped with hand rails. Many pedestrian crossings have sloping curbs.

➡ Newer and recently remodeled hotels, especially chain hotels, have rooms with extra-wide doors and spacious bathrooms.

➡ Interpretive centers at national and provincial parks are usually accessible, and many parks have trails that can be navigated in wheelchairs.

➡ Car rental agencies offer hand-controlled vehicles and vans with wheelchair lifts at no additional charge, but you must reserve them well in advance.

➡ For accessible air, bus, rail and ferry transportation check **Access to Travel** (www.accesstotravel.gc.ca), the federal government's website. In general, most transportation agencies can accommodate people with disabilities if you make your needs known when booking.

➡ Download Lonely Planet's free Accessible Travel guide from http://lptravel.to/AccessibleTravel. Other organizations specializing in the needs of travelers with disabilities:

Access-Able Travel Source (www.access-able.com) Lists accessible lodging, transport, attractions and equipment rental by province.

Mobility International (www.miusa.org) Advises travelers with disabilities on mobility issues and runs an educational exchange program.

Society for Accessible Travel & Hospitality (www.sath.org) Travelers with disabilities share tips and blogs.

Visas

Visitors from certain countries require a visa to enter Canada. Those who are exempt require an Electronic Travel Authorization (eTA; $7), with the exception of Americans. This must be applied for prior to traveling and can be completed online. It usually takes minutes but can take days. See www.cic.gc.ca/english/visit/eta-start.asp.

Currently, visas are not required for citizens of 46 countries – including most EU members, Australia and New Zealand – for visits of up to six months.

To find out if you need an eTA or are required to apply for a formal visa, go to www.cic.gc.ca/english/visit/visas.asp.

Visitor visas – aka Temporary Resident Visas (TRVs) – can now be applied for online at: www.cic.gc.ca/english/information/applications/visa.asp. Single-entry TRVs ($100) are usually valid for a maximum stay of six months from the date of your arrival in Canada.

A separate visa is required for all nationalities if you plan to study or work in Canada.

Visa extensions ($100) need to be filed with the **CIC Visitor Case Processing Centre** (☎888-242-2100; ⏲8am-4pm Mon-Fri) in Alberta at least one month before your current visa expires.

Visiting the USA

Admission requirements are subject to rapid change. The **US State Department** (www.travel.state.gov) has the latest information; you can also check with a US consulate in your home country.

Under the US visa-waiver program, visas are not required for citizens of 38 countries – including most EU members, Australia and New Zealand – for visits of

UNIQUELY CANADIAN CELEBRATIONS

National Flag Day (February 15) Commemorates the first time the maple leaf flag was raised above Parliament Hill in Ottawa, at the stroke of noon on February 15, 1965.

Victoria Day (late May) This day was established in 1845 to observe the birthday of Queen Victoria and now celebrates the birthday of the British sovereign, who's still Canada's titular head of state. Victoria Day marks the official beginning of the summer season (which ends with Labour Day on the first Monday of September). Some communities hold fireworks.

National Aboriginal Day (June 21) Created in 1996, it celebrates the contributions of Aboriginal peoples to Canada. Coinciding with the summer solstice, festivities are organized locally and may include traditional dancing, singing and drumming; storytelling; arts and crafts shows; canoe races; and lots more.

Canada Day (July 1) Known as Dominion Day until 1982, Canada Day was created in 1869 to commemorate the creation of Canada two years earlier. All over the country, people celebrate with barbecues, parades, concerts and fireworks.

Thanksgiving Day (mid-October) First celebrated in 1578 in what is now Newfoundland by explorer Martin Frobisher to give thanks for surviving his Atlantic crossing, Thanksgiving became an official Canadian holiday in 1872 to celebrate the recovery of the Prince of Wales from a long illness.

up to 90 days (no extensions allowed), as long as you can present a machine-readable passport and are approved under the **Electronic System for Travel Authorization** (www.cbp.gov/esta). Note that you must register at least 72 hours before arrival with an e-passport, and there's a $14 fee for processing and authorization.

Canadians do not need visas to enter the USA, though they do need a passport or document approved by the **Western Hemisphere Travel Initiative** (www.getyouhome.gov). Citizens of all other countries need to apply for a US visa in their home country before arriving in Canada.

All foreign visitors (except Canadians) must pay a US$6 processing fee when entering at land borders. Note that you don't need a Canadian multiple-entry TRV for repeated entries into Canada from the USA, unless you have visited a third country.

Volunteering

Volunteering provides the opportunity to interact with local folks and the land in ways you never would just passing through. Many organizations charge a fee, which varies depending on the program's length and the type of food and lodging it provides. The fees usually do not cover travel to Canada. Groups that use volunteers:

Churchill Northern Studies Centre (www.churchillscience.ca) Volunteer for six hours per day (anything from stringing wires to cleaning) and get free room and board at this center for polar bear and other wildlife research.

Earthwatch (www.earthwatch.org) Help scientists track whales off the coast of British Columbia, track moose and deer in Nova Scotia, and monitor climate change in Churchill, Manitoba or the Mackenzie Mountains of the Northwest Territories. Trips last from seven to 14 days and cost from $2250 to $5050.

Volunteers for Peace (www.vfp.org) Offers tutoring stints in Aboriginal communities in Canada's far north, as well as projects in Québec.

World-Wide Opportunities on Organic Farms (www.wwoof.ca) Work on an organic farm, usually in exchange for free room and board; check the website for locations throughout Canada.

Women Travelers

Canada is generally a safe place for women to travel, even alone and even in the cities. Simply use the same common sense as you would at home.

In bars and nightclubs, solo women are likely to attract a lot of attention, but if you don't want company, most men will respect a firm 'no, thank you.' If you feel threatened, protesting loudly will often make the offender slink away – or will at least spur other people to come to your defense. Note that carrying mace or pepper spray is illegal in Canada.

Physical attacks are unlikely, but if you are assaulted, call the police immediately (☎911 except in the Yukon, Northwest Territories and Nunavut) or contact a rape crisis center. A complete list is available from the **Canadian Association of Sexual Assault Centres** (☎800-726-2743; www.casac.ca).

Resources for women travelers include:

Her Own Way (www.travel.gc.ca/travelling/publications/her-own-way) Published by the Canadian government for Canadian travelers, but contains a great deal of general advice.

Journeywoman (www.journeywoman.com) Travel links and tips for women with a section on Canada.

Work Permits

In almost all cases, you need a valid work permit to work in Canada. Obtaining one may be difficult, as employment opportunities go to Canadians first. Before you can even apply, you'll need a specific job offer from an employer, who in turn must have been granted permission from the government to give the position to a foreign national. Applications must be filed at a visa office of a Canadian embassy or consulate in your home country. Some jobs are exempt from the permit requirement. For full details, check with **Citizenship & Immigration Canada** (www.cic.gc.ca).

Employers hiring temporary service workers (for hotels, bars, restaurants, and resorts) and construction, farm or forestry workers sometimes don't ask for a permit. If you get caught, however, you can kiss Canada goodbye.

Finding Work

Students aged 18 to 30 from more than a dozen countries, including the USA, UK, Australia, New Zealand, Ireland and South Africa, are eligible to apply for a spot in the **Student Work Abroad Program** (www.swap.ca). If successful, you get a six-month–to–one-year, nonextendable visa that allows you to work anywhere in Canada in any job you can get. Most 'Swappers' find work in the service industry as waiters or bartenders.

Even if you're not a student, you may be able to spend up to a year in Canada on a 'working holiday program' with **International Experience Canada** (www.cic.gc.ca/english/work/iec). The Canadian government has an arrangement with several countries for people aged 18 to 35 to come over and get a job; check the website for participants. The Canadian embassy in each country runs the program, but basically there are quotas and spaces are filled on a first-come, first-served basis.

Transportation

GETTING THERE & AWAY

Flights, cars and tours can be booked online at www.lonelyplanet.com/bookings.

Entering the Country

Visitors to Canada must hold a valid passport with at least six months remaining before its expiration. Visitors from visa-exempt countries (with the exception of the US) are required to purchase an electronic travel authorization (eTA, $7), similar to the USA's ESTA visa waiver, before departing their home country. Visitors from non-visa-waiver countries must apply for the appropriate visa prior to arriving in Canada.

Note that questioning may be more intense at land border crossings and your car may be searched.

For updates (particularly regarding land-border crossing rules), check the websites for the **US State Department** (www.travel.state.gov) and **Citizenship & Immigration Canada** (www.cic.gc.ca).

Passport

Most international visitors require a passport to enter Canada. US citizens at land and sea borders have other options, such as an enhanced driver's license, permanent resident card or NEXUS card. See **Canada Border Services** (www.cbsa-asfc.gc.ca) for approved identification documents.

Air

Airports & Airlines

Toronto is far and away Canada's busiest airport, followed by Vancouver. The international gateways you're most likely to use:

Calgary (Calgary International Airport; www.ycc.com)

Edmonton (Edmonton International Airport; www.flyeia.com)

Halifax (Halifax Stanfield International Airport; www.hiaa.ca)

Montréal (Montréal Trudeau Airport; www.admtl.com)

Ottawa (Ottawa International Airport; www.ottawa-airport.ca)

St John's (St John's International Airport; www.stjohnsairport.com)

Toronto (Toronto Pearson International Airport; www.torontopearson.com)

Vancouver (Vancouver International Airport; www.yvr.ca)

Winnipeg (Winnipeg International Airport; www.waa.ca)

Air Canada (www.aircanada.com), the national flagship carrier, is considered one of the world's safest airlines. All major global airlines fly to Canada. Other companies based in the country and serving international destinations:

WestJet (www.westjet.com) Calgary-based low-cost carrier serving destinations throughout Canada as well as across the US and Caribbean.

CLIMATE CHANGE & TRAVEL

Every form of transport that relies on carbon-based fuel generates CO_2, the main cause of human-induced climate change. Modern travel is dependent on aeroplanes, which might use less fuel per kilometer per person than most cars but travel much greater distances. The altitude at which aircraft emit gases (including CO_2) and particles also contributes to their climate change impact. Many websites offer 'carbon calculators' that allow people to estimate the carbon emissions generated by their journey and, for those who wish to do so, to offset the impact of the greenhouse gases emitted with contributions to portfolios of climate-friendly initiatives throughout the world. Lonely Planet offsets the carbon footprint of all staff and author travel.

Porter Airlines (www.flyporter.com) Flies around eastern Canada and to US cities, including Boston, Chicago, Washington, DC, and New York.

Air Transat (www.airtransat.com) Charter airline from major Canadian cities to holiday destinations (ie southern USA and Caribbean in winter, Europe in summer).

Land

Border Crossings

There are around 25 official border crossings along the US–Canadian border, from New Brunswick to British Columbia.

The website of the **Canadian Border Services Agency** (www.cbsa-asfc.gc.ca) shows current wait times at each. You can also access it via Twitter (@CBSA_BWT).

In general, waits rarely exceed 30 minutes, except during the peak summer season, and on Friday and Sunday afternoons, especially on holiday weekends. Some entry points are especially busy:

- Windsor, Ontario, to Detroit, Michigan
- Fort Erie, Ontario, to Buffalo, New York
- Niagara Falls, Ontario, to Niagara Falls, New York
- Québec to Rouse's Point/Champlain, New York
- Surrey, British Columbia, to Blaine, Washington

When returning to the USA, check the website for the **US Department for Homeland Security** (http://apps.cbp.gov/bwt) for border wait times.

All foreign visitors (except Canadians) must pay a $6 processing fee when entering the USA by land; credit cards are not accepted.

Bus

Greyhound (www.greyhound.com) and its Canadian equivalent, **Greyhound Canada** (www.greyhound.ca), operate the largest bus network in North America. There are direct connections between main cities in the USA and Canada, but you usually have to transfer to a different bus at the border (where it takes a good hour for all passengers to clear customs/immigration). Most international buses have free wi-fi on board.

Other notable international bus companies (with free wi-fi) include:

Megabus (www.megabus.com) Runs between Toronto and US cities, including New York City, Philadelphia and Washington, DC; usually cheaper than Greyhound. Tickets can only be purchased online.

Quick Coach (www.quickcoach.com) Runs between Seattle and Vancouver; typically a bit quicker than Greyhound.

Car & Motorcycle

The highway system of the continental USA connects directly with the Canadian highway system at numerous points along the border. These Canadian highways then meet up with the east–west Trans-Canada Hwy further north. Between the Yukon Territory and Alaska, the main routes are the Alaska, Klondike and Haines Hwys.

If you're driving into Canada, you'll need the vehicle's registration papers, proof of liability insurance and your home driver's license. Cars rented in the USA can usually be driven into Canada and back, but make sure your rental agreement says so. If you're driving a car registered in someone else's name, bring a letter from the owner authorizing use of the vehicle in Canada.

Train

Amtrak (www.amtrak.com) and **VIA Rail Canada** (www.

TRAIN ROUTES & FARES

ROUTE	DURATION (HR)	FREQUENCY (DAILY)	FARE (US$)
New York–Toronto *(Maple Leaf)*	13	1	$125
New York–Montréal *(Adirondack)*	11	1	$65
Seattle–Vancouver *(Cascades)*	4	2	$52

GREYHOUND BUS ROUTES & FARES

ROUTE	DURATION (HR)	FREQUENCY (DAILY)	FARE (C$)
Boston–Montréal	7-8	4	$77
Detroit–Toronto	5-6	5	$63
New York–Montréal	8-9	6-10	$91
Seattle–Vancouver	4	3-5	$43

viarail.ca) run three routes between the USA and Canada: two in the east and one in the west. Customs inspections happen at the border, not upon boarding.

Sea

Various ferry services on the coasts connect the USA and Canada:

Alaska Marine Highway System (www.ferryalaska.com) Alaska to Port Hardy, BC.

Bay Ferries Limited (www.ferries.ca/thecat) Bar Harbor, Maine, to Yarmouth, NS.

BC Ferries (www.bcferries.com) Bella Bella, Alaska to Prince Rupert, BC.

East Coast Ferries (www.eastcoastferries.nb.ca) Eastport, Maine, to Deer Island, NB.

Victoria Clipper (www.clippervacations.com) Seattle to Victoria, BC.

GETTING AROUND

Air

Airlines in Canada

Air Canada operates the largest domestic-flight network in the country, serving some 150 destinations.

The Canadian aviation arena also includes many independent regional and local airlines, which tend to focus on small, remote regions, mostly in the North. Depending on the destination, fares in such noncompetitive markets can be high.

Air Canada (☎888-247-2262; www.aircanada.com) Nationwide flights.

Air Creebec (☎800-567-6567; www.aircreebec.ca) Serves northern Québec and Ontario, including Chisasibi and Chibougamau, from Montréal and other cities.

Air Inuit (☎888-247-2262; www.airinuit.com) Flies from Montréal to all 14 Inuit communities in Nunavik (northern Québec), including Kuujjuaq and Puvirnituq.

Air Labrador (☎800-563-3042; www.airlabrador.com) Flies mostly within Labrador.

Air North (☎in Canada 867-668-2228, in USA 800-661-0407; www.flyairnorth.com) Flies from the Yukon to British Columbia, Alberta, Northwest Territories and Alaska.

Air St-Pierre (☎877-277-7765, 902-873-3566; www.airsaintpierre.com) Flies from eastern Canada to the French territories off Newfoundland's coast.

Air Tindi (☎867-669-8260; www.airtindi.com) Serves the Northwest Territories' North Slave region.

Aklak Air (☎866-707-4977; www.aklakair.ca) Serves the Northwest Territories' Mackenzie Delta.

Bearskin Airlines (☎800-465-2327; www.bearskinairlines.com) Serves destinations throughout Ontario and eastern Manitoba.

Calm Air (☎204-778-6471, 800-839-2256; www.calmair.com) Flights throughout Manitoba and Nunavut.

Canadian North (☎800-661-1505; www.canadiannorth.com) Flights to, from and within the Northwest Territories and Nunavut.

Central Mountain Air (☎888-865-8585; www.flycma.com) Destinations throughout British Columbia and Alberta.

First Air (☎800-267-1247; www.firstair.ca) Flies from Ottawa, Montréal, Winnipeg and Edmonton to 24 Arctic destinations, including Iqaluit.

Harbour Air (☎800-665-0212; www.harbourair.com) Seaplane service from the city of Vancouver to Vancouver Island, Gulf Islands and the Sunshine Coast.

Hawkair (☎866-429-5247; www.hawkair.ca) Serves northern British Columbia from Vancouver and Victoria.

Northwestern Air Lease (☎877-872-2216; www.nwal.ca) Flies in Alberta and the Northwest Territories.

North-Wright Air (☎867-587-2333; www.north-wrightairways.com) Serves the Northwest Territories' Mackenzie Valley.

Pacific Coastal Airlines (☎800-663-2872; www.pacific-coastal.com) Vancouver-based airline with service to many British Columbia locales.

Porter Airlines (☎888-619-8622; www.flyporter.com) Turboprop planes from eastern Canadian cities to Toronto's more convenient Billy Bishop City Airport downtown.

Provincial Airlines (☎800-563-2800; www.provincialairlines.ca) St John's–based airline with service throughout Newfoundland and to Labrador.

Seair Seaplanes (☎604-273-8900, 800-447-3247; www.seairseaplanes.com) Flies from Vancouver to Nanaimo and the Southern Gulf Islands in British Columbia.

Transwest Air (☎800-667-9356; www.transwestair.com) Service within Saskatchewan.

Westjet (☎888-937-8538; www.westjet.com) Calgary-based low-cost carrier serving destinations throughout Canada, flying to Varadero, Cayo Coco, Santa Clara and Holguín in Cuba.

Air Passes

Star Alliance (www.staralliance.com) members Air Canada, United Airlines and US Airways have teamed up to offer the North American Airpass, which is available to anyone not residing in the USA, Canada, Mexico, Bermuda or the Caribbean. It's sold only in conjunction with an international flight operated by any Star Alliance member airline. You can buy as few as three coupons (from US$399) or as many as 10. Air North has an **Arctic Circle Air Pass** (www.flyairnorth.com) for those traveling around the Yukon and Northwest Territories.

Bicycle

Much of Canada is great for cycling. Long-distance trips can be done entirely on quiet back roads, and many cities (including Edmonton, Montréal, Ottawa, Toronto and Vancouver) have designated bike routes.

➡ Cyclists must follow the same rules of the road as vehicles, but don't expect drivers to always respect your right of way.

➡ Helmets are mandatory for all cyclists in British Columbia, New Brunswick, Prince Edward Island and Nova Scotia, as well as for anyone under 18 in Alberta and Ontario.

➡ The **Better World Club** (www.betterworldclub.com) provides emergency roadside assistance. Membership costs $40 per year, plus a $12 enrollment fee, and entitles you to two free pickups, and transport to the nearest repair shop, or home, within a 50km radius of where you're picked up.

Transportation

By air Most airlines will carry bikes as checked luggage without charge on international flights, as long as they're in a box. On domestic flights they usually charge between $30 and $65. Always check details before you buy the ticket.

By bus You must ship your bike as freight on Greyhound Canada. In addition to a bike box ($10), you'll be charged an oversize charge and GST. Bikes only travel on the same bus as the passenger if there's enough space. To ensure that yours arrives at the same time as (or before) you do, ship it a day early.

By train VIA Rail will transport your bicycle for $25, but only on trains offering checked-baggage service (which includes all long-distance and many regional trains).

Rental

➡ Outfitters renting bicycles exist in most tourist towns.

➡ Rentals cost around $15 per day for touring bikes and $25 per day for mountain bikes. The price usually includes a helmet and lock.

➡ Most companies require a security deposit of $20 to $200.

Boat

Ferry services are extensive, especially throughout the Atlantic provinces and in British Columbia.

Walk-ons and cyclists should be able to get aboard at any time, but call ahead for vehicle reservations or if you require a cabin berth. This is especially important during summer peak season and holidays. Main operators:

Bay Ferries (☎888-249-7245; www.ferries.ca) Year-round service between Saint John, New Brunswick, and Digby, Nova Scotia.

BC Ferries (☎250-386-3431, 888-223-3779; www.bcferries.com) Huge passenger-ferry systems with 25 routes and 47 ports of call, including Vancouver Island, the Gulf Islands, the Sechelt Peninsula along the Sunshine Coast and the islands of Haida Gwaii – all in British Columbia.

Coastal Transport (☎506-662-3724; www.coastaltransport.ca) Ferry from Blacks Harbour to Grand Manan in the Fundy Isles, New Brunswick.

CTMA Ferries (☎418-986-3278, 888-986-3278; www.ctma.ca) Daily ferries to Québec's Îles de la Madeleine from Souris, Prince Edward Island.

East Coast Ferries (☎506-747-2159, 877-747-2159; www.eastcoastferries.nb.ca) Connects Deer Island to Campobello Island, both in the Fundy Isles, New Brunswick.

Labrador Marine (☎866-535-2567, 709-535-0810; www.labradormarine.com) Connects Newfoundland to Labrador.

Marine Atlantic (☎800-341-7981; www.marine-atlantic.ca) Connects Port aux Basques and Argentia in Newfoundland with North Sydney, Nova Scotia.

Northumberland Ferries (☎902-566-3838, 888-249-7245; www.ferries.ca) Connects Wood Islands (PEI) and Caribou, Nova Scotia.

Provincial Ferry Services (www.gov.nl.ca/ferryservices) Operates coastal ferries throughout Newfoundland.

Bus

Buses are generally clean, comfortable and reliable. Amenities may include onboard toilets, air-conditioning (bring a sweater), reclining seats, free wi-fi and onboard movies. Smoking is not permitted. On long journeys, buses make meal stops every few hours, usually at highway service stations.

Greyhound Canada (☎800-661-8747; www.greyhound.ca) is the king, plowing along an extensive network in central and western Canada, as well as to/from the USA. Regional carriers pick up the slack, especially in the east.

LONG-DISTANCE BUS FARES

ROUTE	STANDARD FARE	7-DAY FARE	DURATION (HR)
Vancouver–Calgary	$104	$77	14-17
Montréal–Toronto	$67	$55	8-10
Toronto–Vancouver	$267	$253	65-70

ROAD DISTANCES (KM)

	Banff	Calgary	Edmonton	Halifax	Inuvik	Jasper	Montréal	Ottawa	Québec City	St John's	Toronto	Vancouver	Whitehorse	Winnipeg
Calgary	130													
Edmonton	410	290												
Halifax	4900	4810	4850											
Inuvik	3440	3515	3220	8110										
Jasper	280	415	370	5250	3150									
Montréal	3700	3550	3605	1240	6820	3950								
Ottawa	3450	3340	3410	1440	6620	3770	200							
Québec City	3900	3800	3880	1020	7060	4210	250							
St John's	6200	6100	6150	1480	9350	6480	2530	2730	2310					
Toronto	3400	3400	3470	1790	6680	3820	550	450	800	3090				
Vancouver	850	970	1160	5880	3630	790	4580	4350	4830	7130	4360			
Whitehorse	2210	2290	2010	6830	1220	1930	5620	5390	5840	8150	5450	2400		
Winnipeg	1450	1325	1330	3520	4550	1670	2280	2140	2520	4820	2220	2290	3340	
Yellowknife	1800	1790	1510	6340	3770	1590	5050	4900	5350	7620	4950	2370	2540	2800

These distances are approximate only.

Autobus Maheux (☎888-797-0011; www.autobusmaheux.qc.ca) Service from Montréal to Québec's northwest regions.

Coach Canada (☎800-461-7661; www.coachcanada.com) Scheduled service within Ontario and from Toronto to Montréal.

DRL Coachlines (☎709-263-2171; www.drl-lr.com) Service throughout Newfoundland.

Intercar (☎888-861-4592; www.intercar.qc.ca) Connects Québec City, Montréal and Tadoussac, among other towns in Québec.

Limocar (☎866-700-8899; www.limocar.com) Regional service in Québec.

Maritime Bus (☎800-575-1807; http://maritimebus.com) For New Brunswick, Prince Edward Island and Nova Scotia.

Megabus (www.megabus.com) Service between Toronto and Montréal via Kingston; tickets can only be purchased online.

Ontario Northland (☎800-461-8558; www.ontarionorthland.ca) Operates bus and train routes that service northern Ontario from Toronto.

Orléans Express (☎888-999-3977; www.orleansexpress.com) Service to eastern Québec.

Pacific Coach Lines (☎250-385-4411, 800-661-1725; www.pacificcoach.com) Service between Victoria, Vancouver and Whistler.

Parkbus (☎800-928-7101; www.parkbus.ca) Runs from Toronto to Algonquin, Killarney and other Ontario parks.

Red Arrow (☎800-232-1958; www.redarrow.ca) Serves all the major cities in Alberta, with free wi-fi, snacks, drinks and plug-ins.

Saskatchewan Transportation Company (STC;☎800-663-7181; www.stcbus.com) Service within Saskatchewan.

Reservations

Tickets can be bought online or at bus terminals for Greyhound. Some companies, such as Megabus, take reservations online only. The earlier you buy a ticket online, the cheaper your fare.

Show up at least 30 to 45 minutes prior to departure.

Car & Motorcycle

Automobile Associations

Autoclub membership is a handy thing to have in Canada. The **Canadian Automobile Association** (www.caa.ca) offers services, including 24-hour emergency roadside assistance, to members of international affiliates, such as AAA in the USA, AA in the UK and ADAC in Germany. The club also offers trip-planning advice, free maps, travel-agency services and a range of discounts on hotels, car rentals etc.

The **Better World Club** (www.betterworldclub.com), which donates 1% of its annual revenue to environmental cleanup efforts, offers service throughout Canada and has a roadside-assistance program for bicycles.

Bringing Your Own Vehicle

There's minimal hassle driving into Canada from the USA as long as you have your vehicle's registration papers, proof of liability insurance and your home driver's license.

Driver's Licenses

In most provinces visitors can legally drive for up to three months with their home driver's license. In some, such as British Columbia, this is extended to six months.

If you're spending considerable time in Canada, think about getting an International Driving Permit (IDP), which is valid for one year. Your automobile association at home can issue one for a small fee. Always carry your home license together with the IDP.

Fuel

Gas is sold in liters. Prices are higher in remote areas, with Yellowknife usually setting the national record; drivers in Calgary typically pay the least for gas.

Fuel prices are usually lower in the USA, so fill up south of the border.

Insurance

Canadian law requires liability insurance for all vehicles, to cover you for damage caused to property and people.

- The minimum requirement is $200,000 in all provinces except Québec, where it is $50,000.
- Americans traveling to Canada in their own car should ask their insurance company for a Nonresident Interprovince Motor Vehicle Liability Insurance Card (commonly known as a 'yellow card'), which is accepted as evidence of financial responsibility anywhere in Canada. Although not mandatory, it may come in handy in an accident.
- Car-rental agencies offer liability insurance. Collision Damage Waivers (CDW) reduce or eliminate the amount you'll have to reimburse the rental company if there's damage to the car itself. Some credit cards cover CDW for a certain rental period if you use the card to pay for the rental and decline the policy offered by the rental company. Always check with your card issuer to see what coverage it offers in Canada.
- Personal accident insurance (PAI) covers you and any passengers for medical costs incurred as a result of an accident. If your travel insurance or your health-insurance policy at home does this as well (and most do, but check), then this is one expense you can do without.

Rental

CAR

To rent a car in Canada you generally need to:

- be at least 25 years old (some companies will rent to drivers between the ages of 21 and 24 for an additional charge);
- hold a valid driver's license (an international one may be required if you're not from an English- or French-speaking country);
- have a major credit card.

You should be able to get an economy-size vehicle for about $35 to $70 per day. Child safety seats are compulsory (reserve them when you book) and cost about $15 per day.

Major international car-rental companies usually have branches at airports, train stations and in city centers.

In Canada, on-the-spot rentals often are more expensive than pre-booked packages (ie cars booked with a flight).

Avis (800-437-0358; www.avis.com)

Budget (800-268-8900; www.budget.com)

Dollar (800-800-4000; www.dollar.com)

Enterprise (800-261-7331; www.enterprise.ca)

Hertz (800-263-0600; www.hertz.com)

National (877-222-9058; www.nationalcar.ca)

Practicar (800-327-0116; www.practicar.ca) Practicar often has lower rates. It's also affiliated with Backpackers Hotels Canada and Hostelling International.

Thrifty (800-847-4389; www.thrifty.com)

MOTORCYCLE

Several companies offer motorcycle rentals and tours. A Harley Heritage Softail Classic costs about $210 per day, including liability insurance and 200km mileage. Some companies have minimum rental periods, which can be as much as seven days. Riding a hog is especially popular in British Columbia.

Coastline Motorcycle (250-335-1837, 866-338-0344; www.coastlinemc.com) Tours and rentals out of Victoria and Vancouver in British Columbia.

McScoots Motorcycle & Scooter Rentals (250-763-4668; www.mcscoots.com) Big selection of Harleys; also operates motorcycle tours. It's based in Kelowna, British Columbia.

RECREATIONAL VEHICLES

The RV market is biggest in the west, with specialized agencies in Calgary, Edmonton, Whitehorse and Vancouver. For summer travel, book as early as possible. The base cost is roughly $175 to $280 per day in high season for midsize vehicles, although insurance, fees and taxes add a hefty chunk to that. Diesel-fueled RVs have considerably lower running costs.

Canadream Campers (403-291-1000, 800-461-7368; www.canadream.com) Based in Calgary, with rentals (including one-way rentals) in eight cities, including Vancouver, Whitehorse, Toronto and Halifax.

Cruise Canada (☎800-671-8042; www.cruisecanada.com) Offers three sizes of RVs. Locations in Halifax, and in central and western Canada; offers one-way rentals.

CAR-SHARING

Car2Go (www.car2go.com) operates in Vancouver, Calgary, Montreal and Toronto. It costs $35 to join and then 41 cents per minute or $15 per hour to use a vehicle. You locate the cars with a smartphone app and then can park and leave them anywhere within the designated downtown zone.

Road Conditions & Hazards

Road conditions are generally good, but there are a few things to keep in mind:

- Fierce winters can leave potholes the size of landmine craters. Be prepared to swerve. Winter travel in general can be hazardous due to heavy snow and ice, which may cause roads and bridges to close periodically. **Transport Canada** (☎800-387-4999; www.tc.gc.ca/road) provides links to road conditions and construction zones for each province.
- If you're driving in winter or in remote areas, make sure your vehicle is equipped with four-season radial or snow tires, and emergency supplies in case you're stranded.
- Distances between services can be long in sparsely populated areas such as the Yukon, Newfoundland or northern Québec, so keep your gas topped up whenever possible.
- Moose, deer and elk are common on rural roadways, especially at night. There's no contest between a 534kg bull moose and a Subaru, so keep your eyes peeled.

Road Rules

- Canadians drive on the right-hand side of the road.
- Seat belt use is compulsory. Children who weigh under 18kg must be strapped into child-booster seats, except infants, who must be in a rear-facing safety seat.
- Motorcyclists must wear helmets and drive with their headlights on.
- Distances and speed limits are posted in kilometers. The speed limit is generally 40km/h to 50km/h in cities and 90km/h to 110km/h outside town.
- Slow down to 60km/h when passing emergency vehicles (such as police cars and ambulances) stopped on the roadside with their lights flashing.
- Turning right at red lights after coming to a full stop is permitted in all provinces (except where road signs prohibit it, and on the island of Montréal, where it's always a no-no). There's a national propensity for running red lights, however, so don't assume 'right of way' at intersections.
- Driving while using a hand-held cell phone is illegal in Canada. Fines are hefty.
- Radar detectors are not allowed in most of Canada (Alberta, British Columbia and Saskatchewan are the exceptions). If you're caught driving with a radar detector, even one that isn't being operated, you could receive a fine of $1000 and your device may be confiscated.
- The blood-alcohol limit for drivers is 0.08%. Driving while drunk is a criminal offense.

Hitchhiking

Hitching is never entirely safe in any country and we don't recommend it. That said, in remote and rural areas in Canada it is not uncommon to see people thumbing for a ride.

- If you do decide to hitch, understand that you are taking a small but potentially serious risk. Remember that it's safer to travel in pairs and let someone know where you are planning to go.
- Hitchhiking is illegal on some highways (ie the 400-series roads in Ontario), as well as in the provinces of Nova Scotia and New Brunswick.

Ride-Sharing

Ride-share services link drivers and paying passengers headed in the same direction. **Kangaride** (www.kangaride.com) is a Québec City–based service that is rapidly expanding across Canada. It costs $7.50 per year for membership and $5 per ride (on top of what the driver charges). **Allô Stop** (www.allostop.com) is a similar service operating in Québec; the website is in French.

Local Transportation

Bicycle

Cycling is a popular means of getting around during the warmer months, and many cities have hundreds of kilometers of dedicated bike paths. Bicycles typically can be taken on public transportation (although some cities have restrictions during peak travel times). All the major cities have shops renting bikes. Vancouver, Toronto and Montréal have bike-share programs.

Bus

Buses are the most common form of public transportation, and practically all towns have their own systems. Most are commuter-oriented, and offer only limited or no services in the evenings and on weekends.

Taxi

Most of the main cities have taxis and smaller towns have one or two. They are usually metered, with a flag-fall fee of roughly $2.70 and a per-kilometer charge of around $1.75. Drivers expect a tip of between 10% and 15%. Taxis can be flagged down or ordered by phone.

Train

Toronto and Montréal are the two Canadian cities with subway systems. Vancouver's version is mostly an above-ground monorail. Calgary, Edmonton and Ottawa have efficient light-rail systems. Route maps are posted in all stations.

Tours

Tour companies are another way to get around this great big country.

Arctic Odysseys (☎206-325-1977, 800-574-3021; www.arcticodysseys.com) Experience Arctic Canada up close on tours chasing the northern lights in the Northwest Territories, heli-skiing on Baffin Island or polar-bear spotting on Hudson Bay.

Backroads (☎510-527-1555, 800-462-2848; www.backroads.com) Guided cycling, walking and paddling tours in the Rockies, Nova Scotia and Québec.

Moose Travel Network (☎in eastern Canada 855-741-7318, in western Canada 888-244-6673; www.moosenetwork.com) Operates backpacker-type tours in small buses covering British Columbia, Alberta and beyond.

Road Scholar (☎800-454-5768; www.roadscholar.org) This nonprofit organization offers study tours in nearly all provinces for active people over 50, including train trips, cruises, and bus and walking tours.

Routes to Learning (☎613-530-2222, 866-745-1690; www.youngretired.ca) Formerly known as Elderhostel, this nonprofit group has dozens of educational tours throughout Canada for travelers 55 and over, from walking in the steps of Newfoundland's Vikings to exploring New Brunswick's Acadians or Nova Scotia's lighthouses.

Salty Bear Adventure Tours (☎902-202-3636; www.saltybear.ca) Backpacker-oriented van tours through the Maritimes with jump-on/jump-off flexibility. There's a three-day circuit around Cape Breton, Nova Scotia, and a five-day route that goes around Prince Edward Island.

Trek America (☎in UK 0870-444-8735, in USA 800-221-0596; www.trekamerica.com) Active camping, hiking and canoeing tours in small groups, geared primarily at people between 18 and 38, although some are open to all ages.

Train

VIA Rail (☎888-842-7245; www.viarail.ca) operates most of Canada's intercity and transcontinental passenger trains, chugging over 14,000km of track. In some remote parts of the country, such as Churchill, Manitoba, trains provide the only overland access.

➡ Rail service is most efficient in the corridor between Québec City and Windsor, Ontario – particularly between Montréal and Toronto, the two major hubs.

➡ The rail network does not extend to Newfoundland, Prince Edward Island or the Northwest Territories.

➡ Free wi-fi is available on most trains.

➡ Smoking is prohibited on all trains.

Classes

There are four main classes:

➡ Economy class buys you a fairly basic, if indeed quite comfortable, reclining seat with a headrest. Blankets and pillows are provided for overnight travel.

➡ Business class operates in the southern Ontario/Québec corridor. Seats are more spacious and have outlets for plugging in laptops. You also get a meal and priority boarding.

➡ Sleeper class is available on shorter overnight routes. You can choose from compartments with upper or lower pullout berths, and private single, double or triple roomettes, all with a bathroom.

➡ Touring class is available on long-distance routes and includes sleeper class accommodations plus meals, access to the sightseeing car and sometimes a tour guide.

Costs

Taking the train is more expensive than the bus, but most people find it a more comfortable way to travel. June to mid-October is peak season, when prices are about 40% higher. Buying tickets in advance (even just five days before) can yield significant savings.

Long-Distance Routes

VIA Rail has several classic trains:

Canadian A 1950s stainless-steel beauty between Toronto and Vancouver, zipping through the northern Ontario lake country, the western plains via Winnipeg and Saskatoon, and Jasper in the Rockies over three days.

Hudson Bay From the prairie (slowly) to the subarctic: Winnipeg to polar-bear hangout Churchill.

Ocean Chugs from Montréal along the St Lawrence River through New Brunswick and Nova Scotia.

Jasper to Prince Rupert An all-daylight route from Jasper, Alberta, to coastal Prince Rupert, British Columbia; there's an overnight stop in Prince George (you make your own hotel reservations).

Privately run regional train companies offer additional rail-touring opportunities:

Algoma Central Railway (www.agawatrain.com) Access to northern Ontario wilderness areas.

Ontario Northland (www.ontarionorthland.ca) Operates the seasonal *Polar Bear Express* from Cochrane to Moosonee on Hudson Bay (round-trip $112).

Royal Canadian Pacific (☎877-665-3044; www.royalcanadianpacific.com) A cruise-ship-like luxury line running between and around the Rockies via Calgary.

Rocky Mountaineer Railtours (www.rockymountaineer.com) Gape at Canadian Rockies scenery on swanky trains between Vancouver, Kamloops and Calgary (two days from $1000).

White Pass & Yukon Route (www.wpyr.com) Gorgeous route paralleling the original White Pass trail from Whitehorse, Yukon, to Fraser, British Columbia (round-trip $160).

Reservations

Seat reservations are highly recommended, especially in summer, on weekends and around holidays. During peak season (June to mid-October), some of the most popular sleeping arrangements are sold out months in advance, especially on long-distance trains such as the *Canadian*. The *Hudson Bay* often books solid during polar-bear season (around late September to early November).

Train Passes

VIA Rail offers a couple of passes that provide good savings:

➡ The 'System' Canrailpass (from $699) is good for seven trips on any train during a 21-day period. All seats are in economy class; upgrades are not permitted. You must book each leg at least three days in advance (which you can do online).

➡ The 'Corridor' Canrailpass (from $299) is good for seven trips during a 10-day period on trains in the Québec City–Windsor corridor (which includes Montréal, Toronto and Niagara).

Language

English and French are the official languages of Canada. You'll see both on highway signs, maps, tourist brochures, packaging etc. In Québec the preservation of French is a major concern and fuels the separatist movement. Here, English can be hard to find, and road signs and visitor information is often in French only. Outside Montréal and Québec City, you'll need French at least some of the time.

New Brunswick is the only officially bilingual province. French is widely spoken, particularly in the north and east. It is somewhat different from the French of Québec. Nova Scotia and Manitoba also have significant French-speaking populations, and there are pockets in most other provinces. In the west of Canada, French isn't as prevalent.

The French spoken in Canada is essentially the same as in France. Although many English-speaking (and most French-speaking) students in Québec are still taught the French of France, the local tongue is known as 'Québecois' or *joual*. Announcers and broadcasters on Québec TV and radio tend to speak a more refined, European style of French, as does the upper class. Québecois people will have no problem understanding more formal French.

French sounds can almost all be found in English. The exceptions are nasal vowels (represented in our pronunciation guides by o or u followed by an almost inaudible nasal consonant sound m, n or ng), the 'funny' *u* (ew in our guides) and the deep-in-the-throat *r*. Bearing this in mind and reading the pronunciation guides in this chapter as if they were English, you'll be understood just fine.

WANT MORE?

For in-depth language information and handy phrases, check out Lonely Planet's *French Phrasebook*. You'll find it at **shop.lonelyplanet.com**, or you can buy Lonely Planet's iPhone phrasebooks at the Apple App Store.

BASICS

Hello.	*Bonjour.*	bon·zhoor
Goodbye.	*Au revoir.*	o·rer·vwa
Excuse me.	*Excusez-moi.*	ek·skew·zay·mwa
Sorry.	*Pardon.*	par·don
Yes./No.	*Oui./Non.*	wee/non
Please.	*S'il vous plaît.*	seel voo play
Thank you.	*Merci.*	mair·see
You're welcome.	*De rien.*	der ree·en

How are you?
Comment allez-vous? — ko·mon ta·lay·voo

Fine, and you?
Bien, merci. Et vous? — byun mair·see ay voo

My name is ...
Je m'appelle ... — zher ma·pel ...

What's your name?
Comment vous appelez-vous? — ko·mon voo·za·play voo

Do you speak English?
Parlez-vous anglais? — par·lay·voo ong·glay

I don't understand.
Je ne comprends pas. — zher ner kom·pron pa

ACCOMMODATIONS

Do you have any rooms available?
Est-ce que vous avez des chambres libres? — es·ker voo za·vay day shom·brer lee·brer

How much is it per night/person?
Quel est le prix par nuit/personne? — kel ay ler pree par nwee/per·son

Is breakfast included?
Est-ce que le petit déjeuner est inclus? — es·ker ler per·tee day·zher·nay ayt en·klew

a ... room	*une chambre ...*	ewn shom·brer ...
single	*à un lit*	a un lee
double	*avec un grand lit*	a·vek un gron lee
air-con	*climatiseur*	klee·ma·tee·zer

bathroom	*salle de bains*	sal der bun
campsite	*camping*	kom·peeng
dorm	*dortoir*	dor·twar
guesthouse	*pension*	pon·syon
hotel	*hôtel*	o·tel
window	*fenêtre*	fer·nay·trer
youth hostel	*auberge de jeunesse*	o·berzh der zher·nes

DIRECTIONS

Where's ...?
Où est ...? — oo ay ...

What's the address?
Quelle est l'adresse? — kel ay la·dres

Could you write the address, please?
Est-ce que vous pourriez écrire l'adresse, s'il vous plaît? — es·ker voo poo·ryay ay·kreer la·dres seel voo play

Can you show me (on the map)?
Pouvez-vous m'indiquer (sur la carte)? — poo·vay·voo mun·dee·kay (sewr la kart)

at the corner	*au coin*	o kwun
at the traffic lights	*aux feux*	o fer
behind	*derrière*	dair·ryair
in front of ...	*devant ...*	der·von ...
far (from ...)	*loin (de ...)*	lwun (der ...)
left	*gauche*	gosh
near (to ...)	*près (de ...)*	pray (der ...)
next to ...	*à côté de ...*	a ko·tay der...
opposite ...	*en face de ...*	on fas der ...
right	*droite*	drwat
straight ahead	*tout droit*	too drwa

EATING & DRINKING

A table for (two), please.
Une table pour (deux), s'il vous plaît. — ewn ta·bler poor (der) seel voo play

What would you recommend?
Qu'est-ce que vous conseillez? — kes·ker voo kon·say·yay

What's in that dish?
Quels sont les ingrédients? — kel son lay zun·gray·dyon

I'm a vegetarian.
Je suis végétarien/végétarienne. — zher swee vay·zhay·ta·ryun/vay·zhay·ta·ryen (m/f)

I don't eat ...
Je ne mange pas ... — zher ner monzh pa ...

KEY PATTERNS

To get by in French, mix and match these simple patterns with words of your choice:

Where's (the entry)?
Où est (l'entrée)? — oo ay (lon·tray)

Where can I (buy a ticket)?
Où est-ce que je peux (acheter un billet)? — oo es·ker zher per (ash·tay un bee·yay)

When's (the next train)?
Quand est (le prochain train)? — kon ay (ler pro·shun trun)

How much is (a room)?
C'est combien pour (une chambre)? — say kom·buyn poor (ewn shom·brer)

Do you have (a map)?
Avez-vous (une carte)? — a·vay voo (ewn kart)

Is there (a toilet)?
Y a-t-il (des toilettes)? — ee a teel (day twa·let)

I'd like (to book a room).
Je voudrais (réserver (une chambre). — zher voo·dray (ray·ser·vay ewn shom·brer)

Can I (enter)?
Puis-je (entrer)? — pweezh (on·tray)

Could you please (help)?
Pouvez-vous (m'aider), s'il vous plaît? — poo·vay voo (may·day) seel voo play

Do I have to (book a seat)?
Faut-il (réserver une place)? — fo·teel (ray·ser·vay ewn plas)

Cheers!
Santé! — son·tay

That was delicious.
C'était délicieux! — say·tay day·lee·syer

Please bring the bill.
Apportez-moi l'addition, s'il vous plaît. — a·por·tay·mwa la·dee·syon seel voo play

Key Words

appetiser	*entrée*	on·tray
bottle	*bouteille*	boo·tay
breakfast	*déjeuner*	day·zher·nay
children's menu	*menu pour enfants*	mer·new poor on·fon
cold	*froid*	frwa
delicatessen	*traiteur*	tray·ter
dinner	*souper*	soo·pay
dish	*plat*	pla

SIGNS

Entrée	Entrance
Femmes	Women
Fermé	Closed
Hommes	Men
Interdit	Prohibited
Ouvert	Open
Renseignements	Information
Sortie	Exit
Toilettes/WC	Toilets

food	*nourriture*	noo·ree·tewr
fork	*fourchette*	foor·shet
glass	*verre*	vair
grocery store	*épicerie*	ay·pees·ree
highchair	*chaise haute*	shay zot
hot	*chaud*	sho
knife	*couteau*	koo·to
local speciality	*spécialité locale*	spay·sya·lee·tay lo·kal
lunch	*dîner*	dee·nay
main course	*plat principal*	pla prun·see·pal
market	*marché*	mar·shay
menu (in English)	*carte (en anglais)*	kart (on ong·glay)
plate	*assiette*	a·syet
spoon	*cuillère*	kwee·yair
wine list	*carte des vins*	kart day vun
with	*avec*	a·vek
without	*sans*	son

Meat & Fish

beef	*bœuf*	berf
chicken	*poulet*	poo·lay
fish	*poisson*	pwa·son
lamb	*agneau*	a·nyo
pork	*porc*	por
turkey	*dinde*	dund
veal	*veau*	vo

Fruit & Vegetables

apple	*pomme*	pom
apricot	*abricot*	ab·ree·ko
asparagus	*asperge*	a·spairzh
beans	*haricots*	a·ree·ko
beetroot	*betterave*	be·trav
cabbage	*chou*	shoo
celery	*céleri*	sel·ree
cherry	*cerise*	ser·reez
corn	*maïs*	ma·ees
cucumber	*concombre*	kong·kom·brer
gherkin (pickle)	*cornichon*	kor·nee·shon
grape	*raisin*	ray·zun
leek	*poireau*	pwa·ro
lemon	*citron*	see·tron
lettuce	*laitue*	lay·tew
mushroom	*champignon*	shom·pee·nyon
peach	*pêche*	pesh
peas	*petit pois*	per·tee pwa
(red/green) pepper	*poivron (rouge/vert)*	pwa·vron (roozh/vair)
pineapple	*ananas*	a·na·nas
plum	*prune*	prewn
potato	*pomme de terre*	pom der tair
prune	*pruneau*	prew·no
pumpkin	*citrouille*	see·troo·yer
shallot	*échalote*	eh·sha·lot
spinach	*épinards*	eh·pee·nar
strawberry	*fraise*	frez
tomato	*tomate*	to·mat
turnip	*navet*	na·vay
vegetable	*légume*	lay·gewm

Other

bread	*pain*	pun
butter	*beurre*	ber
cheese	*fromage*	fro·mazh
egg	*œuf*	erf
honey	*miel*	myel
jam	*confiture*	kon·fee·tewr
lentils	*lentilles*	lon·tee·yer
oil	*huile*	weel
pasta/noodles	*pâtes*	pat
pepper	*poivre*	pwa·vrer
rice	*riz*	ree
salt	*sel*	sel
sugar	*sucre*	sew·krer

QUESTION WORDS

How?	*Comment?*	ko·mon
What?	*Quoi?*	kwa
When?	*Quand?*	kon
Where?	*Où?*	oo
Who?	*Qui?*	kee
Why?	*Pourquoi?*	poor·kwa

Drinks

beer	*bière*	bee·yair
coffee	*café*	ka·fay
(orange) juice	*jus (d'orange)*	zhew (do·ronzh)
milk	*lait*	lay
red wine	*vin rouge*	vun roozh
tea	*thé*	tay
(mineral) water	*eau (minérale)*	o (mee·nay·ral)
white wine	*vin blanc*	vun blong

EMERGENCIES

Help!
Au secours! o skoor

I'm lost.
Je suis perdu/perdue. zhe swee pair·dew (m/f)

Leave me alone!
Fichez-moi la paix! fee·shay·mwa la pay

There's been an accident.
Il y a eu un accident. eel ya ew un ak·see·don

Call a doctor.
Appelez un médecin. a·play un mayd·sun

Call the police.
Appelez la police. a·play la po·lees

I'm ill.
Je suis malade. zher swee ma·lad

It hurts here.
J'ai une douleur ici. zhay ewn doo·ler ee·see

I'm allergic to ...
Je suis allergique ... zher swee za·lair·zheek ...

Where are the toilets?
Où sont les toilettes? oo son lay twa·let

SHOPPING & SERVICES

I'd like to buy ...
Je voudrais acheter ... zher voo·dray ash·tay ...

May I look at it?
Est-ce que je peux le voir? es·ker zher per ler vwar

I'm just looking.
Je regarde. zher rer·gard

I don't like it.
Cela ne me plaît pas. ser·la ner mer play pa

How much is it?
C'est combien? say kom·byun

It's too expensive.
C'est trop cher. say tro shair

Can you lower the price?
Vous pouvez baisser le prix? voo poo·vay bay·say ler pree

NUMBERS

1	*un*	un
2	*deux*	der
3	*trois*	trwa
4	*quatre*	ka·trer
5	*cinq*	sungk
6	*six*	sees
7	*sept*	set
8	*huit*	weet
9	*neuf*	nerf
10	*dix*	dees
20	*vingt*	vung
30	*trente*	tront
40	*quarante*	ka·ront
50	*cinquante*	sung·kont
60	*soixante*	swa·sont
70	*soixante-dix*	swa·son·dees
80	*quatre-vingts*	ka·trer·vung
90	*quatre-vingt-dix*	ka·trer·vung·dees
100	*cent*	son
1000	*mille*	meel

There's a mistake in the bill.
Il y a une erreur dans la note. eel ya ewn ay·rer don la not

ATM	*guichet automatique de banque*	gee·shay o·to·ma·teek der bonk
credit card	*carte de crédit*	kart der kray·dee
internet cafe	*cybercafé*	see·bair·ka·fay
post office	*bureau de poste*	bew·ro der post
tourist office	*office de tourisme*	o·fees der too·rees·mer

TIME & DATES

What time is it?
Quelle heure est-il? kel er ay til

It's (eight) o'clock.
Il est (huit) heures. il ay (weet) er

It's half past (10).
Il est (dix) heures et demie. il ay (deez) er ay day·mee

morning	*matin*	ma·tun
afternoon	*après-midi*	a·pray·mee·dee
evening	*soir*	swar
yesterday	*hier*	yair
today	*aujourd'hui*	o·zhoor·dwee
tomorrow	*demain*	der·mun

Monday	*lundi*	lun·dee
Tuesday	*mardi*	mar·dee
Wednesday	*mercredi*	mair·krer·dee
Thursday	*jeudi*	zher·dee
Friday	*vendredi*	von·drer·dee
Saturday	*samedi*	sam·dee
Sunday	*dimanche*	dee·monsh

January	*janvier*	zhon·vyay
February	*février*	fayv·ryay
March	*mars*	mars
April	*avril*	a·vreel
May	*mai*	may
June	*juin*	zhwun
July	*juillet*	zhwee·yay
August	*août*	oot
September	*septembre*	sep·tom·brer
October	*octobre*	ok·to·brer
November	*novembre*	no·vom·brer
December	*décembre*	day·som·brer

TRANSPORTATION

Public Transportation

boat	*bateau*	ba·to
bus	*bus*	bews
plane	*avion*	a·vyon
train	*train*	trun

I want to go to ...
Je voudrais aller à ... zher voo·dray a·lay a ...

Does it stop at ...?
Est-ce qu'il s'arrête à ...? es·kil sa·ret a ...

At what time does it leave/arrive?
À quelle heure est-ce qu'il part/arrive? a kel er es kil par/a·reev

Can you tell me when we get to ...?
Pouvez-vous me dire quand nous arrivons à ...? poo·vay·voo mer deer kon noo za·ree·von a ...

I want to get off here.
Je veux descendre ici. zher ver day·son·drer ee·see

first	*premier*	prer·myay
last	*dernier*	dair·nyay
next	*prochain*	pro·shun

a ... ticket	*un billet ...*	un bee·yay ...
1st-class	*de première classe*	der prem·yair klas
2nd-class	*de deuxième classe*	der der·zyem las
one-way	*simple*	sum·pler
return	*aller et retour*	a·lay ay rer·toor

aisle seat	*côté couloir*	ko·tay kool·war
cancelled	*annulé*	a·new·lay
delayed	*en retard*	on rer·tar
platform	*quai*	kay
ticket office	*guichet*	gee·shay
timetable	*horaire*	o·rair
train station	*gare*	gar
window seat	*côté fenêtre*	ko·tay fe·ne·trer

Driving & Cycling

I'd like to hire a ...	*Je voudrais louer ...*	zher voo·dray loo·way ...
car	*une voiture*	ewn vwa·tewr
bicycle	*un vélo*	un vay·lo
motorcycle	*une moto*	ewn mo·to

child seat	*siège-enfant*	syezh·on·fon
diesel	*diesel*	dyay·zel
helmet	*casque*	kask
mechanic	*mécanicien*	may·ka·nee·syun
petrol/gas	*essence*	ay·sons
service station	*station-service*	sta·syon·ser·vees

Is this the road to ...?
C'est la route pour ...? say la root poor ...

(How long) Can I park here?
(Combien de temps) Est-ce que je peux stationner ici? (kom·byun der tom) es·ker zher per sta·syo·nay ee·see

The car/motorbike has broken down (at ...).
La voiture/moto est tombée en panne (à ...). la vwa·tewr/mo·to ay tom·bay on pan (a ...)

I have a flat tire.
Mon pneu est à plat. mom pner ay ta pla

I've run out of petrol.
Je suis en panne d'essence. zher swee zon pan day·sons

I've lost my car keys.
J'ai perdu les clés de ma voiture. zhay per·dew lay klay der ma vwa·tewr

Where can I have my bicycle repaired?
Où est-ce que je peux faire réparer mon vélo? oo es ker zher per fair ray·pa·ray mon vay·lo

Behind the Scenes

SEND US YOUR FEEDBACK

We love to hear from travelers – your comments keep us on our toes and help make our books better. Our well-traveled team reads every word on what you loved or loathed about this book. Although we cannot reply individually to your submissions, we always guarantee that your feedback goes straight to the appropriate authors, in time for the next edition. Each person who sends us information is thanked in the next edition – the most useful submissions are rewarded with a selection of digital PDF chapters.

Visit **lonelyplanet.com/contact** to submit your updates and suggestions or to ask for help. Our award-winning website also features inspirational travel stories, news and discussions.

Note: We may edit, reproduce and incorporate your comments in Lonely Planet products such as guidebooks, websites and digital products, so let us know if you don't want your comments reproduced or your name acknowledged. For a copy of our privacy policy visit lonelyplanet.com/privacy.

OUR READERS

Many thanks to the travelers who used the last edition and wrote to us with helpful hints, useful advice and interesting anecdotes: Ailidh Cameron, Amanda Kiilerich, Bastian Schnabel, Brian Pritchard, Cristina Rolla, Ellen Archibald, Erica Wijarnako, Gemma Beher, Greg Malcher, Harald Pfannhauser, Heather Monell, Johan van den Berg, Johannes Voit, Kristen Wicks & Christopher Armour, Kristina Disney, Leonie Sage , Linda van Happen, Lucía Canga, Maria del Mar Garcia Fernandez, Marieke Vos, Mark Allard, Miguel Prohaska, Pat Luck, Pirkko Anderson, Rebecca Scott, Susanne Hartigan, Thomas Coquel, Zsuzsanna Gaspar

WRITER THANKS

Korina Miller

Thank you to Alex Howard for inviting me to join this project and to the team of travel-thirsty authors who helped make it great. Thank you to the many Albertans who shared their stories, insight and love for their province. Thanks to Kajsa Erickson for acquainting me with Calgary's wilder side during the height of Stampede; to my parents and daughters, Simone and Monique, for camping out in the Rockies with me; and to Kirk and Bing for keeping the home fires burning. And finally, thanks to my chiropractor, Dr Bob Mabee for straightening me out after driving 4500km in 10 days.

Kate Armstrong

Many thanks to Alexander Howard at LP plus the many locals who gave nothing but Acadian and Maritimes hospitality. Three cheers to those who advised on local tourism: Alison Aiton and Stacey Russell (Fredericton), Jillian MacKinnon (Saint John), Jillian Somers and Colette McLaughlin (Moncton) and Janice Arseneault (Edmunston). Finally, merci to all the helpful Canadian enthusiasts along the way who know that their region is a special one.

James Bainbridge

Thanks to everyone who helped on my long journey from Ottawa's political spires up the hazy shores of Lake Superior. The friendly souls throughout Ontario are too numerous to mention, but old mate Ciprian and new friend Shayne get a special shout out, as does David Peterson for stabling their horse. Back in Cape Town, thanks to my ever-wonderful family, and to everyone who turned up to celebrate my 40th while I was writing up Ontario.

Anna Kaminski

A massive thanks to Alex for entrusting me with three fascinating regions, and to all who helped me along the way, particularly Crystal in Yellowknife, Christine, Don and Patrick in Fort Smith, Gina and John in Fort Providence, Ted Grant for the amazing day in Nahanni, Rachel and Li in Winnipeg, Kylik and Sarah in Inuvik, the wonderful Parks Canada people (Bronwyn, Karen, Jovan) in Iqaluit, Sherry in Valleyview, and Sebastian from Dawson City for picking up a stranded hitchhiker.

Adam Karlin

Thanks to my co-authors, particularly Anna, for feedback and advice; Alexander, our editor, for the same and inviting me on the project; the two French guys in the Gaspé for their podcast skills; Zach, Kate and Dan for roadtripping me into the Eastern townships; Andy and Marie for being wonderful hosts in Montréal; Rachel, who is a perfect partner for discovering the Laurentians; Sanda, for giving Google hangout pep talks. This chapter on Québec is for Gizmo.

John Lee

Special thanks to Maggie for ensuring my sanity and delivering copious amounts of tea during the write-up for this project. Thanks also to our feline companion Max for grooming my beard on a regular basis. And cheers to my buddy Dominic for joining me on that elongated Vancouver Island road trip. Sincere apologies to all my other Vancouver friends and family for being stuck to my keyboard for so long; I'm more than ready for a beer or two now.

Carolyn McCarthy

Many thanks go out to the good people of Newfoundland for their warm welcome and hospitality. My gratitude goes out to Carolyn Cook for her camping gear and adventure know-how, Bernadette Walsh for her total expertise, Terri Coles for her journalistic insights, Kathleen Kearns for her tips, and my hosts Elissa and Mark.

Phillip Tang

Super thanks to Stephen Hu (Ren Jie) for photography, Hamilton geese, backpack goose-chase, dawn language geek-out, inspections, shoppers, and a hot-pot of Toronto smarts. Thanks James Salo for the incredible hospitality and insight spanning Toronto to Tobermory. Thanks Sherman Jones for sharing Elora, Fergus, Kitchener, and travel tales. Thanks to Alexander Howard and Imogen Bannister for sanity checks.

Ryan Ver Berkmoes

The number of folks to thank outnumber Kermode bears but here's a few: Ben Greensfelder, my fearless co-pilot who kept the supply of good beer flowing. In Prince Rupert, I am beyond indebted to Bruce Wishart for literally food folks and fun. And words can't repay the car shuttle service. In Dawson, Tony and the gang almost made me forget my visit. Finally, to Alexis Ver Berkmoes, who I love even more than the giant beaver.

Benedict Walker

Heartfelt thanks to my ever-patient and supportive mother, Trish Walker, to the folks at LP, especially Alexander Howard for giving me this opportunity and my editors, Kristin Odijk and Saralinda Turner. In Canada, love and gratitude to Cherly, the Cowies and Mr Mikey Brown. To my mates Carl, Matt and Baker Paul in NS and to Brittany, Kaylin and Rae-Anne in PEI: thanks all for your friendship, encouragement and local knowledge.

ACKNOWLEDGEMENTS

Climate map data adapted from Peel MC, Finlayson BL & McMahon TA (2007) 'Updated World Map of the Köppen-Geiger Climate Classification', Hydrology and Earth System Sciences, 11, 163344.

Cover photograph: Mother polar bear and her cub, Churchill, Manitoba, Steve Bloom Images/Alamy©

THIS BOOK

This 13th edition of Lonely Planet's *Canada* was researched and written by Korina Miller, Kate Armstrong, James Bainbridge, Anna Kaminski, Adam Karlin, John Lee, Carolyn McCarthy, Phillip Tang, Ryan Ver Berkmoes and Benedict Walker. The previous edition was written by Karla Zimmerman, Celeste Brash, John Lee, Sarah Richards, Brendan Sainsbury, Caroline Sieg, Andy Symington, Ryan Ver Berkmoes and Benedict Walker. This guidebook was produced by the following:

Destination Editor Alexander Howard

Product Editor Jenna Myers

Senior Cartographer Corey Hutchison

Assisting Cartographers Julie Dodkins, Hunor Csutoros

Book Designer Cam Ashley

Assisting Editors Imogen Bannister, Michelle Bennett, Carly Hall, Victoria Harrison, Gabby Innes, Ali Lemer, Kate Mathews, Kate Morgan, Anne Mulvaney, Lauren O'Connell, Kristin Odijk, Charlotte Orr, Susan Paterson, Chris Pitts, Alison Ridgway, Saralinda Turner, Fionnuala Twomey, Simon Williamson

Cover Researcher Naomi Parker

Thanks to Kate Chapman, Joel Cotterell, Grace Dobell, Liz Heynes, Andi Jones, Catherine Naghten, Claire Naylor, Karyn Noble, Martine Power, Kirsten Rawlings, Vicky Smith, Lyahna Spencer, Ross Taylor, Tony Wheeler, Tracy Whitmey, Amanda Williamson

Index

Map Pages **000**
Photo Pages **000**

Map Pages **000**
Photo Pages **000**

D

E

F

Map Pages **000**
Photo Pages **000**

Map Pages **000**
Photo Pages **000**

O

P

Map Pages **000**
Photo Pages **000**

Map Legend

Sights
- Beach
- Bird Sanctuary
- Buddhist
- Castle/Palace
- Christian
- Confucian
- Hindu
- Islamic
- Jain
- Jewish
- Monument
- Museum/Gallery/Historic Building
- Ruin
- Shinto
- Sikh
- Taoist
- Winery/Vineyard
- Zoo/Wildlife Sanctuary
- Other Sight

Activities, Courses & Tours
- Bodysurfing
- Diving
- Canoeing/Kayaking
- Course/Tour
- Sento Hot Baths/Onsen
- Skiing
- Snorkeling
- Surfing
- Swimming/Pool
- Walking
- Windsurfing
- Other Activity

Sleeping
- Sleeping
- Camping

Eating
- Eating

Drinking & Nightlife
- Drinking & Nightlife
- Cafe

Entertainment
- Entertainment

Shopping
- Shopping

Information
- Bank
- Embassy/Consulate
- Hospital/Medical
- Internet
- Police
- Post Office
- Telephone
- Toilet
- Tourist Information
- Other Information

Geographic
- Beach
- Gate
- Hut/Shelter
- Lighthouse
- Lookout
- Mountain/Volcano
- Oasis
- Park
- Pass
- Picnic Area
- Waterfall

Population
- Capital (National)
- Capital (State/Province)
- City/Large Town
- Town/Village

Transport
- Airport
- BART station
- Border crossing
- Boston T station
- Bus
- Cable car/Funicular
- Cycling
- Ferry
- Metro/Muni station
- Monorail
- Parking
- Petrol station
- Subway/SkyTrain station
- Taxi
- Train station/Railway
- Tram
- Underground station
- Other Transport

Note: Not all symbols displayed above appear on the maps in this book

Routes
- Tollway
- Freeway
- Primary
- Secondary
- Tertiary
- Lane
- Unsealed road
- Road under construction
- Plaza/Mall
- Steps
- Tunnel
- Pedestrian overpass
- Walking Tour
- Walking Tour detour
- Path/Walking Trail

Boundaries
- International
- State/Province
- Disputed
- Regional/Suburb
- Marine Park
- Cliff
- Wall

Hydrography
- River, Creek
- Intermittent River
- Canal
- Water
- Dry/Salt/Intermittent Lake
- Reef

Areas
- Airport/Runway
- Beach/Desert
- Cemetery (Christian)
- Cemetery (Other)
- Glacier
- Mudflat
- Park/Forest
- Sight (Building)
- Sportsground
- Swamp/Mangrove

Adam Karlin

Québec Born in Washington DC and raised in the rural Maryland tidewater, Adam has been exploring the world and writing about it since he was 17, and considers it a blessedly interesting way to live one's life – and also good fun.

John Lee

Vancouver, Southern British Columbia Originally from the UK, John moved to British Columbia to study at the University of Victoria in the 1990s. Eventually staying and moving to Vancouver, he started a freelance travel-writing career in 1999. Since then, he's been covering the region and beyond for Lonely Planet plus magazines, newspapers and online outlets around the world. Winner of numerous writing awards, very active on Twitter and a weekly columnist for Canada's *The Globe and Mail* national newspaper, catch up with him at www.johnleewriter.com and @johnleewriter.

Carolyn McCarthy

Newfoundland & Labrador Carolyn specializes in travel, culture and adventure in the Americas. She has written for *National Geographic*, *Outside*, *BBC Magazine*, *Boston Globe* and other publications. A former Fulbright fellow and Banff Mountain Grant recipient, she has documented life in the most remote corners of Latin America. Carolyn gained her expertise by researching guidebooks in diverse destinations. She has contributed to over 30 guidebooks for Lonely Planet, including *Colorado*, *USA*, *Argentina*, *Chile*, *Panama*, *Peru* and the USA National Parks guides. She is also the author of Lonely Planet's *Trekking in the Patagonian Andes*.

Phillip Tang

Toronto, Southern Ontario Phillip grew up on typically Australian *pho* and fish'n'chips. A degree in Chinese and Latin-American cultures launched him into travel and writing about it for Lonely Planet's *Canada, China, Japan, Korea, Mexico, Peru* and *Vietnam* guides. Phillip has made his home in Sydney, Melbourne, London and Mexico City. His travels include most countries in Europe, much of Asia and Latin America, as well as the greatest hits of North America. More pics and words: philliptang.co.uk.

Ryan Ver Berkmoes

Saskatchewan, Northern British Columbia, Yukon Territory Ryan has written more than 110 guidebooks for Lonely Planet. He grew up in Santa Cruz, California, which he left at age 17 for college in the Midwest, where he first discovered snow. All joy of this novelty soon wore off. Since then he has been traveling the world, both for pleasure and for work – which are often indistinguishable. He has covered everything from wars to bars. He definitely prefers the latter. Ryan calls New York City home. Read more at ryanverberkmoes.com and at @ryanvb.

Benedict Walker

Nova Scotia, Prince Edward Island Born in Newcastle, Australia, Ben holds notions of the beach core to his idea of self, though he's traveled hundreds of thousands of kilometers from the sandy shores of home. Ben was given his first Lonely Planet guide *(Japan)* when he was 12. Two decades later, he'd write chapters for the same publication: a dream come true. A communications graduate and travel agent by trade, Ben whittled away his twenties gallivanting around the globe. He thinks the best thing about travel isn't as much about where you go as who you meet: living vicariously through the stories of kind strangers enriches one's own experience. Ben has also written and directed a play, and toured Australia managing the travel logistics for top-billing music festivals.

OUR STORY

A beat-up old car, a few dollars in the pocket and a sense of adventure. In 1972 that's all Tony and Maureen Wheeler needed for the trip of a lifetime – across Europe and Asia overland to Australia. It took several months, and at the end – broke but inspired – they sat at their kitchen table writing and stapling together their first travel guide, *Across Asia on the Cheap*. Within a week they'd sold 1500 copies. Lonely Planet was born.

Today, Lonely Planet has offices in Franklin, London, Melbourne, Oakland, Dublin, Beijing and Delhi, with more than 600 staff and writers. We share Tony's belief that 'a great guidebook should do three things: inform, educate and amuse'.

OUR WRITERS

Korina Miller

Alberta, Plan Chapters, Understand Chapters, Survival Guide Korina grew up on Vancouver Island and has been exploring the globe independently since she was 16, visiting or living in 36 countries and picking up a degree in Communications and Canadian Studies, an MA in Migration Studies and a diploma in Visual Arts en route. As a writer and editor, Korina has worked on nearly 60 titles for Lonely Planet and has also worked with LP.com, BBC, the *Independent*, the *Guardian*, BBC5 and CBC, as well as many independent magazines, covering travel, art and culture. She has currently set up camp back in Victoria, soaking up the mountain views and the pounding surf.

Kate Armstrong

New Brunswick Kate has spent much of her adult life traveling and living around the world. A full-time freelance travel journalist, she has contributed to around 40 Lonely Planet guides and trade publications and is regularly published in Australian and worldwide publications. She is the author of several books and children's educational titles.

James Bainbridge

Ottawa, Northern & Eastern Ontario James is a British travel writer and journalist based in Cape Town, South Africa, from where he roams the globe and contributes to publications worldwide. He has been working on Lonely Planet projects for over a decade, updating dozens of guidebooks and TV hosting everywhere from the African bush to the Great Lakes. The coordinating author of several editions of Lonely Planet's *South Africa, Lesotho & Swaziland*, *Turkey* and *Morocco* guides, his articles on travel, culture and investment appear in the likes of *BBC Travel*, the UK *Guardian* and *Independent*, *Condé Nast Traveller* and *Lonely Planet Traveller*.

Anna Kaminski

Manitoba, Northwest Territories, Nunavut Anna has been a travel writer with Lonely Planet for more than 15 years, and has contributed to numerous guides, most recently regions as far and wide as Costa Rica, Papua New Guinea, Sweden, Great Britain, Spain, Hungary, Vietnam and India. She tweets at @ACKaminski.

OVER PAGE MORE WRITERS

Published by Lonely Planet Global Limited
CRN 554153
13th edition – April 2017
ISBN 978 1 7865 7335 3

10 9 8 7 6 5 4 3 2 1
Printed in Singapore